ENCYCLOPEDIA OF RELIGION

SECOND EDITION

ENCYCLOPEDIA OF RELIGION

2

SECOND EDITION

ATTRIBUTES OF GOD
•
BUTLER, JOSEPH

LINDSAY JONES
EDITOR IN CHIEF

MACMILLAN REFERENCE USA
An imprint of Thomson Gale, a part of The Thomson Corporation

THOMSON
GALE

Detroit • New York • San Francisco • San Diego • New Haven, Conn. • Waterville, Maine • London • Munich

THOMSON

GALE

Encyclopedia of Religion, Second Edition

Lindsay Jones, Editor in Chief

For more information, contact
Macmillan Reference USA
An imprint of Thomson Gale
27500 Drake Rd.
Farmington, Hills, MI 48331-3535
Or you can visit our Internet site at
http://www.gale.com

LIBRARY OF CONGRESS CATALOGING-IN-PUBLICATION DATA

Encyclopedia of religion / Lindsay Jones, editor in chief.— 2nd ed.
p. cm.
Includes bibliographical references and index.
ISBN 0-02-865733-0 (SET HARDCOVER : ALK. PAPER) —
ISBN 0-02-865734-9 (V. 1) — ISBN 0-02-865735-7 (v. 2) —
ISBN 0-02-865736-5 (v. 3) — ISBN 0-02-865737-3 (v. 4) —
ISBN 0-02-865738-1 (v. 5) — ISBN 0-02-865739-X (v. 6) —
ISBN 0-02-865740-3 (v. 7) — ISBN 0-02-865741-1 (v. 8) —
ISBN 0-02-865742-X (v. 9) — ISBN 0-02-865743-8 (v. 10)
— ISBN 0-02-865980-5 (v. 11) — ISBN 0-02-865981-3 (v. 12) — ISBN 0-02-865982-1 (v. 13) — ISBN 0-02-865983-X (v. 14) — ISBN 0-02-865984-8 (v. 15)
1. RELIGION—ENCYCLOPEDIAS. I. JONES, LINDSAY, 1954-

BL31.E46 2005
200'.3—dc22 2004017052

This title is also available as an e-book.
ISBN 0-02-865997-X
Contact your Thomson Gale representative for ordering information.

Printed in the United States of America
10 9 8 7 6 5 4 3 2 1

EDITORS AND CONSULTANTS

Harvard Forum on Religion and Ecology
Ecology and Religion

JOSEPH HARRIS
Francis Lee Higginson Professor of English Literature and Professor of Folklore, Harvard University
Germanic Religions

URSULA KING
Professor Emerita, Senior Research Fellow and Associate Member of the Institute for Advanced Studies, University of Bristol, England, and Professorial Research Associate, Centre for Gender and Religions Research, School of Oriental and African Studies, University of London
Gender and Religion

DAVID MORGAN
Duesenberg Professor of Christianity and the Arts, and Professor of Humanities and Art History, Valparaiso University
Color Inserts and Essays

JOSEPH F. NAGY
Professor, Department of English, University of California, Los Angeles
Celtic Religion

MATTHEW OJO
Obafemi Awolowo University
African Religions

JUHA PENTIKÄINEN
Professor of Comparative Religion, The University of Helsinki, Member of Academia Scientiarum Fennica, Finland
Arctic Religions and Uralic Religions

TED PETERS
Professor of Systematic Theology, Pacific Lutheran Theological Seminary and the Center for Theology and the Natural Sciences at the Graduate Theological Union, Berkeley, California
Science and Religion

FRANK E. REYNOLDS
Professor of the History of Religions and Buddhist Studies in the Divinity School and the Department of South Asian Languages and Civilizations, Emeritus, University of Chicago
History of Religions

GONZALO RUBIO
Assistant Professor, Department of Classics and Ancient Mediterranean Studies and Department of History and Religious Studies, Pennsylvania State University
Ancient Near Eastern Religions

SUSAN SERED
Director of Research, Religion, Health and Healing Initiative, Center for the Study of World Religions, Harvard University, and Senior Research Associate, Center for Women's Health and Human Rights, Suffolk University
Healing, Medicine, and Religion

LAWRENCE E. SULLIVAN
Professor, Department of Theology, University of Notre Dame
History of Religions

WINNIFRED FALLERS SULLIVAN
Dean of Students and Senior Lecturer in the Anthropology and Sociology of Religion, University of Chicago
Law and Religion

TOD SWANSON
Associate Professor of Religious Studies, and Director, Center for Latin American Studies, Arizona State University
South American Religions

MARY EVELYN TUCKER
Professor of Religion, Bucknell University, Founder and Coordinator, Harvard Forum on Religion and Ecology, Research Fellow, Harvard Yenching Institute, Research Associate, Harvard Reischauer Institute of Japanese Studies
Ecology and Religion

HUGH URBAN
Associate Professor, Department of Comparative Studies, Ohio State University
Politics and Religion

CATHERINE WESSINGER
Professor of the History of Religions and Women's Studies, Loyola University New Orleans
New Religious Movements

ROBERT A. YELLE
Mellon Postdoctoral Fellow, University of Toronto
Law and Religion

ERIC ZIOLKOWSKI
Charles A. Dana Professor of Religious Studies, Lafayette College
Literature and Religion

ABBREVIATIONS AND SYMBOLS USED IN THIS WORK

abbr. abbreviated; abbreviation
abr. abridged; abridgment
AD *anno Domini,* in the year of the (our) Lord
Afrik. Afrikaans
AH *anno Hegirae,* in the year of the Hijrah
Akk. Akkadian
Ala. Alabama
Alb. Albanian
Am. *Amos*
AM *ante meridiem,* before noon
amend. amended; amendment
annot. annotated; annotation
Ap. *Apocalypse*
Apn. *Apocryphon*
app. appendix
Arab. Arabic
ʿArakh. *ʿArakhin*
Aram. Aramaic
Ariz. Arizona
Ark. Arkansas
Arm. Armenian
art. article (pl., arts.)
AS Anglo-Saxon
Asm. Mos. *Assumption of Moses*
Assyr. Assyrian
A.S.S.R. Autonomous Soviet Socialist Republic
Av. Avestan
ʿA.Z. *ʿAvodah zarah*
b. born
Bab. Babylonian
Ban. Bantu
1 Bar. *1 Baruch*
2 Bar. *2 Baruch*
3 Bar. *3 Baruch*
4 Bar. *4 Baruch*
B.B. *Bavaʾ batraʾ*
BBC British Broadcasting Corporation
BC before Christ
BCE before the common era
B.D. Bachelor of Divinity
Beits. *Beitsah*
Bekh. *Bekhorot*
Beng. Bengali
Ber. *Berakhot*
Berb. Berber
Bik. *Bikkurim*
bk. book (pl., bks.)
B.M. *Bavaʾ metsiʿaʾ*
BP before the present
B.Q. *Bavaʾ qammaʾ*
Brāh. *Brāhmaṇa*
Bret. Breton
B.T. Babylonian Talmud
Bulg. Bulgarian
Burm. Burmese
c. *circa,* about, approximately
Calif. California
Can. Canaanite
Catal. Catalan
CE of the common era
Celt. Celtic
cf. *confer,* compare
Chald. Chaldean
chap. chapter (pl., chaps.)
Chin. Chinese
C.H.M. Community of the Holy Myrrhbearers
1 Chr. *1 Chronicles*
2 Chr. *2 Chronicles*
Ch. Slav. Church Slavic
cm centimeters
col. column (pl., cols.)
Col. *Colossians*
Colo. Colorado
comp. compiler (pl., comps.)
Conn. Connecticut
cont. continued
Copt. Coptic
1 Cor. *1 Corinthians*
2 Cor. *2 Corinthians*
corr. corrected
C.S.P. Congregatio Sancti Pauli, Congregation of Saint Paul (Paulists)
d. died
D Deuteronomic (source of the Pentateuch)
Dan. Danish
D.B. Divinitatis Baccalaureus, Bachelor of Divinity
D.C. District of Columbia
D.D. Divinitatis Doctor, Doctor of Divinity
Del. Delaware
Dem. *Demaʾi*
dim. diminutive
diss. dissertation
Dn. *Daniel*
D.Phil. Doctor of Philosophy
Dt. *Deuteronomy*
Du. Dutch
E Elohist (source of the Pentateuch)
Eccl. *Ecclesiastes*
ed. editor (pl., eds.); edition; edited by

ʿEduy. *ʿEduyyot*
e.g. *exempli gratia,* for example
Egyp. Egyptian
1 En. *1 Enoch*
2 En. *2 Enoch*
3 En. *3 Enoch*
Eng. English
enl. enlarged
Eph. *Ephesians*
ʿEruv. *ʿEruvin*
1 Esd. *1 Esdras*
2 Esd. *2 Esdras*
3 Esd. *3 Esdras*
4 Esd. *4 Esdras*
esp. especially
Est. Estonian
Est. *Esther*
et al. *et alii,* and others
etc. *et cetera,* and so forth
Eth. Ethiopic
EV English version
Ex. *Exodus*
exp. expanded
Ez. *Ezekiel*
Ezr. *Ezra*
2 Ezr. *2 Ezra*
4 Ezr. *4 Ezra*
f. feminine; and following (pl., ff.)
fasc. fascicle (pl., fascs.)
fig. figure (pl., figs.)
Finn. Finnish
fl. *floruit,* flourished
Fla. Florida
Fr. French
frag. fragment
ft. feet
Ga. Georgia
Gal. *Galatians*
Gaul. Gaulish
Ger. German
Giṭ. *Giṭṭin*
Gn. *Genesis*
Gr. Greek
Ḥag. *Ḥagigah*
Ḥal. *Ḥallah*
Hau. Hausa
Hb. *Habakkuk*
Heb. Hebrew
Heb. *Hebrews*
Hg. *Haggai*
Hitt. Hittite
Hor. *Horayot*
Hos. *Hosea*
Ḥul. *Ḥullin*
Hung. Hungarian
ibid. *ibidem,* in the same place (as the one immediately preceding)
Icel. Icelandic
i.e. *id est,* that is
IE Indo-European
Ill. Illinois
Ind. Indiana
intro. introduction
Ir. Gael. Irish Gaelic
Iran. Iranian
Is. *Isaiah*
Ital. Italian
J Yahvist (source of the Pentateuch)
Jas. *James*
Jav. Javanese
Jb. *Job*
Jdt. *Judith*
Jer. *Jeremiah*
Jgs. *Judges*
Jl. *Joel*
Jn. *John*
1 Jn. *1 John*
2 Jn. *2 John*
3 Jn. *3 John*
Jon. *Jonah*
Jos. *Joshua*
Jpn. Japanese
JPS Jewish Publication Society translation (1985) of the Hebrew Bible
J.T. Jerusalem Talmud
Jub. *Jubilees*
Kans. Kansas
Kel. *Kelim*
Ker. *Keritot*
Ket. *Ketubbot*
1 Kgs. *1 Kings*
2 Kgs. *2 Kings*
Khois. Khoisan
Kil. *Kil'ayim*
km kilometers
Kor. Korean
Ky. Kentucky
l. line (pl., ll.)
La. Louisiana
Lam. *Lamentations*
Lat. Latin
Latv. Latvian
L. en Th. Licencié en Théologie, Licentiate in Theology
L. ès L. Licencié ès Lettres, Licentiate in Literature
Let. Jer. *Letter of Jeremiah*
lit. literally
Lith. Lithuanian
Lk. *Luke*
LL Late Latin
LL.D. Legum Doctor, Doctor of Laws
Lv. *Leviticus*
m meters
m. masculine
M.A. Master of Arts
Ma ʿas. *Maʿaserot*
Ma ʿas. Sh. *Maʿ aser sheni*
Mak. *Makkot*
Makh. *Makhshirin*
Mal. *Malachi*
Mar. Marathi
Mass. Massachusetts
1 Mc. *1 Maccabees*
2 Mc. *2 Maccabees*
3 Mc. *3 Maccabees*
4 Mc. *4 Maccabees*
Md. Maryland
M.D. Medicinae Doctor, Doctor of Medicine
ME Middle English
Meg. *Megillah*
Me ʿil. *Meʿilah*
Men. *Menaḥot*
MHG Middle High German
mi. miles
Mi. *Micah*
Mich. Michigan
Mid. *Middot*
Minn. Minnesota
Miq. *Miqvaʾot*
MIran. Middle Iranian
Miss. Mississippi
Mk. *Mark*
Mo. Missouri
Moʿed Q. *Moʿed qaṭan*
Mont. Montana
MPers. Middle Persian
MS. *manuscriptum,* manuscript (pl., MSS)
Mt. *Matthew*
MT Masoretic text
n. note
Na. *Nahum*
Nah. Nahuatl
Naz. *Nazir*
N.B. *nota bene,* take careful note
N.C. North Carolina
n.d. no date
N.Dak. North Dakota
NEB New English Bible
Nebr. Nebraska

Ned. *Nedarim*
Neg. *Nega'im*
Neh. *Nehemiah*
Nev. Nevada
N.H. New Hampshire
Nid. *Niddah*
N.J. New Jersey
Nm. *Numbers*
N.Mex. New Mexico
no. number (pl., nos.)
Nor. Norwegian
n.p. no place
n.s. new series
N.Y. New York
Ob. *Obadiah*
O.Cist. Ordo Cisterciencium, Order of Cîteaux (Cistercians)
OCS Old Church Slavonic
OE Old English
O.F.M. Ordo Fratrum Minorum, Order of Friars Minor (Franciscans)
OFr. Old French
Ohal. *Ohalot*
OHG Old High German
OIr. Old Irish
OIran. Old Iranian
Okla. Oklahoma
ON Old Norse
O.P. Ordo Praedicatorum, Order of Preachers (Dominicans)
OPers. Old Persian
op. cit. *opere citato,* in the work cited
OPrus. Old Prussian
Oreg. Oregon
'Orl. *'Orlah*
O.S.B. Ordo Sancti Benedicti, Order of Saint Benedict (Benedictines)
p. page (pl., pp.)
P Priestly (source of the Pentateuch)
Pa. Pennsylvania
Pahl. Pahlavi
Par. *Parah*
para. paragraph (pl., paras.)
Pers. Persian
Pes. *Pesahim*
Ph.D. Philosophiae Doctor, Doctor of Philosophy
Phil. *Philippians*
Phlm. *Philemon*
Phoen. Phoenician
pl. plural; plate (pl., pls.)
PM *post meridiem,* after noon
Pol. Polish
pop. population
Port. Portuguese
Prv. *Proverbs*
Ps. *Psalms*
Ps. 151 *Psalm 151*
Ps. Sol. *Psalms of Solomon*
pt. part (pl., pts.)
1Pt. *1 Peter*
2 Pt. *2 Peter*
Pth. Parthian
Q hypothetical source of the synoptic Gospels
Qid. *Qiddushin*
Qin. *Qinnim*
r. reigned; ruled
Rab. *Rabbah*
rev. revised
R. ha-Sh. *Ro'sh ha-shanah*
R.I. Rhode Island
Rom. Romanian
Rom. *Romans*
R.S.C.J. Societas Sacratissimi Cordis Jesu, Religious of the Sacred Heart
RSV Revised Standard Version of the Bible
Ru. *Ruth*
Rus. Russian
Rv. *Revelation*
Rv. Ezr. *Revelation of Ezra*
San. *Sanhedrin*
S.C. South Carolina
Scot. Gael. Scottish Gaelic
S.Dak. South Dakota
sec. section (pl., secs.)
Sem. Semitic
ser. series
sg. singular
Sg. *Song of Songs*
Sg. of 3 *Prayer of Azariah and the Song of the Three Young Men*
Shab. *Shabbat*
Shav. *Shavu'ot*
Sheq. *Sheqalim*
Sib. Or. *Sibylline Oracles*
Sind. Sindhi
Sinh. Sinhala
Sir. *Ben Sira*
S.J. Societas Jesu, Society of Jesus (Jesuits)
Skt. Sanskrit
1 Sm. *1 Samuel*
2 Sm. *2 Samuel*
Sogd. Sogdian
Soṭ. *Soṭah*
sp. species (pl., spp.)
Span. Spanish
sq. square
S.S.R. Soviet Socialist Republic
st. stanza (pl., ss.)
S.T.M. Sacrae Theologiae Magister, Master of Sacred Theology
Suk. *Sukkah*
Sum. Sumerian
supp. supplement; supplementary
Sus. *Susanna*
s.v. *sub verbo,* under the word (pl., s.v.v.)
Swed. Swedish
Syr. Syriac
Syr. Men. *Syriac Menander*
Ta' an. *Ta'anit*
Tam. Tamil
Tam. *Tamid*
Tb. *Tobit*
T.D. *Taishō shinshū daizōkyō,* edited by Takakusu Junjirō et al. (Tokyo,1922–1934)
Tem. *Temurah*
Tenn. Tennessee
Ter. Terumot
Ṭev. Y. *Ṭevul yom*
Tex. Texas
Th.D. Theologicae Doctor, Doctor of Theology
1 Thes. *1 Thessalonians*
2 Thes. *2 Thessalonians*
Thrac. Thracian
Ti. *Titus*
Tib. Tibetan
1 Tm. *1 Timothy*
2 Tm. *2 Timothy*
T. of 12 *Testaments of the Twelve Patriarchs*
Ṭoh. *ṭohorot*
Tong. Tongan
trans. translator, translators; translated by; translation
Turk. Turkish
Ukr. Ukrainian
Upan. *Upaniṣad*
U.S. United States
U.S.S.R. Union of Soviet Socialist Republics
Uqts. *Uqtsin*
v. verse (pl., vv.)
Va. Virginia
var. variant; variation
Viet. Vietnamese

viz. *videlicet,* namely
vol. volume (pl., vols.)
Vt. Vermont
Wash. Washington
Wel. Welsh
Wis. Wisconsin
Wis. *Wisdom of Solomon*
W.Va. West Virginia
Wyo. Wyoming

Yad. *Yadayim*
Yev. *Yevamot*
Yi. Yiddish
Yor. Yoruba
Zav. *Zavim*
Zec. *Zechariah*
Zep. *Zephaniah*
Zev. *Zevaḥim*

* hypothetical
? uncertain; possibly; perhaps
° degrees
+ plus
– minus
= equals; is equivalent to
× by; multiplied by
→ yields

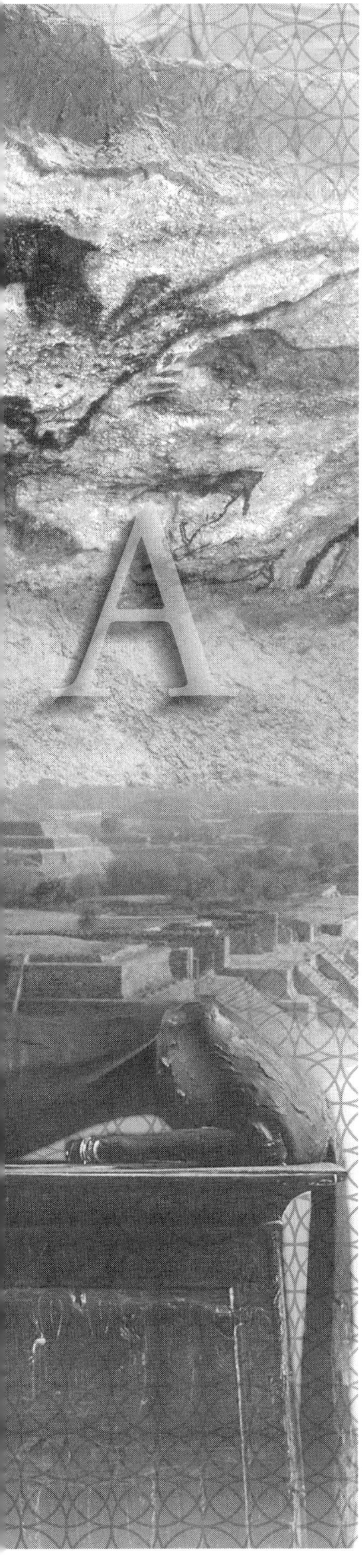

A
CONTINUED

ATTRIBUTES OF GOD

This entry consists of the following articles:

JEWISH CONCEPTS
CHRISTIAN CONCEPTS
ISLAMIC CONCEPTS

ATTRIBUTES OF GOD: JEWISH CONCEPTS

Postbiblical Jewish teachers sensed no incongruity in attributing to God qualities having strong human associations; the rabbis of the Talmud and the Midrash rely on the biblical attributes by which, as they remark, God is called in place of his name. This reliance on biblical attributes should not be taken anachronistically to mean that God is only called just, compassionate, and the like, but that, in reality, his true nature cannot be known, since this kind of distinction between essence and attributes did not surface in Judaism until the more philosophically oriented Middle Ages. God is called by his attributes because he is so described in scripture, which, as God's revealed word, informs humans how God is to be thought about and addressed.

The Hebrew word *middah,* used by the rabbis, corresponds roughly to the word *attribute* and means quality or measure. The medieval distinction between God's attributes and his essence could have had no significance for the spontaneous nature of rabbinic thinking. The term *middot* (pl. of *middah*) denotes the proper limits by means of which each of his qualities finds its expression when required in particular circumstances. A good part of the rabbinic thinking on divine control of the universe consists of the subtle interplay between God's justice and his mercy. For God to overlook sinfulness and wickedness would be for him to betray his quality of justice. As a rabbinic saying has it: "Whoever declares that God is indulgent forfeits his very life" (B.T., *B.Q.* 50a). Yet God's justice is always tempered by mercy. He pardons sinners who return to him in sincere repentance and is ever ready to be entreated to exercise his compassion. God's mercy is extended to human beings who show mercy to one another. A typical rabbinic doctrine is that of mea-

CLOCKWISE FROM TOP LEFT CORNER. Fourteenth-century BCE terra-cotta hedgehog of Aegean Rhyton, from Ugarit, Syria. Louvre, Paris. *[©Erich Lessing/Art Resource, N.Y.]*; Facsimile of prehistoric paintings in Lascaux Cave in southwestern France. Musée des Antiquites Nationales, France. *[©Réunion des Musées Nationaux/Art Resource, N.Y.]*; Ancient Egyptian underworld god Anubis. Cairo Museum. *[©Roger Wood/Corbis]*; Pyramid of the Sun at Teotihuacan, Mexico. *[©Charles & Josette Lenars/Corbis]*; Late-nineteenth-century brass Altar of the Hand shrine from Benin. British Museum, London. *[©HIP/Scala/Art Resource, N.Y.]*.

sure for measure (Soṭ. 1.7–10). To the extent that humans are prepared to go beyond the letter of the law to be excessively generous and forgiving, God can, with justice, be gracious; the more merciful human beings are in conduct with their fellows, the more will God extend to them his sympathy and his pardon (B.T., *R. ha-Sh.* 17a).

The rabbis explore the biblical record, elaborating on the attributes found there. For the rabbis, the teaching that emerges from biblical statements about God is that he is omnipresent, omniscient, and omnipotent, although these abstract terms are never used by the rabbis, who prefer the concrete language favored by the Bible. God is present at all times in the universe, which he fills. Yet reservations are implied about the language used when God's presence (*shekhinah*) in the universe is compared to the human soul filling the body it inhabits (B.T., *Ber.* 10a), with the clear implication that the pervasiveness is spiritual, not spatial. God knows all there is to be known, including all future events (B.T., *San.* 90b), although the idea of God's foreknowledge receives little prominence in rabbinic thought. As in the Bible, so for the rabbis, God possesses unlimited power, but here, too, the consideration of whether the doctrine of God's omnipotence embraces even contradiction had to wait until the rise of medieval theological speculation.

That God is one and eternal is as axiomatic for the rabbis as it is for the biblical authors upon whom they based their views. God is totally unaffected by the passage of time. Nevertheless, the Midrash (*Mekhilta'*, Be-shalaḥ 4) can say that God appeared to the children of Israel at the crossing of the sea in the guise of a youthful warrior, whereas he appeared at Sinai as a venerable sage teaching the Torah to his disciples. In another Midrashic passage (*Ex. Rab.* 5.9) it is said that God's voice at Sinai adapted itself to the temperament and disposition of the individual recipients. God spoke to the young in youthful terms, to the older folk in more mature ways. Men heard the voice speaking in a form suitable to males, women in a form suitable to females. Implied here is the idea, later to be developed more fully, that a distinction is to be made between God as he is in himself and God as he becomes manifest in creation. The differentiation is said to have been only in the way in which the divine revelation had its effect. In God there is no trace of age or sex. God is unchanging and unlimited.

The rabbis do not, however, refuse to allow all attributes of the divine nature to be used. The rabbis, following literally the biblical accounts, seemingly believe that God possesses the attributes of goodness, justice, wisdom, truth, and holiness and that these are not simply metaphors, although God possesses these attributes in a manner infinitely greater than human beings can imagine; human beings can only approximate these attributes in very faint measure in their conduct. The divide between God and humanity is never crossed, but it is the duty of humans to be godlike by trying to make the divine attributes their own insofar as this is possible (B.T., *Shab.* 133b). A person can and should be holy, but he or she can never be holy in the way that God is holy (*Lv. Rab.* 24.9). Humans can pursue the truth and live a life of integrity, but even of Moses it is said that he failed to attain to the fiftieth and highest gate of understanding, that is, of perception of the divine (B.T., *Ned.* 38a). Humans must be compassionate like their maker, but their compassion must not stray beyond its legitimate boundaries. If, for example, someone mourns beyond the period specified by the law when a relative has died, God is said to protest: "Cease from mourning. You are not more compassionate than I" (B.T., *Mo'ed Q.* 27b).

The change that came about in the Middle Ages, when a more systematic theological approach dominated the scene, resulted in a completely fresh examination of the whole question of divine attributes. In their quest for the most refined, abstract formulation, the medieval thinkers tended to speak of God as simple, pure, a complete unity, with neither division nor multiplicity. Their difficulty with the divine attributes found in the Bible and the rabbinic literature was not only because in these God is described in human terms. Even if the attributes could be explained as metaphors, there remained the implication that the realities the metaphors represented were coexistent with God for all eternity, seeming to suggest for many of the thinkers a belief in a plurality of divine beings. For the more thoroughgoing of the medieval thinkers, to ascribe attributes in any positive sense to God was to be guilty of idolatry.

Not all the medieval thinkers saw reason to qualify the older doctrine of attributes. Ḥasdai Crescas (1340–1410/11) refused to accept the notion that to say God is good or wise is to impose limits on his nature or to set up goodness and wisdom as rival deities. Maimonides (Mosheh ben Maimon, 1135/8–1204) and others, however, sensed the difficulties so keenly that they felt themselves obliged to develop the idea of negative attributes. For Maimonides, the attributes referring to God's essence (his unity, wisdom, and existence) are not to be understood as saying anything at all about God's true nature. All that they imply is the negation of their opposites. When God is said to exist, the meaning is that he is not a mere fiction. When he is said to be wise, the meaning is that there is neither ignorance nor folly in him. When it is said that he is one, the meaning is that there is neither plurality nor multiplicity in his being, although the actual nature of that being is beyond all human comprehension, and of it no human language can be used. For Maimonides, the knowledge of God is a constant process of negation. The finite mind can never hope to grasp the divine nature, but the more one knows of what God is not the closer one comes to such perception. Secondary attributes, on the other hand, such as goodness, justice, and mercy, may be used of God even in a positive sense, since these do not refer to his essence but to his activity. Maimonides gives the illustration of God's care for the embryo in the womb. If such care were possible for a human being, one would attribute it to that person's compassionate nature, and in this sense one is permitted to say that God is compassionate.

The qabbalists, in their doctrine of Ein Sof ("the limitless," God as he is in himself) and the *sefirot* (the powers by means of which the godhead becomes manifest), tread a middle road on the question of attributes. The qabbalists, more radical here than the philosophers, do not allow even negative attributes to be used. But for God as he is expressed in the realm of the *sefirot,* even the positive attributes of essence are in order. God can be described positively as existing, as one and as wise, provided it is realized that the reference is to his manifestation in the *sefirot.*

The question of the divine attributes receives little attention in modern Jewish thought, there being a marked tendency to see the whole subject as somewhat irrelevant to living faith.

SEE ALSO Folk Religion, article on Folk Judaism; God, articles on God in the Hebrew Scriptures, God in Postbiblical Judaism; Qabbalah; Shekhinah.

BIBLIOGRAPHY

For the rabbinic period the best treatment is still the section "The Attributes of God," in *The Old Rabbinic Doctrine of God* by Arthur Marmorstein (1927; reprint, New York, 1968), pp. 148–217. For the medieval period, the passages referred to in the index under "Attributes" should be consulted in *A History of Mediaeval Jewish Philosophy* by Isaac Husik (New York, 1916).

New Sources

Dan, Joseph. "The Book of the Divine Name by Rabbi Eleazar of Worms." *Frankfurter Judaistische Beiträge* 22 (1995): 27–60.

Gruenwald, Ithamar. "God the 'Stone-Rock': Myth, Idolatry, and Cultic Fetishism in Ancient Israel." *Journal of Religion* 76 (1996): 428–449.

Hoffman, Joshua, and Gary S. Rosenkrantz. *The Divine Attributes.* Oxford, 2002.

Manekin, Charles H. "Belief, Certainty, and Divine Attributes in the 'Guide of the Perplexed.'" *Maimonidean Studies* 1 (1990): 117–141.

Waldman, Nahum M. "Divine Names." *Jewish Bible Quarterly* 25 (1997): 162–168.

LOUIS JACOBS (1987)
Revised Bibliography

ATTRIBUTES OF GOD: CHRISTIAN CONCEPTS

In the tradition of Christian theology, an attribute of God is a perfection predicted of God in a formal, intrinsic, and necessary way as one of many defining characteristics. These perfections, first discovered as they are reflected in the created universe, are such that their objective concept can be disengaged from all their finite modes of realization, enabling them to be attributed to God as pure perfections within God. Such perfections are numerous and logically interconnected. One among them is given ontological priority as grounding all the others and is understood as the formal constituent of the divine nature; the others, derivative from it, are what are strictly called attributes. Historically, there have been many candidates for the former: goodness (Christian Platonism), being as act (Thomas Aquinas), infinity (Duns Scotus), radical intellection (John of Saint Thomas), omniperfection (nominalism), spirit as *Geist* (Hegel), radical liberty, love, and so forth.

The multiple formalities taken to be attributes are understood as characteristic of God in a way proper to himself, that is, one that transcends all finite modes in which any perfection is found realized in the cosmos. The formalities, as divine, remain unknowable in themselves. Thus, the "knowledge act" on which such predication is based is always analogical or symbolic in kind. This is clearest in the understanding that the many divine attributes are all really identical with divinity and so with each other, but that a formal distinguishing of them is demanded by the inadequacy of human thought in its finite mode of knowing God. Thus, the justice of God really is his mercy in the order of his own being, but both the formalities of justice and mercy are ascribed to him in the human finite order of knowing. The distinctions between the divine attributes, in other words, are distinctions of reason. It became customary to categorize these attributes in various ways, the most significant of which distinguishes entitative attributes from operative ones. The former characterized God in his very being (goodness, eternity, infinity, etc.); the latter characterize his necessary relationship to any world he might summon into being and are grasped by reason as the divine knowing and loving. These latter are attributes only insofar as they are necessarily in God. Thus, love is a divine attribute in that the Christian cannot conceive of God as nonloving, but the termination of that divine activity at this or that creaturely good is not an attribute but something freely chosen by God.

The doctrine concerning the divine attributes originated with the early Church Fathers and continued to develop, with its main architectonic lines unchanged, until the Enlightenment; it was not, for example, matter for dispute between the parties to the Reformation. Obviously, it is a theological construct rather than a direct matter of faith; that is to say, it is the product of reflection upon what God has revealed rather than the immediate content of that revelation. The self-revelation of God articulated in both Old and New Testaments (i.e., the Jewish and the Christian scriptures) is not any metaphysical account of God's essence and its defining characteristics, but a narrative of God's saving history with first Israel, and then, through Jesus Christ, with the world at large. Thus, the Bible offers no doctrine of divine attributes but rather an account of the attitudes God has freely chosen to adopt toward his creatures, his free decisions in the events of revelation and saving grace. In this light, the traditional teaching on the divine attributes assumes something of the character of a natural theology, in the sense that such teaching is neither revealed in a direct of formal way nor immediately derived from what is so revealed, but rather results from rational reflection upon a presupposed concept of what constitutes God's inmost nature. But the illation from characteristic activity to underlying nature or essence is a valid one logically, that is, the manner in which God freely chooses to relate to his creatures is disclosive of what constitutes his nature and attributers. Thus, there is a natural theology operative in the doctrine on the attributes, but it is not one which serves as a criterion for interpreting the Bible. Rather, the very converse is true: the New Testament confession of God as revealed in Jesus the Christ controls any subsequent determination of the attributes of God postulated theologically.

Inherent in the theism wherein the above understanding of the attributes is developed is a strong emphasis on God's transcendence of the world, without any denial of his simultaneous immanence therein. From the time of Hegel and Schleiermacher (in the mid-nineteenth century), emphasis begins to shift to the immanence of God. Classical theism is now confronted with a pantheistic notion of God (in which the world is God's unfolding of himself), or a panentheistic one (in which God and world, without being identical, are correlates each necessary to the other). Insofar as this movement gains momentum, it undercuts the traditional doctrine on the attributes by focusing not only on what constitutes God absolutely, but equally on what constitutes him relatively, that is, insofar as he is determined contingently by creatures. This approach has been adopted notably by process theology, which finds its inspiration in the thought of Alfred Whitehead and Charles Hartshorne. Here, "becoming," rather than "being," is the ultimate category, and God is only partially described in terms of absolute attributes he cannot lack (divine nature as primordial); the full description includes also God's limited but actual determination of his own nature in his action upon and reaction to the world (divine nature as consequent). Differing from this but sharing in some of its basic intuitions are various theologies following the modern stress upon subjectivity and self-consciousness. These tend to historicize the reality of God, viewing it more as event than as being: as the power of the future (Wolfhart Pannenberg), or the promise of a new future (Jürgen Moltmann). Here, the anthropomorphisms of the Old Testament especially are translated, not into a metaphysical scheme taken over from Greek rationalism, but into the categories of universal history. In such thought, the attributes of God are not done away with but are relativized historically—for example, God is no longer characterized as eternal but as infinitely temporal.

SEE ALSO God, articles on God in Postbiblical Christianity, God in the New Testament.

BIBLIOGRAPHY

The most thorough coverage available is in the series of articles under Dieu by various authors in vol. 4 of the *Dictionnaire de théologie catholique,* edited by Alfred Vacant and Eugène Mangenot (Paris, 1911). Another extensive study can be found in W. T. Davison's article "God, Biblical and Christian," in the *Encyclopaedia of Religion and Ethics,* edited by James Hastings, vol. 6 (Edinburgh, 1913). The biblical data are well covered in Karl Rahner's "Theos in the New Testament," in *Theological Investigations,* vol. 1 (Baltimore, 1961). For the thought of the Church Fathers, the best available single work is G. L. Prestige's *God in Patristic Thought* (1936; reprint, London, 1952). A contemporary defense of the classical teaching is to be found in H. P. Owen's *Concepts of Deity* (New York, 1971); a more critical treatment by Richard Swinburne is *The Coherence of Theism* (Oxford, 1977). An expanded treatment of the above article can be found in chapter 6 of my *Knowing the Unknown God* (New York, 1971). For the alternative to classical theism known as process thought, see Alfred North Whitehead's *Process and Reality* (New York, 1929), part 5, chap. 2, "God and the World."

New Sources

Boff, Leonardo. *Trinity and Society.* Translated by Paul Burns. Maryknoll, N.Y., 1988.

Carman, John Breasted. *Majesty and Meekness.* Grand Rapids, Mich., 1994.

Clark, Kelly James, ed. *Our Knowledge of God.* Dordrecht and Boston, 1992.

Gunton, Colin E. *Act and Being.* London, 2002.

Hughes, Gerard H. *The Nature of God.* New York, 1995.

Nnamani, Amuluche Gregory. *The Paradox of a Suffering God.* New York, 1995.

WILLIAM J. HILL (1987)
Revised Bibliography

ATTRIBUTES OF GOD: ISLAMIC CONCEPTS

The word *ṣifah* ("attribute"; pl., *ṣifāt*) is not found in the Qurʾān, but the verbal noun *wasf* does appear there one time (6:139) and the imperfect of the first form of the verb thirteen times in the sense of "to ascribe or uphold a description, to attribute, with the idea of falsehood." This meaning is associated with *Allāh* (God) in 6:100, 23:91, 37:159, 37:180, and 43:82; these verses seem to indicate that every description of God is bound to fail.

In order to avoid certain confusions, one must remember that the Arabic grammatical categories do not correspond to those of Western languages. Arab grammarians divided words (*kalimah;* pl., *kalām*) into three categories: the verb (*fiʿl*), the *ism,* and the particle (*ḥarf*). But the term *ism* does not cover the term *noun* in Western grammar. In fact, the word *ism* includes, among other things, the *maṣdar* (verbal noun), the present and past participles, and the "attribute" (*al-ṣifah al-mushabbahah*), which is the adjective or participle of adjectival value—a situation that could hardly fail to produce a certain variation in the use of the terms "attributes" and "divine names." To cite only one example, E. H. Palmer, in the introduction to his translation of the Qurʾān (*The Qurʾān Translated,* Oxford, 1900, p. lxvii), writes: "His attributes are expressed by ninety-nine epithets in the Qurʾān, which are single words, generally participial forms. . . . The attributes constitute the *asmāʾ al-ḥusnā,* the good names. . . ."

Theologians have worked hard to distinguish between the *ism* and the *ṣifah* by saying that the *ism* designates God insofar as he is qualified—for example, the Powerful or the Knowing—whereas the attribute is the entity in the essence of God that permits one to say that he is powerful or knowing—the Power, the Knowledge. In the course of the development of theology and following discussions among different schools, the *mutakallimūn* (scholastic theologians) refined the notion of the attribute by attempting to distinguish the various relations between the divine essence and the attributes. We shall encounter some of these distinctions below.

EARLY CREEDAL STATEMENTS. The first dogmatic creeds scarcely allude to the problem of the attributes. Historical conditions easily explain this absence: several years after the death of Muḥammad, the expansion of the new religion, with its political and social ramifications, led the heads of the community to express the essential traits of Islam and to condense them into a formula of faith easy to remember. Some of these formulas are found in the *ḥadīth* collections. Their common trait is the absence of any distinction between the ritual obligations and man's relationship to God. Little by little emerges the definition of the five pillars of Islam and then the formula of the Shahādah ("There is no god but God, and Muḥammad is the Messenger of God") by which the convert is integrated into the community. Already, in a way that was not philosophical but real, the unity of God was affirmed: God is one and he is unique. This was the point of departure for what would soon become the problem of the attributes in God.

Dissensions within the nascent Muslim community quickly gave rise to definite points of view, and those who did not accept them were anathematized. One of the first professions of faith, the eighth-century *Fiqh akbar I*, does not yet mention the unity of God, which is not questioned, nor for that matter does the *Waṣīyah* attributed to Abū Ḥanīfah (d. 767). However, with the *Fiqh akbar II*, the problem of the attributes begins; there one finds, in fact, affirmations such as these: God is one; he has no associates; nothing resembles him; God will be seen in heaven; God is "a thing" *(shay')*, without body, without substance, without accidents; God is the Creator before creating (art. 16); it is permissible to use Persian to designate the attributes of God except for the hand (art. 24); the proximity and distance of God are not material (art. 26); all the names of God are equal (art. 27); the Qur'ān is the word of God (art. 3).

EXTREMIST VIEWS: THE *ḤASHWĪYAH* AND THE *ḤANĀBILAH*. The *ḥashwīyah*, the all-too-strict traditionalists, take literally the anthropomorphic passages of the Qur'ān, refusing any interpretation and taking refuge in the mystery of God, in whom the apparent contradictions are resolved.

In one passage of al-Juwaynī (d. 1037), reported by Ibn Asākir (*Tabyīn*, Damascus, 1928–1929, pp. 149ff.; cf. Gardet and Anawati, 1948, pp. 58–59), the author indicates the respective positions of the *ḥashwīyah*, the Muʿtazilah, and the Ashʿariyah with regard to the principal points of doctrine. The *ḥashwīyah* sin through excess: for them the attributes of God are like human attributes. In heaven, God will be seen in the same way sensory things are seen; God is "infused" *(hulul)* in the throne, which is his place; the hand and the face of God are real attributes like hearing and life: the hand is an actual body part; the face is a face in human form; the descent of God to the nearest heaven is a real descent. The eternal Qur'ān is the uncreated word of God, eternal, unchangeable; the individual letters, the ink with which it has been written, are created.

These extreme positions are also those of Ibn Ḥanbal and his disciples. His most important *ʿaqīdah*, or creed (translated by Henri Laoust in *La profession de foi d'Ibn Baṭṭa*, Damascus, 1958, p. 88, and by Allard as cited below), numbers no fewer than twelve pages. The problem of the divine attributes, which is to say, the ensemble of questions concerning God himself, is dealt with toward the end of the dogmatic exposition before the refutation of heretics. Briefly recalling the traditional cosmology, Ibn Ḥanbal continues:

> The throne of the Merciful is above the water, and God is on his throne. His feet rest upon the stool. God knows all that exists in the seven heavens and the seven earths, as well as all that exists between them. . . . He knows what is under the earth and at the bottom of the seas. The growth of trees and that of hair is known to him, as is that of every seed and every plant; he knows the place where each leaf falls. He knows the number of words and the number of pebbles, the number of grains of sand and grains of dust. He knows the weight of the mountains; he knows the actions of human beings, their traces, their words, and their breaths; God knows everything. Nothing escapes him. God is on his throne high above the seventh heaven, behind the veils of lights, of shadows, of water, and of everything that he knows better than anyone. If an innovator or heretic relies upon the words of God such as: "We are nearer to him than the jugular vein" (50:16); "He is with you wherever you are" (57:4); "Three men conspire not secretly together, but he is the fourth of them, neither five men, but he is the sixth of them, neither fewer than that, neither more, but he is with them, wherever they may be" (58:7); or if he bases himself on similarly ambiguous verses, one must say to him: What that signifies is knowledge, for God is on the throne above the seventh heaven and his knowledge embraces everything. God is separate from his creation, but no place escapes his knowledge. The throne belongs to God, and the throne is supported by those who carry it. God is on the limitless throne. God is understanding without being able to doubt, seeing without being able to hesitate, knowing without being able not to know, generous without avarice, long-suffering without haste; he is mindful without forgetting; he is alert without negligence; he is near without anything escaping him; he is in movement, he speaks, he looks, he laughs, he rejoices, he loves and he detests, he displays ill-will and kindness; he becomes angry and he forgives; he impoverishes, gives or gives not. Every night he descends, in

the manner he wishes, to the nearest heaven. "Like him there is naught; he is the All-Hearing, the All-Seeing" (42:11). The hearts of humankind are between two fingers of the Merciful: he turns them over as he desires and engraves on them whatever he wants. He created Adam with his hands and in his image. On the day of resurrection, the heavens and the earth will be in his palm; He will put his feet in the fire and he will disappear, and then he will make the people of the fire come out with his hand. The people of Paradise will look at his face and see it; God will honor them; he will manifest himself to them and give them gifts. On the day of resurrection, humankind will draw near to him and he will be in charge of the reckoning of their actions; he will not confide that to anyone else. The Qur'ān is the word of God, that which he uttered; it is not created. He who claims that the Qur'ān is created is a Jahmī and an infidel. He who says that the Qur'ān is the word of God, but goes no further and does not say that it is uncreated, is of an opinion worse than the preceding one. He who claims that our pronunciation of the Qur'ān and our recitation are created, whereas the Qur'ān is the Word of God, is a Jahmī. And he who does not treat all of those people as infidels is like them. (Qādī Abū al-Husayn, *Ṭabaqāt al-ḥanābilah*, Cairo, 1952, vol. 1, p. 29; trans. Allard, 1965, pp. 99–100)

THE MU'TAZILAH. The first essential thesis of the Muʿtazilah concerns the unity of God and thus the problem of the attributes and their relationship with the essence of God. It is the most important thesis of their doctrine, for it is the source of the others and has served to characterize the Muʿtazilah themselves: *ahl al-ʿadl wa-al-tawḥīd* ("the partisans of justice and unity").

We have already seen that the Qur'ān contains verses describing God in an anthropomorphic manner (6:52, 7:52, 55:27). There are others that insist on the differences between God and all that is created: "Like him there is naught" (42:11, 6:103). The first generations, mostly fideists, had accepted both groups of verses, taking refuge, by way of reconciling them, in the mystery of God and refusing to give any explanations. Contrary to the "corporealists" "whose extreme views we have seen, they were content to say that God had a hand, ears, and face, but not like ours" (see al-Bājūrī, *Ḥāshi-yah... ʿalā Jawharat al-tawḥīd*, Cairo, 1934, p. 76, and the satirical verse of Zamakhsharī, the Muʿtazī).

The Muʿtazilah were radical: in their view, the *via remotionis*, or *tanzīh*, was to be applied in all of its rigor. The Qur'ān itself invites us to do so: in regard to God one must reject all that is created. The anthropomorphic verses? They will be "interpreted" symbolically; if necessary, they will be denied. Similarly, *ḥadīth* that go the wrong way will be rejected. It is necessary to maintain, at whatever cost, the absolute divine unity, strict monotheism. Against the anthropomorphisms of "the people of the *ḥadīth*" and the ʿAlids, they affirmed their agnosticism in regard to the nature of God (see their creed as reported by al-Ashʿarī in his *Maqālāt al-Islāmīyīn*, ed. Ritter, Istanbul, 1929, p. 155). Without going as far as the Jahmīyah, who completely denied the attributes of God, they affirmed that all these attributes were identical with the essence, that they had no real existence. Against the Dahrīyah (materialists), they affirmed a personal creator God.

Likewise, if God is absolutely spiritual, he cannot be seen by the senses; hence the negation of the "vision of God" in the future life, the *ru'yah* of the traditionalists (see al-Jurjānī, *Sharḥ al-Mawāqif*, Cairo, 1907, bk. 8, pp. 115ff.). The absolute transcendence of God in relation to the world leads them to distinguish rigorously between the preeternal *(qadīm)* and that which has begun to be *(muḥdath)* and makes them reject energetically all notion of *ḥulūl* (the infusion of the divine in the created).

The affirmation of a God distinct from the world poses the problem of the relations of God with this world. The Muʿtazilah ask themselves if God's knowledge of things precedes them in existence or is born with them; on the whole they conclude in favor of a "contingent" or "created" divine knowledge of free future things and of the possible in general (see al-Ashʿarī, *Maqālāt*, p. 222 and passim, and al-Khayyāt, *Kitāb al-intiṣār*, ed. Nyberg, Cairo, 1925, p. 126). They study the object, the limits of divine power; they analyze man's power over actions and affirm that he creates them by "generation" (*tawallud;* on which, see Aḥmad Amīn, *Duha*, vol. 3, p. 59; and Ibn Ḥazm, *Fiṣal*, vol. 5, Cairo, 1899/1900, p. 52).

Finally, always with the same concern to suppress every shadow of associationism, they affirmed the *created* character of the Qur'ān, the word of God. In the history of the Muʿtazilah, this thesis has drawn the greatest attention because of its political repercussions. The reasoning of the Muʿtazilah was very simple: God, identical with his attributes, admits of no change; it is thus impossible that the Qur'ān, the word of God in the sense of an attribute, is uncreated, for it is essentially multiple and temporal. The Muʿtazilah did not fail to find texts in the sacred book itself to support their thesis. They concluded that the Qur'ān is a "genre" of words, created by God; it is called "the word of God" because, contrary to our own words, the Qur'ān was created directly.

In his *Lawāmiʿ al-bayyināt fī al-asmā' wa-al-ṣifāt* (Cairo, 1914, pp. 24ff.), Fakhr al-Dīn al-Rāzī (d. 1209) expounds the different groupings of the attributes in accordance with the schools. He sets forth those of the Muʿtazilah in the following manner: For Abū Ḥashim, the attributes are "modes" *(aḥwāl)*, intermediate entities between the existent and the nonexistent. What ensures the reality of these modes is either (1) the divine essence, whether initially *(ibtidā'an)* or by the intermediary of other modes, for in all this it is a matter of essential attributes; or else it is (2) the *maʿānī* found in the divine essence, in which case it is a matter of entitative attributes or of qualification *(maʿnawīyah)*, such as *ʿālim* ("knowing") or *qādir* ("able"). As for operative attributes, they do not constitute a stable state *(ḥālah thābitah)* of the divine essence, nor of the *ma ʿānī*, but they are made up of the pure emanation of effects starting from God.

AL-ASHʿARĪ. It was left to Abū al-Ḥasan al-Ashʿarī (d. 935), a deserter from the Muʿtazilah, to give to it the hardest and one might say the most decisive blows. The doctrine he elaborated would become that of orthodox Islam itself.

A native of Basra, he was for forty years the disciple and then the collaborator of al-Jubbāʾī, the chief of the Muʿtazilah in that city, until one day, suddenly made aware of the dangers that the Muʿtazilah were bringing to Islam, he was "converted" to the true doctrine. He broke publicly with them and consecrated the rest of his life to the refutation of their doctrine.

But at the same time that he attacked his former companions, he took care to put himself in the good graces of the fervent traditionalists, the Ḥanbalī zealots. Their inquisitorial attitude was allied—among the most exalted of them, the *ḥashwīyah*—with a materialization of doctrine that did not fail to disquiet the intelligent believers. And it was precisely to fend off their misdeeds that al-Ashʿarī, upon arriving in Baghdad, decided to write his *Ibānah*, or "elucidation" of the principles of religion. In an apostolic *captatio benevolentiae,* he expressed his admiration for Ibn Ḥanbal out of a desire to show the latter's disciples that one could be a good Muslim without falling into the exaggerations of literalism.

What was al-Ashʿarī's method, and on what bases did this doctor, only yesterday a fervent Muʿtazī, ardent promoter of reasoning, construct his "defense of dogma"? First of all, regarding exegesis of the Qurʾān, he thrust aside the much too drastic *tanzīh* of the Muʿtazilah, which led to *ta ʿṭīl,* the total stripping away of the notion of God (*Ibānah,* Cairo, 1929/30, p. 46; Ibn Ḥazm, *Fiṣal,* vol. 2, pp. 122–126). He had in mind to keep himself within a literal interpretation of the text and thus clearly seems to present himself as a faithful disciple of Ibn Ḥanbal. One should not be too surprised that the creed opening the short treatise of the *Ibānah* explicitly refers to the severe *imām,* covering him with eulogies. This is a literalism peculiar to al-Ashʿarī, for the later Ashʿarīyah were to move away noticeably from the rigid literalism of their founder and thereby draw upon themselves the fire of an Ibn Ḥazm and of the Ḥanābilah themselves (Henri Laoust, *Essai sur . . . Takī-d-Dīn Aḥmad B. Taimiya,* pp. 81–82). Likewise, on the question of "the vision of God," on that of anthropomorphic expressions and attributes (*Ibānah,* p. 45), he entertains opinions that Ibn Ḥanbal would have subscribed to without fear.

That is the al-Ashʿarī of our direct sources, but there is another one: the figure whom his disciples have in mind. For al-Juwaynī (eleventh century), who would become al-Ghazālī's teacher, al-Ashʿarī is not a theologian who rallied to the opinions of Ibn Ḥanbal but a reconciler of two extreme positions. We have a clear testimony in the long extract from al-Juwaynī that Ibn ʿAsākir gives us in his *Tabyīn* (pp. 149ff.). The famous judge shows how his master, in the principal questions, has followed a middle way between the exaggerations of the Muʿtazilah and those of the *ḥashwīyah* who, in truth, were recruited among the Ḥanbalī extremists (see Gardet and Anawati, 1948, pp. 58–59).

Al-Ashʿarī was not the only one to fight the good fight for the triumph of traditional doctrine. One of his contemporaries, al-Māturīdī, propagated in the eastern provinces of the empire the ideas that the author of the *Ibānah* fought for in Baghdad. After epic struggles against the old conservatives on the one hand and the Muʿtazilah on the other, Ashʿarism ended up in triumph. It won its case definitively when the famous Seljuk minister Niẓām al-Mulk created chairs for the new theological doctrine in the schools he founded at Nishapur and Baghdad.

This triumph was marked by the successive development of doctrine; three names indicate the principal stages: the *qāḍī* al-Bāqillānī (d. 1013), al-Juwaynī (Imām al-Ḥaramayn, d. 1085), and finally al-Ghazālī (d. 1111).

AL-BĀQILLĀNĪ. Among al-Bāqillānī's numerous works, it is in his *Kitāb al-tamhīd* that we find the most information on the problem of the attributes and the divine names. He deals with it especially in the chapter on *tawḥīd,* written explicitly against the Muʿtazilah, "for they all affirm that God has no life, no knowledge, no power, no hearing, no vision" (ed. R. C. McCarthy, Beirut, 1957, p. 252).

At the beginning of his treatise, al-Bāqillānī speaks only of the active participles such as *ʿālim* ("knowing"), *qādir* ("able"), and *ḥayy* ("living"), whereas in the chapter on the attributes he seems to affirm that only the substantives employed in language about God designate attributes properly speaking.

In the chapter on the name and the named *(al-ism wa-al-musamma),* a distinction is made between the *names* of God, encompassing all the active participles, and the divine attributes, which are substantives characterizing the essence of God or his action. The attribute is of two sorts: that of essence or that of action. From the divine names one deduces logically the existence of the attributes. To what degree are they really existent in God? To respond in precise fashion to this question, he distinguishes two series of terms: *waṣf* ("description"), *ṣifah* ("attribute"), and *mawṣūf* ("described"), on the one hand, and *tasmiyah* ("nomination"), *ism* ("name"), and *musammā* ("named"), on the other. He defines the attribute *(ṣifah)* as "the thing found in the being described *[mawṣūf]* or belonging to it; that which makes this thing something acquired is the act of description *[waṣf],* which is the quality *[na ʿt]* deriving from the attribute *[ṣifah]*" (p. 213). Much later he will say: "The act of describing is the speech of the person who describes God or someone else as 'being,' 'knowing,' 'living,' 'able,' giving favor and kindness. This act of describing is speech that is heard and its expression; it is different from the attribute subsisting in God and the existence of which entails that God is knowing, able, willing" (p. 214).

In a parallel way al-Bāqillānī gives the following precise details: "The doctrine of the partisans of the truth is that the name *[ism]* is the named *[musammā]* itself, or an attribute tied to it, and that it is other than the fact of giving a name *[tasmiyah]*" (p. 227).

Thus, to explain the realism of the divine names and attributes, al-Bāqillānī distinguishes between the plane of language and that of reality. "Language affects the reality of the speaker, but the moment that speech [name or attribute] is uttered, it refers only to the one spoken of" (Allard). This distinction presupposes a theory of the divine origin of language that allows humans to enter into reality directly, as it is.

In the chapter dealing with name and denomination, al-Bāqillānī gives a classification of the names and attributes, which can be summarized as follows (p. 235, 5–15; Allard, 1965, p. 308):

1. Names that express the named—for example, "thing" *(shay')*, "existent" *(mawjūd)*;
2. Names that express that the named is different from the rest—for example, "other" *(ghayr)*, "different" *(khilāf)*;
3. Names that express an attribute of the named, an attribute that is the form, the composite; an attribute that is an exterior aspect; an attribute that is found in the being itself; an attribute that is an action of this being; an attribute that is not an action.

On the question of the anthropomorphism of the Qur'ān, al-Bāqillānī remains very close to al-Ash'arī: he affirms that God really has a face, and hands, that he is really on his throne. He refuses to interpret these expressions either in a realistic fashion (like the Ḥanābilah) or in an allegorical fashion (like the Mu'tazilah). Similarly, for the "vision of God" (pp. 266–279), al-Bāqillānī insists on God's transcendence: there is no possible explanation for the way that vision will take place any more than there is for the way that divine speech is to be understood.

AL-JUWAYNĪ. With al-Juwaynī a distinction among the divine attributes was made with reference to the notions of the necessary, the possible, and the impossible. In his treatise *Al-irshād*, which became a classic of *kalām*, after an introduction consecrated to the study of the character of reasoning and its nature, the author deals with *tawḥīd*: he proves the existence of God, in particular by the contingency of the world and *a novitate mundi;* then he establishes two large categories: (1) what exists necessarily in God—the attributes, and (2) what is possible—in which he deals with the visibility of God, the creation of human acts, justification and reprobation, prophetology, eschatology, and the imamate.

As regards the attributes, al-Ash'arī spoke of *bi-lā kayf* (lit., "without how"): affirmation of the existence of the attributes while refusing to ask about their mode *(kayf)* so as to safeguard, at one and the same time, the divine transcendence and the explicit assertions of the Qur'ān. Al-Juwaynī goes further: he divides the attributes into *nafsī* ("essential") and *ma'nawī* (of quality, or "entitative" [Allard]). The "essential" attribute is every positive attribute of the subject that resides in the subject so long as it lasts and that does not come from a cause. The qualitative attribute comes from a cause that exists in the subject (*Irshād*, ed. and trans. Jean Dominique Luciani, Paris, 1938, pp. 17–18; trans. p. 39). Next al-Juwaynī sets down the different attributes of God: existence, eternity, subsistence, dissimilarity to all things—in particular the absence of extent, hence the obligation to interpret allegorically those passages of the Qur'ān that presuppose extent.

Then al-Juwaynī affirms that God is not a substance *(jawhar)*, which implies extent, and thus he refutes the Christian doctrines on the Trinity. After that he shows the unicity of God by the argument of "the natural obstacle": if there were two gods, their wills could be discordant. Finally, the seventh chapter is dedicated to the qualitative attributes: God is powerful; he is willing, living, and so forth.

Contrary to most of the *mutakallimūn*, he preserves the system of the "modes" *(aḥwāl)*, which in his opinion resolves the rather delicate problem of the relations of the essence of God with the attributes, the mode being an attribute attached to an existing thing but which is qualified neither by existence nor by nonexistence (pp. 47–48/81–83).

To know the divine attributes we cannot but start with that which is known to us: the invisible can only be known by starting with the visible. The bonds that unite the two are of four kinds: the law of cause (to be knowledgeable in the visible world is a result of knowledge), the law of condition (to be knowledgeable presupposes that one is alive), the law of essence (the essence of the knowing person is to have knowledge), and finally the law of proof (the action of creating proves the existence of the Creator, p. 49/83–84).

AL-GHAZĀLĪ. Of the works of the great theologian al-Ghazālī, I shall confine myself here to only two: the *Iqtiṣād fī al-I'tiqād* (The just mean in belief) and *Al-maqṣad al-aqṣā: Sharḥ asmā' Allāh al-ḥusnā* (The further goal: Commentary on the most beautiful names of God).

In the first book, al-Ghazālī devotes the first four chapters to establishing the nature of *kalām*, its social function, its method, and the category of people it addresses. Then he divides the ensemble of the questions envisaged into four main parts, expressed precisely: since God is the object of *kalām*, one should first of all study him in his essence (first part), then in his attributes (second part); one then should consider God's action, that of his personal acts (third part) and those of his envoys (fourth part). The whole of the work may be summarized as follows:

Preliminaries. The nature of *kalām*; its importance; its methodology.

I. *The Divine Essence.* (1) God exists. (2) He is eternal. (3) He is permanent. (4) He is insubstantial. (5) He is incorporeal. (6) He in nonaccidental. (7) He is undefined. (8) He is not localized. (9) He is visible and knowable. (10) He is one.

II. *The Attributes of God.* (1) The attributes in themselves: life, knowledge, power, will, hearing, sight, speech. (2) The "status" of the attributes: (a) they are not the essence; (b) they are in the essence; (c) they are eternal; (d) the divine names.

III. *The Acts of God* (what God can or cannot do). (1) God can choose (is free) to impose no obligation on his creatures. (2) Or he can choose to impose on them what they cannot do. (3) God does nothing in vain. (4) He can make innocent animals suffer. (5) He can fail to reward one who obeys him. (6) The obligation of knowing God comes from revelation alone. (7) The sending of prophets is possible.

IV. *The Envoys of God.* (1) Muḥammad. (2) Eschatology (and faith). (3) The caliphate. (4) The sects.

The *Maqṣad al-aqṣā* is a small treatise numbering about a hundred pages in the Cairo edition (n. d.), on the attributes and the divine names. A long introduction contains an analysis of the nature of the name and its relations with the named, along with its meaning in reality and in the spirit. Al-Ghazālī distinguishes among the different categories of names—univocal, synonymous, equivocal—and shows how the pious man finds his happiness in this world in attempting to pattern his life on the "divine morality" expressed by the attributes and the names. In the second part, a more or less lengthy account is given to each of the ninety-nine names of God.

(For the development of the doctrine of the divine attributes and the place it occupies in the later theological treatises of al-Shahrastānī, al-Rāzī, al-Bayḍāwī, al-Ījī, al-Jurjānī, al-Sanūsī, and, for the contemporary period, al-Laqānī, al-Bājūrī, and Muḥammad ʿAbduh, see Gardet and Anawati, 1948, pp. 160–174.)

The Falāsifah. In the wake of Aristotelian and Neoplatonic philosophy, al-Fārābī (d. 950) and Ibn Sīnā (Avicenna; d. 1037) elaborated a metaphysical notion of God that attempted to return to the Qurʾanic data. For al-Fārābī as for Ibn Sīnā God is the necessary Being as such; in him essence and existence are identical; he is without cause and the cause of everything; he belongs to no genus nor to any species; he has no contrary in any respect; nothing resembles him. He is the Truth, the pure Good, the pure Intelligence; he is generous; he is life; he is blissful. He knows because he knows himself, and so forth.

But what becomes of the divine attributes in this conception, and what degree of reality do they have outside of the divine essence? In referring more or less explicitly to Aristotelian principles, al-Fārābī, and after him Ibn Sīnā, consider the attributes as properties of the essence, but expressed negatively. The principle is as follows: Certain terms, although applied to creatures, can also be applied to God, but only by taking into account the manner in which one would make the attribution. Insofar as they are applied to creatures, they are accidents of different kinds, but, applied to God, they should be considered properties expressing only action. Moreover, terms that, when applied to created things, are positive in both their form and signification, when applied to God have a negative sense while retaining their positive form. Al-Fārābī would say of the divine attributes, for example, that they fall into two groups: (1) those that designate what belongs to God by virtue of himself and (2) those that designate what has a relation to something else outside of him, that in fact designate an action. As examples of the latter, al-Fārābī mentions justice *(al-ʿadl)* and generosity *(al-jūd)*; as an example of the former, he would say that God is not wise through wisdom that he would have acquired by knowledge of something outside his essence, but rather it is in his own essence that he finds this knowledge. In other words, the nonrelational predicates, such as wisdom, are affirmed of God as if belonging to him in a negative sense: the qualities they express were not acquired from something external to his essence.

In the same manner, Ibn Sīnā explains that the attributes are properties that reveal not the essence of God, but only his existence. Even then they only reveal it in describing the actions of God or his dissimilarity to other things. So much so is this the case that even when the predicates are adjectives of positive form one must interpret them as signifying actions or negations.

One can understand that, under these conditions, al-Ghazālī had a good chance to show that the *falāsifah* (he had in mind al-Fārābī and Ibn Sīnā above all) were practically denying the reality of the distinction between the essence and the attributes; see his exposition of the doctrine of the *falāsifah* on this point and his criticism in *Tahāfut al-falāsifah (Incoherence of the Philosophers).*

With certain reservations, Ibn Rushd (Averroës) adopted Ibn Sīnā's position on the divine attributes and attempted to refute al-Ghazālī's attacks in his *Tahāfut al-tahāfut (The Incoherence of [al-Ghazālī's] Incoherence).*

In conclusion one may say that, from early times down to the present, the divine attributes and names have played an important role in Muslim piety among the educated and the common people alike. The faithful need to address themselves to God, to a living God, and they can only reach him through those descriptions that the Qurʾān has offered, precisely in order to make him accessible to those who invoke him. The Muslim prayer beads *(subḥah)* serve to remind those who hold them while reciting the "most beautiful names of God" that their creator is among them and that he is enveloping them in his protection and mercy. It is no exaggeration to say that the quintessence of Muslim piety finds its best sustenance in this fervent meditation on the attributes and the divine names.

See Also Ashʿariyah; Creeds, article on Islamic Creeds; Muʿtazilah.

BIBLIOGRAPHY

For the general development of Islamic theology, see Louis Gardet's and my *Introduction à la théologie musulmane* (1948; 2d ed., Paris, 1970); J. Windrow Sweetman's *Islam and Christian Theology*, 2 vols. (London, 1942–1947); Harry A. Wolfson's *The Philosophy of the Kalām* (Cambridge, Mass., 1976); and A. J. Wensinck's *The Muslim Creed* (1932; reprint, New York, 1965).

There are many studies on the divine attributes in Western languages. In my article "Un traité des Noms divins de Fakhr al-Dīn al-Rāzī, le *Lawāmi' al-bayyināt*," in *Arabic and Islamic Studies in Honor of H. A. R. Gibb*, edited by George Makdisi (Leiden, 1965), pp. 36–52, I discuss al-Rāzī's seminal work on the subject. For al-Ashʿarī's approach to the question of the attributes of God, Otto Pretzl's *Die frühislamische Attributenlehre* (Munich, 1940) is an important study based on al-Ashʿarī's *Maqālāt al-islāmīyīn*. Other works to be consulted include J. W. Redhouse's "The Most Comely Names," *Journal of the Royal Asiatic Society* 12 (1880): 1–69; Youakim Moubarac's "Les noms, titres et attributs de Dieu dans le Coran," *Le Muséon* 68 (1955): 93–135; Jacques Jomier's "Le nom divin 'al-Raḥmān' dans le Coran," in *Mélanges Louis Massignon* (Damascus, 1957), vol. 2, pp. 361–381; Denise Masson's *Le Coran et la révélation judéo-chrétienne*, 2 vols. (Paris, 1958), especially chapter 21, "Les attributs de Dieu," pp. 15–82; and Michel Allard's *Le problème des attributs divins dans la doctrine d'al-Ašʿari et de ses premiers grands disciples* (Beirut, 1965).

Abraham S. Halkin's "The Hashwiyya," *Journal of the American Oriental Society* 54 (1934): 1–28, is a useful introduction to the doctrines of that group. For more details on the Muʿtazilah, see Richard M. Frank's very technical study, *Beings and Their Attributes: The Teaching of the Basrian School of the Muʿtazila in the Classical Period* (Albany, N.Y., 1978). The doctrines of the *falāsifah* and al-Ghazālī's criticism of them are discussed in Harry A. Wolfson's "Avicenna, Algazali and Averroes on Divine Attributes," in *Homenaje a Millás-Villicrosa*, vol. 2 (Barcelona, 1956), pp. 545–571, and in Ibn Rushd's *Tahāfut al-tahāfut*, which has been translated by Simon van den Bergh as *The Incoherence of the Incoherence*, 2 vols. (Oxford, 1954). On Gnostic and mystical elaborations of the attributes of God, see A. E. Affifi's *The Mystical Philosophy of Muhyid Din Ibnul ʿArabī* (Cambridge, 1939), index 2, and Reynold A. Nicholson's *Studies in Islamic Mysticism* (1921; reprint, Cambridge, 1976), pp. 77–148.

GEORGES C. ANAWATI (1987)
Translated from French by Mary Ann Danner

ATUA. Across Polynesia the word *atua* (or its cognate form) is commonly interpreted as "god," "deity," "supernatural," or "spirit" entity. According to Torben Monberg (1966, p. 36) the *atua* were anthropomorphic (shaped like humans), anthroposocial (able to perceive what humans were doing and to communicate with them), and anthropopsychic (relations were conducted with them as though they had human ways of thinking). E. S. Craighill Handy (1927, p. 88) defined *atua* as personified concepts that embodied desires, needs, hopes, and dreads, or as individualized elements and forces observed in nature.

In some Polynesian groups (e.g., Tokelau, Samoa) a loose distinction is made between *atua* (gods) and *aitu* (spirits). Monberg (1966, p. 58) uses the term *aitu* to refer to lesser gods, while Raymond Firth (1970, pp. 66–69) uses the term *atua* to refer to all supernatural beings. A summary of usages of the word disguises the variations found between island groups. However, a summary can also give the range of meanings associated with this term. Generally, the term *atua* can refer to two major groups of entities: *atua* who have never been human, and those who once were human.

First among the group who were never human are the great creator gods of Polynesian origin stories. Sometimes these major *atua* are seen as sea gods (e.g., Tangaroa) or land gods (e.g., Tane). Under them come what could be called departmental gods—those that have control over the elements, the landscape, and human interactions, such as war or fertility. Both major and lesser deities can manifest beneficent or maleficent characteristics, although actively unpleasant spirits are often associated with specific places on the land. While these *atua* were never human, the chiefly lines of some Polynesian island groups are believed to have descended from them. There are few female *atua* in the Pacific pantheon—Hina, often associated with the moon, Pele of Hawai'ian volcanoes, and the *atua* Fafine (female goddess) of Tikopia—but the majority are male. Gender roles and relations on earth are often reflected in the heavens.

The second group, spirits that were once human, can be important dead ancestors whose significance on earth has been recognized in the supernatural realm and who may even be seen as lesser gods. All humans were believed to have *ora*, or "soul." At death this *ora* goes on to become either *atua* or *aitu*, a continuation of the life force in the spirit realm. These ancestral spirits may play no particular role in the relationship between the living and the dead, or they may feature in the rituals of their descendants, returning to collect the spirits of the newly dead and overseeing the welfare of the family to which they once belonged.

Records of traditional religious beliefs in Polynesia were often collected by the missionaries whose duty it was to extirpate these beliefs. The extent of their understanding varied in quality. Alternatively, accounts were also collected after the conversion of the Pacific to Christianity (Firth writing on Tikopia is an exception) and the stories of traditional gods have sometimes been fitted into a Christian understanding of a supreme god or a trinity. The oral traditions of each island group and their early ethnographies need to be studied carefully to discover the parameters of the term *atua*.

SEE ALSO Mana; Polynesian Religions, overview article; Taboo.

BIBLIOGRAPHY

Firth, Raymond. *Rank and Religion in Tikopia: A Study in Polynesian Paganism and Conversion to Christianity.* London, 1970.

Handy, E. S. Craighill. *Polynesian Religion.* Honolulu, 1927.

Monberg, Torben. *The Religion of Bellona Island: The Concepts of the Supernaturals.* Copenhagen, 1966.

Williamson, Robert W. *Religious and Cosmic Beliefs of Central Polynesia.* Cambridge, U.K., 1933.

JUDITH MACDONALD (2005)

ATUM was the creator god of Heliopolis, the sole progenitor and head of the ancient Egyptian pantheon according to one of the earliest Egyptian cosmogonies. Atum, "the all" or "the complete one," by spitting, vomiting, or masturbating produced Shu and Tefnut, "air" and "moisture," who in turn generated Geb and Nut, "earth" and "sky." This last chthonic pair produced Osiris and Seth, rivals for the rulership of the land, together with their consorts, Isis and Nephthys. Together these nine deities comprised the great Heliopolitan ennead, but probably the greatest function of this pantheon was to provide a genealogy for the Egyptian king, who was equated with Horus, the son of Isis. Horus had to avenge the slaying of his father, Osiris, by his uncle, Seth.

As early as the Old Kingdom (2686–2181 BCE) the sky god, Atum, had been assimilated to the sun god, Re. This new solar deity, Re-Atum, gained or regained a commanding position at the head of the Egyptian pantheon and contributed to some weakening in the myth of divine kingship by clearly subordinating the king to the god by the fifth dynasty. However, the Horus-king was accommodated to the new solar cult by being titled also "Son of Re." At some point the creator god, Atum, was subordinated to Ptah, at least by Memphite priests who described Atum's creation by Ptah as recorded on the Shabaka Stone.

The great temple of Heliopolis, one of the three largest in Egypt, has not survived, and very few finds have been made in its vicinity. The vast amount of religious literature whose origin was Heliopolitan was primarily solar-oriented and had Re as principal god, but the sources are from the fifth dynasty and later. In the solar religion Atum was retained as the old, setting sun, and Khepri was the young, rising sun, but Re was the bright noonday sun. It is probably impossible to estimate the earlier importance of Atum or of the later revivals that may have reawakened interest in this primordial god. The late *Contendings of Horus and Seth* presents Atum as one of the chief judges before whom most of the other senior deities testify on behalf of Horus, while Seth appears to have had the support of the supreme god Re.

BIBLIOGRAPHY

The two volumes of *Studien zum Gott Atum* (Hildesheim, 1978–1979), edited by Karol Mysliwiec as volumes 5 and 8 of the "Hildesheimer ägyptologische Beiträge," offer comprehensive coverage.

LEONARD H. LESKO (1987)

AUGUSTINE OF CANTERBURY (d. 604/5), leader of the first evangelistic mission to the Saxon peoples in southeastern England and first archbishop of Canterbury. Pope Gregory the Great (590–604) had conceived a mission to evangelize the Anglo-Saxons and in 596 chose Augustine, prior of Saint Andrew's monastery in Rome, to lead the expedition. With forty monks and letters of recommendation from Gregory addressed to Catholic leaders across Gaul, Augustine embarked. Within the year he reached the town now called Canterbury, which was the headquarters of the Saxon king Ethelbert (Æthelberht). Augustine was received with surprising hospitality, probably because Ethelbert had married a Christian, Bertha, the daughter of the Frankish king. Ethelbert gave Augustine lodging, land on which the mission could support itself, and freedom to preach and teach. Although Augustine and his men spoke only Latin and had to use interpreters, their message and manner of life were evidently winsome. Within a year several thousand people had requested baptism. Soon after, Augustine crossed the channel to Arles and was consecrated a bishop. Shortly after his return to Canterbury, he baptized Ethelbert, and this act set the stage for a wider Christian influence among the Saxons. In 601, Gregory appointed Augustine archbishop and sent additional helpers with instructions for him to establish his cathedral in the old Roman trade center to the northwest, called Londinium (London), and to appoint twelve suffragan bishops for the area. Augustine chose Canterbury as more feasible, but he did establish a bishop in London and one in Duro Brevis (modern-day Rochester), twenty-four miles west of Canterbury.

Far to the west of Canterbury existed another group of Christians among the Celtic people. According to optimistic instructions from the pope, "all the bishops of Britain" were to be under Augustine's care, a message that revealed Rome to be largely ignorant of the old Celtic church, which the Saxons had driven out of central England. Their church calendar, pastoral organization, and monastic procedures were different from those of Rome. In 604, Augustine arranged a meeting with some of its bishops and sought to harmonize the two groups' differences. The distinctions between the two, however, and the Celts' fear of the Saxons, formed a chasm that seemed unbridgeable. Although unable to unify the church in his day, Augustine contributed to the unity that would come sixty years later.

Limited also was the extent of Augustine's evangelization, but he did bring to Canterbury the Italian monastic tradition, as it was beginning to be modified by the rule of Benedict of Nursia. This monastic practice of daily rounds of worship, meditation, farm work, preaching, works of mercy, and operation of a school for the sons of the leading families of the area was to become an influential instrument in the conversion of England. Augustine died May 26, 604 or 605 and was buried in Canterbury. He left no writings and established only the three dioceses in the southeast, but he laid foundations for the christianization of Anglo-Saxon England.

Bibliography

A history written one hundred years after Augustine is the fundamental source: Bede's *Ecclesiastical History of the English People,* edited by Bertram Colgrave and R. A. B. Mynors (Oxford, 1969), bk. 1, chaps. 23–33. For the times of Augustine and a critical evaluation of the man, see Henry H. Howorth's *Saint Augustine of Canterbury* (London, 1913). Good for historical context and for a reply to accusations that Augustine was a mediocre leader is Margaret Deanesly's *Augustine of Canterbury* (London, 1964).

H. McKennie Goodpasture (1987)

AUGUSTINE OF HIPPO (354–430), Christian theologian and bishop. A creative genius of mystical piety and great philosophical acumen, Augustine wrought a theological-ecclesiological system in which biblical tradition and classical philosophy coalesced. Not only was his thought seminal for the development of Western Christianity, his moral values and personal piety remained norms for medieval and Reformation Europe.

Augustine's life spanned a crucial epoch in state and church. The late Roman Empire was disintegrating, and its collapse would devastate the public sense of political stability and continuity. The Christian church, having weathered persecution, moved into a period of doctrinal and ecclesiastical formation. Punic Africa had no small part in these political and religious affairs, and Augustine's self-proclaimed identity as "an African, writing for Africans. . . . living in Africa" (*Letters* 17.2) must not be overlooked. Indeed, the manner in which Augustine united, in his works and in his person, the various currents of his time has definitely marked Western culture.

Early Life. Augustine, known also as Aurelius Augustinus, was born in Tagaste (present-day Souk-Ahras, Algeria) to a pagan father, Patricius, and a Christian mother, Monica. Monica's influence on Augustine was tremendous. He was convinced that her prayers, piety, and relentless pursuit of his conversion were instrumental in bringing about his life-altering encounter with God. Monica forbade Augustine's receiving infant baptism, but he was given the rite of the cross on the forehead and cleansing salt on the lips.

After early study under local schoolmasters, Augustine was sent, at fifteen, to Madaurus to continue his education. There began a period of profligacy that was to continue when he went to Carthage for advanced study. In that city, he took a concubine and fathered a son, Adeodatus, meaning "gift of God," to whom Augustine referred as "child of my sin." In Carthage, Augustine's education centered primarily on his becoming a rhetorician and lawyer—a field in which he became highly proficient. In later years, according to Philip Schaff, he "enriched Latin literature with a store of beautiful, original, and pregnant proverbial sayings" (*History of the Christian Church,* vol. 3, Grand Rapids, 1950, p. 998).

At this time, Augustine became enamored of Manichaeism, a sect that emphasized an essential dualism of good and evil. Manichaean stress on the evil nature of flesh had far reaching influence on Augustine. The impact of the Manichaean view of sex in his later formulation of the concept of the basic sinfulness of humankind and the weakness of the flesh has not been fully recognized.

In 373, Augustine came upon Cicero's now lost *Hortensius.* This work "inflamed" Augustine with a love of philosophy that continued for a lifetime. Induced by Monica's incessant pleading, prayers, and vivid dreams, Augustine turned to the Christian scriptures, but was gravely disappointed. In comparison to "the stately prose of Cicero," the Bible seemed unworthy. He found sections of *Genesis* crude; he questioned the integrity of certain Old Testament figures. It was philosophy that captured his intellectual curiosity. He proceeded with study of Aristotle's book on the categories.

Augustine returned to Tagaste, where he began teaching rhetoric. Patricius had died, having embraced the Catholic Church at Monica's insistence. Monica refused her son entrance to her home because he had espoused Manichaeism. She continued to pray and was told by a bishop, "It cannot be that the son of these tears should be lost" (*Confessions* 3.12).

In 380, Augustine completed his first book, *De pulchro et apto* (Beauty and Proportion), a work on aesthetics no longer extant. At this time, he gathered about him a group of students who became his intimate friends. Among these were Alypius and Nebridius, who, like Augustine himself, would become priests and bishops in the African church.

Bitter sorrow at the death of a childhood friend prompted Augustine's return to Carthage. There he became interested in the Skeptics (the New Academy) and less enchanted with Manichaeism. A long anticipated dialogue with the celebrated Faustus, Manichaen bishop of Milevis, proved to be utterly disappointing to Augustine. Thus began his disillusionment with and gradual separation from the sect, which he increasingly detested and later acrimoniously attacked.

Unruly students in Carthage occasioned Augustine's decision to leave for Rome, but once there illness overtook him. Upon his recovery he began teaching rhetoric. The position of public orator opened in Milan—where the imperial court frequently resided, and with the aid of friends and associates he secured this important position.

In Milan, Augustine came to know the respected Ambrose (c. 339–397), the patrician bishop of Milan. The latter's skill as rhetorician was legendary, and it was professional interest that drew Augustine to him initially. Ambrose's allegorical interpretation of the Bible gave Augustine a new understanding and appreciation of scripture. Stoic ethics—in which Ambrose was an expert—likewise had lasting effect. Augustine was also fascinated by the use of music—chanting and hymns—in Ambrose's church.

Augustine was soon joined by Monica, several cousins, his brother, students, and his mistress and son. Thus surrounded by a congenial African phalanstery, Augustine and his associates were introduced to Plato via the teachings of Plotinus (205–270). Ambrose was well informed on Plotinus and quoted at length Plotinus's mystical interpretation of Platonic idealism. What clearly appealed most to Augustine was the possibility of combining Platonism with Christian cosmology. Augustine saw the Platonic conception of God—the One as the absolute, the all perfect, from whom emanates the nous (intelligence)—as a key to understanding the "God who was in Christ."

From this beginning Augustine delved deeper into Platonism, reading Plato in Latin translations. In Plato, Augustine found answers to questions on the origin and meaning of evil that had first drawn him to the sect of Mani. Later in his life, Augustine transformed Plato into a near-Christian, combining the Logos doctrine with Platonic idealism, the *Gospel of John* with the writings of Plotinus—in short, reconciling Greek wisdom with Hebrew-Christian faith. A Platonic metaphysics was the result: the absolute Good as center of all reality, transcending thought and concrete being.

Very likely in pursuit of greater wealth and higher position in the society of Milan, it was decided that Augustine's mistress be dismissed and a marriage with a Milanese heiress arranged. This separation was painful to Augustine, but, nonetheless, unable to restrain his sexual desires while waiting for his intended bride, he took another mistress. He was deeply tormented by these conflicts between his actions and ideals. He had been reading the Bible regularly, listening to Ambrose, and discussing with friends the lives of those converted by scriptures. The number who had subsequently realized the need for celibacy particularly struck him.

Events converged during August of 386. The stern ethical demands of Ambrose's preaching joined with Monica's unending pleading that Augustine become a Christian. These, along with an increasing sense of the Platonic idea of personal integrity, were linked with the message of the apostle Paul.

A crisis was at hand. "I was frantic, overcome by violent anger with myself for not accepting your will and entering into your covenant" (*Confessions* 8.8). Suddenly, as he stood in the garden, he heard the voice of a child chanting "Tolle lege" ("Take it and read"). Taking up the Bible, he read the first passage to strike his eye, *Romans* 13:13–14: "not in revelling and drunkenness, not in lust and wantoness, not in quarrels and rivalries. Rather, arm yourselves with the Lord, Jesus Christ; spend no more thought on nature and nature's appetites." Augustine underwent a dramatic conversion, a profound life-transforming experience wherein sexual, willful, and spiritual wrestling resulted in complete surrender to God.

AUGUSTINE THE CHRISTIAN. Marriage plans were dismissed, and Augustine now aimed to become a Christian philosopher. To that end he took his coterie of friends and students, together with Adeodatus and Monica, to Cassiciacum, a country estate north of Milan. Here he engaged in leisurely debate and writing. Works of this period, such as *De beata vita* (On the Happy Life) and *De ordine* (On Order), show Augustine's transition from philosophy toward theology.

In Milan at Easter of 387, along with Adeodatus and Alypius, Augustine was baptized by Ambrose. The decision was then made to go back to Africa, and the family journeyed to Ostia, planning to take a ship for Carthage. At Ostia, Augustine and Monica experienced in their discussions of eternal wisdom moments of towering mystical exaltation. Shortly thereafter, in Ostia, Monica died.

Returning to Rome, Augustine immersed himself in writing. His *De immortalitate animae* (On the Immortality of the Soul) and *De quantitate animae* (On the Greatness of the Soul) clearly reveal a philosopher who is incorporating a new biblically oriented theology into his understanding of the Christian faith.

Once more in his native Africa, Augustine established a lay retreat, a monastery, for philosophical contemplation, based at his small estate at Tagaste. He and his friends aimed to be servants of God. Here he composed *De vera religione* (On True Religion), which takes the Trinity as the foundation for true religion, a theme central to the majority of his works, and sees in Christianity the consummation of Plato's teaching.

At this time, Augustine had no thought of becoming a priest and carefully avoided those towns where priests were needed, but a chance visit to Hippo Regius (present-day Annaba, Algeria) in 391 resulted in his conscription. The aging bishop Valerius probably contrived the scene wherein Augustine was ordained under popular pressure. Such conscription and summary ordination were common in the African church at that time. Immediately after ordination, Augustine requested a leave of absence for intensive study of scripture. He increasingly became a man of the Bible.

Refreshed from his retreat, Augustine took up his duties as parish priest, using Paul as guide and ideal rationale for ministry. He found in Paul his theological mentor. Valerius granted permission for the establishment of a monastery, which became Augustine's seminary for the training of future priests and bishops. Valerius did more—in violation of tradition, which stipulated that when present the bishop always preached: he requested Augustine to deliver the sermon regularly. This practice became a lifelong responsibility, wherein Augustine established himself as master homiletician.

By 392, Augustine was writing to Jerome (c. 347–420) in Bethlehem, asking for Latin translations of Greek texts. After early difficulties with Greek, Augustine had made himself only somewhat proficient; he knew scant Hebrew. The same year he composed numerous biblical commentaries; on Psalms, on the Sermon on the Mount, and on the letters of Paul.

In an unprecedented move, Augustine convinced Valerius that the Catholic Church must bestir itself against

Manichaeans, pagans, and irreligionists of all sorts. In 393, the General Council of Africa assembled in Hippo. Augustine made his address, *De fide et symbolo* (On Faith and the Creed), a stirring call for catholic reform and evangelism. This was the beginning of regular councils in the African church, with Augustine as perennial lecturer.

Valerius, fearing that he might lose his priest to a vacant see, requested that Augustine be made his coadjutor, and Augustine was elevated to episcopacy in 395. Valerius died the following year, leaving Augustine to rule as sole bishop of Hippo.

Two years after becoming a bishop, Augustine, now forty-three, began his *Confessiones,* a treatise expressing gratitude to God in which he employed intimate autobiographical recollections. He wrote with complete candor, revealing to the world his agonizing struggle with himself, his sexual nature, his self-will, and his pride. In this his aim was to give God the glory for his redemption, to create a paean of praise and thanksgiving, rejoicing in the grace of a God who had stooped so low to save so fallen a sinner.

Simultaneously, the *Confessions* was a theological work in which Augustine presented his positions on the Incarnation and the Trinity. In the three concluding books he proffered a study on memory, time, and *Genesis,* weaving the work of the Holy Spirit into the act of creation. He developed in the *Confessions* the theological direction in which he continued to move, emphasizing divine predestination, personal religious experience through conscious conversion, and the direct relationship of the believer to God. Augustine's opus in praise of God, drawing on his spiritual journey, stands as a masterpiece in the world's devotional literature.

THEOLOGICAL CONTROVERSIES. Immediately after taking up his duties as priest in Hippo, Augustine lost no time in launching his attack on his mortal enemies, the Manichaeans. He denounced Manichaean cosmology, the view of humanity and humanity's sin, and especially the concept of God as having human attributes and anatomical features. The error that Augustine repudiated repeatedly was the attribution of evil to deity. The dualistic Manichaeans claimed that good and evil had their origin in two distinct deities. For Augustine, the one true God could not be blamed for the existence of evil.

In 392, Augustine engaged in public debate with the Manichaean bishop Fortunatus. Augustine, the consummate debater, so demolished Fortunatus that the Manichaean did not appear for the third day of the contest. Augustine followed up his victory with a scathing polemic, *Acta contra Fortunatum Manichaeum* (Against Fortunatus the Manichaean), which demonstrated his implacable attitude toward people and causes he thought heretical. He was soon the protagonist for the Catholic position.

Augustine's advocacy of consistent teachings in the church is exemplified by his contributions to ecclesiology. He defined the status and role of the bishop not only as administrator but as teacher, interpreter, and defender of pure doctrine. A bishop was responsible for determining orthodoxy, through use of the pronouncements of councils as well as scripture, and for eradicating heresy. At no point does this issue come into clearer focus than in Augustine's protracted and painful conflict with the Donatists.

Donatism provoked a major schism, almost exclusively affecting the African church, dividing it into warring camps. The Donatists accused the Catholics of having a blemished priesthood and thus no true sacraments. Against this view, Augustine lucidly argued that the efficacy of the sacraments does not depend upon the worthiness of the priest. "My origin is Christ, my root is Christ, my head is Christ," he claimed. "The seed of which I was born, is the word of God . . . I believe not in the minister by whom I was baptized, but in Christ, who alone justifies the sinner and can forgive guilt" (*Against Petilianus* 1.1.7).

Augustine repudiated Donatist insistence that if Catholics were to join the Donatist church they must be rebaptized. It was the universal church that Augustine proclaimed, and baptism does not profit the recipient unless the sinner returns to the true fold. The *esse* (being) of the church is not found in the personal character of the several Christians in it but in the union of the whole church with Christ. The church is not made up of saints as the Donatists held but of a mixed body of saints and more or less repentant sinners. Augustine insisted that weak members must be patiently borne by the church—as in the parable of the wheat and tares. How can there be a full separation of saints and sinners prior to the final judgment?

After two major colloquies in which Augustine led the attack, stringent imperial laws were enacted against the Donatists, banishing their clergy from the country. In 415, they were forbidden to hold religious assemblies on pain of death. Augustine advocated and applauded the use of imperial force to bring such heretics under control.

In his early work *De libero arbitrio* (On Free Will), written between 388 and 396, Augustine endeavored to explain the apparent contradiction of the existence of evil in the world with the goodness of an omnipotent deity. Evil, Augustine assayed, was the result of Adam's free will. God would not permit humans to be completely free without giving them the potentiality of doing wrong or right. From Adam's sin all later humanity inherited the inclination toward evil, thus, all humans since Adam have been sinners. Only God's grace could overcome that propensity. No number of good works chosen freely by latter-day men and women could atone for so grievous a fall. God proffered salvation to those he deigns to give grace, knowing that many would refuse it. For humankind, the possibility of eternal damnation was the price of moral freedom. Divine foreknowledge does not obliterate human freedom. God simply foresees the choice that free moral agents will make.

It was the brilliant Celtic monk Pelagius (d. 418) who confronted Augustine with the fundamental issue of the nature of humankind. Shocked by the gross immorality of culture, Pelagius called for a righteous responsibility on the part of Christian believers. He soon had an enthusiastic following. The Pelagian view was later advocated by Julian, bishop of Eclanum, who became the chief theological adversary of Augustine's later years. Against this school Augustine directed his anti-Pelagian writings, a corpus of some fifteen works. The controversy with Pelagianism occasioned extended debate on questions of human freedom, responsibility, and humanity's relation to God.

Pelagius claimed that what one does, "either laudable or blameworthy," depends upon the individual. Human nature has the inherent capacity for achievement. Augustine, in *De Spiritu et littera (On the Spirit and the Letter)* and later in *De natura et gratia* (On Nature and Grace), insisted that grace alone enables fallen humanity to achieve anything worthy. Freedom is linked with God's grace, not humanity's nature.

God is not, however, in any sense responsible for sin, nor does obedience to God's will nullify human freedom. In *De gratia et libero arbitrio* (On Grace and Free Will) Augustine asserts, "No man . . . when he sins, can in his heart blame God for it, but every man must impute the fault to himself. . . . Nor does it detract from man's own freedom of will when he performs any act in accordance with the will of God" (part 4).

In *De praedestinatione sanctorum* (On the Predestination of the Saints) and *De dono perseverantiae* (On the Gift of Perseverance), Augustine presents grace as independent of human desert. It is a sacred mystery why some are chosen for eternal life and others for eternal death. The mystery of faith and righteousness is hidden in God's eternal wisdom and purpose (a position John Calvin would elaborate in the sixteenth century).

"Know," said Augustine in *Contra Julianum,* "that good will, that good works, without the grace of God . . . can be granted to no one." How much of this position on grace reflects Augustine's personal experience of God's saving power? Augustine had attempted to save himself, through elevated wrestlings with philosophy, and found it could not be done. Humanity cannot save itself. Salvation is God's doing. In gratitude the believer lives. The mind as God's creation is endowed with a natural capacity for remembering, understanding, and willing. When these powers are rightly directed, the self will recognize the true order of being, its relation to God in whose image it is. In the human fallen condition, sin holds this natural capacity in abeyance but can never completely destroy it. Grace awakens the dormant power in humans to see God's image in themselves.

In his discussion of grace, Augustine frequently employed the symbol of the infant—a child in constant need of a parental deity. Pelagius scoffed at such notions; for him, son, warrior, and mature adult were suitable emblems of the person in his relationship to God. Pelagius insisted, "Since perfection is possible for man, it is obligatory"; human nature was created for perfection, and humanity is competent to achieve it. Augustine repeatedly assailed this theme which, for him, struck at the heart of the Christian gospel. Augustine's numerous anti-Pelagian writings testify to the unalterable position that man cannot redeem himself; man cannot depend upon himself for goodness. Whatever virtue exists in human nature is a gift from God.

It is interesting to note that Pelagius and Augustine never met face to face. In 410 Pelagius went to Hippo, hoping to meet Augustine. Indeed, Pelagius had written in advance, but received a cautious reply. When the visit took place, Augustine was conveniently absent. Augustine finally achieved the condemnation of Pelagius and Pelagianism in 431 at the Council of Ephesus.

The sacraments. Attendant to Augustine's view of grace is his concept of the church: the earthen vessel for sacramental grace. For him, the Catholic Church represents, exclusively, the genuine infusion of love by the Holy Spirit. Sacraments are the work of God, and only in the Catholic Church do the sacraments attain their appropriate function; there alone can that attesting love be found.

Sacraments are visible signs representing invisible spiritual reality, outward symbols by which divine matters are exhibited. Communication of the invisible divine reality, of invisible divine power, takes place in the sacraments. The outward symbol, however, has no power to convey to the individual the divine reality unless that person's inner being is sensitive to communion with God. To that end God's grace will assist.

Augustine's list of sacraments holds baptism and the Lord's Supper as preeminent; others are ordination, marriage, exorcism, and the giving of salt to the catechumen. Without the sacraments there is no salvation. "The churches of Christ maintain it to be an inherent principle, that without baptism and partaking of the Supper of the Lord it is impossible for any man to attain either to the kingdom of God or to salvation and everlasting life" (*De peccatorum meritis et remissione;* On the Wages and Remission of Sins 1.34).

Trinity and Christology. Recognized even during his lifetime as a doctor of the Latin church, Augustine clarified numerous points of doctrine. In fact, he established doctrine, not the least of which was his interpretation of the triune deity. "I am compelled to pick my way through a hard and obscure subject," he noted as he embarked on his *De Trinitate* (On the Trinity), an opus written over a period of twenty years (399–419). Primarily in answer to the Arians, Augustine sorted out points at issue that would later become key factors in discussion at the Council of Chalcedon in 451. While *On the Trinity* is unquestionably a definitive work in Christian theology, Augustine's basic suppositions are made lucid in earlier writings, including his letters and sermons. To Nebridius he wrote, "Whatever is done by the Trinity must be regarded as being done by the Father and by the Son and by the Holy Spirit together" (letter 10).

In his view of the Trinity, Augustine emphasized that there are not three Gods but one. These form a "divine unity of one and the same substance in an indivisible equality." In this Trinity "what is said of each is also said of all, on account of the indivisible working of the one and same substance" (*Trinity* 1.4.7, 1.12.25). He established a metaphysical ground for the Christian's threefold experience of God. In the Father, the believer knows God as source of being; in Christ, the redeemer; and in the Holy Spirit, the sanctifier.

Revelation was Augustine's starting point. The first part of *On the Trinity* considers the nature of faith. Citing scripture (especially passages falsely interpreted by the Arians—for example, *John* 14:28, *John* 10:30, *Mark* 13:32), he proves the deity of the Son and his relation to the Father. Augustine argues at length that the Son is in no way subordinate to the Father. Previously, Tertullian and Origen had insisted on subordination of the Son and Holy Spirit to the Father. For Augustine, there "is so great an equality in that Trinity that not only the Father is not greater than the Son, as regards divinity, but neither are the Father and the Son greater than the Holy Spirit" (*Trinity* 8). The Holy Spirit proceeds from Father and Son and enjoys the same essential nature. Relations between the persons of the Trinity are not of degree or order but of causality. The Father is "the beginning of the whole divinity. . . . He therefore who proceeds from the Father and the Son is referred back to Him from whom the Son was born." The Holy Spirit is the unifying principle in the godhead, "a certain unutterable communion of Father and Son." Every theophany is thus a work of the three, even though in such divine manifestations the appearance is frequently that of only one of the persons. This is because of the limitations of the "bodily creature" necessary for a theophany. One cannot repeat the words Father, Son, Holy Spirit simultaneously and without an interval. Accordingly "both each are in each, and all in each, and each in all, and all in all, and all are one."

When speaking of the Trinity, Augustine's Latin term for what the Greeks called *hupostasis* is *persona* ("person"), but he frankly admits the inadequacy of any appellation. Ultimately the key to knowing God—the Trinity—is love, for love itself implies a trinity "he that loves, and that which is loved, and love itself" (*Trinity* 8.10.14). In the final analysis, Augustine himself, after years of contemplation, admits that the human mind may behold the Trinity "only in an enigma." Only when liberated from the restrictions of physical being will humans be able to comprehend completely "why the Holy Spirit is not the Son, although He proceeds from the Father" (*Trinity* 15.24.45).

Augustine declared that the whole of doctrine might be summed up as service to God through faith, hope, and love. This principle underlies his work the *Enchiridion.* Taking the Lord's Prayer as starting point, he develops the theme of Christ as mediator and considers the Incarnation as manifestation of God's saving grace. He explicates the Apostles' Creed and with rare sensitivity assesses the resurrection.

PHILOSOPHY OF HISTORY. On August 24, 410, Alaric invaded Rome. Son of a great Visigoth family, Alaric regarded himself a defender of the empire and a faithful Christian. His sack of Rome lasted only three days, and the city was by no means destroyed, nor was it the end of the Western Empire. The psychological effect, however, was horrendous. "If Rome can perish, what can be safe?" lamented Jerome. Decisiveness and dependability in government were in serious question. It was in response to the charge that abandonment of the ancient Roman deities and widespread acceptance of Christianity had brought about the fall that Augustine, in 413–427, produced *De civitate Dei* (City of God). His immediate assertion was that rather than bringing down the city the Christians had saved it from total ruin. The work proceeds to render his brilliant critique of Greco-Roman culture, drawing illustrative material from the greatest historians and writers. Augustine had enormous respect for and loyalty to that culture yet he believed it to be morally rotten, and he goes to considerable lengths to point out degradation of Roman standards of conduct, life patterns, and sexual behavior. He pictures gross licentiousness and obscenities pertaining to Liber and other deities. By contrast, he depicts the health, vigor, and cleanliness of the Christian life. Thus, as the Pax Romana deteriorated, Augustine became spokesman for a new, fresh, Christian social order.

MORALITY AND ETHICS. *City of God* best illustrates a facet of Augustine seldom recognized: he was a moral rigorist who permitted nothing to stand in the way of either individual or group righteousness. Neither personal relationships nor individual aspirations should be permitted to thwart the doing of God's will. Sinful pleasures were intolerable. It was in part reaction to his profligate past that prompted the complete turnabout in which he became the seer of an ethical, morally upright deity.

Scrupulous observance of the ethical code was required of Augustine's people, especially his clergy. On one occasion, certain members of Augustine's monastery had not complied with the vow of poverty and at death willed large estates to their families. Augustine reacted swiftly and sternly, requiring that all draw up statements of their holdings prior to being admitted to the order. In his monastery, Augustine established a way of life that was to become the prototype for the cenobite. It is claimed that his own widowed sister, abbess of the convent he established in Hippo, was never permitted to converse with her brother save in the presence of a third party. Augustine's moralism must be seen in the context of his ideal of blessedness. It was said of him, "Everyone who lives with him, lives the life described in the *Acts of the Apostles*" (sermon 356).

FINAL YEARS. On September 26, 426, Augustine named his successor, Eraclius, and arranged for the latter to assume responsibility for the practical affairs of the diocese. At that time Bishop Possidius agreed to write a biography of Augustine. His biography captures the spirit of the man Augustine. He tells of daily life in the monastery, stressing the simplicity of the monks' lives, and of Augustine's concern for the poor. Augustine the eminent theologian is barely visible.

May of 429 saw the army of Genseric's Vandals cross from Spain and march through Mauritania, spreading havoc and desolation. Roman rule in Africa collapsed. Augustine spent these concluding years comforting and reassuring his people. *On the Predestination of the Saints* and *On the Gift of Perseverance,* written 428–429, reflect the message that God alone would provide faith and courage for his elect. This became a doctrine of survival.

In 426 Augustine began to correct and catalog his vast literary output in his *Retractiones.* His wish, and that of his fellow bishops, was that whatever befell Hippo, Augustine's library was to be preserved. Fortunately for posterity, it was.

As Vandals were besieging Hippo, Augustine was dying, insisting—perhaps for the first time—that he be alone; he read, in these final hours, the penitential psalms hung on the walls of his room. On August 28, 430, while prayers were being offered in the churches of Hippo, Augustine died. It was designated his day in the lexicon of Roman Catholic saints.

Augustine's place in Western history is not to be contested. He was a man of science (in spite of his deprecation of scientific knowledge) whose power to scrutinize nature was remarkable. He engaged in an unrelenting quest for knowledge that rendered him a keen observer of human nature, and he probed the deep recesses of the human soul. Augustine set the compass for much of the Western Christian culture that followed. His interpretation of Plato dominated most of Christian thought in the West until the rediscovery of Aristotle in the thirteenth century. Humanists of the Renaissance relied upon Augustine. His impress on Reformation leaders is great. Luther followed his conception of grace. A reading of Calvin's *Institutes of the Christian Religion* reveals that second to the Bible, Augustine is the most frequently quoted source. In the eighteenth century, John Wesley studied Augustine diligently, even when he came to differ strongly with him. Indeed, even those who most heartily reject Augustine's anthropology have found it necessary to come to terms with him. Pietistic, sentimental studies of Augustine during the nineteenth and early twentieth centuries are being replaced with frank appreciation not only for his intellectual and spiritual preeminence but also for his profound human qualities.

SEE ALSO Arianism; Autobiography; Donatism; Free Will and Predestination, article on Christian Concepts; Grace; Manichaeism; Merit, article on Christian Concepts; Neoplatonism; Pelagianism; Pelagius; Plotinus; Skeptics and Skepticism.

BIBLIOGRAPHY

Listing all the worthy studies of Augustine would be difficult, if not impossible. The student of Augustine is apt to be overcome by the sheer enormity of the material available. Only a small selection follows.

Works by Augustine

For the serious student, the Latin works are indispensable. A complete collection appears in *Patrologia Latina,* edited by J.-P. Migne, vols. 32–47 (Paris, 1841–1842). In spite of errors and omissions, Migne's edition remains an essential source, but it should be studied along with Palémon Glorieux's *Pour revaloriser Migne: Tables rectificatives* (Lille, 1952). Augustine's collected works can also be found in *Corpus Scriptorum Ecclesiasticorum Latinorum,* vols. 12, 25, 28, 33–34, 36, 40–44, 51–53, 57–58, 60, 63, 74, 77, and 84–85 (Vienna, 1866–1876), which is the product of good critical scholarship.

Splendid translations into modern English, reflecting superior contemporary scholarship, can be found in "The Library of Christian Classics," edited by John Baillie and others, vols. 6–8 (Philadelphia, 1953–1958); "The Fathers of the Church," edited by Roy Joseph Deferrari, vols. 1–15, 17–18, and 35 (New York, 1947–1963); and "Ancient Christian Writers," edited by Johannes Quasten and Walter J. Burghardt, vols. 2, 9, 15, 22, and 35 (Westminster, Md., 1960–). The several texts are strengthened in their overall usefulness by an impressive amount of supportive background data, copious explanatory notes, full bibliographies, and indexes.

Works about Augustine

Classic works by eminent scholars such as Prosper Alfaric, Adolf von Harnack, and Otto Scheel continue to be mandatory reading for the thoughtful student. Among the most recent publications, Karl Adam's *Die geistige Entwicklung des heiligen Augustinus* (Augsburg, 1931) is a superb work with bibliographical references that are especially helpful. *A Companion to the Study of St. Augustine,* edited by Roy W. Battenhouse (New York, 1955), presents a series of scholarly essays, especially helpful as broad, introductory works. Gerald Bonner's *St. Augustine of Hippo: Life and Controversies* (London, 1963) provides a survey of the enormous literary output of Augustine.

Possidius's fifth-century *Sancti Augustini vita scripta a Possidio episcopo* (Kiel, 1832) is the original biography by one who stood in awe of his subject. Filled with human interest stories, it nonetheless should not be missed. Peter Brown's *Augustine of Hippo* (London, 1967) is unquestionably the best biography available. His *Religion and Society in the Age of Saint Augustine* (London, 1972) is of equally fine scholarship and is indispensable for an understanding of the period. My own *Augustine: His Life and Thought* (Atlanta, 1980) is a lively biography, portraying Augustine against the backdrop of the tumultuous age in which he lived. Frederik van der Meer's *Augustine the Bishop* (London, 1961) is an interpretation of Augustine's episcopate and the cultural milieu.

Étienne Gilson's *The Christian Philosophy of Saint Augustine* (New York, 1960) is an outstanding study of the overall thought of Augustine. A wide range of scholarly articles can be found in *Augustine: A Collection of Critical Essays,* edited by Robert A. Markus (Garden City, N. Y., 1972). Ragnar Holte's *Béatitudes et sagesse: S. Augustin et le problème de la fin de l'homme dans la philosophie ancienne* (Paris, 1962) concentrates on Augustine as philosopher. John Burnaby's *Amor Dei: A Study of the Religion of St. Augustine* (London, 1938) is outstanding, especially in interpreting Augustine's theological understanding of love. Pierre Courcelle's *Recherches sur les Confes-*

siones de S. Augustin (Paris, 1950) provides one of the best interpretations of the *Confessions.*

Henri Irénée Marrou's *St. Augustine and His Influence through the Ages* (New York, 1957), Karl Jaspers's *Plato and Augustine* (New York, 1962), and Eugene TeSelle's *Augustine the Theologian* (New York, 1970) are excellent studies of various aspects of Augustine's philosophy and theology. Robert Meagher's *An Introduction to Augustine* (New York, 1978) provides new translations of important passages that are clues to fresh interpretations of Augustine's spiritual life.

Finally, Tarsicius J. van Bavel's *Répertoire bibliographique de Saint Augustin, 1950–1960* (Steenbrugis, Netherlands, 1963) is a useful survey of recent critical studies.

WARREN THOMAS SMITH (1987)

AUGUSTUS (63 BCE–14 CE), Roman emperor. Born Gaius Octavius, he was the grandnephew of Julius Caesar. Adopted by Caesar, and made his chief heir at nineteen, Octavius built upon Caesar's name, charisma, military success, political connections, and fortune. Calculating, opportunistic, an unfailingly shrewd judge of men and circumstances, he emerged in 31 BCE from thirteen years of political chaos and civil war triumphant over Mark Antony and sole master of the Roman world.

Exhausted by the effects of civil war and seeking only peace and a return of order and prosperity, Roman citizens and provincial subjects alike hailed Octavius as a savior sent by divine Providence. He did not fall short of their expectations. To mark the beginning of a new order, he assumed the name *Augustus* in 27 BCE. In a series of gradual steps, he restructured the Roman political system. While preserving the forms of republican government, he in effect established a monarchy, concentrating in his own hands all real power, political, military, financial, and legal. This power was used with great and enduring success to reform the administration of the provinces, the finances of the Roman state, and every aspect of military and civil life. In so doing he laid the basis for two centuries of unparalleled peace and prosperity in western Europe and throughout the Mediterranean world. The golden age of Rome's empire, "the period in the history of the world during which the condition of the human race was most happy and prosperous" (Gibbon), was the supreme legacy of Augustus.

Himself deeply pious, Augustus understood fully the important role that religion plays in securing that unity of shared belief that is essential to the integration and successful functioning of a pluralistic society. Through carefully orchestrated and highly effective propaganda techniques, he projected the image of himself as a divinely sent savior; and the very name he assumed, *Augustus,* evoked in Latin and in its Greek form, *Sebastos,* an aura of divine consecration and charismatic authority.

Augustus undertook a thorough reform of Roman state religion. He restored some eighty-two temples that had fallen into decay and built numerous new ones. He revitalized old cult forms and priesthoods, such as the *lares compitales* and the Fratres Arvales, and instituted new ones, such as Pax Augusta and the Seviri Augustales. He carefully steered public approval of his person and policies into religious channels. Particularly in the Greek provinces of the East, he permitted himself to be worshiped as a god. Roman state cult celebrated the divine element and creative force that resided in Augustus through the cult of the Genius Augusti. Religious reform and innovation were linked to programs of social and moral reform, aimed at restoring traditional Roman values of service and piety toward country, family, and the gods.

The Augustan program tapped the wellsprings of popular piety in an age of religious revival. It mobilized in its service literary and artistic talent of enduring genius: Vergil's *Aeneid,* Horace's *Roman Odes* and *Carmen saeculare,* Livy's history of Rome, and the iconography of the Altar of Augustan Peace (the Ara Pacis) at Rome all celebrated, each in its own medium, the message that the gods themselves had willed the peace-bringing and benevolent rule of Rome and Augustus over the entire human race.

BIBLIOGRAPHY

The best-balanced introduction to Augustus and his achievement is H. H. Scullard's study *From the Gracchi to Nero,* 5th ed. (London, 1983), which includes extensive bibliographical notes. Recent but somewhat superficial accounts of Roman religion in the age of Augustus include *Continuity and Change in Roman Religion,* by J. H. W. G. Liebeschuetz (Oxford, 1979), pp. 55–100, and *Religion and Statecraft among the Romans,* by Alan Wardman (London, 1982), pp. 63–79. For interpretative studies of Augustus's religious policy within the context of traditional Roman religion, see my *Princeps a Diis Electus: The Divine Election of the Emperor as a Political Concept at Rome* (Rome, 1977), pp. 121–130, 189–219, and my following contributions to *Aufstieg und Niedergang der römischen Welt,* vol. 2.17.2, (Berlin and New York, 1981): "The Cult of Jupiter and Roman Imperial Ideology," pp. 56–69; "The Theology of Victory at Rome," pp. 804–825; and "The Cult of Virtues and Roman Imperial Ideology," pp. 884–889.

New Sources

Alföldi, Andreas. "From the Aion Plutonios of the Ptolemies to the Saeculum Frugiferum of the Roman Emperors (Redeunt Saturnia regna VI)." In *Greece and the Eastern Mediterranean in Ancient History and Prehistory. Studies Presented to Fritz Schachermeyer on the Occasion of his Eightieth Birthday,* edited by K. H. Kinzl, pp. 1–30. Berlin, 1977.

Binder, Gerhard. *Saeculum Augustum,* vol. 2, *Religion und Literatur.* Darmstadt, 1988.

Bleicken, Jochen. *Augustus.* Berlin, 1998.

Bowersock, Glen W. "The Pontificate of Augustus." In *Between Republic and Empire: Interpretations of Augustus and His Principate,* edited by Kurt A. Raaflaub and Mark Toher, pp. 380–394. Berkeley, 1990.

Cotton, Hannah M., and Alexander Yakobson. "Arcanum imperii: The Powers of Augustus." In *Philosophy and Power in the Graeco-Roman World. Essays in Honour of Miriam Griffin*, edited by Gillian Clark and Tessa Rajak, pp. 193–209. Oxford, 1992.

Eck, Werner. *Augustus und seine Zeit.* Munich, 1998.

Fishwick, Duncan. "On the Temple of Divus Augustus." *Phoenix* 46 (1992): 232–255.

Huttner, Ulrich. "Hercules und Augustus." *Chiron* 27 (1997): 369–391.

Pollini, John. "Man or God: Divine Assimilation and Imitation in the Late Republic and Early Principate." In *Between Republic and Empire: Interpretations of Augustus and His Principate*, edited by Kurt A. Raaflaub and Mark Toher, pp. 334–363. Berkeley, 1990.

Radke, Gerhard. "Augustus und das göttliche." In *Antike und Universalgeschichte. Festschrift Hans Erich Stier*, edited by Reinhardt Stiehl and Gustav Adolf Lehmann, pp. 257–279. Münster, 1972.

Speyer, Wolfgang. *Das Verhältnis des Augustus zur Religion.* Berlin and New York, 1986.

Syme, Ronald. *The Roman Revolution.* Oxford, 1939.

Whitehorne, John E. G. "The Divine Augustus as Theos Kaisar and Theos Sebastos." *Analecta papyrologica* 3 (1991): 19–26.

Zanker, Paul. *The Power of Images in the Age of Augustus.* Translated by Alan Shapiro. Ann Arbor, Mich., 1988.

J. Rufus Fears (1987)
Revised Bibliography

AUM See OṂ

AUM SHINRIKYŌ, or "Aum Sect of Truth," is a new religious movement based on Buddhism and other Eastern traditions, including Hinduism and Daoism. The movement was founded by Asahara Shōkō, also known as Matsumoto Chizuo (b. 1955), who claims to have attained ultimate enlightenment. Although Aum Shinrikyō presents itself as a Buddhist sect, its main deity is Śiva. This is unusual even in the eclectic and syncretic Japanese religious tradition. Compared to other new religious movements in the main line, at its height Aum was a small group, with only one thousand *shukke* (full-time members who had renounced the world) and ten thousand *zaike* (lay members) in Japan, and more than twenty thousand members in Russia. As of early 2004, twelve Aum members (including Asahara) had received death sentences because of the group's criminal and terrorist activities perpetrated in the name of salvation. Aum Shinrikyō proved to the world how a new religious movement could be a real threat and danger to the contemporary society. In 2001, under the leadership of Jōyū Fumihiro (b. 1962), the group changed its name to Aleph. Reeling from the legal problems and poor public relations resulting from the 1995 sarin gas attack on the Tokyo subway, the sect was radically reformed.

Asahara Shōkō, who suffered from severe eye problems as a child, entered an elementary school and high school for the blind in Kyushu. He went to work in Tokyo after graduating from high school with special training to become a licensed masseur. Asahara then entered cram school in Tokyo to prepare for the university entrance examinations. After he failed, he got married and, with the help of his wife's parents, opened a pharmacy of Eastern medicine in Chiba prefecture.

Asahara's religious interests matured during this period. In the 1980s he was a member of Agonshū, a new religious movement based on the ideas of the Shingon sect of esoteric Buddhism, Kuṇḍalinī Yoga, and the *āgama*, the ancient collections of the Buddha's own words and teachings. Agonshū stressed liberation from individual karma and the attainment of supernatural powers by awakening the *chakras*, the spiritual centers inside the body. Later, Asahara's teaching also emphasized the goal of attaining those powers by yogic practice.

Asahara opened a yoga school in Tokyo in 1983. In either 1984 or 1986 he named his circle Aum Shinsen no Kai (Aum circle of immortals); it is certain that he established the Aum Corporation in 1984. He frequently appeared in New Age magazines during this period, and he published books with such titles as *The Secret Method to Develop Psychic Powers* (1986) and *Beyond Life and Death* (1986). In 1986, Asahara claimed that he had attained "ultimate enlightenment" after meditating in the Himalayas. In 1987, Asahara renamed his group Aum Shinrikyō and transformed his yoga school into a religious body. At the same time he published a book titled *Initiation* (1987), in which he invited people to become members.

In 1989 the Tokyo metropolitan government recognized Aum Shinrikyō as a religious corporation, which gave it tax-exempt status and legal protection. By this time Aum was facing attacks from those who saw it as a dangerous group that recruited minors as monks and stole money from believers. In November 1989, with criticism mounting, Asahara secretly ordered his disciples to kill not only the anti-Aum lawyer of families whose children were Aum members, but also the lawyer's wife and baby boy.

Asahara had a political ambition to become elected to the Japanese diet, and in February 1990 Asahara and twenty-four of his followers stood for election in the general election. Their resounding political defeat was a humiliation for both Asahara and Aum Shinrikyō. Aum Shinrikyō then built facilities in rural Yamanashi and Kumamoto prefectures, and in both sites the group provoked strong opposition, causing Asahara's antipathy toward Japanese society to intensify.

Asahara began publishing books with such titles as *Doomsday* (1989) and *The Truth of the Destruction of Humanity* (1991) that announced a coming armageddon caused by the use of weapons of mass destruction. His apocalyptic eschatological vision intensified during these years, and his disciples worked to facilitate his prophecies. They secretly pursued research into biological weapons and constructed a laboratory in Aum's Yamanashi compound. In 1990 Aum tried to produce poison gas in the Kumamoto compound, and in 1993 Asahara secretly ordered his disciples to produce one thousand machine guns and conduct research on developing chemical weapons. At the same time, he complained that Aum was being persecuted by the Japanese government and American troops, and he claimed that they themselves had suffered from nerve gas attacks.

SARIN GAS ATTACKS. In June 1994 Aum members released sarin gas in Matsumoto, killing 7 and injuring 144. On March 20, 1995, Aum agents released sarin gas on several Tokyo subway trains, killing 12 people and injuring 3,796. Two days later several thousand police officers began systematic raids on Aum facilities. On May 16 Asahara was found hiding in one of the Aum facilities and was arrested. More than one hundred Aum members were arrested that year. The details of the criminal activities of this religious organization were revealed in the subsequent trials.

Asahara is accused of masterminding seventeen crimes in which at least twenty-six people were killed and more than five thousand were injured. The crimes that Asahara and his followers committed fall into the following categories: murder of its own members (thirty-three Aum members are missing); murder of its enemies; and indiscriminate mass murder using nerve gas. Aum members also produced and used illegal drugs like LSD, and they manufactured machine guns. On February 27, 2004, Asahara was convicted and received a death sentence from the Tokyo District Court. His lawyers, who claimed Asahara's innocence and blamed his disciples, appealed to the upper court just before their resignation. It will take a number of years before the Japanese Supreme Court passes the final sentence on him. Aleph announced its deep regret to the victims and vowed to compensate them on the occasion of Asahara's death sentence.

In October 1995 the Tokyo District Court ordered Aum Shinrikyō to disband as a religious corporation because of the danger it posed to the public. Members of the government argued whether or not it was proper to apply existing antisubversive activities laws to Aum Shinrikyō. In January 1997 they decided that this was not necessary because most of the executive members involved in the sarin incidents in Matsumoto and Tokyo had been arrested, eliminating any clear and present danger.

In 1999 there were major changes in Aum Shinrikyō. The organization finally admitted its criminal responsibility, asked for forgiveness, and promised to compensate victims and bereaved families. Two new so-called Aum laws were passed by the national diet. They restrict groups that have committed indiscriminate mass murder and allow the confiscation of the group's property to compensate victims.

At the end of 1999 Jōyū Fumihiro was released from prison. In January 2001, Aum Shinrikyō changed its name to Aleph. As the leader of Aleph, Jōyū began trying to reform the organization's structure and doctrine. The Japanese government decided to keep Aleph under surveillance for three years, but in 2003 the surveillance was extended for three more years. Although many intellectuals pointed out that Aleph was not capable of mass murder, there was almost no public objection to the extension of the surveillance over the organization.

AUM PRACTICES AND WORLDVIEW. In Japan, new religious movements have developed during four distinct periods. The first such development occurred in the waning days of the Tokugawa regime in the late nineteenth century; the second occurred in the Taisho period of the early 1900s; and the third was the period following Japan's defeat in World War II. Aum Shinrikyō and Agonshū were products of the fourth boom of new religious movements, which occurred in the 1970s. The religious movements of the first and the third periods stressed this-worldly merits and popular ethics in daily life. However, the movements that arose during the second and the fourth periods emphasized manipulation of the spirits and personal asceticism for self-cultivation. After the student revolution in the late 1960s and early 1970s, young people experienced a spiritual void and disorientation. New religious movement like Aum Shinrikyō gave some of them a purpose and meaning in life. The average age of Aum's members was around thirty, which was young compared with other new religious movements.

The worldview of Aum Shinrikyō and Aleph is a mixture of Hinduism, Buddhism, and other traditions. According to Aum teachings, human history is devolutionary. People are degenerating from their true selves in *mahānirvāna*, and they are fallen and stuck in the mud of suffering. To be born in this world means that one has bad karma. Every living being transmigrates up and down through the six worlds of being.

Asahara espoused a kind of eschatology from the start. In 1987 he predicted that Japan would arm itself again in 1993 and that there would be a nuclear war between 1999 and 2003 unless Aum Shinrikyō built two branch offices in each country in the world. Then, in 1989, Asahara predicted that the United States president and the secretary general of the Soviet Union would start a war that would put an end to the world. He warned his disciples that more than one-fourth of humankind would die unless Aum Shinrikyō produced accomplished practitioners.

The ultimate purposes of Aum Shinrikyō were the worship of Śiva as the principal god and the saving of every living being from *saṃsāra* based on ancient yoga, original Buddhism, and Mahāyāna Buddhism under the guidance of people who understand and execute Śiva's will. There are three kinds of salvation: to free people from disease, to bring worldly happiness to people, and to lead people to *satori* and *gedatsu*, that is, "self-realization" and "enlightenment," as Aum translated these terms into English. The first two kinds of salvation are this-worldly benefits typical of new religious movement in Japan. The third is an otherworldly ideal that is consistent with traditional Buddhism.

Aum Shinrikyō promoted a plan to transform Japan into Shambhala, a society based on truth, in which people realize themselves according to the truth, understood as the great will of Asahara and Śiva. Later, Aum Shinrikyō tried to make the whole world into Shambhala. This means that Aum Shinrikyō aimed to put the world under its rule.

Aum's system of practice was also a mixture of Buddhism and Yoga philosophy. On the Buddhist side, there was the noble eightfold path, the six perfections of wisdom (*prajñāpāramitās*), and other ideas and practices. On the Yoga side, there was *raja*, *kuṇḍalinī*, *jñāna*, *Mahāyāna*, and astral and causal yoga. In addition to these practices based on self-power, there were also initiations that relied on other-power. Initiations like *shaktīpat* were methods to increase one's spiritual ability through the *gurū*'s charisma or some other source of spiritual power.

It was believed that Aum's superior members removed the bad karma of inferior members by violence or ill treatment. Such behavior was interpreted by Aum as an act of compassion, because it was a means of eliminating the bad karma of members. This idea was taken to extremes, however, with the *poa* (*phowa*) in Aum Shinrikyō's sense. The Tibetan word *phowa* refers to the transference of the dead soul to a higher realm. However, Asahara claimed that a deliberate act of murder by a superior being was also a case of *poa*. To be identical with Asahara (meaning "the cloning of the *gurū*") was also interpreted as liberation and salvation for Asahara's disciples because Asahara was considered the ultimate enlightened one and the embodiment of the true self.

CONCLUSION. Aum Shinrikyō is an ultimate example of a new religious movement that turns violent. Aum's violent acts have had an impact on religion and politics around the world, and they have led to legislation against dangerous groups in a number of countries, especially in Japan and France. For a number of secular people the Aum incident was a serious disappointment and caused disbelief toward religion in general. And it also raised people's awareness toward deviant religious movements in various countries, and Japanese people actually welcomed and supported the arrest of the founders of such groups as Life Space and Hō-no-hana Sanpōgyō in 2000. Because of its use of a chemical weapon (one of the weapons of mass destruction), Aum Shinrikyō also indicated that the activities of a new religious movement could be a matter of public safety. The sect created an apocalyptic connection between religion and violence (as well as terrorism) that foreshadowed the tragedy of September 11, 2001.

SEE ALSO New Religious Movements, overview article, article on New Religious Movements in Japan.

BIBLIOGRAPHY

Several books can be recommended: Ian Reader, *Religious Violence in Contemporary Japan: The Case of Aum Shinrikyō* (Richmond, U.K., 2000), one of the most reliable and critical reviews of the Aum affair; Robert J. Kisala and Mark R. Mullins, eds., *Religion and Social Crisis in Japan: Understanding Japanese Society through the Aum Affair* (Houndmills, UK, and New York, 2001), a good collection of papers and informative essays on reactions to the Aum affair; Susumu Shimazono, *Gendai shūkyō no kanōsei* (Possibility of contemporary religions; Tokyo, 1997), a critical study of the doctrine of salvational violence in Aum Shinrikyō; Shimada Hiromi, *Oumu: Naze shūkyō wa terorizumu wo undanoka?* (Aum: Why did a religion turn to terrorism? Tokyo, 2001), an in-depth study of Aum and the author's personal reflections on the future of religious studies; and Robert Lifton, *Destroying the World to Save It: Aum Shinrikyō, Apocalyptic Violence, and the New Global Terrorism* (New York, 1999), a psychologically informed reflection on the Aum affair, including interviews with former members, which are rare in English-language materials.

MANABU WATANABE (2005)

AUROBINDO GHOSE (1872–1950), yogin, nationalist, poet, critic, thinker, spiritual leader of India. Born in Calcutta (August 15, 1872), Aurobindo Ghose was educated in England from the age of seven to age twenty-one at the insistence of his father, Dr. Krishnadhan Ghose, who had been one of the first Indians educated in England. Having grown up ignorant of Indian culture and religion, Aurobindo neither discovered nor appreciated Indian languages, literature, or history until he returned to India after college, in 1893. He served for a time as a teacher of French and English and as vice principal and acting principal of Baroda College. In 1906 Aurobindo joined the political movement of Indian resistance to British colonial rule and became a prominent voice of the Nationalist party, arguing for complete independence from Britain. Through his articles in periodicals such as *Bande Mataram*, Aurobindo nourished a revolutionary consciousness among Indians by addressing the issues of *swarāj* and *swadeśi* (both centered on self-rule) and boycott. He was open to the use of armed revolt as well as nonviolent means for achieving independence. In this he was flexible and pragmatic: the means of social change were selected on the basis of circumstances, not adherence to an absolute ethical principle.

In 1908 Aurobindo was arrested in connection with an unsuccessful bombing episode against a British district judge. Although he was ultimately acquitted, he spent a year in the Alipore jail during the investigation and trial. During this imprisonment his interest in yoga deepened. In 1910, following "a sudden command from above," Aurobindo moved to French India. He spent the next forty years of his life in Pondicherry, formulating his vision of spiritual evolution and integral Yoga, and refusing to pursue direct involvement in political events.

"Spiritual evolution," or the evolution of consciousness, is the central framework for understanding Aurobindo's thought. *Consciousness* is a rich and complex term for Aurobindo. Consciousness is inherent in all things, in seemingly inert matter as well as plant, animal, human, and suprahuman life. It participates in the various levels of being in various ways. *Sachchidānanda,* literally the highest level of "being, consciousness, and bliss," is also known as the Absolute. The Supermind mediates *sachchidānanda* to the multiplicity of the world. The Overmind serves as delegate of the Supermind. Intuitive Mind is a kind of consciousness of the heart that discerns the truth in momentary flashes rather than in a comprehensive grasp. Illumined Mind communicates consciousness by vision, Higher Mind through conceptual thought. Mind generally integrates reality through cognitive, intellectual, and mental perceptions rather than through direct vision, yet mind is also open to the higher levels of consciousness, for it is basically oriented to Supermind, in which it participates in a derivative way. The Psyche is the conscious form of the soul that makes possible the evolution from ignorance to light. Life is cosmic energy through which the divine is received and made manifest. Matter, the lowest level in Aurobindo's hierarchy of consciousness manifestation, is not reducible to mere material substance, but is an expression of *sachchidānanda* in diminished form.

The hierarchical view of consciousness or spirit must also be seen in a process perspective in which the supreme is seen as continuously being and becoming manifest in these many levels of being. Consciousness liberates itself through an inner law that directs evolution. Spiritual evolution is also seen as a series of ascents from material, physical existence up to supramental existence, in which we are able to reach or true being and fulfillment.

Yoga is a means by which this evolutionary thrust can be consciously assisted. Whereas evolution proceeds slowly and indirectly, yoga functions more quickly and directly. Evolution seeks the divine through nature, while yoga reaches out for the divine as transcendent to nature.

Aurobindo's Integral Yoga is so named because it seeks to incorporate the essence and processes of the old yogas, blending their methods and fruits into one system. It is integral also insofar as it seeks an integral and total change of consciousness and nature, not for the individual alone but for all of humanity and the entire cosmos. Unlike some yogas of the past, Integral Yoga does not seek release from the cycle of birth and death but seeks a transformation of life and existence, by, for, and through the divine. In most yogas, ascent to the divine is emphasized. In Integral Yoga, ascent to the divine is but the first step; the real goal is descent of the new consciousness that has been attained by the ascent.

Disciples, admirers, and advocates of Aurobindo's vision of spiritual evolution and system of Integral Yoga gather in communities throughout the world. Best known are those who have begun construction of Auroville, a city near Pondicherry designed to embody Aurobindo's ideal for a transformed humanity, and the ashram at Pondicherry where Aurobindo himelf lived for forty years.

Bibliography

The complete works of Aurobindo are available in the "Sri Aurobindo Birth Centenary Library," 30 vols. (Pondicherry, 1972–1976). A useful overview of Aurobindo's major works can be found in *Six Pillars: An Introduction to the Major Works of Sri Aurobindo,* edited by Robert A. McDermott (Chambersburg, Pa., 1974). Kees W. Bolle relates Aurobindo's thought, which evidences both Western and Eastern influences, to the Tantric tradition, in *The Persistence of Religion: An Essay on Tantrism and Sri Aurobindo's Philosophy* (Leiden, 1965). A lucid analysis of Aurobindo's philosophy of the world is found in Beatrice Bruteau's *Worthy Is the World: The Hindu Philosophy of Sri Aurobindo* (Rutherford, N.J., 1976). My *The Quest for Political and Spiritual Liberation: A Study in the Thought of Sri Aurobindo Ghose* (Cranbury, N.J., 1976) addresses the relationship between Aurobindo's political (1905–1910) and spiritual (1910–1950) commitments and writings.

New Sources

Heehs, Peter. *Sri Aurobindo, A Brief Biography.* Delhi; New York, 1989.

Kluback, William. *Sri Aurobindo Ghose: The Dweller in the Lands of Silence.* New York, 2001.

Madhusudan Reddy, V. *Seven Studies in Sri Aurobindo.* Hyderabad, India, 1989.

McLaughlin, Michael T. *Knowledge, Consciousness and Religious Conversion in Lonergan and Aurobindo.* Rome, 2003.

Nandakumar, Prema. *Sri Aurobindo, A Critical Untroduction.* New Delhi, 1988.

Umar, M. G. *Sri Aurobindo, Thinker and the Yogi of the Future.* Pondicherry, 2001.

Van Vrekhem, Georges. *Patterns of the Present: From the Perspective of Sri Aurobindo and the Mother.* New Delhi, 2002.

Vrinte, Joseph. *The Perennial Quest for a Psychology with a Soul: An Inquiry into the Relevance of Sri Aurobindo's Metaphysical Yoga Psychology in the Context of Ken Wilber's Integral Psychology.* Delhi, 2002.

June O'Connor (1987)
Revised Bibliography

AUSTRALIAN INDIGENOUS RELIGIONS

This entry consists of the following articles:

AUSTRALIAN INDIGENOUS RELIGIONS: AN OVERVIEW

The opening ceremony of the Sydney Olympic Games began at dusk on September 15, 2000, with a fanfare of charging Aussie stockmen, dignitaries, flags, and anthems. Then the floor of the huge stadium was cleared.

The sound of gulls signaled sea's edge. A golden-haired girl in pink beach dress skipped into the stadium, placed a beach towel down on the sand, and laid back. The Australian television commentator explained: "The opening ceremony tonight is designed to encapsulate the evolution of Australia from its ancient Indigenous origins to a modern twenty-first century society. A wide brown land linked inextricably to the sea. It is now, and always has been, a land of dreams."

Giant marine creatures floated into the stadium. Suddenly and dramatically the "dream girl" rose, swimming her way to the surface many meters above the stadium floor. Stadium Australia was transformed into an ocean in which a deep-sea choreography was performed against the background of a rich symphonic score. The giant screen declared this segment of the opening ceremony to be:

"Réve des profoundeurs oceans. Deep Sea Dreaming."

As the last notes of the deep-sea score were conducted, a deep male voice addressed the audience from the dais. He addressed the world in a language incomprehensible to most. Clap sticks and didgeridoo accompanied his address. The man, his body clad in loin covering and white clay, was unambiguously Aboriginal. Around his neck hung a clear signifier of his power as an Indigenous man. With the spotlight focusing on him the stadium was grounded once more. The giant screen announced this segment of the four-hour opening ceremony: "Awakening."

The young Australian girl who swam in the heights of the stadium and dived to resurface on its sea floor was Nikki Webster, a thirteen-year-old actor and singer born and bred in Sydney. The tall Indigenous performer on the dais was Djakapurra Munyarryun, born in the "remote" settlement of Yirrkala and brought up in the "Top End" region of Arnhem Land in Australia's Northern Territory. Presented in the "Awakening" segment of the Sydney 2000 opening ceremony were many of the themes taken up in this overview article. They will be used to signpost the discussion.

Understanding Indigenous religions in Australia must take relations between people, territory, and history as its starting point. The first major section of this article will outline themes for a continent-wide understanding of Australian Indigenous religions. The discussion will be broad, teasing out underlying themes that resonate but are not necessarily the same in Australia's hundreds of Indigenous religious traditions. Then the article will travel west to the central region of Australia via the Olympic performance of a section of the Seven Sisters Dreaming by Central Desert women. The article will pause to explore a particular example of Central Desert culture: the Warlpiri people. Then the article will track north, as the opening ceremony did, to the Yolngu people, whose homelands are in the north of Australia, in Arnhem Land. From there the article will go south to examine the contested religious heritage of the Ngarrindjeri people, whose homelands are near the capital city of South Australia, Adelaide.

Continental Themes. In his introduction to the "Awakening" segment of the Sydney Opening Ceremony, Ernie Dingo continued: "Over forty thousand years of culture with six hundred Indigenous nations. Over two hundred Aboriginal groups representing over 250,000 Indigenous Australians. This is an awakening."

Indigenous peoples' roots on the continent reach back at least forty to sixty thousand years and possibly longer. The British active colonization of the continent dates back only to 1788. Though the categories and numbers stated by Dingo might be contested in their precise detail by a variety of experts, the sentiment he expressed is important. There is no single Indigenous religion in Australia. There are many. There is no single Australian Indigenous experience. There are many.

Australia is an island continent. It stretches across thirty degrees of latitude in the Southern Hemisphere. The "Top End" of Australia reaches toward Papua New Guinea and Indonesia and is subject to monsoon weather patterns. In the south of the continent the climate is temperate and includes alpine regions that are snow-covered each winter. The center of the continent is a vast area of arid desert subject to extreme heat in the summer months and freezing overnight temperatures in the winter.

Although they belong to many specific cultural groups, Indigenous people in Australia are often described collectively as "Aboriginal" (referring generally to Indigenous people from the mainland and the southern island of Tasmania) or "Torres Strait Islander" (referring to those Indigenous people coming from the hundreds of islands between the tip of the mainland and Papua New Guinea). It has become customary to refer to Indigenous Australians associated with the mainland as Aboriginal people with a capital *A* as a mark of respect for their "proper" status as a group of people. Before the 1970s the term *Aboriginal* was not accorded the status of a proper noun in Australian usage. Since the mid-1990s the referent "Indigenous Australians" has become popular.

The federal, or commonwealth, government has developed (since the late 1960s) an administrative definition of Aboriginal and Torres Strait Islander people by reference to their descent, identification, and community acceptance. Under this definition an Aboriginal or Torres Strait Islander is someone "of Aboriginal or Torres Strait Islander descent who; identifies as being of Aboriginal or Torres Strait Islander origin and who is; accepted as such by the community with which the person associates."

Aboriginal and Torres Strait Islanders are a minority group in Australia. In the 1996 census people identifying themselves as Aboriginal or Torres Strait Islanders comprised 2.1 percent of the total population. Only in the Northern Territory, which arguably was the last outpost of the colonial frontier, did Indigenous people make up a significant proportion of the population as a whole, 27 percent. It is in the Northern Territory and in the more remote or "outback" areas of the states of Western Australia, South Australia, and Queensland that "traditional" practices are understood to continue to underpin everyday life. In the longer-settled "fertile fringe" of the continent, around cities towns and cultivated lands, Indigenous traditional practices are popularly understood to have been disrupted if not destroyed. This sets up a broad "primitivist" dichotomy in popular Australian discourse between remote-traditional societies and settled-nontraditional Indigenous peoples and areas. In reality the circumstances of all Indigenous people in Australia have been transforming since before 1788 in a continuum of history and experience.

National statistics also give Aboriginal and Torres Strait Islanders a number of dubious distinctions that reflect their experiences of colonizing processes. Aboriginal and Torres Strait Islander peoples as a group have worryingly low life expectancies and high levels of illness and disease. They suffer high levels of violence and crime. They are disproportionately imprisoned. They have relatively low educational and employment levels. They have low income levels. And as the High Court of Australia noted in the landmark *Mabo* native title judgment, the homelands of most Aboriginal people in Australia have been alienated from them "parcel by parcel."

Prior to colonization there were probably, as Max Charlesworth suggests in his review of the literature on Aboriginal religion in *Religious Inventions* (1998), around five hundred distinct Aboriginal groups in Australia using more than two hundred distinguishable languages. Each of these groups had its own territory or "country." Each had a specific social system and laws. Each spoke a particular language or dialects of a larger language group. Before European colonization began in 1788, Indigenous people lived as members of hundreds of different cultural and landholding groups across the continent. At the start of the twenty-first century most of Australia's population is urban and most towns and cities can be found in the more fertile coastal fringe of the continent. Indigenous people continue to live across the continent, but many of their traditional homelands have been alienated, and many more Indigenous Australians live in towns and cities than live in the homelands of their ancestors.

It is generally accepted that prior to colonization most Indigenous people on the mainland of Australia were hunter-gatherers. Small groups of relatives, often between five and fifty people or more in the most fertile regions of the continent, moved as extended families, hunting, gathering, and camping in their territories. In rich ecosystems, population densities were higher, and it seems that there Indigenous people were able to be more sedentary, at times moving between winter and summer camps. The area now called Sydney includes such rich cultural and natural areas. In the Torres Strait Islands, Indigenous people were more like their northern Melanesian neighbors and interacted with them in their everyday lives. In arid areas, particularly the inland deserts, population densities were lower, and Indigenous people moved around their territories and, with permission, crossed into those of their neighbors. They hunted with tools made from resources in their local environments or traded in from other groups.

As hunter-gatherers there was little need for complex built structures. Their kin-based society did not give rise to hierarchical political structures. Australia's Indigenous people built simple shelters to sleep under. They camped behind natural windbreaks. Men hunted with simple but sophisticated tools like boomerangs and spears with specialized launchers. They traveled over the water in bark canoes. They netted, trapped, and speared fish. Women were by and large gatherers, harvesting grasses, berries and fruit, small reptiles, insects, mussels, and shellfish. Grinding stones, wooden dishes, and digging sticks were among their key tools across the continent. Sophisticated stone tools were keys to many tasks, including the making of other specialized tools.

Aboriginal people did not hoe and cultivate the land as European settlers came to do. Australia's hunter-gatherers moved lightly over their lands and waters. Though it is a matter of live debate, some scholars are of the view that in many parts of the continent Indigenous people nurtured the productivity of their homelands with incipient "farming" practices. They managed the country with selective burning referred to as "fire stick farming," cultivated practices to nurture the growth of plants for harvesting; engaged in "fish farming" with the construction of eel traps and fishponds; and used dams and weirs to increase natural productivity.

In the "Top End" of the Northern Territory, Yolngu people in Arnhem Land had long-term relations with Macassans from what is now part of Indonesia, probably from the sixteenth century forward. The situation in the Torres Strait Islands was also somewhat different, their practices revealing extensive links with Melanesian peoples. Torres Strait Islanders, by contrast with most mainland Aboriginal peoples, were not predominantly hunter-gatherers. They owned and cultivated gardens and harvested marine life in designated fishing grounds.

Indigenous life in local groups was a complex, intertwined whole. Religion could not be separated from facets of their lives like land ownership and subsistence, or their interactions with others in marriage, trade, and warfare, or their understandings of the cosmos. Each of these facets, now given English-language names, underpinned the rich fabric of people's lives in ways that did not divide them from others.

Central to their existence were people's connections to specific territory. In contemporary times the English term *country* is frequently used to refer to Indigenous territories. Countries included both land and waters (inland and sea). A pivotal idea shared by most if not all Indigenous traditions is that "country" is sacred and imbued with the powerful and immanent spirits of ancestors. "Country" was, before the disruptions of colonization and "settlement," vested in groups of varying sizes and territorial range: clans, tribes, and nations with their own specific understandings of the world, practices, and ways of being.

The Australian continent was crisscrossed by a complex web of religious, marriage, and trading relationships that highlighted and managed the differences between particular peoples, boundaries, beliefs, and practices. Some trade routes moved resources, including the religious resources of myth and ritual, between disparate groups. Other trading relationships operated in much more localized regions.

Ceremonies and rituals brought people together in larger groups when the season or time was ripe. The extended families that were the general basis of Indigenous hunting-gathering life came together usually in the seasons of plenty to undertake larger affairs. These periods might bring hundreds of people together for periods of several weeks. Thus various configurations of landholding groups were usually well represented at these gatherings and indeed needed to be so that the "business" being celebrated would have an "owner," "managers," and "visitors" present to ensure its accuracy and efficacy. Indigenous people undertook rituals to maintain the fertility of country and all the living beings it supported. They performed rites of passage that made people more human and gave them insights into the nature of their world and what it is to be human. In the context of large ceremonial gatherings, marriages were arranged, disputes settled, and valuables traded.

Many Indigenous people were multilingual, understanding as many as a score of languages. Yet no Indigenous person understood or even knew about the many more hundreds of languages beyond that of their homeland and regional neighbors. By the time of the 2000 Sydney Olympics about a hundred Indigenous languages remained in everyday use in Australia. Of these only around twenty had a sufficiently large and concentrated "community of speakers" to make it possible for children to learn them as their first languages. Yolngu Matha, the language in which Djakapurra Munyarryun addressed a global audience in the Sydney "Awakening" ceremony, is one he learned in his own "Top End" homeland. It is among the diminishing number of Indigenous languages that remain strong and vital.

The composition of the "Awakening" segment points to the diversity of Indigenous religious and cultural experience in Australia. Some performers were from the long-settled fertile northern rivers region of New South Wales (the host state commonly abbreviated as NSW); others were from Sydney, the host city. Others, such as women from the Central Desert regions that cross the states of South Australia, Western Australia, and the Northern Territory, the Yolngu people from Arnhem Land, and the Torres Strait Islanders continue to live everyday lives, albeit under conditions different from that of their forebears, through which they maintain a strong connection to their ancestors, their country, and their traditions.

But such locally founded identity is not the experience of most Indigenous people. Australian Bureau of Statistics census figures suggest that in 1996 only 29.1 percent of Aboriginal and Torres Strait Islander people "identif[y] with [a] clan, tribal or language group," and only 31 percent live in their "homelands/traditional country." Most Australian Indigenous people live in cities, towns, and "settled regions." In remote areas the lives of many so-called traditional people are now centered on remote settlements—former mission stations, now small townships with residents from a number of different Indigenous groups and territories. Some of these settlements were established early in the colonial period; others were established after World War II. The focal position of such settlements persists despite a constellation of homeland settlements established when people moved away from service-providing townships to create smaller settlements (often called "outstations") on their homelands in a movement dating from the 1970s. Indigenous settlements and towns provide the basic infrastructure of government services: schools, transport nodes, power, water, sewerage management, water services, and in some communities, television stations and museums. Indigenous Australians in longer and more intensively settled parts of Australia predominantly live in the suburbs of towns and cities. A minority live in "fringe camps" on the peripheries of towns and cities.

Grounds of Being. From the spotlight on Djakapurra Munyarryun addressing the audience on the stadium's dais, attention shifted back to the stadium floor. Nikki Webster in her pink beach dress was again visible as a huddled group of white ochre-daubed dancers parted to make space for her to move. These performers were also recognizably Indigenous. They seemed to pursue the golden-haired girl toward the dais. They moved beside and behind her with their heads down and torsos bent low, clasping their hands behind their backs.

Nikki Webster glanced back at her pursuers with evident uncertainty and concern. Finally the young Australian girl climbed the stairs toward the tall Aboriginal man and was picked up by performers and placed beside him on the dais. She knelt. Looking. Learning. The scene was punctuated by a white cloud as the Aboriginal man clapped his ochre-filled hands above her. The voice of Indigenous commentator Ernie Dingo elaborated: "The deep-sea dream of young Australia is transformed by an undeniable call from an ancient heritage by the Dreamtime spirits of another age, but a culture very much alive."

Ernie Dingo's statement of ancient Indigenous roots and contemporary vitality was significant. So too were references to an ancient heritage of Dreamtime spirits. In this Dingo pointed the audience to what has become the key concept for understanding most Australian Indigenous religious traditions. These concepts link the religious lives of Indigenous people from the forty thousand and more years before the continent's settlement by non-Indigenous people and the two hundred and more years since.

The idea of Dreaming, the Dreamtime, and Dreamtime Spirits has wide usage, is key to understanding Australian Indigenous Religions, and the words are not restricted to Indigenous or non-Indigenous speakers. Though these terms have become general in their usage, they had their origins in the translation of a specific term by a specific group by researchers working in the late eighteenth century.

The concept of the Dreaming can be understood as that transcendent aspect of power through which all key elements of the cosmos—material and immaterial—have their origins and remain connected. The essence of the Dreaming is in the Indigenous principles of formation, order, and knowledge.

Most Indigenous traditions in Australia share basic ideas about the place of Aboriginal people in their cultural world, and it is the "business" of contemporary Indigenous people to continue these ideas in order to maintain that world. Across the continent Indigenous people take as the bedrock of their being (or believe that their ancestors did so in the past) deep ideas of transcendent form and relatedness and the enduring entailments of these connections.

The terms Dreaming, or Dreamtime, mentioned in the Olympic "Awakening" ceremony are used to refer to the "the ancient past" in which all Indigenous life was founded. For many it endures from its ancient formational time into the present and future. The anthropologist W. E. H. Stanner, in *White Man Got No Dreaming* (1979), called it "the everywhen."

As Howard Morphy has suggested in "Empiricism to Metaphysics: In Defense of the Concept of the Dreamtime" (1995), Dreaming is part of a group of related terms that can be found in most if not all Australian Indigenous languages. Such sets of terms refer to ancestral figures, their actions and powers, and sacred things and doings that connect living beings to them.

The ideas behind such sets of terms are thoroughly grounded in the premise that people properly belong to specific areas or "countries" that were created by their own ancestral spirits. Indeed "country" itself was formed long ago as these powerful transcendent beings moved across the landscape or stayed as forms within it. Ancestors left tracks and sometimes their own bodies in the areas through which they moved. These tracks gave the land and waters a form that endures in the early twenty-first century. Thus in some Indigenous traditions mountains are the shelters that ancestors left behind as they traveled. A bend in a river may be a Dreaming figure's elbow or knee or the sweep of a giant ancestral fish. Sand dunes are the kinetic tracks of women who danced in the "Dreamtime" or the windbreaks behind which they camped. Islands are the ossified remains of ancestors or the objects they carried. Ancestors created or were the natural species that fill the land and waters.

Dreamings in the broadest sense then are power-filled landforms, stories, spirits, stars and natural species as well as natural forces like rain, sun, whirlwinds, and waters. They initiated relationships. Contemporary human beings are the descendents of these powerful beings with all the responsibilities of relatedness and enduring connection. Countries are sacred and have particularly sacred places because of their ancestral connections. Specific natural species are kindred: totemic protectors and friends.

Deborah Bird Rose put it this way in *Nourishing Terrains* (1996):

> The Australian continent is criss-crossed with the tracks of the Dreamings: walking, slithering, crawling, flying, chasing, hunting, weeping, dying, giving birth. Performing rituals, distributing the plants, making landforms and water, establishing things in their own places, and making relationships between one place and another. Leaving parts or essences of themselves, looking back in sorrow; and still travelling, changing languages, changing songs, changing skin. They were changing shape from animal to human and back to animal and human again, becoming ancestral to particular animals and particular humans. Through their creative actions they demarcated a whole world of difference and a whole world of relationships which cross-cut difference. (Rose, 1996, p. 35)

Dreaming stories, countries, people, and all living things are differentiated. Although the idea of the Dreaming founds all life, particular people and particular groups of people have rights and responsibilities for specific segments of stories, tracks, movements, and the sacred: dances, designs, and sacred objects. A single person will generally have relationships and therefore responsibilities to a number of specific ancestral figures and tracks. People make those parts of the Dreaming for which they have responsibility manifest in the organization and performance of ritual and the realization of the powers of their "everywhen" in sand, on rock, on bodies, and on canvases. They sing them into power and dance their presence. In doing so they continue the Dreaming and carry out their responsibilities for its endurance.

Living human beings keep particular segments of the Dreaming alive: by keeping the rules of practice laid down by the founding beings, dancing the segments to which they have rights, repeating their actions and their tracks in the landscape, "singing" the country in a language that the spirits of the dead can hear, dancing and re-creating the ancestors and their actions, living in ways that nurture continued life, and guarding the propriety with which others do so.

Social orders were also established in the foundational "everywhen" of the Dreaming, including clans, "skins" (subsections), totems, and other groupings of identity, relationship, and regulation. Particular human groups are allied with natural species or forces and given responsibilities for their vitality and endurance. Religious action is predicated on the cooperation of different groups of people who have different roles in performance and in many regions a critical distinction is made between the "owners" of ritual and the "managers" who must survey proceedings and ensure that things are properly done.

In Indigenous social orders gender is a fundamental point of differentiation as well as cooperation. Males and females have mutually entailed knowledge, roles, and responsibilities in the world. These things were established in the foundational orders of the Dreaming.

Critical stages in human life too were established in formational times and events as well as the rites for human passage: they included in some societies birth rituals, initiation, and mortuary ceremonies. In some traditions human conception was animated as spirits entered a woman in particular places (often those associated with water), enlivening a fetus within her. Such places come to be regarded as the person's "conception place." These connections gave rise to special relationships, rights, and responsibilities. Rituals for maintaining the fertility of country and species more generally were also given to human beings from foundational actions. In this way too laws of living were established and punishments and rewards set down for tradition.

Complex processes of concealment and revelation are pivotal in the life of many Indigenous traditions and practices. Some practices are open and public. Others are restricted. Knowledge, practice, and power in such traditions are frequently layered and segmented. With the pioneering work of Phyllis Kaberry, Catherine Berndt, and Diane Bell has come a deeper understanding of the positions and roles of Indigenous women in their societies. Many Indigenous traditions are organized around age and gender-based divisions of religious cooperation, knowledge, and work. Some matters were restricted to women, some to older women, some to women with several children. These matters and responsibilities are now often referred to as "women's business." Others were restricted to men and are referred to as "men's business." Both sides of business required the complementary participation of the other and entailed negotiations of who knew what story and who could claim knowledge. The balance as to who takes the lead depends on the purpose of the ceremony and varies across the continent.

Rituals, objects, and designs commonly have many meanings in these traditions. Revelation and knowledge of spiritual matters were graduated. Some sacred matters were more narrowly restricted within gendered knowledge. It is not uncommon, for example, for novices in initiation to have less-restricted knowledge about stories or the nature of practices, designs, or the sacred revealed to them while the adepts who bring this knowledge withhold other "inside" meanings. As ritual experience and adeptness is gained, so too is inside knowledge.

But it is also crucial to recognize that knowledge has power in such societies. It is not given away freely. For this reason Eric Michaels, in "Constraints on Knowledge in an Economy of Oral Information" (1985), has written of such systems as forming an "economy of knowledge." Founding practices in which gender, age, ritual status, and divisions of esoteric knowledge were laid down also established the basis of different rights and obligations in these economies of knowledge: to come into and see special sacred places or to turn one's back and stay away, to tell and reenact specific ancestral actions in ritual, to sing but not to dance, to dance but not to sing, to paint bodies or to be painted, to see and hear restricted knowledge, to oversee specific performances by others, to participate in action and constructions but not to gain rights to repeat them in any way.

Another broad feature of Indigenous traditions is an insistence as ideology that things that have come from the Dreaming are unchangingly "everywhen": that the Dreaming and its consequences are not subject to innovation and that "things have been this way for forty thousand years." Yet many traditions also admit the possibility of "rediscovering" things temporarily lost or the gaining of new insight or elaboration in the inspired dreams of living humans. The ambiguity of layered systems of knowledge also makes space for new understandings and sometimes in turn new practices. It is also clear that new rituals, performances, and objects move between groups from time to time and probably that they have long done so. And clearly the Dreaming has also found new ways of life: in the expression of Dreaming designs in paintings on canvas using acrylic paints, for example, and in performances like those at the Olympics, where new groupings of Aboriginal people are linked into an overarching performance message before different and radically enlarged audiences and with performances adjusted for this unprecedented context.

The "Awakening" segment of the Sydney opening ceremony, with its three to four billion viewers worldwide, brought together seven different Indigenous groups and performers from all corners of the Australian continent in an innovative performance of different traditions lasting just over eleven minutes. These different performances were linked to create an innovative "story."

This was far from the first time Indigenous cultural productions went global, though clearly this was Indigenous Australians' largest and most widely based global audience. Australian Indigenous art, based in artists' own Dreamings, had moved out of ethnographic museums into art galleries by the 1980s. Public institutions commission Indigenous art to hang on walls in public view. When Australia's new Parliament House opened in 1988, it featured a commanding forecourt paved with a mosaic by the Western Desert artist Michael Nelson Tjakamarra. The same year the Asia Society in New York hosted the exhibition Dreamings: The Art of Aboriginal Australia. Australian Indigenous art now sells widely and commands high prices in global art markets. Exhibitions of Indigenous art tour the world.

Indigenous cultural performance has also gone global. The Bangara Dance Theatre, whose director, Stephen Page, was codirector of the "Awakening" segment of the Sydney 2000 opening ceremony, has been presenting contemporary Indigenous dance to international and Australian audiences since 1989. The Arnhem Land rock group Yonthu Yindi sings Yolngu messages that are broadcast to large audiences, and Yolngu elders invite influential outsiders to come and learn from them at Garma festivals held in their homelands.

Traditional religious acts and performances, ordinarily set in the country made by Dreamings, have also gone international. Often they are part of the opening of exhibitions of Indigenous art. In "Culture-Making: Performing Aboriginality at the Asia Society Gallery" (1994), Fred Myers has documented the complex negotiations and performances through which sandpaintings were constructed in New York as part of the opening of the 1988 Dreamings exhibition. Men from the small and remote Aboriginal community of Papunya, 160 miles from Alice Springs, traced sandpaintings ordinarily grounded in their remote homelands, albeit adapted to this particular and peculiar audience and context.

In January 2000 Warlpiri people from the Central Desert presented a "One Family corroboree" at the Baptist World Alliance Congress in Melbourne in which they painted strong Warlpiri iconographs on their bodies for their performance of a "Christian *purlapa*" (Christian public ceremony). As Ivan Jordan documents in *Their Way* (2003), the designs they painted on their bodies and the songs and dances they performed were "dreamed" into being in small Central Desert communities.

Indeed as many as 75 percent of the nation's Indigenous people call themselves Christian. Some might be said to have converted from the religious life of their ancestors to Christianity. For many others Christian ideas sit side by side in a now enlarged cosmology in which the forces that founded Indigenous countries and for which human beings have responsibilities include ancestral figures as well as God and Jesus Christ. And understandings about the nature of the human condition are told in stories about the formational actions and powers of Dreaming figures as well as with those drawn from the Bible.

The concept of the Dreaming or Dreamtime has had a central place in Indigenous and popular Australian parlance for many years. It has long been a central though sometimes contested concept in academic analyses of Indigenous religion. The use of these English-language terms originated from a translation of a particular term in a particular Indigenous language group (the Aranda or Arrente) in the late eighteenth century. Their contemporary use carries the danger of homogenization: of concealing cultural difference between the hundreds of Indigenous groups in Australia. This issue will be addressed in the following sections.

But the strength of the English terms' usage, as Morphy has shown, is that these concepts overlap semantic fields or sets of related terms in most if not all Aboriginal languages. Morphy has suggested that the term "signifies a semantic field in Aboriginal languages, the significance of which became relevant in the context of postcolonial Aboriginal discourse. The term fitted a lexical gap in Aboriginal languages, a lexical gap the colonial conditions made it more necessary to fill. It was an anthropological term that was adopted by Aboriginal people because of its salience to them" (Morphy, 1995, p. 178).

If the term *Dreaming* can be traced back to early attempts to understand the terms of Aranda-Arrente religious life, it should be kept in mind, as Morton has noted, that:

> Mythological and ceremonial knowledge . . . has undoubtedly in some sense diminished since the turn of the century: yet initiation continues, dreamings are transmitted and enhanced, and old stories and songs now sit side-by-side with new stories and songs about Jesus and Mary, God and Satan, and Adam and Eve. . . . Some Western Aranda men are now very prominent in the Lutheran Church, but they have not thereby forsaken their countries or their dreamings or their kinsmen. This would quite simply be unthinkable. (Morton 1991, p. 54)

THE AUSTRALIAN POLITICS OF INDIGENOUS RELIGIONS. Nikki Webster, the young Australian star of the opening ceremony, was pursued by clay-daubed "awakening spirits" along the stadium toward the stairs of the dais from which Dkakapurra Munyarryun spoke. She joined him on the dais. Ernie Dingo said: "The young Australian girl is now part of the land's ancient culture, for her too to share. First of all to understand the origins of where it all came from."

Dingo's call was understood by many Australians in the audience to address political debates from the years running up to the Sydney 2000 Olympics. The peak national Indigenous body, the Aboriginal and Torres Strait Islander Commission (disbanded by the Australian government in 2004), said of the Indigenous performance:

> The Sydney Olympics will help shine a spotlight on Aboriginal culture and its historical plight. The attention should prove uncomfortable to the Australian government. The nation has made great strides on the racial front in recent decades, but it is showing some distressing signs of weariness from the progress, and a resistance to march onward. In recent months, the Australian government has ceased cooperating with United Nations human rights monitors looking into the status of Aborigines and has opposed calls for an official apology for past wrongs.

The 1990s began with hope for acknowledgment and reconciliation. A wide-ranging national inquiry of the executive government (the Royal Commission into Aboriginal Deaths in Custody) listened carefully to bereaved Indigenous people as well as a range of other witnesses. The inquiry found that fundamental disadvantage underlay the disproportionate incarceration rates (and consequent high death rates) of Indigenous people in Australia. It recommended systemic change in legal and social institutions and practices. This gave some Indigenous Australians hope for their children's future. It suggested that "reconciliation" between Indigenous and settler Australians might be possible.

Indigenous hopes were raised too in 1992, when the High Court of Australia recognized the prior ownership and native title of the Meriam people of the Torres Strait in the *Mabo* case. The following year an act of the commonwealth (federal) parliament gave Indigenous claimants across the country a right to have their native title claims tested and declared by the federal court (the Native Title Act of 1993). In overturning the doctrine of *terra nullius* (that the continent at settlement was a land without owners and therefore open to be legally taken and colonized), the High Court of Australia noted in its judgment that "Aborigines were dispossessed of their land parcel by parcel, to make way for expanding colonial settlement. Their dispossession underwrote the development of the nation."

The new legislation gave Indigenous people the opportunity to claim native title on crown land—land whose title had not been sold or transferred to others in legal contracts but was still held by "the crown." The primary questions before the courts in native title claims is whether Indigenous claimants were owners of crown land through their own system of custom and law (which would have to be demonstrated) and whether they have maintained their connection with the land they claim. The Native Title Act promised limited access to native title rights and recognition across the nation.

It was the Land Rights (Northern Territory) Act of 1976 that put Australian Indigenous religions squarely on the agenda of public debate in Australia. That act, which was limited in its operation to the Northern Territory, put Aboriginal peoples' religious lives at the heart of their claims to land. A key test in land claims turned on Aboriginal peoples' spiritual affiliation with the land. According to the legislation, it was "Traditional Aboriginal owners" who could make claims for land. But the claimants had to constitute "a local descent group of Aboriginals who have *common spiritual affiliations* to a site on the land, being affiliations that place the group under a *primary spiritual responsibility* for that site and for the land, and are entitled by Aboriginal tradition to forage as of right over that land" (emphasis added).

Ideas about Indigenous beliefs and traditions later underpinned the federal "safety net" heritage act, which offered Indigenous people a way to protect areas or objects of significance to their tradition from destruction or desecration when all other means had been exhausted. In the Aboriginal and Torres Strait Islander Heritage Protection Act of 1984, "Aboriginal tradition" means the body of traditions, observances, customs, and beliefs of Aboriginals generally or of a particular community or group of Aboriginals and includes any such traditions, observances, customs, or beliefs relating to particular persons, areas, objects, or relationships. A critical question then becomes: Who defines tradition and according to what criteria?

Thus, Australian Indigenous religions have been made to count in a number of facets of Australian affairs. This has brought Australian Indigenous religions into a spotlight of controversy and contestation. Indigenous people became by the mid-1990s a target of political skepticism. Some have been accused of fabricating traditions and beliefs they sought to have acknowledged as significant under Australian law. In this context the commentary that "the young Australian girl is now part of the land's ancient culture, for her too to share" had a particular salience.

Particularities: Person and Identity. As Nikki Webster joined Djakapurr Munyarryun on the dais, the Yolngu man continued to sing and address the audience in his own language. Ernie Dingo explained again to television viewers: "Djakapurra, the song man, calls the visitors to listen to the sounds of the earth, to meet an ancient past and awaken the spirits within."

Djakapurra Munyarryun, the key Indigenous performer in the opening ceremony of the Sydney Olympics, is an Aboriginal man. More particularly he is a Yolngu man. *Yolngu* is the term six thousand people in Arnhem Land use to identify themselves to others as Indigenous people.

Djakapurra Munyarryun is a member of a specific Yolngu clan reported to be the Wan'gurri clan. The homelands of the Wan'gurri are Dhalinbuy, inland and roughly southwest of the township of Yirrkala and the Nhulunbuy-Gove area (the site of a large bauxite mine and its associated township).

Yolngu clans like the Wan'gurri are made up of people related to each other through their fathers. They are a group because they share a common ancestor (usually about five generations distant) through their patriline (father's line), but also because they are linked by being created on land by a particular Dreaming ancestral figure and as part of a particular story of creation. Clan members, led by elders, are custodians of specific tracts of country for which they have particular responsibilities. Each clan claims and looks after particular tracts of country (land in coastal areas, the sea) and have a specific set of sacred objects, songs, dances, and designs that are underwritten by the activities of particular ancestral figures.

The Wan'gurri clan of which Djakapurra Munyarryun is a member belongs to the Yirritja moiety. Other Yolngu clans belong to the opposite and complementary Dhuwa moiety. Everything in the Yolngu world is part of one moiety or the other. Yolngu people become a member of their father's moiety at birth (and are such prior to birth in a dead-spirit-to-newborn continuum). In Yolngu tradition they must marry a member of their mother's moiety, for it would be incestuous to marry into the moiety they share with their father. Many Yolngu religious obligations can be discharged only in cooperation with people and clans of the opposite moiety. They require particular ceremonial events to be conducted in the presence of members of both moieties. For example, some dances and designs held by one clan are only to be used under the supervision of members of another clan belonging to the opposite moiety. This is often described as the *yothu-yindi* (child-mother) relationship between an individual's own clan and his or her mother's clan. Thus the duty to observe and supervise the activities of another clan is akin to the responsibility of a mother providing advice and guidance to her child.

When Yolngu people refer to themselves, they frequently use specific terms that identify them with a narrower group of people, such as a specific clan group, that possesses its own language dialect which is associated with one or more homelands and that shares ancestral totems, songs, and designs associated with and bestowed upon them by particular Dreaming ancestors responsible for the creation of their clan lands. More narrowly still Yolngu clan members identify themselves as belonging to a family or particular patriline (which since mission times have come to be identified by distinct surnames). Djakapurra's second name, Munyarryun, is such a name.

In 1991 Djakapurra Munyarryun moved as a young man to Sydney to become a performer and cultural consultant for the Bangarra Dance Theatre. He remained a full-time member of the company until 2002. As a member of Bangarra, Djakapurra Munyarryun embodied long-standing links between the dance company and Yolngu peoples in Arnhem Land, where members of the company traveled, viewed dance in its ceremonial context, and held contemporary dance workshops in local venues. As the Bangarra Dance Theatre web page notes: "Djakapurra contributes far more than dancing, singing and didjeridu playing. He is a creative consultant, linking traditional past and contemporary present as he moves between his remote community, Sydney and international tours that have taken him around the world" (www.bangarra.com.au).

PARTICULARITIES: THE SEVEN SISTERS. The "Awakening Spirits" dance that moved Nikki Webster to join Djakapurra Munyarryun on the podium finished with a puff of dry ochre (a dry white clay powder). As Nikki Webster knelt watching and learning beside the song man, the high pitch of many women's singing voices turned viewers' attention to the other end of the stadium. Television viewers saw from overhead three hundred women proceeding in a pendulous elongated group up the stadium. At ground level the women could be seen entering the stadium with their hands clasped behind their backs. Then, as they hastened down the stadium, they brought their arms to their sides, with elbows bent in a stylized movement. The women wore only black skirts and red headbands. Their breasts were painted with lined designs of white, yellow, and red.

"This, *inma kunga rapaba,*" Ernie Dingo announced, "a dance from central Australia. Dance of the seven emu sisters." At about two-thirds of the way down the length the women stopped their forward movement and bunched into circle, their arms raised in the air, hands cupped and waving above them.

These women, members of the Ngaanyatjarra, Pitjantjatjara, and Yunkunyatjara (or NPY) Women's Council, came to Sydney from homelands in three Australian states, South Australia, Western Australia, and the Northern Territory. They are members of a cultural region sometimes referred to in the ethnographic literature as the "Western Desert" block. Their languages, though distinct, are generally comprehensible to each other. They call themselves by the common term *anangu* (human beings).

The NPY Women's Council has been an important force in local, regional, state, and national politics since it was formed in 1980. The words of a senior member of the council were translated and appeared as subtitles in the film *Minymaku Way.* They read:

> There are many of us living across a huge area of country [in fact the area is 350,000 square kilometers of the interstate desert areas]. Our country belongs to us Anangu people and we have our own ways, our own language and we women want to keep these ways alive, especially while there is so much tragedy in our lives. That is why we formed the Women's Council.

Minymaku Way tells the story of the council's first twenty years. It tells of how the council was formed in 1980 during the fight for land rights, a fight from which women—despite their business and traditions—were silenced and excluded. It tells also of contemporary programs arising out of "worry for families," as the non-Anangu worker Maggie Kavanagh put it. Prominent among Women's Council programs are care for the aged, disability services, domestic violence, nutrition programs, and substance abuse (alcohol, marijuana, and petrol sniffing).

Minymaku Way also tells that a major item on the agenda of the twenty-year anniversary general meeting of the council held at Kanpi (about a seven-hour drive from Alice Springs) was to decide on one song, dance, and body painting for their performance at the opening ceremony of the Olympic Games, a context for them to showcase their strength and culture "for all the world to see." The meeting at Kanpi celebrated the roots of the Women's Council in the singing of the "Land Rights Song" that appeared as subtitles on-screen as the women sang in their own language:

> It is our grandfathers' and our grandmothers' country from a long time ago. Listen everybody! This is our sacred land. This is a really true story. Why don't you listen to us? Listen everybody! Listen everybody! This is our land, our beautiful land.

The decision about what they would perform at the Olympics was a difficult one. Many women from different communities would perform. The audience would primarily be those with no ordinary right to see or hear the performance. It would include men, women, and children. Other Aboriginal people, including some from their own communities, might tune in. One Anangu woman talked about the dilemmas on film: "We have to make a proper choice. Making our songs so public is unusual because normally we keep our songs so private, hidden and separate. We have to consider and discuss which non-fun song, which serious and important song we can present to the people of the world."

The group narrowed their decision down to two possibilities. In the end the decision was made to perform a section of the Seven Sisters story. The other song and dance considered was deemed to be too restricted and sacred to perform for the world.

Maggie Kavanagh sent a message on camera to Stephen Page, the co–artistic director of the "Awakenings" segment of the Olympics opening. She spoke about the negotiations and decisions about which *inma* (song-dance-design relating to a segment of a Dreaming) the women would perform in Sydney. She spoke to the camera in English:

> They have decided on the Seven Sisters and they practiced three parts of the Seven Sisters *inma.* Looks like the one [localized section] they'll agree on is the *kanpi.* . . . *Kanpi* means fat. It is emu fat. The Seven Sisters are traveling [she moved her hands up one after the other in a flowing movement as if to grasp something in the air, bending her elbows in a stylized way as she did so]. You'll see them trying to get the emu fat [with their hands], that's a really prized part of the emu. And it's actually not far from where we are [referring to the *inma's* specific section of country or locale at Kanpi]. The women liked the song, for that particular Seven Sisters song and also the movement. They like the movements. They think it's really good moving-movement for what you want in Sydney.

The Kanpi *inma* of the Seven Sisters Dreaming was taped by David Page and his colleagues from Sydney as the women performed it in song and dance in the landscape to which it referred. *Minymaku Way* showed the women singing the songs relating to the designs they painted on their bodies (though taking out the black so the designs would show better as they danced before a world audience). In the country of the song they danced in a clearing, keeping their forefeet in the sand, marking the country with the story once again and grasping for the emu fat unseen in front of them while others sat beating time with bottles, shoes, and clapping sticks. It was the sounds of their singing that day, clarified in a Sydney studio, that were broadcast for the Sydney performance.

There are many stories and many story lines about the Seven Sisters among Indigenous Australians. These stories concern the Pleiades constellation. Aboriginal people sometimes refer to the stars of the constellation as the "many women or sisters." The "Seven Sisters" is a common usage. This constellation rises and falls in the sky seasonally. Christine Watson is the most recent scholar to canvass the travels and adventures of the Seven Sisters. Spurred by work she did on women's art and ceremony from Balgo in northeastern Western Australia, she describes, in *Piercing the Ground* (2003), how those women's Dreamings are part of a "web of Seven Sisters narratives which traverse mainland Australia, the Torres Strait, and Tasmania, through South Australia to New South Wales and Victoria, parts of them belonging to men's and parts to women's ceremonial practice among the different groups holding the mythology" (Watson, 2003, p. 194).

In the temperate eastern states of Australia documentation from the nineteenth century suggests that the Seven Sisters story was associated with winter and frosts. R. H. Mathews recorded in 1904 that all the stars and star clusters in the sky are named and known in Aboriginal tradition. The stars, he said, are like human beings arranged into kinship systems. Of the Seven Sisters constellation in particular, he wrote, in nineteenth-century parlance:

> The aborigines of the Clarence River have a story that the Pleiades when they set with the sun go away to bring winter; and that when these stars reappear early in the evening in the eastern sky, they are ushering in the warm weather. They are supposed to be a family of young women, whose name was War-ring-garai, and who belonged to the section Wirrakan. . . . Among the Ngeumba blacks, in the cold weather of mid-winter, when the Pleiades rise about three or four o'clock in the morning, the old men take some glowing coals on bark shovels, and cast them towards this constellation as soon as it is visible. This is done to prevent the spirit women, whom these stars represent, from making the morning too cold. The women in the camp are not permitted to look at all at the Pleiades in winter nights, because such conduct would increase the severity of the frost. If a woman transgresses this law, her eyes will become bleary, and she will suffer from uterine troubles. (Mathews, 1904, pp. 279–280)

It is not clear whether all stories across the continent are parts of a wide-ranging whole. It is clear, however, that such Dreamings crossed boundaries and connected a number of different groups. It is more likely that some if not most of the Seven Sisters stories that track around the arid inland, in and out of Western Australia, South Australia, and the Northern Territory, are related and connecting Dreaming stories. Certainly contemporary women make the assertion that this Dreaming connects them to many others across the continent. Most of the reported segments or versions in the cross-border desert regions contain common themes. They tell of a group of women who travel widely, camping, dancing, eating, and spending much of their time trying to escape from the unwelcome and usually illicit advances of a lustful man (and sometimes more). Sometimes the main pursuer has a son.

As with other Dreamings, these women's presence can be seen in the early twenty-first century in the sandhills they used as windbreaks or those they formed as tracks when they danced with their feet in the sand. Particular vegetation marks food they ate or with which the lustful "lover boy" sought to tempt them. Caves point to places where they were raped. In some versions of the myth the women have dogs that protect them and fight off the lecherous man or men. The women move between earth and sky, rising and falling with the seasons as the Pleiades. The lustful man is still to be seen in the sky as Orion or in other traditions the moon. At various points this Dreaming crosses and interacts with other Dreaming tracks.

In her *Nukunu Dictionary* (1992) Luise Hercus recorded an account of the story from a South Australian Nukunu informant, Harry Bramfield. This account makes clear the relationship between events in the story, the stars, and terrestrial landmarks. In Bramfield's account the Seven Sisters

> ran from the east and they came across to Yartnamalka [in the Flinders Ranges], where the Yartnamalka lady is, where the big chunk of clay is in the hills. They ran away from the east and they went west. One of them got crook [ill] at the hill at Yartnamalka, and that is where she stayed, so there is only six of them up there (in the sky) now. The seventh is there at Yartnamalka, that is the landmark. And of course the three brothers—they only had three brothers, they took after them to find them, they traveled and traveled and they too went up into the sky so there is the three brothers chasing the six sisters. (Hercus, 1992)

The Seven Sisters Dreaming is a context for ritual and indeed political cooperation among different groups. Arguably this Dreaming is progressively more celebrated by Aboriginal people in the contemporary context where their special claims have been under a variety of political threats. Whether such issues were at the forefront of decisions made by the women themselves and the ceremony organizers, the dancing of the Seven Sisters at the opening ceremony of the Sydney 2000 Olympics was in many ways a particularly apt choice, for the Seven Sisters is a Dreaming story that links Indigenous groups across the continent and through all of Australia's mainland states.

PARTICULARITIES: THE WARLPIRI OF THE CENTRAL DESERT. What the Sydney Olympic organizers referred to as "Central Desert" Aboriginal people and attributed to the NPY Women's Council includes a large number of distinct Indigenous groups—the Alyawarra (Alywarr), Kaytej (Kaytetye), Pintupi, Ngaanyatjarra, Pintjantjatjara, Yankunytjatjara, Warlpiri, and Warumungu. Their homelands can be found in the remote regions of three different states of Australia: Western Australia, South Australia, and the Northern Territory. To complicate matters, scholars have sometimes distinguished between the Central Desert and Western Desert cultural regions. In this schema Pintupi, Ngaanyatjarra, Pintjantjatjara, and Yunkunytjatjara are groups from the "Western Desert cultural bloc," and Alyawarra (Alywarr), Kaytej (Kaytetye), Warlpiri, and Waramungu are from the so-called Central Desert bloc. In reality these "blocs" are crumbling somewhat. Nowadays people from these regions live in settlements and small townships like Ali Kurang (formerly Warrabri), Yendemu, Lajamanu (once known as Hooker Creek), and Balgo, now known as Wirrimanu.

When Diane Bell worked at the Aboriginal community of Warrabri (Ali Kurang), it comprised Kaytej, Alyawarra, Warlpiri, and Warumungu-Warlmanpa people but was located on Kaytej country, a place associated with dog Dreaming. The community of Yuendumu began its life in 1946, when the government established a "ration depot" near a soak of that name. The depot was situated near several Warlpiri ceremonial sites and came to be used by mainly Warlpiri people but also by Pintupi and Anmatyerre.

Both Bell, in *Daughters of the Dreaming* (1983), and Françoise Dussart, in *The Politics of Ritual in an Aboriginal Settlement* (2000), provide a sense of how Aboriginal life "maps" on to these communities. Their accounts differ in important ways and point up the fact that difference is important for understanding the religious life of Indigenous people in Central Australia. The central part of Warrabri, as Bell experienced it in 1976 to 1978, included a built-up area with an airstrip, powerhouse (for generating electricity), police station, store, sports field, council offices, hospital, and houses surround by a number of camps, each oriented to the "country" of its traditional owners. There were also initiation grounds, "Sorry" camps (for the bereaved), and a number of *jilimi,* or independent women's camps. During Dussart's stay in Yuendumu from 1983 to 1985, that community likewise included the built structures of a remote Australian town: airstrip, powerhouse, council buildings, school, sports facilities, and store as well as a hall, a video-television station building (under construction at the time), a church, a recreation center, a clinic, a morgue, an adult education center, and separate men's and women's museums. Surrounding these "permanently" built structures were the six Aboriginal "camps" with their men's and women's ritual areas. She too found *jilimi* as well as *yampirri,* the quarters of unmarried men, and *yapukarra,* the quarters of married couples.

But these are also communities that keep their Dreamings alive and frequently perform ritual, as the substantial ethnography from this area demonstrates. The languages of these complex settlements refer to the Dreaming similarly: as *Jukurrpa.* Each member of these communities has particular connections to specific *Jukurrpa* as stories, relationships, objects, designs, places, and actions. People sing their Dreamings. They dance them. They draw their designs in the sand. They paint the marks of the Dreaming on their bodies. They recognize their marks on ritual objects. They move about the landscape with its forces, powers, and essences always in mind and with them as guides of where to go and where they must lower their eyes and turn their backs. Aboriginal people are mindful of the rules and laws set down. And for some decades now they have painted their Dreamings onto canvases and sung them as they did so.

All the critical moments in an individual's life are "made manifest" in ritual. Conflicts resolved, lovers are attracted and repelled. Dussart tried to convey the force of ceremony: "In reenacting a Dreaming, ritual performers follow in the footsteps (spiritually and physically) of their Jukurrpa Ancestral Beings" (Dussart, 2000, p. 47).

The Aboriginal groups of the Central Desert regions have extraordinarily intricate systems for specifying membership of a number of groups of relations and orienting one's future marriage preferences. These webs of relatedness are founded in connections to specific tracts of land and through them to specific Dreaming ensembles. Groups of people also have special relationships with natural species, which are often referred to in English as their "totems" or "Dreaming."

Rights and responsibilities to Dreamings are shared by groups of relatives related in specific ways to it. *Kirda* are those related to a particular place, "country," or Dreaming on their "father's" side, from their father and grandfather. They must dance for the country and wear the designs for the Dreamings and places in the country. *Kudrungurlu* are those who are related to the same places, "countries," or Dreaming on the "mothers' father's" side. As Bell notes in *Daughters of the Dreaming* (1983), "they had to sing, paint the *kirda,* and ensure that the Law was correctly followed." Members of each group must be present for ritual performances to be proper. Both must be present and sign off on acrylic paintings of Dreaming segments. In their action one to the other and in respect of the Dreamings for which they hold complementary responsibility, *kirda* and *kurungurlu* help each other carry out their responsibilities.

But all people who are related as *kirda* and *kurungurlu* are not the same. There are two further distinctions that are essential to consider in respect of Central Desert religious life: gender and the restrictions that could be called those of adeptness.

The Warlpiri continue to conduct male initiation ceremonies. Though these are "men's business," women play important roles in this ritual process. Women too have ritual responsibilities.

In *Daughters of the Dreaming,* Diane Bell describes a *yawulyu* ceremony she witnessed in 1976. On average, she said, she saw one such ceremony a week during her stay. These rituals are "women's business" and continue to be a feature of Warlpiri life. Women gather for *yawalyu* in the afternoon and prepare ritual objects and designs. A fire is kept burning throughout the ceremony, and the ashes will be raked over and reused in subsequent rituals.

In Bell's account the first stage entailed the gathering of women and painting of women's bodies and of the sacred boards they hold. While this work goes on, women sing of the *Jukurrpa* ancestors who formed their country and its institutions. When their preparations were finished, "the assembled group had sung for the country where the ochres were quarried; they had sung for the ancestors who were to be celebrated in the dancing; they had provided ritual instruction for those women who were being groomed as future leaders, and they had offered brief guidance regarding the structure of their activities" (Bell, 1983, pp. 12–13).

As the sun was nearly setting, seven women moved some distance from the group of singers. With this the singers emphasized the rhythm of their songs with cupped hand clapping. The song grew stronger, and women from all groups and "countries" were called to attend. When the broader group had gathered, the singers recounted the travels of the ancestors depicted in the painted designs. Then, dancing in a straight line from the northwest came women wearing red and white designs on their bodies.

> They represented the activities of the diamond dove that travelled from Kurinji country through the desert lands. . . . As they neared the seated singers they held aloft the painted boards bearing ideational maps of the sites visited by the diamond dove in its trek south. The songs told of each site, of how the dove tired of travelling, of how the dove cried out for seed. On approaching the claypan known as Pawurrinji, the dove sighted the willy-wagtail, who was feasting on a small marsupial mouse. Women of the black and white designs of the wagtail danced forward to meet the travelling dove people; who then wove in and out of the wagtail ranks, flanking them before joining them in one circle. From where I sat I could see that the patterns traced in the red desert sand by the dancer's feet echoed those on the sacred boards. (Bell, 1983, p.13)

Bell describes how all the dancers then united in a tight circle in front of the seated singers. They presented the painted boards to them. With this the spirits of the birds entered the ground. This was the climax of the performance.

General gaiety followed. Singers were paid for their ritual work, and nonparticipants paid for having seen the ceremony. And singing again of the country, the women began the task of "rubbing down" the boards: "The designs had to be removed and the power with which they were infused during the dancing, absorbed and neutralized" (Bell, 1983, p. 14).

It is *kurdungurlu* who introduce the country with songs. It is they who collect the *kirda* for the ceremony. Both *kirda* and *kurdungurlu* dance. Both sing. But as Bell notes, "they do not sing for themselves."

In *Their Way* (2003) Ivan Jordan describes how, following attempts by missionaries to develop meaningful symbols for their church teaching, Warlpiri Christians came to present Christian symbols and develop Warlpiri Christian rituals. Jordan describes how boards were painted with Warlpiri Christian iconographs, new songs were developed, and finally the first "Christian *purlapa*" (public ceremony) was performed. He describes how in 1977 the Lajamanu and Yuendumu churches met:

> Then it happened. For many days, as daylight disappeared into darkness "big mobs" of people gathered to sing this new corroboree. Often someone came to the door to tell us they were ready to start. . . . As with all traditional corroboree singing, each song had just a few words, maybe five or six, and these words were repeated many times—at least thirty or forty. . . . When it finally happened, the dancing was truly exciting. Firstly, the appropriate symbolism for the body paintings had to be agreed on. . . . Preparation always took hours. . . . Having finished the painting, the right starting positions and dances and gestures were agreed upon after a good deal of group interaction. . . . I can still see those first dancers; dust flying, calloused black feet thudding the ground in perfect timing and harmony with the rising and falling chants of the singers and the echoing clicking of the boomerangs, Japanangka and Napurrula, husband and wife church leaders, were Mary and Joseph. At the appropriate time a suitable baby wrapped in a blanket and lying on a *coolamon* [wooden carrying dish] was produced from the

> crowd. . . . At the conclusion of the *purlapa,* it was usual for the men to begin rubbing the decoration from their bodies, the women quickly don bras, and blouses while Jerry Jangala [a church leader] stood and talked briefly about the story. Jangala would then conclude by praying. After this the people would disappear into the darkness happy and excited that they had not just heard God's story but they had actually danced and sung it. They had danced and sung God's "Business." (Jordan, 2003, pp. 119–121)

Jordan's account resonates in interesting and significant ways with Bell's description of Warlpiri ritual performance.

PARTICULARITIES: KOORI KIDS EMBRACING CULTURE AND COMING TO KNOW. About two-thirds of the way down the stadium the Seven Sisters dancers ceased their forward gait (which we can see, in retrospect, as signifying at some level their pursuit of emu fat). They formed a circle, dancing, swaying on the spot with their cupped hands in the air. The Awakening spirits moved in close to surround the older desert women. Ernie Dingo explained to viewers that the clay-daubed Awakening Spirits dancers came back from the podium to which they had followed the young girl and encircled the tightly bunched performers from the center of Australia. He announced their intent:

> To perform, to take to the heart of Australia the ancient art, the ancient stories of the past and to be embraced by the young Aboriginal culture of today and to share in its history and acceptance without questioning. They are preparing for an awakening, a welcome, and a rebirth in unity, so we can all be as one mob, the youth of today and the ancient culture of years gone by.

The cameras moved from the circled Central Desert women and koori kids to Djakapurra Munyarryun and Nikki Webster on the dais. Dingo continued: "The rebirth has started."

The "Awakening" spirit dancers who "embraced" the desert women were young, Sydney-based Koori performers covered in white clay. "Koori" is a term now widely understood as a collective referent for Aboriginal people in New South Wales and Victoria. Those children were learning about Australian Indigenous culture from this experience. Their dance was choreographed. Until their participation in the Sydney Olympics, many of the koori clan performers of the "Awakening" segment shared with Stephen Page a childhood in which they "had no exposure to our traditional culture."

The Sydney Organising Committee of the Olympic Games (SOCOG) media guide to the opening ceremony described the group brought together for the occasion as the "NSW Nationskoori clan." The SOCOG media guide described this group as one hundred men and women "from seventeen high schools and dance groups, [who] represent the Sydney language groups and the East coast of NSW language groups such as Biripi, Geawegal, Wiradjuri, Bundjalung, Gidbal, Awagakul Dunghutti and Gumbainggir" (SOCOG, p. 27). These Indigenous performers are Aboriginal people whose cultural lives and traditions are generally understood to have been sorely tested and disrupted by the colonial process in which their homelands were "settled" by non-Indigenous Australians.

The "NSW Nationskoori clans," or "Koori clans," as the creative team appears more commonly to have referred to them in film footage, performed dances especially choreographed for the opening ceremony. They performed themes that are emerging as general Indigenous religious ideas across the nation: the complex of ideas that the land and people hold within them the spirit of the land to which, despite disruption, their own spirit remains tied. These are connections they might respect and in performances like this rekindle and nurture. Matthew Doyle, described as the koori clan choreographer, said on camera: "What we were trying to do is represent young Aboriginal people from New South Wales from quite a few different areas." Describing his choreographic process, he continued: "I'm just looking at a couple of different styles of dance, you know, a mixture of some traditional-type movement and some modern and contemporary."

Djakapurra Munyarryun has pointed to the cultural "awakening" of these koori kids in *The Awakenings* film: "When I was watching the kids during the ceremonies . . . they were learning something. Learning something not new, but old" (Roger, 2001).

What was it they were learning? Michael Cohen, a participant-observer of the ceremony and preparations, reported that, "having taught performers the stooped torso and soft lifting of feet involved in the 'spirit dance,' Page constantly reminded the performers of the sacredness of their movements: 'Yes we're gonna do the low [dances]. The ones that hurt. [You've] gotta stay low. [The movements] are circular to keep the spirit internal.'"

The Awakenings shows Stephen Page directing the performers in rehearsal. He told them to move "Like spirits coming through." Page is also reported by Cohen to have told performers in practice, "[Awakening] Spirits, that was good—keeping your hands close to your sacred chests. But now just one problem: you have to try to move fast and still keep the spirit low. You have to try and combine these two energies" (Cohen, p. 166).

As far as one can tell from the available material, the Koori kids were presented with generalized Indigenous ideas about sacredness and spirits in their dancing. They mastered movements the choreographers presented to them with these generalized ideas.

In the film *The Awakenings,* Rhoda Roberts says:

> I think for the North coast group it's a very brave thing to dance in front of traditional people [for whom] ceremony is an everyday part of their lives. And I think we have in some way given a spirit and a soul and about what culture is what they didn't have before they started this little journey for the Olympics. And I think that makes me very proud to see that they are actually proud of their culture. (Roger, 2001)

Cohen reports that Rhoda Roberts told the Awakening spirits performers that the Central Desert women "dance *inma.* They dance bare-breasted. They paint each other. They're sistas [sisters]. I'm asking you to pay respect. I want you to understand. Those other segments [of the opening ceremony]—they've got props, they've got gizmos. But we don't need that cos we've got land. We've got spirit."

It is unlikely that the koori kids were told much detail of the *Kanpi* section of the Seven Sisters myth, whose dance and body paint the desert women displayed but did not fully reveal to the world. But it is clear that the kids learned about spirits and land and their own power as Indigenous people. In *The Awakenings,* Stephen Page calls on performers exhausted by rehearsal: "Wake up now. We're gunna go and meet the respected mother spirit from the Central Desert. Three hundred and thirty women represent one mother earth. We as young children got to respect that. Open our door. Got to welcome. We go and get them when they come. All their paint. We're very lucky" (Roger, 2001). The Koori performers were asked to respect the desert women who represented "mother earth," a concept of Indigenous relationships to land that has been gaining cross-continental currency among Indigenous people who have been distanced from their own local traditions.

But it was not their loss that seems to have been emphasized to these young performers. Rather, organizers emphasized what they had gained by participating and coming in contact with people from remote communities. By the end of their journey some of the koori performers saw the relationship as a two-way exchange. One boy from the Northern Rivers region of NSW put it this way in *The Awakenings:* "They're learning. They can back up what they learned down here and we what we learned here take back [to] where we came from. Show the people there what we learned, people we met" (Roger, 2001). If some Indigenous Dreamings remain embedded and enduring in local contexts, a new sense of general spiritual connection that respects the sacredness of the earth is also developing among Indigenous people in all corners of the nation.

PARTICULARITIES: YOLNGU. The encircling of desert women by koori kids dominated the stadium until the spotlights traced a large oblique cross on the red sands of the stadium floor. Attention turned to colorful dancers with flags emerging from the four corners. They danced into center stage to the sound of didgeridoo and song. Ernie Dingo elaborated for the television audience:

> The wonderful voice of Don Nundihirribala singing the Dhumbala which is the flag song. Flags represented [the relationship] with the Aboriginal community of the top end, of Arnhem Land, when the Macassan traders used to come over four thousand years ago to trade shellfish with cloth and tobacco. Representation of the Numbulwar, Yirrkala, Ramingining, and Maningrida people from Arnhem Land.

In the tropical "Top End" of Australia the country of the Yolngu juts out into the Arafura Sea, and its eastern coast forms one edge of the Gulf of Carpentaria. Yolngu country is rich in resources. Its coastline includes rich mangrove estuaries as well as sandy beaches. Inland the mighty Arnhem Land escarpment juts out of the resource-rich plains and littoral belt. There are three main settlements of Yolngu people in northeast Arnhem Land: Milingimbi, founded in 1922; Yirrkala, founded in 1935; and Elcho Island, founded in 1942. These settlements began their lives as mission stations. Before the establishment of these settlements Yolngu clans were dispersed throughout northeast Arnhem Land. As Morphy has noted in *Ancestral Connections* (1991): "Although the size and structure of communities varied seasonally, for much of the year people lived in bands of around thirty to forty individuals" (Morphy, 1991, p. 40). By the 1970s an "outstation movement" was under way and many people were returning to their ancestral homelands.

Yolngu call their ancestral figures or Dreamings *wangarr.* They tell of them and their formative actions in myths. As Morphy has eloquently shown, Yolngu people live

> in a world that includes both European and Aboriginal institutions, systems of knowledge, languages: they are influenced by both. Yolngu clans have taken on functions and arguably a constitution that they did not have before, and those new functions are going to affect the trajectory the clans have over time. The process is a two-way one, and European institutions in northern Australia must sometimes take account of Aboriginal practices and institutions. (Morphy, 1991, p. 4)

Yolngu openness to other cultures and cultural exchange is not new. The flag dance performed at the opening ceremony relates to the annual visits of Macassans from what is now Suluwasi in Indonesia. They came annually to Arnhem Land on the winds of the northwest monsoon, sailing in praus. They set up camp on Yolngu beaches, gathering and processing bêche-de-mer (sea cucumber) until stopped by government officials in 1907. Ian Keen has noted:

> Many Yolngu religious traditions reflected their relations with the Macassans. . . . Ceremonies represented the practices of Macassans, including their rituals. The subjects of these songs and ceremonies were not merely historical or typical figures but *wangarr* ancestors of the human Macassans. . . . Through the exchange of personal names Macassan names entered the Yolngu lexicon, along with other words. Some Macassan place names [continue to have currency] . . . for the Macassans applied their own names to the landscape of north-east Arnhem Land and declared certain rocks sacred, as sites for offerings to sea spirits. (Keen, 1994, pp. 23–24)

Ian McIntosh suggests that Macassans caused some turbulence in Yolngu life. Memories of interactions between Yolngu and Macassans also focus on the creational being Birrinydji. In "Sacred Memory and Living Tradition" (2000) McIntosh suggests, "Belief in Birrindyji empowers the listener-viewer to transform the nature of relations between the cultural groups and to regain what was deemed to have been lost at the 'beginning of time'" (McIntosh, 2000, p. 144). When a replica of a Macassan prau returned to Yolngu shores in 1988, hundreds of Yolngu performed the ceremonies of Birrinydji for their arrival. McIntosh also notes two kinds of depictions of Macassan themes: some "inside" some "outside" designs. He continues:

> Depictions of praus (sailing craft), trepang-processing sites, the goods obtained through trade with the visitors, the mistreatment or abduction of women by Macassans, or the slaughter of Aboriginal men by firing squad, are "outside." Images such as golden-skinned women working on weaving looms, the performance of corroborees in honour of Allah, and an Arnhem Land creational being who directs Aboriginal men in the making of iron kilns are "inside." "Outside" art deals with specific historical episodes; "inside" art refers implicitly or explicitly with Birrinydji. (McIntosh, 2000, p. 144)

The idea of "inside" and "outside"—open and restricted knowledge and practice—is a fundamental feature of Yolngu religious life. As Keen notes in *Knowledge and Secrecy in an Aboriginal Religion* (1994), "Age, gender, group identity, and kin relation to a group were important determinants of who could impart information about elements of ceremonies, especially secret meanings, and to whom" (Keen, 1994, p. 244). Yet as Annette Hamilton shows, one does not find in Arnhem Land a context in which gender separation is as marked as it is in the desert regions. Rather, she says, "we find a complex conundrum of arrivals and departures, presences and absences, in which women are fully involved. It is sometimes said that women are made present by their absences. This is a neat expression of a much more complex set of connections" (Hamilton, 2000, p. 71).

Keen relates:

> Yolngu conceived of *wangarr* ancestors as beings with human form, but having some of the properties of the beings or entities whose names they took, such as Rock or Honeybee, and as having extraordinary powers. They were active long, long ago in "far off" times. They camped, foraged, made love, quarreled and fought, and bore children, somewhat like humans, but they were involved in extraordinary events and were transformed by them, perhaps into species such as jabirus or entities such as the moon. Some *wangarr* engendered the ancestors of human groups. These were a group's *gulu'kulungu* ancestors. (Keen, 1994, p. 45)

Yolngu views of reproduction include a connection between *wangarr* ancestors, reproductive processes (such as the ancestral spirit menstruating into waters), and the conception of children's spirits. In this understanding of human conception, a child's "image" *(mali)* enters the woman from such waters. The father might then "find" the spirit of his child in a dream or strange experience (Keen, 1994, p. 106). Thus Keen says that in Yolngu belief "the person was, in a sense, born of the *wangarr* ancestor and the waters" (Keen, 1994, p. 107).

Keen notes too that, "from a Yolngu point of view . . . land was not mere dirt; land and waters consisted in part of the bodily substance of the *wangarr* ancestors." Keen has drawn out the connection between country (*Wa:nga*), ancestors (*wangarr*), sacred objects (*rangga,* which were "placed in the country by the ancestors and which were the *ngaraka,* 'bones,' of the ancestor"), and ceremonial grounds (where sacred objects are revealed to novices) (Keen, 1994, pp. 102–103).

> All these things and beings implied links between people, living and dead, country, ancestors, and the ceremonies which followed them. The individual, group, and country were all identified with the bodies and *mali'* ("image," "spirit") of the *wangarr* ancestors. In ceremony a *rangga* sacred object which represented the transformation of a *wangarr* ancestor or a part of an ancestor was its bone and flesh. The "bone country" (*ngaraka wa:nga*) contained the transformed substance as well as the powers of the ancestors. The individual gained both his or her being and powers from the *wangarr.* At a person's death the spirit was believed to return to the waters on his or her country, the domain of the *wangarr* ancestor, and/or to a land of the dead over the sea, and/or to heaven, the spirit home of [the Christian] "God *wangarr.*" But if people performed disinterment and reburial rites the body of the dead was reincorporated with the country and body of the ancestor in its manifestation as a hollow-log coffin. (Keen, 1994, p. 103)

Despite the apparent remoteness of their countries, Yolngu people were subject to alienation from their lands like Indigenous people across the nation. In the 1960s the federal government of Australia granted a mining lease and property rights to a French aluminum company over a large part of northeast Arnhem Land. In 1963 Yolngu people from Yirrkala sent a petition to the federal parliament in Canberra. The Yolngu petitioners demanded that their rights in land be recognized and protected. They sought to be consulted about such developments in their homelands. Significantly the protesting Yolngu did not present their petition to the federal parliament as a mass of signed pages, the traditional form by which Australian parliaments are petitioned. Instead, the Yolngu petition, as Morphy notes, "was attached to a bark painting bordered with designs belonging to the clans whose lands were most immediately threatened by the mining" (Morphy, p. 18). A federal inquiry and a court case followed. Their findings were sympathetic to the Arnhem Landers's plight. Morphy notes, "In the short term the Yolngu had completely failed, but in the process they had helped to create the political environment for granting Aboriginal land rights" (Morphy, p. 31). This case laid the foundation for the passage in 1974 of land rights legislation in the then commonwealth-administered Northern Territory.

PARTICULARITIES: THE NGARRINDJERI AND A CONTESTED SEVEN SISTERS STORY. Veronica Brodie, a woman of Ngarrindjeri and Kaurna descent, says in *My Side of the Bridge* (2002): "You know there's a beautiful Dreaming story that goes with Hindmarsh Island, and that's The Seven Sisters." It is in this area, Brodie says, that the Seven Sisters rise and descend seasonally to the sky world.

One side of Ngarrindjeri country lies where the land of the lower Murray and Coorong Rivers meets the Southern Ocean. This coastal and lakes region forms an area with huge horizons. The land and waters of Ngarrindjeri country fill only the bottom of everyday vistas. On a clear night the sky, punctuated by stars and the soft clouds of the Milky Way, comes down to meet the horizon. In this country it is not a great leap to imagine ancestral figures moving between sky, sea, and land.

South Australia was colonized in 1836. The lands of the Ngarrindjeri people, within a hundred or so miles of Adelaide, the new colony's capital, were settled soon after. Gradually the land was taken, parcel by parcel. Even so many Ngarrindjeri families remained in or near their homelands in the mission established in 1859 at Point McLeay or in fringe camps throughout the region. Some continue to live on their country. Others have moved to major centers and live in homes that blend easily with those of their suburban neighbors.

A century after the colonization period had begun, researchers of Indigenous life, such as Norman Tindale and more briefly Ronald Berndt, undertook work with Ngarrindjeri people. They documented the endurance of significant cultural knowledge a century or so after the process of settlement had begun in earnest. Both researchers recorded myths about the formation of the landscape and of Ngarrindjeri law. Both documented their informants' knowledge of Ngarrindjeri life prior to the arrival of white settlers.

The action of the Murray River dominates the life of the area. As Ronald M. Berndt and Catherine H. Berndt put it:

> The great River Murray that dominated the Narrinyeri [Ngarrindjeri] people was significant not only because of the Ngurunderi myth which was known all over its territory. . . . [T]he River was like a lifeline, an immense artery of a living "body" consisting of the Lakes and the bush hinterland that stretched across towards the Adelaide Hills and over the southern plains and undulating land. This "body" also included the country to the east. . . . Its "legs" spread south-eastwards along the Coorong and south-westwards along Encounter Bay and beyond. The "body," symbolic of Ngurunderi himself, embraced five different environments which merged into one another: salt-water country, riverine, Lakes, bush (scrub) and desert plains (on the east)—a combination that had particular relevance to the socio-economic life of the people. (Berndt and Berndt, 1993, p. 13)

Several versions of this myth have been recorded. This is thought to reflect the orientation of different clans to the story and to the section of it relating to their homelands. The myth tells of the great ancestor Ngurunderi, who traveled in search of two wives who had run away from him. At first a giant cod (*pondi*) traveled before him. The sweep of its tail widened the river in parts. Elsewhere it darted away from him when he threw his spear to create long straight stretches of the river. Other actions of the pair gave form to the swamps, shoals, and wetlands along the way and formed the great lakes at the river's end. When the cod reached Lake Alexandrina, Ngurunderi sought the aid of another ancestral figure, his wives' brother Nepeli. Ngurunderi caught the cod and cut it up with a stone knife. From pieces of *pondi's* body came other fish: boney bream, perch, callop, and mudfish. Ngurunderi made camp but while he was there smelled cooking fish and knew his wives were near. He left his camp to renew his pursuit, but his huts remained as two hills, and his bark canoe rose into the sky to form the Milky Way. More forms came into being in his tracks and wake. The story ends with the drowning deaths of the two wives whose bodies became islands known as the Pages. Eventually Ngurunderi himself entered the spirit world on Kangaroo Island. He dived into the sea and rose to become a star in the Milky Way.

In the late 1980s, by then 150 years after settlement, the South Australian Museum framed an exhibition of Ngarrindjeri culture around the Ngurunderi myth. On display too was a dramatization of the myth by contemporary Ngarrindjeri people. Though knowledge of the Ngurunderi myth was no longer widespread, it had persisted in the memories of a small handful of Ngarrindjeri people. The processes of negotiating the exhibition and its subsequent popularity revived and revitalized existing knowledge of the myth across the Ngarrindjeri nation.

The mighty Murray River winds its way through three states of Australia as it makes its way from the east to the south of the continent. At the end of its journey it spills slowly into one of Australia's great lakes, Lake Alexandrina. Despite barrages and irrigation, the waters of the Murray flow on, channeling out of the lake and around a low-lying island called Kumerangk, or Hindmarsh Island, in the Goolwa Channel. The Murray edges past the small river town of Goolwa. At a place known as the mouth the breakers of the Great South Ocean run onto a sandbar, where a channel ordinarily gives course for the ocean and the fresh water to finally meet.

In May 1995 a group of thirty-five or so Ngarrindjeri women met with an appointee of the national minister responsible for Indigenous affairs. The developer of a marina complex had sought to start building a bridge between Hindmarsh Island and the township of Goolwa. Ngarrindjeri people sought protection of their heritage, which they said would be damaged or destroyed if the bridge work went ahead. The state minister accepted that damage and destruction was entailed in building the bridge but, in the context of a complex web of preexisting obligations, authorized the work to proceed under an act the aim of which was the protection of Aboriginal heritage in South Australia. Ngarrindjeri people petitioned the federal minister to exercise his powers under the Aboriginal and Torres Strait Islander Heritage Protection Act of 1984.

The minister had been informed that in Ngarrindjeri culture the "meeting of the waters" around Kumerangk (Hindmarsh) Island was vital to the fertility and life of *ngatji,* Ngarrindjeri totems. He had also been advised that the area had significance to women in Ngarrindjeri tradition but that the nature of that significance was part of "secret-sacred" traditions.

On a cold day in May 1995 women who were petitioning the federal minister for the protection of their heritage formed a circle on the beach of Kumerangk at the mouth of the river. There with them was the woman appointed to report to the minister. They said this place was important to their fertility and to the survival of their culture. Many wept. Women hugged and held each other. Some said that though they had not known the significance of this place in their tradition before these meetings, they could now feel the significance of the place and felt assured of the rightness of what they were doing. Doreen Kartinyeri, a key figure in their application to the minister, looked out at the mouth and said, "For all the mothers that was, for all the mothers that are, for all the mothers that will be," indicating why she was undertaking this task.

Kartinyeri was later elected the group's spokesperson, authorized to disclose restricted knowledge that underpinned her opposition to the building of the bridge to the minister's reporter. Her disclosures did not occur without immediate opposition. Some Ngarrindjeri women in the group took the position that Ngarrindjeri people should not disclose restricted knowledge to people not entitled by tradition to receive it. Despite the difficult debate about the propriety of divulging restricted traditions, the group of women ultimately authorized Kartinyeri to disclose the restricted knowledge to the minister's reporter. She in turn agreed that she would do her best to protect against its further disclosure. The minister acted to ban the building of a bridge for twenty-five years: the years that would cover perhaps another generation of Ngarrindjeri people.

But that was not the end of the matter. The developers whose bridge and marina project was stymied by this decision sought legal review. Nearly a year later, in May 1995, another group of Ngarrindjeri women went public with claims that the knowledge had been fabricated. Most said simply that they did not have this knowledge themselves and on that basis doubted its veracity. One said she believed she was witness to an insinuation by Ngarrindjeri men that the area of the lower Murray represented "a women's privates" and that this suggestion was the beginning of a process of fabrication. These claims split Ngarrindjeri people and Ngarrindjeri families. They split anthropological opinion. They split opinion across the nation.

The South Australian government called a royal commission into the claims of fabrication. Veronica Brodie reports in *My Side of the Bridge* that the claimant women declined on the first day of hearings to participate in the royal commission's enquiry. Instead, they wrote to Royal Commissioner Iris Stevens as follows:

> We are deeply offended that a Government in this day and age has the audacity to order an inquiry into our secret, sacred, spiritual beliefs. Never before have any group of people had their spiritual beliefs scrutinized in this way. It is our responsibility as custodians of this knowledge to protect it. Not only from men, but also from those not entitled to this knowledge. We have a duty to keep Aboriginal law in this country. Women's business does exist, has existed since time immemorial and will continue to exist where there are Aboriginal women who are able to practice their culture. (Brodie, 2002, p. 151)

The Stevens Hindmarsh Island Bridge Royal Commission found in December 1995 that "the whole of the 'women's business' was a fabrication" intended to prevent the construction of a bridge between the township of Goolwa and Hindmarsh Island.

In 1998 Brodie, with the support of other Ngarrindjeri women, gave Diane Bell permission to publish (in *Ngarrindjeri Wurruwarrin*) the following limited account of her knowledge of the Seven Sisters story and its relevance to the issue of building a bridge to Hindmarsh Island:

> It begins with Ngurunderi's cave which is situated . . . [at Goolwa]. From the cave he looked across to the island. Ngurunderi felt it was his responsibility to look after the sky, the bird life, the waters, because he made the environment and the island. He was the god of the Ngarrindjeri. His connection with the Seven Sisters was that he sent a young man, Orion, after the Seven Sisters to chase them and bring them back. They didn't want to be caught so they headed up to the sky, up and up and over the Milky Way and hid and there became the Seven Sisters. When they want to come back to see their Mum, who is still in the waters—near where the ferry crosses, just a little over towards the mouth, to the south—there has to be a clear way, so they can return and they'll be returning shortly, when it gets cold, that's when they disappear from the sky. Then they come back down and go under the water to be with their mother. Their mother belonged to the Warrior Women of the Island. (Bell, 1998, p. x)

In 1997 the commonwealth government legislated to exclude this area from the protections offered by the Aboriginal and Torres Strait Islander Heritage Protection Act. Ngarrindjeri claimants made appeal to the High Court of Australia, arguing among other things that the Hindmarsh Island Bridge Act breached the Australian constitution and the Commonwealth Racial Discrimination Act of 1975. In April 1998 the High Court ruled to the contrary. The Hindmarsh Island bridge was built. It opened to traffic in March 2001. It has become a curiosity stopover on Australian tourist routes.

Legal questions relating to the matter have now been pursued through a number of state and commonwealth courts in a number of separate cases. In August 2001, after a long-running civil suit for damages, Federal Court judge John Von Doussa found that he was not convinced that the claims of the claimant women were fabricated.

Meanwhile the phrases "secret women's business" and "secret men's business" have entered popular Australian speech. They are used to refer to gender-specific contexts, especially those carrying sexual overtones. Racing boats have these names. Prewedding parties are referred to with these terms. These usages indicate how easily Indigenous religious claims that are brought to bear in Australian law or public life can be disrespected. In the early twenty-first century the controversy and the public skepticism of Aboriginal claims it fuels continue. So too do Ngarrindjeri people endure.

FINALE. This overview of Australian Indigenous religion has traced connections, responses, contestation, and endurance to explore themes that underlie many Indigenous traditions. It has surveyed a range of Australian Indigenous societies and their contexts.

The "Awakening" segment of the Sydney Olympic opening ceremony has provided touchstones for this discussion. This article has moved between specific Dreamings grounded in local places, where they are constantly enlivened in human action, to more diffuse expressions of emerging Pan-Australian Indigenous expressions and beliefs. But the finale of the Olympic journey is still to come.

The Yolngu flag dancers moved into lines running down the stadium. Overhead cameras showed the performers on the stadium floor forming into a colorful design: two separated lines leading like a pathway into a circle open to meet it.

A conch shell heralded the arrival of another group of performers. Drums and rattles beat out an aggressive rhythm. Headdressed and painted dancers in colorful grass skirts formed a phalanx and proceeded, full of rhythmic vitality, in a low hopping and skipping movement down the stadium toward the patterning presences on the floor. Ernie Dingo responded to the energy of the performance: "Ah, this'll get ya' blood boiling. To the Torres Strait. Welcoming the Torres Strait Islanders, brothers and sisters from the north of Queensland and the *admulla,* the rhythm dance to celebrate the energy of the Torres Strait Islands from far north Queensland." The Torres Strait Islanders moved to position themselves kneeling, though still performing, as additional lines in a "pathway" to the circle.

Then a new sound was heard. Jean-clad dancers entered the stadium covered in silver paint. They held boomerangs out from their bodies as they danced. "The red Kangaroo dance welcoming the koori people of New South Wales, the host nation. Welcoming them as the last to come on to the site and [to] dance with the rest of the nation and prepare the unity from the ancient culture to the modern youth of today."

On the dais smoke rose from wooden vessels held high by dancers from the Bangarra Dance Theatre. With Djakapurra Munyarryun they descended the stairs to the stadium floor. The ground pattern broke up. "The smoking ceremony is set up to cleanse the air of all ailment; to cleanse the air of all negativity; to cleanse this meeting place in preparation for rejoicement."

Smoke rose now from forty-four-gallon drums on the stadium floor. Djakkapurra Munyarrun sang again, beating time with his clap sticks.

"Once the cleansing has happened, the spirits are awakened, called by the song man."

On high stilts, spiky headdressed "mimi spirits" loped through and above the smoke billowing from the stadium floor. Ernie Dingo introduced the finale.

"The Bradshaw paintings depicted . . . are the helpers of the Wandjina, the great spirit from the Kimberlies in Western Australia. When the people are one, they'll call the spirits of creation to awaken the spirit, to lead them to a future they want to be."

Then a huge golden fabric was raised. Outlined on it in black was a great fringed head with big black eyes and nose, a Wandjina figure. The figure was raised to form an enormous backdrop. The Wandjina rippled gently in the breeze.

"The great Wandjina spirit who comes from the Kimberley. The eyes. The nose. And no mouth to pass judgment will awaken the spirits around and [give] the people the chance of rejoicement."

The Indigenous performers now mixed together on the floor waving their hands above their heads before the Wandjina. Stilted spirits stepped high among them. The background music rose to a crescendo. Then a barrage of fireworks pierced the night and shot sparks around the stadium. The great Wandjina figure was animated in the light and breeze.

The "Awakening" segment was ending and "Fire" beginning. Ernie Dingo explained: "The rebirthing has started. The land now needs to prepare for a new life. A new life comes in the form of a bush fire, controlled fire which allowed the Aboriginal people [to rid] the land of unwanted life."

The Awakenings film showed Stephen Page, codirector of the segment, on camera high in a control room enjoying the finale. "That's what you call a ceremony!" he said. "Can't have a ceremony without culture" (Roger, 2001).

BIBLIOGRAPHY

Australian Bureau of Statistics. "Statistics. Statistical Profile—Aboriginal Women and Torres Strait Islander Women." Available from http://abs.gov.au/websitedbs.

Australian Bureau of Statistics. "Website Indigenous Statistics Education: Population Information—Distribution of Indigenous People across Australia." Available from http://abs.gov.au/websitedbs.

Bell, Diane. *Ngarrindjeri Wurruwarrin: A World That Is, Was, and Will Be.* North Melbourne, Australia, 1998.

Bell, Diane. *Daughters of the Dreaming.* North Melbourne, 1983; reprint, 2002.

Berndt, Ronald M., and Catherine H. Berndt, with John E. Stanton. *A World That Was: The Yaraldi of the Murray River and the Lakes, South Australia.* Melbourne, Australia, 1993.

Brodie, Veronica. *My Side of the Bridge.* Kent Town, South Australia, 2002.

Charlesworth, Max, ed. *Religious Business: Essays on Australian Aboriginal Spirituality.* Cambridge, U.K., 1998.

Charlesworth, Max, Howard Morphy, Diane Bell, and K. Maddock, eds. *Religion in Aboriginal Australia: An Anthology.* Saint Lucia, Queensland, Australia, 1984.

Davis, Richard, ed. *Woven Histories Dancing Lives: Torres Strait Islander Identity, Culture and History.* Canberra, Australia, 2004.

Dussart, Françoise. *The Politics of Ritual in an Aboriginal Settlement: Kinship, Gender, and the Currency of Knowledge.* Washington, D.C., 2000.

Evatt, Elizabeth. *Review of the Aboriginal and Torres Strait Islander Heritage Protection Act 1984.* Report to the Minister for Aboriginal and Torres Strait Islander Affairs, Commonwealth of Australia, 1996.

Foley, Dennis. "The Cultural Genocide of the Sydney Olympic 2000 Games." Available from http://www.faira.org.au/lrq/archives/199811/stories/the-cultural-genocide.html.

Hamilton, Anette. "Gender, Aesthetics, Performance." In *The Oxford Companion to Aboriginal Art and Culture,* edited by S. Kleinert and M. Neale, pp. 68–75. South Melbourne, Australia, 2000.

Hercus, Luise. *Nukunu Dictionary.* Canberra, Australia, 1992.

Hiatt, Lester R. *Arguments about Aborigines: Australia and the Evolution of Social Anthropology.* Cambridge, U.K., 1996.

Jordan, Ivan. *Their Way: Towards an Indigenous Warlpiri Christianity.* Darwin, Australia, 2003.

Keen, Ian. *Knowledge and Secrecy in an Aboriginal Religion: Yolngu of North-East Arnhemland.* Oxford, 1994.

Kleinert, S., and M. Neale, eds. *The Oxford Companion to Aboriginal Art and Culture.* South Melbourne, Australia, 2000.

McIntosh, Ian. "Sacred Memory and Living Tradition: Aboriginal Art of the Macassan Period in North-East Arnhem Land." In *The Oxford Companion to Aboriginal Art and Culture,* edited by S. Kleinert and M. Neale, pp. 144–145. South Melbourne, Australia, 2000.

Michaels, Eric. "Constraints on Knowledge in an Economy of Oral Information." *Current Anthropology* 26, no. 4 (1985): 505–510.

Morphy, Howard. *Ancestral Connections: Art and an Aboriginal System of Knowledge.* Chicago, 1991.

Morphy, Howard. "Empiricism to Metaphysics: In Defense of the Concept of the Dreamtime." In *Prehistory to Politics: John Mulvaney, the Humanities and the Public Intellectual,* edited by Tim Bonyhady and Tom Griffiths, pp. 163–189. Melbourne, Australia, 1995.

Morphy, Howard. *Aboriginal Art.* London, 1998.

Morton, John. "Country, People, Art: The Western Aranda 1970–1990." In *The Heritage of Namatjira: The Watercolorists of Central Australia,* edited by J. Hardy, J. V. S. Megaw, and M. R. Megaw. Melbourne, Australia, 1991.

Myers, Fred R. *Pintupi Country, Pintupi Self: Sentiment, Place, and Politics among Western Desert Aborigines.* Washington, D.C., 1986.

Myers, Fred R. "Culture Making: Performing Aboriginality at the Asia Society Gallery." *American Ethnologist* 21, no. 4 (1994): 679–699.

Rose, Deborah Bird. *Nourishing Terrains: Australian Aboriginal Views of Landscape and Wilderness.* Canberra, Australia, 1996.

Stanner, W. E. H. *White Man Got No Dreaming: Essays, 1938–1973.* Canberra, Australia, 1979.

Stanner, W. E. H. "The Dreaming." In *White Man Got No Dreaming* (pp. 23-40), Canberra, Australia, 1979.

Stanner, W. E. H. *On Aboriginal Religion* (1966). Oceania Monograph 36. Sydney, Australia, 1989.

Watson, Christine. *Piercing the Ground: Balgo Women's Image Making and the Relationship to Country.* Freemantle, Wash., 2003.

DEANE FERGIE (2005)

AUSTRALIAN INDIGENOUS RELIGIONS: MYTHIC THEMES [FIRST EDITION]

In the positive sense myth is a charter for and a guide to action, though not necessarily socially approved action. Although myth is not always linked directly to religious ritual, the most important myths usually have a two-way, mutually supportive relationship with ritual. A myth may stipulate, explain, or describe a rite or outline a sequence of events that, when translated into ritual action, emphasizes different facets of its mythic counterpart.

As nonliterate peoples, the Aborigines relied almost entirely on oral transmission. Other modes of communication were supplementary and, like spoken languages and dialects, regionally based: hand-sign vocabularies, material representations, body markings, ritual and ceremonial posturing and dance, and gestures and facial expressions. These, like myth, illustrate the crisscrossing of similarity and diversity in traditional Aboriginal culture throughout the continent, as well as the balance between local and outward-looking orientations.

Mythic characters were usually associated with specific sites in the territories of specific groups. They mediated and personalized the relationship between people and the land. But most mythic beings were travelers, not confined to single regions, and however much of their spiritual essence they left behind at sites which now commemorate them, their mythic tracks led outward as well as inward. Along with trade and gift exchanges, which connected persons and groups beyond the ordinary range of social interaction, the mythic beings encouraged a centrifugal perspective, actualized in meetings for religious rituals that focused on the appropriate mythic characters, their sites and tracks, and their sayings, songs, and deeds.

Aboriginal societies were based on religion. Religious rules, authority, and sanctions were dominant, permeating the whole of living and ranging from the highly concentrated secret-sacred dimension through the dimension of the open sacred, or public sacred, to more routine mundane affairs. In themes and in modes of transmission, and in their ritual associations, myths in all regions reflect that span and that coverage.

SACRED CONTEXT OF EVERYDAY LIFE. Many myths contain primary or secondary themes that have a practical bearing on issues of everyday life. These are sometimes regarded as too mundane or too localized to be put in the same category as more obviously sacred myths with potentially universal appeal. Nevertheless, they are set firmly within a religious frame.

Essentially practical and down-to-earth, Aboriginal religion put almost equal importance on human physical well-being and on spiritual matters or nonempirical aspirations. Many religious rites, large and small, were directed to human goals. For example, a multitude of species-renewal rites, performed by different persons or groups at different times and places, tried to ensure that people had enough of all the resources they regarded as necessary for living in their particular area. The rites were designed to achieve through religious means aims that were, in one sense, mundane. And myths were vital ingredients in this process. Mythic characters were responsible for contributing the different "necessities for living"; they also sanctified and sponsored locally available assets by simply using them themselves. Myths, then, were and are storehouses of practical information, rules, and precepts, as well as a source of divine truths.

Some mythic characters created supplies of food or water that had not been there before. For example, the Djanggawul sisters in eastern Arnhem Land urinated to provide fresh water for the local human populations. Several of these waters were so powerfully sacred that access to them was restricted. The Djanggawul also caused trees to grow from their posts, called djuda, but in western Arnhem Land a high proportion of mythic characters are credited with actually "planting" a wide range of vegetation. Sometimes they carried vegetables or fish in long baskets and "poured them out" in what seemed appropriate places. Others, such as one of the many mythic sister pairs who traveled throughout Arnhem Land, shaped goannas and lizards, put them among red ants that bit them into life, then struck them on the head with a spear-thrower to make them move and spread across the land. Still other characters turned into various vegetable foods or into fresh and edible land creatures. An old potential water-peanut man ended his journey (during which he planted many foods) in a billabong near the East Alligator River, where he gradually changed into a water peanut and with his last words urged the people of that region to gather and eat him in his food manifestation.

In a Dieri myth from the Lake Eyre region, one of the *muramura* used songs to make both bitter and pleasant-tasting plants grow. (Howitt, 1904, p. 781). T. G. H. Strehlow, in the narrative myth of Emianga in central Australia, sets out details of edible seed preparation (see below). Ngurunderi, the great mythic personage of the lower Murray River in South Australia, took a fish—a Murray cod—caught by his wives' brother Nepeli in a giant *pondi*, cut it into pieces, and threw the pieces into the river and into the lakes at the river's mouth. As he did so, he named each piece as a different variety of fish, making the waters rich in fish for the human beings who were to come.

On Cape York Peninsula, Hard Yam Woman and Arrowroot Man, descending into their respective sacred sites, took on the shape of roots and uttered instructions on how they should be treated to render them edible (McConnel, 1957, p. 54). Beforehand, they themselves had foraged and hunted for food, as they traveled, the woman digging for roots and the man spearing fish. According to the story, Hard Yam Woman carefully prepared the roots by cooking them with pieces of heated ant-bed (termite mound) and repeatedly washing and rinsing them. She carried a dillybag and bark container and Arrowroot Man had a spear-thrower and a tomahawk as well as spears.

Characters in Aboriginal myths do not often instruct human beings about food and water, nor do they usually transform themselves into food; they are more commonly seen using the resources that are already available. Usually no explanation of how the resources got there is given; it is enough, in these myths, that they are there and can be utilized by the characters whose story it is in the course of their adventures and encounters. That applies to the making or use of tools and other nonedible resources.

In a song series closely related to the Wawalag myth, the boomerang-legged honey spirit man Wudal, or Woial, carries bees in tightly plaited baskets hung from his shoulders; he chops out a honeycomb from a tree with his stone ax and gashes a paper-bark tree with his boomerang to obtain fresh water. (His boomerang legs are a type of bone deformity, said to be a result of early malnutrition.) The Wawalag themselves have baskets and digging sticks; they build a fire and try to cook their food on it and gather paper bark for sleeping mats and stringy bark for a hut. The stone spear blades they carry are referred to in one of the Wudal songs: Ridarngu-speaking men who have dug out and shaped the stone sit around in a circle, wrapping the blades carefully in paper bark, then packing them into baskets.

Metamorphosed stone objects at various sites are the grinding stones, food containers, domestic tools, and fish traps of mythic characters. Other myths throughout the continent tell of the making of spears and shields. In some cases, they say who was responsible; in others, mythic characters simply use the implements. For example, the Djanggawul came on the path of the rising sun in their bark canoe (or raft), but we are not told who made it. Boomerangs were not used or even traded in all regions. Where they were, they were not all the same: not all were returning; not all were used as weapons or clapping sticks for singing or as ritual defloration tools, or in women's secret rites. Similarly, the *didjeridu* (drone pipe) does not appear in inland or Western Desert myths. On the north coast of western Arnhem Land, however, it is mostly an ordinary item of a mythic songman's equipment. According to one *didjeridu* origin myth, after a troublesome mythic character had been killed and buried, people heard a strange new sound coming from underground. Far from being dead, the character had put the end of his abnormally long penis in his mouth and was blowing through it.

Some myths have characters using fire for cooking food and for warmth but make no reference to its origin. The Wawalag sisters, for instance, took it for granted. In other myths, there are characters who are credited with introducing it. Wuragag, in western Arnhem Land, brought it especially from his origin place, somewhere beyond Bathurst and Melville islands, so that people on the mainland would not need to eat their food raw. In other examples fire is a cause of quarrels, as in a simplified children's story from northeastern Arnhem Land in which Crocodile and Frilled (Blanket) Lizard, both men then, fight about fire. Crocodile threw a fire stick at Frilled Lizard, so that he grew small and reddish, taking on his lizard shape; Crocodile slid into the salt water and stayed there.

Theft of fire is a common theme and is often associated with birds. In an account from the Kurnai of Victoria, a "supernatural being called Bullum-baukan stole the fire of the early Kurnai. Narugul, the Crow, and Ngarang, the Swamphawk, having recovered it, Bullum-baukun ascended to the sky by climbing up a cord made of the sinews of the red wallaby." (Howitt, 1904, p. 486). In a Western Desert myth, Old Man Gandju's companions went hunting without him. He covered up their campfires and went away with his own fire stick. When they returned, they tried to make fire but could not. They died of cold and are visible today as a heap of granite stones at their old camping site. Gandju later had his fire stick stolen by two men, but he turned into a fire spirit and burned them to death. On the Daly River, in the Northern Territory, Dog tried to twirl a fire-drill stick to make fire to cook roots, but the stick always broke. He tried to steal a live fire stick from some women who were preparing an oven, but twice they drove him away. Big Hawk, his companion, was also unsuccessful, but Little Chicken Hawk was able to swoop down on a piece of glowing wood and fly off with it. In their camp, Dog had impatiently eaten all his yams raw. That is why dogs eat their food raw today and why they do not talk. (See Berndt and Berndt, 1982, pp. 396–397. Some fire myths in various parts of Australia are discussed by Maddock, 1970).

At one level, the myths of different regions provide two kinds of information. First, they contain details about terrain, vegetable and animal foods, and fresh and salt water, noting how these resources are utilized by mythic characters. Secondly, the artifacts that are mentioned can be located on maps, as in the case of boomerangs and *didjeridu,* indicating where and how they appear in myths—including ceremonial gift exchanges where mythic characters meet, engage in trade, or carry items from one area to another. Subthemes of both kinds, with varying content, are a rich source of data for comparison with the actualities of traditional Aboriginal life—corresponding, in a different dimension, to details of mythic origins and to the manufacture and use of sacred and secret-sacred materials. (Howitt, 1904, contains a wealth of detail on all of these points for southeastern Australia.)

A third kind of information is inseparable from the other two, as far as myths in this and in the secret-sacred dimensions are concerned. In the charter and guide that are set out explicitly or implicitly in the myths, the "what" of natural resources and artifacts does not stand on its own; the issue of "who" is crucial. For example, in the division of labor in everyday hunting and foraging, men use spears, women use digging sticks, and these tools symbolize their roles. Some food containers are specific to women (e.g., wooden carrying dishes throughout the Western Desert and elsewhere), whereas baskets or dillybags are used by women slung from their foreheads, by men slung from their shoulders, occasionally in everyday circumstances but often (as in northern Arnhem Land), when feathered and decorated, as sacred baskets holding sacred objects. This division of labor was ordained in myth, or myths served as a model justifying it for human beings. Other such themes in myth specify or imply who is permitted to eat or to prepare or to handle which foods, in what circumstances, and in what company: the range of food taboos that were a feature of all Aboriginal societies, varying in accordance with age, sex, ritual status, and region. The penalties for breaking such taboos might be imposed either by human agents on the basis of mythic injunctions or directly by supernatural figures who are believed to be able to cause illness or death. The same sorts of rules apply in the case of material objects; but in both cases, the sanctions and the penalties in regard to religious ritual matters are more conspicuous.

Mythic characters also stipulate—through actual statements or through their own example—how people should behave toward one another. They specify the rules for betrothal, marriage, and kinship, as well as the obligations and rights that should apply between particular persons and groups and in relationships involving varying degrees of constraints or taboos. These "social relations" themes, in some instances subthemes, are among the most recurrent in Aboriginal myths.

Regional Patterns. Apart from similarities in general themes, modified by regional distinctiveness in cultural details, there are examples where almost the same myth, or closely related myths, can be found over very great distances. The Kunapipi and Munga-munga, not necessarily under those names, are known in linguistically different populations over wide expanses of country. The rites that go with these mythic complexes have helped keep them largely intact while adapting to various local conditions. That is true also for the Two Men myth and the myth of Malu, the Red Kangaroo Man, in their respective versions throughout the Western Desert and adjacent regions, as well as for the Dingari myth ritual complex.

In some cases myths seem to have spread slowly, through interactions between participants in large religious rituals, whether or not such myths are linked with those particular rituals. A few mythic themes have been reported from almost every part of the continent, with no accompanying references to any traveling rituals or cults—unlike, for instance, the Molonga song series of Queensland or the several Kurangara series of songs and myths ranging from the Kimberley to the north of the Western Desert. The most notable in this respect is the Rainbow Snake theme.

Australia's terrain and vegetation vary a great deal—from arid scrub, sand hills, and rocky hills to rain forests, fresh and tidal rivers, salt lakes, coastal beaches, and mangrove swamps. The populations of birds, mammals, reptiles, fishes, and insects vary accordingly. All of these factors find a place in myth. Even in adjoining regions, however, accounts of the origins of natural phenomena can diverge widely, as do the myths and stories about the sun, moon, and stars in southeast Australia (Howitt, 1904, pp. 427–434). There are also transcontinental differences in mythic statements about stars. Most regions have a number of such statements, at least to the extent of naming a few stars, and in some cases a wide range of individual stars and constellations. These are not conceptualized as material entities in their own right; virtually everywhere, with a few exceptions, the stars and constellations were originally in human or some other terrestrial form, and in their stories they are involved in human situations and show human emotions.

There are some widespread similarities. A falling star, or meteorite, usually presages or indicates a death. Just as common is the theme of a group of young women, often called in English the Seven Sisters, pursued by a man whose advances they reject. They escape into the sky, where they are now visible as the Pleiades; their pursuer, in some versions, is now a star in the constellation Orion. Among the Wotjobaluk of northwestern Victoria (Howitt, 1904, pp. 429–430), Native Cat Man was always chasing the women who are now the Pleiades. "Now he is up in the sky, still chasing them, and still behind." Howitt also (p. 787n.) refers to an Arabana story in which a number of girls become stars in the Pleiades and in the belt of Orion, while the man who tries to follow them is now "the principal star in Scorpio." In a New South Wales example (Parker, 1974, pp. 105–109, 125–127), their pursuer captured two of them before they escaped into the sky; a group of boys who had wanted to marry them, and who died of despair when they could not, are now Orion's Sword and Belt. In various parts of the Great Victoria Desert and in the Western Desert generally, similar myths are known to women as well as to men (White, 1975, pp. 128–130; also, for one part of the story, Berndt and Berndt, 1982, p. 250). In the eastern Kimberley, the Pleiades women were chased by Eaglehawk, now the Southern Cross constellation (Kaberry, 1939, p. 12). But in the north of the Western Desert, by the 1980s Nyirana-Yulana and the women he pursued were regarded by women as "something for men to talk about, not for us."

Although the theme of a sky world, other than stars and clouds, appears in myths throughout the continent, it is more common in the south and southeast (bearing in mind that myth material from the southwest, like information on ritual and religious matters generally, is scarce because so little was recorded before the region's traditional cultures and people succumbed to outside pressures). There are more references to the inhabitants of the sky world and to ropes, vines, and other bridges between the sky and earth. Also, the land of the dead is more often located in the sky. For instance, after his physical death, the great Ngurunderi of the lower Murray River cleansed himself in the sea before going to the sky world to continue his nonearthly life. His canoe had earlier been metamorphosed into the Milky Way.

Another common theme deals with the questions of why and when certain creatures—venomous snakes, sharks, and the like—are dangerous. In a related group of myths, characters appear in the shape of snakes or other such creatures and are respected or feared because of their destructive or punitive powers. They may swallow their victims before regurgitating them (more or less intact in form) or vomiting them (not intact) as parts of the landscape or as sacred relics.

Although regional diffusion of mythic themes, with or without ritual expressions, is significant, the intraregional patterning of myths and related features is perhaps even more important. Traditionally, no myth or ritual or song sequence existed in isolation. Every such item was associated with particular social groups and people, so that there was a mosaic of proprietary rights, responsibilities, tasks, and rewards: a division of verbal and dramatic and song materials, and a division of labor in regard to holding and safeguarding and transmitting them to, and through, appropriate persons. Distinctions along lines of sex and age had a bearing on such transmission, and on rights to know and rights to participate and to transmit. Thus what might seem to be the same myth could actually exist in a number of versions, with levels of complexity in form, content, and interpretation.

Contrasts have been drawn by, for example, Strehlow (1971) between wholly sung and wholly narrative versions of myth, especially in relation to esoteric as against public interpretations. He sets out and contrasts (pp. 147–165) the Northern Aranda Emianga myth in its narrative and song versions, combining "the myth and song of Ljaua women with those of the serpent ancestor (Ljaltakalbala)." (*Ljaua* is a small plant with edible seeds; the deep pool at Emianga was the women's origin site.)

The beginning of the narrative Emianga myth details the women's collection of seeds in wooden dishes and the processes of winnowing and grinding them, shaping them into "meal cakes," cooking, dividing, and eating them. A Willy Wagtail Woman who had come from the same pool later took seeds to her nephew, the huge serpent who had also emerged from the pool; she ground them, gave him an uncooked meal cake, and invited him to return with her for some cooked ones. The rest of the long story tells of his adventures: he swallowed all the people, and their belongings, at a camp of Echidna Men who, secretly goaded by his aunt, had been planning to kill him. He split himself open, let out their bones and their belongings, and sang his own wounds to heal. The same thing happened at a camp of Yam Men. Eventually he swallowed all the Ljaua women and vomited them out as *tjurunga* in the sacred cave at Emianga. Only the Willy Wagtail escaped into a narrow cave. He himself now remains forever inside the deep pool.

Briefly, Strehlow sees Aranda prose myths as giving "a coherent story of the history of a legendary totemic ancestor (or group of ancestors)," complete with place names, mythic tracks, and the rituals instituted by such characters. He distinguishes these from ordinary stories in the Aranda cultural area on the grounds that stories are not tied specifically to sites, ritual expressions, or group ownership and are therefore, he implies, more mobile as well as less sacred.

In any one regional pattern of myth, story, song, and ritual material, every item needs to be considered in relation to the others and to the total context within the social frame. Children who grew up learning their own language, culture, and social relationships without very much intrusion by alien influences were introduced to this pattern of myths through relatively simple examples and were taught to see those examples in connection with others, as part of a pattern. The context of myths and stories was as significant in the learning process as were other contextual features. Relatively simplified (but not contextualized) children's versions of myth are regarded by many traditionally oriented Aborigines as the only suitable versions for most outsiders. The more detailed and elaborate versions they themselves have learned would, they say, not be appreciated or understood.

Traditional stories for children purport to answer some, not all, of the same questions that adult myths raise. Who are we? Where did we come from? Where did it all begin? Why do people die? Where do people go when they die?

In parts of the Western Desert, children's stories may be accompanied by fast-moving scenes drawn in the sand, with sticks or leaves to represent the main characters. They are sometimes dismissed by adults as insignificant because they lack portentous meanings or ritual connections. They are just-so stories about how various creatures assumed their shapes, why they behave as they do, and so on. For example, Marsupial Mole Man, in the north of the Western Desert, changed into a mole after a quarrel with his two wives, who attacked him because he had deceived them and failed to provide them with meat. This story, then, presents children with several obvious themes, including the message of a husband's duty as a hunter, and the incidents are clearly located at specific sites. It is one of several such stories which become more complex as children are judged more competent to deal with them.

In western Arnhem Land, a children's story about the Long-necked Tortoise Woman, Ngalmangii, tells how she and Echidna Woman had quarreled after she had eaten Echidna Woman's baby, left in her care when they were camping together. Her excuse was "I was hungry!" Echidna flung at Tortoise the flat stone she always carried, and Tortoise threw the small bamboo spears she always had with her at Echidna. That is how they took their present shapes. In northeastern Arnhem Land, children are (or were) introduced to the great Djanggawul epic with a shorter account of the travels of the Sun Woman and her small daughter, a story that includes such items as the colorful feathered string symbolizing the rays of the sun.

In these examples there is a transition from simple to less simple versions within a similar range of topics or themes. Another, more significant point is the interconnection between adult myths within the same region. There have been suggestions that "a myth is best interpreted through another myth."

Fate and destiny. Mythic characters proceeding on their journeys are likely to encounter others whose stories lead them in divergent directions. Such meetings may involve conversations and perhaps camping together for a short time and then separating, never to see one another again.

An example of a very brief, single encounter comes in a western Arnhem Land Rainbow Snake myth told to me in 1950 by Gunwinggu-speaking women at Oenpelli. The Snake "arose far away, coming from the north, from the middle [of the] sea. She saw land, and came up out of the sea. No water there! Dry land! She went underneath again, travelling underground, and camp up here at Oenpelli, at this water where we drink. Then she went on to the waterfall, where those two Birds spoke to her." Following the stream, she eventually dug out a deep billabong, set rocks in place to form a cave, and gave birth to an egg, which she put in the sun to harden. The two Birds, whose spirits remain forever at the waterfall, are the only other Dreaming characters noted in her story until an old Dangbun-speaking man, Manyurulbu, "came to that tabu water because he was thirsty. He saw the egg, broke it, cooked it and ate it. Inside the cave she moved in her sleep, feeling something was wrong; she came out, and smelt him. She was weeping, looking for her egg. She took him under the water, then brought him up to the surface and vomited his bones." He "went hard," like rock. He became taboo and was transformed into an eternal spirit presence, *djang*, at that site. The Rainbow

Snake, in the cave above the billabong, watches over the other two eggs that she made and allowed to become hard. (One was stolen during the late 1940s but was returned after a local outcry: people were afraid the Snake might punish them for failing to prevent the theft.) No one is allowed to go to where the Snake is lying.

This is an almost typical Rainbow Snake story. The Snake's meeting with the two Birds has numerous parallels in western Arnhem Land myths in general. The conversation between them is not reported, but it is unlikely, given the Rainbow Snake's reputation, that the Birds told her to move to another site. Usually the Rainbow Snake does not meet animals or human characters as equals: the encounter with the old Dangbun man is more characteristic. Although in the final outcome he also becomes taboo and immortalized at that place, he is less taboo, and less dangerous, than the Snake.

Among the rocks and caves of the western Arnhem Land escarpment, every large hill and even small topographical features are locally compartmentalized, shared among a number of *djang*. One of the exceptions is Wuragag, Tor Rock, who rises as a landmark above the coastal plains. Wuragag "made himself hard" without the intervention of the Rainbow Snake, partly because "he was afraid. He thought some men [other mythic characters] were coming to kill him." He had been the husband of Waramurungundji, the anthropomorphic creative mother of this region, but she left him after he slapped her cheek for referring openly to coitus. After that, she tried unsuccessfully to introduce the rite of circumcision for boys.

A similar venture in the south of the region also failed. An old man, known as Stone Knife Carrier, or Penis *djang*, came traveling from beyond Dangbun territory, circumcising boys along his route. However, the first Gunwinggu boy he tried to circumcise died instantly. Men who had gathered for the ritual turned on him angrily, declaring that the practice was "not for us, we who speak Gunwinggu and Gunbalang" (a language spoken farther north, toward the coast). Traditionally, circumcision was not practiced in western Arnhem Land. The two myths provide a reason, and the Stone Knife Carrier episode ends with a statement about linguistic and cultural boundaries. Waramurungundji was more successful with girls' puberty rites. By teaching her young daughter at puberty, through actions and verbal advice, she showed what should be done at first and subsequent menstrual periods, including the routine behavior of squatting over a heap of hot coals and ashes, frequently changed, avoiding water courses (fresh or salt), and observing social and food taboos.

In western Arnhem Land alone, more than in a number of other regions, the theme of travelers meeting is built into the fabric of many myths, and knowing those myths also involves knowing at least something about all of the characters whose paths cross at or near particular sites. Some travel alone, in pairs, or in small family groups and join others in casual or long-term sweetheart or marital unions—or in hostilities—but in a large proportion of these myths the Rainbow Snake provides a common thread.

Another Rainbow Snake story from the same region leads us to several further points. The venomous snake Bek was once a man. In his travels he came to a mortuary platform, looked at the soles of the corpse's feet to see who it was, and identified it as his uncle. He was upset and angry: "They [someone] killed my uncle!" He went as a death messenger, taking the news. The people (unspecified, but relatives are implied) wept and gashed themselves in grief. He "stood as *gungulor* for them"; the bearer of a death message takes the risk of being attacked by the mourners. He decided to take revenge on them. "I'll damage a Dreaming *djang*, and then that Mai [an oblique reference to the Snake] will come and eat us all!" He used the term *man-djang*; the *man-* prefix usually classifies vegetable foods and plants, but when attached to other substantive forms it indicates an especially sacred or ritually important quality. He found a taboo palm tree and chopped it to pieces. A great rain came and drowned all of those people at that place. But he went into a rotten tree, buried himself inside it, and spat at them all: "You turn into rocks—but as for me, I become a creature!" The narrator added, "Ngalyod bit their heads, ate their noses. Their bones lie about like rocks, but Bek put himself as *djang*; and his spirit remains there, at Maganbang, in Magani."

Bek's vengeful action is one of several such cases in western Arnhem Land myths, but it is only in the realm of myth that there are any reported instances of suicide in traditional Aboriginal Australia. Revenge usually takes the form of direct violence or indirect sorcery, and both of these are found often in myth. Also, like Wuragag, Bek made his own decision about his *djang* transformation; unlike Wuragag, he survives in the form of a living, mobile natural species, still antagonistic to human beings, as well as in a site-linked spirit manifestation. The Rainbow Snake was not directly an agent in his transmutation. The myth includes no reference to any attempt on Bek's part to evade being swallowed by the Rainbow Snake or to plead not to be swallowed, as some mythic characters do; nor is there any mention of the Snake trying to engulf him or being thwarted or defeated, as in cases from coastal areas where a Snake manifestation is killed and cut open to release the victims. However, while in one sense they are victims, in another sense they are not.

Western Arnhem Land is unusual in the high proportion of statements about transformation and intent made by its mythic characters. Many mythic accounts, especially of potential *djang*, open with such statements; others come at the conclusion. The pervasive tone of the *djang* myths is one of destiny and of its inevitability, and the Rainbow Snake is, for most such characters, the main force through which destiny is achieved. A few characters manage to delay the inevitable end, but only temporarily: they might weep or try to escape, but they "couldn't do anything." If, in rare instances, they were helped by a "clever man," an Aboriginal doctor, they eventually "became hard," and their *djang* sites are identified as such.

Without spelling it out, the myths make contradiction here plain. On the one hand, there is the inescapable aspect of fate: the aim of a *djang* character's journey and the choice of the "right place" are predetermined, although the determining agent is not mentioned. On the other hand, the actions that cause the final disaster, as it is often described, are mostly set in a more negative frame even when the Rainbow Snake is not involved. Mythic characters "go wrong" or "do wrong"; they take a wrong turning spatially or in terms of behavior, or someone else "makes them go wrong." Although not defined as such, this contradiction is almost like a contrast between preordained destiny and individual will. It has a parallel in local views on sorcery, which combine the acknowledgment that physical death is the fate of all human beings with the belief that it can be brought about prematurely through human action.

A large range of myths deal with issues of human choice in regard to good and bad behavior in social relationships. They appear in the content of *djang* myths but only as secondary themes. Except in such examples as the Bek myth, they are not shown as causal or precipitating factors in attracting the Rainbow Snake. The Snake is drawn more or less automatically to the following kinds of scenes: when, for example, a goanna or an opossum sizzles and bursts while someone is trying to cook it in a low-lying sandy place during the wet season (or on a flat rock, which is likely to crack); when someone mistakenly kills a daughter or son of the Rainbow Snake; or when someone makes loud noises, allows children to cry, or breaks food or ritual taboos. In the myths, all of these are presented as potentially, but not inevitably, dangerous circumstances: the characters concerned have a measure of choice. Some of them, in their final moments, say, "We went wrong, we shouldn't have done that!"—whereas others, such as Bek, know exactly what they are doing and make a deliberate choice to draw upon a supernatural force to achieve a personal objective. One sociocultural theme implied in the Bek story is, "If someone has an unsatisfied grievance, watch him carefully because he may take a secret revenge." That theme emerges more conspicuously in sorcery accounts, in myth and in everyday life, especially in regard to neglected obligations or a girl's rejection of her betrothed or her husband. Resolution of such conflicts is seen as a human responsibility. As a rule it is only the physical consequences of human action that bring the Rainbow Snake to deal with ordinary people—noise, ground movements, breaches of taboo, damage to taboo sites, and the like.

Myth patterns in local perspective. People throughout western Arnhem Land were traditionally acquainted, at least in outline, with most of the *djang* myth themes and could identify *djang* sites. More significantly, they were aware that the country around them was spiritually alive with thousands of major and minor presences, and they knew that every *djang* site had its story and its specific character(s) and that all of this was documented in myth, supplemented by illustrations in rock art and in bark paintings. Adding to the "living" quality of the whole region were, and are, numerous spirit characters such as the Mimi, whose ancient, stick-thin likenesses, drawn in blood, appear in paintings in the rocky hills and escarpment country. Other spirit beings who can be either friendly or malevolent include the ghost aspects of dead human beings, whose souls have gone to the land of the dead, leaving a third aspect to return to child spirit centers to await reincarnation.

The Rainbow Snake, in swallowing and (among more inland groups) vomiting manifestations, is an important linking theme in regard to the shape of the landscape and, to some extent, of the seascape. The Snake connects land and people and the invisible, supernatural dimension in another way, in the sphere of religious ritual—in the Ubar, for instance, and in the Kunapipi, with their bearing on fertility and on initiation rites and their core of secret-sacred mystique. Other important characters are widely known in western Arnhem Land, not only through their cross-country traveling but also through their position in the same kind of ritual context. Among them are the Nagugur, associated with the Kunapipi rites. In some versions of their myth, they are a father-son pair traveling with their wives; in others, a group of that name, sometimes said to be self-renewing or self-perpetuating. Associated with the Ubar rites is Yirawadbad, a venomous snake man (in one ritual manifestation, a Rainbow Snake); Nadulmi or Narol'mi, a kangaroo man; and Ngaldjorlbu, the Ubar woman. Associated with the Maraiin rites are Lumaluma, the Whale Man, a good and bad character, and, among others, Laradjeidja of the Yiridja moiety and Gundamara of the Dua moiety. (Dua and Yiridja are patrilineal-classifying terms that have been spreading from northeastern Arnhem Land.)

The paths, or tracks, of these and other characters are usually implicit in their myths, but it is the sites that receive most attention. That is the general rule throughout the continent too, but within a certain territorial range people also know and identify the tracks without hesitation, partly because these are paths they themselves are, or were traditionally, likely to use in their own journeys. In the Western Desert, mythic tracks are especially important in respect to what used to be called "conception totemism." The place at which a woman first reported awareness of pregnancy need not be a named site. The crucial question is, On or near what track—*whose* track—did this happen? For instance, was it on or near a Dingari route, a Malu (Red Kangaroo) route, or a Wadi Gudjara (Two Men) route? The answer has implications for the child's religious ritual rights and participation in later life.

Traditionally, the myths of a region—and the sites, paths, and activities they enshrined—made up a living context map, pervaded and highlighted by religious rituals and full of practical information about natural, human, and supernatural resources. The verbal surface of the myths and songs, the visible and audible surface of the rituals, and the material representations that went with both of these never contained all the information available for understanding, interpreting, and acting in relation to them. Even knowing them all *in toto* would not be enough. In an ongoing situation, the social context of discussion—the "running commentary," as Malinowski called it—is an indispensable part of any myth or ritual constellation. Furthermore, to take a single myth or a single ritual sequence out of its larger context of myths or of rites is to ignore what can be vital clues to its meaning. This is not to say that one must have, or must include in one's scrutiny, details of every account in any given region. No Aboriginal person in a traditionally oriented society could do that. But adults in such a society would be aware of the extent and nature of the information and of its relevance, even though some would be more knowledgeable by virtue of age, ritual status, interest, and competence. That kind of awareness is a minimal requirement for students of myth.

Interconnecting themes. An inside perspective on myth should coincide, up to a point, with an outside perspective—recognizing that in neither case can there be a single perspective. Over and above that, however, an outside approach should take into account a wider span of similarities and differences in a larger comparative frame. Such comparisons should begin on a small, regional scale. This frame should go beyond what people take as their own immediate mythic and ritual and social context and include material that they may know or have heard a little about but do not explicitly or consistently bring together.

A useful example in this respect is northeastern Arnhem Land, a fairly compact region for which a great deal of information on myth and ritual has been available since the 1920s. The two most important mythic and ritual sequences there are the Djanggawul and the Wawalag. William Lloyd Warner, from the vantage point of his fieldwork at Milingimbi in the 1920s, attempted a brief comparison of these two great sequences. The significant point is that he made the attempt, even though it reflects some of the difficulties inherent in the exercise. As he noted, the Djanggawul constellation was better known in northeastern Arnhem Land, the Wawalag in the north-central area. That position continues to apply, up to the mid-1980s, with one exception which must have been relevant even in Warner's day. The Djanggawul, traveling from east to west, roughly parallel to the course of their mother, the Sun, did not move very far from the coast. Milingimbi, in the Crocodile Islands, was virtually their last port of call in eastern Arnhem Land. Extensive versions of their myth were still well known there, to both men and women, up to the 1950s, although they have been somewhat attenuated in more recent years. Even in the early 1960s, rumors were circulating on the eastern side that an incarnation of one of the Djanggawul sisters had been seen at Milingimbi—not the routine type of incarnation of child spirits, nor the routine use of personal names drawn from myth, songs, and place names, but a unique superhuman incarnation. The rumors were short-lived. However, the north-central recognition of the Djanggawul's importance is much less marked farther south, where emphasis is on the Wawalag constellation, with its inland overtones, and on the longer-standing inland association with Kunapipi ritual.

Both constellations, Djanggawul and Wawalag, share a common, pervasive theme of fertility of the land and of all its living inhabitants. Within the overall theme, the Djanggawul stress the human component. The two sisters, and on the eastern side they and their brother, produced the first human populations in the region, locating them at specific named sites and telling them what languages (dialects) they should speak, along with other customary rules these new people were to follow. They provided supplies for fresh water and indirectly indicated what foods they were to eat or abstain from. The Wawalag sisters are often referred to in connection with fertility, but this rests mainly on their connection with the Great Python, who swallowed them. They were not traditionally regarded in northeastern Arnhem Land as the very first people or as creators on a large scale, as were the Djanggawul. (Some bark paintings on this theme in the Djanggawul myth show multiple birth scenes on a superhuman numerical scale.) The Djanggawul story includes some "human" touches, such as putting newly born girls onto soft grass and boys onto rougher ground. But the sisters are almost impersonal as contrasted with the Wawalag; although they are not forcibly separated from the children by the Snake, as in the Wawalag case, they continue on their journey toward the setting sun, voluntarily leaving the children behind to fend for themselves.

The Wawalag sisters are sometimes referred to as "the first mothers," but no time sequence is suggested to distinguish them from the Djanggawul in this respect. Certainly in the Wawalag myth the sisters have a more obvious mothering relationship with their child(ren). (In Aboriginal Australia a mother's sister would also be called "mother.") Between them the Wawalag sisters have only two children, three at the most. They care for the children as individuals and try to protect them from the Snake; detailed versions include conversations about looking after the children, and a breast-feeding fireside scene for the new mother. The mother-child relationship is a focal theme in this part of the myth. Also, the Wawalag sisters perform almost no miraculous feats, even though they are bringing with them powerful songs and dances from their inland place of origin. They are more vulnerable than the Djanggawul and have to join with the Great Python before their ritual linkages and also the monsoon rains can be activated. Although there are some obvious similarities as well as contrasts between the two myths, a more detailed inquiry would reveal that they are even more obviously complementary.

Another important constellation in the same region, already noted, is also complementary to the Wawalag myth but less clearly so to the Djanggawul. Like them, it belongs to Dua moiety clans. The central character, himself Dua, is the boomerang-legged honey spirit man, Wudal. His journey from the distant inland toward the Roper River is told in song, not in story-type narrative. It is a riteless myth, made up of images, place names, and short action sequences. Wudal is often described as a single male person. His body is covered with white feathered string, and he wears a headband of kangaroo claws; long baskets full of bees and honey are slung from both shoulders. He moves with a kind of skipping step, partly because the sunbaked rocks are hot under his feet; he pauses at intervals to dance and to tap the sides of his baskets. However, the traveler can be female (*Laglag* is one of the names more often used in that case) or, as in other single or multiple myth examples from other regions, a group of Dreaming men and women. The song sequence details his journey, the creatures encountered on the way, and his own actions. The sequence of some of the songs can vary according to different versions, but it should always end with a song accounting for the redness of the sunset sky. Other explanations for the redness are offered in several song and myth series from both moieties; in one, for instance, the color symbolizes the blood of the Wawalag sisters.

In one song (noted earlier), Yiridja men are making stone spear blades, which are of the Dua moiety; the flakes they chip off in the process are Yiridja, and in kin relationship the blades are like mothers to them. Wudal men are there too. Tired of sitting down, the men stand up and practice throwing their spears and posture with them as if dancing. Later, Dua Wudal men of various subsections (an eightfold division into social categories, widespread through much of Aboriginal Australia) have been hunting and killing Yiridja-moiety kangaroos: the song notes their subsection affiliations, one by one. They return to their home base, a large, freshwater billabong. Leaning their spears against the stringy-bark trees there, they lean forward to look at their reflections in the water, then stoop down to drink, making lapping noises and spitting out some of the water. In the late afternoon they settle down to eat their kangaroo meat, which they like raw, with blood running. They spit as they eat, reddening the sky, causing the red cloud, or sunset.

Other songs have noted the creatures Wudal sees on his travels and at the sacred billabong: colored caterpillars, frilled (blanket) lizards, several kinds of birds, and his own bees. Several songs describe a sacred mound of earth that men have prepared near the billabong. Wudal people, gathered for dancing, speak the untranslatable ritual language, gin-nga, or gidjin, associated with this. On the mound they have erected two painted *djuwei* posts with bark hair, representing two adolescent girls. In the "honey wind" part of the series, Wudal is thirsty and eats honey from his baskets and from the sacred trees at the billabong and kangaroo meat from a separate basket. As he eats, he spits. The spray of saliva rises up, mixing with the spray from the Wudal men and with the crows and the bees. It joins the clouds rising from the smoke of fires sparked by the flaking of the stone spear blades and from fires lit by Wudal with the bark fire stick he always carries. It is "burning grass time." The clouds are dark with rain—Dua rain and wind, the "wind of the honey and the bees," blowing from the sacred billabong.

The songs, each seemingly inconsequential in itself, build up into a coherent pattern with a number of pertinent themes. One is the Wawalag connection. Some of the place names noted in the songs also appear in the Wawalag myth. One, Muruwul, was said to be the "billabong of Wudal, Crow, and the Wawalag." The two *djuwei* posts resemble stylized Wawalag figures and have the same shredded-bark hair. In the Rainbow Snake's song in the Wawalag myth, the sacred mound is equated with the Wawalag sisters' hut that the Snake is preparing to coil around before swallowing them. He also sang the names of places from which the honey wind comes, bringing its Dua-moiety rain. There are other meeting points between the two myths, some explicit, others more oblique. As myths, the two are generally asserted to be separate; and the ritual associations of the Wawalag, as well as the central role of the snake (who has no parallel in the Wudal sequence), help to keep them distinct.

Whatever the details of similarity and difference between them, however, their most salient feature is their complementary involvement in the seasonal cycle. The year is divided into a succession of named seasons, each with its characteristic combination of rainfall, temperature, vegetation growth or decay, availability of various foods, and the behavior of various land and sea creatures. It is not a simple division between wet and dry seasons. The Wawalag-Yulunggul contribution is responsible for the Dua-moiety monsoon from the west and northwest, the principal source of fertilizing rains. The major contribution of the Wudal song sequence *in toto* is the gentler, less ferocious but moderately strong wind and rains, also Dua, that bring relief from the heat at a time when the grasses and foliage of the inland are dry and inflammable. Lightning strikes, as well as deliberate burning-off for hunting and regeneration in selected areas, cause large, billowing smoke clouds. Perhaps just as significant in this seasonal context is the theme of bees and honey. The songs that focus on the bees bring in several singing names of the stringybark: it is *gongmiri* (it has "hands"); it is *mareiin* ("sacred"). Wild honey is a highly desirable food, and the flowering of the eucalyptus signals the development of other foods.

Even though no formally organized rites are attached to this song series, the actual singing and accompanying dancing, though performed in a less emotionally charged atmosphere, are equivalent to such rites. The series is in the category of so-called clan songs, in this case belonging to Dua moiety dialect units such as Djambarbingu and Riraidjingu. The singing in itself affirms and anticipates the coming of the required state of affairs in an almost timeless sequence. The honey wind, then, comes between the west monsoon and the southeast trade winds that bring light rain at the end of the cold weather.

Wudal himself is credited with bringing the subsection system to northeastern Arnhem Land. Of inland origin, the subsection system is now an integral feature of social organization all along the north coast. Boomerangs, however, are not, except in ritual settings such as the Kunapipi, they are still associated with "other" Aboriginal groups. The songs reveal Wudal as a stranger, coming north toward the coast for the first time; the coming of travelers from one area to another is one of the commonest themes in all Australian Aboriginal myths. And he is a benefactor, bringing bees and honey, taking part in stone spear blade preparation and distribution, and strategically sending rain between the deluge of the monsoon and the lighter falls from the southeast.

The complementary relationship between the two patrilineal moieties, Dua and Yiridja, is a subtheme in many myths and song series. They are portrayed as different but interdependent. Everything and everyone of significance is classified in those terms. Even the major mythic figures, the deities, do not stand outside the system: they are either Dua or Yiridja. However, while men's offspring are in the same patrilineal moiety as themselves, women's are not: Yiridja women have Dua offspring, and vice versa. Except for the great Djanggawul, themselves Dua, who made children of both moieties—in a situation where they were formulating, not necessarily conforming with, the rules—myths and songs note this almost zig-zag descent line linking mothers and their offspring. The two moieties are not identified by a single pair of symbols, as are the famous Eaglehawk and Crow of southeastern Australia. They have multiple associations, spread across the whole field of possibilities. Thus, there is a Yiridja shark species, but the large, aggressive Dua shark is more prominent in song and in clan-linked symbolism and oratory. In shark songs, a female Dua shark must have Yiridja offspring: in procreation,"Yiridja comes out of Dua," "Dua comes out of Yiridja." The song and myth references are a reminder that neither moiety can do without the other and that patrilineal rights and obligations are not the only consideration: a person has certain rights also in the myths, songs, and ritual affairs of his or her mother and mother's brothers, including rights to tell and to sing and participate.

The Wudal myth resembles the clan song style of presentation in being sung rather than told, in whole or in parts, as a narrative. The clan songs deal predominantly in imagery and in song words specifying attributes and activities of various creatures and other natural phenomena. Yiridja rain and wind from the southeast are treated in this way in one song sequence, where mythic characters as such play only a minor part. Another popular subtheme in myths and songs purports to answer a twofold question: How do clouds come about, and what (or who) makes rain? Rainmaking rites are virtually lacking in northeastern Arnhem Land, except for the larger seasonal fertility affairs that link the Djanggawul and Wawalag and other myth and ritual complexes. Aside from outstanding figures such as the Lightning Snake, and Larrpan the Cyclone Man (whose long penis is associated with rain and thunder), the image of spitting and spraying out moisture, as in the Wudal songs, recurs in a number of settings. In one song sequence, spray rising from whales in their rare appearances offshore automatically causes clouds, followed by rain. Lighting fires that send up columns of smoke, another Wudal activity, is another way of making clouds and rain, not necessarily in the same area as the fires. There are clan songs about Dua fire and others about Yiridja fire, just as there are distinct song series relating to clouds and rain. Clouds, in named varieties, are either Dua or Yiridja; they come from, pass over, and go toward named places and populations. Clouds of both moieties may meet and pass each other, just as freshwater streams and tidal rivers may contain layers of water belonging to different moieties.

Such images are basic ingredients in the clan songs, whether or not they are explicitly associated with mythic characters. They permeate the myths of this region, with their often poetic language. In varying degrees they also enter into the so-called play stories, the *wogal dou*, that include stories designed mainly for children, such as a version of the Djanggawul myth. These range from the trivial to the portentous or tragic. *Wogal* means "play" but carries an underlying tone of seriousness or purpose; *dou* means "information."

Clouds are more prominent than stars in northeastern Arnhem Land myths and songs. One exception is the evening star, symbolically identified with the large water lily, the lotus, and also associated in song with the death and return to life of the moon. The morning star comes from Bralgu, the mythical island in the Gulf of Carpentaria from which the Djanggawul set out on their epic journey to the Australian mainland. It is also the home of souls of Dua-moiety dead. That theme connects it with the Djanggawul, although the song series that goes with mortuary rites for a dead Dua person is separate from the principal Djanggawul myth. So is the myth that describes what happens to the soul on its voyage to Bralgu and when it reaches there, and that also gives advice on what to expect from the spirit guardians there and how to behave toward them. That myth is supplemented by the account of a Dua-moiety man, Yawalngura, said to have gone to Bralgu by canoe while he was still living and to have returned for just long enough to report his experiences (Warner, 1937, pp. 524–528).

The song imagery begins with a corpse on its mortuary platform, then dwells, in turn, on the creatures that move to and fro between it and Bralgu. One section of the sequence focuses on the morning stars that Bralgu spirits send out to specifically named sites on the mainland and islands of northeastern Arnhem Land. This overall combination of the more conventionalized Djanggawul creation myth, the corroborative report of a living human being, and the song sequence on the topic of a Dua person's final transition to the island from which the Djanggawul embarked on their journey, dwells explicitly on the two dimensions of human life—the spiritual and the physical. The decay of the body is frankly stated, in some detail, but that process is demonstrated to be inseparable from the continuing life of the soul after the death of the body.

Two associated myth complexes make it clear that not all of the soul goes on the voyage. One of these complexes, which is not set out in narrative form but usually as an adjunct to other accounts, emphasizes the theme of reincarnation or continuity. One part of the deceased person's spirit remains in its former country, to animate the fetus of a human being in the appropriate social categories, an event revealed in a dream to the prospective father or father's sister, or other eligible relatives. A third part, the trickster spirit, is the subject of many *wogal dou* and other stories, some of them highly dramatic. Together, the substance of all of these myths and songs makes up a detailed commentary on the transcendental issues of human life and death: how individual people came into being, something about their life on earth as human beings, and what they can expect to happen after that. They do not, however, take up the difficult question of relationships with close relatives and spouses of the opposite moiety. The question is traditionally left unanswered—or, rather, not asked. In the conventional view, people of the Yiridja moiety go to their own land of the dead, an island off the north coast. The Yiridja guardians of the dead also send items to living people on the mainland and offshore islands. The songs tell how these things come bobbing and dancing on the waves, borne by the north and northeast Yiridja winds.

A major theme in all the myths of northeastern Arnhem Land is the relationship between people and their land. When the mythic characters shaped the land, they shaped the sky, the clouds, and the seasons—the total environment that provided a background for themselves and for all the living beings there.

In the Wudal myth as in the Djanggawul and Wawalag, and in eastern Arnhem Land generally, the patterning of cross-references is much more noticeable than in many other parts of Aboriginal Australia. There is a concern with small details, which are not left suspended or clustered loosely but fit together in a variety of coherent shapes. The interlocking of items and themes has been tentatively described as representing a characteristic sociocultural style which finds expression in graphic art such as bark paintings and stylized body designs (C. H. Berndt, 1970, p. 1316). Strehlow notes the same point in stressing the need to examine material from all of the Aranda groups in studying myths in central Australia:

> When looking through a collection of myths that have been gathered in any one of these groups, one feels that one is being led into a wide-spread maze, into a vast labyrinth with countless corridors and passages and sidewalks, all of which are connected with one another in ramifications that at times appear altogether baffling in their complexity and interdependence. (Strehlow, 1947, p. 45)

Precedents and Contrasts. The creative period of the Dreaming is traditionally regarded as the principal, indisputable source of rules and injunctions governing human behavior. This early period is portrayed in myth as an era of development and process: the sociocultural as well as the natural world was taking shape or, rather, being given shape not only by the major deities but also by the host of mythic characters who were, and continue to be, an integral part of the process.

When the lawmaking, lawgiving characters make pronouncements at the end of their earthly journey in the formative era, their myths have already recorded the events leading up to these; they do not merely note the pronouncements but tell how and why they came to be made. The mythic explanation, in many cases, describes the very behavior or situations the rules were supposed to guard against, prohibit, or at least discourage. Even when myths spell out the details of such behavior, they do not always add the warning that it is wrong. In the ongoing traditional Aboriginal scene, the messages believed to be contained in myth did not need to be stated explicitly on any one occasion of telling or singing or ritual enactment. There were other opportunities for that, formal or otherwise; and in any case, the levels of complexity in interpretation varied according to the social and ritual context. The dynamic, continuing aspect of myth has its counterpart in human life: the events set in train by the mythic beings are still in process. To keep things going in the appropriate way, this and that must be done, in religious ritual terms and in everyday social living. Myths were not designed as an intellectual exercise or for aesthetic pleasure or entertainment. They were for use—for information, explanation, and action. Narrative myths, outside the more formalized ritual context, were open to audience participation and questions and comment. Sometimes a narrator would amplify certain passages when he or she considered that some members of the audience needed further information on a topic.

In this living mythology, no myth is taken as a total package, the content of which is to be accepted or rejected *en bloc*. Even where claims are made to that effect, they are largely ideal statements or, rather, statements of principle that take for granted the matters of selection and interpretation that accompany even the most rigid attempts to maintain verbal (and ritual) adherence to an unchanging pattern.

Some precedents are fairly straightforward: in regard to food and material resources, for instance, that are fundamental in making a living. Another set of mythic themes that also seem to have been taken very much as a given recounts the shaping of human and other forms of life. In general, the potential for change was inherent in all of the mythic characters. The shape in which they appeared at the beginning of their respective stories was not necessarily the same as that of their final *appearance*. More often than not, it was quite different, but the emphasis is on the word appearance. They had built into them the program or plan which emphasized the shared quality of all life but accorded them different roles and different shapes in the "web of life" that encompassed them all. However, as far as human shapes were concerned, myths put forward more or less common views as to what a human being should look like (as well as how he or she should behave).

Howitt (1904, pp. 475–476, 484ff.) provides some interesting examples of this. Bat was lonely, because "there was no difference between the sexes," so "he altered himself and one other, so that he was the man and the other was the woman"; he also made fire. In another version the great being Bunjil "made men of clay and imparted life to them," and his brother Bat "brought women up out of the water to be their wives." Among the Yuin, it was the Emu-Wren who shaped incomplete creatures into men and women. On Cape York Peninsula a White Sand Snake Man, wanting a wife, castrated and cut an opening in his younger brother to make him into a woman (McConnel, 1957, pp. 128–130); the same action is also attributed to Moon (p. 28). In the eastern Kimberley an old mythic woman "tried to subincise girls and 'make them into men.' But they developed into young women," and she admitted defeat (Kaberry, 1939, p. 201). The Djanggawul, in contrast, with their dominant position in the mythic scene in northeastern Arnhem Land, adjusted their own shapes to what they considered proper for human beings. All that was needed in their case was clitoris shortening for the sisters and penis shortening for the brother. This episode has an initiatory connotation, just as in the eastern Kimberley version of the subincision attempt. And in fact the bodily operations which are part of so many initiation rituals conform with the same body-shaping, body-marking principles that are implied, if not actually enunciated, in the more comprehensive initial efforts. So are the minor body-marking conventions of cicatrization, nasal septum piercing, and the like. All of these, like hairstyles, rest on mythic edicts or suggestions.

A theme that is more emotionally charged is how, and why, death is the lot of all human beings. In many myths, Moon is somehow connected with this. In one western Arnhem Land myth, simplified as a children's account (because children traditionally learned, quite young, the facts of bodily death), Moon Man and Djabo, Spotted Cat Man, traveling together, succumbed to a sickness that was spreading across the land. Moon was a *margidjbu*, a healer or clever man. He recovered and wanted to revive Djabo, but Djabo didn't trust Moon, so he refused—and died. Because of that, all human beings must die, and their bodies cannot be renewed, but when Moon dies, he always comes back anew after three days. There are many variants on the same theme. This one carries an added message: if you are sick and a *margidjbu* offers to heal you, you must have faith in him and in his treatment to survive. In east Kimberley, Moon originated death and wrong marriage by trying to marry a woman he called mother-in-law. "She and the other women with her attacked him in fury and cut off his organs which changed to stone." Then he declared that after dying he would "come back in five days," but they would not come back (Kaberry, 1939, pp. 128, 199–200). Howitt (1904, pp. 428–429) reports the same kind of edict from southeastern Australia.

Strehlow (1947, pp. 44–45) outlines a different myth among the northern Aranda. Near Ilkakngara, Curlew People emerged from the hard rock: women first, one making an opening in the rock with her nose, then men. The first man lit a fire, but the others were angry and pointed a magic bone against him, so that he died. After he was buried, grieving women danced around his grave, and he began to work his way up through the ground, head first. He had almost freed his shoulders when Magpie, in a rage, thrust a heavy mulga spear into his neck and stamped him down hard into the ground, ordering him to remain there forever. If Magpie had not so forcibly intervened, everyone who died would have come to life again, emerging successfully from the ground. Strehlow notes that other "legends" express the same general idea.

Themes that are more open to debate or to questions of interpretation mostly hinge on matters of social relationships. One is about the nature of participation and control in religious affairs, especially ritual affairs, as between men and women. The key set of questions in mythic terms is, Who first found, owned, or controlled the most sacred religious materials? What happened? and Did that situation change? Outside the field of myth, in the sphere of ordinary human activities, the question is, Who has control now? with the corollary, Who makes decisions about participation? In the great majority of myths such questions do not focus specifically on male-female relations in this respect, but in a substantial minority of examples across the continent they do.

In the Djanggawul myth, the sisters lose their monopoly right to ownership and control of secret-sacred materials when these are stolen from them by men. On Cape York Peninsula, two girls find a bull-roarer and swing it, singing that it is forbidden; they place it in a bloodwood tree, saying "It belongs to us women, really, we have found it! But no matter! We leave it for the men!" (McConnel, 1957, p. 119). In east Kimberley, "some of the female totemic ancestors were given *tjurunga*" by the mythic being Djulargal, but "later these were stolen from them by Porcupine" (Kaberry, 1939, p. 201). In western Arnhem Land, "the *ubar* ritual belonged at first only to women"; Gandagi Kangaroo Man drove the women away, took their sacred emblems, and gathered a group of men to perform the same rites (Berndt and Berndt, 1982, p. 257; 1970, pp. 120–121). The Wawalag brought Kunapipi songs and rites on their journey to the northern Arnhem Land coast, but after being swallowed by the Great Python they taught these, and gave them, to men. An interesting point here is that the Wawalag were swallowed and regurgitated in much the same way as male novices are, symbolically, in initiation rites. But those male novices are recipients of sacred knowledge, whereas the Wawalag were both teachers and donors, and the novices in that episode in their myth were adult men. To compound this issue of "women had it first," many ritual sequences now dominated by men show a preoccupation with the idea, or the ideal, of women, and with female physiological characteristics such as pregnancy and childbirth.

Mythic precedent and substantiation also emphasize the important place of women in the creative era of the Dreaming, even in cases where it is not spelled out. For example, in the Northern Aranda Curlew and Magpie death myth, it was a Curlew woman who first broke through the hard rock to emerge on the earth, followed by other women. Strehlow specifies in other discussions the "majestic" and impressive bearing of mythic women in Aranda myth. Isobel M. White (1974, 1975) has tried, inconclusively, to explain central Australian myths that seem to suggest ritual subordination of women by relating them to similar attitudes and values in everyday living. Others, including Diane Bell (1984), have argued that such interpretations are based on inadequate empirical evidence and that closer scrutiny of both myth and its sociocultural context are needed before any definitive conclusions can be reached. In the past, Aboriginal women's perspectives have rarely been taken into account except at a very superficial level, and in some areas their own secret-sacred rites and myths continue to be unknown to outsiders. That aside, the larger issue of myth interpretation is still controversial and difficult.

Myths from all parts of the continent contain as much bad as good human behavior. The activities of a great many mythic characters do not conform with what was regarded as good behavior by, or for, the people who told and heard their stories. Even in regions where the main deities concentrate on creation in a relatively mild way, such as the Djanggawul (despite their original incest, and the men's theft of sacred paraphernalia), other material dwells on more emotionally rousing events. Among the wogal dou are accounts of aggressive encounters, cruelty, and despair. The trickster Pomapoma (Gwingula), for example, in the course of his adventures, rapes and kills his young mother-in-law in a story which at once deplores his reprehensible actions and presents them in quasi-humorous style. In western Arnhem Land, in a more clearly moralizing or threatening vein, Yirawadbad, in his venomous snake form, kills both his young betrothed wife and her mother because the girl consistently rejected him; he is now dangerous to everyone but especially to girls, and he makes his reason explicit as he surveys the two corpses. In his human form, he went on to be one of the main instigators of the important Ubar ritual; this includes ritual enactment of the scene where, as a snake in a hollow log, he bites the hand of each woman in turn.

Relating such materials to their sociocultural context involves more than simply considering how, and how far, one dimension reflects what takes place in the other. "Mythic beings were both good and bad, and badness was a necessary corollary of goodness." It is as if "an immoral act must occur in order to demonstrate what can be regarded as being moral," but myth and story reflect "the total life situation, in which . . . there is both good and bad . . . [as] part of the inevitable and irreversible framework of existence" (R. M. Berndt, 1970, pp. 220, 223, 244).

A crucial issue, particularly in respect to what Strehlow has called the "amoral" behavior of many central Australian mythic figures, is whether sanctions operate to discourage or prevent or deflect such behavior. How far do the myths themselves serve to deflect it, as a kind of catharsis? This is a complex issue because the myths never exist in a sociocultural vacuum.

To compile a dictionary or an index of themes or motifs in traditional Aboriginal mythology would be a formidable undertaking. But it would be only a beginning in the process of understanding and explanation. In virtually all cases, a spoken or written myth must be heard and seen in relation to the unspoken, unwritten information known to the people to whose mythology it belongs, the shared understandings that are essential in learning what it is about. Discussions and comments help to throw light on these assumptions, but they are not enough without a more complete knowledge of the sociocultural and personal contexts. And the nature of the relevant sanctions and rules is a necessary and salient aspect of that context.

Myths do not consitute a mirror image of Aboriginal societies. They reflect those societies, in their "ought" as well as their "is" dimensions, in a variety of ways, both negative and positive. What the myths in general do reflect is one of the major strengths of Aboriginal religion. It ranges from the mystical and esoteric, the secret aspects of the sacred, the spectacle and exhilaration and drama of ritual events, to the more mundane features of everyday living. There is a place in religion—a significant place—for all of these and for all of the varied roles and circumstances throughout a person's life. The sphere of myth illuminates that place through contrasts and challenges as well as through insistence on continuities.

SEE ALSO Djan'kawu; Gadjeri; Rainbow Snake; Yulunggul Snake.

BIBLIOGRAPHY

Bell, Diane. *Daughters of the Dreaming.* Sydney, 1983. A fairly wide-ranging discussion of Aboriginal women's involvement in mundane and religious affairs in central Australia; also includes details of social structure and social relationships. Aims at achieving a positive balance in regard to Aboriginal women, to counter the negative image which has prevailed in the literature, in the writings of women as well as of men.

Berndt, Catherine H. "Monsoon and Honey Wind." In *Échanges et communications: Mélanges offerts à Claude Lévi-Strauss,* edited by Jean Pouillon and Pierre Maranda, vol. 2, pp. 1306–1326. The Hague, 1970. Includes comments on similarities and interconnections between the Wawalag myth and the Wudal myth-song sequence.

Berndt, Ronald M. "Traditional Morality as Expressed through the Medium of an Australian Aboriginal Religion." In *Australian Aboriginal Anthropology,* edited by Ronald M. Berndt, pp. 216–247. Nedlands, Australia, 1970. A companion article is "Mythic Shapes of a Desert Culture," in *H. Petri Festschrift*, edited by Kurt Tauchmann (Cologne, 1973), pp. 3–31.

Berndt, Ronald M., and Catherine H. Berndt. *Man, Land and Myth in North Australia: The Gunwinggu People.* Sydney, 1970. A general study of Gunwinggu culture and people in western Arnhem Land, incorporating a large number of myths, with discussion of their ritual and sociocultural context.

Berndt, Ronald M., and Catherine H. Berndt. *The World of the First Australians* (1964). Rev. ed., Adelaide, 1985. Includes examples, with discussion, of myths from several regions: first in connection with religious rites; and later, along with a number of stories, in the perspective of oral literature. Many of these were told to either or both authors and translated in the course of firsthand fieldwork with men (Ronald M. Berndt) or women (Catherine H. Berndt). A longer version and discussion of the Gandju Fire myth from the Western Desert appears on pp. 46–49 of my and Ronald M. Berndt's "Aboriginal Australia: Literature in an Oral Tradition," in *Review of National Literatures: Australia*, edited by L. A. C. Dobrez, vol. 2. (New York, 1982), pp. 39–63.

Charlesworth, Max, et al., eds. *Religion in Aboriginal Australia: An Anthology.* Saint Lucia, Australia, 1984. A collection of published articles on various aspects of the topic.

Eliade, Mircea. *Australian Religions: An Introduction.* Ithaca, N. Y., 1973. A useful overview of myth in the context of ritual and of religion generally.

Hiatt, L. R., ed. *Australian Aboriginal Mythology.* Canberra, 1975. A somewhat mixed collection of myths, with examples and analysis and including some controversial as well as some useful discussion.

Howitt, A. W. *The Native Tribes of South-East Australia.* New York, 1904. For all its obvious shortcomings, this is one of the most useful of the compendia put together by early writers on the topic of Australian Aboriginal culture. It includes a large assortment of myths and stories as well as other material.

Kaberry, Phyllis, M. *Aboriginal Women, Sacred and Profane.* London, 1939. Contains a number of myths, and references to others, based on fieldwork in the Kimberley region of Western Australia. Continues to be useful. Kaberry recognized the need to reshape and update the study, but her book remains a classic—virtually the first to look at Aboriginal women's viewpoints and contributions.

McConnel, Ursula H. *Myths of the Munkan.* Melbourne, 1957. Especially useful for its versions of Wik-Mungkan myths from Cape York Peninsula, told to McConnel during her fieldwork there, which she began in the late 1920s. She sets these myths in their living context, but her general discussion and interpretations are less helpful.

Maddock, Kenneth. "Myths of the Acquisition of Fire in Northern and Eastern Australia." In *Australian Aboriginal Anthropology*, edited by Ronald M. Berndt, pp. 174–179. Nedlands, Australia, 1970.

Mountford, Charles P. *The Tiwi: Their Art, Myth and Ceremony.* London, 1958. One of the few accounts of the art and myths of the Tiwi of Bathurst and Melville islands, but more useful for its illustrations and line drawings than for the details of its text.

Parker, Katherine Langloh. *Australian Legendary Tales*: Selected by Henrietta Drake-Brockman; illustrated by Elizabeth Durack. Sydney, 1975. The original volume, with the same title, was first published in London in 1896; the second, *More Australian Legendary Tales*, in London in 1898; later there were two others. This section is designed mainly for children, though it includes some discussion for adults. The editor's discussion and the illustrations (especially the distorted Arnhem Land figures heading the "Seven Sisters" story, p. 105) tend to be misleading.

Spencer, Baldwin. *Native Tribes of the Northern Territory of Australia* (1914). Oosterhout, 1966. A "must" for any student of Aboriginal mythology in context. Equally so are Baldwin Spencer and F. J. Gillen's *The Northern Tribes of Central Australia*, (London, 1904) and their two-volume study *The Arunta* (1927; reprint, Oosterhout, 1966), as well as their *The Native Tribes of Central Australia* (1899; reprint, London, 1938).

Stanner, W. E. H. "On Aboriginal Religion: IV, The Design-Plan of a Riteless Myth." *Oceania* 31 (June 1961): 233–258. This is one part of the author's larger study "On Aboriginal Religion," extending through several volumes of *Oceania* during 1959–1961 and 1963. Here he examines in detail the Murinbata myth focusing primarily on the Rainbow Snake Kunmanggur and on the activities of his son Tjinimin, who raped his two sisters, "mended his own bones" after being dropped onto rocks (p. 243), and had other adventures before killing his father. Stanner considers the myth as " a kind of essay in self-understanding" (p. 247), and "an attempt to systemize a throng of visionary shapes set up by mythopoeic thought over an unknown period, so that in any version at any time only some of the many possibilities are used" (p. 251). He pays special attention to variant versions and expressed doubts, but he does not set the myth or discussion in a wider Australian comparative frame.

Strehlow, T. G. H. *Aranda Traditions.* Melbourne, 1947. This volume of Aranda myths and rites is indispensable to any student of myth. Strehlow's superb presentation and translation of myths and songs is marred only by hints of his strict Lutheran background and his stress on male points of view, which (as he himself suggests here and there) does less than justice to the viewpoints of women.

Strehlow, T. G. H. *Songs of Central Australia.* Sydney, 1971. A magnum, or maximum, opus indeed. Strehlow deliberately included examples and discussion of literature and song from northern Europe to demonstrate that the Aranda material, his primary interest, was equal to any on the world scene. It is detailed, emotional, and scholarly. Also, it contains more positive comments on the place of women in the Aboriginal religions of central Australia than does his 1947 study.

Warner, William Lloyd. *A Black Civilization: A Study of an Australian Tribe* (1938). New York, 1958. Contains a large number of myths and stories, set in their sociocultural and ritual context, but (as Warner acknowledged) without sufficient attention to women's substantial role and status. His story of Yawalngura, the living man who visited the land of the dead, told to him in the Milingimbi area in the late 1920s, is very similar to versions told to Ronald M. Berndt and me in northeastern Arnhem Land in 1946–1947.

White, Isobel M. "Sexual Conquest and Submission in the Myths of Central Australia." In *Australian Aboriginal Mythology*, edited by L. R. Hiatt, pp. 123–142. Canberra, 1975. Takes what some consider to be a negative attitude toward Aboriginal women's role as portrayed in myth and in "real life" circumstances, although she claims that her view is both realistic and positive.

CATHERINE H. BERNDT (1987)

AUSTRALIAN INDIGENOUS RELIGIONS: MYTHIC THEMES [FURTHER CONSIDERATIONS]

By the beginning of the twenty-first century, the role of myths in shaping the imagination of Australian Aborigines had become exceedingly difficult to determine. Various external forces have left their mark on this theme, and these forces have made Aborigines the subject of a project of mythologization that, in turn, has been appropriated by the Australian state. The multimillion-dollar Aboriginal arts industry, for instance, has turned mythic themes visualized on canvas into commodities and icons of national identity. Similarly, the spiritualization of the Aboriginal cosmo-ontology through marketable popularizations and simplifications—whereby Ancestral sites become conflated into "My Mother Earth," for example—has occluded the historical foundation of myths. This process presents a particular historical turn in itself, and raises questions about the likelihood and forms in which mythic themes may endure.

Since the late 1980s anthropologists have rarely centered their work on myths in the narrow sense of story. Following Aboriginal English usages in certain parts of the continent, some ethnographers have replaced the term myth, with its emphasis on narration, with the far more comprehensive expression, Dreaming.

CONTINUITIES, CHANGE, AND CHALLENGES. The constitution of Aboriginal cultures is dynamic and highly heterogeneous. A variety of pre-contact traditions combine with the uneven experience of colonization and the emergent relationships between Aborigines and the wider Australian and international community to form locally-specific forms of sociality and identity. Cultural diversity persists alongside the notion of traditional Aboriginality. Hence, the endurance of the Dreaming is not a question internal to Aboriginal societies alone; it concerns the articulation of relationships across cultural contexts.

At the end of the 1990s, possibly 20,000 out of a total of over 350,000 Aboriginal people were living in so-called remote communities in the Kimberley region, the Western Desert, Central Australia, Arnhem Land, and on Cape York Peninsula. The ceremonial life in these regions has thrived, but manifestations of the Dreaming are also present, if contested, in at least three other fields. One is the Australian legal system. The second is in the world of art. Aborigines use a variety of mediums that engage non-Aboriginal audiences and that are often market-oriented, such as artworks for sale, film, international dance performances, fiction, poetry, and biographical and autobiographical writings. The third is a burgeoning urban New Age movement focusing on Aboriginal spirituality, health and healing. Publications in this field seem to outnumber scholarly works on Aboriginal mythology. The increasing, if appropriative, recognition of Aboriginal traditions is reflected in the expanding cultural tourist industry as well as the growing popularity and rising prices of publications on any theme related to Aborigines.

The fact that in many parts of the Australian continent Aborigines uphold knowledge of mythic traditions that began to evolve long before colonization does not allow us to infer that the same paradigms and meaning structures continue to be relevant. As Ronald and Catherine Berndt have noted in what may be considered the most important compilation of myths in the second half of the twentieth century, *The Speaking Land* (1989), there exists an "incalculable number" of myth-stories in the passive form of "memory culture" (p.13). By itself, this tells us little about the status of mythic themes as an active force in the consciousness and the unconscious of people, or how stories relate to other symbolic systems. Moreover, as John von Sturmer (2002) pointed out, important myths are not recalled, told, or sung in fully elaborate form; they are "called on" in fragments.

It is self-evident that post-contact expressions of the Dreaming are transformations of a worldview that knew only itself. For this reason, anthropologists emphasize the inherently dynamic constitution of the Dreaming that Aborigines consider to be the source of all forms and purposes of being—past, present and future. Scholars point out that the structural potential for change is the very condition for the resilience of the Law and is built into the clan organization (Berndt, 1979); ways of forging totemic identities and rights over country in the domains of ritual and everyday life (Duelke, 1998); a concept of non-biological subjectivity (Petchkovsky et al., 2003); kinetic perceptions of features in the landscape such as rocks that quiver or places that move (Redmond, 2001); and the variety of artistic systems. For instance, in Central Australian Warlpiri communities, designs that totemic Ancestors give to individuals in nocturnal dreams can be painted on canvas for sale or, if accompanied by song, may be incorporated into ritual (Dussart, 2000; Poirier, 1996). People in the Daly River region in northwestern Northern Territory conceive new songs from ghosts in dreams that become efficacious in ceremony (Marett, 2000). Artists in Arnhem Land develop adaptive conceptual structures that encode Dreamings through modifications of painting styles (Morphy, 1991; Taylor, 1996).

Observations about the endurance of the Dreaming furthermore need to address the profound differences in the religious orientation across cultural regions as well as on the level of local communities, especially the heterogeneity of Aboriginal Christianity (Swain and Rose, 1988).

Recognition of Aboriginal identities has become a major issue in the Australian public self-understanding. One indication is the progressive, if contested, legal codification of Indigenous rights over land and cultural knowledge. The political ramifications of establishing mythic traditions that can challenge existing and future forms of land tenure and use have impact on the way Aboriginal custodians handle such knowledge as well as on how anthropologists conceptualize and employ that knowledge. From a wider perspective, the incorporation of Aboriginal identities, cultural property, and land ownership into the framework of state and federal laws creates conflict between Aborigines and others as well as between Aboriginal groups and families.

The 1995 Hindmarsh Island Bridge Affair painfully illustrated such an intragroup disagreement. Some Ngarrindjeri Aboriginal women publicly accused other Ngarrindjeri women of having deliberately fabricated a secret women's tradition pertaining to Hindmarsh Island and the surrounding lower Murray River region in South Australia. The claim made by the accused was aimed at preventing the progress of a marine development project and the building of a bridge on the island. The lengthy legal dispute that ensued relied on anthropological expertise and fuelled a battle over the nature of cultural traditions, secrecy, and the legitimacy of innovative processes. In the male-dominated courts and parliament, the provision that mythological knowledge was restricted to women was a major problem, since the gender-restricted nature of information was also thought to prove the authenticity of the claim. The case deeply divided Ngarrindjeri society and damaged the anthropological profession.

Such difficulties notwithstanding, Aboriginal people have felt encouraged that their role as cultural educators has been acknowledged. Aborigines have long expressed desire to speak for themselves and for their country. With the opening of communication, it has become worthwhile then to survey the many forms in which the Dreaming is conveyed outside the context of ritual and secrecy.

CULTURAL KNOWLEDGE AND SELF-REPRESENTATION. Aboriginal people from very different backgrounds consider it their responsibility to record and often publish certain sections and layers of mythic traditions that have been maintained as part of the local knowledge or reclaimed from external sources. These works are directed at both their own descendants and a wider audience. Often produced in collaboration with former missionaries or anthropologists, the works include documentations of the regional totemic landscape in narrative and photographic form, such as Dorothy Tunbridge's *Flinders Ranges Dreamings* (1988); compilations of myths and legends that may draw heavily on versions recorded by non-Aboriginal researchers; art exhibition catalogs; and biographical and autobiographical accounts that, like *Warlpiri Women's Voices* (1995) or Ruby Langford Ginibi's *My Bundjalung People* (1994), establish identifiable links with country in the context of a history of displacement.

Since the mid-1980s, Aborigines have increasingly held intellectual control over ritual objects, artifacts, paintings, and audio recordings of myths together with research documents that were collected and stored by others. Some communities have begun to establish their own cultural heritage collections, held in local museums and galleries. Anangu (Pitjantjatjara and Yankunytjatjara speakers) in northwest South Australia have developed an interactive digital museum that stores and re-creates myths, family histories, pictorial material, and various historical documents. They have also produced several thousand hours of video recordings of *Inma*, the ritual and song performances of Dreamings.

The movement toward self-representation is in part inspired by the awareness that oral traditions expressing the many links between people and country are at risk of being irretrievably lost for future generations.

Painting. One way of recording and maintaining mythic knowledge is to paint for an international art market. Paintings are possibly the most prolific public expression of mythic themes and forces. For Aboriginal artists, canvas, bark, batik, print, and sculpture present suitable mediums of communicating aspects of the Dreaming outside local contexts. The condensed and multi-dimensional symbolisms that have been developed allow for the control of carefully-guarded knowledge without diminishing the total aesthetic effect necessary to evoke Ancestral presence or Dreaming Power.

The function of paintings as the visual embodiment of Dreamings has solidified Aborigines' links to country even where it is no longer possible to visit the ancestral sites. Until the late 1980s, men dominated the painting movement of the Western and Central Deserts with magnificent pictorial renditions of local totemic sites and the great traveling myths. Some of these early paintings are valued as national cultural heritage on the basis of a triple antiquity: the Dreaming, the modern painting movement, and the seniority of the painter. By the 1990s, women had become fully engaged in making their Ancestral connections visible, often painting bush food Dreamings.

Paintings are also an important form of documenting destructive interferences with the Dreaming brought about by colonization, resource development, and tourism. Two art shows about missionary and mining activities were held on Ngaanyatjarra lands that, together with the accompanying catalogues, *Mission Times at Warburton* (2002) and *Trust* (2003), are powerful examples of how local communities seek to make explicit and preserve their cultural heritage.

SCHOLARLY APPROACHES TO MYTH. For a variety of reasons, the number of scholarly publications specifically concerned with myth has diminished since the 1980s. One of these is that with the growing participation of Aboriginal people in the academic and public domain, it has become necessary to restrict access to secret-sacred knowledge. The primary example of this conflict of intellectual interests is the withdrawal from the market of Charles P. Mountford's massive documentation of Pitjantjatjara myths, *Nomads of the Australian Desert,* in 1976. The Pitjantjatjara Council had made a successful case for an interlocutory injunction on the basis of breach of confidence.

Between the late 1980s and mid-1990s, researchers devoted much attention to the issues of Aboriginality, urban Aboriginal identity, women's rights and rituals, land rights, mining, and racism. Howard Morphy's (1990) brief analysis of the constitutive links between myths and clans in Yolngu society is one of few publications on Aboriginal mythology. With the passing of the *Native Title Act 1993,* however, whereby the occupation of the continent prior to colonization became recognized as common law, the study of myth received a renewed impetus. Partly in response to the controversy in the legal arena about rights over land, and partly in the context of appreciating narratives of resistance, a debate developed on the relationship between myth and history. In an attempt to re-conceptualize Aboriginal ontologies in a way that incorporates the experience of colonization, Aboriginalists began to re-analyze stories they had recorded decades earlier. Following a conference organized by Jeremy Beckett, the journal *Oceania* devoted almost an entire issue (December 1994) to the discussion of how history, human agency, and the Dreaming intersect. This theme was revisited shortly thereafter at another Australian anthropological conference and extended into a comparative framework with Papua New Guinea (Rumsey and Weiner, 2001). Basil Sansom's essays (e.g., 2001) on the subversive aesthetics of the Dreaming are further important contributions in this field.

Anthropologists have generally adopted a holistic and dynamic approach to the meaning of mythic traditions. Deborah Bird Rose (1984, 1992, 1994, 2002) and David Turner (1987) have made especially comprehensive contributions in this field. But despite seeming conceptual affinities, their respective frameworks of interpretation differ profoundly. Both authors seek to establish a contrast between the values and worldview of Aborigines on the one hand, and the Western Christian tradition and modern capitalist society on the other. Yet Rose goes further and aligns Aboriginal cultural notions with extraneous environmental and feminist concerns. This is perhaps most evident in her conceptualization of a "Dreaming ecology" (1992) or "nourishing terrains" (1996, 2002), an emphasis on universal moral principles (1984), gendered places and power, world-creating women, and the bodied existence of all forms of life (1994). Turner's starting point is at the opposite end. Combining anthropological and comparative religious scholarship, he analyses in parallel fundamental aspects of Australian Aboriginal, Canadian Cree and Judeo-Christian ways of life, thinking and symbolizing. He arrives at a classification of cultural systems that emphasizes historically evolved differences of human social organisation. His analysis includes a structuralist interpretation of myths that underscores his characterization of Australian Aboriginal societies as clan-based pluralistic "confederations." In stark contrast to Rose's (1994) assertion that in Dreaming law "there is no category of being . . . which is not bodied" (p. 329), Turner recognizes as the organizing principle of the religious attachment to the land an "abstract eternal jurisdiction" (p. 54). Throughout the 1980s and 1990s, most ethnographic field researchers focused on the contextual, performative and political nature of the Dreaming, in particular its relationship to artistic forms. Exemplary studies include Howard Morphy (1990) and Luke Taylor (1996) on totemic painting traditions in Northeast Arnhem Land and West Arnhem Land respectively; Ian Keen (1994) on the politics of secret knowledge held by Yolngu men in Northeast Arnhem Land; Françoise Dussart (2000) on Warlpiri women's ritual; and Fred Myers (2002) on the intersections between international and local contexts of Pintupi artmaking. Dianne Johnson's (1998) literature-based survey of sky-related myths is significant in being the first contribution towards an Australian Aboriginal ethno-astronomy. The claim by Ngarrindjeri women over a sacred site in the waters around Hindmarsh Island rests on a Seven Sisters Dreaming about the Pleiades (Bell, 1998, pp. 573–89) that occurs in many variations across Australia. A new generation of scholars has begun to analyze the aesthetic forms themselves and how these encode meaning and relate to the structures of the social and mythological imagination (e.g., Biddle 2003; Eickelkamp 2003; Tamisari 1998; Watson 2003).

Three important contributions to Aboriginal mythology explore the classic ethnographies from the late nineteenth and early twentieth centuries. One is the highly contested work by the historian of religion Sam D. Gill (1998), who produced a textual analysis of the scholarly construction of the Central Australian Arrernte and their religious traditions by early ethnographers, including Mircea Eliade and Jonathan Smith. The second is a monograph by Johanna M. Blows (1995) that offers a structuralist and psychoanalytic exegesis of the Eagle-Crow conflict myth based on twenty-six previously recorded text versions mostly from the Darling-Murray River system in the southeast part of the continent. Third, John Morton has analyzed in a number of essays Central Australian and foremost Arrernte creation myths in a framework of Lacanian psychoanalysis, while also strongly drawing on the insights of the early psychoanalytic ethnographer Géza Róheim (e.g., Morton 1993).

REFLECTIONS. Ronald and Catherine Berndt observed that myths are an "immense mirror" (1989, p. 4) for Aboriginal people's self-understanding, but not, according to Catherine Berndt, a mirror of their society. They left untouched the question of how differences between these two symbolic orders, society and the collective self-understanding, are to be perceived.

In contrast, psychoanalytic anthropologists have made this a central point of investigation. For example, Morton (1993, pp. 333–334) identifies Ancestral creation as a process of mirroring or self-reflection—looking to one's own transformation from one species into another, being echoed in a name—that is extended to human identities and the social order. Petchkovsky, San Roque, and Beskow (2003), having worked therapeutically with Central Australian Aborigines near Alice Springs, suggest that a Jungian perspective on the imagination may help to understand better the conditions for self-reflection and for the creation of mythic traditions. They also show the central importance of the active imagination in myths and nocturnal dreams for the sustenance of creativity. Pointing out that the inner imagery process in Aboriginal mythopoesis and dreaming appears to have been changing since at least the 1950s, they cautiously observe that the vividness of dreams in conjunction with ritual may be deteriorating.

Mythic themes endure because people make them, but those themes also make the people. Through the accounting of myths, the Dreamings have become everlasting manifestations that tell of their self-transformations. It may be then that the capacity of their human descendants to sustain a viable image of themselves may likewise depend on the possibilities for creative renewal. As the Warlpiri/Pintupi man Andrew Japaljari put it, "One reason why we [Aboriginal people] can't handle the grog is because we have no Grog Dreaming" (Petchkovsky et al. 2003, p. 224).

BIBLIOGRAPHY

Bell, D. *Ngarrindjeri Wurruwarrin: A World That Is, Was, and Will Be.* Melbourne, 1998.

Berndt, Ronald M., and Catherine H. Berndt, eds. *Aborigines of the West: Their Past and Present.* Forest Grove, Ore., 1979.

Berndt, Ronald M., and Catherine H. Berndt. *The Speaking Land: Myth and Story in Aboriginal Australia.* New York, 1989.

Berndt, Ronald M., and Catherine H. Berndt with John E. Stanton. *A World That Was: The Yaraldi of the Murray River and the Lakes.* Vancouver, 1993.

Biddle, Jennifer. "Country, Skin, Canvas: The Intercorporeal Art of Kathleen Petyarre." *Australian and New Zealand Journal of Art* 4, No. 1 (2003): 61–76.

Blows, Johanna M. *Eagle and Crow: An Exploration of an Australian Aboriginal Myth.* New York, 1995.

Duelke, Britta. *". . . Same but Different . . ." Vom Umgang mit Vergangenheit.* Cologne, 1998.

Dussart, Françoise. *The Politics of Ritual in an Aboriginal Settlement: Kinship, Gender, and the Currency of Knowledge.* Washington, D.C., 2000.

Eickelkamp, Ute. "On the Meaning of Form in Pitjantjatjara Women's Art." In *An Odyssey of Space: The 2000 Chacmool Conference Proceedings,* edited by Andrea Waters, Calla McNamee, L. Steinbrenner, C. Clooney, Geoffrey G. McCafferty. Calgary, Alberta, 2003.

Gill, Sam S. *Storytracking: Texts, Stories and Histories in Central Australia.* New York, 1998.

Ginibi, Ruby Langford. *My Bundjalung People.* Queensland, 1994.

Johnson, Dianne. *Night Skies of Aboriginal Australia: A Noctuary.* Sydney, 1998.

Keen, Ian. *Knowledge and Secrecy in an Aboriginal Religion.* Oxford, 1994.

Marrett, Alan. "Ghostly Voices: some Observations on Song-Creation, Ceremony and Being in NW Australia." *Oceania* 71 (2000): 18–29.

Mission Time in Warburton. Exhibition and catalog, compiled and edited by Vikki Plant and Albie Viegas. Warburton, Western Australia, 2002.

Morphy, Howard. "Myth, Totemism and the Creation of Clans." *Oceania* 60 (1990): 312–328.

Morphy, Howard. *Ancestral Connections: Art and an Aboriginal System of Knowledge.* Chicago, 1991.

Morton, John. "Sensible Beasts: Psychoanalysis, Structuralism, and the Analysis of Myth." *The Psychoanalytic Study of Society* 18 (1993): 317–343.

Mountford, Charles P. *Nomads of the Australian Desert.* Rigby, Australia, 1976.

Myers, Fred R. *Painting Culture: The Making of an Aboriginal High Art.* Durham, N.C., 2002.

Native Title Act (Queensland) 1993. Available from http://www.legislation.qld.gov.au/LEGISLTN/CURRENT/N/NativeTitleQA93_01_.pdf. Also see *A Guide to Australian Legislation Relevant to Native Title.* Native Title Research Unit, AIATSIS, Canberra, 2000.

Petchkovsky, Leon, Craig San Roque, and Manita Beskow. "Jung and the Dreaming: Analytical Psychology's Encounters with Aboriginal Culture." *Transcultural Psychiatry* 40, No. 2 (2003): 208–238.

Poirier, Sylvie. *Les Jardins du Nomade: Cosmologie, Territoire et Personne dans le Désert Occidental Australien.* Muenster, 1996.

Redmond, Anthony. "Places That Move." In *Emplaced Myth: Space, Narrative, and Knowledge in Aboriginal Australia and Papua New Guinea,* edited by Alan Rumsey and James Weiner, pp. 120–138. Honolulu, 2001.

Rose, Deborah Bird. "The Saga of Captain Cook: Morality in Aboriginal and European Law." *Australian Aboriginal Studies* 2 (1984): 24-39.

Rose, Deborah Bird. *Dingo Makes Us Human: Life and Land in an Aboriginal Culture.* Cambridge, U.K., 1992.

Rose, Deborah Bird. "Flesh, and Blood, and Deep Colonising." In *Claiming Our Rites: Studies in Religion by Australian Women Scholars,* edited by Morny Joy and Penelope Magee, pp. 327-341. Adelaide, 1994.

Rose, Deborah Bird. *Country of the Heart: An Indigenous Australian Homeland.* Canberra, 2002.

Sansom, Basil. "Irruptions of the Dreamings in Post-Colonial Australia." *Oceania* 72, No. 1 (2001): 1–32.

Sturmer, John R. von. "Click Go the Designs: Presencing the Now in 1000 Easy Pieces." *Warburton One and Only: Painted Earthenware by Women from the Mirlirrjarra Ceramics Centre.* Sydney, 2002.

Swain, Tony, and Deborah Bird Rose, eds. *Aboriginal Australians and Christian Missions: Ethnographic and Historical Studies.* Bedford Park, South Australia, 1988.

Tamisari, Franca. "Body, Vision and Movement: in the Footprints of the Ancestors." *Oceania* 68 (1998): 249–270.

Taylor, Luke. *Seeing the Inside: Bark Painting in Western Arnhem Land.* Oxford, 1996.

Trust. Exhibition and catalog edited and curated by Jan Turner. Alice Springs, 2003.

Tunbridge, Dorothy. *Flinders Ranges Dreaming.* Canberra, 1988.

Turner, David H. *Life Before Genesis: A Conclusion.* 2d ed. New York, 1987.

Vaarzon-Morel, Petronella, ed. *Warlpiri Women's Voices: Our Lives, Our History /Stories Told by Molly Nungarrayi et al.*; Alice Springs, 1995.

Watson, Christine. *Piercing the Ground: Balgo Women's Image Making and Relationship to Country.* Fremantle, Western Australia, 2003.

UTE EICKELKAMP (2005)

AUSTRALIAN INDIGENOUS RELIGIONS: NEW RELIGIOUS MOVEMENTS

Indigenous new religious movements or cultic developments have a certain exotic appeal for theorists from state societies. But new religious developments in kin-based societies are not dissimilar in role to new political movements in state societies. For kin-based peoples, the ancestral realm is the source of life, knowledge, and power. During the original cosmogonic journeys, ancestral substances and energies were transformed into landforms and water sources. At the end of their journey the ancestors grew tired and merged into the landscape, taking the forms of hills, rocks, and trees. For their human descendants, following the ancestral way ensures protection from unknown and potentially malign outside forces. Breaking ancestral laws can lead to withdrawal of protection, revenge, and calamity. Indigenous people acted on the world and achieved their political and economic goals through religious ritual and activation of ancestral power.

The Western mind compartmentalizes human-world enterprises into separate domains, such as economics, politics, and religion. It reifies "religion" and gives it a sui generis status, setting it above "mundane" spheres of life. But for Aboriginal people and people of other non-Western cultures, human-ancestral interaction is not separate from politics or economics or any other sphere of life.

New religious movements in Aboriginal Australia did not come into being as a result of European colonization. New cults were continually being generated from old religious forms. They were used to legitimize migration and establishment of land claims in new areas and were widely used as alliance-forming mechanisms. For Indigenous people, the new is really just a discovery (or rediscovery) of something that was there from the beginning but had become lost or hidden. Sociocultural practices are "*always* in flux, in a perpetual historically sensitive state of resistance and accommodation to broader processes of influence that are as much inside as outside the local context" (Marcus and Fischer, 1986, p. 78). For I. M. Lewis, new religious movements are the idiom in which those who aspire to positions of leadership compete for power and authority (Lewis, 1971, p. 128). Such movements are often generated by younger people to challenge the established leaders of the central ritual system who are perceived as incompetent to deal with contemporary reality.

Indigenous leaders are expected to be "strong, powerful and dangerous . . . physically vigorous [with] forceful personalities" (Williams, 1987, p. 44). Leaders of new cultic developments, who are generally widely traveled, may attempt to engage with new and stronger forms of power in order to deal with new conditions of life. They, like traditional clever men, attempt to appropriate strange and mysterious powers from faraway places. In the early colonial period some cultic leaders clearly attempted to appropriate European colonial power-knowledge in order to achieve their goals.

OLD AND NEW TYPOLOGIES. Early colonial studies of Indigenous new religious movements reflect European colonial beliefs and values. In this period it was taken for granted by missionaries and social scientists alike that colonized peoples would become like them. Theorists and policy makers saw assimilation as an appropriate goal for Indigenous peoples within a colonial state. Confronted by strange religious phenomena that appeared to be neither Christian nor Indigenous, religious theorists appealed to their traditional frameworks of reference. They classified new religious movements along a pagan-Christian dimension and used descriptive terms from their own religious traditions—*messianism, millenarianism,* and *prophetism*—in order to render the strange cults familiar. Early attempts at categorization proliferated into a bewildering array of typologies, including Neopagan, Hebraist, Sabbatarian, Ethiopian Zionist, syncretist sects, aladuras, prophet healing, Apostolics, revelatory, enthusiastic movements, spiritual churches, and separatist sects (Turner, 1976, p. 13).

Anthropologists entered this discourse in the 1930s and 1940s and, using the terminology of the religious theorists, began to construct their theories of social change. In this colonial period anthropologists saw new religious movements as prime examples of acculturation to the European way of life. These strange hybrid cults, however anticolonialist in theme, were believed to be transitional stages along the road to full acculturation or assimilation. Ralph Linton (1940) set his analysis of new religious movements within this general framework. "Nativistic movements," that is, "organised attempts to revive or perpetuate certain aspects of their native cultures," were believed to be set in motion by the impact of European culture on traditional societies. Linton classified his nativistic movements as revivalistic-magical, revivalistic-rational, perpetuative-magical, and perpetuative-rational (Linton, 1979, pp. 497–501). This began a new spate of typology construction. Anthropologists began to speak of dynamic nativism, passive nativism, reformative nativism, adjustment movements, accommodative movements, transformative movements, crisis cults, denunciatory cults, protest movements, vitalistic movements, and revitalization movements (Burridge, 1969, p. 102). However, these descriptive terms do not refer to types that are mutually exclusive. In the 1970s there was a movement away from synchronic typology construction stimulated by historical research and phenomenological studies (Fernandez, 1978, p. 204). With a new generation of researchers, colonial studies of "millenarian" and "messianic" cults developed into postcolonial studies of anticolonial movements, cultural persistence, and "discourses of resistance."

The concept of the Dreaming is nonmillenarian, nonutopian, and nonhistorical. Localized Dreaming narratives are unable to account for cataclysmic changes (Wild, 1987, pp. 562–563). However, local and regional Dreaming tracks and story lines can be extended indefinitely as new tracks can be discovered, ancestral routes changed, and different routes connected together. Erich Kolig describes a universalizing project that occurred in the Fitzroy Valley region of the Kimberley in the 1970s. Walmajarri people brought the ancestors of local totemic cults together to travel over vast areas along newly interconnected tracks in order to eliminate religious particularism and unify themselves organizationally (Kolig, 1981, pp. 37–43).

Anticolonial movements in Australia occurred most commonly at colonial frontiers—places of extreme violence and dissymmetries of power (Carey and Roberts, 2002). These politico-religious cults were precipitated by failed military resistance, massacres, and catastrophic population decline brought about by introduced diseases, falling birthrates, and high infant mortality. Through participation in religious ritual, Aboriginal people attempted to mobilize powerful ancestral forces to engulf and destroy the colonial invaders.

THE BAIAME *WAGANNA*, 1833–1835. The Baiame *waganna* (dance ceremony) was one of the earliest anticolonial movements recorded in Australia. This traveling cult was precipitated by a catastrophic smallpox epidemic (1830–1831) followed by continuing population decimation. European men on the colonial frontier were usurping Aboriginal men's sexual rights to women. The Wiradjuri spirit beings, Baiame and Tharrawiirgal, were emasculated by European colonial penetration into Wellington Valley. Tharrawiirgal lost his tomahawk (and sent smallpox into the valley in revenge). One of Baiame's wives was stolen by a white man, and he was angered into retaliatory action (Carey and Roberts, 2002, pp. 822–843).

The Baiame *waganna* was performed to access the power of Baiame (who had defeated Tharrawiirgal in an earlier altercation), to protect Wiradjuri people against further smallpox depredations, to enforce nasal septum piercing, and to direct Baiame's anger toward European men and the Aboriginal women who consorted with them. Hilary M. Carey and David Roberts describe the Baiame *waganna* as a "nativist" or "revitalist" movement (Carey and Roberts, 2002, p. 823).

THE MULUNGA CULT, 1890S–1930S. Tony Swain (1993, p. 224–233) traces the Mulunga cult to the Kalkatungu wars in northwest Queensland and the wholesale slaughter of the Kalkadoon warriors in 1884. The traveling cult that spread into South Australia and Central Australia excited the research interests of Walter Roth, Baldwin Spencer, Otto Siebert, and Adolphus Elkin. Performers in this cult not only reenacted the bloody confrontation between colonists and Aborigines but danced out the desired end of this interaction. Dances showed Aborigines being shot down by whites until the "Grandmother," a powerful ancestral being, emerged from the sea to swallow the whites, gesturing in every direction to show that the destruction of whites would be complete. Leaders of the Mulunga cult exhorted adherents to follow the ancestral laws, especially marriage and sexual relations (Carey and Roberts, 2002, p. 835). Siebert saw in the Mulunga cult millenarian and nativistic themes (Kolig, 1989, p. 79).

BANDJALANG PENTECOSTALISM. Bandjalang people on the northern coast of New South Wales were first evangelized by the fundamentalist United Aborigines Mission (UAM). In 1952, as a result of UAM missionary shortages, Aboriginal UAM adherents transferred their allegiance to a Pentecostal fellowship. The Christian God merged with the ancestral being Ngathunggali, the Virgin Mary with Ngathunggali's wife, and Jesus Christ with their son Balugan (Calley, 1964, pp. 50–53). Beginning in the 1950s Bandjalang people developed some elaborate foundation stories from biblical and Dreaming sources. For example, Ngathunggali-God landed on the north coast of New South Wales in a bark canoe. His people, the Bandjalang, are the descendants of Jacob, who set out from the Holy Land in a sailing ship that was wrecked off the coast of New South Wales. The crew safely reached shore, built a bark canoe, and continued on their journey. Twelve tribes of Aboriginal people developed from these "founding fathers." The Bandjalang identified themselves as one of the "lost" tribes of Israel (Calley, 1955, pt. 2, pp. 6–7).

The Old Law was a special revelation of Ngathunggali-God to the Bandjalang. God spoke to Aboriginal people through the clever men. Balugan-Christ was killed by enemies (white people) at Kempsey and is buried on the Arakoon racecourse, from whence he will return to the Bandjalang. The white people, prosperous and powerful, crucified Christ and are rejected by God. The Bandjalang, humble and poor like Christ, are the beloved of God. Aborginal people will go to heaven and white people to hell (Calley, 1964, pp. 52–53).

THE DINGARRI-KURANGGARA SONG CYCLE. New politico-religious developments in northern Australia have been studied by the scholars Ronald M. Berndt, A. Lommel, Erich Kolig, K. P. Koepping, Helmut Petri, Gisela Petri-Odermann, Deborah Bird Rose, Tony Swain, and others. The celebrated Gunabibi traveling cult originated in the Victoria or Roper River regions of the Northern Territory and spread into Arnhem Land, Central Australia, and East Kimberley (Berndt, 1951, p. 233; Meggitt, 1955, p. 401; Petri, 1954, p. 265). In Central Australia and East Kimberley the cult developed into the Gunabibi-Gadjeri complex with masculinist forms and ideologies (Meggitt, 1966, pp. 84–86). This cult complex merged with the wandering Dingarri-Kuranggara song cycle of the Western Desert. Dingarri traditions celebrate the long migrations of Dingarri ancestors through the Western Desert. These migrations ended at Dingarri, a mythical location. The Kuranggara cult emanated highly dangerous life forces that originated in Anangu Pitjantjatjara country.

The Dingarri-Kuranggara song cycle brought the desert *jarnba*, spirits of the dead, into regional prominence. Visible only to initiates, *jarnba* were tall, skeleton-like spirits with menacing faces, horns, and long sexual organs. They could see what was hidden and were able to kill at a distance using sacred boards as rifles that they pointed at their enemies. As the pastoral industry penetrated into the desert regions, the *jarnba*—with ferocious appetites and raging thirst—were sucking the land dry (Koepping, 1988, pp. 401–402; Kolig, 1989, p. 84; Mol, 1982, p. 67). They also acted as fearsome guardians of the anticolonial desert cults, exhibiting fierce aggression toward European encroachments (Petri, 1968, p. 254).

Within the northern pastoral industry, in a context of structural inequality and exploitation, Aboriginal people continued to carry out ceremonial responsibilities for land and people. Aboriginal workers conducted complex negotiations with employers over generations in order to maintain a fragile security of land tenure. People adapted their cultural practices to the seasonal cycle of pastoral work, holding their large ceremonies during the wet season layoff period. However, employers failed to reciprocate in kind. They provided meager accommodation and in the early years paid workers only in clothing, kits, and rations. Even in later years they paid poor wages, avoided compensation payments, and neglected the health of their workers (McGrath, 1997, pp. 3–7).

In the 1930s the Dingarri-Kuranggara cult began to engage with new forms of power to counter the catastrophic effects of colonization. Cultists trafficked in the deadly power of the introduced diseases leprosy and syphilis. The *jarnba* leader had access to European forms of power-knowledge and lived in a white man's house; there he grew leprosy and syphilis from poisonous weeds in his backyard. This toxic power was ritually transferred into ceremonial boards that were distributed throughout Northwest Australia by motor vehicle, steamer, and airplane (Lommel, 1950, p. 23). The song cycle also predicted a reversal of Indigenous gender relationships. At this time women were becoming powerful and dangerous because they associated with white colonial forces and looked like half-castes; it was believed they would live on after death as powerful ghosts, that they would take control of cultic life, and that men would have to do the everyday work (Koepping, 1988, pp. 402–409).

The Dingarri-Kuranggara movement was strongly aggressive and antiwhite, yet it was also an attempt to incorporate European colonial power-knowledge into Indigenous cultic forms. Colonized people do more than just conform to or resist hegemonic forms and practices. They may creatively manipulate the forces of colonization by appropriating and transforming its signifiers according to their own political and cultural needs. Petri (1954, p. 268) regarded the cult as the reaction of younger Aborigines to the increasing incapacity of elders to rally against European encroachment. Cult organizers were named "clerks," "policemen," and "cooks." Petri and Lommel's descriptions of the movement contain nativistic, revivalistic, and antiwhite themes. Kolig finds millenarian, apocalyptic, and cargoistic themes in the Kuranngara cult (Kolig, 1989, pp. 84–85).

THE WOAGAIA-JINIMIN MOVEMENT. Modes of resistance to colonial incursions vary from ritual performance to overtly political (in the Western sense) forms of struggle. From the 1930s Aboriginal people on remote pastoral stations organized to have their working conditions improved. Most governments supported employers' refusal to grant Aborigines award wages, and it was not until the late 1940s that Aboriginal workers attracted significant union support. In 1946, assisted by Don McLeod, a white bore sinker, Aboriginal cattlemen walked off twenty-two stations in the Pilbara. During this strike a number of agitators were jailed. In the mid- to late 1940s McLeod organized Aboriginal mining cooperatives along socialist principles, and in 1949 "the Pindan mob" formed their own company in order to control financial enterprises on their land (McGrath, 2001, p. 144).

Central Australian and West Kimberley people at this time were the recipients of intensive missionization. The Lutheran Church established its missions with Arrernte people of the Macdonnell Ranges, Haasts Bluff, and Simpson Desert in 1877. The Australian Baptist Missionary Society began mission work with Warlpiri people of Central Australia in 1947. Walmajarri people of the northern Great Sandy Desert were influenced by both the United Aborigines Mission (at Fitzroy Crossing from 1952) and the Catholic Church (at La Grange from 1955).

In 1963 the Dingarri-Kuranggara traditions merged with the new Woagaia-Jinimin movement developing out of the Gadjeri-Woagaia cult complex of Central Australia. *Woagaia* is a generic term for several cults introduced into the Kimberley by Warlpiri, Gurindji, Ngadi, and other Central Australian groups (Kolig, 1989, p. 124). On a mission station in Central Australia, Jinimin, the precocious son of an old venerable ancestral being, revealed himself to Aboriginal people as Jesus Christ. This epiphany occurred during the performance of a Woagaia ceremony. Jinimin-Jesus proclaimed himself the protector and preserver of ancestral laws (Petri and Petri-Odermann, 1988, p. 393).

The black-and-white-skinned Jesus favored Aborigines over whites. He proclaimed that the land from the beginning had belonged to Aboriginal people and that he would help them regain their land. The Dingarri ancestors were returning from the mythic land Dingarri in the east. By participating in the Woagaia cult, Aboriginal people would gain the power and strength needed to rally against the colonizers. In order to succeed in their campaign, they must rigorously adhere to ancestral laws. If they did so, the European invaders would be defeated, and Holy Water would fall from heaven to drown all white people and turn Aboriginal skins white. Aborigines would thus regain sovereignty over their lands by becoming white-skinned (Koepping, 1988, p. 404; Kolig, 1989, p. 86; Petri and Petri-Odermann, 1988, p. 393).

In June 1966 stockmen walked off Newcastle Waters Station, followed by two hundred Gurindji workers at Vesteys Wave Hill station. Vesteys, an English cattle company, owned ten stations across the Northern Territory and East Kimberley, controlling a pastoral empire almost the size of Tasmania. One of the richest families in Britain, the Vesteys made more than a billion pounds in the global meat trade, and yet their Aboriginal workers were paid a pittance and lived in substandard conditions. The Gurindji strike that began as a demand for equal wages and working conditions emerged as the politics of an oppressed people who had never relinquished sovereignty over their land. The Gurindji mounted a land claim over their traditional lands and the right to run their community free from exploitation by the Vesteys and from "welfare" control (Jennett, 2001, p. 122).

By 1966 the Woagaia-Jinimin cult—proclaimed as "God's Law"—had spread to the west. Walmajarri people had been migrating in a northwesterly direction from desert areas three hundred kilometers southeast of Fitzroy Crossing since the beginning of the twentieth century. Under Walmajarri direction, Dingarri ancestors were "returning" from the desert to their "true" country in the northwest. The Dreamtime groups were marching along underground routes (which were used to traverse the country of strangers) with camels to carry their *darrugu* (secret-sacred objects). Their leader and protector on this journey was Jinimin-Jesus. The Woagaia-Jinimin traveling cult was used to legitimize the northwesterly migration of Walmajarri people and their establishment of land claims in new areas. It was also an attempt by people who had been marginalized by European colonization to find again "the centre of the world" (Petri and Petri-Odermann, 1970, pp. 251–272).

In the northwestern coastal areas Jinimin-Jesus was black-skinned. Missionaries were accused of falsifying God's message to keep Aboriginal people in bondage. Apocalyptic visions of an end-time deluge continued, and a new Noah appeared at Fitzroy Crossing. This Walmajarri man had discovered a gold-laden ark, sent from heaven by Jinimin, that had been hidden in the land since the Dreaming. At Myroodah-Looma, an Aboriginal "Bible" revealed the ark to be a refuge from the flood that would destroy all whites and the basis of a new Aboriginal world that would be superior to European colonial society (Kolig, 1981, p. 160, 1988, p. 167, 1989, p. 119; Petri and Petri-Odermann, 1988, pp. 393–394).

The 1969 Pastoral Award that granted Aboriginal workers equal wages was followed immediately by a pastoralist countermove to remove Aboriginal people from stations. The pastoralists' strategy was to evict Aboriginal people before they were forced to grant them land or fuller access rights. The 1970s thus saw a new dispossession of pastoral Aborigines, with many forced to live in camps on the fringes of towns. The expulsion coincided with a rise in Aboriginal political consciousness (McGrath, 2001, p. 144).

The Woagaia-Jinimin movement combined Don McLeod's sociorevolutionary ideas, an emerging Land Rights politic, and apocalyptic biblical themes. In ceremonial performance (under the protection of Jinimin-Jesus) the cultists appropriated dangerous colonial powers and harnessed them to their own cause. Apocalyptic forces were projected toward the colonizers, while Noah's ark provided safety and security for Aboriginal people. Erich Kolig (1988, p. 166) sees chiliastic features in the Noah's ark story. For Helmut Petri and Gisela Petri-Oderman (1988, pp. 391–394), the Woagaia-Jinimin cult was a new nativistic-millenarian movement with strong revivalist and revitalistic tendencies.

JULURRU TRAVELING CULT. The Julurru cult that developed out of the Dingarri-Kuranggara and Woagaia ceremonial complexes made its first appearance in the Pilbara region. Tony Swain traces the cult to Don McLeod's Aboriginal lieutenant, who had frustrated leadership ambitions (Swain, 1993, p. 259). Malay ghosts of the sunken ship *Koombana* visited him in dreams and revealed to him their colonial adventures. Julurru—a dangerous Malay or Japanese ghost—traveled through Australia by Afghan camel trains, horse teams, cars, ships, and airplanes. He united disparate Dreaming tracks, tracked wandering Dreamings, and brought them to Dingarri. This fearsome warmonger was also involved in World War II airplane battles, ship sinkings, and bombing raids in Aboriginal country. Through the performance of his traveling cult, Julurru passed his military-technological power-knowledge on to Aboriginal people and asserted the equality of Aborigines and whites in Australia (Kolig, 1989, pp. 120–121; Swain, 1993, p. 261).

In the 1960s and 1970s the cult traveled up the Fitzroy River and into southern Kimberley, where "prisoners" (cult initiates) were held in "gaol" (jail) and guarded by "policemen." Dance sequences included soldier battles, airplane battles, spectacular fire dances, the bombing and sinking of ships, and appearances of Adolf Hitler (Kolig, 1989, p. 122; Swain, 1993, p. 258).

The cult reached Central Australia in the late 1970s. There Julurru assumed a pastoral guise, dressing in stockman garb with a cowboy hat and pistols. He rode a white horse or a motorbike, consumed vast amounts of alcohol, and caused vehicles to crash when drivers failed to assist Aboriginal people (Swain, 1993, pp. 254–255). The cult was embraced by Warlpiri people at Lajamanu during a period of political empowerment—in 1976 the Aboriginal Land Rights (Northern Territory) Act 1976 was passed, and in

1978 Gurindji and Warlpiri people were granted ninety-five thousand square kilometers of land south of Wave Hill. However, the 1979 Julurru ceremony at Lajamanu was attended by a Noonkanbah contingent that resulted in increased understanding of Aboriginal powerlessness in the face of mining interests and increased cynicism about government goodwill toward Aborigines (Wild, 1981, p. 3). Aboriginal people from twenty-six communities assembled at Noonkanbah in April 1980 to prevent the land being mined, engaging in direct political action and in the performance of politico-religious ceremonies.

Stephen Wild sees the Julurru cult, at least in part, as an alliance-forming mechanism operating between Western Desert, Kimberley, and Central Desert Aborigines in the wake of land rights successes and failures. At Lajamanu the cult was managed by relatively young Aboriginal administrators who were politically aware, skilled in negotiations with Europeans, and in control of community transport and communications. The aim of cult leaders at Lajamanu was to replace the old ceremonies with the new (Wild, 1981, p. 14, 1987, p. 565).

Local and regional Dreaming stories were unable to account for the devastation of European colonization. Traveling cults that trafficked in strange and mysterious life forces were unable to generate powers sufficiently dangerous to expel the colonizers. Aboriginal people appropriated narratives available to them from the colonists' repertoires. The Bible—a colonial document—was an excellent source of stories about catastrophe and devastation. The Old Testament God punished wrongdoers with plagues, famines, floods, wars, exile, and slavery. Aboriginal cultists incorporated increasingly dangerous colonial powers into their ceremonial performances and, under the protection of powerful spirit beings, unleashed apocalyptic forces onto their enemies.

More recently Aboriginal people have appropriated "nonreligious" colonial narratives, such as Captain Cook and Ned Kelly stories, to construct discourses of resistance but have used these stories in religious-mythic ways. Aboriginal narratives featuring Captain Cook as the major agent of colonization have been studied in northern Australia by Kolig, Rose, Chips Mackinolty, and Paddy Wainburranga. Captain Cook, like the Dreaming beings, was a lawmaker, but he refused to recognize Aboriginal law. The prior occupancy and ownership of the country was obvious: "You [Captain Cook] been look around, see the land now. People been here, really got their own culture. All around Australia . . . we the one on the land. Sitting on the land, Aboriginal people. You got nothing, all you government . . . we got all the culture. That Dreaming place, important one" (Danaiyairi, in Rose, 1984, p. 34).

Captain Cook carried out his colonizing program by imposing his own immoral law over the top of Aboriginal law. Aboriginal country, its products, and human labor were appropriated by Europeans to enhance their own political and economic well-being—to "make themselves strong" at Aboriginal people's expense. This particular Captain Cook narrative locates responsibility for colonization not in the spirit realm but in European law and practice and finds this law immoral (Rose, 1984, p. 35, 1988, p. 371).

If Captain Cook has been a negative presence in most Aboriginal colonial narratives, Ned Kelly has been given a different focus. In Yarralin stories Ned Kelly and his band of angels came down from the sky. Friends of Aboriginal people, they traveled around the Northern Territory and the Kimberley, shooting the police. Kelly's life story has been conflated with biblical stories about God, Noah, and Jesus. For example, Kelly created dry land after the flood and fed many Aboriginal people with one billy of tea and a small damper. And in one version of the story, he was killed by Captain Cook, buried, and on the third day rose from the dead, ascending to the sky to the accompaniment of a great noise and the shaking of the earth (Rose, 1988, p. 369, 1992, pp. 182–184).

Colonial and postcolonial narratives continue to be generated by Aboriginal people in contemporary Australia. They construct histories of the world by incorporating Dreaming stories, "the old people's stories," and their own life histories into biblical and Australian colonial frameworks (see Beckett, 1993; McDonald, 2001). They (like all human beings) appropriate stories and characters from larger explanatory narratives, reworking them to fit present needs, and inserting into these frameworks their own narratives of the self. These narrative sources are subject to readings, misreadings, rereadings, and interpretations as Aboriginal people move away from colonial towns and reserves to develop their own independent communities. In northern Australia:

> [Aboriginal people's] main goal is a form of segregation that will enable them to achieve the necessary measure of detachment from White hegemony and thus once again give them control over their own existence . . . a separation willed and desired by a politically powerless group so that they may be able to live their own lives, at their own pace, and realizing their own ideals. (Kolig, 1989, p. 33)

SEE ALSO Christianity, article on Christianity in Australia and New Zealand.

BIBLIOGRAPHY

Beckett, J. "Walter Newton's History of the World—or Australia." *American Ethnologist* 20, no. 4 (1993): 675–695.

Berndt, Ronald M. "Influence of European Culture on Australian Aborigines." *Oceania* 21, no. 3 (1951): 227–235.

Burridge, K. *New Heaven, New Earth.* Oxford, 1969.

Calley, Malcolm John Chalmers. "Aboriginal Pentecostalism: A Study of Changes in Religion, North Coast, NSW." M.A. thesis, University of Sydney, 1955.

Calley, Malcolm John Chalmers. "Pentecostalism among the Bandjalang." In *Aborigines Now,* edited by Marie Reay. Sydney, 1964.

Carey, Hilary M., and David Roberts. "Smallpox and the Baiame *Waganna* of Wellington Valley, NSW, 1829–1840: The Earliest Nativist Movement in Aboriginal Australia." *Ethnohistory* 49 no. 4 (2002): 821–869.

Fernandez, James W. "African Religious Movements." *Annual Review of Anthropology* 7 (1978): 195–234.

Jennett, C. "Aboriginal Politics." In *The Australian People: An Encyclopedia of the Nation, Its People, and Their Origins*, edited by James Jupp, pp. 121–127. York, U.K., 2001.

Koepping, K. P. "Nativistic Movements in Aboriginal Australia: Creative Adjustment, Protest, or Regeneration of Tradition." In *Aboriginal Australians and Christian Missions*, edited by Tony Swain and Deborah Bird Rose, pp. 397–411. Bedford Park, South Australia, 1988.

Kolig, Erich. "Captain Cook in the Western Kimberleys." In *Aborigines of the West: Their Past and Their Present*, edited by Ronald M. Berndt and Catherine H. Berndt. Perth, Australia, 1980.

Kolig, Erich. *The Silent Revolution.* Philadelphia, 1981.

Kolig, Erich. "Religious Movements." In *The Australian People: An Encyclopedia of the Nation, Its People, and Their Origins*, edited by James Jupp, pp. 165–167. Sydney, 1988.

Kolig, Erich. *Dreamtime Politics: Religion, World View, and Utopian Thought in Australian Aboriginal Society.* Berlin, 1989.

Lewis, I. M. *Ecstatic Religion.* Middlesex, U.K., 1971.

Linton, Ralph. *Acculturation in Seven American Indian Tribes.* Gloucester, Mass., 1940.

Linton, Ralph. "Nativistic Movements." In *Reader in Comparative Religion*, edited by William A. Lessa and Evon Z. Vogt. New York, 1979.

Lommel, A. "Modern Culture Influences on the Aborigines." *Oceania* 21, no. 1 (1950): 14–24.

Mackinolty, Chips, and Paddy Wainburranga. "Too Many Captain Cooks." In *Aboriginal Australians and Christian Missions*, edited by Tony Swain and Deborah Bird Rose, pp. 355–360. Bedford Park, South Australia, 1988.

Marcus, George E., and Michael Fischer. *Anthropology as Cultural Critique: An Experimental Moment in the Human Sciences.* Chicago, 1986.

McDonald, Heather. *Blood, Bones, and Spirit: Aboriginal Christianity in an East Kimberley Town.* Melbourne, 2001. Author's note: "I thank Melbourne University Press for giving me permission to use extracts from this book."

McGrath, Ann. "The History of Pastoral Co-Existence." In *Annual Report of Human Rights and Equal Opportunity Commission*, edited by M. Dodson. Canberra, 1997.

McGrath, Ann. "The Pastoral Industry." In *The Australian People: An Encyclopedia of the Nation, Its People, and Their Origins*, edited by James Jupp, pp. 141–145. York, U.K., 2001.

Mol, Hans. *The Firm and the Formless.* Waterloo, Ontario, 1982.

Petri, Helmut. *Sterbende Welt in Nordwest-Australien.* Braunschweig, Germany, 1954.

Petri, Helmut. "Australische eingeborenen-religionen." In *Die Religionen der Sudsee und Australiens*, edited by H. Nevermann, E. A. Worms, and H. Petri. Stuttgart, 1968.

Petri, Helmut, and Gisela Petri-Odermann. "Stability and Change: Present-Day Historic Aspects among Aborigines." In *Australian Aboriginal Anthropology*, edited by Ronald M. Berndt. Perth, 1970.

Petri, Helmut, and Gisela Petri-Odermann. "A Nativistic and Millenarian Movement in North West Australia." In *Aboriginal Australians and Christian Missions*, edited by Tony Swain and Deborah Bird Rose. Bedford Park, South Australia, 1988.

Rose, Deborah Bird. "The Saga of Captain Cook: Morality in Aboriginal and European Law." *Australian Aboriginal Studies* 2 (1984): 24–39.

Rose, Deborah Bird. "Jesus and the Dingo." In *Aboriginal Australians and Christian Missions*, edited by Tony Swain and Deborah Bird Rose, pp. 361–375. Bedford Park, South Australia, 1988.

Rose, Deborah Bird. "Ned Kelly Died for Our Sins." *Oceania* 65, no. 2 (1994): 175–186.

Swain, Tony. *A Place for Strangers: Towards a History of Australian Aboriginal Being.* Cambridge, U.K., 1993.

Turner, H. W. "The Approach to Africa's Religious Movements." *African Perspectives* 2 (1976): 13–23.

Wild, Stephen. "A Contemporary Aboriginal Religious Movement of the Western Desert." Paper presented at the AIAS Symposium on Contemporary Aboriginal Religious Movements. Canberra, Australia, 1981.

Wild, Stephen. "Modern Movements." In *The Encyclopedia of Religion*, edited by Mircea Eliade, pp. 562–566. New York, 1987.

Williams, Nancy. *Two Laws: Managing Disputes in a Contemporary Aboriginal Community.* Canberra, Australia, 1987.

HEATHER MCDONALD (2005)

AUSTRALIAN INDIGENOUS RELIGIONS: ABORIGINAL CHRISTIANITY

Aboriginal Theology was a radical movement beginning in the late 1960s and becoming more prominent in the early 1970s. The movement pushed the barriers forward toward the creation of an Indigenous theology that leaned heavily towards Biblical social justice. It was an autonomous post-Western, post-denominational movement that emphasized prophetic obedience, action and liberation. It attempted to hold up Aboriginality (e.g. identity, culture and spirituality) as the guiding principle, and to maintain traditional Aboriginal religion by drawing up Ancestral Narratives [Dreamings], ceremonies, rituals and laws as the divine grounding for contemporary faith and identity. It held traditional practices such as ceremonies and stories as potent reminders of important cosmic and temporal truths. And it embraced Aboriginal Dreaming as a timeless guide for active engagement.

Out of the many Aboriginal Christian leaders involved in the development of Aboriginal Theology, the three most remembered by Aboriginal Christians today are Pastor Don Brady, the Rev. Charles Harris and Pastor David Kirk; these men are considered by Aboriginal Christians as the pioneers of Aboriginal Theology and Church (with reference to the Aborigines Inland Mission, United Aborigines Mission, and the Methodist Church in Queensland). These Aboriginal leaders condemned the dominant white society's subjugation and exploitation of Aboriginal people and also raised important issues of justice and equality. Further, they condemned white missionaries as destructive influences upon the Aboriginal peoples and cultures. In this way they mixed deep faith with political commitment. The impact that these three leaders had on Aboriginal Christian understanding was radical. Historically, missionaries (both Catholic and Protestant) had determined that Aboriginal access to God only could be obtained through them. Now presented to the Aboriginals was a different image of access—a direct connection to God. Aboriginal leaders made clear for all Aboriginal Christians that they themselves had direct access to God, and that their relationship to Jesus Christ was established a long time before the white invasion of their land, through their lived experience with God from time immemorial.

THE REV. DON BRADY. The Rev. Don Brady was a pivotal figure in Aboriginal religious, social and political movements. Indeed, Aboriginal people recognized that his life and ministry were pivotal to the development of Aboriginal Theology. He was the first Aboriginal church leader to lead political marches, calling for the abolition of the racist and oppressive *Queensland Aborigines Act,* which subjected Aboriginal people to inhumane social, economic and health conditions, controlling where they could live and work, whom they could marry, and how far they could advance in school. Brady's ministry was to influence many generations that followed.

Pastor Brady was from Palm Island, the former prison compound in far north Queensland, which was used to contain and control Aboriginal people. He came to the Lord there, and eventually was amongst the first of the male Aboriginal students to receive training through the Aborigines Inland Mission (AIM). He married fellow student Darlene Willis, of Cherbourg, another Aboriginal mission in southern Queensland. They ministered together within AIM for a number of years.

Pastor Brady was a gifted man, who was able to see through the lack of effectiveness of mission practice, program and policy. In the early 1960s, he began a further two years of theological training in the Methodist College at Kangaroo Point. In the late 1960s, Brady worked with the Methodist Church in Queensland in the heart of Brisbane, at Spring Hill. He was enormously popular, particularly among his own Aboriginal people, because his ministry was (w)holistic. Brady was concerned, not only about the spiritual side, but also the physical and emotional sides of people. He had a way of connecting with people—of seeing brokenness and being able to heal it. The appeal of his ministry extended far beyond the bounds of his own Aboriginal community, as many non-Aboriginal people were also drawn to his charisma.

Pastor Brady's prophetic stance grew out of his experiences overseas. He had won a Churchill Fellowship, and had traveled to several communities in the United States and begun to sense a new direction. In his own words, "In Chicago I heard a call, 'Don arise, you are going to do a new thing'" (Brady, 1971, p. 39).

Brady was the first of all the Aboriginal pastors and leaders to combine the application of the Gospel with Aboriginal cultural practice. There were two things for which he stood out: (1) he was right at the cutting edge of "Gospel and culture"; and (2) his emphasis on social justice issues. His ministry demonstrated the priority of Christ for the poor—Christ's identification with the poor. It was Brady's particular ministry in relation to these two factors that worked so well. He tried to bring Aboriginal culture into the church, which enormously affirmed Aboriginal people. Aboriginal church leader, the Rev. Graham Paulson, remembers Brady's influence, and states, "Brady was right at the cutting edge of Methodist ministry with urban Aboriginal people" (Paulson, 1995).

Pastor Brady saw the poverty of his people and heard their cries. He felt that God was on the side of the oppressed and was leading his people out of bondage. He questioned how he could minister to the spiritual needs of Aboriginal people, when they were enslaved by Australian legislation that oppressed them and literally denied them their human dignity and rights. Brady earned the title, "The Punching Parson," by simply going around and picking up those of his homeless people in the parks and other places who were vulnerable to arrest and further abuse by the system. He took them back to a refuge—sometimes having to "knock them out" first, but they always thanked him the next morning. That sort of work, so far as the church was concerned, had never been done before in the history of mission amongst the Aboriginal people.

Brady was a catalyst, in the sense that he created a Black church, challenged the institutions, and began a Black movement—one that was to be felt across all of Australia. He lit the fire in people; he lit the spark, the will to fight, and the need for them to struggle for justice. He instilled in people the hope, the will to live. Brady revealed to Aboriginal Christians that the God of justice, who freed the Israelites from the bondage of Egyptian rule, also was with the Aboriginal people as they struggled for freedom from Western oppression, racist laws and imperialism. Together with other secular Aboriginal movements (such as the Aboriginal Land Rights Movement) throughout the country, Brady brought the force of his Black Church with him, led by the conviction of equality and freedom for all. Black people began to share in the hope that God was on their side, and that God would send the Holy Spirit, the Comforter, to be their strength, hope and courage in the face of the racism inflicted upon them by the white Australian society. He raised the consciousness of his people—that Christ came and died for them, and they too were free, and inheritors of the Kingdom. The pressures on Brady were enormous, because he was the lone voice in the Methodist Church at that time, saying things that Aboriginal people had never heard before.

Brady questioned the political system (such as the Department of Native Affairs in Brisbane), and other policies in his concern for the people, and raised a number of social justice questions. In the process, the conservatives and whites in the Methodist Church began to distance themselves from him. He found himself more and more isolated by the system that had affirmed him from the very beginning—that is, until he began to raise questions of justice in terms of social issues. Increasingly, Brady found himself a lonely and deserted leader. Also, from his conservative beginnings in AIM, some of his former colleagues were sniping at him as well. They could not understand his political leanings and were trying to spiritualize away all the political, social and economic issues.

Brady's belief in doing and bringing the Gospel through Christ's action led to severe repercussions. He was spiritually and emotionally shattered. The church pulled back and 'defrocked' him, and his status and the basis for his drive in the community—that which gave him the basis for justice and morality and integrity—was pulled away from him.

Brady gave his life for what he believed, and in obedience to what God called him to do. And, even though the church turned against him and tried to silence and discredit him, the legacy of his ministry was to be continued and made visible in the lives and ministries of those who were to follow. Brady's efforts were not wasted; on the contrary, his influence lives on in those who have the courage and the conviction to carry the cross today. David Thompson, a lifelong friend of Pastor Brady, describes him as "a man ahead of his time," and "a man of strength, character and vision, who laid the foundations for the future" (Thompson, 1995).

Pastor David Kirk. Pastor David Kirk was another pivotal figure in the development of an Aboriginal organization-fellowship. He grew up in Cherbourg, the mission compound in southeast Queensland. He, like others during his time, grew up under the oppressive authority of the *Queensland Aborigines Act.*

Kirk came to the Lord in Cherbourg, under the ministry of an Aboriginal preacher, Herbie Fisher, and entered the Bible College at Singleton, in N.S.W., in the mid-1950s. He worked with Howard Miles—who later became president of AIM in the Northern Territory—and after he was married, he worked at Caroona, in central New South Wales, with his wife, Dawn Dates. Kirk served for many years with AIM, and the highlight of his ministry was the development of his work at Cherbourg, which he built from nothing under the previous white missionary, to the point where the church became the dominant social institution in the area. There were many operations and programs that had their central focus either in or from the church or from the Christians, and the church was continuously packed. At Cherbourg, he was interested in upgrading secular education, because Queensland's Department of Native Affairs policies still had not changed since his youth. He worked with the community in social programs, toward the improvement of the quality of life of people within Cherbourg.

In the early to mid-1960s, Kirk was asked to serve as Deputy Principal at the Bible College in Singleton. His commitment to social justice was visible through his work of trying to change the system from within. He did not see Aboriginal people being empowered by the system, as there were no Aboriginal leaders participating in the decision-making bodies of the church. They were not in positions of status, nor in positions of power; they were continuously oppressed and kept down by the mission. Kirk felt that because it was called the Aborigines Inland Mission, those whom AIM had trained—the indigenous people themselves—should be at the forefront of running the mission. He spearheaded the drive for as long as he could, before finally leaving the mission. The confrontation was so great that the Aboriginal people and the non-Aboriginal people decided to go their own ways.

Ultimately, at a meeting of the Aboriginal people at Cherbourg twelve to eighteen months later, the Aboriginal Convention decided to form the Australian Aboriginal Evangelical Fellowship. Unbeknownst to them, Kirk's colleagues had been aware of this movement and were leading their own counter-movement amongst the United Aborigines Mission (UAM), a sister Mission of AIM in Western Australia. Both of these had worked together in the initial stages at La Perouse, in Sydney. The Aboriginal Conference in Western Australia formed the Aboriginal Evangelical Fellowship. Within one week of each other, and without prior notice, these two Evangelical Fellowship organizations, independently of each other, had arrived at the same name, with almost the same mandate—one in the east and one in the west. In 1968, they began joint conferences and, finally, in 1970, decided to merge the groups, and formulated the national umbrella, the Aboriginal Evangelical Fellowship of Australia (AEF).

Kirk sought the development of the Aboriginal Church by Indigenous principles. Up until this time he could not see the church being self-supporting, self-governing and self-propagating. However, he began to see evangelism spread within the Aboriginal community (self-propagation), and see the beginnings of self-support. Australian Aboriginals were and still are at the bottom of the ladder of socio-economic development, and what concerned him most, was that the Aboriginal people had no power of decision-making. How could they get out of this mess, if they could not decide for themselves? The teaching of Roland Allen's book, *The Indigenous Church,* was the driving and motivating force for Kirk. He sought to employ the principles of Roland Allen within Cherbourg, but when he went back into the mission the missionaries continued to hold onto control and would not give up their power base.

In 1978, Kirk, along with others, worked to prepare the property and program to become a Bible College. Kirk saw that the mission's policies and programs were not working in truly liberating the Aboriginal people. It was only bringing them so far, but still keeping them in bondage within the mission system. What Kirk wanted was true autonomy. The mission taught that the truly Indigenous church was to be self-governing, but it would not allow the Aboriginal people the opportunity to govern themselves within this system. This caused Kirk to lead his people against the oppressive system. Kirk saw the hypocrisy of the mission, on the one hand teaching self-government in its training program at local church level, and on the other not letting self-government go through all of the other levels of the church's bureaucracy. The whites held on to power within the decision-making and management processes, and marginalized the Aboriginal people. He saw their Westernizing within the context of their missionizing as racism—a form of racism that was very subtle and that they had systematically perpetuated against Aboriginal people for 80 to 90 years, literally dominating all aspects of their lives.

Further, Kirk saw the mission getting money in the name of Aboriginal people, and Aboriginals not being the direct beneficiaries of this income. It was mostly going into building up the mission bureaucracies in which Aboriginal people had no part. He led the charge against the mission, and led the breakaway with the AEF.

Where he sought empowerment for the indigenous people through the establishment of their own churches and institutions, Kirk, however, did not see the need for the development of an Indigenous Theology. He thought that through Aboriginal control, he had achieved indigenization; but, instead, what had in fact been done was the creation of a Black bureaucracy founded upon white theology, missiology, ideology and misogyny. The only thing indigenous about this move was the black people who controlled it. What they all failed to see was they had all internalized their own oppression, as they were Aboriginal people thinking, acting and speaking white. They had not seen the need to incorporate into this new structure, or into the churches, their own identity, culture and theology. Paulson's assessment of Kirk's ministry was that "he was still applying Western theology to Aboriginal situations, rather than conceptualizing a new framework for theology" (Paulson, 1995). Kirk affirmed his culture and identity, but saw these as secondary and separate to his focus. While Kirk had not constructed a theology of liberation, he nevertheless had radicalized the mission. Kirk believed that Aboriginal people should govern their own Christian lives, institutions and theological education, be the preachers and interpreters of the Gospel message in their own churches, and determine the mission and evangelism of and to their own people.

After the first ten years, he began to suffer isolation as some of his colleagues questioned "where he was going" and "where he was leading AEF." Coming with a more conservative theology, they sought to impose their viewpoints. Kirk saw this imposition as detrimental to the cause of pushing ahead for an Indigenous Church. Eventually, as a result of this radical push, Kirk suffered repercussions. Colleagues wrote letters to him, advising that they were cutting themselves off from him because they felt he was too radical. The white missionaries pulled back, accusing Kirk of racism and separatism; they then used their influence over his Aboriginal colleagues to do likewise. Both began to ridicule him together. It was when his own people turned against him, that Kirk found nothing left for which to live. In 1986, feeling so abandoned, Pastor David Kirk took his own life. Kirk's ministry was cut short due to the overwhelming heartache of leadership under these conditions.

The Rev. Charles Harris. The Rev. Charles Harris was a third pivotal figure—the Founder of the Uniting Aboriginal and Islander Christian Congress, and the visionary behind the 1988 March for Justice, Freedom and Hope.

The Rev. Harris was born in Ingham, in north Queensland, during the Depression. He grew up on the fringes of white towns during the time of the *Queensland Aborigines Act* and the "White Australia Policy" (this policy excluded non-Europeans from entry into Australia on the basis of race). Eventually, his father moved the family to the bush near Victoria Station, where they lived in a small "house" with palm tree floorboards, kerosene tin walls and roof, and hessian sugar bags for partitions. The eight children, four boys and four girls, kept warm during the cold winters by wearing the hessian bags. The family lived on what they were able to plant (yam, taro, sweet potato) or keep (fowl), and on the scraps of his mother's cane farmer boss. The children walked two and a half miles to school each day, where they could only afford to have damper with treacle (a syrup). Young Charles would watch the white children eat their nicely cut packed lunches, while he sat over in a corner where no one could see his meager damper and treacle. It was at school that Harris first realized the power of racism to create the hunger and poverty he and his family were experiencing.

During the 1970s and 1980s, Harris completed nearly four years of study in conservative, white, Western theological colleges (including Nungalinya, Wontulp-Bi-Buya and the College in Brisbane), where he remained unaware of the issues of justice and struggle.

In the 1970s, the Rev. Charles Harris followed Brady at the ministry in Brisbane, taking up the mantle of direct ministry with the Aboriginal people at Musgrave Park. His work continued the prophetic stands for justice, eventually culminating in his vision of the Uniting Aboriginal and Islander Christian Congress in 1985. His subsequent writings reveal a true passion and "thirst" for justice.

When he came to work with Pastor Don Brady in the inner city suburbs of Brisbane and the centre at Paddington, however, he encountered a reality that shocked and changed him. While Harris was sitting with the alcoholics in Musgrave Park, God gave him a vision of his own people "crushed beyond hopelessness, just drinking themselves to death, having no hope for the future" (Pattel-Gray, p. 122), and he felt the pain and suffering of the Aboriginal people. There, he met not the imported God, but the Aboriginal God—the One that called him to a radical new vision of a Gospel which liberates, and one that could "break through any barrier and bridge any gap that existed not only in the Aboriginal community, but also in the world" (Pattel-Gray, p. 122). Harris was made aware that the Bible could address current issues, those that affected his people. "Unless the Gospel does address and can address the [current] situation . . . the current issues, then it's not the Gospel to me. It's definitely not the Gospel, it's something that man has imposed upon his fellow man" (Pattel-Gray, p. 122).

In 1980, Harris was ordained to the Christian ministry in the Uniting Church in Australia. During this period, Harris had a vision of a Black, autonomous church, with its own leadership and ministry—a place for Aboriginal people to gather and to share their hopes, faith and ministry. In 1985, as the visionary behind this initiative and under his direction, Harris founded the Uniting Aboriginal and Islander Christian Congress (UAICC), under the umbrella of the Uniting Church in Australia (UCA). What Kirk had envisioned, Harris made a reality for Aboriginal Christians of the UCA. Harris' achievements included not only separate organizational structures, but also securing the economics to sustain national and various state entities throughout Australia. No longer would Aboriginal ministry be in the hands of the West; now, it would be secured firmly in the hands of Aboriginal people—fulfilling the goal of self-determination so sought by Harris. His accomplishments became the impetus behind the Aboriginal Christian movement within the church for a separate Aboriginal ecclesiastical structure, yet with an equal place in the life of the whole church.

During his time of leadership as President of the UAICC, Harris had yet another vision: a March for Justice, Freedom and Hope, which would be a protest against the white Australian bicentennial celebration. This march was to go down in history as the largest protest ever seen. On January 26, 1988—Invasion Day—despite government and general community insensitivity towards the Aboriginal call for a *Year of Mourning,* most of Australia marked a "year of celebrations." For whites, this date (Australia Day) commemorated the claiming of Australia for the "English Crown" by the first British governor of New South Wales. Nevertheless, Aboriginal people managed to draw national and international attention to the hypocrisy of the bicentenary with the March. On Invasion Day—*and for the first time*—thousands of Aboriginals from across the nation met in Sydney and marched to mourn past and present injustices against Aboriginal people and to celebrate the Survival of the Aboriginal Race. As a popular song by an Aboriginal rock band said: *"We Have Survived!"* On that day 20,000 Aboriginals marched for justice, and another 30,000 non-Aboriginals came to march in solidarity with them.

During and after the March, the Aboriginal and white leadership turned against Harris as a result of his radical leadership, which led to a conservative backlash among his peers (both Aboriginal and white), his colleagues feeling threatened by such radicalism. Moves were made to oust Harris from his position.

In the closing months of 1988, while attending a church conference in Taiwan, the Rev. Harris suffered a severe heart attack. Complications led to his being ill for several years afterwards, and in 1993 he passed away. In one of his last interviews, Harris stated, "the ultimate vision is that once again my people, Aboriginal people, the Aboriginal & Islander Nation, will walk tall and again find their dignity that they had before 1788. As they are able to do that they can make a contribution to any world community, any nation throughout the world, any society" (Reid, pp. 19–21).

Brady, Kirk and Harris were pivotal in facilitating the significant developments that were to follow. All three walked the narrow road, and all three paid a high price for their radical stance on justice and their challenges to oppressive racist institutions. Their vision, obedience and leadership pioneered a new way of understanding Christianity, which still is evolving (alongside and in conflict with other, more conservative ways).

Other Leaders. Following the significant achievements of Brady, Kirk and Harris, Aboriginal people saw the rise of several Aboriginal Christian leaders who would also take up the gauntlet and continue to struggle against white oppression of Aboriginal communities, in the hope of securing the equal rights and liberation so desired by Aboriginal people. Yet, this struggle quite often came at a high price.

In 1975, Patrick Dodson became the first Aboriginal person to be ordained a Roman Catholic priest. Like Brady and Harris, his stands for justice were far too threatening for the hierarchical, institutionalized church, and he left both the priesthood and the church. After his departure, Dodson served as Director of the Central Land Council, Commissioner of the Royal Commission into Aboriginal Deaths in Custody, and Chairperson of the (Federal) Council for Aboriginal Reconciliation–all positions which reflect his continuing commitment to justice and equality for all peoples. His writings include: "This Land Our Mother," in the *CCJP Occasional Paper;* and, "The Land Our Mother, the Church Our Mother," in the *Compass Theology Review.*

Others have followed these great leaders with a strong theology and a passion for justice. Father Dave Passi, a Torres Strait Islander priest of the Malo group (which is the traditional religion of the Torres Strait Islander people) is also a fully qualified and ordained priest of the Anglican Church of Australia. He was one of the original plaintiffs in the landmark Native Title (*Mabo*) land rights case, which shattered the white "legal fiction" that the Australian continent was *terra nullius* (or, uninhabited land—ready to be "worked" and colonized). Passi was led by his strong theological commitment to justice.

The Rev. Dhalanganda Garrawurra, of the Uniting Church in Australia, was a former Assistant to the Principal at Nungalinya Theological College in Darwin—this despite the fact that he was denied food rations by Christian missionaries when he did not go to the church on the Aboriginal Reserve as a youth.

The Rev. Trevor Holmes—also of the Uniting Church in Australia—has been at the forefront of the defense of a small parcel of Aboriginal land on the Swan River, in Perth, Western Australia. His theological stand has cost him: psychologically (he has been smeared in the media), physically (he has received death threats and, on numerous occasions, he has been beaten or arrested by police), socially (he is "unpopular" in Perth), and professionally (he is shunned in some white church circles).

Though he probably did not consider himself to be an Aboriginal Christian theologian, Kevin Gilbert nevertheless provides one of the most comprehensive critiques of Christian theology and Christianity itself. His works demonstrate vast knowledge of both the Bible and of Christianity, though he stood at the fringe of Christian hermeneutics. His sharp insights offer a major contribution to Aboriginal theology.

While "Aboriginal Theology" has been passionate about justice and the need for liberation of their people, it nevertheless has failed to address the particular concerns of oppression suffered by the Aboriginal women, youth and the disabled. Indeed, all of the theologies mentioned thus far are weighed down by Western patriarchal structures and sexist attitudes and actions. This endeavor to develop an Aboriginal systemic theology will encompass everything from Aboriginal cosmogony—the timeless oral tradition of Aboriginal Ancestral narratives to the modern written tradition of critical exegetical and hermeneutical work. The goal is to preserve the ancient wisdom of Aboriginal culture and tradition, as well as reinterpret and reformulate more recent Western theological concepts.

SEE ALSO Christianity, article on Christianity in Australia and New Zealand.

BIBLIOGRAPHY

Allen, Roland. *Missionary Methods: St Paul's or Ours?* London, 1912.

Allen, Roland. *Missionary Principles.* London, 1913.

Allen, Roland. *The Spontaneous Expansion of the Church and the Causes Which Hinder It.* London, 1927.

Ansara, Martha. *Always Was, Always Will Be: The Sacred Grounds of the Waugal, Kings Park, Perth, W. A.* Balmain, Australia, 1989, rev. ed., 1990.

Brady, Rev. Don. "Sermon Quotes." *Racism in Australia: Tasks for General and Christian Education: Report of Southport Conference.* Melbourne, 1971, p. 39.

Dodson, Patrick. "This Land Our Mother." *CCJP Occasional Paper* 9 (1973).

Dodson, Patrick. "The Land Our Mother, the Church Our Mother." *Compass Theology Review* 22, no. 1–2 (autumn–winter, 1988): 1–3.

Gilbert, Kevin. *Living Black: Blacks Talk to Kevin Gilbert.* Melbourne, Australia, 1978.

Gilbert, Kevin. "God at the Campfire and That Christ Fella." In *Aboriginal Spirituality: Past, Present, and Future.* Blackburn, Vic., 1996.

Harris, Rev. Charles. "Reconciliation or Whitewash." *Koori Mail* no. 15 (November 6, 1991): 15.

Harris, Rev. Charles. "Indigenisation Key to Our Survival." *Koori Mail,* no. 16 (December 18, 1991): 11.

Harris, Rev. Charles. "Thinking for Ourselves." *Koori Mail,* no. 17 (January 15, 1992): 18, 20.

Harris, Rev. Charles. "Western Christianity a Curse to Indigenous Spirituality." *Koori Mail* no. 20 (February 26, 1992): 19.

Hart, Max. *Story of Fire.* Adelaide, Australia, 1988.

McDonald, Heather. *Blood, Bones, and Spirit: Aboriginal Christianity in an East Kimberley Town.* Melbourne, 2001.

Passi, Dave. "From Pagan to Christian Priesthood." In *The Gospel Is Not Western: Black Theologies from the Southwest Pacific,* edited by Garry W. Trompf, pp. 45–48. Maryknoll, N.Y., 1987.

"Pastor Burns and Spits on Aboriginal Act," *Courier-Mail* (1970): 1.

Pattel-Gray, Anne. *Through Aboriginal Eyes: The Cry from the Wilderness.* Geneva, 1991.

Reid, John. "Only the Truth Will Make Us Free." *Journey* (August 1988): 19–21.

Uniting Church in Australia, commission for Mission. "God's Startling New Initiative: The Uniting Aboriginal and Islander Christian Congress." *Mission Probe* 25 (1984): 4.

ANNE PATTEL-GRAY (2005)

AUSTRALIAN INDIGENOUS RELIGIONS: HISTORY OF STUDY [FIRST EDITION]

The study of Australian Aboriginal religions has been the study of religions without a written record provided by their adherents. We depend on what outsiders to Aboriginal religion have thought worthwhile to commit to writing. Moreover the history of contact in Australia has been a sorry one in the main—Aborigines were dispossessed of land, regarded with contempt, and made socially and politically inferior. The amateur anthropologist A. W. Howitt could observe in 1880 that the frontier was often marked by a line of blood. Indeed, between the late eighteenth century, when European settlement began, and the 1920s, Aboriginal numbers fell so sharply that prophecies of race extinction were neither alarmist by some nor wishful thinking by others. After World War II, in keeping with a new policy of assimilating Aborigines to an ill-defined general Australian standard, there was a great expansion of administrative interference with them. But a more sympathetic attitude toward tradition became prevalent during the 1970s; "self-management" and "self-determination" entered common usage as policy slogans; and a few Aborigines even began to call for sovereignty. In what is now a highly politicized atmosphere, with laws passed or proposed for the grant of land rights, the protection of sacred sites, and the recognition of customary law, it can be an advantage for Aborigines to be—or to appear to be—traditional in outlook and values. It is amid such aftermaths and in such contexts that scholars (mostly anthropologists) have studied Aboriginal religion.

In the course of this strained and unhappy history a remarkable change has occurred in the appreciation of Aboriginal religion. It can best be illustrated by juxtaposing two pairs of quotations. In 1828 Roger Oldfield (pseudonym of the Reverend Ralph Mansfield) wrote that "the religion of the Aborigines, or rather their superstition, is very absurd," and in 1841 another clergyman, Lancelot Edward Threlkeld, described Aborigines as "deluded men" who, "like most ignorant savage tribes, are remarkably superstitious." But by the mid-twentieth century, a number of writers had discussed the status of Aboriginal religion more sympathetically. In 1965, the anthropologist W. E. H. Stanner referred to "the facts that have convinced modern anthropologists that the Aborigines are a deeply religious people."

Such a rise in estimation reflects growing knowledge of and deepening sympathy with Aborigines, but another important cause is the loss of confidence in the validity or usefulness of earlier criteria for distinguishing true religion from false, or religion from superstition and magic. Assertions of Aboriginal religiosity (or spirituality, as it is often called) and studies of aspects of Aboriginal religion have proliferated since the 1950s—coinciding, ironically, with a growing inclusion of Aborigines in the Australian polity and an increasing erosion of the more tangible features of traditional culture. No longer as objectively "other" as they once were, the Aborigines have become subjectively "other" through being credited with a religious dimension largely absent from the secularized society which engulfs them. It would be wrong, however, to imagine that an unbridgeable gulf has opened between earlier and later bodies of opinion. A degree of continuity can be seen even in the writings of Stanner, who worked passionately and to great effect to dispel misperceptions of Aboriginal life and thought.

The Aborigines, he wrote in 1953, have no gods, their afterlife is only a shadowy replica of worldly existence, their ethical insights are dim and coarsely textured, their concept of goodness lacks true scruple, and their many stories about the Dreaming (the far-off creative period when nature and culture were formed) are plainly preposterous, lacking logic, system, and completeness. Does this differ much from Howitt, half a century earlier, who could not see that the Aborigines had any form of religion, and who thought that the supernatural beings in whom they believed showed no trace of a divine nature (being, at most, ideal headmen living in the sky instead of on earth)? Does it differ from Howitt's contemporaries, Baldwin Spencer and F. J. Gillen, in whose monumental works such words as *god, religion,* and *divinity* are conspicuous by their absence, though they saw a religious aspect in the Intichiuma, or totemic increase ceremonies, of central Australia? Yet Stanner insisted not only that Aborigines had made the longest and most difficult move toward the formation of a truly religious outlook, but that they had gone far beyond that first step.

Some of the observed particulars and some of the conclusions drawn from them are much the same as those from the turn of the century. But a good deal of the old theoretical baggage—concern with the order of appearance of magic, religion, and science, for example—has gone overboard in the course of extensive remodeling of our frameworks of perception and interpretation. That Aborigines lack certain features of the religions best known to Europeans no longer seems important. Thus the heat has left the debate over whether Baiame, Daramulun, and other such All-Fathers were supernaturalized headmen, Christian borrowings, or genuine high gods (as maintained, for example, by Spencer's contemporary, the Lutheran missionary and amateur anthropologist Carl Strehlow, regarding the Aranda of central Australia)—indeed, it is doubtful that one can still speak of a debate on this arcane topic. What does seem important is to see the world and humankind in Aboriginal terms, though it be through a glass darkly.

This new imperative has required a considerable broadening in interpretative framework. There would be general agreement with Stanner that a study may be about religion but will not be of it if any of the four categories of experience, belief, action, and purpose is neglected. Aboriginal religion, he argued, draws on a human experience of life and a creative purpose in life, and the study of it cannot, as so often thought, be equated with study of the beliefs and actions (myths and rites) of its adherents. But a deeper insight is also needed. Stanner saw myths, rites, and the images of art as "languages of the mind," beyond which one must go to reach the "metaphysic of life" by which they are cryptically invested. Few would disagree with him that anthropology has so far failed in this last and most ambitious task. There is, indeed, much still to be done in mapping the languages of the mind and in working out their interplay with one another, with the social organization of the people, and with the landscape in which Aboriginal lives are set.

Religion's Luxuriant Growth. Stanner suggested in 1965 that one of the best avenues of study of Aboriginal religion was through the surviving regional cults. In fact, anthropological attention has long tended to focus on them, as can be seen by the studies that Howitt and Robert Hamilton Mathews (1841–1918) made of the Bora, or initiation, ceremonies in southeast Australia and that Spencer and Gillen made of the increase and initiation ceremonies of central Australia. This tradition, as it can justly be regarded, has continued until the most recent times. Some of the more notable examples are Ronald M. Berndt's monographs on the Kunapipi and Djanggawul of northern Australia, A. P. Elkin's papers on the Maraian and Yabuduruwa, also of the north, and M. J. Meggitt's monograph on the Gadjari of central Australia, though there has also been valuable work of a more general nature, such as Catherine H. Berndt's and

Diane Bell's studies of women's religious beliefs and observances.

The popularity of the cult for study stems from the fact that it is in many ways a natural whole—it seems to be self-bounding. Commonly it has a name (Kunapipi or Kuringal, for example), includes a sequence of ritual episodes—the performance of which may stretch over several weeks—and usually one or more cycles of songs, and has attached to it a body of myths and tangible symbols, such as a musical instrument—gong or bull-roarer, for example—which may stand for a mythical founder of the cult and be known by the same name as the cult. An outsider who attends a performance may well be reminded of European plays, operas, or ballets, though it would be wrong to think of a cult as necessarily an enactment of a straightforward story. Some episodes do have a narrative quality, but others can be quite cryptic, and the sequence as a whole is likely to have a variety of stories and significations woven through it. Rather similarly, the songs that make up the accompanying cycle or cycles may be easily translatable, translatable only in fragments, or altogether devoid of any meaning known to the performers. The performers themselves are not self-chosen or selected at random but occupy roles prescribed according to such criteria as sex, degree of initiatory advancement, moiety (where, as is usual, a dual organization exists), totemic identity, or localized group. All of these criteria, and perhaps others as well, can be relevant in the course of a single cult performance. Another typical aspect of a cult is its anchorage in the landscape: myths and songs refer to numerous places, rites are symbolically or actually performed at such places, and the groups and categories of the social order in terms of which the performers are chosen stand in a variety of jurisprudential relations to those places. A cult, then, is virtually a microcosm of Aboriginal culture.

Although a performance can be seen as a many-sided symbolic display, it also achieves certain institutionalized purposes. The Bora ceremonies of the southeast were especially concerned with the advancement of boys to manhood. They included spectacular episodes in which novices were first separated from, and later returned to, mundane life (often personified by their mothers); in the intervening period they suffered a visible mark of advancement in the loss of a tooth through evulsion. In other regions circumcision or subincision might be substituted for or added to tooth evulsion as the preeminent physical sign of manhood.

Throughout much of central and western Australia the maintenance or promotion of fertility in plant and animal nature was aimed at in cult performances. Disposal of the remains of the dead can be an important purpose, as can transformation of spirits of the dead into a state in which they can return to ancestral waters (or other places) and from which they can (in some regions) be reincarnated. Several such purposes can be achieved in a single cult performance. We should not, that is to say, think of there necessarily being a one-to-one correlation of cult and institutionalized purpose. Nor should we think of express purposes as the motives for cult performances. As musical, dramatic, and aesthetic occasions, as mappings-out of landscape and social organization, they can be deeply satisfying for their own sake. This has been brought out especially in the writings of Stanner on the Murinbata of northern Australia, and of T. G. H. Strehlow (1908–1978), the linguist-anthropologist son of Carl Strehlow, on the Aranda.

In spite of seeming to be the natural unit of study, no cult has yet been the subject of a truly comprehensive published work. Howitt and Mathews, for example, concentrated on the sequence of ritual episodes, with the latter also providing detailed descriptions of the shape and dimensions of ceremonial grounds, of the paths between them, and of the objects of art by which they were surrounded. Berndt's Kunapipi monograph runs to 223 pages and his Djanggawul monograph to 320, but both are stronger on myth and song than on ritual description. Elkin on the Maraian, like Meggitt on the Gadjari and Stanner on the cults performed by the Murinbata, neglects the songs (the Yabuduruwa lacks singing). None of these scholars shows, in a really detailed way, how the cults are anchored in landscape and social organization, though all of them are aware of it. In short, even at a purely descriptive level, each of our accounts suffers pronounced weaknesses as well as showing characteristic strengths. It is as though the student of a cult is defeated by the sheer abundance of what it offers to eye, ear, and mind. But even if we had a truly comprehensive account of, say, the Kunapipi or Yabuduruwa, we would still be far removed from an adequate grasp of the religious life of the area concerned, for usually several cults coexist.

In southern Arnhem Land, for example, where religious studies have been made by myself, following on earlier work by Elkin, five cults were extant in the 1960s and 1970s, with others still remembered by some older people. The five, in order of degree of secrecy or importance, were Bugabud, Lorgon, Kunapipi and Yabuduruwa (this pair being ranked about equally), and Maraian. All men and women could expect to take part in each of them—they were not the concern, then, of specialized and mutually exclusive groups of votaries. The dual organization, divided into patrilineal moieties named Dua and Yiridja, imposed its pattern on the set of cults: Bugabud, Lorgon, and Maraian existed in two versions, one for each moiety; Kunapipi was classified as Dua and Yabuduruwa as Yiridja. But in each case performers would necessarily be drawn from both moieties by virtue of a prescribed division of labor and responsibilities.

The acquisition of competence in these cults is part of the protracted process by which individuals rise to full adulthood. However, they also discharge purposes connected with the dead. Bugabud and Lorgon are mortuary cults, in the sense that they are concerned with the bones of a dead person—rites of secondary disposal, as defined early this century by the French comparativist Robert Hertz. Kunapipi, Yabuduruwa, and Maraian are postmortuary in the sense that, the mortal remains having been finally dealt with, they are concerned with transforming the spirit of the dead person into a state in which it may enter its clan waters and later be reborn. How many rites are held for a man—or whether any at all are held—depends on such variables as his standing while alive, and the energy, interest, and degree of influence of his survivors. In addition, mortuary observances can be blocked altogether when, as has become usual, people die in hospitals and are buried in municipal graveyards.

To write an adequate description of such a set of cults would be a mammoth undertaking. But to think of portraying the religious life of southern Arnhem Land by describing discrete cults would be to remain in the condition of theoretical backwardness remarked upon by Kenelm Burridge in 1973. What marks recent advances in the study of religion, he argued, is the transformation of functionalism into some kind of structuralism, by which he meant the abandonment of the concrete institution in favor of the search for the elements of a total semantic field. Institutions would be seen as particular constellations of these elements, and the value of an element would be determined by its position in a constellation. Something like this view is now fairly widely held, and two anthropologists have published substantial approximations of it. Stanner is one, with his perceptive and influential analyses of Murinbata religion. The other is William Lloyd Warner, whose classic study, *A Black Civilization* (New York, 1937), includes a valiant attempt to demonstrate pervasive and recurring themes and symbols in the myths and rites of the Murngin of northern Arnhem Land.

Two examples from southern Arnhem Land may show the importance of being willing to cut across the boundaries of discrete cults. One concerns the spirits of the dead, which are transformed by the performance of postmortuary cults. In their transformed state, they are colored as the rainbow. So were the waters which covered the earth when time began. The transformed spirits can be called by the same name as is used for real rainbows, and this is also the name for certain beings of prodigious power who existed in the Dreaming and may still exist, for example, the well-known Rainbow Snake, here conceived to be plural. Moreover the animal-like beings who acted creatively in the Dreaming and who, in many instances, are ritually celebrated in the cults may be described thusly in order to distinguish them from everyday animals who take the same form but lack marvelous powers. In studying such a pattern of thought and imagery we come to grips with Stanner's "metaphysic of life."

The second example concerns the systematic relation of complementary opposition in design plan between Kunapipi and Yabuduruwa, cults of equal rank but of opposite moiety. Thus one is performed largely by night and the other mostly by day. One is strongly curvilinear in its imagery; the other has a rectilinear emphasis. One is full of singing and is noisy and joyous; the other lacks songs altogether. There are other contrasts as well. The point is that although each cult can, in a sense, be treated as an organized whole, there is another sense in which they are halves of a divided universe, just as the moieties are halves of a divided society. Much in the literature suggests that such contrasts in design plan are common in Aboriginal religious complexes; there may well be equally fascinating patterns of opposition and permutation between cults at different levels of a hierarchy.

It is also clear from the literature that important work can be done in tracing chains of connection between the religious complexes of different areas. Some of the early writers were aware of this possibility—Howitt, for example, in distinguishing eastern and western types of initiation, was recognizing far-flung patterns of similarity and difference—and it has been explored by later writers, including Elkin, Berndt, and Meggitt. The most ambitious effort has come from Worms, who made continent-wide studies of religious vocabulary and also sought to enumerate the "essentials" of Aboriginal religion and to distinguish them from "accidental accretions."

Main Phases of Study. It may seem artificial to distinguish periods in the study of Aboriginal religion, as distinct from recognizing certain enduring problems posed by the material, yet all but a few of the scholars likely to be taken seriously today belong to one of three main groupings. To a great extent the ways in which they have worked their data have been conditioned, if not determined, by fashions and theories of overseas origin—Stanner, Worms, and the younger Strehlow would be notable exceptions.

A first phase, spanning the late nineteenth and early twentieth centuries, is dominated by the names of Howitt, Spencer and Gillen, Mathews, and the elder Strehlow. Except for Strehlow, who concentrated his researches on the Aranda and their Loritja neighbors, these scholars amassed information over very great areas indeed, although Howitt's work mainly concerned the southeast of the continent and Spencer and Gillen's the Northern Territory. Some of the descriptions of ritual dating from this period, which of course preceded the rise of professional anthropology, are as thorough and detailed as any that have been written since, if not a good deal more so. (It should be noted that the elder Strehlow felt constrained as a missionary not to attend cult performances, so his knowledge of ritual was hearsay, but in studying myths and songs he reaped the benefits of long acquaintance with his informants and of a thorough grasp of their language.) An indication of the quantity of data collected by the workers of this phase is given by Spencer and Gillen's first book, *The Native Tribes of Central Australia* (London, 1899). It has eight chapters, totaling 338 pages, on totems, ceremonies, and the like, with some material in other chapters also being relevant to what we would call religion.

A second phase, beginning in the mid-1920s and flowering especially during the 1930s, the first decade of the journal *Oceania*, owed much to the initial impetus given by A. R. Radcliffe-Brown, Australia's first professor of anthropology. Those years saw the advent of professional anthropology, inspired by functionalist ideas and committed to intensive fieldwork in relatively small areas. Yet the harvest of religious data was meager in comparison with what had been collected in the preceding phase. Before World War II the most substantial portrayal of religious life to emerge from the new wave of scholars was Warner's study of the Murngin, but the chapters of *A Black Civilization* devoted to the subject run to barely two hundred pages (including a good deal of interpretation)—fewer than Berndt would later devote to the Kunapipi alone. The strong point of the writers of this period was their sense of the interconnectedness of the institutions that go to make up a culture, and besides Warner a number of them made useful, albeit somewhat limited, contributions to our religious knowledge. Donald F. Thomson, Ralph Piddington, Ursula H. McConnel, and Phyllis M. Kaberry may particularly be mentioned. Except for Warner they have since been greatly overshadowed by Elkin, Stanner, and the younger Strehlow—scholars who were active in research before World War II, but published their best work on religion long after it, thus overlapping the third phase, which indeed they did much to stimulate.

The third phase really got under way with the expansion of anthropology departments in the universities and the foundation of the Australian Institute of Aboriginal Studies in the 1960s. Intellectually it owes a special debt to papers published by Stanner between 1959 and 1967. Stanner's writings, the product of intensive ratiocination and prolonged reflection, best fit his own prescription for study of, and not merely about, religion. But much that he has to say is difficult, if not positively cryptic, and is best tackled by readers who already enjoy a familiarity with Aboriginal thought and ritual. The store of personally gathered field data on which he relies is far less plentiful than that amassed by Ronald M. Berndt and Catherine H. Berndt or by the younger Strehlow, writers whose work has exerted less influence on their fellows.

The third phase is less clearly distinguishable from the second than the second from the first. The greater degree of continuity is partly due to the shared emphasis on intensive fieldwork by professional anthropologists, as well as to the survival into the 1970s of scholars who had already begun to make their mark forty years earlier and to the appearance of a few students of religion (notably the two Berndts and Meggitt, all trained by Elkin) during the intervening period. Apart from a vast increase in the number of persons doing research, the main differences between the two phases consist in an abandonment of old-style functionalism, a rise of approaches influenced in varying degree by forms of structural or symbolic anthropology, and an intense interest in the significance of the landscape in which Aboriginal lives are set. There is still little sign of philosophers or students of comparative religion challenging the ascendancy of anthropologists.

See Also Howitt, A. W.

Bibliography

The best general exposition of Aboriginal religion is Mircea Eliade's *Australian Religions: An Introduction* (Ithaca, N. Y., 1973), which is based on specialized studies and theoretical arguments published before 1965. Another useful account taking an Australia-wide view is the contribution by Worms, with an updating by Petri, in Hans Nevermann, Ernest A. Worms, and Helmut Petri's *Die Religionen der Südsee und Australiens* (Stuttgart, 1968). A comprehensive selection of readings from anthropologists with field experience among Aborigines is *Religion in Aboriginal Australia*, edited by Max Charlesworth, Howard Morphy, Diane Bell, and me (Saint Lucia, Queensland, 1984). The wealth of detail to be found in particular cults is shown by Ronald M. Berndt in his *Kunapipi* (Melbourne, 1951) and *Djanggawul* (London, 1952) but is most superbly demonstrated in T. G. H. Strehlow, *Songs of Central Australia* (Sydney, 1971), which includes texts and translations of a great many songs. Classic older accounts of Aboriginal religion are in A. W. Howitt's *The Native Tribes of South-East Australia* (New York, 1904), and Baldwin Spencer and F. J. Gillen's *The Northern Tribes of Central Australia* (London, 1904). Two recent studies on topical themes are Erich Kolig's *The Silent Revolution* (Philadelphia, 1981), a study of change and modernization in Aboriginal religion, and Diane Bell's *Daughters of the Dreaming* (Melbourne, 1983), which is concerned with the religious roles of women. *Australian Aboriginal Mythology*, edited by L. R. Hiatt (Canberra, 1975), is a good example of the approaches of some of the younger workers in the field; see also *The Rainbow Serpent*, edited by Ira R. Buchler and me (The Hague, 1978), which contains studies of one of the most widespread Aboriginal symbols. The classic theoretical analysis remains Émile Durkheim's *The Elementary Forms of the Religious Life* (1915; reprint, New York, 1965), but it relies on nineteenth- and early twentieth-century research and opinion. The most penetrating modern vision and analysis are from W. E. H. Stanner, whose *On Aboriginal Religion* (Sydney, 1964) and *White Man Got No Dreaming: Essays 1938–1973* (Canberra, 1979) are essential.

Kenneth Maddock (1987)

AUSTRALIAN INDIGENOUS RELIGIONS: HISTORY OF STUDY [FURTHER CONSIDERATIONS]

These "further considerations" highlight the intellectual, political, legal, and administrative frames of reference that have shaped the study of Aboriginal religion throughout its history. Four phases—not necessarily distinct—are emphasized. Early accounts of indigenous religions were framed by philosophical and scientific debates about race in the context of colonialism and the assumption of sovereignty over subject peoples. For much of the nineteenth century the study of Aboriginal religion went hand in hand with "protection" and amelioration in the face of racial (and actual) death or a presumption of disappearance in the face of civilization. This approach merged with the rise of the missionary proto-ethnographer, whose aims of salvage, instruction, and benefit were framed by the active pursuit of religious change.

The development of academic anthropology in the twentieth century was marked by the testing and application of various models of explanation. Its results have had an abiding influence on how Aboriginal cultures are popularly perceived and legally treated. The academy was never isolated from the government policies and practices of its day, however. The study of Aboriginal religion should be viewed in the context of finding (social) scientific answers to a variety of "problems" posed by Aborigines in a modernizing Australia. Late-twentieth-century developments in the legal recognition of land rights and native title provided an unprecedented impetus to the study of Aboriginal religion. They are also contexts in which the history of that study has become crucial, with its record being recalled, reused, and forensically tested in a wider range of settings than ever before. Old ethnographies are being read again, and the archive is being searched as never before either to support or to confound Aboriginal claims to land and identity. It is this that has made the framing of the record—its circumstances, intentions, limitations, and possibilities—so important in the late twentieth century and early twenty-first century.

A New Sovereignty. The earliest pronouncements on an absence of religion among Aborigines cannot be divorced from the simultaneous proclamation of sovereignty over what to the European colonizers were new and unfamiliar lands. Watkin Tench, captain of the Royal Marines, provided one of the earliest accounts of Aboriginal-European relations in the colony of New South Wales. Despite numerous opportunities for "detached observations," Tench could not discern the meanings of Aboriginal ceremonies. He pondered the distance between cultures and what he saw as an Aboriginal perversity (a "fickle," "jealous," and "wavering" disposition) that inhibited the cross-cultural relations that might disclose such meanings. In his *A Complete Account of the Settlement at Port Jackson* (1793), Tench declared that the "indians [*sic*] of New South Wales" in fact did evidence belief in spirits and a superintending deity and possessed a sense of the immortality of some part of their being. In these conclusions Tench aligned Aboriginal belief with what was recognizable as religion to the colonists and therefore to what was ideologically integral to the colonizing process itself. Establishing the media of communication and finding an appropriate framework for interpreting Aboriginal religion remain abiding (and contested) concerns for its study.

A contemporaneous and opposite pronouncement was provided by David Collins, the colony's judge advocate and secretary. Despite providing a detailed record of the Eora people's ceremonies in *An Account of the English Colony in New South Wales* (1798), Collins declared that the Aborigines of Port Jackson possessed no element of religion whatsoever. In this he epitomized the "blindness" noted by W. E. H. Stanner in "Religion, Totemism, and Symbolism (1962)," by virtue of which early observers genuinely could not—regardless of knowledge, learning, or humanism—see the "facts" that later convinced others that Aborigines were indeed a deeply religious people. The earliest, conflicting assessments of Aboriginal religion were framed by philosophical, theological, and scientific debates about where Aboriginal people fitted in an (evolutionary) Great Chain of Being. Such assessments derived from and contributed to the political positioning—racially, morally, and intellectually—of a subject people either expected to disappear or required to acquiesce to the advance of "civilization."

Historically constituted framings of what counts as religion have often been more powerful than direct observation or meticulous recording. More than two centuries of elaborated framings for the study of Aboriginal religion (whether derived from anthropology, history, theology, or missiology) have not necessarily transcended such limitations. As Stanner has pointed out, studying Aboriginal religion is necessarily distinct from its embodied practice as a fundamental orientation to place, kin, and country for Aboriginal people themselves. As an object of study it cannot escape the frames by which it is apprehended, recorded, represented, and represented in a range of settings and to diverse ends. Religion remains a primary vehicle for knowing Aboriginal cultures in Australia and therefore forms the basis for various disciplinary, legislative, and administrative actions brought to bear on Aboriginal people. The problematic "blindness" of the earliest witnesses is not so strange and certainly not easy to transcend. In it one recognizes an abiding separation of purposes despite the enormous progress the history of study has achieved in reducing the interpretive gaps.

Missionary Fields. The substantive body of material on "manners and customs" that derives from nineteenth-century missionary-ethnographers was framed by the conjoined impulses to protection and conversion. Collins reported the devastation wrought by smallpox in 1789, the sites of Aboriginal habitation around Sydney Harbour being filled with the victims' putrid bodies. As Tony Swain, in *A Place for Strangers* (1993), points out, everything known about Aboriginal life in Southeast Australia comes from records made after a massive population decline. By the time missionaries and explorers began recording Aboriginal beliefs in the 1830s, it is estimated that only one-third of the quarter million people in New South Wales and Victoria had survived. By 1850 the figure was down to 4 percent. It was another generation before proto-ethnographic accounts were compiled and then another half century before recognizably modern records of myth, ceremony, and sites became readily available in such works as Alfred William Howitt's *The Native Tribes of South-East Australia* (1904) and R. H. Mathew's approximately 203 scattered journal articles. The gaps and discrepancies represented by this necessarily piecemeal coverage have continuing implications in the early twenty-first century for Aboriginal people who increasingly must rely on such materials in a variety of legislative and bureaucratic settings.

Although lacking in what would later be seen as systematic and "theoretical" examination, the nineteenth century saw an explosion in the recording of Aboriginal religious concepts. Once the Blue Mountains west of Sydney were crossed in 1813, explorers and settlers began noting the "manners and customs" of the "natives" they encountered. It was missionaries, however, who began living with those Aboriginal people who had survived the massive disruption of their lands and kin groups and who assembled the more extensive reports on language, religion, and social relations. Lancelot Edward Threlkeld, for example, conducted extensive language recording among the Awabakal people "settled" on the shores of Lake Macquarie in New South Wales. He was eventually dismissed by the London Missionary Society for spending too much time on ethnographic and linguistic observations and too little on the salvation of Aboriginal souls. Threlkeld initiated a small but strong contingent of missionary observers, including Carl Strehlow, William Ridley, Clamor Schürmann, George Taplin, and J. H. Sexton, whose records remain of considerable significance. Pater Wilhelm Schmidt, though he did not work within Australia himself, was nevertheless instrumental in the collection and study of Australian materials.

The task of studying Aboriginal religious belief (a focus that necessarily predominated over that of religious practice, given the circumstances) was accomplished in tandem with the goal of translating and representing Christian belief for the edification and conversion of people still seen as religiously deficient. Carl Strehlow and Johann Georg Reuther's 1897 *Testamenta Marra: Jesuni Christuni Ngantjani Jaura Ninaia Rarithmalkana Wonti Dieri Jaurani* (The New Testament in the Dieri language) was the first complete translation into an Aboriginal language. It was both vehicle and justification for Reuther's towering linguistic and ethnographic recording, especially of the mythic journeys and geographic creations of ancestral Beings called Muramuras in the far northeast of South Australia. This effort was subsequently repeated by Carl Strehlow among the Arrernte (Arunta, Aranda) to the north and was continued by his son Theodor George Henry Strehlow.

The missionary recorders, more than the anthropologists, were presentient of Émile Durkheim's analytic proposition (in *Les formes élementaires de la vie réligieuse,* 1914; *The Elementary Forms of the Religious Life,* 1915) that religion is society sanctified and that mythology was a primary vessel of Aboriginal spiritual sentiment. It is these images of Aboriginal society and religion being coterminous and of story and songline anchoring belief, people, and place that remain frames of reference for contemporary analyses of Aboriginal religion across Australia.

The Work of the Academy. The great nineteenth-century and early-twentieth-century recordings appeared before anthropology was a recognized academic discipline in Australian universities. The first chair was established at the University of Sydney in 1926. The work of its first incumbent, A. R. Radcliffe-Brown, remains pivotal to debates on the articulation of Aboriginal social organization with traditional land ownership. Its was his successor, Adolphus Peter Elkin, however, who had an abiding influence on the study of myth, legend, and music both through his own works and those of successive Sydney researchers. Outside of Sydney, Adelaide was a center of substantial and enduring work on Aboriginal religion, focused in the South Australian Museum, the Royal Society of South Australia, and the University of Adelaide. Norman B. Tindale had a research base there for his continent-wide studies of tribal boundaries and mythology; Charles Mountford assembled his substantial records of art, myth, and symbolism; and T. G. H. Strehlow produced his incomparable *Songs of Central Australia* (1971).

Throughout the twentieth century other universities emerged or developed, offering intellectual and financial nurturance to the study of Aboriginal religion. Melbourne provided a base for the biologist Donald Thompson, whose work in Cape York, Arnhem Land, and Central Australia is still celebrated in books and exhibitions. The University of Western Australia was home to Ronald Berndt and Catherine Berndt, indefatigable researchers of myth, rite, and story throughout Aboriginal Australia, with a legacy of students and colleagues very much active in the early twenty-first century. Anthropology at the Australian National University, Canberra has also been pivotal in training, research, publication, and debate in all areas relating to Aboriginal religion, including the insertion and translation of such studies into a variety of legislative, policy, and administrative reforms.

The academic framing of Aboriginal religion has involved principally an active, progressive, and critical engagement with theories and ideas coming from a range of developing disciplines. Major threads have included Durkheim's organicism and its reinterpretation via the structural functionalism of Radcliffe-Brown; Claude Lévi-Strauss's structuralism, especially as interpreted through the works of W. E. H. Stanner and Kenneth Maddock; and Sigmund Freud's psychoanalysis, reinterpreted through the Aboriginal data by Géza Róheim and continued in the work of Les Hiatt and John Morton. In his chapter article "The Resurrection of the Hydra," Howard Morphy provides an excellent and nuanced overview of the main ideas that oriented the academic study of Aboriginal religion throughout the twentieth century. Stanner remains the pivotal mid-twentieth-century figure, with his *On Aboriginal Religion* (1966) reissued with commentaries and an "appreciation" in 1989. Stanner's movement away from structural functional interpretation toward symbolism and ontology—highlighting the distinctive moral, emotional, and spatiotemporal dimensions of the Dreaming—remains enormously influential, perhaps best reflected in the oeuvre of Deborah Bird Rose.

The progress of academic study has not been without contestation, of course, and the resulting debates have impacted enormously on understandings of Aboriginal religion. In particular, the rise of Marxist and feminist theories in the 1970s initiated controversies that resonate into the twenty-first century. Exemplifying this period is the work undertaken by Annette Hamilton while a research student at the University of Sydney, and that of Diane Bell while a student at the Australian National University. In challenging academic orthodoxies and overcoming the initial resistance of the anthropology discipline, both these scholars have fundamentally recalibrated the ways in which the lives of Aboriginal men and women must be thought about. Hamilton's 1960s research amongst the Gidjingali people of Arnhem Land challenged previous perspectives—derived from Hiatt and Maddock, amongst others—on support and rivalry amongst cross-sex siblings, the benefits that flow to men and women from marriage bestowal, and issues of male control and female autonomy more generally. In the late 1970s Hamilton again challenged models of male dominance in her PhD research on the economic and religious life of Western Desert Aborigines. In the far northwest of South Australia Hamilton documented men's dependence on women's labor, women's control of key productive technologies (such as grindstones), and a strong and secret female ceremonial domain. Working in the Central Desert region, also in the late 1970s, Bell provided equally challenging evidence of women's active participation in marriage bestowal, exercised in ritual contexts and facilitating control of their sexual choices. Like Hamilton, but with differences reflecting regional variation, Bell also documented a religious realm in which women worked separately to maintain the Dreaming, enact their responsibilities to the land, and manage the health and harmony of their kin groups. When first published in 1983, Bell's *Daughters of the Dreaming* prompted unprecedented reactions to its assertion that Aboriginal women hold such an encompassing ritual responsibility as well as having strong traditions of cultural and religious autonomy. This text remains both pivotal and controversial more than two decades later. In *Arguments about Aborigines* (1996) Hiatt charts the history of these challenges and their effects on reconfiguring academic paradigms. These debates have fuelled a "re-reading" of the traditionalist literature in Francesca Merlan's "Gender in Aboriginal Social Life: A Review," which highlights dominant constructions of gender in the anthropological canon and addresses abiding issues of theoretical bias and ethnographic adequacy. The capacity of these (unresolved) debates to generate innovative accounts of Aboriginal religion as a gendered domain is evidenced by such works as Françoise Dussart's *The Politics of Ritual in an Aboriginal Settlement* (2000) and Christine Watson's *Piercing the Ground* (2003).

But work in the academy was never completely removed from wider historical shifts in the social, economic, and administrative circumstances of Aboriginal life. Elkin's department at the University of Sydney itself functioned in the domain of applied social research both in the Pacific and at home. It had a major role in training officers for Australia's own colonial possession in New Guinea and was supported in part by funds from the commonwealth and state governments to do this. Sir John Hubert Murray, the Australian administrator in New Guinea and the first lieutenant governor of (the renamed) Papua from 1908, warned the new department against preoccupation with mere scientific investigation. This suggests something of the array of institutional and governmental forces at work on the development of academic anthropology across much of the twentieth century.

The anthropological study of Aboriginal life, including religious life, cannot be separated from more practical concerns with welfare and assimilation policy throughout this period. Elkin himself bridged academic and administrative worlds. As a professor from 1934 Elkin and his students forged the academic study of Aboriginal life into a proud and progressive tradition. As editor of the pioneering journal *Oceania* Elkin oversaw publication of much of the research that established (and still supports) the authoritative record of Aboriginal religion. He was chairman of the Australian National Research Council's Anthropology Committee between 1933 and 1948, overseeing the allocation of research funds to address Aboriginal welfare "problems." From 1941 to 1968 he was vice president of the New South Wales Aborigines Protection Board that had the power to intervene directly into people's most intimate daily lives. The academic study of Aboriginal religion developed alongside the application of anthropology to a range of practical and policy concerns. The later decades of the twentieth century saw these domains brought absolutely together.

OUTSIDE THE ACADEMY. The study of Aboriginal people—so problematic for the Australian state, so vulnerable to surveillance and recording—was never of course confined to the academy. A huge compendium of data on Aboriginal religion has been assembled outside of formal research settings by literary scholars, antiquarians, clergy, local historians, poets, humanists, and government officials, such as the police trooper Samuel Gason, stationed on Cooper Creek to facilitate the arrival of pastoralists and missionaries. Out of nine years of close engagement with Aboriginal people, learning local languages, and participating in ceremonies, Gason provided, in *Manners and Customs of the Dieyerie Tribe of Australian Aborigines* (1874), one of the first detailed accounts of traditional life in the eastern central deserts. It is a record that is still used by researchers and Aborigines alike seeking to verify claims to ancestral lands. This pioneering work was not disinterested; it is not separable from its frame of economic, material, psychological, and spiritual transformation being wrought on Aboriginal people by colonial expansion. Gason's aim in publishing his data was to assist the Lutheran missionaries at Lake Killalpaninna (where Reuther was later to make his own collections); Gason hoped that his writings "may be of some assistance to those pious missionaries and others, who are extending so greatly inland this vast continent, civilisation, through its gracious handmaiden, Christianity."

The enigmatic Daisy Bates also deserves mention. Variously a student of anthropology, secular missionary, and unofficial "protector," she lived for decades among Aboriginal people in Western Australia and South Australia including, famously, sixteen years at Ooldea on the east-west railway line. Her prodigious output (something like 274 published articles) contains much of significance to the study of religion, such as her series on astronomy, stellar myths, and associated rituals that appeared in newspapers such as *The Australasian* and *The Sydney Morning Herald* in the 1920s and 1930s. Her manuscripts, letters, and diaries are scattered in libraries but are increasingly sourced by researchers seeking foundational data for use in a variety of heritage and native title contexts.

Such materials have been continually repatriated to more authoritative and institutionalized processes of study and documentation. This is exemplified by the work of Isobel White in collating and editing a portion of Daisy Bates's manuscripts into *The Native Tribes of Western Australia* (1985), published by the National Library of Australia and prompting a reassessment of Bates as a serious fieldworker and scholar rather than a popular commentator. This movement of materials accelerated in the later decades of the twentieth century (and continues to expand in the twenty-first century) in response to significantly changed frameworks of governance, administration, legal recognition, and cultural policy. It is to key moments in this change that this discussion now turns.

LAND RIGHTS. Under the Aboriginal Land Rights (Northern Territory) Act of 1976, Aborigines were able to claim title to land provided they could demonstrate specific relationships to it. The critical test was set out in the definition of "traditional owner," requiring a person to be a member of a "local descent group" and to have "primary spiritual responsibility" for a site on the land. The two were interrelated: to have rights in land recognized, a person had to be a member of a group on the basis of descent and to possess a spiritual connection to sacred sites arising from that membership. Not only did this represent a translation of accumulated anthropological knowledge into legal statute, but it placed Aboriginal religion at the center of political and administrative recognition of Aboriginal rights and aspirations. Evidence and displays of religious attachment to land were presented to administrative inquiries presided over by a specially appointed federal court judge in the form of an aboriginal land commissioner.

The "applied" legal domain of land rights provided an enormous incentive and opportunity for the detailed local "study" and documentation of Aboriginal religious practice in the late twentieth century. In the almost three decades during which claims to land have been made under the Act, a vast body of written and recorded materials has come into existence, including the detailed supporting claim books prepared by anthropologists, linguists, and historians, transcripts of public portions of the hearings themselves, and references in the land commissioner's findings to the demonstration and performance of sacred knowledge. The final reports themselves are emblematic of the insertion of Aboriginal religious knowledge into the Australian public record. In them the commissioner reiterates, as a matter of legal fact, the journeys of ancestral Beings (Dreamings) across the land in question. In the Warumungu Land Claim report, for example, one learns that Jurnkurakurr, site of the Tennant Creek Telegraph Station acquired by the Northern Territory government in 1987 as a monument to white settlement in the region, is the spiritual home of Jalawala (black-nose python), the Mungamunga women, and the snake Kiliriji—all primordial actors creating the broader landscape. The report also details the site-specific travels and cosmological productions of Pirrtangu (flying-fox), Milwayijarra (two snakes), Aakiy (black plum), and Warupunju (fire) together with a host of more minor Dreamings: Nyinkka (grass-tailed lizard), Yarrangarna (dingo), Emu, Crow, Ngappa (rain), Kurtinja (bush turkey), Karli (boomerang), Yukulyari (wallaby), and Mangirriji (plains goanna) among others.

In these reports the learned justice often reviews the anthropological evidence presented to the hearing from all sides (including that coming from parties opposing the claim), testing its usefulness to the legislative framework, assessing its contradictions, and gauging its resonances with the longer published record. In this way the history of anthropological study itself has frequently been reviewed and re-presented as a matter of public record. The Aboriginal past and the history of its study are brought into a continuing relationship that directly influences Aboriginal futures, whatever the outcome of the case. In the following Justice Michael Maurice compares what Sir Baldwin Spencer and Francis Gillen had recorded of Warumungu burial practices with what had been elicited from other anthropological sources and from Aboriginal witnesses during the claim hearing:

> The import of Sir Baldwin Spencer's letter to Sir James Frazer was that many of the practices he had recorded among the tribes he visited, though they involved different types of ritual and different kinds of social institutions, and took different outward forms, expressed a relatively invariant current of ideas . . . . It hardly need be said . . . that these ways of being and thinking, and the social relations in which they are practiced, remain a powerful force in the lives of the Warumungu people today. It is what makes them distinctly different from non-Aboriginal residents of [the town of] Tennant Creek. The same tradition as recorded by Spencer and Gillen, and by the late Professor Stanner, albeit much altered, was the source of the present claims, the conceptions which informed them, and the terms in which they were stated. (Aboriginal Land Commissioner, 1988, p. 129)

Here, in a localized microcosm, the entire history of studying Aboriginal religion is rehearsed and reassessed for the purpose of returning a parcel of land to Aboriginal people for what the commissioner acknowledges to be their continuing economic, social, and political survival.

The engagement of anthropologists as "expert" translators of Aboriginal culture in land claim processes has resulted in some of the most compelling and innovative accounts of religion as a key modality of Aborigines' social, cosmological, political, and practical engagement with the world. Outstanding examples include D. B. Rose's *Dingo Makes Us Human* (1992), Francesca Merlan's *Caging the Rainbow* (1998), and Elizabeth Povinelli's *Labor's Lot* (1993). Each re-envisages the subject of Aboriginal religion as meaning, symbol, and action, and each brings to that study a broader historical, legislative, and political context.

Land rights highlighted the power of anthropological models to frame legal understandings: the act encoded a model of descent through fathers (patriliny), giving rise to rights in land as real property that were often contradicted by Aboriginal evidence. Over time land claim hearings forced the development of more nuanced understandings, prominently through recognition of the roles of "owners" and "managers" expressing the complementary rights and ritual responsibilities inherited through both men and women. Another development was the facilitation of women to give evidence of their gender-restricted secret and sacred responsibilities toward land and the Dreaming. Witnessing ceremonies, visiting sites and seeing sacred objects during the course of a land claim hearing meant that procedures for managing men's restricted knowledge were in place very early, and have been largely unproblematic. Some early land claims acknowledged that women's ceremonies and secrets complemented those of men and played an equally vital role in Aboriginal religious life. For example, in his report on the Alyawarra (Alywarr) and Kaititja (Kaytetye) land claim heard in 1978 Mr. Justice Toohey commented on the forceful display of attachment to land he had witnessed in women's ceremonies and site visits. In other hearings such as the 1988 Jasper Gorge and Kidman Springs land claim, however, women kept their knowledge of sites, songs, dances, designs, and objects secret because their own Dreaming law dictated that no man should see these things. In the Palm Valley claim of 1994 Arrernte women agreed to give evidence on the basis that the land commissioner was the only man present; male lawyers were permitted to read the transcript but not to cross examine the women. This has subsequently raised a number of broader legal and procedural issues regarding the right of a party to choose his or her own legal representative and the capacity of courts to limit that choice on the basis of gender. In the Tempe Downs land claim, also heard in 1994, women achieved some procedural parity with men by giving extensive evidence in restricted sessions resulting in a restricted transcript that was not available to others. In "Preserving Culture in Federal Court Proceedings," Greg McIntyre and Geoffrey Bagshaw survey such ongoing difficulties in reconciling Aboriginal cultural principles of gender-based religious secrecy with the requirements of Australia law.

Land claims became a principal occasion for the display and performance of religious knowledge, not just its recording. Hearings moved out of the court and into the bush, where successive commissioners heard evidence on or near the land being claimed and were witnesses to performances of ritual, dance, and song that sought to convey direct, revelatory knowledge of Aboriginal authority (and in this way perhaps to entail judges, lawyers, and others in relationships of reciprocal obligation and respect). As D. B. Rose pointed out in "Histories and Rituals: Land Claims in the Territory" (1996), such processes themselves became a form of "ceremony for country" that has fed back into the religious life of communities. The interpenetration of Aboriginal and non-Aboriginal worlds and the subsequent changes this has wrought on negotiating public versus restricted ritual performance, managing gendered responsibilities for social and cosmological action, and the seemingly more mundane negotiations of kin group identity and residence are major threads of Dussart's fine-grained ethnography of ritual as politics among Warlpiri people at Yuendumu.

The land claim process also highlighted the dynamic tension between revelation and concealment that is itself a feature of Aboriginal religion. In many circumstances religious knowledge can only be revealed by those who have particular rights to it, to those who have compatible rights to know it and with the consent (and often in the presence) of others in positions to authorize such a transfer. In recognition of this, some Australian legal processes have, in places and for limited purposes, adapted to accommodate Aboriginal cultural principles. Thus whereas land claims have resulted in unprecedented levels of detail about Aboriginal religion being made available, they have also underscored the strict limits and controls that are placed on such knowledge, with portions of the evidence and hearing transcripts in many cases being permanently suppressed. At the same time as there is greater access to Aboriginal religion in diverse contexts (from legal judgments to art exhibitions to Olympic Games ceremonies), the very restrictions placed on that accessibility have become more prominent and more problematic. This theme is explored in papers edited by Christopher Anderson as *Politics of the Secret* (1995), focusing on transactions in men's restricted knowledge, designs, and sacred objects in central and north west Australia, including the history and micro-politics of Aboriginal engagement with a range of non-Aboriginal recorders, collectors and institutions.

The tension between revelation and concealment provides the framework for Ian Keen's *Knowledge and Secrecy in an Aboriginal Religion* (1994), a sustained ethnographic exploration of a specific (Yolngu) religious tradition that highlights the essential ambiguity of cultural meaning and the ongoing necessity for its negotiation. Similar themes are explored in Morphy's *Ancestral Connections* (1991) and Luke Taylor's *Seeing the Inside* (1996), both major monographs on the expression of the Dreaming through art in northeast and western Arnhem Land respectively.

Conflicts over revelation have been played out publicly and acrimoniously in a series of court actions and media trials focused on Aboriginal assertions of sacredness and restriction, Uluru (Ayers Rock), Coronation Hill, and Junction Waterhole in the Northern Territory; Noonkanbah station in Western Australia; and Hindmarsh Island in South Australia being the most prominent examples. Especially in contexts where claims to restricted religious knowledge have come into conflict with development or the desires of the state, some sacred sites have taken on meanings (and have had effects) far beyond the local and often beyond their culturally specific significance to Aboriginal owners. It is in such heightened political arenas that the meaning and peculiar power of sacred sites have become what Ken Gelder and Jane M. Jacobs in *Uncanny Australia* (1998) call "promiscuous," escaping their Aboriginal specificity and their academic or legal framing to disrupt and bring into question the wider Australian population's sense of place and identity. These complex currents of what is known and by whom—and who should control the circumstances of its revelation, even when it is contained in a published record—have themselves redirected the study of Aboriginal religion. They provide the framework for Diane Bell's *Ngarrindjeri Wurruwarrin* (1998), where the voices of Ngarrindjeri women from "settled" South Australia are brought into dialogue with the record of previous ethnographers, asking questions of what was and what was not recorded about their religious traditions and debating what can and cannot be said, even in the twenty-first century.

NATIVE TITLE. The Land Rights Act returned significant tracts of land to Aboriginal people, but it applied only to unalienated crown land in the Northern Territory, and even there significant disparities existed between those who could and could not meet the legal test of traditional ownership. Elsewhere around the country (as in Northern Territory towns), aspirations to land and the recognition of rights were largely unmet. In 1992 a long-running case brought by the Murray Islanders of Torres Strait resulted in the landmark *Mabo* decision by the High Court. In a majority of six to one, the court ruled that, in common law, indigenous rights to land had survived the acquisition of sovereignty by Britain, thus overturning the earlier "fiction" of *terra nullius,* or of Australia as a land belonging to no one. The Commonwealth's Native Title Act of 1993 sought to enact the court's decision in law and opened the way for Aboriginal people across the continent to have their surviving rights recognized. It should be noted that in cases where an Aboriginal land commissioner found existing traditional ownership, the relevant minister could grant an exclusive Aboriginal Freehold Title for that land to be held by a land trust. Under the Native Title Act, a tribunal or court determines whether or not native title exists in relation to a particular area of land or waters, the nature of such rights and interests, and with which other parties they coexist. No land is granted as a result, and only limited rights are conferred on claimant groups. Achieving even that recognition has entailed the production of unprecedented quantities of documentation (in the form of "connection reports" detailing a group or a person's association with country) and a complex but decentralized bureaucracy of registration, assessment, mediation, and determination. Several contested native title cases have proceeded to full hearings in the federal court.

There is no legislative requirement to assess spiritual connection to land in native title. However, this has been a principal register of inquiry, highlighting the way religion has become embedded in the administrative imagining of Aboriginal people and their culture.

In proceedings spanning 1994 to 2002, the Miriuwung and Gajerrong people sought recognition of their native title rights in some three thousand square miles of east Kimberley land straddling the Western Australia and Northern Territory border, including the Ord River irrigation project and the Argyle Diamond Mine. Continuing religious practice was a key element allowing claimants to demonstrate their observance of traditional laws and customs, these being the crucial content for legislative recognition of native title. The judges in the case rejected physical occupation of the land as a necessary requirement for proof of continuing connection. In being found to have upheld traditional laws and customs, ceremonial practices, economic and ceremonial links with other Aboriginal communities as well as possessing knowledge of myths, Dreaming tracks, and sites, the claimants' relationship to the land was determined to have been maintained. The evidence elicited from Aboriginal witnesses was tested against the historical record and the research of anthropologists, archaeologists, and historians who had drawn together diverse written and unpublished ethnographic materials for the purpose of the proceedings. This work was extensively reviewed, compared, and assessed in the court's "Reasons for Judgment." Likewise the judges reviewed the work of Elkin and his student Phyllis Kaberry in the 1920s and 1930s, including the latter's seminal *Aboriginal Women: Sacred and Profane* (1939). Kaberry's field notes, diaries, and genealogies were also before the court. The claimants' case was supported by these materials, and native title was found to coexist with other interests, limited by the rights (to water and minerals, for example) conferred on others.

In another long-running native title case, this one involving land in New South Wales and Victoria, the federal court determined that the most credible source of information about the traditional laws and customs of the Yorta Yorta people is in the writings of a nineteenth-century pastoralist who established a degree of rapport with Aboriginal people and observed their society before its "disintegration." Yorta Yorta assertions concerning the "sacredness" of land, resources, sites, and contemporary cultural practices were dismissed in light of the historical record, but also against those displays of spiritual attachment that Aboriginal people have produced in other judicial inquiries. Evidence of the role of a Christian missionary in disrupting traditional religious practices and suppressing indigenous language did not mitigate assessment of the claimants' inadequate religious expression. Such are the vicissitudes of contemporary inquiries into Aboriginal belief, where the historical record may be as powerful and determinant as anything an Aboriginal person may say or demonstrate.

CONTINUING SIGNIFICANCES. Reuther's labyrinthine compendium of myth, story, and place names from the far northeast of South Australia has been preserved in archives and made available on microfiche (as *The Diari*) by the Australian Institute of Aboriginal and Torres Strait Islander Studies. It has been deployed again by those various players who are required to take account of Aboriginal relations to this area. Thus Reuther's data have been used by the state in assessing the multiple (and sometimes competing) native title claims in this region. Copies of his maps and place name data are held by mining and exploration companies who must enter into negotiations with native title claimants about access to the land. The material is used by anthropologists to frame heritage and native title reports to courts and other tribunals of inquiry. Increasingly it is used by Aboriginal people themselves to become informed of their own history, their associations with place, and to support contemporary expressions of identity through painting and sculpture.

Similarly Taplin's recording of "manners and customs" became the baseline ethnographic record examined by a royal commission looking into the contemporary beliefs of Ngarrindjeri women, whose assertion of sacredness and restriction in respect of a development site embroiled the nation in public debate and speculation. The Berndts' Yaralde material of the 1940s was trawled through in the same inquiry and in a subsequent federal court case to test the beliefs and cultural knowledge of Aboriginal witnesses. Tindale's manuscripts returned from the United States to be co-opted to the same proceedings. To some extent his meticulous recordings conflict with those of the Berndts, each having derived from different informants. Differences of record, methodology, and interpretation fuel academic and public debate; materials once confined to the archives are aired in a new light, forging new interpretations and positionings for anthropologists, historians, and Ngarrindjeri people alike.

Such materials are at play in more ways than at any previous time, ramifying their meanings and multiplying the contexts of their interpretation. The study of Aboriginal religion—together with the history, meaning, and uses of that study—counts like never before in more forums and with more consequences than was ever imagined. Its contestation and its centrality to intellectual life, government policy, and public debate ensures that studying Aboriginal religion has become as necessary and as dynamic as at any time in its long history.

BIBLIOGRAPHY

Aboriginal Land Commissioner. *Land Claim by Alyawarra and Kaititja.* Canberra, Australia, 1979.

Aboriginal Land Commissioner. *Warumungu Land Claim.* Report no. 31. Canberra, Australia, 1988.

Aboriginal Land Commissioner. *Palm Valley Land Claim No. 48.* Report no. 57. Canberra, Australia, 1999.

Anderson, Christopher, ed. *Politics of the Secret.* Sydney, 1995.

Bell, Diane. *Daughters of the Dreaming.* Melbourne, 1983; 2d ed., Saint Leonards, Australia, 1993; 3d ed., North Melbourne, 2002.

Bell, Diane. *Ngarrindjeri Wurruwarrin: A World That Is, Was, and Will Be.* North Melbourne, Australia,1998.

Collins, David. *An Account of the English Colony in New South Wales with Remarks on the Dispositions, Customs, Manners of the Native Inhabitants of that Country.* London, 1798; reprint, Adelaide, Australia, 1971.

Durkheim, Émile. *The Elementary Forms of the Religious Life.* Translated by Joseph Ward Swain. 2d ed. London, 1976.

Dussart, Françoise. *The Politics of Ritual in an Aboriginal Settlement: Kinship, Gender, and the Currency of Knowledge.* Washington, D.C., 2000.

Gason, Samuel. "The Manners and Customs of the Dieyerie Tribe of Australian Aboriginals." In *The Native Tribes of South Australia,* edited by James Dominick Woods, pp. 253–307. 2d ed. Adelaide, Australia, 1879; reprint, 1997.

Gelder, Ken, and Jane M. Jacobs. *Uncanny Australia: Sacredness and Identity in a Postcolonial Nation.* Melbourne, Australia, 1998.

Hamilton, Annette. "Dual Social Systems: Technology, Labour and Women's Secret Rites in the Eastern Western Desert." *Oceania* 51 (1980): 4–19.

Hiatt, L. R. *Arguments about Aborigines.* Cambridge, U.K., 1996.

Howitt, Alfred William. *The Native Tribes of South-East Australia.* London, 1904; reprint, Canberra, Australia, 1996.

Kaberry, Phyllis M. *Aboriginal Women: Sacred and Profane.* London, 1939; reprint, 2004.

Keen, Ian. *Knowledge and Secrecy in an Aboriginal Religion: Yolngu of North-East Arnhem Land.* Oxford, 1994.

McIntyre, Greg, and Geoffrey Bagshaw. "Preserving Culture in Federal Court Proceedings: Gender Restrictions and Anthropological Experts." *Land, Rights, Laws: Issues of Native Title,* 2, issues paper no. 15. Canberra, Australia, 2002.

Merlan, Francesca. "Gender in Aboriginal Social Life: A Review." In *Social Anthropology and Australian Aboriginal Studies: A Contemporary Overview,* edited by R. M. Berndt and Robert Tonkinson, pp. 17–76. Canberra, Australia, 1988.

Merlan, Francesca. *Caging the Rainbow: Place, Politics, and Aborigines in a Northern Australian Town.* Honolulu, Hawaii, 1998.

Morphy, Howard. "The Resurrection of the Hydra: Twenty-Five Years of Research on Aboriginal Religion." In *Social Anthropology and Australian Aboriginal Studies: A Contemporary Overview,* edited by R. M. Berndt and Robert Tonkinson, pp. 241–266. Canberra, Australia, 1988.

Morphy, Howard. *Ancestral Connections: Art and an Aboriginal System of Knowledge.* Chicago, 1991.

Povinelli, Elizabeth A. *Labor's Lot: The Power, History, and Culture of Aboriginal Action.* Chicago, 1993.

Reuther, Johann Georg. *The Diari.* Vols.1–13. Translated by Philipp A. Scherer. AIAS microfiche no. 2. Canberra, Australia, 1981.

Rose, Deborah Bird. *Dingo Makes Us Human: Life and Land in an Aboriginal Australian Culture.* Cambridge, U.K., 1992.

Rose, Deborah Bird. "Women and Land Claims." *Land, Rights, Laws: Issues of Native Title,* issues paper no. 6. Canberra, Australia, 1995.

Rose, Deborah Bird. "Histories and Rituals: Land Claims in the Territory." In *In the Age of Mabo: History, Aborigines, and Australia,* edited by Bain Attwood, pp. 35–53. Saint Leonards, Australia, 1996.

Stanner, W. E. H. "Religion, Totemism, and Symbolism (1962)." In *White Man Got No Dreaming: Essays, 1938–1973.* Canberra, Australia, 1979, pp. 106–143.

Stanner, W. E. H. *On Aboriginal Religion* (1966). Oceania Monograph 36. Sydney, Australia, 1989.

Strehlow, Carl, and Johann Georg Reuther. *Testamenta Marra: Jesuni Christuni Ngantjani Jaura Ninaia Rarithmalkana Wonti Dieri Jaurani.* Tanunda, Australia, 1897.

Strehlow, T. G. H. *Songs of Central Australia.* Sydney, Australia, 1971.

Swain, Tony. *A Place for Strangers: Towards a History of Australian Aboriginal Being.* Cambridge, U.K., 1993.

Taylor, Luke. *Seeing the Inside: Bark Painting in Western Arnhem Land.* New York, 1996.

Tench, Watkin. *A Complete Account of the Settlement at Port Jackson.* London, 1793; reprint, Sydney, Australia, 1961.

Watson, Christine. *Piercing the Ground: Balgo Women's Image Making and Relationship to Country.* Fremantle, Australia, 2003.

White, Isobel, ed. *The Native Tribes of Western Australia by Daisy Bates.* Canberra, Australia, 1985.

RODNEY LUCAS (2005)

AUTHORITY is a constant and pervasive phenomenon in the history of religions. One often speaks of traditional authority, scriptural authority, ecclesiastical authority, or imperial authority based on religious claims. As legitimate power to require and receive submission and obedience, it is found in primitive and archaic religions as well as in founded religions wherever the question of order is involved. At different stages of history, a variety of religions have contributed to the creation and maintenance of order by providing the necessary sources of authority. These sources are diverse, but the following may be counted among the major ones: (1) persons, usually classified into various types of religious leadership such as kings, founders of religions, and other leaders of religious communities, (2) sacred writings, (3) traditions, oral and/or written, constituting doctrinal truths and ethical precepts, (4) religious communities with a priesthood and sacramental rites, and (5) personal experience. The question of the legitimacy of this or that authority has been a cause of tension and conflict in and between individual religions, for any authority recognized as legitimate must be respected and placed in proper order, while a rejected authority must be combated.

AUTHORITY IN PRIMITIVE RELIGIONS. Among many primitive peoples authority is embodied in orally transmitted traditions of the tribal community. Oral traditions reign supreme, imposing a binding authority on the tribal community in which they are preserved. Especially authoritative are myths, as distinguished from legends and fables. Myth carries authority in primitive society for at least three reasons. First, myth is a "true" story, never a fable, a fiction, or a childish fancy tale. Second, it is a sacred story narrating the acts of the gods and other divine beings that took place in the beginning of mythical time. What occurred—in the words of Mircea Eliade—in *illo tempore* ("at this time") represents for the primitive peoples a reality higher and greater than any kind of historical reality known to them. Myth is authoritative because it reveals the "absolute truth" of the events at the beginning of mythical time. And third, this transhistorical reality that occurred in *illo tempore* serves as the exemplary model for the activities of man in primitive society. According to Bronislaw Malinowski, myth functions as the "charter" of established social facts, including religious beliefs and practices, morality, and everyday rules of conduct.

This divinely sanctioned authoritative tradition is transmitted orally from elders to adolescents during rites of initiation. The candidate for these rites undergoes the process of symbolic death and rebirth, and it is precisely in this process of spiritual regeneration that he receives knowledge about the secrets of the tribal tradition: the myths serve as bearers of traditional authority; they tell of the gods and the origin of the world, the names of the gods, the role and origin of the initiation ceremonies, and, of course, codes of morality and rules of conduct. Thus the initiate comes to obtain gnosis, true authoritative knowledge, essential for his life as a human being, that is, knowledge about the higher and greater reality that sustains the order of the primitive society in which he lives.

AUTHORITY IN ARCHAIC RELIGIONS. The rise of the great civilizations in Mesopotamia, Egypt, India, and China during the third and second millennia BCE marked a significant turning point in history. All these civilizations originated and unfolded along rivers. Irrigation systems had to be worked out in order to control nature and produce a good harvest, and this necessity called for the formation of the efficient administrative organization, which was accompanied by the institution of kingship. A system of writing was a sine qua non for this new development.

Under these circumstances, the authority of the oral traditions, which had characterized primitive culture, tended to be replaced by that of written traditions embodied in literary texts. These texts were primarily the creation of royal courts and temples, and those who were engaged in the interpretation and transmission of the texts were scribes and priests. They were professional carriers of the written traditions. In China, for example, government officials were thought to possess magical charisma by virtue of their familiarity with the Confucian classics. These officials made the study, interpretation, and transmission of the words of the master Confucius the focal point of their efforts. Their vision was preeminently political in orientation, and eventually they achieved an extraordinarily stable social order. In India, *brahmans* occupied the authoritative status in society on account of their esoteric knowledge of the Vedas, the Brahmanas, and the many other sacred writings. Not only in China and India, but also in the ancient Near East, the scribes and priests who served as guardians of the written traditions were the chief religious figures vested with authority.

It was the king, however, who exercised supreme authority. In archaic civilizations, the state functioned as a religious community, as a cosmos, and the king was the person supremely responsible for the maintenance of this cosmic order. Imperial authority was sustained by both the kingship ideology, which was grounded in myths, and the celebration of rituals, especially the New Year festival. The ideology used for the legitimation of imperial authority was different from one region to another; that is, the nature of the king's person and his role in the given cosmic order was variously conceived in different societies, depending on their religious outlook on life and the universe.

In ancient Egypt, for example, the king was believed to be divine in essence. His coronation, usually celebrated at the beginning of a new year, signified not an apotheosis but an epiphany, or self-manifestation, of the god. As long as he ruled, the king was identified with the god Horus; in fact, he was Horus incarnate in his earthly existence, but upon his death he was mystically assimilated to Osiris, the god of rebirth and immortality. Egyptian kingship was also intimately associated with the theme of cosmogony. The dais, for example, on which the new king was seated symbolized the hill of sand, the "first" land, which, according to the Egyptian cosmogonic myth, emerged out of the primeval ocean at the time of beginning. Ascension to the royal throne represented a ritual reenactment of the emergence of a cosmos out of chaos, the primeval waters. Thus, the king repeated the act of creation at his enthronement.

In Mesopotamia, too, the king played a part of vital importance in the well-being of the cosmic order. The *Enuma elish*, the Babylonian epic of creation, was recited and reenacted during the New Year festival. The primary purpose of this recitation and ritual reenactment of the cosmogonic myth was the renewal and regeneration of the cosmos; the king, representing the god Marduk on earth, repeated what took place at the time of absolute beginning, as narrated in the myth. However, the king in ancient Mesopotamia was generally not conceived as a divine being. More properly, he was viewed as divine only while he participated in the ceremonies as representative of Marduk. He was essentially a mortal being, not divine; he represented the gods on earth as their "chosen servant."

The king in ancient China was called the "unique man" as well as the "Son of Heaven" (*t'ien-tzu*). The Son of Heaven was one who received the mandate of Heaven (*t'ien-ming*). This notion of the mandate of Heaven implied that imperial authority could not become a permanent possession of the ruler, that Heaven had the complete freedom to confer or withdraw his mandate, just as in ancient Israel God was absolutely free to confer or withdraw his charisma or "gift of grace" from the ruler on earth. The Chinese Son of Heaven obviously had nothing to do with the genealogical concept of kingship, such as in ancient Egypt or Japan, where the king was considered the descendant or incarnation of a certain god; he was simply the earthly representative of Heaven, or heavenly will.

The Chinese king was also conceived as the unique man, one supremely responsible for the maintenance of the cosmic order. He maintained the cosmic order by assisting Heaven in the regulation and harmonization of the yin and yang principles, as best exemplified by his performance in the ceremonial building, the *ming-tang*. This structure was an *imago mundi* ("image of the universe"); it had a square plan symbolizing the earth and was covered by a circular roof, symbolic of the sky. Other features, such as the building's twelve rooms, reflected the cycle of the year. Thus the whole structure was a vast space-and-time diagram, a microcosm. Here the king observed the rituals of worship and sacrifice to Heaven and Earth and myriad spirits in order to secure their favor for the entire universe. When he was to inaugurate the seasons and months, he placed himself in an appropriate room of the building: in the second month of the spring, for example, the king took his position facing east, clothed in green, the color of spring and the east, while in the fall he faced west, clothed in a white ceremonial dress appropriate for the fall and the west. Thus, the king assisted Heaven in guaranteeing the ascendancy of the yang principle in spring, while in the fall he helped the rise of the yin principle. In essence, the Chinese king was expected to be the harmonizer of the cosmic movement.

AUTHORITY IN FOUNDED RELIGIONS. The emergence of Buddhism, Christianity, and Islam is an innovation in the history of religions. While in primitive and archaic religions authority is embodied in the sacred kings as well as in oral or written traditions of the tribal community and state, in these founded religions authority is ultimately derived from the founder of a new community of faith, and/or his religious experience. Consequently, the founded religion, whatever it is, develops its own structure of authority and authoritative tradition, which is distinctively different from that in primitive and archaic religions.

Buddhism. The Buddha's authority was grounded in his conviction that he had discovered the *dharma*, the universal law of existence, through his personal experience of enlightenment. He himself lived in accordance with it, and on his deathbed he urged his disciples to depend on it as the sole guiding principle of life.

But this truth was not self-evident; it was the truth taught and interpreted by the Buddha that his followers accepted. After his death his closest disciples assumed a new responsibility for the successful realization of the Buddhist ideal. Inevitably, important traditions emerged that were transmitted orally until they were put into writing in the first century BCE. These authoritative oral traditions included the memories and interpretations of the Buddha's own teaching concerning the *dharma* and the rules of conduct, the Vinaya, which he had established for the regulation of the *saṃgha*, or Buddhist community.

However, there exists no single canon of scriptures that is universally recognized by all Buddhists. The development of such a canon was impossible because of the decentralized nature of the Buddhist community or the lack of a central ecclesiastical authority to determine orthodoxy. From the beginning of its history, Buddhism allowed its local monastic orders to function as autonomous, self-governing bodies in accordance with the teachings and disciplinary rules that they had inherited. As might be expected, the development of the autonomous monastic orders, or "schools," led to the rise of different versions of the canon without, however, invalidating the importance of the concept of canon or the theoretical unity of the Buddhist community as a whole.

Underneath all this evidence for a virtual absence of the canonical and ecclesiastical authority is the Buddha's insistence on the primacy of self-knowledge, the immediacy of experience, or the personal realization of truth. The canon of scriptures in Buddhism was generally authoritative in concept, but in practice it functioned meaningfully only on the level of particular monastic orders or schools. Moreover, the concept of canonicity itself was often in conflict with the Buddhist belief in the immediacy of the experience of enlightenment.

This general trend, away from the traditional scriptures and toward the exploration of new insights, wisdom, and interpretations, is more evident in Mahāyāna Buddhism, which arose in the first century CE, than in Theravāda, that is, Buddhism in more traditional forms, especially regarding the concepts of the Buddha and the *dharma.* The concept of the Buddha in Mahāyāna has changed so much that he is no longer simply the person who attained enlightenment in the sixth century BCE, but is regarded as a self-manifestation in history of the *dharmakāya*, a cosmic principle immanent in all beings, the ground of all expressions of the eternal Buddha nature. The Buddha preaching on the Vulture Peak, as he does in Mahāyāna scriptures, is not a human teacher talking to a band of his disciples but a transhistorical being addressing himself to representatives of the whole universe. Mahāyāna scriptures purport to be ever-recurring revelations of the eternal universal principle (*dharmakāya*) and tend to be dissociated from the tradition that is deeply rooted in the particular life of the historical Buddha. A scripture is considered useful insofar as it can lead one to the same religious experience that the Buddha himself had during his life. The implication is that scriptures can ultimately be dispensed with. This implication is most evident in Zen Buddhism, which claims to be based on a "special transmission outside the scriptures" and stresses only the immediate personal experience of *kenshō* ("seeing into one's true nature"), or enlightenment.

Christianity. During his public life of ministry, Jesus of Nazareth rejected the authority of the oral Torah in Judaism, which is often referred to in the New Testament as the "tradition of the fathers." For this he substituted his own authority as interpreter of the written Torah (the Mosaic Law), namely, the authority of the one who proclaimed, in word and deed, God's will as well as the imminent coming of the kingdom of God. Jesus thus presented himself as the ultimate source of the new traditions, which were to become authoritative for the emerging church or community of Christians.

After the resurrection of Jesus, his immediate disciples understood the meaning of his life, suffering, and death in the light of the Hebrew scriptures: Jesus was the Messiah (the Christ) and the fulfillment of God's promise. Naturally, the church assumed responsibility for the creation and transmission of the traditions concerning the words and deeds of Jesus Christ. For the primitive Christian community these traditions were the most appropriate and correct interpretations of the written Torah; they were, in effect, the oral Torah of Christianity. It was especially the apostles and Paul—eyewitnesses to the earthly life and to the resurrection of Jesus Christ—who played a vital role in the interpretation and transmission of the traditions, just as in Judaism scribes and rabbis made essential contributions to the transmission of the oral Torah. Here emerged the authoritative apostolic tradition, which was initially transmitted orally, then written down in the various literary forms, and finally codified by the church as the canon of the New Testament. This New Testament took its place beside the canon of the Old Testament. While Protestantism accords supreme authority to the combined Old and New Testament as the sum total of the apostolic tradition, distinguishing it from the postapostolic tradition, Catholicism asserts the ongoing tradition of the church as having equal authority with the apostolic tradition embodied in the scripture. For Catholics there is no fundamental opposition between scripture and tradition; they are manifestations of one and the same thing, the apostolic tradition.

The essence of the Roman Catholic church lies in its institutional character as the objective organ of salvation, which is embodied in tradition, sacraments (seven in number), and priesthood. The church stands for the eternal presence of Jesus Christ in history, and the papacy is based on the founder's explicit designation of Peter as the foundation rock of the church. Roman Catholics claim a direct succession of papal authority from Peter to the present pope, and this claim to legitimacy, which under the pope's sanction extends to the entire Roman Catholic priesthood, is a vital element in grounding the authority of the church. Sacraments are the objective and tangible channels through which God's grace is communicated to the faithful. The objectivism of Roman Catholicism is best exemplified in its interpretation of the Eucharist, namely, the theory of transubstantiation, officially proclaimed as doctrine in 1215. As to the teaching of the church, it is the magisterium (teaching authority) of the church, the pope, who determines the legitimate interpretation of scripture and tradition. From medieval times, membership in the Roman Catholic church has involved submission to papal authority. This is certainly a typical example of institutionalized charisma, and over the centuries it has proved its strength as a source of authority in the lives of its adherents.

Eastern Orthodoxy and Roman Catholicism agree that the church possesses the divinely given infallible authority. Eastern Orthodoxy differs from Roman Catholicism, however, in that its church has no organ of infallibility; the quality of infallibility resides in the mystically conceived church itself, not in any fixed office like that of the Roman Catholic papacy.

The Protestant understanding of authority is inclined more or less toward subjectivism in contrast to the objectivism of medieval Christianity. The Protestant Reformation hinged upon two main principles of complementary importance: justification by faith and the authority of scripture.

The question that most preoccupied Martin Luther was soteriology, that is, the question of personal salvation and its certainty. According to Luther, man is justified before God by faith alone; the church with its priesthood, sacraments, and tradition can by no means guarantee man's salvation. Hence Luther reduced the sacraments to two, baptism and the Lord's Supper. While justification by faith is the "material" principle of the Reformation, scripture alone is its "formal" principle. For Luther, as well as for John Calvin, the Bible, not the church, is the final authority for Christian life. While Calvin in his practice of interpretation seems to accept particular words of the Bible as the revealed word of God, Luther distinguishes between the words of the Bible and the word that God speaks through them: the words of the Bible are the "cradle of Christ." Accordingly, Luther does not support the literal interpretation of the Bible, nor does he find the word of God equally in all its parts, but regards some as inferior in quality. The corollary of the two main principles of the Reformation is the theory concerning the priesthood of all believers: each and every individual is a priest to himself or herself and as such is to serve God by listening to the word of God within the words of the Bible. This emphasis on personal conscience constitutes a great innovation of the Reformation, but it has also opened the way for uncontrolled interpretations of the Bible as well as the proliferation of an ever-increasing number of Protestant denominations and small sects led by conscientious, "inspired" leaders.

Trends away from the Roman Catholic type of objectivism and toward subjectivism are even more evident in many sectarian Protestant communities. They insist on the importance of Bible study, prayer, and the personal experience of salvation and its certainty; and for members of these communities the ideas of sin, salvation, and faith in Jesus Christ assume an intense and vivid personal reality. One of the best examples of this Protestant emphasis is George Fox, the founder of the Society of Friends, also known as the Quakers. Fox organized a community of the faithful without priesthood or sacramental rites. He was convinced that true religion consisted not in the church or in the creeds, but in the personal experience of what he called illumination by the Holy Spirit; the source of final authority for him was the personal experience of the inner light.

Islam. For Muslims the Qurʾān is the immediate and complete revelation of God's message to mankind through Muḥammad. It is the heavenly book of revelation, the word of God par excellence. While controversies have raged among Muslims as to the sense in which this is true, that it is true has never been questioned. The Qurʾān for some Muslims is "created," but for the majority it is not a historical creation; just as the Torah in Judaism is of celestial origin, deriving from the time prior to the creation, the Qurʾān, although composed in Arabic, reflects its heavenly archetype. Thus the Qurʾān is "uncreated," not conditioned by time and history. The Qurʾān is unquestionably the supreme source of authority for the *ummah*, or Muslim community.

The Muslim community has also accepted the *ḥadīth* ("tradition," i.e., the record of the words and deeds) of the prophet Muḥammad as the normative authority for its beliefs and practices. While Muslims do not consider him the savior in the Christian sense of the word, they are firmly convinced that Muḥammad was divinely guided in the years after receiving the revelation; he is God's prophet and apostle and the perfect man, the exemplary model and spiritual guide for humanity. For Muslims, everything Muḥammad said and did during his life is worthy of study and imitation.

Still another tradition, which is accepted as authoritative by the orthodox Muslims (Sunnīs), is the *ḥadīth* of the first four caliphs. In his later years, when he was in Medina, Muḥammad attempted to build up a socioreligious community on the basis of Islamic principles, and after his death this ideal was carried on by his four immediate successors (caliphs), known as the ideal rulers. The Muslim community then was in need of detailed rules for ordering both its communal life and the life of its individual members. These rules of life, called *sharīʿah*, or Islamic law, are based on the interpretation of the Qurʾān and the *ḥadīth*s of Muḥammad and the first four caliphs who followed him.

Significantly, the caliph as head of the community had no pontifical or even priestly functions. His task was not to expound or to interpret the faith, but to serve as the guardian of the public order. The task of interpreting the Qurʾān and *ḥadīth*s and applying them to the actual life of the community was carried out by the *ʿulamāʾ*. They were not priests and claimed no priestly power or authority, but, on account of their learning in the Qurʾān and *ḥadīth*s, played an important role quite analogous to that of the Jewish rabbinate.

While the Sunnīs consider the *ḥadīth* concerning the first three caliphs as one of the sources of authority for Islam, the Shīʿīs have rejected it as such, because they view the three caliphs as illegal usurpers and recognize instead ʿAlī, Muḥammad's cousin and son-in-law, as the first caliph, or, more properly, the first imam. What underlies the Shīʿī contention is the belief that Muḥammad's personal charisma, which he received from God, is transmitted genealogically only in his family tradition. This view is remarkably different from the Sunnī view that Muḥammad's charisma is channeled through the office of caliph regardless of its occupant: while Sunnī orthodoxy is committed to the principle of institutional charisma, the Shīʿīs reject it and uphold the principle of hereditary charisma. Accordingly, the Shīʿīs have replaced the *ḥadīth* of the first three caliphs with the *ḥadīth* of the twelve imams.

In sharp contrast to the caliph, who has no legal authority, the imam is authorized to interpret the *ḥaqīqah*, or inner mysteries, which are hidden in the Qurʾān and *ḥadīth*s. He is endowed with such a spiritual gift because, through the chain of direct transmission, he has received from Muḥammad a body of gnosis, or esoteric knowledge. Consequently, the imam is charged with a power at once political and religious; he is one who rules the community with mercy and justice but who also interprets Islamic law and its inner meanings. Naturally, the Shīʿīs are persuaded that the final authority for Islam is in the hands of the imam himself. According to them, the last, or twelfth, imam, the so-called hidden imam, did not die but entered a prolonged "concealment." One day, so they believe, from that state of concealment he will emerge as the Mahdi ("expected one"), that is, the messiah. Until he comes, a group of leading lawyer-theologians, called *mujtāhid*s, will continue to exercise an extensive authority on matters of religion and law.

TENSION BETWEEN RELIGIOUS AND SECULAR AUTHORITIES. While tension between religious and secular authorities may be present in primitive and archaic cultures, it arises in its sharpest forms only after the emergence of the founded religion. Then it occurs between rival principles, each claiming universal supremacy, and only under particular cultural and historical circumstances.

Islam has rarely experienced tensions analogous to those between church and state in medieval Western Christendom because the Muslim community has been founded on the principle of theocracy, and a distinct ecclesiastical body powerful enough to challenge secular authorities has never existed.

Buddhism knows of no such tensions either, but for different reasons. While it succeeded in establishing a theocratic state in Tibet, in many other Asian countries it has been placed in a defensive position vis-à-vis the indigenous institution of sacral kingship and its ideology; the Buddhist community has either been headed by the king or indirectly put under control of the state. Consequently, it has been constantly exposed to the temptation of soliciting favor from secular authorities. It may be noted, in this connection, that Buddhism developed a theory for peaceful interdependence between its own community and the state: the ideal of the *cakravartin*, a righteous, universal king. Whereas the Buddha was depicted as a universal king in the spiritual domain, who set in motion of wheel of *dharma*, the *cakravartin*, essentially political in nature, was widely expected to appear as a universal king and to turn a wheel of *dharma* in the secular domain. The Buddhist community saw in Aśoka, the third emperor of the great Mauryan kingdom, the realization of the *cakravartin* ideal: he converted to Buddhism, supported its community, sent out missionaries, and governed people in accordance with the *dharma*. To the eyes of the Buddhists, the two wheels of *dharma*, one in the spiritual domain and the other in the secular, should go hand in hand. This theory, a kind of caesaropapism, has exerted enduring influences on Asian countries.

The Christian church in its early centuries had no ambition to stand against the Roman imperial authority. It desired only freedom from persecution. This whole situation was changed by the conversion of Constantine, in the fourth century, and by the subsequent spread of Christianity as the official religion of the Roman Empire. What emerged in the arena of church-state relations was caesaropapism. The Byzantine emperors transformed the church of the Eastern Empire into a state church closely dependent on the imperial government; these emperors claimed the right to control the church and decide any disputes that arose in the ecclesiastical sphere, and the prelates of Constantinople accepted their claims.

In the Western Empire the situation was different. All effective imperial power gradually declined during the early Middle Ages, and this resulted in the emergence of the popes as temporal governors of Rome and its surroundings. Moreover, they abandoned their old allegiance to the Byzantine emperors and formed a new alliance with the Frankish kings. The climax of this Frankish-papal alliance occurred with Leo III's coronation of Charlemagne as emperor of the Romans in 800; thus Leo established the precedent, followed through the Middle Ages, that papal coronation is essential to the making of an emperor, and in so doing he implanted the germ of the idea that empire is a gift to be bestowed by the papacy.

The king's office, however, was conceived to be as sacred as the papacy, a view supported by Old Testament texts; kings were regarded as the Lord's anointed, as ministers of God, and were hailed as vicars of Christ. As such, they aspired to supreme power, both spiritual and temporal. It soon became customary throughout Europe for kings to choose bishops; they gave them great fiefs and invested them with the ring and pastoral staff that symbolized episcopal office. This practice proved beneficial for the kings, but it was a radical departure from the sacred tradition of the church. A measure of this imperial power can be illustrated by an incident that occurred in 1046. When Henry III of Germany arrived in Rome for his imperial coronation, he found there three rival candidates for the papal throne, each claiming to be the rightful pope. Henry settled the issue in high-handed manner: he dismissed all three and installed his own choice. It seemed to Henry that he had as much right to appoint a bishop for Rome as for any other diocese in his territory, and as vicar of God he was also very much aware of his duty to appoint the best man available to such an important office.

The clash between papal theocracy and imperial theocracy became inevitable in 1073 when Hildebrand became Pope Gregory VII and asserted the church's independence from, and indeed its domination over, the imperial power embodied in Henry IV of Germany. Henry could not give up the right of appointing bishops without abandoning all hope of welding Germany into a unified monarchy, and Gregory could not acquiesce in the imperial claims, which included a claim to appoint the popes themselves. The Roman pontiff maintained that as God's vicar he possessed a direct authority—not only spiritual but also political—over all men and all their affairs in the *Corpus Christianum.* He even asserted in the *Dictatus Papae,* issued in 1075, that the pope could depose emperors. Henry then appointed a bishop of Milan and strengthened his position by summoning a council of German bishops, which accused Gregory of gross abuse of papal authority. Gregory replied in 1076 with a decree in which he declared Henry excommunicated and deprived of his imperial authority. Rarely has the history of religions witnessed more direct clashes between religious and secular authorities.

See Also Buddhist Books and Texts, article on Canon and Canonization; Canon; Imamate; Intellectuals; Kingship; Myth; Papacy; Politics and Religion; Scripture; Sunnah; Tradition; Truth.

Bibliography

There are no comprehensive presentations on the theme of authority in the general history of religions based on comparative or typological studies. On the authority of myth in premodern society, see Mircea Eliade's *Myth and Reality* (New York, 1963). This book contains an excellent bibliography. Bronislaw Malinowski has attempted to elucidate the authentic nature and function of myth in primitive society on the basis of his fieldwork among the Trobriand Islanders in New Guinea. See his classic work *Myth in Primitive Psychology* (New York, 1926), which has been reprinted in his *Magic, Science and Religion* (New York, 1948), pp. 93–148.

The best single book on the problem of imperial authority in the ancient Near East remains Henri Frankfort's *Kingship and the Gods: A Study of Ancient Near Eastern Religion as the Integration of Society and Nature* (Chicago, 1948). The eighth International Congress for the History of Religions met in Rome in the spring of 1955 to discuss the theme of kingship. Its proceedings have been published as *The Sacral Kingship* (Leiden, 1959). On imperial authority in ancient China and Japan, see D. Howard Smith's "Divine Kingship in Ancient China," *Numen* 4 (1957): 171–203, and my own "Conceptions of State and Kingship in Early Japan," *Zeitschrift für Religions- und Geistesgeschichte 28* (1976): 97–112. On the structure of authority in the Buddhist community, there is an excellent discussion in Sukumar Dutt's *The Buddha and Five After-Centuries* (London, 1957).

The sources of authority in Islam are succinctly presented in Sir Hamilton A. R. Gibb's *Mohammedanism,* 2d rev. ed. (New York, 1961), which still remains the best introduction to Islam.

The origins and development of the structure of authority in the early Christian church has been masterfully studied by Hans von Campenhausen in *Kirchliches Amt und geistliche Vollmacht* (Tübingen, 1953), translated by J. A. Baker as *Ecclesiastical Authority and Spiritual Power in the Church of the First Three Centuries* (Stanford, Calif., 1969). On scriptural authority in the modern period, there is much useful material in J. K. S. Reid's *The Authority of Scripture: A Study of the Reformation and Post-Reformation Understanding of the Bible* (London, 1957) and in Georges H. Tavard's *Holy Writ or Holy Church: The Crisis of the Protestant Reformation* (London, 1959). Concerning authority in Eastern Orthodoxy, see Georges Florovsky's *Bible, Church, Tradition: An Eastern Orthodox View* (Belmont, Mass., 1972).

On the manifold relations of church and state, a useful comparative and typological study has been presented by Joachim Wach in his *Sociology of Religion* (1944; Chicago, 1962), pp. 287–330. The standard work on the confrontation between papal and secular authorities in the Middle Ages remains Walter Ullmann's *The Growth of Papal Government in the Middle Ages,* 2d ed. (London, 1962). The primary sources relating to the subject have been skillfully assembled by Brian Tierney in *The Crisis of Church and State, 1050–1300* (Englewood Cliffs, N.J., 1964).

New Sources

Abraham, William. "The Offense of Divine Revelation." *Harvard Theological Review* 95 (July 2002): 251–264.

Berkey, Jonathan. *Popular Preaching and Religious Authority in the Medieval Islamic Near East.* Seattle, Wash., 2001.

Engler, Steven. "Religion, Consecration and the State in Bourdieu." *Cultural Studies* 17 (May 2003): 445–468.

Keyes, Charles F., Laurel Kendall, and Helen Hardacre, eds. *Asian Visions of Authority: Religion and the Modern States of East and Southeast Asia.* Honolulu, 1994.

Lincoln, Bruce. *Authority: Construction and Corrosion.* Chicago, 1994.

Siebers, Tobin, ed. *Religion and the Authority of the Past.* Ann Arbor, Mich., 1993.

Stout, Jeffrey. *Democracy and Tradition.* Princeton, 2004.

Wills, Gregory. *Democratic Religion: Freedom, Authority, and Church Discipline in the Baptist South 1785–1900.* New York, 1996.

Manabu Waida (1987)
Revised Bibliography

AUTOBIOGRAPHY.

AUTOBIOGRAPHY. Autobiography is a form of religious literature with an ancient lineage in the Christian, Islamic, and Tibetan Buddhist traditions. It became an increasingly common and significant form of discourse in almost every religious tradition during the twentieth century, and its many forms and recurring themes raise crucial religious issues. This article first discusses Christian and Islamic autobiography, then turns to examples of life writing in Asian and Native American cultures, and finally discusses the religious significance of this literary genre.

The question of how to define autobiography is highly contested. By its most precise and restricted definition, autobiography is, according to Philippe Lejeune's *On Autobiography* (1989), "a retrospective prose narrative that someone writes concerning his own existence, where the focus is the individual life, in particular the story of his personality." Many scholars follow Karl Weintraub in seeing "true" autobiography as tied to the development of the ideas of individuality and historicity, and therefore as an essentially Western form of discourse. Yet there is a great deal of writing that intentionally reveals the author's character in different ways than classical Western autobiography, and these representations of the author's self will be considered here as forms of religious autobiography. In the West, many examples of life writing do not fit all aspects of the traditional definition, such as memoirs of only a portion of a person's life, accounts in poetry, and diaries and journals that reflect day-by-day introspection rather than a retrospective view of an entire life. Many non-Western texts disclose the author's religious experiences, although they are usually less concerned with distinguishing the author's uniqueness or singularity than they are with exemplifying a collective sense of identity, a community's values, or the common human condition. One must be flexible in recognizing the diverse forms of writing about the self in the world's religious traditions and discern both similarities and differences in relation to the classical Western tradition of autobiography. What makes an autobiography religious is the author's attempt to describe and evaluate his or her life from the perspective of the author's present convictions about what is ultimate or sacred.

CLASSIC CHRISTIAN AUTOBIOGRAPHIES. Augustine's *Confessions,* written between 397 and 401, is the fountainhead of Christian autobiography. Augustine (354–430) showed later writers how to interpret the self in relation to the models and norms of Christian tradition, including biblical figures such as Adam, Moses, Jesus, and Paul. Augustine's self-disclosure is indebted to two biblical genres: the Hebrew psalms and Pauline letters. Confession for Augustine denotes both acknowledgment of sin and confession of praise to God. The entire book is directly addressed to God, as Augustine speaks in the second person to the source of all being and the One who knows him better than he knows himself. The most famous sentence in the *Confessions* is essentially a plot summary: "Our hearts are restless until they rest in You." Augustine attempts repeatedly to place his faith in something other than God: his career as a teacher, the Manichee religion, the love of a woman, or his dear friends. Finally, after these idols have failed to satisfy his yearning, and after protracted intellectual struggle, he commits himself to God and attains the serenity that he asserts can come only from a correct understanding and wholehearted trust in God. As a conversion narrative, the *Confessions* became a model for both long-drawn-out religious change and a sudden crisis such as Augustine dramatizes in Book 8. It can be argued that the very nature of autobiography is tied to the structure of the conversion narrative as the story of how the story's protagonist became the narrator of the story, the person whose present understanding provides the norms by which past actions are judged. Yet one must be wary about imposing this paradigm on all texts, especially ones from religious traditions other than Christianity.

Many of the central themes of Christian autobiography are rooted in Augustine's *Confessions.* A searching, self-critical conscience shapes the introspective, moralizing tenor of many later Christian works. Augustine's account of memory and time in Books 10–13 analyzes the deeply problematic nature of self-knowledge and his continuing dependence on God in the act of composition. Augustine showed the interdependence of the writer's life story with central philosophical and theological questions about the nature of truth, agency, textuality, faith, and ultimacy. The theme of providence is a crucial aspect of Augustine's legacy, for he demonstrated how a faithful Christian may discern God's guidance of his life through trials, sin, and suffering.

Among the most important autobiographical works in Christian tradition are the writings of medieval mystics including Teresa of Ávila, Julian of Norwich, Ignatius of Loyola, and Margery Kempe. These works are characterized by an intense focus on the life of prayer and vision to the relative neglect of details of ordinary social life. Abelard (1079–1142) wrote *The History of My Misfortunes* to try to understand his adversities, defend himself against false accusations, and model Christian virtues. In contrast to Augustine's self-accusation, Abelard's work is largely an apology, a defense of his character. Petrarch (1304–1374) composed three imaginary dialogues with Augustine entitled the *Secretum,* examining his own life's pursuits in the light of Christian norms in preparation for death. The essays of Michel de Montaigne (1533–1592) offer a thematic rather than chronological account of the writer and a constantly changing self-awareness rather than a stable and permanent sense of identity. Montaigne is skeptical of religious certainties and understands himself in the light of classical texts rather than the Bible. There is a crucial ethical dimension in Montaigne's criticisms of arrogance and presumptuousness in all areas of life, including matters of religious controversy. He shows how religious and political theories usually neglect the physical realities of human existence, pointing out that even "on the loftiest throne in the world we are still sitting on our own rump."

In the seventeenth and eighteenth centuries, Protestants wrote prolifically in many genres: diaries, captivity narratives, community histories, and conversion accounts. John Bunyan (1628–1688) was the most influential Protestant autobiographer. *Grace Abounding to the Chief of Sinners* (1666) was written while Bunyan was imprisoned for preaching to the Baptist community of Bedford, England. Bunyan never goes through a decisive conversion culminating in final serenity, but instead undergoes a protracted pattern of doubting his salvation, searching the Bible for clues, and being reassured that he is indeed one of the elect. Then the cycle begins again. Bunyan's narrative shows the anxieties that shaped Puritan religious experience, an interest in the mundane details of an ordinary Christian's life, and a relentless Protestant focus on the Bible as the key to interpreting every experience. Later Protestants, including Thomas Shepard, Cotton Mather, Mary Rowlandson, Elizabeth Ashbridge, George Fox, Jonathan Edwards, and John Woolman also sought to discern God's will or providential design for their lives, and they took biblical figures as models or metaphors for their experience. A period of wandering in the wilderness, an episode of being a prodigal son, or entrance into a promised land became the lens for interpreting incidents in their lives. These works are highly introspective, scrupulously probing thoughts and behavior for hints of sin. Puritans and Quakers used their own stories didactically to instruct others about their central convictions and to model the expected pattern of a believer's life.

CHRISTIAN VALUES IN MODERN WESTERN AUTOBIOGRAPHIES. Christian values and beliefs continue to influence many autobiographers with secular concerns. Benjamin Franklin (1706–1790) describes his "scheme of perfection" based on a theory of the virtues and his multifarious endeavors to improve Philadelphia, largely discarding theological convictions. Franklin was a Deist with little interest in doctrine or denominational loyalties. His autobiography shows how Christian moral values could be expressed in practical activity and a narrative of character building, as well as utilitarian and pragmatic modes of thinking that were hostile to an otherworldly orientation.

In *The Confessions* of Jean-Jacques Rousseau (1712–1778), Christian metaphors shape the thought of a man who has moved far from Augustine's self-accusation and dependence on God's mercy. Rousseau imagines a scene at the Last Judgment when he will present his autobiography to God and receive approval for his truthfulness. It is not God, however, but his readers and his own guilty conscience that Rousseau tries to persuade of his essential goodness. His moral standard is not virtuous behavior but sincerity, utter truthfulness about himself: "I have displayed myself as I was, as vile and despicable when my behavior was such, as good, generous, and noble when I was so." Rousseau defiantly challenges any reader to reveal his heart with equal candor and then say, "I was a better man than he." When he describes a number of rather distasteful deeds, Rousseau asserts that it was always an embarrassing social situation that forced him to act against his benevolent inclinations. Human nature is essentially good, he argues, and the errors people make are not attributable to selfishness or sin but to the inhospitable and false environment of modern society, which creates a struggle for status that corrupts the innocent child of nature. Although there are many prior examples of life writing with a focus on nonreligious matters, Rousseau marks the beginning of secular autobiography haunted by spiritual anxieties. The social struggles of the self displace the religious journey of a soul, and it is not movement toward God's salvation but the author's achievements and encounters in society that decisively shape the plot of his story. There is a crucial religious dimension in Rousseau's struggle to understand the meaning of his life in terms of a secular response to the problem of evil. He believes that his explanation of why he is persecuted illumines the fundamental nature of the human condition. If Rousseau abandons the substance of Christian faith, he retains its metaphors and imagery and the yearning for an ultimate judgment and justification of his character. This desire is continually frustrated, and *The Confessions* dramatically displays the increasing paranoia and self-deception that marked Rousseau's final years.

In the nineteenth century many "versions of deconversion," as John D. Barbour puts it in his 1994 work of that title, describe the loss of faith. This experience is often the result of profound religious doubt and moral reflection and is described in terms of Christian motifs such as a central event of crisis, analysis of the subjective experience of faith, and a transition to a new community with a new language for describing oneself and the world. Such writers as Thomas Carlyle, John Ruskin, Leo Tolstoy, and Edmund Gosse wrote powerful accounts of the reasons for which they abandoned a particular form of Christianity and sought meaning elsewhere, as in aesthetic experience. At the turn of the twenty-first century, the theme of deconversion continues to be important in autobiography as writers explore religious doubts, assess the practices of religious communities, and struggle to reconcile belief in historic Christian doctrines with other intellectual and moral convictions, for instance, about scientific theory or the rights of women.

Among the most compelling modern autobiographies by Roman Catholics are John Henry Newman's *Apologia pro Vita Sua* (1864); Dorothy Day's *The Long Loneliness* (1952); and the many letters, journals, and essays by Thomas Merton (1915–1968). Influential Protestant works include medical missionary Albert Schweitzer's *Out of My Life and Thought* (1933); C. S. Lewis's conversion narrative, *Surprised by Joy* (1955); and Dietrich Bonhoeffer's *Letters and Papers from Prison* (1951), a posthumously published collection by a German theologian imprisoned and executed by the Nazis. Conversion narratives continue to be a popular genre, and in recent decades they are often linked to the theme of recovery from various forms of addiction or abuse. Christian women and persons of color address the reasons that they remain committed to a tradition that has frequently been misogynistic and racist. They criticize oppressive aspects of Christian thought and practice and retrieve minority perspectives that may offer a helpful corrective in the ongoing struggle for justice within Christian tradition and in the larger society.

ISLAMIC AUTOBIOGRAPHY. Autobiographical writing in Islamic culture began in the ninth century and is influenced by even older traditions of biography such as the *sīra* (exemplary life story) and *tarjama* (biographical notice included in a larger work). Islamic works of hagiography are especially concerned with the chain of transmission of authority back to the Prophet. Some of the earliest autobiographies composed in Arabic are essentially self-authored examples of these biographical genres. Because Islamic historians valued eyewitness accounts so highly, autobiography was usually seen as a reliable and significant source of knowledge for posterity. In *Interpreting the Self* (2001), Dwight Reynolds identifies over one hundred Arabic autobiographical texts written between the ninth and nineteenth centuries CE and translates thirteen representative works into English.

Often a particular verse from the Qurʾān provided religious justification for self-representation: "And of the blessings of thy Lord, speak!" (93:11). Telling one's story was an act of thanksgiving, gratitude, and praise for the generosity of Allah. Writers often referred to the example of respected figures of the past or traced the spiritual lineage of the author's teaching. Most Islamic autobiographies are highly didactic, and the purpose of moral instruction legitimates depicting the self. Muslim writers often present themselves explicitly as models for the reader's emulation.

As in other traditions, an emphasis on a particular religious theme is often associated with a distinctive category or genre of autobiographical writing. Conversion narratives recount how a Christian or Jew became a Muslim or how a relatively indifferent Muslim was moved to greater piety, ascetic practice, or the Ṣūfī path. Narratives of pilgrimage recount the life-transforming effects of the journey to Mecca. Ṣūfī texts explore mystical states and the ascent through spiritual stations. The Mughal Empire in India yielded numerous autobiographical texts such as the sixteenth-century *Bāburnāmah,* or *Book of Bābur,* written by the founder of that empire.

The most famous classical Arabic autobiography is *al-Munquidh min al-dalāl,* by al-Ghazālī (1058–1111 CE [450-505 AH]). This work recounts a spiritual crisis that has intrigued Western readers and is often compared to Augustine's *Confessions.* Literally translated as "What delivers from error," this work is rendered in a 1992 English translation as *The Confessions of al-Ghazālī.* When al-Ghazālī experienced a total breakdown that left him unable to speak, he undertook a ten-year period of wandering and seclusion. He found serenity in the Ṣūfī emphasis on the heart and intuitive knowledge rather than intellectual argument. Al-Ghazālī correlates his account of his spiritual search with polemical arguments against other Islamic theologians and philosophers.

In the nineteenth and twentieth centuries, Muslim autobiographers were influenced by traditional forms and themes and were also shaped by Western literature, especially the novel. After the Egyptian scholar Tāhā Ḥusayn's *al-Ayyām* (1929; *An Egyptian Childhood* [1932]), it was possible to explore in an author's life the uneasy encounters between Islamic culture and the modern secular world. In the twentieth century, autobiographies such as Muhammad Asad's *The Road to Mecca* (1954) and *The Autobiography of Malcolm X* (1965) were composed in English and European languages by converts to Islam.

HINDUISM. There is virtually no autobiography in Hindu tradition until the twentieth century. Various explanations have been offered for the relative lack of interest in self-representation: the Indian love of philosophy and general absence of historical writing; the cyclical view of time; and the deemphasis on the individual in the search for universal truth. Whatever the explanation, there are few examples of first-person life narratives in classical Hindu tradition, although there are rich personal references and expressions in the writings of *sant*-poets such as Kabir (fifteenth century) and Tukaram (seventeenth century).

Western literary influences and an intended Western audience shape the first modern Hindu autobiographies. Swami Vivekananda (1863–1902), the heir of the mystic Sri Ramakrishna, attained renown at the first World Parliament of Religions in Chicago in 1893. His letters, while not a complete narrative of his life, reveal his distinctive personality to his disciples in the Ramakrishna Mission and to potential supporters both Indian and Western. *Autobiography of a Yogi* (1946), by Paramahansa Yogananda, has been published in many editions and languages. Yogananda (1893–1952) was a Bengali who came to the United States in 1920 and spent many years teaching yoga, lecturing, and promoting his Self-Realization Fellowship. His autobiography focuses on encounters with saints, *gurus,* and yogis who taught and inspired him.

The outstanding example of autobiography by a Hindu is Mohandas Gandhi's *The Story of My Experiments with Truth* (1927). This work was originally written in Gujarati and published in 1925 in weekly installments in a nationalist journal. It was soon translated into English and many other languages and played an important role in the political movement for Indian independence. In the introduction, Gandhi discusses his ambivalent relationship to the Western idea of autobiography. He quotes a friend's doubts about doing this kind of writing:

> "Writing an autobiography is a practice peculiar to the West. I know of nobody in the East having written one, except amongst those who have come under Western influence. And what will you write? Supposing you reject tomorrow the things you hold as principles today, or supposing you revise in the future your plans of today, is it not likely that the men who shape their conduct on the authority of your word, spoken or written, may be misled?"

Gandhi responds that it is not his purpose to write "a real autobiography." Rather, "I simply want to tell the story of my experiments with truth, and as my life consists of nothing but these experiments, it is true that the story will take the shape of an autobiography." His narrative recounts the story of a soul's striving for *satya* (truth), which was Gandhi's "sovereign principle," equated with God. Gandhi orients his life story to the truth as he understands it, yet he also presents his life as an experiment open to revision and further clarification. The writing of a spiritual text that has "the shape of an autobiography" requires the practice of the virtues of truthfulness, humility, courage, and discerning moral judgment. Finally, however, it is a work about *satyagraha* (the force of truth), not personal virtue: "My purpose is to describe experiments in the science of Satyagraha, not to say how good I am."

Autobiographers from Hindu tradition have often used this form of discourse as part of their effort to proselytize in the West. In addition, *dalit* literature by members of "untouchable" castes and conversion stories to other religious traditions voice criticisms of traditional Hindu social structure and raise important questions about what beliefs and practices are central to Hinduism and what may be changed. Autobiography thus plays a powerful role in contemporary ethical critique and reflection on the nature of Hindu identity and society and their controversial relationship to the nation of India.

BUDDHISM. With one significant exception, Buddhist cultures did not produce autobiographical literature until the twentieth century. The reason for this absence has been explained in various ways: the concept of the self is viewed by Buddhists as an illusion; calling attention to oneself is seen as egotistical; and the ideal of sudden enlightenment precludes interest in what leads up to the moment of awakening. These simplistic explanations do not probe deeply enough into the cultural contexts that inhibited Buddhist life writing in India and China and fostered it in Tibet.

Janet Gyatso's *Apparitions of the Self* (1998) examines the Tibetan genre of "secret autobiography" (*rangnam*) as composed by such visionary lamas as Jigme Lingpa (1730–1798). This literary tradition focuses on the way a spiritual master attained liberation through visions, yogic practices, and memories of past lives. Such texts do not record all the factual details that the genre of "outer" autobiography would narrate. Like spiritual autobiography in Puritan and Catholic traditions, *rangnam* deals with what is interior and most important: the ways in which the subject understands ultimate reality as a result of personal experience. In Tibet, visionaries discovered so-called Treasures revealed in previous lives that they retrieve and transmit to disciples. The autobiographical dimension of these texts consists in the visionary's demonstration of his awesome powers, profound meditative experiences, and unique insights into the elusive nature of subjectivity. *Rangnam* legitimized a lama's authority, inspired confidence in disciples, and distinguished among competing interpretations of Buddhist thought.

According to Gyatso, Buddhism nurtured autobiography in Tibet because of particular historical factors that were not present in India or China. Tibet's tradition of self-written life stories dates to the eleventh century. Unlike India and China, where Buddhism never supplanted ancient traditions, Tibet became predominantly Buddhist. Salvation was always a matter of individual self-transformation and was not linked to membership in a clan or group. In this context religious power and prestige were based on individual accomplishments such as celibacy and asceticism, remembering prior lives, and esoteric yogic practices and visions. Biography and autobiography flourished in the competition between charismatic teachers vying for disciples and patronage. Tibetan Buddhist autobiography made possible self-assertion and cultivation of the individual characteristics of a religious leader, even as these texts show the unstable, elusive quality of the states of mind that human beings typically identify with selfhood. The paradox of representing a self that allegedly does not exist challenges modern Western Buddhists to devise new literary strategies to depict their path to awakening. Since everything is constantly changing and the origin of suffering is the desire to cling to what is unstable, Buddhist autobiography, like postmodernist thought in the West, must depend on the idea of the self even as it shows the self to be a projection, illusion, or fiction.

CHINA AND JAPAN. Ancient Chinese autobiographies were modeled after biography and focused on public historical facts rather than intimate self-knowledge. In the Confucian and Daoist traditions the emphasis on self-effacement and modesty discouraged revealing accounts of religious experience. Chan Buddhist narratives are circumspect in their portrayal of enlightenment. The doctrine of sudden enlightenment without long years of practice may have been a factor, as was the lack of a literary tradition providing a model for the personal search for wisdom.

According to Pei-Yi Wu in *The Confucian's Progress* (1990), there was a significant group of Confucian autobiographers during the late Ming period, the sixteenth and early seventeenth centuries. Models for life writing were found in travel literature and in accounts by Buddhist disciples of their masters' sermons, which sometimes described incidents in their lives. Writers such as the Confucian apostate and Buddhist monk Deng Huoqu (1498–c. 1570) and the neo-Confucian Gao Panlong (1562–1626) described quests for self-transformation using metaphors of journey and ascent. In addition, a group of penitential texts written at about the same time confess misdeeds, express self-reproach and remorse, beg forgiveness from a deity, or promise a reformed life.

This flowering of introspective life writing ended with the imposition of Manchu rule in 1644, which brought disapproval and official censorship of the bold literary experimentation associated with the late Ming period. Thereafter, autobiographies took the form of annals charting the stages of an official career until, in the twentieth century, Western practices influenced new kinds of life writing. The author's girlhood struggle to understand the relevance of Chinese myths and "talk-stories" to life in the United States is powerfully conveyed in Maxine Hong Kingston's *The Woman Warrior* (1976).

Japanese life writing dates to the Heian period (794–1185), when diaries were written in Chinese, such as the monk Ennin's account of his travels to China. The native *kana* script, often deemed suitable for women, was used to render emotional life and spiritual musings. Japan has a rich tradition of personal, introspective writing that presents the author's perceptions of the transience of the natural world and human life. What modern scholars call "recluse literature" or "grass-hut literature" (*sōan bungaku*) records a rural writer's contemplations of the vicissitudes of life and the emptiness at the heart of all existence. The most famous is *Hōjōki* (An account of my hut) by Kamo no Chōmei (1156?–1216). Another genre is the official diaries kept by the holders of established positions, including leaders of monastic institutions. Since the Tokugawa period (1600–1868), neo-Confucian values have shaped autobiographies written by the heads of families for their descendents, which describe the duties expected of future generations.

Chinese models influence Japanese accounts of travel to sacred places and to sites made famous in literature. These works take the author's journey through space as a metaphor for human existence and construct the self in relation to literary precedent. The poet Bashō (1644–1694) wrote five travel narratives, the most famous of which has been translated as *The Narrow Road to the Deep North* (1966). Bashō combined haiku and prose narration in describing his physical and spiritual journey through Japan. Bashō studied with a Zen Buddhist priest and was also influenced by neo-Confucianism and the *kami* (Shintō) cults.

Native American Autobiography. As a written text, autobiography is not found in oral cultures such as those of Native American tribes. Yet oral traditions of life narration have influenced the written narratives that American Indians began to produce in great number in the nineteenth century. In *American Indian Autobiography* (1988), H. David Brumble identifies "preliterate traditions" including coup tales, self-examinations to account for misfortune, educational narratives, and stories about the acquisition of healing or visionary powers. The survival and vitality of oral traditions is an important theme in other tribal cultures such as those of Australian aboriginal people. The preservation of threatened cultural knowledge is a significant incentive for life writing in many indigenous cultures and also in displaced or refugee communities such as the Hmong of Laos and other diaspora peoples.

There are more than seven hundred Native American autobiographical narratives. More than half of these documents are "as-told-to" stories edited by white missionaries, anthropologists, and literary scholars. Many of these collaborative works raise controversial questions about the extent of the white editor's contribution. The most famous American Indian autobiography is *Black Elk Speaks* (1932). This narrative tells the story of the life of Black Elk (1863–1950), the Oglala Sioux holy man, from the age of nine until he witnesses the Wounded Knee massacre in 1890. It recounts Black Elk's spiritual visions, important Lakota rituals and healing practices, and the Ghost Dance movement. In a 1979 introduction to this work, Vine Deloria Jr. asserts that *Black Elk Speaks* "has become a North American bible of all tribes." Yet this text reflects the perspective of "editor" John G. Neihardt as much as Black Elk's. It ends with a portrayal of Black Elk as a despairing and defeated man lamenting his failure to make the Lakota spiritual vision relevant to his people at a time of crisis. The narrative does not reveal that Black Elk converted to Roman Catholicism in 1904 and acted for decades as a catechist and missionary on Indian reservations, or that Black Elk continued to believe in the value and relevance of the Lakota worldview. (See Raymond De Mallie's analysis in *The Sixth Grandfather* [1984] of the transcripts of the collaboration between Black Elk and Neihardt.) A very different form of as-told-to autobiography is created when the white editor is an anthropologist. For instance, Paul Radin's *The Autobiography of a Winnebago Indian* (1920) recounts the life of S. B., a convert to the Peyote religion of the Native American Church, and Nancy Oestreich Lurie's *Mountain Wolf Woman* (1961) tells the story of S. B.'s sister, who also had religious experiences with peyote.

In addition to these white-edited "Indian autobiographies" there are "autobiographies by Indians" (Arnold Krupat's distinction) produced by literate Native Americans. The first ones were by Christians, such as *Son of the Forest* (1829) by William Apess (Pequot). Important works of life writing were produced by George Copway (Ojibway) in 1847, Sarah Winnemucca Hopkins (Paiute) in 1883, Charles Eastman (Lakota) in 1902, and Luther Standing Bear (Lakota) in 1928. Subsequently, Native American novelists and poets have created highly complex personal narratives, such as *The Way to Rainy Mountain* (1969), by N. Scott Momaday (Kiowa and Cherokee); *Storyteller* (1981), by Leslie Marmon Silko (Kowa and Cherokee); and the poetry and memoirs of Linda Hogan (Chickasaw) and Joy Harjo (Creek). The dominant religious themes in these works are sacred geography and the importance of a sense of place in human identity; a cyclical view of time as necessary for human well-being; respect for the wisdom of elders and oral traditions; and the importance of reciprocity and harmony with the natural world, in human society, and with the sacred. Like the members of other threatened indigenous cultures (in this regard, too, Australian aboriginal peoples offer significant parallels), many American Indian writers use autobiography to explore the conflict of cultural values within their own lives and to protest against the racism, injustice, and spiritual poverty that they see in the dominant culture.

Spiritual Autobiography. In addition to defining religious autobiography in relationship to specific historical traditions, one can consider certain more ambiguous texts, sometimes called spiritual autobiographies. Particularly in the West, spirituality usually means the personal, experiential aspects of religion in contrast with an organized community's doctrines, institutions, and rituals. Spiritual autobiographies are shaped by particular religious traditions, but the author is usually dissatisfied or looking beyond institutionalized forms of worship and belief. For instance, a genre of spiritual autobiography is American nature writing by such authors as Henry David Thoreau, John Muir, Annie Dillard, Edward Abbey, and Terry Tempest Williams. Another form of spiritual autobiography is writing by contemporary women who attempt to reconcile their apprehension of what is holy with patriarchal religious institutions, and to discriminate within their formative tradition that which is a source of oppression and that which is a liberating resource for women. Spiritual autobiographies are usually ambivalent about the author's original religious tradition, sorting out those elements that the author rejects and those that personal experience helps them to appreciate. Such writers seek an individual path, a personal approach to what is holy, although they also hope to find community.

Contemporary spiritual autobiographers often criticize traditional dualistic contrasts between the sacred and the profane and try to reclaim areas of life rejected by many religious believers as this-worldly. They usually do not seek salvation from ordinary human existence but rather beauty, meaning, and love within it. Spiritual autobiographers are primarily concerned to interpret personal experiences; far less than their predecessors do they advocate particular beliefs, doctrines, or institutional affiliations to their readers. In contrast to most classic religious texts, these writers do not propose to readers a single normative model of belief or affiliation. They demonstrate far greater openness to a variety of legitimate religious options than one would find in most worshiping communities or in the history of religious autobiography. Spiritual autobiographers tend to be open-minded in this pluralistic sense, and their works are open-ended, leaving the impression that the author's search is not completed, but a journey still in progress. Seeking has become more important than finding, and an author may discover meaning even in the process of deconversion, or loss of faith. Scholars disagree about what kinds of writing should be considered as spiritual autobiographies. Does it make sense to see a work as spiritual when the search for self replaces the desire to know God, and when the goal of defining a unique personal identity becomes more important than otherworldly salvation, adherence to orthodox beliefs, or commitment to a community? Is a book a spiritual autobiography if its author is more concerned with literary originality than with fidelity to a received religious tradition? Readers will differ as to whether and how to interpret as spiritual autobiography such diverse texts as Peter Matthiessen's *The Snow Leopard* (1978), Paul Auster's *The Invention of Solitude* (1982), Patricia Hampl's *Virgin Time* (1992), Kathleen Norris's *Dakota* (1993), and Nancy Mairs's *Ordinary Time* (1993).

AUTOBIOGRAPHY AS A RELIGIOUS ACT. Even in religious traditions without a strong legacy of autobiography, first-person life writing became increasingly common and significant during the twentieth century. An example is Judaism, which does not have an ancient tradition of autobiography yet in the twentieth century produced many examples of Holocaust memoirs, accounts of struggles in Israel, and narratives about assimilation into American society. Autobiography seems likely to become even more widely practiced if we expand our definition to include self-representations that use technologies such as tape-recorded oral narratives, personal websites, confessional radio and television programs, and video and digital formats. The reasons for this proliferation of life narratives are many, complex, and religiously significant.

One reason for the prevalence of autobiography is anxiety about personal identity as individuals encounter the possibility of a secular orientation, the loosening of communal loyalties, and the challenge of other faiths and worldviews in an increasingly mobile and interdependent global culture. Autobiographers try to reconcile the ways that personal identity is shaped by membership in communities, including those fostered by religious commitments, and the ways in which identity is singular, distinctive, or unique. Without resolving the complex issue of whether autobiography is tied to the Western concept of the self, one can recognize that all life writing reveals an interplay between communal norms for life stories and individual differentiation. In religious autobiographies the authors believe that both of these pressures—adherence to communal norms and individual searching—bring them closer to what is ultimate. The religious autobiographer finds meaning not only in allegiance to tradition, but in an act of personal interpretation and self-evaluation. Relationship to a religious community takes the form of reinterpretation of one's life story in dialogue, although not necessarily in strict accordance with, a community's norms. The autobiographer discerns in new ways how a religious tradition's symbolic resources and mythic narratives may illumine personal experience, as well as ways that the tradition fails to help in the task of self-understanding or needs to be criticized in terms of other values.

Thus, writing an autobiography is itself a significant religious event and experience in the writer's life. The writing of autobiography raises crucial ethical issues, including the author's struggle with conscience as part of moral self-assessment (see John D. Barbour, *The Conscience of the Autobiographer* [1992]) and the effect of telling one's story on other persons (see Paul John Eakin, ed., *The Ethics of Life Writing* [2004]). Religious autobiography is best conceived of as a testing of the adequacy of a religious community's norms for a life narrative, when not only the communal norms but the testing itself—that is, the writing of one's life story—is believed to be called for by God or that which the author believes to be worthy of ultimate loyalty and trust. Religious autobiography attempts to interpret the life of the writer and reorient the lives of readers in relation to what is ultimate.

BIBLIOGRAPHY

Barbour, John D. *The Conscience of the Autobiographer: Ethical and Religious Dimensions of Autobiography.* London and New York, 1992.

Barbour, John D. *Versions of Deconversion: Autobiography and the Loss of Faith.* Charlottesville, Va., 1994.

Barbour, John D. *The Value of Solitude: The Ethics and Spirituality of Aloneness in Autobiography.* Charlottesville, Va., 2004.

Brumble, David. *American Indian Autobiography.* Berkeley, Calif., 1988.

Caldwell, Patricia. *The Puritan Conversion Narrative: The Beginnings of American Expression.* Cambridge, U.K., 1983.

Delaney, Paul. *British Autobiography in the Seventeenth Century.* New York, 1969.

De Mallie, Raymond J., ed. *The Sixth Grandfather: Black Elk's Teachings Given to John G. Neihardt.* Lincoln, Neb., 1984.

Eakin, Paul John, ed. *The Ethics of Life Writing.* Ithaca, N.Y., 2004.

Fleishman, Avrom. *Figures of Autobiography: The Language of Self-Writing in Victorian and Modern England.* Berkeley, Calif., 1983.

Gyatso, Janet. *Apparitions of the Self: The Secret Autobiographies of a Tibetan Visionary.* Princeton, N.J., 1998.

Jolly, Margetta, ed. *Encyclopedia of Life Writing.* 2 vols. Chicago and London, 2001. This outstanding two-volume encyclopedia contains articles on specific authors, genres of autobiographical writing, particular religious traditions, and themes including conversion, confession, repentance, and spiritual autobiography.

Krupat, Arnold. *For Those Who Come After: A Study of Native American Autobiography.* Madison, Wis., 1985.

Lejeune, Philippe. *On Autobiography.* Edited by Paul John Eakin. Translated by Katherine Leary. Minneapolis, 1989.

Olney, James. *Metaphors of Self: The Meaning of Autobiography.* Princeton, N.J., 1972.

Peterson, Linda. *Victorian Autobiography: The Tradition of Self-Interpretation.* New Haven, Conn., 1986.

Reynolds, Dwight. *Interpreting the Self: Autobiography and the Arabic Literary Tradition.* Berkeley, Calif., 2001.

Shea, Daniel. *Spiritual Autobiography in Early America.* Princeton, N.J., 1968.

Smith, Sidonie, and Julia Watson. *Reading Autobiography: A Guide for Interpreting Life Narratives.* Minneapolis, 2001.

Watkins, Owen. *The Puritan Experience: Studies in Spiritual Autobiography.* New York, 1972.

Weintraub, Karl. *The Value of the Individual: Self and Circumstance in Autobiography.* Chicago, 1978.

Wong, Hertha Dawn. *Sending My Heart Back across the Years: Tradition and Innovation in Native American Autobiography.* New York, 1992.

Wu, Pei-Yu. *The Confucian's Progress: Autobiographical Writing in Traditional China.* Princeton, N.J., 1990.

JOHN D. BARBOUR (2005)

AVALOKITEŚVARA

AVALOKITEŚVARA, a *bodhisattva* especially associated with the principle of compassion, is the most popular figure in the pan-Asian Mahāyāna Buddhist pantheon. Worshiped and invoked in both male and female forms, Avalokiteśvara is considered a potent savior in times of life-threatening dangers, who watches over all beings and heeds their cries of suffering and distress. He responds directly to the pleas of those in great need, while also serving in symbolic manner as the embodiment of the principle of compassion, a fundamental aspect of the Buddhist way of life. In addition to his numerous pan-Asian roles, Avalokiteśvara has played a significant role in distinctive local traditions throughout Buddhist Asia.

The meaning of this *bodhisattva*'s name traditionally has been understood in several ways, emphasizing his sovereignty over the material world and his responsiveness to the calls of suffering humanity. A principal interpretation holds that the name Avalokiteśvara is a compound of Sanskrit *avalokita* and *īśvara,* translated variously as "the lord of what is seen, the lord who is seen" or "the lord who surveys, gazing lord." The celebrated seventh-century Chinese monk-scholar Xianzang upheld this view, translating the *bodhisattva*'s name as Guanzizai ("gazing lord").

An alternate spelling of this name—Avalokitasvara—also existed, as seen in some fifth-century Sanskrit manuscripts and as noted by learned Chinese exegetes such as Chengguan (eighth century). This led to the well-known Chinese translation Guanyin ("he who has perceived sound"). The frequently seen Chinese translation Guanshiyin ("he who perceives the sounds of the world") appears to have a dubious etymological basis, but expresses well the functional quality of the *bodhisattva:* a savior who hears all cries of suffering and responds with potent aid.

Avalokiteśvara has numerous epithets. The most common are Padmapāṇi ("lotus bearer") and Lokeśvara ("lord of the world"), by which he is best known in Southeast Asia. Many epithets related to his specific saving functions are connected to a dizzying panoply of iconographic forms.

ORIGINS. It generally is agreed that the cult to Avalokiteśvara arose in the northwestern borderlands of India. Much scholarly energy has been devoted to determining the "origins" of the *bodhisattva.* Many of these efforts presuppose a diffusionist model for the formation of the Mahāyāna pantheon; they assume that the pantheon was in some way devised or adapted from the various deities of neighboring religious movements. For example, Marie-Thérèse de Mallmann (1948) suggested Iranian antecedents based on Avalokiteśvara's name and functions. Others hold that the pantheon came into being as the deification of early Buddhist principles or of potent moments in the life of Śākyamuni Buddha; for example, Giuseppe Tucci (1948) suggested that Avalokiteśvara is the personification of the compassionate gaze of Śākyamuni. Such views are far distant from the notable intensity of belief in the compassionate lifesaving powers of this deity, as expressed among Buddhist Asians from all levels of society. Mahāyāna scriptural traditions simply hold that Avalokiteśvara is one among many beings having human history whose dedication and spiritual development has led to successful fruition as a bodhisattva.

Principal Scriptural Sources. Among the numerous scriptural sources on Avalokiteśvara, three works are especially important: the *Saddharmapuṇḍarīka Sūtra* (Lotus scripture), various versions of the *Sukhāvatīvyūha Sūtra* (Pure land scripture), and the so-called *Amitāyurdhyāna Sūtra* (Contemplation on Amitāyus scripture). The *Lotus* provides much information on the *bodhisattva*'s lifesaving powers, while the *Pure Land* and the meditation scripture reveal his spiritual kinship to Amitābha Buddha and outline his functions in this context. These aspects both have been essential features of the cult.

The *Lotus* devotes a full chapter to Avalokiteśvara, and this chapter (chapter 25 in Kumārajīva's eloquent fourth-century Chinese translation) not uncommonly has been memorized, recited, and treated as an independent scripture by East Asian devotees. The chapter includes discussion of the *bodhisattva*'s name, the dangers that he can dispel, and the myriad forms in which he may appear to aid devotees.

The *bodhisattva*'s name in this well-known version of the *Lotus* clearly is Avalokitasvara, translated by Kumārajīva as Guanshiyin, or "hearer of the sounds of the world." Śākyamuni Buddha explains in the scripture that this name arises from the *bodhisattva*'s pledge to heed the call of any suffering being who cries out his name and to appear before him in rescue.

The list of dangers and difficulties that the *bodhisattva* can counter is impressive: fire, drowning in a river, being lost at sea, murder, demonic attack, fierce beasts and noxious snakes or insects, legal punishment, attack by bandits, falling from steep precipices, extremes of weather, internecine civil or military unrest, and others. The *bodhisattva* also assists those ensnared by the traditional three poisons of Buddhism: lust, anger, and delusion. Avalokiteśvara also grants children—both male and female—in response to the pleas of barren women. According to the *Lotus,* Avalokiteśvara is a master of skillful means (*upāya*) who is adept at manifesting himself in any suitable form (thirty-three are listed) to convey the deliverance of any being.

The *Pure Land* scriptures, of which several versions are extant in Chinese translation, pair Avalokiteśvara with a *bodhisattva* named Mahāsthāmaprāpta. Both are principal assistants to the Buddha Amitābha, lord of the Western Paradise, a glorious realm free of suffering where diligent questers for enlightenment may be reborn after earthly existence. Among his various functions, Avalokiteśvara guides devotees from earthly deathbed to rebirth in the spirit land. He acts as emissary for the Buddha throughout the various realms of the universe, and he is described as the eventual heir to the throne of this realm. (The *Karuṇāpuṇḍarīka Sūtra,* translated into Chinese in the early fifth century, extends this relationship by explaining that Avalokiteśvara was the first son of Amitābha in an earlier incarnation.)

The meditation scripture provides an extended description of Avalokiteśvara as the focus for one of the stages of a multifaceted visualization practice. Successful accomplishment of this practice leads not only to future rebirth in the Western Paradise, but also to continuous invocation of the principal lords of that land, with the accompanying protection and inspiration they afford. Avalokiteśvara is described as a golden-skinned princely being of enormous stature, wearing a great crown made of wondrous gems within each of which there stands a manifested Buddha. Many-hued rays of light stream forth from his body in a patterned manner; these rays reach into the various realms of existence and send forth manifested Buddhas and *bodhisattvas,* who accomplish his works of compassion. Innumerable rays of soft light extend from his hands, illumining all things, and he is seen to be assisting all beings with these hands.

Paradise. Avalokiteśvara is believed to dwell on a certain mountain from which he attentively hears the rising cries of suffering beings and extends his mystic aid. A version of the *Avataṃsaka Sūtra* (Flower garland scripture) identifies this site as Potalaka Mountain, a name that became well known throughout Buddhist Asia. This mountain has been identified with a number of actual geographical sites in Asia. The seventh-century monk-traveler Xuanzang noted that Potalaka could be found on the Malaya coast, although few who sought the *bodhisattva* had been successful in their quest. From at least the tenth century it was identified as an island off the coast of the southern China seaport of Ningbo, which was named Putuo Shan (Potalaka Mountain) and remains an important pilgrimage center to the present day. In Japan, several sites have been identified as Potalaka: at the Nachi Falls within the Kumano Shrine complex near the ocean on the Kii Peninsula, in the mountains at Nikko, and at the Kasuga Shrine in Nara. In Tibet, the seventeenth-century palace of the Dalai Lama, built upon a hill facing Lhasa and constituting one of the world's great architectural treasures, was named the Potala. Thus, the mountain palace was physically made manifest as the residence of the Tibetan ruler, believed to be the physical embodiment of the *bodhisattva.*

Principal Iconographic Forms and Cultic Activity. Numerous forms of Avalokiteśvara are seen in art and described throughout a wide range of ritual texts, meditation manuals, and scriptures. These range from the simplicity of the Water-Moon form, with the princely *bodhisattva* seated upon Mount Potalaka gazing at the evanescent reflection of the full moon upon a still sea, to the complexity of the eleven-headed, thousand-armed, thousand-eyed images, the multiplicity of features expressing the *bodhisattva*'s extraordinary abilities to seek out and respond to the distress of all beings.

Aryāvalokiteśvara ("noble Avalokiteśvara"), sometimes termed "great compassionate one," is a simple form of the *bodhisattva* bearing in his left hand a lotus flower. Often, especially from the ninth century onward, this form wears a crown or headpiece in which the image of his spiritual father

Amitābha Buddha is depicted. Closely related to this form is the White-Robed (Paṇḍaravāsinī) Avalokiteśvara, the most frequently seen East Asian type from the tenth or eleventh century to the present. With special emphasis on the motherly compassion of the *bodhisattva,* this form most often is depicted as a female seated in meditation or holding a lotus blossom. Caṇḍī, less commonly seen, is another female form, having three eyes and eighteen arms.

Paintings and sculptures depict some of the specialized abilities of the *bodhisattva*: as savior of those subject to life-threatening dangers such as fire, flood, and attack; as benevolent bestower of sons; as guide of souls, leading them in the journey from deathbed to Amitābha's Western Paradise; as a king of healing, in one form holding both a willow branch (as sign of the ability to ward off disease) and a vase of *amṛta* (the nectar of enlightenment), or in another healing form seated upon a roaring lion. Other important forms include Amoghapāśa ("unfailing rope"), holding out a lasso to assist all beings, or the fiercely protective Hayagrīva, horse-headed with dark flames emanating from his body. Avalokiteśvara is also shown paired with Mahāsthāmaprāpta in attendance on Amitābha, performing various functions in the Western Paradise, and he is seen as one among eight or more *bodhisattvas* in numerous types of assembly scenes throughout Mahāyāna art. This vast array of iconographic forms, only touched upon here, provides a sense of Avalokiteśvara's preeminent popularity throughout the Asian Buddhist populace.

An eleven-headed form of the *bodhisattva* is seen in the art of numerous Buddhist lands. These eleven heads may represent an elaboration of the concept of Avalokiteśvara as an all-seeing lord, encompassing views of the four cardinal and the four intermediate directions, as well as the nadir, center, and zenith. In East Asia, this form was first associated with special confession and repentance rites undertaken by lay and monastic practitioners. According to a text translated from Sanskrit into Chinese in the sixth century, the eleven heads are related to an elevenfold vow made by the *bodhisattva* to aid all sentient beings, including pledges to do such things as relieve beings of illness, misfortune, suffering, and worries, free them of unwholesome intentions, and turn their thoughts toward that which is wholesome. Iconographically, the eleven heads should be depicted in the following manner: three heads in the center with a compassionate expression—suited to devotees with predominantly good karma (Skt., *karman*); three heads on the left with an angry expression—directed toward saving beings with unwholesome qualities; three heads on the right with white tusks protruding from the tops of the mouths—to assist people with good karma to find enlightenment; a single face in back with an expression of violent laughter—to reform evil-doers; and a Buddha face on top, preaching the *dharma*—for those capable of following the Mahāyāna path.

The development of this *bodhisattva*'s cult is closely related to his function as extender of life and protector from the hardships and dangers of the world, who, as the *Lotus* puts it, "confers the gift of fearlessness" in the midst of terror and trouble. Based on the records of Chinese travelers to India, there was some worship of Avalokiteśvara in the fourth century at Mathurā, and by the seventh century the cult was widespread throughout India; by this time, according to Xuanzang, images of the *bodhisattva* flanked the "diamond seat" of Śākyamuni Buddha's enlightenment at Bodh Gayā, one of the most sacred sites in the Buddhist world.

In all the coastal areas of Mahāyāna Buddhist countries, Avalokiteśvara has been especially worshiped and invoked for his lifesaving protection of seafarers. This ability, mentioned in the *Lotus Scripture,* is attested to in numerous travel diaries and miracle tales from the fourth century to the present.

As noted above, in East Asia Avalokiteśvara has been the most popular of all Buddhist deities, most especially by virtue of the prominence accorded him in the *Lotus Scripture* traditions. The *Lotus* traditions of the thirty-three types of manifestations of the *bodhisattva* led in Japan to several very important pilgrimage circuits devoted to Kannon (Avalokiteśvara), each having thirty-three stations dedicated to the *bodhisattva.*

Avalokiteśvara (Spyan ras gzigs) is one of the key protective deities of Tibet, and the recitation of his six-syllable Sanskrit mantra, "Oṃ maṇi padme hūṃ," has been a widespread practice among Tibetans. Tibetan myths hold that Avalokiteśvara was the progenitor of the Tibetan people, and they believe that the founder of the first Tibetan dynasty, Srong bstan sgam po (seventh century), was an incarnation of Avalokiteśvara. Similarly, especially since the seventeenth century, the Dalai Lamas, successive temporal rulers and spiritual leaders of Tibet, have been believed to be human incarnations of Avalokiteśvara.

SEE ALSO Bodhisattva Path; Buddhas and Bodhisattvas, article on Celestial Buddhas and Bodhisattvas.

BIBLIOGRAPHY

The most comprehensive Western-language study of Avalokiteśvara is Marie-Thérèse de Mallmann's *Introduction à l'étude d'Avalokiteçvara* (Paris, 1948), which surveys the myriad forms of the *bodhisattva* seen in Indian art. Mallmann's diffusionist views were rejected by Giuseppe Tucci in his "À propos Avalokiteśvara," *Mélanges chinois et bouddhiques* 9 (1948–1951): 173–220. Another diffusionist, Alexander Coburn Soper, has also made a study of the origins and iconography of the *bodhisattva,* relying on Chinese sources; see "The Triad Amitāyus-Amitābha, Avalokiteśvara, Mahāsthāmaprāpta," in his *Literary Evidence for Early Buddhist Art in China* (Ascona, 1959), pp. 141–167. For a valuable study of Chinese perceptions of Avalokiteśvara written by a learned Buddhist practitioner and devotee of the *bodhisattva,* see C. N. Tay's "Guanyin: The Cult of Half Asia," *History of Religions* 16 (November 1976): 147–177. For the so-called *Avalokiteśvara Sūtra,* chapter 25 of the *Lotus,* see *Scripture of the Lotus Blossom of the Fine Dharma,* translated by Leon Hurvitz (New York, 1976). Also helpful is Henri

Maspero's discussion in "The Mythology of Modern China," in *Daoism and Chinese Religion*, translated by Frank A. Kierman, Jr. (Amherst, 1981), pp. 166–171.

New Sources

Bdud joms, Jigs bral ye ses rdo rje, and Matthew Kapstein. "The Royal Way to Supreme Compassion." In *Religions of Tibet in Practice,* edited by Donald S. Lopez, Jr., pp. 69–76. Princeton, 1997.

Campany, Robert F. "The Earliest Tales of the Bodhisattva Guanshiyin." In *Religions of China in Practice,* edited by Donald S. Lopez, Jr., pp. 82–96. Princeton, 1996.

Idema, Wilt L. "Guanyin's Acolytes." In *Linked Faiths,* edited by Jan A. M. De Meyer and Peter M. Engelfriet, pp. 205–226. Boston, 2000.

MacWilliams, Mark W. "Temple Myths and the Popularization of Kannon Pilgrimage in Japan: A Case Study of Oya-ji on the Bando Route." *Japanese Journal of Religious Studies* 24 (1997): 375–411.

Obeyesekere, Gananath. "Avalokitesvara's Aliases and Guises." *History of Religions* 32 (1993): 368–373.

Thang Stong Rgyal Po, and Janet Gyatso. "An Avalokitesvara Sadhana." In *Religions of Tibet in Practice,* edited by Donald S. Lopez, Jr., pp. 266–270. Princeton, 1997.

Yu, Chun-fang. *Kuan-yin: The Chinese Transformation of Avalokitesvara.* New York, 2001.

RAOUL BIRNBAUM (1987)
Revised Bibliography

AVATĀRA. The idea of an *avatāra,* a form taken by a deity, is central in Hindu mythology, religion, and philosophy. Literally the term means "a descent" and suggests the idea of a deity coming down from heaven to earth. The literal meaning also implies a certain diminution of the deity when he or she assumes the form of an *avatāra. Avatāras* usually are understood to be only partial manifestations of the deity who assumes them.

The *avatāra* idea in Hinduism is associated primarily with the god Viṣṇu. One of the earliest references to the idea is found in the *Bhagavadgītā* (c. 200 BCE), where we find a concise statement concerning Viṣṇu's primary intention in assuming different forms:

> Whenever righteousness wanes and unrighteousness increases I send myself forth.
> In order to protect the good and punish the wicked,
> In order to make a firm foundation for righteousness,
> I come into being age after age. (4.7–8)

Theologically an *avatāra* is a specialized form assumed by Viṣṇu for the purpose of maintaining or restoring cosmic order. The form is suited to particular circumstances, which vary greatly, and therefore the different *avatāras* that Viṣṇu assumes also vary greatly. All the *avatāras*, however, perform positive functions vis-à-vis the cosmic order and illustrate Viṣṇu's nature as a deity who is attentive to worldly stability.

Historically the different *avatāras* of Viṣṇu often appear to represent regional, sectarian, or tribal deities who have been subsumed by established Hinduism under the rubric of one of Viṣṇu's many forms. By viewing these regional deities as so many varying forms of one transcendent deity, Hinduism was able to accommodate itself to a great variety of local traditions while maintaining a certain philosophic and religious integrity. This process also obviated unnecessary tension and rivalry among differing religious traditions.

Although the number of Viṣṇu's *avatāras* varies at different periods in the Hindu tradition and in different scriptures, the tradition usually affirms ten *avatāras*. While the sequence in which these *avatāras* is mentioned varies, the following order is common: fish, tortoise, boar, man-lion, dwarf, Rāma the Ax Wielder, Rāma of the *Rāmāyana,* Kṛṣṇa, the Buddha, and Kalki. Traditionally, each *avatāra* appears in order to perform a specific cosmic duty that is necessary to maintain or restore cosmic order. Having performed that task, the *avatāra* then disappears or merges back into Viṣṇu.

Viṣṇu assumed the form of a great fish in order to save Manu Vaivasvata, the progenitor of the human race in this present cosmic age. A great deluge occurred at the beginning of the world, but Manu Vaivasvata was rescued when a giant horned fish appeared in the midst of the waters and bade him tie himself to its great horn. Bearing the seeds of creation for all living species (which the fish had instructed him to collect), the parent of the human race was prevented from drowning.

Viṣṇu appeared in the form of an immense boar when the demon Hiraṇyākṣa took possession of the goddess Pṛthivī (Earth) and carried her away beneath the cosmic waters. Diving into the waters, Viṣṇu battled and defeated Hiraṇyākṣa. Then he placed Pṛthivī on his tusk and lifted her above the waters. In both the fish and boar forms Viṣṇu involves himself dramatically in the cosmic process. He does so in order to preserve an element of order and life in the midst of overwhelming chaos represented by a limitless expanse of water.

Viṣṇu assumed the form of a tortoise when the gods and demons combined their efforts to churn the ocean of milk in order to extract from it the nectar of immortality. Having acquired Mount Meru, the cosmic axis, as a churning stick and Vāsuki, the cosmic serpent, as a churning rope, the gods and demons despaired because they were unable to find a secure base upon which to set the mighty churning stick. At that point, Viṣṇu assumed the form of a gigantic tortoise on whose broad back the gods and demons were able to set the churning stick and thus proceed with their task. In this form Viṣṇu assumes the role of cosmic foundation, that upon which all things securely rest and without which the world would lack stability.

Viṣṇu appeared as a man-lion to uphold the devotion and righteousness of Prahlāda, who was being persecuted by his father, Hiraṇyakaśipu, a demon who was oppressing the world and who violently opposed his son's devotion to Viṣṇu. Because of a special boon that Hiranyakasipu had received, namely, that he would be invulnerable to man and beast, Viṣṇu assumed the form of the man-lion, which was neither man nor beast, and defeated him.

Viṣṇu assumed the form of a dwarf in order to restore the world to the gods. The world had been taken over by Bali, a powerful yet virtuous member of the ordinarily unrighteous race of the *asuras*. Appearing as a dwarf, Viṣṇu asked Bali for a favor, which Bali piously granted. Viṣṇu asked for the territory he could encompass in three strides, and Bali gladly agreed. Then Viṣṇu assumed his cosmic form and traversed the entire universe. He thereby restored the cosmos to the gods.

As Paraśu Rāma (Rāma the Ax Wielder) Viṣṇu chastened the *kṣatriyas*, the warrior class, for the haughty, presumptuous, and overbearing attitudes with which they had oppressed the brahmans. In several bloody campaigns, Paraśu Rāma humbled the *kṣatriyas* and asserted the priority of the brahmans in the social and theological systems.

As Rāma, the hero of the *Rāmāyana* (one of the two great Indian epics), Viṣṇu defeated the demon Rāvaṇa, who had brought the world under his sway. After a long exile and a heroic battle Rāma defeated Rāvaṇa and became ruler of India. He then instituted a reign of virtue, order, and prosperity that has come to assume in the Hindu tradition the place of a golden age. In this *avatāra* Viṣṇu descended to the world to set forth a model of ideal kingship that might serve as an inspiration for all rulers at all times.

As Kṛṣṇa, Viṣṇu descended to the world in order to defeat the demon Kaṃsa, who was oppressing the earth with his wickedness, and to ensure the victory of the Pandava brothers in their war against their cousins, the Kauravas. The story of this battle is related in the other great Hindu epic, the *Mahābhārata.*

As the Buddha, Viṣṇu acted to delude those who already deserved punishment for their bad deeds. Deceived by the Buddha's false teachings, these individuals renounced the Vedas and traditional Hinduism, thus earning punishment in hell or in inferior births. In a number of later texts, Viṣṇu's Buddha *avatāra* is interpreted positively. He is said to have assumed this form in order to teach nonviolence and gentleness to the world.

Kalki is the form that Viṣṇu will assume at the end of this cosmic age. As Kalki he will appear in human form riding a white horse; he will bring the world to an end, reward the virtuous, and punish the wicked.

So popular did the *avatāras* Rāma and Kṛṣṇa become in medieval Hindu devotion that they assumed for their respective devotees the position of supreme deity. For Kṛṣṇa devotees, Kṛṣṇa is the highest expression of the divine and as such is understood not as an *avatāra* himself but rather as the source of all *avatāras*. In this context, Viṣṇu is understood to be a lesser manifestation of Kṛṣṇa. Similarly, devotees of Rāma regard him as the highest expression of the divine.

The *avatāra* idea also came to be applied to other Hindu deities. Śiva and Durga, for example, are said in some later scriptures to assume appropriate forms in order to preserve the world or to bless their devotees. Especially in devotional contexts, *avatāras* no longer function primarily to restore cosmic order. Rather, their *raison d'être* is to bless devotees with the presence of the divine, to rescue devotees from peril, or to reward them for heroic devotion or service.

SEE ALSO Kṛṣṇa; Rāma; Viṣṇu.

BIBLIOGRAPHY

A convenient summary of the principal Sanskrit texts in which the *avatāra* myths are told is found in *Classical Hindu Mythology: A Reader in the Sanskrit Purāṇas*, edited and translated by Cornelia Dimmitt and J. A. B. van Buitenen (Philadelphia, 1978), pp. 59–146. An abbreviated account of the *avatāra* myths may be found in John Dowson's *A Classical Dictionary of Hindu Mythology and Religion, Geography, History, and Literature* (London, 1878), pp. 33–38. Jan Gonda's *Aspects of Early Viṣṇuism* (Utrecht, 1954) discusses some of the *avatāras* in historical context and shows how the development of the *avatāra* theology developed in the Hindu tradition.

New Sources

Gupta, Shakti M. *Vishnu and His Incarnations.* Bombay, 1993.

Krishna, Nanditha. *The Book of Vishnu.* New Delhi; New York, 2001.

Miranda, Prashant. *Avatar and Incarnation: A Comparative Analysis, from Dr. S. Radhakrishnan's Viewpoint.* New Delhi, 1990.

Parrinder, Edward Geoffrey. *Avatar and Incarnation: The Divine in Human Form in the World's Religions.* Oxford; Rockford, Mass., 1997.

DAVID KINSLEY (1987)
Revised Bibliography

AVEMPACE SEE IBN BĀJJAH

AVERROËS SEE IBN RUSHD

AVESTA. Only a small part of the Avesta (MPers., Abastāg; the name probably means "the Injunction [of Zarathushtra]"), the collection of sacred books of Zoroastrianism, has come down to us: about three-quarters of the original texts, whose codification dates to the Sasanid period (third to seventh centuries CE), have been lost. The oldest extant manuscript is from the thirteenth century.

The oral tradition that has permitted the transmission of the texts is therefore very long, especially since significant portions of the Avesta go as far back as the first years of the first millennium BCE. This fact, together with the problems connected with the writing system employed (derived from the Pahlavi alphabet, of Aramaic origin) and with the manuscript tradition, means that the study of the Avesta is philologically among the most difficult and complex.

The selection of texts that has survived—first published by their discoverer, Abraham Hyacinthe Anquetil du Perron, in 1771—was apparently primarily determined by liturgical interests. For the most part, these are the texts that were used for religious services during the period in which the manuscript tradition arose, and they are accompanied by Pahlavi versions. It should be remembered that their language (which, being impossible to locate geographically within the Iranian world beyond a general characterization as eastern Iranian, is simply called Avestan) was no longer understood. Pahlavi versions were, consequently, necessary for an understanding of the text, which was thus strongly influenced by a relatively late exegetical tradition (in any case, not earlier than the Sasanid period). The compilation must have had to meet the requirements of the new Zoroastrian state church to provide—as did the contemporary and rival religions Christianity, Judaism, and Manichaeism—scriptures that would promote the establishment of a solid and rigid orthodoxy. Indeed, the process of selection of the scriptures is mentioned explicitly in the Pahlavi literature.

The surviving texts are highly varied, both in content and in language. Several parts of the *Yasna* are written in a dialect known as Gathic: the *Gāthās*, the five compositions in verse attributed to Zarathushtra (Zoroaster) himself, which constitute chapters 28–34, 43–46, 47–50, 51, and 53; the *Yasna Haptanhāiti*, or Yasna of the Seven Chapters (35–41); the three fundamental prayers of Zoroastrianism, Yenhē Hātam, Ashem Vohu, and Yatha Ahū Vairyō (chap. 27); and the prayer Airyema Ishyō (chap. 55). The other parts of the Avesta are written in a linguistically later Avestan, more or less archaic and also more or less correct. They include the rest of the *Yasna* and the *Nyāyishn*, the *Gāh*, the *Yashts, Sīrōza, Āfrīnagān, Vendidad, Nīrangistān, Hadhōkht Nask, Aogemadaēchā.*

The *Yasna* is the most important section, and not just because the *Gāthās* are inserted in it: these are the seventy-two chapters recited by the priest during the ceremony of the same name (*Yasna*, "sacrifice"). Among these is found the *Hōm Yasht*, the hymn to Haoma (chap. 9–11); the *Fravarānē* ("I profess"), a confession of faith (chap. 12); and the so-called *Bagān Yasht*, a commentary on the three fundamental prayers (chaps. 19–21). But without doubt the most important part of the *Yasna*, and the most beautiful part of the whole Avesta, is the *Gāthās* ("songs") of Zarathushtra. Difficulties of interpretation do not diminish their value: they are the primary source for a knowledge of the doctrines of the prophet. In their literary genre, they are close to the Vedic hymns and testify to the presence in Iran, as elsewhere, of a tradition of Indo-European sacred poetry.

Among the other sections, the *Yashts* (hymns to various divinities) deserve special mention. Several of these hymns or prayers are particularly significant in the history of religions, as they are the most direct evidence of the new faith's adaptation of the older religious tradition. Especially noteworthy are those dedicated to Anāhitā (5); to Tishtrya, the star Sirius (8); to Mithra (10); to the *fravashis* (13); to Verethraghna (14); to Vāyu (15); and to Khvarenah (19).

The *Vendidad* (*vī-daēvo-dāta*, "the law abjuring *daivas*"), the only section that may be an addition to the text, contains, along with mythological parts like the second chapter dedicated to Yima, the king of the golden age, a detailed body of rules for achieving purity. The *Hadhōkht Nask* and the *Aogemadaēchā* are texts dealing with events after death and funeral rites. The other parts are primarily invocations and prayers for the various forms, articulations, and requirements of worship services.

BIBLIOGRAPHY

Editions and Translations of the Avesta or of Its Sections

Bartholomae, C. *Die Gathas des Avesta: Zarathustra's Verspredigten.* Strassburg, 1905. Translated by J. H. Moulton in *Early Zoroastrianism* (1913; reprint, London, 1972), pp. 343–390.

Darmesteter, James. *The Zend-Avesta*, pt. 2, *The Sirozahs, Yashts and Nyayesh.* Sacred Books of the East, vol. 23. Oxford, 1883; reprint, Delhi, 1965.

Darmesteter, James. *The Zend-Avesta*, pt. 1, *The Vendīdād.* 2d ed. Sacred Books of the East, vol. 4. Oxford, 1895; reprint, Delhi, 1965.

Duchesne-Guillemin, Jacques. *Zoroastre: Étude critique avec une traduction commentée des Gâthâ.* Paris, 1948. Translated by Maria Henning as *The Hymns of Zarathushtra* (London, 1952).

Humbach, Helmut. *Die Gathas des Zarathustra.* 2 vols. Heidelberg, 1959.

Humbach, Helmut. *The Gāthās and the Other Old Avestan Texts.* 2 vols. Wiesbaden, 1991.

Insler, Stanley. *The Gathas of Zarathushtra.* Acta Iranica, 3d ser., vol. 1. Leiden, 1975.

Kellens, Jean, and Eric Pirart. *Les textes vieil-avestiques.* 3 vols. Wiesbaden, 1988–1991.

Lommel, Herman. *Die Yäšt's des Awesta.* Göttingen, 1927.

Lommel, Herman. *Die Gathas des Zarathustra.* Edited by Bernfried Schlerath. Basel, 1971.

Mills, L. H. *The Zend-Avesta*, pt. 3, *The Yasna, Visparad, Afrinagan, Gahs and Miscellaneous Fragments.* Sacred Books of the East, vol. 31. Oxford, 1887; reprint, Delhi, 1965.

Smith, Maria W. *Studies in the Syntax of the Gathas of Zarathushtra, Together with Text, Translation and Notes.* Philadelphia, 1929; reprint, Millwood, N.Y., 1966.

Taraporevala, Irach J. S. *The Divine Songs of Zarathushtra.* Bombay, 1951.

Editions and Translations of the Pahlavi Version

Anklesaria, Behramgore Tahmuras, trans. *Pahlavi Vendidād.* Edited by Dinshah D. Kapadia. Bombay, 1949.

Dhabhar, Bamanji Nasarvanji, ed. *Zand-i Khūrtak Avistāk.* Bombay, 1927.

Dhabhar, Bamanji Nasarvanji, ed. *Pahlavi Yasna and Vispered.* Bombay, 1949.

Jamasp, Hoshang, ed. *Vendidâd.* Bombay, 1907. Avestan text with Pahlavi translation, commentary, and glossary.

Kanga, Ervad Maneck F., ed. *Pahlavi Version of Yašts.* Bombay, 1941.

Studies of the Transmission, Transliteration, and Oral Tradition

Altheim, Franz. *Awestische Textgeschichte.* Halle, 1949.

Bailey, H. W. *Zoroastrian Problems in the Ninth-Century Books* (1943). Reprint, Oxford, 1971.

Henning, W. B. "The Disintegration of the Avestic Studies." *Transactions of the Philological Society* (1942): 40–56.

Morgenstierne, G. "Orthography and Sound System in the Avesta." *Norsk tidsskrift for sprogvidenskap* 12 (1942): 38–82.

Widengren, Geo. "The Problem of the Sassanid Avesta." In *Holy Book and Holy Tradition,* pp. 36–53. Manchester, 1968.

General Studies

Christensen, Arthur. *Études sur le zoroastrisme de la Perse antique.* Copenhagen, 1928.

Gershevitch, Ilya. "Old Iranian Literature." In *Iranistik-Literatur.* Leiden, 1968.

Hoffmann, Karl. "Das Avesta in der Persis." In *Prolegomena to the Sources on the History of Pre-Islamic Central Asia,* edited by J. Harmatta, pp. 89–93. Budapest, 1979.

Hoffmann, Karl, and Johanna Narten. *Der sasanidische Archetypus.* Wiesbaden, 1989.

Kellens, Jean. *Zoroastre et l'Avesta ancien.* Paris, 1991.

Kellens, Jean. *Essays on Zarathustra and Zoroastrianism.* Translated and edited by Prods Oktor Skjærvø. Costa Mesa, Calif., 2000.

Meillet, Antoine. *Trois conférences sur les Gâthâ de l'Avesta.* Paris, 1925.

Schlerath, Bernfried. *Avesta-Wörterbuch.* 2 vols. Wiesbaden, 1968.

Schmidt, Rüdiger, comp. *Indogermanische Dichtersprache.* Darmstadt, 1968.

Stausbert, Michael. *Die Religion Zarathustras. Geschichte-Gegenwart-Rituale,* vol. 1. Stuttgart, 2002.

Wesendonk, O. G. von. *Die religionsgeschichtliche Bedeutung des Yasna Haptanhāti.* Bonn, 1931.

GHERARDO GNOLI (1987)
Translated from Italian by Roger DeGaris

AVICENNA SEE IBN SĪNĀ

AVIDYĀ.

AVIDYĀ. *Avidyā* is the conceptual starting point of classical Indian thinking about the nature of existence. The Sanskrit term connotes "ignorance," "false understanding," or "nescience." There are, broadly, two schools of thought on its nature: Sāṃkhya-Yoga and Vedānta. Sāṃkhya locates *avidyā's* genesis in the proximate association of *puruṣa* (spirit) with *prakṛti* (nature), which results in a sequential evolution of qualities and substances, from intelligence, embodiment, and senses to elemental traces of matter. The ensuing multiplicity of "I"-consciousnesses, forgetting the true identity of *puruṣa,* misidentify themselves with *vṛttis,* or the wavering flux of forms and properties of materiality, through a convoluted mix of three ontological aspects *(guṇas):* the lightness *(sattva),* motion *(rajas*), and denseness *(tamas)* of matter. Thus arise certain incongruent life-worlds (self, other, and spheres) with their related domains of being, causality, time-space, motion, mind, askesis, passions, and ends. *Avidyā,* then, is the epistemic foreclosure of access to true consciousness. Yoga attempts to erase this subreptitious affliction through rigorous ascetic, contemplative, and meditative praxis, freeing *puruṣa* from *avidyā's* ontological concealment; set free, the spirit shines in its own effulgence.

Vedānta, on the other hand, proffers a more stringent metaphysical account derived from its fundamental presupposition that *brahman,* the unitary principle underwriting the universe, is without any trace of distinction and differentiation. The challenge is then to account for the heterogeneous recognition of differences among selves and entities. At the cosmic level the explanation is given in terms of *māyā* (illusion-making); at the phenomenal level it turns on the facticity of conscious experiences. *Ātman* (the innermost essence of the individual) is one with *brahman,* and is in its essence pure, impersonal consciousness. But our everyday experiences in waking, sleep, dream, and deep-sleep states belie this fact. This can be explained by the assertion that pure consciousness remains veiled by various adjuncts *(upādhis)* and conditionings. For Śaṅkara (788–820 CE), a philosopher of the Hindu (advaita or non-dualist school) the process itself is more formal (efficient, *nimitta*) than it is material (as in Sāṃkhya-Yoga); it is the function of *adhyāsa* (superimposition or transference). The "subject," revealed as the content of the "I-notion" *(asmatpratyayagocara),* and the "object," revealed as the content of "you" *(yuṣmat-)* or "that," are as radically opposed to each other in nature as darkness is to light, so that neither they nor their attributes can ever be identified with or transformed into each other.

In regular veridical cognition *(jñāna),* perceptual error occurs when the mind, in confusion, projects a residual memory of, say, silver, onto an oblique object, such as a seashell, and thinks it to be mother-of-pearl. This epistemic deception and aligned ignorance *(ajñāna)* about the other are analogically extended to the metaphysical context to account for the more pervasive and fundamental illusion inherent in our existential condition. Hence, owing to the superimposition of spurious concepts upon pure consciousness, the "I-awareness" tends toward differentiation and identifies itself with "nonconscious entities"; thus: "I am a princess"; "I adorn jeweled *mangalsutras*"; "I wear a hat." Śaṅkara frames this contradiction in terms of the "real" and "unreal," respectively. The phenomenological result of this projective transference afflicts all empirical experiences and is described as *avidyā.* The Vedanta philosopher and theologian Rāmānuja (1017–1137) synthesizes Śaṅkara's clinical purism with Sāṃkhya monadology and Yoga's pragmatism. He makes a distinction between substantive consciousness *(dharm-*

ībhūtijñāna) and qualia-consciousness *(dharmabhūta-jñāna).* The false predication of the latter on the former is removed through love, devotion, and surrender (with a touch of alchemy); the individual attains higher stages of self-realization, and ultimately union in Viṣṇu as *māyā*-embodied *brahman.*

Later Vedānta scholastics pondered the ontological status of *avidyā:* on the one hand, if it were "real" then it would compete with the primeval Word *(Śabdabrahman),* which is prior even to manifest consciousness, thereby compromising *ātman/brahman's* singular uniqueness; on the other hand, if it were "unreal" it would lack any efficiency and would stand to be conceptually sublated. This dilemma was resolved by the argument that a higher, second-order witness-consciousness *(śakṣin-dharmībhūta-cit)* persists in and through all levels of experience, unblemished by *avidyā.* Hence, *avidyā* is described as *anirvacanīya,* the inexplicable remainder of that which is "neither real nor unreal." *Avidyā* then becomes a sui generis ontological category, like that of the "Sublime," as the unexceptional precondition for all phenomenal experience.

SEE ALSO Māyā; Prakṛti; Rāmānuja; Śaṅkara; Vedānta.

BIBLIOGRAPHY

Arapura, J. G. "Māyā and the Discourse about Brahman." In *The Problem of Two Truths in Buddhism and Vedānta,* edited by Mervyn Sprung, pp. 109–121. Dordrecht, Netherlands, 1973.

Rāmānuja. *Śrībhāṣya.* Translated by M. Rangacharya et al. Delhi, 1988.

Rao, Srinivasa. *Perceptual Error: The Indian Theories.* Honolulu, 1988.

Śaṅkara. *Brahmasūtrabhāṣya,* vol. 1. Rev. ed. Madras, India, 1981.

Sarasvati, Madhusūdana. *Advaitasiddhi.* Edited by D. Srinivasachar and G. Venkatanaraimha Sastri. Mysore, 1933.

PURUSHOTTAMA BILIMORIA (2005)

AVRAHAM BEN DAVID OF POSQUIÈRES

(c. 1125–1198), known by the acronym Ra'ABaD (Rabbi Avraham ben David). Avraham ben David is best known for his original and versatile contributions to the literature of *halakhah.* He composed commentaries on various types of Talmudic literature: on the Mishnah (e.g., *'Eduyyot* and *Qinnim*); on the Talmud (e.g., *'Avodah Zarah* and *Bava' Qamma'*); and on halakhic midrashim (e.g., *Sifra'*). Further works include *responsa* (Heb., *teshuvot,* decisions concerning the interpretation of application of the law), which reveal his character and method; homiletic discourses (e.g., *Derashah le-Ro'sh ha-Shanah*); codes of rabbinic law; and critical annotations or glosses (*hassagot*) on standard works of rabbinic literature.

The most important and influential of Avraham ben David's codes, which include *Hilkhot lulav* (Laws concerning the palm branch), *Ḥibbur harsha'ot* (A manual on the laws of agency), and *Perush yadayim,* is the *Ba'alei ha-nefesh,* a careful presentation of the laws of uncleanness and purity. The last chapter of his *Sha'ar ha-qedushah* (Gate of holiness) is an ethical-homiletical disquisition that formulates and analyzes the moral norms and religious attitudes that enable one to achieve self-control in sexual matters and attain purity of heart and action.

Avraham ben David is referred to as the *ba'al hassagot* ("author of the glosses") because of the critical scholia and animadversions that he composed toward the end of his life on the *Halakhot* of Yitsḥaq ben Ya'aqov Alfasi, the *Sefer ha-ma'or* of Zeraḥyah ha-Levi, and especially the *Mishneh Torah* of Maimonides. These glosses combine criticism and commentary; they are not exclusively polemical, and their polemical emphasis varies in intensity and acuity. *Hassagot,* a wide-ranging form of writing based on a firm premise and finely honed polemical skill, are refined by Avraham ben David and his Provençal contemporaries into an expressive genre of pointed, precise, and persuasive critique. This genre played an important role in the preservation of the spirit of criticism and intellectual freedom so central to rabbinic literature.

Beyond his literary creations, Avraham ben David contributed significantly to the development of a critical-conceptual approach to Talmudic literature that sought to define with rigor and precision complex concepts discussed fragmentarily in numerous, unrelated sections of the Talmud. Many of his interpretations and innovations were endorsed and transmitted by subsequent generations of Talmudists and incorporated into standard works of Jewish law.

During the lifetime of Avraham ben David the centers of rabbinic learning in southern France provided a home for the transplanted philosophic-scientific-ethical literature of Spanish Jews. At this time, an undercurrent of mystical speculation began to emerge that was to find its expression in medieval qabbalistic literature. Avraham ben David was involved in both these developments. He encouraged and benefited from this newly translated philosophical literature, and his own writing reflects some traces of philosophy and philology in the use of terms, phrases, and concepts from this new literary phenomenon. He is described by later qabbalists (e.g., Yitsḥaq of Acre, Shem Ṭov ben Ga'on, and Menaḥem Recanati, and others from the school of Moses Nahmanides and Shelomoh ben Avraham Adret) as one of the fathers of qabbalistic literature. This is supported by references in the writings of Ra'abad's son, Yitsḥaq the Blind, and Yitsḥaq's nephew, Asher. They depicted him as a mystic who was worthy of receiving special revelations and who actually did receive them. In the absence of explicitly qabbalistic statements in Avraham ben David's own works, our knowledge of his use of doctrines and symbolism of Qabbalah depends on passages quoted by others in his name. These deal with mystical meditations during prayer (*kavvanot*) and the doctrine of the ten *sefirot,* and they reveal an acquaintance with early

Heikhalot terminology and its fusion with contemporary philosophic vocabulary.

BIBLIOGRAPHY

Abramson, Sheraga. "Sifrei halakhot shel ha-Ra'abad." *Tarbiz* 36 (December 1966): 158–179.

Gross, H. "R. Abraham b. David aus Posquières." *Monatsschrift für Geschichte und Wissenschaft des Judenthums* 22 (1873): 337–344, 398–407, 446–459; 23 (1874): 19–29, 76–85, 164–182, 275–276.

Twersky, Isadore. *Rabad of Posquières: A Twelfth-Century Talmudist.* Rev. ed. Philadelphia, 1980. Includes a complete bibliography.

New Sources

Mutius, Hans-Georg von. "Eine nichtmasoretische Vokalisierung im masoretischen Konsonantentext von Jeremia 9,18 bei Abraham Ben David von Posquières (12. Jrh.)." *Biblische Notizen* 100 (1999): 22–26.

Soloveitchik, Haym. "History of Halakhah—Methodological Issues: A Review Essay of I. Twersky's 'Rabad of Posquières' [1962, rev. ed. 1980]." *Jewish History* 5 (1991): 75–124.

Trigano, Shmuel L. "Intention d'amour—les Maîtres de l'âme, de Rabbi Abraham ben David: un guide matrimonial en Languedoc au XIIe siècle." *Pardes* 1 (1985): 149–172.

ISADORE TWERSKY (1987)
Revised Bibliography

AVVAKUM (1620/1–1682), Russian Orthodox archpriest; founding father of the Old Believers; martyr. Avvakum was ordained to the priesthood at the age of twenty-two, serving in the area of Nizhni Novgorod; eight years later he was promoted to be archpriest. By then he had amply demonstrated his zeal as a reformer. Following in the wake of the Muscovite "God-seekers," an influential group of scholarly zealots, he sought to revive liturgical life and public morality. The resentment which this provoked led to his displacement and his first visit to Moscow (1652). There he was welcomed by the leading God-seekers and introduced to the tsar.

The election of Nikon as patriarch of Moscow later that year promised to confirm and revitalize the God-seekers' reforms. However, Nikon proceeded arbitrarily to reform liturgical phraseology and practice, particularly concerning the sign of the cross. Avvakum vociferously objected to these reforms, which he saw as a challenge to the true faith. For if even minor rituals were to change, the whole edifice of related doctrine would be undermined. He was arrested and exiled to Siberia (1653). After many tribulations he was permitted to return to Moscow (1664), but his insistence on the validity and importance of the pre-Nikonian liturgical norms led to renewed exile.

Avvakum and his companions were brought back to Moscow and anathematized at a church council of 1666–1667; he in turn anathematized the council. Thus was confirmed the existence of the Russian church schism, which was to have a decisive influence on the ordering of Russian society over the centuries to come. Avvakum was sent to the arctic outpost of Pustozersk from which he and his companions issued tracts and letters. More important than these was Avvakum's apologetic autobiography composed in 1672 to 1673. It is a masterpiece of Russian literature and one of Europe's great confessional texts.

The accession of a new patriarch of Moscow (Joachim) was probably a decisive factor in taking the state's campaign against the Old Believers a stage further, and Avvakum, together with his three companions, was sent to the stake in April 1682. Avvakum had persuasively presented himself as confessor and prophet in defense of the sacred Orthodox heritage delivered to Moscow, the "third Rome," and he is remembered as a martyr of the old faith.

BIBLIOGRAPHY

Avvakum's autobiography has been reedited from the manuscript by Andrei N. Robinson, *Zhizneopisaniia Avvakuma i Epifaniia* (Moscow, 1963). The most scholarly edition and translation of the text in a Western European language is by Pierre Pascal, *La vie de l'archiprêtre Avvakum écrite par lui-même*, 2d ed. (Paris, 1960). Even so, Robinson utters words of caution about the redaction on which the translation is based. It was also Pascal who provided a magnificent treatment of Avvakum and his times in *Avvakum et les débuts du Raskol: La crise religieuse au dix-septième siècle en Russie*, 2d ed. (Paris, 1963).

SERGEI HACKEL (1987)

AXIS MUNDI, the "hub" or "axis" of the universe, is a technical term used in the study of the history of religions. It comprises at least three levels of reference: the images themselves, their function and meaning, and the experiences associated with them.

Vivid images of the axis of the universe vary widely, since they depend on the particular worldview entertained by a specific culture. Foremost among the images designated by the term *axis mundi* is the cosmic mountain, a sacred place deemed to be the highest point of the universe and perhaps identified with the center of the world and the place where creation first began. Well-known examples of the cosmic mountain are Mount Meru of South Asian cosmology, Haraberazaiti of Iranian tradition, and Himinbjörg of Scandinavian mythology.

The cosmic tree, at whose top abides the celestial divinity, is another frequent image standing for the axis of the world. The roots of such a tree may sink into the underworlds, while its branches traverse the multiple world planes. At the center of the classical Maya vision of the world stood Yaxche, the "first tree," the "green tree," whose place marked the center of all meaningful directions and colors of the universe.

A cosmic pillar may also serve as an *axis mundi.* Such is the case with the Delaware (Lenape) Indians and other Eastern Woodland peoples of North America. The center post of their ceremonial cult house supports the sky and passes into the very hand of the celestial deity. The Milky Way is often viewed as another form of cosmic pillar that supports the heavens and connects them with earth.

Many other images fall under the designation *axis mundi* because they share in the symbolic meaning represented by a cosmic mountain, tree, or pillar that joins heaven, earth, and underworld. This category includes cities, especially imperial capitals deemed "heavenly" sites by virtue of proximity to the divine realm; palaces or temples that continue the imagery of the cosmic mountain (e.g., the Babylonian ziggurat); vines or ropes that pass from heaven to earth; and sacred ladders such as the seven-rung ladder, described by Origen, that brings the candidate in the cult of Mithra through the seven heavens.

None of these images has a static function. They are all places of active passage and transition. As places of dynamic union where beings of quite different natures come together or pass into one another, the images of *axis mundi* may be associated with the coincidence of opposites—that is, the resolution of contradictions by their progress onto a more spiritual plane.

Because the *axis mundi* serves as the locus where cosmic regions intersect and where the universe of being is accessible in all its dimensions, the hub of the universe is held to be a place sacred above all others. It defines reality, for it marks the place where being is most fully manifest. This connection of the *axis mundi* with the full manifestation of being is often expressed as an association with the supreme being to whom the axis provides access. This *axis mundi* is often traversed and its heights attained in a state of ecstasy brought about by spiritual techniques. Hence the term *axis mundi* implies an intersection of planes through which transcendence to other kinds of being may be achieved.

There is a tendency to replicate the image of the *axis mundi* in multiple forms. Such is the case with the cross—the cosmic tree of Christianity. Re-creating the image of the *axis mundi* in the form of village sites, house plans, ritual furnishings, personal ornaments, and even kitchen items tends to identify the universe as a whole with the fullness of being characteristic of action at that sacred place. It ensures that contact with the fullness of reality is everywhere possible. As a result, the meaning and function of the *axis mundi* rest not in abstract and geometrical concepts alone but in everyday gestures that can effect the same transcendence.

All these symbols imply a particular quality of experience. The symbols of *axis mundi* are ambivalent: on the one hand, they connect realms of being but on the other hand they emphasize the distance between such realms. In short, they point to the need for a rupture of planes of existence, for experience of an order quite different from that of the ordinary world.

SEE ALSO Architecture; Mountains; Trees.

BIBLIOGRAPHY

For a wide-ranging discussion of the general concept of *axis mundi,* see Mircea Eliade's *Patterns in Comparative Religion* (New York, 1958), pp. 367–387, which concern the "center of the world," and pp. 265–303, which treat the question of the *axis mundi* manifest as cosmic tree. See also Eliade's *The Sacred and the Profane: The Nature of Religion* (New York, 1959), pp. 20–67, and *Images and Symbols: Studies in Religious Symbolism* (New York, 1961), pp. 27–56, which provide bibliographies tracing the history of this concept in scholarly study of religion.

For contemporary studies representing investigations of specific aspects of *axis mundi,* the following may serve as illustrations: for the image of mountain, I. W. Mabbett's "The Symbolism of Mount Meru," *History of Religions* 23 (August 1983): 64–83; for cosmic tree, Y. T. Hosoi's "The Sacred Tree in Japanese Prehistory," *History of Religions* 16 (November 1976): 95–119; as a city, Werner Müller's *Die heilige Stadt* (Stuttgart, 1961) and Paul Wheatley's *The Pivot of the Four Quarters: A Preliminary Enquiry into the Origins and Character of the Ancient Chinese City* (Chicago, 1971), esp. pp. 411–476. For an examination of the temple as place of union of beings and manifestation of sacred presence, see David Dean Shulman's *Tamil Temple Myths* (Princeton, 1980).

For a consideration of the liturgical function of sacred geography and spatial images when seen as expressions of being, see Kees W. Bolle's "Speaking of a Place," in *Myths and Symbols,* edited by Joseph M. Kitagawa and Charles H. Long (Chicago, 1969), pp. 127–140.

New Sources

Feuerstein, Georg, Subhash Kak, and David Frawley. *In Search of the Cradle of Civilization.* Wheaton, Ill., 1995.

Michell, John, and Christine Rhone. *Twelve-Tribe Nations and the Science of Enchanting the Landscape.* Grand Rapids, Mich., 1991.

Schama, Simon. *Landscape and Memory.* New York, 1995.

LAWRENCE E. SULLIVAN (1987)
Revised Bibliography

ĀYURVEDA. The traditional Hindu system of medicine widely practiced in India, Āyurveda is based on authoritative treatises written in Sanskrit over approximately the past two millennia. Three major classical medical systems have flourished on the Indian subcontinent: Āyurveda among Hindus, Yunānī among Muslims, and Siddha among Tamils in South India. Their reliance on elaborate textual traditions distinguish these three systems from the assorted medical practices offered by astrologers, exorcists, priests, snakebite specialists, and kindred healers in the context of diverse folk traditions. In general, folk practices are associated with a magico-religious understanding of illness, whereas Āyurveda is associated with an understanding of illness that refers to the balance of three physiological principles suggestive of, yet distinct from, the Galenic humors. Such boundaries delimiting classical and folk traditions are not absolute, however, and humoral concepts pervade many folk practices just as magico-religious considerations have at times played a significant role in the practice of Āyurveda.

TEXTS. Major traditions evolving in the context of Hinduism frequently trace their roots to one of the four Vedic Saṃhitās, the earliest canonical texts, and Āyurveda is associated with the *Atharvaveda.* While all four Vedas demonstrate at least a peripheral concern for medical issues, they do so in the context of a decidedly supernatural worldview. At this early stage one finds barely a hint of the later humoral physiology among the charms, prayers, and propitiatory rites suggested for the relief of specified ailments frequently attributed to demons.

The tradition of Āyurveda holds that the medical doctrine was revealed through a series of deities and sages to human physicians who in turn composed the basic texts. According to the *Suśruta Saṃhitā,* the doctrine passed from Indra, chief among the gods, to Dhanvantari, who has come to be regarded as the Hindu god of medicine, and then to Suśruta himself, who composed this treatise. The *Caraka Saṃhitās* states that the doctrine passed to the sage Ātreya Punarvasu, who trained a disciple named Agniveśa, author of the *Agniveśa Tantra* (an Ayurvedic, not a Tantric, text). When this text subsequently fell into disrepair, it was partially restored first by Caraka and later by Dṛḍhabala. Both the *Caraka Saṃhitā,* as revised by Caraka, and the *Suśruta Saṃhitā* are believed to have been written during the first three hundred years CE, and the redaction by Dṛḍhabala is thought to have been made in approximately 500 CE. It is widely accepted that these texts are based on a medical doctrine that was followed for at least several centuries before it was committed to writing, and some scholars claim that the tradition extends back several millennia, although this assertion is disputed by many Indologists. Other major texts include the *Aṣṭāṅgahṛdaya Saṃhitā* of Vagbhata from approximately 600 CE, *Mādhavanidāna* of Mādhava from approximately 700 CE, and *Bhela Saṃhitā,* which may have been contemporaneous with the *Agniveśa Tantra* and hence is the oldest surviving text. The most often cited of these treatises are *Caraka, Suśruta,* and *Vāgbhaṭa,* collectively known as "the great three" (*bṛhat trayī*).

THEORY OF DISEASE AND TREATMENT. According to Āyurveda, most sickness results from an imbalance of one or more of three humors (*tridoṣa*): wind (*vāta*), bile (*pitta*), and phlegm (*kapha*). A patient's illness is determined by the character of the particular disease (*vyādhi*), which is dependent on both the deranged humor and the body substance (*dhātu,* e.g., blood, flesh, fat, bone, etc.) or anatomical part that is affected. Such factors as dietary imbalance, physical and emotional stresses, suppression of natural urges, or the effects of deeds in a previous life (*karmavipāka*) are said to cause the deranged humoral balance in a particular disease or subtype. Although this *tridoṣa* theory has been emphasized, a number of independent external factors are also recognized, including injuries, poisons, and supernatural agencies. Some early Ayurvedic passages employ references to these supernatural agencies as technical terms in order to develop meaningful diagnostic concepts while explicitly denying a supernatural conceptual frame of reference (see, for example, *Caraka Saṃhitā* 2.7.19–23). Other passages refer to demonic possession as it is more popularly understood. Specific classes of demons and deities, generically referred to as *bhūtas,* serve as paradigms for a range of character types and categories of mental disorder based on the well-known traits of *devas, gandharvas, rākṣasas, piśācas,* and others.

Therapy according to Ayurvedic principles is based on the premise that a humoral imbalance must be corrected by either pacifying or eliminating the excited humor. This is accomplished with preparations of herbs, animal products, and heavy metals; decoctions in clarified butter *(ghī)*; dietary adjustments; or by other means. One type of treatment described in the early texts that became especially popular in South India is *pañcakarma*; it involves emesis, purgation, sternutation, medicinal enema, and phlebotomy. Surgery is emphasized in the *Suśruta Saṃhitā.* The texts also specify ritual offerings, the recitation of sacred formulas *(mantras),* and other ritual procedures.

MEDICAL AND SOTERIOLOGICAL PLURALISM. The humoral theory of *tridoṣa* appears to have remained dominant throughout the course of development of the Ayurvedic tradition. In contrast, perhaps due in part to the growing influence of Tantra—the ritualization of otherwise socially unacceptable practices—in the culture at large from the middle of the first millennium CE, later Ayurvedic texts pay increased attention to magico-religious concepts and interventions that resonated with strains not only of Tantric literature but of the mystical aspects of Vedic literature as well. The number of classes of supernatural beings (*bhūtas*) associated with insanity steadily grew from eight in *Caraka* and *Suśruta* to twenty in the thirteenth-century text *Śārṅgadhara Saṃhitā* (1.7.38–39).

To the extent that this conceptual shift from a secular humoral theory toward a supernatural orientation is manifest in the later Ayurvedic compositions, it signifies a reaffirmation of certain aspects of the distinctly different worldview of the *Atharvaveda,* with which the mechanistic physiological theory of *tridoṣa* had made a definite break at an early stage in the development of Āyurveda. In the twentieth century, competition with Western-styled cosmopolitan medicine may have led some advocates of Āyurveda to ignore magico-religious aspects persisting in the tradition in favor of the systematic principles of the *tridoṣa* doctrine, and at the same time to focus on the issue of clinical efficacy of Ayurvedic therapies rather than the validity of the underlying humoral theory of other theoretical premises.

Hybrid ideologies that have emerged in the medically pluralistic setting of India presently complicate any analysis of the relationship between Āyurveda and other therapeutic options, both Western-styled and indigenous, since each system exerts some influence on the evolving conceptualizations of the others. Historically, Āyurveda has also stood in a complex relationship with coexisting traditions in its cultural context. However, it may be stated generally that healing is emphasized in Āyurveda, whereas other Hindu traditions such as Tantra, Yoga, and Indian alchemy (*rasavidyā*), which are primarily concerned with spiritual attainments, have overlapping objectives. Anatomical and physiological principles provide a framework in Āyurveda for understanding sickness and health in the physical body, but in Tantra and Yoga provide a framework for understanding the mystical path leading to the attainment of spiritual objectives. Similarly, although Indian alchemy was concerned with the use of preparations of mercury, other heavy metals, and herbs to restore youth and promote health, such motives were secondary to the primary goal of liberation of the spirit.

A number of philosophical concepts are specified in the Ayurvedic texts, referring to ideas more fully developed in the orthodox systems of Hindu philosophy, mainly Sāṃkhya, but also Nyāya-Vaiśeṣika and the rest. Social and ethical issues are also considered. Medical students are instructed to pledge diligence and purity, in accordance with the traditional values guiding students of the Veda, as they commence training under a guru after a prescribed initiation ceremony. Professional standards for physicians are advocated not only in medical treatises but in other Sanskrit treatises as well, especially in the Nītiśāstra and Dharmaśāstra texts on polity and Hindu law.

SEE ALSO Healing and Medicine, article on Healing and Medicine in Āyurveda and South Asia.

BIBLIOGRAPHY

Primary Sources

Translations of several Ayurvedic classics are available. *The Caraka Saṃhita*, 6 vols., prepared by the Shree Gulabkunverba Ayurvedic Society (Jamnagar, 1949), contains the Sanskrit text, translations into English, Hindi, and Gujarati, and an introductory volume. *Caraka-Saṃhitā: Agniveśa's Treatise Refined and Annotated by Caraka and Redacted by Dṛḍhabala*, 2 vols. (Varanasi, 1981–1983), is a critical edition and translation prepared by R. K. Sharma to facilitate further study of the text and its commentaries. *The Sushruta Samhita*, translated by Kaviraj Kunjalal Bishagratna (Calcutta, 1907–1916) has been reprinted (Varanasi, 1963), but it appears to be based on a Sanskrit text that varies somewhat from current printed editions. While only the first five chapters of *Vāgbhaṭa's Aṣṭāṅgahṛdayasaṃhitā* have been translated into English from the Tibetan version by Claus Vogel (Weisbaden, 1965), printed with the Tibetan and Sanskrit text, there is a complete translation in German by Luise Hilgenberg and Willibald Kirfel: *Vāgbhaṭa's Aṣṭāṅgahṛdayasaṃhitā: Ein altindisches Lehrbuch der Heilkunde* (Leiden, 1941). The work by G. J. Meulenbeld, *The Mādhavanidāna and Its Chief Commentary: Chapters 1–10* (Leiden, 1974), is the only English translation to provide both an Ayurvedic text and commentary, and it also contains useful appendices. Sanskrit editions of all the major texts are available.

Secondary Sources

The classic survey by Julius Jolly, *Medicin* (Strassburg, 1901), has been translated by C. G. Kashikar as *Indian Medicine*, 2d ed. (Delhi, 1977), and it remains a useful source for access to a range of texts on a given topic. The Ayurvedic tradition with reference to its context in the Vedic literature and its relationship to Greek medicine has been analyzed by Jean Filliozat in *La doctrine classique de la médecine indienne: Ses origines et ses parallèles grecs* (Paris, 1949), translated by Dev Raj Chanana as *The Classical Doctrine of Indian Medicine: Its Origins and Its Greek Parallels* (Delhi, 1964). *Asian Medical Systems: A Comparative Study*, edited by Charles Leslie (Berkeley, 1976), contains several noteworthy articles on various aspects of the Ayurvedic tradition, including A. L. Bash-am's survey of the social history of medicine during the classical period, "The Practice of Medicine in Ancient and Medieval India," pp. 18–43, and Charles Leslie's essay on the modernization of Ayurvedic institutions through the nineteenth and twentieth centuries, "Ambiguities of Revivalism in Modern India," pp. 356–367. Yoga, Tantra, and Indian alchemy are discussed in contrast to the objectives of "utilitarian medicine" in Mircea Eliade's *Yoga: Immortality and Freedom*, 2d ed. (Princeton, 1969). A comprehensive study of Indian chemistry and its roots in alchemy, tracing its development from pre-Harappan times through Vedic, Ayurvedic, and Tantric epochs, can be found in *History of Chemistry in Ancient and Medieval India*, edited by Priyadaranjan Ray (Calcutta, 1956).

New Sources

Fields, Gregory P. *Religious Therapeutics: Body and Health in Yoga, Ayurveda, and Tantra.* Albany, 2001.

Kulkarni, P. H. *Ayurveda Therapeutics.* Delhi, 2001.

Zysk, Jenneth G. *Asceticism and Healing in Ancient India: Medicine in the Buddhist Monastery.* New York, 1991.

MITCHELL G. WEISS (1987)
Revised Bibliography

AZTEC RELIGION developed in the capital city of Tenochtitlán in the Valley of Mexico between the fourteenth and sixteenth centuries CE. The Aztec religious tradition combined and transformed a number of ritual, mythic, and cosmic elements from the heterogeneous cultural groups who inhabited the central plateau of Mesoamerica. Seldom has a capital city fit the category of "center of the world" more completely than Tenochtitlán: the high plateau of Mexico is roughly the center of Mesoamerica; the Valley of Mexico is the heart of that plateau; interconnected lakes formed the center of the valley; and Tenochtitlán was constructed near the center of the lakes.

Mexico's central highlands had been the dominant cultural region of central Mesoamerica since the beginning of the common era, when the great imperial capital of Teotihuacán ("abode of the gods") had been established thirty miles north of where Tenochtitlán would later rise. Like Tenochtitlán, Teotihuacán was organized into four great quarters around a massive ceremonial center. Scholars and archaeologists have theorized that the four-quartered city was a massive spatial symbol for the major cosmological conceptions of Aztec religion. In many respects, the cultural and religious patterns of Teotihuacán laid the groundwork for all later developments in and around the Valley of Mexico. The mythologies of successive cultures—the Toltec and the Aztec most prominent among them—looked back to Teotihuacán as their symbolic place of origin and as the source for the legitimacy of their political authority.

Between 1300 and 1521 all roads of central Mesoamerica led into the lake region of the valley from which the magnificent capital of the Aztec arose. When the Aztec's precursors, the Chichimec ("dog lineage"; lit., "dog rope") migrated into the region in the thirteenth century, the valley was held by warring city-states constantly competing for land and tribute. This fragmented world was partly the result of the twelfth-century collapse of the northern Toltec empire centered at the illustrious capital of Tollan ("place of reeds"). The Toltec collapse brought waves of Chichimec and Toltec remnants into the Valley of Mexico, where they interacted with different city-states and religious traditions.

The basic settlement of central Mexico from Teotihuacán times was the *tlatocayotl*, or city-state, which consisted of a capital city surrounded by dependent communities that worked the agricultural lands, paid tribute, and performed services for the elite classes in the capital according to various ritual calendars and cosmological patterns. Occasionally one city-state would grow to large proportions and establish widespread territorial control and integration into some form of tributary empire. Around 1325, a Chichimec group who called themselves *México* settled Tenochtitlán and within a hundred years had organized a political unit with the power to dominate an expanding number of cities and towns in the central valley.

One of the major problems in the study of Aztec religion is the fragmentary nature of the pictorial, written, and archaeological sources associated with Tenochtitlán. The Spanish military conquest of Mexico was accompanied by a sustained campaign to eliminate Aztec symbols, images, screenfolds, and ceremonial buildings, as well as members of the military and priestly elites. Surprisingly, a counter attitude developed among certain Spanish officials and priests, who collected indigenous documents and organized their reproduction in order to enhance missionary work and inform Spanish officials about native religion and life. The result is a spectrum of sources including art and architecture; pre-Columbian screenfolds depicting the ritual, divinitory, historical, and genealogical traditions of different cities; post-Conquest codices sometimes accompanied by Spanish commentary; prose sources dependent on indigenous pictorial and oral traditions; histories written by descendants of Aztec royalty; Spanish eyewitness accounts; and large histories and ritual descriptions by Spanish priests such as Diego Durán, Toribio Motolinía, and Bernardino de Sahagún, who vigorously researched Aztec religion. It is only through a skillful combination of these sources that the complex character of Aztec religion can be discerned.

COSMOGONY AND COSMOLOGY. The general attitude toward the Aztec position in the cosmos is made clear in a poetic fragment about the capital that states:

> Proud of Itself Is the city of México-Tenochtitlán Here no one fears to die in war This is our glory This is your Command Oh Giver of Life Have this in mind, oh princes Who would conquer Tenochtitlán? Who could shake the foundation of heaven? (Miguel León-Portilla, *Pre-Columbian Literatures of Mexico*, 1968, p. 87)

The image of the capital city as the foundation of heaven, which the Aztec conceived of as a vertical column of thirteen layers extending above the earth, points to the cosmological conviction underpinning Aztec religion that there existed a profound correspondence between the sacred forces in the universe and the social world of the Aztec empire. This correspondence between the cosmic structure and the political state was anchored in the capital of Tenochtitlán.

In his important summary of religion in pre-Hispanic central Mexico, H. B. Nicholson (1971) outlines the "basic cosmological sequential pattern" of the Aztec cosmogony found in the myths and historical accounts associated with the México. A summary view reveals that Aztec life unfolded in a cosmic setting that was dynamic, unstable, and finally destructive. Even though the cosmic order fluctuated between periods of stability and periods of chaos, the emphasis in many myths and historical accounts is on the destructive forces which repeatedly overcame the ages of the universe, divine society, and the cities of the past.

This dynamic universe appears in the sixteenth-century prose accounts *Historia de los Mexicanos por sus pinturas* and the *Leyenda de los soles.* In the former, the universe is arranged in a rapid, orderly fashion after the dual creative divinity, Ometeotl, dwelling in Omeyocan ("place of duality") at the thirteenth level of heaven, generates four children, the Red Tezcatlipoca ("smoking mirror"), the Black Tezcatlipoca, Quetzalcoatl ("plumed serpent"), and Huitzilopochtli ("hummingbird on the left"). They all exist without movement for six hundred years, whereupon the four children assemble "to arrange what was to be done and to establish the law to be followed." Quetzalcoatl and Huitzilopochtli arrange the universe and create fire, half of the sun ("not fully lighted but a little"), the human race, and the calendar. Then, the four brothers create water and its divine beings.

Following this rapid and full arrangement, the sources focus on a series of mythic events that constitute a sacred history. Throughout this sacred history, the dynamic instability of the Aztec universe is revealed. The universe passes through four eras, called "Suns." Each age was presided over by one of the great gods, and each was named for the day (day number and day name) within the calendrical cycle on which the age began (which is also the name of the force that destroys that Sun). The first four Suns were called, respectively, 4 Jaguar, 4 Wind, 4 Rain (or 4 Rain of Fire), and 4 Water. The name of the fifth (and last) cosmic age, 4 Movement, augured the earthquakes that would inevitably destroy the world.

The creation of this final age, the one in which the Aztec lived, took place around a divine fire in the darkness on the mythical plain of Teotihuacán (to be distinguished from the actual city of that same name). According to the version of this story reported in Fray Bernardino de Sahagún's *Historia general de las cosas de la Nueva España* (compiled 1569–1582; also known as the Florentine Codex), an assembly of gods chose two of their group, Nanahuatzin and Tecuciztecatl, to cast themselves into the fire in order to create the new cosmic age. Following their self-sacrifice, dawn appears in all directions, but the Sun does not rise above the horizon. In confusion, different deities face in various directions in expectation of the sunrise. Quetzalcoatl faces east and from there the Sun blazes forth but sways from side to side without climbing in the sky. In this cosmic crisis, it is decided that all the gods must die at the sacrificial hand of Ecatl, who dispatches them by cutting their throats. Even this massive sacrifice does not move the Sun until the wind god literally blows it into motion. These combined cosmogonic episodes demonstrate the fundamental Aztec conviction that the world is unstable and that it draws its energy from massive sacrifices by the gods. Large-scale sacrifice became a basic pattern in Aztec religion, a ritual means of imposing or maintaining social and cosmological order.

With the creation of the Fifth Sun, the focus of the sacred history shifts from heaven to earth, where agriculture is discovered and human sacrifice is established as the proper ritual response to the requirements of the gods. In one account, Quetzalcoatl, as a black ant, travels to Sustenance Mountain with a red ant where they acquire maize for human beings. Other accounts reveal the divine origins of cotton, sweet potatoes, different types of corn, and the intoxicating drink called pulque. In still others, we learn that warfare was established so that human beings could be captured and sacrificed to nourish the Sun on its heavenly and nocturnal journey. Typically, a god like Mixcoatl creates four hundred human beings to fight among themselves in order for captives to be sacrificed in ceremonial centers to provide the divine food, blood, for the gods who ensure cosmic life.

Finally, a number of accounts of the cosmic history culminate with the establishment of the magnificent kingdom of Tollan where Quetzalcoatl the god and Topiltzin Quetzalcoatl the priest-king organize a ceremonial capital divided into five parts with four pyramids and four sacred mountains surrounding the central temple. This city, Tollan, serves as the heart of an empire. Aztec tradition states that "from Quetzalcoatl flowed all art and knowledge," representing the paradigmatic importance of the Toltec kingdom and its religious founder.

The spatial paradigm of the Aztec cosmos was embodied in the term *cemanahuac*, meaning the "land surrounded by water." At the center of this terrestrial space, called *tlalxico* ("navel of the earth"), stood Tenochtitlán, from which extended the four quadrants called *nauchampa*, meaning "the four directions of the wind." The waters surrounding the inhabited land were called *ilhuicatl*, the celestial water that extended upward to merge with the lowest levels of the thirteen heavens. Below the earth were nine levels of the underworld, conceived of as "hazard stations" for the souls of the dead, who, aided by magical charms buried with the bodies, were assisted in their quests for eternal peace at the lowest level, called Mictlan, the land of the dead.

The Mesoamerican pattern of quadrapartition around a center was a pervasive organizing principle of Aztec religion. It was used in the Aztec conceptions of temporal order as depicted in the famous Calendar Stone, where the four past ages of the universe are arranged in orderly fashion around the fifth or central age. Recent research has shown that this same spatial model was used to organize the celestial order of numerous deity clusters, the architectural design of palatial structures, the collection of economic tribute in the empire, and the ordering of major ceremonial precincts.

The Pantheon. One of the most striking characteristics of the surviving screenfolds, which present ritual and divinatory information, is the incredible array of deities who animated the ancient Mesoamerican world. Likewise, the remaining sculpture and the sixteenth-century prose accounts of Aztec Mexico present us with a pantheon so crowded that H. B. Nicholson's authoritative study of Aztec religion includes a list of more than sixty distinct and interrelated names. Scholarly analysis of these many deities suggests that virtually all aspects of existence were considered inherently sacred and that these deities were expressions of a numinous quality that permeated the "real" world. Aztec references to numinous forces, expressed in the Nahuatl word *teotl*, were always translated by the Spanish as "god," "saint," or "demon." But the Aztec *teotl* signified a sacred power manifested in natural forms (a rainstorm, a tree, a mountain), in persons of high distinction (a king, an ancestor, a warrior), or in mysterious and chaotic places. What the Spanish translated as "god" really referred to a broad spectrum of hierophanies that animated the world. While it does not appear that the Aztec pantheon or pattern of hierophanies was organized as a whole, it is possible to identify clusters of deities organized around the major cult themes of cosmogonic creativity, fertility and regeneration, and war and sacrificial nourishment of the Sun.

Aztec deities were represented pictorially as anthropomorphic beings. Even in cases where the deity took an animal form, as in the case of Xolotl, the divine dog, or the form of a ritual object, as in the case of Itztli, the knife god, he was disguised with human features like arms, torso, legs, face, and so on. Aztec deities dwelt in the different levels of the thirteen-layered celestial sphere or the nine-layered underworld. The general structuring principle for the pantheon, derived from the cosmic pattern of a center and four quarters, resulted in the quadruple or quintuple ordering of gods.

For instance in the Codex Borgia's representation of the Tlaloques (rain gods), the rain god, Tlaloc, inhabits the central region of heaven while four other Tlaloques inhabit the four regions of the sky, each dispensing a different kind of rain. While deities were invisible to the human eye, the Aztec saw them in dreams, visions, and in the "deity impersonators" (*teixiptla*) who appeared at the major ceremonies. These costumed impersonators, sometimes human, sometimes effigies of stone, wood, or dough, were elaborately decorated with identifying insignia such as conch shells, masks, weapons, jewelry, mantas, feathers, and a myriad of other items.

As we have seen, Aztec religion was formed by migrating Chichimec who entered the Valley of Mexico and established important political and cultural centers there. This process of migration and urbanization informed and was informed by their concept of deity. An outstanding feature of Aztec religion was the tutelary-patron relations that specific deities had with the particular social groups whom they guided during their peregrinations. These patron deities (or *abogados,* as the Spanish chroniclers called them) were represented in the *tlaquimilolli,* or sacred bundles, that the *teomamas* ("godbearers," or shaman-priests) carried on their backs during the long journeys. The *teomama* passed on to the community the divine commandments communicated to him in visions and dreams. These sacred specialists were considered *hombre-dioses* (Span., "man-gods"), whose extraordinary powers of spiritual transformation, derived from their closeness with these numinous forces, enabled them to guide, govern, and organize the tribe during migrations and the settlement of new communities. A familiar pattern in the sacred histories of Mesoamerican tribal groups is the erection of a shrine to the patron deity as the first act of settlement in a new region. This act of founding a settlement around the tribal shrine represented the intimate tie between the deity, the *hombre-dios,* and the integrity of the people. In reverse fashion, conquest of a community was achieved when the patron deity's shrine was burned and the *tlaquimilolli* was carried off as a captive.

This pattern of migration, foundation, and conquest associated with the power of a patron diety is clearly exemplified by the case of Huitzilopochtli, patron of the wandering Méxica. According to Aztec tradition, Huitzilopochtli inspired the Méxica *teomama* to guide the tribe into the Valley of Mexico, where he appeared to them as an eagle on a cactus in the lake. There they constructed a shrine to Huitzilopochtli and built their city around the shrine. This shrine became the Aztec Great Temple, the supreme political and symbolic center of the Aztec empire. It was destroyed in 1521 by the Spanish, who blew up the temple with cannons and carried the great image of Huitzilopochtli away. This colossal image of the Aztec god has never been found.

CREATOR GODS. The Aztec high god, Ometeotl ("lord of duality") was the celestial, androgynous, primordial creator of the universe, the omnipotent, omniscient, omnipresent foundation of all things. In some sources he/she appears to merge with a number of his/her offspring, a sign of his/her pervasive power. Ometeotl's male aspects (Ometecuhtli and Tonacatecuhtli) and female aspects (Omecihuatl and Tonacacihuatl) in turn merged with a series of lesser deities associated with generative and destructive male and female qualities. The male aspect was associated with fire and the solar and maize gods. The female aspect merged with earth fertility goddesses and especially corn goddesses. Ometeotl inhabited the thirteenth and highest heaven in the cosmos, which was the place from which the souls of infants descended to be born on earth. Ometeotl was more "being" than "action." Most of the creative effort to organize the universe was accomplished by the divine couple's four offspring: Tezcatlipoca, Quetzalcoatl, Xiuhtecuhtli, and Tlaloc.

Tezcatlipoca ("smoking mirror") was the supreme active creative force of the pantheon. This powerful, virile numen had many appellations and was partially identified with the supreme numinosity of Ometeotl. Tezcatlipoca was also identified with Itztli, the knife and calendar god, and with Tepeyolotl, the jaguar-earth god known as the Heart of the Hill, and he was often pictured as the divine antagonist of Quetzalcoatl. On the social level, Tezcatlipoca was the archsorcerer whose smoking obsidian mirror revealed the powers of ultimate transformation associated with darkness, night, jaguars, and shamanic magic.

Another tremendous creative power was Xiuhtecuhtli, the ancient fire god, who influenced every level of society and cosmology. Xiuhtecuhtli was represented by the perpetual "fires of existence" that were kept lighted at certain temples in the ceremonial center at all times. He was manifested in the drilling of new fires that dedicated new ceremonial buildings and ritual stones. Most importantly, Xiuhtecuhtli was the generative force at the New Fire ceremony, also called the Binding of the Years, held every fifty-two years on the Hill of the Star outside of Tenochtitlán. At midnight on the day that a fifty-two-year calendar cycle was exhausted, at the moment when the star cluster we call the Pleiades passed through the zenith, a heart sacrifice of a war captive took place. A new fire was started in the cavity of the victim's chest, symbolizing the rebirth of Xiuhtecuhtli. The new fire was carried to every city, town, and home in the empire, signalling the regeneration of the universe. On the domestic level, Xiuhtecuhtli inhabited the hearth, structuring the daily rituals associated with food, nurturance, and thanksgiving.

FERTILITY AND REGENERATION. A pervasive theme in Aztec religion was fertility and the regeneration of agriculture. Aztec society depended on a massive agricultural system of *chinampas* ("floating gardens") that constituted large sections of the city's geographical space. Also, surrounding city-states were required to pay sizable amounts of agricultural goods in tribute to the capital. While many female deities inspired the ritual regeneration of agriculture, the most ancient and widespread fertility-rain god was Tlaloc, who dwelt on the prominent mountain peaks, where rain clouds were thought to emerge from caves to fertilize the land through rain, rivers, pools, and storms. The Aztec held Mount Tlaloc to be the original source of the waters and of vegetation. Tlaloc's supreme importance is reflected in the location of his shrine alongside that of Huitzilopochtli in the Templo Mayor. Surprisingly, the great majority of buried offerings excavated at the temple were dedicated to Tlaloc rather than Huitzilopochtli.

Two other major gods intimately associated with Tlaloc were Chalchiuhtlicue, the goddess of water, and Ehécatl, the wind god, an aspect of Quetzalcoatl. Ehécatl was known as in *tlachpancauh in tlaloques* ("road sweeper of the rain gods"), meaning that Ehécatl's forceful presence announced the coming of the fertilizing rains. Other prominent fertility deities included Centeotl, goddess of maize; Xilonen, goddess of the young maize; Ometochtli, goddess of maguy; and Mayahuel, whose four hundred breasts insured an abundant supply of pulque for ritual drinking.

The most powerful group of female fertility deities were the *teteoinnan*, a rich array of earth-mother goddesses, who were representatives of the usually distinct but sometimes combined qualities of terror and beauty, regeneration and destruction. These deities were worshiped in cults concerned with the abundant powers of the earth, women, and fertility. Among the most prominent were Tlazolteotl, Xochiquetzal, and Coatlicue. Tlazolteotl was concerned with sexual powers and passions and the pardoning of sexual transgressions. Xochiquetzal was the goddess of love and sexual desire and was pictured as a nubile maiden associated with flowers, feasting, and pleasure. A ferocious goddess, Coatlicue ("serpent skirt") represented the cosmic mountain that conceived all stellar beings and devoured all beings into her repulsive, lethal, and fascinating form. Her statue is studded with sacrificed hearts, skulls, hands, ferocious claws, and giant snake heads.

A prominent deity who linked agricultural renewal with warfare was Xipe Totec, whose gladiatorial sacrifice renewed vegetation in the spring and celebrated success on the battlefield. Part of his ceremony, called the Feast of the Flaying of Men, included the flaying of the sacrificial victim and the ceremonial wearing of the skin by the sacred specialist. Xipe Totec's insignia, including the pointed cap and rattle staff, was the war costume of the Méxica emperor.

Ceremony and Sacrifice. Another important facet of Aztec religious practice was human sacrifice, usually carried out for the purpose of nourishing or renewing the Sun or other deity (or to otherwise appease it), thus ensuring the stability of the universe. The mythic model for mass human sacrifice was the story of the creation of the fifth age, in which the gods themselves were sacrificed in order to empower the Sun. Tonatiuh, the personification of that Sun (whose visage appears in the center of the Calendar Stone), depended on continued nourishment from human hearts.

Some of the large-scale sacrificial ceremonies re-created other sacred stories. For example, women and masses of captive warriors were sacrificed in front of the shrine of Huitzilopochtli atop the Templo Mayor. Their bodies tumbled down the steps to rest at the bottom with the colossal stone figure of Coyolxauhqui, Huitzilopochtli's dismembered sister, symbolically reenacting the legendary slaughter of the four hundred siblings at Huitzilopochtli's birth.

Cosmology, pantheon, and ritual sacrifice were united and came alive in the exuberant and well-ordered ceremonies carried out in the more than eighty buildings situated in the sacred precinct of the capital and in the hundreds of ceremonial centers throughout the Aztec world. Guided by detailed ritual calendars, Aztec ceremonies varied from town to town but typically involved three stages: days of ritual preparation, death sacrifice, and nourishing the gods. The days of ritual preparation included fasting; offerings of food, flowers, and paper; use of incense and purification techniques; embowering; songs; and processions of deity-impersonators to various temples in ceremonial precincts.

Following these elaborate preparations, blood sacrifices were carried out by priestly orders specially trained to dispatch the victims swiftly. The victims were usually captive warriors or purchased slaves. Though a variety of methods of ritual killing were used, including decapitation, burning, hurling from great heights, strangulation, and arrow sacrifice, the typical ritual involved the dramatic heart sacrifice and the placing of the heart in a ceremonial vessel *(cuauhxicalli)* in order to nourish the gods. Amid the music of drums, conch shell trumpets, rattles, and other musical instruments, which created an atmosphere of dramatic intensity, blood was smeared on the face of the deity's image and the head of the victim was placed on the giant skull rack *(tzompantli)* that held thousands of such trophies.

All of these ceremonies were carried out in relation to two ritual calendars, the 365-day calendar or *tonalpohualli* ("count of day") consisting of eighteen twenty-day months plus a five-day intercalary period and the 260-day calendar consisting of thirteen twenty-day months. More than one-third of these ceremonies were dedicated to Tlaloc and earth fertility goddesses. Beside ceremonies relating to the two calendars, a third type of ceremony related to the many life cycle stages of the individual. In some cases, the entire community was involved in bloodletting.

Aztec religion, as we have seen, was formed during the rise to empire of a minority population who inherited urban traditions and sociopolitical conflicts of great prestige and intensity. This remarkable tradition came to an abrupt end during the military conquest of Tenochtitlán by the Spanish and the subsequent destruction of ceremonial life. But it is important to note that one of the last images we have of the Templo Mayor of Tenochtitlán before it was blown apart by Spanish cannon is the image of Aztec warriors sacrificing captive Spanish soldiers in front of the shrine to Huitzilopochtli.

See Also Coatlicue; Huitzilopochtli; Human Sacrifice; Quetzalcoatl; Tezcatlipoca; Tlaloc.

BIBLIOGRAPHY

Broda, Johanna. "El tributo en trajes guerreros y la estructura del sistema tributario Mexica." In *Economia, política e ideología en el México prehispanico*, edited by Pedro Carrasco and Johanna Broda. Mexico City, 1978. A valuable study of the pattern and structure of tributary payments to Tenochtitlán during the height of its dominance.

Brundage, Burr C. *The Fifth Sun: Aztec Gods, Aztec World.* Austin, Tex., 1979. The best English-language monograph introduction to Aztec religion; provides an insightful understanding of the Aztec pantheon and human sacrifice.

Carrasco, David. *Quetzalcoatl and the Irony of Empire; Myths and Prophecies in Aztec Tradition.* Chicago, 1982. Utilizing the history of religions approach, the author focuses on the Quetzalcoatl paradigm to study the history of Mesoamerican religions.

López Austin, Alfredo. *Hombre-Dios: Religión y política en el mundo Nahuatl.* Mexico City, 1973. The best Spanish-language account of the interweaving of myth, history, politics, and religious authority in Mesoamerican history.

Matox Moctezuma, Eduardo. *Una visita al Templo Mayor de Tenochtitlán.* Mexico City, 1981. The chief excavator of the Aztec Great Temple describes the fascinating treasures found at the heart of the Aztec empire.

Nicholson, H. B. "Religion in Pre-Hispanic Central Mexico." In *Handbook of Middle American Indians*, edited by Robert Wauchope, vol 10. Austin, Tex., 1971. The classic description of Mesoamerican religion in the central plateau of Mexico during the decades prior to the Conquest.

Pasztory, Esther. *Aztec Art.* New York, 1983. The finest single-volume description and interpretation of Aztec art and its religious significance. Excellent prose accompanied by magnificent photographs.

Townsend, Richard. *State and Cosmos in the Art of Tenochtitlán.* Washington, D.C., 1979. A concise, brilliant interpretation of the monumental art of the Aztec capital of Tenochtitlán in the light of a good understanding of religious realities.

New Sources

Almere Read, Kay. *Time and Sacrifice in the Aztec Cosmos.* Bloomington, Ind., 1998.

Anaya, Rudolfo A., and Francisco A. Lomelí, eds. *Aztlán: Essays on the Chicano Homeland.* Albuquerque, 1989.

Bierhorst, John. *History and Mythology of the Aztecs: The Codex Chimalpopoca.* Tucson, 1992.

Carrasco, David. *Religions of Mesoamerica: Cosmovision and Ceremonial Centers.* San Francisco, 1990.

Markman, Robert H., and Peter T. Markman. *Flayed God: The Mesoamerican Mythological Tradition: Sacred Texts and Images From Pre-Columbian Mexico and Central America.* San Francisco, 1992.

McKeever-Furst, Leslie. *Natural History of the Soul in Ancient Mexico.* New Haven, 1995.

Miller, Mary Ellen, and Karl Taube. *The Gods and Symbols of Ancient Mexico and the Maya: An Illustrated Dictionary of Mesoamerican Religion.* London, 1993.

Pérez Guerrero, Juan Carlos. *Religión azteca.* Madrid, 2000.

DAVÍD CARRASCO (1987)
Revised Bibliography

B

BAAL. The name Baal *(bʿl)* is a common Semitic appellative meaning "lord" that is used as a proper name for the West Semitic storm god in ancient Near Eastern texts dating from the late third millennium BCE through the Roman period. Identified as the warrior Hadd (or Hadad) in the Late Bronze Age texts from Ugarit, Baal is a popular deity in Syro-Palestinian or "Canaanite" religious traditions as a god of storms and fertility. Associated with kingship and oaths, his name appears as a divine witness to international treaties and as a common element in theophoric names. Baal was venerated in West Semitic religious traditions as a powerful god and patron of humanity for over two thousand years.

The character of Baal is most fully described in the Late Bronze Age archives of the ancient Syrian city of Ugarit (modern Ras Shamra), where he is the patron of the royal house and protector of the city. Archaeologists have recovered hundreds of mythological, epic, and ritual texts written in an alphabetic cuneiform script from this coastal site since its rediscovery in 1929. The Baal revealed in these texts is an aggressive and powerful warrior who vies for kingship among the gods. Frequent epithets for Baal in the Ugaritic texts include "Almighty Baal" (*aliyn bʿl*), "the mightiest of warriors" (*aliy qrdm*), "the rider of the clouds" (*rkb ʿrpt*), and "the Prince, lord of the earth" (*zbl bʿl arṣ*). He is the son of the grain god Dagan and the brother of the violent Maiden Anat. Baal dwells on Mount Saphon (*ṣpn*), identified with Jebel el-Aqra (Mons Casius in classical sources), the highest peak in Syria. From here he also controls the winds and storms at sea and acts as the protector of mariners.

As a god of the storm, Baal is depicted as both a divine warrior and the provider of natural fertility in the form of dew and rains. His presence in the heavens is manifested by dark clouds, roaring winds, peals of thunder, and bolts of lightning. Ugaritic myths depict Baal as victorious in battle against the primordial forces of Sea (Yamm) and Death (Mot). He is praised for his defeat of dragons or sea monsters called Litan the Fleeing Serpent, Tunnan, and the seven-headed Twisting Serpent. Baal's distinctive iconography portrays him as a bearded god, wearing a conical hat with two horns, brandishing a mace or battle-ax in his right hand and grasping lightning and thunderbolts in the left. As king (*mlk*) of the gods, Baal rules the cosmos under the authority of El, the grey-bearded patri-

---

CLOCKWISE FROM TOP LEFT CORNER. Eleventh-century black basalt relief depicting the birth of Kṛṣṇa. Indian Museum, Calcutta. *[©Giraudon/Art Resource, N.Y.]*; Female temple figure. Bali, Indonesia. *[©Wolfgang Kaehler/Corbis]*; The Great Buddha in Kamakura, Japan. *[©Edifice/Corbis]*; Buddha sculpture and stupas at Borobudur in Java, Indonesia. *[©Owen Franken/Corbis]*; A mid-nineteenth-century *nahen* (a house partition screen) depicting a squatting bear, from Tlingit, Alaska. Denver Art Museum. *[©Werner Forman/Art Resource, N.Y.]*.

archal leader of the divine assembly. Baal "reigns over the gods," "issues orders to gods and humans," and "satisfies the multitudes of the earth" with his fertilizing rains in Ugaritic poetry. The absence of Baal from the world results in "no dew, no downpour, no swirling of the deeps, no welcome voice of Baal" to break the sweltering heat, according to the Aqhat epic. Baal is also associated with the fertility of the herd, as is mythologically represented in two Ugaritic texts that describe his sexual intercourse with a cow, who then bears a son as his heir.

The myth of Baal's rise to sovereignty over the gods is narrated in the six tablets of the Ugaritic Baal Cycle, which encompasses three main sections. The elderly god El presides over the divine assembly, while a younger god is enthroned as the active king of the cosmos. As the son of Dagan, Baal has a conflicted relationship with El, who resists Baal's rise to power in preference for his own sons' claims to divine kingship. In the cycle's first episode, Baal contends with Yamm (Sea) for dominion among the gods. After defeating Yamm with the help of magic war clubs crafted by Kothar-wa-Hasis, Baal seeks permission from El to build a palace as a symbol of his divine kingship. Kothar, Anat, and El's own consort, Athirat, eventually support Baal in the political intrigue, and his palace is constructed in the second section of the Baal Cycle.

The third section of the Baal Cycle describes Baal's conflict with divine Mot (Death), who challenges Baal's kingship. Mot demands that the storm god "enter the maw of Death" and descend into the underworld. Baal immediately submits to Mot's authority, but the fragmentary text obscures the sequence of events at this point. It remains unclear if Baal actually dies and enters the dreary land of the dead. Regardless, the heavenly gods believe that Baal has died. Anat discovers a corpse "in the pleasant field of Death's Realm" (*ysmt šd šḫlmmt*). There is a burial, copious ritual mourning, and funerary offerings by El and Anat in honor of the fallen Baal. After these events, El and the divine council unsuccessfully seek a replacement for Baal as the king of the gods. Meanwhile, Anat approaches Mot with a pitiful request to release her brother. When her pleas go unheeded for months, Anat violently attacks Mot, chops his body into pieces, and scatters his remains upon the fields for the birds to consume. After more broken text, El has an oracular dream of Baal's return to the earth in which "the heavens rain oil and the wadis run with honey" to relieve the parched furrows of the fields. Baal then returns to the divine assembly, defeats his enemies, and is again seated upon "the throne of his dominion." Later, "in the seventh year," Mot returns to challenge Baal's sovereignty, but the sun goddess Shapsh mediates between the rival gods and resolves their dispute in favor of Baal. The Baal Cycle concludes with the establishment of Baal's kingship over the heavenly gods, the earth, and humanity.

Scholars continue to debate whether Baal is appropriately described as a "dying and rising god" whose annual death and resurrection are cultically reenacted within a seasonal calendar. Certain West Semitic texts also hint at Baal's role in the revivification of the dead in a netherworld existence. Indeed, some scholars identify Baal as the leader of the Rephaim, the underworld shades of deceased kings, but no consensus exists among scholars on this issue. The Ugaritic myth of the voracious "Devourers" also narrates Baal's defeat and seven-year absence from the earth. The fragmentary character of the relevant episodes in the Baal Cycle precludes any definite conclusion, but perhaps Baal is most accurately described as a "disappearing god," similar to certain Hittite traditions. There is no compelling evidence for the ritual reenactment of Baal's annual death and resurrection in any ancient Syro-Palestinian source. Mot's absence for seven years in the Baal Cycle further argues against the alleged seasonal pattern of the conflict between Baal's fructifying rains and Mot's sterile rule during the heat of summer. Yet the seasonal aspects of the drama between the rain god and Mot cannot be denied. With their emphasis on fertility, death, and the politics of divine kingship, the myths of Baal represent the precarious balance of powerful forces at play in the natural, divine, and human realms. In many ways, Baal himself symbolizes the fragility of life, fertility, and political stability in a hostile cosmos.

In the Hebrew Bible, the Phoenician Baal appears as the most prominent divine rival to the Israelite god, Yahweh. Indeed, the two gods share many of the same qualities and epithets. Like Baal, Yahweh is depicted as a god of the storm who sounds his voice in thunder and sends lightning (*Ps.*18:10–16). Yahweh is the rider of the clouds (*Isa.*19:1; *Ps.* 68:5), who dominates the sea (*ym*) and vanquishes primordial dragons or sea monsters, including Tannin and Leviathan the Twisting Serpent (*Ps.* 74:13–14; *Isa.* 27:1; 51:9–10; *Job* 26:12–13). Yahweh is also responsible for human and natural fertility, including the "dew of the heavens and the fat of the earth, the abundance of new grain and wine" (*Gen.* 27:28).

SEE ALSO Dying and Rising Gods.

BIBLIOGRAPHY

Parker, Simon B., ed. *Ugaritic Narrative Poetry.* Atlanta, 1997. Excellent and accessible English translations of the Ugaritic mythological texts.

Schwemer, Daniel. *Die Wettergottgestalten Mesopotamiens und Nordsyriens im Zeitalter der Keilschriftkulturen.* Weisbaden, 2001. See pp. 443–588.

Smith, Mark S. *The Ugaritic Baal Cycle, I.* Leiden, 1994. The first volume of a projected three-volume commentary on the Baal Cycle.

Smith, Mark S. *The Early History of God: Yahweh and the Other Deities in Ancient Israel.* 2d ed. Grand Rapids, Mich., 2002. An excellent introduction with comprehensive bibliographic references to recent work.

Van der Toorn, Karel, Bob Becking, and Pieter W. van der Horst, eds. *Dictionary of Deities and Demons in the Bible.* 2d ed. Leiden, 1999. See the entries by W. Hermann on "Baal," pp. 132–139, and J. C. Greenfield on "Hadad," pp. 377–382.

NEAL H. WALLS (2005)

BAAL, JAN VAN. Jan van Baal (1909–1992), a Dutch anthropologist of religion, studied Indonesian culture, law, and languages at Leiden University and was influenced by J. P. B. de Josselin de Jong's structural ethnology. Van Baal's Ph.D. thesis (1934) about the Marind-anim of New Guinea was based on ethnographic material collected by the Swiss ethnologist Paul Wirtz. Van Baal later became a civil servant in the Dutch East Indies (1934–1949), a prisoner in Japanese concentration camps (1942–1945), an advisor on native affairs to the government of Dutch New Guinea (1946–1953), and the governor of Dutch New Guinea (1953–1958). Van Baal served as professor of cultural anthropology at the University of Utrecht from 1959 to 1973, and he acted until 1969 as director of the Royal Tropical Institute in Amsterdam. He published *Dema,* a thousand-page volume on the Marind-anim of New Guinea in 1966, and a number of articles and books, of which *Symbols for Communication* (1971), *Reciprocity and the Position of Women* (1975), and *Man's Quest for Partnership* (1981) are the most important. Van Baal was admired by many anthropologists, Margaret Mead and Claude Lévi-Strauss among them.

Van Baal's theory is based on the view that religion is a system of symbols by which humans communicate with their universe. These symbols enable individuals to overcome their inner solitude, which is the inescapable result of their inability to solve the existential problem of being subjects opposed to and separated from their universe, as well as being part of that same universe and at the same time functioning in it. Religion enables humans to cope with the contradictions related to human existence itself. The several contradictions inherent in the phenomenon of religion must be connected with contradictions in human existence. These contradictions are the result of the idea of being opposed to the world one lives in. People express their detachment, as well as their feelings of being part of their world, in symbolic activities. The dialectics of "subject to" and "part of" contain the uncertainty of individuals. The ambition of self-realization can bring the individual into conflict with the universe, and it creates a dualism because one's fellow human beings and one's surroundings are used as instruments for self-realization. But, at the same time, the individual wants to be recognized and treated as a partner. Problems of doubt and loneliness, which are the result of this dualism, can only be solved, according to van Baal, when humans manage to remain subject to, as well as part of, the community.

Symbols play a crucial role here, since they can save people from existential solitude, and their analysis is therefore important in van Baal's work. In his Marind-anim ethnography he decodes the meanings of specific symbols and their interrelations within the context of the analysis of a specific culture, religion, or mythology. After this, more general descriptions of processes of symbolization are pointed out by different kinds of classifications. He characterizes the relation between the subject and the symbols he uses as being asymmetrical. The subject is unique and timeless, but the symbols are temporary and infinitely numerous. Moreover, van Baal holds that systems of symbols do not spring from the interaction between individuals and their surroundings, but first of all from the individual.

The basic model of gift exchange and reciprocity described by Marcel Mauss is given great emphasis in van Baal's line of thought. But among the distinctive features of offering and sacrifice he does not include their sacred nature. For him, both sacrifice and offering have one characteristic in common, that of being gifts. The dialectics of the human condition make communication an urgent necessity, and the gift is an attractive and persuasive form for establishing contacts and ameliorating relations. Giving is a symbolic act of communication; it is the symbol that counts, and the notion that offering and sacrifice are sacral acts hardly plays a role. Van Baal objects to a reification of the symbolic content by interpreting it as a magical act; he also objects to the use of the term *sacrifice* for rituals in which every element of the gift or of atonement is absent. For him, giving is participating, and it is essential for a meaningful existence. All communication begins with giving.

Van Baal's description of religion comes down to the acceptance of a non-empirical reality that influences the reality of people's daily life. Opposing the classical comparative method in cultural anthropology, he uses a monographic method that compares only a few religions after a systematic description of each separate religion. In doing so, van Baal wants to exclude ethnocentrism and a priori arguments. He does not make this "overall approach" absolute, and invariably asks himself what is the measure of integration between the elements of a religious system, how far does it link up with other social or cultural institutions, and whether or not its relation with them is strained. When it comes to the question what individual motives underlie the development of religious ideas, van Baal thinks that craving for "communion" is the fundamental motive. A successful ritual makes the participant feel at ease with his world. In his view, being part of a community implies the acceptance of authority, which reduces individual freedom.

In van Baal's work there is no connection between the development of religions and social stratification, religious specialists and charismatic leaders, and there is little analysis of the dynamics of religion and its social components, as can be found in the work of Max Weber. Van Baal's approach is ahistorical and structuralistic, and he is highly critical of phenomenologists like Gerardus van der Leeuw and Mircea Eliade. Van Baal is interested in the conscious ordering, in the role of the participants in the processes of symbolization. Unlike Lévi-Strauss, Baal is not concerned with the analysis of the results of human thought or the discovery of the grammar in them. Instead, he is primarily interested in and looking for the motives in human thought, and he is searching for its message and meaning.

BIBLIOGRAPHY

Selected Works of van Baal

Over Wegen en Drijfveren der Religie. Amsterdam, 1947.

De magie als godsdienstig verschijnsel. Amsterdam 1960.

Dema: A Description and Analysis of Marind-anim Culture. The Hague, 1966.

"The Political Impact of Prophetic Movements." In *International Yearbook for the Sociology of Religion* 5 (1969): 68–88.

Symbols for Communication: An Introduction to the Anthropological Study of Religion. Assen, Netherlands, 1971; 2d ed., 1985.

De Boodschap der Drie Illusies: Overdenkingen over religie, kunst en spel. Assen, Netherlands, 1972.

Reciprocity and the Position of Women: Anthropological Papers. Assen, Netherlands, 1975.

"Offering, Sacrifice, and Gift." *Numen* 23 (1976): 161–178.

"The Role of Truth and Meaning in Changing Religious Systems." In *Official and Popular Religion: Analysis of a Theme for Religious Studies,* edited by Pieter Vrijhof and Jacques Waardenburg, pp. 607–628. The Hague, 1979.

Man's Quest for Partnership: The Anthropological Foundations of Ethics and Religion. Assen, Netherlands, 1981.

"The Language of Symbols." In *L'ethnologie dans le dialogue intercultural* (Ethnologie im dialog, vol. 5), edited by Gerhard Baer and Pierre Centlivres. Freiburg, Germany, 1980.

"The Dialectics of Sex in Marind-anim Culture." In *Ritualized Homosexuality in Melanesia,* edited by Gilbert H. Herdt, pp. 128–166. Berkeley, 1984.

About van Baal's Work

Droogers, A. F. *Boodschap uit het Mysterie: Reacties op de visie van Jan van Baal.* Baarn, Netherlands, 1996.

Kuiper, Y. B. "Religion, Symbols, and the Human Condition: An Analysis of the Basic Ideas of Jan van Baal." In *On Symbolic Representation of Religion: Groninger Contributions to Theories of Symbols,* edited by Hubertus G. Hubbeling and Hans G. Kippenberg, pp. 57–69. Berlin and New York, 1986.

Kuiper, Y. B., and A. de Ruijter. *De Menselijke Conditie: Speurtocht naar Partnerschap.* Groningen, Netherlands, 1982.

W. HOFSTEE (2005)

BAʿAL SHEM TOV (master of the good name), popular designation for Yisraʾel ben Eliʿezer (c. 1700–1760), the founder of the Hasidic movement in eastern Europe, who is also known by the acronym BeSHT (commonly written "Besht"). There are few historically authentic sources that describe the life of the Besht; most information must be gleaned from nineteenth-century hagiography, especially the collection of more than three hundred stories about him, known as *Shivhei ha-Besht* (*In Praise of the Besht;* first printed in 1815), and the works of later Hasidic writers.

Born in the small town of Okopy in the southern Ukraine, Yisraʾel ben Eliʿezer is said to have begun preaching around 1738, after a long period of seclusion in the Carpathian Mountains with his wife. According to other accounts, he served throughout his life as a popular healer, writer of amulets, and exorcist of demons from houses and bodies, which were the traditional roles of a *baʿal shem* (master of the name) or *baʿal shem tov* (master of the good name)—in other words, the master of the name that empowered him to perform what he wished.

In his wandering around many Jewish communities, the Besht came into contact with various circles of pietists. In some cases he was criticized by the rabbis, but his powers as a preacher and magician attracted disciples, including masters of Jewish law and Qabbalah such as Yaʿaqov Yosef of Polonnoye (d. 1782) and Dov Ber of Mezhirich (1704–1772). As Gershom Scholem has suggested, the Besht should be regarded as the founder of the great eastern European Hasidic movement, even though our knowledge of his organizational work is scanty, and even though the first Hasidic center was established only after his death by Dov Ber, who became the leader of the movement.

Although he was not a scholar in Jewish law, the Besht was well versed in Qabbalah and in popular Jewish ethical tradition, on which he relied when delivering his sermons and formulating his theories. He saw the supreme goal of religious life as *devequt* (cleaving), or spiritual communion with God; this state can be achieved not only during prayers but also in the course of everyday activities. In his view, there is no barrier between the holy and the profane, and worship of God can be the inner content of any deed, even the most mundane one. Indeed, the Besht did not insist on following the complicated qabbalistic system of *kavvanot* (intentions) in prayers and in the performance of the Jewish religious commandments, but substituted instead the mystical devotion of *devequt* as the primary means of uplifting the soul to the divine world. His teachings also included the theory that evil can be transformed into goodness by a mystical process of returning it to its original source in the divine world and redirecting it into good spiritual power; this idea was further developed by his followers.

The Besht believed that he was in constant contact with the divine powers and saw his mission as that of correcting and leading his generation. In a letter preserved by Yaʿaqov Yosef (whose voluminous works contain the most important material we have concerning the Besht's teachings), the Besht indicates that he practiced *ʿaliyyat neshamah,* or the uplifting of the soul. In this way, he explained, he communicated with celestial powers who revealed their secrets to him. According to the document, these included the Messiah, who told him that redemption would come when his teachings were spread all over the world (which the Besht interpreted as "in a long, long time").

The Besht was convinced that his prayer carried special weight in the celestial realm and that it could open heavenly gates for the prayers of the people as a whole. His insistence that there are righteous people in every generation who, like himself, carry special mystical responsibilities for their communities laid the foundations for the later Hasidic theory of the function of the *tsaddiq,* or leader, a theory that created a new type of charismatic leadership in the Jewish communities of eastern Europe.

SEE ALSO Hasidism, overview article.

BIBLIOGRAPHY

Dan Ben-Amos and Jerome R. Mintz have translated and edited *Shivhei ha-Besht* as *In Praise of the Ba'al Shem Tov: The Earliest Collection of Legends about the Founder of Hasidism* (Bloomington, Ind., 1970). Gershom Scholem has discussed the Besht in *Major Trends in Jewish Mysticism,* 3d rev. ed. (New York, 1961), pp. 330–334, 348–349. Three papers concerning the Besht and Hasidism are included in Scholem's *The Messianic Idea in Judaism* (New York, 1972), pp. 176–250. Additional bibliographic references accompany his article "Israel ben Eliezer Ba'al Shem Tov" in *Encyclopaedia Judaica* (Jerusalem, 1971).

Several monographs dealing with the Besht and the beginnings of Hasidism were published in the 1990s, some of them concentrated around the historical figure and others on his theology and religious message. Rachel Elior emphasizes the Besht's mystical theology of divine immanence and omnipresence in her *Herut 'al Ha-luhot* (Tel Aviv, 1999), whereas Moshe Idel's *Hasidism between Ecstasy and Magic* (Albany, N.Y., 1995) tries to integrate the Besht and his teachings with medieval mystical-magical models; Immanuel Etkas, in his historical analysis *Ba'al Hashem: The Besht—Magic, Mysticism, Leadership* (Jerusalem, 2000, in Hebrew), emphasizes the Besht's social message and minimizes the magical one. Moshe Rosman's *Founder of Hasidism: A Quest for the Historical Ba'al Shem Tov* (Berkeley, Calif., 1996) presents a critical analysis of the historical sources and a detailed study of contemporary Polish documents.

JOSEPH DAN (1987 AND 2005)

BABA YAGA, known in Russian folklore as a witch and an ogress, is the ancient goddess of death and regeneration of Slavic mythology, with roots in the pre-Indo-European matrilinear pantheon. In Slavic folk tales (mainly Russian), Baba Yaga lives in nocturnal darkness, deep in the woods, far from the world of men. She is variously depicted as an evil old hag who eats humans, especially children, and as a wise, prophetic old woman. In appearance, she is tall, bony-legged, and pestle-headed, with a long nose and disheveled hair. At times she appears as a young woman, at other times as two sisters, one young and one old. Her primary theriomorphic image is that of a bird or a snake, but she can turn instantly into a frog, a toad, a turtle, a mouse, a crab, a vixen, a bee, a mare, a goat, or an inanimate object.

Baba Yaga never walks; she either flies in a fiery mortar or lies in her hut on top of the oven, on a bench, on the floor, or stretched from one end of the hut to the other. The fence around her hut is made of human bones and is topped with human skulls, with eyes intact. The gate is fastened with human legs and arms instead of bolts, and a mouth with sharp teeth serves as a lock. The hut, which is supported on bird's legs and which can turn around on its axis like a spindle, is, in fact, Baba Yaga herself.

Linguistic analysis of Baba Yaga's compound name reveals prehistoric characteristics. *Yaga,* from Proto-Slavic **(y)ega,* means "disease," "fright," and "wrath" in Old Russian, Serbo-Croatian, and Slovene, respectively, and is related to the Lithuanian verb *engti* ("strangle, press, torture"). The early form may be related to Proto-Samoyed **nga,* meaning "god," or "god or goddess of death." The Slavic etymon *baba* means "grandmother," "woman," "cloud woman" (a mythic being who produces rain), and "pelican." The last points to Baba Yaga's avian nature, comparable to that of the archetypal vulture and owl goddess of European prehistory, who represents death and regeneration. In Russian tales, Baba Yaga eats humans by pecking like a bird.

In East Slavic areas, Baba Yaga has a male counterpart, Koshchei Bessmertnyi, "Koshchei the Immortal." His name, from *kost'* ("bone"), bears the notion of a dying and rising god, that is, a deity who cyclically dies and is reborn. In tales in which Koshchei appears, Baba Yaga is either his mother or his aunt. Another male equivalent of Baba Yaga is Morozko ("frost"). Baba Yaga is also the "mother of winds," analogous to the German Frau Holle. Other relatives in current folklore are the Lithuanian goddess Ragana and the Basque vulture goddess, the "Lady of Amboto."

BIBLIOGRAPHY

Shapiro, Michael. "Baba-Jaga: A Search for Mythopoeic Origins and Affinities." *International Journal of Slavic Linguistics and Poetics* 27 (1983).

Toporov, V. N. "Khettskaia SALSU: GI i slavianskaia Baba-Iaga." *Kratkie soobshcheniia Instituta slavianovedeniia* (Moscow) 38 (1963): 28–37.

New Sources

Hubbs, Joanna. *Mother Russia: The Feminine Myth in Russian Culture.* Bloomington, Ind., 1988.

MARIJA GIMBUTAS (1987)
Revised Bibliography

BĀBĪS. Bābīs are the followers of the teaching of Sayyid ʿAlī Muḥammad, known as the "Bāb." Immediately after the Bāb's demise, the name Bābīs was applied to these people for some years; since the 1860s those Bābīs who followed Bahāʾ Allāh, became known as the "people of Bahā" or as Bahāʾī. A minority group that follows Ṣubḥ-i Azal as a successor of the Bāb is known as Azalīs.

SAYYID ʿALĪ MUḤAMMAD, THE BĀB. Born in Shiraz on October 20, 1819, ʿAlī Muḥammad was orphaned as a young boy and subsequently raised by a maternal uncle who, as is indicated by the title Sayyid, is believed to have been a descendant of Muḥammad. ʿAlī Muḥammad earned his early living as a merchant, traveling in Iran and Iraq for his business. In 1840–1841 he visited the famous Shīʿah shrines at Karbala, Iraq, where he came in contact with Sayyid Kāẓim Rastī, the leader of the Shaykhī movement. This movement originated with Shaykh Aḥmad al-Ahsāʾī (d. 1826), whose mystical and philosophical interpretation of Islam was based on the theosophical philosophy of Mullā Ṣadrā Shīrāzī and other Muslim Gnostics, but which was also a dissent from the orthodoxy of the ʿulamāʾ. After studying Shaykhī doctrines for about eight months, ʿAlī Muḥammad returned to Shiraz. In 1842 he married, and he had one son who died as an infant. ʿAlī Muḥammad's relationship with the Shaykhīs during the next two years is not entirely clear, but he was inclined to some of the Shaykhī teachings and also to chiliastic expectations in connection with the hidden (twelfth) *imām* of Shīʿī Islam.

After Sayyid Kāẓim Rastī's death in December 1843, some of the Shaykh's disciples were looking for the expected Mahdi, whose appearance had been predicted for the near future. One of these disciples, Mullā Ḥusayn of Bushrūyah, met with Sayyid ʿAlī Muḥammad in Shiraz on May 22, 1844. In this encounter Sayyid ʿAlī Muḥammad presented himself as the Bāb, the "gate" to the hidden *imām.* Mullā Ḥusayn accepted this claim and thus was the first to recognize the Bāb as his new spiritual leader. That same night the Bāb started composing his first major literary work, a long commentary in Arabic language on the *sūrah* of Yūsuf in the Qurʾān (*Sūrah* 12), the *Qayyūm al-asmaʿ*. Both Bābīs and Bahāʾīs consider this commentary the first revealed work of the Bāb, making it the starting point of a new era. Some of the Shaykhīs and Shīʿī Muslims soon made up an increasing number of disciples of the Bāb, and he designated the foremost eighteen of them as *Ṣurūf al Ṣayy* (letter of the living), among them Mullā Ḥusayn and Qurrat al-ʿAyn.

In September 1844 the Bāb began a pilgrimage to Mecca, and he returned to Shiraz in late spring of the following year. During his pilgrimage journey he maintained the conviction that other Muslims might join his "reforming" view of Shīʿī Islam, a conviction reflected both in some *khuṭbah* read during his pilgrimage journey and also in letters to Muḥammad Shāh. Judging from references in the *Bayān*, the Bāb's central book, the pilgrimage was not a positive experience because he learned that the majority of Muslims did not agree with his views. Back in Shiraz, he was imprisoned for four months. After his release he moved to Esfahan, but in early 1847 he again was put in jail, first at the fortress of Mākhū in Azerbaijan, from where he was transferred to the castle of Chirīq in April 1848. Shortly before this move to Chirīq, the Bāb sent a letter to Mullā Shaykh ʿAlī Turshīzī, presenting himself as the long-awaited twelfth Shīʿī *imām.* For Bāb's followers, foremost among them the *Ḥurūf al-Ḥayy*, this letter marked the clear decision to dissent from the *sharīʿah.*

The leading Bābīs met in July in Badasht, close to the Caspian Sea. The meeting was intended to discuss the consequences of the Bāb's declaration to be the returned *imām* and to make plans to free him from prison. Qurrat al-ʿAyn, well versed in Shīʿī and Shaykhī thinking and a leader of the meeting, fostered a radical position regarding a total and social break with Islam. In addition to unveiling her own position, she also motivated her fellow believers to separate from Muslims, if necessary by force. After the death of Muḥammad Shāh in September 1848, some radical Bābīs hoped for the opportunity to establish a "sacred Bābī state," leading to Bābī uprisings and a "Bābī *jihād*" for the next five years. The Bāb remained in prison, and in 1850 he was given a death sentence. He was executed on July 9, 1850.

FROM THE BĀBĪS TO THE BAHĀʾĪS. The first years after the Bāb's death can be seen as a period of persecution. The Bābīs were responsible for some revolts against the Qajār government that led to an attempt to assassinate Nāṣir al-Dīn Shāh in 1852. As a consequence severe persecution of the Bābīs was renewed, and all the *Ḥurūf al-Ḥayy* were put to death, including Qurrat al-ʿAyn in 1853. The main centers of these Bābī revolts and Muslim persecutions were Mazandaran, Nayriz, and Zanjan. Based on the Bāb's interpretation of *jihād*, Bābīs displayed great heroism, but they were forced to surrender to the Qajār troops.

The Bābī community was then led by Mīrzā Yaḥyā Nūrī, called Ṣubḥ-i Azal (Morning of Eternity), the half brother of Mīrzā Ḥusayn ʿAlī Nūrī, called Bahāʾ Allāh (Bahá'u'lláh according to Bahāʾī orthography). Because Ṣubḥ-i Azal had stayed at Nur at the time of the attack on Nāṣir al-Dīn Shāh, he escaped imprisonment, whereas his half brother Bahāʾ Allāh was jailed in Tehran in the summer of 1852. After some months Bahāʾ Allāh was exiled to Baghdad, at that time part of the Ottoman Empire, rather than Qajār, arriving there on April 8, 1853. Some months earlier Ṣubḥ-i Azal had also settled there. During the early period in Baghdad, in the vicinity of Shīʿī and Shaykhī centers like Nadjaf and Karbala, the Bābīs looked to Ṣubḥ-i Azal as the leader of the community, but tensions between him and his half brother could not be hidden any longer. The main reason for these tensions might have been the quite different characters of the men. Ṣubḥ-i Azal seemed only partly aware of the needs of his community to survive, whereas Bahāʾ Allāh reorganized the community and strengthened it in the late 1860s. From a sociological point of view, therefore, Ṣubḥ-i Azal lost his influence on the Bābīs more and more, whereas Bahāʾ Allāh gained importance as a community leader. Since 1861 the Ottoman government had pressured the Bābī movement, which ended with the exiles of Bahāʾ Allāh and Ṣubḥ-i Azal via Istanbul to Edirne. Before leaving Baghdad, Bahāʾ Allāh, in the presence of some close followers, proclaimed himself a new prophet made manifest by God, thus theologically ending, according to the Bahāʾī interpretation, the Bābī movement as an independent religion. Even though Ṣubḥ-i Azal might have known about this, he was only informed about Bahāʾ Allāh's claim to be "the one whom God shall manifest" in the so-called *surāt al-amr* sent by Bahā᾽ Allāh to his half brother on March 10, 1866. This date marks the definitive break between the Bābī and Bahā᾽ī groups.

While the majority sided with Bahā᾽ī Allāh, a minority followed Ṣubḥ-i Azal, joining him at his exile in Cyprus, where he had been since 1868. On April 20, 1912, Ṣubḥ-i Azal died on the island, and he was buried in Famagusta, according to Muslim practice. Thus it is safe to conclude that the Bābī community on Cyprus could not prosper any longer, whereas some followers of the Bāb still live in Iran as so-called Bābī-Azalīs. During the twentieth century they showed neither further theological development nor large-scale organization, but instead turned into a more static community, preserving the writings of the Bāb and Ṣubḥ-i Azal. Thus they mainly live as a hidden minority, passing on the religious heritage through family lines, often not distinguishable amid their Muslim surroundings. Most probably there are not more than one or two thousand Bābī-Azalīs residing in Iran.

BĀBĪ DOCTRINES. The main source for Bābī doctrine is the *Bayān* (Declaration), the holy book of this religion, written by the Bāb in Persian and Arabic during his imprisonment. Though based on monotheism like Islam, the eschatological thought is changed, as "the day to come" is no more a day in the far future. Rather, anyone who lives with God can enjoy the joy of paradise in a spiritual way even in the present. The universal eschatology will start with "the one whom God will manifest." According to Bābī teaching, no precise date is given for this eschatological event, whereas Bahā᾽īs take it for granted that the Bāb indicated that this would happen in the near future after his demise. On the other hand, Bābī doctrines maintain their traditional bond to Shīʿī Islam, as is the case with *taqīya*, the possibility of hiding one's religious thoughts or convictions in times of crisis or danger. The idea of martyrdom and warlike *jihād* as a means to reach salvation also remain central in Bābī thought.

The *Bayān* also is the foundation of Bābī religious law, thus abrogating Islamic *sharīʿah*. Some of the famous religious laws concern the new direction of the *qiblah*, no longer the Kaʿbah in Mecca but the Bāb's house in Shiraz. Another change in religious ritual law is in connection with the cultic calendar, which divides the solar year into nineteen months with nineteen days each, and four additional days. According to the Iranian solar year, the Bābī year also begins at the spring solstice. Within the new calendar, the month of fasting became fixed at the last month of the Bābī year in March.

Generally speaking, these doctrines and practices have been fixed in the various writings of the Bāb and, to a minor degree, also in the writings of Ṣubḥ-i Azal, whose "Mu᾽tammim-i Bayān" features as the conclusion of the *Bayān*, thus focusing on Ṣubḥ-i Azal's claim (against Bahā᾽ Allāh) that he is the real successor of the Bāb. Further writings by Ṣubḥ-i Azal can be seen as interpretations and elaborations of the Bāb's teachings, mainly written after the split between the Bābīs and the Bahā᾽īs to uphold Bābī doctrine as a religious system of its own, thus focusing on eschatology and the question of the future divine prophet.

SEE ALSO Bahā᾽īs.

BIBLIOGRAPHY

Primary Sources

ʿAbdu᾽l-Bahā. *A Traveller's Narrative Written to Illustrate the Episode of the Bāb.* Translated by Edward G. Browne. Cambridge, U.K., 1891; reprint, Amsterdam, 1975.

Bāb, ʿAlī Muḥammad Shīrāzī. *Le Béyân Arabe.* Translated by Alphonse L. M. Nicolas. Paris, 1905.

Bāb, ʿAlī Muḥammad Shīrāzī. *Le Béyân Persan.* Translated by Alphonse L. M. Nicolas. 4 vols. Paris, 1911–1914.

Bāb, ʿAlī Muḥammad. *Selections from the Writings of the Bāb.* Translated by Habib Taherzadeh. Haifa, Israel, 1976.

Husain, Hamadānī. *The Tārihk-i-Jadīd; or, New History of Mīrza ʿAli Muhammad, the Bāb.* Translated by Edward G. Browne. Cambridge, U.K., 1893; reprint, Amsterdam, 1975.

Nabīl-i-Aʿzam. *The Dawn-Breakers: Nabīl's Narrative of the Early Days of the Bahā᾽ī Revelation.* Edited and translated by Effendi Shoghi. Wilmette, Ill., 1999.

Studies

Amanat, Abbas. *Resurrection and Renewal: The Making of the Babi Movement in Iran, 1844–1850.* Ithaca, N.Y., and London, 1989. Study of the historical and sociological background of the early Bābī period.

Balyuzi, Hasan M. *The Bāb.* Oxford, 1973. Comprehensive biography of the Bāb.

Hutter, Manfred. "Prozesse der Identitätsfindung in der Frühgeschichte der Bahā᾽ī-Religion: Zwischen kontinuierlichem Bewahren und deutlicher Abgrenzung." In *Kontinuität und Brüche in der Religionsgeschichte,* edited by Michael Stausberg, pp. 424–435. Berlin, 2001. Study of the split between the Bābī and the Muslim communities in 1848 and between the Bābī and the Bahā᾽ī communities in 1863–1866 from the pattern of "identity."

MacEoin, Denis. "The Babi Concept of Holy War." *Religion* 12 (1982): 93–129.

MacEoin, Denis. *The Sources for Early Bābi Doctrine and History: A Survey.* Leiden, Netherlands, 1992. Important study of partly unpublished manuscripts for Bābī history.

Stümpel, Isabel. "Ṭāhira Qurrat al-ʿAin." In *Iran im 19. Jahrhundert und die Entstehung der Bahā᾽ī Religion,* edited by Johann Christoph Bürgel and Isabel Schayani, pp. 127–143. Hildesheim, Germany, 1998. Study of the history and personality of Qurrat al-ʿAyn, focusing on her role in the shaping of the Bābī community.

MANFRED HUTTER (2005)

BABYLONIAN RELIGION SEE MESOPOTAMIAN RELIGIONS

BACCHIC GOLD TABLETS SEE ORPHIC GOLD TABLETS

BACHOFEN, J. J. (1815–1887) was a Swiss scholar of mythology and Roman law and history. Through his most famous books, *Gräbersymbolik* (1859) and *Mutterrecht* (Mother right, 1861), Bachofen had a great influence on twentieth-century culture, even in fields not closely related to the history of religions.

LIFE. Johann Jakob Bachofen was born to a patrician family in Basel, Switzerland, on December 22, 1815. His father, Johann Jacob Bachofen, owned a highly successful silk ribbon business that had belonged to the family since 1720. The wealth accumulated by the Bachofens was visible in their immense real-estate holdings, as well as in their rich art collection. Bachofen's mother, Valeria Merian, came from one of Basel's most distinguished families of important businessmen, politicians, and university professors.

Bachofen was brought up to be a pious churchgoing member of the French reformed Christian community. In 1831 he became a student at the *Pädagogium*, the preparatory college of Basel University, which he entered in 1834. Here his most important teacher was Franz Dorotheus Gerlach in Latin, and the two became lifelong friends. From 1835 to 1837 Bachofen studied at Berlin University, attending lectures of the outstanding representative of the historical school of law, Friedrich Karl von Savigny (who influenced him deeply); the romantic geographer Karl Ritter, whose lessons on ancient geography were to be of great importance for Bachofen's conception of matriarchy; the philologists August Böckh and Karl Wilhelm Lachmann; and the historian Leopold von Ranke. In order to deepen his knowledge of Roman law, Bachofen spent the winter semester of 1837–1838 at the University of Göttingen, where he took courses with Gustav Hugo (the founder of the historical school of law and a friend of Savigny) and the classicist Karl Otfried Müller. In 1838, after having achieved his doctoral degree in Basel with a study on Roman law, Bachofen spent a year in Paris taking courses at the *École de Droit* and the *Collège de France* under Pellegrino Rossi, as well as one year in London and Cambridge. By 1840 he had returned to Basel, where he became ordinary professor of Roman law in 1841, appellate judge at the criminal court in 1842 (a post he filled for twenty-five years), and a member of the Basel Senate in 1844. He resigned his university position in 1844 because of a political campaign directed against him by the local press, and in 1845 he gave up his seat in the Senate. He also served briefly on the university governing board (1855–1858), but resigned because of conflict with a colleague. Thereafter Bachofen withdrew completely from academic life.

The turning point in Bachofen's life came during his first journey to Italy in 1842 (a journey followed by others in 1848–1849, 1851–1852, 1863, and 1865). Here, especially while visiting Roman archaeological museums and ancient tombs, he found inspiration for his works on prehistoric, oriental, and pre- or early Roman Italy, and he came to understand the importance of funerary evidence (the *Gräberwesen*) for the study of antiquity. Other archaeological trips reinforced this direct approach to the ancient world: Greece (1851–1852); the British Museum in London (1847 and 1852); the Louvre in Paris (1852, 1860, 1864, and 1865); and Spain and southern France (1861).

After leaving behind his studies on Roman law, which had made him a respected scholar, Bachofen abandoned mainstream classical philology, first in his *Geschichte der Römer* (1851), in which he led a direct attack on the principles of the eminent scholars Barthold Niebuhr and Theodor Mommsen, then in the *Gräbersymbolik* and the *Mutterrecht.* The latter two books, which are inextricably linked, were the result of seventeen years of collecting and organizing a huge amount of literary and archaeological data, most of which remains unpublished.

By the late 1860s Bachofen had started studying the writings of the most important ethnologists and anthropologists of his time: John Ferguson McLennan, Werner Munzinger, John Lubbock, Edward Burnett Tylor, Adolf Bastian, and Lewis Henry Morgan, among others (he read altogether more than six hundred different authors). In these years he planned a revised edition of the *Mutterrecht*, which would have taken into account "the remains of the maternal system surviving in all the peoples of the world," as he stated in a letter to Heinrich Meyer-Ochsner (November 10, 1870). He never managed to fulfill this task, but published these extensive ethnological data in the *Antiquarische Briefe* (1880 and 1886). Bachofen died on November 25, 1887; he was survived by his wife, Louise Elisabeth Burckhardt, whom he had married in 1865, and their twenty-one-year-old son.

OEUVRE. Bachofen's dissertation on Roman law was written in Latin: *De romanorum iudiciis, de legis actionibus, de formulis et de condicione* (1840). His inaugural lecture, "Das Naturrecht und das geschichtliche Recht in ihren Gegensätzen," held on the occasion of his appointment to a professorship at Basel University on May 7, 1841, is important for understanding his Savigny-influenced view of Roman law. Other major works on this topic are *Die lex Voconia und die mit ihr zusammenhängenden Rechtsinstitute* (1843) and *Das römische Pfandrecht* (1847). Bachofen's main treatises on Roman history are the *Politische Betrachtungen über das Staatsleben des römischen Volkes* (published posthumously in 1848) and *Die Geschichte der Römer*, edited with Gerlach (1851).

Bachofen's eventual rejection of scholarly philology and his conversion to a symbolic approach to antiquity is most evident in a letter to Savigny dated September 24–27, 1854 (published as "Eine Selbstbiographie" in *Zeitschrift für vergleichende Rechtswissenschaft* 34, 1916, pp. 337–380). In this context the strong impression exercised on Bachofen by the ancient sites of Italy and Greece is of utmost importance (see

Griechische Reise, written in 1851 and edited 1927 by Georg Schmidt). Other major writings leading to his works on funerary symbolism and gynecocracy are the unpublished *Das alte Italien* (especially the incomplete manuscript 104, written in 1855) and the lecture "Über das Weiberrecht" given in Stuttgart on September 9, 1856 (*Verhandlungen der 16, Versammlung deutscher Philologen, Schulmänner und Orientalisten*, 1857, pp. 40–64). Bachofen's two chief books are *Versuch über die Gräbersymbolik der Alten* (1859) and *Das Mutterrecht: Eine Untersuchung über die Gynaikokratie der Alten Welt nach ihrer religiösen und rechtlichen Natur* (1861), the latter of which he dedicated to his mother, Valeria Merian.

Strongly inspired by Georg Friedrich Creuzer's *Symbolik und Mythologie der alten Völker* (1819–1822), Bachofen's *Gräbersymbolik* conceives myth as "the exegesis of the symbol" (*Gesammelte Werke*, 1943–1967, vol. 4, p. 61). Myth narrates through a series of connected actions what the symbol embodies and unifies. Similar to a discursive philosophical treatise, myth unfolds the profound, impenetrable muteness of the symbol, though respecting and not violating its intrinsic mystery: "to expound the mystery doctrine in words would be a sacrilege against the supreme law; it can only be represented in the terms of myth" (*Gesammelte Werke*, 1943–1967, vol. 4, p. 61). The symbols of funerary art (Bachofen takes into account Greek, Roman, Egyptian, and Microasiatic evidence) are thus capable of revealing the true essence of antiquity, as well as of religion throughout. In the *Gräbersymbolik*, the most significant symbols analyzed are those of the three mysteric eggs and of the rope-weaver Ocnus. The myths arising from them explain the relationships between the cosmic powers of life and death, light and obscurity, spirit and matter, masculine and feminine, and right and left, as well as the duality of Roman power as exemplified by Romulus and Remus (and consul and magistrate).

The symbolic context of the *Gräbersymbolik* also occurs in Bachofen's best-known work, the *Mutterrecht*. Here he presents his theory of the evolution of human society from its beginning to modernity as it develops through three stages of civilization (*Kulturstufen*). According to this scheme, before the stage of patriarchal society, which extends from Homeric antiquity to the present, in prehistoric times there were two earlier and universal stages. The first was that of *haeterism* (or *aphroditism*), a stage of sexual promiscuity and social anarchy very close to the original state of nature. During this stage, humans lived in swamps without any legal and ethical obligation, and women suffered complete domination by every male component of the horde. Since descent could be reckoned only through the mother, women rebelled against this condition of disorderly life and instituted the *mother right*, at once a juridical system, a social order, and a religious view founded on the principle of matrilinearity (in Bachofen's view this matrilinear aspect is particularly evident within the ancient Lycians: see his *Das lykische Volk und seine Bedeutung für die Entwicklung des Alterthums*, 1862).

This second stage, *gynecocracy*, was thus characterized by the nonviolent power of the materfamilias, who endorsed piety, communal peacefulness, and the prosperity of the people and life. This new stage took place within an agricultural milieu, where the worship of chthonic and lunar deities prevailed over that of heavenly and solar ones. The most important divinity was the mother goddess Demeter, who was closely linked to the fertility of earth and women. Towards its end however, this stage degenerated into *amazonism*, that is, the military predominance of women over men. The reaction to the female principle was fulfilled by Dionysian religion, which determined the decline of gynecocracy and gave way to the third and last *Kulturstufe*, that of *patriarchy*.

In patriarchy, the Dionysian principle was soon replaced by the Apollonian, then by Roman law, and finally by Christianity. Humankind organized society in patrilinear families, grouped in cities, kingdoms, and empires. In Bachofen's view, the patriarchal order represented the victory of spirit over matter, of culture over nature, of reason over instinct, but also of arbitrary power over freedom, of social hierarchy over communal unity, of violence over peace. Beneath Apollo, the main divinity of this stage was Zeus, father and king of the Olympian gods, who embodied the spiritual, uranic, and male principle.

The assumption of a gynecocratic, oriental root for Roman history inspired the main work of Bachofen's maturity, *Die Sage von Tanaquil: Eine Untersuchung über den Orientalismus in Rom und Italien* (1870), a book juxtaposed with Theodor Mommen's popular *Römische Geschichte* (1854–1856). The *Antiquarische Briefe vornehmlich zur Kenntnis der ältesten Verwandtschaftsbegriffe* (1880/1886), which are dedicated to Morgan, shed light on the great influence the American scholar had on Bachofen starting from 1874 onwards, inspiring his vast studies on the institution of the avunculate in matrilinear societies (still partly unpublished). The posthumously edited *Römische Grablampen* (1890) shows how in the last weeks of his life Bachofen had returned to study funerary symbolism.

Reception and Influence. During Bachofen's lifetime only his writings on Roman law were appreciated. His works on Roman history and on mythology were criticized or even ignored by most of the scholars of his time. The only specialists who admired Bachofen's work were Meyer-Ochsner, a wealthy private scholar like himself, and Alexis Giraud-Teulon, a French honorary professor at the University of Geneva; Bachofen corresponded with both of them for years. Giraud-Teulon was profoundly influenced by the *Mutterrecht*, whose theories he reformulated in *La mère chez certains peuples de l'antiquité* (1867) and *Les origines du mariage et de la famille* (1884). These works presented Bachofen's ethnosociological conceptions from a scholarly though simplified point of view, making them accessible to anthropologists, ethnologists, and sociologists of the time. Lubbock (*The Origin of Civilization*, 1870) and McLennan (*Studies in Ancient History*, 1876) took great interest in Giraud-Teulon's interpretations of Bachofen's ideas; Morgan even considered the Swiss scholar to be the predecessor of his own theories (*Ancient Society,* 1877). From the end of the nineteenth century until the late 1920s, Bachofen was considered a forerunner of family-evolutionism; most discussed were his conceptions of haeterism and matrilinear gynecocracy. Although these topics were progressively abandoned by scholars, Bachofen's theory of the *Kulturstufen,* closely related to that of the *Kulturkreise,* survived within the ethnology and sociology of the first half of the twentieth century (e.g., that of Leo Frobenius, Oswald Spengler, Adolf Ellegard Jensen, and Wilhelm Schmidt).

Morgan's works and Giraud-Teulon's Bachofen-influenced idea of an original communism influenced Karl Marx (see *The Ethnological Notebooks,* edited by Lawrence Krader, 1972) and Friedrich Engels (*Der Ursprung der Familie, des Privateigenthums und des Staates,* 1884; in the fourth edition of this book in 1891 Bachofen's influence is even stronger). Later this topic was studied also by Paul Lafargue, Heinrich Cunow, Wilhelm Reich, Erich Fromm, Max Horkheimer, and Ernst Bloch.

The work of Bachofen reached its greatest popularity during the 1920s, when it was rediscovered by the *Münchner Kosmiker* Karl Wolfskehl, Alfred Schuler, and Ludwig Klages. Klages's *Vom Kosmogonischen Eros* (1922) introduced a true *Bachofen-Renaissance,* which expanded in a variety of fields, reaching from mythical symbolism (Carl Albrecht Bernoulli, *J. J. Bachofen und das Natursymbol* [1924] and *J. J. Bachofen als Religionsforscher* [1924]; Alfred Bäumler, "Bachofen, der Mythologe der Romantik," an introduction to the renowned anthology of Bachofen's work, *Der Mythus von Orient und Occident,* edited by Bäumler and Manfred Schröter [1926]; and Karl Kerényi, *Bachofen und die Zukunft des Humanismus* [1945]), to psychology (Carl Gustav Jung, who suggested translating Bachofen's work into English in 1967, and Erich Neumann), to literature (Hugo von Hofmannsthal, Gerhard Hauptmann, Walter Benjamin, and Thomas Mann), to ancient history (George Thomson), to city planning (Lewis Mumford), and to feminism (August Bebel, Robert Briffault, Ernest Bornemann, Evelyn Reed, Ida Magli, Marie Louise Janssen-Jurreit, Richard Fester, and Heide Göttner-Abendroth).

SEE ALSO Creuzer, G. F.; Evola, Julius; Family; Feminine Sacrality; Feminist Theology, overview article; Frobenius, Leo; Goddess Worship, overview article; Gynocentrism; Kulturkreiselehre; Patriarchy and Matriarchy.

BIBLIOGRAPHY

A detailed bibliography of Bachofen's printed writings and the literature on his life and works is available in Hans-Jürgen Hildebrandt, *J. J. Bachofen: A Bibliography of the Primary and Secondary Literature* (in English and German; Aachen, Germany, 1988). Most of Bachofen's published and previously unpublished work has been collected in his *Gesammelte Werke,* 8 vols., edited by Karl Meuli and others (Basel, 1943–1967). The remaining (10,000) unedited handwritten pages lying in the Basel University archive are thoroughly described by Johannes Dörmann in his *Archiv J. J. Bachofen auf der Grundlage des Nachlasses J. J. Bachofen* (Basel, 1987; appendix to the *Gesammelte Werke,* vol. 5). Further insight into the *Bachofen-Archiv* is supplied by Emanuel Kienzle, "Nachwort," in *Gesammelte Werke,* vol. 6, pp. 459–477 (1951); Ernst Howald, "Nachwort," in *Gesammelte Werke,* vol. 4, pp. 507–560 (1954); and Philippe Borgeaud, *La mythologie du matriarcat: L'atelier de J. J. Bachofen* (Geneva, 1999). A selection of Bachofen's major work in English translation, with notes, glossary, and bibliography, is *Myth, Religion, and Mother Right: Selected Writings of J. J. Bachofen,* translated by Ralph Mannheim with a preface by George Boas and an introduction by Joseph Campbell (Princeton, 1967; 2d ed., 1992).

The most complete sketch of Bachofen's life and work until 1861 is Karl Meuli's "Nachwort," in *Gesammelte Werke,* vol. 3, pp. 1011–1128 (1948). The years leading to the *Sage von Tanaquil* are covered by Emanuel Kienzle, "Nachwort," in *Gesammelte Werke,* vol. 6, pp. 447–451 (1951), whereas the period after 1870 is examined by Johannes Dörmann's "Bachofens 'Antiquarische Briefe' und die zweite Bearbeitung des Mutterrechts," in *Gesammelte Werke,* vol. 8, pp. 523–602 (1966). The peculiarity of Bachofen's personality within German scholarship has been outlined by Jonathan D. Fishbane, *Mother-right, Myth, and Renewal: The Thought of J. J. Bachofen and Its Relationship to the Perception of Cultural Decadence in the Nineteenth Century* (Ann Arbor, Mich., 1982), and Lionel Gossman, *Basel in the Age of Burckhardt* (Chicago and London, 2000), pp. 111–200, the latter focusing on Bachofen's relationship to Mommsen ("Orpheus Philologus: Bachofen versus Mommsen on the Study of Antiquity," *Transactions of the American Philosophical Society* 73 [1983]: 1–89). Bachofen's studies in the history of Roman law have been examined by Roy Garré, *Fra diritto romano e giustizia popolare: Il ruolo dell'attività giudiziaria nella vita e nell'opera di J. J. Bachofen* (Frankfurt am Main, 1999), and Annamaria Rufino, *Diritto e storia: J. J. Bachofen e la cultura giuridica romantica,* 2d ed. (Naples, 2002). His conception of history was examined by Georg Schmidt, *J. J. Bachofens Geschichtsphilosophie* (Munich, 1929); Johannes Dörmann, "War J. J. Bachofen Evolutionist?" *Anthropos* 60 (1695): 1–48; and Andreas Cesana, *J. J. Bachofens Geschichtsdeutung* (Basel, 1983); his relationship to politics by Max Burckhardt, *J. J. Bachofen und die Politik* (Basel, 1942).

In Germany, Bachofen's success in the second half of the twentieth century owes much to Marxism and feminism (see Uwe Wesel, *Der Mythos vom Matriarchat* [Frankfurt am Main, 1980] and Hartmut Zinser, *Der Mythos des Mutterrechts* [Frankfurt am Main, 1981]); to literature (Walter Muschg, *Bachofen als Schriftsteller* [Basel, 1949]); and to psychology (Adrien Turel, *Bachofen-Freud: Zur Emanzipation des Mannes vom Reich der Mütter* [Bern, 1939]). A comprehensive reconstruction of the *Bachofen-Renaissance* can be found in *Das Mutterrecht von J. J. Bachofen in der Diskussion,* edited by Hans-Jürgen Heinrichs, 2d ed. (Frankfurt am Main, 1987). Other collections include *J. J. Bachofen (1815–1887): Eine Begleitpublikation zur Ausstellung im Historischen Museum Basel,* edited by Barbara Huber-Greub (Basel, 1987) and *Matriarchatstheorien der Altertumswissenschaft,* edited by Beate Wagner-Hasel (Darmstadt, Germany, 1992).

In France, where the *Mutterrecht* had been translated already in 1903 by the Group of Feminist Studies in Paris (a new translation by Étienne Barilier appeared 1996 in Lausanne), the strong criticism of Émile Durkheim prevented Bachofen's work from having any influence within the École Sociologique. In Italy, on the contrary, where most of Bachofen's works have been translated (starting with the anthology *Le madri e la virilità olimpica*, edited by Julius Evola [Milan, 1949]), many scholars have produced important writings on various aspects of the Swiss mythologist (Arnaldo Momigliano, Giampiera Arrigoni, Giulio Schiavoni, Eva Cantarella, and Giampiero Moretti). International conferences on Bachofen took place in 1987 and 1988 (Pisa: "Seminario su J. J. Bachofen," *Annali della Scuola Normale di Pisa* 18 [1988]: 599–887; Rome: "J. J. Bachofen e la discussione sull'origine dello Stato," *Quaderni di Storia* 28 [1988]: 7–139).

ALESSANDRO STAVRU (2005)

BACON, FRANCIS (1561–1626), Lord Verulam, Viscount St. Albans; English statesman, essayist, and philosopher of science. A major political figure in early Stuart England, Bacon drew a visionary picture of the role and practices of the science of the future. This science was to be experimental, and Bacon advocated setting up public institutions for its pursuit. Written in the conviction that science, properly conducted, would lead to the improvement of the material conditions of life, his major works are at the same time philosophical discourses and recommendations for public policy.

Bacon was born of distinguished parents. His father was lord keeper of the great seal to Elizabeth I, and his mother was the niece of Lord Burghley, Elizabeth's lord treasurer. In 1573 he entered Trinity College, Cambridge, and two years later was enrolled briefly as a law student at Gray's Inn. His father's death in 1579 left Francis, the youngest son, comparatively poor, and he embarked on a career in law and politics. In 1584 he became a member of the House of Commons, where he sat until his elevation to the House of Lords in 1618. Despite wide knowledge, great ability, and influential friends, Bacon never achieved high office under Elizabeth, but after the accession of James I in 1603 he became successively king's counsel, solicitor general, attorney general, lord keeper, and lord chancellor. Then, in 1620, he was found guilty of taking a bribe and was removed from public office. He spent the remainder of his life working on a vast project: to provide both a new foundation for knowledge and a program for its acquisition.

This project had occupied him since he first entered Parliament. An essay written in 1584 has not survived, but from 1594 we have *Discourse in Praise of Knowledge*, a contribution to an entertainment devised for Elizabeth. Its themes, the sterility of traditional Aristotelian philosophy on the one hand and the lack of progress in empirical endeavors like alchemy on the other, reappeared in *The Advancement of Learning* (1605); book 1 of this work contains a defense of learning, and book 2 a catalog of the branches of knowledge, with a commentary showing where each is deficient. An expanded version, in Latin, was published in 1623 as *De augmentis scientarum.* Bacon thought of this version as the first section of his "great instauration" of the sciences, of which the second part, *Novum organum* (The new organon), had already appeared (1620). Posthumously published, though written in 1610, was *New Atlantis*; here, in the guise of a traveler's tale, Bacon depicts his ideal scientific community. The science he proposed was to be both experimental and systematic: "The men of experiment are like the ant, they only collect and use; the reasoners resemble spiders, who make cobwebs out of their own substance. But the bee takes a middle course: it gathers its material from the flowers of the garden and of the field, but transforms and digests it by a power of its own" (*Novum organum* 95). Similarly, adherence to proper principles of induction would yield scientific knowledge from experimental findings.

Bacon's methodology of science has been criticized for its rejection of those speculative hypotheses that contribute essentially to progress; he is also faulted for his dismissal of the use of mathematics in science. But these criticisms are made with hindsight: when, in 1662, the Royal Society was founded along Baconian lines, its early members, including speculative natural philosophers like Robert Boyle, were lavish in their praise of him.

In his lifetime, however, the works most widely read were *De sapientia veterum* (Of the wisdom of the ancients, 1610), which puts forward rational reinterpretations of classical fables and mythology, and his *Essays.* The essays, appearing in several editions between 1597 and 1625, are aphoristic in style and worldly in content; like Machiavelli, whom he admired, Bacon sought to describe the political world as it is rather than as it should be. He described the essays as "recreations of my other studies," but they may also be regarded as supplying material for "civil knowledge," a branch of "human philosophy" in Bacon's scheme.

Bacon's views on religion are problematic. Although the first edition of the *Essays* included his *Meditationes sacrae* (Sacred meditations), in the essays themselves religion is viewed merely as a useful social cement, contributing to the stability of the state. And, along with Aristotelian philosophy, Bacon rejected the scholastic tradition within theology. Repeatedly he emphasized the necessity of a divorce between the study of science and of religion: the truths of science are revealed in God's works, the truths of morality and religion by God's word, that is, in sacred scripture. Fact and value become apparently dissociated. But those commentators who claim that Bacon's frequent protestations of faith were either politic or ironical must deal with the recurrence of theological elements within his thought. For example, his inductive system rests on a belief that the surface of nature can be made transparent to us, provided we rid ourselves of the misconceptions ("idols," Bacon calls them) that are the product of our fallen state; proper inductive procedures will, at least partially, restore the "commerce between the mind of man and the nature of things" to its original condition, that is, to its condition before the Fall. Again, Bacon's *New Atlantis* is suffused with a mystical Christianity, which, it has been persuasively argued, owes much to the Rosicrucian movement. Of course, such religious elements are open to reinterpretation, as Bacon's own reinterpretation of the myths of antiquity shows. And although certain eighteenth-century religious ideas, like the "argument from design" for God's existence, are prefigured in Bacon's writings, it was his insistence on the autonomy of science, as well as his systematic ordering of its various components, that earned him the admiration of Enlightenment thinkers like Voltaire and d'Alembert. They rightly saw him as among those who made the Enlightenment possible. For good or ill, he was also a herald, not only of the technological age that succeeded it, but also of the compartmentalization of experience characteristic of our culture.

BIBLIOGRAPHY

The standard edition of Bacon's *Works* (London, 1857–1874) was edited by James Spedding, R. L. Ellis, and D. D. Heath; volumes 1–7 contain the works, together with translations of all the major Latin works into English; volumes 8–14 contain a life, letters, and miscellanea. All important works appear in English in *Philosophical Works,* edited by J. M. Robertson (London, 1905). Noteworthy among editions of individual works is a scrupulously annotated edition of *The Advancement of Learning* and *New Atlantis,* 3d ed., edited by Arthur Johnston (Oxford, 1974). Three interesting and previously untranslated minor works appear in Benjamin Farrington's *The Philosophy of Francis Bacon* (Liverpool, 1964), together with a valuable monograph on Bacon's thought. A useful, albeit adulatory, account of Bacon's philosophy is Fulton H. Anderson's *The Philosophy of Francis Bacon* (1948; reprint, Chicago, 1971); more critical is Anthony Quinton's *Francis Bacon* (Oxford, 1980). Paulo Rossi's *Francis Bacon: From Magic to Science* (Chicago, 1968) offers an intriguing study linking Bacon's thought with the hermetic tradition. Other aspects of Bacon scholarship are covered in *Essential Articles for the Study of Francis Bacon,* edited by Brian Vickers (Hamden, Conn., 1968).

R. I. G. HUGHES (1987)

BACON, ROGER (c. 1214–c. 1292), philosopher and Franciscan friar. Born in the west of England of a wealthy family, for most of his life Bacon alternated between England and France. His first, if not his only, university education was at Oxford, and soon thereafter he pioneered in lecturing on Aristotle's metaphysics and on natural philosophy at Paris. Several Artistotelian commentaries survive from this period, but Bacon was soon to undergo a profound intellectual reorientation, inspired at least partly by another work that he believed to be by Aristotle, the *Secretum secretorum,* a long letter of advice on kingship supposedly written to Alexander the Great.

Bacon's intellectual universe was peopled with heroes and villains. Aristotle was a particularly great ancient hero, while among the few contemporaries admitted to the pantheon were Robert Grosseteste and Adam Marsh. Grosseteste (whom Bacon may not have known personally) had been a lecturer to the Franciscans at Oxford, and Marsh was a Franciscan himself. These men must have been very important in influencing Bacon's somewhat surprising decision to join the Franciscan order, for he was no model of simple humility. Indeed Bacon could be almost as rude about fellow Franciscan intellectuals as about rival Dominicans, such as Albertus Magnus. His relations with his superiors were probably never easy, and it seems certain that he was at least once put under some form of confinement, although the reasons remain obscure. It has been suggested, notably by Stewart C. Easton, that one of the principal reasons for strained relations was his sympathy for the spirituals, the more austere wing of the order, but this view has not been universally accepted.

Both before and after becoming a Franciscan Bacon developed his new approach to philosophy, and in the 1260s his big chance came. His schemes were brought to the attention of Cardinal Guy de Foulques, who in 1265 became Pope Clement IV. Bacon was ordered to produce his writings, but unfortunately there were as yet none fit for dispatch. Bacon, therefore, began to write in a flurry; the results were not only the famous *Opus majus* but also the *Opus minus* and *Opus tertium,* both of which supplemented and summarized the *Opus majus.* Some if not all of these works reached Rome, but there is no evidence of their having provoked any reaction there, and Clement died in 1268. For the rest of his intellectual life Bacon may not unfairly be described as rewriting the same major work, often with great vehemence at what he saw as the increasing ignorance and corruption of his times. Although he never completed a new grand synthesis, he was still at work in 1292. Tradition places his death in the same year.

A cornerstone of Bacon's mature thought is the postulate that all wisdom is included in the scriptures but is in need of explication by means of canon law and philosophy. Thus, while subordinating philosophy to theology Bacon also accorded it immense importance. Moreover, he did not conceive philosophy narrowly but included in its domain—besides its crowning glory, moral philosophy—the study of languages, mathematics, geography, astrology, optics, and alchemy. His emphasis was often empirical, and this, together with the fact that one part of the *Opus majus* is devoted to "experimental science," has led many to portray Bacon as a harbinger of modern experimental science. There is some truth in this, but it is a view that can all too easily lead to anachronism. For instance, it must be remembered that Bacon emphasized that experience was accessible through both external senses and interior illumination, and that revelation was necessary even for philosophical knowledge. Indeed, in his view the plenitude of philosophy had first been revealed to the ancient patriarchs and prophets. It was then transmitted to posterity, with an inevitable decline in quality accompanying the process, the decline only occasionally being arrested by special illuminations to such men as Pythagoras, Socrates, Plato, and Aristotle. Among other means of reversing the decline, according to Bacon, was the study of languages, which would allow ancient texts to be read in the orignal.

Bacon believed that there were six (although at times he appears to allow seven) principal religions, which were astrologically linked to six of the seven planets. The rise and decline of the religions were also correlated with the heavenly motions, so that, for instance, astrology could indicate that the time of the last religion, that of the antichrist, was near at hand. Christianity was one of the principal religions, but was unique in that philosophy could provide conviction of its truth.

Bacon saw preaching to the unconverted as a bounden, but in fact neglected, duty of Christians, and he strongly disapproved of the Crusades, which, he held, shed Christian blood unnecessarily while actually hindering the conversion of Muslims. But even with effective preaching there would still be those who obstinately resisted conversion and would need to be physically repulsed. Here again philosophy came into play, for Bacon was a firm advocate of what in modern terms would be called the application of technology in warfare. Among his proposals was the use of huge burning mirrors to destroy enemy encampments and the use of "fascination" (psychic influence), a phenomenon Bacon believed could be explained naturalistically. The antichrist would be well armed with such weapons, and so it was imperative that Christendom defend itself in similar fashion.

Bacon could often seem suspiciously close to advocating the use of magic. He was very conscious of this, and made strenuous efforts to distinguish philosophy sharply from magic and its appeals to demons. Nevertheless, although some of his "pure scientific" writings had considerable influence (notably those on optics), it is not surprising that he went down to posterity as part of the magical tradition. By the learned he was cited as a defender of what in the Renaissance was called natural magic, but to the public at large he was himself a full-blooded magician who had no compunction about trafficking with spirits. Later this image was transformed into that of a hero of experimental science born centuries before his time; more recent critical scholarship, in its urge to demythologize, has often unjustly muted the individuality and originality of this intellectually turbulent figure.

BIBLIOGRAPHY

The best general introduction to Bacon is Stewart C. Easton's *Roger Bacon and His Search for a Universal Science* (New York, 1952), although Easton perhaps exaggerates Bacon's sympathies for the teachings of Joachim of Fiore. A very useful trilogy for probing the basic structure of Bacon's thought is by Raoul Carton: *L'expérience physique chez Roger Bacon, L'expérience mystique de l'illumination intérieure chez Roger Bacon,* and *La synthèse doctrinale de Roger Bacon* (all, Paris, 1924). *Roger Bacon: Essays,* edited by Andrew G. Little (1914; reprint, New York, 1972), remains of considerable value. A good, up-to-date account of Bacon and his attitude to non-Christians is provided in E. R. Daniel's *The Franciscan Concept of Mission in the High Middle Ages* (Lexington, Ky., 1975).

A. GEORGE MOLLAND (1987)

BĀDARĀYAṆA, reputed author of the *Vedānta Sūtra* (*Brahma Sūtra*), the source text for all subsequent philosophical Vedānta. No biographical information is available; the name may be a convenient surrogate for the process of redaction that eventuated in the present text. Indeed, a recent tradition identifies Bādarāyaṇa with Vyāsa, the eponymous "compiler" of much late Vedic and epic material, including the *Mahābhārata.*

The name *Bādarāyaṇa* occurs in the *Mīmāṃsā Sūtra* (1.5) of Jaimini, there referring to a *ṛṣi* to whose opinion on an important point Jaimini seems to defer. If the *Vedānta Sūtra* is indeed *Bādarāyaṇa*'s, then he also refers to himself in the context of other teachers whose disputations evidently formed the beginnings of early Vedānta speculation (*Vedānta Sūtra* 4.4.5–7).

Modern discussion of Bādarāyaṇa is focused chiefly on the date of the *sūtra* text, on *Bādarāyaṇa*'s "relations" to other post-Upaniṣadic teachers, notably Jaimini, and on the question of which of his many commentators has been most faithful to his thought. Paul Deussen in general prefers Śaṅkara's monistic version, the oldest extant commentary, but others (George Thibaut, Vinayaka S. Ghate, and Louis Renou) have suggested important reservations in this view and have often concluded that Rāmānuja's *bhedābheda* ("difference within unity") more accurately reflects Bādarāyaṇa's original thesis. The discussion is made extremely difficult by the fact, universally admitted, that Bādarāyaṇa's *sūtras,* of an extreme brevity and terseness, are often unintelligible without an explanatory commentary.

Bādarāyaṇa's relation to the *ṛṣi* of the other (Pūrva) Mīmāṃsā, Jaimini, is again not easy to decipher. The names appear in the collections attributed to the other teacher, which has led many to suspect that the two may have been close contemporaries. But the doctrines that they espouse in these stray passages do not seem clearly related to the perhaps later massive schism implied by the existence of the separate text collections to which their names were attached. What is clear is that they were preeminent among the many teachers whose names alone survive. The date of Bādarāyaṇa is also closely tied to that of Jaimini but, like all such early Indian dating, is highly speculative and often circularly argued. If, as Renou concludes, Bādarāyaṇa does directly confront the Buddhist Mahāyāna in several *sūtras* (see 2.2.28–32), then his date cannot be much earlier than the third century of our era. But Jaimini's date is sometimes put back as far as the third century BCE (see, e.g., Jacobi, 1911). Bādarāyaṇa's name had of course become associated with the *sūtra* text by the time of Śaṅkara (early eighth century).

The text itself is composed of 555 *sūtras,* grouped in four major chapters (*adhyāyas*), each with four subdivisions (*pādas*). Commentators have further identified various "topics" within each *pāda,* but the number and boundaries of these differ markedly from one commentator to another. In general, the first chapter is fundamental, treating *brahman* as the one source of the world. It argues that the various Upaniṣadic teachings concerning *brahman* present one doctrine. Much of the discussion in the fourth *pāda* appears directed against the Sāṃkhya. The second chapter refutes speculative objections to the Vedānta theses from the Sāṃkhya, Nyāya, and Bauddha schools and discusses certain problems of "realism," notably whether the world is "caused" or not. The third chapter treats the individual soul (*jīva*) and how it "knows" *brahman.* The final chapter, on "fruits," discusses meditation and the condition of the liberated soul before and after death.

SEE ALSO Mīmāṃsā; Vedānta.

BIBLIOGRAPHY

The *Vedānta Sūtra* has been translated by George Thibaut as *The Vedānta Sūtras of Bādarāyaṇa* in "Sacred Books of the East," vols. 34, 38, and 48 (Oxford, 1890–1904). Thibaut's work contains an extensive introduction to the text. Important secondary sources include Paul Deussen's *Das System des Vedānta* (Leipzig, 1883), translated by Charles Johnston as *The System of the Vedānta* (Chicago, 1912); Hermann Jacobi's *Zur Frühgeschichte der indischen Philosophie* (Berlin, 1911); Vinayaka S. Ghate's *Le Vedānta: Études sur les Brahma-Sūtras et leurs cinq commentaires* (Paris, 1918); and Louis Renou and Jean Filliozat's *L'Inde classique,* vol. 2 (Hanoi, 1953).

New Sources

Adams, George C. *The Structure and Meaning of Badarayana's Brahma Sutras: A Translation and Analysis of Adhyaya.* Delhi, 1993.

Badarayana. *The Vedantasutras of Badarayana: Wth the Commentary of Baladeva Translated by Srisa Chandra Vasu.* New Delhi, 2002.

EDWN GEROW (1987)
Revised Bibliography

BAECK, LEO (1873–1956), rabbi and theologian, representative spokesman of German Jewry during the Nazi era. Born in Lissa, Posen (at that time part of Prussian Germany), a son of the local rabbi, Baeck first pursued his higher education at the university in Breslau and the moderately liberal Jewish Theological Seminary. In order to study with the distinguished scholar of religion Wilhelm Dilthey, Baeck transferred to the university in Berlin, where he earned a doctorate in 1895. Two years later, he was ordained as a rabbi at the Hochschule für die Wissenschaft des Judentums, a leading institution of Liberal Judaism. Baeck then held pulpits in Oppeln (Silesia) and Düsseldorf, and in 1912 he was called to Berlin where, with the exception of a stint as chaplain during World War I, he remained until his deportation to a concentration camp by the Nazis. During his years in Berlin, Baeck assumed a number of increasingly influential positions. In 1913 he joined the faculty of the Hochschule as a docent of Midrash and homiletics. In 1922 he became chairman of the national association of German rabbis, and in 1925 he assumed the presidency of the B'nai B'rith, a fraternal network, in Germany.

When Hitler ascended to the German chancellorship, it was Baeck who had the prescience to declare that "the thousand-year" history of German Jewry had come to an end. Baeck was instrumental in founding the Reichsvertretung der deutschen Juden, an organization that made the most successful attempt in German-Jewish history to unify Jewish defense, welfare, and cultural activities on a nationwide scale. As president of this body, he devoted himself to defending the rights of Jews in Germany, facilitating their emigration, and raising the morale of those still left in Hitler's Reich. A noteworthy example of the last effort was a special prayer composed by Baeck for public recitation on the Day of Atonement (Yom Kippur) in 1935, which included a defiant rejection of Nazi slanders: "In indignation and abhorrence, we express our contempt for the lies concerning us and the defamation of our religion and its testimonies" (*Out of the Whirlwind: A Reader of Holocaust Literature,* ed. Albert Friedlander, New York, 1968, p. 132). Arrested repeatedly by the Nazis for his outspokenness, Baeck persisted in his refusal to flee Germany until every Jew had been rescued. He continued to head the national body of German Jews after it was forcibly reorganized by the government into a council that was accountable to the Nazis. In January 1943 Baeck was deported along with other elderly German Jews to the concentration camp of Theresienstadt. In that "model camp" he served as honorary president of the ruling Jewish council and devoted his time to comforting and teaching his fellow inmates. When the camp was liberated, he still refused to leave his flock until he had been assured of their safety.

Baeck immigrated to London after the war. His last years were devoted to work on behalf of the World Union for Progressive Judaism, teaching at the Hebrew Union College (the Reform rabbinical school in Cincinnati), and organizing the surviving remnants of German Jewry. In England, he served as president of the Council of Jews from Germany. And shortly before his death, Baeck helped found an international research institute for the study of central European Jewry that bears his name (the Leo Baeck Institute).

Baeck's writings reflect his lifelong efforts to defend his people and faith. He achieved early fame by rebutting the anti-Jewish claims of Adolf von Harnack, a liberal Protestant theologian who denigrated Judaism in his book *Das Wesen des Christentums* (The Essence of Christianity). Baeck's first book, a polemical work entitled *Vorlesungen über das Wesen des Judentums* (Lectures on the Essence of Judaism; 1905), continued this defense and boldly proclaimed Judaism superior to Christianity, a claim that won Baeck considerable attention as a champion of German Jewry. Employing the approach to religion developed by his mentor, Dilthey, Baeck attempted to penetrate the underlying psychology of Judaism and understand the Jewish religion in its totality (*Gestalt*).

In subsequent essays and reworkings of his first book, Baeck sharpened the contrast between Judaism and Christianity: the latter, he claimed, was a "romantic religion" that exalted feeling, self-indulgence, dogma, and passivity; Judaism, by contrast, was a "classical religion" imbued with ethical concerns. In Judaism, Baeck saw a religion in which God's mystery and commandment exist as polarities. *Dieses Volk* (This People Israel), a book written in Nazi Berlin and the concentration camp of Theresienstadt, explores the meaning of Jewish existence. Written during the bleakest era of Jewish history, it is a work of optimism that expresses Leo Baeck's belief in the eternity of the Jewish people and their ongoing mission. In defiant rejection of Nazi barbarism, Baeck affirmed the messianic role of the people Israel to heed God's ethical command.

Bibliography

Two of Baeck's most important books have been translated into English: *The Essence of Judaism,* rev. ed. (New York, 1961), and *This People Israel: The Meaning of Jewish Existence,* translated by Albert H. Friedlander (New York, 1965). Several of his major essays appear in *Judaism and Christianity: Essays by Leo Baeck,* translated by Walter Kaufmann (Philadelphia, 1958). There are two book-length studies of Leo Baeck: Friedlander's *Leo Baeck: Teacher of Theresienstadt* (New York, 1968) primarily analyzes Baeck's writings; Leonard Baker's *Days of Sorrow and Pain: Leo Baeck and the Berlin Jews* (New York, 1978), a more popular account, describes, on the basis of extensive interviews, Baeck's communal and wartime activities.

Jack Wertheimer (1987)

BAHĀʾĪS follow the teaching of the Bāb and Mīrzā Ḥusayn ʿAlī Nūrī, later known as Bahāʾ Allāh (Bahá'u'lláh, according to Bahāʾī orthography), the Bāb's successor and "the one whom God shall manifest" (*man yuẓhiruhu Allāh*). The religion spread from Iran and the Middle East all over the world starting at the end of the nineteenth century.

Mīrzā Ḥusayn ʿAlī Nūrī, Bahāʾ Allāh. Born into a noble Tehran family, Mīrzā Ḥusayn ʿAlī Nūrī (1817–1892) and his younger half brother Mīrzā Yaḥyā Nūrī (1830–1912), known as Ṣubḥ-i Azal, came in touch with the Bāb soon after his revelation in 1844. But during the first years neither brother took a dominant position among the Bābīs. At the meeting at Badasht in the summer of 1848, Bahāʾ Allāh supported Qurrat al-ʿAyn's position regarding the abrogation of the *sharīʿah* but did not share her other radical views. During the following year Ṣubḥ-i Azal was designated as the leader of the Bābīs because the Bāb appreciated his knowledge and thought him an able leader to succeed him. During the persecution of the Bābīs following the attempt to assassinate Nāṣir al-Dīn Shāh in 1852, Bahāʾ Allāh was imprisoned in Tehran in a jail known as Siyāh Chāl, the "Black Hole." There for the first time Bahāʾ Allāh became aware of his future mission as a divine messenger. In 1853 Bahāʾ Allāh was exiled to Baghdad, where other Bābīs, including Ṣubḥ-i Azal, already resided.

Although Bahāʾ Allāh accepted the leading position of his half brother, in Baghdad the first tensions between the two became evident, partly fostered by differences in interpreting the *bayān,* which Bahāʾ Allāh saw in a more mystical or ethical light. As a result he left Baghdad on April 10, 1854, to live as a dervish in Kurdistan near Sulaymānīyah for two years. After his return to Baghdad, his influence on the Bābī exiles increased. Famous works authored by Bahāʾ Allāh in those years include mystical books, like the *Seven Valleys,* the *Four Valleys,* and the *Hidden Words* (1858). Theological arguments that the Bāb saw himself as a prophet announced in the Qurʾān are the main contents of the *Book of Certitude* (1862; *Kitāb-i Īqān*). These writings foreshadowed Bahāʾ Allāh as the divine messenger whom the Bāb had foretold.

Shortly before the Ottoman authorities removed him from Baghdad to Istanbul, Bahāʾ Allāh declared himself to be this promised figure on April 8, 1863, in a garden called Bāgh-i Riẓvān (Garden of Paradise) in the precincts of Baghdad. After some months in Istanbul, Bahāʾ Allāh and the other exiles were sent to Edirne, where they stayed for about five years. In the *Surāt al-Amr,* Bahāʾ Allāh informed his half brother officially about his claim to be "the one whom God shall manifest" (*man yuẓhiruhu Allāh*). The writings of Bahāʾ Allāh that originated from the time spent in Edirne make it clear that he was the promised prophet. One of the important writings is the *Kitāb-i Badīʿ* (Wondrous book), but he also wrote letters (*alwāḥ,* tablets) to political leaders during these years. Conflicts arose among the Bābīs, who had to decide whether to side with him or with Ṣubḥ-i Azal. Therefore the Ottoman authorities banished the Bahāʾīs, as the followers of Bahāʾ Allāh were called, to Acre in Palestine, whereas the followers of Ṣubḥ-i Azal, the Azalīs, were banished to Cyprus.

In August 1868 Bahāʾ Allāh and his family arrived at Acre, where Bahāʾ Allāh was imprisoned for the next nine years before he was allowed to move to a country house at Mazraʿah. In 1880 he moved to Bahjī near Haifa. During more than two decades in Palestine, Bahāʾ Allāh was revered by his followers, who came from as far away as Persia to catch sight of him for a moment. He finished the most holy text of the Bahāʾīs, the *Kitāb-i Aqdas,* in 1873. This book primarily relates to sacred and civil laws for the Bahāʾīs, thus abrogating the Bāb's *bayān* for the legal aspects of the religion. The Arabic texts of the *Kitāb-i Aqdas* are meant to be stylistically close to the classical style of the Qurʾān. Further letters to individual Bahāʾīs and political leaders as well as other writings also originated in these years. Close to the end of his life, Bahāʾ Allāh wrote *Epistle to the Son of the Wolf* (*Lawḥ-i Ibn Dhiʾb*), which reflects the main topics of Bahāʾī teachings and aspects of its history once more. The *Kitāb-i ʿAhd*, Bahāʾ Allāh's will, set out that his son Abbas Effendi, better known as ʿAbd al-Bahāʾ (Servant of the Glory [of God]), would be his only legitimate successor and the infallible interpreter of his father's books. On May 29, 1892, Bahāʾ Allāh died at Bahjī.

FURTHER HISTORICAL DEVELOPMENTS. According to Bahāʾī tradition, ʿAbd al-Bahāʾ (ʿAbduʾl-Bahā according to Bahāʾī orthography) was born in the same night when Sayyed ʿAlī Muḥammad declared himself in Shiraz to be the Bāb to the hidden Imām on May 23, 1844. He was close to his father from the days of his childhood, and at least since the period of Bahāʾ Allāh's imprisonment in Acre, he was the person who maintained contact between Bahāʾ Allāh and the community. In the *Kitāb-i ʿAhd* he was bestowed the title *markaz-i ʿahd* (the center of the covenant), thus marking his elevated position within the Bahāʾī faith. But ʿAbd al-Bahāʾ never was considered a prophet, only the interpreter of Bahāʾ Allāh's revelation. During the first years of ʿAbd al-Bahāʾ's leadership, the Bahāʾīs faced another crisis as another son of Bahāʾ Allāh, Muḥammad ʿAlī, contested ʿAbd al-Bahāʾ's position. It took about one decade to settle this dispute.

During these years ʿAbd al-Bahāʾ's activities to further the religion were restricted to the area of Acre. But Bahāʾīs from the Middle Eastern countries went to Acre, thus strengthening the bonds between the "center of the covenant" and his followers. In 1898 the first American Bahāʾī pilgrims arrived in Acre; the Bahāʾī faith had been known in the United States since 1894. ʿAbd al-Bahāʾ was imprisoned for participating in the revolt of the Young Turks against the Ottoman government, but with his formal release from prison in 1908, the situation changed. In 1909 the Bāb's corpse was buried in his shrine on Mount Carmel, thus making this shrine, in addition to Bahāʾ Allāh's grave at Bahjī, a center for Bahāʾī pilgrimage. In 1910 ʿAbd al-Bahāʾ set out for his first missionary journey to Egypt. During the following year he visited Europe, and in 1912–1913 he traveled on missions to Europe and the United States. In 1912 the foundation stone for the "house of worship," the first building of its kind in the West, was laid at Wilmette, Illinois.

With these missionary journeys, the Bahāʾī faith became an international religion, and ʿAbd al-Bahāʾ's encounters with Westerners also brought new topics into his writings interpreting the revelations of his father. At least in his speeches delivered in the West, ʿAbd al-Bahāʾ increased references to Christianity and reduced references to Islam. ʿAbd al-Bahāʾ's presence in the United States stimulated the first wave of growth of the American Bahāʾī community, and he continued to send tablets to America after his departure. The Bahāʾī faith had started in the United States in 1894, when Ibrahim George Kheiralla (1849–1929), a native of Lebanon, converted the first Americans to the faith. Several American converts spread the religion during the first decade of the twentieth century, helping establish the communities in India, Burma, and Tehran and introducing the religion to Paris and London. Therefore ʿAbd al-Bahāʾ was impressed by the efforts of the still small American community during his visit. In his "Tablets of the Divine Plan" (1914–1916), he advised the American community regarding how to spread the new religion throughout America. ʿAbd al-Bahāʾ admonished the American Bahāʾīs to arrange interracial or multiethnic marriages as an expression of the Bahāʾī doctrine of the unity of humans.

The Bahāʾī religion broadened and developed on a social level, which led to the humanitarian involvement of ʿAbd al-Bahāʾ and other Bahāʾīs during World War I. In appreciation ʿAbd al-Bahāʾ was knighted by the British government in 1920. ʿAbd al-Bahāʾ died on November 28, 1921, in Haifa and is buried in the Bāb's shrine.

ʿAbd al-Bahāʾ was succeeded by his grandson Shoghi Effendi Rabbani, born in 1897. Under Shoghi Effendi's leadership Bahāʾī communities existed in about twenty-two countries, from the Middle East to Europe, the United States, India, and Burma. Shoghi Effendi was educated at Oxford University, and in 1936 he married Mary Maxwell, also known as Rūḥīyah Khānum (d. 2000). Shoghi Effendi is the infallible interpreter of Bahāʾ Allāh's and ʿAbd al-Bahāʾ's writings and the "guardian of the cause of God" (*walī-yi amr Allāh*). His main achievements included establishing the administrative and institutional structure of the Bahāʾī religion. Whereas most of the Bahāʾī organizations are only indicated in short and general terms in Bahāʾ Allāh's *Kitāb-i Aqdas*, Shoghi Effendi laid out the details. During his period as guardian, the number of National Spiritual Assemblies increased, thus creating a firm and uniform basis for the Bahāʾī communities in different countries. These assemblies, later renamed National Houses of Justice, are headed by the Universal House of Justice, the governing body of all the Bahāʾīs worldwide, which was planned by Shoghi Effendi. The Universal House of Justice is a body of nine men elected to five-year terms by representatives from the National Spiritual Assemblies. No elections took place during Shoghi Effendi's lifetime. In 1951 he named the first twelve Bahāʾīs to the Hand of the Cause, assigning them special tasks in teaching and missionary activities. Until his untimely death on November 4, 1957, Shoghi Effendi appointed further "Hands," raising the total number to twenty-seven.

As Shoghi Effendi did not leave any will at his death, the Hands of the Cause assumed management of the religion and arranged the first election of the Universal House of Justice during the Riẓvān festival in April 1963, one hundred years after Bahāʾ Allāh proclaimed himself the *man yuẓhiruhu Allāh* in the Riẓvān garden in Baghdad. The Universal House of Justice has subsequently led the religion with both legislative and executive powers and also with the task of commenting on the writings of the Bāb, Bahā' Allāh, 'Abd al-Bahā', and Shoghi Effendi. However, the Universal House of Justice does not interpret Bahā' Allāh's scripture because 'Abd al-Bahā' and Shoghi Effendi were the definitive interpreters of those writings. Therefore, the Universal House of Justice's infallibility is restricted to the juridical level and does not include the theological level, where only the writings from the Bāb to Shoghi Effendi are definitive.

In the early twenty-first century the Bahā'īs number close to six million in more than two hundred countries all over the world. The number of adherents rose significantly in the late twentieth century from a little more than one million at the end of the 1960s to six million by end of the century. But the growth of the religion is not equally distributed. In Europe and North America the number is relatively stagnant, whereas in India, South America, and sub-Saharan Africa the Bahā'īs attract large numbers of new converts. In Iran the situation of the Bahā'īs has been critical through the ages, as they have faced increasing persecutions. Bahā'īs sometimes face persecution in other Muslim countries as well, as the Bāb's and Bahā' Allāh's claims to bring revelation even after the prophet Muḥammad are considered apostasy by Muslims.

The number of Bahā'īs in the United States in the early twenty-first century is about 142,000 members with about 1,200 Local Spiritual Assemblies. About fifteen thousand Bahā'īs live in Canada. A rough estimate is about one-third of these members were raised as Bahā'īs, whereas approximately half of them may have been raised in a Christian confession or denomination. The Bahā'ī faith experienced a major influx between 1969 and 1972, when about fifteen thousand rural African Americans joined the religion, motivated by the Bahā'ī doctrine of racial equality. Also several hundred Native Americans in the Lakota and Navajo reservations embraced the faith in the late twentieth century.

BELIEFS AND PRACTICES. The central focus of Bahā'ī theology is the idea of a threefold unity—there is only one God, all the divine messengers are one, and humankind is one. The strict monotheism of the Bahā'īs brings them in line with older Jewish and Christian monotheism but most closely to Islam. This monotheistic trait clearly reflects the idea that there is only one religion, which develops according to human evolution. Therefore it is necessary that divine messengers and prophets appear in the course of time, but every prophet or divine manifestation brings the eternal religion, clothed in new garb. This evolutionary idea within Bahā'ī faith is not totally new, as Manichaeism in Iran and Muslim groups have held similar views. But Bahā' Allāh's contribution lies in the concept that the Bahā'ī religion is part of this cyclical evolution. Thus for Bahā'īs in the future, but according to the *Kitāb-i Aqdas* not before "a thousand years," a new divine manifestation will appear to bring new knowledge from the one God, revealed in a way that is more suitable for the spiritual state of development of humankind then.

As the one God is unchangeable but society changes, divine messengers appear, but they are also thought to be one at a spiritual level. They "seal" the period of every earlier religion, thus keeping up the Muslim idea of Muḥammad as "seal of the prophets" (*khātam al-nabīyīn*) but reducing it only to the period of Islam as religion in its worldly (or social or materialistic) form. An absolute "seal" exists for every kind of revelation that brings (the unchangeable) divine knowledge anew.

The third aspect of "oneness" relates to humankind. All people, men and women as well as different races, are considered one. Therefore Bahā'īs not only proclaim their religion but also take actions to reduce differences among societies or disadvantages among people based on their race or sex. The Bahā'ī the theological idea of the unity of humankind encourages social engagement to improve living conditions, for example, in less-developed countries or to give equal chances for education both to women and men, and they participate in projects for global peace or global ethics. Such attempts to reach unity among humans by preserving cultural values and differences as a kind of "unity within pluralism" make the Bahā'ī religion attractive to a growing number of people.

For the individual believer, the prophet is the appointed representative of God in the created world. Whoever knows this has obtained all good in the world, as is stated at the beginning of the *Kitāb-i Aqdas*. Thus living as a Bahā'ī is a continuous journey toward God, and heaven and hell are symbols for coming close to God or being separated from him. As already indicated by the Bāb's teachings and taken up by Bahā' Allāh, eschatology is no longer something of the future, but with the appearance of God's new prophet on earth, eschatology, as predicted in earlier religions, has been realized. To behave according to this eschatological closeness to God, in ethical as well as cultic terms, is one of the main tasks for each Bahā'ī.

Though elaborate rituals are not known within the Bahā'ī community, some religious practices are noteworthy. Every believer is obliged to pray daily and to take part in the Nineteen-Day Feast that marks the beginning of every Bahā'ī month according to the cultic calendar, made up of nineteen months with nineteen days each and four intercalculary days, a practice adopted from the Bābīs. The main festivals, the nine holy days of the Bahā'ī faith, commemorate central events of the history of the religion: the Riẓvān festival (April 21 to May 2), the day of the Bāb's declaration (May 22), the birthdays of the Bāb (October 20) and Bahā' Allāh (November 12) and the days of their deaths (July 9 and May 29, respectively), the New Year festival (March 21) at the spring equinox according to the solar calendar, the Day of the Covenant (November 26), and the day of 'Abd al-Bahā''s death (November 28). The Houses of Worship are buildings dedicated only for devotions and readings from the Bahā'ī Scripture. The month of fasting ('Ala) in March and the *qiblah*, the direction during individual prayer to Bahā'

Allāh's shrine in Bahjī, retain phenomenologically some links to practices in Shīʿī Islam. But on the whole the Bahāʾī faith, though evolving with the Bābīs from a Muslim background, clearly defined its own doctrines and practices.

See Also Bābīs.

Bibliography

Primary Sources

ʿAbd al-Bahāʾ. *Some Answered Questions.* Wilmette, Ill., 1982.

ʿAbd al-Bahāʾ. *Paris Talks.* London, 1995.

Bahāʾ Allāh. *Kitāb-i-Īqān* (The book of certitude). Wilmette, Ill., 1950.

Bahāʾ Allāh. *Gleanings from the Writings of Bahāʾuʾllāh.* Translated by Shoghi Effendi. Wilmette, Ill., 1951.

Bahāʾ Allāh. *The Hidden Words of Bahāʾuʾllāh.* Wilmette, Ill., 1954.

Bahāʾ Allāh. *The Seven Valleys and the Four Valleys.* Wilmette, Ill., 1978.

Bahāʾ Allāh. *Tablets of Bahāuʾllāh, Revealed after the Kitāb-i-Aqdas.* Wilmette, Ill., 1988.

Bahāʾ Allāh. *The Kitāb-i-Aqdas: The Most Holy Book.* Haifa, Israel, 1992.

Shoghi Effendi. *God Passes By.* Wilmette, Ill., 1944.

Shoghi Effendi. *The World Order of Bahāʾuʾllāh: Selected Letters.* Wilmette, Ill., 1991.

Secondary Sources

Åkerdahl, Per-Olof. *Bahāʾī Identity and the Concept of Martyrdom.* Uppsala, Sweden, 2002. A Study on the shaping of Bahāʾī identity and theology.

Balyuzi, Hasan M. *Bahāʾuʾllāh: The King of Glory.* Oxford, 1980. Biography of Bahāʾ Allāh that is partly hagiographical.

Buck, Christopher. *Symbol and Secret: Qurʾan Commentary in Bahāʾuʾllāh's Kitāb-i Īqān.* Los Angeles, 1995. Excellent study in the Kitāb-i Īqān.

Bushrui, Suheil. *The Style of the Kitāb-i-Aqdas: Aspects of the Sublime.* Bethesda, Md., 1995. Excellent study of the literacy and theology of the central book of the Bahāʾīs.

Cole, Juan R. I. *Modernity and the Millennium: The Genesis of the Bahaʾi Faith in the Nineteenth-Century Middle East.* New York, 1998. Analysis of the historical situation leading to the rise of the Bahāʾī religion.

Hollinger, Richard, ed. *Community Histories.* Los Angeles, 1994. Collection of articles on the history of the religion in America.

Hutter, Manfred. *Die Bahāʾī: Geschichte und Lehre einer nachislamischen Weltreligion.* Marburg, Germany, 1994. Concise presentation of the history and doctrine.

McMullen, Michael, *The Bahāʾī: The Religious Construction of a Global Identity.* New Brunswick, N.J., 2000. Focuses on the Bahāʾī community of Atlanta in relation to the general situation of the Bahāʾī faith in the United States.

Momen, Moojan, ed. *Scripture and Revelation.* Oxford, 1997. Collection of essays on Bahāʾī literature.

Saiedi, Nader. *Logos and Civilization: Spirit, History, and Order in the Writings of Bahāʾuʾllāh.* Bethesda, Md., 2000. In-depth study of the theology of the main writings of Bahāʾ Allāh.

Schaefer, Udo. *Beyond the Clash of Religions: The Emergence of a New Paradigm.* Prague, Czech Republic, 1995. Survey of Bahāʾī relations to other religions and an outline of Bahāʾī theology.

Smith, Peter. *A Short History of the Bahāʾī Faith.* Oxford, 1996. Well-balanced introduction to history and doctrine.

Smith, Peter, and Moojan Momen. "The Bahāʾī Faith 1957–1988: A Survey of Contemporary Developments." *Religion* 19 (1989): 63–91. Detailed study of the growth of the Bahāʾī religion from a sociological perspective.

Manfred Hutter (2005)

BAḤYE IBN PAQUDA (second half of the eleventh century), also known as Baḥya; Jewish moral philosopher. Virtually nothing is known of Baḥye's life, except that he probably lived in Saragossa and served as a *dayyan,* a judge of a Jewish court. His Hebrew poems, only a few examples of which are extant, were highly regarded by at least one medieval critic. All are on religious themes, and most were composed to serve in the liturgy. His two best-known poems, intended for private devotion, are both appended to his magnum opus, a treatise on the inner life of religion written in Arabic and titled *Al-hidāyah ila farāʾid al-qulūb* (Right guidance to the precepts of the hearts). Composed sometime between 1050 and 1090, this work, in the Hebrew translation by Yehudah ibn Tibbon titled *Ḥovot ha-levavot* (The duties of the hearts, 1161), became one of the most influential religious treatises in Judaism.

Baḥye was heir to a Judeo-Arabic religious tradition in which the rabbinic Judaism of the Talmud and the Geonim had been synthesized with Islamic rationalistic theology (*kalām*). This synthesis had received its definitive formulation in the writings of Saʿadyah Gaon (882–942), which had become authoritative for the educated elite class of Jews in Arabic-speaking countries such as Spain. To this synthesis, Baḥye contributed a new element: the traditions of Islamic asceticism and mysticism. His work is replete with sayings, exempla, and technical terminology derived from the writings of earlier Muslim mystics, ascetics, and moralizers; the very structure of his book has Islamic antecedents. Some of his materials have been traced to specific Islamic authors such as al-Muḥāsibī, and parallels to passages in his work are found in the writings of Abū Ḥāmid al-Ghazālī (d. 1111). Although Baḥye cites many passages from the Bible, rabbinic literature, and the writings of the Geonim in support of the thesis that the true function of religious practice is to enable humanity to develop its inner life toward spiritual perfection and love of God, he was the first Jewish writer to develop these principles into a complete spiritual program.

Baḥye's treatise begins with an introduction in which he defines and explains the distinction between "duties of the limbs" and "duties of the heart," between outward (*ẓāhir*) and inward (*bāṭin*) piety, derived ultimately from the disciples of the early Muslim mystic Ḥasan al-Baṣrī (d. 728). The body of the book consists of ten chapters, each on a different inward virtue. Reason, the Torah, and the rabbinic tradition all teach that the true worship of God is through the intention that accompanies the observances dictated by religious law. Yet most people feel secure that they fulfill God's will through formal obedience to religious law, while neglecting the spiritual development that is the purpose of the system.

Thus, most Jews believe that they fulfill the obligation to acknowledge God's existence and unity by passive assent and by ritual recitation of the Shema' in their daily prayers. This sort of formal compliance with a religious duty *(taqlīd)* is, in Baḥye's opinion, adequate only for children, the uneducated, and the feebleminded. An adult of normal intellectual capacity is obliged, first, to grasp the meaning of God's unity in its logical and philosophical essence, as far as the human mind is able to grasp it. Accordingly, Baḥye devotes his first chapter to a restatement of the definitions and proofs of God's existence and unity that had been advanced by Sa'adyah and other *kalām* writers.

Second, one must grasp the meaning God's existence and unity has for one's relations both to God and to one's fellow humans. Since God is not accessible to direct observation, humanity can learn about God's relationship to the world only by studying nature, in which God's actions are evident, and by studying humans, the microcosm. The study of nature makes humans aware of God's work in the world and brings them closer to knowledge of God. It further has the effect of instilling in individuals a profound gratitude, the attitude that makes for the perfect fulfillment of the duties of the heart.

The constituent elements of humans are the body and the soul; as taught by the Neoplatonists, the soul is foreign to the body, being celestial in origin. It was placed in the body by God's will, both as a trial for it and to help the body. For all its yearning to return to its source, the soul is in constant danger of being diverted from its mission because of love of pleasure and love of power. With the help of reason and revelation, however, the soul can purify itself and, after the death of a body, complete its journey.

In order to achieve the soul's desired end, it is necessary to practice certain virtues, to each of which Baḥye devotes a chapter: worship, trust, sincerity, humility, repentance, self-examination, asceticism, and love of God. These virtues flow spontaneously from the gratitude to the creator felt by the thoughtful believer. While the organization of these virtues as a series of degrees of perfection is derived from the writings of such Muslim mystics as Abū Ṭālib al-Makkī (d. 996), Baḥye does not accept their concept of progressive mystic ascension toward illumination. In fact, Baḥye's demands and expectations are quite moderate. Thus, "trust" does not mean that people should neglect their work and expect God to provide them a living, but that they should pursue their livelihood modestly and conscientiously, knowing that it is not their work that provides their living but God's will. Likewise, "asceticism" does not mean extreme self-abnegation and mortification, and it has no intrinsic value. The closest to "the moderation of the law" are those who are not outwardly distinguishable from others.

Finally, there is no conception in Baḥye's thought of mystical union with God. The love of God results from the soul's natural yearning to rejoin its source, but while the soul can perfect and purify itself, it cannot fulfill its desire while attached to the body. The "lover" keeps a respectful distance from the "beloved." Baḥye's mysticism is thus fully compatible with rabbinic Judaism.

See Also Jewish Thought and Philosophy, article on Premodern Philosophy.

Bibliography

Baḥya ben Yosef ibn Pakuda. *The Book of Direction to the Duties of the Heart.* Edited and translated by Menahem Mansoor with Sara Arenson and Shoshana Dannhauser. London, 1973.

Goldrich, Amos. "Hameqorot ha'arviim ha'efshariim shel hahavhana bein ḥovot haeivarim vehovot halevavot." *Teuda* 6 (1987–1988): 179–208.

Safran, Bezalel. "Baḥya ibn Paquda's Attitude toward the Courtier Class." In *Studies in Medieval Jewish History and Literature,* edited by Isadore Twersky, pp. 154–197. Cambridge, Mass., 1979.

Sifroni, A. *Sefer ḥovot ha-levavot be-targumo shel R. Yehudah ibn Tibbon.* Jerusalem, 1927–1928.

Vajda, Georges. *La théologie ascétique de Baḥya ibn Paquda.* Paris, 1947.

Yahuda, A. S., ed. *Al-hidāya 'ila fara'id al-qulūb des Bachja ibn Jōsēf ibn Paqūda, aus Andalusien.* Leiden, 1912.

Raymond P. Scheindlin (1987 and 2005)

BAKHTIN, M. M.

BAKHTIN, M. M. Mikhail Mikhailovich Bakhtin (1895–1975) was a literary critic, philosopher, and leading Russian humanist. He was banished in 1929 to Kazakhstan, but his work was rediscovered after World War II and introduced to Europeans by Julia Kristeva and others. To Bakhtin, perhaps more than anyone, is owed the current attention to intertextuality, the otherness of others' voices, insistence on the moral and epistemological significance of differences, and "dialogism."

A classically trained linguist, Bakhtin challenged Russian formalist followers of Ferdinand de Saussure, insisting that basic speech units are not phonemes or words but specific, often "double-voiced," utterances instantiating historical matrices. Apprised of developments in the arts, sciences, and philosophy by fellow members of "the Bakhtin circle," he anticipated Ludwig Wittgenstein on "private language," dismissed as "monological" all religious and secular ideological systems, and rejected formulaic dialectics.

Bakhtin made his name with a 1929 study of Fyodor Dostoevsky. According to Bakhtin, Dostoevsky, unlike Leo

Tolstoy, did not direct readers to a single moralizing conclusion but initiated open-ended conversations among his characters concerning bourgeois crises of faith, love, crime, and punishment. Dostoevsky's journalistic/Christian authorial voice allowed them their conflicting (often inner) voices, giving his novels a "polyphonic" form, avoiding psychologism and capturing the rich realism of everyday discourse.

Adapting Henri Bergson on organic temporal processes and Hermann Cohen's neo-Kantian ethico-aesthetic holistic judgments, Bakhtin found the same dialogical imagination exercised in age-old folkloric critiques of establishment pretensions in Miguel de Cervantes, William Shakespeare, Charles Dickens, and Dostoevsky. Unconstrained by classical literary canons, Bakhtin believed that the prose of modern novelists, not poetry, best communicates orientational pluralism.

According to Bakhtin, François Rabelais first textualized oral satirical traditions, embodying Renaissance resistance to the hegemony of medieval Christendom. Rabelais used accepted, grotesque medieval tropes and bawdy carnivalesque humor to ridicule inquisitors who pretended to eternal verities while pursuing mundane goals. His countercultural apocalypticism undermined homogenizing dogmatism. Rabelais worked prototypically, honoring the specifics of his historical locale (his "chronotope"), working through national and international conflicts to a global conception of liberating truth.

Bakhtin's study covertly critiqued Stalinism, expecting the dissonance of social injustices and insights prompted by multilingual encounters to foster public, not just private, reforms. Gods and tyrants are dethroned by laughter.

In his earliest, more phenomenological studies, Bakhtin examined the complexity of authorial artistry and asymmetries of self–other relations. People theorize about their background, but they never see it, nor others theirs. Recognizing "transgredience" (not transcendence) in one's experience breaks with both classical and modern single-consciousness models of knowing (God's or the individual ego's) and mind–body dualism. No theories are final, all boundaries in "threshold" situations are permeable. Inside–outside dichotomies miss the "outsideness" of every thought, and one's dialogical dependence on others for true wholes. Actual texts embody simultaneously many contexts. Both sciences and humanities interweave descriptions and evaluations. Neither authorial intention nor reader responses alone determine dialogically realized meanings.

Such conclusions, reworked in many notes on form, content, material, style, genre, and representational discourse, constitute an independent Russian contribution to postmodernism. Bakhtin's influence on religious studies remains mostly indirect. In the 1970s Robert Polzin pioneered in applying Bakhtinian ideas to the Deuteronomic histories, and later Gavin Flood followed Bakhtin "beyond phenomenology."

Most Christian commentators agree that Bakhtin's sense of overlapping meanings and contrasting, simultaneous perspectives was influenced by Orthodox iconography based on a kenotic two-natures Christology and paradoxical space–time conceptions of quantum physicists. Not logocentric, Bakhtin insisted that the world is in our words and words are of the world. Living languages are "unfinalizable" philosophies of life. Because human operative judgments realize some freedom in weighing alternatives, people are without alibi for their lives, answerable to themselves, others, and their environment, which address them on many levels. Bakhtinian answerability is a richer notion than Heideggerian authenticity, affirming both individual responsibility and corporate accountability.

Despite his circumstances, Bakhtin de-emphasized the dark side of human nature. He agreed with Thomas Mann that hell is lack of being heard. Wisely, he generally let Dostoevsky and Rabelais speak for him on Christianity, denying that individuals own ideas. In all discourse, Bakhtin came to regard God as the "Super-Addressee," the basis for the human drive for perfect understanding, a third or fourth voice on the dialogical edge of consciousness, impersonally called "the voice of conscience" but not just a regulative idea. Bakhtin dismissed talk of absolute values and "the collective unconscious" as abstractions. Actual consummating responses must be concretely personal. He remarked that Ludwig Feuerbach misread the double-voiced import of incarnation, while the church drained the blood out of history. Ethico-aesthetically, in the artistry of making a life, what I must be for the other, God (however named) is for me.

Bakhtinian dialogism is opposed to any dichotomizing between the sciences and the humanities in the study of religion and to treating religion in isolation from the texture of, or reducing it to, either its ideal or its material aspects.

SEE ALSO Literature, articles on Critical Theory and Religious Studies, Literature and Religion.

BIBLIOGRAPHY

Bakhtin, Mikhail. *Problems of Dostoevsky's Poetics* (Russian, 1929, 1963). Edited and translated by Caryl Emerson. Minneapolis, 1984.

Bakhtin, Mikhail. *Rabelais and His World* (Russian, 1940). Translated by Hélène Iswolsky. Bloomington, Ind., 1984.

Bakhtin, Mikhail. *The Dialogic Imagination: Four Essays.* Edited by Michael Holquist; translated by Caryl Emerson and Michael Holquist. Austin, Tex., 1981.

Bakhtin, Mikhail. *Speech Genres and Other Late Essays.* Edited by Caryl Emerson and Michael Holquist; translated by Vern W. McGee. Austin, Tex., 1986.

Bakhtin, Mikhail. *Art and Answerability: Early Philosophical Essays.* Edited by Michael Holquist and Vadim Liapunov; translated by Vadim Liapunov. Austin, Tex., 1990.

Bakhtin, Mikhail (and/or Voloshinov, V. N.). *Marxism and the Philosophy of Language.* Translated by Ladislav Matejka and I. R. Titunik. London, 1986. Influential 1929 book by a member of the Bakhtin circle, sometimes attributed to Bakhtin, but more Marxist than his other writings.

Coates, Ruth. *Christianity in Bakhtin: God and the Exiled Author.* Cambridge, UK, 1998. Discusses Bakhtin's relation to Marxism.

Felch, Susan M., and Paul J. Contino, eds. *Bakhtin and Religion: A Feeling for Faith.* Evanston, Ill., 2001. Mostly theological.

Gardiner, Michael, ed. *Mikhail Bakhtin.* 4 vols. London, 2003. To date, four volumes of many important articles have been published on Bakhtin's context and relation to such authors as Cassirer and Buber.

Green, Barbara. *Mikhail Bakhtin and Biblical Scholarship: An Introduction.* Atlanta, 2000. Includes a bibliography.

Haynes, Deborah J. *Bakhtin and the Visual Arts.* Cambridge, U.K., 1995. Gives Russian nuances.

PETER SLATER (2005)

BAKONGO SEE KONGO RELIGION

BALARĀMA is a Hindu god, the elder brother of the god Kṛṣṇa. He is sometimes considered as the third of the three Rāmas, and thus the eighth *avatāra* of Viṣṇu; at other times he appears as an incarnation of the serpent Śeṣa or Ananta. He is also known by the names Baladeva, Balabhadra, Bala, and Halāyudha. Legends of Balarāma are found in the Brahmanical and Jain literature. He is mentioned along with Kṛṣṇa in the *Mahābhārata,* especially in its sequel *Harivaṃśa,* in the *Bhāgavata Purāṇa,* and other Vaiṣnava Purāṇas.

The birth of Balarāma was extraordinary. When a disembodied voice predicted that the demon Kamsa would be killed by the eighth child of his sister Devakī, Kamsa vowed to kill her male children. Balarāma was conceived as the seventh child of Devakī and was saved from Kamsa when he was transferred to Rohiṇī's womb by the *yogamāyā* (magical power) of Viṣṇu. Balarāma was thus born of Rohiṇī. Another story narrated in the *Mahābhārata* accounts for his white color. Viṣṇu, extracted one of his white hairs and sent it to Devakī's womb; the hair then was born as Balarāma.

Balarāma and Kṛṣṇa are always together and are in perfect contrast with each other: Balarāma is white, whereas Kṛṣṇa is black; Balarāma is the all-masculine figure with the powerful plowshare as his weapon, whereas Kṛṣṇa's beauty is described as graceful and feminine, dark in color, and attractive to women.

Once, while intoxicated, Balarāma called the river Yamunā (personified as a goddess) to come to him so that he could bathe. When she did not comply with his wish, he plunged his plowshare into the river, pulling the waters until Yamunā surrended.

Balarāma married the daughter of King Raivata. The king, who thought that his daughter was so beautiful that she could not be wed to a mortal, took her to the world of Brahmā to seek advice. Brahmā advised the king that Balarāma was the most suitable bridegroom for her. The visit with Brahmā took many aeons, and by the time they returned, mankind had grown smaller. Balarāma found Revati so tall that he shortened her with his plowshare before marrying her.

Balarāma was an expert of three weapons: the plow, the mace, and the club. He taught the use of the mace to Duryodhana. Balarāma disapproved of Kṛṣṇa's role in the *Mahābhārata* war and wanted the cousins, the Kauravas and the Paṇḍavas, to make peace. When the cousins were fighting, Balarāma refused to take sides and went on a pilgrimage. He was indignant when in the final mace battle Bhīma hit Duryodhana on his thighs, against all propriety. Balarāma vowed to kill Bhīma and could only be pacified by Kṛṣṇa.

Although addicted to liquor himself, Balarāma prohibited intoxicants in the holy city of Dvārakā. After the battle of Kurukṣetra the Yādavas of Dvārakā were involved in a drunken brawl and killed each other. Balarāma sat in deep meditation and the serpent Śeṣa, of whom Balarāma was an incarnation, came from his mouth and entered the ocean.

According to the Jain *Harivaṃśa Purāṇa,* Balarāma watched over Kṛṣṇa, and also helped his brother, who was raised by Yaśodạ, to visit his real mother, Devakī. When Devakī saw Kṛṣṇa, her breasts spontaneously flowed with milk. In order to protect her identity, Balarāma poured a jar of milk over her.

SEE ALSO Avatāra; Kṛṣṇa.

BIBLIOGRAPHY

Further information on Balarāma can be found in *Srimad Bhagavatam,* 2 vols., translated by N. Raghunathan (Madras, 1976).

New Sources

Bigger, Andreas. *Balarama im Mahabharata: seine Darstellung im Rahmen des Textes und seiner Entwicklung Beiträge zur Indologie Bd. 30.* Wiesbaden, 1998.

VELCHERU NARAYANA RAO (1987)
Revised Bibliography

BALDR is an important god in Scandinavian mythology. Evidence for the worship of Baldr is limited to a few place-names; the name was not used as a personal name during the Middle Ages. Baldr's story has several parts: his death; an attempt to reverse his death; his funeral; vengeance for his death; and his return after Ragnarǫk (the final battle between the gods and the giants). Of these, only the funeral is recounted in skaldic poetry, although a detail of the vengeance occurs there. In Eddic poetry, Snorri Sturluson's *Edda,* and the *Gesta Danorum* of Saxo Grammaticus the full story emerges, often with quite varying forms.

From the *Húsdrápa* of Úlfr Uggason, a skaldic ekphrasis of carvings inside a building in western Iceland from circa

985, five stanzas survive dealing with Baldr's funeral. A stanza of Kormákr Ǫgmundarson (Icelandic, tenth century) says that Óðinn used magic on Rindr, a reference to his siring of the avenger Váli.

In Eddic poetry, *Baldrs draumar* (Baldr's dreams) is wholly about the Baldr story, and the story is important in the *Codex Regius* version of the poem *Vǫluspá,* although it is lacking in the Hauksbók version of the poem. Two stanzas of *Lokasenna* (Loki's quarrel) also refer to the story: Loki, a giant who often helped the gods, takes credit for Baldr's absence.

Baldrs draumar is set in motion by Baldr's bad dreams. Óðinn rides Sleipnir to the realm of Hel and poses four questions to a dead seeress: Who is to die? Answer: Baldr. Who will kill him? Answer: Hǫðr. Who will avenge him? Answer: Óðinn will sire an avenger. The name is missing in the manuscript, but the alliteration requires one in initial *V-*, presumably Váli. The fourth question is obscure. The seeress does not answer it but states that she now knows her interlocutor to be Óðinn. He in turn says that she is the mother of seven monsters.

The *Codex Regius* version of *Vǫluspá* tells of Baldr's "hidden fate," and of the deadly weapon, mistletoe (a motif that has never been satisfactorily explained). Hǫðr kills Baldr and an avenger is soon born. Further stanzas discuss vengeance taken on a figure much like Loki. Much later in the poem, in the description of the aftermath of Ragnarǫk, Baldr and Hǫðr return.

Snorri Sturluson knew *Vǫluspá*, and his version of the story, though much fuller, also agrees with the bare outline as set forth in *Baldrs draumar.* Baldr's bad dreams lead Frigg, his mother and Óðinn's consort, to extract oaths from all creatures and matter not to harm him. Thereafter, the gods honor Baldr by casting weapons at his invulnerable body. Loki cannot bearthis, and disguised as a woman he learns from Frigg that mistletoe has not sworn the oath. Loki makes a dart out of mistletoe and helps Hǫðr, here presented as Baldr's blind brother, to throw it at Baldr. Baldr falls dead, and the gods are struck silent. Frigg thereafter dispatches Hermóðr, another son of Óðinn, to Hel to try to get Baldr back. The funeral is held. Hermóðr returns from Hel without Baldr, but with gifts and with a deal: if everything will weep for Baldr, Hel will release him. Everything does weep, except an old giantess in a cave, thought to be Loki. Baldr stays dead until after Ragnarǫk. Loki flees to a mountaintop fastness, where he invents the fishing net. This he burns when he sees the gods approaching, for his plan is to change himself into a salmon. Kvasir recognizes the form of the net in the ashes, and the gods make one and capture Loki. They bind him in a cave, where he will remain bound until Ragnarǫk.

Saxo's version is set in Danish prehistory. Høtherus and Balderus, son of Odin and a demigod, vie to rule Denmark and to marry Nanna, the foster-sister of Høtherus. In the last of a series of battles, Høtherus finally kills Balderus with an ordinary weapon. Othinus learns through prophecy that he can sire an avenger with Rinda, a Rostaphian princess. After failing to win the girl in various guises, he returns dressed as a woman, and when she falls ill he is to treat her. He binds her to her bed and rapes her. The avenger, Bous, kills Høtherus and himself dies a day later. For his shameful acts the gods exile Othinus from Byzantium for almost ten years.

All the sources stress that Baldr is Óðinn's son, that he dies, and that he is avenged. Baldr's return is found only in *Vǫluspá* and Snorri's *Edda.* These facts subvert the older interpretations, such as those of James Frazer or Gustav Neckel, of Baldr as a dying god like Baal or Tammuz, one whose regular resurrection is associated with annual cycles of fertility. The emphasis on vengeance makes it clear that Baldr is far more than a Nordic adaptation of Christ (Bugge), and it also weakens Georges Dumézil's proposed parallel from the *Mahābhārata,* the circumstances surrounding the war between the Paṇḍava and Duryodhana. Jan de Vries argued that the story has to do with initiation into the cult of Óðinn, and he was certainly correct in locating the myth in the realm of Óðinn, although his reading does not take into account all the aspects of the myth. Nor does Margaret Clunies Ross do so in her emphasis on the issue of dynastic succession.

In *Vǫluspá* and Snorri's *Edda,* the death of Baldr leads directly to Ragnarǫk, and even in Saxo there is a sea battle in which Høtherus defeats all the gods, although it occurs before Baldr's death. Given the emphasis in *Vǫluspá's* description of Ragnarǫk as a time when brother kills brother, murderers are about, and oaths are broken, Baldr's death can easily be read in that poem as the beginning of Ragnarǫk. Baldr's is the first death of a god, and since the cosmos was created with the body of a murdered giant, this killing upsets the usual order of the mythology. The hierarchical superiority of the gods over the giants ends, and the two groups destroy each other. The ensuing world order brings peace, and Baldr and Hǫðr are reunited.

In the Scandinavian context, the accounts that make Baldr and Hǫðr brothers indicate a flaw in the system of blood feud (Lindow, 1997), for when Óðinn sires an avenger, the vengeance he takes still leaves Óðinn with an unavenged son, now Hǫðr. A killing within a family poses an insurmountable problem in such a system, and since the gods created the cosmos by killing a maternal relative, this problem was present from the beginning. The gods' solution was to deny maternal kinship relations, but that denial ultimately fails. So too does Óðinn's attempt to counter Loki's giant patrimony by swearing blood brotherhood with him. Only myth can resolve this problem, and it does so by reuniting Baldr and Hǫðr in a new world order after Ragnarǫk.

SEE ALSO Eddas; Germanic Religion; Loki.

BIBLIOGRAPHY

Bugge, Sophus. *Studien über die Entstehung der nordischen Götter- und Heldensagen.* Translated by Oscar Brenner. Munich, 1889. Argues influence of the Christ story.

Clunies Ross, Margaret. *Prolonged Echoes: Old Norse Myths in Medieval Icelandic Society,* vol. 1, *The Myths.* Odense, Denmark, 1994. Discusses the problem of the slaying within a family; the dynastic implications.

Dumézil, Georges. *Gods of the Ancient Northmen.* Berkeley, Calif.,1973. Adduces Indo-European analogues.

Frazer, James George. *The Golden Bough: A Study in Magic and Religion,* part 7, *Balder the Beautiful.* 2 vols. 3d ed. New York, 1990. Famous study seeking association with annual rituals of invigoration.

Lindow, John. *Murder and Vengeance among the Gods: Baldr in Scandinavian Mythology.* Helsinki, 1997. Analyzes the problem of slaying within a family in the context of a society that uses blood feud to resolve disputes.

Neckel, Gustav. *Die Überlieferungen vom Gotte Balder.* Dortmund, Germany, 1920. Argues connection with the Middle Eastern dying gods.

Vries, Jan de. "Der Mythos von Balders Tod." *Arkiv för nordisk filologi* 70 (1955): 41–60. Argues a ritual association with the cult of Óðinn and a mythological association with the introduction of death.

JOHN LINDOW (2005)

BALINESE RELIGION. Eight degrees south of the equator, toward the middle of the belt of islands that form the southern arc of the Indonesian archipelago, lies the island of Bali, home of the last surviving Hindu-Buddhist civilization of Indonesia. A few kilometers to the west of Bali is the island of Java, where major Hindu-Buddhist kingdoms flourished from the time of Borobudur (eighth century) until the end of the sixteenth century, when the last Javanese Hindu kingdom fell to Islam. Just to the east of Bali is the Wallace Line, a deep ocean channel marking the biogeographical frontier between Asia and the Pacific. The Wallace Line is also a cultural frontier: journeying eastward from Bali, one leaves the zone of historical Asian civilizations and enters a region of tribal peoples. Bali is the last stepping-stone from Asia to the Pacific.

The preservation of Hindu-Buddhist kingdoms on Bali centuries after their disappearance elsewhere in the region is largely the result of geography. The island is not only remote but quite small—172 kilometers east-west by 102 kilometers north-south. The fertile valleys that form the heartland of Balinese civilization face southward, toward a largely untraveled sea. Behind them lies an arc of steep jungle-covered mountains, a natural barrier to Java and the busy seas to the north. Balinese kingdoms nestled along the south coast, each of them so tiny that a man could easily ride across an entire "kingdom" in half a day on horseback. The Balinese attitude toward the world beyond their shores is nicely illustrated by the complaints of the first European ambassadors to Bali, who frequently could not even obtain an audience with a Balinese prince—the Balinese were simply too preoccupied with their own affairs!

SOURCES OF BALINESE RELIGION. Evidence for the nature of prehistoric Balinese religion comes from three sources: archaeology, historical linguistics, and comparative ethnography. Linguistically, Balinese belongs to the Malayo-Polynesian language family, itself derived from Proto-Austronesian, which is thought to have been spoken by Southeast Asian peoples around six thousand years ago. Proto-Austronesian-speakers on Bali had words for many religious concepts: nature gods, such as a sky god; ancestral spirits (who were probably thought to inhabit mountaintops); a human soul, or perhaps multiple souls; and shamanistic trance. Such beliefs and practices remain widespread in Indonesia, reflecting the influence of Malayo-Polynesian culture. The vocabulary of Proto-Austronesian reflects a Neolithic culture; the advent of the Metal Age in Bali is marked by a magnificent bronze kettledrum, the "Moon of Pejeng." Stylistically related to similar "Dong-son" drums found over much of eastern Indonesia and Vietnam, the Balinese drum is distinguished by its large size (186 x 150 cm) and splendid ornamentation. The discovery of a casting mold used to make the drum in a nearby village proved that the drum was created by indigenous Balinese metalsmiths, some time between the second century BCE and the second century CE.

Fifty-three stone sarcophagi, tentatively dated to the same era as the "Moon of Pejeng," provide additional evidence for a sophisticated Metal Age culture in Bali with well-developed social ranking and elaborate funerary rituals. Hewn from stone with bronze tools and ornamented with protruding knobs decorated with stylized human heads, they contain human skeletons of both sexes along with bronze arm and foot rings, carnelian beads, and miniature socketed bronze shovels. Even more impressive are the stepped stone pyramids of this era, reminiscent of Polynesian *marae,* which apparently served as temples to the ancestors and nature gods, and perhaps also as monuments for important chiefs. Thus, by the first millennium CE Balinese society was organized into sedentary villages ruled by chiefs. The major economic occupation was wet-rice agriculture, supported by small-scale irrigation. The economy supported craft specialists, such as metalworkers and builders of megaliths.

Sometime in the early first millennium of the common era, Bali came into contact with Indian civilization and thus with the Hindu and Buddhist religions. The nature of this contact and the ensuing process of "indianization" has long been a subject of scholarly debate. At one extreme, J. C. van Leur maintained that "hinduization" was wholly initiated by Southeast Asian rulers who summoned Indian brahmans to their courts, creating merely a "thin and flaking glaze" of Indic culture among the elite (van Leur, 1955). At the other extreme, R. C. Majumdar postulated wholesale colonization of Southeast Asia by Indian exiles. Between these two poles, nearly every conceivable intermediate position has been staked out, and there is as yet no consensus as to which is most likely, although there is no persuasive evidence for large-scale colonization by Indian exiles (Majumdar, 1963).

In Bali, the first clear indication of "indianization" is entirely of a religious nature, consisting of several sorts of physical evidence: stone sculptures, clay seals and ritual apparatus, and a series of stone and copperplate inscriptions. The sculptures closely resemble Central Javanese sculptures of the same era (both Hindu and Buddhist), while the clay seals contain Mahāyāna formulas duplicated in the eighth-century Javanese temple Candi Kalasan. However, it is important to note that these objects show no evidence of Javanese influence (whether conceptual or stylistic); they are obviously Indian and seem to have appeared in both Java and Bali at about the same time.

The first inscriptions appear in the ninth century CE and are the earliest written texts discovered in Bali. They were written by court scribes in two languages, Sanskrit and Old Balinese, using an Indian alphabet. Inscriptions in Sanskrit proclaim the military triumphs of Balinese rulers, and were addressed to the (Indic) world at large. They are not unique to Bali, for similar inscriptions are found throughout the western archipelago—monuments intended to validate the authority of rulers in the idiom of Indian theories of kingship. Such validation was essential because of the cosmological significance of kings, according to the Hindu and Buddhist medieval traditions. Inscriptions in Old Balinese, by contrast, were addressed very specifically to particular villages or monasteries, and they document the interest of the rulers in supporting a variety of Hindu and Buddhist sects. To explain the process of indianization in Bali, it is tempting to postulate the conversion of a powerful Balinese chief to some Hindu or Buddhist sect, who then zealously promoted the new faith among his subjects—except that the inscriptions clearly reveal patronage for a multitude of sects. No single group was given precedence; all were encouraged, suggesting that a ruler's enthusiasm for Indian ideas went deeper than the doctrinal differences that divide sect from sect. The texts specifically mention Tantric and Mahāyāna Buddhism, the major schools of Śaiva Siddhānta and Vaiṣṇava Hinduism, and the cults of Sūrya and Gaṇeśa. Early sculptures include *dhyāni* Buddhas, Padmapāṇi (Avalokiteśvara) and Amoghapāśa, Viṣṇu on Garuḍa, Viṣṇu as Narasiṃha, and Śiva in many forms including Ardhanāri, quadruplicated as the *catuḥkāyas*, and accompanied by Durgā, Gaṇeśa, and Guru.

Most of the 250 known inscriptions, which date from the ninth through the fourteenth century, direct the inhabitants of particular villages to provide various kinds of assistance to the monks and monasteries, including taxes, hospitality, labor, and military defense against sea raiders. Through the inscriptions we can trace the development of an intricate web of ties linking indianized courts and Hindu and Buddhist monasteries to the villages. As early as 1073 CE, a royal inscription describes the population as divided into the four castes of the Indian *varṇa* system (*brāhmaṇa, kṣatriya, vaiśya,* and *śūdra*). The inscription is significant not as proof that the Balinese had managed to magically recreate the Hindu caste system, but as evidence of the ruler's desire to impose the Indian ideal of caste on his kingdom.

In time, the Balinese came to identify their own sacred mountain, Gunung Agung, with the mythical Mount Meru, center of the "Middle World" of Indic cosmology. The old Balinese nature gods were perhaps not so much nudged aside as reincorporated intothe new Indic pantheon. The great earth serpent Anantaboga was symbolically buried in the Balinese earth, his head beneath the crater lake of Batur near the island's center, his tail just touching the sea at Keramas. But the old gods were not entirely eclipsed. The most popular character of contemporary Balinese epics, and star of the shadow play (*wayang*), is the ancient buffoon Twalen, who usually plays the servant of the Hindu gods. Like the Balinese themselves, he is pleased to serve the splendid Hindu gods. But in reality, as everyone knows, Twalen is older and more powerful than all the Hindu gods. From time to time in the stories, when the gods have gone too far astray, he ceases to play the aging buffoon and reveals his true powers as "elder brother" to Siwa (Skt., Śiva), the supreme Hindu god.

LIVING TRADITIONS. At some time between the fourteenth and nineteenth centuries, the monastic tradition of Bali came to an end, and the various competing sects of Hinduism and Buddhism fused into what is now perceived as a single religion, called Bali Hindu or, more accurately, Āgama Tīrtha, the Religion of Holy Water. The vast majority of the Balinese adhere to this religion. Bali Hindu is officially sanctioned by the Indonesian government, which insists that all of its citizens belong to some recognized religion. Consequently, in recent years there has been some attempt to include tribal religions from other islands such as Sulawesi (Celebes) under the Bali-Hindu umbrella.

The ultimate source of religious knowledge for the Balinese remains ancient Hindu and Buddhist texts, some still written in Sanskrit, the majority in Kawi (Old Javanese) and Balinese. As in India, high priests are invariably brahmans who have studied this literature extensively. Various types of lesser priests are also recognized, belonging to the other castes, most of whom have made at least some study of the written sources for their religion. Some priests and healers do not go through a course of study but are instead "chosen by the gods" directly in trance rituals. Even these priests revere the palm leaf *lontar* manuscripts. All books, and the written word itself, are consecrated to the goddess of wisdom, Sarasvatī. She alone among the gods has no special shrines. Instead, on her festival day all books and libraries are given offerings for her, because they are her temples.

No one knows, as yet, how many manuscripts exist in Balinese libraries, but the number is certainly in the thousands. The entire literature of Classical Javanese, which eventually boasted over two hundred distinct metrical patterns and which flourished for a millennium, would have been lost to the world but for the painstaking efforts of generations of Balinese literati, who had to recopy the entire corpus onto fragile palm-leaf manuscripts about once each century. Western scholars have only begun to examine this vast and rich literary tradition.

In considering the significance of these texts for Balinese religion, it is important to pay attention to the ways in which they are read and used. The Balinese approach to the activity of reading, and the "life of texts in the world," is quite different from that of the modern West. Balinese "reading groups" (*sekehe bebaosan*), for example, gather to read the ancient texts, either informally or to "embellish" a worthy gathering of people preparing for a ritual or temple festival. A reader intones a line from the text in its original language; if he strays from the correct metrical pattern, the line may have to be repeated. Then another reader will propose a spontaneous translation into modern colloquial Balinese. He pauses, in case anyone cares to suggest a better translation or a different interpretation. Once the meaning has been agreed upon, the first reader will recite the next line. The Balinese words for these "readings" are perhaps best rendered into English as "sounding" the texts, in both senses of turning letters into sounds, and searching for their meaning. "Sounding the texts" brings written order into the world, displaying the Logos that lies behind mundane reality. Words themselves may have intrinsic power, as is hinted in the poem that begins "Homage to the god . . . who is the essence of written letters . . . concealed in the dust of the poet's pencil."

RITUAL LIFE. It is possible to participate fully in Balinese religion all one's life without reading a single line from a *lontar* manuscript. Moreover, one is never called upon to make a public declaration of faith, either in a particular god or the efficacy of a particular ritual. Religion, for the Balinese, consists in the performance of five related ritual cycles, called *yajña*. Broadly speaking, the five *yajña* are sacrifices, and thus founded on ancient brahmanic theology. However, the details of the *yajña* are unique to Bali. The five *yajña* are

1. *déwa yajña* (sacrifices to the gods)
2. *būta yajña* (sacrifices to the chthonic powers or "elements")
3. *manuṣia yajña* (rites of passage)
4. *pitṛ yajña* (offerings to the dead)
5. *ṛṣi yajña* (consecration of priests)

Déwa yajña. Offerings to the gods (*déwa yajña*) are made in temples. The importance of these temples goes far beyond what we usually think of as religion, for temples provide the basic framework of Balinese economic and social organization. Classical Bali was a civilization without cities, in which important institutions such as irrigation networks, kinship groups, or periodic markets were organized by specialized temple networks. Most of these temple networks continue to function today. For example, consider the "irrigation" or "water temples." Each link in an irrigation system, from the small canal feeding one farmer's fields to the headwaters of a river, has a shrine or temple. The festivals held in these temples determine the schedule of "water openings" (flooding of the fields) for fields downstream. Later festivals mark the major events of the farmer's calendar: planting, transplanting, appearance of the milky grain (panicle), pest control, and so forth. The rituals of water temples synchronize farming activities for farmers using the same irrigation canals, and perhaps more important, allow higher-level temples to stagger cropping cycles to maximize production and minimize pest damage.

In similar ways, the Balinese version of a Hindu caste system was organized through temple networks—to belong to a caste translated into participating in the festivals of "caste temples," from the family shrine for the ancestors, through regional caste "branch temples," to the "origin temples" for whole castes or subcastes. Each Balinese temple has a specific purpose—it is part of an institutional system—and draws its membership exclusively from members of that institution. A Balinese worships only in the temples of the institutions he belongs to, which usually amount to half a dozen or more, including village temples, kinship or caste temples, water temples, and perhaps others as well.

Physically, Balinese temples consist of open rectangular walled courtyards with a row of shrines at one end. This architectural plan owes more to ancient Malayo-Polynesian megalithic shrines than to Indian temple design, and within the temple, space is ordered along a continuum, also Malayo-Polynesian in origin.

The gods are not believed to be continuously present in the temples but to arrive for only a few days each year as invited guests to temple festivities.

Members of the congregation prepare the temple and bring offerings for the gods, "not merely a fruit and a flower," as Margaret Mead observed, "but hundreds of finely wrought and elaborately conceived offerings made of palm leaf and flowers, twisted, folded, stitched, embroidered, brocaded into myriad traditional forms and fancies" (Belo, 1970, p. 335). Priests invite the gods to descend into their shrines with incense, bells, and prayers in Sanskrit. Worshipers kneel and pray for a few seconds, flicking flower petals toward the shrines of the gods, and are rewarded with a blessing of holy water from a temple priest. The remainder of the festival, which may last for days, is occupied with artistic performances for the amusement both of the gods and the human congregation. It was these performances that led Noël Coward to complain that "It seems that each Balinese native / From the womb to the tomb is creative." Temple festivals adhere to rigid schedules, based on the extremely complex Balinese permutational calendar. The gods must appear on a particular day, and at a given moment they must depart. Since the gods partake only of the essence of their offerings, the end of a temple festival is the beginning of a feast, for each family retrieves its offerings and shares the edible portions with friends and clients.

Būta yajña. *Būta,* usually translated into English as "demon," actually is the Balinese version of the Sanskrit word for "element of nature" (*bhūta*). It is therefore an oversimplification to describe the rituals of *būta yajña* as "demon offerings." Every important ritual, such as a temple festival, begins with *būta yajña* offerings as a purification or cleansing. Usually, these offerings require some form of blood sacrifice to satisfy the raw appetites of the elemental powers. All Balinese "demons" may take form either in the outer worlds (*buana agung*) or the inner world of the self (*buana alit*). A strong Tantric element in Balinese religion suggests that demons are essentially psychological projections but differs from Western psychology in insisting that "demonic" forces are part of the intrinsic constitution of both inner and outer reality.

Demons (*būta*) are the raw elements from which the higher realities of consciousness and the world are created. If their energy is not contained, they quickly become destructive. The purpose of *būta yajña* may be made clearer by considering the supreme *būta yajña* ceremony, called Eka Dasa Rudra, last held in 1979. The year 1979 marked the beginning of a new century acccording to the Balinese Icaka calendar. In order for the new century to begin auspiciously, it was felt necessary to complete all unfinished *būta* rituals, such as cremations, and then hold a gigantic ceremony at Bali's supreme temple, Besakih, to transform all of the accumulated demonic energies of the prior century into divine energies, to begin a new cycle of civilization in a phase of growth rather than decline. Nearly all Balinese participated in the yearlong preparations for Eka Dasa Rudra, which climaxed at the moment the old century ended, in a ceremony at Besakih temple involving over 100,000 people.

Manuṣia yajña. *Manuṣia yajña* are rites of passage, fitted to the Balinese belief in reincarnation. Twelve days after birth, an infant is given a name, and offerings are made to the four birth spirits (*kanda empat*) who have accompanied him. After three 35-day months, the child and his spirits are given new names, and the child's feet are allowed to touch the earth for the first time, since before this time he is considered still too close to the world of the gods. More offerings are made for the child's 210-day "birthday," at puberty, and finally in the climactic ceremony of tooth filing, which prepares the child for adulthood. The six upper canine teeth and incisors are filed slightly to make them more even, symbolically reducing the six human vices of lust (*kāma*), anger (*krodha*), greed (*lobha*), error (*moha*), intoxication (*mada*), and jealousy (*matsarya*). The *manuṣia yajña* cycle ends with the performance of the marriage ceremony.

Pitṛ yajña. These rituals are the inverse of *manuṣia yajña:* they are the rituals of death and return to the world of the gods, performed by children for their parents. The Balinese believe that people are usually reincarnated into their own families—in effect, as their own descendants—after five or more generations. The rituals of preparing the corpse, preliminary burial, cremation, and purification of the soul ensure that the spirits of one's parents are freed from earthly attachments, are able to enter heaven, and eventually are able to seek rebirth. Cremation is regarded as a major responsibility, costly and emotionally charged since the cremation bier proclaims both the wealth and the caste status of the family of the deceased. After these rituals are completed, the souls of the departed are believed to begin to visit their family shrines, where they must receive regular offerings, so the *pitṛ yajña* ritual cycle is never really finished.

Ṛṣi yajña. While the other four *yajña* involve everyone, the ceremonies of the consecration of priests (*ṛṣi yajña*) are the exclusive and esoteric provenance of the various priesthoods. In general, each "caste" has its own priests, although "high priests" (*pedanda*) are invariably brahmans. Buddhist traditions are kept alive by a special sect of high priests called *pedanda bodha.* The greatest of the *ṛṣi yajña* is the ceremony of consecration for a new *pedanda,* during which he must symbolically undergo his own funeral as a human being, to reemerge as a very special kind of being, a Balinese high priest.

SEE ALSO Megalithic Religion, article on Historical Cultures; Music, article on Music and Religion in Southeast Asia; Southeast Asian Religions, article on Insular Cultures.

BIBLIOGRAPHY

The most influential modern scholar of Balinese religion is Clifford Geertz. Several of his important essays are collected in *The Interpretation of Cultures* (New York, 1973), and his analysis of cosmology and kingship is presented in *Negara: The Theatre State in Nineteenth-Century Bali* (Princeton, 1980). Translations of Balinese texts on religions are provided in the many publications of Christiaan Hooykaas, including *Cosmogony and Creation in Balinese Tradition* (The Hague, 1974) and *Surya-Sevana: The Way to God of a Balinese Siva Priest* (Amsterdam, 1966). Many important essays from the 1930s by scholars such as Margaret Mead and Gregory Bateson are collected in *Traditional Balinese Culture,* edited by Jane Belo (New York, 1970). Belo also provides excellent descriptive accounts in *Bali: Temple Festival* (Locust Valley, N.Y., 1953) and *Trance in Bali* (New York, 1960). Opposing theories on the "indianization" of Bali are presented in J. C. van Leur's *Indonesian Trade and Society: Essays in Asian Social and Economic History* (The Hague, 1955) and in R. C. Majumdar's *Ancient Indian Colonization in South-East Asia* (Calcutta, 1963). Rites of passage are nicely evoked in Katherine Edson Mershon's *Seven Plus Seven: Mysterious Life-Rituals in Bali* (New York, 1971). Many important articles by Dutch scholars of the colonial era have been translated into English in *Bali: Studies in Life, Thought, and Ritual* (The Hague, 1960) and a second volume entitled *Bali: Further Studies in Life, Thought, and Ritual* (The Hague, 1969), both edited by J. L. Swellengrebel.

One of the most delightful books describing the relationship of the performing arts to religion is Beryl de Zoete and Walter Spies's *Dance and Drama in Bali* (1938; reprint, Oxford, 1973). A worthy successor is I. M. Bandem and Frederick

De Boer's *Kaja and Kelod: Balinese Dance in Transition* (Oxford, 1981). Urs Ramseyer's survey of *The Art and Culture of Bali* (Oxford, 1977) is a beautifully illustrated encyclopedia of Balinese religious art by a Swiss anthropologist. My *Three Worlds of Bali* (New York, 1983) provides an introduction to the role of religion and art in shaping the evolution of Balinese society.

New Sources

Barth, Fredrik. *Balinese Worlds.* Chicago, 1993.

Hauser-Schäublin, Brigitta. *Traces of Gods and Men: Temples and Rituals as Landmarks of Social Events and Processes in a South Bali Village.* Berlin, 1997.

Howe, Leo. *Hinduism & Hierarchy in Bali.* Oxford, 2001.

Lansing, J. Stephen. *Priests and Programmers: Technologies of Power in the Engineered Landscape of Bali.* Princeton, 1991.

Ottino, Arlette. *The Universe Within: A Balinese Village through Its Ritual Practices.* Paris, 2000

Rubinstein, Raechelle. *Beyond the Realm of the Senses: The Balinese Ritual of Kakawin Composition.* Leiden, 2000.

Stuart-Fox, David. *Pura Besakih: Temple, Religion and Society in Bali.* Leiden, 2002.

Suryani, Luh Ketut and Gordon D. Jensen. *Trance and Possession in Bali: A Window on Western Multiple Personality, Possession Disorder, and Suicide.* New York, 1993.

J. STEPHEN LANSING (1987)
Revised Bibliography

BALLGAMES

This entry consists of the following articles:

MESOAMERICAN BALLGAMES
NORTH AMERICAN INDIAN BALLGAMES

BALLGAMES: MESOAMERICAN BALLGAMES

Scholars employ the phrase "Mesoamerican ballgame" to refer to a diverse number of sport or ritual activities involving the use of a ball. All Mesoamerican peoples practiced "the ballgame" in one form or another. The three best-known forms of the game are the hipball, handball, and stickball variants.

TEMPORAL AND REGIONAL DIVERSITY. Mesoamerica is an ethnically, linguistically, and geographically varied region that is identifiable by shared cultural traits and religious beliefs which date to the pre-Columbian era (i.e., prior to the sixteenth century, which brought European contact). This culturally distinctive area encompasses the contemporary political boundaries of Mexico (excluding the northern, desert region), Belize, Guatemala, Honduras, and El Salvador. Mesoamerican ballgames reflect the diversity of the cultural and geographic environment in which they originated. The Mesoamerican ballgame also had strong ties with the ballgames of peoples of the North American Southwest and Caribbean.

Mesoamerican ballgames varied both temporally and regionally. Temporal variations appear to be related to fluctuations in popularity, to regionally specific and other developments, and to the particular socio-political and religious context and significance attributed to the game. Regional distinctions may also, in some cases, have had some relationship with ethnicity and identity. Scholars generally concur (with differences in interpretation on the specific points) that from their inception, which occurred at least as early as the Early Formative period (1200–900 BCE), all forms of the Mesoamerican ballgame shared fundamental ideological associations with creation mythology and with beliefs about the cycles of life and death, rain and fertility, and the cosmos.

Of all known Mesoamerican ballgames, the historic, artistic, and archaeological record has provided the most detailed information about the hipball game, and it is thus this form of the game that is most popularly thought of as "the" Mesoamerican ballgame. However, the hipball game also had numerous forms, dependent upon period, cultural and architectural context, costuming, equipment, and modes of play, across time and space in Mesoamerica. The hipball game was fully developed by the Early Formative period in the Socomusco region (the southern coastal plain and piedmont of the Isthmus of Tehuantepec and northern Guatemala, respectively), and the Veracruz-Tabasco Gulf Coast region associated with the Olmec civilization. In Nahuatl, the language of the Mexica (Aztec) people of the later Postclassic period (thirteenth to early sixteenth centuries CE), the hipball game was known as *ollama* or *ullama* (from *olli*, the word for rubber, which is related to the term *ollin*, meaning "movement"). The hipball game is still played today in Sinaloa state, in northwestern Mexico, although without the protective equipment of antiquity, and in an open field, rather than a court. Of the other relatively well-known forms of ballgame, the stick-ball game is particularly associated with the Teotihuacan culture of Central Mexico, and the handball game is best known at the site of Dainzu, Oaxaca state, Mexico.

EQUIPMENT. Different forms of the ballgame employed different types of paraphernalia. Common to all pre-Columbian hipball games was the use of padding around the waist and hips. This padding was used to propel the ball with greater force than was possible with an unpadded hip, while offering protection to the body during the course of this physically intensive game. Hip and waist protectors were probably made of padded cotton, leather, wicker, or wood. The only surviving pre-Columbian hip pads are the well-known, often elaborately carved, stone "yokes" (misnamed because of their physical appearance). These are particularly associated with the cultures of the Gulf Coast of Veracruz and Tabasco states, from the Formative through the Terminal Classic periods (c. 900 BCE to c. 900 CE), although examples are known elsewhere in Mesoamerica. Some stone yokes were functional, but a larger number were evidently ceremonial and symbolic.

Other stone hipball game paraphernalia survive from the Gulf Coast region. Carved stone *hachas*, so called because of the axe-like shape of many of these objects, were inserted into the yokes as chest protectors, or to project the ball. John Scott has suggested that those carved with twisted human faces were worn by victorious players of ritual games to represent the severed heads of players they had defeated. The stone *palmas* (referring to their palm-frond shape) were also carved with elaborate iconography related to religious or ritual components of the game, including references to the supernatural world and human sacrifice. *Palmas* were also inserted into the hip-pad for the same purposes as *hachas*. Mary Ellen Miller and Karl Taube also suggest that *palmas* were displayed in ballcourts as architectural decoration. Stone *manoplas* (handstones), often referred to in the literature as "knuckledusters," are more generally found throughout Mesoamerica. These were employed to project the ball in some forms of the hipball game, might have also been used in a ritual variant of the handball game and, according to Karl Taube and other researchers, were evidently employed as actual knuckledusters ("brass knuckles") in ritualized one-on-one boxing combats. Hipball players also wore loin coverings and knee pads on one knee, to protect their bodies when they slid onto their upper thighs or when they dropped to one knee to check the ball during the course of the game.

Ritualized versions of the hipball game are are distinctive in their use of ceremonial costuming, including elaborate headdresses, jewelry, and ornate forms of equipment. Ceremonial costuming often referenced the underlying beliefs associated with the ballgame; however, it is important to note that these are very specific and not recoverable though generalizations. For example, Classic Maya nobles, at sites such as Yaxchilan, Chiapas state, Mexico, are shown in some ritual games sporting the net kilt and other costume elements associated with the Maya Maize God, whose actions were emulated by Maya rulers to retain and underscore their sociopolitical and spiritual success.

Stickball games were also known in Mesoamerica. Players are depicted with bat-like or field hockey-like sticks, striking a soft-ball-sized ball in a defined, open field. Stickball players are represented in pre-Columbian art wearing loin cloths, head coverings, bands around the knees, and—in elaborated forms of the game—with fancy dress elements. Although the stickball game was particular to Central Mexico, especially the great city and culture of Teotihuacan, Theodore Stern has documented this ballgame variant elsewhere in Mesoamerican and the Caribbean. A modern form of the stickball game is played in Michoacán state, Mexico, using simple wooden bats. This game is played at night, with the ball set on fire at the beginning of the game as a symbolic reference to the sun.

Handball games are known throughout Mesoamerica from the Formative through the Classic periods. At the Late Formative site (c. 200 BCE to c. 200 CE) of Dainzu, in Oaxaca, carved stone slabs represent handball players wearing grilled helmets, gauntlet-like gloves, padded clothing over the torso and legs, thick knee pads on both knees, and sandals. Such full-body covering suggests a particularly energetic and perhaps dangerous form of ballgame. The contemporary Mixtec ballgame (*Juego de Pelota Mixteca*), known principally in Oaxaca, may descend from the Dainzu handball game.

BALLS. The hipball game used a rubber ball that was as much as a foot or more in diameter and which may have weighed seven or more pounds when solid. However, proportionately much larger balls are represented in Maya art of the Classic period (300 to 900 CE). The Terminal Classic (c. 800 to 1200 CE) carved stone panels lining the Great Ballcourt at Chichén Itza depict very large balls with skulls at the center. Some scholars propose that both sets of images might be taken literally: overly large, hollow-core balls might have been used in some Maya hipball games, whereas the skulls of sacrificed individuals may have been used to form ball cores in ritual games (although no known examples survive). The earliest known surviving rubber balls were excavated from the offerings of El Manati, Veracruz, at a spring site sacred to the Formative Olmec civilization of the Gulf Coast. The largest and most spherical of these are ten inches in diameter, and have been dated by the excavators to around 1600 BCE.

Stickball and handball games probably used small, solid rubber balls. However, some researchers have suggested that for ritualized handball games, the rubber balls may have been replaced with stone spheroids. The rubber used to make the various balls came from any of the several rubber-producing plants and trees found throughout Mesoamerica and the North American Southwest. In Mesoamerica, rubber was used not only for the ballgame, but in offerings, particularly to rain deities, and for medicinal purposes.

BALLCOURTS. Ballgame courts, fields, and the structures on which ritual ballgames were enacted, reflect some of the diversity of Mesoamerican ballgames, although these features tend to share general characteristics.

The best-known form of Mesoamerican ballcourt is the masonry court designed for hipball games. The earliest versions of these structures date to approximately 1400 BCE and are found in the Socomusco and Gulf Coast regions, although there may be examples dating as early as the fifth century BCE. Early Soconusco and Gulf Coast Olmec heartland courts were formed by two parallel earthen mounds flanking and delineating a central playing court.

In general, Late Formative and Classic period hipball courts have playing alleys and end zones laid out in a shape similar to the capital letter "I." The court's boundaries are defined by two parallel platform mound structures. The alley walls are sloped and typically have benches along the sides. Three markers are commonly located down the axial center of the alley. Specialized superstructures containing steambaths and other preparatory facilities were built atop the platform mounds. In most cases, spectators were probably seated along platforms and structures located around, and outside of, each end zone. Postclassic (c. 900 to 1521 CE) ballcourts generally have perpendicular side walls with stone ring markers.

Mary Ellen Miller and Stephen Houston, and others including David Friedel, Linda Schele, and Joy Parker, have identified symbolic courts used for ritualized ballgames. These ritual courts comprise temple stairways such as that of the war monument Temple 33, at the Maya site of Yaxchilan, and patios such as the Classic period East and West Courts of Copan, Honduras. They may also include the Formative period sunken court of Teopantecuanitlan, Guerrero state, Mexico.

Stickball and handball games employed defined, open playing fields. Eric Taladoire has suggested that one form of formal court may have been used for the handball game as played in Oaxaca during the Formative period.

The Rules. The rules of Mesoamerican ballgames were specific to each particular game, and, although broadly understood by researchers, have not been recovered in detail. Most ballgames were played with two competing teams facing each other at either end of the playing field or court. In hipball, points were scored by hitting the ball toward the alley markers, the end zones, or the rings on the alley walls. The ball typically was hit with the thighs, buttocks, and upper arms. Bare hands or *manoplas* were employed only to set the ball into motion, since the use of the hands to strike the ball was not permitted, except in the case of handball games. Athletic vigor, physical intensity, and a high degree of competition seem to characterize all Mesoamerican ballgames. In addition, it is evident that both men and women played the ballgame.

Social, Political, and Religious Significance. Mesoamerican ballgames were generally conducted within one of two broad contexts: sport and ritual. As pure sport, pre-Columbian ballgames were not unlike football, soccer, and baseball as they are known today. Outstanding athletes were highly regarded, and could even achieve star-like status. Communities competed with one another through their teams. Betting on the games is known to have been popular at the time of Spanish contact, with desirable items, such as fine cotton shirts, being wagered on favorite teams or players. pre-Columbian ballgames are distinctive from contemporary occidental ball sports, however, in the complexity of meaning attached to them, and their symbolic connection to the events of creation and universal cycles.

Surviving Mesoamerican creation stories tell of primordial beings playing life-and-death ballgames in mythical time. For example, the sixteenth-century Quiché Maya community book, *The Popol Vuh*, and Classic period Maya hieroglyphic texts, recount how the legendary Hero Twins were summoned to the Underworld to play a deadly ballgame with the Underworld deities. The Twins survived several trials, defeated the Underworld gods, and resurrected their father, the Maize God, in the ballcourt, which is named as the place of sacrifice (and the locus of rebirth or renewal). This tradition explains how corn was brought into the world and provides a metaphor for the life cycle of birth, death, and regeneration as it is dramatically experienced by agrarian societies in this geographic region, with its distinctive rainy and dry seasons. Certain ballgames were thus directly associated with rain deities, and with the coming of the rains and subsequent fertility of the earth.

Very early on, Mesoamerican ballgames were linked to political authority and the fundamental role of rulers as providers for their communities. If there were natural disasters such as drought and famine, or political and military defeats, the legitimacy of an individual's rule could seriously be called into question. At such times, some ballgames came to serve as public spectacles, full of courtly pomp and circumstance, for the ritual reenactment of warfare and success on the battlefield. Captives were made to play staged, fixed, "games" that were essentially mock combats with predetermined outcomes. The end result of these events was the sacrifice and, frequently, decapitation and dismemberment of defeated players. In some cases, severed heads, taken as trophies in these ritualized ballgames, were displayed on nearby skull racks, known by the Nahuatl term *tzompantlis.*

Since the earliest scholarship in Mesoamerica, researchers have noticed that, in certain ballgames, the movement of the ball was associated with the movement of cosmic bodies, particularly the sun. It is clear, however, that these associations were very particular and were framed in specific cultural ways, dependent upon the time and location of the game.

Popularized misconceptions of the Mesoamerican Ballgame suggest that the winners of ritualized games were the ones to be sacrificed. No substantiated or credible academic evidence supports this belief, nor does the idea conform in any way to the scholarly and indigenous understanding of pre-Columbian cultures in Mesoamerica.

The Mesoamerican ballgame was a central component of Mesoamerican society and culture. Indeed, ballcourts, which could be strategically located on community boundaries or on the periphery of major centers, often functioned as the loci for ritual and interaction between social and political entities, including alliance building, trade, and exchange.

See Also Sports and Religion.

Bibliography

Bernal, Ignacio, and Andy Seuffert. *The Ball Players of Dainzú.* Graz, Austria 1979.

Borhegyi, Stephan F. de. *The Pre-Columbian Ballgames: A Pan-Mesoamerican Tradition.* Contributions in Anthropology and History, vol. 1. Milwaukee, 1980.

Coe, Michael. "The Hero Twins: Myth and Image." In *The Maya Vase Book*, edited by Justin Kerr. New York, 1990.

Filloy, Laura. "Rubber and Rubber Balls in Mesoamerica." In *The Sport of Life and Death: The Mesoamerican Ballgame*, edited by E. Michael Whittington. New York, 2001.

Friedel, David, Linda Schele, and Joy Parker. *Maya Cosmos: Three Thousand Years on the Shaman's Path.* New York, 1993.

Leyenaar, Ted, and Lee Parsons. *Ulama: The Ballgame of the Mayas and Aztecs, 2000 B.C.–A.D. 2000.* Leiden, 1988.

Miller, Mary Ellen, and Stephen D. Houston. "Stairways and Ballcourt Glyphs: New Perspectives on the Classic Maya Ballgame." *Res* 14 (1987): 47–66.

Miller, Mary Ellen, and Karl Taube. *The Gods and Symbols of Ancient Mexico and the Maya.* London and New York, 1993.

Orr, Heather. "Stone Balls and Masked Men: Ballgame as Combat Ritual, Dainzu, Oaxaca." *Ancient America* 5 (2003): 73–104.

Scarborough, Vernon L., and David R. Wilcox, eds. *The Mesoamerican Ballgame.* Tucson, 1991.

Scott, John. "Dressed to Kill: Stone Regalia of the Mesoamerican Ballgame." In *The Sport of Life and Death: The Mesoamerican Ballgame,* edited by E. Michael Whittington. New York, 2001.

Stern, Theodore. *The Rubber-Ball Game of the Americas.* New York, 1949.

Taladoire, Eric. "Could We Speak of the Super Bowl at Flushing Meadows? La Pelota Mixteca: A Third Prehispanic Ballgame and Its Possible Architectural Context." *Ancient Mesoamerica* 14, no. 2 (July 2003): 319–342.

Taube, Karl. "American Gladiators." Paper presented at the 8th Annual Maya Weekend, U.C.L.A., 2001.

Tedlock, Dennis, trans. and comm. *Popul Vuh: The Definitive Edition of the Mayan Book of the Dawn of Life and the Glories of Gods and Kings.* New York, 1996.

Uriarte, Maria Teresa. "Unity in Duality: The Practice and Symbols of the Mesoamerican Ballgame." In *The Sport of Life and Death: The Mesoamerican Ballgame,* edited by E. Michael Whittington. New York, 2001.

HEATHER S. ORR (2005)

BALLGAMES: NORTH AMERICAN INDIAN BALLGAMES

Throughout what is now the United States and Canada, First Nations historically have engaged in a variety of games that incorporate a ball. Such activities often appear in narrative traditions, and many communities continue such games in the early twenty-first century. These include shinny, racket or lacrosse-type games, double ball, and ball racing and feature both single-gender and mixed-gender participation.

Given that for many people the term *game* carries with it associations with frivolity and leisure—both "not work" and "not serious"—the nature of these activities must be stressed. Native American games can be quite serious endeavors, in certain cases requiring a great deal of preparation, and the outcomes can have economic, political, and social ramifications beyond the playing field. Games can provide opportunities for expressions of cultural values and ideals and may incorporate other traditional activities, and thus they can radiate potent symbolic meanings for participants and observers.

Because the activities of many cultures do not fit easily within the rubric of "religion" and because community members themselves may not isolate and identify particular activities as "religious," it is necessary to assert here that certain of the "games" discussed in this article should be understood as "religious," based upon commonly held definitions in the academic study of religion. Thus supernatural beings or "other-than-human persons," to use A. Irving Hallowell's term (1975) can be explicitly honored or referenced by the playing of certain games as well as beseeched for assistance in preparation for and during the contests (Hallowell, 1975, p. 145). Religious and medicinal specialists can be employed to prepare teams and influence the outcome, while certain games themselves are said to be ceremonial activities or rituals.

SHINNY, BALL THROWING, AND BALL RACING. Though there are a variety of ballgames, mention will be made here only of those that contain some religious referent. Shinny is a team game in which a ball is raked or propelled toward a goal with a stick not unlike that used in hockey. Although the hands may not be used, the ball may be kicked. According to Stewart Culin, author of the encyclopedic *Games of the North American Indians* (1975), the game was the most widespread of the ballgames and "frequently referred to in the myths" yet was "commonly played without any particular ceremony" (Culin, 1975, pp. 562, 617). Culin recorded the names of more than fifty groups that once played the game. Though most often played by women, it also has been played by men as well as by men and women together and against one another.

Shinny is known as *tabegasi* in the Ponca language, the root word *tabe,* or ball, being the same in the Osage and Omaha languages (Howard, 1971, pp. 10, 14). According to an account from the early 1970s, the Ponca version pitting teams of men against one another still retained some amount of ceremony having to do with the balls and the choosing of teams. The keeper of the game was an individual from the Nikapashna clan, members of which also supervised hunting and warfare activities at one time (Fletcher and La Flesche in Howard, 1971, p. 14). In some instances, for example, among California peoples such as the Yurok, Hupa, Karuk, and Tolowa, this game is said to have been played by the first beings on earth and taught to humans (Gendar, 1995, pp. 19–20).

The Lakota ballgame *tapa wankayeyapi* ("throwing the ball upward") was one of the *Wicoh'an Wakan Šakowin* (Seven Sacred Rites) given to the people by *Ptehincalaskawin* (White Buffalo Calf Woman). A young girl tossed a ball to participants standing at the four directions, with the ball symbolizing knowledge and the attempts of the participants symbolizing the struggle against ignorance (Powers, 1977, p. 103; St. Pierre and Long Soldier, 1995, p. 28). It is not currently performed.

Ball races were run by communities in the present-day southwestern United States and in adjacent areas of California and Mexico. Groups such as the Keres people of the Acoma community, the Zunis, and the Hopi people engaged in spring kick-ball or kick-stick races to secure rain (Culin, 1975, p. 668). These races pitted two individuals or teams against one another; the first to kick a ball or stick around a course and return to the starting point was the winner.

RACKET GAMES. In North America ballgames that employ a racket and ball are the most prevalent of those that reference supernatural beings, employ religious and medicinal specialists, are part of ceremonies, are linked to other ritual activities, or are self-contained rituals. Many communities along the eastern seaboard of North America, across the inland southeast, in the Great Lakes region, and to the immediate west in what is now the United States once played the game along with certain communities in present-day California, Mexico, and the Pacific Northwest region of North America. Generally speaking, racket games are considered the precursors of the sport of lacrosse; versions played by peoples in the present-day northeastern United States and in southeastern Canada are routinely cited as the specific forerunners of that sport.

Historically, lacrosse-type activities commonly termed "ballgames" have been integral cultural elements for many Native American peoples, though they have functioned differently from community to community. Rituals in and of themselves for some groups, a part of religious festivals for others, and at the center of ceremonial complexes in still other communities, the ballgames almost always have been major social events. In some cases they have been instruments of healing, and in other cases they have been primarily social events.

There are two major categories of lacrosse-type activity: single- and double-racket games. These categories correspond broadly to regional areas, with the single-racket game being played throughout what is now the northeastern United States and to an area west of the Great Lakes. Nations in the Haudenosaunee (Iroquois) Confederacy continue to play the single-racket version, as do surrounding nations such as the Huron and Passamaquody. The racket used is typically over a yard in length and is crooked at one end; webbing is fitted from here to the straight portion of the stick to form a large triangular pocket. It is the model for the stick used in the popularized sport of field lacrosse. Groups in the Great Lakes region, such as the Ojibwas, Santee Dakotas, Menominees, Potowatomis, and Winnebagos (among others), also used one racket; however these were shorter, straight pieces of wood curved at the end to form a small circle, which was webbed to create a pocket. Though information is somewhat limited on the Dakota version of the game, there are several accounts of Yankton and Santee games as well as paintings and drawings of players that support the conclusion that the game was a regular feature of life at least throughout the nineteenth century.

The double-racket game was and is prevalent in what is now the southeastern United States. It has long been standard among nations such as the Cherokee, Choctaw, Chickasaw, Yuchi, and Seminole and among those of the Muskogee (Creek) Confederacy. The rackets used in this game are usually two to three feet long and are formed from single pieces of wood bent and dried to form oval shapes at one end, which are then webbed with rawhide or other materials to form pockets. Despite individual particularities, broad regional similarities historically have resulted in ballgames between First Nations, such as those between Cherokee and Muskogee (Creek) communities or between confederated nations, for example, the Mohawk and Seneca (Mooney, 1890, p. 107; Culin, 1975, p. 591).

In both the single- and the double-racket versions, the object of the game is to score goals, which can be achieved by players crossing a threshold while in possession of the ball. This can be a goal line between two posts, some other goal marking, or a single goal post that must be circled completely. The rules of a particular contest dictate what actions are allowable; in some cases goals can be scored by throwing the ball over the goal line.

In all versions the rackets must be used to propel the ball, and players cannot pick the ball up off the ground with their hands; in certain versions, players can use their hands to carry or throw the ball once they have retrieved it. Games can feature rough play, including wrestling and body blocking. In the games between teams of men, players usually wear little or no protective equipment, and often, especially in the Southeast, players wear only short pants—no shirts or shoes. A distinguishing aspect of many versions of this contest, both single- and double-racket, is that the object is to bring the ball back to one's own goal, not penetrate the goal of the opponent, as is the case in other goal-oriented physical activities.

While for the most part this is a male activity, in some communities women's teams compete against each other. Selected versions of the game, such as those on Cherokee Nation dance grounds in Oklahoma, are played around a central pole, the object being to hit a target at the top to score points. Single-pole contests routinely feature teams of men wielding rackets against women who are allowed to use their hands.

Wagering on the men's games once was widespread. In the nineteenth century and early twentieth century religious and governmental authorities discouraged certain Southeastern communities' ballgames (particularly those of the Cherokees and Choctaws). They objected to the wagering, the inherent violence of the contests, and the unruly crowd behavior that became more frequent with the influx of spectators from outside the participating communities. Wagering has been eliminated or much reduced in most contemporary contests.

Single-racket games. In 1636 the Jesuit father Jean de Brébeuf wrote about the Huron game in the area then known as New France. This account of a ballgame is the earliest written by a European yet located and appears in the *Relations* of the Jesuit fathers. Brébeuf noted that a Huron medico-religious specialist ("sorcerer") might prescribe a game of "crosse" for the benefit of the entire nation or for a sick individual, and that sometimes a person would dream that a game was necessary for their recovery (Brébeuf in Culin, 1975, p. 589).

The Six Nations of the Haudenosaunee (Iroquois) Confederacy have maintained their specific ballgame traditions while participating in other forms of the game. Scholars generally agree that the sport of lacrosse derived from their games, and many of the early stick makers were members of confederacy nations. Haudenosaunee teams in the early twenty-first century participate both in field and box lacrosse as well as in the classic version.

The Onondaga term for the single-racket lacrosse-type ballgame is *dehuntshigwa'es*, meaning "they (men) hit a rounded object" (Vennum, 1994, p. 72). Onondaga games between clan groupings or teams of older and younger players last until a predetermined number of goals have been won and feature uneven teams; the number of players determines the length of the field (Vennum, 1994, pp. 6–7). They have been employed to heal sickness and comfort the sick and dying. This was the case in 1815, when Onondaga people held a ballgame for the dying Seneca prophet Handsome Lake, and accounts from the late twentieth century suggest the same use (Vennum, 1994, pp. 6–7, 222; Oxendine, 1988, p. 10). The game is played in the afterworld, and players make arrangements to bring sticks with them for those future contests (Vennum, 1994, p. 7).

A mid-twentieth-century account stated that the ballgame called *gatci·''kwae* ("beating the mush") was the central element of the Cayuga Nation's Thunder Rite, a one-day ceremony in the middle of the summer (Speck, 1949, p. 117). Games were played to honor the Seven Thunders, called "Grandfathers," for "continuation of the service which they render mankind as agents of the Great Spirit," and which team won or lost was not important (Speck, 1949, pp. 117, 118). At the conclusion of the game players sang the War Dance or Thunder Song and went into the longhouse, where they gave thanks to the Seven Thunders and other forces in the universe in a manner similar to the way in which the Thanksgiving Address was made during the Midwinter Ceremony (Speck, 1949, pp. 117, 118). According to one 1960s source, the players "personify the seven thunder gods"; on rare occasions when a sick person had dreamed of the game, Cayuga teams played it during the Midwinter Ceremony (Eyman, 1964, pp. 18–19).

Writing at the turn of the twentieth century, the anthropologist Lewis Henry Morgan rendered the name of the single-racket game as *O-tä-dä-jish'-quä-äge* and recounted a tradition stating that the war that resulted in the Eries being expelled from New York around 1654 originated in "a breach of faith or treachery" during a ballgame against the Senecas (Morgan, 1901, pp. 280, 282). Other terms used by individual members of the Six Nations include *Ga-lahs* (Oneida) and *Tewaarathon* (Mohawk). Among the Oneidas it is considered a "rite sacred to the Thunders" and is said to have been played for Hayewat-ha, "to console him for the loss of his children" during the founding of the confederacy ("Lacrosse: An Iroquois Tradition"). The Mohawks consider it pleasing to the Creator, a means of thanksgiving, and a way "to call the Creator's attention to the efforts of the medicine people" (North American Indian Travelling College in Fisher, 2002, p. 23).

According to one source from the early twentieth century, the Menominee ballgame and warfare are related activities that came from the thunders; thus the "game was supposed to resemble a battle" (Densmore, 1932, p. 35). Traditional narratives detail the origin of the game and the implements, including the racket, which is shaped like a war club (Densmore, 1932, pp. 36–37). A 1925 account reported that a Menominee man who dreamed of the thunders held a lacrosse game to receive help promised by them, a process termed "playing out a dream"; such dreams promised health or success, and medicinal specialists could prescribe games (Densmore, 1932, p. 27). In these games, one of which Frances Densmore witnessed in 1925, the dreamer did not play and the outcome did not affect the dreamer's chances of achieving what he sought. One source noted that to "cure illness, the Menominee still play the game in the spring, before the first thunder" (Vennum, 1994, p. 33). There also are accounts of Ojibwe and Potawatami games played to achieve similar results (Vennum, 1994, p. 33; Oxendine, 1988, p. 8).

Double-racket games. The Cherokee double-racket ballgame *anetso* (*a:ne:tso*) is known also as "da·na·wah? u·sdi'" (as rendered by the anthropologist Raymond D. Fogelson), or "little war" (Fogelson, 1962, p. 2). There is a similar term for the game among towns of the Muskogee or Creek Confederacy, rendered by the anthropologist Mary R. Haas as *"hółłi icósi"* ("younger brother to war") (Haas, 1940, p. 483). In the Cherokee language, the phrase "to play a ball game" has a figurative meaning of engaging in battle (Mooney, [1900] 1982, p. 384)

Anetso once was the occasion for a great deal of wagering, and the community at large participated in pregame activities, such as night dances. Currently members of the Eastern Band of Cherokee Indians continue their ballgame tradition with a series of annual games during the Cherokee Fall Fair. The Cherokee games match townships against one another or are scrimmage exhibitions between squads from the same township. The ballgame is a rough contest, with frequent wrestling and body blocking. The games are to twelve points, and teams usually consist of ten to twelve players who have undergone several weeks of training and preparation for the week's series of games.

In addition to a rigorous practice schedule, the training regimen typically includes *amó:hi atsv?:sdi* ("going to water," ritual bathing or laving) and interaction with a medico-religious specialist. Though not always employed, the following actions can and have been performed: scarification, ingestion or application of medicinal substances, dancing, fasting, avoidance of certain foods, and for men, avoidance of contact with women and children for specified periods of time. Movements to and from the field are ritualized as well. Finally, medico-religious specialists can perform a variety of activities, including some of a divinatory nature, before and during the match.

Teams of women have begun competing during the Cherokee Fair, and there are differing opinions as to whether this is a new innovation or a revival of a custom as old, or possibly even older, than the men's contest. The women's games follow the same rules as the men's; only their wardrobe differs, as they wear shirts. Many other communities have reinvigorated the men's ballgame as well; for example, members of the Mississippi Band of Choctaw Indians play their version of the game, *kapucha toli,* during annual fairs.

GENERAL OBSERVATIONS. Some commentators have suggested that there once was a formal link between ballgames and warfare for both southeastern and northeastern nations, and as noted above, there are several accounts of intertribal matches in both oral traditions and historical texts. While some evidence suggests that ballgames have been used to settle disputes, there is no definitive evidence to support the conclusion that such games once were surrogates for war. There is evidence that these activities once were training for warfare, and there are historical accounts of games being used to lure an enemy into a trap. One well-known example is a 1763 game of *bagga'adowe* between Ojibwa and Ottawa villages outside the British Fort Michilimackinac in present-day Michigan. The soldiers guarding the fort were drawn outside to view the contest, when suddenly the Ojibwa players attacked and captured the fort. On the whole, research suggests that ballgames have expressed a range of social, political, religious, and economic meanings dependent on cultural and historical contexts.

There are many Native American cultural narratives featuring games of ball between nonhuman beings and humans or in some cases between nonhuman beings in a time before humans inhabited the earth. For example, in the Cherokee narrative tradition there are accounts of ballgames played by supernatural beings (the Sons of Thunder) and games between teams of birds and four-legged animals as well as famous games between Cherokee teams and teams from other nations. There also are Choctaw, Muskogee, Seminole, Mohawk, and Onondaga narratives of similar games between birds and animals. In all of them the pivotal character, the bat, was rejected by one or both of the teams before being allowed to play. The narratives differ regarding such details as which team finally accepted the bat and why, but the team that did so always won in the end.

Though not as widespread as they once were, ballgames continue to be viable cultural traditions in many First Nations communities and are undergoing some amount of revitalization in others.

SEE ALSO Sports and Religion.

BIBLIOGRAPHY

Blanchard, Kendall. *The Mississippi Choctaws at Play: The Serious Side of Leisure.* Urbana, Ill., 1981.

Culin, Stewart. *Games of the North American Indians.* New York, 1975. Originally published as part of the *Twenty-Fourth Annual Report of the Bureau of American Ethnology, 1902–1903,* Washington, D.C., 1907.

Densmore, Frances. *Menominee Music.* Smithsonian Institution Bureau of American Ethnology Bulletin 102. Washington, D.C., 1932.

Eyman, Frances. "Lacrosse and the Cayuga Thunder Rite." *Expedition* 6, no. 4 (1964): 15–19.

Fisher, Donald M. *Lacrosse: A History of the Game.* Baltimore and London, 2002.

Fogelson, Raymond D. "The Cherokee Ball Game: A Study in Southeastern Ethnology." Ph.D. diss., University of Pennsylvania, Philadelphia, 1962.

Gendar, Jeannine. *Grass Games and Moon Races: California Indian Games and Toys.* Berkeley, Calif., 1995.

Haas, Mary R. "Creek Inter-Town Relations." *American Anthropologist* 42, no. 3 (July–September 1940): 479–489.

Hallowell, A. Irving. "Ojibwa Ontology, Behavior, and World View." In *Teachings from the American Earth: Indian Religion and Philosophy,* edited by Dennis Tedlock and Barbara Tedlock, pp. 141–178. New York, 1975. First published in *Culture in History: Essays in Honor of Paul Radin,* edited by Stanley Diamond (New York, 1960).

Howard, James H. "The Ponca Shinny Game." *Indian Historian* 4, no. 3 (Fall 1971): 10–15.

Iroquois Nationals Lacrosse team website. Available from http://www.iroquoisnationals.com.

"Lacrosse: An Iroquois Tradition." Available from www.oneidanation.net.

Mooney, James. "The Cherokee Ball Play." *American Anthropologist* o.s. 3 (1890): 105–132.

Mooney, James. *Myths of the Cherokee and Sacred Formulas of the Cherokees.* Nashville, Tenn., 1982. "Myths of the Cherokee" was originally published as the *Nineteenth Annual Report of the Bureau of American Ethnology, 1897–1898,* pp. 3–576, Washington, D.C., 1900; "Sacred Formulas of the Cherokees" was originally published in the *Seventh Annual Report of the Bureau of American Ethnology, 1885–1886,* pp. 301–397, Washington, D.C., 1891.

Morgan, Lewis Henry. *League of the Ho-dé-no-sau-nee or Iroquois,* vol. 1. Edited by Herbert M. Lloyd. Rev. and enlarged ed. New York, 1901.

North American Indian Travelling College. *Tewaarathon (La Crosse) Akwesasne's Story of Our National Game.* Cornwall Island, Ontario, 1978.

Oxendine, Joseph B. *American Indian Sports Heritage.* Champaign, Ill., 1988; reprint, with a new afterword by the author, Lincoln, Neb., 1995.

Powers, William K. *Oglala Religion.* Lincoln, Neb., 1977; reprint, 1982.

Salter, Michael A. "Meteorological Play-Forms of the Eastern Woodlands." In *Studies in the Anthropology of Play: Papers in Memory of B. Allan Tindall,* edited by Phillips Stevens Jr., pp. 6–28. Cornwall, N.Y., 1978.

Salter, Michael A. "Play in Ritual: An Ethnohistorical Overview of Native North America." In *Play and Culture,* 1978 Proceedings of the Association for the Anthropological Study of Play, edited by Helen B. Schwartzman, pp. 70–91. West Point, N.Y., 1980.

Speck, Frank G., in collaboration with Alexander General (Deskáheh). *Midwinter Rites of the Cayuga Long House.* Philadelphia, 1949; reprint, with an introduction by William N. Fenton, Lincoln, Neb., and London, 1995.

St. Pierre, Mark, and Tilda Long Soldier. *Walking in the Sacred Manner: Healers, Dreamers, and Pipe Carriers: Medicine Women of the Plains Indians.* New York, 1995.

Vennum, Thomas, Jr. *American Indian Lacrosse: Little Brother of War.* Washington, D.C., 1994.

MICHAEL J. ZOGRY (2005)

BALTIC RELIGION

This entry consists of the following articles:

AN OVERVIEW
NEW RELIGIOUS MOVEMENTS
HISTORY OF STUDY

BALTIC RELIGION: AN OVERVIEW

Latvians, Lithuanians, and Old Prussians constitute the Baltic language and cultural unit. The Old Prussians, who lived in the territory of the present-day Kaliningrad district and eastern Germany, were conquered during the period of eastward German expansionism from the ninth to the fourteenth century. They were assimilated progressively and disappeared completely in the seventeenth century. Latvians and Lithuanians have preserved their national identities to this day. At one time or another since the Crusades of the eleventh century, all these peoples have been subject to German, Polish, Russian, and Swedish colonization. This fact is of special significance since it has affected our understanding of the elements of the ancient religious systems that have been preserved. As colonies, the three national groups were subject to extensive political and economic exploitation. Although formally Christianized, they continued their traditional ways of religious life despite colonial restrictions.

The Baltic peoples have inhabited their present territory from the middle of the second millennium BCE. At that time, however, their territory extended farther east, to Moscow, and southwest, across the banks of the Vistula. Living on the fringe of eastern Europe, they were virtually unknown to the West, and thus were able to remain relatively untouched by the influence of Christianity up to the seventeenth century. As early as the first millennium BCE, these isolated peoples, untouched by foreign developments, had developed from a hunting and fishing culture to an agrarian one. The structure of agrarian society and its routine determined the development of the belief system and the structure of cultic life.

The Baltic peoples came to the attention of European linguists at the end of the eighteenth century. These linguists were especially interested in the Vedic language and literature of ancient India. In their attempt to build a bridge to the living European languages, they discovered that the closest European affinity to the Vedic language—both etymologically and, to some extent, lexically—existed with the Baltic language group, especially Lithuanian. (Comparative linguists of the twentieth century, such as Alois Walde, Julius Pokorny, Antoine Meillet, and Hans Krahe, have devoted particular attention to Baltic languages.) Interest in the languages generated interest in the ethnogenesis of the Baltic peoples. This subject fascinated scholars as late as the nineteenth century. It became apparent that the geographic isolation of these peoples had not only allowed, but had furthered, an unhindered and uninterrupted development free from external influence. But their rather late appearance in the European arena and their previous isolation have fostered a great deal of guesswork about their linguistic and ethnic origins and kinships. Until recent times there has been great confusion on this subject. The Baltic languages were often erroneously classified as Slavic, although linguists (e.g., Jānis Endzelīns, Wolfgang Schmid, and Vladimir Toporov) had long known that they are no more closely related to the Slavic language group than to the Germanic or any other Indo-European language group originating from their common Indo-European base, whereas the Estonian language belongs to the Finno-Ugrian language group and has a completely different history behind it.

Any investigation of the Baltic religion must touch upon the central problem of sources, of which there are three types: archaeological evidence, folklore, and historical documents. The archaeological evidence can easily be surveyed since these peoples have always lived in the same region. Excavations have unearthed artifacts from the second millennium BCE that present a clear picture of material culture, though not of religious life. (On the territory of Latvia, archaeologists Jānis Graudonis, Ēvalda Mugurēvičs, Juris Urtāns, Raisa Deņisova, Ilga Zagorska, Egīls Šņore, and Anna Zariņa discovered important artifacts during the 1990s). There is no evidence of gods and their cults. The burial rites and belief systems connected with these rites have been carefully researched by such scholars as Marija Gimbutas and Francis Balodis, but evidence from historical documents is meager. The earliest documents are from the tenth century, when Germans and Danes attacked the eastern shore of the Baltic Sea. There is mention of contact with the Balts but little further information. The situation remained almost unchanged up to the beginning of the seventeenth century, when more elaborate descriptions were written by leading clergymen, including, for example, Paul Einhorn and certain Jesuit priests.

Despite the dearth of archaeological evidence and historical documentation, the folklore materials of these peoples is one of the richest in all of Europe. Songs (*dainas*), stories, tales, proverbs, and beliefs have been recorded. The diversity of these sources has, however, proved to be a stumbling block, because each type of source has required a particular investigatory method. As a result, objective investigation of Baltic religion was slow to come. At first, there was a tendency to approach the topic ideologically, from both Christian and Marxist points of view. Then, during the period of national awakening in the latter half of the nineteenth century, came a tendency to create pseudo-gods and figments of imagination, as well as an attempt to raise the national consciousness of the former colonial nations by finding "precedents" in the primary ethnic tradition. Scholarship since the 1960s (e.g., that of Jonas Balys, Marija Gimbutas, Lena Neuland, and Haralds Biezais) has become more scientifically accurate.

SKY GODS. Of all the Baltic gods in heaven, the most prominent is Dievs. Linguists agree that etymologically the Latvian name *Dievs* (Lithuanian, Dievas; Old Prussian, Deivas) has common origin with the names of such gods as the ancient Indian Dyaus and the Greek Zeus, which are in turn derived from the Indo-European root **dyeu-* and its derivatives. The meaning of words derived from this root is "the heavens." Older scholarship sought to establish a semantic connection between this root and the daytime sky or light, but this contention lacks proof, and one must therefore assume that the meaning "the heavens" is more precise, as Grace Hopkins (1932) has argued. The original identity of Dievs then becomes clearer from his name. The nature of, and the psychological motives behind, the god's development from a phenomenon of nature to a personification and, later, to a personal god is, however, a source of contention. Despite these uncertainties, it is clear that Dievs is closely connected with the heavens.

The first written evidence of the Baltic gods comes from "Germania" by the Roman historian Tacitus (55–120 CE) where he mentions that "aists" (Balts) worship the Mother of gods (mater deorum). In "Rhymed Chronicles" (Livlaendische Reimchronik, 1290) the god of thunder Perkun is mentioned as being of highest authority.

Cardinal Valenti in his chronicles written in 1604 and based greatly on "Statuta provincialia consilii Rigensis" (1428) provided the evidence that the Balts worshiped a god of heaven: "Credono un Dio Supremo, che chiamano Tebo Deves" ("They believe in a high god, called Tebo Deves"). Tebo Deves is a corrupted form of *debess dievs* ("sky god"). That same year the Jesuit Janis Stribins, in his discussion of ancient Latvian religion, noted that the Balts claim "Habemus Deum q[ui] habetet [sic] curam coeli" ("We have a god, who in the sky takes care"). The pantheon of ancient Baltic gods is also described by Einhorn in his "History of Latvia" (*Historia Lettica,* 1649). Though these documents offer only fragmentary evidence, they do show that the Balts worshiped a god of heaven (Dievs). Folklore materials, which allow one to delve deeper into the essence, function, and attributes of this god, support the claim.

The anthropomorphic character of Dievs has been carefully described and compared to that of other divinities. He is clad in a silver overcoat, gray jacket, and hat; he is girded with a decorated belt and wears mittens; and in certain situations he also has a sword, though this is probably a later development. His dress resembles that of a prosperous farmer.

That Dievs has his abode in the heavens is self-evident from his name. The heavens resemble a mountain, and this mountain is his farm. Herein lies one of the peculiarities of Baltic religion. The gods are closely associated with horses, and horses have a special significance in the activities of Dievs: he appears as a horseman and often rides in a chariot down the mountain. It appears that in this association with horses the motifs of very ancient Indo-European myths have been preserved.

The homestead of Dievs consists of several buildings. In addition to the house there are stalls and barns for horses and cows, a threshing barn for drying grain, a storage room, and a sauna. The sources make no mention of castles, which are very common in other religions. From the configuration of the homestead one can conclude that Dievs oversees a large farmstead: the buildings are encircled by large fields, meadows, and forests. Dievs needs the help of the members of his own family, especially his sons, the number of whom varies, to work this farm, but others participate in the labors as well, plowing, harrowing, planting, and reaping the grain and hay. Special attention is devoted to the cultivation of hops and barley, from which beer is brewed. (Beer, the "drink of the gods," is the traditional drink of Baltic sacral feasts.) The inhabitants of the heavenly mountain not only work together, they celebrate feasts together, especially marriages, and they gather together in the sauna.

Indo-European creator gods are usually so mighty and distant that they retreat to a realm removed from humans and turn into a type of god referred to as *deus otiosus* (god at leisure). Other gods, whose function is to monitor the daily lives of humans, take their place. This is not, however, the case in the religion of the Balts. Instead, the Baltic gods follow an agricultural way of life that corresponds to that of the Baltic farmer. This is not only a formal analogy. Dievs, who dwells in heaven, is a neighbor of the farmer on earth. At times of the most important decisions, the farmer meets and consults with Dievs, just as farmers meet and consult among themselves. Dievs rides down on a horse or, more frequently, in his chariot. These visitations coincide with key events in the agricultural calendar and represent cyclic time perception.

Dievs usually appears in the spring, at the beginning of the agricultural year. His participation in planting is described in beautiful myths. He accompanies the farmer and advises him so that the field will be evenly sown. When the horses are led out to the first night watch, he accompanies the farmer, accepts his due in the sacral feast, and spends the entire night with the farmer, tending the fire and protecting the horses. In many of the planting myths, Dievs leaves the night watchers after sunrise but forgets his mittens. Dievs has an even more significant role in the fall, after the harvest and threshing. Once again a sacral meal is shared and Dievs participates in ecstatic song and dance. At these times the boundary between the transcendental god and the earthbound farmer becomes blurred.

From time to time, Indo-European gods display universal qualities, which are revealed in creation stories and in myths describing the establishment of the world order, including individual and societal norms of morality. The role of Dievs as creator is expressed in the words *laist* (to give birth to), *likt* (to determine fate), and *dot* (to provide for), all of which are words that describe his function. Everything is the creation of Dievs and corresponds to this threefold activity. The act of creation is final and unalterable, and the same is true of the world order. Human beings are subject to the laws of nature as they were ordained in the act of creation. Dievs, therefore, in his function as creator, is almighty. Humans are subject to fate, especially in the realm of morality, but this does not lead to resignation and quietism, although such moods exist as undeniable undercurrents in Baltic religion. Humans accept the moral laws of the universe as set down by Dievs as a framework for his life. Within this framework, however, human beings are free to determine and order their lives in concordance with their moral outlook and practical needs; therefore, they experience freedom of choice and assume responsibility for their actions. Human morality is practically determined: human beings must do all to further their well-being, and "the good" is whatever aids them in achieving this goal.

The cult of Dievs is not so formalized as are the cults of gods of heaven in other religions. As we have seen, Dievs actively participates at the most important junctures in the life of the farmer. He even shares in the sacrificial feasts, but there is no evidence that goods were sacrificed to him in order to ensure his benevolence. That can be concluded only indirectly. One can best describe the nature and function of Dievs metaphorically: he is the neighbor of the farmer, the grand farmer living on the mount of heaven.

A second important god of heaven is Saule, the personification of the sun. This name is also derived from an Indo-European root (*sauel-*, and variants). Unlike personifications of the sun in other traditions, Saule is a female deity. Saule is close to Sūrya of the Vedic tradition, where Sūrya is the feminine counterpart to the masculine sun god, although proof for this contention is not conclusive. There could be other explanations for the feminine gender of Saule, such as the fact that the sun is usually a female deity for people living in the north, where the climate is mild and nourishing, while further to the south, where the climate is more harsh, the sun god takes on a neutral gender (as in Russian), and becomes masculine even farther south. In Latvian tradition Saule dwells with the moon god Mēness, who is masculine and who requires a feminine counterpart. In certain situations Saule is also referred to as Saules māte (mother sun) and as Saules meita (daughter of the sun).

Descriptions of Saule's appearance are incomplete. A white shawl and one or more silver brooches, which secure the shawl, are mentioned in the sources. Occasionally she wears a wreath. Otherwise she appears in peasant dress. If the texts are vague about Saule's appearance, they do provide insight into her life both on the mount of heaven and in the midst of the farmers during their labors and festivals. She is the personification of gaiety, especially at the betrothal of her daughters, when all the gods of heaven join in her rejoicing. But there are also times of discord. Conflicts with the farmer arise as a result of harm done by the Dieva dēli (sons of god) to the Saules meitas (daughters of the sun) during play. The most frequent cause of this discord is the destruction of the latter's playthings. More serious conflicts arise between Saule and Dievs when the Dieva dēli remove the rings of the Saules meitas. This is part of an ancient betrothal tradition, during which the girl is abducted. Then for three days Saule and Dievs accuse one another of wrongdoing. Saule also has conflicts with other gods of heaven, especially Pērkons (thunder). She lives the life of an ordinary landlady and oversees her daughters' spinning and weaving, but after her linen has been put in the sun to dry, Pērkons comes and ruins the work with rain, and so Saule has good reason to be angry. Apart from these minor conflicts, harmony reigns on the mount of heaven. Saule provides sunlight and brightness for the others. The gods' harmony in the common labors, in love, and in gaiety can easily be compared to that of the Olympian gods.

Saule and Dievs are neighbors, and both oversee their farmsteads. Saule also has her own horses; in this she is similar to Apollo, who is depicted in frescoes with his chariot and four horses. Sometimes she rides across the sky in her chariot; she also crosses the sea in a boat. The steersman and oarsmen are her servants. Saule begins her ride at dawn and finishes at sundown, when the oars are thrown into the boat and the passengers disembark. At times, however, Saule begins her boat ride in the evening, and rides in the night unseen. This latter myth gives rise to the question of the Baltic conception of the form of the universe. As we have seen, the heavens have the form of a mountain. They are subject to the same laws of nature as the earth is, but only gods may dwell there. The belief that Saule travels by boat as well as by chariot indicates some kind of connection between the sea and the heavens.

The Balts do not appear to be overly concerned about the composition of the world, or at least no trustworthy record of such speculation has been found. The universe, however, is assigned two levels: the heavens and the earth. This becomes evident when one looks closely at several word forms. The word for "world" is *pasaule* (Latvian), a compound form consisting of *pa* and *saule*. *Saule*, the substantive, means "the sun"; with the prefix *pa* it means "below the sun." Thus *pasaule* means "everything that is under the sun." The adjectival form is *pasaulīgs*, meaning "profane" or "not sacred." A synonym for *pasaule* is *šīsaule*, a compound that is formed with the demonstrative pronoun *šī* and means "all that can be seen in sunlight." The antithesis of *šīsaule* is *viņasaule*, a compound that is formed with the demonstrative pronoun *viņa* and implies all that is still in the realm of the sun but cannot be seen.

This dualistic worldview is at the base of Baltic religion. The tradition concerning Saule's traveling developed further and is crucial to the Baltic understanding of death. Saule travels by chariot or by boat in the visible world during the day, but in the invisible one at night. Similarly, the dead continue to live a life in the invisible world, just as the sun does at night. The land of the dead is located just beyond the horizon, in the place where the sun sets.

In addition to the concepts of the mountain of heaven and the dualistic cosmos there is in the Baltic myths a *saules koks* (tree of the sun). It grows on the mount of heaven and is often referred to as an oak, a linden, or an apple tree. The difference between this tree and common trees on earth is symbolized by its gold or silver color. No mortal has ever seen this tree, although many youths have set out to search for it, only to return unsuccessfully in old age. A magical round object, often compared to a pea or an apple, rolls down its branches. The *saules koks* on the mount of heaven is one of the oldest elements of Baltic religion. It seems that this tree is the "center of the world," as Mircea Eliade has pointed out, but it is also the "tree of life." Whether the latter idea developed under the influence of Christianity is hard to determine. It certainly could stem from an older tradition in which Saule is the mother and source of life.

A cult surrounding Saule is not fully described in the sources. A few strands of tradition suggest her begetting and nurturing role. Similar to Dievs, she too comes down from the mountain to aid the farmer: she raises her skirt and inspects his fields. This tradition has caused some scholars to speculate about the existence of a belief that the baring of sexual organs improved fertility. The texts, however, provide inconclusive evidence. Saule could also have raised her skirt to avoid breaking or flattening the stalks. She does, at any rate, promote fertility. The result of her walk across the field is wholesome grain and a plentiful harvest.

The most significant element of the cult of Saule is the celebration of the summer solstice, in which everyone on the farmstead takes part. After the setting of the sun a fire is lit in a bucket and raised on top of a pole. A feast and dancing around the fire follow, and special songs of praise are sung. The major components of the feast are cheese and newly brewed beer. At this time shepherds become the center of attention. This has led August Bielenstein, a prominent linguist and ethnologist, to conclude that the summer solstice festival began as a celebration commemorating the breeding of livestock. The origin of this festival is obscure, but today it is a celebration of the sun. The feast continues through the entire night, lasting until dawn. Those who retire early are believed to be subject to evils and to encounter failure in the next year. This celebration of the sun is a fertility rite of sorts. The authors of Christian chronicles were especially critical of it, accusing celebrants of sexual excesses. Indeed, promiscuity is allowed during the festival and at times even encouraged. A sexual act performed in a field was believed to improve the field's fertility.

Mēness, the moon god, is also among the gods of heaven. The Latvian word for "moon," *mēness* (Lithuanian, *menulis*; Old Prussian, *menins*), derives from the Indo-European root **me-*, meaning "a measure of time." The measure of time was an apt designation for Mēness, who periodically disappears from the sky and then reappears in it once again. No substantial evidence in Baltic sources proves that Mēness was originally a feminine deity. As a full-standing member of the mount of heaven, he, too, has his own farmstead there, along with his family, sons, servants, and horses. His horses are represented by the morning and evening stars. Like Saule, Mēness travels through the sky by boat, and at times he even accompanies her. He has close ties to Saule: he is her untiring suitor.

In other religions the moon has a special connection with water and fertility, but this is not true in Baltic religion. Instead, Mēness is the god of war, and the stars are his troops, which, like a true general, he counts and leads. These metaphors reveal Mēness's true function: he is worshiped before battle, and his symbol appears in insignia of war. Although Mēness is frequently mentioned in the sources, his cult, like that of the other gods, is not fully described. Only sparse evidence of it remains, and none proves that offerings were made to him. The cult disappeared completely during the period of Christianization.

The two groups identified in Latvian as Dieva dēli (sons of god) and Saules meitas (daughters of the sun) are among the most interesting of the Baltic gods of heaven. As early as 1875, Wilhelm Mannhardt observed:

> Already Welcker and Preller have pointed to the close similarity between the Greek Dioscuri and the Indian Aśvins. The analogy is even closer with the Latvian *Dieva Dēli* found in the sun songs. The Aśvins are sons of Dyaus, heaven, *divo nāpata*. . .One can easily conclude from the Vedic texts that they are personifications of the morning and evening stars, which never appear at the same time. (Mannhardt, 1875; trans. Biezais)

Although this contention was based on scanty evidence in Mannhardt's time, additional evidence has since been gathered and analyzed. As a result, it can be shown that the Vedic Divo Napāta (i.e., the Aśvins), the Greek Dioskouroi (i.e., the Dioscuri), and the Baltic Dieva dēli are not only typologically parallel but are also historically connected. They differ only inasmuch as they developed in different cultural settings.

A closer comparison reveals some more unusual parallels. Although the discussion about the nature and function of the Vedic and Greek "sons of god" continues, the Baltic materials provide a clear answer: the Dieva dēli are the morning and evening stars. Whereas the Vedic and Greek gods represent hypostases of the differentiated functions or traits of the primary gods, this is not true of the Baltic gods. Rather, their social background is stressed, and their functions are expressed in terms of family relationships. Like the Aśvins, the Baltic "sons of god" or "sons of heaven," the Dieva dēli are the suitors of the Saules meitas, and they are their active marriage partners. There is no evidence, however, to prove that the Dieva dēli are twins, as are the Aśvins.

Just as the function of Dievs is transferred to his sons, so is the function of Saule transferred to her daughters. The Vedic Divo Duhitā (daughter of heaven), Sūryasya Duhitā (daughter of the sun), and the goddess Sūrya (the feminine aspect of the sun), like the Greek Helen (a daughter of Zeus), and Phoebe and Hilaeria (the Leucippides, daughters of Leucippus), correspond to the Baltic Saules meitas, although scholars disagree about their original connection. The designation *Saules meitas* is not original, since *meita* is a rather late loanword from German. The most ancient designation, meaning "daughter of heaven," has been preserved in Lithuanian, *dieva dukryte.* This designation might refer to dawn, as do the names of the Vedic goddess Ušas and the Greek goddess Ēōs.

Heavenly nuptials are central to Baltic myths about heaven. Dievs, Mēness, or Pērkons may be the bridegroom, and Saule is the bride. For linguistic reasons, in some contexts it is hard to determine who participates in the marriage, Saule or her daughter, for Saule is regarded as a maiden and is sometimes referred to as Saules meita. However, this circumstance does not alter the marriage procedure. A peculiarity of the event is that all the gods take part, each performing his or her specific role, which can be traced to ancient Baltic marriage traditions. The abduction and auctioning of the bride is an integral part of the ritual. The ceremony concludes with a feast of song and dance on the mount of heaven. Scholars have observed that these elements establish a connection with an old stratum of Indo-European marriage traditions.

The most unusual part of the marriage ceremony is the gathering of the gods in the sauna, which, as mentioned above, is a part of the heavenly farmstead. (Baltic ethnographic traditions reveal that the sauna was a place not only for washing but also for birthing and for sacral feasting. The Baltic sauna had the same status as a holy place or precinct, like a church in the Christian tradition.) Folklore materials reveal the procedure by which gods prepare the sauna: a fire is lit, special birch whisks are brought in, and water is drawn. The gods split up these chores, with lesser gods performing special tasks. The gathering of gods has special significance, since this is not just an occasion for bathing but also the preparation for a wedding. Special attention is paid to the Saules meitas, who await the Dieva dēli, their suitors. In the sauna the most fitting partner is chosen. All the gods are guests in the sauna, not owners of it. The matron of the sauna, Pirts māte (sauna mother), is the hostess. Latvian peasants have traditionally prepared offerings to her to guarantee her benevolence at the time of birthing. After the visit to the sauna, members of the farmstead left a whisk and a vessel with clean water so that Pirts māte could also bathe.

The gods of heaven described above correspond roughly to other Indo-European gods. They are especially similar to the Vedic and Greek gods, but they also have some unique qualities and functions that developed in the Baltic social structure. The primitive world of Baltic farmers is reflected in the conceptions and functions of their gods.

Gods of Prosperity and Welfare. As one can see from an analysis of the essence and function of the Baltic gods, it is clear that they were an integral part of the daily life cycle. This is especially true of a particular group of gods whose special function was to protect and guarantee the welfare of humans. These gods can be subdivided into two groups: fertility gods and determiners of fate. The most prominent of the second group is Laima, whose name means "fortune." She occupies a central place among the Baltic gods, but unlike the gods of heaven, she is not removed from the realm of human activity; she lives on earth and is involved in the minutest details of everyday life. Kārta, another goddess of fate, fulfills similar functions and has evolved into an independent hypostasis. Her name, derived from the verb *kārt* (to hang), is proof of this. Laima's most basic function is to determine and fix the birth of a child, which involved hanging a cradle, as ethnographic traditions show. From this function developed an independent goddess, Kārta, and with her an entire cult. Under the influence of the Christian church her function was assumed by Saint Thecla (Latvian, Dēkla).

The major fertility goddess is Zeme (Lithuanian, Žemýna), a very different type of goddess. Her name means "earth," and she is commonly referred to as Zemes māte (earth mother, mother of the earth). She plays a variety of roles that, over time, have developed into independent hypostases; tradition has it that she has seventy sisters. Some of them have very special functions, indicated by their descriptive names: Dārzu māte (mother of the garden), Lauku māte (mother of the fields), Meža māte (mother of the forest), and Linu māte (mother of flax). These descriptive names point to a specific place or plant that is under each mother's protection. The same is true of Lazdu māte (mother of the hazel), Sēņu māte (mother of mushrooms), and Briežu māte (mother of elk). The role of each particular mother is expanded: they are transformed from purely fertility goddesses to protectors in general, as indicated by such names as Pirts māte (mother of the sauna), Uguns māte (mother of fire), and Pieguļas māte (mother of the night watch). Morphologically related are the goddesses designated as Nāves māte (mother of death), Kapu māte (mother of the grave), Smilšu māte (mother of sand), and Veļu māte (mother of the dead). In many names the word *māte* is used to mean not only "mother" but also "goddess," as in, for example, the names Saules māte and Laimas māte, designating the mother goddess of the sun and the mother goddess of fortune.

The question of the character and role of these mothers has not been adequately investigated. Two schools of thought are current. One maintains that the development of the mothers is a thoroughly Baltic phenomenon; the other (upheld by Jonas Balys) maintains that it occurred under the influence of the cult of the Virgin Mary. If the mothers are judged by their functions, it must be concluded that they are closely connected with the annual agricultural cycle and that, as guarantors of fertility in the fields and for livestock, they are an outgrowth of the Christian church. It must be noted, however, that many of the mothers—among them, those designated as Vēja māte (mother of the wind), Ziedu māte (mother of blossoms), and Dzīparu māte (mother of colored wool)—are the products of poetic fantasy. These lack any cult and are the products of mythopoetic processes.

The annual reports of the Society of Jesus contain many references to pagan traditions among the Balts against which the Jesuits waged war. One such report from the beginning of the seventeenth century mentions Ceroklis, a god whose name is derived from the verb *cerot*, meaning "to sprout several stalks [*ceri*] from one seed or root." This name, suggestive of grains such as rye and wheat, implies a bountiful harvest. One must assume that from this natural process the god Ceroklis, a fertility god, developed.

A special fertility god is Jumis. The etymological connection between his name and the Vedic stem is not clear. The name could be related to *yama* (pair, or twins) or to *yuti* (conjunction, or connection). But the differences overshadow the connections between these terms. In Baltic religion the meaning of the word *jumis* is clear: two ears of grain, stalks of flax, or vines or branches bearing fruit that have grown together. Therefore the god with this name is the one who brings a double dose of fertility. After reaping, the final sheaf is completed and designated as Jumis, the god of fertility of the field. If the final sheaf is not reaped, the uncut ears of grain are bound or weighed down by a rock. Whether the sheaf is cut or not, the basic rationale is the same: the sign of fertility is left intact in the field. With this sign, thanks are expressed and the next year's grain harvest is guaranteed. Jumis is believed to remain in the field and to hibernate below the sod or underneath a rock. Around him an entire cultic ritual has developed. The abandoning of Jumis in the field is accompanied by song and dance, a cultic feast, and offerings, which continue inside the house when the reapers return home. The final sheaf may also be brought home, and Jumis can be put to rest either in the granary or in the form of a wreath in a central place within the living quarters. The grain of this wreath is mixed with the grain to be planted in the spring. Jumis has many of the same functions as the fertility gods of other religions, and his rituals resemble theirs.

It can be concluded that Baltic religion has two major conceptions of gods. One concerns the gods of heaven and their various functions. They are personifications and deifications of certain processes of nature, but they are also determined by the social structure of the farmstead and the daily life of the farmer. The farmer acquires the foundation for all of his life from the sky god Dievs. The other concept is closely connected with the life cycle and welfare of the individual. The gods associated with this concept determine the fate of humans from birth to death. This aspect is very practically determined: humans regard the gods as their equals, as beings with whom they can discuss problems but whom they can also censure. Nevertheless a total equality is never developed, since humans remain dependent on the gods. The gods do what humans cannot. For this reason the gods become universalized, and moral qualities are attributed to them. At the center of this religious moral system is the idea of the good, described in terms of the social context on a cosmic level.

BIBLIOGRAPHY

Adamovičs, Ludvigs. "Senlatviešu reliģija." In *Vēstures atziņas un tēlojumi*, pp. 45–115. Riga, Latvia, 1937. A concise survey of the main traits of Baltic gods but without an analysis of sources.

Akmentiņš, Roberts, et al. *Mitoloģijas enciklopēdija.* 2 vols. Riga, Latvia, 1994. Encyclopedia of mythology.

Ankrava, Sigma. *Vai Lāčplēsis bija karalis Artūrs?* Riga, Latvia, 2000. Was Bearslayer the King Arthur?—a study in comparative mythology.

Bauer, Gerhard. *Gessellschaft und Weltbild im baltischen Traditionsmilieu.* Heidelberg, Germany, 1972.

Beresnevečius, Gintaras. *Baltu religines reformos.* Vilnius, 1995.

Bertuleit, Hans. "Das Religionswesen der alten Preussen mit litauisch-lettischen Parallelen." *Prussia* 25 (1924).

Biezais, Haralds. *Die Religionsquellen der baltischen Völker und die Ergebnisse der bisherigen Forschungen.* Uppsala, Sweden, 1954. An annotated bibliography of sources and studies through 1953.

Biezais, Haralds. *Die Hauptgöttinnen der alten Letten.* Uppsala, Sweden, 1955.

Biezais, Haralds. *Die Gottesgestalt der lettischen Volksreligion.* Uppsala, Sweden, 1961.

Biezais, Haralds. "Baltische Religion." In *Germanische und baltische Religion*, edited by Åke Ström and Haralds Biezais, pp. 307–391. Stuttgart, Germany, 1965.

Biezais, Haralds. *Die himmlische Götterfamilie der alten Letten.* Uppsala, Sweden, 1972.

Biezais, Haralds. *Lichtgott der alten Letten.* Uppsala, Sweden, 1976. The works listed in this volume are surveys of Baltic religion based on critical analyses of the sources.

Brastiņš, Ernests. *Latvju dievadziesmas.* 2d ed. Würzburg, Germany, 1947. A selected collection of *dainas* (songs) concerning the sky god Dievs.

Clemen, Carl C., ed. *Fontes historiae religionum primitivarum, praeindogermanicum, indogermanicum minus notarum.* Bonn, Germany, 1936. A collection of selected Greek and Roman sources.

Dunbavin, Paul. *Picts and Ancient Britons: An Exploration of Pictish Origins.* Long Eaton, U.K., 1998.

Gaižutis, Algirdas, ed. *Senoves baltu simboliai.* Vilnius, 1992. Symbols of ancient Balts.

Gimbutas, Marija. *The Balts.* London, 1963. See pages 179–204 for a short, popular survey of Baltic religion.

Hopkins, Grace Sturtevant. *Indo-European *Deiwos and Related Words.* Philadelphia, 1932. A valuable etymological and semantic study of names of Indo-European sky gods.

Ivinskis, Zenonas. *Senoves lietuviuh religijos bibliografija.* Kaunas, Lithuania, 1938. The best complete bibliography of Baltic religion up to 1938.

Johansons, Andrejs. *Der Schirmherr des Hofes im Volksglauben der Letten.* Stockholm, 1964. Valuable as a collection of material, but the speculative construction of "house god" is false.

Kokare, Elza. *Latviešu galvenie mitoloģiskie tēli folkloras atveidē.* Riga, Latvia, 1996. Major Latvian mythological figures as depicted in folklore.

Kursīte, Janīna. *Latviešu folklora mītu spogulī.* Riga, Latvia, 1996. Latvian folklore as reflected by myth.

Kursīte, Janīna. *Mītiskais folklorā, literatūrā,* mākslā. Riga, Latvia, 1999. The mythical in folklore, literature, and art.

Mackova, Jolanta. *Atraktā debess.* Riga, Latvia, 1995. Latvian symbols.

Mannhardt, Wilhelm. "Die lettischen Sonnenmythen." *Zeitschrift für Ethnologie* 7 (1875): 73–330. Out of date but still important as a standard study of solar mythology.

Mannhardt, Wilhelm. *Letto-preussische Götterlehre.* Riga, Latvia, 1936. The best sourcebook on Baltic religion.

Neuland, Lena. *Jumis die Fruchtbarkeitsgottheit der alten Letten.* Stockholm, 1977. A basic study of the fertility cult with extensive analyses of sources and bibliography.

Pisani, Vittore. *Le religioni dei Celti e dei Balto-Slavi nell'Europa precristiana.* Milan, Italy, 1950. A brief comparative survey marred by linguistic shortcomings.

Rudzīte, Anta, ed. *Latviešu tautas dzīvesziņa.* 4 vols. Riga, Latvia, 1990. Latvian world perception.

Skrīvele, Kristīne, ed. *Latvian Tales of Magic.* Riga, Latvia, 2001.

Šmits, Pēteris. *Latviešu tautas ticējumi.* Riga, Latvia, 1941. Latvian folk beliefs.

Straubergs, Kārlis. *Latviešu buramie vārdi.* 2 vols. Riga, Latvia, 1939–1941. Latvian magic formulae.

Straubergs, Kārlis. *Latviešu tautas paražas.* Riga, Latvia, 1944. Latvian customs.

Toporov, Vladimir. *Baltu mitologijos ir ritualo tyrimai: Rinktinel Toporov.* Vilnius, 2000.

Velius, Norbertas. *Senoves baltu pasauležiūra.* Vilnius, 1983. The world perception of ancient Balts.

Velius, Norbertas. *Suzeistas vejas.* Vilnius, 1987. Lithuanian symbols.

Velius, Norbertas, ed. *Lietuviu mitologija.* Vilnius, 1997. Lithuanian mythology.

Velius, Norbertas, ed. *Baltu religijos ir mitologijos šaltinai* (Dictionary of Baltic religion and mythology), 4 vols. Vilnius, 1996–2001.

Zicāns, Eduards. "Die Hochzeit der Sonne und des Mondes in der lettischen Mythologie." *Studia Theologica* 1 (1935): 171–200. Important as a supplement to Wilhelm Mannhardt's solar mythology.

HARALDS BIEZAIS (1987)
SIGMA ANKRAVA (2005)

BALTIC RELIGION: NEW RELIGIOUS MOVEMENTS

In the context of Baltic religion, the designation "modern movements" refers to different movements in the Baltic lands, organized or unorganized, aiming at a revival or restoration of the autochthonous pre-Christian religions, as well as at a fusion of these religions with esoteric, metaphysical, theosophical, astrological, or environmentalist teachings and practices. The polysemantic term *Baltic* is used here as an ethnic denominator, with the modern Balts—Lithuanians and Latvians—as the primary focus, but with some attention paid also to Prussians and other Baltic-related groups.

LITERARY AND SYMBOLIC CONSTRUCTIONS OF BALTIC PAGANISM. Among Baltic peoples, ideas about "genuine, inherited, local, natural" religion as opposed to "borrowed, superimposed, alien, artificial" Christianity were formulated in the second half of the nineteenth century, during the period of gradual transition from patriarchal to modern society soon after the abolishment of serfdom. This concept of natural, local religion was reinforced in public discourse by different means, among them the Latvian epic *Lāčplēsis* (Bear-slayer) by Andrejs Pumpurs (1841–1902), with its national hero Lāčplēsis opposed to the Black Knight, symbolizing the crusaders and, henceforth, the forceful Christianization of Latvia. At that time, some remnants of pagan practices still existed in remote rural areas, and this served as a conceptual permit to treat the revived religions as a continuation of a tradition.

The quest for a national identity created a demand for proof that the Baltic peoples were as developed culturally as other Europeans, especially the older nations. That was one of the reasons why certain efforts were taken to construct mythological pantheons as impressive as those of the ancient Greeks. By the end of the nineteenth century, a significant amount of research on Baltic mythology was published, and many facts about the ancient worldview and religion became broadly known. Still, most of the essential topics were studied insufficiently, and some of the analyses of these topics were quite controversial; for that reason, the missing elements, not necessarily documented in historical or ethnographical sources, were re-created in literature. Those new creations at times permeated serious studies, as with Teodoras Narbutas's *Lithuanian Mythology,* the first volume of his fundamental historical work *Dzieje starożytne narodu litewskiego* (1835–1841).

Such a process took another direction in Latvia, where writers, poets, and publicists created new gods and goddesses in their literary works. In the opening part of his epic, Pumpurs created a pantheon in which well-known Latvian gods were featured along with deities from Prussian sources (and some invented deities as well). More or less invented pantheons are found in the publications of Juris Alunāns (1832–1864), but especially in the works of Miķelis Krogzemis-Auseklis (1850–1879) and Jēkabs Lautenbahs-Jūsmiņš (1847–1928). Thus, in the poetry of Auseklis one finds the names of almost sixty deities and spirits, of which only five—Dēkla, Laima, Lauma, Pērkons, and Ūsiņš—are taken from Latvian folklore texts. Two are from Lithuanian and seven are from Prussian sources, while the rest are invented by Auseklis or taken from uncertain sources and transformed to suit the stylistics of his romantic works.

Those mythologies, like the fundamental folklore collections published at the end of the nineteenth century, became one of the cornerstones of the new constructed national identity. As such, they did not promote ritual practice, but rather served as a symbolic marker of ethnicity. Those few practical activities that did occur still preserved their symbolic nature. Thus, for instance, the Lithuanian publicist Jonas Gediminas Beržanskis-Klausutis (1862–1936) tried to obtain written acknowledgment from the Russian imperial administration that he was *Krivių Krivaitis*—the successor of pagan Baltic priestly tradition. (Unconfirmed sources report that Beržanskis-Klausutis succeeded in getting such recognition shortly before the First World War.)

RELIGIOUS MOVEMENTS IN THE FIRST HALF OF THE TWENTIETH CENTURY. The Prussian Lithuanian writer, mystic, and philosopher Wilhelm Storosta-Vydūnas (1868–1953) tried to synthesize theosophy with the Lithuanian pantheist tradition. Vydūnas was attracted by theosophy because he perceived it as a form of nonorthodox philosophical religiosity. For him, theosophy was a doctrine that declared none of the religions to be superior, claiming instead that all expressed the same esoteric truth through different languages. This was a crucial discovery for Vydūnas, opening up the possibility of honoring the old Lithuanian religion. He contributed to the justification of Lithuanian paganism through his dramatic works (the trilogy *Amžina ugnis* ["eternal fire"]), and through historical and philosophical writings. Particularly important in his writings has been the concept of *Romuva*—the pagan Baltic (originally, Prussian) sanctuary. Among the activities initiated by Vydūnas was the celebration of *Rasos*—the pagan Lithuanian midsummer solstice—by the Rambynas hill. The Tilsit Lithuanian singing society, led by Vydūnas from 1895, was at the core of those celebrations, and performed more or less regularly until 1935, when the society was closed by the Nazis.

Soon after the First World War and the subsequent formation of the Baltic nation-states, ideas began to circulate concerning the form that the revived or renewed religions should take, and about how to organize them, but these proposals did not meet with much success and were not realized. Juris Lecs wrote a book on ancient Latvian religion and ethics and tried to organize a non-Christian congregation. The theologian Jānis Sanders (1858–1951) attempted to reform Christianity: he sought to abandon the Old Testament, to check and correct the Gospels by comparing them to the Greek originals, to view the teaching of Jesus in the light of Vedanta, and to shape Christian ritual in a way he supposed to be specifically Latvian. In 1930 he founded the Latvian Christian Society, which became the Latvian Christian Congregation in 1937, but was not much noticed by the public. The writer Eduards Meklērs (1884–1973) planned to establish a new, syncretic religion, comprised of elements of all world religions but with a sanctuary in Latvia and with Latvian forms of worship. Considerable were the efforts of the Lithuanian writer and publisher Domas Šidlauskas-Visuomis (1878–1944), who tried to revive the Romuva or Visuoma faith and religion, inspired by the ideas and writings of Vydūnas. During the second decade of the twentieth century he formulated the doctrinal basis for this religion, later partly published in the United States. But his repeated efforts to register Visuoma as a religion in 1926 were stymied. In spite of good publicity, his sermons were not permitted after 1927, and his lectures at the public university were banned in 1930. During the first half of the 1930s he organized Rasos celebrations in the vicinity of Sartai Lake in northeastern Lithuania. Not incidentally, he referred to the place of celebration as Romuva—a name meaning "natural sanctuary" for him—thus hoping to make it the central location of the revived religion.

DIEVTURI. Latvian Dievturība could be considered the most successful effort to put the revived religion into organized and legally recognized forms. Dievturība was founded by Ernests Brastiņš (1892–1942), an artist, publicist, and researcher, together with Karlis Bregžis-Marovskis (1895–1958?). They initiated the development of the doctrine, coined the terms *Dievturība* (Latvian religion) and *Dievturi* (adepts of Dievturība—literally, "those who keep their God"), and published the first manifesto in the brochure *The Restoration of Latvian Religion* in 1925. The new religious organization was registered under the name Latvju Dievtuŗu Draudze (Community of Latvian Dievturi) in 1926. Following disagreements between the two leaders, Brastiņš in 1929 founded and registered a new organization, Latvijas Dievtuŗu Sadraudze (Congregation of Latvian Dievturi), which kept its status as a religious organization until 1935, after that time continuing as a public organization. Latvju Dievtuŗu Draudze, which had become Bregžis-Marovskis's organization, ceased to exist at the beginning of the 1930s.

In the following years Brastiņš did the basic work to establish doctrines based on the ancient mythology, and to shape rituals and social practices. He published selections of Latvian folk-song texts, which were intended to serve as canonical texts revealing different aspects of the religion. The church's doctrine was published in the form of a catechism in *Dievtuŗu cerokslis* (1932), in which questions related to theology, religious life, ethics, and ritual were discussed. According to this publication, Latvians have worshiped only one God, Dievs; their religion has been monotheistic, or, more exactly, henotheistic. Dievs is progenitor of everything, and He is omnipotent. Dievs is one, but dual—He is spirit and matter, Father and Mother, the good and the bad simultaneously. Māra is a goddess representing the material aspect of Dievs, while Laima is the aspect of Dievs connected with causality, fate, and fortune. Brastiņš described humans as being threefold—they consist of *augums* (body), *velis* (astral body), and *dvēsele* (soul). The body is composed of rough matter and is subject to destruction; the astral body is formed of thin, subtle matter and enters *Veļu valsts* (the world of shades) after death, staying there until it gradually disappears; the soul is imperishable, eternal, and reaches Dievs's abode after death. The moral norms of Dievturība were expressed as imperatives, the most important of which is "Be good!" Humans were presumed to be naturally good, because that was Dievs's intention, and any deviation from that was considered to be a mistake.

Dievturi propagated the use of vernacular names for calendar months (these are still are in use in Lithuania). Additionally, they used their own method of reckoning time: for the adepts of Dievturība the starting point was "the period of the formation of Aryans (meaning Indo-Europeans)," which was assumed to be some 10,000 years ago. To mark this, a *1* was added to the year of the Christian era, so that, for example, 11926 corresponds to 1926 CE.

According to the statute of the Congregation of Latvian Dievturi, membership in the church was open to Latvian nationals of both sexes. There was an elected *Dižvadonis* (Grand Leader) at the head of the organization, while the regional sections were permitted their own leaders. Also, no ordained priests were intended; instead, there could be only the performers of ritual actions. The movement gained ground during the 1930s, its members and supporters being mostly intellectuals—students, artists, academics, and teachers. The congregational activities included meetings, holy services, calendar celebrations, and life-cycle celebrations such as weddings and funerals. The Congregation of Latvian Dievturi published their magazine *Labietis* (The good, noble man), from 1933 until 1940. Before that, Bregžis-Marovskis also published a magazine, *Dievturu Vēstnesis,* from 1928 until 1929, as well as his version of Dievturība's doctrine, *The Teaching of Latvian Religion* (1931).

RELIGIOUS MOVEMENTS DURING THE SOVIET AND NAZI OCCUPATIONS. The devotees of Baltic paganism can be characterized as the modelers of a new, national faith that was intended to support national statehood and lay a new, firm spiritual foundation for it. After the occupation of the Baltic countries by the U.S.S.R., pagan movements were claimed to be of a chauvinistic character, and thus inherently inimical to the ideas of communism and internationalism. They were destroyed and their members persecuted. Brastiņš was deported and shot dead in a Russian prison in 1942.

These movements partly survived in exile and in secret during the whole occupation period, but the story of this requires a special study, as only a few facts are known concerning their status during the Soviet period. Stasys Jameikis, the follower of Šidlauskas-Visuomis, tried to organize some religious activities even under the extreme conditions of life in a Soviet forced labor camp. Certain elements of Dievturi's rituals, or at least some outward signs, were present at weddings and funerals when nonconformist pagans were participants.

The first initiatives to revive the Dievturi movement in exile were started in Germany by 1944, and in Sweden by the beginning of the 1950s. The most vigorous development of the movement occurred in the United States starting at the end of 1940s, under the leadership of Ernests Brastiņš's brother Arvīds. Arvīds Brastiņš became the Grand Leader in 1947, and he kept this position until his death in 1984. The religion has been registered as the Latvian Church Dievturi in Illinois. To meet congregational needs, a church complex named Dievsēta was built in Wisconsin. The magazine *Labietis* was relaunched in 1955, and has been published continuously since then. Smaller groups of Dievturi emerged at different periods in Canada, Australia, and Great Britain. The exile Dievturi church was by led by Jānis Palieps from 1985 until 1990; by Marģers Grīns, the son-in-law of Arvīds Brastiņš, until 1995; by Juris Kļaviņš until 2000; and, since 2000, by Palieps again.

NEW RELIGIOUS MOVEMENTS IN THE SECOND HALF OF THE TWENTIETH CENTURY. A resurgence of ethnically based religiosity in the Baltics emerged at the end of the 1960s, a development that should be viewed in the context of global cultural changes. The new religious movements were less uniform, less dogmatic; they displayed much more interest in the preservation of nature and of cultural heritage. At the same time, these movements were much more open to other traditions and influences; they were essentially pantheistic. Most of the neopagans displayed marked interest in folk tradition and folklore in general; therefore they can often be viewed as the extremist wing of folklore movements.

One of the characteristics of most Lithuanian and Latvian religious movements in the modern period is the presence of pan-Baltism. This encompasses the study of the traditions of kindred peoples—Lithuanians, Latvians, Curonians, Prussians, Yatvings—with the goal of finding a quintessential primitive spirit, which would embody the ancient heritage when followed consciously. Feelings of ethnic kinship have led to closer cooperation between modern Balts, as well as between Balts and neighboring peoples—Poles, Belarussians, German Prussians—who are presumed to have inherited certain aspects of ancient Baltic religion.

ROMUVA. Lithuanian Ramuva (Romuva) was revived in 1967 as the Association for the Study of Local Culture. Its first and most important activity was the organization of Rasos celebrations, which involved an ever-increasing number of participants. A strong impulse for the movement's development was provided by Professor Marija Gimbutas (1921–1994), who visited Lithuania in 1968 and delivered one or (most likely) two lectures on Baltic history and mythology at Vilnius University. The association was dissolved and the Rasos celebrations stopped in 1971 after the group was accused of becoming increasingly nationalistic and of being involved in religious activity, but the organization was reborn in 1988 as the Association for Lithuanian Ethnic Culture. To distinguish between cultural and religious activities, a new organization—the Community of Baltic Faith Romuva—was officially registered in 1992. Additionally, a terminological distinction was agreed upon: *Romuva* would refer to the religion, and *Ramuva* to the much broader movement of preservation, study, practice, and dissemination of ethnic culture. As of 2001, twelve regional Romuva organizations had emerged in Lithuania, with a collective membership of about two thousand members and numerous supporters. There are Romuva organizations in Canada, Russia, and the United States. Vilija Witte, a member of the Canadian Romuva, published six issues of the magazine *Sacred Serpent* in Canada in 1994–1995, with a focus on traditional Baltic culture, old beliefs, and indigenous Lithuanian religion.

The Romuva faith emphasizes the sacredness of nature and of humans first and foremost. The contact of adepts with the divine is based on tradition and personal experience. Traditional Lithuanian gods—Dievas, Laima, Perkūnas, Žemyna—are preferred, but not mandatory. One of the core concepts of the faith is *Darna* (harmony); believers aspire to inner harmony, endeavor to create harmony at home and in the community, pursue harmony with ancestors, and seek harmony with the universe—with life and with the divinities. The essential moral concept is *Dora.* This encompasses respect for Nature, for all expressions of life. It asks for a confident and loving attitude towards the world, refusing violence and vengeance. On account of its doctrine of *Dora* and the traditional toleration of other faiths in the Grand Duchy of Lithuania, Romuva claims it does not negate other religions. This claim is perhaps best understood in light of its very flexible doctrinal formulations, with their emphasis on the experience of the divine. Humans (male *žmogus,* female *žmona*) are children of the Earth *(Žemė),* and therefore are responsible for other life forms. There is no essential difference between the status of men and women, and the dominant view is that both can participate in all rituals and on all hierarchical levels.

The three biggest Romuva communities joined to make the Union of the Religion of Ancient Balts in 2001. Restoring the priestly class, a circle of ritual elders *(Vaidilų Ratas)* was established, and the highest priest *(Krivis)* was chosen and ordained in 2002. The new *Krivis,* Jonas Trinkūnas (b. 1939), was given the name Jaunius after an elaborate ritual on the Gediminas hill, which is believed to be the burial place of Grand Duke Gediminas of the fourteenth century, one of the last pagan rulers of the Grand Duchy.

Following these developments, a public discussion has been sparked concerning the validity of the *Krivis* institution. Arguments in favor of it cite the continuation of pagan practices up until the twentieth century, and claim that "native or ethnic religiosity" is a significant constituent part of modern Lithuanianness. Additionally, a discussion was initiated in Parliament in 2001 on the question of whether or not the Religion of Ancient Balts should be recognized as a traditional religion, alongside Catholicism, Russian Orthodoxy, Judaism, and others. As of 2003 there has been no resolution to this issue.

Romuva has initiated the organization of the World Congress of Ethnic Religions (WCER)—an institution consisting of "ethnical and/or traditional and/or native religious groups." It is primarily concerned with the protection and development of ethnic cultures, religions, and identities, and the "ethnic religions" are defined as "surviving ancient religions, such as Hinduism, or animism of various other cultures, as well as religions in the process of restoration, such as the Icelandic *Asatru,* Latvian *Dievturi,* Lithuanian *Romuva* and others." The objectives of the WCER, as stated in its regulations, are to:

1. Spread educational knowledge about ethnic cultures and their religions, while propagating mutual trust and tolerance for the peoples of Europe and the entire world.
2. Through education, propagation and the organization of support for the appropriate projects . . . preserve ethnic cultures and religions, safeguard them from extinction and propagate such ideas.
3. Unify people and organizations engaged in ethnocultural and ethno-religious activities within Lithuania and outside its borders.
4. Fight against religious discrimination.
5. Undertake other kinds of activities concerning ethnic culture and ethnic religions.

The first Congress was held in Vilnius, Lithuania, in 1998, and several countries were represented there: Belarus, Belgium, the Czech Republic, Denmark, France, Germany, Greece, India, Latvia, Lithuania, Norway, Poland, Russia, Sweden, Ukraine, and the United States. Six congresses were arranged by the fall of 2003, all in Lithuania. A newsletter, the *Oaks,* has been published since 1999.

DIEVTURI: CONTEMPORARY DEVELOPMENTS. The Dievturi organization was restored officially in 1990, shortly before the regaining of Latvian national independence. A few years later, in 1995, the Latvian parliament recognized it as one of the traditional religions of Latvia.

The Congregation of Latvian Dievturi has sections and regional organizations: according to the 2001 census, their number is twelve, with the total number of members exceeding six hundred. There have been significant changes in the approach to leadership questions within the community. The first Grand Leader after the restoration was Eduards Detlavs (1919–1992); it was his initiative to drop this title. From 1992 to 1995, Dievturi in Latvia accepted the leadership of Marģers Grīns, who was the head of the Dievturi church in exile. He was followed by Jānis Brikmanis and, since 1998, by Romāns Pussars (b. 1932). Simultaneously, Grīns has been regarded as the Dievturi's highest authority globally.

The main forms of Dievturi's religious activities are congregational meetings, celebration of calendar holidays, and life-cycle celebrations—weddings, funerals, and so on. The Dievturi church has the right to register marriage, and in

2001 four couples availed themselves of this possibility. Members of the Dievturi church organize summer camps and lecture courses, and have effectively tried to introduce Latvian folklore, mythology, and ethics teaching into the curriculum of general education schools. The magazine *Dievtuŗu Vēstnesis* was published from 1989 until 1996.

Two opinions of what Dievturība is have emerged recently in public discourse. According to the first, it is a religion, practiced by members of the Dievturi church. The other position tends, in reaction to the decreasing significance of the Dievturi church, to treat a much broader spectrum of modern folkloric expression as part of Dievturība practice.

Movements and Groups with Marginal Religious Involvement. The Latvian folklore movement was started in the second half of the 1970s as a grassroots effort seeking the preservation, study, practice, and dissemination of ethnic culture. While concentrating on songs, dances, and calendar and life-cycle celebrations, folklorists occasionally performed rituals, incantations, and offerings to deities, claiming to do these things "as they used to be done in the olden days."

This approach to religion, as well as the doctrine of Dievturi giving higher status to nation than to God, has been criticized by Modris Slava (b. 1946), the leader of the Latvijas Viedas Sadraudzība (Latvian Fellowship for Spiritual Knowledge)—a theosophical circle with the aim of interpreting Latvian (and more generally, Baltic) religion from a theosophical viewpoint. According to Slava, the spiritual life of a society has three hierarchical levels: spiritual knowledge *(Vieda)* on the top, spiritual practice or religion *(Līga)* thereafter, and paganism or remnants of previously existing religious systems on the bottom. Through the adaptation of supranational spiritual knowledge to specific national conditions, a national religion emerges. Slava concludes, however, that Dievturība does not possess the requisite spiritual knowledge and is therefore on the level of paganism. Because of this statement and later frictions, the two organizations—Dievturi and Latvijas Viedas Sadraudzība—have, despite initial intentions to cooperate in the field of recreating Latvian/Baltic religion, distanced themselves from each other more and more.

The fellowship of Lithuanian pagan faiths Senasis Žynys (The Old Sorcerer) has emerged in the 1990s as a circle centered around Andželika Tamaš—a controversial person claiming to be a successor of Baltic Selonian sorcerers. Some issues of the newsletter *Senasis Žynys* have been published in Lithuania, presenting the fellowship's vision of a Baltic worldview, religion, symbolism, and healing *(Gaiva)*. The group has tried to register as a religious community at the Ministry of Justice, but so far with little success. Tamaš has a group of followers in Latvia, too, led by Uldis Zandbergs and closely related to another spiritual community.

This related community is the center of spiritual culture known as Baltais Aplis (The White Circle). Since its foundation in 1991, the center has been led by the painter Lilita Postaža (b. 1941). Aiming at the promotion of personal freedom and spiritual development, they practice Hindu, Agni Yoga rituals, combining them with Baltic religious and magic ceremonies—solstice celebrations and offerings to deities.

Certain aspects of Baltic religion are present in several groups having no official status or institutionalized form—practitioners of different energy and healing arts, paleoastronomers, and environmentalists and the green movement. Particularly interesting is the Pokaiņi phenomenon in Latvia. Pokaiņi Forest, located close to the town of Dobele in southern Latvia, received public attention in the second half of 1990s due to the efforts of publicist and paleoastronomer Ivars Vīks (1933–2002), and of Rasma Rozīte, follower of the teaching of Babaji and an active member of Baltais Aplis. Pokaiņi was claimed to be an ancient healing and ritual place, a doorway to Shambhala, providing intense radiation of cosmic energy. This hilly, forested spot with numerous stone piles, scattered in an area of about four hundred hectares, has become a place of healing, worship, and pilgrimage not only for Latvians but for visitors from other countries as well, more than a thousand of whom visit weekly in season.

See Also Saule.

Bibliography

Biezais, Haralds. "Dievturi—nacionālie romantiķi—senlatvieši." *Ceļš* 1, no. 44 (1992): 43–59.

Brastiņš, Ernests. *Dievtuŗu cerokslis jeb teoforu katķisms.* Riga, Latvia, 1932.

Brastiņš, Ernests. *Tautai, Dievam, Tēvzemei.* Riga, Latvia, 1993.

Dārdedzis, Jānis. *Latvju dievestība: Īss pārskats.*/ Latvian Religion: An Outline. New York, 1968.

Glodenis, Donatas. "New and Non-Traditional Religious Movements in Lithuania." A paper presented at the fourteenth international CESNUR conference "New Religiosity in the 21st Century," August 29–31, 2000, Riga. Available from http://www.cesnur.org/conferences/riga2000/glodenis.htm.

Klotiņš, Arnolds. "The Latvian Neo-Folklore Movement and the Political Changes of the Late Twentieth Century." *World of Music* 44, no. 3 (2002): 107–130.

Krumina-Konkova, Solveiga. "Maybe Shambhala Is Here: Esoteric Quests in Latvia Today." A paper presented at the CESNUR 2003 international conference "Religion and Democracy: An Exchange of Experiences between East and West," April 9–12, 2003, Vilnius. Available from http://www.cesnur.org/2003/vil2003_krumina.htm.

Muktupāvels, Valdis. "Baltu mitoloģija." *Sarunas IV* (2003): 142–155.

Pumpurs, Andrejs. *Lāčplēsis.* Introduction and comments (in Latvian) by Jāzeps Rudzītis. Riga, Latvia, 1988.

Ramoškaitė-Sverdiolienė, Živilė. "Archaic Folklore Elements in Contemporary Everyday Life." In *Contemporary Folklore: Changing World View and Tradition,* edited by Mare Kõiva, pp. 79–85. Tartu, Estonia, 1996.

Saivars, Juris. "Kā atbildēt dievturiem." *Mantojums* 1 (1997): 49–90.

Slava, Modris. "The Situation of Spiritual Culture and Problems in Latvia" (in Latvian). *Viedas Vēstis* 3 (1991): 1–2.

Šorys, Juozas. "Continuation of the *Krivis* Institution" (in Lithuanian). *Liaudies kultūra* 1 (2003): 12–20.

Trinkūnas, Jonas. *Baltų tikėjimas: Lietuvių pasaulėjauta, papročiai, apeigos, ženklai.* Vilnius, 2000.

Wiench, Piotr. "Neopaganism in Central-Eastern Europe." Available from http://vinland.org/heathen/pagancee/.

VALDIS MUKTUPĀVELS (2005)

BALTIC RELIGION: HISTORY OF STUDY

Although the concepts of pre-Christian Baltic religion have not been systematized, they can be reconstructed using several sources that contain pre-Christian elements. These sources include: artifacts found in archaeological digs; folklore texts, in particular Latvian and Lithuanian formulaic folk songs, riddles, and magic incantations; written texts, such as medieval chronicles; records of witch trials from the sixteenth century to the first half of the eighteenth century; church visitation records; written accounts of travelers; geographical descriptions of the Baltic territories; and archaic elements retained in language, in particular in toponyms and hydronyms.

The earliest written records that provide information about the Baltic pre-Christian religion are found in *Germania* 45, written during the first century CE by the Roman historian Publius Cornelius Tacitus, who mentions that the Aestii, a term coined by him to refer to the "people of the East," worshiped the mother of God (Lat., *matrem deum venerantur*). The Anglo-Saxon traveler Wulfstan visited the Prussian seashore between the years 887 and 901, and his description of that journey offers various items of information about the Prussian concepts of death and burial. There are several chronicles that also provide significant, although not systematically recorded, material about the early religious concepts. For instance, Adam of Bremen (d. 1081) in his chronicles has supplied testimony of the existence of fortune-tellers and prophets among the Baltic peoples. Relatively substantive information about Baltic religious concepts may also be found in *Henrici chronicon Livonia* (Chronicle of Henricus de Lettis), written during the first quarter of the thirteenth century, which describe various historic events in the Baltics occurring from 1180 to 1227.

At the end of the twelfth century, German merchants together with Christian missionaries settled in Latvia. In 1201, Bishop Albert built a fortified castle in the city of Riga, and a year later he founded the Order of the Livonian Knights to combat the pagan religion practiced by the Balt and Finno-Ugrian peoples. At about the same time, Christianization by sword of another Baltic population, the Prussians, began and lasted for several centuries. A significant information source for Prussian religious concepts is Petrus de Dusburg's *Chronicon terrae Prussiae* (Chronicle of the land of Prussia, 1326), as well as *Preussische Chronik* (Prussian chronicles, published only in the nineteenth century) by Simon Grunau (d. 1530). Chronicles and other historical sources name the major Prussian deities: Swāikstiks (the sun god), Perkūns (the god of thunder), Puskaītis (the god of the forests), and Pekols (the god of the netherworld and animals). Petrus de Dusburg's *Chronicon* mentions *romow*, the principal Prussian sanctuary, which was also worshiped and recognized as the most important in Lithuania and Latvia, part of Livonia. From these chronicles we learn that the oak-encircled sanctuary was ruled over by the Prussian high priest, called *Krive krivaitis*, and that the Prussians burned one-third of their spoils of war there as a sacrifice to their gods. Located in the center was an evergreen oak, in whose branches were located images of the three main deities.

The traveler Ghillebert de Lannoy (1385–1414) was in Livonia from 1413 to 1414 and wrote in his travel accounts, among other things, about the burial traditions of the Latvian Curonian tribe, specifically that the dead were burned in a bonfire built of oak. If smoke climbed directly to heaven, the dead soul was said to travel directly to the gods, but if the smoke blew sideways, then the dead soul was lost.

Information about the ways the Balts and the Finno-Ugrian tribe prophesized the future and discerned future events before critical moments in life is to be found in the *Henrici chronicon Livonia.* Using these same methods the Latgallians (a Latvian tribe) made their decision to become Christians according to the Russian or Latin precepts, and in a similar fashion the Zemgallians, also known as the Semigallians, and Curonians of Latvia, sought answers from their pagan gods about the outcome of their battles. Another ancient form of fortune-telling is described in the *Reimchronik* (Rhymed chronicles; c.1250–1300), where a Lithuanian military leader, finding himself captive, discovers the fate of his soldiers in the field by gazing at an animal's shoulder blade as if at some sort of film screen.

In his history of Poland, the Polish chronicler Ioannes Długoszius (or Johannes Długosz, 1415–1480) provides material about Lithuanian pagan rituals and deities. Following the style that was popular at that time in Europe, Długosz does not call the Lithuanian deities by their Lithuanian names, but, depending on their function, assigns to them their respective Greek and Roman names—Vulcanus, Jupiter, Diana, Silvanus, and Aesculapius.

In 1589, Salomon Henning (1528–1589), the duke of Courland and Gotthard Ketler's advisor in spiritual matters, wrote that the Latvians of Courland (Kurzeme) and Semigallia (Zemgale) worshiped as deities the sun, the stars, and such animals as the toad. Henning also wrote that the people themselves had the ability to turn into werewolves. He describes an incident that he himself witnessed in which the country folk fed milk to toads and snakes until they grew fat and swollen; when they were chopped in two, milk flowed from their bodies. Old women then came running, wailing and screaming that their "mother of milk" had been killed.

The sixteenth-century German historian and cosmographer Sebastian Münster (1489–1552) in his book *Cosmographia* (1544; supplemented in 1550) claims that even though the Latvian and Estonian peasants of Livonia had Christian names, they were ignorant and did not understand Christ's teachings. According to Münster these same people worshiped not only heavenly bodies as deities but also special trees and stones. Münster also describes marriage and burial practices of the time, claiming that food and drink, as well as money, were buried with the dead in a grave.

In 1581 a Polish chronicler of Italian origin, Alexander Guagnini (1534–1614), described celebration customs and Lithuanian and Latvian folk songs, both in terms of their content and how they were sung. Similar accounts of Lithuanian and Latvian folk beliefs, celebrations, and rituals can be found in the chronicles of Maciej Stryjkowsky (1547–c. 1590), published in 1582. An important source of information about religious beliefs, specifically regarding the deities and sanctuaries of the Zhemaitian tribe of Lithuania and Latvia during the first half of the seventeenth century, is a book written in 1615 by the historian Jan Lasicki (or Joannes Lasicius, 1534–1599). In this book Lithuanians are depicted as not wanting to hew down trees that their fathers and forefathers considered to be holy. Lasicki also describes in this work Lithuanian and Latvian marriage and burial practices.

The Catholic priest Fabricius Dionysius, who died during the first half of the seventeenth century, wrote of the snake being perceived as divine and of the worship and feeding of milk to dead souls (called *gari* in Latvian) in his series of books *Livonicae historiae compendiosa*, published posthumously in 1795. He also suggests that abstract concepts associated with Christianity and morality could not be expressed in the Latvian language, thus such words as *virtue* (Lat. *virtutem*), *integrity* (Lat. *probitatem*), and *piety* (Lat. *devotionem*) could not be communicated. The Latvian language is, in fact, characterized by forceful and well-developed concrete concepts, while the abstract philosophical and generalized religious terminology developed only during the nineteenth century in conjunction with the Latvian national awakening and cultural renaissance period. A significant source of information on Latvian folk beliefs of the first half of the seventeenth century is to be found in the works of Courland's governor Paul Einhorn's (d. 1655) *Wiederlegung der Abgotterey und nichtigen Aberglaubens* (Refutation of idolatry and erroneous superstition, 1627) and *Historia Lettica* (Latvian history, 1649), in which he describes Latvians as "*semi-christiani oder ethnico-christiani*" (semi-Christian or ethno-Christian) and as stubbornly resisting the observance of Christian church rituals while practicing semipagan family rituals and traditions at weddings, burials, and christenings. He also reports that at Christmas they performed a rite involving the pulling of an oak log and celebrated a special *bluķa* (log) night prior to Christmas. Also popular among Latvians is the summer solstice, known as Jāņi or the midsummer's eve celebration, the paying of homage to dead souls in autumn, and the worship of chthonic deities, among them the female deities Māra, Laima, and Dēkla.

The Catholic Jesuit priest Johannes Stribing, during his 1606 visit to inspect the operations of the Catholic Church among Latvians (Latgallians), wrote that Latvians continued to believe not only in one God the Lord, but also in their own heavenly and earthly deities. They made offerings and sacrifices to their gods at holy trees. The most valuable offerings were to Ūsiņš (the god of horses) and Māršа (the goddess of cows). Stribing also wrote that Latvians (Latgallians particularly) made a distinction between a masculine holy tree (oak) and a feminine holy tree (linden). Accordingly, men made their offerings under the oak tree, while women did so under the linden. Even such pagan rites as the feeding of dead souls took place at a special dead souls celebration in November. Stribing reports that Latvians believed in gods of fate, and he describes how they tried through various maneuvers to determine their own fate. As an example, he describes how a young Latvian woman who, trying to forecast what lies in her future and how long she will live, poured melted beeswax into cold water.

The information about the deities and religion of the Baltic peoples that is found in chronicles and travel records written by foreigners contains errors and imprecise facts as a result of a lack of understanding of local languages, as well as distortion due to a Christian perspective from which everything associated with pre-Christian beliefs is seen as abnormal or strange. Taking into account the imprecision and, in some cases, fabrications, these chronicles, as well as later records, remain valuable sources of information about the deities and religious concepts of the Balts. In most cases, these sources can be verified by comparison with information drawn from Lithuanian or Latvian folklore texts describing mythical folk songs, folk beliefs, magic incantations, and so on.

Since Christian religious precepts were introduced in Latvia through force and disseminated in foreign languages (Latin, German, or Polish), for a long time they did not make a meaningful impression but remained at the level of a formal religion. Perhaps because of this, even as late as the seventeenth and eighteenth centuries one can find in written sources, especially visitation records and Jesuit reports about the state of religious belief among the peasants, condemnation of certain pagan practices and rituals, such as paying homage to trees or feeding milk to toads or snakes.

In the seventeenth and eighteenth centuries a relatively large number of people wrote about Baltic pre-Christian religious concepts, but for the most part these works reflect collected eyewitness accounts or information compiled in the preceding centuries. The most noteworthy author of that time was Matthäus Prätorius (1636–1704), who wrote about Prussian religion and culture, and the linguist and writer Gotthard Friedrich Stender (1714–1796), who, in a special supplement to a Latvian grammar text published in 1783, tried to determine which deities were worshiped by the ancient Latvians.

Until the nineteenth century, Baltic religious concepts were studied primarily by Baltic writers, cultural scholars, historians, and theologians of German or Polish origin, but in the nineteenth century scholars of Latvian and Lithuanian origin, fluent in the local languages, became involved in this research. They had the advantage of being able to dialogue freely with Latvian and Lithuanian peasants who, to a large extent, were the people who transmitted the living oral tradition, as well as various taboos linked to this or that sacred item or activity.

In the second half of the nineteenth century, two areas of Baltic religion were explored simultaneously. One was associated with Baltic mythology and consisted of the extensive collection, interpretation, and publishing of Baltic folk songs, fairy tales, and legends. The second dealt with the collection of oral folk texts, as well as artifacts gathered in archaeological digs. The most significant nineteenth-century research into Baltic mythology was done by the Latvian scholar Jēkabs Lautenbahs (1847–1928), who published a study on the Laimas, the three Baltic goddesses of fate, basing his research on the rich source material of Latvian and Lithuanian folk songs and fairy tales. In 1896 Lautenbahs also published the first comprehensive comparative study on Lithuanian and Latvian mythological concepts, which he arrived at through an analysis of folk songs. In 1901 his extensive research on Latvian religion and pagan deities appeared in German in the journal *Magazin.* Drawing on Latvian and Lithuanian mythological folk songs and the available, though limited, material on Prussian deities, Lautenbahs tried to pull together a comprehensive compilation of the pantheon of deities of the three Baltic peoples.

Also published in *Magazin* were a series of essays by the Latvian minister and mythology scholar Roberts Kārlis Auniņš (Robert Karl Auning, 1834–1914). These essays dealt with the hitherto little researched Using (German) or Ūsiņš (Latvian), the god of light whose responsibilities included guardianship of men and their horses and who was associated with the spring equinox. Another subject appearing for the first time in published research was the *pūķis,* literally "dragon," which in Latvian mythology is linked to wealth and well-being and not to evil, as in many foreign mythologies. These essays aroused much interest and a great wave of discussion about the Latvian deities of light.

Of note in the field of Latvian and Prussian mythology is the work of the German scholar Johann Wilhelm Emanuel Mannhardt (1831–1880) on the sun myths of the Baltic peoples (published in 1875) and the Latvian and Prussian deities (published only in 1936). Mannhardt's research, following mythological or solar-research school practices, was the most extensive in Europe at the time. It included Latvian and Prussian mythology interpreted within the context of Indo-European religious and mythological concepts. Mannhardt's studies greatly influenced some of the early broader-based researchers, specifically Lautenbahs. It should be noted that Lautenbahs was not only on the teaching staff of the University of Tartu (then called Dorpat) but he was also a poet who wrote a series of epic poems with mythological themes based on Lithuanian and Latvian folk songs, legends, and fairy tales, with the intent of reconstructing epics lost in distant antiquity. During the second half of the nineteenth century, Latvian writers and folklore researchers searched for and tried to piece together and restore seemingly lost fragments of grand epics. They also sought the deities and ancient religious concepts that were forgotten under conditions of captivity and violence during the Latvian peoples' seven hundred years of subjugation beginning in the thirteenth century.

Intensive restoration or reconstruction work on the ancient pagan deities was begun in the mid-nineteenth century, coincident with the start of a strong Latvian nationalistic movement and the Romantic movement in literature and art. Latvian folklore texts of the time contained references to a relatively long and seemingly adequate list of pre-Christian deities. This list included Dievs (the god of heaven); Velns (the chthonic god of the underworld); Saule (the sun goddess); the daughters of Saule; the sons of Dievs, including Ūsiņš; Mēness (the lunar deity); Pērkons (the god of thunder); Māra (the goddess of the earth), who incorporated features of the great archetypal mother linked to death and rebirth; Laima, Dēkla, and Kārta, the three deities of fate; Jumis, a twin deity linked to fertility; and many spirits, including more than one hundred archaic female maternal spirits, each with its own significant sphere of influence in nature, such as Vēja māte (mother of the winds), Meža māte (mother of the forests), and Lauka māte (mother of the fields). The scholars of the second half of the nineteenth century thought this long list of deities found in folklore sources was inadequate and proceeded to reinstate deities they considered forgotten over the passage of time. Thus, writers of the Romantic period, along with folklore enthusiasts, introduced many new deity names into the field. Later, in the first half of the twentieth century, this nineteenth-century folklore and mythology research came under criticism and was called the "creation of the Olympus of pseudo gods."

How were these new deities created? The first and most common approach was to take deities from the neighboring peoples, especially the ones appearing in Lithuanian and Prussian folklore, and to conclude that Latvians must have had the same deities, but that they had been lost with the passage of time. Thus, in the nineteenth century the following appeared on the list of Latvian deities: Anšlavs (the god of light, phonetically adapted from the Prussian Aušauts), Antrimps (the god of health, from the Prussian Autrīmps, god of the sea), Potrimps (from the Prussian Patrīmps, god of the rebirth of spring and fertility), and a series of other deities borrowed from Prussian mythological sources. The second source for the creation of new deity names and functions was ancient Greek and Roman mythology. Totally new deities with new functions were invented in response to areas of importance to nineteenth-century Latvian peasants. Most were modeled after ancient Greek or Roman deities. In the Olympus of newly invented Latvian deities appeared Krūģis (the god of fire and blacksmiths, drawn from the Roman god Vulcanus and the Greek god Hephaistos). Just as quickly as this process of inventing new deities started in the middle of the nineteenth century, it ended at the end of the century when realism replaced romanticism in literature.

The next wave in broader-based research into Latvian and Baltic religion began just before the proclamation of Latvia's independence as a nation in 1918. This wave is associated with the linguist, cultural historian, and folklorist Pēteris Šmits (1869–1938). In 1918 he became the first to publish a comprehensive and systematic study into Latvian mythology, with a second edition in 1926. In this study Šmits examines Latvian deities as they were revealed in various folklore and historical sources. Whereas nineteenth-century researchers had looked for ways to expand the list of Latvian deities, inventing them if they did not exist, Šmits's approach to Latvian folklore material was characterized by great scrupulousness and perhaps too excessive a skepticism. Šmits was knowledgeable about Latvian fairy tales and legends, having served as editor of the fifteen-volume *Latviešu pasakas un teikas* (Latvian fairy tales and legends), published between 1925 and 1937, complete with commentaries and compiled according to the Finnish folklorist Antti Aarnes's system. Šmits was also an expert in folk songs and folk beliefs. Under his editorship, four volumes of Latvian folk songs and four volumes of Latvian folk beliefs were published in the 1930s.

In his writing, Šmits attempts to find a credible explanation and basis for Latvian mythological deities. However, the research method he used, while applicable for the natural sciences, often restricted the parameters of Šmits's field of study. Influenced by the Finnish school, which focused on geographic elements in the comparative study of folklore, Šmits tried to determine the initial place of origin for both deities and folksong motifs. He thus arrived at some curious conclusions, proposing that the chthonic deity Māra was not a genuine Latvian deity, but rather derived from Germans or Russians, who themselves had lost traces of the goddess in antiquity. The result was a paradox. On the one hand, Russians of that period seemingly knew nothing about the paranormal being *zmeja* Marina (snake Marina), uncovered by Šmits in some obscure Russian sources. On the other hand, following Šmits's hypothesis, *zmeja* Marina became popular among Latvians for some reason. There is no documented proof that Latvians had previously ever mentioned or known a deity by this name. It is likely that the adopted *zmeja* Marina subsequently fused with the Virgin Mary worshiped in the Catholic Church, to become the deity Māra of later times.

Šmits, like the majority of the religion researchers of the 1920s and 1930s, was guilty of an overzealous search for foreign models for Māra, as well as for other Latvian deities and myths. This pertains as well to his approach to religious terminology. Upon finding a related root form in the Russian or German language, Šmits almost automatically assumed that Latvians had borrowed the word—for example, *baznīca* (church) or *krusts* (cross). However, despite his several exaggerations about deity names and assumed foreign sources for religious terms, as well as his view on the Christian influence on Latvian mythology, Šmits did provide in his research a generally coherent overview of the Latvian mythological system, which included a comprehensive description of the cult of the dead and related customs of the period, such as offerings and sacrifices.

At the turn of the twentieth century, researcher Mārtiņš Bruņenieks (1866–1950) published several essays about Latvian deities based on the animism theory. In his opinion, all or almost all gods and spirits in Latvian folklore were animated from dead souls and from the worship of departed ancestors. Another extensive treatise, *Senlatviešu reliģija* (The religion of ancient Latvians, 1937) was published by the Lutheran theologian and folklore researcher Ludvigs Adamovičs (1884–1941), who was exiled in Russia. Citing folklore as well as historical sources, Adamovičs's study explores in depth various topics, including Latvian cults and rituals in ancient times, in particular the fertility cult practiced during the summer solstice and the autumnal cult of dead souls; the Latvian concept of soul (*dvēsele*, from the verb *dvest*, literally translated as "to breathe"); the world of the dead and its inhabitants and patrons; sanctuaries and ritual celebrations; and communal festivities of ancient times. In his work, Adamovičs focuses on the ancient belief in spirits, attempting to list by function the many "mothers" to be found in Latvian folklore—the ambivalent female guardian spirits who determined success or failure in various spheres of human activity and nature. These spirits included the mother of berries, the mother of mushrooms, the mother of bees, the mother of the sea, and the mother of night. Adamovičs categorizes deities into deities of heaven and light (Dievs, Pērkons, Mēness, Saule, Auseklis), deities of fate (Laima, Dēkla, Kārta), and agricultural deities (Ūsiņš, Māršala, Jumis). Even though, like Šmits, Adamovičs traces without substantiation Māra and some other deities and religious concepts back to Christianity, his study continues to be the most comprehensive research to date on the ancient Latvian religious system.

Several other significant studies of the 1920s and 1930s deserve mention, specifically a study of Baltic sanctuaries by Kārlis Straubergs (1890–1962), research into possible totemism traces in Latvian folklore by Arveds Švābe (1888–1959), and a study of Latvian masks used in connection with beliefs in magic by Jānis Alberts Jansons (1892–1971).

After 1940, during the Soviet occupation of Latvia, in-depth research into mythology, and religious concepts in particular, was not feasible. However, such research continued with Latvians in exile. Of note is research done in Sweden by Andrejs Johansons (1922–1983) into Latvian water spirits and the ancient snake cult, and a study of the cult of the dead by Kārlis Straubergs. Research into Latvian religious concepts was taken to a new level by the theologian and historian Haralds Biezais (1909–1995). Living in exile in Sweden beginning in 1944, Biezais published a series of studies in German, including systematic comparative studies of Latvian female goddesses (1955), gods of light (1976), and the gods of heaven viewed as prototypes of the ancient family (1972). Biezais's scientific reconstruction of mythological beings and deities is immaculately done and includes comparative foreign material. To date, his research is considered to be the most comprehensive overview of the Latvian religious system in terms of factual content and documented testimony. However, his research is perhaps not as comprehensive as it might have been had he also explored the much broader oral folklore tradition, instead of taking the somewhat pedantic approach by which only that which is recorded in writing has research value.

Vaira Vīķe-Freiberga, an eminent folklorist and scholar, lived and worked in exile in Canada until the end of 1990, when she returned to live in Latvia. Her work on Latvian concepts of magic as expressed in oral incantations and her study of ancient Latvian religion, including extensive comparative analysis of Latvian deities vis-à-vis the hypotheses of Robert Graves, Georges Dumézil, and Algirdas Greimas, have been published in Latvian, English, and French. Vīķe-Freiberga has published the most comprehensive research into the Latvian (Balt) sun cult and the various aspects—cosmological, chronological, and meteorological—of the sun in Latvian folklore.

Lithuanian folklorist and ethnologist Jonas Balys, working in exile in Germany and later in the United States, continued research into mythology, publishing systematic studies of Lithuanian and Latvian folklore in encyclopedias in German and English, as well as specific research about the Baltic god of thunder and his adversary, the chthonic devil god (Latvian, Velns; Lithuanian, Velnias). A fellow Lithuanian, Marija Gimbutas, also working in exile in the United States, published an overview of Balt religious beliefs based on artifacts from archaeological digs.

When, due to ideological prohibition during the Soviet period, research into mythology ceased in Latvia and also partially in Lithuania, Vladimir Toporov and Vjačeslav Ivanov, two adherents of the Moscow school of structuralism (a method of analysis practiced in twentieth-century social sciences and humanities), published a series of studies about Baltic mythology in various periodicals in Russia. They also wrote a series of articles, *Balto-slavjanskie issledovanija* (Balt-Slav research), first published in 1970, in which they look at Balt and Slav mythology, folklore, and language on a comparative basis.

Research into Baltic religion resumed during the 1980s, first in Lithuania and then in Latvia. In Lithuania the most significant work was by Norbertas Vėlius (1938–1996). A disciple of the structuralism movement, he used its system of analysis to explore links with the religious concepts of other Indo-European peoples. While the majority of his many studies were published in Lithuanian, the quintessence of Vėlius's research can be found in his book *The World Outlook of the Ancient Balts* (1989). Vėlius's goal in *Baltų religijos ir mitologijos šaltiniai* (Baltic religious and mythological sources, 1996/2001) was to consolidate source data on Baltic religion and mythology both in the original language and in translation into Lithuanian. Several scholars have continued the comparative research in Balt mythology and religion begun by Vėlius. Nijolė Laurinkienė has published monographs about the Lithuanian god of thunder, and Gintaras Beresnevičius has published a series of monographs about Lithuanian and Prussian religious concepts, as well as broader-based research on Baltic religious concepts. The methodology, both structural and comparative, used by these scholars is similar to the one used in the monographs *Latviešu folklora mītu spogulī* (Latvian folklore in the mirror of mythology, 1996) and *Mītiskais folklorā, literatūrā un mākslā* (The mythical in folklore, literature, and art, 1999) by the Latvian mythology researcher and scholar Janīna Kursīte, wherein the author reexamines Latvian deities within a broader context and deals with subjects previously ignored or minimally researched, such as amulets and talismans, the symbolism of dreams, and the concept of a sacral landscape.

In both Lithuania and Latvia at the turn of the twenty-first century, research in Baltic mythology started to show a marked tendency to focus on comparative aspects, to critically reevaluate the role of chronicles from the Middle Ages, and to incorporate oral materials into the reconstruction of Prussian, Lithuanian, and Latvian mythology within the global context. Thus, new themes have appeared in research on Baltic religion, themes that were previously ignored or only considered from one point of view, such as the view that the Christian beliefs of the Latvian people are a (new) symbiotic religious structure formed from a fusion of Christian and pagan religious concepts.

BIBLIOGRAPHY

Adam of Bremen. *History of the Archbishops of Hamburg.* Bremen. N.Y., 1959.

Adamovičs, Ludvigs. *Senlatviešu reliģija: Vēstures atziņas un tēlojumi,* pp. 45–115. Riga, Latvia, 1937.

Adamovičs, Ludvigs. *Zur Geschichte der altlettischen Religion.* Studia Theologica, vol. 2. Riga, Latvia, 1940.

Auning, Robert Karl. "Ueber den Uhsin-Mythus." *Magazin* 20 (1905): 3–5.

Balys, Jonas. *Lietuvių tautosakos skaitymai.* 2 vols. Tübingen, Germany, 1948.

Balys, Jonas. "Parallels and Differences in Lithuanian and Latvian Mythology" In *Spiritus et veritas,* pp. 5–11. Eutin, Germany, 1953.

Balys, Jonas. "Latvian Mythology." In *Standard Dictionary of Folklore, Mythology, and Legend,* pp. 607–608 and 631–634. New York, 1972.

Balys, Jonas and Haralds Biezais. "Baltische Mythologie." In *Wörterbuch der Mythologie*, edited by Hans William Haussig. Stuttgart, 1965.

Beresnevičius, Gintaras. *Dausos: Pomirtinio gyvenimo samprata senovės lietuvių pasaulėžiūroje.* Vilnius, 1990.

Beresnevičius, Gintaras. *Baltų religinės reformos.* Vilnius, Lithuania, 1995.

Beresnevičius, Gintaras. *Trumpas lietuvių ir prūsų religijos žodynas.* Vilnius, 2001.

Bertuleit, Hans. "Das Religionswesen der alten Preussen mit litauisch-lettischen Parallelen." In *Sitzungsberichte der Altertumsgesellschaft* 25, pp. 9–113. Königsberg, 1924.

Biezais, Haralds. *Die Hauptgöttinnen der alten Letten.* Uppsala, Sweden, 1955.

Biezais, Haralds. *Die Himmlische Götterfamilie der alten Letten.* Uppsala, Sweden, 1972.

Biezais, Haralds. *Lichtgott der alten Letten.* Stockholm, 1976.

Biezais, Haralds, and Ake Ström. "Baltische Religion." In *Germanische und Baltische Religion,* pp. 309–384. Stuttgart, 1975.

Bonnefoy, Yves, comp. "Baltic Myths and Religion Categories." In *American, African, and Old European Mythologies,* pp. 251–253. Chicago and London, 1993.

Bregžis, Kārlis. *Baznīcu vizitāciju protokoli.* Riga, Latvia, 1931.

Bruņenieks, Mārtiņš. *Senlatviešu reliģiskais pasaules uzskats.* Riga, Latvia, 1930.

Bruņenieks, Mārtiņš. *Senlatviešu Laima.* Riga, Latvia, 1930.

Dundulienė, Pranė. *Senovės lietuvių religija ir mitologija.* Vilnius, 1990.

Einhorn, Paul. *Wiederlegung der Abgotterey und nichtigen Aberglaubens.* Riga, Latvia, 1627.

Einhorn, Paul. *Historia Lettica: Das ist Beschreibung der lettischen Nation.* Dorpat, Estonia, 1649.

Fabricius, Dionysius. *Livonicae historiae compendiosa series, curante Gustavo Bergmann.* Stanno Ruiensi, 1795.

Gimbutas, Marija. *The Balts.* London and New York, 1963.

Gimbutas, Marija. "Perkūnas/Perun, the Thunder God of the Balts and the Slavs." *Journal of Indo-European Studies* 1, no. 4 (1973): 466–478.

Gimbutas, Marija. "The Lithuanian God Velnias." In *Myth in Indo-European Antiquity,* edited by Gerald James Larson, pp. 87–92. Berkeley and Los Angeles, 1974.

Gimbutas, Marija. "Baltic Laima." In *The Language of the Goddess: Unearthing the Hidden Symbols of Western Civilization,* pp. 11–113. San Francisco, 1989.

Gimbutas, Marija. "The Baltic Religion." In *The Living Goddesses,* pp. 197–215. Berkeley, 1999.

Greimas, Algirdas J. *Apie dievus ir žmones: Lietuvių mitologijos studijos.* Chicago, 1979. Translated by Milda Newman as *Of Gods and Men: Studies in Lithuanian Mythology.* Bloomington, Ind., 1992.

Grunav, Simon. *Preussische Chronik: Im Auftrage des Vereins für die Gescichte der Provinz Preusse.* Leipzig, Germany, 1876–1896.

Guagnini, Alessandro. *Sarmatiae Europeae descriptio.* Spirae, 1581.

Ivanov, Vjačeslav. "O mifopoėtičeskih osnovah latyšskih dajn." In *Balto-slavjanskie issledovanija 1984,* pp. 3–28. Moscow, 1986.

Ivanov, Vjačeslav, and Vladimir Toporov. "Baltijskaja mifologija v svete sravnitel'no–istoričeskih rekonstrukcij indoevropejskih drevnostej." In *Zeitschrift für Slavistik* 19, no. 2 (1974): 144–157.

Ivinskis, Zenonas. *Senovės lietuvių religijos bibliografija.* Kaunas, Lithuania, 1938.

Jansons, Jānis Alberts. *Die lettischen Maskenumzüge.* Riga, Latvia, 1933.

Jansons, Jānis Alberts. *Maģija latviešu tautas tradīcijās.* Riga, Latvia, 1937.

Jaskiewitcz, Walter. "A Study in Lithuanian Mythology." *Studi baltici* 9 (1952): 65–106.

Johansons, Andrejs. *Der Wassergeist und der Sumpfgeist.* Stockholm, 1968.

Jonval, Michel. *Les chansons mythologiques lettonnes.* Paris, 1929.

Kiaupa, Zimantas, Ain Mäesalu, Agu Pajur, and Gvido Straube. *The History of the Baltic Countries.* Avita, Estonia, 1999.

Lasicius, Jan. *De Diis Samagitarum caeterorumque Sarmatarum et falsorum Christianorum.* Basileae, 1615.

Laurinkienė, Nijolė. *Senovės lietuvių dievas Perkūnas.* Vilnius, 1996.

Laurinkienė, Nijolė. "Šventovė Prūsijoje baltų ritualų ir mitologinės tradicijos kontekste." In *Nuo kulto iki simbolio,* pp. 33–55. Vilnius, 2002.

Lautenbahs, Jēkabs. *Očerki iz istorii litovsko–latyšskogo narodnogo tvorčestva.* Jurjev, 1896.

Lautenbahs, Jēkabs. "Über die Religion der Letten." *Magazin* 20, no. 2 (1901): 101–273.

Mannhardt, Wilhelm. "*Die lettischen Sonnenmythe.*" In *Zeitschrift für Ethnologie* 7. Berlin, 1875.

Mannhardt, Wilhelm. *Letto-Preussische Götterlehre.* Riga, Latvia, 1936.

Matossian, Mary Kilbourne. "Vestiges of the Cult of the Mother Goddess in Baltic Folklore." In *Baltic Literature and Linguistics,* edited by Arvids Ziedonis, et al., pp. 119–127. Columbus, Ohio, 1973.

Pisani, Vittore. *Le religioni dei Celti e dei Balto-Slavi Nell' Europa precristiana.* Milan, 1950.

Puhvel, Jaan. "The Baltic Pantheon." In *Baltic Literature and Linguistics,* edited by Arvids Ziedonis, et al., pp. 99–109. Columbus, Ohio, 1973.

Russow, Balthasar. *Chronica der Prouintz Lyfflandt: Scriptores rerum Livonicarum.* Riga, Latvia, and Leipzig, Germany, 1846.

Šmits, Pēteris. *Latviešu mītoloģija.* Riga, Latvia, 1918.

Šmits, Pēteris, ed. *Latviešu pasakas un teikas.* 15 vols. Riga, Latvia, 1925–1937.

Straubergs, Kārlis. *Lettisk folktro om de döda.* Stockholm, 1949.

Stryjkowsky, Maciej. *Ktora przedtym nigdy światla nie widziała Kronika Polska, Litewska, Žmodzka y wszystkiey Rusi Kijowskiey, Moskiewskiey.* Krolewiec, Prussia, 1582.

Švābe, Arveds. *Raksti par latvju folkloru.* Riga, Latvia, 1923.

Toporov, Vladimir. "Zametki po baltijskoj mifologii." In *Balto-slavjanskij sbornik*, pp. 289–314. Moscow, 1972.

Vėlius, Norbertas. *Mitinės lietuvių sakmių būtybės.* Vilnius, 1977.

Vėlius, Norbertas. *Chtoniškasis lietuvių mitologijos pasaulis.* Vilnius, 1987.

Vėlius, Norbertas. *The World Outlook of the Ancient Balts.* Translated by Dalija Tekorienė. Vilnius, 1989.

Vėlius, Norbertas. *Baltų religijos ir mitologijos šaltiniai.* Vilnius, 1996 (vol. 1), 2001 (vol. 2).

Vīķe-Freiberga, Vaira. "The Major Gods and Goddesses of Ancient Latvian Mythology." In *Linguistics and Poetics of Latvian Folk Songs: Essays in Honour of the Sesquicentennial of the Birth of Kr. Barons*, pp. 91–113. Kingston, Ont., and Montreal, 1989.

Vīķe-Freiberga, Vaira. *Trejādas saules.* 3 vols. Riga, Latvia, 1997–2002.

JANĪNA KURSĪTE (2005)
Translated by Margita Gailītis and Vija Kostoff

BALTIC SANCTUARIES. There are two types of Baltic sanctuaries. The first and most important type is the pagan sanctuary, which no longer exists but which has survived in countless legends, documented accounts, and evidence of sacrifice rituals from archaeological digs. In addition, records of seventeenth- and eighteenth-century Catholic Church visitations and some toponyms that have survived to this day suggest that sacrifice to pagan gods and spirits was still being practiced in certain places at that time. The second type is the Catholic sanctuary. This type pertains to present-day Lithuania, which is entirely Catholic, and to Latgale, the eastern region of Latvia, which is also Catholic, in contrast to the rest of Protestant Latvia. Christian sanctuaries were frequently superimposed in the Baltic Catholic region in places where pre-Christian sanctuaries had already existed; in some cases these pre-Christian sanctuaries were simply reactivated as Christian ones during Christian times. Although German missionaries, merchants, and crusaders brought Christianity into Latvian territory as early as the thirteenth century, Latvians remained fundamentally pagan well into the seventeenth century.

Latvia's inhabited territory in the thirteenth century included Livonia. At that time the Prussian peoples had not succeeded in joining together to create a strong and independent nation and had thus come under the power of the Teutonic Order—a religious military order, also known as Teutonic Knights, established in the southeastern Baltic lands from the thirteenth century until the mid-sixteenth century. As a consequence, the Prussian peoples had been Christianized. The fate of another Baltic group, the Lithuanians, was different in that Mindaugas, a Lithuanian prince, established an independent Lithuanian nation in 1240. Unable to maintain the upper hand in ongoing battles with Lithuania's neighbors, however, Mindaugas was forced to seek the help of the Teutonic Order. In gratitude for the order's support, in 1251 Mindaugas and his followers became Christians, and in 1253 he was crowned king with a crown sent from Rome by the pope. Subsequently, the Baltic peoples ruled by King Mindaugas, particularly the Zhemaits, rebelled against the crusaders and their forced conversion to Christianity. Mindaugas renewed his struggle against his former ally, the Teutonic Order, and eventually was slain in 1263. At this point people throughout Lithuania began turning back to their old pagan beliefs, and the wars with the German crusaders did not abate during the thirteenth century and even into the fourteenth century. During this period the Teutonic Order blocked trade activity between Lithuania and western Europe, forcing Lithuania's kings to seek compromise solutions regarding both trade and religion issues. Despite the strong resolve of the common people and the aristocracy throughout most of the fourteenth century to resist the government's desire to convert the nation to Christianity (and thus put an end to the onslaught by the crusaders). Lithuania was officially Christianized in 1387, in line with the tenets of the Catholic faith. On a practical level, however, Lithuanians maintained strong pagan beliefs, particularly the pagan worship of sacred places, as evidenced by the survival to the present day of a good number of place-names that pertain to ancient Balt sanctuaries.

During the thirteenth century, Prussians also engaged in ongoing and merciless struggles with the Teutonic Order. Because their territory extended the farthest west, the Prussians suffered the most on the battlefield against the order. However, on the religious front, which included the worship of pagan sanctuaries, they were able to maintain their beliefs and practices well into the beginning of the eighteenth century, when a massive epidemic of the plague struck their entire territory and wiped out many of the Prussians who had remained faithful to their pagan and linguistic identity.

The vocabulary of Prussians, Lithuanians, and Latvians has common root forms that pertain to pre-Christian sanctuaries. One of them is the root **elk-/*alk-*, which means sanctuary. Traditionally, such a sanctuary was a designated deciduous tree forest, but it could also be a hill, river, lake, cliff, or cave. Until World War II one could find in East Prussia, and even today in Latvia and Lithuania, toponyms and hydronyms relating to sanctuaries, which indicate that sanctuaries once existed in those locations. Examples include Alkayne, Alkeynen, and Alkebirge in East Prussia (the Kaliningrad region of modern Russia and northeastern Poland); Elkupis and Elkus in Lithuania; and Elka, Elkasgals, Elkas Grava, Elkas Purvs, Elkezers, Elkleja, and Elkazeme in Latvia. With the advent of Christianity into the Baltic territory, the root form **elk-/*alk-* was used in words designating pagan worship symbols in the form of wood or stone sculptures, pre-Christian faith in general, and pre-Christian divinities, such as the Latvian *elka dievi.* From an etymological point of view the root form **elk-/*alk* is related to the concept of curve, bend, or turn. We see this root in the Prussian word *alkunis* (elbow) and in *elkonis*, the Latvian counterpart. For the ancient Baltic peoples the concept of curving and bending was linked to foretelling of the future; it was the ability, through the language of symbols and intuition, to see around corners. In other words, by looking straight ahead a person could see only objects linked to the profane material world, but by looking in an indirect manner (as through fortune-telling) one could see that which was hidden in both people and things. The pre-Christian meaning of *elks, alke,* or *alkas* for the Baltic peoples was that of the sanctuary where they worshiped gods and brought gifts to the images of those gods. The Lithuanian term *alkas* designated a hill overgrown with trees or, in a historic context, a hill where sacrifice with its accompanying rituals has taken place.

Another important sanctuary concept for the Baltic peoples is contained in the root form **rom-*. For Lithuanians, it was *romuva/romove*; for Latvians, *ramava*; and for Prussians, *romow/romowe.* There are few documented records, other than legends, about this type of sacrifice ritual in Latvian and Lithuanian sanctuaries. However, the term *romow* is mentioned in many and varied sources, starting with Petrus de Dusburg's *Chronicon terrae Prussiae* (Chronicle of the land of Prussia, 1326), as the principal sanctuary for Prussians, and it is recognized as such also in Lithuania and Latvia. It was in this sanctuary that the Prussians burnt a third of the spoils of war as a sacrifice to their gods. During special celebrations the sacrifice consisted of various animals, with a white horse and a goat singled out as favorites. The *romow* sanctuary was encircled by large oak trees with an evergreen oak bearing the image of three of the principal gods at its center. The three Prussian gods represented three cosmic zones—the heavens (Perkūns, the god of thunder), earth (Patrīmps, god of fertility), and the underworld (Patuls, god of the underworld). Typically, one *romow* is mentioned in regard to the Prussians. However, toponymy shows that in the territories inhabited by Prussians, in addition to the main and most important *romow,* there were smaller less significant *romows* in each neighborhood. According to an ancient legend, before the attack by the German Teutonic Order on western Prussia's Heiligenbeil (the town of Mamonovo in today's Kaliningrad region of Russia), there existed in the sanctuary an oak, which was supposedly always green, both in summer and winter. The leaves of the tree were considered medicinal, and people applied them to ailing parts of the bodies of humans and animals alike. The tree's canopy was so dense that no snow or rain could penetrate it. Even in Latvia and Lithuania you can still find toponyms with the root form **rom-*, which shows that similar sanctuaries existed throughout the inhabited Baltic territory.

Dusburg's *Chronicon terrae Prussiae* makes a connection between the word *romow* and the city of Rome by comparing the power of the *romow's* high priest (*Krive krivaitis*) to that of the pope. However, *romow* does not derive from the city name *Rome.* The origin is rather in the Indo-European root form **rem-*, meaning "to be at peace" or "to be peaceful." In Latvian this concept is expressed by the word *rāms* (calm, peaceful), as in the folk song "Rāmi, rāmi Dieviņš brauca / No kalniņa lejiņā" ("Calmly, calmly Dievs [dim.] rode / From the hill down to the valley"), and in Lithuanian as *ramus* or *romus* (peaceful, silent). Peace and calm in *romow's* sacred grove, described in a mythical Latvian folksong as "when no leaf stirred" (*ne lapiņa nečabēja*), was seen as a universal manifestation of a cosmic order. A special ritual of cosmic order was conducted by the *Krive krivaitis.* Typically, ordinary mortals were not allowed to enter the *romow* sanctuary, and those who were allowed in were not permitted to touch anything. In this sense the *romow* sanctuary was perceived in the way paradise is by Christians; that is, the sanctuary knew no chaos and was in total harmony with the cosmos. It is interesting to note that the Latvian language has a related root verb, *ramīt,* which means "to grieve" or "to mourn the dead" in the sense of allowing the spirit to leave this world: *aizlaist no šīs saules viņsaulē* (literally, "to leave this sun to go to the nether sun") and "be at peace."

A variety of *romow* source materials also indicate that the oak trees that typically populated the sanctuary were evergreen. However, the climate in Prussia, Lithuania, and Latvia is such that there is usually snow in winter. Therefore, deciduous trees, including oak trees, would lose their leaves in autumn. One school of thought suggests that on the sanctuary's sacred oak trees grew the evergreen mistletoe, which is considered by the Baltic people, as well as by Romans, Germans, Scandinavians, and others, to be linked to immortality and fertility. It is mistletoe that guarantees one's resurrection after death. Mistletoe is the "golden bough" mentioned in Scandinavian and German source material and also by Vergil, who describes the blossoming of the miraculous "golden bough" upon Aeneas's entry into the underworld.

Many toponyms include **kriv/*kreiv-*, a prolific root form in all Baltic languages. Examples include the word *Krywyen* in Prussian, mentioned in written sources dating back to 1419; *Krivonys, Krivičiai, Krivai* and *Kreivupė* in Lithuanian; and *Krīvi, Krīviņa, Krivaši, Krievaiņi, Krievaceļš,* and *Krievapurvs* in Latvian. As with the root **elk-/*alk-*, the meaning of these words is linked to the concept of indirect, not straight, crooked. The Latvian archaic *krievs* and the Lithuanian *kreivas* both mean "crooked," and *kryvuoti* means "to stumble" or "to walk in a crooked fashion." Similarly, *kreivakis* refers to someone who is cross-eyed. This root word can be found as well in *Krive krivaitis,* whose symbol of spiritual power was a crooked staff. He was also considered the priest of fire, who along with his disciples maintained the eternal flame.

A relatively large number of pre-Christian sanctuary names have as their root **svent-*, which can be traced back to the Indo-European **kuen-*. In Prussian the comparative form is *swints,* in Lithuanian *šventas,* and in Latvian *svēts.* Many Baltic hydronyms are also formed from the same root. Examples in Prussian are the names *Swent* (a river), *Swentyn* (a lake mentioned in literary sources dating back to 1297), *Swyntheynen* (another lake mentioned in a 1340 source), and

Swentegarben (mentioned in 1351). Lithuanian language examples pertain both to the names of bodies of water and hills, as in *Šventas, Šventėlis, Šventė, Švenčius, Švenčiukas, Šventā, Šventupė, Šventežeris, Šventākalnis,* and *Šventrāgis.* In Latvian, the root form can be found primarily in the names of rivers and lakes, but in some isolated cases it also appears in the names of inhabited regions. Examples include the rivers *Svēte, Svētupe, Sventa,* and *Sventāja/Šventoji* (a river on the Latvian and Lithuanian border); the lakes *Sventes* and *Svētavas*; and the inhabited regions of *Svente* and *Svenči.* One can conclude that for the Baltic peoples the epithet *svēts* (sacred, holy) was closely tied to the idea of certain rivers, lakes, and springs that had been specifically identified as sacred. The root form's association with the names of hills or mountains is less frequent, and it is even less common in names of forests or groves. One can therefore hypothesize that the Latvian *svēts* and the Lithuanian *šventas,* in their various forms in hydronyms, symbolized for the Balts a certain brilliance, shininess, or brightness, and ultimately a supernatural light.

Throughout Latvia certain hills were considered sanctuaries known as the *zilie kalni* (blue hills). Records have survived that show nine such blue hills were or still are in existence on Latvian soil. The most important of these is the blue hill located not far from the city of Valmiera. In ancient times, this hill was considered sacred and was widely known for its spring waters, to which were ascribed countless miraculous healing powers. It was forbidden to break off even the smallest branch of a tree in the hill's grove. A severe punishment awaited anyone who disobeyed this edict. People from near and far flocked to the sacred hill on June 23, midsummer's eve. Seventeenth-century literary sources describe several trials of witches who held secret meetings on the blue hill outside Valmiera. For instance, during a 1636 trial in Riga a woman confessed that she and her mother had attended a secret gathering on the blue hill. Both were found to be witches by the court and were burned to death. The following year, a trial took place in Riga regarding five individuals from the village of Liepupe who had met on the blue hill in order to cast a curse on their neighbors' flax and barley. Even in the twentieth century certain stories about Valmiera's blue hill lend this particular sanctuary special status among all the blue hill sanctuaries. In the 1970s, during the Soviet period, a widely known healer nicknamed Blue Hill Marta (Marta Rācene, 1908–1992) lived near the blue hill sanctuary. Many eyewitness accounts have been recorded about her supernatural healing powers. A common denominator among all the blue hill sanctuaries is the existence of a spring of healing waters and the profusion of rare and protected plants. Today, Valmiera's sanctuary is more of a tourist attraction than a sacred place. But when, towards the end of 1990, a proposal was put forth to build a gigantic garbage dump at the base of Valmiera's blue hill, protests were heard throughout the country objecting to the defiling of ancient sacred places. Obviously, the principle of protecting sacred sites has survived to the present day.

The symbiosis of pre-Christian and Christian sanctuaries in Catholic Lithuania is most evident, from the sixteenth century on, in the affixing of images of Christ or other sacred symbols on vertical posts with crosses called *kryžius* in Lithuanian. At first these crosses were made exclusively from wood, and in later times from both metal and wood, at an initial height of 1.5 to 2 meters, and eventually extending to several meters high. Frequently, a special fence encircled the crosses, and colorful flowers were either planted at the base of the cross or cut flowers were placed below the cross. In May, people still gather at these crosses to sing songs in honor of the Virgin Mary. Since the nineteenth century, people who have survived some serious illness or disability, or who hope to guard against one, flock to the Hill of the Crosses (Kryžių kalnas) near the Lithuanian town of Šiauliai, bringing with them homemade crosses of various shapes, sizes, and materials. Several attempts were made during the Soviet period to remove these crosses. For example, in 1961, following an edict from the Communist Party's Central Committee, more than two thousand such crosses were removed from the hill, but people secretly replaced them with new crosses. Since Lithuania regained its independence in the early 1990s, more than 100,000 new crosses have been placed on the hill. Today, the Hill of the Crosses is one of the most popular sanctuaries and it is visited by a large number of people from Lithuania and other countries, who come to pray and place their own homemade crosses. The location has also become a major tourist attraction.

Findings from archaeological digs indicate that in the pre-Christian period a place called Aglona, in the western part of Latvia, was a pagan sanctuary. Vague records and legends point to the existence of a nearby spring with healing powers. In the seventeenth century a Catholic Dominican cloister and cathedral were built on this site. In the eighteenth century the cathedral inherited a painting of the Virgin Mary by an anonymous artist. In time, Catholics started to attribute miraculous powers to this painting, including the power to answer prayers and grant good health and protection during crises. Even during the Soviet occupation of Latvia (1940–1941 and 1945–1991), when the practice of Christian faith and church attendance were considered major crimes against the state, Aglona Cathedral was the secret destination of many pilgrims. The biggest pilgrimage (approximately 100,000 people) takes place annually on August 15 (the Feast of the Assumption of the Virgin Mary to heaven) when Catholics from Latvia and neighboring Lithuania and Poland, as well as people of other faiths, descend on Aglona. To this day, visitors to Aglona make sure they also seek out the nearby spring.

See Also Sacred Space; Sanctuary; Shrines.

Bibliography

Dundulienė, Pranė. *Medžiai senovės lietuvių tikėjimuose.* Vilnius, 1979.

Kursīte, Janīna. "Nacionālā ainava 19. gadsimta latviešu literatūrā un mākslā." In *Mītiskais folklorā, literatūrā, mākslā,* pp. 358–379. Riga, Latvia, 1999.

Mačiulis, Dainius. "Kryžių kalno ir ji supančio krastovaizdžio istorinė raida." In *Kryžių kalno istorinė raida ir jo išlikimo problemos,* pp. 41–53. Šiauliai, Lithuania, 2000.

Širmulis, Alfrėdas. *Lietuvių liaudies memorialiniai paminklai.* Vilnius, 1999.

Straubergs, Kārlis. *Latvju sakrālā pasaule.* Ludwigsburg, Germany, 1948.

Straubergs, Kārlis. "Latviešu kultavietu vārdi." In *In honorem Endzelini,* pp. 138–149. Chicago, 1960.

Šturms, Eduards. *Elka kalni un pilskalni Kursā: Pagātne un tagadne.* Riga, Latvia, 1936.

Šturms, Eduards. "Baltische Alkhügel: Conventus primus historicorum Balticorum." *Acta et relata* 8 (1937): 16–18.

Šturms, Eduards. "Die Alkstätten in Litauen." *Contributions of the Baltic University, Hamburg* 3 (1946): 82–102.

Urbonienė, Skaidrė. "Mažosios architektūros paminklų geležinės viršūnės: Antkapiniai geležiniai kryžiai." *Etnografija* 12 (2002): 23–27.

Urtāns, Juris. *Latvijas senās svētnīcas.* Riga, Latvia, 1993.

Urtāns, Juris. "Velna vārds Latvijas vietās un vietvārdos." *Latvijas Vēsture* 11 (1993/1994): 55–61.

Vaitkevičius, Vykintas. *Senosios Lietuvos šventavietės.* Vilnius, 1998.

Vaitkevičius, Vykintas. *Alkai: baltų šventviečių studija.* Vilnius, 2003.

Vaitkunskene, Laima. *Kul'tovye mesta–"alkvetes" v mogil'nike Pagribis Šilal'skogo rajona Drevnosti Litvy i Belorussii.* Vilnius, 1988.

JANĪNA KURSĪTE **(2005)**
Translated by Margita Gailītis and Vija Kostoff

BALUBA SEE LUBA RELIGION

BAMBARA RELIGION.

The Bambara, the most important Mande group, number about 1.5 million people. They are agriculturists who live in the Republic of Mali on both sides of the Niger River, from the capital city of Bamako northeast to Mopti. Bambara agriculture and religion are closely intertwined. For example, the Bambara high god is conceived of as a grain from which three other divine "persons," and finally, the whole of creation, are born. Bambara theology and religion are complex. Deep religious speculations exist among the Bambara sages and are transmitted orally without codification.

THE SUPREME BEING AND THE CREATION. The Bambara believe in one god, Bemba, or Ngala, who is the creator of all things and has, in a way, created himself as a quaternity. This quaternity consists of Bemba himself, Mousso Koroni Koundyé (or Nyale), Faro, and Ndomadyiri; the last three correspond to the four elements—air, fire, water, and earth. Before the creation Bemba was named Koni and was, in a sense, "thought" (*miri*) dwelling in a void; he is also the "void" itself (*lankolo*). Accordingly, he cannot be perceived by humans using their usual senses. His existence is manifested as a force: a whirlwind, thought, or vibration that contains the signs of all uncreated things.

Bemba realized the creation of the world in three stages, each corresponding to one of the three other divine beings. In the first stage, called *dali folo* ("creation of the beginning"), the naked earth is created. God is known as Pemba in this stage, and he manifests himself in the form of a grain, from which grows an acacia (*Balanza*). This tree soon withers, falls to the ground, and decays. One oblong beam, however, called Pembélé, survives. An avatar of God, Pembélé kneads the rotten wood with his saliva and forms Mousso Koroni Koundyé ("little old woman with a white head"), who becomes the first woman and his wife. Although she is associated with air, wind, and fire, Mousso Koroni Koundyé engenders plants, animals, and human beings. But because her person is unbalanced, her creations are produced in haste, disorder, and confusion.

The second stage, called *dali flana* ("second creation"), brings order and equilibrium to the previous creation. It is conducted under the authority of the deity Faro, an androgynous being issued from the breath of Bemba and identified with water, light, speech, and life. Faro gives every creature and thing a place in the world, a physical space, as well as a position in relation to other beings and things. He stops short of differentiating between things, however.

Differentiation of creation belongs to Ndomadyiri, the heavenly blacksmith, who is the eponymous ancestor of all blacksmiths. His principal task is to separate and distinguish things from each other, to make, in a sense, a comprehensible "speech" from the thought of creation. He is associated with the earth (from which food originates) and with trees (which produce remedies for ill health).

Thus the supreme being of the Bambara exists first as a sort of repository of energy and then manifests itself as four "persons" who generate the creation by each performing a different phase of activity. In this way the creation proceeds from confusion to clarity, from the unintelligible to the intelligible.

ANCESTOR WORSHIP AND THE DASIRI CULT. Only those who led exemplary lives and died in a "natural" way (not due to any sorcery) can become ancestors. An ancestor must have reached an advanced age upon death and lived a life that is beyond reproach ethically, religiously, socially, and intellectually. One generation must separate the living and the dead before the rites of ancestor worship can be celebrated.

Nonfermented foodstuffs (e.g., fresh water, saliva, kola nuts, and mixtures of millet flour and water) are offered to appease the ancestor. These often precede more sophisticated offerings such as sorgo beer and blood. The beer is meant to "excite" the ancestor and to make him shake off his indolence toward living persons. The blood, usually obtained from sacrificed chickens or goats, represents the communion of the living and the dead. The place of worship differs according to the ancestor, but both sides of the entrance door to the hut are a preferred spot.

The founding ancestor is held in higher esteem than all other ancestors. His preeminence appears in the cult of the *dasiri*, a group of *genius loci*, or spiritual places, chosen by the founding ancestor when he created the village. One finds in each agglomeration two sorts of *dasiri*: a fixed one (e.g., tree, rock), which functions as the *axis mundi* of the village; and a mobile one, embodied in a wild or domestic animal (except birds). Offerings are made to the *dasiri* each time a community member encounters difficulties or a significant household event takes place. Sacrificial victims are always white, a color that symbolizes calmness and peace.

INITIATORY SOCIETIES AND SPIRITUAL LIFE. Bambara religious life is mostly fulfilled during the epiphanies, or ritualistic manifestations, of the six initiatory societies: the N'domo, Komo, Nama, Kono, Tyiwara, and Korè. Together they give their members a complete (according to the Bambara ideal of perfection) intellectual, moral, and religious education.

The N'domo, open exclusively to noncircumcised children, teaches the origin and destiny of human beings. The highlight of the annual N'domo ceremonies is a sacred play featuring an androgynous child dancer who maintains complete silence while he performs. Dressed so that not one part of his body is visible, the dancer wears a wooden mask with human features and horns. The N'domo comprises five classes, each representing one of the five other initiation societies. Passage from one stage to another prefigures the adept's access to the Komo, Nama, Kono, Tyiwara, and Korè. In its structure as well as in its ceremonies, the N'domo attempts to answer, in a symbolic way, the following questions: What is man? Where does he come from? What is his destiny? Its answers are: He is androgynous; he comes from God; his fate is to return to God.

After their initiation into the N'domo, Bambara boys are circumcised. The operation has a double goal: to suppress their femininity (represented by the foreskin) and thus guide them to seek the opposite sex in marriage and to introduce the spirit to knowledge. Once these goals have been met, the boys are entitled to seek entry to the Komo society, whose purpose is to reveal to them the mysteries of knowledge.

Komo initiation societies consist of dances performed by masked individuals and sacrifices offered at the society's various altars. The Komo dance mask represents a hyena. Its jaws emphasize the animal's crushing force, which symbolizes knowledge. It should be noted that knowledge, as presented in the Komo, constitutes an entity in itself, independent and distant from man and "descending" upon him when he acquires it. For this reason, the Komo mask is worn on top of the head, like a helmet, and not on the face.

The Nama teaches its adepts about the union of spirit and body, of male and female, and of good and evil. Initiation ceremonies are particularly concerned with the union of a man and woman in matrimony and with the duality of good and evil (evil is symbolized by sorcery). The third society, the Kono, deals with the problems of human duality in greater depth. It examines the union of thought and body, a union that gives birth to the conscience.

The Tyiwara, the fourth society, is meant to teach its adepts about agriculture and work in the fields. It confers special significance on the relationship between the sun and the nurturing earth. At its annual festival, the growth of edible plants, and of vegetation in general, is ritually mimed by two dancers in a performance invested with cosmic symbolism.

The Korè is the last of the initiation societies. It bestows knowledge of man's spiritualization and divinization; an initiate learns how to resemble God, that is, how to become "immortal." Its vast program of initiation is conducted over several weeks for two consecutive years. The society marks the final attainment of the knowledge that assures salvation. The term *salvation* should not be interpreted here in its Christian sense; salvation, for the Bambara, consists of the ability to return to earth by being reborn within one's own clan lineage. The reincarnations continue as long as one's descendants preserve one's memory and cult. The Korè's ceremonies are held every seven years.

The Bambara believe that by following the exigencies of their religion—by not only assisting at religious ceremonies but also participating in them—they can vanquish death and become equal to God. This kind of immortality, proposed to the faithful by the Korè, exemplifies the spiritual finality of Bambara religion, whose aim is to make the believer participate in the deity's essence. The faithful Bambara is not meant to enjoy the presence of God eternally, however: his destiny is to be continually reincarnated so that he can return to his clan. His postmortem contact with God is like a brief, gentle "touch"; he will not be attached permanently to the creator until all reincarnations within the clan cease.

BIBLIOGRAPHY

To the best of my knowledge, the most complete and current survey of Bambara religion remains my own work *The Bambara*, "Iconography of Religions," sec. 7, fasc. 2 (Leiden, 1974). It not only offers a rich and original analysis of Bambara iconography but also provides a fresh view of the rites and institutions of these people. My *Sociétés d'initiation bambara: Le N'domo, le Korè* (Paris, 1960) is an essential study of two of the Bambara initiatory societies and the mystical life, and my *Antilopes du soleil: Art et rites agraires d'Afrique noire* (Vienna, 1980), which treats the Tyiwara, is a penetrating study of the religious role of the Bambara bestiary. Germaine Dieterlen and Youssouf Cissé's *Les fondements de la société d'initiation du Komo* (Paris, 1972) is a remarkable introduction to the inquiries on the Komo. For brilliant studies of some of the Bambara creation myths, see the following works: Solange de

Ganay, "Aspects de mythologie et de symbolique bambara," *Journal de psychologie normale et pathologique* 42 (April-June 1949): 181–201 and "Notes sur la théodicée bambara," *Revue de l'histoire des religions* 135 (1949): 187–213; Solange de Ganay and Dominique Zahan, "Un enseignement donné par le *komo*," in *Systèmes de signes: Textes réunis en hommage à Germaine Dieterlen* (Paris, 1978), pp. 151–185; Germaine Dieterlen, *Essai sur la religion bambara* (Paris, 1951); and also by Dieterlen two articles in the *Journal de la Société des Africanistes*, "Mythe et organisation sociale au Soudan Français," vol. 25, nos. 1–2 (1955): 39–76 and "Mythe et organisation en Afrique occidentale," vol. 29, nos. 1–2 (1959): 119–138.

New Sources

Cissé, Youssouf. *La Confrérie des Chasseurs Malinke et Bambara: Mythes, Rites et Recits Initiatiques.* Paris, 1994.

Dieterlen, Germaine. *Essai sur la Religion Bambara.* 2nd edition. Brussels, 1988.

Djata, Sundiata A. *The Bamana Empire by the Niger: Kingdom, Jihad and Colonization, 1712–1920.* Princeton, N.J., 1997.

DOMINIQUE ZAHAN (1987)
Translated from French by Eva Zahan
Revised Bibliography

BANARAS. The city of Banaras, also known in India as Vārāṇasī, is one of the most important and ancient of the sacred places of India. Such places are called *tīrthas*, "crossings" or "fords." Many *tīrthas*, like Banaras, are located geographically on the banks of India's rivers and were, indeed, fords where ferries plied the river. As places of pilgrimage, however, such *tīrthas* are seen primarily as spiritual fords, where one might safely cross over to the "far shore."

Banaras is located on the bank of the Ganges River in North India, at a place where the river curves northward, as if pointing back toward its Himalayan source. The river itself is considered holy, having fallen from heaven upon the head of Lord Śiva, who tamed the goddess-river in his tangled ascetic's hair before setting her loose to flow upon the plains of North India. In Banaras great stone steps called *ghāṭs* lead pilgrims from the lanes of the city down to the river's edge to bathe. To the north and south of the city, smaller rivers named the Varaṇā and the Asi, respectively, join the Ganges, thus providing a popular etymology for the city's ancient name Vārāṇasī.

Another of the ancient names of this place is Kāśī, which means "shining, luminous." Kāśī is also the name of one of the North Indian kingdoms that rivaled one another from about the eighth to sixth century BCE. The city of Vārāṇasī seems to have been the capital of the kingdom of Kāśī. Located on the high Rājghāṭ plateau overlooking the Ganges, this city, known as both Vārāṇasī and Kāśī, maintained a degree of importance for many hundreds of years, through the period of the Maurya and Gupta empires. Perhaps the height of its prestige was in the late eleventh and early twelfth centuries, when it was one of the administrative capitals of the Gāhaḍavāla kings of the Ganges Plain. Throughout its long history, however, the political significance of the city and its surrounding kingdom could not compare with its religious importance.

As a place of religious significance, Banaras was not only a "city" but a forest, which stretched beyond the small urban center and attracted sages and seekers to its forest hermitages. It was to these rural environs of Banaras, to a place called Sarnath, that the Buddha came following his enlightenment at Bodh Gayā. There he encountered his former companions in asceticism and preached his first sermon to them. Until the late twelfth century, much of the area south of the Rājghāṭ plateau, which today is the center of urban Banaras, was still an extensive forest, filled with pools and rivulets, and dotted with temples and shrines. In the Purāṇas, it is called the Ānandavana, the "forest of bliss." Even today, when Banaras *brahmans* speak of ancient Banaras, they refer to the time when this city was the Ānandavana.

In the time of the Buddha, the most popular form of worship in this part of North India was the worship of what might be called "life-force" deities, such as *yakṣas*, *yakṣīs*, and *nāgas*. Such deities were propitiated with offerings called *bali*, which often included wine or meat. These deities were known for their strength, which they could use in either harmful or beneficent ways. With the rise of theism, whether Buddhist, Śaiva, or Vaiṣṇava, these life-force deities were gathered into the entourage of the great gods. In Banaras, it was Śiva who rose to preeminence and, according to mythological tradition, attracted the allegiance and even the devotion of many *yakṣas*. They became his *gaṇas* ("flocks, troops") and *gaṇeśas* ("troop leaders") and were appointed to positions of great responsibility within the precincts of Śiva's city.

The mythology of Banaras, including the stories of Śiva's connection to this city, is found in the Purāṇas in a genre of praise literature called *māhātmya.* The most extensive of such *māhātmyas* is the *Kāśī Khaṇḍa,* an entire section of the voluminous *Skanda Purāṇa.* One myth tells of the divine hierophany of Śiva in this place. Here, it is said, Śiva's fiery pillar of light *(jyotirliṅga)* burst from the netherworlds, split the earth, and pierced the sky—a luminous and fathomless sign of Śiva. Kāśī is not only the place where that *liṅga* of light is said to have split the earth, but in a wider sense, Kāśī is also said to be the *liṅga* of light—an enormous geographical *liṅga,* with a radius of five *krośas* (about ten miles). Even today pilgrims circumambulate Kāśī on the Pañcakrośī Road, a five-day pilgrimage circuit around the whole of the city.

There are countless shrines and temples of Śiva in Kāśī, each containing a *liṅga,* which, according to Saiva theology, is a symbol *(pratīka)* of that fathomless light of Śiva. It is said that in Kāśī there is a *liṅga* at every step; indeed, the very stones of Kāśī are Śiva *liṅgas*. Within this wider array, however, there are several temples that have special fame as sanctuaries of Śiva. The most significant of these *liṅgas* are

Oṃkāreśvara, Viśveśvara, and Kedāreśvara, which traditionally centered the three *khaṇḍas*, or "sectors," of Banaras—north, central, and south. Oṃkāreśvara was of great importance in ancient Kāśī, but was damaged during the early Muslim destruction of the city and has never regained its former prominence. Viśveśvara (modern-day Viśvanātha) rose to preeminence and popularity around the twelfth century, and later continued to hold its position and reputation despite repeated Muslim devastation. Finally, Kedāreśvara anchors the southern sector of Kāśī. Its original home and prototype even today is the shrine of Kedār in the Himalayas, but it is one of the many *liṅgas* from elsewhere in India that have an important presence in this sacred center. The three *khaṇḍas* centered by these temples also have traditional circumambulatory routes that take the pilgrim through the most important temples and *tīrthas* of each sector.

In another mythic sequence from the *Kāśī Khaṇḍa,* Śiva populated the city of Vārāṇasī with the entire pantheon of gods. At that time, Śiva dwelt in his barren Himalayan home with his new bride, Pārvatī. He surveyed the entire earth for a suitable abode for the two of them. Seeing the beautiful Kāśī, he set about the task of evicting its ruling king, Divodāsa, so that he could have the city for himself. One by one, Śiva sent the various gods and demigods to Kāśī to find some way to force the king to leave. Not only did each god fail, but all the gods were so entranced with the city itself that they remained there without reporting to Śiva. Finally, with the help of Viṣṇu, Śiva succeeded in evicting King Divodāsa. The city into which he triumphantly entered was full of the gods.

As a sacred center, then, Kāśī is not only the city of Śiva, but also a *maṇḍala* containing the entire divine population of the Hindu pantheon. There are the twelve *ādityas*, "suns"; sixty-four *yoginīs*, "goddesses"; and eight *bhairavas*, the "terrible ones," led by Kāla Bhai-rava, the divine governor of the city. There are fifty-six *gaṇeśas*, protectively situated around the city in seven concentric circles at the eight compass points. Lord Brahmā and Lord Viṣṇu are there, both of whom have prominent locations within the city.

In addition to assigning a place to each of the gods, the city of Banaras has a place within its precincts for each of the other great *tīrthas* of India. India's twelve *jyotirliṅgas*, its seven sacred cities, and its sacred rivers and lakes all have symbolic locations in Kāśī. Banaras, then, is a microcosm of India's sacred geography.

The intensity of power that comes from the symbolic gathering of gods, *tīrthas*, and sages in this one place has made Banaras India's most widely acclaimed place of pilgrimage. While it is visited for the benefits associated with pilgrimage in this life, Kāśī is most famous as an auspicious place to die; a popular phrase is "Kāśyām maranam muktiḥ" ("Death in Kāśī is liberation"). According to tradition, those who die within the precincts of the holy city are certain to be instructed by Śiva himself at the time of death: in Banaras, Śiva's teaching is said to carry one across the flood of *saṃsāra* to the "far shore" of immortality.

See Also Nāgas and Yakṣas; Pilgrimage, article on Hindu Pilgrimage; Śiva.

Bibliography

Eck, Diana L. *Banaras: City of Light.* New York, 1982. A study of the city of Banaras, based on its traditional literature in the Sanskrit Purāṇas and its modern sacred geography and patterns of pilgrimage.

Sherring, Matthew A. *The Sacred City of the Hindus: An Account of Benares in Ancient and Modern Times.* London, 1868. A consideration of the temples and legends of Banaras by a nineteenth-century British missionary.

Sukul, Kuber Nath. *Vārāṇasī down the Ages.* Patna, India, 1974. A study of the religious history and spiritual life of Banaras, including consideration of its saints, fairs, festivals, and arts.

New Sources

Parry, Jonathan P. *Death in Banaras.* Cambridge; New York, 1994.

Diana L. Eck (1987)
Revised Bibliography

BANTU RELIGIONS

See CENTRAL BANTU RELIGIONS; EAST AFRICAN RELIGIONS, *ARTICLE ON* NORTHEASTERN BANTU RELIGIONS; INTERLACUSTRINE BANTU RELIGIONS; SOUTHERN AFRICAN RELIGIONS, *ARTICLE ON* SOUTHERN BANTU RELIGIONS

BAPTISM.

The word *baptism* comes from the Greek *baptein,* which means to plunge, to immerse, or to wash; it also signifies, from the Homeric period onward, any rite of immersion in water. The frequentative form, *baptizein,* appears much later (Plato, *Euthydemus* 227d; *Symposium* 176b). The baptismal rite is similar to many other ablution rituals found in a number of religions, but it is the symbolic value of baptism and the psychological intent underlying it that provide the true definition of the rite, a rite usually found associated with a religious initiation.

Pre-Christian Religions. The purifying properties of water have been ritually attested to ever since the rise of civilization in the ancient Near East. In Babylonia, according to the *Tablets of Maklu,* water was important in the cult of Enki, lord of Eridu. In Egypt, the *Book of Going Forth by Day* (17) contains a treatise on the baptism of newborn children, which is performed to purify them of blemishes acquired in the womb. Water, especially the Nile's cold water, which is believed to have regenerative powers, is used to baptize the dead in a ritual based on the Osiris myth. This ritual both assures the dead of an afterlife and rids them of blemishes that may not be taken into the other world. Baptism of the dead is also found among the Mandaeans (cf., the *Book of John*), and a similar rite is mentioned on Orphic tablets (*Orphicorum fragmenta,* 2d ed., Otto Kern, ed., Berlin, 1963, p. 232).

The property of immortality is also associated with baptism in the Greek world: according to Cretan funeral tablets, it was associated especially with the spring of Mnemosyne (memory). A bath in the sanctuary of Trophonios procured for the initiate a blessed immortality even while in this world (Pausanias, *Description of Greece* 9.39.5). Greek religious sanctions did impose a number of lustral ablution rites for the removal of sins, but these rites were only preliminary to the principal rites of the mysteries. Thus, the bath in the sea with which the initiation rites of the great Eleusinian mysteries began was simply a physical purification, accompanied by the sacrifice of a piglet. This was true as well of the immersion of the followers of the god Men Askaenos, near Antioch in Pisidia, and of the ablutions required of the Corybantes and of the followers of the Thracian goddess Cotyto, who were called *baptai* ("the baptized ones"). In all these cases, baptism was only a preamble, as the *Magic Papyrus* of Paris testifies (43): "Jump into the river with your clothes on. After you have immersed yourself, come out, change your clothes, and depart without looking back." Such a rite marked the beginning of an initiation; this practice was required to put the neophyte in the state of purity necessary for him to receive the god's oracle or an esoteric teaching.

In Hellenistic philosophy, as in Egyptian speculation, divine water possessed a real power of transformation. Hermetism offered to man the possibility of being transformed into a spiritual being after immersion in the baptismal crater of the *nous*; this baptism conferred knowledge on man and permitted him to participate in the gnosis and, hence, to know the origins of the soul. Having received baptism, the gnostic "knows why he has come into existence, while others do not know why or whence they are born" (*Corpus Hermeticum* 1.4.4). Egyptian cults also developed the idea of regeneration through water. The bath preceding initiation into the cult of Isis seems to have been more than a simple ritual purification; it was probably intended to represent symbolically the initiate's death to the life of this world by recalling Osiris' drowning in the Nile (Apuleius, *Metamorphoses* 11.23.1).

In the cult of Cybele, a baptism of blood was practiced in the rite of the *taurobolium*: the initiate went down into a pit and was completely covered with the blood of a bull, whose throat was cut above him. At first, the goal of this rite seems to have been to provide the initiate with greater physical vitality, but later it acquired more of a spiritual importance. A well-known inscription attests that he who has received baptism of blood is *renatus in aeternum,* that he has received a new birth in eternity (*Corpus inscriptionum Latinarum* 6.510). In other inscriptions associated with the *tauro-bolium,* the word *natalicium* seems to be the exact equivalent of the Christians' *natalis,* suggesting that the day of the baptism of blood is also the day of a new and spiritual birth. However, the fact that this baptism was repeated periodically shows that the idea of complete spiritual regeneration was not originally associated with it. Only under the influences of Christianity and the Mithraic cult does the idea of an atonement for past sins through shed blood appear; henceforth, it was possible to believe that the *taurobolium* procured the hope of eternity, and that the Mithraic bull sacrifice was a redeeming act that gave the initiate a new life.

The liturgical use of water was common in the Jewish world. Mosaic law imposes the performance of ablutions before ritual entry into sacred areas; likewise, it describes the chief impurities that water can erase (*Nm.* 19:1–22; *Lv.* 14, 15, 16:24–28). Under Persian influence, rites of immersion multiplied after the exile. Some prophets saw in the requirement of physical purity a sign of the necessity of inner and spiritual purification (*Ez.* 36:25–28). The Essenes linked the pouring forth of the divine life in man to purification by baptism in flowing water. They practiced a baptism of initiation that brought the neophyte into the community at Qumran after a year's probation. However, the rite did not produce any magical effects, for, as the *Manual of Discipline* asserts, a pure heart was necessary for the bath to be effective, and an impure man who receives it merely soils the sanctified water (*Manual of Discipline* 6.16–17, 6.21).

Toward the beginning of the Christian era, the Jews adopted the custom of baptizing proselytes seven days after their circumcision, the rabbis having added the impurity of converted gentiles to the chief impurities enumerated in the Torah. After their baptism, new converts were allowed access to the sacrifices in the Temple. A series of specific interrogations made it possible to judge the real intentions of the candidate who wished to adopt the Jewish religion. After submitting to these interrogations, he was circumcised and later baptized before witnesses. In the baptism, he was immersed naked in a pool of flowing water; when he rose from the pool, he was a true son of Israel. Clearly a rite of unification with the community of believers, this baptism developed under the influence of the school of Hillel and emphasized the importance of a new birth. "Every proselyte," says the Babylonian Talmud, "is like a newborn child" (*Yev.* 22a, 48b, 62a, etc.).

The ministry of John the Baptist in the Jordanian desert was connected with this baptist movement, which symbolically linked immersion in a river of flowing water to the passage from death to a new and supernatural life. To achieve the erasing of sin that is closely tied to inner conversion, John administered a baptism of water, but by doing so in the water of the Jordan itself, not in the ritual water of purified pools, John made a clear departure from official practice. This departure was all the more striking because his baptism appears to be a substitute for the *ḥaṭa't,* the sacrifice for sin, and is not a rite of unification with the Israelite community but rather a sign of divine pardon and of the advent of the messianic era. Not surprisingly, John drew down upon himself the fierce hatred of the scribes and Jewish authorities (Josephus Flavius, *Jewish Antiquities* 18.116–119).

The Mandaeans take their baptismal practice directly from the example of John, whom they consider the perfect gnostic; they administer baptism in the flowing water of a symbolic Jordan. "Be baptized with the flowing water I have brought you from the world of light," says the *Right Ginza* (19.24). Mandaean baptism is followed by a sacred meal where a blessing is given to bread and water mixed with wine, considered the sustenance of divine beings; in addition, the Mandaeans practice baptism of the dead. Johannine and Christian rites of baptism do not, however, have their origin in these practices, as was thought at the beginning of the twentieth century. Rather, Jewish and Christian influences create the numerous ritual similarities found in Mandaean practice, including the white garments with which recipients of Mandaean baptism are clothed. "Clothe yourselves in white, to be like the mystery of this flowing water," says the *Right Ginza.*

The same influences were felt by the Elkesaites, who at the beginning of the second century abolished the fire of the patriarchal sacrifice and substituted for it a baptism by water that both remits sin and brings the neophytes into a new religion. Their baptismal ritual takes place in the flowing water of a brook or river after invocations are addressed to earth, air, oil, and salt. This sort of baptism also becomes a method of physical healing and appears again in numerous Baptist sects of the modern period.

Christian Baptism. John baptized Jesus, like others who came to him, in the waters of the Jordan, but the manifestations of the Father and the Holy Spirit during Jesus' baptism give it a completely new dimension (*Mk.* 1:9–11). Jesus' baptism also inaugurated his public ministry, and he later gave his disciples the mission of baptizing in the name of the trinitarian faith—a mission that they carried out even before their master's death (*Mt.* 28:19, *Jn.* 4:1–2). The apostles continued to practice the baptism of water of the type administered by John; but they emphasized the necessity of an inner conversion preceding the profession of the trinitarian faith, the focus of the new belief.

It was Paul who first defined the theological and symbolic significance of Christian baptism, joining the neophyte's ritual descent into water to Christ's death and rebirth to a new and spiritual life through his resurrection (*Rom.* 6:3–4). Sin is not carried away by the flowing water but by the Lord's death and resurrection; through baptismal immersion, the Christian is able to participate in this new existence (*Col.* 2:12). In *Titus* 3:5, Paul describes baptism as the gift of "a bath of regeneration and renewal"; the baptismal water is at once the water of death in which the old, sinful man is immersed and the water of life from which he emerges renewed. In fact, Paul rediscovers the meaning of a very ancient symbolism of death and resurrection found in archaic initiation rituals a symbolism that has been admirably analyzed by Mircea Eliade (*Images et symbols: Essais sur le symbolisme magico-religieux,* Paris, 1952, pp. 199–212; *Traité d'histoire des religions,* Paris, 1949, pp. 64–65).

Every detail of the Christian ritual is intended to symbolize birth to a new life in Jesus Christ: nudity (at least for men) during immersion; conferral of new names on the neophytes, who are also given new, white garments; imposition of the sign of the cross, understood as the seal (*sphragis*), mentioned in *Revelation;* and the dispensation of a drink of milk and honey to the newly baptized. Ever since the *First Letter of Peter,* new Christians have been compared to little children (*1 Pt.* 2:2), a comparison frequently represented in the early Christian art of the catacombs; in another early symbol, they are likened to "little fish, so named for our great Ichthus, Jesus Christ, who is born in water and remains alive by living there" (Tertullian, *On Baptism* 1.3). Old Testament prototypes of baptism—the Flood, the crossing of the Red Sea, the crossing of the Jordan, and entrance into the Promised Land—are evoked in catechesis even by the first generations of Christians, who recognized in them the passage through the water of life and death (cf. *1 Cor.* 10:1–2). As Chrysostom explained in the fourth century, "Baptism represents death and the sepulcher but also resurrection and life. Just as the old man is buried in the sepulcher, so we immerse our heads in water. At the moment when we come out of the water, the new man appears" (*Homilies* 25.2). Christian representations of baptism were also enriched by other symbols drawn from the Old Testament, notably the deer drinking at the spring, from Psalm 42, and the Good Shepherd surrounded by his sheep, from Psalm 23 (*Ps.* 23, 42:25). Both these psalms were sung during the Easter Vigil by candidates for baptism.

Christian baptismal practice is founded on the commandment of Jesus himself to his disciples (*Mt.* 28:19). Its administration during the first centuries of the church took place at Easter night and Pentecost and was limited to bishops, the heads of the Christian communities. Reception of baptism seems often to have been put off until the moment of death by neophytes who were reluctant to accept the full consequences of inner conversion; and infant baptism, though possible, was probably not practiced in the early period of the church (cf. *Mt.* 19:14, *Acts* 16:33, *1 Tm.* 2:4). As the gateway to the sacraments, baptism opened the way into the church community, and prayers and rites increasingly describe it as the entrance to a holy place, the opening of the different routes offered by the faith.

The church was especially concerned, however, to organize a period of probation during which the catechumens were prepared to receive the sacrament through prayer, fasting, and doctrinal instruction. The *Didache,* in chapter 7, clearly asserts the duty of candidates to live according to evangelical precepts and to renounce evil in all its forms. As a number of patristic texts attest, the baptismal ritual was quickly enriched through such additions as interrogations (like those preceding Jewish baptism), a triple renunciation of the devil (recalling Jesus' triple renunciation during his temptations), a triple immersion (representing the Trinity), the anointing of the neophyte with the holy chrism, and the laying on of hands by the bishop or priest (Tertullian, *Against Praxeas* 26; *On Baptism;* Hippolytus, *Apostolic Tradition*).

Because it was the sacrament that indicated entrance into the life of faith and the community of the church, baptism was also considered a means to inner enlightenment. In the Eastern church, those who were initiated into the Christian mysteries by baptism were called the "enlightened," for, as Gregory of Nazianzus explains, the baptismal rite opens the catechumen's eyes to the light that indicates God's symbolic birth in man (Discourse 40: *On Baptism*). In this view, the bishop theologian merely continues a long tradition begun by Paul. "Awake, sleeper," the apostle writes in *Ephesians,* "and Christ will shine upon you"—an admonition he repeats in the *Letter to the Hebrews* (*Eph.* 5:14, *Heb.* 6:4, 10:32). Writing of baptism in the second century, Justin Martyr speaks of the "bath that is called enlightenment" (*First Apology* 61); in the following century, Clement of Alexandria wrote: "Baptized, we are enlightened; enlightened, we are adopted; adopted, we are made perfect; perfect, we become immortal" (*Pedagogue* 1.6.26). Thus, in the early church, baptism was clearly understood as the initiation required for a man to recognize the divine light and to participate in eternal life while still in this world.

But because it was also the fundamental rite of entry into the church community, baptism was quickly claimed as a prerogative by several rival churches, each of which called itself orthodox and accused the others of heresy and schism. Modifications of baptismal rites by the various sects were inevitable. After the second half of the fourth century, the Anomoeans, exponents of a doctrine akin to Arianism, rejected triple immersion, the symbol of a Trinity equal in all its members, a doctrine they contested; for the same reason, they even modified the baptismal formula that had been fixed by scripture (*Mt.* 28:19). What is more important, from the third century on, the Arians insisted upon the invalidity of a rite of baptism conferred by a heretic or schismatic, a view given great importance by the Donatists. The Arians denied the validity of Catholic baptism, and in Italy (especially in Milan) and Vandal Africa they required rebaptism (cf. Michel Meslin, *Les Ariens d'Occident,* Paris, 1967, pp. 382–390). Arians and Donatists alike did not believe that a person could be brought within the church community by a minister who was personally alien to it and did not share its faith; they held that baptism was valid only if it was accompanied by a pure intention in the person who administered it, who had also to belong to the true church. They refused to accept the Catholic view that the rite of baptism is in itself the canal of an omnipotent divine grace that completely surpasses a channel for qualities of the individual who administers it.

From the sixth century on at the latest, the Catholic church permitted the baptism of children, the engagement to follow the faith being taken in their name by adult Christians. The custom of baptizing infants soon after birth became popular in the tenth or eleventh century and was generally accepted by the thirteenth (Thomas Aquinas, *Summa theologiae* 3.68.3). In the fourteenth century, baptismal ritual was simplified, and a rite of spiritual infusion, in which water is poured on the head of a child held above the baptismal font, replaced baptism by immersion.

After 1517, the questions posed by the practice of the baptism of small children served as a major foundation for dissident Christian movements stemming from the Reformation. To adherents of these movements, an uncompromising interpretation of the doctrine of individual justification by faith alone implied that the rite of entry into the Christian community had to be restricted to adults who were conscious of their salvation through Christ and who asked to be baptized. The dissidents formally denied the validity of baptism given to nonresponsible children and required those who had received such baptism to be rebaptized as adults, thus earning the name Anabaptists (*Wiedertäufer*). Going even further, Thomas Müntzer (1485–1525), one of the "prophets of Zwickau," affirmed that individual inspiration by the Holy Spirit determined a person's conduct and demonstrated the unique rule of faith. Along with this demand for religious discipline, the Anabaptist movement, especially in Germany, developed a revolutionary ideology, preached radical egalitarianism, community of property, and even polygamy, and actively supported the German Peasants' Revolt. Denounced and condemned by Luther, Calvin, and Zwingli, Müntzer was executed at Mülhausen, and the Anabaptists were subjected to a pitiless repression. Nevertheless, their movement survived in northern Europe and expanded during the seventeenth and eighteenth centuries in Holland, where the Mennonites still practice adult baptism by immersion and advocate a policy of nonviolence that denies them participation in public office or military service.

In 1633, a group of English Baptists immigrated to North America, beginning the development in the New World of a number of Baptist sects and churches, whose members founded their belief on the theological baptism of Paul (cf. *Rom.* 6:4, *Col.* 2:12) and insisted upon a return to strict apostolic practice. These sects and churches have in common the practice of baptism by immersion administered in the name of the Trinity only to adults who believe and confess their faith in Jesus Christ; in addition, from their distant Anabaptist origins, a majority retains the doctrine of the freedom of each confessional community to interpret the scriptures and the Christian faith.

SEE ALSO Ablutions; Purification; Water.

BIBLIOGRAPHY

Beasley-Murray, G. R. *Baptism in the New Testament.* New York, 1962.

Beirnaert, Louis. "La dimension mythique dans le sacramentalisme chrétien." *Eranos-Jahrbuch* (Zurich) 17 (1949): 255–286.

Drower, Ethel S., trans. *The Canonical Prayerbook of the Mandaeans.* Leiden, 1959.

Gilmore, Alec, ed. *Christian Baptism.* Chicago, 1959.

Lundberg, Per. *La typologie baptismale dans l'ancienne église.* Leipzig, 1942.

Malaise, Michel. *Les conditions de pénétration et de diffusion des cultes égyptiens en Italie.* Leiden, 1972.

Meslin, Michel. "Réalités psychiques et valeurs religieuses dans les cultes orientaux (premier-quatrième siècles)." *Revue historique* 512 (October–December 1974): 289–314.

Payne, Ernest A. *The Fellowship of Believers: Baptist Thought and Practice Yesterday and Today.* 2d ed., enl. London, 1952.

Reitzenstein, Richard. *The Hellenistic Mystery Religions* (1927). Translated by John E. Seeley. Pittsburgh, 1978.

Rudolph, Kurt. *Die Mandäer.* 2 vols. Göttingen, 1960–1961.

Thomas, Jean. *Le mouvement baptiste en Palestine et en Syrie.* Gembloux, 1935.

MICHEL MESLIN (1987)
Translated from French by Jeffrey C. Haight and Annie S. Mahler

BAPTIST CHURCHES. As with most denominational names, the term *Baptist* began as a pejorative nickname. It first appeared as *Anabaptist,* or "rebaptizer," because in the sixteenth century, when this group arose in Western Christendom, virtually all persons had already been baptized as infants. Thus, these rebaptizers were scandalously denying the validity of that first baptism, setting themselves up as a truer church, if not indeed as the true church. Gradually, as infant baptism became less prevalent and as alternative modes of worship grew more widespread, this still young denomination adopted the shortened form of *Baptist,* both as a convenient distinction and as a point of honor. (New England churches in the seventeenth century and early eighteenth century gradually progressed from simply "the Church of Christ" to "the Church of Christ in Gospel Order" to "the Church of Christ Baptized upon Profession of Their Faith" to "the Baptized Church of Christ" to, finally, the Baptist Church.) To be sure, the new subject of the baptism (namely the adult, or "believer") and not originally the mode of baptism (whether by sprinkling, pouring, or immersing) stood out as the most glaring liturgical innovation of this politically powerless and socially suspect group. Although not preserved in the denominational designation, the other feature of the early Baptist movement that most alarmed contemporaries was the Baptists' novel notion that civil government had no responsibility, and indeed no right, to enforce a religious conformity. As one of their seventeenth-century opponents wrote, Anabaptists "deny Civil Government to be proved of Christ" (Featley, 1646).

ORIGINS. As used by their enemies, the word *Anabaptist* was calculated to have an unnerving effect upon all who believed in a well-ordered society, for the term suggested that English rebaptizers of the seventeenth century were of a piece with the most radical continental rebaptizers of the century before. Thus every fanaticism, every antinomianism, every vagary of the Reformation's bloodiest days could be laid at the doorstep of those English Separatists opposing infant baptism. History, to say nothing of the specific individuals involved, was by this indiscriminate name-calling badly served, for modern Baptists have only the most tenuous connection with the radical reformers of the sixteenth century. (Modern Mennonites may be more accurately seen as lineal descendants of the Reformation's left wing.) English and American Baptists, who in the twentieth century accounted for nearly 90 percent of all Baptists worldwide, emerged from the Puritan agitations of Elizabethan and Jacobean England.

Sharing many of the Puritan concerns about a Church of England still too papist, still too engrossed with civil enforcement and ecclesiastical preferment, these separating Puritans early distinguished themselves by insisting that the church be a voluntary society. That voluntarism had two critical components: (1) the insistence that members choose their church rather than be born into it; this voluntary act was testified to by the act of baptism, which was both obedient to Christ's command and declarative of one's personal, uncoerced confession of faith; and (2) the conviction that the covenant of believers to work and worship together was a private agreement with which the state had nothing to do, for conscience must be left free. As Thomas Helwys (c. 1550–c. 1616), one of that first generation of English Baptists, wrote, "the King is a mortal man and not God, therefore [he] hath no power over the immortal souls of his subjects, to make laws and ordinances for them, and to set spiritual lords over them."

The leadership of Helwys and two others, John Smyth (d. 1612) and John Murton, proved decisive in the first two decades of the seventeenth century as the English General Baptists (that is, non-Calvinist, affirming an unrestricted or general atonement for humankind) grew from a scarcely visible knot of believers in 1609 to around twenty thousand members by 1660. Despite this impressive showing, however, the major strength of the modern Baptist churches came from a somewhat later development of the 1630s: the rise of the Particular Baptists (of Calvinist orientation, affirming a limited or particular redemption for humankind). Under the leadership of John Spilsbury in the decade following 1633, a single church became mother to six more. By the time seven such churches existed in and around London, these Calvinist Baptists had also reintroduced the ancient Christian practice of baptism by immersion, this mode being preferred as a more suitable symbol of one's burial with Christ followed by one's new birth or resurrection from that death to walk in a wholly new life. One of the members of Spilsbury's group, Mark Lucar (d. 1676), immigrated to America, settling in Newport, Rhode Island. There he introduced the "new baptism" to New England's scattered Anabaptists, as they were still called. Lucar, arriving sometime before 1648, also helped strengthen ties between American and English Baptists as the two groups together labored to make clear the unfairness of the broad application of the "Anabaptist" label. (New England continued to legislate against Anabaptists.) In this endeavor they were much assisted by the moderate, well-reasoned, properly Calvinist London Confession of 1644.

Baptist growth in America lagged behind that of England in the seventeenth century and early eighteenth century. Roger Williams (1603?–1683) gave the infant denomination both a geographical base and a theological thrust when in 1636, as an exile from Puritan Massachusetts Bay Colony, he made his way on foot to a territory at the head of the Narragansett Bay. After a careful and conscientious purchase of land from the Indians, he named the first settlement Providence in gratitude to God for having delivered him safely from the Puritans, the Indians, and the rigors of his fourteen-week exposure to the New England winter. The colony of Rhode Island, founded on the principle of a "full liberty in religious concernments," as well as on a hot hatred of the "Bloudy Tenent of Persecution" (the title of Williams's 1644 London publication), received into its midst all manner of religious pariahs: Baptists, Quakers, Ranters, Fifth Monarchists, Gortonists, and many others. Yet only in a limited sense did Rhode Island become a Baptist stronghold. By the end of the seventeenth century, Quakers dominated the colony politically, while Baptists had separated into Calvinist, Arminian (Six Principle), and Seventh-day factions. Williams, moreover, had remained within the Baptist fold only briefly; the leadership of the Providence church quickly passed into other hands. In Newport, on the other hand, the more enduring leadership of John Clarke (1609–1676; assisted by Lucar, Obadiah Holmes [1607–1650], and Joseph Torrey) gave the infant denomination a firm if tiny base in the New World.

EXPANSION IN NORTH AMERICA. The great growth of Baptists in North America (and by extension in the world) followed the eighteenth century's Great Awakening, that Calvinist explosion of evangelical zeal and intense religious experience. Even though Baptists were not prime leaders in the movement, they were the prime beneficiaries of it. Churches separating from the Congregational establishments in New England often moved from a halfway house called "Separatist" to a new denominational home called "Baptist." For example, the eminent pastor, theologian, historian, and civil libertarian Isaac Backus (1724–1806) followed this path. Moreover, the Awakening, even if it did not make an itinerant ministry respectable, did make such traveling evangelism both popular and pervasive. John Leland (1754–1841), a New Englander transplanted to Virginia, is an instructive example of such a ministry: irregular, unauthorized, ill-supported, and enormously effective. The names of Backus and Leland also point to a rhetoric that during the Revolutionary period served to identify Baptists with the cause of liberty, both civil and ecclesiastical. In the South, where the Church of England had for so long enjoyed a legal monopoly, Baptists seized upon the discomfort of a church so swiftly disestablished and so widely under suspicion to make major conquests among farmers, artisans, and even gentry.

After the American Revolution, Baptists also made phenomenal advances among the nation's blacks. Using a persuasive preaching style, an accessible theology, an appealing baptismal ritual, and an ecclesiology that granted freedom from white rule, the Baptist message found ready hearers among both enslaved and free blacks. By the end of the nineteenth century, black Baptists had formed their own national organizations, publishing boards, and mission societies. By the mid-twentieth century, approximately two-thirds of America's black Christians were Baptists, and one-third or more of all of America's Baptists were black. Like their white counterparts, however, blacks found it difficult to maintain organizational or theological unity.

The pattern of increasing diversity had been set by the white Baptists. Even before the nineteenth century began, some Baptists, disturbed by the prevailing Calvinist orientation of their denomination, chose to emphasize people's free will: Free Will Baptists thus maintained a separate identity until early in the twentieth century. Others in the new nation, fearing that Baptists would aspire to national status with all the evils that bureaucracy and hierarchy implied, resisted the creation of national societies and boards, preferring to remain in smaller, more local, more nearly autonomous units. In the bitter conflict over slavery, more specifically over the appointment of a slaveholding missionary, white Baptists split along geographical lines in 1845, and the Southern Baptist Convention was organized in Augusta, Georgia. (A national organization of Baptists dated back only to 1814, so denominational unity in the United States enjoyed but a brief life.) The Southern Baptist Convention, with its base initially in the states of the southern Confederacy, moved aggressively to the West, to the North, and to "foreign fields," becoming the largest single Baptist entity in the world. By the mid-twentieth century it had also become the largest Protestant denomination in the United States. The northern group (originally the Northern Baptist Convention, now the American Baptist Churches, USA), with about three-fourths the number of churches as the southern group at the time of separation, found itself repeatedly depleted in the twentieth century by separations and schisms—most of them related to the conflict between modernists and fundamentalists. As a consequence, by the late twentieth century the Southern Baptist Convention outnumbered its northern counterpart by about ten to one. Although the other major Protestant groups that divided over slavery reunited—the Methodists in 1939 and the Presbyterians in 1983—the Baptists have shown little sign of returning to a single fold. In fact they continued to divide and subdivide into the twenty-first century. Southern Baptists divided over questions of theology and denominational control, with moderates forming such new groups as the Alliance of Baptists, the Cooperative Baptist Fellowship, and Baptists Committed.

In 2000 the northern and southern "halves" had an aggregate membership of around nineteen million, while the two oldest black denominations had a combined membership of eight to ten million. This leaves uncounted some four or five million Baptists in the United States who are scattered among a wide variety of other organizations. Most of these groups affirm a strict congregational polity (eschewing any national superstructure or headquarters), a rigid biblical theology (rejecting all critical study of the biblical text itself), and their own special hold on "the faith once delivered to the saints" (opposing all ecumenical ventures, even with other Baptist bodies). The Baptist family in the United States is large—Protestantism's largest by far in the nation, as it approaches thirty million—but as in many another large family, some members do not speak to other members.

WORLDWIDE. Outside the United States, the Baptist churches are unevenly, and often sparsely, scattered. One may speak most conveniently in terms of continents rather than individual nations in offering estimates of membership: in Africa and Europe, about 1 million in each; in Asia, about 1.5 million; and in Central and South America, something less than 1 million. In Canada, to which New England Baptists began to migrate in the late eighteenth century, there are between 100,000 and 200,000 Baptists. By the beginning of the twenty-first century, Baptists worldwide numbered over forty million, with over thirty million in the United States.

The former Soviet Union (counted in the European total) constitutes something of a special case as the Baptist presence there is both highly visible and highly vulnerable. Baptists entered Russia from several points of departure in the late nineteenth century, but they encountered severe opposition from the czars and the Russian Orthodox Church. In the USSR that opposition intensified as Baptists, true to an ancient heritage, found any interference or regulation by the state intolerable. With the collapse of the Soviet Union in 1989, new Baptist groups were established in a variety of newly formed eastern European countries. These groups included the Baptist Unions of Lithuania, Georgia, Romania, and Latvia. New churches and seminaries were formed, and many of the unions affiliated with the European Baptist Federation and the Baptist World Alliance. The latter is the primary international fellowship of Baptists, funding programs and promoting church interaction throughout the world.

In England the General Baptists of the seventeenth century lost either zeal or identity or both, and many of that number merged with the Universalists. The Calvinist or Particular Baptists maintained both zeal and identity, but in the face of a powerful and sometimes repressive national church, the numbers of these dissenters never approached that of their coreligionists in the United States. In 2000, Baptists in the British Isles (England, Ireland, Scotland, and Wales) numbered a little over 200,000.

Because of their belief in a threefold immersion (separately in the name of the Father, the Son, and the Holy Spirit), German Baptists received the nickname of "Dunkers" (or "Dunkards"). Known officially since 1908 as the Church of the Brethren, these Baptists originated in Germany early in the eighteenth century. Fleeing from persecution there, however, they immigrated virtually en masse to America, settling in Pennsylvania, the Virginia backcountry, and the Midwest. Although distinguished by liturgical emphases on the Love Feast and the ceremonial washing of each other's feet, these German Baptists attract most public attention by their consistent witness for peace and their choice of alternative service rather than military enlistment. Their membership in 2000 neared 200,000. One other sizable group of distinctive ethnic heritage, the (Swedish) Baptist General Conference, dropped its ethnic label in 1945; in 2000 its membership in the United States exceeded 130,000.

Across nearly four centuries and six continents, the Baptist churches have multiplied in variety nearly as much as in number. Yet it is possible to point to broad features generally characteristic of the entire group. The first broad feature is voluntarism, which places Baptists squarely in the free-church tradition. Membership is by choice; creeds are to emerge from below and not to be handed down from above; covenants are ideally arrived at by the local congregations and periodically revised; and worship follows no fixed form, without service books or a canon of prayers. That voluntarism also sees its integrity and spontaneity as fatally compromised whenever the state intrudes into the realm of religious conscience. Voluntarism has its weaker side in becoming the passive reflection of a surrounding culture, in surrendering slowly and unthinkingly to what one author has called the "cultural captivity of the churches" (Eighmy, 1972). The second broad feature is Pietism, which places its first priority on the personal and direct encounter with God. Such individualism protects against an autocratic or coldly impersonal structure, but it can also lead to a chaotic splintering where, as Ralph Waldo Emerson (1803–1882) said, every man is his own church. Pietism ensures a zeal; it does not always carry with it a corresponding bounty of knowledge and public responsibility.

The Baptist movement's third broad feature is evangelism, which in some times and places has been seen as the totality of the Baptist effort. Special classes and techniques in "soul winning" have been developed, and the revival meeting became standard fare in most Baptist churches, whether large or small, urban or rural. This evangelistic emphasis has also been responsible for a heavy investment in missions, both at home and abroad. In the opening of the American West, such men as Isaac McCoy (1784–1846) and John Mason Peck (1789–1858) played major roles. Abroad, the path cut in the early nineteenth century by Adoniram Judson (1788–1850) and Luther Rice (1783–1836) was traveled by thousands, both male and female, in succeeding decades. Yet there is also a strong antimission strain in Baptist history, institutionalized in several Primitive Baptist bodies, both black and white.

The fourth broad feature is sectarianism, which has kept most Baptists on the fringes of the ecumenical movement. The transition from sect to denomination is uneven and to some degree unpredictable. A mid-nineteenth-century movement known as Landmarkism represents the sectarian extreme; it held that true Baptist churches have existed from the apostolic age and only the true local church has a valid ministry, valid sacraments, and biblical authenticity. The American Baptist Association, with about one million members in the 1980s, constitutes the contemporary manifestation of a sectarianism that rejects all ecumenical endeavors, is strongly suspicious of Roman Catholicism, and deeply resents those Baptist churches that behave in a more "denominational" way.

SEE ALSO Anabaptism; Williams, Roger.

BIBLIOGRAPHY

Two books on English Baptists that provide not only good historical background but excellent insight into contemporary life and thought are H. Wheeler Robinson's *The Life and Faith of the Baptists,* rev. ed. (London, 1946), and Ernest A. Payne's *The Fellowship of Believers: Baptist Thought and Practice Yesterday and Today,* rev. ed. (London, 1952). These two works have been reprinted together under the title *British Baptists* (New York, 1980). A worldview is provided in Bill J. Leonard's *Baptist Ways: A History* (Valley Forge, Pa., 2003), whereas Samuel S. Hill Jr. and Robert G. Torbet reviewed the American scene in *Baptists North and South* (Valley Forge, Pa., 1964). On the Southern Baptist Convention specifically, see Jesse C. Fletcher, *The Southern Baptist Convention* (Nashville, Tenn., 1994). Two works on Baptist development in early America made giant historiographical strides over most previous efforts. William G. McLoughlin's *New England Dissent, 1630–1833,* 2 vols. (Cambridge, Mass., 1971), and C. C. Goen's *Revivalism and Separatism in New England, 1740–1800* (New Haven, Conn., 1962). Finally, for an informed view of alternative ecclesiological styles among Baptists, see Winthrop Still Hudson, ed., *Baptist Concepts of the Church* (Chicago, 1959).

Other sources cited in the article include John Lee Eighmy, *Churches in Cultural Captivity: A History of the Social Attitudes of Southern Baptists* (Knoxville, Tenn., 1972), and Daniel Featley, *The Dippers Dipt, or the Anabaptists Duck'd and Plung'd over head and eares, at a disputation in Southwark* (London, 1646).

EDWIN S. GAUSTAD (1987)
BILL LEONARD (2005)

BAR AND BAT MITSVAH SEE RITES OF PASSAGE, *ARTICLE ON* JEWISH RITES

BARDAISAN (or Bardesanes) of Edessa (154–222 CE) was a philosopher, an ethnographer, and the first Syriac Christian theologian, later regarded as unorthodox.

Only a few events are known about the life of Bardaisan (Bar Dayṣān, or "son of [the local river] Dayṣān"). He attended the court of the king of Edessa, Abgar VIII (176–211), and probably fled from Edessa to Armenia after Abgar IX was taken prisoner by the Romans in 216. Bardaisan had a son who introduced metrical hymns in Syriac, which were imitated by later Syriac poets. Edessene Christianity of his time did not have a hierarchical structure, but was divided into various groups, such as the Jewish-Christians, the "orthodox" Christian minority, the Gnostics, and the Marcionites, who later came into conflict with Bardaisan and his school.

What can be ascribed to Bardaisan shows his familiarity with both Greek philosophy (Platonism, Stoicism) and Hellenistic astrological and ethnographic culture (works on India and Armenia are mentioned by some sources). In Edessa, Bardaisan founded a circle in which scientific and religious questions were freely debated. Only in the fifth century did Bishop Rabbula succeed in eradicating the Bardesanites from Edessa.

The sources for the doctrines of the Bardesanites include *The Book of the Laws of the Countries,* preserved in Syriac and probably written in that language, and quoted by later Greek authors in an ancient Greek version. This work has the literary form of a dialogue between Bardaisan and his disciples and deals with the relation between free will and fate. In the dialogue, Bardaisan declares that two factors affect human life: (1) nature *(kyānā),* namely, the natural constitution (to be born, grow up, procreate, grow old, and die); and (2) fate *(ḥelqā);* that is, the accidents that can either reinforce or oppose the natural constitution (e.g., wealth, poverty, illness). Humans, whose bodies undergo the influence of both nature and fate, in their quality of God's images are provided with free will *(ḥērūtā),* which is placed in the intellect—a conception in which Jewish and Christian elements are mingled with Aristotelian philosophy. To prove this assumption, Bardaisan delivers a speech, well known in late antiquity, where, by describing the customs and the laws of different peoples (including Jews and Christians), he shows their independence from fate. The last sentences indicate that fate and its elements are part of the order imposed by God after a crisis that took place among the original entities.

The Bardesanite sources also include the antiheretical works of Ephraem of Syria (306–373); that is, *Prose Refutations* and *Hymns against Heresies,* to be compared with four cosmogonic traditions, preserved by Syriac authors from the sixth to the tenth centuries, describing the Bardesanite doctrine of the origin of the world. According to these sources, from eternity there are four entities *(ītyē)*—light, wind, fire, and water—in a wandering state (*Gn.* 1:2). Some disciples of Bardaisan maintain the atomic nature of the entities. God resides over the entities as their lord; darkness underlies them. For a reason independent from God—either the breath of the wind or an accidental *(šegmā)* event *(gedšā)*—the entities begin to damage each other. Darkness arises, partially defiling the entities. The "word of thought" *(mēmrā d-tarʿītā),* corresponding to the middle Platonic and Stoic logos (or, according to Bardaisan's disciples, a set of three kinds of spiritual atoms), is sent by God to separate darkness from the entities. From what is still defiled, the logos establishes the world in such a way as to be progressively purified. Ephraem mentions the "diffusion of life," which apparently is a spiritual element, whose connections with the logos are not clear. He reports that, according to Bardaisan, the human body is created by the archons of fate and is destined to dissolution—the soul is a corporeal but light element, whereas the intellect is a fragment of the divinity. The resurrection is therefore spiritual. Before the coming of the savior, human souls were imprisoned in the astrological regions because of Adam's sin; afterward, only pure souls and intellects can reach God.

Ephraem's *Hymn against Heresies* 55 quotes Bardesanite verses mentioning the following Gnostic figures: the father and the mother of life (compared to, or identified with, the sun and the moon), who beget (through sexual union) the son of life as well as two female figures—the holy spirit and the youthful spirit. The youthful spirit, who is destined for a wedding feast, calls upon God in the words pronounced by Christ on the cross (*Mt.* 27:46). The father of life and the mother of life also beget the paradise and several astrological entities.

Later heresiological accounts, written in Syriac and Arabic by Christian and Muslim authors, testify to the reduction of Bardesanite doctrine to a strict dualism similar to Manichaean dualism. These sources also report Bardesanite mythology and a theory of seven atomic entities, which are also mentioned by Ephraem.

Although the astrological and mythological aspects of Bardesanite thought influenced the culture of such later dissident groups as the Audians (fourth century) and the Sabians of Ḥarran (sixth century onward), Manichaeism appears to be more sensitive to Bardaisan's theological speculations. Mani's (216–273) lost work *The Book of Mysteries* was directed against Bardaisan's ideas about the human soul. Other differences can also be detected between Bardaisan and Mani. For Bardaisan, for example, darkness is not an active principle, as it is for Mani, and Bardesanite anthropology is apparently more optimistic than Manichaean anthropology. However, a partial reception of Bardesanite ideas by Mani seems certain, and includes the three periods of cosmic history (the original situation, crisis and mixing, and final separation), the formation of the world as an instrument of purification, and the two couples, the father and mother of life and the sun and moon.

There are two main controversial issues about Bardesanite doctrines: (1) the ideological unity of Bardesanite texts; and (2) their relationship with the Gnostic family. Some scholars, for whom *The Book of the Laws of the Countries* reflects Bardaisan's own ideas, maintain the ideological unity of all Bardesanite texts (despite differences of language) and deny their Gnostic character. Others, disqualifying the authenticity of the dialogue as a document of Bardaisan and regarding it as a late and catholicizing product, interpret the other fragments as a clear witness to Bardaisan's close proximity to Gnosticism. A possible third interpretation sees Bardesanite texts as the product of different authors who support in varying ways an anti-Marcionite theology adverse to systems that divide God the creator too sharply from God the savior, based on the assumption that the original crisis took place not within God, but within a distinct principle (the entities) subordinated to him.

SEE ALSO Ephraem of Syria; Gnosticism; Mani; Marcion.

BIBLIOGRAPHY

The standard reference book about Bardaisan, his life, his school, and his writings, with a listing of the essential editions of the sources, is Han J. W. Drijvers, *Bardaiṣan of Edessa* (Assen, Netherlands, 1966). On the Syriac sources see Alberto Camplani, "Note bardesanitiche," *Miscellanea marciana* 12 (1997): 11–43. On the Arabic sources see Georges Vajda, "Le témoignage d'al-Māturidī sur la doctrine des Manichéens, des Daysanites, et des Marcionites," *Arabica* 13 (1966): 1–38 and 113–128; and Wilferd Madelung, "Abu 'isa al-Warraq über die Bardesaniten, Marcioniten, und Kantäer" in *Studien zur Geschichte und Kultur des vorderen Oriens: Festschrift für Bertold Spuler,* edited by Hans R. Roemer and Albrecht Noth, pp. 210–224 (Leiden, 1981). On Porphyrius's Greek quotations from a work on Indian customs, see Franz Winter, *Bardesanes von Edessa über Indien: Ein früher syrischer Theologe schreibt über ein fremdes Land* (Innsbruck, 1999). On the philosophical collocation of *The Book of the Laws of the Countries* see Albrecht Dihle, "Zur Schicksalslehre des Bardesanes" in *Kerygma und Logos: Festschrift für Carl Andresen,* edited by Adolf Martin Ritter, pp. 123–135 (Göttingen, Germany, 1979), reprinted in *Antike und Orient: Gesammelte Aufsätze,* edited by Viktor Pöschl and Hubert Petersmann, pp. 161–173 (Heidelberg, Germany, 1984).

For a general presentation of the critical debate on Bardesanite thought, see Alberto Camplani, "Rivisitando Bardesane: Note sulle fonti siriache del bardesanismo e sulla sua collocazione storico-religiosa," *Cristianesimo nella Storia* 19 (1998): 519–596. Representatives of the unitarian and antidualistic interpretation of Bardesanite texts, apart from Han J. W. Drijvers, include Edmund Beck, "Bardaisan und seine Schule bei Ephräm," *Le Muséon* 91 (1978): 271–333; and Javier Teixidor, *Bardesane d'Edesse: La première philosophie syriaque* (Paris, 1992). Representatives of the Gnostic interpretation include the following scholars: Taeke Jansma, *Natuur, lot en vrijheid: Bardesanes, de filosoof der Arameeër en zijn images* (Wageningen, Netherlands, 1969); Barbara Aland-Ehlers, "Bardesanes von Edessa—ein syrische Gnostiker," *Zeitschrift für Kirchengeschichte* 81 (1970): 334–351; and Prod O. Skjærvø, "Bardesanes" in *Encyclopaedia Iranica,* edited by Ehsan Yarshater, vol. 3, pp. 780–785 (London and New York, 1989).

ALBERTO CAMPLANI **(2005)**

BARDESANES SEE BARDAISAN

BAR-ILAN, ME'IR (1880–1949), born Me'ir Berlin; one of the foremost leaders of the religious Zionist movement Mizraḥi. A native of Volozhin, Russia, he was the son of Naftali Berlin, the head of the famous Volozhin *yeshivah* (rabbinic academy). Bar-Ilan joined the religious Zionist movement and attended many Zionist congresses from 1905 onward. In 1911, he became the secretary of the Mizraḥi movement and moved to Berlin. In 1915, he immigrated to the United States, and in 1925 he settled in Jerusalem, where he remained until his death.

As the Mizraḥi representative, Bar-Ilan held many important positions in the Zionist movement before the creation of the State of Israel. He edited the religious Zionist Hebrew weekly *Ha-ʿIvri* from 1910 through 1921 and was editor in chief of the Tel Aviv daily *Ha-tsofeh* from 1938 to 1949.

In both his political activities and his writings, Bar-Ilan tried to create a central role for Orthodox Jews in Jewish nationalism. He rejected the notion of separation of synagogue and state, but he also rejected the more extreme religious arguments against any cooperation with the secular nationalists. He argued for inculcation of traditional religious values through the educational system. He believed that only by education, not by coercion, could the Orthodox win the struggle with the secularists over the final status of religion in the Jewish state. His position can be summed up in the Mizraḥi slogan that he coined: "The Land of Israel for the people of Israel according to the Torah [God's law] of Israel."

Bar-Ilan's position on the relationship between religion and state in Israel remains substantially that of the present religious Zionist party, the Mafdal (National Religious Party). The Bar-Ilan University near Tel Aviv, which was founded in 1955 to wed traditional Jewish learning with modern academic scholarship, was named after him.

Bibliography

In addition to Zvi Kaplan's article on Bar-Ilan in *Encyclopaedia Judaica* (Jerusalem, 1971), further biographical information can be found in Moshe Krone's *Ha-Rav Me'ir Bar-Ilan* (Jerusalem, 1954) and in *The Zionist Idea,* edited by Arthur Hertzberg (Philadelphia, 1959), pp. 546–555.

New Sources

Shemesh, David. *Ha-Rav Me'ir Bar-Ilan: demuto shel manhig.* Jerusalem, 1979.

David Biale (1987)
Revised Bibliography

BARLAAM OF CALABRIA (c. 1290–c. 1350), humanist, philologist, and theologian; one of the forerunners of the Renaissance. Barlaam was born in Seminara commune, Calabria, a Greek by ethnic descent and language, and a member of the religious groups that still preserved the memory of their Orthodox Christian past in southern Italy. With the passage of time the inhabitants of the region were obliged to submit to Rome, but they felt themselves to be Orthodox as a result of their long tradition. The religious duality of the Greek communities of southern Italy explains the oscillation in Barlaam's advocacy of the two competing traditions. He was possessed of a sentimental love of Orthodoxy on account of his Greek ancestry, but as a theologian and philosopher, he was influenced by Western Scholasticism.

In 1326, traveling from Italy to the Greek peninsula, Barlaam doffed the clothes of a Western monk and put on Greek monastic dress. He stayed in Thessalonica several years and strengthened his reputation as a philosopher. Barlaam later settled in Constantinople, where he soon gained the confidence of ecclesiastical and political circles, especially of the emperor Andronicus III Palaeologus, who gave him a professorial chair at the university. No one had any doubts about the sincerity of his Orthodox convictions. He was made abbot of the Monastery of Our Savior, and two confidential missions on behalf of the emperor were entrusted to him. During the years 1333–1334, Barlaam undertook to negotiate the union of churches with the representatives of Pope John XXII. For this occasion he wrote twenty-one treatises against the Latins in which he opposed papal primacy and the *filioque* doctrine. In 1379, he was sent to the exiled Pope Benedict XII at Avignon to suggest a crusade against the Turks and to discuss the union of churches, but he was not successful.

A reaction against Barlaam was not late in coming on both the philosophical and theological fronts. In a public discussion with Nikephoros Grigoros, Barlaam was defeated. More serious was his defeat in the area of theology by the spiritual leader Gregory Palamas. Because of his Western theological presuppositions, Barlaam was not able to understand the mystical-ascetical tradition of the East, and therefore he criticized it, with the result that he was condemned in Constantinople at the synod of 1341, and both he and his followers were formally anathematized there at the synods of 1347 and 1351. After his condemnation, he returned to the West and adhered to Roman Catholicism; he was subsequently ordained a bishop by the pope, a fact that was interpreted in the East as a confirmation of the suspect role he had played in the ranks of the Greek church.

Barlaam's theological works include eighteen anti-Latin treatises, antihesychastic writings (*On Light, On Knowledge,* and *Against the Messalians,* all of which are lost), and treatises and letters supporting Western theology such as *Advisory Discourse* and the draft of the *Discourse to Pope Benedict XII.* In his antihesychastic works Barlaam held that knowledge of worldly wisdom was necessary for the perfection of the monks and denied the possibility of the vision of the divine life. In addition to theological works, Barlaam also composed philosophical, astronomical, and mathematical works. Among these are his *Ethics according to the Stoics,* a treatise on calculating the eclipses of the sun, six books on arithmetic, and a paraphrase of the second book of Euclid's *Elements.*

A product of both East and West, Barlaam influenced the culture of both. Petrarch and Boccaccio were his pupils, and there is no doubt that he contributed to the strengthening of the current that led to the Italian Renaissance. On the other hand, Barlaam's interest in the hesychast dispute resulted in the development of a lively theological movement in the fourteenth century in Constantinople and Thessalonica. One of its consequences was the formulation of the mystical-ascetical teaching of the Orthodox church by Gregory Palamas.

Barlaam overestimated the significance of philosophy (especially of Greek philosophy) for theology, asserting that only through philosophy could humanity arrive at perfection. He thus denied the renewing power of the Holy Spirit, which makes saints even out of uneducated people, as it made the fishermen apostles. Being a humanist, Barlaam placed emphasis on created means of salvation (e.g., philosophy and knowledge) and reduced the role of the grace of the Holy Spirit.

BIBLIOGRAPHY

Works by Barlaam

Giannelli, Ciro. "Un progetto di Barlaam per l'unione delle chiese." In *Miscellanea Giovanni Mercati*, vol. 3, "Studi e Testi," no. 123. Vatican City, 1946. See pages 157–208 for excerpts from his writings.

Migne, J.-P., ed. *Patrologia Graeca*, vol. 151. Paris, 1857. Includes excerpts from the *Discourse to Pope Benedict XII* and the *Advisory Discourse*.

Schiro, Giuseppe, ed. *Barlaam Calabro: Epistole greche*. Palermo, 1954.

Works about Barlaam

Christou, Panagiotis C. "Barlaam." In *Threskeutikē kai ēthikē enkuklopaideia*, vol. 3, cols. 624–627. Athens, 1963.

Jugie, Martin. "Barlaam de Seminara." In *Dictionnaire d'histoire et de géographie ecclésiastiques*, vol. 6, cols. 817–834. Paris, 1932.

Meyendorff, John. "Un mauvais théologien de l'unité au quatorzième siècle: Barlaam le Calabrais." In *L'église et les églises, 1054–1954*, vol. 2, pp. 47–65. Chevetogne, 1955.

THEODORE ZISSIS (1987)
Translated from Greek by Philip M. McGhee

BARTH, KARL (1886–1968), Swiss Reformed theologian, described by Pope Pius XII as the greatest theologian since Thomas Aquinas, and certainly the most influential of the twentieth century. Barth stands as a prophetic voice in the tradition of Athanasius, Augustine, and Calvin, calling the Christian church back to the Bible and to its foundation in Jesus Christ. This message sounded forth powerfully in his first book, *Romans* (especially in the largely rewritten second edition of 1921), which drew widespread attention. Barth later said that in writing this book he was like a man in a dark church tower who accidentally trips, catches hold of the bell rope to steady himself, and alarms the whole countryside. As a result, he was called to university chairs in Göttingen (1921), in Münster (1925), and in Bonn (1930). From this latter post he was dismissed in 1935 because of his refusal to take an oath of loyalty to Hitler and because of his leading role in the *Kirchenkampf*, the struggle against the Nazi attempt to control the German Evangelical church. He returned to his native Switzerland to a professorship in Basel, where he taught for the rest of his long life until his death in 1968, drawing students from all over the world to his classrooms and publishing his lectures in his massive *Church Dogmatics*.

Barth was born in Basel on May 10, 1886, the son of Fritz Barth, a professor of church history and New Testament in Bern. In Bern Barth received his earliest education, and there, on the eve of his confirmation, he "boldly resolved to become a theologian" out of an early eagerness to understand his faith and see its relevance for the twentieth century. He commenced his university studies in Bern, where, while receiving a solid grounding in Reformed theology, he began to study the theoretical and practical philosophy of Immanual Kant, whose "Copernican revolution" in the theory of knowledge and ethics awakened Barth to an acute awareness of the question of our knowledge and service of God. At the same time he developed his early and lifelong interest in the theologian Friedrich Schleiermacher, whose analysis of religious experience and desire to commend religion to its "cultured despisers" had dominated German theology since his death in 1834. Like Schleiermacher, Barth was later to interpret Christian dogmatics as the function of the Christian church, scrutinizing scientifically the content of the Christian faith, but unlike Schleiermacher he saw, not religious experience in general, but the revelation of God in Jesus Christ, attested in holy scripture, as the criterion of truth.

Barth expressed a desire to study at Marburg with Wilhelm Herrmann (1846–1922), the leading Kantian theologian in Europe, but under his father's influence he went first to Berlin to spend a semester under Adolf von Harnack, the most outstanding church historian and liberal theologian of the day, before returning to complete a third year in Bern. In 1907 he enrolled in Tübingen to study under the conservative New Testament theologian Adolf Schlatter, before spending a final year in Marburg. Herrmann defined faith in terms of "inner experience" which has its "ground" in the "inner life of Jesus" and is awakened in man's conscience by the influence of Jesus, the so-called Jesus of history of the nineteenth-century liberal quest. Although influenced by Herrmann, Barth came to feel that his conception conflicted with the New Testament and Reformed understanding of the Christ of faith and with the church's creeds, and that it was more the product of modern individualistic bourgeois liberal idealism and Kantian philosophy than of sound New Testament scholarship. He also felt that the very nature and possibility of a scientific approach to Christian theology was being called into question by the philosophical and historical presuppositions of the "culture-Protestantism" of the day, wherein theology and relativizing historicism, religion, and culture were fused, obscuring the gospel through "reverence before history" and reducing Christian theology to a branch of the general philosophy of religion.

These questions assumed acute importance for Barth once he was ordained to the pastoral ministry and sought to take seriously the exposition of the Bible and the preaching of the gospel, while also taking full account of critical biblical scholarship. It was during his time as a pastor in Safenwil, Switzerland (1911–1921), that his theological position underwent a drastic change. On the one hand, when World War I broke out, he was deeply disturbed by the "Manifesto of the Intellectuals," "the black day" he called it, when ninety-three scholars and artists, including his own teachers Harnack and Herrmann, supported the war policy of Kaiser Wilhelm II, which seemed to him to call into question his colleagues' understanding of the Bible, history, and dogmatics. Was this where the synthesis of (German) culture and religion was leading the Christian church? On the other hand, in his industrial parish, he became acutely aware of the issues of social justice, poor wages, factory legislation, and trade union affairs. In 1915 he became a member of the Social Democratic party, but unlike his Christian Socialist friends, he refused to identify socialism with the kingdom of God.

Throughout his life Barth endeavored to interpret the gospel and examine the church's message in the context of society, the state, war, revolution, totalitarianism, and democracy, over against the pretensions of man to solve the problems of his own destiny, without the judgment of the message of the cross and the resurrection of Jesus Christ. Toward the end of his life he could write, "I decided for theology, because I felt a need to find a better basis for my social action." The fundamental question was how to relate what the Word of God in the Bible says about the sovereignty and transcendence of God, grace, the coming of the Kingdom, the forgiveness of sins, and the resurrection of the dead with human problems. Barth voiced his concern over the bankruptcy of much contemporary religion and theology in his commentary on *Romans* (*Der Römerbrief*, 1919), where the influence of Kierkegaard, Dostoevskii, Franz Overbeck, Johann Christian Blumhardt, and Christoph Blumhardt in their attacks on institutionalized Christianity is evident. In this book, which was described by a Roman Catholic theologian as "a bombshell in the playground of the theologians," Barth seeks to summon the church back to the living God of the Bible, before whom are exposed the pretensions of human religion or piety, the proud sinful attempts to assert oneself without God. Salvation is God's gift, and the Kingdom must break in "vertically from above," summoning humankind to radical response and decision, that God's righteous purposes might be fulfilled in the world.

Barth used Paul's letter to the Romans for a critique of philosophical idealism, romanticism, and religious socialism. If his concern was that the church should listen to the divine word of judgment on our political and intellectual towers of Babel, his concern throughout his life was also to assert "that there is joy with God . . . and that the Kingdom on earth begins with joy." Together with his lifelong friend Eduard Thurneysen (1888–1974), he discovered in the Bible "a strange new world, the world of God," which is the kingdom of God, established by God and not man. Like Luther, he was gripped by the Pauline message of the righteousness of God, which calls into question all human righteousness.

Only by listening to the Word of God and recognizing God's prior righteousness can we regain a proper foundation for culture, morality, state, and church. Theologically this means we must ground Christian dogmatics in the Word of God and seek to interpret God out of God, as he reveals himself in Christ in the scriptures, and not subsume him under our prior generic concepts, categories, and ideologies. The task of theology is to allow revelation to shine in its own light. The inner meaning of the resurrection of Christ, who as creator and redeemer is lord over all, is not just a word of hope for the future, but the action of God in vindicating his righteous purposes in history and giving us a pledge of the triumph of God's righteousness in the world. Far from belittling the need for social action, the resurrection, as God's act in establishing the Kingdom, should be for us a summons to participate in this event and engage in social action with a passion for God's righteousness. There must be no divorce between justification and justice.

There were distinctive stages in Barth's theological development, in each of which he wrestled with the polarities of God and man. Nineteenth-century liberal thought too readily presupposed an inward continuity between the divine and the "highest" and "best" in human culture, positing that knowledge of God is given in the depths of the human spirit in human self-understanding and inward religious experience. Barth rejected this view early in his ministry, saying that we do not talk about God by "talking about man in a loud voice." At first, like Herrmann, he identified conscience with the voice of God, but increasingly he argued that the voice of God is heard only in scripture, in encounter with Christ, the living Word. During the period of the so-called dialectical theology or theology of crisis, stemming from the second edition of Barth's *Romans*, and under the influence of Kierkegaard's critique of Hegel, Barth stressed "the infinite qualitative difference between God and man." God meets us in the moment of crisis and decision, creating his own point of contact and summoning us to radical obedience. As he wrote in his preface, "If I have a system, it is limited to a recognition of what Kierkegaard called the 'infinite qualitative distinction' between time and eternity and to my regarding this as possessing negative as well as positive significance: 'God is in heaven, and thou art on earth'" (Barth, 1933, p. 10).

The chasm between God and man can be bridged by God alone, and not by man. The Word of the cross means that God says no to our human sin and pride and pretensions, while in grace God says yes to his own good creatures in a word of forgiveness. If in this early period Barth, like the early Luther, stressed God's "no" (i.e., God's righteousness as God), his later message, like that of the later Luther, became more powerfully a "yes": God's righteousness as a triumph of grace through the vicarious humanity of Jesus Christ. In the manner of the great medieval theologians, Barth saw that there are elements of negation and affirmation in all human knowledge of God, leading him to see an analogy of "relation," but not of "being," between God and man grounded in grace.

In 1927 Barth began writing *Christian Dogmatics*, intending to expound all the main Christian doctrines, by grounding all he had to say on God's self-revelation in Jesus Christ. The first volume was entitled *Christian Doctrine in Outline, Volume I: The Doctrine of the Word of God, Prolegomena to Christian Dogmatics*. In it he argues that possibility of Christian knowledge of God is grounded on the actuality of the revelation in Jesus, as he makes himself known to faith by the Holy Spirit. Such a revelation is trinitarian in character, having a triadic pattern. God makes himself known as Father in Jesus Christ the Son, and to us by the Holy Spirit. The doctrine of the Trinity thus unfolds from the fact that "God reveals himself as the Lord." As such, this doctrine is the starting point and grammar for all Christian knowledge of God, and not merely an appendix, as in Schleiermacher.

Within this self-revelation of the triune God we can distinguish three forms of the one Word of God: the eternal Word incarnate in Jesus Christ, the written Word in the witness of the Bible to that primary Word, and the Word of God as proclaimed in the church. The task of Christian dogmatics is to be faithful to this Word, and therefore to examine the content of the church's preaching by tracing it back to its source in God, by the standard of holy scripture, and under the guidance of its creeds and confessions.

The reviewers of this first volume criticized Barth for so casting the gospel into the language of an immediate timeless encounter with God that he was in danger of dehistoricizing the gospel and transposing theology into a new philosophical mold. Barth took this criticism seriously, having himself seen this development of dialectical theology in Rudolf Bultmann, and gave himself to examining the question of method in theology by a careful study of Anselm's *Proslogion*. In 1931 he published his results in *Fide quaerens intellectum* (Faith seeking understanding). From Anselm he had learned that the Word of God has its own rational content in God. The polarity of God and man must be interpreted, not so much in the language of an existential encounter between God and man in the crisis of faith, but primarily in terms of the given unity of God and man in Jesus Christ, the incarnate Lord, in whom God has come—not simply *in* a man, but *as* a man—in a once and for all reconciling act in which we are called to participate through the Holy Spirit.

Barth's approach in the future was to build all theology on the reality of the Word of God in Jesus Christ. This led him to turn from his *Christian Dogmatics* to a new work entitled *Church Dogmatics*, which he began in 1932 and which occupied him for the rest of his life (resulting in thirteen part-volumes). In *Church Dogmatics* he argues that all we know and say about God and about humankind is controlled by our knowledge of Jesus Christ as "true God and true man." From this dogmatic starting point, Barth expounds the four intersecting areas of Christian doctrine: the doctrine of the Word of God (vol. 1), of God (vol. 2), of creation (vol. 3), and of reconciliation (vol. 4). (A fifth volume, dealing with redemption [eschatology], remained unwritten at the time of his death.) Each of these doctrines is expounded in a trinitarian framework in terms of a double movement, a God-manward movement and a man-Godward movement in Jesus Christ, revealing a bipolarity in every doctrine. Fundamental to his whole theology is the axiom by which the ancient church expounded the doctrine of an "ontological Trinity," that what God is toward us in Jesus Christ, he is "eternally and antecedently in himself." By looking at Jesus Christ through the Holy Spirit, we know the heart of the eternal Father. In Jesus Christ we see the inner meaning of creation as well as of redemption, for Christ is the one by whom and for whom all things were created, and in redemption we see brought to fulfillment God's filial purposes for the whole human race. Consequently, our anthropology as well as our theology must be built on this christological foundation, not on any "natural theology," on any independent concept of "orders of creation," or on any purely empirical concept of man.

Barth was concerned to unpack the implications of this Christ-centered perspective in every area of life. It proved highly significant in his outspoken opposition to Hitler, to the persecution of the Jews, and to the so-called German Christians who sought to justify National Socialism and its racist policies by an appeal to the natural orders of creation. Barth felt that this was a betrayal of the Christian understanding of grace by its appeal to sources of revelation other than that given to us in Jesus Christ. God's election of Israel for a vicarious role among the nations finds its fulfillment in Jesus Christ, the Jew in whom God has broken down the barriers between the Jews and all other ethnic groups (the gentiles). Christ as Lord is head over church and state, and to him alone we owe supreme loyalty in both spheres. The state must be interpreted not just in terms of the orders of creation and preservation (as he had earlier thought), but in terms of the orders of redemption. This found explicit formulation in the *Barmen Declaration* of 1934, largely written by Barth. For this stand he was deprived of his university chair in Bonn, but his theological insights and interpretation of the political scene gained him enormous prestige. Barth saw himself standing in the tradition of the ancient fathers of the church like Irenaeus and Athanasius, and of the Protestant reformers like Luther and Calvin, engaging in lifelong dialogue with liberal Protestantism on the left and Roman Catholicism on the right, both of which he felt weakened the emphasis of the Bible that God accepts us by grace alone in Jesus Christ.

BIBLIOGRAPHY

The best and most authoritative biography is Eberhard Busch's *Karl Barth: His Life from Letters and Autobiographical Texts* (London, 1976). On the early period of the so-called dialectical theology, the most influential work was Barth's *The Epistle to the Romans*, translated by Sir Edwyn C. Hoskyns (Oxford, 1933). The significance of this work is discussed in Thomas F. Torrance's *Karl Barth: An Introduction to His Early Theology, 1910–1931* (London, 1962). Barth's *Protestant Theology in the Nineteenth Century*, translated by Brian Cozens and John Bowden (Valley Forge, 1973), is invaluable for understanding his European theological background. The book that marked his transition to the later period of the *Church Dogmatics* is his *Anselm: Fides Quaerens Intellectum; Anselm's Proof of the Existence of God*, translated by I. W. Robertson (Richmond, 1960). In the Gifford Lectures given in Aberdeen, Barth expounded the 1560 Scots Confession in *The Knowledge of God and the Service of God*, translated by J. L. M. Haire and Ian Henderson (London, 1938). His massive exposition of Christian doctrine is set out in *Church Dogmatics*, 4 vols., edited by Geoffrey W. Bromiley and Thomas F. Torrance (Edinburgh, 1956–1969). Very readable is Barth's short *Evangelical Theology*, translated by Grover Foley (New York, 1963).

JAMES B. TORRANCE (1987)

BASILICA, CATHEDRAL, AND CHURCH.

[*This entry focuses specifically on Christian houses of worship.*]

Over the centuries Christians have employed different terms to denominate their religious buildings, and *basilica*, *cathedral*, and *church* are but three of many. The word *church*, deriving ultimately from the Greek *kuriakos* ("of the Lord") designates a building belonging to God and, in a sense, God's dwelling. A church where the bishop's throne (cathedra) is located is called a cathedral, while *basilica* refers to a class of Roman public buildings predating Christianity, particularly those with royal association. In usage the three terms overlap. During the early centuries of the Christian era, a cathedra was placed in a basilica, and it was not until the eighth century that the word *cathedral* itself became current. From the Middle Ages on, the word *church* has been applied to parish churches, but it is also proper to speak of the Cathedral Church of Saint John the Divine (New York City) or of the Holy and Undivided Trinity Church (Bristol, England). The terms themselves provide no clue to the forms that the edifices may take; rather, they are the result of a host of factors, including the need to provide for certain functions as well as stylistic and aesthetic influences, the availability of materials, patronage, and climatic conditions.

ORIGINS: THE HOUSE-CHURCH. The first Christians were Jews who quite naturally continued to attend synagogue and, when possible, the Temple in Jerusalem; in addition, they had their own distinctive celebration which took the form of a meal. Jesus had enjoyed table fellowship with his followers during his ministry, at the last supper, and, so it was reported, after his resurrection. The Lord's Supper, soon to be called the Eucharist, or thanksgiving, was interpreted as a remembrance and renewal of the communion experienced at these gatherings. The only architectural provision required for such a service was a dining room, so Christians in the apostolic age met in private houses: at Ephesus in the home of Aquila and Prisca, at Laodicea in the home of Nymphas, and at Colossae in the home of Philemon. The property concerned would vary from single-family buildings up to four stories high, common in the East, to apartments arranged horizontally as in the tenements of Rome.

In the third century the church took the step of acquiring, either by purchase or by gift, houses of its own, and at Dura-Europos on the Euphrates there is an actual example of a house modified for use by a Christian congregation. Built shortly after the year 200, it underwent alteration in 231, when the room across the courtyard opposite the street was enlarged by knocking down a wall, and a dais was inserted, probably for the bishop's chair. West of the atrium there was a chamber, possibly for the use of catechumens, and by the entrance was another chamber for initiation. The alterations did not affect the character of the house as an example of local domestic architecture or the character of the Eucharist as a domestic event within the family of Christians. It is not surprising therefore, that several writers of the period, such as Minucius Felix and Arnobius, asserted, "We have no temples and no altars." The situation was to change dramatically in the early fourth century.

THE NATURE OF THE BASILICA. The conversion of the Roman emperor Constantine I in the year 313 conferred on Christianity a new role: as the state religion, it was now charged with ensuring the well-being of the empire; its worship, replacing the pagan sacrificial system, was to obtain the divine favor; the preeminence of the ruler was to be recognized and safeguarded; the identity of the populace as citizens of Rome was to be fostered. Christianity, as it were, went public, and the unpretentiousness of the private dining room was out of keeping. Consequently, when Constantine wrote to Bishop Macarius of Jerusalem in 326 or 327 concerning his project of adorning the site of the Holy Sepulcher, he instructed him to build a basilica. This term referred to a type of Roman structure that combined religious overtones with the criteria of an official building; it was a large meeting hall, often containing an effigy of the emperor. The Christian basilica belonged to the same genus: it was a monumental public edifice where devotion to God as emperor of heaven was substituted for the imperial cult.

Initially there was no uniform plan for basilicas, but by the end of the fourth century there were sufficient common features to constitute a recognizable form. Apart from Mesopotamia, where the basilican hall was transverse, one entered through a narrow side into a rectangle, the nave, flanked usually by one aisle on either side. At the opposite end there was a triumphal arch leading to a semicircular apse; at the center back of the apse was the bishop's throne, with seats for the presbyters to the right and left and the altar in front of them framed by a triumphal arch. This interior had all the characteristics of a path. Continuity and directionality were ensured by floor patterns, by the advancing row of columns, and by the succession of windows. The altar at the end of the central axis provided the terminal and goal of what Christians (themselves a pilgrim people) often called the royal highway. Architecturally, then, the Christian basilica was a structure whose walls molded and defined space as a continuum that found its climax in the altar as the center of the eucharistic action. The altar was seen as a symbol of Christ, the mediator between God and man, the meeting place of heaven and earth, so it testified to the historical specificity in time and space of the New Testament revelation.

As centers of the state religion, Christian basilicas replaced the pagan temples and thus acquired the character of holy places that had not been associated with the earlier house-churches. This character was reinforced when, since there was nothing in the New Testament about church buildings, recourse was had to the Old Testament and to the account of the Jerusalem Temple in particular for guidance. Saint Peter's in Rome, for example, would appear to have deliberately followed Solomon's model, not only with part corresponding to part but with the orientation (the apse or Holy of Holies at the west end) and even the proportions identical.

Differences of detail between one basilica and another did not affect the building's essential nature as a sacred area and a path. The apse might protrude, as in the western half of the Mediterranean, or be enclosed to create side chambers, as in the Middle East. The outer walls might be carried up to the level of those of the nave, thus making a clerestory impossible and necessitating windows that opened into the aisles and the apse, as in Asia Minor. A forecourt or atrium was frequent, but it was not indispensable. An external porch might be favored, as in Italy, or incorporated into the structure to create a narthex, where the catechumens had their place, as in Greece. The roof might be steep-pitched, made of wood or stone, even domed. A side chamber for initiation might be provided, as was often the case in North Africa and Palestine, or there could be a detached baptistery adjacent to it, as in France or Austria. No matter what the variations, the basilica met the needs of Christian congregations so well that it was not modified in any important particular for a thousand years and was still the recognizable prototype of the more elaborately planned churches of the later Middle Ages.

CHURCHES OF THE MIDDLE AGES IN THE WEST. Two factors above all had striking effects on architecture in the Middle Ages: a growing distinction between priests and laity and the definition of the essential role of the priests to be that of offering the sacrifice of the Mass. During the patristic period up to about 1000 CE, the place of the clergy had been demarcated by low balustrades or chancelli, but by the Middle Ages these had developed into chancel screens that virtually shut the priest off from the congregation. Indeed, by that time many churches consisted of two rooms, as the sanctuary became a chamber separate from the nave. The altar ceased to be freestanding, and the celebrant stood with his back to the body of the church. If there were more than one priest, additional altars and side chapels were introduced: there was no longer one altar, as had been the case in the basilica. For larger churches and cathedrals, there were additional factors at work.

Cathedrals. By the Middle Ages, parish churches ceased to have a bishop's throne, and even cathedrals no longer gave it prominence—as the high altar was no longer freestanding, the cathedra was pushed to one side. A large number of cathedrals were under the direction of monks, for whom a fenced-off choir was fitted into the building for the saying of the divine office. A self-contained unit constituting an independent place was thus inserted into a system of paths. Since many of the religious were ordained, the need for extra altars for each priest to celebrate the daily Mass was more pronounced than in the parish church, and an abundance of small chapels was created. This multiplication of altars was also encouraged by the practice of celebrating votive masses (masses offered with special intentions), culminating in the chantry chapels, which were separate structures endowed for masses on behalf of the dead. Some chapels opened off transepts, others radiated from the ambulatory encircling the east end. This later arrangement, known as the chevet, was also the outcome of two other influences: pilgrimages and the cults of the saints. Attention had to be given to the location and means of housing the sacred relics and to the circulation space necessary for the crowds who came to honor them. Some relics were enshrined within the altars, some in crypts; the ambulatory facilitated movement, as did galleries, and consequently many pilgrimage centers, such as Santiago de Compostela, present a much more complex plan than that of the basilica. In elevation, too, there were differences, largely the outcome of stylistic change.

Romanesque, Gothic, and Renaissance. Although adapted for Christian use, the early Christian basilica is best categorized as an example of Roman architecture, apart from the virtual neglect of the potentialities of the original Roman vault: the walls and ceiling had a space-shaping function producing a carefully proportioned interior that was an uninterrupted continuum of flowing space. After the year 1000, something essentially new in church design emerged when the vault came into its own. The vault had three effects: it determined the shape and form of the supports, which had to be much larger than the columns of the basilica because the burden was greater; it united ceiling and walls; and it created a series of bays, that is, individual spatial units. This last feature of the Romanesque style attenuated the west-to-east drive. The whole remained a path or system of paths, but it now constituted a place in itself; a focus for gathering with a character of its own. It declared that instead of advancing to meet God—the message of the basilica—the faithful live in God and are embraced by God.

The nature of the Gothic style, which succeeded Romanesque particularly in England, France, and Germany from the mid-twelfth to the early fifteenth century, was similarly determined by the vault, but now the round Roman arch was replaced by a pointed one, derived possibly from mosque architecture, familiar through the Crusades and the reconquest of Spain from the Muslims, and adopted for aesthetic reasons rather than, as nineteenth-century art historians believed, for its structural convenience. The pointed arch and the corresponding crisscrossing ribs turned the vault into a composition of triangles and diamonds; diagonality became prominent. The effect was to turn the supports into two juxtaposed V's, one jutting out into the nave and the other into the aisle, so replacing the flatness of Romanesque with projection. Verticality became the predominating factor, but this heavenward movement was balanced by a horizontal progression in that the bays were no longer independent but interlocked, and the nave became a way from expectancy to fulfillment. Every Gothic church or cathedral corresponded in a sense with one of the greatest literary creations of the age, namely the *Commedia* of Dante, who recounted how he was led ever onward and upward to the beatific vision.

A further stylistic change took place at the beginning of the fifteenth century with a rebirth of classical culture. This development derived from a careful study of the writings and ruins of ancient Rome, coupled with an imaginative recreation of that past era as a "golden age" in which consolation and refreshment could be sought. The entire Roman architectural vocabulary was pressed into service to articulate the walls and later the three-dimensional shapes of the buildings. There was an overriding concern for proportion and harmony. The intention was to make churches to human scale because human beings are in the image of God, to create an architecture in which they could move naturally. Hence the change from the dominating verticality of the Gothic style to horizontality. There was no longer the propulsion of the early Christian drive to the east or the slow progression of Romanesque bays. In a Renaissance church one is at ease because one is the measure of it all. There is peace and serenity since the whole is a single self-contained hall; there is minimal movement, and the church is best perceived as a place, concentrated in form, reality comprehensible in shape, limited in size, a focus for assembly and quite evidently to be experienced as an interior volume, in contrast to a surrounding exterior. These characteristics of place apply even more precisely to the churches of Eastern Orthodoxy.

THE CHURCHES OF EASTERN ORTHODOXY. For the first flowering of the Byzantine style, from which all later Orthodox buildings derive, it is necessary to return to the sixth century, when there was a decisive break with the basilican tradition. Just as later the combination of the Roman groin vault with the basilica was to produce the Romanesque church, under the emperor Justinian (527–565) it was the alternative form of Roman vault, the dome, that became favored in the East. Ideologically the dome was perceived as a symbol of heaven and so was regarded as suitable for tombs, baptisteries, and martyria. When the cult of the saints came to the parish churches, the dome came with it, and preference was given to a centralized plan constructed according to the baldachin principle. A baldachin, or ciborium, is a dome carried on four columns. No load-bearing walls are needed between these four columns, and so the spaces can be perforated, replaced by columnar screens, or simply eliminated, reducing the enveloping system to a mere skin stretched on a skeleton. Churches of this type are planned from the top downward, that is, the lower parts exist simply for the dome and would be meaningless without it. The general effect is that of a hanging architecture: the vault has no apparent weight of its own; the columns are conceived not as supports but as pendulous roots; the space radiates downward. Heaven, represented by the dome, condescends to earth, which corresponds to the flat pavement: incarnation is given architectural expression. But this is incarnation understood not in the sense of the divine veiled in human flesh but in the sense of the material transfigured, because in and through it the divine is made visible. The mosaics, which ideally should clothe every surface within a Byzantine church, as in Saint Mark's in Venice, affirm this transfiguration: while remaining themselves, the natural substances become spirit-bearing; the material reality is integrated with the divine life that pours down from above, and glory is made visible.

While the dome was the characteristic feature of such churches, there was some variety in substructure, but the most popular became a quincunx. This is divided into nine bays, with a central large square dominated by the principal dome. This domed square is abutted by four rectangular bays that are usually barrel-vaulted, and at each of the four corners there is a small square, usually domed. To provide for the liturgy, an apse appears at the east end, generally flanked by side chambers, while at the west end there is a porch or narthex; galleries too are common. External decoration was much increased, and domes of different sizes and height were juxtaposed, as seen at the Church of Saint Sophia in Novgorod. Beginning in Russia toward the end of the fourteenth century, a solid screen—the iconostasis—covered with pictures of the saints and scenes from the Bible, shuts off the sanctuary, thus entirely blunting any suggestion of a horizontal axis or of a path. These churches then became holy places with all the features they require: union with the divine in wrapt contemplation tends to replace the movement associated with pilgrimage. Gradually this uniform architectural vocabulary began to break down in certain areas such as Bulgaria and Russia. Plans then became more diversified when, for example, a centralized sanctuary was fused with a basilica-type nave.

THE COUNTER-REFORMATION AND BAROQUE. It was in 1054 that the eastern and western halves of Christendom split in the Great Schism, but even more fragmentation was to come in the sixteenth century with the Protestant Reformation, which had profound effects on churches and cathedrals. First to be noted is the Roman Catholic Church reaction to the Protestants—the Counter-Reformation—which found artistic expression in the Baroque style.

With the Counter-Reformation in full spate in the latter half of the sixteenth century, church buildings began to convey ecclesiastical self-assurance and authority. Power and exuberance were embodied in physical structures. Facades acquired a new propaganda function, both proclaiming the confidence of the church in an awe-inspiring manner and seeking to persuade and entice those who regarded them to come inside. The interior was equally designed to impress: the use of the oval plan, combining the centralized effect of a circle with an eastward thrust, produced dynamic tension that allowed no repose. There was a planned movement through space; in the drive to the high altars, the aisles, which might have distracted from the importance of the nave, were reduced to a series of side chapels, and the transepts, likewise, to mere bulges.

On the main altar there was now a tabernacle, or receptacle, for the reserved sacrament. To celebrate this localized presence of the divine, the church borrowed from both the court and the theater. This was the period of the emergence of nation-states, each with its own monarch enjoying magnificent apartments and ceremonial. Since God is the king of kings, his residences were to display even more splendor—all the visual arts being fused to achieve this—while the liturgy became the etiquette of the heavenly ruler. At the same time the Mass became the religious equivalent of the principal artistic creation of the age, namely the opera. The main devotional act was now the exposition of the reserved sacrament: the displaying, at the end of a magnificent scenographic approach, of the consecrated Host to the assembly.

Within this divine theater, every worshiper was assigned an active role. One was made aware that the earthly interior was in communication with heaven above since the vast illusionistic ceiling paintings denied enclosure and gave access to the throne of God. This was the style that spread throughout the Roman Catholic Church, becoming even more decorative than in Italy when it passed to Spain and its colonies in the New World, where miners and slave owners sought to honor God and thank him for the treasures they believed he had bestowed on them.

The Churches of Protestantism. One of the organs of the Counter-Reformation had been the Council of Trent (1545–1563), which reaffirmed many medieval theological ideas, among them the view that the essence of Christian priesthood is to offer the sacrifice of the Mass. Protestants reacted strongly against this position, emphasizing the fellowship aspect of the Eucharist and the importance of preaching while lowering the barrier between clergy and laity. These three factors were to have important results in the building of churches, but in the early decades after the Reformation few new structures were erected; rather, the main architectural activity consisted in adapting those buildings taken over, for example, by the Calvinists and Anglicans. The former destroyed rood screens, brought the pulpit into the midst of the congregation, and similarly advanced the baptismal font. The latter used the nave for the ministry of the word, using the second of the two medieval rooms, the sanctuary, for the ministry of the sacrament.

As time passed and additional churches were planned, Protestants in general tended to favor some kind of centralization to express the idea of the gathered congregation. Lutherans brought table, pulpit, and font together to produce the *Prinzipalstück*, or triple liturgical focus, at the east end. Anglicans approved of the auditory church devised by Christopher Wren (1632–1723): elongated chancels and prominent side aisles were suppressed to produce a single volume of such a size that all present could both hear and see what was taking place. Other denominations adopted plans that were both modest and domestic in character; many an early Quaker meetinghouse, for example, is externally indistinguishable from a private dwelling: in a sense the wheel had come full turn. Stylistically the buildings followed the current fashion, although preference began to be given to the restrained classicism that had been popularized by Wren and which in England represented the influence of the Renaissance as mediated through the Italian architect Andrea Palladio (1508–1580). Baroque, with its implicit triumphalism, did not appeal to the heirs of the Reformation, but most if not all were eventually to succumb to architectural revivalism.

The Gothic Revival in England. Once the task of the architect was conceived to be the reproduction of the styles of a former age, then there appeared to be no reason why any one epoch should be given preference. In Germany, for example, the *Rundbogenstil* (Romanesque style) was favored. In England there is the Church of Saint Mary at Wilton, Wiltshire (1840–1846), complete with freestanding Italianate campanile. It is, however, the Gothic style that most commended itself in the end. The adherents of this late eighteenth-century style rested their case on a number of vigorously argued but largely untenable beliefs. First, they held that national churches should promote whatever is the main national style, and this they identified in Great Britain as Gothic—in ignorance of the fact that it had originated in France. Second, they maintained that every religion produces its own architectural style that best expresses its character; Greek temples, for example, were deemed to embody paganism and therefore to be unsuited for Christianity. Wedded to this consideration was a third conviction that architecture mirrors the spirit of the age in which it is produced and that consequently, the Gothic of the thirteenth century, which was held to be the "age of faith" is to be recognized above all others as the Christian style.

The Gothic revival appealed to many because of a contemporary emphasis on spirituality, on sacramentality, on ritual rather than preaching, and on the visual and decorative elements that went with that emphasis. From 1839 to 1845, the Cambridge Camden Society, with the *Ecclesiologist* as its organ, campaigned all over England for the restoration of existing churches that did not conform to its ecclesiastical canons, and for the designing of new churches with extended chancels, screens, and a clear division of sanctuary from nave. Three-decker pulpits were reduced to a single level; box pews were replaced by benches all facing the altar; the empty space in the architectural choir was filled with a robed singing choir.

Beginning with Anglicanism but soon influencing Roman Catholicism, this movement quickly spread to affect all denominations. Methodism and Congregationalism in particular followed suit, though probably more for social than theological reasons: they wanted their buildings to look like "churches." Inside, however, their arrangement remained more "protestant" in that it featured a central pulpit on a rostrum and galleries, thus laying stress on the word rather than the sacrament and giving the building something of the appearance of an auditorium.

Gothic revivalism was to spread throughout the world—from the United States to Australia, from New Zealand to Iran. Failing to distinguish the gospel from its embodiment in Western cultural forms, Christians rejected indigenous architecture as primitive and even essentially pagan. Hence there appeared in Kuala Lumpur in Malaysia a complete Gothic cathedral, and a similar alien immigrant enshrines the tomb of the apostle Thomas in Madras, India.

Church Buildings in the Twentieth Century. Revivalism continued into the twentieth century, although it was being hotly contested by many architects. Indeed, it was not until the 1920s that the ideals of the modern movement in architecture began to be related to those of the liturgical movement within Roman Catholicism. The technical achievements of the modern movement were first utilized in the reinforced concrete church of Le Raincy near Paris (1923). The principles of the liturgical movement found expression in the hall of the Catholic Youth Movement headquarters at Schloss Rothenfels-am-Main in Germany (1828). This was a large rectangular space devoid of decoration and furnished with a hundred black cubical stools. For a liturgical celebration a provisional altar was set up, the faithful on three sides of it, and the president completed the circle by facing them across the table. This arrangement embodied the principles that the Mass should be the central Christian act of devotion, that it should be intelligible, with a unity of word and sacrament, and that it should be corporate. The space for the altar and that for the congregation were united in a single volume. When this was translated into parish church terms—for example, in the Church of Corpus Christi in Aachen, Germany (1928–1930), which was to have a potent influence on design throughout the decade before World War II—it resulted in a narrow rectangle with the altar somewhat isolated. Because the fundamental concept was that the building should be planned from the altar outward, this article of furniture was required to be a large, static object that constituted the visual and monumental focus of the entire space. The persistence of this view into the 1960s is evidenced by the chapel of Saint John's Abbey in Collegeville, Minnesota (1963).

The main characteristic of the period prior to Vatican II, in all denominations, was the progressive abandonment of the rectangular plan in favor of a design based on the square, as seen in the Church of Saint James the Fisherman, Cape Cod, Massachusetts, or Saint Paul's Church, Bow Common, London (1960). At the same time, experimentation was at its height, leading to a great variety of shapes and often, under the influence of Le Corbusier's pilgrimage chapel at Ronchamp, northeastern France (1950–1955), to asymmetry. There was, in fact, a temptation for architects to seek to display their individual genius in buildings that were monumental in conception.

The tenets of the liturgical movement, already operative within and outside the Roman communion—they were visibly embodied in the North Christian Church, Columbia City, Indiana (1964)—were fully endorsed by Vatican II, which began its sessions in October 1962. A complete break with the monumental image was now promoted; church buildings were expected to be at the "service" of the congregation. The altar was no longer regarded as the unique pole. To integrate word and sacrament, emphasis was now also placed on the pulpit or lectern and the teaching chair. A growing ecumenical consensus and an acceptance of common principles so influenced church buildings that many could not now be identified in denominational terms. It is possible to visit churches in Switzerland or the United States and be unaware of which belong to the reformed tradition and which to the Roman Catholic. Nevertheless, differences may be detected; Unitarians, for example, generally lay less stress on sacraments than do Episcopalians. As a result, Unitarian churches are likely to limit or even to give no prominence at all to the altar, instead emphasizing the pulpit; this was the case with Frank Lloyd Wright's influential design for the Unity Temple (now Unitarian Universalist Church) in Oak Park, Illinois, as long ago as 1904–1906.

Since 1970 the architectural scene has not remained static. There has been a recognition that a variety of buildings are needed for use as pastoral centers or to accommodate small groups, medium-sized congregations, and large assemblies. Indeed, what some would regard as bizarre designs have been realized; such was the drive-in church planned by Richard Neutra in 1959 for the Garden Grove community of Orange City in southern California, which was superseded by Philip Johnson's crystal cathedral opened in September 1980. The importance of mobility and flexibility has been acknowledged, with a consequent effect on furnishings and seating. The responsibility of the Christian community, not only to its own members but to the larger community within which it is set, has also led to the development of the idea of the multipurpose church, that is, one that accommodates not only worship but also other services for those in the neighborhood who are in need.

Reuse and reordering have also become important issues. The decline in attendance at worship in some areas and the movement of population in others (especially from the inner city) have made many churches virtually redundant. Some churches of little architectural or townscape interest have been demolished, while others have been adapted as libraries, museums, cultural centers, even dwelling places. Where a viable liturgical life is being maintained, there is often the need to redesign the interior of a building that was originally planned to accommodate hieratic forms of worship now regarded as belonging to the past. Beliefs, worship practices, and architecture continue to march in inextricable partnership, sometimes, but by no means always, producing less-than-major monuments, sometimes creating works of considerable beauty, in all cases and in all periods representing varying and valid traditions within the Christian denominations.

SEE ALSO Architecture; Monastery; Pilgrimage, articles on Eastern Christian Pilgrimage, Roman Catholic Pilgrimage in Europe, and Roman Catholic Pilgrimage in the New World; Relics; Religion; Shrines; Tombs; Worship and Devotional Life, article on Christian Worship.

BIBLIOGRAPHY

Blunt, Anthony, et al. *Baroque and Rococo: Architecture and Decoration.* London, 1978.

Conant, Kenneth J. *Carolingian and Romanesque Architecture, 800 to 1200.* 3d ed. Harmondsworth, U.K., 1973.

Davies, J. G. *The Secular Use of Church Buildings.* New York, 1968.

Davies, J. G. *Temples, Churches and Mosques. A Guide to the Appreciation of Religious Architecture.* New York, 1982.

Debuyst, Frédéric. *Modern Architecture and Christian Celebration.* London, 1968.

Frankl, Paul. *Gothic Architecture.* Harmondsworth, U.K., 1962.

Hammond, P. *Liturgy and Architecture.* London, 1960.

Kennedy, Roger G. *American Churches.* New York, 1982.

Krautheimer, Richard. *Early Christian and Byzantine Architecture.* Harmondsworth, U.K., 1965.

Murray, Peter. *The Architecture of the Italian Renaissance.* London, 1963.

New Sources

Anderson, William. *The Rise of the Gothic.* London, 1985.

Binding, Günther, and Uwe Dettmar. *High Gothic: The Age of the Great Cathedrals.* Cologne and New York, 1999.

Branham, Joan Rebekah. "Sacred Space in Ancient Jewish and Early Medieval Christian Architecture." Ph.D. Diss., Emory University, 1993.

Dragan, Radu, and Augustin Loan. *Symbols and Language in Sacred Christian Architecture.* Translated by Christina Ilina Salajanu. New York, 1996.

Greenacre, Roger. *The Sacrament of Easter.* Grand Rapids, Mich., 1995.

Hill, Stephen. *The Early Byzantine Churches of Cilicia and Isauria.* Aldershot, U.K., 1996.

Kieckhefer, Richard. *Theology in Stone: Church Architecture from Byzantium to Berkeley.* Oxford and New York, 2004.

Mancinelli, Fabrizio. *Catacombs and Basilicas: The Early Christians in Rome.* Translated by Carol Wasserman. Florence, 1981.

Scott, Robert A. *The Gothic Enterprise: A Guide to Understanding the Medieval Cathedral.* Berkeley, Calif., 2003.

White, L. Michael. *Building God's House in the Roman World: Architectural Adaptation among Pagans, Jews, and Christians.* Baltimore, 1990.

White, L. Michael. *The Social Origins of Christian Architecture.* 2 vols. Valley Forge, Pa., 1997.

J. G. DAVIES (1987)
Revised Bibliography

BASIL OF CAESAREA (c. 329–379), called "the Great"; Christian theologian, bishop of Caesarea (modern Kayseri, Turkey), and one of three great Cappadocian fathers of the church (together with his friend, Gregory of Nazianzus, and his younger brother, Gregory of Nyssa).

Basil was born into a deeply Christian family of high social standing and extensive possessions. His grandmother Macrina, his parents Basil and Emmelia, his older sister Macrina, and his younger brothers Gregory of Nyssa and Peter of Sebaste are venerated as saints in both the Eastern Orthodox and Roman Catholic churches. Basil received a Christian education from childhood; his father, who was a rhetor, also gave him the beginnings of his secular training. After the early death of his father, Basil continued his secondary education in Caesarea (c. 345–347) and then pursued further studies in rhetoric and philosophy in Constantinople (c. 348–350), where he was probably a student of the famous pagan rhetor Libanius. Finally, he studied, together with Gregory of Nazianzus, in Athens (c. 350–355). Returning home, Basil seems to have taught rhetoric for a short time, but soon gave up a promising worldly career for the Christian ascetic ideal.

In accordance with the fourth-century custom of late baptism—even in fully Christian families—Basil was baptized and ordained a reader of scripture in Caesarea by Bishop Dianius, undertook a tour of monastic settlements in Syria, Mesopotamia, Palestine, and Egypt (c. 356–357), and then joined his mother and his sister Macrina in a semi-eremitical type of asceticism on a family estate at Annesi in Pontus. Dianius's successor, Eusebius, ordained Basil a priest (c. 364), and he soon became the actual leader of the diocese. After the death of Eusebius (c. 370), Basil was elected bishop of Caesarea and as such became metropolitan of Cappadocia. He fulfilled his office in an exemplary manner and extended his pastoral care to all aspects of the life of the church. He led the faithful, especially through his sermons, to a deeper understanding of their Christian faith. He supported the needy with social institutions, financed in great part from the selling of his possessions. He gave direction to the thriving, but often "sectarian" monastic movement and integrated it within the Christian community as a whole. He worked unceasingly against doctrinal and political divisions within the Eastern church and between Eastern and Western Christianity. Consumed by hard discipline and labors, he died on January 1, 379.

Because of the respect he enjoyed during his lifetime, Basil's works have been relatively well preserved. They reveal both his own quest for Christian perfection and his concerns as leader of the church. The *Philokalia*, apparently published posthumously, is an anthology of excerpts from Origen's writings, compiled by Basil and Gregory of Nazianzus during their retirement in Annesi. It reflects their critical assimilation of the theology of Origen and preserves many of his texts in the original Greek. In this same period he composed the *Moralia*, an anthology of more than 1,500 verses of the New Testament, distributed under eighty headings (rules), as guidelines for a perfect Christian life; it is directed, for the most part, to all believers, not only to monks and clergy. It was originally published with a preface, *On the Judgment of God*, to which Basil later added a second preface, *On the Faith*. During Basil's years as a priest he composed his "little" *Asceticon* (preserved in the Latin translation of Rufinus); the full version (the "great" *Asceticon*), completed during his later years as a bishop, consists of fifty-five "longer rules," or systematic regulations of the cenobitic life (i.e., monastic life in a community) and 313 "shorter rules," or practical answers to the questions emerging in such communities.

Basil's numerous letters (366 of which have been preserved) cover his life from the time of his return from Athens and contain precious information on the history of the church in the fourth century. His sermons are more difficult to date; some were preached during his priesthood, but the majority during his episcopate. Particularly famous are the nine *Homilies on the Hexaemeron* (i.e., on the story of creation in six days according to *Genesis*).

The most important of his dogmatic works are *Against Eunomius* (c. 364), a refutation of extreme Arianism (books 4 and 5 are not by Basil), and his substantial treatise *On the Holy Spirit* (c. 375), which is directed against those who denied that equal glory is to be given to the third person of the Trinity. The small treatise *On the Spirit*, a radical rewriting in the sense of the Christian Trinity of *Ennead* 5.1 of Plotinus ("founder" of Neoplatonism, c. 205–270), is probably not by Basil, although it seems to have influenced him. Particularly revered from the time of the European Renaissance is Basil's short treatise, *To the Young, on How They Might Derive Benefit from Greek Literature*, written probably in the last years of his life.

Basil's theology is both "theoretical" (i.e., contemplative) and "practical" (i.e., giving guidance for life). The strife-torn situation of the contemporary church, according to him, results primarily from the failure of Christians to live according to their faith (see *On the Judgment of God).* Only the grace of Christ and the guidance of the Holy Spirit can accomplish salvation, but in order to receive this, one should live according to God's precepts as manifested in the gospel, especially the two greatest commands, the love of God and of neighbor. Insisting on fidelity in practice, Basil was equally concerned with the purity of faith. He defended the divinity of the Son against the denial of the Arians (especially Eunomius), and the equal glory of the Holy Spirit against the so-called Pneumatomachians ("fighters against the spirit"), even though, to the disappointment of his friends, he did not demand an explicit confession of the divinity of the Holy Spirit. Clearly asserting, however, both the unity of the divine essence (*ousia*) and the distinction of the three persons (*hupos-taseis:* that is, Father, Son, and Holy Spirit), Basil anticipated the definitive formulation of the trinitarian faith by the Council of Constantinople (381).

Basil had a profound and far-reaching influence on both Eastern and Western Christianity. His trinitarian faith, further clarified by the other two great Cappodocians, became normative for subsequent Christianity, and a basis for overcoming the divisions of the church that arose from the trinitarian controversies. Eastern monasticism, of crucial importance throughout the history of the church, still follows (with modifications) the rule of Basil, which was also one of the important resources of Western monasticism. The so-called "Liturgy of Saint Basil," still in use in the Eastern church, originated in his practice and writings. There can be no doubt that his life and teaching have been a source of inspiration for many Christians through the ages.

BIBLIOGRAPHY

Works by Basil of Caesarea

The only complete edition of the works of Basil in the original Greek with parallel Latin translation is that prepared by Julien Garnier and Prudentius Maran in 3 volumes (Paris, 1721–1730), reprinted in J.-P. Migne's *Patrologia Graeca*, vols. 29–32 (Paris, 1857, 1886). The photomechanical reprints of these volumes (Turnhout, 1959–1961) contain new introductions by Jean Gribomont, giving a survey of all editions and translations of Basil's works, with information on authenticity and chronology. A complete listing of Basil's works, indicating the best edition for each, with information as to authenticity, is given in Maurice Geerards's *Clavis Patrum Graecorum*, vol. 2 (Turnhout, 1974), pp. 140–178.

Basil's works can be found in English translation in *Letters and Selected Works*, translated by Blomfield Jackson, "Select Library of Nicene and Post-Nicene Fathers," 2d series, vol. 8 (1886; reprint, Grand Rapids, Mich., 1978–1979); *The Ascetic Works*, translated by W. K. L. Clarke (London, 1925); *Letters*, 4 vols., edited and translated by Roy J. Defarrari, "Loeb Classical Library" (Cambridge, Mass., 1926–1934), volume 4 of which also contains the *Address to Young Men on Reading Greek Literature* (pp. 363–435); *Ascetical Works*, translated by Monica Wagner, "Fathers of the Church," vol. 9 (Washington, D.C., 1950); *Letters*, translated by A. C. Way, "Fathers of the Church," vols. 13, 28 (Washington, D. C., 1951–1955); *Exegetic Homilies*, translated by A. C. Way, "Fathers of the Church," vol. 46 (Washington, D. C., 1963); and *Saint Basil on the Value of Greek Literature*, edited and translated by Nigel G. Wilson (London, 1975).

Works about Basil of Caesarea

Basil of Caesarea: Christian, Humanist, Ascetic; A Sixteen-Hundredth Anniversary Symposium, 2 vols., edited by Paul Jonathan Fedwick (Toronto, 1981), contains papers presented at an international symposium held in Toronto, June

10–16, 1979, on all major aspects of Basil's life, works, thought, and influence, by leading specialists, with extensive bibliography.

David L. Balás (1987)

BATAK RELIGION. The Batak societies, located around Lake Toba in North Sumatra, are among the more than three hundred ethnic minorities of Indonesia. Batak religion, like Batak culture as a whole, is ethnically diverse, syncretic, changing, and bound at once to both village social organizational patterns and the monotheistic national culture of Indonesia. Like many religious traditions of Indonesia, Malaysia, and the Philippines, Batak myths and rituals focus on the yearly cycle of rice cultivation activities and the local kinship system. Batak religions tie these two realms to a larger cosmological order, which is then represented in various religious art forms (traditional house architecture, village spatial layout, and wood sculpture) and ritual activities (dances, oratory, and gift-giving ceremonies). Batak kinship revolves around marriage alliances that link together lineages of patrilineal clans, called *marga.* This marriage system, which involves ritually superior and "holy" wife-providing lineages and their ritually subordinate, "mundane" wife-receiving lineages, is much celebrated in the indigenous Batak religions. Many village rites of passage, for instance, are largely occasions for eulogizing this asymmetrical marriage alliance system through hours of ritual oratory. Beyond these very localized ethnic patterns, however, Batak religious life extends outward into the world religions: the large majority of homeland Batak and virtually all migrants to cities in Sumatra and Java are Muslim or Christian. In fact, the Batak are stereotyped in Indonesia as uncommonly pious monotheists; both the southern Batak Muslim pilgrim to Mecca and the Toba Batak Protestant minister are stock characters in the national *dramatis personae* when members of other ethnic groups think of these Sumatran peoples. In this monotheistic environment, Batak village religion has undeniably lost some of its social and symbolic scope. However, through an inventive reinterpretation of symbols, other sectors of village belief and ritual continue to thrive in new forms.

There are six major Batak societies in the homeland region around Lake Toba. These societies are similar in village social structure and subsistence base (paddy rice farming with some dry field agriculture) but speak different dialects of Batak and have distinct ritual systems. These societies are commonly called the Toba Batak, Karo Batak, Pakpak and Dairi Batak, Simelungun Batak, Angkola and Sipirok Batak, and the Mandailing Batak (although some "Batak" rarely call themselves Batak). Their pre-monotheistic religions are impossible to reconstruct in detail from current evidence because Islam and Christianity have reshaped village ritual and folk memories of the past so thoroughly. It is common, for instance, for committed Muslim and Christian Batak to speak disparagingly of their "pagan" ancestors, who believed in populous spirit worlds before they "discovered that there was only one God." In other words, "traditional Batak religion" is in large part a figment of the contemporary Batak imagination. It is safe to say, however, that the Batak religions practiced before the 1820s (when Islam entered the southern Angkola and Mandailing homelands) and the 1850s and 1860s (when Protestant Christianity was introduced to Angkola and the Toba region by Dutch missionaries and the German Rheinische Mission Gesellschaft) shared many symbolic complexes with the related indigenous religions of Kalimantan's Dayaks, Sulawesi's highland societies, and the people of eastern Indonesia.

In all these regions, certain assumptions about the nature of the universe permeated village religion. Binary oppositions between life and death, humans and animals, the village and the forest, metal and cloth, masculinity and femininity, and warfare and farming were recurrent themes in ritual and myth. Both human and agricultural creativity and fertility were thought to come from the temporary, intensely powerful union of such complementary opposites as life and death, masculinity and femininity, and so on. Also important was the notion that the two opposing categories were aboriginally one. Ritual often endeavored to unite for a moment the binary opposites and then control the resulting release of power from the center. (For instance, at Batak weddings the bride-giving faction bestows ritual textiles on their bride-receivers while the latter bestow counter-gifts of metal and livestock. Such exchanges foster fertility in the marriage.) The Batak societies took these familiar pan-Indonesian concepts and fit them to their particular social structure. Toba origin myths, for instance, tell of a first human, Si Raja Batak, who fathered two sons (Guru Tateabulan and Raja Isumbaon), who in turn fathered the ancestors of the major Toba patrilineal clans. Related myths tell of the origin of farming and weaving and link clan clusters to certain valleys and upland regions. Other Toba myths warn of the consequences of clan incest and marriages that violate the asymmetrical alliance rules (men should not marry women from lineages that serve as their traditional wife-receivers).

All Batak religions had extensive soul concepts and generally posited a personal soul that could fragment when startled and escape from a person's head to wander haplessly in the countryside until recalled to his body in special soul-capture ceremonies. *Datu* or *gurū* were diviner-sorcerers who performed such religious cures and also served the village chiefs as "village protection experts" in times of warfare, epidemic, or crop failure. Sacrificial rituals were central to the *datu*'s protective tasks; in a few areas there may have been occasional ritual cannibalism (a point that is hotly debated among Batak today). Common myth images include magic numbers, constellations of stars, the magic colors red, white, and black, the *baringin* tree (the banyan tree seen as the cosmic tree uniting the layers of the Batak cosmos), the *singa* (a powerful monster that is part human, part water buffalo, and part crocodile or lizard), the cosmic serpent Naga Padoha, the hornbill, and aboriginal boy-girl twins. In Toba and Karo such images animated an extensive range of art forms, including carved wooden sorcerers' staffs, textiles, funerary masks, and megalithic monuments. These art forms, and the larger religions surrounding them, also drew on Indian beliefs; like many Indonesian cultures the Batak came into contact with Hinduism and Buddhism via possible trading colonies near Barus, a temple community near Portibi, and through influence from the indianized ancient kingdoms of south Sumatra.

Contact with the monotheistic religions varies considerably from Batak society to society. Karo is an area of fairly recent conversions, with many animists. In this mixed Muslim and Protestant region, Christian proselytizing gained some converts in the 1930s, but the major switch to monotheism has come since 1965 as a result of the national government's identification of Indonesian patriotism with belief in a monotheistic religion. Toba is overwhelmingly Protestant; the original, German-sponsored missionary church, the HKBP (Huria Kristen Batak Protestan), has its headquarters in Tarutung. During the Padri Wars in the 1820s Minangkabau Muslims brought their religion to the southern Angkola and Mandailing homelands; today, Mandailing is entirely Muslim while Angkola is about 10 percent Protestant and 90 percent Muslim.

During the Suharto regime, the HKBP church has splintered into the parent church and a number of bickering class- and ethnicity-based new denominations. In religiously mixed areas, members of the churches tend to align themselves with Muslim families along class lines. In Angkola, for instance, where pre-national society was divided into an aristocracy, commoners, and slave descendants, Muslims from noble families often find political allies among highborn Christians. Early conversions in the 1850s and 1860s brought large numbers of slave descendants into the church, while later Dutch colonial policy led to favoritism for village chiefly lineages that became Christian. This policy has left southern Batak Christianity argumentative and faction-ridden.

In Angkola, members of the same social class often emphasize their common heritage "in the *adat*" (village custom) over their differences in monotheistic religion. Because *adat* encompasses much village ritual, this leads to much syncretism. In Muslim Mandailing and Christian Toba, by contrast, *adat* is often seen as conflicting with monotheistic religion. In all Batak societies, the area where *adat* meets monotheism promises to remain an important growing edge of culture in the coming decades.

See Also Southeast Asian Religions, article on Insular Cultures.

Bibliography

There is a large literature in Dutch, English, and Indonesian on the Batak societies. Toenggoel P. Siagian's "Bibliography on the Batak Peoples," *Indonesia* 2 (October 1966): 161–184, is a valuable guide to the main research before the mid-sixties, and the bibliographies in *Beyond Samosir: Recent Studies of the Batak Peoples of Sumatra,* edited by Rita Smith Kipp and Richard D. Kipp (Athens, Ohio, 1983), provide references to the mid-1980s, a period of much American anthropological fieldwork in the area. Jacob Cornelis Vergouwen's *The Social Organization and Customary Law of the Toba-Batak of Northern Sumatra* (1933), translated by Jeune Scott-Kemball (The Hague, 1964), remains the premier descriptive ethnography of a Batak culture, with much information on non-monotheistic rituals and beliefs. Some articles and monographs by anthropologists reflect a shift in research toward Batak symbol systems: Rita Smith Kipp's "The Thread of Three Colors: The Ideology of Kinship in Karo Batak Funerals," in *Art, Ritual, and Society in Indonesia,* edited by Judith Becker and Edward M. Bruner (Athens, Ohio, 1979), discusses Karo religion in its marriage alliance context; I discuss religious syncretism and change in *Adat, Islam, and Christianity in a Batak Homeland* (Athens, Ohio, 1981). Two major collections of anthropological essays on similar religious and social systems from other regions of Indonesia provide invaluable comparative material: *The Flow of Life: Essays on Eastern Indonesia,* edited by James Fox (Cambridge, Mass., 1980), and *The Imagination of Reality: Essays in Southeast Asian Coherence Systems,* edited by A. L. Becker and Aram A. Yengoyan (Norwood, N.J., 1979).

New Sources

Becker, Dieter, ed. *Mit Worten kocht man keinen Reis: Beiträge aus den Batak-Kirchen auf Nordsumatra.* Wuppertal, 1987.

Goes, Beatriz van der. "Beru Dayang: The Concept of Female Spirits and the Movement of Fertility in Karo Batak." *Culture Asian Folklore Studies* 56, no. 2 (1997): 379–405.

Kipp, Rita Smith. *Dissociated Identities: Ethnicity, Religion, and Class in an Indonesian Society.* Ann Arbor, Mich., 1993.

Kipp, Rita Smith, and Susan Rodgers, eds. *Indonesian Religions in Transition.* Tucson, 1987.

Steedly, Mary Margaret. *Hanging without a Rope: Narrative Experience in Colonial and Postcolonial Karoland.* Princeton, 1993.

Susan Rodgers (1987)
Revised Bibliography

BATHS in a religious context are sacred places where people bathe not for hygienic purposes, but rather to spiritually re-create themselves in both mind and body. Spiritual bathing may take place in sacred spaces in nature, for example in hot springs or in the water of a sacred river such as the Ganges or Nile, or in buildings made out of stone (Roman baths) or wood (saunas).

Sauna is a Finnish and Sami word for a building where one bathes for the purpose of cleansing body and mind. It has somewhat varied meanings, including commercial and erotic ones, in communities without a history of sauna culture. Sauna has been part of the Finnish life cycle for thousands of years—and, at the dawn of the third millennium, it still is, both in Finland, with its 2.2 million saunas for 5.2 million people (in 2004), and among expatriate and emigrant Finns.

Saunas in the form of log building are characteristic of the peasant architecture of Finnish-related and Slavic peoples living in northern Eurasian forest territories. Throughout its traditional area it is still central to ethnic religion and cultural habits. The sauna as a building and as a heated construction has undergone various changes, but as it has been adapted into new milieus, including urban environments, many sauna-related habits and rituals have shown remarkable strength not only in surviving but also in being revived as a form of socially shared group behavior among youth, adults, and environmentalist societies.

There are bathing traditions reminiscent of the Finnish sauna on other continents, for example, the traditions surrounding the Roman, Turkish, and Celtic bath, the Japanese *furo,* and the Native American sweat lodge (such as the Lakota *inipi*). What is common to all of them is the feeling that bathing is not just a cleansing experience, but a spiritual one, as well as the bath's intimate connection to various life stages and rituals. In all these traditions, baths have also played a part in solving various personal crises. In *inipi, furo,* and sauna mind and body are purified—re-created, as it were, to enable the person to face the challenges life presents. On all three continents sacred baths are the subject of various religious narratives, including certain Japanese Buddhist texts, Native American initiation songs, and the poems of the *Kalevala,* the Finnish national epic.

At the core of the sauna is the *kiuas* (lit., "stones in a hot heap"), around which the early sauna, in a depression in the earth, and subsequently the smoke sauna were created. Over time, saunas developed from mere heaps of stones covered by skin or cloth to the electrically powered sauna stoves presently found in private homes and hotels. The public sauna was an important part of Finnish community life and shared urban culture before its almost complete disappearance after World War II. In Tokyo the *furo* is faring better; public facilities for this type of bath amount to well over a thousand. In the United States, the formerly forbidden sweat lodge has been undergoing a revival as an expression of Native American identity.

The Finnish sauna began its spread abroad at an early stage. In 1638 a colony called New Sweden was established in Delaware on the eastern seaboard of America, with several hundred Forest Finns among its approximately 1,000 inhabitants. Smoke cabins were among the typical constructions built by the early settlers. The so-called pioneer house found along the coast throughout New England was neither German nor Dutch in origin, but was instead based on the Finnish smoke sauna; a log timber house it served frequently as a model for other constructions. The propagation of Finnish sauna has continued to this day. For example, for Finnish United Nations peacekeeping forces around the world the construction of saunas at their bases is among the first tasks.

For Finns today, the sauna is more a national than a religious symbol, just as the *furo* symbolizes the modern Japanese way of life and the *inipi* the revived consciousness of Native American identity. Symbols have their importance, however, all the more so for small nations that feel compelled to change as a result of domination by major cultures. *Sauna* is the most popular Finnish loanword, and even quite recently has been borrowed by several new languages. Along with the sauna buildings drawn by Alvar Aalto and other well-known Finnish architects, the word itself has made its way all around the world, even though rituals and beliefs associated with Finnish sauna have not always been transmitted with it.

For Finns, the sauna has been a sacred place. Traditionally, it was visited once a week, on Saturday evening. To heat a smoke sauna for several sessions was a whole day's operation, an operation demanding its own expertise in the selection of kindling, the laying of the kindling, and the adding of firewood; above all, it required patience, as heating the sauna and binding the birch switches took a great deal of time. The taking of sauna itself entailed certain ritual behavior observed with religious zeal. An oral proverb has it that one should conduct oneself in a sauna as in church—reverently. Visits to saunas were governed by many rules of conduct: it was important not to be rowdy, to curse, gossip, speak evil, break wind, or make noise in a sauna.

The spirit of *löyly,* the vapor rising from the water splashed over the stones of the sauna stove, is the main element in folk beliefs related to Finnish sauna, along with a belief in the manifold healing effects of the birch switches used in saunas. It is still a Finnish custom to greet the *löyly* spirit as the guardian of the holy space either through gestures or words before entering the door, crossing the threshold, or mounting the benches. Adults and older children were expected to bless themselves as they entered saunas. This was both to express reverence for the sacred space and to guard against harm: while people were naked, with all their pores open and exuding sweat, they were defenseless against the evil eye and envy. When a sauna was inaugurated, reference was often made to the power of Väinämöinen the wise man, a sage and a shaman who is the central figure in the *Kalevala;* the *löyly* itself was even said to be "Väinämöinen's sweat."

Löyly establishes a connection between the sauna or sweat-shed and the other worlds, both above and below, as well as in the Hereafter. The steam rising from the stove, like the smoke issuing from the open fire, the door of the smoke sauna, the flue, or the chimney, creates a symbolic connection between the sacred space of the sauna and its people (microcosm) and the sphere of the Hereafter and its inhabitants (macrocosm). An individual healing event occurring within the sauna and concerning the health of an individual is thus linked to the entire universe. Myths based on a connection to the gods, the departed, and various spirits are recounted and intoned in the *löyly* of the sauna, or by the campfires.

The word *löyly* is older than *sauna.* A term with Finno-Ugric origins, it does not only refer to the steam rising from the sauna stove. *Löyly* and its variants (Estonian, *leil;* Hungarian *lélek*) can also refer to a person's soul and to the span of a human life, which in ancient beliefs was held to last from the first breath to the last. The "departure of *henki* 'breath'" (which in Finnish is synonymous with the word for spirit) was thus the end of physical life, the perceptible sign of death.

However, *löyly* is only one of the appellations for "soul" in the Finno-Ugric languages. Another is *itse,* "self" (in Hungarian, *iz*), which refers to social rather than physical life and death. The "self" of a person has a different life span than their *löyly.* A person acquires this "self" at a later stage than their *löyly,* and it lasts longer. A child acquires the status of "having a self" when they are given a name. Only then are they deemed to have a social existence; their name endows them with a right to inherit and, among the Sami, with their own reindeer mark of identification. The "self" does not expire when the spirit departs, but only two to three years later. Then the person is considered dead as an individual. The Finnish word *henki* (Estonian, *hing*) refers to a third soul, which is thought to be immortal. In the shamanic belief system, this third soul is the soul of the shaman traveling outside the human body to the realm of death, generally in the form of an animal, such as a fish, snake, bear, reindeer, or bird.

The sauna was generally the first building a Finnish settler built, designating thereby both the limits of his territory and his sacred space in nature. Building a sauna involves a thorough knowledge of timber construction, the right types of wood to use, and the appropriate time for felling trees. As with all buildings with a fireplace of some sort, there was, according to folk beliefs, a spirit watching to see that customs were observed and infringements punished. Thus the first person to light a fire had to be chosen with care, as it was he who would, according to the superstition, assume the position of *saunatonttu, saunanhaltija,* or spirit of the sauna.

Problem-free heating of the sauna and the correct way of making birch switches was taught by one generation to the next. Expertise in the effects of taking saunas is a special branch of traditional Finnish-Karelian folk medicine, reserved for those versed in cupping, bleeding, and healing joints. When a healer was called to a sauna or when an injury was being healed at home, very special attention had to be paid to the heating of the sauna and to other operations. Wood from alder trees was to be used for the logs. This ensured the greater efficacy of the cures effected in the sauna. According to a well-known Finnish proverb encapsulating the effectiveness of saunas, "What tar, alcohol, or sauna cannot help is fatal indeed."

In central Finland there was at one time a custom of laying a table for the spirits of the farmhouse kitchen before departing for the sauna: "While the people of the house bathed the spirits took to the table." There are many ways in which saunas have been connected to the cycles of the agricultural year. Many important farming tasks were performed in saunas: the softening of flax, the smoking of meat, and the brewing of beer and the like in the malt sauna. Annual chores lasting for days involved younger and older family members spending time together in saunas reciting poems and songs and telling tales and riddles as everyone worked at the job in hand.

For Finns, the sauna has been associated with all life cycle events, from birth to death. During the marking of various rites of passage, the sauna normally becomes the exclusive province of women. Only in such cases where the transition from one state to another is considered by the community to be infelicitous for one reason or another—for example, if the child or patient is very sick—would the intercession of a male witch, sage, or folk healer be called for. Such a crisis situation requires the most potent religious leader of the locality or family, be they woman or man.

Until World War II, Finnish women mostly gave birth in saunas. The midwife was referred to as the "sauna wife" and the mother-to-be as the "sauna woman." "Sauna time" among the womenfolk might last as much as a week before the child was triumphantly carried into the farmhouse. This process was associated with precautionary measures against disease and the evil eye, as in Protestant Finland both the child, who was "without self," having no name, and the woman, who was deemed "unclean" because she had not yet made the church visit that occurred six weeks after a birth, were considered to be in a precarious state. On reaching adulthood women went to the sauna. Girls of marriageable age were bathed and slapped with birch branches by older women who recited incantations on procuring love. Traditional Finnish wedding ceremonies known as *antilas* involved the bathing by family members of the girl to be given in marriage. After the ablutions, in a delicate ritual performed in the sauna by the married women of the family, the girl's hair, which had so far been worn loose, was plaited and a "wife's cap" was placed on her head together with the other symbols of a married woman. In the sauna, in the company of married women, the girl was also initiated into how different life would be at her husband's home and told what it would be like under the eagle eye of her mother-in-law. She was then completely "away from the paternal home," to which she would only be able to return to visit relatives the first August following the birth of a son—which could mean a two- to three-year period of separation from her childhood home.

For women, there were more transitions marked in the sauna than there were for men: transitions from girl to bride-to-be, from bride-to-be to a woman given in marriage, from a woman given in marriage to a wife, from a wife to a "breeding" mother, then to one who suckled an infant. Within the extended family, various family members became specialists in the different functions associated with these life-cycle rituals.

The sauna was also connected to funeral rites. In some rural areas, there was a custom that after death the corpse was carried into the sauna on a board, where women of the family specialized in the task washed it. In family-oriented communities it was important that all those with a role in the rituals—the wailing women, and those who washed the body, spoke the ritual words, and made the coffin—should be family members. If someone was asked to perform such a function it was tantamount to a last wish, and it would be improper to decline. Once the corpse had been washed with soap reserved for that purpose, it would be dressed and lifted onto a laying-out board in the threshing building. The last voyage toward the cemetery started from the threshold of the sauna.

Despite widespread assumptions to the contrary, research into ancient Finnish folk traditions indicates that mixed bathing in saunas was practiced in only a few communities. In most communities men and women took their own turns. Taking saunas together as a family group is a more recent phenomenon. In earlier years, the farmer would visit the sauna with his farmhands once the work in the fields was done, whereas the farmer's wife would go to the sauna with the maids after milking. Because the men's turn was first, the women's turn on the eve of the Sabbath might well continue until the beginning of the Sabbath. Sunset was the delimiting factor until it was superseded by the six o'clock church bells announcing the arrival of the Sabbath; by this point the women were supposed to have left the sauna.

In Finnish oral folklore saunas were pictured as sometimes being a hard and dangerous place, and thus people were afraid to go to them alone. There are many stories about encountering the spirit of the sauna and finding it in a wrathful mood. Such an apparition was believed to be a punishment for infringements against the Sabbath. Following the men's and women's sauna turns, there was a third turn, that of the spirit of the sauna. In most cases the person experiencing something strange is a lone woman or a group of women bathing together. Sometimes it is a question of an obviously erotic dream; the last woman to go to bathe falls asleep on the bench and feels or sees a hairy male creature who, after throwing water on the stones, comes to touch, hug, or caress her.

As in the home, the threshing building, the cow house, or other buildings with a fireplace, the spirit of the sauna is believed to be like the first one to kindle a fire. Thus even today people try to find a "nice, mild" person, such as a kindly old woman or man, to kindle the first fire, to ensure good luck in their home. These kinds of ancient traditions have survived until recently in accordance with the ancient belief that the most suitable personality for a sauna spirit is that of a playful, blithe child. Another custom is to honor family members and friends, both those still alive and the deceased, by mentioning their names in turn when pouring water, *löyly,* on the stones. This ceremony lasts as long as new names are remembered by the bathers.

SEE ALSO Finnish Religions; Finno-Ugric Religions; Karelian Religion; Shamanism; Tuonela.

BIBLIOGRAPHY

Alho, Olli. "Sauna." In *Finland: A Cultural Encyclopedia,* edited by Hildi Hawkins and Päivi Vallisaari. Helsinki, 1997.

Edelsward, Lisa Marlene. *Sauna as Symbol: Society and Culture in Finland.* New York, 1991.

Konya, Allan. *The International Handbook of Finnish Sauna.* London, 1973.

Ministry for Foreign Affairs. *Sauna: A Finnish National Institution.* Helsinki, 2001.

Peltonen, Jarno, and Matti Karjanoja, eds. *Sauna: Made in Finland.* Helsinki, 1997.

Pentikäinen, Juha, ed. *The Finnish Sauna, the Japanese Furo, the Indian Inipi: Bathing on Three Continents.* Helsinki, 2001.

Sytula, Charles M. *The Finnish Sauna in Manitoba.* Ottawa, 1977.

Teir, Harald, et al., eds. *Sauna Studies. Papers Read at the VI International Sauna Congress in Helsinki on August 15–17, 1974.* Vammala, Finland, 1976.

Viherjuuri, H. J. *Sauna: The Finnish Bath.* Brattleboro, Vt., 1965.

JUHA PENTIKÄINEN (2005)

BAUBO figures in the myth of the ancient Greek goddess Demeter as the perpetrator of an obscene spectacle that causes the goddess to laugh and that marks the end of her long period of mourning. The myth of Demeter tells of her inconsolable grief at the loss of her daughter Persephone (or Kore) and of her wanderings in search of her. The aged Demeter finally comes out of mourning in the town of Eleusis, where she suddenly bursts into laughter. A double tradition relates how obscene words and gestures diverted and comforted this holy mother.

In the Homeric *Hymn to Demeter* (192–211), it is the maiden Iambe who cheers up the goddess with dirty jokes. The hymn says nothing about the specific content of these obscenities, but the effectiveness of Iambe's words is certain. Indeed, Demeter laughs, comes out of mourning, and ends her fast by accepting and drinking *kukeon* (a beverage made of wheat, water, and pennyroyal), which is offered to her by her hostess, Metanir, the wife of King Keleos.

In the writings of the Church Fathers, Baubo plays a role comparable to Iambe's. But whereas Iambe succeeds in comforting the goddess by telling jokes, Baubo does so not by words but by an obscene gesture: she suddenly lifts her gown to reveal her genitals. This indecent unveiling provokes laughter in the grieving mother, who then accepts and drinks the kukeon that Baubo offers her. Christian polemicists, who attribute the story of the obscene gesture to the Orphics, preserve two versions of the incongruous scene. Clement of Alexandria (*Protrepticus* 2.20.1–1.21.2) and Eusebius of Caesarea (*Praeparatio evangelica* 2.3.31–35) relate that the young Iacchos was found beneath Baubo's raised garment, laughing and waving his hand. Arnobius (*Adversus nationes* 5.25–26) presents a different, more detailed version in which Baubo's unveiled genitals, because of a cosmetic operation, look like the face of a baby.

This "spectacle" (*theama, spectaculum*) has given rise to numerous interpretations. In general, historians have understood it as an etiological myth justifying fertility rites, and certain specialists have recognized in Baubo the mythic memory of the manipulation of sexual articles at Eleusis. Baubo has also been associated, often confusedly, with anything obscene in the ancient world, particularly with obscene words and objects that evoke female sexuality.

Some earthenware figurines found at the beginning of the twentieth century in the temple of Demeter and Kore (fourth century BCE at Priene, in Ionia, have been identified with Baubo. These "Baubos of Priene" merge the head, the belly, and the female sexual organ, with the genitals immediately below the mouth.

SEE ALSO Demeter and Persephone.

BIBLIOGRAPHY

Devereux, Georges. *Baubô: La vulve mythique.* Paris, 1983. Ethnopsychiatric approach, carried on by Tobie Nathan, *Psychanalyse païenne,* Paris, 1988.

Graf, Fritz. *Eleusis und die orphische Dichtung Athens in vorhellenistischer Zeit.* Berlin, 1974.

Olender, Maurice. "Aspects de Baubô: Textes et contextes antiques." *Revue de l'histoire des religions* 202 (January–March 1985): 3–55. English translation in *Before Sexuality. The Construction of Erotic Experience in the Ancient Greek World,* edited by David Halperin (Princeton, 1990).

Olender, Maurice. "Les manières de Baubô." In *Masculin et féminin en Grèce ancienne,* edited by Nicole Loraux. Paris, 1986.

Picard, Charles. "L'épisode de Baubô dans les mystères d'Éleusis." *Revue de l'histoire des religions* 95 (March–June 1927): 220–255.

For an interpretation from the religious-historical point of view and a full bibliography see further Giovanni Casadio, *Vie gnostiche all'immortalità,* Brescia, 1997, pp. 62–64, esp. n. 151.

MAURICE OLENDER (1987)
Translated from French by Kristine Anderson
Revised Bibliography

BAUER, BRUNO

BAUER, BRUNO (1809–1882), left-wing Hegelian critic of the Bible, Christianity, and Prussian society. Bauer began his career as a conservative (right-wing) Hegelian theologian. His earliest writings on the Old Testament (1838) argued that the Hebraic idea of a deity distinct from creation gradually developed toward the Christian doctrine of the immanence of God and humanity. As a Hegelian, he interpreted this to mean that the finite had become conscious of itself as infinite. In an essay of 1840 he also argued that the union of the Reformed and Lutheran churches in 1818 further confirmed the Hegelian view that the Prussian state had become the embodiment of true spiritual life.

Appointed to the faculty of Bonn University in 1839, he turned his attention to the New Testament and wrote what is now considered his most important work: *Kritik der evangelischen Geschichte der Synoptiker.* In it he tried to show that biblical criticism could advance the self-consciousness of humanity by extracting the kernel of truth in the Christian narratives—that is, that human self-consciousness is divine—from the contradictions resulting from the historical form of those narratives. He treated the New Testament Gospels as purely human documents and as literary products of the creative imagination of the authors, therefore concluding that they record little about the real Jesus but much about the mentality of the early church.

Dismissed from the faculty at Bonn, he returned in bitterness to Berlin and wrote attacks on Christianity, the Prussian state, and even Hegel. He came to believe that unremitting, rational criticism, unallied with any political party and without presuppositions of any kind, could bring about a transformation of society. Scornful of revolutionary action in 1848, he became disillusioned with Prussia until the advent of Bismarck. Although he returned to the problem of the origins of Christianity in later works, his views were largely ignored. He spent his last years working in his family's tobacco shop.

BIBLIOGRAPHY

Unfortunately, not only is there no edition of Bauer's entire work, but there are no English translations of major individual works. His two best-known and most influential works, so far as New Testament criticism is concerned, are *Kritik der evangelischen Geschichte der Synoptiker,* 3 vols. (Leipzig, 1841–1842), and *Kritik der Evangelien und Geschichte ihres Ursprungs,* 4 vols. in 2 (Berlin, 1851–1855). His attack on Christianity is best represented by *Das entdeckte Christentum,* now reprinted in an edition by Ernst Banikol (Jena, 1927).

There are surprisingly few books on Bauer. Recommended are Dieter Hetz-Eichenrode, *Der Junghegelianer Bruno Bauer im Vormärz* (Berlin, 1959), Douglas Moggach, *The Philosophy and Politics of Bruno Bauer* (Cambridge, 2003), and Zvi Rosen, *Bruno Bauer and Karl Marx: The Influence of Bruno Bauer on Marx's Thought* (The Hague, 1977). There is a fine discussion of Bauer and his significance for Christian thought in Karl Löwith's *From Hegel to Nietzsche: The Revolution in Nineteenth-Century Thought* (Garden City, N.Y., 1967). Nor should one neglect Albert Schweitzer's discussion of Bauer's critical work in *The Quest of the Historical Jesus,* 2d ed. (1911; reprint, London, 1952). Other helpful secondary sources are *The Young Hegelians* by William J. Brazill (New Haven, 1970), which contains very useful bibliographies, and *From Hegel to Marx: Studies in the Intellectual Development of Karl Marx* by Sidney Hook (New York, 1936).

VAN A. HARVEY (1987 AND 2005)

BAŪLS SEE BENGALI RELIGIONS

BAUR, F. C. (1792–1860) was a German Protestant theologian, biblical scholar, and church historian. Ferdinand Christian Baur is best known as the leader of the "Tübingen school" and the practitioner of an allegedly Hegelian historial method. He was perhaps the most important German theologian between Friedrich Schleiermacher and Albrecht Ritschl. Over the years he has suffered from caricature and neglect, but reappraisal was made easier in the 1960s when selected works by him began to reappear in a new edition.

Baur was born in Schmiden, near Stuttgart, and educated mainly at Blaubeuren seminary and the University of Tübingen. In 1817 he returned to Blaubeuren as a teacher, and his thinking changed radically from the supernaturalism of the so-called Old Tübingen School to the conviction, learned from Schleiermacher, that Christianity cannot be studied in isolation from other religions, as though it alone had a divine origin. He moved in 1826 to a chair at his old university, Tübingen, where he remained until his death.

At Tübingen Baur led the secluded life of a dedicated academic. But he became embroiled in two famous literary debates. The first was occasioned by the attempt of Johann Adam Moehler, of the Catholic theological faculty, to specify in his symbolics (1832) the doctrinal differences between Roman Catholics and Protestants. The second erupted when David Friedrich Strauss, one of Baur's former students from Blaubeuren, published his notorious *Life of Jesus* (1835) and was dismissed from his lectureship at Tübingen. Baur protested against the dismissal, but he endorsed neither Strauss's method nor his conclusions.

Unlike Strauss, Baur did not believe that criticism had proved the books of the New Testament to be virtually worthless as sources for reconstructing Christian origins. The documents themselves, according to Baur, give plain evidence of the historical situation through which they should be interpreted, namely, the clash between Jewish Christianity and gentile Christianity, which was later to be harmonized in the old Catholic church. The historical worth of the sources can be appraised by determining each author's "tendency," or theological proclivity, against this background of conflict. Baur concluded that John's gospel must be set aside in any serious attempt to write the history of the primitive church, that Matthew's is the earliest of the Gospels that have come down to us, and that Paul most likely wrote only four of the letters attributed to him *(Galatians, 1 Corinthians, 2 Corinthians,* and *Romans).* Further, while he rejected Schleiermacher's belief that in Christ the ideal became actual, he thought it possible, against Strauss, to trace the way in which the Christ of ecclesiastical dogma developed out of Jesus' own self-consciousness.

His critics read Baur's New Testament work as a doctrinaire application of the Hegelian dialectic of thesis, antithesis, and synthesis. Similarly, in his series of learned works in the history of dogma they discovered more speculation than history. Baur replied that objective history can be written only by one who first determines history's object—that is, what it is all about. The historian who is interested in something more than a senseless jumble of facts must take his point of departure from the thinking of his own day, and that meant, for Baur, the Hegelian vision of history as the progress of Mind through time in the medium of ideas. Church history, in particular, must start from the idea of the church, which is the idea of the reconciliation of God and man.

Whatever the merits of his Hegelianism, Baur was a scholar of massive erudition and a highly sophisticated methodologist. He held that history without philosophy is "eternally dumb," and that the only way to understand Christian doctrines is to trace their development in a process that has already begun within the New Testament itself. History, philosophy, constructive theology, and New Testament studies, Baur believed, belong together in a single grand enterprise.

BIBLIOGRAPHY

Baur's literary output was enormous. Of his greatest work, *Geschichte der christlichen Kirche,* 5 vols. (1853–1863; reprint, Leipzig, 1969), only the first volume was translated into English: *The Church History of the First Three Centuries,* 2 vols., translated from the third edition and edited by Allan Menzies (London, 1878–1879). The second edition of his major study of Paul (1866–1867) appeared in English as *Paul the Apostle of Jesus Christ, His Life and Work, His Epistles and His Doctrine: A Contribution to a Critical History of Primitive Christianity,* 2 vols., translated by Allan Menzies and Eduard Zeller (London, 1875–1876). Baur's survey of the epochs of church historiography (1852) and the introduction to his posthumously published lectures on the history of dogma (1865–1867) are translated in Peter C. Hodgson's *Ferdinand Christian Baur on the Writing of Church History* (New York, 1968). Hodgson's *The Formation of Historical Theology: A Study of Ferdinand Christian Baur* (New York, 1966) is a comprehensive guide to Baur's life and work. For the debate with Moehler, see Joseph Fitzer, *Moehler and Baur in Controversy, 1832–38: Romantic-Idealist Assessment of the Reformation and Counter-Reformation* (Tallahassee, Fla., 1974).

New Sources

Evans, William B. "The Tübingen School: A Historical and Theological Investigation of the School of F. C. Baur." *Journal of the Evangelical Theological Society* 36 (1993): 247–249.

Morgan, Robert. "Ferdinand Christian Baur." In *Nineteenth Century Religious Thought in the West,* edited by Ninian Smart et al., vol. 1, pp. 261–289. Cambridge, UK, 1985.

B. A. GERRISH (1987)
Revised Bibliography

BAYḌĀWĪ, AL- (died sometime between AH 685 and 716, or 1286 and 1316 CE), fully, Abū Saʿīd ʿAbd Allāh ibn ʿUmar ibn Muḥammad ibn ʿAlī Abū al-Khayr Naṣīr al-Dīn al-Bayḍāwī; Islamic religious scholar and judge. Born in Bayḍā᾽, near the city of Shiraz in Persia, al-Bayḍāwī was educated in the religious sciences in Baghdad and spent most of his life following in his father's footsteps in Shiraz as the chief justice of the province of Fārs. He belonged to the Shāfiʿī legal school (*madhhab*) and was a follower of the tradition of al-Ashʿarī in theology. He wrote some twenty works on various subjects, including jurisprudence, law, grammar, theology, and the Qur᾽anic sciences. While all of these works were written in Arabic, he also produced a world history in his native Persian.

Al-Bayḍāwī's fame and reputation rest mainly upon his commentary (*tafsīr*) on the Qur᾽ān, titled *Anwār al-tanzīl wa-asrār al-ta᾽wīl* (The lights of the revelation and the secrets of the interpretation). This work examines the Qur᾽ān phrase by phrase in an attempt to present, concisely yet comprehensibly, the conclusions of earlier commentators in such a way as to express al-Bayḍāwī's own understanding of the orthodox Sunnī interpretation of the Qur᾽ān in his time. His main sources of interpretational information are the famous philosopher and Qur᾽anic commentator Fakhr al-Dīn al-Rāzī (d. 1209) and the Muʿtazilī theologian al-Zamakhsharī (d. 1144). The latter author was clearly more important for al-Bayḍāwī, whose commentary may be viewed to a great extent as a simplified summary of his predecessor's work, condensing what was found to be most essential in grammar, meaning, and textual variants. Omitted most of the time, although sometimes overlooked and allowed to remain, are statements that reflect al-Zamakhsharī's rationalist theological views. For example, in interpreting *sūrah* 3:8, "Our Lord, make not our hearts to swerve, after that thou hast guided us," al-Zamakhsharī takes "make not our hearts to swerve" to mean "do not withhold your grace from us after having already granted it to us," with the emphasis placed upon the notion of God's grace coming after man has acted to deserve it. Al-Bayḍāwī rejects this free-will, rationalist position, substituting the interpretation that since God does lead people astray, they must pray to God for the divine gift of guidance and grace.

Because of its concise nature, al-Bayḍāwī's commentary has proved valuable over the centuries for quick reference, although certainly not for full analysis. For this reason it has been widely read in the Muslim world and has attracted a large number of supercommentaries, and soon after Europeans made learned contacts with Islam it became the best-known Qur᾽ān commentary in the West. Representing what is best described as the consolidation of traditionalism in the field of Qur᾽anic interpretation, al-Bayḍāwī's *tafsīr* has been the basic textbook for all students of the subject in East and West alike.

BIBLIOGRAPHY

Anwār al-tanzīl wa-asrār al-ta᾽wīl has been edited and published numerous times both in the Islamic world and in Europe; the standard edition of the Arabic text is that edited by H. O. Fleischer (Leipzig, 1846–1848). Sections of the work are available in English translation, although they are often not completely understandable without at least some knowledge of Arabic. The commentary on *sūrah* 12, the story of Joseph, has appeared twice in translation, by Eric F. F. Bishop and Mohamed Kaddal in *"The Light of Inspiration and the Secrets of Interpretation," Chrestomathia Baidawiana: Translation of Surat Yusuf with Baidawi's Commentary* (Glasgow, 1957) and by A. F. L. Beeston in *Baiḍāwī's Commentary on Sūrah 12 of the Qur᾽ān* (Oxford, 1963). The commentary on *sūrah* 3 was translated by D. S. Margoliouth in *Chrestomathia Baidawiana: The Commentary of El-Baidāwī on Sura III* (London, 1894). The best place to start in order to experience al-Bayḍāwī's commentary in English is probably Kenneth Cragg's *The Mind of the Qur᾽ān: Chapters in Reflection* (London, 1973), which includes the commentary on *sūrah* 112. All of these works also provide some basic overview of al-Bayḍāwī and his significance. A number of articles by Lutpi Ibrahim have appeared on al-Bayḍāwī and his theological relationship to al-Zamakhsharī: "Al-Bayḍāwī's Life and Works," *Islamic Studies* (Karachi) 18 (1979): 311–321; "The Concept of Divine Justice According to al-Zamakhsharī and al-Bayḍāwī," *Hamdard Islamicus* 3 (1980): 3–17; "The Relation of Reason and Revelation in the Theology of al-Zamakhsharī and al-Baiḍāwī," *Islamic Culture* 54 (1980): 63–74; "The Concept of *Iḥbāṭ* and *Takfīr* According to az-Zamakhsharī and al-Bayḍāwī," *Die Welt des Orient* 11 (1980): 117–121; and "The Questions of the Superiority of Angels and Prophets between az-Zamakhsharī and al-Bayḍāwī," *Arabica* 28 (1981): 65–75.

ANDREW RIPPIN (1987)

BAY ÜLGEN SEE ÜLGEN

BEARS. Bears are a significant presence in the religious lives of various peoples in the Americas, Europe, and Asia. For thousands of years bears and humans have lived within the same habitat and competed for the same foods but not without encounters leading to one killing the other. Thus it has long been in the best interest of each species to give the other a wide berth of space.

By maintaining a safe distance from the brown bear, the Cahuilla people of California allowed these bears greater presence in their religious lives. Ironically by avoiding physical closeness, the Cahuilla brought the grizzly religiously nearer, such that an encounter with the bear incited a confrontation with ancestors, supernatural powers, and wisdom. The Cahuilla believed their safety relied on an ability to converse with the big bear, which they called "great-grandfather," and so they talked to the bear in a soothing tone, asking it to recognize their peaceful intentions. They also believed that after death some people would be reborn as great bears.

However, this example does not encapsulate the diversity of the bear's religious presence to many peoples throughout the world. In fact *bear* is a generalized term that does not account for differences between the eight species of bears in the world. Nor does it take into account habitat diversity that can influence behavior differences—based on variations in climate, availability of foods, and landscape—between bears of the same species. Indeed a bear's symbolic meaning to humans living alongside it is influenced both by species diversity and habitat diversity. Whereas this may initially seem more appropriate for ecology than religion, those who seek an adequate understanding of the religious significance of bears must first account for the type of bear and the aspects of this bear's habitat. They must also account for the religious aspects of the people sharing the bear's habitat. Thus not only the physical and biological characteristics of the bear itself but also the characteristics of the bear's habitat and the characteristics of a culture's experiences with the bear are primary for adequately determining the bear's symbolic meaning. Consequently these same aspects are also essential for identifying common religious themes that can be cross-culturally attributed to bears.

SPECIES DIVERSITY AND RELIGIOUS SIGNIFICANCE. There are eight species of bears in the world. They are the American black bear, the Asiatic black bear, the brown bear, the giant panda, the polar bear, the sloth bear, the spectacled bear, and the sun bear.

The Asiatic black bear is also known as a moon bear. It inhabits China, Tibet, southern Russia, Afghanistan, Pakistan, Indochina, and southern Japan. It has been identified as a "helping spirit" for some shamans of Asia, such as the Ostyaks, who sought to acquire health and strength as well as the power to heal and give strength to others. But perhaps more than other bears, the Asiatic black bear plays an important role in traditional medicine. It is first mentioned in a pharmaceutical report written in China in the fifth century. Bear paw soup was reputed to confer health; the bear's gallbladder, dried and crushed into a fine powder, is supposed to treat heart disease, headaches, and abdominal pain. There is also evidence that bear meat gave people strength. But the Asiatic black bear's greatest significance is as a symbol of rebirth. As a hibernator, which disappears in midwinter and reappears every spring, it has often been a symbol of immortality, particularly in prehistoric cultures, because every spring the bear is reborn. It is also believed that the bear derives its immortal powers from the eternal cycles of the moon. Ironically though it is called "moon bear" because of the white, yellow, or orange crescent on its chest, there are similarities between the moon bear's name and the birth-rebirth symbolism of the lunar cycle.

The American black bear, populating much of North America, has symbolic and ceremonial importance to such cultures as the Ojibwa and the Cherokee. But in identifying the black bear in a religious context, one will note conflicting descriptions of this species among various peoples. This is because the American black bear varies widely in size and color, and it can therefore be confusing to those who are unaware of these variations. In fact black bears native to the Floridian wetlands are about half the size of the salmon-feeding black bears of British Columbia and therefore pose different degrees of reverential fear to the people living near them. And because the bears in Florida hibernate much less (if at all some years), there are disparities in how much this bear cross-culturally symbolizes rebirth.

In addition to size variations, the black bear is not always black. It also appears as cinnamon, chocolate, light blond, grayish-blue, and even white. In various native myths, particularly those originating in the northwestern United States and Canada, there are references to "black," "brown," "glacier," "blue," and "white" bears. Such reports of a "glacier" or "white" bear, as is witnessed in the study of the Kwakiutl, Tlingit, Kitasoo, and Gitgaát peoples, may seem odd because these cultures are not northern enough to regularly encounter the polar bear. Yet these references are really to black bears. Here the blue bear or "glacier bear" is a black bear that inhabits central Alaska and the Yukon and once roamed glaciers that have long since receded. The white bear, Kermode bear, ghost bear, or spirit bear is only found in three isolated areas off the coast of British Columbia and lives so remotely and reclusively that its numbers and origins are shrouded in mystery that goes as far back as the Kitasoo and Gitgaát peoples' cosmologies, which state that these bears are "white bear people" made by the creator. The story also says that when the great glaciers retreated northward, the creator made the spirit bear to remind the people that the lush rainforest was once white with ice and snow. The creator then proceeded to set aside an island paradise for these "white bear people," where they could live in peace forever, and on that special island the creator made every tenth bear white.

Thus considering these variations in color, it seems likely that there are variations in the bears' religious significance to native peoples as well. Nevertheless the association of this bear, like its Asiatic cousin, with strength, magic, good luck, healing powers, and immortality remains a widely common theme. In many cases American black bears are also considered to be ancestors reborn as bear people. This can be witnessed in the Tlingits' reference to the bear as "my father's brother-in-law" and the Lapps' euphemism for the bear as "sacred man," "old man of the mountains," and "old man with the fur garment." This ancestral link naturally gives way to many indigenous people associating wisdom, respect, and guidance to bear ancestors, and it is through this link and the bears' association (as a hibernator) with birth and rebirth that some people believe that, upon their death, they will be reborn as bear people.

The brown bear once extended in North America as far south as Mexico and also inhabits Russia, northern Japan, central Asia, and Europe. The Alaskan brown bear, the Kodiak bear, the grizzly bear, the bear of the Ainu people, the bears integral to Basque celebrations in Spain, the Russian bears inhabiting the Kamchatka Peninsula, and the extirpated bears of Mexico, California, and the southwestern United

States all belong to the same species of brown bear. But variations in diet throughout the vast range of this species (which are linked to differences in habitat) have naturally resulted in variations in the bear's religious significance.

The giant panda inhabits the forests and bamboo jungles of central China. It was first mentioned in Chinese literature two thousand years ago and it was often captured and entombed with emperors in royal mausoleums. The giant panda is also mentioned in the *Shih-King,* the Book of Odes, and is known as *beishung,* the harmless bear of all bears. The panda was considered supernatural—partly because of its black and white markings—to many aboriginals of China, including the Lolo. Because it feeds on bamboo, the panda did not directly compete with these peoples and was ritually hunted only for its powerfully significant pelt. For these people donning the panda skin meant becoming the panda and inheriting its powers. However, unlike other species, pandas were rarely hunted until Westerners offered money for them.

The polar bear or sea bear is located in the northern regions of Canada, Alaska, Siberian Russia, Greenland, and Scandinavian Europe. It has long been integral to shamanic initiations of native peoples in the northern regions. Among the Ammasilik peoples, the shaman initiate stood for long hours in a snow hut meditating until he or she apparently fell dead and remained lifeless for three days and three nights. During this period some initiates dreamed of a polar bear devouring their flesh until nothing remained but the skeleton. Because dismemberment and the reduction of the body to a skeleton were parts of the mystical experience that illustrated that the initiate had received the gift of shamanic powers, it can be argued that it was the polar bear, as a guardian spirit, that mediated the shamanic gift to the initiate. By withdrawing to solitude and rejecting one's body, the spirits could manifest themselves to the shaman initiate in the form of a polar bear who dismembered the person's body until there was nothing left but the skeleton, resulting in his or her "death." Upon his or her death, the way for that person's rebirth was revealed. Thus for many northern peoples, the polar bear symbolizes a real and direct connection with the beyond—as perhaps the helping spirit that guides the person through death to the underworld and then serves as the manifestation of rebirth as a shaman.

The sloth bear is known to inhabit Nepal, Sri Lanka, Bhutan, and Bangladesh, but it is most widespread in the dry and deciduous forests of India. Living in the tropics, this bear does not hibernate, and so there is little religious birth-rebirth significance tied to it. Also known as the lip bear, the sloth bear's significance is in its medicinal powers, especially the magical potency attributed to its penis bone. Despite its docile name, many local people in jungle areas have attributed a fear-based reverence and wisdom to the sloth bear, because, although usually timid and preoccupied with diligent termite digging, it is known to attack savagely when surprised or sometimes at night when someone gets too close.

The spectacled bear is the largest carnivore in South America and the second largest mammal. The Andean peoples attributed magical and curative powers to the spectacled bear. There is evidence that the Incan civilization attributed the powers of strength, healing, and longevity to the spectacled bear. In Venezuela the fat from a ritually hunted bear is used to heal rheumatic problems, and the bear's bones are ground up and mixed with milk and then given to infants to strengthen them. Often when the Incans killed the bear, its blood was immediately consumed to help the hunter become bearlike. Even the spectacled bear's scat (feces) was believed to carry magical powers. Thus many peasants fed and continue in the twenty-first century to feed bear droppings to their cattle with the belief that their animals will become stronger.

The sun bear or honey bear is about half the size of the average American black bear. It is the smallest of the eight bear species and the least known. It inhabits the lowland forests of Southeast Asia from Malaysia and Indonesia westward as far as India, and it is greatly threatened in southern China, Myanmar, Cambodia, Laos, Borneo, and Vietnam. The sun bear's religious significance is in its power to heal (its gallbladders are said to heal bruises and broken bones), and whereas not much is known about this least studied of the eight bear species, future research on shamanism in this region may reveal more about the sun bear's religious significance.

Habitat Diversity and Religious Significance. Not only do fluctuations in bear color result in variations in symbolic meaning, but variations in a bear's habitat may also affect its religious significance. For instance, the diet of the grizzly in the Rocky Mountains of western North America consists largely of vegetation. Similar diets can be attributed to brown bears in Europe and Asia. Yet the diets of brown bears inhabiting the Pacific coasts include a greater percentage of prey, resulting in their larger size and, not surprisingly, a fiercer reputation. Additionally because of the coastal region's milder climate, food sources are generally more abundant, causing a denser population of bears in these regions as opposed to the mountainous areas. This increases the chance of an encounter by coastal peoples with brown bears than by people living inland.

Along the Pacific Coast, big bears dominated the scene before Europeans arrived. According to the Yokuts, the grizzly bear's ferocious disposition was clearly evident even in death, when the muscle fibers bristled erect. The fears that resulted from the sheer presence of such a powerful animal and the gruesome stories that were passed on describing human encounters with these great bears resulted in a religious significance that often emphasized fear, strength, and bad superstitions. Among the Luiseño the grizzly was a great avenger of the god Chungichnish; the Luiseño warned that Chungichnish would ascend to the stars after his death and send bears down to punish those who were faithless. Likewise the Pomo believed that faithless people would have to stay behind after death in the bodies of miserable and tormented grizzlies, forever roaming the wilderness to be hated and loathed by all who saw them. The Wintun shared a similar belief and therefore would not eat big bears for fear of absorbing lost souls. In fact the Wintun also believed that thunder and lightning were destructive twins born of a grizzly bear woman and that the rippling of the moon's reflection on the water was caused by a grizzly who must run eternally around the lunar orb.

In contrast, the Thompson peoples of British Columbia considered the birth of twins to be one of the greatest blessings that could come to a tribe, and the children were treated from birth like royalty and called "grizzly bear children." They were considered to have within them courage, healing powers, and control over the weather—all considered to be unique magical powers of the great bear. Likewise the Blackfoot in Montana and Alberta also held the grizzly, the "unmentionable one," in reverent esteem. Blackfoot legends attribute to the bear the power to heal wounds and make warriors wise and brave. In addition various tribes honored the grizzly bear as their ancestor, as is evidenced by its name as "chief's son" by the Cree, "old man" by the Sauk, and "elder brother" by the Menominee. Whether or not these people had the nerve to hunt the bear or were afraid of it and stayed out of its way, the bear appeared to be more like them than any other animal.

For many people, like various Apache groups and the Navajo, the brown bear was to be avoided, because they believed it possessed sinister supernatural powers, and they thought that contact with the bear, its tracks or feces, or even a place where it had noticeably been could cause deadly "bear sickness." Yet for such people as the Kato, who did not avoid brown bears and sought them in ritualistic hunts, the hide became essential for the "bear shaman," who made war on the human enemies of their specific tribe. In many Californian tribes, bear shamans were thought to be invulnerable or at least to possess the power of returning to life, because their power was derived from the grizzly bear.

For those people who were brave enough to hunt the brown bear, there were even fewer tribes who ate them. For instance, the Yurok would not eat grizzlies simply because grizzlies ate people. Yet for those few tribes that did feed on grizzlies, like the Atsugewi, the hunted grizzly was eaten only if it was known that it had not killed a human. This is probably because of the bear's humanlike gestures and its similarities to humans when it is skinned. In fact, many (especially the Wintun) believed that eating a grizzly was an act of cannibalism.

Numerous examples like these support the widespread belief that many peoples considered grizzlies to be ancestors who were heroes, fierce warriors, bear shamans, or chiefs reborn as bear people. In fact the Wintun and the Nomlaki peoples were known to bury some of their dead in grizzly bear fur with the belief that they would be reborn as bears. The Chumash, living near the Valley of the Bears in California, believed that all who died there would become grizzlies.

COMMON THEMES OF RELIGIOUS SIGNIFICANCE. Considering the eight species of bears in the world, the wide range of habitat, and the diversity of religious cultures, it is not easy to generalize the bear's religious significance. However, strength, wisdom, courage, the power to heal, and ancestral kinship seem to be religiously significant characteristics both among bears of the same species living in different areas and among all eight species of bears throughout the world. Yet the symbolism of birth-rebirth and immortality are generally only traceable to the four hibernating bears: the Asiatic and American black bears, the brown bear, and the polar bear. Even more specific are the symbolic variations related to a bear's diet, especially if bears had to compete with people for the same food from the same places, which often resulted in people regarding bears with intense fear-based reverence and considering them to be bad omens.

SEE ALSO Ainu Religion; Khanty and Mansi Religion; Lord of the Animals; Tunguz Religion.

BIBLIOGRAPHY

Barrett, Samuel Alfred. *Pomo Bear Doctors.* Berkeley, Calif., 1917.

Brown, David. *The Grizzly in the Southwest: Documentary of an Extinction.* Norman, Okla., 1985. Emphasizes the European influence on the extinction of the brown bear in the American Southwest. However, a few sections discuss the significance that the grizzly has to some native people of the Southwest, particularly the Apache, Navajo, and Comanche. In addition, the reference section includes valuable listings of archived documentations about the first European encounters with Native Americans and bears.

Campbell, Joseph. *Historical Atlas of World Mythology,* vol. 1: *The Way of the Animal Powers.* New York, 1983. A popular source for building parallels between the significance of bears and the religious lives of various peoples.

Eliade, Mircea. *Shamanism: Archaic Techniques of Ecstasy.* Translated by Willard R. Trask. Princeton, N.J., 1964. This remains a definitive source for understanding basic commonalities for bear shamanism.

Rockwell, David. *Giving Voice to Bear: North American Indian Myths, Rituals, and Images of the Bear.* Niwot, Colo., 1991. This is an introductory source for myths, rituals, and images of the bear in North America.

Servheen, Christopher, Stephen Herrero, and Bernard Peyton. *Bears: Status Survey and Conservation Action Plan.* Gland, Switzerland, 1999. A detailed book about the eight different species of bears. An excellent source for understanding and identifying which "bears" are most likely being addressed in religious literature, myths, and folklore.

Shepard, Paul, and Barry Sanders. *The Sacred Paw: The Bear in Nature, Myth, and Literature.* New York, 1985. A good source for reviewing the religious significance of bears, with recognition of the variations that occur among the different bear species. Although there are many themes that have since been updated, this book is most valuable for its reference index on bear mythology, natural history, and literature. Its index is perhaps one of the most extensive to date on the religious significance of bears, and therefore it is not only an excellent introductory source on bear religious attributions but also a solid library on literature about bear ceremonialism, myths, and legends throughout the world.

Storer, Tracy I., and Lloyd P. Tevis. *California Grizzly.* Berkeley, Calif., 1955. A good source on the diversity of influences the grizzly has had on the numerous tribes of California. However, the language is generally exclusive, and there is more emphasis placed on the grizzly's ferocity toward humans than its role as an object of ancestral reverence.

LEON CHARTRAND (2005)

BEAUTY is said to be a property of an object that produces an aesthetic pleasure; this pleasure is a subjective response to a beautiful object, often, but not always, in nature. For example, the beauty of a rose produces an aesthetic pleasure. Immanuel Kant thought other objects beautiful to the degree they conform to objects in nature (Kant, 1953, paras. 42–45). The question is whether this subjective response to a beautiful object can be spontaneous and universally communicable.

Certain philosophers have argued that pleasurable enjoyment of beautiful artistic creations is not originally spontaneous, but needs to be cultivated as a cognitive disposition. This cultivation involves attending to an object (or subject) to recognize its (or her) beauty. Beauty's recognition is similar to the cultivation of the moral virtues of justice and goodness. A virtue achieves truth to the degree that it acquires its distinctive form of perfection; perfection is the goal (*telos*) for the cultivation of virtues. If the disposition for beauty is a human cognitive capacity, then once beauty is acquired in its true form it would be universally communicable. Ideally, beauty would produce aesthetic pleasure spontaneously in all those human subjects whose cognitive dispositions are cultivated for their own perfection.

What is the measure of this perfection? Is there a perfect form of beauty for every natural and created object? Or is this merely a subjective matter? If the latter, how can we agree about what is beautiful? Is perfection of the human form measured against an aesthetic, moral, or divine standard? Religion has concerned itself with beauty precisely because of the inability of human beings to recognize or create perfection. Despite our apparent inability, we desire beauty in fair countenance (or justice), in human relationships (or love), and in orderly action (or goodness). In various dimensions of human experience, we long for perfect order and so crave beauty. If we turn this around, evidence of beauty as perfect order in nature serves to support imperfect human beings in proving the necessity of a divine creator.

BEAUTY IN WESTERN PHILOSOPHY. As a concept, beauty has a history of meanings and uses. Beauty's meaning changes in relation to the variability of human conceptions of nature, as well as the variability of human values. Beauty's use in political, moral, and religious philosophy links it with the cultivation of a range of dispositions that can become settled states of character. As with the virtues of political justice, moral goodness, and religious love, the real existence of beauty may be doubted, while dispositions are fragile and corruptible. Nevertheless, human beings still seek to achieve the experience of aesthetic pleasure, as well as other forms of perfection. Although justice, goodness, and love are often lacking in our global world, we seek them. We recognize and create beauty in the sense of the French *reconnaître*; that is, gratefully acquired knowledge of what is true, legitimate, or proper to one's own nature. This complex sense of recognition (of beauty) resonates with Western political, moral, and theological concerns.

For a sense of the history of the concept of beauty, consider ancient Greek philosophy. Plato recommends a deliberate ascent away from sensuous nature. The human soul aspires to be united with divine love in the apprehension of truth, to become the perfect form of love. Beauty is seen in this perfection. But a strictly Platonic account is inadequate for understanding significant conceptions of beauty, especially those built upon beauty's relation to sensuous nature.

A concrete, contemporary understanding of beauty's "exile" from human experiences of art, morality, and religion could rescue this concept (cf. Steiner, 2001). Good reasons exist for beauty's exile from (much) twentieth-century experience, including a failure of human self-understanding and spiritual development. A less obvious reason is beauty's close association with the idealized female subject who has dominated the Western imagination—whether in the Virgin Mary, the fragile innocence of the maternal figure of femininity, or the perfect (sexualized) form of the female body. As female consciousness gained a critical edge in twentieth-century societies, so did the recognition that the female body had been objectified, even idolized, as an erotic object. The objectification of this subject of beauty became exclusive in taking on the form of a specific gender-type, as well as idealizing the qualities of a specific race, class, and religion.

The extent of this objectification, by both men and women, is evident in the degree to which women's self-image is determined by a culture's fetish of beauty. This is when women do not actually see their own selves in representations of female beauty but are seen in terms of what others think they should look like. Beauty becomes the opposite of anything natural, free, or creative. Instead it is bound up with oppressive images of the female subject. Contemporary aesthetics has not generally treated beauty as a central concern. Yet it is possible to find serious endeavors to restore beauty to what is still thought to be its rightful place in the pleasurable enjoyment of nature, artistic creations, and human love.

To write about beauty is to tell a story about values for human beings. Values, including love (*caritas*), and such acquired dispositions as truth, goodness, and justice, have been portrayed in myths, in representations of relationships between men, women, and the divine. Philosophers and theologians have turned to the poets and the artists of their age to imagine in myth what is not seen but is experienced. Beauty is only truly seen when human vision (and therefore lived experiences) is not determined by oppressive ideals and images. Even ancient myths about beauty involve struggle and concealment until, ideally, the seeing that attends to an "other" achieves a revelation of truth and goodness.

One ancient myth that has been restored to prominence in contemporary discussions of love, pleasure, and beauty is the story of Psyche and Cupid. *Cupid* is the Latin name of the ancient figure of love, represented in this myth by a male god; *Psyche* is the Greek name for a human soul, represented by the female subject who appears trapped in a beautiful body, alienated from others by their envy of her beauty. Psyche's beauty does not bring happiness, but its opposite. The envy of others causes Psyche to suffer the tricks and trials of human and divine subjects. Then Cupid and Psyche become lovers, and Psyche learns to be trustworthy, face-to-face with love in the presence of beauty. In the end, Psyche becomes divine, loving freely and eternally (see Apuleius, 1998; Gilligan, 2002).

GENDERING BEAUTY AND THE SUBLIME. An adequate historical account of the Western concept of beauty should consider the gender associated with the beautiful and the sublime at the end of the eighteenth and beginning of the nineteenth centuries. New gendered readings aligned the beautiful with feminine virtues, and the sublime with masculine ones. At this point, the sublime—in place of beauty—becomes associated with the divine. Why would the divine be associated with one or the other? God, as perfect, would fulfill the human desire for fairness of countenance, whether as the beautiful or the sublime. Again, turning this around, philosophical awareness of perfection in nature, including human nature, gives grounds for the existence of a (maximally) great creator of this perfect design. But why would Enlightenment-era religion replace the beautiful with the sublime? The conception of the divine must represent absolute greatness and perfection; hence, the sublime, as greater than beauty in sensuous nature or in its imitation, is taken to represent inexpressible perfection and greatness.

Jean-Jacques Rousseau's eighteenth-century account of the different moral educations of men and women in *Émile* (1762) maintains the above gendered distinction. Kant's *Observations on the Feeling of the Beautiful and the Sublime* (1764) follows Rousseau, while Mary Wollstonecraft's *Vindication of the Rights of Woman* (1792) responds critically to this gendering of beauty. The following is disputed: "The fair sex has just as much understanding as the male, but it is a *beautiful understanding* whereas ours should be a *deep understanding*, an expression that signifies identity with the sublime" (Kant, 1960, p. 78). A positive reading of Kant's claim acknowledges a certain level of equality—in understanding—between the male and female sexes. However, the gendered differences between beautiful and deep understandings have negative implications when read alongside Kant's assertion that "The virtue of a woman is a beautiful virtue. That of the male sex should be a noble virtue. Women will avoid the wicked not because it is un-right, but because it is ugly; and virtuous actions mean to them such as are morally beautiful. Nothing of duty, nothing of compulsion, nothing of obligation!" (Kant, 1960, p. 81). At first glance women seem freed from the constraints of duty—but this would imply excluding them from moral autonomy, i.e., from acting for the sake of duty alone. Additional gendered connotations differentiate men from women by the ability to distance themselves from sensuous nature and move closer to the divine. This crucial difference shapes later associations of women with nature. Women's beauty as a gift of nature becomes increasingly problematic as science and technology seek to dominate nature as unruly and threatening rather than orderly and nurturing.

Kant's gendering of beauty affects subsequent accounts of aesthetic education in profound ways, but it equally affects theological accounts of divine greatness as the sublime. The problematic tradition of the gendering of beauty and the sublime continues today. The nineteenth-century German idealist Friedrich Schiller passed on this tradition by reinforcing the gendered differences of Kant's moral virtues. The twentieth-century French postmodernist Jean-François Lyotard ensures that absolute beauty is unobtainable for women while men struggle for the divine—by transcending the chaotic and corrupting forces of nature—in the sublime.

LIMITS OF THE HUMAN AND THE DIVINE. The upshot of Kantian aesthetics in modern and postmodern literature culminates in a monstrous sublime. When human desire and delight go beyond their proper limits, human creations become monstrous. At the extreme, the yearning connoisseur of beauty fails tragically to be worthy of this perception. Without the mutual exchange between creator and creature, between lover and beloved, monstrous forms of creativity manifest human unworthiness. Instead of harmony, integrity, and splendor, the one-sided endeavor to create human "beauty" results in the monstrous sublime of death and destruction, "where by its size it defeats the end that forms its concept" (Kant, 1952, p. 100).

In contrast, the mutual exchange of love in beauty had been lifesaving, as a new creation and a fragile intimation of the divine. Positive qualities are undermined by the monstrous (sublime), which is imaginatively represented by the Enlightenment myth of a new Prometheus in Mary Shelley's *Frankenstein* (1818). Shelley's story about a man-made creature explores the tragedy and distortions of a scientific "man" who replaces divine with human creations, religion with science, and love with technology; the outcome is truly horrific. The Romantic idea of human creativity cannot be sustained without mutual love and justice. These virtues, sustained by something transcendent of both men and women, ensure that creativity does not result in self-destruction by a chaotic and violent nature.

How do men and women acquire those necessary virtues that are not theirs at birth? One answer is to return to the ancient allegory of love. Its lesson is that we have to be inspired to *see* the beautiful as something to love; perception of beauty in the beloved that renders her or him desirable is an experience inspired by perfect(ed) love. The allegory represents Cupid with the power to transform humans from mere mortals without erotic aspirations to midwives—or philosophers—who yearn for what they perceive as good. In this allegory, love is motivated neither by desire nor by beauty perceived independent of love. Instead, the very perception of the beloved as good is dependent on, first of all, the true vision of love. The lover, then, beholds the beautiful countenance of her beloved. This vision of beauty takes the two lovers outside of themselves as subjects.

Iris Murdoch describes this ability to *see beauty* as "unselfing." Her account recalls aspects of Plato's and Kant's accounts of beauty, yet it also reflects Murdoch's unique vision of attentiveness to the reality of love and beauty:

> It is important too that great art teaches us how real things can be looked at and loved without being seized and used, without being appropriated into the greedy organism of the self. This exercise of *detachment* is difficult and valuable whether the thing contemplated is a human being or the root of a tree or the vibration of a color or a sound. Unsentimental contemplation of nature exhibits the same quality of detachment: selfish concerns vanish, nothing exists except the things which are seen. Beauty is that which attracts this particular sort of unselfish attention (Murdoch, 1970, p. 65).

"What counteracts [blinding self-centered aims and images]. . .is *attention to* reality inspired by, consisting of, love" (Murdoch, 1970, p. 67, italics added). And "the most obvious thing in our surroundings which is an occasion for 'unselfing'. . .is beauty" (Murdoch, 1970, p. 84). This occasion for unselfing generates an attitude for seeing beauty in all its colors, shapes, and sizes. Although Murdoch's writing predates the postmodern challenges to the racial and ethnic biases of Anglo-American philosophy, her attitude for seeing beauty resonates with the more contemporary words of the African American cultural and feminist critic bell hooks: "'We must learn to see.' Seeing is meant metaphysically as heightened awareness and understanding, the intensification of one's capacity to experience reality through the realm of the senses" (hooks, 1990, pp. 111–112).

CULTIVATION OF BEAUTY AND A NEW AESTHETIC. Hooks proposes "an aesthetic of blackness," picturing beauty in the eyes of those women and men who take time to see and pay attention to the racial and material locations that shape and define their perceptions, feelings, and relationships. Specifically, "a radical aesthetic acknowledges that we are constantly changing positions, locations, that our needs and concerns vary, that these diverse directions must correspond with shifts in critical thinking" (hooks, 1990, p. 111).

To stand the test of time, beauty joins justice in seeking equality in fair relationships. The allegory of love presents an ultimate vision of the human soul (Psyche) becoming divine and immortal in a marital union of equality with the god of love (Cupid) in the presence of beauty that in turn begets pleasure. In this way, beauty constitutes an opportunity for self-revelation and exchanges of power between the self and another. Yet, in reality, beauty remains dangerously bound up with oppressive ideals, images, and symbols. At the same time, world religions have generated significant contexts in which divine love can raise the human soul above the death that haunts the natural world. This tension is problematic, since a spiritual ascent to love in the presence of beauty is not an ideal to which human beings can aspire unaided. The difficulty is to see a spiritual ascent in a sensorial descent, rising towards the transcendent even in descending.

A CONTEMPORARY THEOLOGICAL AESTHETICS. The danger in developing religious symbolism to conceive love of beauty as a form of salvation is evident in the aesthetic theology of the twentieth-century Swiss theologian Hans Urs von Balthasar. When the beauty of God radiates from every created form, the values of truth and goodness become inseparable from beauty's aesthetic value. But in placing beauty at the center of his symbolic story of salvation, von Balthasar makes the male gender central. Salvation in the form of beauty is limited by the gendered symbolism of his Christology, reinforcing the exclusion of the female body. Von Balthasar's objectification of the female body forces not beauty, but woman herself, into exile. What are the implications for his theology of beauty?

To be fair, von Balthasar has done more than other twentieth-century Christian theologians to restore beauty to a central place: he conceives Jesus Christ as the revelation of the form of God as absolute truth, goodness, and beauty. Von Balthasar gives a complex unity to this divine form; the beauty of divine revelation comes to perfection in Christ as the central form of God's glory. Beauty exists not merely for aesthetic pleasure, but as a moral and truthful challenge to conversion (von Balthasar, 1982–1991, vol. 1, p. 209). When beauty, truth, and goodness come together, the glory of God is revealed. The crucial question is whether the human need for spiritual perception of the form of beauty can be perfectly satisfied by von Balthasar's theological aesthetics.

Tina Beattie raises doubts about von Balthasar's Christology, exposing the danger in images of beauty that fail to represent the equality and mutuality of men and women in divine love. Beattie's critique of von Balthasar's symbolism begins by explaining how gender functions metaphorically and analogically. Next, Beattie shows how the female body in von Balthasar's complex sexual metaphysics is rendered redundant by the symbolism of Christ and the church. Only the male sex is necessary for the performance of the story of Christ, whose personae includes all variety of masculine and feminine qualities. This exclusion of the female body creates an asymmetry between men and women. On the one hand, motherhood and femininity are detached from the female body by, for instance, the symbolism of the church as mother, where both men and women can symbolize the mother church. On the other hand, their possession of a female body excludes women from performing any role associated with the essential masculinity of Christ. Due to their female bodies, women are reduced to the biological role of reproduction; *men* can represent *both* feminine and masculine qualities, while their male bodies allow men to perform roles associated exclusively with the masculinity of Christ (as in the priesthood, administration of sacraments, etc.). Thus, the symbolism of von Balthasar's Christology renders the male body essential for salvation, and the female body inessential.

Although von Balthasar's aesthetics respond to the control of the world by technological forces and masculine values of aggression, power, and war, any acknowledgment of the need for maternal feminine values, in order to avoid violence and exploitation, is undermined by the Catholic Church (of which von Balthasar plays a prominent part) being resolutely committed to the exclusion of women from positions of visibility and social-ethical influence. Can von Balthasar's Christology make sense of absolute beauty, goodness, and truth while his symbolism enshrines a vicious association between the female body, sex, death, and violence? If the female body represents Eve as the devil's gateway, whereby the threatening impurity of female flesh drags the male spirit into its chaotic depths of death and disintegration, then the devaluation of woman, nature, and ultimately, beauty is inevitable.

CONCLUSION. The artist Marlene Dumas captures the female body's association with death—displacing beauty—in a dramatic reformulation of the *pietà*, in which a male subject holds a female corpse (see Dumas's 1993 painting, *The Image as Burden*). Instead of the *pietà* with Mary holding the dead body of her male son Christ, a male mourner carries the dead body of the female subject. This reverses the traditional portrait of beauty. Can the female body and nature represent the source of life, not death, in a rebirth of beauty? One positive response refigures the allegory of love, offering hope for a new story of salvation for men and women.

The story of Psyche and Cupid can guide a symbolic reconfiguration of sexed and gendered subjects. Psyche is saved when, as the new Venus, (i.e., the soul of beauty), she (or he) replaces Cupid's mother and creates a new relationship as the beautiful one who is equal in love to her (or his) lover. In being transformed from human to divine, Psyche freely unites with divine love, Cupid, creating a relation of equality for love in beauty. At the same time, this love involves an unselfing in attending to the other self; hence, beauty is seen in the other's differences. The moral psychologist Carol Gilligan suggests that paying particular attention to our gendered relationships in the light of the birth of pleasure is (still) needed. Gilligan herself discovers the seeds for this new account in refiguring Psyche and Cupid.

Psyche as the soul of the (female) mortal becomes a divine subject in love. Psyche and Cupid together create a new fluidity of pleasure; this renders possible delight in the beautiful. These lovers pay attention to each other in a loving gaze. The fluidity of pleasure moves in between material differences of sex and gender, enabling beautiful interchanges. Giving birth to pleasure in the beauty of love transforms human relationships: this fairness, as another term for beauty, remains forever divine.

SEE ALSO Aesthetics; Architecture; Art and Religion; Human Body, article on Human Bodies, Religion, and Gender; Music.

BIBLIOGRAPHY

Apuleius. *The Golden Ass or Metamorphoses.* Translated by E. J. Kenney. Harmondsworth, U.K., 1998. An inspiring second-century story about Cupid and Psyche creates an allegory of love, beauty, and the metamorphoses of human and divine identities.

Beattie, Tina. *God's Mother, Eve's Advocate: A Marian Narrative of Women's Salvation.* Bristol, U.K., 1999; London, 2002. This feminist text criticizes and reconfigures the theological imagery of Eve and Mary, rewriting the story of salvation to include the integrity of the female body.

Gilligan, Carol. *The Birth of Pleasure: A New Map of Love.* London, 2002. The psychological study of intimate human relationships takes on new significance as it tells a story about the birth of pleasure, locating the shared feelings that shape human love.

hooks, bell. "An Aesthetic of Blackness: Strange and Oppositional." In *Yearning: Race, Gender, and Cultural Politics,* pp. 103–113. Boston, 1990. A brief but significant article, challenging conceptions of beauty and contending that beauty's function and purpose cannot be separated from material life, metaphysical perception, or political passion.

Kant, Immanuel. *The Critique of Judgement.* Translated by James Creed Meredith. Oxford, 1952. This third *Critique* (1790) contains a historically pivotal account of beauty, separating beauty's aesthetic value from moral and metaphysical philosophy, while carving out a universal role for the delight (in the beautiful) that communicates a shared feeling of aesthetic pleasure.

Kant, Immanuel. *Observations on the Feeling of the Beautiful and the Sublime.* Translated by John T. Goldthwait. Berkeley, 1960. Published in 1764, this work connects femininity and beauty, masculinity and the sublime.

Murdoch, Iris. *The Sovereignty of Good.* London, 1970. Three philosophical lectures addressing different aspects of the concept of the good tackle the selfishness and illusions that obscure reality and present beauty as the occasion for "unselfing."

Plato. *Symposium.* Translated by Alexander Nehamas and Paul Woodruff. Indianapolis, 1989. The classic dialogue on love and beauty.

Scarry, Elaine. *On Beauty and Being Just.* Princeton, 1999. A gem that redirects discussions of beauty towards justice.

Shelley, Mary. *Frankenstein, or The Modern Prometheus.* 1818; reprint, London, 1985. A novel that portrays imaginatively and critically the excess of human (exclusively male) creativity, going beyond its limits for love and beauty, in the reproduction of a monstrous creature.

Steiner, Wendy. *Venus in Exile: The Rejection of Beauty in Twentieth-Century Art.* Chicago, 2001. This study critically documents the difficulties resulting from an equation of beauty with the female subject, seeking to rescue the beautiful exile in reciprocal forms of aesthetic pleasure.

von Balthasar, Hans Urs. *The Glory of the Lord: A Theological Aesthetics.* 7 vols. Edited by Joseph Fessio and John Riches, and translated by Erasmo Leiva-Merikakis. Edinburgh, 1982–1991.

PAMELA SUE ANDERSON (2005)

BEDE (c. 673–735), usually called "the Venerable"; Northumbrian monk and scholar. Bede's whole life was associated with the twin monasteries of Wearmouth and Jarrow, founded by Benedict Biscop in 673–681. It is difficult to improve on the summary of his life supplied by Bede himself in introducing the list of his works provided in the final chapter of his *Ecclesiastical History of the English People:*

> I was born on the lands belonging to this monastery and at the age of seven was given by my family to the most reverend Benedict [Biscop] and to Ceolfrid [his successor] to be educated. From that time onward I have lived my whole life in this same monastery, devoting all my time to the study of the scriptures. While observing the regular monastic discipline and singing the daily office in church, I have always taken delight in learning, teaching, and writing. In my nineteenth year I became a deacon, and in my thirtieth a priest. . . . And from the day of my priestly ordination to this, my fifty-ninth year [731], I have composed the following works on Holy Scripture, either for my own use or that of my brethren, drawing for this purpose on the works of the holy Fathers, and at times adding comments of my own to clarify their meaning and interpretation.

Bede then adds a list that, in addition to scriptural works, also contains lives of saints, histories, grammatical works, poetry, and treatises on computation.

Bede's *Ecclesiastical History of the English People*—basically a religious history written for Christian believers—is a remarkable work, able to win the admiration even of modern-day historians who may not share Bede's religious beliefs. It demonstrates Bede's scholarly gifts, his fine Latinity, his concern to find trustworthy sources, his dexterity in the use of these sources, and his sobriety of judgment even when handling miraculous elements. The *Ecclesiastical History* is also noteworthy for its introduction of *anno Domini* as a means of dating events in the common era, a practice that became customary throughout the Western world.

Although Bede is most famous in modern times for the *Ecclesiastical History*, it was his scriptural comentaries that were best known and most used in his own day and among medieval writers of later generations, not all of whom employed their typically allegorical method of interpretation with Bede's characteristic restraint. His works were so well respected and so often copied that most of them have survived. His numerous borrowings from the Fathers testify to the magnificent collection of books Benedict Biscop had accumulated in Rome and transported all the way to Northumbria.

Bede's writings display the working of a lively and inquiring mind, fascinated not only by problems of scripture but also by those of the natural world. Taken in their chronological order his works allow us to discern a constantly growing scholarly maturity, as well as an attractive and winning personality. Bede's work on the calendar deserves special mention. The controversy over the date of Easter was particularly acute in his time since it pitted Roman against Celtic usage. Bede tried to put order into the controversy through a work, *De temporum ratione*, whose modern editor remarks that it still remains "the best introduction to the ecclesiastical calendar."

We possess a moving eyewitness account of Bede's last days in a letter written by one of his disciples, Cuthbert, to another, Cuthwin. He continued working and teaching to the end. One of his last tasks—left incomplete—was a translation of John's gospel into Old English. He died on May 26, 735.

BIBLIOGRAPHY

The edition of Bede's works by J. A. Giles (1834–1844) was reprinted in *Patrologia Latina*, edited by J.-P. Migne, vols. 90–95 (Paris, 1850–1851). New editions of most of Bede's works have since appeared in *Corpus Christianorum, series latina*, vols. 118–122 (Turnhout, 1955–1969). For the Latin text of the *Ecclesiastical History*, Bertram Colgrave and R. A. B. Mynors's edition (Oxford, 1969) supersedes that of Charles Plummer (Oxford, 1896), although Plummer's historical notes retain much value.

The bibliography on Bede is large, especially in the form of articles in scholarly journals. Special mention should be made of Peter Hunter Blair's *The World of Bede* (London, 1970); *Bede, His Life, Times and Writings: Essays in Commemoration of the Twelfth Centenary of His Death*, edited by Alexander Hamilton Thompson (Oxford, 1935); and *Famulus Christi: Essays in Commemoration of the Thirteenth Centenary of the Birth of the Venerable Bede*, edited by Gerald Bonner (London, 1976). The best general introduction to Bede's *Ecclesiastical History* remains Jackson J. Campbell's "Bede," in *Latin Historians*, edited by T. A. Dorey (New York, 1966). Numerous aspects of Bede and his background have been examined in the "Jarrow Lectures" (1958–), a series too little known but published yearly by the rector of Jarrow (Saint Paul's Rectory, Jarrow, England).

PAUL MEYVAERT (1987)

BEGGING SEE ALMSGIVING; MENDICANCY

BEING SEE ONTOLOGY

BEIT HILLEL AND BEIT SHAMMAI

BEIT HILLEL AND BEIT SHAMMAI were two early Jewish schools of thought, or "houses" (*beit,* from Hebrew *bayit,* means "house of"), named after Hillel and Shammai, leading sages of Jerusalem in the latter half of the first century BCE and in the early first century CE. The schools actually represented two distinct approaches to the study of the oral law that were prevalent from the time of Hillel and Shammai until the beginning of the second century. While very few adherents of either school are known by name, it appears that the Shammaites managed to achieve dominance sometime before the destruction of the Temple in 70 CE. According to some scholars, the "Eighteen Matters" that Beit Shammai is said to have decreed despite the objections of Beit Hillel (J.T., *Shab.* 1.4, 3c, and parallels) refer to measures instituted during the first revolt against Rome (66–70 CE) in order to assure the separation of Jews and Gentiles. In any event, Beit Hillel clearly emerges as the more influential school at Yavneh, where the sages of Israel convened after 70 CE. The Jerusalem (Palestinian) Talmud (*Ber.* 1.7, 3b) relates that a "heavenly echo" went forth at Yavneh and declared that the *halakhah* ("law") would henceforth be in accordance with Beit Hillel. Actually, the more than three hundred controversies between the two schools that have been preserved in Talmudic literature, many of which date to the Yavnean period, attest to what must have been a protracted struggle for ascendance before Beit Hillel prevailed in the early second century.

Though the Hillelites and Shammaites are said to have practiced love and friendship toward each other and even intermarried despite differences over marital law (B.T., *Yev.* 14b), it is clear that the rabbis regarded the schools as distinct factions. Thus the many controversies between Beit Hillel and Beit Shammai are attributed to the increase in the number of students of Hillel and Shammai "who did not wait upon [their masters]" sufficiently, which in turn led to the creation of two Torahs (Tosefta *Ḥag.* 2.9 [MS Vienna] and parallels), or, according to another version, two "parties," or *kittot* (J.T., *Ḥag.* 2.2, 77d). The tannaim generally considered Beit Shammai to be the school with the stricter viewpoint, calling attention to the few instances where this was not so (*ʿEduy.* 4, 5).

Modern scholars have tried to clarify further the differences between the schools. The usual explanation is that the schools assumed the characteristics of Hillel and Shammai themselves, with Hillel representing the ideals of kindness, forbearance, and conciliation and Shammai, their opposites. Unfortunately, too few direct controversies between the two sages have been recorded to discern whether these characteristics played any major role in their differences.

Another theory is that there were socioeconomic differences between the schools; that is, that Beit Shammai expressed the attitudes of the upper classes and Beit Hillel, those of the lower. For example, when Beit Shammai maintained that on the eve of the Sabbath or a festival one should first recite the benediction over the day and then that over the wine and Beit Hillel contended that the wine should be blessed first (*Ber.* 8.8), each school's position may reflect its socioeconomic background. The wealthy commonly used wine at their meals, and so its use in no way indicated the festive nature of the Sabbath or festival. For the poor, however, the presence of wine at the table suggested the specialness of the day, so Beit Hillel decided that the benediction over it had to be recited first.

Some writers have maintained that the two schools had distinct hermeneutical approaches. For example, Beit Shammai tended to be more literal in its exegesis, explaining the verse "when thou liest down and when thou risest up" (*Dt.* 6:7) to mean that the Shemaʿ should be recited in the evening while reclining and in the morning while standing. Beit Hillel understood the intention to be that the Shemaʿ is said at the time when people are accustomed to lie down and when they arise (*Ber.* 1.3).

Still others have suggested that Beit Hillel insisted that a valid act had to be accompanied by intention, whereas Beit Shammai emphasized the deed itself. A common example pertains to the law that foods consumed on a festival must be prepared the day before. The question arose as to whether an egg laid on the festival day could be eaten (*Beits.* 1.1). Beit Shammai permitted its consumption because it viewed the egg as having been readied, albeit by the hen, the day before. Beit Hillel however, regarded this preparation as inadequate since no one could have anticipated that the egg would actually be laid on the festival day.

Finally, it has been suggested that Beit Hillel analyzed texts and concepts and broke them down into smaller components in order to understand them, while Beit Shammai emphasized the context and the whole. This understanding is actually an elaboration of the hermeneutical and intention-versus-deed explanations.

No one theory accounts for all or even most of the disputes between the two schools, so it must be concluded that aside from the generally strict perspective of Beit Shammai and the leniency of Beit Hillel, no general underlying principle can be discerned.

SEE ALSO Hillel.

BIBLIOGRAPHY

The disputes between the houses are presented and evaluated in volume 2 of Jacob Neusner's *The Rabbinic Traditions about the Pharisees before 70,* 3 vols. (Leiden, 1971). See also the "Bibliographical Reflections" in volume 3 (pp. 320–368) of Neusner's work. Alexander Guttmann considers the relation of Hillel and Shammai to the schools and discusses the different approaches of Beit Hillel and Beit Shammai in his *Rabbinic Judaism in the Making: A Chapter in the History of the Halakhah from Ezra to Judah I* (Detroit, 1970), pp. 59–124.

The socioeconomic understanding of the controversies is presented in Louis Ginzberg's "The Significance of the Halakhah for Jewish History," in his *On Jewish Law and Lore* (1955; reprint, New York, 1979), pp. 77–124. For the claim that the Hillelites had an "atomic-nominalistic" tendency, see Isaiah Sonne's "The Schools of Shammai and Hillel Seen from Within," in *Louis Ginzberg Jubilee Volume* (New York, 1945), pp. 275–291. The "Eighteen Matters" are discussed in Solomon Zeitlin's "Les 'dix-huit mesures,'" reprinted in his *Studies in the Early History of Judaism,* vol. 4 (New York, 1978), pp. 412–426.

STUART S. MILLER (1987)

BELIEF SEE DOUBT AND BELIEF; FAITH; KNOWLEDGE AND IGNORANCE

BELLARMINO, ROBERTO (1542–1621), Jesuit theologian, controversialist, and cardinal; canonized saint of the Roman Catholic church. Roberto Francisco Romulo Bellarmino was born at Montepulciano in Tuscany on October 4, 1542. His father was an impoverished nobleman. His mother was a sister of Marcello Cervini, papal legate at the Council of Trent and later Pope Marcellus II (1555). Bellarmino entered the Society of Jesus in 1560. He studied philosophy at the Roman College and theology at Padua. He was frail as a youth and suffered from uncertain health all his life. As a student he was much devoted to literature and even wrote some poetry, most of which he later destroyed.

In 1569 Bellarmino was sent by his Jesuit superiors to Louvain in Flanders. The following year he was ordained priest by the bishop of Ghent and assumed his duties as lecturer in theology at the Jesuit house associated with the university. He was an immediate success in this capacity, so much so that by the end of his sojourn at Louvain, in 1576, he was offered prestigious positions at Paris and Milan. He was recalled instead to Rome, where a special chair of theological controversy was established for him at the Roman College. The lectures he delivered there, confuting all the leading Protestant spokesmen, were published in 1586 under the title *Disputationes de controversiis Christianae fidei adversus hujus temporis haereticos* (Lectures concerning the controversies of the Christian faith against the heretics of this time), a manual that soon became the standard of Roman positive, as distinguished from scholastic, theology. It had to pass first, however, through the displeasure of the imperious Pope Sixtus V, who threatened to put *Disputationes* on the Index of Forbidden Books because it argued that the pope's temporal jurisdiction is only indirect. Bellarmino was spared this embarrassment by the death of Sixtus in August 1590.

In 1591 Bellarmino was appointed spiritual director of the Roman College and a year later its rector. In 1595 he became Jesuit provincial in Naples, where he lived for three years until he was chosen by Clement VIII to be the papal theologian and grand penitentiary, a post that carried with it a red hat. Bellarmino was created cardinal under the title of Santa Maria in Via on March 3, 1599.

In the midst of his various administrative duties, Bellarmino continued to publish works in defense of Catholic doctrine and piety, as well as works on the Fathers, scriptural studies, and liturgy. All these books taken together amount to a considerable corpus, most conveniently consulted in the twelve large volumes edited by J. Fèvre in 1874.

Inevitably, Bellarmino was drawn into the sharp quarrel between the Jesuits and the Dominicans over the problem of the relation between grace and free will. It has been said that Bellarmino's position on this issue displeased the pope, who, for whatever reason, sent him off to be archbishop of Capua in 1602. When Clement died in March 1605, Bellarmino resigned his see, and Pope Paul V named him librarian of the Vatican. He remained active in the Curia Romana for the rest of his life and took an intellectual's part in many of the great events of the time, including the Venetian interdict (1606), the literary controversies with James I of England (1607–1609), and the debate on Gallicanism (1610–1612), which was the occasion for his celebrated treatise on the powers of the pope, *De potestate summi pontificis in rebus temporalibus* (Concerning the powers of the supreme pontiff in temporal matters). In 1615 he was involved in the first curial interrogation of Galileo, a man for whom he had great regard and whom he treated with marked respect.

The process of Bellarmino's canonization began in 1627, six years after his death, but because of what was conceived to be his minimizing views about the papacy, it was not consummated until 1930. Roberto Bellarmino, personally austere, pious, and kindly, set the highest tone for the positive theology of the Counter-Reformation, not only because of his erudition and industry, but also because of the amiability and courtesy he brought to his controversial writings—characteristics rare indeed in his tumultuous era.

BIBLIOGRAPHY

The best short study of Bellarmino's life and work is Xavier-Marie Le Bachelet's entry, "Bellarmin, François-Robert-Romulus," in *Dictionnaire de théologie catholique* (Paris, 1932). Somewhat effusive but nevertheless useful is James Brodrick's *The Life and Work of Blessed Robert Francis Cardinal Bellarmine,* 2 vols. (London, 1928). E. A. Ryan's *The Historical Scholarship of Saint Bellarmine* (Louvain, 1936) examines the centerpiece of the subject's controversial writings. For a recent treatment of one of Bellarmino's controversies within his own communion, see Gustavo Galeota's *Bellarmino contra Baio a Lovanio* (Rome, 1966).

MARVIN R. O'CONNELL (1987)

BEMBA RELIGION. The Bemba, also known as Awemba, inhabit the northeastern part of Zambia between lakes Tanganyika, Mweru, Malawi, and Bangweulu. According to oral traditions, three sons of the Luba king, Mukulumpe, who had fallen out with their father, led a migration of people from what is now the Shaba Province of southern Zaire to what became the Bemba territory. The royal clan of the Bemba traces its descent to these brothers and to their sister, Bwalya Chabala. By the mid-seventeenth century, the Bemba were established in their present territory. A paramount chief, or *citimukulu* (a title associated with Mukulumpe's sons), ruled the Bemba with the assistance of local chiefs, also of the royal clan, whom he appointed to govern the various districts under Bemba control.

The matrilineal clan structure of the Bemba can be traced to Bwalya Chabala's central role in the migrations from Shaba. According to tradition, the sons of Mukulumpe, after wandering in exile from their father's kingdom, realized that they needed the assistance of a royal woman to found their clan, so they went back to their father's compound and secretly carried Bwalya Chabala away with them. She is often mentioned as the person who brought the seeds and plants used in Bemba agriculture. In their tradition of a woman founding the royal clan as well as introducing agricultural knowledge, the Bemba assert the intimate connection between the principle of matrilineal descent and the fertility of the land. Bwalya Chabala's honored place in Bemba traditions can be seen in a sacred burial place, not far from the present-day Bemba capital, associated with her. Offerings of cloth and flour are brought to her burial shrine. A basket, which is said to be hers, hangs in the relic house of the *citimukulu*. Flour from this basket is used in several Bemba religious ceremonies.

Like other central African ethnic groups, the Bemba acknowledge a high god known as Lesa. Among the neighboring Lamba people, Lesa is thought to have been a man who lived on earth and helped his people. For the Bemba, however, Lesa was never a person. He is a creator god who controls the rains and the power of fertility manifested in humans, animals, and agriculture. He is the source of the creative power in the roots and shrubs that the Bemba use in healing and religious rituals. There is no organized cult associated with Lesa, and the Bemba do not ordinarily solicit his assistance. When serious problems of community-wide concern arise, however, they organize collective rituals to ask Lesa for help. These are particularly common in times of severe drought.

Spirits of the ancestors play a more central role in the day-to-day existence of the Bemba. Rituals are performed to seek assistance from the ancestors and to ensure that their considerable influence over the lives of the living becomes a force for good. Some of these ancestral spirits (*mipashi*) are considered benign; others, called *fiwa*, are more dangerous. The *fiwa* are the spirits of those who died with a sense of grievance or injury and who trouble their descendants until the wrong is corrected.

When a pregnant woman feels the child moving in her womb, she knows that the *mupashi* of an ancestor has entered her body. After the child is born, the identity of this ancestor is ascertained by divination. The child's *mupashi* is believed to guard him wherever he goes and remains as a guardian for his descendants after he dies.

For every man or woman who dies there is a special succession ceremony (*kupyamika*) in which a close relative assumes the dead man's bow or the dead woman's girdle. By doing so, the relative assumes some of the personal characteristics of the deceased as well as his or her position in the kinship system. Thus a young boy who is appointed in this way to succeed a dead man will thereafter address his fellow villagers using the same forms the deceased would have used; the villagers, in turn, will regard the boy as the husband of the dead man's widow and will speak of him as such.

The Bemba's paramount chief is said to succeed to the *mipashi* of his matrilineal ancestors, which dates back to the founding siblings. During the chief's succession ceremony, he is given a number of material objects associated with the *mipashi;* it is through these sacred relics that the *citimukulu* acquires power over his domains. This power can be weakened, however, by any failure of the chief to fulfill ritual obligations or to adhere to a series of sexual avoidances associated with his office. The ritual objects (*babenya*) inherited by the chief are kept in special spirit huts in the capital where they are looked after by hereditary "councillors" (*bakabilo*), who also trace their ancestry to the foundation of the Bemba state. The shrines are also guarded by "wives of the dead," who are direct descendants of the wives of former chiefs. The approximately four hundred *bakabilo* are responsible for purifying the paramount chief before he approaches the spirit huts and for protecting him from harmful influences. They prevent the ritually impure from approaching the chief and guard his power by quickly removing from the capital anyone who is in imminent danger of dying.

Traditionally, when a paramount chief was at the point of death, the *bakabilo,* who traced their membership in the royal clan by paternal descent and were therefore ineligible to succeed him, gathered in the royal hut to ensure that the necessary rituals were carried out precisely as dictated by tradition. Their leader determined when the *bakabilo* should strangle the paramount chief. The *bakabilo* had to be careful to do this at the proper moment, for to strangle the king too soon would have been considered murder and to wait too long might have allowed the royal *mipashi* to escape, with devastating consequences for the entire kingdom. (The Bemba *citimukulu* may be seen as conforming to James G. Frazer's model of a "divine king.") After the death of the *citimukulu,* the *bakabilo* removed the ritual objects associated with the office and took them to a neighboring village for safekeeping until the succession ceremony took place.

The burial of the chief had to be done according to strict ritual procedures to ensure that the spiritual power of the office was not weakened. The corpse was washed by the three senior women—the chief's mother, his senior sister, and his head wife—then placed in the fetal position upon a platform made of branches. Hereditary royal buriers completed the rituals by pouring a special bean sauce over the body at dawn and at noon. The skin of a newly sacrificed bull was wrapped around the body, followed by a special cloth. At the end of a yearlong mourning period and after the millet had been harvested, the chief's remains were moved to the sacred burial place (*mwalule*). Before the *bakabilo* set out for the burial place, the senior widow was slain in sacrifice. On their way to the burial site, the *bakabilo* sacrificed all the chickens and goats that they encountered. Commoners were supposed to hide from the burial procession. The chief's wives and servants were buried with his remains. Ivory tusks and other valuable goods were placed on top of his grave, which was guarded by the "wives of the dead."

The hereditary burier of the *citimukulu,* who was in charge of the royal burial ground, was known as *shinwalule* ("lord of the burial ground"). In addition to playing a prominent role in the succession ceremonies of the new chief, the *shinwalule* performed a variety of rituals associated with rain and the fertility of the land.

One of the most important Bemba rituals is the female initiation ceremony, Chisungu, held shortly after the onset of menstruation. Between one and three girls take part in the ceremony. During her first menstruation, a girl undergoes an individual purification rite designed to "bring her to the hearth" or "show her the fire," because it is believed that her condition has made her "cold." (Fire is often used in Bemba rituals to purify a person who has passed through a dangerous or impure condition.) Medicines treated with fire play an important part in the girl's purification ritual.

The actual Chisungu ritual is held at a convenient time relatively soon after the menstrual purification ritual. Chisungu is a nubility rite in the sense that it is less concerned with the physical transformations of puberty than with the social changes necessary for a woman to be ready for marriage. Normally the girl is already betrothed; the ritual is designed to protect the couple from the dangers associated with their first act of sexual intercourse and to establish the rights of the future husband to engage in sexual relations. It is also a time when women elders teach younger women the religious and social responsibilities of women in their community. The rite entails no physical operation but involves singing and dancing both within the village and in the bush. There is no comparable ritual for boys.

Bibliography

For background history of the Bemba, see Andrew D. Roberts's *A History of the Bemba* (Madison, Wis., 1973). The following of my own works should also be consulted: "The Bemba of North-Eastern Rhodesia," in *Seven Tribes of British Central Africa,* edited by Elizabeth Colson and Max Gluckman (Oxford, 1951), pp. 164–193, gives a preliminary treatment of Bemba religion; *Land, Labour and Diet in Northern Rhodesia* (Oxford, 1939) contains accounts of religious ceremonies related to the economic life of the people; "Keeping the King Divine" in *Proceedings of the Royal Anthropological Institute of Great Britain and Ireland* (1968) draws on information provided by hereditary bearers of the *citimukulu;* and *Chisungu,* 2d edition (London, 1982), examines this important female initiation ceremony. A. H. Muenya's "The Burial of Chitimukulu Mubanga," *African Affairs* 46 (1947): 101–104, offers an eyewitness account of the burial of a recent *citimukulu.*

New Sources

Badenberg, Robert. *The Body, Soul and Spirit Concept of the Bemba in Zambia: Fundamental Characteristics of Being Human in an African Ethnic Group.* Bonn, 1999.

Davoli, Umberto. *The Dancing Elephant: A Collection of the Tales of the Bemba People.* Ndola, Zambia, 1992.

Hinfelaar, Hugo F. *Bemba-Speaking Women of Zambia: A Century of Religious Change, 1892–1992.* Leiden and New York, 1994.

James, Eric. *Moment of Encounter.* New York, 1984.

Moore, Henrietta L. *Cutting Down Trees: Gender, Nutrition and Agricultural Change in the Northern Province of Zambia 1890–1990.* Portsmouth, N.H., 1994.

Richards, Audrey Isabel. *Chisungu: A Girl's Initiation Ceremony among the Bemba of Zambia.* London and New York, 1988.

AUDREY I. RICHARDS (1987)
Revised Bibliography

BENARAS SEE BANARAS

BENCHŌ (1162–1238), also known as Shōkōbō; posthumous name, Ben'a; founder of the Chinzei branch of the Japanese Jōdo (Pure Land) sect, the dominant branch of this sect. He is presently counted the second patriarch of the Jōdoshū.

Born in the province of Chikuzen in northern Kyushu, Benchō became a novice monk at the age of seven. At the age of twenty-two he left Kyushu and entered the head Tendai monastery of Enryakuji on the northeastern outskirts of Kyoto, then the capital of Japan. After six years of study there under the erudite scholar-monk Hōchibō Shōshin he returned to Chikuzen. Three years later, deeply shocked by the death of his stepbrother, he underwent a religious crisis in which he came to feel keenly the impermanence of things. On a trip to Kyoto in order to obtain a statue for a pagoda he had helped to reconstruct, Benchō met Hōnen and became his disciple. After delivering the statue to Chikuzen he returned to Kyoto in 1199 to study the Nembutsu (Chin., *nianfo*) teachings under Hōnen.

Five years later he returned again to Kyushu, and from this time on was active in propagating the Pure Land Nembutsu teachings throughout the northern portion of Kyushu. Among his many disciples was Ryōchū (1198–1287), who was designated the heir of Benchō's transmission when the latter gave official sanction to Ryōchū's work, *Ryōge matsudai nembutsu jushuin shō.* Ryōchū was later instrumental in establishing Benchō's lineage as the dominant branch among the many offshoots of Hōnen's teaching.

Benchō held that practices other than the Nembutsu (the recitation of the words "Namu Amida Butsu") do not fundamentally accord with Amida's Original Vows (*hongan*). However, he did state that it was possible to attain birth in the Pure Land through non-Nembutsu practices insofar as they are performed in good faith. Thus he held that both Nembutsu and non-Nembutsu are qualitatively identical in that they can be the cause of birth in the Pure Land. He also emphasized the idea of "unperturbed mind at the deathbed" (*rinjū shōnen*). For Benchō, it is of utmost importance to recite the Nembutsu with an undisturbed mind at the time of one's death. Under these circumstances, the practitioner is said to be able to see the Buddha arriving to lead him to the Pure Land. This deathbed vision of the Buddha is considered crucial to one's birth in the Pure Land and eventual enlightenment there. Finally, Benchō placed strong emphasis on the actual recitation of the Nembutsu. This ultimately places him among the ranks of those who advocate "many-calling" (*tanen*), the constant repetition of the Nembutsu, and "self-power" (*jiriki*), the position that the Nembutsu is recited through one's own conscious effort.

SEE ALSO Hōnen; Jōdoshū; Nianfo.

BIBLIOGRAPHY

Hōnen to sono monka no kyōgaku. Kyoto, 1972. Sponsored by Ryukoku Daigaku Shinshu Gakkai.

Kodo Yasui. *Hōnen monka no kyōgaku.* Kyoto, 1968.

BANDO SHŌJUN (1987)

BENDIS.

BENDIS. In Greek testimonies, this South Thracian goddess is known variously as Bendis, Béndis, or Mendis. Her name is uncontroversially explained as deriving from Indo-European **bhendh-*, "bind." She was probably a goddess of marriage whose function it was to watch over marital bindings.

As early as 429/8 BCE, Bendis was the object of a state cult in Athens. In the ceremonies called Bendideia, which took place on the nineteenth or twentieth of the month Thargetion, two processions took place, one composed of the rich and influential Thracians of Piraeus, the other of Athenians. The Bendideion, or temple of Bendis, was situated on the hill Munychia.

The Bendideia, as described in Plato's *Republic* (327a–c), was spectacular but did not contain any hint of the orgiastic character that is typical of rites performed in worship of a great goddess. Bendis was commonly identified with the Greek Artemis; it is therefore puzzling that Herodotus, who was very well acquainted with the Athenian Bendis, fails to mention her name in connection with the Thracian Artemis (*Histories* 4.33 and 5.7). Perhaps Herodotus had in mind another Thracian goddess, not Cotys, however, to whom the same objection would apply.

On reliefs and small statues, Bendis is represented as wearing Thracian garments and a pointed (Phrygian) cap. Her attributes are often a sacrificial cup in the right hand and a spear in the left hand. On Bythinian coins, however, she is represented as holding two spears in her right hand and a dagger in her left hand. On coins from Kabyle, she bears two torches, or one torch and a *patera.* Torches were also the attribute of the Greek goddess Hekate, with whom Bendis has also been often identified.

A temple consecrated to Bendis or Mendis existed in 188 BCE on the western shore of Hebros. Later testimonies mention another temple in Egypt, near Ptolemais. Her name is attested as an anthroponyme in both Thrace and Greece.

Notwithstanding her prominent role at Athens, Bendis is not to be considered an important divinity. The cult of Diana among the Roman soldiers in Dacia and south from the Danube does not necessarily have anything to do with Bendis.

BIBLIOGRAPHY

For further discussion, see Zlatozava Goceva's essay "Der Bendiskult und die Beziehungen zwischen Thrakien und Klein-asien" in *Hommages à Maarten J. Vermaseren,* edited by Margaret B. de Boer and T. A. Edridge (Leiden, 1978), vol. 1, pp. 397–404.

New Sources

Best, J., Jr. "Bendis." *Hermeneus* 35 (1964): 122–128.

Blomart, Alain. "Identité culturelle, altérité et religions étrangères: exemples antiques de Mithra, Bendis et la Mère des dieux." *Itaca* 16–17 (2000–2001): 9–22.

Cerkezov, Valentin. "Iconography of the Thracian Goddess Bendis in the Tombstones with a funeral feast from Southern Thrace." *Eirene* 33 (1997): 53–66.

Ducrey, Pierre. "Quelques reliefs et dessins rupestres de Philippes de Macédoine." In *Mélanges d'histoire ancienne et d'archéologie offerts à Paul Collart* (Lausanne, Switzerland, 1976): 147–160.

Gerasimova-Tomova, V. "Sur le culte de Bendis en Thrace et le vêtement de femme thrace." *Arch(Sofia)* 22 (1980): 27–34.

Masson, Olivier. "Les noms théophores de Bendis en Grèce et en Thrace." *Museum Helveticum* 45 (1988): 6–12

Planeaux, Christopher. "The Date of Bendis' Entry into Attica." *Classical Journal* 96 (2000–2001): 165–192.

Popov, D. "Essence, origine et propagation du culte de la déesse thrace Bendis." *Dialogues d'Histoire Ancienne* 2 (1976): 289–303.

IOAN PETRU CULIANU (1987)
CICERONE POGHIRC (1987)
Revised Bibliography

BENEDICT, RUTH

BENEDICT, RUTH (1887–1948) was an American cultural anthropologist. Ruth Fulton grew up in a Baptist household in New York State. After four years at Vassar (1905–1909), schoolteaching, and marriage to Stanley Rossiter Benedict in 1914, she enrolled in the anthropology department at Columbia University. In 1923 she earned a doctorate under the aegis of Franz Boas.

On field trips to the Pueblo Indians between 1924 and 1926, Benedict elaborated on ideas about religion that she had formulated in prose sketches, poetry, and early anthropological writings. The significance of Zuni theocracy and ceremonialism is conveyed in her *Patterns of Culture* (1934). Through the 1930s, Benedict taught at Columbia, edited the *Journal of American Folk Lore,* and began to compare myths employed in primitive societies with the dreams of utopia current in complex societies. During World War II, at the Office of War Information, Benedict was assigned to work on Japan, a society whose beliefs and behaviors contrasted sharply with those of her own society. *The Chrysanthemum and the Sword* was published in 1946; Benedict died two years later.

According to Benedict, religion stems from human perception of a "wondrous power, a voltage with which the universe is believed to be charged" ("Religion," *General Anthropology,* p. 630). In an attempt to manipulate this power, people invent practices and accompanying beliefs; these constitute religion. People perceive "extraordinary power" either as a property of things (*mana*) or as analogous to human will and intention (animism). Each perception produces a distinct dogma and practice.

Benedict's interpretation centered on the individual, who needs reassurance and the security of knowing he or she can influence their own fate. Such psychological factors shape the universal elements of religion: vision, ceremonialism, ethical sanction, and dogma. All of these guide the individual through known and unknown forces. Because Benedict argued that religions exist to comfort human beings, she rejected the "cold," distant Christian God, the absolutist "good versus evil" of Western religions, and the abstract theologies of most stratified, literate societies. The Zuni religion was her model: gods resemble humans, humans dance as gods, religion is down-to-earth and sensual.

Religions also, in Benedict's view, express human imaginativeness. The capacity to envision a world beyond the ordinary provides the content of religion; in religion, humans symbolize their highest ideals. Whatever the precise form—quest, prayer, poem—dreaming represents an imaginative redoing of reality that can direct social change.

Benedict assumed that the human urge to control daily events precipitates fantasies, which are elaborate, imaginative transformations of culturally available means and ends. Her argument about religions echoes her theory of myth: Just as myths give the plain details of everyday life an extraordinary character, so religion accords the mundane daydream a supernatural quality. The impulse to alter present conditions expands into a "desire to remodel the universe," although Benedict did not outline the process. An attempt to manipulate the "forces of the universe" is, by her definition, religious.

For Benedict, the dream had to be tied to reality. Cut loose from substantive, secular concerns, dream becomes delusion and the seed of mass deception. Benedict offered no way of ensuring the link to reality except her own faith that individual demands and the daily pressures of existence keep religions accountable. Reflecting human vulnerability and creativeness, religion is also a "technique for success" and a mode of survival. A religion that failed to perform these functions, Benedict hoped, would be rejected. This point illustrates a movement typical of Benedict's anthropology, from the psychological to the cultural: individual need leads to social phenomenon.

Benedict's view of religion fitted her humanistic and relativistic anthropology. Humanism provided the universal aspect: human response to perception of a "wondrous power" is an attempt to control and to comprehend this power. The one impulse issues in acts (prayer, ritual, liturgy), and the other issues in articulation (symbols, myths, theologies). Relativism emerged in her claim that religious content must be tied to the stuff of everyday life. The diversity of religions proves how thoroughly perceptions of the extraordinary are linked to the ordinary; the "supernatural" (or spiritual) has no meaning apart from the "natural" (for Benedict, the "cultural").

Although her writings do not offer a fully developed theory of religion, Benedict does provide insight into human religiosity. The humility, imaginativeness, pragmatism, and hope in humans gave birth to religions. In freeing religion from a specific kind of behavior and content, Benedict offered a concept with cross-cultural application. Her statements on religion reiterated her general anthropological theory: shared dilemmas of human existence produce a variety of cultural solutions.

BIBLIOGRAPHY

My book *Ruth Benedict: Patterns of a Life* (Philadelphia, 1983) contains a bibliography including all of Benedict's published writings, archival sources, and works of significance to her anthropology, as well as secondary sources relevant to her life and works. Here follows an annotated list of Benedict's more important works.

The Concept of the Guardian Spirit in North America. Menasha, Wis., 1923. Benedict's dissertation was a comparative discussion of the guardian spirit complex in North American Indian tribes. She explored notions of "vision," the links of vision to everyday life, and the importance of imagination. She also showed how borrowed traits are altered to fit an existing culture.

Tales of the Cochiti Indians. Washington, D.C., 1931. A collection of myths and tales from a Pueblo tribe, the volume anticipated Benedict's theory, articulated in later works, that myths and tales are two sides of one coin. The volume also contains an early version of the "compensation" theory she later outlined in *Zuni Mythology.*

Patterns of Culture. Boston, 1934. Benedict's best-known book presents portraits of Zuni, Dobu, and Kwakiutl cultures in order to urge changes in contemporary American culture. Saying that "culture is personality writ large," she argued that cultures acquire personality traits, that individuals are "molded" to their cultures, and that conformity can be variously suppressive of individual expression in different societies.

Zuni Mythology. 2 vols. New York, 1935. The introduction to and summary of these two volumes explicated a theory of myth. For Benedict, myths are "compensatory," a way of making up for the constraints and the failures of everyday life. Myths are also "wishes" for a better social order and for a "redesigned universe." The former she called "tales" and the latter, because of their religious content, "myths." The volumes contain a large number of Zuni stories.

"Religion." In *General Anthropology,* edited by Franz Boas. Boston, 1938. In this chapter of Boas's text, Benedict presented her theory of religion. The chapter is not entirely satisfactory; she focuses less on religious phenomena than on individual psychology and cultural diversity. The attempt to develop a cross-cultural definition of religion somewhat weakens the explanatory force of her theory.

The Chrysanthemum and the Sword. Boston, 1946. This book, the product of inquiries made during World War II, is an elegant portrait of Japanese society and individuals. Benedict's discussions of honor, debt, obligation, and childrearing are still classic, and her evocation of a unique Japanese "personality" has not been equaled even by anthropologists who have done the fieldwork Benedict could not do for her study.

New Sources

Babcock, Barbara A. "Not in the Absolute Singular." In *Women Writing Culture,* edited by Ruth Behar and Deborah A. Gordon, pp. 104–130. Berkeley, Calif., 1995.

Caffrey, Margaret M. *Ruth Benedict: Stranger in This Land.* Austin, Tex., 1989.

JUDITH S. MODELL (1987)
Revised Bibliography

BENEDICTINES. The Order of Saint Benedict (O.S.B.) is not a centralized religious order like the Franciscans, Dominicans, or Jesuits but rather a confederation of congregations of monks and nuns who follow the rule of Benedict of Nursia (c. 480–547). Each monastery is an autonomous community bound to other monasteries of the same congregation by loose juridic ties and associated with the rest of the confederation through common commitment to the rule. Benedict himself is known to have founded monasteries at Subiaco, Monte Cassino, and elsewhere in central Italy. Because of its wisdom and moderation his rule was also adopted in many of the other monasteries of Latin Christendom. Its widespread implementation was also fostered by the missionary zeal of the early Benedictine monks and by papal patronage.

Gregory the Great helped spread the influence of the rule in 596 when he sent Benedictine monks to evangelize the Anglo-Saxons. Augustine, their monastic leader, became the first archbishop of Canterbury, and their success also resulted in the development of schools and a flourishing scholarship, as seen especially in the work of the Venerable Bede (c. 673–735). Anglo-Saxon monks subsequently took up missionary work in Frisia and also in central Germany, where Boniface (673–754) firmly established monastic life according to the rule of Benedict. In the eighth and early ninth centuries, however, many monasteries fell into the hands of lay abbots, and consequently serious abuse and decadence crept into monastic life. Reform was initiated by Benedict of Aniane (c. 750–821), who insisted on a more literal observance of the rule; his approach to monasticism spread to other abbeys in Aquitaine. When Louis I, "the Pious," succeeded Charlemagne as emperor of the Holy Roman Empire in 814, Benedict was installed as superior of all monasteries in the empire. At Aachen in 817, the Frankish abbots agreed on a uniform discipline and encouraged a liturgy that was more elaborate and solemn than that provided for in the rule. As a result manual labor declined in importance. Such uniformity was not consonant with the spirit of the rule. Because more attention was given to external monastic structures than to the spirit of the rule, the Frankish attempt at reform was ultimately a failure. A new regularity of discipline was imposed in the Frankish houses during the first half of the ninth century and was accompanied by the development of scholarship, as indicated by the writings of Smaragdus, Paschasius Radbertus, Ratramnus, and Rabanus Maurus. However, the collapse of the empire in 843 resulted in a further decline in monastic life and discipline.

The tenth century saw a successful revival of Benedictinism, above all at Cluny, a monastery founded in 910 by William of Aquitaine and placed directly under papal patronage. Three distinguished and long-lived abbots, Majolus (abbot from 954 to 994), Odilo (994–1048), and Hugh (1049–1109), directed that house very effectively, establishing a high level of observance. They also established numerous other foundations so that in the twelfth century Cluny included a network of almost fifteen hundred monasteries, although many of them were very small houses. In reaction against the highly structured, economically wealthy, politically powerful, and liturgically elaborate form of monasticism that prevailed at Cluny and its larger daughter houses, other monastic families also developed during the eleventh century. These included the Camaldolese, the Vallumbrosans, the Carthusians, and the Cistercians, all of whom stressed a return to the basic elements of Benedict's rule, especially manual labor, corporate poverty, silence, prayer, and penitence.

Monasticism was corrupted by the feudal system in the late Middle Ages; the observance of poverty and simplicity of life became particularly difficult to maintain. Popes Innocent III (d. 1216), Honorius III (d. 1227), and Gregory IX (d. 1241) sought reform, above all by having recourse to the Cistercian institution of the general chapter. In 1215 the Fourth Lateran Council mandated triennial provincial chapters that were to elect visitators to oversee the implementation of legislated reform measures, but this program was generally carried out only in England. In 1336 Benedict XII organized all Benedictine monasteries into thirty-two provinces and also prescribed a triennial chapter and visitation. Unfortunately, there was no way to implement this legislation effectively.

The institution that is known today as a Benedictine congregation was inaugurated in the fifteenth century by Luigi Barbo. In 1408 he became the abbot of Santa Giustina at Padua, where he established regular discipline. This attracted so many candidates that he went on to found new monasteries and reform existing ones, all of which were joined into a congregation in 1419. All of the Italian and Sicilian monasteries also eventually joined this congregation, which became known as the Cassinese Congregation when the abbey at Monte Cassino joined the congregation in 1504.

The Protestant Reformation destroyed about eight hundred of the approximately three thousand monasteries extant in Europe at the time. As a result of the Council of Trent (1545–1563), the congregational system was imposed on those monasteries that survived, and exemption from episcopal control was extended to all houses. By the eighteenth century Benedictine monasticism was generally in a healthy state, but it soon declined again as a result of the Enlightenment, the French Revolution, and widespread secularism. However, recovery and expansion followed during the nineteenth century. In 1833 Prosper Guéranger restored Benedictine life at Solesmes in France, prosperous houses developed in Germany at Metten in 1830 and at Beuron in 1863, and Boniface Wimmer, a monk of Metten, brought Benedictine monasticism to the United States in 1846. In 1888 Pope Leo XIII revived the Benedictine College of Sant'Anselmo in Rome, which had been founded by Innocent XI in 1687 as an international college for young Benedictine monks. The office of abbot primate was created in 1893. Elected by the Benedictine abbots of the world, the primate serves as head of the College of Sant'Anselmo and acts as an official representative of Benedictines to the Holy See; although he has no jurisdiction over individual abbeys throughout the world, he is a symbol of moral unity among Benedictines. On March 21, 1952, Pius XII approved the codification of the *Lex Proprio*, a particular code of law that governs the confederation of congregations. It is reviewed regularly at the congress of abbots held in Rome every four years.

The history of Benedictine women has not been well chronicled because of the scarcity of manuscript evidence. It seems that the Benedictine rule was first adopted in English convents in the seventh century, at the time the nuns Hilda and Etheldreda both ruled over double monasteries. When Boniface went as a missionary to Germany he was assisted by a distinguished group of nuns, including Lioba, Walburga, and Thekla. In the thirteenth century significant mystical writings were produced in Germany by Gertrude the Great; Mechthild of Hackeborn, and Mechthild of Magdeburg; it is not known, however, whether they were Benedictines or Cistercians. Post-Reformation nuns included Gertrude More (1606–1633); she achieved a high degree of holiness under the direction of Dom Augustine Baker while a member of the English community exiled at Cambrai in France. That community returned to Britain and finally settled at Stanbrook, near Worcester, in 1983. It is probably the most distinguished abbey of Benedictine nuns. Those nuns who came to the United States from Germany and Switzerland in the nineteenth century were forced to give up their solemn vows as nuns because of their apostolates outside the monastic enclosure; the majority of the women in the communities they founded are now Benedictine Sisters of pontifical jurisdiction.

In addition to the traditional life of work and prayer carried on within the enclosure of the monastery, Benedictine men and women engage in various ministries, including education, scholarship, health care, retreats, and parochial and missionary work. According to 2004 statistics, approximately eight thousand monks belong to twenty-one congregations. There are approximately 16,000 nuns and sisters, many of whom work in diverse apostolates and live outside the monastery.

SEE ALSO Bendict of Nursia; Cistercians.

BIBLIOGRAPHY

A good introductory account of the Benedictines is to be found in Edward Cuthbert Butler's *Benedictine Monachism,* 2d ed. (1924; reprint, New York, 1961). *St. Benedict's Disciples,* edited by D. H. Farmer (Leominster, U.K., 1980), is a broad collection of essays on the past and present achievements of Benedict's followers, and through them of Benedict himself. *Saint Benedict: Father of Western Civilization,* prepared under the direction of Pieter Balsetier (New York, 1981), is a comprehensive and generously illustrated volume exploring many aspects of the Benedictine contribution to Christian humanism through art and architecture, as well as through scholarship. Statistical information can be found in *Catalogus monasteriorum O.S.B.,* 16th ed. (Rome, 1985), and J. P. Müller's *Atlas O.S.B.: Index monasteriorum* (Rome, 1975).

New Sources

Kardong, Terrence. *The Benedictines.* Wilmington, Del., 1988.

Posset, F. "Palate of the Heart." In *Augustine: Biblical Exegete,* edited by Frederick van Felteren and Joseph C. Schnaubelt, pp. 252–278. New York, 2001.

Wright, J. R. "An Olivetan Benedictine Breviary of the Fifteenth Century." In *A Distinct Voice,* edited by Jacqueline Brown and William P. Stoneman, pp. 143–154. Notre Dame, Ind., 1997.

R. KEVIN SEASOLTZ (1987)
Revised Bibliography

BENEDICT OF NURSIA (c. 480–547), Christian saint, monastic founder, and spiritual leader. Best known as the author of the monastic rule still followed by Benedictine and Cistercian monks and nuns. Benedict is looked upon as the father of Western monasticism because of the widespread influence of his rule. Book 2 of the *Dialogues* of Gregory the Great, written about 593–594, is the only source of information on the details of Benedict's life. Although the primary purpose of the *Dialogues* is moral edification rather than biography in the modern sense, Gregory's work provides facts that conform to the general history of sixth-century central Italy; hence most scholars agree that the core of Gregory's information is basically reliable. His account of Benedict, however, concentrates mainly on miracles and encounters with demons.

Benedict was born in the Umbrian province of Nursia, northeast of Rome, into what the *Dialogues* describe as "a family of high station." The world of his time was in many ways chaotic. The Roman Empire, already crumbling from within, was overrun by barbarians in the fifth century. In the sixth century Italy was devastated by war, famine, and plunder as Justinian I, the Byzantine emperor, attempted to reclaim control of the area. When Benedict was sent to Rome as a youth to study liberal arts, he was repelled by the immorality of the city; in about 500 he sought solitude, first at Enfide (modern-day Affide) and then at Subiaco, where he lived an eremitical life in a hillside cave. Sustained by the ministrations of a neighboring monk who brought him bread, he spent three years as a hermit but then reluctantly agreed to become the abbot of a nearby community of monks. Tensions between Benedict and the community, however, culminated in an attempt by members of the community to poison him. Benedict returned to Subiaco, where he was pursued by so many disciples that he established twelve small monasteries in the area. Because of the jealous opposition of a local priest, he migrated in about 525 to Casinum, approximately eighty miles south of Rome. Together with a small group of monks Benedict built his famous monastery, Monte Cassino, on the top of that imposing mountain in the central Apennines in place of a pagan shrine that he had destroyed.

The *Dialogues* portray Benedict in his relations with various personalities, including Totila, king of the Ostrogoths. Once a year he met with his sister Scholastica, who lived near Monte Cassino with a community of nuns. Benedict does not seem to have been ordained a priest. After founding the monastery he spent the rest of his life at Monte Cassino where he wrote the rule for monks, which has diffused his influence throughout the world for more than fourteen centuries. According to tradition, he died on March 21, 547. In about 590, Lombards ransacked the monastery at Monte Cassino and left it abandoned until it was reconstituted under Petronax of Brescia in about 720.

There are two traditions concerning Benedict's relics. One maintains that they were translated to the abbey of Saint-Benoït-sur-Loire in France some time during the seventh century; the feast of the translation of the relics has been celebrated on July 11. According to the other tradition the relics were discovered at Monte Cassino in about 1069 by Abbot Desiderius, the future Pope Victor III. On October 24, 1964, Pope Paul VI declared Benedict the patron saint of Europe.

In Gregory's *Dialogues* Benedict's life is set out in four successive stages: confrontation with evil, or temptation; spiritual triumph, in which Benedict's virtue is demonstrated; a new situation in which his influence is shown more widely; and finally a fresh confrontation with the power of evil occasioned by this new position of influence. In this way Benedict's life unfolds as a search for God or a pilgrimage in which he finds God through temptations and trials. Benedict, as his name implies, is a man "blessed by God." His life illustrates the pattern set out in the rule itself, which invites the disciple to enter by the narrow gate in order to enjoy the freedom of living in the wide expanse of God. It also illustrates the paradox that fruitfulness emerges out of apparent sterility, that life comes forth from death.

It is the rule rather than the *Dialogues* that reveals Benedict's religious concerns. Impressive scholarship has been devoted to the question of the originality of the rule; the issue is in many ways of secondary importance. What is significant is that Benedict wisely took what he thought was good from existing rules and practices, evaluated that material in the light of his own experience, and blended the elements to form a balanced, positive, and flexible synthesis. The result is a clear code designed for a cenobitic rather than an eremitic form of monasticism: it combines sound spiritual teaching with pastoral details covering most aspects of community life. As Gregory noted, the rule is "outstanding for discretion." While setting out clear principles, it leaves much to the abbot's discernment.

The basic spiritual values affirmed by the rule are humility and unconditional obedience to God. Liturgical prayer, called the "work of God" in the rule, is to be carried out with a profound sense of God's presence, but that same awareness is also to permeate the whole of a monk's monastic life. A sense of the holiness of God generates a sense of compunction in the monk because of his sinfulness, but that awareness of weakness inspires confident trust in God's loving mercy rather than anxious fear.

Silence should prevail in the monastery so that the monk may be recollected and attentive to the word of God, especially during prayerful reading in which he is formed in accordance with the scriptures and the Christian monastic tradition. The monk's relationship of obedience with God is expressed especially through his relationship with his abbot, who is described in the rule as a sacrament of Christ. The abbot, however, is to reflect not only God's justice but his loving mercy as he "tempers all things so that the strong may have something to strive for and the weak may not recoil in dismay." The monk's relationship with God is also reflected in his relations with the other monks in the community as he shares all things in common, renounces self-will, forgives offences, and shows compassion for the weaknesses of others. Stability in the community provides the monk with his basic asceticism and supports and challenges him as he pursues his commitment to an ongoing conversion of life.

Work, whether manual or intellectual, is also an integral part of Benedict's vision of the monastic life. The rule proposes a set time for work not only because Benedict distrusted idleness but also because he wanted work to be kept in proportion with prayer and holy reading. Work is always situated in a communal context; it is not to degenerate into activism nor to promote self-sufficiency and arrogance. Pursued with an attitude of profound reverence for creation, work is meant to be a humanizing experience in which the monk serves both God and the community.

The rule of Benedict promotes a spirituality that is both broad and simple. Because of its flexibility and adaptability, it is capable of incorporating various local traditions. Whenever and wherever the rule is authentically incarnated in monastic men and women, both as individuals and communities, it results in a life that is biblical, contemplative, rooted in a community life of work and prayer, and productive of holiness and peace.

SEE ALSO Benedictines; Cistercians.

BIBLIOGRAPHY

The best critical edition of Gregory's *Dialogues* in Latin and French translation is edited by Adalbert De Vogüé, *Dialogues: Gregoire le Grand*, 3 vols. (Paris, 1978–1980). The rule of Benedict in Latin and French translation with extensive introduction, notes, and bibliography has also been edited by De Vogüé, *Le règle de Saint Benoît*, 7 vols. (Paris, 1971–1977). The final volume is available in English translation: *The Rule of Saint Benedict, a Doctrinal and Spiritual Commentary*, translated by John Hasbrouck (Kalamazoo, Mich., 1983). *RB 1980: The Rule of St. Benedict in Latin and English with Notes*, edited by Timothy Fry (Collegeville, Minn., 1981), is the best Latin edition of the rule accompanied by an English translation; it also contains excellent essays on specific topics in the rule. A balanced contemporary theology of Benedictine monasticism can be found in *Consider Your Call: A Theology of Monastic Life Today*, by Daniel Rees and others (Kalamazoo, Mich., 1980).

R. KEVIN SEASOLTZ (1987)

BENGALI RELIGIONS.

This entry treats Bengal—which corresponds to the Indian state of West Bengal and the country of Bangladesh—as a region in which different religious traditions, from approximately the eighth century to the present, have coexisted, intertwined, and sometimes battled, creating a distinctive context for the study of religion in South Asia. While historically the two "great traditions" have been and continue to be Brahmanical Hindu and Islamic, Bengal has also been highly pluralistic, home to Buddhists, Jains, Parsis, Jews, Christians, Sikhs, and lightly Hinduized tribal peoples, as well as, more recently, Hindus and Muslims who identify as Marxists or secular humanists. This entry proceeds synthetically by proposing thirteen perspectives on Bengal's uniqueness, on what sets "Bengali religions" off from religious traditions elsewhere in the subcontinent.

BENGAL AS THE LAST INDIAN STRONGHOLD OF BUDDHISM. The first regional state in Bengal was established by the Mahāyāna Buddhist dynasty of the Pālas (750 to the mid-twelfth century). Under their rule, centered in Bihar, Bihar and Bengal were unified culturally and politically through religious and economic ties to the outside via trade routes and pilgrims; a great literary activity in Sanskrit (Buddhist intellectual strongholds in Bengal were located in Chittagong, Comilla, Maldah, and Rajshahi, and reflected a vibrant mix of Buddhist traditions (Mahāyāna, Sthavira, Sarvāstivāda, and Vajrayāna); and a common artistic tradition of sculptures and bronzes. Under the late Pālas and Senas (eleventh to early thirteenth centuries), the latter of whom dominated all of Bengal at the time of the Turkish conquest in 1202, the center of gravity began to change, both physically and in terms of religious patronage: political attention shifted from western Bihar to eastern Bihar and Bengal, and Brahmanical Hindu religion became more popular. One can chart this movement east through the artistic record: early Pāla art is Buddhist and found chiefly in Bihar, whereas late Pāla and Sena art is principally Hindu, favoring ornate statues of Sūrya and Viṣṇu, located in Bengal. It is also important to note that the Pāla period was responsible for cultural linkages between Bengal and Nepal and Tibet, through the transmission north of Tantric (Vajrayāna) Buddhist texts and practices.

Scholars are divided as to the reasons for the decline of Buddhism in India—viable proposals include the weak links between Buddhist institutions and Buddhist laity; the fact that life-cycle rites were left in the hands of *brahman* priests; the incorporation by Hindus of Buddha as an incarnation of Viṣṇu; the appeal of Hinduism to the late Pālas and Senas; and the loss of distinctiveness between Brahmanical and Buddhist traditions in the eyes of the laity—but it is certain that in Bengal it lasted longer than anywhere else. (The last Buddhist edifice in South India was constructed in the sixth century and the last Ellorā Buddhist temple in Maharashtra in the eighth century; Gandhara monasteries in the northwest were devastated by the Hunas in the sixth century, and by the ninth century in Kashmir, Buddhist and Śaiva institutions had comingled). Today, indigenous tribal remnants of such Buddhist communities, the Chakmas, Marmas, and Baruas, live mostly in the rural areas of the Chittagong Hill Tracts in eastern Bangladesh, but they comprise less than one percent of the total population of that country, and they perceive their traditional lifestyles and religious freedom to be threatened when an Islamicizing climate is dominant in the government.

LATE, LIGHT ARYANIZATION. A second curious feature of the Bengali religious framework is the region's slow incorporation into the Brahmanical orbit. After an early, Vedic period of scorn—from the time of the *Aitareya Brāhmaṇa* Bengal was said to be a place of exile, lying outside the boundary of Aryan civilization—the area began slowly to be included in it, first under the Guptas from the fourth century and then later in the post-Gupta period with the introduction into the region of *brahmans* from elsewhere in India. This process of Brahmanization is encapsulated in a legend about five *brahmans* who were brought to Bengal from Kanauj by the mythical King Ādisura in order to render the country respectable (dates for this importation of specialists vary from the eighth to the eleventh centuries). These dates may in fact represent approximate beginning and ending points of the diffusion of north-India-derived upper-caste customs into Bengal. That Bengal never achieved the level of cultural refinement considered desirable elsewhere is indicated by the common disparagement of the Bengali *brahman* for his uncouth habits, such as fish- and meat-eating.

Caste in West Bengal represents its own further anomalies. Of the approximately 75 percent Hindus in West Bengal and 10 percent in Bangladesh, less than 10 percent are *brahmans*; most of the rest are *śūdras*, divided into "clean" and "unclean" categories. The two highest groups of the former are the *vaidyas* (traditional physicians) and *kāyasthas* (traditional clerks); these, together with the *brahmans*, constitute the gentle classes, or *bhadralok* (literally, "refined people"), who distinguish themselves from the lower orders, the *chotolok* (literally, "small people"), in Hindu society.

Because of Bengal's peripheral geographic status and the late, relatively flexible structure of its caste system, outsiders—whether ethnic, religious, or cultural—have typically been able to settle and thrive there. This was true of the early Buddhists, and also accounts in large measure for the deep embedding of Islam in the region.

THE ROOTING OF ISLAM IN BENGAL. Ever since the first Indian census of 1872, when the British initially noticed the surprisingly large number of Muslims living in the Bengal Presidency, the problem of accounting for their size has been a scholarly puzzle. Muslims remain even today the largest religious community among Bengalis (86 percent of Bangladesh and 24 percent of West Bengal). Most are Sunnī of Ḥanafī orientation, the few Shīʿah deriving from Persian officials of the late Mughal period; although there must have been a long history of mixed exogenous and indigenous parentage, the majority of Bengal's Muslims are converts, and hence of Bengali ethnic background.

As Richard Eaton (1993) has argued, old-style theories purporting to explain such large numbers of Muslims do not convince: people did not convert "by the sword" or for the "benefits" of political patronage; if either of these had been true, the majority of Muslims in the subcontinent today would either live around the sultanate and Mughal capitol of Delhi, or in Bengal they would be concentrated in the regions surrounding the old Muslim strongholds at Murshidabad or Dhaka, which they do not and are not. Indeed, the Mughals were condescending toward Bengal and hence discouraged conversion. Nor can one have recourse to the theory of conversion for social uplift, since the Hindu system of caste oppression was lighter than elsewhere in north India and since egalitarianism was not the main message of Islam as preached in the medieval period. Instead, Eaton argues, one must look to the geography and frontier nature of the region in a period of expansionism under the Mughals after 1574. Needing workers to clear and domesticate the lands in the east, where the rainfall is up to three times heavier than in the west, the Mughal representatives (*nawābs*) and their land-owning dependents sent in local adventurers to plow and reclaim the land, and to settle and populate it. Such people were typically Muslim holy men (local judges, *pīrs* [popular mystics], and *shaikhs* [teachers]), who taught Islam by example and whose memories were hallowed by those with whom they worked. Such a historical perspective discounts four outmoded conceptions about Bengal and Islam: we now know that the Mughal period was not one of decline, Islam is not monolithic, Muslims are not primarily urban, and the emergence of a noticeable community of Muslims does not necessitate as a precondition a political regime encouraging conversion.

THE RISE OF THE BENGALI LANGUAGE. Much, though not all, of what is distinctively Bengali in terms of religion is articulated textually in the Bengali language, which developed, after the late-Pāla breakaway from Magadhan/Bihari influence, around the twelfth century. Indeed, the earliest specimen of religious literature preserved in Bengali derives from this period: the *Caryāpadas*, or mystic poetic literature usually classed by experts as expressing a nonsectarian Tantric viewpoint. Discovered in 1907 by Hariprasad Sastri, the *Caryāpadas* and other *Caryā*-related texts uncovered since that time are the only texts extant from this earliest period.

What is usually called "the medieval period" of literature, from the fifteenth to the eighteenth centuries, contains three major literary genres, parallel for both Hindus and Muslims. The first are poems built around epic stories, such as Kṛttivāsa's Bengali version of the *Rāmāyaṇa* (from the early fifteenth century) and the *Jangnāma* stories, focused on battles like that fought against the Muslim heroes Ḥasan and Ḥusayn at Karbala, from the end of the fifteenth century. The second genre are poems, songs, and sayings on the Vaiṣṇava and Ṣūfī theme of love in separation, most famously captured through the love story of Rādhā and Kṛṣṇa. Third, on the Hindu side, are the long narrative poems, or *maṅgal-kāvyas*, praising the auspicious merits of various local deities, with a view to publicizing their worship. Examples include Bijaya Gupta's *Manasāmaṅgal*, from 1494, and Bipradāsa's *Manasābijay*, from 1495, both about the snake goddess Manasā; the late-sixteenth century *Caṇḍīmaṅgal* by Mukundarāma Cakrabartī; a spate of *Śītalāmaṅgals* and *Dharmamaṅgals* from the late seventeenth century; and even the sophisticated *Annadāmaṅgal* by the famed Bengali poet Bhāratcandra Rāy, from the mid-eighteenth century. The corresponding Islamic narratives consist of stories about heroes, with the same mix of the supernatural, miraculous, and fantastic that one finds in the *maṅgal-kāvya* literature.

Because of the ambivalence with which Bengal as a region was viewed, first by the Brahmanical mainstream and then by the ruling Muslim elite, Bengali as a language never developed a prestige market. In other words, there is almost no court poetry in Bengali comparable to that written in Persian and Sanskrit. In addition, there is a near complete lack of secular literature before the eighteenth century, and not until the nineteenth century did Bengali even garner sufficient interest to generate grammars and dictionaries. Nevertheless, perhaps because of the fluidity of the medieval vernacular medium, the seeds of distinctively Bengali forms of Vaiṣṇava, Śākta, and Islamic religiosity were sewn.

GAUḌĪYA VAIṢṆAVISM, THE BENGALI VARIETY OF DEVOTION TO RĀDHĀ AND KṚṢṆA. While one can trace Bengali interest in Viṣṇu to Pāla- and Sena-period art of the eleventh to twelfth centuries, it is the tradition associated with (1) Jayadeva, the twelfth century court poet of Lakṣmaṇa Sena and author of the Sanskrit *Gītagovinda,* where Rādhā makes her first major literary debut, (2) the masterpoets Caṇḍīdāsa and Vidyāpati of the fourteenth to fifteenth centuries, and especially (3) Caitanya (1486–1533), considered the dual incarnation of Rādhā and Kṛṣṇa, that has endured as the most characteristic form of Vaiṣṇava devotionalism in Bengal (or Gaur/Gauḍ; hence Gauḍīya Vaiṣṇavism). Caitanya, who introduced an ecstatic singing tradition centered on the name of Kṛṣṇa, was the subject of many biographies, the most famous of which is the *Śrīcaitanyacaritāmṛta* by Kṛṣṇadāsa Kavirāja, of the early seventeenth century. Caitanya's example led to a burgeoning of devotional poetry centered on Rādhā and Kṛṣṇa, and it inspired his chief intellectual disciples, the Gosvāmins of Vrindavan, to elaborate and categorize the aesthetic and devotional principles of that new religiosity—of particular merit in this regard is Rūpa Gosvāmin's early sixteenth century *Ujjvalanīlamaṇi.* In his own person Caitanya knit Nadia, his birthplace in Bengal, to Puri, Orissa, site of the Jagannātha Temple, where he spent the last twenty years of his life, and Vrindavan, in present-day Uttar Pradesh, where he sent the Gosvāmins to establish pilgrimage centers at the sites of Kṛṣṇa's various life stories.

Caitanya's influence also extended to art and architecture, the most striking example of which are the terra-cotta temples of Vishnupur in south-western Bengal. Constructed by Hindu chieftains who in the wake of the collapse of the sultanate in 1575 were looking for symbolic ways to establish their authority, the two-storied structures, heavily indebted to sultanate art forms, were sites for both Sanskritization of the new Vaiṣṇavism and protest against an authority structure dictated solely by *brahman* priests. Perhaps the most visible Western outgrowth of the Bengali Gauḍīya Vaiṣṇava tradition are the followers of the International Society for Krishna Consciousness (ISKCON), whose founder, A. C. Bhaktivedanta Swami Prabhupada (1896–1977), was a devotee of Kṛṣṇa in the tradition of Caitanya.

BENGAL AND THE BRAHMANICAL PREOCCUPATION WITH GODDESSES. Structurally, Muslims and Vaiṣṇavas have tended historically to occupy the same social position in Bengali society: among the lower middle castes of cultivators, artisans, and service providers. By contrast, the preferred deities of *brahmans, vaidyas,* and *kāyasthas,* as well as of the lowest castes and tribes, are goddesses. These range from folk and rural deities like Biṣaharī and Manasā (serpent goddesses), Ṣaṣṭī (the protectress of children), Śītalā (the goddess of smallpox), and Caṇḍī (a popular form of Durgā), to the more universalized Kālī (the demon-slayer who stands astride Śiva), Durgā (the killer of the buffalo demon Mahiṣa), and Umā (the Bengali name for Pārvatī, Śiva's gentle wife). Starting as early as the eighth century and extending to the eighteenth century in the Sanskrit *Upapurāṇas* from Bengal, one can see an avid interest by *brahman* authors with local goddess cults—an indirect acknowledgment of their prior preeminence in the region. Such authors identified these folk deities with Śakti and Śiva, making Śiva Caṇḍī's and Śītalā's husband, Manasā's father, and Ṣaṣṭī's father-in-law. Similarly, in the eighteenth century, many of the landowning *rājās* or self-made gentry under the Mughal representatives patronized Śākta deities, festivals, temples, literature, and devotees. Famous examples of goddess-worshipping devotees supported by the noted Śākta enthusiast Rājā Kṛṣṇacandra Rāy of Nadia (1728–1782) were the brilliant court poet Bhāratcandra Rāy (1712–1760) and Rāmprasād Sen (1718–1775), the first in a long line of folk poets to write devotional poetry (called *Śyāmāsaṅgīt*) to Kālī, Durgā, and Umā. Scholars speculate that the reason for this interest among the upwardly mobile in martial goddesses has to do with their own ambitions: the ostentatious patronage of strong, bellicose deities, especially those whose worship had been undercut during the sultanate period, was seen in the Mughal and post-Mughal periods as an expression of political aspiration and muscle.

Kṛṣṇa- and Kālī-centered traditions have long been at loggerheads in Bengal, with competition and cooption the dominant strategies for mutual containment. The Caitanya cult has tended to downplay Śākta deities as impure or barbaric (due, in part, to their association with blood sacrifice), whereas the Śāktas have been more inclined to embrace Kṛṣṇa by claiming that he is none other than the Goddess in a different form. The saintly figure of Ramakrishna (1836–1886), a priest in Calcutta's famed Kālī temple at Dakṣiṇeśvar, was a living example of such theological accommodation, for he attempted to experience the divine in all forms, realizing ultimately that all were the same Mother Goddess.

That Durgā's yearly festival, or Durgā Pūjā, has now become synonymous with Bengali religious culture and identity, regardless of caste, region, or economic status, is proof of the success of the upper-caste Brahmanical project. Other goddesses with popular and universally celebrated annual festivals are Kālī and Sarasvatī; more regional goddesses, like Jagaddhātrī and Śītalā in the Hulgi and Howrah districts of West Bengal, respectively, also follow the festival model of their more famous sisters. As Kunal Cakrabarti notes, "a common orientation towards the regional goddesses makes Bengal a cult region" (2001, p. 309).

TANTRA AND BENGAL. Along with Kashmir, Tamil Nadu and Kerala in South India, Nepal, and Tibet, Bengal is noted for its Tantric tradition. While the origins of Tantra are still a hotly debated issue among scholars—does it derive from the non- or pre-Aryan substratum? To what degree can one find hints of Tantra in Vedic literature? Does Buddhist Tantra predate Hindu Tantra, or *vice versa*?—from the eighth century, in the Pāla period, Tantra flourished in Bengali religious contexts at both elite and popular levels. Although a Tantric perspective can be applied to the cult of any deity, even including Kṛṣṇa, from the medieval period in Bengal, Tantric texts tended to focus on goddesses and to prescribe specific meditation techniques, hymns, philosophical interpretations, and rituals for their worship. The overall concern in Tantra is to integrate the world into, not separate it from, the perspective of salvation, and the Tantric adept tames the deity in question through transmuting her into inner energy in meditation, receives associated spiritual powers, and learns a monistic method of homologizing his own body, the outside world, and the cosmos with the deity. Significant Śākta Tantras for Bengal include Lakṣmaṇadeśika's *Śāradātilaka Tantra* (eleventh century), the *Kulārṇava Tantra* (1000–1400), the *Kālī Tantra* (c. fifteenth century), Sarvānandanātha's *Sarvollāsa Tantra* (sixteenth century), the *Śāktānanda Taraṅgiṇī* and *Tārārahasya* of Brahmānanda Giri (mid-sixteenth century), Pūrṇānanda Giri's *Śyāmārahasya* and *Śrītattvacintāmaṇi* (sixteenth century), Kṛṣṇānanda Āgamavāgīśa's *Tantrasāra* (seventeenth century), and Raghunātha Tarkavāgīśa Bhaṭṭācārya's *Āgamatattvavilāsa* (1687). There are also sizeable Buddhist and Śaiva Tantric literatures in Bengal, as well as Vaiṣṇava and even Ṣūfī texts influenced by indigenous Tantric patterns.

HUMANISM AND DOMESTICATION OF DIVINITY. Tapan Raychaudhuri has characterized one of the dominant traits of Bengali Hindu religious sensibility as a "domesticated religiosity, a pervasive sense of belief in and adoration of multiple deities as well as other supernatural beings, not all very benign, inspired by an ardent hope that faithful worship and observance of ritual duties would ensure the well-being, *mangal*, of all one cared for" (1996, p. 97). There is ample evidence for this claim as far back as the Bengali *maṅgal-kāvyas*, whose deities are local, ambiguous, greedy for devotees, and sometimes—as Edward C. Dimock has argued in his essays on Śītalā—even outwardly repulsive, although to a devotee such masks hide their true benevolence or mercy (*dayā*). This tendency to endow gods and goddesses with human, almost fallible characteristics is also present in the devotional poetry focused on Kālī, who is chided for her unmotherliness, and even in that centered on Kṛṣṇa, who in Baḍu Caṇḍīdāsa's *Śrīkṛṣṇakīrtana* from the fifteenth or sixteenth century acts like a *maṅgal-kāvya* deity, not above moral reproach. In the same vein, in the eighteenth and nineteenth centuries, lower-class women used songs about Rādhā and Kṛṣṇa as vehicles for airing their grievances against men. Kṛttivāsa's *Rāmāyaṇa* presents readers with a good-natured, not necessarily divine Rāma, and peppers Rāma's story with references to Bengali marriage rituals, Kulīn polygamy, food types, musical instruments, and even place names. Following in this trajectory, the female poet Candrāvatī, in her seventeenth century Bengali *Rāmāyaṇa*, centers the action on Sītā, whose emotions are just like those of a Bengali woman. Continuing into the colonial period, one finds the same tendency to domesticate, Bengali-ize, and humanize divinity in the person of the famed poet Michael Madhusudan Datta (1824–1872). His Bengali version of the *Rāmāyaṇa*, the *Meghnādkāvya*, casts Rāvaṇa and his son Meghnād as the heroes—and he heightens their pathos by the typically Bengali imagery of love in separation, portraying their eventual fall as an indication of universal human frailty. Likewise, the illustrious Bengali novelist, Bankimcandra Chatterjee (1838–1894), presents in his *Kṛṣṇacaritra* (Acts of Kṛṣṇa) an idealized, humanized Kṛṣṇa as a model for modern Indians.

PRIDE IN REGIONAL IDENTITY. Another theme common to Bengali religious traditions is the consistent attempt, in the person of local rulers, to use religious and other symbolism to assert their independence from north Indian centers. One can see this from the first sultanate government under Muḥammad Bakhtyār in 1203 at Lakhnauti, through the nearly two-century period from the Ilyās Shāhī dynasty at Pandua and Gaur in 1342 to the nominal take-over by the Mughals in 1526, to the state governments of East and West Bengal in the twentieth and twenty-first centuries. For example, sultanate rulers asserted their autonomy by patronizing mosque styles different from those customary in Delhi, minting coins with local Bengali imagery, and giving encouragement to folk and popular Hindu traditions over classical, Sanskrit ones. Under the *nawābs* in the early eighteenth century when the Mughal empire was unraveling, this same impulse led to the conscious aggrandizement of Hindu estates by men wishing to build their own power bases in Bengal; Murshid Quli Khan (*nawāb* 1704–1725) cultivated the *rājās* of Burdwan, Nadia, and Rajshahi to create a buffer between him and claimants to the Mughal throne in Delhi.

During the decades before independence, Bengali nationalists who were still mourning the loss of the centrality of Calcutta, which had been demoted from the capitol of British India in 1911, attempted to differentiate themselves from the politics associated with Delhi and Mohandas Gandhi (1869–1948); C. R. Das (1870–1925), head of the short-lived Swaraj Party (1922–1925), challenged the politicians of his day in an attempt to bring Bengal back to center stage: "You cannot delete Bengal!" A string of other Bengali nationalists—the "extremist" Bipincandra Pal (1858–1932), the litterateur Rabindranath Tagore (1861–1941), the radical humanist M. N. Roy (1887–1954), and the Indian National Army leader Netaji Subhascandra Bose (1897–1945)—also disagreed with Gandhi's policies, whether for his mixing of politics and religion or for his adherence to a Vaiṣṇavized doctrine of nonviolence. After independence in 1947, the passionate commitment by Bengalis in East Pakistan to their language and culture contributed to the split from West Pakistan and the creation of Bangladesh in 1971; in a parallel movement, West Bengal since the 1970s has been ruled by the Communist Party of India (Marxist), which in many cases has distanced itself from politics in Delhi at "the center." Hence, in spite of or perhaps because of their vantage point from the periphery of the subcontinent, Bengalis have always wished to maintain a significant, unique perspective.

BENGAL AS AN EARLY TESTING GROUND FOR INDIAN RELATIONSHIPS TO CHRISTIAN MISSIONS. As the seat of British power until 1911, Bengal was the "nerve center" of political, commercial, and intellectual developments in India from the early nineteenth century. One of these developments involved the relationship between Hinduism and Christianity, and many elite Bengalis, especially Hindus, were at the forefront of such an exploration. While some became famous converts to Christianity (Krishna Mohan Banerjea [1813–1885], Lal Bihari De [1826–1894], Protap Chandra Majumdar [1840–1905], and Brahmobandhab Upadhyaya [1861–1907]), and others derided and fought against Christian diatribes from a conservative Hindu viewpoint (see Richard Young's work [1981] on several *paṇḍits*' reactions to John Muir's anti-Hindu tracts after 1839), many Hindu intellectuals preferred to remain Hindu but to engage Christian ideas, finding in them common ground for a postulation of universal truth. For example, Rammohan Roy (1772–1833), often called "the Father of Modern India" for his role in the so-called Bengal Renaissance, was one of the first to enter into dispute in English over issues of Christian doctrine and interpretation. After the publication in 1820 of his *The Precepts of Jesus: The Guide to Peace and Happiness*, he was challenged over a three-year period by the Baptist missionary Joshua Marshman, who did not approve of Roy's attraction to Christian Unitarianism and its emphasis on the unity of a merciful, rational God, an ethical Jesus, and social reform, and who denounced Roy's assertion that while Jesus' moral teachings were fine, doctrines such as the atonement were not. This public disagreement soured Roy on the missionaries, and led him in 1828 to leave the Unitarians in order to found the Brāhmo Sabhā, which eventually became the Brāhmo Samāj (Society of Theists). The Brāhmo Samāj attracted an elite group of Hindus who professed monotheism, shunned image worship and blood sacrifice, and decried the evils of caste discrimination.

Two other noted examples of Hindus appropriating Christian imagery for their own ends are Keshab Chandra Sen (1838–1884), founder of the syncretistic New Dispensation in 1881, who, although he championed an "Asiatic Christ," never quoted the Bible and had no use for Christianity, and Swami Vivekananda (1863–1902), who, in an inclusivist, almost triumphalistic interpretive move, saw in the New Testament evidence for the three levels of Vedānta: Dvaita, or dualism (Jesus calls God his father); Viśiṣṭādvaita, or qualified nondualism, in which God dwells in us as if separate ("I am in the Father and the Father is in me"); and Advaita, or monism, the highest truth ("I and the Father are One"). Yet Vivekananda believed that Jesus' death was a mirage and, like Roy, that the miracles are a stumbling block to true faith.

Indigenous Christians comprise about half of one percent of the population of West Bengal and a third of one percent of that of Bangladesh, according to the 2001 census. They are a diverse group: Roman Catholics, through Portuguese influence in the sixteenth century; Baptists, descended from converts made by the Baptist Mission founded in Serampore in 1793; and Lutherans, Anglicans, Presbyterians, Seventh-day Adventists, and Jehovah's Witnesses, most of whom trace their origins to nineteenth-century Western missions. Anglo-Indians, those descended from a British or European father and Indian mother, are also a significant element of the multi-denominational Christian population in Bengal. Because of the colonial legacy and, in India because of the memory of Nobel Prize winner Mother Teresa (1910–1997), Christians are more influential—and more controversial—than their small numbers might imply. In the 1990s, for instance, with debates about Christian *dalit* inclusion in constitutional provisions for benefits, the 1999 murder of missionary Graham Staines in Manoharpur, Orissa, by an alleged Hindu nationalist sympathizer, and the accusations by Hindu nationalist politicians that political separatism in Christian-majority states like Mizoram (85 percent in 2001) and Nagaland (87 percent in 2001) is linked to religious preaching, Christians throughout India, and also in West Bengal, felt beleaguered. The same is often true in Bangladesh as well, in periods when the drive for a more complete Islamicization is pushed through to state policy.

It is worth noting that since the nineteenth century Calcutta (Kolkata) has been home to one of India's three communities of Jews, the Baghdadi Jews, who arrived in India as a result of opportunities opened up by the British. However, their numbers today have dwindled drastically (in the 1991 census they compromised one-twentieth of one percent of the population of West Bengal), and only one synagogue remains functional in Kolkata as of 2004. Other small religious groups, the Jains (0.05 percent in 2001) and the Sikhs (0.08 percent in 2001), who are Gujaratis, Rajasthanis, and Panjabis by background, live in the state primarily for business purposes.

DEBATES ABOUT IDOLATRY, OBSCENITY, AND POLITICIZED RELIGION. Probably because of the early nineteenth-century Brāhmo critique of image worship, influenced from its inception by the strict monotheism of Islam, many elite Bengalis, Hindus, and Muslims, over the last two hundred years have spoken out against idolatry in any form. One sees this, for instance, in the Unitarian leanings of Rammohan Roy, who coined the term for idolatry (*pauttalikatā*, derived from the Bengali word for "doll"); in the writings of Isvaracandra Vidyasagar (1820–1891), who was concerned with ethicizing and universalizing *dharma*, emphasizing purity of mind over outward ritual; in Swami Vivekananda's patronizing attitude to image worship as a lower step along the spiritual path; in the poetry by Kazi Nazrul Islam (1899–1976), who denounced idolatry; in Rabindranath Tagore's repudiation of ritual in his poetry collection *Gītāñjali*, blood sacrifice to the goddess Kālī in his play *Bisarjan*, and country-worship in his works on nationalism; and in the consistent disavowal of dead religious ritual and superstition in the novels and stories of Saratcandra Chatterjee (1876–1938). Sumanta Banerjee (1989) explains that this condemnation of the "folk religion" of the lower classes for its lack of sensitivity to Upaniṣadic monism was one way in which, after the 1820s, the *bhadralok* sought to define and elevate themselves in the context of their new role as cultural mediators between India and the West. Another was their championing of a prudish, almost Victorian sensibility, according to which the traditions of popular religion, such as the esoteric and often Tantric Vaiṣṇava Sahajiyās, Auls, Bauls, Kartābhajās, and Ṣūfīs, were viewed as participating in dubious moral practices and hence as embarrassing. Bankimcandra Chatterjee was outspoken in his disapproval of the frank eroticism in Bhāratcandra's *Annadāmaṅgal* and of the sensuality displayed in normative devotional poetry centered on Kṛṣṇa and Rādhā (he preferred the martial Kṛṣṇa of the *Bhagavadgītā*). Although one can certainly lay this concern to prove one's religion as "respectable" at the feet of the British, it is also undeniable that the sanitizing instinct was alive and well before colonial influence: consider Caitanya's disciples, the Gosvāmins, who tried to demonstrate in the sixteenth to seventeenth centuries, via several theological somersaults, that Rādhā and Kṛṣṇa were not adulterers.

These puritanical diatribes against image worship did not last in Bengal, however; at least among Hindus they largely fell victim, in the nationalist period after 1905, to a politicized revival of traditional and religious fervor, expressed in a peculiarly Bengali idiom: Śāktism. Thus even though Bankimcandra was by nature morally conservative, his novels attempted to arouse Hindu pride and to remove humiliation. "Bande Mātaram!," or "Hail to the Mother!," the song identifying the motherland with the Mother Goddess that he embedded within his novel *Ānanda Maṭh* (1882), became a political slogan during the protests from 1905 to 1907 against the first partition of Bengal. Political extremists of the period went further, using temples as rallying places, taking oaths in front of Hindu deities to buy only India-made (*svadeśī*) items, and glorifying caste and caste rituals as natural and beneficial. Aurobindo Ghose (1872–1950), who before his retirement into spiritual seclusion in 1910 was a Bengali revolutionary, wrote a didactic play called *Bhawani Mandir*, in which he follows Bankimcandra in homologizing the Goddess to the nation. The British even noted with alarm that Kālī was being employed as an incitement to the violent sacrifice of "white goats." Much later, Bengali political leader Subhascandra Bose, a staunch critic of Gandhi for the latter's reliance on nonviolence, extolled a self-sacrificing love for Bengal closely entwined with his own devotion to blood-demanding Durgā.

Although, because of the Communist Party's strict policy of secularism, the politicized equation of the land with the Goddess is not much in evidence in West Bengal today, it is alive elsewhere in India in the form of *deśabhakti*, or devotion to the country, which can be traced back to Bankimcandra's Bengali articulations. *Deśabhakti* and *Rāmabhakti* form the twin backbones of Hindu nationalist ideology.

To What Extent Can One Be Bengali and Muslim at the Same Time? Another characteristic of the Bengali religious context is related to the third theme mentioned above: Islam and the process of its embedding in the region. A striking feature of premodern Islam is the disjuncture between a folk Bengali variant of Islam, based on and in conversation with indigenous roots, and an urban elite variant, with ties outside Bengal either to north India or to Persia, Arabia, and the regions of central Asia beyond the Khyber Pass. The latter group, called the *ashrāf* (literally, "noble people"), cultivated a high Perso-Islamic culture and literature in Arabic, Persian, and Urdu, and ignored the Bengali traditions of their lower-class coreligionists, the *ātrap* (literally, "mean people"). In the medieval period from the thirteenth to the nineteenth centuries, such folk traditions were highly syncretistic, pragmatic, and influenced by the surrounding Hindu culture. For example, Hindus and Muslims both worshipped the composite Hindu-Muslim figure of Satya Pīr, for Hindus a form of Viṣṇu who acts like a *maṅgal-kāvya* deity and for Muslims a moral exemplar or hero; in the deltaic areas near the Bay of Bengal, they joined, again, in the reverence for Dakṣiṇ Rāy and Baḍa Ghazi Khān, who in Kṛṣṇarāma Dāsa's 1686 *Rāymaṅgal-kāvya* are co-authorized by a figure that is half-Kṛṣṇa and half-Muḥammad to offer protection against tigers and crocodiles.

Other examples of a liberal, flexible premodern Islam can be seen in Ṣūfī texts, such as Saiyid Sultan's *Nabī-vaṃśa* (1654), where yogic and Tantric parallels are forged with Ṣūfī imagery; in the lineages of Baul singers, many of which are mixed Hindu and Muslim; and in intercommunity social customs, such as those relating to kinship, marriage, and even naming practices. Such commonalities make sense in the context of the fact that the vast majority of Bengali Muslims are converts, from the same stock as their tribal and Hindu neighbors.

Although there are sporadic examples of continuing syncretistic trends after the nineteenth century—for instance, Nazrul Islam's attempt in the 1920s to forge a nonsectarian message equally applicable to a Hindu and Muslim audience—from the anti-partition period in 1905 one finds evidence of maturing Islamic reform movements, particularly the Tariqah-i-Muḥammadīya, based on the prior teachings of Shah Waliullah (1703–1762), and the Farā'idī movement, founded a century earlier by Ḥājjī Sharī'at Allāh of Faridpur (1781–1840). Fueled by agrarian unrest against Hindu landlords and responding to the cry of "Islam in danger!," both groups wished to purge the Muslims of eastern Bengal of Hindu influences, dress, and names; of syncretistic attitudes promulgated by local Ṣūfīs and *pīrs*; of folk customs such as the veneration of tombs, the celebration of the Shīʿī festival of Muḥarram, and the exorcisms performed by local *mullahs*; and even of the Sanskrit-derived vocabulary in Bengali language. "Displacing" Hindu elements with Muslim ones was the agenda. By the 1920s, such calls were becoming increasingly successful, and many Bengali Muslims took to this "Ashrafization" process (the Muslim equivalent to what happens in Sanskritization) with increasing vigor. By 1938, when Jinnah, on behalf of the Muslim League, demanded that "Bande Mātaram" be dropped as the nationalist anthem, the more accommodative strategy of Nazrul Islam, who in the early 1920s had written poems like "Ānandamayī," in which he pleaded with Durgā to save her sons, and "Vidrohi," which exhorted rebellion through combined Muslim and Hindu images of martial strength, was politically outmoded.

It was not until after the formation of Pakistan that Bengalis in East Pakistan began to vocalize once again, in the face of increasing persecution and attempts at cultural obliteration by the dominant, Urdu-championing wing of their bifurcated country, that their Muslim identity was in no way inconsistent with their Bengali origins; indeed, the creation of Bangladesh in 1971 was a direct result of such a conviction. Since the formation of Bangladesh, however, a slow process of Islamization has inexorably proceeded: under General Ziaur Rahman (1976–1981), "secular" was dropped from the constitution and replaced by "absolute faith in Allah"; Hussain Mohammed Ershad (1982–1990) was responsible for the addition of the Eighth Amendment, "Islam is the State Religion"; and Jamāʿat-i-Islāmī spokespeople continue to press for *sharīʿah* law to become the law of the land. When parties aligned with the Jamāʿat-i-Islāmī have come to power in Dhaka, minority communities—Hindus, Buddhists, Christians, and tribals—have feared oppression and reported state-promoted endeavors to use cultural differences and linguistic divergences as a means for justifying harassment. In the eyes of many secular or liberal-minded citizens, those for whom Bangladeshi identity is neither equated with being Muslim nor exclusive of non-Muslims, such Islamicizing trends are a departure from the vision of the country for which its founders fought in the late 1960s.

BENGALI RELIGIOUS COMMUNITIES IN THE DIASPORA. It is difficult to know exactly how many Indian Bengalis and Bangladeshis—whether Hindu, Muslim, Christian, or otherwise—live abroad in the diaspora, as published estimates vary. According to the 2000 United States census, "Asian Indians" make up 0.6 percent of the United States population; of these, people described as "Bengalese" form one of five subcategories. Similarly, "Other Asians," at 0.5 percent of the population, include Bangladeshi, Pakistani, Sri Lankan, Indonesian, and Burmese peoples. Of the approximately three million Muslims judged to be living in the United States, the largest subgroup is South Asian, with Bangladeshis slightly trailing Pakistanis. The number of Muslims from India who have emigrated to the United States—mostly from Hyderabad and Bihar, not West Bengal—is one-tenth of the non-Muslim Indian immigrant population, roughly equivalent to their proportional size in India.

Most Bengali immigrants, whether Hindu or Muslim, Indian or Bangladeshi, arrived in the United States after the Immigration and Naturalization Act of 1965, which liberalized American immigration policies. They came and come for a variety of reasons, including educational and economic opportunities, violence at home, and a desired freedom of political and religious expression. Once here, not surprisingly, immigrants retain strong ties with their homelands, facilitated by ease of travel and transnational communications networks. One can see this in the types of religious groups they have organized. For instance, the first thing Bengali Hindus tend to do is to form cultural associations to sponsor the annual celebration of Durgā Pūjā (and, if they are big and wealthy enough, Kālī and Sarasvatī Pūjās). North American cities in which there is a sizeable Hindu Bengali population, such as Toronto and Washington, D.C., have also raised money to build Kālī temples. In addition, Bengali associations offer activities geared toward training second-generation youth, like classes in Bengali language, dance, and the singing of Rabindra-saṅgīt. In all of this, the imitation of the model "back home" is extremely significant, and much ritual paraphernalia, including personnel, is brought directly from South Asia to sacralize the diaspora celebrations. Bangladeshi Hindus, although they may join West-Bengali-run associations, have tended to form their own groups, partly because of different socio-economic backgrounds and partly because, for the Bangladeshi Hindu, cultural celebration cannot be divorced from political reality. Sensitized to the plight of Hindus in Bangladesh who are perceived as being threatened when Islamicizing governments hold power in Dhaka, they use Durgā Pūjā festivities in the United States as a means of raising awareness and garnering support for the straightened circumstances of their coreligionists back home. This is not something that West Bengalis can readily identify with.

While West Bengali and Bangladeshi Muslims have often made common cause with one another, as also with Muslims from Pakistan, Egypt, Syria, Iran, and Lebanon, they too have founded groups that speak to concerns specific to their lands of origin. The Association of Indian Muslims in America, for example, raises money to help beleaguered and persecuted Muslims in India, and a whole host of Bangladeshi organizations endeavors to keep alive Bengali Muslim culture, festival traditions such as ʿĪd al-Fiṭr, and devotional musical events, to which Bengali poets are invited from the subcontinent.

There is some overlap of communities and religious traditions in these diasporic contexts—for instance, Bengali Muslim artists singing at Durgā Pūjā cultural events, or Hindus attending fast-breaking meals at the close of each day of Ramaḍān—but the degree to which such communal harmony prevails in North America depends to some extent on what is happening in the subcontinent: whether India and Bangladesh are on friendly terms, or whether Muslims or Hindus, respectively, are perceived as being maltreated at home. What oils the relationship between the two separate diaspora groups is, of course, their dual pride in the Bengali language, which, until a momentous point in history wrenched the two halves of Bengal apart, united its people.

SEE ALSO Buddhism, article on Buddhism in India; Caitanya; Christianity, article on Christianity in Asia; Dīvālī; Durgā Hinduism; Goddess Worship, article on The Hindu Goddess; Hindi Religious Traditions; Indian Religions, article on Rural Traditions; International Society for Krishna Consciousness; Jayadeva; Kṛṣṇaism; Marathi Religions; Ramakrishna; Tamil Religions; Tantrism, overview article; Varṇa and Jāti.

BIBLIOGRAPHY

Although somewhat dated, the two-volume *History of Bengal,* edited by R. C. Majumdar and Jadunath Sarkar; Vol. 1: *The Hindu Period,* edited by R. C. Majumdar (Dacca, Bangladesh, 1943); Vol. 2: *The Muslim Period,* edited by Jadunath Sarkar (Dacca, Bangladesh, 1948), is still useful, if supplemented by current studies on individual subjects. Likewise, for comprehensive introductions to Bengali literature, Asitkumār Bandyopādhyāy's *Bāṅglā Sāhityer Itivṛtta,* 5 vols. (Calcutta, 1955) and Sukumar Sen's *History of Bengali Literature,* 3rd ed. (New Delhi, 1979) remain invaluable.

Excellent studies on Islam include Rafiuddin Ahmed, *Bengal Muslims, 1871–1906: A Quest for Identity* (Delhi, 1996); Rafiuddin Ahmed, ed., *Understanding the Bengal Muslims: Interpretative Essays* (New Delhi, 2001); Richard M. Eaton, *The Rise of Islam and the Bengal Frontier, 1204–1760* (Berkeley, Calif., 1993); Abdul Karim, *Social History of the Muslims in Bengal, down to A.D. 1538* (Dacca, Bangladesh, 1959); Asim Roy, *The Islamic Syncretistic Tradition in Bengal* (Princeton, N.J., 1983); Tony K. Stewart, *Fabulous Females and Peerless Pīrs: Tales of Mad Adventure in Old Bengal* (New York, 2004); and Mamatjur Rahman Tarafdar, *Husain Shahi Bengal, 1494–1538 A.D.: A Socio-Political Study* (Dacca, Bangladesh, 1965). Ahmed Sharif, Anisuzzaman, and Rafiqul Islam have each written voluminously in Bengali on aspects of Bengali Muslim literature and culture.

For monographs and translations pertaining to the Gauḍīya Vaiṣṇava tradition, see the overview studies of Ramakanta Chakravarti, *Vaiṣṇavism in Bengal, 1486–1900* (Calcutta, 1985), and Sushil Kumar De, *Early History of the Vaiṣṇava Faith and Movement in Bengal, from Sanskrit and Bengali Sources* (Calcutta, 1962); the translations of Edward C. Dimock Jr., *The Caitanya Caritāmṛta of Kṛṣṇadāsa Kavirāja: A Translation and Commentary,* edited by Tony K. Stewart (Cambridge, Mass., 1999), Edward C. Dimock Jr. and Denise Levertov, trans., *In Praise of Krishna: Songs from the Bengali* (Chicago, 1981), and Barbara Stoler Miller, trans., *Love Song of the Dark Lord: Jayadeva's Gītagovinda* (New York, 1977); the study of Rādhā in Bengali Vaiṣṇava conceptions by Sumanta Banerjee, *Appropriation of a Folk-heroine: Radha in Medieval Bengali Vaishnavite Culture* (Shimla, India, 1993); and descriptions of Vishnupur and Vaiṣṇava art and architecture in Pika Ghosh's *Temple to Love: Architecture and Devotion in Seventeenth-Century Bengal* (Bloomington, Ind., 2004) and Ákos Östör's *The Play of the Gods: Locality, Ideology, Structure, and Time in the Festivals of a Bengali Town* (Chicago, 1980).

Further reading on the Śākta and Tantric traditions should include two excellent studies of the Sanskrit literature: Kunal Cakrabarti, *Religious Process: The Purāṇas and the Making of a Regional Tradition* (New Delhi, 2001), and Teun Goudriaan and Sanjukta Gupta, *Hindu Tantric and Śākta Literature* (Wiesbaden, Germany, 1981). Essays on individual regional deities, such as Śītalā, Manasā, and Caṇḍī, may be found in Edward C. Dimock Jr., *The Sound of Silent Guns and Other Essays* (Delhi, 1989), and Ralph W. Nicholas, *Fruits of Worship: Practical Religion in Bengal* (New Delhi, 2003). For information on and translations of the Śākta devotional poetry tradition, see Rachel Fell McDermott, *Mother of My Heart, Daughter of My Dreams: Kālī and Umā in the Devotional Poetry of Bengal* (New York, 2001) and *Singing to the Goddess: Poems to Kālī and Umā from Bengal* (New York, 2001); Malcolm McLean, *Devoted to the Goddess: The Life and Work of Ramprasad* (Albany, N.Y., 1998); and Clinton B. Seely and Leonard Nathan, trans., *Grace and Mercy in Her Wild Hair: Selected Poems to the Mother Goddess by Ramprasad Sen,* 2d ed. (Prescott, Ariz., 1999). For studies of Śākta saints, see Jeffrey J. Kripal, *Kālī's Child: The Mystical and the Erotic in the Life and Teachings of Ramakrishna,* 2d ed. (Chicago, 1999), and June McDaniel, *The Madness of the Saints: Ecstatic Religion in Bengal* (Chicago, 1989). For lists of Bengali Buddhist Tantras, see S. C. Banerji, *Tantra in Bengal: A Study in its Origin, Development, and Influence,* 2d ed. (New Delhi, 1992). The Tantric impact on Ṣūfī texts is discussed by Asim Roy, *The Islamic Syncretistic Tradition,* cited above.

Various types of folk and popular religion—for instance, the Bauls, Sahajiyās, and Kartābhajās—have been discussed in the following: Sumanta Banerjee, *Logic in a Popular Form: Essays on Popular Religion in Bengal* (Calcutta, 2002); Shashibhusan Dasgupta, *Obscure Religious Cults* (Calcutta, 1962); Edward C. Dimock Jr., *The Place of the Hidden Moon: Erotic Mysticism in the Vaiṣṇava-sahajiyā Cult of Bengal* (Chicago, 1966) and *The Thief of Love: Bengali Tales from Court and Village* (Chicago, 1963); E. Alan Morinis, *Pilgrimage in the Hindu Tradition: A Case Study of West Bengal* (Delhi, 1984); Jeanne Openshaw, *Seeking Bauls of Bengal* (Cambridge, U.K., 2002); Tapan Raychaudhuri, "Transformation of Religious Sensibilities in 19th Century Bengal (I)" in *Ramakrishna Mission Institute of Culture Bulletin* (Calcutta, March 1996): 96-100; and Hugh B. Urban, *The Economics of Ecstasy: Tantra, Secrecy, and Power in Colonial Bengal* (New York, 2001).

The colonial period, from roughly the early eighteenth to the mid-twentieth centuries, has garnered tremendous interest among scholars of Bengal. A few titles germane to the study of religion include the following. For the interplay between Hindu *zamīndārs,* Śāktism, and the conditions of early British power, see David L. Curley, "Maharaja Krisnacandra, Hinduism, and Kingship in the Contact Zone of Bengal," in *Rethinking Early Modern India,* edited by Richard B. Barnett (New Delhi, 2002), pp. 85–117; and John R. McLane, *Land and Local Kingship in 18th Century Bengal* (Cambridge, UK, 1993). For elite and popular contexts of eighteenth- to nineteenth-century Calcutta, see Sumanta Banerjee, *The Parlour and the Streets: Elite and Popular Culture in Nineteenth Century Calcutta* (Calcutta, 1989); and David Kopf, *The Brahmo Samaj and the Shaping of the Modern Indian Mind* (Princeton, N.J., 1979) and *British Orientalism and the Bengal Renaissance: The Dynamics of Indian Modernization, 1773–1835* (Berkeley, Calif., 1969). Sumit Sarkar's study of the first partition of Bengal is still a classic: *The Swadeshi Movement in Bengal, 1903–1908* (New Delhi, 1973).

Recommended monographs on famous Bengali writers and religious leaders include Shamita Basu, *Religious Revivalism as Nationalist Discourse: Swami Vivekananda and New Hinduism in Nineteenth Century Bengal* (New Delhi, 2002); Michael Madhusudan Datta, *The Slaying of Meghanada: A Ramayana from Colonial Bengal*, translated with an introduction by Clinton B. Seely (New York, 2004); Brian A. Hatcher, *Idioms of Improvement: Vidyāsāgar and Cultural Encounter in Bengal* (Calcutta, 1996); Tapan Raychaudhuri, *Europe Reconsidered: Perceptions of the West in Nineteenth Century Bengal* (Delhi, 1988); and Sumit Sarkar, *An Exploration of the Ramakrishna Vivekananda Tradition* (Shimla, India, 1993). For types of Hindu response to Christian teaching, see Julius J. Lipner, *Brahmabandhab Upadhyay: The Life and Thought of a Revolutionary* (Delhi, 1999); and Richard Fox Young, *Resistant Hinduism: Sanskrit Sources on Anti-Christian Apologetics in Early Nineteenth-century India* (Leiden, 1981).

Comparative data on Hindu and Muslim class, marriage, and kinship patterns may be found in Lina M. Fruzzetti, *Gift of a Virgin: Women, Marriage, and Ritual in a Bengali Society* (New Brunswick, N.J., 1982); Lina M. Fruzzetti and Ákos Östör, *Kinship and Ritual in Bengal: Anthropological Essays* (New Delhi, 1984); Ronald B. Inden and Ralph W. Nicholas, *Kinship in Bengali Culture* (Chicago, 1977); and Manisha Roy, *Bengali Women*, 2d ed. (Chicago, 1996).

RACHEL FELL MCDERMOTT (2005)

BENNETT, JOHN G. John Godolphin Bennett (1897–1974) was a British industrial scientist, mathematician, thinker, and visionary mystic who embodied the model of the perennial spiritual searcher. He combined scientific research with studies of Asiatic languages and religions. His legacy lives on through his books and recorded lectures about "The Work" which he received from the enigmatic Greek Armenian spiritual teacher George Ivanovich Gurdjieff (1866?–1949) and which formed the foundation of his religious convictions. Bennett's contact with Gurdjieff convinced him that it is not enough to know intellectually more: what matters is to be more—that is, to have "presence." It was the search for the key to "being" that drove him to work on himself in order to be free from vanity and self-love, so that he could "live to the full inwardly as well as outwardly," as he wrote in his autobiography *Witness* (34). Outwardly, he experienced a life of political intrigue and scientific creativity. Inwardly, he awoke to ever-deeper visions of a dimension that he called "eternity." Bennett's four-volume book, *The Dramatic Universe* (1956–1966), testifies to his considerable intellectual powers and his lifelong commitment to the possibility of integrating all human knowledge. His inner story has historical roots, and its review includes major spiritual teachers of the twentieth century.

Born to an American mother from New England and an English father, Bennett did not consider his life to have truly begun until his near-death out-of-body experience in battle at the age of twenty-one during World War I. Shortly after the war, he awoke, for the first time, to a vision of a fifth dimension that he called "eternity," which took thirty years for him to create concepts to explain. After the war he married and fathered a daughter, but he separated from his family to pursue political intrigues in Turkey. In 1920–21 he worked as an Intelligence agent of the British government in the War Office in Constantinople, present-day İstanbul, where half a dozen races and four religious groups converged in the aftermath of the Great War and the Russian revolution. Working in the thick of Turkish politics at this center of great ferment and change, Bennett was entrusted with every kind of secret and consulted about the highest government appointments and activities, including the disarmament of the Turkish army. He spoke, read, and wrote Turkish constantly and worked to resolve political issues with the English, French, Italians, Turks, Circassians, Kurds, Greeks, Armenians, Russians, Arabs, and Jews.

In Constantinople, Bennett witnessed the death of an epoch as the sultanate was overthrown and the Ottoman Empire gave way to the modern and secular Turkish Republic. Here, Bennett had his first contact with Islam and Muslim mystics, or Sufis, who had an impact on him and with whom he reconnected later in his life. Also here in 1920, he met Peter D. Ouspensky (1878–1947) and Gurdjieff, who became his spiritual teachers, and Winifred Beaumont, who became his second wife and shared his life of spiritual search until her death nearly forty years later. Gurdjieff inspired Bennett to dedicate his life to awakening a "permanent unchanging I" beyond the stream of consciousness of ordinary existence. From him, Bennett learned about the possibility of the transformation of a human being. Three years later, in 1923 Bennett went to Gurdjieff's Institute for the Harmonious Development of Man at the Chateau le Prieuré in Fontainebleau-Avon near Paris, where he spent thirty-three life-transforming days. This brief experience convinced him that he must learn to understand with his heart and his body, not just his mind. He realized he could learn to be by training his body to work for a spiritual aim. Gurdjieff demonstrated that it is not enough to know that another world exists: one must be able to enter that world at will.

In 1941 Bennett acquired an estate near London called Coombe Springs where he attempted to reconstruct Gurdjieff's ideas about the "Work," conducting experiments with one hundred students at a time that continued for twenty years. It was during these years that he outlined the four volumes of *The Dramatic Universe.* While Bennett remained in touch with Ouspensky and his wife Sophia Grigorevna in

London, where they studied and taught the principles of Gurdjieff's Work, twenty-five years passed before he reconnected with Gurdjieff in Paris. In the remaining eighteen months of Gurdjieff's life Bennett traveled between London and Paris to be with him despite his professional commitment at the coal company Powell Duffryn and his responsibility for group work at Coombe Springs. In the summer of 1949 he spent a month with Gurdjieff in Paris, which experience was a turning point in his spiritual growth. In 1958 following the death of his second wife, he married Elizabeth Howard, who was a follower of Gurdjieff's Work and they raised a family of two sons and two daughters.

In 1956 Bennett pursued the teachings of "Pak" Subuh (1901–1987), who transmitted a method for the awakening of conscience called "the *latihan*." This was a spiritual practice resembling some states of meditation. It induced powerful psychic and spiritual experiences that varied in intensity and effect. Many practitioners of *latihan* were terrified by a pitiless awakening to feelings of conscience, while others were deeply moved by healing feelings of ecstasy and bliss. With its emphasis on submission to the will of God and its reliance on a single practice, the *latihan* seemed to be the antithesis of Gurdjieff's methods for spiritual awakening, causing many of Bennett's students to leave him. By 1962 Bennett became disillusioned with the passivity of this teaching and returned to exercises in self-discipline. In 1961–63 he was attracted to the teachings on Right Living developed by the 135-year-old Hindu saint Shivapuri Baba, whom he visited in Nepal. In 1971 Bennett acquired Sherborne House near London and established the International Academy for Continuous Education, an "experimental" Fourth Way school, where he conducted experiments with students to apply the techniques he had learned throughout his life for awakening from conditioned existence. Shortly before he died, he also made arrangements for starting another experimental school at Claymont Court in the Shenandoah Valley of West Virginia.

At this point it is difficult to assess Bennett's historical impact. He is almost completely ignored by the academic community. While his ideas continue to influence small groups who work with them, little formal documentation about these groups is available, and some feel that they are already dissolving as those who knew Bennett retire and die. Although Bennett tried to make his ideas accessible to all, the complexity and depth of his vision remain anomalous and inaccessible to most readers. His major work, *The Dramatic Universe,* was Bennett's valiant attempt to resurrect the profound simplicity of the original Pythagorean teaching. It is possible that the core of this wisdom will be collated and integrated within the Neoplatonic and Neo-Pythagorean traditions at some future point.

SEE ALSO Gurdjieff, G. I.; Ouspensky, P. D.

BIBLIOGRAPHY

Works by Bennett

The Dramatic Universe, vol. 1, *The Foundations of Natural Philosophy* (London, 1956) explains the domain of facts: a six-dimensional description of the natural world. In it, Bennett proposes two additional dimensions beyond the traditional four dimensions of space and time. In the fifth dimension of "eternity," time stops but life goes on as a quality of energy in which nothing happens but everything constantly changes. The sixth dimension is called *hyparxis,* or the patterns of eternal recurrence that link potentialities in eternity with manifestations in time.

The Dramatic Universe, vol. 2, *The Foundations of Moral Philosophy* (Charles Town, W.Va., 1961) describes Bennett's ethical insights and aesthetic vision through the use of multi-term systems. These systems take the form of invisible value-structures that can be apprehended by empathetic feeling. Bennett called these structures *monads, dyads, triads, tetrads, pentads, hexads, septads, octads, enneads* and *docecads.*

The Dramatic Universe, vol. 3, *Man and His Nature* (London, 1966) investigates the nature of human existence.

The Dramatic Universe, vol. 4, *History* (London, 1966) sketches a theory of history.

Gurdjieff: A Very Great Enigma. York Beach, Maine, 1973.

Intimations: Talks with J. G. Bennett at Beshara. Gloucestershire, U.K., 1975.

Transformation. Charles Town, W.Va., 1978.

Idiots in Paris. With Elizabeth Bennett. Bath, 1980.

The Way to be Free. New York, 1980.

Witness: The Autobiography of John Bennett. Charles Town, W.Va., 1983.

Energies: Material, Vital, Cosmic. Charles Town, W.Va., 1989.

Is There Life on Earth? An Introductin to Gurdjieff. Santa Fe, 1989.

The Masters of Wisdom: An Esoteric History of the Spiritual Unfolding of Life on This Planet. Santa Fe, 1995.

Secondary Sources

Blake, Anthony G. E. *The Intelligent Enneagram.* Boston, 1996.

BRUCE W. MONSERUD (2005)

BERBER RELIGION. It is difficult to refer with any sort of precision to "Berber religion" per se, even as it is difficult to speak about a "Berber people." The term *berber*—originally a derogatory name (cf. Gr. *barbaroi,* Eng. *barbarians*) applied by outsiders—designates the rather heterogeneous, indigenous population of North Africa extending from the Siwa Oasis in the western Egyptian desert to Morocco, Mauretania, and even as far as the great bend of the Niger River. These people, who have been in the region since prehistoric times, exhibit varying physical features, customs, and social organizations. They are united mainly by language. But even the language itself is highly variegated and is subdivided into a number of mutually unintelligible dialects and many localized vernaculars. In addition to language, another trait that has characterized the Berbers as a whole throughout history has been a strong spirit of local political, social, and cultural independence in the face of domination by civilizations that have imposed themselves upon the Maghreb (the Arabic name for western North Africa): Carthaginians, Romans, Vandals, Byzantines, Arabs, and, for a relatively short time, modern Europeans.

ANCIENT BERBER RELIGION. Echoes of prehistoric Berber religiosity may be found in rock paintings and carvings from the Neolithic period. Many of these depictions are difficult to interpret, but some seem to indicate clearly the veneration of certain animals and perhaps even fetishism. The numerous animal sculptures in hard rock must certainly be idols. These include rams, bulls, and antelopes. By Punic and Roman times, however, zoolatry seems to have been a thing of the past. Augustine of Hippo singles out the Egyptians as animal worshipers, but he does not mention his fellow North Africans in this regard (*Sermons* 198.1).

Throughout the first half of the twentieth century, leading European scholars (e.g., Gsell, Basset, Bel, and Gautier) generally held that the Egyptian cult of Amun-Re was widespread across the Maghreb in antiquity. They based this supposition upon the iconography of a few rock drawings discovered in Algeria and upon the popularity in Carthage of the Punic deity Baal-Hammon, who was identified with Zeus-Amun of the Siwa Oasis. This interpretation, however, has been called into serious question by Gabriel Camps, who has argued that the depictions are of sacrificial animals with ornamental bonnets and not sun disks on their heads. The ram god of Siwa does not seem to have played any special role among the ancient Berbers beyond Libya.

If any deity enjoyed extensive popularity in classical times, it was Saturn. The omnipresence of depictions of this god and his associations with the Punic Baal-Hammon are evidence that he was the real master of the region. One of his iconographic representations, showing him seated on a lion (his animal attribute) and holding a serpent (the symbol of death and fertility), has continued in folk religion down to the present. Rabbi Ephraim Enqawa of Tlemcen, a Jewish saint, who is venerated throughout the Berber regions of southern Morocco, is invariably depicted in the same fashion.

From Punic times onward, it seems that foreign gods were borrowed and syncretized with local North African deities. However, it is difficult to isolate the native Berber divinities from the overlay of official Punic and Roman religion. Because of its essentially popular character, Berber religious practice receives only occasional mention in classical sources or early Christian writings.

Most of the *dii Mauri* (i.e., Mauretanian gods), for whom some fifty-two names survive, were local spirits. Many of these have recognizably Berber names, such as Varsissima (Berb., *war ism,* "the nameless one") and Macurgum (Berb., *imqqor, amqran,* "the great one"), both members of the pantheon of seven deities worshiped at Vaga (modern Béja in Tunisia).

Natural phenomena were the main focuses of Berber veneration, and nature worship has continued to be the core of Berber religiosity into the modern era despite the official overlay of Islam. Writing nearly two thousand years apart, both Herodotus (*Histories* 4.188) and Ibn Khaldun (*'Ibar* 6.94) relate that the Berbers worshiped the sun and the moon, although in what way is not known. Inscriptions from the Roman period mention a god, Ieru, whose name corresponds to the Berber *ayyur* or *ior* ("moon"). Latin dedications to the sun have been found in Tunisia and Algeria, and Spanish writers report that the Guanches (the Berber natives of the Canaries) worshiped the sun, one of whose names was Amen, which in certain Tuareg dialects still means "lord" or "god."

Rocks, mountains, caves, and springs were frequently places of sanctity for the ancient Berbers, as they have continued to be for their modern descendants. Few of the spirits inhabiting these holy spots had names; they were impersonal forces, like so many of the *jnun* of later Berber folk belief.

On the basis of archaeological evidence, it seems that the Berbers of antiquity had a well-developed funerary cult. Decorated rock-cut tombs, funeral altars, and tumuli—all with votive offerings—have been found throughout the region. Among the Numidians, charismatic rulers were venerated as gods after their death, a practice that had its parallel in the widespread saint and marabout cults of later Christian and Islamic times.

BERBER RELIGION IN CHRISTIAN TIMES. During the early centuries of the common era, when Christianity began to spread throughout the Roman empire, many Berbers in the urbanized parts of North Africa adopted the Christian faith. However, Berber particularism frequently imparted to their Christianity an individualistic stamp. The cult of local martyrs was very strong and widely diffused. Many of the practices and votive offerings reflected earlier funerary cults. Certain customs from this period, such as the partaking by women of ritual meals at the grave site, continued after islamization.

Adherence to heretical schisms was another manifestation of Berber individualism. In addition to Donatism, which was an indigenous North African movement, there were active communities of Montanists, Pelagians, Arians, and Manichaeans. As in the pre-Christian era, there was a great deal of syncretizing of native religious traditions with the adopted religion of the dominant culture.

BERBER RELIGION IN ISLAMIC TIMES. According to Arab historians, the Berber tribes of North Africa submitted to Muslim rule and accepted Islam at the end of the seventh century, after more than fifty years of fierce resistance. This mass conversion was due more to political interest than to religious conviction. Since Arab settlement outside the few urban centers was very sparse indeed, the islamization of much of the interior and outlying regions must have been nominal at best. According to orthodox Muslim tradition, the Berbers seceded from Islam no fewer than twelve times. As late as the eleventh century, the Andalusian geographer al-Bakrī mentions Berber tribes who worshiped a stone idol named Kurzah (or Gurzah), which may be related to a Berber deity of Roman and Christian times known as Gurzil. Even in the major towns, Berber particularism made itself felt quite early by the widespread adherence to Khārijī sectarianism, whose egalitarian doctrines had great appeal in the wake of Arab domination and oppression.

New Berber religions appeared during the Middle Ages; influenced by Islam, they adopted aspects of its external form but remained native in language, rite, and usage. The earliest of these was the religion of the Barghawāṭah, who inhabited the Atlantic coastal region of eastern Morocco. During the eighth to twelfth centuries, they adhered to the faith of their prophet, Ṣāliḥ, as propagated and led by his descendants. The Barghawāṭah worshiped one god, Yākush, and had a Berber scripture consisting of eighty chapters. Their religion was highly ascetic and had a strict moral code. In contrast to Islam's five daily prayers, it had ten (five daily and five nightly). There were numerous food taboos: fish, animal heads, eggs, and cocks were all forbidden (some of these have modern parallels among particular families in Morocco for whom eating a taboo food is considered "inauspicious"—Berb., *tteath;* Arab., *ṭīrah*). The charisma of the prophet, Ṣāliḥ's family was a central element in Barghawāṭah communal life. As in the case of the late marabouts, their spittle was considered to have great spiritual and curative powers.

Another new Berber religion influenced by Islam was that of Ḥā-Mīm, who appeared among the Ghumārah tribe in the Rif province of northern Morocco during the tenth century. He too produced a Berber scripture, and had dietary taboos similar to those of the Barghawāṭah. However, Ḥā-Mīm's religion had only two daily prayers, at sunrise and sunset. An important place was accorded to Ḥā-Mīm's paternal aunt and sister, both of whom were sorceresses. According to al-Bakrī and Ibn Khaldūn, the Ghumārah sought their aid in times of war, drought, and calamity.

The Muslim reform movements of the Almoravids in the eleventh and twelfth centuries and of the Almohads in the twelfth and thirteenth centuries, although properly speaking a part of Islamic religious history, nevertheless show certain important affinities with the independent religious movements of the Barghawāṭah and Ghumārah. Tribal or regional Berber identity is very strong in all of them. In each instance the role of the charismatic leader is paramount (in the case of the Almoravids and Almohads this is truest at the early stages of their respective movements).

Although Islam had no rivals as the official religion among the Berbers from the thirteenth century onward, many native Berber rites continued to be practiced within the Maghrebi Islamic context. These are particularly apparent in the highly developed cults of saints both living and dead, in the veneration of such natural phenomena as springs, caves, rocks, and trees, and in numerous rituals linked to agriculture and the seasons. Many Berber groups have retained a solar calendar alongside the Muslim one, which, because it is not only lunar but not intercalated, is of little use to farmers and pastoralists.

Certain dates of the solar year have traditionally been marked by widespread religious observances. For example, New Year's Day—called variously ʿĪḍ Ennayr (Feast of January); Asuggwas Ujdid (New Year); Byannu, Bu-ini, Bubennāni, or Bumennāni (all apparently from the Latin *bonum annum*); and ʿĪḍ n-Ḥagūza (Feast of the Old Woman); is commonly celebrated with special meals, with household rites to ensure a good year, and, in some regions of Morocco and Algeria, with carnivals and bonfires.

Another important celebration in the solar cycle is the summer solstice, called variously *l-ʿanṣra, l-ʿanṣart,* and *tʿaynsāt* (Arab., *anṣārah*). It is celebrated all over Morocco and Algeria with bonfires, fumigation with braziers, and water rites that include ritual bathing, sprinkling, and water fights. The Jews of North Africa have incorporated playful water fights into the celebration of Shavu'ot, which takes place only a few weeks before the *ʿanṣrah.* (It should be noted that the very word *ʿanṣrah* has been linked by some scholars to the Hebrew *ʿatseret,* or "holy convocation," a term used to describe Shavuʿot.)

Although Islam has its own rogatory ceremony for rain in time of drought—the *istisqāʾ* ritual—the Berbers throughout North Africa have in addition their own practices for seeking divine intervention at such times of crisis. One ceremony involves the use of dolls called *tislātin* (sg., *taslit,* "bride"). These are frequently made from ladles or stirring sticks and are carried about by women and children who chant and pray. Even the North African Arabs who perform this ritual call the little effigies by their Berber name, which seems to underscore its autochthonous character.

In conclusion, it should be emphasized that, because of the many conquests of North Africa over the last three millennia and its domination by outside civilizations, it is extremely difficult to identify in many instances what is indigenous Berber religious practice. Even in those parts of the Maghreb where there has been a reassertion of Berber ethnic identity (e.g., in the Algerian Kabylia region), the primary emphasis has been ethnolinguistic and not religious. Islam—whether practiced normatively or not—still commands the Berbers' fundamental religious allegiance.

See Also Christianity, article on Christianity in North Africa; Islam, article on Islam in North Africa.

Bibliography

There is no single work devoted to the history of Berber religion as a discrete entity, although there is an enormous literature on Maghrebi Islam and on popular beliefs and rituals. Berber religion receives extensive treatment within this broader context.

Though somewhat outdated in part, Alfred Bel's *La religion musulmane en Berbérie,* vol. 1 (the only volume to appear; Paris, 1938), remains the best survey of Berber religious history from antiquity through the later Islamic Middle Ages. An important bibliography precedes each chapter. The chapter on religion in Gabriel Camps's *Berbères: Aux marges de l'histoire* (Paris, 1980), pp. 193–271, goes a long way toward updating and correcting Bel and is especially good for the pre-Islamic periods. Edward A. Westermarck's *Ritual and Belief in Morocco,* 2 vols. (1926; reprint, New Hyde Park, N.Y., 1968), remains a classic source of information on popular religion in Morocco. In addition to a wealth of descriptive detail, the book offers much comparative data. Another valuable survey of popular religious practice is Edmond Doutté's *Magie et religion dans l'Afrique du Nord* (Algiers, 1909).

There are many studies on saint veneration in North Africa. The best dealing with holy men in a Berber society is Ernest Gellner's *Saints of the Atlas* (London, 1969). For a comparison of Muslim and Jewish saints, see my study "Saddiq and Marabout in Morocco," in *The Sepharadi and Oriental Jewish Heritage,* edited by Issachar Ben-Ami (Jerusalem, 1982), pp. 489–500.

New Sources

Aki'o Nakano. *Ethnographic Texts in Moroccan Berber (Dialect of Anti-Atlas).* Tokyo, 1994.

Benyounès, Arav. *Berberes, Hier et Aujourd'hui = Imazighen Idelli Ass-a.* Hull, Quebec, 1997.

Haddadou, Mohand Akli. *Le Guide de la Culture Berbere.* Paris, 2000.

Kratochwil, Gabi. *Die Berber in der Historischen Entwicklung Algeriens von 1949 bis 1990.* Berlin, 1996.

NORMAN A. STILLMAN (1987)
Revised Bibliography

BERDIAEV, NIKOLAI (1874–1948), Russian philosopher and spiritual thinker. Nikolai Alexandrovich Berdiaev is one of the distinguished Christian existential philosophers of the twentieth century. His major themes were freedom, creativity, and eschatology. Born in Kiev, he died seventy-four years later in Clamart, a suburb of Paris, without realizing his desire to return to his homeland. Yet Berdiaev was first and foremost a Russian and a mystic, despite his indebtedness to the West.

Berdiaev's life can be divided almost evenly into three quarter-centuries: the years in Kiev, the years in Vologda, Saint Petersburg, and Moscow, and the years abroad in exile (primarily France). Berdiaev was the scion of a privileged family. His father held high military honors; his mother, born Princess Kadashev, had French royal blood. The family's means and status were quite comfortable; yet Berdiaev was restless. From his early youth he was disposed to regard the world about him as illusory, and to consider himself a part of another, "real" world. The child's consciousness of his spiritual aptitude—an eschatological and mystical yearning—was later to find expression in his principal works. He spoke of his early outlook in his autobiography, *Dream and Reality: An Essay in Autobiography* (1949): "I cannot remember my first cry on encountering the world, but I know for certain that from the very beginning I was aware of having fallen into an alien realm. I felt this as much on the first day of my conscious life as I do at the present time. I have always been a pilgrim" (p. 1).

Berdiaev's pilgrim personality is revealed in the following significant works (all available in English translation): *The Meaning of the Creative Act* (1916), *Dostoevskii* (1923), *Freedom and Spirit* (1927), *The Destiny of Man* (1931), *Solitude and Society* (1934), *The Origin of Russian Communism* (1937), *Slavery and Freedom* (1939), and *The Realm of Spirit and the Realm of Caesar* (1951). Throughout these works, he philosophized as an existentialist on the concrete human condition from a Christian perspective that was at times mystical and nonlogical.

Berdiaev's insights, reinforced by personal example, made him both a lonely and a prophetic figure among his contemporaries. He identified himself as belonging to the Russian intelligentsia of the turn of the century, who were permanently in search of truth. He inherited the traditions of both the Slavophiles and the westernizers, of Chaadaev, Khomiakov, Herzen and Belinskii, and also of Bakunin and Chernyshevskii. He saw himself in the line of Dostoevskii and Tolstoi, as well as of Vladimir Solov'ev and Nikolai Fedorov. In summarizing the traditions that influenced him he declared, "I am a Russian, and I regard my universalism, my very hostility to nationalism, as Russian" (*Dream and Reality,* p. xiv).

Appointed professor of philosophy at Moscow University in 1920, Berdiaev was expelled from the Soviet Union two years later for his unwillingness to embrace orthodox Marxism. His subsequent break with Marxism was inevitable. He questioned Marxist subordination of individuality and freedom in its worship of the collective. Furthermore, he found the Marxist view of reality too limited, denying any world other than a temporal-materialistic existence. For Berdiaev, life in one world was flat; he believed that the human spirit seeks transcendence—a striving toward the unlimited and the infinite. To live only in the realm of Caesar is to deny the realm of the spirit. Such restriction was contrary to his ideas of freedom, creativity, and hope. Only a Christian outlook, as embodied in his Russian Orthodox tradition, could satisfactorily embrace both heaven and earth and point to his understanding of the kingdom of God.

As a pilgrim philosopher, Berdiaev viewed the human task as stewardship toward God's End (eschatology); it was a view that called for a complete reevaluation of one's present values and style of life. For him the Christian outlook was far more revolutionary than Marxism.

The Christian gospel for Berdiaev pointed to an ethic of redemption culminating in the coming of the kingdom of God, a kingdom based on love rather than rights and rules. However, he felt strongly that the truth of the spiritual life cannot conform completely to earthly life. For him, there never had been, nor could there be, a Christian state, Christian economics, Christian family, Christian learning, or Christian social life. In the kingdom of God and in the perfect divine life there is no state, no economics, no family, no teaching, nor any other aspect of social life governed by law.

Berdiaev's vision of the Kingdom often led to misunderstandings throughout his lifetime. As a consequence, he was viewed as a maverick philosopher, with no desire for disciples to institutionalize his thoughts. The basic idealism in his thinking led Berdiaev to a serious devaluation of this world, a view that was more spiritualistic (gnostic-Manichaean) than biblical. Nevertheless, his lasting influence as a Christian philosopher and prophetic spirit lies in his ability to stimulate dialogue among divergent cultures and patterns of thought.

BIBLIOGRAPHY

Calian, Carnegie Samuel. *Berdyaev's Philosophy of Hope: A Contribution to Marxist-Christian Dialogue.* Minneapolis, 1968. Contains a complete list of Berdiaev's works.

Clarke, Oliver Fielding. *Introduction to Berdyaev.* London, 1950.

Lowrie, Donald A. *Rebellious Prophet: A Life of Nicholai Berdyaev.* New York, 1960.

Spinka, Matthew. *Nicolas Berdyaev, Captive of Freedom.* Philadelphia, 1950.

CARNEGIE SAMUEL CALIAN (1987)

BERENGAR OF TOURS (c. 1000–1088), rector of the schools of Saint-Martin in Tours and sometime archdeacon of Angers. Berengar was at the center of a eucharistic controversy in his own day and subsequently lent his name to a cluster of positions that more or less closely resembled his. He stands at one pole of a tension that has recurrently characterized Western thinking on the sacrament.

In 1059, under duress, Berengar took an oath formulated by Humbert, cardinal bishop of Silva Candida, to the effect that "the bread and wine which are laid on the altar are after consecration not only a sign [*sacramentum*], but the true body and blood of our Lord Jesus Christ, and they are physically [*sensualiter*] touched and broken by the hands of the priests and crushed by the teeth of the faithful, not only in a sign [*sacramento*] but in truth." The oath of 1059 passed into canonical collections as orthodox doctrine, but its crudity embarrassed most later theologians.

Returning from Rome to Tours, Berengar repudiated and attacked the oath of Humbert and defended his own position that Christ's body and blood were received by the faithful figuratively rather than naturally. This time Lanfranc of Bec led the opposition with his *On the Lord's Body and Blood,* to which Berengar replied in *On the Holy Supper, against Lanfranc.* Berengar took a "spiritual" view of salvation, in which the mental memory of the Lord's life, passion, and resurrection apparently did not entail an earthly reception of Christ's physical body, which was in fact incorruptibly located in heaven. "Eternal salvation is given us if we receive with a pure heart the body of Christ, that is, the *reality* of the sign [*rem sacramenti*], while we are receiving the body of Christ in sign [*in sacramento*], that is, in the holy bread of the altar, which belongs to the temporal order" (Beekenkamp, 1941, vol. 2, p. 158).

At a Roman council in 1079, Gregory VII secured the reconciliation of Berengar by a considerably modified oath:

> The bread and wine which are placed on the altar . . . are converted substantially into the true, proper, life-giving flesh and blood of Jesus Christ our Lord and after the consecration are, not merely in sacramental sign and power, but in the property of nature and truth of substance, the true body of Christ, which was born of the Virgin, and which as an offering for the salvation of the world hung upon the Cross, and sits at the right hand of the Father, and the true blood of Christ, which flowed from his side. (J.-P. Migne, ed., *Patrologia Latina* 150.411)

Berengar's account of the Roman council shows him still trying to interpret the late insertion of *substantialiter* in his own sense.

Berengar never ceased to quote Augustine: "That which you see on the altar is bread and wine, but faith insists that the bread is the body of Christ, and the wine is his blood." Berengar's interpretation of that principle, though rejected by the Roman Catholic church, finds clear echoes in the "receptionism" of parts of the Reformed tradition.

BIBLIOGRAPHY

Berengar's chief work was respectively introduced and edited by W. H. Beekenkamp in two volumes: *De avondmaalsleer van Berengarius van Tours and De Sacra Coena adversus Lanfrancum* (The Hague, 1941). Necessary corrections have been made by R. B. C. Huygens in "À propos de Bérengar et son traité de l'eucharistie," *Revue bénédictine* 76, nos. 1–2 (1966): 133–139.

The background and sequel to the Berengarian controversy are described in Gary Macy's *The Theologies of the Eucharist in the Early Scholastic Period* (Oxford, 1984); see especially pages 1–72. An account of the affair is also given in Margaret T. Gibson's *Lanfranc of Bec* (Oxford, 1978). Roman Catholic scholars tend to stress the inadequacy of Berengar in terms of the later teaching of the Fourth Lateran Council, Thomas Aquinas, and the Council of Trent, as does Jean de Montclos in *Lanfranc et Bérenger: La controverse eucharistique du onzième siècle* (Louvain, 1971). On the other hand, a sympathetic appreciation of Berengar is offered by the Protestant A. J. Macdonald in *Berengar and the Reform of Sacramental Doctrine* (London, 1930).

GEOFFREY WAINWRIGHT (1987)

BERGSON, HENRI (1859–1941), French philosopher. Born in Paris and educated at Lycée Condorcet and École Normale Supérieure, Bergson taught at three lycées and the École Normale Supérieure before he was invited to the Collège de France in 1900, where he lectured until 1914, formally retiring in 1921. His popular lectures influenced listeners from a wide variety of disciplines. He served as the first president of the Commission for Intellectual Cooperation of the League of Nations. In 1927, already awarded France's highest honors, Bergson received the Nobel Prize for literature.

Although born Jewish, Bergson was increasingly attracted to Roman Catholicism. While declaring his "moral adherence" to Catholicism and requesting that a priest pray at his funeral, Bergson refused to abandon his fellow Jews in the face of Nazi anti-Semitism.

Bergson began his career as a disciple of Herbert Spencer, whose evolutionism exalted science and the individual. In the 1880s, however, Bergson decided that science provided an incomplete worldview, for its concept of time could not account for the experience of duration. From this disagreement came his first book, *Essai sur les données immédiates de la conscience* (1889; translated as *Time and Free Will,* 1910). He next examined the relationship of mind to body in *Matière et mémoire* (1896; *Matter and Memory,* 1911). *L'évolution créatrice,* his most famous work, appeared in 1907 (*Creative Evolution,* 1911). In it he expounded a nonmechanistic portrait of biological evolution, propelled toward higher levels of organization by an inner vital impulse *(élan vital). Les deux sources de la morale et de la religion* appeared in 1932 (*The Two Sources of Morality and Religion,* 1935). These four books constitute his major works.

In *Two Sources* Bergson distinguished between static and dynamic morality. The first, a morality of obligation, sanctions behavior consistent with an ordered community. The second, a morality of attraction, issues from mystical experience. The vital impulse, communicated from God through the mystic to others, generates a dynamic morality guided by a vision of humanity as a whole. Whatever his earlier views, by 1932 Bergson was affirming a transcendent God of love who is creatively involved in human existence.

Because many found Bergson's thought liberating, his influence in the early twentieth century was important and widespread. Although he regarded science very seriously, there was still room in Bergson's universe for intuition as well as reason, for morality and religion as well as mechanics, for organic communities as well as isolated individuals. A gifted writer, he bridged the worlds of literature, philosophy, and science.

Bergson was a seminal thinker, prompting others to move beyond his own conclusions. There were few disciples and no one to transform his essays into a polished system. The American philosopher William James and the Jesuit philosopher of science and religion Pierre Teilhard de Chardin borrowed much and yet departed from him at significant points.

Bergson's influence continues among existentialists who borrow his distinction between conventional and "higher" morality and continues within various process theologies that abandon classical theism to find both divine and human creativity at work in an evolving world.

BIBLIOGRAPHY

The best introduction to Bergson's philosophy is the volume edited and introduced by Harold A. Larrabee, *Selections from Bergson* (New York, 1949). In addition to excerpts from Bergson's major works, it contains all but ten pages of his brief *Introduction to Metaphysics* (*Introduction à la métaphysique,* Paris, 1903). Translated by T. E. Hulme in 1913, this work, perhaps the best place to begin reading Bergson himself, has also been published separately with an introduction by Thomas Goudge (New York, 1955). Bergson's complete writings are available in one volume, *Œuvres* (Paris, 1959), introduced by Henri Gouhier and edited by André Robinet. P. A. Y. Gunter's *Henri Bergson: A Bibliography* (Bowling Green, Ohio, 1974) lists 4,377 entries: 470 refer to letters, articles, and books by Bergson himself, while 3,907 entries, some annotated, refer to essays on Bergson by various other authors. A brief introduction to Bergson's thought can be found on pages 49–83 of *French Philosophy in the Twentieth Century* by Gary Gutting (Cambridge, U. K., 2001).Three studies of his philosophy are Vladimir Jankélévitch's *Henri Bergson* (Paris, 1959; in French), Daniel Herman's *The Philosophy of Henri Bergson* (Washington, D.C., 1980), and A. R. Lacey, *Bergson* (London, 1989). Jankélévitch's book contains a chapter entitled "Bergson et le judaïsme." Herman's relatively brief interpretive essay surveys major topic in Bergson's thought while focusing on the role of finality in his philosophy. Lacey's purpose is to state and assess Bergson's main arguments. *The New Bergson* (Manchester, England, 1999), edited by John Mullarkey, gives evidence of a renewed engagement with Bergson's philosophic ideas.

DARRELL JODOCK (1987 AND 2005)

BERNARD OF CLAIRVAUX (1090–1153), monastic reformer, abbot of the Cistercian monastery of Clairvaux, France. Bernard is known principally through four biographical accounts written in his own century (which contain more legend than fact), through other writings of his contemporaries, and through his own works. Born to a noble family at the château of Fontaine, near Dijon, Bernard was educated by the canons of Saint-Vorles, Châtillon. At about the age of twenty he decided to commit himself to monastic life at the recently founded abbey of Cîteaux, which he entered in 1113. In 1115 he was sent to found the abbey of Clairvaux. So many recruits came that in 1118 he founded another abbey, and he continued to found one or more each year for a total of about seventy monasteries.

By 1125 Bernard had written three treatises: *The Steps of Humility, In Praise of the Virgin Mother,* and *Apologia to*

Abbot William. His reputation spread. Around 1127 he wrote *On the Behavior and Duties of Bishops* and *On Grace and Free Choice; On Loving God* was composed between 1126 and 1141, and *In Praise of the New Knighthood* between 1128 and 1136. In 1133 he traveled to Italy to settle the schism in the papacy between Innocent II and Anacletus II. In about 1135 Bernard began the long series of sermons *On the Song of Songs,* leaving the last sermon, the eighty-sixth, unfinished at his death. In 1139 he began to participate in the controversy then raging over the writings of Abelard, as is particularly illustrated by his Letter 190, "Against the Errors of Abelard." At this time he wrote the treatise *On Conversion* for the students in Paris. Before 1144 he dedicated to some Benedictine monks *On Precept and Dispensation.* He also took an active part in church politics, first in the combat against the heresies of the Cathari in the south of France, and then in Flanders, the Rhineland, and Bavaria, to rally men for the Second Crusade, initiated in 1146 by Eugenius III, the first Cistercian pope, for whom Bernard wrote *Five Books on Consideration.* After 1148 he penned *The Life and Death of Saint Malachy,* a biography of the bishop of Armagh who died at Clairvaux. About five hundred of Bernard's many letters are extant, as are numerous sermons on various subjects. Bernard died at Clairvaux on August 20, 1153 and was canonized by Alexander III in 1174.

Bernard was essentially a monk and a reformer, and his way of being both was determined by his character. His extremely artistic literary style tended to conceal his natural spontaneity. One senses deep conflict in this man: a tendency to be aggressive and domineering versus a will to be humble, to serve only "the interests of Jesus Christ." By constant examination of his motivations Bernard acquired a certain self-control. Occasionally charity gave way to passion; however, his humanity toward all won him more friends than enemies.

Bernard reformed monasticism by introducing greater poverty and austerity among the monks of the older orders, such as those at Cluny and Saint-Denis. He encouraged the new orders, the Regular Canons and the Carthusians. He strove for similar reform in the papacy, in the Curia Romana, and among bishops, clergy, and laity. He continued the institutional reform of Gregory VII by a spiritual reform in favor of interiority.

In the controversies over Abelard, historians have detected a conflict between personal rather than doctrinal points of view. Bernard and Abelard were in basic agreement on most points of doctrine and especially on the necessity of the appeal to reason, but Bernard, ill informed about the details of Abelard's teachings, won the support of the clergy of his day more by the form of his presentation of Christian dogma than by his criticism of Abelard.

In the political field, and especially in connection with the continual warfare of his day, Bernard defended nonviolence and made every effort to bring about reconciliation. About the pagan Wendes he said, "We must persuade to faith, not impose it." Elsewhere, he pointed out that the faithful of the Eastern and the Western churches were united by faith. Further, he defended the persecuted Jews of the Rhineland.

Bernard's theology had its roots in his own spiritual experience and in scripture, which served as the norm of interpretation for experience. He affirmed that the Holy Spirit, who inspired the sacred authors, gives understanding to their readers. His style is a tapestry of biblical quotations and allusions, often worded as they are found in the liturgy or in the writings of the fathers of the church. He borrowed very little from profane authors.

His doctrine is founded on the idea that the image of God in man has been dimmed by sin but not effaced. This image is restored when grace gives true self-knowledge or humility. In Jesus Christ, God became imitable. The Holy Spirit enables us to share in the salvation brought by Christ by keeping alive in us his "memory"—through meditation, in the celebration of the "mysteries" (the sacraments), in the liturgy, and by following his example. Within the church—Christ's bride—ascesis and prayer lead to union with God, to peace and joy.

BIBLIOGRAPHY

The best critical edition of Bernard's writings is *Sancti Bernardi Opera,* 8 vols., edited by Jean Leclercq, C. H. Talbot, and H. M. Rochais (Rome, 1957–1977). English translations are available in the "Cistercian Fathers Series" (Kalamazoo, Mich.). For historical orientation, see N.-D. d'Aiguebelle's *Bernard de Clairvaux* (Paris, 1953), volume 3 in the series "Commission d'histoire de l'Ordre de Citeaux." For discussions of Bernard's thought, see *Saint Bernard théologien,* edited by Jean Leclercq (Rome, 1953), volume 9, nos. 3–4, of the series "Analecta Sacri Ordinis Cisterciensis," and Gillian Evans's *The Mind of Saint Bernard of Clairvaux* (Oxford, 1983). An analysis of Bernard's work and influence is my own *Bernard of Clairvaux and the Cistercian Spirit,* translated by Claire Lavoie (Kalamazoo, Mich., 1976).

JEAN LECLERCQ (1987)

BERNDT, CATHERINE H. (1918–1994). Born Catherine Helen Webb on May 8, 1918, in Auckland, New Zealand, Catherine Berndt grew up in households rich in the sounds and stories of many places and in the company of strong, supportive women. From her maternal grandparents and their siblings, Catherine heard of their early life in Nova Scotia. She heard tales of Scotland from her "great-aunt" Catherine, who had informally adopted Catherine's mother and in whose house Catherine was born. It was to this house that her mother returned with her three children after Catherine's parents separated and her father went to Australia. Her parents reconciled when she was about ten, and, in her father's house in Wellington, Catherine had access to libraries that reflected his interests in travel and anthropology. In her great-aunt's house in Auckland she read Celtic history and heard, in her great-uncle James's lilting singing, the rhythms of the Scottish lowlands. Missionaries visiting the Webbs at both locations brought tales of faraway places. Her later research interests in women's religious lives, race relations, social change, oral and children's literature, myths, and her exploration of a number of languages, at university and in the field, resonate with these early experiences.

During her undergraduate years, 1936–1939, at Victoria University College (now Victoria University), Wellington, Catherine studied classics and majored in Latin. She learned from fellow Maori students of their struggles, and later, in 1986, was proud to discover her Maori forebears. In getting an education Catherine enjoyed the unfailing support of her female kin. Her great-aunt cared for her during the first years of her postprimary education. Then, after her great-aunt fell ill, Catherine's younger sister moved to keep her company. Catherine's mother, wanting her daughter to have the university education denied to her, considered anthropology a good field and, with a fourth child born after another reconciliation, moved the family to Dunedin so that Catherine could complete a one-year certificate of proficiency in anthropology at the University of Otago. There, H. D. Skinner (1886–1978), director of the Otago Museum, encouraged Catherine to pursue her anthropological interests in Australia. In 1940, shortly after her mother's death, Catherine headed to Sydney to work with Professor A. P. Elkin (1891–1979), and there she met fellow student Ronald M. Berndt (1916–1990), whom she married in 1941, beginning a remarkable partnership spanning five decades and research in a number of indigenous communities in Australia and New Guinea.

Catherine Berndt's contribution to the study of the religious lives of Aboriginal women across Australia, particularly in Balgo, Victoria River Downs, Oenpelli, and Ooldea, reinforced and expanded upon the earlier pioneering work of Phyllis Kaberry (1910–1977) in the Kimberleys. Berndt documented the separate and secret religious lives of Aboriginal women, the richness of their songs and myths, the wide range of their religious activities, and the complementarity of the genders. It is a great loss to the field that much of Catherine Berndt's remarkable research remains inaccessible. (The field notebooks of Ronald and Catherine Berndt are under a thirty-year embargo in the Anthropology Museum at the University of Western Australia. In her publications Berndt often notes that they are sketches only and that further research is needed.)

Berndt's first fieldwork in Ooldea in the west of South Australia—where, along with her husband, she studied the impact of transcontinental railway on the local population—set the stage for much that would follow. She wrote of women's knowledge of the land and rituals associated with marriage, pregnancy, spirit children, and childbirth; of women's "secret life, in which men have no share, [that] centres round the ancestral myths and songs told by the old women" (Berndt and Berndt, 1942–1945, p. 230); and emphasized that women had "no feeling of inferiority in regard to religion" (p. 260).

In subsequent fieldwork and publications, Berndt mapped the diversity of women's religious activities and teased out common themes. In "Women's Changing Ceremonies in Northern Australia"—her 1949 M.A. thesis (with first class honors from the University of Sydney), published in 1950 in *L'Homme* and praised by Claude Levi-Strauss (b. 1908) for its contribution to the sociology of religion and attention to the dynamism of Aboriginal society—Berndt argues that, on the whole, culture contact in the Victoria River Downs region of the Northern Territory and Western Australia was having a "discouraging and deleterious" effect on women's ceremonial life (p. 9). Relying solely on female informants, Berndt set out three categories of ceremonies: ones in which men and women participate as equals, those in which women's roles are supplementary, and those kept secret by women, at which men are not present. Her 1965 article on women's secret life explores their songs, designs, dancing, and myths against the background of the historical and theoretical literature, in particular Durkheim's sacred-profane dichotomy. In "Digging Sticks and Spears; or, The Two-Sex Model," written in 1970, Berndt characterizes gender relations in Aboriginal society as facilitating women's independence within a societal framing of interdependence.

The Berndts' research of the early 1940s among the Yaraldi (Ngarrindjeri) of the Lower Murray region of South Australia, a people whose contacts with outsiders reach back to the 1800s, is ambivalent regarding the extent of women's secret religious traditions and has been subject to critical scrutiny in the context of a major court case.

Following their 1951–1952 fieldwork in Papua New Guinea, the Berndts, from 1953 to 1955, studied under Raymond Firth (1901–2002) at the London School of Economics, where they also completed their dissertations. Catherine Berndt's dissertation on myth in action, written in 1955, remains unpublished.

Catherine Berndt had a complicated relationship with feminism and feminist scholars. She had little time for what she termed "militant feminists," and she celebrated her "separate but together" fieldwork style with her husband. Catherine was raised to believe in the equality of the sexes, but, in common with a number of other talented women scholars, she never held a tenured position. In 1956 the Berndts moved to the University of Western Australia, Perth, and together they established the anthropology department: Ronald as senior lecturer and then in 1963 as foundation professor, and Catherine as visiting tutor and later as visiting lecturer.

Catherine Berndt was the recipient of numerous grants and awards, including a Winifred Cullis grant from the International Federation of University Women (1954–1955), a travel grant from the Wenner-Gren Foundation, and the New South Wales Premier's Special Children's Book Award for *Land of the Rainbow Snake,* shared with illustrator Djoki Yunupingu. She was a foundation member of the Australian Institute of Aboriginal Studies (now the Australian Institute of Aboriginal and Torres Strait Islanders Studies) and, in 1982, was elected a fellow of the Academy of Social Sciences in Australia. In 1987 she received the Order of Australia and an honorary doctorate from the University of Western Australia, where a prize is awarded annually in her name to the female whose Ph.D. thesis made the most outstanding contribution to social anthropological knowledge of Aboriginal Australia.

SEE ALSO Berndt, Ronald.

BIBLIOGRAPHY

Berndt, Catherine H. "Women's Changing Ceremonies in Northern Australia." *L'Homme* 1 (1950): 1–88.

Berndt, Catherine H. "Mythology in the Eastern Central Highlands of New Guinea." Ph.D. diss., London School of Economics, London, 1955.

Berndt, Catherine H. "Women and the 'Secret Life.'" In *Aboriginal Man in Australia,* edited by Ronald M. Berndt and Catherine H. Berndt, pp. 238–282. Sydney, 1965.

Berndt, Catherine H. "Digging Sticks and Spears; or, The Two-Sex Model." In *Women's Role in Aboriginal Society,* edited by Fay Gale, pp. 39–48. Canberra, Australia, 1970.

Berndt, Ronald M., and Catherine H. Berndt. *A Preliminary Report of Field Work in the Ooldea Region, Western South Australia.* Sydney, 1942–1945.

Berndt, Ronald M., Catherine H. Berndt, and John E. Stanton. *A World That Was: The Yaraldi of the Murray River and the Lakes, South Australia.* Melbourne, Australia, 1993.

Kaldor, Susan. "Catherine H. Berndt." In *Women Anthropologists: A Biographical Dictionary,* edited by Ute Gacs et al., pp. 8–16. New York, 1988.

Tokinson, Robert, and Myrna Tokinson. "Obituary. Catherine Helen Berndt." *Australian,* May 25, 1994.

Von Doussa, John. "Reasons for Decision." August 21, Chapman v Luminis Pty Ltd (No. 5) Federal Court of Australia, 1106, No. SG 33 of 1997. 2001.

DIANE BELL (2005)

BERNDT, RONALD (1916–1990), an Australian anthropologist, was the first to transcribe, translate, and analyze Aboriginal stories and songs; he also wrote extensively on social organization, sexuality, poetry and song, art and material culture, as well as social change and acculturation within Aboriginal societies. Born in Adelaide, South Australia, to an Australian-born Huguenot mother and a German father he was attracted to anthropology at an early age. Fascinated with the Great Pyramids of Egypt, he even taught himself to read hieroglyphics as a child.

His interest in ethnology and in Aboriginal culture led him first to pursue local field research. In 1940 he entered the University of Sydney as a student of Professor A. P. Elkin, earning a diploma of anthropology (1943), bachelor of arts (1950), and master of arts in anthropology, first class (1951). While at the university he also met New Zealander Catherine Helen Webb (1918–1994), whom he married in 1941 (Stanton, 1994).

The Berndts' very close professional partnership spanned almost five decades; neither of their achievements can be considered apart from the other's. The extent and breadth of their fieldwork were exceptional, and their publication record reflects this. They first worked together in South Australia at Ooldea from 1940 to 1941, continuing the research Berndt began there in 1939; they then went to the Murray Bridge area to for two years, followed by a year in the Northern Territory at Birrundudu.

It was, however, during his thirty-three years of work in Arnhem Land (1946–1979) that Berndt's most detailed descriptions of Australian Aboriginal life were focused and for whose publications he is best known: *Kunapipi* (1951), *Djanggawul* (1952), *An Adjustment Movement in Arnhem Land* (1962), and *Love Songs of Arnhem Land* (1976). The Berndts also carried out pioneering fieldwork at Balgo Hills on the northern edge of Australia's Western Desert (1951–1981) as well as in highland New Guinea (1951–1953). The latter work formed the bases of their respective doctoral theses from the London School of Economics in 1955.

Berndt was trained within the British structural-functionalist tradition, taught first by Elkin and then supervised by Firth in London. The dominant anthropological and sociological school of the mid-1940s through the early 1970s, structural-functionalism taught that societies are an interrelated collection of groups that must maintain order and balance to function smoothly. In this view, shared norms and values form the basis of society, and social order rests on tacit agreements between groups and organizations. As a student of this method, Berndt pursued a holistic approach to gaining an understanding of Australian Aboriginal societies.

Berndt was preoccupied with all aspects of Aboriginal religious life; it was his point of convergence in articulating the nature of these societies (see, for example, his *Australian Aboriginal Religion,* 1974). By the start of the twenty-first century, however, his contribution to the wider understanding of Aboriginal religion had been little evaluated. The 2004 republication of *Djanggawul* and *An Adjustment Movement in Arnhem Land,* two of his major works, was expected to provoke such an assessment.

The scope of Berndt's fieldwork in Australia added a more global vision to his perspective on the nature and articulation of Aboriginal societies—their commonalities as well as their divergences. The couple's best-known work, *The World of the First Australians* (1964), sought to explore the transformations, as well as the consistencies, of Aboriginal social practices. It became the classic reference for students and others, continuously in print for over forty years and often found as the sole volume on Aboriginal Australia in many of the world's libraries.

For Berndt, Aboriginal religion found tangible expression in both sacred and secular art. It was through these media, he believed, that social relations were most clearly expressed, and the tenets of religious experience most substantively uttered, affirmed, and transmitted to oncoming generations.

Writing of Aboriginal art decades before its renaissance in the 1970s and its widespread acceptance within the international art world a decade later, Berndt avowed the primacy of the religious experience in the daily lives of Aboriginal people, past and present (1964). Indeed, he saw the widespread distribution of contemporary expressions of artistic creativity as a demonstration of the enduring power of Aboriginal knowledge to communicate, challenge and shape the future (1973, 1982).

Collecting such material expressions of cultural diversity and local perspectives throughout his lifetime (Stanton, 1990), the works he and his wife donated to the University of Western Australia form the unique collection at the core of the museum founded in 1976 to house those works. In 1980 the museum was renamed the Berndt Museum of Anthropology in recognition of their contributions to Australian and world anthropology.

SEE ALSO Berndt, Catherine H.

BIBLIOGRAPHY

Berndt, Ronald. *Kunapipi: A Study of an Australian Aboriginal Religious Cult.* Melbourne, 1951.

Berndt, Ronald. *Djanggawul: An Aboriginal Religious Cult of North-eastern Arnhem Land.* London, 1952.

Berndt, Ronald. *An Adjustment Movement in Arnhem Land.* Paris, 1962.

Berndt, Ronald. *Australian Aboriginal Religion.* Leiden, 1974.

Berndt, Ronald. *Love Songs of Arnhem Land.* Melbourne, 1976.

Berndt, Ronald, ed. *Australian Aboriginal Art.* Sydney, 1964.

Berndt, Ronald, and Catherine H. Berndt. *A Preliminary Report on Fieldwork in the Ooldea Region, Western South Australia.* Oceania Bound Offprint. Sydney, 1945.

Berndt, Ronald, and Catherine H. Berndt. *The World of the First Australians.* Sydney, 1964.

Berndt, Ronald, and Catherine H. Berndt. *End of an Era: Aboriginal Labour in the Northern Territory.* Canberra, 1987.

Berndt, Ronald, and Catherine H. Berndt, with John E. Stanton. *Aboriginal Australian Art: A Visual Perspective.* Melbourne, 1982.

Berndt, Ronald, and Catherine H. Berndt, with John E. Stanton. *A World that Was: The Yaraldi of the Murray River and the Lakes, South Australia.* Melbourne, 1993.

Berndt, Ronald, and E. S. Phillips. *The Australian Aboriginal Heritage: An Introduction through the Arts.* LP Recording. Australian Society for Education through the Arts/Ure Smith. Sydney, 1973.

Berndt, Ronald, and John E. Stanton. *Australian Aboriginal Art in the Anthropology Research Museum of the University of Western Australia.* Nedlands, Australia, 1980.

Stanton, John. "Obituary: Ronald Murray Berndt 14 July 1916–2 May 1990." *Australian Aboriginal Studies* (1990): 95–99.

Stanton, John. "Obituary: Catherine Helen Berndt 1918–1994." *Australian Aboriginal Studies* (1994): 93–96.

JOHN E. STANTON (2005)

BERSERKERS. The Old Norse term *berserkr* was used to identify certain fierce warriors with animal characteristics. According to Old Norse literature, particularly the later sagas, berserkers howled like animals in battle and bit their shields. They felt no blows and had unnatural or supernatural strength, which gave way to languor after battle. The earliest attestation of the term, however, which occurs in the poem *Haraldskvæði* (attributed to two different poets), presents *berserks* as the shock troops of King Harald Fairhair at the Battle of Hafrsfjörðr (end of ninth century):

> 8. They [the warships] were laden with men and with white shields with western spears and Welsh [French] swords: berserks wailed, battle had begun for them, *ulfheðnar* ["wolf skins"] howled, irons shook. 20. About the gear [service?] of berserks I want to ask, tasters of carrion-sea [blood], how it is for the ones who go into the army, battle-brave men. 21. They are called *ulfheðnar* who in battle bear bloodied shields; they redden spears when they come to battle: there they work in common; among champions alone I think would conceal himself The wise king, Among those who hack at shields.

In this tradition, at least, it is clear that there was little difference between berserkers and *ulfheðnar.* For this reason, many scholars understand the term *berserkr* as "bear-shirt," and they take both terms to refer to shape-changing in the manner of werewolves and man-bears, or perhaps to animal cloaks the warriors may have worn. Others, however, have ignored this passage and argued that the word *berserkr* means "bare-shirted" and refers to the berserkers' lack of armor. Explanations of the *berserksgangr* ("going berserk") include self-induced or group ecstasy, psychosis, or lycanthropy.

In Norse mythology berserkers are associated primarily with the god Óðinn. In his *Ynglingasaga*—a euhemerized account of the origin of the royal line of the Ynglingar that constitutes the first saga in his famous *Heimskringla* (c. 1230)—the Icelandic mythographer Snorri Sturluson gives an explicit description of the *berserksgangr* and attributes it specifically to Óðinn warriors (chap. 6). Óðinn also is master of the *einherjar,* dead warriors who inhabit Valhǫll, spending their days in battle, their evenings in feasting and drinking.

The religious complex suggested by these and other data is that of an ecstatic warrior cult of Óðinn, whose name, coming from the Proto-Germanic term **woþanaz,* appears to mean "leader of the possessed." This cult probably involved strict rules of initiation, similar perhaps to those attributed by Tacitus to the Chatti (*Germania* 30). Óðinn's association with the *einherjar* may also imply worship of the dead within this cult. Its central moment, however, was presumably some form of religious ecstasy.

Iconographic evidence for this cult includes cast-bronze dies from Torslunda, Sweden, which show dancing warriors with theriomorphic features.

BIBLIOGRAPHY

Fredrik Grøn's *Berserksgangens vesen og arsaksforhold* (Trondheim, Norway, 1929) treats the phenomenology of the *berserksgangr.* Hans Kuhn's "Kämpen und Berserkir," originally published in 1968 and reprinted in his *Kleine Schriften,* vol. 2 (Berlin, 1971), pp. 521–531, emphasizes possible Roman influence, especially gladiator traditions. In *Kultische Geheimbünde der Germanen,* vol. 1 (Frankfurt am Main, Germany, 1934), Otto Höfler has offered the fullest treatment of the relationship between berserkers and the Óðinn cult, *Männerbünde,* and worship of the dead, arguing the existence of a mystery cult that left traces in later folklore phenomena such as the Wild Hunt. Chapter 6, "Images of the Animal Guardians," in Stephen O. Glosceki's *Shamanism in Old English Poetry* (New York and London, 1989) relates berserkers and the iconographic evidence for the Germanic warrior cult to shamanism and animism. Kris Kershaw, *The One-Eyed God: Odin and the (Indo-) Germanic Männerbünde* (Washington, D.C., 2000), adduces the Indo-European evidence.

JOHN LINDOW (1987 AND 2005)

BERTHOLET, ALFRED (1868–1951), Swiss Protestant theologian, scholar in Old Testament and comparative religion. Bertholet was born in Basel, where he got his primary and secondary school education and enrolled at the university in order to study Protestant theology. He continued his studies at the universities of Strassburg and Berlin. His principal lecturers were Carl von Orelli, Bernhard Duhm, and Adolf von Harnack. After two years as minister to the German-Dutch parish in Leghorn he returned to Basel; there he obtained his doctorate in 1895 and became an assistant professor in 1896; from 1905 he occupied the chair of Old Testament, and extended his studies to the history of religions. After spending some years in Tübingen (1913) and Göttingen (1914–1928) he became professor at the University of Berlin, where he went into retirement in 1936, although he lectured until 1939. From 1945 until his death he was visiting professor of the history of religions at his home university in Basel. He died in the hospital of Münsterlingen, Switzerland.

Bertholet was appointed doctor *honoris causa* of the universities of Strassburg and Lausanne and of the Faculté Libre de Théologie Protestante de Paris. He was a fellow of the academy of Göttingen and an honorary member of the American Society of Biblical Literature and Exegesis. He organized and was secretary general of the international congress for the history of religions held in Basel in 1904. In 1938 he was the first historian of religions to be elected a fellow of the Prussian Learned Society (Preussische Akademie der Wissenschaften). With Gerardus van der Leeuw and C. Jouco Bleeker, he was one of the initiators of the Amsterdam congress for the history of religions in 1950.

The works of Bertholet, all written in German, include both Old Testament studies and investigations in the field of comparative religion. Among his contributions to the study of the Old Testament are commentaries and a history of the civilization of biblical Israel. His Old Testament thesis *Die Stellung der Israeliten und Juden zu den Fremden* (1896) was concerned with the relations of the Israelites and Jews to foreign peoples. His numerous writings on the subject of "foreign" religions, chiefly published in the series "Sammlung gemeinverstandlicher Vorträge und Schriften aus dem Gebiet der Theologie und Religionsgeschichte" (Tübingen), are concerned with themes of religious phenomenology and especially with the relationship of dynamism to personalism. These works prove Bertholet to be one of the founders of the phenomenology of religion. Bertholet was also active in stimulating the work of other scholars, and in editing many well-known works in the history of religions.

BIBLIOGRAPHY

Further details of Bertholet's life and work can be found in the *Festschrift Alfred Bertholet zum 80. Geburtstag gewidmet* (Tübingen, 1950), edited by Walter Baumgartner and others. This volume, which includes a useful bibliography compiled by Verena Tamann-Bertholet, should be supplemented by Leonhard Rost's "Alfred Bertholet, in Memorium," *Theologische Literaturzeitung* 77 (1952): 114–118.

GÜNTER LANCZKOWSKI (1987)

BERURYAH (second century CE), one of the few famous women in rabbinic Judaism of late antiquity. Rabbinic tradition states that she was the daughter of Ḥananyah ben Teradyon, and the wife of Me'ir.

In rabbinic sources Beruryah appears several times among the scholars who reestablished the Sanhedrin in the Galilean town of Usha after the Bar Kokhba Revolt. She is mentioned twice in the Tosefta (in Tosefta, *Kelim,* Bava' Metsi'a' 1.6 by name and in Tosefta, *Kelim,* Bava' Qamma' 4.17 as the daughter of Ḥananyah ben Teradyon) and seven times in the Babylonian Talmud.

Beruryah's contemporary importance lies in her prominence as one of the only female scholars accepted in the male-dominated rabbinic culture. David Goodblatt (1977) believes that Beruryah exemplifies the possibility, though quite uncommon, that a woman might receive formal education within rabbinic society. Goodblatt argues, however, that the traditions that ascribe rabbinic learning to Beruryah appear to be late accounts that do not reflect the situation in

Roman Palestine, where Beruryah is said to have lived, but rather the situation in Sasanid Baylonia, where the traditions were formulated during the process of Talmudic compilation.

Whether historical or not, rabbinic tradition portrays Beruryah as a sensitive yet assertive figure. The Talmud recounts anecdotes illustrating her piety, compassion, and wit. In one source she admonishes her husband Meʾir not to be angry with his enemies and not to pray for their deaths. Instead, she suggests, he should pray that their sins cease and that they repent (B.T., *Ber.* 10a). When two of her sons died one Sabbath she delayed telling her husband until Saturday night when he had finished observing the Sabbath in peace (*Midrash Mishlei* on *Prv.* 31:10). The Talmud also recounts Beruryah's sharp tongue. When Yose the Galilean asked her for directions on the road she derided him for speaking too much with a woman (B.T., *ʿEruv.* 53b).

The drama of her life climaxes in the so-called Beruryah Incident. A story preserved by the eleventh-century exegete Rashi (in his commentary to B.T., *ʿA.Z.* 18b) says that Beruryah mocked a misogynistic rabbinic tradition that labeled women as flighty. To test her own constancy, Meʾir sent one of his students to tempt her to commit adultery. According to the legend, she committed suicide after submitting to the student's advances.

BIBLIOGRAPHY

David M. Goodblatt, in "The Beruriah Traditions," in *Persons and Institutions in Early Rabbinic Judaism*, edited by William S. Green (Missoula, Mont., 1977), pp. 207–229, translates and analyzes all the materials relating to Beruryah in rabbinic literature.

New Sources

Bacon, Brenda. "How Shall We Tell the Story of Beruriah's End?" *Nashim* 5 (2002): 31–239.

TZVEE ZAHAVY (1987)
Revised Bibliography

BESANT, ANNIE. Annie Besant (1847–1933) was a British activist with many facets to her life: Anglican; atheist and Freethinker; socialist; Theosophist; educator, reformer, and politician in India; and prophetic announcer of the coming World-Teacher and New Civilization. Besant's monism and her desire to serve humanity were the unifying themes in her diverse efforts. She accomplished pioneering and influential work in Britain and India, and exerted an international influence in her political and religious work. As the second president of the Theosophical Society (1907–1933), Besant popularized Theosophical concepts around the world through her lectures and writings, putting the concepts articulated by Helena P. Blavatsky into accessible language.

Besant possessed a progressive millennial outlook, believing that human effort guided by superhuman agents or forces (when she was an atheist she defined them as Nature and Evolution; when she became a Theosophist they were the Masters and the Solar Logos) could create the millennial condition of collective well-being on Earth. In 1908 Besant added messianism to her thought, and groomed a young Indian, J. Krishnamurti, to be the physical vehicle for the Lord Maitreya, a messiah who would usher in the millennial New Civilization. Besant believed that Krishnamurti as the World-Teacher would present a teaching that would become the next world religion, and thus raise humanity's awareness of spiritual unity and create the "New Civilization." Much of Besant's progressive millennialism, including its messianic themes, were perpetuated in the written works of Alice Bailey (1880–1949), another British Theosophist. Bailey was among the first to use the terms New Age and the Age of Aquarius, making Annie Besant an important source for the New Age movement.

EARLY LIFE. Annie Wood was born and raised in London by parents with a predominantly Irish background. She was raised in the Anglican faith and received an education in the home of a maiden lady. She married Frank Besant, an Anglican priest, in 1867. They had a son and a daughter, but the marriage failed, in part due to her intellectual questioning and rejection of Christian doctrines and the Bible. The couple separated but a divorce was never granted.

ATHEISM AND SOCIALISM. After a brief passage through theism, Besant found an intellectual home in Charles Bradlaugh's National Secular Society in 1874, where she became an atheist and Freethinker. Besant and Bradlaugh had a close relationship. She became a vice-president of the National Secular Society, and she and Bradlaugh formed the Freethought Publishing Company. Besant became a noted public speaker, questioning Christianity and the Bible and advocating social reform and women's rights. In 1877 Besant became the first woman to be prosecuted for disseminating information on birth control when she and Bradlaugh were prosecuted for publishing a pamphlet on contraception. Besant subsequently published her own booklet on contraception that was translated and sold internationally.

In the late 1870s Besant studied science at London University, but did not receive a degree. Besant's atheism was a monistic materialism—she believed that the one universal substance was matter—but she had a lively interest in the study of world religions and philosophies, as manifested in a magazine titled *Our Corner* she founded in 1883.

In 1885 Besant joined the Fabian Society of socialists, and maintained her commitment to nonrevolutionary socialism for the rest of her life. In 1888 Besant and Herbert Burrows organized the Bryant & May match girls strike, and subsequently the strikes of other workers, marking the formation of the trade union movement.

THEOSOPHY. Besant joined the Theosophical Society in 1889 after reviewing Helena P. Blavatsky's *The Secret Doctrine* (1888). The two thick volumes of *The Secret Doctrine* titled "Cosmogenesis" and "Anthropogenesis" purport to reveal the secrets of progressive evolution of consciousness in the universe and humanity. Blavatsky claimed that his complex philosophy was revealed to her by elusive Masters of Wisdom, described as men in physical bodies possessing highly evolved awareness who directed evolution on this planet. Besant went to meet Blavatsky, then residing in London. She took the ailing Blavatsky, who was much beleaguered by critics skeptical of the existence of the Masters and their appearances and communications, into her home, where she resided until the end of her life. Becoming a Theosophist marked Besant's shift from monistic materialism to a monism that affirmed the reality of a spiritual dimension to life. Theosophy's assertion that spiritual reality could be investigated and confirmed by the development of new faculties of perception appealed to her rationalism.

When Blavatsky died in 1891 a power struggle ensued within the Theosophical Society, with Besant and Henry Steel Olcott, the Society's president, on one side, and William Q. Judge on the other. Judge led the American Section in its succession from the Theosophical Society. His organization was inherited by Katherine Tingley upon Judge's death in 1896, and she created the Point Loma community of Theosophists. A new American Section of the Theosophical Society was built up, boosted by lecture tours by Annie Besant, which is now called the Theosophical Society in America. Besant was elected the second president of the international Theosophical Society, headquartered in Adyar, Chennai (Madras), in 1907 after Olcott's death.

WORK IN INDIA. Annie Besant first visited the international headquarters of the Theosophical Society in India in 1893, and she made the country her home in 1895. In India Besant worked to build Hindu pride and worked for educational and social reform and Indian Home Rule. Olcott had worked to revive Buddhism in Sri Lanka (then Ceylon) in an attempt to counteract the demoralizing effects of colonialism and Christian missionaries. Besant was determined to do the same for Hinduism in India. She believed that she had been a Hindu in previous incarnations and regarded India as her homeland.

Among the schools founded by Besant and other Theosophists in India were the Central Hindu College for boys, which was founded in 1897 and in 1916 became the Benares Hindu University, and the Central Hindu Girls' School, founded in 1904. In 1914 Besant began speaking out for social reform in India and working for Indian Home Rule within the British Commonwealth. Besant believed that a self-ruling India as part of the Commonwealth would contribute to the ultimate unity of humanity in the New Civilization. She founded daily and weekly newspapers to promote her political efforts. She also founded associations to promote patriotism among young Indians, and started the Indian Boy Scouts Association. In 1916 Besant founded her Home Rule League. She also worked for women's rights in India, and in 1917 helped found the Women's Indian Association and later the All-India Women's Conference.

As a result of her work for Home Rule, Besant and some of her colleagues were interned in 1917 by the colonial government. Besant's internment increased the Indian public's awareness of the agitation, and at age seventy Besant was elected president of the Indian National Congress. She promptly turned the office into a base for political activism. Historian Nancy Fix Anderson has written that Besant was the "primary instigator of the organised Indian nationalist movement," and that she worked "for a sense of inclusive Indian identity" (p. 36). Besant's career as Indian politician was quickly eclipsed by that of Mohandas Gandhi, who called for complete independence from the British empire, which Besant opposed.

THE WORLD-TEACHER. In 1908, just after becoming president of the Theosophical Society, Besant and her colleague in psychic investigations, Charles W. Leadbeater, began lecturing on the imminent appearance of the Lord Maitreya, the Master who was said to hold the office of the bodhisattva. Drawing on Buddhist and Christian expectations, Besant and Leadbeater added messianism to the progressive millennialism of Theosophy. Besant adopted a twelve-year-old Indian boy, J. Krishnamurti, and raised him to be the vehicle of the World-Teacher *(jagadguru)*. She believed that Krishnamurti as the World-Teacher would present teachings that would become a new religion and raise humanity's awareness of spiritual unity, thereby creating the millennial New Civilization. Besant created an international organization known as the Order of the Star in the East, with about thirty-thousand members who anticipated the coming of the World-Teacher. She purchased a home for Krishnamurti in Ojai, California, along with additional land she named the Happy Valley. Besant believed that the "new race" of aware human beings would develop in southern California, Australia, and New Zealand. The many New Age and Theosophical groups that continue in the Ojai valley carry on Besant's expectations.

Beginning in 1922, Krishnamurti had experiences that led him to conclude that his consciousness had blended with that of the Lord Maitreya. He began speaking publicly as the Lord Maitreya in 1925. Eventually, however, Krishnamurti concluded that people were not hearing his Zen-like message advocating personal effort in achieving "choiceless awareness," and instead were relying on him for salvation. In 1929 Krishnamurti dissolved the Order of the Star and distanced himself from the Theosophical Society and his role as the World-Teacher. Krishnamurti never denied being the World-Teacher, and he went on to become an internationally known teacher. Annie Besant maintained her faith in Krishnamurti as the World-Teacher until her death in 1933.

CONCLUSION. The stages of Annie Besant's life were held together by her commitment to the service and betterment of humanity and by her monism. She was a strong believer in the Victorian doctrine of progress, believing that humans working according to a higher plan could create a collective salvation on Earth (the millennial kingdom). She found it frustrating that despite all her hard work society remained imperfect. So in 1908 she added messianism to her progressive millennialism; the World-Teacher would accomplish the New Civilization. After Krishnamurti distanced himself from her messianic plans in 1929, the Theosophical Society gave up messianism while maintaining its progressive millennial orientation, although many individual Theosophists remained intensely interested in Krishnamurti's teachings. Annie Besant's hope for a New Civilization accomplished by a critical mass of people developing a consciousness of spiritual unity under the guidance and influence of Masters, and including the possible return of the Christ, continues to influence the New Age movement, especially through the writings of Alice Bailey, a former member of the Theosophical Society.

See Also Blavatsky, H. P.; Judge, William Q.; Theosophical Society.

Bibliography

Anderson, Nancy Fix. "'Mother Besant' and Indian National Politics." *Journal of Imperial and Commonwealth History* 30, no. 3 (2002): 27–54. Describes Besant's impact on the Indian Home Rule movement.

Besant, Annie. *Autobiographical Sketches.* London, 1885. Initial autobiographical account written prior to becoming a Theosophist.

Besant, Annie. *Annie Besant: An Autobiography.* London, 1908. Revision of *Autobiographical Sketches* after her conversion to Theosophy.

Jayakar, Pupul. *Krishnamurti: A Biography.* San Francisco, 1986. The first biography of Krishnamurti that revealed he thought of himself as the World-Teacher until the end of his life.

Nethercot, Arthur H. *The First Five Lives of Annie Besant.* Chicago, 1960.

Nethercot, Arthur H. *The Last Four Lives of Annie Besant.* Chicago, 1963. These two books by Nethercot remain the most thoroughly researched biographical treatments.

Sloss, Radha Rajagopal. *Lives in the Shadow with J Krishnamurti.* London, 1991. An eye-opening biography of Krishnamurti.

Wessinger, Catherine Lowman. *Annie Besant and Progressive Messianism.* Lewiston, N.Y., 1988. An intellectual biography of Besant that traces her evolving millennialism.

Wessinger, Catherine Lowman. "Annie Besant and the World-Teacher: Progressive Messianism for the New Age." *Quest* (spring 1989): 60–69. Short description of Besant's progressive millennialism and her influence on the New Age movement.

Catherine Wessinger (2005)

BESHT See BAʿAL SHEM TOV

BETH, KARL

BETH, KARL (1872–1959), German historian of religions and Christian thinker. Karl Beth studied at the University of Berlin in the 1890s (under Adolf von Harnack, Otto Pfleiderer, and Wilhelm Dilthey), where he obtained his Ph.D. in 1898 with a dissertation entitled "Die Grundanschuungen Schleiermachers in seinem ersten Entwurf der philosophischen Sittenlehre"; he became an instructor of systematic theology at Berlin in 1901. Five years later he moved to Vienna and served at the university there, first as a lecturer and from 1908 onward as a full professor. The political developments that in 1938 brought an end to his academic career in Europe led him to emigrate to the United States in the following year. He served on the faculty of Meadville-Lombard Theological School in Chicago from 1941 to 1944, teaching the history of religions, a field that was a primary concern for him at several points in his life.

As early as 1901 in his inaugural address at Berlin, he argued that the study of the general history of religions—not merely the study of the religious environment of early Christianity—was necessary for understanding and defining the essence of Christianity. Shortly after he gave this address, he received a travel stipend that enabled him to visit areas around the Mediterranean under Greek and Turkish control, and the acquaintances he made with Christians living in these regions led to his publication of an account of Eastern Orthodox Christianity that opened the way for a new understanding of it among European Protestants (*Die orientalische Christenheit der Mittelmeerländer,* 1902; see also his article "Orthodox-anatolische Kirche" and several related entries in the second edition of *Religion in Geschichte und Gegenwart,* 1929–1932).

In the decade following 1902 much of Beth's work focused on the issue of Christianity and modern thought (e.g., *Das Wesen des Christentums und die moderne historische Denkweise,* 1904, and *Die Moderne und die Prinzipien der Theologie,* 1907). During this period he also dealt with specific issues such as the significance of the notion of evolution for Christian theology (comparing it, in *Der Entwicklungsgedanke und des Christentum,* 1909, with the significance of the idea of *logos* fifteen hundred years earlier) and with historical-critical questions regarding Jesus (in *Hat Jesus gelebt?,* 1910).

In the following years some of his major studies were again in the history of religions, particularly his book on religion and magic, *Religion und Magie bei den Naturvölkern: Ein religionsgeschichtlicher Beitrag zur Frage nach den Anfängen der Religion* (1914), in which he stresses *Ehrfurcht* ("reverence" or "awe") as a constituent element of religion, draws a sharp contrast between religion and magic, and assumes the existence of a historical stage preceding both. (He rejected James G. Frazer's hypothesis that magic was the forerunner of religion.) Also significant were his *Einführung in die vergleichende Religionsgeschichte* (1920) and his study on faith and mysticism (particularly within Christianity), *Frömmigkeit der Mystik und des Glaubens* (1927).

A third major field of involvement for Beth was the psychology of religion. He helped to establish the Research Institute for Psychology of Religion in Vienna in 1922, was editor of the *Zeitschrift für Religionspsychologie* from 1927 to 1938 (during which period he published more than twenty articles in that journal), and was instrumental in the organization of the First International Psychology of Religion Congress, held in Vienna in 1931 on the theme of the psychology of unbelief.

BIBLIOGRAPHY

Sources of biographical data include Beth's autobiographical essay in *Die Religionswissenschaft der Gegenwart in Selbstdarstellungen,* vol. 2, *Karl Beth,* edited by Eric Strange (Leipzig, 1926), and Erwin Schneider's article "Das Lebenwerk Karl Beths," in *Theologische Literaturzeitung* 78 (1958): 695–698, which is followed by an extensive bibliography of Beth's publications.

WILLEM A. BIJLEFELD (1987)

BEVERAGES. In addition to their nutritional role, all beverages are invested with a certain amount of symbolic and affectional content, and it seems likely that there is no beverage that has not taken on a profound religious significance somewhere or other in the world. Intoxicants and hallucinogens seem particularly well suited to this role, given the ways in which they open up startling new areas of experience to those who imbibe them, including ecstasy, enthusiasm, and vision. Yet it is not just those drinks that are most extraordinary in their effects that come to be celebrated in myth, ritual, and sacred speculation, for often those drinks that are most ordinary—that is, most commonly used as a part of the normal diet and most unremarkable in their physiological and neurological effect—come to be invested with religious significance. Thus, for instance, among the Maasai and other cattle-herding peoples of East Africa, cow's milk is a staple part of the diet, but it is nevertheless regarded with the greatest of respect, for unlike virtually all other food items, milk can be obtained without causing the death of any living thing, animal or vegetable. For this reason, milk is set in marked contrast to beef, a food which has the same source as milk—cattle—but the procurement of which entails the violent death of the animal from which it is taken. The equation is explicitly drawn: milk is to meat as life is to death, and the two are not to be mixed within the same meal. The same prohibition is encountered in rabbinic law (itself an extension of the biblical prohibition, stated in *Exodus,* against cooking a kid in its mother's milk), perhaps arrived at by a similar line of reasoning.

To be sure, milk is understood as a perfect or paradisiacal fluid in many passages of the Hebrew scriptures, as for instance in those that refer to Israel as "the land of milk and honey" (*Ex.* 3:8 et al.), honey being—like milk—a nourishing and delicious food that may be obtained without doing violence to any living thing. Greek and Roman ritual also employed this symbolism, albeit in different fashion, for a libation offering of a fluid composed of milk and honey, called *melikraton,* had the power to reanimate the dead (*Odyssey* 10.519), while a potion known as *hermesias* was drunk by women before conception and while nursing in order to obtain children who were "excellent in soul and beautiful of body," that beverage being a symbolically charged mixture of milk, honey, pine nuts, myrrh, saffron, and palm wine (Pliny, *Natural History* 24.166).

In the *hermesias* concoction, we have come a long way from the simplicity and familiarity of milk, although the associations of milk—maternal nurturance and the gift of life—provide the symbolic starting point for a grander elaboration. Another simple beverage that came to be invested with a profound religious significance is tea, the preparation, distribution, and consumption of which are regarded as constituting nothing less than a master art and a way of knowledge and liberation in Japan, as is expressed in the common term *chadō* ("the way of tea"); the second element, *dō,* is the Japanese equivalent of the Chinese word *dao,* a term reserved for a select set of religio-aesthetic pursuits: painting, poetry, calligraphy, archery, flower arranging, and above all, tea. Originally used as a medicine in China, tea later came to be a more common beverage, the highly ritualistic preparation of which—with twenty-four carefully specified implements—was already systematized by Lu Yü (d. 804) in his *Ch'a ching* (Classic of tea). Although there are indications that some tea may have come to Japan as early as the ninth century, its serious introduction came with Eisai (1141–1215), the founder of the Rinzai sect of Zen Buddhism in Japan, who also brought tea seeds and a knowledge of tea ceremonial with him after a period of study in China.

Although it is obvious from the title of Eisai's work on the art of tea—*Kissayōjōki* (The account of drinking tea and prolonging life)—that he was interested in the medico-physiological effects of the drink, this never became a major part of the Japanese celebration of tea. Rather, as developed and explicated by such renowned tea masters as Daiō (1235–1308), Nōami (1397–1471), Ikkyū (1394–1481), Shukū (1422–1502), and above all Rikyū (1521–1591), it is the utter simplicity, serenity, and austere beauty of the tea ceremony (*cha no yu*) that were the foremost concerns. For within the small tearooms, meticulously cleansed of all impurities and equipped with perfectly chosen utensils and decorations, tea masters sought to create nothing less than a perfect microcosm, a thoroughly harmonious environment in which one might take refuge from the tribulations of the external world and encounter the buddha-nature that lies beyond the conflicts and fluctuations of life in the material world. Along these lines, the tea master Takuan observed:

> The principle of *cha-no-yu* is the spirit of harmonious blending of Heaven and Earth and provides the means for establishing universal peace. . . . The way of *cha-no-yu,* therefore, is to appreciate the spirit of a naturally harmonious blending of Heaven and Earth, to see the pervading presence of the five elements by one's fireside, where the mountains, rivers, rocks, and trees are found as they are in nature, to draw the refreshing water from the well of Nature, to taste with one's own mouth

> the flavor supplied by nature. How grand this enjoyment of the harmonious blending of Heaven and Earth! (Suzuki, 1959, p. 278)

Yet for all that the tea ceremony possesses a cosmic dimension and can be nothing less than a vehicle for full enlightenment, these lofty significances notwithstanding, it remains always also a celebration of the simple pleasures of the drink of tea. A celebrated poem of Rikyū, the greatest of all the recorded tea masters, stresses this point:

> The essence of the tea ceremony is simply to boil water, To make tea, And to drink it—nothing more! Be sure you know this. (Ludwig, 1974, p. 41)

In contrast, intoxicants are rarely regarded with such utter serenity and simplicity, given the drama, power, and even violence of their transformative effects. "Ale," observes one Icelandic text, "is another man" (*Jómsvikingasaga* 27). One may consider, for instance, the hallucinogenic decoction of vines called *yagé*, used throughout the upper Amazon; its use has been described at length by Gerardo Reichel-Dolmatoff (1975 and 1978). *Yagé* is ritually consumed; it produces nausea, vomiting, and diarrhea but also—aided by such other stimuli as torchlight and musical rhythms—induces brilliant visions that take regular and predictable forms to which interpretations based on mythic references are attached.

According to Reichel-Dolmatoff, the visions produced by *yagé* unfold in different stages, an initial phase of phosphenic patterns (i.e., colors and geometric shapes only) being followed by one or more coherent images of a hallucinatory nature. Indigenous interpretation of the first phase attaches specific iconographic meanings to given shapes—a diamond with a point in it represents an embryo in the womb, for example—and also makes use of color symbolism. Yellow and white are thus considered cold colors, and—more importantly—the embodiment of seminal and solar fertilizing energy. Red is considered hot, being associated primarily with the womb, fire, and menstrual blood. Finally, blue is an asexual color, being also morally ambiguous. A "good" vision in this first phase depends upon a proper balance of red and yellow, which is to say, of male and female, hot and cold principles.

Interpretation of the visions within the hallucinatory phase is somewhat more complex, and Reichel-Dolmatoff (1975) emphasizes the social nature of these visions and their imputed meanings: "The individual hallucinations do not constitute a private world, an intimate or almost secret experience; they are freely discussed, and anyone will ask questions and solicit answers." There is, then, a process of feedback, or reinterpretation and elaboration. This feedback process continually refers visions to the creation myths in order to make sense of them, myths which tell of the primordial incest of the Sun and his daughter. Through one's visions, one is felt to return to the time and place of creation, becoming a witness to and a participant in these events. Moreover, the ritual consumption of *yagé* is itself understood as a sexual experience of an incestuous and creative nature, for the *yagé* vessel is homologized to the mother's body, its opening to her vagina, and its interior to her womb. To drink *yagé* is thus to enter into sexual relations with one's mother and also to reenter her womb, becoming an embryo once more. Ultimately, as one emerges from the trance induced by the drug, one is felt to be reborn, re-created, renewed.

The myth of the creation of *yagé* is also of interest, for it exhibits a different kind of feedback process whereby details of the drug's physiological effects are appropriated to construct a mythic narrative. The story tells of the entrance of a primordial Yagé Woman into the first *maloca,* where the first ancestors of all the peoples of the Amazon were gathered. Yagé Woman gave birth to a child outside the *maloca,* and carried the infant inside. There, this child—who is *yagé* personified —shone radiant, white and yellow and red, those colors which are first seen during the phosphenic phase of *yagé* visions. Upon seeing this child, those gathered all experienced the various sensations brought on by *yagé*: nausea, bewilderment, and a sense of "drowning." According to Reichel-Dolmatoff's informants, the entrance of Yagé Woman and her child into the *maloca* is the high point of the myth, but there follows a curious episode. When Yagé Woman asked who was the father of the babe, all the assembled men claimed this honor, and fought over the rights to the child. Finally, all turned upon him and dismembered him, each taking a different part of his body. These bodily members then became the different vines used by the different peoples of the Amazon to prepare their own particular forms of *yagé.*

This same motif—the creation of an intoxicant from the body of a primordial divine being—is found in numerous other religious traditions, not least of which is the foundation of the Christian Eucharist. For at the end of the last supper, according to the Synoptic Gospels, Jesus gave wine to his disciples, saying: "Drink of it, all of you; for this is my blood of the covenant, which is poured out for many for the forgiveness of sins. I tell you I shall not drink again of this fruit of the vine until that day when I drink it new with you in my Father's kingdom" (*Mt.* 26:27–29 and parallels). Throughout the history of the church, there has been disagreement as to how literally this passage ought to be interpreted, a disagreement which is at the heart of the theological debate over transubstantiation in the Mass.

Another account in which intoxicants derive from a quasi-sacrificial victim is the Iranian story of the origin of wine, which tells how the vine came into being from the blood of the primordial bovine when that animal was killed. Crushing grapes thus constitutes a reenactment of the bull's death, and the wine thereby produced is seen to be nothing less than the blood of the bull, which bestows the bull's strength, energy, and vital force upon one who drinks it (*Zādspram* 3.46), just as one who drinks sacramental wine takes Christ's essential nature and very blood within his or her own body, given a full-blown theory of transubstantiation.

Yet again one encounters a myth of intoxicants created from the blood of a murdered primordial being in the Norse account of the origin of mead, a story related by the god of poetry, Bragi, in response to the question "Whence came the art called poetry?" (*Skáldskaparmál* 2). The story begins at that moment when the two major groups of gods, the Æsir and Vanir, concluded their treaty of peace by spitting into a single vat and letting their saliva mingle. From the mixture, there grew a man by the name of Kvasir—who himself incarnates an intoxicant known in Russia as *kvas*, if his name is any indication—an individual gifted with exceptional wisdom, indeed, omniscience itself. Kvasir was subsequently murdered by two dwarfs, who mixed his blood with honey and made from it the first mead, a mead so powerful that it is said that "whoever drinks from it becomes a poet or a scholar."

Other stories pursue the fate of this "mead of poetry," telling how it fell first into the hands of the dwarves, then giants, from whom it was finally rescued by the wisest of gods, Odin himself, who assumed the form first of a serpent and then of an eagle in order to gain the precious mead. This myth of the mead's theft has important correspondences to myths elsewhere in the Indo-European world (see, for instance, the Indic text *Ṛgveda* 4.26) but it is that portion of the story that recounts the origin of the mead which provides a religious rationale and legitimation for its miraculous effect: that is, mead can bestow knowledge and inspiration because in origin and essence it is nothing less than the blood of the wisest of men and also the spittle of the gods.

The highly formalized, even solemn, consumption of mead, beer, ale, and/or wine has been a regular feature of banquets in Europe since antiquity, and may be seen to have a ritual origin and significance. As we have seen, such drinks as these are often felt to partake of divinity, and also demonstrably enable those who imbibe to transcend the limits of their ordinary human condition, bestowing upon them extraordinary powers of speech, intellect, physical strength, and well-being. Such potent fluids are also regularly offered as sacrificial libations, through which the same gifts are conferred upon gods, demigods, spirits of the dead, or the natural order itself.

Nowhere, however, have intoxicating drinks been elevated to a loftier position of religious significance than among the Indo-Iranian peoples, who knew both a profane intoxicant known as *surā* in India and *hurā* in Iran and a sacred drink (Indic *soma*, Iranian *haoma*), the latter of which was invested with both the status of a deity and a stunningly complex set of symbolic elaborations. At the most concrete level, this beverage—prepared by pressing the sap from a specific plant to obtain a juice that is mixed with water, milk, or honey in different ritual contexts—had powerful hallucinogenic effects, but beyond this, it was understood to be an all purpose intensifier, which enhanced all human capabilities, giving health to the sick, children to the barren, eloquence to the poet, vision and insight to the priest, strength to the warrior, and long life to any who may drink it. Going still further, it was claimed that *soma* or *haoma* could grant freedom from death (Skt., *amṛta*, literally "nondeath"; often incorrectly translated as "immortality") both to gods and to humans, as for instance, in the exultant *Ṛgveda* 8.48.3:

> We have drunk soma; we have become free from death.
> We have gone to the light; we have found the gods!
> What now can joylessness do to us? What, truly, can the
> evil of mortality do, o you who are free from death?

Going further still, *soma* and *haoma* were considered nothing less than the universal life essence, the fluid that vivifies and invigorates all living beings. Moreover, the sacrificial offering of this elixir came to be regarded as the means to effect circulation of life energy throughout the entire cosmos. For in the last analysis, *soma* and *haoma* were not merely drinks, nor were they the plants from which drinks were made; rather, they were only temporary forms or incarnations of the life essence, of which there were many others. To pursue but one line of analysis found in the Indic manuals of esoteric speculation upon sacrificial ritual, we see that the juice extracted from some plants, when poured into the sacrificial fire, ascends to heaven in the form of smoke. This smoke coalesces to form clouds, from which the rains pour down to earth. Smoke, clouds, and rain—like *soma* juice—are all forms of the universal energizing fluid, and when rain falls upon the earth it brings forth plants (among them *soma*, the "king of plants," but all the others as well). These plants, in turn, are eaten by grazing animals. Having passed through rain and plants, in the bodies of male animals the elixir becomes semen, and in females, milk, both of which are but further transformations of *soma*. By eating plants, drinking water or milk, humans also absorb *soma* into their bodies, gaining life and energy thereby. But in all its various forms, *soma* is ultimately and inevitably destined for the sacrificial fire, for not only are plants, water, and milk offered along with the *soma* liquid proper, but the cremation fire is also a fire of sacrifice that returns the life fluids left in the corpse to the cosmic cycle.

This is but one system of symbolic speculation centering on *soma;* numerous others have also enjoyed currency, such as that which homologized the waxing moon to a vessel filled with the sacred fluid and the waning moon to a libation for the benefit of all the waters and plants (see, e.g., *Śatapatha Brāhmaṇa* 11.1.5.3). Ultimately, the symbolic importance of *soma* came to overshadow its use as an intoxicant, such that it mattered relatively little when either supplies of the original *soma* plant were cut off or the knowledge of its original identity was lost. For centuries the soma sacrifice has been performed with a substitute, the *Ephedra* plant, which has no hallucinogenic effect whatsoever, but which is treated with the same reverence as was its more potent predecessor. Although numerous attempts have been made to identify the original plant—the psychotropic mushroom *Amanita muscaria* being the most recent candiate—most Indologists consider it unlikely that it will ever be located.

In Iran, the *haoma* cultus developed somewhat differently, but Iranian data support the same general conclusion as do those from India: the symbolic possibilities of the drink were far more important than its physiological effects in the long run. The earliest mentions of *haoma* in any Iranian text are ringing condemnations of the intoxicating beverage. These are two verses within the most ancient and prestigious portions of the Avesta, attributed by the Zoroastrian tradition and most modern scholars to Zarathushtra himself (*Yasna* 32.4 and 48.10). In the latter of these, the speaker calls directly to Ahura Mazdā, the Wise Lord, pleading, "When will you strike down this piss of an intoxicant, with which the Karapan-priests and the wicked lords of the lands evilly cause pain?"

Expert opinion is divided on whether this implies a blanket condemnation of *haoma*, or only a rejection of certain abuses of the drink. What is clear is that by the Achaemenid period *haoma* once again stood at the center of Iranian cult, as is attested by hundreds of inscriptions at Persepolis. Later Zoroastrian texts also grant a privileged position to *haoma* as a sacred beverage, an elixir of life, and a deity who is celebrated with his own hymn, the famous *Hōm Yasht* (*Yasna* 9–11), a text that deserves much more careful and detailed study than it has received to date. This hymn appears to be a highly successful attempt to rehabilitate the *haoma* cultus, purifying it of the unseemly elements that led to Zarathushtra's denunciation while retaining many aspects of its symbolic significance, and reintegrating it into Zoroastrian worship. And to this day, the solemn preparation, consumption, and offering of *haoma*—now a drink devoid of intoxicating effect—is the central Zoroastrian ritual.

To these few examples, countless others might well be added, not least of which would be the clear magico-religious symbolism evident in advertisements for commercial soft drinks, as for instance "Come alive with Pepsi Cola," a slogan ineptly translated for the Taiwanese market as "Pepsi brings your ancestors back to life."

SEE ALSO Elixir; Haoma; Psychedelic Drugs; Soma.

BIBLIOGRAPHY

To date, there is no satisfactory general summary of the variety of religious uses and significances of beverages. Rather, the literature exists in scattered form, most of it in languages other than English.

On the symbolic value of milk among the Maasai, see John G. Galaty's "Ceremony and Society: The Poetics of Maasai Ritual," *Man* 18 (June 1983): 361–382. On milk in antiquity, see Karl Wyss's *Die Milch im Kultus der Griechen und Römer* (Giessen, 1914), and specifically on milk and honey, note the still useful article of Hermann Usener, "Milch und Honig," *Rheinisches Museum für Philologie* 57 (1902): 177–195. On wine, see Karl Kirchner's *Die sakrale Bedeutung des Weines im Altertum* (Giessen, 1910).

Regarding the Japanese tea ceremony, several useful treatments are available. A. L. Sadler's *Cha-no-yu, the Japanese Tea Ceremony* (Rutland, Vt., 1962) provides a detailed description, but little in the way of analysis or interpretation. For these, see D. T. Suzuki's *Zen and Japanese Culture*, 2d ed., rev. & enl. (1959; reprint, Princeton, 1970), pp. 269–328; and Theodore M. Ludwig's "The Way of Tea: A Religio-Aesthetic Mode of Life," *History of Religions* 14 (1974): 28–50. For another excellent example of the religious valorization of a familiar beverage, see G. Mantovani's "Acqua magica e acqua di luce in due testi gnostici," in *Gnosticisme et monde hellénistique*, edited by Julien Ries (Louvain, 1982), pp. 429–439.

For use of intoxicants in the Amazon, the best sources to date are the writings of Gerardo Reichel-Dolmatoff, especially *The Shaman and the Jaguar* (Philadelphia, 1975) and *Beyond the Milky Way: Hallucinatory Imagery of the Tukano Indians* (Los Angeles, 1978). On the Germanic usage and mythology of mead, see the splendid work of Renate Doht, *Der Rauschtrank im germanischen Mythos* (Vienna, 1974).

On myths of the theft of an "immortality fluid," see the diverging interpretations in Adalbert Kuhn's *Die Herabkunft des Feuers und des Göttertranks* (Berlin, 1859); Georges Dumézil's *Le festin d'immortalité* (Paris, 1924); and David M. Knipe's "The Heroic Theft: Myths from Rgveda IV and the Ancient Near East," *History of Religions* 6 (May 1967): 328–360. On fluids of immortality in general, but with primary emphasis on the Greco-Roman world, the old work of W. H. Roscher, *Nektar und Ambrosia* (Leipzig, 1883), retains value.

There are numerous discussions on *soma* and *haoma*, the most valuable for its attention to the rich symbolism of these cult beverages being Herman Lommel's "König Soma," *Numen* 2 (1955): 196–205. The attempt to identify soma with the mushroom *Amanita muscaria* was made in R. Gordon Wasson's *Soma: Divine Mushroom of Immortality* (New York, 1968) but has been soundly refuted in John Brough's "Soma and Amanita Muscaria," *Bulletin of the School of Oriental and African Studies* 34 (1971): 331–362.

New Sources

Armstrong, David E. *Alcohol and Altered States in Ancestor Veneration Rituals of Zhou Dynasty China and Iron Age Palestine: A New Approach to Ancestor Rituals.* Lewiston, N.Y., 1988.

Bologne, Jean-Claude. *Histoire morale and culturelle de nos boissons.* Paris, 1991.

Elkart, Martin. *The Secret Life of Food: A Feast of Food and Drink History, Folklore, and Fact.* New York, 1991.

Graham, Patricia Graham. *Tea of the Sages: The Art of Sencha.* Honolulu, 1988.

Kueny, Kathryn. *The Rhetoric of Sobriety: Wine in Early Islam.* Albany, 2001.

Poo, Mu-chou. *Wine and Wine Offerings in the Religion of Ancient Egypt.* New York, 1995.

Saoshitsu, Sen. *The Japanese Way of Tea: From Its Origins in China to Sen Rikyu.* Translated by V. Dixon Morris. Honolulu, 1998.

Tanaka, Sen'O. *The Tea Ceremony.* New York, 1977.

BRUCE LINCOLN (1987)
Revised Bibliography

BEZA, THEODORE (1519–1605), Reformed theologian and successor to John Calvin as moderator of the Venerable Company of Pastors in Geneva, Switzerland. Born Théodore de Bèze and raised in Paris, he was trained as a lawyer (at Orléans) but preferred the company of humanists. His first publication, *Poemata*, evidenced considerable poetic talent. Upon his conversion from Catholicism to Protestantism in 1548, Beza fled France and, as a professor of Greek, joined Pierre Viret at the academy in Lausanne, Switzerland. Meanwhile, the French Parlement declared Beza an outlaw, confiscated his goods, and burned his effigy in Paris. It was at Lausanne that Beza wrote *A Tragedie of Abraham's Sacrifice* (1559; Eng. trans., 1575), the first biblical tragedy (a genre later utilized by Racine), as well as his theologically significant *Tabula praedestinationis* (1555), translated the following year as *A Briefe Declaraccion of the Chiefe Poyntes of the Christian Religion, Set Forth in a Table of Predestination.* The subject of predestination created such heated disputes that Viret and Beza left Lausanne in 1558. John Calvin then appointed Beza rector of the newly founded Academy of Geneva, a post that he held formally from 1559 to 1562, but Beza effectively directed the academy until he retired as professor of theology in 1599. Beza began three other significant works in Lausanne, which he continued in Geneva: the completion of the translation of the *Book of Psalms*, begun by the French poet Clément Marot; his New Testament commentaries; and his *Confession of the Christian Faith* (Fr., 1559; Lat., 1560). Beza's confession of faith was translated into every major European language and had a wide influence as a simple expression of Reformed belief.

In 1561, Beza was the primary spokesman for the French Reformed churches at the Colloquy of Poissy, summoned by Catherine de Médicis in the vain hope of preventing the bloody Wars of Religion, which broke out in 1563. In 1564, the dying Calvin designated Beza to succeed him as moderator of the Venerable Company of Pastors in Geneva, and Beza began his long career as the most influential pastor of the Genevan church and therefore of the Reformed French churches, for which Geneva trained pastors. From 1564 to 1599, Beza held the only regular chair in theology at the academy. His work included lectures, sermons, polemical and systematic publications, and numerous colloquies with Lutherans and Roman Catholics. Beyond his professorial and pastoral duties in Geneva, Beza advised the French Huguenot leaders, including Henry of Navarre (Henry IV), traveled to defend Reformed theology and church discipline, and, almost singlehandedly, kept the academy functioning during the sieges of Geneva by Savoy.

Out of his efforts to assist the Huguenots came his *On the Right of Magistrates* (1574), an important treatise for the history of political theory that supported the God-given right of the people through their magistrates to rebel against royal leaders if these latter were seriously misleading and mistreating the people. While with the Huguenot troops, Beza discovered what was at that time considered the oldest extant New Testament manuscript (the Codex Bezae), which Beza later sent to Cambridge University in an effort to gain Queen Elizabeth's support for the Huguenots and for plague-ridden and besieged Geneva.

As has been true of Calvin studies, Beza scholars dispute the degree to which the doctrine of predestination underlies all of Beza's theology. Scholars also disagree on the influence of Beza's work on the development of Reformed scholasticism in the seventeenth century. Beza's original contribution regarding the doctrine of the Lord's Supper, in which he taught the presence of Christ through the category of "relation" rather than of "substance," went unnoticed until the 1960s. Beyond dispute, however, is the contribution Beza made to the stability of the church and the Academy of Geneva for nearly forty years following Calvin's death.

BIBLIOGRAPHY

Beza's works are largely unavailable except as rare books. Most of his major treatises were rapidly translated into English and can be found in sixteenth-century editions. Beza collected his own most significant theological treatises in three volumes: collectively titled *Theodori Bezae Vezelii*, they are *Vol. tractationum theologicarum* (Geneva, 1570); *Vol. alterum tractationum theologicarum* (Geneva, 1573); and *Vol. tertium tractationum theologicarum*, 3 vols. in 1 (Geneva, 1582). Beza's correspondence is being meticulously edited in Geneva and published by Librairie Droz, 24 vols. to date (Geneva, 1960–).

A bibliography of Beza's works, which omits his biblical commentaries, has been gathered in Frédéric L. Gardy's *Bibliographie des œuvres théologiques, littéraires, historiques et juridiques de Théodore de Bèze* (Geneva, 1960). The standard biography is Paul F. Geisendorf's *Théodore de Bèze* (Geneva, 1967).

JILL RAITT (1987)

BHAGAVADGĪTĀ.

The *Bhagavadgītā* is perhaps the most widely read and beloved scripture in all Indian religious literature. Its power to counsel and inspire its readers has remained undiminished in the almost two thousand years since its composition.

The *Bhagavadgītā* (Song of the Blessed Lord) is sacred literature, holy scripture—it is a text that has abundant power in its persistence and its presence. The pious Hindu, even if his piety is mild, will inevitably have access to the book or will be able to recite, or at least paraphrase, a few lines from it. The devout turn to it daily; they read it ritually, devotionally, with a sense of awe. The text is intoned during the initiation ceremony wherein one becomes a *saṃnyāsin* (renunciant); teachers and holy men expound upon it; professors translate it and write about it; the more humble listen to the words that, though heard countless times before, remain vibrant. The text is read by all Hindus, esteemed by Śaivas as well as by Vaiṣṇavas, venerated by the lower caste as well as by the high, savored by villagers as well as by the more urbane. Many times each day in India the consoling words of the *Gītā* are read or whispered into the ear of someone who, with eyes looking to the south in fear or hope or both, awaits death: "And whoever remembers Me alone when leaving the body at the time of death attains to My status of being" (8.5).

One may dispute whether the *Bhagavadgītā* teaches the dualistic Sāṃkhya philosophy or the nondualistic Vedānta, whether it is a call to action or renunciation; but what is beyond dispute is that it teaches devotion to god as a means to liberation, whether that liberation is understood as release from the world or freedom in the world: "Hear again My supreme word, the most secret of all: thou are greatly beloved by Me, hence I will speak for thy good. Center thy mind on Me, be devoted to Me, sacrifice to Me, revere Me, and thou shalt come to Me. I promise thee truly, for thou art dear to Me" (18.64–65).

The Text in Context. The *Bhagavadgītā* occupies a very small part of the *Mahābhārata*—it is but one of the Hundred Minor Books of that enormous epic, that elephantine tale of the great war between the Kauravas and the Pāṇḍavas, two descendant branches of the Kurus, the Lunar Race. Yudhiṣṭhira, the righteous leader of the Pāṇḍavas, having lost his family's portion of the kingdom to the Kauravas in a crooked game of dice, was forced, together with his four brothers, into forest exile for thirteen years. Afterward Yudhiṣṭhira asked for the just return of the kingdom, or at least five villages, one for each of the brothers. When this was refused, the great war became inevitable.

Both armies sought allies. Kṛṣṇa, the princely leader of the Vṛṣṇis, another branch of the Lunar Race, in an attempt to remain neutral and loyal to both families, offered his troops to the Kauravas and his service as charioteer and counselor to his friend Arjuna, one of Yudhiṣṭhira's younger brothers.

The battle was ready to begin: "Conches and kettledrums, cymbals and drums and horns suddenly were struck and the sound was tumultuous" (1.13). Suddenly, seeing his own kinsmen—teachers, fathers, uncles, cousins, and in-laws—arrayed for battle, Arjuna decided that he was unable to fight. Realizing that to kill them would destroy the eternal laws of the family and uncaring as to whether or not he himself would be slain, "Arjuna cast away his bow and arrow and sank down on the seat of his chariot, his spirit overcome by grief" (1.47).

In this dramatic setting the teachings of the *Bhagavadgītā* begin. Kṛṣṇa must show Arjuna why he must fight in this terrible war and, in so doing, he reveals the nature of reality and of himself. Military counsel becomes spiritual instruction; the heroic charioteer discloses his divinity. Kṛṣṇa-Vāsudeva is God, the highest reality and eternal self, beyond the world and yet of it as a preserver, creator, and destroyer. In the midst of the theophany Arjuna cries out: "Thou art the imperishable, the highest to be known; Thou art the final resting place of this universe; Thou are the immortal guardian of eternal law; Thou are the primal spirit" (9.18).

By the time the *Bhagavadgītā* was incorporated into the story of the great war (probably during the third century BCE), a conception of this world as a dreadful, burning round of death, a tedious prison in which we are trapped by transmigration, had taken hold and with it renunciatory ideals and impulses for liberation challenged more ancient, hieratic ideals of ritual action and aspirations for heavenly domains. The *Gītā* provided a synthesis of conflicting ideals and past and present norms. It harmonized Brahmanic values with a warrior's code, reconciled a traditional pantheism with a seemingly new theistic religiosity, and coalesced a variety of differing and potentially dissentient philosophical trends. This synthetic or syncretic quality of the text invested it with a pan-Indian appeal that it has retained.

Ancient Indian religious literature was formally classified as either a "revelation" (*śruti*—that which has been sacramentally "heard," the eternally existent Veda) or a "tradition" (*smṛti*—that which has been "remembered" from ancient times—the epics, Purāṇas, and various sūtras and *śāstras*). As a book within the *Mahābhārata*, the *Bhagavadgītā*, like Kṛṣṇa's later discourse, the *Anugītā*, and like the other didactic and philosophical portions of the epic, has the technical status of *smṛti*. But the *Bhagavadgītā* has attained the functional status of a gospel. Śaṅkara (eighth century), the major proponent of the Advaita Vedānta school of philosophy, quite typically begins his exegesis of the text with the comment that the *Gītā* contains the very quintessence of the Veda and that a knowledge of it leads to *mokṣa*, liberation from the bonds of worldly existence. Rāmānuga (eleventh century), who qualified the nondualistic position of Vedānta in order to expound his theology of a supreme and loving god, understood the *Gītā* as the actual revelation of the word of that god under the mere pretext of a discourse with Arjuna. And the Bengali saint Ramakrishna (1836–1886), like so many other modern commentators, declared the book to be "the essence of all scriptures" (*The Gospel of Sri Rāmakrishna*, New York, 1949, p. 772). The *Bhagavadgītā*, particularly after the great flowering of the devotional strain within the Hindu tradition, became accepted as revelation within tradition. The text transcended its context.

The Philosophy of the Text. The individual human being, according to the *Bhagavadgītā*, is at once natural (a product of nature caught up in lawlike relations and filled with desires and longings) and spiritual (an embodiment of the divine). The individual is not, however, a walking dualism, for the spiritual aspect is one's higher nature and one must come to realize that one's natural existence, taken in itself, is only provisional and has meaning only from the standpoint of the spiritual.

The individual human being, Kṛṣṇa tells Arjuna early on in the text, is immortal. Possessed of an eternal, unchanging spirit, a person can only appear to be an autonomous actor in the natural world. This appearance derives from an ignorance of the true self. Normally identifying himself as an ego self-sufficiently working within the conditions of his psychophysical nature, a person must reidentify himself at a deeper level of integrated selfhood and thereby understand his true role as a social being.

Following the already traditional understanding of the ideal organization of society into classes (*varṇa*s), the codified stages of life (*āśrama*s) and aims in life (*puruṣārtha*s), the *Bhagavadgītā* places much emphasis on one's need to follow or fulfill one's *dharma* ("social duty" or "role") as it is defined relative to one's place in the larger social order. The universe is sustained by *dharma.* Ideally each person works out his social career according to the dictates of his own nature (*svadharma*) as this is itself a product of past experience. *Dharma, karman* ("action" or "work"), and *saṃsāra* ("rebirth") belong together: action carried over innumerable lives must be informed by a sensitivity to the obligations one has in virtue of one's interdependence with others. Arjuna is a member of the warrior class and must fulfill the duties of this social position—he must fight.

But what is the nature of reality that makes this both possible and imperative? The *Gītā*'s answer to this is that reality, in its essence, is the presence of a personalized *brahman,* something higher than the impersonal *brahman,* the absolute reality described in the Upaniṣads. "There are two spirits in this world," Kṛṣṇa explains, "the perishable and the imperishable." The perishable is all beings and the imperishable is called *kūṭastha* ("the immovable"). But there is another, the Highest Spirit (*puruṣottama*), called the Supreme Self, who, as the imperishable Lord, enters into the three worlds and sustains them. "Since I transcend the perishable and am higher even than the imperishable, I am renowned in the world and in the Veda as the highest Spirit" (15.16–18).

This "Highest Spirit" then is not the nonpersonal, undifferentiated, unchanging *brahman* of Advaita Vedānta, but rather that being who while enjoying its status as a supreme reality, actively engages worlds of its creation. It has its higher and lower statuses as creative spirit and as the manifest natural world.

In its analysis of the lower status of the divine, the *Gītā* draws heavily upon the Sāṃkhya system of thought. Nature (*prakṛti*) is seen as an active organic field constituted by various strands (*guṇa*s), which can best be understood as energy systems. Everything in nature, and particularly every individual human being, is constituted by a combination of these forces. *Sattva* represents a state of subtle harmony and equilibrium which is exhibited as clear intelligence, as light. At the other extreme is darkness, *tamas,* the state of lethargy, of heaviness. In between is *rajas,* agitation, restlessness, passion, the motivating force for actions. The *puruṣa* ("the individual spirit") caught up in *prakṛti,* is driven by the *guṇa*s and is deluded into thinking that, as a given phenomenal fact, it is their master and not their victim.

The aim of human life in the *Bhagavadgītā* is to attain a self-realization that "I" am not a separate, autonomous actor but that "I" am at one with a divine reality, and that my ultimate freedom comes from bringing my actions into accord with that reality. "Everyone," the *Gītā* says, "is made to act helplessly by the *guṇa*s born of *prakṛti*" (3.5). "I" can become a true actor only when my actions get grounded in a divine will. Freedom (*mokṣa*) is thus not a transcendence of all action but rather calls for my being a social persona fulfilling my *dharma* without ego-attachment, at one with the divine.

The realization of this aim of life is at the heart of the *Bhagavadgītā*'s teaching, and has been the most controversial among both modern and traditional interpreters of the text. Following Śaṅkara, whose commentary is one of the oldest to have survived, many have argued that the central yoga put forward by the *Bhagavadgītā* is the way of knowledge, *jñānayoga*: it alone provides the insight into reality that allows for genuine self-realization. Taking the position of Rāmānuja, others have argued that *bhaktiyoga,* the discipline of devotion, remains the highest way for the *Gītā*; *bhakti,* in his understanding of the text, provides the basis for a salvific relationship between the individual person and a loving god with absolute power and supremacy over the world. Still others have seen the *Gītā* as a gospel of works, teaching most centrally *karmayoga,* the way of action—of acting without attachment to the fruits of one's acts. This multiplicity of interpretations results from the fact that the *Bhagavadgītā* does extol each of these ways at various times. Each discipline or respective integration is said to have value. The text combines and assimilates the central features of the various paths.

The yoga of the *Bhagavadgītā* demands that actions be performed without attachment to their results, for otherwise, with attachment, comes bondage, not freedom. Actions, the *Gītā* says, must be performed as sacrifice (*yajña*), which means that actions must be performed in a spirit of reverence, with loving attention to the divine. But to do this one must understand how nature, as the lower status of the divine, acts according to its own necessity and that the individual actor is merely an expression of the *guṇa*s. This understanding is the work of a preliminary *jñāna*—intellectual, philosophical analysis—which must then develop into a deeper insight into the nature of the self, one which allows for that discrimination between the higher and lower nature of both the human and the divine. It is only with this *jñāna* that actions can be carried out according to one's *dharma,* for that insight brings a fundamental axiological change. One sees the value of everything relative to the supreme value of reality itself. But according to the *Bhagavadgītā,* this knowledge is not sufficient for the realization of complete freedom, as it fails to provide a motivation or justification for any particular action. *Jñāna* must then recombine with *bhakti* at its highest level, which has as its object the divine in its own deepest personal nature. "Those who renounce all actions in Me and are intent on Me," Kṛṣṇa reveals, "who worship Me with complete discipline and meditate on Me, whose thoughts are fixed on Me—these I quickly lift up from the ocean of death and rebirth" (12.6–7). With the realization that one is entirely at one with an active, creative spiritual vitality, one can then imitate the divine—one can act according to *its* nature and realize thereby one's destiny. One rises above the ocean of death.

With such awareness Arjuna announced that his confusion and despair had passed. He picked up his bow and arrows: "I stand firm with my doubts dispelled; I shall act by Thy word" (18.73). The battle on the field of righteousness began.

THE PERSISTENCE OF THE TEXT. By the eighth century the *Bhagavadgītā* had become a standard text for philosophical and religious exposition. The normative commentary of Śaṅkara generated subcommentaries and inspired responses, new interpretations, new commentaries and more subcommentaries. Rāmānuja's theistic exegesis set forth devotional paradigms for understanding the text which were to be elaborated by medieval Vaiṣṇava scholiasts. These latter commentators do not seem to have distinguished between the heroic Kṛṣṇa-Vāsudeva of the *Mahābhārata* and the originally distinct, erotic Kṛṣṇa-Gopāla of the Puranic and literary traditions. With the amalgamation of various Kṛṣṇas into one supreme God, the cool and detached *bhakti* of the *Bhagavadgītā* became subsumed into the emotional and passionate *bhakti* exemplified by the milkmaid lovers of Kṛṣṇa, the cowherd in the *Bhagavata Purāṇa.* The meaning of the text changed—Madhva's commentary (thirteenth century) explains that Kṛṣṇa, the supreme lord, can only be approached or apprehended by the way of *bhakti* which is love (*sneha*), a love that is attachment.

Unabashedly classifying the overtly Vaiṣṇava *Bhagavadgītā* with their own ritual texts, the Agamas, Śaiva exegetes produced their own corpus of commentarial literature. In the *Gītārthasaṅgraha* of the Kashmir Śaiva philosopher Abhinavagupta (eleventh century), which purports to reveal the "hidden meaning of the text," Kṛṣṇa is described as a protector of *dharma* and a guide to a *mokṣa* which is explicitly defined in the prefatory verses as "merger in Lord Śiva."

Beyond the exegetical tradition, the *Bhagavadgītā* became the prototype for a genre of devotional literature in which an Arjuna-like student is urged by a particular sectarian deity to absorb himself in the worship of that deity. So in the *Śivagītā* (eighth century), for example, Rāma is too disconsolate over his separation from Sita to go into battle with Rāvaṇa; Śiva counsels and instructs him just as Kṛṣṇa did Arjuna. In the *Īśvaragītā* (ninth century) Śiva explains the paths to self-realization, the methods of liberation, to ascetics in a hermitage, in more or less the same words as were uttered in the prototype. The form and style of the original *Bhagavadgītā* seem to have imbued these later *gītās* with authority and legitimacy. Many of these texts are embedded within the Purāṇas (e.g., the *Śivagītā* in the *Padma Purāṇa*, the *Īśvaragītā* in the *Kūrma Purāṇa*, the *Devigītā* in the *Devībhāgavata Purāṇa*). The later Purāṇas commonly give quotes from, résumés of, or eulogistic references to, the *Bhagavadgītā*; the *Padma Purāṇa* (eighth century) contains a glorification of the book, the *Gītāmāhātmya*, a paean to the text as the perfect distillation of supreme truth. The text about devotion became itself an object of devotion. It is carried like a talisman by many a wandering holy man.

Throughout Indian history the *Bhagavadgītā* has provided social theorists with axioms whereby political issues and problems could be understood in religious and traditional terms. Bal Gangadhar Tilak (1856–1920), one of the most important nationalist leaders of the modern Hindu renaissance, for example, while in prison in Mandalay for sedition, wrote the *Gītā rahasya*, an interpretation of the ancient text as a revolutionary manifesto, a call to the Indian people to take up arms against the British. Gandhi, on the other hand, who first became acquainted with the *Bhagavadgītā* through British Theosophists in London, asserted, without a trace of self-consciousness, that the *Bhagavadgītā* taught nonviolence. He urged his followers to read it assiduously and to live by it. He often referred to the book as *Mother Gita*, and would say, "When I am in difficulty or distress, I seek refuge in her bosom" (*Harijan*, August, 1934).

The *Bhagavadgītā* changes with each reader, fluctuates in meaning with each successive generation of interpreters, which is to say, it lives. This vitality constitutes its sacrality.

Caitanya (1486–1533), the ecstatic founder of Bengal Vaisnavism, once came upon a man reading the *Bhagavadgītā* aloud in a temple, and as he read everyone laughed at him, for he mispronounced all of the words. The man himself was weeping and trembling, and Caitanya asked him which words made him cry so. "I don't know the meaning of any of the words," the man confessed, "but as I sound them out I see Kṛṣṇa in Arjuna's chariot. He is holding the reins in his hands and he is speaking to Arjuna and he looks very beautiful. The vision makes me weep with joy." Caitanya smiled: "You are an authority on the *Bhagavadgītā.* You know the real meaning of the text" (*Caitanyacaritāmṛta* of Kṛṣṇadāsa Kavirāja, *Madya-līlā* 9.93–103).

It has not always been important for readers or hearers of the *Bhagavadgītā* to understand all the words; rather, what has been crucial for many Hindus has been to feel or experience the text, to participate in it, to allow the *Bhagavadgītā* to sanctify their lives and console them in death.

SEE ALSO Abhinavagupta; Arjuna; Bhakti; Caitanya; Devotion; Dharma, article on Hindu Dharma; Kṛṣṇaism; Madhva; Mahābhārata; Rāmānuja; Sāṃkhya; Śaṅkara; Vaiṣṇavism; Vedānta; Yoga.

BIBLIOGRAPHY

The passages from the *Bhagavadgītā* cited in this article are from the translation of the text by Eliot Deutsch (New York, 1968). Since Charles Wilkins published his *The Bhăgvăt-gēētā, or, Dialogues of Krēēshnă and Ărjŏŏn in Eighteen Lectures, with Notes* in 1785 literally hundreds of translations of the text have been made into European languages.

Gerald J. Largon has thoughtfully surveyed the stylistic and interpretive trends as exemplified by many of these translations in "The Song Celestial: Two Centuries of the *Bhagavad Gītā* in English," *Philosophy East and West* 31 (October 1981): 513–541. Of the readily available translations, Franklin Edgerton's (1925; reprint, Oxford, 1944) is the most literal, so literal in its attempt to preserve the Sanskrit syntax, in fact, that, for the sake of balance, it was originally published together with Sir Edwin Arnold's transformation of the text into Victorian poesy (Cambridge, Mass., 1944). Though Edgerton's always reliable translation is difficult to read, his lengthy commentary is masterful scholarship. The interpretive notes that accompany the translation by W. Douglas P. Hill (London, 1927) remain an important contribution to the literature. Étienne Lamotte's *Notes sur la Bhagavadgītā* (Paris, 1929) is a fine example of rigorous exegesis and reflection.

R. C. Zaehner's lucid translation (Oxford, 1969) is a pleasure to read and his analyses are as judicious as they are sensitive; Zaehner introduces the insights of Śaṅkara and Rāmānuja where they are appropriate and he admits his penchant for the theistic interpretation of the latter. For a more detailed understanding of Rāmānuja's understanding of the text, see J. A. B. van Buitenen's *Rāmānuja on the Bhagavadgītā* (The Hague, 1953). Van Buitenen's own translation, *The Bhagavadgītā in the Mahābhārata* (Chicago, 1981), is heroic scholarship, translation at its best, and his introductory essay is no less insightful. The very important exegesis of Śaṅkara has been translated into English by Allādi Mahadeva Sastri: *The Bhagavad-Gita with the Commentary of Srî Śaṅkarachârya*, 5th ed. (Madras, 1961). And the interesting commentary of Abhinavagupta, the *Gītārthasaṅgraha*, has been well translated into English and perceptively introduced by Arvind Sharma (Leiden, 1983).

For significant examples of modern Indian interpretations of the text, see *The Gospel of Selfless Action, or the Gita According to Gandhi*, edited and translated by Mahadev Desai (Ahmadabad, 1948); *Śrimad Bhagavadgītā Rahasya*, edited by B. G. Ti-lak (Poona, 1936); and Aurobindo Ghose's *Essays on the Gita* (Calcutta, 1926).

New Sources

Chaturvedi, Laxmi Narayan. *The Teachings of Bhavagad Gita.* New Delhi, 1991.

Lipner, Julius, ed. *The Fruits of Our Desiring: An Enquiry into the Ethics of the Bhagavadgita for Our Times: Essays from the Inaugural Conference of the Dharam Hinduja Institute for Indic Research, Cambridge University.* Calgary, 1997.

MacKenzie, Matthew D. "The Five Factors of Action and the Decentring of Agency in the Bhavagad Gita." *Asian Philosophy*, 11 (November 2001): 141–151.

Patel, Ramesh. *Philosophy of the Gita.* New York, 1991.

Rambachan, Anatanand. *The Hindu Vision.* New Delhi, 1992.

Sartwell, Crispin. "Art and War: Paradox of the Bhavagad Gita." *Asian Philosophy* 3 (1993): 95–103.

Teschner, George. "Anxiety, Anger and the Concept of Agency in the Bhavagad Gita." *Asian Philosophy* 2 (1992): 61–78.

Verma, C. D. *The Gita in World Literature.* New Delhi, 1990.

ELIOT DEUTSCH (1987)
LEE SIEGEL (1987)
Revised Bibliography

BHAIṢAJYAGURU, the Buddha named Master of Healing, is an important member of the Mahāyāna Buddhist pantheon. He has been worshiped predominantly in East and Central Asian traditions of Buddhist practice.

Concepts of healing played a fundamental role in early Buddhism: Śākyamuni Buddha was sometimes given the epithet "supreme physician," and the Buddhist teachings were termed the "king of medicines" for their ability to lead beings out of suffering. In early Buddhist teachings, as in later times, the enlightenment process was equated with the healing process. Further, many monks were healers and physicians; such persons played a significant role in the spread of Buddhist teachings. Thus, when the Mahāyāna pantheon began to take form in the centuries directly before and after the beginning of the common era, several key figures were associated especially with healing abilities, both metaphorical and literal. Master of Healing ultimately was viewed as the most important figure of this group.

The principal scripture written about this Buddha, entitled *Scripture on the Merits and Original Vows of the Master of Healing, the Lapis Lazuli Radiance Tathāgata*, is a work that eventually became best known in the Chinese version translated by Xuanzang in 650 CE (T.D. no. 450). As in other works of this type, most likely composed in the early centuries of the common era in the northwest borderlands of India, the historical Buddha Śākyamuni serves as a pivot between the human realms and celestial spheres, in this instance revealing to his listeners the existence of the enlightened celestial being Bhaiṣajyaguru. Following a pattern often seen in such texts, the Buddha and his pure land are described, his vows to aid all beings are detailed, and various methods are explicated for invoking his beneficent force. Here, Master of Healing is described as lord of a spirit realm located to the east, a land named Pure Lapis Lazuli, with level ground made of that radiantly blue stone, marked by roads of gold and various structures built of precious substances. Like the celestial fields of other Buddhas such as Amitabha, this realm is a refuge from suffering; it is an ideal site to listen without distraction to the pure principles taught by its lord, the Master of Healing, in association with the two leaders of his *bodhisattva* assembly, Sunlight (Sūryaprabha) and Moonglow (Candraprabha).

Master of Healing's twelve vows, first made when he set out to gain enlightenment, cover a wide range of benefits to sentient beings. The most widely known is the sixth vow, a pledge to alleviate the sickness and suffering of all beings. The fulfillment of this pledge forms the subject of much of the scripture. Yet, while Master of Healing has pledged to aid all beings who are sick and suffering, he must be called upon in order to invoke this potent aid. According to the scripture, methods of effective invocation range from the simple expedient of calling out his name to special rites involving prayer and worship before his image. In the case of life-threatening disease, a complex rite is outlined in the scripture (and described in great detail in special ritual texts) in which forty-nine cartwheel-shaped lamps are burned before seven images of the Buddha for forty-nine days, with many other ritual acts performed in units of seven or forty-nine. The number seven (and its square, forty-nine) is especially important in the Buddhist healing cults, most likely relating to the number of days in the intermediate state (*antarābhava*) between death and rebirth.

A fundamental feature of the healings bestowed by Bhaiṣajyaguru is the transformation of *karman*, that is, a concern for eradicating the patterned causes as well as the visible symptoms of suffering. This sense of transformation pervades the scriptural and ritual traditions associated with the cult. In this context, Master of Healing is especially important for his work in assisting beings to reach a momentous spiritual turning point known as the "aspiration to attain enlightenment," at which the drifting life is cast aside in order to seek spiritual fulfillment.

Standard images of Master of Healing depict him as a seated Buddha in monk's garb, either having skin the rich blue color of lapis lazuli or having a golden complexion with a halo and mandorla of lapis lazuli-colored rays. The Buddha holds a bowl or covered medicine jar on his lap with his left hand, while his right hand, resting on his right knee with palm outward, offers the medicinal myrobalan fruit; sometimes he is standing, holding the medicine jar in his left hand, with right hand upraised in the gesture of the banishment of fear. He is flanked by his *bodhisattva* assistants, Sunlight and Moonglow, who stand in princely garb. Encircling them are twelve *yakṣa* generals, each of whom is said to command seven thousand troops, all in aid of the Buddha's healing work. In some East Asian traditions, these twelve generals are clearly depicted as lords of the twelve hours of the day and the twelve years of the Jupiter-based cycle. The cosmic wholeness of this scene is striking: with lapis lazuli at the center that radiates like the depths of space, together with the two luminaries who are encircled by lords of time, it points to the profound nature of internal and external healing provided by this Buddha.

A somewhat later tradition, introduced to China in the early eighth century and eventually popular among Tibetans and Mongolians, focuses on seven brothers identified as healing Buddhas, the senior physician among them being Bhaisajyaguru. This group is often depicted with Śākyamuni Buddha, thus turning back to the roots of the Healing Buddha cult in the early tradition of Śākyamuni as spiritual healer.

See Also Celestial Buddhas and Bodhisattvas; Healing and Medicine.

Bibliography

The only extended study of Bhaiṣjyaguru is my *The Healing Buddha* (Boulder, Colo., 1979), which includes full translations from Chinese scriptures on this Buddha. This work provides a cross-cultural view of the cult, emphasizing its scriptural foundations and iconographic manifestations. Further information specific to the context of Chinese practice traditions can be found in my "Seeking Longevity in Chinese Buddhism: Long Life Deities and Their Symbolism," in *Myth and Symbol in Chinese Tradition*, edited by Norman Girardot and John S. Major, a special issue of the *Journal of Chinese Religions* 13 (1985). A comprehensive cross-cultural essay on Buddhist medical theory and healing traditions is admirably set forth in Paul Demiéville's "*Byō* (Disease)," in *Hōbōgirin*, fasc. 3 (Paris, 1937), pp. 224–270; Mark Tatz has translated this monographic study into English under the title *Buddhism and Healing: Demiéville's Article "Byō" from Hōbōgirin* (Lanham, Md., 1985).

New Sources

Hassnain, F. M., and Tokan Sumi. *Bhaisajya-guru-sutra: Original Sanskrit Text with Introduction and Commentary*. New Delhi, 1995.

Willemen, Charles. "The Medicine Buddha Bhaisajyaguru." In *Oriental Medicine: An Illustrated Guide to the Asian Arts of Healing*, edited by Jan Alphen and Anthony Aris, pp. 261–265. Boston, 1997.

Williams, Paul. *Mahāyāna Buddhism: The Doctrinal Foundations*. London, 1989.

Raoul Birnbaum (1987)
Revised Bibliography

BHAKTI. The Sanskrit term *bhakti* is most often translated in English as "devotion," and the *bhaktimārga*, the "path of devotion," is understood to be one major type of Hindu spiritual practice. The *bhaktimārga* is a path leading toward liberation (*mokṣa*) from material embodiment in our present imperfect world and the attainment of a state of abiding communion with a personally conceived ultimate reality. The word *devotion*, however, may not convey the sense of participation and even of mutual indwelling between the devotees and God so central in *bhakti*. The Sanskrit noun *bhakti* is derived from the verbal root *bhaj*, which means "to share in" or "to belong to," as well as "to worship." *Devotion*, moreover, may not suggest the range of intense emotional states so frequently connoted by *bhakti*, most of which are suggested by the inclusive English word *love*. God's love, however, whether answering or eliciting the devotee's love, is denoted with other words than *bhakti*. Thus *bhakti* is the divine-human relationship as experienced from the human side.

While *bhakti* is sometimes used in a broad sense to cover an attitude of reverence to any deity or to a human teacher, the *bhaktimārga* is understood to be a "path" of exclusive devotion to a divine or human figure representing or embodying ultimate reality, a path whose goal is not this-worldly benefits but supreme blessedness. Those who follow the path believe that ultimate reality is the personal Lord (Īśvara) who both transcends the universe and creates it. *Bhakti* is thus theistic and can be distinguished, not only (1) from those religious movements that deny the reality of Īśvara (including those of Buddhists and Jains), but also (2) from polytheistic beliefs in a number of deities within a divine cosmos, and

(3) from philosophies that see Īśvara as an ultimately illusory appearance of the reality that transcends personal qualities, *nirguṇa brahman.*

In practice the boundaries of the *bhaktimārga* are indistinct and its forms are many and diverse, and it is differently defined by various sectarian communities. Nonetheless, there are some important common features found in different expressions of *bhakti,* and there is a discernible "history" of *bhakti* during the last fifteen hundred to two thousand years.

Modern historical approaches to Indian religion generally recognize some traces of *bhakti* in a few of the classical Upaniṣads and see it strikingly present in large sections of the epics (including notably the *Bhagavadgītā*). The earliest devotional poetry is considered that in praise of the Tamil god Murukan̲, beginning about 200 CE, followed between the fifth and ninth centuries by the works of many poets in two distinct bodies of Tamil poetry, one in praise of Śiva, the other in praise of Viṣṇu. According to the traditional accounts, however, the Tamil poet-saints are scattered through the first five thousand years of the fourth and most degenerate age, the *kaliyuga.* This traditional dating fits a frequent theme, that *bhakti* is an easier path to salvation appropriate to an age of diminished spiritual capacities, but another theme sometimes crosses this: the assertion that the triumph of bands of singing and dancing devotees marks the breaking of the power of the demon Kali, and thus the end of Kali's evil age and the restoration of the age of spiritual perfection.

From a modern historical standpoint the flowering of *bhakti* is the coming together of considerably earlier theistic tendencies in three major religious traditions of ancient India: (1) the sacrificial cult of the invading Aryans and the recitation by *brāhmaṇa* priests that became the foundation of the Vedas; (2) the practice of bodily mortification and spiritual withdrawal by individuals and groups known as *śramaṇas,* probably continuing traditions of earlier inhabitants of India but soon adopted and adapted by some of the Aryans; and (3) the pre-Aryan cults of spirits and village goddesses inhabiting trees and rocks and protecting special places or special groups.

All three traditions were subject to one type of reinterpretation that emphasized the great results of effective practice and a second type of reinterpretation that concentrated on the intuitive knowledge of the deities or ultimate powers of that tradition. There was also a third type of reinterpretation, however, that ascribed omnipotence to a particular deity, more or less personally conceived, and advocated single-minded devotion to this supreme deity. In the case of the Vedic tradition it was increasingly Viṣṇu who was regarded as both the essential core and the lord of the sacrifice. Some of the *śramaṇas* sometimes regarded Śiva as the great yogin, paradoxically lord of fertility and sexual plenitude as well as of sexual abstinence. The more popular and polytheistic traditions have also had their *bhakti* forms, in which local goddesses are conceived as manifestations of the Mother, the great Power (Śakti) whose devotees sing her praises as the giver of both destruction and well-being.

Those who worship Viṣṇu (in any of his incarnations but particularly as Kṛṣṇa and Rama) as the supreme deity are known as Vaiṣṇavas; likewise those who accord the supreme place to Śiva are called Śaivas, and those who are devotees of the Goddess, conceived not as the subordinate consort of Śiva but as the ultimate Power, are termed Śāktas. Each "sect" is in practice divided into a large number of groups marked by allegiance to particular forms of the supreme deity, to particular lineages of teachers and teachings in characteristic sectarian organizations, which usually include some form of initiation.

The major forms of *bhakti* are described by Hindus themselves, not only by their special relation to particular forms of deity, but also according to the various moods of the devotee. The classifications vary slightly; some are closely related to classical Indian aesthetic theory according to which a particular raw emotion (*bhāva*) is transformed in drama into a refined mood or essence (*rasa*). Each combination of *bhāva* and *rasa* uses a particular human relationship: servant to master or child to parent (respectful subordination), friend to friend (joking familiarity), parent to child (maternal affection and concern), and beloved to lover (combining elements of the other three relationships in passionate love). Individual devotees as well as larger sectarian movements differ in their personal preference and doctrinal ranking among these relationships, but all are generally accepted as appropriate devotional stances.

When passionate attachment to the Lord is stressed, *bhakti* is a striking contrast to yoga and other ascetic paths to salvation that stress detachment and the overcoming of all passions, positive as well as negative. Yet many forms of *bhakti* also stress the detachment from all worldly beings that must accompany attachment to the Lord, or, like the *Bhagavadgītā,* which speaks of *bhaktiyoga,* they use the language of ascetic philosophy to extol the path of *bhakti.*

The *bhakti* movements generally stand religiously in between the more extreme ascetic paths and popular Hindu religiosity. (Less extreme forms of asceticism are often incorporated within the *bhakti* movements.) *Bhakti* generally shares the ascetic concern for *mokṣa:* release from finite existence and the realization of transcendent beatitude. What is primary, however, is communion with the Lord, and if *bhaktas* think of *mokṣa* as anything else than such communion, they will reject it as a goal that would deprive them of the very communion for which they fervently yearn.

A few *bhaktas* make the total commitment of time and style of life characteristic of Hindu "renouncers," spending whole days in chanting and singing the praise of their Lord. Most, however, must find time for their devotion in the midst of their daily occupations, whether high or low, but may become "full time" devotees temporarily during a lengthy pilgrimage. Their being *bhaktas* is sometimes shown by the sectarian marks on their foreheads or by other signs that they have been initiated into a particular community.

Bhakti often shares with popular Hinduism the basic ritual of *pūjā:* worship of the deity in some image form with vegetables, fruits, and flowers, which are spiritually consumed—or worn—by the deity and then returned to the worshiper as *prasāda,* material substance filled with the Lord's grace. Such *pūjā* may take place in one's home shrine or local temple, or it may be done as the culmination of a lengthy and arduous journey to a center of pilgrimage. Most Hindus perform such *pūjā* in order to win the deity's favor for some request, or, in the case of a vow (*vrata*), to fulfill a promise made at the time of a request since favorably answered. True *bhaktas*, however, perform the very same ritual acts in a different spirit: in thanksgiving for divine gifts freely granted, in petition for the supreme gift of God's presence, sometimes expressed as the privilege of doing God some service, in obedient performance of duties to the deities God has ordained, which include sacrificial worship for the maintenance of the universe. *Bhaktas* recognize that the Lord they serve also grants worldly gifts to those who seek them, and moreover, even grants requests made to lower deities. This means that they often can practice common Hindu forms of worship and support temple establishments. On the other hand, some *bhakti* movements have at one time been or continue to be sharply critical of popular religion and/or the temple establishment. This was strikingly true of the Vīraśaiva poets in Karnataka from the twelfth to the fourteenth century CE. In North India Kabīr and Nānak (the first Sikh *gurū*) were sharply critical both of popular piety and of the religious establishments, Hindu as well as Muslim.

There are also distinctive *bhakti* rituals: the singing (sometimes communal) of hymns and chants, the performance of dramas, dances, and recitals of the heroic deeds or erotic sports of Viṣṇu's incarnations or of the mysterious appearances of Lord Śiva. Stories about the Lord may thus lead to stories about the great *bhaktas*. The recounting of their lives is almost as popular as the singing of their songs.

Here, too, there is a strong difference in emphasis between devotional and ascetic paths, for the distinctive rituals of *bhaktas* are generally not reserved for the few qualified initiates but open to all, whatever their motives or their qualifications in the socioreligious hierarchy. This egalitarian thrust of *bhakti,* although it has not always penetrated in practice to the untouchables, is usually praised in song and story. It is not the equality of modern Western individualism, but the openness to a divine seeking that transcends or even reverses the order of human society, sometimes precisely because humility is the necessary qualification for receiving the Lord's grace.

Bhakti means not only "sharing" with God but also some form of sharing or mutual participation among God's devotees. While there is a heroic loneliness in the lives of some of the great *bhaktas* corresponding to or even combined with the physical and spiritual isolation of more extreme asceticism, the dominant note in *bhakti* is community, between generations as well as among fellow devotees of the same generation. Within this devotional community there is usually both a hierarchical relationship between teacher and disciple and a more egalitarian relationship between fellow disciples.

The English word *movement* is particularly appropriate for most *bhakti* movements, for there is a spiritual movement between the divine and the human, an emotional movement affecting or even engulfing any particular community of devotees, and a movement through time celebrated in sacred story. The stories about the *bhakti* saints help to define particular devotional communities and sometimes to extend them. While the sacred history of many devotional movements is of interest only to their own members, there has also been, especially in North India since the fifteenth century, a combination of hagiographies known as the *Bhaktamāla* (The garland of devotees). The present evil age, the *kaliyuga,* is considered to be the one, in the vast recurring cycle of the four ages, in which the human capacity to live rightly is at its lowest. Yet this cycle of stories assumes that the present age is also the *bhaktikāla,* the time for devotion. The worst of times becomes the best of times for those who join together in fervent praise. Those who remember the Lord (as continuously as the flow of oil, in Rāmānuja's definition of *bhakti*) have already in this life a foretaste of the eternal communion that is their final goal and, in many Vaisnava communities, the expected goal at the end of their present earthly life. *Bhaktas* thus share in a movement from eternity through time back to eternity.

Philosophically, Vaisnava *bhakti* has expressed itself in a range of positions between the "pure nondualism" (*śuddhādvaita*) of Vallabha and the "dualism" (*dvaita*) of Madhva, and Śaiva *bhakti* ranges from the monistic philosophy of Kashmir Śaivism to the dualistic or pluralistic position of the Tamil Śaiva Siddhānta, yet almost all of these philosophical positions agree both on the infinitely superior quality of the divine reality and on some kind of subordinate reality for finite souls and material things.

The common goal of communion with the Lord can also be understood more or less monistically. One classification distinguishes between four degrees of communion: (1) *sālokya,* being in the same heaven with a continuous vision of the Lord; (2) *sāmīpya,* residing close to the Lord; (3) *sārūpya,* having the same form, understood to be the privilege of the Lord's intimate attendants, whose external appearance is similar to the Lord's; and (4) *sāyujya,* complete union through entering the body of the Lord.

In terms of religious practice and religious experience there is a somewhat comparable range of positions between the affirmation of the constant divine presence both within finite realities and surrounding them, on the one hand, and the lamenting of God's absence from the devotee's experience in this present life. The typical *bhakti* position is somehow to affirm both God's presence and God's absence, but there is considerable difference in emphasis, not only between different sects and different individuals, but also within the experience of the same *bhakta*. The moments of experienced union (*saṃśleṣa*) and anguished separation or desolation (*viśleṣa* or *viraha*) alternate, but the *bhakta*'s experience is still more complicated: the realization of the fleeting character of the experience of union may intrude into it, while, on the other hand, the grief at separation is sharpened by the memory of previous shared delight. That grief itself, if it passes the moment of despair, expresses itself as a passionate yearning for a new moment of divine presence or as a more serene confidence in the final goal of unending communion with God.

Those who express a devotion of passionate attachment to the Lord, especially when the Lord is conceived as Kṛṣṇa, are sometimes dissatisfied with merely spiritual union after this earthly life. They yearn for the Lord's physical embrace of their present embodied selves. *Bhaktas* differ as to whether such union of the human devotee's body with the Lord's body is possible. Within this life, however, ecstatic moments of perceived union are fleeting. Permanent union brings with it an end to the *bhakta*'s life in this world, as is dramatically portrayed in the stories of the merger of two of the Tamil Vaisnava saints (Āṇṭāl and Tiruppāṇ Āḻvār) into the Lord's image incarnation, Ranganātha. Similar stories are told of the Rājpūt woman saint Mīrā Bāī, absorbed with Kṛṣṇa's image at Dvarka, and of Caitanya, who, according to the local Oriya tradition in Puri, was absorbed into the image of Jagannātha.

For the more monistic *bhakti* that regards permanent union as the end of the finite self's distinct personal existence, the state of separation may actually be preferred as ensuring the continued bittersweet experience of the Lord's absence. Certainly for *bhaktas* in many schools and sects, the moments of absence are conveyed in poetry of great intensity and beauty. There our common human experience of separation from the infinite source of being is transfigured by the special experience of that rare human being who has felt the divine presence or known the divine rapture and then experienced even more intensely the pain of separation from this incredibly beautiful and desirable Lord.

In the South Indian Vaisnava *bhakti* of Rāmānuja, however, separation and union are coordinated in a hierarchical vision in which the Lord enters the heart of all finite beings as their inner controller, without obliterating the distinct existence and moral responsibility of the finite person. Here longing for God and belonging to God are not alternatives but mutually reinforcing coordinates in intensifying the *bhakta*'s experience.

From an outside vantage point the meaning of *bhakti* may be conveyed by two questions. One is a theological question: how can the infinite Lord be independent of all finite reality and yet be dependent on his devotees? Most *bhaktas* affirm both propositions. The second is the corresponding anthropological question: how can the *bhakta* be both the humble servant and the intimate companion of the Lord—not only the Lord's instrument but the Lord's bride? Since we recognize that these are no more than an outsider's "translation" of the *bhaktas*' own questions, we must add a third, what we might call a hermeneutical question: how can the outside student of Hindu *bhakti* (whether non-Hindu or non-*bhakta*) understand any particular form of Hindu *bhakti?* How can divine-human "sharing" be understood without sharing in it? While most of the Hindu tradition would find it difficult to imagine such external understanding as the question implies, and those in the Western Platonic tradition would reject the separation of loving and knowing, most Western study of religion in general and of Hindu *bhakti* in particular assumes that reasonable understanding is possible—enough to write this article, for example—*without* personally participating as a scholar in the *bhakta*'s experience. The very nature of *bhakti* as experienced participation, however, is a continuing challenge to the strong tendency of Western notions of understanding, especially the Western effort to "capture" all human experience in carefully crafted objective concepts.

To understand an alien experience we need to remember partially similar experiences familiar to us. *Bhakti* has both appealed to and puzzled Western students because they see in its central features Western monotheism combined with other elements that seem different or even totally alien. Many features of Hindu *bhakti* are also found in the more popular aspects of Jainism and Buddhism, and Pure Land Buddhism has incorporated much of *bhakti* at its very core. The Indian expressions of both Islam and Christianity, moreover, have developed their own *bhakti* poets and saints. In the case of Islam, *bhakti* has provided a bridge for a mutual interpenetration with Hindu piety that has given the piety of Muslims in South Asia a distinctive character; yet Islamic and Hindu *bhakti* did not merge. In the case of Christianity in the modern era, *bhakti* provided the basic vocabulary for Christian prayer and hymnody in most modern Indian languages, yet Christian *bhakti* has usually been so distinctive as to be unaware of its debt to the Hindu tradition. Perhaps *bhakti*, although distinctively Hindu, may be appropriated and developed, if not by the proud at least by the humble, in a great variety of religious and cultural communities.

SEE ALSO Bhagavadgītā; Caitanya; Devotion; Īśvara; Kabīr; Mīrā Bāī; Mokṣa; Nānak; Poetry, article on Indian Religious Poetry; Pūjā, article on Hindu Pūjā; Rāmānuja; Śaivism, article on Vīraśaivas; Yoga.

BIBLIOGRAPHY

Dhavamony, Mariasusai. *Love of God according to Śaiva Siddhanta.* Oxford, 1971.

Hardy, Friedhelm. *Viraha Bhakti: The Early Development of Kṛṣṇa Devotion in South India.* Oxford, 1981.

Hawley, John Stratton. *Sūr Dās: Poet, Singer, Saint.* Seattle, 1984.

Hawley, John Stratton, and Donna M. Wulff, eds. *The Divine Consort: Rādhā and the Goddesses of India.* Berkeley, 1982.

Hein, Norvin J. "Hinduism." In *A Reader's Guide to the Great Religions*, edited by Charles J. Adams, pp. 106–155. New York, 1977. See pages 126–140.

Ramanujan, A. K., trans. *Speaking of Śiva.* Harmondsworth, 1973.

Ramanujan, A. K., trans. *Hymns for the Drowning.* Princeton, 1981.

Schomer, Karine, and W. H. McLeod, eds. *The Sants: Studies in a Devotional Tradition of India.* Berkeley and Delhi, 1985.

Yocum, Glenn E. *Hymns to the Dancing Śiva.* New Delhi and Columbia, Mo., 1982.

Zelliot, Eleanor. "The Medieval Bhakti Movement in History: An Essay on the Literature in English." In *Hinduism: New Essays in the History of Religions*, edited by Bardwell L. Smith, pp. 143–168. Leiden, 1976.

New Sources

Bhakti Religion in North India: Community Identity and Political Action. Edited by David N. Lorenzen. Albany, 1995.

Devotion Divine: Bhakti Traditions from the Regions of India: Studies in Honour of Charlotte Vaudeville. Edited by Diana L. Eck and Françoise Mallison. Groningen, 1991.

Haberman, David L. *Acting as a Way of Salvation: A Study of Raganugabhakti Sadhana.* New York, 1988.

Love Divine: Studies in Bhakti and Devotional Mysticism. Edited by Karel Werner. Durham indological series no. 3. Richmond, Surrey, 1993.

Tripathi, S. K. *Music and Bhakti.* Varanasi, 1993.

John B. Carman (1987)
Revised Bibliography

BHĀVAVIVEKA (c. 490–570 CE), also known as Bhavya or (in Tibetan) Legs ldan 'byed pa; Indian Buddhist philosopher and historian, and founder of the Svātantrika-Mādhyamika school. Born to a royal family in Malyara, in South India (although some Chinese sources claim it was in Magadha, in North India), Bhāvaviveka studied both *sūtra* and *śāstra* literatures during his formative years. Having excelled in the art of debate, especially against Hindu apologists of the Sāṃkhya school, he is said to have been the abbot of some fifty monasteries in the region of Dhanyakata, in South India. His chief influences were the writings of Nāgārjuna (second century CE), the founder of the Mādhyamika, and treatises on logic from the traditions of Buddhism (especially Dignāga's works) and Hinduism (especially the *Nyāyapraveśa*). His chief philosophical contribution was his attempt at formulating a synthesis of Mādhyamika dialectics and the logical conventions of his time.

As all of Bhāvaviveka's works are lost in the original Sanskrit and preserved only in Tibetan translations, the scholarly world came to know of him only through Candrakīrti (c. 580–650 CE), who refuted Bhāvaviveka's position in the first chapter of the *Prasannapadā.* It could therefore be argued that current understanding of the Mādhyamika in general has suffered from a one-sided perspective that relies solely on Candrakīrti's rival school, the Prāsaṅgika-Mādhyamika. However, contemporary scholarship no longer neglects Tibetan sources, and thus a more balanced approach has ensued, one that reads Nāgārjuna's seminal writings through the commentaries of both the Prāsaṅgikas and the Svātantrikas.

Nagarjuna, especially as read through the commentaries of Buddhāpalita (c. 470–550 CE), was characterized by many Indian philosophers as a *vaitaṇḍika,* a nihilist who refused to assume any thesis (*pratijñā*) in the course of the ongoing dialogue between Hindu thinkers of various schools and the Buddhists. While Mādhyamika thought had not asserted any claim about ultimate truth/reality (*paramārthasatya*), Bhāvaviveka's independent reasoning (*svatantra-anumāna*) was applied to conventional truth/reality (*saṃvṛtisatya*) as a means of rescuing logico-linguistic conventions (*vyavahāra*) from a systematic negation (*prasaṅga*) that opened the school to charges of nihilism. While Bhāvaviveka accepted the Mādhyamika view that ultimately (*paramārthataḥ*) no entities could be predicated with any form of existence, he was willing to employ such predication on a conventional level. In order to maintain the reality and utility of traditional Buddhist categories for talking about the path of spiritual growth while denying the ultimate reality of such categories, he employed a syllogistic thesis (*pratijñā*), a philosophic strategy that was nearly incomprehensible to scholars of the Mādhyamika, who knew this school only through Candrakīrti's Prāsaṅgika systematization.

In order to affirm a thesis on the conventional level while denying it ultimately, Bhāvaviveka creatively reinterpreted the key Mādhyamika doctrine of the two truths (*satyadvaya*). In his *Madhyamārthasaṃgraha,* he propounds two levels of ultimacy: a highest ultimate that is beyond all predication and specification (*aparyāya-paramārtha*), in conformity with all Mādhyamika teachings, and an ultimate that can be inferred logically and specified meaningfully (*paryāya-paramārtha*); this latter level was a bold innovation in the history of Mādhyamika thought. Of course, such a distinction was operative only within the realm of conventional thought. Again one must employ Bhāvaviveka's crucial adverbial codicil, *paramārthataḥ,* and follow him in claiming that such a distinction, like all distinctions, is ultimately unreal although conventionally useful.

Bhāvaviveka's two main philosophic contributions—his affirmation of a thesis on a conventional level and his reinterpretation of the two-truths doctrine—are evaluated diversely by contemporary scholars. Those unsympathetic to him see his work as an unhappy concession to the logical conventions of his day, a concession that dilutes the rigor of the Mādhyamika dialectic. Those with more sympathy see his contributions as a creative surge that rescued Buddhist religious philosophies from those dialectical negations that threatened the integrity of the Buddhist path itself.

Within the evolved Tibetan Buddhist tradition, Bhāvaviveka is especially known for two other contributions. His refutations of the rival Yogācāra school are considered to be among the clearest ever written. The fifth chapter of his *Tarkajvālā,* the "Yogācārattvaviniścaya," refutes both the existence of the absolute and the nonexistence of the conventional, both seminal Yogācāra positions.

He is also the forerunner of the literary style known as *siddhānta* (Tib., *grub mtha'*), which became enormously popular within Tibetan scholarly circles. A *siddhānta* text devotes ordered chapters to analyzing the philosophic positions (*siddhāntas*) of rival schools, both Buddhist and Hindu. His *Tarkajvālā* contains systematic critiques of the positions held by the Hinayana and the Yogācāra, both Buddhist schools, and the Sāṃkhya, Vaisesika, Vedānta, and Mīmāṃsā schools of Hindu philosophy.

Bhāvaviveka was also a keen historian. His *Nikāyabhedavibhaṅgavyākhyāna* remains one of the most important and reliable sources for the early history of the Buddhist order, and for information on the schisms within its ranks.

See Also Buddhist Philosophy; Mādhyamika; Śūnyam and Śūnyata.

Bibliography

The most important philosophical works by Bhāvaviveka are his commentary on Nagarjuna's *Mūlamadhyamakakārikā,* the *Prajñāpradīpa;* his verse work, the *Madhyamakahṛdayakārikā,* with the autocommentary the *Tarkajvālā;* his *Madhyamārthasaṅgraha;* and his *Karatalaratna.* All these works can be found in volumes 95 and 96 of *The Tibetan Tripiṭaka,* edited by D. T. Suzuki (Tokyo, 1962). Bhāvaviveka's work on the history of the Buddhist order, the *Nikāyabhedavibhaṅgavyākhyāna,* is included in volume 127.

Bhāvaviveka's biography can be found in Khetsun Sangpo's *Rgya gar paṇ chen rnams kyi rnam thar ngo mtshar padmo'i 'dzum zhal gsar pa* (Dharamsala, India, 1973). Perhaps the most definitive study of Bhāvaviveka is Malcolm David Eckel's "A Question of Nihilism: Bhāvaviveka's Response to the Fundamental Problems of Mādhyamika Philosophy" (Ph.D. diss., Harvard University, 1980). Shotaro Iida's *Reason and Emptiness: A Study in Logic and Mysticism* (Tokyo, 1980) studies Bhāvaviveka from the perspective of medieval Tibetan sources. Louis de La Vallée Poussin's essay "Bhāvaviveka," in volume 2 of *Mélanges chinois et bouddhiques* (Brussels, 1933), pp. 60–67, is the statement of classical Buddhology on the subject. Kajiyama Yuichi's "Bhāvaviveka and the Prāsaṅgika School," *Nava-Nalanda-Mahavihara Research Publication* 1 (n.d.): 289–331; my own "An Appraisal of the Svātantrika-Prasamgika Debates," *Philosophy East and West* 26 (1976): 253–267; Peter Della Santina's "The Division of the Madhyamika System into the Prāsaṅgika and Svātantrika Schools," *Journal of Religious Studies* 7 (1979): 40–49; and Ichimura Shohei's "A New Approach to the Intra-Mādhyamika Confrontation over the Svātantrika and Prāsaṅgika Methods of Refutation," *Journal of the International Association of Buddhist Studies* 5 (1982): 41–52, exemplify contemporary scholarship. One important source was unavailable to this author: Donald Lopez's "The Svātantrika-Mādhyamika School of Mahāyāna Buddhism" (Ph.D. diss., University of Virginia, 1982).

Nathan Katz (1987)

BHAVE, VINOBA (1895–1982), Indian social and religious reformer. Vinayak Narhari Bhave was closely associated with Mohandas Gandhi, who bestowed upon him the affectionate epithet Vinoba (Mar., "brother Vino"). He is generally acclaimed in India as the one who "stepped into Gandhi's shoes." As a young man Bhave studied Sanskrit and the Hindu religious tradition in Varanasi. It was here that he read accounts of Gandhi's patriotic speeches. Attracted by Gandhi's ideas, Bhave joined Gandhi as his disciple in 1916 and soon became one of his close associates. In 1921 Gandhi had Bhave move to a new ashram (retreat center) in Wardha in the state of Maharashtra. Here he began experimenting with many Gandhian ideas designed to implement self-rule for India. His main goal was to engage in village service for the benefit of the Indian masses. As a result, he became a skillful farmer, spinner, weaver, and scavenger. Many of these activities were later incorporated into several of his plans for the moral and spiritual uplift of all humanity. Impressed with his political and religious dedication, his spiritual way of life, and his belief in nonviolent methods of social action, Gandhi chose him in 1940 as the first *satyāgrahī* (one who uses nonviolent means to bring the opponent to the point of seeing the truth) in a protest against British rule.

After India's independence Bhave emerged from the shadow of his teacher as he began his *pad yātrā* ("journey on foot") to meet the people of India. The famous Bhoodān ("land gift") movement was born when on one such journey he sought a donation of land in order to distribute it among the landless poor. Later he designed a program to collect fifty million acres of land for the landless. For the rest of his life, he tirelessly worked for *grām swarāj* ("village self-rule") to free the people from the rich and the powerful. He retreated to his ashram in Paunar, near Wardha, in 1970 and died there in 1982.

Influences. Bhave's influence was greatest in his promotion of Gandhian principles. He became the chief exponent of the Sarvodaya ("welfare of all") movement and executed Gandhi's nonviolent philosophy through a series of activities known as "constructive works." These included such programs as promotion of *khādī* ("self-spun cloth"), *naī talīm* ("new education"), *strī śakti* ("woman power"), cow protection, and *śānti senā* ("peace brigade"). He created the Sarva Seva Sangha ("society for the service of all") in order to carry out the work of Sarvodaya, and served as its spiritual adviser. Bhave also launched a series of movements connected with the Land Gift movement in order to tackle the problem of exploitation of the farmers by their landlords. Although through these movements he sought to accomplish socioeconomic reform, for him they were part of a spiritual struggle to establish *rām rāj* ("kingdom of God") through *grām swarāj*. To this end, he adopted and promoted the Gandhian model of Sarvodaya. Bhave took the concept of "giving" (*dān*) further and asked that people donate their money, labor, intellect, and life for the work of Sarvodaya.

Bhave organized village councils (*grām sabhās*) to oversee the village development program. His aim was not only to bring self-sufficiency to the villages but also to establish a nonviolent society based on religious ideals. Through the constructive programs of Sarvodaya, Bhave sought to create a moral force in Indian society. The aim of his movement was not to promote the greatest good for the greatest number, but the greatest good for all people. The goal of Sarvodaya philosophy can be summarized as follows: in the social realm it advocates a casteless society, in politics it shares a democratic vision of the power of the people, in economics it promotes the belief that "small is beautiful," and in religion it asks for tolerance for all faiths. Its final goal is to promote peace for all humankind.

The failure of many of Bhave's plans to come to fruition ultimately led to dissension in the Sarvodaya. In the 1960s Jai Prakash Narayan, a Marxist-turned-Gandhian activist and an associate of Bhave, sought to steer the Sarvodaya movement in other directions. The controversy arose over the issue of whether Sarvodaya workers should participate in politics in order to initiate change in Indian society. Disenchanted with Bhave's nonpartisan religious approach and the slow moving program of *grām swarāj*, Narayan began taking an active part in contemporary politics. By the 1970s this led to a serious split within the organization of the Sarva Seva Sangha (the work agency of Sarvodaya) and the parting of ways of these two giants of the Gandhian movement. The conflict brought into focus various ideological differences that existed within the Sarvodaya movement. However, Bhave's supporters continued to maintain that his was a movement to "change the hearts of the people" through moral force and nonpartisan alliances. Since Bhave's death, many programs for social reform are still being carried out within the Sarvodaya movement by the *lok sevaks* ("servants of the people") whom he inspired.

SEE ALSO Gandhi, Mohandas.

BIBLIOGRAPHY

Vinoba Bhave wrote relatively few books. However, many of his talks and speeches have been compiled into books and pamphlets. Most of these works are published by the Sarva Seva Sangha. The majority of his writings deal with the Bhoodān and Gramdan movements, but he also wrote on a variety of topics related to Sarvodaya. His major English titles include *Bhoodān Yajna* (Ahmadabad, 1953), *Swaraj Sastra: The Principles of a Non-Violent Political Order*, translated by Bharatan Kumarappa (Wardha, 1955), *From Bhoodan to Gramdan* (Tanjore, 1957), *Thoughts on Education*, translated by Marjorie Sykes (Madras, 1959), *Talks on the Gita* (New York, 1960), *Democratic Values* (Kashi, 1962), and *Steadfast Wisdom*, translated by Lila Ray (Varanasi, 1966).

There are numerous secondary sources on Bhave. For a detailed biography, *Vinoba: His Life and Work* (Bombay, 1970) by Shriman Narayan is considered most authoritative. *Vinoba and His Mission* (Kashi, 1954) by Suresh Ramabhai is less biographical, but it gives a thorough description of the origin and progress of the movement started by Bhave. Vasant Nargolkar's *The Creed of Saint Vinoba* (Bombay, 1963) attempts to analyze Sarvodaya as interpreted by Vinoba. Among recent works, *Selections from Vinoba*, edited by Vishwanath Tandon (Varanasi, 1981), presents the "essential Vinoba." Finally, *Vinoba: The Spiritual Revolutionary*, edited by R. R. Diwakar and Mahendra Agrawal (New Delhi, 1984), presents Vinoba Bhave as others see him. It contains a series of articles by several scholars and close associates of Bhave covering a variety of topics dealing with Vinoba Bhave's thought.

ISHWAR C. HARRIS (1987)

BIANCHI, UGO. Ugo Bianchi (1922–1995) was an Italian historian of religions. Born at Cavriglia (Arezzo) of a Tuscan mother and Roman father who was a parastatal employee, he attended primary and secondary school in Rome. He then studied in the Faculty of Arts at the University of Rome, graduating in 1944 with a degree in the history of religions, under the mentorship of Raffaele Pettazzoni. Subsequently, he completed specialized studies of Roman religion (1947), ethnology (1949–1951) and ancient history (1951–1956) at the same university. After receiving the degree of *libero docente* (teaching qualification for university) in 1954 and a professorship in 1958, Bianchi attained the chair (professorship) of history of religions at the University of Messina (1960–1971). Subsequently, he taught at the University of Bologna (1970–1974) and the University of Rome (1974–1995). Given his deep Christian and Catholic convictions, he was logically chosen for teaching the same discipline at the Università Cattolica del Sacro Cuore in Milan (1974–1991) and religious ethnology at the Urbanian University of Propaganda Fide in Rome (1977–1995). Because of his independence, however, he never became an official figure of the Catholic establishment (although for a short time he was a consultant of the Vatican Secretariat for the Non-Christians).

Bianchi's entire life was dedicated to his family (he married Adriana Giorgi in 1956 and had four children), to the teaching of a host of disciples, to scholarly research, to the elaboration of historically founded typologies (with the cooperation of international specialists convened in conferences), and to the promotion of the study of religions in scholarly organizations both national (he was first secretary and then president of the Società italiana di storia delle religioni for thirty-five years) and international. Elected a member of the International Committee of the International Association for the History of Religions (IAHR) at the organization's 1965 congress at Claremont, California, he became a member of the IAHR executive board in 1975 at the Lancaster, England, Congress after the retirement of Angelo Brelich and Alessandro Bausani. In 1980 at Winnipeg, Canada, he was elected IAHR vice president, and in 1990 he became president of the IAHR at the Rome congress of which he had been the convener. In 1967 and again in 1992 he was involved in events concerning university competitions that caused serious problems in the Italian academy, hampering cooperation among scholars of religion for years to come. These circumstances, however, did not diminish his indefatigable activity. He was a tenacious man with adamantine convictions and a quasi-missionary vocation for organizing the field of religious studies.

OEUVRE. The years between the time he received his first degree in 1944 to the time when he won tenure in 1959 were marked by hectic activity. It was during these years, at the height of the Cold War, that Pettazzoni—a secular scholar who was nevertheless mindful of the autonomy of religious phenomena—left his onerous legacy as historian of religions to the Catholic Bianchi, the communist Ernesto de Martino, and the maverick leftist Angelo Brelich. Bianchi studied cult-related aspects of Roman religion (a minor but never entirely neglected interest in his subsequent activity). But most of all he dedicated himself to investigating fundamental features of theology and mythology in Greece, Iran, and the ancient Near East by pinpointing the three interconnected areas around which he would later focus his reflection: Fate, Humankind, and Godship, as indicated in the subtitle of his first monograph, *Dios aisa* (1953), as well as in the title of his monograph on Zoroastrianism, *Zaman i Ohrmazd* (Time-Fate as determined by the supreme divinity; 1958). At the same time, Bianchi, starting from—but going beyond—the analysis and the results of the Religionsgeschichtliche Schule and of historical ethnology (as practiced by the Vienna and Frankfurt Schools), endeavored to represent "religious dualism" as an almost universal historical typology in the work, *Il dualismo religioso* (1958), which was destined to become a classic in the field.

As a corollary of this wide-ranging research, he produced a type of guide to the history of religions with a title representative of his particular frame of mind, *Problemi di storia delle religioni* (Problems of the history of religion; 1958). The word *problems* is appropriate because each topic is approached in an argumentative manner, even though none is left without answers (answers that generally reflect original views that Pettazzoni regarded as "too personal" (so read the minutes of the competitive exam of 1958 for the professorship). A similar style characterizes the booklet *Teogonie e cosmogonie* (Theogonies and cosmogonies; 1960), which discusses in a cross-cultural key recurrent motifs of mythology (trickster, cosmogonic egg, and so on), in close debate with the views of his predecessors (i.e., Pettazzoni, Mircea Eliade, Leo Frobenius and his school), which he counteracts with proposals of his own. In the following years he had an ever-growing concern for determining a typology of religious phenomena and a methodology of the history of religions.

Besides research on specialized topics, he produces three general surveys that summarize his experience in his respective fields: *Storia dell'etnologia* (History of ethnology; 1964; 2d ed., 1971); *La religione greca* (Greek religion; 1962; 2d ed., 1971); and *The History of Religions* (1975). He dedicated the latter years of his life mainly to promoting conferences on the themes for which he cared most: Gnosticism (1966); Mithraism (1978); the soteriology of Oriental cults in the Roman Empire (1979); asceticism in early Christianity (1982); and the concept of religion (1990). Bianchi had a clear-cut scholarly agenda in mind: he sought papers that avoided both pointless erudition and theoretical verbiage that was not supported by hard evidence. As a result, all of these conferences marked a milestone in their respective fields of scholarly research.

LEGACY. Bianchi applied to the study of religious phenomena the historical-comparative method inherited from his mentor, Pettazzoni, a method that was only partially equivalent to that adopted by his fellow disciples Angelo Brelich (1913–1977), Vittorio Lanternari (1918–), and Dario Sabbatucci (1923–2003). He opposed this method to radical historicism (with its entailed form of reductionism) and phenomenology, both of which have, said Bianchi, "a univocal conception of religion located within a preconceived frame of reference" (1987, vol. 6, p. 400). Instead, according to Bianchi, the frame of reference inside which religious phenomena should be placed and studied is that of a "historical typology of religions," "a multidimensional map of the actual religious terrain" (1987, vol. 6, p. 402). Such a map, if well structured and used with due caution, will prevent the scholar from falling into the double trap set by the a priori constructions of phenomenology on the one hand and the no less a priori reductionism of historicism on the other. What is needed to avoid these opposing traps when approaching religious subjects is recourse to two opposing "holisms." For one thing, the historian of religions must advocate cultural holism; that is, he must, as Bianchi wrote, study all phenomena "within the specific contexts that give them their full meaning" (1987, vol. 6, p. 402). For another, Bianchi continued, he must also take note of religious holism, that is, of "those partial (analogical, not properly univocal) 'religious' continuities which cross, not always in the same direction, the limits of the different cultures" (1991, p. 260).

In practice, Bianchi's method, when applied to an idiographic analysis of historico-religious phenomena, pursued the typically nomothetic aim of providing a very accurate definition of the different kinds of religious experience to be tackled. The first definition at which he worked unceasingly is precisely the definition of religion itself. On the one hand, when his epistemological interest prevails, he defines religion in a merely operative way: religion in itself is an "analogon," not an univocal concept. In other words, Bianchi conceives religion as a "concrete (i.e., historical) universal, studied by history, rather than as a generic universal resulting from a theoretic option" (Bianchi, *History of Religions,* 1975, p. 200; cf. pp. 6 and 214–215). On the other hand, when his existentialist animus emerges, he recurs to an Eliadean formula, religion as "rupture de niveau," (break of level) which he explains as a relationship "with a supra and a prius" (above and before) (*Problemi di storia delle religioni*, 1958, pp. 116–117) or as a concern "with the widespread human tendency to identify a 'beyond'" (1994, p. 920). It is, therefore, tangibly clear that Bianchi's historicist empiricism adjusted itself to a certain amount of a priori hermeneutics, despite his explicit denials.

All the multifarious subjects investigated by Bianchi essentially converged on a single problem: the problem of destiny, evil, and salvation—in other words, the problem of humanity's relationship with God, or theodicy, to which Bianchi dedicated his last course of lectures at Rome University in 1991 and 1992. In his painstaking handling of all the themes connected with this triadic concern, he practically turned his attention to all the religious words of the ancient Mediterranean region, offering meticulous contributions to very specific subjects a synthesis of which is given in his *Prometeo, Orfeo e Adamo* (1976). Most influential was his definition of the category of dualism as a widespread phenomenon with ethnic roots all over the world. Dualism means the doctrine of the two principles that, coeternal or not, cause the existence of that which exists or seems to exist in the world. Despite all the criticisms it has drawn, his typology is still valid in historical research. Also notable, notwithstanding a certain rigidity, is the three-pronged typology that he applied to some conspicuous religious phenomena of antiquity. The triad comprises mysticism, mystery cults, and mysteriosophy, where the last two types are alternative specifications of the first one, which is more inclusive. Last, but not least, the investigation of the origin and definition of Gnosticism is perhaps the topic that, more than any other, made Bianchi famous in the academic world. At the same time, however, it garnered him his harshest criticism.

Bianchi's system for testing and ultimately perfecting his definitions and typologies was gathering around itself senior and junior scholars who might contribute fresh materials and discussions on subjects whose scope Bianchi firmly delimited. During his life he managed to organize as many as thirteen conferences, and he succeeded in having the proceedings of all of them published. In sum, apart from the importance of his personal contribution to the study of Mesopotamian, Iranian, Egyptian, Greek, Roman, and Christian religions, Bianchi has represented in the history of twentieth-century religious studies the figure who advances science using both dialogue and steadfastness as his weapons.

See Also Brelich, Angelo; History of Religions.

Bibliography

The following books of Bianchi can be mentioned: *Dios aisa. Destino, uomini e divinità nel'epos, nelle teogonie e nel culto dei Greci* (Rome, 1953); *Zaman i Ohramzd. Lo zoroastrismo nelle sue origini e nella sua essenza* (Turin, 1958); *Il dualismo religioso. Saggio storico ed etnologico* (Rome, 1958); *Problemi di storia delle religioni* (Rome, 1958; German transl. Göttingen, 1964); *Teogonie e cosmogonie* (Rome, 1960); *Storia dell'etnologia* (Rome, 1964; 2d ed. 1971); *La religione greca* (Turin, 1975); *The History of Religions* (Leiden, 1975); *The Greek Mysteries* (Leiden, 1976); *Prometeo, Orfeo e Adamo. Tematiche religiose sul destino, il male, la salvezza* (Rome, 1976); *Selected Essays on Gnosticism, Dualism and Mysteriosophy* (Leiden, 1978); *Saggi di metodologia della storia delle religioni* (Rome, 1979). He has been the main editor of twelve collectaneous works. To be cited: *Le origini dello gnosticismo* (Leiden, 1967); *Storia delle religioni* (5 vol.; Turin, 1971; still one of the best handbooks of history of religions); *Problems and Methods of the History of Religions* (Leiden, 1972); *Mysteria Mithrae* (Leiden and Rome, 1979); *La soteriologia dei culti orientali nell'impero romano* (Leiden, 1981); *La tradizione dell'enkrateia* (Rome, 1985); *Transition Rites: Cosmic, Social and Individual Order* (Rome, 1986); *The Notion of "Religion" in Comparative Research* (Rome, 1994); *Orientalia sacra urbis Romae. Dolichena et Heliopolitana* (Rome, 1996). See also two articles which are important from the methodological point of view: "History of Religions," in this *Encyclopedia of Religion*; "Between Positivism and Historicism: The Position of R. Pettazzoni," in *Religionswissenschaft und Kulturkritik*, ed. by H. G. Kippenberg and B. Luchesi, Marburg, 1991, pp. 259–263. A complete and well-organized bibliography was compiled by his son Lorenzo Bianchi, "Bibliografia di Ugo Bianchi," in *Ugo Bianchi. Una vita per la storia delle religioni*, edited by Giovanni Casadio (Rome, 2002), pp. 469–496.

In the above-mentioned volume, topics of the history of ancient religions and methodological issues to which Bianchi dedicated his attention are analyzed critically by specialists, disciples and colleagues (e.g., Sanzi, Giuffré, Casadio, Chiodi, Antes, Mander, Panaino, Albanese, Aronen, Pachis, Gasparro, Ciattini, Cerutti, Brezzi, Terrin, Giusti, Spineto, Gothoni). The aim is to contribute to the methodological debate on the study of religion by pointing out the interrelation between the historical data and the motivations behind the interpretive discourse. There are other critical evaluations of aspects of his work and methodology, and more general profiles (especially in the form of obituaries). The following are worth mentioning. Franco Bolgiani, *Il dualismo in storia delle religioni* (Turin, 1974), points out the difficult balance between history and phenomenology in Bianchi's interpretation of dualism. Ursula King, "Historical and Phenomenological Approaches," in F. Whaling (ed.), *Contemporary Approaches to the Study of Religion*, vol. 1, *The Humanities* (Berlin, New York, and Amsterdam, 1984), pp. 83–85 and 97–98, is superficial in her criticism. Aldo Natale Terrin, "Ugo Bianchi," in P. Poupard (ed.), *Grande dizionario delle religioni* (Assisi and Turin, 1988), pp. 215–216, writes from the point of view of phenomenology. Julien Ries, "Un régard sur la méthode historico-comparative en histoire des religions," in G. Sfameni Gasparro (ed.), *Agathe Elpis. Studi storico-religiosi in onore di Ugo Bianchi* (Rome, 1994), pp. 121–148, describes accurately Bianchi's method and sympathizes with it. Likewise, Kurt Rudolph, "In memoriam Ugo Bianchi," *Numen* 42 (1995): 225–227, is unanimous in his approach. Giovanni Filoramo, "In memoria di Ugo Bianchi," *Rivista di storia e letteratura religiosa* 32 (1996): 487–489, is appreciative but with some nuance (see also in

Filoramo and Carlo Prandi, *Le scienze delle religioni*, Brescia, 1997, pp. 57–59 and 305–306). Giulia Sfameni Gasparro, "Ricordo di Ugo Bianchi: tappe di un percorso scientifico," in *Destino e salvezza. Itinerari storico-religiosi sulle orme di Ugo Bianchi*, edited by Gasparro (Cosenza, 1998), pp. 15–36 (see also "Ugo Bianchi and the History of Religions," in *Themes and Problems of the History of Religions in Contemporary Europe*, edited by Gasparro, Cosenza, 2003, pp. 19–30) gives an exhaustive presentation from the viewpoint of a faithful disciple.

GIOVANNI CASADIO (2005)

BIBLICAL EXEGESIS

This entry consists of the following articles:

BIBLICAL EXEGESIS: JEWISH VIEWS

The shift from rabbinic hermeneutics to medieval exegesis is marked by discrimination between different types of interpretation. It has been suggested, though not established, that this occurred, in the Arabic-speaking world, under the impetus of Karaism which, by rejecting the authority of rabbinic tradition, forced proponents and opponents alike to consider the literal meaning of the biblical text. The development of Arabic grammar and rhetoric may also have encouraged systematic study of the literal meaning.

The first major figure of medieval biblical exegesis is the Babylonian rabbinic leader Saʿadyah Gaon (d. 942), who, like his successors, engaged in translation into Arabic and commentary written in the same language. Saʿadyah insisted on literal interpretation, but discussed four circumstances in which deviation from the obvious literal meaning of the biblical text is justified: (1) when the literal meaning contradicts reason (e.g., "God is a consuming fire" [*Dt.* 4:24] must be interpreted metaphorically); (2) when the literal meaning contradicts sense-experience (e.g., Eve was not the "mother of all living beings" [*Gn.* 3:21] but rather the mother of human life); (3) when the literal meaning contradicts another biblical passage (e.g., "Thou shalt not test the Lord" seemingly contradicts "Test me and see," thus necessitating reinterpretation); (4) when the literal meaning contradicts the oral tradition (e.g., "Thou shalt not seethe a kid in its mother's milk" [*Ex.* 23:19, 34:26; *Dt.* 14:21] is to be interpreted in conformity with the rabbinic view that this verse refers to all cooking of milk with meat).

The polemical thrust in Saʿadyah's exegesis manifests itself in various ways. For example, his insistence that *Psalms* is a prophetic rather than a devotional book is meant to controvert Karaite dismissal of rabbinic liturgy as a superfluous innovation.

Saʿadyah and the writers who succeeded him over the next century, under the sway of Islam, were to a great degree eclipsed, whether because they wrote in Arabic rather than Hebrew or as a result of their prolixity, by the popularity of Avraham ibn ʿEzraʾ. In fact, what influence they exerted was largely due to their citation by Ibn ʿEzraʾ. Included among these are commentators like Shemuʾel ben Ḥofni (d. 1013), Yehudah ibn Balʿam, Mosheh ha-Kohen ibn Giqatilla; grammarians like Yehudah ibn Hayyuj and Yonah ibn Janah; and Karaite exegetes like Yefet ben ʿEli, who are generally treated neutrally by Ibn ʿEzraʾ, except with regard to crucial polemical texts such as *Leviticus* 23:15, which divided the Karaites from the Rabbinites.

The peripatetic Ibn ʿEzraʾ wrote on almost all of the Bible, often writing multiple commentaries on the same book, not all of which have been published. Occasionally engaging in philosophical asides (e.g., *Ecclesiastes* 5 and 7), he is nonetheless committed to the straightforward interpretation of the text, governed by the principles of grammar. He is often skeptical of Midrashic elaboration upon the narrative, typically remarking, "If it is a tradition, we shall accept it." Regarding legal matters, he asserts his agreement with the oral law whenever its views are no less plausible than possible alternatives; otherwise, he accepts the oral law only as a normative legal tradition that has been attached to the verse.

The quest for exegetical simplicity led Ibn ʿEzraʾ to criticize some earlier approaches to the text. Thus he rejects Ibn Jannaḥ's view that the same Hebrew word can express contradictory meanings, as well as his willingness to transpose words or to substitute words for those in the text. By the same token, he sees no need to employ the rabbinic listing of *tiqqunei soferim* (euphemistic emendations of phrases referring to God). He is troubled neither by variations of phrase, so long as the meaning is conserved (for example, he considers the differences between *Exodus* 20 and *Deuteronomy* 4 insignificant), nor by orthographical inconsistencies.

Ibn ʿEzraʾ has been regarded as a precursor of the Higher Criticism which began with Barukh Spinoza (1632–1677). Several cryptic passages in his commentary (e.g., on *Gn.* 12:7, *Dt.* 1:2) allude to anachronisms in the Torah that have since been interpreted either as signs of a post-Mosaic hand (as first suggested by Yosef Bonfils in the fourteenth century) or as consequences of prophetic familiarity with the future. Attention has also been given his obscure remarks about the postexilic historical setting of *Isaiah* 40–66.

FRANCO-GERMAN EXEGESIS. The commentary of Rashi (Shelomoh ben Yitsḥaq, 1040–1105) to the Torah is the most influential work of Jewish exegesis. Combining philological sensitivity with generous quotations from rabbinic literature, it became, at the popular level, almost inseparable from the biblical text itself: until the nineteenth century no text of the Pentateuch was published with any commentary that did not include Rashi's as well. Rashi's popularity, as well as his laconic presentation, inspired hundreds of supercommentaries. The most important of these (e.g., Eliyyahu Mizraḥi and Yehudah Löw in the sixteenth century, David ha-Levi in the seventeenth, and the eclectic Shabbetai Bass) constitute a significant contribution to biblical exegesis in their own right. The contemporary leader of Lubavitch Hasidism, Menaḥem Mendel Schneerson, has devoted the lion's share of his voluminous output to an investigation of Rashi's nuances.

Rashi several times distinguishes the literal meaning (*peshaṭ*) from the homiletical (*derash*), identifying his own method, despite its heavy use of *aggadah,* with the former (e.g., on *Gn.* 3:8). His interpreters have generally inferred from this that all comments not explicitly labeled as Midrashic (and perhaps even these) are evoked by some peculiarity in the text that Rashi seeks to resolve. Reworking of and deviation from standard rabbinic exegesis occur both in narrative and in legal passages (for the latter, see, for example, *Exodus* 23:2). In his philology, Rashi is limited by his dependence on those grammarians who wrote in Hebrew (Menaḥem ben Saruq and Dunash ibn Labrat), employing, for example, the doctrine of the two-letter root, later superseded by the idea of a three-letter root. Among Rashi's predecessors, mention must also be made of Menaḥem ben Ḥelbo.

Among Rashi's contemporaries and successors, Yosef Qara᾽ and Shemu᾽el ben Meir (Rashbam) are the most influential. The latter, who was Rashi's grandson, reflected on the innovation in the study of *peshaṭ* (see digression at *Genesis* 37:2): earlier generations, in their piety, had been concerned with the legal and moral lessons of scripture, leaving room for the "ever new facets of *peshaṭ* that are every day discovered." Rashbam is more reluctant than Rashi to erect his exegesis on rabbinic tradition, and he is more prone to seek exegetical alternatives in the legal passages (e.g., his preface to *Exodus* 21). Thus he asserts that day precedes night in *Genesis* 1:5, in contradiction to the halakhic exegetical tradition.

Other Franco-German scholars of note are Yosef Bekhor Shor, Eliʿezer of Beaugency, and Rashbam's brother Yaʿaqov Tam (primarily for his grammatical remarks). Their works were overshadowed by Rashi's and did not enjoy wide circulation. More often republished are various collections of tosafistic exegetical works (e.g., *Daʿat zeqenim*) that are homiletical in nature and often refer to Rashi. Also noteworthy are the many biblical exegetical comments found in *tosafot* to the Talmud. A significant manifestation of biblical study is found in Jewish-Christian polemical literature, such as the anonymous *Sefer nitstsaḥon yashan.*

MEDIEVAL PHILOSOPHICAL EXEGESIS. Philosophical concerns play a role in the work of Saʿadyah (who participates in Kalam philosophy) and the Neoplatonist Ibn ʿEzra᾽. Baḥye ibn Paquda's ethical treatise *Duties of the Heart* and Yehudah ha-Levi's *Kuzari* also contain remarks pertinent to biblical study. It is, however, with the *Guide of the Perplexed* of Moses Maimonides (Mosheh ben Maimon; 1135/8–1204) that the philosophical approach to scripture becomes central. Maimonides' doctrine of religious language leads him to reinterpret anthropomorphisms and anthropopathisms more rigorously than his predecessors. In addition to his interpretations of such sections as *Genesis* 1, *Ezekiel* 1, and *Job,* his concern for the symbolic functions of biblical imagery finds expression in an elaborate doctrine of prophecy and a tendency to allegorize many narratives. Lastly, his views on the "reasons for the commandments" occasionally emphasize the literal sense of the text at the expense of its normative application (e.g., the literalist rationale for the *lex talionis* in *Guide* 3.41), and more than occasionally justify the commandments in utilitarian terms relevant to the historical situation of Israel at the time of Moses (e.g., the purpose of the incense is fumigation of the Temple; many sacrificial and agricultural commandments are intended to counteract idolatrous practices).

The philosophical emphasis in Jewish biblical commentary flourished during the thirteenth to fifteenth centuries. Maimonides' views spread in commentaries on the Prophets and *Psalms* written by both David Kimḥi (known as Radak; early thirteenth century) and Menaḥem Me᾽iri (late thirteenth century) of Provence. His terminology and concerns deeply affect the work of the antiphilosopher Yitsḥaq Arama (early fifteenth century) and the more ambivalent exegete and commentator on the *Guide,* Isaac Abravanel. Maimonides is also discussed by Moses Nahmanides (Mosheh ben Naḥman, thirteenth-century Spain) and the exegetical tradition stemming from him. Yosef Albo's *Sefer ha-ʿiqqarim* (Book of principles), in which the greatest doctrinal affinity is to Albo's teacher Ḥasdai Crescas, a trenchant critic of Maimonides, should be cited for several homiletical sections.

The prolific Yosef ibn Kaspi (fourteenth-century Provence and Spain) displays a Maimonidean interest in the allegorization of prophetic stories (e.g., Jonah and the fish) along with strikingly original speculations (e.g., on the differences between *Samuel, Kings,* and *Chronicles*).

Levi ben Gershom (Gersonides; fourteenth-century Provence), a major Jewish philosopher, and more consistent an Aristotelian than Maimonides, is a major biblical commentator as well. Limiting divine providence, he offered rationalistic explanations of the stopping of the sun by Joshua and maintained that it was not Lot's wife but Sodom that became a pillar of salt. Like Maimonides before him, he interprets the *Song of Songs* as an allegory of God and the individual soul, not, as Rashi and Ibn ʿEzra᾽ did, as an allegory of God's relationship with the Jewish people. Following Maimonides, he unraveled the speeches of Job and his friends as presentations of philosophical positions on providence. Gersonides affixed to his commentaries a list of *toʿaliyyot* ("lessons") to be derived from scripture.

ECLECTIC COMMENTARIES: THIRTEENTH–FIFTEENTH CENTURIES. David Kimḥi combines philological-grammatical perspicuity with liberal quotations from rabbinic literature, discussions of the Targum and its variants, fealty to Maimonides, and references to Rashi, Ibn ʿEzra᾽, Yosef Kimḥi, who was his father, and his brother Mosheh (author of pseudo-Ibn ʿEzra᾽ on *Proverbs* and *Ezra-Nehemiah*). Given the paucity of Rashi on Prophets, it is not surprising that Kimḥi is perhaps the most popular of medieval exegetes on the

Prophets. A polemical contention with Christianity frequently comes to the fore, for example, contra the christological reading of the Immanuel prophecy (*Is.* 7). He evinces serious concern for variations in the received Masoretic text.

Nahmanides, like Rashi, is a major Talmudist who devoted himself to a commentary on the Torah; its impact over the centuries is second only to Rashi's. He attends to philology and law and comments on theological issues and psychological factors. Reaching the Land of Israel in his old age, he is occasionally able to draw upon an acquaintance with its geography and *realia.* A qabbalist, he is the first major commentator in whose work qabbalistic hints are common. Thus, by the fourteenth century, in the aftermath of Maimonides and Nahmanides, we encounter the fourfold division of biblical interpretation—PaRDeS—in which *remez* (hint) and *sod* (esoterica) join the familiar *peshaṭ* and *derash.* Nahmanides frequently quotes and discusses Rashi, particularly in legal sections, less frequently, Ibn ʿEzraʾ, toward whom he adopts an attitude of "open rebuke and hidden love." He cites Maimonides, sometimes lauding his views, but on several crucial matters he disagrees sharply, for example, on the meaning of the sacrificial cult (*Lv.* 1:9) and the role of angels in prophecy (*Gn.* 18:1).

Nahmanides also employs typological interpretation to explain apparent superfluities in *Genesis.* While this method has its roots in Midrash ("the acts of the fathers are a sign for the sons"), it does not enjoy the popularity among Jewish medieval commentators that it attained in Christian exegesis. Of the Spanish commentators of import who flourished in the fourteenth and fifteenth centuries, several were strongly influenced by Nahmanides. Baḥye ben Asher includes a larger quota of homiletical and qabbalistic material. Yaʿaqov ben Asher's *Perush ha-ṭtur ha-arokh* avoids such digressions. Nissim of Gerona, whose *12 Derashot* (Twelve homilies) and commentary to *Genesis* 1–23 are occasionally critical of Nahmanides, nonetheless belongs to his sphere of influence.

Isaac Abravanel (Spain and Italy, d. 1508) represents the last stage of classic medieval commentary. Loquacious in style, he makes liberal use of the work of his predecessors, ranging over the philological, philosophical, and homiletical approaches. His psychological-political sense is keen; his philosophy, while tending toward fideism, is rooted in an extended and passionate involvement with Maimonides' *Guide;* philological originality, however, is not his strong suit. His prefaces to the biblical books are more elaborate than his predecessors', often devoting detailed attention to the authorship and provenance of the text; here he is willing to challenge rabbinic ascriptions, for example, attributing the *Book of Joshua* to Samuel instead of Joshua.

Abravanel makes use of such Christian scholars as Jerome and Nicholas of Lyra. His piety finds clear expression in his eschatological emphasis. Against Ibn Giqatilla, who interpreted most prophecies of redemption as references to the Second Temple period, and Ibn ʿEzraʾ, who took a middle view, Abravanel is eager to read all such prophecies as messianic and is quick to respond to christological interpretations (e.g., *Is.* 7, 34).

The Sixteenth–Eighteenth Centuries. The centuries following the expulsion of the Jews from Spain have been erroneously characterized as a stagnant era for Jewish biblical study. M. H. Segal, in his survey of Jewish Bible study, includes only the *Metsuddat David* and *Metsuddat Tsion* (by the Altschuler family, late seventeenth-century Germany), a generally unoriginal selection from Rashi, Ibn ʿEzraʾ, and Kimḥi that became a standard accompaniment to the study of the Prophets and Hagiographa. Jewish exegesis of this period, unlike that of Rashi, Ibn ʿEzraʾ, Maimonides, and Kimḥi, does not exercise an impact on Christian scholarship. It innovates little of value as regards philology and grammar, beyond the achievements of the medievals (more specifically, the eleventh–thirteenth centuries). Moreover, the lack of willingness to develop alternatives to previous commentaries and rabbinic tradition brings innovation in reading the legal sections to a virtual standstill (despite the isolated examples culled by contemporary scholars). Typical of this change, which reflects the failure of the leading Talmudists of the period to make the Bible a major preoccupation, is Ibn Kaspi's preface to *Exodus* 21, in which he disclaims his own competence and defers to Rashi's exegesis of the legal matters.

Pace Segal, however, one cannot gainsay several contributions of the period. ʿOvadyah Sforno (sixteenth-century Italy), writing on the Torah and other biblical books, stresses both literal and philosophical interpretation. He follows Nahmanides in regarding the stories of *Genesis* as a typological "blueprint" of history. He is particularly concerned about the placement of legal sections among narrative units (e.g., the laws pertinent to the Land of Israel that follow the story of the spies, *Nm.* 15). Other major figures generally present their comments within a homiletical framework, with a not-infrequent mystical tendency. Efrayim of Luntshits's *Keli yaqar,* the work of a sixteenth-century Polish preacher, and the mystically oriented *Or ha-ḥayyim* of Ḥayyim ibn Attar (eighteenth-century Morocco) have become enshrined in many editions of *Miqraʾot gedolot,* the standard rabbinical Bible textbook, as have excerpts from the commentaries of the sixteenth-century Greek preacher Mosheh Alshekh. The aforementioned works find their continuation in nineteenth- and twentieth-century homiletical literature, of which the most outstanding examples are the classic works of the Hasidic movement, such as Yaʿaqov Yosef of Polonnoye's *Toledot Yaʿaqov Yosef* and Elimelekh of Lizhensk's *Noʿam Elimelekh* in the eighteenth century, and *Sefat emet* (by Alter of Gur) or *Shem mi-Shemuʾel* (by Shemuʾel of Sochatchov) in the late nineteenth to early twentieth century.

It should be noted that this period also marks the heyday of the major supercommentaries on Rashi, which apparently offered an outlet to rabbis interested in extending the medieval methods of study.

Traditional Developments in the Modern Period. Beginning in the late eighteenth century there is a renewal of interest, evident from several Torah commentaries, in the interaction between traditional rabbinic exegesis and extra-traditional exegesis. This renewal may derive from increased availabililty of the full panoply of rabbinic exegesis (i.e., *Sifra'*, *Mekhilta'*, *Sifrei*, the Jerusalem Talmud, and eventually *Mekhilta' de Rabbi Shim'on* and *Sifrei Zuṭa'*), which drew attention to hermeneutical results other than those preserved in the Babylonian Talmud. Whatever its sources, it is clearly motivated by a desire to defend the authenticity of the oral law against its skeptical ("enlightened" or Reform) detractors by showing the connection between the "text and tradition" (the title of Ya'aqov Mecklenburg's nineteenth-century commentary *Ketav ve-ha-qabbalah*).

One may distinguish between two types of works produced by these authors. The eastern Europeans, such as Eliyyahu ben Shelomoh Zalman, known as the gaon of Vilna (now Vilnius; d. 1796), Naftali Tsevi Berlin (d. 1892), and Me'ir Simḥah of Dvinsk (now Daugavpils; d. 1926) often present their own novel interpretations. Those who were most exposed to the aforementioned external challenges, in Germany (Mecklenburg and Samson Raphael Hirsch) or Romania (Malbim), are reluctant to propose legal interpretations contrary to tradition. Eliyyahu ben Shelomoh Zalman's treatment of the Bible is displayed in his commentary to *Proverbs*, to sections of other books, and in notes to others. He seeks an integration of all dimensions of Torah study, from the literal to the mystical. This involves the unification of oral and written laws but also precipitates an awareness of the differences between them. As an example of the latter one may point to his comment on *Leviticus* 16, where he recognizes two strata: 1–28 (referring to Aaron and oblivious to the Day of Atonement) and 29–34 (referring to the high priest and specifying the Day of Atonement). Both are, of course, Mosaic: the former pertaining to Aaron's priesthood; the latter, to the period after his death. Like his eastern European successors, he interprets many verses as allusions to the value of Torah study.

Berlin, in his *Ha'ameq davar* on Torah as well as his commentaries to halakhic *midrashim* and the *Shei'ltot* of Aḥa'i Gaon (eighth century), continues to cultivate both the unification and differentiation of *peshaṭ* and *derash*. His work on narrative sections is distinguished by psychological perspicuity that is enhanced rather than diminished by his reliance on the qabbalistic typology that identifies the patriarchs with particular *sefirot*. Me'ir Simḥah's *Meshekh ḥokhmah* is valued both for its insightful homiletical pieces and for his comments on, and alternatives to, classic rabbinic tradition.

Connected with these developments are such works as Barukh Epstein's *Torah temimah,* an anthology of rabbinic material with eclectic notes (1903) and Menaḥem Mendel Kasher's *Torah shelemah,* a heavily annotated encyclopedia work of the same nature. In addition one must note the aforementioned Hasidic exegesis and the homiletical literature produced by the Musar movement (e.g., Natan Finkel's *Or ha-tsafun*), generally interpreting the text in the light of Midrash to derive a lesson illustrative of rigorous moral standards. There is also a quasi-exegetical literature seizing the text as an opportunity for halakhic analysis (e.g., *Beit ha-Levi* by the nineteenth-century Yosef Dov Soloveichik; *Tsafenat pa'aneaḥ* by the early-twentieth-century Yosef Rosin). Samson Raphael Hirsch, who as rabbi in Frankfurt contended with Reform, maintained in his German commentaries to Torah and *Psalms* that the written law was dependent on the oral, as a set of notes is dependent on the lecture. Rabbinic hermeneutic, then, is less a matter of correct philology than of access to a code. In seeking to interpret the text, both narrative and legal, and justify tradition regarding the latter, Hirsch resorted to an idiosyncratic etymological method (occasionally used by Mecklenburg as well), whereby phonetically similar consonants are interchanged in order to locate the "essential" meaning of the word. Hirsch strongly criticized Maimonides' approach to "reasons for the commandments." Instead he offered a system of symbolic interpretation in which, for example, the upper half of the altar represents the higher nature of man, while the lower half symbolizes the lower aspects of human nature. Hirsch's rationales, unlike those dominant in the medieval literature, sought to explain not only the general purpose of the laws but their particular features as well, including those that are derived through rabbinic interpretation.

In contrast with Hirsch, Malbim proclaimed rabbinic hermeneutics to be the correct grammar of biblical Hebrew. From his premise about the perfection of biblical Hebrew he concludes that the Bible contains no redundancies of style or language: every seeming redundancy must be explained. Thus, Malbim (following Eliyyahu ben Shelomoh Zalman and others) discovers many fine distinctions among the synonyms in biblical parallelism, rejecting the approach of Kimḥi and the *Metsuddot* that "the content is repeated in different words." Malbim's identification of rabbinic exegesis with philology is symbolized in his commentary to biblical law, where his independent commentary becomes, instead, a commentary to the corpus of halakhic *midrashim,* insofar as the latter provides the literal meaning of scripture.

Illustrative of the differences between Malbim and some of his major medieval predecessors is his treatment of *qeri* (vocalization) and *ketiv* (Masoretic text). Ibn 'Ezra' had viewed the *qeri* as instructive of how the *ketiv* is to be read. Kimḥi had proposed that *qeri*/*ketiv* in the Prophets generally reflects alternative textual traditions, both of which were retained by the editors ("the men of the Great Assembly") out of uncertainty. Abravanel had gone so far as to suggest that the plethora of *qeri*/*ketiv* in *Jeremiah* derives from that prophet's orthographic deficiencies. For Malbim, however, both *qeri* and *ketiv* are divinely ordained and so must be interpreted.

Both Hirsch and Malbim had enough awareness of biblical criticism to address such problems as the doublets in biblical narrative through literary analysis. They are both oblivious, however, to the data provided by comparative Semitics or knowledge of the ancient Near East. David Tsevi Hoffmann (d. 1922), the last great traditional biblical exegete of western Europe, is fully aware of contemporary biblical scholarship and its ancillary disciplines. In his German commentaries to *Leviticus, Deuteronomy,* and *Genesis* and in *Die wichtigsten Instanzen gegen die Graf-Wellhausensche Hypothese* he marshaled his arguments against non-Mosaic dating of the Torah. A leading Talmudic authority, he concentrated on biblical law, attempting to establish that the laws ascribed to the P and D sources could best be understood within the context of Israel's desert experience, in the order narrated by the Torah, and that these laws were available in their present form during the First Temple period.

Enlightenment and Its Aftermath. The second half of the eighteenth century also marks the entry of Jewish exegesis into the world of general European culture. The founding father of the Jewish Enlightenment was Moses Mendelssohn (d. 1786), whose elegant German translation of the Torah was the first by Jewish hands; the translation was accompanied by a commentary (the *Bi'ur*) authored by Mendelssohn and his associates. This commentary follows in the footsteps of the classical medieval exegetes but is quite conservative in accepting rabbinic tradition regarding the legal sections; it is also concerned with aesthetic features of the text. That the *Bi'ur* was banned in many Orthodox circles had little to do with its content.

Nineteenth-century scholars like the Italian Shemu'el David Luzzatto (d. 1865) accepted the principles of contemporary biblical scholarship—up to a point—reluctant as they were to apply critical results to the text of the Torah. Luzzatto was willing to propose emendations outside the Torah. He stoutly resisted the thesis of postexilic authorship for *Isaiah* 40–66 on internal, not merely theological, grounds (though, by the turn of the century, Hoffmann's Orthodox colleague Jakob Barth recognized internal evidence for the later dating). Resistance to the Documentary Hypothesis continued, beyond Orthodox circles, into the twentieth century. The German Liberal rabbi Benno Jacob insisted on the literary integrity of the Torah and rejected textual emendation. The notes to British Chief Rabbi Joseph Hertz's popular English translation of the Pentateuch contain a lively attack on Higher Criticism. Umberto Cassuto and M. H. Segal, both professors at the Hebrew University in Jerusalem, rejected the Documentary Hypothesis without accepting the Orthodox position: Cassuto spoke of the post-Mosaic writing down of oral traditions, while Segal posited a significant number of interpolations. Their stances have been furthered by their more conservative student Y. M. Grintz. Such views maintain an attraction and influence among Jewish students of the Bible.

Contemporary Trends. Philosophical and literary contributions have also affected contemporary study. Yeḥezkel Kaufmann's insistence on the radical success of biblical monotheism is a theological as well as historical thesis. The literary sensitivity exhibited by Martin Buber and Franz Rosenzweig's German translation, particularly the notion of *Leitworten,* and Buber's own biblical studies have exerted an important influence, as has Me'ir Weiss's method of "total-interpretation." It is too early to assess the impact of Abraham Joshua Heschel's *The Prophets,* André Neher's theological studies, or Joseph B. Soloveitchik's (mostly unpublished) existential homilies.

The last generation has also seen a revival of interest, on the part of Jewish biblical scholars, in traditional exegesis. The teaching and writing of Nehama Leibowitz have made the traditional corpus attractive beyond the Orthodox camp. This development has further encouraged literary and theological concerns. It is not surprising to find scholars like Moshe Greenberg and Uriel Simon who, like Segal before them, combine research in the Bible with research in the history of exegesis. Thus the turn toward literature and, to a lesser extent, theology and the significant place accorded to Jewish exegesis have created a scholarly style that transcends, to some degree, the gap in belief between Orthodox and non-Orthodox.

Within the modern Orthodox community, two developments must be marked. The *Da'at miqra'* series (which does not include the Torah) offers a semipopular commentary that incorporates the data of modern investigations into the framework of traditional scholarship. The somewhat idiosyncratic work of Mordecai Breuer proclaims that the Torah, from a human point of view, speaks in multiple voices whose relation to one another must be clarified, along the lines of Hoffmann. Breuer also seeks to investigate textual variants with an eye to grasping the meaning of the canonized text.

Bibliography

While several modern exegetical works have appeared in Western languages, such as those of Samson Raphael Hirsch and David Hoffmann, which were published in German, most of the primary literature has appeared in Hebrew. However, several primary sources are available in English translation. A mildly bowdlerized translation of Rashi's commentary on the Pentateuch was prepared and annotated by M. Rosenbaum and A. M. Silbermann under the title *Pentateuch with Targum Onkelos, Haphtaroth and Rashi's Commentary,* 5 vols. (New York,1934). C. B. Chavel's *Ramban (Nachmanides): Commentary on the Torah,* 5 vols. (New York, 1971–1976) is a complete and annotated translation of Nahmanides' commentary on the Pentateuch.

Other medieval biblical exegetes whose works have been translated into English include Avraham ibn 'Ezra' on *Isaiah* (*The Commentary of Ibn Ezra on Isaiah,* translated by Michael Friedländer, vol. 1, London, 1873); David Kimḥi's commentary on *Isaiah* (*The Commentary of David Kimḥi on Isaiah* [1926], translated by Louis Finkelstein, reprinted, New York, 1966), as well as his work on *Hosea* (*The Commentary of Rabbi David Kimhi on Hosea* [1929], translated by Harry Cohen, reprinted, New York, 1965), and on *Psalms,* chaps. 120–150 (*The Commentary of Rabbi David Kimḥi on Psalms CXX-CL,* translated by Joshua Baker and E. W. Nicholson, Cambridge, 1973); Levi ben Gershom's commentary on *Job* (*Commentary of Levi ben Gerson on the Book of Job,* translated by A. L. Lassen, New York, 1946).

A complete listing of all editions of exegetical works written prior to 1540 is to be found in M. Kasher and Jacob B. Mandelbaum's *Sarei ha-elef,* 2d ed., 2 vols. (Jerusalem, 1978). Nehama Leibowitz's studies on each book of the Pentateuch have been translated into English and adapted by Aryeh Newman in six volumes (Jerusalem, 1972–1980) and provide an excellent guide to traditional Jewish commentary. Moshe Greenberg's *Understanding Exodus* (New York, 1969) integrates a generous amount of traditional exegesis.

M. H. Segal's *Parshanut ha-miqra',* 2d ed. (Jerusalem, 1971) is a fine survey of Jewish exegesis. Ezra Zion Melamed's *Mefarshei ha-miqra',* 2 vols. (Jerusalem, 1975), covers Rashi, Shemu'el ben Me'ir, Ibn 'Ezra', Kimḥi, Nahmanides, and the exegesis of rabbinic Targum in detail.

Some aspects of exegesis between Sa'adyah and Ibn 'Ezra' are dealt with by Uriel Simon in *Arba' gishot le-sefer Tehillim* (Ramat Gan, Israel, 1982). The exegesis of the medieval Franco-German Jewish scholars is described by Samuel Pozananski in his edition of Eli'ezer of Beaugency's *Perush Yeḥezqe'l ve-Terei 'Asar* (Warsaw, 1909).

An extensive bibliography of recent literature can be found in the *Entsiqeloppedyah miqra'it* (Jerusalem, 1982), in the lengthy entry on biblical exegesis that appears in volume 8 (pp. 649–737).

SHALOM CARMY (1987)

BIBLICAL EXEGESIS: CHRISTIAN VIEWS

Biblical exegesis involves the interpretation, explanation, and exposition of the Bible's various books, in relation either to the time of their composition, or to their meanings for readers in subsequent centuries. The basis of biblical exegesis is translation and the detailed study and explanation of grammatical meaning. It has been linked in the modern period with the elucidation of the historical context of biblical texts, though there is nothing in the word that would confine it to such study. Indeed, the cognate verb (*exegesato*) is found in the New Testament at *John* 1:18, where Christ is described as one who explains or expounds the unseen God (cf. *Heb.* 1:1). *John* 1:18 suggests a definition broader than mere verbal paraphrase or grammatical explanation, as it asserts that the practical demonstration of meaning—through living out the meaning of biblical words—is equally, if not more, important.

Christian exegesis is not a homogeneous entity. There are clearly discernible methodological strands in the history of Christian biblical interpretation, but there are also many features that Christian exegesis shares with other religious traditions (especially Judaism). This has remained so throughout the history of the church. There is not much that can be called distinctively Christian, other than those very deliberate attempts to relate passages from the Hebrew Bible to the person and work of Jesus Christ (e.g., *Matt.* 1:23).

TYPES OF CHRISTIAN EXEGESIS. In the earliest phase of exegesis the main strands of doctrine and ethics were established and we find interpretation oscillating between the contrasting approaches of the literal and the allegorical. In the medieval period much of this polarity was continued, but one major development arose as a result of the interpretation of Apocalypse and the departure from the Augustinian consensus found in the work of Joachim of Fiore (twelfth century) and his successors in which the Bible as whole offered a philosophy of history which reflected the trinitarian nature of God. By the time of the Reformation a distinct preference had developed for the plain sense of Scripture over the manifold meanings that had been worked out in medieval exegesis, itself largely dependent on the work of the patristic period. Scripture, within Protestantism, moved from being one important component in discerning the divine will to become the central means of Christian life and thought. At the Enlightenment, the importance of human experience and intellectual reflection and the expansion of historiography at the time of the Enlightenment reflected a resistance to authoritative texts and institutions, and led to a shift from studying the literal meaning of texts to considering them within their supposed historical contexts.

Literal exegesis. Literal exegesis of scripture is in fact a limited enterprise in which the basic tasks, such as consultation of the best manuscripts and accurate construal and translation of passages in the original, enable a reader to know what the text actually says and means. The task of understanding meaning almost always moves beyond the literal through recourse to analogies, such as parallels drawn from other texts, whether inside or outside the Bible, or through historical reconstruction.

Figurative and allegorical exegesis. There has always been a dialectic between literal interpretation and those forms of interpretation in which another referent becomes a factor. This latter kind of interpretation presupposes that the letter of the text points to another level of reality and other dimensions of meaning. The literal sense of Scripture yields a "deeper," "transcendent" meaning in the contrast between two cities and two covenants (e.g., *Gal.* 4:24). Paul refers to this kind of method in *2 Corinthians* 3:6 as a contrast between the letter and the spirit. Allegorical exegesis, therefore, involves the ability of the interpreter to discern in a piece of biblical text subject matter different from the apparent subject, even though it may be suggested by the latter.

Textual and social context. Context in exegesis can be provided by something as basic as reference to the occurrence of synonyms, or thematic parallels, in a single document or in multiple parts of the Bible. In the modern period, however, context is also understood in a broader sense as, firstly, the situation of the original writer and recipients, and, secondly, the effects of social context on the interpreter. The impact of social situation upon exegesis is something already deeply rooted in Jewish exegesis, as the application of the Torah in new circumstances led to interpretative approaches that either amplified, or were determined by, social context. Consciousness of the extent to which social context influences interpretation has been a feature of all exegesis influenced by the theology of liberation.

From Christian tradition to ancient history. The modern period witnessed a significant shift at the end of the eighteenth century with the rise of the historical method. This meant that a method of interpretation based on the received wisdom of the Christian tradition was over time replaced with a form of interpretation that either had only loose ties to the earlier tradition, or rejected it completely. In the place of traditional exegesis, there emerged an interpretative approach in which the exegesis of specific biblical texts was based primarily on establishing relationships between those texts and others that were contemporaneous with them. The emergence of the historical method as a hegemonic mode of biblical interpretation in the academy and then the church meant that there was a significant caesura with earlier patterns of interpretation. That difference is more apparent than real, however, as some of the underlying interpretations at work are quite similar, in that historical study is driven by a desire to ascertain what really went on and not to rely on what the text actually says.

AUTHORITY. It is because the biblical writings have been deemed to be fundamental for the existence of the Christian religion that their interpretation has been a matter of central significance from the very start. In one important respect, however, largely determined by the form of the biblical material, neither Judaism nor Christianity has been able to resort to their authoritative texts as unambiguous sources of authority in matters of doctrine and ethics. Even legal texts are too imprecise to allow readers to know exactly what is required of adherents: How does one know how to keep the Sabbath holy when all one is give is a general command with little detail regarding what is involved? Much of Jewish tradition is an attempt to relate contemporary circumstance to a tradition of case law and scripture. With its connections to the Jewish Bible so loose, early Christianity could never become a religion of the book. Other factors were always required (tradition, a rule of faith, even charismatic or prophetic inspiration) to guide readers as they sought to use the Bible in connection with their religion.

EXEGESIS AND THE LIFE OF FAITH. In the modern period there has often been a tense relationship between church and academy in regards to the interpretation of the Bible. For most of Christian history the interpretation of the Bible was part of the life of faith. That is not to suggest that it was an uncritical activity. There was, however, a widespread recognition that the interpretation of Scripture was not an end in itself but part of an education in the life of faith. The study of the Bible was for the purpose of hearing God addressing the church and also the individual. A variety of interpretative techniques contributed to the fulfillment of this goal, in order that even the most apparently inhospitable parts of scripture could provide a means whereby the believer could be addressed by God. This is well illustrated by some famous lines that summarize Christian exegesis: "The literal sense teaches what happened, allegory what you are to believe, the moral sense what you are to do, anagogy [interpretation] where you are going" (Nicholas of Lyra, thirteenth century). The point of the interpretation of Scripture is also well illustrated in the following quotation from Augustine's *De doctrina christiana:*

> The student who fears God earnestly seeks his will in the Holy Scriptures. Holiness makes him gentle, so that he does not revel in controversy; knowledge of languages protects him from uncertainty over unfamiliar words and phrases, and a knowledge of certain essential things protects him from ignorance of the significance and detail of what is used by way of imagery. . . . Once close consideration has revealed that it is uncertain how a passage should be punctuated and articulated, we must consult the rule of faith, as it is perceived through the plainer passages of the scriptures and the authority of the church (iii.1).

CHRISTIAN IDENTITY AND THE JEWISH BIBLE. A major issue in nascent Christianity was difference from other Jews and the contrasting interpretations of shared scriptural texts. The messianism which lies at the heart of Christian belief and which stresses qualitative difference and discontinuity always has the effect of downplaying the importance of the past in its preference for the new and the revelatory. The title *New Testament* indicates something of this character. It suggests a relationship to another covenant that is now considered obsolete and underlines the newness of what is being offered (*1 Cor.* 11:25; *2 Cor.* 3; *Heb.* 8–9; cf. *Exod.* 24 and *Josh.* 24). It also reveals a primary concern with the relationship of its convictions to the traditions of the past (see, e.g., *Matt.* 1:1; *Acts* 28:25ff.; *Rom.* 9–11). In early Christian writings this is dealt with in various ways: with Christ comes the "end" (*telos*) of the Law (*Rom.* 10:4), promise and fulfillment (*1 Cor.* 10:11; *Matt.* 1:23), or obsolescence (*Hebrews*). Other passages contrast one dispensation in the divine purposes with the new, decisive one in Christ (*Luke* 16:16), posit essential continuity between Christians and the traditions with the clear assumption that Jews had misunderstood those tradition (*Acts* 7), claim that literal interpretation or application of the Bible is misguided (*Epistle of Barnabas*), or dismiss the Bible as the product of an inferior divinity (Marcion). Because of the belief that the Jewish scriptures found their fulfillment in Jesus, the meaning of the Hebrew text was thereby reduced to a reference to Christ. While there is often the sense that the scriptures have already been fulfilled in Christ and the church, there can also be a degree of open-endedness, such as is found in *1 Corinthians* 9:8–12, in which the biblical text can have an ongoing application to the life of the reader without the fulfillment in Christ closing down interpretative possibilities.

In the New Testament there is a tension between the belief that a messianic deliverer has already come, thereby fulfilling the scriptures, and the belief that the final coming to establish what he has already started is still awaited. This tension is at the heart of much of the theology and interpretation of Christianity and it is this tension, or dialectic, which in various forms can be seen to be characteristic of Christian exegesis down the centuries. It is exemplified in the *Gospel of John* in which tension between past revelation on the one hand and present or future revelation on the other hand is left unresolved in the departing words of Jesus (*John* 14:26; 16:13). The bulk of the Spirit-Paraclete's sayings are retrospective: the Paraclete's role is to point to Jesus, but there is some evidence of continuing inspiration (e.g., *John* 16:13). In Christian history there have always been many movements that have stressed the importance of present inspiration in preference to the patient interpretation of words from the past. One such was Montanism, which in the second century claimed to represent the ongoing activity of the Spirit-Paraclete in their own prophetic activity—and was thereby the pioneer of many similar claims throughout the history of the church (e.g. in the claims to new revelation and spiritual renewal found in the radical Franciscan movement of the thirteenth century and in the Radical Reformation). In Christian exegesis there is a constant dialectic between the announcing of something new and the fact that what is new is going to follow the contours of what has been said and done by Jesus. This retrospective element has always pushed Christian interpreters back to their scriptures and to the events to which they bear witness. The importance of that underlying historical referent has always been a matter for debate: Did it matter whether the events described actually took place, or is the story itself of value as a means of moral or spiritual improvement? Such matters were central to debates between emerging Christian orthodoxy, whose adherents wanted to hang onto the historical referent, and those who saw the words themselves as of more existential than historical import.

There is obviously a close relationship between the theological ideas and practices outlined in the New Testament and what one finds in the Hebrew Bible. The extent of the relationship has been a mater of debate, however. There are those who maintain that one cannot understand the New Testament without an intimate knowledge of the original context of elements taken from the Hebrew Bible, whereas others assume that the original context of material alluded to does not determine the meaning of a New Testament passage. The evidence suggests that New Testament writers were much more constrained by their convictions about the new life in Christ than by the actual details of the text of the Hebrew Bible. The scriptural texts are made to serve the emergence of a different kind of religion. Scriptural passages had become part of a different religious system, which subtly shifted the meaning of the original scriptural texts. Christians gave Scripture a new meaning, appropriate to their own time, reusing it in new and creative ways, to provide a way of understanding present experience that could be at variance with the Scriptures' original purpose. The New Testament writers (and even more so their readers) were not, therefore, engaged in an exegesis of the Scriptures detached from the practice of faith. Earlier scriptures had to be read in the light of convictions about Jesus Christ. God spoke directly through Spirit in revelations (*1 Cor.* 14:26), and Scripture and tradition provided a secondary support for insight obtained by other means.

The Foundations. The earliest Christian interpretations of the Bible take many forms. The true meaning of the text is demonstrated in relation to the key stories of the emerging Christian tradition (e.g., *Matt.* 1:23). This has its analogies in the Jewish interpretative tradition as is evident in treatment of the Dead Sea Scrolls, especially the Habakkuk Commentary (1 Qp. *Hab.*), in which the meaning of the prophetic oracles, opaque to the original writer, is now revealed to an inspired interpreter. An apologetic, Christological concern became a hallmark of attempts—from the writings of Justin (second century) onwards—to prove that the Christian message had its origins in the prophetic material of the past.

Typology and allegory were both used to serve these ends. Typology is the juxtaposition of types (including people, institutions, or events), and is employed in exegesis when a biblical scene or figure is taken up and viewed as an interpretative analogy for a contemporary belief or practice. The relationship between type and antitype is suggested by the accumulation of points of correspondence between two (or more) narratives. The type and the antitype are not identical and cannot be one and the same person, institution, or event, since, by definition, typology is describing one thing in terms of another. The correspondences can be based on difference as well as similarity. Thus Paul in *1 Corinthians* 10 can see an analogy between what had happened to the disobedient people of Israel in the wilderness and the Corinthian Christians with whom he has to deal. The type functions, therefore, as a warning to readers not to pursue a path similar to that followed in the original story. Typological exegesis became a favorite device as analogies between the Old and New Testaments were taken up as a way of asserting divine providence.

Allegory differs from typology in one key respect. Whereas typology depends for its success on the interplay between figures or incidents—Isaac and Christ, for example, or the serpent lifted up by Moses versus the Son of man being lifted up in *John* 3:14—allegory opens up another, "deeper" level of meaning latent within a text's literal sense. In the complex reference to allegorical exegesis made by Paul in *Galatians* 4:24, the Sarah-Hagar story of *Genesis* 16 and 21 becomes a gateway into another understanding: what the text really means is that the two women represent two covenants or two cities, Sinai and the new covenant, or two cities, the Jerusalem below and the Jerusalem above. The literal sense of the text in allegorical exegesis becomes a signifier of another dimension of meaning. This device, already thoroughly explored in the writings of the Jewish philosopher Philo Judaeus (first century CE), has been taken up by Christian writers down the centuries as they seek to find meaning in some of the most unlikely and problematic places in the scriptures.

In the New Testament there is a concerted attempt to offer a reading of the Hebrew Bible that challenges the accepted understanding of its meaning. What Paul offers in the *Letter to the Galatians,* for example, is a reading of the Abraham story that harnesses it to the convictions of a minority community as it struggles for its identity. The true children of Abraham are not the Jewish nation (which turns out to be the children of Hagar, who is ejected from Abraham's home). The Christians are the children of promise (*Gal.* 3:29). In this approach to the *Genesis* account we see a way of entering into the Scriptures that becomes central for subsequent interpretation. What is essential for interpreting the biblical text is not so much attention to the details, as it is the fundamental conviction that experience of the Christ is the foundation on which the text should be read (*2 Cor.* 3:6).

Such attitudes are paralleled elsewhere in the New Testament, not least in the deconstruction of the sacrificial system in the *Letter to the Hebrews* and particularly in the early-second-century text the Letter of Barnabas, in which an acceptance of Jewish laws and institutions as literal expectations of the divine will is rejected in favor of figurative interpretation. There were similar radical rereadings of the Bible in the Gnostic texts, in which there emerged a complete rejection of the theological value of the Jewish scriptures, which were seen as the product of some lesser divine being. The Christian church rejected such a radical solution, and yet the roots of such radicalism lie deep within the New Testament. Because the early Christian writers continued to use the Hebrew Bible, however freely, in the service of their ethics and community identity, rather than relying solely on present revelation and authoritative advice, the Jewish scriptures became a fundamental focus of the emerging theological tradition, albeit in a manner in which literal interpretation was always subordinated to the figurative.

As we have seen, from the very beginning of Christian exegesis the Jewish scriptures were mined to enable readers to understand that what had happened in Jesus had been predicted by ancient writers in the divinely inspired scriptures. Thus, we find that the famous description of the suffering prophetic figure in *Isaiah* 53 is seen in *Acts* 8:32–34 and *1 Peter* 2:21–23 as a prediction of the sufferings of the messiah. The appeal to the Bible was not unproblematic, however, as the way in which passages were interpreted by Christians, as referring either to their identity as the people of God or to the events of Christ's life, was rejected by most Jews. Whatever its exact relationship to history, the Dialogue of Justin with Trypho represents the Christian side of the debate: in it, a Christian writer seeks to prove why it is that contemporary Jewish interpretation of the shared scriptures is misguided. The second century proved to be a critical one for Christian attitudes toward what would later be termed the Old Testament. The relativizing of its significance in parts of the New Testament, such as the *Letter to the Galatians* and the *Letter to the Hebrews,* inevitably raised the question of whether the scriptures had much or indeed any importance for the new revelation. In the mid-second century this question was raised with peculiar clarity by Marcion of Sinope (d. c. 160), who not only contrasted the two revelations but also formed a collection of authoritative writings to support the superiority of the new revelation in his Gospel (the *Gospel of Luke*) and Apostle (a collection of Paul's letters which omitted the Pastoral Epistles). Later judgments of Marcion have been based on the polemic of his opponents (as none of his own writings are extant). Marcion picked up on important themes in the New Testament (not least in *Acts* 7) and in texts like the *Epistle of Barnabas* to argue the qualitative difference of the revelation in Christ. This view has always been an integral part of Christian exegesis. Marcion's opponents in the emerging orthodoxy refused, however, to let go of the Jewish scriptures as an essential framework for the Christian message and for the understanding of salvation history.

The tradition of figurative and allegorical exegesis was pioneered in particular by Origen (c. 185–254), one of the founders of the Alexandrian school of exegesis. Despite his reputation as an allegorical exegete, Origen was a careful philologist, who made use of the best critical methods of his day (as evidenced, for example, in his Hexapla, a critical comparison of different versions of the Old Testament). In many ways, he anticipates modern exegesis. For all his critical brilliance, however, Origen was not interested in philological or historical analysis for its own sake, but in how it could serve a more important goal: the training of the soul so as to lead it back to God. He emphasizes the *usefulness* of Scripture, that is, how it can benefit the human soul. Origen sees the Scriptures both as a record of God's revealing himself to the saints in the past and as the locus of divine pedagogy in the present, the way the divine Logos addresses individual souls and gradually leads them up to perfection. In *On First Principles* 4:1–3, he speaks of three different levels of meaning in scripture: literal, moral, and allegorical—corresponding to body, soul, and spirit (*1 Thess.* 5:23). The most important meaning is the spiritual. Not all Biblical texts exist on all three levels, but all have a spiritual meaning. The Holy Spirit deliberately places difficulties in the text in order to point the reader toward the spiritual meaning, and this meaning can be understood only with the help of divine assistance—the interpreter must have the "mind of Christ" (*1 Cor.* 2:16).

The excesses of allegorical interpretation led to a significant reaction. Followers of the so-called Antiochene school of exegesis (e.g., Theodore of Mopsuestia, c. 350–428) sought to drag Christian biblical interpretation back to the letter of the text. Antiochenes had a concern with literal sense that included reference to historical context as well as purely spiritual exposition. This concern with literal sense was affirmed in medieval exegesis by exegetes such as Hugh of Saint-Victor (d. 1142), who in his *Didascalion* stressed literal meaning, reference to Jewish history, and the Hebrew text of the Bible (he also worked out elaborate techniques for memorization and the imaginative meditation on Scripture). Origen's influence is evident in the exegetical work of Jerome who developed facility in Hebrew. An important example of early Christian interpretation is Augustine's *De doctrina christiana,* in which both literal and figurative exegesis are discussed, along with the need for criteria in determining between readings of biblical texts.

The issue of criteria soon became important in the developing tradition of Christian exegesis, particularly as emerging orthodoxy sought to distinguish its own approach to Scripture from rival interpretations. Appeal to visionary experience, such as we find in Paul's *Letter to the Galatians* (1:12–16), was declared inadequate by the orthodoxy, even as secret revelation as a source of authority became a favorite means in what have come to be known as *Gnostic* scriptures. In the face of conflicting interpretations of the Scriptures, there emerged the *rule of faith,* a concise summary of the basic articles of the faith, the origins of which can be found in New Testament passages.

As in Jewish exegesis (for example, the rules [*middoth*] attributed to Hillel), Christian interpreters formulated exegetical rules to assist with interpretation and to set the bounds of interpretative possibility. Often these were formulated in connection with the interpretation of Apocalypse, which throughout the history of interpretation had presented problems for interpreters because of the allusiveness of its figurative language. The earliest set of exegetical rules was developed by Tyconius, the great fifth-century Donatist exegete. The exegesis of Tyconius had a profound effect on Augustine: Tyconius claims that a biblical text has a dual perspective, as is appropriate for a Bible with two testaments. His interpretation of Apocalypse and his general biblical interpretation were closely intertwined. The seven interpretative rules outlined in his *Book of Rules* allow the possibility of multiple references in Scripture. For Tyconius, the biblical text is a tool that facilitates moral and spiritual discernment. His method allows him to apply even obviously eschatological passages to the present life of the church as present and future are always mingled. Seeing the world as divided into two opposed societies, he finds references this duality throughout Scripture. The struggle between the demonic and the divine is evident in both the individual and society.

The Reformation saw a reaction against dominant trends in exegesis that in some ways resembled the earlier reaction against the allegorical exegesis of Origen. John Calvin's (1509–1564) commentaries take up grammatical and historical matters, with careful attention paid to context. Martin Luther's (1483–1546) interpretative concerns are more overtly theological and interpretative, as he sought to find a basic principle for interpreting scripture. The emphasis on the letter of the text as opposed to deeper spiritual or moral readings forms the heart of the protestant reaction to the exegetical methods that had been developed over centuries. This reaction often took the form of a vigorous rejection of the variety of exegetical methods. Luther stressed the importance of the plain statement of the gospel, with what constituted the heart of the Christian message and by which all else in the Bible and Christian interpretation should be judged. For him the letters of Paul and the Gospel of John offered the essence of Scripture. On the radical wings of the Reformation Anabaptist, interpreters like Hans Denck (1495–1527) went further and anticipated the modern tendency to question the propriety of obedience to the letter of the text of the Bible as the cornerstone of the Christian religion in favor of engagement with the spirit of the text—which suited their conviction that scripture was only a witness to the Living Christ at work in the hearts and lives of all people.

With the coming of the Enlightenment, a significant shift occurred away from the long tradition of interpretation based on ecclesiastical teaching, towards a focus on historical contextualization that drew on ancient texts written contemporaneously with the Bible. There are a variety of reasons for this change. A move away from reliance on the Vulgate necessitated knowledge of Greek literature to enable the translation of biblical texts. The Christian tradition of Hebrew scholarship led to an appreciation of the value of certain parts of the corpus of rabbinic literature, whether for apologetic or illustrative purposes. The awareness of the different manuscript traditions of the Greek Bible emerged and with it a realization that the Holy Scriptures were a mélange of texts with a multitude of differences. This was accompanied by a growing interest in texts that were contemporaneous with the New Testament. Thus, for example, the Apocalypse of Enoch, brought back from Ethiopia, where it had been preserved by the Ethiopian Church, was first published at the beginning of the nineteenth century. The points of contact of parts of this book with the New Testament gospels has meant that it has been a pivotal text in New Testament exegesis ever since.

By far the most important aspect of Enlightenment thinking, in relation to the ways in which biblical text was interpreted, was the growing suspicion of authoritative institutions. The primacy of history and human reason as a basis for theology led to a very different enterprise which needed to be undertaken from first principles. It was no longer sufficient to accept the Bible's authority on the basis of tradition, as it too needed to be vindicated by human reason. This new attitude, when taken in the context of philological and historical developments, led to a growing recognition that the parts of the Bible were historically various and by no means homogenous.

The interpretation of the Pentateuch, for example, represents a typical feature of Enlightenment criticism. Recognition of differences and tensions within the text of *Genesis* did not only start with modernity. Philo Judaeus in the first century CE noted the differences between the creation narratives (*Gen.* 1 and 2 in his *Allegorical Interpretation of the Laws*). Such differences provided him with a reason to engage in a theological disquisition, rather than tempting him to offer an explanation that resorts to source criticism. The modern interpreter would explain the differences as stemming from the collation of texts coming from very different periods and with multiple sources and different agendas. Thus, *Genesis* 1 is an account of the creation which represents the interests of priestly groups at the time of the Exile in Babylon in the sixth century BCE, whereas the creation in *Genesis* 2 is a story which emerged in the court of the Judean kings three or four centuries earlier.

Enlightenment biblical criticism further considered questions that had been raised for centuries about different parts of Scripture (for example about the Pauline authorship of *Hebrews* and the Johannine authorship of the Apocalypse). Differences between texts that were attributed to Paul, particularly the difference in vocabulary and tone between the so-called Pastoral Epistles (*1* and *2 Tim.* and *Titus*) and the mainstream Pauline texts like *Romans* 1 and 2 *Corinthians* and *Galatians,* led to questions being raised about Pauline authorship of the former. Similarly apostolic authorship of the gospels was widely questioned, with the central problem being the difference in style, chronology, and content between the first three gospels (often called the Synoptic Gospels because their material can be examined "synoptically" in parallel columns) and the Gospel of John. This problem remains at the heart of modern criticism and the understanding of the relationship between the two streams of tradition seems scarcely any nearer resolution.

Typical of modern historical interpretation has been the fascination with the search for the real Jesus behind the gospel narratives. G. E. Lessing (1729–1781) published the fragments of a work on reason and the Bible by H. S. Reimarus (1694–1768), which helped initiate a new age in interpretation of the gospels. While the variety of attempts to recover the Jesus of history has been testimony to the ongoing interest in the subject, there has been a basic similarity in the kinds of portraits that have been constructed. Such portraits have often involved sophisticated source analysis, and a concerted attempt to reconstruct the earliest writings of Christianity that bear witness to Jesus.

The basic outlines of the various modern interpretations of the historical Jesus were already in place by the beginning of the twentieth century. There have been three major ways of construing the Jesus of history in the modern period. First (and most venerable, as it is the hypothesis of Reimarus) is the view that Jesus was a Jewish messianic pretender, whose attempts to bring about God's kingdom on earth led to his execution at the hands of the Romans. Second is the view that Jesus was a prophet of the end of the world. Third is the picture of Jesus as a teacher, or holy man, who was part of a nonconformist fringe in Second Temple Judaism.

Interest in history led to another important development in modern interpretation. The various texts seemed to open a window onto the life and disputes of the religious communities which produced them and to whom they were addressed. Thus, in the Hebrew Bible the period of the Exile, when the elite of Jerusalem ended up in forced exile in Babylon, was seen as a period of great soul-searching and intellectual creativity—during which the traditions of the past were examined and systematized and the disasters of previous decades understood in the light of the primary theological convictions. In the New Testament the hints of difficulties that emerge briefly in Paul's letters were regarded as a symptom of an underlying tension between different strands of Christianity in the earlier period. In the hands of Ferdinand Christian Baur and his Tübingen school of the mid-nineteenth century, these hints revealed tensions between a form of Christianity linked with Peter and James, which maintained the basic contours of Jewish practice, and a different form of religion pioneered by Paul, which has a looser relationship to Jewish law. Here conflict was the motor of religious development, a concept in part inspired by Hegelian views of history. The various books in the New Testament could be plotted according to where they stood in this ideological struggle, or, as in the case of texts like Luke and Acts, how they contributed to the reconciliation between these antithetical positions.

This kind of exegesis of biblical texts has provided the basis of much modern interpretation. Literary remains form the basis of imaginative reconstructions of the life of communities. Characters in narratives become ciphers for different groups. In this approach the fabric of the text and its form become a kind of window through which (with varying degrees of distortion) the situation behind the text, that other story which allegory seeks to expose, can be laid bare. The gospels contain indications that we cannot read them without attention to another level of meaning (*Matt.* 28:15 is a good example). It is that other story which an interpretation suspicious of the credibility of religious texts, for whatever reason, has been intent on laying bare.

In another respect the contrasting emphasis between the words and that to which they bear witness has been a thread that links the first century and the modern world. The two giants of modern biblical interpretation, Karl Barth and Rudolf Bultmann, differed over the emphasis they gave to the words of scripture. The former saw them as witnesses to the Divine Word who in some way stood behind the text (e.g. *Church Dogmatics* 1/1: 125–6), whereas Bultmann considered that the words themselves were the very medium of that meeting with the Divine Word. There has always been a need to move beyond the detail of the text to grasp the essential thrust of the texts' meaning. In modern criticism this has taken a very distinctive turn. *Sachkritik* is a form of interpretation in which a reading of a text is offered in the light of what its modern interpreter deems to be its essential subject matter: the interpreter, therefore, tells us what the text is really about. Thus, the interpreter grasps the nature of the book and by focusing on particular verses to interpret the whole, offers other readers insight into what the critic considers the fundamental subject matter.

Another distinctive aspect of the Enlightenment's historical study of the Bible, and one that, arguably, has thrown the most light on its interpretation, was the location of the Bible in the study of the history of religions. Much of this study has concentrated on the history of ideas, so that biblical creation myths are compared with those from Babylonia, or the gospel parable with the multitude of examples that are to be found in the corpus of Jewish rabbinic literature. What emerged in the last decades of the twentieth century, however, was a greater concern with the social implications of those ideas. With the emergence of a Marxist approach to the study of ideology, less emphasis has been placed on the influence of individual ideas and more on social movements and the complex interests and power relations which lead to the triumph of particular ideas and of particular social and economic forces that supported them. Thus, critic Karl Kautsky's (1854–1938) work on the origins of Christianity differs markedly from much mainstream biblical exegesis in the way in which he tries to interpret the early Christian texts within the context of the socioeconomic history of the Greco-Roman world.

In an environment in which the human origin of biblical texts was being asserted more and more, there was a need to reassert their divine authority, particularly in the case of Protestants, for whom the central authority of the Bible was crucial for the maintenance of religious community. In one sense, of course, the authority of the texts themselves was common to both sides of the argument. The extraordinary character of the engagement with the Bible was a recognition of its authority and of its dominance in culture and theology. However, a stronger argument for biblical authority was necessary to justify a subservience of human will to the letter of Scripture. Some conservative views of the inspiration and authority of the Scriptures maintain the infallibility of the words of human authors as the means by which Almighty God chose to communicate with humanity, thereby guaranteeing the necessity of human interpreters to attend to the exact meaning of these words as the vehicle of divine truth.

So far nothing has been written explicitly about hermeneutics and yet the preceding pages have all been about hermeneutics. Hermeneutics is the study of the principles of interpretation, and is best used as a way of describing a critically reflective activity concerned with the interpretation of texts. The interpretation of the Bible has played a significant if not central role in the history of hermeneutics, as the reflection on reading and interpretation of texts (or for that matter any artifact) was given impetus by discussions about the authority of the Bible, and by questions raised by its interpretation. From the very start of Christian exegesis, hermeneutics was a vital issue, as the early Christians sought to understand their own relationship with the scriptures that they shared with the Jews. Modern hermeneutics has become largely independent of biblical interpretation, however, even if it owes its origins to debates about the interpretation of the Bible. Key interpreters like Paul Ricoeur and Hans Georg Gadamer (1900–2002) have recognized the importance of the interpretation of the Bible in the history of critical reflection on the different ways of reading.

There has been a gradual recognition that the history of influence has a crucial part to play in the understanding of Christian exegesis of the Bible. The important work of Gadamer has stressed the way in which any reading contains within it some traces of the previous history of the interpretation of that text. The understanding of the original setting of the text has always, therefore, to be seen within the context of the contribution of culture and received wisdom as that which has conditioned the present form of interpretation. A glance at most modern interpretations of biblical texts reveals how little attention is given both to the pre-Enlightenment interpretation of these texts and to the wider cultural appropriation of the texts in non-religious writing and other media, which collectively exhibit an influence whose importance for exegesis should not be neglected. In reaction, there have arisen a variety of attempts to reacquaint exegesis with the history of interpretation and the history of the effects of the text, as both are seen as crucial components of the exegetical task. This has in part been an appeal to tradition (though the appeal to tradition is always double-edged as tradition itself, like the notion of what is a classical text, is a highly controverted concept). An openness to the varieties of effects of biblical texts also puts Christian exegesis in touch with wider intellectual currents in the humanities, so that literature, art, and music become part of its purview.

There have been moves away from the preoccupation with biblical text as witness to ancient history and toward an engagement solely with the text itself—with its structure and form and with the issues that the readers themselves bring to their interpretation. This reflects a suspicion of the difficulties attendant on much of the historical reconstruction that has been regarded as an indispensable basis for exegesis. It has led to interpretations in which the text itself is deemed to be the focus of meaning, without reference to external sources of comparison. This kind of textual analysis does not take into consideration any data external to the text, such as the intention of the author or the nature of the likely audience, any events to which the text refers, or the sources which might lie behind the text as we now have it. In this kind of interpretation the exposition of a text's meaning is worked out through contrasts and connections within the text, through the exploration of characters and the way they interact.

Another reaction to historical exegesis appeared in the last decades of the twentieth century with the emergence of a variety of contextual theologies in the developing nations, and with the formation of an influential feminist interpretation. It should be noted that to label this kind of theology *contextual* is to make a false distinction between supposedly neutral exegesis and committed exegesis, as all interpretation has a context and a tradition of interpretation which conditions its approach. What has emerged in liberationist exegesis and feminist and related interpretations is a conscious avowal of the importance of the ways in which readers' contexts determine exegesis.

Liberation theology emerged from Roman Catholic theology based on the Second Vatican Council, and the encyclicals associated with it. It developed in the context of the emergence of the Basic Ecclesial or Christian Communities (the CEBs). In the basic communities the Bible has become a catalyst for the exploration of pressing contemporary issues. Understanding the Bible takes place in the dialectic between the Bible as a witness to the memory of the struggles for justice of the people of God on the one hand and the issues of the contemporary world on the other. Thus, the emphasis is not placed on the text's meaning in itself, but rather on the meaning the text has for the people reading it. It is an interpretation that is passionate and committed and challenges a widespread view that exegesis is primarily about letting the text speak for itself, unencumbered by contemporary issues. Connections are made between contemporary demands and bible stories. This can take various forms. Bible study can go straight to the text with no concern for its original historical context. This method Clodovis Boff describes as an example of *correspondence of terms*, in which persons or events function in a kind of typological relationship with scriptural analogies. Alternatively, bible study may also include outlines of the historical and social contexts of biblical texts, so that the struggles facing the people of God at another time and place may be discerned. The experience of poverty and oppression is regarded as being as important a text as Scripture itself. In this approach to the Bible, which is rooted in the needs of the people, there emerges an authentic Christian praxis leading to the transformation of society. So, exegesis is not neutral, and participation in the struggle for a better life is key to the discovery of the meaning of texts. Practice itself stimulates understandings that would only with difficulty have emerged through the calm reflection of academy or church. The implication is that academic analysis might not, in some instances at least, offer the best or most appropriate understanding of a text, and that one who is engaged in the struggle for political justice for the poor and outcast might, in certain circumstances, better capture the spirit of the text. This way of reading the Bible has affinities with earlier methods in the opportunity offered for an imaginative interface between the biblical text and the existential situation of the interpreters.

The exponents of this kind of exegesis, which stresses the conscious recognition of the events of one's life and the circumstances in which one lives as ingredients in the exegetical process, attach great interpretative importance to the fact that what one undergoes and learns thereby informs the understanding of the text. In different ways this has been key to all kinds of feminist exegesis and Black Theology. Sometimes this has led to a much more critical attitude towards the liberative value of the text. Using historical tools of analysis, liberationists have sought to disentangle and describe the ways in which the liberative traditions in the Bible have been taken up and employed by the elite in the service of a more repressive and restrictive religion, whose effects on society have been deleterious and from which an enlightened, liberative reading can hope to emancipate people. Feminist exegesis, for example, has patiently explored the occasional inclination in the texts to reclaim the voice of women in historical situations in which women were denied or were losing power. Such liberative approaches have many antecedents long before the twentieth century where interpretation of the Bible has been at the heart of struggles for justice among radical groups throughout the history of the church.

Christian exegesis of the Bible at the beginning of the twenty-first century is increasingly polarized. The principal positions, however, share much in common with earlier approaches in the history of exegesis. On the one hand, there is an appeal to the letter of the Bible as the basis for doctrine and ethics. On the other hand, there is a willingness to allow for a modern interpretative framework in which the insights of the modern world are given their theological due. Appeals to Christian exclusivism appear ever more fragile in an increasingly multicultural world. Nevertheless, the claim to exclusiveness underlying the key element of Christian doctrine, the coming of the messiah in the person of Jesus, seems to leave little room for debate. In one respect, however, the New Testament does leave open the door for a more liberal and inclusive approach. Fundamental to the understanding of the Christian revelation is the belief that Christians live by faith, not by sight, and that in this age one "sees in a glass darkly" and not yet "face to face." That suggests the possibility of an approach to difference that may seem excluded by some of the more assertive claims of contemporary Christianity.

BIBLIOGRAPHY

Barr, James. *Holy Scripture: Canon, Authority, Criticism.* Oxford, 1983.

Barton, John. *People of the Book? The Authority of the Bible in Christianity.* London, 1988.

Bauman, Clarence. *The Spiritual Legacy of Hans Denck: Interpretation and Translation of Key Texts.* Leiden, 1991.

Boff, Clodovis. *Theology and Praxis: Epistemological Foundations.* Translated by Robert R. Barr. Maryknoll, N.Y., 1987.

Bradstock, Andrew, and Christopher Rowland. *Radical Christian Writings: A Reader.* Oxford, 2002.

The Cambridge History of the Bible. Vol. 1, *From the Beginnings to Jerome*, edited by Peter Ackroyd and Christopher Francis Evans; vol. 2, *The West from the Fathers to the Reformation,* edited by G. W. H. Lampe; vol. 3, *The West from the Reformation to the Present Day*, edited by S. L. Greenslade. Cambridge, U.K., 1963–1970.

Carruthers, Mary. *The Book of Memory: A Study of Memory in Medieval Culture.* Cambridge, U.K., 1990.

Ebeling, Gerhard. *Luther: An Introduction to His Thought.* Translated by R. A. Wilson. London, 1972.

Fowl, Stephen E., ed. *The Theological Interpretation of Scripture.* Oxford, 1997.

Gottwald, Norman K., and Richard A. Horsley. *The Bible and Liberation: Political and Social Hermeneutics.* Maryknoll, N.Y., 1993.

Houlden, J. L., ed. *The Interpretation of the Bible in the Church.* London, 1995.

Kovacs, Judith, and Christopher Rowland. *Revelation: The Apocalypse of Jesus Christ.* Oxford, 2004.

Kümmel, Werner Georg. *The New Testament: The History of the Investigation of Its Problems.* Translated by S. McLean Gilmour and Howard C. Kee. London, 1973.

Lubac, Henri de. *Medieval Exegesis: The Four Senses of Scripture.* 2 vols. Translated by Mark Sebanc and E. M. Macierowski. Grand Rapids, Mich., 2000.

McGinn, Bernard. *The Calabrian Abbot: Joachim of Fiore in the History of Western Thought.* London, 1985.

McKim, Donald K. *Historical Handbook of Major Biblical Interpreters.* London, 1998.

Metzger, Bruce M. *The Canon of the New Testament: Its Origin, Development, and Significance.* Oxford, 1987.

Morgan, Robert, with John Barton. *Biblical Interpretation.* Oxford, 1988.

Murray, Stuart. *Biblical Interpretation in the Anabaptist Tradition.* Kitchener, Ont., Canada, 2000.

O'Neill, J. C. *The Bible's Authority: A Portrait Gallery of Thinkers from Lessing to Bultmann.* Edinburgh, 1991.

Pagels, Elaine. *Adam, Eve, and the Serpent.* London, 1988.

Thiselton, Anthony C. *New Horizons in Hermeneutics.* Grand Rapids, Mich., 1992.

Young, Frances M. *Biblical Exegesis and the Formation of Christian Culture.* Cambridge, U.K., 1997.

CHRISTOPHER ROWLAND (2005)

BIBLICAL LITERATURE

This entry consists of the following articles:

HEBREW SCRIPTURES
APOCRYPHA AND PSEUDEPIGRAPHA
NEW TESTAMENT

BIBLICAL LITERATURE: HEBREW SCRIPTURES

The terms *Hebrew scriptures* and *Hebrew Bible* are synonyms here restricted to that received, definitive corpus of ancient literature, written in Hebrew except for some sections in Aramaic (*Genesis* 31:47, *Jeremiah* 10:11, and parts of *Daniel* and *Ezra*), that has been traditionally accepted by Jews and Christians alike as having been divinely inspired and, as such, authoritative in shaping their respective faiths and practices.

The word *Bible* is ultimately of Greek derivation and passed into many languages of the world through the medium of Latin. It meant simply "the Books" *par excellence*, the way in which the Jews of the Hellenistic world referred to their sacred scriptures, apparently in literal translation into Greek of the earliest known Hebrew designation current in Palestine. This latter is already reflected in *Daniel* 9:2.

Other names for the corpus that were current in ancient times are "Holy Books" and "Holy Writings." More specific to Jews is the Hebrew term *miqra'*, widely used in the Middle Ages, but most likely going back to *Nehemiah* 8:8. Literally meaning "reading," this name underscores the fact that the public reading of the scriptures constituted the core of the Jewish liturgy. Another term commonly used among Jews is *tanakh*, the acronym (TaNaKh) composed of the initial consonants of the names of the three parts into which the Hebrew Bible is customarily divided: the Torah (Pentateuch), the Nevi'im (Prophets), and the Ketuvim (Writings, Hagiographa).

Among Christians, the Hebrew Bible has traditionally been referred to as the Old Testament (i.e., Covenant), in contradistinction to the New Testament—theological appellations based upon a Christological interpretation of *Jeremiah* 31:30–34. In recognition of the partisan nature of this title, and under the impact of the ecumenical movement of recent times, many scholars have increasingly preferred instead to refer to the Hebrew Bible or Hebrew scriptures.

CANON. As generally used in scholarly parlance, the term *canon* relates particularly to the received and definitively closed nature of the sacred corpus. The noun derives from the Greek *kanōn*, itself borrowed from a Semitic word meaning "cane" or "measuring rod." The word was employed figuratively in Classical Greek, a usage adopted by the church fathers in the fourth century for a norm of faith or doctrine and applied by them to the collection of sacred scriptures.

The completed canon of the Hebrew Bible exerted a profound influence, first upon the Jewish people that produced it, and then upon a large section of the rest of humanity. It was the major factor in the preservation of the unity of the Jews at a time of desperate national crisis after the destruction of their state in the year 70 (or 68) CE and their subsequent wide dispersion. The wholly new and unique experience of Judaism as a book-centered religion became the direct inspiration for Christianity and its New Testament, while both religions served as the acknowledged analogue for the rise and development of Islam, based upon its own sacred book, the *kanōn.*

Contents. The tripartite division of the Hebrew Bible roughly describes its variegated contents, although, admittedly, some of the books of the third part would not be out of place in the second.

The Torah. More fully called the Torah of Moses, the Torah comprises the first five books of the biblical canon, usually known in English as the Pentateuch: *Genesis, Exodus, Leviticus, Numbers,* and *Deuteronomy.* These names, derived from the Greek, may translate Hebrew titles that were current among the Jews of Palestine. They more or less epitomize the subject matter of the books. Another system of designation, long in popular use among Jews, and probably earlier than the foregoing, is based upon the opening words of each book, a practice characteristic of ancient Mesopotamian literature: *Bere'shit, Shemot, Va-yiqra', Be-midbar,* and *Devarim.*

The Hebrew term *torah*, usually, but inaccurately, rendered "law," means "instruction, teaching." In the present context, the Pentateuch comprises a continuous narrative from the creation of the world to the death of Moses in which is embedded a considerable amount of legal and ritual prescription. *Genesis* constitutes a distinct work within the Torah corpus in that its first eleven chapters deal with universal history up to the birth of Abraham, and the rest of the book is devoted to the fortunes of a family, the ancestors of the people of Israel. *Deuteronomy*, too, forms a discrete entity, in that it is largely the summarizing discourses of Moses and is marked by its own characteristic style and theological tendency. The intervening three books deal with two generations of the people of Israel from the period of the Egyptian oppression and the Exodus through the wanderings in the wilderness. This section makes up the bulk of the Torah literature and comprises the record of the Egyptian oppression, the liberation, and the arrival at Mount Sinai (*Ex.* 1–18), God's self-revelation to Israel at this site with the divine legislation mediated there through Moses (*Ex.* 19–*Nm.* 10:10), and the events of the people's wanderings in the wilderness until they arrive at the plains of Moab ready to cross the Jordan River into the Promised Land (*Nm.* 10:11–chap. 36).

It is not certain how this corpus was materially preserved in early times. Two separate systems have survived. For convenience of study, the material was written on five separate scrolls, but for ideological reasons, in order both to delimit the Torah as a closed corpus and to emphasize its being a distinct unified composition, the Torah was also written on a single scroll. It is solely in this form that it has played a role in the Jewish synagogal liturgy.

The Nevi'im. The prophetic corpus naturally divides into two parts. What has come to be known as the Former Prophets continues the historical narrative of the Torah, beginning with Joshua's succession to leadership of Israel after the death of Moses and the conquest of Canaan, and closing with the destruction of the First Temple in Jerusalem, the end of the monarchy, and the Babylonian exile of the Judeans up to the year 560 BCE. This material is contained in the books of *Joshua*, *Judges*, *Samuel*, and *Kings*. They are incorporated into the prophetic corpus because they contain much information about the activities of prophets, and particularly because they constitute, in reality, a theological interpretation of the fortunes of the people of Israel presented from the perspective of prophetic teaching and judgment.

The second part of the Nevi'im, the Latter Prophets, comprises the works of the literary prophets in Israel and Judah from the eighth to the fifth centuries BCE. These are *Isaiah*, *Jeremiah*, and *Ezekiel*, and "the Book of the Twelve," known in English as the Minor Prophets: *Hosea*, *Joel*, *Amos*, *Obadiah*, *Jonah*, *Micah*, *Nahum*, *Habakkuk*, *Zephaniah*, *Haggai*, *Zechariah*, and *Malachi*. It should be noted that the adjective *minor* characterizes only the relative brevity of these works, and is by no means intended to be a judgment on their degree of importance.

The Ketuvim. The Writings, often also called Hagiographa in English, are actually a miscellany of sacred writings of several genres of literature, as the nonspecific nature of the name indicates. There is religious poetry (*Psalms* and *Lamentations*); love poetry (the *Song of Songs*); wisdom or reflective compositions (*Proverbs*, *Job*, and *Ecclesiastes*); historical works (*Ruth*, *Esther*, *Ezra-Nehemiah*, and *Chronicles*); and apocalypse (*Daniel*).

Tripartite canon. It is widely held that the tripartite nature of the canon represents three successive stages of canonization of the separate corpora. Repeated reference to this threefold division comes from the literature of the period of the Second Temple. *Ben Sira* 39:1, probably written around 180 BCE, mentions the "law of the Most High, the wisdom of all the ancients . . . , and . . . prophecies." About fifty years later, Ben Sira's grandson, who translated the work into Greek, writes in his prologue about "the law and the prophets and the others that came after them," which last are also called "the other books of our fathers" and "the rest of the books," while *2 Maccabees* (2:2–3, 2:13) has reference to "the law, the kings and prophets and the writings of David." In Alexandria, Egypt, the Jewish philosopher Philo Judaeus (d. 45–50 CE) mentions, besides "the law," also "the prophets and the psalms and other writings" (*De vita contemplativa* 3.25). The Jewish historian Josephus Flavius (37–c. 100 CE) tells of the Pentateuch of Moses, the "prophets" and "the remaining books" (*Against Apion* 1.39–41). Similarly, in the New Testament, the *Gospel of Luke* speaks of "the law of Moses and the prophets and the psalms" (24:4). This persistent allusion to the threefold division of the Hebrew scriptures, and the lack of any uniform title for the third collection of writings, in addition to the heterogeneous nature of that corpus, all argue in favor of two closed collections—the Torah and the Prophets—with a third being somewhat amorphous and having no uniform name, undoubtedly a sign of its late corporate canonicity.

Of course, the closing of a corpus tells nothing about the canonical history of the individual books within it. Some parts of the Ketuvim, such as the *Psalms*, for instance, would most likely have achieved canonical status before some of those included within the Nevi'im.

Samaritan canon. The religious community centered on Nablus (ancient Shechem) that calls itself Benei Yisra'el ("children of Israel") or Shomrim ("keepers," i.e., of the truth), and that is known by outsiders as Samaritans, claims to be directly descended from the Israelites of the Northern Kingdom who escaped deportation at the hands of the Assyrian kings who destroyed it in 722/1 BCE (*2 Kgs.* 17:5–6, 17:24–34, 17:41). Their canon consists solely of the Pentateuch, excluding the Prophets and the Writings. This fact has not been satisfactorily explained. The older view, that the final breach between the Samaritans and the Jews occurred in the time of Ezra and Nehemiah (fifth century BCE), before the canonization of the rest of the Hebrew Bible, is no longer tenable because both documentary and archaeological evidence leads to the conclusion that the schism was the culmination of a gradual process of increasing estrangement. A major step was the construction of a Samaritan shrine on Mount Gerizim early in the Hellenistic period; the destruction of the temple on that site by John Hyrcanus in 128 BCE completed the rupture.

Canon at Qumran. The discovery of a hoard of more than five hundred manuscripts in the region of the sectarian settlement at Khirbat Qumran, northwest of the Dead Sea, has raised the question of the nature of the biblical canon recognized by that community, which came to an end about 70 CE. The question is legitimate both in light of the variant canon preserved by the Greek Septuagint, as discussed below, and because copies of extrabiblical books, apocryphal and pseudepigraphical works such as *Tobit*, *Ben Sira*, the *Letter of Jeremiah*, *1 Enoch*, and *Jubilees*, not to mention the sect's own productions, were included among the finds.

A variety of factors combine to render a decisive conclusion all but impossible in the absence of a list that would determine contents and sequence. This lack is aggravated by the practice at that time of writing each biblical book on a separate scroll, and by the very fragmentary form of the overwhelming majority of extant scrolls. Furthermore, since the manuscripts had generally been hidden in the caves in great disorder, we cannot be sure whether we are dealing with a living library or a *genizah*, a storeroom of discarded works.

The following items of evidence are pertinent to the discussion: (1) With the exception of *Esther*, fragments of all the books of the Hebrew Bible have turned up; hence the Qumran canon would have included at least almost every book of the Hebrew Bible. (2) The category of Qumran literature known as the *pesharim*, or contemporizing interpretations of prophetic texts, is, so far, exclusively restricted to the books of the standard Hebrew canon. (3) The Manual of Discipline (*Serekh ha-yaḥad*, 1QS IX:11) expresses the hope for the renewal of prophecy, the same as is found in *1 Maccabees* 4:46. This suggests that the Qumran community recognized a closed corpus of prophetic literature. (4) The great psalms scroll (11QPs[a]), on the other hand, exhibits not only a deviant order of the standard psalms, but also contains other compositions, largely deriving from Hellenistic times. This scroll circulated in more than one copy, and several other Qumran manuscripts of psalms also vary in sequence and contents. At first glance it would seem that this phenomenon proves that the Qumran community could not have had a concept of a closed canon. However, it may be pointed out that the compiler of 11QPs[a] certainly was dependent on a Hebrew book of psalms much the same as that of the Hebrew Bible, and he may simply have been putting together a liturgical collection, not creating or copying a canonical work. Moreover, the caves of Qumran have yielded numerous psalters that contain only known canonical psalms, apparently without any deviation from the standard sequence. (5) As to the presence of noncanonical works, we have no means of knowing whether these had authority for the community equal with that of the standard Hebrew canonical books. (6) In sum, the evidence so far at hand does not justify the assumption that Qumran sectarians had a concept of canon different from that of their Palestinian Jewish brethren, although the opposite too cannot be proven.

Alexandrian canon (Septuagint). To meet the needs of worship and study, the populous Hellenized Jewish community of Alexandria produced a Greek translation of the Hebrew Bible known as the Septuagint, begun in the third century BCE and completed before about 132 BCE. As it has come down to us, it differs from the traditional Hebrew Bible (the canonized books of the Masoretic text) both in content and form, and often textually (see "Greek Translations," below). It includes works that rabbinic Judaism rejected as noncanonical, and in it the books of the Prophets and Writings are not maintained as separate corpora but are distributed and arranged according to subject matter: historical books, poetry and wisdom, and prophetic literature. This situation has given rise to a widely held hypothesis of an Alexandrian or Hellenistic canon; that is to say, the Septuagint is said to represent a variant, independent concept of canon held by Diaspora Jewry. Alternatively, it is suggested that it derives from a rival canon that circulated in Jewish Palestine itself.

The evidence for either view is indecisive. First of all, it must be remembered that all extant complete manuscripts of the Septuagint—the Sinaiticus, the Alexandrinus, and the Vaticanus—are Christian in origin and are not earlier than the fourth century CE. There is a gap of at least four hundred years in our knowledge, which fact raises the possibility that the divergencies in content and arrangement from the traditional Hebrew Bible may have originated with the church. Moreover, there is no uniformity in the Greek manuscripts themselves in respect to the additional books included. Furthermore, the separate collections of the Torah and the Prophets were definitely known in Alexandria in the second century BCE, as is clear from the prologue to *Ben Sira* (which even speaks of their translation into Greek), as well as from *2 Maccabees* 2:13 and 15:9. At the same time, Ben Sira, his grandson who wrote the prologue, and Philo clearly distinguish between the books that make up the Hebrew Bible and other works of Jewish origin. In short, the problem of the origin of the contents and sequence in the Greek Bible cannot be solved in the present state of our knowledge.

Christian canon. The Christian canon of the Jewish scriptures differs in three ways from the Bible of the Jews. First, its text is not that of the received Hebrew, usually called the Masoretic text, but is based on the Greek and Latin versions. This fact is grounded in historical, not theological considerations. The early church functioned and missionized in a Greek-speaking environment, and thereafter took over the Jewish scriptures in their most readily available and convenient form, namely the (Greek) Septuagint version. Later, the Latin translation became authoritative. Second, although all the books officially recognized as canonical by the Jews were also accepted by the Christian church, many segments of the latter also included within its canon additional Jewish works that date from the days of the Second Temple. These, generally termed "deuterocanonical" by theologians of the Roman Catholic Church, are books of historical and didactic content, composed in Hebrew or Aramaic. They were not sectarian in origin, and they circulated widely in both Palestine and the Greek-speaking Jewish Diaspora in their original language and in Greek translation long after the close of the Hebrew canon. Such books were often included in early manuscripts of the Septuagint, not as a separate group but appropriately interspersed among the undoubtedly canonical works. The books in question are *2 Ezra* (called *3 Esdras* in the Vulgate), *Tobit*, *Judith*, additions to *Esther*, the *Wisdom of Solomon*, *Ben Sira*, *1 Baruch*, together with the *Letter of Jeremiah*, additions to *Daniel*, and *Maccabees*. It is to be noted that *Esther*, *Judith*, *Wisdom*, *1* and *2 Maccabees*, *1 Baruch*, chapters 1–5, and the Septuagint additions to *Daniel* and *Esther* have not yet turned up among the Dead Sea finds.

The presence of the extra compositions in the manuscripts of the Septuagint long engendered controversy, and their status remained ambivalent. The authors of the New Testament books were certainly familiar with them and used them, but it remains a fact that New Testament citations from them are minimal. Further, the early lists of the Fathers emphasize a twenty-two-book canon identical with that of the Jews. In general, the Western church held the deuterocanonical books in high esteem, while the Eastern church downgraded them. The synods of the North African church held at Hippo (393 CE) and Carthage (397, 419 CE) confirmed the practice of the Western church. The powerful influence of the church theologian Augustine (354–430) weighed heavily in according the entire Septuagint equal and identical divine inspiration with the Hebrew Bible. The additional books remained in the Latin Vulgate, which became the official version of the Roman Catholic Church at the Council of Trent (1545–1563).

On the other hand, the Latin father Jerome (347–420) did not recognize them as authoritative scripture, although he did concede them to be "ecclesiastical" or spiritually edifying, and he did translate them into Latin. The Syrian church utilized only the Jewish canon. It later succumbed to the influence of the Septuagint, a move resisted by the Nestorian (Chaldean or East Syrian) branch. In the Greek Orthodox church, the question remains unresolved to the present day, while it was not until the nineteenth century that the theologians of the Russian Orthodox Church unanimously excluded the extra books from the canon.

The period of the Reformation and the Protestant appeal to the authority of the Hebrew Bible generated a renewed attack on their canonicity. John Wyclif (c. 1330–1384), forerunner of the Reformation, who initiated the first English translation of the Bible, omitted them entirely. Martin Luther, in his debates with Johann Maier of Eck (1519), denied their canonical status. His translation of the Bible (1534) included them as a group between the two Testaments, with the following rubric: "Apocrypha: these are books which are not held equal to the sacred Scriptures and yet are useful and good for reading." Luther's view became standard Protestant doctrine. The Thirty-Nine Articles of Religion of the Church of England (1563) asserted their worth for private study and edification but denied them any doctrinal value; and the Westminster Confession (1647), which established the confession of faith of English-speaking Presbyterians, definitively decreed that they were not divinely inspired, are to be excluded from the canon of scripture, and are devoid of authority. The King James Bible of 1611 had grouped the apocryphal books together before the New Testament, but in 1827 the British and Foreign Bible Society decided not to circulate the Apocrypha in whole or part.

The third way in which the Christian canon diverges from the Jewish canon relates to the order of the books. The Hebrew tripartite division, clearly attested in *Luke* 28:44, was disregarded, and the contents were regrouped, as in the manuscripts of the Septuagint, according to literary categories—legal, historical, poetic-didactic, and prophetic. It is possible that the church selected one of the pre-Christian rival traditions already current in Palestine and the Diaspora. At any rate, the variant sequence was best suited to express the claim of the church that the New Testament is the fulfillment of the Hebrew scriptures of the Jews. The closing of the canon with Malachi's prophecy of the "day of the Lord" to be heralded by the return of Elijah provides a transition to the New Testament with John the Baptist as the new Elijah acclaiming his Messiah.

Number of books. Until the sixth century CE, it was customary among Jews for the scribes to copy each biblical work onto a separate scroll. The number of books in the biblical canon therefore relates to the number of scrolls onto which the completed Hebrew Bible was transcribed, and which were physically kept together as a unit. Josephus (*Against Apion* 1. 39–41, ed. Loeb, p. 179) is emphatic that there were no more than twenty-two such. What is not clear is whether this figure was arrived at by conjoining books, such as *Judges* and *Ruth*, and *Jeremiah* and *Lamentations*, or whether two books were not yet included in his canon, perhaps the *Song of Songs* and *Ecclesiastes*. The former suggestion seems more likely because this figure of twenty-two biblical books represents a widespread tradition in Palestine to which there are many Christian witnesses for several hundred years. It appears in a Hebrew-Aramaic list of titles that derives from the first half of the second century CE, and is repeated by several church fathers, such as Melito, bishop of Sardis in western Asia Minor (d. 190), Origen, theologian of Caesarea in southern Palestine (c. 185–c. 254), Eusebius, bishop of Caesarea (c. 260–339), who equates it with the number of letters of the Hebrew alphabet, Cyril, bishop of Jerusalem (d. 386), and the celebrated scholar Jerome. All of the aforementioned either visited Palestine or lived there for many years, and there can be no doubt that they reflect contemporary local

Jewish practice. They all include the *Song of Songs* and *Ecclesiastes* in the canon.

A variant tradition counting twenty-four books eventually prevailed among Jews. This is first found in *2 Esdras* 14:45, written circa 100 BCE. The books are listed by name in a text that antedates 200 BCE cited in the Babylonian Talmud (*B.B.* 14b). Thereafter, this figure is explicitly given, and it becomes standard in rabbinic literature (cf. B.T., *Ta'an.* 5a). Whether the number has any significance is uncertain. In the case of Homer's *Odyssey* and *Iliad*, which are also each divided into twenty-four books, the division came about in the third century BCE because a scroll of more than a thousand verses was found to be too cumbersome to handle, and twenty-four is the number of letters in the Greek alphabet. It is of interest that the Old Babylonian bilingual lexical series known as Har-ra-Hubullu is inscribed on twenty-four tablets, the Mesopotamian *Epic of Gilgamesh* on twelve tablets, the Greek *Theogony* of Hesiod comes in twelve parts, and the old Roman law code was eventually codified as the Twelve Tablets (of wood). At any rate, in Jewish tradition, the biblical books become twenty-four by treating all the twelve Minor Prophets as one, since they were written on a single scroll, and by regarding *Ezra* and *Nehemiah* as a single work.

English Bibles (English version) have thirty-nine books because *Samuel*, *Kings*, and *Chronicles* are divided into two books each for reading convenience, and *Ezra* and *Nehemiah* are counted as separate works, as is each of the twelve Minor Prophets.

CANONIZING PROCESS. The available sources are silent about the nature and identity of the validating authorities, about the criteria of selectivity adopted in respect of the books included and excluded, and about the individual crucial stages in the history of the growth of the Hebrew biblical canon. This deficiency is aggravated by the fact that the literature that has survived represents at least six hundred years of literary creativity, in the course of which Israelite society underwent far-reaching, indeed metamorphic, change, much of it convulsive. Such a state of affairs militates against the likelihood of uniformity in the processes involved or of unbroken consistency in the considerations that swayed decisionmaking about individual works and collections of works. For these reasons, any reconstruction of the history of the phenomenon of the canonization of biblical literature must of necessity remain hypothetical.

Nonetheless, it should be noted that well before the year 1000 BCE, the libraries of the temples and palaces of Mesopotamia had organized the classical literature into a standardized corpus in some kind of uniform order and with a more or less official text. In similar manner, by order of Peisistratus, tyrant of Athens, the Homeric epics were codified in the sixth century and endowed with canonical authority. The idea of a canon was thus well based in the ancient world. There is every reason to assume that in Israel, too, temples served as the repositories of sacred texts from early times, and that the priests and scribes played an important role in the preservation and organization of literature. Hence, the formation of the biblical canon should not be viewed as a late development in Israel but as an ongoing process that is coextensive with the biblical period itself.

The definition of *canon* should, furthermore, be extended beyond the purely historical, external, formal aspects relating just to the end result of a process, to which it is usually restricted. In Israel, the conviction that the texts record the word of God or were divinely inspired, however these concepts were understood, would have been a decisive factor in their preservation. For the same reason, they would have been periodically read or recited, and the very force of repetition would inevitably and powerfully have informed the collective mind and self-consciousness of the community. This, in turn, would have subtly shaped and reshaped both the existing literature and new compositions in a continual process of interaction between the community and its traditions. A text that appears to be directed to a specific situation in time and space acquires a contemporizing validity and relevance that is independent of such restrictive dimensions and develops a life of its own.

The earliest testimony to the canonizing process of the Torah literature comes from *Exodus* 24:1–11, which describes how Moses mediated the divine commands to the entire people assembled, how the people orally bound themselves to obedience, how Moses then put the stipulations into writing, and how a cultic ceremony was held at which the written record of the covenant just made was given a public reading. This was followed by a collective pledge of loyalty to its stipulations.

Another important text is *Deuteronomy*, chapter 31 (verses 9–13, 24–26). Here, too, Moses writes down the Teaching (Torah), this time entrusting the document to the ecclesiastical authorities for safekeeping, with provision for its septennial national public reading in the future. What is then called "this book of the Torah" is placed beside the ark of the covenant. In this case, the sanctity of the book is taken for granted, as is its permanent validity and authority, independent of the person of Moses.

The only other record of a preexilic public reading of Torah literature comes from near the end of the period of the monarchy. *2 Kings* 22–23 (cf. *2 Chr.* 34) recounts the chance discovery of "the book of the Torah" in 622 in the course of the renovations being carried out at the Temple in Jerusalem at the initiative of Josiah, then king. The scope of this work cannot be determined from the narrative, but the royal measures taken as a consequence of the find prove beyond cavil that it at least contained *Deuteronomy.* What is of particular significance is that it had long been stored in the Temple, that its antiquity, authenticity, and authority were recognized at once, and that its binding nature was confirmed at a national assembly. The ceremony centered upon a document that had already achieved normative status, but the impact of the event—the thoroughgoing religious reformation that it generated and sustained ideologically—left an indelible imprint on the subsequent literature and religion of Israel and constituted a powerful stimulus to the elevation of the Torah literature as the organizing principle in the life of the people. In this sense, the developments of 622 are an important milestone in the history of canonization. Between this year and 444 the process gathered apace. It is reasonable to assume that it was consummated in the Babylonian exile after 587/6, for it is impossible to explain the extraordinary survival of the small, defeated, fragmented community of Israelites, bereft of the organs of statecraft, deprived of its national territory, living on alien soil amid a victorious, prestigious civilization, other than through the vehicle of the book of the Torah, which preserved the national identity.

In the period of the return to Zion (the Land of Israel) and beyond, after 538 BCE, the convention of attributing the entire Torah to Moses is frequently attested—in *Malachi, Ezra-Nehemiah, Daniel,* and *Chronicles.* It also appears in *Joshua* (8:32, 23:6) and in *1 Kings* (2:3) and *2 Kings* (14:6, 23:25), but many scholars maintain that these references result from a later revision of these works. At any rate, by the year 444 the "Torah of Moses" had received popular acceptance. *Nehemiah* 8–10 records that in that year a public, national assembly took place in Jerusalem at which the people requested that "the scroll of the Torah of Moses with which the Lord had charged Israel" be read to them. This was done by Ezra, who is himself described as "a scribe, expert in the Torah of Moses," "a scholar in matters concerning the commandments of the Lord and his laws to Israel . . . a scholar in the law of the God of heaven" (*Ezr.* 7:6, 7:11–12, 7:21). It is quite evident that the stress is on the teaching, dissemination, interpretation, and reaffirmation of the Torah, long popularly recognized and accepted, not on its promulgation anew. Ezra had been commissioned by the Persian king Artaxerxes I "to regulate Judah and Jerusalem according to the law of God," which was in his care (*Ezr.* 7:14). True, the texts do not define the scope of this literature, but it can be safely assumed that it was little different from the Pentateuch that has come down to us, for the author of *Chronicles* who composed his history about 400 repeatedly refers to the "Torah of Moses," and it can be shown that this phrase in context applies comprehensively to the entire Pentateuch.

In the Pentateuch itself, however, there is no statement unambiguously asserting Mosaic authorship of the entire work, nor can the use of the term *torah* be shown to refer comprehensively to the complete Pentateuch. Rather, its applicability changes considerably, being variously restricted to an individual law, to a specific and limited collection of traditions, or to a large literary unit. The background to the tradition ascribing the authorship of the Pentateuch to Moses lies in the fact that, in biblical literature, Moses is the divinely chosen individual through whose instrumentality a social-religious revolution is effectuated. He is the leader *par excellence,* preeminent beyond compare; his is the only name associated with the term *torah;* he is the sole mediator of the word of God to the people; all laws are presented as divine communications to Moses; there are no collections of binding laws outside of the Torah. He is also the first person to whom the act of writing is ascribed. There can be no doubt that in a very real sense the Pentateuch would have been unthinkable were it not for his activity.

Compilation and Redaction. The composite nature of the biblical, especially the Pentateuchal, literature has long been recognized (see *Nm.* 21:14, *Jos.* 10:13). By the application of analytical criteria of consistent variations in style, phraseology, and theological viewpoint, of doublets and inconsistencies, of breaks in continuity with the obvious presence of connectives that conjoin separate homogeneous sections, critical research has concentrated on the disentanglement and isolation of the constituent literary strands.

The early founders of modern biblical criticism were Barukh Spinoza (1632–1677) and Jean Astruc (1684–1766). In the course of the nineteenth century, several important contributions were made by Wilhelm M. L. De Wette, Wilhelm Vatke, and Heinrich Ewald. It was Julius Wellhausen, however, who popularized what is known as the Documentary Hypothesis. He systematized and developed the work of his predecessors in several influential treatises: *Die Composition des Hexateuchs* (Berlin, 1876), *Geschichte Israels* (Berlin, 1878), and *Prolegomena zur Geschichte Israels* (Berlin, 1883).

The Documentary Hypothesis isolated four primary collections of traditions (sources) that it labeled J (because it employs the divine name *Jehovah,* in Hebrew, *YHVH*), E (because it uses *Elohim* for God), D (Deuteronomy), and P (Priestly). The isolation of the D and P sources, each with its distinctive content, style, and perspective, was less complicated than determining the literary parameters of J and E, on which there has been much difference of opinion. It became clear that the provenance, historical setting, and chronological sequence of these sources would yield the materials for reconstructing the history of the religion of Israel in biblical times. Accordingly, J, which was believed to have originally constituted the skeleton of the continuous narrative of *Genesis* through *1 Kings,* chapter 2, was assigned to the period of the united Israelite kingdom of David and Solomon in the tenth century and was thought to have derived from Judea. E was considered to be northern Israelite or Ephraimite from the ninth to eighth centuries. It was fused with J to become JE. D was regarded as the product of the reformation of Josiah in 622, and P as having been compiled in the Babylonian exile, between 587 and 560. The entire Pentateuch was taken to have reached its final form before Ezra's journey to Jerusalem in 458.

This hypothesis, with its evolutionary presuppositions, has been considerably modified since its systematic presentation in the nineteenth century. The major sources have themselves been dissected, and serious challenge has been posed to the dating and sequence of the reconstructed documents. Furthermore, it has been recognized that a distinction must be made between the age of the traditions, which may be of great antiquity, and the time of their assemblage and final editing. It has been noted that literary strands become interwoven, and sources tend to interact one with another, thus making the identification of the original documents far less secure. In addition, the creative work of the redactor(s) has come to be increasingly appreciated as an important factor in the development of biblical literature by scholars engaging in "redaction criticism."

Scholars of the school of "tradition criticism" have also paid attention to the process by which traditions were preserved and transmitted. It has been pointed out that much of the written material may well have had an oral prehistory. Traditions would have been recited in a cultic context at local and regional shrines, such as Bethel, Shiloh, Shechem, and Jerusalem (cf. *Dt.* 27:1–10). A series of major themes, like the divine promises to the patriarchs, the Exodus, the covenant of Sinai, and the wanderings in the wilderness would have been given public expression on sacral occasions to form the core of the Israelite religion. These units of tradition would become the focus of expansive tendencies, would be written down, assembled, and serve as the building blocks of extensive and complex narratives presented in a continuous form. The nature and characteristic properties of oral tradition, poetic or prose, its antiquity, reliability, and tenacity, its vicissitudes in the course of transmission, and the kinds of transformation it undergoes when reduced to writing have all been the subjects of intensive study, for they have direct bearing on the understanding of the development of biblical literature.

Finally, it has been acknowledged that any analysis that ignores the primary nature and function of the material must be incomplete. The formation of the scriptures was not motivated by literary, aesthetic considerations, or by the desire to write objective history. Rather, the literature is essentially religious, its purposes being theological interpretation and didactic function. This fact imposes considerable restraint on the simple application to it of the accepted literary-critical method.

The Bible and the Ancient Near East. The recovery of the languages and cultures of the lands of the ancient Near Eastern world demonstrate that the people of Israel arrived on the scene of history rather late, long after the great civilizations of Mesopotamia, Egypt, and the Hittite area had already passed their prime and produced a classical literature. Moreover, it is clear that this region, often referred to as the Fertile Crescent, constituted a cultural continuum, although, to be sure, each constituent, local entity possessed its own distinctive features. It is not surprising, therefore, that there exist numerous, close affinities in subject matter and form between the biblical writings and the literatures of the ancient Near East. This phenomenon is not necessarily to be explained in terms of dependency or borrowing, but more likely as a result of the sharing of a common cultural heritage. Furthermore, correspondences and parallels are not the same as identity. Contrast is as important a dimension as similarity, and it is the former that accords the Israelite productions their claim to singularity.

This point is illustrated by the fact that whereas all the diverse literary genres of the Bible are to be found in the neighboring cultures, the reverse is not the case, and the omissions are highly instructive. The huge literature belonging to the worlds of astrology and magic, omens, divination, and the like, and the considerable body of mythical texts, have no counterpart in the Hebrew scriptures (although the texts preserve evidence of these customs) because they are incompatible with Israel's fundamental monotheism. Moreover, it is apparent that what was drawn upon from the common Near Eastern stock was thoroughly refined and reshaped to bring it into conformity with the national religious ideology.

The primeval history in *Genesis*, chapters 1–11, well exemplifies this situation. The genealogies, for instance, belong to the same type of document as the Sumerian king-list, but they are used both as connectives to bridge the gap between narrative blocks and for theological purposes. Thus, ten generations are delineated to span the period between Adam and Noah, and another ten between Noah and Abraham, the symmetry being intended to convey the idea that history is the unfolding of God's predetermined plan for humankind. The Flood story has manifold and detailed points of contact with the corresponding episode in the Mesopotamian *Epic of Gilgamesh* and with its parent version, the Atrahasis epic. But the biblical version has a singularly didactic function and is uniquely placed within a spiritual and moral framework.

The law collection in the Pentateuch is another case in point. No less than six law codes have survived from the ancient Near East, the earliest probably deriving from about seven hundred years before Moses. All these, plus innumerable documents of law-court proceedings, leave no doubt of the existence of a common legal culture in the area that found expression in a similarity of content, legal phraseology, and literary form that Israel shared. Nevertheless, the scriptural exemplar features some fundamental and original departures from the general norm. The source and sanction of law are conceived in Israel to be entirely the revelation of divine will. The law is taken to be the expression of the covenant between God and Israel. There is no dichotomy, as elsewhere, between the secular and the religious. Social, moral, ethical, and cultic precepts are all equally and indiscriminately encompassed within the realm of the law. Also, there is an overwhelming preoccupation with the human person and with human life, and a lesser concern with matters of property, which is the reverse of the situation in the traditional codes. Finally, the biblical laws are encased within a narrative framework and are not isolated documents.

The genre that was truly an international phenomenon is that of biblical wisdom literature. It deals with observations on human behavior and the world order, drawn from experience. One such category has the individual as its focus of interest and is essentially pragmatic and utilitarian, containing precepts for success in living. Its artistic forms are mainly the maxim, the proverb, the pithy question, and the riddle. The other is reflective in nature and is more concerned with the human condition, and with the wider issues of divine-human relationships. Here the literary unit is much longer. Both Egypt and Mesopotamia produced an extensive body of literature of this type, and the analogues with *Proverbs*, *Job*, and *Ecclesiastes* are striking. Yet here, again, although these latter are mostly devoid of national or special Israelite content, they are distinctive in their uncompromising monotheism, in the absence of dream interpretation as an attribute of the sage, and in their insistence on the fear of the Lord as being the quintessence of wisdom.

The *Book of Psalms* and the rich psalmody of Egypt and Babylon are closely related in both style and motifs. Both can be categorized under the more or less same limited number of literary genres. Although no Canaanite psalm has yet been recovered, the abundance of affinities with the poetry from ancient Ugarit (modern Ras Shamra) by way of poetic form, fixed pairs of words, the use of stereotyped phrases and of parallelism, is impressive. It is clear that biblical psalmody did not arise in cultural isolation from the neighboring civilizations. However, unlike the Mesopotamian psalms, the Hebrew scriptural compositions do not contain any cult-functional information, nor do they feature spells and incantations. Moreover, their conspicuous citation of history is unique, as are the spiritual experience and the soul-life of the Israelites that they mirror.

Historical Complexity of the Text. The model for printed editions of the Hebrew Bible was the second "Great Rabbinic Bible" published at Venice by Daniel Bomberg, 1524–1525, and edited by Ya'aqov ben Hayyim ibn Adoniyyah. All printed editions, as well as all extant medieval Hebrew manuscripts of the Bible—the earliest deriving from the ninth century CE—represent a single textual tradition, known as the Masoretic ("received") text (MT). This standard text comprises three distinct elements: the Hebrew consonants, vocalization signs, and accentuation marks. The last two components are relatively late additions. Their purpose is to preserve the proper traditional pronunciation and cantillation of the text for purposes of study and synagogue lectionary.

This normative uniformity notwithstanding, there is abundant evidence for a far more complex history of the Hebrew consonantal text than is suggested by the aforementioned manuscripts and the printed editions. Several different categories of testimony bear witness to an earlier era of textual transmission that was characterized by much diversity.

1. *Internal evidence* is represented by the duplication of several passages within the scriptures. These duplicates may display differences in content and arrangement, linguistic or grammatical variants, and orthographic diversity, testifying to the existence of divergent texts of one and the same composition as early as the period of the formation of biblical literature itself.
2. *Citations from the scriptures* are found in the Jewish literature of Second Temple times, such as the extracanonical books, the works of Philo Judaeus and the writings of Josephus, as well as in the New Testament. In all these sources, there can be no doubt that the citations, though in translation, often present genuine variant readings from an underlying Hebrew text that is independent of the Masoretic text and of the Septuagint.
3. *The Samaritan Pentateuch* exhibits many variants from the Masoretic text, the great majority of which relate to insignificant details, and even its manuscripts are not uniform. Although many of the disagreements are clearly the result of sectarian or dogmatic redactions and exegetical and editorial expansions, there remain several genuine variants, a goodly number of which coincide with Septuagint readings.
4. *Several ancient translations* were made directly from the original texts. None of these is identical in every respect with the Masoretic Hebrew. They are important because they were made prior to the emergence of one authoritative Hebrew text. (See "Aramaic Translations" and "Greek Translations" below.)
5. *Rabbinic sources* which supply rich and varied data make up the fifth type of testimony. Traditions, essentially anomalous ones, and hence of plausible credibility, have been preserved relating to the activities of the scribes in transmitting the sacred texts. These tell of "scribal corrections" and of divergent readings in different scrolls. In addition, there are reports of the existence of an official Temple model scroll from which other scrolls were corrected and of a class of "book-correctors" whose salaries were paid from Temple funds (e.g., B.T., *Ned.* 376, *Ket.* 106a; J.T., *Ta'an.* 4.2, 5.1; J.T., *Suk.* 3.2, *Sheq.* 4.3). A medieval source has retained a list of textual variants deriving from a Torah scroll deposited in the Severus Synagogue (or public building) in Rome and said to have been taken to Rome from Jerusalem after the destruction of the Second Temple, circa 70 CE (*Midrash Bere'shit Rabbati*, ed. C. Albeck, Jerusalem, 1940, p. 209, 45.8). Rabbinic literature also contains hundreds of citations from the Hebrew Bible that feature variants from the Masoretic text. While many of these may be discounted as having been caused by lapse of memory on behalf of the tradent or by the errors of medieval scribes, many also represent genuine variants. In addition, there are several examples of rabbinic exegesis based on consonantal texts not identical with the Masoretic text (see B.T., *San.* 4b).
6. *The Dead Sea Scrolls* are the last and most important, because the most direct, type of evidence. They consist of the Hebrew scrolls and fragments found in the Judean desert in modern-day Israel, which are now the earli-

est extant manuscripts of the period extending from the second half of the third century BCE to the fall of Jerusalem to the Romans in 70 (or 68) CE. The oldest of these antedate by about a thousand years the earliest Hebrew Bible manuscripts hitherto known. Some 180 separate manuscripts of biblical books have come to light in various states of preservation, together with thousands of fragments. Every book of the Hebrew Bible, except *Esther,* is represented, several in multiple copies. Some Pentateuchal books, as well as *Job* fragments, are written in the Paleo-Hebrew script, a derivative of the ancient Hebrew script in use prior to the Babylonian exile of 587/6 BCE.

The great importance of these scrolls and fragments lies in the fact that they supply unimpeachable evidence for a degree of textual diversity that exceeds the limited three major witnesses previously known: the Masoretic text, the Septuagint, and the Samaritan Pentateuch. In fact, each biblical book displays a variety of individual texts that agree now with one of the above versions, now with another. It is to be emphasized, however, that none of the Hebrew scrolls from Qumran so far published can be seen to be actually identical in all respects with either the Septuagint or the Samaritan tradition. Particularly interesting and instructive are the direct citations from the Pentateuch found in the Qumran "Temple Scroll." These often agree with the Septuagint and occasionally with the Samaritan against the Masoretic text, but they differ from both more frequently than they agree with them.

Development of the Masoretic Text. Examination of the evidence from the Judean desert yields the general conclusion that the profusion of variants increases in proportion to the antiquity of the manuscripts and decreases with the progression of time. Further, this diminution of variants works overwhelmingly in favor of the textual tradition close to that which eventually came to be known as Masoretic. This tradition is characterized, in the main, by a very conservative approach to the consonantal text that expresses itself in a minimum of expansiveness and harmonization. Difficult readings and archaic spellings and grammatical forms are carefully preserved. *Matres lectionis,* that is, the use of the weak letters (alef, he', vav, and yud) as vowel indicators, is sparsely employed. In the hoards of manuscripts from the Judean desert, the Masoretic-type exemplars are more numerous than the other text traditions. For instance, there are present no less than fourteen copies of *Isaiah* that are very close to our received Hebrew version.

These facts unmistakably point to the high prestige enjoyed by this particular tradition. Since there is no evidence for the biblical scrolls being a product of the Qumran community, this situation must reflect the text-type that eventuated in the Masoretic text, which was not only present very early at Qumran but was also already highly and widely esteemed in Palestine in Second Temple times. This implies its patronage by powerful and respected circles that could only have been located in the Temple at Jerusalem.

By the end of the first century CE this text tradition became authoritative and displaced all others. The process is clearly visible in the phenomenon of a revision at this time of the Septuagint to bring it into conformity with the proto-Masoretic text (see below, "Greek Translations"). The biblical manuscripts found at Masada are all but identical with our received texts from Wadi Murabbaat, deriving from the period of Bar Kokhba Revolt (132–135 CE).

The manuscript evidence for the development of a single authoritative text can be supplemented by secondary testimony. The recorded disputes between the Sadducees and the Pharisees never once center on or reflect differences in the text of scripture. Similarly, the Christians in the times of the New Testament do not claim a superior or different text from that used by the Jews. Also, early Christian-Jewish polemics frequently involved differences between Jewish and Christian citations of the Bible, but it was the Hebrew text of the Jews as against the Latin version of Jerome, not versus a different Hebrew existing text, that was the subject of dispute. This is in accord with another phenomenon of major importance. No differences of opinion regarding biblical readings appear in rabbinic literature, only varying interpretations of the same text. In fact, the above-cited rabbinic material that bears witness to the one time existence of divergent texts constitutes at the same time testimony to the tendency to reduce the plurality of readings; it communicates a desire to produce conformity to one text.

The above-mentioned existence of Temple-supported "book-correctors," of a model scroll kept in the Temple court, and of a hermeneutical derivation of a legal decision from the presence of a redundant conjunctive letter vav ("and") in the biblical text (*Soṭ.* 5.1) by a scholar who belonged to the generation of the destruction of the Temple—all presuppose a text fixed unalterably in spelling and content. The same conclusion is to be drawn even more emphatically from the reports of the literary activity of the *sofrim* (official scribes). This term is interpreted to mean "tellers" by the rabbis because the *sofrim* kept count of the number of letters in the Torah and marked its middle consonant, its middle words, and its middle verse to ensure the exact transmission of the Hebrew text. They did the same for the *Book of Psalms* (B.T., *Ḥag.* 15b, B.T., *Kid.* 30a).

Two other sources confirm that the concept of an official, fixed scriptural text was well rooted in Jewish learned circles. The Greek *Letter of Aristeas* (late second century BCE), which purports to tell of the origin of the Septuagint, knows of inaccurate copies of the Torah and reports an official Alexandrian request of the high priest in Jerusalem to supply an accurate Hebrew copy from which a Greek translation may be made. In the same vein, Josephus boasts that the Jews have always venerated their scriptures to the degree that none would dare to add, to remove, or to alter a syllable of the text (Josephus, *Against Apion,* 1.6, 1.8).

The process by which the Masoretic text type achieved supremacy over all others and eventually supplanted them entirely is unclear. There is absolutely no evidence for an official promulgation on the subject by rabbinical authorities. The most plausible explanation for the phenomenon is that the very concept of a sacred canon of scripture on the basis of which Jewish communities established their identity, and the reading and studying of which formed the core of the organized public liturgy, would naturally tend toward the promotion of a stabilized, normative text. The specific text favored by scholarly and hierarchical circles in Second Temple times would acquire high prestige and serve as a model for less elitist groups. The trend toward uniformity would be hastened by the destruction of the Temple and the ever-widening Jewish Diaspora because a common text would act as a vital cohesive force. Laymen would cease to order and scribes would desist from copying any but the "official" text. All others would be discarded, and, being written on organic material, would perish—except for chance preservation in unusually favorable environmental conditions such as obtain in the Judean desert.

Aramaic Translations. The extensive imperial campaigns of the Assyrian kings during the eighth and ninth centuries BCE began the process that culminated in the Aramaization of the Jewish people. Arameans and Chaldeans came to constitute a significant and powerful segment of the population under Assyrian domination. The diffusion of Aramaic was doubtless facilitated by the convenience and efficiency of the alphabet as opposed to the cumbersome cuneiform writing. The Aramaic language finally became the language of diplomacy and international trade throughout the neo-Assyrian empire (see *2 Kings* 18:26). The fall of the northern kingdom of Israel in 722 to the Assyrian armies, and the subsequent large-scale population exchanges carried out by the conquerors, brought into Samaria and the Galilee various ethnic groups that seem to have had Aramaic as a common language. The importance of Aramaic was further enhanced during the days of the neo-Babylonian empire (626–539 BCE). The destruction of the southern kingdom of Judah in 587, and the resultant Babylonian exile, soon caused a weakening of Hebrew and the adoption of Aramaic as the vernacular of the exiles. The return to Zion in the late sixth century BCE meant an influx into Judaea of Aramaic-speaking Jews who reinforced the existing bilingual situation. Throughout the Persian empire (539–333 BCE), Aramaic was the official language of the administration, and by the end of the period it was most likely the vernacular of a majority of Jews. While Hebrew still enjoyed pride of place as a literary language, this situation changed with the deteriorating fortunes of the organized Jewish rebellions against Roman rule in Palestine. The center of Jewish life shifted at the end of the first century from Judaea, where Hebrew had still managed to maintain its hold, to the Galilee, where Aramaic was the dominant language. The Jewish communities of Palestine and the widespread Diaspora of the East were now thoroughly Aramaized. The emergence of Aramaic translations of the Hebrew scriptures was an inevitable development.

These Aramaic translations are known as *targumim* ("translations"; sg., *targum*). Their origins are ascribed in rabbinic sources to the time of Ezra and Nehemiah (fifth century BCE). *Nehemiah* 8:8 is adduced in support of this thesis (J.T., *Meg.* 4.1, 74d et al.). This tradition undoubtedly preserves a historical kernel, for the process certainly arose in connection with the public liturgical lectionary, most likely with the glossing in Aramaic of difficult Hebrew words and phrases. In the course of time, there arose the institution of the *meturgeman*, the official translator into Aramaic who stood beside the one who read the scriptural portion in Hebrew. According to rabbinic sources, the Aramaic had to be rendered extemporaneously, without the aid of a written text and without even a glance at the Torah scroll. The purpose was to ensure the exclusive authority of the original Hebrew text, and to prevent it from being superseded by a translation.

The existence of established Targums for private use is attested for the period of the Second Temple. The *Genesis Apocryphon* from Qumran is a typical aggadic Targum, that to *Job* from the same locale is a literal exemplar. The Greek translation of *Job*, probably made during the first century BCE, concludes with an addendum that seems to point to the existence of an earlier "Syriac" (probably Aramaic) Targum to that book. Another early written Targum to *Job* is mentioned in rabbinic sources (Tosefta, *Shab.* 13.2–3 et al.). Jesus' citation of *Psalms* 22:1 in Aramaic, rather than in Hebrew, at his crucifixion (*Mt.* 27:46, *Mk.* 15:34) testifies to a well-rooted tradition of Aramaic translation of *Psalms*, but whether it existed in oral or written form cannot be determined.

The almost total aramaization of the Jews of Palestine and the eastern Diaspora, and the unremitting retreat of Hebrew as a spoken language, made the Aramaic Targums to the scriptures a vital and effective tool of mass education. All resistance to their commitment to writing broke down. Some achieved official recognition to the extent that the private reading of the Targum together with the Hebrew text was actually prescribed (B.T., *Ber.* 8a–b).

Pentateuchal Targums. Targums to all books of the Hebrew Bible except *Daniel* and *Ezra-Nehemiah* have survived. Three that translate the Pentateuch are particularly important.

Targum Onkelos. Targum Onkelos was the official and single universally accepted Targum to the Torah. The ascription of its authorship is based on a passage in the Babylonian Talmud that refers to "Onkelos the proselyte" (B.T., *Meg.* 3a). From the corresponding passage in the Palestinian Talmud (J.T., *Meg.* 1.11, 71c) it is clear that the original reference was to the Greek translation of Aquila, a name pronounced "Onkelos" in the dialect of Babylonia. Because nothing was known about this Greek version in the East, that translation was there confused with the one to the Torah in Aramaic.

Identifying the dialect of Targum Onkelos presents a problem. It shares features characteristic of both Eastern and Western Aramaic, and is close to Middle Aramaic (200 BCE to 200 CE), whose place of origin seems to have been Palestine, which would point to a Palestinian provenance for Targum Onkelos. This conclusion is reinforced by linguistic evidence. In addition, its *aggadah* and *halakhah*, or homiletical and legal traditions, show unmistakable influence of the school of the Palestinian rabbi ʿAqivaʾ ben Yosef.

On the other hand, Targum Onkelos vanishes from Palestinian Jewish records for many hundreds of years after the end of the third century CE. It exhibits morphological features that are typical of Eastern Aramaic, and it was the official Targum of the academies of Babylon. It was transmitted with a Babylonian vocalization and a *masorah*, a text-critical apparatus that, written in the margins of the manuscript, reflects the Babylonian traditions regarding the form of the text, the spelling of words, directions for pronunciation, and other lexicographic details.

In light of the above data, it seems safe to assume that this Targum originated in Palestine and was brought to Babylon at the end of the second century CE. There it underwent a local, systematic redaction and was given official ecclesiastical recognition. It is a work composed of numerous and varied layers that represent a time span of hundreds of years.

Generally speaking, Targum Onkelos was executed with great care as a straightforward, literalistic rendering of the Hebrew source. It departs from this approach in the difficult poetic sections of the Pentateuch, as well as in those passages in which its pedagogic goals, namely, the Aramaic translation as an instrument for mass education, required change or expansion. Here it incorporated oral traditions, halakhic and aggadic, and it used circumlocutions and euphemisms to avoid misunderstanding on the part of the public as to the monotheistic concept of God, changing anthropomorphisms and anthropopathisms, and texts that might be misconstrued as suggesting direct physical contact between man and God.

Targum Onkelos was first printed at Bologna in 1482. The Sabbioneta text of 1557 served as the basis of Abraham Berliner's edition (Leipzig, 1877). A new edition, based on old Yemenite manuscripts and printed texts, was edited by Alexander Sperber in 1959.

Targum Jonathan. A second popular Targum to the Pentateuch was the Targum Jonathan (Heb., Yonatan). The name is a misnomer arising from a mistaken interpretation of an abbreviation, "T. Y.," which actually denotes Targum Yerushalmi (Jerusalem Targum). An earlier, widespread name for this translation was Targum of the Land of Israel. This Targum is also characterized by an aversion to anthropomorphisms, but it is free and expansive, replete with aggadic and halakhic material. Biblical toponyms are modernized. Its history is problematic. Internal evidence for its dating ranges from mention of the high priest John Hyrcanus (135–104 BCE) in the Targum to *Deuteronomy* 33:1, to mention of the "six orders of the Mishnah" (Targ. Jon., *Ex.* 26:9) that were edited only around 200 CE, to the presence of Khadījah, wife of Muḥammad (some texts read "Ayesha," another of his wives) and Faṭimah, his daughter (Targ. Jon., *Gn.* 21:21), to references to Ishmael and Esau as masters of the world (Targ. Jon., *Gn.* 49:26, *Dt.* 33:2), which can only refer to Islam and Byzantium of the seventh century CE at the earliest. A reference to Constantinople in the Targum on *Numbers* 24:19 seems to allude to the war of the caliph Sulaymān against the Byzantine capital in 716–718 CE.

A curious feature of this Targum is the number of passages in which the exegesis contradicts normative rabbinic *halakhah* (e.g., Targ. Jon., *Lev.* 18:21, cf. *Meg.* 4.9), and in several cases agrees with that of Philo and the sect of Karaites (eighth century CE on). As a result it is extremely hazardous to date this version. Its language is essentially Galilean Aramaic, and its origins certainly go back to Second Temple times. Innumerable accretions and the influence of Targum Onkelos on it have vastly complicated the task of reconstructing the history of its transmission.

Targum (Pseudo-) Jonathan was first printed at Venice, 1591. A British Museum manuscript was edited by Moses Ginsburger (Berlin, 1903) and published in a corrected edition by David Rieder (Jerusalem, 1974).

Neofiti 1. An early sixteenth-century manuscript known as Neofiti 1 represents a third Galilean Aramaic Targum to the Pentateuch. Discovered in the Vatican Library in 1956 by Diez-Macho, it has since been published in five volumes (1968–1978). The codex is complete and well preserved. It features a large number of marginal and interlinear variants and notes written in rabbinic script by different hands, the source of which may well be parallel readings in various Targums, since they often coincide with fragments preserved in the Cairo Genizah.

The dating of this Targum presents complex problems. Linguistic and other aspects point to the early centuries CE. It undoubtedly contains valuable textual variants paralleled in other ancient versions. It differs, however, in orthography, grammar, and the extent of paraphrastic material from the other Galilean Targums, and there is good reason to believe that the original underwent later revision. Another Palestinian Aramaic translation exists that is sometimes referred to as Targum Yerushalmi or Fragmentary Targum. It was first printed in the Bomberg Rabbinic Bible of 1517–1518, and subsequently, with additions, by Moses Ginsburger (Berlin, 1899). These fragments cover only about 850 of the 5,845 verses of the Pentateuch, and it is not clear whether it was ever complete.

The Samaritan Targum (or Targums). The Samaritan community produced for its own use a Targum based upon its recension of the Pentateuch. The dialect is that of the area of Shechem and the central highlands, very close to Galilean Aramaic. Linguistic criteria suggest an original date of composition sometime between the second and third centuries CE. Generally, the Samaritan Targum is characterized by extreme literalism even to the extent of reproducing anthropomorphisms.

A serious problem is the fact that the Samaritans never produced a definitive edition of their Targum, with the result that every manuscript exhibits its own peculiarities, the variants frequently reflecting changes and developments in their Aramaic dialect. Moreover, the later scribes, who did not know Aramaic, introduced numerous errors into their copies.

The first edition printed in the West was that of the Paris Polyglot (1645), but it is now clear that it was made from a decidedly inferior manuscript dating to 1514. Walton's London Polyglot of 1657 (vol. 6) reprinted this, but with numerous corrections. A version based on various manuscripts found in the Samaritan synagogue in Shechem was begun by Heinrich Petermann in 1872 and completed by Caroli Vollers in 1893, but the copies used were unreliable.

Targum to the Prophets. Traditionally, the official Targum to the Prophets is ascribed to Jonathan son of Uzziel, based on a single Talmudic passage (B.T., *Meg.* 3a), which also makes him a contemporary of Haggai, Zechariah, and Malachi (sixth century BCE). However, another rabbinic text (B.T., *Suk.* 28a) has him a student of Hillel the Elder (end of first century BCE–beginning of first century CE). It has been noted that the name *Jonathan* (*Yonaton*) is a Hebrew rendering of the Greek name *Theodotion.* One of the second-century Greek versions of the Bible was executed by a certain Theodotion, and it is conjectured that in Babylonian Jewish circles he was confused with Jonathan ben Uzziel, who was then credited with translating the Prophets into Aramaic.

The Aramaic of the Targum to the Prophets is close to biblical Aramaic and to the Palestinian Jewish dialect. Its affinities with the *Pesher Habakkuk* (a commentary on *Habakkuk*) from Qumran and the exegetical traditions it shares in common with Josephus testify to the antiquity of some of its layers. At the same time, a definite dependence on Targum Onkelos to the Torah can be established. In assessing the date of Targum Jonathan's composition, account must also be taken of the fact that the Babylonian Talmud contains numerous citations of Aramaic renderings of passages from the Prophets, which are identical with those in Targum Jonathan, and which are given in the name of the Babylonian amora Yosef ben Ḥiyya' (d. 333 CE). These indicate that they were composed at least a generation earlier (B.T., *San.* 94b et al.).

It is possible that Yosef ben Ḥiyya' may have been connected with one of the revisions. At any rate, it is certain that the Targum is not the work of a single individual or of one period but has undergone much revision over a long period of time, until it reached its definitive form, by the seventh century CE.

The style of the Targum, especially to the Latter Prophets, is paraphrastic and expansive, probably because of the difficulties in translating the poetic oratory, which is replete with figurative language. It shares with Targum Onkelos to the Torah the general aversion to anthropomorphisms. Fragments of the Targum from Codex Reuchlinianus were edited by Paul de Lagarde as *Prophetae Chaldaice* (1872). A critical edition of the Targum Jonathan to the Prophets was published by A. Sperber (1959, 1962).

Citations from another Palestinian Targum to the Prophets appear in the biblical commentaries of Rashi (Shelomoh ben Yitsḥaq, 1040–1105) and David Kimḥi (c. 1160–c. 1235) and in the rabbinic dictionary of Natan ben Yeḥi'el of Rome (1035–c. 1110), known as the *Arukh,* as well as in the above-mentioned Codex Reuchlinianus. They have been collected by Lagarde and Sperber. While the Aramaic is Palestinian, the influence of the Babylonian Talmud upon this Targum is clear.

Targums to the Ketuvim. Ever since the Venice edition of 1518, rabbinic Bibles have carried Targums to all the books of the Ketuvim (Hagiographa) except *Daniel, Ezra,* and *Nehemiah.* Lagarde edited the series in *Hagiographa Chaldaice* (1873), and a critical edition was published by Sperber in 1964. These Targums are composed in the Palestinian Aramaic dialect, and presumably originate in Palestine. Each is distinctive, and there is no uniformity of style. None of them ever became authoritative or underwent formal redaction. Those to *Psalms* and *Job* share in common several distinctive features.

Rabbinic sources make clear that a Targum to *Job* already existed in Second Temple times (Tosefta, *Shab.* 13.2 et al.). The remains of such a one have been recovered from Qumran Cave 11, but whether it has any relationship to the former cannot be determined. The language of this Targum is close to biblical Aramaic and seems to go back to the late second century BCE.

The Targum to *Job* that appears in the printed editions has no relation to the preceding and appears to be a compilation from different periods. The Targum to *Proverbs* is unique in that it bears strong resemblance to the Peshitta, or Syriac version, leading to the most likely conclusion that both renderings go back to a common, older, Aramaic translation or to the influence of a Jewish transliteration of the Peshitta into Hebrew characters.

There are Targums to the Five Scrolls, but these are so expansive and paraphrastic that they are more collections of *midrashim* than true Targums. They were edited with an introduction by Bernard Grossfeld in 1973.

GREEK TRANSLATIONS. The history of the Jewish community in Egypt can be traced back at least to the beginning of the sixth century BCE. There Jews spoke Aramaic and knew Hebrew, but the influx of Greek-speaking settlers had far-reaching effects on their cultural life. With the conquest of Egypt by Alexander the Great, the local Jewish population was swelled by a great wave of immigration attracted there by the opportunities afforded by the Ptolemies. The Jews concentrated mainly in Alexandria, where they formed an autonomous community with its own synagogues and sociocultural institutions, and where they came to form a significant segment of the population. They soon adopted Greek as their everyday language.

By the third century BCE, both liturgical and educational considerations dictated the need for a Greek translation of the scriptures, at least of the Pentateuch. The version known as the Septuagint was revolutionary in its conception, its execution, and its impact. No lengthy Eastern religious text had previously been translated into Greek, nor had a written translation of the Jewish scriptures been made hitherto. The Septuagint was one of the great literary enterprises of the ancient world, and it served to fashion and shape a distinctively Jewish-Hellenistic culture, which attempted to synthesize Hebraic and Greek thought and values. Eventually, it became a powerful literary medium for the spread of early Christianity throughout the far-flung Greek-speaking world, thereby transforming the culture and religion of a goodly segment of humanity.

The Septuagint ("seventy") received its Latin name from a legend current among the Jews of Alexandria that it was executed by seventy-two scholars in seventy-two days. Originally applicable only to the translation of the Pentateuch, this abbreviated title was gradually extended to the complete Greek rendering of the entire Jewish scriptures. In the course of time, the origins of the Septuagint came to be embroidered in legend and enveloped in an aura of the miraculous. The *Letter of Aristeas*, Philo's *Moses* (II, v–vii, 25–40) and rabbinic writings (e.g., B.T., *Meg.* 9a; *Avot de Rabbi Natan*, ms. b, 37) are the principal witnesses to this development, whereby the initiative for the translation was said to have come from Ptolemy II Philadelphus (r. 285–246 BCE).

The fullest and most popular version of the legend is that found in the first of the above-mentioned sources. That the *Letter* is a fiction is apparent from internal evidence, and it has been shown to have been composed by a hellenized Jew writing in the second half of the second century BCE, about a hundred years after the publication of the original Septuagint. It is certain that it was the needs of the Alexandrian Jewish community that called forth the translation in the course of the third century BCE. It is not impossible, however, that the project did receive royal approval, given the known interest and activities of the Ptolemies as patrons of culture. Furthermore, it is quite likely that the translators did come from Palestine and worked in Egypt.

The Greek of the Septuagint is essentially the Koine, that form of the language commonly spoken and written from the fourth century BCE until the middle of the sixth century CE by the Greek-speaking populations of the eastern Mediterranean. Hence, the Septuagint stands as a monument of Hellenistic Greek. However, it is distinctive in many ways. It abounds with lexical and syntactical Hebraisms and is often indifferent to Greek idiom. Neologisms are comparatively rare, but the translators frequently forced the meaning of common Greek words by using a standard rendering of a Hebrew term without regard to context. Further, Aramaic was still widely used, and the translators sometimes gave Aramaic rather than Hebrew meanings to certain words. On occasion, they rendered the original by Greek words that were similar in sound but quite dissimilar in meaning. Quite clearly they injected Palestinian exegetical traditions into their translations. All in all, the Septuagint was generally competently rendered. If its style is not consistent throughout, this is partly due to the multiplicity of translators and partly to the revolutionary nature of the undertaking in that the translators had neither experience nor real precedent to fall back on.

The rest of the Greek Bible displays a wide variety of styles and techniques ranging from the literal to the free and the paraphrastic. This is due to the piecemeal nature of the translations, to the long period of time it took to complete the entire scriptures—several hundred years—and to the fact that the books of the Prophets and Hagiographa were apparently privately executed. At least, no traditions about them have been preserved. The result was considerable fluctuations in the quality of the translations.

The Septuagint as it has come down to us often reflects readings at variance with the Masoretic Hebrew text. Two factors complicate the scholarly use of this version as a tool for biblical research. The first relates to its early external form, the second to its textual history.

With the spread of Christianity and the pursuit of missionary and polemical activity on the part of the church, the inconvenience of the traditional scroll format for the sacred books became more and more pronounced. The church, therefore, early adopted the codex or "leaf-book" format for its Bible, perhaps being additionally motivated by a conscious desire to differentiate its own from Jewish practice, which adhered to the scroll form for study purposes until at least the sixth century CE. Those who produced the early codices of the Greek Bible must have had great difficulty in assembling uniform copies of the individual scrolls that made up the scriptural canon. Accordingly, various scrolls of a heterogeneous nature were used by the copyists for their archetypes. A badly copied scroll might have been the only one available to the compiler.

The second factor concerns the tendency of later scholars to rework the original Greek translation. Scholars reworked translations because the manuscripts before them had been poorly made, or because the literary quality of the Greek rendering was deemed to be in need of improvement, or, what is most important, because the Greek reflected an underlying Hebrew text at variance with that current at the time, so that editors would attempt to bring the translation in line with the current Hebrew. As a result, multiple text traditions of the Septuagint arose, and the problem of recovering the pristine translation is a formidable one. Each book of the Septuagint must first be individually examined both in terms of its translation technique and style and of its own textual history and transmission. As a result, a rendering that appears to reflect a variant Hebrew text may turn out to be nothing of the sort and may be accounted for on quite different grounds. On the other hand, the Qumran scrolls often clearly display a Hebrew reading that the Septuagint translators must have had before them.

The problems relating to Septuagint studies are exacerbated by the large number of witnesses available, consisting of citations in the works of Philo Judaeus, Josephus, the writers of New Testament, and the Church Fathers; the manuscripts of the Septuagint itself; and the acknowledged revisions of it. Many of the variant quotations may, in fact, be independent personal renderings of the authors or not even be original to the works cited, having been tampered with by later copyists or editors. In the case of the New Testament, there is also the possibility of their having been rendered into Greek from an Aramaic version rather than the Hebrew. Nevertheless, there still remains a respectable residue of genuine Septuagint quotations that differ from the manuscripts. As to these last, the material is very extensive and stretches from the middle of the second century BCE (with the Dead Sea Scrolls material) to the age of printing.

The turning point in the production of Greek Bibles comes in the fourth century CE attendant upon the conversion to Christianity of Constantine (c. 280–337) and the conferring upon that religion of a privileged position in the Roman Empire. An order from Constantine in 332 for fifty vellum Bibles for use in the new churches he was erecting in Constantinople afforded an immense stimulus to the creation of the great and handsome Greek Bibles known technically as majuscules or uncials ("inch high") because of the practice of the scribes to employ capital-size letters without ligatures. The three most important codices of this type that have come down to us in a reasonably complete state are the Codex Sinaiticus (usually designated for scholarly purposes by *S* or by the Hebrew letter alef), the Codex Alexandrinus (given the siglum *A),* and the Codex Vaticanus (indicated by the initial *B).* The Sinaiticus, executed in the fourth century CE, is not complete and in places has been seriously damaged by the action of the metallic ink eating through the parchment. Despite the often careless orthography, the manuscript is witness to a very early text tradition. The Vaticanus, also produced in the fourth century, is nearly perfect and constitutes the oldest and most excellent extant copy of the Greek Bible, even though it is not of uniform quality throughout. It was used as the basis of the Roman edition of 1587, the commonly printed Septuagint. The Alexandrinus, containing practically the entire Bible, was probably copied in the early fifth century. Its text is frequently at variance with that of the Codex Vaticanus. It too has suffered damage from corrosive ink.

Up to the eighth century, only uncials were produced, but thereafter appear the minuscules, written in small-size cursive writing. From the eleventh century, this type completely replaces the other. The minuscules were mainly intended for private reading, and hundreds are extant. Their value for Septuagint studies is small.

The adoption of the Septuagint instead of the Hebrew as the Bible of the church was itself a source of discomfort to Greek-speaking Jews. That the Greek rendering frequently departed from the by then universally recognized Hebrew text constituted additional and decisive cause for its rejection by the synagogue. Doubtless, the conviction on the part of the Jews that Christological changes had been introduced into the original Septuagint also played a role. This reversal of attitude to the Septuagint on the part of the Jewish religious authorities is strikingly reflected in rabbinic literature. The Palestinian minor tractate *Soferim* (1.7) asserts, "The day that the Torah was rendered into Greek was as disastrous for Israel as the day in which the Golden Calf was made, for the Torah could not be adequately translated."

On the Christian side, the lack of uniformity and consistency within the Greek manuscripts themselves were to be an embarrassing disadvantage to Christian missionaries in their theological polemics with Jews. This situation would be exacerbated by the discrepancies between the translation used by Christian disputants and the Hebrew text, which was the only authoritative form of the scriptures recognized by Palestinian Jews. Exegetical debate could proceed only on the basis of a mutually acknowledged text, which in this case had to be the only Hebrew text tradition accepted by the Jews.

All the aforementioned factors led to conscious attempts by Jews and Christians to revise the Septuagint in order to bring it into closer harmony with the Hebrew. In the second century CE, three systematic revisions of the Greek translation took place, namely, those of Aquila, Theodotion, and Symmachus. Aquila, a Jewish proselyte from Pontus, Asia Minor, apparently worked under rabbinical supervision (J.T., *Meg.* 1.11, 70c). He adopted a mechanical, artificial technique of consistently using fixed Greek equivalents for Hebrew terms, and he coined words or forms to this end. This extreme literalness, to the extent of reproducing even minutiae of the original, yielded a recension that was often alien to one who knew no Hebrew. Aquila's motivation was to underline the authority of the standardized consonantal Hebrew text and to produce a Greek version that would be absolutely faithful to it. His work replaced the Septuagint in the synagogues of Greek-speaking Jews, and was used there for the lectionaries well into the sixth century CE. It has survived only in part.

It is not certain whether Theodotion was an Ebionite Christian or a Jewish proselyte. At any rate, he, too, displays excessive literalness. At times, he even transliterates Hebrew words into Greek letters, possibly for the benefit of Jews. His translation was not preserved in Jewish circles, but was highly regarded by the church. His Greek was readable, and his *Daniel* was incorporated into the Septuagint, displacing the inferior original Greek version of that book.

The third revision in the course of the second century CE was done by Symmachus. His origins are obscure. While he used the existing translations, his work has an independent quality about it. The style of the Greek is superior to that of the other two. He also exhibits a tendency to soften anthropomorphisms, as well as a marked influence of rabbinic exegesis. Very little of his work has survived.

The climax of a process of revision for the benefit of Christian missionaries and polemicists against the Jews was the work of the great church theologian of Caesarea, Origen (c. 185–257). He attempted both to provide a textbook for the study of Hebrew and to reduce the variety of Septuagint versions to order, taking as his base the standardized Hebrew text current among the Palestinian Jewish communities of his day. This was a bold step, for it made the Hebrew text superior to, and more authoritative than, the Septuagint, which the church had officially adopted and canonized. To achieve his goal, he arranged texts in six parallel columns. This bulky work, the product of prodigious industry, has come to be known as the Hexapla ("sixfold").

The first column of the Hexapla, the consonantal text-in Hebrew characters, has wholly vanished, but the second, a Greek transliteration of the former, testifies to the fact that it was practically identical with the Masoretic Hebrew text. Origen's aim was apparently to indicate how to vocalize the consonants of the first column. Aquila's translation for the third column was the logical sequence since it was closest to the current Hebrew text, and that of Symmachus came next, apparently because it seems to have been based to a large extent upon Aquila, and it made that rendering more intelligible.

It is in the fifth column, a revised Septuagint, that Origen invested his main energies. In attempting to produce a "corrected" Greek translation, in the sense that it would faithfully represent the Hebrew of his first column, he devised a system for indicating to the reader the substantive differences between the latter and the Septuagint, and for remedying the "defects." The codex of Origen's Hexapla vanished completely sometime in the seventh century. However, his "restored" Septuagint text had been independently published and received wide circulation. In this way it considerably influenced subsequent copies of the Septuagint. Unfortunately, future scribes either neglected or carelessly reproduced the system of critical symbols, with the result that the text became chaotic and Origen's work was ruined.

One other edition of the Greek Bible is that of the Christian theologian Lucian of Antioch (c. 240–312). Lucian was heir to a still earlier Greek version that can now be shown, on the basis of Qumran readings, to have reflected an ancient Hebrew text. Where *Samuel* and *Kings* are concerned, at least, the "Proto-Lucian" was an early Jewish revision of the original Greek translation of which both Theodotion and Aquila seem to have known, if not the original itself, as some have claimed. At any rate, Lucian apparently revised this version on the basis of Origen's fifth column.

TRANSLATIONS BASED ON THE SEPTUAGINT. The great prestige that the Septuagint acquired as the official, authoritative Bible of the church generated a number of secondary translations as Christianity spread to non-Greek-speaking lands and the churches had to accommodate themselves to the native language. Whereas the early translations had been the work of scholars who knew Hebrew, this was now no longer a requirement. The Greek itself served as the base for subsequent translations. Such was the case in respect to the Coptic, Ethiopic, Armenian, Georgian, Gothic, and Old Latin versions, all of which have little bearing on the history of the Hebrew text but are of lesser or greater importance for the study of the Septuagint itself.

The most important of all the secondary renderings of the Bible is the Latin. This language advanced with the expansion of Roman power, first throughout Italy, then into southern Gaul and throughout the Mediterranean coastal regions of Africa. In Rome itself, Greek remained the cultural language of the church until the third century, but in the African communities Latin was very popular, and it is most probable that the earliest translations thereinto emanated from these circles. The needs of the liturgy and the lectionary dictated renditions into the vernacular, which at first remained oral and by way of interlinear glosses. It is not impossible but cannot be proven that the earliest such efforts were made by Jews directly from the Hebrew. At any rate, by the middle of the second century CE, an Old Latin version, in the colloquial form of the language, based on the Septuagint, was current. Whether we are speaking here of a single text or a plurality of translations is a matter of dispute because of the great variety of readings to be found in extant manuscripts and citations. These divide roughly into African and European types, but it must be remembered that the two interacted with each other.

Despite the fact that the Old Latin is a translation of a translation, and for that reason must be used with extreme caution for text-critical studies, it is nevertheless important since it was made from a pre-Hexaplaric Greek text. For example, it has much in common with the Lucianic recension and with the Vatican and Sinaitic codices. In the case of *Job* and *Daniel*, it has renderings that presuppose a Greek reading that has not otherwise been preserved and that, in turn, indicates an original Hebrew text not identical with that received. The psalms, in particular, are significant for the numerous texts available as a consequence of their having been used in the liturgy, although they were frequently reworked.

Vulgate of Jerome. By the close of the fourth century, the confused state of the Old Latin texts had become acute, a source of embarrassment to the church in the lands of the West where Latin was the language of the intelligentsia and of literature. A stable and standardized Bible in that language was a desideratum. At the papal initiative of Damasus I (c. 382), Jerome undertook to revise the Old Latin version.

The Roman Psalter (384), a limited revision of the *Psalms* based on the Greek, seems to have been the first fruit of Jerome's labors in the Hebrew scriptures, although his authorship has been disputed by some scholars. This version was officially adopted into the church liturgy at Rome. It was soon generally superseded by the Gallican Psalter, so called because it was first accepted by the churches of Gaul. This was Jerome's revision of the Old Latin on the basis of the fifth column of the Hexapla, a rendering therefore very close to the Hebrew text of his day. This version, produced in Bethlehem, achieved preeminent status and is the one included in editions of the Vulgate to the present time, even though the fresh translation from the Hebrew more accurately reflects the original.

Jerome's involvement with Origen's Hexapla convinced him of the superiority of the Hebrew text over the Greek, and he set about creating a fresh Latin translation of the Hebrew scriptures, directly from the Hebrew text (the *Hebraica veritas*, the "Hebrew truth"). Doubtless, another motivation was the recognition that Christian theological polemic with Jews could not be conducted on the basis of a text, the Septuagint in this case, which had no authority for one of the parties.

Jerome completed his translation in 405, having enjoyed the assistance of both Jewish converts to Christianity and rabbinical scholars. Indeed, elements of rabbinic tradition and exegesis are embedded in his work, and it is evident that he was also influenced by Aquila's translation. Conscious of the implications of his audacious disregard of the Septuagint that the church had canonized, Jerome was careful to employ the terms and phrases of the Old Latin that had achieved wide currency, particularly those in the New Testament that had doctrinal coloration.

The new Latin translation, known since the sixteenth century as the Vulgate, or "common" edition, met with strenuous opposition, especially on the part of Augustine, but owing to its elegance and superior intelligibility it made headway, so that by the eighth century its preeminence was undisputed. However, because the Vulgate existed for several centuries side by side with the Old Latin, the two versions interacted with each other so that the manuscripts of the Vulgate became corrupted. Various attempts in the Middle Ages to produce a corrected and revised edition are recorded, but none gained lasting success.

The invention of printing finally made possible the long-sought goal of a standardized text, but this goal was not achieved at once. Jerome's Vulgate may have the distinction of being the first book printed from movable type to issue from Gutenberg's press at Mainz (1456), but it took almost another century of sporadic attempts at revision before a definitive, official edition was achieved. The achievement of a definitive edition was an outgrowth of the decision of the Council of Trent in 1546 to proclaim Jerome's Vulgate to be the authoritative Bible of the Catholic Church. The hastily prepared three-volume edition of Sixtus V (1590), the "Sixtine Bible," proved to be unsatisfactory, and it was soon replaced by the "Clementine Bible" of 1592, promulgated by Clement VIII. This latter remained the one official text of the church until the twentieth century.

In 1907, a new critical edition of the Vulgate was commissioned by Pius X, and the task of preparation was entrusted to the Benedictine order. About eight thousand manuscripts were consulted, and it began to appear in 1926. By 1981, fourteen volumes had been published covering most of the books of the Hebrew Bible. A two-volume edition based on the foregoing was issued at Stuttgart in 1975, with a second edition in 1980.

The importance of the Vulgate as a major factor in the cultural and religious life of Western civilization cannot be overestimated. For a thousand years, it was the Bible of the churches of western Europe and served as the base at first for all translations into the respective developing vernaculars.

Syriac versions. Syriac is an Eastern Aramaic dialect within the Semitic group of languages that was current in southeastern Turkey and the Euphrates Valley. It was an important literary and liturgical language within the Christian church from the third century until the Arab Muslim invasion of the area. The Hebrew Bible was several times translated into Syriac, the many renderings necessitated by dialectic and theological considerations.

It is quite likely that there existed an early Syriac rendering that was the basis of the many later versions, most of which are extant only as fragments. The one complete translation to survive is the standard and most important recension, known since the ninth century as the Peshitta. This term means the "simple [version]," a designation it acquired either because of its popular style or, more likely, to contrast it with the more complicated renderings that were equipped with a text-critical apparatus. Ever since the third century, the Peshitta has been the official Bible of the Syrian church, common in one form or another to all its different branches.

The Peshitta is theoretically of the utmost significance for the textual criticism of the Hebrew Bible, since it was executed directly from the original long before the fixing of the Hebrew masoretic system, and because it is in a language closely related to Hebrew, in contrast to the Greek versions. This importance, however, is diminished by the facts that the version possesses a long complex history as yet imperfectly reconstructed, that the hundreds of manuscripts housed in the Western libraries display a large number of variants, and that all existing printed editions are unreliable.

No early trustworthy data about the provenance and date of the Peshitta or of the identity of the translators have been handed down. Weighty evidence has been adduced to prove both a Jewish and a Christian origin. If the former, the work would have originated in a Syriac-speaking community that maintained close relationships with Jerusalem. This immediately suggests the district of Adiabene in the upper region of the Tigris, situated between the rivers Great Zab and Little Zab, where a Jewish kingdom existed in the first century CE (Josephus, *Antiquities* 20.2.1–20.4.3, Loeb ed. XX.17–

96). On the other hand, a Christian provenance can also be argued, since Christianity early took firm hold in the region of Adiabene, which already had Christian bishops by 123 CE. The ecclesiastical authorities, in preparing a version of scripture for the needs of the local Christian community, could have made use of earlier Jewish Aramaic translations and could have entrusted the task to Jewish Christians, whose presence in the area is attested. There is also the possibility that the Christian elements may be the result of the later redaction of an earlier Jewish work. It is impossible to generalize about the nature of the translation, which is the work of many hands and different periods and which lacks consistency.

Early in the fifth century, the Syriac church experienced a schism, dividing into Nestorians in the East and Jacobites in the West, with each group developing its own form of the Peshitta. Because of the relative isolation of the former, politically and geographically, in the area of Nisibin in southern Anatolia, the Eastern or Nestorian texts are regarded as having been less vulnerable to revisions on the basis of Hebrew or Greek sources.

The most important Peshitta manuscripts are those copied before the tenth century when the standardized Syriac biblical *masorah* was finally fixed.

A Syriac version that is second in importance only to the Peshitta is the Syro-Hexapla. This is a rendering of the Septuagint version of the fifth column of Origen's Hexapla. It was commissioned to serve political and theological ends, and it was most likely executed in a Syrian monastery in Egypt by Paul, bishop of Tella, together with associates, and completed in 617. It never achieved its purpose of displacing the Peshitta, but it has its own inherent worth and is most valuable as a tool for reconstructing the lost column of the Hexapla on which it was based.

Another version of the Syriac Bible is the Syro-Palestinian. This version has only partially survived. Its script is distinctive, in that it used the Estrangela ("round script") type, as is also its dialect, which is a West Palestinian Aramaic spoken by a Christian community in certain areas of the Judean hills. This is a development of the dialect spoken by Jews who converted to Christianity around the year 400, and who intermingled with the Melchite church. The version bears close affinities with Jewish Aramaic Targums. Moshe H. Goshen-Gottstein together with H. Shirun assembled all printed remnants of this version as well as some unpublished material. The Pentateuch and the Prophets in Hebrew characters appeared in 1973.

Still another Syriac version, the Philoxenian, was commissioned by the leader of the Jacobite Monophysite church, Philoxenus, bishop of Mabbug-Hierapolis, near Aleppo, Syria, in 507–508. This version was not a revision of the Peshitta, but a new translation based on the Lucianic version of the Greek. Only fragments of *Isaiah* and *Psalms* have survived.

Finally, there is the attempt of Jacob (c. 640–708), bishop of Edessa, to modernize and popularize the style of the Syro-Hexapla while retaining the text-form of the former. For the first time, chapter divisions were introduced, and the Syrian Masoretic apparatus was utilized.

Arabic translations. Jewish and Christian communities existed in the Arabian Peninsula many centuries before the dawn of Islam, engaging in missionary activities among the pagan Arabs, often in competition with one another. In Yemen, in southwestern Arabia, the last of the Himyarite rulers, Dhū Nuwās, even converted to Judaism (517 CE). The buffer state of Al-Hīrah was a center of Arab Christianity between the third and sixth centuries. The Jews used their Hebrew Bible, the Christians either the Syriac or Greek translations. Since both religious communities were well integrated into Arabian life and culture, while retaining their distinctiveness, it seems plausible that at least parts of the Bible had been rendered into Arabic, if only in oral form, in pre-Islamic days, much the same way as Aramaic oral renderings long antedated the first written translations in that language. It was the Muslim invasions of western Asia and the concomitant Arabization of the populace that prompted the systematic, written translation of the Bible into Arabic. The foremost Christian scholar and translator, Ḥunayn ibn Isḥāk (Johannitus, 808–873), is said to have produced such a version, basing himself on the Septuagint, but if there was such a version, it has not survived.

The first and most celebrated translation made directly from the Hebrew was that of Saʿadyah Gaon (882–942), leader of Babylonian Jewry. It has come down only in Hebrew script, and its appearance constituted a major turning point in the development of Judeo-Arabic culture. Saʿadyah tried to conform in his style to the genius of the Arabic language. He sought to eliminate anthropomorphisms and he rendered geographical names into contemporary usage.

The impact of Saʿadyah's translation was immense. It has continued to enjoy high prestige and to be read weekly by Yemenite Jews to the present day. It even influenced the Samaritan and Karaite communities, both of which produced their own Arabic versions of the Hebrew scriptures. The first Samaritan translator of the Pentateuch, Abū Saʿīd (thirteenth century), based himself on it; at the end of the tenth century, the foremost Karaite scholar, Yafet ben Eli, rendered the entire Bible anew into Arabic, which translation remained the standard text for all Karaite communities in the East. It, too, was indebted to Saʿadyah, even though its style and language were updated, more popular, and excessively literal.

Christian translations were generally not made from the Hebrew but were variously based on the Greek, Syriac, Latin, and Coptic versions, sometimes on more than one. In the sixteenth century, attempts were made to assemble a complete Bible in Arabic, but the different translators individually used different versions as their base. The resulting codex was a mixed text. The Paris Polyglot of 1629 first featured an almost complete Arabic text of the Bible, which was followed by the London Polyglot of 1657, but here again the result was a mixed text.

In the course of the nineteenth and twentieth centuries, as a result of renewed interest in the Arab world on the part of Western powers, Protestant and Catholic organizations set about producing translations into modern Arabic for missionary purposes. The most frequently used is that by the American Protestant mission in Beirut, completed in 1864, and made from the Hebrew. The most widely used Catholic translation is that in three volumes (1876–1880) made by the Jesuits in Beirut with the assistance of Ibrāhīm al-Yāzijt.

In sum, the Arabic translations, apart from that of Saʿadyah, are relatively late and are mostly secondary, so that they have no value for textual studies of the Hebrew original. They are, however, useful sources for the history of biblical exegesis, as well as witnesses to the earlier translations such as the Greek, the Aramaic, and the Syriac.

See Also Biblical Exegesis, article on Jewish Views; Canon; Chanting; Dead Sea Scrolls; Israelite Law; Israelite Religion; Oral Tradition; Prophecy, article on Biblical Prophecy; Psalms; Samaritans; Wisdom Literature, article on Biblical Books.

Bibliography

The most reliable and comprehensive work on the Bible is *The Cambridge History of the Bible*, 3 vols., edited by Peter R. Ackroyd (Cambridge, 1963–1970). It summarizes the current state of scholarship in nontechnical language and each chapter is written by a specialist in the field. The excellent bibliographies are arranged by topic. For more concise introductions to the issues and approaches involved in the contemporary study of the Hebrew scriptures there are Herbert F. Hahn's *The Old Testament in Modern Research*, 2d exp. ed., with a survey of recent literature by Horace D. Hummel (Philadelphia, 1966), and John H. Hayes's *An Introduction to Old Testament Study* (Nashville, 1979). The latter work notes only items in English in the useful bibliographies that precede each chapter. Two most frequently used comprehensive traditional introductions to the Bible containing extensive bibliographies are Otto Eisfeldt's *The Old Testament: An Introduction*, translated from the third German edition by Peter R. Ackroyd (New York, 1965), and Georg Fohrer's *Introduction to the Old Testament* (Nashville, 1968).

Two classic works on the history of the canon are Frants Buhl's *Canon and Text of the Old Testament*, translated from the German by John Macpherson (Edinburgh, 1892), and H. E. Ryle's *The Canon of the Old Testament: An Essay on the Gradual Growth and Formation of the Hebrew Canon of Scripture*, 2d ed. (London, 1892). Both contain ample references to and quotations from rabbinic and patristic sources. *The Canon and Masorah of the Hebrew Bible*, edited by Sid Z. Leiman (New York, 1974), provides an indispensable collection of thirty-seven essays by as many scholars relating to various aspects of the biblical canon; all but four are in English. The work lacks an index. Leiman's original contribution to the subject is *The Canonization of Hebrew Scripture: The Talmudic and Midrashic Evidence* (Hamden, Conn., 1976). Extensive citations from rabbinic literature are given both in their original form and in translation. The work is enhanced by copious notes, bibliography, and indexes.

The new concept of canon as a process is explicated by James A. Sanders in his *Torah and Canon* (Philadelphia, 1972) and in his essay "Available for Life: The Nature and Function of Canon," in *Magnalia Dei', The Mighty Acts of God: Essays on the Bible and Archaeology in Memory of G. Ernest Wright*, edited by Frank Moore Cross et al. (Garden City, N.Y., 1976), pp. 531–560. *Introduction to the Old Testament as Scripture* by Brevard S. Childs (Philadelphia, 1979) seeks to describe the form and function of each book of the Hebrew Bible in its role as sacred scripture, and to understand the literature in that context. It contains detailed bibliographies. Contemporary concerns with canonical criticism are examined by James Barr in his *Holy Scripture, Canon, Authority, Criticism* (Philadelphia, 1983).

Ernst Würthwein's *The Text of the Old Testament*, translated from the German by Peter R. Ackroyd (Oxford, 1957), is a useful key to the critical apparatus of the Kittel edition of the Hebrew Bible. The text is illustrated by forty-four plates. The most detailed and readable work is that by Bleddyn J. Roberts, *Old Testament Text and Versions* (Cardiff, 1951). However, some of the data need to be updated in light of research into the Dead Sea Scrolls. The best all-around discussion of these last-mentioned is *The Ancient Library of Qumrân and Modern Biblical Studies*, rev. ed. (Garden City, N.Y., 1961), by Frank Moore Cross. This work is supplemented by a collection of scholarly essays assembled by the same author together with Shemaryahu Talmon in *Qumran and the History of the Biblical Text* (Cambridge, Mass., 1975). Paul E. Kahle's *The Cairo Genizah*, 2d ed. (New York, 1959), examines and evaluates the impact of the hoard of manuscripts found in the bibliocrypt of the synagogue in Old Cairo and in the caves of Qumran on the scholarship relating to the history of the biblical Hebrew text and the ancient translations, as well as on the ancient pronunciation of Hebrew. The history and critical evaluation of the methodology of textual criticism is given by M. H. Goshen-Gottstein in "The Textual Criticism of the Old Testament: Rise, Decline, Rebirth," *Journal of Biblical Literature* 102 (September 1983): 365–399.

A basic introduction to the Greek versions, their history, character, and the problems they present, is provided by the collection of thirty-five essays assembled by Sidney Jellicoe, *Studies into the Septuagint: Origins, Recensions, and Interpretations* (New York, 1974). Another important work for nonspecialists is Bruce M. Metzger's *Manuscripts of the Greek Bible: An Introduction to Greek Palaeography* (Oxford, 1981). Of a more technical and advanced nature is Imanuel Tov's *The Text-Critical Use of the Septuagint in Biblical Research* (Jerusalem, 1981). Henry Barclay Swete's *An Introduction to the Old Testament in Greek*, 2d ed. (Cambridge, 1902), still remains standard. Harry M. Orlinsky's essay "The Septuagint as Holy Writ and the Philosophy of the Translators," *Hebrew Union College Annual* 46 (1975): 89–114, contributes important insights into the nature of this version. *A Classified Bibliography of the Septuagint* by Sebastian P. Brock, Charles

T. Fritsch, and Sidney Jellicoe (Leiden, 1973) is an indispensable scholarly tool.

For Targumic studies, there is Bernard Grossfeld's *A Bibliography of Targum Literature*, 2 vols. (Cincinnati, 1972–1977).

The Bible and the Ancient Near East: Essays in Honor of William Foxwell Albright, edited by G. Ernest Wright (Garden City, N.Y., 1961), contains fifteen studies by as many different scholars summarizing the course taken by scholarly research in various areas of Near Eastern studies bearing on the Bible. J. B. Pritchard has edited a superb collection, *Ancient Near Eastern Texts relating to the Old Testament*, 3d ed. (Princeton, 1969), which gives translations of pertinent texts drawn from all genres of literature, together with brief introductory notes and also indexes of names and biblical references. This collection is supplemented by *The Ancient Near East in Pictures relating to the Old Testament*, 2d ed. (Princeton, 1969), by the same author, which is arranged by topics, and is equipped with a descriptive catalogue giving in concise notation the significant details of each picture, and an index. *Near Eastern Religious Texts relating to the Old Testament*, edited by Walter Beyerlin, translated from the German by John Bowden (London, 1978), is more restricted in scope, but includes several texts available only since 1969. The accompanying notes are fuller than in the preceding work. Another useful collection of this type, though far more limited in scope, and less up to date, is D. Winton Thomas's *Documents from Old Testament Times* (New York, 1961). Theodor H. Gaster's *Myth, Legend, and Custom in the Old Testament* (New York, 1969) is a comparative study based on James G. Frazer's *Folk-Lore in the Old Testament*, 3 vols. (London, 1919). The copious notes are especially valuable. A concise yet comprehensive introduction to the geographical and historical settings of the Hebrew Bible is provided by Martin Noth in his *The Old Testament World*, translated by Victor I. Gruhn (Philadelphia, 1966). Frederick G. Kenyon's *Our Bible and the Ancient Manuscripts*, revised by A. W. Adams, with an introduction by Godfrey R. Driver (New York, 1965), is particularly useful for a survey of the ancient versions.

NAHUM M. SARNA (1987)

BIBLICAL LITERATURE: APOCRYPHA AND PSEUDEPIGRAPHA

Well known are the documents canonized as the Hebrew scriptures (Old Testament) and dated from approximately 950 to 165/4 BCE. Less well known are the bodies of writings cognate to the Hebrew scriptures, called the Apocrypha and the Pseudepigrapha, and written by Jews during the Hellenistic and Roman periods. Closely related to the thirty-nine Old Testament books canonized by Jews and Christians and sometimes related to the twenty-seven New Testament books canonized by Christians, these documents were very influential and were frequently considered inspired by many Jewish and Christian communities. When the canons of scripture were closed, first by Jewish and then by Christian authorities, these writings were not included, and they quickly began to lose their influence and importance. Consequently, these documents are usually preserved only in late manuscripts that are translations of lost originals. Since the discovery of the Dead Sea Scrolls and the renewed appreciation of the diversities of thought at the time, scholars have agreed that the history of Early Judaism (250 BCE–200 CE) and Early Christianity (first–fourth centuries) cannot be written without consulting these bodies of so-called extracanonical writings, the Apocrypha and Pseudepigrapha.

THE APOCRYPHA. The Apocrypha has been variously defined, for there is, of course, no set canon of either the Apocrypha or the Pseudepigrapha. The word *apokrypha* is a transliteration of a Greek neuter plural that means "hidden." By the fourth century CE the term *apocrypha* no longer denoted hidden esoteric secrets (cf. *Daniel* 12:9–10 and *4 Ezra* 14:44–48), but it was often used to name a category of discarded, heretical books. Jerome (c. 342–420), however, used the term to denote extracanonical, not heretical, documents. This position is the one adopted by Protestants today; Roman Catholics, since the Council of Trent (during session 4 on April 8, 1546), consider these works "deuterocanonical" and inspired, as do most Eastern Christians. These books are in the official Catholic canon because they are in the Vulgate (of the thirteen works in the Apocrypha, *2 Ezra*, which is *3 Esdras* in the Vulgate, is not included in the Catholic canon).

Since the first century CE, Jews and Christians have had widely divergent opinions regarding the Hellenistic literature collected into the Apocrypha and Pseudepigrapha of the Hebrew scriptures. It is essential now, while appreciating the varying status of each work in different religious denominations, to establish a set list of books in each collection, without delving into normative value judgments. It is best to limit the documents included in the Apocrypha to those contained in the fourth-century Greek codices of the Hebrew scriptures (these codices of the Septuagint contain more documents than the Hebrew scriptures) and to include documents occasionally found in some expanded collections of the Apocrypha under the larger collection called the Pseudepigrapha. The Apocrypha, then, contains thirteen writings, and the Pseudepigrapha contains fifty-two documents. In the following discussion, these writings will be arranged according to loosely defined genres and then presented according to the most probable chronological order.

The thirteen works in the Apocrypha have been dated by experts over a wide period, from the fourth century BCE to the late first century CE; most scholars today correctly date all of them from circa 300 BCE to 70 CE, when the Temple was burned by the Romans. Almost all were written in a Semitic language, except the *Wisdom of Solomon* and *2 Maccabees*, which were probably written in Greek. There probably is a consensus that none was written in Babylon, that all but two were written in Palestine, and that these two, the *Wisdom of Solomon* and *2 Maccabees*, were written in Egypt. In contrast to the Pseudepigrapha, the Apocrypha contains no examples of three literary genres—namely, apocalypses, testaments, and prayers, psalms, and odes. (The expanded Apocrypha, however, does include an apocalypse, *4 Ezra*, a prayer, the *Prayer of Manasseh*, and a psalm, Psalm 151.)

Legends, romantic stories, and expansions of the Hebrew scriptures. Nine documents of the Apocrypha can be regarded as forming a group of legends, romantic stories, and expansions of the Hebrew scriptures: the *Letter of Jeremiah, Tobit, Judith, 2 Ezra,* the additions to *Esther,* the *Prayer of Azariah and the Song of the Three Young Men, Susanna, Bel and the Dragon,* and *1 Baruch.*

Letter of Jeremiah. The *Letter of Jeremiah,* probably composed in Hebrew or Aramaic, is the oldest writing in the Apocrypha. A Greek fragment dating from around 100 BCE was found in Qumran Cave VII, and this discovery only disproves conjectures regarding a late date, such as Edgar J. Goodspeed's claim in *The Story of the Apocrypha* (Chicago, 1939, p. 105) that the *Letter of Jeremiah* was written late in the first century CE. Carey A. Moore (1977, pp. 327–329) concludes that the *Letter of Jeremiah* reflects the social setting of Palestine in the late fourth century BCE. A date between 323 and 100 BCE seems possible; perhaps around 300 is most likely (see Antonius H. J. Gunneweg, *Der Brief Jeremias,* Gütersloh, 1975, p. 186). A Palestinian provenience is relatively certain (not Alexandrian, as Goodspeed contends in *The Story of the Apocrypha,* p. 105).

The document is "a letter" (*epistole*) pseudonymously attributed to Jeremiah (verse 1); it contains seventy-two or seventy-three verses. The work is not a letter but a passionate sermon or plea to fellow Jews not to fear or worship idols; it is inspired by *Jeremiah* 10:1–16 (cf. *Isaiah* 44:9–21 and *Psalms* 115:3–8, 135:15–18), which is also a polemic against idolatry. The literary facade may have been stimulated by Jeremiah's letter to the exiles in Babylon (*Jer.* 29:1–23).

Tobit. Written in a Semitic language, probably Aramaic, around 180 BCE, and in Palestine—not in Egypt (*pace* D. C. Simpson, in Charles, 1913, p. 185)—*Tobit* is not a historical book, as some earlier critics claimed. It is a romantic story that attempts to edify the reader and to illustrate that God is efficacious and helps the righteous. The author fills the text with striking anachronisms: the tribe of Naphtali was exiled by Tiglath-pileser, not Shalmaneser (*Tb.* 1:2); Shalmaneser's successor was Sargon, not Sennacherib (*Tb.* 1:15); Nineveh was captured by Nabopolassar and Cyaxares, not Nebuchadrezzar and Ahasuerus (*Tb.* 14:15). These errors may have served to warn the attentive reader that the work is intended to be taken not as a history but as a folktale, or fictional short story. Likewise, the angel Raphael's declaration that he appears before men not corporally but in a vision (*Tb.* 12:19) may indicate the author's refusal to play on the credulity of the simple, or it may perhaps reflect a theology that is against belief in angels. The author is learned, borrowing from the Hebrew scriptures (the Pentateuch and the Prophets especially), from the Pseudepigrapha (notably from Ahiqar, who is mentioned explicitly in *Tobit* 1:21–22, 2:10, 11:18, and 14:10), and perhaps from the fable of the Grateful Dead (Simpson, in Charles, 1913, p. 188; Pfeiffer, 1949, pp. 269–271).

Combining two ancient folk legends, those of the Grateful Dead and the Dangerous Bride, the author, in fourteen chapters, weaves a deeply religious story. Tobit, a righteous man in exile in Nineveh, risks the king's wrath and certain death by collecting the corpses of fellow Israelites and giving them an honorable burial. Forced to sleep outside, because of his impurity one night, he is blinded by sparrows' dung. After an altercation with Anna, his wife, he prays to God to die. Also praying to die on that same day is Sarah, whose seven bridegrooms had perished on their wedding night, slain by Asmodeus, a demon (his name means "destroyer").

Remembering ten talents of silver (a wealthy sum) he had left in Media with a certain Gabael, Tobit sends his son Tobias to Gabael. In words reminiscent of a "testament," Tobit instructs his son regarding his duties to his parents and to the Law and avows practical wisdom regarding daily life. Tobias sets off on his journey accompanied by Raphael (whose name means "God heals"), God's angel disguised as an Israelite. He captures a fish and removes its gall, heart, and liver. With these magical potents and Raphael's advice and help, Tobias successfully defeats Asmodeus. He then marries Sarah, at whose home they rested. Raphael collects Tobit's money. Tobias and Sarah return to Nineveh, with Tobit's talents and half of Sarah's father's wealth. Tobias heals his father's eyesight with the gall of the fish. Offered half the riches, Raphael respectfully declines, affirming that prayer and alms are superior to riches, and reports that God had sent him, one of the seven angels, to heal Tobit and Sarah (*Tb.* 3:17). Raphael ascends; Tobit and Anna live a full life and are honorably buried by their son, who moves from (wicked) Nineveh to Ecbatana, Sarah's hometown.

Judith. The dramatic and didactic story of Judith was written in Hebrew around 150 BCE in Palestine, not in the Diaspora (not Antioch, *pace* Solomon Zeitlin in *The Book of Judith,* Leiden, 1972, p. 32). The sixteen chapters can be divided into a description of the attack upon the Jews by Holofernes, the general of the Assyrian king Nebuchadrezzar (chaps. 1–7), and then the deliverance of the nation by God through Judith, who decapitates Holofernes (chaps. 8–16). Judith is reminiscent of numerous biblical heroines, notably Jael (*Jgs.* 4:17–22, 5:2–31), Deborah (*Jgs.* 4:4–5:31), and Esther (esp. *Est.* 2:15–8:17).

This literary masterpiece—a classic example of an ancient short story—was written in order to encourage fellow Jews to resist the evil enemy, and to exhort them to obey the Law strictly (see especially Achior's prophecy and celebration of the people "in the hill country," *Jdt.* 5:5–21). God's efficaciousness depends upon observance of the Law. Since the story circulated shortly after the beginning of the Maccabean revolution, which began in 167 BCE, it would have served to encourage the Jews who not only faced superior military forces but were weakened internally by the bewitching attractiveness of Greek culture. God is proclaimed in Judith's song as "the Lord who shatters wars" (*Jdt.* 16:2). During the early decades of the Maccabean revolution this thought characterized those zealous and faithful to the Law; they would have been encouraged also by Judith's victorious shout: "With us still is God, our God, to effect power in Israel and strength against our enemies" (*Jdt.* 13:11).

2 Ezra (1 Esdras in the Septuagint, 3 Esdras in the Vulgate). Probably written in Hebrew or Aramaic, this work is a reproduction and rewriting of parts of the Hebrew scriptures, especially *2 Chronicles* 35:1–36:23, all of *Ezra,* and *Nehemiah* 7:38–8:12. Although very difficult to date, the work may derive from the late second century, or around 150–100 BCE. It certainly must predate 100 CE; Josephus Flavius used it, and not the Septuagint parallels, as his source for the period 621–398 BCE in his *Jewish Antiquities* (esp. 11.1.1–11.5.5).

Although this document is, of all the apocryphal writings, the one most closely connected to the Hebrew scriptures, it contains one section that is without parallel therein. This passage, chapters 3:1–5:6, is not dependent on any biblical book, and it may be a rewriting and adaptation of an earlier Babylonian tale. It describes a great feast after which three young guardsmen attempt to ascertain which of three potents is strongest: wine, the king, or women. To these answers a fourth is appended at the end of the chapter (4:33–41; plus 4:13b); it shifts the answer from "women" to "truth" and has all the earmarks of being a Jewish editorial addition in order to bring the climax of the account to an acceptable Jewish affirmation: "Great is truth, and strongest of all" (cf. Vulgate: "Magna est veritas et praevalet").

While the purpose of the nine chapters in the document is unclear, some characteristics are notable. The author elevates Ezra and refers to him as "high priest" ("Esdras ho archiereus," 9:40; cf. 9:49). He puts considerable emphasis on the Temple and its cult, which is reflected in the numerous references to the Temple and in the magnification of Zerubabel, the winner of the contest, who is the only guardsman identified (4:13; 4:13b is an editorial addition). Zerubabel is linked closely with King Darius, who commends him as "the wisest" (*sophoteros,* 4:42) and rewards him by providing for the rebuilding of the Temple (see Myers, 1974, pp. 8–15).

Additions to Esther. The additions to *Esther* are not a separate book; they are six extensive expansions to the Greek version of the *Book of Esther:*

A. Mordecai's dream and his exposure of a conspiracy against King Artaxerxes (1:1a–1r or 11:2–12:6),

B. a letter by Artaxerxes, who orders the extermination of the Jews (3:13a–13g or 13:1–7),

C. prayers by Mordecai and Esther (4:17a–17z and 5:2a–2b or 13:8–15:16),

D. Esther's radiant and successful audience before the king (5:1a–1f., 5:2a–2b or 15:1–16),

E. a second letter by Artaxerxes, who rescinds his former edict and praises the Jews (8:12a–12x or 16:1–24), and

F. the interpretation of Mordecai's dream (10:3a–3l or 10:4–11:1).

These additions amount to 107 verses not found in the Hebrew scriptures.

Four of these additions reflect a Hebrew original, but additions B and E, the two letters, were probably composed in Greek (see Moore, 1977, p. 155). Modern scholars tend to accept the authenticity of the ending of the additions, which dates them before 114 BCE and situates them in Jerusalem ("In the fourth year of Ptolemy and Cleopatra's reign . . . the preceding Letter of Purim . . . had been translated by Lysimachus, son of Ptolemy, [who is among those Egyptians living] in Jerusalem," 31 or 11:1). Moore (1977, pp. 161, 165–167) argues (unconvincingly) that the letters, additions B and E, postdate 114 and may have originated in Alexandria. The date of the Hebrew sections (A, C, D, and F) is now an open issue: do they appreciably predate 114 BCE? Hans Bardtke in *Historische und legendarische Erzählungen: Zusätze zu Esther* (Gütersloh, 1973, p. 27), argues that the date of the additions to *Esther* is between 167 and 161 BCE, because *2 Maccabees* 15:36, which refers to "Mordecai's day," probably postdates these additions, and the celebration on this day was for the defeat and death of Nicanor in 161.

The purposes of these imaginative additions seem clear. First and foremost, they supply the religious dimension so singularly lacking in *Esther.* Second, they provide color and detail to the story. Third, they contain a strong apologetic for Judaism (see especially E and F): "We find the Jews are not evildoers, but they are governed by the most just laws. . . . Permit the Jews to live by their own laws."

Prayer of Azariah and the Song of the Three Young Men. Three additions to *Daniel* are collected into the Apocrypha. Two of these, the story of Susanna and the story of Bel and the dragon, are separate, self-contained works in the *Daniel* cycle; the third, the *Prayer of Azariah,* like the additions to *Esther,* should be read as an insertion of sixty-eight verses into the *Book of Daniel*; in the Septuagint these verses are numbered from 3:24 to 3:90 (hence, the addition begins after 3:23).

All three additions were probably written originally in Hebrew, or possibly in Aramaic, and not in Greek as many early scholars concluded. The date of the additions is difficult to discern; in their present form all, of course, must postdate 164/5, the date of the *Book of Daniel.* A date between 164/5 and 100 BCE is a reasonable guess for all three additions, provided we acknowledge the possibility that one or more, especially *Bel and the Dragon,* could have been added in the early decades of the first century BCE. The three additions are probably from different times. It is possible that all three, or portions of them, originally reflected a setting different from their present place in the Septuagint. In the second century BCE there probably existed two rival versions of *Daniel* in Hebrew, one that is represented in the present Hebrew Bible (Masoretic text), and the other a later Hebrew recension, which was translated into Greek (of which today there are two recensions, the Septuagint and the Theodotion).

Two caveats are necessary. First, these additions may originally have been composed without *Daniel* in mind; Moore (1977, pp. 26–29) argues that parts of the *Prayer of Azariah* come from the liturgy of the Temple or the synagogue, and that *Susanna* and *Bel and the Dragon* originally had "nothing at all to do with the prophet Daniel" (esp. pp. 26, 109). Second, while this possibility deserves careful examination, these three additions are now clearly related to *Daniel* and should be studied in light of the Danielic cycle, represented by previously unknown documents found among the Dead Sea Scrolls, especially the *Prayer of Nabonidus* (4QPsDan ar a–c; cf. 4QPsDan Aa, 4QPrNab ar). A Palestinian provenience seems most likely for the additions.

The *Prayer of Azariah*, clearly composed in Hebrew (see Otto Plöger, *Züsatze zu Daniel*, Gütersloh, 1973, p. 68), emphasizes that there is only one God and that he is always just. This addition to *Daniel* shifts the focus from the evil king and his golden idol to three potential martyrs and their faithfulness in prayer.

Susanna. The colorful tale of Susanna, told in only sixty-four verses (in the Theodotion), may originally have been independent of the Danielic cycle and is perhaps considerably earlier than the *Book of Daniel.* It describes how a beautiful woman, Susanna, is brought to court, because she refuses to submit to two aroused influential men (elders, *presbuteroi*, and judges, *kritai*), who approached her while she was bathing. Her scream and the men's lies land her in court. There her fate is sealed; the people and judges condemn her without hearing her. As she is being led to be stoned, the Lord hears her cry (verse 44) and arouses a youth, Daniel, who asks the judge to cross-examine the accusors. The story illustrates how God hears and helps the faithful and virtuous woman, and it demonstrates the wisdom of God in Daniel. This story, however, does not permit us to claim unequivocally either that witnesses were privately cross-examined in court in the second century BCE or that the worth of the individual—even women—was accorded first priority in courts in Hellenistic Judaism.

Bel and the Dragon (Bel and the Snake). This story of forty-two verses contains two separate tales. The first, one of our earliest examples of a detective story, describes how Daniel, by pointing out footprints in the ashes he had strewn on the floor of a temple, reveals to the king that the priests, their wives, and children had been eating the food offered to Bel, the Babylonian idol. The king recognizes he has been duped, becomes enraged, sees the secret doors used by the priests, and orders their deaths. Daniel is told to destroy the idol and its temple. The second story tells how Daniel destroys an idol, which is shaped like a great dragon (*drakōn*, v. 23), and is subsequently thrown into a lions' den. He survives, and Habakkuk, with angelic aid, zooms to Babylon and feeds Daniel. The king releases Daniel and casts his enemies into the pit. The shout of the king is significant for the purpose of these two stories: "You are great, O Lord God of Daniel, and there is no other but you" (v. 41). These stories lack the polish and brilliance of *Tobit* and *Judith;* their purpose is to ridicule idolatry and affirm the importance of worshiping God alone.

1 Baruch. O. C. Whitehouse (in Charles, 1913, pp. 572–573) argued that *1 Baruch* had been written in Greek; but his editor, R. H. Charles, appended a significant footnote (pp. 573–574) in which he claimed it had been composed in Hebrew. Modern scholars have concluded that at least parts of this document were composed in Hebrew, others in Hebrew or perhaps Greek. Although the precise date of the document in its present form is unknown, there is wide agreement that it dates from the second or first centuries BCE. W. O. E. Oesterley (*An Introduction to the Books of the Apocrypha*, New York, 1935, p. 260) and Whitehouse (in Charles, 1913, p. 575) were certainly wrong to have dated *1 Baruch* after 70 CE. The provenience may be Palestinian.

The document is a composite: 1:1–3:8 is a prose composition and contains a confession of sins and a plea for God's compassion after the destruction of Jerusalem (cf. *Deuteronomy* 28–32 and *Daniel* 9:4–19); 3:9–4:4, by another writer, is in poetry and praises wisdom (cf. *Ben Sira* 24 and *Job* 28:12–28); 4:5–5:9, probably by the second writer, describes how Jerusalem's lament was heard. In *The Poetry of Baruch: A Reconstruction and Analysis of the Original Hebrew Text of Baruch 3:9–5:9* (Chico, Calif., 1982), David G. Burke argues that the second section, the poem on wisdom, is the earliest portion of the work and that the compilation dates somewhere from 180 to 100 BCE; he also attempts to reconstruct the original Hebrew of 3:9–4:4. This document is an example of Hellenistic Jewish theology, but noticeably absent are references to a messiah, eschatological or apocalyptic ideas, beliefs in a resurrection, and any signs of a dualism.

Wisdom and philosophical literature. Two books in the Apocrypha are from the wisdom school of Hellenistic Judaism, but while each is written by a single author, they are very different. *Ben Sira*, written in Hebrew, is by a conservative traditionalist from Palestine, perhaps even Jerusalem. The *Wisdom of Solomon*, written in Greek, is by a liberal thinker, thoroughly open to and influenced by non-Jewish ideas and philosophy—reminiscent to a certain extent of Philo Judaeus of Alexandria and *4 Maccabees;* it comes from Egypt, probably Alexandria.

Ben Sira (Sirach, Ecclesiasticus). The author addressed his work to fellow Jews and wrote it probably around 180 BCE. Fragments of the Hebrew original of 39:27–43:30 were discovered in 1964 in an eastern casemate wall at Masada. These twenty-six leather fragments must predate 74 CE, the date of the destruction of Masada, and paleographically they are from circa 125–25 BCE; they are middle or late Hasmonean (see the facsimiles in Yigael Yadin, *The Ben Sira*

Scroll from Masada, Jerusalem, 1965, pls. 1–9 and pp. 2–11). The Qumran fragments of *Ben Sira* (2QSir) are also approximately of the same date; they are late Hasmonean or early Herodian (see M. Baillet in *Les "Petites Grottes" de Qumrân,* Oxford, 1962, p. 75 and pl. 15). Also, the Hebrew text of *Ben Sira* 51 (11QPs^{a}Sirach; see J. A. Sanders, ed., *The Psalms Scroll of Qumrân Cave 11,* Oxford, 1965, pp. 79–85, cols. 21 and 22) has been found in a Qumran manuscript dating from the first half of the first century CE. It is now certain that *Ben Sira* predates the first century BCE. Moreover, the Hebrew original must antedate the Greek translation (in the Septuagint) made by Ben Sira's grandson in Egypt not long after 132 BCE (see the prologue to *Ben Sira* in the Septuagint by the grandson, who refers to "the thirty-eighth year of the reign of Euergetes"). Finally, most scholars date the work to around 180, which seems reasonable, because in 50:1–24 the author refers to Shimʿon (i.e., Simon II, 219–196 BCE) as if he had died recently (note the Hebrew of 50:24, *ye'amen ʿim Shimʿon ḥasdo;* see the text in Moses H. Segal, *Sefer ben Sira' ha-shalem,* Jerusalem, 1958, ad loc.).

A work of fifty-one chapters, *Ben Sira* is an apology for Judaism and is directed against the encroachments from Greek religion and culture. In particular, note the claim that Wisdom found a home in Israel and not in other nations (24:1–12). Some characteristic ideas in this long and major work are the following. The author believes in one God (explicit monotheism in 36:1–5) who is all-knowing (42:18), eternal (18:1), holy (23:9), just (35:12–13), and merciful (2:11, 48:20, 50:19). Ben Sira does not advocate an afterlife (17:27–28); immortality is through a son (30:4). Sin began with a woman (*me-ishshah teḥillat ʿavon,* 25:24) and death then appeared; but the author is not affirming the concept of original sin or predestination. He rather affirms man's essential freedom to obey the Law because of the inclination (*be-yad yitsro,* 15:14) given to man by God (see the brilliant discussion "Sin and Death" by E. E. Urbach in *The Sages: Their Concepts and Beliefs,* 2 vols., Jerusalem, 1979, vol. 1, pp. 420–422). He reveres the Temple and the priests (45:6–25) and elevates the Law (viz. 9:15). Wisdom is both personified and divine (viz. 24:3–5). Noticeably absent are beliefs in angels and the coming of a messiah.

G. H. Box and W. O. E. Oesterley (in Charles, 1913, p. 283) argued that this document "in its original form, represented the Sadducean standpoint." Today, scholars are far more reluctant to assign the text, in any form, to the Sadducees. It is certain that many ideas in *Ben Sira* are similar to those attributed by Josephus to the Sadducees (*Antiquities* 18.1), but does that factor indicate that the document comes from the Sadducees? Would a Sadducean document have been accepted at Qumran, and at Masada?

Wisdom of Solomon. Addressed to non-Jews, to whom the author often accommodates his thought, and written probably in the first half of the first century CE (Winston, 1979, pp. 20–25) or conceivably as early as 100 BCE (Pfeiffer, 1949, p. 327; Metzger, 1957, p. 67), this document reflects the intriguing blend of ancient Israelite and Jewish wisdom traditions with earlier and contemporary Greek philosophy and Egyptian reflective thought. The influence of non-Jewish ideas often replaces earlier Jewish perspectives; for example, many scholars, notably Metzger (1957, p. 75) and Chrysostome Larcher (*Études sur le livre de la Sagesse,* Paris, 1969, pp. 43, 91, 104), correctly claim that the Platonic conception of the soul's immortality, and not the Jewish idea of the resurrection of the body (see esp. *2 Maccabees* 14:37–46) is presented in *Wisdom of Solomon* 3:1–19 (viz., verses 1 and 4: "But the souls of the righteous . . . their hope [is] full of immortality"; cf. also 1:15, 5:15, 8:13–20). As in *Ben Sira,* Wisdom has now become personified in Jewish thought; she even appears to be hypostatic (see 7:21–8:21). Winston (1979, p. 4) divides the document into three sections (1:1–6:21, Wisdom's Gift of Immortality; 6:22–10:21, Wisdom's Nature and Power and Solomon's Quest for Her; and 11:1–19:22, Wisdom in the Exodus) and distinguishes two "excursuses" (11:15–12:22, On Divine Mercy, and 13:1–15:19, On Idolatry).

Quasi-historical books. It has been customary to refer to *1 Maccabees* and *2 Maccabees* as historical works; R. H. Charles (1913) arranged them, along with *2 Ezra* (*3 Esdras* in the Vulgate) and *3 Maccabees,* under the heading "Historical Books"; he put *Tobit* and *Judith* under the heading "Quasi-historical Books Written with a Moral Purpose." Today we recognize that *Tobit* and *Judith* are romantic and didactic stories, and that *1 Maccabees* and especially *2 Maccabees* are far too tendentious and selective to be labeled anything more than "quasi-historical."

1 Maccabees. The sixteen chapters of *1 Maccabees* were written in Hebrew, in Palestine, perhaps Jerusalem, shortly before the end of the second century BCE. They recount the military exploits of the Maccabees and the history of Judaism from the incursions by Antiochus IV Epiphanes (176–165 BCE) and the zealous rejection of paganism by Mattathias to the rule of John Hyrcanus I (135/4–105/4 BCE). As Jonathan A. Goldstein (1976) has emphasized, the author of *1 Maccabees* held strong theological views: he is fervently pro-Hasmonean and is impressively silent about—and probably rejected—beliefs in immortality and resurrection. In contrast to the author of *2 Maccabees,* he apparently disavows the value of martyrdom in prompting God to action, and he clearly accepts the twelve-month Babylonian lunar calendar.

2 Maccabees. The fifteen chapters of *2 Maccabees,* compiled by an unknown author, are an epitome (or abridgment) of a lost five-volume work (which is our only example of the "pathetic history" genre) by Jason of Cyrene (*2 Mc.* 2:19–32), of whom we otherwise know nothing. The epitomist probably wrote in Greek in Alexandria—or possibly in Jerusalem—shortly after 124 BCE or early in the first century BCE; he wrote for a sophisticated, informed Jewish audience.

This abridged history of Jason's tomes, which emphasizes the holiness of the Jerusalem Temple (see Elias Bickerman, *The God of the Maccabees,* Leiden, 1979, p. 21), is often fundamentally different from *1 Maccabees.* It presents the clearest examples of the Jewish belief in the resurrection of the body (see esp. 7:1–42, 12:43–45, and 14:37–46). Martyrdom by faithful Jews is efficacious, moving God to act and ensuring military victories (7:37–38, 8:3–7). Miracles are employed to explain major events.

Perhaps the most significant difference between *1 Maccabees* and Jason's work, according to *2 Maccabees,* is that the former legitimizes the Hasmonean dynasty but the latter tends to disparage it (see 10:19–23, 12:39–43, and Goldstein, 1976, pp. 27–34). Robert Doran argues in *Temple Propaganda: The Purpose and Character of 2 Maccabees* (Washington, D.C., 1981) that the epitomist was anti-Hasmonean, because he rejected the late Hasmonean use of mercenary troops and attributed military success to God rather than to the Maccabees.

The larger part of *2 Maccabees,* 3:1–15:36, is commonly called the Epitome. The Epitome covers Jewish history from circa 180; it gives prominence to the high priest Onias III (d. 170 BCE) and to the defeat and death of Nicanor in 161. It thereby corresponds to *1 Maccabees* 1:10–7:50.

Appreciably different from the Epitome are the two letters that begin *2 Maccabees.* The first letter (1:1–10a) was probably written in Hebrew or Aramaic (the most likely language for official communications at that time), as both Charles Cutler Torrey (1945, pp. 78–79) and Jonathan A. Goldstein (1976, p. 35) have concluded. It appears to be an authentic letter from Jewish authorities in Jerusalem to Jews in Egypt (*2 Mc.* 1:1). While it dates from 124 BCE, it also quotes in verses 7–8 an earlier letter of 143/2 BCE. The purpose of the letter is to urge the proper celebration of Ḥanukkah (verse 9), and it may have been propaganda against Onias's temple at Leontopolis, as Goldstein (1976, p. 35) argues.

The character of the second letter (1:10b–2:18) continues to be debated among scholars. Probably no part of it is authentic (*pace* Arnaldo Momigliano, *Prime linee di storia della tradizione Maccabaica* [1931], Amsterdam, 1968, pp. 81–94), and probably it was not written in Aramaic (*pace* Torrey, 1945, pp. 78–79). It was most likely written in Greek and is inauthentic (Goldstein, 1976, p. 36; Martin Hengel, *Judaism and Hellenism,* Philadelphia, 1974, vol. 1, p. 100, vol. 2, p. 69; Christian Habicht, *Historische und legendarische Erzählungen: 2. Makkabäerbuch,* Gütersloh, 1976, pp. 170, 199–207). The date assigned to this forged letter and its possible provenience are uncertain; it may be as early as 103 BCE (Goldstein, 1976, p. 36) or as late as 60 BCE (Bickerman, *Studies in Jewish and Christian History,* Leiden, 1980, pp. 136–158), and it may derive from Jews in either Jerusalem or Alexandria.

Goldstein (1976, p. 36) suggests that both letters are anti-Oniad propaganda and that they were prefaced to the Epitome shortly after 78 or 77 BCE in order to create a liturgical text that would be proper for the celebration of Hanukkah and serve for that festival as *Esther* does for Purim.

It is difficult to identify or categorize the epitomist himself. Only 2:19–2:32 and 15:37–39, derived neither from letters nor from Jason of Cyrene, appear to have originated with him.

2 Maccabees is, therefore, a recital through prophetic perspectives of the highlights in Jewish history of the second century BCE. This deliberate alteration of history by theology tends to cast *1 Maccabees* as more reliable for a reconstruction of the paradigmatic and historic events by the Hasmoneans.

THE PSEUDEPIGRAPHA. The Pseudepigrapha has been inadvertently defined incorrectly by the *selections* from this corpus published in German under the editorship of Emil Kautzsch in *Die Apokryphen und Pseudepigraphen des Alten Testaments,* 2 vols. (Tübingen, 1900), and in English under the editorship of R. H. Charles in *The Apocrypha and Pseudepigrapha of the Old Testament,* 2 vols. (Oxford, 1913). Charles's edition of the Pseudepigrapha contains all the documents in Kautzsch's collection plus four additional writings: *2 Enoch, Ahiqar,* a Zadokite work, and *Pirke Aboth* (*Pirqei avot*). The last two works belong, respectively, among the Dead Sea Scrolls and the rabbinic writings. All the others and many more, to a total of fifty-two writings plus a supplement that contains thirteen lost Jewish works quoted by the ancients, especially Alexander Polyhistor (c. 112–30s BCE), are included in *The Old Testament Pseudepigrapha,* 2 vols., edited by James H. Charlesworth (Garden City, N.Y., 1983–1984).

The fifty-two main documents in *The Old Testament Pseudepigrapha (OTP)*—which is not a canon of sacred writings but a modern collection of Jewish and Christian writings from circa 200 BCE to 200 CE—can be organized in five categories: (1) apocalyptic literature and related works; (2) testaments, which often include apocalyptic sections; (3) expansions of biblical stories and other legends; (4) wisdom and philosophical literature; and (5) prayers, psalms, and odes. (See *The Pseudepigrapha, Arranged by Category,* below.) To represent the corpus of the Pseudepigrapha within the confines of this relatively short article demands that comments on each category of writings be brief and sharply focused.

THE PSEUDEPIGRAPHA, ARRANGED BY CATEGORY:

Apocalyptic Literature and Related Works

1. Ethiopic *Apocalypse of Enoch* (*1 Enoch*)
2. Slavonic *Apocalypse of Enoch* (*2 Enoch*)
3. Hebrew *Apocalypse of Enoch* (*3 Enoch*)
4. *Sibylline Oracles*
5. *Treatise of Shem*
6. *Apocryphon of Ezekiel*
7. *Apocalypse of Zephaniah*
8. *Fourth Book of Ezra* (*4 Ezra*)
9. *Apocalypse of Ezra*
10. *Vision of Ezra*
11. *Questions of Ezra*

12. *Revelation of Ezra*
13. *Apocalypse of Sedrach*
14. Syriac *Apocalypse of Baruch* (*2 Baruch*)
15. Greek *Apocalypse of Baruch* (*3 Baruch*)
16. *Apocalypse of Abraham*
17. *Apocalypse of Adam*
18. *Apocalypse of Elijah*
19. *Apocalypse of Daniel*

Testaments

1. *Testaments of the Twelve Patriarchs*
2. *Testament of Abraham*
3. *Testament of Isaac*
4. *Testament of Jacob*
5. *Testament of Job*
6. *Testament of Moses*
7. *Testament of Solomon*
8. *Testament of Adam*

Expansions of Biblical Stories and Other Legends

1. *Letter of Aristeas*
2. *Jubilees*
3. *Martyrdom and Ascension of Isaiah*
4. *Joseph and Aseneth*
5. *Life of Adam and Eve*
6. *Pseudo-Philo*
7. *Lives of the Prophets*
8. *Ladder of Jacob*
9. *Fourth Book of Baruch* (*4 Baruch*)
10. *Jannes and Jambres*
11. *History of the Rechabites*
12. *Eldad and Modad*
13. *History of Joseph*

Wisdom and Philosophical Literature

1. *Ahiqar*
2. *Third Book of the Maccabees* (*3 Maccabees*)
3. *Fourth Book of the Maccabees* (*4 Maccabees*)
4. *Pseudo-Phocylides*
5. *Syriac Menander*

Prayers, Psalms, and Odes

1. Five More Psalms of David (Psalms 151–155)
2. *Prayer of Manasseh*
3. *Psalms of Solomon*
4. *Hellenistic Synagogal Prayers*
5. *Prayer of Joseph*
6. *Prayer of Jacob*
7. *Odes of Solomon*

Apocalyptic literature and related works. Nineteen pseudepigrapha can be grouped in the category of apocalyptic literature and related works (see *The Pseudepigrapha, Arranged by Category*). These nineteen works cover three overlapping chronological periods.

1. Antedating the burning of Jerusalem by the Romans in 70 CE, the great watershed in the history of Early Judaism (250 BCE–200 CE), are *1 Enoch*, some of the *Sibylline Oracles*, the *Apocrypha of Ezekiel*, and perhaps the *Treatise of Shem*.
2. After 70, the great varieties of religious thought in Judaism waned markedly as religious Jews, with great anxiety, lamented the loss of the Temple and pondered the cause of their defeat. *4 Ezra*, *2 Baruch*, *3 Baruch*, and the *Apocalypse of Abraham* are characterized by an intense interest in theodicy. *4 Ezra* is very pessimistic; its author finds it difficult to see any hope in his remorse. *2 Baruch* is much more optimistic than *4 Ezra;* the Temple was destroyed by God's angels because of Israel's unfaithfulness (7:1–8:5), not by a superior culture or the might of the enemy.
3. Later works are documents 3, some of 4, 9, 10, 11, 12, 13, 18, and 19, ranging in date from the lost purported Jewish base of (or traditions in) the *Apocalypse of Adam* in the first or second century CE to the *Apocalypse of Daniel* in the ninth. These works are important for an understanding of Early Judaism only because they apparently preserve some edited works and record some early Jewish traditions.

The most important pseudepigraphon in this group is the composite book known as *1 Enoch.* It is preserved in its entire, final form only in Ethiopic, although versions of early portions of it are preserved in other languages; of these the most important are the Greek and Aramaic. The Qumran Aramaic fragments, because of their paleographic age, prove that portions of *1 Enoch* date from the third, second, and first centuries BCE.

In *The Books of Enoch: Aramaic Fragments of Qumrân Cave 4* (Oxford, 1976), J. T. Milik not only published the *editio princeps* of the Aramaic fragments of *Enoch*, but he also claimed that chapters 37–71 must be Christian and postdate 260 CE. He obtained this surprising conclusion because of the absence of these chapters at Qumran, the striking similarity to the New Testament concepts of the Son of man and the Messiah, and the author's imagined reference to the "events of the years 260 to 270 CE" (p. 96). These arguments are erroneous, and they have been rightly rejected by all specialists. The absence of fragments at Qumran is not so significant as Milik claims; the striking parallels to the New Testament are due either to a shared culture or to influences from

1 Enoch 37–71 upon Jesus or the New Testament authors; the historical events of the third century CE are *not* reflected in *1 Enoch.* Moreover, all manuscripts of *1 Enoch* attest that chapters 37–71 move climactically to the elevation of Enoch as son of man (in 71:14, the angel says to Enoch, "You are the son of man."). Hence, all of *1 Enoch* is Jewish and predates 70.

1 Enoch consists of five works that were composed over three centuries. In chronological order they are *Enoch's Astronomical Book* (*1 Enoch* 72–82), from the third century BCE; *Enoch's Journeys* (*1 Enoch* 1–36), from pre-160 BCE; *Enoch's Dream Visions* (*1 Enoch* 83–90), from pre-160 BCE), *Enoch's Epistle* (*1 Enoch* 91–105), from the second or first century BCE; and *Enoch's Parables* (*1 Enoch* 37–71), from pre-70 CE. Addenda (*1 Enoch* 106–108) are of uncertain date.

Some of the chapters that begin and end the divisions in *1 Enoch* were added or edited as the separate works were brought together into one document; this composite work circulated in Palestine before 70. While the precise dates for these sections of *1 Enoch,* or *Books of Enoch,* are debated, it is clear that the ideas they contain, such as the advocation of a solar calendar, were characteristic of some Jews from the third century BCE to the first century CE. *1 Enoch* is one of our major sources for Hellenistic Jewish ideas on cosmology, angelology, astronomy, God, sin, and mankind.

Example: "Then an angel came to me [Enoch] and greeted me and said to me, 'You, son of man, who art born in righteousness and upon whom righteousness has dwelt, the righteousness of the Antecedent of Time will not forsake you'" (*1 En.* 71:14; trans. E. Isaac in *OTP).*

Testaments. Eight testaments, some of which include apocalyptic sections, make up a second group of pseudepigrapha (see *The Pseudepigrapha, Arranged by Category*). Of these, only the *Testament of Job* and the *Testament of Moses* clearly predate 70 CE. The *Testament of Adam,* in its present form, may be as late as the fifth century CE. The *Testament of Solomon* is earlier, perhaps from the third centruy CE. The *Testament of Isaac* and the *Testament of Jacob* were possibly added in the second or third century to the *Testament of Abraham,* which in its earliest form probably dates from the end of the first century or the beginning of the second century CE.

The most important—and most controversial—document in this group is the *Testaments of the Twelve Patriarchs.* Marinus de Jonge (for bibliographic data, see Charlesworth, 1981) has argued that this document is a Christian composition that inherits much Jewish tradition, both oral and written. Most scholars have concluded that, while the extant document is Christian, the Christian passages are clearly interpolations and redactions added to a Jewish document that dates from the second or first century BCE. This documents consists of twelve testaments, each attributed to a son of Jacob and containing ethical instruction often with apocalyptic visions.

Example: "A copy of the words of Levi: the things that he decreed to his sons concerning all they were to do, and the things that would happen to them until the day of judgment. . . . I, Levi, was born in Haran and came with my father to Shechem. . . . There I again saw the vision as formerly. . . . And now, my children, I know from the writings of Enoch that in the end time you will act impiously against the Lord . . . your brothers will be humiliated and among all the nations you shall become the occasion for scorn. For your father, Israel, is pure with respect to all the impieties of the chief priests [who laid their hands on the savior of the world (*sōtēra tou kosmou.*)], as heaven is pure above the earth; and you should be the lights of Israel as the sun and the moon" (*T. Levi* 1:1, 2:1, 8:1, 14:1–3; trans. H. C. Kee in *OTP;* brackets denote the Christian interpolation).

Expansions of biblical stories and legends. The documents in the Hebrew Bible, because of their recognized divine authority and revered antiquity, profoundly affected the daily and religious life of Jews in the Hellenistic world. The three divisions of the Hebrew Bible—the Torah (Law), Prophets, and the Writings—moved toward canonicity during the years from 300 BCE to 200 CE. Almost all Jewish religious writings were categorically shaped on the literary norms, theological perspectives, and semiotic language already developed in the Hebrew Bible. Of the many ramifications caused by the normative force of the biblical books, one is singularly represented by the documents that expand upon the biblical stories, supplying details and providing answers—often through pictorially rich narratives—to questions aroused by careful and repeated readings of the sacred books. Thirteen documents fall into this category (see *The Pseudepigrapha, Arranged by Category*).

These thirteen documents represent Jewish expansions of stories in the Hebrew scriptures over many centuries. The *History of Joseph,* in a class by itself, is late, and perhaps reached its final form in the sixth century CE. Five writings, documents 8–12, date from the late first century to the late second century. The *History of the Rechabites,* however, was extensively expanded and reworked by early Christians; its present form in Syriac, and perhaps in Greek, was not complete until around the sixth century.

In this group the most important writings for Hellenistic Judaism are documents 1–7. Almost all these predate the destruction of Jerusalem in 70. The *Martyrdom and Ascension of Isaiah* is a significant exception; it continued to be expanded and was redacted by Christians up until about the fourth century. *Joseph and Aseneth* has been a controversial writing; while it has been dated by some scholars as early as the second century BCE, it probably dates from the early decades of the second century CE (see Charlesworth, 1981; Denis, 1970; and especially C. Burchard in *OTP*). *Jubilees* was probably composed in the years between 163 and 140 BCE.

Example: "And in the eleventh jubilee Jared took for himself a wife. . . . And she bore a son for him in the fifth week. . . . And he called him Enoch. This one was the first who learned writing and knowledge and wisdom. . . . And who wrote in a book the signs of the heaven according to the order of their months, so that the sons of man might know the (appointed) times of the years according to their order, with respect to each of their months" (*Jub.* 4:16–17; trans. Orval Wintermute in *OTP*).

Wisdom and philosophical literature. Mankind's search for understanding and wisdom crosses all boundaries, including the fictitious divides of centuries and the fluctuating contours of nations. Five pseudepigrapha constitute a Hellenistic Jewish record of humankind's insights into wisdom and present practical ethical rules and aphorisms for enlightened actions (see *The Pseudepigrapha, Arranged by Category*). *Syriac Menander*, as a collection, seems to date from the third century CE (see T. Baarda in *OTP*), but *Pseudo-Phocylides* and *4 Maccabees* date from the first century CE, and perhaps the former from even the first century BCE (see P. W. van der Horst in *OTP*). *3 Maccabees* was clearly composed in the first century BCE. *Ahiqar* is very early, dating from the fourth or even fifth century BCE, but it influenced the author of *Tobit* around 180 BCE.

Examples: "The love of money is the mother of all evil" (*Ps-Phoc.* 42; trans. van der Horst in *OTP*). "Long hair is not fit for boys, but for voluptuous women" (*Ps-Phoc.* 212; trans. van der Horst in *OTP*). "Do not laugh at old age, for that is where you shall arrive and remain" (*Syr. Men.* 11–12; trans. T. Baarda in *OTP*). "For reason [*logismos*] is the guide of the virtues and the supreme master of the passions" (*4 Mc.* 1:30; trans. H. Anderson in *OTP*).

Prayers, psalms, and odes. The Davidic Psalter, the hymnbook of the Second Temple, was gradually considered closed during the centuries that preceded the destruction of the Temple. Other poetic compositions were completed during the years from the conquests of Alexander the Great in 336–323 BCE until the final defeat of Shimʿon Bar Kokhba in 135 CE. Many of these were incorporated into various pseudepigrapha to accentuate or illustrate a point or to raise the confessional level of the narrative. Others were collected into "hymnbooks" or "prayer books" that may be grouped as a fifth, and final, category of pseudepigrapha (see *The Pseudepigrapha, Arranged by Category*). The *Odes of Solomon*, the earliest Christian "hymnbook," is modeled on the poetic style of the Davidic Psalter; it dates from the late first century or the beginning of the second century CE. The *Prayer of Joseph* and the *Prayer of Jacob* are Jewish compositions from perhaps as early as the first century CE. The "Hellenistic Synagogal Prayers," preserved in books 7 and 8 of the *Apostolic Constitutions*, are Christian in their present form, but they may well be remnants of Jewish prayers that date from the early centuries CE. The *Psalms of Solomon*, which seems to represent the piety of a circle of Jews living in Jerusalem, was certainly composed in the second half of the second century BCE. The *Prayer of Manasseh* is very difficult to date, but it probably comes from the turn of the eras. The Davidic Psalter itself was expanded with "Five More Psalms of David" (psalms 151–155), which date from various time periods, ranging from the third century (151) to the second or first century BCE (152–155). The original language of Psalms 151, 154, and 155 is Hebrew; the others were composed in a Semitic language (Hebrew, Aramaic, or Syriac).

Example: "O Lord, do not condemn me according to my sins; / For no one living is righteous before you" (Psalm 155 [11OPs^a 155]; trans. Charlesworth in *OTP*).

SEE ALSO Apocalypse, overview article and article on Jewish Apocalypticism to the Rabbinic Period.

BIBLIOGRAPHY

The Apocrypha

The best bibliographical guide to the Apocrypha is Gerhard Elling's *Bibliographie zur jüdisch-hellenistischen und intertestamentarischen Literatur, 1900–1970,* "Texte und Untersuchungen," no. 106, 2d ed. (Berlin, 1975). An important introduction to parts of the Apocrypha and Pseudepigrapha, with insightful comments regarding their sources and historical setting, is George W. E. Nickelsburg's *Jewish Literature between the Bible and the Mishnah: A Historical and Literary Introduction* (Philadelphia, 1981). See also Robert H. Pfeiffer's *History of New Testament Times with an Introduction to the Apocrypha* (New York, 1984). A careful, well-written, and authoritative introduction (but a little dated now) is Bruce M. Metzger's *An Introduction to the Apocrypha* (New York, 1957). An earlier work is Charles C. Torrey's *The Apocryphal Literature: A Brief Introduction* (1945; reprint, London, 1963). Reliable introductions to the Apocrypha, from Roman Catholics who consider these books deuterocanonical, can be found in *The Jerome Bible Commentary*, edited by Raymond E. Brown, Joseph A. Fitzmyer, and Roland E. Murphy (Englewood Cliffs, N.J., 1968).

Critical Greek editions of the Apocrypha have been appearing in the Cambridge and Göttingen editions of the Septuagint. A handy Greek edition of the Apocrypha is Alfred Rahlfs's *Septuaginta*, 2 vols. (Stuttgart, 1935; reprint of 8th ed., 1965). A classic work on the Apocrypha is volume 1 of *The Apocrypha and Pseudepigrapha of the Old Testament in English: With Introductions and Critical and Explanatory Notes to the Several Books*, edited by R. H. Charles (Oxford, 1913). More recent and excellent translations are those in *The Jerusalem Bible* (Garden City, N.Y., 1966), which is translated by Roman Catholics, and in *The New Oxford Annotated Bible with the Apocrypha: Revised Standard Version*, exp. ed., edited by Herbert G. May and Bruce M. Metzger (New York, 1977).

The best current commentary series is the Anchor Bible. Volumes 41–44 (Garden City, N.Y., 1976–1983) include Jonathan A. Goldstein's *I Maccabees* (vol. 41, 1976) and *II Maccabees* (vol. 41A, 1983), Jacob M. Myers's *I and II Esdras* (vol. 42, 1974), David Winston's *The Wisdom of Solomon* (vol. 43, 1979; reprint, 1981), and Carey A. Moore's *Daniel, Esther, and Jeremiah: The Additions* (vol. 44, 1977). Also valuable, especially because the Greek text is printed opposite the English translation, is *Jewish Apocryphal Literature*, 7 vols., edited by Solomon Zeitlin (Leiden, 1950–1972). The fruit of the best German scholarship on the Apocrypha and Pseudepigrapha has been appearing in fascicles in the series titled

"Jüdische Schriften aus hellenistisch-römischer Zeit" (JSHRZ), edited by Werner Georg Kümmel (Gütersloh, 1973–). Valuable tools for those who know Greek are Christian Abraham Wahl's *Clavis librorum veteris testamenti apocryphorum philologica* (1853; reprint, Graz, 1972) and Edwin Hatch and Henry A. Redpath's *A Concordance to the Septuagint and the Other Greek Versions of the Old Testament, including the Apocryphal Books*, 2 vols. (1897–1906; reprint, Graz, 1972). A model computer-produced reference work is now available for the Apocrypha (and part of the Pseudepigrapha): Bruce M. Metzger et al., *A Concordance to the Apocrypha- Deuterocanonical Books of the Revised Standard Version* (Grand Rapids, Mich., 1983).

The Pseudepigrapha

Charlesworth, James H. *The Pseudepigrapha and Modern Research with a Supplement*. Chico, Calif., 1981. This book succinctly introduces the documents in the Pseudepigrapha and provides a bibliography of publications from 1960 until 1979. All publications mentioned in this article are cited with complete bibliographic data.

Charlesworth, James H., ed. *The Old Testament Pseudepigrapha*. 2 vols. Garden City, N.Y., 1983–1985. This massive collection contains introductions to and English translations of fifty-two writings classified as pseudepigrapha and of thirteen other documents included in a supplement. The introductions by the editor clarify the problems in defining "apocalypses," "testaments," "expansions of the 'Old Testament,'" "wisdom and philosophical literature," and "prayers, psalms, and odes."

Denis, Albert-Marie. *Introduction aux pseudépigraphes grecs d'Ancien Testament*. Leiden, 1970.

Nickelsburg, George W. E. *Jewish Literature between the Bible and the Mishnah: A Historical and Literary Introduction*. Philadelphia, 1981.

Sparks, H. F. D., ed. *The Apocryphal Old Testament*. Oxford, 1984. A selection of some documents usually placed in the Pseudepigrapha.

New Sources

Anderson, Bernhard W., ed. *The Books of the Bible*. Vol. 2: *The Apocrypha and the New Testament*. New York, 1989.

Charlesworth, James H. *Authentic Apocrypha*. North Richland Hills, Tex., 1998.

Charlesworth, James H. *The Old Testament Pseudepigrapha and the New Testament*. Harrisburg, Pa., 1998.

Collins, John J. *Jewish Wisdom in the Hellenistic Age*. Louisville, Ky., 1997.

DeSilva, David Arthur. *Introducing the Apocrypha*. Grand Rapids, Mich., 2002.

Jones, Ivor H. *Apocrypha*. London, 2003.

Mendels, Doron. *Identity, Religion, and Historiography*. Journal for the Study of Pseudepigrapha Supplement Series, 24. Sheffield, UK, 1998.

Meurer, Siegfried. *The Apocrypha in Ecumenical Perspective*. Translated by Paul Ellingworth. Reading, UK, 1991.

Russell, David Syme. *The Old Testament Pseudepigrapha*. London, 1987.

Russell, David Syme. *Divine Disclosure: An Introduction to Jewish Apocrypha*. Minneapolis, 1992.

Scott, J. Julius. *Jewish Backgrounds of the New Testament*. Grand Rapids, Mich., 2000.

Vanderkam, James C. and William Adler, eds. *The Jewish Apocalyptic Heritage of Early Christianity*. Assen, Netherlands and Minneapolis, 1996.

JAMES H. CHARLESWORTH (1987)
Revised Bibliography

BIBLICAL LITERATURE: NEW TESTAMENT

The New Testament is a collection of twenty-seven books written by over a dozen authors with diverse theological convictions. The books were written between circa 50 CE and 150 CE. Along with the Hebrew Bible, they are the normative scriptures of the Christian churches. They gained that status only after a long and complex process; the shape of the collection took definitive form for most churches only in the fourth century.

Neither Jesus nor the early Christians knew anything of a New Testament. Their Bible was the Jewish Bible alone. Originally, Christian traditions were oral, and a preference for the oral over the written lived on into the second century. But during the last thirty or so years of the first century CE, traditions about Jesus came to be transmitted in written sources that were read at Christian gatherings. Concurrently, some communities began to use several Pauline epistles in their gatherings. Gradually, then, theological and moral authority came to be embodied in written Christian texts. However, since different writings were read in different places, and because the diversity in the early church was considerable, there was often disagreement over which texts to privilege.

THE FOUR GOSPELS AND *ACTS*. Jesus did not to our knowledge write anything. He was an oral preacher, with a repertoire of parables, aphorisms, exhortations, and example stories. If, as the Gospels have it, he sent out followers to preach what he preached (see *Lk.* 10:2–12), they must have learned much the same repertoire, so oral transmission of the Jesus tradition must have begun before Jesus' death.

After Jesus' crucifixion, his disciples continued to recite his words, and they also began to tell stories about him. Unfortunately, the roads along which the tradition moved to the written Gospels, who moved it, and how much it changed along the way, cannot be recovered. The tradition was sometimes used in moral exhortations, other times in polemical and apologetical settings, other times in gatherings for worship. While the tradition was not fixed word-for-word, it likewise did not have the character of an amorphous folk tradition. Beyond such generalities, however, it is not known how the tradition was handled.

Sometime in the second century, for reasons unknown, the Gospels of *Matthew, Mark, Luke,* and *John* began to circulate as a collection. This fact troubled some because these four present distinctly different pictures of Jesus and sometimes contradict each other. So some preferred to read only one gospel. In the middle of the second century, in Rome, Marcion used a version of Luke's gospel. Shortly thereafter, Tatian composed his *Diatessaron,* which turned four books into one. Many eastern churches accepted this harmony as canonical for three centuries thereafter. By the beginning of the third century, however, many churches were reading the fourfold collection.

Historically, most Christians, being more interested in Jesus than the evangelists, have sought to downplay the differences between the four Gospels. Modern scholarship has instead highlighted them, emphasizing that the Gospels are not just the product of their subject but also of their authors and their creative theological traditions, so that the Gospels tell us about the church as well as Jesus. By including, excluding, arranging, rewriting, offering commentary, and creating materials, each writer reflects a particular theological tradition that should not be flattened for harmony with the other writers.

The synoptic problem and *Q*. *Matthew, Mark,* and *Luke* are known as "the synoptics." They are sufficiently similar that one can place them side by side and view most of their contents synoptically, at the same time. They share many sayings and stories and often the order of those stories and sayings. About 55 percent of *Mark* is in *Luke,* and about 90 percent of *Mark* is in *Matthew;* often there is word-for-word agreement (compare, for example, *Mt.* 3:7–10 with *Lk.* 3:7–9). While it is impossible to prove that such agreements do not derive from careful memorization of the same oral tradition, most scholars take the extensive agreements to indicate a literary relationship.

The consensus that emerged in Germany, England, and the United States at the end of the nineteenth century, and that held for most of the twentieth century, is that *Mark* was the first written gospel, and that Matthew and Luke, independently of each other, both knew and used *Mark.* Matthew and Luke also had access to a lost text known as *Q.* This last was mostly a collection of sayings of Jesus not unlike the apocryphal *Gospel of Thomas.*

It is not hard to find dissenters. Some important scholars have characterized *Q* not as a written source but as a series of tractates or even oral sources. Others have explained the data by arguing that *Mark* used both *Matthew* and *Luke,* or that *Mark* came first, after which Matthew expanded *Mark,* after which Luke used both. Still, the most common view remains that Matthew and Luke independently used *Mark* and *Q.* Among the reasons, which are suggestive rather than demonstrative, are these:

(1) Texts in *Mark* but not in *Matthew* include: *Mark* 3:21 (Jesus' family seeks to restrain him because some think him mad); 8:22–26 (Jesus heals a blind man who then sees, but only imperfectly, and Jesus has to heal him a second time); 9:49 (Jesus says "everyone will be salted with fire"); 11:16 (Jesus forbids vessels to be carried in the temple); and 14:51–52 (a young man runs away naked when Jesus is arrested). On the theory of Markan priority, Matthew omitted these items. On the theory of Matthean priority, Mark added them. The latter is less likely, for the items catalogued are all potentially embarrassing, of uncertain meaning, or not theologically significant. It is easier to imagine someone dropping them than adding them.

(2) If Mark used *Matthew,* he decided not to reproduce the story of the virgin birth, the tale of the magi, the sermon on the mount, and other portions that seem memorable, entertaining, and edifying. It is unclear what would have motivated Mark to not include them.

(3) Jesus spoke Aramaic, and *Mark* exhibits more traces of this fact, containing as it does several Semitic words or phrases missing from both *Matthew* and *Luke: Boanerges* (3:17); *talitha cum* (5:41); *korban* (7:11); *rabbouni* (10:51); and *abba* (14:36).

(4) *Matthew's* Christology, being higher than *Mark's,* seems later. Jesus is called "Lord" only once in *Mark* but a full nineteen times in *Matthew.* In *Mark* 1:32–33 and 3:10, Jesus heals "many," but the Matthean parallels have him healing "all." Several times in *Mark,* Jesus asks questions, all of which are missing from *Matthew* (see *Mk.* 5:9, 30; 8:12; 9:12, 16, 33; 10:18; and 14:14). Again, whereas *Mark* 6:5 says Jesus "could do no deed of power" in Nazareth, *Matthew's* "he did not do many deeds of power there" (13:58) not only implies that he worked some miracles but further avoids the implication, near to hand from *Mark,* that maybe Jesus tried but failed.

Regarding *Q, Matthew* and *Luke* alone share about 230 verses in common. It is unlikely that Matthew took them from Luke, for *Matthew* does not show clear knowledge of Luke's editorial work, and there are no obvious reasons for Matthew to omit memorable parts of *Luke,* such as the tales of the rich man and Lazarus (16:19–31) and the prodigal son (15:11–32). Similarly, it is unlikely that Luke copied Matthew, because *Luke* does not show clear knowledge of Matthew's editorial work, and there are no obvious reasons for Luke having omitted memorable parts of *Matthew,* such as Herod's slaughter of the infants (2:1–21) or the fuller version of the Lord's Prayer (6:9–13).

If *Matthew* and *Luke* are independent of each other, the non-Markan traditions they share came to them through oral tradition or in writing. Favoring a written text is the fact that most of the common material occurs in four large blocks that are in the same order in the two gospels: the sermon on the mount or plain (*Mt.* 5-7; *Lk.* 6:17–49); missionary directives (*Mt.* 10; *Lk.* 9, 10); polemic against leaders (*Mt.* 23; *Lk* 11); and eschatological matters (*Mt.* 24:28, 37–40; *Lk.* 17: 20–37).

Although *Q* remains hypothetical, this has not prevented attempts to recover its text, date it, reconstruct its stages of composition, and so on. Particularly intense has been the debate over whether *Q* reflects a faith that did not have as its center the death and resurrection of Jesus. Because there is no evidence that the document contained a passion narrative or described Jesus' resurrection, this is possible. But *Q*'s silence can also be explained by its genre as a collection of sayings of Jesus, which need not be a full-length mirror of its community's convictions.

Matthew. Papias, a bishop in Asia Minor, wrote in the early second century: "Now Matthew made an ordered arrangement of the oracles in the Hebrew [or Aramaic] language, and each one translated [or interpreted] it as he was able." These words and the traditional title *According to Matthew*—added at an early but uncertain date—show that some attributed this gospel to the disciple named in *Matthew* 9:9 and 10:3. Most now doubt the tradition. Papias and others after him consistently associated Matthew's authorship with a Semitic text, but *Matthew* is in Greek and seems unlikely to be a translation from Hebrew or Aramaic. Furthermore, it is unlikely that a Semitic document, such as Papias speaks of, would have incorporated, as *Matthew* seems to have done, the Greek *Mark* almost in its entirety.

The author of *Matthew,* whatever the name, was probably a Jew. Some of the biblical quotations seem to be translated from the Hebrew specifically for the gospel (2:18, 23; 8:17; 12:18–21). There is, further, concentrated focus on the synagogue (e.g., 6:1–18; 23:1–39), as well as affirmation of the abiding force of the Mosaic law (5:17–20). And *Matthew* alone records Jesus' prohibitions against mission outside Israel (10:5; 15:24) and shows concern that eschatological flight not occur on a Sabbath (24:20).

Majority opinion holds that *Matthew* appeared in the last quarter of the first century CE A later date is excluded because Christians writers from the first part of the second century, such as Ignatius of Antioch and Papias, show knowledge of *Matthew,* which accordingly must have been composed before 100 CE. An earlier date is excluded because *Matthew* 22:7 seems to betray knowledge of the fall of Jerusalem in 70 CE. An origin in Antioch in Syria is a common guess, but it is no more than a guess.

The primary structure of the gospel is narrative followed by discourse followed by narrative followed by discourse, and so on:

1–4: Narrative—the main character introduced.

5–7: Discourse—Jesus' demands upon Israel.

8–9: Narrative—Jesus' deeds within and for Israel.

10: Discourse—extension of ministry through words and deeds of others.

11–12: Narrative—negative response.

13: Discourse—explanation of negative response.

14–17: Narrative—founding of new community.

18: Discourse—instructions to the new community.

19–23: Narrative—commencement of the passion.

24–25: Discourse—the future: judgment and salvation.

26–28: Narrative—conclusion: the passion and resurrection.

Matthew not only often quotes the Jewish Bible, it also draws upon it to create typologies that order and add details to the story. In chapters 1 to 5, for instance, the text again and again directs the informed reader to the foundational story in *Exodus,* and so teaches that Jesus is a new lawgiver whose advent inaugurates a new exodus. Herod's order to do away with the male infants of Bethlehem (2:16–18) is like Pharaoh's order to do away with every male Hebrew child (*Ex.* 1). The quotation of *Hosea* 11:1 in *Matthew* 2:15 evokes thought of the exodus, for in its original context "Out of Egypt I have called my son" concerns Israel. Jesus, like Israel, is exiled to Egypt and then returns to the land. *Matthew* 2:19–21 borrows the language of *Exodus* 4:19–20 so that just as Moses, after being told to go back to Egypt because all those seeking his life have died, takes his wife and children and returns to the land of his birth, so too with Jesus: Joseph, after being told to go back to Israel because all those seeking the life of his son have died, takes his wife and child and returns to the land of his son's birth. When Jesus passes through the waters of baptism and then goes into the desert to suffer temptation, Matthew again recalls the exodus (cf. especially *Dt.* 8:2–3). Jesus, whose forty-day fast reminds one of Moses' forty-day fast (*Ex.* 24:18), is, like Israel, tempted by hunger (*Ex.* 16:2–8), tempted to put God to the test (*Ex.* 17:1–4; cf. *Dt.* 6:16), and tempted to idolatry (*Ex.* 32). On each occasion *Matthew* quotes from *Deuteronomy*—from 8:3 in *Matthew* 4:4, from 6:16 in *Matthew* 4:7, and from 6:13 in *Matthew* 4:10. After all this, Jesus goes up on a mountain, where he delivers the sermon on the mount, perhaps Christianity's most important source of ethical direction. In this he discusses the Sinai commandments of Moses (5:17–48) and delivers his own imperatives. Jesus is a new Moses.

Mark. This gospel is traditionally ascribed to John Mark. *Acts* mentions him several times, claiming that believers met in his mother's house in Jerusalem and that he was the cause of a falling out between the apostles Paul and Barnabas (*Mk.* 12:12, 25; 13:5; 15:37, 39). This man also appears in Paul's letters, where he is a coworker (*Col.* 4:10; *2 Tm.* 4:11; *Phlm.* 24), as well as in *1 Peter* 5:13, which associates him with Peter.

It is not known when early *Mark* gained its title, but the gospel was attributed to Mark in the early second century CE Papias defended Mark this way:

> The Presbyter said this: Mark, having become the interpreter of Peter, accurately wrote what he remembered, although not in order, the things said and done by the Lord. . . .Mark erred not in recording what he remembered. For he took forethought for one thing, not to omit any of the things that he had heard nor to state any of them falsely.

Proponents of Markan authorship have asked why anyone would, without good reason, attribute a gospel to someone as relatively obscure as John Mark. Why not Peter himself?

Many, nonetheless, doubt the tradition. The gospel itself nowhere purports to come from John Mark or otherwise associates itself with Peter. It furthermore makes no claim to pass on eyewitness information, nor does it contain any evidence of such; if the work had been written by a Mark even less important than John Mark, tradition might have turned one into another.

Early tradition says that *Mark* was composed shortly before or after Peter's death. As Peter was probably martyred in the 60s, the tradition is not here far from the modern consensus, which places *Mark* shortly before or after 70 CE. One reason for the consensus is that if Matthew and Luke knew *Mark*, and if they appeared before the end of the first century, *Mark* must be earlier. Another reason is that *Mark* 13 seems to reflect the circumstances of the late 60s and maybe the destruction of the temple in 70 CE.

According to Clement of Alexandria in the last quarter of the second century, the gospel was composed in Rome. This fits the conventional ascription to John Mark, because tradition has Peter moving to Rome and because *1 Peter* 5:13 associates John Mark and Peter with Rome (represented by Babylon). Many scholars still find a Roman origin plausible and think that the gospel's emphasis upon suffering may reflect the trying conditions of Christian life in Rome in and after Nero's days. But the gospel itself contains no statement about where it was written, and other scholars believe that Galilee or somewhere else is no less likely.

Regarding *Mark*'s audience, probably most were Gentiles. This follows from *Mark* 7:3–4: "For the Pharisees, and all the Jews, do not eat unless they thoroughly wash their hands, thus observing the tradition of the elders; and they do not eat anything from the market unless they wash it; and there are also many other traditions that they observe, the washing of cups, pots, and bronze kettles." Apart from the problem that this statement may not be wholly accurate, it would make little sense for an author to inform Jews about Jewish customs. The gospel is, nevertheless, firmly rooted in Jewish culture and tradition. It begins by citing the Bible (*Mk.* 1:2–3) and continues to quote from and allude to the Scriptures throughout. Jesus' God is explicitly the God of Abraham, Isaac, and Jacob (*Mk.* 12:26). And all of the main characters are, with the exception of Pilate, Jews.

Unlike *Matthew*, *Mark* is not organized in any obvious way. Material is sometimes arranged by topic, sometimes by geography, sometimes by chronology. The parables in chapter 4 and the collection of eschatological materials in chapter 13 display a topical interest, whereas a geographical interest emerges in chapter 1, which brings together events that take place in Capernaum, as well as in the latter chapters, which bring together all of the stories about Jesus in Jerusalem. (Contrast John's gospel, in which Jesus goes up to Jerusalem several times.) The main outline of the book, however, is chronological: Jesus is baptized; then he engages in his public ministry; then he goes up to Jerusalem; then he has a last supper with his disciples; then he is arrested; then he is put on trial; then he is crucified; and then he is buried.

Like *Matthew* and *Luke*, *Mark* consists mostly of small units that could stand alone. More often than not paragraphs have an introduction and a conclusion and do not require a context to be understood. Evidently most of the paragraphs once functioned as isolated units. Mark was then largely responsible for the geographical and chronological placement that the stories and sayings now possess.

Mark's ending is problematic. *Mark* 16:9–20 cannot, for both literary and textual reasons, be original. Scholars debate whether the book's original ending was lost or whether it ended at 16:8, without recounting a resurrection appearance. Most recent experts have favored the view that *Mark* exists in its entirety. But one may ask whether the current consensus, which favors 16:8 as the original, ambiguous, mysterious ending, is popular partly because it appeals to modern sensibilities, which are often suspicious of neat closure and happy endings.

Luke-Acts. *Luke* and *Acts*—the New Testament's two longest books—are now separated. Originally, however, as the two prefaces imply (*Lk.* 1:1–4; *Acts* 1:1–2), they were volumes one and two of the same work, which scholars call *Luke-Acts*. Whether the two volumes first appeared together, or whether *Acts* was a sequel that appeared sometime after the gospel, is unknown. In any case, both works are from the same author, and *Acts* continues the story of *Luke*. A brief outline might look something like this:

Volume 1, *Luke:* How Christianity began with Jesus in Galilee and Jerusalem.

1–12. The coming of Jesus (infancy, youth).

3–4:13. The call of Jesus (baptism, temptation).

4:14–9:50. The Galilean ministry (teaching, miracles).

9:51–19:48. The road to Jerusalem (teaching, miracles).

20–24. The end in Jerusalem (passion, resurrection).

Volume 2, *Acts*: How the apostles carried the gospel from Jerusalem to Rome.

1–12. From Jerusalem to Antioch.

13–28. From Antioch to Rome.

Jesus is the central character in volume 1; Peter in chapters 1–12 of volume 2; and Paul in chapters 13–28 of volume 2. Both volumes cover approximately the same amount of time, about thirty years.

Apart from the traditional title for the gospel (*According to Luke* or *The Gospel according to Luke*), the earliest testimony to authorship comes from Irenaeus and Tertullian in the latter part of the second century. Both associate the gospel with the common name "Luke." Tradition identified him with a native of Antioch in Syria. *Colossians* 4:14 calls him a physician and implies his Gentile status. *2 Timothy* 4:11 identifies him as a coworker of Paul. Some scholars think that the tradition is right, for a number of reasons. (1) Several portions of *Acts* use the first person plural ("we"): 16:10–17; 20:5–15; 21:1–18; and 27:1–28:16. As these "we" sections, which are rich with detail, are unlikely to be a fictional literary device, either the author incorporated a source ostensibly composed by one of Paul's companions or the author was such a companion. In favor of the latter is the fact that these sections do not differ in style from the rest of *Acts*. (2) Those sections, taken at face value, imply that their author was one of the four individuals who traveled with Paul to Rome—Titus, Jesus Justus, Crescens, or Luke. (3) Why would tradition latch onto Luke if he were not the author? Why not rather pick the better known and more important Titus? (4) Although the author of *Acts* probably did not know Paul's epistles, *Acts* does know many things that those epistles confirm, such as that Paul did not stay long in Thessalonica (*Acts* 17; cf. *1 Thes.*), or that Paul visited Athens but had no substantial ministry there (again *Acts* 17; cf. *1 Thes.* 3:1; the epistles make no other mention of Athens), or that Paul had exceptional success in Ephesus (*Acts* 19; cf. *1 Cor.* 16:8, 9).

There remain, however, many who reject the traditional ascription. The "we" passages do not make Luke any more likely a candidate for authorship than Titus or the other companions. Perhaps the tradition inferred Lukan authorship from the latter part of *Acts* and picked the wrong individual. It is, moreover, possible that the author took the "we" sections from a source and rewrote them, which would explain why their style matches the rest of the book. Those who hold this view typically underline the differences between *Acts* and the historical Paul as known from his letters. Many have thought it impossible, for instance, to reconcile the Paul of *Galatians* with the Paul of *Acts* 16:3, who has Timothy circumcised. Yet why Luke's being a companion of Paul entails that he agreed with Paul on everything or that he wrote nothing but sober history does not appear. The tradition, then, could be correct, even if the case for it falls short of demonstration.

The date of *Luke-Acts* raises important questions about interpretation. The usual line is that *Luke-Acts* had to have been written after Paul's death in the 60s because *Luke* 21:20 shows knowledge of the destruction of Jerusalem in 70 CE But some find a difficulty here. *Acts* ends by relating that Paul lived for two years in Rome in prison (28:30–31). Could the author have concluded without narrating Paul's fate? Deaths are important events in *Luke-Acts*, which relates the crucifixion of Jesus (*Lk.* 23), Judas's suicide (*Acts* 1), and Stephen's martyrdom (*Acts* 7). So if the author knew about Paul's martyrdom, should we not expect its narration? Since it is absent, maybe it had not yet happened. Maybe *Acts* was written at the end of the two-year period in *Acts* 28, and so in the mid-60s.

This argument has persuaded only a minority, in part because there are other explanations for the ending on the assumption that Paul was dead when *Luke-Acts* appeared, such as: (1) A third volume was planned and, for whatever reason, never completed. (2) The author did finish, and the conclusion is one or more of the pastoral epistles. Some ancient narratives come with epistles from the hero. (3) The author wanted to present a favorable picture of Christianity to the Romans and so did not want to relate that the emperor had Paul executed. (4) The author's purpose is reached in chapter 28. *Acts* 1:8 speaks of the gospel going to the ends of the earth, and that is what the author cares about, not Paul's biography (which is why the book says nothing of his early life). Once the gospel goes to Rome, the story is over. *Luke* also says nothing about the fates of Peter or James, the brother of Jesus, nor does he tell the gruesome story of the beheading of John the Baptist. (5) The true verdict about Paul is reached in the sea storm episode in chapter 27. Here God vindicates the apostle. The subsequent earthly verdict is irrelevant. (6) Ending with Paul's death would have created an aesthetic imbalance. *Luke* ends not with death but resurrection. If the second book ended with a death without resurrection, it would have seemed anticlimactic.

Luke and *Acts* both address themselves to "Theophilus" (*Lk.* 1:1; *Acts* 1:1) whose identity is not known. He was perhaps Luke's literary patron or publisher. Some have suggested that he was a non-Christian Roman official, and that *Luke-Acts* was intended to correct official misapprehensions about Christianity. The word *theophilus* itself, however, means "lover of God" or "loved by God," and some have supposed him entirely fictional: *Luke-Acts* addresses itself to those who love God.

Luke-Acts seems to be for Gentile Christians. The author prefers Greek terms to Hebrew terms (e.g., the Greek *master* instead of *rabbi*, and *truly* instead of *amen*). Jesus' controversy with the Pharisees over things clean and unclean (*Mark* 7) is, moreover, omitted, as are derogatory uses of the word *Gentile* (contrast *Mt.* 5:47; 6:7).

Regarding the purpose of *Luke-Acts*, the preface fails to allude to any specific occasion or crisis that might have called it forth. "I too have decided" is the only stated motive, and for the rest *Luke* 1:1–4 is formulated in frustratingly general terms. Attempting to be more specific, some have proposed that the writer wished to show Christianity to be politically harmless. After Nero, Christians became a political problem, and it is striking that in *Luke-Acts* Roman officials repeatedly pronounce Christian figures to be politically innocent (*Lk.* 23:4, 14, 22; *Acts* 16:39; 17:6–9; 18:12–17; 19:37–41; 23:29; 25:25; 26:31–32). Another suggestion is that the author wanted to show Christianity to be rooted in Judaism, which the empire tolerated as a legal religion. *Luke* 1–2 opens the story by painting a picture of pious Jews, and the rest of *Luke* is about Jesus the Jew and his mission to Israel. *Acts* begins in Jerusalem, its hero calls himself a Pharisee (23:6), and Christianity is labeled a "sect" or "party" of Judaism (24:5, 14; 28:11).

The chief literary feature of *Luke-Acts* may be parallelism. Both *Luke* and *Acts* open with a preface to Theophilus (*Lk.* 1:1–4; *Acts* 1:1–2). Both narrate the descent of the Spirit upon those who have been praying (*Lk.* 3:21–22; *Acts* 1:14, 24; 2:1–13). Both have opening sermons that feature prophetic fulfillment and the rejection of Jesus (*Lk.* 4:13–30; *Acts* 2:14–40). Both follow this with stories of healing the lame (*Lk.* 5:17–26; *Acts* 3:1–10), conflict with Jewish leaders (*Lk.* 5:29–6:11; *Acts* 4:1–8:3), a centurion asking for help (*Lk.* 7:7–10; *Acts* 10), Pharisaic criticism of Jesus (*Lk.* 7:36–50; *Acts* 11:1–18), and so on. Not only does *Acts* replay *Luke,* but *Acts* 13–28 often parallels *Acts* 1–12, and *Luke* is quite fond of piling up parallels between sympathetic characters—John the Baptist and Jesus, Stephen and Jesus, Paul and Jesus, Peter and Paul. There are several explanations for this literary phenomenon, which has parallels in both Greek and Jewish sources, but one motive is a desire to set Jesus up as a moral model, whom others emulate.

John. "According to John" became affixed to the gospel sometime during the second century, at the end of which Irenaeus wrote: "All the elders that associated with John the disciple of the Lord in Asia bear witness that John delivered it [John's gospel] to them. For he remained among them until the time of Trajan" (who ruled 98–117); "afterwards [after the writing of the other gospels] John, the disciple of the Lord, who also reclined on his bosom, published his gospel, while staying at Ephesus in Asia."

This John is the brother of James, son of Zebedee. *Mark* 1:16–20 recounts his call to discipleship, and elsewhere in *Mark* he belongs to an inner circle around Jesus (3:17; 5:37; 9:2; 14:33). *Acts* presents him as a companion of Peter and as an evangelist and leader of the church (4:1, 13, 23; 8:14–17). *Galatians* 2:9 refers to him, along with James the brother of Jesus and Peter, as one of the pillars of the Jerusalem church.

The Fourth Gospel nowhere mentions John by name (although 21:2 refers to "the sons of Zebedee"). John's gospel does, however, speaks of "the disciple that Jesus loved": 13:23–25; 19:25–27; 20:2; 21:7, 20. It also refers to a "witness" to Jesus (19:35; 21:24), as well as someone it calls "the other disciple" (18:15–16; 20:2–10). Chapter 20 identifies this "other disciple" with the beloved disciple, and 19:35 implies that the beloved is the "witness."

Putting everything together, the beloved disciple belongs to Jesus' inner group. He is present at the last supper (*Jn.* 13), Mary is entrusted to him (*Jn.* 19:25–27), and he is among the group in 21:2, which includes Peter, Thomas, Nathaniel, the sons of Zebedee, and two other unnamed disciples. He is clearly not Peter. Nor can he be James (*Acts* 12:2 has James martyred very early); and since he belongs to Jesus' inner circle, tradition identified him with John, son of Zebedee. The identification is consistent with the gospel's knowledge of pre-70 Jerusalem (see, e.g., *Jn.* 4:5; 5:2; 9:7; 19.13).

One difficulty with the tradition is that John's gospel was not widely used in the second century, which is odd if it was known as the work of an apostle. Furthermore, the "we" of 21:24 cannot be the beloved disciple himself. So perhaps the book was published anonymously and became attached to John's name because the church felt the need to give the document apostolic authority. This might have been especially important given the differences between John and the synoptics, which have always been obvious.

It seems likely that John's gospel was the product of a long process and that more than one person was involved in its editing. This would account for 21:24, where the author speaks in the first-person plural and appears to be different from the beloved disciple, and for 19:35, which speaks of the beloved disciple in the third person. In this case, the beloved disciple, whether John or not, could have been a follower of Jesus who was thought of as the source and guarantee of the tradition behind the gospel.

Whether the author of *John* knew the synoptics is disputed. One possibility is that the author did know them and wanted to supplement them, correct their omissions, and so on. This would make sense of all that is present in *John* but not the synoptics. It does not, however, explain the many overlaps. Common to *John* and the synoptics are, among other things, the cleansing of the temple, the feeding of the five thousand, the walking on the water, the entry into Jerusalem, the anointing of Jesus, the arrest of Jesus, the denials of Peter, the trial before Pilate, the crucifixion, the burial by Joseph of Arimathea, and the discovery of empty tomb. So others have imagined that the author wanted to correct the synoptics. One can interpret *Matthew* and *Luke* as doing this to *Mark.* But then one could also consider the option that the author wanted to replace or oust the synoptics.

Still another option is that *John*'s author did not know the synoptics at all. Yet *John* appeared some time after *Mark* (see below), and there are overlaps with Luke's gospel in particular that may suggest literary contact. Both gospels tell us that Satan entered into Judas (*Lk.* 22:3; *Jn.* 13:27), that Peter cut off the right ear of a servant (*Lk.* 22:50; *Jn.* 18:10), that Jesus' tomb was new (*Lk.* 23:53; *Jn.* 19:41), that there were two angels at the tomb (*Lk.* 24:4; *Jn.* 20:12), that there were resurrection appearances in Jerusalem (*Lk.* 24; *Jn.* 20), and that the risen Jesus invited the disciples to touch him (*Lk.* 24:36; *Jn.* 20:19). Even if, however, *John*'s author knew one or more of the synoptics, use of an independent tradition remains plausible. Apart from traditions going back to the beloved disciple and perhaps the synoptics, John's gospel probably incorporates a traditional passion narrative, a collection of numbered miracle stories designed to show Jesus' messianic status (scholars dub this the "Signs Source"), and various oral traditions.

Most now date *John* to between 80 and 100 CE. Tradition has *John* written after the other gospels, during the time of Trajan (98–117 CE). Such a late date is consistent with both 21:18–19, which probably presupposes the tradition about Peter's martyrdom, and 21:22–23, which reflects eschatological disillusionment when the last of Jesus' disciples had died (some believed that Jesus would return before all of his disciples had passed on; see *Mk.* 9:1). A date later than this is prohibited by an early second-century papyrus fragment containing *John* 8:31–33 and 8:37–38. A date in the 90s or shortly after the turn of the century seems plausible.

Scholars have offered an array of suggestions concerning *John*'s purpose: (1) To record the testimony of the beloved disciple, an eyewitness to Jesus. (2) To supplement, correct, or displace the synoptics. (3) To discourage Christians from maintaining contact with the Jewish synagogue. This would explain the emphasis upon how Jesus replaces Jewish institutions. Again and again *John* uses "the Jews" in a disparaging way. (4) Maybe *John* counters Christians who denied the physical reality of Jesus. Such people were certainly around not long after *John* was written, and if 1:14 emphases that the "word" became flesh, 19:34 speaks of the blood and water coming from Jesus' side. (5) Maybe *John* encourages Christians. *John* 20:31 can be read as an invitation to continue to believe, and most of *John* 13–17 functions to edify believers and build up their faith.

John's differences from the synoptics raise questions about its status as a historical source. The gospel presents Jesus as the Logos (1:1–18) and has Jesus regularly speak in long discourses with a central theme. *John*'s Jesus uses certain words and expressions repeatedly that are rare in the synoptics (e.g., "to love," "I am," "life"). Only *John* clearly teaches Jesus' preexistence and deity (see especially 1:1–18), and only *John*'s Jesus makes clear public statements about himself (e.g., 6:35: "I am bread of life"; 8:12: "I am the light of the world"; 10:30: "I and the Father are one"). In the synoptics, Jesus favors parables and aphorisms; in *John*, these are rare. In the synoptics, Jesus celebrates Passover; in *John*, the Passover lamb is slaughtered as Jesus is being crucified. In the synoptics, Jesus enters the temple at the end of his ministry; in *John*, Jesus does this at the beginning. In the synoptics, the central theme of Jesus' proclamation is the "kingdom of God"; in *John*, Jesus uses the term only twice. In the synoptics, Jesus is preoccupied with future eschatology; in *John*, Jesus focuses on the present (see, e.g., 5:25; 6:47; 16:11). In the synoptics, Jesus goes to Jerusalem once; in *John*, he goes three times, and the public ministry lasts at least three years.

The synoptic picture of Jesus is closer to history than *John*'s portrait. Not only does *John*'s higher Christology reflect later developments, but *John*'s author was not much concerned to differentiate his own words from those of Jesus. There are places, such as the end of *John* 3, where modern editors cannot even agree on where a quotation from Jesus ends and the editor's words begin. Because comparison with the synoptics proves that there are traditional words of Jesus embedded in *John*, the long discourses may have developed from reflection upon those words; they may indeed be something like homilies upon them.

The Letters Attributed to Paul. Thirteen New Testament letters purport to come from Paul. When one adds that he is the major figure in *Acts*, he clearly dominates half of the New Testament. One wonders whether Paul was as important in his own time as his prominence in the canon implies, or whether his canonical importance exaggerates his initial significance and influence. Whatever the answer, the collection of letters assigned to him must be the primary source for his life and thought. Although Paul's self-perception and accounts of events cannot be taken at face value, they must be deemed more reliable than the flattering presentation in *Acts*, whoever authored it.

Of the thirteen canonical Pauline epistles, scholars recognize seven as undoubtedly from Paul: *Romans, 1 Corinthians, 2 Corinthians, Galatians, Philippians, 1 Thessalonians,* and *Philemon*—all of which come from the second half of his ministry, circa 50 CE and later. The authorship of *2 Thessalonians* and *Colossians* are disputed. Most scholars think that *Ephesians* and the so-called pastoral epistles—*1 Timothy, 2 Timothy, and Titus*—were written in Paul's name after his death.

Romans. Paul wrote this essay in letter form, his most systematic product, during his last visit to Corinth, probably in 56 or 57 CE He was on his way to Jerusalem with money he had collected for the church there. Little is known about Christianity in Rome at that time. Paul was not the founder of the church, which consisted of both Jews—the Jewish population of Rome was substantial—and Gentiles. *Romans* 1:13 and 11:13 imply that Gentile Christians outnumbered Jewish Christians.

The occasion and purpose of the letter are cloudy. Local circumstances could have called it forth. Perhaps Paul had heard reports of conflict between Jewish and Gentile Christians and wished to help. Yet given that most of the letter has a general character and addresses issues that do not seem specific to the Roman church, it is more common to see *Romans* in a broader context. Maybe the letter is Paul's attempt to clarify his own mind about certain matters, especially in view of his upcoming visit to Jerusalem and the trouble he anticipated there, although the suggestion that Paul wanted a copy of *Romans* sent to Jerusalem is not demonstrable. More persuasive are attempts to read *Romans* as a sort of introduction to Paul himself, sent to prepare the way for his coming to the empire's capital (see 1:10–11; 15:15, 20, 24, 28–29). Paul was a controversial figure about whom rumors must have flourished, and if he planned on going to Rome and using it as a missionary base for his work in Spain, he may have felt a need to explain clearly what he was all about and so recommend himself.

The original form of *Romans* is problematic. The doxology, 16:25–27, is missing in some ancient manuscripts, and the preceding 16:24 ("The grace of the Lord Jesus Christ be with you all. Amen.") is unlikely to be pristine. Some textual authorities put 16:25–27 immediately after chapter 14, or immediately after chapter 15; others put it in both places, and it is altogether missing from still others. A few Latin manuscripts omit 15:1–16:23, and the third-century church father Origen says that the second-century heretic, Marcion, removed the last two chapters. In addition, some textual authorities do not name Rome in 1:7 and 15.

Several accounts of the data are possible. (1) Paul composed a letter to the Roman church, containing everything except 16:24–27. He then reissued the letter, omitting the last two chapters, which contain much personal material. He also excised "Rome" from 1:7 and 15, thus creating a treatise for a larger audience. (2) Paul turned a general letter into a letter for Rome. Originally he composed a general essay, which he then revised for the Roman community in particular by naming Rome in 1:7 and 15 and adding chapter 16 or chapters 15 and 16. (3) Perhaps Paul sent chapters 1 to 15 to Rome and afterward added chapter 16, sending the enlarged, expanded letter to Ephesus, which is associated with many of the people *Romans* 16 names. (4) Maybe chapter 16 is an independent Pauline letter, sent to Ephesus, and someone other than Paul preserved it by tacking it onto the end of *Romans.* (5) Origen may have been right: someone omitted the last two chapters. Since 14:23 does not work well as an ending, someone added the doxology in 16:25–27.

After the introduction in 1:1–15, *Romans* 1:16–3:20 indicts humanity's sin and guilt. The chapters are unremittingly bleak, and among the most pessimistic evaluations of the human condition in ancient literature. Such pessimism is the foil for 3:21–8:39, with its thesis in 3:21–31. This large section presents the solution to humanity's plight, which is the grace of God in Jesus Christ, to be appropriated by faith. Paul's presentation of this solution involves a critique of the Jewish Torah, but the attack is less sweeping and more moderate than in *Galatians.* Paul is in *Romans* inclined to say positive things about the law. Perhaps the strident statements in *Galatians* had proved to be too extreme even in Paul's own eyes.

Romans 9:1–11:36, which historically has been a theological battleground for debates over free will and predestination, addresses the problem of Israel, which was occasioned by the failure of so many Jews to accept the Christian Gospels. How could Israel not embrace the messiah? What of God's promises to Israel? The logic of these three chapters is tortured because Paul's reduction of salvation to Christology resists harmonization with his biblically inspired faith in the redemption of Israel.

Romans 12:1–15:13, which at points echoes sayings attributed to Jesus, outlines Paul's ethic. His critique of the Torah disallows him from simply citing its ethical imperatives as authoritative, even though his counsels are for the most part taken over from Jewish tradition. He in effect reinvents the law by grounding proper behavior in Christian theology.

Christians have often found in *Romans* an account of Judaism as a religion of salvation based on works, of a legalism unconnected to God's grace. Jewish sources, whether biblical, intertestamental, or rabbinic, do not support this view, which is a caricature due not only to a misreading of Paul but also to Paul's tendentious generalizations. The apostle offers neither an objective account of Jewish life under the law nor an insider's sympathetic understanding, but rather pens polemic in the service of his cause. His arguments, in the final analysis, issue from his seeing matters through the eyes of his Gentile converts. Some in the early church desired those converts to undergo circumcision and otherwise follow Jewish customs. Paul instead sponsored a theology according to which Gentiles fully participate in redemption, and he disagreed fervently with those who urged that those born outside the covenant with Abraham needed, in addition to their faith in Jesus Christ, to undergo circumcision and embrace other distinctive Jewish practices. It was this conflict regarding Gentiles that led to Paul's sweeping generalizations about the law. He could have been fairer to Judaism had he simply affirmed that the Torah was never intended for Gentiles, or if he had not treated the law as a whole but rather argued for its partial observance (which is what in fact most Christians have done ever since). Paul, however, took another course, and the outcome is no guide to how Judaism looked and felt to its practitioners.

The Corinthian correspondence. The Corinthian correspondence supplies the most valuable information available about early Gentile Christianity. The letters, although a record of what happened to one church, presumably reflect the sorts of problems faced by Gentile converts everywhere in the Roman world.

Corinth is located near the isthmus that links the Peloponnesus to mainland Greece. In Paul's day it was the capital of the province of Achaia and a cosmopolitan seaport. Paul founded the Christian community there and spent two years ministering in the area (see *Acts* 18).

To read *1* and *2 Corinthians* is to hear only one side of the conversation, so much remains hidden. But from the letters and *Acts* 18 one can reconstruct a sequence of events into which it is possible to place *1* and *2 Corinthians.*

Paul first visited Corinth in 50 or 51 CE During his extended stay, he made converts, began a house church, and handed down Christian traditions. He did not, however, remain the only Christian leader known to the Corinthians. Apollos and probably Peter came to Corinth soon after his departure (*1 Cor.* 1:12; 9:4–5).

After leaving Corinth, Paul sent to the Corinthians a letter no longer extant (unless *2 Corinthians* 6:14–7:1, which badly disrupts its present context and seems secondary, preserves part of it). *1 Corinthians* 5:9 refers to this letter: "I wrote to you in my letter not to associate with immoral men." In part as a response to this lost letter, the Corinthians wrote their own letter to Paul, to which most of *1 Corinthians* (composed 52–55 CE) is a point-by-point reply. *1 Corinthians* 7:1 (on marriage and divorce), 25 (on virgins), 8:1 (on food offered to idols), 12:1 (on spiritual gifts), 16:1 (on the collection for the church in Jerusalem), and 12 (on Apollos) all open with the phrase, "Now concerning," and in each case Paul is responding to Corinthian queries. He even at points seems to quote the Corinthians: "All things are lawful" (6:12; 10:23); "It is well for a man not to touch a woman" (7:1); and "All of us possess knowledge" (8:1).

The various topics that *1 Corinthians* addresses are not all clearly related to each other; they cannot be traced to one central theological idea. Rather, there was a host of issues. Some Corinthians valued other teachers more than Paul (*1 Cor.* 1:11–16; 3:10–4:20). Some thought the apostle insufficiently sophisticated (3:1–9). One man was living with his stepmother (5:1–13). Some believers had taken others to court (6:1–8). There were questions about divorce as well as virginity, which some Corinthians reckoned a superior state (7:1–40). There was debate over whether believers could eat food consecrated to pagan idols (8:1–11:1). Some women—virgins wishing to display their equality with men?—were worshiping without head coverings (11:2–16). The common meal of the community was fractured by cliques, probably according to social status (11:17–34). Ecstatic gifts were creating disorder in worship and becoming an inordinate source of pride (12:1–14:40). *1 Corinthians* 14:33b(34)–36, with its prohibition of women speaking in church, may be an interpolation; it contradicts 11:2–16, where women pray and prophesy. In addition, some Corinthians evidently had an anthropology that made bodily resurrection unnecessary and unwanted (15:1–58).

1 Corinthians was followed by a "painful visit" (see *2 Cor.* 2:1; 12:14; 13:1). Clearly the letter had not worked its intended result. Perhaps already by the time of the second visit, Jewish Christian teachers, with letters of commendation from Jerusalem, had arrived and were offering criticism of Paul (see *2 Cor.* 3:1; 11:4–6, 22–23).

After the failure of his second visit, Paul sent from Ephesus through Titus a "severe letter" (see *2 Cor.* 3–4, 9; 7:8). Some have identified this letter with *2 Corinthians* 10–13; others believe it has been lost. Whatever the truth, this severe letter was followed by *2 Corinthians* 1–9 (chapters 8 and 9 should probably not be considered separate letters, occasional opinion to the contrary). Titus had returned with good news (*2 Cor.* 7:2), which explains Paul's thanksgiving and confidence in much of *2 Corinthians.* He is irenic, however, only in chapters 1–9. Chapters 10–13 are defensive and polemical and reflect a different situation. If *2 Corinthians* 10–13 was sent before chapters 1–9, it apparently met a favorable response, given the relief and gratitude expressed in *2 Corinthians* 1–9. If *2 Corinthians* 10–13 was sent after chapters 1–9, then *2 Corinthians* 1–9 must have met an unsympathetic hearing. In either case, Paul determined to visit Corinth for a third time (see *2 Cor.* 12:14; *Acts* 10:1–2). What happened then is not known.

Galatians. Paul preached in Galatia, where an infirmity perhaps delayed his departure (4:13). He founded several house churches there. After Paul left Galatia, other Christian teachers arrived. Although these were, like Paul, Jewish Christians, they regarded him as promoting an inferior brand of Christianity, and he viewed them as enemies of his proclamation. Their theology can be partly inferred from *Galatians* 4:10 ("You are observing special days, and months, and seasons, and years") and 6:12–13 ("They want you to be circumcised so that they may boast about your flesh"). They demanded that Gentile Christians observe Jewish practices.

Despite scholarly ingenuity, many questions remain unanswered. It is unclear whether the teachers with whom Paul disagreed were closely connected with either James or those whom Paul debated in Jerusalem according to 2:3–6. Nor is it known whether, in addition to the Jewish Christians who imposed circumcision, other agitators promoted an antinomianism (some see this in 5:13–6:10). How the Galatians responded to Paul's passionate pleas is a mystery—although his conviction that Gentiles should not be circumcised eventually became the dominant position of the church.

Commentators dispute whether Paul wrote to Celts living in the northern part of Roman Galatia or whether his converts lived in the southern section of the province, where most were not Celts. There is also debate over the date of composition. Some think *Galatians* was written in 49 or 50 CE. Others believe a date in the later 50s better fits the evidence. The issues are complex and involve deciding whether the meeting in Jerusalem in *Galatians* 2 should be equated with the council of *Acts* 15 or instead with the episode in *Acts* 11:29–30. The tendency of modern scholarship is to favor the northern destination, the later date, and the equation of *Galatians* 2 with *Acts* 15.

The introduction, *Galatians* 1:1–9, contains, uncharacteristically for a Pauline letter, a rebuke (1:6–9). Notably missing is any thanksgiving. *Galatians* 1:10–2:21 follows with an autobiographical defense (the starting point for any reconstruction of Pauline chronology). Here Paul stresses the divine origin of his ministry, his independence from Jerusalem, others' recognition of his ministry, and Peter's hypocrisy in dealing with Gentile Christians. In 3:1–5:1, Paul offers arguments from experience (3:1–5), from Scripture (3:6–9; 4:21–31), and from Christology (3:10–4:20) to buttress his understanding of a law-free gospel and to impeach those with another point of view. The last major section, 5:2–6:10, which conceives of the moral struggle as a battle between "spirit" and "flesh," contains exhortations; Paul at least did not feel that his theology entailed ethical indifference. It is noteworthy that 6:2 refers to "the law of Christ." While the expression remains susceptible to various interpretations, Paul cannot, despite the seeming implication of his polemic, do without some sort of "law."

Ephesians. This letter opens with a salutation (1:1–2) and a long thanksgiving (1:3–23). *Ephesians* 2:1–10 follows with an account of the saving benefits that have come to those with faith in Christ, who were formerly captive to "the prince of the power of the air." *Ephesians* 2:11–22 displays the collective nature of those benefits though an exposition of the church as a manifestation of the new humanity, in which the differences between Jew and Gentile no longer count. *Ephesians* 3:1–13, which sounds like a retrospective paean, not an authentic self-evaluation, testifies to Paul and his distinctive role in disseminating God's revelation throughout the world. Then, in 3:14–21, the author seemingly reverts to the prayer of chapter 1, asking that the recipients may be strengthened, grounded in love, and filled with knowledge of "the love of Christ." *Ephesians* 4:1–6:20 explores the behavioral implications of the preceding theology. Believers are to seek unity among themselves (4:1–16), lay aside pagan habits (4:17–5:20), observe proper rules for the household (5:21–6:9), and live in truth, righteousness, peace, faith, and prayer (6:10–20).

Paul did not write *Ephesians*. There is an uncharacteristic absence of personal data, and the concerns are not those of a concrete community. Much of the vocabulary and style are also un-Pauline. Decisive against the traditional attribution is the dependence upon *Colossians*. Readers may compare, to illustrate this, *Ephesians* 1:15–17 with *Colossians* 1:3–4, 9–10; *Ephesians* 4:31–32 with *Colossians* 3:8, 12; and *Ephesians* 6:5–9 with *Colossians* 3:22–4:1. Notably, the traditional text of *Ephesians* 1:1, with "the faithful who are at Ephesus," is secondary. Originally, the recipients were unnamed.

Given that Christian writers of the first half of the second century clearly knew *Ephesians*, it was presumably written not long after Paul's death. That it was composed to introduce a collection of the apostle's epistles is an intriguing if unproven suggestion. In any case, *Ephesians* is someone's meditation on Paul and a development of his theology and ethics. The place of composition cannot be determined.

Philippians. Paul wrote this letter to his first European converts, the Christians of Philippi in Macedonia (see *Acts* 16). At the time of writing, Paul was in prison (*Phil.* 1:12–26). Whether this was his Roman imprisonment (see *Acts* 28), as most used to think, is uncertain. The date in this case would be the early 60s. Some think rather of Caesarea, where Paul was a prisoner in the late 50s CE according to *Acts* 23–24, or of Ephesus, where, despite the silence of *Acts*, Paul may have been a prisoner for a time (c. 56 CE).

To judge from *Philippians* 2:25–29 and 4:18, the *Philippians* sent Epaphroditus to Paul with a gift, presumably of money. *Philippians* is Paul's happy response. He takes the occasion to return his thanksgiving for the Philippians, to whom he seems particularly attached (1:3–11). He describes his circumstances and entertains the possibility of his own death (1:12–26), offers ethical admonitions (1:27–2:18), shares news (2:19–3:1), warns against proponents of circumcision (3:2–11), commends himself as an example for emulation (3:12–4:1), gives counsel regarding Euodia and Syntyche (4:2–3), calls for rejoicing in all things—poignant given his circumstances (4:4–13)—and thanks the Philippians for their gift (4:14–20).

The tone of chapter 3 differs from the tone of chapters 1 and 2. Common, then, is the proposal that *Philippians* is a conflation of two letters, one consisting perhaps of 3:1b–4:20 or 23, the other of 1:1–3:1a (+ 4:21–23). Even more popular has been the suggestion that *Philippians* combines three originally separate letters: a polemical letter in 3:1b–4:3 + 4:8–9; a letter of thanks for the Philippians' gift in 4:10–20 or 23; and a longer letter in 1:1–3:1a + 4:4–7 + (perhaps) 21–23. It is hard to know how to evaluate such proposals. Authentic letters of Paul do contain some abrupt shifts. Many have not been compelled to deny the unity of the letter.

Colossians. The authorship of *Colossians* continues to be disputed, although perhaps most authorities now doubt that Paul wrote it. The opponents are unlike any in other authentic letters. (The problem in Colossae cannot be identified with the problem in Galatia.) Jesus' cosmic role in creation and redemption is distinctive, as is the church's participation in his cosmic authority. The eschatology is more realized than what is otherwise found in Paul. And there are some stylistic peculiarities. Some scholars, however, maintain that *Colossians* is distinctive because of the unique situation it addresses and because Paul allowed a secretary some compositional freedom or even assigned its composition to an associate.

Colossae was a small town about a hundred miles east of Ephesus in Asia Minor. *Colossians* 1:7 implies that Paul's associate, Epaphras, founded the church there. If *Colossians* came from Paul, he wrote it at the same time he sent *Philemon* (see below). If it is a pseudepigraphon, written in the last quarter of the first century, the author gave the work the appearance of authenticity by borrowing personal details from *Philemon*.

Colossians opposes Christians who sponsor a "philosophy" (2:8), observe Jewish food laws and a Jewish calendar (2:16), value visionary experiences (2:18), and venerate angels or participate in the angel's heavenly liturgy (2:18). There is no consensus concerning the Colossians' identity and the source of their convictions. Commentators have thought of Christians enamored of Hellenistic philosophy, or of people who mixed their Christianity with a pagan mystery cult, or of mystical Jewish visionaries, perhaps related to those who composed many of the Dead Sea Scrolls, or of Jewish Christians on the path toward Gnosticism.

1 Thessalonians. According to *Acts* 17, Paul, Silas, and Timothy founded the church in Thessalonica, Macedonia's capital. Because of opposition, they soon left. Anxious about his converts, Paul sent Timothy back to the Thessalonians. When Timothy subsequently returned to Paul with news, Paul wrote *1 Thessalonians* from Corinth (probably only a few months after he left). The letter is full of gratitude for how well the Thessalonians, despite suffering, have fared. Although *1 Thessalonians* is the earliest extant of Paul's letters (c. 50 CE), it was written after he had been a Christian for approximately fifteen years, so it need not reflect an immature theology.

The first three chapters are mostly personal. *1 Thessalonians* 4:1–12 offers general exhortations. *1 Thessalonians* 4:13–18 explains that Christians who have died will share in

Jesus' return. Evidently Paul had preached an imminent second advent. When more than one Thessalonian Christian died, there was dismay. Such dismay may well have been exacerbated by non-Christians who attributed the deaths to supernatural vengeance. Paul in any event had not said much about the general resurrection, probably because his converts' ancestors were not Christians. *1 Thessalonians* 5:1–11, with close parallels in *Matthew* 24 and *Mark* 13, presents the Parousia (Second Coming) as near and sure to come suddenly.

2 Thessalonians. This letter depicts the eschatological judgment (1:5–12) and outlines events on the day of the Lord (2:1–12). Between the eschatological teaching in chapters 1 and 2 is an appeal "not to be quickly shaken in mind or alarmed, either by spirit or by word or by letter, as though from us, to the effect that the day of the Lord is already here" (2:1–2). The nature of this conviction is unclear. Is it a spiritualized or fully realized eschatology? Is it belief in a very near end? Is it the conviction that certain events in the eschatological scenario, including the punishment of enemies, have already taken place?

Unlike *1 Thessalonians,* the Pauline authorship of *2 Thessalonians* is controversial. Many are suspicious of the extensive overlap between *1* and *2 Thessalonians,* which they take as a sign of the latter copying the former (compare, for example, *2 Thes.* 3:8 with *1 Thes.* 2:9). Questions are also raised by *1 Thessalonians* 3:17 ("This greeting is with my own hand. This is the mark in every letter of mine"), which may imply a collection of Paul's letters. Further questions are raised by the length of the sentences, which are longer than is Paul's wont, and by the eschatological scenario in chapter 2, which stands in tension with *1 Thessalonians* 4–5 (in *1 Thessalonians* the day comes like a thief; in *2 Thessalonians* it follows a well-defined series of events). This last consideration, however, does not count for much because Paul is elsewhere inconsistent and because ancient eschatological discourses often display contradictions.

If Paul wrote *2 Thessalonians,* he wrote it after *1 Thessalonians,* perhaps after several return visits. He was concerned about discouragement brought by persecution and by the failure of some to continue working for a living. If Paul did not write *2 Thessalonians,* then someone late in the first century, in a context of persecution, sought in his name to impart eschatological instruction and encouragement.

The pastorals. *1 Timothy, 2 Timothy,* and *Titus,* collectively known as the pastoral epistles, address themselves not to communities but to two leaders that Paul left in charge of churches, Timothy in Ephesus and Titus on Crete. Like the correspondence between Paul and Seneca, the pastorals are pseudepigrapha. Someone wrote them in Paul's name at the end of the first or the beginning of the second century.

1 Timothy consists mostly of two sorts of material. Chapters 2, 3, 5, and 6 concern themselves with church administration—with the ordering of public worship (2:1–15), for instance, and with the behavior of women and widows (5:3–16)—as well as with more general moral guidance. Chapters 1 and 4 counter false teaching. It is most likely that an early form of Gnosticism is the target. The author's opponents occupy themselves with "myths" (1:4), practice some sort of asceticism (4:3), and possess what the pastor calls a false *gnosis,* or knowledge (6:20). *1 Timothy* 6:18 suggests not only a knowledge of *1 Corinthians* 9 but also seemingly quotes *Luke* 10:7 as "scripture," a circumstance impossible in Paul's lifetime.

2 Timothy, which has more claim that *1 Timothy* or *Titus* to be from someone who knew Paul, purports to be composed from a Roman prison (1:16–17), with Paul's death near (4:6–8). *2 Timothy* 2:14–3:9 warns against false doctrine, including the conviction that the resurrection is past (2:17–18). The exact nature of this realized eschatology is unknown, although it proponents may be Gnostics, who sometimes spoke of a present resurrection (as in the *Treatise on the Resurrection* from Nag Hammadi).

Titus, addressed to a Gentile companion of Paul known from *2 Corinthians, Galatians,* and *2 Timothy,* but not *Acts,* consists primarily of instructions on the appointment of leaders and exhortations to defend sound doctrine. It largely replays *1 Timothy.* Chapter 1 focuses on elders and bishops in the context of "rebellious people, idle talkers and deceivers, especially those of the circumcision" (1:10). Chapter 2 offers advice for older men, older women, younger men, and slaves (2:1–10) and concludes with a general summary of Christian behavior. Chapter 3 continues to outline the Christian response to God's actions in Jesus Christ and then ends with personal details intended to add verisimilitude to the letter (3:12–15).

Philemon. Although the brief letter is cryptic about some things, it seems best to follow the conventional view that Onesimus, the slave of the Christian Philemon, had run away from his master. Onesimus then sought an advocate in Paul, who wrote and flattered Philemon in the hope of reconciling him to Onesimus upon the latter's return. But what exactly Paul was asking Philemon to do is unclear, and there is no way of finding out what did in fact happen. Did Paul want Onesimus to turn around and come back to him, or did he expect Onesimus to stay with Philemon? Or was he willing to let Philemon decide that? And did Paul expect Philemon to treat Onesimus differently thereafter, or even to manumit him? The latter possibility seems doubtful. One should not forget that Christians who supported the slave trade appealed to Philemon; they observed that Paul nowhere in this or other letters does much to undermine slavery.

Paul wrote *Philemon* in prison. The parallels in personal matters it shares with *Colossians* imply that, if the latter is authentic, the two letters were sent to Colossae at the same time (note *Col.* 4:9). If Paul wrote from Ephesus, the date would be circa 56. If he wrote from Rome, a date in the early 60s would be required.

***HEBREWS* AND THE CATHOLIC EPISTLES.** Following the Gospels and Paul, the New Testament contains eight additional letters. These had a harder time making it into the canon. *Hebrews* comes first because of its mistaken ascription to Paul; it serves as a conclusion to the Pauline collection. The remaining seven letters are traditionally assigned to four authors—James, Peter, John (compare the order of *Gal.* 2:9), and Jude. Unlike the Pauline epistles, the titles identify the authors rather the recipients (e.g., "The Epistle of James" versus "To the Romans"). The general character of these letters encouraged the conviction that they address the church universal. From the fourth century on they have collectively been known as the "Catholic epistles."

Hebrews. While often in the past attributed to Paul (although not in the West until the fourth century), this rhetorically polished work, so heavily indebted to Platonism, was originally anonymous. No contemporary scholar believes that Paul wrote it, although at points the author shows a knowledge of Pauline thought. Some have guessed that it was written by a member of Paul's circle, but Origen's comment that "only God knows" stands. The book is not, despite the epistolary ending, formally a letter, and the title, "To the Hebrews," cannot be original. The date of composition was probably between 60 and 90 CE. Some have insisted that it must come from before the destruction of Jerusalem in 70 CE, for the author uses the present tense for activities in the temple (7:27–28; 8:3–5; etc.). But many rabbinic texts composed long after 70 also speak of the temple as though it were still standing. A date before 90 is required by the fact that *1 Clement,* probably written in the 90s, quotes from *Hebrews.* The places of writing and destination are unknown (although Jerusalem and Rome have been common proposals for the latter).

Despite the traditional title, the first readers need not have been Jews. A Gentile or mixed readership is possible. The concerns vocalized, such as that its readers are "sluggish" (6:12), or that some Christians are no longer meeting together (10:25), do not allow us to say anything concrete about the recipients or their situation. All that is know of the recipients is that they had suffered affliction (10:32–34). If the author was combating particular opponents, there is no way detect who they were.

There are three highly structured discourses. *Hebrews* 1:5–4:16 argues for Jesus Christ's superiority over angels and Moses. *Hebrews* 5:1–10:39 presents Jesus as a great high priest whose invisible heavenly realities mirror the priestly duties of Jewish tradition. This section famously develops the parallels between Jesus and Melchizedek, whose fleeting presence in the story of Abraham scarcely prepares readers for what they find here. *Hebrews* 11:1–13:19 then contains calls to faith and moral exhortations.

James. *James* is an enigma. The identity of its author is unknown, as are the date and place of composition. The book moreover does not develop as an argument but instead seems to touch on loosely related topics. Its purpose remains unclear. Equally unclear is the sort of Christianity it represents.

Tradition assigns the book to James, Jesus' brother. While one cannot rule out his authorship entirely, it is more likely that the book is a pseudepigraphon. The good Greek, the possible dependence upon *1 Peter,* the fact that nothing but the title and opening line of the book link it to James, and the work's long struggle for canonical acceptance all go against the conventional ascription.

The date, on the theory of pseudonymity, is hard to guess. While there are possible contacts with works from the early second century (*1 Clement; Shepherd of Hermas*), there is no clear knowledge of *James* until the beginning of the third century, when Origen refers to it. There are three papyrus scraps of *James* from the third century. Although maybe most scholars now date *James* to the end of the first century, a later date is possible.

James displays several anomalous features. One is its reluctance to be explicitly Christian. Jesus is mentioned only twice, in 1:1 and 2:1, and the relevant clause in 2:1 has often, because of its grammatical awkwardness, been reckoned an interpolation. The obviously Christian elements are so sparse that a few have claimed the text was originally Jewish; Christian hands then added the references to Jesus in 1:1 and 2:1. But this cannot be right. *James* borrows too heavily from traditions that were specifically Christian for it to be non-Christian in origin. The teaching on oaths in 5:12, for instance, clearly reproduces the same tradition that lies behind *Matthew* 5:34–37, which presumably goes back to Jesus and which in any event was handed down through Christian channels. Chapter 2, moreover, is almost certainly polemic directed at Paul or people influenced by him: *James* looks like a Christian document.

Even if *James* must be Christian, Jesus' crucifixion is not alluded to. Nor is anything said about his resurrection or exaltation. The deeds of Jesus, so important for the synoptic evangelists and John, also fail to put in an appearance, and one searches in vain for any remark upon Jesus' character or his status as a moral model—a striking omission given the appeals to other moral models. The tradition of his words is alluded to, perhaps often, but the author never says "This comes from Jesus." *James* likewise has nothing to say about baptism, the Lord's Supper, the Holy Spirit, or fulfilled prophecy. Martin Luther speculated that *James* was written by a Jew who did not know much about Christianity.

Another striking feature of *James* is that it is written to "the twelve tribes in the diaspora." While commentators often equate the twelve tribes with the church, this is not convincing. Certainly nothing demands a Gentile audience; much suggests a Jewish one. *James* 2:21 calls Abraham "our father" without any hint that the expression has a transferred sense. The readers gather in a "synagogue" (2:2). In 2:19, their faith is embodied in the Shema' ("You believe that God is one"; see *Dt.* 6:4). The writer calls God "the Lord Sabaoth" without explanation (5:4). And all the moral exemplars are from Jewish tradition—Abraham, Rahab, the prophets, Job, Elijah. More than this, parts of *James* do not seem to address believing Christians. *James* 4:1–10 demands that readers submit themselves to God, resist the devil, cleanse their hands, purify their minds, mourn and weep, and humble themselves. These individuals are called "adulterers" (4:4) and "sinners" (4:8). They are full of covetousness (4:2) and are friends of the world and enemies of God (4:4). They are even guilty of murder (4:2). *James* 4:13–5:6 upbraids the rich who are about to suffer eschatological misery, people who have "condemned and murdered the righteous one, who does not resist you" (5:3–6).

One explanation of *James* is that it addresses a fictional audience (the twelve tribes) and that it represents a distinctive sort of Jewish Christianity still trying to make its way within the synagogue. James condemns persecutors and communicates that Jesus' followers are not apostates but faithful members of the synagogue who live according to the Jewish moral tradition, keep the Torah, and oppose those who want to divide faith from works. One might further attempt to relate *James* to one of the groups Johannine scholarship has detected behind the scenes of John's gospel—Jews who attended synagogue and believed in Jesus but did not proselytize. Such crypto-Christians, as they have been called, promoted tolerance.

The most controversial part of *James* has been 2:14–26. These verses, which discuss faith and works, are likely aimed against the perceived teaching of Paul. Many believe the argument is misdirected because Paul and *James* use the word *faith* differently. For Paul, *faith* is trust in Jesus Christ. In *James*, it is intellectual assent. While the latter may exist without good works, the former, so it is claimed, cannot. Whatever the theological truth, *James* may be less a response to the historical Paul than a reaction to a later version of Paulinism, which someone perceived as disconnecting ethics from faith.

1 Peter. This collection of exhortations and moral and religious guidance has no clear outline or developed argument. It addresses itself to "the exiles of the Dispersion in Pontus, Galatia, Cappadocia, Asia, and Bithynia, chosen and destined by God the Father and sanctified by the Spirit for obedience to Jesus Christ" (1:1–2). As the readers are Gentiles (1:14, 18, 21; 2:10, 25; 4:3), "the Dispersion" must stand for the church in exile from the pagan world in Asia Minor. The letter's chief aim is to offer encouragement to Christians who are suffering social ostracism for their faith.

The work attributes itself to Peter and claims to come from Rome. (In *1 Pt.* 5:13, as in *Rev.*, Babylon represents Rome). If this is the truth, it must have been penned before Peter's death in the mid-60s. But Petrine authorship should be doubted. The Greek is better than one would expect from a Galilean fisherman. If one responds that Sylvanus (see *1 Pt.* 5:12) was commissioned to write it and is responsible for the language, nothing apart from the title and the claim of the opening verse ties the letter to Peter. The work betrays no first-hand knowledge of Jesus. And if one were going to write in someone else's name, one could hardly do better than Peter. Other pseudonymous works, such as the *Gospel of Peter* and the *Apocalypse of Peter*, circulated under his name.

1 Peter probably appeared not long after Peter's death. For one thing, the letter was known to Polycarp and Papias in the first half of the second century. For another, the view of the Roman Empire is less critical than in *Revelation*, which probably appeared in the last decade of the first century. A date between 70 and 90 CE is likely.

2 Peter. Presenting itself as a follow-up to *1 Peter* (see 3:1), this letter contains three main sections. *2 Peter* 1:3–21 mixes exhortations to holiness with a defense of the author's authority. *2 Peter* 2:1–22 attacks false teachings with language that in large part reproduces *Jude* (but out of anxiety omits *Jude*'s borrowing from extra-canonical material). *2 Peter* 3:1–18 defends the author's eschatological convictions.

2 Peter, despite its claims, is not Peter's work. As in the case of *1 Peter*, the good Greek is not that of a Galilean fisherman. Even more importantly, although Peter died in the mid-60s, the author of *2 Peter* 3:15–16 knows a collection of Paul's letters, which cannot have been in existence so early. It is telling that there is no solid evidence for *2 Peter* until the beginning of the third century, in the work of Origen, who observes its disputed status; *2 Peter* is not widely cited or discussed until the fourth century (when Jerome writes that most reject it because its style is inconsistent with *1 Peter*'s style). A letter known to come from Peter would not have met with such a tepid reception.

2 Peter may not have come into circulation until the middle of the second century. Consistent with such a late date is the problem of the third chapter. *2 Peter* 3:4 counters scoffers who ask, "Where is the promise of his coming? For ever since the fathers fell asleep, all things have continued as they were from the beginning of creation." Such disillusionment is unlikely to have arisen until the first generation of Christians had died. Also harmonizing with a second-century date is the real possibility that *2 Peter* opposes Gnostics. The author's adversaries spin "clever myths" (1:16) and reject traditional eschatology (3:3–10). They interpret the Jewish Bible in unacceptable ways (1:21), and they find support for their theology in their own interpretation of Paul (7:15–18).

The three Johannine epistles. The titles to *1*, *2*, and *3 John* assign them to the same person, traditionally identified as John the disciple of Jesus. Many early Christian writers, however, including Origen, Eusebius, and Jerome, thought otherwise. They believed that *2* and *3 John*, which attribute themselves to "the Presbyter," had a different author than *1 John*. Some moderns have also thought this. A few have even thought of three different authors.

Whether or not *1 John*, which is not formally a letter, ever circulated apart from the other two, which formally are letters, its author never uses a name or title. But the tradition is likely correct to assign all three letters to one individual. The common style and vocabulary are striking. The parallels are such that the choice is either a common author or deliberate imitation.

Scholars do not often assign these letters to the apostle John. The books themselves do not name their author, and their content does not establish apostolic authorship. As for their relationship to John's gospel, it is possible that the person who wrote *1, 2,* and *3 John* was also involved in the publication of the gospel. There are certainly intriguing thematic overlaps, and the opening of *1 John* recalls the opening of the gospel (see 1:1–3). Both texts also speak about walking in darkness (*1 Jn.* 1:6–7; 2:10–11; *Jn.* 8:12; etc.), use the expression "little children" (*1 Jn.* 2:1, 12, etc.; *Jn.* 13:33), refer to a new commandment (*1 Jn.* 1:2–8; *Jn.* 13:34), teach that the world, ignorant of God, hates the followers of Jesus (*1 Jn.* 3:1, 13; *Jn.* 7:7; etc.), and associate water, blood, and Spirit (*1 Jn.* 5:6; *Jn.* 19:30, 34).

Yet there are also differences. For example, *John* uses the inferential particle *oun* ninety-four times; *1 John* never uses it. And if, in *John,* Jesus is the *logos,* or "word," in *1 John, logos* is rather the author's message. So the many similarities exist alongside significant differences. Perhaps there was some sort of group or school, the members of which shared an insider language. One common view is that the publication of the *Gospel of John* helped precipitate a crisis, which the epistles, from another author or not, reflect. Maybe the epistles are something like a late epilogue to the gospel, an attempt at correct commentary.

Whatever the relationship to John's gospel, the epistles reflect a crisis. Some people had left the community (*1 Jn.* 2:18–19), denying the real humanity of Jesus (see *1 Jn.* 4:1–3; *2 Jn.* 7). If John's gospel intended to correct an emerging docetism, it did not convert everyone. Perhaps some readers of *John,* observing the high Christology and the "I am" statements, did not reckon Jesus to be a real human being. The author of *1 John* instead emphasized that Jesus came in the flesh (1:1; 4:2). It may also be that some readers of *John* came away with the notion that it is possible to be without sin (see *Jn.* 8:31ff.), or that eschatology is wholly realized in the present, and that *1 John* responded by recognizing the reality of sin (1:8, 10) and forwarding a literal, future eschatology (3:2–3).

The reason *1 John* talks so much about love is that its goal is reconciliation. To judge by *2* and *3 John,* this reconciliation was not achieved. *2 John* shows us that some people left the community, and *3 John* shows us that there were rival communities. *2 John* counsels avoiding contact with the group that has left (vv. 10–11). The situation of *3 John* is harder to pin down. It is addressed to named individuals and encourages hospitality for certain missionaries. But the identities of Demetrius in verse 12 and Diotrephes in verses 9–10 remain unclear. Is Diotrephes a theological opponent of the Presbyter? Is he an independent figure not on the side of the Presbyter or his opponents? Is he a bishop? Whatever the answers, *3 John* indicates that the problems reflected in *1* and *2 John* remained unresolved.

Jude. Containing only twenty-five verses, *Jude* appears to be a sermon in letter form. Although it opens with a salutation (vv. 1–2), it ends not with greetings but with a doxology, perhaps designed for public reading (vv. 24–25). In between is an exposé of false teachers. These teachers are said to be "ungodly" (v. 4), to sponsor licentiousness (v. 4), to reject authority and slander angels (v. 8), to "feast without fear" (v. 12), and to grumble, boast, and flatter (v. 16). From the author's point of view, the teachers set up divisions and are worldly (v. 19). In condemning these people, the author manages, in a very short space, to refer to a host of traditions—the exodus from Egypt (v. 5), the sin of the Sons of God in *Genesis* 6 (v. 6), Sodom and Gomorrah (v. 7; see *Gn.* 19), a tale about the burial of Moses (vv. 8–9, probably from the lost ending of *The Testament of Moses*), Cain's murder of Abel (v. 11; see Gn. 4:9), the story of Balaam's ass (v. 11; see *Nm.* 22–24), Korah's rebellion (v. 11; see *Nm.* 16), a prophecy of Enoch (vv. 14–15; the author here quotes the extra-canonical *1 Enoch* 1:9), and a prophecy of "the apostles": "In the last time there will be scoffers, indulging their own ungodly lusts" (v. 18). In each case the author draws analogies between the past and his own present. Thus his opponents are like Cain, like the Sons of God who erred, like those who rebelled in the desert, and so on.

The identity of *Jude's* opponents is unknown. Suggestions are numerous. Maybe they were Gnostics, or maybe Essenes, or maybe Pauline antinomians, or maybe Jewish antinomians. *Jude,* assuming that its recipients already know who these people are, does not introduce them. It rather traffics in polemic, which is uninterested in objective description. Yet giving caution its due, and on the assumption that the letter has particular people in view, they may well have been antinomians who engaged in sexual activities disturbing to the author.

The letter claims to be from Jude, "the brother of James." Although the New Testament knows several people by these names, tradition has usually thought of Jude, the brother of James and Jesus (*Mt.* 13:55; *Mk.* 6:3). In favor of this is Jude's seeming obscurity, the apparent use of the Hebrew as opposed to the Greek Bible in verse 12 (this agrees with the Hebrew of *Prv.* 25:14, not the Greek), and the lack of any firm evidence for a late date for the letter. Yet one cannot rule out the use of a pseudonym. The appeal to "remember the predictions of the apostles of our Lord Jesus Christ" in verse 17 may be a retrospective glance from a later age. Also, it is not known when Jude the brother of Jesus died, and so it cannot be determined how early the composition would have to be if authentic. Perhaps, furthermore, Jude was an important figure in some sectors of Jewish Christianity, and in that context a pseudepigraphon in his name made sense.

The *Revelation* to John. The book is from a certain John (1:1). Tradition, despite the stylistic differences between *Revelation* and John's gospel, which prohibit common authorship, identified him with John the son of Zebedee, one of the twelve disciples (so thought Justin Martyr, for instance, in the middle of the second century). The Apocalypse, however, does not require this identification, and internal evidence to support it is lacking. John was a popular name in the first century, and the New Testament knows several Johns.

Church tradition and most modern historians date the book to the time of the Roman emperor Domitian, circa 90 to 95 CE. Some have instead argued for a date during Nero's reign, sometime shortly before 70 CE. Both periods saw Christians persecuted, and *Revelation* was seemingly written in a time of suffering. According to 1:9, the seer is in exile, on the island of Patmos off the coast of Asia Minor. *Revelation* 2:13 refers to the recent execution of a certain Antipas. *Revelation* 3:10 speaks of a soon-approaching time of trouble, and 6:10 has dead saints crying out to God to avenge their blood.

Until modern historical criticism, there were basically four different ways of interpreting the Apocalypse. (1) On the "futurist" reading, *Revelation* is primarily a divinely inspired prophecy about the end of the world and the events preceding that end. With the exception of the first few chapters—especially the letters to the seven churches in chapters 2 and 3—the entire work is about the latter days and the second coming of Christ. (2) According to the "historicist" view, *Revelation* is an outline of church or human history. It begins in the first century and maps out in chronological fashion the course of events until the second advent. (3) The "preterist" view holds that John was completely preoccupied with the events of his own day, as opposed to the future consummation. (4) A few, taking an "idealist" view, have tried to divorce *Revelation* from history. For them, the book is not about the course of history or the end of history but theological principles or ideas. In other words, it is timeless. Its symbols refer not to events in the everyday world but to the eternal order.

Each approach is deficient. The futurist makes the book irrelevant and unintelligible to its first readers. The historicist is wrong because the Apocalypse belongs to a recognized literary genre, and the other members of this genre cannot bear a historicist reading. The preterist view is untenable because *Revelation* is without question about the latter days. As for the idealist view, it is perfectly valid so long as the interpreter does not pretend to be recovering the intention of the author, which was something other than the communication of large theological ideas.

Revelation is an enigma to contemporary readers unfamiliar with the literary category to which it belongs. The ancients, however, would have recognized it as an apocalypse, a well-known literary genre in ancient Judaism and early Christianity. More than a few old Jewish and Christians books are filled with strange beasts, with number symbolism, with descriptions of the end of the world (thought of as near), with accounts of heavenly journeys, with pictures of God's throne, and with prophecies of a shattered planet. *1 Enoch, 2 Enoch, 4 Ezra, 2 Baruch,* and the *Apocalypse of Abraham* are examples. *Revelation* should be interpreted in the same way that these other books are interpreted. Moreover, anyone unfamiliar with the genre will be unable to understand the Apocalypse correctly, and it makes no more sense to plot the future of the world by reading *Revelation* than it does by reading its literary cousins.

EARLY NONCANONICAL LITERATURE. For convenience, early Christian works outside the canon may be divided into three groups.

New Testament apocrypha. This is a large, ill-defined collection of texts, many of which mimic New Testament models. They come from different places, different times, and different authors. Most of them date from the second to fourth centuries. The category is purely retrospective. It groups texts that, although in some times and places reckoned authentic or authoritative, failed to win their way into the canon. But their status before the closing of the canon was often unclear. That some of them exist in several languages is testament to their popularity. Among them are papyrus fragments of unknown gospels, gospels used by various groups of Jewish Christians (e.g., the *Gospel of the Hebrews,* the *Gospel of the Ebionites,* the *Gospel of the Nazoraeans*), and infancy gospels (e.g., the *Protevangelium of James,* the *Infancy Story of Thomas*). Christians never ceased to create new stories about Jesus and the sayings of Jesus. Although most of the material in the apocryphal gospels is post-first century and so less helpful than the canonical Gospels for reconstructing the historical Jesus, contemporary scholars are more inclined than their predecessors to see early traditions independent of the canon in some of the extra-canonical sources.

There are also apocryphal letters (e.g., the *Epistle of Paul to the Laodiceans* and the *Epistle of Titus,* both parasitic upon Paul's correspondence) and apocryphal acts (e.g., the *Acts of John,* the *Acts of Peter,* the *Acts of Paul).* Some of the latter appear to have been particularly popular. Equally well known were some apocryphal apocalypses, especially the *Apocalypse of Peter* and the *Apocalypse of Paul*—both canonical still in the sixth century in some places—which contributed so much to popular ideas about the afterlife.

The Nag Hammadi library. In 1945, thirteen Coptic papyrus codices from the fourth century CE were discovered near Nag Hammadi, Egypt. Presumably from an old Christian monastery, they contain fifty-two tractates, only fourteen of which were already known (including a fragment of Plato's *Republic*). The majority are Gnostic texts attributed to important individuals known from the New Testament. Included are apocryphal gospels (e.g., the *Gospel of Truth* and the *Gospel of the Egyptians*), acts (e.g., the *Acts of Peter and the Twelve Apostles* and the *Acts of Peter*), apocalypses (e.g., the *Apocalypse of Paul* and the *First Apocalypse of James*), and several writings that purport to pass on secret revelations of the risen Jesus (e.g., the *Apocryphon of James* and the *Apocryphon of John*).

The most interesting and controversial document is the *Gospel of Thomas.* It contains 114 sayings of Jesus, some of them already known from the synoptics. As Origen rejected its authority, and as there exist Greek fragments from not long after 200 CE, a date no later than the second century is demanded. Some who fail to find in *Thomas* any knowledge of the synoptics, but rather take it to be independent of the canon, date *Thomas* as early as the first century.

The apostolic fathers. This designation is a modern one and includes over a dozen writings from the first and second or third centuries: *1 Clement,* a letter written by the bishop of Rome at the end of the first century; *2 Clement,* a homily from the second century by an unknown author; seven epistles from Ignatius, a bishop of Antioch martyred before 117 CE; the *Epistle of Polycarp to the Philippians,* written by a bishop of Smyrna martyred in 155 CE; the *Didache,* an anonymous, influential church order perhaps written in the late first century; the *Epistle of Barnabas,* an anonymous second-century treatise featuring allegorical exegesis of the Jewish Bible; the *Shepherd of Hermas,* a second-century apocalypse; the *Martyrdom of Polycarp,* the earliest account of Christian martyrdom; and the Epistle to *Diognetus,* an apology from the third century or the late second century. Most of these books were received as authoritative writings by some early Christians, while others who did not put them on the same level as the Gospels and Paul nonetheless found them edifying and worth reading in churches.

The Canon of the New Testament. The Greek word *canon* means first "reed" and then "measuring stick" or "norm." The church has used the term to refer to its authoritative writings. Although Christians consider the New Testament to be the norm of their faith, it was not precisely defined until the fourth century.

The first step toward the later canon probably occurred during the last quarter of the first century, when someone collected letters attributed to Paul. In the apostle's own lifetime, his correspondence, which typically addresses specific problems of specific communities, probably did not circulate widely. Some writers in the first half of the second century, however, must have known collections. Clement of Rome (c. 96), Ignatius (c. 110), and Polycarp (d. 155) all quote from or allude to several of Paul's epistles. The extent of the collections they knew is unclear, but each knew at least several letters.

In the middle of the second century, the controversial Roman theologian Marcion used a collection of Paul's epistles with this order: *Galatians, 1* and *2 Corinthians, Romans, 1* and *2 Thessalonians, Ephesians* (which Marcion knew as "To the Laodiceans"), *Colossians, Philippians,* and *Philemon.* The pastoral epistles (*1* and *2 Timothy* and *Titus*) are missing.

The pastoral epistles were also not in the other early collections, which usually took one of two forms. One had this order: *1* and *2 Corinthians, Romans, Ephesians, 1* and *2 Thessalonians, Galatians, Philippians, Colossians,* and *Philemon.* The other had: *Romans, 1* and *2 Corinthians, Ephesians, Galatians, Philippians, Colossians, 1* and *2 Thessalonians,* and *Philemon.* Both collections ordered the texts according to decreasing length, the difference being that the first counts both *1* and *2 Corinthians* and *1* and *2 Thessalonians* as single books.

It is not know who first published a collection of Paul's letters, nor is anything known about subsequent revisers. Perhaps the process was a haphazard affair, with no guiding hand, no definitive moment. Perhaps smaller collections grew into larger collections over time. Yet it could also be that a devoted follower of Paul, sometime after his death, collected several of his epistles and published them as a collection.

Little is also known regarding the emergence of the fourfold Gospels. Numerous gospels circulated in the early church, and there is probably no explanation as to why most churches ended up with the four they did. One can say no more than that the collection reflects the preferred liturgical practice of many churches at the end of the second century. Initially, various churches must have used just one gospel. This seems confirmed by the early papyri P^{52} and P^{66}, which contain only *John.*

Early in the second century, things changed. Papias knew both *Mark* and *Matthew* as authoritative texts. A bit later, Justin Martyr knew *Matthew* and *Luke* and probably *Mark.* By the last quarter of the second century, *Matthew, Mark, Luke,* and *John* were together liturgical texts in many places.

The latter half of the second century was also the period during which many Christians began to think of the Gospels and Paul as together constituting an authoritative corpus, along with the Old Testament and a few other Christian writings. *Acts* seems to have been universally accepted. But it seems impossible to generalize about *Hebrews, James, 1* and *2 Peter, 1, 2, and 3 John, Jude,* and *Revelation,* except that their status was uncertain.

The earliest discussion of a collection of New Testament books beyond the four Gospels appears in the so-called Muratorian canon. Although extant only in a seventh-century Latin manuscript, it was (despite some recent debate) originally composed in Rome in the late second or early third century. The beginning, although lost, clearly mentioned *Matthew* and *Mark.* The author, in discussing what books the churches read, listed the following: *Luke* (cited as "the third book of the Gospel"), *John, 1* and *2 Corinthians, Galatians, Romans, Ephesians, Philippians, Colossians, 1* and *2 Thessalonians, Philemon, Titus, 1* and *2 Timothy, Jude, Revelation,* two epistles of John (one of which must be *1 John*), the *Apocalypse of Peter* (which the author says some do not accept), and the Shepherd of Hermas (which the author regards as inspired but not apostolic). Also mentioned are letters to the Laodiceans and the Alexandrians, which are dismissed as forgeries.

The Muratorian canon is typical of what one finds from the end of the second century on, namely, recognition of the four Gospels, recognition of Paul's epistles, recognition of several additional books, uncertainty and disagreement over others. Many did not know or questioned the authority of *Hebrews, James, 2 Peter, 2* and *3 John, Jude,* and *Revelation.* Only in the fourth century do statements that match today's canon appear.

In discussing the content of the canon, theologians often discussed authorship, date, doctrine, and church tradition. The latter two were the decisive factors. Many wanted a collection that did not support the doctrines of Marcion or the Gnostics or Montanists. No less important was the actual practice of the churches. Later theologians for the most part justified after the fact what most communities, for reasons that escape easy generalization, had long been reading.

THE TEXT OF THE NEW TESTAMENT AND TEXTUAL CRITICISM. None of the original Greek New Testament survives. The documents presumably wore out. The earliest extant text is a tiny fragment of John's gospel known as P^{52}. Dated on the basis of its handwriting to around 125 CE, it contains parts of *John* 18. The next witnesses are all fragmentary papyri from Egypt that date to around 200.

The oldest copies of the New Testament as a whole are from the fourth century, the two most famous being *Codex Sinaiticus* and *Codex Vaticanus* (although the latter lacks *Hebrews,* some of Paul's letters, and *Revelation*). These are all on parchment (the skins of sheep and goats). Their good quality reflects the prosperity of the fourth-century church, which could afford better copies of its scriptures after the legalization of Christianity. Before this period, Christians had often suffered persecution, and many of their books were burned.

No two extant manuscripts of the New Testament are exactly alike. So scholars have to reconstruct likely originals. Current editions of the Greek New Testaments do not reproduce any ancient manuscript but are rather the product of a committee's vote.

There are two types of variants. First are unintentional changes due to errors of sight or hearing. These include misreading a single letter (e.g., some manuscripts of *Luke* 6:43 have *karpos,* "fruit," instead of *karphos,* "speck"); *homoioteleuton* (a scribe passing from one occurrence of a series of letters to another—as when some witnesses move from the first occurrence of "in the kingdom of heaven" in *Matthew* 5:19 to the second occurrence, omitting the words in between); simple reversal of two words; hearing one word instead of another; *dittography* (writing the same word twice); or its opposite, *haplography* (writing a word once when it should be written twice).

While unintentional errors fill the manuscripts, many variants arose from intentional alterations. There are stylistic changes, due to a scribe seeking to improve the Greek. There are doctrinal changes, due to someone wanting to make a theological text more acceptable. Some who believed in Mary's perpetual virginity omitted part of *Matthew* 1:25 so that it no longer implies the resumption of conjugal relations. Someone else added a testimony to the Trinity in *1 John* 5:7: "There are three that testify in heaven, the Father, the Word, and the Holy Spirit, and these three are one." There are liturgical changes, which make a text more suitable for public reading. Thus "amen" concludes each of the four Gospels in some witnesses, and there are doxologies added to the Lord's Prayer in *Matthew* 6:13, which otherwise ends with "but deliver us from evil." There are changes of clarification, such as the addition to *Matthew* 1:22, which turns "This all happened in order to fulfill the word of the Lord through the prophet, saying. . ." into "This all happened in order to fulfill the word of the Lord through the prophet Isaiah, saying. . . ." There are also changes due to correction. Thus the erroneous reference in *Mark* 2:26 to Abiathar is dropped in some manuscripts.

Although an earlier reading is better than a later one, all other things being equal, typically other things are not equal. Internal evidence must accordingly be considered. A reading that fits an author's style and vocabulary is preferable to one that does not. It also seems reasonable to prefer hard readings because scribes tended to iron out difficulties. "The only begotten God" in *John* 1:18 could supply an illustration of this: the phrase is so strange that one can understand it being altered.

The chief criterion, however, is this: the best reading explains the other readings. When faced with variants, one wants to tell a story that explains how, beginning with one text, the other texts came into being. A simple example of this is *Luke* 11:2, which introduces the Lord's Prayer. The address in some witnesses is simply "Father." In others it is "Our Father who art in heaven." It is easy to see why someone familiar with *Matthew's* version of the Lord's Prayer, which has dominated liturgical usage, assimilated *Luke* to *Matthew* by expanding the shorter address into the longer. Again, while some witnesses to *Matthew* 5:22 forbid anger unconditionally, others forbid anger that is "without a cause." As the church father Cassian already observed, someone added the qualification. It relaxes an otherwise impossible imperative and brings Jesus into line with scriptures in which God and Jesus get angry.

Most of the variants in the textual tradition are insignificant and do not change the sense. Further, even without the original Greek texts, it is presumably possible to reconstruct something close to what circulated in the first century. There are, however, some cases in which the stakes are theologically significant. One is the ending of the *Gospel of Mark,* already discussed. Another is *John* 7:53–8:11, the story of the woman caught in adultery. This has been a liturgical text for centuries, and it is in all contemporary translations of *John* (although it is typically set apart in some way). But it is more than suspect. Many manuscripts, including most of the older ones, omit it. Others mark the passage with asterisks. It is also missing from many Latin texts and some of the other versions and does not appear to have been known to a number of the Church Fathers. The earliest Greek commentator to write upon it lived in the eleventh century, and he declares that it is not found in the most accurate copies. Some manuscripts put *John* 7:53–8:11 after *Luke* 21, others after *John* 21. Augustine of Hippo argued that someone removed the text because Jesus' treatment of adultery seemed overly generous. Yet when one considers that the passage contains words and phrases not typical of *John,* the conclusion that it is not original is inevitable. Where it came from is not known. Apart from whether it contains a historical memory, the text is nonetheless a favorite of many Christians, and knowledge of its secondary nature does not seem likely to erase its canonical status.

Ancient Versions and Modern Translations. Although Jesus spoke Aramaic, all of the New Testament documents were composed in Greek. Beginning in the second century, the spread of Christianity required translating the Greek into other languages. The resultant versions are important not only for doing textual criticism but also because they help show us what text types were dominant in what regions. Eastern translations include:

Syriac. In the latter part of the second century, Tatian, a native of Mesopotamia who studied in Rome, produced the *Diatessaron,* a harmony of the canonical Gospels. Containing fifty-five chapters, it was designed for liturgical use. Although popular for centuries (and translated into Arabic, Latin, Persian, and other languages), it did not entirely displace the four Gospels, which also circulated in Syriac (the so-called Old Syriac). In the fifth century a Syriac version of the New Testament, lacking only *2 Peter, 2* and *3 John, Jude,* and *Revelation,* was published. This, known as the *Peshitta,* was revised in the sixth and seventh centuries, when the missing five books were added.

Coptic. Bohairic and Sahidic were the two chief dialects of Coptic, the last stage of the Egyptian language. The New Testament was translated into Sahidic no later than the early third century, and into Bohairic (still the language of Egyptian Christians today) a bit later.

Armenian. Although Christianity arrived in Armenia in the third century, it appears that a translation into Armenian (perhaps from the Syriac) was not made until the fifth century. Included in the Armenian canon are a third letter of Paul to the Corinthians and a letter supposedly written by the Corinthians to Paul.

There were also translations into Georgian (fifth century), Ethiopic (maybe as early as the fourth century), Arabic (eighth century?), and Persian (fourth or fifth century). Among the more important Western translations are the following:

Old Latin. This refers not to a single translation but to a variety of Latin translations made prior to Jerome's Vulgate in the late fourth century. Although ecclesiastical tradition is silent on the subject, it seems likely that some Latin translations were made in second-century North Africa, others in third-century Rome. No complete copy of the New Testament in Old Latin exists.

The Vulgate. In 382, Pope Damasus commissioned Jerome to standardize the Latin text. Jerome's version eventually replaced the Old Latin versions, thus earning its name, which means "popular" or "common." It became the liturgical text of the Roman Catholic Church and stamped all subsequent Christian language in the West.

Gothic. Ulfilas, a missionary to the Goths along the lower Danube, translated the Bible into Gothic in the last half of the fourth century. Ulfilas created the Gothic alphabet for this purpose. As the Ostrogothic kingdom fell in the sixth century, and as the Gothic language died not long thereafter, few manuscripts of the Gothic Bible exist.

The New Testament, or portions of it, have at this point in history been translated into over two thousand languages, and for many modern languages there are several contemporary translations. In the English-speaking world, there is no lack of sound translations. Unfortunately, new versions continue to appear not because of new discoveries, but mostly for marketing reasons.

See Also Apostles; Biblical Exegesis, article on Christian Views; Canon; Gospel; Marcionism; Nag Hammadi.

Bibliography

An introduction that presents the conclusions of contemporary scholarship is Raymond E. Brown, *An Introduction to the New Testament* (New York, 1997). Dated but more detailed is Werner Georg Kümmel, *Introduction to the New Testament,* translated by Howard Clark Kee, rev. ed. (Nashville, 1975). Comparison of Helmut Koester, *Introduction to the New Testament,* 2 vols., 2d rev. ed. (New York and Berlin, 1995, 2000), with Luke Timothy Johnson and Todd C. Penner, *The Writings of the New Testament: An Interpretation,* rev. ed. (Minneapolis, 2003), shows the distances that often separates scholars. As a way of determining how much really is and is not new in contemporary work, it is instructive to read some of the older introductions, the best of which is James Moffatt, *An Introduction to the Literature of the New Testament,* 3d ed. (Edinburgh, 1918). For interesting introductions to the Gospels in particular see Helmut Koester, *Ancient Christian Gospels: Their History and Development* (Philadelphia and London, 1990), and E. P. Sanders and Margaret Davies, *Studying the Synoptic Gospels* (London and Philadelphia, 1989).

Collections of extra-canonical books include J. K. Elliott, ed., *The Apocryphal New Testament: A Collection of Apocryphal Christian Literature in an English Translation* (Oxford, 1993); Wilhelm Schneemelcher, ed., *New Testament Apocrypha,* 2 vols., English translation edited by R. McL. Wilson (Louisville, Ky., 1991); Kirsopp Lake, *The Apostolic Fathers,* 2 vols.

(London and Cambridge, Mass., 1912); and James Robinson, ed., *The Nag Hammadi Library in English* (New York, 1977).

On the canon see Harry Y. Gamble, *The New Testament Canon: Its Making and Meaning* (Philadelphia, 1985), and Bruce M. Metzger, *The Canon of the New Testament: Its Origin, Development, and Significance* (Oxford, 1987).

An excellent introduction to textual criticism is Kurt Aland and Barbara Aland, *The Text of the New Testament: An Introduction to the Critical Editions and to the Theory and Practice of Modern Textual Criticism,* translated by Erroll F. Rhodes, 2d ed. (Leiden and Grand Rapids, Mich., 1989). Also useful is Bruce M. Metzger, *The Text of the New Testament: Its Transmission, Corruption, and Restoration,* 3d ed. (New York, 1992). On the nature of ancient Christian books and the subject of literacy, Harry Y. Gamble's *Books and Readers in the Early Church: A History of Early Christian Texts* (New Haven and London, 1995) is important.

The most helpful introduction to the various ancient versions is the authoritative Bruce M. Metzger, *The Early Versions of the New Testament: Their Origin, Transmission, and Limitations* (Oxford, 1977). For later translations and for the whole history of the Bible in the West, the three-volume *Cambridge History of the Bible* (Cambridge, U.K.) is indispensable: P. R. Ackroyd and C. F. Evans, eds., *From the Beginnings to Jerome* (1970); G. W. H. Lampe, ed., *The West from the Fathers to the Reformation* (1969); S. L. Greenslade, ed., *The West from the Reformation to the Present Day* (1963).

For various contemporary approaches to the New Testament see A. K. M. Adam, *What Is Postmodern Biblical Criticism?* (Minneapolis, 1995); John H. Elliott, *What Is Social-Scientific Criticism?* (Minneapolis, 1993); John H. Hayes, ed., *The Dictionary of Biblical Interpretation,* 2 vols. (Nashville, 1999); George A. Kennedy, *New Testament Interpretation through Rhetorical Criticism* (Chapel Hill, N.C., 1984); Steven L. McKenzie and Stephen R. Haynes, eds., *To Each Its Own Meaning: An Introduction to Biblical Criticisms and Their Application,* 2d ed. (Louisville, Ky., 1999); Stephen D. Moore, *Poststructuralism and the New Testament: Derrida and Foucault at the Foot of the Cross* (Minneapolis, 1994); Norman Perrin, *What Is Redaction Criticism?* (Philadelphia, 1969); David Rutledge, *Reading Marginally: Feminism, Deconstruction and the Bible* (Leiden, 1996); Elizabeth Schlüsser Fiorenza, *Bread Not Stone: The Challenge of Feminist Biblical Interpretation,* rev. ed. (Boston, 1995) and *But She Said: Feminist Practices of Biblical Interpretation* (Boston, 1992); and Fernando F. Segovia and Mary Ann Tolbert, eds., *Reading from this Place,* 2 vols. (Minneapolis, 1995).

The two standard histories of critical New Testament scholarship are Werner Georg Kümmel, *The New Testament: The History of the Investigation of Its Problems,* translated by S. McLean Gilmour and Howard C. Kee (Nashville, 1972), and Stephen Neill and Thomas Wright, *The Interpretation of the New Testament 1861–1986,* 2d ed. (Oxford, 1988).

DALE C. ALLISON, JR. (2005)

BIBLICAL RELIGION SEE ISRAELITE RELIGION

BIBLICAL TEMPLE.

[*This entry is a discussion of the history, activities, and structure of the biblical Temple.*]

The Hebrew Bible records various temples dedicated to God throughout ancient Israel. Recent archaeological discoveries generally have corroborated the record, while at the same time raising new questions about the character, functions, and locations of temples of the biblical period. Foremost among these temples were the First and Second Temples built in Jerusalem.

HISTORY AND DESIGN. The First Temple was built between 960 and 950 BCE during the reign of Solomon; it was destroyed in 587/6 with the Babylonian conquest of Judah. The Second Temple was built on the site of the First in 516, and was destroyed by the Romans in 70 CE. However, both Temples underwent periodic renovations, expansion, and even restructuring, so that in describing temples we are speaking of an ongoing process, rather than of single events. Furthermore, the term *Temple* is ambiguous since it may designate either the building specifically, the focus of cult activity, or the entire complex of buildings, gates, and walls that together constitute the institution. For the purposes of this article, *Temple* refers to the building, *Temple complex* to the institution.

Most of the physical changes that the two Temples underwent at various times came in response to corresponding changes in the urban environment that were brought about, in turn, by changing political circumstances. Increased population density and the fluctuating political status of Jerusalem stimulated a tendency to protect, even barricade, the Temples against the outside. To a degree, and according to conditions, such efforts may have been vital to defense. More consistently, however, they expressed specific religious attitudes: the Temple and cult were to be shut off from the sounds and movements of the world around.

Temples in antiquity generally were intended to be prominent, to stand out in relation to the environment. They were often located on the summits of hills, and if construction intensified in the area either the temple was elevated, or the courtyards and buildings in the vicinity were downgraded.

Solomon's Temple (The First Temple). The Temple of Solomon gained preeminence as a result of political and religious movements, most notably the conquest of the northern kingdom of Israel by the Assyrians, and the drive, for both religious and political causes, to eliminate local and regional temples. David, founder of the united Israelite kingdom, had made Jerusalem (more precisely, the City of David on Mount Zion) his capital after conquering it around 1000 BCE; he confirmed royal sponsorship of the cult of the Ark of the Covenant by bringing the Ark to the city, while at the same time sanctioning the city as his royal seat (*2 Sm.* 6–7).

The best functional definition of the Temple complex that eventually arose on Mount Zion is preserved in *Amos* 7:13, which originally applied to Bethel, not Jerusalem. Bethel was the most important cult center of the northern kingdom in the eighth century, and the priest of Bethel admonished Amos not to speak against the king at Bethel: "Don't ever prophesy again at Bethel; for it is a king's sanctuary and a royal domain." Indeed, the Temple was initially only one component of a royal acropolis built on the northern summit of Mount Zion.

As described in *1 Kings* 6–8, Solomon's Temple was an oblong, stone structure, reinforced by cedar beams. The interior was divided by a wooden partition into two sections: the *heikhal* (great hall), encountered upon entering the building through swinging wooden doors, followed by the *devir* ("shrine"), the holiest section of the Temple, sometimes called the Holy of Holies. The shrine was raised higher than the floor of the great hall, and was set upon a huge rock, known later in the Jewish tradition as *even ha-shetiyyah* ("the foundation stone") and in Arabic as *al-sakhrah* (the "rock"), over which the Dome of the Rock was later built.

There were no interior columns, for the roof rested on large beams, and rows of windows punctuated two walls of the Temple. The facade of the Temple included a portico (*ulam*) extending the width of the building, in front of which stood two massive, ornamental columns, *yakhin* and *bo'az*, that were probably insignia of the Davidic monarchy. The Temple lay on an east-west axis.

The design of Solomon's Temple points to Syrian and Phoenician models. The temple at Tell Tuʿeimat (ancient Kunulua) on the Syrian coast is often mentioned by archaeologists, as are temples at Zinjirli in Northwest Syria, and at Carchemish and Byblos. The Kunulua temple was also an oblong structure, divided into three parts: portico, hall, and shrine. An earlier prototype may have been the late Bronze Age temple at Hazor in Galilee, dating from between the sixteenth and the thirteenth centuries.

What is unusual about Solomon's Temple is its east-west orientation. Some have suggested that this was to allow the sun's rays to penetrate the Temple; others have speculated that the alignment was to allow the sun, at certain times of the year, to shine through two successive doorways into the shrine itself.

The interior doors were paneled with cedar, as was the ceiling, and both were extensively decorated with floral motifs and cherubs, overlaid with gold. In the windowless shrine stood the Ark, and hovering over it were two cherubs, whose combined wingspan reached from one wall to the other. In the great hall, facing the entrance to the shrine, stood the incense altar, made of cedar wood and overlaid with gold, and two rows of five lampstands, ten in all, hammered of solid gold.

Abutting three of the outer walls of the Temple was a network of stone chambers three stories high, called the *yatsiʿa*, through which one proceeded from chamber to chamber, climbing to the higher stories. Although the biblical text fails to specify the *yatsiʿa's* function, it undoubtedly was used for storing consecrated materials and for priestly preparations. The structure reached halfway up the Temple's walls, so that the great hall's windows on the north and south walls were not blocked.

The Temple was surrounded by an enclosed courtyard (*ḥatser*), in the center of which, facing the entrance to the Temple, stood the altar for burnt offerings. The Temple had three gates, on the east, north, and south. Upon entering to the right and again in front of the Temple was a huge bronze reservoir, the *yam* ("sea"), and ten mobile basins—all ornamented with beasts of burden, as if to indicate that these animals carried the sea and the basins.

As described in *1 Kings*, the Temple was more exposed initially than in later periods. A comparison of Solomon's Temple complex with the visionary descriptions of the Temple complex in *Ezekiel* 40–48 shows how the process of insulating the Temple from the outside world had proceeded from the tenth century to the early sixth century, prior to the Temple's destruction in 587/6. Serious doubt exists as to how realistic the descriptions of *Ezekiel* are, given their visionary, literary context, but they probably reveal somewhat how the Temple complex appeared in its last years.

Two periods of major renovation were the reign of Hezekiah in the late eighth and early seventh centuries, and the reign of Josiah in the late seventh century. Hezekiah's projects undoubtedly were motivated by the growth of the population of Jerusalem after the fall of the northern kingdom of Israel in 722, which left the Temple as the only national religious center.

2 Kings 22 tells of Josiah's Temple renovations. Both he and Hezekiah were, of course, devout Yahvists; Josiah, in particular, had a lasting impact on the historical importance of the Temple. However, not only pious, Yahvistic kings were motivated to undertake Temple renovation. Ahaz, Hezekiah's father and hardly a devout, Yahvistic monarch, installed an additional altar, modeled after one he had seen in Damascus, and he built a passageway leading from his palace to the Temple (*2 Kgs.* 16). Even Manasseh, characterized as wicked, who ruled during much of the seventh century, may not have neglected the Temple; indeed, Nahman Avigad's excavations in Jerusalem's upper city reveal the extent of Manasseh's construction efforts.

By the time of Ezekiel the Temple is described as enclosed in two courtyards; there were now three sets of gatehouses, so that the Temple was approached by mounting three staircases; the burnt offering altar was elevated, and numerous stores were near the walls and gates (*Ez.* 40–48).

The Second Temple. Returning Judahite exiles, under their Davidic king Zerubbabel, rebuilt the Temple of Jerusalem on its original site pursuant to the edict of Cyrus II (the Great), issued in 538. Despite opposition from Samaritan leaders and other causes of delay, the Second Temple was dedicated in 516, its design resembling that of the First Temple. Measurements in *Ezra* 6:3, however, indicate that there may have been an upper story or attic above the ceiling of the Temple, as in later times, causing it to loom larger over the surrounding area than the First Temple.

As far as we know, no administrative buildings were located in the Temple complex, an absence that is understandable given the changed status of Jerusalem from capital of a sovereign kingdom to provincial temple city, one of many such entities throughout the Persian Empire.

Since its inception, the Second Temple had been devoid of certain artifacts once considered essential to the sanctity of the First. For instance the shrine held neither ark nor cherubs. (These cultic objects are missing in Ezekiel's descriptions of the First Temple.) Also missing were the two ornamental columns in front of the portico, since they symbolized royal authority and the Jews no longer had their own king. Yet even though no attempt was ever made to fashion a new ark (or cherubs), the empty shrine nevertheless was believed to be the domicile of the God of Israel.

Nehemiah 7:2 describes a fortress, *birah*, built in the northwest corner of the acropolis. (It is also mentioned in the *Letter of Aristeas* in the third century BCE.) In Herod's time it was renamed the Antonia and heavily fortified.

Records from the Persian period (538 to around 330 BCE) are sparse, but once Hellenistic sources begin to appear, more information emerges. The writings of Josephus Flavius, a Jewish historian of the first century CE, early tractates of the Mishnah, and passages in the New Testament all afford considerable information. Josephus, in *Against Apion*, refers to a certain Hecateus of Abdera who visited the temple in Jerusalem in the late fourth century BCE; from the third century come descriptions in the *Letter of Aristeas*, and Yehoshu'a son of Sirah (*Ben Sira*) mentions that Shim'on ha-Tsaddiq (Shim'on the Just) undertook Temple renovations around 200. The recently discovered Temple Scroll, a pre-Herodian, Hebrew document, preserves detailed plans for a Jewish temple, and archaeological excavations in the Temple complex area have yielded additional material of interest.

Two periods appear to be times of major renovations and structural changes in the Temple: one following the Maccabean liberation of the Temple in 164, and the other, beginning about 20 BCE when Herod undertook the rebuilding of the entire Temple complex, a project that continued virtually until the destruction in 70 CE. From 164 the Hasmonean (Maccabean) rulers maintained a degree of political autonomy, after ridding the Temple of the heterodox artifacts and cult practices introduced by the Hellenizing priesthood of Jerusalem in the period leading up to the persecutions of Antiochus IV. During the Hasmonean period, construction began on a series of archways leading to the Temple, connecting it to the city of Jerusalem. These are better known from the Herodian period.

Herod, descendant of the Idumeans who converted to Judaism, was a favorite of the Romans. His monumental Temple project was motivated by both his desire to rule over a majestic polis of the Roman Empire, and at the same time be accepted by the religious leaders of the Jews. The accommodation struck by Herod produced a Temple complex conceived along Roman lines that nonetheless retained the traditional Temple building, by now probably heightened considerably.

Extensive archaeological excavations in the Temple mount area, initiated under the direction of Benjamin Mazar in 1968, have provided new information. It seems that Herod's Temple preserved earlier Temple design but the dimensions were considerably enlarged, including its height.

The inner area of Herod's Temple complex was prohibited to Gentiles, and it was bounded by a balustrade called the *soreg*. Josephus mentions that inscriptions in Greek and Latin were posted at intervals warning Gentiles not to pass beyond that point; two examples of these inscriptions have been discovered in modern times.

A visitor moving from east to west would perceive that the walled area of the temple was composed of two main sections. First, he would pass through the Beautiful Gate into the women's court and proceed up a staircase through the Nicanor Gate to the court of Israel, where male worshipers assembled. (Men and women did not worship together.) The court of Israel was set off in the eastern section of the inner court, and there was no wall separating it from the priests' court where the altar of burnt offerings stood. This entire walled section contained various chambers, including the Chamber of Hewn Stone, where the Sanhedrin, the high court of the Jews, convened prior to approximately 30 CE.

The altar for burnt offerings was situated in front of the Temple, slightly to the south of the staircase leading to the portico. In the Herodian period it was a raised altar reached by a ramp called the *kevesh*. Sacrificial animals were slaughtered in the northern front section of the court of priests, and a laver stood near the southern wall. The portico facade itself is described as exceedingly impressive and ornate; however, it included a golden eagle that aroused intense opposition because many Jews regarded the eagle as a pagan symbol.

The entire Temple mount, some of it resting on pillars, was enclosed by a high wall called the *ḥeil*. It undoubtedly served as a fortification, along with the Antonia fortress. The Temple mount had massive retaining walls, some of which have been exposed in recent archaeological excavations. (One is the so-called Western Wall.) On the periphery of the Temple mount were porticos, the best known of them being the royal portico, built along the southern side of the outer courtyards. This royal portico, which is profusely praised by Josephus, has been identified with the *ḥanuyyot* ("stores") mentioned in the Mishnah (*Ta'an.* 1.6). The Temple mount's outer dimensions prior to the destruction are estimated at 1,550 meters, an area twice the size of Trajan's forum in Rome.

The two Temples of Jerusalem, built on the same spot, had the cumulative effect of sanctifying that place for all subsequent generations of Jews.

The Cult of the Temples of Jerusalem. Information on the conduct of worship in the Temples of Jerusalem comes from several kinds of sources, all of which are problematic in one way or another. Most of the detailed descriptions of cultic praxis in biblical times come from the priestly codes of the Pentateuch, known as the P source. This source projects the sacrificial cult back to the time of the Sinai migrations, prior to Israelite settlement in Canaan. Historically these codes of practice, found primarily in *Exodus, Leviticus,* and *Numbers,* belong to a much later period and probably reflect the Jerusalem Temple cult. It is difficult, however, to as certain whether the cult of the First or Second Temple is being described. While the P source, as we have it, is more logically the product of the early postexilic period, the time of Persian domination (538–c. 330 CE), much of it, especially as pertains to types of sacrifices and their essential modes of presentation, was probably in effect in Judah in the latter part of the monarchic period, prior to the Babylonian exile. Today, the dating of the P source is a matter of considerable disagreement among scholars, with a substantial number favoring a preexilic provenance.

The *Letter of Aristeas* and the *Book of Ben Sira* contain a good deal of information from pre-Maccabean times about the Second Temple. For the Herodian period and thereafter (about the last one hundred years of the Temple), considerable information is preserved in the writings of Josephus. The Mishnah and Tannaitic literature may also be employed for the Herodian period even though they were not compiled until the early third century CE. *Megillat ta'anit* and the books of the New Testament also contain authentic information on Temple worship. It is warranted to assume a high degree of conservatism in the religious practice of ancient Jerusalem.

Structure of the cultic worship. The public cult of Jerusalem was, from earliest times, structured around a daily regimen, wherein the major sacrifice was offered in the morning, and a less elaborate one offered before sunset. This was the ancient Near Eastern pattern, according to which the day was defined as the daylight hours. This was the time frame for most worship, although certain types of ritual were conducted at night, magic and penitential worship for the most part. The daytime schedule expressed the basic aim of worship: the need to secure God's blessings and help in the practical pursuits of life, in the activities of each day.

Thus, the Bible tells us that Ahaz, king of Judah, instructed the priests of Jerusalem to offer "the burnt offering of the morning and the grain offering of the evening" (*2 Kgs.* 16:15). The late afternoon came to be referred to as the time "of the ascent of the grain offering" (*1 Kgs.* 18:29, 18:36). In *Ezekiel* 46:12–15, both a burnt offering and a grain offering were to be sacrificed each morning, but there is no mention of a second burnt offering later in the day, as is required by the laws of the Torah (*Ex.* 29:38–46; *Nm.* 28:1–8). It is likely, therefore, that the Torah codes which project two daily burnt offerings are postexilic, as suggested by Roland de Vaux.

On Sabbaths, new moons, and festivals, additional or perhaps special sacrifices were offered. The Mishnah, especially in tractate *Tamid,* describes the daily regimen of the Second Temple, including the procedures for assignment of priests to various duties.

Basic kinds of sacrifices. *Leviticus* 1–3 and 5–7 outline the three basic types of sacrifices offered on the altar of burnt offerings:

1. *'Olah,* functionally translated as "burnt offering" or "holocaust," was a sacrifice burned to ash, no part of which was eaten by the priest or donors. Literally, *'olah* means "that which ascends [in smoke]." An *'olah* could consist of a bull, a sheep or goat, or certain birds. The donor of the sacrifice laid his hands on the animal's head and, following a set formula, assigned it as an *'olah;* the Mishnah (*'Arakh.* 5.5) preserves examples of such formulas used during the late Second Temple. The priest then slaughtered the animal, flayed it, washed certain internal organs, and decapitated and sectioned it. The blood of the sacrifice was then splashed on the altar. The *'olah* was also termed an *isheh* (offering by fire), a more general term for all burnt offerings, as well as a *qorban* ("offering").
2. *Minḥah* (grain offering) consisted of semolina wheat flour, finely ground, mixed with oil and frankincense into a dough. A scoop of the dough was burned on the altar, while the remainder was baked or cooked some other way. Any grain offering burned on the altar had to be made of unleavened dough (*matsah*). The reason for this restriction is not known. Portions of the *minhah* were eaten by the priests.
3. *Zevaḥ shelamin* ("a sacred gift of greeting"; sometimes termed a "peace offering"). The term *zevaḥ* seems to mean "sacred meal," or "food." Such an offering could consist only of a bull, sheep, or goat. It too was assigned by the donor; its blood was splashed on the altar. But, in contrast to the first two kinds of sacrifice, this offering was shared with the donors. The altar received certain of the internal organs and the fat adhering to them, whereas the meat was divided between priests and donors and then boiled in pots (*1 Sm.* 2:13). In addition, libations of wine usually accompanied the major sacrifice (*Nm.* 15:1–16, 15:22–31).

Sacrifice as a mode of worship. The sacrificial regimen just outlined represents the outcome of a long process of development; left unanswered are questions about the history and meaning of sacrifice.

There were two basic sacrificial modes in biblical Israel: the presentation and the burnt offering. In the presentation offering, the deity is portrayed as looking upon the offering and accepting or rejecting it. Such offerings, once "set" or placed before God, were usually assigned to the priests who would partake of them. Examples include the offering of first fruits (*Dt.* 26:1–11); the "bread of display," placed on tables in the Temple for a week and then given to the priests (*Lv.* 24:5–9, *1 Sm.* 21:7); the leavened loaves of the thanksgiving offering (*Lv.* 6:11–13); and the offering of the sheaf from the new grain crop (*Lv.* 23:11, 23:17). Therefore, to a degree mode relates to substance, and presentations tended to consist of grain and fruits, very much in keeping with sacrifice in other ancient Near Eastern countries.

With the burnt offering, the deity is portrayed as inhaling the aromatic smoke of the sacrifice, typical of an incense offering—a kind of sacrifice in its own right (*Ex.* 30:7f, *Lv.* 6:12–15, *Is.* 1:13). Historically, the burnt offering may have originated in northern Syria, for it is known that it was adopted and widely used by the Hittites. It may not have been native to Canaan, although current research into this question is inadequate.

What is clear from biblical literature is the progressive ascendancy of the burnt offering in the public cult and in private donations. This can be traced in the adaptation of certain modes of sacrifice. The grain offering is a case in point. As prescribed in *Leviticus* 2 it can be analyzed as the accommodation of what was originally a presentation offering: only a scoop of dough was burned on the altar, the rest was given to the priests after having been offered first to the deity.

Yet another instance of accommodation is implicit in the term *tenufah* (raised offering). Before certain offerings were placed on the altar, they were held up and carried about for the deity to view (*Lv.* 10:4).

Procedures whereby offerings initially having nothing to do with the altar were adapted to the prevailing mode are also evident with respect to animal sacrifices. According to the old mode of sacrifice, the paschal lamb was roasted whole over an open fire without employing the altar (*Ex.* 12 and 13). But as prescribed in *Deuteronomy* 16:7 and like all other sacrifices of the *zevaḥ* variety, it was to be boiled in pots, with certain parts burned on the altar.

Generally, most sacrificial types and modes existed quite early in the biblical period, and some are mentioned independently by eighth-century prophets. What changes perceptibly is the elaborateness of composite, public rituals, such as those performed at festivals, or in purifying the Temple. The liturgical calendar in *Numbers*, chapters 28 through 29, shows the growth of a frequent and detailed sacrificial activity since an earlier period in *Leviticus* 23.

Certain very ancient sacrifices were revived after long periods; one was the water libation, mentioned in connection with David's early years (*1 Sm.* 23:16), and which figured in Elijah's confrontation with the Baal priests somewhere in the Carmel mountain range (*1 Kgs.* 18). It was revived in the early rabbinic period (*Sheq.* 6:3).

Interacting with mode and substance was motivation, the reason for the sacrifice. There were several types of sacrifices whose objective was expiation, through purification; two major ones were the *ḥaṭṭa't* ("sin offering") and the *asham* ("guilt offering"). The *asham* in particular had a votive aspect, and it could be donated in other than a sacrificial form (as silver, for instance), especially since the priesthood at different times preferred different kinds of revenue. The *asham*, as a sacrifical offering, had no role in the public cult, but the *ḥaṭṭa't* was used in Temple purification in rites such as those described for the Day of Atonement (*Lv.* 16). These sacrifices resembled others in substance, and usually consisted of large or small cattle, except that allowances were made for less expensive offerings from donors with limited means so as not to deny them expiation.

Private and public worship intersected in the Temple. Individuals donated public sacrifices; the Temple was a place to pronounce vows and fulfill pledges; new mothers, in accordance with *Leviticus* 12, brought pigeons and doves to the Temple following their specified periods of seclusion. Scattered among the legal discussions of the Talmudic sages are beautiful descriptions of celebrations in the late Second Temple period; for example, the description of the offering of first fruits in Jerusalem, as first commanded in *Deuteronomy* 20:1–11, and later recorded in the Mishnah, tractate *Bikkurim*, chapter 3.

Once consecrated, sacrificial materials became susceptible to defilement, and could not be left unused. Not only would certain foodstuffs spoil, which was a practical consideration, but there was always the fear that impurity would affect the entire Temple complex or, put another way, that demonic forces would contaminate sacrifices.

Sacrificial blood was utilized in the Temple cult in special ways. As such, blood from sacrifices was considered taboo, as was all blood from cattle, sheep, and goats used as food (*Gn.* 9:4; *Lv.* 3:17, 17:10f.; *Dt.* 12:16f.). In most sacrifices, the blood was splashed on the sides of the altar, and in some cases on the horns atop the altar. In certain expiatory rites, such as those performed in Temple purification, blood was also dabbed on the interior incense altar, on the curtains at the entrance to the great hall and the shrine, and even on the Ark and cherubs. Blood, as the vital fluid of living creatures, was to be returned to the earth, and the blood splashed on the sides of the altar would therefore be allowed to run down into the earth. What had once been a blood libation to chthonic powers became an offering to God. Other uses, such as dabbing blood on cult objects (and occasionally people), seem to have been intended to ward off demonic forces. Salt was applied to offerings to drain off residual blood after slaughter (*Lv.* 2:13), and the method of slaughter, later described in the Mishnah (*Ḥul.* 2.4), was to cut the jugular vein. An entire order of the Mishnah, *Qodashim* ("Sacred Things"), is devoted to procedures of sacrifice in late Second Temple times.

Apart from sacrifices, the Temple cult always included prayers and song, and probably dance as well (or at least orchestrated movement). The *Psalms* were first prayers, and one tradition has it that the Levites were the singers (*Ez.* 2:41, *Neh.* 7:44, *1 Chr.* 15:10), at least at the time of the Second Temple. This tradition is reflected in the captions of certain psalms that associate them with Levitical clans. But prayer and song were not regarded as the main events or even as sufficient modes of worship: only sacrifice and its rituals were ultimately efficacious. The *tamid* or daily sacrificial offering that in the Second Temple was burned twice each day was the mainstay of the cult, and when it was suppressed by decree great anxiety overtook Jewish people everywhere.

FUNDING AND ADMINISTRATION. Temple building and maintenance, the public cult, and the support of Temple personnel all required large outlays of funds. Who bore the costs? As with other matters pertaining to the Temples of Jerusalem, we are reliant primarily on the Hebrew Bible, since we lack contemporary documentation in the form of administrative records, such as those that have survived from the major ancient temples of Syria-Mesopotamia, or the inscribed ancient wall reliefs, for instance, that we find in Egypt. With the Hellenistic period, documentation begins to appear, and in the Roman period Jewish writings become available. Together these sources provide more specific information on the operation of the Second Temple.

In itself, the biblical record is complex and often confusing: the Torah tells one story, and the historical books of Hebrew scriptures—*Samuel, Kings, Ezra, Nehemiah, Chronicles*—another. The Torah gives little indication as to the role of the monarchy in biblical Israel, never venturing beyond stating the eventuality of a monarchy. Nor is there evidence of governmental taxation, only gifts to God—tithes, priestly emoluments, voluntary and obligatory sacrifices, and so forth. The various documentary sources of the Torah project legislation into the days of Moses, before the Israelite settlement of Canaan, when there was no king and no temple in Jerusalem. Historically misleading, all matters concerning the major temples of the land were controlled by the monarch, once established, in both Judaea and northern Israel. Although priestly groups probably originated independent of the monarchy, retaining traditional prerogatives, they nonetheless operated under royal jurisdiction for most of the preexilic period.

The contrast between the laws of the Torah, which provide so much detail on the performance of the cult, and the historical books of the Hebrew Bible, which contain little on these subjects but considerable information on governmental administration, can be demonstrated by the case of the tithe. The tithe amounted to one-tenth of the annual yield of grain and fruit, as well as an equal percentage of any increase in herds and flocks. In the Torah, such tithes are represented as cult dues or religious duties owed to the Levitical priests and the needy, without any governmental involvement in the process (*Dt.* 14:22–29, 15:19–23; *Lv.* 27:30). In contrast, the statement of royal jurisdiction preserved in *1 Samuel* 8 (especially verse 15) refers to the fact that kings are the ones who impose tithes on crop yield. Projecting back to Moses, so characteristic of the Torah, often masks the realities of royal administration that obtained during the preexilic period, as well as the realities of priestly administration under foreign rulers in the postexilic period.

Funding in the Second Temple. The preferred method of studying Temple funding would be to begin with the Hellenistic period, for which we have contemporary evidence, and work backward. Elias Bickerman (1976) has clarified this subject for the Ptolemaic and Seleucid periods in Judaea and Jerusalem (c. 312–363 CE) in a study of the mission of Heliodorus to the Temple of Jerusalem, as recounted in *2 Maccabees* 3 and as known well in later literature and art.

In later times, maintaining the Temple and cult in Jerusalem was a royal responsibility; tax revenues were allocated for this purpose, augmented by gifts from the nobility. Under the Romans (63 BCE–70 CE) the system was more complicated, as will become apparent.

The principle of royal sponsorship also applied during the earlier Achaemenid period (538–330 BCE); both Hebrew and Aramaic versions of the edict of Cyrus II of 538 BCE have been preserved (*Ezr.* 1:2–3, 6:6–12). Of particular relevance are statements of the Aramaic version, in *Ezra* 6:8–9, relevant to the funds and materials required for the restoration of the public cult in Jerusalem:

> The expenses are to be paid to these men [the Judean elders] with dispatch out of the resources of the king, derived from the taxes of the province of Beyond the River, so that the work not be interrupted. They are to be provided daily, without fail, whatever they need of young bulls, rams and lambs as burnt offerings for the God of Heaven and wheat, salt, wine and oil, at the order of the priests in Jerusalem.

Further back in history, similar information about the funding of the First Temple under the national Judahite kings can be found.

Ezekiel 45 contains a statement on the prerogatives of the *nasi'* ("prince"; literally, "the one elevated, raised" above the people), Ezekiel's term for the future ruler of the restored Judahite community. It is not certain when this chapter was composed, but it is probably warranted, as in the matter of Temple design, to regard it as expressing the principle of royal funding in effect during the last days of the First Temple.

The chapter begins by designating a quarter inside Jerusalem to be set aside for the Temple complex (*Ez.* 45:1–8). Verses 9 through 17 establish standards of weights and measures, and specify a system of taxation based on percentage of annual yield. Verses 16–17 are particularly relevant:

> The entire population must pay this levy to the *nasi'*. It shall then be the responsibility of the *nasi'* to provide the holocausts, grain offerings and libations on the pilgrimage festivals, on New Moons and Sabbaths, on all the appointed celebrations of the House of Israel.

This passage has been variously interpreted by biblical historians, such as Jacob Jiver, who was undoubtedly correct in seeing it as reflecting royal sponsorship. In accounting terms royal sponsorship was a form of indirect funding. Taxes collected by government agents (sometimes priests served in this capacity) were partially or fully allocated to the Temple. Direct Temple funding came from the people, and was specifically earmarked for Temple use. The *nasi'*, a civil authority although he had sacral functions, was made responsible for the entire Temple restoration, and it was he who collected taxes for the Temple project and the public cult.

But Ezekiel's vision never materialized, because during the postexilic period Temple funding became a function of foreign kings, and indeed the Davidic king Zerubbabel did not retain authority very long. Morton Smith has correctly understood the statement in *Zechariah* 6:12–13 as an official, prophetic endorsement of Zerubbabel as sponsor of the rebuilt Temple of Jerusalem, with the authority of the high priest less precisely defined. He notes, however, that king and high priest are often addressed together, as coleaders of the people (*Hg.* 1:1, 1:12, 1:14, 2:2; *Zec.* 3–4), and by placing two crowns in the Temple, their joint authority was memorialized. As time goes on, with priestly administration of the Temple under Persian jurisdiction as the everyday reality, much less is said in scripture about a Davidic restoration. So in effect Ezekiel's recast vision embodies the principle of royal sponsorship as it operated in the period of the First Temple. Further, *Samuel* and *Kings* clearly describe the First Temple as a royal agency, but say little about taxation other than that labor forces were conscripted for Temple projects and other royal enterprises.

Funding in the First Temple. One way to investigate Temple funding in the preexilic period is to discuss the royal and Temple treasuries, both mentioned in *1 Kings* 12:19, 14:26, and elsewhere, as separate agencies under royal control. We often read of "sanctuary weight" but hardly ever of royal standards of weights and measures. And yet, in a single, random passage (*2 Sm.* 14:26), we read of *'even ha-melekh* ("the royal weight"), which tells something about the degree to which even the historical chronicles mask administrative reality in a preoccupation with religious concerns.

Several biblical chronicles tell how Judahite kings, both "upright" in God's sight and those who "did what was evil," appropriated Temple treasures for other than cult purposes (*2 Kgs.* 18:15–16). In speaking of these acts, an assertion of royal authority over the Temple, *Kings* usually refers to Temple treasures as "sacred gifts" (*qodashim*) donated by the various Judean kings and their ancestors, as if to imply that they, in turn, had the right to expropriate them.

Chapters 12 and 22 in *2 Kings* are particularly informative on the subject of Temple funding during the period of the Judahite monarchy. Chapter 12 tells of Joash, a king who ruled in the late ninth century BCE, who used Temple treasures for tribute. The chapter's present arrangement has the confrontation with the Aramean king, Hazael, after Temple renovations undertaken by Joash, as seen in verses 18 and 19, yet it is quite logical to regard the renovations mentioned in verses 1 through 17 as actually taking place subsequent to Joash's payment to Hazael.

Payments to Hazael left Temple coffers empty. The chapter opens with an edict issued by Joash to the priests: all silver brought into the Temple as votaries was to be collected by the priests and used for Temple renovation. This was apparently an exceptional measure, and the priests were lax to resort to votaries for this purpose, expecting instead royal allocations to cover their cost. After a time the king, seeing that repairs had not been made, summoned the chief priest of the Temple and, prevailing over the priest's objections, insisted that his edict be carried out. The priest installed a collection box near the altar where all donors were to deposit their votaries. At appropriate intervals the priest would tally donations, in the presence of the royal scribe, and the silver would be melted down into ingots; these, in turn, were paid out to craftsmen working on the Temple who apparently were so trustworthy that no accounting system was required for them. A freeze was placed on the manufacture of cultic vessels of silver and gold in order that all available funds could be used for needed repairs. The only exemption, for penalties brought to the Temple by worshipers in need of expiation, was granted so that atonement would not be delayed.

2 Kings 22 describes a similar situation under Josiah, king of Judah, in the late seventh century BCE; both chapter 12 and this chapter are drawn from the same kind of royal chronicles. Again, all silver, this time collected by the Temple gatekeepers, was to be melted down into ingots to pay Temple workers. Josiah's coffers were also empty after the long period of Manasseh's reign.

Both chapters report that the king had jurisdiction over the Temple, royal scribes supervised Temple accounting procedures, and craftsmen were paid by royal order. In part records were preserved to credit Judean kings for proper maintenance of the First Temple of Jerusalem and for attending to necessary repairs. And yet they also point to another fairly constant source of Temple revenue and serve to link the historical books of the Hebrew Bible to the laws of the Torah.

Sacred vessels and sacrificial offerings were regularly donated (or "devoted") to the Temple by individual Israelites and their families. Votaries mentioned in *2 Kings* 12, in fact, are the subject of Torah legislation in *Leviticus* 27, where specific payments are determined separately for men and women by age group. Such devotions often assumed large proportions. The writings of Josephus and rabbinic sources describe large-scale devotions from prominent Diaspora Jews, such as Helene, the queen of Adiabene. These donations were usually prompted by the motive of sponsorship.

The priesthood, for its part, relied on popular support, which, however, was not always adequate to sustain the priests and their families. People were exhorted to pay tithes and vows on time and to devote sacrifices; indeed, the Torah sets down the dues payable to the Levitical priesthood and includes a whole schedule of offerings (*Nm.* 18).

Fiscal responsibilities. The main problem here is to determine who bore responsibility for the Temples of Jerusalem—the government (so to speak), or the private sector. No persistent policy of support by the private sector is evident until late Hasmonean or early Roman times. Basing his work on Bickerman's, Jiver meticulously surveyed the background of this development, showing that the first reference to popular funding of the Temple is found in the writings of Josephus (*Jewish Antiquities* 18:312), who tells of the annual head tax of one-half shekel (at times, equal to two Roman drachmas); *Matthew* 17:24 through 17:27 speaks about the collection of this tax in Capernaum, in the early first century CE. In the Mishnah (*Sheq.* 1:3–6) the tax is called *terumat ha-lishkah* ("the levy of the bureau," for the bureau in the Temple complex where it was collected); it was used mainly to fund the *tamid* or daily sacrifice that was the mainstay of the public Temple cult. It was not accepted from Gentiles, thereby excluding them from any role in supporting the cult. But more specifically, at some prior time Jewish religious leaders decided that the cult should be supported "by all Israel," and not by foreign rulers—Herodian or Roman. This decision is first recorded in the *scholia,* or comments, affixed to *Megillat ta'anit,* concerning a dispute involving the early Pharisees. The text states that Boethusians (perhaps the Sadducees, or some other anti-Pharisaic sect) claimed:

> The *tamid* sacrifices may be brought from private contributions: one person may offer it for one week, another may offer it for two weeks, and still another for thirty days. The Sages [Pharisees] retorted: "You are not permitted to act in this way, because this sacrifice may only be contributed by all Israel . . . and all of them [the sacrifices] are to come from the 'levy of the bureau.' " When they [the Pharisees] prevailed over them and defeated them, they instituted that all should weigh out their shekels and deposit them in the bureau, and *tamid* sacrifices were henceforth offered from popular funds. (quoted in Lichtenstein, 1931–1932, p. 325)

We cannot date the enactment of which this passage speaks, but historically it may have been the result of Pharisaic displeasure with the later Hasmoneans; some scholars trace it to the reign of Salome Alexandra (76–67 BCE). Whatever the case, Jewish communities from all over the Diaspora contributed their shekels.

The policy of refusing royal support was based on several Torah traditions that speak of all Israelites as contributing to the building of the Tabernacle in the Sinai wilderness. These traditions have baffled biblical historians, who have searched for a historical situation that could account for them. Since no such principle is known for either the First Temple or the Second, both of which relied on royal funding, the question remains as to when popular funding came to function as a system.

The Torah traditions are preserved primarily in the priestly sources of *Exodus* and *Numbers.* Beginning with *Exodus* 30:11 through 16, a law required every adult Israelite male to contribute one-half shekel "to Yahveh" to support the Tabernacle; it was to be collected in the course of a census.

In its context, this law was formulated as a one-time obligation. *Exodus* 25 and the following chapters appealed to all Israelites to contribute voluntarily to the construction of gold and silver objects for the Tabernacle, valuable fabrics, and the like. This fund-raising effort was very successful, and sufficient materials were donated. The half-shekel was for the "service" of the Tabernacle, to support its sacrifical cult. Of course it is possible that in *Exodus* 25 and 30 parallel traditions on funding exist: one recording a fixed tax, the other a voluntary contribution.

Either way, these traditions, reinforced by *Numbers* 7, which tells that the chieftains of the twelve tribes contributed identical vessels and sacrificial materials for the dedication of the Tabernacle, quite clearly idealize popular support for the Temple and its public cult. Nonetheless, all Israelites participated in its support, making it an institution of and for the people, even though it was conducted by the priesthood.

Since it is virtually out of the question to date these Torah traditions to the late first century BCE, it is difficult to identify their historical situation. Most likely Julius Wellhausen and others were right in attributing the head tax of *Exodus* 30 with the period of Nehemiah, the late fifth century BCE; he was a Jew who served for two terms under the Persians as governor of Judah. In *Nehemiah* 10 is a record of a popular assembly, or "constitutional convention," that some historians date to around 438 BCE, although *Nehemiah* may have been written considerably later.

Under Nehemiah the people, along with priestly leaders and civil officials, assembled in Jerusalem and pledged to fulfill the Torah of Moses. In fact, however, they also instituted some new marriage restrictions, reinforced the observance of the Sabbath, and assumed certain financial obligations in support of the Temple cult. They pledged one-third shekel a year in support of the cult and cast lots to determine who would provide wood for the altar fire. In addition, they promised to pay tithes, redeem firstlings and firstborns by remitting their set value to the Temple, and offer first fruits of the harvest—all of which brought profit to the Temple.

It is reasonable to see the priestly traditions as the institutionalization of a temporary policy change that occurred in the late Persian period when the economic fortunes of the Empire declined, threatening the continuity of the cult. According to the *Book of Nehemiah,* especially chapter 5, taxes were heavy and Jewish leaders had to help matters along. With the conquest of Alexander the Great, and the initiation of Ptolemaic and Seleucid rule in Jerusalem and Judaea, the economic situation improved substantially, and royal sponsorship functioned well once again.

The Torah traditions also correlate with other references to popular responsibility for the public cult in *Ezra* and *Chronicles,* although these references reach into the fourth century BCE. (See *Ezra* 1:4, an addendum to the Cyrus Edict, also *Ezra* 3:5, 8:28; *2 Chronicles* 31:14, 35:8.)

2 Chronicles 24:4 through 14 is a late recasting of *2 Kings* 12, discussed earlier. In this version, Joash orders the priests and Levites to travel to every town in Judaea to collect silver for Temple repairs, from "all Israel." When the Levites fail to do their part, he rebukes them (*2 Chr.* 24:6). Thus, this preexilic chronicle's version of Temple votary expropriation was recast as the record of a tax collected throughout the land from all the people.

The Torah traditions, whenever composed, became epitomes ultimately of a democratic ideal—the liberation of the Temple cult from royal domination. The Jews took charge of the Temple and limited the authority of foreign kings over the conduct of religious life. Perhaps for the first time, these kings, who had spent a fortune on the Temples from taxes collected from the people, were no longer permitted to claim exclusive sponsorship of the worship of God.

The Torah speaks of "consecrations" to the Temple (*Lv.* 27), with an assured 20 percent profit on "redemptions" of land or real estate so designated. Land was also permanently bequeathed to the Temple, making it the beneficiary of private estates. More than likely, the Temple served as a channel for tax exemptions.

The Mishnah describes how the Temple operated on a day-to-day basis in Herodian times and prior to its destruction. Like the prophet Jeremiah before him, Jesus certainly had reason to object to the atmosphere of the marketplace that characterized the Temple complex, but such was the nature of holy cities everywhere. Great numbers of sacrificial animals, as well as large quantities of incense, flour, wine, and oil, were stocked in the Temple stores; priests and their agents attended to the business of the Temple, selling to worshipers the goods that they required and collecting various payments. Priests were assigned to Temple duty, usually of a week's duration. Ancient records of these tours (*mishmarot*) have been discovered in recent archaeological investigations, such as those at Beit She'an. The Temple proper was inspected every morning; a daily duty roster was used, with one priest placed in charge of work assignments each day; treasurers kept Temple accounts. Indeed, the Temple complex was the very hub of Jerusalem.

TEMPLE FUNCTION AND PHENOMENOLOGY. Throughout biblical literature, the temple of Jerusalem is called *beit YHVH* ("the House of Yahveh"). This role emerges clearly from *1 Kings* 8, a mixed text that presents both an early statement on the functions of this house and a later postexilic reinterpretation. Its primary function is best conveyed in verses 12 and 13: "Then Solomon spoke: Yahveh has chosen to abide in dense cloud. I have accordingly built for You a royal house, a dais for Your eternal enthronement."

The Temple served as an earthly residence for God and was designed to replicate his celestial estate. In the heavens, God is enveloped by dense cloud (*2 Sm.* 22; *Ps.* 18, 97:2; *Jb.* 38:9); his heavenly throne room was, in graphic terms, an arrested version of his chariot, fashioned as a winged sphinx and cherub (*Ez.* 28:14, *Ps.* 18:11). God rode his chariot across heaven, as "rider amid the clouds" (*Ps.* 68:5) and as "Yahveh of the [heavenly] hosts, seated astride the cherubim" (*1 Sm.* 4:4, *2 Sm.* 6:2)—a projection now recognized as a very ancient Near Eastern image known in Ugaritic mythology.

Also basic to celestial depictions is the obscurity that afforded protection from view and access. Moses climbed Mount Sinai, "into the dense cloud where God is" (*Ex.* 20:21); God had descended there to communicate with Moses, a dramatic move in keeping with other visible manifestations of the deity (*2 Sm.* 20:10, *Ps.* 18:10).

The Temple was a divine palace. In the ancient Near Eastern tradition of inverting reality, earth was perceived as a replica of heaven, yet poets and writers depicted heaven according to what they knew on earth—an inversion seemingly endemic to the human imagination. The earthly residence of God in Jerusalem contained a shrine without windows, a dark room; in it the Ark served as God's footstool, and his throne was formed by the arched, winged cherubs. He was present, but invisible, and immaterial. On those rare occasions that the high priest entered the shrine, he bore incense, partly to protect himself, but also to cloud the immediate area of the shrine where the deity was thought to be seated (*Lv.* 16:13).

The term for great hall, *heikhal*, goes back to Sumerian *egal* ("big house"); Akkadian *hekallu*, and Ugaritic *hkl*. The Egyptian title *pharaoh* (*pr*) literally means "big house," the ruler who lives in a palace. The great hall was a veritable audience room or parlor, where priests (perhaps originally worshipers as well) offered gifts to the resident divine monarch. There was a table for presentations and an incense altar, so that the air would be sweetened for God's pleasure. The cedar-paneled walls and ceiling were decorated with motifs suitable for a divine residence—cherubs and floral motifs. Here was an effort to simulate a heavenly "garden," such as described in *Ezekiel* 27–28. Such decorations were not thought to contradict the ban on iconography so basic to Israelite monotheism (*Ex.* 20:4, *Dt.* 5:8). And, like a palace, the Temple had a portico, so that one would not enter into the presence of the deity abruptly.

Offerings. In the open-air courtyard stood the altar of burnt offerings, facing the entrance of the Temple. Every day sacrifices were burned on this altar, and other installations and artifacts were also present to serve the priests' needs.

The classic plan of Solomon's Temple and of all its successors represented the integration of two originally separate concepts: that of a house, closed and covered by a roof, and that of an open-air encampment. Within the "house" gifts were presented to the deity, and his "looking upon" them with favor constituted his acceptance of them. Normally, such gifts were assigned to the priests, who partook of them in a sacred meal.

The offerings of incense inside the great hall point to another kind of divine response—inhalation. In this respect, incense and the burnt offerings of animals, birds, and grain belonged together on the outdoor altar. Therefore, two modes of sacrifice took place in the great hall: presentation, which was intended to evoke a visual response from God, and aromatic smoke, intended for inhalation by the deity. A description of the open-air ceremony will help us to understand the phenomonology of incense offerings. On the altar of burnt offerings were placed parts of animals and fowl and scoops of dough that were reduced to ash by the fire. The smoke ascended heavenward, there inhaled by God and in this manner accepted by him. When God disapproved of the worshipers or the manner of their worship, he angrily refused to inhale the aromatic smoke of their burnt offerings (*Am.* 5:21, *Lv.* 26:31).

The open-air altar was oriented vertically and the effects of the rite directed heavenward, which helps explain the preference for mountaintops and high places. As the sacrificial rite began, God was thought to be in heaven, not yet present; once the smoke rose to heaven, it was hoped that he would be attracted by the sweet aroma, and come to his worshipers (*Ex.* 20:24). Once God drew near he could be entreated and petitioned for the blessings of life. This was the basic phenomenology of the open-air burnt offering. In liturgical terms it was a form of invocation, and this seems to be the original function of the burnt offering referred to as *ʿolah* (literally, "that which *ascends,*" in aromatic smoke, to heaven).

The presentation clearly had a horizontal orientation. The deity was perceived as already present in his "house." This is the basic difference between a "house" and the open-air setting. The Temple "house" was God's permanent residence, affording him shelter and the necessities of life (so to speak), whereas an altar or *bamah* ("high place") was a site visited by him on occasion. Consequently, it is likely that the incense offering was originally an open-air ritual. Archaeological evidence seems to suggest this; many incense stands have been found in front of temples, or outside their entrances. But it is also reasonable to assume that the venue of the incense offering was, in certain instances, shifted to the Temple's interior.

Structure. As a projection of differing patterns of human habitation, the typical temple plan—including both an open-air court and a closed, covered "house"—combines the encampment and the town, the pastoral and the more settled, agricultural bases of economic life into one expression.

Wood was preferred for temple architecture, particularly the fine, aromatic cedar from Lebanon. The Sumerian king Gudea used cedar wood in his temple, built more than a thousand years before Solomon's Temple. In many areas of the ancient Near East there seems to be an almost symbolic preference for wood, persisting long after stone and mud brick became the functional materials for construction. In the earliest temple tombs of Egypt, wooden motifs were retained long after stone was used. It was conventional to romanticize more ancient modes of construction, while for practical purposes utilizing stronger, more lasting materials.

The huge reservoir, *yam* ("sea"), located in the courtyard also had its particular meaning; in Mesopotamian temples similar reservoirs were called *apsu* ("the deep"). Aside from their practical purposes, their names reflect a common cosmic or mythological concept. *Zechariah* 14:8 states that the Temple rested on the fountainhead of the earth and was connected to the deep wellsprings. As in heaven, where gods lived at the junctures of cosmic streams, so too on earth the divine palace was associated with water. The manmade reservoir was called "sea" to symbolize the purifying and fructifying properties of "living water."

Gods normally desired an earthly house or palace built by worshipers (usually their king) more fervently than they desired altars and high places. This desire is beautifully expressed (and with considerable pathos) in ancient Near Eastern literature from Sumer to Ugarit. Biblical historiography reports this suprisingly sophisticated attitude as attributed to the God of Israel when he, in effect, initially refuses David's offer to build a temple in his honor. He states that only when the Davidic dynasty is established and the conquest of the promised land accomplished will he insist on a "house." In *2 Samuel* 7 "house" (*bayit*) undergoes an ingenious semantic transaction: both David's dynasty and the Temple are houses, and only when David's dynasty is established, in the days of his son, will the time be right to build God his house.

The Temple is thus a royal project par excellence, a fact further demonstrated by the other components of Solomon's acropolis. The two pillars in front of the portico (*yakhin* and *boʿaz*) were apparently royal insignia, although the precise meaning of their names remains elusive. The hall of justice demonstrates the judicial role of the king, as the one responsible for establishing justice in the land, and as a court of last resort for the redress of grievances. The king, chosen by God to rule in his name, exercised judicial authority over the Temple complex; documents were stored for safekeeping near the Temple, as was the practice in other temples. Oaths were pronounced in God's name, often in his presence, that is in the Temple (*Ex.* 21:7). Priests served as judges as well as cultic officiants, determining innocence or culpability according to a code of instruction (a *torah*), and the king was commanded to consult God's law in arriving at his judgments (*Dt.* 17:18–20). This set of functions is articulated in *Deuteronomy* 17:8f.:

> If a case is too baffling for you to decide . . . you shall promptly repair to the place which the Lord your God will have chosen, and appear before the Levitical priests, or the magistrate in charge at the time and present your problem.

Reference to the "the place which the Lord your God will have chosen" is *Deuteronomy*'s way of referring to the central temple of the land, ultimately identified as the Temple of Jerusalem.

Until soon before the Roman destruction of the Second Temple in 70, the Sanhedrin convened in a chamber of the inner Temple complex; around 30 CE it moved out to the portico, in the outer Temple area.

Sanctity. The Temple area itself was considered sacred space; this very ancient notion that certain spaces are sacred goes back to animism, the belief that power (or "life") is immanent in mountains, rivers, trees, and the like. Biblical statements on the subject of sanctity rarely (if ever) define it as immanent, but rather as property attributed to a certain place, object, person, act, or time. It was therefore important to know how and when a particular site had become sacred in the first place. A story or poem that relates how a place became sacred is known as *hieros logos,* and the Bible presents quite a few examples. A classic example is found in *Genesis* 28, which tells how Bethel, the major cult center of the northern kingdom of Israel, first achieved its sanctity: the partriarch Jacob once spent the night there and experienced a theophany.

The sanctity of Jerusalem is recounted in several biblical sources. In addition to the historiographies and oracles of *2 Samuel* 6 and 7 and the chronicle of *1 Kings* 8, a *hieros logos* in *2 Samuel* 24 relates that David, after fighting many battles, angered God by conducting a census and imposing new conscriptions and taxes on the already weary people of Israel. God's anger was unleashed in a plague that at the critical moment was stopped when David confessed his sinfulness. This confession took place in front of a threshing floor owned by Aravnah, the Jebusite, most probably the Canaanite ruler of Jerusalem. Realizing that the spot was propitious, David obeyed a prophetic order to worship the God of Israel there. He purchased the facility from Aravnah, as well as sacrificial animals, insisting on making full payment. He then offered sacrifices to God. In addition, the episode of Abraham and the king of Salem, Melchizedek (*Gn.* 14:18–20), has been interpreted as a veiled allusion to Jerusalem, in that Salem is traditionally equated with [Jeru]salem. This is further suggested by Psalm 110, wherein Melchizedek is praised and promised the priesthood of Zion.

In other words, biblical literature preserves stories about the sanctity of Jerusalem (and Zion) as the divinely chosen site for the Temple, just as it does for other similar sites, such as Bethel, Shiloh, and elsewhere. While these accounts seem to sanction changing political realities, in terms of religious phenomenology they explain the basis for the sanctity of certain "spaces." In the case of Jerusalem, we have an entire genre of psalms in which the divine selection of Jerusalem (Zion) is recounted (for example, Psalms 48, 78, and 122).

Historically, however, sites like Bethel were sacred to the Canaanites before sanctification by the Israelites, as is evident from the intensive archaeological excavations that have been carried out at Bethel, Shechem, and other sites. Information about pre-Israelite Jerusalem is less precise, but there are indications of cultic history there as well. The Israelites, notwithstanding their distinctive religion, were not averse to appropriating sacred space and worshiping the God of Israel where others had worshiped pagan gods. Sanctity of space seems to have cut across religious and national boundaries, and once attributed to a space, no matter by whom, such sanctity was permanent.

The Jerusalem Temple complex was a sacred space in which the farther one penetrated, the greater the sanctity, and, accordingly, the greater the restrictions on those who may enter and the greater the degree of purity required. Precise information is lacking on the "graduated" sanctity of the First Temple of the kind available on the Second Temple in its later period. The priestly writings of the Torah, projecting an elaborate system of purity and describing a Tabernacle with demarcated zones of graduated sanctity, may not have reflected the First Temple in detail, but rather the postexilic Temple. Nevertheless, it is quite certain that in principle there were, from the outset, limitations on who could enter the Temple, and there were rites of purification for all who desired entry. It is reasonable to conclude that only priests who were consecrated could enter the Temple, or stand in the courtyard near the Temple, although Judean kings may not have always respected this rule. Sacrificial animals and other materials used in worship had to conform to certain specifications; cult artifacts were also subject to specific standards, and in this connection the introduction of pagan or otherwise improper cult objects into the Temple or its courtyards defiled the sanctity of the Temple. certain kings were guilty of such acts of defilement, and others—the more upright in God's sight—piously removed the improper cult objects from the Temple and its courts, thus restoring its condition of purity.

Whereas the preexilic prophets concentrated their denunciations on paganism and on social evils for which no ritual remedy existed (*Isaiah* 1 is a good example), early postexilic prophets, taking their cue from Jeremiah, Ezekiel, and "Second Isaiah," begin to attack the problem of defilement more pointedly. Thus, the *Book of Malachi* insists on ritual purity and quite explicitly condemns improper sacrifice. It is reasonable to place the elaborate priestly regimen of *Exodus, Leviticus,* and *Numbers* in the early postexilic period, when the Temple became the center of the restored Judean community, and certainly by the end of the fourth century BCE the degree of ritual stringency with respect to sacred spaces had increased considerably, as can be gathered from *1* and *2 Chronicles,* and from passages of *Ezra* and *Nehemiah*—all literary products of that century.

This priestly tradition was the basis for the later rabbinic codification of law relating to the Temple and cult, preserved primarily in the Mishnah and other tannaitic sources. In other words, early rabbis utilized the complete Torah, drawing on it selectively to produce a regimen of purification.

With the changing designs of both the First and Second Temples of Jerusalem, progressively, the Temple and its inner courts were further protected or barricaded against the outside world by the addition of more walls, gates, and courtyards. Since a great deal is known about the Herodian temple, it is possible to be specific on the subject of "graduated" sanctity. The design of the structure prohibited entry to gentiles beyond a balustrade that encircled the inner Temple complex: this then was the first graduation. Such a restriction is actually presaged in principle in the priestly writings of the Torah; *Ezekiel* 44:63 is the first to mention explicit opposition to the presence of Gentiles within the Temple, in a passage that is exilic at the very earliest.

Within the compound open to all Jews, the next graduation pertained to the exclusion of women. There is no explicit evidence from preexilic sources that women were excluded from those areas of the Temple complex that were open to men. Even if the laws of *Leviticus* 12 are preexilic (which is less likely than some suppose), the exclusion would have affected menstruating women and new mothers, and only for a limited length of time. But little information exists on the status of women and sacred space until late in the postexilic period; it is known, however, that women were never considered legitimately acceptable as priests, although they undoubtedly served in that capacity under heterodox sponsorship.

The next graduation pertained to the priesthood itself. In the Herodian Temple complex, the court of Israel was not separated by a wall from the court of the priests, but probably by a marker. Opposed to the increasingly greater emphasis on purity was the ancient notion that the donor of the sacrifice, the Israelite who offered the gift to God, should "appear" before him and stand in his presence (*Ex.* 23:17). According to priestly law, the donor was to lay his hands upon the sacrifice (*Lv.* 1:4), so no wall or absolute barrier could stand between donor and altar.

Beyond the court of Israel was the court of the priests and the Temple itself. The shrine, the Holy of Holies, was out of bounds to priests, even to the high priest for the most part. Only when ritual purification of the Temple was obligatory could the high priest penetrate its space. We do not know how early in the biblical period the laws of *Leviticus* 16 detailing the purification of the Temple were in force, but prior to the end of the Persian period at the very latest there was an annual day of purification, Yom Kippur.

Following any defilement, purification of the Temple complex and its ground was both possible and necessary (*2 Kgs.* 18, and 23; *1 Mc.* 1). Depending on the material of construction, many cultic vessels had to be destroyed, and sacrificial materials—meat and other foodstuffs—usually were not susceptible to purification and had to be likewise eliminated. Generally people could be purified, certainly as long as the Temple cult was in operation. Ultimately, the Temple complex and grounds withstood all the defilements recorded in literature and retained their sanctity through the ages.

Sanctification of space could also be affected by a ritual process, usually based on "mythic" models. At the first level, Israelites visited sites thought to be holy; in all cases, however, formal consecration was required. Jacob anointed the foundation stone of the temple at Bethel and offered sacrifices on an altar (*Gn.* 28). Usually there were specific recitations and celebrations, proclaiming the sanctity of the site; the process was then inverted and a myth created: it was declared that God had chosen the site and manifested himself there. But the myth was never quite sufficient, however, and communal sanctification was required.

Pilgrimage. There is no clearer demonstration of how the notion of sacred space worked than the religious pilgrimage. Important, often obligatory, the pilgrimage supported the belief that worshiping God at a sacred site is more efficacious than worship elsewhere.

In biblical Israel the three annual festivals—*matsot* in the early spring, the spring grain harvest, and the autumn fruit harvest—were all referred to as *ḥag*, which means "pilgrimage." On these occasions an Israelite was required to appear before God, bearing gifts, at a proper pilgrimage center (*Ex.* 23, 34). *1 Samuel* 1 tells the story of a family undertaking an annual pilgrimage to Shiloh, in the Ephraimite mountains. The occasion was not a scheduled religious festival but instead an annual clan gathering.

Throughout most of the preexilic period, there were temples and altars throughout the Land of Israel. An open-air cult site was called *bamah* ("high place") in Judaea and *maqom* ("cult site") in northern Israel. Political and demographic realities determined their relative prominence as pilgrimage centers.

HETERODOXY AND CENTRALIZATION OF THE CULT. Experience with local and regional temples, high places, and altars, both in Judah and in northern Israel, was usually troublesome from the point of view of piety because of the almost inevitable tendency to introduce pagan elements into the ritual. There were even temples dedicated to pagan gods. These trends were regularly denounced by the prophets, such as the northern Israelite Hosea. *1* and *2 Kings*, since they reveal a strong pro-Judahite bias, tell less about heterodoxy in Judah and Jerusalem, although there must have been similar problems there as well.

1 Kings 18:4 tells that Hezekiah, king of Judah after the fall of the northern kingdom of Israel, removed the *bamot.* However, no record of a follow-up exists and historians assume that the efforts of this "upright" king were not effective, especially since, following Hezekiah, his son Manasseh, who reigned for many years, pursued a decidedly heterodox policy. The next attempt to remove the *bamot*, an issue that pervades *1* and *2 Kings*, was during the reign of Josiah (*2 Kgs.* 22, 23). In response to the horrendous execrations found in an old document that had been deposited in the Temple, Josiah closed down the local and regional cult sites in the towns of Judah, ordering all the priests to report to Jerusalem. He destroyed what remained of the temple and necropolis of Bethel, the major cult site of the erstwhile northern kingdom. Josiah further proclaimed a celebration of the paschal sacrifice in the Temple of Jerusalem for the first time, thereby altering in a basic way the relevance of what had been a domestic, clan-centered sacrifice.

To understand just how the site of the temples of Jerusalem eventually became the unique sacred space in Jewish religion, the background and consequences of Josiah's (and Hezekiah's) edicts need to be discussed. One of the major preoccupations of modern Bible scholarship has been to define the historical relationship between the events recorded in *2 Kings* 22 and 23 and the doctrine in *Deuteronomy* 12 and 16. The narrative setting of *Deuteronomy* is projected back into the presettlement period of Israelite history, a projection consistent with Torah traditon. Chapters 12 and 16 state that once the Israelites have securely settled in their land, they must discontinue their customary practice of offering sacrifice at cult sites throughout the land and paying tithes locally, and they must do all of these things only at a central temple, to be built in a town selected by God.

At first, modern scholars tended to regard this doctrine of cult centralization as a seventh-century Judahite movement, a reaction to the heterodox policies of Manasseh. H. L. Ginsberg (1982) has made a good case for regarding the core of *Deuteronomy*, wherein this doctrine is expounded, as the product of the mid- to late eighth century, in northern Israel. He compares the language of *Hosea* and *Deuteronomy*, showing the unique correspondences, and argues that the doctrine of cult centralization grew out of the extreme dissatisfaction of northern Israelite prophets and leaders with the cults of the many local altars operating there, and eventually with the major temples of Dan and Bethel as well. They sought a solution in the form of a new, central temple, perhaps in Shechem on Mount Gerizim, which was still sacred to the Samaritans. *Deuteronomy* never refers to Jerusalem, even by allusion, but after the fall of the northern kingdom, it was logical to identify the proper site of the central temple as Jerusalem and to evoke the myth of Jerusalem's selection by God. So, some forty years before the Babylonian destruction (c. 622), Josiah taught this doctrine by devout priests who had educated him, acted in fulfillment of *Deuteronomy's* doctrine. In the short run he probably failed to remove all local cult sites, but in the long run he succeeded.

The real motivations behind cult centralization as a means of control over religious worship can only be guessed at. From the beginning of the monarchy, there were at least two factions or "parties" in Judah and the northern kingdom: what Morton Smith (1971) called "the Yahveh-alone" party, and a party that accepted Yahveh as the national god of Israel but saw no reason not to allow (or even sponsor) worship of other gods as well.

In 587/6 BCE the Babylonians conquered all of Judah and destroyed the Temple of Jerusalem. At that point religious life, both in the devastated land and among the exiles in Babylonia, Egypt, and elsewhere, could have gone one of two ways. Sacrificial worship might have been undertaken at substitute sites, which would have been the normal course. As it happened, Jewish leadership opposed substitute sites and insisted on a restoration theology—sacrifice would be resumed only at the site of a rebuilt Jerusalem Temple, as God had promised.

There were several Jewish temples in the Diaspora—the best known were one near Heliopolis, a suburb of Cairo, and one at Aswan (Elephantine) in Upper Egypt. There is also evidence of temples in Transjordan and possibly elsewhere in the Land of Israel. But in the main the Jewish religious leadership during the exilic period opposed such worship, and a clue to this policy may be preserved in *Ezekiel* where the elders of Israel approached Ezekiel in Babylonia and apparently inquired of him as to whether it would be proper to erect an altar to the God of Israel while in exile. The unequivocal response of the prophet: only when God restores his people to his holy mountain and to the Land of Israel will he once again be worshiped by sacrifice. Meanwhile, God would be present among the exiles, and there was no need for a temple in exile (*Ez.* 20:40–44).

During the period of the Second Temple, the religious pilgrimage and support of the priesthood and cult of Jerusalem became mainstays of Jewish religious life throughout the expanding Diaspora. The statements in *Deuteronomy* about being distant from the central temple (*Dt.* 12:21) took on a new, somewhat pathetic interpretation: dispersed Jews must attend upon the cult of Jerusalem's Temple. *Tobit*, a pseudepigraphica work probably writen well before the Maccabean period, relates that Tobit made regular pilgrimages to Jerusalem and contributed his dues to the Temple (*Tb.* 1). The Jewish military colony of Elephantine, active in the fifth century BCE, which had its own temple, nevertheless maintained a steady relationship to the Temple of Jerusalem, as is known from the archives of that community.

During the period of the Second Temple, the Jewish synagogue came into being as a local institution devoid of any cultic status, strictly speaking. Jews in Israel and Diaspora communities assembled at synagogues for prayer and the reading of sacred writ, to attend to communal matters, and to celebrate in their own way Sabbaths and festivals, while the cult of the Temple of Jerusalem was in full operation. The true and sufficient worship of the God of Israel took place in the Temple, and delegations of pilgrims were dispatched to Jerusalem to attend the offering of sacrifices as representatives of the far-flung communities (*Taʿan*, chap. 4).

In *1 Kings* 8 great emphasis is placed on prayer and song as forms of religious devotion. Prayers are heard by God in heaven when recited at the Temple. Prayer assumed an importance it did not have in the preexilic Temple, although the psalms, many of them preexilic in origin, show evidence that prayer and sacrifice coexisted even in earlier periods.

From praying "at" the Temple to praying elsewhere "toward" or "facing" it is a fascinating step in religious phenomenology, having relevance not only to postbiblical Judaism but to Christianity and Islam as well. Islam substituted Mecca for Jerusalem but insisted that in every mosque in the world the *qiblah* ("niche") be oriented toward a central spot, the focus of pilgrimage. Daniel, the wise seer of the exile, turned toward Jerusalem thrice daily when praying to God while in exile (*Dn.* 6:11).

Throughout the centuries, Jewish pilgrims attempted and often succeeded in visiting the site of the Temple in Jerusalem, but in fact Judaism accommodated itself to the loss of the Temple—to living without sacred space. It is still too soon to speculate on the effects upon the Jewish religion of the modern resettlement of Israel, except to take note of the renewed importance of sacred space, as identified with Jerusalem.

SEE ALSO Altar; Iconography, article on Jewish Iconography; Israelite Religion; Levites; Music, article on Music and Religion in the Middle East; Pilgrimage, article on Contemporary Jewish Pilgrimage; Priesthood, article on Jewish Priesthood; Psalms; Rabbinic Judaism in Late Antiquity; Sacrifice; Synagogue; Tithes.

BIBLIOGRAPHY

Th. A. Busink's *Der Tempel von Jerusalem: Von Salomo bis Herodes*, 2 vols. (Leiden, 1970–1980), is the most exhaustive study, encyclopedic in nature, on the two temples of Jerusalem, providing discussion of everything from design and architecture to function, with numerous references to recent scholarly investigations. These volumes are replete with comparative evidence and are amply illustrated. The results of recent excavations in the area of the Temple mount are summarized, along with a survey of the physical history of Jerusalem by the leader of the excavations, Benjamin Mazar, in *The Mountain of the Lord* (Garden City, N.Y., 1975). This volume is well illustrated and synthesizes the archaeological and the textual evidence. It is popular in presentation but authentic. As a companion to Mazar's volume, the reader is referred to Nahman Avigad's *Discovering Jerusalem* (Nashville, 1983), a fascinating and well-illustrated report of the archaeologist's recent discovery of the upper city of Jerusalem, whose buildings, public and private, help to define the relation of the city to the Temples of Jerusalem, both in the preexilic and postexilic periods.

Henri Frankfort's *The Art and Architecture of the Ancient Orient* (New York, 1969) remains the most penetrating treatment of temple architecture and its relation to meaning and function in the ancient Near East. Using examples drawn from Syria—Mesopotamia and Egypt—Frankfort analyzes the physical development of major temples, and his insights shed light on the temples of Jerusalem as well.

On the subject of cult and ritual and the phenomenology of worship in biblical Israel, two works, based on differing methods, may be consulted: Menahem Haran's *Temples and Temple-Service in Ancient Israel* (Oxford, 1978) and my own *In the Presence of the Lord* (Leiden, 1974). A collection of studies on various forms of sacrifice and their religious significance is provided in Jacob Milgrom's *Cult and Conscience: The Asham and the Priestly Doctrine of Repentence* (Leiden, 1976). An earlier work, highly influential in its impact on present-day cultic studies, is G. B. Gray's *Sacrifice in the Old Testament* (1925), which I have reissued with a prolegomena (New York, 1971).

Recent encyclopedias offer informative "state of the field" investigations. The *Encyclopedia of Archaeological Excavations in the Holy Land*, 4 vols., edited by Michael Avi-Yonah (Englewood Cliffs, N. J., 1975–1978), is a heavily illustrated reference work that will lead the reader to information on the modern exploration of ancient sites in biblical lands.

The *Encyclopaedia Judaica*, 16 vols. (Jerusalem, 1971), contains many easily located and informative articles on Jerusalem, the Temple, cult and ritual, with extensive bibliography. For those who read Hebrew, volume 5 of the *Encyclopedia Biblica*, edited by Haim Beinart and Menahem Haran (Jerusalem, 1968), contains a series of articles by Menahem Haran and Samuel Yeivin under "Miqdash" that are unexcelled for sound scholarly judgment, breadth of view, and attention to detail.

Several specialized studies contribute to our understanding of the foundations of the two Temples of Jerusalem. The administration and funding of the Second Temple under the Seleucids is incisively clarified in Elias J. Bickerman's "Heliodore au Temple de Jerusalem," in his *Studies in Jewish and Christian History* (Leiden, 1976), pp. 151–191. The movement toward cult centralization, as reflected in *Deuteronomy*, is explored with new insights by H. L. Ginsberg in his *The Israelian Heritage of Judaism* (New York, 1982). Ginsberg traces this religious movement to northern Israel of the eighth century, and shows how it eventually overtook Judaea, as well. The political implications of the Temples and their priesthoods are investigated by Morton Smith in *Palestinian Parties and Politics That Shaped the Old Testament* (New York, 1971).

The phenomenology of the Temple as a house built for God is explored in my "On the Presence of the Lord in Biblical Religion," *Religions in Antiquity: Essays in Memory of Erwin Ramsdell Goodenough*, edited by Jacob Neusner (Leiden, 1970), pp. 71–87.

The reader will also want to consult ancient sources outside the Bible, referred to in this article. The best available English translation of the Mishnah is Herbert Danby's *Mishnah* (Oxford, 1933). The writings of the ancient historian Josephus Flavius, translated by Henry St. J. Thackeray and Ralph Marcus, are available in volumes 1–5 and 7 of the "Loeb Classical Library" (Cambridge, Mass., 1950–1961). *Apocrypha and Pseudepigrapha of the Old Testament*, 2 vols., edited by R. H. Charles (Oxford, 1913), includes such works as *Ben Sira. Aristeas to Philocrates*, or the *Letter of Aristeas*, has been edited and translated by Moses Hadas (New York, 1951). The *Ta'anit Scroll* (*Die Fastenrolle*) has been edited by Hans Lichtenstein in "Die Fastenrolle: Eine Untersuchung zur Judisch-Hellenistis-chen Geschichte," *Hebrew Union College Annual* 8–9 (1931–1932): 257–351. A newly discovered Hebrew document, named the *Temple Scroll*, dating from the pre-Herodian period, and containing plans for a Jewish temple and laws for its cult has been published in a three-volume English edition, translated and edited by Yigael Yadin (Jerusalem, 1977).

New Sources

Bahat, Dan. "Below the Temple Mount." *BAIAS* 16 (1998): 97–104.

Barker, Margaret. *The Gate of Heaven: The History and Symbolism of the Temple in Jerusalem.* London, 1991.

Berman, Joshua. *The Temple: Its Symbolism and Meaning Then and Now.* Northvale, N.J., 1995.

Collins, John Joseph. *Jerusalem and the Temple in Jewish Apocalyptic Literature of the Second Temple Period.* International Rennert Guest Lecture Series, no. 1. [Ramat Gan, Israel], 1998.

Elior, Rachel. "The Jerusalem Temple: The Representation of the Imperceptible." *Studies in Spirituality* 11 (2001): 126–143.

Hayward, C.T.R, ed. *The Jewish Temple: A Non-biblical Sourcebook.* London and New York, 1996.

Mazar, Eilat, and Benjamin Mazar. *Excavations in the South of the Temple Mount: The Ophel of Biblical Jerusalem.* Publications of the Institute of Archaeology, the Hebrew University of Jerusalem. Jerusalem, 1989.

McCormick, Clifford Mark. *Palace and Temple: A Study of Architectural and Verbal Icons.* Beihefte zur Zeitschrift für die alttestamentliche Wissenschaft, no. 313. Berlin, 2002.

Schmidt, Francis. *How the Temple Thinks: Identity and Social Cohesion in Ancient Judaism.* Translated by J. Edward Crowley. Biblical Seminar, no. 78. Sheffield, 2001.

Schwartz, Max. *The Biblical Engineer: How the Temple in Jerusalem Was Built.* Hoboken, N.J., 2002.

BARUCH A. LEVINE (1987)
Revised Bibliography

BINDING. The motif of binding is widespread in the history of religions, in both the so-called primitive religions and in the religions of both ancient and modern higher civilizations. Its many, complex transpositions, often quite original, vary according to the cultural milieu and the historical moment of which they are the expressions.

Drawing on extraordinarily rich examples taken from the most diverse civilizations, phenomenologists of religion have called attention to the enormous sacred potential that is polarized around acts of physical and symbolic binding, to the concretization of this potential in the form of knots, and to the importance of the opposing act of loosening a bond. In many traditional cultures, important mythical events are believed to be the result of the fastening or loosening of bonds. Actions of binding and loosing frequently occur at the center of rituals, both cultic rituals that involve superhuman beings, and autonomous rituals that are efficacious in themselves, such as the so-called rites of passage, rites of purification, and, above all, magic.

The agents of these actions of binding and loosing vary according to circumstances. They may be superhuman beings of the most diverse kinds, whether located at the time of origins (as, for example, the creator, the first man, the *dema,* the trickster, the culture hero, the totemic ancestor, and so on), or believed to be still acting in the present (as, for example, the supreme being, the earth mother, fetishes, spirits, ancestors, polytheistic gods, or the god of monotheistic religions). Or it may be ordinary mortals who bind and loose, especially those who belong to a specialized sacred group (priests, shamans, wizards, magicians, etc.). The materials with which the bond is made are extremely diverse but generally may be distinguished as either concrete or abstract. Equally numerous are the ends that the binding or loosing action is intended to serve, whether positive or negative. This variety has been well illustrated in the works of Arnold van Gennep, Gerardus van der Leeuw, and Mircea Eliade.

Scholarly interest in binding began in the first half of the nineteenth century, when scholars such as Jacob B. Listing (1847) and Peter Guthrie Tait (1879) became interested in the question of knots. It was James G. Frazer, however, who finally brought the problem to the attention of historians of religion in the first decade of the present century. In the wake of his studies of the concept of taboo and the binding action it exercised, Frazer (1911) saw the need to broaden the scope of his research to include the special type of restraint constituted by the bond as such, its varieties and its functions. Given Frazer's predominant interest in magic, it is not surprising that he interpreted bonds as magical impediments. Despite the problems involved with such an emphasis on the magical—itself inadequately conceived as prior to or even opposed to religion—Frazer's work had the merit of interpreting sacred bonds in terms of the specific historical circumstances in which they are found, showing that the significance of a bond is relative to the positive or negative nature of what it restrains. This latter aspect of Frazer's work unfortunately left little trace in the works of his successors, such as Isidor Scheftelowitz (1912) and Walter J. Dilling (1914). Today this historical dimension to the study of bonds and binding, initially opened up by the great English scholar, remains to be developed.

The less positive side of Frazer's theory, namely the emphasis on magic, has by contrast provided the direction for more recent studies. This can be seen in the case of Georges Dumézil. Dumézil's researches, carried out in the 1930s, were based upon studies of deities of the Vedic religion of ancient India, Varuṇa most especially, but also Mitra, Vṛtra, Indra, Yama, and Nirṛti. These deities were believed to possess snares or at least to be endowed with the ability to bind their enemies and ensnare evil human beings. Accepting the thesis of the magical value of binding *in toto* and uncritically, Dumézil identified a structure of magical binding within the royal function of ancient Indo-European culture, a function that was itself associated with magic.

Dumézil's findings were based largely on Indo-European cultures. A decade later, however, Eliade, in an elegant effort to reinterpret Dumézil's conclusions, demonstrated the presence of what he called the "binding complex" in other civilizations as well, both higher civilizations (for example, in the Semitic world) and in primitive ones, and on several different planes: cosmological, magical, religious, initiatory, metaphysical, and soteriological. Although he initially followed the Frazer-Dumézil line, Eliade soon departed from it, distancing himself from the conflicts over the presumed necessity of interpreting every binding action exclusively in terms of magic or in strict accordance with French trifunctionalism. Beyond the diverse historical forms assumed by the binding motif in the most diverse cultural surroundings, Eliade attempted to identify an archetypal form of binding that would find different realizations on an infinite variety of levels. In the process, he demonstrated that it was possible to interpret the various forms of binding in nonmagical terms. At the same time, however, his work was indicative of the problematic status that the question of binding continues to have in historical comparative studies. Although there are particular studies concerning this or that type of sacred bond that are founded on a rigorously historical basis, in general the scholarly world continues to address the issue merely on the phenomenological level, thereby leaving the question of the historical foundations of the binding motif unresolved.

On the properly historical level, however, it seems possible, and indeed necessary, to establish the precise relation between the sacred value of the bond and the type of reality that lies at the origin of this value; to explain why such a phenomenon arises, and under what circumstances.

The fact that sacred bonds are known in even the most archaic cultures suggests that we should seek an answer to these questions in primitive societies before confronting them on the level of higher civilizations, with their more abstract symbolism. To take only one example, an observation made by Raffaele Pettazzoni in his comparative study of the confession of sins contributes more to our understanding of the "snares" used by the Vedic god Varuṇa than does the sophisticated tri-functional theory of Dumézil. Pettazzoni noted how often primitive peoples try to concretize their sins in the form of knots, tied in various kinds of material (ropes, lianas, vegetable fibers, etc.). He went on to interpret the Vedic motif of binding as "the primitive idea of evil-sin as a fluid wrapping the sinner like the meshes of a net" (*La confessione dei peccati*, vol. 1, Bologna, 1929, p. 230).

It is characteristic of the religions of primitive peoples that sacred bonds, of whatever type they may be and whatever their function, are viewed in a way that is not at all dissimilar to the normal, concrete bonds used in the most varied circumstances of everyday life: the means by which a shaman attempts to "capture" the soul of a sick person to bring it back to the body is an ordinary lasso, of the type ordinarily used to stop a running animal or to prevent it from straying off. Similarly, among the Aranda, an ordinary rope represents the means by which the Tjimbarkna demons tie up at night men whom they want to harm. Akaanga, the lord of the dead for the Aranda inhabitants of Harvey Island, Australia, is believed to capture the deceased by means of a real net, of the kind used by fishermen. There are many such examples.

The same parallel between sacred and ordinary bonds is found in the mythologies of primitive peoples. Here the lassos, traps, nets, and so forth, with which the sun, moon, or clouds are captured, or with which one snares the spirits, are the same as those with which on other occasions poles are tied together in the construction of a hut, wild animals are captured, and fish caught. There is nothing extraordinary in these bonds, except for the increase in power that their use normally confers on the person who employs them.

These facts should lead us to reflect on the enormous importance that fibers used for weaving and spinning, ropes, lassos, nets, and other means of binding have for peoples with a technology that is still at a rudimentary level. Such simple materials and implements are needed for the capture and domestication of animals, and for making weapons, garments, utensils, containers, pottery, and so on. These are the tools and instruments by which the labor potential of *homo faber* can be significantly increased beyond its natural limits, so as to enable the social group to establish greater control over reality, especially over those sectors that most closely concern economic interests and that would otherwise be too difficult to master. There is nothing strange, therefore, in the constant tendency of primitive cultures to transpose the techniques and the tools used to perform a binding action onto a superhuman level. The main goal of this transposition is to strengthen their supposedly extraordinary nature and to place their beneficial effects under the care of the supernatural beings who are often believed to be the source of these marvels. In this way their use can also be protected from possible risks by means of appropriate ritual practices.

Spinning and weaving provide numerous examples of such transposition. These techniques in particular involve the activity of binding and tying (one thinks of the countless loops, weaves, and knots to be found in even a tiny piece of fabric). For example, among the Bambara of Mali, the spindle and the batten, originally the possessions of Faro, the lord of the waters, were granted by him to human beings, whom he also instructed in their use. Thus the first work of a weaver cannot be used, but must be thrown into the river in honor of the superhuman being. The Dogon, on the other hand, link the invention of spinning and weaving directly with the myth of the origin of the world. Among the Ashanti various sacred precautions are taken to protect weaving. It is usually exclusively reserved for men, or else for women who have passed menopause; the work cannot be begun or finished on Friday, the day on which, according to tradition, the use of weaving had been introduced into the land; menstruating wives of weavers must not touch the loom or speak to their husband for the entire duration of the period of impurity; and in the case of adultery with another weaver, a goat must be sacrificed on the loom. In the so-called weaving schools found among the Maori of New Zealand, the technical procedures and the sacred practices are taught at the same time. The sacred practices must be scrupulously observed throughout the work in order to increase the weaver's skill. Weavers must be initiated into the profession by a priest, and are required to follow various alimentary taboos and protect their work from the harmful gaze of strangers, in order to prevent the loss of their own inventiveness and mastery.

In addition to spinning and weaving, other specific binding actions, such as the working of fibers and wicker to produce ropes, baskets, nets, traps, and so forth, are projected onto the sacred plane. In the beginning they are the exclusive property of superhuman beings of various kinds, who decide at a certain point to transmit the practice to human beings. The Athapascan-speaking Wailaki of northwestern California relate that the culture hero Kettanagai taught people to weave ropes, baskets, and fishing nets after the flood. Among the Diegueño of southern California the art of working wicker through weaving was included in the comprehensive knowledge that exploded from the head of the primordial serpent and spread throughout the world. The Hopi, for their part, maintain that Spider Woman, a superhuman being connected for several reasons with spiders, and who had directly collaborated in creation, taught the Indians to spin and weave cotton. Among the eastern Pomo (north central California), Marunda first created men by weaving his own hair and, immediately thereafter, wicker; he then taught the art of working wicker to humanity.

The ever closer relationship that is being established by the comparative history of religions between the sphere of work and the sphere of the sacred in the explanation of the activity of binding may furnish us with the possibility of going back to quite precise and concrete historical roots, and to the corresponding economic substrata of all types of bonds, temporarily bypassing the complex and sophisticated symbolism with which they are often associated in higher civilizations. This more complex symbolism, once condemned to obscurity through the now outmoded label of "magical," may itself finally find a more fitting, definite, and substantial clarification.

Thus we may expect to find that behind the "snares" so skillfully manipulated by this or that god in the Indo-European, Indo-Iranian, or Semitic areas (zones with a pastoral economy in antiquity) in order to prevent deviations from the just order of things stand the actual snares (or lassos) with which the society of primitive stockbreeders, during their continual migrations in search of new pastures, maintained control over their herds, the almost unique source of their subsistence. Snares stood, therefore, as a precious guarantee of the proper course of reality.

See Also Knots; Webs and Nets.

Bibliography

For research on the extent to which binding is associated with religious activity, three works dating from the 1910s are still indispensable: James G. Frazer's *The Golden Bough*, 3d ed., rev. & enl., vol. 3, *Taboo and the Perils of the Soul* (London, 1911); Isidor Scheftelowitz's *Das Schlingen- und Netzmotiv im Glauben und Brauch der Völker* (Giessen, 1912); and Walter J. Dilling's "Knots," in the *Encyclopaedia of Religion and Ethics*, edited by James Hastings, vol. 7 (Edinburgh, 1914).

Rich in examples of the use of sacred bonds are Arnold van Gennep's *Les rites de passage* (Paris, 1909), translated as *The Rites of Passage* (Chicago, 1960); Gerardus van der Leeuw's *Phänomenologie der Religion* (Tübingen, 1933), translated as *Religion in Essence and Manifestation*, rev. ed. (New York, 1963); and Mircea Eliade's *Patterns in Comparative Religion* (New York, 1958). More detailed studies are two now-classic works of Georges Dumézil, *Ouranós-Váruna* (Paris, 1934) and *Mitra-Varuṇa*, 4th ed. (Paris, 1948), and Mircea Eliade's "The 'God Who Binds' and Symbolism of Knots," in his *Images and Symbols: Studies in Religious Symbolism* (New York, 1961), chap. 3.

Reinterpretations of the concept of magic in rigorously historical terms can be found in *Il mondo magico*, by Ernesto de Martino (Turin, 1948), and in *Magia: Studi di storia delle religioni in memoria di Raffaela Garosi*, edited by Paolo Xella et al. (Rome, 1976). Enrico Cerulli discusses the sublimation at the sacred level of the arts of spinning and weaving in "Industrie e tecniche," in *Ethnologica*, vol. 2, *Le opere dell'uomo*, edited by Vinigi Grottanelli (Milan, 1965). On the theme of binding action and bonds, see both Raffaele Pettazzoni's *Miti e leggende*, 4 vols. (Turin, 1948–1963), and G. M. Mullett's *Spider Woman Stories* (Tucson, 1979).

Giulia Piccaluga (1987)
Translated from Italian by Roger DeGaris

BIOETHICS. Bioethics as a discipline clearly did not begin fully developed, and its origins are somewhat unclear. Very remote origins can be traced to late medieval discussions in Roman Catholicism concerning what means were required to preserve life in the face of illness. These discussions, commented on by the majority of theologians, initiated the famous distinction between ordinary and extraordinary means of preserving life. The assumption was that all had an obligation to preserve their own lives because life was a gift of God and while humans exercised stewardship over life, they had no dominion over it. Thus the question became "does proper stewardship mandate doing everything possible to preserve life?" The clear consensus throughout the Middle Ages was that it did not: one did not need to be a hero and submit to any number of painful and marginally useful treatments, nor did one have to bankrupt one's self or one's family, nor did one have to move to a better climate, or seek out the best and most healthful foods. If one would be embarrassed by a physical examination, one could decline the exam. Thus began a long conversation over the problem of the ethical management of one's death.

In various religious communities this tradition continued in pastoral counseling: the provision of theological guidance to those in various crises, spiritual, moral, or medical. Pastoral counseling in some form was an element of all denominations, more formal in some and more individualized in others. But the reality of religious institutions both reflecting on and expressing their concern for the sick and dying ensured that questions of significance related to medical practice would be an important part of the tradition.

Thus in the United States, the real locus of the beginning of bioethics as a discipline, when questions about the application of new technologies in medicine began to come to the fore, particularly issues of death and dying—the use and removal of ventilators, the distribution of the scarce resource of the kidney dialysis machine—theologians were receptive and, because of the religious bioethics tradition, did not have to begin from square one. A conversation was already in place and new questions could be brought in and the conversation furthered.

The first formal structuring of bioethics took place at the Hastings Center—founded in 1971 and originally known as the Institute for the Study of Ethics and the Life Sciences. While these developments occurred under the direction of the center's founders, a philosopher and a psychiatrist, the majority of the individuals in the first groups invited to meetings were theologians or people in religious studies, or clergy. While the perspectives brought to the table were sectarian, the discussions were surprising ecumenical and nondoctrinaire. This mix of participants also characterized the first Presidential Bioethics Commission.

Philosophers were also part of this early mix but their entry was more difficult, perhaps because many philosophers were, at that time, trained in the analytic tradition and were more interested in problems of theory. Thus the turn to practice was a little complicated and was not fully validated until the development of the field called applied philosophy, another birth accomplished only under difficult circumstances. While theory has always been part of theological reflection, people in theology and the ministry in particular were used to discussion of cases and were immediately attuned to the specifics of the problems brought to bioethics.

Following the foundation of the Hastings Center and then of the Kennedy Institute of Ethics, bioethics saw a blossoming of undergraduate courses and bioethics centers nationwide. These centers were staffed by individuals who had theological or philosophical training, but were typically not versed in the sciences or the new developments in medicine and technology. Thus one of the first functions of both of these bioethics centers was to offer summer courses in the new field to get people scientifically and technically up to speed. Eventually these people found their way into medical schools and programs in medical ethics and medical humanities became an established part of the medical curriculum.

These developments were quickly followed by the creation of graduate courses, journals, conferences, graduate programs, and a professional society: the American Society of Bioethics and Humanities. This society, as the premier professional bioethics organization, is reflective of major changes in the field. Only a minority of the society's members comes from theology or religious studies backgrounds. The majority comes from the social sciences, medicine, literature, anthropology, and so on. Although there have been sessions on religion at the society's meetings, they are not a standard feature of conventions. People in theology or religious studies seem to do much of their professional work in bioethics through special sessions or programs in associations such as the American Academy of Religion, the Society of Christian Ethics, the Society of Jewish Ethics, and other denominational professional societies.

While many individuals at work in the field of bioethics are theologians or in the field of religious studies, the discipline seems to have moved from these to other academic disciplines as new questions are examined and new discussions established. This shift may also reflect a growing secularization and pluralism within American culture and a greater interest in the public policy dimensions of bioethical debates, debates in which religious perspectives are seen as particularly divisive. Thus the religious perspective, though the inspiration for many of the early discussions in bioethics, has now moved to the side as new disciplines bring their perspectives forward.

A Shift in Context. Probably one of the largest shifts in bioethics has been from clinical perspectives to public policy issues. The early decades of bioethics were centered on the clinical experience of the physician-patient relationship. In part this was because of the case-oriented nature of bioethics' theological background, but it was also because the physician-patient relationship was the dominant locus of the practice of medicine. Here the discussion, from both theological and philosophical perspectives, centered on the values of the patient and the physician, how they complemented each other, how they clashed, whose would take priority, and how were both of their value sets to be respected in practice. In these discussions, principles were appealed to as well, whether theological or philosophical. But the focus of the discussion was always the individual patient and the individual physician. Both theology and philosophy were comfortable with this framework.

The problem now is that both the field and the critical questions in bioethics have moved from a primary emphasis on the physician-patient dyad to how that dyad is understood within the context of a variety of public policy issues, relating to such complexities as the variety of health insurance plans, hospital organization, research agendas, the funding of public and private health-care delivery systems, and the requirements of care for a variety of specialized populations: the newborn, the disabled, the incompetent, the aging. A major focus is now on what could be termed institutional bioethics, in that the questions have to do with issues of justice within the system of health care itself and with what services are available and to whom and how are they delivered.

Needless to say, such questions give rise to a variety of competing values-based positions regarding priority of needs, equitable distribution of resources, and ease of access to various programs. While religious communities are both providers of health care and participants in these discussions, the public debate is complicated by the presence of a variety of competing actors: insurance companies, HMOs, advocacy groups for various diseases and programs, and the Social Security, Medicare, and Medicaid programs to name just a few. While all recognize that values are at the center of the debate, the pluralistic nature of U.S. society is a complicating factor precisely because of the competition of values originating from so many different communities.

While it is the case that a variety of forms of national health care exist in many other countries, many of these plans are beginning to experience crises stemming from the need for increased funding, a demand for improved services and better and more rapid access to them, and the pressures put on such systems by the needs of an expanding population of aging citizens. Additionally, due to recent immigration into Europe, the problems associated with pluralism are beginning to be experienced there, and this will undoubtedly have an impact on various national health-care systems. Many of the debates in the United States will soon be part of the discussion in Europe.

EMBRYONIC STEM CELL RESEARCH: AMERICAN PERSPECTIVES. One particularly contentious debate in the field of bioethics concerns the question of at what developmental stage human life becomes subject to morally and legally mandated protections. In the United States, this debate was brought into focus by the 1973 U.S. Supreme Court case *Roe v. Wade.* This decision decriminalized abortion in the first trimester, permitted some state regulation of abortion within the second trimester, and permitted more regulation in the final trimester. It set off both a firestorm of debates and about 1.3 million abortions per year in the United States, though these figures vary by the year. The debate has been complicated by the introduction of a variety of fetal diagnostic technologies, including preimplantation genetic diagnosis, and of prenatal technologies such as amniocentesis and ultrasound. Additionally, part of the practice of in vitro fertilization (IVF) is the freezing of embryos not immediately used to achieve a pregnancy. Their status and disposition has been the subject of moral, religious, clinical, court, and public policy debates. Finally, given the possibilities of embryonic stem cell research, new questions are being raised: can human embryos be generated expressly for research purposes, are human embryos generated by cloning morally the same as those generated in the customary way, and might frozen embryos be used in this research? The public policy of the Bush administration enunciated in August 2002 was a political finesse that permitted federally supported research on already existing lines of cells derived from embryos, but prohibited the creation of any new cell lines for research from either embryos in storage in IVF clinics or embryos generated expressly for such research. Originally scientists thought that there might be some sixty-three such cell lines available for research but the actual number of useable lines is around ten. Many hailed this decision as an appropriate compromise that permitted some research to go forward but also protected human life by prohibiting the future destruction of embryos for this project. Additionally, in 2003 and 2004, the states of California and New Jersey passed legislation permitting embryonic stem cell research, thus setting a precedent for other resolutions regarding the permissibility of such research as well as the funding of it.

In general, religious communities in the United States have varied considerably in their reaction to this solution. The most conservative is the Roman Catholic community, which prohibits absolutely any direct abortion or any procedure that involves killing the embryo, though it does permit research designed to benefit the fetus. This leads to the position that any research predicated upon the destruction of human embryos is totally prohibited, regardless of whether the cell lines are already in existence or generated and destroyed for a specific research project. This position is shared by the Orthodox Bishops of America for precisely the same reason: the sacredness of human life from its inception. The other religious denominations typically approve of some abortions under certain circumstances, though this moral approval is given reluctantly.

Many other denominations tend to be conservative on the use of the embryo in research, typically arguing against the embryo's being reduced to an object and its possible commodification. Officials in the Methodist Church have suggested a moratorium on embryonic stem cell research and already deplore the use of research that produces what they call waste embryos. The Presbyterian Church, which both recognizes the moral status of the embryo/fetus and also supports a woman's right to abortion, affirms the use of fetal tissue and embryonic stem cells from surplus embryos from IVF for research that could lead to lifesaving breakthrough in medicine. They require a proportion between the significance of the research and the destruction of the embryo.

Judaism affirms the traditional doctrine of stewardship by acknowledging that our bodies are on loan to us from God. This then generates a corresponding obligation to seek cures for diseases. However, in Judaism, as in Christianity, one finds a variety of positions. The more liberal position argues that because abortions are permitted, based on the Talmudic teaching that for the first forty days the fetus is as water, one could argue that the destruction of the fetus is not murder. Such destruction would be possible as one way of fulfilling the obligation to seek cures for serious diseases. Other experts within Judaism are more conservative in their position on abortion. Therefore, they do not support the destruction of embryos for research. Because of their concern for protecting human life, these experts would limit such research with stringent regulations. Still others respond that such limitations on research, though intended to protect human life, also erect barriers to curing disease, relieving pain and suffering, and promoting health.

Public policy implications. This debate has complicated the public policy process of deciding on whether embryos can be used in research in at least two ways. First, there is great controversy over who is appointed to various commissions. Second, there is debate within the commissions themselves. And both are subsets of the critical litmus test in U.S. politics: one's position on the moral status of the human embryo. The goal in appointing national commissions is to achieve balance or adequate representation of particular positions, especially those that represent the main constituencies of the one doing the appointing. That process then creates problems for the commission in its deliberations, frequently manifest by lopsided votes or minority reports, or by the final recommendations not being accepted or being left to languish. The main problem is that the politicization of the process inhibits genuine debate and research that might prove profitable for the country as a whole. Additionally, while the individuals chosen for such panels or commissions are generally qualified, the main criterion guiding their selection is their advocacy of a particular viewpoint.

EMBRYONIC STEM CELL RESEARCH: EUROPEAN PERSPECTIVES. In Europe the situation is somewhat different and is a function of the developing policies of the European Union (EU) and of how the legislation of individual countries within the EU relate to them. The situation is also complicated by the political situations and religious traditions of various countries. And the situation is very dynamic.

The nub of the issue is the question of whether human embryos can be generated for research or whether only surplus embryos from IVF clinics can be used. In November 2003, the European Parliament, in a 298-242 vote with 21 abstentions, voted to permit the use of EU funds for experimenting on human embryos that were no older than fourteen days and were from IVF clinics. In the Parliament's Environmental Committee, amendments to ban human embryonic stem cell research were blocked. The European Union Industry Committee, in a 28-22 vote with 2 abstentions, permitted the use of such cells for research under strict conditions. In addition, this committee stated that the funding should depend both on the contents of the research proposals and the legal framework of the individual country. Additionally, the committee ruled that priority should be given to adult stem cells; it also permitted the funding of research using embryonic or fetal cells from spontaneous or therapeutic abortions. In December 2003, the EU voted not to permit the use of EU money on research using new human embryos.

With respect to individual members of the EU early in the twenty-first century, Belgium, Denmark, Finland, Greece, the Netherlands, Sweden, and the United Kingdom permit taking cells from surplus embryos for research. However, Austria, Germany, France, Ireland, and, under some circumstances, Spain prohibit such obtaining of these cells. Luxembourg, Italy, and Portugal have no specific legislation as of 2004. Nonetheless, Italy is proposing legislation to prohibit any research on generating embryos for research and the destruction of human embryos. Spain, however, appears to be ready to permit obtaining cells from surplus embryos from IVF if donor consent is obtained. Germany permits the use of human embryos for research only if the cells have been imported and if the research is critical and no alternatives to human embryonic stem cells are available.

Background. In Europe in general, there has been relatively strong resistance to a variety of forms of genetic engineering, whether applied to humans, animals, or crops. This movement has been particularly strong in Germany, an understandable position given the eugenic dimension of the National Socialist Party. Other countries, including Ireland, have constitutions that give strong protection to early human life. England permits both cloning for therapeutic purposes (generating embryos for therapy in the donor of the cell) and the use in research of human embryos and cells from them so long as embryos are no more than fourteen days old.

The Commission of European Bishops' Conferences has criticized the actions of the EU with respect to stem cell research. The conference recommends the prohibition of EU funds for research on human embryos and embryonic stem cells primarily because of the intrinsic value of human life at all stages of development. Thus such material should not be used for research, regardless of any good ends to which the research might be put. Additionally the bishops argue that there is yet to be found any clear evidence for any therapeutic benefits from such research.

The cultural and religious situation in Europe is moving from positions of relative homogeneity to that of pluralism. This is due to population changes resulting from immigration, the changing status and level of political power of the Catholic Church in historically Catholic countries, and pressure from various groups, both governmental and private, to advance the participation of the EU in genetic research. At stake are religious and cultural values as well as vast economic consequences. The final resolution of the specific issue of the use of human embryos in research as well as the larger question of the reconfiguration of religious and cultural values in the EU is yet to be determined. But this resolution will present a major case study in how such resolutions are brokered.

CONCLUSIONS. The beginnings of bioethics occurred within the context of religion broadly understood. Various denominations had pursued bioethical questions for long periods of their history, but typically within the context of pastoral counseling or the resolution of particular cases at the bedside. As bioethics became more of an academic discipline, the orientation shifted from a religious perspective to a more philosophical one. However, as public policy issues related to bioethics began to be debated, religious issues came to the fore once again, both in terms of the content of policy proposals and in terms of the selection process that determined the membership of bioethics committees.

In the United States at the present time, there is a significant debate over the place of religion in discussions of public policy. But the terms of the debate are far from clear. Some buttress their arguments by appealing to the so-called traditional Christian heritage of the United States. Others point out the difficulties of that position in light of the United States' current religious heterogeneity. Yet others argue that religion is being marginalized in favor of a secularized society through attempts to eliminate religious voices from the debate. Others still argue that religious positions or institutions are being favored by the government through voucher programs and public funding of some religiously based charities. Just who is on what side of the debate seems occasionally to vary from case to case, the result being an increasing cacophony in the public arena.

What is clear is that, in Western culture, religion is important for many citizens and that believers expect some degree of coherence between their beliefs and their social life. Religion is not simply a private belief system; it has personal and social behavioral implications. Additionally, we assume that religious bodies, as well as individual representatives of those bodies, have the right to participate in public debate over public policy. And while in theory many will agree that one's religious beliefs should not be a litmus test for participation in office or committees, those beliefs are in fact becoming increasingly important in nominating processes and elections.

Nonetheless, bioethics should not shed or attempt to eliminate its religious heritage. That heritage has been exceptionally helpful in the analysis and resolution of many questions in bioethics. What needs to be added to this heritage is a new chapter of ecumenical reasoning and of dialogue between all religious traditions. What is also needed is a focused reflection on the process of conducting public policy debates, with respect to the religious traditions represented, to the merging of these traditions, and to the public presentations of the positions of these traditions. The contribution of these traditions to the public debate is important not only because of the inherent value of their positions, but also because religious viewpoints may bring out or highlight facets of the public policy debate that might be missed or undervalued by others. Such a contribution will be made, however, only when the religious traditions can articulate these positions in a language and style accessible to a broad public. This is the challenge for the new religiously based bioethics.

Bibliography

Catholic News Service. "European Bishops Oppose EU Funding of Stem-Cell Research." Available at www.cwnews.com/news.

CellNews. "EU to Fund Stem-Cell Research Despite Split." Available at www.geocities.com/giantfideli.

Cole-Turner, Ronald, ed. *Beyond Cloning: Religion and the Remaking of Humanity.* Harrisburg, Pa., 2001.

Council of Europe. "Convention for the Protection of Human Rights and Dignity of the Human Being with Regard to the Application of Biology and Medicine: Convention of Human Rights and Biomedicine." Available at www.conventions.coe.int/treaty/en/treaties.

Davis, Dena S., and Laurie Zoloth, eds. *Notes from a Narrow Ridge: Religion and Bioethics.* Hagerstown, Md., 1999.

Hanson, Mark J., ed. *Claiming Power over Life: Religion and Biotechnology Policy.* Washington, D.C., 2001.

Holland, Suzanne, Karen Lebacqz, and Laurie Zoloth, eds. *The Human Embryo Stem Cell Debate: Science, Ethics, and Public Policy.* Cambridge, Mass., 2001.

Mackler, Aaron L. *Introduction to Jewish and Catholic Bioethics: A Comparative Analysis.* Washington, D.C., 2003.

Peters, Ted. *For the Love of Children: Genetic Technology and the Future of the Family.* Louisville, Ky., 1996.

Post, Stephen G., editor-in-chief. *The Encyclopedia of Bioethics.* 3d ed. New York, 2003.

Shannon, Thomas A., and James J. Walter. *The New Genetic Medicine: Theological and Ethical Reflections.* Lanham, Md., 2003.

Verhey, Allen, ed. *Religion and Medical Ethics: Looking Back, Looking Forward.* Grand Rapids, Mich., 1996.

Walter, Jennifer K., and Eran P. Klein, eds. *The Story of Bioethics: From Seminal Works to Contemporary Exploration.* Washington, D.C., 2003.

Thomas A. Shannon (2005)

BIOGRAPHY. The subject here is best termed *sacred biography,* which most precisely designates the written accounts of lives of persons deemed to be holy, although its usage is extended also to oral traditions concerning such figures. The reason for allowing this wider usage is clear: in most contexts it was oral traditions that not only preceded but also largely shaped the later, written versions. The category of sacred biography is bounded on one side by mythology—that is, narratives concerning gods and other beings thought to be supernatural—and on the other side by biography, efforts to reconstruct credible accounts of the lives of ordinary human beings. It might also be defined as a genre that mixes myth and biography: unlike the former, its subjects are held even today to have actually lived but, unlike the latter, the received versions of their lives are often heavily mythologized.

Whereas mythology will usually tell only of random deeds of deities in a largely episodic and nonconsecutive manner, the subjects of a sacred biography will tend to be treated as persons whose life stories need to be told as discrete and continuous lives. The subject of a sacred biography will tend to be treated as someone whose life story can be told from birth to death and, to that degree at least, as it would be treated in a secular biography. The difference from the latter, however, lies in the degree to which such a subject will be represented as carrying out a divinely planned mission, being the possessor of a "call" or visions authenticating such a mission, and having either infallible knowledge or supernatural powers. Individual instances of this genre differ in the degree to which they exemplify either the empirical or the mythological sides of the spectrum, but some degree of combination is present in all. Most sacred biographies are written either about the founders of the major religions or about saints—in which case this rubric overlaps with hagiography. In order to illustrate the genre our consideration here will focus upon sacred biographies of the founders.

History of the Designation "Sacred Biography." The detection or designation of sacred biography as a genre of oral and written literature with its own structure and rules was initially a concomitant of that nineteenth-century scholarship which, under the aegis of positivist expectations and the use of an objective historical method, had sought to disentangle the incontrovertible "facts" of the life of Jesus of Nazareth from the overlay both of pious fabrications and Christological dogma. The intention of this process of winnowing and reconstruction was captured best in Albert Schweitzer's phrase "the quest of the historical Jesus." To some extent Schweitzer's work, while not terminating the search for verifiable facts, did signal the end of the nineteenth-century scholars' confidence that they could simply circumvent or dispense with the piety and Christology of the early Christian community and thereby disclose the "facts" of Jesus' life. When twentieth-century scholarship abandoned that part of the earlier "quest," it became possible to see that the Gospels are not merely flawed or failed biographies but a form of devotional literature of the early church, and, to that extent, examples of a genre with its own intentions and norms. As a result scholars came to see the rubric of sacred biography as discrete and legitimate for the first time. They recognized that the documents in question ought not merely to be sifted through for the purpose of separating fact from fiction, but that they had to be subjected to the more sophisticated type of analysis known as "form criticism."

With this perspective such studies could also become comparative and cross-cultural for the first time. Important in this development was Martin Dibelius's *Die Formgeschichte des Evangeliums* (Tübingen, 1919), translated as *From Tradition to Gospel* (New York, 1935). Dibelius referred to a "law" at work in such biographies and noted that there existed "many points of agreement between Buddha-legends and Jesus-legends" as well as between the saints of otherwise very different traditions. He claimed that this was a "law of biographical analogy leading to formulations constantly renewed" rather than a pattern that arose from cultural borrowing or diffusion. As examples he noted that various traditions separately articulate "a fixed idea of the life of the holy man: such a man may neither be born nor die without the significance of the event being proclaimed from heaven." Likewise his calling is announced in his youth and he has divine powers at his disposal throughout his life.

Although Dibelius arrived at this formulation through his analysis of the literary form of the Christian Gospels, his attribution of intrinsic value to sacred biography implicitly recognized that the early Christian community had quite properly had the decisive role in shaping the account of the life of Jesus according to its own ideals and expectations; modern scholars neither could nor should simply circumvent the contributions of the church in an attempt to reconstruct an "objective" biography of its founder.

This shift in attitude coincided with the embryonic development of the sociology of religion. Joachim Wach interpreted and applied Max Weber's concept of charisma and its routinization in his *Sociology of Religion* (Chicago, 1944). He discussed in some detail the founders of the great religions and took note that the term *founder* "does not denote any intrinsic quality or activity of the personality but refers to the historical and sociological effect of his charisma." He went on to state that "virtually all the founders became objects of religious veneration themselves." Although Wach tended to give causal priority to the founder and his teaching, he went further than others before him in recognizing an element of *reciprocal* generation in this phenomenon: at least in a sociological sense, the religious community creates its founder almost as much as the founder creates the community. Therefore, the message of the founder will often tend to be "implemented by miraculous acts, such as healing, feeding, transforming matter, etc." In this "hagiographical development" will be illustrated "the specific personal charisma which designates the man of God in an unmistakable and uninterchangeable way."

Wach, who brought a detailed knowledge of many religious traditions to his comparative efforts, tried as much as possible to retain the particularity of the separate traditions. His focus on the social matrix of religious traditions also led him to emphasize the relationship that each founder of a major religion had to his own circle of disciples. His 1924 essay on this topic shows how central it was in his thinking (Eng. trans., "Master and Disciple: Two Religio-Sociological Studies," *Journal of Religion* 42, 1962, pp. 1–21). The importance of this essay is that it reconstructs the psychological and social interaction between a master and his disciples—precisely the element that would seem to have frequently been the prelude to a later mythic embellishment of the deceased master's life in the form of sacred biography.

Although Mircea Eliade did not specifically elaborate a new theory of sacred biography, his discussions of the paradigmatic and exemplary nature of sacred time had a deep impact upon many scholars working on biographical materials of the past. This influence is clearly evident in the most comprehensive study of this topic to date, namely, *The Biographical Process: Studies in the History and Psychology of Religion*, edited by Frank E. Reynolds and Donald Capps (The Hague, 1976).

Sacred Biography and the Great Founders. The crucial importance of the concept of sacred biography in modern scholarship is that it has forced attention to certain kinds of materials that had tended to be slighted, dismissed, or regarded as uninteresting to intellectual historians and positivist text critics. It acknowledges that the formation of the major religions and religiously based philosophies was not merely the result of individual geniuses and their ideas but equally the product of social groupings and the projection of their shared ideals onto that person who, precisely through this reciprocity, was coming to be regarded as the "founder" of the new community. In the section above we looked at the process through which the Christian Gospels came to be gradually recognized as such a form of sacred biography. But a similar process was present in the formation of the received "lives" of the founders of the other major religions as well, and we focus here upon the Buddha, Muḥammad, and Confucius by way of illustration.

Although the scholarly study of Buddhism in nineteenth-century Europe made great strides in linguistic and textual matters, the recognition of the received biographies of the Buddha as a form of sacred biography was comparatively late. The reason for this was that scholarship on the life of the Buddha tended to oscillate between the two positions just beyond the boundaries of the sacred biography spectrum: pure mythology on one side and "factual" biography on the other. Advocates of the former, scholars working mostly with Sanskrit texts, saw the Buddha's life story as a variety of myth—solar myth in this case. The two principal proponents of this view were Émile Senart in his *Essai sur la légende du Bouddha, son caractère et ses origines* (Paris, 1882) and Hendrik Kern in his *Der Buddhismus und seine Geschichte in Indien* (Leipzig, 1882–1884). Their position was strenuously opposed by T. W. Rhys Davids and others in England who, working with and usually trusting the antiquity and reliability of the newly discovered Pali texts, were convinced that, with the carrying out of requisite analyses, the authentic life of the Buddha could be extracted from these sources. Although their materials were many and various, the scholars of the London school of Pali studies saw their task as different from that of their counterparts working on the life of Jesus, inasmuch as the Pali texts tended to present the Buddha—especially in his adult years—as an unparalleled but fully human teacher, not as an incarnate deity performing miracles. In that sense their texts themselves resembled ordinary biography much more than mythology.

Posed in this way between the alternatives of myth on one side and ordinary biography on the other, scholars working on the life of the Buddha had difficulty recognizing the presence and integrity of sacred biography in their texts. Only with the collapse of the solar-myth hypothesis and the gradual recognition that the Pali sources were more complex and mythicized than had been previously assumed did it finally become possible to see the life of the Buddha as a variety of sacred biography. Edward J. Thomas's *The Life of Buddha as Legend and History* (London, 1927) makes some tentative steps in that direction. By the middle of the twentieth century scholars had generally accepted the fact that, even though the Buddha had existed and had lived within a detectable time frame, it was impossible to ignore the role that the ideals of the early *saṃgha* (the Buddhist order) had played in shaping and elaborating the received narratives of their founder's life. To that extent the impassable presence of sacred biography has been recognized even though individual scholars differ considerably in their analyses of the process of its composition and its movement from oral tradition to scripture.

Once the sacred biographies of the Buddha could be seen not merely as excrescences to be scaled off but as research topics with their own intellectual importance, the relationship of these to the specific cultural matrix of India could be studied as well. In particular, the Indian presupposition that life involves multiple lives could be positively assessed: the Jātakas, tales of the earlier lives of the Buddha, could be studied as part of the later sacred biographical tradition.

Quite soon after the death of Muḥammad in 632—at least by the eighth century—biographies appeared that demonstrated the growing tendency to idealize the Prophet as sinless and capable of performing miracles. Throughout most subsequent history the received accounts of the life of Muḥammad were clearly in the genre of sacred biography. Beginning with William Muir's *The Life of Mahomet and History of Islam, to the Era of Hegira* (London, 1861), this view was challenged, especially by Ignácz Goldziher's *Muhammedanische Studien* (Halle, 1888–1890). The Qurʾān itself was subjected to analyses in order to locate reliable data for the reconstruction of what European scholars regarded as a verified account of the life of Muḥammad. This was much to the consternation of Muslims, for whom the Qurʾān is special and divinely derived revelation, not a source among other sources for a critical study of the Prophet's life. The first reaction to this approach on the part of Muslim scholars themselves came in the last quarter of the nineteenth century in the form of many new biographies of Muḥammad, works clearly intended to state the facts of his life correctly from within the faith-framework of Islam. Although these biographies did tend to stress the prophetic in Muḥammad's life and to play down the miraculous, to many Western scholars they nevertheless seem continuous in some sense with the classical sacred biographies' tendency to idealization.

Within this context the study of sacred biographies of Muḥammad has been relatively difficult. Tor Andrae, best known for his *Mohammed: The Man and His Faith* (London, 1936), contributed earlier and substantially to this topic in his *Die person Muhammeds in lehre und glauben seiner gemeinde* (Stockholm, 1918). Distinguished by its skillful use of comparative materials, Andrae's book amply demonstrated the growth of legends that formed over time around the person of the Prophet—so much so that as a superhuman exemplary figure he eventually came to have status almost equal to that of the Qurʾān for some Muslims. More recent studies include *Divine Word and Prophetic Word in Early Islam* by William A. Graham (Paris, 1977), a work that uses and adapts Eliade's conception of "sacred time" to insist that later Muslims looked back on the whole period of Muḥammad's life as such a paradigmatic age even though it was historical time as well. Graham notes that, although passages in the Qurʾān distinguish mortal Muḥammad from immortal God, the tradition also includes materials showing that "the divine authority of [Muḥammad's] role as God's Apostle was a major factor in the tendency to divinize his person" and that as such he became "the paradigm for Muslim life" (p. 23). In an important essay Earle H. Waugh focuses upon later (Ṣūfī) materials but also uses Eliade's studies of shamanism to analyze the legends concerning Muḥammad's Miʿrāj as a form of shamanic ascension. He also explores the exemplary role of these legends in the spiritual life of individual Ṣūfīs ("Following the Beloved: Muhammed as Model in the Ṣūfī Tradition," in Reynolds and Capps, 1976, pp. 63–85). Perhaps what makes the study of sacred biography in the Islamic tradition both difficult and fascinating is the fact that its very existence—suggesting as it does the apotheosis of the founder—could only exist and develop in some state of tension with Islamic orthodoxy's insistence upon the uncompromisable transcendence of God.

The study of sacred biography as it exists in the Chinese cultural context has presented scholars with very different kinds of problems. Because there remain serious questions about any historical fact underlying the accounts of the life of Laozi, the reputed founder of Daoism, it is best here to restrict our consideration to Confucius (511–479 BCE). If sacred biography is characterized by the forging together of myth and history, accounts of the life of Confucius certainly tend to remain closer to the history side of this combination. In addition, since the *Analects* (*Lun-yü*) clearly shows that Confucius himself turned attention away from the gods and spirits and toward man and society, modern scholars, sensing this way of thought to be remarkably consonant with the temper of the modern West, have tended to find the subsequent sacralization of Confucius within China to be intellectually uninteresting at best and reprehensible at worst. It is not incidental, therefore, that the latter of these views informs the approach taken in what remains to date the most important and influential biographical study, H. G. Creel's *Confucius: The Man and the Myth* (New York, 1949), republished as *Confucius and the Chinese Way* (New York, 1960).

There was indeed a tradition of sacred biography that grew up around the figure of Confucius, but his apotheosis was shaped by distinctly Chinese cultural norms. This is shown in the fact that the Master's apotheosis was expressed through the extension of his sagacity rather than his power; in a work such as the *K'ung-tzu chia yü* (Discourses of the Confucian school) of the third century BCE, Confucius is presented as infallible, not as a miracle worker. In a similar fashion the *Tso chuan*, which was composed around 300 BCE, attributes to him not supernatural deeds but knowledge of arcane and supernatural matters—things that seem rather far removed from the Confucius of the *Analects*. Also in the *Tso chuan* his lineage is presented as derived from that of the Sage-Kings of archaic times; some scholars such as D. C. Lau (in his translation *The Analects*, London, 1979) do not find this exceptionable, but Creel judged it to be so. If it was, in fact, part of the developing sacred biography of Confucius, it also shows the imprint of the pattern of the culture. In subsequent centuries, especially in the writings of what was called the New Text school, Confucius was viewed as having received a mandate from Heaven and was often also treated as a supernatural being (See Donald J. Munro's *The Concept of Man in Early China*, Stanford, 1969, p. 40).

The cult of Confucius increased over the centuries, often to the neglect of his writings. As late as the early twentieth century Kang Yuwei (1858–1927) advocated Confucianism as a state religion for China. Although much less work has been done on Confucius than on the other founders considered above, the tradition of reverence for him as a founder presents difficult but important problems for any theory of the nature of sacred biography. It demonstrates that, whatever tendency may exist for sacred biography to develop around a figure who comes to be recognized as a religious founder, that development occurs in distinctive *cultural* patterns. Confucius's life is certainly presented as a paradigmatic one, but he is the exemplar of the teacher and sage. There seem to be specific cultural restraints—perhaps even derived from the doctrinal content of the *Analects* itself to the exfoliation of the mythic dimension in this case. Wach's explication of the master-disciple relationship may well be the most useful methodological tool to apply in connecting the sacred biographies of Confucius with those of the other founders of the great religions.

Recent Directions in Scholarship. Current scholarship shows a marked tendency to focus upon the varieties of sacred biographical composition found within a specific cultural context. The research tradition that began it all—namely, the one initially concerned with the Gospels and the quest for the historical Jesus—remains in the forefront in terms of detailed and innovative studies. The scope has been widened to include a variety of types of hagiography and sacred biography found throughout the Hellenistic period extending to late antiquity. Although Eliade's point about sacred biographies being paradigmatic and exemplary is widely accepted and employed, there is increasing attention to both intertextuality in these matters and to the particularity of special kinds of idealized figures within a given cultural context. One example is the hypothesis that there exists a connection between the Gospels and the aretalogies of the Greco-Roman period—proposed especially by Morton Smith in his "Prolegomena to a Discussion of Aretalogies, Divine Men, the Gospels, and Jesus" (*Journal of Biblical Literature* 90, 1971, pp. 174–199) and Jonathan Z. Smith in his "Good News Is No News: Aretalogy and Gospel" (in *Christianity, Judaism, and Other Greco-Roman Cults*, edited by Jacob Neusner, Leiden, 1975, vol. 1, pp. 21–38).

Also important is the growing attention to the combination of religious with sociopolitical aspirations in every specific community that projected its ideals onto its founder or its saints. Not only the specific social matrix of the community that shaped its sacred biographies but also the history of such popular piety deserves attention. In his critique of the "two-tiered model" that has long relegated popular piety to the inferior status of something that is always and everywhere the same, Peter Brown (*The Cult of the Saints: Its Rise and Function in Latin Christianity*, Chicago, 1981) charts a direction that could be profitably followed by students of sacred biography generally. Another important new study—again focused on the Greco-Roman world—is Patricia Cox's *Biography in Late Antiquity: A Quest for the Holy Man* (Berkeley, 1983). Especially valuable is her discussion of paradigms of the divine sage in that period.

Aside from Frank E. Reynolds and Donald Capps's *The Biographical Process* and Michael A. William's *Charisma and Sacred Biography* (1982), real comparative work on this genre seems nonexistent in recent literature. (This is in keeping with the concentration of recent studies upon intertextuality and the continuities within a specific cultural area.) Perhaps after this phase of scholarship has attained its objectives, new energies and techniques can again be directed toward comparative work on sacred biography.

SEE ALSO Autobiography; Buddha; Confucius; Heroes; Jesus; Muḥammad; Myth; Oral Tradition; and Sainthood; Schweitzer, Albert.

BIBLIOGRAPHY

Brown, Peter. *The Making of Late Antiquity.* Cambridge, Mass., 1978.

Dungan, David L., and David R. Cartlidge, eds. and trans. *Sourcebook of Texts for the Comparative Study of the Gospels.* 4th ed. Missoula, Mont., 1974. See part 1, "Selections of Popular Religious Biographies."

Hadas, Moses, and Morton Smith. *Heroes and Gods: Spiritual Biographies in Antiquity.* Freeport, N.Y., 1970.

Jaspers, Karl. *Socrates, Buddha, Confucius, Jesus: The Paradigmatic Individuals.* New York, 1962.

Reynolds, Frank E., and Donald Capps, eds. *The Biographical Process: Studies in the History and Psychology of Religion.* The Hague, 1976. Includes an extensive bibliography on this and related topics. See especially Joseph M. Kitagawa's "Kūkai as Master and Savior" (pp. 319–341) and my "The Death and 'Lives' of the Poet-Monk Saigyo: The Genesis of a Buddhist Sacred Biography" (pp. 343–361).

Scholem, Gershom. *Sabbatai Sevi: The Mystical Messiah, 1626–1676.* Princeton, 1973.

Waugh, Earle H. "Images of Muḥammad in the Work of Iqbal: Tradition and Alterations." *History of Religions* 23 (1983): 156–168.

Williams, Michael A., ed. *Charisma and Sacred Biography.* Chico, Calif., 1982.

Wright, Arthur F. "Biography and Hagiography: Huei-chiao's Lives of Eminent Monks." In *Silver Jubilee Volume of the Zinbun-Kagaku-Kenkyūsho,* pp. 383–432. Kyoto, 1954.

Wright, Arthur F. "Sui Yang-Ti: Personality and Stereotype." In his *Confucianism and Chinese Civilization,* pp. 158–187. New York, 1964.

New Sources

Ashton, Gail. *The Generation of Identity in Late Medieval Hagiography: Speaking the Saint.* New York, 2000.

Greer, Allan, and Jodi Bilinkoff, eds. *Colonial Saints: Discovering the Holy in the Americas, 1500–1800.* New York, 2003.

Hahn, Cynthia J. *Portrayed on the Heart: Narrative Effect in Pictorial Lives of Saints from the Tenth through the Fifteenth Century.* Berkeley, 2001.

Heffernan, Thomas J. *Sacred Biography: Saints and Their Biographies in the Middle Ages.* New York, 1988.

Mooney, Catherine M., ed. *Gendered Voices: Medieval Saints and Their Interpreters.* Philadelphia, 1999.

Schober, Juliane, ed. *Sacred Biography in the Buddhist Traditions of South and Southeast Asia.* Honolulu, 1997.

Sharpe, Richard. *Medieval Irish Saints' Lives: An Introduction to Vitae Sanctorum Hiberniae.* New York, 1991.

Szarmach, Paul. *Holy Men and Holy Women: Old English Prose saints' Lives and Their Contexts.* Albany, 1996.

WILLIAM R. LAFLEUR (1987)
Revised Bibliography

BIRDS are primarily the epiphanies of the gods and spirits, but they also appear as messengers of the heavenly divine beings. They announce new situations in advance and serve as guides. Moreover, birds symbolize man's soul or spirit as it is released from the body in ecstasy or in death; the bird is a symbol of absolute freedom and transcendence of the soul from the body, of the spiritual from the earthly. Hence, a bird is often associated with divinity, immortality, power, victory, and royalty.

Birds and bird-masked figures are clearly attested as early as the Paleolithic period. In the cave painting at Lascaux in the Dordogne, dating from approximately 15,000 BCE, a bird-masked person is depicted as falling backward before a bison confronting him. At his feet lies his spear-thrower, and the spear that he has discharged has pierced the bison's body. Quite close to them is a bird perched on a pole. Most scholars interpret this scene as depicting a hunting tragedy: wearing a bird mask, the hunter has been killed by the bison. The mask may have been used as a device to enable the hunter to approach his prey without being noticed. The bird on a pole may represent the soul of the dead man or the totem and mythical ancestor of the tribe to which he belongs. For other scholars, the scene presents the shamanic trance. The man wearing a bird mask is a shaman; he lies unconscious while his soul has departed for the ecstatic journey to the world beyond. A companion on this spiritual journey is his helping spirit, here symbolized by the bird on a pole. The bison is possibly a sacrificial animal.

Although it is still uncertain whether shamanism originated in the Paleolithic period, birds undoubtedly occupy a very important place in the spiritual world of hunters generally and of northern Eurasia in particular, where shamanism has been a dominant magico-religious force. In fact, the shaman of Inner Asia and Siberia receives help from the spirits of wild animals and birds when undertaking an ecstatic journey. Bird spirits (especially those of geese, eagles, owls, and crows) descend from heaven and enter the shaman's body to inspire him as he beats his drum, wearing the shamanic costume of the bird type. Otherwise, they move into his drum or sit on his shamanic costume. This is precisely when shamanic ecstasy occurs; the shaman is transformed into a spiritual being, a bird in his inner experience. He moves, sings, and flies like a bird; his soul leaves the body and rises toward the heavens, accompanied by bird spirits. This motif of the ascending bird spirit has been revalorized by Daoism on a new spiritual plane: in the *Zhuangzi*, dating from the third century BCE, for example, a huge bird named Peng appears as the symbol of the soaring spirit that enjoys absolute freedom and is emancipated from mundane values and concerns. When a shaman dies among the Yakuts, the Tunguz, and the Dolgans, it is customary to erect on his tomb poles or sticks with a wooden bird at each tip. The bird symbolizes the soul of the departed shaman.

Birds appear in the myths of creation that center on the theme of the cosmogonic dive or the earth diver. In the beginning, when only the waters exist, aquatic birds (ducks, swans, geese, or swallows) dive to the bottom of the primeval ocean to fetch a particle of soil. Birds dive sometimes by God's order and sometimes by their own initiative, but in some variants God transforms himself into a bird and dives. This motif of the diving bird, common among such Altaic peoples as the Buriats and the Yakuts, is also found among the Russians and such Uralic peoples as the Samoyeds, the Mansi, the Yenisei, and the Mari. Earth divers also appear in a certain number of Indian cosmogonic myths of North America. The result of the courageous dive is always the same: a small particle of soil that has been brought up grows miraculously until it becomes the world as it is today. In Finnish and Estonian cosmogonic myths, God flies down as a bird onto the primeval ocean and lays on it the cosmic eggs from which the world emerges. This motif is also found in Indonesia and Polynesia.

Myths of kingship in northern Eurasia are often imbued with the symbolism of birds. According to the Mongolians, a golden-winged eagle gave them the *yasa*, or basic rules of life on the steppes, and helped them to establish the foundation of the Mongol empire by installing Chinggis Khan on the royal throne. Japanese myths tell how a crow (or raven) and a golden kite flew down as messengers of the heavenly gods and served Jimmu, the first mythical emperor of Japan, as guides in his march through the mountains to Yamato, where he established his imperial dynasty. The Hungarians have the tradition that the Magyars were guided by a giant *turul* (falcon, eagle, or hawk) into the land where Árpád founded the Hungarian nation. The *turul* is known as the mythical ancestor of the Árpáds.

These myths of creation and kingship reveal the prominent role played by birds in the formation of the cosmic order. As an epiphany of a god, demiurge, or mythical ancestor, a bird appears in the beginning of the world, and its appearance serves as an announcement of the creation of the universe, of the alteration of the cosmic structure, or of the founding of a people, a dynasty, or a nation. The eagle in Siberia, as well as the raven and thunderbird in North America, is especially invested with the features of the culture hero. Often described as the creator of the world, the bird is the divine being who familiarizes the people with knowledge and techniques, endows them with important cultural inventions, and presents them with the rules of life and social institutions.

In the ancient Near East and the Greco-Mediterranean world, birds are charged with a complex of symbolic meanings. Here, as elsewhere, the bird is essentially an epiphany of deity. In the Near East the dove usually symbolizes the goddess of fertility by whatever name she is known, and in Greece it is especially an epiphany of Aphrodite, the goddess of love. The eagle is a manifestation of the solar deity, as is clearly illustrated by the winged sun disks of Mesopotamia and later of Persia. The eagle is often represented as engaged in fighting with the snake or dragon. This archaic motif, attested in the Near East, India, and the southern Pacific, shows the tension that exists between the celestial solar principle and that of the maternal chthonic forces, but it also reveals man's inextinguishable aspiration for universal oneness or wholeness, which can be achieved by the cooperation and synthesis of conflicting powers.

The bird, and particularly the dove, often symbolizes love as an attribute of the goddess of fertility. In the cults of Dumuzi and Adonis, the goddess appears as a mother who laments over her son's captivity in the underworld and descends there to rescue him, to raise him from the dead. It is possible that the dove's moaning contributed to making it the special symbol of the goddess of love in the ancient Near East. In Greece the dove is an epiphany of divinity, but divinity in its amorous aspect, as can be seen from the dove's association with Aphrodite. In the Greco-Mediterranean world the dove has never lost this erotic connotation.

The eagle, the king of birds, is inseparably associated with royalty as well as with the solar deity. Indeed, royalty has never severed its symbolic ties with the sun and the eagle. In the Near East certain coins depict Hellenistic kings wearing a tiara with a pair of eagles on it facing the sun between them. In utilizing these symbols, the kings declare that they are divine by nature or deified. The divinity of the Roman emperor is expressed through the symbolism of Sol Invictus ("the invincible sun") and the eagle.

More generally, birds in the ancient Near East also signify the immortal souls of the dead. This celebrated image seems to have survived in Islam, where it is believed that the souls of the dead will remain as birds until the Day of Judgment. In Greece, images of the dove on graves may symbolize the soul of the departed, the divinity coming to help the departed, or the soul now in divine form. In Syria, the eagle depicted on tombs is the psychopomp, who leads the soul of the deceased to heaven. On Egyptian tombs the soul of the dead is represented as an androcephalic bird. However, soul birds (hawks, ducks, or geese) in Egypt have more than one function, usually in connection with the mummy. Certainly they are immortal souls, but they also symbolize divine presence and protection; birds bring all sorts of nourishment to the corpse to revive it. Thus in Egypt as elsewhere, the bird is both the soul of the departed and the divinity, regardless of what bird is depicted. The peacock, which in the Greco-Roman world may have symbolized man's hope for immortality, is of Indian origin. In Buddhism not only the peacock but also the owl and many other birds appear as epiphanies of the Buddhas and *bodhisattvas,* preaching the message of enlightenment and compassion. The *bodhisattva* Mayūrāsana, for example, is usually portrayed riding on a peacock.

In Judaism the dove and the eagle, the two most important birds, seem to have kept much the same symbolic values intact although they have been given specific Jewish colorings. The dove depicted on Jewish tombstones, in the wall paintings of Jewish catacombs, and on the ceilings of synagogues signifies Israel the beloved of God, the individual Israelite, or the salvation and immortality given to the faithful by God. In rabbinic tradition, too, the dove symbolizes not only the soul departing at death, but especially Israel the beloved. Moreover, the dove serves as the psychopomp. The eagle is equally multivalent; it is an epiphany of God of the power of God, but it is symbolic also of man's hope for eternal life and immortality.

The Christian symbolism of the dove and the eagle has also undergone a process of revalorization. The dove signifies the Holy Spirit in the baptism of Jesus, but is also becomes the erotic and impregnating force in the Annunciation. The motif of soul birds is well attested in early Christian literature and iconography. The soul becomes a dove at baptism; it identifies thereby with the Holy Spirit, the dove of Jesus' baptism. As a dove, the soul of the departed becomes immortal, soaring up to heaven at death, especially at martyrdom. The eagle as a Christian symbol is bound up with a complex of ideas and images. For early Christians the eagle was symbolic of John the Evangelist because at the beginning of his gospel it is implied that John has risen to the heights of the genealogy of the Logos. But the eagle also symbolizes Jesus Christ himself, and it is believed that as an eagle Christ has accompanied John on his flight in quest of visions. Moreover, the eagle represents the Logos itself, just as in Judaism it signifies God or his power. Finally, the eagle depicted on Christian sarcophagi is inseparably associated with the hope for eternal life, light, and resurrection; it serves as the escort of the souls of departed Christians into immortal life with God.

In Islamic literature and folklore, the symbolism of birds abounds. Farīd al-Dīn ʿAṭṭar's famous epic *Manṭiq al-ṭayr* (Conversation of the birds) uses the imagery of birds as human souls that journey through the seven valleys and, at the end of the road, discover their identity with the Simurgh, the divine bird that "has a name but no body," a perfectly spiritual being. The Turkish saying "Can kuşu uçtu" ("His soul bird has flown away"), uttered when someone dies, expresses the same concept. And throughout Persian and Persianate poetry and literature, one finds repeatedly the image of the nightingale *(bulbul)* in love with the radiant rose *(gul),* representing the soul longing for divine beauty.

Birds are not yet deprived of symbolic meanings. Dreams of flying birds still haunt us. In his masterpiece *Demian,* Hermann Hesse has given new life to bird symbolism when he speaks of the "bird struggling out of the egg." Modern man's aspiration for freedom and transcendence has also been admirably expressed by the sculptor Constantin Brancusi through images of birds.

SEE ALSO Cocks; Eagles and Hawks; Owls; Swans.

BIBLIOGRAPHY

The supreme importance of ornithomorphic symbolism and shamanism in the religious life of Paleolithic hunters has been stressed by Horst Kirchner in his article "Ein archäologischer Beitrag zur Urgeschichte des Schamanismus," *Anthropos* 47 (1952): 244–286. On the shaman's ecstasy and his transformation into a bird, there is much useful material in Mircea Eliade's *Shamanism: Archaic Techniques of Ecstasy* (New York, 1964). The bird type of the shamanic costume is illustrated in two works by Uno Harva (formerly Holmberg): *The Mythology of All Races,* vol. 4, *Finno-Ugric, Siberian* (Boston, 1927), and *Die religiösen Vorstellungen der altaischen Völker* (Helsinki, 1938). On the cosmogonic myths of the earth-diver type in which birds play a prominent role, see Mircea Eliade's "The Devil and God," in his *Zalmoxis, the Vanishing God: Comparative Studies in the Religions and Folklore of Dacia and Eastern Europe* (Chicago, 1972), pp. 76–130. On birds and kingship in Inner Asia and North Asia, see my article "Birds in the Mythology of Sacred Kingship," *East and West,* n.s. 28 (1978): 283–289. The symbolism of birds in Judaism has been admirably studied by Erwin R. Goodenough in *Pagan Symbols in Judaism* (New York, 1958), volume 8 of his *Jewish Symbols in the Greco-Roman Period.* The best single book by a folklorist on folk beliefs and customs concerning birds is Edward A. Armstrong's *The Folklore of Birds: An Enquiry into the Origin and Distribution of Some Magico-Religious Traditions,* 2d ed., rev. & enl. (New York, 1970).

New Sources

Estela Núñez, Carmen. "Asai, a Mythic Personage of the Ayoreo." *Latin American Indian Literatures* 5 (Fall 1981): 64–67.

Luxton, Richard N. "Language of the Birds: Tales, Texts and Poems of the Interspecies Communication." *Latin American Indian Literatures Journal* 3, no. 1 (Spring 1987): 61–62.

Seligmann, Linda J. "The Chicken in Andean History and Myth: The Quechua Concept of Wallpa." *Ethnohistory* 34 (Spring 1987): 139–170.

Waida, Manabu. "Problems of Central Asian and Siberian Shamanism." *Numen* 30 (December 1983): 215–239.

MANABU WAIDA (1987)
Revised Bibliography

BIRTH. The mystery associated with birth forms a central motif in every religion. The motif may be appreciated in its irreducible physical form or may become a highly abstract symbol or ritual. Religiously, birth is not regarded as merely a physiological process, or even a ritualized physiological event, but is associated with the evolution and transcendence of spiritual powers or the soul. Transmuted through myth, ritual, and symbol, the concept of birth becomes a major cipher for understanding existence and expressing wonder at creation.

Most religions explore the motif of birth through these three areas of myth, ritual, and symbol. Mythic narratives about important births or mythic figures who give birth are found in most religious traditions, and these myths shed light on the theological and ethical importance of rituals surrounding birth and rebirth. The ritual concerning physical childbirth itself makes this physiological event a religious experience. A third important motif is symbolic rebirth. Many religions speak of the central transformations in the religious life as rebirth. Whether as a collective initiation or as a solitary conversion, members of most religions are expected to undergo a second birth, which sometimes closely duplicates the first, physiological birth. At other times it is intended to undo the inadequacies of the first birth, so that there is an opposition between physiological birth and spiritual or social rebirth. This kind of second birth can often involve great tension or even hostility between women and men. This second birth can be so abstract that the way in which it duplicates one's first birth is unclear.

PRIMAL RELIGIONS. Statues of pregnant women dating from the Paleolithic period are important as indicators of the earliest attachment of religious significance to birth. Found in archaeological sites from Spain to Russia, these statues date from about 25,000 BCE on. Since they are found in the remains of old settlements and dwellings, they are thus assumed to be part of domestic religion. Although the exact use and significance of these figures cannot be determined, it seems undeniable that they reflect and express concern with birth specifically and with feminine energy in general as central existential and religious symbols.

For the Neolithic period, the evidence for a religion centered on goddesses and for a matrifocal society in Old Europe between 6500 and 3500 BCE is convincingly presented by Marija Gimbutas (1982). According to Gimbutas, the appropriate collective title for the goddesses is "the Goddess-Creatrix in her many aspects." Among the most important of these aspects is "the life-giving goddess, her legs widely parted" (p. 176). Reliefs of this goddess found in the temples of the Anatolian village of Çatal Hüyük (excavated and reported by James Mellaart) have become especially well known. Contemporary interpreters of this culture have suggested that one may contemplate the impact of entering a religious sanctuary and finding the large, central, elevated image of the Great Birth-Giver with widely parted legs. Such sanctuaries were common in Çatal Hüyük for at least a millennium. In addition, according to Gimbutas, the schematic diagram for this birth-giving goddess was widespread in Old Europe.

The religious significance of birth in primal religions can also be studied in the context of the present ethnographic data. Rituals surrounding first and second birth have been minutely described and analyzed for many societies. Small-scale societies provide reference points for many classic analyses of birth and rebirth ritual. The links between these rituals of birth and mythologies about birth have not been thoroughly studied, but many small-scale societies also possess a significant mythology concerning births.

Physiological birth is the occasion for rituals in almost all small-scale societies. The well-known pattern for transition rituals—withdrawal, seclusion, and return—is evident in the activities surrounding physiological childbirth. In this case there is an especially close connection between physiological requirements and ritual elaboration. Other transition rituals do not carry the same physiological necessity for withdrawal and seclusion, which strengthens the hypothesis that the experience of giving birth is the model upon which other transition rituals are based. This observation also intensifies the impression that the religious meaning of birth extends far beyond physiological childbirth, which is nevertheless one of the most powerful and pervasive root metaphors of religion.

The pattern of withdrawal, seclusion, and return can take many forms and can include other ritual details. The withdrawal may begin some time before the actual delivery, or it may begin only with the onset of labor, as among the !Kung of southern Africa. The seclusion may be short and solitary, an unusual pattern found among the !Kung and, among them, only for uncomplicated deliveries. Usually the woman giving birth is secluded with appropriate relatives and helpers. Though there are exceptions, as among the inhabitants of Tikopia and the Marquesas, one of the most reliable generalizations that can be made about childbirth seclusion in primal religions is the absence of men. Usually their absence is not merely an accident or a practical arrangement but rather a deeply felt religious requirement. However, the woman's husband may participate vicariously in childbirth through practicing couvade, a series of work and food taboos, physical symptoms, and seclusion. These practices are especially associated with South American Indians. While male absence from childbirth is a general requirement, exceptions are sometimes made in special circumstances such as a difficult delivery; then the shaman or the father may attempt to help the delivery.

After childbirth, the seclusion for the woman continues usually for at least a few days and frequently for a month or more. During this seclusion period, both mother and child receive special treatment and are subject to special restrictions. In most cases, during the entire period of the withdrawal, seclusion, and return, normal routines of eating, working, and human association are disrupted. Normal activities or associations may be restricted to protect either the mother and child or those with whom the mother comes in contact or both. On the other hand, the mother may also be indulged with special foods, a lighter workload, and the solicitous companionship of her friends and relatives. Generally, some ritual elaboration of physiological childbirth seems to be universal among the women of primal cultures.

Almost all of the observances of childbirth outlined above are found among the Aboriginal Australians. The ethnographic literature on these groups concentrates heavily on the second birth, or initiation, as the important birth. In fact, many analyses of Australian Aboriginal religion suggest that physiological birth is the low point in the life cycle relative to membership in the sacred or religious community, and that this situation begins to change only with a second or so-called real birth during initiation. For the birth-giver, however, childbirth is definitely a religious experience that also serves to advance her ritual status. She experiences and practices all the rituals associated with participation in a sacred ceremony and thus emulates models from the mythic Dreaming that sanction her experience and behavior.

For members of many primal religions, birth is believed to be something that must be reexperienced at least once, especially by men. Frequently, for this purpose, boys are forcibly removed from their familiar surroundings, isolated from women, subjected to painful ordeals and physical operations, and taught secret lore that only men may know (although, in fact, women often surreptitiously find out these secrets). When the boys are reintegrated into the society, they have become "men" through the agency of their male initiators.

Though there are exceptions, as among the Mende of West Africa, this process of a prolonged and tedious rebirth is more typically expected of males than of females. Some scholars analyze this male rebirth ritual as a symbolic gesture whereby boys enter the masculine realm and are freed of the feminine world in which they had previously lived. The second-birth ceremonies of Australian Aborigines may also be seen as experiences that serve as a transition from profane to sacred status. This analysis suggests that the second symbolic birth is the *real* birth, and that male initiation is needed to accomplish what women cannot do when they give birth. This analysis stresses the differences and tensions between the two modes of birth—that given by women and that given by men—and focuses often on male-female tension and hostility in the culture. However, other analyses emphasize the continuity between first and second births and see the second birth as a duplication rather than an undoing of the first birth. More significantly, the male initiators finally experience vicarious childbirth in a kind of delayed couvade as they duplicate the pattern of childbirth. This kind of analysis stresses the extent to which the ceremonies of male second birth are based on awe of, not scorn for, the women's accomplishment in giving birth.

Aboriginal Australian male ceremonies of second birth give clear evidence for the dual meaning of second birth as both a transformation of boys into men and as a birth-giving experience for men. During the ceremonies, boys are carried about by men in the same way that women carry babies. After the initiation operation, the boys are taught a new language, and the men engage in the same purificatory and healing practices as do women after childbirth like the mythic sisters of the Dreaming. The operation itself is symbolic of severing the umbilical cord. In other ceremonies, a trench, symbolizing a uterus, is dug on sacred ritual ground and boys are made to lie in it until the proper time for their emergence, which is indicated by the correct sequence in the dance dramas conducted by the men. In some ceremonies, men ritually wound themselves and correlate their blood with the blood that flows in childbirth.

Many primal religions focus on mythic births and birth-givers. No mythological system among primal religions is devoid of female personalities and activities that focus on birth and rebirth. Among the Aborigines of Australia, there are several well-known mythologies of birth-givers, who are also models for current ritual practices that both women and men engage in. Ronald M. Berndt has reported on two major myth cycles in *Kunapipi* (Melbourne, 1951) and *Djanggawul* (Melbourne, 1952). The Djanggawul epic concerns a brother and two sisters who travel together; the sisters are perpetually pregnant and constantly give birth, assisted by their brother. The other epic concerns two sisters, the Wawalag, one of whom is pregnant and gives birth. The sisters reveal their experiences to men through dreams that become the basis for the men's ritual drama that accompanies second birth. In some Aboriginal mythologies, the ritual process of second birth is itself identified with the great All-Mother or Birth-Giver.

Indian Religions. In the Indian religious context, especially in Indian folk religions, childbirth remains an occasion for religious observances. These rituals follow familiar patterns of withdrawal, seclusion, return, and disruption of normal daily routines. Usually both women and men take part in some birth observances, though the rituals are much more extensive for women. Indian childbirth practices are characterized by uniquely Hindu notions and practices of ritual purity and pollution and are colored by the highly patriarchal character of the Indian family.

The childbirth rituals of an Indian village have been described in a study by Doranne Jacobsen (1980). Though restrictions on food and activity during pregnancy are minimal, with the onset of labor the woman giving birth is separated from others. It is believed that during labor and for a short period immediately following childbirth, the woman and her baby are in a highly polluted and polluting state, similar to the state of people in the lowest untouchable classes. Anyone who contacts the mother and child contracts this pollution, so the two are carefully isolated. Only the midwife, who belongs to a very low class because of the polluting nature of her work, and one married female relative stay with the woman. This childbirth pollution extends to a lesser extent to all members of the husband's family. They also observe some of the restrictions incumbent upon one in a state of pollution and undergo purificatory practices.

The delivery is followed by a series of ceremonies gradually reintegrating the woman and child into the ongoing life of the village. On the evening of the birth girls and women gather in the courtyard of the house to sing. After three days, the level of pollution is lessened when the woman is given purifying baths; she then begins to have limited contact with her household. After ten days, in an important women's ceremony, the woman and her baby leave the house momentarily for the first time, and the mother blesses the family water pots and water supply. For the next month, the woman is still in a transitional state, participating in some of the family's activities, but not cooking or participating in worship services for the deities. Usually the pollution period ends about forty days after the birth, when the mother performs a ceremony at the village well at night, symbolically extending her fertility to the village water supply and completing her reintegration into the community.

This transition period in the woman's life is significant not only for her but for her entire family and community. Both male and female members of her husband's family, who often make the young wife's life very difficult, recognize the new mother's ritual status and must change their behavior appropriately. For the new mother herself, the forty-day seclusion is not so much a period of liability and deprivation as a period of healthful rest and indulgence. She receives special foods, attention, and a new, respected status in her husband's family, especially if she has just given birth to her first son. These rituals surrounding childbirth support and validate women's vital role in a society that often expresses ambivalence toward women and projects strong male dominance.

Second symbolic birth is important in some Indian castes and some religious groups. During the Vedic period (c. 1500–900 BCE) and in those castes that are still heavily involved in rituals and privileges having Vedic antecedents, second birth is an important affair. During Vedic times it was important in its own right; in contemporary Hinduism it is more important because of the privileges associated with being eligible to undergo a second birth.

The upper levels of Hindu society call themselves "twice-born"; their second birth gives them privileges, status, and responsibilities unavailable to the rest of the population. The privileges include the right to study the Vedic sacred texts and to practice religious ceremonies derived from Vedic models. The visible symbol of this status is a cotton cord worn by men across the left shoulder and resting on the right hip. A boy's second birth occurs when he is invested with this sacred thread, receives a sacred verse from his mentor, and undertakes, for at least a few moments, the ascetic discipline of a religious student.

The ancient texts regarding this initiation ceremony regard it as a second birth conferred by the male preceptor. The preceptor transforms the boy into an embryo, conceiving him at the moment when he puts his hand on the boy's shoulder. The preceptor becomes the boy's mother and father and symbolically carries him in his belly for three nights; on the third day the boy is reborn as a member of the privileged twice-born group. After his initiation the twice-born man can perform further sacrifices, which also begin with an initiation involving return to embryonic status and rebirth. Some Indian cultic traditions that still rely heavily on initiation continue to employ these motifs. For example, some Buddhist initiations begin with a series of rites in which the neophyte, deliberately compared to an infant, is washed, dressed, decorated, taught to speak, given a name, and so on.

However, though the theme of second birth occurs in the Indian contexts, many of the great soteriological themes of the Indian tradition do not rely on metaphors of birth and rebirth. Neither Hindu yoga nor the Buddhist Eightfold Path are a process of second birth; neither Hindu *brahman* nor Buddhist *nirvāṇa* results from second birth. They destroy delusion and result in insight and understanding. Images of maturation and death, rather than images of birth and rebirth, more accurately describe this attainment of an otherworldly attitude.

In the Indian context both stories of mythic birth and images of great birth-givers are ambiguous. The two most familiar birth stories, that of the Buddha and that of Kṛṣṇa, are highly unusual. Rather than serving as paradigms of birth-giving, they tell of the extraordinary futures awaiting the infants Buddha and Kṛṣṇa. Goddesses are numerous and important, but they are never simple mother goddesses. Though the creative power of the goddesses is stressed, none of the great goddesses of Hindu mythology experiences a pregnancy and delivery with which a human female could identify, not even Pārvatī, the wife of Śiva and the mother of two of his children. But the veneration of symbols of male and female sexuality is widespread. Temple reliefs of goddesses, naked, hands on hips, knees turned outward to display their sex, recall the Creatrix of Çatal Hüyük. As Sakti, vital energy, she is the energy that fuels the entire phenomenal world. Moreover, without the touch of her energizing dancing feet even the greatest god, Śiva, is a mere *sava* or corpse.

MONOTHEISTIC RELIGIONS. In the ancient Near East, the concept of monotheism involved the suppression of the goddess as the legitimate symbol of divine creativity and resulted in her replacement by a solitary sovereign, an abstract and nonsexual, though male, creator. Many mythologies from the third millennium onward display an increasing attempt to present males as primordially creative, even as the first birth-givers. They become pregnant and give birth, despite their anatomical limitations. Even if they are not directly involved in birth-giving, they are depicted as performing creative acts. Perhaps the most dramatic account of this reversal occurs in the creation epic of ancient Mesopotamia (mid-second millennium BCE). The older generation of gods are the primordial parents Apsu and Tiamat. After Apsu is killed by younger gods, Tiamat engages in battle against the younger gods. The battle is a confrontation between Marduk, a young male hero, and Tiamat, the Original Mother. He kills her and creates the cosmos out of her lifeless body. The gender identification of the two protagonists, though often ignored, is extremely significant. It is also found in one of the most important myths of Western culture, the creation of the female (Eve) out of the male (Adam).

Against this mythological background, physiological childbearing is not an especially important or religiously valued activity in monotheistic religions. The pains of childbirth are explained as punishment for Eve's curiosity and disobedience; the most noteworthy birth, Jesus' virgin birth, can no more be a model for ordinary women than can the births of the Buddha or Kṛṣṇa. Throughout the centuries, though women have been exhorted to bear children and even have been declared saved by their childbearing (*1 Tm.* 2:15), their childbearing has neither been given value by significant religious rituals nor been utilized as a significant symbol in the mythological system. In the Christian, Jewish, and Muslim traditions, childbirth has nevertheless been surrounded by folk rituals, taboos, and superstitions. Even in modern secular societies, the activities surrounding childbirth are highly ritualized, as has been pointed out by several anthropological analyses of modern Western cultures. These rituals are changing at present, as indicated by the growing popularity of home births, birthing centers, and so on, and by much more direct participation of fathers in the childbirth process than is found in most other societies.

In the context of these Western religious traditions, mothering as an activity has been a more significant religious symbol than birth itself, as is evidenced by the madonna-and-child imagery that is popular in Christian piety. Scholars are beginning to notice aspects of motherly energy in the symbolism of the divine. Yahveh of the Hebrew scriptures is also depicted as a mother eagle. The word for his mercy (*raḥamim*) derives from the word meaning "womb" (*reḥem*); some suggest that the phrase "merciful father" could be translated as "motherly father." The words for his spirit may be masculine or feminine, while the word for his wisdom is definitely feminine, as is *shekhinah,* the term for his presence on earth. In medieval times Christ was depicted as being motherly and feminine. Anselm, in his ontological proof of the existence of God, pictured Christ as a mother hen, an image that appears in the Bible (*Mt.* 23–37, *Lk.* 13–34).

Second birth has remained a central motif in monotheistic religions, especially in Christianity. Physiological birth by itself is insufficient to initiate a person into complete membership in the religious community, which is accomplished by the second and *real* birth. In Judaism and Islam the circumcision ritual does not stress, or even recognize, circumcision as rebirth. In Judaism it is simply "entry into the covenant," and is the first religiously significant event, but is not modeled on an earlier birth.

In Christianity, the necessity of second birth has been especially strong. The contrast between the "Old Adam" and the "New Man" is deeply built into the Christian symbol system. Transition from one birth to the other is a necessary individual experience, verified in baptism, or more recently, in the psychological experience of being "born again." Inasmuch as baptism is performed by a traditionally all-male clergy, the ritual resembles the second births performed by men in other religions. However, rebirth is not a duplication of physiological childbearing but instead emphasizes the need to die to the "old life." In Christianity, everyone, whether female or male, needs to be individually reborn. In this way the Christian understanding of true rebirth departs significantly from other traditions. However, this rebirth occurs through the ritual agency of a male clergy and is almost always understood as a rebirth into the graces of a male monotheistic deity. Perhaps in no other context is the need to be reborn so strongly felt yet so strongly removed from the arenas of feminine symbolism and replication of female activity.

See Also Couvade; Initiation; Prehistoric Religions.

Bibliography

Literature about rituals of birth and rebirth as well as the mythology and symbolism of the Great Birth-Giver is scattered in many sources. Only rarely, or not at all, are such materials easily found in a few sources. Two classic discussions of transition rituals are Mircea Eliade's *Rites and Symbols of Initiation: The Mysteries of Birth and Rebirth* (New York, 1958) and Arnold van Gennep's *The Rites of Passage* (Chicago, 1960). More recent books that include significant comparative discussions of birth rituals include Martha Nemes Fried and Morton H. Fried's *Transitions: Four Rituals in Eight Cultures* (New York, 2001) and Sheila Kitzinger's *Women as Mothers: How They See Themselves in Different Cultures* (New York, 1978).

The Old European religion is discussed in Marija Gimbutas's *The Goddesses and Gods of Old Europe, 6500–3500 B. C.* (Berkeley, 1982) and in Anne Barstow's "The Prehistoric Goddess," in *The Book of the Goddess: Past and Present,* edited by Carl Olson (New York, 1983). The ceremonies of birth and rebirth among Aboriginal Australians are summarized in my essay "Menstruation and Childbirth as Ritual and Religious Experience among Native Australians," in *Unspoken Worlds,* edited by Nancy Auer Falk and me (San Francisco, 2001), where Doranne Jacobson's "Golden Handprints and Red-Painted Feet: Hindu Childbirth Rituals in Central India" can also be found. Rebirth ceremonies are described in David G. Mandelbaum's *Society in India,* 2 vols. (Berkeley, 1970), and Abbé Jean Antoine Dubois's *Hindu Manners, Customs and Ceremonies,* 3d ed. (1906; reprint, Oxford, 1968). The many qualities of Hindu goddesses and mythic birth-givers can be seen in N. N. Bhattacharyya's *The Indian Mother Goddess,* 2d ed. (Columbia, Mo., 1977), and in *The Divine Consort,* edited by John Stratton Hawley and Donna Marie Wulff (Berkeley, 1982).

Shifts in the core symbolism of the ancient Near East become apparent when the older worldview is first studied. Diane Wolkstein and Samuel Noah Kramer present a moving portrait in *Inanna: Queen of Heaven and Earth* (New York, 1983). The prebiblical shifts in symbolism are presented by Thorkild Jacobsen's *The Treasures of Darkness* (New Haven,

1976), and the struggle to enforce the biblical shift in symbolism is discussed by Raphael Patai's *The Hebrew Goddess* (New York, 1967). For symbolism of second birth in Christianity, see Marion J. Hatchett's *Sanctifying Life, Time and Space* (New York, 1976) and Joseph Martos's *Doors to the Sacred* (New York, 1982). Finally an older source containing much valuable information, including chapters on Palestine and the church, is E. O. James's *The Cult of the Mother Goddess* (New York, 1959).

RITA M. GROSS (1987 AND 2005)

BĪRŪNĪ, AL- (AH 362–442/973–1051 CE), more fully known as Abū Rayḥān Muḥammad ibn Aḥmad al-Bīrūnī; Muslim scientist and polymath. Among the most brilliant, eclectic, and fertile minds produced by Islamic civilization in its peak middle period, al-Bīrūnī is a genius to be compared to but two contemporary Muslim literati, Ibn Sīnā (Avicenna; d. 1037), the medical philosopher, with whom he maintained an intermittent correspondence, and Firdawsī (d. 1020), author of the heralded and often illustrated Persian epic, the *Shāh-nāmah.* Firdawsī shared with al-Bīrūnī the unhappy fate of being a scholar-prisoner in the court of the Turkic warrior Maḥmūd of Ghaznah (r. c. 1000–1030).

LIFE. Al-Bīrūnī's life illustrates the keen interest that Persian-Turkic dynasts of the tenth and eleventh centuries had in promoting scientific learning and literary productivity. It also reveals the extent to which all scholars, like all branches of scholarship, were dependent on the taste—and sometimes the whim—of powerful political patrons. While official support allowed al-Bīrūnī to travel widely, to gather disparate data, and to develop a broad network of contacts in Central and South Asia, certain of his patrons, especially Maḥmūd, may have impeded as much as they aided his intellectual undertakings. Only kings and princes, in his view, "could free the minds of scholars from the daily anxieties for the necessities of life and stimulate their energies to earn more fame and favor," but, he adds, "the present times are not of this kind. They are the very opposite, and therefore it is quite impossible that a new science or any new kind of research should arise in our days. What we have of sciences is nothing but the scanty remains of bygone better times" (E. C. Sachau, trans., *Alberuni's India,* vol. 1, p. 152).

Despite that harsh judgment, al-Bīrūnī's biography serves to highlight the manner in which a genius, though subject like other mortals to political strictures and the vagaries of fate, nonetheless maximizes the narrow opportunities provided him. Born near Khorezm, just south of the Aral Sea in modern Uzbekistan, he studied under eminent local scientists. Though he favored mathematics and astronomy, he gained competence and even renown in several fields. Political disturbances constantly uprooted him; from 995 until 1004 he found employment under patrons of the Samanid and Ziyarid dynasties. After his return to Khorezm in 1004, he was caught up in diplomatic as well as academic pursuits until 1017, the date of the Ghaznavid conquest of his native region. Pressing al-Bīrūnī into his royal entourage, Maḥmūd sent him first to Ghaznah (Afghanistan) and then to parts of India during prolonged military compaigns there. Maḥmūd died in 1030, but al-Bīrūnī remained in Ghaznah, where he served first under Maḥmūd's son and successor, Masʿūd, and then under weaker dynasts, until his own death in 1051.

WORKS. Al-Bīrūnī's scholarship transcends the limiting circumstances of his life and reveals a mind of broad interests and encyclopedic learning. He was first and foremost an empiricist, fascinated by discoveries of the physical world derived through precise observation and careful calculation. Benefiting from the comprehensive curricular resources available to the intellectual elite of the eastern Muslim world by the eleventh century, he studied and wrote about astronomy, mathematics, geology, pharmacology, languages, and geography. He also concerned himself with history, philosophy, and religion. During his lifetime al-Bīrūnī wrote approximately thirteen thousand pages of publishable text, most of it highly technical in nature. This may be sorted out into 138 titles, although some have said he wrote 146 or even 180 independent volumes. Only 22, however, are known to have survived: most were written in Arabic, his preferred scholarly language, although some also exist in Persian versions. Among the most notable are the following:

1. *Al-āthār al-bāqiyah ʿan al-qurūn al-khāliyah* (Vestiges of bygone days), his first major work, completed around 1000 but subsequently revised. In it al-Bīrūnī sets forth a comparative chronology of the eras and festivals of various ethnic and religious groups.
2. *Qānūn al-Masʿūdī* (The canon Masʿudicus), compiled over several years but dedicated in 1031 to Maḥmūd's son and successor, Masʿūd. It is the most systematic and comprehensive of his numerous works on astronomy and includes an appendix on astrology that leaves little doubt about his personal distaste for it as a pseudoscience, despite its popularity among his coreligionists.
3. *Kitāb taḥqīq mā lil-Hind min maqbūlah lil-ʿaql aw mardhūlah* (The book confirming what pertains to India, whether rational or despicable), often simply known as the *India,* composed in 1030. This work is based on al-Bīrūnī's study of Sanskrit scientific texts and his conversations with Indian pandits whom he met while forced to accompany Maḥmūd on military campaigns against their patrons. Neither the *Āthār* nor the *Qānūn* nor any of his extant works can surpass the *India's* sheer breadth of learning and novel sense of cosmopolitan objectivity.

Al-Bīrūnī's work as a comparative religionist is rated high on the scale of his total scholarly output primarily because of the *India.* In it he not only distances himself from his warlike patron, Maḥmūd, for whose brutality he expresses barely veiled contempt, but he also attempts to understand what it was that made Indians think as they did; he prejudges neither the truth nor the falsehood of their religious beliefs and ritual practices. If the *India* reveals any weakness, it is al-Bīrūnī's constant preference for literary evidence over ethnographic observation and his predilection to posit the underlying metaphysical unity of Hindu, Greek, and Muslim elites, with disregard bordering on disdain for the views of nonelites. But the shortcomings of the *India* pale in comparison with its achievement, a vast, unprecedented, and unrepeated compendium that details the cultural traits of a conquered people from the point of view of one of their conquerors.

Al-Bīrūnī's vast erudition and innovative scholarship should have commended his works to Muslims of his own and later generations. Unfortunately, he stands out as an exception to his time rather than a model for others to respect or emulate. His scientific work did gain him a reputation as the outstanding authority in fields as diverse as astronomy, geology, and pharmacy, yet his contribution as a comparativist inspired no Muslim successors. It remained for nineteenth-century European scholars to rediscover al-Bīrūnī's legacy as a cultural historian and to spark an interest in the further study of him, both among educated Muslims and Western scholars of Islam. One mark of al-Bīrūnī's continued success is the large number of his extant writings that have been edited, published, and translated since the 1930s, some of them by Soviet scholars laying claim to a native son.

BIBLIOGRAPHY

While there is no dearth of secondary literature on al-Bīrūnī, there is a dearth of essays providing a competent overview of the range and significance of his writings for the study of religion. The best introductory article to all aspects of his life and work is E. S. Kennedy's "al-Biruni," *Dictionary of Scientific Biography* (New York, 1970), vol. 2, pp. 147–158. Less critical, especially on his attitude toward astrology, but otherwise valuable is Seyyed Hossein Nasr's *An Introduction to Islamic Cosmological Doctrines: Conceptions of Nature and Methods Used for Its Study by the Ikhwān al-Safa', al-Bīrūnī, and Ibn Sīnā* (Cambridge, U.K., 1964), pp. 107–174. For an assessment of his religious data in the *Āthār* and *India*, see Arthur Jeffery's "Al-Biruni's Contribution to Comparative Religion," in *Al-Biruni Commemoration Volume* (Calcutta, 1951), pp. 125–160, now to be supplemented by more recent articles in *The Scholar and the Saint: Studies in Commemoration of Abu'l-Rayhan al-Bīrūnī and Jalal al-Din Rūmī*, edited by Peter J. Chelkowski (New York, 1975), pp. 1–168; *Biruni Symposium: Iran Center, Columbia University*, edited by Ehsan Yarshater and Dale Bishop (New York, 1983); and select papers from *Al-Bīrūnī Commemorative Volume* (Karachi, 1979), edited by Hakim Mohammed Said. An attractive abridgement of Edward C. Sachau's translation of the *India* has been done, with introduction and notes, by Ainslie T. T. Embree (New York, 1971). Soviet scholarship can be traced by reference to M. S. Khan's "A Select Bibliography of Soviet Publications on Al-Biruni," *Janus* 62 (1975): 279–288.

A fuller appreciation of his contribution to the Muslim study of non-Muslim religions must be derived from unpublished or incomplete studies, such as Michael H. Browder's "Al-Biruni as a Source for Mani and Manichaeism" (Ph.D. diss., Duke University, 1982) and Shlomo Pines and Turia Gelblum's "Al-Bīrūnī's Arabic Version of Patañjali's Yogasūtra," a text that preceded and informed his evaluation of Brahmanic beliefs in the *India*, published seriatim in the *Bulletin of the School of Oriental and African Studies* 29, no. 2 (1966): 302–325 (chap. 1), 40, no. 3 (1977): 522–549 (chap. 2), and 46, no. 2 (1983): 258–304 (chap. 3).

BRUCE B. LAWRENCE (1987)

BISṬĀMĪ, ABŪ YAZĪD AL-

BISṬĀMĪ, ABŪ YAZĪD AL- (Abū Yazīd) Ṭayfūr, born ʿĪsā b. Surūshān, better known as Bāyazīd (or Abū Yazīd) Bisṭāmī, famed as the "King of the Gnostics" (*Sulṭān al-ʿārifīn*), is perhaps the most famous of early Persian Ṣūfīs, widely renowned for his ecstatic sayings and extraordinary spiritual discourses. Born in 777–778, he passed in most of his life in Bisṭām, located in the modern-day province of Simnān in northern Iran, where he died in 848 or 875.

SCHOOL, STATURE, AND SAYINGS. His master in Sufism was reputedly Abū ʿAlī al-Sindī, an illiterate sage. His antinominian utterances, such as his claim to have visited the Almighty's court, only to find it devoid of all Muslim scholars (*ʿulamāʾ*) and jurisprudents (*fuqahā*), his derogatory reference to scholars specializing in traditions of the Prophet as "dead men who narrate from the dead," his assertion that "I am greater" upon hearing the Muslim call to prayer, "*Allāh akbar*" (God is supreme!), and his claim to have had his own interiorized version of the Prophet's "ascension" (*Miʿrāj*), did not endear him to formalistic clerics. He was accordingly exiled several times from his native Bisṭām.

His large circle of Ṣūfī acquaintances and associates (some of whom with he exchanged legendary correspondences) included many of the foremost Ṣūfīs of his day. He was also acquainted with Sarī Saqaṭī (d. 871) whose nephew and disciple Abū'l-Qāsim al-Junayd (d. 910) later commented on Bāyazīd's sayings. Several famous Ṣūfī women featured among his associates as well, including Fāṭima of Nīshāpūr (d. 838), of whom he confessed, "In my life I encountered one true man and one true woman—and that was Fāṭima of Nīshāpūr. There was not any station on the way about which I told her that she had not already experienced." Yet Bāyazīd's unmarried state, explicitly outlined in such early sources as Qushayrī's *Risāla*, sets him at odds with the majority of Ṣūfīs.

Since he authored no written works, the main sources for later accounts of Bāyazīd are isolated collections of sayings and tales (all of uncertain authenticity) narrated by close companions and relatives several generations later. Many of these were recorded by Abū'l-Faḍl Muḥammad b. Sahlajī (d. 984) in his *Kitāb al-nūr min kalimāt Abī Ṭayfūr*. The two other important sources of sayings are Abū Naṣr al-Sarrāj's (d. 988) *Kitāb al-lumaʿ fī'l-taṣawwuf*, and Rūzbihān Baqlī Shīrāzī's (d. 1209) *Sharḥ-i shaṭhiyyāt*, which features fifty of Bāyazīd's paradoxes.

A century after his death a Bāyazīdian school came into being, and some two centuries later this school's contours became intellectually formalized in ʿAlī Hujwīrī's (d. 1071) *Kashf al-maḥjūb*, a Persian manual of Ṣūfī teachings and doctrine, in which Bāyazīd's followers are classified as comprising a separate school of thought known as the Ṭayfūriyya and described as advocates of rapture (*ghalabat*) and intoxication (*sukr*), as opposed to Junayd's "school of Sobriety (*ṣaḥw*)."

Bāyazīd's Herculean stature still dominates the pantheon of Muslim mystics. He was, as Louis Massignon remarks, "a figure without peer. . . the model of the perfect Muslim ascetic." Rūmī, among others, has said, "If a drop of Bāyazīd's faith were to fall into the ocean, the ocean itself would be drowned in that drop" (*Mathnawī*, ed. Nicholson, V: 3394), which seems to be a paraphrase of Abū Saʿīd ibn Abī'l-Khayr's (d. 440/1048) hyperbolic tribute, "I see the 18,000 worlds as full of Bāyazīd, yet nowhere therein can 'Bāyazīd' be found," cited by ʿAṭṭār (*Tadhkirat*, pp. 160–161). Hujwīrī notes that Junayd said of Bāyazīd that, "he is among us [the Ṣūfīs] as Gabriel is among the angels." Rūzbihān believed the abode of the esoteric lore of the Ṣūfīs could only be found through the dynamic leadership of Bāyazīd's paradoxical words (*Sharḥ-i shaṭḥīyyāt*, p. 78). Ibn ʿArabī referred to Bāyazīd more often than any other early Ṣūfī. Many great mystics have been celebrated as "the Bāyazīd of their age."

Bāyazīd's memory was kept alive by a cult of patronage centered around his tomb actively supported by the political elite. The Mongol Īl-Khān ruler Öljeitü (r. 1304–1316) reconstructed his tomb and named three of his sons (Bisṭām, Bāyazīd, and Ṭayfūr) after him. In fifteenth-century India a certain "Ṭayfūriyyya Order" appeared, claiming descent from Bāyazīd. It soon branched off into various suborders, of which the best known was the "Shaṭṭāriyya," established in India by ʿAbdu'llāh Shaṭṭārī (d. 1428) Another Ṭayfūrī branch was the ʿIshqiyya centered in Iran. Finally, a Bisṭāmiyya branch appeared in Ottoman Turkey.

BĀYAZĪDIAN MYSTICAL THEOLOGY. Bāyazīd is placed by Ibn ʿArabī (*Futūḥāt*, III, 34.11) among the *malāmatī* Ṣūfīs who constitute the highest category of saints, willingly enduring humiliation and incurring blame for the sake of their beliefs in order to subdue their own pride and conceit. Complementing and balancing the need to call down public blame upon oneself, with the Ṣūfīs of this school vying with one another for the title of greatest sinner on the one hand, Bāyazīdian teaching also aspires paradoxically on the other toward a kind of apotheosis that is grounded in the key Ṣūfī doctrines of annihilation (*fanā'*) and mystical drunkenness (*sukr*). Bāyazīd claimed that his self-identity, his individuality, was annihilated in God's Self-identity, so that he contemplated God directly through God's own eye (Rūzbihān, *Sharḥ*, p. 115). The same Bāyazīd who confessed that one should stand before God as if one is a "Zoroastrian infidel" about to convert to Islām (Sahlajī, *Al-Nūr*, p. 69), and who even went so far as to say that he had prayed for thirty years imagining himself a Zoroastrian (infidel) about to sever his cincture (*zunnār*) and recant, in the same breath could also give voice to the "blasphemous" claim, "Glory be to me! How great is my majesty!" and could tell God: "Thy obedience to me is greater than my obedience to Thee!" He even said to a disciple, "It is better for you to see me once than God a thousand times!" Beneath the cloak of exterior humility and outward abasement an interior exaltation of the Spirit is revealed. "The reality of esoteric sapience (*ḥaqīqat-i maʿrifat*)," he thus explained, lies in "being annihilated under the omniscience of God and becoming eternally subsistent upon the wide expanse of God, without any self or creature. In this wise, the mystic is a perishable being (*fānī*) who is eternal (*bāqī*), an eternal being who is perishable, a dead person who is living, a living person who is dead, a veiled person who is visibly exposed, and a manifest being who is hidden from sight." (ʿAṭṭār, *Tadhkirat*, p. 199)

The theory that an Indian origin could be found for Bāyazīd's doctrine of *fanā'* in the Buddhist doctrine of *nirvāṇa*, or Vedāntin ideas, espoused by earlier scholars such as Max Horten, R. A. Nicholson and R. C. Zaehner, has been definitively rejected by modern scholarship and has long since demolished by a number of scholars, including A. J. Arberry (1962), Muhammad Abdur Rabb (1971), and more recently by Michael Sells (2002).

The secret of Bāyazīd's continuing popularity lies in the power of his paradoxes to foster a kind of transcendental Ṣūfī ecumenism, with Muslim faith representing a kind of higher esoteric, interiorized religion, in contrast to exoteric Islam. To illustrate this higher form of faith, Rūmī recounts the tale of a "pagan" Zoroastrian who refused to convert to the form of "Islām" offered him by his "Muslim" neighbor (which, he objected, is so empty that it "chills the love of anybody with even a mite of potential faith"), since he claimed to be a follower of the interior spirit of Bāyazīd's faith, which he asserted to be "superior to all other faith" (*Mathnawī*, V: 3361–2). A saying of Bāyazīd confirms the *malāmatī* sentiments of his "pagan Zoroastrian" follower precisely: "The infidelity of adepts with high aspiration (*ahl-i himmat*) is nobler than the Islam of egotists (*ahl-i maniyyat*)" (Hujwīrī, *Kashf*, p. 541).

BIBLIOGRAPHY

Böwering, Gerhard. "Besṭāmī (Basṭāmī), Bāyazīd." In *Encyclopædia Iranica*, edited by Ehsan Yarshater, vol. 3, pp. 182–186. London, 1982. Scholarly overview of Bāyazīd's life and thought.

Lājvardī, Fāṭima. "Bāyazīd Bisṭāmī." *Dā'irat al-maʿārif-i buzurg-i islāmī.* Tehran, 1992, XI: 313–321. Thorough discussion of his life and teachings.

Meddeb, Abdelwahab. *Les Dits de Bistami (shatahāt).* Paris, 1989. An abridged French translation of his ecstatic sayings taken from Sahlajī's text.

Rabb, Muhammad ʿAbdur. *The Life, Thought and Historical Importance of Abū Yazīd al-Bisṭāmī.* Dacca, 1971. An excellent historical overview of the saint in Islamic history and thought.

Ritter, H. "Abū Yazīd al-Bisṭāmī." In *Encyclopædia of Islam,* 2d ed., vol. 1, pp. 162–163. Leiden, 1999. Scholarly overview of Bāyazīd's life and thought.

Sells, Michael. "The Infinity of Desire: Love, Mystical Union, and Ethics in Sufism." In *Crossing Boundaries: Essays on the Ethical Status of Mysticism,* edited by G. William Barnard and J. J. Kripal, pp. 184–229. New York, 2002. On the controversy surrounding possible Hindu influences on his teachings.

LEONARD LEWISOHN (2005)

BLACK ELK (1863–1950) was a Lakota spiritual leader known in Lakota as Hehaka Sapa. Few American Indian spiritual leaders have gained greater national and indeed international recognition than this Oglala Lakota. Although Nicholas Black Elk was well known by his own people as a holy person *(wicasa wakan),* it was the poetic interpretation given to his life in *Black Elk Speaks* (1932) by John G. Neihardt that caught the imagination of a much wider public. A second book, on the seven rites of the Lakota, was dictated at Black Elk's request to Joseph Epes Brown. This work, *The Sacred Pipe* (1953), further stimulated interest in the man and his message, which became, especially during the 1960s, meaningful symbols for a generation seeking alternate values.

Of the Big Road band of Lakota, Black Elk was born in December 1863 on the Little Powder River in present-day Wyoming. During this time his people hunted west of the Black Hills (Pa Sapa in Lakota) until 1877, when they were forced to move east to their present reservation at Pine Ridge in South Dakota. At thirteen Black Elk was present at General George Custer's defeat at the Battle of the Little Bighorn. He remembered the murder at Fort Robinson of his relative, the great warrior and spiritual leader Crazy Horse, and recalled the years when his people sought refuge with Sitting Bull's band in Canada. He was also present at the tragic massacre at Wounded Knee (1890), which nearly ended the revivalistic Ghost Dance movement.

Against that background of traumatic historical events, Black Elk at the age of nine received the first of a long series of sacred visionary experiences that set him upon a lifelong quest to find the means by which his people could mend "the broken hoop" of their lives, could find their sacred center, where "the flowering tree" of their traditions could bloom again. This first of many vision experiences was of terrifying Thunder Beings, the powers of the West; whoever received their power was obliged to become a *heyoka,* or sacred clown. Shaken by his experience, Black Elk could not bring himself to reveal the vision until he reached the age of seventeen. Then he confided it to the holy man Black Road, who instructed Black Elk in the spring of 1881 to enact part of his visionary experience, the Great Horse Dance, so that the people might share in the power of his vision.

It was in part his mission to find a means to help his people that led Black Elk to join Buffalo Bill's Wild West Show in 1886. He appeared in New York and then in England in 1887–1888 for the Golden Jubilee of Queen Victoria, whom he apparently met. He subsequently joined another western show and toured France, Germany, and Italy, finally returning to South Dakota in 1889.

Shortly after his return Black Elk married Katie War Bonnet, and they soon had children. From 1889 to about 1904 Black Elk gained much respect among his people as a curer, spiritual counselor, and ceremonial leader. It was also during this time that Black Elk was introduced to the Ghost Dance. He gained new inspiration through the similarities between the dance and his own vision: dancers surrounded a sacred pole seeking promises of renewal. After Wounded Knee and the end of the Ghost Dance, Black Elk turned his back on white culture, pursuing his work as a traditional Lakota holy man. During one healing ceremony on the Pine Ridge Reservation, a priest broke into the ceremony, destroying his sacred objects and accusing Black Elk of doing the work of Satan. Black Elk's patient recovered, but the priest died shortly thereafter in a riding accident.

Despite this experience, in 1904, following the death of his wife, Black Elk sought out the teachings of the Catholic Church. Shortly thereafter Black Elk became an important figure in the local parish, working as a catechist. While Black Elk's conversion was certainly sincere, the decision was also pragmatic. As a catechist of the church, Black Elk was able to maintain his social role as traditional Lakota spiritual leader. Further, with the suppression of traditional men's and women's sacred societies, a central feature of classical Lakota religious and cultural life, Lakota community and social structure were threatened. Catholic men's and women's societies offered an alternative, providing many of the same social and cultural functions.

As a catechist in the Society of Saint Joseph, Black Elk continued his traditional role as holy man: counseling and advising the people, praying and singing for them, instructing children, visiting the sick, and coordinating spiritual societies. As most priests were rarely able to visit outlying communities and spoke little Lakota, they relied heavily on such catechists as Black Elk, who soon became one of the most influential figures in reservation religious life. His work as a catechist also supplied him with financial support and other resources, resources that he immediately distributed to those in his community who were in need, a gesture characteristic of a traditional Lakota spiritual leader.

As Julian Rice argues, Black Elk's life work and cooperation with Neihardt and Brown can also be understood through the lens of traditional Lakota spiritual leadership. As a holy man and religious leader, whether traditionalist or Catholic, Black Elk's obligation was to the protection and well-being of his people. Throughout his labors, as a *yuwipi* ceremonialist, a catechist, or as a collaborator with Neihardt and Brown, Black Elk worked for his people's cultural and spiritual survival.

Black Elk knew something of the power of the printed word. He was thus willing to give in his two books details of his visions as well as accounts of the rites and metaphysics of his people. However, Raymond DeMallie has argued that Neihardt's *Black Elk Speaks* presents an inaccurate image of Black Elk. Neihardt viewed the Lakota as players in a tragic epic, in which Native people were vanishing before the destructive march of civilization. He placed Black Elk within this tragic story when he wrote: "With running tears I must say now that the tree has never bloomed. A pitiful old man, you see me here, and I have fallen away and have done nothing. Here at the center of the world, where you took me when I was young and taught me; here, old, I stand, and the tree is withered, Grandfather, my Grandfather!" (p. 273).

However, the transcript of Black Elk's actual words to Neihardt is not so bleak, instead presenting a man determined to work for his people's renewal, and his hope that through sharing his vision this might be accomplished:

> At that time I could see that the hoop was broken and all scattered out and I thought, "I am going to try my best to get my people back into the hoop again. . . . You know how I felt and what I really wanted to do is for us to make the tree bloom. On this tree [of life] we shall prosper . . . therefore we shall go back into the hoop and here we'll cooperate and stand as one . . . our families will multiply and prosper after we get this tree to blooming." (DeMallie, 1984, p. 294)

Black Elk sought the means for this cultural renewal within both traditional Lakota spirituality and the Catholic Church. Contemporary scholars disagree over the degree to which Black Elk's conversion was merely pragmatic, a recognition of the need to survive in a rapidly changing world. Most agree that his conversion was likely sincere but that Black Elk was able to accommodate both religious traditions without inner conflict. Some see him as a sophisticated ecumenicalist, negotiating both religious systems and incorporating them within his life's work.

Until the end of his life, Black Elk maintained a commitment to the Catholic Church and to traditional Lakota spirituality, seeing them as inherently compatible and describing the Six Grandfathers of the Lakota tradition as One, as Wakan Tanka, as the Great Spirit. When he died on August 19, 1950, in his log cabin at Manderson, South Dakota, there was for him no contradiction in the fact that he was holding a Christian rosary as well as a Lakota sacred pipe, which he had never given up smoking in the ceremonial manner. Whether Catholic or traditionalist, Black Elk worked for the well-being of his people, for their survival as a nation, and for the renewal of the sacred tree. The widespread popularity of his legacy, among both American Indians and non-Indians, and the subsequent revitalization of traditional ceremonies across the reservations by younger Native people, attest that Black Elk still speaks.

SEE ALSO Lakota Religious Traditions; Native American Christianities.

BIBLIOGRAPHY

Brown, Joseph Epes, ed. *The Sacred Pipe: Black Elk's Account of the Seven Rites of the Oglala Sioux.* Norman, Okla., 1953.

DeMallie, Raymond J., ed. *The Sixth Grandfather: Black Elk's Teachings Given to John G. Neihardt.* Lincoln, Nebr., 1984.

Kehoe, Alice Beck. *The Ghost Dance: Ethnohistory and Revitalization.* Fort Worth, Tex., 1989.

Neihardt, John G. *Black Elk Speaks: Being the Life Story of a Holy Man of the Oglala Sioux* (1932). Rev. ed. Lincoln, Nebr., 1979.

Rice, Julian. *Black Elk's Story: Distinguishing Its Lakota Purpose.* Albuquerque, N.Mex., 1991.

JOSEPH EPES BROWN (1987)
SUZANNE J. CRAWFORD (2005)

BLACKFEET RELIGIOUS TRADITIONS.

The name Niitsitapiiksi, referring to the Blackfoot Native American people, means "Real People," as in honest, good, true beings. This is the general collective term that encompasses the different divisions of the Blackfoot Confederacy who presently reside on four different reservations, three of which are in Alberta, Canada, and one which is in northwest Montana. The Montana division is called the Southern Piegan or Blackfeet, Aamskaapipiikani, while the Northern Peigan, Aapatohsipiikani and Blood, Kainai and Siksika (the Blackfoot proper) divisions reside in Canada. The entire Confederacy can be referred to with Niitsitapiiksi or Blackfoot, so for simplicity, this chapter uses this designation. The term "Blackfeet" has often been attributed to accounts of stories about the burnt prairies that stained moccasins with soot, but the Blackfoot trace the origin of the name to a sacred story of a man with three sons to whom he gave each a gift. Present population of the entire confederacy has estimates that vary widely, generally falling somewhere between 25,000–50,000 depending on how reservation resident status, enrolled vs. non-enrolled, official census tabulations, etc. are counted.

Niitsitapii (Blackfoot) religion is not so much a "religion" as a way of life, a collection of lessons, most learned from the natural environs, including plants, animals, the weather, the seasons, and the dimensions that involve—or house—the spiritual and the spirits. The meanings and the semantics of terms typically used to describe religious life and belief are appropriate, in given degrees, only to the "way of being" expected of those who practice the Niitsitapii (Blackfoot) spiritual traditions. The creation of the universe happened in a series of stages even though the central energy emanated from the central Giver-of-Life.

THE BLACKFOOT COSMOGONY: BETWEEN THE LAND AND THE SKY. Niitsitapii (Blackfoot) traditions consider that people have skills and attributes that allow them to survive, but people must learn to request assistance from those who have been here for much longer and therefore know the world well. The act of sacrifice has a key role in Niitsitapii (Blackfoot) spiritual life because the reciprocal and symbiotic relationships and properties that are the general rule of life apply to humans as well. Improving individual abilities to interact with the unseen forces of the universe means that an accumulation of information about this skill becomes part of the Niitsitapii (Blackfoot) repository of skills. The complex of stories about the origin and continuation of the Niitsitapii (Blackfoot) take place within the traditional homeland of the Niitsitapii (Blackfoot) at specific locations. They bind the learning of each generation of Niitsitapii (Blackfoot) in the teaching the earth, the sky, and all of the elements in between offer. The stories anchor the people's history and identity in their surroundings, stellar and earthbound, where every aspect of the space and the beings in it is occupied by the Creator's energy.

Individual sites and locations, the keystones of the culture and religious or spiritual orientation throughout the traditional Niitsitapii (Blackfoot) homeland, provide the foundation for the spiritual and religious life of the people. These sites are coordinated with astral reference points—star beings in the sky—and the exchanges recorded in the stories between them give rise to a complex matrix of relationships among elements, directions, beings, and forces that the Niitsitapii (Blackfoot) must learn to understand and with which they must interact appropriately. The relatives that inhabit different sites within the Niitsitapii (Blackfoot) homeland have over time offered assistance and encouraged the building of a life for the Niitsitapii (Blackfoot) people. Protecting the homeland is important because these relationships took a long time to build and because they continue into the present and future.

Stories and Oral Tradition. Niitsitapii (Blackfoot) terms for persons that emphasize concepts central to the way of being that is reinforced in Niitsitapii (Blackfoot) traditions of the spirit include Sun (painted, with Sun Dogs), Creator, Life-Giver, World-Maker, Grandfather; Napi, Old Man; Moon(s), Night Light, Old Woman, Grandmother; Morning Star, Early Riser; Backbone of the World; Thunder; Rivers and Creeks (the water system and life within boundaries); Cold Maker; Winds (including the Chinook "Snow-Shrinker"); Celestial Beings (different constellations); Above Persons, Ground Persons, Below Persons; Ground of Many Gifts (that is, a homeland that is all alive, filled with persons in different shapes and forms); "Helpers" (when seeking pity and assistance); Dream (Nitsokan); Cosmic Clock (to which humans pace their lives); Energies (animate-inanimate, manifested-potential, earth-sky, shadow-light, life-death). All of these play central roles in stories about creation, as do Scarface, the Woman-Who-Married-the-Star, Blood-Clot, and others.

In the traditional context Niitsitapii (Blackfoot) spiritual traditions were taught initially and primarily as stories. Through these sacred narratives the young were introduced to the important roles of certain elements or energies that are deemed powerful or that contain or have access to even more powerful sources of energy. The Niitsitapii (Blackfoot) stories introduced the complex relationships of these energies and described their roles in the creation of the universe and world. Within the stories are multiple levels in an uneven and unpredictable hierarchy of powers, but constants are recognized as well and prayed to for guidance and strength. The stories orient listeners, beginning as young children, to the variable nature of the universe and tell of the long-standing observations of the cycles and patterns of nature in which they are rooted. In their observation as in their telling and retelling, the stories ground listeners in the natural surroundings and encourage them to remain sensitive to other dimensions or sources of existence intimately interrelated with their living selves in physical manifestations of being.

Throughout the stories there are warnings, examples, and notifications of helpers and sources of strength. Various types of beings communicate with each other, and they help the child learn that the world, this combination of sources of life energy, existed long before humans were brought into it and that attention to the details of the powers that were interacting and balancing each other before humans arrived is essential for continued survival. The stories, in their retelling, take the listener into the time of the original occurrence described and allow the listener to experience firsthand, as the first person to experience the story would have. Not only does the Niitsitapii (Blackfoot) language have the grammatical structure to accommodate such movement in time, it also requires it, because the spoken form of the stories conveys firsthand experience to the listener, who becomes a participant. This ability to have the listener essentially relive the experiences of those who came before is why storytelling is not simply about relating events or emotions as experienced by someone else but is the act of placing the listener in the role of the actor and protagonist, the main player in the story, the focus of the event.

The Niitsitapii (Blackfoot) origin stories essentially encapsulate the rules for proper living within an extensive but not unbounded moral universe, where everyone has intention, emotion, action, and choice about how to interact. The spiritual-religious levels reinforce the moral code laid out in the stories. The stories tell of physical challenges that are also understood to be spiritual journeys and relate seemingly individual experiences that are understood to comment on the broader communitywide level. Most significantly the stories codify layered interpretations that range from the most basic of human needs and desires to the complex workings of the natural world, such as the rhythms of the celestial beings, which in turn guide the systems and cycles of creation that humans map themselves into and ties these altogether. Patterns are attended to, cycles observed, and distinctions made between the usual and the unusual, but all are included in the interrelated stories. The stories keep in order the songs that are the communicative force among the elements, persons, and levels of the universe. It is a universe that communicates with all, sometimes directly, sometimes through intercessors and intermediaries, and listens.

The stories reveal relationships that are important to attend to, that make up a whole, an extended description of the timeless and reiterating, returning nature of nature itself and of our connection to it. They remind one to try to live in sync with those patterns set by the earlier relatives before one's arrival. They show that the physical dimension or aspect of who one is constitutes, mirrors, or reveals opportunities for growth at that unseen level and that in life these energies must be balanced. The stories that bind the bundles are a bound bundle themselves, held together by links and transfers that make their most recent participant the recently initiated.

Niitsitapii (Blackfoot) Language. In physical culture the language communicates a visual picture, a perception, or a description of action that takes place in the moment of speaking, the full meaning of which is explained by the physical context. The language shares these descriptive duties by separating inanimate and animate beings, classified by some as having gender, although they then have to place nouns as being either animate or inanimate. Celestial beings, together with plants and animals, are animate.

The sign language used by the Niitsitapii (Blackfoot) also makes use of spatial orientation as a foundational principle, as does the syllabary system. The writing on rocks also relates stories. The placing of stones in particular shapes tells stories, which can then be read, telling of significant events that affect the entire community, that is, they are told by the community members to signal that some important event took place there. The orthography of lodge paintings and other expressions of the universe's forces also expresses this localizing order. A rich vocabulary is contained in each. All action has boundary and orientation, which is how one knows what happened. Above Ones, Below Ones, and All Four Directions, the origin stories, are based in the same rules. Patterns are sought and utilized in visual dimensions, with these depictions rooted in the oral patterns that set rhythm and segment, order and beauty to the storytelling. In songs and prayers, the vibration of creation is repeatedly re-created.

Dreams, Visions, and Acknowledgment of the Invisible Universe. The stories that have formed over a long period of varied interactions the foundational structures and values of the Niitsitapii (Blackfoot) way of being have several sources. One essential source is in the people's communications through times of increased awareness, which are also of varied forms and of different degrees. Whether they are classified as dreams, visions, or near-death experiences, they can occur under several possible conditions and, depending upon the reasons, are difficult to even see as belonging to any specific category defined by the English language. It is more accurate to simply say that the ways the sacred forces of the universe communicate to or through people are unique and not entirely predictable. Given this general observation, precedent—even when established generations ago by a third party—is granted great weight in such considerations. The observations of innumerable individuals who have lived an experience with the sacred powers that surround us and inhabit the entire universe are naturally recorded and repeated so the rest of the people might get a chance to grow from that experience. The stories frame the boundaries, physical and nonphysical, that form the basis of the Niitsitapii (Blackfoot) way of being in life and create a backdrop upon which to interpret the slightest significance of the movements of the natural world. Interpreting energies (for example, light and dark), the roles of the celestial beings, and the cycles of the life system within which the Niitsitapii (Blackfoot) were created was traditionally recognized as a highly valued skill that not everyone had the abilities for, but that was nonetheless respected and encouraged.

Ceremonial Bundles and Ceremonies. The many inhabitants of the Niitsitapii (Blackfoot) homeland continue to offer support and relationship with the Niitsitapii (Blackfoot) by serving as intermediaries, keeping the Niitsitapii (Blackfoot) reminded of healthy pathways in life. The stories that literally ground the Niitsitapii (Blackfoot) to the homeland and explain the history of the first relationships between the Niitsitapii (Blackfoot) and the rest of the natural forces of the universe are housed in groupings that were gathered together in the form of bundles. All bundles, even those known to only their individual keepers as personal bundle with unique obligations and regulations, have in common the practice uniting various dimensions through their contents. Each article has a role and a story that are part of the larger Niitsitapii (Blackfoot) narrative. Niitsitapii (Blackfoot) religious-spiritual traditions were created in a specific physical context and environmental setting, where animal forms from each of the relevant realms—underwater, earth, and sky—all relate to one another and interact with human forms as well. The energies that form the bundle function as a condensed conduit for communications and exchanges between the living, physical world and the unseen dimensions.

Bundles can range from a single individual's personal bundle, which may not necessarily ever be transferred, to larger community-held bundles that circulate among, and are cared for by, different members of the Niitsitapii (Blackfoot) community. There are also society bundles kept by individuals and transferred to new society members and cared for by different members of the ever-changing society membership. Some examples of the larger bundles include the Sun Dance (Turnip) Bonnet Bundle, the Beaver Bundle, and the Medicine Pipe Bundle. There has always been a variety of types of bundles, all simultaneously created and used to express the spiritual life of the Niitsitapii (Blackfoot).

The Niitsitapii (Blackfoot) View of the Universe. The Niitsitapii (Blackfoot) origin stories, which are replete with detailed encounters of life with the celestial beings recognized as having played key roles in the creation of the Niitsitapii (Blackfoot) world, are recorded in several ways throughout the Niitsitapii (Blackfoot) lifeways. The constant transfer of energy between celestial and other beings on earth and through the flow of the cosmos has been charted and recorded by bundle keepers, a tradition based on a close watch of the transitions, directions, risings, respective speeds, and patterns of movement in the celestial realm. To better observe these celestial movements and messages, observatories are located within the traditional homeland. Such sites are not ideal for habitation but are specifically associated with the observatory purposes of Niitsitapii (Blackfoot) bundle keepers and ceremonial leaders. Their observations and experiences became the focus of the central ceremonies and religious rites practiced by the Niitsitapii (Blackfoot).

The definition of the earthbound physicality of human nature was originally designed from the earth, given form, purpose, and its source of identity in the relationship with the earth as proof of a conjoined past and of sustenance for a similar future. Because traditionally there is no strict separation between the sacred and everyday realms, the sacred could be seen depicted and represented all over sacred and everyday items as reminders of sacred pacts, covenants, and obligations with those powers. Several examples include patterns depicted in the oldest-known forms in rock art distributed throughout the homeland (such as in Writing-on-Stone), in picture writing in the rocks (patterned after the sign language), quill and beadwork designs, feathers and other articles used in headdresses, body paint, lodge-cover designs, and designs on ceremonial items. These designs demonstrate how the structure of the Niitsitapii (Blackfoot) universe and the order of powers within it are simultaneously hierarchical and fluid, structured and unpredictable, multidimensional and seemingly simplistic to the uninitiated. The origin stories are inextricably linked to the explanations of the ceremonial and establish a clear familial and kin relationship to the people, so every Niitsitapii (Blackfoot) is aware of the human's connection to the rest of the creative forces of the universe. The stories and the ceremonies and celebrations they support help humans connect to the underlying consciousness of the universe. The articles, objects, and structures used in the ceremonies are tools and memory devices to assist this endeavor. The universe's energies expect recognition, respect, and reciprocity. Attention is paid to the sources of power, such as the sun, and to those who are endowed with the same power, spread throughout various dimensions and elements, and offer it to humans to use, who then have the power to decide whether it will be used to heal or hurt, to extend a productive and vibrant way of life, or to pursue directions that weaken and kill. These forms work together to help humans maintain harmony with the spirit world in their work through the renewal of commitments and vows.

Practice as a Way of Life: Cycles, Paradigms, and People. Following an introduction through stories and storytelling, children were traditionally encouraged to witness and to be active participants in the religious-spiritual life of the community. Numerous religious-spiritual-social societies that incorporated youngsters on through to those well advanced in age were also rooted in stories and in the practices indicated by them. Formal initiation is still a prerequisite. Individual children are selected to receive special pipes or other articles, which they hold, in formal ceremonies. Therefore even as a more informal, familial setting was and still is a source of religious training and exposure, the traditional social structure of the community includes formal recognition and practices, areas and contexts where spiritual protocols are taught in settings that emphasize the interrelatedness of purposes and the compound lessons to be acquired in order to live life well. These societies are based on the observation that learning—spiritual and otherwise—takes time. The group authorizes individual members. Some of these include the Horns, the Brave Dogs, the Buffalo Women's Society, the Prairie Chickens, the Doves, the Mosquitoes, and several others that traditionally include young children.

There was traditionally no "religious" consciousness separate from that of a moral philosophy that allows younger generations to live in good relations with each other and to be good people. Preferably training involved a combination of the individual and the community on the levels both of the religious-social societies and of the larger Niitsitapii (Blackfoot) community. Instead of strict adherence to a doctrine, Niitsitapii (Blackfoot) spiritual traditions encouraged unique contributions and awareness that, when brought back to the group, strengthen the overall knowledge and awareness of the larger community. Individual attainment of access to knowledge or spiritual gifts, such as those revealed in unique visions or dreams (among other ways) are brought into the matrix, to the already extant and fully operating intricate web of spiritual communications and exchanges. Exchanges can be mediated by representatives from the natural, nonphysical world who might reveal themselves in the form of an animal or a storm, among other things. The process of learning to be a contributing member of the societies includes creating a fully human being who understands that the world is composed of a balance between the physical manifestations of life and the nonphysical powers that are in constant communication and sharing. Through the accumulation of lived experiences over an untold amount of time, a number of interactions occur that let the people know what and with whom the Niitsitapii (Blackfoot) share their home. A complete existence is one that acknowledges the balance of the universe. Humans are powerful enough to recognize and even manipulate this balance.

There is redundancy and coupling and pairing, repetition and recycling, and returning and refreshing in all Niitsitapii (Blackfoot) spiritual-religious practices. There is emphasis placed on actions of participation in the spiritual life instead of on the question of faith itself. There is the imperative to repeat, renew, and refresh instead of establishing completion. There is a focus on caretaking and the well-being of the group. There is careful consideration and selection of individuals who would accept the duties and put the needs of the community in a place of priority. There is agency and purpose in those energies that inhabit the space all share. The orientation offered by the stories and the ceremonial life underscores the imperative to seek connections to the larger order of things. Humans live in a unique position of having the ability to seek to understand the cycles of the world or to ignore and destroy the cycles and themselves in the process. The spiritual life of the Niitsitapii (Blackfoot) people, just as for each individual Niitsitapii person, is part of a longer, more extended life of the spirit world that cycles and recycles all its energies. There are circles within circles that extend out into the natural world from humans. The visible manifestations of vibrations in water and the invisible that move through the air as sound waves are the sorts of energies that the Niitsitapii (Blackfoot) met through re-creations of the same shapes surrounding the traditional homeland and into which every aspect of the world was tied. Being attentive and sensitive to the rhythms of the universe and learning to live within them is the traditional Niitsitapii (Blackfoot) focus. The circular formation of the growth pattern of a small plant, for example, would be emulated in the shape of the family dwelling and then in a camping arrangement, in a dance pattern, and in the largest community gathering during the most sacred celebrations and in innumerable ideals and protocols in Niitsitapii life. There is an order to the world; what matters is how good one is at learning to live with its apparently unpredictable and predictable aspects and the delicate balance that results.

Challenges and Constants. Since the arrival of the Europeans, the traditional Niitsitapii (Blackfoot) religious-spiritual life has suffered a great deal though it has been continued and carefully maintained through the determined efforts and constant struggle of those Niitsitapii (Blackfoot) knowledgeable about the traditions. Whether trader, missionary, military, or otherwise, the Niitsitapii (Blackfoot) resistance to incursions into the Niitsitapii (Blackfoot) way of being in life has been well documented and has historically been a notable characteristic of the people. Before policies to exterminate then rehabilitate the Niitsitapii (Blackfoot) and before the combination of government and military forces with diverse economic interests—furs, gold, precious metals, water, land, and a variety of natural resources—that initially spread diseases and justified massacres, the nonnatives that visited the Blackfoot were interested in capturing the Niitsitapii (Blackfoot) soul. The killing and abduction of those who continued to practice the traditions were seen as a necessary step in ridding the future of "heathens" and "devil worshippers" who were and are presently considered morally corrupt. They were supported by the outlawing of ceremonies and the societies that sponsored them and by the imprisonment of Niitsitapii (Blackfoot) who refused to give up the old way of life into modern times. State-supported denominations have long vied for membership and control, resulting in the splitting of families—and by extension the entire community—into several distinct religious factions. Intermarriage for the sake of gaining economic and political advantage, false representation in negotiations with governments, violated and ignored treaty guarantees, and the forced indoctrination and relocation of the Niitsitapii (Blackfoot) people from the traditional homeland have compounded this initial negative effect on the traditional life.

Despite the numerous challenges to the Niitsitapii (Blackfoot) spiritual-religious traditions, there are those for whom, through their continuing practice and the accompanying sacrifices, the Niitsitapii (Blackfoot) way of life survives. The Niitsitapii (Blackfoot) way is not concerned with instructing a fixed perception of the sacred in which one must believe; it is precisely about seeking the best routines and awareness that enable one to experience firsthand the sacred powers of the universe. Knowledge of the Niitsitapii (Blackfoot) language teaches an orientation in the world that is rooted in the land, location, and spatial orientation in unique ways. It binds the landscape of the traditional homeland to those living in it and to the recognition of the traditional Niitsitapii (Blackfoot) observations.

Bibliography

The works that speak to Niitsitapii (Blackfoot) religious-spiritual orientations and concerns come from a range of disciplines, levels, and specialties and are of varying quality.

Bullchild, Percy. *The Sun Came Down: The History of the World as My Blackfoot Elders Told It.* San Fransisco, 1985. Contains many versions of Creation stories as told by a Blackfoot and is controversial because of influences from other religious beliefs.

Calf Robe, Benjamin Augustine, Adolf Hungry Wolf, and Beverly Hungry Wolf. *Siksika: A Blackfoot Legacy.* Invermere, British Columbia, 1979. The story of Ben Calf Robe's life. A Siksika elder, he relates information about his education, life, and the Blackfoot spiritual traditions and his role in them, as well as the history of his people.

Dempsey, Hugh A., ed. *Mike Mountain Horse: My People the Bloods.* Calgary, Alberta, 1979. The story of Mike Mountain Horse's life. A Kainai, he relates his education, his involvement in his people's traditions, political and spiritual, as well as explaining the life of his ancestors and their beliefs.

Ewers, John C. *The Blackfeet: Raiders on the Northwestern Plains.* Norman, Okla., 1958. A combination of history and explanation of religious and cultural practices of the Blackfoot people, documenting the early history (what is known of it in the literature) to the reservation realities.

Frantz, Donald G. *Blackfoot Grammar.* Toronto, 1991. The first comprehensive grammar of the Blackfoot language, that explains ideology and intent behind the language.

Grinnell, George Bird. *Blackfeet Indian Stories.* Old Saybrook, Conn., 1913. A compilation of some stories that are central to the Blackfoot spiritual beliefs and practices.

Grinnell, George Bird. *Blackfoot Lodge Tales: The Story of a Prairie People.* Lincoln, Neb., 1962. A compilation of some stories that are central to the Blackfoot spiritual beliefs and practices.

Hernandez, Nimachia. "Mokakssini: A Blackfoot Theory of Knowledge." Ph.D. diss., Harvard University, Cambridge, Mass., 1999. This work focuses on the Blackfoot Star Stories and on interviews with elders about them to articulate the uniquely Blackfoot conception of the cosmos and of how these form the basis for the Blackfoot spiritual/religious/ philosophical practices.

Hungry Wolf, Beverly. *The Ways of My Grandmothers.* New York, 1980. The story of Beverly Hungry Wolf's grandmothers, literally, in which she enfolds the history of her people's material and cultural traditions, together with the sacred Blackfoot stories.

Hungry Wolf, Beverly. *Daughters of the Buffalo Women: Maintaining the Tribal Faith.* Skookumchuck, British Columbia, 1996. The story of Beverly Hungry Wolf's grandmothers, literally, in which she enfolds her people's history, including schooling.

Lokensgard, Kenneth Hayes. "Gift and Commodity: Sociocultural Economies, Indigenous Religions, and Academic Exchange Practices." Ph.D. diss., Syracuse University, Syracuse, N.Y., 2001. This work delves into the meaning of the Blackfoot place on the transfer of spiritual power, and of how these function in the economic and social realms of the Blackfoot.

McClintock, Walter. *The Old North Trail.* London, 1910. A recounting of Walter McClintock's time with the Blackfoot, in which he includes the personal histories of some Blackfoot elders, also including the sacred stories they shared with him.

Pepion, Donald Duane. "Blackfoot Ceremony: A Qualitative Study of Learning." Ph.D. diss., Montana State University-Bozeman, Bozeman, Mont., 1999. Using interviews with Blackfoot elders as a basis of investigation of the Blackfoot understanding of learning and its relationship to the spiritual life, this work focuses on the Blackfoot traditions as methods for teaching.

Reeves, Brian O. K., and Sandra Leslie Peacock. *The Mountains Are Our Pillows: An Ethnographic Overview of Glacier National Park.* Glacier National Park, Mont., 2001. Archeological findings are brought together with Blackfoot sacred stories, revealing a long-standing and deep interrelationship between the environment and the Blackfoot spiritual-religious practices.

Uhlenbeck, C. C. *A Concise Blackfoot Grammar, Based on Material from the Southern Peigans.* New York. 1978. Grammatical explanations based on Blackfoot stories. Some of the earliest versions of Blackfoot stories recorded.

Uhlenbeck, C. C. *An English-Blackfoot Vocabulary, Based on Material from the Southern Peigans.* New York, 1979. Grammatical explanations based on Blackfoot stories. Focus on the Blackfoot versions of stories.

Wissler, Clark, and David C. Duvall. *Mythology of the Blackfoot Indians.* Norman, Okla., 1995. Comprehensive and very detailed accounts of the sacred stories of the Blackfoot, and of the ceremonies they support.

NIMACHIA HERNANDEZ (2005)

BLACK MUSLIMS SEE AFRICAN AMERICAN RELIGIONS, *ARTICLE ON* MUSLIM MOVEMENTS; ELIJAH MUHAMMAD; MALCOLM X

BLACK THEOLOGY. African Americans have a long, rich history of spiritually based advocacy for social change. African Americans read their religious texts through their experience. Consequently there is a long tradition of interpreting the Christian gospel in ways that reflect God's involvement in the struggles of oppressed peoples. This tradition is documented in several places, most notably in the life and work of David Walker (1785–1830), particularly in the classic *Walker's Appeal in Four Articles* (1829); Frederick Douglass (1817–1895); and Howard Thurman (1900–1981), particularly his classic text *Jesus and the Disinherited* (1949).

Black Theology as it is largely understood in the early twenty-first century refers to the movement initiated by James Cone (b. 1938) at Union Theological Seminary in New York and later taken up by his students and a successive generation of thinkers. It is a contextual liberation theology that draws its strength and focus from the historic African American struggle for freedom in North America as it was primarily, although not exclusively, manifested in and through the black church. In this sense it must not be thought of as in anyway an exhaustive or definitive account of African American religious reflection, reflection on African American religious or Christian experience or African American theology. Black Theology is therefore one among a variety of orientations to African American thought on Christian experience in particular and religious experience in general. "Most of us in this school of black theology have contended that we belong to a radical, but honorable and widely recognized, tradition in the African American community. Moreover we believe that this orientation, while not the only one, has been the most distinctive, persistent, and valuable part of the religious heritage of African Americans in the United States" (Cone, 2001, p. 147).

Although Black Theology is largely identified with the work of James Cone and his followers, other thinkers and theologians in what is referred to as the first generation, such as J. Deotis Roberts, Gayraud Wilmore, Joseph R. Washington, Albert B. Cleage, and Major Jones, played a prominent role in the founding of the movement and have continued (with the exception of perhaps Cleage) to exercise considerable influence in the early twenty-first century. Contributing to the formation of the Black Theology movement, they helped shape its substantive and methodological agenda. While other prominent African American scholars and thinkers, like Charles Long, a historian of religion; Cecil Cone, a theologian (and brother of James Cone); Vincent Harding, a historian; William R. Jones, a philosopher; and C. Eric Lincoln, a sociologist, all made valuable contributions to the formation of Black Theology, serving as invaluable resources for the standard interpretation of African American history as the history of resistance if not revolt and as interlocutors raising critical issues with respect to the methodology, epistemological status of, and interpretive claims on the nature of black religious experience as employed in Black Theology, they cannot be identified as

"Black Theologians." All of these thinkers operated effectively in the long-standing tradition of academic reflection on African American and religious experience within their respective fields of study.

Origins of Black Theology. Black Theology arose from the ferment of the late 1960s as many African American clergy, scholars, and activists, disillusioned by the pace of social change in regard to the condition of the African American masses, moved from the integrationist perspective that served as the touchstone of the Civil Rights movement toward an affirmation of black power (i.e., black self-determination, cultural affirmation, political empowerment, and racial pride) and the identity politics of the early 1970s. The Black Theology movement was the Christian theological response to and expression of the burgeoning African American self-affirmation that crystallized during the period. The movement came in answer to the fundamental challenge posed by many in the African American community who saw in Christianity the epitome of not only American but also Western spiritual hypocrisy. Christianity's historical complicity in African American slavery, suffering, and oppression and the occlusion of the African American encounter with Christianity in the grand narrative of American church history and theology as well as its failure to respond courageously, aggressively, and positively to the ongoing struggle of the late 1960s read like a balance sheet on the moral and spiritual bankruptcy of the Christian faith.

There is a sense in which Black Theology can be read as an outcome of the larger problematic of Christianity's confrontation with modernity, rendering it more or less a variation on a theme. Classically conceived, this problematic is twofold, involving, first, the search for justice and, second, the encounter with science. Black Theology has yet to take on the issue of science in any meaningful sense, although the issue is implicated at least at the epistemological level inasmuch as it employs a particular understanding of history and an implicit metaphysics, moves into more dialogue with the social sciences, and attempts a more rigorous social analysis to substantiate claims and make purportedly objective statements about the sociocultural location of African Americans.

More to the point, however, is the issue of social justice. In spite of the efforts of some theologians to take the challenge for social justice seriously, European American theology remained strangely and disturbingly silent on the issue of race. The theological concern with social justice in the dominant theology prior to the rise of Black Theology made only passing reference to African Americans or their plight. Given the centrality of race and its concomitant ideologies in the shaping of modernity, from the role played by slavery in the Western articulation of capitalism, colonialism, and imperialist expansion to American Jim Crow, South African apartheid, institutionalized poverty, and second-class citizenship in the second half of the twentieth century, all sanctioned and justified by the dominant Christianity and grounded in its theological articulation. The failure of European American theology to figure in the utter centrality of race fatally compromised its legitimacy and forfeited all pretensions to universality. The centrality of race and the elimination of the epithet *social* from this new proclamation of the Gospel effectively and fundamentally distinguished the movement from previous articulations of the "Social Gospel."

Is Christianity the "white man's" religion? Are there resources in the Christian faith as experienced by black people for a liberating praxis, or is it the instrument of subjugation some of the more radical and educated voices in the black community have claimed it to be? Can Christianity become the vehicle for freedom, or should it be tossed to the dustbin of history with all the other lies and deceptions heaped upon the backs of the oppressed to keep them bent in bondage? These were the questions no serious-minded African American Christian could ignore. It was the genius of the first generation Black Theologians not only to resist the temptation to sidestep the issues with an apologetic for the failures of historical Christianity but to lead the charge in proclaiming them. Secondly, they turned to a rigorous examination of the African American tradition, confirming both its uniqueness and its affirmation of black humanity. They discovered that not only could African American Christianity provide a liberating vision and praxis for the oppressed but in fact it already had.

Black Theology's Message. Joseph R. Washington, in a ninety-degree turn from his earlier work, *Black Religion* (1964), where he argued that the solution to the Negro problem in Christianity was full-scale integration and assimilation into the "theologically grounded" white church, now argued in *The Politics of God* (1967) that the black church's mission was to bring the message of equality, freedom, and true democracy to the United States. As the new "suffering servant," the black person "bound" to the white person through slavery has been called to the task "not only of being released from bondage but of releasing [their] captors from their shackles as well" (Washington, 1967, p. 157). More than this prescriptive imputation of meaning to the struggle, the sheer identification of a stream of African American folk Christianity with the religion of freedom, equality, and justice was a major contribution. In addition Washington articulated what would become a major theological criterion or hermeneutical lens for evaluating the religious contributions of African Americans in Black Theology. "The authenticity of the Spirituals resides in their expression of the love and drive for freedom and equality with and for all men. The inauthenticity of the spirituals are those expressions of escape from this world" (Washington, 1967, p. 157). Later James Cone examined the spirituals as an expression of the spirit of liberation but dropped the qualifier "all men," affirming their exclusive relevance in Black Theology to black people.

In response to the internal critique from many African Americans and the external assumption of many whites that African Americans and their Christian faith was historically essentially quietistic and accommodatingly otherworldly, people such as Vincent Harding (*There Is a River*) and Gayraud Wilmore (*Black Religion, Black Radicalism*) uncovered a long, unbroken story of resistance and rebellion that ran through the black tapestry of African American history like a scarlet thread, beginning before the ships made shore in the Americas and continuing through the modern-day Civil Rights movement. The river Harding wrote of may not have always raged beyond its prescribed borders, but even contained the powerful current and strong undertow continued its flow wide and deep.

Black Theology and Black Power, published in 1969, was James Cone's first firm and fearless statement of the convergence of black power and Christian thought at an academic level. This revolutionary statement exploded expectations in the white church that African American Christians would aid and abet their comfortable conformity with the historically oppressive, traditional power structure and the more gradualist and conservative elements in the African American community. In Cone's *Black Theology and Black Power* and in another two of his books, *A Black Theology of Liberation* (1970) and *God of the Oppressed* (1975), which came in relatively quick succession, Black Theology proclaimed with a joyful and liberating resonance, particularly to those trapped in a paralyzing tension, that there was no conflict between black self-affirmation and self-determination, in a word black liberation, and the Gospel of Jesus Christ. In fact the struggle for black liberation as defined by black power advocates was the mandate of the Gospel, and its emergence was a contemporary manifestation of the liberating activity of the Jesus revealed in New Testament Scripture. Since God was the God of the oppressed, always on the side of the oppressed, and Jesus Christ was his self disclosure and a living historical presence, then he manifests himself amid the oppressed. In the United States, African Americans were the oppressed, and hence Jesus Christ would not only be among them in their struggle for freedom but would manifest himself in them and their struggle. Jesus Christ revealed himself in the black faces affirming their freedom. In the United States therefore Jesus was black.

Other voices forcefully entered the fray emphasizing other aspects of Black Theology, some at least implicitly and others explicitly critical of Cone. Black Theology for Cone was theology of, by, and for black people. J. Deotis Roberts insisted upon the preeminence of the theme of reconciliation. The emphasis on reconciliation was essential to preserve the doctrinal integrity of Black Theology, given its claim to be Christian and normative. In addition to reconciliation Roberts feared an unhealthy isolation of Black Theology as it divorced itself, through a kind of ideological separatism, from the larger Christian theological tradition. "If we unwisely mark off a little space for our operation as black scholars, most white scholars will gladly let us operate only within these bounds. There will be no need to admit the black theologian to the comprehensive field of theology. Some of us have fought too long and hard to give up this territory now" (Roberts, 1971, pp. 19–20). Major J. Jones, continuing in this vein with some unique contributions and further elaboration, radicalized the approach to "reconciliation" in his *Christian Ethics for Black Theology* (1974), arguing that the concept presupposed "an ideal prior relationship" that blacks and whites did not share. In this work, while critically examining the Black Theology project, he suggested grounds for building "a totally new relationship that has never heretofore existed between black and white people in America" (Jones, 1974, p. 8).

Although Black Theology's essential critique of the white church gained wide acceptance, its constructive theological program drew heavy but primarily constructive criticism from several different quarters. Those that criticized Black Theology were no less committed to the struggle for African American liberation. They did not, however, accept James Cone's theological method, the rationality of his claims, or his interpretation of the essential nature of African American religious experience in which his theology claimed to be grounded. Nor did they accept the claim that it was somehow free of the traditional conceptual entanglements, challenges, and demands of academic accountability of the "white" theological tradition. Charles Long, in *Significations* (1986), and Cecil Cone, in a more strictly theological vein in *The Identity Crisis in Black Theology* (1975), argued that African American religious experience had to be more broadly interpreted in order to remain true to the nature of the "religious," the sources themselves, as well as maintain the theoretical integrity of theological method. Black Theology came under fire for reducing religious experience primarily to a selective interpretation of black church history. Many critics of Black Theology argue that its method is primarily tautological in that it formulates its conclusions, then shapes the interpretation of the sources it claims to be based on to fit them, dismissively excising or devaluing those dimensions of the experience that remain recalcitrant. In a word, critics have claimed that Black Theology has forced African American religious experience onto the procrustean bed of a quasi-political ideology in view of the methodological prominence of "black power."

A second generation of Black Theologians is attempting to meet some of these and other challenges by (1) broadening their reach into the sources, such as slave narratives, African American literature, and other cultural artifacts (see, for instance, *Cut Loose Your Stammering Tongue: Black Theology in the Slave Narratives* (2003), edited by Dwight N. Hopkins and George C. L. Cummings); (2) widening the scope of Black Theology by engaging in conversation with other third world and liberation theologies; and (3) placing themselves in dialogue with indigenous African religious traditions (see Josiah U. Young and Will Coleman).

There were other earlier attempts to respond to the limitations of the black theological vision, but these have garnered little attention, ironically, because of the academic ascendancy of the one particular vein. One such instructive effort, *Black Theology II: Essays on the Formation and Outreach of Contemporary Black Theology* (1987), edited by Calvin E. Bruce and William R. Jones, remains a valuable contribution to the ongoing development of the black theological project.

WOMANIST THEOLOGY. One of the most promising developments in the movement has been the emergence of Womanist Theology. The womanist perspective distinguishes itself by challenging the traditional neglect of black women's experience by black (and white) men in the academy and the church. In addition to challenging the neglect of their experience, they critique the openly oppressive nature of the black church, given the disproportional numbers of women who make up black congregations and their virtual absence in leadership roles in local congregations and denominational hierarchies. Womanists also distinguish themselves from white feminists, challenging their implicit and explicit racism, while affirming their distinctive contribution to the larger feminist dialogue (see *White Women's Christ and Black Women's Jesus: Feminist Christology and Womanist Response* [1989] by Jacquelyn Grant). The term *womanist* was derived from Alice Walker's definition of the term, which is comprised of a distinctive African American cultural inflection. Although some "Womanist" Theologians have expressed uneasiness about being identified too closely with a label that carries what many women in the black church consider morally ambiguous baggage, the term has become ensconced in the discourse as the recognized designation. Other notable figures in the Womanist movement are Delores S. Williams, Kelly Brown Douglas, Cheryl J. Sanders, M. Shawn Copeland, and Emily Townes. While the broader themes of Womanist Theology bring coherence to the movement, there are significant differences in approach, theoretical inflection, and theological sensibility (see *Introducing Womanist Theology* [2002] by Stephanie Mitchem).

SEE ALSO Liberation Theology.

BIBLIOGRAPHY

For a rich textured history of the beginning and later development of Black Theology through an assemblage of primary texts, consult Gayraud S. Wilmore and James H. Cone, eds., *Black Theology: A Documentary History, 1966–1979* (Maryknoll, N.Y., 1979), and James H. Cone and Gayraud S. Wilmore, eds., *Black Theology: A Documentary History,* 2d ed. (Maryknoll, N.Y., 1993). See also James H. Cone, *My Soul Looks Back* (Nashville, Tenn., 1982) and *Risks of Faith: The Emergence of a Black Theology of Liberation, 1968–1998* (Boston, 1999); and M. Shawn Copeland, "Black, Hispanic/Latino, and Native American Theologies," in *The Modern Theologians: An Introduction to Christian Theology in the Twentieth Century,* edited by David F. Ford (Cambridge, Mass., 1997).

Significant texts in the formation and development of the first generation of Black Theology are Joseph R. Washington, *Black Religion: The Negro and Christianity in the United States* (Boston, 1964) and *The Politics of God* (Boston, 1967); and James H. Cone, *Black Theology and Black Power* (New York, 1969) and *A Black Theology of Liberation* (Philadelphia, 1970). For valuable secondary material on Cone's 1970 text and the development of Black Theology, see Cone, *A Black Theology of Liberation: Twentieth Anniversary Edition* (Maryknoll, N.Y., 2001), *The Spirituals and the Blues: An Interpretation* (San Francisco, 1972), *God of the Oppressed* (New York, 1975); J. Deotis Roberts, *Liberation and Reconciliation: A Black Theology* (Philadelphia, 1971) and *Black Theology in Dialogue* (Philadelphia, 1987); Gayraud S. Wilmore, *Black Religion and Black Radicalism* (Garden City, N.Y., 1972); Major J. Jones, *Christian Ethics for Black Theology: The Politics of Liberation* (Nashville, Tenn., 1974); and James J. Gardiner and J. Deotis Roberts, eds., *Quest for a Black Theology* (Philadelphia, 1971).

Second-generation efforts to explicate Black Theology and expand its intellectual and social range include Dwight N. Hopkins, *Introducing Black Theology of Liberation* (Maryknoll, N.Y., 1999), *Black Theology USA and South Africa: Politics, Culture, and Liberation* (Maryknoll, N.Y., 1989), *Down, Up, and Over: Slave Religion and Black Theology* (Minneapolis, Minn., 2000), and with George C. L. Cummings, eds., *Cut Loose Your Stammering Tongue: Black Theology in the Slave Narratives* (Louisville, Ky., 2003); Josiah U. Young III, *Pan-African Theology: Providence and the Legacies of the Ancestors* (Trenton, N.J., 1992), *Dogged Strength with the Veil: Africana Spirituality and the Mysterious Love of God* (Harrisburg, Pa., 2003); and Will Coleman, *Tribal Talk: Black Theology, Hermeneutics, and African/American Ways of "Telling the Story"* (University Park, Pa., 2000). For an alternative vision, see Calvin E. Bruce and William R. Jones, eds., *Black Theology II: Essays on the Formation and Outreach of Contemporary Black Theology* (Lewisburg, Pa., 1978).

Critical responses to the Black Theology movement from within the African American community include Cecil Wayne Cone, *The Identity Crisis in Black Theology* (Nashville, Tenn., 1975); William R. Jones, *Is God a White Racist: A Preamble to Black Theology* (Boston, 1998); Charles H. Long, *Significations: Signs, Symbols, and Images in the Interpretation of Religion* (Philadelphia, 1986); and Dale P. Andrews, *Practical Theology for Black Churches: Bridging Black Theology and African American Folk Religion* (Louisville, Ky., 2002). For an engaging and positive assessment, see Theo Witvliet, *The Way of the Black Messiah: The Hermeneutical Challenge of Black Theology as a Theology of Liberation* (Oak Park, Ill., 1987).

For an introduction and overview of the Womanist development, see Stephanie Y. Mitchem, *Introducing Womanist Theology* (Maryknoll, N.Y., 2002). Additional important works include Jacquelyn Grant, *White Women's Christ and Black Women's Jesus: Feminist Christology and Womanist Response* (Atlanta, Ga., 1989); Emilie M. Townes, ed., *A Troubling in My Soul: Womanist Perspectives on Evil and Suffering* (Maryknoll, N.Y., 1993) and *Embracing the Spirit: Womanist Perspectives on Hope, Salvation, and Transformation* (Maryknoll, N.Y., 1997); Diana L. Hayes, *And Still We Rise: An Introduction to Black Liberation Theology* (New York, 1996); Delores S. Williams, *Sisters in the Wilderness: The Challenge of Womanist God-Talk* (Maryknoll, N.Y., 1995); Kelly Brown Douglas, *The Black Christ* (Maryknoll, N.Y., 1994); Cheryl J. Sanders, *Ministry at the Margins: The Prophetic Mission of Women, Youth, and the Poor* (Downers Grove, Ill., 1997); and Cheryl J. Sanders, ed., *Living the Intersection: Womanism and Afrocentrism in Theology* (Minneapolis, Minn., 1995) and.

MATTHEW V. JOHNSON, SR. (2005)

BLADES, such as those of swords, knives, axes, scythes, scissors, and saws, are instruments for cutting things apart. As hierophanies of divine power, blades manifest the instrumental function of intentional or purposeful cutting, dividing, separating, splitting, cleaving, or articulating.

The divine cutting power epiphanized by blades acts creatively or constructively when it differentiates a primordial entity; multiplies one into many by cutting something into parts; releases or receives some fructifying substance by cutting something open; orders a confused state by dividing it into parts; or purifies or brings something to its perfected form by cutting away a nonessential admixture. The same cutting power acts in a negating, limiting, or destructive way when it brings about a premature end by cutting off further development, by establishing an impassable boundary, or by destroying the necessary integrity or organic unity required for the continuance of something.

Blades are manmade instruments designed for implementing conscious intentions; they require craft for their manufacture and both training and discipline for their use. This quality of consciousness enables them to symbolize the divine intellect, purpose, will, judgment, craft, cunning, or wisdom that wields or guides the cutting power.

Blades manifest their divine power in all domains of existence—agriculture, warfare, civil administration, service to the gods, and meditative disciplines. For instance, cutting power in the form of the sickle is an attribute of divinities connected with agriculture as a sacred institution. The ancient Italian god of seedtime and harvest, Saturnus, carries a sickle. The Greek earth goddess, Gaia, invented the sickle and urged her son Kronos to castrate his father with it because he was preventing her children from coming into the light.

Cutting power in the form of a sword is an attribute of divinities connected with meditative disciplines. In Hinduism, for example, the sword Nandaka ("source of joy"), which is held by the god Viṣṇu represents pure knowledge (*jñāna*), whose substance is wisdom (*vidyā*). The flaming sword of knowledge is the powerful weapon that destroys ignorance. Generally, in whatever domain of existence the divine cutting power manifests itself it does so as the sacred blade of a numinous agent who wields the blade and whose essential nature is represented by it.

Blades as attributes of the ruling gods of the sky in various religious traditions manifest cutting power in both its constructive and its negative connotations. The blades of the sky gods have their natural analogue in the phenomenon of lightning. For example, the Vedic ruler of heaven, the cloud-dwelling god Indra, is deity of space, dispenser of rain, thrower of the thunderbolt (*vajra*), and principle of lightning—the energy of cosmic and animal life, which is stored as the semen (*vīrya*) of all beings. When the priest of Indra brandishes the ritual wooden sword (*sphyha*), he is regarded as raising the thunderbolt used by Indra to behead Vṛtra, the dragon (or demon) that caused drought. In the epic *Mahābhārata*, Indra's thunderbolt is equated with the penis, and in the Tantras it is equated with sexual power as the fundamental energy.

According to Ananda Coomaraswamy, "the Japanese sword, Shinto, royal, or samurai, is in fact the descendant or hypostasis of the sword of lightning found by Susa-no-Wo-no-Mikoto in the tail of the Dragon of the Clouds, whom he slays and dissevers, receiving in return the last of the daughters of the Earth, whose seven predecessors have been consumed by the Dragon" (*Selected Papers*, Princeton, 1977, vol. 1, p. 434).

Lightning is also a metaphor expressive of the flashing sword of judgment wielded by Yahveh. "I have posted a sword at every gate to flash like lightning, polished for havoc" (*Ez.* 21:20). After Adam and Eve are expelled from the Garden of Eden, Yahveh posts "the cherubs, and the flame of a flashing sword, to guard the way to the tree of life" (*Gn.* 3:24).

The ax is also an attribute of sky gods. Indra is incarnated as the god Rāma-with-the-Ax, Parasic-Rāma. Rāma's ax is the cutting power in the service of reestablishing the proper social order by means of war. Rāma was given the ax and trained in its use by Śiva, the god or principle of disintegration, dispersion, and annihilation. Zeus is another example of a sky god whose warrior power is represented by the ax. At the time of his birth on Mount Ida in Crete the mountain brought forth the Kouretes, youths armed with battle-axes and shields, who danced around the divine child to conceal his cries from Kronos, his murderous father. The birthplace of Zeus on Crete is also a major site of the cult of the double ax. Apparently the double ax itself was worshiped, and in later representations Zeus is shown shouldering the ax.

Blades are attributes of sun gods and solar heroes. These blades have their natural analogue in the form and activity of sunbeams and rays of sunlight. The Babylonian sun god, Shamash, who was a judge, lawgiver, and fertility deity, is depicted holding a saw with which to cut decisions. His heroic and kingly agent, Gilgamesh, carries a battle-ax and a sword with which he kills both the monster Huwawa, who rules the wilderness, and the Bull of Heaven, sent against him by the goddess Ishtar, whose seduction he rejects. In general, the blades associated with sun gods and solar heroes manifest the divine cutting power serving the interest of establishing the human order, civilization, and kingship.

Swords are almost universally found as a part of royal regalia, for the sovereign is the temporal counterpart of the divine principle that rules through cutting power. For example, there are five swords in the regalia of the British monarch: the sword of state, a smaller sword substituted for it that is used during the coronation ceremony, the sword of spiritual justice, the sword of temporal justice, and the sword of mercy, which has a blunted tip.

Scissors are particularly connected with the power of terminating or cutting something off. For example, the Moirai or goddesses of fate in the pre-Olympian Greek religion spun and determined the length of the threads of human lives. One of them, Atropos, snipped off the threads with scissors. In Hindu iconography the goddess Kālī is sometimes depicted with scissors, which she uses to snip the thread of life.

Kālī or Mahā-Kālī, the transcendent power of time that dissociates all things, is often shown holding a sword, which represents the destructive power of time to cut off life. The sword is also an instrument of sacrifice in the rites of Kālī.

Blades are also attributes of gods of the underworld. For instance, Yama, the Hindu sovereign of the infernal regions and judge of the dead, carries a sword, an ax, and a dagger. The name *Yama* means "binder, restrainer." When Yama is identified with the principle of time (Kālā) he is shown as an old man carrying a sword and shield, as this concept has to do with endings.

In the biblical *Book of Revelation* (15:14–16) the end of time is represented by the image of the Son of man appearing on a cloud with a sickle in his hand. "Then another angel . . . shouted aloud to the one sitting on the cloud, 'Put your sickle in and reap: harvest time has come and the harvest of the earth is ripe.' Then the one on the cloud set his sickle to work on the earth. . . ." The judging Word of the Lord is also represented in the image of the Son of man with the double-edged sword coming from his mouth (*Rv.* 1:16).

Thus the divine cutting power manifested in blades works toward a multiplicity of ends in all domains of existence. Depending upon the context in which it appears, the blade traditionally symbolizes the instrument of creativity, liberation, justice, power, authority, fertility, purification, enlightenment, punishment, death, execution, destruction, martyrdom, and limitation.

Bibliography

Further discussion can be found in Alain Daniélou's *Hindu Polytheism* (New York, 1964).

New Sources

Evangelista, Nick. *The Encyclopedia of the Sword.* Westport, Conn., 1995.

Harris, Victor, and Nobuo Ogasawara. *Swords of the Samurai.* London, 1990.

Irvine, Gregory. *The Japanese Sword: The Soul of the Samurai.* London, 2000.

Pierce, Ian. *Swords of the Viking Age.* Rochester, N.Y., 2002.

Pleiner, Radomir. *The Celtic Sword.* New York, 1993.

Richard W. Thurn (1987)
Revised Bibliography

BLASPHEMY

This entry consists of the following articles:

JEWISH CONCEPT
CHRISTIAN CONCEPT
ISLAMIC CONCEPT

BLASPHEMY: JEWISH CONCEPT

There is no one standard Hebrew term for blasphemy, indicating that blasphemy—namely, speaking impiously or irreverently about God or sacred things—is not recognized as a distinct, prohibited category of speech in traditional Judaism. In fact, some activities or statements that might appear to members of different religious traditions as blasphemous toward God are part and parcel of Judaism. Thus, although one might think that arguing with God is a blasphemous activity, the precedent of Abraham's bargaining with God before the destruction of Sodom and Gomorrah (*Gn.* 18:16–33) legitimized the Jewish convention of disputing with God, most notably in modern Hasidism. Some medieval Christians found certain rabbinic utterances about God to be blasphemous, but this was partially the result of a Christian desire to find reasons to outlaw the Talmud (the accusation of blasphemy was used as a justification for Christian censorship of Jewish books). Jews, however, accepted the ostensibly objectionable statements, even if they sometimes appeared to be peculiar, as a legitimate part of Judaism (although they were often explained allegorically by Jewish rationalists). Although one cannot say that Judaism allows complete freedom of speech, it would seem that the rabbis were more concerned with language that offended humans (e.g., idle and malicious gossip) than with language that might have been taken as offensive to God.

There are, however, certain actions that the Jewish tradition might consider a type of blasphemy, some of which are more culpable than others. These actions can be categorized, from the more specific and punishable to the more general and unenforceable, as: (1) cursing God and God's name; (2) using God's name in vain, pronouncing it illicitly, or destroying its written form; (3) saying inappropriate things about God; and (4) acting in a manner that would bring disrepute upon the God of Israel (and, therefore, upon the people of Israel).

Cursing God. The holiness of God's name was such that an offense against that name was considered a severe crime. The gravity of the act was so great that a euphemism was often used to describe the transgression—for example, cursing God was referred to as "blessing God." The first mention of the prohibition in the Bible (*Ex.* 22:27) links reviling God (*Elohim*) with the cursing of a ruler (*nasi*), but no punishment is prescribed, and Jewish tradition has generally, but not unanimously, understood *Elohim* in this passage to mean *judges* and not *God.* A more specific reference occurs when, as a result of an altercation in the desert camp of the Israelites, the son of an Israelite woman and an Egyptian man enunciated the Name (*ha-shem,* presumably the tetragrammaton, YHVH) and cursed. Moses did not know what to do with the miscreant, but God informed him that the community was to put him to death by stoning after those who heard the curse placed their hands on the head of the sinner. Furthermore, those who curse God (*Elohim*) are culpable, and those who enunciate the name of YHVH are to be punished by stoning. The fact that the offender was not a full Israelite did not mitigate the severity of the crime, since the law applied to both the native born and strangers. The sentence was then carried out (*Lv.* 24:10–23). Commentators are divided as to the exact nature of the offense for which this half-Israelite/half-Egyptian was executed—was it, for instance, pronouncing the name, cursing it, or both? In any event, it would appear that the man committed a transgression specifically against God's name, an act that could be construed as blasphemy and that was punishable by death.

The Bible provides other examples of this offense. When King Ahab fell into a deep depression after being unsuccessful in convincing Naboth the Jezreelite to sell him his ancestral vineyard, Ahab's wife Jezebel conspired to have Naboth executed by inciting false witnesses to accuse him of having cursed (literally, blessed) God (*Elohim*) and the king (*melekh*). This would indicate that the prohibition of *Exodus* 22:27 was enforced as a capital offense (*1 Kgs.* 21:1–17). Job's wife thought Job's troubles would be over if he "cursed [literally, blessed] God and died" (*Jb.* 2:9).

The consequences of cursing God were felt not only by the executed malefactors, but also by those who heard the curse and by the community. The accusation against Naboth was accompanied by a call to public fasting (*1 Kgs.* 21:9, 12). When the Assyrian army commander came to the besieged Jerusalem and made highly unflattering statements about the God of Israel (YHVH), and said them in Hebrew (literally, Judean) so that the beleaguered people would understand him, his Israelite interlocutors rent their garments (*2 Kgs.* 18:37; *Is.* 36:22). The punishment for the Assyrians was a plague that destroyed their army, wiping out 185,000 soldiers (*2 Kgs.* 19:35; *Is.* 37:36).

The Bible, then, seems to consider offensive speech against God serious and actionable both by human courts and by God. Hellenistic Jewish literature described such offensive speech with the Greek term *blasphemy* and understood the concept as including any offense against the sovereignty of God. The Septuagint used the word *blasphemy* in its translation of a number of biblical passages that have reference to reviling or insulting God (*2 Kgs.* 19:4, 6, 22; *Is.* 52:5; *Ez.* 35:12; *Dn.* 3:29). The Syrian-Greek attempt to eradicate Judaism and replace it with idolatry is seen by the author of *2 Maccabees* as a form of blasphemy. After the author described the deadly illness of King Antiochus as divine punishment for his sins, he wrote: "So the murderer and blasphemer, having endured the most intense suffering, such as he had inflicted on others, came to the end of his life by a most pitiable fate" (*2 Mc.* 9:28). In the wars between the Syrian-Greeks and the Judeans, the former are portrayed as uttering insults about the God of Israel, namely blaspheming, and this action inspired the Maccabees to fight more fiercely (*2 Mc.* 10:34–35; 12:14–15). Judah Maccabeus prayed to God that his contemporary blasphemers suffer the fate of the 185,000 Assyrian troops who had attacked Jerusalem (*2 Mc.* 15:22–24).

This expansive use of the concept and term of *blasphemy* was not adopted by the rabbis of the Talmud, who had a more limited view of the crime of offensive speech against God, restricting it specifically to cursing God. They also made it almost impossible to execute someone for this action. In general, although the Bible prescribes capital punishment for a number of crimes, rabbinic law was instrumental in limiting the possibility of judicial executions. In order to put someone to death, the offense must have been committed before two eyewitnesses who had previously warned the criminal explicitly against the act and had received his acknowledgment of their warning. In the case of cursing God, the rabbis added further restrictions, including the fact that the case is a capital one only if God's personal name, the tetragrammaton, was used both as the one who curses and the accursed. In rabbinic parlance, this meant that the miscreant must say something in the form of "May Yossi smite Yossi," in which *Yossi* is used as a euphemism for the divine name. The euphemism is used until the very end of the judicial procedure, but since a person could not be executed on the basis of an accusation consisting only of a euphemism, the eldest witness would then be asked to say exactly what he had heard. At this point, the judges rend their garments irreparably, and the younger witnesses say: "I also heard it like this" (Mishnah *Sanhedrin* 7:5). A Talmudic rabbi opined that hearing other names of God cursed did not require tearing the garments, since "if that were the case, one's garments would be full of rents" (Babylonian *Sanhedrin* 60a).

It is unclear whether this punishment was ever carried out by rabbinic courts, since by the time of the editing of the Mishnah (c. 200 CE), Jews no longer had authority to impose capital punishment upon malefactors. Medieval discussions of this capital offense were certainly theoretical and do not reflect applied case law. Maimonides (d. 1204), whose code dealt with all of Talmudic law, whether it was pertinent in his own day or not, extended the capital prohibition to the main substitute for the tetragrammaton (ADNY), whereas cursing God using other holy names was forbidden but not actionable by a human court (*Mishneh Torah,* Laws of Idolatry, 2:7–10). Later codes, which are not as inclusive and do not treat of capital offenses, omit this prohibition all together, but they do obligate those who hear God's name cursed, even if only a substitute for that name (and perhaps even in a foreign language), to rend their garments (*Shulhan Arukh,* Yoreh De'ah, 340:37).

USING GOD'S NAME IN VAIN, PRONOUNCING IT, OR DESTROYING IT. The third commandment reads: "You shall not take the name of the Lord your God in vain, for the Lord shall not clear one who takes His name in vain" (*Ex.* 20:7; *Dt.* 5:11). The Jewish exegetical tradition generally understands this prohibition as using God's name for making a false oath and not necessarily as solely misusing God's name (Maimonides, *Book of Commandments,* Negative Commandment 62). The exact nature of what false oaths are is also a matter of dispute, although some would understand the prohibition as any unnecessary use of God's name when swearing. Avraham ibn Ezra (d. 1167) noted that this injunction is the most violated of the Ten Commandments, which is the cause of the continued exile. The violation is so widespread that even if one points out to people that they are swearing by God's name, they will swear by God's name that they are not doing so (*Long Commentary on Exodus,* 20:7).

A different prohibition is pronouncing God's name. The tetragrammaton was understood as God's personal name, and, therefore, it was imbued with particular holiness. Pronunciation of the name became increasingly rare, and, according to later sources, by the Second Temple period it was articulated only once a year on Yom Kippur in the Temple's Holy of Holies. In general usage, the tetragrammaton is replaced by *Adonai* (Lord) or *Ha-Shem* (the Name); someone who attempts to pronounce the tetragrammaton by its letters is said not to have a portion in the world to come (Mishnah *Sanhedrin* 10:1). Today, there is no agreement as to the correct pronunciation of the tetragrammaton, and therefore the prohibition is more or less moot, even though there are some who would forbid attempts at saying the name lest one come up with the correct pronunciation. Because of the perceived holiness of divine names, observant Jews generally refrain from any full pronunciation of these names, even those used instead of the tetragrammaton, except in specific ritual actions. As alternate divine names or notations become widespread, they too are imbued with sanctity, and there is a tendency to seek further substitution for them.

Because of the sanctity of the divine name, it is forbidden to destroy its written form. This is the reason why Jewish written materials that include divine names are generally buried (in a *geniza,* a special repository for this material) rather than destroyed. Maimonides lists seven such names that are not to be destroyed, and anyone who erases even one letter of these names is punished by lashes (*Mishneh Torah,* Laws of the Foundations of the Torah, 6). Just as one does not pronounce divine names in everyday speech, one also does not write divine names fully for fear of profaning them. There is a difference of opinion as to whether this caution is to be applied to divine names in languages other than Hebrew, but the most stringent employ substitute formulations and spellings even in non-Hebrew writing and speech. It is also incumbent to treat both a Torah scroll and traditional Jewish books with reverence lest one show disrespect to God by demeaning the divine word.

SAYING INAPPROPRIATE THINGS ABOUT GOD. Before one can prohibit blasphemy as a form of saying inappropriate things about God, one must first determine what exactly it is that is inappropriate to say. Since Judaism has always placed greater stress on observance of the law rather than on correct beliefs, there is a wide latitude in Jewish theology and no central authority to decide on questions of faith. Thus, it is difficult to define that which is inappropriate to say about God. For instance, Maimonides wrote that one who says that there is one God, but that God has body and form, is a heretic who has no portion in the world to come. This statement was highly criticized by Rabbi Avraham ben David of Posquières (RABaD, d. 1198) as unfair to those "greater and better" than Maimonides who held such views (*Mishneh Torah,* Law of Repentance, 3:6). Obviously, one person's blasphemy can be someone else's deep-seated pious belief. The Middle Ages witnessed a large number of controversies between rationalist and more conservative Jews as to which statements about God are meant literally and which are to be taken allegorically.

The medievals debated the question of heresy as well. Although there are many terms in post-biblical Hebrew for *heretic* (the Bible, itself, does not mention the concept of heresy), there is no agreement in rabbinic or medieval literature as to what makes one a heretic. The rabbis deny a place in the world to come to someone who negates the beliefs in the divinity of the Torah or the resurrection of the dead, or to the Epicurean (Hebrew, *apiqoros*—apparently one who denies divine providence, but traditionally one who is disrespectful to the sages; Mishnah *Sanhedrin* 10:1). Although this statement cannot necessarily be used to define the rabbinic view of heresy, it did influence medieval discussions of Jewish dogmatics. Maimonides' Thirteen Principles were formulated as part of his commentary on this statement, and they seem to be based upon them. Other authors of dogmatic systems, however, did not always use them as a means of identifying heretics, and Judaism never achieved unanimity as to the parameters of heresy. There were also disagreements as to the status and culpability of the inadvertent heretics (those who are unaware of the heresy of their beliefs). Thus, in the absence of clear definitions of heresy, there could be no identification of heretical statements with blasphemy.

ACTING IN A MANNER THAT WOULD BRING DISREPUTE UPON THE GOD OF ISRAEL. The Torah provides remedies for those who transgress God's law unintentionally, but the *Book of Numbers* (15:30) states that intentional disobedience by a native-born Israelite or by a stranger is considered a form of insulting God *(giduf)* and is punishable by excision (*karet*), a sanction that is apparently a divine, rather than human, punishment. Since this verse seems to expand unreasonably the sanction of excision, in contrast to other biblical punishments, the rabbis generally restricted its application to the prohibition of idolatry. In fact, the prophet Ezekiel cited Israelite idol worship as an example of this type of insult to God, and he predicted that God would punish the people for their sin, forcing them to acknowledge the sovereignty of God (*Ez.* 20:27–44).

More broadly, the Bible enjoins Jews to sanctify God's name and to refrain from desecrating it (e.g., *Lv.* 22:32). This has been interpreted in the Jewish tradition as the responsibility Jews have to act in such a way as not to bring discredit upon God and Israel, God's people. Sanctification of God's name can include such actions as doing business honestly (so that the non-Jew is impressed by the influence God has on everyday transactions and on Jewish honesty), or being willing to die rather than convert to another religion (so that the non-Jew is impressed by the Jewish loyalty to God's religion). Conversely, actions that bring dishonor upon God (a Jew's acting dishonestly in business or not choosing death over coerced conversion) are understood as desecrating God's name and bringing dishonor upon Israel. It is difficult, however, to define clearly either sanctification or desecration of God's name, and human punishment for the latter would thus be hard to enforce. In general, desecration of God's name is more a moral category than a legal one, and it is not punished, for instance, as cursing God is. Yet, desecrating God's name in the ways mentioned might be considered, by extension, a form of blasphemy.

Jewish law provides outlines as to how one is to act to prevent public desecration of God's name. Thus, even if one may generally transgress a commandment under duress (except for the prohibitions of idolatry, murder, and adultery and incest), if that duress is public, for the purpose of offending God and the people of Israel, then Jews are enjoined not to violate minor proscriptions as well, even at the pain of death. Sanctification of God's name is one of the most important commandments that a Jew can perform, and as such it is almost the exact opposite of the offense of blasphemy.

See Also Heresy.

Bibliography

There is no comprehensive study of blasphemy in the Jewish tradition. Leonard W. Levy's *Blasphemy: Verbal Offense against the Sacred, from Moses to Salman Rushdie* (Chapel Hill, N.C., 1993), contains very little Jewish material, only reinforcing the statement made here that blasphemy is not an important concept in Judaism. A discussion of biblical terms for *cursing* is found in Herbert Chanan Brichto, *The Problem of "Curse" in the Hebrew Bible* (Philadelphia, 1963), but it omits *giduf*, one of the terms that is often translated as "blasphemy." Menachem Kellner's *Dogma in Medieval Jewish Thought: From Maimonides to Abravanel* (Oxford, 1986) reviews Jewish views of the principles of Judaism and heresy, illustrating that there was no one Jewish position on this question.

Daniel J. Lasker (2005)

BLASPHEMY: CHRISTIAN CONCEPT

The word *blasphemy* derives from a Greek term meaning "speaking evil," but in the Christian religious tradition the word refers to verbal offenses against sacred values or beliefs. A seventeenth-century Scottish jurist epitomized blasphemy by calling it "treason against God." The concept of blasphemy has never remained fixed. It has ranged from the ancient Hebrew crime of cursing the ineffable name of God to irreverent statements that outrage the religious sensibilities of others. What is deemed blasphemous varies from society to society and may differ with time and place, but whatever is condemned as blasphemy is always regarded as an abuse of liberty and reveals what a society cannot and will not tolerate. Blasphemy constitutes a litmus test of the standards a society feels it must enforce to preserve its religious peace, order, morality, and above all, salvation. Wherever organized religion exists, blasphemy is taboo.

Yet Christianity holds no monopoly on the concept of blasphemy. Every society will punish the rejection or mockery of its gods. Because blasphemy is an intolerable verbal violation of the sacred, it affronts the priestly class, the deep-seated beliefs of worshipers, and the basic religious values that a community shares. Punishing the blasphemer may serve any one of several social purposes in addition to setting an example to warn others. Punishment is also supposed to propitiate the offended deities by avenging their honor, thereby averting their wrath in the shape of earthquakes, infertility, lost battles, floods, plagues, or crop failures. Public retribution for blasphemy also vindicates the witness of believers, reaffirms communal values, and avoids the snares of toleration. Toleration sanctions the offense, inviting others to commit it, and sheds doubt on orthodox truths.

Periclean Greece cherished liberty yet prosecuted its blasphemers. Anaxagoras the philosopher, by imagining a superior intellect that had imposed a purposeful order on the physical world, insulted the Greek gods; Phidias the sculptor, by carving a figure of himself on the shield of his colossal statue of Athena, profaned her; Euripides the tragic poet seemed to doubt the sanctity of oaths witnessed by the gods; Alcibiades the general supposedly mocked the sacred rites honoring Demeter, the grain goddess; Protagoras the mathematician and Diagoras the poet confessed to agnosticism. Finally, Socrates, whose trial for blasphemy is the best known in history next to that of Jesus, was charged with corrupting the youth by disbelieving in the gods of the state and advocating deities of his own.

Christendom's concept of blasphemy derived from the Mosaic injunction of *Exodus* 22:28, which declares, "You shall not revile God." The precedent for punishing blasphemy as a crime is in *Leviticus* 24:16, where one who cursed the name of the Lord was put to death by stoning. None of the Old Testament references to the commission of blasphemy quotes the actual crime for fear of repeating it. The Hebrew scriptures distinguished blasphemy from other offenses against religion, in contrast to the Septuagint. Where, for example, Greek usage showed a preference for *blasphemy* and used that term somewhat loosely, the Hebrew scriptures referred more precisely to "idolatry" or "sacrilege," as in *Isaiah* 66:3 and *1 Maccabees* 2:6, or sometimes to "speaking anything against God," as in *Daniel* 3:29. On the other hand, the term for "blasphemy" in the Hebrew scriptures is *linqov*, which means "to specify, enunciate, or pronounce distinctly"; but *Leviticus* 24:10–23 uses it in conjunction with *qillel*, which means "curse." The word cannotes also "to pierce [the name of God], rail, repudiate, derogate, speak disrespectfully, denounce, insult, and abuse." The blasphemy of Rab-Shakeh in *2 Kings* 18–19 shows the offense to mean speaking disrespectfully of God, doubting his powers, and comparing him to idols. However, only cursing the personal name of the Lord merited the death penalty; for a lesser blasphemy, the punishment was probably excommunication. To curse was a far more serious offense than in our time. "God damn," a familiar curse, is today mere profanity; in the biblical sense, to curse meant uttering an imprecation in the name of God for the purpose of calling upon his power to perform an evil deed. Although the Septuagint tends to use *blasphemy* as a broad term for any offenses against religion, with the exception of *Ben Sira* 3:16 no Greek-Jewish text uses the word or any form of it that is not God-centered. Only God can be blasphemed in Jewish thought. And nowhere in Old Testament or Greek-Jewish sacred books is *blasphemy* a synonym for *heresy*. Indeed, no equivalent for the concept of heresy exists in the pre-Christian era. Christianity, though greatly influenced by Greek-Jewish texts, would use the two terms *blasphemy* and *heresy* as equivalents and as more than a God-centered offense. Not until Christianity began did the meaning of *blasphemy* change.

The New Testament retained the God-centeredness of the Mosaic code but expanded the concept of the offense to include the rejection of Jesus and the attribution of his miracles to satanic forces. Although only Mark and Matthew depict a formal trial and condemnation of Jesus by the Sanhedrin, all four evangelists employ the motif that the Jewish rejection of Jesus was blasphemy. Readers understand that whenever the Gospels depicted the Jews as describing Jesus as blasphemous for performing some miracle, or healing on the Sabbath, or forgiving sins, none of which constituted the crime of blasphemy in Jewish law, the Jews by their rejection, and not Jesus, were blasphemous. Thus in the climax of the trial scenes before the Sanhedrin, those who found Jesus guilty were blasphemers because they did not recognize him as the Son of God and the Messiah. Jesus' answer to Caiaphas in *Mark* 14:62 ("I am") should be understood as post-Easter theology, but it became the basis for a new, expanded concept of blasphemy in Christian thought.

For four centuries after the crucifixion, many different interpretations of Christianity competed with each other as the true faith, producing accusations of blasphemy. Jesus, having joined God as a divine majesty in Christian thought, though not in Arianism, became a target of blasphemers or, rather, the basis for leveling the charge of blasphemy against variant professors of Christianity. Cursing, reproaching, challenging, mocking, rejecting, or denying Jesus Christ became blasphemy. Posing as Jesus, claiming to be equal to him, or asserting powers or attributes that belonged to him, became blasphemy. Ascribing evil or immoral inspiration to any work of God or of the Holy Spirit that moved Jesus also became blasphemy, as did any denial or renunciation of the faith, and any discord, false beliefs, or dissent from Jesus' teachings. Denying the incarnation or calling the Son of God a human being only resulted in the same charge. Blasphemy was a concept of primary concern to Christians, as well as a vile epithet with which to blacken religious enemies. During the four centuries it took for Christianity to define itself and develop its faith, every faction accused its opponents as blasphemers. In time, heresy, which originally meant a factionalism arising from the willful choice of an untrue faith, became not just a form of blasphemy that exposed the true faith to contention; it became a term that eclipsed blasphemy. A point implicit in the deutero-Pauline epistles became explicit in *2 Clement,* which stated that blasphemy means "you do not do what I desire" and therefore consists of anything that contravened ecclesiastical authority. This viewpoint became a fixed position in Christian thought.

Any religious view contrary to church policy was blasphemy, a form of heresy, but the doctrine of the Trinity became the focal point in the controversy over blasphemy. The conflict between Arians and Athanasians involved more than a dispute over the right faith; it concerned the right road to salvation for all Christians. The authority of the church, when backed by the coercion of the state, settled the controversy by fixing on the Nicene Creed, which ultimately became the test of orthodoxy. Constantine's decrees against Arians and Arian books eventually led to the Theodosian Code of 438, enthroning Catholic Christianity as the exclusive religion of the empire, and Christians began persecuting each other. Heresy then superseded blasphemy as the great crime against Christianity. Unfreighted with Old Testament origins, heresy was more flexible and spacious a concept than blasphemy and had as many meanings. Both Athanasius and Augustine freely intermixed accusations of blasphemy and heresy, as if the two terms were interchangeable. But heresy became the encompassing term, because the church faced abusive criticism and competing doctrines about the faith, not abusive speech about God. Augustine developed a theory of persecution that lasted more than a millennium. Blasphemers, he wrote, "slay souls," causing "everlasting deaths." Rape, torture, and death were nothing compared to rejection or corruption of the pure faith. The church persecuted "out of love," he declared, "to save souls." Toleration intensified the heretic's damnation and passed his guilt to church and state for allowing him to contaminate others, multiplying his eternal fate among the faithful. Those who knew the revealed truth yet permitted disloyalty to it committed a greater crime than those who rejected it. Indulging willful error in a matter of salvation betrayed the faith and risked the worst calamity in the hereafter. Blasphemy, Augustine wrote, was the most "diabolical heresy."

Theologians who discussed blasphemy in the times of Bede, Gratian, Aquinas, Bernard Gui, and Bellarmine said nothing significantly different from Augustine. Aquinas regarded blasphemy as saying or thinking something false against God; he therefore understood it as a species of unbelief meriting death. But he also condemned all heresies as blasphemy: heretics, he thought, ought to be punished for crimes worse than treason or murder because they victimized God, not merely other human beings. According to Aquinas, "heretics . . . blaspheme against God by following a false faith."

Protestants during the Reformation had to reinvent the crime of blasphemy on the fiction that it was distinguishable from heresy. Because "heresy" was the Catholic description for Protestantism, Protestant leaders tended to choke on the word *heretic* and preferred to describe as "blasphemy" anything they disliked or disagreed with, just as the church had used "heresy." Luther, for example, impartially if promiscuously condemned as blasphemies Anabaptism, Arianism, Catholicism, Judaism, and Islam. Any denial of an article of Christian faith as he understood it was blasphemy. So too, sin was blasphemy, opposing Luther was blasphemy, questioning God's judgments was blasphemy, persecution of Protestants by Catholics was blasphemy, Zwinglian dissent from Lutheranism was blasphemy, missing church was blasphemy, and the peasantry's political opinions were blasphemy. Luther abused and cheapened the word, but he certainly revived and popularized it. It became part of the Protestant currency. In 1553 Calvin's Geneva executed Michael Servetus, the first systematic antitrinitarian theorist, for his "execrable blasphemies" that scandalized the Trinity and entailed the murder of many souls. Of all the blasphemy cases of the sixteenth century the strangest was that of Ferenc Dávid, the head of the Unitarian church in Transylvania. His allies, the Socinians, denounced and prosecuted him as a blasphemer because of his belief that Christians should not worship Christ. In 1579 the Hungarian Diet convicted him of blasphemy and sentenced him to life imprisonment.

During the seventeenth century blasphemy increasingly became a secular crime. The state began to supplant the church as the agency mainly responsible for instigating and conducting prosecutions. The connection between religious dissent and political subversion and the belief that a nation's religious unity augmented its peace and strength accounted in part for the rising dominance of the state in policing serious crimes against religion. Governments intervened more frequently to suppress nonconforming sectarians and intellectuals. Although Rome had charged Giordano Bruno with blasphemy and burned him for heresy in 1600, Protestant precedents were not without some influence. The church condemned for heresy, the state increasingly for blasphemy, even in Catholic states. On the continent, blasphemy prosecutions continued into the present century, although the death penalty for the crime was abandoned during the eighteenth century.

In England the prosecution of heresy as a capital crime had begun to die out in the reign of Elizabeth. The earliest Protestant codification of ecclesiastical law in England (1553) had the first separate section on blasphemy. Elizabeth burned five or six Arians and Anabaptists whose crimes included the beliefs that Christ was not God and that infant baptism was unnecessary. The last English executions for religion occurred in 1612; both victims were antitrinitarians, the principal targets of suppression throughout the century. John Biddle, the Socinian father of English Unitarianism, was persecuted for seventeen years and finally died in prison in 1662.

In 1648 Parliament had enacted a statute against blasphemy that reached the doctrines of Socinianism but not those of Ranterism, a phenomenon of the disillusioned and defeated political left that turned to religion for expression. Ranters believed that, as God's grace is unbounded, nothing is sinful. Antinomian sentiment run amok into religious anarchy, the Ranters were seditious, obscene, and blasphemous in ways as flagrantly offensive as possible. A 1650 act against blasphemy cataloged Ranter beliefs but punished them lightly compared to Scotland, which carried out the death penalty. The Ranters, believing that life should be enjoyed, recanted easily and disappeared. Unlike the Socinians or the Quakers, they did not have the stuff of martyrs.

George Fox, the founding Quaker, who was prosecuted for blasphemy four times, and his followers endured violent persecution. Their belief in the Christ within seemed blasphemous. In 1656 James Nayler, then the greatest Quaker, was convicted by Parliament for blasphemy because he reenacted Jesus' entry into Jerusalem on Palm Sunday as a sign of the imminent Second Coming. Nayler was savagely beaten and imprisoned. The first person imprisoned for blasphemy after the Restoration was William Penn, accused of antitrinitarianism.

In 1676 John Taylor, a farmer who really blasphemed ("Religion is a cheat" and "Christ is a bastard"), was convicted by the King's Bench. Chief Justice Matthew Hale delivered an opinion that made Taylor's case the most important ever decided in England; he ruled that the secular courts had jurisdiction of blasphemy and could punish blasphemers, because Christianity is part of the law of the land and the state has to prevent dissolution of government and religion. After the crime of nonconformity died in consequence of the Toleration Act of 1689, blasphemy remained an offense punishable by the state. A blasphemy act of 1698 targeted antitrinitarians, showing that England still regarded them as execrable atheists.

English precepts about blasphemy made the Atlantic crossing. Virginia's first code of laws (1611) specified death for anyone blaspheming the Trinity or Christianity, and most other colonies followed suit. But the actual punishments consisted of fines, branding, whipping, banishment, and prison. Massachusetts regarded Quakers as blasphemous but inflicted the death penalty, technically, for defiance of banishment decrees. In the eighteenth century, the Age of Enlightenment, blasphemy prosecutions on both sides of the Atlantic diminished. All the American colonies produced only half a dozen convictions, and the worst sentence was boring through the tongue and a year in prison. In Great

Britain, where there were a dozen convictions, the cases involved important defendants, serious legal issues, and heavier sentences. In one case the first minister to call himself a Unitarian was convicted for writing a book that temperately argued the subordination of Christ to God. A biblical scholar who mocked literal interpretations of miracles lost his appeal when the high court of Britain relied on the judgment in Taylor's case. As the century closed, a series of blasphemy prosecutions began against the publishers and sellers of Thomas Paine's *Age of Reason.*

The number of blasphemy cases peaked in England and the United States in the first half of the nineteenth century. Between 1821 and 1834 English trials produced seventy-three convictions. The defendants, who in the past had professed to be believing Christians, increasingly became agnostics, deists, and secularists who relied on freedom of the press more than freedom of religion, with as little success. In the American cases the courts maintained the legal fiction that the law punished only malice, never mere difference of opinion. The law aimed, that is, not at what was said but the way it was said; the judicial cliché on both sides of the Atlantic rested on the doctrine that manner, not matter, determined criminality. That seemed so in an important New York case of 1811 *(People v. Ruggles),* in which the court ruled that only Christianity could be blasphemed and judged guilty the defendant, who had declared that Jesus was a bastard, his mother a whore. Such malicious blasphemy found no protection in constitutional guarantees of freedom of expression or separation of church and state. But in the leading American case *(Commonwealth v. Kneeland),* decided in 1838 in Massachusetts, arguments based on liberty of conscience and press failed even though the defendant was a pantheist who declared in language devoid of scurrility that he did not believe in God, Christ, or miracles. The view that received no judicial endorsement in the nineteenth century was that espoused in 1825 by two old men, John Adams and Thomas Jefferson, who agreed that blasphemy prosecutions conflicted with the principle of free inquiry; Jefferson also sought to prove that Christianity was not part of the law of the land and that religion or irreligion did not belong to the cognizance of government. In 1883 the Lord Chief Justice of England supposedly liberalized the law by holding that decency of expression would exempt from prosecution even an attack on the fundamentals of Christianity—a fairly subjective test. Moreover, the decencies of controversy were also subjective in character. Indeed, the authors of most of the books of the Old and New Testaments as well as many leading saints and the originators of most Protestant denominations and sects gave such offense that they would not have passed the legal tests that prevailed in England and America.

In the twentieth century, blasphemy prosecutions have dwindled in number. In 1977 Massachusetts refused to repeal its three-hundred-year-old act against blasphemy, even though the last prosecutions in that state were conducted in the 1920s and had failed. But in the same year a prosecution succeeded in London, the first in over half a century. In the United States no prosecution has occurred since 1968, despite laws against blasphemy, and no prosecution ending in a conviction could survive judicial scrutiny on appeal, given the contemporary interpretations of First Amendment freedoms by the Supreme Court. Blasphemy prosecutions, relics of the Anglo-American world, are becoming obsolete even elsewhere in Christendom. People seem to have learned that Christianity is capable of surviving without penal sanctions and that God can avenge his own honor.

See Also Cursing.

Bibliography

Theodore Albert Schroeder's *Constitutional Free Speech Defined and Defended in an Unfinished Argument in a Case of Blasphemy* (1919; New York, 1970) is, despite its misleading title, a comprehensive history by a passionate, freethinking radical lawyer who opposed any restraints on expression. Not factually accurate, it is nevertheless a still useful pioneering work. Gerald D. Nokes's *A History of the Crime of Blasphemy* (London, 1928) also has a misleading title. It is a brief and narrowly legalistic study of English cases only, but is well executed. Leonard W. Levy's *Treason against God: A History of the Offense of Blasphemy* (New York, 1981) is easily the fullest treatment of the concept from Moses to 1700; covering religious thought as well as legal history, it is oversympathetic to victims of prosecution, according to reviewers. A promised sequel will bring the subject up to date. Levy's *Blasphemy in Massachusetts: Freedom of Conscience and the Abner Kneeland Case* (New York, 1973) reprints the major primary sources on the most important American case. Roland Bainton's *Hunted Heretic: The Life and Death of Michael Servetus* (Boston, 1953) is the best introduction to the most important blasphemy case of the Reformation. Donald Thomas's *A Long Time Burning: The History of Literary Censorship in England* (New York, 1969) is a vivid account that views the subject of blasphemy against a broad canvas. William H. Wickwar's *The Struggle for the Freedom of the Press, 1819–1832* (London, 1928) is a splendid, scholarly book that recounts prosecutions for blasphemy in England at a time when they peaked in number. George Holyoake's *The History of the Last Trial by Jury for Atheism in England* (1851; London, 1972) is a short autobiographical account by a freethinking victim of a prosecution. Hypatia Bradlaugh Bonner's *Penalties upon Opinion: Or Some Records of the Laws of Heresy and Blasphemy* (London, 1912) is a short account by an opponent of all blasphemy prosecutions and the daughter of the victim of one. William Wolkovich's *Bay State "Blue" Laws and Bimba* (Brockton, Mass., n. d.) is a well-documented study of a 1926 prosecution. Alan King-Hamilton's *And Nothing But the Truth* (London, 1982) is a judge's autobiography containing a chapter on a noted blasphemy case in England.

Leonard W. Levy (1987)

BLASPHEMY: ISLAMIC CONCEPT

Offering insult (*sabb*) to God, to the prophet Muḥammad, or to any part of the divine revelation is a crime in Islamic religious law, fully comparable to blasphemy. In the Christian tradition, blasphemy properly denotes mockery or *lèse majesté* of God. There is no exact equivalent to *blasphemy* in the Islamic tradition, although the Qurʾanic phrase "word of infidelity" (*kalimat al-kufr*) comes fairly close. From the viewpoint of Islamic law, blasphemy may be defined as any verbal expression that gives grounds for suspicion of apostasy (*riddah*). In theological terms, blasphemy often overlaps with infidelity (*kufr*), which is the deliberate rejection of God and revelation; in this sense, expressing religious opinions at variance with standard Islamic views could easily be looked upon as blasphemous. Blasphemy can also be seen as the equivalent of heresy (*zandaqah*), a pre-Islamic Persian term used in reference to the revolutionary teachings of Mani and Mazdak; in this sense, it can mean any public expression of teachings deemed dangerous to the state. Thus, in describing the Islamic concept of blasphemy, it is necessary to include not only insulting language directed at God, the Prophet, and the revelation, but also theological positions and even mystical aphorisms that have come under suspicion.

Blasphemy in Early Islam. During his own lifetime, the prophet Muḥammad (d. AH 10/632 CE) encountered strong opposition from the leaders of the Arab clans of Mecca when he preached the worship of the one God and attacked the traditional polytheism of the Arabs. Most frequently, this opposition took the form of verbal disputes and abuse, by which the pagan leaders rejected and ridiculed the Qurʾanic teachings on the unity of God and the resurrection. Muḥammad's opponents, moreover, mocked his claim to be an inspired prophet and accused him variously of being possessed, a soothsayer, a magician, a poet, or an unscrupulous power-seeker. From the beginning, as the Qurʾān attests, the blasphemous language of the Prophet's opponents thus consisted of calling divine revelation a lie (*takdhīb*). Insult to the Prophet was particularly blasphemous, since Muḥammad was the chief medium of that revelation. Among Muḥammad's opponents the Qurʾān (*sūrah* 111) singles out Abū Lahab above all as destined to punishment in hellfire; according to traditional accounts, the Qurʾān turns back on Abū Lahab the very words that he had used to curse Muḥammad. The followers of Muḥammad who killed two poets who had written satires on the Prophet evidently considered this kind of mockery to be blasphemy. The Qurʾān stresses the opposition that previous prophets experienced, as in the notable case of the pharaoh who called the revelation to Moses a lie, saying, "I am your highest Lord" (79:24). As a rejection of divine lordship, this saying is usually considered to be the height of blasphemy. Within the early Islamic community itself, the "hypocrites" (*munāfiqūn*) uttered blasphemous jests about God and the Prophet (9:65–66). Such mockery constituted infidelity (*kufr*) after professing faith (*īmān*) and invalidated whatever good deeds they might have previously performed (5:5).

Blasphemy in Islamic Law. Building upon the descriptions of and pronouncements on blasphemy found in the Qurʾān and the example (*sunnah*) of the Prophet, the various legal schools have elaborated upon the nature, conditions, and punishments for blasphemy. Jurists describe it as the expression of denigration (*istikhfāf*), contempt (*ihānah*), or scorn (*ḥaqārah*) for God, the Prophets, the Qurʾān, the angels, or the traditional religious sciences based on revelation. The legal handbooks of the Ḥanafī school, in particular, offer numerous examples of blasphemous sayings, usually classified under the heading of "words of infidelity" (*kalimāt al-kufr;* see *sūrah* 9:74). Since most of the classical collections of case-judgments (*fatāwā*) of this school derive from Iranian and Central Asian jurists of the eleventh and twelfth centuries, the blasphemous sayings are usually given not in Arabic but in Persian, which was the spoken language of those regions. The sayings, many of which were doubtless uttered in levity or in the heat of emotion, are generally wisecracking remarks, oaths, and imprecations of an intemperate or irreligious nature. Some examples are borderline cases, which are judged ambiguous or declared innocent. Later works, which include several separate monographs on "words of infidelity," give even larger collections of examples, with special prominence for those remarks that give offense to religious scholars as a class. An insult to religious scholarship is equivalent to rejection of religious knowledge and, hence, gives the lie to divine revelation. Under the same heading, the handbooks also include acts of sacrilege, such as donning the clothing of Jews or Zoroastrians, or participating in non-Islamic religious festivals. To claim that forbidden acts are permitted, or to invoke the name of God while committing sins, is blasphemy. A very small proportion of blasphemous statements (primarily in Ḥanafī texts) concern doctrinal matters, such as the formula used to declare oneself as a faithful worshiper.

Legal authorities agree that the conditions for blasphemy include adulthood, lack of duress, and being of sound mind, and it is immaterial whether the offender is a Muslim or not. Accidental blasphemy is, in general, not excused, although Ḥanafī jurists allow suspicious statements to be construed innocently if a legitimate case can be made for the interpretation. The Mālikī school permits an excuse to be made for one who has converted to Islam from another religion, but otherwise views blasphemy as entailing apostasy (*riddah*).

The punishment for blasphemy differs somewhat from one school to another. The Ḥanafīyah define blasphemous statements as acts of infidelity (*kufr*) and strip the blasphemer of all legal rights: his marriage is declared invalid, all religious acts worthless, and all claims to property or inheritance void. The death penalty is a last resort that most authorities try to avoid, especially if some element of accident or doubt is present. Repentance, however, restores all previous rights, although it is necessary to renew marriage. A few cases are mentioned in which a woman uttered blasphemies as a stratagem to annul her marriage, with the intention of repenting later to regain her other rights. The Mālikīyah, treating blasphemy as apostasy, call for immediate execution of the offender; as in cases of apostasy, they do not offer the chance to repent. An exception is made for female blasphemers, who are not to be executed but punished and encouraged to repent. In cases of minor blasphemies, or cases supported by only a single witness, the Mālikīyah prescribe a discretionary punishment in place of the death penalty.

Blasphemy in Islamic Theology and Philosophy. As indicated above, certain doctrinal propositions found their way into the lists of blasphemous statements. One of the earliest credal documents in Islam, the *Fiqh Akbar I* attributed to the jurist Abū Ḥanīfah (d. 767), includes two blasphemous statements about the prophets and God and calls them infidelity. But with the development of theological dogma, there was a tendency for scholars to label opposing doctrinal positions as forms of infidelity, even though only highly abstract arguments were involved. The legal consequences of such accusations were quite serious, as noted above, so it was natural that cooler heads insisted on moderating the use of such anathemas in theological debate. The great religious thinker Abū Ḥāmid al-Ghazālī (d. 1111) clarified this problem by removing infidelity (and hence blasphemy) from the realm of doctrine altogether. Insisting that infidelity is strictly a legal matter, al-Ghazālī defined it as calling the Prophet a liar in any respect; this is to equate infidelity with blasphemy. He further stipulated that no one who prays toward Mecca and repeats the Muslim confession of faith should be accused of infidelity, unless there is clear proof regarding a matter essential to the faith. In doctrinal terms, there are only three teachings that al-Ghazālī regards as infidelity in this sense. These teachings, all drawn from the works of philosophers such as Ibn Sīnā (Avicenna, d. 1037), are the doctrines that (1) the world is eternal and not God's creation; (2) God does not know particulars; and (3) the resurrection is not bodily but spiritual. Although al-Ghazālī enumerates many other doctrines that he considers objectionable, these alone appear to contradict the Prophet and divine revelation on essential matters (creation, divine omniscience, and eschatology). Thus teaching these doctrines is a blasphemous act punishable by death. It is worth noting that the Andalusian philosopher Ibn Rushd (Averroës, d. 1198) disputed al-Ghazālī's findings on both doctrinal and legal grounds, and later Iranian philosophers, such as Mullā Ṣadrā (d. 1637), certainly upheld similar theses. Although the doctrines of Greek philosophy seem far removed from the scurrilous insults that generally constitute blasphemy, certain of these teachings were potentially in serious conflict with the traditional Islamic understanding of revelation. Insofar as philosophy could be seen as calling the Prophet a liar, it constituted blasphemy.

Blasphemy in Ṣūfī Mysticism. The concept of blasphemy is applied rather differently in the case of mysticism. The growing Ṣūfī movement, which was centered on meditative practices that interiorized the Qurʾān and the ritual prayer, distinguished itself also by creating a technical vocabulary to express the states of mystical experience. Legalists challenged this innovation as a departure from the usage of the Qurʾān. More suspicious still were the ecstatic sayings (*shaṭḥīyāt*) that uncontrollably burst forth from the mystics. Ṣūfīs such as Abū Yazīd (Bāyazīd) al-Bisṭāmī (d. 874) and al-Ḥallāj (executed in 922) were notorious for such sayings as the former's "Glory be to Me! How great is My Majesty!" and the latter's "I am the Truth." Such proclamations appeared to be pretensions to divinity or prophecy, and readily fell into the category of blasphemy. Other sayings of this type criticized mechanical performance of ritual, made light of the punishments of hell, and, in general, made claims of great audacity.

Since Islamic law did not take formal cognizance of the existence of mystical states, the legal reaction to ecstatic sayings was not systematic. Certain Ṣūfīs, such as Nūrī (d. 907), ʿAyn al-Quḍāt (d. 1131), and the above-mentioned al-Ḥallāj, were put on trial and even executed, but such trials were heavily politicized and did not reflect correct juridical procedure. Contrary to popular opinion, however, Ṣūfīs such as al-Ḥallāj were not executed on account of their utterances; historical accounts reveal a mixture of charges, including radical Shiism, philosophical atheism, pretension to divinity and prophecy, and libertinism. Al-Ḥallāj was formally accused of maintaining the legitimacy of private ritual that could substitute for pilgrimage to Mecca. The Ḥanafī legal textbooks give a few examples of blasphemous statements that savor of mysticism. These generally consist of claims to know the unseen (*ghayb*), the assertion that only God exists, and the recognition of the omnipresence of God. Authentic ecstatic sayings were far more audacious than these examples cited by the jurists. One of the few jurists to review ecstatic sayings in detail was Ibn al-Jawzī (d. 1200), who severely criticized these utterances in his polemical treatise, *The Devil's Delusion.* Later jurists frequently criticized the theosophical writings of the Andalusian Ṣūfī Ibn al-ʿArabī (d. 1240) as blasphemous; he drew fire, in particular, for upholding the validity of Pharaoh's confession of faith, though it was made even as the waters of the Red Sea fell upon him (10:90). This was not so much a contradiction of the Qurʾān as it was a rejection of the dominant learned opinion.

Some authorities attempted a compromise on the subject of ecstatic sayings by considering them the products of intoxication (*sukr*). As such, they were like the ravings of a madman and hence were not punishable as blasphemy. From this point of view, ecstatic sayings were neither accepted nor condemned. Ṣūfīs, on the other hand, maintained that they were symbolic of inner experiences and could only be understood by those who had attained to esoteric knowledge. Legalists were thus incapable of the spiritual exegesis (*taʾwīl*) that alone could provide the correct interpretation of ecstatic sayings. A significant minority of legal scholars accepted this distinction and so excused ecstatic sayings from the charge of blasphemy, on the grounds that they were symbolic.

Bibliography

The Qurʾanic references to the Meccans' verbal criticism of Muḥammad are conveniently listed and discussed in W.

Montgomery Watt's *Muhammad at Mecca* (London, 1953), pp. 123–131. For the legal status of blasphemy insofar as it relates to apostasy, see Rudolph Peters and Gert J. J. de Vries's "Apostasy in Islam," *Die Welt des Islams*, n.s. 17 (1976–1977): 1–25, especially pages 2–4. Most of the legal treatises dealing with blasphemy remain unedited in manuscript form, but a French translation from the *Mukhtaṣar* by the Mālikī jurist Sīdī Khalīl (d. 1374) has been made by Léon Bercher, "L'apostasie, le blasphème et la rébellion in droit Musulman malékite," *Revue tunisienne* 30 (1923): 115–130 (occasioned by the controversy over the "naturalized" Tunisian Muslims who became subject to French instead of Islamic law). Other important legal discussions of blasphemy and apostasy can be found in David Santillana's *Istituzioni di diritto musulmano malichita con riguardo anche al sistema sciafiita*, vol. 1 (Rome, 1925), pp. 167–170 (Mālikī and Shāfiʿī); Eduard Sachau's *Muhammedanisches Recht nach Schafiitischer Lehre* (Stuttgart, 1897), pp. 843–846; and Neil B. E. Baillie's *A Digest of Moohummdan Laws*, 2 vols. (Lahore, 1965) (see the index for *apostacy* and *apostate*). A. J. Wensinck discusses the *Fiqh Akbar I* in *The Muslim Creed: Its Genesis and Historical Development*, 2d ed. (New Delhi, 1979), pp. 102–124. Al-Ghazālī's treatise on heresy and blasphemy has been translated by Richard Joseph McCarthy in *Freedom and Fulfillment* (Boston, 1980), pp. 145–174. Ibn al-Jawzī's censure of blasphemy of Ṣūfism has been translated by David S. Margoliouth in "'The Devil's Delusion' of Ibn al-Jauzi," *Islamic Culture* 10 (1936): 363–368 and 21 (1947): 394–402. An analysis of the legal criticisms of Ṣūfī sayings is available in my book *Words of Ecstasy in Sufism* (Albany, N.Y., 1985), in which see especially part 3.

CARL W. ERNST (1987)

BLAVATSKY, H. P. Helena Petrovna Blavatsky (1831–1891) was the principal founder of the modern theosophical movement. Blavatsky, née von Hahn, was born in Ekaterinoslav, Russia, of distinguished parentage. Her father, of German descent, was an army officer. Her mother, a popular novelist, died during Helena's childhood. Helena was raised largely on the estate of her maternal grandfather, then civil governor of Saratov. An unusual and gifted child, she read widely in her grandfather's library, taking a special interest in science and occultism. She also enjoyed riding vigorously with her father's regiment. In 1849 she married the middle-aged Nikifor Blavatsky, vice-governor of Yerevan, but quickly left him to make her way to Constantinople and, by her own account, to travel the world in pursuit of esoteric teachings, culminating with study and initiation in Tibet in the late 1860s under the tutelage of mahatmas (highly evolved teachers). Much of this period of her life is undocumented. But she asserted throughout her mature life that her work and teaching were guided by her mahatmas, and this is a key facet of her character. She was also by all accounts a colorful and unforgettable person, capable of tempestuous outbursts and great kindness, possessed of what many perceived as remarkable psychic talents, set apart by a certain air of mystery.

Helena Blavatsky came to America in 1873, where she met Henry Steel Olcott (1832–1907), a lawyer, journalist, and student of spiritualism. He, Blavatsky, and others founded the Theosophical Society in New York in 1875, an organization initially devoted to the investigation of occult lore, both Eastern and Western. In 1877 Blavatsky's first book, *Isis Unveiled*, was published, based on her occult study and experience.

Then, in 1878, she and Olcott departed for India, believed to be a reservoir of the wisdom she was seeking. She remained in India until 1885. Those were years of rapid growth for the theosophical movement, but also of much controversy related especially to a critical report on Blavatsky published by the Society for Psychical Research in 1885. Returning to Europe that year, Blavatsky settled in London in 1887. Despite failing health, she produced several more major works before her death in 1891: *The Secret Doctrine* in 1888, and *The Key to Theosophy* and *The Voice of the Silence* in 1889. *The Secret Doctrine* presents, often in mythopoeic language, the fullest and most mature articulation of her outlook, tracing through two large volumes the evolution of the universe, the solar system, the world, life, and humanity by the interaction of matter and consciousness from the first light through various "root races" to its present state and beyond. *The Key* summarizes theosophical basics in question-and-answer form. *The Voice* is a guidebook for "the few" who follow a path of altruistic mysticism.

The underlying theme of Blavatsky's work was the recovery of what she often called "the ancient wisdom": primordial lore about the manifestation and inner nature of the universe and humanity. She believed that in recent centuries this wisdom had been largely obscured by dogmatic religion and doctrinaire materialistic science, being preserved only in a scattering of esoteric groups and reservoirs of ancient truth such as Tibet. However, certain adept teachers, those also called mahatmas or masters, were prepared to instruct select candidates in the path to this almost forgotten learning. These adepts were largely real persons living in out-of-the-way places on earth, but able to communicate psychically with one another and with students like Blavatsky.

Blavatsky's theosophy could be termed an enhanced naturalism. She said that the universe works by law and evolves naturally out of original oneness from within. But, in contrast with the prevailing scientific view, as she perceived it, that process includes consciousness, which has coexisted with matter eternally and is evolving with it. In her more picturesque hermetic language, the inner essence of each individual is the "monad" or "pilgrim," an entity of refined consciousness traveling from life to life, world to world, and state to state as it descends into the realm of experience and ascends upward again toward ultimate unity.

The ethical dimension of Blavatsky's teaching must be underscored. Especially in her later writings, she emphasized that her evolutionary outlook and the ancient wisdom concealed everywhere indicated the "brotherhood" of all humanity, the importance of kindness and justice, and the evil of dogmatism and persecution. The early theosophical movement clearly had a place in the reformism of the Progressive Era in areas like feminism, education, anticolonialism, and child and animal welfare.

The influence of Blavatsky and her Theosophical Society is difficult to assess precisely, but it is increasingly recognized as a significant element within twentieth-century modernism in art, music, and poetry. The tribute she paid to Eastern and other submerged religions and cultures in the heyday of European imperialism by describing them as important custodians of ancient wisdom played a role in subsequent spiritual revivals and national independence movements from Ireland to India and Sri Lanka. Theosophy was no less important in popularizing Eastern religious concepts such as karma and reincarnation in the West. Some aspects of her philosophy hinted at forthcoming insights in relativity, quantum, and evolutionary theory. More narrowly, her work has had a powerful impact on all later occult, esoteric, and New Age ideologies. Finally, as a woman of strong and independent personality, exercising international spiritual leadership outside established institutions, she could be considered a feminist prototype.

Blavatsky aroused intense controversy in her lifetime, and she has continued to do so ever since. Charges of psychic fraud and plagiarism have been made but not conclusively substantiated. In the end she must be assessed by the historical significance of her movement and the inherent worth of her teachings.

See Also Besant, Annie; Theosophical Society.

Bibliography

Besant, Annie. "Theosophical Society." In *Encyclopedia of Religion and Ethics,* edited by James Hastings, vol. 12, pp. 300–304. Edinburgh and New York, 1908–1926. A concise summary of theosophical teaching and the early history of the Theosophical Society by a major disciple of Blavatsky.

Blavatsky, H. P. *Collected Writings.* 15 vols. Edited by Boris de Zirkoff. Wheaton, Ill., 1966–1991. Together with her major books, the fundamental sources.

Caldwell, Daniel, comp. *The Esoteric World of Madame Blavatsky.* Wheaton, Ill., 2000. A collection of first-hand personal impressions of Blavatsky by contemporaries of hers, the majority friendly but some negative.

Cranston, Sylvia (Anita Atkins). *HPB: The Extraordinary Life and Influence of Helena Blavatsky, Founder of the Modern Theosophical Movement.* 3d rev. ed. Santa Barbara, Calif., 1998. A modern sympathetic biography, uncritical but notable for its extensive documentation of Blavatsky's impact on modern art and letters.

Gomes, Michael. *The Dawning of the Theosophical Movement.* Wheaton, Ill., 1987. An empathetic scholarly study of Blavatsky and early theosophy in context.

Gomes, Michael. *Theosophy in the Nineteenth Century: An Annotated Bibliography.* New York, 1994. An essential resource.

Meade, Marion. *Madame Blavatsky: The Woman Behind the Myth.* New York, 1980. A biography from an independent perspective, sometimes speculative as to psychological motivation.

Oltramare, Paul. "Theosophy." In *Encyclopedia of Religion and Ethics,* edited by James Hastings, vol. 12, pp. 304–325. Edinburgh and New York, 1908–1926. Largely on theosophy as a general category in the history of religion, but refers to Blavatsky briefly from a critical perspective.

Washington, Peter. *Madame Blavatsky's Baboon: A History of the Mystics, Mediums, and Misfits Who Brought Spiritualism to America.* London, 1993; New York, 1995. An entertaining portrait of Blavatsky and others by an "outsider," presenting Blavatsky as a colorful eccentric.

Robert S. Ellwood (2005)

BLEEKER, C. JOUCO

BLEEKER, C. JOUCO (1898–1983), Dutch historian of Egyptian religion and leading figure in the field of phenomenology of religion. Claas Jouco Bleeker was born in Beneden Knijpe, the Netherlands, and attended school in Leeuwarden. He went on to study theology at the University of Leiden. There he specialized in Egyptology and the history of religions, chiefly under the tutelage of W. Brede Kristensen, whose work influenced him greatly. He continued his studies at the University of Berlin, and in 1929 he received his Th.D. from the University of Leiden for his thesis *De beteekenis van de Egyptische godin Ma-a-t* (The Significance of the Egyptian Goddess Maat). In 1925 Bleeker began a career as a minister in the Dutch Reformed church, serving first in the town of Apeldoorn. He held pulpits in various Dutch cities until 1946 when he was appointed professor of the history of religions and the phenomenology of religion at the University of Amsterdam. He remained in that post until his retirement in 1969.

Bleeker's interest both in the religion of ancient Egypt and in religious phenomenology continued throughout his life. His writings on Egyptian religion consist for the most part of studies of individual deities, such as *Die Geburt eines Gottes: Eine Studie über den ägyptischen Gott Min und sein Fest* (The Birth of a God: A Study on the Egyptian God Min and His Festival; 1956), and research on particular aspects of Egyptian religious life, such as *Egyptian Festivals: Enactments of Religious Renewal* (1967).

His work in the field of phenomenology was strongly influenced by Kristensen and Gerardus van der Leeuw. Bleeker was concerned with establishing phenomenology of religion as a distinct scholarly discipline that would examine the meaning of religious phenomena in the light of their realized "essence." He understood religion to be structured in terms of "(a) a holy vision of the Supreme Being or of the being and the will of the Deity, (b) a holy path that a man must pursue in order to be freed from his sin and suffering, and (c) a holy action that the believer must carry out in the cult and in his personal religious life" (*The Rainbow,* 1975, p. 8). He proposed three main objectives for phenomenology of religion. First, it must seek to understand individual phenomena that appear in all or many religious systems, such as prayer (this type of inquiry he called "theōria"). Second, it must try to discover the inner laws that determine the structure of a particular religion ("logos"). Finally, it should attempt to elucidate the way in which religions develop and evolve ("entelecheia").

Bleeker viewed the study of religion as an examination of humanity's varied relationships with God, and he attempted to understand humankind in light of its various attitudes toward divinity. Furthermore, he believed that the science of religion could engender greater mutual respect and understanding among religious groups holding widely differing opinions.

An able and energetic administrator, Bleeker served as secretary-general of the International Association for the History of Religions from 1950 to 1970. From 1960 to 1977 he edited the I. A. H. R.'s review *Numen* and supervised that journal's supplementary monograph series "Studies in the History of Religions." With Geo Widengren he coedited the important, two-volume hand-book *Historia Religionum* (1969–1971). He also oversaw the publication of the proceedings of several important international conferences.

Upon his retirement Bleeker was honored with a festschrift, *Liber Amicorum* (1969). Thereafter, until the time of his death, he remained active as a scholar, organizer, and editor.

BIBLIOGRAPHY

The fullest account of Bleeker's life is J. H. Kamstra's "In Memoriam: Prof. Dr. C. J. Bleeker," *Nederlands theologisch tijdschrift* 38 (January 1984): 67–69 (in Dutch). See also the obituary by R. J. Zwi Werblowsky in *Numen* 30 (December 1983): 129–130. For assessments of Bleeker's contribution to scholarship, see Geo Widengren's "Professor C. J. Bleeker, A Personal Appreciation" in the festschrift *Liber Amicorum: Studies in Honour of Professor Dr. C. J. Bleeker* (Leiden, 1969), pp. 5–7, and J. G. Platvoet's "The Study of Rites in the Netherlands," in *Nederlands theologisch tijdschrift* 37 (July 1983): 177–188.

A complete bibliography of Bleeker's works up to 1969 may be found in the *Liber Amicorum.* To this list may be added *Hathor and Thoth: Two Key Figures in Ancient Egyptian Religion* (Leiden, 1973). Many of Bleeker's articles are collected in two volumes: *The Sacred Bridge: Researches into the Nature and Structure of Religion* (Leiden, 1963) and *The Rainbow: A Collection of Studies in the Science of Religion* (Leiden, 1975).

M. HEERMA VAN VOSS (1987)

BLESSING.

Blessing is one of the most common religious acts in all belief systems. It is the beginning and the end of almost all rituals, including funeral services. Blessing manifests in worldly activities and common speech, in which it may be imperceptibly embedded, as well as in highly aspired religious contexts. Blessing nurtures hope and wards off fear; it is a companion and assurance in time of peace and a consolation and hope in time of crisis. Blessing is indispensable in celebrations, initiations, rituals, sacrifices, and rites of passage.

The process of blessing involves the act of blessing, its content, the means, the agent who has the power to grant the blessing, and the recipient who requests and receives the blessing. The act of blessing forms a bond between the supreme beings and the faithful. The contents of blessing reveal the hopes and fears of humankind.

GENERAL NOTIONS. Etymologically, the verb *to bless* comes from the word *blood*, suggesting the use of blood in consecration. Blessing thus directly invokes the ritual of consecration. When the Bible was translated into English, *to bless* was derived from the Hebrew word *berakh,* which was earlier translated into Greek as *eulogia* and into Latin as *benediction.* In the process of translation we find at least three meanings of what is supposedly the same word: consecration, eulogy, and benediction. In addition to these, there are common expressions that we usually consider to be blessings: Happy Birthday; Happy New Year; Merry Christmas; may God protect you; peace be with you; long live the king; with this truth; may you attain liberation. These phrases show that *blessing* has a broader meaning than that used in the process of translating the Bible.

Common and technical usages in different traditions reveal a wide range and many shades of meaning for the word *blessing.* Blessing can be an act or just an expression to convey good will or favor, frequently invoking God, gods, or a supreme being. One may assign to *blessing* three primary meanings: an act or rite of granting and receiving favor, with or without divine power; the expression of human aspiration towards goodness; and praise to a supreme and powerful entity. In order to cover all traditions, *supreme entity* is used here to mean superhuman authority, be it God, gods, holy men, or revered objects. There is no simple boundary among these three meanings. They are in a sense derived from the one concept that there is a benign power able to confer benefits upon humanity, individually or collectively.

Since God, gods, and holy persons are sources of goodness and mercy, offering praise to them can be a blessing automatically. Consecrated objects are blessed; that is, empowered to bring benefits. Blessing, in the sense of accord or approval, suggests that what has been proposed will advance shared aims for good. In all these meanings there is the undeniable presence of religious elements, such as belief in a supreme entity or in the efficacy of morality and ethics.

Among communicative speeches, which could include blessing, thanking, congratulating, or cursing, blessing is positive and creative. But blessing is not confined to words alone; the act of blessing involves semantic, social, psychological, and other elements. It should therefore be defined as a whole process of creating something beneficial.

The Components of Blessing. Within the process of blessing one can discern three elements: verbal, nonverbal, and religious actions. These rites are not distinct from each other, but rather act as coefficients. The third element is the most important, since without it blessing would not be effective.

Verbal elements. Blessing expressed through language is in fact the end-product of the process, the last to appear. But since it is the most obvious, we shall consider this aspect first. Blessing can embed in everyday language even without obvious religious context or intention. Whether the actual statement of blessing is embedded or independent, what is important is that it is a complete act, an attempt to do something by speaking. We can say that a blessing is an act done by speaking: it is a *speech-act.* Verbal statements like "to bless," "to promise," "to pronounce," "to wish," and "to vow" have the quality of performing or realizing themselves when uttered. The actualization of what is pronounced is not crucial. If circumstances are favorable it will materialize, but the act of blessing is complete in itself. These favorable circumstances, the *felicity conditions*, may consist of various elements according to circumstances.

But a speech-act cannot be the whole blessing. Speech has thought as its basis and it must have a semantic base. There are psychological and semantic elements in communicative situations involving blessings, curses, vows, oaths, and so on. If one describes the act of blessing as performative, then one might describe the pre-blessing state—the psychosemantic or thought state—as generative. Speech-acts show the speaker's attitude toward the good and bad things of life. The blessing must be said in context, otherwise how could we distinguish a blessing from a curse? The situation is contextually dependent.

The relation between benefactor and beneficiary or between benefactor and petitioner or supplicant, whether blessing is sought for oneself or for another, can be explained through the background of the supplicant. The content and the process of blessing can be generalized or universalized from the point of view of the benefactor, since a powerful entity is usually considered to be omnipresent, omnipotent, and omniscient. From the point of view of the petitioner, blessing is specific and personal. Humanity is always imperfect, which is why blessing is needed.

Nonverbal elements. Nonverbal elements accompany, surround, and evolve with or around blessing. They comprise a wide range of objects, places, persons, and phenomena. Everything worshiped, everything believed to be sacred and to have the power to bless, can be subsumed in this category. To attempt an inventory would be a superfluous endeavor: some examples will suffice to show how vast the nonverbal elements of blessing can be.

Signs, symbols, emblems, or diagrams which are deemed sacred and auspicious can be an instant blessing. The swastika, the Eight Auspicious Symbols of Indian tradition, sacred initials, anagrams, the cross, and others have long been used as devices of blessing. Images of founders (buddhas, Jain *Tīrthaṅkaras,* Jesus, Laozi, Confucius), deities, *bodhisattvas,* and saints, no matter whether they are painted, sculpted, or otherwise produced, are empowered to bless by consecration rites, myths, auspiciousness of the location, connection with relics, and so on. To witness these objects is to be blessed; a wish made in their presence is sure to be granted. Pilgrimages, miracles, and oracles reinforce the reputation of these special images, relics, and shrines: the process of empowerment is continuing and relational.

Natural features like the Ganges River, the Himalayas, caves, or even an island such as Delos are seen as sources of blessing, and have been popular destinations for pilgrimage since ancient times. Myth and legend, images and relics reinforce the holy or sacred status of these geographic locations. For the Hindu, the Ganges River is a blessing: to merge into the Ganges is to liberate oneself from suffering and sins, which is one of the most sought-after blessings. The complexities of social activities that center upon the Ganges demonstrate how a sacred locality can loom large in religion and belief and develop into a socioeconomic phenomenon.

Blessing is signified physically by gestures like raising or extending the right hand with palm open, the *varadamudrā.* Blessings are usually accompanied by verbal elements or verbal symbolism such as the sacred syllable *Oṃ* or a *mantra.* Verbal embodiments of blessing, even when muttered or inscribed, generate the power of protection and benediction. Music and dance are commonly used in ritual. In many cultures, for example Indian or Thai, there are specific songs or tunes auspicious for blessing, and there is also blessing by means of music: the music itself is sacred and is a blessing when played.

Nonverbal elements mainly concern the benefactor or situations favorable to giving a blessing. They mediate or enhance the blessing, as is evident in ritual, which usually incorporates symbolism, icons, and the concept of sacred space. In ritual the verbal and the nonverbal elements unite. Ritual is performed by religious experts, priests, monks, or shamans, within a consecrated space, using implements, gestures, words, music, and chants. Nonverbal elements are also used to transfer blessings. In some cases, such as in Armenian tradition, fragments from an old Bible are inserted into a new one as a blessing. The blessing is transferred by means of nonverbal empowerment.

The religious elements of blessing. The religious element is the most important component of blessing, since without it the other elements, verbal or nonverbal, cannot become a blessing. These elements are something already produced. To use a linguistic term, this is a surface structure. The religious element is in the deep structure of blessing. It must be present before a blessing is performed, and not cease to exist afterward. We can hear a blessing when it is uttered, we can perceive its surroundings with our senses. But the mystic power, which is the most fundamental element in the production of a blessing, is intangible. That power exists because we believe in the power of the blessing, and that is why blessing is deemed to be religious. Human beings assume that there is an entity or, in some cultures, entities, that possess or generate power and transform it into a blessing; but the power and process of transformation is intangible and unquantifiable.

The transcendental power. Generally, all religions worship and venerate something as sacred and powerful. The names might be different but the concept, and thus the relation between the ultimate entity and humanity, is more or less comparatively the same among people of different faiths. The sacred or the transcendental entity can take many forms. It can be represented by a panoply of gods and goddesses, as in Indian and Chinese religions. It can be a pervasive and universal essence, as in the concept of *ātman-paramātman* in Indian philosophy. It can be a one and only God as in Judaism, Christianity, and Islam. In religions like Jainism and Buddhism, where God or gods do not play the role of supreme power, the founders themselves—the Jinas, the buddhas and the buddhas-to-be, and the *bodhisattvas*—because of the wisdom, purity, and mercy gained from their enlightenment, take the position of the ultimate.

It is true that in some forms of belief, such as monism, the supreme power is both fearful and graceful, as it encompasses and is the same as chaos and the cosmos. This pervasive power manifests in various forms to answer the needs of humanity, but it is, in whatever form, refuge to the faithful. Since this power is transcendental and blissful it is always available for supplication and always ready to bless. The ways and means to approach and ask favor from the power and how the power is to be transferred to the supplicants vary.

The divine or the sacred can transfer a blessing to human beings at will and without intermediary. However, in practice a blessing is usually transferred with some form of mediation. Two main intermediaries are common in most traditions (this is especially prominent in Catholicism). First, ritual or sacrifice, with its accessories and liturgical procedures in which words or speech-acts form a vital role; second, the agents who perform the ritual, who can be priests, monks, shamans, kings, or leaders, or the senior male or female members of a community or family. It should be noted that in Buddhism ritual is meant to bless and is performed mostly with words: chanting of the sacred texts or praises to the Three Gems and the *dharma.* It is a blessing ritual, not a ritual in which blessing forms a part.

Power of the word: divine origin and origin of the world. Speech possesses power because it is unique to humans, so much so that it is thought to be divine or of divine origin. Language, as a vehicle of thought and emotion, is not totally explicable. It is not actually known how the power of communication works, but language and thought are clearly not separable. Words carry not only significative and suggestive, but also mystic, meaning. Words can convey not just the content but also the power and the mystic elements embodied in God and blessing. In some traditions, like the Indian, speech is the outcome of thought, or the inner language system, of a person, which originates in the universal langue. It is the bridge connecting the abstract and the concrete.

Words express, reveal, and expose reality. They are equal to the essence of the universe itself. In other words they are equal to god. In Vedic tradition the word *vac* (word or speech) is said to be the origin and the essence of this universe. The ultimate word is *brahman* (the essence of the universe.) And in the New Testament, the same concept is propounded: "In the beginning was the Word, and the Word was with God, and the Word was God" (*John* 1:1). Words in themselves are thus divine and have power. Speech-acts such as blessings, curses, and vows are more intensified by psychological processes than normal significative ones. Since speech is powerful, blessing has the potential to be efficacious.

Words are more powerful if they stem from the ultimate power and are considered to be the words of god or the Truth, realized or seen by sages such as Vedic seers or the Buddha. Holy texts like the Bible, the Qurʾān, or the Buddhist canon are considered to be blessings by themselves. They are the words of power. Words can also become more powerful through encrypted forms. Mantras, sacred syllables, chanting in a reversed order, or syllables set in diagrams are examples of this type. They can bless and act as blessings. These words of power are closely related to the action-oriented blessing. To listen, chant, read, copy, or propagate the chosen words lead to happiness, a blessing gained by action.

FORMS AND CONTENTS OF BLESSINGS. The three elements—verbal, nonverbal, and religious—evolve into different forms to express a blessing. Blessing can be simple and personal or ritualized and public, both in verbal and nonverbal form. The act of blessing usually involves a benefactor, a petitioner, and a beneficiary. In this case, one can say that blessing acts as a tie between humanity and the supreme power or the sacred. It is a search for the benign qualities in a supreme entity and an effort to transfer them.

Blessing can be expressed in various forms of speech. In relation to a benefactor, a blessing is expressed in eulogy, praise, or prayer. Praise and prayer breathe life into the sacred and make the sacred real and present. In relation to the supplicant who requests something from a powerful entity, blessing conveys favors and is a gift from the sacred to humankind. Here blessing can take the form of an invocation or supplication. It marks the relationship between the sacred and humanity as benevolent, in contrast to the malevolence of evil. In ritual it takes the form of benediction.

Language formulas also reflect how the faithful receive a blessing. Invocation and praises to god or the transcendental power are the most common formulas. They are mixed into common speech to the point that they have often become exclamation words. They are personal, since one can invoke and praise a powerful entity by oneself. But they can also be ritualized and liturgical. In this case, blessing is sought through participation in ritual. Catholic liturgies usually end with a blessing, the benediction. The central activity of Buddhist rituals for auspicious occasions is the chanting of *paritta* or *raksa* text, selected auspicious and protective blessings, by monks. Even a funeral rite ends with stanzas of blessing.

As a supplication, blessing is related to wishes for oneself or for another. Wishes for others may be expressed through vows and strong altruistic intentions. When the wish is for oneself, the activity is mainly on the beneficiary's part. This is generally an activity-oriented blessing, in which the petitioner asks the sacred for help in doing something. In other cases something is done or promised which will make the recipient worthy of blessing, or a vow is made to do something to express gratitude to the sacred if the wish is granted. The petitioner may go to any sanctuary, or one associated with a specific need or wish. In strong monotheistic traditions like Christianity or Islam, total submission to God is the most meritorious act and is a form of blessing in itself: if one acts as God or the Prophet has prescribed, one is saved and blessed.

Participation in religious ritual and sacrifice are also considered meritorious. In traditions where there is no divine authority, the path laid down by the founder is the way to blessedness. In Buddhism the emphasis is on good *karma,* the cultivation of meritorious deeds by body, speech, and mind. Blessing is instantaneous when one does something good. In this case even an inferior in age, position, or spiritual attainment can bless a superior. This phenomenon is not limited to Buddhism but can be observed in all religions. One can bless priests or rabbis for the good they have done by wishing them long life or good health, for example. This is blessing through gratitude or thankfulness. In Islam, performing the *zakāt* as prescribed is a blessing in itself. We may say that in these cases rituals have been transformed into moral acts. In theistic religions moral acts function as intermediaries because they are prescribed by God, who alone has the power to bless.

Generally speaking, the content of blessings is what one wishes for and asks from the Ultimate. Blessing can have general content, unspecified and at the same time universal, as in expressions like "Bless you," "God bless," and "May good merit protect you." In religious ceremonies blessing is pervasive—everyone who participates is blessed, and participants can direct the blessing to whatever end they like. When blessing is more specific in content it can be classified as material or spiritual. The first category comprises all that is tangible: wealth, health, prosperity, progeny, longevity, and protection. Examples of spiritual blessing are found in several traditions. In *Ephesians* 1:3, spiritual blessing is mentioned: "Blessed be the God and Father of our Lord Jesus Christ, who has blessed us with every spiritual blessing." In Buddhism it is common to wish for the ultimate blessing of liberation from suffering, which, ironically, is only possible through an arduous spiritual journey.

BLESSINGS IN MAJOR RELIGIOUS TRADITIONS. The four major religious traditions each have their own version of blessing, governed by their individual natures. Judeo-Christian and Islamic tradition exemplifies strong monotheistic principles. The Indic religion is a challenge to classify because it embraces all conceivable types of religion: polytheistic, henotheistic, monotheistic, and monistic. In the Buddhist tradition, gods and goddesses play some roles but are not essential. The Chinese tradition can be called mystically pragmatic or naturalistic, and the mystic forces of nature elements play an essential role.

Judaic, Christian, and Islamic traditions share the concept of the One God, the Almighty, the Creator, who has absolute, transcendental power over what he has created. God is thus the source of all blessings. The power to bless is the nature of God, but God himself is also considered a blessing. He is evoked before any ritual can commence so that the ritual can become a blessing.

Judaic traditions. The word *blessing* in these traditions is derived from the Semitic root *brk* (to bless). The derivations of the root evolve into various shades of meaning in these traditions, which reflect their thinking on blessing. The Hebrew scriptures emphasize the principle of God as the sole source of blessings. He created humans and bestowed various blessings on them. Of course he punished them from time to time, but less frequently than he blessed them. Forms of the word *berakhah* (blessing) appear 398 times in the Hebrew Bible. In Jewish tradition blessings are bestowed upon the Chosen People, the people of God. But since all human beings come from the same ancestor, the tradition extends blessings to all of humanity. And only through God's blessings can one attain salvation.

Blessing can also be transferred to humanity by means of an intermediary—a family head, king, or priest—charged with a mission. When the Hebrew religious institutions were established and the religious organization refined, the content and intermediary of blessings were codified:

> And the Lord spoke to Moses, saying, Speak to Aaron and his sons, saying, This is the way you shall bless the children of Israel. Say to them: the Lord bless you and keep you; the Lord make His face shine upon you and be gracious to you; The Lord lift up His countenance upon you and give you peace. So they shall put My name on the children of Israel, and I will bless them. (*Num.* 6:22–27)

But this is not the only means by which the Jewish people ask for blessing and bless. Blessings as both a means of praising God and of requesting his favor blend into every aspect of Jewish life.

Berakhah (blessing), widely rendered in liturgical literature as *benediction,* has a fixed formula in Jewish liturgy. It must contain the words *baruch atta adonai elohenu melech ha'olam baruch* (Blessed art thou Lord, our God, King of the Universe). *Berakhah* can be found throughout every form of the Jewish liturgy.

Jewish daily life starts with blessing from the moment of waking up. There are blessings for every activity: washing one's hands before a meal, saying grace before and after a meal, even smelling fragrant trees or bark. Blessings are spoken over wine and over specially prepared food. In domestic and public rituals of worship, blessing, in the sense of praising and supplicating, pervades the liturgical sequences. Through blessing, activities, no matter how mundane, are sanctified, and the relationship between God and his people is confirmed.

In public worship there are two essential components in the liturgical sequence that show *berakhah* as the core and the focal point of the liturgy: the praise, *shevah,* which has the Confirmation of the Faith as its focal point, and the prayer, *tefillah* or *ʿamida.* They both contain *berakhah,* but it is in the prayer that blessing has a special status. Evidence shows that both *sh'maʿ* and *ʿamida* originated in the sacrificial rites performed in the Temple of Solomon before its destruction in 70 CE.

There are several terms used for *tefillah.* It may be called *ʿamida,* because it is recited while standing; or *sh'moneh ʿesreh,* because it has eighteen blessings or benedictions (even when the nineteenth is added, the name stands). It consists of nineteen benedictions. These include three benedictions called praise, thirteen petitions, and three thanksgivings. In regular daily services all are recited, first silently by each individual so sinners can atone without embarrassment, then repeated aloud by the reader. At festive occasions the petitions are replaced by an appropriate blessing.

The *sh'maʿ* and *ʿamida* are the core of Jewish liturgy; in fact they can be considered instrumental in holding the religion together. The Confirmation of the Faith holds Israel to be a nation no matter how far and wide the Jews spread over the world. Blessings accompanying the *sh'maʿ* stress that Jews are the Chosen People blessed by God. In *ʿamida* blessing shines forth with its whole range of meanings, be it praise, petition, or thanksgiving. It establishes God as the sole resource, power, and refuge of humankind.

Christian traditions. The Christian tradition is similar to the Jewish in that God is the source of all blessings. The word *berakhah* is translated as *eulogia* in Greek and *benediction* in Latin, carries the meaning of "speak well" or "good words." This can be interpreted in two ways: towards God, the good words are praises, while towards human beings, they are gifts from God. There is parallelism here: Jesus is the gift of god to humankind, he is the *eulogia* and through him the *eulogia* passes to humankind. Jesus' communication to God is direct, thus his words, as praises and petitions to God, are the most effective. This direct communication with God was continued by the Apostles and later by the priests of the church. Thus in Christianity blessings are passed along by means of ritual officiated over by the designated officers of God. The most common blessing used by Jesus, *pax vobis* (peace be with you), has become part of all the sacraments.

Islamic traditions. In the pre-Islamic Arab world the root *brk* has two meanings: "to bless" and "to crouch." The second meaning, as a noun, *baraca,* alludes to the crouching camel and to mating, which suggests a fertility cult. The meaning is further extended to signify wealth and all desirable things. But in the uncompromising monotheistic view of Islam, the meaning of the word *baraca* and *al baracat,* the plural form, is restricted to blessings from God. It is God's mercy that makes blessing possible. Anyone who is totally submissive to his will, will be blessed.

Indic traditions. In Indic tradition the word for blessing, *vara,* is derived from the root *vr* (to choose). The concept of blessing has its root in *yajna,* sacrifice to gods and goddesses. Sacrifice is officiated over by priests to please the gods, and the *yajamana,* the person who sponsors the sacrifice, chooses the blessing to receive. The way to obtain something through the action of sacrifice is called *karma.* The arrangement and the sequences of sacrifices, which in later periods become more elaborate and complex, are seen as the means by which the universe is regulated. In this sense sacrifice can be called *dharma,* the upholder of the universe.

On a personal level, the act of sacrifice is further internalized and becomes a moral act, good or bad, which will entail a result. It can also be an act done to please the gods in the form of *tapas* (penance). This is one of the most popular ways to obtain divine blessing, and appears abundantly in Indian literature. At times, the blessing that was chosen had a negative effect on other people or even upset the universe, and the gods were obliged to convene to try to save the situation.

When ethics and morality are emphasized, good actions, the *kusalakarma* or *dharma,* in the sense of the upholder of society, are the source of blessings. In orthodox Indic tradition, *dharma* in this sense means action as prescribed by the gods for the four classes, or *varna* (Brāhmaṇ, the priests; *kṣatriya,* the warriors; *vaiśya,* the merchants and craftmen; *śūdra,* the serfs). Those who act according to the divine rule sustain the goodness and peace in this world and are blessed by the gods.

Another aspect of blessings in Indic tradition is the intimacy between gods and man. There are many gods, goddesses, local spirits, and sacred places to which the Indian will go for blessings. Images of gods and goddesses, whether in a temple or private shrine, are worshiped daily as if they were alive; they are clothed and fed and offered ornaments, music, and fragrances.

Words are crucial in all of these rituals. In Vedic times the correct pronunciation of the mantra of the Veda was at the heart of a sacrifice. When it is internalized and intensified in the mind, action is considered to be a genuinely efficacious power. When uttered solemnly, words, blessings, and curses become real and have a real effect. Words uttered by holy or virtuous individuals and the Truth expressed through words are especially potent.

Blessings penetrate into all actions in Indian life. No activity can begin if the blessing of the gods is not first invoked. In the morning the *Savitṛ* stanza must be recited before any activity is undertaken. In Indic tradition, as well as in Southeast Asian traditions such as those of the Thai, Burmese, and Khmer, literary works start and end with blessing stanzas, which confer auspiciousness and protection to the writer, listener, and reader. The performing arts and fine arts begin with homage to the teachers to express gratitude, to obtain blessings, and to ward off all obstacles and mishaps.

Buddhist traditions. Buddhist practice follows the same line as mainstream Indic tradition. Buddhists propitiate buddhas and *bodhisattvas* as well as gods and goddesses for good fortune and protection. They have *paritta* or *raksa* text, the blessing literature, which they chant or have monks chant in ceremonies for blessing. Monks, or even lay people by virtue of their high moral status, can also be the source of blessings.

Chinese traditions. The Chinese concept of blessing and the blessed state stems from harmony among the three realms of the universe: Heaven, Earth, and Man. Heaven is the source of blessings through the king or emperor, who has the right and duty to propitiate Heaven by performing sacrifices according to the treatises. The ideal state is expressed by the balance between the two forces of yin and yang and the Five Elements. Since these elements are the components of the universe, they arrange themselves in various shapes and forms. The elements take turns to preside over Earth and human beings. One must know which element is predominant at a specific moment or period in order to act in harmony with that element and to gain thereby the energy and blessing in full force.

The same concept applies to feng shui practice, which is the art of drawing on natural forces to gain favor and blessings. Sacrifice is the key to harmony. The king or emperor performs sacrifices for the blessing of the state and his people. Heaven blesses through the medium of the emperor; this was the role of a priest-king in ancient times. In a household, the head of the family performs sacrifices to ancestral and other gods to maintain the harmony of the family.

Language, both spoken and written, plays a special role in the Chinese tradition of blessing. Auspicious characters, singly or in combination, such as those for fortune, longevity, and promotion, confer blessings in their own right. Auspicious characters, graphic designs, and phrases represented in calligraphy are affixed inside and outside of buildings to bring blessings. They may be represented in forms other than calligraphy, appearing in paintings or decorative arts as symbols derived from homonyms of auspicious words. A picture of a bat stands for fortune because *bat* and *fortune* are homonyms. These visual representations confer instantaneous and constant blessings.

The primary blessings in Chinese thought are *fu* (felicity), *lu* (prosperity or promotion), and *shou* (longevity). They are represented in calligraphy, in personified form, and by symbols on almost everything, from the architectural elements of a house or a town to the decorations on utensils such as plates, cups, and bowls. As a result, the Chinese live amid a landscape of blessings.

Blessing can be considered the act of giving blessing, the blessing itself, and the process by which blessing is transferred. Language and complex systems of communication are believed to belong only to humankind; they enable humans to control society and their environment and thus express or embody power. They convey meaning and transmit knowledge, emotion, and thought. Words uttered intentionally, like blessings, are moral and social acts by themselves. Intensified by mental and spiritual factors they are invested with potency both in the minds of the speakers and the audience. Words of god, pertaining to god or gods or the sacred, are endowed with power by themselves.

Blessings are an essential part of life. Even in religions where they must be granted only by God and through the intermediacy of authorized representatives, adherents bless each other when they are on good terms and curse each other when on bad terms. They even bless God, whether or not he can be or needs to be blessed. Blessings represent creative, benign, or even saving forces. They help reconcile us with this imperfect world. They are a primary consolation, since they express the hopes of humankind. They manifest the benign relationship between the sacred and the human. In a sense, blessing breathes life into the sacred and the supreme and makes them vivid and real in human life.

BIBLIOGRAPHY

Regrettably not a single book has been written solely on blessing. The word is found in dictionaries and encyclopedias, most of which deal with blessing in Catholicism; see for example "benediction" in *Encyclopedie Catholique* (Paris, 1948), pp. 1405–1416; see also *Livre des benediction, rituel romain,* (Paris, 1995), p. 5–13. For a general introduction one may consult articles in the *Encyclopedia of Religion and Ethics,* edited by James Hastings, (Edinburgh, 1913) and the *Encyclopedia of Religion.* A brief entry on blessing in terms of the phenomenology of religion is found in G. van der Leeuw, *La religion dans son essence et ses manifestations, phenomenologie de la religion* (Paris, 1970), p. 59. The theory of the speech-act found its definitive form in John L. Austin, *How to Do Things with Words* (Oxford, 1962). Further ideas on the subject can be found in books on cognitive linguistics. For linguistic analysis of blessing in a particular language, James A. Matisoff, *Blessings, Curses, Hopes, and Fears: Psycho-Ostensive Expressions in Yiddish* (Stanford, Calif., 2000), is the only example. The relationship between human being, language, and gesture is discussed in Jean Poirier, ed., *Histoire des moeurs,* vol. 2 (Paris, 1991). For nonverbal elements of blessing, there is no direct source, and one must turn to works on ritual, such as Roy A. Rappaport, *Ritual and Religion in the Making of Humanity* (Cambridge Studies in Social and Cultural Anthropology, Cambridge, Mass., 1999) and John R. Bowen, *Religions in Practice: An Approach to the Anthropology of Religion* (Boston, 2002), chap. 9, "Objects, Images,

VISUAL NARRATIVE

Storytelling may be one of the most universal of human behaviors. Representing events in a series of episodes allows storytellers and their audiences to explain a state of affairs, to trace the historical development of a people, to limn the portrait of a hero, or to account for the status of a ruler, city, or natural order. Storytelling ascribes causation to events, provides access to the past, bestows meaning on the present, and offers counter-narratives to prevailing or rival accounts.

Images work closely with oral and written narratives, sometimes as external scaffolding or supportive prompts. This can involve little or even no imagery. Some Native American winter counts are no more than abstract patterns, unlike the late pictographic example reproduced here **(a)**, which consists of symbolic devices that demarcate tribal history and lore among the Brulé Lakota. This example, produced in the early twentieth century, replicates the notation that was traditionally painted on buffalo hides, and adds numeric dating beneath the pictographs. An *aide de memoire*, the winter count assists the narration of tribal memory but is not a linguistic system in the manner of Egyptian hieroglyphics. The winter count supplements oral culture by prompting patterns of verbal discourse, such as song and chant, in the setting of dance and ceremonial discourse.

Images also commonly provide less pictographic prompts to narrative, such as paintings and sculptures of the nine

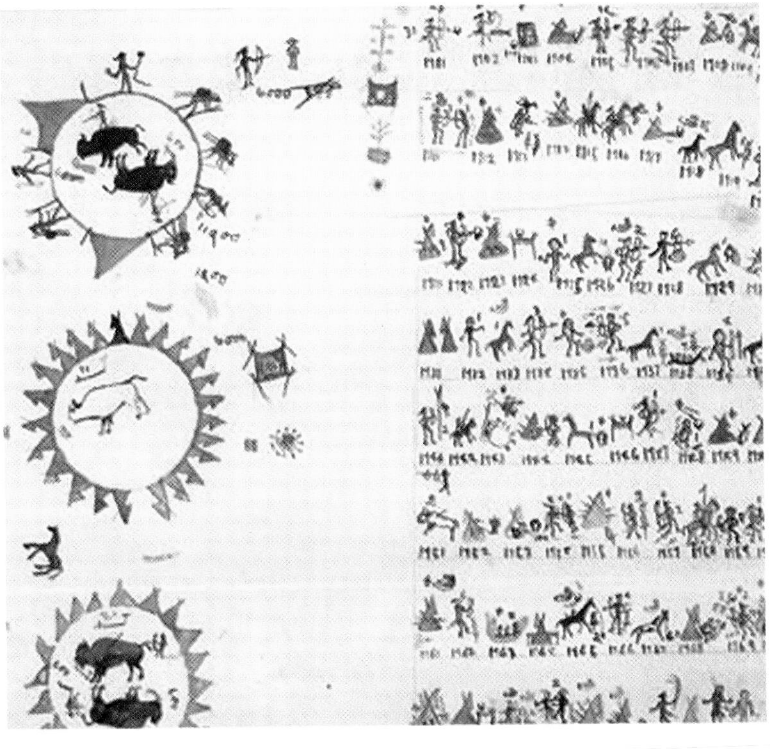

(a) Detail from a winter count by Battiste Good, watercolor on paper, c. 1907. *[Library of Congress]*

great events of the Buddha's life (**b**). In these works, artists do not seek to render a seamless succession of episodes, but surround the key event of the life of the historical Buddha—the moment of his triumph over Māra, the god of illusion, a decisive victory symbolized by the Buddha's touching the earth, calling it as witness to his many lives of karmic ascent. Nine key events are visualized in a pictorial shorthand, organized as a compendium of the principal episodes in the Buddha's life, and framing the central representation of his enlightenment. This gathering of representations assists Buddhist teachers and students in recounting not only the historical life of the Buddha, but the meaning of his teaching. Narrative in this sense is not a neutral recounting of events, but a highly interpretative reading of the founder's life.

Storytelling of any sort is invariably interpretative

(b) LEFT. *Buddha Shakyamuni and Scenes from the Life of Buddha*, copper with traces of gilding, twelfth century, Nepal. *[Los Angeles County Museum of Art, gift of Mr. and Mrs. Michael Phillips]* **(c)** BOTTOM LEFT. Roman marble sculpture of Laocoon and his sons, believed to be a first-century CE copy of a first- to second-century BCE Greek original. *[©Araldo de Luca/Corbis]* **(d)** BOTTOM RIGHT. Roman copy of a fifth-century BCE Greek relief of Hermes, Orpheus, and Eurydice. *[©Alinari/Art Resource, N.Y.]*

and not merely descriptive, because it consists necessarily of a selection and weighting of particular events, as well as their integration, into a series of episodes that culminates in a state of affairs that offers a perspective that the viewer/listener is presumed to accept as compelling in the sense of being cautionary, explanatory, aesthetically pleasing, or inspirational.

But images operate differently than words. Unless they are presented on the pages of a book or scroll, or organized as dense grids of individual events, or seen in succession across the broad surfaces of walls or ceilings, an image is largely unable to unfold temporally since a viewer stands in front of it and sees all of it at once in sweeping scans. Consequently, images often present single selections from a narrative that focus the viewer's attention on a particular episode that is considered by teachers or patrons or the devout as especially significant or as emblematic of the entire narrative **(a, d, e, f, g)**. For example, the sculpture of Laocoon and his sons **(c)** writhing in agony in the coils of a serpent sent by Athena to prevent the priest's discovery of the Greeks hidden within the wooden horse left at

(e) Kṛṣṇa steals the clothes of the *gopīes* in a Pahari school illustration from the *Bhāgavata Purāṇa*, Kangra, Himachal Pradesh, 1780. *[©Art Resource, N.Y.]*

(f) Contemporary print depicting Gurū Gobind Gingh addressing his khālsā. *[Reproduced by permission of Oxford University Press India, New Delhi. W. H. Mcleod, Popular Sikh Art]*

Troy was probably taken from the second book of Vergil's *Aeneid.* The sculpture does not purport to represent the entire narrative, but singles out a dramatic instance within it, the heroic struggle of a man against a fate doled out by an unsympathetic deity. In that sense, however, the image captures a view conveyed by the fateful story of Vergil's epic. The nobility of humankind, registered unforgettably in the monumental masculinity of Laocoon's body, is caught up in the larger force of a destiny from which Laocoon, priest of Apollo and son of Priam, king of Troy, is unable to extricate himself. Not only does the narrative image signal the story and something of its lesson, but it offers aesthetic satisfaction as its end or purpose, combin-

(**g**) Gary Kapp, *That Ye May Know,* oil on canvas, 1996. *[©1996 Gary Kapp]*

ing the two for greater effect as a conveyer of the famous narrative. As this sculpture tells the story of human fate, the human condition is gendered as a heroic but doomed male struggle.

This highly selective, emblematic treatment of narrative informs many different instances of narrative religious art. In a great deal of art around the world, the practice is often to signify a narrative by the minimal means of portraying no more than its principal characters. A Roman relief **(d)** portraying three figures of Greek mythology—Hermes, Orpheus, and Eurydice—is a good example of this. Viewers learn little about the original story by looking at these three figures. Indeed, if one did not know the narrative, the image might be unidentifiable. (In fact, the Greek names inscribed above each figure were misidentifications added much later.) Orpheus has turned to look back to see that his dead wife, Eurydice, follows him from Hades, but in doing so he seals her fate, which is to return to the realm of the dead, taken there by the god Hermes, whose task it is to conduct souls to the underworld. With this narrative in mind, the many gestures of the image can be unfolded from the narrative's highly encapsulated state—the loving touch of Orpheus, his wistfully inclined head facing the other two, echoed visually in their opposing stances, and Hermes's fateful grip of the woman's wrist.

By contrast, some visual narratives enumerate virtually each moment of a textual narrative, as in the case of the large and very elaborate sculptural programs mounted on the exterior of many Hindu temples **(h)**. Literally hundreds of figures combine to narrate the long and intricate stories of such important deities as Viṣṇu or Śiva. In other cases, images may accompany printed text **(f, i, j)**, fashioning a symbiotic dependence of word and image upon one another, even in some instances creating a synergy in

(h) LEFT. Detail of figures adorning the exterior of the Kandariya Mahādeva Temple, Khajuraho, Madhya Pradesh, India, c. 1025–1050. *[©Wolfgang Kaehler/Corbis]* **(i)** BOTTOM LEFT. Illustration in ink depicting the first meeting between the Incas and the Spanish in Peru, from *El primer nueva corónica y buen gobierno* by Felipe Guamán Poma de Ayala, 1613. *[The Art Archive/Archaeological Museum Lima/Dagli Orti]* **(j)** BOTTOM RIGHT. Carved stone stele of Ameny and family, from the twelfth dynasty of ancient Egypt (c. 1938–1756 BCE), found near the Temple of Osiris in Abydos. *[Courtesy Ashmolean Museum, University of Oxford]*

which the resultant meaning is greater than its textual or visual parts taken alone. An example is Felipe Guamán Poma's extensively illustrated chronicle of colonial Peru **(i)**. Guamán's voluminous text is densely illustrated by full-page drawings of instances like the one depicted here. The visual narrative allowed him to describe the initial encounter of the Spanish and Incan cultures in such detail as the contrasting costumes and headgear of each group. The nuanced use of gesture signals the complexity and simultaneity of their attempts at communication and the easy confusion and misunderstandings that ensued.

Yet the time, expense, and space required for such narrative density of imagery can be too demanding and limiting. More commonly, narrative imagery operates with greater economy by relying on different forms of evocation—on synecdoche, with a part standing for the whole; on emblem, a highly condensed configuration of symbols or narrative cues; or on conflation, the juxtaposition of different narrative scenes in a single pictorial field **(k)**. Allowing one episode from an entire narrative to stand for the whole is evident in several of the images reproduced here **(c, d, e, f)**. Evoking a narrative by the use of emblematic signals works well in images that are intended to convey a great deal of highly prized or even secret information, material that is shared only among the literate, privileged, or initiated **(a, b, j, l, m)**. Such

(k) TOP. *The Tribute Money* (1427), fresco, by Masaccio in Brancacci Chapel, Santa Maria del Carmine, Florence, Italy. *[©Sandro Vannini/Corbis]* **(l)** RIGHT. Masonic Chart, chromolithograph 1851–1864. *[Courtesy American Antiquarian Society]*

(m) Detail of libationers, from a fresco cycle in the Villa of the Mysteries in Pompeii, Italy, c. 50 BCE. *[©Massimo Listri/Corbis]*

imagery presupposes a distinctive literacy among viewers, relying sometimes on elaborate codes for its proper "reading" or interpretation. The narrative in these instances need not be a story as much as a narrated set of meanings, teachings, ritual moments, and states of experience. Finally, conflation is a pictorial device for condensing into one visual field more than a single episode. Masaccio achieved this in his fresco titled *The Tribute Money* **(k)** when he portrayed three different moments: the central crowd gathered about Christ, a depiction of Peter finding a coin in a fish (to the left), and Peter paying the tribute to the tax collector (on the right).

Bibliography

Adorno, Rolena. *Guamán Poma: Writing and Resistance in Colonial Peru.* 2d ed. Austin, Tex., 2000.

Brilliant, Richard. *Visual Narratives: Storytelling in Etruscan and Roman Art.* Ithaca, N.Y., 1984.

Desai, Vishakha N., and Darielle Mason. *Gods, Guardians, and Lovers: Temple Sculptures from North India A.D. 700–1200.* New York and Ahmadabad, India, 1993.

Karetzky, Patricia E. *Early Buddhist Narrative Art: Illustrations of the Life of the Buddha from Central Asia to China, Korea, and Japan.* Lanham, Md., 2000.

Kessler, Herbert L., and Marianna Shreve Simpson, eds. *Pictorial Narrative in Antiquity and the Middle Ages.* Washington, D.C., and Hanover, N.H., 1985.

Maurer, Evan M. *Visions of the People: A Pictorial History of Plains Indian Life.* Minneapolis, 1992.

DAVID MORGAN (2005)

and Worship"; pilgrimage and blessing is discussed briefly in chap. 13, "Place and Pilgrimage," in the same work. For more general concepts on geography and religion see Chris C. Park, *Sacred Worlds: An Introduction to Geography and Religion* (London, 1994), especially chap. 8, "Sacred Places and Pilgrimage." Philosophical and religious analysis of the power of words, mainly expounded in Indian philosophy, is found in "Les pouvoir de la parole dans le Rgveda," in Louis Renou, *Études Vediques et Panineennes,* vol. 1 (Paris, 1955) and the *Encyclopedia of Indian Philosophy,* vol. 5 (Delhi, 1990). For a good introduction to the anthropological approach see John R. Bowen, *Religions in Practice: An Approach to the Anthropology of Religion* (Boston, 2002), chap. 11, "Sacred Speech and Divine Power." For Jewish liturgy see Abraham Z. Idelsohn, *Jewish Liturgy and Its Development* (New York, 1995) and Nicholas de Lange, *Judaism* (Oxford, 2003). For other terms used for blessing in Indian literature, especially in the Vedic period, see Jan Gonda, *Prayer and Blessing: Ancient Indian Ritual Terminology* (Leiden, 1989). For the Buddhist tradition see Peter Skilling, "The Raksa Literature of the Sravakayana," *Journal of the Pali Text Society* 14 (1992): 109–182. For a brief introduction to Chinese tradition see Edward L. Shaughnessy, ed., *China: The Land of the Heavenly Dragon* (London, 2000).

PRAPOD ASSAVAVIRULHAKARN (2005)

BLONDEL, MAURICE

BLONDEL, MAURICE (1861–1949), French Roman Catholic philosopher. Blondel was born at Dijon and educated at the École Normale Supérieure, where he was a pupil of Léon Ollé Laprune, to whom he dedicated his thesis, published as *L'action,* which he presented at the Sorbonne in 1893. He was professor of philosophy at Aix-en-Provence from 1897 to 1927. *L'action* aroused much interest and controversy because of its originality. Blondel claimed that from purely philosophical premises he had reached theological conclusions. Unlike the positivists, who were dominant in the university, and the scholastics, who controlled the theological schools, Blondel worked from a subtle analysis of what was involved in human experience, and maintained that it pointed to, and in the end required, the supernatural. Thus by what was known as "the method of immanence" he arrived at the transcendent. By "action" he did not mean only activity but all that is involved in the human response to reality, including affection, willing, and knowing.

Blondel was not a lucid writer, and his teaching was regarded as complicated and obscure. He spent the rest of his life in trying to clarify his meaning and seeking to distinguish his ideas from those of others with which they were liable to be confused. He waited for many years before publishing a revised edition of *L'action,* which, with other works, won for his thought a widespread influence in France. Most important among these other works were *Le problème de la philosophie catholique* (The problem of Catholic philosophy; 1932), *La pensée* (Thought; 1934), *L'être et les êtres* (Being and beings; 1935), and *La philosophie et l'esprit chrétien* (Philosophy and the spirit of Christianity; 1944–1949). One of his closest collaborators was Lucien Laberthonnière, but eventually Blondel fell out with him, as he did with most of his contemporaries. He was involved in the modernist movement and obviously desired a renewal of the church's teaching, but he insisted that he did not share the views of modernists such as Alfred Loisy, Édouard Le Roy, and Friedrich von Hügel. Though sometimes threatened with ecclesiastical censure, he avoided it, and indeed received a certificate of orthodoxy from Pope Pius X.

BIBLIOGRAPHY

In addition to *L'action* (1893; reprinted in 2 vols., Paris, 1936), *The Letter on Apologetics, and History and Dogma* (New York, 1964), and the other works mentioned above, several volumes of Blondel's correspondence have been published. In English there is the *Correspondence of Pierre Teilhard de Chardin and Maurice Blondel,* translated by William Whitman (New York, 1967), and *Maurice Blondel and Auguste Valensin, 1899–1912,* 2 vols. (Paris, 1957). None of Blondel's major works has been translated into English.

A comprehensive 240-page Blondel bibliography was produced by René Virgoulay and Claude Troisfontaines, *Maurice Blondel; Bibliographie analytique et critique* (Louvain, 1975). The following works about Blondel can be recommended: Frédéric Lefèvre's *L'itinéraire philosophique de Maurice Blondel* (Paris, 1928); Paul Archambault's *Vers un réalism intégral: L'œuvre philosophique de Maurice Blondel* (Paris, 1928); Henri Bouillard's *Blondel and Christianity* (Washington, D.C., 1970); and René Virgoulay's *Blondel et le modernisme: La philosophie de l'action et les sciences religieuses* (Paris, 1980). Blondel's work is also discussed in Bernard M. G. Reardon's *Roman Catholic Modernism* (Stanford, Calif., 1970) and in Gabriel Daly's *Transcendence and Immanence: A Study in Catholic Modernism and Integralism* (Oxford, 1980).

ALEC VIDLER (1987)

BLOOD

BLOOD. Among the religions of the world one finds many ambivalent or contradictory attitudes toward blood. Blood is perceived as being simultaneously pure and impure, attractive and repulsive, sacred and profane; it is at once a life-giving substance and a symbol of death. Handling blood is sometimes forbidden, sometimes mandatory, but usually dangerous. Rites involving blood require the intervention of individual specialists (warriors, sacrificers, circumcisers, butchers, or executioners) and always the participation of the group or community.

In many primitive societies, blood is identified as a soul substance: of men, of animals, and even of plants. The Romans said that in it is the *sedes animae* ("seat of life"). In pre-Islamic times, Arabs considered it the vegetative, liquid soul that remains in the body after death, feeding on libations. For the Hebrews, "the life of the flesh is in the blood" (*Lv.* 17:4).

The spilling of blood is often forbidden. This ban applies to certain categories of humans and animals: sacrificial victims, royalty, game, and so on. The Iroquois, the Scythians (Herodotus, 4.60–61), and the old Turco-Mongols, as well as the rulers of the Ottoman empire, forbade shedding the blood of persons of royal lineage. There is reason to believe that the Indian Hindu religions that have abolished sacrifices, and the feasting that goes with sacrifice, have done so more to avoid the shedding of blood than to comply with the dogmas of nonviolence and reincarnation. According to *Genesis* 9:4, the eating of raw meat is forbidden: "But you must not eat the flesh with the life, which is the blood, still in it." The Islamic tradition has similar restrictions.

Attitudes toward blood can be divided into two general categories: toward the blood of strangers, foreigners, or enemies and toward the blood of members of one's own community.

The blood of enemies usually is not protected by any taboo. It has been suggested that one justification for war is the perceived necessity of shedding blood in order to water the earth. One frequently encounters the idea that the earth is thirsty for blood—but only for licit blood. It can refuse blood that is not licit or cry out for vengeance against such illicit bloodshed, as the biblical passages *Isaiah* 26:21 and *Job* 16:18 illustrate. In pre-Columbian America blood was essential to the survival of the Sun, and in other countries it was demanded by the gods.

The killing of enemies is sometimes mandatory. Among the Turkic peoples in ancient times and again during the Islamic period in the sixteenth century, an adolescent did not acquire his adulthood, his name, and thus his soul until he committed his first murder. Killing—and being killed—has been the *raison d'être* for the Ojibwa and Dakota Indian tribes, as well as, to a certain extent, the Muslim "martyrs" of holy war and the Japanese samurai. At one time, a bloody death at the hand of an enemy seemed more to be envied than a natural death. However, concerning the caste of Hindu warriors in India, it was believed that one whose vocation was killing awaited his own immolation.

The blood of the enemy is rarely dangerous, even though the qualities and strengths of the soul remain in it. In antiquity people attempted to appropriate these qualities of blood by drinking it or washing themselves in it. Herodotus (17.64) notes that the Scythians drank the blood of the first victims they killed.

Within the community, however, attitudes toward blood and killing are different. Members of the community are connected by consanguinity, and they share collective responsibility for one another; the blood of each is the blood of all. The group's totemic animals may be included in this community, which is connected to the animals by adoption or alliance. A stranger can enter the group through marriage or "blood brotherhood," a custom practiced among the Fon of West Africa and among Central Asian peoples. Relations between blood brothers can be established in various ways, often through the juxtaposition of cuts made in their wrists or by pouring a few drops of blood into a cup, mixing it with wine (called "the blood of the vine" in antiquity), and drinking it. The Turkic peoples, Scythians, and Tibetans used the tops of skulls for drinking cups.

Murder within the community is forbidden. To kill one's relative is tantamount to shedding one's own blood; it is a crime that draws a curse that lasts for generations. When Cain murdered Abel, Abel's "blood cried out for vengeance," and Cain's descendants suffered as a result. When Oedipus unknowingly killed his father, he gouged out his own eyes to confess his blindness, but his punishment fell upon his children. After Orestes executed his mother, Clytemnestra, he was followed by the Furies, spiritlike incarnations of blood. The death of the just and innocent brings vengeance. King David protested: "I and my kingdom are guiltless before the Lord forever from the blood of Abner. . . . Let it rest on the head of Joab, and on all his father's house" (*2 Sm.* 3:28–29). According to Matthew, after the sentencing of Jesus to be crucified the Jews cried: "Let his blood be upon us and upon our children" (27:25).

A murder between families or between clans is a grave wrong that must be avenged by killing the guilty party. The latter, who in turn becomes the victim, will have his own avenger from among his relatives. Thus develops the cycle of vendetta killing, which can be broken only by "paying the blood price." Vendetta killing is found in ancient Greece, pre-Islamic Arabia, modern Corsica, and among the Nuer of the Sudan. The Jewish and Muslim demands of "an eye for an eye" may be similar to this phenomenon.

Under certain circumstances killing is perceived as a creative act, especially in the realm of the gods, where suicide or parricide sometimes leads to birth or new life. Mesopotamian and Babylonian cosmogonies feature gods who were slain in order to give life. The Greek Kronos severed the testicles of his father Ouranos (Sky) with a billhook while the latter lay in a tight embrace with Gaia (Earth). The blood of Ouranos's genital organs gave birth to new beings and, according to some traditions, to Aphrodite herself. This kind of suicide—relinquishing a part to preserve the whole—was sometimes magnified into a supreme act of love or redemption: Odin gave up one eye for the sake of supernatural "vision"; Attis emasculated himself; Abraham was prepared to slit the throat of his only son; Jesus accepted death voluntarily.

Some kinds of sacrifice are centered around blood. Blood is the drink of the gods or the drink shared by mortals with the gods. Blood sacrifices are varied in form and function. In Jewish sacrifice (abolished since the destruction of the Temple), the victim is not human but animal; its death has reconciliatory and expiatory value. In Muslim sacrifices, the gift of meat is the price paid by the genuinely guilty; there is no blessing or grace expected, and reconciliation and expiation are not involved.

In the Christian concept of sacrifice, the slitting of an animal's throat is abolished, and the animal is replaced by the "Lamb of God," Jesus on the cross. Crucifixion and asphyxiation, although not bloody in themselves, are perceived as fundamentally bloody. The sacrifice (at least, as it is understood outside Protestantism) is renewed daily; it is both expiatory and redemptory. The sacrifice is accompanied by a communal meal (Eucharist) where the believer is invited to eat bread, symbolizing the body of Christ, and to drink wine, symbolizing his blood. Charles Guignebert has noted that the bread has been of less interest than the wine; the wine "is the symbolism of blood that dominates in the Eucharist . . . and affirms its doctrinal richness" (Guignebert, 1935, p. 546). Christ, who offers the cup to his disciples, says, "This is the blood of the new testament that is shed for many for the remission of sins."

Judaism had already established that the covenant between God and his people was one of blood, of circumcision and sacrifice. Moses sprinkled the people with the blood of sacrificed bulls, saying, "Behold the blood of the covenant which the Lord hath made with you" (*Ex.* 24:8).

The idea of establishing a covenant through blood is found in many cultures. People create covenants among themselves as well as between their gods and themselves. Some peoples in Central Asia, in Siberia, and on the steppes of eastern Europe cut a dog or other animal in two to seal a treaty or to take a solemn oath, thus guaranteeing their loyalty. The protective force of blood is illustrated in the covenant between God and Israel in *Exodus* 13:7–13; the Israelites, remaining in their homes, which were marked with blood, were spared from the death that struck the Egyptians. A similar idea is expressed in Indonesia when the doors and pillars of houses are smeared with blood during sacrifices of domestic dedication.

Blood can eliminate flaws and weaknesses. In Australia, a young man would spread his blood on an old man in order to rejuvenate him. Some Romans, in honor of Attis, emasculated themselves and celebrated the *dendrophoria* by beating their backs, hoping thus to escape the disease of death and to wash themselves of its stain. Similarly, Shīʿī flagellants relive the martyrdom of Ḥusayn ibn ʿAlī, grandson of the prophet Muḥammad.

The most common type of self-inflicted wound is circumcision. In the female the incision of the clitoris sometimes corresponds with this rite. Male circumcision is required in Hebrew tradition, where it is the sign of a covenant with God. It is common also in Islam. Many explanations have been given for this almost universal rite. It is seen primarily as a manifestation of the desire to eliminate any traces of femininity in the male. It is doubtful that circumcision is an attempt to imitate the menses. If the sexual act is considered a defilement, the removal of the foreskin could, in effect, rid the sexual organ of impurity transmitted from the mother. Yet there are some societies where the circumcised male is considered to be as impure as the menstruating female and where he is treated as if he were one.

The menses are universally considered the worst impurity, due to the involuntary and uncontrollable flowing of blood. Menstruating women are believed to pose great dangers to men, and for this reason many peoples of New Guinea, Australia, Polynesia, Africa, Central Asia, and the Arctic have feared them and imposed innumerable bans on them. One finds similar fears in the Hebrew (*Lv.* 20:18), Islamic, and Hindu traditions. Researchers have not yet properly emphasized the implications of the interruption of menstruation during pregnancy; one can surmise that the fetus, believed to be fed with the impure blood, acquires this impurity, which has to be removed at birth. The impurity only indirectly appears to be a function of the sexual act or of the vaginal bleeding at delivery.

SEE ALSO Circumcision; Clitoridectomy; Human Sacrifice; Mortification; Omophagia; Revenge and Retribution; Sacrifice.

BIBLIOGRAPHY

Nearly all works on the history of religions mention blood, but there are no valuable monographs on the subject other than G. J. M. Desse's *Le sang dans le rite* (Bordeaux, 1933). The reader is referred also to Lucien Lévy-Bruhl's *The "Soul" of the Primitive* (New York, 1928) and to Mircea Eliade's *Rites and Symbols of Initiation* (New York, 1958). Numerous facts on the topic are found in Bronislaw Malinowski's *Sex and Repression in Savage Society* (London, 1927) and *Crime and Custom in Savage Society* (New York, 1926). W. Robertson Smith's *Lectures on the Religion of the Semites*, 3d ed. (London, 1927), is still fundamental in the study of sacrifice. Charles Guignebert discusses the symbolism of blood as found in the Christian Eucharist in *Jesus* (London, 1935). On circumcision, see B. J. F. Laubscher's *Sex, Custom and Psychopathology* (London, 1937). On blood brotherhood, see Georges Davy's *La foi jurée* (Paris, 1922). Bruno Bettelheim's *Symbolic Wounds: Puberty Rites and the Envious Male* (Glencoe, Ill., 1954) and Paul Hazoumé's *Le pacte de sang au Dahomey* (Paris, 1937) are also worth consulting.

New Sources

Jean-Paul Roux has published *Le sang. Mythes, symboles et réalités* (Paris, 1988), which is the only monograph tackling this subject in a cross-cultural perspective. There is a plentiful bibliography but the approach is old-fashioned and the style not very scholarly. An indispensable tool for any further research is represented by the imposing series "Sangue e antropologia," edited for nine years in twenty two volumes by Francesco Vattioni under the auspices of the Centro Studi Sanguis Christi (Rome, 1981–1996). Philologists, historians and theologians present and discuss a host of materials related to blood functions and symbolism in various cultural contexts, with focus on Christianity in Biblical and patristic times.

JEAN-PAUL ROUX (1987)
Translated from French by Sherri L. Granka
Revised Bibliography

BOAS, FRANZ (1858–1942), German-American anthropologist, was born at Minden, Prussian Westphalia, on

July 9, 1858, the son of Jewish parents of comfortable means, both of whom were assimilated into German culture. His education was largely at the local state school and gymnasium. He seems not to have had significant Jewish religious instruction. His mother, Sophie Meyer Boas, who had been part of a circle of liberal and Marxist intellectuals dedicated to the revolutionary principles of 1848, was a major influence in his youth. He studied the sciences at the universities of Heidelberg (1877), Bonn (1877–1879), and Kiel (1879–1881), but he decided upon geography as a career. Shortly after receiving his doctorate, he left for a twelve-month expedition to Baffin Island, studying local geography and anthropology. He qualified as a university instructor at Berlin in 1886 but never taught, instead going to the United States, where he undertook a research trip to the Northwest Coast, whose native peoples became the subjects of his most intensive ethnological scrutiny. He worked for a number of scholarly institutions in the United States and Canada from 1887 until 1896, when he found secure employment in New York City at the American Museum of Natural History and Columbia University. He left the museum in 1906 but continued at Columbia until his retirement in 1936. In his later years he became increasingly involved in public affairs, speaking out especially against racialist ideas. He died in New York on December 22, 1942.

Boas published in a wide range of anthropological fields, exercising a dominating influence on American anthropology both in his own right and through a network of associates and former students, including A. L. Kroeber, Paul Radin, Alexander Goldenweiser, Robert H. Lowie, Ruth Benedict, Leslie Spier, J. R. Swanton, and Margaret Mead. Many of these, Radin and Lowie in particular, were more systematically concerned with religion than he.

Boas was himself a rationalist without conscious religious views. One of the mainsprings of his intellectual life was the search for an explanation of the "psychological origin of the implicit belief in the authority of tradition," a belief foreign to his own mind, and thus for an explication of how "the shackles that tradition has laid upon us" might be recognized and then broken. Alongside this, however, went a relativist's tolerance of the beliefs and values of others.

Boas's anthropological methodology was so strongly particularistic that his religious descriptions usually have little generalizing value in themselves; his approach was so concerned with the integrated totality of a culture that religion often seems to occur only as a by-product in his work. However, the enormous amount of material, especially texts, that he published on mythology, ceremonialism, and secret societies contains rich material for the study of beliefs, and his shorter treatments, including the religion entry in the *Handbook of American Indians* and his discussion of esoteric doctrines and the idea of future life among primitive tribes, are valuable.

The fundamental concept bearing on the religious life of the North American Indians, Boas wrote, was a belief in the existence of a "magic power," the "wonderful qualities" of which are believed to exist in objects, animals, humans, spirits, or deities and that are superior to the natural qualities of humans. The actions of the Indians were regulated by the desire to retain the good will of powers friendly to them and to control those that were hostile. Taboos, guardian spirits, charms, offerings and sacrifices, and incantations were all means to these ends. Boas also clearly associated religion with social structure in totemic kinship groups, in ceremonialism, and in explanatory mythology.

BIBLIOGRAPHY

Boas's publications are numerous and scattered. He collected some essays into *Race, Language and Culture* (New York, 1940), including "The Idea of the Future Life among Primitive Tribes" and "The Ethnological Significance of Esoteric Doctrines." George W. Stocking, Jr., edited another collection, including the essay "The Religion of American Indians," in *The Shaping of American Anthropology, 1883–1911: A Franz Boas Reader* (New York, 1974), with a fine introduction. Some of Stocking's other studies of Boas are in his *Race, Culture, and Evolution,* 2d ed. (Chicago, 1982). Boas's *Kwakiutl Ethnography* (Chicago, 1966) is, with *The Social Organization and the Secret Societies of the Kwakiutl Indians* (1897; reprint, New York, 1970), his most important discussion of the Kwakiutl. Ake Hultkrantz's *The Study of American Indian Religion* (New York, 1983), contains a discussion of Boas and his students on the subject. See also Boas's "An Anthropologist's Credo," in *The Nation* 147 (27 August 1938): 202.

New Sources

Hyatt, Marshall. *Franz Boas, Social Activist: The Dynamics of Ethnicity.* New York, 1990.

Williams, Vernon J. *Rethinking Race: Franz Boas and His Contemporaries.* Lexington, Ky., 1996.

DOUGLAS COLE (1987)
Revised Bibliography

BOATS.

It is not surprising that those who live by the sea or on a river often visualize a person's last journey as being undertaken in a boat. One enounters the use of boats in the burial rites of such peoples as well as in their mythology. Although boats figure in strikingly similar ways in the rituals and mythologies of peoples from all over the globe, their exact significance in a given culture or religion and the precise relationship between their cultic use and their appearance in myth are often far from clear. In some cases a specifically religious significance may be lacking, or the actual use of boats in the cult may bear no discernible relation to their role in mythology. These thoughts should be kept in mind as one considers individual cases of the use of boats or boat symbolism in the history of religions.

THE MYTHIC FERRY ACROSS THE WATERS OF DEATH. The use of a boat to cross the waters of death is fairly common in the ancient Near East and in classical antiquity. The Assyrian version of the well-known Babylonian *Epic of Gilgamesh*

(c. 1200 BCE) provides a particularly striking example. The tenth episode of the epic describes the hero's long and arduous attempt to reach Utanapishtim, the Akkadian Noah, and obtain the secret of immortality. In order to do so Gilgamesh must cross the sea and the Waters of Death, something no mortal has ever done. Only Shamash, the sun god, is able to cross the sea. However, with the help of Urshanabi, Utanapishtim's boatman, Gilgamesh manages to cross the waters in a boat equipped with 120 stout, ferruled punting poles, each 60 cubits in length. Since the Waters of Death must not be touched by human hands, each pole can be used for only a single thrust. As the final pole is used, Gilgamesh and Urshanabi arrive at the dwelling of Utanapishtim, the keeper of the plant of immortality.

Most of the elements contained in later accounts of the journey to the otherworld can be found in the Gilgamesh epic. Thus one can understand the enthusiasm of the German Assyriologist Peter Jensen (1861–1936), who thought he could detect traces of it in all subsequent epic writings.

In classical antiquity one finds a boat being used by Charon, the ferryman of the underworld. According to ancient Greek belief, first documented in the fragmentary epic *Minyas* and in paintings found at Delphi, Charon used a boat to ferry the dead across the rivers of the underworld to the gates of Hades, which were guarded by Kerberos. Vergil, in the sixth canto of the *Aeneid,* describes Charon's repulsive appearance and adds that his services are reserved for the dead alone. It was customary to bury the dead with an obol (a small coin) for Charon left in the mouth to make sure that he would perform the necessary service. Charon has survived in neo-Grecian Christian belief as the figure Charos.

The description of Charon's boat was detailed by the Greek satirist Lucian. In *The Downward Journey,* Lucian has Charon describe his vessel to Hermes, who has just delivered to him more than three hundred souls ready for the crossing: "Our ship is ready and very well prepared for putting to sea. It is bailed out, the mast is raised, the sail is ready hoisted and each of the oars is furnished with its thong. Nothing prevents us, as far as I am concerned, from weighing anchor and taking off."

EGYPTIAN GRAVE BOATS. Boats and ships were part of Egyptian burial gifts since earliest times. The simple clay representations of boats found in prehistoric times were replaced, during the Old Kingdom period (c. 3000–2200 BCE), by reliefs or by references to boats in the sacrificial lists. Near the end of the sixth dynasty (c. 2350–2260 BCE), representations of boats in wall decorations gave way to simple sculptures, including model ships complete with crews and cabins where the dead rested. Sailboats were to be used for the journey up the Nile toward the south, rowboats for the journey downstream toward the north. During the New Kingdom period (c. 1569–1085 BCE), the use of such models was discontinued for all but the royal tombs.

The primary function of these boats was to facilitate the continued journeys of the dead to specific places in the otherworld, just as they had facilitated journeys in life. The presence of war ships and hunting boats suggests a continuity between this life and the next. There was also a belief in a journey to the west. A model boat or the ceremonial "formulas for bringing a ferry" were believed to guarantee that the deceased would successfully reach his goal. Some of the boats found in or around the tombs lack equipment and in all probability were intended not as burial gifts but for use during the funeral ceremonies.

As worship of Osiris, god of the dead, gained ground, boats acquired yet another function: to take the dead to Busiris and Abydos, the shrines of Osiris, so that they could partake of the life-giving blessings of the god. During the journey, the mummy rested on a bier under a canopy while a priest made offerings of incense and read from the sacred texts. Still later, the deceased acquired a superhuman quality, assuming an Osiris-like form during the course of the journey.

Toward the end of the Old Kingdom, models of the two sun boats—the ships in which the eye of the day traveled across the evening and morning sky—made their appearance. These are known from Tutankhamen's tomb dating from the New Kingdom period. From the *Book of Going Forth by Day* (often called the *Book of the Dead*) it is known that these particular burial gifts expressed the desire to be united with Re, the sun god, and to accompany him in his sun boat. According to texts found in the pyramids, the dead king would thus be able to share in the governance of the world. Later this privilege was extended to commoners, and the sun boats were laden with food offerings to be shared among the fellow travelers.

SHIP BURIALS. Boats and ships constitute the most frequently encountered images in the Bronze Age rock carvings of central and southern Sweden (c. 1600–500 BCE). Interpretation is difficult because no written sources exist from this period or the one immediately following. The images consist of two parallel lines that curve upward at the ends and are joined by cross strokes, one of which sometimes terminates in an animal head. The fact that several contain men obviously handling paddles argues against the theory that these images actually represent sleds. Occasionally, depictions of a steering oar or helmsman are found. The ships may be outrigged canoes or, in the case of the carvings found in northern Scandinavia, skin boats similar to the Inuit (Eskimo) kayaks. It is unclear, however, whether these images represent real boats, cultic objects associated with solar worship, or even scenes from mythology.

Ships and other objects represented in these rock carvings are also found in Bronze Age graves. The end of this period marks the appearance of both ship graves and ship settings (stones erected spaced so that they form the outline of a ship's deck). The island of Gotland in the Baltic contains around three hundred such ship settings from the late Bronze Age. After an interval of about a thousand years, ships were once more used as funeral symbols on memorial stones found on the same island. They remained in use until the end of the pagan era. These memorials stem mainly from the late Iron Age (c. 400–1050 CE). The dead were sometimes buried in boats, or a ship setting was erected either on top of the actual grave or as a memorial over an empty grave. All kinds of equipment were buried with the dead for use in the other-world.

At about the same time, boat burials came into use in Sweden, Norway, and, through Norse invaders, in East Anglia. Seventh-century grave fields containing unburned boats have been uncovered in the Swedish province of Uppland (Vendel, Valsgärde, Ultuna, and Tuna in Alsike). The dead that the boats contain—in all probability they were wealthy yeomen and heads of families—have been equipped with costly weapons and ample provisions. Ordinary family members, by contrast, were cremated and their remains buried in mounds in a routine fashion. Numerous boat graves have also been found along the Norwegian coast—at the ancient trading center by the Oslo Fjord, for instance. However, the best-known Norwegian ship graves are in Oseberg and Gokstad in the southern part of the country. The ships found here are lavishly equipped seagoing vessels, leading one to suspect that the dead men were kings. The same applies to the famous Sutton Hoo find made in Suffolk in 1939, which also dates from the seventh century.

By 1970 Michael Müller-Wille had found a total of 190 Norse graves that contained boats. Graves containing burned boats or ships, however, are most numerous in Scandinavia (where a total of 230 have been found) and in the territories colonized by Norsemen, for example, in Knoc y Doonee, Parish of Andreas, and Balladoolee, Parish of Arbory, on the Isle of Man, and on Colonsay in the Hebrides. Evidence from the Hebrides makes it clear that women followed their men in death. A ship grave also has been discovered on the Île de Groix off the Brittany coast. Only a few cases of ship burial are known from Denmark (e.g., Ladby, c. 900 CE). Five boat graves from the tenth century have been found so far in Iceland.

Thus there is a wealth of Norse archaeological material attesting to the custom of real boat burial, a custom unique to Europe and limited both chronologically and geographically to a single ethnic group. Similar customs in the Near East and among North American Indians do not include burial of the actual boat. Nevertheless the significance of the Norse practice remains unclear. What can be the explanation for this way of burying the dead (or at least the most prominent among the dead)? Icelandic literary sources mention the practice of placing the dead in a ship that was then covered with a burial mound, but they offer no explanation of why this was done.

One could reasonably assume that boat graves are in some way tied to the notion of a voyage on the water. Norse mythology in fact knows several worlds of death, all of which are reached by a long journey. The Icelandic epic poet Snorri Sturluson (c. 1179–1241) relates that the wicked go to Hel and thence to Misty Hel (Niflhel, Niflheimr). The journey passes north through deep and dark valleys, and the traveler must be well equipped. Nastrand ("the shore of corpses") and the Land of Death, surrounded by rushing rivers, lie to the north. Still, neither the journey to the underworld nor the way to Valhǫll calls for sailing ships. The ships of the dead that are sometimes set ablaze and launched, such as those mentioned in *Beowulf,* the *Ynglingasaga,* the *Skjoldungasaga,* and the *Gylfaginning,* all trace their origins to Celtic legends and are thus not thought to be associated with Norse burial customs. Nor may any sure conclusions be drawn from the early medieval German usage of the words *naufus* or *naucus* ("ship") alongside *truncus* ("trunk"), used to denote a coffin. These may well be terminological relics of the ancient custom of boat burial but only the terms survive.

One must conclude, therefore, that the Norse sources ultimately fail to explain the purpose behind boat burials. While the introduction of the boat into burial customs is certainly an interesting innovation, it may well have been intended merely as an addition to such other burial paraphernalia as weapons and food. Such boats do not necessarily have to be understood as burial ships designed to carry the dead to a distant and unknown land.

There is some evidence, however, that at least in some instances the funeral boat was understood as such. A famous and detailed eyewitness account of the funeral of a Norse chieftain on the banks of the Volga in 922 CE was given by an Arabian diplomat, Ibn Faḍlān, a member of a delegation sent by a caliph in Baghdad to the Bulgars along the Volga. According to Ibn Faḍlān's description, all the grave offerings were first placed in a ship, then, as a final offering, a servant woman was brought forward to follow her master into death. Before being killed, she looked three times over a kind of door frame to see what was awaiting her and told the men who lifted her that she could see her father, her mother, and her dead relatives. The last time she was lifted she added: "I can see my master, seated in Paradise, and Paradise is green and fair. . . . He is calling me; send me to him." She was then killed by an old woman known as "the angel of death," and everything was subsequently consumed by a fire lit by the nearest kinsman. A mound was built up over the site and crowned by a wooden monument. Ibn Faḍlān also reported that the Norsemen deride the Arabs for giving their dead to the earth and the worms: "We burn him in a moment, so that he enters paradise at once. . . . His master, out of love for him, sent him the wind to carry him off in an hour."

Although this description has been colored by Ibn Faḍlān's Islamic preconceptions and by his manner of presentation, the purpose of the funeral rites is clear, even though the role played by the ship remains uncertain. Does the wind refer to the breeze fanning the flames or to a sailing wind? If the latter is the case, it may be concluded that, at least in this case, the burial ship was indeed intended to carry the dead to the otherworld, although this may not have been its only purpose. In addition to the report by Ibn Faḍlān, other studies confirm a link between eschatological myth and burial rites among the Norse.

Among certain North American Indians, burial customs involving boats and a journey to the land of the dead have been documented. For instance, the typical grave of the Twana and other Coast Salish Indians consists of a canoe suspended on poles or on an elevated platform. A grieving husband traditionally spends four days and four nights near the canoe, waiting for his wife to depart for the otherworld. According to a Twana tale, the inhabitants of the realm of the dead come in a canoe to claim the newly deceased. Late at night it is said that one can hear their paddles in the water as they come to carry away their new companion.

The same vivid imagination characterizes a song from an entirely different part of the world, the Trobriand Islands, north of the eastern point of New Guinea. The tale is told of a warrior's sweetheart who, fearing that her lover has fallen in battle, waits by the shore to greet him in his spirit boat as he travels to the otherworld.

In Late Megalithic cultures, there is a belief among certain island people that their ancestors had arrived at their present location by canoe, having come across the sea from the west. On the Tanimbar Islands in Indonesia, for instance, this belief is reflected in the roofs of the ceremonial huts, which are shaped like canoes and have gables that are referred to as "stems" and "sterns." Canoes and stone or wooden representations of canoes also figure prominently in burial rites. The underlying thought is that the spirits of the dead journey across the sea in a spirit boat to the land of their ancestors in the west. The organization of the community itself is modeled on that of a ship's crew, exactly as it is in ancient Scandinavia.

Throughout central Polynesia the dead are placed in canoes or canoe-shaped coffins or receptacles. Robert W. Williamson (1977) speculates that the spiritual essence of the visible canoe was intended to carry the soul on its journey to the spirit land called Hawaiki. The voyage could be undertaken symbolically as well in miniature boats containing bones and images of the dead person. In the case of inhumation and cremation, the grave on land could be shaped like a ship, or pictures of ships could be carved on top of the memorials. The canoe was also used as an instrument for the removal of a dead person's sins.

CELTIC TALES OF SEA JOURNEYS TO MYTHICAL LANDS. The Celtic imagination is especially fertile when it comes to depicting the adventures of the deceased on the way to their final resting place. This place is represented as an earthly Elysium—the abode of the gods—a notion that is clearly derived from Classical Greek sources. This paradise on earth has many names, such as Magh Mór ("great plain"), Magh Mell ("plain of delights"), Tír na nÓg ("land of the young"), Annwn ("abyss"), and Tír nam Béo ("land of the living"). Tales are told of a sea voyage (*imram*) to various scattered islands, often involving a magic ship or vessel. In what is possibly the earliest of these tales, the *Voyage of Bran* (eighth century), the hero sails from one marvelous island to another: the Land beneath the Waves, the Island of Laughter, and the Island of Women. Other islands are mentioned in the *Voyage of Maeldúin* (ninth to eleventh century), in which the voyager builds the boat himself. The same elements, combined with other motifs, are also found in the widespread account of the *Navigation of Saint Brendan* (c. tenth century), where the journey ends in the Land of Promise, or Paradise. In this case, the story is obviously colored by Christian legends. The role of the seagoing vessel appears to have faded in the medieval visionary literature and in the extracanonical apocrypha and apocalypses, possibly because of its pagan connotations.

Medieval allegories, ballads, and romances, as well as historical legends, contain stories about magic ships, often rudderless and unpiloted. Marie de France, the earliest known French female writer (twelfth century), describes such a ship in her lay *Guigemar.* Its sails are made of silk, the timbers of ebony, and it contains a sumptuous bed in a pavilion. It carries a wounded hero to a castle in an ancient town where he encounters a fairy endowed with healing powers. This same motif of a rudderless boat is found in *Beowulf* where Scyld (Skjold), the founder of the Danish dynasty of the Skjoldunger, is said to arrive as a child in an unpiloted ship. He also departs for an unknown destination in a burial ship. The story appears to be patterned on the theme of the journey to the otherworld but may also reflect notions connected with ship burials.

SHIP SYMBOLISM. Ship symbolism was very highly developed in the Hellenistic world, a fact that helps explain its importance in Christian sources. But the Greeks did not go to sea with undiluted joy. "The sea is an evil thing, seafaring is a hazardous and dangerous undertaking," declares the Greek rhetorician Alciphron; "the sailor is the neighbor of death." But the danger, though mortal, was nevertheless considered wonderful and tempting, worthy of men who are like gods. Courage, hope, and joy characterize the names of the Athenian ships—names that might as easily refer to the ship of the church—and they are always feminine: *Salvation, Grace, Bringer of Light, Blessed, Victorious, Virgin, Dove, Savior, Providence, Help,* and *Peace.*

Allusions to ships are frequent in classical literature. The ancient ship of Theseus, in which the planks of the hull are successively exchanged, is compared by Plutarch to the human body that is also in a process of constant renewal. Meleager, the Greek epigrammatist (first century BCE), turns this image the other way around and refers to his beloved in her old age as an old frigate: the various members of her withered body are compared with nautical precision to the different parts of a ship. Love is like a hazardous voyage; the cunning Greek or Roman "turns his sheet windward"; death overtakes one "with swelling sails." To act to one's own detriment was expressed by the ancient Greek or Roman as "drilling holes through the hull." To give up a fight was "to take down the sail"; from beginning to end was "from fore to aft."

An expression still in use, "to be in the same boat," is borrowed from Cicero. A good ship is necessary for the voyage through life.

Three classical images are of special importance and exerted a strong influence on the development of Christian symbolism: the ship of state, the ship of the soul, and the ship of the world. In the shared fate of the crew and in their dependence on their captain—reflected in such expressions as "our governor" and "to be at the helm"—the Greek sailors saw a clear allegorical reference to their own city-state. The Greek lyrical poet Alcaeus wrote around 600 BCE of "the storm-tossed ship of state." He is echoed by many, Horace among them. The Greek writers of tragedy, Aeschylus and Sophocles, used the same symbols, which entered the field of political philosophy through Plato: all is well on a ship where all obey the captain (*nauklēros*), while nothing but misfortune awaits a ship where the captain is ignorant and each sailor wants to be in command. The human body too is likened to a ship where the soul and reason are the helmsman, and the eyes and ears constitute the lookout. Cooperation is vital, just as governors and governed must cooperate in a good state. Aristotle maintains that the common goal of all good citizens, regardless of their tasks and rights, must be a good voyage (that is, the welfare of the state). Nautical symbols are found in Demosthenes, Plutarch, and Cicero, as well as in the writings of emperors and church fathers.

The idea of the body as the ship of the soul is based on the image of a hull under construction: the spine is likened to the keel, the frame timbers represent the ribs, and the place of the helmsman is the head (see Ovid, *Metamorphoses* 14.549–554). This comparison between the human body and a ship later becomes important in the characterization of the ship as a symbol of the church. The church fathers perceived Noah's ark as a symbol of the church and interpreted it in terms of the human body. In this way, the images of the mystical body of Christ and the ship of the church were able to merge. What applies to the church as the collectivity of the redeemed applies as well to the individual soul, itself conceived of as a vessel, a *navicula animae.*

The relationship between body and soul, which in Platonism and Neoplatonism is likened to the dependence of a ship on its captain, is a recurring image in the Christian sermon. Death is spoken of as a shipwreck. The emperor Constantine talks of the flotsam of the body on the underworld river Acheron. In the image of Charon and his ferry, death becomes a voyage to the other side. The fluidity of such symbolism allows the images to merge independently of any restraints imposed by logic. This in turn leads to the Christian reference to "the blessed haven."

The Stoic philosopher Chrysippus claims that reason (*logos*) governs humanity like a ship. Plutarch further develops this metaphor: the governing part of the soul is itself governed by God like a rudder, or it listens like an experienced helmsman to the divine captain. Jerome, in commenting on Psalm 103, is therefore able to preach to his attentive monks: "Who among us is such a sturdily built ship that he is able to escape this world without going down or running aground on a rock—if he wants to reach salvation, the right sense (*sensus*) must be his pilot." The philosophical *logos* has thereby been replaced by reason enlightened by faith, and Christ as the true Logos becomes the real pilot of the soul. The ascetic tradition refers to "the ship of the soul," "the ship of the heart," and "the ship of life." Augustine gives further impetus to the notion of Christ dwelling in the heart as in a ship.

The divinely governed world is also likened to a ship. Although worshiping the thing created is as reprehensible as mistaking the ship for its captain, it is nevertheless possible to deduce the builder from the ship. Platonic, Neoplatonic, and Stoic thought lends itself especially well to adoption and christianization. The large eye, which is still painted on the bows of Mediterranean boats, is interpreted by ancient philosophers and Christians alike as a symbol of Providence. Furthermore, the ship of the world must perish one day; only the ship of the church will survive.

The image of the ship of the church or of salvation can be further extended so that the cross becomes the mast and the yard, a spiritual wind fills the sails, and Christ himself is at the helm. The account of Odysseus, fettered to the mast in order not to succumb to the sirens' song, is also easily christianized. The ship of salvation sails across the sea of time, past all temptations, toward the heavenly haven.

BIBLIOGRAPHY

Arbman, Holger. "Begravning." In *Kulturhistorisk Leksikon för Nordisk Middelalder,* vol. 1. Copenhagen, 1956.

Baldwin, B. "Usituma! Song of Heaven." *Oceania* 15 (March 1945): 201–238. Includes a canoe and a war song from the Trobriand Islands, where the author served as missionary.

Bar, Francis. *Les routes de l'autre monde: Descentes aux enfers et voyages dans l'au-delà.* Paris, 1946. A good short survey treating European folklore, Asian, American, Near Eastern, and classical material, Jewish and Christian apocrypha, Norse and Celtic stories, medieval literature on visions, and parodies from antiquity.

Bonnet, Hans. *Reallexikon der ägyptischen Religionsgeschichte.* Berlin, 1952.

Davidson, Hilda R. Ellis, ed. *The Journey to the Other World.* Totowa, N.J., 1975. See pages 73–89. The South Sea and Egypt are touched on as an introduction to the Norse material. Caution is needed.

Foote, Peter, and David M. Wilson. *The Viking Achievement: The Society and Culture of Early Medieval Scandinavia.* New York, 1970. A chapter on religion treats the ship burials.

Fredsjö, Åke, Sverker Janson, and C.-A. Moberg. *Hällristningar i sverige.* Stockholm, 1956. A short critical survey of Swedish rock carvings written by trained archaeologists.

Hultkrantz, Åke. *The North American Indian Orpheus Tradition: A Contribution to Comparative Religion.* Stockholm, 1957. Tales of the recovery of a beloved person from the land of the dead.

Meuli, Karl. *Gesammelte Schriften,* 2 vols. Basel, 1975.

Müller-Wille, Michael. *Bestattung im Boot: Studien zu einer nordeuropäischen Grabsitte.* Neumünster, Germany, 1970. Outstanding scientific monograph.

Müller-Wille, Michael, David M. Wilson, Hayo Vierck, and Heinrich Beck. "Bootgrab." In *Reallexikon der Germanischen Altertumskunde,* edited by Johannes Hoops, vol. 3. Berlin and New York, 1978. A concentrated, well-documented survey with an extensive bibliography.

Patch, Howard R. *The Other World according to Descriptions in Medieval Literature.* Cambridge, Mass., 1950. A reliable study starting with Oriental and classical material, as well as Celtic and German mythology.

Pritchard, J. B., ed. *Ancient Near Eastern Texts relating to the Old Testament.* 3d ed. Princeton, 1969. Contains Egyptian, Sumerian, and Akkadian myths of death and the otherworld.

Rahner, Hugo. *Symbole der Kirche: Die Ekklesiologie der Väter.* Salzburg, 1964. Half of this learned, voluminous work of a patristic scholar contains the Christian symbolism of the ship and its classical background.

Strömberg Krantz, Eva. *Des Schiffes Weg mitten im Meer: Beiträge zur Erforschung der nautischen Terminologie des Alten Testaments.* Lund, 1982. Study of the nautical terminology of the Israelites and of the small traces in it of their contact with seafaring people ever since their entrance into Palestine.

Turville-Petre, E. O. G. *Myth and Religion of the North: The Religion of Ancient Scandinavia.* New York, 1964.

Vendel Period Studies. Stockholm, 1983. A multi-author work of twenty specialists that was connected with an exposition in Stockholm of the boat graves from Vendel, Valsgärde (Sweden), and Sutton Hoo (England). A good, popular summary of the actual state of research. Contains a rich bibliography.

Vroklage, Bernardus A. G. "Das Schiff in den Megalithkulturen Südostasiens und der Südsee." *Anthropos* 31 (1936): 712–757. The author belongs to the Kulturgeschichtliche Schule.

Wachsmuth, Dietrich. *Pompimos ho daimon: Untersuchung zu den antiken Sakralhandlungen bei Seereisen.* Exp. ed. Berlin, 1967. A very substantial study of all religious rites in connection with classical seafare.

Williamson, Robert W. *Religious and Cosmic Beliefs of Central Polynesia* (1933). 2 vols. New York, 1977. A careful, systematic survey based on an extensive literature.

CARL-MARTIN EDSMAN (1987)
Translated from Swedish by Kjersti Board

BOCHICA was a major deity of the Muisca (Chibcha) Indians of the highlands around Bogotá, Colombia, at the time of the Spanish conquest, in the sixteenth century. Early Spanish chroniclers report varying mythical dates for Bochica's appearance in Muisca territory. He was called by several names or titles, one of which means "sun," another "disappearing one." Said to be a foreigner from the east (i.e., present-day Venezuela), he appeared as an old man with a waist-length beard, long hair, and a mantle. He preached and taught virtuous behavior, religious ritual, and crafts, particularly spinning, weaving, and cloth painting. Traveling to the west through the Muisca region, then eastward again, he arrived at Sogamoso, on the eastern Muisca border. There, according to different accounts, he died, disappeared, or became the Sun. At the time of the Conquest, there was an important Temple of the Sun at Sogamoso. One Muisca myth tells that the world was created there, and one of Bochica's titles was "messenger of the creator."

Bochica combines the culture hero, sun, and transformation aspects characteristic of many New World gods. He was the patron of chieftains and goldsmiths, the latter perhaps because of his association both with the sun and with craft. Worked gold was offered to him. When an angry local god once caused a destructive flood, so a tale relates, the Muisca people appealed to Bochica, who appeared on a rainbow to strike and shatter a rock with his golden staff, releasing the floodwaters from the Bogotá plateau and creating the great Tequendama waterfall, one of the wonders of the South American landscape.

According to one set of mythical stories, a beautiful goddess taught the people promiscuity, pleasure, and dancing—the opposite of Bochica's instructions. In some accounts, she was the Moon, or was changed by Bochica into the Moon; because she was evil, she was permitted to shine only at night. She was sometimes called the wife of the Sun (presumably Bochica). In one tale, the goddess was turned by Bochica into an owl.

BIBLIOGRAPHY

The best summary in English of early source material on Bochica is A. L. Kroeber's "The Chibcha," in the *Handbook of South American Indians,* edited by Julian H. Steward, vol. 2 (Washington, D.C., 1946). In Spanish, José Pérez de Barradas's *Los Muiscas antes de la Conquista,* vol. 2 (Madrid, 1951), quotes the chroniclers, with references. Harold Osborne's *South American Mythology* (London, 1968) publishes material taken largely from Kroeber, without citation of early sources; it is the most comprehensive recent discussion.

New Sources

Arango Cano, Jesús. *Mitiología en América Precolombina: México—Aztecas, Colombia—Chibchas, Perú—Incas.* Bogotá, 1989.

ELIZABETH P. BENSON (1987)
Revised Bibliography

BODHIDHARMA (fl. c. 480–520), known in China as Damo and in Japan as Daruma; traditionally considered the twenty-eighth patriarch of Indian Buddhism and the founder of the Chan (Jpn., Zen) school of Chinese Buddhism.

THE "HISTORICAL" BODHIDHARMA. Accounts of Bodhidharma's life have been based until recently on largely hagiographical materials such as the *Jingde chuandeng lu* (1004). However, the discovery of new documents among the Dunhuang manuscripts found in Central Asia at the turn of this century has led Chinese and Japanese scholars to question the authenticity of these accounts. The oldest text in which Bodhidharma's name is mentioned is the *Luoyang qielan ji*, a description of Buddhist monasteries in Luoyang written in 547 by Yang Xuanzhi. In this work, a monk called Bodhidharma from "Po-ssu in the western regions" (possibly Persia) is said to have visited and admired the Yongning Monastery. This monastery was built in 516 and became a military camp after 528. Consequently, Bodhidharma's visit must have taken place around 520. But no other biographical details can be inferred from this, and the aged western monk (he was purportedly one hundred and fifty years old at the time) bears no resemblance to the legendary founder of Chinese Chan.

The most important source for Bodhidharma's life is the *Xu gaoseng zhuan*, a work written by Daoxuan in 645 and revised before his death in 667. It states that Bodhidharma was a brahman from southern India. After studying the Buddhist tradition of the Greater Vehicle (Mahāyāna), Bodhidharma decided to travel to China in order to spread Mahāyāna doctrine. He arrived by sea at Nanyue, in the domain of the Liu Sung dynasty (420–479), and later traveled to Lo-yang, the capital of the Northern Wei (386–534). In Lo-yang, he attempted to win converts, apparently without great success. Nonetheless, he eventually acquired two worthy disciples, Huike (487–593) and Daoyou (dates unknown), who studied with him for several years. He is said to have transmitted the *Laṅkāvatāra Sūtra*, the scripture he deemed best fitted for Chinese practitioners, to Huike. Bodhidharma seems also to have met with some hostility and slander. Daoxuan stresses that Bodhidharma's teaching, known as "wall-gazing" (*biguan*), or as the "two entrances" (via "principle," *liru*, and via "practice," *xingru*), was difficult to understand compared to the more traditional and popular teachings of Sengchou (480–560). Daoxuan concludes by saying that he does not know where Bodhidharma died. In another section of the text, however, Daoxuan states that Bodhidharma died on the banks of the Lo River. That Bodhidharma's teachings evoked hostility in China is evident from the fact that after his death, his disciple Huike felt it necessary to hide for a period. Since the locale mentioned is known to have been an execution ground, it is possible that Bodhidharma was executed during the late Wei rebellions.

Although Daoxuan's account is straightforward, succinct, and apparently fairly authentic, it presents some problems. Most important, it presents two different, almost contradictory, images of Bodhidharma—as a practicer of "wall-gazing," intent on not relying on the written word, and as a partisan of the *Laṅkāvatāra Sūtra*. Daoxuan clearly has some difficulty in reconciling his divergent sources. Primarily, he draws on the preface to the so-called *Erru sixing lun* (Treatise on the two entrances and four practices), written around 600 by Bodhidharma's (or Huike's) disciple Tanlin (dates unknown) and on information concerning the reputed transmission of the *Laṅkāvatāra Sūtra*. This latter had probably been given to Daoxuan by Fachong (587?–665), an heir of the tradition. In any case, at the time of Daoxuan's writing, Bodhidharma was not yet considered the twenty-eighth patriarch of Indian Buddhism.

In Daoxuan's time, a new school was developing on the Eastern Mountain (Dongshan, in modern Hunan) around the *dhyāna* masters Daoxin (580–651) and Hongren (601–674). The latter's disciples, Faru (638–689), Shenxiu (606–706), and Huian (attested dates 582–709), spread this new teaching, known as the "Dongshan doctrine," in the region of the Tang capitals (Ch'ang-an and Luoyang). Faru's epitaph and two historiographical works of this metropolitan Chan written in the first decades of the eighth century, the *Chuan fabao ji* and the *Lengqie shizi ji*, succeeded in linking the Dongshan tradition to the *Laṅkāvatāra* tradition. Bodhidharma and Huike were defined in these texts as the first two Chinese patriarchs of the Chan school and Daoxin and Hongren were designated the fourth and fifth patriarchs. The missing link was conveniently provided by an obscure disciple of Huike, Sengcan (d. 606)—baptized "third patriarch." Having established its orthodoxy and spiritual filiation, the new Chan school, popularly known as the Damo zong (Bodhidharma school) or the Lengqie zong (*Laṅkāvatāra* school), quickly developed as the main trend of Chinese Buddhism and its "founder" Bodhidharma accordingly acquired legendary status.

The Legend of Bodhidharma within the Chan Sect. About 150 years after Bodhidharma's death, his legend had already grown considerably. His Indian origin plus the very scarcity of information available from the *Xu gaoseng zhuan* seem to have been the essential factors in Bodhidharma's posthumous assumption of the status of "first patriarch" of the new Chan school. In 686, Faru settled at Song Shan, near Luoyang (in modern Henan). Song Shan was already a Buddhist stronghold; Sengchou, Bodhidharma's lucky rival, had once studied under another Indian monk named Fotuo (dates unknown) at Song Shan. Fotuo was revered by the Northern Wei emperor, Xiaowen di (r. 471–499), who, after moving the capital to Luoyang in 496, had the Shaolin Monastery built for him at Song Shan. It seems that later, in Faru's circle, an amalgam was made of the legends of Fotuo, Sengchou, and Bodhidharma. This may be the reason why Bodhidharma became associated with the Shaolin Monastery. According to the *Chuan fapao ji*, Bodhidharma practiced wall-gazing at Song Shan for several years. He thus became known as the "wall-gazing brahman," the monk who remained without moving for nine years in meditation in a cave on Song Shan (eventually losing his legs, as the popular iconography depicts him). There he also met Huike, who, to show his earnestness in searching for the Way, cut off his own arm. (The *Chuan fapao ji* severely criticizes Daoxuan for claiming that Huike had his arm cut off by bandits.) This tradition, fusing with the martial tradition that developed at Song Shan, resulted in Bodhidharma becoming the "founder" of the martial art known as Shaolin boxing (Jpn., Shōrinji *kempō*).

Bodhidharma's legend continued to develop with the *Lidai fabaoji* (c. 774), the *Baolin* (801), and the *Zutang ji* (Kor., *Chodangjip*, 952), and reached its classical stage in 1004 with the *Jingde chuangdeng lu.* In the process, it borrowed features from other popular Buddhist or Daoist figures such as Baozhi or Fuxi (alias Fu Dashi, "Fu the Mahāsattva," 497–569, considered an incarnation of Maitreya). But its main aspects were already fixed at the beginning of the eighth century. For example, the *Chuan fabao ji* contains the following account concerning Bodhidharma's "deliverance from the corpse" (a typical Daoist practice): On the day of his death, he was met in the Pamir Mountains by Songyun, a Northern Wei emissary on his way back from India. After his arrival in China, Songyun told Bodhidharma's disciples of his encounter. The disciples, opening their master's grave, found it empty except for a single straw sandal. Bodhidharma returning to his home in the western regions on one sandal has become a standard motif in Chan iconography.

Another important—if somewhat later—motif is Bodhidharma's encounter with Liang Wudi (r. 502–549) on his arrival in China. This story, which became a favorite theme of Chan "riddles" or *gongan* (Jpn., *kōan*), has its prototype in Fuxi's encounter with Liang Wudi. In both cases, the emperor failed to understand the eminence of the person he had in front of him.

It is also noteworthy that many early Chan works formerly attributed to Bodhidharma have recently been proved to have been written by later Chan masters such as Niutou Farong (594–657) or Shenxiu (606–706). That so many works were erroneously attributed to Bodhidharma may be due simply to the fact that the Chan school was at the time known as the Bodhidharma school, and that all works of the school could thus be considered expressive of Bodhidharma's thought. Whatever the case, these works have greatly contributed to the development of Bodhidharma's image, especially in the Japanese Zen tradition. Further confusing the issue is the "discovery," throughout the eighth century, of epitaphs supposedly written shortly after his death. In fact, these epitaphs were products of the struggle for hegemony among various factions of Chan.

Bodhidharma in Popular Religion. The *Genkōshakusho*, a well-known account of Japanese Buddhism written by a Zen monk named Kokan Shiren (1278–1346), opens with the story of Bodhidharma crossing over to Japan to spread his teachings (a development of the iconographic tradition representing him crossing the Yangtze River). In Japan, Bodhidharma's legend seems to have developed first within the Tendai (Chin., Tiantai) tradition brought from China at the beginning of the Heian period (794–1191) by the Japanese monk Saichō (767–822) and his disciples. One of them in particular, Kōjō (779–858), was instrumental in linking the Bodhidharma legend to the Tendai tradition and to the legend of the regent Shōtoku (Shōtoku Taishi, 574–622), who was considered a reincarnation of Nanyue Huisi (515–577), one of the founders of the Tiantai school (notwithstanding the fact that Shōtoku was born before Huisi died). In his *Denjutsu isshin kaimon*, a work presented to the emperor, Kōjō mentions the encounter that took place near Kataoka Hill (Nara Prefecture) between Shōtoku and a strange, starving beggar—considered a Daoist immortal in the version of the story given by the *Kojiki.* Kōjō, arguing from a former legendary encounter between Huisi and Bodhidharma on Mount Tiantai in China, and from Bodhidharma's prediction that both would be reborn in Japan, has no difficulty establishing that the beggar was none other than Bodhidharma himself.

This amalgam proved very successful and reached far beyond the Tendai school. Toward the end of the Heian period a Zen school emerged from the Tendai tradition, and its leader, Dainichi Nōnin (dates unknown), labeled it the "Japanese school of Bodhidharma" (Nihon Darumashū). This movement was a forerunner of the Japanese Zen sect, whose two main branches were founded by Eisai (1141–1215) and Dōgen (1200–1253) at the beginning of the Kamakura period (1192–1337). This eventually led to the publication of a *Daruma sanchōden* (Biography of Bodhidharma in the Three Kingdoms [India, China, and Japan]) during the Edo period.

But it is in popular religion that Bodhidharma's figure developed most flamboyantly. Early in China, Bodhidharma not only borrowed features from Daoist immortals but became completely assimilated by the Daoist tradition; there are several Daoist works extant concerning Bodhidharma. In Japan, Bodhidharma's legend developed in tandem with that of Shōtoku Taishi; a temple dedicated to Daruma is still to be found on the top of Kataoka Hill. The Japanese image of Daruma, a legless doll known as *fuku-Daruma* ("Daruma of happiness"), presides over many aspects of everyday life (household safety, prosperity in business, political campaigns, etc.). This figure, impressed on every child's mind, has come to play an important role in Japanese art and culture.

See Also Chan; Liang Wudi; Shotoku Taishi.

Bibliography

Demiéville, Paul. "Appendice sur 'Damoduolo' (Dharmatra[ta])." In *Peintures monochromes de Dunhuang* (*Dunhuang baihua*), edited by Jao Tsong-yi, Pierre Ryckmans, and Paul Demiéville. Paris, 1978. A valuable study of the Sino-Tibetan tradition that merged Bodhidharma and the Indian translator Dharmatrata into a single figure, which was subsequently incorporated into the list of the eighteen legendary disciples of the Buddha.

Dumoulin, Heinrich. "Bodhidharma und die Anfänge des Chʿan-Buddhismus." *Monumenta Nipponica* (Tokyo) 7, no. 1 (1951): 67–83. A good summary of the first Sino-Japanese re-examinations of the early Chan tradition.

Sekiguchi Shindai. *Daruma no kenkyu.* Tokyo, 1967. An important work, with an abstract in English, on the Chinese hagiographical tradition concerning Bodhidharma.

Yanagida Seizan. *Daruma.* Tokyo, 1981. The most recent and authoritative work on Bodhidharma. It examines the historical evidence and the development of the legend in Chan (Zen) and in Japanese popular religion and also provides a convenient translation in modern Japanese of Bodhidharma's thought as recorded in the *Erru sixing lun.*

New Sources

Broughton, Jeffrey L. *The Bodhidharma Anthology: The Earliest Records of Zen.* Berkeley, 1999.

Faure, Bernard. *Le Traité de Bodhidharma, première anthologie du bouddhisme Chan.* Aix-en-Provence, 1986.

Faure, Bernard. "Bodhidharma as Textual and Religious Paradigm." *History of Religions* 25, no. 3 (1986): 187–198.

McRae, John. "The Antecedents of Encounter Dialogue in Chinese Ch'an Buddhism." In *The Kōan: Texts and Contexts in Zen Buddhism,* edited by Steven Heine and Dale S. Wright, pp. 46–74. New York, 2000.

Welter, Albert. "Mahakasyapa's Smile: Silent Transmission and the Kung-an (Koan) Tradition." In *The Kōan: Texts and Contexts in Zen Buddhism,* edited by Steven Heine and Dale S. Wright, pp. 75–109. New York, 2000.

BERNARD FAURE (1987)
Revised Bibliography

BODHISATTVA PATH.

A *bodhisattva* (Pali, *bodhisatta*) is a person who, according to Buddhism, is on the path to attaining the status of an enlightened being. More specifically the term is commonly used for one on the path to becoming a fully enlightened buddha. The "path of the *bodhisattva*" is usually known in Sanskrit as the *bodhisattvamārga* (*bodhisattva*-path), the *bodhisattvayāna* (bodhisattva-vehicle), or the *bodhisattvacaryā* (*bodhisattva*-conduct). It is the path followed by such a person from the time he or she first attains *bodhisattva* status until reaching the "fruit of the path," commonly full buddhahood.

There is no significant difficulty with the meaning of *bodhi.* This derives from the Indo-Aryan root *budh-*, from which the word *buddha* also derives, literally "awakening," or "enlightenment." The real problem is with *sattva.* This commonly means in Sanskrit a "[sentient] being," an "essence," or sometimes "courage." Thus a *bodhisattva* would be an "enlightenment being," "one who has enlightenment as essence," or occasionally perhaps an "enlightenment hero." And that is how the term is regularly glossed in Buddhist Sanskrit sources. But it is not clear how it relates to one that has not yet attained the goal of enlightenment. K. R. Norman (1990–1996, p. 87) suggests that *bodhisattva* may have been "back-formed" as part of sanskritization of Middle Indo-Aryan (such as Pali) expressions. Thus the Middle Indo-Aryan *bodhisatta* has been sanskritized as *bodhisattva.* There are other possible alternatives, however, and these alternatives fit better with explanations given for the etymology of *bodhisatta* in Pali commentaries. The Sanskrit of *bodhisatta* could equally be *bodhisakta* (directed toward enlightenment), or it could be *bodhiśakta* (capable of enlightenment). Clearly these etymologies make better sense.

Buddhism divided fairly early into a number of monastic ordination traditions, identified by different Vinayas, monastic codes. Thus one can speak of, for example, Theravāda, Sarvāstivāda, Mahāsaṃghika, or Dharmaguptaka traditions. In looking at texts deemed authoritative for each of these monastic traditions, one finds discussions of the *bodhisattva* path and the gradual evolution of a common or preferred "school" position. The details of those, however, may not be identical.

As Buddhism developed, it came to refer to three types of enlightenment. There is the enlightenment of those who heard and followed the teaching of the Buddha (i.e., "hearers," *śrāvakas*), attaining *nirvāṇa,* becoming an *arhat* (Pali, *arahant*), and thus putting an end to all types of suffering. One has also the enlightenment of a shadowy group of "solitary buddhas" called *pratyekabuddhas* (Pali, *paccekabuddhas*). Finally, there is the supreme, full enlightenment of a buddha. How the enlightenment of a buddha differs was a point of dispute, but no one denied that in certain important respects it was different. Since *bodhi* means "enlightenment" and three types of enlightenment have been identified, the term *bodhisattva* was therefore also recognized as having application to persons on each of these three "vehicles."

Although *bodhisattva* is commonly used colloquially for a person on just the third of these paths, to full buddhahood, where texts want to make this point explicit the word *bodhisattva* is linked with *mahāsattva.* A Buddha-to-be is a *bodhisattva mahāsattva.* One significance of this is that if Norman's use of the Pali etymologies is correct, the *mahā* (great) in *mahāsattva* might entail "one directed toward the great" or "one capable of the great." If so then "the great" must be buddhahood. It is not clear how early this *bodhisattva mahāsattva* usage occurred, although it is found in fairly early Mahāyāna scriptures. It allows the hypothesis that *mahā* in Mahāyāna should also be taken as referring to "the great," that is, buddhahood (compare *mahābodhiyāna* in Dhammapāla's c. sixth-century *Caryāpiṭaka* commentary). Thus Mahāyāna would be in origin etymologically the "Vehicle [which leads to] the Great," that is, buddhahood.

The path of the *bodhisattva* in this sense is central to Mahāyāna theory and practice. For Mahāyāna, all who can should have buddhahood as their goals, as did the Buddha himself. Because no Buddhist tradition would hold that to be enlightened as an *arhat* or as a *pratyekabuddha* is as distinguished as becoming a buddha, the Mahāyāna can be contrasted with a *yāna* that is by definition inferior, a *Hīnayāna.* To translate *hīna* as "small" or "lesser" would be to miss the point. Those who disagree that it is necessary or even possible that all now should aim to become buddhas follow regular, mainstream Buddhism as *śrāvakas* aiming for enlightenment (to become *arhats*), without a Mahāyāna understanding of what it should all be about. They consider themselves simply to be following the teaching of the Buddha, the way to enlightenment, the end of all suffering. Following some other contemporary scholars, this article refers to the non-Mahāyāna position as "Mainstream Buddhism."

Little is known about how specifically Mahāyāna doctrinal schools developed and were transmitted in India. It would be better to think (at least at this stage) in terms of various discussions in a number of different Mahāyāna texts, some of which gradually came to influence each other. Thus one should not expect to find a single *bodhisattva* path, even in Mahāyāna. To the extent to which texts know of each other there may be mutual influences, positive or negative. How far and in what way that was the case in India is still a subject of research. Outside India, in Tibet, for example, as synthesizing schools of Buddhism developed, attempting to make sense of all this Buddhist and particularly Mahāyāna material, sources were harmonized and molded to create the *bodhisattva* path of that school, eventually more or less accepted by all school members.

This article will first describe how the *bodhisattva* and his or her path is seen in Mainstream Buddhism and will focus on material preserved in Pali associated with the Theravāda tradition. By far the most important sources are in the *Khuddaka Nikāya* section of the canon. These are the *Buddhavaṃsa* (Chronicle of buddhas) by Buddhadatta, *Caryāpiṭaka* (Basket of conduct) by Dhammapāla, and *Nidānakathā* (Story of the origins) attributed to Buddhaghosa, with their associated commentaries (fifth and sixth centuries CE).

These discussions of the career of a *bodhisattva* are placed firmly within a descriptive account of the actual career as a *bodhisattva* of Gautama (Pali, Gotama) Buddha, "our" Śākyamuni. The *Buddhavaṃsa* recounts that Gautama constructed a miraculous jewel-walk in the sky. This is because, so the commentary relates, there were those who grumbled that he was still a young chap and therefore could not be anything that special. Gautama points out that actually it takes an enormous amount of time to become a buddha. It was four "incalculable" aeons plus a hundred thousand aeons ago that, as the accomplished Brahmin ascetic Sumedha, Gautama-in-a-previous-life, had fallen on his face in the mud before a previous buddha, Dīpaṃkara, out of deep respect and admiration and in order to save that buddha from muddy feet. At that time Sumedha vowed that he too would become a Buddha:

> (54) If I so wished I could burn up my defilements today. (55) What is the use while I (remain) unknown of realizing dhamma here? Having reached omniscience, I will become a Buddha in the world with the devas. (56) What is the use of my crossing over alone, being a man aware of my strength? Having reached omniscience, I will cause the world together with the devas to cross over. (57) By this act of merit of mine towards the supreme among men I will reach omniscience, I will cause many people to cross over. (Horner, pt. 3, 1975, p. 14)

The *Buddhavaṃsa* explains that at this fortunate time various factors had come together through *karma* to make realistic aspirations to buddhahood possible:

> (59) Human existence, attainment of the [(male)] sex, cause [possibility of becoming an *arhat*], seeing a Teacher [a Buddha], going forth [as a renunciate], attainment of the special qualities [spiritual attainments], and an act of merit [sacrificing even one's own life for the Buddhas], and will power. (Horner, pt. 3, 1975, p. 15; commentary paraphrased from Buddhadatta, 1978, pp. 133–134)

Dīpaṃkara predicts that Sumedha will indeed, many aeons hence, become the Buddha Śākyamuni. And a buddha's prediction, Sumedha reflects, cannot be mistaken. Others at that time, hearing this, are delighted. If they fail to attain enlightenment under Dīpaṃkara, they can always attain it in the future with Śākyamuni.

The following points are notable. The story of Sumedha's vow under Dīpaṃkara is intended (a) to engender respect for Śākyamuni and (b) to encourage present followers who had failed to gain enlightenment in his presence with the possibility of enlightenment in the future under the next buddha. This will be Metteyya (Sanskrit, Maitreya), already predicted by Śākyamuni. In addition the *bodhisattva* makes a firm vow. His vow takes place in the presence of a previous buddha, who is able to predict the future success of the vow. Commentaries make it clear that it is not enough to take the vow in the presence of a substitute, like the Buddha's relics. Thus at this time the *bodhisattva* had reached an irreversible stage. But what had led to this? Later Pali works describe even earlier stages when, for example, a *bodhisattva* first conceives the idea of becoming a buddha. The notion of earlier stages had already been formalized in, for example, another important Mainstream Buddhist source, the Sanskrit *Mahāvastu* (The great topic) of the Mahāsāṃghikas. First, there is the "natural" stage, when the *bodhisattva*-to-be lives a normal virtuous life before conceiving the wish to become a buddha. Then there is the "resolving," when the vow is first conceived, then that of "living in conformity" with it. Finally, the *bodhisattva* is declared "irreversible" (Mahāvastu, 1949–1956, vol. 1, p. 1 n. 2, 39–46). The *Mahāvastu* also mentions ten successive "stages" (*bhūmi*) of a *bodhisattva*'s career to buddhahood (see Mahāyāna below).

Sumedha took the vow out of concern to help others as well as himself but also perhaps out of some sort of recognition that, under the circumstances that had come about, the highest fame and glory were fitting for him. It was, one might say, his duty. Had Sumedha not taken the vow of a bodhisattva at that time he would have wasted a precious opportunity, and crucially Śākyamuni buddha would never have existed.

All the sources, but particularly the *Caryāpiṭaka* and commentary, then describe the many rebirths of Sumedha between his vow and eventual fruition as Śākyamuni. During this time there were twenty-three further buddhas. The *bodhisattva* renewed his vows under each of them but also developed those qualities necessary to become a buddha. These are listed as ten and are called "perfections" (Pali, *pāramī* or *pāramitā*). In the Pali sources they are giving, morality, renunciation, wisdom, energy, patience, truth telling, resolute determination, loving kindness, and equanimity. Dhammapāla reduced these to six: giving, morality, patience, energy, meditation, and wisdom. It has been suggested that this shows Mahāyāna influence, but this scheme of the perfections is also found in Mainstream Buddhist sources like the *Abhidharmakośa.* All of these perfections are to be acquired by each Buddhist practitioner. It is the degree of perfection that distinguishes a buddha.

With the plan of the rebirths of Sumedha, in which he develops the perfections, are recounted enjoyable stories of heroic virtue. For example, the *bodhisattva* was reborn as the prince Vessantara. In that life he particularly practiced the perfection of generosity. He gave everything away when asked, even his wife and children. In some lives the *bodhisattva* was an animal, like the virtuous monkey king. Thus popular fables with moral purpose were assimilated into Buddhist pedagogy. These "rebirth stories" are the *Jātaka* tales, and throughout the Buddhist world they really tell the path of the *bodhisattva.*

Crucially this whole account is entirely descriptive, within the context of admiration for the success and sheer goodness of Śākyamuni (and by implication the similar acts that led to past buddhas and will lead to future buddhas). No one denies that the concern of followers of Śākyamuni should be their own acquisition of freedom from all suffering, that is, *nirvāṇa.* There is no indication that anyone else need currently take the vow of a *bodhisattva.* Indeed they cannot, because a buddha is no longer around to confirm the vow. The next buddha, Metteyya (Sanskrit, Maitreya), is already predicted and "in process."

Yet there is instability in this account of Sumedha. It is quite clear that Sumedha could have become an enlightened *arhat* there and then. So why did he take the *bodhisattva* vow? The suggestion is that factors came together that might otherwise be wasted (there would now be no Śākyamuni) and that Sumedha sought the greater glory, perhaps precisely out of a sense of duty. He was also astonished by the sheer magnificence of Dīpaṃkara, and he wanted to save more people than just himself. Overwhelmingly there is a feeling of moral justification, in Buddhist terms preeminently compassion. The soteriological thrust of early Buddhism, in common with other contemporary Indian soteriologies, was toward freedom through knowing (Williams and Tribe, 2000, pp. 17–18). Yet with the account of Sumedha emerges a suggestion that it is actually in some way better to become a buddha, and this must be for reasons not of knowing but of virtue. Sumedha wished to help others in such a way that immediate freedom for himself was left behind. There is something better than immediate spiritual freedom. Almost all the perfections are matters of moral qualities, virtue. The *Jātaka* tales are accounts of heroic virtue. The liberation of a buddha must be significantly higher than, morally better than, that of an *arhat.* And the ways in which this is the case must relate to altruism, for there is nothing more to gain for oneself than becoming an *arhat.* If that is the case, then perhaps, some thought, all should try to aim for buddhahood, that is, take the vow of a *bodhisattva.*

The Mahāyāna goes beyond the descriptive account of the *bodhisattva*'s path as a description of Śākyamuni's previous lives in order to generate respect for the buddha and hope for the future, to a prescription. Because buddhahood is much better than being an *arhat* in ways that actually count, all who can should surely take the *bodhisattva* vow. It makes no sense in this Mahāyāna context to talk, as do some older books, of the *bodhisattva* postponing enlightenment. The *bodhisattva* renounces the goal of ever becoming an *arhat* in favor of attaining as quickly as possible a much superior buddhahood.

Textual evidence shows that the earliest Mahāyāna notion of *bodhisattvas* was as a group one should actually join. But there is an obvious problem. How is one to do this, given that the vow has to be taken in the presence of a buddha? There is currently no buddha around, and the next will not appear for a long time. Crucial here was the development of the notion that buddhas are still around and still active on behalf of sentient beings. One can verify this, it was argued, because it is possible to see them in visions and receive new teachings from them (Williams, 1989, 29–31; Williams and Tribe, 2000, pp. 108–111). If buddhas are still around even after their apparent deaths, everything changes. This makes sense too of the claimed superiority of buddhas over *arhats* in key matters relating to their liberation.

In any relatively comprehensive discussion of a Mahāyāna *bodhisattva* path the root source has to be the *Daśabhūmika Sūtra* (Ten stage scripture). This can be supplemented with Indian exegetical texts like the *Abhisamayālaṃkāra* (Ornament for the realizations) and the commentaries by Haribhadra (late eighth century CE), Asaṅga's (c. fourth century CE) *Mahāyānasūtrālaṃkāra* (Ornament for the Mahāyāna Scriptures) and *Bodhisattvabhūmi* (Stages for the *bodhisattva*), the *Madhyamakāvatāra* (Supplement to the middling) and the commentary by Candrakīrti (seventh century), Śāntideva's *Bodhicaryāvatāra* (Introduction to the conduct that leads to enlightenment; eighth century CE), and summaries of practice such as Kamalaśīla's three *Bhāvanākramas* (Stages of cultivation; eighth century) and Atiśa *Bodhipathapradīpa* (Lamp for the path to enlightenment; eleventh century). Because of the limitation of space, however, this article follows the typical late Indian Mahāyāna scheme of the first *Bhāvanākrama.*

As befits the prescriptive Mahāyāna schema, where the earlier stages in particular have direct relevance to conduct, Kamalaśīla starts his account well before the *bodhisattva* has reached the stage of irreversibility or any prediction by a buddha. It is assumed of course that the aspiring *bodhisattva* is already an ardent Buddhist with a good practical appreciation of basic Buddhist tenets and practice, such as morality and renunciation. Note incidentally that historically the thesis (favored particularly by Japanese scholars) that the role of the *bodhisattva* in Mahāyāna had anything to do in India with the significance and aspirations of the laity is now doubted. In practice Mahāyāna path builds on existing patterns of morality and monastic renunciation rather than ignoring, negating, or superseding them. The aspiring *bodhisattva,* Kamalaśīla says, needs to strive in three things: compassion (*karuṇā*), the "awakening mind" (*bodhicitta*), and meditative cultivation. The basis of all is compassion. It is compassion that generates the motivation that leads one to undertaking the *bodhisattva* path. It is therefore compassion that produces Mahāyāna affiliation. Thus the *bodhisattva* practices systematic meditations calculated to create a deep sense of universal compassion for others. When compassion becomes perfect, it is called "great compassion" (*mahākaruṇā*).

Eventually the *bodhisattva* conceives the deep yearning to obtain perfect buddhahood for the sake of all sentient beings. This is the "arising of the awakening mind" (*bodhicittotpāda*). It is a completely self-transforming, deep revolution in the mind from selfishness to altruism in its highest degree. It is hymned extensively and beautifully in Śāntideva's *Bodhicaryāvatāra,* chapter one. Both Kamalaśīla and (famously) Śāntideva refer to two types of awakening mind. First is the aspiration, that is, the yearning intention, for buddhahood. Second, there is actually engaging in the *bodhisattva* path through making a vow and, over an enormously long period of time, acquiring the stocks of merit and wisdom necessary to become a buddha. The *bodhisattva*-to-be thus takes a vow to buddhahood. Kamalaśīla speaks of formally taking this vow in the presence of a master who holds the vow (and who as the *guru* is to be seen as a buddha). If there is no master available, significantly it can be taken in the presence of all the buddhas and advanced *bodhisattvas* who, from a Mahāyāna perspective, are still present throughout all directions.

This leads to a *bodhisattva* who truly practices as a *bodhisattva.* The practice is one of equal development in the means (of helping all sentient beings) and wisdom (seeing things the way they really are) without neglecting either. This requires mastery of meditative cultivation. The *bodhisattva* acquires "calm abiding" (*śamatha*), an ability to steady the mind on a meditation subject perfectly and at will. He or she masters the various trance states, with the possible acquisition of supernormal powers and ability in meditation to visit and see buddhas. He or she also applies a calm, steady mind to analyzing reality until coming to an understanding of the true nature of things through meditative "insight" (*vipaśyanā*). This true nature is described as "emptiness" (*śūnyatā*), the complete absence anywhere of any sort of intrinsic existence. Eventually it becomes possible to place the mind steadily and one-pointedly in meditation on this true nature, the way things really are, but within the context of a compassion that will not lead to abandoning sentient beings and falling into the path of an *arhat.* Thus one aims for a "not-settled-down *nirvāṇa*" (*apratiṣṭhitanirvāṇa*), constantly engaged in benefiting beings.

The path from now on is organized in accordance with a path structure familiar from Mainstream Buddhism, such as the Sarvāstivāda (but not Theravāda). This is the five paths, and all the attainments of the way to buddhahood (typically spoken of as the thirty-seven principles conducive to enlightenment) are plotted onto this scheme in due order.

The first path is the path of accumulation (*sambhāramārga*). Kamalaśīla says little about this path. It initially occurs with the full arising of the awakening mind and is described as having three progressive phases. Through increasing depth in meditation, of integrating calm abiding and insight into the nature of reality, one reaches the path of preparation (*prayogamārga*). This has four progressive phases of meditative achievement (further subdivided), known as warmth, climax, patience, and highest mundane thing. It leads to direct nonconceptual insight into the true nature of things. At this point one attains the path of seeing (or vision, *darśanamārga*). As part of the *bodhisattva* path the *bodhisattva* is finally a noble one (*ārya*), no longer an ordinary worldling, and can inter alia control his or her rebirths. But the *bodhisattva* still has far to go. Directly seeing the true nature of reality is in a sense just the beginning. The *bodhisattva* is only doing all this in order to become a buddha and benefit others. From now on a *bodhisattva* animated by deep compassion, who also sees directly the true nature of things, may act in ways not in keeping with legalistic "lower" moral codes.

On attaining the path of seeing, the third of the five paths, the *bodhisattva* also attains the first of the ten *bodhisattva* stages (*bhūmi*), the Stage of Joy. The sequential attainment of the six or ten Mahāyāna perfections (*pāramitās*) is grafted onto these stages. Thus at the first *bhūmi* the *bodhisattva* strives and attains the perfection of giving. Therefore for a *bodhisattva* giving and the other perfections are embedded in the achieving in meditation of direct nonconceptual insight into the true nature of things. This is no ordinary giving. That is why it becomes, at its highest degree, the "perfection of giving."

The following nine *bodhisattva* stages all occur on the fourth of the five paths, the path of cultivation (or contemplation, *bhāvanāmārga*). Thus the corresponding perfection brings the:

Stainless Stage: morality

Luminous Stage: patience

Radiant Stage: energy

Difficult to Conquer Stage: meditation

Face-to-Face Stage: wisdom

Gone Afar Stage: skill in means

Immovable Stage: vow

Good Stage: power

Cloud of Dharma (Teaching) Stage: gnosis (*jñāna*)

Four further perfections are added to the basic six of Sanskrit Buddhism, correlating to the last four *bodhisattva* stages (compare also the Pali ten).

At the seventh stage a *bodhisattva* is said to become irreversible. The last three stages are thus termed "pure." At the tenth stage the *bodhisattva* appears on a lotus seat, surrounded by other *bodhisattvas* and buddhas, light rays fill the sky, and he (there is little evidence in Indian Buddhism that it could be a woman) is consecrated to full buddhahood. A tenth-stage bodhisattva is extraordinary. For example, he can emanate innumerable forms to help others or place whole world systems inside each pore of his skin. It is at this level that commonly Mahāyāna practitioners locate *bodhisattvas* like Avalokiteśvara (the Bodhisattva of Compassion) or Mañjuśrī (the Bodhisattva of Wisdom), iconically represented bodhisattvas to whose compassionate care prayers for help can be made.

Becoming a buddha is to attain the fifth path, the path of no more learning (*aśaikṣamārga*). Kamalaśīla observes that even buddhas could not fully tell of the wonderful qualities possessed by buddhas for the welfare of all sentient beings.

This description of the path of the *bodhisattva* has been in accordance with exoteric Indian sources. But in later Indian Buddhism esoteric Tantric materials and practices begin to emerge. Two elements in Tantric doctrine taken as a whole make considerable difference to the *bodhisattva* picture. First, through certain Tantric practices it is possible to follow the whole *bodhisattva* path from beginning to end in just one lifetime. Second, no matter how much one practices the path described above, it becomes necessary to engage in Tantric practice to attain full buddhahood. Great summas of Buddhism, concentrating on the *bodhisattva* path and integrating Tantra at the appropriate point, are found particularly in Tibet. An example would be the *Lam rim chen mo* (Greater stages of the path) by Tsong kha pa (late fourteenth century and early fifteenth century). This tendency to shorten (or even sideline) the lengthy *bodhisattva* path is also found in some East Asian Buddhist traditions, such as Zen.

See Also Amitābha; Buddha; Buddhism, Schools of, article on Mahāyāna Philosophical Schools of Buddhism; Iconography, article on Buddhist Iconography; Jñāna; Karuṇā; Merit, article on Buddhist Concepts; Pāramitās; Prajñā; Śāntideva; Soteriology; Stupa Worship.

Bibliography

Beyer, Stephan V. *The Buddhist Experience: Sources and Interpretations.* Encino, Calif., 1974. Includes a translation of the first *Bhāvanākrama.*

Bodhi, Bhikkhu. *A Treatise on the Pāramīs.* Kandy, Sri Lanka, 1996. Partial translation of Dhammapāla's commentary on *Cariyāpiṭaka.*

Buddhadatta. *The Clarifier of the Sweet Meaning (Madhuratthavilāsinī).* Translated by I. B. Horner. London, 1978. Translation of Buddhadatta's commentary on *Buddhavaṃsa.*

Cleary, Thomas, trans. *The Flower Ornament Scripture: A Translation of the Avatamsaka Sutra.* Vol. 2. Boulder, Colo., and Boston, 1984–1987. Includes the *Daśabhūmika Sūtra* translated from the Chinese.

Horner, I. B., trans. *The Minor Anthologies of the Pali Canon.* Part 3, *Chronicle of Buddhas (Buddhavaṃsa); Basket of Conduct (Cariyāpiṭaka).* London, 1975.

Jayawickrama, N. A., trans. *The Story of Gotama Buddha.* Oxford, 1990. The *Nidānakathā.*

Mahāvastu. *The Mahāvastu.* 3 vols. Translated by J. J. Jones. London, 1949–1956.

Norman, K. R. *Collected Papers.* 6 vols. Oxford, 1990–1996.

Śāntideva. *The Bodhicaryāvatāra.* Translated by Kate Crosby and Andrew Skilton. Oxford, 1996.

Sinor, Denis, ed. *Studies in South, East, and Central Asia.* Delhi, 1968. Includes the *Daśabhūmika Sūtra* translated from the Sanskrit by Megumu Honda.

Tucci, Giuseppe, ed. *Minor Buddhist Texts.* Part 2. Rome, 1956–1958. An English summary of *Bhāvanākrama.*

Williams, Paul. *Mahāyāna Buddhism: The Doctrinal Foundations.* London and New York, 1989.

Williams, Paul, with Anthony Tribe. *Buddhist Thought: A Complete Introduction to the Indian Tradition.* London and New York, 2000. Contains a full bibliography.

Paul Williams (2005)

BODILY MARKS.

The human body is constantly altered by natural and cultural processes. These alterations leave visible traces, which in many societies are associated with religious ideas, beliefs, and forces. Biological growth itself leaves marks on the body. Adolescence brings changes in physical structure to members of both sexes. Aging alters the coloring and density of body hair. Firm flesh wrinkles; teeth drop out. Furthermore accidents at work and play mar, scar, mutilate, and deform the body. Such biological and accidental changes may in many cultures be evidence of the operation of invisible beings or powers, such as deities, ancestors, or witchcraft. Or compensatory, supernormal powers may be attributed to the lame, to the malformed, to the blind, and to albinos. Just as certain kinds of diviners may read hidden meanings in such natural phenomena as the flight of birds or the spoor of foxes in sand, so too may the will of invisible entities be read into the natural marks left on the body by growth, illness, and violent mishap.

But nature lags far behind culture in the use of the body as a "canvas," as manipulable material for the expression of meaning. Clothing, headgear, ornaments, and regalia are of course salient agencies for the situational communication of personal and social identity, religious and secular values, and social status. Masks too have similar functions. Such external coverings indicate cultural transformations, particularly those of a transitory and repeatable character. It must be stressed, however, that in ritual settings in many cultures the same concepts and beliefs may be expressed by the marking of the body and by its clothing and masking. Ritual enlists many sensory codes, nonverbal and verbal, and orchestrates them to convey many-layered messages about the meaning of the human condition.

Bodily marking proper may be divided into two main types. The first, permanent marking, involves surgical or quasi-surgical operations on the surface of the body by means of cutting or piercing instruments, such as knives, needles, or razors. The general purpose here is to leave indelible marks on the body, mute messages of irreversible status change, permanent cultural identity, or corporate affiliation. The second category, temporary marking, includes the application to the body of decorations through such media as chalk, charcoal, paint, or other substances that can readily be washed or dusted off. In a sense such bodily marks are less durable than clothing, but when they are used in ritual contexts, they may convey more tellingly important aspects of the cosmological order.

Radical alteration of the genitalia is common to many cultures. It should be noted, however, that such operations, both in preindustrial societies and among adherents of some of the major historical religions, take place in a religious context, often to mark an important stage of the patient's life cycle. Symbolic action reinforces the surgical message that the patient, also an initiate, is undergoing an irreversible change in status and mode of being as culturally defined. Religious as well as cultural definitions and evaluations—gender, age, social segmentation, and cultic, tribal, and national affiliation—are given permanent expression precisely in the surgical refashioning of those bodily parts through which the very existence of the patient's group is genetically transmitted.

Many authorities hold that, generally speaking, tattooing has flourished most among relatively light-skinned peoples, whereas scarification and cicatrization are mostly found among dark-skinned peoples because raised scars and keloids are more easily seen as pattern elements than the darker pigments. In contrast to body painting, however, all forms of piercing, cutting, or cauterizing the body involve contact with nerve endings resulting in pain, hence their not infrequent association with initiatory ordeals, in which respect they find common ground with such practices as genital excision, scourging, and knocking out teeth. Neuroscience may someday discover the precise effects on the central nervous system and on such concomitant psychological functions as memory and sexuality that are produced by these often prolonged operations on the subcutaneous neuronic network.

With the spread of Western culture, many societies that formerly practiced surgical bodily marking in religious contexts have abandoned these customs. Certainly the three major religions "of the book"—Judaism, Christianity, and Islam—have interdicted tattooing since early times. Body marking was forbidden to Jews by God in the Torah (*Lv.* 19:28; *Dt.* 14:1). In 787 CE a Roman Catholic council forbade tattooing. Tattooing was also forbidden by Muḥammad. Nevertheless tattooing has been frequently practiced, for therapeutic or decorative reasons, by nominal adherents of these three religions: for example, by Bosnian Catholics, where it may be a survival of an ancient puberty rite (reported by Mary Durham, 1928, pp. 104–106), by Muslims in the Middle East (exhaustively discussed in Henry Field, 1958), and (rarely) among Middle Eastern and North African Jews.

TATTOOING. European explorers during the fifteenth to eighteenth centuries were struck by the marks they found on the bodies of the peoples they encountered in hitherto unknown lands. Captain John Smith in Virginia and Captain James Cook in Polynesia (who coined the term *tattoo* from the Tahitian word *tattau*, meaning "to mark") were struck by this form of body marking "by inlaying the Colour Black under their skins in such a manner as to be indelible" (Cook, 1893, p. 93). European explorers found tattooing in general practice among the Maori of New Zealand and most other Polynesian islands. The custom was also common throughout New Guinea, Melanesia, Micronesia, the Malay Archipelago, and the Malay Peninsula. On mainland Asia certain peoples of India, Burma, and the fringes of Tibet employed tattooing. Some African groups, including the Nama Khoi, also practiced the art. Tattooing was relatively frequent among North and South American Indians.

Tattooing resembles painting, with the face and body as canvas, while scarification resembles sculpture or woodcarving. Both processes can be painful, but tattooing seems to be less so than scarification, though a full design may take longer to apply. Perhaps the relative quickness of scarification and cicatrization is one of the reasons they figure so prominently in rites of passage and other religious and therapeutic rituals, because they literally mark a sharp contrast between the initiate's previous and subsequent state and status. Nevertheless if such rites include a lengthy period of seclusion from the mundane domain, the slower, more cumulative operation of tattooing may proceed at a more leisurely pace.

Full-body tattooing may take years to complete and may be accomplished in several ritually significant stages. Wilfrid D. Hambly (1925) reported, for example, that among the Motu Koita of New Guinea tattooing played a prominent role in rituals celebrating the physical development of the female body. At about five years old, the hands and forearms were tattooed. Between five and ten years of age, the chin, nose, lower abdomen, and inner thighs were tattooed as they lost their infantile appearance and grew firmer. At puberty, the breast, back, and buttocks were tattooed as they took on adult contours. During marital rites and then at motherhood, the final designs were placed. Each phase of maturation had its own design. Indeed the Motu believed that tattooing not only signified growing up but even helped to cause it (Hambly, 1925, p. 32).

In a religious context, as distinct from a purely decorative context, tattoo marks are clearly symbolic. Hambly, for example, showed how the tattooing of initiates in girls' puberty rituals among the Omaha of North America was originally associated with rites devoted to the sun, the dominant power in their universe. The Omaha deified day and night as the male and female cosmic powers, akin to the Chinese opposition of yang and yin. At the apogee of solar ritual, a nubile girl was the focus of ritual dances, painting, and tattooing. She was tattooed with a disk representing the sun and a star standing for night. Four points on the star signified the four life-giving winds. The two marks together expressed the message that night gives way to the sun, a presage of the girl's marriage. The tattoos were believed to confer life energy and potential fecundity on the developing woman during this liminal phase. If her tattoo sores did not heal quickly, this was thought to indicate the displeasure of spirits because she had been unchaste (Hambly, 1925, pp. 83–84). This example illustrates how ritual tattooing inscribes—or one might even say incarnates—cosmological ideas and forces, leaving a permanent impress, both subjectively and objectively.

There is archaeological evidence for puncture tattooing in the Middle East at least as early as the second millennium BCE. Puncture marks on mummy skins with duplicate signs painted on figurines have been found in Nubian burials from this period. Just as in preliterate societies, the polytheistic cultures of the eastern Mediterranean world saw tattooing as an efficacious means of communication between the invisible and visible domains, here regarded as divine and human. For example, the pharaoh Akhenaton (Amenhotep IV) is represented in reliefs as bearing the name Aton on his body. Although Akhenaton was reared in a polytheistic tradition, he tried to develop a solar monotheism and encouraged naturalistic art at the expense of symbolism. Hence his tattoo was a name, not a symbol. The great monotheistic religions went even further in forbidding the marking of symbols of deities on the body. Field (1958, p. 4) supplied further evidence of rapport between humans and deities effected by tattooing. The symbol of the goddess Neit, for example, was tattooed on the arms and legs of Libyan captives figured on the tomb walls of Seti I (1318–1304 BCE). Even in modern North Africa a tattoo pattern called Triangle of Tanit has been identified as the symbol of the Carthaginian goddess Tanit, who was perhaps the Libyan goddess Ta-Neit taken over by the Carthaginians. Field also mentioned that the devotees of Dionysos were stamped with that god's symbol, the ivy leaf. In Syria-Palestine the worshipers of the moon goddess Mylitta were tattooed with her figure or symbol on their hands or the backs of their necks.

Subsequently, despite religious interdictions, both Christians and Muslims bore tattoos as evidences of pilgrimages to the sacred places. This practice apparently derived from the time of the Crusades. Coptic pilgrims were tattooed with the word *Jerusalem* with the date of the visit beneath it or a standardized religious emblem. Moses Maimonides (1135/8–1204), commenting on the prohibition against tattooing in *Leviticus*, reiterated the central Judaic argument against idolatry as its motive force, whereas other scholars in his tradition stressed the integrity of the human body made in the express image and likeness of God as justification for the ban.

In the cultural history of tattooing, certain main trends are discernible. In antiquity and in many of the reports of travelers in the early modern period, tattooing in preindustrial societies dominantly relates the tattooed person to a social group or category (totemic clan, age or sex category, secret society or warrior association, unmarried or married categories, the widowed, and the like). Sometimes the tattooing process is embedded in an encompassing ritual process. In other instances, as discussed, cumulative tattooing may operate independently from rites of passage, stressing individual development rather than collective affiliation. As societies increase in scale and grow more complex and the division of economic and social labor becomes more refined, tattooing becomes more a matter of individual choice and serves the purpose of self-expression, stressing the decorative rather than the religious and corporate functions. Instead of classing individuals together, homogenizing them symbolically, it now differentiates them. An antinomian character invests tattooing. As the technology of the art develops (for example, the invention of the electric tattooing needle), the designs and colors multiply, allowing considerable scope for self-expression and for making statements about the self not only to others but also to oneself, indelibly imprinting a complex image of one's identity upon one's body.

In societies where tattooing is strongly interdicted or frowned upon for religious or political reasons, tattooing comes to mark and identify not only recalcitrant individuals but also marginal groups that otherwise have few means to display identity in mainstream society. A considerable literature exists on tattooing among such diverse categories as enlisted men in World Wars I and II, criminals, prostitutes, homosexuals, juvenile delinquents, and motorcycle gangs such as the Hell's Angels.

In Japan, where the art of tattooing (*irezumi*) has been long established and may have had, as in Polynesia, ritual connections, the practice fell under interdict in the late Tokugawa period, but it was strongly revived after 1881, when it ceased to be a penal offense. According to Robert Brain, the Japanese—who embroider the whole body with artistic designs, the equivalent of a suit of clothes to a culture that has never hallowed the nude—"use tattooing to give personality to the naked body. . . . Even the bare skin, incorporated into the overall design, acquires an appearance of artificiality" (Brain, 1979, p. 64). The designs are traditional and include the dragon, "giver of strength and sagacity," the horse and the carp (mutations of the dragon), epic heroes such as Yoshitsune, Chinese sages, and the gods whose deeds are recorded in the *Kojiki* and *Nihongi* (*Nihonshoki*). In Japan it has often been difficult to distinguish, in Western style, the religious from the aesthetic and social. Contemporary tattooed men and women wear on their bodies subtle and beautiful expressions of a continuous tradition that links deity, nature, and humankind.

As tattooing became detached from its earlier religious contexts, it seems to have become increasingly associated with the magical protection of individuals and with curative rites performed in cases of individual affliction. Field (1958) provided innumerable examples of tattooing in Syria, Iraq, Iran, Kuwait, Saudi Arabia, Palestine, Baluchistan, and West Pakistan used as prophylaxis, cure, and subsequent prevention of a variety of diseases and ailments, mostly thought to be due to supernatural causes, such as the evil eye, witchcraft, or demons. Therapeutic tattooing is found in many cultures. For example, the Sarawak Kaya of Borneo believe that sickness is caused by the soul leaving the body. A ritual therapist, the *dayong*, is called in to perform a ritual, including dancing and incantations, to recall the patient's soul to its body. After he is sure the soul is back, the *dayong* tattoos an emblem on the patient to keep it from straying again. Similar uses are found cross-culturally in abundance.

Mention should be made of the growth of tattooing in the United States, particularly in California during the late 1970s. After World War II the practice subsided, but because of the influence of the "counterculture" of the late sixties, the role of electronic media in bringing the practices of other cultures into the American home, extensive tourism, a general emphasis on individuality (in dress, sexual mores, art, and religion), and improvements in the techniques of professional tattooing, there has been a marked revival in the art. In the early twenty-first century tattoos along with body piercing became such an integral part of American popular culture that, for many youths, obtaining a tattoo became something of a rite of passage into adulthood. As such the ancient connection with religion has not been forgotten. In addition at the Fifth World Convention of Tattoo Artists and Fans, held in Sacramento, California, in 1980, the prize tattoo was "a large back mural, which included the Virgin of Guadalupe, set on a bed of bright roses, framed in the lower corners by a skull face and a human face, and in the upper, by flowing angels" (Govenar, 1981, p. 216).

Scarification and Cicatrization. Whereas tattooing is the insertion of pigment under the skin and involves pricking instruments ranging from thorns, fish spines, cactus spikes, shells, and bones to steel and electric needles, scarification and cicatrization are more drastic ways of marking the body. Many anthropologists equate these terms, but strictly speaking scarification is the operation of marking with scars, whereas cicatrization is the subsequent formation of a scar at the site of a healing wound, that is, the healing process. It might be useful to distinguish *scarification*, the production of long cuts, from *cicatrization*, the deliberate formation of keloids, sharply elevated, often round or oval scars due to the rich production of collagen in the dermal layer. David Livingstone, in his *Last Journals of David Livingstone in Central Africa* (1874), gave the classic definition of keloid formation when writing of the Makwa, who have double lines of keloids on the face: "After the incisions are made, charcoal is rubbed in, and the flesh pressed out, so that all the cuts are raised above the level of the surface" (Livingstone, 1874, vol. 1, p. 33). In many parts of sub-Saharan Africa cicatrization follows the work of two instruments: a hooked thorn to raise the skin and a small blade to slice it. The more the skin is raised, the more prominent the resulting keloid.

In many preindustrial societies the cicatrization process is embedded in a complex ritual sequence. In *The Drums of Affliction* (Victor Witter Turner, 1968) Edith Turner reported such a ritual sequence among the Ndembu of Zambia. During the seclusion phase of a girl's puberty ritual, the initiate is cicatrized by a woman skilled in the work. The girl is said to feel much pain while the incisions are made, but after the operation she is allowed to revile the operator in compensation, just as boys are permitted to swear at the circumciser during the corresponding male initiation rites. Groups of horizontal incisions converge on the navel from either side, like several sentences of braille. Other keloids are made beneath the navel toward the pubes and on the small of the back. Black wood ash mixed with castor oil is rubbed into the cuts. The raised cicatrices beside the navel constitute a kind of erotic braille and are "to catch a man" by giving him enhanced sexual pleasure when he plays his hand over them. Initiates who can stand the pain are also cicatrized on the mid-chest above the breast line. Two parallel cuts, known by a term signifying "to deny the lover," are made. The first keloid, to the left, represents the initiate's premarital lover, the second, to the right, her husband-to-be. The girl is told never to mention her lover's name to her husband, for the two men should "remain friends" and not fight each other.

Although tattooing, cicatrization, and scarification have much in common, may be combined in various ways, or may each be applied in different contexts in the same society, it may be broadly concluded that tattooing, like body painting, lends itself well to decorative use and personal art. The body becomes a canvas on or under the skin of which may be depicted naturalistic scenes and portraits, abstract designs, and symbolic patterns. Cutting and scarring flesh too may result in aesthetic effects of a quite sophisticated character but also constitutes a visible record of incarnate religious forces and a sacred chronicle of a culture's life-crisis ceremonies. Here the incised body itself proclaims carnally the disciplines involved in the cultural definition of its age, gender, and communal and structural identifications and alliances. In certain societies these marks are believed to be inscribed on the ghost or spirit after death, enabling the gods or spirits to recognize the membership and status of the deceased and to send him or her to an appropriate place of posthumous residence. It is interesting that the Roman Catholic and Orthodox branches of Christianity have sublimated similar beliefs, while condemning body marking itself, in the notion that sacraments of baptism, confirmation, and ordination confer indelible marks upon the soul.

Body Painting. Of the many languages of bodily adornment, several may coexist in a single culture. Terence S. Turner (1977) pointed out, for example, that the Chikrí, a Ge-speaking group in central Brazil, possess elaborate body painting, adorn themselves with earplugs, lip plugs, and penis sheaths, and put on cotton leg and arm bands in ritual contexts. Turner argued that such body adornments are a kind of symbolic language. Body painting is a code that expresses a wide range of information about social status, sex, and age. More than this, wrote Turner, it "establishes a channel of communication *within* the individual, between the social and biological aspects of his personality" (Terence S. Turner, 1977, p. 98).

Color symbolism is most important here, especially the colors red, black, and white, all of which are used in determinate ways. Red is always applied on bodily extremities, forearms and hands, lower legs and feet, and the face. Black is used on the trunk and the upper parts of the limbs as well as for square cheek patches and borders along the shaved areas of the forehead. Black face paintings, executed with great care, are often covered immediately by a heavy coat of red that renders them almost invisible. This practice may be explained by the symbolic values of the colors. Red, according to Turner, represents energy, health, and "quickness," both in the sense of swiftness and of heightened sensitivity. Black, per contra, is associated with transitions between clearly defined states or categories, with liminal conditions, or with regions where normal, precisely defined structures of ideas and behavioral rules are "blacked out." Black also means "dead" and is adjectivally applied to a zone of land outside the village, separating it from the wild forest, that is used for graveyards and seclusion camps for groups undergoing rites of passage. The Chikrí see death itself as a liminal phase between life and complete oblivion. Ghosts survive for one generation in the village of the dead before they "die" once more, this time forever. White represents the pure, terminal state of complete transcendence of the normal social world, for white is the color of ghosts, and white clay is the food of ghosts. The Chikrí paint over the black designs with red to make a symbolic statement, clearly uninfluenced by aesthetic considerations. According to Turner, the black designs represent the socialization of the intelligent part of the person, which is then energized by the biological and psychic life force represented by the thick red overpainting.

Turner's conclusion that body painting at this general level of meaning "really amounts to the imposition of a second, social 'skin' on the naked biological skin of the individual" (Terence S. Turner, 1977, p. 100) has a wide cross-cultural range of applications. The etymological link between *cosmos* and *cosmetics* has often been noted; both derive from the Greek term meaning "order, ornament, universe." When the face and body are painted with designs and colors, the cosmeticized ones are living links between the individual and the sociocultural order with which he or she is temporarily identified. But as with tattooing, in complex industrial societies body painting may assume an antinomian function; bizarre and extravagant designs may betoken rebellion against a society's most cherished values. Or it may become merely an expression of personal vanity and love of adornment.

Marks of Supernatural Election. A considerable literature exists on bodily marks that are believed to be signs of election to high religious status. These must be distinguished from blemishes or birthmarks taken to be indications of reincarnation. In many sub-Saharan societies, for example, recently born infants are carefully inspected for marks corresponding to conspicuous scars and moles found on some deceased relative. Among the Ndembu of Zambia, a child was called Lupinda because marks resembling scratches on his thigh were similar to the scar marks of a leopard-inflicted wound on the thigh of his mother's brother, the great hunter Lupinda. It was expected that the boy, Lupinda reborn, would likewise excel at the chase. Similar beliefs have been reported among the Haida and Tlingit of northwestern North America.

In the great historical religions founders, prophets, saints, and notable teachers of the faith are sometimes associated with supernaturally generated bodily characteristics. For example, it is reported that when Siddhārtha Gautama, who became the Buddha, was born, his body bore the thirty-two auspicious marks (*mahapu-rusa laksanani*) that indicated his future greatness besides secondary marks (*anuvyañjanani*). The Indian poet Aśvaghoṣa, who wrote his *Buddhacarita* (Life of the Buddha) in the second century CE, mentioned some of these marks: the sign of a wheel on one foot, webbing between his fingers and toes, and a circle of hair between his eyebrows. In Islam too there is a tradition of a person bearing bodily marks signifying divine election. Muḥammad's son-in-law ʿAli predicted that the Mahdi, the "divinely guided one," would come to restore justice and righteousness to the world and that he would be recognized by certain bodily traits, among them a balding forehead and a high, hooked nose. A birthmark on his right cheek, a gap between his front teeth, and a deep black beard were also predicted. Muḥammad Aḥmad, who was believed to be the Mahdi by many living in the Sudan during the nineteenth century, was said to have all the looked-for attributes.

Christianity also has its tradition of bodily marks divinely imposed. For Christians the term *stigmata* refers to wounds some people bear on the hands and feet and occasionally on the side, shoulder, or back that are believed to be visible signs of participation in Christ's passion. Francis of Assisi (1181/2–1226) is said to have been the first stigmatic. Since his time the number has multiplied. Historically the stigmata have taken many different forms and have appeared in different positions on the body, hands, and feet of stigmatics. For example, Francis's side wound was on the right, while that of the celebrated modern stigmatic Padre Pio (1887–1968) was on the left. For the Catholic Church stigmata do not by themselves indicate sanctity. Of the several hundred stigmatics listed since the thirteenth century, only sixty-one have been canonized or beatified. Herbert Thurston (1933), an authority on this phenomenon, was extremely reluctant to attribute stigmatization to a miracle. Other theologians are ready to await the verdict of neuroscientific research to settle the problem. Moreover C. Bernard Ruffin, a Lutheran minister, has pointed out that "for every genuine stigmatic, whether holy or hysterical, saintly or satanic, there are at least two whose wounds are self-inflicted" (Ruffin, 1982, p. 145).

SUMMARY. In many societies birthmarks, blemishes, deformities, and other natural signs have been regarded as visible indicators of the permanent or transient presence of invisible, preternatural forces and influences, whether of a magical or religious character. They may be linked with notions of reincarnation, illness caused by spirits or witches, election to a priestly or shamanic role, or the marking of basic group identity. However, the deliberate shaping of the body as an artifact by cultural means is the most widely practiced marker of group identity, an identity that in the simpler societies is also religious identity. Here the body becomes a deliberately created badge of identity. Both permanent and temporary changes are made for this purpose. In addition to the means described above, one might cite tooth filing, piercing or otherwise changing the shape of ears, nose, tongue, and lips, and changes made in the body's extremities, such as hair, feet, fingers, and nails. Although discussion of clothing, the identifying medium for all kinds of religions in all cultures, is beyond the scope of this article, as is detailed discussion of the relationship between aesthetic and ritual bodily marking, it is clear that the body, whether clad or unclad, painted or unpainted, smooth or scarred, is never religiously neutral. It is always and everywhere a complex signifier of spirit, society, self, and cosmos.

SEE ALSO Circumcision; Clitoridectomy; Clothing; Human Body; Masks; Nudity.

BIBLIOGRAPHY

Brain, Robert. *The Decorated Body.* London, 1979. A readable cross-cultural description by an anthropologist of the decoration of the human body.

Caplan, Jane, ed. *Written on the Body: The Tattoo in European and American History.* Princeton, N.J., 2000. An excellent cultural history of the tattoo in Europe and North America from early Greek and Roman antiquity to contemporary Euro-America.

Cook, James. *Captain Cook's Journal during His First Voyage Round the World, in H.M. Bark "Endeavour," 1768–1771.* Edited by William J. L. Wharton. London, 1893.

DeMello, Margo. *Bodies of Inscription: A Cultural History of the Modern Tattoo Community.* Durham, N.C., 2000. An ethnography of contemporary tattooing in the United States written by a female anthropologist who is also a member of the tattoo community.

Durham, Mary Edith. *Some Tribal Origins, Laws, and Customs of the Balkans.* London, 1928.

Field, Henry. *Body-Marking in Southwestern Asia.* Papers of the Peabody Museum of Archaeology and Ethnology, Harvard University, vol. 45, no. 1. Cambridge, Mass., 1958.

Fisher, Angela. *Africa Adorned.* London, 1984. A beautiful collection of photographs cataloging the various forms of African body adornment, both temporary and permanent.

Gell, Alfred. *Wrapping in Images: Tattooing in Polynesia.* Oxford, 1993. A comparative analysis of tattooing in Polynesia based on a comprehensive survey of both written and visual documentary sources that attempts to demonstrate the role tattooing played in constructing a distinctively Polynesian type of social and political being.

Govenar, Alan B. "Culture in Transition: The Recent Growth of Tattooing in America." *Anthropos* 76 (1981): 216–219.

Hambly, Wilfrid D. *The History of Tattooing and Its Significance: With Some Account of Other Forms of Corporal Marking.* London, 1925. Reprint, Detroit, 1974. Still the classic study on tattooing.

Livingstone, David. *Last Journals of David Livingstone, in Central Africa, from 1865 to His Death.* London, 1874.

Rubin, Arnold, ed. *Marks of Civilization: Artistic Transformations of the Human Body.* Los Angeles, 1988. A scholarly collection of ethnographic essays, photographs, and drawings that focus on the divergent ways human beings have used bodily marks to inscribe the human body with social and cultural meaning. It also contains an extensive bibliography on bodily marks categorized by geographical region, including Euro-America.

Ruffin, C. Bernard. *Padre Pio: The True Story.* Huntington, Ind., 1982. A critical, sober, essentially nonhagiographical account of the life of the best-known stigmatic of the twentieth century. The medical evidence about his stigma is thoroughly discussed.

Strathern, Andrew, and Marilyn Strathern. *Self-Decoration in Mount Hagen.* Toronto, 1971. A comprehensive account of body decoration and its meaning in a single society, that of Mount Hagen, New Guinea.

Thurston, Herbert. "The Problem of Stigmatization." *Studies* 22 (1933): 221–232.

Turner, Terence S. "Cosmetics: The Language of Bodily Adornment." In *Conformity and Conflict,* 3d ed., edited by James P. Spradley and David W. McCurdy, pp. 91–108. Boston, 1977. A seminal article on bodily adornment among the Chikrí of Brazil. The author deciphers the complex code underlying various modes of decoration to reveal their meaning and suggests that body decorations have similar functions in all societies.

Turner, Victor Witter. *The Drums of Affliction.* Oxford, 1968.

VICTOR TURNER (1987)
EDITH TURNER (2005)

BODY SEE HUMAN BODY

BODY PAINTING SEE BODILY MARKS

BOEHME, JAKOB (1575–1624), Protestant visionary and theologian. Born into a Lutheran farming family in the village of Alt Seidenberg near Görlitz, Saxony, Boehme was apprenticed to a shoemaker following his elementary education. In 1599 he became a citizen of Görlitz, where he opened a shoemaking business and married. Boehme was early associated with various religious groups in the city, and through them he encountered the work of the alchemist Paracelsus (1493–1541) and the nature mystic Valentin Weigel (1533–1588). He also shared with his religious associates an interest in Qabbalah.

In 1600 Martin Moller (d. 1606) came to the city as Lutheran pastor and formed the Conventicle of God's Real Servants, which Boehme joined following a religious conversion. Deeply concerned with the problem of theodicy, Boehme in 1612 completed *Aurora,* but when a copy of the manuscript fell into the hands of the local Lutheran pastor, the book was confiscated and the author banned from further writing. Seven years later, as the result of an illumination, Boehme broke his silence with the publication of *On the Three Principles of Divine Being,* a work abounding in alchemic imagery, which was to shape the form of his arguments for the next several years. In 1620 there appeared *On the Three-fold Life of Man, On the Incarnation, Six Theosophical Points,* and *Six Mystical Points.* Other major works followed quickly, including, *Concerning the Birth and Designation of All Being, On Election to Grace,* the large commentary on *Genesis* titled *Mysterium magnum,* and the various tracts that make up *The Way to Christ.* As a result of these publications, Boehme was involved in bitter controversy, and suffered exile for a short time. He died in Görlitz on November 17, 1624.

In an attempt to solve the problem of theodicy, Boehme began with the nothing (unknown even to itself), which, as a single unified will, wills a something. In this act of willing, the Son is begotten. In this begetting the nothing discovers the something within itself, which is itself the ground of the abyss. Simultaneously the will proceeds from the Son as Holy Spirit to an eternal contemplation of itself as wisdom (Sophia).

In this contemplation are conceived the various possibilities of being present in the Word (the Son) and created by it. The will of the nothing looks out to the something as light (love) and returns into itself as a desiring fire (wrath). In the knowledge that results, eternal nature has its being. The two fused principles of fire and light reflect in themselves a third, the being of the universe, which is progressively manifested through seven properties: harshness; attraction; dread; the ignition of fire, which is the basis of sensitive and intellectual life; love, which overcomes the individualism of the first four; the power of speech; and speech itself. All properties are present in all being. Further, the seven properties can be categorized according to three principles. The first three properties represent the fire (wrath) principle. The fifth and sixth properties represent the light (love) principle. The seventh property represents the third principle (being of the universe). The fourth property is the center on which all turn. All beings of the third principle are free and can turn to either of the first two principles, thereby upsetting the balance. Searching for the controlling fire of light, Lucifer refused to accept the light principle within himself and as a result fell.

At the moment of Lucifer's fall, temporal creation came into existence. At its height stood Adam, a perfect balance of the four elements fire and light, male and female. But Adam, too, chose to know the principles separately and fell. In the loss of the balance, these four elements were awakened and male and female divided. Thereafter human beings have chosen the fiery origin that, untempered by light, love, or the spiritual water of the new life, would destroy each individual human being. In his mercy, however, God fully revealed the light element in the New Man, Christ, in whose perfect balance each human being can once more live in harmony with the divine contemplation, the virgin Sophia.

Following Boehme's death, his disciples, chief among whom was Abraham von Franckenberg (1593–1649), spread his ideas throughout Europe. The Silesian poet Angelus Silesius (Johann Scheffler, 1624–1677) used Boehme's images extensively in his poetry before and after his conversion from Lutheranism to Roman Catholicism. By 1661 Boehme's works appeared in English translation, and under the direction of Jane Leade (1623–1704) the Philadelphian Society was founded in London on Boehmist principles. In England alone Boehme's influence can be traced in the seventeenth century to persons of such stature as the Cambridge Platonist Benjamin Whichcote, the poet John Milton, and the physicist Isaac Newton, and in the eighteenth century to the spiritual writer William Law and the visionary poet William Blake. In the Low Countries, Boehme's thought was popularized by the most important of his editors and students, Johann Georg Gichtel (1638–1710), and by radical Quietists such as Antoinette Bourignon (1616–1680) and Pierre Poiret (1646–1719).

SEE ALSO Alchemy; Sophia.

BIBLIOGRAPHY

Boehme, Jakob. *Sämmtliche Schriften.* 10 vols. Edited by Will-Erich Peuckert. Stuttgart, 1955–1960.

Koyré, Alexandre. *La philosophie de Jacob Boehme* (1929). Reprint, New York, 1968. The fullest introduction to Boehme's thought.

Peuckert, Will-Erich. *Das Leben Jakob Böhmes* (1924). Reprint, Stuttgart, 1961. A detailed biography of Boehme.

Stoudt, John Joseph. *Sunrise to Eternity.* Philadelphia, 1957. The best introduction to Boehme's life and thought in English.

Thune, Nils. *The Behmenists and the Philadelphians.* Uppsala, 1948. A limited but useful outline of the Boehmist heritage.

PETER C. ERB (1987)

BOETHIUS (c. 475–c. 525), more fully, Anicius Manlius (Torquatus) Severinus Boethius, late Roman philosopher, theologian, and statesman. Because of the paucity of sources concerning Boethius's life, no more than the most shadowy biographical sketch is possible. A member of one of the great Roman families, Boethius was almost certainly born at Rome. The Rome in which he lived had lost much of its importance—imperial control had given way to the reign of the barbarian king Odoacer about the time of his birth—but the prestige of the Anician family remained intact, as shown by the consulship of Boethius's father in 487. Upon completing his schooling, which he presumably received at Rome, Boethius continued his education by studying philosophy, probably at Alexandria, but possibly in his native city. Of his public life, it is known only that he served as consul in 510 and that, about 523, he became master of offices, one of the highest civil officials in the court of the Ostrogothic king of Italy, Theodoric. While master of offices, Boethius was implicated in a treasonable conspiracy with the Eastern emperor, which apparently centered upon a plot to overthrow Theodoric. Although Boethius resolutely maintained his innocence, he was imprisoned. During his imprisonment he wrote *On the Consolation of Philosophy*, his most famous work, which he completed only shortly before his execution.

Much more important than his public career, which was not unusual for a person of his standing, was his literary career. In one of his early works, he described his projected program of philosophical writings: in a world in which the Latin West was rapidly losing its knowledge of Greek, Boethius wished to translate into Latin all the works of Plato and Aristotle and to show, through a series of commentaries on these works, that there was no essential conflict between the Platonic and Aristotelian traditions. He did not realize this plan in its entirety, but he did translate a number of the logical works of Aristotle (the so-called *Organon*) and wrote (or possibly only translated from the Greek) several commentaries on these writings. In doing so, he rendered a very important service to the early medieval West by providing the only Latin translations of Aristotle available until the gradual introduction of the "new learning" in the late Middle Ages.

Despite his failure to translate any of the works of Plato, Boethius did provide the medieval world with one of its most important source books of Neoplatonic thought, *On the Consolation of Philosophy*, one of the most widely read books of the Middle Ages. Cast in the form of a cosmological revelation by Lady Philosophy to the imprisoned and perplexed Boethius, the *Consolation* presents a highly sophisticated and systematic Neoplatonic worldview. The curious fact that Boethius, who was certainly a Christian, looked to Neoplatonism rather than to Christianity to console him is inexplicable.

Boethius's chief creative contribution to the intellectual tradition of the West comes in his five brief Christian theological works. Although these works are highly Augustinian in their content, Boethius established his independence from Augustine in matters of terminology and method. In *On the Trinity*, he employed the term *theology* for the first time as a technical Christian term denoting the philosophical inquiry into the nature of God. Methodologically, his contribution lies in the use of formal Aristotelian demonstrative logic for the first time in the service of Christian theology. In doing so, he anticipated the fundamental character of the Thomistic method of "scientific" theology by some five and one-half centuries.

BIBLIOGRAPHY

Most of Boethius's works have not been translated into English, but *The Theological Tractates* and *The Consolation of Philosophy*, translated by H. F. Stewart and E. K. Rand, are widely available in a Loeb Classical Library edition (Cambridge, Mass., 1926). The best work in English on Boethius's writings in general is Pierre Courcelle's *Late Latin Writers and Their Greek Sources*, translated by Harry E. Wedeck (Cambridge, Mass., 1969). For specific discussion of the Christian theological works, see my study titled "Boethius Conception of Theology and His Method in the Tractates" (Ph.D. diss., University of Chicago, 1974).

A. RAND SUTHERLAND (1987)

BON. There are two organized religious traditions in Tibet: Buddhism and a faith that is referred to by its Tibetan name, Bon. Since its introduction into Tibet in the eighth century, Buddhism has been the dominant religion; in the person of the Dalai Lama, present-day Tibetan Buddhism has an articulate and internationally respected spokesman.

The Bon religion is much less well known, although the number of its adherents in Tibet is by all accounts considerable. In the West, the traditional view of Bon has been less than accurate. It has been characterized as "shamanism" or "animism," and as such, regarded as a continuation of what supposedly were the religious practices prevalent in Tibet before the coming of Buddhism. It has also been described in rather unfavorable terms as a perversion of Buddhism, a kind of marginal countercurrent in which elements of Buddhist doctrine and practice have either been shamelessly copied or inverted and distorted in a manner that has been somewhat imaginatively compared with satanic cults. It was only in the mid-1960s that a more accurate understanding of this religion emerged (first and foremost thanks to the efforts of David L. Snellgrove), so that Bon is now recognized as closely related to the various Buddhist schools in Tibet (in particular the Rnying ma pa [Nyingma pa] order) and yet possessed of an identity of its own that justifies its status as a distinct religion.

PROBLEMS OF DEFINITION. An adherent of the Bon religion is called a Bonpo, again using the Tibetan term. A Bonpo is "a believer in *bon*," and for such a believer the word *bon* signifies "truth," "reality," or the eternal, unchanging doctrine in which truth and reality are expressed. Thus *bon* has the same range of connotations for its believers as the Tibetan word *chos* (corresponding to the Indian word *dharma*) has for Buddhists.

A problem, however, arises when one is confronted with the fact that an important group of ritual experts in pre-Buddhist Tibet were likewise known as *bonpos*. It is possible that their religious practices were styled Bon (although scholars are divided on this point); certainly their practices were so designated in the later, predominantly Buddhist historiographical tradition. Be that as it may, their religious system was essentially different not only from Buddhism, but also, in certain important respects, from the Bon religious tradition as practiced in later centuries. For example, the pre-Buddhist religion of Tibet gives the impression of being preoccupied with the continuation of life beyond death. It included elaborate rituals for ensuring that the soul of a dead person was conducted safely to a postmortem land of bliss by an appropriate animal—usually a yak, a horse, or a sheep—which was sacrificed in the course of the funerary rites. Offerings of food, drink, and precious objects likewise accompanied the dead. These rites reached their highest level of elaboration and magnificence in connection with the death of a king or a high nobleman; as was the case in China, enormous funerary mounds were erected, and a large number of priests and court officials were involved in rites that lasted for several years. The purpose of these rites was twofold: on the one hand, to ensure the happiness of the deceased in the land of the dead, and on the other, to obtain their beneficial influence for the welfare and fertility of the living.

The term *Bon* refers not only to these and other religious practices of pre-Buddhist Tibet, but also to the religion that apparently developed in close interaction with Buddhism from the eighth century onward and that still claims the adherence of many Tibetans. It is with the latter religion that this article is concerned. The Bonpos claim that there is an unbroken continuity between the earlier and the later religion—a claim that, whatever its historical validity, is significant in itself.

The matter is further complicated by the fact that there has always existed a vast and somewhat amorphous body of popular beliefs in Tibet, including beliefs in various techniques of divination, the cult of local deities (connected, above all, with certain mountains), and conceptions of the soul. In Western literature, such beliefs are frequently styled "Bon," and reference is made to "Bon animism" and other supposedly typical Bon attributes. This has, however, no basis in Tibetan usage, and since this popular, unsystematized religion does not form an essential part of Buddhism or Bon (although it is, to a large extent, sanctioned by and integrated into both religions), an appropriate term for it is the one coined by Rolf A. Stein, "the nameless religion."

THE BONPO IDENTITY. Although limited to Tibet, Bon regards itself as a universal religion in the sense that its doctrines are true and valid for all humanity. For this reason it styles itself G'yung drung Bon, "Eternal Bon." According to its own historical perspective, it was introduced into Tibet many centuries before Buddhism and enjoyed royal patronage until it was supplanted and expelled by the "false religion" (Buddhism) coming from India.

Before reaching Tibet, however, it is claimed that Bon prospered in a land known as Zhang-zhung and that this country remained the center of the religion until it was absorbed by the expanding Tibetan empire in the seventh century. There is no doubt as to the historical reality of Zhang-zhung, although its exact extent and ethnic and cultural identity are far from clear. It does, however, seem to have been situated in what today is, roughly speaking, western Tibet, with Mount Kailash as its center.

The ultimate homeland of Bon, is, however, to be sought farther to the west, beyond the borders of Zhang-zhung. The Bonpos believe that their religion was first proclaimed in a land called Rtag gzigs (Tazik) or 'Ol mo lung ring. Although the former name suggests the land of the Tajiks in Central Asia, it has so far not been possible to identify this holy land of Bon in a convincing manner.

In Rtag gzigs, so the Bonpos claim, lived Ston pa Gshen rab (Tonpa Shenrap), a fully enlightened being who was, in fact, nothing less than the true Buddha of our world age. The Bonpos possess a voluminous biographical literature in which his exploits are extolled. Without entering into details, or discussing the many problems connected with the historical genesis of this extraordinary figure, one may at least note that his biography is not closely related to the biographical traditions connected with Śākyamuni, the Buddha on whose authority the Buddhists base their doctrines. Ston pa Gshen rab was a layman, and it was as a prince that he incessantly journeyed from his capital in all directions to propagate Bon. It is remarkable that this propagation also included the institution of innumerable rituals, the supervision of the erection of temples and stupas, and the conversion of notorious sinners. His numerous wives, sons, daughters, and disciples also played a significant role (in a way for which there is no Buddhist parallel) in this soteriological activity. It was only late in his life that he was ordained as a monk, and at that point in his career he retired to a forest hermitage. On the other hand, Ston pa Gshen rab is considered to have been a fully enlightened being from his very birth, endowed with numerous supernatural powers. His importance in the Bon religion is crucial; it is he who—directly or indirectly—lends authority to the religious literature of the Bonpos, and he is the object of their intense devotion.

RELIGIOUS BELIEFS AND PRACTICES. In the same way as the Buddhists of Tibet divide their sacred scriptures into two vast collections, the Bonpos also—probably since the middle of the fourteenth century CE—possess their own Bka' 'gyur (Kanjur, texts considered to have been actually expounded by Ston pa Gshen rab) and Brten 'gyur (Tenjur, later commentaries and treatises), comprising in all approximately three hundred volumes. Since the middle of the nineteenth century wooden blocks for printing the entire collection have been available in the principality of Khro bcu in the extreme east of Tibet, and printed copies of the canon were produced until the 1950s. (The blocks were destroyed during the Cultural Revolution.) The Bka' 'gyur and Brten 'gyur have been reconstituted and printed editions have been published in Tibet.

A common division of the Bonpo Bka' 'gyur is the fourfold one into Sūtras (*mdo*), Prajñāpāramitā texts (*'bum*), Tantras (*rgyud*), and texts dealing with the higher forms of meditation (*mdzod*, lit. "treasurehouse"). The Brten 'gyur is divided into three basic textual categories: "External," including commentaries on the Vinaya, the Abhidharma, and the Sūtras; "Internal," comprising the commentaries on the Tantras and the rituals focusing on the major Tantric deities, as well as the cult of *ḍākinīs*, *dharmapālas*, and worldly rituals of magic and divination; and finally, "Secret," a section that treats meditation practices. A section containing treatises on grammar, architecture, and medicine is appended.

For the sake of convenience, the Indian (Buddhist) terms corresponding to the Tibetan have been used here, but it must be kept in mind that although the Bonpos employ the same Tibetan terms as the Buddhists, they do not accept their Indian origin, since they trace, as explained above, their entire religious terminology to Zhang-zhung and, ultimately, to Rtag gzigs.

As this review of Bonpo religious literature indicates, the doctrines they contain are basically the same as those of Buddhism. The concepts of the world as suffering, of moral causality and rebirth in the six states of existence, and of enlightenment and Buddhahood are basic doctrinal elements of Bon. Bonpos follow the same path of virtue and have recourse to the same meditational practices as do Buddhist Tibetans.

In the early fifteenth century—and indeed even earlier—the Bonpos began to establish monasteries that were organized along the same lines as those of the Buddhists, and several of these monasteries developed into large institutions with hundreds of monks and novices. The most prestigious Bonpo monastery, founded in 1405, is Sman ri (Menree) in central Tibet (in the province of Gtsang, north of the Brahmaputra River). Fully ordained monks, corresponding to the Buddhist *dge slong* (Gelong; Skt., *bhikṣu*), are styled *drang srong* (a term that in Tibetan otherwise translates *ṛṣi*, the semidivine "seers" of the Vedas). They are bound by all the rules of monastic discipline, including strict celibacy.

Over the centuries the monastic life of Bon has come increasingly under the influence of the tradition of academic learning and scholastic debate that characterize the dominant Dge lugs pa (Geluks pa) school, but the older tradition of Tantric yogins and hermits, constituting an important link between the Bonpos and the Rnying ma pas, has never been quite abandoned.

An important class of religious experts, which likewise finds its counterpart in the Rnying ma pa tradition, consists of the visionaries—both monks and laymen—who reveal "hidden texts." During the Buddhist persecution of Bon in the eighth and ninth centuries, the Bonpos claim, their sacred texts were hidden in caves, buried underground, or walled up in certain temples. Later (apparently from the tenth century onward) the texts were rediscovered—at first, it would seem, by chance, and subsequently through the intervention of supernatural beings who would direct the chosen *gter ston* ("treasure finder") to the site. Later still, texts would be revealed in visions or through purely mental transference from divine beings. The greater part of the Bon Bka' 'gyur and Brten 'gyur consists of such "rediscovered" or supernaturally inspired texts. "Treasure finders" have been active until the present, and indeed may be said to play an important role in the revival of religious activities in Tibet today, as texts that were hidden for safekeeping during the systematic destruction of the 1960s and 1970s are once more being removed from their hiding places.

As is the case in Tibetan religion generally, these texts are particularly important in that they serve, in an almost literal sense, as liturgical scores for the innumerable and extremely complex rituals, the performance of which occupies much of the time and attention of the monks. Many of these rituals do not differ significantly from those performed by the Buddhists, except that the deities invoked—although falling into the same general categories as those that apply to the deities of Mahāyāna Buddhism—are different from the Buddhist ones. They have different names, iconographical characteristics, evocatory formulas (mantras), and myths. A systematic study of this pantheon has, however, only just begun, and likewise, our knowledge of the rituals of the Bonpos is still extremely incomplete.

The laypeople are confronted by many of these deities, impersonated by monks, in the course of mask dances. The lay Bonpos have the same range of religious activities as Tibetan Buddhist laypeople: the practice of liberality toward monks and monasteries (in exchange for the performance of rituals); the mechanical multiplication of prayers by means of prayer flags and prayer wheels; and journeys of pilgrimage to the holy places of Bon, such as Mount Kailash in the western Himalayas, or Bon ri ("mountain of Bon"), in the southeastern province of Rkong po (Kong po).

THE DIFFUSION OF BON. Both Buddhists and Bonpos agree that when Buddhism succeeded in gaining royal patronage in Tibet in the eighth and ninth centuries, Bon suffered a serious setback. By the eleventh century, however, an organized religious tradition, styling itself Bon and claiming continuity with the earlier, pre-Buddhist religion, appeared in central Tibet. It is this religion of Bon that has persisted to our own times, absorbing doctrines and practices from the dominant Buddhist religion but always adapting what it learned to its own needs and its own perspectives. This is, of course, not just plagiarism, but a dynamic and flexible strategy that has ensured the survival, indeed the vitality, of a religious minority.

Until recent years, much has been made in Western literature of the fact that the Bonpos perform certain basic ritual acts in a manner opposite to that practiced by the Buddhists. Thus, when circumambulating sacred places and objects or when spinning their prayerwheels, the Bonpos proceed counterclockwise rather than following the (Indian and Buddhist) tradition of *pradakṣiṇā*, or circumambulation "toward the right." For this reason, it has been said of Bon that "its essence lay largely in contradiction and negation," and Bon's "willful perversions and distortions" have been pointed out. The error of such views cannot be too strongly emphasized. The Bonpos are conscious of no element of "contradiction and negation" in their beliefs and practices but regard their religion as the pure path to liberation from suffering and rebirth. It is true that down through the centuries Bonpo historiographers have generally regarded the introduction of Buddhism into Tibet as a catastrophe, which they have ascribed to the accumulated collective "evil karma" of the Tibetans. On the other hand, conciliatory efforts have not been lacking; thus one source suggests that Ston pa Gshen rab and Śākyamuni were really twin brothers.

It is difficult to assess just how large the Bonpo community of Tibet is. Certainly the Bonpos are a not insignificant minority. Particularly in eastern Tibet, whole districts are populated by Bonpos. Scattered communities are also to be found in central and western Tibet, particularly in the Chumbi Valley (bordering Sikkim) and among nomads. In the north of Nepal, too, there are Bonpo villages, especially in the district of Dolpo. At a point in history that remains to be determined precisely, Bon exerted a strong influence on the religion of the Nakhi people in Yunnan Province in southwestern China; with this exception, the Bonpos do not seem to have engaged in missionary enterprises. In India, Bonpos belonging to the Tibetan refugee community have established (since 1968) a large and well-organized monastery in which traditional scholarship, rituals, and sacred dances are carried on with great vigor. Since 1980, when religious life was revived in Tibet itself, the Bonpos there have rebuilt several monasteries (albeit on a reduced scale), installed monks, and resumed—to the extent that prevailing conditions permit—many aspects of traditional religious life. It would thus seem that there is good reason to believe that Bon will continue to exist, and even, with certain limits, to flourish.

SEE ALSO Buddhism, Schools of, article on Tibetan and Mongolian Buddhism; Dge lugs pa; Tibetan Religions, overview article.

BIBLIOGRAPHY

A well-illustrated introduction to Bon for the nonspecialist is Christian Baumet, *Tibet's Ancient Religion Bon* (Bangkok/Trumbull, Conn., 2002). When it was published in 1950 and for many years thereafter, Helmut Hoffman's *Quellen zur Geschichte der tibetischen Bon-Religion* (Wiesbaden, 1950) was the most reliable and comprehensive study of Bon, based as it was on all sources available at the time. Since 1960, Tibetan Bonpo monks in exile have collaborated with Western scholars. The first major work to result from this entirely new situation was *The Nine Ways of Bon: Excerpts from the gZi-brjid*, edited and translated by David L. Snellgrove (1967; reprint, Boulder, 1980), in which doctrinal material from the important fourteenth-century Bon text *Gzi brjid* was presented for the first time. In the following year, David L. Snellgrove and Hugh E. Richardson presented a historical framework for the development of Bon in *A Cultural History of Tibet* (1968; reprint, Boulder, 1980) that has since been generally accepted. An excellent presentation of Bon was also given by Anne-Marie Blondeau in her article "Les religions du Tibet," in *Histoire des religions*, edited by Henri-Charles Puech, vol. 3 (Paris, 1976), pp. 233–329.

An important survey of the Bon religion is Samten G. Karmay's "A General Introduction to the History and Doctrines of Bon," *Memoirs of the Research Department of the Tōyō Bunko*, no. 33 (1975): 171–218 (also printed as a separate booklet, *The M. T. B. Off-prints Series*, no. 3; Tokyo, 1975). The same scholar has also translated a history of Bon written by the Bonpo scholar Shar rdza Bkra shīs Rgyal mtshan (1859–1935) in 1922 under the title *The Treasury of Good Sayings: A Tibetan History of Bon* (London, 1972).

On Bon literature, see Per Kvaerne's "The Canon of the Bonpos," *Indo-Iranian Journal* 16 (1975): 18–56, 96–144, and Samten G. Karmay's *A Catalogue of Bonpo Publications* (Tokyo, 1977). The monastic life of Bon (based on information from Sman-ri monastery) is outlined in Kvaerne's "Continuity and Change in Tibetan Monasticism," in *Korean and Asian Religious Tradition*, edited by Chai-shin Yu (Toronto, 1977), pp. 83–98. On meditational practices, see Kvaerne's "'The Great Perfection' in the Tradition of the Bonpos," in *Early Ch'an in China and Tibet*, edited by Whalen Lai and Lewis R. Lancaster (Berkeley, 1983), pp. 367–392.

A detailed description of a Bonpo ritual has been provided in Per Kvaerne's *Tibet, Bon Religion: A Death Ritual of the Tibetan Bonpos* (Leiden, 1984). The same book analyzes the extensive iconography connected with that particular ritual. The biography of Ston pa Gshen rab has been studied intensively on the basis of the *Gzi-rjid* and a series of paintings in Per Kvaerne's "Peintures tibétaines de la vie de *sTon-pa-gçen-rab*," *Arts asiatiques* 41 (1986).

A general survey of the iconography of Bon is provided in Per Kvaerne, *The Bon Religion of Tibet. The Iconography of a Living Tradition* (London, 1995; reprint, 2001).

PER KVAERNE (1987 AND 2005)

BONAVENTURE, religious name of Giovanni di Fidanza (c. 1217–1274), Italian scholastic theologian, minister general of the Friars Minor, cardinal bishop of Albano, doctor of the church, and Christian saint.

LIFE AND WORKS. Information concerning the early life of Bonaventure is scant. His parents were Giovanni di Fidanza, who was a doctor in Bagnoregio in Tuscany, and Maria di Ritello. Bonaventure himself tells that he was cured of a serious childhood illness through his mother's prayer to Francis of Assisi. After early schooling at the Franciscan friary in Bagnoregio, Bonaventure began his studies at the University of Paris in 1235. After earning a master of arts degree, he entered the Franciscan order (Friars Minor), probably in 1243, pursuing the study of theology first under the Franciscan masters Alexander of Hales and John of La Rochelle and later under Odo Rigaldi and William of Meliton.

After he received a bachelor of scripture degree in Paris in 1248, Bonaventure began lecturing on the Bible. Although not all his commentaries survived, those on *Luke* and *John* remain important sources for his early theological viewpoints. After giving his courses on the *Sentences* of Peter Lombard between 1250 and 1252, he was ready to receive the licentiate and the doctorate in theology. Although there is some debate concerning the exact date of his formal acceptance into the masters' guild, there is strong evidence indicating that he functioned as regent master at the school of the Friars Minor at Paris from 1253 to 1257. During this period, he composed at least three well-known sets of disputed questions: *On Evangelical Perfection, On Christ's Knowledge*, and *On the Mystery of the Trinity.* Because of his election as minister general, Bonaventure had to resign his university post to take up the pressing tasks of administration. Even though he no longer lectured at the university, he made Paris his headquarters and preached frequently to the students and masters gathered there.

During his first years as minister general of the Friars Minor, Bonaventure produced three works that are important sources for his system of thought: a concise handbook of theology called the *Breviloquium* (1257), a brief tract titled *Retracing the Arts to Theology* (date unknown), and a synthesis of his speculative and mystical theology known as *The Journey of the Mind to God* (1259). Most of the writings coming from his years as minister general are directly religious or ascetical in nature, including many sermons, letters, and regulations for the friars, two lives of Francis of Assisi, and the *Defense of the Mendicants* (c. 1269). Of particular importance for insight into the development of Aristotelianism are three sets of conferences held for the friars of Paris: *On the Ten Commandments* (1267), *On the Seven Gifts of the Holy Spirit* (1268), and *On the Six Days of Creation or the Illuminations of the Church* (1273). The final set of conferences was left unfinished when Bonaventure was named cardinal bishop of Albano by Pope Gregory X in 1273.

Bonaventure left Paris to help with preparations for the Council of Lyons, which convened on May 7, 1274, and he took an active part in the council until his unexpected death on July 15, 1274. Canonized by Sixtus IV in 1482, he was declared a doctor of the church by Sixtus V in 1588 with the title "Seraphic Doctor."

THEOLOGICAL TEACHING. Although not a stranger to philosophy, Bonaventure is known primarily as a theologian. He acknowledged philosophy as a legitimate and important level of reflection, but he believed that it must be transcended by speculative theology and finally by mystical union with God. Bonaventure's theology was influenced not only by the spirituality of Francis of Assisi and the thought of Augustine but also by Dionysius the Areopagite, Boethius, Joachim of Fiore, Richard of Saint-Victor, Aristotle, and Ibn Gabirol (Avicebron).

Bonaventure's theological system is strongly Christocentric. While his early *Commentary on John* describes a view emphatically centered around the Word, his final work, *Collations on the Six Days of Creation,* reveals a system for which the Word as incarnate is the point of departure for theological reflection. While Christ is the historical foundation of Christian theology, reflection on Christ reveals the ontological foundation of theology, which is the triune God.

Doctrine on God. Bonaventure is deeply Augustinian in his conviction that the existence of God cannot be denied (*Opera,* vol. 1, p. 155; vol. 5, pp. 45–51). Human reason can be called on either to affirm or to deny the existence of God. Bonaventure develops three approaches that he sees not as philosophical demonstrations but as spiritual exercises that make one aware of the closeness of God to the human spirit. Any doubt concerning the existence of God can arise only from some deficiency in the human subject. Ultimately, knowledge of God is not an affair of the intellect alone. Love pushes beyond reason. The knowledge of God through love is the goal to which the intellectual analysis is directed and to which it is subordinate (*Opera,* vol. 3, pp. 689, 775).

Bonaventure's theology of the Trinity begins with the New Testament perception of God as a mystery of goodness and love. This theme is developed into metaphysical reflection on the nature of goodness and love by drawing on the insights of Dionysius the Areopagite, Richard of Saint-Victor, Aristotle, and the *Liber de causis,* an influential Neoplatonic work of uncertain authorship. This perception of God as supreme love that is necessarily triune is the highest level of metaphysical insight available to the human mind in this world. Open to us only through revelation, it leads us beyond philosophical metaphysics, which is constrained to reflect on the supreme reality under the name of being (*Opera,* vol. 5, p. 308). As supreme, self-communicative goodness and love, God is conceived as *plenitudo fontalis,* an overflowing fount of being and life that first flows into the two internal emanations through which the Son is generated and the Spirit is breathed forth, then flowing outward into creation. Peculiar in Western trinitarian theology is the emphasis given to the primacy of the Father within the Trinity. As the Trinity is first with respect to the created world, the Father is first with respect to the divine persons (*Opera,* vol. 5, p. 115).

Christology. From the centrality of Christ in the spirituality of Francis of Assisi, Bonaventure moves to systematic reflection on Christ as the center. The core of the Christological mystery is that in Christ the center of reality has become incarnate and has been made historically visible. The theme of the center becomes ever more important in Bonaventure's thought, finding its most extensive development in his *Collations on the Six Days of Creation.* The Son who from eternity is the center of the Trinity mediates all the divine works of creation, illumination, and consummation. When the Son became incarnate in Jesus, he assumed his place as the center of the created universe and its history.

The concept of Christ as center is grounded in Bonaventure's understanding of exemplarity. As a metaphysical concern, exemplarity is the question of the original reality in whose likeness all the copies in creation are formed. The Platonic influence in Bonaventure's thought is apparent in his conviction that exemplarity is the most basic metaphysical question. The Word is the most compact expression of the original divine reality, copies of which are scattered throughout the created cosmos. When the Word becomes incarnate in a particular human being, that human being provides the crucial key to unlock the mystery of reality. As the incarnate Word, Jesus is both the temporal and the eternal exemplar (*Opera,* vol. 8, pp. 242–243). Therefore, his moral teaching and example have normative significance in the search for authentic human existence. For Bonaventure, spirituality is above all the journey of the human soul to God. This journey is made through the person of Christ, who mediates grace to the soul and draws the human person to respond to God by shaping human life in terms of the normative values that have been lived and taught by Christ.

Creation and salvation. Creation and salvation are symbolized by the two sides of a circle whereby Bonaventure expresses the spiritual journey that is the mainspring of world history. Emanation and return (*egressus* and *reditus*) speak of the origin and finality of creation. These paired concepts indicate that in Bonaventure's system creation and salvation are inseparably related. Creation is the movement of finite being from nothing toward that fullness of life that constitutes salvation. Salvation is the actualization of the deepest potential latent in finite reality by reason of the creative love of God.

Bonaventure's understanding of creation coheres with his understanding of God as *plenitudo fontalis.* Since God is the fullest abundance of being, creation is like an immense river that flows from the fecund love of God. Emanating from the depths of the Father through the mediation of the Son and the Spirit, creation circles back to its point of origin. Emanation is always a movement toward return.

The world of created reality takes shape in a hierarchical order based on degrees of Godlikeness. The faintest reflection of God is found in the shadow (umbra) or vestige (*vestigium*) at the level of inorganic substances and lower forms of life. By nature, man is an image (*imago*) principally because of his soul. As the image is reformed by grace, it becomes a likeness (*similitudo*) of God. An angel, by reason of its purely spiritual nature, is also a similitude. Bonaventure employs the doctrine of Dionysius the Areopagite on the angelic and ecclesiastical hierarchies as a means of elaborating the structure of the angelic world and the mediatorial nature of the church.

To the enlightened eye, the entire created world may become a road that leads the human person to God and thus to the fulfillment of creation's destiny. The return of creation to God (technically, *reductio*), which takes place in and through the spiritual journey of humanity, is above all the work of the illumination and grace mediated through Christ. The redemptive process, begun decisively in Christ, includes the overcoming of sin (satisfaction) and the completion of the creative work of God (cosmic fulfillment). The theology of redemption is the elaboration of the return of an incomplete and fallen creation to God.

Spiritual life. Bonaventure has long been regarded as one of the masters of the spiritual life. Reflecting the spirituality of Francis of Assisi, the spiritual doctrine of Bonaventure is centered around Christ as mediator of grace and interior teacher of the soul. Christ's historical life and teaching manifest the basic values by which human life is transformed in its response to God's grace. As risen Lord, Christ functions as a hierarch, exercising the three hierarchical acts of purgation, illumination, and perfection, which Bonaventure draws from Dionysius the Areopagite (*Opera,* vol. 8, pp. 3–27). Through its response to Christ's action, the soul becomes hierarchized as the disorder of sin is replaced by order. The goal of the spiritual journey is contemplative union in love with God. All philosophical and theological reflection is subordinate to this end. Bonaventure follows Dionysius in describing a level of ecstatic, loving contact with God that transcends all purely intellectual knowledge of God. At this point, apophatic theology and silence are appropriate (*Opera,* vol. 5, pp. 312–313).

The doctrine of the soul's journey integrates the spirituality of Francis into the broader context of Augustinian and Dionysian mysticism. Finally, the journey of the individual soul is integrated into the journey of the church, and Francis of Assisi becomes the model of the destiny of the church as *ecclesia contemplativa.*

Theory of knowledge. While Bonaventure agrees with Aristotle that knowledge of the external world is dependent on sensation, he attempts to integrate elements of Aristotle's empiricism with Augustine's doctrine of illumination. Convinced that the experience of certitude can be accounted for neither in terms of mutable objects nor in terms of the mutable human mind, Bonaventure suggests a mode of divine cooperation whereby the human mind is elevated by the light of the divine ideas and thus is able to arrive at certitude even though all the objects of experience are mutable (*Opera,* vol. 5, p. 23). The divine ideas function as a regulatory and motivating influence that illumines the mind so that it can judge in accord with the eternal truth. Illumination is involved especially in the full analysis of finite being, which leads ultimately to absolute being. Such analysis, or reduction, is possible only if the human mind is aided by that being that is "most pure, most actual, most complete and absolute" (*Opera,* vol. 5, p. 304).

Though the soul is dependent on the senses for knowledge of the external world, it enjoys a relative independence of the senses in its knowledge of itself and its own activity. Thus Bonaventure departs from the Aristotelian view that there is nothing in the intellect that is not first in the senses, and he incorporates into his theory of knowledge the way of interiority inherited from Augustine and found in a variety of mystical systems.

Theology of history. Among the great theologians of history, Bonaventure is one of the most consistently apocalyptic. Influenced by Joachim of Fiore's theory of exegesis, Bonaventure interpreted Francis of Assisi as a positive sign of the dawning of a new contemplative age. The adulteration of the wine of revelation by the water of philosophy was seen as a negative sign of apocalyptic import. To Bonaventure it seemed that his own time was experiencing the crisis of the "sixth age" of history. This would be followed by an age of full revelation and peace prior to the end of the world, an age in which the Holy Spirit would lead the church into the full realization of the revelation of Christ, making all rational philosophy and theology superfluous.

INFLUENCE. Bonaventure's theological views were instrumental in consolidating late-thirteenth-century opposition to radical Aristotelianism. In the context of the controversy concerning Thomas Aquinas's philosophy, Franciscans, including John Pecham, Roger Marston, William de la Mare, Walter of Bruges, Matthew of Aquasparta, and others, developed a form of neo-Augustinianism that drew much inspiration from the work of Bonaventure. It is hardly possible, however, to speak of a Bonaventurian school in the fourteenth century. The founding of the College of Saint Bonaventure at Rome by Sixtus V in 1587 was intended to foster Bonaventurian studies. The most significant contribution of the college was the first complete edition of the works of Bonaventure (1588–1599). An attempted Bonaventurian revival in the seventeenth century met with little success. The College of Saint Bonaventure at Quaracchi, near Florence, founded in the late nineteenth century, produced the critical edition of Bonaventure's works, which provides the basis for the many studies that appeared in the twentieth century.

The influence of Bonaventure as a master of the spiritual life has been extensive, especially in Germany and the Netherlands during the late Middle Ages. The *Soliloquy* and the *Threefold Way* were widely disseminated in vernacular translations and influenced Germanic education, piety, and theology for centuries. In *Bonaventura deutsch* (Bern, 1956), Kurt Ruh calls Bonaventure "an essential factor in the history of the German mind" (p. 295).

BIBLIOGRAPHY

The most complete and reliable edition of Bonaventure's works is the critical edition published as *Opera omnia,* 10 vols. (Quaracchi, 1882–1902).

Of the English translations available, those being published in the series "Works of Saint Bonaventure," edited by Philotheus Boehner and M. Frances Laughlin (Saint Bonaventure, N.Y., 1955–), are most useful because of their scholarly introductions and commentaries. This series has published *Retracing the Arts to Theology,* translated by Emma Thérèse Healy (1955); *The Journey of the Mind into God,* translated by Philotheus Boehner (1956); and *Saint Bonaventure's Disputed Questions on the Mystery of the Trinity,* translated by me (1979). A five-volume series of translations by José de Vinck entitled *The Works of St. Bonaventure* (Paterson, N.J., 1960–1970) provides no commentary. Three sermons on Christ with commentary offering an orientation to the Christology of Bonaventure are found in my edited volume *What Manner of Man?* (Chicago, 1974). Ewert H. Cousins's *Bonaventure* (New York, 1978) provides fresh translations of *The Soul's Journey,* the *Tree of Life,* and the *Life of Saint Francis* with an introduction relating the spiritual doctrine to Bonaventure's theology.

Jacques Guy Bougerol's *Introduction to the Works of Bonaventure* (Paterson, N.J., 1964) is a useful resource for information on the sources, chronology, and stylistic characteristics of Bonaventure's writings.

John Francis Quinn's *The Historical Constitution of Saint Bonaventure's Philosophy* (Toronto, 1973) gives a full historical account of the modern controversy concerning Bonaventure's philosophy together with an excellent bibliography. On the philosophical aspects of Bonaventure's thought, Étienne Gilson's *The Philosophy of Saint Bonaventure* (Paterson, N.J., 1965) is still the classic exposition. Examining the inner structure of Bonaventure's thought from the perspective of archetypal thought-patterns, Ewert H. Cousins's *Bonaventure and the Coincidence of Opposites* (Chicago, 1978) offers a challenging and controversial analysis.

An excellent resource for Bonaventure's trinitarian theology is Konrad Fischer's *De Deo trino et uno* (Göttingen, 1978). A full, systematic exposition of Christology emphasizing the synthesis of spirituality and speculative thought is presented in my book *The Hidden Center* (New York, 1981). Joseph Ratzinger's *The Theology of History in Saint Bonaventure* (Chicago, 1971) is an important study of the mature work of Bonaventure and its relation to Joachim of Fiore. The first four volumes of *S. Bonaventura, 1274–1974,* edited by Jacques Guy Bougerol (Grottaferrata, 1973–1974), include discussion of iconography and articles on philosophy, theology, and spirituality. Volume 5 contains the most extensive and up-to-date bibliography.

ZACHARY HAYES (1987)

BONES have long been a major object of concern in burial, sacrificial, and divination practices throughout the world. Indeed, this role has been so significant that a number of theories have been developed to explain their prominence. In the earlier part of the twentieth century, many of these theories were based upon evolutionary claims: several scholars hypothesized that the rituals involving bones emerged from earlier hunting cultures, and that the continuing prevalence of bones in the rituals of agricultural societies represented a survival of these earlier beliefs.

Particular emphasis in many of the theories about bones was based on ethnographic evidence from northern Eurasia and northern America, where several hunting societies believed that after they killed an animal, its bones should be treated with ritual care (for instance, buried, hung in trees, thrown into the sea). If done properly, the animal would then be reborn from the bones. The single most famous example of these beliefs is the bear ceremonial, practiced among the Inuit, Saami, and Ainu, among others (see Hallowell, 1926).

Building upon this evidence, figures such as Adolf Friedrich, Karl Meuli, Joseph Henninger, and Walter Burkert argued that these were probably widespread Paleolithic beliefs, and that sacrificial, burial, and divination practices in cultures throughout the world should accordingly be explicated as remnants of these early rituals. Henninger (1971), for example, used this argument to analyze the proscription against breaking the bones of the Passover lamb. Meuli (1946) and Burkert (1983) attempted to explicate ancient Greek sacrificial practice along these lines as well. Combining archaeological data of bone assemblages with the ethnographic record of hunting societies in Siberia, Meuli and Burkert hypothesized that early hunters perhaps felt guilt over killing for food, so they would gather the bones of the killed animals to help restore the animals to life. Accordingly, Meuli and Burkert argued, the ancient Greek sacrificial practice of offering the bones of a slaughtered animal to the gods should be understood as a survival of these earlier hunting rituals.

The problems with such theories are twofold. To begin with, the ethnographic record necessitates a qualification of some of the assumptions made by these scholars concerning hunting rituals. Although it is true that several hunting societies practice rituals to ensure the rebirth of the animals they kill, these rituals are not necessarily focused predominantly upon the bones. With the Algonquian Cree, for example, depositing bones in a mortuary is a crucial part of their ritual practices, but equally important is the consumption of the animals' flesh because the cycle of reincarnation for animals includes the phase of passing through humans (Brightman, 1993). Among the Kwakiutl, as well, a constant concern was to recycle the souls of the animals one killed, but the animals' skins were at least as important as the bones for this recycling process (see in particular Goldman, 1975, and Walens, 1981).

The second problem with the theories mentioned above is that arguments of survival are often insufficient. Even if a given ritual were to survive from an earlier period, it is still important to understand the meanings that the ritual has for the people who practice it. Because of this, scholars have more recently shifted the focus to analyses of the symbolic associations of rituals in particular cultures. According to this reading, the explanation for the importance of bones in religious practices throughout the world would lie in something simpler than survival from earlier hunter-gatherer practices. The fact that bones survive long after the flesh decays has perhaps made bones—to paraphrase Lévi-Strauss (1963, p. 89)—good to utilize in ritual actions dealing with human afterlife, as well as with sacrifices and divinations to immortal or long-lived gods.

ANCIENT GREEK SACRIFICE. In terms of Greek sacrificial traditions, the most significant attempt to analyze the meanings of the ritual acts has been undertaken by Jean-Pierre Vernant and Marcel Detienne. According to Vernant (1989) and Detienne (1989), the code of early Greek sacrifice can rather be explained with reference to the cultural concerns expressed in Hesiod's *Theogony.* There, sacrifice is presented as a recapitulation of the actions of Prometheus. According to Hesiod, Prometheus killed an ox and split it into two portions: the meat and the bones. In order to fool Zeus, Prometheus then disguised both portions—wrapping the bones in fat to make them look appetizing, and hiding the meat in the ox's stomach to make it look unappetizing. He kept the meat for himself, and offered the disguised bones to Zeus. As a punishment for the trick, Zeus kept fire away from Prometheus, and Prometheus had to steal it in order to cook the meat. Zeus in turn gave humanity women and death. The acts of Prometheus thus won humanity autonomy from the gods, but they also condemned humanity to mortality and a life of labor, as opposed to the immortality of the gods. According to Vernant and Detienne, Greek sacrificial practice is symbolically a repetition of the acts of Prometheus: the offering of bones to the gods thus underscores that gods do not need to eat, while humans, who require sustenance to survive, consume the meat. The sacrificial meal is thus both a communion between gods and humanity as well as a recapitulation of the tragic separation of humanity from the immortal life of the gods. Here, then, the practice of utilizing bones in sacrifice is explicated not through survivals of earlier hunting rituals but rather through the symbolic associations with bones in the culture in question.

BONES IN MORTUARY PRACTICES. Much scholarship has also been undertaken to study the meanings of bones in mortuary practices. A particularly rich area for the study of these practices is Southeast and East Asia, where one finds a strong distinction made between flesh, seen as the inheritance of the mother, and the bones, seen as the inheritance of the father (Lévi-Strauss, 1969, pp. 393–405). In patrilineal cultures that support such a distinction, the goal is often to define ancestors solely in terms of the bones. This has led to the practice of "secondary burial." After the dead have been buried, they are later dug up again and reburied. The crucial issue here is that during the first internment, the flesh—a pollution that needs to be eradicated—decomposes. The society is then free to bury the bones—associated with the patrilineal line—in a way that ensures the continuity of the patrilineal line freed from the pollution of flesh.

Burial practices of this sort have been described in south China. As James Watson has described among rural Cantonese of the New Territories, Hong Kong, the goal of a family is to maintain the patriline. Marriage is exogamous, so females are brought in from other lineages in order for a patriline to continue. Because the patriline is associated with the bones, the flesh that the females contribute is seen as bringing in a dangerous pollution to the family as well. After death, therefore, the goal is to eradicate this flesh and define the ancestor exclusively in terms of the bones. The corpse is first placed in a coffin. Just before the coffin is taken out of the village, the daughters and daughters-in-law of the deceased rub their hair against the coffin, thus absorbing the pollution of the decaying flesh. The coffin is then buried. Then, after roughly seven years (and after the flesh has fully decomposed), the bones are exhumed. The bones are cleaned of every last scrap of flesh and are then placed in a ceramic urn. An auspicious location is determined, and the bones are reburied in a tomb. If done properly, the bones are then believed to bring fertility and good luck to the descendants.

The Merina of Madagascar, as described by Maurice Bloch (1971), also practice secondary burial, but with somewhat different cultural concerns. When a death occurs, the dead person is simply buried on a hillside near the place where the death occurred. This first burial represents the death of the individual. After the corpse has decomposed, the remains are then exhumed. Unlike the Cantonese, however, effort is made to recover not just the bones but also some of the powdered remains of the flesh. The difference here presumably is due to the fact that, unlike the exogamous Cantonese, the Merina are endogamous: because the mother of the deceased came from within the same kin group, the Merina do not feel the need to define the flesh as a nonlineage pollution requiring full eradication (Bloch and Parry, 1982, pp. 20–21). The decomposed corpse would then be moved to a communal ancestral tomb in the land of the deceased's kin group. For the reburial, the corpses of the other ancestors were taken out and—together with the corpses of the recently deceased—danced with joyously, then reburied in the communal tomb. This communal secondary burial in the ancestral land represents the collectivity and continuity of the ancestral line.

In other burial practices, the goal is to have the soul escape from the confines of the bones. In Hindu practices in Benares, as described by Parry (1982), proper death is believed to occur when the chief mourner cracks open the skull of the corpse to release the vital breath. Following this, the entire body of the corpse is cremated, and the ashes are thrown into the Ganges. The goal, in short, is the complete destruction of the body. Death is thus symbolically presented as though the deceased had renounced his or her own body. Parry argues that the goal is to present each individual death as a recapitulation of the beginning of the cosmos, in which Viṣṇu generated the world through a self-sacrifice. The mortuary practice is thus presented symbolically as part of a regeneration of life.

In all of these mortuary practices, reproduction is indeed crucial—the reproduction of the patriline, the kin group, or the world as a whole. Bones play a crucial role in this reproduction. Yet bones are not necessarily seen as the basis of that reproduction. The particular meanings attached to bones vary dramatically across cultures, and the ways that bones are utilized vary as well with the forms of reproduction that the rituals seek to create.

SCAPULIMANCY. Similar points made regarding mortuary practices could also be made with regard to divination practices of scapulimancy. During the late period of the Chinese Shang dynasty (c. 1500–1050 BCE), divinations to ancestors were made through the use of the scapula of oxen and the carapaces of turtles (see Keightley, 1978). Heat was applied to the bones, and the diviner then read the resulting cracks in the bones to foretell the future. The divinations themselves were then carved into the bone. Similar forms of scapulimancy (without the carved inscriptions) have been recorded in Mongolia (see in particular Bawden, 1959), Tibet, Japan, and Siberia (Cooper, 1936). It was also practiced in North America among Algonquin speakers, who would utilize the caribou or hare shoulder blade or grouse sternum (Speck, 1935, p. 139; Tanner, 1979, pp. 117–124), as well as among northern Athabaskan speakers (Cooper, 1936).

Because scapulimancy is practiced in many of the same cultures across northern Eurasia and the Americas that scholars looked to for examples of hunting rituals concerning bones, attempts have been made to connect scapulimancy to beliefs associating bones with rebirth. Mircea Eliade, for example, proposed that bones were used for divination because they symbolized everything pertaining to the future of life (Eliade, 1964, pp. 164–165). While this remains a hypothesis worth exploring, other explanations have been attempted as well. Bogoras (1907, pp. 487–488), for example, points out that the Chukchi of Siberia treated the scapula used for divination as world maps. Keightley, in part inspired by Bogoras, has suggested that Shang divination bones may have also had the same symbolic associations (2000, pp. 93–96). Further research on the meaning of bones in the numerous cultures that practice scapulimancy would well repay the efforts.

SEE ALSO Death; Relics; Sacrifice.

BIBLIOGRAPHY

Bawden, C. R. "On the Practice of Scapulimancy among the Mongols." *Central Asiatic Journal* 4 (1959): 1–44. A detailed study of Mongolian scapulimancy.

Bloch, Maurice. *Placing the Dead: Tombs, Ancestral Villages, and Kinship Organization in Madagascar.* London, 1971. An exemplary analysis of mortuary practice in relation to kinship organization, focused on the Merina of Madagascar.

Bloch, Maurice, and Jonathan Parry. "Introduction: Death and the Regeneration of Life." In *Death and the Regeneration of Life,* pp. 1–44. Cambridge, U.K., 1982. Penetrating discussion of mortuary practices from a comparative standpoint.

Bogoras, W. G. *The Chukchee Religion.* Memoirs of the American Museum of Natural History 11.2. Leiden and New York, 1907. A classic study of Chukchi religion.

Brightman, Robert. *Grateful Prey: Rock Cree Animal-Human Relationships.* Berkeley, Calif., 1993. An excellent ethnography of an Algonquian Cree group.

Burkert, Walter. *Homo Necans: The Anthropology of Ancient Greek Sacrifical Ritual and Myth.* Translated by Peter Bing. Berkeley, Calif., 1983. An attempt to link Greek sacrificial practice to hypothetical Paleolithic hunting practices.

Cooper, John M. "Scapulimancy." In *Essays in Anthropology Presented to A. L. Kroeber,* edited by Robert H. Lowie, pp. 29–43. Berkeley, Calif., 1936. A comprehensive study of the geographical range of the practice of scapulimancy.

Detienne, Marcel. "Culinary Practices and the Spirit of Sacrifice." In *The Cuisine of Sacrifice among the Greeks,* edited by Marcel Detienne and Jean-Pierre Vernant, pp. 1–20. Translated by Paula Wissing. Chicago, 1989. A superb study of the symbolic associations of bones and flesh in Greek sacrificial practice.

Eliade, Mircea. *Shamanism: Archaic Techniques of Esctasy.* Translated by Willard R. Trask. Princeton, 1964. A classic study of shamanism from a comparative standpoint.

Friedrich, Adolf. "Knochen und Skelett in der Vorstellungswelt Nordasiens." *Wiener Beiträge sur Kulturgeschichte und Linguistik* 5 (1943): 189–247. A highly influential study of North Asian bone symbolism.

Goldman, Irving. *The Mouth of Heaven: An Introduction to Kwakiutl Religious Thought.* New York, 1975. An excellent study of Kwakiutl religion.

Hallowell, A. I. "Bear Ceremonialism in the Northern Hemisphere." *American Anthropologist* 28 (1926): 1–175. A classic study of the bear ceremony.

Henninger, Joseph. "Neure Forschungen zum Verbot des Knochenzerbrechens." In *Studia Ethnograpica et Folkloristica in honorem Béla Gunda,* pp. 673–702. Debrecen, Hungary, 1971. An attempt to see the prohibition against breaking bones in various rituals as resulting from a survival of early hunting beliefs concerning the reanimation of undamaged bones.

Keightley, David N. *Sources of Shang History: The Oracle-Bone Inscriptions of Bronze Age China.* Berkeley, Calif., 1978. An introduction to the study of Chinese oracle-bone inscriptions.

Keightley, David N. *The Ancestral Landscape: Time, Space, and Community in Late Shang China (ca. 1200–1045 B.C.).* Institute of East Asian Studies. Berkeley, Calif., 2000. A comprehensive analysis of the world of Shang China as seen through the oracle-bone materials.

Lévi-Strauss, Claude. *Totemism.* Translated by Rodney Needham. Boston, 1963. An influential attempt to analyze how cultures utilize aspects of the natural world for social purposes.

Lévi-Strauss, Claude. *The Elementary Structures of Kinship.* Translated by James Harle Bell, John Richard von Sturmer, and Rodney Needham. Boston, 1969. A structural analysis of kinship.

Meuli, Karl. "Griechische Opferbräuche." In *Phyllobolia* (Festschrift Peter Von der Mühll), pp. 185–288. Basel, 1946. A controversial thesis arguing that aspects of Greek sacrificial practice involving bones should be understood as survivals of Paleolithic beliefs.

Parry, Jonathan. "Sacrificial Death and the Necrophagous Ascetic." In *Death and the Regeneration of Life,* edited by Maurice Bloch and Jonathan Parry, pp. 74–110. Cambridge, U.K., 1982. A penetrating analysis of Hindu mortuary practices in Benares.

Speck, Frank G. *Naskapi: The Savage Hunters of Labrador Peninsula.* Norman, Okla., 1935. A classic ethnography of an Algonquian-speaking group.

Tanner, Adrian. *Bringing Home Animals: Religious Ideology and Mode of Production of the Mitsassini Cree Hunters.* New York, 1979. An excellent ethnography of the religion of an Algonquian Cree group.

Vernant, Jean-Pierre. "At Man's Table: Hesiod's Foundation Myth of Sacrifice." In *The Cuisine of Sacrifice among the Greeks,* edited by Marcel Detienne and Jean-Pierre Vernant, pp. 21–86. Translated by Paula Wissing. Chicago, 1989. A penetrating reading of Hesiod in conjunction with Greek sacrificial practice.

Walens, Stanley. *Feasting with Cannibals: An Essay on Kwakiutl Cosmology.* Princeton, 1981. Excellent study of Kwakiutl religion.

Watson, James. "Of Flesh and Bones: The Management of Death Pollution in Cantonese Society." In *Death and the Regeneration of Life,* edited by Maurice Bloch and Jonathan Parry, pp. 155–186. Cambridge, U.K., 1982. A superb study of the social meanings of Cantonese mortuary practices.

MICHAEL J. PUETT (2005)

BONHOEFFER, DIETRICH (1906–1945), Lutheran pastor, theologian, and martyr. The sixth of eight children, Bonhoeffer was raised in Berlin in the upper-middle-class family of a leading neurologist. He received his doctorate in theology from the University of Berlin. A student of Adolf von Harnack, Bonhoeffer was deeply influenced by the writings of the young Karl Barth. From 1930 to 1931, he studied at Union Theological Seminary in New York with Reinhold Niebuhr. He then returned to Berlin, teaching theology and becoming student chaplain and youth secretary in the ecumenical movement.

As early as 1933 Bonhoeffer was struggling against the Nazification of the churches and against the persecution of the Jews. Disappointed by the churches' nonaction against Nazism, he accepted a pastorate for Germans in London. However, when the Confessing church (i.e., Christians who resisted Nazi domination) founded its own seminaries, he returned to Germany to prepare candidates for ordination, a task he considered the most fulfilling of his life. As a result of this work, he was forbidden to teach at the University of Berlin. In 1939, after conflicts with the Gestapo, he accepted an invitation to the United States, again to Union Theological Seminary. After four weeks, however, he returned to Germany, convinced he would be ineffectual in the eventual renewal of his nation were he to live elsewhere during its most fateful crisis. He then became an active member of the conspiracy against Hitler. On April 5, 1943, he was imprisoned on suspicion. After the plot to assassinate Hitler failed, Bonhoeffer was hanged (on April 9, 1945), along with five thousand others (including three other members of his family) accused of participating in the resistance.

Bonhoeffer's writings have been widely translated. His early work reflects his search for a concrete theology of revelation. His first dissertation, "Sanctorum Communio," published in Germany in 1930 (also under that title in London, 1963; and as *The Communion of Saints*, New York, 1963), relates the revelational character of the church to its sociological features. An original statement at the time, it remains evocative. His second dissertation, "Act and Being," was written in 1931 against a background of such opposing philosophies as Kantian transcendentalism and Heideggerian ontology. This work tries to reconcile an existential theological approach with an ontological one. According to Bonhoeffer, these approaches work themselves out in the church, in which revelational contingency and institutional continuity merge.

Turning to the actual life of the church and to criticism of it, Bonhoeffer, in 1937, published his controversial *The Cost of Discipleship* (New York, 1963). Asserting that "cheap grace is the deadly enemy of our Church," this work, which is based on the sermon on the mount, critiques a Reformation heritage that breaks faith and obedience asunder. In *Life Together* (New York, 1976), Bonhoeffer's most widely read book, the author considers experiments to renew a kind of monastic life for serving the world. In 1939 Bonhoeffer began to write a theological ethics, the work he intended to be his life-work, but he completed only fragments of it (*Ethics*, New York, 1965). These fragments reveal Bonhoeffer as moving beyond a situational ethic to a Christ-centered one.

The most influential of Bonhoeffer's posthumous publications has become *Letters and Papers from Prison* (New York, 1972). Among his daily observations was a vision of a future Christianity ready for "messianic suffering" with Christ in a "nonreligious world." To Bonhoeffer "religion" was a province separated from the whole of life—providing cheap escapism for the individual—and a tool in the hands of the powers that be for continuing domination of dependent subjects. Bonhoeffer was critical of Western Christianity because of its complicity with the Holocaust; his letters reveal his conviction that a life with Christ means "to exist for others." It was his belief in a "religionless Christianity"—that is, a praying church that responds to Christ out of the modern (not sinless) strength of human beings and their decisions—that enabled Bonhoeffer to begin to write a revised theology of "Jesus, the man for others," and to participate in the conspiratorial counteraction against the deadly forces of Hitler.

Bonhoeffer's thought emerged from his cultural heritage of German liberalism. He suffered when he experienced its weakness in the face of Nazism. He rethought this heritage within a Christocentric theology, thus becoming a radical critic of his contemporary church and of contemporary theology because they seemed to him to touch only the insignificant corners of life.

The originality of Bonhoeffer's thought may be summarized in three ways. First, by employing biblical and modern criticism of religion, he gave to theology and piety epochal stress on the idea that the God who is not of this world posits a requisite "this-worldliness" of faith, which is not, however, absorbed by immanentism. Second, Bonhoeffer's words and deeds teach that each generation must discern its own particular means to express its contribution to faith and action. Third, in areas where developments press toward a "confessing church," Bonhoeffer challenges Christians to analyze and to resist ideological syncretism with any zeitgeist, whether the result is a Greek, a Teutonic, or an American Christ.

His influence is worldwide for two reasons. First, his life as theologian and thinker was sealed by martyrdom. Second, Bonhoeffer's legacy has stimulated ecumenism beyond his own national, spiritual, and institutional borders, including influence among Roman Catholics and Jews who see in him a Christian theologian who never cheaply evaded controversial issues.

BIBLIOGRAPHY

For a comprehensive listing of primary and secondary literature, see Clifford J. Green's "Bonhoeffer Bibliography: English Language Sources," *Union Seminary Quarterly Review* (New York) 31 (Summer 1976): 227–260. This admirable work is continually revised and amended in *The News Letter* of the English Language Section of the International Bonhoeffer Society for Archival Research.

In addition to the works by Bonhoeffer mentioned in the article, see three collections of letters, lectures, and notes titled *No Rusty Swords* (New York, 1965), *The Way to Freedom* (New York, 1966), and *True Patriotism* (New York, 1973). For works about Bonhoeffer, see my *Dietrich Bonhoeffer: Theologian, Christian, Contemporary*, 3d abr. ed. (New York, 1970); André Dumas's *Dietrich Bonhoeffer: Theologian of Reality* (New York, 1971); Clifford J. Green's *The Sociality of Christ and Humanity: Dietrich Bonhoeffer's Early Theology, 1927–1933* (Missoula, Mont., 1972); and Keith W. Clements's *A Patriotism for Today: Dialogue with Dietrich Bonhoeffer* (Bristol, 1984).

EBERHARD BETHGE (1987)

BONIFACE (673–754), the most distinguished in the group of English missionaries who, in the eighth and succeeding centuries, felt impelled to cross the seas and to preach the gospel to the peoples of the continent of Europe who were still non-Christians. Winfrith, to whom the pope, as tradition has it, gave the name Boniface in 722, was a missionary, founder of monasteries, diffuser of culture, and church organizer. Born in Devonshire, he was introduced to monastic life at an early age. Here he grew up in an atmosphere of strict observance of the Benedictine rule and acceptance of the vivid culture which was spreading abroad from

Northumbria. His many gifts would have assured him of a distinguished career in the growing English church but he felt within himself an intense inner call to carry the gospel to the as yet non-Christian world.

Two attempts at missionary work with Willibrord in Friesland led to nothing, perhaps because of temperamental differences between the two. In 719, Winfrith made the journey to Rome and received a commission from the pope as missionary to the Frankish lands. This commission was later strengthened by his consecration as bishop. Before long the missionary convictions of Boniface became firmly settled on three points: that the missions of the Western church must be controlled and directed by the central authority in Rome, that religious houses both for men and women must be founded to supply the necessary continuity of Christian life in a period of almost ceaseless military disturbance, that regular dioceses must be founded and supplied with loyal and well-trained bishops.

The first period of Boniface's work was marked by notable successes in Hesse and Thuringia. At Geismar he dared to fell the sacred oak of Thor. This episode was understood by the people of the time as a conflict between two gods. When Boniface felled the oak and suffered no vengeance from the resident Germanic god, it was clear that the God whom he preached was the true God who alone is to be worshiped and adored.

Boniface was successful in securing the confidence and support, first of the all-powerful Frankish ruler, Charles Martel, who in 732 defeated the Muslims at the battle of Tours, and, after Charles's death in 741, of Martel's sons Carloman and Pépin. This helped Boniface greatly in his work of restoring or creating order in the churches in the dominions of the Franks, the goal of his second period of the work. He was successful in creating four bishoprics in Bavaria, where churches existed but without settled order. He also called into being four dioceses in the territories to the east of the Rhine. During this period he brought in many colleagues, both men and women, and founded a number of religious houses. His favorite was Fulda (744), where he was buried, and which for more than a thousand years was a great center of church life in Germany.

Until 747 Boniface had been a primate and archbishop without a diocese. In 747 he was appointed archbishop of Mainz. In the meantime his influence had extended westward, until it was felt in many parts of what is now France. In 742 he was able to hold a synod of the French churches, commonly known as the German Council, and in 744 an even more important meeting at Soissons. It is to be noted that the decrees of the earlier council were issued in the name of Carloman and became the law of the church as well as of the state.

Two special features of the work of Boniface are to be noted. Boniface was too busy to become an accomplished scholar but was deeply concerned for the spread of culture and used his monasteries as centers for the diffusion of knowledge. He himself wrote Latin clearly and elegantly, coming between the over-elaborate style of Aldhelm (d. 709) and the rather flat scholastic Latin of the Middle Ages. Frank Stenton has called him the one great writer produced by the early schools of southern England and a man of individual genius.

The part played by women in the development of the church in this period is astonishing. At a time at which the vast majority of women were illiterate, the religious houses of England produced a number of aristocratic and highly cultivated nuns, a number of whom Boniface brought over to Europe to be the abbesses of his newly founded monasteries. To Leobgytha (Leoba), abbess of Tauferbischofsheim, he was bound, as the letters exchanged between them show, in a relationship of specially affectionate friendship. She survived him by more than a quarter of a century, and when she died in 780, she was buried near her venerable friend at Fulda, in accordance with her earnest desire.

In 752, Boniface, feeling that his work was done, and perhaps wearied by the increasing opposition of the Frankish churchmen to the English dominance, resigned all his offices and returned as a simple missionary to Friesland, where he had begun his missionary career. Great success marked the first year of this enterprise. But on June 4, 754, Boniface and his companions found themselves surrounded by a band of pagans, determined to put a stop to the progress of the gospel. Boniface forbade armed resistance, and he and fifty-three of his followers met their death with the quiet fortitude of Christian martyrs.

The English are accustomed to speak of these years as "the dark ages," but, as the eminent German church historian K. D. Schmidt once remarked, "to us this was the period of light, when the light of the Gospel and of Christian civilization came to us." Boniface, the apostle of Germany, was one of those burning and shining lights.

BIBLIOGRAPHY

The primary authority is the large collection of the letters of Boniface, to be found in Latin, *Bonifacius: Die Briefe des heiligen Bonifacius and Lullus*, vol. 1 (Berlin, 1916), admirably edited by Michael Tangl. A good many of these letters are available in English in *The Anglo-Saxon Missionaries in Germany*, edited and translated by Charles H. Talbot (New York, 1954). For those who read German the outstanding modern work is Theodor Schieffer's *Winfrid Bonifatius und die christliche Grundlegung Europas* (Darmstadt, 1972). In English the pioneer work is William Levison's *England and the Continent in the Eighth Century* (Oxford, 1946). Among more popular works, Eleanor S. Duckett's *Anglo-Saxon Saints and Scholars* (New York, 1947), pp. 339–455, can be specially recommended as both scholarly and readable.

STEPHEN C. NEILL (1987)

BONIFACE VIII (Benedetto Gaetani, c. 1235–1303), pope of the Roman Catholic church (1294–1303). Connected by family relationship not only with the earlier popes Alexander IV and Nicholas III but also with the Orsini and Colonna families, Gaetani studied law at Bologna, worked as a notary at the Curia Romana, served on embassies to France and England, discharged the office of papal legate in France, and by 1291 had become cardinal priest of San Martino. A capable, experienced, and energetic administrator, he was by temperament bold, hardheaded, formidably stubborn, and, at least in his latter years, prone to damaging outbursts of irascibility that some have attributed in part to painful bouts with "the stone." Unfortunately, the juxtaposition of his energetic pontificate with the brief (and chaotic) reign of his predecessor, the devout hermit-pope Celestine V, proved to be a case of the wrong men in a crucial role at the wrong time and in the wrong sequence. The troubles besetting the two pontificates are usually taken to mark the great turning point in the fortunes of the late medieval papacy.

Certainly, the difficulties and disputes that marked the reign of Boniface VIII have served to obscure for posterity the pope's more positive achievements. These were real enough. His reordering of the curial fiscal and administrative system, his publication in 1298 of the *Liber sextus*, a legal compilation supplementary to the decretals of Gregory IX, his sponsorship in 1300 of the Jubilee Year at Rome, his decisive ruling of that same year on the relationship between the diocesan clergy and the clergy of the mendicant orders, his foundation in 1303 of a *studium generale* at Rome—all had important, and some of them enduringly positive, consequences. Nonetheless, even such unquestionably positive achievements sometimes generated problems for Boniface. Thus, the increase in financial support and papal prestige stemming from the enormous flow of pilgrims to Rome during the Jubilee may well have bolstered Boniface's self-assurance and encouraged him to be too unyielding in his subsequent dealings with the French king. Similarly, while they were impartially and carefully framed, the measures he introduced to remedy the dissension and disorder in diocesan government spawned by the extensive exemptions and privileges previously granted to the mendicant orders nevertheless succeeded in alienating many of the friars. Yet again, his tightening of the papal fiscal system after the chaos of the previous pontificate, and, within the papal territories, his success in suppressing disorder, enforcing papal control, and extending the property holdings of his Gaetani kin led him into a fatal conflict with the landed interests of the powerful Colonna family.

Problems with Philip IV, king of France, had begun already in 1296 and centered on the right of monarchs to tax the clergy of their kingdoms. Hostilities between Philip and Edward I of England had broken out in 1294, and even in the absence of papal consent the two kings had taken it upon themselves to tax their national churches. Responding to a protest launched by the French Cistercians, Boniface moved in the bull *Clericis laicos* (February 24, 1296) to proscribe (in the absence of explicit papal permission) all lay taxation of the clergy. In the prevailing climate of opinion, with lay sentiment in the two kingdoms favoring the monarchs and some of the clergy inclining to support them too, threats of excommunication proved to be of no avail. The prestige of the papacy had fallen too low to permit the successful deployment of such spiritual weaponry—so low, indeed, that in 1297, confronted also by the combined opposition in Italy of the Colonna family and the Spiritual Franciscans, Boniface was forced to compromise on the question of taxation and in effect to concede the principle he had attempted to establish.

That concession, however, did not prevent his reacting with great firmness when in 1301 Philip IV arrested Bernard of Saisset, bishop of Pamiers, tried him, threw him into prison, and demanded that the pope endorse those actions. Boniface responded by issuing the bulls *Salvator mundi* and *Ausculta fili*, demanding the bishop's release, revoking the taxing privileges earlier granted to the French king, and commanding attendance of the French bishops at a council to be held at Rome in November 1302 in order to consider the condition of religion in France.

Defeated by a Flemish army at Courtral in the summer of 1302, Philip adroitly used the excuse of a national emergency to prohibit attendance of the French bishops at the Roman council. The abortive nature of that assembly, however, did not prevent Boniface from issuing in November 1302 the bull *Unam sanctam*, a rather derivative document but one culminating with the famous declaration "It is altogether necessary to salvation for every human creature to be subject to the Roman pontiff." Philip's response was even more forceful. Rallying national opinion during the spring of 1303 at a series of assemblies in Paris, and echoing the old Colonna call for convocation of a general council to judge the pope, Philip also authorized his adviser Guillaume de Nogaret to lead an expedition to Italy to seize the person of the pope and bring him back for judgment.

Hence evolved the extraordinary chain of events leading up to the "outrage of Anagni" on September 7, 1303: the attack on the papal palace by Nogaret and Sciarra Colonna, the humiliation of the aged pope, his subsequent rescue by the citizens of Anagni, and his demise soon after at Rome. French pressure by no means ended with his death, and Boniface VIII has since been portrayed as the pope who, while advancing some of the most ambitious claims ever made for the power of the medieval papacy, contrived also to precipitate its decline.

BIBLIOGRAPHY

Boase, T. S. R. *Boniface VIII.* London, 1933.

Digard, G. A. L. *Philippe le Bel et le Saint-siège de 1285 à 1304.* 2 vols. Paris, 1936.

Digard, G. A. L., et al. *Les registres de Boniface VIII.* 4 vols. Paris, 1904–1939.

Dupuy, Pierre, ed. and trans. *Histoire du différend d'entre le Pape Boniface VIII et Philippe le Bel.* Paris, 1655.

Rivière, Jean. *Le problème de l'église et de l'état au temps de Philippe le Bel.* Paris, 1926.

Scholz, Richard. *Die Publizistik zur Zeit Philipps des Schönen und Bonifaz VIII* (1903). Reprint, Amsterdam, 1962.

FRANCIS OAKLEY (1987)

BOOK SEE CANON; SCRIPTURE

BOOTH, WILLIAM (1829–1912), English evangelist, founder of the Salvation Army. William Booth was born on April 10, 1829, in Nottingham, England, the only son of the four surviving children of Samuel and Mary Moss Booth. The elder Booth, an unsuccessful building contractor, and his wife were no more than conventionally religious, but William, intelligent, ambitious, zealous, and introspective, was earnest about Christianity from an early age. He was converted at the age of fifteen and two years later gave himself entirely to the service of God as the result of the preaching of James Caughey, a visiting American Methodist revivalist. From the age of thirteen until he was twenty-two Booth worked as a pawnbroker's assistant, first in Nottingham and after 1849 in London. His zeal for souls and compassion for the poor drove him to preach in the streets. In 1852 he became a licensed Methodist minister. Although Booth had been forced by his father's financial ruin to withdraw from a good grammar school at age thirteen, he read avidly, sought instruction from older ministers, and developed an effective style in speech and writing. In 1855 he married Catherine Mumford, a woman of original and independent intelligence and great moral courage, who had a strong influence on him. They had eight children.

In 1861 Booth began to travel as an independent evangelist, sometimes appearing with Catherine, who publicly advocated an equal role for women in the pulpit. In 1865 the couple established a permanent preaching mission among the poor in the East End of London, in a place where Booth had conducted an especially effective series of meetings. This new endeavor, which soon included small-scale charitable activities for the poor, was known for several years as the Christian Mission. In 1878 the mission was renamed the Salvation Army.

The military structure suggested by the new name appealed to the Booths and to the co-workers they attracted to their work. Booth remained an orthodox Methodist in doctrine, preaching the necessity of repentance and the promise of holiness—a voluntary submission to God that opened to the believer a life of love for God and for humankind. A premillennialist as well, he was convinced that the fastest way to complete the work of soul winning that would herald the return of Christ was to establish flying squads of enthusiasts who would spread out over the country at his command. The General, as Booth was called, saw evangelism as warfare against Satan for the souls of individuals; the militant tone of scripture and hymns was not figurative to Booth and his officers, but literal reality. The autocracy of military command was well suited to Booth's decisive and uncompromising personality; and it appealed both to his close associates, who were devoted to him and who sought his counsel on every matter, and to his more distant followers, the "soldiers" recently saved from sin, most of them uneducated, new to religion, and eager to fit themselves into the great scheme.

William and Catherine were convinced from the beginning of their work in London that it was their destiny to carry the gospel to those untouched by existing religious efforts. To them this meant the urban poor. Their sympathy led them to supplement their evangelism by immediate and practical relief. They launched campaigns to awaken the public to the worst aspects of the life of the poor, such as child prostitution and dangerous and ill-paid piecework in neighborhood match factories. Soup kitchens, men's hostels, and "rescue homes" for converted prostitutes and unwed mothers became essential parts of the Army's program.

In 1890 William Booth published *In Darkest England and the Way Out,* which contained a full-fledged program to uplift and regenerate the "submerged tenth" of urban society. The heart of the scheme was a sequence of "city colonies" (urban missions for the unemployed), "land colonies" (retraining in agricultural skills), and "overseas colonies" (assisted emigration to one of Britain's colonies). The book also explained the existing programs and promised many new schemes in addition to the colonies: the "poor man's lawyer," the "poor man's bank," clinics, industrial schools for poor children, missing-persons inquiries, a "matrimonial bureau," and a poor-man's seaside resort, "Whitechapel-by-the-Sea." The *Darkest England* scheme, which was widely endorsed, represents an important turning point in public support for the Army.

Booth would not have claimed to be a saint in any conventional sense, and there are certainly controversial aspects to his life and work. Always overworked and chronically unwell, he often had strained relationships with his close associates, especially after the death of Catherine in 1890. Many of his statements about the Army overlooked the fact that much of its program was not original. He offered no criticism of the basic social and political structure that surrounded him, and his confidence in the desirability of transferring the urban unemployed to the more healthful and "natural" environment of the country was romantic and impractical. Yet the fact remains that Booth combined old and new techniques of evangelism and social relief in an immensely effective and appealing program. He displayed great flexibility in adapting measures to the needs of the moment, altering or eliminating any program, however dear to him, if its effectiveness diminished. He abandoned anything in the way of theology (such as sacraments) or social theory that might confuse his followers or dampen their zeal for soul winning and good works.

Guileless and unsentimental, Booth showed a rare and genuine single-mindedness in the cause of evangelism. His last public message, delivered three months before his death on August 20, 1912, is still cherished by the Army that is his most fitting memorial. The concluding words of the message were these: "While there yet remains one dark soul without the light of God, I'll fight—I'll fight to the very end!"

SEE ALSO Salvation Army.

BIBLIOGRAPHY

William Booth and the early Salvation Army are gradually receiving attention from serious scholarship. Roy Hattersley, *Blood and Fire: William and Catherine Booth and Their Salvation Army* (New York, 1999) is excellent on economic and social issues and is a good introduction. St. John Ervine, *God's Soldier: General William Booth,* 2 vols. (New York, 1935) and Harold Begbie, *The Life of General William Booth, the Founder of the Salvation Army,* 2 vols. (New York, 1920) held the field of serious biography until recently, and are still almost indispensable. William Booth's *In Darkest England and the Way Out* (1890; reprint, London, 1970) is important for an understanding of Booth and his work. The best biography of Catherine Booth is Roger A. Green, *Catherine Booth: A Biography of the Cofounder of The Salvation Army* (Grand Rapids, 1996). Commissioner Frederick de Latour Booth-Tucker, *The Life of Catherine Booth, the Mother of the Salvation Army,* 2 vols. (London, 1892), by Booth's son-in-law, remains an Army classic.

EDWARD H. MCKINLEY (1987 AND 2005)

BORNEAN RELIGIONS. From earliest times, the coasts of Borneo have been visited by travelers going between ancient centers of civilization in Asia. Since the sixteenth century Islam has slowly spread from coastal trading centers, such as Brunei in the north and Banjarmasin in the south. Immigrant Chinese have brought the practices of their homeland, and in the last century Christian missionaries have been increasingly successful in the interior, prompting syncretic revivalist cults. This article, however, is concerned with the indigenous religions of the great island. Many of these have passed out of existence or are imminently about to do so without being studied in depth. The existing data indicate wide variation in belief and practice. Nevertheless, there are features widely characteristic of Bornean religions, and it is these that are summarized here.

ETHNIC DIVERSITY. All the indigenous peoples of Borneo speak Austronesian languages, but they exhibit bewildering ethnic diversity. There is still no generally agreed upon taxonomy, and many of the most familiar ethnic terms are vague. In the south and west there are large, politically fragmented populations that nevertheless manifest considerable cultural uniformity. Examples of these are the Ngaju and Iban, both numbering some hundreds of thousands. To the north the terrain is mountainous and the rivers difficult to navigate. Here are found many small groups, each at most only a few thousand strong. The ethnic diversity is of immediate consequence for religions, because the religions are rooted in the local community and contribute to much of its identity.

THE GENERAL CONCEPT OF RELIGION. Many of the cultures of interior Borneo lack the concept of a separate domain of religion. Instead, ritual observance is incorporated into a spectrum of prescribed behaviors that includes legal forms, marriage practices, etiquette, and much else. All of these are matters of collective representations shared by autonomous communities. Such communities often consist of a longhouse with a few hundred inhabitants and are separated from neighboring villages by tracts of jungle. There is no notion of conversion to another religion; if an individual moves to another community—for instance, as the result of a marriage—he or she simply adheres to the ritual forms of that place. Significantly, members of a community often exaggerate their ritual peculiarity. An outside observer readily identifies items shared with neighboring groups, but the patterns of distribution are complex, reflecting migration and borrowing over many centuries.

The religions of interior Borneo are rich in both ritual and cosmology. In perhaps the best known account, Schärer (1963) describes the subtle notions of the godhead found among the Ngaju, replete with dualistic aspects of upper world and underworld, multilayered heavens, and complex animal and color symbolism. Other peoples have comparably extensive spirit worlds. Because of the archaeologically attested antiquity of contact with India, some authors have discerned elements of Hindu belief. Schärer (1963, p. 13) attributes one of the names of the Ngaju supreme deity to an epoch of Indian influence. In the north there are features of the religion—for instance, in number symbolism—that may indicate influence from China, but there is no overall similarity to Indian or Chinese religions.

THE PROMINENCE OF MORTUARY RITUAL. One element of ancient Southeast Asian provenance is a central feature of many Bornean religions: that is, a focus on death and, in particular, on secondary treatment of the dead. This mortuary complex has been associated with Borneo at least since the publication of Robert Hertz's classic essay (1907). By no means did all interior peoples practice secondary disposal in recent times. The custom is found across much of the southern third of the island but has only a scattered distribution further north. Stöhr (1959) surveys the variety of death rites across the island. Where secondary treatment occurs, it is part of an extended ritual sequence, often the most elaborate of that religion (Metcalf, 1982). The occurrence of secondary treatment also draws attention to the importance of the dead in indigenous cosmologies. Other life-crisis rituals are generally celebrated on a smaller scale, one that does not involve the participation of entire communities.

AGRICULTURAL RITES. Major calendrical rituals are usually coordinated with the agricultural cycle. This is especially true among the Iban, who speak of the soul of the rice in anthropomorphic terms, and focus rites upon it at every stage of cultivation (Jensen, 1974, pp. 151–195). In some areas, however, notably the northwestern subcoastal belt, reliance on hill rice is relatively recent. In these areas, where sago is produced, rice ritual is less prominent.

HEAD-HUNTING RITES. Head-hunting is another practice commonly associated with Borneo. Formerly prevalent, it usually occurred in the context of warfare or as an adjunct to mortuary rites. Frequently heads were required in order to terminate the mourning period for community leaders. In contrast to other parts of Southeast Asia, heads were the focus of much ritual. Hose and McDougall describe the techniques of warfare and head-hunting found among the Kayan and Kenyah of central northern Borneo, and also the large festivals periodically held to honor the heads (Hose and McDougall, 1912, vol. 1, p. 159; vol. 2, pp. 20–22, 41, 47).

RITUAL SPECIALISTS. Even in societies with little technological and political specialization, ritual specialists are important. But there is great variation in the particular combinations of roles played by priest, shaman, and augur. Women often play a major part. Among the Dusun of northern Borneo, for example, priestesses officiate at all major rituals (Evans, 1953, p. 42). Often in association with death rites there are psychopomps to conduct the deceased to the land of the dead. In all of this, ritual languages are prominent. Often the major function of priests and priestesses is to recite long chants that deal with mythical events. These chants are complexly structured in terms of parallel phraseology; even prayers uttered by laymen in small family rituals display formal structure (Evans, 1953, pp. 42–56). Ritual is often accompanied by the sacrifice of chickens, pigs, or buffalo.

Shamanism is found everywhere and typically involves the recovery of errant souls through séances. Concomitantly, theories of illness usually focus on soul loss, in which all manner of nonhuman, malign agencies are implicated. Yet there is often a complementary theory of illness that results from the infraction of primordial taboo. Although not entirely absent, there is remarkably little concern with witchcraft.

RITUAL AND SOCIAL DIFFERENTIATION. Some societies of interior Borneo are hierarchically stratified, while others are egalitarian. But even in the latter, major public rituals are closely bound up with the forms of leadership and social control. There is a dearth of rites of prestation, in which wealth passes between similar collectivities. This may in part be a result of social organization that is predominantly cognatic, that is, lacking groups defined by fixed rules of descent. In large-scale festivals, however, leaders coordinate the efforts of entire communities in order to feed guests and erect monuments.

BIBLIOGRAPHY

Evans, Ivor H. N. *The Religion of the Tempasuk Dusuns of North Borneo.* Cambridge, U.K., 1953. Describes in list format the beliefs and ceremonies of a subgroup of the extensive but culturally varied Dusun people of Sabah. The major emphasis is on folklore and mythology.

Hertz, Robert. "A Contribution to the Study of the Collective Representation of Death" (1907). In *Death and the Right Hand,* two of Hertz's essays translated from the French by Rodney Needham and Claudia Needham. New York, 1960. A brilliant essay by a prominent student of Émile Durkheim concerning the significance of mortuary rites, particularly secondary treatment of the dead. Hertz utilized published sources, and much of his data came from the Ngaju of southern Borneo.

Hose, Charles, and William McDougall. *The Pagan Tribes of Borneo.* 2 vols. London, 1912. Despite the title, these volumes mostly concern the people of central northern Borneo, particularly the Kayan. Based on Hose's years of experience as a government officer. Contains much useful information; most of that on religion is in volume 2.

Jensen, Erik. *The Iban and Their Religion.* Oxford, 1974. A readable ethnographic account based on Jensen's seven years among the Iban as an Anglican missionary and community development officer. Emphasizes world view, cosmology, and longhouse festivals.

Metcalf, Peter. *A Borneo Journey into Death: Berawan Eschatology from Its Rituals.* Philadelphia, 1982. Describes in detail the elaborate mortuary ritual sequence, involving secondary treatment of the dead, in a small ethnic group of central northern Borneo. Shows how these rites reflect Berawan concepts of the soul in life and death.

Schärer, Hans. *Ngaju Religion: The Conception of God among a South Borneo People* (1946). Translated from the German by Rodney Needham. The Hague, 1963. Schärer was a missionary with the Baseler Mission in southern Borneo for seven years and later studied under J. P. B. de Josselin de Jong at Leiden. His account of Ngaju cosmology is impressive, but he unfortunately gives little idea of the social or ritual context.

Stöhr, Waldemar. *Das Totenritual der Dajak.* Ethnologica, n.s. vol. 1. Cologne, 1959. A compendium of sources on death practices from the entire island. Contains no analysis but is useful as a guide to bibliography.

New Sources

Appell, Laura W.R., and George N. Appell. "To Do Battle with the Spirits: Bulusu' Spirit Mediums." In *The Seen and the Unseen: Shamanism, Mediumship and Possession in Borneo,* edited by Robert L. Winzeler Williamsburg, Va., 1993.

Guerreiro, Antonio J. "Contexte et Metaphore: A Propos du Mythe Kayan de l'Introduction de la Nuit (Borneo)." *Anthropos* 84, no. 4–6 (1989): 487–505.

Kershaw, Eva Maria. *A Study of Brunei Dusun Religion: Ethnic Priesthood on a Frontier of Islam.* Phillips, Maine, 2000.

Rousseau, Jerome. *Kayan Religion: Ritual Life and Religious Reform in Central Borneo.* Leiden, 1998.

Schneider, William M. and Mary-Jo Schneider. "Selako Male Initiation." *Ethnology* 30 (1991): 279–291.

PETER METCALF (1987)
Revised Bibliography

BORROMEO, CARLO (1538–1584), reforming archbishop of Milan, cardinal, and canonized saint of the

Roman Catholic church. Carlo Borromeo, second son of Count Gilberto Borromeo and Margherita de' Medici, was born at Arona, northwest of Milan, on October 2, 1538. From 1552 he attended the University of Pavia, where he received a doctorate in civil and canon law in 1559. At the end of that year his maternal uncle, Gian Angelo de' Medici, was elected Pope Pius IV and immediately bestowed upon his twenty-one-year-old nephew the archbishopric of Milan, a collection of other wealthy benefices, and a cardinal's hat. Borromeo, however, proved by his seriousness and personal austerity to be an atypical beneficiary of nepotism; thus when his elder brother died heirless and his family attempted to persuade him to revert to lay status, marry, and assume the noble title, he refused and instead had himself secretly ordained a priest July 17, 1563.

Borromeo's most significant role in the pontifical government of his uncle was his work as liaison between the Curia Romana and the third session of the Council of Trent (1560–1563). Afterward he served on various postconciliar commissions and oversaw the preparation of the *Catechism of the Council of Trent*—not so much a catechism in the ordinary sense as a doctrinal manual for the use of parish priests. This book was completed in 1564 and published in 1566.

Among the most important reforms of the Council of Trent was the requirement that bishops reside in their dioceses, but Pius IV would not allow his nephew to fulfill this obligation. Borromeo did however visit Milan in September and October of 1565, during which time he summoned and presided over his first provincial council. Recalled to Rome to assist at his uncle's deathbed, he participated in the conclave that followed and was instrumental in the election of his fellow-reformer, Pius V, on January 8, 1566.

Borromeo returned to Milan in April 1566 and labored there for the rest of his life. He became during those years the ideal of the Counter-Reformation bishop, not only because his own spiritual life was rich and deep and in accord with the ascetic principles of his time, but also because he reconstructed his great diocese and province along the lines mandated by the Council of Trent. He was present everywhere to oversee the moral reform of clergy, laity, and religious, either through tireless journeys of episcopal visitation or through the six provincial and eleven diocesan synods he held during his tenure. He founded six seminaries and a special missionary college to train priests to work in nearby Switzerland. He established hundreds of catechetical centers, which by the time he died were serving regularly more than twenty thousand children. He founded orphanages, hospitals, and homes for abandoned women. In his educational projects he worked closely with the new Society of Jesus. He was punctilious in carrying out his pastoral duties and careless of his personal safety, notably during the plague years of 1570 and 1576.

Borromeo's severity earned him enemies as well as adherents. In 1569 a friar attempted to assassinate him. He was constantly at odds with the Spanish authorities who governed the duchy of Milan, and particularly with the redoubtable viceroy, Requesens, whom he excommunicated. But Borromeo never heeded opposition, and during his relatively short span of years he established the model of the Tridentine bishop, a model destined to perdure for nearly four centuries. He was canonized on November 1, 1610.

BIBLIOGRAPHY

Borromeo's own works, especially letters and devotional literature, are in *Opere complete di S. Carlo Borromeo,* 5 vols., edited by J. A. Sassi (Milan, 1747–1748). His reform legislation is found in *Acta ecclesiae mediolanensis,* 2 vols. (Lyon, 1683). The standard life is Andrée Deroo's *Saint Charles Borromée, cardinal, réformateur, docteur de la pastorale* (Paris, 1963); a popular treatment is Margaret Yeo's *A Prince of Pastors: St. Charles Borromeo* (New York, 1938). A particularly incisive treatment of Borromeo's work is Roger Mols's "Saint Charles Borromée, pionnier de la pastorale moderne," *Nouvelle revue théologique* 79 (1957): 600–622.

MARVIN R. O'CONNELL (1987)

BRAHMĀ is the creator in Hindu mythology; sometimes he is said to form a trinity with Viṣṇu as preserver and Śiva as destroyer. Yet Brahmā does not have the importance that creator gods usually have in mythology, nor is his status equal to that of Śiva or Viṣṇu. Though Brahmā appears in more myths than almost any other Hindu god, as the central figure in quite a few, and as a bit player in many more, he was seldom worshiped in India; at least one important version of the myth in which Śiva appears before Brahmā and Viṣṇu in the form of a flaming phallus explicitly states that Brahmā will never again be worshiped in India (to punish him for having wrongly sworn that he saw the tip of the infinite pillar). Brahmā's ability to create is little more than an expertise or a technical skill that he employs at the behest of the greater gods; he is called upon whenever anyone is needed to create something, or even to create a pregnant situation—to give power to a potential villain so that the action of the conflict can unfold. But if one were to create a functional trinity of gods who wield actual power in Hindu mythology, one would have to replace Brahmā with the Goddess.

Brahmā's mythology is derived largely from that of the god Prajāpati in the Brahmāṇas. Unlike Brahmā, Prajāpati is regarded as the supreme deity, and he creates in a variety of ways: he casts his seed into the fire in place of the usual liquid oblation; he separates a female from his androgynous form and creates with her through incestuous intercourse; or he practices asceticism in order to generate heat, from which his children are born. In this way he creates first fire, wind, sun, moon; then all the gods and demons (the *devas* and *asuras*, who are his younger and older sons); then men and animals; and then all the rest of creation. In the epics and Purāṇas, when Brahmā takes over the task of creation he still uses these methods from time to time, but his usual method is to create mentally: he thinks of something and it comes into existence. While he is under the influence of the element of darkness (*tamas*) he creates the demons; under the influence of goodness (*sattva*) he creates the gods. Or he may dismember himself, like the Ṛgvedic cosmic man (Puruṣa), and create sheep from his breast, cows from his stomach, horses from his feet, and grasses from his hairs. Paradoxically (or perversely), he usually employs less abstract methods (such as copulation) to produce the more abstract elements of creation (such as the hours and minutes, or the principles of logic and music).

Brahmā's name is clearly related both to *brahman*, the neuter term for the godhead (or, in earlier texts, for the principle of religious reality), and to the word for the priest, the *brahmāṇa*. In later Hinduism Brahmā is committed to the strand of Hinduism associated with *pravṛtti* ("active creation, worldly involvement") and indifferent, or even opposed, to *nivṛtti* ("withdrawal from the world, renunciation"). He therefore comes into frequent conflict with Śiva when Śiva is in his ascetic phase, and competes with Śiva when Śiva is in his phallic phase. Brahmā's unilateral attachment to *pravṛtti* may also explain why he alone among the gods is able to grant the boon of immortality, often to demon ascetics: he deals only in life, never in death. This habit unfortunately causes the gods serious problems in dealing with demons, who are usually overcome somehow by Śiva or Viṣṇu. Immortality (or release from death) is what Brahmā bestows in place of the *mokṣa* (release from rebirth and redeath) that Śiva and Viṣṇu may grant, for these two gods, unlike Brahmā, are involved in both *pravṛtti* and *nivṛtti*. This one-sidedness of Brahmā may, finally, explain why he failed to capture the imagination of the Hindu worshiper: the god who is to take responsibility for one's whole life must, in the Hindu view, acknowledge not only the desire to create but the desire to renounce creation.

See Also Indian Religions, article on Mythic Themes; Prajāpati; Śiva.

Bibliography

The best study of Brahmā is Greg Bailey's *The Mythology of Brahmā* (Oxford, 1983), which also contains an extensive bibliography of the secondary literature. Many of the relevant texts are translated in my *Hindu Myths* (Baltimore, 1975), pp. 25–55, and interpreted in my *Śiva: The Erotic Ascetic* (Oxford, 1981), pp. 68–77 and 111–140.

New Sources

Mishra, Rajani. *Brahma-Worship, Tradition and Iconography.* Delhi, 1989.

Nagar, Shanti Lal. *The Image of Brahma in India and Abroad.* Delhi, 1992.

Wendy Doniger (1987)
Revised Bibliography

BRAHMAN.

In the Vedic hymns the neuter noun *bráhman* denotes the cosmic principle or power contained in the priestly or inspired utterance. As such, it came to be viewed as embodied in the Veda when the latter was fixed in a body of texts. The masculine form of the word, *brahmán*, denotes the priest who knows and speaks such utterances; in the later standardized Vedic ritual he is one of the four main priests who, mostly silently, oversees and rectifies errors in the sacrificial proceedings. The derivative term *brāhmaṇa* has two denotations. One indicates the Vedic prose texts that expound the *śrauta* ("solemn") ritual; these texts are also known in English as the Brāhmaṇa. The other indicates a person of the first of the four *varṇa*s, or "castes"; in English this becomes *brahman* or *brahmin*. Finally, Brahman or Brahmā is a name for the creator god in Hinduism.

Etymology. Notwithstanding many and various attempts to establish the linguistic derivation of *brahman*, the question remains unsettled. The old equation with Latin *flamen* has been vigorously and repeatedly championed by Georges Dumézil. Louis Renou suggests derivation from the root *barh* (or *brah*), which would mean to speak in riddles. Jan Gonda wants to derive *brahman* from the root *bṛh* ("to be strong"), a view that he finds supported by the ancient Indian exegetes and that has the advantage of bringing together the two largely interchangeable Vedic divinities Bṛhaspati and Brahmaṇaspati. Paul Thieme, rejecting Gonda's reliance on traditional Indian exegesis, starts from a basic meaning of "form(ing), formulation" and pleads for connecting it with Greek *morphē*. These, as well as other proposed etymologies, run into formal or semantic difficulties. Much depends on the view one takes of the basic meaning. Consensus tends to look for the basic meaning in the sphere of (sacred) word or formulation, as is in accordance with abundant textual evidence. The main problem, however, is the multi-interpretability of the element *brah*, which keeps frustrating attempts to arrive at a satisfactory solution.

Mythology. In the Brāhmaṇas and especially in the Upaniṣads, *brahman* comes to designate the impersonal eternal principle and first cause of the universe. It plays, however, no distinct role in Vedic cosmogony. Its connection—under the form of the god Brahmā—with the cosmogonic myth of the golden germ or egg (*hiranyagarbha*) is post-Vedic. In the *Laws of Manu* (1.5ff.) the golden egg is said to have arisen from Brahmā's seed, which he deposited in the primordial waters. After remaining in this embryonic state, Brahmā is born from the golden egg as the cosmic man, Puruṣa-Nārāyaṇa. The essential point of this and similar passages is that Brahmā as the single principle and cause of the universe is "self-existent" (*svayaṃbhū*) and therefore can only put the cosmogonic process into motion by reproducing himself. In the same line of self-reproduction we find the motif of Brahmā's incest with his daughter, Vāc ("speech")—a motif transferred from the Vedic creator god Prajāpati, lord of creatures. Though fused with the cosmic man, Puruṣa, and with Prajāpati, he has not given rise to a cosmogonic myth specific to him. In Hindu cosmology he is either a presiding but inactive deity—not unlike the brahman priest in the sacrificial ritual—or a demiurge who comes into his own only in the second stage of the cosmogony, when the phenomenal world starts its deployment. He is then seated on the lotus that grows out of Viṣṇu's navel, or, again, he is born from the cosmic egg (*brahmāṇḍa*).

In the Hindu pantheon, Brahmā is united, as the static center, with the dynamic supreme deities Viṣṇu and Śiva in the *trimūrti*, the triple form of the divine. Iconographically, he is represented with four bearded heads and four arms. His attributes are the four Vedas, the water vessel, the offering ladle, the rosary (emblems of the brahman), the lotus, and the scepter (or bow), while his mount is the *haṃsa* or goose. The otherwise abundant Hindu mythology does not, however, give much attention to Brahmā, nor is there clear evidence of a cult. In essence, *brahman* remained an abstract concept that was elaborated in the Upanisads and the monistic Vedānta philosophy.

SEMANTIC DEVELOPMENT. Hermann Oldenberg summarized the general meaning of *brahman* (neuter) as the sacred formula and the magic power inherent in it ("die heilige Formel und das sie erfüllende Fluidum der Zauberkraft"; 1917, vol. 2, p. 65). Although this is consistent overall with Vedic usage, it still leaves a large distance between sacred formula and the later meaning of *principium omnium*. Moreover, the Vedic *brahman*, far from being eternal and immutable, is said to be made or "carpented." Gonda's view of *brahman* as "power," derived from the verbal root *bṛh* ("to be strong"), is useful but too general to answer the problem in more precise terms. Thieme's analysis leading to "form(ing), formulation" (*Formung, Gestaltung, Formulierung*) as the original meaning, especially in the sense of (improvised) poetic formulation and later (stereotyped) truth formulation, goes a long way toward filling the gap. Renou, apart from the doubtful etymology proposed by him, draws attention to a particular dimension of the formulation. In his view, *brahman* is distinguished by its enigmatic or paradoxical nature. The *brahman*, then, is the formulation of the cosmic riddle, a riddle that cannot be solved by a direct answer but only formulated in paradoxical terms that leave the answer—the (hidden) connection (*bandhu, nidāna*) between the terms of the paradox—unexpressed. In Renou's felicitous phrase, the *brahman* is the "énergie connective comprimée en énigmes" (1949, p. 43).

Yet another element must be taken into account in fixing the semantic range of *brahman*, namely, the verbal contest. This element is preserved, albeit in fixed and ritualized form, in the Brahmodya of the Vedic ritual, especially in the horse sacrifice, or Aśvamedha. It consists of a series of rounds of verbal challenges and responses. In each round two contestants put riddle questions to each other. The point of the riddle contest is to show that one has "seen" or understood the hidden "connection" by responding with a similar, if possible even more artfully contrived, riddle. The one who holds out longest and finally reduces his opponent to silence is the winner, the true *brahman*, holder of the hidden connection. Hence the importance of silence stressed by Renou. In the elaborate Brahmodya of the horse sacrifice the last round is concluded by the brahman priest who asserts himself, apparently as the winner, with the words: "This *brahman* is the highest heaven of speech" (*brahmāyaṃ vācaḥ paramaṃ vyoma*). In the last resort, then, man as a contestant must place himself in the open gap of the unresolved cosmic riddle and vindicate himself as the live "connection" that holds together the cosmos.

The original Brahmodya, therefore, is not an innocuous riddle game but a matter of life and death. This still transpires in the Brahmodya-like debates of the Upaniṣads, where the losing contestant who fails to submit to his superior opponent and goes on challenging him has to pay for his boldness with his life or, more precisely, with his head. As a contest, the Brahmodya takes its place among other contests, such as chariot races, surviving in fixed, ritualized form. In fact, the Vedic sacrifice itself appears originally to have been a perilous and violent contest for the goods of life. However, the Vedic sacrificial ritual, as the prose texts describe it, is a perfectly peaceful and all but obsessively ordered procedure that has no place for adversaries and real contests. It is the exclusive affair of an individual sacrificer.

This fundamental change is expressed in interesting fashion in a ritualistic myth relating the decisive sacrificial contest between Prajapati and Mrtyu, or Death (*Jaiminīya Brāhmaṇa* 2.69–2.70). Prajāpati wins his final victory by his "vision" of equivalence that enables him to assimilate his adversary's sacrificial panoply and thereby to eliminate him once and for all. "Since then," the text concludes, "there is no sacrificial contest anymore." But this also meant that the formulation of the cosmic life-death riddle with its hidden connection was replaced with flat and artless statements of equivalence, establishing the identification of the elements of macro- and microcosmos with those of the standardized ritual. Thus the so-called "four *hotṛ*" (*caturhotṛ*) formulas are still said to be "the highest hidden *brahman* of the gods" and their original context appears indeed to have been the verbal contest. However, in the way these formulas are given in the texts, they are no more than a string of simple identifications—"Thinking is the ladle, thought is the ghee, speech is the altar . . ."—without mystery or enigma, to be learned and recited by rote. The dynamic tension of the hidden connection has collapsed into flat and static identification. The uncertain outcome of the contest has been replaced by the ritualistic knowledge of him "who knows thus" (*ya evam veda*), namely the identifications that concentrated the whole of the universe in the ritual proceedings and, ultimately, in the single sacrifice.

In the context of the ritual's development and fixation the *brahman* evolves from the visionary formulation of the cosmic riddle to comprise the immutably fixed corpus of Vedic texts. From the subjective truth of the visionary poet it has become the objective truth of the suprahuman, transcendent law of the universe, realized in the ritual and underpinned by identification. This also meant that the function of the *brahman* (masc.), that is, the speaker or knower of *brahman* (neuter), was narrowed down to that of the mostly silent *brahman* priest in the ritual, while the *brāhmaṇa* became (ideally) the human carrier of the Veda (hence the scriptural stress on its oral preservation and transmission by the brahman).

At the same time, the *brahman* kept up its intimate connection with speech, which gave rise to the later speculations on the primordial utterance as the cosmic principle (*śabda-brahman*) and to philosophy of language, as well as to grammatical description.

On the other hand, identification made it possible to concentrate the whole of the spoken and acted proceedings of the ritual in the person of the single sacrificer, who in this way internalizes the whole of the ritual, that is, the transcendent cosmic order, and so becomes identical with *brahman*. This was already prefigured in the *brahman* who, as we saw, identifies himself with "the highest heaven of speech." Here the development leads over to the Upanisadic doctrine of the unity of *ātman*, the principle of individuation or the individual "soul," and *brahman*, which gave rise to the monistic philosophy of the Vedānta.

SEE ALSO Brahmā; Priesthood, article on Hindu Priesthood; Upaniṣads; Varṇa and Jāti; Vedānta.

BIBLIOGRAPHY

The most original view of *brahman* is presented by Louis Renou (with the collaboration of Liliane Silburn) in "Sur la notion de brahman," *Journal asiatique* 237 (1949): 7–46, reprinted in his *L'Inde fondamentale* (Paris, 1978). Jan Gonda's *Notes on Brahman* (Utrecht, 1950) brings in anthropological materials concerning power concepts. He is criticized by Paul Thieme, who presents a balanced view of the semantic development, in "Brahman," *Zeitschrift der Deutschen Morgenländischen Gesellschaft* 102 (1952): 91–129, reprinted in Thieme's *Kleine Schriften*, vol. 1 (Wiesbaden, 1971). For a discussion of Gonda's and Thieme's views, see also Hanns-Peter Schmidt's *Bṛhaspati und Indra* (Wiesbaden, 1968), pp. 16–22, 239ff. The element of verbal contest is stressed in my essay "On the Origin of the Nāstika," *Wiener Zeitschrift für die Kunde Sud- und Ost-asiens* 12–13 (1968–1969): 171–185, which has been revised and reprinted in my *The Inner Conflict of Tradition* (Chicago, 1985). For the equation of *flamen* and *brahman*, see Georges Dumézil's *Flamen-Brahman* (Paris, 1935); see also the *Revue de l'histoire des religions* 38 and 39 for Dumézil's responses to criticism. For Oldenberg's views, see his *Die Religion des Veda* (Stuttgart, 1917) and his *Kleine Schriften* (Wiesbaden, 1967), pp. 1127–1156. A critical survey of the various etymologies is to be found in Manfred Mayrhofer's *Kurzgefasstes etymologisches Wörterbuch des Altindischen*, vol. 2 (Heidelberg, 1963), pp. 453–456.

The philosophical developments and the concept of *sabdabrahman* are discussed in Madeleine Biardeau's *Théorie de la connaissance et philosophie de la parole dans le brahmanisme classique* (Paris, 1964).

New Sources

Myers, Michael W. *Brahman: A Comparative Theology*. Richmond, 2001.

JAN C. HEESTERMAN (1987)
Revised Bibliography

BRĀHMAṆAS AND ĀRAṆYAKAS. The Brāhmaṇas are the oldest Indian Sanskrit prose texts, usually dated from the first half or the middle of the last millennium BCE. Their chronology, like that of most classical Indian texts, is uncertain and hinges on equally uncertain external factors such as the dates for the *Ṛgveda*, for the grammarian Pāṇini, and for the Buddha; moreover, the time span between their first formulation and their final redaction may have been considerable. The word *brāhmaṇa* means a statement on *brahman*, that is, on the cosmic importance or meaning of the Vedic sacrificial ritual, whether of each individual act (*karman*) and formula (*mantra*), or of the combination of such acts and formulas that constitute a particular sacrifice. *Brāhmaṇa* then becomes the generic term applied to such collections of statements or commentaries. As a class of texts, they deal in a step-by-step, rite-by-rite manner with the whole of the *śrauta* ("solemn") ritual. Together with the usually metrical *mantras*, the prose Brāhmaṇas constitute the *śruti* (whence the adjective *śrauta*), the corpus of the "revealed" Veda.

The Brāhmaṇas follow the division of the four Vedas and the corresponding parts of the ritual—*Ṛgveda*, recitation; *Yajurveda*, performance; *Sāmaveda*, chanting; and *Atharvaveda*, officiating. The central and oldest group of Brāhmaṇas are those of the *Yajurveda*, which is concerned with the overall scheme of the ritual process. In the older versions or *śākhās* ("branches") of the *Yajurveda*, the *mantra* and Brāhmaṇa parts are intermingled in the Saṃhitās of the relevant "branch" (*Kāṭhaka*, *Maitrāyaṇī*, and *Taittirīya Saṃhitās* together forming the *Kṛṣṇa* or "Black" *Yajurveda*). In the younger *Śukla* or "White" *Yajurveda*, the Saṃhitā with the *mantras* pertaining to the ritual acts is separated from the Brāhmaṇa (the *Śatapatha Brāhmaṇa*), as is also the case with the *Ṛgveda* and the *Sāmaveda*, while the *Atharvaveda* has appended to its Saṃhitā (which stands apart from the basic threefold Veda) a Brāhmaṇa that is only loosely connected and derivative. In this way the Brāhmaṇas developed into a separate class or genre characterized by a standardized expository prose style. As a genre they remained, however, tied up with the *śrauta* ritual and came to a halt with the ultimate institutionalization of the associated ceremonies. On the other hand they spawned the productive genre of the Upaniṣads, which originally were part of the Brāhmaṇa literature but eventually turned away from the ritual to treat meta-ritualistic and esoteric speculation.

The ritualistic thought of the Brāhmaṇas owes its origins to a fundamental change in worldview that gave rise to a new conception of sacrifice. Though direct and coherent information on the ritual of sacrifice preceding the Brāhmaṇa texts is lacking, they do contain in their explanations many scattered and archaic but telling references that allow us to reconstruct a rough outline of previous ritual practices. In fact, the Brāhmaṇa authors show themselves to be aware of restructuring the sacrifice within the context of a new, rationalized system of ritual. The old pattern of sacrifice was intimately bound up with conflict, contest, and battle, corresponding with the mythological motif of the enmity and combat between the conquering gods (*devas*) and their adversaries, the lordly *asuras*. The agonistic sacrificial festival was the central institution in an essentially tragic-heroic worldview. Its destructive violence is preserved in hypertrophic form in the all-embracing epic war of the *Mahābhārata*. The constant threat of sacrally sanctioned violence, death, and destruction provided the impetus for the intensive reflection on sacrifice and the construction of the *śrauta* ritual expounded in the Brāhmaṇas.

The main thrust of this new exposition of ritual practice served to remove the agonistic festival with its unsettling dangers and uncertain outcome from its central position and to replace it with the absolutely failsafe order of a mechanistic, rational rite. To this end, sacrifice was taken out of its agonistic context. This meant the exclusion of the adversary from the place of sacrifice. With that, sacrifice became a strictly personal affair of the individual sacrificer (acting in perfect unison with the priestly technicians of the ritual engaged by him for the purpose). Hence the striking absence of *sacra publica* from the *śrauta* ritual. Even in the royal rituals the king is just a single sacrificer and as such no different from a commoner. In other words, sacrifice was desocialized and set apart in a separate sphere of its own, transcending the social world. Outside society the sacrificer creates his own conflict-free, perfectly ordered universe, subject only to the absolute rules of the ritual.

Mythologically, this ritualized *agon* is expressed in the identification of the sacrificer with the creator god Prajāpati, the Lord of Creatures, who personifies the monistic conception of sacrifice, being himself both victim and sacrificer. Through sacrifice Prajāpati makes the beings go forth from his dismembered body, recalling the relatively late *Ṛgveda* hymn (10.90) that celebrates the cosmogonic sacrifice by the gods of Puruṣa, the Primordial Being. In this respect Prajāpati supersedes the warrior-god Indra and his cosmogonic martial exploits. The outcome no longer depends on prowess in the sacrificial contest involving martial arts such as charioteering and verbal skills, but on unerring knowledge of the complicated but systematic (and therefore readily learnable) body of ritual rules.

In contrast to the poetic or visionary metaphor, which was based on numerical equivalence (*sampad*, *saṃkhyāna*), the mainstay of Brahmanic thought in elaborating the ritual system was identification in uncomplicated "this-is-that" terms. Elements of the ritual (*mantras*, recitations, chants, acts, ritual implements, the place of sacrifice and its various parts) are identified with those of the universe and of the self. In this way the course of the universe, of man, and of his life are reduced to the denominator of the ritual. In the last resort it is the sacrificer who, through his identification with Prajāpati, the God-Sacrifice, integrates the ritually ordered universe in himself. We are here on the threshold of the Upanisadic doctrine of the identity of the *ātman*, the self, with the *brahman* (*principium omnium*)—a doctrine that announces itself already in a passage of the *Śatapatha Brāhmaṇa* (10.6.3.1–2).

It is possible to view the Brāhmaṇas' conception of sacrifice as "a piece of magic pure and simple," enabling the sacrificer to obtain fulfillment of his wishes—cattle, progeny, prestige, power, health, long life—and indeed the texts are effusive in promising such rewards to the sacrificer. It is, however, a subtly different matter when, as is frequently the case, heaven and immortality are brought in. The problem of death appears as the central motif of the Brahmanic cosmico-ritual system, which is aimed at escaping from the cyclic life-death alternation (the dreaded "re-death," *punarmṛtyu*) by making for oneself an immortal body in the hereafter in accordance with the transcendent order of the ritual. Although the ritual system of the Brāhmaṇas remains open to magic interpretation, this should not obscure their rigorously systemic reflection on the sacrifice resulting in the maximization of the structuring capacity of ritual and the construction of an absolute, comprehensive, and exhaustive system of rules. In this sense we can speak of a "science of ritual" (cf. Hermann Oldenberg's view of the Brāhmaṇas as "vorwissenschaftliche Wissenschaft"). Although the term *brāhmaṇa* refers primarily to the ritual's cosmic importance, expressed in the form of identifications, the *śrauta* tradition gives pride of place to the system of rules as such. Thus the Brāhmaṇas are already characterized early on as ritual injunctions (*codanā*), while the explanatory discussions (*arthavāda*)—including the statements of the cosmic importance of the rites, illustrated by mythological tales and relations of past events—are qualified as secondary, a mere "remainder." Only the pure systematics of the ritual count. In the final analysis, the potential for magic is rejected. The ritual system stands by itself, divorced from mundane reality and unaffected by its uses or abuses.

At this point the development of the ritual bifurcates. On the one hand, the doctrine of the Brāhmaṇas gave rise to the prescriptive handbooks, the Śrautasūtras, and ultimately, via the meta-rules contained in them, to the classical Mīmāṃsā school of jurisprudence. On the other hand, the statements on *brahman*, that is, the cosmic importance of the rites contained in the *arthavāda* parts, prefigure the musings of the Upaniṣads, which go on to form the final series of anskrit prose commentaries and speculation classified as Vedānta, the "conclusion of the Veda."

Āraṇyaka, literally pertaining to the wilderness (*araṇya*), is the name of a loosely defined class of texts that form part of or are attached to the Brāhmaṇas. Their distinctive trait is that the material contained in them—both *mantra* and Brāhmaṇa—is traditionally qualified as secret or dangerous and therefore has to be studied outside the settled community (*grāma*) in the wilderness while submitting to restrictive rules of behavior (*vrata*). Why these texts should be so classified is not explained. Although the Āraṇyakas vary in their contents, they are mainly concerned with the Mahāvrata, originally a New Year festival with agonistic and orgiastic features, and with parts of the ritual concerning the fire, especially the Pravargya (milk offering), featuring an earthen pot brought to glowing temperature in the fire, while funerary rites also occur. The latter item might explain the putatively secret or dangerous nature of the Āraṇyakas, but funerary rites as such do not form a commonly shared or preeminent part of these texts. Perhaps their common denominator could be found in that their contents were still recognized as being specifically bound up with life outside the settled community, that is, not, as has been erroneously thought, the life of the ascetic (*vānaprastha*), but of the nomadic warriors of old setting out with their fires and cattle into the wilds. An indication to this effect may be contained in the formulas giving the names of the divine warriors, the Maruts, and in those celebrating the dread forms or bodies (*ghorā tanvaḥ*) of the fire. Since systematization of the ritual was aimed at the exclusion of the warrior and his deeds, the relevant traditions were relegated to the margin of the ritualistic Brāhmaṇas. On the other hand, the wilderness was of old the typical locus of revelatory vision, which therefore became associated with the warrior. The links between wilderness, warrior, and vision may have been the original basis for the reputation of danger and secrecy attached to the Āraṇyakas, while their marginalization may explain the mixed and disjointed nature of their contents (to which later materials may have been added) as hallowed remnants of the otherwise discredited world of the warrior that could not be easily fitted into the ritual system. For the same reasons, however, it would seem that the Āraṇyakas offered the proper slot for attaching the Upaniṣads to the ritualistic Brāhmaṇas. In this respect it is interesting that in their form the Upaniṣads recall an important aspect of the warrior-and-seer phenomenon, namely the verbal contest (*brahmodya*) on the hidden cosmic connection.

SEE ALSO Brahman; Prajāpati; Upaniṣads; Vedas; Vedism and Brahmanism.

BIBLIOGRAPHY

A general survey of the Brāhmaṇa and Āraṇyaka literature is to be found in Jan Gonda's *Vedic Literature* (Wiesbaden, 1975), pp. 339–432.

The classic studies of the Brāhmaṇa texts are Sylvain Lévi's *La doctrine du sacrifice dans les Brâhmaṇas* (1898; 2d ed., Paris, 1966) and Hermann Oldenberg's *Die Weltanschauung der Brāhmaṇa-Texte* (Göttingen, 1919). The proto-scientific nature of these texts has recently been emphasized again in Frits Staal's P. D. Gune Memorial Lectures, *The Science of Ritual* (Poona, 1982); see also his "The Meaninglessness of Ritual," *Numen* 26 (1979): 2–22, which, however, passes over the Brāhmaṇa explanations based on cosmic identifications; see my own comment in *Festschrift R. N. Dandekar* (Poona, 1984).

For the Āraṇyakas see Hermann Oldenberg's still valuable "Āraṇyaka," *Nachrichten von der Kgl. Gesellschaft der Wissenschaften zu Göttingen* (1915), pp. 382–401, reprinted in *Kleine Schriften*, edited by Klaus Janert (Wiesbaden, 1967), pp. 419–438. Louis Renou's "Le passage des brāhmaṇa aux upaniṣads," *Journal of the American Oriental Society* 73 (1953): 138–144, traces the linkage between Brāhmaṇa, Āraṇyaka, and Upaniṣads.

Translations include Julius Eggeling's *The Śatapatha-Brāhmaṇa*, 5 vols. (1882–1900; reprint, Delhi, 1963); Arthur Berriedale Keith's *The Veda of the Black Yajus School Entitled Taittirīya-Sanhitā*, 2 vols. (1914; reprint, Delhi, 1967), and *Rigveda Brahmaṇas* (1920; reprint, Delhi, 1971); and Willem Caland's *Pañcaviṃśa Brāhmaṇa* (Calcutta, 1931) and *Das Jaiminīya-Brāhmaṇa in Auswahl* (Amsterdam, 1919). Of the Āraṇyakas Keith has translated the Śānkhyāna (London, 1908) and the Aitareya (Oxford, 1909).

JAN C. HEESTERMAN (1987)

BRĀHMO SAMĀJ.

The Brāhmo Samāj, also known as Brāhma Samāj and Brāhmo (or Brāhma) Sabhā, was the first modern Hindu reform movement. It was founded in Calcutta in 1828 by Ram Mohan Roy (1772–1833). As an expression of the social and religious views of a small but influential group of westernized Indians, the Brāhmo Samāj ("congregation of *brahman*") sought to create a purified form of Hinduism, a Hindu *dharma* free of all Puranic elements such as temple rituals and image worship. Led by a series of prominent Bengali intellectuals, the movement was a major factor in shaping Hindu responses to both secular and Christian influence from the West and thus helped pave the way for the so-called Hindu Renaissance in the late 1800s. The Brāhmo Samāj, along with the Ārya Samāj, was one of the most important religio-political influences in the Independence movement, the Brāhmo Samāj being a reform movement and the Ārya Samāj tending toward a revitalistic concern for the religious heritage of the Vedas mediated through new social and theological forms.

The Hindus involved in the Brāhmo Samāj were not broadly representative of the Bengal Hindu population, but instead belonged to a group of castes and families that had prospered in the late eighteenth and early nineteenth centuries after Mughal domination had given way to rule by the British East India Company. The Bengalis who gained money and land during this difficult economic period were mainly those who served as suppliers, agents, or bankers for the British. In the early period of company rule, those who were prepared to take this westernizing route to new wealth were mostly Hindus from a few select castes, and it was they and their descendants who provided the leadership and most of the membership of the Brāhmo Samāj.

The initial Indian response to British rule in Bengal was strongly influenced by caste and religious factors. Muslims deprived of political power and related social privileges largely withdrew from involvement with their conquerors, while Hindu response was divided between what were known in Bengal as *kulīna* and non-*kulīna* castes. In the unique Bengal hierarchy, the highest status was given to five *kulīna* ("superior") brahman castes and three *kulīna* castes of *kāyasthas* (traditional writer/clerical castes of *śūdra* origin). Faced with British rule these *kulīna* castes remained aloof, as they previously had from Muslim rulers, in order to preserve their ritual purity. The upper echelons of non-*kulīnas*, however, were less concerned about purity and were in many cases accustomed to relations with non-Hindu rulers. Members of these castes, whose ranks included the non-*kulīna* brahman families of Roy and Tagore as well as non-*kulīna* *kāyasthas* and *vaidyas*, recognized the benefits of working with the British, and using this involvement to their advantage, they had emerged by the early 1800s as wealthy entrepreneurs and landowners more receptive than other Bengalis to Western social and religious influences.

The newly affluent non-*kulīna* Hindus formed a natural constituency for Hindu reform. They were wealthy, but within the traditional Hindu system they had to accept religious leadership from *kulīnas*. Although attracted to Western culture, most were unwilling to reject Hinduism in favor of Christianity—a choice increasingly urged on them after the British East India Company opened Bengal to Christian missionaries in 1813. If they were to acquire Western culture, retain their Hindu identity, and also improve their religious status, a new form of Hinduism in which they could set the terms and take the leading role was necessary. Thanks to the genius of Ram Mohan Roy, this need was met by the creation of the Brāhmo Samāj in 1828.

The son of a non-*kulīna brahman* and himself a successful entrepreneur, Roy had a passion for reason and universality that led him by 1815 to reject Hindu polytheism and image worship in favor of the monotheism of the early Vedānta texts, the Upaniṣads and the *Brahma Sūtra*, which he interpreted as teaching the worship of *brahman* as the sole creator and supporter of the universe. Applying his standards to Christianity, he concluded that Jesus' ethical teachings had universal validity, though he rejected trinitarian theology. For a brief period in the early 1820s he aligned himself with the Unitarian movements in England and America, but when he saw that Hindus could not satisfy their spiritual and religious needs by becoming Unitarians, he founded the Brāhmo Samāj as a Hindu counterpart.

As Roy conceived it, the Brāhmo Samāj was a rational and ethical expression of Vedantic monotheism, reformist rather than radical in its ideas and goals. One radical element, however, was the assumption of religious leadership by Roy himself, a worldly self-taught non-*kulīna* who rejected traditional priestly authority. Once this example was accepted, the way was open for a new type of religious leader. In Bengal, this meant the recognition of upper non-*kulīnas* such as the Tagores, the Sens, and the Dutts as valid religious guides, and it was they in fact who provided leadership for most of the new religious movements throughout the nineteenth century.

Roy's successors in Brāhmo leadership, Debendranath Tagore (1817–1905) and Keshab Chandra Sen (1838–1884), converted the fledgling enterprise into a vital movement for religious and social reform. Between 1843 and 1858, Tagore recruited hundreds of new members, codified Brāhmo teachings, and campaigned actively against Christian proselytizing. Sen, the son of a Vaiṣṇava *vaidya* banker, expanded the efforts for social reform and brought the movement national attention with his charismatic missionary activities. Most significantly, as non-*kulīnas*, both men reinforced Roy's principle that religious authority rests on reason and ability and not on priestly caste.

By the time Sen died, the Brāhmo Samāj had largely completed its mission, having met the initial impact of Christianity and Western culture and having shown how they could be used to strengthen Hinduism instead of destroying it. In the process, the movement created a new and lasting religious model that could release the creative energies of a class of people who formerly had been patrons rather than leaders in the Hindu system. Although the Brāhmo Samāj survived as an independent organization, the energies of that class after 1884 were largely expressed in other movements of religious, social, and political reform. Such nonpriestly religious leaders as Vivekananda and Gandhi, however, were certainly both beneficiaries and worthy successors to Roy's initial vision.

SEE ALSO Ārya Samāj; Gandhi, Mohandas; Roy, Ram Mohan; Sen, Keshab Chandra; Vivekananda.

BIBLIOGRAPHY

The Brāhmo Samāj has inspired a massive literature from Ram Mohan Roy to the present. The best work on the movement as a whole is David Kopf's *The Brāhmo Samāj and the Shaping of the Modern Indian Mind* (Princeton, 1979). J. N. Farquhar's *Modern Religious Movements in India* (New York, 1915) gives an interesting early description of the Brāhmo Samāj in the context of other nineteenth-century Indian religious developments. Two recent and more analytic studies of the religious views of the movement and its founder are provided in Spencer Lavan's "The Brahmo Samaj: India's First Modern Movement for Religious Reform" and in James N. Pankratz's "Rammohun Roy," in *Religion in Modern India*, edited by Robert D. Baird (New Delhi, 1981), pp. 1–25, and pp. 163–177. The standard source for more detailed information on Roy is Sophia Dobson Collet's *The Life and Letters of Raja Rammohun Roy*, 3d ed. rev., edited by Dilip Kumar Biswas and Prabhat Chandra Ganguli (Calcutta, 1962), and many of his important writings have been collected in the single-volume edition of *The English Works of Raja Rammohun Roy*, edited by Kalidas Nag and Debajyoti Burman (Calcutta, 1958). Narayan Chaudhuri's *Maharshi Devendranath Tagore* (New Delhi, 1973) provides a good description and evaluation of Tagore's contributions to the Brahmo movement, and Meredith Borthwick's *Keshub Chunder Sen: A Search for Cultural Synthesis* (Calcutta, 1977) gives an excellent scholarly assessment of his successor. The unique and complex caste system of Bengal is explained in detail in Ronald B. Inden's *Marriage and Rank in Bengali Culture* (Berkeley, 1976).

New Sources

Takeuchi, Keiji. *The Philosophy of Brahmo Samaj: Rammohun Roy and Devendranath Tagore.* Calcutta, 1997.

THOMAS J. HOPKINS (1987)
Revised Bibliography

BRAINWASHING (DEBATE). The current debate over brainwashing (the term is used here generically to refer to mind control, coercive persuasion, or thought reform unless otherwise stipulated) is best understood in the broader context of recurrent concerns through Western history over powerful, illicit sources of influence on individual loyalty and commitment. Brainwashing is a contemporary version of such historic concerns. These anxieties have periodically assumed crisis proportions when there have been extreme sociocultural tensions that have given rise to allegations of the existence of subversive forces and the marshaling of countersubversion campaigns, with the objective of controlling specific types of contested relationships. As in the case of its predecessors, the contemporary debates over brainwashing embody these related elements. The evidence in both the historical and contemporary episodes supports the conclusions that concerns about powerful, illicit sources of influence are pronounced during periods of sociocultural tension and that certain types of relationships have repeatedly been at issue. However, there is little support for the existence or efficacy of subversive forces as depicted in brainwashing ideologies.

Extreme sociocultural tensions are likely to occur during unsettled periods when a society experiences conflict between alternative, incompatible organizing principles or is moving from one set of organizing principles to another. In Western history, the movement from premodern to modern to postmodern social structures has yielded a succession of these unsettled periods. During such moments the major social forms that orient individual and institutional patterns stand in opposition to one another and therefore yield contradictory behavioral imperatives. It is during unsettled periods that subversion fears are most likely to surface. Throughout history, subversives have appeared in various forms, such as gods, fate, demons, and witches. What such subversives purportedly have in common has been their tendency to work in a secret, conspiratorial fashion with malevolent intent to corrupt individuals' natural essence or purpose, variously conceived as free will, soul, or sanity. American history is replete with subversion fears, such as allegations of the transformation of early settler captives into savages by American Indians, colonial-era witchcraft possession, mesmerism of converts by Mormons, and imprisonment of nuns in Catholic convents. Although the term *brainwashing* had yet to be coined, these earlier forms are related to more modern forms in which the real or imagined subversive agents are Communists, mafioso, religious cult leaders, extraterrestrials, satanists, and terrorists.

The debate over brainwashing and its predecessor forms has centered on forces influencing individual-group relationships. Over the last several centuries, the culturally appropriate form of individuality has increasingly emphasized autonomy, voluntarism, and self-directedness. Individuals are deemed autonomous to the extent that they are not subject to external constraint through coercion, accident, miracle, or nature. Voluntarism is presumptively present when individuals orient their motives and intent in a goal-directed fashion by exercising choice. Self-directedness involves the pursuit of goals that reflect external self-interest or internal self-fulfillment. Relational involvement in any context that may compromise these attributes, particularly those outside of relationships in support of legitimate institutional mandates, are likely to be contested.

The focus of this entry is on allegations of brainwashing in the case of contemporary religious movements. The historical context for the current debate is cold war era disputation over alleged Communist brainwashing. There also have been a number of other related events and episodes in which brainwashing has been alleged that have contributed to broad public acceptance of the reality of brainwashing and to the availability of brainwashing as an explanation for troubling events.

COMMUNIST BRAINWASHING. The term *brainwashing* originated in the cold war division of nations into socialist and capitalist blocs. The historic tensions between those two forms of political and economic organization were reflected in high levels of militarization, a succession of regional wars, and an ongoing threat of nuclear conflagration. The English term *brainwashing* derives from a Chinese counterpart (*si xiang gai zao*) that roughly translates into English as "to cleanse (or wash clean) thoughts" and refers to sociopolitical attitude correction. During the cold war era, American government officials were confronted by a series of disquieting events: public confessions by dissidents during Soviet show trials, apparent conversions by individuals who were subjected to Chinese revolutionary universities, and collaborationist statements and actions by American prisoners of war during the Korean War. It was a Central Intelligence Agency (CIA) operative and journalist, Edward Hunter, who in 1953 coined the term *brainwashing* to account for apparent cases of conversion or collaboration with Communist regimes. During the 1950s and 1960s the CIA undertook its own research on brainwashing, conducting experiments that involved the use of pain, sensory deprivation, and hypnosis on a variety of subjects. While these experiments were successful in psychologically destabilizing subjects, they did not result in implanting new attitudes and values. The CIA version of brainwashing theory permeated popular culture, most notably in the 1962 film, *The Manchurian Candidate.* In that film, Communist captors attempt to turn an American prisoner of war into a robotlike agent through the use of programming by hypnosis and drugs.

Two major studies of Communist brainwashing published in 1961 were particularly influential in shaping later conceptions of the process—Edgar Schein's *Coercive Persuasion* and Robert Lifton's *Thought Reform and the Psychology of Totalism.* In his study of Korean War prisoners and the Chinese indoctrination program, Schein identified three processes in coercive persuasion: (1) unfreezing (displacing the individual's former identity); (2) changing the identity; and (3) refreezing (establishing a new identity). However, Schein criticized the crude CIA brainwashing model, argued that preexisting individual beliefs and values were relevant to the impact of coercive persuasion techniques, and concluded that the Korean and Chinese techniques had been ineffective in producing an attitude change in the targeted individuals. Schein was careful to draw a distinction between conformity to captors' demands during incarceration and actual conversion. On the basis of his research, he could find no cases of conversion. He further argued that there were significant similarities between Communist indoctrination programs and the social pressures generated by such mainstream Western entities as educational institutions, psychotherapy, religious orders, and religious revivals.

The most influential model remains Lifton's theory of thought reform. Lifton studied twenty-five Westerners and fifteen Chinese who were imprisoned and subjected to thought reform programs and subsequently migrated to Hong Kong. On the basis of those cases, Lifton developed eight "themes" that are integral to ideological totalism, which is produced by a combination of extreme ideology and extreme individual character traits. Conditions fostering ideological totalism include the following:

1. Milieu control (controlling internal communication and eliminating external communication);
2. Mystical manipulation (manipulating individuals' perceptions of their own behavior);
3. The demand for purity (moral polarizing of insiders and outsiders);
4. The cult of confession (using confession rituals to expose unacceptable relationships and actions);
5. Sacred science (propounding totalitarian ideology as absolute truth);
6. Loading the language (utilizing emotionally laden concepts that impede critical thought);
7. Doctrine over person (interpreting reality and other persons through group ideology);
8. Dispensing of existence (elevating the group and its ideology as the highest value).

Lifton's theory does not rely simply on the compliance generated by a totalistic situation, as he also argues that some individuals are more predisposed to seek or accept totalistic solutions. To the extent that thought reform occurs, then, it is the product of an interaction between individual predispositions and a totalistic situation. In the cases that Lifton studied, however, thought reform was not very successful. All of the forty individuals Lifton studied did indeed collaborate with their jailers in various ways (such as signing public statements condemning the United States or confessing to germ warfare). However, only two maintained these positions once they were outside of the control of Communist officials, and Lifton found totalistic predispositions in both cases.

Further evidence of the relative lack of success of brainwashing programs can be found in the aggregate statistics on the impact of these programs on American prisoners during the Korean War. Only about half of captured American soldiers survived the brutal conditions to which they were subjected in internment camps. Facing the prospect of starvation and torture, about one-third of the survivors collaborated with their captors. However, only twenty-one of the nearly 4,500 Americans held at the end of the war refused repatriation; several years later eleven members of that group requested repatriation. This defection rate is roughly comparable to the rate for other wars. By contrast to American prisoners of war, about ninety thousand captured North Korean and Chinese soldiers refused repatriation.

In the case of allegations of Communist brainwashing, then, it is clear that there were tensions between capitalist and socialist states that at various times rose to crisis levels, and those tensions produced mutual fears of subversion. However, there is little evidence to support the CIA version of brainwashing, and the agency's own brainwashing experiments were unsuccessful. Independent research by Lifton and Schein produced evidence of collaboration under duress but no evidence of an overpowering psychotechnology that produced lasting transformation of beliefs and attitudes. Lifton's work, in particular, has continued to be influential as a model of totalistic environments and processes. Furthermore, the generic concept of brainwashing has been incorporated into American popular culture. Both formal theories and informal cultural beliefs have created a reservoir of credibility for brainwashing that served as the basis for its introduction into the disputes involving new religious groups in the 1970s.

CULTIC BRAINWASHING. The controversy over new religious movements (NRMs), popularly referred to as *cults,* is most immediately a product of the 1960s countercultural period. As political and social countercultural movements dissipated, alienated young adults began seeking alternative forms of protest. A wave of new movements, some of which immigrated to the West following the rescinding of Asian immigration exclusion legislation and some domestic groups that had languished in relative obscurity, suddenly began attracting converts. Although characteristics of converts varied by movement, in general the first recruits to NRMs were white, middle-class, well-educated young adults. The movements quickly drew attention from families of converts, established churches, and scholars studying religion and social movements.

Opposition to new religions soon mounted as the groups challenged educational, political, occupational, religious, and familial institutions. There were two major wings to the opposition, both of which sought to distinguish between legitimate churches and pseudo-religious "cults." The religious opposition groups involved in the countercult movement existed long before the cult controversy and typically challenged sectarian Christian and non-Christian churches. When new movements appeared, countercult organizations simply added them to their list of opponents. The countercult movement, which drew its strength largely from the ranks of conservative denominational groups, regarded new movements as a spiritual threat because they propagated heretical doctrines. Religious countercult groups were more likely to regard recruits to NRMs as deceived rather than brainwashed. The secular anticult associations were founded by family members of NRM converts. Anticult ideology sought to distinguish cults from legitimate groups on the basis that the former employed brainwashing techniques. Brainwashing in this context typically refers to a deliberate, potent program of indoctrination and control that reduces individual autonomy, voluntarism, and self-directedness.

As initially formulated, anticult ideology depicted NRMs as rapidly growing; unprecedented in their organization, tactics, and destructiveness; and capable of dramatically altering individual beliefs and behaviors and of creating long-term emotional damage to anyone subjected to them. The earliest brainwashing theories were developed by deprogrammers who sought to reverse the effects of cultic "programming" and thereby extract individuals from new religions. These crude and easily disproved theories alleged that individuals were rendered powerless by some combination of hypnosis, sleep deprivation, relentless indoctrination, altered diet, and extreme isolation.

Much more influential was the work of psychologist Margaret Singer who provided the foundation of anticult brainwashing theory, as well as expert witness testimony in many cases based on brainwashing allegations. Singer identified six conditions that she argued are integral to the brainwashing process:

1. Preventing the individual from becoming aware of the group's control or change program;
2. Controlling the individual's environment by limiting and shaping information and contacts;
3. Creating a sense of fear, dependence, and powerlessness in the individual;
4. Eradicating the individual's old attitudes and behavior;
5. Instilling new attitudes and behavior in the individual;
6. Creating a closed logical system through which the individual processes information.

Although Singer's theories were the most influential within anticult circles and judicial forums, there were a variety of other theories ranging from cybernetic trauma to manipulative use of trance and hypnotic states to relational disorders.

More recently, there have been efforts to reorient brainwashing theory. For example, Benjamin Zablocki has argued that brainwashing is better understood as a technique for retaining (rather than obtaining) members, that it may be effective on only a small number of individuals, and that individuals may participate voluntarily in the process. All of these theories share in common a focus on group-induced, deleterious effects on individuals affiliated with religious movements. While they admit some measure of both individual and group influence, the latter is asserted to be more powerful and determinative of outcomes.

NRMs quickly attracted the attention of scholars in the social sciences and religious studies because their appearance and growth during the 1970s appeared to contravene established theories among social scientists predicting the continued secularization of Western societies. Affiliation to (and later disaffiliation from) new religions, based on studies of members, has been by far the most researched aspect of new religions. The vast majority of published findings have employed conversion or affiliation theories that do not presume the illegitimacy of the groups or the manipulative practices inherent in brainwashing models. In mainstream scholarly work, affiliations of individuals with new religions have been interpreted as the product of ongoing countercultural protest, youthful experimentation with alternative lifestyles, or tensions surrounding the transition from adolescence to adulthood, rather than the subversive power of cults. The conversion process is described not in terms of powerful brainwashing techniques but rather in terms of such processes as adherents' adoption of a new symbolic identity, a strengthening of one set of ties to a social network with a corresponding weakening of ties to another network, and role playing and experimentation by individuals searching for meaning in their lives.

There have been a number of major studies of movements associated with brainwashing allegations, including the Unification Church, the Family (originally the Children of God), and the International Society for Krishna Consciousness (ISKCON or Hare Krishnas). These studies include three books on Unificationism—John Lofland's *Doomsday Cult* (1966), David Bromley and Anson Shupe's *Moonies in America* (1979), and Eileen Barker's *The Making of a Moonie* (1984); four books on the Family—David van Zandt's *Living in the Children of God* (1991), Ruth Wangerin's *The Children of God* (1993), James Chancellor's *Life in the Family* (2000), and William Bainbridge's *The Endtime Family* (2002); and two books on the Hare Krishnas—E. Burke Rochford's *Hare Krishna in America* (1985) and Larry Shinn's *The Dark Lord* (1987). The clear implications in these works are that there is no single process of affiliation but rather a variety of kinds of conversion with different dynamics—the personal transformation associated with religious movements may be limited or pervasive, and whatever transformation does occur is a product of both individual volition and group socialization.

Furthermore, these and many other studies challenged basic assumptions of the brainwashing approach. They found that, contrary to the expectations of brainwashing models, the recruitment rates of NRMs were very low while turnover rates were very high. They questioned how such diverse, unrelated groups all could have discovered and implemented brainwashing techniques at precisely the same moment. They also found that organizations within the same movement used different recruitment and socialization practices, and movements changed these practices frequently. Based on movement membership patterns, they concluded that movement recruitment success declined rather than improved over time, a finding difficult to reconcile with brainwashing theory. Finally, they reported that movements displayed a pervasive pattern of factionalism, schism, and conflict, a pattern inconsistent with the compliance that would be predicted by a brainwashing explanation.

The debate over brainwashing became legal disputation when the anticult movement initiated a program to "rescue" members of new religious groups who allegedly had been brainwashed. The process of reversing the effects of putative cultic programming was called *deprogramming.* The procedure was devised by Theodore "Ted" Patrick, who deprogrammed members of many movements. As practiced by Patrick and others, deprogramming bore a striking resemblance to the brainwashing process it was designed to reverse. NRM members were physically abducted, held in isolation for extended periods, and bombarded with ideology and pressure from deprogrammers, former NRM members, and family members. The process was relatively successful, particularly with recent affiliates who lacked strong group ties, but it soon encountered legal problems due to a reliance on coercive restraint. Anticult groups therefore sought legal warrant for deprogramming by obtaining guardianship and conservatorship orders that awarded parents custody of NRM converts based on assertions of brainwashing. This strategy succeeded until religious groups began legally contesting the conservatorships.

Subsequently, anticult organizations encouraged and sometimes orchestrated civil suits against religious groups by former members who had disaffiliated and agreed to "exit counseling." Suits were initiated on grounds that individuals had been brainwashed and were suffering from an infliction of emotional distress or post-traumatic stress syndrome. The litigation strategy avoided problems of coercive restraint and allowed the introduction of expert witnesses who testified to cultic brainwashing practices. This strategy produced a number of favorable trial verdicts, although verdicts often were modified or reversed by appellate courts.

Litigation gradually undermined the viability of cases based on brainwashing assertions, but there were divergent outcomes in some cases. Access to conservatorships based on allegations of cultic brainwashing was dramatically reduced following *Katz v. Superior Court* (1977). After a California judge had granted legal custody of five adult members of the Unification Church to their parents, a California court of appeals overturned the order based in part on the conclusion that inquiry into coercive persuasion involved a constitutionally impermissible investigation of the legitimacy of a religious faith. The later anticult strategy of bringing civil suits against NRMs on the basis that brainwashing involved the intentional infliction of emotional distress also was gradually eroded as successes became more problematic. *Molko and Leal v. Holy Spirit Association* (1983) exemplifies these mixed results. Two former members of the Unification Church, David Molko and Tracey Leal, sued the church for damages suffered as a result of brainwashing after having been successfully deprogrammed. Molko and Leal's complaints were rejected by the trial court, and expert testimony on brainwashing was rejected on the grounds that it lacked scientific standing. However, in 1988 the California Supreme Court reversed the lower court ruling in asserting that the constitution did not preclude brainwashing claims in cases of fraud involving flagrant deception.

Another major case involving infliction of mental distress as a result of brainwashing was brought against the International Society for Krishna Consciousness. In *Robin George v. ISKCON* (1983), brainwashing charges were dismissed by a Los Angeles court after several appeals, and the suit was finally settled in 1993. An important federal case was *U.S. v. Fishman* (1990). In that case Steven Fishman claimed that his fraudulent activities were the result of the debilitating influence of his membership in the Church of Scientology. The judge ruled against allowing mind-control testimony in the trial on the basis that it did not possess scientific standing. Psychologist Singer was the most active and influential anticult expert witness in brainwashing cases. Forensic psychologist Dick Anthony played a pivotal role in convincing courts to exclude Singer's testimony in a number of these cases. These and other cases made presenting brainwashing claims increasingly problematic.

The brainwashing debate spilled over into professional societies as well, most notably the American Psychological Association (APA). In 1983 the APA formed the Deceptive and Indirect Methods of Persuasion and Control (DIMPAC) task force headed by Singer to evaluate the status of such theories. Although the task force was dominated by psychologists sympathetic to anticult brainwashing theories, the APA's Board of Social and Ethical Responsibility rejected the DIMPAC report. Other professional associations also debated the brainwashing issue, but none has endorsed brainwashing theory.

While brainwashing theory has not fared well in U.S. legal and political forums, it has had an impact in Europe and the People's Republic of China. A number of European governments proposed controls over new religions in the wake of the 1994 murder/suicides by the Solar Temple in Switzerland and Canada. American anticult officials consulted with European governmental officials, who made anticult brainwashing theory a key component of reports and legislation. In 1998, France established a new office, the Mission Interministérielle de Lutte les Sectes (Interministerial commission to make war on sects) to monitor *sectes* (cults). A key defining characteristic of *sectes* is "mental manipulation" (a parallel to brainwashing). In the People's Republic of China, anticult representatives have consulted with government officials concerning efforts to suppress Falun Gong, which Chinese officials refer to as a dangerous cult.

OTHER EPISODES AND EVENTS. There has been a succession of other occurrences that have provided popular legitimation for brainwashing. In 1973 the term *Stockholm syndrome* was coined after four Swedish bank employees, who were held hostage for six days by bank robbers, resisted police efforts to free them and publicly defended their captors. The hostages continued to express support for the robbers, and two female captors subsequently became engaged to their captors. According to the Stockholm syndrome theory, hostages may bond with their captors when their lives are in imminent danger, when they are unable to escape the situation, when they do not have access to alternative sources of information, and when the captors are humane. Like brainwashing theories, the Stockholm syndrome is vigorously debated. Nonetheless it has been invoked to account for a variety of contested behaviors, including abused wives who do not support feminism, parents who are unable to win their children's loyalty in custodial disputes, and liberal Israelis who are conciliatory toward Palestinians.

One of the most celebrated events related to brainwashing involved the kidnapping of the Hearst publishing empire heiress Patty Hearst by the Symbionese Liberation Army (SLA) in 1974. Hearst was confined to a closet for an extended period, raped, and subjected to SLA indoctrination. She resurfaced months later as Tania, apparently now a convert to the SLA since she participated with the group in a bank robbery and did not attempt to escape when she had obvious opportunities to do so. After her capture, Hearst's defense team argued that she collaborated with her captors because she had been terrorized and had continuously feared for her life. The jury rejected this argument, however, and Hearst was convicted and imprisoned. She later received a presidential pardon.

Finally, brainwashing was a core element of the Satanism scare that swept through North American and Europe during the 1980s. Proponents claimed the existence of an international, underground cult of satanists who engaged in a range of nefarious activities. Most horrific were the claims that satanists sought enhanced personal power by absorbing the life energy of young children in ritual sacrifices. Brainwashing, drugs, and hypnosis were all allegedly used to maintain control over children. The most significant legal cases emanated from child-care facilities where satanic activity was believed to be occurring. In these cases the testimony of very young children under the care of therapists was pivotal in gaining criminal convictions. Ultimately these cases were discredited as evidence mounted that the biographies of ritual abuse survivors had been fabricated, therapists had implanted memories of abuse in impressionable children, and no victims of satanic rituals were to be found. A series of academic books and reports by investigatory commissions and police agencies unanimously concluded that allegations of underground satanic cults were baseless. Analyses concluded that satanic cults symbolically represented a widely experienced sense of vulnerability and danger among American families by high rates of child sexual abuse; increasing participation of women in the labor force; and unreliable, expensive child-care facilities.

Like their historical predecessors, contemporary episodes of brainwashing allegations have involved claims that culturally illicit groups possessed the capacity to undermine culturally appropriate expression of autonomy, voluntarism, and self-directedness. Brainwashing allegations involving Communists, cultists, and satanists all reflect this pattern. Theory and research on these episodes indicate that allegations of brainwashing occurred in response to sociocultural tensions and that culturally appropriate autonomy, voluntarism, and self-directedness were the behaviors at issue. In each case, social science research has not supported the overwhelming psychotechnology theories, and the judicial system and professional social science associations have likewise declined to grant brainwashing explanations scientific standing.

EMERGING DEVELOPMENTS. Rejecting brainwashing as a general explanation for individual and collective conduct requires offering an adequate alternative explanation for the dynamics of highly regulated or conformist situations. Many questions remain unanswered. There is little doubt that some group contexts complicate and may compromise individuals' ability to sustain culturally appropriate autonomy, voluntarism, and self-directedness. Once the presumption of the existence of an overpowering psychotechnology (brainwashing) by groups has been rejected, the question of how actual uniformities in behavior in diverse groups occur becomes open to explanation. Social scientists are now beginning to explore these issues. For example, the brainwashing model's assertion that behavioral uniformities are the product of the personality characteristics of a manipulative charismatic leader is being displaced by a more complex analysis of charisma as a social construction. In this emerging analysis, charismatic influence is understood as the product of interactive forces that include internal challenges to leadership, pressures to demonstrate charismatic competence, influences by inner circle leadership on the charismatic leader, and external constraints on charismatic legitimacy.

Similarly, there is active investigation of the conditions under which religious movements become involved in violent confrontations with their host societies. Challenging the logic that new religious movements are inherently unstable and prone to violence, there is an emerging consensus that such extreme outcomes involve both internal and external influences to varying degrees. High tension between a movement and the established social order can produce polarization such that each side poses an inherent threat to the other. Under these conditions, factors such as secretive actions on both sides, centripetal and centrifugal forces within the movement or control groups, and the disempowerment of third parties that might mediate conflict are likely to destabilize an already volatile situation. For these and other important questions, simplistic answers are gradually giving way to more complex analyses.

While the specifics of explanations for extreme behavioral uniformities remain to be determined, it appears likely that satisfactory explanations will include sociocultural conditions, organizational characteristics of the groups, dynamics of relationships within the groups, and personality predispositions of individual members. It is also likely that there will be continuing debate over issues of conformity and control because these are inherently normative matters and the cultural norms are constantly changing. There is every reason, then, to expect that there will be no final resolution to the question of what types of organizations may shape individual autonomy, voluntarism, and self-directedness, and what influence processes they may legitimately exercise.

SEE ALSO Anticult Movements; Cults and Sects; Deprogramming; Law and Religion, article on Law and New Religious Movements.

BIBLIOGRAPHY

Anthony, Dick. "Religious Movements and Brainwashing Litigation: Evaluating Key Testimony." In *In Gods We Trust: New Patterns of Religious Pluralism in America*, 2d ed., edited by Thomas Robbins and Dick Anthony, pp. 295–343. New Brunswick, N.J., 1990. Interdisciplinary essays on contemporary religion in the West, with an emphasis on NRMs.

Bainbridge, William S. *The Endtime Family: Children of God.* Albany, N.Y., 2002. A sympathetic case study of the Family based on survey data and personal interviews.

Barker, Eileen. *The Making of a Moonie: Choice or Brainwashing?* Oxford, 1984. A classic study of Unificationism in England, examining conversion and brainwashing models of NRM affiliation.

Bromley, David G., and J. Gordon Melton, eds. *Cults, Religion, and Violence.* Cambridge, U.K., 2002. Interdisciplinary analyses of the relationship of NRMs and violence focusing on the major cases of the 1990s.

Bromley, David G., and James T. Richardson, eds. *The Brainwashing/Deprogramming Controversy: Sociological, Psychological, Legal, and Historical Perspectives.* Lewiston, N.Y., 1983. Essays offering analysis and critique of the brainwashing model and the practice of deprogramming.

Bromley, David G., and Anson Shupe. *Moonies in America: Cult, Church, and Crusade.* Beverly Hills, Calif., 1979. A participant, observation-based study of the early development of the Unificationist Movement in the United States.

Chancellor, James. *Life in the Family: An Oral History of the Children of God.* Syracuse, N.Y., 2000. A participant observation study of the Family conveying the movement's development from a member's perspective.

Hunter, Edward. *Brain-washing in Red China: The Calculated Destruction of Men's Minds.* Rev. ed. New York, 1953. A highly influential, journalistic account of the process and effects of brainwashing.

Lifton, Robert J. *Thought Reform and the Psychology of Totalism: A Study of "Brainwashing" in China.* New York, 1961. One of the most systematic and influential studies of thought reform.

Lofland, John. *Doomsday Cult: A Study of Conversion, Proselytization, and Maintenance of Faith.* Englewood Cliffs, N.J., 1966; rev. ed., New York, 1977. The earliest social science study of Unificationism in the United States.

Long, Theodore, and Jeffrey K. Hadden. "Religious Conversion and the Concept of Socialization: Integrating the Brainwashing and Drift Models." *Journal for the Scientific Study of Religion* 22 (1983): 1–14. A theoretical attempt to bridge brainwashing and socialization theories.

Richardson, James, Joel Best, and David Bromley, eds. *The Satanism Scare.* Hawthorne, N.Y., 1991. Interdisciplinary essays analyzing the 1980s Satanism scare in North America and Europe.

Rochford, E. Burke, Jr. *Hare Krishna in America.* New Brunswick, N.J., 1985. A participant observation study of the early Krishna Consciousness movement in California.

Saliba, John A. *Social Science and the Cults: An Annotated Bibliography.* New York, 1990. The most comprehensive bibliography on NRMs, organized by topic.

Sargent, William. *Battle for the Mind: A Physiology of Conversion and Brain-Washing.* Garden City, N.Y., 1957. An analysis of influence techniques employed in religion, therapy, medicine, and politics.

Schein, Edgar H. *Coercive Persuasion: A Socio-psychological Analysis of the "Brainwashing" of the American Civilian Prisoners by the Chinese Communists.* New York, 1961. A study of brainwashing during the Korean War that reports POW compliance but not conversions.

Shinn, Larry. *The Dark Lord: Cult Images and the Hare Krishnas in America.* Philadelphia, 1987. A participant observation study of Hare Krishna history, theology, and ritual with extensive description of the conversion and deprogramming processes.

Shupe, Anson, and David G. Bromley. *The New Vigilantes: Deprogrammers, Anti-cultists, and the New Religions.* Beverly Hills, Calif., 1980. A study of the ideology and organization of the anticult movement during its formative period in the United States.

Singer, Margaret, with Janja Lalich. *Cults in Our Midst.* San Francisco, 1995. A forceful argument for the dangers of cults and brainwashing by one of the anticult movement's major proponents.

Snow, David, and Richard Machalek. "The Sociology of Conversion." *Annual Review of Sociology* 10 (1984): 167–190. A systematic review of theories of conversion with an emphasis on NRMs.

van Zandt, David. *Living in the Children of God.* Princeton, 1991. A participant observation study of the organization and development of the Family.

Wangerin, Ruth. *The Children of God: A Make-Believe Revolution?* Westport, Conn., 1993. An anthropological and mildly critical study of the organization and development of the Family.

Zablocki, Benjamin, and Thomas Robbins, eds. *Misunderstanding Cults: Searching for Objectivity in a Controversial Field.* Toronto, 2001. A collection of essays presenting contrasting views of brainwashing theory in a debate format.

David G. Bromley (2005)

BRANCH DAVIDIANS.

On February 28, 1993, the United States Bureau of Alcohol, Tobacco, and Firearms (ATF) staged a raid on the home and church of a millennialist, sectarian group outside of Waco, Texas. The thoroughly bungled attempt to serve a search warrant took the lives of four ATF agents and six members of the millennialist group and led to a fifty-one day siege that climaxed with a devastating fire that claimed seventy-four more lives. Although many of the people within the Mount Carmel Center simply saw themselves as students of the Bible, particularly the apocalyptic message of the book of *Revelation,* they became known to the public as Branch Davidians and followers of the self-proclaimed messiah, David Koresh.

Beginnings. The group that gathered around Koresh had a long history in the Waco area, and an even longer history before that. With only a few exceptions, Koresh's disciples had religious roots in the Seventh-day Adventist tradition, which itself grew out of the Millerite movement of the mid-nineteenth century. After painstaking study of the scriptures, William Miller (1782–1849) had come to the conclusion that the second coming of Jesus Christ would occur sometime between March 21, 1843, and March 21, 1844. When the second date passed without incident, the Millerites recalculated the date to October 22, 1844. The failure of Jesus to reappear on that second date provoked what came to be known as the "Great Disappointment," but it only diffused rather than decreased the general Adventist fervor. By the end of 1845, a small group of New Hampshire Millerites had begun to observe the Sabbath on the seventh day, Saturday, and to fashion a new understanding of Miller's prophecy. Led by Joseph Bates, James White, and Ellen G. Harmon, who would marry White in 1846, the group argued that October 22, 1844, had in fact been a crucial date for human salvation, because Jesus Christ had entered the heavenly temple on that day in preparation for the final judgment. His return would happen at an unspecified time in the future.

To their observance of the seventh-day Sabbath, Bates and the Whites added another distinctive theological tenet. They believed that God's will is revealed progressively and that each new generation could expect to receive its "present truth" or "new light." That doctrine introduced a dynamism into the Seventh-day Adventist tradition that would contribute to the schisms that eventually produced Koresh's group of Branch Davidians.

From Davidians to Branch Davidians. The Davidian Adventists, precursors to the Branch Davidians, originated in 1929 in the teaching of Victor Houteff. A Bulgarian immigrant to the United States, Houteff became a Seventh-day Adventist in 1918. His intensive study of biblical prophecy led him to two conclusions that conflicted with orthodox Adventist doctrine. First, he indicted the church for having become complacent and far too "worldly." Houteff believed that his divinely appointed task was to purify the church from within and to gather the 144,000 "servants of God" mentioned in *Revelation* 7 to wait for the imminent arrival of Jesus Christ. In addition, Houteff concluded that the coming Kingdom of God would be a literal, physical, millennial rule on earth, centered in the holy land of Palestine. Houteff's teaching attracted some of his fellow Adventists, but church elders quickly barred him from teaching and in 1934 officially removed him from membership.

Forced out of the mother church, Houteff named his movement the Davidian Seventh-day Adventists to emphasize their belief in the imminent restoration of a Davidic messianic kingdom in Palestine whose practices would closely follow those of traditional Judaism. Houteff came to see himself as the seventh and final link in a line of reformers including Martin Luther, Miller, and Ellen White. As relations between his group and the main body of Adventists worsened, Houteff excoriated the denomination as a heathen, apostate group; in 1935 he moved the Davidians to an isolated 189-acre parcel of land outside Waco and named their settlement Mount Carmel. Although the anticipated move to the holy land never materialized, Houteff led Bible studies every night and eventually conducted a vigorous proselytization program that sent out tracts to thousands of Seventh-day Adventists and sent missionaries to Adventist groups throughout the world.

When Houteff died in 1955, he was succeeded by his wife, Florence. Convinced that the end would come in 1959, she urged Davidians and Adventists all over the world to assemble at the new Mount Carmel Center near Elk, Texas, which the group had recently purchased. In April 1959 some nine hundred Davidians were gathered there. But, in an outcome reminiscent of the "Great Disappointment" of Miller's time, their expectations were frustrated. The numbers of faithful then quickly dwindled, and Florence Houteff herself moved away and became inactive.

Out of the infighting among those remaining in the 1960s, Ben Roden and his wife, Lois, eventually took control of the Mount Carmel property and became the leaders of the handful of stalwarts who still lived there. Like Miller, Ellen White, and Houteff before him, Ben Roden believed that he had a prophetic calling. He portrayed himself as the anointed "Branch" mentioned by Zechariah (*Zech.* 3:8; 6:12) who was to organize the theocratic kingdom in preparation for Christ's return. Roden revivified the group, adding the biblical festivals of Passover, Pentecost, and Tabernacles to their ritual calendar and renewing Houteff's publishing and missionary programs. On his death in 1978, Roden was succeeded by his wife as leader of the Branch Davidians, now a distinct offshoot from Houteff's movement.

Like her predecessors, Lois Roden also claimed special revelations. She taught that the Holy Spirit was a feminine figure and that the coming messiah would fully embody the female aspects of the divinity. Roden actively spread her new version of the Branch Davidian message through extensive missionary travels and the publication of a magazine named *SHEkinah,* after the feminine Hebrew word for the spirit or presence of God. Lois Roden was the leader of the Branch Davidians when David Koresh, then known as Vernon Howell, joined in 1981. Koresh's embrace of Lois Roden's teachings, the possibility that they formed an intimate personal relationship, and her implicit recognition of Koresh as her successor, sparked the enmity of Lois's son George, who had tried to establish himself in a leadership position during his mother's travels. Even before Lois's death in 1986, relations between George Roden and Koresh were hostile; by 1987 they flared into violence over George's bizarre challenge to Koresh that he could resurrect a long-dead member of the community. When Koresh and his armed followers tried to secure evidence of George Roden's grotesque practices, a gun battle erupted between the two groups. In the ensuing trial, Koresh's accomplices were found not guilty and the jury split on the question of Koresh's guilt, with the judge declaring a mistrial. After an unrelated incident, George Roden was found guilty of murder, declared insane, and sentenced to a state mental hospital. Koresh paid the back taxes on the property and his group took over the Mount Carmel Center.

THE BRANCH DAVIDIANS UNDER DAVID KORESH. Koresh's leadership of the Branch Davidians was founded on his ability to interpret the Bible. Many of those who lived with him at the Mount Carmel Center explicitly cited his unparalleled exegetical ability as the reason why they had taken up residence. Koresh's characteristic mode of teaching was the oral Bible study, often lasting several hours or more, in which he recited many portions of the text from memory, wove them together into a single apocalyptic scenario, and exhorted his students to prepare themselves for the coming end. Although much of his teaching resembled that of many other Christian millennialists, Koresh saw things in the Bible that no one before him had. Most notably, he saw himself. As a consequence of a 1985 experience of ascent into the heavens that happened while he was in Jerusalem, Koresh became convinced that he was the Lamb of God described in *Revelation* 4 and 5 as the only one who could open the scroll sealed with seven seals. Koresh also referred to himself as a "Christ," a person anointed by God to undertake a specific mission. He understood his calling to include not only preaching the message of the seven seals but also enacting the apocalyptic events foretold in that message.

In his Bible studies, Koresh impressed upon his students the imminence of the end and urged them to be ready to fight on behalf of God at the battle of Armageddon. Koresh expected the events prophesied in *Revelation* to unfold in the land of Israel very soon. But in the meantime, in the daily life of the Mount Carmel community, Koresh's authority depended less on his claim to the extraordinary experience of ascent into the heavens than it did on his repeated ability to make sense of the message of *Revelation* in his Bible studies. He frequently challenged his students to provide alternative readings of the text that they all shared; every time they accepted his interpretation, his authority was reinforced. The daily Bible studies were Koresh's most important tool for maintaining and enhancing his power, authority, and status within the group. It is an indication of his confidence in his mission, persuasiveness, and interpretive facility that Koresh maintained his position, but it is also an indication of his followers' deep yearning for a thorough renovation of the world that they continued to accept Koresh's teaching about the seven seals and to find in it the promise of their own salvation.

Koresh's hold on his followers could be breached, however. When Koresh proclaimed a "new light" revelation in 1989 that enjoined celibacy on all of his male followers and reserved all females for mating with him in order to produce children who would inherit an exalted status in the coming Kingdom of God, several members left the group. One of them, Marc Breault, would later be instrumental in spreading damaging information about Koresh both to media outlets and the United States government.

The February 28, 1993, assault unsettled the Branch Davidians' expectations. In some ways it seemed that the forces of "Babylon" had indeed begun the apocalyptic battle, but not where it was anticipated. During the fifty-one day siege, in addition to striving unfruitfully to explain his theological system to a series of negotiators sent in by the Federal Bureau of Investigation (FBI), Koresh attempted to fit the unfolding events into his scenario of the end. In an April 14 letter to his attorney, Koresh claimed that he had finally received "word from God" that he could write down his message of the seven seals and share it with the world. In that letter Koresh promised to finish his commentary as quickly as he could and then to come out of Mount Carmel to answer any questions about his actions. The FBI agents in command, however, did not take the offer seriously; the final assault was quickly authorized, and early on the morning of April 19, 1993, the sequence of events that initiated the catastrophic fire commenced. One of the nine people who escaped the flames carried with her a computer diskette of Koresh's unfinished work.

REVIEWING THE SIEGE. The siege that dramatically forced the Mount Carmel community out of its decades of obscurity was not inspired by theological issues. Acting on allegations that the residents of Mount Carmel were illegally turning semiautomatic weapons into automatic machine guns, the ATF had conducted surveillance of Mount Carmel and had begun planning to serve its search warrant. The affidavit in support of the warrant also included allegations that children were being abused by members of the group and that methamphetamines were being manufactured in Mount Carmel. In the later stages of their preparations, agents of the ATF were worried that the group would react negatively to a forthcoming investigative report by the *Waco Tribune-Herald* that cast Koresh as the "Sinful Messiah" who brainwashed his followers, sexually exploited women and young girls, and maintained a large, threatening arsenal.

The ATF's planning, the FBI's conduct of the siege, and the media's coverage of the ongoing drama were all influenced by powerful stereotypes developed by the American anticult movement over the previous two decades. Building primarily on the example of the 1978 murder/suicide of 914 people at the Peoples Temple Agricultural Mission in Jonestown, Guyana, a loose confederation of aggrieved parents, moral entrepreneurs, concerned mental health professionals, and other sympathizers had aggressively marketed the notion that all new religious movements or "cults" were led by dangerously unstable con men who destroyed the mental freedom of their members and could easily lead them to their death. The anticult caricatures so thoroughly shaped public and governmental understandings of the Branch Davidians that it still remains difficult to come to a balanced understanding of the siege and its aftermath, even after multiple government, academic, and other investigations, as well as several court cases.

In that context, the question of whether the Branch Davidians were illegally converting firearms largely fades into the background. Even if they were, the violation is typically punishable by a simple fine. Also, survivors of Mount Carmel vigorously dispute the claim that they were training for an apocalyptic war. They assert that the weapons were the lucrative hobby of a few members who sold them at gun shows for a profit. The affidavit's assertions about drug manufacturing have been totally discredited. But the accusations of child abuse have gained increasing support as the extent of Koresh's sexual involvement with young girls has come to light. Proper investigation and prosecution of those charges, however, would involve agencies other than the ATF.

The ATF has been severely criticized for both its planning and execution of the initial raid and for its failure to attempt to take Koresh into custody during his frequent trips off the property. Similarly, the FBI has been criticized for failing to take Koresh's religious concerns seriously and for quickly deciding that they were merely "Bible babble," but reorganizations within the bureau and the conduct of subsequent encounters, such as the 1996 Montana Freemen standoff, suggest a growing FBI sensitivity to religious factors. On the other hand, the anticult movement has seized upon "Waco" and subsequent events, such as the 1997 Heaven's Gate suicides and the 1995 Aum Shinrikyō attack in Tokyo, as further proof that all "cults" are prone to violence and must thus be constantly monitored and militantly opposed. In the minds of many, and despite more nuanced analyses, the Branch Davidians have been indelibly identified as a "cult" and Koresh stands as the paradigm of the manipulative "cult" leader who exploited his followers for his own gain.

After David Koresh. Although the April 19, 1993, fire virtually obliterated the Branch Davidian community, several people have tried to keep it alive. What remains of Mount Carmel has become both a memorial and a contested site. Though she no longer lives on the property, Amo Paul Bishop Roden, the former wife of George Roden, has abandoned neither her claims to Mount Carmel nor her claims of leadership of the Branch Davidians. Clive Doyle, who survived the fire in which his daughter died, lives in a trailer on the Mount Carmel site and leads a small group of survivors, but the claim of those faithful to Koresh to legal ownership of the property remains unsettled. Despite his own difficult economic circumstances, Doyle has helped erect a small chapel at Mount Carmel and to conduct the annual memorial services. From prison, Livingstone Fagan—who left Mount Carmel during the siege and, after a controversial 1994 trial, began serving a forty-year prison sentence (later reduced to fifteen) for his actions on February 28—continues to represent Koreshian orthodoxy in his self-published writings, including *Mt. Carmel: The Unseen Reality* (1994). Fagan remains convinced of Koresh's messianic mission and limits his own contribution to re-presentation and clarification of Koresh's message. Another imprisoned Branch Davidian, Renos Avraam (writing as the "Chosen Vessel"), has claimed divine approval to further develop Koresh's message of the seven seals. Appealing to the familiar Adventist concept of "present truth" or "new light," the Chosen Vessel emphasizes the limitations and inaccuracies of Koresh's message and claims that his book reveals the necessary new understanding of the imminent end. Both Fagan and the Chosen Vessel retain the apocalyptic expectations that have been so central to the Adventist and Branch Davidian traditions, but the Chosen Vessel claims an insight that eclipses even Koresh's. The development of Branch Davidian thought and practice after Koresh is fluid and multifaceted; some wait for Koresh's imminent resurrection, while others put forward innovative interpretations of his teaching about the seven seals. By all accounts, however, there has not been a substantial influx of converts into the movement since 1993.

Beyond the small circles of surviving and newly converted Branch Davidians and their sympathizers, the destruction of the Mount Carmel Center and the near extinction of the community have had other reverberations. Orthodox Seventh-day Adventist have reviewed events to see if they could identify why faithful Adventists would accept Koresh as a self-proclaimed messiah. Members of several other new religious movements have tried to distance themselves and their groups from association with Koresh's abusive leadership in order to insulate themselves from public criticism and potential governmental intervention. Some more extreme advocates of the right to bear arms have made the Branch Davidians into symbols of the damaging effects of the United States government's efforts to curtail individual freedoms. Most noteworthy among the latter group is Timothy McVeigh, who was executed in 2001 for his role in the 1995 bombing of the Alfred P. Murrah federal building in Oklahoma City. McVeigh explicitly characterized his actions as revenge for what the government had done at Waco.

The Branch Davidians did not cease to exist after the trauma of the destruction of the Mount Carmel Center. Some of the survivors have struggled to rebuild their lives and to stay together as a worshiping community, despite their radically diminished membership. Writing from prison, their theologians have endeavored to keep the message of the seven seals alive, even as they have contended over its adequacy for the present time. For some Seventh-day Adventists, the events at Waco provide a cautionary tale about the consequences of accepting false messiahs. For other new religious movements the destruction of the Mount Carmel Center raises the specter of the awesome power of the state to crush religious innovation. And for the shadowy and overlapping subcultures of self-styled patriots, constitutionalists, militia members, and other denizens of the radical right, the Branch Davidians' fate remains the embodiment of their worst fears about a rogue government turning its military might against its own citizens. The remaining Branch Davidians continue to voice their own millennial hopes, and they also serve as a point of reference for the millennial expectations of others.

SEE ALSO Aum Shinrikyō; Heaven's Gate; Koresh, David; New Religious Movements, overview article, articles on New Religious Movements and Violence, New Religious Movements and Millennialism; Seventh-day Adventism; White, Ellen Gould.

BIBLIOGRAPHY

Docherty, Jayne Seminare. *Learning Lessons from Waco: When the Parties Bring Their Gods to the Negotiating Table.* Syracuse, N.Y., 2001. A thorough treatment of the negotiations between the FBI and the Branch Davidians.

Faubion, James D. *The Shadows and Lights of Waco: Millennialism Today.* Princeton, 2001. An anthropologist's self-reflective study of Amo Paul Bishop Roden's relationship to the Mount Carmel site and the Branch Davidian movement.

Gallagher, Eugene V. "'Theology Is Life and Death': David Koresh on Violence, Persecution, and the Millennium." In *Millennialism, Persecution, and Violence: Historical Cases*, edited by Catherine Wessinger, pp. 82–100. Syracuse, N.Y., 2000. Includes an analysis of Koresh's Bible studies and his unfinished manuscript.

Gallagher, Eugene V. "The Persistence of the Millennium: Branch Davidian Expectations of the End after 'Waco.'" *Nova Religio* 3 (2000): 303–319. Examines the writings of Livingstone Fagan and the Chosen Vessel.

Hall, John R. *Apocalypse Observed: Religious Movements and Violence in North America, Europe, and Japan.* New Brunswick, N.J., 2000. Sets the events at Waco in comparative and theoretical perspective.

Hamm, Mark S. *Apocalypse in Oklahoma: Waco and Ruby Ridge Revenged.* Boston, 1997. Traces the impact of Waco on the radical right.

Haus, Cari Hoyt, and Madlyn Lewis Hamblin. *In the Wake of Waco: Why Were Adventists among the Victims?* Hagerstown, Md., 1993.

Lewis, James R., ed. *From the Ashes: Making Sense of Waco.* Lanham, Md., 1994. An early collection of essays including some primary documents.

Moore, Carol. *The Davidian Massacre: Disturbing Questions about Waco Which Must Be Answered.* Franklin, Tenn., 1995. A thorough critique of the government's actions by a libertarian activist.

Reavis, Dick J. *The Ashes of Waco: An Investigation.* New York, 1995. A journalist's vivid account.

Swett, Mark, ed. *Waco Never Again!* An exhaustive electronic archive of writings from Branch Davidians. Includes transcripts of Koresh's Bible studies, Fagan's works, and other materials. Available at http://home.maine.rr.com/waco.

Tabor, James D., and Eugene V. Gallagher. *Why Waco? Cults and the Battle for Religious Freedom in America.* Berkeley, Calif., 1995. Contains Koresh's unfinished commentary on the seven seals, and a thorough presentation of Branch Davidian theology.

Thibodeau, David, and Leon Whiteson. *A Place Called Waco: A Survivor's Story.* New York, 1999. An insider's story that disputes many accepted interpretations of what happened inside Mount Carmel.

Wessinger, Catherine. *How the Millennium Comes Violently: From Jonestown to Heaven's Gate.* New York, 2000. Provides the best short description of the events of the siege and attempts to isolate factors that promote violent interactions.

Wright, Stuart A., ed. *Armageddon in Waco: Critical Perspectives on the Branch Davidian Conflict.* Chicago, 1995. An important collection of essays on the history, context, and interactions of the Branch Davidians with law enforcement, the media, and the courts.

EUGENE V. GALLAGHER (2005)

BRANDON, S. G. F. (1907–1971), English historian of religions and of the early Christian church. Born in Devonshire, Samuel George Frederick Brandon was trained for the priesthood of the Church of England at the College of the Resurrection, Mirfield, during which time he also studied history at the University of Leeds. He was graduated in 1930 and was ordained two years later. After seven years as a parish priest in the west of England, he became in 1939 a chaplain in the British army, serving in the European and North African campaigns and taking part in the Dunkirk evacuation. He remained in the regular army until 1951, when he was appointed professor of comparative religion at the University of Manchester despite a lack of previous academic teaching experience; he held the post until his death.

Brandon's work centered on two areas. The first and more controversial was the early history of the Christian church. Here he took with the utmost seriousness the older theory of a conflict in the early church between a Petrine, Jewish group and a Pauline, gentile community, the latter gaining the upper hand only after 70 CE. This was the theme of his first book, *The Fall of Jerusalem and the Christian Church* (1951). Over a decade later he returned to the subject of Christian origins in *Jesus and the Zealots* (1967) and *The Trial of Jesus of Nazareth* (1968), in which he emphasized that Jesus had been executed by the Romans for sedition, and drew parallels between Jesus' followers and the violent anti-Roman movements of the time. Coming as they did at a highly volatile period in Western religious history, these books gained him a considerable (and to Brandon, unwelcome) radical following, and much international attention, owing to reports in *Time, Newsweek,* and other newsmagazines.

Brandon's other major interest was centered on the belief that religion is a human response to the inexorable passage of time. His thesis was stated in *Time and Mankind* (1951), and was repeated in various ways in such books as *Man and His Destiny in the Great Religions* (1962), *History, Time, and Deity* (1965), and *The Judgment of the Dead* (1967). Wider interests were revealed in *A Dictionary of Comparative Religion* (1970), planned, edited, and to a great extent written by him, and in his last work, published after his death, *Man and God in Art and Ritual* (1975). Here the focus shifted to iconography, but the underlying theme remained that of history and time.

In 1970 Brandon was elected general secretary of the International Association for the History of Religions, but his unexpected death a little more than a year later prevented him from exercising any permanent influence on that organization.

Despite his years as a parish priest and chaplain, after 1951 Brandon virtually lost touch with the church, and as a professor he had no interest in Christian apologetics. He was a historian pure and simple, who saw Western religion as having been in irreversible decline since the high Middle Ages, and who believed that understanding of religious traditions could be gained only from a study of their origins. His view of the interrelations of religion and the sense of time was undoubtedly valid; however, being uninterested in psychology, philosophy, or phenomenology—or in methodological questions generally—he seldom carried his investigations far enough. Although he was a disciplined scholar and a fastidious writer, his mind lacked flexibility, and his short academic career can now be seen as having marked the end of the era of traditional comparative religion in Britain. In the area of Christian origins, his views were too controversial to win ready acceptance, but it was important that he drew attention to the political setting of early Christianity, a field in which much work remains to be done.

BIBLIOGRAPHY

Sharpe, Eric J. "S. G. F. Brandon, 1907–1971." *History of Religions* 12 (August 1972): 71–74.

Sharpe, Eric J. "Comparative Religion at the University of Manchester, 1904–1979." *Bulletin of the John Rylands Library* (Manchester) 63 (Autumn 1980): 144–170.

Sharpe, Eric J., and J. R. Hinnells, eds. *Man and His Salvation: Studies in Memory of S. G. F. Brandon.* Manchester, 1973. Includes a personal appreciation of Brandon by H. C. Snape, a summary of Brandon's contribution to scholarship by E. O. James, and a bibliography of Brandon's works.

Simon, Marcel. "S. G. F. Brandon, 1907–1971." *Numen* 19 (August-December 1972): 84–90.

ERIC J. SHARPE (1987)

BREAD. We learn from the *Epic of Gilgamesh* that bread was offered to the gods over five thousand years ago. Since that time, wherever grain has been cultivated, bread has held a place of honor in rituals. Bread is the staff of life and often, as in the Lord's Prayer, stands for food in general.

Raised bread was invented by the Egyptians, who made it the basis of their administrative system. Although the Israelites used bread in many of their religious rites and the Greeks honored a bread goddess, it was Jesus who exalted bread to the highest religious value when he said, "This is my body."

In early agricultural societies, the first fruits of the harvest were offered to the gods (cf. *Lv.* 23:15–22). For the harvest feast, Shavu'ot, the Feast of Weeks, the Israelites were instructed to bring two loaves of bread made of wheaten flour as an oblation to Yahveh. Because the festival occurred fifty days (seven weeks) after Passover, it came to be known by the Greek name *Pentecost* and commemorated the giving of the Law at Sinai.

Ḥag ha-Matsot, the Feast of Unleavened Bread, was one of the three great agricultural festivals celebrated by the Israelites after they settled in Canaan. Originally a rite of thanksgiving at the beginning of the grain harvest, it was later linked to the nomadic pastoral feast of Passover as a historical commemoration of Israel's deliverance from Egypt. For seven days, only unleavened bread was eaten, as a sign of a new beginning (cf. *1 Cor.* 5:6–8).

Somewhat similar to first fruits was the "bread of the presence" (shewbread), which the Israelites laid out before the Holy of Holies in the Temple (*Lv.* 24:5–9). Twelve cakes of pure wheaten flour, representing the twelve tribes of Israel and their unending covenant with Yahveh, were placed on a table in two lines. Each Sabbath they were replaced and then eaten by the priests. Because incense was burned while the loaves were being replaced, scholars have viewed the bread as either a sacrificial or a thanks offering.

From the seventh century BCE, the Greeks celebrated the mysteries of Demeter, the bread goddess of Eleusis, whose cult was the established religion of Athens. Demeter was also the intercessor in the realm of the dead. Her two roles were complementary, for grain must die in the earth before it regenerates. Little else is known about the Eleusinian mysteries because adherents took a vow of secrecy.

Bread was among the food offerings that the ancient Egyptians provided for their deceased. An incantation in the *Book of Going Forth by Day* was to be recited if an enemy challenged the deceased's right to bread. In the *Book of Tobit* (4:18), Tobias is told to "be generous with bread and wine on the graves of virtuous men."

The ritual use of bread may have originated as an offering of nourishment to the deity. But since the God of the Israelites refused all nourishment (*Jgs.* 13:16), the loaves became a symbol of communion between Yahveh and his people. In cultures where bread was the staple of life, it was natural that communion be symbolized by the sharing of bread, since eating together has always been a sign of fellowship.

Bread was elevated to a symbol of supreme importance when Jesus spoke of himself as the "bread of life" that would give eternal life to those who believed in him, quite unlike the manna that the followers of Moses fed upon in the desert (*Jn.* 6). In New Testament accounts of sharing bread at a meal, a recurrent series of words (*took, gave thanks* or *blessed, broke,* and *gave*) describes the actions of Jesus at the Last Supper when he instituted the Eucharist. By the ritual act of breaking bread (*Acts* 2:42, 20:7) and eating it, Christians would become one with Christ and his Father in heaven.

The bread that becomes the body of Christ has an interesting parallel among the Aztec, who made a doughlike paste from the crushed seeds of the prickly poppy and molded it into a figure of the god Huitzilopochtli. The ritual involved "god-eating": the bread body was broken into pieces and eaten.

Bread presented by the faithful for the Eucharist but not used for that purpose was called the *eulogia.* The bishop blessed it and had it distributed to catechumens and to absent members of the community. By the fourth century, Christians were sending the *eulogia* to one another as a symbol of their union. Hippolytus of Rome (170–235) pointed to another sign of the special unity that bound early Christians together when he spoke of the bread of exorcism that should be given to catechumens in place of eucharistic bread.

Bread as a symbol has also had negative aspects. The good wife does not eat the "bread of idleness" (*Prv.* 31:27). The ungodly "eat the bread of wickedness" (*Prv.* 4:17). The "bread of deceit" has a sweet taste but leaves the mouth full of gravel (*Prv.* 20:17). Yahveh, when angry with his people, sends the "bread of adversity" (*Is.* 30:20) or the "bread of tears" (*Ps.* 80:5). These expressions evolved from a recollection of God's curse on Adam, who was to earn his bread by the sweat of his brow (*Gn.* 3:19).

SEE ALSO Leaven.

BIBLIOGRAPHY

Borgen, Peder. *Bread from Heaven: An Exegetical Study of the Concept of Manna in the Gospel of John and the Writings of Philo.* Leiden, 1965. A careful study of John's sixth chapter in relation to Jewish concepts about the "bread from heaven."

Jacob, Heinrich E. *Six Thousand Years of Bread: Its Holy and Unholy History.* Garden City, N.Y., 1944. A popular history that should be used with caution.

New Sources

Broshi, Magen. *Bread, Wine, Walls, and Scrolls.* New York, 2001.

Douglas, Mary. "The Eucharist: Its Continuity with the Bread Sacrifice of *Leviticus*." *Modern Theology* (April 15, 1999): 209–224.

Kelly, Tony. *The Bread of God: Nurturing a Eucharistic Imagination.* Linguori, Mo., 2001.

JAMES E. LATHAM (1987)
Revised Bibliography

BREATH AND BREATHING.

The concept of breath figures prominently in the development of thought in many religions. Egyptian *ka,* Hebrew *nefesh* and *ruah,* Greek *psuchē* and *pneuma,* Latin *anima* and *spiritus,* Sanskrit *prana,* Chinese *qi,* Polynesian *mana,* and Iroquoian *orenda* all demonstrate that the theme of breath has had a major place in humanity's quest for religious understanding. Moreover, theological conceptions of breath have led many of the world's traditions to feature respiratory exercises in their religious disciplines, especially in Asia and among groups influenced directly or indirectly by practices from the Indian subcontinent.

BREATH AND THE RELIGIOUS UNDERSTANDING OF HUMANITY. The centrality of breath in defining humanity has focused on understanding what it is that gives humans life and under what circumstances humans define their own deaths. Moreover, the theme of breath, along with related notions of vitality and energy, has been associated with views of the soul and with questions regarding the mortal and immortal aspects of human life.

Greek views. Although the theme of breath is seldom mentioned by Plato and Aristotle, some of their predecessors, for whom the universe was a quasi-living organism, saw air, wind, or breath as central to the definition of the soul. Pre-Socratic philosophers identified two qualities of the soul, movement and knowledge. Empedocles, for example, believed that because the soul knows all natural things, and because natural things can be analyzed into four constituent parts—fire, air, water, and earth—the soul must be made up of a combination of these four elements, together with the principles of love and strife.

Diogenes, taking up the position of the Ionians (one of whom, Anaximenes, described the soul as having an airlike nature that guides and controls the living being), credited air itself with sentience and intelligence. For Diogenes, air was the element most capable of originating movement, because it was the finest element in grain; in this characteristic, he thought, lay the grounds of the soul's own powers of knowing and of originating movement. Moreover, he stated, the internal air in the body had an important role in the functioning of each of the sense organs. Similarly, some of the Pythagoreans believed that the particles in the air, or the force that moved them, were soul, and Heraclitus declared that the soul as first principle was a "warm exhalation" of which everything else was composed.

Of the words Plato used for "soul," including *nous, sōma, psuchē,* and *genesis, psuchē* was the closest to a concept that incorporated breath. In Homer, *psuchē* refers to the life that is lost at death, as well as to the shade or wraith that lives on. Like the ancient Egyptian *ka* ("breath"), the "double" of humanity that was born with humans but survived death and remained close to the tomb, the Homeric soul was an airy, ethereal entity identified with the breath of life. In Plato, however, *psuchē* designates a comprehensive personal soul, the divine aspect of humanity that is the seat of rational intelligence and moral choice, entirely separate from the body. Although, from the beginning of Greek philosophy, *psuchē* referred to the "life force" in all its psychosomatic connotations, it was not always related to breath per se. Because Greek philosophy placed such a premium on the intellectual life of the soul, the "breath of life" came to be relegated to a place of little stature.

Biblical views. In the Bible, the role of breath rests on several concepts: *ruaḥ, neshamah, nefesh, psuchē,* and *pneuma.* Of these, *nefesh* and *psuchē* refer specifically to the individual as the subject of life, while *ruaḥ* and *pneuma* refer to a more generic understanding of breath as a symbol of life and even as life itself.

The Hebrew term *ruaḥ* means "breath, wind," or "spirit." As a concept of nature, it refers to the winds of the four directions, as well as to the wind of heaven. For humans as a species, *ruaḥ* is a general principle, covering such things as the physical breath that issues from the mouth and nostrils, words carried forth on this breath, animated emotions (such as agitation, anger, vigor, courage, impatience, bitterness, troubled disposition, discontent, uncontrollable impulse, and jealousy), and, occasionally, mental activity and moral character. *Ruaḥ* is also the spirit in humans that gives them life; because this spirit is created and preserved by God, it is thus understood to be God's spirit (the *ruaḥ elohim* of *Genesis* 1:2), which is breathed into humans at the time of creation. Biblical literature sees evidence of God's spirit in such phenomena as prophecy (whereby human beings utter instructions or warnings), ecstatic states of frenzy and possession, and situations of authority through which divine wisdom is revealed.

The term *neshamah,* although used considerably less often than *ruaḥ,* nevertheless carries many of the same meanings: the breath of God as wind (hot, cold, life creating, or life destroying), the breath of humans as breathed into them by God, and breath as found in every living thing.

The individual soul of humans is usually designated by the term *nefesh.* From a root probably meaning "to breathe" (cf. Akkadian *napashu,* "expand"), *nefesh* occasionally designates the neck or throat (which opens for breathing), but is more often the concrete sign of life, the breathing substance, and then the soul or inner being, in man. Moreover, since the living are distinguished from the dead by breath, *nefesh* indicates the individual, the person or "I," which after death goes to She'ol. As the life force in individual beings, *nefesh* is mentioned in referring to both animals and humans, and is that which makes flesh alive. The relation between *neshama,* as "breath," and *nefesh,* denoting "person," is seen in *Genesis* 2:7: "Then the Lord God formed man of dust from the ground, and breathed into his nostrils the breath [*neshamah*] of life; and man became a living being [*nefesh*]." This belief in the unity of body and soul is continued from the biblical period into later Jewish philosophy.

Like *ruaḥ, pneuma* in the New Testament denotes "spirit," and it refers both to the Holy Spirit and the spirit of an individual person, as well as to the evil spirits or demons that are responsible for mental illness. Although it has the same psychosomatic implications as *ruah,* its ties to the notion of breath are less obvious.

The New Testament term *psuchē,* on the other hand, although it continues to carry the old Greek sense of life force, corresponds more to the Hebrew notion of breath of life than it does to its use in Plato or the pre-Socratics. Like *nefesh, psuchē* is the individual soul, the "I" that feels, loves, and desires, and that lives only because it has been infused with breath. Nevertheless, under Greek influence, the *nefesh*-become-*psuche* concept was gradually opposed to the mortal body and used to designate the immortal principle in humans.

Breath is of little importance in later Christian investigations of the soul. Tertullian, however, relying on the Stoic tradition, emphasized the union of soul and body, and said that the soul is "born of the breath of God, immortal, corporeal, and representable"—though it was only Adam's soul that was created by God, as all others have come into being by an act of generation.

Islamic views. Arabic terms related to breath parallel the Hebrew. In pre-Qur'anic poetry, for example, *nafs* is the "self" or "person" and *rūḥ* is breath and wind. Beginning with the Qur'ān, *nafs* takes on the additional meaning of "soul," while *rūḥ* comes to refer to an angel, or heavenly messenger, or to a special divine quality. The two words are eventually synonymous in post-Qur'anic literature, where they refer equally to the human spirit, to angels, and to *jinn* (supernatural beings). The term *nafas,* "breath" and "wind," is cognate to *nafs* through its root and to *rūḥ* in some meanings. It first appears in Islamic literary history in the early poetry.

Classical Islamic philosophy gives a central role to breath in the perfection of humanity within the cosmos. According to Ibn Sina, God created the left side of the heart, the main organ of breathing, to be a source and storehouse for breath, which is the rallying point for the faculties of the soul and the conveyor of these faculties to various parts of the body. Breath begins as a divine emanation moving from potentiality to actuality, proceeding without interruption until each form is complete and perfect. There is one breath that acts as the origin of the others; this principal breath arises in the heart and moves throughout the body, giving its parts their proper temperament. It is identified with the force of life itself and is thus the link between the bodily and spiritual aspects of an individual's being. The principal breath of humans, then, makes possible the perfect equilibrium and balance of the elements—a condition necessary for the manifestation of the divine.

Hindu views. The Sanskrit term *prāṇa* is a word of broad import that can refer to breath, respiration, life, vitality, wind, energy, and strength. In general, it is used in the plural to indicate the vital breaths in the body, but is also related to speculation about the individual soul. Early Indian literature proposed a variety of notions about the relation between human breath (*prāṇa*), its natural correlate the atmospheric wind, and the cosmic order. The most important of these equated the atmospheric wind with the breath of Puruṣa, the cosmic man (*Ṛgveda* 10.90.13) who was, like the Egyptian god Amun, a deity manifest in the wind and, as breath, the mysterious source of life in men and animals.

Indian medical theory, the basis for *haṭhayoga,* identifies five *prāṇas* operative within the body: *prāṇa,* the "breath of the front," or thoracic breath, which ensures respiration and swallowing; *udāna,* the "breath that goes upward," which produces speech; *samāna,* "concentrated breath," which provides air to the internal "cooking" fire for digesting food; *apāna,* the "breath that goes downward," or abdominal breath, which controls the elimination of urine and feces; and *vyāna,* the "diffused breath," which circulates throughout the entire body and distributes the energy derived from food and breath. The general process of inhalation and exhalation is referred to by the compound *prāṇāpānau.*

In addition, there are five subsidiary "winds" or *vāyūs*: *nāga,* which relieves abdominal pressure through belching; *kūrma,* which controls the movements of the eyelids, thereby preventing foreign matter and bright light from entering the eyes; *kṛkara,* which controls sneezing and coughing, thereby preventing substances from passing up the nasal passages and down the throat; *devadatta,* which provides for the intake of extra oxygen into the tired body by causing a yawn; and *dhanaṃjaya,* which remains in the body after death, often bloating up the corpse.

There is some debate about the relation of yogic *prāṇa* to the cosmic forces in the universe. In modern literature on yoga, *prāṇa,* even in the compound *prāṇāyāma,* "the restraint of breath," is often interpreted as a subtle psychic force or cosmic element. This is not borne out by the early texts, however, and Patañjali, who provided the first real exposure to yoga, uses the term *prāṇāyāma* to refer only to respiratory movements. Later *haṭhayoga* texts do use the word *prāṇa* to indicate a subtle psychic force, but this is the force awakened by the process of *prāṇāyāma* and not *prāṇāyāma* itself.

The Brāhmaṇas and Upaniṣads equate breath, as "vital breath," with the *ātman* or soul (cf. German *Atem,* "breath") and with *brahman,* the cosmic essence. The vital air in the upper part of the body is here thought to be immortal and to be the inspirer of thoughts. Moreover, it is by the breath of his mouth that Prajapāti created the gods and by the *prāṇa* of his lower body that he created the demons. Finally, in the Vedic sacrifice, bricks for the altar are sniffed by the sacrificial horse, who thereby bestows "breath" upon them—explained as a "sniff-kiss" in which the horse transfers beneficent power to ritual objects.

Chinese views. In ancient China, each person was thought to have two souls, both composed of very subtle matter: the *hun* ("air soul") came from the upper air and was received back into it at death, while the *po* ("earth soul") was generated by the earth below and sank back at the end to mingle with it. Of the two, it was the *hun* that was the object of ancestor worship. This two-part system corresponded to the *yinyang* equilibrium, the *hun* soul being the *yang* aspect, in which the spiritual dominates, and the *po* being the *yin* aspect, in which the demonic dominates. In later tradition, the *hun* soul was thought to give rise to the seminal and mental essences, while the *po* was responsible for the existence of the flesh and bones of the body.

BREATH AND RELIGIOUS DISCIPLINES. Many of the major religious traditions are familiar with some type of respiratory practice. The oldest known and most comprehensive of these breathing disciplines is that of Hindu yoga, from which the disciplines of Jainism and Buddhism are derived. Some scholars have suggested that other traditions as well (particularly Daoism and Islam) have been influenced, at least in part, by Indian practices.

Hindu yoga. The Indian science of respiratory discipline, *prāṇāyāma,* fits within the larger complex of Hindu yoga, the most important type of which, for understanding breath control, is *haṭhayoga.* In general, yoga has as its goal the steady control of the senses and mind, leading to the abolition of normal consciousness and to freedom from delusion. *Prāṇāyāma,* the rhythmic control of the breath, is the fourth in the traditional eight states of yoga, coming after *āsana,* posture, and before *pratyāhāra,* withdrawal of the senses. Its main purpose is to change the ordinarily irregular flow of breath—which can be upset by indigestion, fever, cough, and cold, or by emotions like fear, anger, and lust—by bringing the breath under conscious control so that its rhythm becomes slow and even and respiratory effort is eliminated. By means of *prāṇāyāma* not only are the lungs cleansed and aerated, the blood oxygenated, and the nerves purified, but longevity as well as subtle states of consciousness leading to spiritual release are promoted. Although *prāṇāyāma* came to be a yogic exercise of great importance, Patañjali allots only three *sūtras* to it (1.34, 2.29, 2.49). The technical details for *prāṇāyāma* were then elaborated in the commentaries of Vyāsa, Bhoja, and Vācaspati Miśra, and especially in the classical works on *haṭhayoga.*

Although extraordinary feats resulting from respiratory discipline have been documented in numerous sources, including submersion in water or burial alive for unbelievable lengths of time, more frequent mention is made of the dangerous results of improper breathing. Practitioners are cautioned to undertake *prāṇāyāma* only under the instruction of a knowledgeable teacher, and to proceed with the exercises very slowly at first and according to their own capacity; otherwise they will incur disease or even death. By improper practice of *prāṇāyām,* for example, a pupil can introduce disorders into his system, such as hiccups, wind, asthma, cough, catarrh, pains in the head, eyes, and ears, and severe nervous irritation; by proper practice, however, one is freed from these and most other diseases. The classic example of improper respiratory discipline is that of the nineteenth-century Hindu saint Rama-krishna. When he was young, Ramakrishna's practice of yoga almost always ended in blackout. He later developed bloodshot eyes, then bleeding of the gums, and finally the cancer of the throat from which he died. In this regard, the classical tradition holds that when *prāṇāyāma* is too intensive, that is, when the body becomes overloaded with *prāṇa,* colored flames dance before the eyes and blackout inevitably occurs.

The respiratory rhythm of *prāṇāyāma* is measured in units of time called *mātrāprāmāṇa,* one *mātrā* being the time necessary for one respiration. This rhythm is achieved by harmonizing the three basic activities of inhalation (*pūraka*), retention of breath (*kumbhaka*), and exhalation (*recaka*). The most favored proportion of *pūraka* to *kumbhaka* to *recaka* is 1:4:2, although other traditions recommend 1:2:2 (for beginners) or an equal measure for all three parts. Still another tradition recommends that beginners not practice *kumbhaka* at all. Although this particular terminology is not used by either Patañjali or Vyāsa, it is traditional in *haṭhayoga* texts, where *kumbhaka* alone can sometimes refer to all three respiratory processes. A more detailed analysis describes two different states of "breath retention," *antara kumbhaka,* when breathing is suspended after full inspiration (the lungs being full), and *bāhya kumbhaka,* when breathing is suspended after full exhalation (the lungs being empty).

The technique of *prāṇāyāma* is thought to transform the natural processes already at work in the body. It is believed that every living creature breathes the prayer "So'ham" ("The immortal spirit, he am I") with each inward breath, and "'Hamsah" ("I am he, the immortal Spirit") with each outgoing breath. This unconscious repetitive prayer goes on throughout life, and is to be brought into full consciousness through the discipline that begins with breathing.

Prāṇāyāma should be undertaken only when the third stage of yoga has been mastered, for it is only when correct posture has been achieved and complete relaxation has set in that breath can be made to flow freely. The student of *prāṇāyāma* should be sure that the bowels and bladder are empty, and especially that the stomach has little or no food in it when he or she begins the practice: for the physical culturist, *prāṇāyāma* should take place at least one half hour before the next meal and four and a half hours after the last; for the spiritual culturist, one meal a day is best, but at least six hours should have elapsed since the last meal was eaten. For serious students, *prāṇāyāma* should be practiced four times a day (early morning, noon, evening, and midnight), with a count of eighty cycles per sitting. The best seasons to begin are spring and fall, when the climate is equable, and the best place to practice is one that is well ventilated but without a strong draft. Traditionally *prāṇāyāma* was performed on a carpet of *kuśa* grass covered with a deer hide and then with a clean thick cloth, but current rules prescribe a folded blanket on the floor. The eyes should be fixed in a special gaze (usually directed ahead or at the tip of the nose), while the mind is passive but alert. The breathing itself is directed through the nostrils only, not through the mouth. Specific rules for *prāṇāyāma* differ according to the authority in question, but in most treatises, special respiratory rules are given for pregnant women and those just completing childbirth.

Breath is made to flow through the yogin's body by an elaborate system of controls designed to prevent internal damage: the *bandhas* are postures in which certain organs or parts of the body are contracted and controlled; the *nāḍīs* are tubular channels in the body through which the breath energy flows; and the *cakras* are the flywheels controlling the body's machinery. The three most important *bandhas* are the *jālandhara bandha* ("chin lock"), whereby the chin is pressed against the chest and the abdomen is withdrawn; the *uḍḍīyāna bandha* ("raising of the diaphragm"), whereby the diaphragm is pulled up and the abdominal organs are brought against the back and held toward the spine; and the *mūla bandha* ("anal contraction"), whereby the sphincter muscle is tightened. These postures affect what most authorities believe are the seventy-two thousand *nadis*, along which the breath or life current flows to all parts of the body. Some *nāḍīs* are more important than others, the single most important being the *suṣumna,* identified with the spinal cord. The breath energy flowing through the *nāḍīs* is then regulated by the *cakras*, control points placed at crucial locations in the body.

Respiratory discipline is central in bringing about the unification of consciousness, the goal of yoga. From an early period, mind and breath were held to be intimately connected, and the arousal or cessation of one was known to affect the other. Patañjali, for example, recommended *prāṇāyāma* for achieving equanimity and inner peace, and Bhoja noted that through the suspension of sense activity, breath control could bring about single-pointed concentration (the fifth stage of yoga, *pratyāhāra*). The classical image used here is that of the chariot, according to which the mind is a chariot yoked to a pair of powerful horses, one of which is breath (*prāṇa*), the other, desire. The chariot moves in the direction of the more powerful animal; if breath prevails, desires are controlled, but if desires prevail, breath becomes irregular. Through *prāṇāyāma*, which ensures the controlled progress of the chariot, the advanced yogins can penetrate the four basic structures of consciousness—waking, sleeping with dreams, sleeping without dreams, and the *tuīya* state—thereby unifying all four within themselves.

With the development of Tantrism, the yogic disciplines of posture and breath control were combined with sexual practices that served to unite the practitioner with cosmic energy or *śakti*, as symbolized by the great goddess. According to Tantric texts, the object of *prāṇāyāma* is to arouse *kuṇḍalinī*, the divine cosmic force in the body, symbolized by a coiled and sleeping serpent that lies dormant in the lowest nerve center (*cakra*) at the base of the spinal column. Once aroused by *prāṇāyāma*, this energy rises up through the spinal column, piercing each *cakra* on its way until it reaches the head and there unites with the supreme soul.

Buddhist meditation. For Therāvada Buddhists, respiratory discipline is counted as part of the contemplation of the body—*ānapānasati* ("mindfulness of breathing"). The Pali canon describes the meditation as "mindfully he breathes in, mindfully he breathes out," and then enumerates sixteen ways in which mindful breathing can be practiced. The work begins with developing an awareness of "breathing in a long breath, breathing out a long breath, breathing in a short breath, breathing out a short breath," and continues through the practices until discursive thinking has been cut off and full concentration attained. Unlike yogic breathing techniques, however, Buddhist mindfulness of breath does not hold or control the breath but lets it come and go naturally, with the goal only to become fully aware of all states of the breathing process.

In Tibetan Buddhism, breathing is a part of the complex process of visualization by which a deity is mentally created in front of the practitioner out of his internal psychic elements. Tibetan Buddhists believe that breath or vitality in the body enters not only through the nose but also through the eyes, ears, mouth, navel, male or female organ, anus, and head and body hair pores. Since these "winds" act as a mount or basis for consciousness, the mind's scattering is stopped when they are restrained. Visualization, therefore, can proceed only when vitality (or breath) and exertion (or distraction) have been controlled. To achieve the mental stability needed for visualization, meditators are advised to practice "wind yoga," that is, to hold their breath—"hold the wind"—while simultaneously holding their mind on the divine body that is the object of meditation. When they can no longer retain the breath, they should let it out gently, see themselves clarified as the deity, and then hold their breathing again, keeping in mind, as before, one aspect of the deity. It is only when the mind is thus stabilized that the divine body will appear.

Daoist yoga. In China, breathing exercises go back to an early period. Laozi and Zhuangzi were familiar with a "methodical breathing," and a Chou dynasty inscription, dating from as early as the sixth century BCE, prescribes a precise collection and circulation of the breath inside the body that is designed to achieve long life. Also known were archaic shamanic techniques that imitated the movements and breathing of animals—a practice reflected later in the Daoist notion that the deep and silent breathing of ecstasy is like the breathing of animals in hibernation.

Unlike the many alchemical practices of Chinese tradition, which use aphrodisiacs to restore sexual activity, Daoist yoga aims primarily at restraining and rechanneling the sexual urges of the body. Through the regulation of breathing and other yogic techniques, the practitioner learns to sublimate the generative force that produces sexual fluid, and to prevent this fluid from following its normal course of satisfying desires and producing offspring. The correct method of breathing is essential in Daoist yoga, for it serves to circulate an inner fire through a microcosmic orbit and so immobilize the generative force, causing the genital organ to retract and stopping the drain of vitality caused by the emission of semen.

The ultimate purpose of stemming the generative force is to obtain *chang sheng* ("long life"), a state understood as a material immortality of the body. The practitioner begins by holding the breath through a period of 3, 5, 7, 9, and 12 normal respirations, then up to 120 or even more. To attain immortality, however, one must hold the breath through 1,000 respirations. The practitioner will, in the end, enter a state of serenity characterized by the qualities of *nianchu* ("thoughtlessness"), *xizhu* ("breathlessness"), *mozhu* ("pulselessness"), and *mie jin* ("unmindfulness of worldly existence").

Daoist respiratory disciplines are not, like *prāṇāyāma*, preliminary or auxiliary exercises in meditation to prepare the yogin for spiritual concentration but, rather, techniques that actually accomplish the purpose of the yoga itself: the indefinite prolongation of bodily life. The question whether there may be a historical relation between Daoist and Indian practices has not been resolved. Some scholars believe that Neo-Daoism borrowed from Tantric yoga practices. Others have noted that Daoism must have taken the notion of a physiological role of breath from India, for ancient Chinese medicine—Daoism's most likely source—had no such notion. Whatever the case, the results of both yogas are, in some instances, very similar, for the Daoist's ability to enter the water without drowning or walk on fire without being burned resemble Indian yogic powers or *siddhis*.

The aim of the breathing exercises is to try to return to the type of breathing experienced by the embryo in the womb; when the umbilical cord was cut at birth, this initial type of breathing was replaced by breathing through the nostrils. During the practice, inspiration and expiration are kept as quiet as possible, and breath is held closed up in the body—"swallowed," some texts say—until it is intolerable, and then let out through the mouth. "Embryonic breathing" or "immortal breathing" is thus a restoration of profound fetal breathing; it wipes out all postnatal conditions so that prenatal vitality can be transmuted and the seed of immortality nurtured. As a stage in the quest for immortal breath, the embryonic breathing of Daoism is not merely a checking of respiration, but an internal circulation of vital principles whereby the individual can remain completely airtight. If, however, breathing through the nostrils and mouth is used (and used randomly) in advanced stages of this yoga, then the psychic center in the heart will burst and the practitioner will become deranged.

Central to the yogic endeavor of Daoism is the theory of the five vital breaths located in the heart, spleen, lungs, liver, and kidneys that keep these organs functioning, and without which the body perishes. These vitalities have their source in the brain, and when they converge again in the head into one vitality, a golden light is made manifest. This system of vital breaths is held to correspond to the interaction in the body of the five basic elements: heart (fire), spleen or stomach (earth), lungs (metal), liver (wood), and kidneys (water).

The vital breaths are linked to one another by a network of eight main psychic channels that, when clear, have two distinct roles: the unimpeded flow of the generative force and the unrestricted circulation of the vital breaths. This network contains a microcosmic orbit with four cardinal points: at the root of the penis, where the generative force is gathered; at the top of the head; and at the two points between them in the spine and in the front of the body, where the generative force is cleansed and purified during the microcosmic orbiting.

Dysfunctional breathing in Daoism is designated by the "nine unsettled breaths." They are caused by anger, which lifts the breath, and fear, which lowers it; joy, which slows it down; grief, which disperses it; terror, which throws it out of gear; thinking, which ties it up; toil, which wastes it; cold, which collects it; and heat, which scatters it.

Islamic prayer. The Muslims belonging to the school of Ibn al-ʿArabi practiced a technique comparable to the *prāṇāyāma* of Hinduism. In breathing out, the words *lā-ilāha* ("There is no god") are formed, while the inward breath coincides with the words *illā Allāh* ("but God"), resulting in a profession of faith. Breath control is practiced by Islamic mystics in *dhikr* ("remembrance"), a practice dedicated to the glorification of God that repeats certain fixed phrases in a ritual order, either out loud or in the mind, and is accompanied by certain breathing and physical movements. Although it is not known exactly when methods of breath control (*ḥabs-i dam,* "keeping one's breath in recollection") were adopted into Sufism, there is a twelfth-century text prescribing the following: the breath is "emitted above the left breast (to empty the heart); then the word *lā* is exhaled from the navel (against the sexual demon); then *ilāha* is uttered on the right shoulder, and *illā* at the navel; finally *Allāh* is strongly articulated in the empty heart."

For the Ṣūfī, every breath that goes out without remembering God is "dead," while every breath that goes out in recollection of the Lord is "alive" and connected with him. In *dhikr* one is enjoined not to speak much but rather, in a variant form of the above text, to say, three times in one breath, "Lā ilāha illā Allāh" from the right side and then, having brought the breath down to the heart, to bring forth "Muḥammad rasūl Allāh" from the left side. The importance of breath regulation in *dhikr* to the advanced Ṣūfī is seen in the following example from Pashto poetry: "Thy every breath is a pearl and a coral of inestimable price / Be careful, therefore, and guard every respiration well!" Directions are given in various texts for the exact count and duration of the respiratory cycle in *dhikr,* and some sources state that the experienced mystic is often able to hold his breath for almost three hours. *Dhikr* is also used for healing purposes. Even in the early twenty-first century the recitation of the *Fātiḥah* or some other prayer, together with a "breathing upon" the sick, is common in the Muslim world.

The extent to which the breath control used by Ṣūfīs in their *dhikr* developed under the influence of Indian practices is not certain. It is known that regulated breathing existed among the Ṣūfīs of eastern Iran before Sufism spread to India, but in the later period when there was contact with India, yogic practices undoubtedly further colored numerous aspects of Ṣūfī life.

Christian prayer. Respiratory techniques similar to those used in Hindu yoga can be found in the Christian tradition of hesychasm. Hesychasm is a type of prayer in Eastern Christianity based on a control of physical faculties and a concentration on the Jesus Prayer to achieve peace of soul and union with God. Although the earliest descriptions of the hesychastic method of contemplation go back at least to the fifth century, to John of Jerusalem, the earliest datable combination of the Jesus Prayer with respiratory techniques is in the writings of Nikephoros the Solitary (fl. 1260). Nikephoros writes: "Sit down, compose your mind, introduce it—your mind, I say—into your nostrils; this is the road that the breath takes to reach the heart. Push it, force it to descend into your heart at the same time as the inhaled air. When it is there, you will see what joy will follow."

The traditional breath control that begins hesychastic contemplation is used, like *prāṇāyāma,* to prepare for mental prayer, that is, to bring about a "return of the mind." In a quiet cell, with the door closed, one sits in the corner and presses the (bearded) chin against the upper part of the chest, much as in the *jālandhara bandha* of Hindu yoga. One then directs the eye—and with it all the mind—to the navel, and compresses the inspiration of air in the nose so that normal breathing does not come easily, all the while ceaselessly repeating the Jesus Prayer: "Lord Jesus Christ, Son of God, have mercy on me!" This exercise prepares one for the attainment of absolute quietude of the soul and for the experience of divine light.

See Also Buddhist Meditation; Inspiration; Life; Meditation; Prāṇa; Samadhi; Yoga.

Bibliography

Good summaries of the role of breath in biblical theology can be found in *The Interpreter's Dictionary of the Bible,* 4 vols., edited by George A. Buttrick (New York, 1962), under such headings as "man," "soul," and "spirit." Likewise, important discussions of breath and the soul in Christian and Jewish theology appear in the *New Catholic Encyclopedia,* 17 vols. (New York, 1967), and in the *Encyclopaedia Judaica,* 16 vols. (Jerusalem, 1971). David B. Claus's *Toward the Soul: An Inquiry into the Meaning of* ΨυΧή *before Plato* (New Haven, Conn., 1981) is an important, but often very technical, survey of the development of the concept "psyche" in pre-Socratic thought. Jean Gouillard's *Petite Philocalie de la prière du cœur* (Paris, 1953), on the tradition of hesychasm, has a good bibliography and an excellent sampling of textual translations. On the respiratory technique in Islamic *dhikr,* see Louis Gardet's "La mention du nom divin, *dhikr,* dans la mystique musulmane," *Revue Thomiste* (Paris) 52 (1952): 642–679 and 53 (1953): 197–216.

The best book on *haṭhayoga* is B. K. S. Iyengar's *Light on Yoga (Yoga Dipika)* (New York, 1966). It has an excellent introduction and detailed yet accessible sections on *prāṇāyāma.* Svami Kuvalayānanda's *Prāṇāyāma,* 4th ed. (Bombay, 1966), is a comprehensive handbook on the breathing process and respiratory technique in Hinduism. Kuvalayānanda's work also appears in the quarterly journal *Yoga-Mīmāṁsā* (Lonavla, Poona District, India, 1924–), which contains vast scientific information on actual laboratory and clinical experiments done on yogic breathing. Hans-Ulrich Rieker's excellent translation of the *Haṭhayogapradīpikā* called *The Yoga of Light,* translated from the German by Elsy Becherer (New York, 1971), describes the combination of the two yogic paths *haṭha* and *rāja,* and makes special reference to the arousal and control of the *kuṇḍalinī.* Mircea Eliade's *Patañjali and Yoga* (New York, 1969) and *Yoga: Immortality and Freedom,* 2d ed. (Princeton, N. J., 1969), contain excellent summaries of respiratory techniques in various traditions, as well as abundant bibliographic references. Finally, for those who may wish to go directly to the source, Georg Feuerstein's recent translation of *The Yoga-Sūtras of Patañjali* (Folkestone, U.K., 1979) has an exceedingly helpful commentary.

A good introduction to breathing and mindfulness meditation in Buddhism is Bhikkhu Khantipālo's *Calm and Insight: A Buddhist Manual for Meditators* (London, 1981). For a basic sourcebook on breathing in Daoist yoga, see *Daoist Yoga, Alchemy, and Immortality,* translated by Charles Luk (Kuan Yulu) (London, 1970); the classic article on the topic is, of course, Henri Maspero's "Les procédés de 'nourrir le principe vital' dans la religion taoïste ancienne," *Journal asiatique* 229 (1937): 177–252, 353–430.

Ellison Banks Findly (1987 and 2005)

BRELICH, ANGELO (1913–1977), was an Italian historian of religions. After completing his academic studies in Hungary under Károly Kerényi and Andreas Alföldi, Brelich became the assistant to the chair of history of religions at the University of Rome, a chair then held by Raffaele Pettazzoni, whom he succeeded as professor ordinarius in 1958. His first publication, *Aspetti della morte nelle iscrizioni sepolcrali nell'Impero romano* (Aspects of Death in the Sepulchral Inscriptions of the Roman Empire; 1937), was based upon a thorough exploration of the *Corpus inscriptionum Latinarum* and anticipated Brelich's future interest in methodological reflection. There followed in 1949 *Die geheime Schutzgottheit von Rom* (The Secret Protecting Deity of Rome) and *Vesta,* which show the strong influence of his teacher Kerényi and bear witness to Brelich's own search for scientific originality. In these two books, which were conceived as a unit, Brelich distinguishes between "analytical research," aimed at delineating the fundamental elements of themes present in a divine figure, and "historical research," which is concerned with the figure's specific content and further developments.

A new period in Brelich's studies began in the 1950s. *Tre variazioni romane sul tema delle origini* (Three Roman Variations on the Theme of Origins; 1955) emphasizes the theme of historical creativity. Unlike the evolutionist notion of survival (i. e., the notion of vestigial cultural elements surviving merely as erratic blocks in the living stream of more recent cultural formations), Brelich's notion of historical creativity implies the validation of elements already found within different mythological and religious horizons on the part of new, emerging cultural-historical settings. Brelich also makes use of a basic opposition between primordial chaos or "non-order" and the order that results from the organization of the cosmos. These methodological principles recur in the volume *Gli eroi greci* (The Greek Heroes; 1958), where Brelich advocates the inclusion of the study of the religions of the classical world within the problematic of the history of religions. In the same book, Brelich also reflects on the type of the hero, especially as the object of a funerary cult and in its connection with cosmogonic themes. He was later to alter those views expressed here, however, because of the radicalization of his analytic hermeneutics.

During this period Brelich became deeply interested in polytheism, which had been a rather neglected topic in the field of comparative, cultural-historical studies. He saw in polytheism a religious phenomenon typical of the archaic "high cultures" such as were found in Japan, India, Mesopotamia, Egypt, and Greece, as well as in Central America and Peru. He believed that the polytheistic conception of "god" or deity was to be distinguished from both the ghosts of animism and the *dei otiosi* ("idle gods") of some nonliterate cultures. Polytheism for Brelich is a *sui generis* phenomenon and the proper object of historical research aimed at discovering its structure and *raison d'être* in the religious history of humankind.

Guerre, agoni, e culti nella Grecia arcaica (Wars, Ritual Competitions, and Cults in Archaic Greece; 1961) marked

Brelich's growing interest in initiatory institutions. These institutions are central to his *Paides e Parthenoi* (1969), which is a study of the way in which tribal initiation rites were adapted to use in the Greek polis once their original purpose had been lost. Here again is seen Brelich's interest in historical creativity. He showed less interest in soteriological and eschatological aspects of these institutions.

Brelich left unfinished a complex history of the cult of Jupiter, a history that was to trace Jupiter's development from the status of an Indo-European prepolytheistic heavenly being to that of the head of an entire pantheon, noting especially the political implications of this development. As for his view of religion as a general phenomenon, Brelich's introduction to Henri-Charles Puech's *Histoire des religions* (1970) seems to indicate that he accepted functionalist explanations.

BIBLIOGRAPHY

A notable work by Brelich not mentioned in the text is his posthumously published *Storia delle religioni: Perche?* (Naples, 1979). Two memorial volumes for Brelich have appeared. They are *Perennitas: Studi in onore di Angelo Brelich,* edited by Giulia Piccaluga (Rome, 1980), and *Religioni e civiltà: Scritti in memoria di Angelo Brelich* (Bari, 1982).

UGO BIANCHI (1987)

BRETHEREN OF PURITY SEE IKHWĀN AL-ṢAFĀʾ

BREUIL, HENRI

BREUIL, HENRI (1877–1961), French scholar of prehistoric humans. Henri-Édouard-Prosper Breuil was born in Mortain, Manche. As a youth, he developed an interest in natural history and the history of early humankind, which he pursued during his years at the seminary of Issy. Ordained a priest in 1900, he devoted the rest of his scholarly life to human paleontology. Breuil was introduced to Paleolithic studies by Émile Cartailhac, with whom in October 1902 he opened the Altamira cave in Spain, and his studies of Paleolithic art and artifacts were furthered by Édouard Iette and Joseph-Louis Capitan. In these early stages, Breuil's work was actively supported by Prince Albert of Monaco.

After having taught from 1905 to 1910 at the University of Fribourg, Breuil became professor of prehistoric ethnography at the Institut de Paléontologie Humaine in Paris. From 1929 to 1947 he served as professor of prehistory at the Collège de France. During his career, Breuil taught also in Lisbon (1941–1942) and Johannesburg (1942–1945). He traveled extensively in Europe and southern Africa, and even journeyed to China, searching for survivals of Paleolithic humans.

Through his global studies of Paleolithic cave art and the tools and techniques of Paleolithic craftsmen, Breuil greatly increased our knowledge of the conditions of life and the creative work of Paleolithic people. He drew attention, for example, to the religious aspects (i.e., the symbolic and possible ritual functions) of paintings such as that of "the Sorcerer" in the cave of Les Trois Frères, discovered in 1916 in southern France. He was also interested in the religious meaning of funerary practices and their hieratic manifestations, to which he ascribed a common origin. Breuil gave the first scholarly description of the famous caves of Lascaux (1940). In his thinking about human evolution (and the evidences for such evolution that he found in humanity's early religious history), Breuil envisaged a developing cosmic order moved by energy. Pierre Teilhard de Chardin, who for some time was associated with Breuil, developed these ideas more systematically.

BIBLIOGRAPHY

Most of Breuil's publications are descriptions of the more than eighty painted caves he studied in France and Spain and the hundreds of rock paintings he investigated in Spain, Ethiopia, and southern Africa. An excellent example of these descriptions is his *Les peintures rupestres schématiques de la Péninsule ibérique,* 4 vols. (Lagny-sur-Marne, 1932–1935). Breuil's more extensive works, done in collaboration with other scholars, include *Afrique* (Paris, 1931), which Breuil edited with Leo Frobenius and which contains Breuil's essay "L'Afrique préhistorique" (pp. 60–119), and *Les hommes de la pierre ancienne* (Paris, 1951). A significant example of Breuil's works on the religion of early humanity is his piece "Pratique religeuses chez les humanités quaternaires," in *Scienza e civiltà* (Rome, 1951), pp. 47–73. Among Breuil's books that have been translated into English, the following should be mentioned: *Rock Paintings of Southern Andalusia,* written with M. C. Burkitt and Montagu Pollock (Oxford, 1929); *The Cave of Altamira at Santillana de Mar,* written with Hugo Obermaier (Madrid, 1935); *Beyond the Bounds of History: Scenes of the Old Stone Age* (London, 1949); and *Four Hundred Centuries of Cave Art* (Montignac, 1952). A bibliography of Breuil's writings is contained in *Hommage à l'abbé Henri Breuil pour son quatre-vingtième anniversaire,* compiled by G. Henri-Martin (Paris, 1957).

Publications on Breuil's life and work include "Recollections of the Abbé Breuil" by Mary Boyle and others, *Antiquity* 37 (1963): 12–19; Alan H. Brodrick's *The Abbé Breuil: Prehistorian* (London, 1963); and Nicolas Skrotzky's *L'abbé Breuil* (Paris, 1964).

JACQUES WAARDENBURG (1987)

BRIDGES

BRIDGES. All over the world, in different religions and cultures, there are vivid descriptions of a perilous way that the dreamer, the ecstatic visionary, or the deceased has to follow on his journey to the otherworld. One of the perils may be a bridge leading across a chasm, a rapacious stream, or the void. Success in crossing the bridge may depend on the traveler's own behavior during life or on the sacrifices he or his surviving relatives have performed. Ethical qualifications are not always needed.

Parallel with these eschatological ideas, actual bridge-building on earth has been connected with sacrifices and with religious, folkloric, and magical conceptions. At times, the construction of a tangible bridge—whether for day-to-day use or for ritual use only—is related to the soul's passage to the afterlife. Finally, the bridge in itself has often been a very useful symbol to signify the transcendence of the border between two realms or the ascension from a lower to a higher dominion.

HISTORY. One of the striking characteristics of the bridge as symbol is its universality among traditions from all over the world.

Indo-Iranian religions. In the Hindu religion, from the *Ṛgveda* (9.41.2) onward, the bridge occurs as a link between earth and heaven, the world of illusion (*māyā*) and reality. The sacrifice terminology and the lofty speculations of the Upanisads use it in a figurative rather than a literal sense, though the popular imagination might suppose the latter to be the case. Just as the gods enter the heavenly world by means of the "southern fires" (*dakṣiṇās*) in the Agnicayana ritual, using them as steps and ladders, so the sacrificer "crosses a bridge and enters into the world of heaven" (*Yajurveda, Kāṭhakam* 28.4). It is necessary to make a ladder or a bridge with sacrificial gifts in order to ascend into that heavenly realm.

On the other hand, this luminous *brahman* world is attained by recognition of *ātman,* the spiritual reality. To the extent that this universal self is conceived of as a person, God himself is called "the highest bridge to immortality" (*Svetāśvatara Upaniṣad* 6.19). That bridge, God, in itself is not ethical, but all evil is excluded from the *brahman* world: "Therefore, if blind people go over the bridge they receive their sight, if wounded, they are cured; therefore, if the night crosses the bridge, it is turned to day" (*Chāndogya Upaniṣad* 8.4.1).

According to Herman Lommel (1930, pp. 264ff.), the greatest significance of the ancient Indian bridge is that it holds two worlds, heaven and earth, apart. But, speaking of the Nāciketas fire—"the bridge of the sacrificers to that eternal highest *brahman*"—Lommel does not mention some later lines where the road is described as the "sharp edge of a razor, difficult to pass over" (*Kāṭhaka Upaniṣad* 3.14). The bridge, however, is not explicitly mentioned in this connection.

A comparison of the Indian and Iranian sources reveals common as well as differing conceptions of the bridge and of the whole structure of ideas to which it belongs. The paradisiacal delights of the virtuous are pictured in a very concrete way in *Kauṣītaki Upaniṣad* 1.4: "Five hundred nymphs [*Apsaras*] go to meet him, one hundred with fruit in their hands, one hundred with ointment in their hands, one hundred with wreaths, one hundred with raiment, one hundred with fragrant powder in their hands" (Lommel, p. 270).

Space does not allow a thorough account here of the Iranian sources with their various chronologies, varying content, and difficulties of philological interpretation (cf. Lommel, pp. 263ff., with Nyberg, 1966, pp. 180ff.). Some general ideas may be summarized, however, with the help of a present-day specialist.

In ancient Iran, the ceremonies of the first three days after death were regarded as very important for the soul of the dead person. It had to be protected against evil powers and had to be strengthened before the dangerous journey to the otherworld. Originally, at least, princes, warriors, and priests might hope to come to a luminous paradise with all its delights. The "crossing of the Separator" (Av., Chinvatō Peretu) was imagined as passing over a bridge that began on top of Mount Harā and ended on the road to Heaven. Only worthy souls, perhaps those who had given rich offerings, could reach the heavenly way; the others fell down into the subterranean Hell (Boyce, 1979, pp. 13ff.).

Zarathushtra taught that everyone had the possibility of gaining Paradise and that the successful passing of the bridge depended on the moral qualities of the departed, not on social rank or costly sacrifices. Three godly judges weigh the soul's good and bad thoughts, words, and deeds. If the good are heavier, the bridge is made broader, and the soul can pass, accompanied by a beautiful maiden, Daēnā, its own heavenly double or good conscience. Otherwise, the bridge gets as narrow as a blade edge, and the soul is propelled into the place of torment by an ugly hag (Boyce, 1979, p. 27). The classical sources of this short abstract are the ritual law contained in the Younger Avesta, *Vendidad* 19.28–32, combined with the fragment of the *Hadhōkht Nask* belonging to the same canon, composed in pre-Christian times and supplemented with later Pahlavi literature, from the ninth century CE (*Mēnōg i Khrad* 2; *Bundahishn* 30), as quoted in detail by Nyberg (pp. 180ff.; cf. Duchesne-Guillemin, 1973, pp. 333ff.).

Judaism and Islam. Probably through Iranian influence, a similar conception appears in Judaism. It has been mistakenly cited as existing in the Jewish apocalypse of Ezra (*2 Esdras* 7:8ff., end of first century CE). There, according to Silverstein (1952, pp. 95f.), the bridge, whose width accommodates only a single person's feet, becomes broader when the righteous cross it and narrower for the sinners. But this passage actually refers to two different ways (not bridges), one belonging to this earthly world, the other to the heavenly one. The ordeal of crossing the bridge over the Valley of Jehoshaphat, which according to Jewish eschatology occurs in the Last Judgment, is of a later date.

The corresponding eschatological ideas in Islam also seem to be dependent on Iranian tradition, perhaps with a Jewish intermediary. The Islamic name of this bridge is Ṣirāṭ, which simply means "way." Thus it has been possible to discover the bridge in Qurʾanic passages concerning the afterlife that refer only to a way (36:66, 37:23f.). But the later tradition (*ḥadīth*) describes a real bridge, "thinner than a hair and sharper than the edge of a sword," which leads the dead over Hell's uppermost part, Jahannam. Out of compassion or in recognition of the good deeds of the person concerned, God makes it possible for believers to pass over the bridge. The just and those who have received forgiveness come over without mishap, while sinful Muslims plunge down into Hell and remain there for a limited time in a sort of purgatory. Unbelievers, however, remain in those portions that function as places of punishment. Gabriel stands before the bridge and Michael upon it; they question those who pass over about the lives they have led (Gardet, 1968, p. 87).

According to a tradition that goes back to Ibn Masʿūd, everyone must cross the bridge. In accordance with their works, they do it more swiftly or more slowly: as the wind, as a bird, as a fine horse or a camel, as a running person, or as a person walking only on the big toes, who is immediately shaken off into the fire by the sharp, slippery bridge bristling with barbs. In his passage, the walker is also attacked by angels with fiery pitchforks (Jeffery, 1962, p. 247). The bridge may be arched, ascending for a thousand years, running level for a thousand, and descending for a thousand years. In this tradition, the gate of Paradise is opened only if the deceased gives the right answers. Then he is accompanied over the now soft and level bridge by an angel (Coomaraswamy, 1944/1945, p. 203, with references).

Christianity. In the literature of classical antiquity and in the Bible, no soul-bridge is known. But the classical writer of the Syrian church, Ephraem (fourth century), speaks of the cross of Christ as a bridge leading over the terrible abyss with its menacing fire. This river or sea of fire as an obstacle on the journey of the soul can be transcended in other ways, too; the righteous may even pass through it without being damaged. Because of their vividly striking descriptions, it is sometimes difficult to say whether these passages are to be taken literally or figuratively (Edsman, 1940, pp. 121ff.; cf. pp. 52ff.).

In medieval Russian spiritual songs, which represent popular religion, the language is very realistic (Edsman, 1959, pp. 106ff.). In medieval times, the world of folk imagery knew well the perilous bridge. It also has a place in the literature of Christian visionaries, with its roots in the ancient church's rich outpouring of apocalyptic descriptions of the hereafter. To a great extent, these descriptions are found in the extracanonical apocrypha; these, in turn, are descended from Judaism and Iran.

However, the classic Christian image of a bridge, which has been very influential throughout history, is contained in the *Dialogues* of Gregory I (c. 540–604). The framework is the same as in the famous vision of Er in the last book of Plato's *Republic:* one who seems to be dead revives and tells those around him what he has experienced. In Gregory's story, it is a certain soldier who tells of a bridge under which a dark and stinking river runs, but that leads to the heavenly green meadows and shining mansions inhabited by men in white clothes. Any wicked person who tries to go over the bridge tumbles down into the river, whereas the righteous pass safely across. The soldier also saw a fight between angels and demons over a person who had slipped on the bridge so that half his body was hanging over the edge (*Dialogues* 4.36). As Howard Rollin Patch (1950, pp. 95f.) points out, Gregory quotes *Matthew* 7:14 as part of his interpretation: "For very narrow is the path which leads to life." This quotation, in turn, demonstrates the technique of combining biblical and extrabiblical source material.

The bridge motif occurs in many different categories of medieval literature and belongs to Celtic and Germanic mythology also (Patch, 1950; Dinzelbacher, 1973). It can have greater or lesser importance in the Christian representations of the general topography of the otherworld, where the account of the soul's union with the Savior on the other shore may outweigh the description of the horrors on the way (Dinzelbacher, 1978). Moreover, the eschatological ideas were combined with the practical construction of a bridge; this was considered a pious work that was also helpful for the future fate of the builder. Frequently, a bridge had its own chapel for prayers and often its own hospital. Papal and episcopal indulgences encouraged such construction. Consequently, legacies became common, and bridge-building brotherhoods were founded beginning at the end of the twelfth century (Knight, 1911, p. 856; Boyer, 1967, p. 798).

Buddhism. That the soul-bridge also turns up in Buddhism is hardly surprising, since Buddhism is a daughter religion of Hinduism. As conceptions of an afterlife influenced by Islam can be found in the great stretches of Central Asia into which the Muslim religion has penetrated (Paulson, 1964, 152f.; cf. Eliade, 1964, pp. 482ff.), so a corresponding eschatology has followed Buddhism into East Asia. But here a new feature is observed. Even though people have tried in various ways in the different religions to affect the fate of deceased persons (for example, during the Christian Middle Ages, by accomplishing the actual construction of a bridge as a spirit-gift for the deceased), it is only in "northern" Buddhism that there is found a comprehensive symbolic bridge-building ceremony combined with the funeral. One of the classical Sinologists, J. J. M. de Groot, has written in careful detail about the Buddhist rites for the dead in Amoy, which lies in Fukien opposite Taiwan (1885, pp. 97ff.). According to de Groot, the bridge ceremony that takes place in connection with these rites is based on a quotation from a relatively late description of Hell. According to the latter, no less than six bridges of different materials lead from the underworld to the world of rebirth. There, the souls are sorted out, and their impending fates in the six different forms of existence are decided in detail.

The rites for the dead are intended to help the souls over some of these bridges. If a deceased person has not completely atoned for his crimes by enduring the torments of Hell or has not, through the actions of clergy, been freed from his remaining punishment, he has to plunge down into the pit, which is filled with snakes and writhing monsters. Therefore, in the room where the rites for the dead are being carried out, the priests build a temporary bridge out of boards that are laid upon chairs or out of a long bench without a back. The soul-bridge is also provided with railings of bamboo and cloth or paper, sometimes even with an overhead canopy. As soon as the ceremony, which is called "the beating of Hell," is completed, they undertake "the crossing of the bridge." The happy completion of this is reported to the powers of the underworld, so that they will not be able to hinder the soul in its progress.

Just as the variations in such rituals are numerous, the afterlife concepts that lie behind them also change. Thus, Nai-ho Bridge ("the bridge without return") is also found in the popular color illustrations that the Jesuit father Henri Doré reproduced in his instructive and comprehensive work on what he calls "superstitions" in China (1914, pp. 194f., fig. 52). The text quoted by Doré describes the picture exactly: souls receive the wine of forgetfulness from the ten underworld judges before they continue to what is also called the Bridge of Pain, which goes over a red foaming stream in a hilly region. When the souls have read a text on the conditions of existence, they are seized by two devils, Short Life and Quick Death, who hurl them into the stream. They are swept out through the stream into new existences to live as men, four-footed animals, birds, fish, insects, or worms. As late as after World War II such ceremonies were carried out both in mainland China (Hsu, 1948, p. 165) and on Taiwan.

Ritual Sacrifices. The Latin word *pontifex* is composed of the noun *pons* and the verb *facere,* and it signifies "he who makes or builds bridges." One cannot prove historically that the incumbents of this ancient Roman office literally had such a function. However, the etymology, which existed as early as the Roman librarian and scholar Varro (116–27 BCE), is disputed both in antiquity and among modern researchers. Evidently an old Indo-European meaning is hidden in *pons,* giving it the sense of a "path" or "way," not necessarily over a river (Szemler, 1978, cols. 334ff.).

Discussing the various interpretations of the term *pontifices* and rejecting that of "bridge builders," the Greek writer Plutarch (b. 46?–d. around 119 CE) gives us the arguments of those who defend that theory: the name refers to the sacrifices performed at the very ancient and sacred bridge Pons Sublicius over the Tiber, which were necessary to prevent a sacrilegious demolition of the entirely wooden construction (*Numa* 9.2). The Roman poet Ovid (43 BCE–17 CE) makes reference to this ceremony, at which the Roman high priest, *pontifex maximus,* officiated together with the first Vestal: "Then, too, the Virgin is wont to throw the rush-made effigies of ancient men from the oaken bridge" (*Fasti* 5. 621f.). This ancient festival in the middle of May is also mentioned by another historian, Dionys of Halikarnassos (fl. 20 BCE). Dionys already understands that the puppets are a substitute offering for men (1.38.3).

The purpose of this and corresponding sacrifices is interpreted in different ways by both ancient and modern authors. According to James G. Frazer, the river god must be propitiated when humans intrude into his domain and transcend a border. Or, as Eliade (1957) explains, any building, to withstand its hardships, ought to have a life and soul that are transferred to it by a bloody sacrifice.

A Greek folk song, "The Bridge at Arta," which speaks of this matter, has become famous. The song describes how people keep on building the bridge for three years, but the last span is never finished because what is built by day collapses by night. When the builders begin to complain, the demon or *genius loci,* perhaps originally the river god, lets his voice be heard: he tells the people that unless they sacrifice a human life, no wall is securely founded. They are not, however, to give an orphan child, a traveler, or a foreigner but instead the construction foreman's beautiful wife. From one of the Ionian islands, Zante (Gr., Zákinthos), there is the tale that, as late as the second half of the nineteenth century, the people had wanted to sacrifice a Muslim or a Jew at the building of the more important bridges. There is also a legend that a black person was walled up in an aqueduct near Lebadea in Boeotia (Lawson, 1910, pp. 265f., 276f.; Armistead and Silverman, 1963). In 1890, China's department of public works paid the price of ten pounds for a human bridge sacrifice, if one is to believe a highly respected English reference work (Knight, 1911, p. 850). In Western countries sacrificial ceremonies at the building of bridges have survived as only partly understood reminiscences; they take the form of children's games (Knight, 1911, p. 852; Edsman, 1959).

Symbolism. In Christian metaphorical language, life is likened to a pilgrimage. One is not to become so captivated with the joy of traveling, whether by wagon or ship, that one forgets the destination. It is a matter of using the world, not of enjoying it. Augustine conveys this theme in *On Christian Doctrine* (1.4), while in his discourses on the *Gospel of John* (40.10) he speaks of the world as a lodging where one has temporarily stopped over during one's journey.

This metaphor can easily be reformulated using the bridge symbol. One can then consider a saying of Jesus that is lacking from the New Testament, a so-called agraphon, that has survived in Islamic tradition. It is best known through the inscription that, in 1601, Emperor Akbar caused to be affixed at the chief entrance to the great mosque in Fathepur Sikri in North India: "Jesus, peace be upon him, has said: 'The world is a bridge, walk over it, but do not sit down on it.'" The saying can be traced through Islam as far back as the seventh century (Jeremias, 1955).

Among the extremes of modern psychoanalytical interpretations of the bridge is the Freudian-inspired theory that the bridge constitutes a phallic symbol, with all that suggests about sexual fantasies, castration complexes, and incest (Friedman, 1968). A different interpretation is found in the writings of Hedwig von Beit, who was inspired by C. G. Jung to apply his categories to research into fairy tales. The bridge, which divides two land areas, would thus reflect a psychic situation in which a gap in consciousness occurs or where a transition is occurring to another area. It is at just such a point that the "demons" of the unconscious are free to make an appearance (Reimbold, 1972, pp. 66f., pp. 71f.).

Mircea Eliade, who has also been influenced by Jung, gives a phenomenological interpretation of the bridge symbol in the initiation of shamans among the Mongolian Buriats of southern Siberia. A climbing ceremony is involved in which the candidate climbs nine birches that are tied together with a rope and called a "bridge." Eliade interprets the red and blue ribbons, which further bind this arrangement with the yurt, as a symbol of the rainbow. This would lend support to the interpretation that Eliade gives to the whole ceremony: it is a visualization of the shaman's heavenly journey, his rite of ascension. Therefore, the initiation of the Mongolian shaman can be connected with the crossing of the Chinvat Bridge in ancient Iranian eschatology, which also constitutes a test or an initiation. But both pertain to an even larger framework: the reinstitution of the paradisiacal antiquity when humans and gods could converse with each other without difficulty, thanks to the bridge that then connected them (Eliade, 1964, pp. 116ff.; cf. Berner, 1982). Eliade has treated this theme in his fiction, in a tale entitled "Bridge" (1963) included in his collection *Phantastische Geschichten* (1978), as Berner has pointed out. Eliade's critics, in turn, consider a hermeneutic of this kind fantastic; other specialists (e.g., Blacker, 1975) have found his interpretation confirmed by their own material.

SEE ALSO Chinvat Bridge; Pontifex.

BIBLIOGRAPHY

Armistead, Samuel G., and Joseph H. Silverman. "A Judeo-Spanish Derivate of the Ballad of the Bridge of Arta." *Journal of American Folklore* 76 (January-March 1963): 16–20. Contains a rich bibliography.

Berner, Ulrich. "Erforschung und Anwendung religiöser Symbole in Doppelwerk Mircea Eliades." *Symbolon* 6 (1982): 27–35.

Blacker, Carmen. "Other World Journeys in Japan." In *The Journey to the Other World,* edited by Hilda R. Ellis Davidson, pp. 42–72. Totowa, N.J., 1975.

Boyce, Mary. *Zoroastrians: Their Religious Beliefs and Practices.* Boston, 1979.

Boyer, Marjorie Nice. "Bridgebuilding." In *New Catholic Encyclopedia,* vol. 2, p. 798. Washington, D.C., 1967.

Coomaraswamy, Luisa. "The Perilous Bridge of Welfare." *Harvard Journal of Asiatic Studies* 8 (1944/1945): 196–213.

Dinzelbacher, Peter. *Die Jenseitsbrücke im Mittelalter.* Vienna, 1973.

Dinzelbacher, Peter. "Ida von Nijvels Brückenvision." *Ons Geestelijk Erf* 52 (June 1978): 179–194.

Doré, Henri. *Recherches sur les superstitions en Chine,* vol. 2. Shanghai, 1914.

Duchesne-Guillemin, Jacques. *La religion de l'Iran ancien.* Paris, 1962. Translated as *Religion of Ancient Iran* (Bombay, 1973).

Edsman, Carl-Martin. *Le baptême de feu.* Uppsala, 1940.

Edsman, Carl-Martin. "Själarnas bro och dödens älv." *Annales Academiae Regiae Scientiarum Upsaliensis* 3 (1959): 91–109.

Eliade, Mircea. "Bauopfer." *Die Religion in Geschichte und Gegenwart,* 3d ed., vol. 1, p. 935. Tübingen, 1957.

Eliade, Mircea. *Shamanism: Archaic Techniques of Ecstasy* (1951). Rev. & enl. ed. New York, 1964.

Friedman, Paul. "On the Universality of Symbols." In *Religions in Antiquity: Essays in Memory of Erwin Ramsdell Goodenough,* edited by Jacob Neusner, pp. 609–618. Leiden, 1968.

Gardet, Louis. *Islam* (1967). Cologne, 1968.

Groot, J. J. M. de. "Buddhist Masses for the Dead." In *Actes du Sixième Congrès International des Orientalistes tenu en 1883 à Leide,* vol. 4, pp. 1–120. Leiden, 1885.

Hsu, Francis L. K. *Under the Ancestors' Shadow: Chinese Culture and Personality* (1948). Enl. ed. Stanford, 1971.

Jeffery, Arthur, ed. *A Reader on Islam: Passages from Standard Arabic Writings Illustrative of the Beliefs and Practices of Muslims.* The Hague, 1962.

Jeremias, Joachim. "Zur Überlieferungsgeschichte des Agraphon: Die Welt ist eine Brücke; Zugleich ein Beitrag zu den Anfängen des Christentums in Indien." *Nachrichten der Akademie der Wissenschaften in Göttingen* 4 (1955): 95–103.

Knight, G. A. Frank. "Bridge." In *Encyclopaedia of Religion and Ethics,* edited by James Hastings, vol. 2. Edinburgh, 1911.

Lawson, John Cuthbert. *Modern Greek Folklore and Ancient Greek Religion: A Study in Survivals* (1910). Reprint, New York, 1964.

Lommel, Herman. "Some Corresponding Conceptions in Old India and Iran." In *Dr. Modi Memorial Volume,* pp. 260–272. Bombay, 1930.

Nyberg, H. S. *Die Religionen des alten Iran.* 2d ed. Osnabrück, 1966.

Patch, Howard Rollin. *The Other World According to Descriptions in Medieval Literature.* New York, 1950. See the index, s. v. *Bridge.*

Paulson, Ivar. "Jenseitsglaube der finnischen Völker: In der wolgafinnischen und permischen Volksreligion." *Arv* 20 (1964): 125–164.

Reimbold, Ernst T. "Die Brücke als Symbol." *Symbolon* 1 (1972): 55–78.

Silverstein, Theodore. "Dante and the Legend of the Miʿraj: The Problem of Islamic Influence on the Christian Literature of the Otherworld." *Journal of Near Eastern Studies* 11 (1952): 89–110, 187–197.

Szemler, G. J. "Pontifex." In *Real-encyclopädie der klassischen Altertumswissenschaft,* supp. vol. 15, cols. 331–396. Munich, 1978.

CARL-MARTIN EDSMAN (1987)
Translated from Swedish by David Mel Paul and Margareta Paul

BRIGHID (c. 454–c. 524) was an early medieval Irish Christian saint celebrated as a virgin and miracle worker and the founder of an important monastic community at Kildare. According to early annals, she died in 524 CE at the age of seventy. However, that date is best understood as evidence of the tradition that holds Brighid to be a younger contemporary of Saint Patrick rather than as a precise record. Although Brighid has always been associated with the province of Leinster, in southeastern Ireland, she was also, from at least as early as the seventh century, revered along with Saint Patrick and Colmcille as one of the principal patrons of all Ireland. With the movement of Irish monks in the eighth and ninth centuries, the cult of Brighid spread throughout much of Europe. The spelling *Brighid* is the Middle Irish form of the Old Irish *Brigit*, the modern Irish *Bríd*, and the English *Brigid*.

EARLY RECORDS. The earliest surviving records of Brighid's life date from the seventh century, more than a hundred years after her death; both accounts are in Latin, one anonymous and the other composed by Cogitosus. The former describes her birth to a slave woman who was the concubine of a nobleman; her infancy and early childhood with the druid to whom her mother was sold; her eventual return to her father's home; her resistance to his efforts to arrange a marriage for her; her consecration of her virginity; and her travels throughout Ireland with the women who gathered around her, doing good and performing miracles. Her birth and infancy are said, in this life, to have been accompanied by many portents of her future greatness, and it is of considerable interest that druids as well as Christian bishops recognize them.

The miracle stories give considerable emphasis to Brighid providing food and drink: turning water into milk on some occasions and into beer on others, making butter out of nettles and bacon out of bark, feeding a large crowd on "twelve loaves, a little milk, and one sheep," and producing salt from a stone. Although they are certainly modeled to some extent on accounts of Christ's multiplication of the loaves and fishes and transformation of water into wine in the New Testament, the multiplicity of these stories suggests that abundance and hospitality were qualities associated from a very early date with Saint Brighid's cult.

The early lives also represent Brighid as having extraordinary sympathy with animals. In one of these stories, a wild boar that is being hunted joins her herd of swine and becomes tame. In another, a man has been condemned to die and his family to be enslaved because he has killed a king's pet fox, mistaking it for an ordinary one. At Brighid's behest, a wild fox plays tame and performs tricks just long enough for the king to accept it as a replacement for his lost pet and free the man; then it flees the court and returns to the wild. Several miracle stories involve both her empathy with animals and her liberal provision of food, as when she feeds a substantial portion of bacon to a hungry dog but when it is time to serve her human guests finds the total quantity of meat to be undiminished. As Cogitosus has it, "It is plain that the whole order of beasts, flocks and herds was subject to her rule" (De Paor, 1993, pp. 207–224).

CHRISTIAN AND PRE-CHRISTIAN TRADITIONS. The association of Saint Brighid with food and with animals may reflect aspects of a pre-Christian Irish goddess called Brigit or Bríg. Traces of this figure are faint in the written record, as one might expect them to be in early medieval Irish literary culture, since it was the product of Christian monasteries. A tenth-century list of terms deemed already archaic identifies Brigit as a goddess once worshiped by poets and the sister of two other Brigits, one a healer and one a smith, but it is rather Bríg *briugu*, a legendary hospitaler or innkeeper mentioned briefly in a seventh-century Irish law tract, who might more readily be imagined to have had affinities with the saint as she came to be represented in Christian hagiography. The name of the goddess Brigantī (Exalted One) appears in inscriptions and in the name of the British people known to the Romans as the Brigantes. Quite possibly cognate with *Brighid* or *Bríg*, this name suggests that Brighid may represent the Irish version of a goddess revered by various Celtic-speaking peoples. Since Brigantī was the tutelary goddess of the Brigantes, so was Saint Brighid understood to be the guardian of the Irish province of Leinster. In the anonymous early life, known as the *Vita Prima*, she appears leading the king of Leinster into battle, "with her staff in her right hand and a column of fire blazing skywards from her head" (Connolly, 14–49, at 41).

Many practices are associated with Brighid and with February 1, her feast in the Christian calendar, which was also the pre-Christian festival of *Imbolc*. The Brighid's Day customs, well attested into the second half of the twentieth century and surviving into the twenty-first century, include weaving crosses of rush that can be hung over the byre to protect livestock and in the home to protect the family, and particularly its women; making a figure or doll representing Brighid, the *brídeog*, which is carried around a village and welcomed into each home; and preparing the *brat Bhríde*, or Brighid's cloak, a piece of cloth left outdoors overnight to receive the saint's blessing and then employed throughout the following year to protect and heal humans and animals. Numerous springs or wells regarded as having curative properties are associated with Brighid, and many prayers and charms in Irish and Scottish Gaelic tradition invoke her name.

The explicit linking of the Christian saint and the pre-Christian goddess may be traced to 1900, when Brighid in her two aspects was adopted as the patron of *Inghinidhe na hÉireann* (Daughters of Ireland). Since 1993, several organizations have developed a cult of this dual Brighid; their practices center on maintaining a perpetual flame at Kildare, which was inspired by a twelfth-century account of such a fire tended by women and by Brighid herself, and on the two holy wells in the area associated with Brighid. Brighid's feast is observed at Kildare with a candlelight procession and vigil. These groups place a strong emphasis on women's spirituality, but they are by no means exclusively composed of women.

SEE ALSO Celtic Religion, overview article.

BIBLIOGRAPHY

The early lives of Saint Brighid are available in English translation in Sean Connolly, "Vita Prima Sanctae Brigitae: Background and Historical Value," *Journal of the Royal Society of Antiquaries of Ireland* 119 (1989): 5–49; Liam de Paor, trans., "Cogitosus's Life of St Brigid the Virgin," in *Saint Patrick's World* (Dublin and Notre Dame, 1993), pp. 207–226; and Donncha Ó hAodha, ed. and trans., *Bethu Brigte* (Dublin, 1978). A complete catalogue of the early documents pertaining to Saint Brighid can be found in James F. Kenney, *The Sources for the Early History of Ireland: Ecclesiastical; An Introduction and Guide* (New York 1929; reprint, New York 1966), pp. 356–363. For Saint Brighid's importance in the early Irish Christian church, see Christina Harrington, *Women in a Celtic Church: Ireland 450–1150* (Oxford, 2002), and for a thorough and intelligent analysis of the evidence for the pre-Christian goddess, see Kim McCone, *Pagan Past and Christian Present in Early Irish Literature* (Maynooth, Ireland, 1990), especially pp. 162–166. Séamas Ó Catháin, *The Festival of Brigit: Celtic Goddess and Holy Woman* (Dublin, 1995), especially pp. 1–26, provides a good introduction to the folklore and customs associated with Brighid and Saint Brighid's Day. See also Catherine McKenna, "Apotheosis and Evanescence: The Fortunes of Saint Brigit in the Nineteenth and Twentieth Centuries," in *The Individual in Celtic Literatures*, edited by Joseph F. Nagy (Dublin, 2001), pp. 74–108, and Catherine McKenna, "Between Two Worlds: Saint Brigit and Pre-Christian Religion in the *Vita Prima*," in *Defining the Celtic*, edited by Joseph F. Nagy (Dublin, 2002), pp. 66–74.

CATHERINE MCKENNA (2005)

BRINDAVAN SEE VṚNDĀVANA

BROADCASTING, RELIGIOUS SEE RELIGIOUS BROADCASTING

BROWNE, ROBERT (c. 1550–1633), leading Protestant Separatist from the Church of England in the reign of Elizabeth I. Although he finally conformed, his teaching anticipated much in later Independency, or Congregationalism. He was born at Tolesthorpe in Rutlandshire. For about twenty years after leaving Cambridge, he was an active Separatist. On receiving the bishop's license to preach in 1579, he threw it in the fire, asserting that he preached "not as caring for or leaning on the Bishop's authority, but only to satisfy his duty and conscience." He helped gather a dissenting congregation in Norwich in 1518 and was frequently imprisoned. In 1582 he was in exile in Holland.

During exile, he wrote the tracts that later became influential among more radical Protestants in which he insisted on the voluntary nature of church membership. The best-known is *A treatise of Reformation without Tarying for Anie* (1582). *A Booke which Sheweth the life and Manner of All true Christians* (1582) is the first outline of an Independent church polity.

Browne was a contentious individualist who frequently had to be rescued from trouble by his kinsman Lord Burghley. He fell out with his fellow Separatists Henry Barrow and John Greenwood over the eldership. In 1586, he became master of Saint Olave's School in Southwark but continued to minister to dissenting congregations. In 1591, however, Burghley presented him with the living of a church in Northamptonshire, where he remained for the rest of his life. He appears to have continued to be contentious even in conformity, because he died in Northampton jail after assaulting a constable.

Browne is best thought of as a precursor rather than a founding father of the later Congregational churches. The word *Brownists* became a general term of abuse for English Protestants who favored a democratic church polity.

BIBLIOGRAPHY

Little book-length literature is available other than an edition of Browne's writings in Albert Peel and Leland H. Carlson's *The Writings of Robert Harrison and Robert Browne* (London, 1953). See also Champlin Burrage's *The True Story of Robert Browne, 1550?–1633, Father of Congregationalism* (Oxford, 1906).

DANIEL JENKINS (1987)

BRUNNER, EMIL (1889–1966), Swiss Protestant theologian. Brunner was a critic of liberalism and secularism. His writing on knowledge and faith was influenced by Kant; his stress on religious experience by Kierkegaard and Husserl; and his stress on God's transcendence and the need for vigorous social and political action by Luther and Calvin.

Brunner anticipated Martin Buber's notion of the I-Thou relationship, elucidating throughout his *Dogmatics* the encounter between humanity and God as humanity's most significant existential experience. In *The Divine Imperative*, Brunner argues that the source of Christian ethics lies in God's imperative. He deemed personhood to be the center of human-divine interaction, deploring the reductionism of positivism and behaviorism. Although sympathetic to philosophy, he opposed its attempts to stand in judgment of theology, as well as attempts by Paul Tillich and others to use such philosophical terms as *being* and *ground of being* in reference to God. In contrast to Barth, Brunner asserted that even sinful man can attain some knowledge of God but that, apart from the Christian revelation, this knowledge has no salvific value.

Brunner's theology is rich in the areas of ethics and sociopolitical thought. We are told in his *The Divine Imperative, Christianity and Civilization*, and *Justice and the Social Order* that God's command is to love and that the person who has faith in Jesus Christ responds to God's love by living a life of hope and love in "orders of creation"—the family, the economy, the state, the culture, and the church. Though the New Testament contains no blueprint for a socio-economic-political order, Brunner believed that human institutions could be informed by love and by justice in the service of God.

BIBLIOGRAPHY

Brunner's three-volume *Dogmatics* (Zurich, 1946–1960) is the definitive statement of his theology. The first two volumes have been translated into English by Olive Wyon, and the third by David Cairns and T. H. L. Parker (Philadelphia, 1950–1962). Crucial to an understanding of Brunner's ethics and his Reformed stance is *Das Gebot und die Ordnungen* (Tübingen, 1932), translated by Olive Wyon as *The Divine Imperative* (Philadelphia, 1947). The existentialist and personal aspects of Brunner's thought are best exhibited in *Wahrheit als Begegnung* (Berlin, 1938), translated by Amandus W. Loos as *The Divine-Human Encounter* (Philadelphia, 1943), and *Der Mittler* (Tübingen, 1927), translated by Olive Wyon as *The Mediator: A Study of the Central Doctrine of the Christian Faith* (Philadelphia, 1947). For a critical evaluation of all Brunner's works, see my *The Theology of Emil Brunner* (New York, 1962). This volume contains works by Brunner, interpretative essays, replies to these essays by Brunner, and a complete bibliography.

CHARLES W. KEGLEY (1987)

BRUNO, GIORDANO (1548–1600), Italian philosopher. Bruno was a brilliant and encyclopedic though erratic thinker of the Italian Renaissance, a man who synthesized and transformed thought in terms of the situation of his own times. Born in Nola, Bruno joined the Dominican order in Naples at the age of fifteen. He was expelled for his views on transubstantiation and the immaculate conception and fled Rome about 1576. After wandering over half of Europe, he finally returned to Italy, only to be imprisoned by the Roman Inquisition for his cosmological theories and burned as a heretic, the "martyr of the Renaissance."

Bruno was strongly influenced by the German philosopher Nicholas of Cusa and the latter's theory of the "coincidence of opposites," namely, that the infinitely great coincides with the infinitely small, and that God relates to the world as does one side of a piece of paper to the other side (panentheism). Drawing on Neoplatonic philosophy in developing his theories about the universe, Bruno rejected Aristotle's conception of the structure of the universe, held to a theory of animate monads, taught the relativity of space, time, and motion, and maintained that the universe is infinite in extension and eternal in its origin and duration.

Bruno was a prolific author and, especially in his Italian works, a beautiful writer, though some of his Latin works were prolix and confused. He had obsessions, such as his preoccupation with mnemonic theories, and he was easily distracted by strange thinkers like Ramón Lull (c. 1235–1315). Among Bruno's better-known works are *On Heroic Rages*, expounding a Neoplatonic theodicy cast in mythical form, describing the soul's ascent to God as its return to the original and highest unity; *An Ash Wednesday Conversation*, discussing the Copernican heliocentric theory; *On the Infinite Universe and Worlds*, an ecstatic vision of a single infinite universe; *The Expulsion of the Triumphant Beast*, an allegory dealing mostly with moral philosophy; and *On the Beginnings, Elements and Causes of Things*, his cosmic philosophy. Bruno's writings influenced Jakob Boehme, Spinoza, Leibniz, Descartes, Schelling, and Hegel.

BIBLIOGRAPHY

Virgilio Salvestrini's *Bibliografia delle opere di Giordano Bruno* (Pisa, 1926) is an excellent comprehensive bibliography of Bruno's works, including references to him by other writers. The best book in English on Bruno is Dorothea Waley Singer's *Giordano Bruno: His Life and Thought with Annotated Translation of His Work "On the Infinite Universe and Worlds"* (New York, 1968). An authoritative treatment of his thought is Giovanni Gentile's *Giordano Bruno e il pensiero del rinascimento*, 2d ed. (Florence, 1925). Irving Louis Horowitz's *The Renaissance Philosophy of Giordano Bruno* (New York, 1952) offers a general introduction to his natural philosophy or ontology and an analysis of the interactions of his philosophical system and method. Frances A. Yates's *Giordano Bruno and the Hermetic Tradition* (London, 1964) relates his thought to the mystical and Platonic tradition.

LEWIS W. SPITZ (1987)

BUBER, MARTIN (1878–1965) was a Jewish philosopher and educator. Born in Vienna to Carl and Elise Buber, he was raised by his paternal grandparents, Salomon and Adele Buber, following the breakup of his parents' marriage. He studied at universities in Vienna; Leipzig, Germany; Zurich, Switzerland; and Berlin. In 1904 he received a Ph.D. from the University of Vienna, writing his dissertation on Nicholas of Cusa (1401–1464) and Jakob Boehme (1575–1624). In 1899 Buber married Paula Winkler, a well-known German writer, with whom he had two children.

During his late teens and early university years, Buber experienced a sense of alienation from Judaism and the Jewish community. The newly formed Zionist movement opened the way to a renewed connection to the Jewish community. Embracing Zionism as a form of Jewish spiritual renewal, Buber began to write extensively on Judaism and Jewish nationalism. From 1901 to 1904 he edited the official journal of the Zionist movement, *Die Welt*.

A five-year (1904–1909), intensive engagement with the sources of Hasidism, an eastern European movement of Jewish religious renewal, helped revive Buber's connection to the religious and spiritual dimensions of Judaism. In Hasidism, which he first encountered as a child living with his grandparents in central Europe, Buber experienced a spiritual energy that he considered missing from most forms of Jewish life. This five-year period of study resulted in two volumes in German, *The Tales of Rabbi Nachman* (1906) and *The Legend of the Baal-Shem* (1908). These were followed by volumes of essays and translations, including *For the Sake of Heaven* (1945), *Tales of the Hasidim* (1947), and *The Origin and Meaning of Hasidism* (1960), which first appeared in Hebrew, and *Hasidism and Modern Man* (1958). Other early writings include studies in mysticism, *Ekstatische Konfessionen* (1909) and *Reden und Gleichnisse des Tschuang-Tse* (1910), as well as two collections of essays on Jewish national and religious renewal, *Die Jüdische Bewegung* (2 vols., 1916–1920) and *Reden über das Judentum* (On Judaism, 1923). He also edited a monographic series on social thought, *Die Gesellschaft* (1904–1912), and a journal, *Die Jude* (1916–1924), that focused on Jewish history and culture.

Buber taught at the University of Frankfurt from 1923 to 1933 and had a powerful spiritual impact on Jewish youth. Active in Jewish cultural life, he also lectured at the Frankfurt Jüdische Lehrhaus directed by Franz Rosenzweig (1886–1929). During the 1930s Buber's lectures and writings served as an important source of spiritual inspiration for the besieged German Jewish community. In 1938 Buber immigrated to Palestine, where he served as professor of social philosophy at the Hebrew University in Jerusalem and actively engaged in adult education. Buber was a founder and active participant in Brit Shalom and Ihud, movements for Arab-Jewish rapprochement. A staunch advocate of a binational state in Palestine, he wrote and lectured on its behalf.

PHILOSOPHY OF JUDAISM. Buber's imaginative reading of Hasidism served as an important foundation for his distinctive interpretation of Judaism and religion. He was particularly drawn to Hasidism's emphasis on the hallowing of the everyday. Rather than seek the sacred in special places, moments, or ritual practices, Hasidism, according to Buber, found it in everyday encounters with other people, animals, and nature. As he read them, the Hasidic teachings provided a viable path whereby his generation could bridge the gulf between the sacred and the profane.

Buber did not consider becoming a member of a Hasidic community to be a viable possibility. Rejecting Orthodoxy, he espoused spontaneous, experiential "religiosity" over static, institutionalized "religion." Eschewing the formal rabbinic practices and structures of classical Hasidism, he instead encouraged an existential engagement with Hasidic teachings as a path of religious renewal for Jews and non-Jews alike.

Taking issue with both Jewish historical scholarship and rationalist Jewish theology, Buber emphasized the mystical and mythic components of Judaism. Gershom Scholem (1897–1982), a leading modern scholarly interpreter of Jewish mysticism, objected to Buber's interpretations of Hasidism. His criticisms and Buber's response resulted in one of the most significant debates among modern Jewish scholars concerning the interpretation of religion in general and Judaism in particular. Diverging from the canons of Western academic scholarship, Buber, according to Scholem, produced a subjective, idiosyncratic, misleading representation of Hasidism. Ignoring such basic sources of Hasidic teachings as liturgical texts and biblical commentaries, Buber focused exclusively on the Hasidic tales. Moreover, ignoring the nihilistic tendencies in Hasidic teachings, Buber, according to Scholem, focused solely on Hasidism's affirmation of everyday life. Finally, swayed by his own anarchistic tendencies, Buber had neglected the central role of formal religious practices *(halakhah)* in Hasidism.

Responding to Scholem in "Interpreting Hasidism," Buber distanced himself from conventional historical scholarship that "addresses the past as an object of knowledge with the intention of advancing the field of historical knowledge" (Buber, 1963, p. 218). To Buber the study of the past was important not for its own sake, but because of its power in assisting people to confront the spiritual crisis of the present. While never explicitly denying the validity of historical inquiry, Buber considered it an ineffective way to address the spiritual demands of the present.

To Buber, Hasidism incorporated a spiritual power that could help the modern person overcome the alienation that separated people from one another, from the world of nature, and from the divine. More than a system of theological concepts and ritual practices, Hasidism, argued Buber, was a way of life. As such, its dynamic power is best revealed through tales and legends that emerged out of life situations.

Biblical writings provided another important foundation for Buber's interpretation of Judaism. In such works of biblical interpretation as *Kingship of God* (1932), *Moses* (1945), *Prophetic Faith* (1942), and *On the Bible* (1968), Buber sought to recover the living situations from which the biblical text emerged. While his biblical writings reveal a great appreciation for critical scholarship, his primary concern was to engage the Bible as a living record of Israel's ongoing dialogue with God. In his German translation of the Hebrew Bible, Buber, together with his collaborator Rosenzweig, sought to recover the sensuous, poetic force of the spoken language. (The first volumes of this translation were published in 1925; following Rosenzweig's death, Buber finally completed it in 1962.)

PHILOSOPHY OF RELATION AND DIALOGUE. Following in the tradition of existential philosophers (Søren Kierkegaard [1813–1855], Friedrich Nietzsche [1844–1900]) and German social theorists (Ferdinand Julius Tönnies [1855–1936], Georg Simmel [1858–1918], Max Weber [1864–1920]), Buber believed that modern society and culture estranged people from their authentic selves, and from other persons, nature, and God.

After World War I, Buber's philosophical orientation increasingly privileged interpersonal encounters over individual mystical experiences. His neologism *das Zwischenmenschliche* (the interhuman) reflects his effort to uncover and represent a unique, overlooked dimension of human life. In

Ich und Du (I and thou, 1923) he sought to formulate a philosophy that highlighted the fundamental importance of this realm and to elucidate the relations that derive from it.

Buber's philosophical discourse may be understood in terms of Richard Rorty's distinction between normal and edifying philosophers. Like Kierkegaard and Nietzsche, Buber's basic concern was not to construct a philosophical system but to render visible the alienating forms of contemporary society and provide an alternative way of thinking and relating. In evaluating Buber's edifying philosophy, the question is not whether or not it accurately mirrors reality, but whether or not it can transform one's life and relations to other persons, the divine, and the nonhuman world. Buber distinguished between two basic modes of relation, "I-You" and "I-It." The I-It mode is characterized by a practical, goal-oriented, instrumentalist perspective. In it, people relate to others according to their usefulness and value. From a detached stance, people measure and type others in terms of their own needs and objectives. Whereas this mode of relation may be appropriate to technological and practical endeavors, Buber denounced the extent to which the I-It mode had come to dominate human relationships. In social relationships, rather than relate to others as unique beings, the modern person tends to reduce them to the status of objects or tools, valuing them solely for their use in helping one fulfill his or her own goals and purposes.

A major concern of Buber's was to formulate an alternative to the dominant I-It form of human relationship. This alternative, which he referred to as the I-You mode, is marked by direct, nonpurposive relations. In the I-You mode one relates to the other as an end (You), rather than a means (It). In so doing people accept, confirm, and nurture the unique qualities of the other. Such relations infuse lives with meaning and purpose.

Whereas structured, ordered I-It relations perdure, I-You relations are fleeting and fluid and cannot be planned. When they do occur, they quickly revert back to I-It relationships: "Every you in the world is doomed by its nature to become a thing, or at least to enter into thinghood again and again" (Buber, 1970, p. 69).

According to Buber, people are as they relate: "In the beginning is the relation" (Buber, 1970, p. 69). Through I-You relations, people actualize their humanity. In later writings Buber grounded the I-You relation in a person's basic wish "to be confirmed as what he is, even as what he can become, by men; and the innate capacity to confirm his fellow men in this way" (Buber, 1965, p. 68). In genuine dialogue, rather than frame the other in terms of one's own needs, one accepts, affirms, and confirms the other as the person that he or she is and can become. In a series of writings, *Between Man and Man* (1947) and *Knowledge of Man* (1965), Buber sought to formulate a philosophical-anthropological grounding for his philosophy.

Buber and the Dao. Buber's encounter with the teachings of ancient China provides an important context for understanding his philosophy. In particular, he seriously engaged and was influenced by the *Dao de jing* and *Zhuangzi,* two fundamental texts of Daoism. As early as 1914 Buber produced a pioneering German translation of and commentary to sections of *Zhuangzi.* A series of unpublished lectures on the *Dao de jing,* delivered in 1925 in Ascona, Switzerland, reveals important connections between the teachings of this text and Buber's philosophical views. Several articles, published at different periods of his life, provide further examples of his attraction to, as well as his reservations about, the Chinese teachings. Buber's attraction to, and use of, concepts drawn from Chinese teachings distinguished him from other Jewish philosophers of the twentieth century. More recent studies in Chinese philosophy have enhanced our understanding of the connections between Buber's philosophy and Daoist teachings. These studies help to clarify the importance of concepts such as *wu-wei* to Buber's understanding of human relations.

As formulated in the concept *wu-wei,* one accommodates oneself to the other's values and perspectives, doing nothing to impose one's own views. *Wu-wei,* like I-You relations, contrasts sharply with dominant Western modes of relation, where effectiveness is measured in terms of power and goals. Both *wu-wei* and I-You conceive of human relationships based upon noninterference.

The I-You relation, like *wu-wei,* emphasizes "action without doing, action through nonaction" (Buber, 1967, 190). Both concepts provide a major alternative to the prevailing Western conceptions of action and relation. In each people engage the other not by imposing themselves on him or her but by helping him or her actualize his or her inherent qualities.

Buber's description of the I-You relationship as "election and electing, passive and active at once" (Buber, 1970, p. 62) is no less applicable to *wu-wei.* In both instances, while seemingly passive, one acts with one's whole being while refraining from imposing on or interfering with the other or the world around one. In both cases action is spontaneous rather than calculated and natural rather than forced.

Religious Faith and the Eternal You. In his writings on religious faith, elaborated in such texts as *I and Thou* (1923), *Two Types of Faith* (1951), *Eclipse of God* (1952), and *Good and Evil* (1953), Buber emphasized the centrality of divine-human relation. Although he admitted the possibility of direct divine-human encounters, he situated the primary locus of genuine religious life in the realm of the "interhuman." I-You relations between persons, when extended, "intersect in the Eternal You" (Buber, 1970, p. 123). As he made clear in his Hasidic writings, one lives religiously by hallowing the beings that one encounters, human and nonhuman alike. In confirming their unique qualities and potentials, nurturing the divine spark in each of them, one actualizes God in the world.

Speaking of the divine as the "Eternal You," Buber denied that people could relate to it through the objectifying I-It mode. Revelation, in his view, occurs when one directly encounters a "presence," receiving a ground of meaning that one must translate into action. Moments of divine-human encounter, like all significant moments of relation, elude conceptual speech and are best conveyed through myth and poetry.

Genuine relation both presupposes and fosters genuine community, characterized by authentic relations between members and between members and leader. Like his mentor, the Romantic socialist and anarchist Gustav Landauer (1870–1919), Buber advocated a community based on "utopian socialism," that is, mutual ownership and mutual aid.

JUDAISM AND GENUINE COMMUNITY. To Buber the Jewish people's unique vocation is to actualize true community in daily life. Israel fulfills its responsibility as a specific nation by actualizing in its social life genuine, nonexploitative, confirming relations between people. As conveyed in the Bible, the Jews, a people united by common kinship, fate, and memory, accepted this task as an obligation. In Buber's view the Israeli kibbutz, a unique social experiment, stands out as one of history's most successful efforts to establish genuine community based upon mutual responsibility.

To live as a Jew means to dedicate oneself to actualizing genuine relation in all spheres of life. Rejecting all prepackaged recipes, norms, and principles, Buber emphasized the people of Israel's continuing responsibility to draw anew the "line of demarcation" separating just from unjust action.

For Buber, the Arab-Jewish conflict is the greatest test of the Jewish people's ability to actualize its vocation. His efforts on behalf of Arab-Jewish rapprochement can best be understood in terms of his philosophy of relation. A major figure in a small group of Jews espousing such rapprochement, he advocated a binational state in which Jews and Arabs would live together as two culturally autonomous people with absolute political equality. With the establishment of the State of Israel in 1948, he reluctantly abandoned this idea, accepting a separate Jewish state as a necessary outcome of historical realities. An active critic of the policies of the new state, he repeatedly rebuked Israel's political leaders for approaching Arab-Jewish relations in terms of power politics rather than genuine relations between persons.

Buber viewed the State of Israel as a microcosm of general humanity. Like Israel, all nations share a responsibility to actualize true community and dialogue in people's daily lives. Acceptance of this responsibility is a prerequisite for world peace. Criticizing both the centralization of power in the modern nation-state and the existential mistrust that permeates modern society, Buber envisioned a network of decentralized communities grounded in mutual production and direct relations between people.

INFLUENCE. Buber's influence among European Jewish youth was great. In Israel, however, most of his fellow Jews, religious and secular, considered his unique synthesis of religious existentialism and cultural nationalism unacceptable. Consequently his influence was limited to small groups of intellectuals and kibbutz members. In the United States many rabbis were put off by his strongly anti-institutional orientation to religion. He had a great impact, however, on a small but significant group of Jewish theologians, including Will Herberg (1902–1977), Arthur A. Cohen (1928–1986), and Eugene B. Borowitz (b. 1924). His impact on Christian theologians, such as Paul Tillich (1886–1965) and H. Richard Niebuhr (1894–1962), was extensive, and his writings were widely read in Christian seminaries.

Beyond the borders of the religious community, Buber's teachings had a strong impact on psychiatrists such as R. D. Laing, Irvin Yalom, and Leslie Farber; on philosophers such as Gabriel Marcel, Phillip Wheelwright, and Ernst Becker; and on the anthropologist Victor Turner. Deeply attracted by the political implications of Buber's philosophy of relation, Dag Hammarskjöld (the secretary general of the United Nations from 1953 to 1961) was, at the time of his death, engaged in translating Buber's writings into Swedish.

SEE ALSO Jewish Thought and Philosophy, article on Modern Thought.

BIBLIOGRAPHY

A comprehensive bibliography of Buber's writings is Margot Cohn and Rafael Buber, *Martin Buber: A Bibliography of His Writings, 1897–1978* (Jerusalem and New York, 1980). Other important works by Buber are *Israel and the World: Essays in a Time of Crisis,* 2d ed. (New York, 1963), which includes important essays on Judaism, the Bible, and Zionism; *A Believing Humanism: My Testament, 1902–1965,* translated and with an introduction and explanatory comment by Maurice S. Friedman (New York, 1967); *Pointing the Way,* translated, edited, and with an introduction by Friedman (New York, 1957); *I and Thou,* translated by Walter Kaufmann (New York, 1970); and *The Knowledge of Man* (New York, 1965). A valuable collection of writings on the Arab question is *A Land of Two Peoples: Martin Buber on Jews and Arabs,* edited with an incisive introductory essay and notes by Paul R. Mendes-Flohr (New York, 1983). A collection of Buber's writings in English is *The Martin Buber Reader,* edited by Asher D. Biemann (New York, 2002). An important selection of Buber's correspondence, drawn from the three-volume German edition, is *The Letters of Martin Buber: A Life of Dialogue,* edited by Nahum N. Glatzer and Mendes-Flohr with a biographical overview by Grete Schaeder (New York, 1991). In addition to Schaeder's biographical essay, the specifics of Buber's life, previously available only in German in Hans Kohn's fine study *Martin Buber: Sein Werk und seine Zeit* (Cologne, Germany, 1961), are now available in Friedman's three-volume biography, *Martin Buber's Life and Work* (New York, 1981–1983), a work marred by its hagiographic approach. Friedman's *Martin Buber: The Life of Dialogue,* 3d ed. (Chicago, 1976), was one of the early introductions to Buber's thought. Schaeder's *The Hebrew Humanism of Martin Buber,* translated by Noah J. Jacobs (Detroit, Mich., 1973), emphasizes the aesthetic and humanistic dimensions of Buber's writings, traced biographically. Important criticisms, with Buber's responses, are in Paul Arthur Schilpp and Friedman, eds., *The Philosophy of Martin Buber* (La Salle, Ill., 1967); and Sydney Rome and Beatrice Rome, eds., *Philosophical Interrogations,* pp. 15–117 (New York, 1964).

For discussions of Buber's philosophy, see the proceedings of the Buber Centenary Conference, held in 1978 at Ben-Gurion University in Israel, in Haim Gordon and Jochanan Bloch, eds., *Martin Buber: A Centenary Volume* (New York, 1984). On Buber and Daoism see Jonathan R. Herman, *I and Tao: Martin Buber's Encounter with Chuang Tzu* (Albany, N.Y., 1996); and J. J. Clarke, *The Tao of the West: Western Transformations of Taoist Thought* (London and New York, 2000). Works enabling a wider appreciation of the impact of Chinese thought on Buber include David L. Hall and Roger T. Ames, *Thinking from the Han: Self, Truth, and Transcendence in Chinese and Western Culture* (Albany, N.Y., 1998); and *Dao de jing: Making This Life Significant: A Philosophical Translation,* translated with commentary by Roger T. Ames and David L. Hall (New York, 2003). Valuable critical insights into Buber's life and thought as they relate to modern Jewish culture are provided in several articles by Ernst Simon, including "Martin Buber and German Jewry," *Yearbook of the Leo Baeck Institute* 3 (1958): 3–39; "The Builder of Bridges," *Judaism* 27 (Spring 1978): 148–160; and "From Dialogue to Peace," *Conservative Judaism* 19 (Summer 1965): 28–31. These and other articles on Buber are in Simon's Hebrew work, *Ye'adim, tsematim, netivim: Haguto shel Mordekhai Martin Buber* (Tel Aviv, 1985). An insightful effort to situate Buber's interpretive approach is Steven Kepnes, *The Text as Thou: Martin Buber's Dialogical Hermeneutics and Narrative Theology* (Bloomington, Ind., 1992). For further discussion and analysis, see Laurence J. Silberstein, *Martin Buber's Social and Religious Thought: Alienation and the Quest for Meaning* (New York, 1989).

LAURENCE J. SILBERSTEIN (1987 AND 2005)

BUCER, MARTIN (1491–1551), Christian humanist and reformer. Best known as the chief reformer of the Free Imperial City of Strasbourg, Bucer illustrates the combining of Martin Luther's evangelical theology with aspirations and traditions that predated the Reformation. A Dominican, Bucer was thus trained in the *via antiqua* of Thomas Aquinas but early fell under the spell of Erasmian humanism. Meeting and hearing Luther for the first time at the Heidelberg Disputation (1518) led him to become increasingly dissatisfied with his vocation and finally to secure release from his vows. He thus arrived in Strasbourg (1523) as a dispossessed and married cleric who could only appeal to that city's authorities for protection from the episcopal court. Friends arranged a position for him; he led in the efforts to abolish the Mass (1529), to erect a new church (1533–1534), and to construct the city's policy of mediation in the Sacramentarian Controversy. Eventually he became president of the Company of Pastors, but he was forced because of his opposition to the Interim (a temporary religious settlement arranged by Charles V) to flee to England, where he participated in the revision of *The Book of Common Prayer* shortly before his death. Ostensibly he appeared to have broken decisively with the intellectual and religious traditions that predated his encounter with Luther.

Bucer was thoroughly evangelical—and a follower of Luther—in the basic outline of his theology, but prior allegiances were apparent in his actions. At colloquies with representatives of Rome in the 1540s, he agreed to a theory of "double justification," according to which a Christian cooperates with God after the gift of salvation, a claim that may hark back to Thomas. In the Sacramentarian Controversy, although he was an early adherent to Zwingli's spiritualist view of the elements and later agreed with Luther in the Wittenberg Concord (1536), he consistently argued that the true meaning of the Lord's Supper was communion among the believers and with Christ. His mediatory efforts both flowed directly from this view and reflected the earlier influence of Erasmus and northern humanism.

These prior traditions and aspirations showed through most clearly in the sort of reformation Bucer promoted and the manner in which he did so. Like many others who translated Luther's theology into practice, Bucer sought a thorough reform of all of Christian society, as is well summarized in his posthumously published *De regno Christi,* dedicated to Edward VI. Outlined there is the program he followed throughout his entire career. Not only did he advocate that the Mass be abolished and proper Christian worship and doctrine be put in its place. He also helped found schools that had the humanist educational program at the heart of the curriculum. He laid the groundwork for creating in Strasbourg and elsewhere an educated clergy, who in turn made religion even at the popular level a matter of the mind as well as of the heart. And he helped to establish civil authority over relief for the poor and over marriage and morals. Finally, throughout his career he sought to tame the turbulent reform movement by working with the Christian magistrates, as he called the princes and city councils, so that peace might prevail and Christian society flourish.

BIBLIOGRAPHY

Martin Bucer's works are collected in *Martin Bucers deutsche Schriften,* edited by Robert Stupperich (Gütersloh, 1960–), and in *Martini Buceri opera Latina,* edited by François Wendel (Paris, 1954–). See also *Correspondance de Martin Bucer,* edited by Jean Rott (Leiden, 1979–). A good English biography is Hastings Eells's *Martin Bucer* (1931; New York, 1971). For bibliography, see *Bibliographia Bucerana,* by Robert Stupperich (Gütersloh, 1952), and *Bucer und seine Zeit,* edited by Marijn de Kroon and Friedhelm Krüger (Wiesbaden, 1976).

JAMES M. KITTELSON (1987)

BUDDHA. Etymologically, the Sanskrit/Pali word *buddha* means "one who has awakened"; in the context of Indian religions it is used as an honorific title for an individual who is enlightened. This metaphor indicates the change in consciousness that, according to Buddhism, is always characteristic of enlightenment. It suggests the otherness and splendor associated with those named by this epithet in various Buddhist traditions. *Buddha* is also related etymologically to the Sanskrit/Pali term *buddhi*, which signifies "intelligence" and "understanding." A person who has awakened can thus be said to be "one who knows."

Within the traditional Buddhist context *buddha* is an appellative term or title—that is, a term or title that is inclusive in character. As with all titles of office (e.g., king), the term *buddha* denotes not merely the individual incumbent but also a larger conceptual framework. As an appellative, *buddha* describes a person by placing him or her within a class, instead of isolating and analyzing individual attributes. It emphasizes the paradigm that is exhibited, rather than distinctive qualities or characteristics.

The designation *buddha* has had wide circulation among various religious traditions of India. It has been applied, for example, by Jains to their founder, Mahāvīra. Definition of the inclusive category has varied, however, and *buddha* has been used to describe a broad spectrum of persons, from those who are simply learned to those rare individuals who have had transforming and liberating insight into the nature of reality. Buddhists have, in general, employed the term in this second, stronger sense.

Buddhists adopted the term *buddha* from the religious discourse of ancient India and gave it a special imprint, just as they have done with much of their vocabulary. It seems, however, that the early Buddhists may not have immediately applied the term to the person—the historical Gautama—whom they recognized as the founder of their community. In the accounts of the first two Buddhist councils (one held just after Gautama's death, the other several decades later) Gautama is spoken of as *bhagavan* ("lord," a common title of respect) and *śāstṛ* ("teacher"), not as *buddha.* However, once the term *buddha* was adopted, it not only became the primary designation for Gautama but also assumed a central role within the basic structure of Buddhist thought and practice.

We will begin our discussion by focusing on the question of the historical Buddha and what—if anything—we know about him and his ministry. This issue has not been of particular importance for traditional Buddhists—at least not in the way that it is formulated here. But it has been of major significance for modern scholars of Buddhism, and it has become of great interest to many contemporary Buddhists and others who have been influenced by modern Western notions of history.

We will then turn to the term *buddha* as it has been employed within the various traditions that constitute classical Buddhism. As an appellative term utilized in classical Buddhist contexts, *buddha* has had three distinct, yet interwoven, levels of meaning. It has referred, first of all, to what we will call "the Buddha"—otherwise known as the Gautama Buddha or the Buddha Śākyamuni ("sage of the Śākyas"). Most Buddhists recognize Gautama as the buddha of our own cosmic era and/or cosmic space, and they honor him as the founder of the existing Buddhist community. As a perfectly enlightened being, Gautama is understood to have perfected various virtues (*pāramitās*) over the course of numerous lives.] These prodigious efforts prepared Gautama to awake fully to the true nature of reality just as other Buddhas had awakened before him. The preparation also gave him—as it did other Buddhas—the inclination and ability to share with others what he had discovered for himself. Following his Enlightenment, Gautama became a teacher who "set in motion the wheel of Dharma" and oversaw the founding of the Buddhist comunity of monks, nuns, laymen, and laywomen.

The second level of meaning associated with *buddha* as an appellative term has to do with "other buddhas." Many buddhas of different times and places are named in Buddhist literature. Moreover, anyone who attains release (*mokṣa, nirvāṇa*) from this world of recurring rebirths (*saṃsāra*) can be called—in some contexts at least—a buddha. Buddhas, then, are potentially as "innumerable as the sands of the River Ganges." But all buddhas are not equal: they possess different capabilities according to their aspirations and accomplishments. The enlightened insight of some is greater than that of others. Some attain enlightenment only for themselves (e.g., *pratyekabuddha*), others for the benefit and welfare of many (e.g., *samyaksaṃbuddha*). Some accomplish their mission through their earthly careers, others through the creation of celestial buddha fields into which their devotees seek rebirth.

Finally, the term *buddha* as an appellative has a third level of meaning that we will designate as buddhahood—a level that provides its widest conceptual context. This level is constituted by the recognition that the Buddha and other buddhas are, in a very profound sense, identical with ultimate reality itself. Consequently, Buddhists have given the more personal and active connotations associated with the Buddha and other buddhas to their characterizations of absolute reality as *dharma* (salvific truth), *śūnyatā* ("emptiness"), *tathatā* ("suchness"), and the like. At the same time, the term *buddhahood* has on occasion given a somewhat depersonalized cast to the notions of the Buddha and other buddhas. For example, early Buddhists, who were closest to the historical Buddha, were reluctant to depict Gautama in anthropomorphic forms and seem to have intentionally avoided biographical structures and iconic imagery. They used impersonal and symbolic representation to express their perception that the Buddha whose teachings they had preserved was fully homologous with reality itself. In some later traditions the pervading significance of this third level of meaning was expressed through the affirmation that the Buddha's impersonal and ineffable *dharmakāya* ("*dharma* body") was the source and truth of the other, more personalized manifestations of Buddhahood.

THE HISTORICAL BUDDHA. The scholars who inaugurated the critical study of Buddhism in the late nineteenth and early twentieth centuries were deeply concerned with the question of the "historical Buddha." But their views on the subject differed radically. The field was largely divided between a group of myth-oriented scholars, such as Émile Senart, Heinrich Kern, and Ananda Coomaraswamy, and a group of more historically oriented philologists, such as Hermann Oldenberg and T. W. and C. A. F. Rhys Davids. The myth-oriented interpreters placed emphasis on the study of Sanskrit sources and on the importance of those elements in the sacred biography that pointed in the direction of solar mythology; for these scholars, the historical Buddha was, at most, a reformer who provided an occasion for historicizing a classic solar myth. In contrast, the historically oriented philologists emphasized the texts written in Pali, as well as those elements in these texts that they could use to create (or reconstruct, in their view) an acceptable "historical" life of the Buddha. From the perspective of these scholars, the mythic elements—and other supposedly irrational elements as well—were later additions to a true historical memory, additions that brought about the demise of the original Buddhism of the Buddha. Such pious frauds were to be identified and discounted by critical scholarship.

More recently, scholars have recognized the inadequacy of the older mythic and historical approaches. Most scholars working in the field at present are convinced of the existence of the historical Gautama. The general consensus was well expressed by the great Belgian Buddhologist Étienne Lamotte, who noted that "Buddhism would remain inexplicable if one did not place at its beginning a strong personality who was its founder" (Lamotte, 1958, p. 707). But at the same time scholars are aware that the available tests provide little information about the details of Gautama's life.

The difficulties involved in saying anything significant about the historical Buddha are illustrated by the lack of certainty concerning the dates of his birth and death. Since different Buddhist traditions recognize different dates, and since external evidence is slight and inconclusive, scholars have ventured diverging opinions.

Two chronologies found in Buddhist texts are important for any attempt to calculate the date of the historical Buddha. A "long chronology," presented in the Sri Lankan chronicles, the *Dīpavaṃsa* and the *Mahāvaṃsa*, places the birth of the historical Buddha 298 years before the coronation of King Aśoka, his death 218 years before that event. If we accept the date given in the chronicles for the coronation of Aśoka (326 BCE), that would locate the Buddha's birth date in 624 BCE and his death in 544. These dates have been traditionally accepted in Sri Lanka and Southeast Asia and were the basis for the celebration of the 2500th anniversary of the Buddha's death, or *parinirvāṇa*, in 1956. However, most modern scholars who accept the long chronology believe, on the basis of Greek evidence, that Aśoka's coronation took place around 268 or 267 BCE and that the Buddha's birth and death should therefore be dated circa 566 and circa 486, respectively. These later dates are favored by the majority of Buddhologists in Europe, America, and India.

A "short chronology" is attested to by Indian sources and their Chinese and Tibetan translations. These sources place the birth of the Buddha 180 years before the coronation of Aśoka and his death 100 years before that event. If the presumably reliable Greek testimony concerning Aśoka's coronation is applied, the birth date of the Buddha is 448 and the date of his death, or *parinirvāṇa*, is 368. This short chronology is accepted by many Japanese Buddhologists and was spiritedly defended by the German scholar Heinz Bechert in 1982.

Although there seems to be little chance of resolving the long chronology/short chronology question in any kind of definitive manner, we can say with some certainty that the historical Buddha lived sometime during the period from the sixth through the fourth centuries BCE. This was a time of radical thought and speculation, as manifested in the pre-Socratic philosophical tradition and the mystery cults in Greece, the prophets and prophetic schools of the Near East, Confucius and Laozi in China, the Upaniṣadic sages and the communities of ascetic wanderers (*śramaṇas*) in India, and the emergence of "founded" religions such as Jainism and Buddhism. These intellectual and religious movements were fostered by the formation of cosmopolitan empires, such as those associated with Alexander in the Hellenistic world, with the Qin and Han dynasties in China, with Darius and Cyrus in Persia, and with the Maurya dynasty in India. Urban centers were established and soon became the focal points around which a new kind of life was organized. A significant number of people, cut off from the old sources of order and meaning, were open to different ways of expressing their religious concerns and were quite ready to support those engaged in new forms of religious and intellectual endeavor.

The historical Buddha responded to this kind of situation in northeastern India. He was a renouncer and an ascetic, although the style of renunciation and asceticism he practiced and recommended was, it seems, mild by Indian standards. He shared with other renunciants an ultimately somber view of the world and its pleasures, and he practiced and recommended a mode of religious life in which individual participation in a specifically religious community was of primary importance. He experimented with the practices of renunciants—begging, wandering, celibacy, techniques of self-restraint (yoga), and the like—and he organized a community in which discipline played a central role. Judging from the movement he inspired, he was not only an innovator but also a charismatic personality. Through the course of his ministry he gathered around him a group of wandering mendicants and nuns, as well as men and women who continued to live the life of householders.

Can we go beyond this very generalized portrait of the historical Buddha toward a fuller biography? Lamotte has advised caution, observing in his *Histoire* that writing the life of the historical Gautama is "a hopeless enterprise" (p. 16). There are, however, a few details that, though they do not add up to a biography, do suggest that there is a historical core to the later biographical traditions. These details are presented in almost identical form in the literature of diverse Buddhist schools, a reasonable indication that they date from before the fourth to third centuries BCE, when independent and separate traditions first began to develop.

Some of these details are so specific and arbitrary or unexpected that it seems unlikely that they were fabricated. These include the details that Gautama was of the *kṣatriya* caste, that he was born in the Śākya clan (a more distinguished pedigree could have been created), that he was married and had a child, that he entered the ascetic life without the permission of his father, that his first attempts to share the insights that he had gained through his Enlightenment met with failure, that his leadership of the community he had established was seriously challenged by his more ascetically inclined cousin, and that he died in a remote place after eating a tainted meal. But these details are so few and disconnected that our knowlege of the historical Buddha remains shadowy and unsatisfying. In order to identify a more meaningful image of Gautama and his career we must turn to the Buddha who is explicitly affirmed in the memory and practice of the Buddhist community.

THE BUDDHA. The general history of religions strongly suggests that the death of a founder results in the loss of a charismatic focus. This loss must be dealt with if the founded group is to survive. In his classic article "Master and Disciple: Two Religio-Sociological Studies," Joachim Wach suggests that "the image" of the beloved founder could produce a unity sufficient for the group to continue (*Journal of Religion* 42, 1962, p. 5).

Each founded religion has developed original ways of preserving the image of their master: Christians with the Gospels and later artistic expressions, Muslims with *ḥadīth* and *Miʿrāj* stories of Muḥammad's journeys to heaven, and so on. Buddhists, it seems, have addressed this crisis with the assumption—explicitly stated in the words of a fifth-century CE Mahāyāna text known as the *Saptaśatikāprajñāpāramitā*—that "a Buddha is not easily made known by words" (Rome, 1923, p. 126). This recognition has not proved to be a restraint but has instead inspired Buddhists to preserve the image of Gautama through the creation and explication of epithets, through a variety of "biographical" accounts, and through a tradition of visual representation in monumental architecture and art. The image of the founder became, in Joachim Wach's phrase, "an objective center of crystalization" for a variety of opinions concerning the nature and significance of his person.

The creative preservation of the image of the Buddha was closely related to evolving patterns of worship—including pilgrimage, contemplation, and ritual—in the Buddhist community. This reminds us that the various ways of portraying the Buddha are the result of innumerable personal efforts to discern him with immediacy, as well as the product of the desire to preserve and share that image.

Epithets. Certainly one of the earliest and most ubiquitous forms in which Buddhists have expressed and generated their image of Gautama Buddha was through the medium of epithets. For example, in the *Majjhima Nikāya* (London, 1948, vol. 1, p. 386), a householder named Upāli, after becoming the Buddha's follower, acclaims him with one hundred epithets. The Sanskrit version of this text adds that Upāli spoke these epithets spontaneously, as an expression of his faith and respect. Over the centuries the enumerations of these and other epithets focused on the extraordinary aspects of the Buddha's person, on his marvelous nature. In so doing they became a foundation for Buddhist devotional literature, their enunciation a support of devotional and contemplative practice.

Countless epithets have been applied to the Buddha over the centuries, but *buddha* itself has been a particular favorite for explanation. Even hearing the word *buddha* can cause people to rejoice because, as the Theravāda commentary on the *Saṃyutta Nikāya* says, "It is very rare indeed to hear the word *buddha* in this world" (London, 1929, vol. 1, p. 312). The *Paṭisambhidā*, a late addition to the Theravāda canon, explored the significance of the word *buddha* by saying that "it is a name derived from the final liberation of the Enlightened Ones, the Blessed Ones, together with the omniscient knowledge at the root of the Enlightenment Tree; this name 'buddha' is a designation based on realization" (*The Path of Purification*, translated by Ñyāṇamoli, Colombo, 1964, p. 213). Sun Chou, a fourth-century Chinese writer, explicated the *buddha* epithet in a rather different mode, reminiscent of a Daoist sage: "'Buddha' means 'one who embodies the Way'. . . . It is the one who reacts to the stimuli (of the world) in all pervading accordance (with the needs of all beings); the one who abstains from activity and who is yet universally active" (quoted in Erik Zürcher's *The Buddhist Conquest of China*, Leiden, 1959, p. 133).

Particular epithets accentuate specific qualities of the Buddha that might otherwise remain unemphasized or ambiguous. Thus the epithet "teacher of gods and men" (*satthar devamanussānāṃ*) is used in the *Mahāniddesa*, another late canonical text in the Theravāda tradition, to display the Buddha as one who helps others escape from suffering. The techniques used—exploiting ordinary polysemy and puns and deriving elaborate etymologies—are favorites of Buddhist commentators for exposing the significance of an epithet.

> He teaches by means of the here and now, of the life to come, and of the ultimate goal, according as befits the case, thus he is Teacher (*satthar*). "Teacher (*satthar*)": the Blessed One is a caravan leader (*satthar*) since he brings home caravans. Just as one who brings a caravan home gets caravans across a wilderness. . . gets them to reach a land of safety, so too the Blessed One is a caravan leader, one who brings home the cara-

vans; he gets them across. . . the wilderness of birth. (Ñyāṇamoli, p. 223)

Some of the epithets of the Buddha refer to his lineage and name: for example, Śākyamuni, "sage of the Śākya tribe," and his personal name, Siddhārtha, "he whose aims are fulfilled." Some refer to religio-mythic paradigms with which he was identified: *mahāpuruṣa* means "great cosmic person"; *cakravartin* refers to the "universal monarch," the possessor of the seven jewels of sovereignty who sets in motion the wheel of righteous rule. Some—such as *bhagavan*—convey a sense of beneficent lordship. Others—such as *tathāgata* ("thus come," or "thus gone")—retain, at least in retrospect, an aura of august ambiguity and mystery.

Various epithets define the Buddha as having attained perfection in all domains. His wisdom is perfect, as are his physical form and manner. In some cases the epithets indicate that the Buddha is without equal, that he has attained "the summit of the world." André Bareau concluded his study "The Superhuman Personality of the Buddha and its Symbolism in the *Mahāparinirvāṇa-sūtra*," which is largely an examination of the epithets in this important text, by stating that through these epithets the authors "began to conceive the transcendence of the Buddha. . . . Perfect in all points, superior through distance from all beings, unique, the Beatific had evidently taken, in the thought of his followers, the place which the devotees of the great religions attributed to the great God whom they adored" (*Myths and Symbols*, ed. Charles H. Long and Joseph M. Kitagawa, Chicago, 1969, pp. 19–20).

The epithets of the Buddha, in addition to having a central place in Buddhist devotion, are featured in the *buddhānusmṛti* meditation—the "recollection of the Buddha." This form of meditation, like all Buddhist meditational practices, had as its aim the discipline and purification of the mind; but, in addition, it was a technique of visualization, a way of recovering the image of the founder. This practice of visualization by contemplation on the epithets is important in the Theravāda tradition, both monastic and lay, and it was also very popular in the Sarvāstivāda communities in northwestern India and influential in various Mahāyāna traditions in China. It was instrumental in the development of the Mahāyāna notion of the "three bodies" (*trikāya*) of the Buddha, particularly the second, or visualized, body that was known as his *saṃbhogakāya* ("body of enjoyment").

Biographies. Like the tradition of uttering and interpreting epithets that extolled the exalted nature and virtues of the Buddha, the tradition of recounting biographical episodes is an integral part of early Buddhism. Episodic fragments, preserved in the Pali and Chinese versions of the early Buddhist literature, are embedded in sermons attributed to the Buddha himself and illustrate points of practice or doctrine. Such episodes are also used as narrative frames to provide a context indicating when and where a particular discourse was taught. It appears certain that other episodic fragments were recounted and generated at the four great pilgrimage centers of early Buddhism—the sites that were identified as the locations of the Buddha's birth, of his Enlightenment, of the preaching of his first sermon, and of his death, or *parinirvāṇa*. Some of the scattered narratives do seem to presuppose a developed biographical tradition, but others suggest a fluidity in the biographical structure. Thus, a crucial problem that is posed for our understanding of the biographical process in the Buddhist tradition is when and how a more or less fixed biography of the Buddha actually took shape.

The most convincing argument for the very early development of a comprehensive biography of the Buddha has been made by Erich Frauwallner (1956). Frauwallner argues, on the basis of a brilliant text-critical analysis, that a no longer extant biography of the Buddha, complete up to the conversion of the two great disciples, Śāriputra and Maudgalyāyana, was written approximately one hundred years after the Buddha's death and well prior to the reign of King Aśoka. This biography, he maintains, was composed as an introduction to the *Skandhaka*, a text of monastic discipline (Vinaya) that was reportedly confirmed at the Second Buddhist Council held at Vaiśālī. Appended to the *Skandhaka*, according to Frauwallner, was an account of the Buddha's death, or *parinirvāṇa*, and of the first years of the fledgling monastic community. Frauwallner contends that all subsequent Buddha biographies have been derived from this basic ur-text. The fragmentary biographies found in the extant Vinaya literature of the various Buddhist schools indicate a crumbling away of this original biography; later autonomous biographies are versions cut from the original Vinaya context and subsequently elaborated.

A different argument has been made, also on the basis of close text-critical study, by scholars such as Alfred Foucher, Étienne Lamotte, and André Bareau. They have argued that there was a gradual development of biographical cycles, with only a later synthesis of this material into a series of more complete biographies. According to this thesis, the earliest stages of the development of the Buddha biography are the fragments in the sūtra and Vinaya texts, which show no concern for chronology or continuity. The Sūtra literature emphasizes stories of the Buddha's previous births (*jātaka*), episodes leading up to the Enlightenment, the Enlightenment itself, and an account of his last journey, death, and funeral. André Bareau states that the biographical material in the sūtras was "composed for the most part of episodes taken from separate traditions, from which the authors chose with complete freedom, guided only by their desire to illustrate a particular point of doctrine" (Bareau, 1963, p. 364). The Vinaya texts, on the other hand, focus on the Buddha as teacher and incorporate—in addition to accounts of the events associated with his Enlightenment—narratives that describe the early days of his ministry, including an account of the conversion of his first disciples. The air of these Vinaya fragments seems to be to confer authenticity on the monastic rules and practices set forth in the rest of the text.

The oldest of the surviving autonomous biographies is the *Mahāvastu,* an unwieldly anthology written in Buddhist Hybrid Sanskrit about the beginning of the common era. Other more tightly constructed biographies were produced soon after the *Mahāvastu*—notably, the *Lalitavistara,* which played an important role in various Mahāyāna traditions; the *Abhiniṣkramaṇa Sūtra,* which was especially popular in China, where at least five Chinese works were, nominally at least, translations of it; and the very famous and popular *Buddhacarita,* attributed to Aśvaghoṣa. Much later, between the fourth and fifth centuries, still another autonomous biography, known as the Vinaya of the Mūlasarvāstivādins, was given its final form. This voluminous compendium of biographical traditions provided later Mahāyāna schools with a major source for stories about the Buddha and his career.

These new autonomous biographies continued to incorporate stories that had developed at the pilgrimage sites associated with the Buddha's birth and great renunciation, his Enlightenment, and his first sermon. For example, in the *Lalitavistara* an episode is recounted that is clearly related to a specific shrine at the Buddhist pilgrimage site at Kapilavastu—namely, the story in which the Buddha's charioteer leaves him and returns to the palace in Kapilavastu. What is more, these new autonomous biographies also continued to exhibit structural elements that had been characteristic of the biographical segments of the older Vinaya literature. For example, all of the early autonomous biographies (with the exception of the "completed" Chinese and Tibetan versions of the *Buddhacarita*) follow the Vinaya tradition, which ends the story at a point soon after the Buddha had begun his ministry.

These new autonomous biographies testify to three important changes that affected the traditions of Buddha biography during the centuries immediately following the death of King Aśoka. The first is the inclusion of new biographical elements drawn from non-Buddhist and even non-Indian sources. The autonomous biographies were the products of the cosmopolitan civilizations associated with the Śātavāhana and Kushan (Kuṣāṇa) empires, and therefore it is not surprising that new episodes were adapted from Greek and West Asian sources. Somewhat later, as the autonomous Buddha biographies were introduced into other areas, changes were introduced to accentuate the Buddha's exemplification of new cultural values. Thus, in a fourth-century Chinese "translation" of the *Abhiniṣkramaṇa,* great emphasis was placed on the Buddha's exemplification of filial piety through the conversion of his father, King Śuddhodana.

The second important change exhibited by these new autonomous biographies was the ubiquitous inclusion of stories about the Buddha's previous lives (*jātaka*) as a device for explicating details of his final life as Gautama. This is particularly evident in the *Mahāvastu* and in certain versions of the *Abhiniṣkramana Sūtra,* in which, according to Lamotte, "the Jātakas become the prime mover of the narration: each episode in the life of the Buddha is given as the result and reproduction of an event from previous lives" (Lamotte, 1958, p. 725).

The third discernible change is the increasing placement of emphasis on the superhuman and transcendent dimensions of the Buddha's nature. Earlier narratives refer to the Buddha's fatigue and to his susceptibility to illness, but in the autonomous biographies he is said to be above human frailties. There is a tendency to emphasize the Buddha's superhuman qualities, not only of mind, but also of body: "It is true that the Buddhas bathe, but no dirt is found on them; their bodies are radiant like golden amaranth. Their bathing is mere conformity with the world" (*Mahāvastu,* trans. J. J. Jones, London, 1949, vol. 1, p. 133). As a function of this same emphasis on transcendence, the Buddha's activities are increasingly portrayed in the modes of miracle and magic. With the emergence and development of Mahāyāna, new narratives began to appear that portrayed the Buddha preaching a more exalted doctrine, sometimes on a mountain peak, sometimes in a celestial realm, sometimes to his most receptive disciples, sometimes to a great assembly of *bodhisattvas* (future buddhas) and gods.

Whereas the Mahāyāna accepted the early autonomous biographies and supplemented them with additional episodes of their own, the Theravāda community displayed a continuing resistance to developments in the biographical tradition. For almost nine centuries after the death of Gautama, the various elements of the Buddha biography were kept separate in Theravāda literature. But in the fifth century CE, about half a millennium after the composition of the first autonomous biographies, the Theravādins began to create their own biographical genres. These brought together and synthesized, in their own, more restrained style, many of the previously fragmented narratives.

Two types of Buddha biographies have had an important impact and role in the later history of the Theravāda tradition. The model for the classical type is the *Nidānakathā,* a text that serves as an introduction to the fifth-century *Jātaka Commentary* and thus continues the pattern of using biography to provide a narrative context that authenticates the teaching. It traces the Buddha's career from the time of his previous birth as Sumedha (when he made his original vow to become a buddha) to the year following Gautama's Enlightenment, when he took up residence in the Jetavana Monastery. Subsequent Theravāda biographies, based on the *Nidānakathā,* continued the narration through the rest of Gautama's ministry and beyond.

The second type of Theravāda biography—the chronicle (*vaṃsa*) biography—illustrates a distinctive Theravāda understanding of the Buddha. From very early in their history the Theravādins had distinguished between two bodies of the Buddha, his physical body (*rūpakāya*) and his body of truth (*dharmakāya*). After the Buddha's death, or *parinirvāṇa,* the *rūpakāya* continued to be present to the community in his relics, and his *dharmakāya* continued to be present in his teachings. In the fourth to fifth centuries

CE the Theravādins began to compose biographical chronicles that focused on these continuing legacies. These begin with previous lives of the Buddha, then provide an abbreviated account of his "final" life as Gautama. They go on to narrate the history of the tradition by interweaving accounts of kings who maintain the physical legacy (in the form of relics, stupas, and the like) with accounts of the monastic order, which maintains his *dharma* legacy (in the form of proper teaching and discipline). Examples of this type of biographical chronicle are numerous, beginning with the *Dīpavaṃsa* and *Mahāvaṃsa* and continuing through many other *vaṃsa* texts written in Sri Lanka and Southeast Asia.

Throughout the premodern history of Buddhism, all of the major Buddhist schools preserved biographies of the Buddha. And in each situation, they were continually reinterpreted in relation to contemporary attitudes and experiences. But in the modern period, a new genre of Buddha biographies has been introduced. This new type of biography has been influenced by Western scholarship on Buddhism and by Western attempts to recover the historical Buddha, who had—from the modernist perspective—been hidden from view by the accretions of tradition. New, largely urbanized elites throughout the Buddhist world have sought to "demythologize" the Buddha biography, deleting miraculous elements of the Buddha's life and replacing them with an image of the founder as a teacher of a rationalistic ethical system or a "scientific" system of meditation or as a social reformer committed to the cause of democracy, socialism, or egalitarianism. This new genre of Buddha biography has appeared in many Buddhist contexts and has made an impact that has cut across all the traditional lines of geographical and sectarian division.

Visual representations. The images of the founder that Buddhists have generated and expressed visually are more enigmatic than the images presented in epithets and biographies. The history of Buddhist monumental architecture, art, and sculpture does not neatly fit such accustomed categories as "mythologization" or "divinization." Furthermore, the association of various kinds of visual representation with veneration and worship challenges many stereotypes about the secondary place of cult activity in the Buddhist tradition. The situation is further complicated by the fact that the function and significance of visual representations of the Buddha are only explained in relatively late Buddhist literature, after both doctrine and practice had become extremely complex.

The most important of the very early visual representations of the Buddha was the burial mound, or stupa (Skt., *stūpa*). The interment of the remains of kings and heroes in burial mounds was a well-established practice in pre-Buddhist India. Buddhists and Jains adopted these mounds as models for their first religious monuments and honored them with traditional practices. In the Pali *Mahāparinibbāna Suttanta* and its parallels in Sanskrit, Tibetan, and Chinese, the Buddha gives instructions that his funeral rites should be performed in the manner customary for a "universal monarch" (*cakravartin*), an epithet that was applied to the Buddha. After his cremation his bones were to be deposited in a golden urn and placed in a mound built at the crossing of four main roads. Offerings of flowers and garlands, banners, incense, and music characterized both the funeral rites themselves and the continuing worship at a stupa.

As Buddhism developed, the stupa continued to serve as a central visual representation of the founder. Seeing a stupa called to memory the greatness of the Buddha and—for some at least—became equivalent to actually seeing the Buddha when he was alive. Since the Buddha's physical remains could be divided, replicated, and distributed, new stupas containing relics could be constructed. They became a focal point for worship wherever Buddhism spread, first within India and then beyond. What is more, the stupa had symbolic connotations that exerted a significant influence on the way in which the Buddha was perceived. For example, stupas had a locative significance through which the Buddha was associated with specific territorial units. They also came increasingly to represent a cosmology and cosmography ordered by Buddhist principles, thus symbolically embodying the notion of the Buddha as a cosmic person.

The later literature explains that a stupa is worthy of worship and reverence not only because it contains a relic or relics but also because its form symbolizes the enlightened state of a Buddha, or Buddhahood itself. In some texts the stupa is described as the *dharmakāya*, or transcendent body, of the Buddha, and each of its layers and components is correlated with a set of spiritual qualities cultivated to perfection by a Buddha. Such symbolic correlations made evident what, in some circles at least, had been long accepted, namely, the notion that the stupa represents the Buddha's spiritual, as well as his physical, legacy.

The beginnings of Buddhist art are found on post-Aśokan stupas, such as those found at Bhārhut, Sāñcī, and Amarāvatī. These great stupas and their gates are decorated with narrative reliefs of events from the Buddha's life and with scenes of gods and men "rendering homage to the Lord." The Buddha is always depicted symbolically in these reliefs, with emblems appropriate to the story. For example, in friezes depicting scenes associated with his birth he is often represented by a footprint with the characteristic marks of the *mahāpuruṣa* (the cosmic man destined to be either a *cakravartin* or a Buddha). In scenes associated with his Enlightenment he is often represented by the bodhi tree under which he attained Enlightenment, or the throne on which he was seated when that event occurred. When the subject is the preaching of his first sermon he is often represented by an eight-spoked wheel that is identified with the wheel of *dharma.* When the subject is his death, or Pāramitās *parinirvāṇa,* the preferred symbol is, of course, the stupa.

The motivation for this aniconic imagery is not clear, especially since the friezes abound with other human figures. However, it is probable that abstract art was more adaptable to contemplative uses that we have already seen emphasized in connection with the epithets of the Buddha and with the symbolic interpretation of the stupa. It may also be that these aniconic images imply a conception of the Buddha as a supramundane being similar to that of the docetic portrayals found in the autonomous biographies that appear somewhat later. This suggests that at this time Buddhism may have been richer in its concrete reality, in its practice, than in its doctrine, as it took centuries for a doctrinal understanding of the significance of these first representations to be formulated in the literature.

The stupa and other aniconic symbols emblematic of the Buddha have remained an integral component of Buddhist life in all Buddhist areas and eras. Toward the end of the first century BCE, however, another form of visual representation began to appear, namely, the anthropomorphic image that subsequently assumed paramount importance in all Buddhist countries and sects. The first of these images are contemporary with the autonomous biographies of the Buddha, and like these texts, they appropriate previously non-Buddhist and non-Indian motifs to express Buddhist conceptions and experiences. At Mathurā, in north-central India, where the first statues seem to have originated, sculptors employed a style and iconography associated with *yakṣas*, the popular life-cult deities of ancient India, to create bulky and powerful figures of the Buddha. At Gandhāra in northwestern India, another major center of early Buddhist image-making, the artists sculpted the Buddha images quite differently, appropriating Hellenistic conventions introduced into Asia by the Greeks, who ruled the area in the centuries following the invasions of Alexander the Great.

A great many styles have developed for the Buddha image; and just as at Mathurā and Gandhāra, local conventions have been fully exploited. There has been a continuity, however, to all these creations: the Buddha image has consistently served a dual function as both an object of worship and a support for contemplation. It seems clear that the basic form of the image was shaped by conceptions of the Buddha as *lokottara* (supramundane), *mahāpuruṣa*, *cakravartin*, omniscient, and so on, and standardized iconography was used to convey these various dimensions. The sculpted (and later painted) image was both an expression of, and an aid for, the visualization of the master and the realization of his presence.

If aniconic symbols lend themselves especially well to contemplative uses, anthropomorphic images seem more appropriate to emotion and prayer, as well as to worship as such. In fact, the patterns of veneration and worship that developed in connection with Buddha images show a strong continuity with the ancient devotional and petitionary practices associated with the *yakṣas* and other folk deities. Throughout Buddhist history the veneration and worship of Buddha images have involved sensuous offerings of flowers, incense, music, food, and drink, and have often been closely tied to very immediate worldly concerns.

Later Buddhist literature explains that the Buddha image is worthy of honor and worship because it is a likeness of the Buddha. Popular practice often ascribes a living presence to the statue, whether by placing a relic within it or by a ritual of consecration that infuses it with "life." Thus the image of the Buddha, like the stupa, is both a reminder that can inspire and guide and a locus of power.

OTHER BUDDHAS. The representations of the Buddha in epithet, biography, and image have been shared in their main outlines by the great majority of Buddhist schools. However, the recognition of other buddhas, the roles other buddhas have played, and the evaluation of their significance (and hence the role and significance of Gautama himself) have varied greatly from one tradition to another.

Buddhas of the past and future. Quite early, Gautama is perceived as one of several buddhas in a series that began in the distant past. In the early canonical literature, the series of previous buddhas sometimes appears as a practically anonymous group, deriving probably from the recognition that Gautama could not have been alone in achieving enlightenment. It is thus not surprising that in texts such as the *Saṃyutta Nikāya* the interest in these previous buddhas focuses on their thoughts at the time of enlightenment, thoughts that are identical with those attributed to Gautama when he achieved the same experience.

The most important early text on previous buddhas is the *Mahāvadāna Sutta*, which refers to six buddhas who had appeared prior to Gautama. This text implicitly contains the earliest coordinated biography of the Buddha, for it describes the pattern to which the lives of all buddhas conform. Thus, describing the life of a buddha named Vipaśyin, Gautama narrates that he was born into a royal family, that he was raised in luxury, that he was later confronted with the realities of sickness, aging, and death while visiting a park, and that he subsequently took up the life of a wandering mendicant. After Vipaśyin realized the truth for himself, he established a monastic order and taught what he had discovered to others. In the narratives of the other Buddhas, some details vary; but in every instance they are said to have discovered and taught the same eternal truth.

There is clear evidence that buddhas who were thought to have lived prior to Gautama were worshiped in India at least from the time of Aśoka through the period of Buddhist decline. In the inscription, Aśoka states that he had doubled the size of the stupa associated with the Buddha Konākamana, who had lived earlier than Gautama and was his immediate predecessor. During the first millennium of the common era, successive Chinese pilgrims recorded visits to Indian monuments dedicated to former buddhas, many of them attributed to the pious construction activities of Aśoka.

The *Buddhavaṃsa* (Lineage of the buddhas), which is a late text within the Pali canon, narrates the lives of twenty-four previous buddhas in almost identical terms. It may be that the number twenty-four was borrowed from Jainism, which has a lineage of twenty-four *tīrthaṃkaras* that culminates in the figure of the founder, Mahāvīra. The *Buddhavaṃsa* also embellished the idea of a connection between Gautama Buddha and the lineage of previous buddhas. It contains the story that later came to provide the starting point for the classic Theravāda biography of Gautama—the story in which the future Gautama Buddha, in his earlier birth as Sumedha, meets the previous Buddha Dīpaṃkara and vows to undertake the great exertions necessary to attain buddhahood for himself.

According to conceptions that are closely interwoven with notions concerning previous buddhas, the appearance of a buddha in this world is determined not only by his own spiritual efforts but also by other circumstances. There can only be one buddha in a particular world at a given time, and no buddha can arise until the teachings of the previous buddha have completely disappeared. There are also cosmological considerations. A buddha is not born in the beginning of a cosmic aeon (*kalpa*) when human beings are so well off and live so long that they do not fear sickness, aging, and death; such people, like the gods and other superhuman beings, would be incapable of insight into the pervasiveness of suffering and the impermanence of all things and therefore would not be prepared to receive a buddha's message. Furthermore, buddhas are born only in the continent of Jambudvīpa (roughly equivalent to India) and only to priestly (*brāhmaṇa*) or noble (*kṣatriya*) families.

The idea of a chronological series of previous buddhas, which was prominent primarily in the Hīnayāna traditions, accentuates the significance of Gautama by designating him as the teacher for our age and by providing him with a spiritual lineage that authenticates his message. This idea also provides a basis for hope because it suggests that even if the force of Gautama's person and message has begun to fade, there remains the possibility that other buddhas are yet to come.

The belief in a future buddha also originated in the Hīnayāna tradition and has played an important role in various Hīnayāna schools, including the Theravāda. The name of this next buddha is Maitreya ("the friendly one"), and he seems to have come into prominence in the period after the reign of King Aśoka. (Technically, of course, Maitreya is a *bodhisattva*—one who is on the path to buddhahood—rather than a buddha in the full sense. However, the degree to which the attention of Buddhists has been focused on the role that he will play when he becomes a buddha justifies consideration of him in the present context.)

According to the Maitreyan mythology that has been diffused throughout the entire Buddhist world, the future buddha, who was one of Gautama Buddha's disciples, now dwells in Tuṣita Heaven, awaiting the appropriate moment to be reborn on earth, where he will inaugurate an era of peace, prosperity, and salvation. As the buddha of the future, Maitreya assumed many diverse roles. Among other things he became an object of worship, a focus of aspiration, and a center of religio-political interest both as a legitimator of royalty and as a rallying point for rebellion.

The wish to be reborn in the presence of Maitreya, whether in Tuṣita Heaven or when he is reborn among humans, has been a sustaining hope of many Buddhists in the past, and it persists among Theravādins even today. The contemplation and recitation of the name of Maitreya inspired devotional cults in northwestern India, Central Asia, and China, especially between the fourth and seventh centuries CE. But in East Asia his devotional cult was superseded by that dedicated to Amitābha, a Buddha now existing in another cosmic world.

Celestial and cosmic buddhas. The recognition that there could be other buddhas in other world systems described in Buddhist cosmology builds on implications already present in the idea of past and future buddhas. Like the first buddhas of the past, the first Buddhas associated with other worlds are largely anonymous, appearing in groups to celebrate the teaching of the Buddha Gautama. The many epithets of the Buddha were sometimes pressed into service as personal names for individual buddhas who needed to be identified.

The idea of buddhas existing in other worlds comes to the fore in the early Mahāyāna literature. It was first employed, as in the *Saddharmapuṇḍarīka Sūtra* (Lotus of the true law), to authenticate new teachings, just as the tradition of former buddhas had done for the teachings of the early community. In the course of time, some of these buddhas came to be recognized individually as very powerful, their worlds as indescribably splendid and blissful. They were buddhas in superhuman form, and their careers, which were dedicated to the saving of others, lasted for aeons. Their influence was effective beyond their own worlds, and they could provide assistance—through the infinite merit they had accumulated—to the inhabitants of other world systems, including our own. The traditions that have focused attention on these buddhas have inevitably deemphasized the importance of Gautama Buddha by removing his singularity in human experience and by contrasting him with more powerful buddhas who could make their assistance and influence immediately and directly available.

While the number of such coexisting celestial buddhas is, in principle, infinite, and a great number are named in Buddhist literature, distinct mythological, iconic, and devotional traditions have only developed in a few cases. Amitābha ("boundless light") is one of the most important of the buddhas who did become the focus of a distinctive tradition. Originating in Northwest India or Central Asia, his appeal subsequently spread to China, Tibet, and Japan. Amitābha rules over a paradise that contains all the excellences of other buddha lands. He offers universal accessibility to this Pure Land (called Sukhāvatī), granting rebirth to those who practice the Buddha's determination to be reborn in it, and even to those who merely recite his name or think of him briefly but with faith. In the Amitābha/Pure Land traditions, which have had continuing success in China and Japan, we see a concentration on patterns of contemplation, visualization, and recitation first developed in connection with the epithets of the Buddha.

Another celestial buddha who came to hold a position of importance in the Buddhist tradition is Bhaiṣajyaguru, the Master of Medicine. Bhaiṣajyaguru rules over his own paradisiacal realm, which, in contrast to Amitābha's western paradise, is traditionally located in the east. Unlike Amitābha, he does not assist human beings in reaching final liberation, nor does he even offer rebirth in his land. Rather, the repetition or rememberance of his name relieves various kinds of suffering, such as sickness, hunger, and fear. The ritual worship of his statue brings all things that are desired. In the cult dedicated to Bhaiṣajyaguru—popular in China and Japan, where it was often influenced by Amitābha traditions—we see a magnification of the patterns of worship that had originally coalesced around the stupa and the Buddha image.

In other contexts, conceptions of integrated pantheons of buddhas were developed and exerted widespread influence. For example, in the traditions of Esoteric Buddhism a strong emphasis was placed on a primordial, central buddha. He was taken to be the essence or source of a set of buddhas who were positioned in the form of a cosmic *maṇḍala* ("circle") that was vividly depicted in iconography and ritual, for example, in the *tanka* paintings of Tibet. In certain Indo-Tibetan traditions the central buddha was Vajradhara ("diamond holder") or sometimes, when the emphasis was more theistic, the Ādi ("primordial") Buddha. In other Indo-Tibetan traditions the central buddha was Vairocana ("resplendent"), who also served as the preeminent buddha in the Esoteric (Shingon) tradition of Japan, where he was identified with the all-important solar deity in the indigenous pantheon of *kami.* In both cases—the one associated with Vajradhara and the Ādi Buddha and the one associated with Vairocana—the pantheon encompassed other Buddhas (and sometimes their "families"), who were identified with subsidiary cosmic positions. These included the east, a position often occupied by Akṣobhya ("imperturbable"); the south, often occupied by Ratnasambhava ("jewel-born"); the west, often occupied by Amitābha; and the north, often occupied by Amoghasiddhi ("infallible success"). In both cases the pantheon had a macrocosmic reference to the universe as a whole and a microcosmic reference in which the Buddhas of the pantheon were homologized with the mystic physiology of the human body.

Living buddhas. In addition to the Buddha, *pratyekabuddhas*, previous buddhas, the future buddha, celestial buddhas, and cosmic buddhas, still another kind of buddha was recognized by some Buddhists—what we shall call a "living buddha." Living buddhas are persons in this world who have, in one way or another, achieved the status of a fully enlightened and compassionate being. In some cases these living buddhas have attained buddhahood through various, usually Esoteric, forms of practice; in others they are incarnations of a buddha, ordinarily a celestial buddha, already included in the established pantheon. The presence of living buddhas tends, of course, to diminish to a new degree the significance of Gautama Buddha (except in rare cases where it is he who reappears). However, their presence also reiterates with new force two characteristic Mahāyāna-Vajrayāna emphases: that the message of the Buddhas continues to be efficaciously available in the world and that the community still has direct access to the kind of assistance that only a buddha can provide.

Like the notions of previous buddhas and the buddhas of other worlds, the concept of living buddhas began to be elaborated in a context in which a new kind of teaching and practice was being introduced. In this case the new teaching and practice was Esoteric in character and was focused on ritual activities that promised to provide a "fast path" to buddhahood. Thus the new kind of buddha—the living Buddha—was both a product of the new movement and a mode of authenticating it. The analogy between the earlier development of the notion of celestial buddhas and the later development of the notion of living buddhas can be carried further. Just as only a few celestial buddhas received their own individual mythology, iconography, and devotional attention, so too a limited number of living buddhas were similarly singled out. It is not surprising that many of these especially recognized and venerated living buddhas were figures who initiated new strands of tradition by introducing practices, revealing hidden texts, converting new peoples, and the like. A classic example of a living buddha in the Tibetan tradition is Padmasambhava, the famous missionary from India who is credited with subduing the demons in Tibet, converting the people to the Buddhist cause, and founding the Rnying ma pa order. An example of the same type of figure in Japan is Kūkai, the founder of the Esoteric Shingon tradition, who has traditionally been venerated both as master and as savior.

The notion of living buddhas as incarnations of celestial buddhas also came to the fore with the rise of Esoteric Buddhism. In this case there seems to have been an especially close connection with Buddhist conceptions of kingship and rule. In both the Hīnayāna and Mahāyāna contexts, the notion of the king as a *bodhisattva,* or future buddha, was ancient; in the case of the rather common royal identifications with Maitreya, the distinction between the king as an incarnation of the celestial *bodhisattva* and the king as a living buddha had been very fluid. With the rise of the Esoteric Buddhist traditions a further step was taken. Thus, after the Esoteric tradition had been firmly established in the Khmer (Cambodian) capital of Angkor, the king came to be explicitly recognized and venerated as Bhaiṣajyaguru, Master of Medicine. Somewhat later in Tibet, the Panchen Lamas, who have traditionally had both royal and monastic functions, were identified as successive incarnations of the buddha Amitābha.

BUDDHAHOOD. The epithets, biographies, and images of Śākyamuni and other Buddhas weigh the distinctiveness of each Buddha against his inclusion within a series or assembly of similar beings. However, as the appellative character of the term *buddha* suggests, at the level of buddhahood each tradition has affirmed the ultimate identity of all those they have recognized as buddhas. Even the Theravādins, who have consistently given pride of place to Gautama, have acknowledged this final level at which differentiations are not relevant. The same is true for those movements that focus primary attention on Amitābha or Mahāvairocana. The consensus of Buddhists in this respect is voiced by the *Milindapañha* (The questions of King Milinda), a Hīnayāna text dating from the beginning of the common era: "There is no distinction in form, morality, concentration, wisdom, freedom. . . among all the Buddhas because all Buddhas are the same in respect to their nature" (London, 1880, p. 285).

This initial consensus concerning the ultimate identity of all buddhas notwithstanding, the actual delineation of buddhahood has varied significantly from one Buddhist tradition to another. This third level of meaning of the term *buddha* has always been discussed in connection with questions concerning the nature and analysis of reality. Early Buddhists believed that a buddha awoke to and displayed the causal process (*pratītya-samutpāda*, codependent origination) that perpetuates this world, allowing himself and others to use those processes to end further rebirth. The early Mahāyāna, especially in the Prajña-paramita literature, saw buddhahood as awakening to the absence of self-nature in all things (*śūnyatā*) and proclaimed this absence as the ultimate reality (*tathatā*). Later Mahāyāna schools, such as the Yogācārins, held a more idealistic worldview; for them buddhahood was the recovery of an originally pure and undefiled mind. The Huayen (Jpn., Kegon) school, an East Asian tradition based on the *Avataṃsaka Sūtra*, posited the infinite mutual interaction of all things and developed a striking conception of a universal, cosmic buddha who is all-pervasive. In such contexts buddhahood itself became an alternative way of describing reality.

Between the consensus about the identity of all buddhas and the diversity of interpretations, there are at least two different languages in which buddhahood has traditionally been conceived and described. The first is the identification of buddhahood in terms of the special characteristics associated with a buddha. The second is the discussion of the buddha bodies that make up buddhahood. These two clusters of concepts allow us to see patterns of continuity in the midst of the very different ways in which buddhahood has been understood.

Buddhist scholasticism developed subtle catalogs of the unique powers and qualities of a buddha, culminating in lists of *āveṇika dharmas* (special characteristics). These special characteristics vary in number from 6 to 140, depending on the text and context. What interests us here is not the multitude of qualities and powers that are mentioned but, rather, the fact that these qualities and powers are often grouped under four major headings. These four headings are conduct and realization, which apply to the attainment of buddhahood, and wisdom and activity, which apply to the expression of buddhahood.

Throughout Buddhist history these four dimensions of buddhahood have been interpreted in different ways. For example, Hīnayānists have tended to emphasize motivated conduct as a means to the realization of buddhahood, whereas Mahāyānists and Vajrayānists have tended to stress that buddhahood (often in the form of buddha nature) is in important respects a necessary prerequisite for such conduct. Similarly, Hīnayānists have often recognized a certain distance between the attainment of wisdom and a commitment to compassionate activity, whereas in the Mahāyāna and Vajrayāna traditions the stress has been placed on the inseparable fusion of wisdom on the one hand and the expression of compassion on the other. These differences notwithstanding, the four basic dimensions are present in virtually all Buddhist conceptions of buddhahood.

When we turn to the way buddhahood has been expressed through the language of buddha bodies, we discern the same sort of continuity in the midst of difference. In the early Buddhist literature (e.g., *Dīgha Nikāya*, vol. 3, p. 84) the Buddha is described as having a body "born of *dharma*," that is, a *dharmakāya*. In this early period, and in the subsequent Theravāda development, the notion that Gautama possessed a *dharmakāya* seems to have served primarily as a metaphor that affirmed a continuity between the personal realizations that he had achieved and truth or reality itself. In some later Hīnayāna traditions such as the Sarvāstivāda, and in the Mahāyāna, the notion of *dharmakāya* took on a stronger meaning. It served as a primary means through which an increasingly transcendent vision of buddhahood could subsume the inescapable fact of Gautama's death. According to such texts as the *Saddharmapuṇḍarīka*, the *dharmakāya* is the true meaning of buddhahood; buddhas such as Gautama who appear, teach, and die among human beings are mere manifestations. In this early Mahāyāna context, however, the correlated notions of buddhahood and *dharmakāya* are still conditioned by their close association with philosophical conceptions such as *śūnyatā* ("emptiness") and *tathatā* ("suchness").

The *dharmakāya* is given a more ontological cast in other Mahāyāna and Vajrayāna traditions. In these cases, *dharmakāya* denotes a "ground" or "source" that is the reality that gives rise to all other realities; this provides the basis for a new understanding of the whole range of buddha bodies. buddhahood comes to be explicated in terms of a theory of three bodies. The *trikāya* ("three bodies") are the *dharmakāya*, the primal body that is the source of the other two; the emanated *saṃbhogakāya* ("enjoyment body"), a glorious body seen in visions in which buddhas of other worlds become manifest to devotees in this world; and the "magical" and ephemeral *nirmāṇakāya*, the physical body in which Gautama, for example, appeared among his disciples.

In some Mahāyāna and Vajrayāna contexts, this more ontological conception of the buddhahood and *dharmakāya* was also connected with the important soteriological notion of a buddha nature, or *tathāgata-garbha* (*tathāgata* is an epithet for a buddha, *garbha* means "womb"), which is the source and cause of enlightenment as well as its fruit. In these traditions, buddha nature, or *tathāgata-garbha*, is taken to be the *dharmakāya* covered with defilements. Enlightenment, and therefore buddhahood, is the recovery of this pure, original state of being that is identical with ultimate reality itself. In other Mahāyāna and Vajrayāna contexts, even the dichotomy between purity and defilement is transcended at the level of buddhahood.

CONCLUSION. In the course of our discussion of *buddha* as an appellative term we have distinguished three basic levels of meaning—those associated with Gautama Buddha, with other buddhas, and with buddhahood as such. However, it is important to note that Buddhist usage has always held the three levels of meaning closely together, with the result that each level has had a continuing influence on the others. Thus, even though a distinction between the different denotations of *buddha* is helpful for purposes of interpretation and understanding, it cannot be drawn too sharply.

In fact, these three meanings represent three different modes of reference that, according to some Indian theories of denotation, are common to all names. The word *cow*, for example, refers to individual cows ("a cow"), the aggregation of cows, and the quality of "cowness" common to all cows. There are obvious parallels to the uses of *buddha*. It might be helpful for those unfamiliar with such theories to think of *buddha* in terms of set theory: individual buddhas are members of subsets of the set of buddhahood. Just as mathematical sets exist without members, so buddhahood exists, according to the affirmation of Buddhists, even when it is not embodied by individual buddhas.

SEE ALSO Amitābha; Bhaiṣajyaguru; Bodhisattva Path; Buddhas and Bodhisattvas; Buddhism, Schools of; Buddhist Ethics; Buddhist Philosophy; Cakravartin; Cosmology, article on Buddhist Cosmology; Huayan; Iconography, article on Buddhist Iconography; Karuṇā; Mahāvairocana; Mahāvīra; Maitreya; Merit, article on Buddhist Concepts; Millenarianism, article on Chinese Millenarian Movements; Nianfo; Nirvāṇa; Padmasambhava; Pāramitās; Prajñā; Pratītya-samutpāda; Pure and Impure Lands; Stupa Worship; Śūnyam and Śūnyatā; Tathāgata; Tathāgata-garbha; Tathatā; Upāya; Yogācāra.

BIBLIOGRAPHY

Scholarship that is available in European languages generally treats the different levels of meaning of the appellative *buddha* in isolation. The interrelations among the different levels of meaning still remain largely unexplored.

Two books by Edward J. Thomas, if read in conjunction, can serve as a suitable introduction to the subject. *The Life of Buddha as Legend and History* (1927; 3d rev. ed., London, 1949) remains the standard work on the biography of the Buddha in English. *The History of Buddhist Thought* (1933; 2d ed., New York, 1951) surveys the development of ideas of other buddhas and buddhahood against the backdrop of the Indian Buddhist tradition. Thomas, however, does not include any of the developments in Tibet or East Asia, and his work has a definite bias in favor of the Pali tradition. A useful supplement for Tibet is David L. Snellgrove's *Buddhist Himālaya* (Oxford, 1957), which provides an introduction to the Vajrayāna interpretations. East Asian innovations were largely in connection with the meaning of buddhahood. They may be approached through Junjirō Takakusu's *The Essentials of Buddhist Philosophy*, edited by Wing-Tsit Chan and Charles A. Moore (Honolulu, 1947), although, as the title suggests, Takakusu is not primarily concerned with Buddhological patterns as such.

Heinz Bechert's important article "The Date of the Buddha Reconsidered," *Indologica Taurinensia* 10 (1982): 29–36, provides helpful summaries of the arguments favoring the long and short chronologies for calculating the date of the Buddha, although his conclusion in favor of the short chronology is by no means definitive. The cultural context of the historical Buddha is outlined by Padmanabh S. Jaini in his "*Śramaṇas:* Their Conflict with Brāhmaṇical Society," in *Chapters in Indian Civilization*, rev. ed., edited by Joseph W. Elder (Dubuque, 1970) vol. 1, pp. 39–81. This article should be read together with J. A. B. van Buitenen's "Vedic and Upaniṣadic Bases of Indian Civilization," which immediately preceeds it in the same volume (pp. 1–38).

A helpful starting point for the study of the Buddha biography is Frank E. Reynolds's "The Many Lives of Buddha: A Study of Sacred Biography and Theravāda Tradition" in *The Biographical Process*, edited by Reynolds and Donald Capps ("Religion and Reason Series," vol. 11, The Hague, 1976). It provides a survey of the patterns of interpretation that have developed in connection with the Buddha biography in Western scholarship, as well as an overview of the relevant Hīnayāna and later Theravāda texts.

The most important recent research on the biographies of the Buddha is written in French. An argument for successive stages in the development of the Buddha biography is found in Étienne Lamotte's *Histoire du bouddhisme indien* (Louvain, 1958), pp. 707–759, in which Lamotte responds to Erich Frauwallner's thesis that there was a very early, complete biography. Frauwallner presented this thesis in *The Earliest Vinaya and the Beginnings of Buddhist Literature* (Rome, 1956). An indispensable aid to serious work on the Buddha biography is André Bareau's *Recherches sur la biographie du Buddha dans les Sūtrapitaka et les Vinayapiṭaka anciens*, 2 vols. (Paris, 1963–1971). In these volumes Bareau documents and improves upon Lamotte's arguments in favor of a gradual development of the biographical cycles.

Alfred Foucher presents a composite biography of the Buddha from the beginning of the common era in *The Life of the Buddha according to the Ancient Texts and Monuments of India*, abridged translation by Simone B. Boas (Middletown, Conn., 1963). Foucher also includes an introduction that is of particular importance because it highlights the significance of early Buddhist pilgrimages in the development of the biographical tradition.

Several of the autonomous biographies, as well as some later biographies from Tibet, China, and Southeast Asia, have been translated into European languages. The most readable is Aśvaghoṣa's *Buddhacarita, or, Acts of the Buddha,* 2 vols. in 1, edited and translated by Edward H. Johnston (Calcutta, 1935–1936; 2d ed., New Delhi, 1972). This translation should be supplemented by Samuel Beal's translation of the Chinese version of the same text, *The Fo-Sho-hing-tsan-king: A Life of Buddha by Asvaghosha Bodhisattva* (Oxford, 1883; reprint, Delhi, 1966).

The role of the stupa as a preeminent Buddha symbol in Buddhist thought and practice is introduced in the collection *The Stūpa: Its Religious, Historical and Architectural Significance,* edited by Anna Libera Dallapiccola in collaboration with Stephanie Zingel-Ave Lallemant (Wiesbaden, 1980). Gustav Roth's article in this collection, "Symbolism of the Buddhist Stupa," is especially significant for its investigation of the symbolic interpretation of the stupa in Buddhist literature. A convenient and beautiful survey and appraisal of the visual representations of the Buddha throughout the Buddhist world is *The Image of the Buddha,* edited by David L. Snellgrove (London, 1978).

Modern research on "other Buddhas" is much less extensive than the research focused on the biographies and symbols associated with Gautama. Those interested in short, well-done introductions to Akṣobhya, Amitābha (Amita), and Bhaiṣajyaguru should consult the *Encyclopaedia of Buddhism,* edited by G. P. Malalasekera (Colombo, 1968). Vairocana is discussed by Ryūjun Tajima in his *Étude sur le Mahāvairocana sūtra (Dai-nichikyō),* (Paris, 1936). Material on "living buddhas" can be gleaned from various sections of Giuseppe Tucci's *The Religions of Tibet,* translated from the Italian and German by Geoffrey Samuel (Berkeley, 1980).

A work of monumental importance for the study of the concept of the Buddha and of Buddhism in general, is Paul Mus's *Barabaḍur,* 2 vols. (1935; reprint, New York, 1978). It is perhaps the only academic work that exploits the full potential of the appellative character of the term *buddha.* It contains seminal discussions of Buddhology in early, Hīnayāna, and Mahāyāna traditions; of the symbolism of the stupa and the relics; of celestial and cosmic Buddhas; and of the origin of Pure Land symbolism and thought. Unfortunately, this ponderously long work has not been translated, and the French is extremely difficult.

Readers seeking more specialized references (e.g., available translations of biographical texts or studies of particular developments) should consult the annotated entries in Frank E. Reynolds's *Guide to Buddhist Religion* (Boston, 1981), especially section 8, "Ideal Beings, Hagiography and Biography," and section 9, "Mythology (including Sacred History), Cosmology and Basic Symbols."

New Sources

Bechert, Heinz, ed. *The Dating of the Historical Buddha. Die Datierung des historischen Buddha.* 3 vols. Göttingen, 1991–1997.

Hallisey, Charles. "Roads Taken and Not Taken in the Study of Theravada Buddhism." In *Curators of the Buddha,* edited by Donald Lopez, pp. 31–62. Chicago, 1995.

Khoroche, Peter. *Once the Buddha Was a Monkey: Ārya Śūra's Jātakamālā.* Chicago, 1989.

Ohnuma, Reiko. "The Story of Rupavati: A Female Past Birth of the Buddha." *Journal of the International Association of Buddhist Studies* 23, no. 1 (2000): 103–45.

Payne, Richard Karl, and Kenneth Tanaka, eds. *Approaching the Land of Bliss: Religious Praxis in the Cult of Amitabha.* Honolulu, 2003.

Schober, Juliane, ed. *Sacred Biography in the Buddhist Traditions of South and Southeast Asia.* Honolulu, 1997.

Schopen, Gregory. "Burial *Ad Sanctos* and the Physical Presence of the Buddha in Early Indian Buddhism: A Study in the Archaeology of Religions." In *Bones, Stones, and Buddhist Monks. Collected Papers on the Archaeology, Epigraphy, and Texts of Monastic Buddhism in India,* pp. 114–147. Honolulu, 1997.

Schopen, Gregory. "The Buddha as an Owner of Property and Permanent Resident in Medieval Indian Monasteries." In *Bones, Stones, and Buddhist Monks. Collected Papers on the Archaeology, Epigraphy, and Texts of Monastic Buddhism in India,* pp. 258–289. Honolulu, 1997.

Sponberg, Alan, and Helen Hardacre, eds. *Maitreya, the Future Buddha.* New York, 1988.

Strong, John S. *The Buddha: A Short Biography.* Oxford, 2001.

FRANK E. REYNOLDS (1987)
CHARLES HALLISEY (1987)
Revised Bibliography

BUDDHADĀSA. Phra Dhammakosājān (1906–1993), better known by his self-designated monastic name, Buddhadāsa Bhikkhu ("Servant of the Buddha"), was one of the most influential Thai monks of the twentieth century. Born on May 21, 1906, as Nguam Panich, Buddhadāsa spent three years as a temple boy at Wat Pum Riang, a monastery in his home town, where he learned to read and write and was introduced to Buddhist teachings and rituals. After completing his primary schooling and beginning lower secondary education in Chaiya, south Thailand, his father's untimely death forced him to work in his family's business at age sixteen. Ordained a Buddhist monk in 1926, by 1928 he had passed the third and final level of the monastic curriculum and was invited to teach at the royally sponsored Wat Boromathat monastery in Chaiya.

After two years residency in Bangkok to study Pali (1930–1932), he became disenchanted with rote learning, the noise and distractions of the city, and the lax behavior of Bangkok monks. He returned home in the spring of 1932, the year Thailand's government changed from an absolute to a constitutional monarchy, where subsequently he established a forest monastery, Suan Mokkhabalārāma ("The Garden of Empowering Liberation"), known simply as Suan Mokkh. There, with the help and encouragement of his brother, Dhammadāsa, he founded a quarterly periodical, *Buddhasadana,* through which he captured the attention of the Thai Buddhist intelligentsia and rapidly gained a reputation for his intellectual prowess, his ability as a teacher, and his innovative interpretations of Theravāda doctrine. By 1937 his history of the Buddha's life was being used as a textbook at the Thammayut monastic university, Mahāmakut. In 1940 Buddhadāsa gave a series of lectures at the Buddhadhamma Association in Bangkok that attracted wide attention. His plain language unencumbered with technical monastic jargon, and his rational, demythologized interpretation of Buddhist teachings appealed to the growing urban, educated elites.

The Garden of Empowering Liberation. Suan Mokkh continued to expand, moving to its present site in 1944. The center combines aspects of early Buddhist forest practice with modern methods of propagating the *dhamma.* The resident monks live in simple wooden structures (*kuṭī*) with fewer amenities than are found in wealthy urban monasteries. Monks observe the traditional precepts of monastic life (*vinaya*), devote much of their day to study and meditation, and shun the ceremonial rituals that demand the attention of the typical Thai monk. In seemingly stark contrast to these traditions that emulate the lifestyle of the early *saṅgha* is the "Spiritual Theater" equipped to teach the *dhamma* using modern audiovisual technology. Copies of bas-reliefs from Sāñcī and Barhut adorn the exterior walls, while the interior walls are covered by mural paintings inspired not only by Buddhism but by other religious traditions as well. The building embodies Buddhadāsa's universalist vision that the highest goal of all religions is to transform selfish egoism into compassionate altruism.

In the decade prior to Buddhadāsa's death in 1993, he directed the establishment of a training center ancillary to Suan Mokkh, the International Dhamma Hermitage, where monthly meditation retreats are conducted in English. He also had plans to develop two other training centers, one for women (*dhammamata*) and another to train monks from all over the world in the practical application of the Buddha's teaching to the solution of global problems.

***Nirvāṇa*, Rebirth, and the Buddha.** Buddhadāsa's teachings have become the central platform of reformist Buddhism in Thailand for both monks and laity. Several noted Thai social activists, including Sulak Sivaraksa and Dr. Prawet Wasi, acknowledge their indebtedness to his example and interpretation of the *buddhadhamma.* His books are taught in monastic and secular universities, and he remains one of the most widely published and read Buddhist authors in the country. A severe critic of mainstream Thai Buddhism's self-serving preoccupation with merit-making rituals, he characterizes ceremonials whose intent aims at worldly personal gain as nothing but religious materialism. For Buddhadāsa, *nirvāṇa* is not an unachievable ideal but liberation from egoistic preoccupation, whether seen as a temporary cessation of the idea of "I" and "mine" (*tadaṇga-nibbāna*)—a mental peace that accompanies a state of meditative calmness—or a permanent state achieved through vigilant awareness that leads to the total elimination of the "I" idea.

Buddhadāsa's innovative teaching offers a counterpoint to the conventional Thai Theravāda understanding of rebirth (*saṃsāra*) and *nirvāṇa.* For him both are mental events: *saṃsāra* the everyday mind conditioned by the repeated arising and cessation of the "I" idea, and *nirvāṇa* the total elimination of that condition. In a similar vein, Buddhadāsa argues that devotion to the person of the Buddha, either as a historical being or as represented in images and relics, distorts the true significance of the Buddha, namely, the truth (*dhamma*) he realized at his awakening. Consequently, for Buddhadāsa, true devotion to the Buddha is the achievement of the mind of the Buddha, namely, the *dhamma,* not worshiping the person of the Buddha in the hope that the Blessed One will grant boons in the manner of a Hindu deity. Buddhadāsa's demythologized approach to the Buddha, *nirvāṇa,* rebirth, and other concepts is based on a Madhyāmikan epistemology that distinguishes between ordinary language (Thai, *phassā khon*) and truth-language (Thai, *phassā tham*). Within this framework, a *phassā khon* understanding of the Blessed One obscures the true meaning of the Buddha as the *dhamma,* namely, the universal law of causality (*idapaccayatā*).

Personal Liberation, the Just Society, and the Natural Order. Buddhadāsa's lectures and writings, published in seventy-two volumes, span a period of sixty years and are so wide-ranging that they have yet to be systematized. However, the legacy of his ethical thought can be distilled into three broad themes: personal liberation (Thai, *chit wāng*), the just society (Thai, *thamika sankhom niyom*), and the natural order (Thai, *kot thamachāt*). First and foremost, Buddhadāsa was committed to the central importance of the liberation of the individual from attachment to self. In his talks and essays he continually refers to the liberated mind and heart (*chit wāng*), overcoming selfishness (Thai, *mai hen kae tua*), and other Thai and Pali terms related to liberation from egocentrism (Thai, *tua kū khong kū*). He asserts that the core of the Buddha's teaching is epitomized not by the oft-quoted phrase, "Refrain from evil, do only good, purify the mind," or even the four noble truths, but by the statement in the *Majjhima Nikāya* (Collection of middle-length discourses), "Nothing whatsoever should be clung to" (*sabbe dhammā nālaṃ abhinivesāya*).

In one of his seminal writings, *Tu Kū Khong Kū* (Me and mine) Buddhadāsa makes the provocative, iconoclastic claim that the realization of not-self (Pali, *anattā*) negates the need to speak about the Buddha, the *dhamma,* the *saṃgha,* or any point of doctrine or event in the history of Buddhism. Where Buddhadāsa departs from conventional Theravāda wisdom is not in his emphasis on nonattachment and the liberation from craving (Pali, *tanhā*), but in the unique way in which he formulates and universalizes it. In Buddhadāsa view, liberation is the business of all Buddhists, not just monks; it is not something that one achieves only after many lifetimes but is attainable here and now; and, in an even more radical vein, liberation (Thai, *khwam wāng*) is the realization of our original condition unobscured by the taints or defilements (Pali, *kilesa*) that result from our preoccupation with gain and loss, love and anger, hatred and fear. Our original mind freed from defilement is a state of emptiness (Pali, *suññatā*), the normal or normative (Pali, *pakati*) state of things. When the mind attains to this condition it is in a state of buddhahood; that is, the mind knows the true nature of things.

Armed with truth and nonattachment we are able to act in a manner of open mutual regard. Only when we transcend our own ego-centeredness are we able to realize the common condition of all beings, that we are subject to the same process of birth, old age, suffering, and death, and to perceive that everything in the world is conditioned by the same universal natural law (Pali, *paṭicca samuppāda, idapaccayatā*). The just society that results is a dhammically governed society (Thai, *thamika sangkhom niyom*), a community grounded in the *dhamma* in which all members restrain their acquisitive self-interests and act on behalf for the mutual benefit of all. Such a community operates according to three complementary principles: the good of the whole, restraint and generosity, and respect and loving kindness. A dhammically grounded, mutually cooperative society, then, promotes a lifestyle of simplicity, moderation, and nonviolence. Buddhadāsa contends that the Buddhist philosophy of the Middle Way (Pali, *majjhimā patipadā*) supports such a cooperative society, as does the example of the life of the Buddha and the early *saṅgha.*

Buddhadāsa's utopian vision of the just society includes not only the human community but also the total natural and physical environment (Pali, *dhammajāti*; Thai, *thamachāt).* Everything is incontrovertibly linked together in the process of dependent co-arising; the human body, human society, and the entire cosmos operate according to this universal, dhammic, principle. The core of Buddhadāsa's ecological hermeneutic, consequently, is an identification of the *dhamma* with nature, and it was his sense of the liberating power of nature-as-*dhamma* that inspired him to found Wat Suan Mokkh. It is by understanding the natural order of things (*dhamma-idapaccayatā, pakati*) that human beings are enabled to truly comprehend the lesson of self-forgetting. In Buddhadāsa's biocentric spirituality, being attuned to the lessons of nature is tantamount to being at one with the *dhamma.* By inference, conversely, the destruction of nature implies the destruction of the *dhamma*; hence, caring for (Thai, *anurak*) and conserving the natural world is, for Buddhadāsa, not only an environmental imperative but a profoundly spiritual act.

Buddhadāsa's death on July 8, 1993, was a significant event of national mourning. Although Thailand does not celebrate a "Buddhadāsa Bhikkhu Day," his birth and death anniversaries are commemorated with lectures and symposia, and in anticipation of the one hundredth anniversary of his birth in 2006, twenty-five workshops have been scheduled and dozens of publications planned. While Buddhadāsa is no longer physically present, he noted in his own poetic necrology that he will continue to live on in his teaching:

> Even when I die and the body ceases,
> My voice still echoes in comrades' ears,
> Clear and bright, as loud as ever.
> Just as if I never died, the *Dhamma*-body lives on.

BIBLIOGRAPHY

Gabaude, Louis. *Une herméneutique bouddhique contemporaine de Thaïande: Buddhadasa Bhikkhu.* Paris, 1988.

Jackson, Peter A. *Buddhism, Legitimation, and Conflict: The Political Functions of Urban Thai Buddhism.* Singapore, 1989.

Jackson, Peter A. *Buddhadasa: A Buddhist Thinker for the Modern World.* Rev. ed. Chiang Mai, Thailand, 2003.

Santikaro Bhikkhu. "Buddhadasa Bhikkhu: Life and Society through the Natural Eyes of Voidness." In *Engaged Buddhism: Buddhist Liberation Movements in Asia,* edited by Christopher S. Queen and Sallie B. King, pp. 147–193. Albany, N.Y., 1996.

Sivaraksa, Sulak, ed. *Radical Conservatism:Buddhism in the Contemporary World, Articles in Honour of Bhikkhu Buddhadasa's 84th Birthday Anniversary.* Bangkok, 1990.

Sivaraksa, Sulak, ed. *The Quest for a Just Society: The Legacy and Challenge of Buddhadasa Bhikkhu.* Bangkok, 1994.

Swearer, Donald K. "Bhikkhu Buddhadāsa's Interpretation of the Buddha." *Journal of the American Academy of Religion* 64 (1996): 313–336.

Swearer, Donald K. "The Hermeneutics of Buddhist Ecology in Contemporary Thailand: Buddhadāsa and Dhammapiṭaka." In *Buddhism and Ecology: The Interconnection of Dharma and Deeds,* edited by Mary Evelyn Tucker and Duncan Ryūken Williams, pp. 21–44. Cambridge, Mass., 1997.

Swearer, Donald K., ed. *Me and Mine: Selected Essays of Bhikkhu Buddhadāsa.* Albany, N.Y., 1989.

DONALD K. SWEARER (2005)

BUDDHAGHOSA (fl. fifth century CE), one of the greatest Buddhist commentators. Participating in the Buddhist heritage as it neared completion of its first millennium, Buddhaghosa is most acclaimed for providing a commentarial and interpretive structure for the Theravāda tradition. He took the many strands of contemporary Buddhist teachings and traditions, both oral and written, and through patience and methodical scholarship wove them together to produce the standard Theravāda orientation for interpreting the teachings of the Buddha. He accomplished this by coordinating, collating, translating, and editing the vast, imposing body of the Theravāda canon.

Very little about the life of Buddhaghosa can be established definitely. That he was held in great esteem in the Theravāda tradition is seen in the *Buddhaghosuppatti,* a late Pali text of uncertain origin, date, and authorship, which presents a legendary account of his life and work. The *Mahāvaṃsa,* the chronicle of Sri Lanka written and preserved by the monastic community there, provides some information about this figure, but in a section (chap. 37, vv. 215ff.)

considered to have been written seven to eight centuries after his life. From the silence regarding biographical information about such a prolific commentator, one may infer that his enormous industry and productivity were the consequence of a consistently self-effacing purpose. His foremost aim was to provide a commentarial framework in the language of the canonical texts that would contribute to a clearer understanding of the canonical teachings and ensure the continuity of these teachings and interpretations for posterity.

Although an old Burmese tradition has claimed that Buddhaghosa was a native of Thaton, in lower Burma (a position generally discredited, but argued anew on occasion), it appears that Buddhaghosa was from India, but opinions vary as to whether he came from the region of Bodh Gayā or from Andhra, or from an area farther to the south, around Kāñcīpuram.

Buddhaghosa received his ordination into the monastic order, came to Sri Lanka, and resided either at the Mahāvihāra in Anurādhapura or in nearby monastic dwellings. His purpose there was to study the Theravāda exegetical tradition. When he arrived in the early fifth century, he found approximately twenty-five sources forming a multifaceted collection of commentarial literature written in Sinhala, the predominant language of Sri Lanka. At least one additional commentarial source seems to have been preserved in a Dravidian language. These sources had developed over several centuries and by the end of the first century CE had reached the state in which Buddhaghosa found them.

It was against this historical background that Buddhaghosa wrote in Pali the *Visuddhimagga* (The path of purity), his first literary effort in Sri Lanka. This encyclopedic work, structured upon a cardinal tripartite theme in the Buddhist heritage—virtue (Pali, *sila*), concentration (*samādhi*), and wisdom (*paññā*)—demonstrates Buddhaghosa's talent in arranging the complex details of the Buddhist teachings at his disposal. He brought together details drawn from practically all of the canonical Pali texts, a few postcanonical works, and several Sinhala commentarial sources. His classic work remains the scholar's gateway to a Theravāda perspective on the canonical teachings and through which those canonical teachings subsequently passed into the continuing tradition.

Buddhaghosa continued his labor to assure a wider dissemination of the received commentarial interpretations of Sri Lanka by translating into Pali the Sinhala exegetical literature on many of the canonical texts. The chronological order of his works remains uncertain, however. He drew from his sources to provide a commentary on the Vinaya Piṭaka, the voluminous *Samantapāsādika.* He also provided a particular commentary, the *Kaṅkhāvitaraṇī*, on a portion of the Vinaya known as the *Pātimokkha.* He further provided commentaries on the four sections of the Sutta Piṭaka: the *Sumaṅgalāvilasinī* on the *Dīgha Nikāya;* the *Papañcasūdanī* on the *Majjhima Nikāya;* the *Saratthappakāsinī* on the *Saṃyutta Nikāya;* and the *Manorathapūraṇī* on the *Aṅguttara Nikāya.* Each work testifies, in its prologue, that it represents a translation of the Sinhala commentaries established by Mahinda, who is said to have brought the *buddhadhamma* to Sri Lanka in the middle of the third century BCE; these commentaries were preserved in the Mahāvihāra.

Although the point remains open to debate, it appears that Buddhaghosa also wrote commentaries on the seven texts comprising the third major division of the Pali canon, the Abhidhamma Piṭaka: on the *Dhammasaṅganī* he provided a commentary called *Atthasālinī*; on the *Vibhaṅga*, the *Sammohavinodanī*; and on the remaining five texts, one work called *Pañcappakaraṇaṭ-ṭhakathā.* The commentaries note that they are based on the older Sinhala commentaries and follow the tradition of interpretation endorsed at the Mahāvihāra.

A few years after completing these commentaries, political turmoil disrupted the calm of the Mahāvihāra when Anurādhapura was overrun by invaders. This probably was the cause of Buddhaghosa's departure from Sri Lanka and the reason he did not complete commentaries on all the canonical texts. The weight of tradition says that he returned to India, although some accounts claim that he left Sri Lanka for lower Burma. Additional commentaries have been ascribed to Buddhaghosa, but they were probably the work of others. Buddhaghosa was followed by other notable commentators, namely Buddhadatta, Dhammapāla, Upasena, and Mahānāma.

SEE ALSO Theravāda.

BIBLIOGRAPHY

Adikaram, E. W. *Early History of Buddhism in Ceylon* (1946). Reprint, Colombo, 1953.

Law, Bimala Churn. "Buddhaghosa." In *Encyclopaedia of Buddhism*, edited by G. P. Malalasekera, vol. 3, fasc. 3. Colombo, 1973. A condensation of his *The Life and Work of Buddha-ghosa* (1923; reprint, Delhi, 1976).

Malalasekera, G. P. *The Pali Literature of Ceylon* (1928). Reprint, Colombo, 1958.

Ñyāṇamoli, trans. *The Path of Purification (Visuddhimagga) by Bhadantācariya Buddhaghosa.* 2d ed. Colombo, 1964.

New Sources

Crosby, Kate. "Uddis and Acikh: Buddhaghosa on the Inclusion of the Sikkhapada in the Pabbajja Ceremony." *Journal of Indian Philosophy* 28, no. 5–6 (2000): 461–477.

Hamilton, Sue. "From the Buddha to Buddhaghosa: Changing Attitudes Toward the Human Body in Theravada Buddhism." In *Religious Reflections on the Human Body,* edited by Jane Marie Law, pp. 46–63. Bloomington, Ind., 1995.

Smart, Ninian. "What Would Buddhaghosa Have Made of The Cloud of Unknowing." In *Mysticism and Language,* edited by Steven T. Katz, pp. 103–122. New York, 1992.

JOHN ROSS CARTER (1987)
Revised Bibliography

BUDDHAPĀLITA (c. 470–540), Indian Buddhist dialectician belonging to the Madhyamaka (Mādhyamika) school. According to the Tibetan historian Tāranātha, Buddhapālita (Tib., Sangs rgyas skyangs; Chin., Fo-hu; Jpn., Butsugo) was born at Haṃsakrīḍa (Ngang pas rtse ba) in the South Indian district of Tambala. Having taken religious ordination there, he learned much about the scriptures of Nāgārjuna from Saṃgharakṣita (Dge' dun bsrung ba), a disciple of Nagāmitra (Klu'i bshes gnyen). He attained the highest knowledge through intense meditation and had a vision of Mañjuśrī. Residing in the Dantapurī monastery, he delivered many sermons on the Dharma and composed commentaries on treatises by such authors as Nāgārjuna and Āryadeva. Finally, he attained the miraculous powers (*siddhi*). More or less the same account of his life is given in Buston's *Chos 'byung* (History of Buddhism) and Sum pa mkhan po's *Dpag bsam ljon bzang*, although these works exist only in fragments.

Buddhapālita is one of the traditionally reported "eight commentators" on Nāgārjuna's *Mūlamadhyamakakārikā*, the seven others being Nāgārjuna himself, Bhāvaviveka, Candrakīrti, Devaśarman, Guṇaśrī, Gunamati, and Sthiramati (the last four commentators are Yogācāras). According to tradition, he composed commentaries on many Madhyamaka treatises, but only one has survived: the (*Buddhapālita*) *Mūlamadhyamakavṛtti*. The original Sanskrit text is actually lost; the work is only preserved in the Tibetan translation made by Jñānagarbha and Klu'i rgyal mtshan in the beginning of the ninth century. This commentary is one of the six extant commentaries on the *Mūlamadhyamakakārikā*, the five others being: (1) the *Akutobhayā* (Derge edition of the Tibetan Tripiṭaka 3829, hereafter cited as D.; Beijing edition of the Tibetan Tripiṭaka 5229, hereafter cited as B.); (2) Qingmu's (Piṅgala?) *Zhonglun* (T.D. no. 1824); (3) Bhāvaviveka's *Prajñāpradīpa* (D. 3853, P. 5253); (4) Sthiramati's *Dasheng zhong guan shilun* (T.D. no. 1567); (5) Candrakīrti's *Prasannapadā* (Sanskrit ed. by L. de La Vallée Poussin in Bibliotheca Buddhica 4; D. 3860, P. 5260).

Buddhapālita's commentary consists of twenty-seven chapters in accordance with its basic text the *Mūlamadhyamakakārikā*. Chronologically, it was composed between the *Akutobhayā* and the *Prajñāpradīpa*. It incorporates most of the *Akutobhayā*'s passages; the last five chapters are almost identical. Chapter titles in Buddhapālita's commentary are the same as those of the *Akutobhayā* and the *Prajñāpradīpa* (perhaps because the translators of these three commentaries are the same: Jñānagarbha and Klu'i rgyal mtshan), but they differ slightly from the titles of Candrakīrti's *Prasannapadā* (particularly chapters 2, 3, 7, 11, 13, 15, 18, and 20). Buddhapālita's titles thus represent an older text of the *Mūlamadhyamakakārikā*, which was known to these translators before the revision by Pa tshab Nyi ma grags (b. 1055) and his collaborators when they translated the *Prasannapadā*. The main authorities cited by Buddhapālita in his commentary are Nāgārjuna (*Mūlamadhyamakakārikā*), Āryadeva (*Catuḥśataka*), Rāhulabhadra (*Prajñāpāramitāstotra*), and 'Phags pa 'jigs med (Āryābhaya?).

Buddhapālita's main philosophical methodological approach consisted of his explaining the philosophy of Nāgārjuna by the method of *prasaṅgavākya* (*reductio ad absurdum*). That is, without himself maintaining any thesis or proposition to be established, he tried to point out the necessary but undesired consequences resulting from a non-Madhyamaka opponent's thesis. This method was strongly criticized by Bhāvaviveka, who wanted to make use of independent inferences (*svatantrānumāna*) to prove the Madhaymaka standpoint, but it was later defended by Candrakīrti. The Tibetan doxographers accordingly classified Buddhapālita with Candrakīrti as members of the Prāsaṅgika (Thal 'gyur ba) school, while Bhāvaviveka was classed in the Svātantrika (Rang rgyud pa) school.

SEE ALSO Mādhyamika.

BIBLIOGRAPHY

Lindtner, Christian. "Buddhapālita on Emptiness." *Indo-Iranian Journal* 23 (1981): 187–217.

Ruegg, David S. *The Literature of the Madhyamaka School of Philosophy in India.* Wiesbaden, 1981.

Saito, A. "A Study of the Buddhapālita-Mūlamadhyamakavṛtti." Ph.D. diss., Australian National University, 1984.

New Sources

Ames, William. "Bhavaviveka's Own View of His Differences with Buddhapalita." In *The Svatantrika-Prasangika Distinction: What Difference Does a Difference Make?*, edited by Georges B. J. Dreyfus and Sara L. McClintock, pp. 41–66. Boston, 2003.

Ames, William L. "Buddhapalita's Exposition of the Madhyamaka." *Journal of Indian Philosophy* 14, no. 4 (1986): 313–348.

Heine, Steven. "Visions, Divisions, Revisions: The Encounter Between Iconoclasm and Supernaturalism in Koan Cases about Mount Wu-t'ai." In *The Kōan: Texts and Contexts in Zen Buddhism*, edited by Steven Heine and Dale S. Wright, pp. 137–167. New York, 2000.

MIMAKI KATSUMI (1987)
Revised Bibliography

BUDDHAS AND BODHISATTVAS

This entry consists of the following articles:

CELESTIAL BUDDHAS AND BODHISATTVAS
ETHICAL PRACTICES ASSOCIATED WITH BUDDHAS AND BODHISATTVAS

BUDDHAS AND BODHISATTVAS: CELESTIAL BUDDHAS AND BODHISATTVAS

The term *bodhisattva* occurs frequently in early Buddhist literature, usually referring to Śākyamuni Buddha prior to the time of his enlightenment, which he achieved as he sat under the famous bodhi tree (Skt., *bodhivṛkṣa,* "tree of enlightenment") a few miles south of Gayā in modern Bihar. *Bodhisattva* means literally "enlightenment being," or, according to a theory that *bodhisattva* is a slightly mistaken Sanskrit spelling of the early dialectical form *bodhisatta* (as preserved in Pali), it could have originally meant "intent upon enlightenment." Whatever the literal meaning (and most scholars would favor the first one), a *bodhisattva* is a living being, usually human but not necessarily so, who has set out on the long path toward Buddhahood, which in accordance with the general Buddhist acceptance of the Indian theories concerning continual rebirth (or transmigration) was calculated to lead the aspirant through a very long series of different lives.

Large collections of such legendary life stories *(jātaka)* were made in the early Buddhist period, illustrating the heroic self-sacrifice of the future Buddha Śākyamuni in his progress toward his last life (also told in legendary style), when his purpose was finally revealed to the world. As Śākyamuni was never regarded as the one and only Buddha, but rather as one in a whole series (seven are named in early texts, but the number is gradually much extended), each of whom appears in a separate world age, it was inevitable that his followers should come to expect a future Buddha for the next world age. Thus, a new *bodhisattva,* Maitreya ("loving kindness"), appears as the first of the many other "great beings," who later extend the Buddhist pantheon to infinity. The cult of Maitreya is certainly attested among the followers of the early Buddhist sects, later referred to disparagingly as Hīnayānists, and his appearance seems to mark the beginning of the considerable devotion that came to be directed toward these celestial beings.

It should be borne in mind that the distinctions between the so-called Mahāyānists and Hīnayānists were not so clear-cut in the early centuries CE as they appear to be later. The same mythological concepts concerning the nature of a Buddha and a *bodhisattva* (a future Buddha) remain fundamental to Buddhism in all its forms, and it can easily be shown that all the later extravagant developments of the Mahāyāna are traceable to tendencies inherent in the earliest known forms of Buddhism. The Mahāyānists differed in their philosophical assumptions and the manner in which they applied the *bodhisattva* theory to normal religious life. For them, the *bodhisattva* career was the only genuine path toward enlightenment, which they distinguished from the goal of *nirvāṇa,* interpreted by them as the limited selfish aspiration of the early disciples. At the same time they followed the same forms of monastic discipline (Vinaya) as their Hīnayāna brethren, often living together in the same monastic compound until doctrinal disputes led them to set up separate communities of their own. Thus freed, the Mahāyānists began to go their own way, but there would appear to have been no very noticeable iconographic changes in their monasteries until several centuries later.

The well-known caves of Ajantā were probably occupied by Buddhist communities up to the eighth century CE, and there is scarcely any image or painting there that might displease a determined adherent of the older sects. The only celestial *bodhisattva* apart from Maitreya to be painted at Ajantā is Avalokiteśvara ("the lord who looks down in compassion"), and he may be quite convincingly interpreted as the future Buddha Śākyamuni, who looked down in compassion from the heaven called Tuṣita ("joyful") before finally agreeing to be born in our world for the benefit of its inhabitants. None of the many Buddha and *bodhisattva* images surviving at Ajantā in carved stone can be identified as particular celestial Buddhas and *bodhisattvas.* Numerous *bodhisattvas* are named in Mahāyāna sūtras from the first century CE onward, but a rather more limited number achieved generally accepted iconographic forms, namely those who were especially popular as distinct beings and those who were fitted into *maṇḍalas* and related iconographic patterns.

The earliest iconographic pattern, which resulted in the eventual appearance of three leading *bodhisattvas,* is probably the triad of images representing Śākyamuni Buddha flanked by two attendants. According to early accounts, Śākyamuni was attended by Indian divinities at his birth. Originally, these two attendants may have been thought of as Brahmā and Indra, but they came to be accepted as Buddhist divinities by the simple method of giving them new Buddhist names. They thus become identified as Padmapāṇi ("lotus-holder") and Vajrapāṇi ("*vajra*-holder"). Padmapāṇi comes to be identified with Avalokiteśvara, who also holds a lotus flower, and thus becomes a great *bodhisattva* in his own right. Vajrapāṇi's rise to fame is very much slower, since through the earlier Mahāyāna period he continues to be regarded as Śākyamuni's personal attendant, his function and duties merely being extended to protect all other *bodhisattvas.*

It is not until we reach the early Tantric period as represented by the *Mañjuśrīmūlakalpa* that Vajrapāṇi appears as a powerful *bodhisattva* in his own right, but still as a member of a triad. By this time (perhaps the fifth to the sixth century CE) many non-Buddhist divinities were being spontaneously accepted into the Buddhist fold; they were being accepted for the straightforward reason that those who became supporters of the monks or who even became Buddhist monks themselves did not need to renounce their devotion to other divinities, whose existence and capabilities were never denied either by Śākyamuni himself or by his followers. Local divinities decorate Buddhist stupas (Skt., *stūpas*) from at least the second century BCE onward, and as already noted, the great Hindu divinities were soon incorporated as Buddhist "converts." This process continued throughout the whole history of Indian Buddhism and goes far to explain the existence of so many celestial beings in the ever more elaborate Buddhist pantheon.

In the *Mañjuśrīmūlakalpa* these divinities are grouped into various "families," of which the three chief ones are those of the Buddha or Tathāgata, the Lotus, and the Vajra. Divinities who were already accepted as fully Buddhist were placed in the Buddha's family, while gentle divinities due for conversion were placed in the Lotus family under the leadership of Avalokiteśvara; fierce divinities, whose conversion was supposed to be troublesome, were placed under the command of Vajrapāṇi, who was able to subdue them with his powerful *vajra* ("thunderbolt"). Since it was suitable that the original Buddha family should be headed by a *bodhisattva* just like the other two, this position was assigned to Mañjuśrī ("gentle and glorious one," also known as Mañjughoṣa, "gentle voice"), who appears in early Mahāyāna sūtras as Śākyamuni's chief spokesman. His origin is obscure but it is significant that he is later linked with Sarasvatī, the Hindu goddess of speech, taking her *mantra* ("Oṃ vāgīśvari muṃ") as his own. It must be emphasized that none of these great *bodhisattvas* has a "history" in the modern sense: they are all mythological creations.

CELESTIAL BUDDHAS. While the cult of a celestial *bodhisattva* as a Great Being of heavenly associations clearly has its roots in the early cult of Śākyamuni, who was appealed to as both Buddha and *bodhisattva*, its full implications were developed from approximately the first century CE onward by those who began to adopt specific Mahāyāna teachings. Śākyamuni was traditionally acclaimed as the one and only Buddha of our present world age, and early legends tell how he made the vow, when he was a *brahman* boy named Megha or Sumegha, before a previous Buddha, Dīpaṃkara, to follow the self-sacrificing *bodhisattva* path toward Buddhahood. It must be emphasized that the later concepts never had the effect of negating the earlier ones, and despite the change of viewpoint that I am about to explain, the cult of Buddhas of the past, as well as of the future, was never abandoned. The "Buddhas of the three times" (past, present, and future) are frequently mentioned in Mahāyāna literature and their cult has continued in Tibetan Buddhism to this day.

The change that takes place in Mahāyāna theories results from their perhaps more realistic view of the nature of the cosmos. The early Buddhists viewed the world as a closed system, comprising four main island-continents arranged around a central sacred mountain, known as Meru, identified with Mount Kailash in western Tibet. Mahāyāna teachings, on the other hand, were greatly affected by views that envisaged the universe as whole galaxies of world systems, extending endlessly throughout all the directions of space. It followed logically from this that there should also be Buddhas operative in all these other world systems. One of the earliest disputes that arose between Mahāyānists and those who held to the earlier views concerns precisely the problem of whether there can be more than one Buddha at a time, and it is clear that they argue against different cosmological backgrounds. Mahāyāna ideas on the nature of such myriads of world systems may be learned from the reading of any of the Mahāyāna sūtras, where Buddhas, surrounded by *bodhisattvas*, continue to preach simultaneously in their various "buddha fields" *(buddhakṣetra).*

Not all such worlds are fortunate enough to have a Buddha at any particular time. Those that do are divided generally into two classes, known as "pure" or "impure." The pure fields contain only those beings who are on the way to Buddhahood, that is, *bodhisattvas*, while the impure fields contain beings of all kinds at all stages of spiritual advance and decline. The manner in which *bodhisattvas* may travel miraculously from one buddha field to another is well illustrated in the important Mahāyāna sūtra, the *Vimalakīrtinirdeśa* (The teaching of Vimalakīrti), where the question is understandably raised as to why Śākyamuni should have elected to be born in an impure field rather than a pure one. His superiority is acknowledged by visiting *bodhisattvas* from a pure field, who exclaim: "The greatness of Śākyamuni is established; it is wonderful how he converts the lowly, the wretched and the unruly. Moreover, the Bodhisattvas who are established in this mean Buddha-sphere (i.e., our world) must have inconceivable compassion" (Lamotte, 1976, pp. 204–218).

Śākyamuni's essential identity with all other Buddhas is often asserted, sometimes subtly, sometimes quite explicitly, as in chapter 15 of the *Saddharmapuṇḍarīka Sūtra (Lotus of the True Law Scripture).* In another sūtra, the *Śūraṃgamasamādhi* (Lamotte, 1965, pp. 267–270), the *bodhisattva* Dṛḍhmati asks Śākyamuni how long his life will last. Śākyamuni tells him to go and ask another buddha named Vairocana ("resplendent one"), who presides over a world system named Well Adorned, which is to be reached in the eastern direction by crossing over thirty-two thousand buddha fields. Having traveled there he is told by that Buddha: "My length of life is exactly the same as that of the Buddha Śākyamuni, and if you really want to know, the length of my life will be seven hundred incalculable world ages." Returning to Śākyamuni, the inquiring *bodhisattva* says: "In so far as I understand the words of the Lord, I would say that it is you, O Lord, who are in the world-system named Well Adorned, where with another name you work for the happiness of all living beings."

So many different kinds of Buddha manifestations are taken for granted in the Mahāyāna sūtras that scholarly efforts have been made to reduce them to some order. The best account of such attempts will be found in Louis de la Vallée Poussin's translation of the *Cheng weishi lun,* Xuanzang's compilation of ten major commentaries to Vasubandhu's *Triṃśikā* (La Vallée Poussin, 1929, vol. 2, p. 762).

The simplest scheme, which gradually gained general acceptance, envisages an "Absolute Buddha Body" (the *dharmakāya* of early Buddhist tradition) manifesting itself as various "glorious bodies" (*saṃbhogakāya,* "body of enjoyment") to high-ranking *bodhisattvas* in celestial spheres, and as various "human bodies" (*nirmāṇakāya,* "manifested body"), which need not necessarily be human but are usually conceived as such, in impure Buddha fields like our own world. Later Tantric tradition suggests the existence of a fourth, supreme body, known as *svābhāvikakāya* ("self-existent"), but earlier this is used as an alternative name for the Absolute Body *(dharmakāya).* We shall note later the tendency to arrive at ever-more-transcendent states of buddhahood, when a sixth, supreme buddha is placed above the set of five cosmic buddhas. To these we must now give attention as the production of later Mahāyāna speculation and as the foundation of the whole class of *tantras* known as Yoga Tantras.

Just as buddha manifestations, conceived in a diachronic time sequence in accordance with the earlier conceptions of buddhahood, came to be represented by a triad of Buddhas, referred to as the Buddhas of the Three Times, namely Dīpaṃkara, Śākyamuni, and Maitreya (in this later context he is referred to as Buddha and no longer as *bodhisattva*), so those other buddha manifestations, conceived synchronically as existing simultaneously in all directions throughout space in accordance with later Mahāyāna conceptions of the universe, came to be symbolized by the Five Buddhas of the cosmos, representing the center and the four cardinal points. These have been popularly referred to as *dhyāni-buddhas* ("meditational buddhas"), a term that Brian Hodgson (1800–1894) seems to have heard used locally in Nepal but that appears to have no traditionally established justification. In the few sūtras and the many *tantras* and their commentaries in which they are referred to, they are known simply as the Five Buddhas *(pañcabuddha)* or the Five Tathāgatas *(pañcatathāgata)* with no other ascription. If such is required, then the term *Cosmic Buddhas* seems appropriate, in that their primary function is to represent buddhahood in its cosmic dimension, as symbolized in the fivefold *maṇḍala.*

As may be expected, this set of five buddhas evolved gradually, and we find at first various sets of names, some of which become gradually stabilized. Two fairly constant ones from the start are Amitābha ("boundless light") or Amitāyus ("boundless life") as the Buddha of the West, and Akṣobhya ("the imperturbable") as the Buddha of the East. It has been suggested with great plausibility that the Buddha of the West was first accepted as an object of devotion by the Buddhists of the far northwest of the Indian subcontinent as a result of Persian cultural and religious influence, since light and life are essential characteristics of the chief Zoroastrian divinity, Ahura Mazdā. This hypothesis is borne out by the very special devotion shown to this particular Buddha in Central Asia and especially in China and Japan, where a particular constellation of sects (known generically as Pure Land) is devoted to his cult. There is no indication that any such special cult developed elsewhere in India, where Amitābha/Amitāyus remains simply one of the Five Buddhas. Judging by the very large number of images found, the most popular buddha, certainly in northeastern India, where Buddhism survived until the early thirteenth century, is Akṣobhya, the Buddha of the East. Iconographically he is identified with Śākyamuni Buddha, who was challenged at the time of his enlightenment by Māra, the Evil One (the Satan of Buddhism), to justify his claim to buddhahood. Śākyamuni called the earth goddess to witness his claim by tapping the ground with the fingers of his right hand, and she duly appeared to give testimony, to the total discomfiture of Māra. A buddha image formed in this style became the typical image of Bodh Gayā (south of Gayā) in eastern India, where Śākyamuni showed himself imperturbable *(akṣobhya)* despite the assaults of the Evil One.

The geographical choice of this particular buddha (Akṣobhya) as the Buddha of the East in the later formulation of the set of five is not difficult to understand, being the obvious one because of his popularity in the eastern region. The central buddha came to be identified with the buddha image, which must have been typical of another famous place of pilgrimage, the Deer Park (now known as Sārnāth, a few miles from Vārāṇasī), where Śākyamuni was believed to have preached his first sermon. The gesture of preaching is symbolized by the two hands linked in front of the chest in order to suggest a turning wheel, the "wheel of the doctrine," which Śākyamuni is said to have turned, just as the chariot wheels of a universal monarch (*cakravartin,* "wheel-turner") turn throughout the world.

A buddha's supremacy in the religious sphere was equated in very early Buddhist tradition with the supremacy of the quasi-historical but mainly mythological concept of a "universal monarch," with the result that a *bodhisattva* is generally idealized as a kind of crown prince; thus it is in princely garments that he is generally portrayed. In particular, Mañjuśrī, Śākyamuni's spokesman in early Mahāyāna sūtras, is referred to specifically as the prince *(kumārabhūta).* It is not surprising that as central Buddha of the set of five, the preaching Śākyamuni comes to be referred to as Vairocana ("resplendent one"), the very buddha of vast age with whom he claims identity in the *Śūraṃgamasamādhi Sūtra.* The full name of that particular buddha is in fact Vairocana-raśmipratimaṇḍita-vikurvanarāja ("resplendent one, adorned with light-rays, transformation-king"). The remaining two buddhas, placed to the south and to the north, become generally stabilized in this configuration as Ratnasambhava ("jewel-born"), presumably symbolizing Śākyamuni's boundless generosity, and Amoghasiddhi ("infallible success"), symbolizing his miraculous powers.

Summarizing these various kinds of Buddha manifestations, one may make the following observations:

1. The state of Buddhahood is essentially one and only, or, to use a safer term, nondual, and nonmanifest in any way whatsoever: such is the Absolute Body of Buddhahood.
2. The various stages at which this Absolute Body may assume apparently manifested form have been explained as various grades of buddha bodies, of which the Glorious Body, or Body of Enjoyment, and the Human Body, or Manifested Body, are the other two terms in more general use.
3. According to the earliest Buddhist beliefs, buddhas manifest themselves in a kind of historical sequence, each one presiding over a different world age.
4. According to the later Mahāyāna theories, Buddhas are

manifest all the time in all the directions of space, presiding over their individual buddha fields.

These various concepts, which may appear to an outsider as in some measure conflicting, are retained by those who were responsible for the later formulations, while in general the "historical" buddha Śākyamuni continues to hold the center of the stage.

BODHISATTVAS AND GODDESSES. Large numbers of *bodhisattvas* are mentioned in the Mahāyāna sūtras as residing in various Buddha fields, but very few of these come to receive a special cult as great individuals. The three primary ones, Mañjuśrī, Avalokiteśvara, and Vajrapāṇi, have already been mentioned. These are later identified as the "spiritual sons" of the three primary Buddhas, Śākyamuni (alias Vairocana), Amitābha, and Akṣobhya. The concept of Five Buddhas causes the number of buddha "families," previously three, to be extended to five, and thus two more leading *bodhisattvas* are required to complete the set. They are known as Ratnapāṇi ("jewel-holder") for the Jewel family of Ratnasambhava, and as Viśvapāṇi ("universal holder") for the Sword or Action family of Amoghasiddhi. Both these are latecomers and their artificial nature is suggested by their names.

In the early Mahāyāna sūtras we find various *bodhisattvas* named, such as the student Sadāprarudita ("always weeping"), whose story is told in the Perfection of Wisdom literature, or Dṛḍhamati ("firm-minded"), who is the main spokesman in the *Śūraṃgama Sūtra,* or again the *bodhisattva* Dharmākara ("expression of the *dharma*"), who sets the conditions for his own buddha field through a long series of vows, the fulfillment of which is a precondition for his becoming the buddha Amitābha. None of these achieves individual fame except for the last as the buddha Amitābha, of whom he is little more than a formative shadow, like the *brahman* boy Megha who eventually became the buddha Śākyamuni. Vimalakīrti, already mentioned above, gains a popular following in Central Asia and in China. Of others so far not mentioned there is the one-time *bodhisattva* Bhaiṣajyaraja ("king of medicine"), named in *The Lotus of the True Law* (see Kern, 1963, pp. 378ff.), whom we find soon elevated to the rank of buddha with the name of Bhaiṣajyaraja. In certain sets of divinities, the *bodhisattva* Ākāśagarbha ("womb of space") replaces Ratnapāṇi as chief of the Jewel family; neither of these leading *bodhisattvas* appears to attract any special cult. Paralleling Ākāśagarbha, at least in name, is the *bodhisattva* Kṣitigarbha ("womb of the earth"). Perhaps by the mere chance form of his name, Kṣitigarbha achieved enormous success in Central Asia and China as the one who controls the welfare of the dead. By far the most popular of all the "great gods" of Buddhism is Avalokiteśvara, who also assumes the name of Lokeśvara ("lord of the world"), normally Śiva's title in Hindu tradition. It is possible that his name was a deliberate parody of Śiva's title, with the syllables changed sufficiently to give the new meaning of "lord who looks down (in compassion)." It remains doubtful if any image of him can be identified specifically before the sixth century, unless we include the lotus-holding (Padmapāṇi) attendant by Śākyamuni's side, already referred to above. However, by the sixth century his cult is well established, as attested by an entire sūtra, the *Kāraṇḍavyūha,* compiled in his honor. It is here that the well-known *mantra* "Oṃ maṇipadme hūṃ" ("O thou with the jeweled lotus") can be firmly identified for the first time. This *mantra,* like the one of Mañjuśrī, is in the form of a feminine vocative for reasons that should become immediately clear.

Feminine divinities first appear within the Buddhist pantheon as handmaidens of the great *bodhisattvas*, whom they accompany in much the same way that Indian princes were usually depicted with a small circle of lady companions. Thus we may note that in the *Mañjuśrīmūlakalpa* (Macdonald, 1962, pp. 107ff.) Avalokiteśvara is surrounded by Pāṇḍaravāsinī ("white-clad"), Tārā ("savioress"), Bhrukuṭi ("frowning"), Prajñāpāramitā ("perfection of wisdom"), Tathāgata-locanā ("Buddha-eye"), and Uṣṇāṣarājā ("lady of the wisdom-bump"). We shall meet with some of these again within the scheme of the fivefold *maṇḍala,* but already two and possibly three look forward to devotional cults of their own, since they become the great goddesses of Buddhism. The goddess Prajñāpāramitā represents the fundamental wisdom of Mahāyāna philosophy, as a divine concept corresponding in many respects to Sancta Sophia of Christian tradition. Even more popular is Tārā, whose flourishing was assured by the salvific assurance conveyed by her name. She was soon recognized as the feminine counterpart (not a partner in the Tantric sense) of Avalokiteśvara. Tārā is his feminine expression, just as Sarasvatī becomes the feminine expression of Mañjuśrī. Thus we may note that since the *mantra* of a great divinity is also his expression (his *vidyā* or special knowledge, as it is often called), his *mantra* too assumes a feminine form. Tārā became so important that many other feminine divinities came to be regarded as her various forms. Thus she appears as Bhrukuṭi when she wishes to show her displeasure, or in the triumphant form of Uṣṇīśasitātapatrā ("lady of the wisdom-bump with the white parasol") when she becomes manifest with a thousand arms and a thousand heads, arranged in paintings so as to appear as a high, elaborate headdress, so that she is in no way grotesque. Here, she corresponds to the eleven-headed, thousand-armed form of Avalokiteśvara.

These more complex forms may clearly be related to subsequent Tantric developments, where the central divinity of the *maṇḍala* may be conceived of as comprising in his person all his various directional manifestations, from four to a thousand. Fluctuation in sex is not uncommon in the early stages of elaboration of this vast and complex pantheon; as is well known, in later Chinese Buddhist tradition Avalokiteśvara (Kuan-yin) merges with Tārā so as to become a feminine divinity. Returning to the *Mañjuśrīmūlakalpa,* we may note that just as Avalokiteśvara is surrounded by benign goddesses (except possibly for Bhrukuṭi), so Vajrapāṇi is surrounded by fierce ones, named Vajrāṅkuśī ("lady of the *vajra* hook"), Vajraśṛṅkhalā ("lady of the *vajra* fetter"), Subāhu ("strong-armed one"), and Vajrasenā ("lady of the *vajra* army"). It is sometimes difficult to draw a line between *bodhisattvas* and great goddesses, but Tārā in her various manifestations is as great as the greatest of *bodhisattvas*. She is saluted as the mother of all Buddhas, and in time Śākyamuni's human mother was duly seen as one of her manifestations.

The travelogue of the famous Chinese pilgrim Xuanzang, who visited monasteries throughout Central Asia and the Indian subcontinent between 629 and 645, well illustrates the extent of popular devotion accorded the images of certain great *bodhisattva* figures during the seventh century CE. Himself a scholarly Mahāyāna philosopher, Xuanzang was nonetheless pleased to hear of the miraculous powers of such images, mentioning in particular those of Maitreya, Avalokiteśvara, and occasionally Mañjuśrī and the great goddess Tārā; on many occasions he offered devout prayers to them on his own account. One may also mention that Xuanzang was equally interested in the cult of *arhats* ("worthy ones"), those early disciples of Śākyamuni Buddha, who, having achieved *nirvāṇa,* were often believed to continue in some kind of suspended existence in remote mountain places. More wonderful tales of *arhats*, tales certainly learned from his Mahāyānist brethren in India, are retold in his account than stories about *bodhisattvas*. In fact, the continuing cult of *arhats* (Chin., *lo-han*), which spread through Central Asia to China, survives in a set of sixteen or eighteen Great Arhats well known to Tibetan Buddhists. These earlier traditions provide an interesting link, all too often ignored, between Hīnayānists and Mahāyānists. Thus, the Buddhist world of the early centuries CE was peopled with a large variety of celestial beings, among whom certain favorite *bodhisattvas* were only just beginning to come to the fore.

Tantric Buddhism, at least in its higher aspirations, may be described as a system of practices, either of ritual yoga or of physical and mental yoga, by means of which the practitioner identifies himself with his tutelary divinity, who is identified both with the practitioner's own teacher and with the goal of final enlightenment. One of the main means toward such an objective is the *maṇḍala* or mystic circle of divinities who symbolize existence at all its various levels, the essential sameness of which the pupil must learn to experience through the guidance of his teacher *(guru). Maṇḍalas* are described in earlier *tantras*, where a "three-family" arrangement predominates, but it is not until the so-called Yoga Tantras, with their fivefold arrangement of *maṇḍalas*, begin to appear that the new symbolism can be worked out effectively.

In the earlier Tantras there is a gradation of importance in the various families: the Buddha or Tathāgata family predominates; the Lotus family with its gentle divinities comes next; the Vajra family of Vajrapāṇi and his fierce children comes last. However, in the Yoga Tantras Vajrapāṇi comes right to the fore as the chief representative of Śākyamuni, alias Vairocana. He is also called Vajradhara ("holder of the *vajra*") and Vajrasattva ("*vajra* being"), names that at a later stage of Tantric development refer exclusively to a sixth, utterly supreme Buddha. The main *tantra* of the Yoga Tantra class is the *Sarvatathāgatatattvasaṃgraha* and here the chief *maṇḍala* is known as the Vajradhātu maṇḍala, the Maṇḍala of the Adamantine Sphere, where *bodhisattvas* with Vajra names, all essentially manifestations of Vajrapāṇi, form circles around the Five Buddhas and the four Buddha goddesses. Although *maṇḍala* means circle, the main divinities may also be arranged around a central square within the main circle, since this square, which is usually provided with four elaborate doorways, represents the sacred palace in which the main divinities dwell.

Next in importance after the Five Buddhas are the four Buddha goddesses, who occupy the subsidiary directions of space, namely Locanā, Māmakī ("my very own"), Pāṇḍaravāsinī, and Tārā. They are usually interpreted as symbolizing the four main elements (earth, water, fire, and air), while the fifth (space) coalesces with supreme Buddhahood at the center. In later *tantras* a fifth, central Buddha goddess is named Vajradhaātvīśvarī ("lady of the adamantine sphere"), but she does not appear in *maṇḍalas* of the Yoga Tantra class normally, since these coupled male-female divinities (known as *yab-yum,* "father-mother" in Tibetan) do not form part of their symbolism. Apart from the sixteen Great Bodhisattvas, all with Vajra names, we may draw attention to the eight lesser goddesses of the offerings, arranged farther out from the center in the intermediate directions, and the four door guardians at the four main entrances. The eight goddesses of the offerings are mere symbols, as their names indicate at once:

1. Vajralāsyā, or Vajra Frolic
2. Vajradhūpa, or Vajra Incense
3. Vajramālā, or Vajra Garland
4. Vajrapuṣpā, or Vajra Flower
5. Vajragīti, or Vajra Song
6. Vajrālokā, or Vajra Lamp
7. Vajranṛtyā, or Vajra Dance
8. Vajragandhā, or Vajra Scent

The names of the four door guardians, beginning with the eastern one, may be interpreted as Vajra Hook, Vajra Noose, Vajra Fetter, and Vajra Bell.

The possible variations within this fundamental pattern are considerable. Thus, the sixteen *bodhisattvas* fall into four groups of four, being allocated in these sets to the four directional Buddhas. The leaders of these four groups are directly identifiable with the chief *bodhisattvas*, already mentioned above, as well as with others who have not yet been mentioned. Such names are generally interchangeable within the

Vajra family, which in the Yoga Tantras is closely associated with the so-called family of All Buddhas. Among the names not met before in this article we draw attention especially to Samantabhadra ("all good"), from whom Vajrapāṇi is said to arise. Since it is also used as a title of Vairocana, the central buddha, it is not surprising that it is used later as one of the names of a sixth, supreme buddha.

Other *tantras* of the Yoga Tantra class, while generally retaining all the Buddha goddesses, the sixteen *bodhisattvas*, and lesser divinities, introduce different names and iconographic forms for the Five Buddhas themselves. As devised by Tantric masters in India (presumably from the seventh century onward) from a wide choice of names, to which others could be added as one pleased, the combinations, at least in theory, are infinite. Mañjuśrī in a four-headed and eight-armed manifestation may replace Śākyamuni at the center, and a highly complex *maṇḍala,* which includes the eight Uṣṇīṣa Buddhas as well as the four directional Buddhas together with the sixteen Great Bodhisattvas and a host of lesser divinities, is known as Dharmadhātu Maṇḍala, or the Maṇḍala of the Dharma Sphere, of which a fine example survives in the eleventh-century monastery of Sumda in Zangskar.

HORRIFIC BUDDHAS. As a result of Śaiva influence transmitted through Tantric yogins of northeast India, celestial Buddhas of horrific appearance become acceptable tutelary divinities in Mahāyāna communities from perhaps the ninth century onward. Most of the *tantras* that describe these divinities provide their own special *maṇḍalas*, with Heruka, Hevajra, Śaṃvara, Caṇḍamahāroṣaṇa, and other such horrific figures clasping their equally horrific feminine partners as they dance on corpses at the center of their circle of *yoginīs*. *Bodhisattvas* are rare in such company. Of the strange Buddha figures just named, only Caṇḍamahāroṣaṇa has male divinities in the four directions, who are all manifestations of Acala ("imperturbable"), a variant of Akṣobhya's name. Claiming superiority over all previous *tantras*, their propagators asserted the existence of a sixth, supreme Buddha, who subsumed the fivefold set, and with whom their particular tutelary divinity is identified. He is usually given the name of Vajrasattva ("*vajra* being") or Vajradhara ("*vajra*-holder"), both of which are titles of Vajrapāṇi in the earlier Yoga Tantras, as has already been noted.

Special mention should be made of the *Guhyasamāja* ("secret union") *Tantra,* for although this *tantra* was later grouped together with the others just mentioned as a so-called Anuttarayoga Tantra ("*tantra* of supreme yoga"), it adheres much more firmly to the fivefold scheme, and although Akṣobhya is made central Buddha of the set of five, the sixth, supreme Buddha is known as Great Vairocana (Mahāvairocana). *Tantras* of the "Old School" (Rñiṅ-ma-pa) of Tibetan Buddhism are to a large extent based on the fivefold scheme of Yoga Tantras with the addition of fierce divinities of the Heruka type. Their supreme Buddha, as in the case of those heterodox Tibetan Buddhists, the Bon-pos, is named Samantabhadra, a title also earlier closely connected with Vajrapāṇi.

FINAL SURVEY. While we have pointed out that far too stark a contrast is often drawn between Mahāyāna Buddhism of the early centuries CE with the already developed Buddhism accepted by their Hīnayānist brethren, there is no doubt that the contrast must have been very stark indeed during the last few centuries of Buddhist life in northern India (from the tenth to the twelfth century), concentrated mainly in Kashmir in the far northwest and in Bihar, Bengal, and Orissa in the east. While the monasteries continued to practice the same ancient monastic rules, one of which was adopted by the Tibetans from the eighth century onward (namely that of the order known as Mūlasarvāstivāda, particularly strong in Central Asia and northern India), the cult of Buddhas, *bodhisattvas*, greater and lesser goddesses, and various attendant beings had developed in the manner described above, introducing many new iconographic forms into the temples and covering the walls with murals of the kind that now only survive in the old temples of Ladakh and western Tibet (tenth to thirteenth century). Although no such murals survive in India (those of Ajantā up to the eighth century are the only ones remaining), the close relationship between the early Tibetan paintings and the original Indian ones, now lost, is proved by the many that still can be seen in the form of miniature paintings on manuscripts of the Pāla dynasty, which ruled in eastern India during the last Buddhist period. These have survived in Nepal and Tibet, where they were subsequently carried.

It would seem that it was not so much the Mahāyāna that was responsible for the great divergence that develops between the cults of the "early" schools (Hīnayāna) and later Buddhism, despite the very important role that celestial *bodhisattvas* play in Mahāyāna sūtras. As noted already, very few of these can be identified iconographically before the sixth or even the seventh century, namely Maitreya, Avalokiteśvara, Mañjuśrī, the great goddess Tārā, and finally Vajrapāṇi, who begins to come to the fore only at the end of this Mahāyāna period. Vajrapāṇi has the best-documented "career" of all Buddhist divinities and it is he (or rather his cult) that results in the Vajrayāna. He appears together with Padmapāṇi ("lotus-holder"), flanking Śākyamuni in several surviving iconographic examples, and the identification of Padmapāṇi with the favorite *bodhisattva* Avalokiteśvara must have suggested a higher status for Vajrapāṇi as well. This he receives in the earliest *tantras*, but he still heads the lowest of the three families, for it is clearly taught that those who receive consecration in his Vajra family cannot perform rites in the two higher families.

It is only in the Yoga Tantras, which become well-known from the eighth century onward, that Vajrapāṇi comes fully to the fore as the leading *bodhisattva,* for all the *maṇḍalas* are based on the Vajradhātu Maṇḍala, even those of the Buddha (or All Buddhas) family. It is thus from this time on that one may correctly speak of a Vajrayāna, as distinct in many ways from the Mahāyāna. All the later *tantras*, which came to be classed as Tantras of Supreme Yoga, belong effectively to the Vajra family. It is even said that Vajrapāṇi himself taught them on the instructions of Śākyamuni Buddha, for although the Yoga Tantras and all earlier ones together with all Mahāyāna sūtras are explicitly taught as the word of the Buddha (i.e., Śākyamuni) himself, there was some understandable hesitancy in attributing the Yogini Tantras, as they were earlier called, directly to him. Moreover, as related above, the sixth, supreme Buddha of these *tantras* is named as Vajrasattva or Vajradhara, titles that are applied exclusively to Vajrapāṇi in the Yoga Tantras. Thus with these exclusive titles and with a slightly developed iconographic form he attains the highest possible rank in the Buddhist pantheon. It has already been pointed out that no later development ever nullifies earlier ones, with the result that Vajrapāṇi continues to fulfill all the roles described above.

Mañjuśrī also becomes the representative of supreme buddhahood in the Dharmadhātu Maṇḍala; later he receives a form expressing the union of "means" *(upāya)* and wisdom in that he clasps his feminine partner to his breast in the manner of all the great Tantric divinities of this class of *tantra.* Known as Mañjuvajra, he is in essence identical with Vajradhara/Vajrasattva. On the other hand, Avalokiteśvara remains the most popular of the great *bodhisattvas*, especially in his triumphant eleven-headed thousand-armed form. But despite his close relationship with Tārā, his feminine counterpart, neither he nor she is even thought to have lost their virginity. It is interesting to note how all the great *bodhisattvas*, despite iconographic changes, preserve their most essential attributes throughout the whole history of Buddhism. Being a powerful queller of the foe, it is Vajrapāṇi who forcibly converts the great gods of Hinduism, thus becoming their leader and finally the representative of all terrible divinities who are raised to high Buddhist rank. Mañjuśrī remains the representative of pure Buddhist teaching (despite his aberrational form as Mañjuvajra): when the followers of Tsong Kha pa (1357–1419) look for a suitably holy lineage for the leader of the reformed Tibetan Dge lugs pa ("yellow hat") order, they identify him as an incarnation of this particular *bodhisattva.* Avalokiteśvara remains popular for his unbounded compassion for the sufferings of all living beings. In order to save living beings, he is prepared to be born in any of the wretched places of existence, among suffering animals or tormented spirits, and even in the regions of hell. It was thus not difficult to suggest that he might also deliberately appear on earth as a recognizable incarnation. Since the Tibetans, in accordance with their pre-Buddhist beliefs, accepted their early kings (those from the sixth to the ninth century) as divine representatives from the heavens, it is not at all surprising that the king during whose reign Buddhism was first introduced into the country (namely Sron brstan sgam po, d. 650?) should have been retrospectively regarded as an incarnation of the *bodhisattva* Avalokiteśvara.

When the fifth Dalai Lama reunited Tibet under his rule in 1642 this same distinction was claimed for him, and since then all succeeding Dalai Lamas, while being theoretically reincarnations of their predecessors, are at the same time honored as incarnations of Avalokiteśvara. Other interesting high incarnations are those of the Grand Lama of Bkra śis lhun po (Tashilhunpo), who is identified traditionally with the buddha Amitābha, and the abbess of Bsam-sdings Monastery (now presumably destroyed), near the Yar 'brog (Yamdrok) Lake, who is identified with the boar-headed partner of the horrific Tantric Buddha Cakrasaṃvara, known as Vajravārāhī ("adamantine sow"), a sufficient indication that such "converted" Hindu divinities were in practice accorded *bodhisattva* rank.

From the above comments it should be clear that it is difficult to draw distinctions in late Indian Buddhism and in Tibetan religion, which inherits the greater part of Indian Buddhist traditions, between *bodhisattvas* and other divinities who are effectively raised to *bodhisattva* rank. Thus, to my knowledge the position of the four chief goddesses, Locanā, Māmakī, and so forth, as well as that of the feminine partners of the great Tantric divinities (who are themselves manifestly accorded full buddha rank) is scarcely definable in traditional Buddhist terms. They are all said to be manifestations of the Perfection of Wisdom, at least according to the later Tantric theories, and thus an associate buddha rank must be assumed for them. Clearer distinctions, however, continue to remain between buddhas and *bodhisattvas*, in accordance with the ideas prevalent during the earliest Buddhist period. According to purist theories, once a *bodhisattva* achieves enlightenment and thereby becomes a buddha ("enlightened") he effectively passes beyond the realm of imperfect living beings. The fact that Śākyamuni Buddha continued to work for the good of others during the forty-five years that elapsed between his enlightenment at the age of thirty-five and his decease *(parinirvāṇa)* at the age of eighty created a philosophical problem for the philosophers of the early schools. Only as *bodhisattva* can there be no doubt of his ability to respond to the needs of lesser beings. It may be for this reason that some early Buddha images are inscribed as *bodhisattva* images, for Śākyamuni in the earliest period could be regarded as both buddha and *bodhisattva.*

The cult of Maitreya as future buddha soon supplied the need for a *bodhisattva,* who could still assist living beings so long as he had not entered the impassive state of Buddhahood. His cult was followed by that of Avalokiteśvara, the "lord who looks down (in compassion)," doubtless suggested by Śākyamuni's previous existence in the heavens, when as *bodhisattva* he had looked down on suffering living beings. The whole *bodhisattva* doctrine represents a remarkable aspect of Buddhist religion, expressing a degree of compassionate concern for others that is either far less developed or lacking altogether in other Indian religious traditions. The distinction between a buddha who represents an ideal state still to be achieved and a *bodhisattva* who assists one on the way there remains fairly clear throughout the whole history of Buddhism. Only rarely can a buddha become an object of prayer and supplication. One well-known exception is Amitābha, the Buddha of the West. But one may note that his cult, so strong in China and Japan, is based upon the *Sukhāvatīvyūha Sūtra,* which lists the many aspirations of the monk Dharmākara toward achieving buddhahood in a buddha paradise, where he may still be available for the solace of living beings in the most marvelous manner possible. This particular Buddha cult may therefore be regarded as exceptional.

SEE ALSO Amitābha; Arhat; Avalokiteśvara; Bodhisattva Path; Buddha; Buddhism, Schools of, articles on Esoteric Buddhism, Mahāyāna Philosophical Schools of Buddhism; Cosmology, article on Buddhist Cosmology; Kṣitigarbha; Mahāvairocana; Maitreya; Maṇḍalas, article on Buddhist Maṇḍalas; Mañjuśrī; Nirvāṇa; Pure and Impure Lands; Soteriology; Tārā; Tathāgata.

BIBLIOGRAPHY

References

Beal, Samuel, trans. *Si-yu-ki: Buddhist Records of the Western World* (1884). Reprint, Delhi, 1969.

Conze, Edward, trans. and ed. *Buddhist Scriptures.* Harmondsworth, 1959.

Conze, Edward, trans. *The Large Sūtra of Perfect Wisdom.* Berkeley, 1975.

Dayal, Har. *The Bodhisattva Doctrine in Buddhist Sanskrit Literature* (1932). Reprint, New Delhi, 1975.

Hodgson, Brian H. *Essays on the Languages, Literature and Religion of Nepal and Tibet* (1874). Reprint, New Delhi, 1972.

Kern, Hendrik, trans. *Saddharmā-Puṇḍarīka, or The Lotus of the True Law* (1884). Reprint, New York, 1963.

Lamotte, Étienne, trans. and ed. *La concentration de la marche héroïque.* Brussels, 1965. A translation of the *Śūraṃgamasamādhi Sūtra.*

Lamotte, Étienne, trans. *The Teaching of Vimalakīrti.* London, 1976. A translation of the *Vimalakīrtinirdeśa Sūtra,* rendered from Étienne Lamotte's *L'enseignement de Vimalakīrti* (Louvain, 1962).

La Vallée Poussin, Louis de, ed. and trans. *Vijñaptimātratāsiddhi: La Siddhi de Hiuan-tsang.* 2 vols. Paris, 1928–1929.

Macdonald, Ariane, trans. *Le maṇḍala du Mañjuśrīmūlakalpa.* Paris, 1962.

Skorupski, Tadeusz. *The Sarvadurgatipariśodhana Tantra: Elimination of All Evil Destinies.* Delhi, 1983.

Snellgrove, David L. *Indo-Tibetan Buddhism, Indian Buddhists and Their Tibetan Successors.* Boston and London, 1986.

Snellgrove, David L., and Tadeusz Skorupski. *The Cultural Heritage of Ladakh.* 2 vols. Warminster, 1977–1980.

Tucci, Giuseppe. *Indo-Tibetica.* 4 vols. Rome, 1932–1941.

Further Reading

Bhattacharyya, Benoytosh. *The Indian Buddhist Iconography* (1924). 2d rev. ed. Calcutta, 1958.

Getty, Alice. *The Gods of Northern Buddhism* (1914). Reprint, Oxford, 1963.

Mallmann, Marie-Thérèse de. *Introduction à l'iconographie du tântrisme bouddhique.* Paris, 1975.

Snellgrove, David L., ed. *The Image of the Buddha.* London, 1978.

Tucci, Giuseppe. *Tibetan Painted Scrolls.* 2 vols. Translated by Virginia Vacca. Rome, 1949.

DAVID L. SNELLGROVE (1987)

BUDDHAS AND BODHISATTVAS: ETHICAL PRACTICES ASSOCIATED WITH BUDDHAS AND BODHISATTVAS

Buddhas and *bodhisattvas* represent exalted images of ethical perfection in Buddhism. In the midst of the kaleidoscopic complexity of Buddhist ethical thought and practice, the presence of buddhas and *bodhisattvas* serve as a universal focal point across traditions.

Buddhist ethics conceives of buddhas and *bodhisattvas* within a hierarchy of distinct categories of ethical actors. These categories are permeable and this hierarchy is not fixed; as ethical transformation occurs, over lifetimes or in some rare cases in a single lifetime, an actor's position is elevated (or potentially deescalated) in this ideational ordering of the ethical universe. It is a general truth that Buddhist traditions highly value the difference between ethical actors. While all beings have a future potential for enlightenment—and in some traditions an inherent capacity for buddhahood—the potential to live in the company of those with greater capacities than oneself—epitomized in the figure of the *kalyāṇamitra,* or beautiful friend—is a primary condition enabling ethical transformation.

The fluidity in this hierarchy is expressed in many ways, such as the debates over which category of being represents the highest ideal of ethical perfection: a buddha or a *bodhisattva.* Mahāyāna traditions have sometimes been characterized (and criticized) for elevating *bodhisattvas* over buddhas because *bodhisattvas* have postponed their full enlightenment for the sake of others, while the buddhas have entered into *nirvāṇa* before all beings have been freed from *saṃsāra.* Whereas the enlightened powers of the Celestial Bodhisattvas may be difficult to distinguish from buddhas, ordinary *bodhisattvas*—that is, *bodhisattvas* at lower stages (*bhūmis*) of the path—may be imperfect in many regards because their own transformations are still taking place.

The conceptions of buddhas and *bodhisattvas* in Buddhist ethical practices are shaped to a significant degree by the Buddhists who stand in relationship to these enlightened beings. buddhas and *bodhisattvas* are the heroes of Buddhist traditions; their extraordinary acts of compassion mitigate suffering in the world. They are also role models for escaping the suffering of *saṃsāra* for oneself and for others. The intercession of buddhas and *bodhisattvas* is sought because of both their power as heroes and their accessibility as role models.

BUDDHAS AND *BODHISATTVAS* AS MORAL HEROES. The originating moment of the *bodhisattva* path—the arising of *bodhicitta*—is nothing short of heroic. The aspiration for enlightenment is a vow to free all beings from suffering; the enormity of this commitment is unparalleled—the weight of the world's suffering rests upon the bodhisattva's shoulders. The power of this vow is captured by Śāntideva, an Indian monk believed to have lived in the seventh and eighth centuries CE. In his exposition of the *bodhisattva* path—the famous *Bodhicaryāvatāra*—he writes: "As long as space abides and as long as the world abides, so long may I abide, destroying the suffering of the world"(Crosby & Skilton, 1995:143). Making the vow is an ethical act that recreates a person as a *bodhisattva* and sets the ethical course they will follow. While the ability to actualize this commitment is far in the future—indeed, potentially numerous lifetimes in the future—the intention to realize this goal establishes the *bodhisattva* as a particular and extraordinary category of ethical actor. The obligations and challenges of this *bodhisattva* identity can at first evoke fear and self-doubt as well as determination, as Śāntideva so evocatively articulates. Buddhas and *bodhisattvas* serve as both inspiration and protection for *bodhisattvas* undergoing the process of ethical transformation as they move through the stages of the path.

Heroic actions of buddhas and *bodhisattvas*. Buddhas and Celestial *Bodhisattvas* actualize the power of their vows through ethical actions that appear nothing short of miraculous. The heroics of buddhas and *bodhisattvas* also lay in the miraculous, superhuman qualities of their actions. As fully enlightened beings, buddhas are perfectly ethical; thus ethics and soteriology are significantly intertwined. Among the perfections (*pāramitās*) cultivated on the bodhisattva path is a specific virtue, *śilā*, often translated as morality. Yet all the *pāramitās*, including vigor (*vīrya*), meditation (*dhyāna*), and wisdom (*prajñā*) are resources for the ethical life.

Buddhas' enlightened status enables them to act with absolute morality. This is modeled in some traditions, such as Chan or Zen, as perfect responsiveness—an enlightened being instantaneously responds exactly as a situation demands. These actions, however, may not always be understood by those without an enlightened perspective. Actions by buddhas and *bodhisattvas* can actually appear to be contrary to moral prescriptions and ethical values. A famous example of this is the parable told by the buddha in the *Saddharmapuṇḍarīka, Lotus Sūtra,* in which a rich man lies to his children in order to get them out of a burning house. His actions are viewed not as a deception, but as *upāya*, a skillful means to most effectively teach the Dharma to beings in its most effective form.

The extraordinary quality of a buddha's or *bodhisattva's* actions raises the question of whether imitation is desirable or possible. Take for example the extraordinary act of *dāna* (giving) in the buddha's penultimate lifetime as a *bodhisattva,* when he was born as the prince Vessantara. He gives away not only his kingdom's auspicious white elephant, but also his two children and his wife. Different versions of the Vessantara *jātaka* emphasize the outrageousness of these actions, as well as the high stakes for everyone involved—his children beg to be released from bondage from the cruel, torturous Brahmin, his wife writhes in physical and psychic agony upon discovering the loss of her children, and even Vessantara is tormented by the effects of his boundless generosity.

Vessantara's actions take place, from this perspective, on a normal moral stage. His actions, regardless of intent or motivation for the future attainment of buddhahood, cause pain. In fact, as Buddhist commentators from a variety of time periods have argued, his actions are not unquestionably ethical. The *bodhisattva's* actions are so different in degree from the norm of ethical practices so as to be a different kind of ethical action altogether. Because of this, the story is not meant to inspire imitation, but rather devotion. While the Vessantara story may be a source of inspiration for the ethical life, the actions it describes must be translated into a human morality. So, whereas it is not moral for a person to give away a child or a spouse in every circumstance, it is a valid moral choice, for instance, to give one's children to the *saṅgha.*

Heroic actions inspiring imitation. In certain instances extraordinary Buddhists have directly imitated the heroic actions of buddhas and *bodhisattvas.* A powerful example can be found in the self-immolation of Vietnamese monks during the Vietnam War—a dramatic demonstration of both commitment to Buddhist tradition and to the power of Buddhist ethical practices as a form of protest. As William LaFleur has argued, this modern-day act had precedence in the story of the Bodhisattva Bhaisajyaguru, in the *Saddharmapuṇḍarīka,* who devotedly lights himself on fire as offering to the buddhas. The heroics in both cases—historical and textual—draw stark distinctions between the ethical agents capable of such extraordinary acts, and the more ordinary beings, who, although perhaps awed, might also have confused these actions different not only in kind but also in degree from the standards for Buddhist ethical life.

Heroic actions inspiring devotion. Devotion inspired by the heroics of buddhas and *bodhisattvas* alike is an important resource for ethical cultivation. Buddhist traditions value celebrating the good deeds of others as beneficial and efficacious for generating merit, as well as engendering gratitude towards buddhas and *bodhisattvas.* The descriptions of the celebratory responses to the heroics of buddhas and *bodhisattvas* are among the most beautiful narrations in Buddhist literature, in which a whole universe—animals, humans, gods and goddesses, as well as the material world—responds with cheers of adulation, showers of flowers, and skies filled with rainbows. Lotus flowers arise from the earth to accept the tiny foot of the newborn baby who strides in each direction at his birth announcing his destiny to become the buddha. Thus, Buddhist traditions posit a world that is not ethically neutral; it is a moral world in which people live.

It would be a mistake to assume that devotion is transcended at a certain stage of ethical or spiritual development.

Many Buddhist traditions emphasize that the experience of enlightenment should create a heightened sense of gratitude towards the buddhas. In his autobiography, *Itsumadegusa*, Hakuin, a seventeenth century Rinzai Zen monk, describes his commitment to teaching other monks as a way to repay the debt he felt he owed to the buddhas and his lineage patriarch. Many other examples from various Buddhist traditions emphasize the gratitude enlightened beings feel as they reflect upon the care they received at every stage of their own process of transformation. This gratitude necessitates a reciprocal devotion to caring for others.

BUDDHAS AND BODHISATTVAS AS ETHICAL ROLE MODELS. Devotion for buddhas and *bodhisattvas*, inspired by their super-human achievements, is not antithetical to the desire to form oneself in their image. As ethical role models, buddhas and *bodhisattvas* are paradigms of virtues—their paths to enlightenment become the templates for ethical transformation.

It is important to ask what people would have been likely to view the buddhas and *bodhisattvas* as role models for their own practices and goals. The bodhisattva path, systematized in different forms by Buddhist traditions, is the most basic model for attaining the achievements of buddhas and *bodhisattvas*. Each stage of the path is a form of ethical practice. The arising of *bodhicitta*, the practice of the perfections and the movement through stages of the path, entail commitments, obligations, and increasing resources for ethical life. A general assumption in scholarship—informed to a significant degree by rhetoric in Mahāyāna sūtras—posits an extreme contrast between the exclusivity of the Hīnayāna conception of the *bodhisattvas* path with the Mahāyāna ideal of a universal path open to all beings. Indeed, the polemic term *Hīnayāna* (lesser vehicle) directly represents the Mahāyāna critique that these early Buddhist traditions—the Therāvada being the only one now extant among them—settled for the less ethically robust figure of the *arhant*, a being, according to the Mahāyāna critics, who attains enlightenment for his or her own benefit alone.

Textual evidence suggests a historical development of the *bodhisattva* ideal and path in both Mahāyāna and Theravādin traditions. Recent studies by scholars such as Paul Harrison and Jan Nattier argue that the Mahāyāna ideals of a universal path were not present in early formulations of the Mahāyāna in the first centuries of the Common Era. In early sūtras the *bodhisattva* ideal and the practitioners who modeled themselves after it were an exclusive minority of male monastic practitioners and even fewer male householders. If the Mahāyāna universal imperative of buddhahood broadened in conception and practice over time, these ideals were not absent from Theravādin traditions either. Theravādin traditions developed a more inclusive category of the *bodhisatta* (the Pali form of the Sanskrit word "*bodhisattva*") in the medieval period, expanding narrative traditions to include a fuller accounting of the *bodhisatta* path of Gautama as well as a more populous pantheon of additional *bodhisatta* who will become buddhas following the next buddha, Metteyya. While Theravādin descriptions of *bodhisattas* remained primarily hagiographical, and primarily (although not exclusively) tied to the *jātaka* lifetimes of Gotama, some systematic formulations of a *bodhisatta* path did emerge in the Theravādin commentarial and post-commentarial literature. Inscriptions and colophons from different parts of the Theravādin world suggest that practices paralleled the broadening of textual representations as some adherents conceived of their own future lifetimes, if not their present ones, as embarking upon the *bodhisattva* path.

Models for ethical transformation. Fascinating temporal issues are raised when we consider buddhas and *bodhisattvas* as ethical role models. From one perspective these figures offer an inspiring vision of the ethical being they aspire to become in the future, often a future lifetime, as it seems impossible for many Buddhists to attain this level of perfection in their present conditions. This future-orientation is powerfully at play in the bestowal of a prediction, *vyākaraṇa*, that is a condition of buddhahood for every *bodhisattva*. In order to become a buddha, a *bodhisattva* must first receive a prediction of their future buddhahood directly from another buddha. In this prediction a buddha describes the details of the *bodhisattva's* future biography when buddhahood will finally be attained. The buddha significantly models this future to be fulfilled by the *bodhisattva*. The prediction powerfully shapes the present as well as the face-to-face encounter between buddha and *bodhisattva*, narrated for example in the Pali *Buddhavaṃsa*, gives the *bodhisatta* a vision of the perfect being he will become in the future.

The bridging of present reality with future ideals is accomplished in a variety of practices directed at generating and experiencing the virtues and powers of enlightened beings. Through the recitation of the buddha's names in the practice of *buddhānusmṛti* (remembrance of the buddha) the qualities of the buddha described in these honorific titles begin to be embodied by the practitioner. The Vajrayāna practice of deity yoga leads the meditator to an experience of identification with a buddha during the course of the visualization.

As Buddhist traditions have changed in different times and places so too have the imaginations of how to best follow the ethical imperatives for *bodhisattvas* and buddhas. In the post-modern, global Buddhist world, the imitation of classical ideals has continued. For example, throughout the Theravādan world ordination ceremonies include a reenactment of the buddha's departure from his palace as he began his six-year struggle for enlightenment. Imitation has also given way to adaptation as Buddhists re-imagine what actions best emulate the compassion of buddhas and *bodhisattvas*. The Engaged Buddhist movement, led by figures like the Vietnamese monk Thich Nhat Hanh, image a universal practice of the *bodhisattva* path. Engaged Buddhism advocates a broad range of social conscious living such as participation in peace rallies, prison advocacy, and even recycling as *bodhisattva* acts.

THE INTERCESSION OF BUDDHAS AND *BODHISATTVAS*. As moral heroes and ethical role models, buddhas and *bodhisattvas* intercede in the lives of others in order to extinguish suffering in its endless varieties and support individuals and communities in their ethical practices. Acts of intercession illuminate the heroic depths of buddhas' and *bodhisattvas'* compassion—a compassion that is active and effective. Important Buddhist conceptions of ethical agency underlie the many different ways buddhas and *bodhisattvas* contribute to the ethical lives of others. For the devotee, the petition to a buddha or *bodhisattva* and the confidence in their response underlies two basic conceptions of Buddhist ethics: first, that while existence is governed by the first noble truth of the ever-present reality of suffering, this suffering can be alleviated by the compassionate intervention of buddhas and *bodhisattvas*; and following directly from this, Buddhist ethics demands that the ethical person conceive of their dependence on others for their own well-being. Communal agency is prioritized over autonomy. Beings depend upon the aid of others in order to reach the heights of ethical perfection as buddhas and *bodhisattvas*—a perfection that is desired in order to more effectively aid others in turn.

While every *bodhisattva* makes a generalized vow to alleviate suffering, buddhas and Celestial Bodhisattvas are differentiated by their individualized vows to address suffering with particular forms of compassion. As a *bodhisattva,* Amitābha Buddha, for example, vowed to become Buddha of Infinite Light, of Infinite Life, and to create a Pure Land, Sukhāvatī, where all beings who said his name would be reborn. In his or her variety of regional, gendered and iconographic forms, the Celestial Bodhisattva Avalokiteśvara is the hero among heroes who saves beings in the saṃsāric world from suffering in whatever form it takes. This *bodhisattva's* interventions, such as granting a child to the infertile, or rescuing the shipwrecked from certain death, display the ever-ready responsiveness of the *bodhisattva* to the particularities of suffering. These examples of intercession are responses to petitions for aid made by engaging in devotional activities such as reciting a *mantra* or a sūtra, or leaving offerings at a *bodhisattva* shrine. The methods for invoking a buddha's or *bodhisattva's* aid is in some cases precisely defined, as in the *Bhaiṣajyaguru sūtras*—the sūtras of the Medicine Buddha—that instruct the devotee how to rid oneself of physical illness.

A decidedly different conception of the un-requested intervention of a buddha or *bodhisattva* is seen as a response to the ethical achievements of particular actors. In these instances, a buddha or *bodhisattva* intervenes to support and encourage the dedicated practitioner striving for ethical fulfillment. In Japan, for example, the Bodhisattva Jizō, often disguised as a young monk, appears to support the beneficial activities of those desiring to follow an ethical path, such as a monk on austere retreat or a devotee leaving offerings at a shrine. In these instances, it is precisely in response to the already present ethical qualities that the *bodhisattva* intervenes in order to promote the success of further ethical development. Jizō's concealed identity in these narratives emphasizes both the worthiness of the person receiving his aid, as well as the intent of the *bodhisattva* to encourage the success of that person, rather than to primarily draw attention to the *bodhisattva's* power and virtues.

Buddhas and *bodhisattvas* as ethical refuges. Buddhas and *bodhisattvas* may also directly intercede in moments of crisis in order to prevent a being from causing physical and karmic harm to themselves or others. In many narratives they are imagined as the final refuge for beings who have found no other resources to redress their suffering. The concept of a buddha, and by extension, a *bodhisattva,* as one of three Refuges has a heightened ethical significance in stories, found in every Buddhist tradition, which describe the precise ways buddhas and *bodhisattva* prevent harm and bring relief. There are countless examples of these forms of intercession. For example, in the famous story of Aṅgulimāla, a moral young man is commanded by his teacher to make him a necklace out of 1,000 fingers. Just as he is about to complete his necklace by murdering his own mother, the Buddha miraculously intervenes, preventing the heinous sin of matricide and setting Aṅgulimāla on an ethical course ultimately ending in enlightenment.

Moral challenges directly confronting ethical self understanding can find a resolution through the intervention of buddhas and *bodhisattvas,* who can re-establish conceptions of integrity for ethical actors. People who perceive themselves as harming others can, through a separate set of actions directed towards a buddha or *bodhisattva,* either redress the particular wrong committed or establish their moral worthiness. Practices from various traditions and time periods show how recourse to interaction with buddhas and *bodhisattvas* provides a redemptive space for those who have faced and perceived failure in an ethical crisis. One might think of the devotional programs of the legendary King Asoka as, in part, a response to the warfare of his early reign; or the trials of the Tibetan yogi, Milarepa—designed by his teacher Marpa, a living buddha—to cleanse the karma produced in his murderous youth; or the modern Japanese practices of mizuko kuyō, where devotional offerings are made to the Bodhisattva Jizō—the caretaker of dead children—by those who have had an abortion. These forms of intervention for redressing or establishing ethical identity are inherently complex religious-social phenomena, as illuminated by this final example where gender, economic, and political factors—as well as ethical ones—are at play.

The ethical formulation of dependency arguably reaches its fullest form in the thinking of Shinran, the twelfth- and thirteenth-century founder of Jōdo Shinshū. In his teachings, the only possibility for ethical action is to give oneself over completely to the Other power of Amida Buddha, who, as the Bodhisattva Dharmakara, vowed to end the suffering of all beings and to bring all who say his name to enlightenment through rebirth in his Pure Land, Sukhāvatī. It is the recognition of one's own complete inability to act ethically that enables the compassion of Amida to transform one into an ethical actor. According to Shinran's thought, the devotee neither inspires nor invokes Amida's compassion; rather, Amida is the sole agent in bringing about the ethical formation of his devotees. Without Amida, Shinran estimated, he was completely without options for leading an ethical life.

This emphasis on the power of a buddha to shape the ethical life of beings is not exclusive to Pure Land traditions. While not articulated with the same direct emphasis as with Shinran, there is, in the Theravādin traditions, for example, the conception that the presence of a buddha—through physical proximity in his lifetime or through his relics after his *parinibbāna*—can change people's destinies. Hagiographical accounts of the buddha's teaching career are filled with stories of the multitudes of people who quickly attained arahatship upon receiving the Dharma from the Buddha.

In addition to these generalized patterns, narratives also depict personalized encounters with the Buddha Gautama. The evocative story of Pattācāra, recorded in the Pali *Therīgīthā*, describes how the Buddha's intercession changes the ethical destiny of a woman whose grief at the loss of her entire family renders her insane, wandering naked as an outcast from society. The Buddha becomes literally her last refuge; he is the only one who clearly perceives her naked ravings as an exposure of suffering. The encounter brings sanity, a new family in the *saṅgha*, and ultimately, enlightenment. Attaining enlightenment is not the ultimate goal for Buddhist ethical life; rather, it is to continue to aid others, both through acts of heroic intervention and, like Pattācāra, by serving as an inspiring role model for others.

See Also Buddha; Buddhism, articles on Buddhism in Japan and Buddhism in Tibet; Buddhism, Schools of, article on Tibetan and Mongolian Buddhism; Celestial Buddhas and Bodhisattvas.

Bibliography

For a translation and useful introduction to Santideva's *Bodhicaryāvatāra*, see Kate Crosby and Andrew Skilton, *Bodhicaryavatara* (Oxford, 1995). An engaging introduction to the Pure Land traditions of Shin Buddhism and Shinran's teachings on issues of ethical agency can be found in Taitetsu Unno's *River of Fire, River of Water* (New York, 1998). Among the many studies of the *bodhisattva* path, Paul Harvey's *An Introduction to Buddhist Ethics* (Cambridge, U.K., 2000) provides a useful overview of ethical conceptions of buddhas, *bodhisattvas* and the *bodhisattva* path. There are several excellent introductions to Buddhism containing insightful chapters on conceptions and roles of buddhas and *bodhisattvas* in Buddhist traditions, such as Donald S. Lopez's *The Story of Buddhism* (San Francisco, 2000). For a brief but helpful discussion of practices of self-immolation practiced, see William R. Lafluer's *Buddhism* (Upper Saddle River, N.J., 1988). For historical studies of early Mahāyāna movements and *bodhisattva* practices see Paul Harrison, "Who Gets to Ride on the Great Vehicle? Self Image and Identity among the Followers of the Early Mahāyāna," *Journal of the International Association of Buddhist Studies* 10, no. 1: 67–89. See also Jan Nattier's *A Few Good Men: The Bodhisattva Path according to the Inquiry of Ugra* (Honolulu, Hawai'i, 2003).

Karen Derris (2005)

BUDDHISM

This entry consists of the following articles:

BUDDHISM: AN OVERVIEW

[*This article attempts to identify certain of the elements and structures that have constituted the Buddhist tradition as it has evolved over the past twenty-five hundred years. It traces a complex of social and ideological formations that have allowed it to develop from a small religious community to a "universal" religion associated with empire, to an important component in the several cultures of Buddhist Asia, to a tradition faced with the problems raised by modernity and contact with the West.*]

The concept of Buddhism was created about three centuries ago to identify what we now know to be a pan-Asian religious tradition that dates back some twenty-five hundred years. Although the concept, rather recent and European in origin, has gradually, if sometimes begrudgingly, received global acceptance, there is still no consensus about its definition. We can, however, identify two complementary meanings that have consistently informed its use. First, it groups together the thoughts, practices, institutions, and values that over the centuries have—to use a phrase coined by the French Buddhologist Louis de La Vallée Poussin—"condensed around the name of the Buddha." The implicit conclusion of this usage is that Buddhism is, in short, whatever Buddhist men and women have said, done, and held dear. Second, the concept suggests some unifying character or order in the overwhelming diversity encompassed by the first usage. The beginning of this ordering process has often been to consider Buddhism as an example of larger categories, and thus Buddhism has been variously labeled a religion, a philosophy, a civilization, or a culture. It must be admitted, however, that no single ordering principle has been found that takes full account of the data included within the first meaning. This admission stands as a rebuke of the limitations of our current understanding, and as a continuing challenge to go further in our descriptions and explanations.

When the first meaning of Buddhism, which emphasizes its encompassment of accumulated traditions, is placed in the foreground, the resulting conception is indeed comprehensive. The further scholarship proceeds, the more comprehensive this conception becomes, because Buddhists have done in the name of the Buddha almost everything that other humans have done. Buddhists have, of course, been concerned with living religiously, some with the aim of salvation, and they have created traditions of belief and practice that help to realize these aspirations. But they have been concerned with much more as well. Buddhists have built cities sanctified by monuments dedicated to the Buddha and they have cultivated their crops using blessings that invoke his name. They have written self-consciously Buddhist poems and plays as well as highly technical works of grammar and logic that begin with invocations to the Buddha. They have commended nonviolence, but they have also gone to war with the name of Buddha on their lips. They have valued celibacy, but have also written erotic manuals and rejoiced in family life, all in the name of Buddha. Buddhists have created subtle philosophical concepts, such as the absence of self (*anātman*), which are contravened by other ideas and values they have held. Like other human beings, Buddhists have been inconsistent and even contradictory, and they have been both noble and base in what they have said and done.

Although most scholars have at some level accepted this first conception of Buddhism as a diverse cumulative tradition, few have been content to allow this encompassing notion to prevail. They have sought to discover what ideals and values have inspired Buddhists, or to formulate generalizations that will help us to see the behavior of individuals as distinctively Buddhist. Some scholars have singled out a pattern, an idea, or a cluster of ideas that they felt was important enough to provide continuity through Buddhist history, or at least sufficient to suggest a coherence to the variety. Important candidates for this "key" to Buddhism are the purported teaching of the founder of Buddhism, Gautama, which provides an essence that has unfolded over the centuries; the monastic organization *(saṃgha),* whose historical continuity provides a center of Buddhist practice and a social basis for the persistence of Buddhist thought and values; the closely related ideas of nonself and emptiness *(anātman, śūnyatā),* realized through insight, which are said to mold Buddhist behavior; and the goal of *nirvāṇa* as the purpose of life. While such patterns and notions are very important for Buddhist sociology and soteriology, they also omit a great deal. Moreover, we can see that the element that is singled out as important is often distictive to Buddhism only in comparison with other religions or philosophies and cannot serve as a core that informs the entire corpus of Buddhist beliefs, rituals, and values.

Scholars have also sought to identify the characteristic order of Buddhism by dividing the cumulative tradition into more manageable parts, whether by chronology, by school, or by country. Some scholars, following the Buddhist historians Bu ston (1290–1364) and Tāranātha (1574–1608), have divided Buddhism into three periods, mainly along philosophical lines. A first phase, represented by the early Theravāda (Way of the Elders) and Sarvāstivāda (All Things Are Real) schools, emphasized the no-soul idea and the reality of the constituents (*dharmas*) of the world. A middle phase, represented by the Mādhyamika (Middle Way) school, introduced the idea of the ultimate emptiness *(śūnyatā)* of all phenomena. A third period, represented by the Vijñānavāda (Consciousness Only) school, was philosophically idealistic in character. The limitations of this philosophical division are severe in that it only touches certain aspects of Buddhism and acknowledges no significant development after the fifth century CE.

Other scholars have elaborated a schema based on polemical divisions within the Buddhist community. They have focused attention on three great Buddhist "vehicles" (*yāna*) that are characterized by different understandings of the process and goal of salvation. The Hīnayāna, or Lesser Vehicle, elaborated a gradual process of individual salvation, and in that context distinguished among the attainment of an *arhat*, the attainment of a *pratyekabuddha* (one who achieves enlightenment on his own but does not become a teacher), and the attainment of a fully enlightened Buddha who teaches others the way to salvation. The Theravāda and Sarvāstivāda schools mentioned above are two of the major schools that are included under the Hīnayāna rubric. The term *Hīnayāna* was in its origins a pejorative name coined by the adherents of a new movement, self-designated as the Mahāyāna, or Great Vehicle, which generated new texts and teachings that were rejected by the Hīnayānists.

Like the adherents of the Hīnayāna, the Mahāyānists elaborated a gradual path of salvation lasting over many lifetimes, but their emphasis was different in two very important and related respects. They held that an individual's soteriological process could be aided and abetted by what some Mahāyāna schools came to designate as "other-power," and they recognized, ultimately, only one soteriological goal—the attainment of fully realized Buddhahood. The Vajrayāna (Diamond Vehicle), which is also known as Mantrayāna (Sacred Sounds Vehicle), Esoteric Buddhism, or Tantric Buddhism, accepted the basic approach and goal of the Mahāyāna, but felt that individual realization could be accomplished more quickly, in some cases even in this present life. The Vajrayānists described the practices that lead to this attainment in texts called *tantras* that were not accepted by either the Hīnayāna or the Mahāyāna schools. Although this Hīnayāna/Mahāyāna/Vajrayāna schema is probably the most common one used by scholars to divide Buddhism into more manageable segments, it too has serious drawbacks. It underestimates the significance of developments after the first millennium of the common era and it tends to overemphasize certain traits therein as extreme differences, beyond what is warranted by history.

Finally, scholars have recognized that Buddhism has always been deeply shaped by its surrounding culture. The Buddhist tradition has been more accretive in its doctrine and practice than the other great missionary religions, Christianity and Islam. It has shown an enduring tendency to adapt to local forms; as a result we can speak of a transformation of Buddhism in various cultures. The extent of this transformation can be seen in the difficulty that the first Western observers had in recognizing that the religion they observed in Japan was historically related to the religion found in Sri Lanka. This cultural division of Buddhism into Tibetan Buddhism, Chinese Buddhism, and so forth has been most successfully applied to the more recent phases of Buddhist history, especially to contemporary developments. Its dangers are, of course, quite obvious: above all, it conceals the Buddhist tradition's capacity to transcend the boundaries of culture, politics, and nationality.

The general trends of scholarship on Buddhism in this century have been within such accepted divisions of the cumulative tradition, with the result that our sense of Buddhism's historical continuity has been greatly obscured. Theodore Stcherbatsky, a Soviet Buddhologist, is in this regard a representative example. He adopted Bu ston's tripartite "philosophical" division of Buddhist history and, in his *Conception of Buddhist Nirvāṇa* (Leningrad, 1927), commented on the transition between the first phase and the second phase as follows: "the history of religions has scarcely witnessed such a break between new and old within the pale of what nevertheless continued to claim common descent from the same religious founder" (p. 36). Similar statements pointing to radical discontinuity have been made from the perspective of the soteriological and cultural forms of Buddhism as well.

The investigation of each segment of the Buddhist cumulative tradition is now generally done in isolation from other segments. This strategy has had remarkable success in our discovery of the imprint of Buddhist thought and practice in areas far beyond the monasteries, beyond the level of elite groups. In small domains scholars have begun to see patterns in the full extent of phenomena grouped under the name of Buddhism. At the same time, contemporary scholarship often risks missing the forest for the trees. Our advances in particular areas of research may be at the price of the scholar's unique vision of Buddhism as a pan-Asian tradition.

As is often the case in the study of religion, however, the scale of investigation is decisive. This article will discuss Buddhism on a general level and will highlight continuities rather than disjunctions within the tradition. These continuities cannot be found in any static essence or core threading its way through all of Buddhist history. They will be traced here by following certain elements that have been preserved in a changing series of structures, expanded to meet new needs, and brought into relation with new elements that are continuously being introduced. We will, in other words, identify various elements and successive structures that have constituted Buddhism as it developed from a small community of mendicants and householders in northeastern India into a great "universal" religion associated with empire, civilization, and culture in various parts of Asia, and ultimately with "modernity" and the West as well.

BUDDHISM AS SECTARIAN RELIGION. Buddhism began around the fifth or fourth century BCE as a small community that developed at a certain distance, both self-perceived and real, from other contemporary religious communities, as well as from the society, civilization, and culture with which it coexisted. Thus, we have chosen to characterize the Buddhism of this period as "sectarian."

It is quite probable that Buddhism remained basically a sectarian religion until the time of King Aśoka (third century BCE). Whether this was a period of approximately two hundred years, as some scholars, dating the death of the Buddha around 486 BCE, maintain, or of approximately one hundred years (accepting a death date around a century later) as others contend, it was by all accounts a crucial period in which many elements and patterns were established that have remained fundamental to subsequent phases of Buddhist thought and life. Despite the importance of this early phase of Buddhist history our knowledge about it remains sketchy and uncertain. Three topics can suggest what we do know: the source of authority that the new Buddhist community recognized, the pattern of development in its teaching and ecclesiastical structures, and the attitude it took toward matters of political and social order. In discussing these three topics we shall identify some of the main scholarly opinions concerning them.

One primary factor that both accounts for and expresses Buddhism's emergence as a new sectarian religion rather than simply a new Hindu movement is the community's recognition of the ascetic Gautama as the Buddha ("enlightened one") and of the words that he had reportedly uttered as a new and ultimate source of sacred authority. The recognition of the Buddha's authority was based on an acceptance of the actuality and relative uniqueness of his person and career, and of his enlightenment experience in particular. It was based on the conviction that through his enlightenment he had gained insight into the *dharma* (the Truth). This included the aspect of truth that he had formulated more "philosophically" as, for example, in the teaching concerning the dependent co-origination (*pratītya-samutpāda*) of the various elements that constitute reality, and also the aspect of truth he had formulated more soteriologically, as summarized, for example, in the classic delineation of the Four Noble Truths (that reality is permeated with suffering, that desire is the cause of suffering, that the cessation of suffering is a possibility, and that there is a path that leads to a cessation of suffering). Finally, the Buddha's authority was based on the confidence that the teachings and actions that had flowed from his enlightenment had been accurately transmitted by those who had heard and seen them.

From certain stories preserved in the tradition it seems that there were some challenges to the Buddha's authority. For example, there are numerous reports that even during his own lifetime a more ascetically inclined cousin named Devadatta tried to take over leadership of the new movement. Such challenges were successfully met by the Buddha and by those who carried on the tradition. As a result, later controversies concerned not so much the authority of his teachings and actions as their content and correct interpretation.

There is less scholarly agreement concerning the more specific content of the early Buddhist teaching and about the closely related question of the structure of the early Buddhist community. Three conflicting interpretations have been set forth, each defended on the basis of detailed text-critical research. Some scholars have maintained that early Buddhism was a movement of philosophically oriented renouncers practicing a discipline of salvation that subsequently degenerated into a popular religion. A second group has contended that Buddhism was originally a popular religious movement that took form around the Buddha and his religiously inspiring message, a movement that was subsequently co-opted by a monastic elite that transformed it into a rather lifeless clerical scholasticism. A third group has argued that as far back as there is evidence, early Buddhist teaching combined philosophical and popular elements, and that during the earliest period that we can penetrate, the Buddhist community included both a significant monastic and a significant lay component. This argument, which is most convincing, has included the suggestion that the philosophical/popular and monastic/lay dichotomies should actually be seen as complements rather than oppositions, even though the understandings of the relative importance of these elements and their interrelationships have varied from the beginning of the Buddhist movement.

By the time of the Second Buddhist Council, held in the city of Vaiśālī probably in the fourth century BCE, the Buddhist community already encompassed two competing assemblies whose members espoused positions that correspond to the modern scholarly group of those who associate the "original" or "true" Buddhism with an elite monastic tradition, and those who associate it with a more democratic and populist tradition. A split occurred at or shortly after the Second Council: those who adhered to the former position came to be known in Sanskrit as Sthaviravādins (Pali, Theravādins; the proponents of the Way of the Elders), while those who adhered to the latter position came to be known as the Mahāsāṃghikas (Members of the Great Assembly).

The third area of discussion about early Buddhism has focused on its sectarian character. While it is not disputed that during the pre-Aśokan period the Buddhist community was a specifically religious community only tangentially involved with issues of political order and social organization, it is less clear whether this distance was a matter of principle or simply an accident of history. Some scholars have argued that early Buddhists were so preoccupied with individual salvation, and the early monastic order so oriented toward "otherworldly" attainments, that early Buddhism's sectarian character was intrinsic, rather than simply circumstantial. While individualistic and otherworldly strands played an important role in some segments of the early Buddhist community, there are balancing factors that must also be taken into account. Early Buddhists were concerned to gain royal patronage and were often successful in their efforts; they appropriated royal symbolism in their depiction of the Buddha and his career; they maintained their own explicitly anti-Brahmanic conception of kingship and social order, in the *Aggañña Sutta*, for example; and they encouraged a respect for authority and moral decorum conducive to civil order and tranquillity. Thus, within the sectarian Buddhism of the early period, there were a number of elements that prepared the way for the "civilizational Buddhism" that began to emerge during the reign of King Aśoka.

BUDDHISM AS CIVILIZATIONAL RELIGION. Buddhism has never lost the imprint of the sectarian pattern that characterized its earliest history, largely because the sectarian pattern has been reasserted at various points in Buddhist history. But Buddhism did not remain a purely sectarian religion. With the reign of King Aśoka, Buddhism entered a new phase of its history in which it became what we have chosen to call a "civilizational religion," that is, a religion that was associated with a sophisticated high culture and that transcended the boundaries of local regions and politics. By the beginning of the common era Buddhism's civilizational character was well established in various areas of India and beyond. By the middle centuries of the first millennium CE, Buddhism as a civilizational religion had reached a high level of development across Asia. However, the signs of the transition to a new stage had already begun to appear by the sixth and seventh centuries CE.

History and legend of the Aśokan impact. Aśoka (r. circa 270–232 BCE) was the third ruler in a line of Mauryan emperors who established the first pan-Indian empire through military conquest. In one of the many inscriptions that provide the best evidence regarding his attitudes and actual policies, Aśoka renounced further violent conquest and made a commitment to the practice and propagation of *dharma.* In other inscriptions Aśoka informs his subjects concerning the basic moral principles that form his vision of the *dharma;* he mentions related meditational practices that he commends to his subjects as well as festivals of *dharma* that he sponsored. He also tells of sending special representatives to ensure that the *dharma* was appropriately practiced and taught by the various religious communities within his realm.

It would seem from Aśoka's inscriptions that the *dharma* that he officially affirmed and propagated was not identical to the Buddhist *dharma,* although it was associated with it, especially insofar as Buddhist teaching impinged on the behavior of the laity. However, the inscriptions give clear evidence that if Aśoka was not personally a Buddhist when he made his first commitment to the *dharma,* he became so soon thereafter. His edicts indicate that he sponsored Buddhist missions to various areas not only within his own empire, but in the Greek-ruled areas of the northwest and in Sri Lanka to the south. They indicate that he maintained a special interest in the well-being and unity of the Buddhist *saṃgha*, that he was concerned to emphasize the importance of Buddhist texts that dealt with lay morality, and that he undertook a royal pilgrimage to the sites associated with the great events in the Buddha's life.

Aśoka's actual policies and actions represent only one aspect of his impact in facilitating the transition of Buddhism from a sectarian religion to a civilizational religion. The other aspect is evidenced in the legends of Aśoka that appeared within the Buddhist community in the period following his death. These legends vary in character from one Buddhist tradition to another. For example, the Theravādins present an idealized portrait of Aśoka and depict him as a strong supporter of their own traditions. Another widely disseminated Aśokan text, the *Aśokāvadāna*, composed in Northwest India probably in a Sarvāstivāda context, depicts an equally imposing but more ambivalent figure, sometimes cruel in behavior and ugly in appearance. But all of the various Aśokan legends present in dramatic form an ideal of Buddhist kingship correlated with an imperial Buddhism that is truly civilizational in character.

During the Aśokan and immediately post-Aśokan era there are at least three specific developments that sustained the transformation of Buddhism into a civilizational religion. The first, a realignment in the structure of the religious community, involved an innovation in the relationship and balance between the monastic order and its lay supporters. Prior to the time of Aśoka the monastic order was, from an organizational point of view, the focus of Buddhist community life; the laity, however important its role may have been, lacked any kind of independent institutional structure. As a result of the Aśokan experience, including both historical events and the idealized example he set as lay participant *par excellence* in the affairs of the *saṃgha*, the Buddhist state came to provide (sometimes as a hoped-for possibility, at other times as a socioreligious reality) an independent institution that could serve as a lay counterpoint and counterbalance to the order of monks. In addition, this realignment in the structure of the Buddhist community fostered the emergence of an important crosscutting distinction between monks and laypersons who were participants in the imperial-civilizational elite on the one hand, and ordinary monks and laypersons on the other.

The transformation of Buddhism into a civilizational religion also involved doctrinal and scholastic factors. During the Aśokan and post-Aśokan periods, factions within the monastic community began to formulate aspects of the teachings more precisely, and to develop those teachings into philosophies that attempted to explain all of reality in a coherent and logically defensible manner. As a result, the literature in which the community preserved its memory of the sermons of the Buddha (the sūtras) and of his instructions to the monastic order (Vinaya) came to be supplemented by new scholastic texts known as Abhidharma ("higher Dharma"). Given the philosophical ambiguities of the received traditions, it was inevitable that contradictory doctrines would be put forward and that different religio-philosophical systems would be generated. This led to controversies within the community, and these controversies led to the proliferation of Buddhist schools and subschools, probably in conjunction with other more mundane disputes that we do not have sufficient data to reconstruct. Some sources list a total of eighteen schools without any consistency in names. The institutional and ideological boundaries between groups and subgroups were probably very fluid.

Developments in the areas of symbolism, architecture, and ritual were also significant components in the transformation of Buddhism into a civilizational religion. Some changes were related to the support Buddhism received from its royal and elite supporters. For example, royal and elite patronage seems to have been crucial to the emergence of large monastic establishments throughout India. Such support was also a central factor in the proliferation of stupas (Skt., *stūpas*), memorial monuments replete with cosmological and associated royal symbolism that represented the Buddha and were, in most cases, believed to contain a portion of his relics. These stūpas were an appropriate setting for the development of Buddhist art in which the Buddha was represented in aniconic forms such as a footprint, a Bodhi ("enlightenment") Tree, a royal throne, the wheel of the *dharma*, and the like. Merit making and related rituals proliferated and assumed new forms around these stupas. Pilgrimages to the sacred sites associated with the great events of the Buddha's life became more popular. The veneration and contemplation of stupas and other symbolic representations of the Buddha became increasingly widespread. Moreover, the notion of merit making itself was expanded so that it came to include not only merit making for oneself but the transfer of merit to deceased relatives and others was well.

Imperial Buddhism reasserted and transcended. Despite the importance of Aśoka to the history of Buddhism, the imperial order that he established persisted only a short time after his death. Within fifty years of his death (i. e., by the year 186 BCE), the Buddhist-oriented Mauryan dynasty collapsed and was replaced by the Śuṅga dynasty, more supportive of Brahmanic Hindu traditions. The Buddhist texts claim that the Śuṅgas undertook a persecution of Buddhism, although the force of any such persecution is rendered dubious by the fact that Buddhism and Buddhist institutions continued to flourish and develop within the territory ruled by the Śuṅgas. Moreover, Buddhism emerged as a dominant religion in areas outside northeastern India where the Śuṅgas were unable to maintain the authority and prestige that their Mauryan predecessors had enjoyed.

During the three centuries from the second century BCE through the first century CE Buddhism became a powerful religious force in virtually all of India, from the southern tip of the peninsula to the Indo-Greek areas in the northwest, and in Sri Lanka and Central Asia as well. New polities seeking to secure their control over culturally plural areas emulated Aśoka's example and adopted Buddhism as an imperial religion. This happened in Sri Lanka, probably when Duṭṭhagāmaṇī brought about the unification of the island kingdom in the mid-second century BCE. It happened in central India when the rising Śātavāhana dynasty became a supporter of the Buddhist cause. It happened to some extent in northwestern India when certain Greek and invading Central Asian kings converted to Buddhism. And it happened more fully in northwestern India during and after the reign of King Kaniṣka (first to second century CE), who ruled over a vast Kushan empire that extended from northern India deep into Central Asia. By this time Buddhism had also begun to penetrate into trading centers in northern China and to spread along land and sea routes across Southeast Asia to South China as well.

A major aspect of the transformation of Buddhism into a fully civilizational religion was the differentiation that occurred between Buddhism as a civilizational religion and Buddhism as an imperial religion. During late Mauryan times the civilizational and imperial dimensions had not been clearly differentiated. However, by the beginning of the common era Buddhism had become a civilizational religion that transcended the various expressions of imperial Buddhism in particular geographical areas. As a direct correlate of this development, an important distinction was generated within the elite of the Buddhist community. By this period this elite had come to include both a truly civilizational component that maintained close international contacts and traveled freely from one Buddhist empire to another and beyond, as well as overlapping but distinguishable imperial components that operated within the framework of each particular empire.

At this time Buddhist texts and teachings were being extended in a variety of ways. In some schools, such as the Theravāda and the Sarvāstivāda, canons of authoritative texts were established, but even after this had occurred new elements continued to be incorporated into the tradition through commentaries. In the case of the Sarvāstivādins, a huge collection of commentaries known as the *Mahāvibhāṣā* was compiled at a Buddhist council held by King Kaniṣka. In other schools the Pitakas themselves were still being enriched by the incorporation of a variety of new additions and embellishments. There also began to appear, on the fringes of the established schools, a new kind of sūtra that signaled the rise of a new Buddhist orientation that came to be known as the Mahāyāna. The earliest of these were the *Prajñāpāramitā Sūtras,* which put forward the doctrine of *śūnyatā* (the ultimate "emptiness" of all phenomena) and proclaimed the path of the *bodhisattva* (future Buddha) as the path that all Buddhists should follow. Before the end of the second century CE the great Buddhist philosopher Nāgārjuna had given the perspective of these sūtras a systematic expression and thereby established a basis for the first of the major Mahāyāna schools, known as Mādhyamika.

This extension of Buddhist traditions of texts and teachings was accompanied by two other developments that also contributed to their civilizational efficacy. During this period the older Buddhist schools (hereafter collectively called the Hīnayāna) that had previously limited themselves to the oral transmission of tradition, and the newly emerging Mahāyāna fraternities as well, began to commit their versions of the Buddha's teaching to writing. Some Buddhist groups began to translate and write their most authoritative texts in Sanskrit, which had become the preeminent civilizational language in India.

The rapid development of Buddhism led to major changes in Buddhist ways of representing the Buddha and relating to him ritually. Some Hīnayāna schools produced autonomous biographies of the Buddha. The most famous of the biographies is the *Buddhacarita* (Acts of the Buddha), by Aśvaghoṣa, written in refined Sanskrit in a classic literary form (*kavya*). The Hīnayāna schools provided the context for the production of anthropomorphic images of the Buddha, which became a major focal point for sophisticated artistic expression on the one hand, and for veneration and devotion on the other. These schools also made a place within the Buddhist system for a new and very important figure who became a focus for new forms of devotional practice and, in later phases of Buddhist history, new forms of religio-political symbolism and activity as well. This new figure was the future Buddha Maitreya ("the friendly one"), who was believed to be residing in the Tusita Heaven awaiting the appropriate time to descend to earth. By the beginning of the common era other buddhological trends were beginning to surface that were exclusively Mahāyāna in character. For example, sūtras were beginning to appear that focused attention on a celestial Buddha named Amitābha ("infinite light") and portrayed practices of visualization that could lead to rebirth in the western paradise over which he presided.

Closely associated developments were taking place at the level of cosmology and its application to religious practice. In the Hīnayāna context the most important development was probably the rich portrayal of a set of six cosmological *gatis*, or "destinies" (of gods, humans, animals, *asuras* or titans, hungry ghosts, and beings who are consigned to hell), which depicted, in vivid fashion, the workings of *karman* (moral action and its effects). These texts, which were probably used as the basis for sermons, strongly encouraged Buddhist morality and Buddhist merit-making activities. Other Hīnayāna works of the period suggested the presence of a vast expanse of worlds that coexist with our own. In the new Mahāyāna context this notion of a plurality of worlds was moved into the foreground, the existence of Buddhas in at least some of these other worlds was recognized, and the significance of these Buddhas for life in our own world was both affirmed and described. Finally, there are indications that during this period both Hīnayāna and Mahāyāna Buddhists increasingly employed exorcistic rituals that depended on the magical power of various kinds of chants and spells (*paritta* in Pali, *dhāraṇī* in Sanskrit).

Buddhism as Pan-Asian Civilization. From the second to the ninth century, Buddhism enjoyed a period of immense creativity and influence. Prior to the beginning of the sixth century, Buddhist fortunes were generally on the rise. Buddhism flourished in Sri Lanka, India, and Central Asia. Through already familiar processes involving its introduction along trade routes, its assimilation to indigenous beliefs and practices, and its adoption as an imperial religion, Buddhism became firmly entrenched in both northern and southern China and in many parts of Southeast Asia. After about 500 CE, these well-established dynamics of expansion continued to operate. Buddhism became the preeminent religion in a newly unified Chinese empire, it continued its spread in parts of Southeast Asia, and it was established in important new areas, first in Japan and then in Tibet. However, during this latter period its successes were coupled with setbacks, and by the middle of the ninth century the era of Buddhism as a pan-Asian civilization was rapidly drawing to a close.

The geographical expansion of Buddhism was both a cause and an effect of its civilizational character. But Buddhism's role as a pan-Asian civilization involved much more than a pan-Asian presence. Buddhist monasteries, often state supported and located near capitals of the various Buddhist kingdoms, functioned in ways analogous to modern universities. There was a constant circulation of Buddhist monks, texts, and artistic forms across increasingly vast geographical areas. Indian and Central Asian missionaries traveled to China and with the help of Chinese Buddhists translated whole libraries of books into Chinese, which became a third major Buddhist sacred language alongside Pali and Sanskrit. In the fifth century Buddhist nuns carried their ordination lineage from Sri Lanka to China. Between 400 and 700 a stream of Chinese pilgrims traveled to India via Central Asia and Southeast Asia in order to visit sacred sites and monasteries and to collect additional scriptures and commentaries. Some of these, such as Faxian, Xuanzang, and Yijing, wrote travel accounts that provide information concerning Buddhist civilization in its fullest development. In the sixth century Buddhism was formally introduced into Japan; in the following century Buddhists from Central Asia, India, and China made their way into Tibet. Beginning in the eighth and ninth centuries monks from Japan visited China in order to receive Buddhist training and acquire Buddhist texts. These are only a few illustrations of the kind of travel and interaction that characterized this period.

While Buddhism was reaching its apogee as a civilizational religion, the teachings of the Hīnayāna tradition were further extended and refined. New commentaries were produced in both Sanskrit and in Pali. During the fifth century these commentaries were supplemented by the appearance of two very important manuals, Vasubandhu's *Abhidharmakośa*, composed in the Sarvāstivāda-Sautrāntika context in Northwest India, and Buddhaghosa's *Visuddhimagga* (Path of Purification), written in the Theravādin context in Sri Lanka. Moreover, many Hīnayāna themes remained basic to the other Buddhist traditions with which it coexisted. Most Buddhists continued to recognize the Buddha Gautama as an important figure, and to focus attention on the single-world cosmology that posited the existence of three realms—the realm beyond form associated with the most exalted gods and the highest meditational states, the realm of form associated with slightly less exalted gods and meditational states, and the realm of desire constituted by the six *gatis* previously mentioned. This latter realm was especially prominent as the context presumed by pan-Buddhist teachings concerning karmic retribution and the value of giving, particularly to the members of the monastic community.

Within the Mahāyāna tradition this period of Buddhist efflorescence as a civilizational religion was characterized by a high level of creativity and by a variety of efforts toward systematization. In the earlier centuries the Mahāyānists produced a rich and extensive collection of new sūtras, including the *Saddharmapuṇḍarīka Sūtra* (Lotus of the true law), the *Mahāparinirvāṇa Sūtra*, the *Laṅkāvatāra Sūtra*, and the *Avatamsaka Sūtra*. With the passage of time, voluminous commentaries were written on many of these sūtras in India, Central Asia, and China. These *sūtras* and commentaries developed new teachings concerning the emptiness of the phenomenal world, the storehouse consciousness (*ālaya-vijñāna*), and the "embryo of the Tathāgata" (*tathāgata-garbha*). These teachings were given scholastic forms in various Mahāyāna groups such as the Mādhyamika and Yogācāra schools, which originated in India, and the Tiantai and Huayan schools, which originated in China. In addition, these sūtras and commentaries recognized a vast pantheon of Buddhas and *bodhisattvas* (future Buddhas) and acknowledged the existence of a plurality, even an infinity, of worlds. Some went on to affirm the reality of an eternal, cosmic Buddha whom they took to be the ultimate source of these innumerable Buddhas, *bodhisattvas*, and worlds (and of all else as well). Some of these texts highlighted various kinds of soteriological help that particular Buddhas and *bodhisattvas* could provide to those who sought their aid. In addition to Maitreya and Amitābha, mentioned above, other Buddhas and *bodhisattvas* who became particularly important include Bhaiṣajyaguru (the Buddha of healing), Avalokiteśvara (the *bodhisattva* exemplar of compassion), Mañjuśrī (the *bodhisattva* patron of the wise), and Kṣitigarbha (the *bodhisattva* who specialized in assisting those who suffer in hell).

By the second half of the first millennium CE a new strand of Buddhist tradition, the Vajrayāna, or Esoteric Vehicle, began to come into the foreground in India. This new vehicle accepted the basic orientation of the Mahāyāna, but supplemented Mahāyāna insights with new and dramatic forms of practice, many of them esoteric in character. The appearance of this new Buddhist vehicle was closely associated with the composition of new texts, including new sūtras (e.g., the *Mahāvairocana Sūtra*), and the new ritual manuals known as *tantras*. By the eighth and ninth centuries this new vehicle had spread through virtually the entire Buddhist world and was preserved especially in Japan and in Tibet. But before the process of systematization of the Vajrayāna could proceed very far the infrastructure that constituted Buddhist civilization began to break down, thus at least partially accounting for the very different form that this tradition took in Tibet and in Japan, where it became known as Shingon.

During the period of its hegenomy as a pan-Asian civilization, Buddhism retained a considerable degree of unity across both the regional and text-oriented boundaries that delimited particular Buddhist traditions. In each cultural area and in each of the three *yānas* there were ascetics and contemplatives who practiced Buddhist meditation; there were ecclesiastics and moralists whose primary concern was Buddhist discipline; there were monks and laypersons who were involved in Buddhist devotion; and there were those who took a special interest in Buddhist magic and exorcism. These diverse groups and individuals shared—and many realized that they shared—beliefs, attitudes, and practices with like-minded Buddhists in distant areas and other *yānas*.

Moreover, during the period of its ascendancy as a civilizational religion, Buddhism provided a successful standard of cultural unification such that other religious traditions, including the Hindu in India, the Manichaean in Central Asia, the Daoist in China, the Shinto in Japan, and the Bon in Tibet, responded to it with their own innovations shaped by Buddhist ideas and values. During this period, in other words, Buddhism set the standards, religious, philosophical, artistic, and so on, to which a whole range of other Asian traditions were forced to respond. Buddhism also served as a civilizational religion by encompassing other elements—logic, medicine, grammar, and technology, to name but a few—that made it attractive to individuals and groups, including many rulers and members of various Asian aristocracies who had little or no interest in the spiritual aspect of religion.

Buddhism as Cultural Religion. For more than a thousand years, from the time of King Aśoka to about the ninth century, Buddhism exhibited a civilizational form that began as pan-Indian and ultimately became pan-Asian in character. Like the sectarian pattern that preceded it, this civilizational pattern left an indelible mark on all subsequent Buddhist developments. Buddhism never completely lost either its concern for inclusiveness or its distinctively international flavor. But beginning in about the fifth century the civilizational structure suffered increasingly severe disruptions, and a new pattern began to emerge. All across Asia, Buddhism was gradually transformed, through a variety of historical processes, into what we have chosen to call "cultural religion."

The period of transition. Buddhist civilization, which characteristically strove for both comprehensiveness and systematic order, was dependent on the security and material prosperity of a relatively small number of great monasteries and monastic universities that maintained contact with one another and shared common interests and values. This institutional base was, in fact, quite fragile, as was demonstrated when historical events threatened the well-being of these monasteries and their residents. New developments arose within the Buddhist community as a result of these vicissitudes, developments that eventually transformed Buddhism into a series of discrete cultural traditions.

Some indication of these developments can be seen quite early, even as Buddhist civilization was at the peak of its brilliance. Events in Central Asia during the fifth and sixth centuries were not favorable to the Buddhist kingdoms along the Silk Route that connected Northwest India and northern China. These kingdoms were invaded and in some cases conquered by different nomadic peoples such as the Huns, who also invaded India and the Roman empire. The Chinese pilgrim Xuanzang, who visited Sogdiana in 630, saw only ruins of Buddhist temples and former Buddhist monasteries that had been given over to the Zoroastrians.

The instability in the crucial linking area between India and China during the fifth and sixth centuries seems to have been sufficient to weaken Buddhism's civilizational structure. For the first time we see the emergence of new Buddhist schools in China that are distinctively Chinese. The appearance of synthetic Chinese schools like Tiantai and Huayan suggests a continuation of the civilizational orientation. These schools sought to reconcile the divergent views found in Buddhist literature through an extended elaboration of different levels of teaching. This is, of course, characteristic of Buddhism as a civilizational religion, but the manner of reconciliation reflects a style of harmonization that is distinctively Chinese.

The increasing importance of Tantra in late Indian Buddhism and the success of the Pure Land (Jingtu) and Chan (Zen) schools in China during the Sui and Tang period (598–907) are further indications that the Buddhist tradition was becoming more local in self-definition. Chinese Buddhism had a new independent spirit in contrast to the earlier India-centered Buddhism. Moreover, the new movements that emerged at that time seem to be the result of a long development that took place apart from the major cosmopolitan centers. Far more than in the past, expressions of Buddhism were being made at all levels of particular societies, and there was a new concern for the interrelation of those levels within each society.

During the last centuries of the first millennium CE, Buddhist civilization developed a new, somewhat independent center in China that reached its peak during the Sui and Tang dynasties. Thus, when Buddhist texts and images were introduced into Japan during the sixth century they were presented and appropriated as part and parcel of Chinese culture. The new religion gained support from the prince regent, Shōtoku Taishi, who wanted to model his rule after that of the Buddhist-oriented Sui dynasty. Chinese Buddhist schools such as Huayan (Jpn., Kegon) also prospered in the Nara period in Japan (710–784) as Chinese cultural influence continued to flourish.

The two centers of Buddhist civilization, China and India, also competed with each other, as can be seen in a situation that developed in Tibet. Buddhism had been brought to Tibet by King Sroṅ bstan sgam po (d. 650), who established the first stable state in the area. Buddhist texts were translated into Tibetan from both Sanskrit and Chinese. A later king, Khri sroṅ lde btsan (755–797), officially adopted Buddhism as the state religion and determined to resolve the tension between Indian and Chinese influence. He sponsored the famous Council of Lhasa, in which a Chinese party representing a Chan "sudden enlightenment" point of view debated an Indian group that advocated a more gradualist understanding of the Buddhist path. Both sides claimed victory, but the Indian tradition gained predominance and eventually translations were permitted only from Sanskrit.

During the ninth and tenth centuries the two Buddhist civilizational centers in India and China were themselves subject to attack, both internally and externally. The combination of Hindu resurgence and Muslim invasions led to the effective disappearance of the Buddhist community in India by the thirteenth century. Repeated invasions by Uighurs and Turkic peoples, as well as official persecutions and the revival of the Confucian tradition, resulted in a decisive weakening of institutional Buddhism in China.

The processes of acculturation that had first become evident in the sixth century in India and China repeated themselves beginning in the tenth century in Japan, Korea, Tibet, Sri Lanka, and Southeast Asia. In each of these areas distinct cultural forms of Buddhism evolved. There was a reorganization of the Buddhist community with an increased emphasis on the bonds between elite and ordinary Buddhists in each particular area. There was a renewed interest in efficacious forms of Buddhist practice and the Buddhist schools that preserved and encouraged such practice. Within each area there was a development of Buddhist symbols and rituals that became representative of distinct Buddhist cultures, particularly at the popular level.

In Central Asia the Buddhist community had no success in surviving the Muslim expansion. Buddhism had some limited success in India during the last centuries of the first millennium. It benefited from extensive royal and popular support in northeastern India under the Pāla dynasty from the eighth to the twelfth century, but Hindu philosophy and theistic (*bhakti*) movements were aggressive critics of Buddhism. Hardly any distinct Buddhist presence continued in India after the last of the great monasteries were destroyed by the Muslims. In China there was more success, although the Confucian and Daoist traditions were powerful rivals. As a result of persecutions in the ninth century, Buddhism lost its distinctively civilizational role, but it continued as a major component of Chinese religion, becoming increasingly synthesized with other native traditions. In Sri Lanka, Southeast Asia (except for Indonesia and the Malay Peninsula, where Buddhism suffered the same fate that it suffered in India), Japan, Korea, and Tibet (from whence it eventually spread to Mongolia), areas where Buddhism did not have to compete with strongly organized indigenous traditions, it was successful in establishing itself as the dominant religious tradition. The religious creativity of these areas, once the periphery of the Buddhist world, resulted in a Buddhist "axial age" that dramatically transformed the tradition as a whole.

Monastic order, royal order, and popular Buddhism. The transformation of Buddhism from a civilizational religion to a cultural religion depended on a fundamental realignment in the structure of the Buddhist community. As a civilizational religion, Buddhist community life had come to include a largely monastic elite that traveled extensively, was multilingual, and operated at the civilizational level; an imperial elite made up of monks and laypersons associated more closely with royal courts and related aristocracies; and a less exalted company of ordinary monks and laypersons living not only in urban areas but in the countryside as well. In Buddhism's zenith as a civilizational religion the central organizing relationship was that between the largely monastic civilizational elite and the imperial elites, consisting of kings, queens, and other high-placed members of the laity on the one hand, and the monks whom they supported on the other. The ordinary members of the laity and the less exalted monks played a role, of course, but in most areas at most periods of time they seem to have been somewhat distanced from the mainstream of Buddhist community life. With the transformation of Buddhism into a cultural religion, however, this situation was drastically altered.

One aspect of this transformation was major changes that took place at three different levels: monastic, imperial, and popular. The demise of the monastic network through which the civilizational aspect of Buddhism had been supported and maintained was decisive. To be sure, there were elements of the monastic community that never lost their international vision, and travel and exchanges between specific cultural areas was never totally absent, particularly between China and Japan, China and Tibet, and Sri Lanka and mainland Southeast Asia. Nevertheless, it would be difficult to speak of a pan-Asian Buddhist elite after the ninth or tenth century.

The pattern at the imperial level was altered by the loss of monastic power and influence coupled with increased state control in monastic affairs. During the period that Buddhism was an effective civilizational religion its great monasteries functioned practically as "states within the state." Monasteries commanded extensive resources of land and labor and were often actively involved in commercial enterprises. This public splendor made the monasteries inviting targets, especially after their usefulness as civilizational centers had declined. If the monasteries were not simply destroyed, as they were in India and Central Asia, they were often deprived of their resources, as occurred at one time or another in virtually every Buddhist area. With the decline of monastic influence at the imperial level, the control of the state over monastic affairs inevitably increased. In China and Japan, and to a lesser extent in Korea and Vietnam, state control became thoroughly bureaucratized. In Sri Lanka and the

Theravāda areas of Southeast Asia, state control was implemented more indirectly and with considerably less efficiency by royal "purifications" of the *sangha*. Specific local conditions in Tibet led to a unique situation in which monastic and royal functions became so tightly interlocked that they were often completely fused.

The demise of the international Buddhist elite and the weakening of the large and powerful establishments were counterbalanced by a strengthening of Buddhist life at the grass-roots level. Smaller, local institutions that for a long time had coexisted with the great monasteries took on new importance as focal points in Buddhist community life. For example, smaller so-called merit cloisters (*kung-te yüan*) supported by wealthy laymen were significant components in the development and life of Chinese Buddhism. In Sri Lanka and Southeast Asia the emergence of cultural Buddhism was closely associated with monks who were called *gāmavāsins* (village dwellers) and who strengthened Buddhist influence among the people in the major cities and in the more distant provinces as well. In contrast to civilizational Buddhism, in which the crucial structural alignment was that between the civilizational elite and the monks and laity at the imperial level, the crucial structural alignment in cultural Buddhism was between the monks and laity of the imperial or state elites, who were located primarily in the capital cities, and the ordinary people who inhabited local monasteries and villages.

The preeminence of practice. The era of comprehensive Buddhist philosophizing and the formulation of original systems of thought came to an end, for the most part, with the demise of Buddhism as a civilizational religion. There continued to be philosophical innovations, and some of the great systems that were already formulated were adjusted to meet new circumstances. However, the real creativity of Buddhism as a cultural religion came to the fore in schools and movements that emphasized efficacious modes of Buddhist practice.

A major component in the development of various Buddhist cultures is the ascendancy of schools or movements that combined a strong emphasis on the importance of discipline (particularly although not exclusively the monastic discipline) with an accompanying emphasis on meditation. In China and Japan, Chan and Zen, with their emphasis on firm discipline and meditative practices such as "just sitting" and the contemplation of *kung-an* (Jpn., *kōan*; enigmatic verses), are representative of this kind of Buddhist tradition. These were the schools that became more prominent as Mahāyāna Buddhism emerged as a cultural religion in East Asia, and they continued to exert influence on the various East Asian political and aesthetic elites from that time forward. The Āraññikas, or "forest-dwelling monks," represented an analogous orientation and played a similar role in Sri Lanka and subsequently in Southeast Asia. The Āraññikas appeared on the Sri Lankan scene in the ninth and tenth centuries as a group of monks who had chosen to withdraw from the wealthy monasteries of the capital, to adopt a strictly disciplined mode of life, and to devote themselves to study and/or meditation. In the twelfth century the Āraññikas led a major reform in Sri Lanka and in subsequent centuries they extended their reform movement throughout the Theravāda world, which included not only Sri Lanka but also Burma, Thailand, Cambodia, and Laos. The Āraññikas in the Theravāda world, like the Chan and Zen practitioners in East Asia, were closely affiliated with the elite segments of the various societies in which they were active. A similar kind of emphasis was placed on discipline, study, and meditation in Tibet, where the Vajrayāna tradition was established by Atīśa, the monk who in the eleventh century inaugurated the "second introduction" of Buddhism into the country. In the fifteenth century another infusion of discipline-oriented reform was provided by reformers who established the Dge lugs pa, the so-called Yellow Hats, which became the preeminent Tibetan (and Mongolian) school subsequently headed by the well-known line of Dalai Lamas.

Each expression of Buddhism as a cultural religion generated, as a kind of counterpoint to its more elitist, discipline-oriented schools and movements, other schools and movements that focused on more populist forms of devotional or Esoteric (Tantric) practice. In the East Asian Mahāyāna areas the most important development was the increasing prominence of the Pure Land schools in the early centuries of the second millennium CE. The Chinese Pure Land schools remained in close symbiosis with the practitioners of Chan and retained a relatively traditional mode of monastic practice. Their Japanese counterparts, however, became more differentiated and considerably more innovative. During the Kamakura period (1185–1333) a number of new, distinctively Japanese Pure Land and related schools were founded by charismatic leaders such as Hōnen, Shinran, and Nichiren; these schools took on a distinctively Japanese cast. For Nichiren, the Pure Land was Japan itself.

Although less important than Pure Land and related kinds of devotion, Esoteric or Tantric modes of religion also were a significant part of cultural Buddhism in East Asia. In China the Esoteric elements were closely related to influences from the Vajrayāna tradition in Tibet as well as interactions with forms of indigenous Daoism. In Japan more sophisticated Esoteric elements persisted in the Tendai (Chin., Tiantai) and Shingon schools, while more rustic and indigenous elements were prominent in groups that were integrated into these schools, for example, the Shūgendō community that was made up of mountain ascetics known as *yamabushi*.

In Sri Lanka in the twelfth and thirteenth centuries (the period of Hōnen, Shinran, and Nichiren in Japan) devotional religion also seems to have been influential in the Buddhist community, generating new genres of Buddhist literature that were written primarily in Sinhala rather than Pali. Although no specifically devotional "schools" were formed, a whole new devotional component was incorporated into the Theravāda tradition and subsequently diffused to the

Theravāda cultures in Southeast Asia. Similarly, there were, as far as we know, no "schools" that were specifically Esoteric or Tantric in character. However, there is some evidence that indicates that Esoteric elements played a very significant role in each of the premodern Theravāda cultures. This kind of influence seems to have been particularly strong in northern Burma, northern Thailand, Laos, and Cambodia.

In Tibet and Mongolia, as one would expect given their Vajrayāna ethos, the primary counterpoints to the more discipline-oriented traditions were the schools, such as the Rnying ma pa and Bka' brgyud pa, that emphasized the performance of Esoteric and Tantric rituals in order to achieve worldly benefits and to proceed along a "fast path" to salvation. However, just as in the other Buddhist cultures devotion was supplemented by recourse to Esoteric and Tantric techniques, so in Tibet and Mongolia Esoteric and Tantric techniques were supplemented by the practice of devotion.

Another important component of Buddhism as a cultural religion was the mitigation, in some circles at least, of traditional distinctions between monks and laity. This trend was least evident in the more discipline-oriented contexts, but even here there was some movement in this direction. For example, in the Chan and Zen monasteries, monks, rather than being prohibited from engaging in productive work as the Vinaya had stipulated, were actually required to work. In the Pure Land schools in Japan, and in some of the Esoteric schools in Japan and Tibet, it became permissible and common for clergy to marry and have families. Also, certain kinds of monastic/lay and purely lay associations played important roles in China and Japan. These included both straightforward religious associations devoted to the various Buddhist causes, and, particularly in China, a number of secret societies and messianically oriented groups. Even in Sri Lanka and Southeast Asia tendencies toward the laicization of the monastic order can from time to time be observed, but in these strongly Theravāda areas the process was always thwarted by royal intervention before the innovations could take root.

The pervasiveness of ritual. Alongside the particular schools and movements that characterized Buddhism as a cultural religion there were also modes of Buddhist practice that, although influenced by those schools and movements, were more pervasively involved in Buddhist cultures as such. Pilgrimage was in the forefront of these practices.

Virtually every instance of Buddhism as a cultural religion had its own particular patterns of Buddhist pilgrimage. In many cases these pilgrimage patterns were a major factor in maintaining the specificity of particular, often overlapping, religious and cultural complexes. In some contexts these pilgrimage patterns delimited Buddhist cultural complexes that supported and were supported by particular political kingdoms. An example of this situation was the Sinhala pattern, in which there were sixteen major sites systematically distributed throughout all of Sri Lanka. In other situations, for example in Southeastern Asia, these patterns often delimited Buddhist cultural complexes that cut across political divisions.

Many of the sites that were the goals of major Buddhist pilgrimages were mountain peaks or other places that had been sacred from before the introduction of Buddhism and continued to have sacred associations in other traditions that coexisted with Buddhism. Through pilgrimage practices at these sites Buddhism assimilated various deities and practices associated with local religious traditions. At the same time, of course, the Buddhist presence imbued those deities and practices with Buddhist connotations. In Japan, Buddhas and *bodhisattvas* became virtually identified in many situations with indigenous *kami* (divine spirits). In China great *bodhisattvas* such as Kṣitigarbha, Mañjuśrī, and Avalokiteśvara became denizens of sacred mountains that were popular pilgrimage sites, and in those pilgrimage contexts underwent a thoroughgoing process of sinicization. Stūpas, footprints, and other Buddhist objects of pilgrimage in Southeast Asia became, for many who venerated them, representations in which the Buddha was closely associated with indigenous spirits (e.g., *nats* in Burma, *phī* in Thailand, etc.) who served as the local guardians or protectors of Buddhist institutions.

Wherever Buddhism developed as a cultural religion it penetrated not only the sacred topography of the area but also the cycle of calendric rites. In China, for example, the annual cycle of Buddhist ritual activities included festivals honoring various Buddhas and *bodhisattvas*, festivals dedicated to significant figures from Chinese Buddhist history, a great vegetarian feast, and a very important "All Soul's" festival in which the Chinese virtue of filial piety was expressed through offerings intended to aid one's ancestors. While these rituals themselves involved much that was distinctively Chinese, they were interspersed with other festivals, both Confucian and Daoist, and were supplemented by other, lesser rituals associated with daily life that involved an even greater integration with non-Buddhist elements. In Sri Lanka the Buddhist ritual calendar included festivals honoring events of the Buddha's life; a festival that celebrated the coming of Mahinda, Aśoka's missionary son, to establish Buddhism in Sri Lanka; a festival in the capital honoring the Buddha relic that served as the palladium of the kingdom; and the monastic-centered *kathin* (Pali, *kaṭhina*; giving of robes) ceremony that marked the end of the rainy season. These Buddhist rituals were interspersed with non-Buddhist celebrations that were, in this case, largely Hindu. These large-scale rituals were supplemented by more episodic and specialized rites that involved an even wider variety of indigenous elements such as offerings to local spirits. In the Tibetan cultural area the Buddhist calendar encompassed great festivals sponsored by monasteries in which the introduction of Buddhism to Tibet was celebrated as the Buddhist defeat of indigenous demons, as well as festivals honoring Buddhist deities (e.g., Tārā) and Tibetan Buddhist heroes (e.g., Padmasambhava). The Tibetan Buddhist calendar also included other large- and small-scale rituals in which Buddhist and indigenous shamanistic elements were combined.

Buddhism in its various cultural expressions also became associated with life cycle rites, especially those of the male initiation into adulthood and those associated with death. The Buddhist involvement in male initiation rites was limited primarily to Southeast Asia. In many Buddhist countries children and young men were educated in the monasteries, but only in Southeast Asia did temporary initiation into the order, either as a novice (as in Burma) or at a later age as a full-fledged monk (as in central Thailand), become a culturally accepted necessity for the attainment of male adulthood. Buddhist involvement in funerary rituals was, on the other hand, a phenomenon that appeared again and again all across Asia. For example, in the Theravāda countries where Buddhism has been the dominant cultural religion elaborate cremations patterned after the ceremony reportedly performed for the Buddha himself have become the rule for members of the royal and monastic elites. Simpler ceremonies, based on the same basic model, were the norm for those of lesser accomplishment or status. Even in cultures where Buddhism coexisted with other major religions on a more or less equal basis, Buddhists have been the preferred officiants in the funerary context. The prime example is China, where Buddhists developed elaborate masses for the dead that were widely used throughout the whole of society. Originally introduced into China by the now defunct Zhenyan (Vajrayāna) school, these masses for the dead were adapted to their new Chinese environment and became an integral component of Chinese Buddhist culture.

All across Asia Buddhism expressed itself as a cultural religion through different kinds of ritual at different levels of society. It was through these ritual forms, more than in any other way, that it became an integral component in the life of different Asian peoples, molding cultures in accordance with its values and being itself molded in the process. Once Buddhism became established as a cultural religion, it was these rituals that enabled it to maintain its position and influence, and to do so century after century on into the modern era.

Buddhism in the Modern World. The beginnings of European mercantilism and imperialism in the sixteenth century initiated a chain of events that continue to stimulate and to threaten the Buddhist community in its parts and as a whole. Traditional social and economic patterns on which the various Buddhist cultures depended were disrupted and eventually displaced by new patterns. These new patterns inextricably linked individual Buddhist societies to a global community and especially to the West. As a result, all of the profound transformations that have occurred in European civilization in the last three centuries, the advent of rationalism, scientific materialism, nationalism, relativism, technology, democracy, and communism, have challenged Buddhists in Asia just as they have challenged religious men and women in Europe and the Americas.

The modern encounter of cultures and civilizations has not been monolithic. Three stages can be identified in Buddhist Asia. The first was the arrival of missionaries with traders in various parts of Asia. These missionaries came to convert and instruct, and they brought printing presses and schools as well as Bibles and catechisms. There was a missionary onslaught on Asian religious traditions, including Buddhism, in Sri Lanka, Southeast Asia, China, and Japan. This onslaught was sometimes physically violent, as in the Portuguese destruction of Buddhist temples and relics in Sri Lanka, but for the most part it was an ideological assault. A second stage was more strictly colonial, as some European powers gained control over many different areas of the Buddhist world. Some Buddhist countries, such as Sri Lanka, Burma, and the Indochinese states, were fully colonized while others, such as Thailand, China, and Japan, were subjected to strong colonial influences. In virtually every situation (Tibet was a notable exception), the symbiotic relationship between the political order and the monastic order was disrupted, with adverse effects for Buddhist institutions.

The twentieth-century acceptance of Western political and economic ideologies, whether democratic capitalism or communism, represents a third stage. Buddhists in China, Mongolia, Tibet, and parts of Korea and Southeast Asia now live in communist societies, and the future of Buddhist communities in these areas looks bleak. Capitalism has been dominant in Japan, South Korea, Sri Lanka, and parts of Southeast Asia (Thailand being the prime example), and greater possibilities for the Buddhist tradition are presumed to exist in these areas. But capitalism, as well as communism, has undercut the claim that Buddhist thought and values are of central significance for contemporary life. Buddhist monuments and institutions are in many cases treated as museum pieces, while Buddhist beliefs are often banished to the sphere of individual opinion. In many situations Buddhism is deplored as backward and superstitious, and is for that reason criticized or ignored. As Edward Conze noted in his *A Short History of Buddhism* (London, 1980), "One may well doubt whether capitalism has been any more kind to Buddhism than communism" (p. 129).

Despite the difficulties that Buddhists have faced, they have responded creatively to the turmoil of recent history. They have engaged in many efforts to adapt to their changing environment, just as they have done repeatedly in the past. Thus far, however, they have drawn on their traditional heritage for suitable models, and their varied responses can thus be grouped as cultural, civilizational, and sectarian.

Cultural responses. The initial responses to European civilization were cultural in character, and often reactionary. Some Buddhist kingdoms, after an initial exposure to elements of European civilization, attempted to isolate themselves as a way of preserving their cultural identity. This was done in Japan, Korea, and Tibet, and was attempted in China. In other cases, Buddhist revivals were inspired by the missionary challenges. In Sri Lanka and China, Buddhist intellectuals responded to the efforts of Christian missionaries to criticize Buddhism with their own spirited apologetics. These intellectuals readily adopted the methods and instruments of the Christian missionary, the printing press and the school, as well as his militancy, to promote the Buddhist cause. Some processes that began in the period of Buddhist culture, especially the mitigation of distinctions between monks and laity, were also stimulated by these innovations. Modern technology, such as improved modes of transportation, also made it easier for more people to engage in traditional practices like pilgrimage.

The Buddhist revivals often were inspired by cultural loyalism. To choose Buddhism as one's religious identity in the face of the Christian challenge also meant that one was choosing to be Sinhala, Thai, or Chinese. It was an emphatic denial that things Chinese, for example, were inferior, even if this was suggested by the power and prestige of Christianity and European civilization.

The association between Buddhism and cultural loyalism has been strongest in Sri Lanka and Southeast Asia. Buddhists, both laity and monks, were actively involved in the local independence movements. In these contexts Buddhism has been given a sharply defined nationalistic character by drawing on both the heritage of indigenous Buddhist culture and the example of Aśoka's imperial religion. Buddhism has been used as an instrument for national integration in postcolonial politics and elements of Buddhism have been appropriated by emerging civic religions in Sri Lanka, Burma, and Thailand.

The colonial disestablishment of Buddhism in Sri Lanka and Southeast Asia, and its analogues in Qing-dynasty China and Meiji Japan, altered again the lay-monk relationship and encouraged the emergence of an active lay leadership. Monasteries, deprived of government maintenance and generally without sufficient resources of their own, found it necessary to cultivate the support of local patrons. A larger number of people from various economic and social levels thus became actively involved in religious affairs focusing on the monasteries. This, of course, often led to controversy, with further segmentation of the monastic communities resulting. It also created an environment in which laity and monks could come together in new kinds of associations, much as had happened in the development of Buddhist cultures. Some of the strikingly successful "new religions" of Japan and Korea, such as Reiyūkai (Association of the Friends of the Spirit) and Won Buddhism, are products of this environment.

The disestablishment of Buddhism also encouraged the development of an active lay leadership among the new urban elites who were most influenced by European civilization. These elites introduced "reformed" interpretations of elements of the Buddhist tradition in order to bring those elements into harmony with the expectations of European civilization. Modern reformers' interpretations of the Buddha's biography have emphasized his humanity and his rational approach to the problem of human suffering. Some modernists have sought to relate Buddhist thought to Western philosophical perspectives and also to scientific patterns. Many Buddhist reformers have stressed the relevance of Buddhist teachings to social and ethical issues.

Civilizational responses. The encounter between European civilization and Buddhist cultures encouraged a new awareness among Buddhists of their common heritage. New contacts among Buddhists began on a significant scale, and, as a result, there was also a renewed sense of Buddhism as a civilizational religion.

This sense that Buddhism could again be a civilizational standard that could encompass the conflicting ideologies present in modern Asia and the world had great appeal to the new urban elites. In many countries Buddhist apologists maintained that Buddhism could be the basis for a truly democratic or socialist society and, as a nontheistic religion, could be the basis for world peace and unity. Sōka Gakkai (Value Creation Society), a Japanese "new religion" stemming from the Nichiren tradition, for example, presents an understanding of Buddhism as the "Third Civilization," which can overcome the opposition of idealism and materialism in thought and, when applied to the economy, can bring about a synthesis of capitalism and socialism.

New missionary efforts to Asian countries such as India, Indonesia, and Nepal, where Buddhist influence had waned, and to the West have been encouraged by this view of Buddhism as "the supreme civilization" and the antidote to the spiritual malaise generated by European civilization.

Sectarian developments. New sectarian developments in the modern period have resulted from the expansion of Buddhism, through missionary work, and from Buddhist losses that have occurred through the encounter with European civilization. These developments are evidence that the idea of a new Buddhist civilization remains, as yet, more an aspiration than a reality.

Sectarian developments resulting from expansion can be seen in the establishment of Buddhism in the West, which has been accomplished at a certain distance from the mainstream communities, whether among immigrant groups or among intellectuals and spiritual seekers disaffected by Western cultures and religious traditions. Another sectarian development resulting from expansion is the neo-Buddhist movement among *harijans*, or scheduled castes, in India, led by B. R. Ambedkar.

A resurgence of sectarian patterns, resulting from Buddhist losses, can be seen in totalitarian communist areas. These developments tend to be pragmatic and defensive in character. Buddhists have attempted to isolate their community from the mainstream of communist society and thus avoid criticism and attack, but these efforts have rarely been successful. Sectarian isolation, however, has often been enforced by new communist governments as a way of weakening and discrediting Buddhist influence. Through a combination of criticism of Buddhist teaching by communist ideology and the radical disestablishment of Buddhist monasteries, communist governments have been able to divest Buddhist leaders and institutions of their cultural power and influence very quickly. This has occurred in the Soviet Union, Mongolia, North Korea, Vietnam, and with special ferocity in Cambodia (Kampuchea) and Tibet.

The Tibetan experience provides a tragic example of a new sectarian development in Buddhism. Buddhist institutions and leaders have been subject to a brutal attack as part of the effort to incorporate Tibet into the People's Republic of China. This has often taken the form of sinicization, with Buddhism being attacked because of its central place in traditional Tibetan culture. Following the Chinese invasion of 1959, thousands of Tibetans, including the Dalai Lama, fled the country. They have established refugee communities in North America, Europe, and India, where they are trying to preserve the heritage of Tibetan Buddhist culture.

Finally, the growth of millenarian movements among Buddhists in the modern period, especially in Burma, Thailand, and Vietnam, may be described as sectarian developments resulting from Buddhist losses. Like so much else of Buddhism in the modern period, Buddhist millenarian movements were transitory responses to crises of power and interpretation within the Buddhist community.

CONCLUSION. Buddhism as a whole has not yet developed a distinctive character in the modern period. On the contrary, there is a great deal of continuity between the historical development of Buddhism and the current responses and innovations. Thus the sectarian, civilizational, and cultural patterns continue to exert a predominant influence in the evolution of Buddhist tradition.

At the same time, we can see that Buddhism, like other world religions, participates in a modern religious situation that is, in many respects, radically new. Buddhism has thus come to share certain modern elements with other contemporary religions. We can see such elements in the search for new modes of religious symbolism, as is found in the writings of the Thai monk Buddhadasa and the Japanese Kyoto school of Buddhist philosophy. We can also see these common elements in the preoccupation with the human world and this-worldly soteriology that is emerging in many Buddhist contexts. A modern Sinhala Buddhist, D. Wijewardena, expressed this attitude in a polemical tract, *The Revolt in the Temple* (Colombo, 1953), by saying that Buddhists must pursue "not a will-o'-the-wisp Nirvana secluded in the cells of their monasteries, but a Nirvana attained here and now by a life of self-forgetful activity . . . [so that] they would live in closer touch with humanity, would better understand and sympathize with human difficulties" (p. 586).

This diversity, representing both tradition and present situation, reminds those of us who would study and understand Buddhism and Buddhists that, in the end, the decisive meaning of our concept of Buddhism must be that of cumulative tradition. Our concept must remain open-ended to allow for future transformations of the Buddhist tradition for as long as men and women associate their lives with the name of Buddha.

SEE ALSO Ālaya-vijñāna; Ambedkar, B. R; Amitābha; Arhat; Aśoka; Atīśa; Avalokiteśvara; Bhaiṣajyaguru; Bodhisattva Path; Buddha; Buddhaghosa; Buddhas and Bodhisattvas, article on Celestial Buddhas and Bodhisattvas; Buddhism, Schools of, article on Mahāyāna Philosophical Schools of Buddhism; Buddhist Books and Texts; Buddhist Ethics; Buddhist Meditation; Buddhist Philosophy; Buddhist Religious Year; Cakravartin; Chan; Chinese Religion, overview article; Confucianism; Cosmology, article on Buddhist Cosmology; Councils, article on Buddhist Councils; Dalai Lama; Dge lugs pa; Dharma, article on Buddhist Dharma and Dharmas; Duṭṭhagāmaṇī; Eightfold Path; Faxian; Folk Religion, article on Folk Buddhism; Four Noble Truths; Hōnen; Huayan; Iconography, article on Buddhist Iconography; Indian Religions, overview article; Islam, article on Islam in Central Asia; Japanese Religions, overview article; Jingtu; Jōdo Shinshū; Jōdoshū; Kamalaśīla; Karman, article on Buddhist Concepts; Kingship, article on Kingship in East Asia; Korean Religion; Kṣitigarbha; Language, article on Buddhist Views of Language; Mādhyamika; Mahāsāṃghika; Mahāsiddhas; Maitreya; Mañjuśrī; Merit, article on Buddhist Concepts; Millenarianism, article on Chinese Millenarian Movements; Missions, article on Buddhist Missions; Monasticism, article on Buddhist Monasticism; Mongol Religions; Mountains; Nāgārjuna; Nats; New Religious Movements, article on New Religious Movements in Japan; Nichiren; Nichirenshū; Nirvāṇa; Padmasambhava; Pilgrimage, article on Buddhist Pilgrimage in South and Southeast Asia; Pratītya-samutpāda; Priesthood, article on Buddhist Priesthood; Pūjā, article on Buddhist Pūjā; Pure and Impure Lands; Reiyūkai Kyōdan; Saṃgha, overview article and articles on Saṃgha and Society; Sarvāstivāda; Sautrāntika; Shingonshū; Shinran; Shōtoku Taishi; Shūgendō; Sōka Gakkai; Soteriology; Soul, article on Buddhist Concepts; Southeast Asian Religions, article on Mainland Cultures; Stupa Worship; Śūnyam and Śūnyatā; Tārā; Tathāgata; Tathāgata-garbha; Temple, articles on Buddhist Temple Compounds; Tendaishū; Theravāda; Tiantai; Tibetan Religions, overview article; Turkic Religions; Vasubandhu; Vinaya; Worship and Devotional Life, articles on Buddhist Devotional Life; Xuanzang; Yijing; Yogācāra; Zen; Zhenyan.

BIBLIOGRAPHY

"A Brief History of Buddhist Studies in Europe and America" is provided by J. W. de Jong in two successive issues of *Eastern Buddhist*, n. s. 7 (May and October 1974): 55–106 and 49–82, which he has brought up to date in his "Recent Buddhist Studies in Europe and America 1973–1983," which appeared in the same journal, vol. 17 (Spring 1984): 79–107. One of the few books that treats a significant theme within this fascinating scholarly tradition is G. R. Welbon's *The Buddhist Nirvāṇa and its Western Interpreters* (Chicago, 1968).

Among the book-length introductory surveys of Buddhism, the second edition of Richard H. Robinson and Willard L. Johnson's *The Buddhist Religion* (Encino, Calif., 1977) is, overall, the most satisfactory. The only modern attempt to present a full-scale historical survey by a single author is to be found in the Buddhism sections of Charles Eliot's three-volume work *Hinduism and Buddhism*, 3d ed. (London, 1957), taken together with his *Japanese Buddhism* (1935; reprint, New York, 1959). Although these books are seriously dated (they were first published in 1921 and 1935, respectively), they still provide a valuable resource. Five other important works that attempt cross-cultural presentations of a particular aspect of Buddhism are Junjirō Takakusu's *The Essentials of Buddhist Philosophy*, 3d ed., edited by Wing-tsit Chan and Charles A. Moore (Honolulu, 1956); Paul Mus's wide-ranging *Barabuḍur: Esquisse d'une histoire du bouddhisme fondée sur la critique archéologique des textes*, 2 vols. (Hanoi, 1935); Robert Bleichsteiner's *Die gelbe Kirche* (Vienna, 1937), which was translated into French and published as *L'église jaune* (Paris, 1937); W. Randolph Kloetzli's *Buddhist Cosmology* (Delhi, 1983); and David L. Snellgrove's edited collection *The Image of the Buddha* (London, 1978).

Many of the most important studies of the early, sectarian phase of Buddhism in India extend their discussions to the later phases of Indian Buddhism as well. This is true, for example, of Sukumar Dutt's *Buddhist Monks and Monasteries of India* (London, 1962) and of Edward Conze's *Buddhist Thought in India* (Ann Arbor, 1967). For those interested in Buddhist doctrines, Conze's book may be supplemented by David J. Kalupahana's *Causality: The Central Philosophy of Buddhism* (Honolulu, 1975), which focuses on sectarian Buddhism, and Fredrick J. Streng's *Emptiness: A Study in Religious Meaning* (New York, 1967), which examines the work of the famous early Mahāyāna philosopher Nāgārjuna.

A historical account that is focused more exclusively on the sectarian period and the transition to civilizational Buddhism is provided by Étienne Lamotte in his authoritative *Histoire du bouddhisme indien: Des origines á l'ère Saka* (Louvain, 1958). A somewhat different perspective on the same process of development is accessible in three closely related works that can profitably be read in series: Frank E. Reynolds's title essay in *The Two Wheels of Dhamma*, edited by Frank E. Reynolds and Bardwell L. Smith, "AAR Studies in Religion," no. 3 (Chambersburg, Pa., 1972); John C. Holt's *Discipline: The Canonical Buddhism of the Vinayapiṭaka* (Delhi, 1981); and John Strong's *The Legend of King Aśoka: A Study and Translation of the Aśokāvadāna* (Princeton, 1983).

Good books that treat Buddhism as an international civilization are hard to come by. Three that provide some assistance to those interested in the topic are Trevor O. Ling's *The Buddha: Buddhist Civilization in India and Ceylon* (London, 1973); Erik Zürcher's *The Buddhist Conquest of China: The Spread and Adaptation of Buddhism in Early Medieval China*, 2 vols. (Leiden; 1959); and René Grousset's *In the Footsteps of the Buddha*, translated by J. A. Underwood (New York, 1971). Works that focus on the process of acculturation of Buddhism in various contexts include Hajime Nakamura's *Ways of Thinking of Eastern Peoples*, the revised English translation of which was edited by Philip P. Wiener (Honolulu, 1964); Alicia Matsunaga's *The Buddhist Philosophy of Assimilation* (Tokyo and Rutland, Vt., 1969); and Kenneth Chen's *The Chinese Transformation of Buddhism* (Princeton, 1973).

Studies of particular Buddhist cultures are legion. Some valuable studies focus on Buddhism in the context of the whole range of religions that were present in a particular area. Good examples are Giuseppe Tucci's *The Religions of Tibet*, translated by Geoffrey Samuel (Berkeley, 1980), and Joseph M. Kitagawa's *Religion in Japanese History* (New York, 1966). Other treatments of particular Buddhist cultures trace the Buddhist tradition in question from its introduction into the area through the period of acculturation and, in some cases, on into modern times. Two examples are *Religion and Legitimation of Power in Sri Lanka*, edited by Bardwell L. Smith (Chambersburg, Pa., 1978), and Kenneth Chen's comprehensive *Buddhism in China* (Princeton, 1964). Finally, some interpretations of particular Buddhist cultures focus more narrowly on a specific period or theme. See, for example, Lal Mani Joshi's *Studies in the Buddhistic Culture of India* (Delhi, 1967), which deals primarily with Buddhist culture in Northeast India during the seventh and eighth centuries; Daniel Overmyer's *Folk Buddhist Religion: Dissenting Sects in Late Traditional China* (Cambridge, Mass., 1976); and William R. La Fleur's *The Karma of Words: Buddhism and the Literary Arts in Medieval Japan* (Berkeley, 1983).

There is also a myriad of books and articles that consider the development of Buddhism in the modern period. The most adequate overview of developments through the early 1970s is provided in *Buddhism in the Modern World*, edited by Heinrich Dumoulin and John Maraldo (New York, 1976). In addition, there are two excellent trilogies on particular traditions. The first, by Holmes Welch, includes *The Practice of Chinese Buddhism, 1900–1950* (1967), *The Buddhist Revival in China* (1968), and *Buddhism under Mao* (1972), all published by the Harvard University Press. The second, by Stanley J. Tambiah, includes *Buddhism and the Spirit Cults in North-East Thailand* (1970), *World Conqueror and World Renouncer: A Study of Buddhism and Polity in Thailand against a Historical Background* (1976), and *The Buddhist Saints of the Forest and the Cult of Amulets* (1984), all published by the Cambridge University Press.

For those interested in pursuing the study of Buddhism in a cross-cultural, thematic manner, Frank E. Reynolds's *Guide to the Buddhist Religion* (Boston, 1981), done with the assistance of John Holt and John Strong, is a useful resource. It provides 350 pages of annotated bibliography of English, French, and German materials (plus a preface and 65 pages of index) organized in terms of eleven themes, including "Historical Development," "Religious Thought," "Authoritative Texts," "Popular Beliefs and Literature," "Social, Political and Economic Aspects," "The Arts," "Religious Practices and Rituals," and "Soteriological Experience and Processes: Path and Goal."

FRANK E. REYNOLDS (1987)
CHARLES HALLISEY (1987)

BUDDHISM: BUDDHISM IN INDIA

A contemporary visitor to the South Asian subcontinent would find Buddhism flourishing only outside the mainland, on the island of Sri Lanka. This visitor would meet small pockets of Buddhists in Bengal and in the Himalayan regions, especially in Ladakh and Nepal, and as the dominant group in Bhutan and Sikkim. Most of the latter Buddhists belong to the Mahāyāna and Vajrayāna forms of Buddhism and represent denominations and orders of Tibetan and Nepalese origin. Buddhists may also be found in the subcontinent among Tibetan refugees (mostly in Himachal Pradesh and Bangalore), among the Ambedkar Buddhists of Maharashtra, and among pilgrims and missionaries flocking to the sacred sites of India. The diversity of manifestations is not new, but the specific forms are not representative of what Indian Buddhism was in the past.

ORIGINS. Approximately twenty-five hundred years ago the founder of the Buddhist religion was born into the Śākya tribe in a small aristocratic republic in the Himalayan foothills, in what is today the kingdom of Nepal. In his youth he descended to the Ganges River valley in search of spiritual realization. After several years of study at the feet of spiritual masters he underwent a profound religious experience that changed his life; he became a teacher himself, and lived for the rest of his adult life as a mendicant peripatetic. His worldview and personal preoccupations were shaped in the cultural milieu of India of the sixth century BCE; the religious communities that trace their origin to him developed their most distinctive doctrines and practices in Indian soil.

Sources and setting. Unfortunately, we do not possess reliable sources for most of the history of Buddhism in its homeland; in particular, we have precious little to rely on for its early history. Textual sources are late, dating at the very least five hundred years after the death of the Buddha. The archaeological evidence, abundant as it is, is limited in the information it can give us. A few facts are nevertheless well established. The roots of Indian Buddhism are to be found in the "shramanic" movement of the sixth century BCE, which owes the name to its model of religious perfection, the *śramaṇa*, or wandering ascetic. The *śramaṇas* set religious goals that stood outside, and in direct opposition to, the religious and social order of the *brāhmaṇas* (brahmans), who represented the Indo-Aryan establishment. Most of the values that would become characteristic of Indian, and therefore Hindu, religion in general were shaped by the interaction of these two groups, especially by a process of assimilation that transformed the Brahmanic order into Hindu culture.

The appearance of two major shramanic religions, Buddhism and Jainism, marked the end of the Vedic-Brahmanic period and the beginning of an era of cross-fertilization between diverse strata of Indian culture. This new age, sometimes called the Indic period, was characterized by the dominant role of "heterodox" or non-Hindu religious systems, the flourishing of their ascetic and monastic orders, and the use of the vernaculars in preference to Sanskrit.

We can surmise that this new age was a time of social upheaval and political instability. The use of iron had changed radically the character of warfare and the nature of farming. The jungle was cleared, farmland could support a court bureaucracy, and palaces and city walls could be built. A surplus economy was created that made possible large state societies, with concentrated populations and resources, and consequently with heightened political ambition.

The Buddha must have been touched directly by these changes: shortly before his death the republic of the Śākyas was sacked by the powerful kingdom of Kośala, which in turn would shortly thereafter fall under the power of Magadha. At the time of the Buddha sixteen independent states existed in north-central India, a century later only one empire would rule in the region, and in another hundred years this empire, Magadha, would control all of northern India and most of the South. The unity of the empire was won at a price: political and social systems based on family or tribal order crumbled; the old gods lost their power.

As the old order crumbled, the brahmans claimed special privileges that other groups were not always willing to concede. Those who would not accept their leadership sought spiritual and moral guidance among the *śramaṇas*. Although recent research has shown that the interaction between these two groups was more complex than we had previously imagined, it is still accepted that the shramanic movement represented some of the groups displaced by the economic and political changes of the day, and by the expansion of Brahmanic power. The *śramaṇas*, therefore, were rebels of sorts. They challenged the values of lay life in general, but especially the caste system as it existed at the time. Thus, what appeared as a lifestyle designed to lead to religious realization may have been at the same time the expression of social protest, or at least of social malaise.

The shramanic movement was fragmented: among the shramanic groups, Buddhism's main rival was Jainism, representing an ancient teaching whose origin dated to at least one or two generations before the Buddha. A community of mendicants reformed by Vardhamāṇa Mahāvīra (d. around 468 BCE) shortly before the beginning of Buddha's career, Jainism represented the extremes of world denial and asceticism that Buddhism sought to moderate with its doctrine of the Middle Way. Buddhists also criticized in Jainism what they saw as a mechanistic conception of moral responsibility and liberation. Another school criticized by early Buddhists was that of Makkhali Gosāla, founder of the Ājīvikas, who also taught an extreme form of asceticism that was based, strangely, on a fatalistic doctrine.

We have to understand the shramanic movements as independent systems and not as simple derivations or reforms of Brahmanic doctrine and practice. One can find, nevertheless, certain elements common to all the movements of the age: the *śramaṇas*, called "wanderers" (*parivrājakas*), like the forest dwellers of Brahmanism, retired from society. Some sought an enstatic experience; some believed that particular forms of conduct led to purity and liberation from suffering; others sought power through knowledge (ritual or magical) or insight (contemplative or gnostic); but most systems contained elements of all of these tendencies.

Among the religious values formed during the earlier part of the Indic age, that is, during the shramanic period, we must include, above all, the concept of the cycle and bondage of rebirth (*saṃsāra*) and the belief in the possibility of liberation (*mokṣa*) from the cycle through ascetic discipline, world renunciation, and a moral or ritual code that gave a prominent place to abstaining from doing harm to living beings (*ahiṃsā*). This ideal, like the quest for altered states of consciousness, was not always separable from ancient notions of ritual purity and spiritual power. But among the shramanic movements it sometimes took the form of a moral virtue. Then it appeared as opposition to organized violence—political, as embodied in war, and religious, as expressed in animal sacrifice.

The primary evil force was no longer envisioned as a spiritual personality, but as an impersonal moral law of cause and effect (*karman*) whereby human actions created a state of bondage and suffering. In their quest for a state of rest from the activities of *karman*, whether the goal was defined as enstasy or knowledge, the new religious specialists practiced a variety of techniques of self-cultivation usually known as *yogas*. The sustained practice of this discipline was known as a "path" (*mārga*), and the goal was a state of peace and freedom from passion and suffering called *nirvāṇa*.

As a shramanic religion, Buddhism displayed similar traits but gave to each of these its unique imprint. The conception of rebirth and its evils were not questioned, but suffering was universalized: all human conditions lead to suffering, suffering has a cause, and that cause is craving, or "thirst" (*tṛṣṇā*). To achieve liberation from the cycle of rebirth one must follow the spiritual discipline prescribed by the Buddha, summarized in the Eightfold Path. The follower of Buddhism was expected to renounce the lay life and become a wandering ascetic, an ideal epitomized by the spiritual career of the founder.

Most shramanic groups made provisions for their lay supporters, essentially members of the community who by circumstance or choice could not follow the wanderer's path. Buddhist laymen could begin moving in the right direction—with the hope of being able to renounce the world in a future birth—by "taking refuge" (*śaraṇa-gamana*), that is, by making a confession of faith in the Buddha, his teachings, and his monastic order, and by adopting five fundamental moral precepts (*pañcaśīla*): not to deprive a living thing of life, not to take what is not given to you, not to engage in illicit sexual conduct, not to lie, and not to take intoxicating drinks.

The Three Jewels. Perhaps all we can say with certainty about the roots of Buddhist doctrine and doctrinal continuity in Buddhism is that the figure of the Buddha and his experience dominate most of Buddhist teachings. If we wish to understand Buddhism as a doctrinal system, we can look at its oral and written ideology—including its scriptures—as the effort of diverse Buddhist communities to explore and define the general issues raised by the Buddha's career. These include questions such as the following: Does the Buddha "exist" after liberation? Is the experience of awakening ineffable? Which of the two experiences, awakening or liberation, is the fundamental one?

On the other hand, if we wish to understand Buddhism as a religion rather than as a system of doctrines, its focus or fulcrum must be found in the religious communities and their objects of veneration. The early community was represented primarily by the gathering of mendicants or monks called the *saṃgha*, held together by ascetic or monastic codes (*prātimokṣa*) attributed to the Buddha himself, and by the objects of worship represented by (1) the founder himself as the "Awakened One" (*buddha*); (2) his exemplary and holy life, his teachings and his experience (*dharma*); and (3) the community (*saṃgha*) itself, sustained by the memory of his personality and teaching. These objects of veneration are known as the "Three Treasures" (*triratna*), and the believer's trust in these ideals is expressed, doctrinally and ritually, in the "Three Refuges" (to rely on the Buddha, the Dharma, and the Sangha). To this day, this formula serves at once as an indication of the meaning of monastic ordination and a lay confession of faith.

Buddha. No Western scholar today would claim to know the exact details of the founder's biography, or for that matter the exact content of his teachings. The above is merely an educated guess based on formulations from a time removed by several centuries from their origins. Scholars agree, nevertheless, on the historicity of the founder. That is to say, though they may doubt the accuracy of the information transmitted in traditional "biographies" (beginning with his personal name, Siddhārtha Gautama) or in legends about the Buddha's sermons, Western scholars accept the existence of an influential religious figure, called Śākyamuni ("the sage of the Śākya tribe") by his disciples, who at some point in the sixth century BCE founded in the Ganges River valley the community of wandering mendicants that would eventually grow into the world religion we now call Buddhism.

Scholars generally tend to accept the years 563 to 483 BCE as the least problematic, if not the most plausible, dating for the life of Gautama Buddha. (Other dating systems exist, however, that place his life as much as a century later.) Assuming, moreover, that the legend is reliable in some of its details, we can say that the history of the religion begins when Śākyamuni was thirty-five (therefore, in about 528), with his first sermon at Sārnāth (northeast of the city of Vārāṇasī).

Before and after his enlightenment, Śākyamuni followed the typical career of a wanderer. At twenty-nine he abandoned the household and sought a spiritual guide. An early legend claims that Śākyamuni actually studied under two teachers of the age, Āḷāra Kālāma and Udraka Rāmaputra. From such teachers the young ascetic learned techniques of meditation that he later rejected, but the imprints of which remain in Buddhist theories of meditation. Dissatisfied with what he had learned, he tried the life of the hermit. Finally, after six years of struggle, he "awakened" under a pipal tree (*Ficus religiosa*) near the border town of Uruvilvā (Bodh Gayā).

His first sermon was followed by forty-five years of wandering through the Ganges River valley, spreading his teachings. Although tradition preserves many narratives of isolated episodes of this half century of teaching, no one has been able to piece together a convincing account of this period. For the tradition this was also a time for the performance of great miracles, and historical accuracy was never an important consideration.

At the age of eighty (c. 483), Siddhārtha Gautama, the Buddha Śākyamuni, died near the city of Kuśināgara. To his immediate disciples perhaps this fading away of the Master confirmed his teachings on impermanence, but the Buddha's death would soon come to be regarded as a symbol of his perfect peace and renunciation: with death he had reached his *parinirvāṇa*, that point in his career after which he would be reborn no more. His ashes, encased in a reliquary buried in a cairn, came to stand for the highest achievement of an awakened being, confirming his status as the one who had attained to truth, the Tathāgata—an epithet that would come to denote ultimate truth itself.

Dharma. The first preaching, known as the "First Turning of the Wheel of Dharma" (or, in the West, the "Sermon at Banaras" or the "Deer Park Sermon"), symbolizes the appearance in history of the Buddhist teaching, whereas Śākyamuni's enlightenment experience, or "Great Awakening" (*mahābodhi*), which occurred in the same year, represents the human experience around which the religion would develop its practices and ideals. This was the experience whereby Śākyamuni became an "Awakened One" (*buddha*). His disciples came to believe that all aspects of Buddhist doctrine and practice flow from this experience of awakening (*bodhi*) and from the resultant state of freedom from passion, suffering, and rebirth called *nirvāṇa*. The teachings found in the Buddha's sermons can be interpreted as definitions of these two experiences, the spiritual practices that lead to or flow from them, and the institutions that arose inspired by the experience and the human beings who laid claim to it.

However, it is difficult, if not impossible, to surmise which, if any, among the many doctrines attributed by tradition to the founder are veritably his. Different Buddhists, even when they can agree on the words, will interpret the message differently. Although most would find the nucleus of Śākyamuni's teachings in the "First Sermon," especially in the doctrine of the Four Noble Truths allegedly preached therein, a host of other doctrinal statements compete for the central position throughout the history of Buddhism in India and beyond. Moreover, a number of texts that can claim great antiquity are not only silent about the Four Noble Truths but actually do not seem to presuppose them in any way. The same can be said about other doctrines that would become central to the development of Buddhist doctrinal speculation, for instance, the principle of conditioned arising (*pratītya-samutpāda*) and the analysis of the human personality into its constituent parts (*skandhas*, etc.).

It is difficult to determine to what extent early Buddhism had an accompanying metaphysics. Some of the earliest strata of Buddhist literature suggest that the early community may have emphasized the joys of renunciation and the peace of abstention from conflict—political, social, and religious—more than a philosophical doctrine of liberation. Such are the ascetic ideals of one of the earliest texts of the tradition, the *Aṭṭhakavagga* (*Suttanipāta*). The mendicant abstains from participating in the religious and metaphysical debates of brahmans, *śramaṇas*, and sages. He is detached from all views, for

> Purity is not [attained] by views, or learning, by knowledge, or by moral rules, and rites. Nor is it [attained] by the absence of views, learning, knowledge, rules, or rites. Abandoning all these, not grasping at them, he is at peace; not relying, he would not hanker for becoming. (*Suttanipāta* 839)

There is in this text a rejection of doctrine, rule, and rite that is a critique of the exaggerated claims of those who believed they could become pure and free through ritual, knowledge, or religious status. The lonely ascetic seeks not to become one thing or the other and avoids doctrinal disputes.

If such statements represent some of the earliest moments in the development of the doctrine, then the next stage must have brought a growing awareness of the need for ritual and creed if the community was to survive. This awareness would have been followed in a short time by the formation of a metaphysic, a theory of liberation, and a conscious system of meditation. In the next strata of early Buddhist literature these themes are only surpassed in importance by discussions of ascetic morality. The ascetic ideals of the early community were then expanded and defined by doctrine—as confession of faith, as ideology, and as a plan for religious and moral practice. The earliest formulations of this type are perhaps those of the Eightfold Path, with its triple division into wisdom, moral practice, and mental concentration. The theoretical or metaphysical underpinnings are contained in the Four Noble Truths and in the Three Marks (impermanence, sorrow, and no-self), both traditionally regarded as the subject matter of the Buddha's first sermons.

Saṃgha. With the first sermon the Buddha began a ministry that would last forty-five years. During this period he established a religious order—perhaps only a mendicant order in its beginnings—and trained a number of distinguished disciples who would carry on the teaching after the founder's death. Tradition preserves the names of many of his disciples and immediate heirs to his teaching: Kauṇḍinya, the first convert to be admitted into the Buddha's religious order (*saṃgha*); Yasa, the first householder to receive full lay initiation with the Three Refuges; Śāriputra, the master of wisdom; Maudgalyāyāna, the great thaumaturge; Upāli, the expert in the monastic code; Ānanda, the Buddha's cousin and beloved disciple; Mahāprajāpati, the first woman admitted into the monastic order; and Mahākāśyapa, who undertook to preserve the Buddha's teaching and organized the First Council. The Buddha's disciples represented a wide spectrum of social classes. Yasa was the son of a wealthy guild master; Upāli, a humble barber; Śāriputra, a brahman; Ānanda, a member of the nobility (*kṣatriya*). Among the early followers we find not only world renouncers but believers from a variety of walks of life; King Bimbisara, the wealthy banker Anāthapiṇḍika, the respectable housewife Viśākhā, and the courtesan Amrapālī, for instance.

Although the Buddhist monastic community was an integral part of Indian society, serving as an instrument of legitimation and cohesion, it also served on occasions as a critic of society. Especially in its early development, and in particular during the period of the wandering mendicants, the *saṃgha* was a nonconformist subgroup. The variety of social classes represented by the roster of early disciples in part reflects the fluid state of Indian society at the time; but it also reflects the Buddha's open opposition to the caste system as it existed then. Although the challenge was religious and political as well as social, the Buddha's critique of Brahmanism made his order of mendicants an alternative community, where those who did not fit in the new social order could find a sense of belonging, acceptance, and achievement. Buddhist reforms and institutions would waver in their function as rebels and supporters of social order until Buddhism ultimately became absorbed into Hinduism during the centuries following the first millennium of the common era.

We can surmise that the earliest community did not have a fixed abode. During the dry season the Buddhist *śramaṇas* would sleep in the open and wander from village to village "begging" for their sustenance—hence their title *bhikṣu*, "mendicant" (fem., *bhikṣuṇī*). They were persons who had set forth (*pravrajyā*) from the household to lead the life of the wanderer (*parivrājaka*). Only during the rainy season would they gather in certain spots in the forest or in special groves provided by lay supporters. There they would build temporary huts that would be dismantled at the end of the rainy season, when they would set out again in their constant wandering to spread the Buddha's Dharma.

The main ideals of the mendicant life of the "wanderers" is expressed in a passage that is presented as the creed or code (the Prātimokṣa) recited by the followers of the "former Buddha" Vipaśyin when they interrupted the wandering to meet and renew their common ideals:

> Enduring patience is the highest austerity, *nirvāṇa* is the highest condition—say the Buddhas. For he who injures another is not a true renouncer, He who causes harm to others is not a true ascetic. Not to do any evil, to practice the good, to purify one's own mind: This is the teaching of the Buddhas. Not to speak against others, not to harm others, and restraint according to the rule (*prātimokṣa*), Moderation in eating, secluded dwelling, and the practice of mental cultivation (*adhicitta*): This is the teaching of the Buddhas. (*Mahāpadāna Suttanta*)

These verses outline important aspects of the early teaching: the centrality of *ahiṃsā*, the two aspects of morality—abstention and cultivation—and the practice of meditation, all in the context of a community of ascetics for whom a life of solitude, poverty, and moderation was more important than the development of subtle metaphysics.

Probably—and the earliest scriptures suggest this—the first aspect of Buddhist teachings to be systematized was the rule, first as a confession of faith for dispersed communities of mendicants, soon as a monastic rule for sedentary ascetics. Also at an early stage, the community sought to systematize its traditions of meditation, some of which must have been pre-Buddhistic (the Buddha himself having learned some of these from his teachers). Thus, Buddhist techniques of meditation represent a continuation of earlier processes of yoga, though we cannot be certain as to the exact connection, or the exact content of the early practices.

The first of these developments brought the community closer together by establishing a common ritual, the recitation of the rule (*prātimokṣa*) at a meeting held on the full and new moon and the quarter moons (*uposatha*). The second development confirmed an important but divisive trait of the early community: the primary source of authority remained with the individual monk and his experience in solitude. Thus, competing systems of meditation and doctrine probably developed more rapidly than differences in the code.

THE CENOBIUM. As India moved into an age of imperial unity under the Maurya (322–185) and Śuṅga dynasties (185–73), the Buddhist community reached its point of greatest unity. Although the *saṃgha* split into schools or sects perhaps as early as the fourth century BCE, differences among Buddhists were relatively minor. Transformed into a monastic brotherhood, Buddhism served a society that shared common values and customs. Unity, however, was shortlived, and Buddhism, like India, would have to adapt rapidly to new circumstances as the first invasions from Central Asia would put an end to the Śuṅga dynasty in 175. Until then, however, during the approximately three hundred years from the death of the founder to the beginning of the age of foreign invasions, Buddhist monks and laymen began the process of systematization that defined the common ground of Indian Buddhism in practice, scripture, and doctrine.

The primary element of continuity became the Prātimokṣa, the rules for the maintenance of the community and the liturgical recitation thereof; differences in this regard would be more serious than differences of doctrine. Thus the Second Council, which is supposed to have caused the most serious split in the history of the community, is said to have been called to resolve differences in the interpretation and formulation of minor details in the monastic regulations. In order to justify and clarify the rules that held the community together a detailed commentary of the Prātimokṣa rules had to be developed. The commentary, attributed to the Buddha himself, eventually grew into the *Vinaya*, an extensive section of the canon.

But the full development of the monastic code presupposes a sedentary *saṃgha.* We can surmise that not long after the Buddha's death the retreat for the rainy season began to extend into the dry season, perhaps at the invitation of the lay community, perhaps owing to dwindling popular support for the mendicant wanderers. Soon the temporary huts were replaced by more or less permanent structures built of wood, and the community of wanderers became a cenobium. The stone and gravel foundation of one of the earliest monasteries remains in the vicinity of Rājagṛha (Bihar). These are the ruins of the famous "Jivaka's Mango Grove" (Jivakāmravaṇa) Monastery, built on a plot of land donated to the order at the time of the Buddha. In its early history it may have been used only during the rainy season, but it already shows the basic structure of the earliest monasteries: living quarters for the monks and a large assembly hall (perhaps for the celebration of the Uposatha).

As the community settled down, rules and rituals for regulating monastic life became a necessity. At least some of the items in the *Prātimokṣa* section of the *Vinaya* and some of the procedural rules discussed in the *Karmavācanā* may go back to the time of the Buddha. The rule and the procedures for governing the *Saṃgha* are clearly based on republican models, like the constitution of the Licchavis of Vaiśālī, which is praised in the canonical texts. If this admiration goes back to the founder, then we can say that the Buddha ordered his community of wandering mendicants on the political model provided by the disappearing republics of North India. Such a rule would encourage order and harmony on the one hand, and peaceful disagreement and individual effort on the other. It provided for mutual care and concern in matters of morals, but lacked a provision for a central authority in political or doctrinal matters.

The common doctrinal ground. The Buddha realized the true nature of things, their "suchness" (*tathatā*), and therefore is one of those rare beings called *tathāgatas.* Yet, whether there is a *tathāgata* to preach it or not, the Dharma is always present, because it is the nature of all things (*dharmatā*). Four terms summarize this truth known by the *tathāgatas*: impermanence, sorrow, no-self, *nirvāṇa.* The first implies the second, for attachment to what must change brings sorrow. Our incapacity to control change, however, reveals the reality of no-self—nothing is "I" or "mine." The experience of no-self, on the other hand, is liberating; it releases one from craving and the causes of sorrow; it leads to peace, *nirvāṇa.*

These principles are summarized also in a doctrine recognized by all schools, that of the Four Noble Truths: sorrow, its cause, its cessation, and the path leading to cessation. Buddhist tradition, therefore, will spend much of its energy in understanding the causes of suffering and the means to put an end to it, or, in doctrinal shorthand, "arising" and "cessation." Since cessation is in fact the obverse of arising, a proper understanding of arising, or causation, becomes central to Buddhist speculation in India. The most important doctrine for this aspect of the religion is the principle of dependent arising (*pratītya-samutpāda*): everything we regard as "the self" is conditioned or compounded; everything conditioned depends on causes and conditions; by understanding the causes of our idea of the self and of the sorrow that this idea brings to us we can become free of suffering. This doctrine is summarized in a stanza that has become one of the best known Buddhist creeds throughout Asia:

> The Tathāgata has proclaimed the cause,
> as well as the cessation,
> of all things (*dharma*) arising from a cause.
> This is the Great *Śramaṇa*'s teaching. (*Mahāvastu* 2.62; Pāli *Vinaya* 1.40)

Abstract theories of causation were perceived as having an ultimately soteriological meaning or function, for they clarified both the process of bondage (rebirth forced upon us as a consequence of our actions) and the process of liberation (freedom from rebirth by overcoming our ignorance and gaining control over the causes of bondage). Liberation was possible because the analysis of causation revealed that there was no reincarnating or suffering self to begin with.

Impermanence and causation were explained by primitive theories of the composition of material reality (the four elements) and mental reality (the six senses, the six types of sense objects, etc.) and, what is more important, by the theory of the constituents (*skandhas*) of human personality. These notions would become the main focus of Buddhist philosophy, and by the beginning of the common era they were being integrated into systematic treatments of the nature of ultimately real entities (*dharma*).

Although the themes of impermanence and causation will remain at the heart of Buddhist philosophical speculation for several centuries, from the religious point of view the question of no-self plays a more important role. At first seen as an insightful formulation of the meaning of awakening and liberation, the doctrine of no-self raised several difficulties for Buddhist dogma. First, it was not at all obvious how moral (or karmic) responsibility could be possible if there was no continuous self. Second, some Buddhists wondered what was the meaning of liberation in the absence of a self.

Closely related to these issues was the question of the nature and status of the liberated being. In other words, what sort of living being is a *tathāgata*? Some Buddhists considered the *tathāgata* as a transcendent or eternal being, while others saw him as someone who by becoming extinct was nonexistent; still others began to redefine the concept of liberation and no-self in an attempt to solve these questions and in response to changes in the mythological or hagiographic sphere. These issues are an essential part of the changes in doctrine and practice that would take place during the age of invasions, culminating in the emergence of Mahāyāna Buddhism.

Worship and ritual. The most important ritual of the monastic community continued to be Upavasatha or Uposatha, a gathering of the *saṃgha* of a given locality or "parish" (*sīmā*) to recite the rules of the Prātimokṣa. These meetings were held at every change in the moon's phase. A similar ceremony, but with greater emphasis on the public confession of individual faults, was held at the end of the rainy season. At this time too was held the *kaṭhina* ceremony, in which the monks received new robes from the lay community. Other rituals, such as the ordination ceremony, had a more limited impact on the community at large, but were nevertheless important symbols of the status of the religious specialist in society at large.

Above all other rituals, one of shramanic origin offered continued reinforcement of the ties that bound the religious order with the laity. The *bhikṣu,* as his title indicates, was expected to receive his sustenance from the charity (*dāna*) of pious laymen and laywomen. Accordingly, the monks would walk the villages every morning to collect alms. By giving the unsolicited gift the layperson was assured of the merit (*puṇya*) necessary to be reborn in a state of being more favorable for spiritual or material progress. According to some traditions, the monk received the benefits of helping others gain merit; but some believed the monk could not gain merit except by his own virtue.

In the early stages lay followers were identified by their adherence to the fivefold moral precept (*pañcaśīla*) and the formal adoption of the Three Refuges. These practices continued throughout the history of Indian Buddhism. It is also likely that participation of lay members in Upavasatha meetings with the *saṃgha* was also an early and persistent practice.

At first the cenobitic life of the monks probably had no room for explicit acts of devotion, and the monk's religion was limited to a life of solitude and meditation. The early monastic ruins do not show evidence of any shrine room. It was essential to have the cells open onto a closed courtyard, to keep out the noise of the world; it was essential to have an assembly hall for teaching and the recitation of the Prātimokṣa; a promenade (*caṅkrama*) for walking meditation was also necessary. But there were no shrine rooms.

With the institutionalization of Buddhism, however, came new forms of lay and monastic practice. The monastic brotherhood gradually began to play a priestly role; in tandem with the lay community, they participated in nonmonastic rituals, many of which must have been of pre-Buddhist origin. One practice that clearly was an important, nonascetic ritual, yet characteristic of Buddhism, was the worship of the relics of the Buddha and his immediate disciples. The relics were placed in a casket, which was then deposited in a cairn or tumulus (stupa, *caitya*), to which the faithful would come to present their offerings. Already by the time of Aśoka (mid-third century BCE) we find evidence of a flourishing cult of the relics, often accompanied by the practice of pilgrimage to the sacred sites consecrated by their role in the life of Śākyamuni—especially the birth place, the site of the Great Awakening, the site of the First Sermon, and the spot where the Buddha was believed to have died. Following an ancient custom, tumuli were built on these spots—perhaps at first as reliquaries, later as commemorative monuments. Monasteries near such sites assumed the role of shrine caretakers. Eventually, most monasteries became associated with stupas.

Aśoka erected columns and stupas (as many as eighty thousand, according to one tradition) marking the localities associated with the life of the Buddha as well as other ancient sacred sites, some associated with "former Buddhas," that is, mythical beings believed to have achieved Buddhahood thousands or millions of lives before the Buddha Śākyamuni. The latter practice and belief indicates the development of a new form of Buddhism, firmly based on the mythology of each locality, that expanded the concept of the Three Treasures to include a host of mythical beings who would share in the sanctity of Śākyamuni's experience and virtue and who were therefore deserving of the same veneration as he had received in the past.

The cairn or tumulus eventually became sacred in itself, whether there was a relic in it or not. Chapels were built to contain the *caitya.* The earliest surviving examples of these structures are built in stone and date from the first or second century BCE, but we can surmise that they existed in wood from an earlier date. These "*caitya* halls" became the standard shrine room of the monastery: a stylized memorial tumulus built in stone or brick, housed in an apsidal hall with a processional for the ritual circumambulation of the tumulus.

Reliefs at the *caitya* hall at Bhājā in western India (late Śuṅga, c. end of the second century BCE) suggest various aspects of the cult: the main form of worship was the ritual of circumambulation (*pradakṣiṇa*), which could be carried out individually or in groups. The stupa represented the sacred or cosmic mountain, at whose center was found the *axis mundi* (now represented by the Buddha's royal parasol); thus the rite of circumambulation expressed veneration for the Buddha and his teaching, while at the same time it served as a symbolic walking of the sun's path around the cosmic mountain.

Stupas were often erected at ancient sacred sites, hills, trees, the confluence of streams, which in many cases were sacred by virtue of non-Buddhist belief. Thus, pre-Buddhist practice, if not belief, survived side by side, and even within, Buddhist liturgy and belief. There is ample evidence of a coexisting cult of the tree (identified with the "Tree of Awakening"), of forest spirits (*yakṣas*) and goddesses (*devatā*), and the persistence of Vedic deities, albeit in a subordinate role, beside a more austere, and presumably monastically inspired, cult of aniconic symbolizations of Buddhahood: the tree and the throne of enlightenment standing for the Great Awakening, the stupa representing the *nirvāṇa,* the wheel representing the doctrine of the Buddha. But one must not assume that the implied categories of "high tradition" and popular cult were mutually exclusive.

The councils and the beginning of scriptural tradition. The First Council, or Council of Rājagṛha, if a historical fact, must have served to establish the Buddhist *saṃgha* and its doctrine for the community of the Magadhan capital. In all probability the decisions of the Council were not accepted by all Buddhists. Further evidence of disagreement, and geographical fragmentation is found in the legend of the Second Council, one hundred years after the Buddha's death.

Since the early community of wanderers, there had been ample room for disagreement and dissension. But certain forces contributed to maintaining unity: the secular powers, for instance, had much at stake in preserving harmony within the *saṃgha*, especially if they could maintain some kind of control over it. Thus, as the legends have it, each of the three major councils were sponsored by a king: Ajātaśatru, Kālāśoka, and Aśoka, respectively. Within the *saṃgha*, there must have been interest groups, mainly conservative, seeking to preserve the religion by avoiding change—two goals that are not always conciliable. There must have been, therefore, a strong pressure to recover the ideal unity of the early community (as we have seen, probably a fantasy), by legislation. These efforts took two forms: in the first place, there was the drive to establish a common monastic code, in the second place, there was the drive to fix a canon of scriptures. Both tendencies probably became stronger toward the beginning of the common era, when a number of political factors recreated a sense of urgency and a yearning for harmony and peace similar to the one that had given rise to the religion.

The most important result of the new quest for harmony was the compilation and redaction of scriptures. Transmitted and edited through the oral tradition, the words of the Buddha and his immediate disciples had suffered many transformations before they came to be compiled, to say nothing of their state when they were eventually written down. We have no way of determining which, if any, of the words contained in the Buddhist scriptures are the words of the founder: in fact we have no hard evidence for the language used by the Buddha in his ministry. Scholars have suggested an early form of Māgadhī, since this was probably the lingua franca of the kingdom of Magadha, but this is at best an educated guess. If it is correct, then none of the words of the Buddha have come to us in the original language.

Although the Theravādin tradition claims that the language of its canon, Pali, is the language spoken by the Buddha, Western scholars disagree. Evidently, the Pali canon, like other Buddhist scriptures, is the creation, or at least the compilation and composition, of another age and a different linguistic milieu. As they are preserved today, the Buddhist scriptures must be a collective creation, the fruit of the effort of several generations of memorizers, redactors, and compilers. Some of the earliest Buddhist scriptures may have been translations from logia or sayings of the Buddha that were transmitted for some time in his own language. But even if this is the case, the extant versions represent at the very least redactions and reworkings, if not creations, of a later age.

Since the *saṃgha* was from the beginning a decentralized church, one can presume that the word of the Buddha took many forms. Adding to this the problem of geographical isolation and linguistic diversity, one would expect that the oral transmission would have produced a variegated textual tradition. Perhaps it is this expectation of total chaos that makes it all the more surprising that there is agreement on so many points in the scriptures preserved to this day. This is especially true of the scriptures of the Theravāda school (preserved in Pali), and fragments of the canon of the Sarvāstivāda school (in the original Sanskrit or in Chinese translation). Some scholars have been led to believe, therefore, that these two traditions represent the earliest stratum of the transmission, preserving a complex of pericopes and logia that must go back to a stage when the community was not divided: that is, before the split of the Second Council. Most scholars tend to accept this view; a significant minority, however, sees the uniformity of the texts as reflecting a late, not an early stage, in the redaction of the canon.

The early canon, transmitted orally, must have had only two major sections, Dharma and Vinaya. The first of these contained the discourses of the Buddha and his immediate disciples. The Vinaya contained the monastic rules. Most Western scholars agree that a third section, Abhidharma, found in all of the surviving canons, could not have been included in early definitions of canonicity, though eventually most schools would incorporate it in their canon with varying degrees of authority.

Each early school possessed its own set of scriptural "collections" (called metaphorically "baskets," piṭaka). Although eventually the preferred organization seems to have been a tripartite collection of "Three Baskets," the Tripiṭaka, divided into monastic rules, sermons, and scholastic treatises (Vinaya, sūtra, Abhidharma), some schools adopted different orderings. Among the collections that are now lost there were fourfold and fivefold subdivisions of the scriptures. Of the main surviving scriptural collections, only one is strictly speaking a Tripiṭaka, the Pali corpus of the Theravādins. (The much later Chinese and Tibetan collections have much more complex subdivisions and can be called Tripiṭakas only metaphorically.)

THE AGE OF FOREIGN INVASIONS. The decline and fall of the Maurya dynasty (324–187) brought an end to an age of assured support for Buddhist monastic institutions. Political circumstances unfavorable to Buddhism began with persecution under Puṣyamitra Śuṅga (r. about 187–151). The Śuṅga dynasty would see the construction of some of the most important Buddhist sites of India: Bhārhut, Sāñcī, and Amarāvatī. But it also foreshadowed the beginning of Hindu dominance. The rising cult of Viṣṇu seemed better equipped to assimilate the religion of the people and win the support of the ruling classes. Although Buddhism served better as a universal religion that could unite Indians and foreign invaders, the latter did not always choose to become Buddhists. A series of non-Indian rulers—Greek, Parthian, Scythian (Saka), Kushan—would hesitate in their religious allegiances.

Among the Greek kings, the Buddhist tradition claims Menander (Milinda, c. 150 BCE) as one of its converts. The Scythian tribe of the Sakas, who invaded Bactriana around 130 BCE, roughly contemporaneous with the Yüeh-chih conquest of the Tokharians, would become stable supporters of Buddhism in the subcontinent. Their rivals in South India, the Tamil dynasty of the Śātavāhana (220 BCE–236 CE), sponsored in Andhra the construction of major centers of worship at Amarāvatī and Nāgārjunīkoṇḍa. The Yüeh-chih (Kushans) also supported Buddhism, though perhaps less consistently. The most famous of their rulers, Kaṇiṣka, is represented by the literature as a pious patron of Buddhism (his dates are uncertain; proposed accession in 78 or 125 CE). During the Kushan period (c. 50–320 CE) the great schools of Gandhāra and Mathurā revolutionized Indian, especially Buddhist, art. Both the northern styles of Gandhāra and Mathurā and the southern school of Andhra combined iconic and aniconic symbolization of the Buddha: the first Buddha images appeared around the third century of the common era, apparently independently and simultaneously in all three schools.

The appearance of schools and denominations. Any understanding of the history of composition of the canons, or of their significance in the history of the religion, is dependent on our knowledge of the geographic distribution, history, and doctrine of the various sects. Unfortunately, our knowledge in this regard is also very limited.

Developments in doctrine and in scholastic speculation. As the original community of wandering mendicants settled in monasteries, a new type of religion arose, concerned with the preservation of a tradition and the justification of its institutions. Although the "forest dweller" continued as an ideal and a practice—some were still dedicated primarily to a life of solitude and meditation—the dominant figure became that of the monk-scholar. This new type of religious specialist pursued the study of the early tradition and moved its doctrinal systems in new directions. On the one hand, the old doctrines were classified, defined, and expanded. On the other hand, there was a growing awareness of the gap that separated the new developments from the transmitted creeds and codes. A set of basic or "original" teachings had to be defined, and the practice of exegesis had to be formalized. In fact, the fluidity and uncertainty of the earlier scriptural tradition may be one of the causes for the development of Buddhist scholasticism. By the time the canons were closed the degree of diversity and conflict among the schools was such, and the tradition was overall so fluid, that it was difficult to establish orthodoxy even when there was agreement on the basic content of the canons. In response to these problems Buddhists soon developed complicated scholastic studies.

At least some of the techniques and problems of this early scholasticism must go back to the early redactions of the sūtra section of the canon, if not to a precanonical stage. The genre of the *mātṛkā*, or doctrinal "matrices," is not an uncommon form of sūtra literature. It is suggested in the redaction of certain sections of the Pali and Sarvāstivādin canons, is found in early Chinese translations (e.g., the *Dharmaśarīraka Sūtra* and the *Daśottara Sūtra*), and continues in Mahāyāna *Sūtra* literature. It is a literary form that probably represents not only an exegetic device but an early technique of doctrinal redaction—a hermeneutic that also served as the basis for the redaction of earlier strata of the oral transmission.

The early sects. Given the geographical and linguistic diversity of India and the lack of a central authority in the Buddhist community one can safely speculate that Buddhist sects arose early in the history of the religion. Tradition speaks of a first, but major, schism occurring at (or shortly after) the Second Council in Vaiśālī, one hundred years after the death of the founder. Whether the details are true or not, it is suggestive that this first split was between the Sthaviras and the Mahāsāṃghikas, the prototypes of the two major divisions of Buddhism: "Hīnayāna" and Mahāyāna.

After this schism new subdivisions arose, reaching by the beginning of the common era a total of approximately thirty different denominations or schools and subschools. Tradition refers to this state of sectarian division as the period of the "Eighteen Schools," since some of the early sources count eighteen groups. It is not clear when these arose. *Faut de mieux*, most Western scholars go along with classical Indian sources, albeit with a mild skepticism, and try to sort out a consistent narrative from contradictory sources. Thus, we can only say that if we are to believe the Pali tradition, the Eighteen Schools must have been in existence already in the third century BCE, when a legendary Moggaliputtatissa compiled the *Kathāvatthu*. But such an early dating raises many problems.

In the same vein, we tend to accept the account of the Second Council that sees it as the beginning of a major split. In this version the main points of contention were monastic issues—the exact content and interpretation of the code. But doctrinal, ritual, and scholastic issues must have played a major role in the formation of separate schools. Many of the main points of controversy, for instance, centered on the question of the nature of the state of liberation and the status of the liberated person. Is the liberated human (*arhat*) free from all moral and karmic taint? Is the state of liberation (*nirvāṇa*) a condition of being or nonbeing? Can there be at the same time more than one fully awakened person (*samyaksaṃbuddha*) in one world system? Are persons already on their way to full awakening, the *bodhisattvas* or future Buddhas, deserving of worship? Do they have the ability to descend to the hells to help other sentient beings?

Among these doctrinal disputes one emerges as emblematic of the most important fissure in the Buddhist community. This was the polemic surrounding the exalted state of the *arhat* (Pali, *arahant*). Most of the Buddhist schools believed that only a few human beings could aspire to become fully awakened beings (*samyaksaṃbuddha*), others had to content themselves with the hope of becoming free from the burden of past *karman* and attaining liberation in *nirvāṇa*, without the extraordinary wisdom and virtue of Buddhahood. But the attainment of liberation was in itself a great achievement, and a person who was assured of an end to rebirth at the end of the present life was considered the most saintly, deserving of the highest respect, a "worthy" (*arhat*). Some of the schools even attributed to the *arhat* omniscience and total freedom from moral taint. Objections were raised against those who believed in the faultless wisdom of the *arhat*, including obvious limitations in their knowledge of everyday, worldly affairs. Some of these objections were formalized in the "Five Points" of Mahādeva, after its purported proponent. These criticisms can be interpreted either as a challenge to the belief in the superhuman perfection of the *arhat* or as a plea for the acceptance of their humanity. Traditionally, Western scholars have opted for the first of these interpretations.

The controversies among the Eighteen Schools identified each group doctrinally, but it seems unlikely that in the early stages these differences lead to major rifts in the community, with the exception of the schism between the two trunk schools of the Sthavira and the Mahāsāṃghika; and even then, there is evidence that monks of both schools often lived together in a single monastic community. Among the doctrinal differences, however, we can find the seeds of future dissension, especially in the controversies relating to ritual. The Mahīśāsakas, for instance, claimed that there is more merit in worshiping and making offerings to the *saṃgha* than in worshiping a stupa, as the latter merely contains the remains of a member of the *saṃgha* who is no more. The Dharmaguptakas replied that there is more merit in worshiping a stupa, because the Buddha's path and his present state (in *nirvāṇa*) are far superior to that of any living monk. Here we have a fundamental difference with both social and religious consequences, for the choice is between two types of communal hierarchies as well as between two types of spiritual orders.

Developments in the scriptural tradition. Apart from the Theravāda recension of the Pali canon and some fragments of the Sarvāstivādin Sanskrit canon nothing survives of what must have been a vast and diverse body of literature. For most of the collections we only have the memory preserved in inscriptions referring to *piṭakas* and *nikāyas* and an occasional reference in the extant literature.

According to the Pali tradition of Sri Lanka, the three parts of the Tripiṭaka were compiled in the language of the Buddha at the First Council. The Second Council introduced minor revisions in the *Vinaya*, and the Third Council added Moggaliputtatissa's *Kathāvatthu*. A few years later the canon resulting from this council, and a number of extracanonical commentaries, were transmitted to Sri Lanka by Mahinda. The texts were transmitted orally (*mukhapāṭhena*) for the next two centuries, but after difficult years of civil war and famine, King Vaṭṭagāmaṇī of Sri Lanka ordered the texts written down. This task was carried out between 35 and 32 BCE. In this way, it is said, the canon was preserved in the original language. Although the commentaries were by that time extant only in Sinhala, they continued to be transmitted in written form until they were retranslated into Pali in the fifth century CE.

Modern scholarship, however, questions the accuracy of several points in this account. Pali appears to be a literary language originating in Avantī, western India; it seems unlikely that it could be the vernacular of a man who had lived in eastern India all his life or, for that matter, the lingua franca of the early Magadhan kingdom. The Pali texts as they are preserved today show clear signs of the work of editors and redactors. Although much in them still has the ring of oral transmission, it is a formalized or ritualized oral tradition, far from the spontaneous preaching of a living teacher. Different strata of language, history, and doctrine can be recognized easily in these texts. There is abundant evidence that already at the stage of oral transmission the tradition was fragmented, different schools of "reciters" (*bhāṇaka*) preserving not only different corpuses (the eventual main categories of the canons) but also different recensions of the same corpus of literature. Finally, we have no way of knowing if the canon written down at the time of Vaṭṭagāmaṇī was the Tripiṭaka as we know it today. There is evidence to the contrary, for we are told that the great South Indian scholar Buddhaghosa revised the canon in the fifth century when he also edited the commentaries preserved in Sinhala and translated them into Pali, which suggests that Pali literature in general had gone through a period of deterioration before his time.

Most scholars, however, accept the tradition that would have the Pali canon belong to a date earlier than the fifth century; even the commentaries must represent an earlier stratum. However late may be its final recension, the Pali canon preserves much from earlier stages in the development of the religion.

Of the Sanskrit canon of the Sarvāstivāda school we only possess a few isolated texts and fragments in the original, mostly from Central Asia. However, extensive sections survive in Chinese translation. This canon is supposed to have been written down at a "Fourth Council" held in Jālandhara, Kashmir, about 100 CE, close to the time when the same school systematized its Abhidharma in a voluminous commentary called the *Mahāvibhāṣa*. If this legend is true, two details are of historical interest. We must note first the proximity in time of this compilation to the date of the writing down of the Pali canon. This would set the parameters for the closing of the "Hīnayāna" canons between the first century BCE and the first century CE. Second, the close connection between the closing of a canon and the final formulation of a scholastic system confirms the similar socio-religious function of both activities: the establishing of orthodoxy.

Developments in practice. The cult at this stage was still dominated by the practice of pilgrimage and by the cult of the *caitya*, as described above. However, we can imagine an intensification of the devotional aspect of ritual and a greater degree of systematization as folk belief and "high tradition" continued to interact. Sectarian differences probably began to affect the nature of the liturgies, as a body of liturgical texts became part of the common or the specific property of different groups of Buddhists. Among the earliest liturgical texts were the hymns in praise of the Buddha, especially the ones singing the many epithets of the Awakened One. Their use probably goes back to the earliest stages in the history of monastic ritual and may be closely connected with the practice of *buddhānusmṛti*, or meditation on the attributes of the Buddha.

Pilgrimage sites and stupas. Many Buddhist practices and institutions remain apparently stable in the subcontinent until the beginnings of the common era. The monuments of Bhārhut and Sāñcī, for example, where we find the earliest examples of aniconic symbolism, represent a conservative Buddhism. Other signs of conservatism, however, confirm a continuous nonliterary cult. The oldest section at Sāñcī, the east gateway, dating from perhaps 90 to 80 BCE, preserves, next to the illustrated Jātakas, the woman and tree motifs, *yakṣas* and *yakṣīs* (with the implied popular cult of male and female fertility deities), and the aniconic representations of the wheel, the footprint, the throne, and the tree. The most advanced or innovative trait is the increasing iconographic importance of the previous lives of the Buddha, represented in the reliefs of Jātakas. These indicate a developed legend of the Buddha's past lives, a feature of the period that suggests the importance of past lives in the cult and in the future development of Mahāyāna. The most important cultic development of the pre-Mahāyāna period, however, was the shift from the commemorative ritual associated with the stūpa and the aniconic symbol to the ritual of worship and devotion associated with the Buddha image. After the beginning of the Christian era major developments in practice reflect outside influence as well as new internal developments. This is the time when the sects were beginning to commit to writing their sacred literature, but it is also the time of foreign invasions. These may have played a major role in the development of the Buddha image. Modern scholarship has debated the place of origin of this important cultic element and the causal factors that brought it about. Some, following Foucher, proposed a northwestern origin, and saw the Buddhas and *bodhisattvas* created under the influence of Greco-Roman art in Gandhāra (Kushan period) as the first images. Others, following Coomaraswamy, believed the first images were created in Andhra, as part of the natural development of a South Indian cult of the *yakṣas*, and in the north central region of Mathurā. Be that as it may, the Buddha image dominates Buddhist iconography after the second century CE; stupas and Jātaka representations remain but play a secondary role. There seems to be, especially in Mathurā art, an association between the Buddha image and solar symbolism, which suggests Central Asian or Iranian influences on Buddhism and may be closely related to the development of the new doctrinal conceptions, such as those that regarded the Buddha as "universal monarch" (*cakravartin*) and lord of the universe, and Buddhas and *bodhisattvas* as radiant beings. The abundance of *bodhisattva* images in Gandhāra, moreover, suggests the beginning of a gradual shift towards a conception of the ideal being as layman, or at least a shift in the way the *bodhisattva* was conceived (from merely an instance of a Buddha's past to the central paradigm of Buddhahood). As a balance to the growing importance of the past lives of the Buddha, the process of redacting the scriptures also brought about the necessity of formulating a biography of the Buddha. The first "biographies" appear at the beginning of the common era, perhaps as late as the second century CE. Partial biographies appear in the literature of the Sarvāstivādins (*Lalitavistara*) and Lokottaravādins (*Mahāvastu*). The first complete biography is a cultured poem in the *kāvya* style, the *Buddhacarita* of Aśvaghoṣa. This is also a time when noncanonical literature flourished. Poets wrote Buddhist dramas and poetical recastings of canonical parables and legends. Aśvaghoṣa, for instance, wrote a drama on the life of Śāriputra, and a poem narrating the conversion of Nanda (*Saundarānanda*). Developments in the literary tradition perhaps should be seen as reflecting other strata of the living tradition. Thus, the vitality of the Jātaka tradition is seen in its appearance as a literary genre in the Jātakamālā of Āryaśūra (fl. c. 150 CE). This classical poet is sometimes identified with Mātṛceṭa, who in his works (e.g., *Śatapañcaśatka*) gives us a highly cultured reflection of the hymns of praise (*stotras*) that must have been a regular part of the Buddhist cult of the day. In these hymns we already see the apotheosis of the Buddha figure, side by side with the newly redefined *bodhisattva* ideal.

Mystics and intellectuals. The development of devotional Buddhism did not obscure the ascetic and contemplative dimensions of the religion. The system of meditation contained in the Nikāyas probably achieved its final form during this period. Diverse techniques for the development of enstasy and insight were conflated first in the canonical *Sūtra* literature, then in the Abhidharmic texts. Side by side with the development of popular and monastic cults a new elite of religious specialists appeared, seeking to follow the Buddha's path through systematic study into the scriptures. They belonged to the tradition of the *mātṛkās* and composed treatises purporting to treat the "higher" Dharma (*abhidharma*)—or, what is perhaps the more correct etymology, treatises "on the Dharma." Although the analysis of meditational categories was an important aspect of these traditions, the scholar-monks were not always dedicated meditators. In fact, many of them must have made scholarship the prime objective of their religious life, leaving the practice of meditation to the forest monks. For the scholars, the goal was to account for the whole of Buddhism, in particular, the plethora of ancient doctrines and practices found in the canon. Above all, they sought to define and explain the ultimately real components of reality, the *dharmas*, into which one could analyze or explode the false conception of the self. This critique was not without soteriological implications. The goal was conceived at times as ineffable, beyond the ken of human conception. Thus canonical literature describes the liberated person, the *arhat*, as follows:

> When bright sparks fly
> as the smith beats red-hot iron,
> and fade away,
> one cannot tell where they have gone.
>
> In the same way, there is no way of knowing
> the final destination of those who are truly free,
> who have crossed beyond the flood, bondage, and desire,
> obtaining unshakable bliss. (*Udāna*, p. 93)

But side by side with the tradition of ineffability, there was a need to define at the very least the process of liberation. For the gradual realization of selflessness was understood as personal growth. Accordingly, a set of standard definitions of liberation was accompanied by accepted descriptions of the stages on the path to liberation, or of degrees of spiritual achievement. The canonical collections already list, for instance, four types of saints (*āryapudgala*): the one who will be reborn no more (*arhat*); the one who will not come back to this world, the "non-returner" (*anāgamin*); the one who will return only once more (*sakṛdāgamin*); and the one who has entered the path to sainthood, the "stream-enterer" (*srotāpanna*). Canonical notions of levels or hierarchies in the path to liberation became the focus of much scholastic speculation—in fact, the presence of these categories in the canons may be a sign of scholastic influence on the redaction of the scriptures. The construction of complex systems of soteriology, conceived as maps or detailed descriptions of the path, that integrated the description and analysis of ethical and contemplative practices with philosophical argumentation, characterized the Abhidharmic schools. This activity contributed to the definition of the doctrinal parameters of the sects; but it also set the tone for much of future Buddhist dogmatics. The concerns of the Abhidharmists, ranging from the analysis of enstasy and the contemplative stages to the rational critique of philosophical views of reality, had a number of significant doctrinal consequences: (1) scholars began devising "maps of the path," or theoretical blueprints of the stages from the condition of a common human being (*pṛthag-jana*) to the exalted state of a fully awakened being (*samyaksaṃbuddha*); (2) Buddhist scholars engaged other Indian intellectuals in the discussion of broad philosophical issues; (3) various orthodox apologetics were developed, with the consequent freezing of a technical terminology common to most Buddhists; (4) the rigidity of their systems set the stage for a reaction that would lead to the creation of new forms of Buddhism.

THE SECTS AND THE APPEARANCE OF MAHĀYĀNA. Most of the developments mentioned above overlap with the growth of a new spirit that changed the religion and eventually created a distinct form of Buddhist belief and practice. The new movement referred to itself as the "Great Vehicle" (Mahāyāna) to distinguish itself from other styles of Buddhism that the followers of the movement considered forms of a "Lesser Vehicle" (Hīnayāna).

The early schools outside India. If we accept the general custom of using the reign of Aśoka as the landmark for the beginning of the missionary spread of Buddhism, we may say that Buddhism reached the frontiers of India by the middle of the second century BCE. By the beginning of the common era it had spread beyond. In the early centuries of the era Mahāyāna and Hīnayāna spread in every direction; eventually certain areas would become predominantly Mahāyāna, others, predominantly Hīnayāna.

Mahāyāna came to dominate in East and Central Asia—with the exception of Turkistan, where Sarvāstivādin monasteries flourished until the Muslim invasion and conversion of the region. Hīnayāna was slower to spread, and in some foreign lands had to displace Mahāyāna. It lives on in a school that refers to itself as the Theravāda, a Sinhala derivative of the Sthavira school. It spread throughout Southeast Asia where it continues to this day.

The Great Vehicle. The encounter of Buddhism with extra-Indian ethnic groups and the increasing influence of the laity gradually transformed the monastic child of shramanic Buddhism into a universal religion. This occurred in two ways. On the one hand, monasticism adapted to the changing circumstances, strengthened its ties to the laity and secular authorities, established a satisfactory mode of coexistence with nonliterary, regional forms of worship. Both Mahāyāna and Hīnayāna schools participated in this aspect of the process of adaptation. But Buddhism also redefined its goals and renovated its symbols to create a new synthesis that in some ways may be considered a new religion. The new style, the Mahāyāna, claimed to be a path for the many, the vehicle for the salvation of all sentient beings (hence its name, "The Great Vehicle"). Its distinctive features are: a tilt toward world affirmation, a laicized conception of the human ideal, a new ritual of devotion, and new definitions of the metaphysical and contemplative ideals.

The origins of Mahāyāna. The followers of Mahāyāna claim the highest antiquity for its teachings. Their own myths of origin, however, belie this claim. Mahāyāna recognizes the fact that its teachings were not known in the early days of Buddhism by asserting that Śākyamuni revealed the Mahāyāna only to select *bodhisattvas* or heavenly beings who kept the texts hidden for centuries. One legend recounts that the philosopher Nāgārjuna had to descend to the underworld to obtain the Mahāyāna texts known as the "Perfection of Wisdom" (Prajñāpāramitā).

Western scholars are divided on the question of the dates and location of the origins of Mahāyāna. Some favor an early (beginning of the common era) origin among Mahāsāṃghika communities in the southeastern region of Andhra. Others propose a northwestern origin, among the Sarvāstivādins, close to the second and third centuries CE. It may be, however, that Mahāyāna arose by a gradual and complex process involving more than one region of India. It is clear that Mahāyāna was partly a reform movement, partly the natural development of pre-Mahāyāna Buddhism; still in another sense, it was the result of new social forces shaping the Indian subcontinent.

The theory of a southern origin assumes that the Mahāsāṃghika monastic centers of Andhra continued to develop some of the more radical ideals of the school, until some of these communities saw themselves as a movement completely distinct from other, so-called Hīnayāna schools. This theory also recognizes external influences: the Iranian invaders as well as the non-Aryan substratum of southern India, the first affecting the mythology of the celestial *bodhisattvas*, the second incorporating non-Aryan concepts of the role of women into the mainstream of Buddhist religious ideals.

For the sake of clarity one could distinguish two types of causes in the development of Mahāyāna: social or external, and doctrinal or internal. Among the first one must include the Central Asian and Iranian influences mentioned above, the growing importance of the role of women and the laity, especially as this affected the development of the cultus, and the impact of the pilgrimage cycles. The foreign element is supposed to have introduced elements of light symbolism and solar cults, as well as a less ascetic bent.

Doctrinal factors were primarily the development of the myth of the former lives of Śākyamuni and the cult of former Buddhas, both of which contributed to a critique of the *arhat* ideal. The mythology of the Buddha's former lives as a *bodhisattva* led to the exaltation of the *bodhisattva* ideal over that of the *arhat.* The vows of the *bodhisattva* began to take the central role, especially as they were seen as an integral part of a developing liturgy at the center of which the dedication of merit was transformed as part of the exalted *bodhisattva* ideal.

It seems likely, furthermore, that visionaries and inspired believers had continued to compose sūtras. Some of these, through a gradual process we can no longer retrace, began to move away from the general direction of the older scholastic traditions and canonical redactors. Thus it happened that approximately at the time when the older schools were closing their canons, the Mahāyāna was composing a set of texts that would place it in a position of disagreement with, if not frank opposition to, the older schools. At the same time, the High Tradition began to accept Mahāyāna and therefore argue for its superiority; thus, a Mahāyāna *śāstra* tradition began to develop almost at the same time as the great Sarvāstivādin synthesis was completed.

In the West, the gap between Mahāyāna and Hīnayāna is sometimes exaggerated. It is customary to envision Mahāyāna as a revolutionary movement through which the aspirations of a restless laity managed to overcome an oppressive, conservative monastic establishment. Recent research suggests that the opposition between the laity and the religious specialists was not as sharp as had hitherto been proposed. Furthermore, it has become apparent that the monastic establishment continued to be a powerful force in Indian Mahāyāna. It seems more likely that Mahāyāna arose gradually and in different forms in various points of the subcontinent. A single name and a more or less unified ideology may have arisen after certain common aspirations were recognized. Be that as it may, it seems evident that the immediate causes for the arising of this new form of Buddhism were the appearance of new cultic forms and widespread dissatisfaction with the scholastic tradition.

Merit, bodhisattvas, and the Pure Land. Inscriptional evidence shows that the doctrine of merit transference had an important role in the cultus even before the appearance of Mahāyāna. Although all Buddhists believe that virtuous thoughts and actions generate merit, which leads to a good rebirth, it appears that early Buddhists believed that individuals could generate merit only for themselves, and that merit could only lead to a better rebirth, not to liberation from the cycle of rebirth. By the beginning of the common era, however, some Buddhists had adopted a different conception of merit. They believed that merit could be shared or transferred, and that it was a factor in the attainment of liberation—so much so that they were offering their own merit for the salvation of their dead relatives.

Dedication of merit appears as one of the pivotal doctrines of the new Buddhism. Evidently, it served a social function: it made participation in Buddhist ritual a social encounter rather than a private experience. It also contributed to the development of a Buddhist high liturgy, an important factor in the survival of Buddhism and its assimilation of foreign elements, both in and outside India.

This practice and belief interacted with the cult of former Buddhas and the mythology of the former lives to create a Buddhist system of beliefs in which the primary goal was to imitate the virtue of Śākyamuni's former lives, when he was a *bodhisattva* dedicated to the liberation of others rather than himself. To achieve this goal the believer sought to imitate Śākyamuni not as he appeared in his last life or after his enlightenment, when he sought and attained *nirvāṇa,* but by adopting a vow similar to Śākyamuni's former vow to seek awakening (*bodhi*) for the sake of all sentient beings. On the one hand, this shift put the emphasis on insight into the world, rather than escape from it. On the other hand, it also created a new form of ideal being and object of worship, the *bodhisattva.*

Contemporary developments in Hindu devotionalism (*bhakti*) probably played an important role in the development of Buddhist liturgies of worship (*pūjā*), but it would be a mistake to assume that the beginnings of Mahāyāna faith and ritual can be explained adequately by attributing them merely to external theistic influences. For instance, the growth of a faith in rebirth in "purified Buddha fields," realms of the cosmos in which the merit and power of Buddhas and *bodhisattvas* create an environment where birth without suffering is possible, can be seen as primarily a Buddhist development. The new faith, generalized in India through the concept of the "Land of Bliss" (the "Pure Land" of East Asian Buddhism), hinged on faith in the vows of former *bodhisattvas* who chose to transfer or dedicate their merit to the purification of a special "field" or "realm." The influence of Iranian religious conceptions seems likely, however, and one may have to seek some of the roots of this belief among Central Asian converts.

Formation of a new scriptural tradition. With the new cult and the new ideology came a new body of scriptures. Mahāyāna sūtras began to be composed probably around the beginning of the Christian era, and continued to be composed and redacted until at least the fifth or sixth century CE. Unlike the canons of the earlier schools, the Mahāyāna scriptures do not seem to have been collected into formal, closed canons in the land of their origin—even the collections edited in China and Tibet were never closed canons.

In its inception Mahāyāna literature is indistinguishable from the literature of some of the earlier schools. The *Prajñāpāramitā* text attributed to the Pūrvaśailas is probably an earlier version of one of the Mahāyāna texts of the same title; the *Ratnakūṭa* probably began as part of a Mahāsāṃghika canon; and the now lost *Dhāraṇī Piṭaka* of the Dharmaguptaka school probably contained prototypes of the *dhāraṇī-sūtras* of the Mahāyāna tradition. The Mahāyānist monks never gave up the pre-Mahāyāna Vinaya. Many followed the Dharmaguptaka version, some the Mahāsāṃghika. Even the Vinaya of a school that fell squarely into the Hīnayāna camp, the Sarvāstivāda, was used as the basis for Mahāyāna monastic rule.

Still, the focus of much Mahāyāna rhetoric, especially in the earlier strata of the literature, is the critique of non-Mahāyāna forms of Buddhism, especially the ideal of the *arhat*. This is one of the leading themes of a work now believed to represent an early stage in the development of Mahāyāna, the *Raṣṭrapālaparipṛcchā*, a text of the *Ratnakūṭa* class. In this text, the monastic life is still exalted above all other forms of spiritual life, but the *bodhisattva* vows are presented for the first time as superior to the mere monastic vows.

It is difficult, if not impossible, to establish with any degree of certainty the early history of Mahāyāna literature. It seems, however, that the earliest extant Mahāyāna *sūtra* is the *Aṣṭasāhasrikāprajñāpāramitā*, or its verse rendering, the *Ratnaguṇasaṃcayagāthā*. Both reflect a polemic within Buddhism, centering on a critique of the "low aspirations" of those Buddhists who chose not to take the vows of the *bodhisattvas*. The *Ratnaguṇa* defines the virtues of the *bodhisattva*, emphasizing the transcendental insight or "perfect wisdom" (*prajñāpāramitā*) that frees him from all forms of attachment and preconceived notions—including notions of purity and world renunciation. An important aspect or complement of this wisdom is skill in means (*upāyakauśalya*)—defined here as the capacity to adapt thought, speech, and action to circumstances and to the ultimate purpose of Buddhist practice, freedom from attachment. This virtue allows the *bodhisattva* to remain in the world while being perfectly free from the world.

The *Aṣṭasāhasrikā* treats these same concepts, but also expands the concept of merit in at least two directions: (1) dedication of merit to awakening means here seeing through the illusion of merit as well as applying merit to the path of liberation; and (2) dedication of merit is an act of devotion to insight (wisdom, *prajñā*). As the goal and ground of all perfections (Pāramitā), Perfection of Wisdom is personified as the Mother of All Buddhas. She gives birth to the mind of awakening, but she is present in concrete form in the Sacred Book itself. Thus, the *Aṣṭasāhasrikāprajñāpāramitā Sūtra* is at the same time the medium expressing a sophisticated doctrine of salvation by insight and skill in means, the rationalization of a ritual system, and the object of worship.

Another early Mahāyāna text, the *Saddharmapuṇḍarīka* (Lotus Sutra), also attacks the *arhat* ideal. This *sūtra* is considered the paradigmatic text on the developed Buddhology of the Mahāyāna: the Buddha is presented as a supernatural being, eternal, unchanging; at the same time he is Buddha by virtue of the fact that he has become free from all conceptions of being and nonbeing. The Buddha never *attained* awakening or *nirvāṇa*—because he is Buddhahood, and has been in awakening and *nirvāṇa* since eternity, but also because there is no Buddhahood or *nirvāṇa* to be attained.

The widespread, but clearly not exclusively popular, belief in the Land of Bliss (Sukhāvatī) finds expression in two texts of the latter part of the early period (c. first to second century CE). The two *Sukhāvatī* sūtras express a faith in the saving grace of the *bodhisattva* Dharmākara, who under a former Buddha made the vow to purify his own Buddha field. The vows of this *bodhisattva* guarantee rebirth in his Land of Bliss to all those who think on him with faith. Rebirth in his land, furthermore, guarantees eventual enlightenment and liberation. The Indian history of these two texts, however, remains for the most part obscure.

The attitude of early Mahāyāna sūtras to laity and to women is relatively inconsistent. Thus, the *Ugradattaparipṛcchā* and the *Upāsakaśīla*, while pretending to preach a lay morality, use monastic models for the householder's life. But compared to the earlier tradition, the Mahāyāna represents a significant move in the direction of a religion that is less ascetic and monastic in tone and intent. Some Mahāyāna sūtras of the early period place laypersons in a central role. The main character in the *Gaṇḍavyūha*, for instance, is a young lay pilgrim who visits a number of *bodhisattvas* in search of the teaching. Among his teachers we find laymen and laywomen, as well as female night spirits and celestial *bodhisattvas*. The *Vimalakīrtinirdeśa* is more down-to-earth in its exaltation of the lay ideal. Although not without its miraculous events, it represents the demythologizing tendencies of Mahāyāna, which are often carried out to the extreme of affirming that the metaphoric meaning of one doctrine is exactly its opposite.

The Development of Mahāyāna. Although Buddhism flourished during the classical age of the Guptas, the cultural splendor in which it grew was also the harbinger of Hindu dominance. Sanskrit returned as the lingua franca of the subcontinent, and Hindu devotionalism began to displace the ideals of the Indic period. Mahāyāna must have been a divided movement even in its inception. Some of the divisions found in the Hīnayāna or pre-Mahāyāna schools from which Mahāyāna originated must have carried through into Mahāyāna itself. Unfortunately, we know much less of the early sectarian divisions in the movement than we know of the Eighteen Schools. It is clear, for instance, that the conception of the *bodhisattva* found among the Mahāsāṃghikas is different from that of the Sarvāstivādins. It appears also that the *Prajñāptivādins* conceived of the unconditioned dharmas in a manner different from other early schools. However, though we may speculate that some of these differences influenced the development of Mahāyāna, we have no solid evidence.

As pre-Mahāyāna Buddhism had developed a scholastic system to bolster its ideological position, Mahāyāna developed special forms of scholarly investigation. A new synthesis, in many ways far removed from the visionary faith underlying the religious aspects of Mahāyāna, grew in the established monasteries partly as a critique of earlier scholastic formulations, partly due to the need to explain and justify the new faith. Through this intellectual function the monastery reasserted its institutional position. Both monk and layman participated in giving birth to Mahāyāna and maintaining its social and liturgical life, but the intellectual leadership remained monastic and conservative. Therefore, Mahāyāna reform brought with it an element of continuity—monastic institutions and codes—that could be at the same time a cause for fossilization and stagnation. The monasteries would eventually grow to the point where they became a burden on society, at the same time that, as institutions of conservatism, they failed to adapt to a changing society.

Still, from the beginning of the Gupta dynasty to the earlier part of the Pāla dynasty the monasteries were centers of intellectual creativity. They continued to be supported under the Guptas, especially Kumāra Gupta I (414–455), who endowed a major monastery in a site in Bihar originally consecrated to Śāriputra. This monastic establishment, called Nālandā after the name of a local genie, probably had been active as a center of learning for several decades before Kumāra Gupta decided to give it special recognition. It would become the leading institution of higher learning in the Buddhist world for almost a thousand years. Together with the university of Valabhī in western India, Nālandā represents the scholastic side of Mahāyāna, which coexisted with a nonintellectual (not necessarily "popular") dimension, the outlines of which appear through archaeological remains, certain aspects of the sūtra literature, and the accounts of Chinese pilgrims.

Some texts suggest a conflict between forest and city dwellers that may in fact reflect the expected tension between the ascetic and the intellectual, or the meditator and the religious politician. But, lest this simple schema obliterate important aspects of Buddhist religious life, one must note that there is plentiful evidence of intense and constant interaction between the philosopher, the meditator, and the devotee—often all three functions coinciding in one person. Furthermore, the writings of great philosophical minds like Asaṅga, Śāntideva, and Āryadeva suggest an active involvement of the monk-*bodhisattva* in the social life of the community. The nonintellectual dimensions of the religion, therefore, must be seen as one aspect of a dialectic that resolved itself in synthesis as much as rivalry, tension, or dissonance.

Mahāyāna faith and devotion, moreover, was in itself a complex phenomenon, incorporating a liturgy of the High Tradition (e.g., the *Hymn to the Three Bodies of the Buddha*, attributed to Aśvaghoṣa) with elements of the nonliterary and non-Buddhist religion (e.g., pilgrimage cycles and the cult of local spirits, respectively), as well as generalized beliefs such as the dedication of merit and the hope of rebirth in a purified Buddha Land.

Developments in doctrine. In explaining the appearance of Mahāyāna, two extremes should be avoided carefully. On the one hand, one can exaggerate the points of continuity that link Mahāyāna with pre-Mahāyāna Buddhism; on the other, one can make a distinction so sharp that Mahāyāna appears as a radical break with the past, rather than a gradual process of growth. The truth lies somewhere between these two extremes: although Mahāyāna can be understood as a logical expansion of earlier Buddhist doctrine and practice, it is difficult to see how the phenomenon could be explained without assuming major changes in the social fabric of the Indian communities that provided the base for the religion. These changes, furthermore, are suggested by historical evidence.

The key innovations in doctrine can be divided into those that are primarily critiques of early scholastic constructs and those that reflect new developments in practice. In both types, of course, one should not ignore the influence of visionary or contemplative experience; but this aspect of the religion, unfortunately, cannot always be documented adequately. The most important doctrine of practical consequence was the *bodhisattva* doctrine; the most important theoretical development was the doctrine of emptiness (*śūnyatā*). The first can be understood also as the result of a certain vision of the concrete manifestation of the sacred; the second, as the expression of a new type of mystical or contemplative experience.

The bodhisattva. In pre-Mahāyāna Buddhism the term *bodhisattva* referred primarily to the figure of a Buddha from the time of his adoption of the vow to attain enlightenment to the point at which he attained Buddhahood. Even when used as an abstract designation of an ideal of perfection, the value of the ideal was determined by the goal: liberation from suffering. In the teachings of some of the Hīnayāna schools, however, the *bodhisattva* became an ideal with intrinsic value: to be a *bodhisattva* meant to adopt the vow (*praṇidhāna*) of seeking perfect awakening *for the sake of living beings*; that is, to follow the example set by the altruistic dedication of the Buddha in his former lives, when he was a *bodhisattva*, and not to aspire merely to individual liberation, as the *arhat*s were supposed to have done. The Mahāyāna made this critique its own, and the *bodhisattva* ideal its central religious goal.

This doctrinal stance accompanied a shift in mythology that has been outlined above: the belief in multiple *bodhisattvas* and the development of a complex legend of the former lives of the Buddha. There was likewise a change in ritual centered around the cult of the *bodhisattva*, especially of mythical *bodhisattvas* who were believed to be engaged in the pursuit of awakening primarily, if not exclusively, for the sake of assisting beings in need or distress. Closely allied with this was the increasing popularity of the recitation of *bodhisattva* vows.

Whereas the *bodhisattva* of early Buddhism stood for a human being on his way to become a liberated being, the *bodhisattva* that appears in the Mahāyāna reflects the culmination of a process of change that began when some of the Hīnayāna schools extended the apotheosis of the Buddha Śākyamuni to the *bodhisattva*—that is, when they idealized both the Buddha and the spiritual career outlined by the myth of his previous lives. Mahāyāna then extended the same religious revaluation to numerous mythical beings believed to be far advanced in the path of awakening. Accordingly, in its mythology Mahāyāna has more than one object of veneration. Especially in contrast to the more conservative Hīnayāna schools (the Sarvāstivāda and the Theravāda, for instance), Mahāyāna is the Buddhism of multiple Buddhas and *bodhisattvas*, residing in multiple realms, where they assist numberless beings on their way to awakening.

Accordingly, the early ideal of the *bodhisattva* as future Buddha is not discarded; rather it is redefined and expanded. As a theory of liberation, the characteristic position of Mahāyāna can be summarized by saying that it emphasizes *bodhi* and relegates *nirvāṇa* to a secondary position. Strictly speaking, this may represent an early split within the community rather than a shift in doctrine. One could speculate that it goes back to conflicting notions of means to liberation found among the shramanic religions: the conflict between enstasy and insight as means of liberation. But this analysis must be qualified by noting that the revaluation of *bodhi* must be seen in the context of the *bodhisattva* vow. The unique aspiration of the *bodhisattva* defines awakening as "awakening for the sake of all sentient beings." This is a concept that cannot be understood properly in the context of disputes regarding the relative importance of insight.

Furthermore, one should note that the displacement of *nirvāṇa* is usually effected through its redefinition, not by means of a rejection of the basic concept of "freedom from all attachment." Although the formalized texts of the vows often speak of the *bodhisattva* "postponing" his entrance into *nirvāṇa* until all living beings are saved, and the Buddha is asked in prayer to remain in the world without entering *nirvāṇa*, the central doctrine implies that a *bodhisattva* would not even consider a *nirvāṇa* of the type sought by the *arhat*. The *bodhisattva* is defined more by his aspiration for a different type of *nirvāṇa* than by a rejection or postponement of *nirvāṇa* as such. The gist of this new doctrine of *nirvāṇa* can be summarized in a definition of liberation as a state of peace in which the liberated person is neither attached to peace nor attached to the turmoil of the cycle of rebirth. It is variously named and defined: either by an identity of *saṃsāra* and *nirvāṇa* or by proposing a *nirvāṇa* in which one can find no support (*apratiṣṭhitanirvāṇa*).

As noted above, in the early conception a *bodhisattva* is a real human being. This aspect of the doctrine is not lost in Mahāyāna, but preserved in the belief that the aspiration to perfect awakening (the *bodhicitta*) and the *bodhisattva* vow should be adopted by all believers. By taking up the vow—by conversion or by ritual repetition—the Mahāyāna Buddhist, monk or layperson, actualizes the *bodhicitta* and progresses toward the goal of becoming a *bodhisattva*. Also uniquely Mahāyāna is the belief that these human aspirants to awakening are not alone—they are accompanied and protected by "celestial *bodhisattvas*," powerful beings far advanced in the path, so perfect that they are free from both rebirth and liberation, and can now choose freely if, when, and where they are to be reborn. They engage freely in the process of rebirth only to save living beings.

What transforms the human and ethical ideal into a religious ideal, and into the object of religious awe, is the scale in which the *bodhisattva* path is conceived. From the first aspiration to awakening (*bodhicitta*) and the affirmation of the vow to the attainment of final enlightenment and liberation, countless lives intervene. The *bodhisattva* has to traverse ten stages (*bhūmi*), beginning with the intense practice of the virtue of generosity (primarily a lay virtue), passing through morality in the second stage, patience in the third, then fortitude, meditation, insight, skill in means, vows, powers, and the highest knowledge of a Buddha. The stages, therefore, correspond with the ten perfections (*pāramitā*). Although all perfections are practiced in every stage, they are mastered in the order in which they are listed in the scheme of the stages, suggesting at one end of the spectrum a simple and accessible practice for the majority of believers, the human *bodhisattva*, and at the other end a stage clearly unattainable in the realm of normal human circumstances, reserved for semidivine Buddhas and *bodhisattvas*, the object of worship. Although some exceptional human beings may qualify for the status of advanced *bodhisattvas*, most of these ideal beings are the mythic objects of religious fervor and imagination.

Among the mythic or celestial *bodhisattvas* the figure of Maitreya—destined to be the next Buddha of this world system after Śākyamuni—clearly represents the earliest stage of the myth. His cult is especially important in East Asian Buddhism. Other celestial *bodhisattvas* include Mañjuśrī, the *bodhisattva* of wisdom, the patron of scripture, obviously less important in the general cultus but an important *bodhisattva* in monastic devotion. The most important liturgical role is reserved for Avalokiteśvara, the *bodhisattva* of compassion, whose central role in worship is attested by archaeology.

Emptiness. The doctrine of emptiness (*śūnyatā*) represents a refinement of the ancient doctrine of no-self. In some ways it is merely an extension of the earlier doctrine: the denial of the substantial reality of the self and what belongs to the self, as a means to effect a breaking of the bonds of attachment. The notion of emptiness, however, expresses a critique of our common notions of reality that is much more radical than the critique implicit in the doctrine of no-self. The Mahāyāna critique is in fact unacceptable to other Buddhists, for it is in a manner of speaking a critique of Buddhism. Emptiness of all things implies the groundlessness of all ideas and conceptions, including, ultimately, Buddhist doctrines themselves.

The doctrine of emptiness was developed by the philosophical schools, but clearly inspired by the tradition of the Mahāyāna sūtras. Thus we read: "Even *nirvāṇa* is like a magical creation, like a dream, how much more any other object or idea (*dharma*). . .? Even a Perfect Buddha is like a magical creation, like a dream. . ." (*Aṣṭasāhasrikā*, p. 40). The practical correlate of the doctrine of emptiness is the concept of "skill in means" (*upāya*): Buddhist teachings are not absolute statements about reality, they are means to a higher goal beyond all views. In their cultural context these two doctrines probably served as a way of making Buddhist doctrine malleable to diverse populations. By placing the truth of Buddhism beyond the specific content of its religious practices, these two doctrines justified adaptation to changing circumstances and the adoption of new religious customs.

But emptiness, like the *bodhisattva* vows, also reflects the Mahāyāna understanding of the ultimate experience of Buddhism—understood both as a dialectic and a meditational process. This experience can be described as an awareness that nothing is self-existent. Dialectically, this means that there is no way that the mind can consistently think of any thing as having an existence of its own. All concepts of substance and existence vanish when they are examined closely and rationally. As a religious experience the term *emptiness* refers to a direct perception of this absence of self-existence, a perception that is only possible through mental cultivation, and which is a liberating experience. Liberation, in fact, has been redefined in a way reminiscent of early texts such as the *Suttanipāta*. Liberation is now the freedom resulting from the negation of all assumptions about reality, even Buddhist assumptions.

> The cessation of grasping and reifying,
> calming the plural mind—this is bliss.
>
> The Buddha never taught any thing/doctrine [*dharma*]
> to anyone anywhere. (*Madhyamakakārikā* 25.24)

Finally, emptiness is also an affirmation of the immanence of the sacred. Applied to the turmoil of the sphere of rebirth (*saṃsāra*), it points to the relative value and reality of the world and at the same time transforms it into the sacred, the experience of awakening. Applied to the sphere of liberation (*nirvāṇa*), emptiness is a critique of the conception of liberation as a religious goal outside the world of impermanence and suffering.

Other views of the Absolute. Mahāyāna developed early notions of the supernatural and the sacred that guaranteed an exalted status to the symbols of its mystical and ethical ideals. Its notion of extraordinary beings populating supernal Buddha fields and coming to the aid of suffering sentient beings necessitated a metaphysic and cosmology that could offer concrete images of a transcendent sacred. Accordingly, the abstract, apophatic concept of emptiness was often qualified by, or even rejected in favor of, positive statements and concrete images.

Pre-Mahāyāna traditions had emphasized impermanence and no-self: to imagine that there is permanence in the impermanent is the most noxious error. Mahāyāna introduced the notion of emptiness, urging us to give up the notion of permanence, but to give up the notion of impermanence as well. Within the Mahāyāna camp others proposed that there was something permanent within the impermanent. Texts like the [*Mahāyāna*] *Mahāparinirvāṇa Sūtra* asserted that the Buddha himself had taught a doctrine of permanence: the seed of Buddhahood, innate enlightenment, is permanent, blissful, pure—indeed, it is the true self, present in the impermanent mind and body of sentient beings.

The *tathāgata* as object of worship was associated with "suchness" (*tathatā*), his saving actions were seen as taking effect in a world formed in the image of the dharma and its ultimate truth (*dharmadhātu*), and his form as repository of all goodness and virtue represented his highest form.

A doctrine common to all Mahāyānists sought to establish a link between the absolute and common human beings. The Tathāgata was conceived of as having several aspects to his person: the human Buddha or "Body of Magical Apparition" (*nirmāṇakāya*), that is, the historical persons of Buddhas; the transcendent sacred, the Buddha of the paradises and Buddha fields, who is also the form that is the object of worship (*saṃbhogakāya*); and the Buddha as Suchness, as nonduality, the *tathāgata* as embodiment of the *dharmadhātu*, called the "Dharma Body" (*dharmakāya*).

Developments in practice. The practice of meditation was for the Mahāyānist part of a ritual process beginning with the first feelings of compassion for other sentient beings, formulating the vow, including the expression of a strong desire to save all sentient beings and share one's merit with them, followed by the cultivation of the analysis of all existents, reaching a pinnacle in the experience of emptiness but culminating in the dedication of these efforts to the salvation of others.

Worship and ritual. The uniquely Mahāyāna aspect of the ritual is the threefold service (*triskandhaka*). Variously defined, this bare outline of the essential Mahāyāna ritual is explained by the seventh-century poet Śāntideva as consisting of a confession of sins, formal rejoicing at the merit of others, and a request to all Buddhas that they remain in the world for the sake of suffering sentient beings. A pious Buddhist was expected to perform this threefold ritual three times in the day and three times in the night.

A text known as the *Triskandhaka*, forming part of the *Upālipariprcchā*, proves the central role of confession and dedication of merit. The act of confession is clearly a continuation of the ancient Prātimokṣa ritual. Other elements of continuity include a link with early nonliterary tradition (now integrated into scripture) in the role of the dedication of merit, and a link with the general Buddhist tradition of the Three Refuges.

More complicated liturgies were in use. Several versions remain in the extant literature. Although many of them are said to be "the sevenfold service" (*saptavidhānuttarapūjā*), the number seven is to be taken as an abstract number. The most important elements of the longer liturgies are the salutation to the Buddhas and *bodhisattvas*, the act of worship, the act of contrition, delight in the merit of others, and the dedication of merit. Xuanzang, the seventh-century Chinese pilgrim to India, describes, albeit cursorily, some of the liturgies in use in the Indian monasteries of his time.

Most common forms of ritual, however, must have been less formalized and less monkish. The common rite is best represented by the litany of Avalokiteśvara, preserved in the literature and the monuments. In its literary form it is a solemn statement of the *bodhisattva*'s capacity to save from peril those who call on his name. But in actual practice, one can surmise, the cult of Avalokiteśvara included then, as it does today in East Asia, prayers of petition and apotropaic invocations.

The basic liturgical order of the literary tradition was embellished with elements from general Indian religious custom, especially from the styles of worship called *pūjā*. These included practices such as bathing the sacred image, carrying it in procession, offering cloth, perfume, and music to the icon, and so forth.

Ritual practices were also expanded in the monastic tradition. For instance, another text also going by the title *Triskandhaka* (but preserved only in Tibetan translation) shows an intimate connection between ritual and meditation, as it integrates—like many monastic manuals of meditation—the typical daily ritual cycle with a meditation session.

Meditation. The practice of meditation was as important in the Mahāyāna tradition as it had been before. The maps of the path and the meditation manuals of Mahāyāna Buddhists give us accounts, if somewhat idealized ones, of the process of meditation. Although no systematic history of Mahāyāna meditation has been attempted yet, it is obvious that there are important synchronic and diachronic differences among Mahāyāna Buddhists in India. Considering, nevertheless, only those elements that are common to the various systems, one must note first an element of continuity with the past in the use of a terminology very similar to that of the Mahīśāsakas and the Sarvāstivāda, and in the acceptance, with little change, of traditional lists of objects and states of contemplation.

The interpretation of the process, however, and the definition of the higher stages of contemplation differed radically from that of the Hīnayāna schools. The principal shift is in the definition of the goal as a state in which the object of contemplation (*ālambana*) is no longer present to the mind (*nirālambana*). All the mental images (or "marks," *nimitta*, *saṃjñā*) that form the basis for conceptual thought and attachment must be abandoned through a process of mental calm and analysis, until the contemplative reaches a state of peaceful concentration free of mental marks (*ānimitta*), free of conceptualizations (*nirvikalpa-samādhi*).

These changes in contemplative theory are closely connected to the abandonment of the *dharma* theory and the doctrine of no-self as the theoretical focus of speculative mysticism. One may say that the leading theme of Mahāyāna contemplative life is the meditation on emptiness. But one must add that the scholastic traditions are very careful to define the goal as constituted by both emptiness and compassion (*karuṇā*). The higher state of freedom from conceptions (the "supramundane knowledge") must be followed by return to the world to fulfill the vows of the *bodhisattva*—the highest contemplative stage is, at least in theory, a preparation for the practice of compassion.

The new ethics. The *bodhisattva* ideal also implied new ethical notions. Two themes prevail in Mahāyāna ethical speculation: the altruistic vow and life in the world. Both themes reflect changes in the social context of Buddhism: a greater concern, if not a stronger role for, lay life and its needs and aspirations and a cultural context requiring universal social values. The altruistic ideal is embodied in the *bodhisattva* vows and in the creation of a new set of ethical rules, commonly known as the "Bodhisattva Vinaya." A number of Mahāyāna texts are said to represent this new "Vinaya." Among these, the *Bodhisattvaprātimokṣa* was especially important in India. It prescribes a liturgy for the ritual adoption of the *bodhisattva* vows, which is clearly based on the earlier rites of ordination (*upasaṃpadā*). Although the Mahāyāna Vinaya Sūtras never replaced in India the earlier monastic codes, they preserved and transmitted important, and at times obligatory, rites of monastic and lay initiation, and were considered essential supplements to traditional monastic Vinaya.

THE HIGH TRADITION AND THE UNIVERSITIES. The most important element in the institutionalization of Mahāyāna was perhaps the establishment of Buddhist universities. In these centers of learning the elaboration of Buddhist doctrine became the most important goal of Buddhist monastic life. First at Nālandā and Valabhī, then, as the Pāla dynasty took control of East Central India (c. 650), at the universities of Vikramaśīla and Odantapurī, Mahāyāna scholars trained disciples from different parts of the Buddhist world and elaborated subtle systems of textual interpretation and philosophical speculation.

The Mahāyāna synthesis. Although eventually they would not be able to compete with more resilient forms of Buddhism and Hinduism, the Mahāyāna scholars played a leading role in the creation of a Mahāyāna synthesis that would satisfy both the intelligentsia and the common believers for at least five hundred years. Devotion, ritual, ethics, metaphysics, and logic formed part of this monument to Indian philosophical acumen. Even as the ruthless Mihirakula, the Ephthalite ("White") Hun, was invading India from the northwest (c. 500–528) and the Chalukya dynasty was contributing to a Hindu renaissance in the southwest (c. 550–753), India allowed for the development of great minds—such distinguished philosophical figures as Dignāga and Sthiramati, who investigated subtle philosophical issues. Persecution by Mihirakula (c. 550) was followed by the reign of one of the great patrons of Buddhism, Harṣa Vardhana (c. 605–647). Once more Buddhism was managing to survive on the seesaw of Indian politics.

Schools. The scholastic tradition of Mahāyāna can be divided into three schools: Mādhyamika (Madhyamaka), Yogācāra, and the school of Sāramati. The first two dominated the intellectual life of Mahāyāna in India. The third had a short-lived but important influence on Tibet, and indirectly may be considered an important element in the development of East Asian Buddhism.

Mādhyamika. The founder of this school can also be regarded as the father of Mahāyāna scholasticism and philosophy. Nāgārjuna (fl. c. 150 CE) came from South India, possibly from the Amarāvatī region. Said to have been the advisor to one of the Śātavāhana monarchs, he became the first major philosopher of Mahāyāna and a figure whose ideas influenced all its schools. The central theme of his philosophy is emptiness (*śūnyatā*) understood as a corollary of the pre-Mahāyāna theory of dependent origination. Emptiness is the Middle Way between affirmations of being and nonbeing. The extremes of existence and nonexistence are avoided by recognizing certain causal relations (e.g., the path and liberation) without predicating a self-existence or immutable essence (*svabhāva*) to either cause or effect. To defend his views without establishing a metaphysical thesis, Nāgārjuna argues by reducing to the absurd all the alternative philosophical doctrines recognized in his day. For his own "system," Nāgārjuna claims to have no thesis to affirm beyond his rejection of the affirmations and negations of all metaphysical systems. Therefore, Nāgārjuna's system is "the school of the Middle" (*madhyamaka*) both as an ontology (neither being nor nonbeing) and as a logic (neither affirmation nor negation). In religious terms, Nāgārjuna's Middle Way is summarized in his famous statement that *saṃsāra* and *nirvāṇa* are the same.

Three to four centuries after Nāgārjuna the Mādhyamika school split into two main branches, called Prāsaṅgika and Svātantrika. The first of these, represented by Buddhapālita (c. 500) and Candrakīrti (c. 550–600), claimed that in order to be faithful to the teachings of Nāgārjuna, philosophers had to confine themselves to the critique of opposing views by *reductio ad absurdum.* The Svātantrikas, on the other hand, claimed that the Mādhyamika philosopher had to formulate his own thesis; in particular, he needed his own epistemology. The main exponent of this view was Buddhapālita's great critic Bhāvaviveka (c. 500–550). The debate continued for some time but was eclipsed by other philosophical issues; for the Mādhyamika school eventually assimilated elements of other Mahāyāna traditions, especially those of the logicians and the Yogācārins.

Mādhyamika scholars also contributed to the development of religious literature. Several hymns (*stava*) are attributed to Nāgārjuna. His disciple Āryadeva discusses the *bodhisattva*'s career in his *Bodhisattva-yogācāra-catuḥśataka,* although the work deals mostly with philosophical issues. Two anthological works, one attributed to Nāgārjuna, the *Sūtrasamuccaya,* and the other to the seventh-century Śāntideva, the *Śikśāsamuccaya,* became guides to the ritual and ethical practices of Mahāyāna. Śāntideva also wrote a "guide" to the *bodhisattva*'s career, the *Bodhicaryāvatāra,* a work that gives us a sampling of the ritual and contemplative practices of Mādhyamika monks, as well as a classical survey of the philosophical issues that engaged their attention.

Yogācāra. Approximately two centuries after Nāgārjuna, during the transition period from Kushan to Gupta power, a new school of Mahāyāna philosophy arose in the northwest. The founders of this school, the brothers Asaṅga (c. 310–390) and Vasubandhu (c. 320–400), had begun as scholars in the Hīnayāna schools. Asaṅga, the elder brother, was trained in the Mahīśāsaka school. Many important features of the Abhidharma theories of this school remained in Asaṅga's Mahāyāna system. Vasubandhu, who converted to Mahāyāna after his brother had become an established scholar of the school, began as a Sautrāntika with an extraordinary command of Sarvāstivādin theories. Therefore, when he did become a Mahāyānist he too brought with him a Hīnayāna scholastic grid on which to organize and rationalize Mahāyāna teachings.

The school founded by the two brothers is known as the Yogācāra, perhaps following the title of Asaṅga's major work, the *Yogācārabhūmi* (sometimes attributed to Maitreya), but clearly expressing the centrality of the practice of self-cultivation, especially through meditation. In explaining the experiences arising during the practice of yoga, the school proposes the two doctrines that characterize it: (1) the experience of enstasy leads to the conviction that there is nothing but mind (*cittamātratā*), or the world is nothing but a perceptual construct (*vijñaptimātratā*); (2) the analysis of mind carried out during meditation reveals different levels of perception or awareness, and, in the depths of consciousness, the basis for rebirth and karmic determination, a storehouse consciousness (*ālaya-vijñāna*) containing the seeds of former actions. Varying emphasis on these two principles characterize different modes of the doctrine. The doctrine of mind-only dominates Vasubandhu's *Viṃśatikā* and *Triṃśikā*; the analysis of the *ālaya-vijñāna* is more central to Asaṅga's doctrine. Since both aspects of the doctrine can be understood as theories of consciousness (*vijñāna*), the school is sometimes called Vijñānavāda.

One of the first important divisions within the Yogācāra camp reflected geographical as well as doctrinal differences. The school of Valabhī, following Sthiramati (c. 500–560), opposed the Yogācārins of Nālandā, led by Dharmapāla (c. 530–561). The point at issue, whether the pure mind is the same as the storehouse consciousness, illustrates the subtleties of Indian philosophical polemics but also reflects the influence of another school, the school of Sāramati, as well as the soteriological concerns underlying the psychological theories of Yogācāra. The debate on this point would continue in the Mādhyamika school, involving issues of the theory of perception as well as problems in the theory of the liberated mind.

Tathāgata-garbha theory. Another influential school followed the tendency—already expressed in some Mahāyāna sūtras—toward a positive definition or description of ultimate reality. The emphasis in this school was on the ontological basis for the experience and virtues of Buddhahood. This basis was found in the underlying or innate Buddhahood of all beings. The school is known under two names; one describes its fundamental doctrine, the theory of *tathāgata-garbha* (the presence of the Tathāgata in all beings), the other refers to its purported systematizer, Sāramati (c. 350–450). The school's emphasis on a positive foundation of being associates it closely with the thought of Maitreyānatha, the teacher of Asaṅga, to whom is often attributed one of the fundamental texts of the school, the *Ratnagotravibhāga*. It may be that Maitreya's thought gave rise to two lines of interpretation—*tathāgata-garbha* and *cittamātratā*.

Sāramati wrote a commentary on the Ratnagotravibhāga in which he explains the process whereby innate Buddhahood becomes manifest Buddhahood. The work is critical of the theory of emptiness and describes the positive attributes of Buddhahood. The *bodhisattva*'s involvement in the world is seen not so much as the abandonment of the bliss of liberation as it is the manifestation of the Absolute (*dharmadhātu*) in the sphere of sentient beings, a concept that can be traced to Mahāsāṃghika doctrines. The *dharmadhātu* is a positive, metaphysical absolute, not only eternal, but pure, the locus of ethical, soteric, and epistemological value. This absolute is also the basis for the *gotra*, or spiritual lineage, which is a metaphor for the relative potential for enlightenment in living beings.

The logicians. An important development in Buddhist scholarship came about as a result of the concern of scholastics with the rules of debate and their engagement in philosophical controversies with Hindu logicians of the Nyāya school. Nāgārjuna and Vasubandhu wrote short treatises on logic, but a creative and uniquely Buddhist logic and epistemology did not arise until the time of Dignāga (c. 480–540), a scholar who claimed allegiance to Yogācāra but adopted a number of Sautrāntika doctrines. The crowning achievement of Buddhist logic was the work of Dharmakīrti (c. 600–650), whose *Pramāṇavārttika* and its *Vṛtti* revised critically the whole field. Although his work seems on the surface not relevant for the history of religion, it is emblematic of the direction of much of the intellectual effort of Mahāyāna scholars after the fifth century.

Yogācāra-Mādhyamika philosophers. As India moved away from the security of the Gupta period, Mahāyāna Buddhist philosophy gradually moved in the direction of eclecticism. By the time the university at Vikramaśīla was founded in the eighth century the dominant philosophy at Nālandā was a combination of Mādhyamika and Yogācāra, with the latter as the qualifying term and Mādhyamika as the core of the philosophy. This movement had roots in the earlier Svātantrika Mādhyamika and like its predecessor favored the formulation of ontological and epistemological theses in defense of Nāgārjuna's fundamental doctrine of emptiness. The most distinguished exponent of this school was Śāntirakṣita (c. 680–740); but some of his theories were challenged from within the movement by his contemporary Jñānagarbha (c. 700–760). The greatest contribution to religious thought, however, came from their successors. Kamalaśīla (c. 740–790), a disciple of Śāntirakṣita who continued the latter's mission in Tibet, wrote a number of brilliant works on diverse aspects of philosophy. He traveled to Tibet, where he wrote three treatises on meditation and the *bodhisattva* path, each called *Bhāvanākrama*, which must be counted among the jewels of Indian religious thought.

New scriptures. The philosophers found their main source of inspiration in the Mahāyāna sūtras, most of which did not advocate clearly defined philosophical theories. Some sūtras, however, do express positions that can be associated with the doctrines of particular schools. Although scholars agree that these compositions are later than texts without a clear doctrinal affiliation, the connection between the sūtras and the schools they represent is not always clear.

For instance, some of the characteristic elements of the school of Sāramati are clearly pre-Mahāyānic, and can also be found in a number of sūtras from the *Avataṃsaka* and *Ratnakūṭa* collections. However, Sāramati appealed to a select number of Mahāyāna sūtras that clustered around the basic themes of the school. Perhaps the most famous is the *Srīmālādevīsiṃhanāda*, but equally important are the

[*Mahāyāna*] *Mahāparinirvāṇa Sūtra,* the *Anūnatvāpūrṇatvanirdeśa,* and the *Dhāraṇīrāja.*

A number of Mahāyāna sūtras of late composition were closely associated with the Yogācāra school. Although they were known already at the time of Asaṅga and Vasubandhu, in their present form they reflect a polemic that presupposes some form of proto-Yogācāra theory. Among these the *Laṅkāvatāra* and the *Saṃdhinirmocana* are the most important from a philosophical point of view. The first contains an early form of the theory of levels of *vijñāna.*

Decline of Mahāyāna. It is difficult to assess the nature and causes of the decay of Mahāyāna in India. Although it is possible to argue that the early success of Mahāyāna led to a tendency to look inward, that philosophers spent their time debating subtle metaphysical, logical, or even grammatical points, the truth is that even during the period of technical scholasticism, constructive religious thought was not dormant. But it may be that as Mahāyāna became more established and conventional, the natural need for religious revival found expression in other vehicles. Most likely Mahāyāna thinkers participated in the search for new forms of expression, appealing once more to visionary, revolutionary and charismatic leaders. But the new life gradually would adopt an identity of its own, first as Tantric Buddhism, eventually as Hinduism. For, in adopting Tantric practices and symbols, Mahāyāna Buddhists appealed to a symbolic and ritual world that fit naturally with a religious substratum that was about to become the province of Hinduism.

The gradual shift from Mahāyāna to Tantra seems to have gained momentum precisely at the time when Mahāyāna philosophy was beginning to lose its creative energy. We know of Tantric practices at Nālandā in the seventh century. These practices were criticized by the Nālandā scholar Dharmakīrti but apparently were accepted by most distinguished scholars of the same institution during the following century. As Tantra gained respectability, the Pāla monarchs established new centers of learning, rivaling Nālandā. We may say that the death of its great patron, King Harṣa, in 657 signals the decline of Mahāyāna, whereas the construction of the University of Vikramaśīla under Dharmapāla about the year 800 marks the beginning of the Tantric period.

Tantric Innovations. As with Mahāyāna, we must assume that Tantra reflects social as well as religious changes. Because of the uncertainties of the date of its origin, however, few scholars have ventured any explanation for the arising of Tantra. Some advocate an early origin for Tantra, suggesting that the literature existed as an esoteric practice for many centuries before it ever came to the surface. If this were the case, then Tantra must have existed as some kind of underground movement long before the sixth century. But this theory must still explain the sudden appearance of Tantrism as a mainstream religion.

In its beginnings, Buddhist Tantra may have been a minority religion, essentially a private cult incorporating elements from the substratum frowned upon by the Buddhist establishment. It echoed ancient practices such as the critical rites of the *Atharvaveda* tradition, and the initiatory ceremonies, Aryan and non-Aryan, known to us from other Brahmanic sources. Starting as a marginal phenomenon, it eventually gained momentum, assuming the same role Mahāyāna had assumed earlier; a force of innovation and a vehicle for the expression of dissatisfaction with organized religion. The followers of Tantra became the new critics of the establishment. Some asserted the superiority of techniques of ritual and meditation that would lead to a direct, spontaneous realization of Buddhahood in this life. As wandering saints called *siddhas* ("possessed of *siddhi,*" i. e., realization or magical power), they assumed the demeanor of madmen, and abandoned the rules of the monastic code. Others saw Tantra as the culmination of Mahāyāna and chose to integrate it with earlier teachings, following established monastic practices even as they adopted beliefs that challenged the traditional assumptions of Buddhist monasticism.

The documented history of Tantra, naturally, reveals more about the second group. It is now impossible to establish with all certainty how the substratum affected Buddhist Tantra—whether, for instance, the metaphoric use of sexual practices preceded their explicit use, or vice versa. But is seems clear that the new wandering ascetics and their ideology submitted to the religious establishment even as they changed it. Tantra followed the pattern of cooperation with established religious institutions set by Mahāyāna in its relationship to the early scholastic establishment. Tantric monks would take the *bodhisattva* vows and receive monastic ordination under the pre-Mahāyāna code. Practitioners of Tantra would live in the same monastery with non-Tantric Mahāyāna monks. Thus Tantric Buddhism became integrated into the Buddhist high tradition even as the *siddhas* continued to challenge the values of Buddhist monasticism.

Although it seems likely that Tantric Buddhism existed as a minority, esoteric practice among Mahāyāna Buddhists before it made its appearance on the center stage of Indian religion, it is now impossible to know for how long and in what form it existed before the seventh century. The latter date alone is certain because the transmission of Tantra to China is marked by the arrival in the Chinese capitals of Tantric masters like Śubhākarasiṃha (arrives in Ch'ang-an 716) and Vajrabodhi (arrives in Lo-yang 720), and we can safely assume that the exportation of Tantra beyond the Indian border could not have been possible without a flourishing activity in India. Evidence for an earlier origin is found in the occasional reference, critical or laudatory, to *mantras* and *dhāraṇīs* in the literature of the seventh century (Dharmakīrti, Śāntideva) and the presence of proto-Tantric elements in Mahāyāna sūtras that must date from at least the fourth century (*Gaṇḍavyūha, Vimalakīrtinirdeśa, Saddharmapuṇḍarīka*).

Tantra in general makes use of ritual, symbolic, and doctrinal elements of earlier form of Buddhism. Especially the apotropaic and mystical formulas called *mantras* and *dhāraṇīs* gain a central role in Tantrayāna. The *Mahāmāyūrī*, a proto-Tantric text of the third or fourth century, collects apotropaic formulas associated with local deities in different parts of India. Some of these formulas seem to go back to parittas similar to those in the Pali canonical text *Āṭāṇātiya Suttanta* (*Dīgha Nikāya* no. 32). Although one should not identify the relatively early, and pan-Buddhist, genre of the *dhāraṇī* and *paritta* with the Tantrayāna, the increased use of these formulas in most existing forms of Buddhism, and the appearance of *dhāraṇī-sūtras* in late Mahāyāna literature perhaps marks a shift towards greater emphasis on the magical dimension of Buddhist faith. The Mahāyāna sūtras also foreshadow Tantra with their doctrine of the identity of the awakened and the afflicted minds (*Dharmasaṅgīti, Vimalakīrtinirdeśa*), and innate Buddhahood (Tathāgatagarbha sūtras).

Varieties of Tantra. Whatever may have been its prehistory, as esoteric or exoteric practice, the new movement—sometimes called the third *yāna*, Tantrayāna—was as complex and fragmented as earlier forms of Buddhism. A somewhat artificial, but useful classification distinguishes three main types of Tantra: Vajrayāna, Sahajayāna, and *Kālacakra* Tantra. The first established the symbolic terminology and the liturgy that would characterize all forms of the tradition. Many of these iconographic and ritual forms are described in the *Mañjuśrīmūlakalpa* (finished in its extant form c. 750), the *Mahāvairocana Sūtra*, and the *Vajraśekhara* (or *Tattvasaṃgraha*) *Sūtra*, which some would, following East Asian traditions, classify under a different, more primitive branch of Tantra called "Mantrayāna." The Sahajayāna was dominated by long-haired, wandering *siddhas*, who openly challenged and ridiculed the Buddhist establishment. They referred to the object of their religious experience as "the whore," both as a reference to the sexual symbolism of ritual Tantra and as a challenge to monastic conceptions of spiritual purity, but also as a metaphor for the universal accessibility of enlightenment. The *Kālacakra* tradition is the farthest removed from earlier Buddhist traditions, and shows a stronger influence from the substratum. It incorporates concepts of messianism and astrology not attested elsewhere in Buddhist literature.

Unfortunately, the history of all three of these movements is clouded in legend. Tibetan tradition considers the Mantrayāna a third "turning of the wheel [of the dharma]" (with Mahāyāna as the second), taking place in Dhānyakaṭaka (Andhra) sixteen years after the enlightenment. But this is patently absurd. As a working hypothesis, we can propose that there was an early stage of Mantrayāna beginning in the fourth century. The term *Vajrayāna* could be used then to describe the early documented manifestations of Tantric practice, especially in the high tradition of the Ganges River valley after the seventh century.

Sahajayāna is supposed to have originated with the Kashmirian yogin Lūi-pa (c. 750–800). The earliest documented Sahajayānists are from Bengal, but probably from the beginning of the ninth century. Regarding the *Kālacakra*, Western scholarship would not accept traditional views of its ancient origins in the mythic land of Shambhala. It must be dated not earlier than the tenth century, probably to the beginning of the reign of King Mahīpāla (c. 974–1026). Its roots have been sought in the North as well as in the South.

The Vajrayāna. The Vajrayāna derives its name from the centrality of the concept of *vajra* in its symbolism. The word *vajra* means both "diamond" and "cudgel." It is therefore a metaphor for hardness and destructiveness. Spiritually, it represents the eternal, innate state of Buddhahood possessed by all beings, as well as the cutting edge of wisdom. The personification of this condition and power is Vajrasattva, a deity and an abstract principle, which is defined as follows:

> By *vajra* is meant emptiness;
> *sattva* means pure cognition.
>
> The identity of these two is known
> as the essence of Vajrasattva. (*Advayavajra Saṃgraha*, p. 24)

Behind this definition is clearly the metaphysics of Yogācāra-Mādhyamika thought. Vajrasattva stands for the nondual experience that transcends both emptiness and pure mind. In religious terms this principle represents a homology between the human person and the essence of *vajra*: in the human body, in this life, relative and absolute meet.

The innate quality of the nondual is also represented by the concept of the "thought of awakening" (*bodhicitta*). But innate awakening in Vajrayāna becomes the goal: enlightenment is present in its totality and perfection in this human body; the thought of awakening is awakening:

> The Thought of Awakening is known to be
> Without beginning or end, quiescent,
> Free from being and nonbeing, powerful,
> Undivided in emptiness and compassion. (*Guhyasamāja* 18.37)

This identity is established symbolically and ritually by a series of homologies. For instance, the six elements of the human body are identified with different aspects of the body of *Mahāvairocana*, the five constituents of the human personality (*skandhas*) are identified with the five forms of Buddha knowledge.

But the most characteristic aspect of Tantric Buddhism generally is the extension of these homologies to sexual symbolism. The "thought of awakening" is identified with semen, dormant wisdom with a woman waiting to be inseminated. Therefore, wisdom *(prajñā)* is conceived as a female deity. She is a mother *(jananī)*, as in the Prajñāpāramitā literature; she is the female yogi *(yoginī)*; but she is also a low-caste whore *(ḍombī caṇḍālī)*. Skillful means (*upāya*) are visualized as her male consort. The perfect union of these two (*prajñopāya-yuganaddha*) is the union of the nondual. Behind the Buddhist interpretation, of course, one discovers the non-Aryan substratum, with its emphasis on fertility and the symbolism of the mother goddess. But one may also see this radical departure from Buddhist monkish prudery as an attempt to shock the establishment out of self-righteous complacency.

Because the sexual symbolism can be understood metaphorically, most forms of Buddhist Tantra were antinomian only in principle. Thus, Vajrayāna was not without its vows and rules. As *upāya*, the symbols of ritual had as their goal the integration of the Absolute and the relative, not the abrogation of the latter. Tantric vows included traditional monastic rules, the *bodhisattva* vows, and special Tantric rules—some of which are contained in texts such as the *Vinayasūtra* and the *Bodhicittaśīlādānakalpa.*

The practice of the higher mysteries was reserved for those who had mastered the more elementary Mahāyāna and Tantra practices. The hierarchy of practice was established in systems such as the "five steps" of the *Pañcakrama* (by the Tantric Nāgārjuna). Generally, the order of study protected the higher mysteries, establishing the dividing line between esoteric and exoteric. Another common classification of the types of Tantra distinguished external daily rituals (Kriyā Tantra), special rituals serving as preparation for meditation, (Caryā Tantra), basic meditation practices (Yoga Tantra), and the highest, or advanced meditation Tantras (Anuttarayoga Tantra). This hermeneutic of sorts served both as an apologetic and a doctrinal classification of Tantric practice by distinguishing the audience for which each type of Tantra was best suited: respectively *śrāvakas*, *pratyekabuddhas*, Yogācārins, and Mādhyamikas.

Elements of Tathāgata-garbha theory seem to have been combined with early totemic beliefs to establish a system of Tathāgata families or clans that also served to define the proper audience for a variety of teachings. Persons afflicted by delusion, for instance, belonged to Mahāvairocana's clan, and should cultivate the homologies and visualizations associated with this Buddha—who, not coincidentally, represents the highest awakening. This system extends the homologies of *skandhas*, levels of knowledge, and so forth, to personality types. This can be understood as a practical psychology that forms part of the Tantric quest for the immanence of the sacred.

The Sahaja (or Sahajiyā) movement. Although traditional Sahaja master-to-disciple lineages present it as a movement of great antiquity, the languages used in extant Sahaja literature belong to an advanced stage in the development of New Indic. These works were written mostly in Apabhrāṃśa (the *Dohākośa*) and early Bengali (the *Caryāgīti*). Thus, although their dates are uncertain, they cannot go as far back as suggested by tradition. Scholars generally agree on a conjectural dating of perhaps eighth to tenth century.

Works attributed to Sahaja masters are preserved not only in New Indian languages (Saraha, c. 750–800, Kāṇha, c. 800–850, Ti-lo-pa, c. 950–1000); a few commentaries exist in Sanskrit. The latter attest to the influence of the early wandering *siddhas* on the Buddhist establishment.

The basic doctrinal stance of the Sahaja movement is no different from that of Vajrayāna: sahaja is the innate principle of enlightenment, the *bodhicitta,* to be realized in the union of wisdom and skillful means. The main difference between the two types of Tantra is in the lifestyle of the adept. The Sahajiyā was a movement that represented a clear challenge to the Buddhist establishment: the ideal person was a homeless madman wandering about with his female consort, or a householder-sorcerer—either of which would claim to practice union with his consort as the actualization of what the high tradition practiced only in symbolic or mystical form. The Vajrayāna soon became integrated into the curriculum of the universities, controlled by the *Vinaya* and philosophical analysis. It was incorporated into the ordered program of spiritual cultivation accepted in the monasteries, which corresponded to the desired social and political stability of the academic institutions and their sponsors. The iconoclastic staints of the Sahaja, on the other hand, sought spontaneity, and saw monastic life as an obstacle to true realization. The force of their challenge is seen in quasi-mythic form in the legend that tells of the bizarre tests to which the *siddha* Ti lo pa submitted the great scholar Nā ro pa when the latter left his post at Vikramaśīla to follow the half-naked madman Ti lo pa.

This particular Tantric tradition, therefore, best embodied the iconoclastic tendencies found in all of Tantra. It challenged the establishment in the social as well as the religious sphere, for it incorporated freely practices from the substratum and placed women and sexuality on the level of the sacred. In opposition to the bland and ascetic paradises of Mahāyāna—where there were no women or sexual intercourse—Tantrism identifies the bliss of enlightment with the great bliss (*mahāsukha*) of sexual union.

The Kālacakra Tantra. This text has several features that separate it from other works of the Buddhist tradition: an obvious political message, suggesting an alliance to stop the Muslim advance in India, and astrological symbolism and teachings, among the others. In this work also we meet the concept of "Ādibuddha," the primordial Buddha, whence arises everything in the universe.

The high tradition, however, sees the text as remaining within the main line of Buddhist Tantrism. Its main argument is that all phenomena, including the rituals of Tantra, are contained within the initiate's body, and all aspects of time are also contained in this body. The concept of time (*kāla*) is introduced and discussed and its symbolism explained as a means to give the devotee control over time and therefore over the impermanent world. The *Sekoddeśaṭīkā*, a commentary on part of the *Kālacakra* attributed to Nā ro pa (Nāḍapāda, tenth century), explains that the time (*kāla*) of the *Kālacakra* is the same as the unchanging *dharmadhātu,* whereas the wheel (*cakra*) means the manifestations of time. In *Kālacakra* the two, absolute and relative, *prajñā* and *upāya*, are united. In this sense, therefore, in spite of its concessions to the substratum and to the rising tide of Hinduism, the *Kālacakra* was also integrated with mainline Buddhism.

Tantric literature. The word *tantra* means "thread" or "weft" and, by extension, "text." The sacred texts produced as the new dispensation, esoteric or exoteric, were called Tantras, and formed indeed a literary thread interwoven with the secret transmission from master to disciple. Some of the most difficult and profound Tantras were produced in the early period (before the eighth century); the *Mahāvairocana*, *Guhyasamāja*, the earlier parts of the *Mañjuśrīmūlakalpa*, and the *Hevajra*. By the time Tantra became the dominant system and, therefore, part of the establishment, a series of commentaries and authored works had appeared. Nāgārjuna's *Pañcakrama* is among the earliest. The Tantric Candrakīrti (ninth century) wrote a commentary on the *Guhyasamāja*, and Buddhaguhya (eighth century) discussed the *Mahāvairocana*. Sanskrit commentaries eventually were written to fossilize even the spontaneous poems of the Sahaja saints.

Tantra and the high tradition. Thus, Tantra too, like its predecessors, eventually become institutionalized. What arose as an esoteric, intensely private, visionary and iconoclastic movement, became a literary tradition, ritualized, often exoteric and speculative.

We have abundant evidence of a flourishing Tantric circle at Nālandā, for instance, at least since the late seventh century. Tantric masters were by that time established members of the faculty. Especially during the Pāla dynasty, Tantric practices and speculation played a central role in Buddhist universities. This was clearly the period of institutionalization, a period when Tantra became part of the mainstream of Buddhism.

With this transformation the magical origins of Tantra were partly disguised by a high Tantric liturgy and a theory of Tantric meditation paralleling earlier, Mahāyāna theories of the path. Still, Tantric ritual and meditation retained an identity of their own. Magic formulas, gestures, and circles appeared transformed, respectively, into the mystical words of the Buddhas, the secret gestures of the Buddhas, and charts (*maṇḍalas*) of the human psyche and the path.

The mystical diagram (*maṇḍala*) illustrates the complexity of this symbolism. It is at the same time a chart of the human person as it is now, a plan for liberation, and a representation of the transfigured body, the structure of Buddhahood itself. As a magic circle it is the sphere in which spiritual forces are evoked and controlled, as religious symbol it is the sphere of religious progress, experience, and action. The primitive functions remain: the *maṇḍala* is still a circle of power, with apotropaic functions. For each divinity there is an assigned meaning, a sacred syllable, a color, and a position within the *maṇḍala*. Spiritual forces can thus be evoked without danger. The sacred syllable is still a charm. The visualization of Buddhas is often inseparable from the evocation of demons and spirits. New beings populate the Buddhist pantheon. The Buddhas and *bodhisattvas* are accompanied by female consorts—these spiritual sexual partners can be found in explicit carnal iconographic representations.

Worship and ritual. Whereas the esoteric ritual incorporated elements of the substratum into a Buddhist doctrinal base, the exoteric liturgies of the Tantric high tradition followed ritual models from the Mahāyāna tradition as well as elements that evince Brahmanic ritual and Hindu worship. The daily ritual of the Tantric Buddhist presents a number of analogies of Brahmanic *pūjā* that cannot be accidental. But the complete liturgical cycle is still Buddhist. Many examples are preserved, for instance, in the Sanskrit text *Ādikarmapradīpa*. The ritual incorporates Tantric rites (offering to a *maṇḍala*, recitation of *mantras*) into a structure composed of elements from pre-Mahāyāna Buddhism (e.g., the Refuges), and Mahāyāna ritual (e.g., confession, vows, dedication of merit).

More complex liturgies include rites of initiation or consecration (*abhiṣeka*) and empowerment (*adhiṣṭhāna*), rites that may have roots going as far back as the *Atharvaveda*. The burnt-offering rites (homa) also have Vedic and Brahmanic counterparts. Elements of the substratum are also evident in the frequent invocation of *yakṣas* and *devatās*, the propitiation of spirits, and the underlying sexual and alchemical symbolism.

Meditation. The practice of Tantric visualization (*sādhana*) was even more a part of ritual than the Mahāyāna meditation session. It was always set in a purely ritual frame similar to the structure of the daily ritual summarized above. A complete *sādhana* would integrate pre-Mahāyāna and Mahāyāna liturgical and contemplative processes with Tantric visualization. The meditator would first go through a gradual process of purification (sometimes including ablutions) usually constructed on the model of the Mahāyāna "sevenfold service." He would then visualize the mystical syllable corresponding to his chosen deity. The syllable would be transformed into a series of images that would lead finally to clear visualization of the deity. Once the deity was visualized clearly, the adept would become one with it. But this oneness was interpreted as the realization of the nondual; therefore, the deity became the adept as much as the adept was turned into a deity. Thus, the transcendent could be actualized in the adept's life beyond meditation in the fulfillment of the *bodhisattva* vows.

Tantric doctrine. Tantric symbolism was interpreted in the context of Mahāyāna orthodoxy. It is therefore possible to explain Tantric theoretical conceptions as a natural development from Mahāyāna. The immanence of Buddhahood is explicitly connected with the Mahāyāna doctrine of the identity of *saṃsāra* and *nirvāṇa* and the teachings of those Yogācārins who believed that consciousness is inherently pure. The magical symbolism of Tantra can be traced—

again through explicit references—to the doctrine of the *bodhisattva* as magician: since the world is like a dream, like a magical apparition, one can be free of it by knowing the dream as dream—knowing and controlling the magical illusion as a magician would control it. The *bodhisattva* (and therefore the *siddha*) is able to play the magical trick of the world without deceiving himself into believing it real.

One should not forget, however, that what is distinctively Tantric is not limited to the externals of ritual and symbolism. The special symbolism transforms its Mahāyāna context because of the specifically Tantric understanding of immanence. The Buddha is present in the human body innately, but the Buddha nature is manifested only when one realizes the "three mysteries," or "three secrets." It is not enough to be free from the illusion of the world; one becomes free by living *in* illusion in such a way that illusion becomes the manifestation of Buddhahood. Tantra seeks to construct an alternative reality, such that a mentally constructed world reveals the fundamental illusion of the world and manifests the mysterious power of the Buddha through illusion. The human body, the realm of the senses, is to be transformed into the body of a Buddha, the senses of a Buddha.

The body, mind, and speech of the Buddha (the Three Mysteries) have specific characteristics that must be recognized and reproduced. In ritual terms this means that the adept actualizes Buddhahood when he performs prostrations and ritual gestures (*mudrās*); he speaks with the voice of the Buddha when he utters *mantras*; his mind is the mind of the Buddha when he visualizes the deity. The magical dimension is evident: the power of the Buddha lives in the formalized "demeanor of a Buddha." But the doctrine also implies transforming the body by a mystical alchemy (rooted in substratum sexual alchemy) from which is derived the soteriological meaning of the doctrine: the ritual changes the human person into a Buddha, all his human functions become sacred. Then this person's mind is the mind of an awakened being, it knows all things; the body assumes the appearance appropriate to save any living being; the voice is able to speak in the language of any living being needing to be saved.

The Decline of Buddhism in India. With Harṣa's death Indian Buddhism could depend only on the royal patronage of the Pāla dynasty of Bihar and Bengal (c. 650–950), who soon favored the institutions they had founded—Vikramaśīla (c. 800), Odantapurī (c. 760). The last shining lights of Nālandā were the Mādhyamika masters Śāntirakṣita and Kamalaśīla, both of whom participated actively in the conversion of Tibet. Then the ancient university was eclipsed by its rival Vikramaśīla, which saw its final glory in the eleventh century.

Traditionally, the end of Indian Buddhism has been identified with the sack of the two great universities by the troops of the Turk Muḥammad Ghūrī: Nālandā in 1197 and Vikramaśīla in 1203. But, although the destruction of Nālandā put an end to its former glory, Nālandā lingered on. When the Tibetan pilgrim Dharmasvāmin (1197–1264) visited the site of the ancient university in 1235 he found a few monks teaching in two monasteries remaining among the ruins of eighty-two others. In this way Buddhism would stay on in India for a brief time, but under circumstances well illustrated by the decay witnessed by Dharmasvāmin—even as he was there, the Turks mounted another raid to further ransack what was left of Nālandā.

For a long time scholars have debated the causes for the decline of Buddhism in India. Although there is little chance of agreement on a problem so complex—and on which we have precious little evidence—some of the reasons adduced early are no longer widely accepted. For instance, the notion that Tantric Buddhism was a "degenerate form" of Buddhism that contributed to or brought about the disappearance of Buddhism is no longer entertained by the scholarly community. The image of a defenseless, pacifist Buddhist community annihilated by invading hordes of Muslim warriors is perhaps also a simplification. Though the Turkish conquerors of India were far from benevolent, the Arabs who occupied Sindh in 711 seem to have accepted a state of peaceful coexistence with the local population. Furthermore, one must still understand why Jainism and Hinduism survived the Muslim invasion while Buddhism did not.

Buddhist relations with Hindu and Jain monarchs were not always peaceful—witness the conquest of Bihar by the Bengali Śaiva king Śaśīṅka (c. 618). Even without the intervention of intolerance, the growth of Hinduism, with its firm roots in Indian society and freedom from the costly institution of the monastery, offered a colossal challenge to Buddhism. The eventual triumph of Hinduism can be followed by a number of landmarks often associated with opposition to Buddhism: the spread of Vaiṣṇavism (in which the Buddha appears as a deceptive *avatāra* of Viṣṇu); the great Vaiṣṇava and Śaiva saints of the South, the Āḻvārs and Nayānars, respectively, whose Hindu patrons were openly hostile to Buddhism and Jainism; the ministry of Śaṅkara in Mysore (788–850), a critic of Buddhism who was himself accused of being a "crypto-Buddhist"; and the triumph of Śaivism in Kashmir (c. 800).

But the causes for the disappearance of Buddhism were subtle: the assimilation of Buddhist ideas and practices into Hinduism and the inverse process of the Hinduization of Buddhism, with the advantage of Hinduism as a religion of the land and the locality. More important than these were perhaps the internal causes for the decline: dependence on monastic institutions that did not have broad popular support but relied exclusively on royal patronage; and isolation of monasteries from the life of the village community, owing to the tendency of the monasteries to look inward and to lose interest in proselytizing and serving the surrounding communities.

The disappearance of Buddhism in India may have been precipitated by the Muslim invasion, but it was caused primarily by internal factors, the most important of which seems to have been the gradual assimilation of Buddhism into Hinduism. The Muslim invasion, especially the Turkish conquest of the Ganges Valley, was the *coup de grace;* we may consider it the dividing line between two eras, but it was not the primary cause for the disappearance of Buddhism from India.

BUDDHIST REMNANTS AND REVIVALS IN THE SUBCONTINENT. After the last days of the great monastic institutions (twelfth and thirteenth centuries) Indian Buddhism lingered on in isolated pockets in the subcontinent. During the period of Muslim and British conquest (thirteenth to nineteenth century) it was almost completely absorbed by Hinduism and Islam, and gave no sign of creative life until modern attempts at restoration (nineteenth and twentieth centuries). Therefore, a hiatus of roughly six hundred years separates the creative period of Indian Buddhism from its modern manifestations.

Buddhism of the frontier. As the Turk occupation of India advanced, the last great scholars of India escaped from Kashmir and Bihar to Tibet and Nepal. But the flight of Buddhist talent also responded to the attraction of royal patronage and popular support in other lands. The career of Atīśa (Dīpaṃkara Śrījñāna, 982–1054), who emigrated to Tibet in 1042, is emblematic of the great loss incurred by Indian Buddhism in losing its monk-scholars. He combined extensive studies in Mahāyāna philosophy and Tantra in India with a sojourn in Sumatra under the tutorship of Dharmakīrti. He had studied with Bodhibhadra (the successor of Nā ro pa when the latter left Vikramaśīla to become a wandering ascetic), and was head master (*upādhyāya*) of Vikramaśīla and Odantapurī at the time of King Bheyapāla. He left for Tibet at the invitation of Byaṅ-chub-'od, apparently attracted by a large monetary offer.

The migration of the Indian scholars, and a steady stream of Tibetan students, made possible the exportation of Buddhist academic institutions and traditions to Tibet, where they were preserved until the Chinese suppression of 1959. The most learned monks were pushed out to the Himalayan and Bengali frontiers in part because the Indian communities were no longer willing to support the monasteries. Certain forms of Tantra, dependent only on householder priests, could survive, mostly in Bengal and in the Himalayan foot-hills. But some Theravādin Buddhists also survived in East Bengal—most of them taking refuge in India after the partition, some remaining in Bangledesh and Assam.

Himalayan Buddhism of direct Indian ancestry remains only in Nepal, where it can be observed even today in suspended animation, partly fused with local Hinduism, as it must have been in the Gangetic plain during the twelfth century. Nepalese Buddhists produced what may very well be considered the last major Buddhist scripture composed in the subcontinent, the *Svayaṃbhu Purāṇa* (c. fifteenth century). This text is an open window into the last days of Indian Buddhism. It reveals the close connection between Buddhist piety and non-Buddhist sacred localities, the formation of a Buddhist cosmogonic ontology (the Ādibuddha), and the role of Tantric ritual in the incorporation of religious elements from the substratum. Nepalese Buddhism survives under the tutelage of married Tantric priests, called *vajrācaryās*. It is therefore sometimes referred to as "Vajrācaryā Buddhism."

Buddhism of Tibetan origin survives in the subcontinent mostly in Ladakh, Sikkim, and Bhutan, but also in Nepal. Perhaps the most significant presence in modern India, however, is that of the Tibetan refugee communities. The Tibetan diaspora includes about eighty thousand persons, among which are several thousand monks. Some have retained their monastic robes and have reconstructed in India their ancient Buddhist academic curricula, returning to the land of origin the disciplines of the classical universities. So far their impact on Indian society at large has been insignificant and their hope of returning to Tibet dwindles with the passing of time. But the preservation, on Indian soil, of the classical traditions of Nālandā and Vikramaśīla is hardly a trivial accomplishment.

Attempted revival: The Mahābodhi society. Attempts to revive Buddhism in the land of its origin began with the Theosophical Society, popularized in Sri Lanka in the early 1880s by the American Henry S. Olcott. Although the society eventually became the vehicle for broader and less defined speculative goals, it inspired new pride in Buddhists after years of colonial oppression. The Sinhala monk Anagārika Dharmapāla (1864–1933; born David Hewavitarane) set out to modernize Buddhist education. He also worked untiringly to restore the main pilgrimage sites of India, especially the temple of Bodh Gayā, which had fallen in disrepair and had been under Hindu administration for several centuries. To this end he founded in 1891 the Mahābodhi Society, still a major presence in Indian Buddhism.

Ambedkar and "Neo-Buddhism." The most significant Buddhist mass revival of the new age was led by Dr. Bhimrao Ramji Ambedkar (1891–1956). He saw Buddhism as the gospel for India's oppressed and read in the Buddhist scriptures ideals of equality and justice. After many years of spiritual search, he became convinced that Buddhism was the only ideology that could effect the eventual liberation of Indian outcastes. On October 14, 1956, he performed a mass "consecration" of Buddhists in Nagpur, Maharashtra. The new converts were mostly from the "scheduled caste" of the *mahārs*. Although his gospel is in some way on the fringes of Buddhist orthodoxy, Buddhist monks from other parts of Asia have ministered to the spiritual needs of his converts, and inspired Indian Buddhists refer to him as "Bodhisattva Ambedkar."

Other aspects of modern Buddhism. The most fruitful and persistent effort in the rediscovery of Indian Buddhism has been in the West, primarily among Western scholars. The achievements of European scholars include a modern critical edition of the complete Pali canon, published by the Pali Text Society (founded in London in 1881), and the recovery of original texts of parts of the canon of the Sarvāstivāda. The combined effort of Indian, North American and European historians, archaeologists, and art historians has placed Indian Buddhism in a historical and social context, which, though still only understood in its rough outlines, allows us to see Buddhism in its historical evolution.

Japanese scholarship has also made great strides since the beginning of the twentieth century. The publication in Japan of three different editions of the Chinese canon between 1880 and 1929 may be seen as the symbolic beginning of a century of productive critical scholarship that has placed Japan at the head of modern research into Indian Buddhism.

Another interesting phenomenon of the contemporary world is the appearance of "neo-Buddhists" in Europe and North America. Although most of these groups have adopted extra-Indian forms of Buddhism, their interest in the scriptural traditions of India has created an audience and a demand for research into India's Buddhist past. The Buddhist Society, founded in London in 1926, and the Amis du Bouddhisme, founded in Paris in 1928, both supported scholarship and encouraged the Buddhist revival in India.

In spite of the revived interest in India of the last century, the prospects of an effective Buddhist revival in the land of Śākyamuni seem remote. It is difficult to imagine a successful living Buddhism in India today or in the near future. The possibility of the religion coming back to life may depend on the reimportation of the Dharma into India from another land. It remains to be seen if Ambedkar and Anagārika Dharmapāla had good reasons for hope in a Buddhist revival, or if in fact the necessary social conditions for the existence of Indian Buddhism disappeared with the last monarchs of the Pāla dynasty.

SEE ALSO Ahiṃsā; Ājīvikas; Āḻvārs; Ālaya-vijñāna; Ambedkar; Amitābha; Amoghavajra; Arhat; Āryadeva; Asaṅga; Aśoka; Atīśa; Avalokiteśvara; Avatāra; Bengali Religions; Bhakti; Bhāvaviveka; Bodhisattva Path; Buddha; Buddhapālita; Buddhism, Schools of, overview article and articles on Mahāyāna Philosophical Schools of Buddhism; Buddhist Ethics; Buddhist Studies; Cakravartin; Candrakīrti; Councils, article on Buddhist Councils; Dharma, article on Buddhist Dharma and Dharmas; Dharmakīrti; Dharmapāla; Dignāga; Eightfold Path; Folk Religion, article on Folk Buddhism; Four Noble Truths; Goddess Worship, article on The Hindu Goddess; Gosāla; Hindu Tantric Literature; Iconography, article on Buddhist Iconography; Indian Religions; Inner Asian Religions; Islam, articles on Islam in Central Asia and Islam in South Asia; Jainism; Kamalaśīla; Karman, article on Buddhist Concepts; Karman, article on Hindu and Jain Concepts; Karuṇā; Kṛṣṇaism; Mādhyamika; Mahāsāṃghika; Mahāsiddhas; Mahāvīra; Maitreya; Maṇḍalas, article on Buddhist Maṇḍalas; Mañjuśrī; Mantra; Marathi Religions; Meditation; Missions, article on Buddhist Missions; Moggaliputtatissa; Mokṣa; Monasticism, article on Buddhist Monasticism; Nāgārjuna; Nāgas and Yakṣas; Nirvāṇa; Pāramitās; Pilgrimage, article on Buddhist Pilgrimage in South and Southeast Asia; Prajñā; Pratītya-samutpāda; Priesthood, article on Buddhist Priesthood; Pūjā; Pure and Impure Lands; Śaivism, overview article and article on Nayānars; Saṃgha; Saṃnyāsa; Saṃsāra; Śaṅkara; Śāntarakṣita; Śāntideva; Sarvāstivāda; Sautrāntika; Śīlabhadra; Soul, article on Buddhist Concepts; Sthiramati; Stupa Worship; Śubhākarasiṃha; Śūnyam and Śūnyata; Tantrism; Tathāgata; Tathāgata-garbha; Tathatā; Temple, articles on Buddhist Temple Compounds; Theosophical Society; Theravāda; Upāya; Vaiṣṇavism, overview article; Vajrabodhi; Vasubandhu; Vedism and Brahmanism; Worship and Devotional Life, article on Buddhist Devotional Life in Southeast Asia; Yoga; and Yogācāra.

BIBLIOGRAPHY

Bareau, André. "Le bouddhisme indien." In *Les religions de l'Inde,* vol. 3, pp. 1–246. Paris, 1966. In addition to this useful survey, see Bareau's "Le bouddhisme indien," in *Histoire des religions,* edited by Henri-Charles Puech vol. 1, (Paris, 1970), pp. 1146–1215. Bareau has written the classical work on the question of the dating of the Buddha's life, "La date du Nirvāṇa," *Journal asiatique* 241 (1953): 27–62. He surveys and interprets classical documents on the Hīnayāna schools in "Les sectes bouddhiques du Petit Véhicule et leurs Abhidharmapiṭaka." *Bulletin de l'École Française d'Extrême-Orient* 50 (1952): 1–11; "Trois traités sur les sectes bouddhiques dus à Vasumitra, Bhavya et Vinitadeva," *Journal asiatique* 242–244 (1954–1956); *Les premiers conciles bouddhiques* (Paris, 1955); *Les sectes bouddhiques de Petit Véhicule* (Saigon, 1955); "Les controverses rélatives à la nature de l'arhant dans le bouddhisme ancien," *Indo-Iranian Journal* 1 (1957): 241–250. Bareau has also worked extensively on the "biography" of the Buddha: *Recherches sur la biographie du Bouddha,* 3 vols. (Paris, 1970–1983); "Le parinirvāṇa du Bouddha et la naissance de la religion bouddhique," *Bulletin de l'École Française d'Extrême-Orient* 61 (1974): 275–300; and, on a more popular but still scholarly bent, *Le Bouddha* (Paris, 1962).

Basham, A. L. *The Wonder That Was India.* London, 1954. This is the most accessible and readable cultural history of pre-Muslim India. A more technical study on the religious movements at the time of the Buddha is Basham's *History and Doctrine of the Ājīvikas* (London, 1951).

Beal, Samuel. *Travels of Fa-hian and Sung-Yun, Buddhist Pilgrims from China to India (400 A. D. and 518 A. D.).* London, 1869. The travel records of two early pilgrims. See also Beal's *Si-yu-ki: Buddhist Records of the Western World,* 2 vols. (London, 1884). Translation of Xuanzang's accounts of his travels to India.

Bechert, Heinz. "Zur Frühgeschichte des Mahāyāna-Buddhismus." *Zeitschrift der Deutschen Morgenländischen Gesellschaft* 113 (1963): 530–535. Summary discussion of the Hīnayāna roots of Mahāyāna. On the same topic, see also "Notes on the Formation of Buddhist Sects and the Origins of Mahāyāna," in *German Scholars on India,* vol. 1 (Varanasi, 1973), pp. 6–18; "The Date of the Buddha Reconsidered," *Indologica Taurinensia* 10 (1982): 29–36; "The Importance of Aśoka's So-called Schism Edict," in *Indological and Bud-*

dhist Studies in Honour of Prof. J. W. de Jong (Canberra, 1982), pp. 61–68; and "The Beginnings of Buddhist Historiography," in *Religion and Legitimation of Power in Sri Lanka,* edited by Bardwell L. Smith (Chambersburg, Pa., 1978), pp. 1–12. Bechert is also the editor of the most recent contribution to the question of the language of Buddha and early Buddhism, *Die Sprache der ältesten buddhistischen Überlieferung / The Language of the Earliest Buddhist Tradition* (Göttingen, 1980).

Bechert, Heinz, and Georg von Simson, eds. *Einführung in die Indologie: Stand, Methoden, Aufgaben.* Darmstadt, 1979. A general introduction to indology, containing abundant materials on Indian history and religion, including Buddhism.

Bechert, Heinz, and Richard Gombrich, eds. *The World of Buddhism.* London, 1984. This is by far the most scholarly and comprehensive survey of Buddhism for the general reader. Indian Buddhism is treated on pages 15–132 and 277–278.

Demiéville, Paul. "L'origine des sectes bouddhiques d'après Paramartha." In *Mélanges chinois et bouddhiques,* vol. 1, pp. 14–64. Brussels, 1931–1932.

Demiéville, Paul. "A propos du Concile de Vaiśālī." *T'oung pao* 40 (1951): 239–296.

Dutt, Nalinaksha. *Aspects of Mahāyāna Buddhism and Its Relation to Hīnayāna.* London, 1930. Although Dutt's work on the development of the Buddhist sects is now largely superseded, there are no comprehensive expositions to replace his surveys. His *Mahāyāna Buddhism* (Calcutta, 1973) is sometimes presented as a revision of *Aspects,* but the earlier work is quite different and far superior. Most of Dutt's earlier work on the sects, found hidden in various journals, was compiled in *Buddhist Sects in India* (Calcutta, 1970). See also his *Early Monastic Buddhism,* rev. ed. (Calcutta, 1960).

Dutt, Sukumar. *The Buddha and Five After-Centuries.* London, 1957. Other useful, although dated, surveys include *Early Buddhist Monachism* (1924; new ed., Delhi, 1960) and *Buddhist Monks and Monasteries in India* (London, 1962).

Fick, R. *The Social Organization in Northeast India in the Buddha's Time.* Calcutta, 1920.

Frauwallner, Erich. "Die buddhistische Konzile." *Zeitschrift der Deutschen Morgenländischen Gesellschaft* 102 (1952): 240–261.

Frauwallner, Erich. *The Earliest Vinaya and the Beginnings of Buddhist Literature.* Rome, 1956.

Frauwallner, Erich. "The Historical Data We Possess on the Person and Doctrine of the Buddha." *East and West* 7 (1956): 309–312.

Fujita Kotatsu. *Genshi jōdoshisō no kenkyū.* Tokyo, 1970. The standard book on early Sukhāvatī beliefs.

Glasenapp, Helmuth von. "Zur Geschichte der buddhistischen Dharma Theorie." *Zeitschrift der Deutschen Morgenländischen Gesellschaft* 92 (1938): 383–420.

Glasenapp, Helmuth von. "Der Ursprung der buddhistischen Dharma-Theorie." *Wiener Zeitschrift für die Kunde des Morgenlandes* 46 (1939): 242–266.

Glasenapp, Helmuth von. *Buddhistische Mysterien.* Stuttgart, 1940. Discusses most of the theories on early Brahmanic influence on Buddhist doctrine.

Glasenapp, Helmuth von. *Buddhismus und Gottesidee.* Mainz, 1954.

Gokhale, Balkrishna Govind. *Buddhism and Aśoka.* Baroda, 1948. Other of this author's extensive writings on the social and political contexts of early Buddhism include "The Early Buddhist Elite," *Journal of Indian History* 43 (1965): 391–402; "Early Buddhist View of the State," *Journal of the American Oriental Society* 89 (1969): 731–738; "Theravāda Buddhism in Western India," *Journal of the American Oriental Society* 92 (1972): 230–236; and "Early Buddhism and the Brahmanas," in *Studies in History of Buddhism,* edited by A. K. Narain (Delhi, 1980).

Gómez, Luis O. "Proto-Mādhyamika in the Pāli Canon." *Philosophy East and West* 26 (1976): 137–165. This paper argues that the older portions of *Suttanipāta* preserve a stratum of the tradition that differs radically from the dominant themes expressed in the rest of the Pāli canon, especially in its Theravāda interpretation.

Grousset, René. *The Civilizations of the East,* vol. 2, India. London, 1931. One of the best surveys of Indian history. See also his *Sur les traces du Bouddha* (Paris, 1957) for a modern expansion and retelling of Xuanzang's travels.

Horner, I. B. *Early Buddhist Theory of Man Perfected.* London, 1936. A study of the *arhat* ideal in the Pāli canon. See also Horner's translation of the dialogues between King Menander and Nāgasena, *Milinda's Questions* (London, 1964), and *Women under Primitive Buddhism* (1930; reprint, Delhi, 1975).

Horsch, P. "Der Hinduismus und die Religionen der primitivstämme Indiens." *Asiatische Studien / Études asiatiques* 22 (1968): 115–136.

Horsch, P. "Vorstufen der Indischen Seelenwanderungslehre." *Asiatische Studien / Études asiatiques* 25 (1971): 98–157.

Jayatilleke, K. N. *Early Buddhist Theory of Knowledge.* London, 1963. Discusses the relationship between early Buddhist ideas and śramanic and Upaniṣadic doctrines.

Jong, J. W. de. "A Brief History of Buddhist Studies in Europe and America." *Eastern Buddhist* 7 (May 1974): 55–106. (October 1974): 49–82. For the most part these bibliographic surveys, along with the author's "Recent Buddhist Studies in Europe and America: 1973–1983," *Eastern Buddhist* 17 (1984): 79–107, treat only the philological study of Indian Buddhism. The author also tends to omit certain major figures who are not in his own school of Buddhology. These articles are nonetheless the most scholarly surveys available on the field, and put forth truly excellent models of scholarly rigor.

Joshi, Lal Mani. *Studies in the Buddhistic Culture of India.* Delhi, 1967. Indian Buddhism during the middle and late Mahāyāna periods.

Kajiyama Yūichi. "Women in Buddhism." *Eastern Buddhist* 15 (1982): 53–70.

Kajiyama Yūichi. "Stūpas, the Mother of Buddhas, and Dharma-body." In *New Paths in Buddhist Research,* edited by A. K. Warder, pp. 9–16. Delhi, 1985.

Kimura Taiken. *Abidammaron no kenkyū.* Tokyo, 1937. A survey of Sarvāstivāda Abhidharma, especially valuable for its analysis of the *Mahāvibhāṣa.*

Lamotte, Étienne. "Buddhist Controversy over the Five Propositions." *Indian Historical Quarterly* 32 (1956). The material collected in this article is also found, slightly augmented, in Lamotte's *magnum opus*, *Histoire du bouddhisme indien des origines à l'ère Śaka* (Louvain, 1958), pp. 300–319, 542–543, 575–606, 690–695. This erudite work is still the standard reference tool on the history of early Indian Buddhism (to circa 200 CE). Unfortunately, Lamotte did not attempt a history of Indian Buddhism for the middle and late periods. He did, however, write an article on the origins of Mahāyāna titled "Sur la formation du Mahāyāna," in *Asiatica: Festschrift Friedrich Weller* (Leipzig, 1954), pp. 381–386; this is the definitive statement on the northern origin of Mahāyāna. See also *Der Verfasser des Upadeśa und seine Quellen* (Göttingen, 1973). On early Buddhism, see "La légende du Buddha," *Revue de l'histoire des religious* 134 (1947–1948): 37–71; *Le bouddhisme de Śākyamuni* (Göttingen, 1983); and *The Spirit of Ancient Buddhism* (Venice, 1961). Lamotte also translated a vast amount of Mahāyāna literature, including *Le traité de la grande vertu de sagesse*, 5 vols. (Louvain, 1944–1980); *La somme du Grand Véhicule d'Asaṅga*, 2 vols. (Louvain, 1938); and *L'enseignement de Vimalakirti* (Louvain, 1962), containing a long note on the concept of Buddha field (pp. 395–404).

La Vallée Poussin, Louis de. *Bouddhisme: Etudes et matériaux.* London, 1898. One of the most productive and seminal Western scholars of Buddhism, La Vallée Poussin contributed to historical studies in this and other works, as *Bouddhisme: Opinions sur l'histoire de la dogmatique* (Paris, 1909), *L'Inde aux temps des Mauryas* (Paris, 1930), and *Dynasties et histoire de l'Inde depuis Kanishka jusqu'aux invasions musulmanes* (Paris, 1935). Contributions on doctrine include *The Way to Nirvāṇa* (London, 1917); *Nirvāṇa* (Paris, 1925); "La controverse du temps et du pudgala dans la *Vijñānakāya*," in *Études asiatiques, publiées à l'occasion du vingt-cinquième anniversaire de l'École Française d'Extrême-Orient*, vol. 1 (Paris, 1925), pp. 358–376; *La morale bouddhique* (Paris, 1927); and *Le dogme et la philosophie du bouddhism* (Paris, 1930). On Abhidharma, see "Documents d'Abhidharma," in *Mélanges chinois et bouddhiques*, vol. 1 (Brussels, 1931–1932), pp. 65–109. The Belgian scholar also translated the most influential work of Abhidharma, *L'Abhidharmakosa de Vasubandhu*, 6 vols. (1923–1931; reprint, Brussels, 1971). His articles in the *Encyclopaedia of Religion and Ethics*, edited by James Hastings, are still of value. Especially useful are "Bodhisattva (In Sanskrit Literature)," vol. 2 (Edinburgh, 1909), pp. 739–753; "Mahāyāna," vol. 8 (1915), pp. 330–336; and "Councils and Synods (Buddhist)," vol. 7 (1914), pp. 179–185.

Law, B. C. *Historical Gleanings.* Calcutta, 1922. Other of his numerous contributions to the early history of Buddhism include *Some Kṣatriya Tribes of Ancient India* (Calcutta, 1924), *Tribes in Ancient India* (Poona, 1943), and *The Magadhas in Ancient India* (London, 1946).

Law, B. C., ed. *Buddhistic Studies.* Calcutta, 1931. A collection of seminal essays on the history and doctrines of Indian Buddhism.

Legge, James. *A Record of Buddhist Kingdoms.* Oxford, 1886. English translation of Fa-hsien's accounts.

Majumdar, R. C., ed. *History and Culture of the Indian People*, vols. 2–5. London, 1951. A major survey of the periods of Indian history when Buddhism flourished.

Masson, Joseph. *La religion populaire dans le canon bouddhique Pāli.* Louvain, 1942. The standard study on the interactions of high tradition Buddhism with the substratum, not superseded yet.

Masuda Jiryō. "Origins and Doctrines of Early Indian Buddhist Schools." *Asia Major* 2 (1925): 1–78. English translation of Vasumitra's classical account of the Eighteen Schools.

May, Jacques. "La philosophie bouddhique de la vacuité." *Studia Philosophica* 18 (1958): 123–137. Discusses philosophical issues; for historical survey, see "Chūgan," in *Hōbōgirin*, vol. 5 (Paris and Tokyo, 1979), pp. 470–493, and the article coauthored with Mimaki (below). May's treatment of the Yogācāra schools (including the school of Sāramati), on the other hand, is both historical and doctrinal; see "La philosophie bouddhique idéaliste," *Asiatische Studien / Études asiatiques* 25 (1971): 265–323.

Mimaki Katsumi and Jacques May. "Chūdō." In *Hōbōgirin*, vol. 5, pp. 456–470. Paris and Tokyo, 1979.

Mitra, Debala. *Buddhist Monuments.* Calcutta, 1971. A handy survey of the Buddhist archaeological sites of India.

Mitra, R. C. *The Decline of Buddhism in India.* Calcutta, 1954.

Nagao Gadjin. "The Architectural Tradition in Buddhist Monasticism." In *Studies in History of Buddhism*, edited by A. K. Narain, pp. 189–208. Delhi, 1980.

Nakamura Hajime. *Indian Buddhism: A Survey with Bibliographical Notes.* Tokyo, 1980. Disorganized and poorly edited, but contains useful information on Japanese scholarship on the development of Indian Buddhism.

Nilakanta Sastri, K. A. *Age of the Nandas and Mauryas.* Varanasi, 1952. See also his *A History of South India from Prehistoric Times to the Fall of Vijayānagar* (Madras, 1955) and *Development of Religion in South India* (Bombay, 1963).

Oldenberg, Hermann. *Buddha, sein Leben, seine Lehre, seine Gemeinde* (1881). Revised and edited by Helmuth von Glasenapp. Stuttgart, 1959. The first German edition was translated by W. Hoey as *Buddha, His Life, His Doctrine, His Order* (London, 1882).

Paul, Diana. *The Buddhist Feminine Ideal: Queen Srimala and the Tathāgatagarbha.* Missoula, Mont., 1980. See also her *Women in Buddhism* (Berkeley, 1980).

Prebish, Charles S. "A Review of Scholarship on the Buddhist Councils." *Journal of Asian Studies* 33 (February 1974): 239–254. Treats the problem of the early schools and the history and significance of their Vinaya. Other works on this topic include Prebish's "The Prātimokṣa Puzzle: Facts Versus Fantasy," *Journal of the American Oriental Society* 94 (April-June 1974): 168–176; and *Buddhist Monastic Discipline: The Sanskrit Prātimokṣa Sūtras of the Mahāsāṅghikas and the Mūlasarvāstivādins* (University Park, Pa., 1975).

Prebish, Charles S., and Janice J. Nattier. "Mahāsāṅghika Origins: The Beginning of Buddhist Sectarianism." *History of Religions* 16 (1977): 237–272. An original and convincing argument against the conception of the Mahāsāṃghika as "liberals."

Rhys Davids, T. W. *Buddhist India.* London, 1903. A classic, although its methodology is questionable. Also of some use, in spite of its date, is his "Sects (Buddhist)," in the *Encyclopaedia of Religion and Ethics*, edited by James Hastings, vol. 11 (Edinburgh, 1920), pp. 307–309.

Robinson, Richard H. "Classical Indian Philosophy." In *Chapters in Indian Civilization,* edited by Joseph Elder, vol. 1, pp. 127–227. Dubuque, 1970. A bit idiosyncratic, but valuable in its attempt to understand Buddhist philosophy as part of general Indian currents and patterns of speculative thought. Robinson's "The Religion of the Householder Bodhisattva," *Bharati* (1966): 31–55, challenges the notion of Mahāyāna as a lay movement.

Robinson, Richard H., and Willard L. Johnson. *The Buddhist Religion: A Historical Introduction.* 3d rev. ed. Belmont, Calif., 1982. A great improvement over earlier editions, this book is now a useful manual, with a good bibliography for the English reader.

Ruegg, David S. *The Study of Indian and Tibetan Thought.* Leiden, 1967. The most valuable survey of the main issues of modern scholarship on Indian Buddhism, especially on the early period. The author has also written the definitive study of the Tathāgata-garbha doctrines *in La théorie du tathāga-tagarbha et du gotra* (Paris, 1969). See also on the Madhyamika school his "Towards a Chronology of the Madhyamaka School," in *Indological and Buddhist Studies in Honour of J. W. de Jong* (Canberra, 1982), pp. 505–530, and *The Literature of the Madhyamaka School of Philosophy in India* (Wiesbaden, 1981).

Schayer, Stanislaus. "Precanonical Buddhism." *Acta Orientalia* 7 (1935): 121–132. Posits an early Buddhism not found explicitly in the canon; attempts to reconstruct the doctrines of Buddhism antedating the canon.

Schlingloff, Dieter. *Die Religion des Buddhismus.* 2 vols. Berlin, 1963. An insightful exposition of Buddhism, mostly from the perspective of canonical Indian documents.

Snellgrove, David L., ed. *Buddhist Himālaya.* Oxford, 1957. Although the context of this study is modern Himalayan Buddhism, it contains useful information on Buddhist Tantra in general. Snellgrove's two-volume *The Hevajra Tantra: A Critical Study* (London, 1959) includes an English translation and study of this major Tantric work. In *The Image of the Buddha* (Tokyo and London, 1978) Snellgrove, in collaboration with other scholars, surveys the history of the iconography of the Buddha image.

Stcherbatsky, Theodore. *The Central Conception of Buddhism and the Meaning of the Word "Dharma"* (1923). Reprint, Delhi, 1970. A classic introduction to Sarvāstivādin doctrine. On the Mādhyamika, Stcherbatsky wrote *The Conception of Buddhist Nirvana* (Leningrad, 1927). On early Buddhism, see his "The Doctrine of the Buddha," *Bulletin of the School of Oriental Studies* 6 (1932): 867–896, and "The 'Dharmas' of the Buddhists and the 'Guṇas' of the Sāṃkhyas," *Indian Historical Quarterly* 10 (1934): 737–760. Stcherbatsky categorized the history of Buddhist thought in "Die drei Richtungen in der Philosophie des Buddhismus," *Rocznik Orjentalistyczny* 10 (1934): 1–37.

Takasaki Jikidō. *Nyoraizō shisō no keisei—Indo daijō bukkyō shisō kenkyū.* Tokyo, 1974. A major study of Tathāgata-garbha thought in India.

Thapar, Romila. *Asoka and the Decline of the Mauryas.* London, 1961. Controversial study of Aśoka's reign. Her conclusions are summarized in her *History of India,* vol. 1 (Baltimore, 1965). Also relevant for the study of Indian Buddhism are her *Ancient Indian Social History: Some Interpretations* (New Delhi, 1978), *Dissent in the Early Indian Tradition* (Dehradun, 1979), and *From Lineage of State* (Bombay, 1984).

Thomas, Edward J. *The Life of the Buddha as Legend and History* (1927). New York, 1960. Still the only book-length, critical study of the life of Buddha. Less current, but still useful, is the author's 1933 work *The History of Buddhist Thought* (New York, 1975).

Varma, V. P. *Early Buddhism and Its Origins.* New Delhi, 1973.

Vetter, Tilmann. "The Most Ancient Form of Buddhism." In his *Buddhism and Its Relation to Other Religions.* Kyoto, 1985.

Warder, A. K. *Indian Buddhism.* 2d rev. ed. Delhi, 1980. One of the few modern surveys of the field, this work includes a bibliography of classical sources (pp. 523–574). Unfortunately, the author does not make use of materials available in Chinese and Tibetan translation.

Watanabe Fumimaro. *Philosophy and Its Development in the Nikāyas and Abhidhamma.* Delhi, 1983. The beginnings of Buddhist scholasticism, especially as seen in the transition from Sūtra to Abhidharma literature.

Watters, Thomas. *On Yuan Chwang's Travels in India.* 2 vols. London, 1904–1905. Extensive study of Xuanzang's travels.

Wayman, Alex. *The Buddhist Tantras: Light on Indo-Tibetan Esotericism.* New York, 1973. Not a survery or introduction to the study of Indian Tantra, but a collection of essays on specific issues and problems. Chapter 1.2 deals with the problem of the early history of Tantra. See also Wayman's *Yoga of the Guhyasamājatantra: The Arcane Lore of Forty Verses; A Buddhist Tantra Commentary* (Delhi, 1977). In his "The Mahāsāṅghika and the *Tathāgatagarbha* (Buddhist Doctrinal History, Study 1)," *Journal of the International Association of Buddhist Studies* 1 (1978): 35–50, Wayman discusses possible connections between the Mahāsāṃghika subsects of Andhra and the development of Mahāyāna. His "Meditation in Theravāda and Mahīśāsaka," *Studia Missionalia* 25 (1976): 1–28, is a study of the doctrine of meditation in two of the leading schools of Hīnayāna.

Winternitz, Moriz. *Geschichte der indischen Literature,* vol. 2. Leipzig, 1920. Translated as *A History of Indian Literature* (Delhi, 1983). Largely dated but not superseded.

Zelliot, Eleanor. *Dr. Ambedkar and the Mahar Movement.* Philadelphia, 1969.

New Sources

Davidson, Ronald M. *Indian Esoteric Buddhism: A Social History of the Tantric Movement.* New York, 2002.

Gellner, David. *Monk, Householder, and Tantric Priest: Newar Buddhism and Its Hierarchy of Ritual.* Cambridge, 1992.

Gombrich, Richard. *Theravāda Buddhism: A Social History from Ancient Benares to Modern Colombo.* London and New York, 1988.

Gombrich, Richard, and Gananath Obeyesekere. *Buddhism Transformed: Religious Change in Sri Lanka.* Princeton, N.J., 1988.

Hirakawa Akira. *A History of Indian Buddhism: From Śākyamuni to Early Mahāyāna.* Translated and edited by Paul Groner. Honolulu, 1990.

Ray, Reginald A. *Buddhist Saints in India: A Study in Buddhist Values and Orientations.* New York, 1994.

Schopen, Gregory. *Bones, Stones, and Buddhist Monks: Collected Papers on the Archaeology, Epigraphy, and Texts of Monastic Buddhism in India.* Honolulu, 1996.

Schopen, Gregory. *Buddhist Monks and Business Matters: Still More Papers on Monastic Buddhism in India.* Honolulu, 2004.

Snellgrove David. *Indo-Tibetan Buddhism.* 2 vols. Boston, 1987.

Williams, Paul, with Anthony Tribe. *Buddhist Thought: A Complete Introduction to the Indian Tradition.* London, 2000.

LUIS O. GÓMEZ (1987)
Revised Bibliography

BUDDHISM: BUDDHISM IN SOUTHEAST ASIA

Conventional wisdom labels the Buddhism of Southeast Asia as Theravāda. Indeed, customarily a general distinction pertains between the "southern," Theravāda, Buddhism of Southeast Asia, whose scriptures are written in Pali, and the "northern," Sanskrit Mahāyāna (including Tantrayāna), Buddhism of Central and East Asia. A Thai or a Burmese most likely thinks of the Buddhism of his country as a continuation of the Theravāda tradition, which was allegedly brought to the Golden Peninsula (Suvaṇṇabhūmi) by Aśoka's missionaries Sona and Uttara in the third century BCE. But modern scholarship has demonstrated that prior to the development of the classical Southeast Asian states, which occurred from the tenth or eleventh century to the fifteenth century CE, Buddhism in Southeast Asia—the area covered by present-day Burma, Thailand, Vietnam, Cambodia (Kampuchea), and Laos—defies rigid classification. Both archaeological and chronicle evidence suggest that the religious situation in the area was fluid and informal, with Buddhism characterized more by miraculous relics and charismatic, magical monks than by organized sectarian traditions. In short, the early period of Buddhism in Southeast Asia was diverse and eclectic, infused with elements of Hindu Dharmśāstra and Brahmanic deities, Mahāyāna Buddhas such as Lokeśvara, Tantric practices, Sanskrit Sarvāstivādin texts, as well as Pali Theravāda traditions.

The classical period of Southeast Asian Buddhism, which lasted from the eleventh to the fifteenth century, began with the development of the monarchical states of Śrīvijaya in Java, Angkor in Cambodia, Pagan in Burma, Sukhōthai in Thailand, and Luang Prabang in Laos, and culminated in the establishment of a normative Pali Theravāda tradition of the Sinhala Mahāvihāra monastic line. Hence, by the fourteenth and fifteenth centuries the primary, although by no means exclusive, form of Buddhism in Burma, Thailand, Laos, and Cambodia was a Sinhala orthodoxy that was dominated doctrinally by "the commentator" (Buddhaghosa) but enriched by various local traditions of thought and practice. By this time, what is now Malaysia and Indonesia, with the exception of Bali, had been overrun by Islam, and the popular religion there was an amalgamation of animism, Brahmanic deities, and the religion of the Prophet. The colonial interregnum, which infused Western and Christian elements into the religious and cultural milieu of Southeast Asia, gradually challenged the dominance of the Indian Buddhist worldview and its symbiotically related institutional realms of kingship (*dhammacakka*) and monastic order (*sāsanacakka*). From the nineteenth century onward Buddhism in Southeast Asia has faced the challenges of Western science; provided cultural and ideological support for modern nationalist movements; offered idiosyncratic, sometimes messianically flavored, solutions to the stresses and strains of political, economic, and social change; and formulated doctrinal innovations challenging the Abhidammic orthodoxy of Buddhaghosa that characterizes the Sinhala Theravāda.

The following essay will examine Buddhism in Southeast Asia in terms of its early development, the establishment of a normative Theravāda orthodoxy, and the diverse responses of this tradition to the challenges of the modern period. The future of Buddhism in Southeast Asia may not hang in the balance; nevertheless, it does appear to be problematic. Political events in Cambodia (Kampuchea) and Laos have threatened the very foundations of institutional Buddhism in those countries. Thailand's rapid and widespread modernization and secularization have undermined many traditional aspects of the religion (*sāsana*), and internal political strife in Burma has had severe, detrimental effects on the *sangha* (Skt., *saṃgha*). Our attention to Southeast Asian Buddhism should not ignore its fragility or its potential contribution to the continuing self-definition and self-determination of these civilizations.

EARLY DEVELOPMENT. From its earliest beginnings to the establishment of the major monarchical states, Buddhism in Southeast Asia can only be characterized as diverse and eclectic. Its presence was felt as part of the Indian cultural influence that flourished throughout the area. During these early centuries Buddhism competed successfully with indigenous forms of magical animism and Brahmanism, undoubtably becoming transformed in the process. Its propagation probably followed the same pattern that was seen in Central and East Asia, with which we are more familiar: Padmasambhava-type monks subjugating territorial guardian spirits; monks accompanying traders and bringing in objects of power and protection, such as relics and images, as well as a literary tradition in the forms of magical chants in sacred languages and also written texts. We glean something of this pattern from Buddhist chronicles in Pali and in Southeast Asian vernacular languages of a later time. When the *Sāsanavaṃsa* of Burma or the *Mūlasāsana* of Thailand relates the story of the Buddha's visit to these countries to establish the religion, we interpret myth in historical terms, reading "the Buddha" to mean "unnamed Buddhist monks" who were bearers of a more advanced cultural tradition. While the chronicles, more so than the early inscriptions, paint a picture of dubious historical accuracy, they correctly associate Buddhism with a high continental way of life in contrast to the less sophisticated life of tribal peoples. Buddhism, then, abets the development of a town or urban culture, provides symbols of translocal value, and articulates a worldview in which diverse communities can participate and find a new identity, a language in which they can communicate, and institutions in which an organized religious life can be pursued and systematically taught.

Such a general description of the early centuries of Buddhism in Southeast Asia does not preclude the establishment of identifiable Buddhist traditions in the area. These include not only strong Pali Theravāda tradition but also other Buddhist sects and schools representing Mahāyāna and Tantric traditions. Pali inscriptions found in Hmawza, the ancient Pyu capital of Śrīkṣetra in lower Burma, indicate the existence of Theravāda Buddhism by the fifth or sixth century CE. Their Andhra-Kadamba script points to connections with Kāñcīpuram, Negapatam, and Kāverīpaṭṭanam in South India. The Chinese traveler Yijing, who visited Shih-li-cha-to-lo (Śrīkṣetra, or Prome) in the seventh century, mentions the presence of not only Theravādins (Āryasthaviras) but also the Āryamahāsāṃghika, Āryamūlasarvāstivāda, and Āryasammatīya schools. We know of the Mahāsāṃghikas as among the forerunners of the Mahāyāna tradition. While their original home was in Magadha, their tradition established itself in parts of northern, western, eastern, and southern India. The Amarāvatī and Nāgārjunikoṇḍa inscriptions, for instance, mention the Mahāsāṃghikas and state that their canon was written in Prakrit. The three other sects are Hīnayāna schools. The Mūlasarvāstivāda, according to one tradition, was one of the seven branches of the Sarvāstivādin tradition and was widespread in India, although it was especially strong in the north, whence it was propagated under the aegis of King Kaniṣka during the late first century CE. Its canon was written in a Buddhist Hybrid Sanskrit. The Sammatīya sect, also known as the Vātsīputrīya or Vajjipattaka, came from Avanti, but inscriptions point to its presence in Sārnāth during the fourth century and in Mathurā during the fifth century. The great early seventh-century ruler Harṣavardhana is thought to have supported the Sammatīyas in the early part of his reign. Hence, the four sects whose presence in the Prome area was attested to by Yijing are all associated with important Indian Buddhist centers and with the reigns of powerful monarchs reputed to have been supporters of various Buddhist sectarian traditions.

Evidence of the diverse nature of sectarian Buddhism during the formative period of Southeast Asian history comes from Burmese and other sources in both mainland and insular Southeast Asia. The Tang dynastic chronicles (seventh to tenth century CE) state that Buddhism flourished in the P'iao (Pyu) capital of Shih-li-cha-to-lo (Śrīkṣetra) in the eighth and ninth centuries. Archaeological and sculptural evidence of the same period from Prome and Hmawza portray the Buddha in scenes from the Jātakas and from popular commentarial stories. Terracotta votive tablets depicting scenes from the life of the Buddha and of the Mahāyāna *bodhisattvas* have also been found, as well as inscriptions written in Sanskrit, Pali, mixed Pali and Sanskrit, and Pyu written in South Indian alphabets. Evidence from ruined stupas in Hmawza, which date from the fifth to the eighth century, reinforce the claim to a strong but diverse Buddhist presence.

The Mon, or Talaing, lived south of the Pyu, occupying the coastal area of lower Burma, with flourishing centers at Pegu (Haṃsavatī) and Thaton (Sudhammavatī). This region, known as Rāmaññadesa in Burmese and Thai chronicles, extended over much of present-day Thailand; one major Mon center was as far north as Haripuñjaya (present-day Lamphun). In Nakorn Prathom, thirty miles southwest of Bangkok, archaeological evidence points to a flourishing Mon Buddhist culture in the region known as Dvāravatī, in which forms of both Hīnayāna and Mahāyāna Buddhism were present. Amarāvatī-style Buddha images in the vicinity of Nakorn Prathom and Pong Tuk date from the fourth to fifth century CE, and images of both early and late Gupta are also found there. While Mon-Dvāravatī Buddhism in Thailand and lower Burma lacked the homogeneity attributed to it by later chroniclers, both archaeological and textual evidence suggest a strong Pali Theravāda presence, especially in comparison to that found in Pagan.

Pagan, near the sacred Mount Popa on the Irrawaddy Plains of upper Burma, had become the locus of power of the Mrammas, a Tibeto-Dravidian tribe who eventually dominated and consequently named the entire region. During the tenth and eleventh centuries, the Buddhism present among people of the Pagan-Irrawaddy River basin seems to have been dominated by an eclectic form of Mahāyāna Tantrism similar to that found in esoteric Śaivism or in animistic *nāga* cults. According to the Burmese chronicles, the monks of this sect, who are referred to as Ari, rejected the teachings of the Lord Buddha. They believed in the efficacy of magical *mantras* over the power of *karman* and propagated the custom of sending virgins to priests before marriage. In addition to numerous figures of Mahāyāna *bodhisattvas*, such as Avalokiteśvara and Mañjuśri, findings include remnants of murals that depict deities embracing their consorts.

According to the *Hmannān mạha yazạwintawkyī* (Glass Palace Chronicle, begun 1829) of Burma, the country's political and religious history was changed by the effect of Shin Arahan, a charismatic Mon Theravāda monk from Thaton, on the Burmese ruler Aniruddha (Anawratha), who ascended to power in Pagan in 1044 CE. According to this account, Shin Arahan converted Aniruddha to a Theravāda persuasion, advising him to secure relics, *bhikkhus* (monks), and Pali texts from Manuha (Manohari), the king of Thaton. Manuha's refusal became the excuse for Aniruddha's invasion of Thaton, the eventual subjugation of the Mons in lower Burma, and the establishment of Theravāda under Kyanzittha (fl. 1084–1113) as the dominant, although by no means exclusive, Buddhist sect.

As part of the Indian cultural expansion into "greater India," Mahāyāna, Tantric, and Hīnayāna forms of Buddhism were established in other parts of mainland and insular Southeast Asia from the fifth century onward. Guṇavarman is reputed to have taken the Dharmaguptaka tradition from northern India to Java in the fifth century, and by the seventh century Buddhism was apparently flourishing in the Sumatra of Śrīvijaya. An inscription from 684 CE, for instance, refers to a Buddhist monarch named Jayanāsā. I-ching, who spent several months in Java on his return to China in order to copy and translate Buddhist texts, indicates that both Hīnayāna and Mahāyāna forms of Buddhism were present at that time. Indonesia was also visited by Dharmapāla of Nālandā University and by two prominent South Indian monks, Vajrabodhi and Amoghavajra, both adherents of a Tantric form of Buddhism. Two inscriptions from the late eighth century refer to the construction, under the aegis of Śailendra rulers, of a Tārā temple at Kalasan and an image of Mañjuśrī at Kelunak. The Śailendras were great patrons of the North Indian Pāla form of Mahāyāna Buddhism.

The rulers of Champa, in southern Annam (Vietnam), also patronized Buddhism. According to Yijing, the dominant tradition in Champa was that of the Āryasammatīya *nikāya*, but the Sarvāstivādins were also present. Amarāvatī-style Buddha images and monastery foundations from the ninth century have been discovered in Quang Nam Province, and an inscription of the same period from An-Thai records the erection of a statue of Lokanātha and refers to such Mahāyāna deities as Amitābha and Vairocana.

Although Hinduism was initially the dominant religion in Cambodia, there is some evidence of Buddhism from the fifth century CE. Jayavarman of Fu-nan sent representatives to China in 503 CE who took as gifts a Buddha image; and an inscription by Jayavarman's son, Rudravarman, invokes the Buddha. In the eleventh century Sūryavarman was given the posthumous Buddhist title of Nirvāṇapada, and Jayavarman VII, the Khmer empire's greatest monarch and builder of Angkor Thom, patronized Buddhism of the Mahāyāna variety. A Pali inscription from 1308, during the reign of Śrīndravarmadeva, refers to a Hīnayāna form of Buddhism, and a Chinese source from about the same time refers to Hīnayāna Buddhism as flourishing in Cambodia at that time.

The evidence cited supports the contention that throughout much of Southeast Asia Buddhism was present as part of the larger Indian cultural influence. Various sources, ranging from testimony of Chinese and indigenous chronicles, diaries of Chinese monk-travelers, as well as a large amount of archaeological and inscriptional evidence, support the contention that both Mahāyāna and Hīnayāna forms of Buddhism existed side by side, dependent on such factors as the particular regional Indian source and the predilection of a given ruler. Clearly, before the emergence of the major classical Southeast Asian states, no standard form of Buddhism existed.

It is also true that various types of Buddhism in this period competed with autochthonous forms of animism as well as Brahmanic cults. Were the early states in Burma, Cambodia, Thailand, and Indonesia—such as Fu-nan, Champa, Śrīkṣetra, Dvāravatī, and so on—Buddhist or Hindu? Or were these great traditions themselves so accommodated and transformed by the Southeast Asian cultures that they qualified the labels "Buddhist" and "Hindu" almost beyond recognition? Although rulers in these preclassical states may be characterized as Hindu or Buddhist and their brand of Buddhism defined by a given sect or school, in all probability they supported a variety of priests, monks, and religious institutions and worshiped various gods and spirits ranging from territorial guardians to Viṣṇu, Śiva, and Vairocana. In some cases we are prone to assign labels when, in reality, the diversity of the situation makes labeling a problematic enterprise at best. Such a qualification does not mean that we are unable to make certain claims about the nature of Buddhism in Southeast Asia in the formative period; however, evidence supporting the presence of particular Buddhist schools and sects should be understood within the general framework of the varied and eclectic nature of Buddhism in this era.

CLASSICAL PERIOD. While diversity and eclecticism continue to mark the character of Buddhism during the period of the foundation of the classical Southeast Asian monarchical states, homogeneity of form and institutional orthodoxy began to emerge during this period. On the one hand, Buddhism and Hinduism contributed to the development of the nature and form of Southeast Asian kingship. On the other hand, the symbiotic relationship that developed between the monarchy and the Buddhist *sangha* tended to support a loose religious orthodoxy. Historically, this orthodoxy follows the Sinhala Theravāda tradition and accompanies the ascendancy of the Burmese and the Tai in mainland Southeast Asia. Vietnam, Malaysia, and Indonesia, however, depart from this pattern: Vietnamese culture was strongly influenced by China, and Malaysia and Indonesia were affected by the advent and spread of Islam during the thirteenth century. We shall first examine Buddhism at the level of the nature and form of classical Southeast Asian kingship and then trace the emergence of Sinhala Theravāda Buddhism as the normative tradition in Burma, Thailand, Cambodia, and Laos after the thirteenth century.

Buddhism and monarchy. The relationship between Buddhism and the rise of the monarchical states in the classical period of Southeast Asian history is customarily referred to as symbiotic, that is, one of mutual benefit. Rulers supported Buddhism because it provided a cosmology in which the king was accorded the central place and a view of society in which the human community was dependent on the role of the king. Ideologically, Buddhism legitimated kingship, providing a metaphysical rationale and moral basis for its existence. The Buddhist *sangha*, in turn, supported Southeast Asian monarchs because the material well-being, success, and popularity of institutional Buddhism depended to a significant degree on the approval, support, and largess of the ruling classes.

The Theravāda picture of the cosmos, set forth classically in the *Aggañña Suttanta* of the *Dīgha Nikāya*, depicts the world as devolving from a more perfect, luminous, undifferentiated state to a condition of greater opacity and differentiation. Imperfection results because differences in sex, comeliness, size of rice fields, and so on engender desire, greed, lust, and hatred, which, in turn, lead to actions that destroy the harmony and well-being of the inhabitants of the world. Recognizing the need to correct the situation, the people select a person whose comeliness, wisdom, virtue, and power enable him to bring order to this disharmonious, chaotic situation. That person, the ruler or king, is referred to in the text as *mahāsammata* because he is chosen by the people. He is *rāja* (king) because he rules by the Dhamma, and he is also *khattiya*, or lord of the fields, responsible for maintaining the economic and political order. Social order is dependent upon the righteous ruler, who creates and maintains the fourfold social structure (the traditional Indian *varṇa* hierarchy). Such a peaceful and harmonious situation also allows for the sustenance of *bhikkhus*, who seek a higher, nonmundane end, that is, *nibbāna* (Skt., *nirvāṇa*). The ruler, then, is responsible for the peace, harmony, and total well-being of the people, which includes the opportunity to pursue a religious or spiritual life.

Buddhism's contribution to the classical conception of Southeast Asian kingship is particularly noteworthy in its emphasis on Dhamma and on the role of the ruler as a moral exemplar. The king is a *cakkavattin*, one whose rule depends upon the universal Dhamma of cosmic, natural, and moral law. His authority stems from the place he assumes in the total cosmic scheme of things. But his power and, hence, his effectiveness rest on his virtue. While the king rules by strength of arms, wealth, intellect, able ministers, and the prestige of his own status, his embodiment of the Dhamma and, hence, his ability to rule depend on his maintenance of the ten *rājadhammas*: liberality, good conduct, nonattachment, straightforwardness, mildness, austerity, suppression of anger, noninjury, patience, and forbearance. The ideal king should cleanse his mind of all traces of avarice, ill will, and intellectual confusion and eschew the use of force and weapons of destruction. These moral virtues represent the highest ideals of Theravāda Buddhism, an overlapping of two "wheels" (*cakka*), or realms: the mundane (*ānācakka, lokiya*) and the transmundane (*sāsanacakka, lokuttara*), or the ideals of the political leader (*cakkavattin*) and the religious exemplar (Buddha).

This symbiotic relationship between political and religious leadership roles takes a particular mythic pattern in many of the classical Southeast Asian chronicles, such as the *Jinakālamālipakaraṇaṃ* (The Sheaf of Garlands of the Epochs of the Conqueror), a pattern also present in the Pali chronicles of Sri Lanka (e.g., the *Mahāvaṃsa*). Essentially, the chroniclers hold that the Budda sacralizes a region by visiting it. He frequently converts the indigenous populations and teaches them the Dhamma. To be sure, the monastic authors had a vested interest in establishing the precedence of Buddhism in the land, but the Buddha's visits to such places as the Tagaung kingdom of Burma and Haripuñjaya in northern Thailand serve the additional purpose of grounding a later interrelationship between Buddhism and kingship. In the northern Thai chronicles, for example, when the Buddha visits the Mon-Lava state of Haripuñjaya in the Chiangmai Valley, he predicts that his bone relic will be discovered by King Ādicca (ĀdTarāja), one of the principal twelfth-century monarchs of this state. This tale not only points to royal support of the *sāsana*, it makes the king the symbolic actualizer of the tradition, which he celebrates by building a *cetiya* for the relic. Furthermore, the Buddha in effect engenders the monarch with the power necessary to rule, a magical potency inherent in the relic. The *cetiya* reliquary mound thus functions as a magical center, or *axis mundi*, for the kingdom. In Haripuñjaya, alliances between the northern Tai kingdom of Lānnā and other states were sealed in front of the magical center. The Emerald Buddha image has played a similar role in Lao and Tai religious history, with various princes of the kingdom swearing fealty to the reigning monarch who possessed it.

The nature of the interrelationship between Buddhism and classical monarchical rule in Southeast Asia manifests itself architecturally in the great *cetiya* or stupa (Skt., *stūpa*) monuments of Borobudur, Angkor, Pagan, and other ancient capitals. The earliest of these, Borobudur, was constructed on the Kedu Plain outside of present-day Jogjakarta on the island of Java in the mid-eighth century CE under a dynasty known as the Śailendras, or "kings of the mountain." The monument's strong Mahāyāna influence is reflected in bas-reliefs that depict stories from the *Lalitavistara, Divyāvadāna, Jātakamālā,* and *Gaṇḍavyūha*. The seventy-two perforated, hollow stupas on the top of three circular platforms cover seated images of the Buddha Vairocana. Scholars have argued that the monument, as a cosmic mountain, connects royal power with the Dharma, the basis of all reality; it may also synthesize an autochthonous cult of "kings of the mountain" with the Ādibuddha, or universal Buddha nature. In support of this connection it is speculated that Śailendra inscriptions use the Sanskrit term *gotra* to signify both "line of the ancestors" as well as "family of the Buddha," thereby identifying the Śailendra ancestral line with that of the Tathāgata.

Angkor, in Cambodia, has been even more widely studied as a source for understanding the interrelationships between Southeast Asian kingship and religion, especially regarding the *devarāja* (god-king) concept. It may be that this concept originated in Fu-nan, a Chinese term derived from the Mon-Khmer *bnam*, meaning "mountain" and possibly referring to a cult of a national guardian spirit established by the founder of the state. In the early ninth century the Khmer ruler Jayavarman II built on this background, adopting Śaivism as the state religion and thus requiring that the king be worshiped as a manifestation of Śiva. This identification was symbolized by a *liṅga* that was set upon the central altar of a pyramidal temple as an imitation of Mount Meru and the center of the realm. The *devarāja* cult took on Mahāyāna Buddhist forms under Sūryavarman I in the early eleventh century and under Jayavarman VII (1181–1218), who constructed the great Bayon Temple, in which Jayavarman and Lokeśvara appear to be identified, at Angkor Thom at the end of the twelfth century. It can be inferred that in the tradition of the *devarāja*, Suryavarman and Jayavarman became *buddharājas*, or incarnate buddhas.

Other classical Southeast Asian capitals and major royal and religious monuments exhibit the influence of both Hindu and Buddhist worldviews. The remains of over five thousand stupas can be seen at the site of ancient Pagan, an area covering sixteen square miles. It was unified by Aniruddha (1040–1077) and the commander of his forces and successor, Kyanzittha (fl. 1084–1113). The Schwezigon Pagoda, possibly begun by Aniruddha but certainly completed by Kyanzittha, enshrines three sacred Buddha relics, symbolizing the power of the *cakkavattin* as the defender of the sacred order of things (*dhamma*). Other stupas, such as the Mingalazedi, which was completed in the late thirteenth century, reflect the basic macro-micro cosmological symbolism of Borobudur; it has truncated pyramidal and terraced bases and a central stairway on each side. The Ānanda Temple, the stupa that dominated Pagan, was constructed by Kyanzittha in the late eleventh century and combines both cosmic mountain and cave symbolism: an ascetic's cave in which the Buddha meditates and a magical *axis mundi* that empowers the entire cosmos. A small kneeling image facing the large Buddha image in the temple is thought to represent Kyanzittha, corroborating inscriptional claims that he saw himself as a *bodhitsatta* and *cakkavattin.*

The mythic ideal of the *cakkavattin* is embodied in the moral example of Aśoka Maurya. Similarly, the *cakkavattin* of the Suttas provides the legendary charter for the idealized kingly exemplar of the Southeast Asian Theravāda chronicles. Aśoka was the moral exemplar *par excellence*, in whose footsteps, so say the chronicles and inscriptions, the monarchs of Burma, Thailand, and Laos follow. Aśoka's conversion divides his biography into two halves—the first tells of warring, wicked Aśoka (Pali, Caṇḍāsoka) and the second of the just, righteous Aśoka (Pali, Dhammāsoka). Similarly Aniruddha kills his brother to become the ruler of Pagan but then becomes a patron of Buddhism, and Tilokarāja (1441–1487) of Chiangmai revolts against his father but then devotes much of his attention to the prosperity of the Buddhist *sangha*. Southeast Asian rulers are also reputed to have called councils, as did Aśoka, in order to purify the *sangha* and regularize the Tipiṭaka. These activities, which supported Buddhism, represented ways the monarch could uphold his reputation for righteousness in ruling the state and in his dealings with the people. In his famous 1292 inscription, Rāma Kham-haeng (Ramkhamhaeng) of Sukhōthai says that the king adjudicates cases of inheritance with complete impartiality, does not kill or beat captured enemy soldiers, and listens to the grievances of his subjects. This paternalistic model of the dhammically righteous king is obviously indebted to the Aśoka model.

Dominance of Sinhala Theravāda Buddhism. The shift to a Sinhala Theravāda orthodoxy in what became, in the true sense, Buddhist Southeast Asia (Burma, Thailand, Laos, and Cambodia) took place gradually from the late eleventh to the early thirteenth century and onward. This development reflected several factors: the decline of Buddhism in parts of Asia that had influenced the Southeast Asian mainland; the rising influence of Sri Lanka under Vijayabāhu I (1055–1110) and Parākramabāhu I; the consolidation of power by the Burmese and Tai; an increasing interrelationship among Sri Lanka, Burma, and Thailand; and the spread of popular Theravāda practice among the general population of mainland Southeast Asia. The general outline of the story of the establishment of Sinhala Theravāda Buddhism in Southeast Asia is reasonably clear, although disparities between epigraphic and chronicle sources make historical precision difficult. Consequently, scholars disagree on dates, and historical reconstructions keep on changing.

Pali Theravāda and Sanskrit Hīnayāna forms of Buddhism were present at a relatively early time. Pali inscriptions found in central Thailand and lower Burma and associated with Mon culture support this claim, as does chronicle testimony, such as the story of Aniruddha's excursion into Rāmaññadesa to secure Pali scriptures. Inscriptional evidence makes it reasonable to assume that the roots of Mon Theravāda lay in the Kāñcīpuram area along the east coast of India. Even the popular Burmese tradition that holds that Buddhaghosa, who has been associated with Kāñcī, either came from Thaton or went there after visiting Sri Lanka may contain a kernel of historical truth, namely, the spread of Kāñcī Theravāda Buddhism into the Mon area. The presence of Pali Theravāda Buddhism among the Mon, who strongly influenced both the Burmese and Tai, provides the religio-cultural backdrop to the eventual consolidation of Sri Lankan forms of Theravāda Buddhism. As we shall see, both the Burmese and the Tai assimilated elements of Mon culture: its religion, legal traditions, artistic forms, and written script. Mon Theravāda, in effect, mediated Sinhala Theravāda. On the one hand, Theravāda Buddhism from Sri Lanka provided continuity with Mon religio-cultural traditions; on the other, it enabled the Burmese and Tai to break away from a Mon religio-cultural dominance. We must now explore some of the details of this story of cultural transformation and religious consolidation.

Burma. Contact between Burma and Sri Lanka dates from the establishment of the Pagan era by Aniruddha. Because of the disruption of Sri Lanka caused by wars with the Cōḻas in the mid-eleventh century, Vijayabāhu I, knowing of the strength of the Mon Theravāda traditions, sought help from Aniruddha to restore valid ordination. Aniruddha responded by sending a group of monks and Pali scriptures to Sri Lanka. In turn, Aniruddha requested, and was sent, a replica of the Buddha's tooth relic and a copy of the Tipiṭaka with which to check the copies of the Pali scriptures acquired at Thaton. The tooth relic was enshrined in Pagan's Schwezigon Pagoda, which became Burma's national palladium. Although archaeological evidence calls into question the chronicler's claim regarding the acquisition of the entire Pali Tipiṭaka, the tale might well be interpreted to indicate the growing importance of Sinhala Buddhism, not simply because the texts were more authoritative, but because the alliance between the king and the new sectarian tradition legitimated his authority over the Mon religio-cultural tradition.

Sinhala Buddhism flourished during the reign of Narapatisithu (1173–1210), and the Mahāvihāra tradition became normative at this time. Sinhala Buddhism, in particular the Mahāvihāra tradition, gained position partly through visits of distinguished Burmese monks to Sri Lanka. Panthagu, successor to Shin Arahan as the nominal head of the Pagan Buddhist *sangha,* visited the island in 1167. The Mon monk Uttarajīva Mahāthera followed in his predecessor's footsteps by journeying to Sri Lanka in 1180 with a group of monks that included a Mon novice named Chapaṭa, who was to figure most prominently in establishing the precedent authority of the Mahāvihāra. Chapaṭa and four others remained in Sri Lanka for ten years and were reordained as Mahatheras in the Mahāvihāra lineage. Their return to Burma marked the permanent establishment of Sinhala Buddhism in mainland Southeast Asia and brought about a schism in the Burmese Buddhist *sangha* between the Theravāda school of Thaton and Kāñcī, characterized by Shin Arahan's orthodoxy; and the Sinhala Theravāda tradition. When Chapaṭa returned to Pagan, Narapatisithu requested that he and the other four Mahatheras reordain Burmese monks of the Shin Arahan tradition, thereby establishing the superior legitimacy of the Sinhala orthodoxy over the Mon form of Theravāda. The chronicles refer to the Shin Arahan tradition as the "early school" (*purimagaṇa*) and to Chapaṭa's Sīhaḷa Sangha simply as the "late school" (*pacchāgaṇa*). Owing to disciplinary and personal reasons, the *pacchāgaṇa* was to divide into several branches each loyal to one or another of the Mahātheras who had returned from Sri Lanka. One point of dispute among the branches was whether gifts could be given to particular monks or to the *sangha* at large.

The Sīhaḷa order was introduced to lower Burma at Dala, near Rangoon, by Sāriputta, who bore the title Dhammavīlasa, meaning a scholar of great repute. This tradition is referred to as the Sīhaḷapakkhabhikkhu Sangha, in contrast with the Ariyārahanta-pakkhabhikkhu Sangha, which represents the Mon Theravāda tradition. The chronicles also call this school the Kambojasanghapakka on the grounds that it was headquartered near a settlement of Kambojans (Cambodians). This title may reflect historical fact or refer to the earlier Theravāda of the Mon-Khmer areas to the east (i.e., Dvāravatī), which found its way into lower Burma. The Sīhaḷa Sangha was also introduced to Martaban by two Mon monks, Buddhavaṃsa Mahāthera and Mahāsāmi Mahāthera, who had been reordained in Sri Lanka. According to the Kalyāṇī inscriptions of Pegu, by the thirteenth century six Buddhist schools—the Mon Ariyārahanta and five Sīhaḷa sects—existed in Martaban. Sectarianism in Burmese Theravāda has continued into the modern period and contrasts with the relative homogeneity of Theravāda Buddhism in Thailand.

Buddhism prospered during the reign of Narapatisithu (1173–1210). Many beautiful temples were built under his sponsorship (e.g., Sulamani, Gawdawpalin), and Pali scholarship flourished. For example, Chapaṭa (also known as Saddhammajotipāla) wrote a series of famous works dealing with Pali grammar, discipline (Vinaya), and higher philosophy (e.g., *Suttaniddesa, Sankhepa-vaṇṇanā, Abhidhammatthasangha*), and Sāriputta wrote the first collection of laws composed in Rāmaññadesa, known as the *Dhammavīlasa* or *Dhammathāt.* The shift away from a dominant Mon influence that occurred during Narapatisithu's reign is also reflected in the architectural style and the use of Burmese in inscriptions.

Thailand. The development of Buddhism among the Tai followed roughly the same pattern as in Burma. As the Tai migrated from southwestern China into the hills east of the Irrawaddy (home of the Shans), the upper Menam Plain (the Siamese), and farther east to the Nam U (the Lao), and as they gradually moved into the lowland area dominated by the Mons and the Khmers, they came into contact with Theravāda and Mahāyāna forms of Buddhism as well as with Brahmanism. After Khubilai Khan's conquest of Nan-chao in 1254 caused ever greater numbers of Tai to push south, they began to establish domination over the Mon and Khmer and to absorb elements of these more advanced cultures. As was the case in Burma, Mon Buddhism in particular became a major influence on the Tai as they extended their sway over much of what we now know as modern Thailand. This influence is seen in the establishment of two major Tai states in the late thirteenth and fourteenth centuries, Sukhōthai and Chiangmai.

Both Sukhōthai and Chiangmai became powerful centers of Tai settlement under the leadership of the able rulers Rāma Khamhaeng (r. c. 1279–1299) and Mengrai respectively. Sukhōthai, which had been a Khmer outpost from at least the time of Jayavarman VII, became an independent Tai state in the middle of the thirteenth century. Two Tai chieftains, Phe Mu'ang and Bang Klang Hao, seized Śrī Sajanalāya and drove the Khmer governor from Sukhōthai. Bang Klang Hao was installed as ruler of Sukhōthai with the title Indrāditya. Indrāditya's third son, Rāma Khamhaeng, was to become Sukhōthai's greatest monarch and one of the exemplary Buddhist kings of Tai history. During his reign, which extended over the last two decades of the century, Rāma Khamhaeng asserted his sway over a large area extending from Haṃsavatī (Pegu) to the west, Phrae to the north, Luang Prabang to the east, and Nakorn Sri Dhammaraja (Nagara Śrī Dharmarāja; Ligor or Tambraliṅga) to the south. Nakorn Sri Dhammaraja, although dominated by Śrīvijaya from the eighth to the twelfth century and later by the Khmer, was an important center of Theravāda Buddhism by the eleventh century. Prior to Rāma Khamhaeng's ascendance to power in Sukhōthai, Chandrabhānu of Nagara Śrī Dharmarāja had sent a mission to Sri Lanka, and the *Cūlavaṃsa* reports that Parākramabāhu II invited Dhammakitti Mahāthera, a monk from Nagara Śrī Dharmarāja, to visit Sri Lanka. Rāma Khamhaeng, who was well aware of the strength of Theravāda Buddhism at Nagara Śrī Dharmarāja, invited a Mahāthera from the forest-dwelling tradition (*araññaka*) there to reside in Sukhōthai. Rāma Khamhaeng's famous 1292 stela inscription refers to various religious sanctuaries in Sukhōthai, including the *araññaka* monastery (Wat Taphan Hin), a Khmer temple (Wat Phra Phai Luang), and a shrine to the guardian spirit of the city, Phra Khaphung. In short, while we have definitive evidence that Rāma Khamhaeng supported Theravāda Buddhism, religion in thirteenth-century Sukhōthai was varied and eclectic.

During the reigns of Rāma Khamhaeng's successors—his son Lö Tai (1298–1347), and his grandson Lü Thai (1347–1368/74?)—Sinhala Buddhism became normative. According to the *Jīnakālamāli*, a Sukhōthai monk named Sumana studied under, and received ordination from, a Sinhala Mahāthera, Udumbara Mahāsāmi, who was resident in Martaban. Sumana returned to Sukhōthai to establish the Sīhaḷa Sangha there, and, along with his colleague Anōmadassī, he proceeded to spread the Sīhaḷa order throughout much of Thailand (Ayuthayā, Pitsanulōk, Nān, Chiangmai, and Luang Prabang). King Lü Thai, in particular, was noted for his piety and his support of Buddhism. He brought Buddha relics and images and established Buddha "footprints" (*buddhapada*) in an effort to popularize Buddhist practice throughout his realm. A Buddhist scholar of note, he was particularly known as the author of the *Traibhūmikathā* (Verses on the Three Worlds), thought to be the first systematic Theravāda cosmological treatise.

About the same time that Sinhala Buddhism was coming into its own in Sukhōthai, it was also being spread to Tai states to the north and northeast, namely, Chiangmai and Luang Prabang. Chiangmai was established as the major Tai state in northern Thailand by Mengrai, who expanded his authority from Chiangsaen to encompass Chiangrai, Chiangkhong, and Fāng. He subjugated the Mon-Lava center of Haripuñjaya in 1291 before founding Chiangmai in 1296. According to both inscriptional and chronicle evidence, Sumana Mahāthera brought the Sinhala Buddhism he had learned from his preceptor in Martaban to Chiangmai in 1369 at the invitation of King Küna (1355–1385). Küna built Wat Suan Dọk to house the Buddha relic brought by Sumana, and Sinhala Buddhism gained favored status over the Mon Theravāda traditions of Haripuñjaya. As in the case of Sukhōthai and Pagan, Sinhala Buddhism functioned not only as a means to build continuity with the Mon Theravāda tradition over which the Tai and the Burmese established their authority but also as a means to assert their unique religio-cultural traditions.

The apogee of the development of the Sīhaḷa order in Chiangmai was reached during the reigns of Tilokarāja, one of the greatest of the Tai monarchs, and Phra Mu'ang Kaew (1495–1526). Tilokarāja legitimated the overthrow of his father, Sam Fang Kaen, through the support of the Mahāvihāra order, which had been brought to Chiangmai in 1430. According to the Mūlasāsana of Wat Pa Daeng in Chiangmai, the center of this sect, this tradition was brought to Thailand by a group of thirty-nine monks from Chiangmai, Lopburi, and lower Burma who had visited Sri Lanka in 1423 during the reign of Parākramabāhu VI of Kotte. They returned to Ayutthayā, a Tai state that subjugated Sukhōthai under the Indrarāja in 1412, and dominated central Thailand until they were conquered by the Burmese at the end of the eighteenth century. According to the northern Tai chronicles, members of this mission spread throughout central and northern Thailand, reordaining monks into the new Sīhaḷa order. Tilokarāja made this Wat Pa Daeng-Mahāvihāra group the normative monastic tradition in Chiangmai at a general council in 1477. The Pa Daeng chronicles depict Tilokarāja as a great supporter of the *sangha* and as a righteous and exemplary monarch in the Aśokan mode. During the reign of Tilokarāja's successor, Phra Mu'ang Kaew, Pali Buddhist scholarship in Chiangmai flourished. The *Māṅga-ladīpaṇi*, a Pali commentary on the *Māṅgala Sutta*, was written at this time and is still used as the basis of higher-level Pali studies, and the most important northern Tai chronicle, the *Jīnakālamālipakaraṇa*, also dates from this period.

Contemporaneous with the apogee of Buddhism in Chiangmai was the reign of Dhammaceti (1472–1492), who ruled Burma from Pegu, in the lower part of the country. According to the northern Tai and Burmese chronicles as well as the Kalyāṇī inscriptions, during Dhammaceti's reign there were several religious missions to Sri Lanka from Pegu and Ava, and Sīhaḷa monks, in turn, visited Burma. Burmese monks were reordained and visited sacred shrines on the island. Like Tilokarāja, Dhammaceti wanted to unify the *sangha* and used the new ordination to unite Buddhists in the Pegu kingdom. Monks from all over lower Burma, Ava, Tougoo, from the Shan kingdoms, Thailand, and Cambodia came to Pegu to be ordained during what the chronicles portray as the "golden age" of lower Burma.

Cambodia and Laos. Theravāda Buddhism was introduced to Cambodia by the Mon of the lower Menam Chaophraya River valley. In the eleventh and twelfth centuries, Theravāda also existed alongside Mahāyāna forms of Buddhism as well as Brahmanism. Mahāyāna Buddhism certainly received royal patronages in the eleventh century, and

Jayavarman VII, the builder of the Bayon Temple at Angkor Thom, was identified with the Buddha Lokeśvara in the divine-royal symbiosis of the Khmer *devarāja/buddharāja* cult. Yet, typical of the classical Southeast Asian monarchs, Jayavarman's patronage of Mahāyāna Buddhism was not exclusive. According to the Kalyāṇī inscriptions and *The Glass Palace Chronicle*, a Cambodian monk, possibly Jayavarman's son, was part of the Burmese mission to Sri Lanka in the twelfth century. There was certainly an influx of Mon Buddhists from the Lopburi region in the face of Tai pressure in the thirteenth and early fourteenth centuries. Testimony of Chau Ta Kuan, a member of a late-thirteenth-century mission to Angkor, indicates that Theravāda monks were present in the Khmer capital during that period. The *Jīnakālamāli* account of the Chiangmai mission to Sri Lanka in 1423 CE includes reference to eight Khmer monks who brought the Sīhaḷa order of the Mahāvihāra to Cambodia.

The development of Buddhism in Laos was influenced by both Cambodia and Thailand. According to the Lao chronicles, Jayavarman Parmesvara (1327–1353) helped Phi Fa and Fa Ngum establish the independent kingdom of Lān Chāng, which earlier had been under the political hegemony of Sukhōthai. An inscription at Wat Keo in Luang Prabang refers to three Sinhala Mahātheras—including Mahāpasaman, Fa Ngum's teacher at Angkor—who went from Cambodia to Lān Chāng as part of a religious mission. Certainly, from the late fourteenth century onward, Buddhism in Laos and Cambodia was primarily influenced by the Tai as a consequence of their political dominance in the area. Even in the modern period, Theravāda sectarian developments in Thailand were reflected in Cambodia and Laos, and prior to the Communist revolution, monks from Cambodia and Laos studied in the Buddhist universities in Bangkok.

Summary. During the period that marks the rise of the classical Southeast Asian states, Buddhism existed in many guises. Pali Theravāda was introduced principally through the Mon of Dvāravatī and lower Burma and was considered a "higher" culture appropriated by the Burmese and the Tai. A strong Mahāyāna Buddhist presence is apparent not only in Śrīvijaya and Angkor but also in Pagan and the early Tai states. Furthermore, these forms of Buddhism competed with, and were complemented by, autochthonous animistic cults and Brahmanism. Buddhism made a decisive contribution to the conception of Southeast Asian kingship and monarchical rule through its ideal of the *dhammarāja*, who was not only represented by King Aśoka in India but by such Southeast Asian monarchs as Kyanzittha, Rāma Khamhaeng, and Tilokarāja.

Sri Lanka played the decisive role in the increasing dominance of Theravāda Buddhism in mainland Southeast Asia. Several factors contributed to this development, but I have singled out two: the rise to power of the Burmese and the Tai, who appropriated the Theravāda Buddhism of the Mon; and their subsequent adoption of Sinhala Buddhism as a way of establishing their own distinctive cultural and religious identity. While Sīnhala influence can be traced to the eleventh century, the Sīhala order only became dominant with the rise and development of the classical states from the mid-twelfth to the end of the fifteenth century. Sinhala Buddhism contributed to the legitimation of the ruling monarchies through its worldview, interpretation of history, monastic institution, education, and language; however, just as important, it became the religion of the masses through the worship of relics and sacred images and through the development of popular syncretic cults.

Vietnam has been largely excluded from the story of the development of the classical Buddhist Southeast Asian states because of the predominance of Hinduism among the Chams during early Vietnamese history and the overwhelming cultural influence of China on the country. Until the eleventh century the Vietnamese were effectively a group within the Chinese empire, and they looked to China for cultural inspiration even after they achieved independence under the Ly dynasty (1009–1224). Mahāyāna Buddhism was certainly part of the Chinese cultural influence, and the Chan (Viet., Thien) school, allegedly first established in 580 CE by Ti-ni-da-lu'u-chi, was the major Buddhist tradition in Vietnam. The elite eventually came to prefer Confucianism, but Buddhism continued to be important among the masses.

SOUTHEAST ASIAN BUDDHISM IN THE MODERN PERIOD. The classical Southeast Asian religio-cultural synthesis, of which Theravāda Buddhism has been a major component, has given the cultures of Burma, Thailand, Cambodia, Laos, and Vietnam a unique sense of identity and has sustained them to the present. Faced with Western imperialistic expansion from the seventeenth century onward and the challenge of modernity, the classical religious worldview, institutional structures, and cultural ethos have been changed, modified, and reasserted in a variety of ways. We shall examine how Buddhism has adapted to this challenge, its role in the development of the modern nation-state, and what the most recent trends suggest for the future of Buddhism in the region.

The condition of Southeast Asian Buddhism in the modern period reflects, to a large degree, the forces unleashed during the colonial period, especially during the nineteenth and twentieth centuries. Although modern religious histories of Burma, Thailand, and Indochina differ because of internal factors as well as the uniqueness of their colonial experiences—just as the Enlightenment fundamentally challenged the medieval synthesis of Christian Europe—the last century and a half has called into question the traditional Buddhist-Brahmanic-animistic synthesis of Southeast Asia and, consequently, the institutions and values associated with that worldview. The challenge to the classical worldview, and to the traditional moral community that was based on it, occurred on many fronts. Throughout the region the educational role of the *sangha* has been undermined by Western education. The status of the monk as one who was educated and as an educator and the significance of what was traditionally taught have also suffered. In Burma, the destruction of the institution of Buddhist kingship in 1885, as well as the relatively open posture of the British toward Buddhism, left the *sangha* in disarray, without the authority and direction the king traditionally provided. Thailand's rapid urbanization over the past fifty years has dramatically changed the village or town milieu that has historically informed and supported Buddhist religious practice. The communist revolutions in Laos, Cambodia, and Vietnam have displaced Buddhism as the fundamental mediator of cultural values. These are but a few of the challenges that Southeast Asian Buddhism has faced in the modern and contemporary periods.

Modernization and reform. The eve of the assertion of colonial power in the Buddhist countries of Southeast Asia found them in differing states and conditions. The Burmese destruction of Ayutthayā in 1767 provided the Thai (the designation applied to Tai living in the modern nation-state) the opportunity to establish a new capital on the lower Chaophraya River at present-day Bangkok. Because of its accessibility to international commerce the new site was much better situated for the new era about to dawn; the new dynastic line was better able to cope with the increasing impact of Western influence and was also committed to building a new sense of national unity. The Burmese, on the other hand, tired of wars under Alaungpaya and his son, were beset by religious and ethnic fractionalism. They were disadvantaged by the more isolated location of their capital (Ava, Amarapura, and then Mandalay), and governed by politically less astute rulers such as King Bagyidaw, who lost the Arakan and lower Burma to the British in the Anglo-Burmese Wars. Cambodia, in the eighteenth and early nineteenth centuries, basically fell victim to either the Thai or the Vietnamese until the French protectorate was established over the country in the 1860s. The Lao kingdoms of Luang Prabang and Vientiane were subject to Thai dominance in the nineteenth century until King Norodom was forced to accept French protection in 1863. Only in the 1890s were the French able to pacify Cochin China, Annam, and Tongkin, which, together with Cambodia, were formed into the Union Indochinoise in 1887. With the rest of Buddhist Southeast Asia disrupted by the colonial policies of France and Great Britain, Thailand's independence and able leadership under Mongkut (Rāma IV, 1851–1868) and Chulalongkorn (1868–1910) abetted religious modernization and reform, making Thailand the appropriate focus for this topic.

The classical Thai Buddhist worldview had been set forth in the *Traibhūmikathā* of King Lü Thai of Sukhōthai. In one sense this text must be seen as part of Lü Thai's program to reconstruct an administrative and political framework and to salvage the alliance structure that had collapsed under the policies of his predecessor. In laying out the traditional Buddhist stages of the deterioration of history, Lü Thai meant to affirm the meaningfulness of a karmically calculated human life within a given multitiered universe. As a Buddhist sermon it urges its listeners to lead a moral life and by so doing to reap the appropriate heavenly rewards. Within its great-chain-of-being framework of various human, heavenly, and demonic realms, the text focuses on a central figure, the universal monarch, or *cakkavattin*, exemplified by the legendary king Dharmaśokarāja. Lü Thai's traditional picture of the world, the role of the king, the nature of karmic action, and the hope of a heavenly reward provide a rationale for Sukhōthai political, social, and religious order. That King Rāma I (1782–1809), who reestablished the fortunes of the Thai monarchy, commissioned a new recension of the *Traibhūmi* testifies to its longevity and also to its utility as a charter for order and stability during yet another time of political and social disruption.

The worldview of the *Traibhūmi* was soon to be challenged by the West, however. European and American missionaries, merchants, and travelers came to Bangkok in the 1830s and 1840s, and by 1850 Thailand, or Siam, had signed commercial treaties with several Western nations. Led by Mongkut, who was crowned king in 1851, and by Chao Phraya Thiphakorawong, his able minister of foreign affairs, the Siamese noble elite proved to be interested in and open to Western technology and culture. A pragmatic type of scientific empiricism began to develop among them, leading even the devout Mongkut to articulate a demythologized Buddhism somewhat at odds with the traditional *Traibhūmi* worldview. This critique was formally set forth in 1867 in Chao Phraya Thiphakorawong's *Kitchanukit* (A Book Explaining Various Things), which explains events not in terms of traditional cosmological and mythological sources but using astronomy, geology, and medicine. For example, he argues that rain falls not because the rainmaking deities venture forth or because a great serpent thrashes its tail but because the winds suck water out of clouds; illness, he says, is caused not by a god punishing evil deeds but by air currents. Although the explanations were inaccurate, they were naturalistic rather than mythological or religious. The *Kitchanukit* presents Buddhism as primarily a system of social ethics; heaven and hell are not places but have a moral or pedagogical utility; *kamma* (Skt., *karman*) is not an actual causal force but a genetic principle that accounts for human diversity. Mongkut's successor, his son Chulalongkorn, moved even further from the mythic cosmology of the traditional Southeast Asian Buddhist worldview, declaring the *Traibhūmi* simply an act of imagination.

Modernization of the Thai Buddhist worldview was accompanied by a reform of the Buddhist *sangha*, led initially by Mongkut and continued during the reign of Chulalongkorn. Before his coronation in 1851 Mongkut had been a monk for twenty-five years. During that time his study of the Pali scriptures and his association with Mon monks of a stricter discipline convinced him that Thai Buddhism had departed from the authentic Buddhist tradition. He advocated a more serious study of Pali and Buddhist scripture as well as the attainment of proficiency in meditation. His efforts at religious reform resulted in an upgrading of monastic discipline in an effort to make it more orthodox. The group of monks who gathered around Mongkut at Wat Bovornives called themselves the Thammayut ("those adhering to the doctrine") and formed the nucleus of a new, stricter sect of Thai Buddhism. With its royal origins and connections, the Thammayut, or Dhammayuttika, sect has played a very influential role in the development of modern Thai Buddhism. In 1864 the Khmer royal family imported it to Cambodia, where it played a similar role. Its impact in Laos, however, was less significant.

The development of a reformist Buddhist tradition that embodied Mongkut's ideals brought about further changes in the monastic order, especially as the *sangha* became part of the policies and programs of Mongkut's son Chulalongkorn. At the same time that he implemented reforms designed to politically integrate outlying areas into the emergent nation-state of Thailand, Chulalongkorn also initiated policies aimed at the incorporation of all Buddhists within the kingdom into a single national organization. As a consequence, monastic discipline, as well as the quality of monastic education, improved throughout the country. A standard monastic curriculum, which included three levels of study in Buddhist history, doctrine, and liturgy, and nine levels of Pali study, was established throughout the country. In addition, two Buddhist academies for higher studies were established in Bangkok.

The modernization and reform of Buddhism in Thailand in the late nineteenth and early twentieth centuries stand out, but the Thai case must be seen as part of a general trend in all the Southeast Asian Buddhist countries. In the area of text and doctrine a new scripturalism, epitomized by the new redaction of the Tipiṭaka in conjunction with the general Buddhist council held in Burma in 1956 and 1957, has emerged. Doctrinal reinterpretation has followed three major lines: an emphasis on the ethical dimensions of the tradition at the expense of the supernatural and mythical; a rejection of magical elements of popular thought and practice as incompatible with the authentic tradition; and a rationalization of Buddhist thought in terms of Western categories, along with an apologetic interest in depicting Buddhism as scientific. Some apologists, such as U Chan Htoon of Burma, have claimed that all modern scientific concepts preexisted in Buddhism. Others make less sweeping claims but cite specific correlations between such Buddhist doctrines as interdependent co-arising (*paṭicca samuppāda;* Skt., *pratītya-samutpāda*) and Einstein's relativity theory. Generally speaking, Buddhist apologists have attempted to prove that Buddhism is more scientific than other religions, particularly Christianity; that the empirical approach or methodology of Buddhism is consistent with modern science; and that science proves or validates particular Buddhist teachings.

Institutional modernization and reform have also taken place along the lines that we have examined in some detail in regard to Thailand. Cambodia, for example, not only adopted the Dhammayuttika sect from Thailand but also reorganized the *sangha* along national lines. In Laos and Burma various Buddhist organizations and associations with reformist intent emerged, often under lay leadership.

Buddhism and the modern nation-state. Buddhism proved to be a crucial factor during the end of the colonial and the postcolonial periods, as Burma, Thailand, Cambodia, Laos, and Vietnam became modern nation-states. On the one hand, Buddhism contributed decisively to the development of the new nationhood; on the other, it resisted in various ways changes forced upon traditional Buddhist thought and practice. We shall first examine the Buddhist contributions to the national independence movements and to the maintenance of national identity and unity; second, we shall explore Buddhist resistance to pressures put on the tradition by the organization of the modern nation-state.

Historically, Buddhism played an important role in the definition of the classical Southeast Asian states. It was inevitable, therefore, that it would be a crucial factor in the redefinition of these states. In those cases, for example, in which a country was dominated by a colonial power, nationalist movements grew out of, or were identified with, a religious base or context. Take Burma as a case in point. Buddhism provided the impetus for the independence movement that arose there during the first decades of the twentieth century. The YMBAs (Young Men's Buddhist Association) of Rangoon and elsewhere in Burma quickly assumed a political role. The first issue of major consequence was the "no footwear" controversy of 1918. The YMBAs argued that Europeans, in keeping with Burmese custom, should be prohibited from wearing shoes in all pagodas; accordingly, the British government allowed the head monk of each pagoda to decide the regulations applying to footwear. During the next decade the nationalist cause was led primarily by the General Council of Burmese Associations and by such politically active monks as U Ottama, who was imprisoned for urging a boycott of government-sponsored elections, and U Wisara, who became a martyr to the independence movement when he died during a hunger strike in a British jail.

When U Nu became prime minister in January 1948, following Aung San's assassination, he put Buddhism at the heart of his political program. Although he rejected Marxism, he espoused a Buddhist socialism. In essence, he believed that a national community could be constructed only if individuals are able to overcome their own self-acquisitive interests. Sufficient material needs should be provided for everyone, class and property distinctions should be minimized, and all should strive for moral and mental perfection. The state was to meet the material needs of the people and Buddhism their spiritual needs. To this end he created a Buddhist Sasana Council in 1950 to propagate Buddhism and to supervise monks, appointed a minister of religious affairs, and ordered government departments to dismiss civil servants thirty minutes early if they wished to meditate. In 1960 U Nu committed himself and his party to making Buddhism the state religion of Burma, an unpopular move with such minorities as the Christian Karens. This attempt was one of the reasons given for General Ne Win's coup in March 1962, which deposed U Nu as prime minister. While in many ways naive and politically unrealistic, U Nu's vision of Buddhist socialism harked back to an earlier vision of the political leader as one who ruled by *dhamma* and who would engender peace and prosperity by the power of his own virtue. But such a vision proved incompatible with the political realities of the 1960s.

Buddhism figured prominently in other Southeast Asian countries, both as a basis of protest against ruling regimes and as an important symbolic component of political leadership. In the 1960s politically active Vietnamese monks contributed to the downfall of the Diem regime, and afterward the United Buddhist Association, under the leadership of Thich Tri Quang and Thich Thien Minh, remained politically active. In Cambodia, Prince Sihanouk espoused a political philosophy based on Buddhist socialism and was the last Cambodian ruler to represent, although in an attenuated way, the tradition of classical Southeast Asian Buddhist rule.

In addition to providing the inspiration for political independence movements, contributing to a political ideology with uniquely Buddhist features, and being the motivating force challenging political power structures, Southeast Asian Buddhism has been used to promote political unity within the boundaries of the nation-state. U Nu's hope that making Buddhism the state religion would promote national unity was naive; it did not take into account the contending factions within the Buddhist *sangha* and the presence of sizable non-Buddhist minorities who feared they might be threatened by covert, if not overt, pressure from the Buddhist majority.

In Thailand the centralization of the Thai *sangha* under King Chulalongkorn and his able *sangharāja*, Vajirañāṇa, not only improved monastic discipline and education but also integrated the monastic order more fully into the nation-state. Chulalongkorn's successor, Vajiravudh (1910–1925), made loyalty to the nation synonymous with loyalty to Buddhism; in effect, he utilized Buddhism as an instrument to promote a spirit of nationalism. In particular, he glorified military virtues and identified nationalism with the support of Thai Buddhism. He founded the Wild Tigers Corps, resembling the British Territorial Army; the Tiger Cubs, a branch of the corps, was later assimilated into the Boy Scout movement. Both encouraged loyalty to nation, religion (i.e., Buddhism), and the king.

Buddhism has continued to be an important tool in the government's policy to promote national unity. In 1962 the Buddhist Sangha Act further centralized the organization of the monastic order under the power of the secular state. In the same year the government organized the Dhammadhuta program, and in 1965 the Dhammacarika program. The former supported Buddhist monks abroad and those working in sensitive border areas, especially the northeastern region of the country, while the latter has focused on Buddhist missions among northern hill tribes.

Buddhism, however, has not only functioned as a kind of "civil religion," contributing to the definition and support of the new Southeast Asian nation-states in the postcolonial period. It has also resisted the kind of accommodation and change brought on by the new nationalism. In some cases this resistance has been generated by the desire to maintain traditional religious practices and more local autonomy; in others, it has come in the form of armed rebellion and messianic, millenarian movements. As an example of the former we cite Khrūbā Sīwichai, a northern Thai monk of the early twentieth century, and of the latter we cite the Saya San rebellion (1930–1931) in Burma.

While the vast majority of the Buddhist *sangha* in Thailand cooperated with the central government's attempts in the early twentieth century to standardize monastic organization, discipline, and education, there were a few notable exceptions. Khrūbā Sīwichai of the Chiangmai region of northern Thailand was one of them. He ran into problems with the *sangha* hierarchy because he ordained monks and novices according to northern Thai custom although he had not been recognized as a preceptor by the national order. He also singlehandedly raised vast sums of money to rebuild monasteries that had fallen into disrepair and to construct a road, using manual labor, to the famous Mahādhātu Temple on Doi Sutēp Mountain, overlooking Chiangmai. Because of his success in these enterprises, miraculous powers were attributed to him. In 1919, however, he was ordered to report to Bangkok to answer charges of clerical disobedience and sedition, but high Thai officials, fearing the repercussions that punishment of Khrūbā Sīwichai might have, intervened on his behalf. Although eventually Sīwichai submitted to the laws of the Thai national monastic order, *sangha* officials tacitly agreed to permit the northern clergy to follow some of its traditional customs.

Other, more radical Buddhist responses to the emerging nation-state developed in various parts of Southeast Asia and usually centered on a charismatic leader who was sometimes identified as an incarnation of the *bodhisattva* Maitreya. In Burma several rebellions in the early twentieth century aimed to overthrow British rule and to restore the fortunes of both Burmese kingship and Burmese Buddhism. One of these was led by Saya San, who had been a monk in the Tharrawaddy district in lower Burma but disrobed to work in a more directly political way to overthrow the British. Saya San's movement had a strongly traditional religious and royal aura, and much of his support came from political monks associated with nationalistic associations (*wunthanu athins*) that had formed in the 1920s. Saya San was "crowned" as "king" in a thoroughly traditional Burmese manner in a jungle capital on October 28, 1930. An armed group was trained and the rebellion launched toward the end of December. As the conflict spread throughout lower Burma and into the Shan States, the British army was called in to help the police forces repress the rebellion. Only after eight months of fighting did the warfare end.

Recent trends. The chapter on Southeast Asian Buddhism's future within the context of the modern nation-state has yet to be closed. The disestablishment of the *sangha* in Cambodia and Laos has shaken, but by no means rooted out, the tradition, even though Pol Pot's genocidal regime attempted such wholesale destruction in the aftermath of American withdrawal from the war in Indochina. Laos and Cambodia, however, have experienced a breakdown of the traditional religio-cultural synthesis. This is taking place more slowly in Thailand and even in Burma, which has been much more isolated from Western influences since the early 1960s. The political and economic contexts of Southeast Asian Buddhism, in short, have obviously affected the state of Buddhism in Southeast Asia. The trends that have emerged seem paradoxical, if not contradictory. We shall examine three sets or pairs: increasingly active lay leadership and the veneration of monks to whom supernatural powers are ascribed; a revival of meditation practice and an emphasis on active political and social involvement; rampant magical, syncretic ritual practice and insistence on the purity of the authentic teaching.

The modern period has seen increased lay leadership at various levels of religious life. The YMBAs of Burma and the Buddhist "Sunday schools" that have arisen in Thailand have obviously been influenced by Western Christian models. Lay associations have developed for various purposes. For example, prior to the revolution Cambodia had the Buddhist Association of the Republic of Cambodia (1952), the Association of Friends of the Buddhist Lycée (1949), the Association of Friends of Religious Welfare Aid Centers, the Association of Religious Students of the Republic of Cambodia (1970), the Association of the Buddhist Youth of Cambodia (1971), and so on. Buddhist laity have also been actively involved in the worldwide Buddhist movement. Most notable of the laity groups are the World Fellowship of Buddhists, which has headquarters in Bangkok, and the World Council of Churches, which holds interreligious dialogue consultations.

The increasingly significant role of the laity in a religious tradition noted for the centrality of the monk reflects many developments in modern Southeast Asian countries, not the least of which is the spread of secular, Western education among the elites. Coupled with this phenomenon, however, we find a polar opposition—a persistent cult of the holy man to whom supernatural powers are attributed. In some instances the holy monk becomes a charismatic leader of a messianic cult (e.g., the Mahagandare Weikzado Apwegyoke in Burma), while in others the form of veneration is more informal and generalized (e.g., Phra Acharn Mun in Thailand). In many cases the holy monk makes few, if any, miraculous or supernatural claims, but these will be ascribed to him by his followers. Hagiographic literature, describing cosmic portents of the monk's birth, extraordinary events during his childhood, and other characteristics of this genre, will often emerge. While the monk as miracle worker is not a new phenomenon in Theravāda Buddhism, it has persisted to the present time and, some observers claim, has been on the upswing in the contemporary period.

Meditation has always been the *sine qua non* of Buddhist practice, but traditionally it was the preserve of the forest-dwelling (*araññavāsī*) or meditating (*vipassana dhura*) monk. In the modern period, meditation has been more widely practiced as part of the routines of ordinary Buddhist temples and, more particularly, in meditation centers that either include or are specifically for lay practice. The lay meditation movement was especially strong in Burma under the leadership of such meditation masters as U Ba Khin and Ledi Sayadaw (1856–1923). Westerners have been particularly attracted to some of Southeast Asia's renowned meditation teachers, such as Acharn Cha of Wat Pa Pong in Ubon Ratchathani. Some meditating monks have also gained reputations not only for their method of meditation or for holiness but for the attainment of extraordinary powers as well.

While meditation has become a lay as well as monastic practice in contemporary Southeast Asian Buddhism, this development has not precluded a movement to formulate a strong, activist social ethic. The Vietnamese Zen monk Thich Nhat Hahn attempted to work out a Buddhist solution to the military conflict in his country during the 1960s, and there has been a widespread interest in formulating a Buddhist theory of economic development that is critical of Western capitalism but not necessarily indebted to Marxism. Buddhists have also acted to solve particular social problems, such as drug addiction, and have spoken out strongly against the proliferation of nuclear arms. Southeast Asian Buddhists have also joined with members of other religious groups, both within their own countries as well as in international organizations, to work for such causes as world peace and basic civil rights for all peoples. Buddhist interpreters, such as the Thai monk Bhikkhu Buddhadāsa, have referred to Buddhism as a practical system of personal and social morality.

Buddhadāsa has also been strongly critical of conventional Thai Buddhist religious practice, which has stressed merit-making rituals. These are aimed at obtaining personal benefit and propitiating various supernatural powers for protection or good luck. In his writings and at his center in Chaiya, southern Thailand, he emphasizes the importance of overcoming greed and attachment. *Nibbāna,* for Buddhadāsa, is the state that is achieved when egoism is overcome. This is the goal of all Buddhists, not just monks. Indeed, he argues, this is the purpose of all religions. Buddhadāsa's critique reflects the magical nature of popular Buddhist ritual practice not only in Thailand but, more generally, in Southeast Asian Buddhism, the goal of which is to improve one's life materially through the mechanism of gaining merit or improving one's karmic status. Buddhadāsa's proposal that such teachings as *nibbāna* and *anatta* (not-self), which represent the essence of the Buddha's teachings, must be part of every Buddhist's religious practice exemplifies an interest on the part of many contemporary Buddhist thinkers to restore the kernel of the authentic tradition, which has often been hidden beneath layers of cultural accretions. Thus, while the popular religious ethos is syncretic and emphasizes the attainment of worldly goals, various apologists in Burma and Thailand are attempting to make the core of the tradition a part of the understanding and practice of the Buddhist populace at large. Some critical observers have referred to this trend as a "protestantizing" of Southeast Asian Buddhism.

The contemporary ethos of Buddhism in Southeast Asia reflects an ancient heritage but also points in new directions. It is difficult to predict how the *sangha* will fare under the Marxist regimes in Laos and Cambodia or, for that matter, in the urban and increasingly materialistic environment of Bangkok and Chiangmai. Can the Theravāda monk maintain his place in society when his education cannot compare with that of the elite? Can Buddhism effectively address problems of overpopulation, prostitution, malnourishment, and economic exploitation? To what extent can the tradition change with the times and retain its identity? These and other questions face a religion that has not only been fundamental in the identity of the Burmese, Thai, Laotians, Cambodians, and Vietnamese but has also contributed much to world culture.

SEE ALSO Amoghavajra; Aśoka; Buddhism, Schools of, article on Tantric Ritual Schools of Buddhism; Burmese Religion; Cakravartin; Dharmapala; Khmer Religion; Kingship, article on Kingship in East Asia; Lao Religion; Mongkut; Pilgrimage, article on Buddhist Pilgrimage in South and Southeast Asia; Saṃgha, articles on Saṃgha and Society; Southeast Asian Religions, article on Mainland Cultures; Thai Religion; Theravāda; Vajrabodhi; Vietnamese Religion; Worship and Devotional Life, article on Buddhist Devotional Life in Southeast Asia.

BIBLIOGRAPHY

Works on Buddhism in Southeast Asia include text translations and doctrinal studies, histories of the development of Buddhism in various Southeast Asian countries, anthropological treatments of popular, village Buddhism, and studies of Buddhism and political change. Georges Coedès's studies, *The Indianized States of Southeast Asia*, edited by Walter F. Vella and translated by Susan Brown Cowing (Canberra, 1968), and *The Making of South-East Asia*, translated by H. M. Wright (Berkeley, 1966), are standard treatments of the region, as is Reginald Le May's *The Culture of South-East Asia* (London, 1954). The classic study of Southeast Asian religion and kingship is Robert Heine-Geldern's *Conceptions of State and Kingship in Southeast Asia* (Ithaca, N. Y., 1956). A readable, general study of the history of Theravāda Buddhism in Southeast Asia and its present teachings and practices is Robert C. Lester's *Theravada Buddhism in Southeast Asia* (Ann Arbor, 1973). My *Buddhism and Society in Southeast Asia* (Chambersburg, Pa., 1981) is an analysis of Theravāda Buddhism in terms of the themes of syncretism, political legitimation, and modernization. The theme of Buddhism and political legitimation is discussed in several seminal articles in *Buddhism and Legitimation of Power in Thailand, Laos, and Burma*, edited by Bardwell L. Smith (Chambersburg, Pa., 1978).

The monumental work on the early Pagan period is Gordon H. Luce's *Old Burma—Early Pagán*, 3 vols. (Locust Valley, N. Y., 1969–1970). Two of the important Burmese chronicles have been translated: *Hmannān mạha yazạwintawkyī: The Glass Palace Chronicle of the Kings of Burma*, translated by Pe Maung Tin and G. H. Luce (London, 1923); and Pannasami's *The History of the Buddha's Religion* (*Sāsanavaṁsa*), translated by B. C. Law (London, 1952). Standard treatments of both Pali and Sanskritic Buddhism in Burma are Nihar-Ranjan Ray's *An Introduction to the Study of Theravāda Buddhism in Burma* (Calcutta, 1946), and his *Sanskrit Buddhism in Burma* (Calcutta, 1936). A more recent study is Winston L. King's *A Thousand Lives Away* (Cambridge, Mass., 1964). Two standard anthropological studies are Melford E. Spiro's *Buddhism and Society: A Great Tradition and its Burmese Vicissitudes*, 2d. ed. (Berkeley, 1982), and Manning Nash's *The Golden Road to Modernity* (New York, 1965). Nash was also the general editor of *Anthropological Studies in Theravada Buddhism* (New Haven, 1966), which contains valuable articles on Burmese and Thai Buddhism by Nash, David E. Pfanner, and Jasper Ingersoll. E. Michael Mendelson's *Sangha and State in Burma*, edited by John P. Ferguson (Ithaca, N. Y., 1965), although difficult going is a mine of information. Buddhism and the early nationalist period are studied in Emanuel Sarkisyanz's *Buddhist Backgrounds of the Burmese Revolution* (The Hague, 1965), and Donald E. Smith's *Religion and Politics in Burma* (Princeton, 1965).

The standard Thai history with much information about Thai Buddhism is David K. Wyatt's *Thailand: A Short History* (New Haven, 1984); Kenneth E. Wells's *Thai Buddhism: Its Rites and Activities* (Bangkok, 1939), while somewhat dated and rather dry is still very useful. One of the major northern Thai chronicles, Ratanapanya's *Jinakālamālīpakaranam*, has been translated by N. A. Jayawickrama as *The Sheaf of Garlands of the Epochs of the Conqueror* (London, 1968). Frank E. Reynolds and Mani B. Reynolds have translated the major Thai cosmological treatise, *Trai Phūmi Phra Rūang*, as *Three Worlds according to King Ruang* (Berkeley, 1982). Prince Dhani-Nivat's *A History of Buddhism in Siam*, 2d ed. (Bangkok, 1965), provides a brief historical overview of the development of Buddhism in Thailand. Much recent, significant work on Thai Buddhism has been done by anthropologists; see especially Stanley J. Tambiah's *World Conqueror and World Renouncer* (Cambridge, 1976) and several articles by Charles F. Keyes, for example, "Buddhism and National Integration in Thailand," *Journal of Asian Studies* 30 (May 1971): 551–567. Historians of religion have also contributed to our knowledge of Thai Buddhism. Frank E. Reynolds has written several articles including, "The Holy Emerald Jewel: Some Aspects of Buddhist Symbolism and Political Legitimation in Thailand and Laos," in *Religion and Legitimation of Power in Thailand, Laos, and Burma*, edited by Bardwell L. Smith (Chambersburg, Pa., 1978), pp. 175–193. I have analyzed a major northern Thai monastery in *Wat Haripuñ-*

jaya: A Study of the Royal Temple of the Buddha's Relic, Lamphun, Thailand (Missoula, Mont., 1976).

French scholars have made the major contribution to the study of Buddhism in Laos, Cambodia, and Vietnam. Louis Finot's "Research sur la littérature laotienne," *Bulletin de l'École Française d'Extrême-Orient* 17 (1917) is an indispensable tool in the study of Lao Buddhist literature. Marcel Zago's *Rites et cérémonies en milieu bouddhiste lao* (Rome, 1972) provides a comprehensive treatment of Lao religion, although Charles Archaimbault's "Religious Structures in Laos," *Journal of the Siam Society* 52 (1964): 57–74, while more limited in scope is very useful. Lawrence Palmer Brigg's "The Syncretism of Religions in Southeast Asia, especially in the Khmer Empire," *Journal of the American Oriental Society* 71 (October-December 1951): 230–249, provides a survey of the development of religion in Cambodia. Adhémard Leclère's classic study, *Le bouddhisme au Cambodge* (Paris, 1899) remains the standard work. The classic study of Vietnamese religion is Leopold Michel Cadière's *Croyances et pratiques religieuses des Viêtnamiens*, 3 vols. (Saigon, 1955–1958), but more accessible is the brief sketch in the trilingual volume by Chanh-tri Mai-tho-Truyen, *Le bouddhisme au Vietnam, Buddhism in Vietnam, Phat-giao Vietnam* (Saigon, 1962). Thich Thien-An's *Buddhism and Zen in Vietnam in Relation to the Development of Buddhism in Asia*, edited by Carol Smith (Los Angeles, 1975), studies the development of Buddhist schools from the sixth to the seventeenth century. Thich Nhat-Hanh's *Vietnam: Lotus in a Sea of Fire* (New York, 1967) puts the Buddhist situation in the 1960s into historical perspective.

Interested readers may also wish to consult the following works: Heinz Bechert's three-volume study, *Buddhismus, Staat und Gesellschaft in den Ländern Theravāda-Buddhismus* (Frankfurt, 1966–1973); *Religion in South Asia*, edited by Edward B. Harper (Seattle, 1964), especially the articles by Michael Ames and Nur Yalman; and *Religion and Progress in Modern Asia*, edited by Robert N. Bellah (New York, 1965).

New Sources

Blackburn, Anne. *Buddhist Learning and Textual Practice in Eighteenth-Century Lankan Monastic Culture.* Princeton, 2001.

Collins, Steven. *Nirvāṇa and Other Buddhist Felicities: Utopias of the Pali Imaginaire.* Cambridge, 1998.

Gombrich, Richard, and Gananath Obeyesekere. *Buddhism Transformed: Religious Change in Sri Lanka.* Princeton, N.J., 1988.

Holt, John. *Buddha in the Crown: Avalokiteśvara in the Buddhist Traditions of Sri Lanka.* Oxford, 1991.

Holt, John C., Jacob N. Kinnard, and Jonathan S. Walters, eds. *Constituting Communities: Theravāda Buddhism and the Religious Cultures of South and Southeast Asia.* Albany, 2003.

Klima, Alan. *The Funeral Casino: Meditation, Massacre and Exchange with the Dead in Thailand.* Princeton, N.J., 2002.

Strong, John. *The Legend and Cult of Upagupta: Sanskrit Buddhism in North India and Southest Asia.* Princeton, N.J., 1992.

Swearer, Donald K. *The Buddhist World of Southeast Asia.* Albany, 1995.

Tannenbaum, Nicola. *Who Can Compete Against the World? Power-Protection and Buddhism in Shan Worldview.* Ann Arbor, 1996.

Trainor, Kevin. *Relics, Ritual, and Representation in Buddhism: Rematerialising the Sri Lankan Theravada Tradition.* Cambridge, 1997.

DONALD K. SWEARER (1987)
Revised Bibliography

BUDDHISM: BUDDHISM IN CENTRAL ASIA

Central Asia is not a clearly defined term. In a narrower sense, it refers to the region previously known as Eastern or Chinese Turkestan, as the Tarim Basin, or as Sinkiang (Xinjiang), lying between the towns of Kashgar in the west and Dunhuang in the east. In a wider sense, it also refers to the former Soviet republics, now independent states, of Middle Asia, generally known as Western Turkestan, and to the whole Tibetan plateau in the south. Here it is meant to include Eastern Turkestan, i.e., the present Xinjiang Uighur Autonomous Region in the People's Republic of China, and those parts of the Middle Asian republics where traces of Buddhism have been found.

During the period of its maximum spread, Buddhism became a major religious and cultural factor not only in India and in East and Southeast Asia, but also in Afghanistan and in large parts of Central Asia. In the northwest, it reached Merv in present-day Turkmenia, Termez at the southern border of Uzbekistan, and Qurġan-tübä in southern Tadjikistan. Although written sources and excavations attest to its presence even farther north, for instance in Samarkand, in Quvā near Fergana, and in Aq Bešim near Frunse, in these areas it did not gain the popularity it did south of the Amu Darya (Oxus). Following old trade routes, monks and merchants brought Buddhism from the northwest of the Indian subcontinent into Central Asia and farther east to China. In all those regions, it was the vigorous spread of Islam that finally replaced the various other religious movements, to the extent that Buddhism disappeared from western Central Asia before the turn of the millennium and was continually driven back in the east. From about the fifteenth century, followers of Buddhism were no longer found, and therefore a description of its history is now based on archaeological remains and on such historical sources as, for instance, the travel accounts of the Chinese Indian pilgrims Faxian (fifth century), Xuanzang (seventh century), Huizhao (eighth century), and others. These written sources are few, and it is mainly such impressive monuments as the two stone statues of the standing Buddha in Bāmiyān, formerly 174 and 115 feet (53 and 35 meters) high (but in 2001 destroyed by the Taliban), or large cave monasteries like Dunhuang with its overwhelming wealth of fascinating wall paintings, which bear witness to the former splendor and importance of Buddhism, as no traces of it are preserved in the present-day cultures of the area.

Although an ever-growing number of publications, mainly on the Buddhist art and literature of the region, continues to appear, the history of Buddhism in Central Asia remains fragmentary. One of the basic difficulties is that Central Asia never formed a political unity during the first millennium CE. A multitude of ethnic groups faced frequent changes of the ruling powers, and powerful neighbors like the Sassanids in the west, the Tibetans in the south, or the Chinese in the east continually sought to establish political and economical influence, often by force and military campaigns. Nomadic tribes from the northern steppes often invaded the area, sometimes causing considerable destruction, as in the case of the White Huns (Hephtalites) on their way through Afghanistan to India, but sometimes becoming sedentary and adopting the local cultures, as in the case of the Uighurs. Powerful empires like those of the Kushans, Tang-dynasty China, or imperial Tibet never succeeded in bringing the whole of Central Asia under their sway. Buddhism offered one of the few uniting elements of the area. However, Buddhism itself did not appear as a uniform phenomenon, but was spread in various forms and school traditions and thereby contributed to the diversity of the whole picture. The situation of the various cultures, especially in the oasis towns along the Silk Road, must have been very complex and is probably best characterized by the modern term "multicultural." Members of very different ethnic groups and cultures-Chinese, Indians, Sakas, Sogdians, Tibetans, Tocharians, Uighurs, to name only the most important ones-lived together and followed various different religious traditions, including Buddhism, Manichaeism, Zoroastrianism, Nestorian Christianity, while the ethnic borders were never identical with linguistic, religious, or political borders.

BEGINNINGS. Buddhism reached Central Asia from the northwest of the Indian subcontinent. Its spread into Afghanistan must have begun not later than the third century BCE when the Indian dynasty of the Mauryas, and especially their most important ruler Aśoka (c. 268–233 BCE), succeeded in uniting major parts of India and advancing the northwestern border of their empire up to Kabul and Kandahār in Afghanistan. This extension is well documented by the famous stone inscriptions placed by Aśoka in various parts of the empire. Such inscriptions are preserved in northwest Pakistan (in Shābāzgaṛhī and Mānsehrā) and in Afghanistan (in Kandahār, in Lampāka, and at the river Laghmān). The inscriptions suggest that Aśoka supported the various religious movements in his empire, but especially Buddhism, to which he appears to have been personally inclined. Since in Buddhist scripture he is depicted as one of the foremost supporters of the faith, it may be concluded that the development of Buddhism, from an ascetic movement mainly situated in northeast India to a universal religion, accelerated during his reign and that the political stability achieved by the Mauryas favored its spread, especially along the trade routes.

Apart from these inscriptions, very few traces of the presence and spread of Buddhism during that period remain. Well-known is the Dharmarājika stupa in the old town of Taxila, a large excavation in Pakistan; the stupa is dated to the time of the Mauryas. This situation changed around the beginning of the common era, when another great empire arose in the northwest and guaranteed an enduring period of peace and stability. In the first century CE, the dynasty of the Kushans united the northwest and established an empire that included Afghanistan and reached from Bactria into northern India and Eastern Turkestan. Trade routes became safe and allowed long-distance trade that facilitated the exchange and spread of both material and non-material cultural goods. Like Aśoka before him, Kaniṣka the Great (first half of the second century CE), the most important ruler of the Kushan dynasty, is described as a devoted supporter of Buddhism in Buddhist sources. No external indications are preserved that could confirm the Buddhist picture of Kaniṣka, as the inscriptions do for Aśoka, but he appears to have built stupas and a monastery near Kāpiśī (Begram). Although the Kushan rulers also supported other religions, the tradition connected with Kaniṣka suggests that Buddhism flourished under the Kushans. Within the varied pantheon depicted on his coins, there is also the figure of a standing Buddha. As far as datable archaeological remains are preserved, only very few monasteries seem to go back to this period, which hints at the possibility that institutionalized Buddhism was less widespread than is often supposed.

ART. As an extremely important innovation, the representation of the Buddha in human form was created during the reign of the Kushan dynasty. Previously, the Buddha had been represented in art only aniconically, for instance by a wheel to symbolize the first teaching. It is still a matter of debate whether the first Buddha figure was created in Mathurā in northern India or in Gandhara, a region in northern Pakistan, but many scholars now believe that the step from aniconic to iconic representation was taken in Gandhara. By fusing Greco-Roman forms with Indian contents, artists in Gandhara created a distinctive style that influenced Indian art and became the model for Buddhist art in Central and East Asia. It is well known that Apollo served as a model for the Buddha, as did Herakles for Vajrapāṇi, a non-human attendant of the Buddha, or Tyche/Fortuna for the goddess Hāritī. Greeks had been living in Bactria and Gandhara since the Indian campaign of Alexander the Great in the fourth century, and the influence of Hellenistic, and then Roman, culture continued until the first centuries CE.

Gandharan art attests to the importance of the cult of *bodhisattvas,* probably Siddhārtha (the Buddha before his enlightenment) and definitely Maitreya (the future Buddha), but despite an overwhelming richness of surviving sculptures, there are very few that can be indisputably connected with Mahāyāna Buddhism and its specific Buddhas and *bodhisattvas.*

THE KUSHANS. The Kushans adopted Bactrian, a Middle Iranian language, for their coins and for inscriptions, but they also used Gandhari, a Middle Indian language written in Kharoṣṭhī script, for administrative purposes. Kushan influence extended well into Central Asia and administrative documents written in Gandhari and dating from the period between 200 and 320 have been found in the kingdom of Shan-shan (Kroraina), which stretched from the Niya River, a short distance east of Khotan as far as Lob Nor. At the same time, Gandhari was the language used by the Dharmaguptakas, a school of mainstream Buddhism. Translations of scriptures of this school into Chinese are known from the beginning of the fifth century, but until recently only one text was known in its Indian original, the famous manuscript of the *Dharmapada,* found more than a hundred years ago in Khotan and probably to be dated to the second or third century CE. Since the 1990s, however, a steadily growing number of Dharmaguptaka texts has been found in Afghanistan. They attest to the importance of this school in the Kushan Empire, and they support the thesis that the Dharmaguptakas were among the first to bring Buddhism to the south and east of Central Asia.

Another school of mainstream Buddhism apparently flourishing in the Kushan Empire was that of the Sarvāstivādins. Originally, they also must have used a Middle Indian language, but they adopted Sanskrit for their commentaries and their poetical literature and then gradually sanskritized their canonical literature. They spread mainly along the northern route of the Silk Road, and the cave monasteries in the oases of Kučā, Karašahr and Turfan became strongholds of the Sarvāstivāda. It is difficult, if not impossible, to date this process. An Shigao, the first known translator of Buddhist texts into Chinese active around 140 CE, apparently used Sarvāstivāda versions, but he came from Parthia in the west of Central Asia. A large amount of manuscript fragments has been found in the monasteries along the northern route, and the oldest of them date to the second century CE, but these are palm-leaf manuscripts imported from India. The oldest Sanskrit manuscripts actually written in Central Asia probably date to the fifth century; they are written on paper, a material introduced from China, but not used in India and Afghanistan at that time.

FORMS OF BUDDHISM. The spread and distribution of various forms of Buddhism in Central Asia has to be reconstructed from the manuscript finds and the reports of the Chinese pilgrims to India. The evidence suggests a clear divide between Buddhism on the northern and southern branches of the Silk Road. Between Kashgar at the western end of the Tarim Basin and Anxi at its eastern end the Silk Road divided into two routes, which followed the mountain ranges from oasis to oasis and skirted the terrible Takla Makan desert. The northern route followed the Tianshan and connected the oases of Tumšuq, Kučā, Karašahr, Turfan, and Hami, while the southern route led along the Kunlun to Khotan and then on to Niya, Mirān, and Dunhuang. Most of the monks in the monasteries on the northern route followed mainstream Buddhism in the form of the Sarvāstivāda school. The overwhelming majority of Sanskrit manuscripts found there belongs to the canonical and postcanonical literature of the Sarvāstivādins. The work represented by the largest number of manuscripts is the *Udānavarga,* a very popular collection of verses allegedly spoken by the Buddha. Next comes the *Prātimokṣasūtra,* the confession formulary of the Buddhist monks. The number and order of its rules are school-specific, and the frequency of this text serves as one of the main arguments for determining the school affiliation of the monasteries along the northern route. Fragments of the corresponding text for the Buddhist nuns point to the possible existence of nunneries, but the fragments are very few and none of the spots where they were found have been proven to be convents for nuns. Besides works from the Sarvāstivāda *Vinaya* (the collection of rules of the Buddhist order), a few from that of the Mūlasarvāstivādins have also been found, and altogether three texts from the canon of the Dharmaguptakas. Interestingly enough, the latter are no longer written in Gandhari, but in Sanskrit, apparently under the influence of the Sarvāstivādins. A certain number of fragments of *Mahāyānasūtras* has come to light, but they belong to no more than thirty manuscripts, most of which have been found in the oases of Šorčuq and Toyoq farther east.

Khotan, on the contrary, must have been an a leading center of Mahāyāna Buddhism, since nearly all of the Sanskrit texts found there belong to sūtras of the "Great Vehicle." The precise date of Buddhism's initial establishment in Khotan is unknown. According to Chinese sources, there was a Buddhist community in Khotan by the second century CE. Zhu Shixing, who studied Prajñāpāramitā literature in the Chinese city of Luoyang in the third century, went west in search of the *Pañcaviṃśatisāhasrikā-prajñāpāramitā-sūtra,* which he found in Khotan. Mokṣala, who translated this work into Chinese in 291, was a Khotanese, and another Khotanese, Gītamitra, took a copy of the same text with him to the Chinese capital Chang'an in 296. Thus, Khotan was already a well-established center of Mahāyāna studies in the third century. None of the manuscripts found in Khotan, however, belongs to this early period. Most of them date from the seventh to the tenth centuries, and they contain either Sanskrit texts or translations from Sanskrit into Khotanese, an Iranian language. Common are manuscripts of the *Prajñāpāramitāsūtras,* the *Suvarṇabhāsottamasūtra,* the *Saṃghāṭasūtra,* and the ubiqitous *Saddharmapuṇḍarīkasūtra,* which, amazingly, was never translated into Khotanese. One of the most famous manuscripts from Central Asia is the so-called Kashgar manuscript of the *Saddharmapuṇḍarīkasūtra.* Originally, it comprised 459 leaves, 447 of which are preserved in full or in fragments and are now distributed over the collections in St. Petersburg, London, Berlin, Dalian (China), and New Haven, a not-at-all uncharacteristic example of the fate of many manuscript finds, especially those from Khotan and from Dunhuang.

LANGUAGES. Indian languages, and from the fifth century onwards, only Sanskrit, remained the "church language" (Nattier, 1990) in Central Asia, and the percentage of Indian texts among the literature is absolutely remarkable. In the western part, in Bactria, Sogdiana, and Afghanistan, no translations into any of the vernaculars have been found so far. Two Buddhist texts in Bactrian, which came to light among the finds from Afghanistan in the 1990s, are possibly not translated, but may have been originally composed in Bactrian. The Sogdians played a very important role in the transmission of Buddhism to the east, since from the third century onwards they took over the long-distance trade and built up a network of trade posts from Samarkand far into China. But when they finally started to translate Buddhist scriptures into their own language, they did so not from Sanskrit originals, but from Chinese. In Eastern Turkestan, however, the situation was different: Sanskrit texts are found side by side with translations into the vernaculars, and they remained in use until the end of Buddhism in the area. Texts in Tocharian, the easternmost Indo-European language, which have been found mostly in Kuča, Karašahr, and Turfan, belong to the literature of the Sarvāstivādins and suggest that it was mainly the Tocharians who continued to use the original Sanskrit texts of that school. Many bilinguals and Sanskrit manuscripts with Tocharian glosses confirm this supposition. To a certain extent, this also holds true for the literature of the Uighurs. After the fall of their empire in the Orkhon Basin further northeast, parts of this Turkish tribe had settled from 840 onwards in the oases of Kuča, Karašāhr, and Turfan, but also in Hami and in the Gansu corridor. In Xočo in the oasis of Turfan, a Uighur kingdom was established, which existed from approximately 850 to 1250. The Uighurs also used Sanskrit, but from the eighth or ninth century onwards they translated a growing number of texts, mostly of Mahāyāna affiliation, from Chinese into Uighur.

INDIGENOUS DEVELOPMENTS. Very different from the development in China, and later in Tibet, it appears that none of the Central Asian forms of Buddhism succeeded in establishing an important indigenous literary tradition based on the received canonical literature. There are very few independent works in the vernaculars; a famous example is a work in Khotanese, provisionally called the "Book of Zambasta" after the person who commissioned it, a voluminous verse-summary of Buddhism, which probably dates from the seventh century. Remarkably enough, its author complains that "The Khotanese do not value the [Buddhist] Law at all in Khotanese. They understand it badly in Indian. In Khotanese it does not seem to them to be the Law. For the Chinese the Law is in Chinese. . . . To the Khotanese that seems to be the law whose meaning they do not understand at all" (Emmerick, 1968, p. 343ff.). This clinging to Sanskrit as the authoritative medium of religious literature may have been one of the reasons for the comparatively small number of indigenous works in the vernaculars.

One of the most important works from the northern route is the *Maitreyasamitināṭaka,* the "dramatical description of the meeting with [the future Buddha] Maitreya" in twenty-seven chapters. Although the text pretends to be of Indian origin, it was probably composed in Karašāhr in Tocharian and then translated into Uighur under the title *Maitrisimit.* It attests to the important position of the cult of Maitreya in Central Asian Buddhism. This cult was practiced equally by followers of mainstream and of Mahāyāna Buddhism, and significantly a whole chapter of the "Book of Zambasta" is devoted to Maitreya. As in the case of Amitābha, the most popular meditation Buddha in Central Asia, an Iranian origin or at least influence has been much discussed. Although both figures display certain elements that are also found with Iranian gods, these elements can just as easily be explained with reference to the Indian background.

One of the most important sites in the region is the monastery Qianfo-dong ("caves of the thousand Buddhas") near Dunhuang. The Indo-Scythian Dharmarakṣa, one of the great translators of Buddhist texts into Chinese, was born there around 230 CE, and one of his Chinese disciples founded a large monastery there. The caves are famous for their excellently preserved wall paintings, but one of them contained another surprise for the European scholars who came there in the first decade of the twentieth century. The local attendant led them to a previously walled-off chamber, which concealed a sensational collection of manuscripts. They had been hidden probably before 1035 when Dunhuang was conquered by the Tanguts, since no Tangut texts are found there. The chamber contained forty to fifty thousand manuscripts, most of them Chinese and Tibetan, the latter dating to the eighth and ninth centuries when the Tibetan empire occupied most of Eastern Turkestan. Besides the Chinese and Tibetan manuscripts, the library included texts in Uighur, Sanskrit, Tocharian, Khotanese, and Sogdian (in the last two cases most of what survives in these languages was found at Dunhuang).

Although the Tibetan texts from Dunhuang are of singular importance for the early history of Tibet, the Tibetan occupation made little mark on Central Asian Buddhism. Only the Uighurs translated Buddhist texts from Tibetan into their own language, but when they started to do so it was after the turn of the millennium and at a time when Tibet had long lost all political influence in Central Asia. This was very different with Chinese Buddhism. During the first centuries CE, it was mainly monks from Central Asia who brought the new religion to China and who became instrumental in acquainting the Chinese with Buddhism by translating the texts. Without such outstanding figures like the famous Kumārajīva, Buddhism would probably never have made a lasting impact on Chinese culture. As a son of an Indian father and a local princess, Kumārajīva was born in Kuča and brought to Chang'an at the beginning of the fifth century. With him, a new translation technique was developed, which finally succeeded in presenting Buddhism in a literary form acceptable to Chinese taste. From the time of the Tang dynasty, however, the relationship was partly reversed. Buddhist literature was no longer imported from Central Asia; instead, Chinese translations of what were originally Indian texts were now translated into Khotanese, Sogdian, and Uighur.

In the western part of Central Asia, Buddhism had practically disappeared by the end of the first millennium. Around 950, it came to an end in Khotan when the rulers decided to embrace Islam. Only on the northern route of the Silk Road did Buddhism survive for a few more centuries, although it must already have been in decline at that time. Around the end of the fifteenth century, at the latest, it finally disappeared from the Turfan oasis when the ruler of Xočo withdrew his support of the local monks.

BIBLIOGRAPHY

To date, a comprehensive history of Buddhism in Central Asia remains a desideratum. Despite its promising title, Boris A. Litvinsky, *Die Geschichte des Buddhismus in Ostturkestan* (Wiesbaden, 1999), is utterly disappointing. A survey of the history of Eastern Turkestan is given in Luciano Petech's "The Silk Road, Turfan and Tun-huang in the First Millennium A.D." in *Turfan and Tun-huang, The Texts: Encounter of Civilizations on the Silk Route,* edited by Alfredo Cadonna, pp. 1–13 (Florence, 1992). A very good historical study of the early phase is still offered by John Brough, "Comments on Third-Century Shan-shan and the History of Buddhism," *Bulletin of the School of Oriental and African Studies* 28 (1965): 582-612 (= *Collected Papers.* Edited by Minoru Hara, J.C. Wright. London, 1996: 276–307). The history of the Tibetan influence is treated in Christopher I. Beckwith's *The Tibetan Empire in Central Asia: A History of the Struggle for Great Power among Tibetans, Turks, Arabs, and Chinese during the Early Middle Ages.* Princeton, 1987.

Buddhism among single ethnic groups is treated in Hans-Joachim Klimkeit's "Buddhism in Turkish Central Asia," *Numen* 37 (1990): 53–69; and Georges-Jean Pinault's "Aspects du bouddhisme pratiqué au nord du désert du Taklamakan, d'après les documents tokhariens," *Bouddhisme et cultures locales,* edited by Fumimasa Fukui and Gérard Fussman, pp. 85–113. Paris, 1994. Jan Nattier's "Church Language and Vernacular Language in Central Asian Buddhism," *Numen* 37 (1990): 195–219, is a judicious study on the complex linguistic situation of Buddhist literature. Useful surveys of this literature in the various languages are Johan Elverskog, *Uygur Buddhist Literature.* Turnhout, 1997; Ronald E. Emmerick, *A Guide to the Literature of Khotan.* 2d rev. ed. Tokyo, 1992; Klaus T. Schmidt, "Zur Erforschung der tocharischen Literatur. Stand und Aufgaben," *Tocharisch. Akten der Fachtagung der Indogermanischen Gesellschaft,* edited by Bernfried Schlerath, pp. 239–283. Berlin, 1994; and David A. Utz, *A Survey of Buddhist Sogdian Studies.* Tokyo, 1978. The most detailed general survey is still provided by Lore Sander, "Buddhist Literature in Central Asia," *Encyclopaedia of Buddhism,* edited by G. P. Malalasekera, vol. 4, pp. 52–75. Colombo, Sri Lanka, 1979. This article, however, contains many inaccuracies of detail and must be used with caution. There are a vast number of either very general or very detailed studies of Buddhist art in Central Asia, but no comprehensive account. This gap is only partly filled by Marianne Yaldiz, *Archäologie und Kunstgeschichte Chinesisch-Zentralasiens (Xinjiang).* Leiden, 1987. See also R. E. Emmerick's *The Book of Zambasta* (London, 1968), pp. 343ff.

JENS-UWE HARTMANN (2005)

BUDDHISM: BUDDHISM IN MONGOLIA

Buddhism in Chinese, Central Asian, Kāśmiri, and Tibetan forms influenced Mongolia's ancient and medieval nomadic empires in varying degrees. From 1580 to 1920 Tibetan-style Buddhism dominated Mongolia and touched every aspect of life. Communist antireligious campaigns destroyed this hegemony, but after 1985 liberalization led to a renewed religious revival. The Mongolian plateau can be divided into Mongolia proper (Outer Mongolia, now the independent State of Mongolia) to the north, and Inner Mongolia (now an autonomous region in China) along the borders of China proper. From the fourth century on, the Mongolic-speaking Xianbi in Inner Mongolia and north China patronized Chinese Buddhism. The Kitans, another branch of the Xianbi, whose Mongolic language has been partly deciphered, became avid patrons and practitioners of Chinese Buddhism under their Liao dynasty (907–1125). Many rulers of the Türk empires, which dominated Mongolia proper from 552 to 745, also patronized Buddhist monks from the Central Asian oasis states and from China.

By the twelfth century, Mongolia and Inner Mongolia were occupied by a variety of Turkic and Mongolic-speaking tribes, and Buddhist influence had virtually disappeared. The unification of the plateau by Chinggis Khan (Genghis, r. 1206–1227) and his conquests brought the Mongols again in touch with Buddhism among the Uighurs of the Central Asian oases (in today's eastern Xinjiang) and in northern China. In 1219 Chinggis Khan granted tax exemption to all Buddhist clerics. Buddhism, alongside Christianity, Daoism, and Islam, became one of the four favored religions of the Mongol empire. Until 1253, the khans chiefly patronized Chinese *dhyāna* (Zen) monks.

With the conquest of the Xi (western) Xia or Tangut dynasty in northwestern China completed in 1227, the Mongols learned of its long-standing ties with Tibetan Buddhist clerics. In 1240 the Mongols first reconnoitered Tibet to find a Tibetan cleric. In 1247, the first Tibetan Buddhist lama came to the court of a Mongol prince. Mongol expansion also brought contact with Kāśmiri monks.

In 1251 a new branch of Chinggis Khan's family seized power. Möngke Khan (r. 1251–1259) began actively patronizing Tibetan and Kāśmiri Buddhist leaders of several different lineages. Möngke's brother Qubilai Khan (r. 1260–1294) made 'Phags pa Lama, of the Tibetan Sa skya pa monastic order, the chief cleric of the empire. From then on, the imperial family of the Mongols in China, as well as many aristocratic Mongol clans, regularly received tutoring and Tantric initiations from Sa skya pa and other Tibetan Buddhist hierarchs.

The Mongols adopted the Uighur script under Chinggis Khan. In the late thirteenth and early to mid-fourteenth centuries, the Mongols in China sponsored many Buddhist translations. Although the translations were generally made from Tibetan texts, the translators were strongly influenced by Uighur Buddhist terminology. The translations of Chos-gi-Odsir (fl. 1307–1321) were particularly famous. A Nepalese artist, Aniga (1244–1278), invited to Qubilai's court, began a school of Nepalese-influenced Inner Asian Buddhist artwork. Surviving monuments of the era include the White Pagoda in central Beijing. Mongol princes also patronized other religions and 'Phags pa Lama and succeeding court chaplains participated in the Mongol ancestral cults maintained at court. Buddhist clergy served as astrologers and diviners.

After 1260, the Mongol dominions in the Middle East, Eastern Europe and Kazakhstan, and in Central Asia broke away from the power of the great khans in East Asia. The local Mongol rulers continued to patronize Buddhist monks, called *baqshi*, who were sometimes Tibetan, Kāśmiri, or Chinese, but mostly Uighur. This patronage in the Mongols' western domains ceased after successive waves of Islamization from 1295 to 1335.

Although the Mongol great khans were expelled from China in 1368, they continued to rule on the Mongolian plateau in the name of the Chinggisid dynasty. Buddhist monks were appointed as court chaplains at least through 1455, but after that the influence of Buddhism declined. Particularly after the reign of Dayan Khan (1480?–1517?), the ancestral cult of Chinggis Khan became the focus of court religious life.

From the 1550s on, Mongols expanded into Kökenuur (Qinghai) in northeastern Tibet where they again came in contact with Tibetan Buddhist clerics. At the same time, Altan Khan (1508–1582), in Höhhot of modern Inner Mongolia, gave refuge to millenarian Buddhists fleeing persecution in China. After making peace with China in 1571, however, Altan Khan extradited the millenarian leaders and instead turned to Tibetan lamas. The Second Conversion that made Mongolia a pervasively Buddhist country began in 1578 when Altan Khan and the Chinggisid nobility of southwestern Inner Mongolia met the Third Dalai Lama of the new Dge lugs pa, or Yellow Hat, order of Tibetan Buddhist monks.

In Tibet itself, the passionately convinced Dge lugs pa adherents fought fierce opposition in order to purge Buddhism of noncanonical tantras and practices. The embattled Dge lugs pa saw the Mongol conversion as a chance to create a purely Yellow Hat society. Mongol rulers converted to Dge lugs pa Buddhism, destroyed shamanist ancestral figures, and severely punished shamanist sacrifices. As Dge lugs pa missionaries expanded to eastern Inner Mongolia and Mongolia proper during the seventeenth century, they also struggled tenaciously against adherents of older Buddhist orders, particularly the Sa skya pa. The missionary endeavor of the Dge lugs pas paid off in 1642 when Güüshi Khan, ruler of the western Oirat Mongols (from today's northern Xinjiang) invaded Tibet, destroyed the enemies of the Yellow Hats, and enthroned the Fifth Dalai Lama as Central Tibet's secular and religious ruler. By 1700, non-Yellow Hat Buddhism had essentially disappeared from Mongolia. Shamanism was more tenacious, but by 1800 it survived in institutionalized form only on the eastern and northern fringes of the Mongolian plateau. From 1800 on, another wave of Dge lugs pa missionary activity converted many Buriat Mongols in southern Siberia.

During the Second Conversion, noblemen dedicated their children to monastic life. Monastic institutions rapidly took shape all over Mongolia. In 1639 the son of a Chinggisid nobleman became the first of the line of Jibzundamba Khutugtus, the most holy Mongolian Buddhist incarnate lama lineage. This First Jibzundamba Khutugtu, named Zanabazar (1635–1723), also become a major political leader who led the Mongols of Mongolia proper into submission to the Manchu Qing dynasty (1636–1912). He was also one of the great sculptors of the Buddhist artistic tradition. Translation of the Buddhist scriptures culminated in the complete translation of the Tibetan Buddhist canon, first of the Bka' 'gyur (the canonical sutras and tantras), in 1628 to 1629 and then of the Bstan 'gyur (the canonical Indian commentaries) in 1749.

By the 1830s virtually every aspect of Tibetan monastic culture had been transplanted to Mongolia. With only a few exceptions, Mongolian Buddhist services were carried on in Tibetan language. In the 1918 census of Mongolia proper, about 45 percent of the Mongolian male population had received some monastic education and hence were considered lamas. Only about a third of these, however, actually lived in monasteries as celibate lamas. The rest left the monasteries in their late teens and became married householders, performing all normal lay duties. Nuns (*chibagantsa*) were almost always widows or unmarried older women who took vows; no organized nunneries are known. Incarnate lamas and major monasteries also had lay subjects, called *shabi* (disciples). Mongolia's present capital, Ulaanbaatar, developed around the monastery of the Jibzundamba Khutugtu. Other major monasteries include Erdeni Zuu in central Mongolia and Badgar Juu in Inner Mongolia.

Mongolian Buddhist literature was first nurtured by translated Indian and Tibetan works. Many Mongolian scholars wrote in Tibetan on Buddhist philosophy, tantra, astrology, medicine, and grammar. In the eighteenth century, the Third Mergen Gegeen Lubsang Dambi Jalsan (1717–1766) designed a Mongolian-language liturgy that incorporated local Mongolian deities and spirits. He also began the tradition of writing didactic poetry and devotional songs in Mongolian; many of his songs are still sung today. This tradition reached its height with the wild poet and incarnate lama Danzin Rabjai (1803–1856).

Lay Mongolian religious life revolved around a number of cults such as that of the *oboo* (cairns), the "White Old Man" (*tsagan ebügen*), and the rituals of the household fire, particularly that of the Lunar New Year. Many scholars have seen these as "survivals of shamanism," yet they were completely integrated into Mongolian Buddhist practice. In fact, the *oboo* cult actually seems to have been introduced into

Mongolia from Tibet in the seventeenth to eighteenth centuries. Poems and sermons addressed to the laity castigated social evils such as hunting, blood sacrifices, alcohol, smoking, and youthful romance, while advocating filial piety, frugality, and obedience to authorities in religion and state.

After the Manchu Qing dynasty changed its policy to sinicizing the Mongols in 1901, the Eighth Jibzundamba Khutugtu (1870–1924) declared Mongolia proper independent in 1911. Under his theocratic rule from 1911 to 1919, clerical privileges in Mongolia expanded to unprecedented levels. Several monuments of Buddhist architecture were built, including the temple housing the 80-foot high statue of Avalokiteśvara and the Green Palace.

In southeastern Inner Mongolia, the Chinese-influenced writer Injannashi (1837–1892) had sharply criticized Buddhist lamas for their ignorant and arrogant rejection of the world. This criticism, reflecting a long-standing Confucian critique of Buddhism, developed in the early twentieth century into an anticlerical ethos that pervaded the new schools movement in eastern Inner Mongolia. By contrast, many Buriat Mongols of southern Siberia clung strongly to Buddhism in resisting Tsarist Russia's policies of Russification and Christianization. After 1917, the lama Agwang Dorzhiev (1853–1938) and the secular intellectual Tsyben Zhamtsarano (1881–1942) strongly advocated the compatibility of Buddhism with modern science and socialism.

In independent Mongolia, a Soviet-supported leftist regime was installed in 1921. When the Eighth Jibzundamba Khutugtu died in 1924, Mongolia was declared a People's Republic. In 1929, mass anti-Buddhist campaigns began among the Buriat Mongols of southern Siberia and in Mongolia proper. Popular support for the monasteries remained strong and religiously based insurrections in Mongolia in 1932 forced a temporary reversal. Between 1936 and 1939, however, pressure from Moscow resulted in the complete destruction of institutional Buddhism in Mongolia and Siberia. In Mongolia, perhaps 50,000 lamas were arrested or shot.

After 1944 one monastery was reopened in Mongolia proper and two in Buriatia. Education of children in religious tenets was prohibited. Lamas were prohibited from performing any religious functions outside the monasteries. All lamas were expected to marry. In 1947 the Chinese Communists came to power in Inner Mongolia. After a period of limited religious tolerance, anti-Buddhist persecution began there in 1958, which resulted in the destruction of all Buddhist institutions after 1966.

In 1979 liberalization in China allowed Inner Mongolian monasteries to open again. By the 1990s, Buddhist monasteries again enjoyed a qualified toleration, although the Communist party still controlled education and public discourse. After 1989, the collapse of the Soviet bloc brought full religious freedom to Mongolia proper for the first time. Old Buddhist monasteries are being rebuilt, often with funds from India, Japan, and the Mongolian government. Child-monks are being trained in new religious schools. At the same time, Buddhism faces new competition from evangelical Christian missionaries. Among the Buriat Mongols, Christian missions are much more limited, but Western-based advocates of non-Dge lugs pa, non-traditional forms of Buddhism have brought new divisions.

Bibliography

Atwood, Christopher P. "Buddhism and Popular Ritual in Mongolian Religion: A Reexamination of the Fire Cult." *History of Religions* 36 (1996): 112–139. Challenges the "shamanist survival" theory of Mongolian popular religion.

Bawden, C.R., trans. *Tales of an Old Lama.* Tring, 1997. Describes the monastic life and atmosphere in the period from 1900 to 1921.

Berger, Patricia, and Theresa Tse Bartholomew, eds. *Mongolia: The Legacy of Chinggis Khan.* San Francisco, 1995. Introduces Mongolian Buddhist art, focusing on Zanabazar's sculptures. Extensive bibliography.

Heissig, Walther. *The Religions of Mongolia.* Translated by Geoffrey Samuel. Berkeley, Calif., 1980. Surveys the sixteenth–seventeenth centuries' Second Conversion and aspects of the popular pantheon from the perspective of "shamanist survivals." Extensive bibliography.

Hyer, Paul, and Sechin Jagchid. *A Mongolian Living Buddha: Biography of the Kanjurwa Khutughtu.* Albany, N.Y., 1983. Describes life in an Inner Mongolian monastery between 1915 and 1949.

Lattimore, Owen, and Fukiko Isono. *The Diluv Khutagt: Memoirs and Autobiography of a Mongol Buddhist Reincarnation in Religion and Revolution.* Wiesbaden, Germany, 1982. Memoir of an active figure in the theocratic regime who was later tried for counterrevolutionary activities in 1930.

Miller, Robert James. *Monasteries and Culture Change in Inner Mongolia.* Wiesbaden, Germany, 1959. Surveys Inner Mongolian Buddhist institutions.

Moses, Larry William. *Political Role of Mongol Buddhism.* Bloomington, Ind., 1977. A useful survey of the antireligious campaigns, despite the absence of post-1990 revelations.

Pozdneyev, Aleksei M. *Religion and Ritual in Society: Lamaist Buddhism in Late 19th-Century Mongolia.* Translated by Alo Raun and Linda Raun. Bloomington, Ind., 1978. By far, the fullest description of clerical life in nineteenth-century Mongolia, by a sympathetic Russian Mongolist.

Zhukovskaia, N.L. "Revival of Buddhism in Buryatia: Problems and Prospects." In *Anthropology and Archeology of Eurasia* 39, no. 4 (Spring 2000–2001): 23–47. Describes the conflicts in modern Buriat Mongol Buddhism.

CHRISTOPHER P. ATWOOD (2005)

BUDDHISM: BUDDHISM IN TIBET

Religion pervades many aspects of Tibetan life and culture, and the dominant, institutional religious system of Tibet is Buddhism (*sangs rgyas kyi bstan pa*). The Tibetan Bon religion, in its organized, clerical dimension, is a form of Buddhism whose first human teacher, Ston pa Gshen rab (Tönpa Shenrab), is always referred to by the Bon po as a buddha (*sangs rgyas*) who lived long before Śākyamuni. Bon, like the other forms of Buddhism in Tibet, embraces a wide-ranging sphere of cultural and religious activity, whose elaborate traditions of ritual, art, and learning derive from both indigenous sources and the ancient religious matrices of India, Iran, and China.

Besides the originally "foreign" traditions of Buddhism and Bon, Tibetan religions embrace a broad range of beliefs, practices, and specialist practitioners that appear to be of autochthonous origin. These may be found in both Bon po and Buddhist settings as well as in some contexts in which sectarian affiliation is left unclear. At issue are the elements of Tibetan religious life that constitute what R. A. Stein has called the "nameless religion," in preference to the misleading designation of "popular religion." What is at stake here is not a distinction between the beliefs of the general populace and those of the religious or social elite. In actual practice, the nameless religion, centering on the cults of local divinities and spirits, the harmony or conflict between humans, and the invisible forces with which they must interact, is the concern of persons belonging to all strata of Tibetan society, and it is in fact almost named Buddhism or Bon, depending upon the contexts in which it occurs. For the purposes of the present survey, however, the point of focus must be restricted to Tibetan Buddhism as represented in the historical and doctrinal traditions of the major Buddhist orders apart from Bon, with some attention too to the role of Buddhism in Tibetan society overall.

TIBETAN BUDDHIST BEGINNINGS. It is not clear when, exactly, Tibetans made their first contact with the Buddhist religion. Indigenous tradition holds that in the time of the legendary king of the Yar lung principality, Lha Tho tho ri (Lha Thotori, c. fourth century CE), Buddhist scriptures and images miraculously fell onto the palace or else that these objects were carried there by a central Asian Buddhist monk. Though these tales must be considered as legends, it is not implausible that some knowledge of Buddhism may have found its way to Tibet during this late period of its prehistory for the Tibetan plateau was by then surrounded on all sides by lands in which Buddhism was well established as a religious and cultural system: Nepal and India to the south, China to the east, the Silk Road states to the north, and the Iranian world to the west.

History proper begins in Tibet with the emperor Srong btsan sgam po (Songtsen Gampo, c. 617–649), who politically unified the peoples occupying the Tibetan plateau and whose armies then penetrated deep into the surrounding territories. The Tibetan system of writing was also developed at this time. The emperor's marriage to the Chinese princess of Wencheng (d. 678) was accompanied by the installation in his capital, Lhasa, of a precious image of Śākyamuni Buddha brought from China as part of her dowry and said to have been originally manufactured in India as an exact likeness of the Buddha himself. The statue, known as the *Jowo* (Lord), remains Tibet's holiest object of pilgrimage. Later accounts relate that the monarch also married a Nepalese Buddhist princess, Bhṛkuṭī, and that, inspired by the devotion of his two foreign queens, Srong btsan sgam po and the inner circle of his court embraced the Indian religion. Indeed, the emperor was regarded in later times as a Tibetan emanation of the regal *bodhisattva* of compassionate love, Avalokiteśvara.

Though Srong btsan sgam po may have extended some degree of official tolerance to Buddhism, at least in order to accommodate his Chinese bride and her court, it is unlikely that the alien faith made much progress in Tibet before another half century or more had passed. In the time of the ruler Khri 'Dus srong (Trhi Düsong, d. 704), a temple was founded in the region of Gling, in far eastern Tibet, perhaps in connection with military campaigns in the southeastern part of the Tibetan Empire, aimed at subjugating the Buddhist kingdom of Nanzhao (in modern Yunnan). Nevertheless, it was only during the reign of Khri 'Dus srong's noted successor Khri Lde gtsug btsan (Trhi Detsuktsen, 704–755) that there is clear evidence of Buddhist advances in central Tibet. Once again, it was a Chinese princess who played an instrumental role in supporting the faith.

The princess of Jincheng arrived in Tibet in 710, two years before her then six-year-old husband-to-be was granted his regal title. She is said to have been much saddened by the absence of Buddhist funerary rites for the deceased nobility and so introduced the Chinese Buddhist custom of conducting rites for the dead during a period of seven weeks of mourning. This practice later gave rise to the belief, famed in such works as the so-called *Tibetan Book of the Dead,* that forty-nine days intervene between death and rebirth. The princess also invited to central Tibet Khotanese monks, who formed the first community of the *saṃgha* in that land. However, following the death of the princess in 739, probably due to an outbreak of the plague, there was a sharp anti-Buddhist reaction, and the foreign monks were expelled.

The last years of Khri Lde gtsug btsan's reign were marked by grave factional conflict among the nobility, resulting finally in the monarch's assassination. When his thirteen-year-old son was placed on the throne in 755, the factions dominating the court were implacably hostile to Buddhism. The young emperor, Khri Srong lde'u btsan (Trhi Songdetsen, 742–c. 797), nevertheless became imperial Tibet's greatest ruler as well as an unparalleled Buddhist benefactor. In the monarch's own surviving edicts, it was written that during the early years of his reign Tibet faced severe epidemics, afflicting both humans and livestock. When no other viable solution appeared, he rescinded the ban on the practice of Buddhist rites and matters rapidly turned for the better. As a result, he himself adopted the Buddhist religion and undertook to study its teachings in depth. His conversion took place in 762, when he was just twenty years of age.

It is sometimes thought that the adoption of Buddhism by the Tibetan court pacified the formerly warlike Tibetan people and thus contributed to the decline and fall of the empire. Research, however, makes clear that Tibet continued aggressive policies of imperial expansion long after Buddhism became a key aspect of Tibetan imperial ideology. Buddhism, in this context, provided the empire with the symbolic means to represent itself throughout its domains and to its neighbors as embodying a universal spiritual and political order.

Khri Srong lde'u btsan went on to construct Tibet's first Buddhist monastery, Bsam yas (Samye, c. 779), and invited the learned Indian monk Śāntarakṣita to ordain the first officially recognized Tibetan Buddhist monks. Henceforth, the Tibetan Buddhist monastic community adhered to the Vinaya of the Indian Mūlasarvāstivāda order as the basis for its monastic code. The court also sponsored the translation of Buddhist canonical scriptures, and the hundreds of texts translated into Tibetan by the imperial translation committees may be counted among the greatest achievements of the art of translation in world history. The Tibetan translation canon, later organized into the complementary collections of the *Kanjur* (*bka' 'gyur,* "translated scriptures") and *Tanjur* (*bstan 'gyur,* "translated commentaries"), preserves numerous Indian and Chinese texts now unavailable elsewhere.

The foundation of Bsam yas is said also to have involved the intercession of Padmasambhava, a renowned Tantric adept from Oḍḍiyāna in northern India, whose services were required to quell the hostile spirits and divinities of Tibet and to win their allegiance to Buddhism. Together, the king Khri Srong lde'u btsan, the monk Śāntarakṣita, and the adept Padmasambhava are popularly revered as the trinity of the Tibetan conversion and represent three of the major constituents of the Tibetan Buddhist world: patron, monk, and Tantric adept.

During the 780s, Khri Srong lde'u btsan's armies conquered Dunhuang, a major center of Chinese Buddhism. The Chinese Chan master Moheyan was invited to central Tibet and became involved in a debate or discussion at Bsam yas with Śāntarakṣita's disciple, the Indian philosopher Kamalaśīla. Their debate may well have led to a draw, but later tradition reviles Moheyan as representing an irrational doctrine of mystical intuition and regards Kamalaśīla's emphasis upon the gradual cultivation of the virtues of a *bodhisattva* as the enduring paradigm to be emulated by Tibetan Buddhists. The Tibetan occupation of Dunhuang in any event broadened Tibet's relations with Chinese Buddhism. The preservation there of numerous Tibetan manuscripts, which first became known in Europe through the work of the British explorer Marc Aurel Stein in 1907, provides the richest source of Tibetan documentation for the religious life of the late first millennium.

DECLINE AND RENAISSANCE. Under Khri Srong lde'u btsan's successors, Khri Lde srong btsan (r. 804–815) and Khri Ral pa can (Trhi Relpacen, r. 815–838), Buddhist monasteries and schools continued to flourish with royal support. In the reign of U'i dum btsan (Üdumtsen, popularly known as Glang Dar ma [Lang Darma], "Ox Dharma," 838–842), state sponsorship of the monasteries was reduced or withdrawn, perhaps for fiscal reasons. Later tradition, however, recounts that there was a persecution of Buddhism culminating in Glang Dar ma's assassination in 842 by the Buddhist monk Lha lung Dpal gyi rdo rje (Lhalung Pelgi Dorje). The collapse of the Tibetan Empire soon followed, and Tibet remained without central authority for a full four hundred years. Though much of Buddhist activity was curtailed, some traditions of study and practice nevertheless survived, and the Tantric traditions appear actually to have flourished following the empire's fall. Monastic Buddhism, however, virtually disappeared in central Tibet for more than a century and was preserved among Tibetans solely in what had been the empire's far eastern districts, in the modern Chinese provinces of Qinghai and Gansu. It was here, at some time during the mid-tenth century, that a young Bon po converted and received Buddhist ordination. Known to posterity as Bla chen Dgongs pa rab gsal (Lachen Gongpa Rapsel), the "great lama whose spirit was clear," he later ordained a group of seekers from central and western Tibet, thus sparking the late-tenth-century monastic revival movement that came to be called the "later promulgation of the teaching" (*bstan pa phyi dar*).

Tibet had now entered a new period of economic and political development and change. Throughout much of the Tibetan world, local lords struggled for supremacy, and religious authority was no less contested than temporal power. Seekers and adventurers looked for authoritative sources of Buddhist teaching in India and Nepal, traveling there in search of *gurus,* scriptures, and esoteric lore. These developments were particularly prominent in western Tibet, where the great translator Rin chen bzang po (Rinchen Zangpo, 958–1055) was patronized by the devout monarch of the Gu ge Kingdom, Ye shes 'od (Yeshe-ö), who was concerned to purify Tibetan Buddhism from what he regarded as the corrupt forms of Tantrism that had emerged during the post-imperial period. At the royal monastery of Tho ling, one of a number of religious establishments newly founded in Gu ge's domains, a translation academy was created, where Indian Buddhist scholars were invited to collaborate with Rin chen bzang po and his disciples. The Tibetan Buddhist translations, particularly of Tantric materials, produced from this time on became known as the "new translations" (*gsar 'gyur*) in contradistinction to the "former translations" (*snga 'gyur*), whose Tantric texts some believed to be apocryphal or corrupt. Tho ling continued to flourish long after Ye shes 'od's decease, and in 1042 his successor Byang chub 'od (Changcup-ö) invited the renowned Bengali scholar and adept Dīpaṃkaraśrījñāna, known to posterity as Atīśa, to teach there. Three years later Atīśa traveled to central Tibet, where he continued to augment his Tibetan following until his death at Snye thang, not far from Lhasa, in 1054.

Atiśa appears in Tibetan accounts to have been an enthusiastic, generous, and saintly teacher, austere but at the same time humorous and good-natured, learned but more concerned with the quality of practice than with scholarship per se. His successors, above all those affiliated with the line of his lay disciple 'Brom ston Rgyal ba'i 'byung gnas (Dromtön, 1004–1064), came to be known as Bka' gdams pa (Kadampa), "adherents of the scriptures and precepts," the first such named Tibetan Buddhist order. 'Brom ston founded the seat of the order at the monastery of Rwa sgreng (Reting), to the north of Lhasa, in 1057. Buddhist philosophical education came to flourish at some Bka' gdams pa centers as well. Especially notable in this regard was the monastery of Gsang phu (Sangphu), founded in 1071, where Rngog Blo ldan shes rab (Ngok Loden Sherab, 1059–1109) established a formal curriculum emphasizing debate and scholastic study, which formed the model for all later Tibetan monastic education.

The renewal of Buddhist activity was marked by intermittent tensions due to a variety of factors: competing lines of transmission, regional and clan affiliations, relations between preexisting Tibetan Buddhist traditions and newly imported Indian teachings, orientations favoring monastic scholarship versus Tantrism and yoga, and competition for patronage among them. It was in this setting that the *guru*, or lama (*bla ma*), began to emerge as a focal point of religious and political authority. Though foreigners have sometimes followed the Chinese in using the word *lama* to refer to Tibetan monks in general, it is a term that retains for Tibetans a special reference to the religious teacher who guides the spiritual life of the individual and often the practical life of the community as well.

Despite the reticence evinced by some factions toward aspects of Tantrism, particularly ritualized sex and violence, it was precisely during this same period that new efforts were made to translate and transmit Buddhist Tantric traditions. These efforts moreover reflected important changes within the Indian Buddhist Tantrism itself: roughly, a shift to systems emphasizing internal yoga over external ritual, which were often strongly eroticized in symbolism and sometimes in practice as well. Indian Tantric adepts active at this time claimed to possess particularly efficacious means for the swift attainment of spiritual powers of various kinds, including and culminating in enlightenment. Hence, the claims on the part of Tibetan masters to continue the authoritative transmission of such esoteric knowledge in Tibet came to play a special role in authenticating new sources of power, prestige, and authority.

Though the age of the new Tantric translations is generally said to have begun with Rin chen bzang po, it is one of his junior contemporaries who is regarded as the first great proponent of these innovative forms of Indian Buddhist Tantrism. 'Brog mi Śākya ye shes (Drokmi, 993–1050) was, like most who entered the *saṃgha* in Tibet during the late tenth century and early eleventh century, ordained within monastic traditions stemming from the indigenous tenth-century monastic revival. But after years of study in Nepal and India, he established his own monastic center and translation academy at Myu gu lung (Nyugulung), where he collaborated with the Indian Tantric master Gayadhara. His most renowned contribution to later Tibetan Buddhism was the transmission of a system of Tantrism and yoga based upon the *Hevajratantra* that came to be the central esoteric tradition of the Sa skya pa (Sakyapa) order, founded by the aristocratic 'Khon (Khön) household in 1073.

Among those who studied with 'Brog mi was Mar pa Chos kyi blo gros (Marpa, 1012–1096), who was sent to study translation when his parents found him otherwise impossible to control. Eventually he rebelled against his teacher's exactions, for 'Brog mi's tutelage did not come cheap, and set out to make his own way among the celebrated masters of India. Famed as the leading Tibetan successor of the renowned Indian *siddhas* Nāropa and Maitrīpa, he attracted many disciples, who, with their successors, came to be known as Bka' brgyud pa (Kagyüpa), "adherents of the oral lineage." Most famous among them was Mi la ras pa (Milarepa, 1040–1123), the great Tibetan mystical poet. The latter's disciple Sgam po pa (Gampopa, 1079–1153) sought to harmonize the esoteric teachings of Mar pa's tradition with the ethical instructions of the Bka' gdams pa, thus "mingling the two streams." The several monastic orders of the Bka' brgyud pa stem from among his disciples and played an important role in later Tibetan religious and political life.

The new infusion of Indian Buddhist teaching during this period gave rise to a large number of new Tibetan Buddhist sects and schools, focusing on both philosophical and Tantric teachings. At the same time, the reassertion of the Bon and Rnying ma pa (Nyingmapa) traditions was advanced by means of rediscovered "treasures" (*gter ma*), texts, and religious objects said to have been cached by famous teachers in ancient times and now recovered. Among the Rnying ma pa, their concealment was mostly attributed to Padmasambhava. By means of their revelation, Nyang ral Nyi ma 'od zer (Nyangrel Nyima Özer, 1124–1196) and the later "treasure revealers" (*gter ston*) elaborated an abundant and influential body of ritual, historical, and legendary literature. Here the memory of the Tibetan Empire of the seventh to ninth centuries is transformed to become a national religious myth in which the emperor Srong btsan sgam po figures as the worldly presence of the *bodhisattva* Avalokiteśvara and his Chinese and Nepalese brides as that of the savioress Tārā. Padmasambhava himself is now transfigured to become the "Precious Guru" (*Gu ru Rin po che*) of the Tibetan people overall. A famous later example of the *gter ma* literature is the so-called *Tibetan Book of the Dead*, the book of "liberation by hearing in the intermediate state" (*Bardo Thödröl*). This fourteenth-century revelation reflects in part the ancient Tibetan religious concern with the safe passage of the deceased.

LATER DEVELOPMENTS. In 1204 the Kashmiri scholar Śākyaśrī arrived in Tibet with a retinue of learned followers.

Their visit did much to catalyze a new enthusiasm for Indian scholarship. Kun dga' rgyal mtshan (Kunga Gyaltsen, 1182–1251), an heir to the 'Khon family of Sa skya and later famed as Sa skya Paṇḍita, was among those inspired to devote himself to the advancement in Tibet of Indian intellectual traditions. Contemporaneously, much of Eurasia experienced the devastating upheaval of the Mongol conquest, which had begun with the rise of Chinggis Khan (d. 1227). By the end of the third decade of the century, prophecies began to appear warning of an impending Mongol attack on Tibet. These proved true when in 1239 an army commanded by Dorta the Black swept into central Tibet, sacking the temple of Rwa sgreng. The Mongols, however, withdrew without consolidating their rule in Tibet. In 1246 Sa skya Paṇḍita embarked on a mission to the Mongol ruler, Godan Khan, and remained among the Mongols until his death. His visit established a precedent for Mongol relations with Tibet and for the eventual adoption of Buddhism by the Mongols. Sa skya Paṇḍita's nephew 'Phags pa (Phakpa, 1235–1280) later became the Tibetan preceptor of Kublai Khan. As the preeminent Tibetan clergyman in the eastern Mongol Empire (the Chinese Yuan dynasty), he would be instrumental in the establishment of Sa skya pa preeminence in Tibet under the Mongols.

Members of non–Sa skya pa orders also maintained relations with the Mongol lords: examples are the second Karma pa hierarch, Karma Pakshi (1206–1283), and his successor, Karma pa III Rang byung Rdo rje (Rangjung Dorje) (1284–1339). The Karma pas, who headed one of the prominent Bka' brgyud pa orders, were instrumental in creating Tibet's unique form of ecclesiastical succession, in which a child is identified as the reborn emanation (*sprul sku*) and legal heir of a deceased master. During the period of the Mongol–Sa skya pa hegemony, Tibetan Buddhist scholastic philosophy also came into flower, thanks in part to Sa skya Paṇḍita's example. The many famous figures active during this period included the Bka' gdams pa scholiast Bcom ldan rig ral (Comden Raldri, early fourteenth century), the celebrated canonical editor Bu ston (Butön, 1290–1364), the promulgator of the Jo nang pa (Jonangpa) order's controversial "extrinsic emptiness" (*gzhan stong*) doctrine, Dol po pa (1292–1361), and the redactor of the Great Perfection system, Klong chen Rab 'byams pa (Longchen Rabjampa, 1308–1363).

Toward 1350, under the leadership of Ta'i Si tu Byang chub rgyal mtshan (Tasi Changcup Gyaltsen, 1302–1364) of the Phag mo gru pa (Phakmotrupa) order, a Bka' brgyud pa offshoot, Tibet was freed from the Sa skya pa–Mongol regime. It was during the period of Phag mo gru pa dominance that followed that Rje Tsong kha pa Blo bzang grags pa (Je Tsongkhapa, 1357–1419) founded the Dga' ldan (Ganden) monastery to the east of Lhasa (1409), which emerged as the main seat of a new order, best known as Dge lugs pa (Gelukpa), the "adherents of virtue." Though Tsong kha pa was greatly revered for his vast learning and rigorous standard of practice, relations between his disciples and some representatives of the older orders grew increasingly contentious. The fifteenth and sixteenth centuries witnessed intensive doctrinal debate between the Dge lugs pa and their Sa skya pa and Bka' brgyud pa rivals.

The connection between Tibetan Buddhism and imperial China, which had been formed under China's Mongol rulers during the Yuan dynasty, did not come to an end after that dynasty fell in 1368. An example may be found in the relationship between one of the greatest Ming emperors, Yongle (r. 1403–1424), and the fifth Karma pa hierarch De bzhin gshegs pa (Dezhinshekpa, 1384–1415). Though the Ming dynasty is often regarded as a period of Karma pa dominance in Sino-Tibetan affairs, the Ming emperors were by no means exclusive in their allegiance to a single Tibetan school. Tsong kha pa's disciple, Byams chen Chos rje (Jamchen Chöje, 1352–1435), for instance, who established Se ra Monastery near Lhasa in 1419, traveled to the Chinese capital and enjoyed an enthusiastic reception at the court, where he was showered with honors and gifts.

Throughout the fifteenth century, Tsong kha pa's successors continued to found important new monastic establishments, gathering the patronage and support of leading princes and powerful families. One of those who succeeded in this way was Dge 'dun grub (Gendündrup, 1391–1474), founder of the Bkra shis lhun po (Tashi Lhünpo) monastery in Gtsang (Tsang) province. This had significant political ramifications during the seventeenth century, when the rulers of Gtsang came to favor the Dge lugs pa's rivals, above all, the Karma pas. Dge 'dun grub and his successor, Dge 'dun rgya mtsho (Gendün Gyatso, 1476–1542), were, however, primarily famed for their learning and sanctity, and under their guidance Bkra shis lhun po soon became the preeminent Dge lugs pa institution in Gtsang and the base for the expansion of the order throughout western Tibet.

During the sixteenth century, important powers in central Tibet were allied with the Dge lugs pa, while the kings of Gtsang in the west supported hierarchs of the Bka' brgyud pa, Jo nang pa, and other orders. Dge 'dun rgya mtsho's successor, Bsod nams rgya mtsho (Sonam Gyatso, 1543–1588), at this time became a missionary to the Mongols, and on winning the allegiance of the chieftain Altan Khan (1578) of the Tumed tribe, he received the Mongolian title Dalai Lama (oceanic guru). Because the title was bestowed posthumously on his predecessors, he became the third in the line. The connection forged with the Mongols encouraged the renewed interest of the Mongolian leadership in Tibetan affairs, and in 1642 Gushri Khan of the Khoshot tribe conquered all of Tibet, establishing the fifth Dalai Lama (1617–1682) as ruler of the reunified realm. The kingdom of Gtsang was suppressed together with the religious traditions it had favored, above all the Jo nang pa, who were banned from all but a few Tibetan territories outside the sphere of the Dalai Lama's control. The government of the fifth Dalai Lama strongly supported the development of mass monasticism in all parts of the country, and new Dge lugs pa establishments were founded everywhere. Many centers of the older orders and of the Bon religion were now required to become Dge lugs pa.

The fifth Dalai Lama forged Tibet's unique political system, based in principle upon a reciprocal relationship between the religious and secular branches of government (*chos srid gnyis ldan*), with the Dalai Lama or his regent directing the affairs of state. This system required that monastic hierarchs and officials be directly involved in most offices of the Tibetan government. The authority of the Great Fifth's regime was given concrete form in the imposing Potala Palace, a large complex of government offices, shrines, and residences. His tutor, the Paṇchen bla ma Blo bzang chos rgyan (Lozang Chögyen, 1567–1662), a distinguished scholar, rose to prominence at this time as well. Thereafter, the successive rebirths of the Panchen Lamas were recognized at Bkra shis lhun po, where they often wielded considerable political power. The Panchen Lamas were officially second in rank to, but sometimes actually rivaled, the Dalai Lamas themselves.

The Manchu rulers of China's Qing dynasty (1644–1911) became directly involved in Tibetan affairs in opposition to the renewed Mongol power in Tibet, and the fifth Dalai Lama visited the court soon after the new dynasty's inception. Tibet was soon a focal point of competition between Manchus and Mongols in their struggle for hegemony in central Asia. The controversial sixth Dalai Lama, Tshangs dbyangs rgya mtsho (Tshangyang Gyatso, 1683–1706), a libertine who preferred the company of women to the life of a monk, was forcibly removed from office and died under mysterious circumstances enroute to the Chinese capital. In 1717 the Mongolian Dzungar tribe invaded Tibet, bringing renewed civil war and intersectarian violence. During the 1720s, the Manchus sought to consolidate their rule over large parts of the eastern Tibetan provinces of Amdo and Kham. Leading Dge lugs pa hierarchs from Amdo, such as the Qianlong emperor's teacher Lcang skya Rol pa'i rdo rje (Jangkya Rölpe Dorje, 1717–1786), came to play an important role in the religious affairs of the Manchu Empire.

The political turmoil in central Tibet throughout much of the seventeenth and eighteenth centuries contributed to a remarkable shift in Tibet's cultural geography. Whereas central Tibet had been, throughout the preceding centuries, the unrivaled heart of Tibetan religious life, it became now the tendency for masters of eastern Tibetan origin to devote much of their energy to activities in or near their native districts. The eastward displacement of cultural activity had many causes and consequences. Thus, for example, the civil wars of the seventeenth century made an exile of the tenth Karma pa, Chos dbyings rdo rje (Chöying Dorje, 1605–1674), a talented painter and patron of the arts, and led him to spend much of his career in the far southeast of Tibet, in what is now Yunnan. The patronage of his order by important princes in Khams encouraged his followers to regard the east as their true base, so that in succeeding centuries the major center of learning and culture in the Karma pa order was Dpal spungs (Pelpung) monastery, in the eastern principality of Sde dge (Derge). With the patronage of the rulers of Sde dge, eastern Tibetan Karma pa and Sa skya pa masters contributed to the foundation of Tibet's greatest publishing house, the Sde dge Printery, whose eighteenth-century edition of the Tibetan Buddhist canon is considered one of the masterworks of traditional Tibetan printing. At the same time, some of the Dge lugs pa monasteries in eastern Tibet for the first time also became important centers of learning in their own right, particularly in Amdo. The best-known examples were no doubt Sku 'bum (Kumbum), near Tsong kha pa's birthplace not far from the city of Xining (Qinghai province), and Bla brang Bkra shis 'khyil (Labrang Tashikhyil), founded by 'Jam dbyangs bzhad pa (Jamyang Zhepa, 1648–1721) in southern Gansu.

Nineteenth-century Khams became home to a dynamic movement often characterized as "eclectic" or "universalist" (*Ris med*), which sought to defuse the intense sectarianism that had often plagued Tibetan Buddhism. The encyclopedic writings of 'Jam dbyangs Mkhyen brtse'i dbang po (Jamyang Khyentse, 1820–1892) and 'Jam mgon kong sprul (Jamgön Kongtrül, 1813–1899) became in some respects a new canon for the adherents of this movement. One of their disciples, Mi pham rnam rgyal (Mipham Namgyal, 1846–1912) also elaborated a new scholastic curriculum emphasizing the doctrinal standpoint of the Rnying ma pa order. Though the thirteenth Dalai Lama (1876–1933) was sympathetic to the goals of the eclectic movement, some factions within the Dge lugs pa leadership were not. Prominent among them was Pha bong kha pa Bde chen Snying po (Phabongkhapa Dechen Nyingpo, 1878–1941), whose visions of the spirit Rdo rje shugs ldan (Dorje Shukden) seem to have entailed a commitment to oppose actively the other schools of Tibetan Buddhism and the Bon religion. There has been, as a result, a continuing legacy of sectarian dispute among Tibetans to the early twenty-first century.

ESSENTIAL BELIEFS AND DOCTRINES. The several orders and schools of Tibetan Buddhism have a great many particular doctrines and precepts, which impart to them each a distinctive character. Here, however, only salient features of the common heritage of Tibetan Buddhism will be considered.

Like many Buddhist traditions, Tibetan Buddhism emphasizes the impermanence of conditioned reality and the resulting inevitability of suffering and death. Living beings who have not achieved *nirvāṇa* (*myang 'das*), that is, the enlightenment of a buddha, are subject to a perpetual, painful round of rebirth, or *saṃsāra* (*'khor ba*), their condition in any given lifetime, whether human, divine, or infernal, being determined by the impetus of their past meritorious and demeritorious *karma* (*las*). Tibetan Buddhism therefore stresses the necessity of gaining merit (*bsod nams*) through donations to monks and religious institutions, offering of lamps and incense, recitation of scriptures, performance of prostrations and circumambulations, "ransoming" of animals from the butcher, and many other types of religiously valued actions. One must turn from worldly activities to religion by taking refuge in the Three Precious Jewels (*dkon mchog gsum*): the Buddha, his teaching (*chos*), and the religious community (*dge 'dun*). Often one's lama is added to this universal Buddhist trinity as a fourth refuge.

Tibetan Buddhists are encouraged not to seek *nirvāṇa* for themselves alone but to cultivate compassion (*snying rje*) for all living beings. One is to embark upon the Great Vehicle, the Mahāyāna (*theg chen*), that is, the path of a *bodhisattva (byang chub sems dpa')*, and to develop the virtues of charity, self-restraint, patience, diligence, meditation, and insight. This last is, above all, insight into the radically contingent nature of conditioned things, that is, their emptiness (*stong nyid*). To comprehend this difficult concept through reason is among the central concerns of Tibetan Buddhist philosophy and is a source of considerable debate.

MONASTIC INSTITUTIONS AND EDUCATION. The institutional heart of Tibetan Buddhism is the monastery. Mass monasticism was encouraged in traditional Tibetan society, particularly after the consolidation of political power by the fifth Dalai Lama. This was justified ideologically by the notion that the monk was in an especially privileged position to avoid evil and to achieve merit, so that by maximizing monasticism, the maximum merit accrued to Tibetan society as a whole and especially to those individuals and families who most contributed to the monastic system by dedicating sons to the religious life and who used their wealth to support religious activities. Nomadic groups in the east often felt this to be a particularly urgent matter, for the merit earned by supporting good monks and their monasteries was believed to counterbalance the burden of sin that one acquired through actions prohibited by the system of religious ethics, especially the slaughter of animals, that were nevertheless unavoidable in a nomadic livelihood. Although worldly life was thought to be inevitably ensnared in various evils, a family could still better itself spiritually by committing some sons to the clergy. And if those sons achieved religious distinction, this could sometimes also impact favorably upon the status of the family concerned.

The monastery fostered a concentration of cultural resources, serving as a center for education and for the cultivation of the arts (though in most cases, only a minority of the monks participated in these pursuits). Significantly too the monastery absorbed surplus labor. Whenever the rate of fertility outpaced the expansion of economic activity, monasticism provided a socially valued alternative to production. For religious girls and women, nunneries also existed, though nuns appear to have been less numerous than monks and seldom had access to resources for more than a rudimentary education.

Most monks entered the monastery as children and did so at the wish of their parents. Such children were granted the essential vows of the Buddhist novitiate and became eligible to receive full ordination as *bhikṣu* (*dge slong*) only in later adolescence. Rudimentary alphabetization seems to have been relatively widespread among monks and nuns, though the numbers able or inclined to pursue a higher education in Buddhist philosophy, or in such disciplines as medicine, art, or astrology, were few. The majority of the monks participated when possible in prayer services sponsored by lay patrons, who offered tea, butter, grain, and cash to the assembled congregation. Monks also pursued economic or administrative activities required for their own support or for that of the monastic community. They therefore were regularly involved in commerce and in various trades. Larger monasteries had their own complex bureaucracies, in which some offices were filled according to merit and ability and others occupied by incarnates (*sprul sku*) groomed for the task since childhood.

Some monasteries housed colleges where advanced studies could be pursued by those who were motivated to do so. Aspirant monk-scholars sometimes traveled for months across the whole of the Tibetan world to enter an especially famous college. Besides the economic and ritual functions of the monastery therefore, almost the entire apparatus of Tibetan formal education was concentrated within the monasteries as well. Literacy in traditional Tibet was a preeminently religious affair, and so, not surprisingly, the clerical services of trained monks were required by the old Lhasa government and by the administrations of the eastern Tibetan principalities as well.

It has become customary to characterize the intellectual life of the Tibetan monastic colleges as a type of scholasticism. From the late eleventh century onward, the Tibetan colleges emphasized a highly rationalized approach to Buddhist doctrine, over and against one dominated exclusively by faith. The curriculum of the colleges required the careful study of Indian Buddhist philosophical writings, with the epistemological and logical works of Dharmakīrti (c. 600) supplying the major methodological organ. Other required topics included the monastic code or Vinaya (*'dul ba*), the "meta-doctrine" or Abhidharma (*chos mngon pa*), the Perfection of Wisdom or Prajñāpāramitā (*phar phyin*), and the teaching of the Middle Way (*dbu ma*), that is, the Mādhyamika dialectic of the Indian philosopher Nāgārjuna. In the Dge lugs pa colleges, those who completed this curriculum were awarded the title of *dge bshes*, "spiritual benefactor" (equivalent to the Sanskrit *kalyāṇamitra*).

Among the most contentious of topics for doctrinal debate was the relationship between the Mādhyamika teaching of emptiness and the positive conception of a "buddha nature" pervading living beings and forming the basis for their potential to achieve enlightenment. While some interpreted the latter as just a metaphorical description of emptiness, the proponents of "extrinsic emptiness," following the teaching of the Jo nang pa master Dol po pa, argued that the absolute, in its proper nature, was not intrinsically empty at all but embodied instead the plenitude of the attributes of the Buddha's enlightenment.

TANTRISM AND YOGA. Tibetan Buddhism was especially influenced by the esoteric Indian teachings of Vajrayāna, the "Vajra Vehicle" (*rdo rje theg pa*), so-called because the primary symbol of this branch of Mahāyāna Buddhism is the *vajra* (*rdo rje*), a ritual implement at once symbolizing the diamond-like clarity and unalterabilty of mind as emptiness and its lightning-like brilliance. Vajrayāna Buddhism has its own authoritative texts, called Tantras (*rgyud*), which are primarily manuals of ritual and esoteric lore. Among the major topics treated in the Tantras is *abhiṣeka* (*dbang*), the consecration or "empowerment" whereby a disciple is initiated into a sphere of meditation called a *maṇḍala* (*dkyil 'khor*), which is most often represented as a heavenly palace. This is the residence of the deity, who is the focal point of the initiate's meditation and who is invoked by means of special formulas called *mantras* (*sngags*). The central deity may be male, female—in which case she is sometimes referred to as a *ḍākinī* (*mkha' 'gro ma*), a term also used to describe women who are Tantric adepts—or a couple in union and is often surrounded by a retinue of divine attendants, arranged symmetrically throughout the *maṇḍala*. Avalokiteśvara (*spyan ras gzigs*) in particular was identified as the national patron-deity and became the focus of a much-elaborated cult. Of central importance is the recitation of Avalokiteśvara's famous six-syllable *mantra, Oṃ Maṇipadme Hūṃ,* invoking the divinity as the "bearer of jewel and lotus. " The ubiquitousness of this formula in Tibetan religion—it is often uttered aloud while turning a prayer wheel containing the *mantra* written many times on a paper scroll—was noted even by medieval European visitors to Tibet.

The systems of meditation taught in the Tantras are referred to as yoga (*rnal 'byor*), or "union," for yoga is a discipline said to unite the adept with the realization of ultimate reality. This unification of the enlightened mind and the absolute is symbolized by the depiction of deities as couples in sexual embrace. Besides those types of yoga concerned with the visualization of *maṇḍala* and deity and the recitation of the *mantra,* there are also more advanced disciplines involving visualizations and exercises in which one's body is conceived as a network of subtle channels and energies, the skillful manipulation of which is believed to hasten the adept's progress toward enlightenment and also to lead to the acquisition of uncanny, magical abilities: clairvoyance, miraculous flight, and the resurrection of the dead. These advanced techniques of yogas are often described in terms of six doctrines (*chos drug*):

1. Inner Heat (*gtum mo*), whereby the adept learns to master the subtle physical energies of the body;
2. Body of Apparition (*sgyu lus*), through which the illusion-like nature of experience becomes known;
3. Dream (*rmi lam*), whereby one achieves the ability to consciously explore the possibilities revealed during dreams;
4. Radiant Light (*'od gsal*), referring to the luminous dimension of the mind;
5. Transference (*'pho ba*), the means to cause one's consciousness to leave the body abruptly at the moment of death and to seek rebirth in a pure realm;
6. Intermediate State (*bar do*), which here refers primarily to the state of consciousness in the course of migration between death and rebirth.

The first four doctrines enable one to attain enlightenment swiftly during this very lifetime, the last two to achieve it at death. Adepts who have attained the goals of this esoteric path are called *siddha* (*grub thob*), "accomplished" or "perfected," because they have attained *siddhi* (*dngos grub*), the mundane or supermundane powers and realizations that are especially cultivated on the path of the Vajrayāna.

The highest teachings of Tibetan Tantric Buddhism are those relating to the abstract realization of the ultimate nature of mind. For the Rnying ma pa tradition, these are represented primarily by the Great Perfection (*rdzogs chen*) teaching, while for the Bka' brgyud pa and Dge lugs pa, the Great Seal (*phyag chen*) system in the tradition of Mar pa is preeminent. Although there are many special points of emphasis, particular to each of these approaches to the absolute, the words of Klong chen Rab 'byams pa summarize their common orientation:

> The luminous nucleus is the absolute truth, permanent, stable, not subject to change or transformation, quiescent, undeceiving, the essence of gnosis that accords with the ground from beginning to end and is free from all the limits of intellectual elaboration. It should be known to be by nature neither stained, nor being stained, nor about to be stained by any of the principles of mind or mental events, and like unto the taintless orb of the sun.

PILGRIMAGES, FESTIVALS, AND RITUAL CYCLES. Among the many characteristic religious activities in which virtually all Tibetans at some time or other participate, pilgrimage is particularly prominent. Pilgrimage was traditionally one of the central phenomena contributing to, and perhaps even to some extent engendering, the cultural unity of Tibet. Pilgrimage, among other things, promoted trade in both goods and information. It brought persons from distant parts of the Tibetan world into direct contact with one another and thus militated to some extent against divisive regional tendencies.

Among the many famous Tibetan places of pilgrimage, most Tibetans regarded the religious shrines of Lhasa to be particularly important to visit. There, in the ancient Tibetan capital, they could behold and be blessed by contact with the Jowo Śākyamuni image residing in the central temple that was thought to have been brought from China by the princess of Wencheng. The pilgrims who flocked to Lhasa brought offerings for the temples and monks and also frequently engaged in trade to finance their journeys. Thus, besides its purely religious significance, pilgrimage also came to play an important role in the Tibetan economy.

The capital, however, was not the sole center of pilgrimage. In fact, there was a sort of national pilgrimage network in Tibet, whose routes, extending the length and breadth of the country, joined great and small temples and shrines as well as caves, mountains, valleys, and lakes that were imbued with sacred significance. In far western Tibet, the greatest pilgrimage center was undoubtedly Mount Kailash, regarded popularly as being substantially identical with the world-mountain, the *axis mundi.* As such it was a major destination for both Hindus and Buddhists. Other important centers of pilgrimage included Tsa ri, where a great procession that convened once every twelve years was said to purge even the taint of murder, and Mchod rten Nyi ma (Chöten Nyima), to the north of Sikkim, where incest pollution could be cleansed.

Related in some respects to the pilgrimage cycles are the festivals of Tibetan Buddhism. The celebration of the Buddha's enlightenment (*sa ga zla ba,* equivalent to the Vesakh of Theravāda Buddhism) is marked by fasting and communal prayer. The Tibetan New Year requires the performance of extensive rites on behalf of the protective divinities and is the occasion for the convening of the Great Prayer Festival (*smon lam chen mo*) in Lhasa. The tenth day of each lunar month is consecrated to the *guru* and, among the Rnying ma pa in particular, is a time for communal feast rituals and sometimes also the elaborate masked dances known as *'cham.*

TIBETAN BUDDHISM IN THE PEOPLE'S REPUBLIC OF CHINA. When the course of events in China turned decisively in favor of the communists after World War II, some Tibetan modernists felt that the revolutionary programs of the Communist Party offered them the best opportunity for modernization and reform. An example was the celebrated monk-scholar Rdo bis Shes rab rgya mtsho (Dobi Sherab Gyatso, 1884–1968), who after allying himself with the Chinese Nationalists during the 1930s, later turned to the Communists. In 1952, two years after China assumed control of Tibet, he became the first chairman of the Chinese Buddhist Association. His attempt to find a common ground between the policies of the party and the interests of Tibetan Buddhism came to represent in some measure the norm among educated Tibetan clergy during the 1950s, when both the Dalai Lama and the Panchen Lama embraced the hopeful idea that Mao Zedong's revolution had room for their religion and indeed that the ethical concerns of Mahāyāna Buddhism for universal well-being would be realized by the dawning socialist order.

Soon, however, the promise of a harmonious relationship between Chinese Communism and Tibetan Buddhism came undone. As the monasteries were considered by China's leadership to be among the centers of resistance to the implementation of Communist programs and also to be giving shelter to rebels in the eastern Tibetan province of Khams, they became increasingly prone to direct attack, and in 1956 a number of eastern Tibetan monasteries were subjected to aerial bombardment. These circumstances were deeply shocking to Tibetan sensibilities and led to the flight of large numbers of eastern Tibetans to central Tibet. With the events surrounding the Lhasa Uprising of 1959 and the subsequent flight of the Dalai Lama to India, the steadily worsening relations between the Tibetan Buddhist establishment and the Chinese government spun altogether out of control. The Dalai Lama and many religious Tibetans fled into exile in India, and many who remained behind were persecuted and imprisoned. By 1962 both the tenth Panchen Lama and Shes rab rgya mtsho, the two leading Tibetan clerics remaining in China, openly expressed their disillusionment and were subsequently dismissed from their posts. The assault on religion intensified throughout the 1960s and during the Cultural Revolution (1966–1976), when all but a few of the thousands of Tibetan temples and monasteries were razed, their artistic treasures and libraries destroyed or plundered. Tens of thousands of monks and nuns were forced to undergo "reeducation," and many perished under extraordinarily harsh conditions or suffered prolonged maltreatment in prison.

The conclusion of the Cultural Revolution and the consolidation of Chinese power by Deng Xiaoping in 1978 brought great changes to cultural and religious affairs. A visit to Tibet in 1980 by the party secretary Hu Yaobang clearly signaled that cultural redevelopment was now possible. In view of new policy directives, a dramatic revival of Tibetan Buddhism now ensued, which took many different forms. At its most basic level, it meant that ordinary believers could now engage publicly once more in a variety of devotional and ritual activities: performance of prostrations, circumambulations, offerings, and prayers at temples and other sacred sites; erecting prayer flags and stone walls with prayers carved upon them; copying and distributing prayer books and religious icons. The small number of temples and monasteries that had survived in more or less usable condition began to be refurbished and reopened, and efforts were made to rebuild some that had been destroyed. As the monasteries reopened, the few aged monks who remained were joined by numbers of young new recruits. The reinception of religious festivals and pilgrimages was also a development welcomed by both monks and laypersons.

The revival that began in the late twentieth century continued into the twenty-first century and even attracted non-Tibetan, Chinese converts to Tibetan Buddhism, but it has nevertheless been marked by repeated tensions with the Chinese political leadership. Most dramatically, a series of demonstrations in support of the exiled Dalai Lama, staged by monks in Lhasa beginning in 1987, led to rioting that culminated in the declaration of a state of emergency in 1989. Subsequently, the government's view of the Dalai Lama steadily hardened, and after a period during which the expression of purely religious devotion to him was tolerated, any explicit manifestation of loyalty to him became treated as fundamentally political in nature.

In 1989 the highest-ranking Buddhist hierarch who had remained in Tibet after 1959, the Panchen Lama, died suddenly, and his passing led to new disputes between Chinese authorities and the partisans of the Dalai Lama. This received worldwide attention when, on May 14, 1995, the Dalai Lama and the Tibetan government-in-exile announced the discovery of the young incarnate Panchen in Tibet. The Chinese responded harshly: the acting abbot of Tashi Lhünpo monastery, Chadrel Rinpoche, was arrested in Chengdu, Sichuan, and Gendun Choekyi Nyima, the young boy who had been recognized as the Panchen Lama by the Dalai Lama, was detained with his family. Shortly thereafter, his recognition was rejected by the Chinese government, and a lottery was held on November 29, 1995, to choose a new Panchen Lama from among several officially approved candidates.

The Dalai Lama, a Nobel Peace Prize laureate in 1989, remained of course the best-known symbol of Tibetan aspirations in the world at large and also for Tibetans themselves. During the late 1980s and the early 1990s, photographs of the Dalai Lama were so ubiquitous as to be seen plentifully in temples, homes, shops, and markets. In reaction to the Panchen Lama affair, the Communist Party launched a campaign in April 1996 to remove such images from view, particularly from public and otherwise high prestige venues, such as schools and the homes and offices of Tibetan officials. With the beginning of the new millennium, the Dalai Lama's government-in-exile and the Chinese leadership cautiously resumed efforts to settle their differences through negotiation. These seem to have made little progress so far, and Buddhism in the Tibetan autonomous region remains hampered by severe restrictions placed on religious recruitment, livelihood, and education.

SEE ALSO Bon; Buddhism, Schools of, article on Tibetan and Mongolian Buddhism; Dalai Lama; Dge lugs pa; Mahāsiddhas; Pilgrimage, article on Tibetan Pilgrimage.

BIBLIOGRAPHY

Blondeau, Anne-Marie. "Les religions du Tibet." In *Histoire des Religions,* edited by Henri-Charles Peuch, vol. 3. Paris, 1970. Now dated in respect of some particulars but nevertheless offers a still useful overview.

Cabezón, José Ignacio, and Roger R. Jackson, eds. *Tibetan Literature: Studies in Genre.* Ithaca, N.Y., 1996. Provides useful surveys of the main classes of Tibetan religious writings.

Demiéville, Paul. *Le concile de Lhasa: Une controverse sur le quiétisme entre bouddhistes de l'Inde et de la Chine au VIIIe siècle de l'ère chrétienne,* Vol. 7: *Bibliothèque de l'Institut des Hautes Études Chinoises.* Paris, 1952. Magisterial study of Dunhuang Chinese sources on the Chan master Moheyan's mission in Tibet.

Dreyfus, Georges. *The Sound of Two Hands Clapping.* Berkeley, Calif., 2003. Invaluable exploration of Tibetan monastic education.

Dudjom Rinpoche, and Jikdrel Yeshe Dorje. *The Nyingma School of Tibetan Buddhism: Its Fundamentals and History.* Translated by Gyurme Dorje and Matthew Kapstein. Boston, 1991. A Tibetan master's synthesis of Rnying ma pa doctrinal and historical traditions.

Goldstein, Melvyn C., and Matthew T. Kapstein, eds. *Buddhism in Contemporary Tibet: Religious Revival and Cultural Identity.* Berkeley, Calif., 1998. Survey and case studies of the post–Cultural Revolution revival of Tibetan Buddhism through the early 1990s.

Kapstein, Matthew T. *The Tibetan Assimilation of Buddhism: Conversion, Contestation, and Memory.* Oxford, 2000. Includes studies of the formation of some of the major Tibetan Buddhist myth-historical traditions.

Karmay, Samten Gyaltsen. *The Great Perfection: A Philosophical and Meditative Teaching of Tibetan Buddhism.* Leiden and New York, 1988. A valuable study of the earliest known works of the Great Perfection system.

Klimberg-Salter, Deborah E. *Tabo: A Lamp for the Kingdom.* New York, 1998. Thorough art historical study of one of the major temples founded by Ye shes 'od and Rin chen bzang po, with a valuable historical contribution by Luciano Petech.

Lopez, Donald, Jr., ed. *Religions of Tibet in Practice.* Princeton, N.J., 1997. Provides translations, with brief introductions, of texts on many aspects of religious life in Tibet.

Obermiller, E. *History of Buddhism (Chos-zbyung) by Bu-ston,* Part 1: *The Jewelry of Scripture,* Part 2: *The History of Buddhism in India and Tibet.* Suzuki Research Foundation Reprint series 5. Heidelberg, 1931–1932. Translation of a key fourteenth-century historical and doctrinal treatise.

Roerich, George, trans. *The Blue Annals.* Delhi, 1976. Translation of 'Gos lo Gzhon nu dpal's celebrated history of Tibetan Buddhism through the early fifteenth century.

Samuel, Geoffrey. *Civilized Shamans: Buddhism in Tibetan Societies.* Washington, D.C., and London, 1993. A wide-ranging anthropological investigation of Tibetan Buddhism as a cultural system.

Smith, E. Gene. *Among Tibetan Texts.* Boston, 2001. A leading Tibetanist's introductions to a wide range of major textual sources.

Snellgrove, David. *Indo-Tibetan Buddhism: Indian Buddhists and Their Tibetan Successors.* Boston, 1987. Detailed survey of esoteric Buddhism and its history in India, Nepal, and Tibet.

Snellgrove, David, and Hugh Richardson. *A Cultural History of Tibet.* New York and Washington, D.C., 1968. Accessible survey, though now dated.

Snellgrove, David, and Tadeusz Skorupski. *A Cultural History of Ladakh.* 2 vols. Boulder, Colo., 1977–1980.

Sørensen, Per K. *Tibetan Buddhist Historiography: The Mirror Illuminating the Royal Genealogies.* Wiesbaden, 1994. Critically annotated translation of a famous fourteenth-century retelling of the legends of the early Tibetan Empire.

Stein, R. A. *Tibetan Civilization.* Translated by J. E. Stapleton Driver. Stanford, Calif., 1972. A fine general account of Tibet as a civilizational sphere.

Tucci, Giuseppe. *The Religions of Tibet.* Translated by Geoffrey Samuel. Berkeley, Calif., and Los Angeles, 1980. The renowned Italian Tibetanist's survey of Tibetan religions.

Vitali, Roberto. *The Kingdoms of Gu.ge Pu.hrang.* Dharamsala, 1996. Thorough account of the history of the main kingdoms of western Tibet.

MATTHEW T. KAPSTEIN (2005)

BUDDHISM: BUDDHISM IN CHINA

First imported from India and Central Asia around the first century CE, Buddhism in China is an evolving hybrid of Chinese and foreign elements. As a social organization with significant implications for the proper ordering of the world, Buddhism has had a long, complicated relationship with the Chinese state, both the imperial dynastic system and the modern Republican and Communist states that began in the twentieth century. Buddhist conceptions of rebirth and salvation, mythologies of buddhas, *bodhisattvas,* and other figures as well as Buddhist art and temple life have attracted people from all social classes. Philosophers have wrestled with Buddhist understandings of emptiness, enlightenment, and sagehood. Buddhist rituals, formed partly in relation to Daoist traditions, are diffused throughout much of Chinese popular religion. Even during those eras when the institutional presence of Buddhism in the form of temples, monks, and nuns has been small, its influence on Chinese culture has remained strong.

A Hybrid of Chinese and Foreign. Both in its origin and later development, Buddhism in China constituted a mixture of foreign and native elements. The first Buddhists in China were immigrants. Before entering the Chinese Empire ruled by the Han dynasty (206 BCE–220 CE), they grew up in lands to the west: parts of India ruled by the Kushan dynasty (an Indo-Scythian ethnic group, called Yuezhi in Chinese, that ruled from 128 BCE to 450 CE), and smaller Central Asian kingdoms like Parthia and Sogdiana. The texts they memorized, or in some cases carried with them, were composed in Sanskrit, forms of *prakrit,* or other Indo-Iranian languages of the Silk Road. When these travelers first arrived in Dunhuang (modern Gansu province, China), the westernmost garrison town in Chinese territory, and proceeded to the capital city of Luoyang (Henan province), they probably could not speak Chinese. Before they developed proficiency in the spoken language, they relied on translators. Thus to explain their beliefs to their Chinese hosts, foreign monks depended on local go-betweens, Chinese-born interpreters whose cultural presuppositions inevitably influenced how they articulated what their guests were trying to say. The first Buddhists in China had even less control over how their message was conveyed in written form. Most of them never mastered Classical Chinese, which differs significantly from the spoken language in both grammar and lexicon (comparable to the difference between Latin and the Romance vernacular languages). For the first several centuries, translation was usually a process conducted by a committee with numerous overseers, none of whom was capable of judging the result against the original.

The vocabulary developed by foreign monks and their local assistants advertises this mixture of cultural influences. Some foreign terms were translated by Chinese words that had a preestablished frame of meaning. *Dharma,* for instance, was rendered by the Chinese word for "law," "principle," or "method" (*fa*). Another translation strategy was to use Chinese words that mimicked the sound of the foreign word but made no sense in Chinese. *Buddha,* for instance, was pronounced in Chinese as *Fotuo* (or abbreviated as *Fo*), which attempts to reproduce the phonetics of the original Indic word. The significance of the second method of translation is that Chinese Buddhists chose to maintain an audible trace of the non-Chinese nature of their religion.

Chinese Buddhists often celebrate that theirs is a foreign faith, meaning that its founder and earliest patriarchs lived outside of China. These facts are both undeniable and misleading. Already in the Han dynasty, Buddhist monks were criticized for worshiping a foreign god, following doctrines unattested in the Chinese classics, dressing in barbarian fashion, and destroying the foundation of the Chinese kinship system. Rather than disavowing their foreign origins, Buddhists responded by claiming that even Chinese figures like Laozi (sixth century BCE) had left China to gain enlightenment as a disciple of Śākyamuni Buddha. They explained that the meaning of the Buddha's golden speech could be accurately conveyed in Chinese translation, that monks followed the more noble among the barbarian habits, and that the ultimate devotion to one's parents was bringing Buddhist salvation to one's ancestors rather than begetting offspring. The controversy over the foreign nature of Chinese Buddhism was never fully settled. *Native* and *foreign* (or the various words authors used for *Chinese* and *Indian*) were continually redefined in relation to each other; they were rhetorical claims rather than fixed identities.

The interdependence of the notions of India and China also casts doubt on the model of Sinification (making Chinese), often used to conceptualize the history of Chinese Buddhism. In general terms it might make sense to say that over a span of two thousand years, Buddhism in China was made more Chinese, or that the tradition was uprooted from Indian soil and transplanted in China. The problem is that the two parties engaged in this imagined process—"India" and "China"—were themselves undergoing constant change. One of the more interesting features of Chinese Buddhism is that it provides such a helpful lens for bringing this history of intercultural redefinition into better focus. The metaphor of transplantation is faulty because the two soils in which the plant grew were not inert media or simply defined cultures. Rather, they were city-states, kingdoms, and empires the definition of which was changing and often contested. Furthermore models of Sinification, transmission, and transplanting assume that the religion transmitted between cultures was sufficiently stable to be identified as an Indian tradition at one moment and a Chinese tradition at another point in time. Yet neither in India nor in the various oasis empires of Central Asia was Buddhism defined by a single canon or governing body. In China too Buddhism might best be considered plural rather than singular. The hybrid nature of Chinese Buddhism thus means that the model of Buddhism being made more Chinese is simplistic at best and misleading at worst.

Buddhism and Political Authority. In both theory and practice, the Buddhist movement in China intersected frequently with political power. Even when Buddhists defined their ultimate purpose as the achieving of *nirvāṇa* (literally, "extinction") or enlightenment, they made strong claims about the social world in which that goal was pursued. Like Buddhists elsewhere, Chinese Buddhists considered morality to be the foundation of religious practice. Most Chinese authors appreciated that traditional Buddhist thought accepted the government and social order as givens. Chinese audiences were also receptive to some of the standard Buddhist models for political authority, especially the ideal of the *cakravarti-rāja* or "wheel-turning king," the monarch who achieves dominion over the entire world through his support of the *dharma*. King Aśoka, who ruled the Mauryan Empire in India from circa 270 BCE to 230 BCE and sent relics and monks abroad to disseminate Buddhism, was a living symbol for some Chinese emperors. Such ideals were a powerful supplement and at times an alternative to the Confucian symbolism of imperial rule. Buddhist models of divine kingship were especially attractive to groups, such as female emperors and rulers of non-Chinese origin, who were normally left out of traditional political theory.

Despite their differences, the paradigms of imperial sovereignty offered by Buddhists, Daoists, and Confucians all stipulated that the emperor should behave as the ritual master of the cosmos. As son of heaven (*tianzi*, ancient parlance for the emperor), the divine monarch was supposed to bring harmony to the world by ordaining the proper ceremonies, including sacrifices to heaven and earth, rites to guarantee good harvests, and observances to assure victory in war. Emperors drew ecumenically from the ritual repertoires offered by shamans and by specialists in Buddhism, Daoism, and Confucianism. From the emperor's perspective, as ritual techniques for rainmaking or blessing the nation, any of these traditions served as well as the others.

Buddhism also played a significant role in the private religious life of the ruler. In their personal as opposed to political lives, emperors behaved like other people: they got sick and needed curing, they were concerned with the afterlife and the fate of their ancestors, and they made donations to religious establishments. Many emperors turned to both Buddhism and Daoism, simultaneously or in succession, for this side of their religious lives. They followed the ceremony of becoming a lay Buddhist, ransomed themselves to Buddhist monasteries, practiced meditation, sought longevity, and built temples to honor their parents.

Buddhism had inescapable political implications in yet another sense by virtue of the large-scale social organization it proposed: a community of monks and nuns dependent on lay donors for support. In China the state vested in itself the right to encourage, limit, or destroy any social institution outside the family whose membership attracted significant numbers or whose organizers even hinted at rebellion. The successive dynasties placed Buddhist and Daoist monastic institutions under the control of various branches of the government. By licensing institutions and practices, the government could simultaneously offer support, exercise power, and take advantage of the religion's popularity. The state limited the number of monks and nuns, sold ordination certificates, established state-supported monasteries and nunneries, drafted statutes governing monastic behavior, defined the Buddhist canon, and distributed copies of the canon throughout the empire. At the other extreme, the government proscribed books, melted down statues, forcibly returned clerics to lay life, redistributed temple landholdings, banned religious organizations, and put their leaders to death.

CONTINUING TRENDS. Beginning around 400 CE the basic foundation of Buddhist belief and practice was well established and has remain recognizable as such into the twenty-first century. The fundamental characteristics of Chinese Buddhism described here apply to people from all walks of life, including those—the vast majority—who would never have identified themselves as exclusive followers of any single religious tradition. (Variations over time and the activities of monks, elite laypeople, and the state are discussed in the following sections.)

The basic worldview of premodern Buddhism proved difficult but not impossible to translate into Chinese terms. The cosmology of continual rebirth was depicted in paintings of the six paths in which sentient beings are reborn: gods in heaven, demigods or *asuras*, humans, animals, hungry ghosts, and beings in hell. Preachers explained how people are reborn in accordance with their deeds (*karma*). Many rituals aimed for rebirth in paradises overseen by buddhas or in the heavens of the gods. This proximate result was supposed to be followed by the ultimate goal: having a direct encounter with a buddha and achieving enlightenment or *nirvāṇa*. Chinese Buddhists were concerned with the question of what exactly carried over from one lifetime to the next. Answers included canonical explanations (one's deeds, one's consciousness, or the five "bundles" [*skandha*] of psychophysical existence) as well as ideas about the yin and yang aspects of the person drawn from ancient Chinese cosmology. The basis of Buddhist practice was morality (*śīla*), followed by the cultivation of concentrative states (*samādhi*) and the development of wisdom (*prajñā*). Specific ethical duties varied from one group to the next. Although everyone was supposed to follow the same guiding principles, there was an ascending series of disciplines. Laypeople adhered to the five precepts, which prohibited the taking of life, stealing, illicit sexual relations, lying, and consuming alcohol. Novices undertook 5 more, fully ordained monks usually observed 250 regulations (348 for nuns), and ascetic monks and hermits were even more severe. The critique of egocentric clinging, analysis of perception, discussion of the path, and philosophy of language in Chinese Buddhism brought the tradition into sustained dialogue with pre-Buddhist Chinese philosophy. Chinese Buddhist writings on emptiness, nonduality, two levels of truth, and buddha-nature are as rich and complex as those in any Buddhist culture.

Chinese Buddhism offers devotees a responsive pantheon of gods and spirits. In theory buddhas are the most majestic and powerful of all beings. Having spent many lifetimes perfecting themselves, they have become "enlightened ones" (buddhas). Each buddha exercises dominion over an entire world or buddha-country. Śākyamuni (the historical Buddha, fifth-century BCE India) lived as a prince, renounced his birthright, achieved enlightenment, and spent fifty years teaching others. Beings who resided in India during his time were particularly fortunate, since hearing a buddha preach or simply being in his presence has a transformative effect on believers, more efficacious than trying to reach enlightenment on one's own. The next buddha who will be reincarnated in this world will be Maitreya, who now resides in Tuṣita Heaven. Amitābha (or Amitāyus) is a currently existing buddha who presides over a distant realm of bliss in the west, known as a "Pure Land" (Chinese, *jingtu*; Japanese, *jōdo*) in the Sino-Japanese tradition. Another important buddha is Mahāvairocana, a cosmic figure who functions as the ontological ground or essence for all manifestations of buddhahood. Just below buddhas are *bodhisattvas*, beings dedicated to becoming buddhas. They define themselves as *bodhisattvas* by taking a formal series of vows in the presence of a buddha. Often serving as saints to people in need, *bodhisattvas* have discrete functions or specializations. Avalokiteśvara (Chinese, Guanyin; Japanese, Kannon; Tibetan, Chenrezi), arguably the most popular *bodhisattva* in China, assures mothers of safe childbirth; Bhaiṣajyaguru (Chinese, Yaoshiwang) is especially invoked in curing rites; Kṣitigarbha (Chinese, Dizang; Japanese, Jizō) rescues beings reborn in hell. *Bodhisattvas* often reincarnate themselves in different guises to make their compassion more effective. Laypeople also modeled their own actions after those of the *bodhisattva* and committed themselves in ceremonies to lesser versions of the *bodhisattva* vows. Ranking significantly below *bodhisattvas* are gods who, in the Buddhist conceptual world, are only temporarily powerful and happy, since they will suffer demotion in their next life. Many gods reside in the heavens, like the gods living in Indra's palace atop Mount Sumeru. Less-powerful gods populate the terrestrial world, inhabiting trees, rocks, caverns, and lakes. All such beings can be converted to serve the Buddhist cause. Biographies, hagiographies, and miracle tales—genres that blend into each other—record the exemplary lives and unusual deeds performed by all these beings treading the path to enlightenment.

Because of its implications for the fate of the ancestors, the rebirth cosmology in which Buddhism was bundled has always been a prime concern for Chinese Buddhists. Religious rituals carried out in the home and a reverence for the ancestors were hallmarks of early Chinese social life. Buddhism preached the acceptance of impermanence and valorized the example of the Buddha, who approached his own special death (*nirvāṇa* rather than another lifetime of suffering) with equanimity. Buddhists accepted the traditional Chinese value of filial piety (*xiao*) but redefined its practice. Priests argued that deathbed rituals, funerals, rites of commemoration, and other pious acts performed by descendants on behalf of their ancestors were more effective when carried out in a Buddhist context, with offerings made to buddhas and *bodhisattvas* and payments given to the *saṃgha.*

Buddhism had a tremendous influence on rituals aimed at increasing good fortune and reducing bad luck. At all levels of society, there were Buddhist versions of rituals, performed by monks as well as unlicensed practitioners, for curing illness, prolonging life, vanquishing spirits, and foretelling the future. Buddhist ideas and ritual structures permeated other forms of Chinese religion. The cross-fertilization between Buddhist and Daoist versions of important rituals was particularly strong.

One religious structure that set Buddhism apart from other Chinese religions was monasticism, a special community of ascetics clearly demarcated from normal social life. Monks and in lesser number nuns were supposed to leave their families, remain celibate, give up worldly conveniences, dedicate themselves full-time to spiritual cultivation, and serve as paragons of the highest Buddhist ideals. Such theories usually came into conflict with realities, political and otherwise. The *saṃgha* itself was organized into ranks and administered by officers, monks and nuns did not fully divorce themselves from their families, monasteries and temples were frequented by lay visitors, and the Buddhist Church possessed great wealth that required careful corporate management. Sometimes the Daoist Church developed a similar monastic structure.

Although one can assume that most Buddhists in China reflected on their beliefs and thought about their religious practice, the overwhelming weight of evidence about Chinese Buddhism was produced by and for a tiny but powerful minority, the literate elite. With that caveat in mind, what was the self-understanding of well-educated Chinese Buddhists as contained in traditional Buddhist canons? The core of the canon consisted of faithful translations of any words attributed to the Buddha or his Indian followers, organized into the traditional three baskets (*tripiṭaka*; Chinese, *sanzang*) of sūtra, Vinaya, and *abhidharma.* In addition it contained an astonishing variety of books written in China: apologetic literature defending Buddhism, biographies, text criticism and bibliographies, encyclopedias, commentaries, essays, miracle tales, genealogies, local histories, debates with Daoists, official documents submitted to the throne, and chronicles of the fate of Buddhist institutions under imperial governance. Buddhist authors wanted to prove that Buddhism, like other noble Chinese traditions, possessed a hallowed historical record and was led by models worthy of emulation, ranging from buddhas, *bodhisattvas,* and *arhats* to local patriarchs, pure monks, and sagacious emperors.

Owing to the decentralization of the welter of texts brought into their country from the West, Chinese thinkers devoted themselves to making sense of the history and diversity of Buddhism. The problem of doctrinal classification gave rise to various attempts to "divide the teachings" (*pan-*

jiao). Since all teachings were understood as the infallible word of the Buddha, each text and philosophical movement was assigned to a specific time-period and audience of Śākyamuni's preachings. Followers of the Tiantai School (named for its monastic home, Mount Tiantai, in Zhejiang) placed the *Lotus Sūtra* at the apex of Buddha's pronouncements, while proponents of Huayan ("Flower Adornment") Buddhism (named after the text, the *Avataṃsaka* [Chinese, *Huayan*] *Sūtra*) believed that their text was the most subtle and profound. In keeping with Buddhist ideas of inclusivity, these interpretations of religious pluralism tended to privilege one school over another by portraying it not as the sole truth but as best adapted to its audience's needs.

Another important paradigm invoked by Chinese Buddhists to make sense of Buddhist history was that of lineage. Like the lines of descent that define Chinese kinship groups, a Buddhist lineage consists of current male members who trace their spiritual authenticity through successive generations of patriarchs. Especially but not exclusively used by the Chan (Japanese, Zen) School, the idea of patriarchal succession solved several problems. It located the sacred origin of current Buddhist leaders in the legendary heroes of the past; it linked China to India; it wrapped male authority in the guise of ineffable religious experience; it answered critics who impugned Buddhism's antiquity; and it helped solidify the identity of various Chinese schools (not really "sects" in the Protestant or modern Japanese sense) in relation to each other.

ORIGINS. Legends written long after the fact illuminate what later generations thought was important about the enculturation of Buddhism. According to some, Confucius (551–479 BCE) knew of the Buddha, and Laozi left China to study with him. Other accounts speak cryptically of a foreign magician carrying the implements of the Buddhist wanderer, a staff and begging bowl, when he visited China in 317 BCE. Some stories claim that the first Buddhist missionaries had been sent by King Aśoka. Another late source explains the chance discovery of sixty scrolls of Sanskrit texts in China by hypothesizing that they had been hidden intentionally to escape the burning of books carried out under the first Qin emperor, Shihuangdi (r. 221–210 BCE). Military records of the defeat of a Xiongnu army (a nomadic group in ancient northern China) in 120 BCE talk about the local people bowing and offering incense to a golden statue. Another legend states that in 2 BCE a man named Jinglu received oral instruction in Buddhism from a royal visitor to China sent by the Yuezhi. The most famous and one of the oldest stories about the origin of Chinese Buddhism is that Emperor Ming (r. 58–75 CE) dreamed of a golden deity and dispatched a mission to the Yuezhi; the embassy returned bearing the first Buddhist text to reach Chinese soil, perhaps accompanied by monks and statues.

It is most likely that Buddhist monks, texts, and images began to trickle into China sometime in the middle of the Han dynasty (206 BCE–220 CE), the dynasty that gives its name to the dominant ethnic group in China as well. During the stable years of that dynasty, China was run by a centralized bureaucracy. Emperor Wu (r. 140–87 BCE) in particular was responsible for extending Han influence into Central Asia, sending emissaries all the way to Bactria in 138 BCE. The military ventures and trade missions of the first few centuries were responsible for securing the overland route between China and the West. It was via this Silk Road that Buddhism and other Western traditions first entered China. By the end of the Han dynasty, Buddhist communities composed of foreign monks, native monks, and local lay supporters had been established in at least three areas: the capital of Luoyang (Henan) in central China, Pengcheng (modern Datong, Shanxi) in the east, and the Tonkin region (now Vietnam, ruled by China 111 BCE–939 CE) in the far south. Monks followed a celibate lifestyle and practiced the semimonthly communal confession and recitation of the *prātimokṣa* rules, and laypeople observed periodic fasting. Buddhist statues were installed in public temples, sometimes alongside icons of Daoist deities. Han dynasty Buddhists also knew the rudiments of the biography of Śākyamuni. Buddhist philosophy of the time was already quite diverse, represented in early texts like the *Sūtra in Forty-Two Sections* and *Mouzi's Essay Resolving Doubts*. Scores of sūtras were translated by An Shigao (fl. 148–170 CE), a Parthian interested in meditation techniques and numbered lists of doctrines, and by Lokakṣema (Chinese, Zhi Loujiaqian, fl. 167–186 CE), a Yuezhi monk who propagated early Mahāyāna texts.

NORTHERN AND SOUTHERN BUDDHISM. Even after the dissolution of Han rule, Buddhism continued to grow in influence and numbers, as exemplified by the massive translation effort of Dharmarakṣa (Chinese, Zhu Faohu, fl. 265–313), a Yuezhi who was raised in Dunhuang. Under increasing military pressure from strong nomadic groups to the north, the unified Chinese Empire broke apart decisively in the early fourth century. From 317 until 589 CE the north was governed by a succession of strong regimes of various non-Han groups, especially the Tabgatch (Chinese, Tuoba), whereas south China was ruled by numerous Han aristocratic families. The bifurcation of political authority had important consequences for Buddhism.

In the south the landowning gentry extended the philosophical and literary experimentation that had begun at the end of the Han in a movement known as "dark learning" (*xuanxue*). The southern capital of Jiankang (modern Nanjing, in Jiangsu) was home to new reflections on texts by Laozi and Zhuangzi and on the *Book of Changes*. One of the most famous monks of the time, Zhi Dun (also known as Zhi Daolin, 314–366 CE), was interested in Buddhist understandings of the perfection of wisdom (*prajñāpāramitā*), wrote commentaries on *Zhuangzi*, and offered a new analysis of the Chinese notion of principle (*li*). Another member of a southern aristocratic family, Huiyuan (334–416 CE), wrote on Buddhist philosophy and the practice of seeking a good rebirth and championed the independence of the *saṃgha* from state authority. The fortunes of organized Buddhism in the south rose to their highest symbolic level under Emperor Wu of the Liang dynasty (r. 501–549 CE), who sponsored Buddhist ceremonies, promoted vegetarianism and social welfare, and oversaw the construction of lavish Buddhist temples.

In north China non-Han rulers frequently employed Buddhist resources to build a strong centralized government. The Central Asian monk Fotudeng (d. 349 CE) served the Later Zhao dynasty (328–352) for nearly twenty years and was famous for performing ceremonies to bring rain during times of drought and to assist the empire in warfare. Dao'an (312–385 CE) influenced many aspects of Buddhist philosophy. He wrote on meditation and emptiness, compiled a catalog of the translation of Buddhist texts into Chinese, led ceremonies for people seeking rebirth in Tuṣita Heaven, composed rules for monastic life, and suggested that the famous monk of Kucha, Kumārajīva (Chinese, Jiumoluoshi, 350–409/413 CE), be invited to China. With state support, Kumārajīva assembled a translation team said to number one thousand in the capital of Chang'an, where he rendered many texts, including key treatises of the Mādhyamika school. Kumārajīva's translation idiom and literary style, as seen in his *Lotus Sūtra* and *Vimalakīrti Nirdeśa*, soon became the dominant form of Chinese Buddhist writing. His Chinese disciple, Sengzhao (373–414 CE), wrote unparalleled essays on the meaning of emptiness (*śūnyatā*; Chinese, *kong*). In institutional terms one of the most important developments in the north was the monk Tanyao's (fl. 470 CE) creation of two social structures under the Northern Wei dynasty (493–534 CE). After a period of state support for Daoism and the mass migration of families uprooted by warfare, Tanyao reasoned that the resources of Buddhism should be used to relieve poverty and encourage agricultural production. He proposed that families be grouped into units called *saṃgha*-households that would send grain to monasteries, which would in turn distribute food to the poor and the general populace in times of drought. He also founded buddha-households, work units of criminals and slaves attached to Buddhist monasteries who worked in the temple or farmed its land.

CENTRALIZED COSMOPOLITAN DYNASTIES. Traditional histories view the Sui (581–618 CE) and Tang (618–907 CE) dynasties as a golden age or high point of Buddhism in China. This interpretation puts too much emphasis on dynastic structures, underplays social history, and privileges certain kinds of doctrinal innovation in Buddhism. Nevertheless there are good reasons for considering these three centuries as China's Buddhist age.

The capital cities of Chang'an and Luoyang were home to a large national bureaucracy of officials recruited increasingly through a publicly administered examination, and they were also the destination of diplomats, armies, Buddhist monks, entertainers, and merchants from most of Eurasia. The Tang court maintained contacts with Arab rulers and sought Indian scholars knowledgeable in mathematics, medicine, and astronomy. To most people outside of India—Uighurs and other Central Asian ethnicities, Tibetans, Koreans, and Japanese—the center of the Buddhist world was not India but China. The Japanese prelate Genbō (d. 746 CE) traveled to China and returned to Japan with over five thousand scrolls of Buddhist scripture, paving the way for later pilgrims like Kūkai (774–835 CE), Ennin (794–864 CE), and Dōgen (1200–1253). Buddhism dominated public religious life but did not blot out other traditions: Christianity in its Persian (Nestorian) form, Islam, and the Iranian religions of Zoroastrianism and Manichaeism were also known in some cities.

The ruling house of the Tang declared its descent from Laozi and officially claimed in 637 CE that the stability of the empire rested on the Daoist-inspired principle of effortless action (*wuwei*). This ostensive affiliation, however, never outweighed the value, personal and political, that the government saw in Buddhist rituals. Buddhist symbolism also played a crucial role in the career of Wu Zhao (624–705 CE), who had been empress (wife of Emperor Gaozong, r. 650–684 CE) but who seized control of the government, instituted a new dynasty (Zhou), and assumed the title of emperor in the year 690 CE. As a female monarch, Empress Wu could not easily draw on Confucian ideology to justify her rule. Instead, she turned to a variety of Buddhist regalia: she was portrayed as a incarnation of Maitreya and as a cakravartin king.

The most famous translator of Sanskrit scripture into Chinese was the Chinese monk Xuanzang (c. 600–664 CE). He was already considered a master of Buddhist philosophy when he embarked for India in 629 CE in search of authoritative texts and teachers. He traveled throughout Central Asia and India, studying intensively at the great center of Buddhist scholasticism, Nālandā (Bihar State, India), before returning to China in 645 CE. He carried back hundreds of texts and a knowledge of Sanskrit that few if any Chinese monks have ever matched. He translated seventy-three works into Chinese in a style known for its philological precision, and he composed a record of his journey detailing the geography, politics, and religious life of China's western neighbors. His exploits as an explorer also made him famous, and one thousand years later his legend was crystallized in the much-beloved vernacular novel *Journey to the West* (*Xiyou ji*, also known as *Monkey*).

One of Xuanzang's most influential contemporaries was Daoxuan (596–667 CE). Daoxuan was an expert on the Vinaya, and he set new standards in the compilation of biographies, miracle tales, apologetic literature, and catalogs of the Buddhist canon. Rather than following Xuanzang's overland route, the Chinese monk Yijing (635–713 CE) traveled by sea to South and Southeast Asia. After more than twenty years abroad, he returned and translated fifty-six separate books, many of them devoted to monastic discipline. Amoghavajra (Bukongjingang, 705–774 CE), who was probably born in Ceylon (Sri Lanka), came to China and translated nearly eighty texts, including a key scripture on the *Vajradhātu Maṇḍala* and many shorter Tantric ritual books.

The Sui and Tang were Buddhist dynasties also in the sense that literary, artistic, and philosophical production was dominated by explicitly Buddhist work in hitherto unprecedented ways. The poet Wang Wei (701–761 CE) employed what could be considered a Buddhist poetics and inculcated an attitude toward nature that draws heavily from Buddhist ideas. Even the most famous anti-Buddhist writer, Han Yu (768–824 CE), who wrote a memorial protesting Emperor Xianzong (r. 805–820 CE) honoring the Buddha's finger relic, was influenced by the tradition he criticized. Han Yu believed the bone had dangerous powers, and his attempt to resuscitate Confucian ideas and revitalize classical prose depended on Buddhist versions of orthodox transmission. The writing of miracle tales, many of which concerned icons, assumed the validity of reincarnation. The popular practice of storytelling with pictures (evidenced in "transformation texts," *bianwen*) was inspired by notions of the salvific intervention of buddhas and *bodhisattvas.* Paintings of paradise scenes and icons of Buddhist deities could be found everywhere. Wu Daozi (also known as Wu Daoxuan, fl. 710–760 CE), a highly placed court painter, was famous for the Buddhist subject matter he chose. His contemporaries report that his renderings of hell struck terror into viewers and that he carried out the act of painting in an inspired, theatrical manner. Buddhist metaphors were so well known that they rarely required explanation: a bubble meant evanescence, a lotus flower symbolized purity amid filth, silence was a reference to Vimalakīrti's understanding of wisdom. The debates of the age were dominated by Buddhist problems like sudden versus gradual approaches to enlightenment, the mechanics of rebirth in paradise, and the effectiveness of spells (*dhāraṇī* and *mantra*).

Written sources dating from the Tang dynasty also provide unambiguous evidence of the spread of Buddhist celebrations, especially in temples, that may have started earlier. Temples, which were not isolated enclaves of monastics in the first place, were especially busy during annual festivals. The yearly cycle included the emperor's birthday, the imperial ancestors' memorial days, the lantern celebration of the new year (around January 15), the Buddha's birthday (February 8 or April 8), and the ghost festival (July 15). Rituals involving the offering of a gift to the *saṃgha* and the participation of monks and nuns were carried out for life-cycle events (safe childbirth, weddings, building houses, curing illness, deathbed rites, funerals, memorial services) or at the behest of the individual practitioner (for commissioning statues or attending lectures). Tang dynasty manuscripts also supply the first detailed evidence of the formation of societies or loose congregations at the local level, groups that came together for semimonthly meetings, to hear monks preach, or to help members of the group with funeral expenses.

The Formation of Sectarian Identity. Like the early Tang emperors, the first emperors of the Song dynasty (Northern Song, 960–1127; Southern Song 1127–1279) were lavish patrons of Buddhism. In many ways, however, the society they ruled and the religion they supported were quite different from those of earlier centuries. Wet rice cultivation became dominant, and the population of the south outnumbered that of the north. The gentry families who had controlled access to power declined at the same time that the use of paper money grew, a merchant class arose, and more and more people lived in cities. Wood-block printing, first used for the reproduction of Buddhist spells, led to the dissemination of all kinds of books. All of these changes meant that the general public to which Buddhism spoke and the wealthy classes whose support it sought were fundamentally different from its former clientele. The government virtually rescinded the tax-exempt status of the monkhood and made larger profits for the state through the sale of ordination certificates. The revival of Confucian thought among officials like Zhu Xi (1130–1200), although not yet constituting an official orthodoxy, began to offer comprehensive philosophical alternatives to Buddhist systems of thought.

Buddhist responses to this changing world resulted in a clearer definition of the relationship between elite Buddhism and other traditions as well as the drawing of clearer lines separating the various schools of Buddhism from each other. The very notion of a strong sectarian identity came into existence at this time through the writing of Chan histories, beginning with *The Record of the Transmission of the Flame [or Lamp] Compiled in the Jingde Era* (*Jingde chuandeng lu,* 1004). Earlier literature had portrayed connections between masters and disciples as contending lineages that could coexist simultaneously. Song sources, however, advance the claim that the orthodox tradition originated at a single point (Śākyamuni smiling or wordlessly passing a flower to Kāśyapā) and continued in a mind-to-mind transmission with only one patriarch per generation. The "records of discourse" (*yulu*) detailing the words and deeds of masters were put together during the Song. Dahui Zonggao (1089–1163) emphasized sustained meditation on the phrase "No" (a response to the question of whether dogs possess buddha-nature), and full collections of past examples of "public cases" (*gongan*; Japanese, *kōan*) were rendered in classic form in anthologies like *The Blue Cliff Record* (*Biyan lu,* 1125).

The Chan myth of patriarchy assumed that the Song dynasty form of identifiable Chan monasteries had begun during the Tang. The vague notion of a Buddhist "school" (*zong*) was forged into a more exclusive sense of identity also in response to the new institutional structures implemented under the Song. The government exercised formal control over a system of public monasteries divided into three classes, Vinaya (*lü*), teachings (*jiao*), and meditation (*chan*), the greatest number of which was the latter. In this atmosphere even proponents of Tiantai ideas followed the dominance of Chan and portrayed their patriarchs as single pearls in an unbroken strand rather than as abbots of strong local monasteries. Such a conception underlies the new genre of Buddhist history writing in Zhipan's (fl. 1258–1269) *Comprehensive Record of Buddhas and Patriarchs (Fozu tongji),* which was also influenced by developments in secular historiography. Genealogical exclusivity was even extended to the Pure Land tradition, which received its first formal list of unbroken patriarch succession from Tiantai writers in the thirteenth century. It should not be forgotten, however, that although sectarian rigidity existed as both rhetoric and institution, it was not universal. Most of Buddhist practice—attending festivals, making offerings to buddhas and *bodhisattvas,* seeking assistance at the local temple, praying for the salvation of one's parents—remained generic. Even the liturgies collected by self-avowed followers of the Tiantai school like Zunshi (964–1032) incorporated the practices of local cults. Buddhists of every persuasion continued to draw on Buddhist ideas that, though associated with one particular school or another, belonged to all: the one mind (Chan), Amitābha Buddha's vows (Pure Land), three thousand worlds in one moment of thought (Tiantai), and the realm of true reality (Huayan).

DYNASTIES OF NON-HAN RULE. Beginning in the tenth century three foreign, originally nomadic groups ruled as Chinese dynasties over portions of north China: the Khitan (Liao dynasty) from 946 to 1125, the Jurchen (Jin dynasty) from 1115 to 1234, and the Tangut (Western Xia dynasty) from 1038 to 1227. After that the Mongols, whose quadripartite dominance over Eurasia extended from Kiev and Bucharest in the west to Korea and Taiwan in the east, conquered all of China and established the Yuan dynasty (1206–1368). Whereas other dynasties could claim that China was a multiethnic and religiously plural empire, during the Yuan dynasty the already diverse Chinese polity was one portion of an even more diverse empire of global proportions. Europeans, the most famous of whom was Marco Polo (c. 1254–1324), traveled to and wrote about the Chinese part of the Mongol Empire, and Muslims from the Middle East and Central Asia directed financial administration for the Yuan government at the local level. Many traditions prospered in China under the Yuan. Despite the banning of all Daoist scriptures except the *Dao de jing* in 1281, four different Daoist movements flourished: Complete Perfection (Quanzhen), Grant Unity (Taiyi), Greatness of Perfection (Zhenda) in the north, and Correct Unity (Zhengyi) in the south. Mongol educators wittingly aided the institutionalization of Confucianism when they turned the *Four Books* (the *Analects* of Confucius, *Mencius, The Great Learning,* and *The Doctrine of the Mean*) with Zhu Xi's commentaries into the basis for the civil service examination in 1313.

Qubilai (Chinese reign name Shizu, r. 1260–1294) was instrumental in placing Tibetan Buddhist clergy at the apex of the Yuan religious establishment. He received consecration (*abhiṣeka*) into the cult of Hevajra (Tibetan, Dges pa rdo rje) in 1253 and named the Tibetan prelate Blo gros rgyal mtshan (Lodro Gyaltsen, the 'Phags pa bla ma, 1235–1280) the imperial preceptor in 1260. Tibetan Buddhism became the new state religion, existing on top of Chinese Buddhist practices and those of other religious traditions. Buddhist symbolism proved amenable to many foreign groups who never forgot that Buddhism itself had begun outside of China. Buddhist mythology, in addition to offering models like the cakravartin monarch, easily accommodated the protector deities, shamanistic practices, and styles of ancestor veneration of the northern nomads. This complicated process of cultural mixing is apparent in the temple architecture, tomb building, and art that survives from these periods. Under the Xia dynasty the Chinese Buddhist canon was written in Tangut script, while the Yuan emperors sponsored both the printing of the Chinese canon and the translation of the Tibetan canon into Mongolian.

BUDDHISM IN LATE IMPERIAL CHINA. Although many events can be used to demarcate important breaks in the history of China between the fourteenth and twentieth centuries, long-term trends are also apparent during this period. One continuity is the threat to imperial sovereignty emanating from the millenarian mythology embedded in some forms of Buddhism and other religions. Daoism, Buddhism, and Manichaeism (and later Christianity) all contained subtraditions positing an imminent cataclysm of cosmic proportions and the replacement of the current regime with a new order ruled by a divine king. Buddhist versions of this eschatology, known since the fourth century, focused on the impending incarnation of Maitreya as a ruler. Already during the Yuan dynasty, Maitreya belief took new social and literary forms. This was a time of growth for sectarian groups—voluntary organizations of laypeople not based on family ties or attendance at temples but rather defined by Buddhist belief and practice. Their members read and recited a relatively new form of vernacular sacred text, "precious scrolls" (*baojuan*), which mixed mythology, moral guidance, and elements from a variety of religious traditions. Movements like the White Cloud (Baiyun) remained utterly conventional in insisting that members observe all forms of political authority. Other groups, such as the White Lotus (Bailian), frequently sought the immediate installation of new, purified regimes or were suppressed by the government for being suspected of rebellion. The man who became the first Ming emperor, Zhu Yuanzhang (1328–1398), was a local leader of one such movement in Anhui. His military success allowed him to wrest control from the Mongols and other adversaries and be enthroned as the Hongwu emperor (r. 1368–1398) of the Ming dynasty (1368–1644). The succeeding Qing dynasty (1644–1911) was founded by the Manchu people of the northeast, descendants of the Jurchens. Their leader was considered an incarnation of the bodhisattva Mañjuśrī, and all of the Qing emperors made significant visits to the temple complex on Mount Wutai (Sanxi province), where Mañjuśrī was believed to have manifested himself. With Qing imperial support, the Buddhist canon was translated into Manchu in 1790. Following the pattern of earlier dynasties, emperors regulated and manipulated Buddhist institutions, and the Ming and Qing ruling houses accorded political office to the highest ranking *bla mas* and other monastic authorities in Tibet and Mongolia.

Another important pattern of late imperial times is the seeming dissolution of distinctively Buddhist elements into Chinese society. During these centuries traces of Buddhism could be found almost everywhere yet not always recognized as such. Perhaps because it was so pervasive, the Buddhism of this period has received the least amount of scholarly research. The conceptual underpinnings of the ethical system of late imperial popular religion were heavily Buddhist. Although human centered, the worldview of Chinese religion had been englobed by a wider framework that included other species (animals) and forms of life (gods, hell beings). Every act, large or small, was thought to carry moral consequences, and ideas of *karma* were expressed in notions like "planting good roots" for future rebirths. Other myths, symbols, and rituals that derived from Buddhism had become a part of generic religious practice in annual festivals, rites of curing, exorcism, funerals, and pilgrimage. Buddhist monastic leaders like Yunqi Zhuhong (1535–1615) exhorted their elite followers to practice the releasing of life (freeing animals bound for the butcher), to adopt a vegetarian diet, and to refrain from wearing silk (the production of which kills silkworms) whenever possible. They promoted the joint practice of Chan-style meditation and the chanting of Amitābha Buddha's name, and they sought rapprochement among all schools of thought. Even outspoken proponents of Confucian learning launched ideas that had been heavily influenced by Buddhism. Wang Yangming (formally named Wang Shouren, 1472–1529) shifted the focus of Confucian discourse from principle *(li)* to the power of the mind and the process of moral thinking. Much as Buddhists predicated the achieving of enlightenment on the inborn capacity to become a buddha, Wang believed that ethical discernment was possible because of every person's "innate knowledge" (*liangzhi*). One piece of common wisdom in late imperial times was the slogan that "the three teachings are one" (*sanjiao heyi*). Different interpretations of the claim were offered—that Confucianism, Daoism, and Buddhism seek a common goal, or stem from the same metaphysical ground, or form three distinct stages of cultivation—but the basic idea (often called *syncretism*) was pervasive.

Increasingly during the Ming and Qing dynasties, Buddhism existed in a world that knew various forms of Christianity. Portuguese traders talked about their faith in the early 1500s, and a variety of European orders dispatched priests to China. Matteo Ricci (1552–1610), the most famous Jesuit in China, formulated a strategy for the propagation of Christianity after learning from the example of Buddhist missionizing. During his first years in China, Ricci adopted the dress of Buddhist monks; the two orders of monks did, after all, share a celibate lifestyle. Ricci soon felt the need, however, to distance himself from the role of ritual specialist and the suspicions cast on monks by the highest classes. He changed into the robes of the scholar, couched his message in terms derived from the Confucian classics, and drew on ancient Chinese precedents to castigate Buddhism, Daoism, and the practices of popular religion. A more pervasive Christian influence began in the early nineteenth century, when Protestant missionaries first arrived in China. They aimed at the lower strata of society and worked at the local level. They formed congregations by preaching about Jesus, translating the Bible into the spoken language, disputing Buddhist ideas of reincarnation, and railing against belief in spirits.

BUDDHISM IN MODERN CHINA. Buddhism was never insulated from the cataclysms shaking Chinese society from the 1850s to the twenty-first century: Western military incursions, imposition of treaties and reparations, unprecedented natural disasters, the overthrow of the imperial system of governance in 1911, the founding of the Republic of China in 1912, civil war and rule by warlords, warfare and eventually occupation of most of China by Japan between 1937 and 1945, the victory of Mao Zedong's (1893–1976) Communist Party and the establishment of the People's Republic of China in 1949, continuing upheaval and the Great Proletarian Cultural Revolution (1966–1976), the opening to foreign capital in 1978, and economic expansion and internationalization beginning in the 1990s. Propelled into the modern world so violently and in such a relatively short period of time (by comparison to Europe), China has offered many solutions to the problem of how to understand "modernity." Chinese from all walks of life debated what form government should take, what place in the world order China should occupy, and what roles science and religion should play in modern society. The answers have been complicated and varied. Intellectuals like Hu Shi (1891–1962) distinguished between unscientific, tradition-bound schools of thinking and rational, practical, Sinified forms of religious thought—including some forms of Buddhism—that could be harnessed to modernity. Monks like Taixu (1890–1947), theorizing the proper social functions of Buddhism, advocated turning away from involvement in funerals and memorial services and focusing on more this-worldly concerns. Buddhist clerics in China debated the contradictions involved in armed resistance against the Japanese military, just as their Japanese brethren came to grips with and often contributed to the Japanese colonial enterprise.

Modern China provides an interesting testing ground for the interaction between Buddhism and Communism. Marxist thought in general treats religion as a superstructure of the pre-Communist state. From this perspective Buddhism is an ideology used to camouflage real suffering in the world, which is caused by ownership of the means of production (land) by the gentry and the consequent alienation of the masses. Following Mao's exhortation, Marxist philosophers viewed Buddhist monks as a nonproductive class and criticized Buddhist idealism for its opposition to a materialist concept of history. The earliest land reforms in the 1940s began to expropriate the economic basis of the monastic livelihood, and the Cultural Revolution targeted monks, nuns, teachers, doctors, and other counterrevolutionaries for harsh reeducation. Nevertheless freedom of religious belief is guaranteed in the Chinese constitution, adopted in 1954. Under new policies in the post-Mao era, private belief in any of five recognized religions (Daoism, Buddhism, Islam, Catholicism, and Protestantism) is allowed. The Chinese Buddhist Association (Zhongguo fojiao xiehui), founded in 1953, is the government-supervised organization of clergy and laypeople. Under its auspices Buddha relics have been exchanged with other Buddhist countries, and intra-Asian missions have been sponsored. Having claimed political dominance over Tibet for centuries, the Chinese army took control of Tibet in 1959; the government formally recognized the authority of the Panchen Lama and derecognized the Dalai Lama, who escaped to India. For Tibetan Buddhists as well as Buddhist believers from other officially recognized minority groups (like those in Yunnan, Sichuan, Qinghai, and Xinjiang provinces), state entitlements are supposed to include the practice of traditional religion. How the government weighs this right against its perception of the overarching authority of the state to condone or extirpate any form of social action remains to be seen.

The future of Chinese Buddhism will depend increasingly on forms of Buddhism outside the Chinese mainland. Taiwan was ruled by the Japanese from 1895 to 1945, and the Nationalist Party (Guomindang or Kuomintang [KMT]) fled there in 1949. The Nationalists consciously distinguished their religious policies from those of their Communist foes and supported the practice of many forms of Chinese religion, including Buddhism. Many organized groups proliferated after the liberalization of laws regarding civic organizations in 1989, and religious revivals continued after the Nationalists lost the presidency in the 2000 elections. Taiwan in the late twentieth century saw the growth of many Buddhist organizations, including the Tzu Chi Foundation (or Buddhist Compassion Relief Merit Association [Fojiao ciji gongde hui]), founded by the nun Zhengyan (b. 1937), which emphasizes medical care, social welfare, and disaster relief; Buddha's Light International Association (Foguangshan), a broad-based, comprehensive organization of laypeople and clerics led by the monk Xingyun (b. 1927); and Dharma Drum Mountain (Fagushan), founded by the monk Shengyan (b. 1931), whose educational complex in northern Taiwan includes a Buddhist seminary, university, library, museum, and conference center. All three of these associations have branches active in other countries, Asian and Western, and they carry out exchanges with Buddhist groups in China.

Buddhist movements comprising laypeople and monastics continue to proliferate in the Chinese communities of Southeast Asia and the West. Just as Buddhism was originally carried into China from abroad, the undecided fate of Buddhism in China is now bound up with forms of Buddhism practiced elsewhere.

See Also Amoghavajra; Aśoka; Avalokiteśvara; Bhaiṣajyaguru; Buddhism, Schools of, article on Chinese Buddhism; Chinese Religion, overview article; Huiyuan; Kṣitigarbha; Kumārajīva; Nirvāṇa; Politics and Religion, articles on Politics and Buddhism and Politics and Chinese Religion; Taixu; Xuanzang; Yijing; Zhu Xi.

Bibliography

Kenneth Ch'en, *Buddhism in China: A Historical Survey* (Princeton, N.J., 1964), remains a good comprehensive, one-volume survey of the field, despite its slim treatment of the period from 907 to the twenty-first century, titled "Decline." Erik Zürcher, "Perspectives in the Study of Chinese Buddhism," *Journal of the Royal Asiatic Society* 2 (1982): 161–176, offers trenchant comments on the most important historiographical problems confronting the field. Bunyiu Nanjio, trans., *A Catalogue of the Chinese Translation of the Buddhist Tripitaka, the Sacred Canon of the Buddhists in China and Japan* (1883; reprint, San Francisco, 1975) is a translation of the table of contents of the official Ming dynasty canon. Paul Demiéville, "Les sources chinoises," in *L'Inde classique*, edited by Louis Renou and Jean Filliozat (Paris, 1953), vol. 2, pp. 398–463, surveys the standard modern scholarly canon, *Taishō shinshū daizōkyō*. An overview of Chinese history that emphasizes Buddhism is Jacques Gernet, *A History of Chinese Civilization*, 2d ed., translated by J. R. Foster and Charles Hartman (Cambridge, U.K., 1996).

For the early centuries, the standard study is Erik Zürcher, *The Buddhist Conquest of China: The Spread and Adaptation of Buddhism in Early Medieval China*, 2 vols., rev. ed. (Leiden, 1972). See also Paul Demiéville, "Philosophy and Religion from Han to Sui," in *The Cambridge History of China*, vol. 1: *The Ch'in and Han Empires, 221 BC–AD 220*, edited by Denis Twitchett and Michael Loewe (Cambridge, U.K., 1986), pp. 808–872; and Helwig Schmidt-Glintzer, *Das Hung-ming chi und die Aufnahme des Buddhismus in China* (Wiesbaden, Germany, 1976).

For Buddhist practice during the medieval period, see Edward L. Davis, *Society and the Supernatural in Song China* (Honolulu, 2001); Jacques Gernet, *Buddhism in Chinese Society: An Economic History from the Fifth to the Tenth Centuries*, translated by Franciscus Verellen (New York, 1995); Li-ying Kuo, *Confession et contrition dans le bouddhisme chinois du Ve au Xe siècle* (Paris, 1994); Stephen F. Teiser, *The Ghost Festival in Medieval China* (Princeton, N.J., 1988); and Stephen F. Teiser, *"The Scripture on the Ten Kings" and the Making of Purgatory in Medieval Chinese Buddhism* (Honolulu, 1994). The place of Buddhism in Chinese culture is discussed in Alan Cole, *Mothers and Sons in Chinese Buddhism* (Stanford, Calif., 1998); John Kieschnick, *The Eminent Monk: Buddhist Ideals in Medieval Chinese Hagiography* (Honolulu, 1997); and Peter N. Gregory, ed., *Sudden and Gradual: Approaches to Enlightenment in Chinese Thought* (Honolulu, 1987).

On the range of Buddhist philosophy, see Bernard Faure, *The Rhetoric of Immediacy: A Cultural Critique of Chan/Zen Buddhism* (Princeton, N.J., 1991); Bernard Faure, *The Will to Orthodoxy: A Critical Genealogy of Northern Chan Buddhism*, translated by Phyllis Brooks (Stanford, Calif., 1997); Jamie Hubbard, *Absolute Delusion, Perfect Buddhahood: The Rise *and Fall of a Chinese Heresy* (Honolulu, 2001); Ming-Wood Liu, *Madhyamaka Thought in China*, (Leiden, 1994); John R. McRae, *Seeing through Zen: Encounter, Transformation, and Genealogy in Chinese Chan Buddhism* (Berkeley, Calif., 2003); Julian Pas, *Visions of Sukhāvatī: Shan-tao's Commentary on the Kuan Wu-Liang-Shou-Fo Ching* (Albany, N.Y., 1995); Michel Strickmann, *Mantras et mandarins: Le bouddhisme tantrique en Chine* (Paris, 1996); and Brook Ziporyn, *Evil and/or/as the Good: Omnicentrism, Intersubjectivity, and Value Paradox in Tiantai Buddhist Thought* (Cambridge, Mass., 2000).

On Buddhism from the Song through the Ming dynasties, see Peter N. Gregory and Daniel A. Getz Jr., eds., *Buddhism in the Sung* (Honolulu, 1999); Yifa, *The Origins of Buddhist Monastic Codes in China: An Annotated Translation and Study of the Chanyuan Qinggui* (Honolulu, 2002); Ruth W. Dunnell, *The Great State of White and High: Buddhism and State Formation in Eleventh-Century Xia* (Honolulu, 1996); Chün-fang Yü, "Ming Buddhism," in *The Cambridge History of China*, vol. 8: *The Ming Dynasty, 1368–1644*, pt. 2, edited by Denis Twitchett and Frederick W. Mote (Cambridge, U.K., 1998), pp. 893–952; Herbert Franke and Denis Twitchett, eds., *The Cambridge History of China*, vol. 6: *Alien Regimes and Border States* (Cambridge, U.K., 1995); Chün-fang Yü, *The Renewal of Buddhism in China: Chu-hung and the Late Ming Synthesis* (New York, 1981); and Timothy Brook, *Praying for Power: Buddhism and the Formation of Gentry Society in Late-Ming China* (Cambridge, Mass., 1993).

The nineteenth and twentieth centuries are discussed in Charles Brewer Jones, *Buddhism in Taiwan: Religion and the State, 1660–1990* (Honolulu, 1999); Don A. Pitmann, *Toward a Modern Chinese Buddhism: Taixu's Reforms* (Honolulu, 2001); Holmes Welch, *The Practice of Chinese Buddhism, 1900–1950* (Cambridge, Mass., 1967); Holmes Welch, *The Buddhist Revival in China* (Cambridge, Mass., 1968); Holmes Welch, *Buddhism under Mao* (Cambridge, Mass., 1972); Stuart Chandler, *Establishing a Pure Land on Earth: The Foguang Buddhist Perspective on Modernization and Globalization* (Honolulu, 2004); and Daniel L. Overmyer, ed., *Religion in China Today*, China Quarterly Special Issues, n.s. 3 (Cambridge, U.K., 2003).

For the interactions between Buddhism and Daoism, see Stephen R. Bokenkamp, "Sources of the *Ling-pao* Scriptures," in *Tantric and Taoist Studies in Honour of R. A. Stein*, edited by Michel Strickmann, vol. 2: *Mélanges chinois et bouddhiques* 21 (Brussels, 1983), pp. 434–486; Stephen F. Bokenkamp, "Stages of Transcendence: The *Bhūmi* Concept in Taoist Scripture," in *Chinese Buddhist Apocrypha*, edited by Robert E. Buswell Jr. (Honolulu, 1990), pp. 119–148; Livia Kohn, *Monastic Life in Medieval Daoism: A Cross-Cultural Perspective* (Honolulu, Hawaii, 2003); Robert H. Sharf, *Coming to Terms with Chinese Buddhism: A Reading of the Treasure Store Treatise* (Honolulu, 2002); Michel Strickmann, *Chinese Magical Medicine*, edited by Bernard Faure (Stanford, Calif., 2002); and Erik Zürcher, "Buddhist Influence on Early Taoism: A Survey of Scriptural Evidence," *T'oung Pao* 66, nos. 1–3 (1980): 84–147.

Buddhism and sectarian religion are the subject of Daniel L. Overmyer, *Folk Buddhist Religion: Dissenting Sects in Late Traditional China* (Cambridge, Mass., 1976); and Barend ter Haar, *The White Lotus Teachings in Chinese Religious History* (Leiden, 1992). For relations between Buddhism and the state, see Charles D. Orzech, *Politics and Transcendent Wisdom: "The Scripture for Humane Kings" in the Creation of Chinese Buddhism* (University Park, Pa., 1998); Antonino Forte, *Political Propaganda and Ideology in China at the End of the Seventh Century: Inquiry into the Nature, Authors and Function of the Tunhuang Document S. 6502 Followed by an Annotated Translation* (Naples, Italy, 1976); Stanley Weinstein, *Buddhism under the T'ang* (Cambridge, U.K., 1987); and Patricia Berger: *Empire of Emptiness: Buddhist Art and Political Authority in Qing China* (Honolulu, 2003).

On important Buddhist deities, see Raoul Birnbaum, *The Healing Buddha* (Boulder, Colo., 1979); Françoise Wang-Toutain, *Le bodhisattva Kṣitigarbha en Chine du Ve au XIIIe siècle* (Paris, 1998); and Chün-fang Yü, *Kuan-yin: The Chinese Transformation of Avalokiteśvara* (New York, 2001).

On Buddhist art, see Stanley K. Abe, *Ordinary Images* (Chicago, 2002); Sarah E. Fraser, *Performing the Visual: The Practice of Wall Painting in China and Central Asia* (Stanford, Calif., 2004); Angela Falco Howard, *Summit of Treasures: Buddhist Cave Art of Dazu, China* (Trumbull, Conn., 2001); and Marsha Weidner, *Latter Days of the Law: Images of Chinese Buddhism, 850–1850* (Lawrence, Kans., and Honolulu, 1994).

English translations of important sūtras include Leon Hurvitz, trans., *Scripture of the Lotus Blossom of the Fine Dharma (The Lotus Sūtra)* (New York, 1976); Burton Watson, trans., *The Lotus Sutra* (New York, 1993); Luis O. Gómez, trans., *The Land of Bliss: The Paradise of the Buddha of Measureless Light, Sanskrit and Chinese Versions of the Sukhāvatīvyūha Sutras* (Honolulu, 1996); Red Pine, trans., *The Diamond Sutra: The Perfection of Wisdom* (Washington, D.C., 2001); Burton Watson, trans., *TheVimalakirti Sutra* (New York, 1996); and Thomas Cleary, trans., *The Flower Ornament Scripture: A Translation of the Avatamsaka Sutra*, 3 vols. (Boulder, Colo., and Boston, 1984–1987). For works composed in China, see Robert E. Buswell Jr., ed., *Chinese Buddhist Apocrypha* (Honolulu, 1990); Neal Donner and Daniel B. Stevenson, *The Great Calming and Contemplation: A Study and Annotated Translation of the First Chapter of Chih-i's "Mo-ho chih-kuan,"* (Honolulu, 1993); Philip B. Yampolsky, trans., *The Platform Sutra of the Sixth Patriarch* (New York, 1967); Burton Watson, trans., *The Zen Teachings of Master Lin-chi: A Translation of the Lin-chi lu* (New York, 1999); and Thomas Cleary, trans., *No Barrier: Unlocking the Zen Koan; A New Translation of the Zen Classic Wumenguan (Mumonkan)* (New York, 1993). For popular literature influenced by Buddhism, see Victor H. Mair, trans., *Tun-huang Popular Narratives* (Cambridge, U.K., 1983); Anthony C. Yu, trans., *The Journey to the West*, 4 vols. (Chicago, 1977–1983); and Daniel L. Overmyer, *Precious Volumes: An Introduction to Chinese Sectarian Scriptures from the Sixteenth and Seventeenth Centuries* (Cambridge, Mass., 1999).

STEPHEN F. TEISER (2005)

BUDDHISM: BUDDHISM IN KOREA

In any examination of the Korean Buddhist tradition, it is essential to recall that in no way was Korea isolated from neighboring regions of Northeast Asia. During its prehistory, Korean culture was most closely akin to that of the seminomadic tribes of the Central and North Asian steppes. From the Warring States period (403–221 BCE) on, however, when refugees from the northern Chinese states of Yan, Qi, and Zhao immigrated to the peninsula to escape the ravages of the mainland wars, Han civilization began to eclipse that indigenous culture at an ever-increasing pace. It is for this reason that Korean Buddhism must be treated as part and parcel of a larger East Asian Buddhist tradition. Indeed, Korea's later appellation as the "hermit kingdom" notwithstanding, there was in fact an almost organic relationship between the Korean, Chinese, and, during its incipient period, the Japanese Buddhist traditions. Admittedly, the Silk Route afforded China closer ties with the Buddhism of India and Central Asia, and China's overwhelming size, both in territory and population, inevitably led to its domination of the doctrinal trends within East Asian Buddhism. This does not deny, however, that Korean exegetes working on both the peninsula and the Chinese mainland made seminal contributions to the development of what are commonly considered to be distinctively "Chinese" schools of Buddhism, such as Tiantai, Huayan, and Chan. At the same time, many Chinese Buddhist theological insights were molded into new forms in Korea, innovations comparable to the Chinese syntheses of Indian and Central Asian Buddhist teachings. Hence, any appraisal of characteristically East Asian developments in the Buddhist tradition cannot neglect to take into account the contributions made by Koreans.

THREE KINGDOMS BUDDHISM (C. LATE FOURTH CENTURY–668 CE). According to such traditional Korean historical sources as *Samguk sagi* (Historical record of the Three Kingdoms), *Haedong kosŭng chŏn* (Biographies of eminent Korean monks), and *Samguk yusa* (Memorabilia and mirabilia of the Three Kingdoms), Buddhism was transmitted to Korea from the Chinese mainland during the (Korean) Three Kingdoms period. The introduction of Buddhism into Korea is presumed to have occurred in 372 CE, when King Fujian (r. 357–384) of the Former Qin dynasty (351–394) sent a monk-envoy, Shundao (Kor., Sundo), to the Koguryŏ court with scriptures and images. Former Qin hegemony over the remarkably cosmopolitan region of eastern Turkistan had brought Chinese culture into intimate contact with Indian, Iranian, and Hellenistic civilizations, ultimately engendering a new, sinified form of Buddhism. Fujian's defeat, in 370, of the Former Yan state, which had for decades laid siege to Koguryŏ, initiated close ties between Fujian and his Koguryŏ contemporary, King Sosurim (r. 371–383). These contacts allowed this vibrant northern Chinese culture, which included the Buddhist religion, to be introduced into Korea. While a paucity of information remains by which we can evaluate the characteristics of the Buddhism of this early period, it is probable that it was characterized by thaumaturgic practices, a symbiotic relationship between the ecclesia and the state, Maitreya worship, and the study of scriptures affiliated with the Mahāyāna branch of Buddhism. A monastery is said to have been erected for Sundo in 376, the first reference to a formal Buddhist institution on Korean soil.

Sundo was followed in 384 by the Serindian monk Maranant'a (*Mālānanda; *Kumārānandin), who is reputed to have come via sea to Paekche from the Chinese state of Eastern Jin (317–420). His enthusiastic reception by the royal court initiated the rapid diffusion of Buddhism throughout the Paekche kingdom. Less than a year after his arrival a monastery had been founded on Mount Han for Maranant'a and the first Korean natives ordained as Buddhist monks. In both Koguryŏ and Paekche, there is evidence that such schools as Samnon (Mādhyamika), Sarvāstivāda Abhidharma, Nirvāṇa, Satyasiddhi, and Ch'ŏnt'ae (Chin., Tiantai) flourished, though few works from this period are now extant. Of vital importance for the dissemination of Buddhism throughout East Asia, however, was Paekche's nautical skill, which made the kingdom the Phoenicia of medieval East Asia. Over its well-developed sea lanes, Paekche began in 554 to dispatch Buddhist doctrinal specialists, psalmodists, iconographers, and architects to Japan, thus transmitting to the Japanese the rudiments of sinified Buddhist culture and laying the foundation for the rich Buddhist culture of the Asuka and Nara periods. Silla expansion throughout southern Korea also prompted massive emigration of Koreans to Japan (where they were known as *kikajin*), and many of the cultural and technical achievements of early Japan—such as the development of paddy fields, the construction of palaces and temples, and town planning—were direct results of the expertise introduced by these successive waves of emigrants. These advancements ultimately paved the way for Japan's first constitution, purportedly written by Prince Shōtoku in 604, and led to the Taika reform of 646, which initiated a sinified bureaucracy in Japan.

It was not until 529, following the martyrdom of Ich'adon (Pak Yŏmch'ŏk), that Silla, the last of the three kingdoms to consolidate its power, officially embraced Buddhism. Political exigencies were probably the catalyst for the acceptance of Buddhism in Silla. The Silla nobility, who continued their drive for peninsular unification, found strong incentive to embrace Buddhism in an effort to accommodate the newly conquered Koguryŏ and Paekche aristocracy, which had embraced Buddhism long before. The vital role played by the Buddhist religion as a conduit through which Chinese civilization was introduced into Silla closely parallels the sinification of non-Chinese tribes that occurred throughout Chinese history.

Three Kingdoms Buddhism seems to have been a thoroughgoing amalgamation of the foreign religion and indigenous local cults. Autochthonous snake and dragon cults, for example, merged with the Mahāyāna belief in dragons as protectors of the Dharma, forming the unique variety of *hoguk pulgyo* ("state-protection Buddhism") that was thereafter to characterize Korean Buddhism. One of the earliest examples of this amalgamation was the vow of the Silla king

Munmu (r. 661–681) to be reborn as a sea dragon after his death in order to guard his country and its new faith from foreign invasion. Buddhism and the state subsequently evolved a symbiotic relationship in which the monks entreated the buddhas and *bodhisattvas* to protect the state and the state provided munificent support for the dissemination of the religion throughout the empire. Many of the most visible achievements of the Korean church throughout its history, such as the xylographic carvings of the Buddhist canon undertaken during the succeeding Koryŏ dynasty, were products of this concern with state protection. Buddhist monks also sought to demonstrate correspondences between Korean ancestral heroes and the new religion, thereby accelerating the assimilation of the religion among Koreans. Attempts were made, for example, to prove that Hwanin, the Celestial Emperor, was identical to Śakro Devāṇām Indra (Chesŏk-ch'ŏn), the Indian and Buddhist king of the gods, and that Tan'gun, the progenitor of the Korean race, was the theophany of Śrī Mahādevī (Kilsang-ch'ŏn). Vestiges of the dispensations of previous buddhas were alleged to have been uncovered in Korea, and the advent of the future Buddha, Maitreya, was prophesied to occur in the south of the peninsula. Modern-day visitors to a Korean monastery will notice on the perimeter of the campus shrines devoted to the mountain god or to the seven stars of the Big Dipper, the presence of which is indicative of the synthesis of common sinified culture with Buddhism.

One of the most prominent institutions of Three Kingdoms Buddhism that is commonly assumed to have been indicative of this interaction between Buddhism and indigenous Korean culture was the Hwarang (Flower Boy) movement. According to the *Samguk sagi,* this movement was instituted around 576 by the Silla king Chinhŭng (r. 540–575), and was patterned upon a more primitive association of shamanesses. The formation of the Hwarang movement is considered to have been part of the expansionist policies of the Silla court, and was intended to instill in the sons of nobility a regard for ethical virtues and an appreciation of refined culture. A later Silla writer relates that they were trained in Confucian filial piety and national loyalty, Daoist quietism, and Buddhist morality. The prominent religious orientation of the Hwarang as related in this and other accounts militates against the popular notion that it was a paramilitary organization. The group aesthetic celebrations—such as singing and dancing out in the open—that are commonly associated with the Hwarang has suggested to a number of scholars the shamanistic activities of initiation journeys and pilgrimages. While the Hwarang's Buddhist affinities are far from certain, their eventual identification with Maitreya assured that tradition would regard the movement as one intended to disseminate the Buddhist faith among Koreans.

UNIFIED SILLA BUDDHISM (668–935). After the unification of the peninsula under the Silla banner in 668, the fortunes of the new religion expanded on an unprecedented scale. It was during this period that the major schools of scholastic Buddhism that had developed in China were introduced into Korea. The doctrinal teachings that had begun to be imported during the Three Kingdoms period were consolidated during the Unified Silla into five major ideological schools: the Kyeyul-chong, which stressed the study and training in Buddhist monastic discipline (Vinaya); the Yŏlban-chong, which promulgated the teachings of the *Mahāparinirvāṇa Sūtra;* the Pŏpsŏng-chong (Dharma Nature), a uniquely Korean school of Buddhism that stressed a synthetic outlook toward Buddhist doctrine; the Wŏnyung-chong, which was the early Korean branch of the Flower Garland (Kor., Hwaŏm; Chin., Huayan) school; and the Pŏpsang-chong, derived from on the "consciousness-only" (*vijñāptimātratā*) teachings of Yogācāra. Some of the greatest achievements of early Korean philosophy occurred during this period, and such important scholiasts as Wŏnhyo (617–686) and Ŭisang (625–702) forged approaches to Buddhist philosophy that would become the hallmarks of the Korean church from that time onward. Korean exegetes working in China also played major roles in the development of Chinese schools of Buddhism. Both Wŏnhyo and Ŭisang were important vauntcouriers in the Huayan school, as reflected in their influence on the systematizer of the Chinese Huayan school, Fazang (643–712). Wŏnch'uk (613–696), a close disciple of Xuanzang (d. 664), was a prominent exegete in the Chinese Faxiang school, whose commentaries on such texts as the *Saṃdhinirmocana Sūtra* exerted profound influence on early Tibetan Buddhism.

It was during this era of ardent scholarly activity that one of the most characteristic features of the mature Korean Buddhist tradition developed: that of "ecumenism" or "synthesis." From the inception of Buddhism in East Asia, the religion had formed around a number of disparate scriptural and commentarial traditions that had developed first in India and later in Central Asia. For this reason, the Chinese church became characterized by a loosely structured sectarianism. The various extremes each of these factional divisions took led to an attempt, begun first in China and considerably refined later in Korea, to see these various approaches, each ostensibly Buddhist yet each so different, in some common light, so as to find some means by which their discordant elements could be reconciled. Certain features of the Korean tradition contributed to the synthetic tendency of the religion. Owing to the smaller size of Korea and its monastic population, there was little hope that Buddhism could continue as a stable and influential force within the religious arena if it was divided into contentious factions. In addition, the constant threat of foreign invasion created the need for a unified, centrally organized ecclesiastical institution. The quest to discover the common denominators in all of these sectarian interpretations—and subsequently to use those unifying elements in order to establish an interdenominational approach (*t'ong pulgyo*) to the religion that could incorporate all elements of Buddhist philosophy and practice—was to inspire the efforts of all major Korean Buddhist philosophers. This attitude prompted the Koreans to develop what remains one of the more ecumenical traditions of Buddhism to be found anywhere is Asia.

One of the most momentous developments in the history of Korean Buddhism occurred during the Unified Silla period: the introduction of the Chan teachings, known in Korea as Sŏn. The earliest transmission of Sŏn to the peninsula is attributed to the monk Pŏmnang (fl. 632–646), a Korean who is said to have trained with the fourth patriarch of the Chinese Chan school, Daoxin (580–646). While little is known of Pŏmnang's life or thought, there are indications that he attempted to combine the teachings of two distinct Chinese Chan lineages—that of Bodhidharma (c. fifth century), Huiguo (487–592), and Sengcan (d. 606) and that of Daoxin and Hongren (688–761)—with the synthetic *tathāgata-garbha* theory of the *Dasheng qixin lun* (Awakening of Faith). A successor in Pŏmnang's lineage eventually founded the Hŭiyang-san school, the oldest of the Korean Sŏn schools. During the eighth and ninth centuries, other Korean adepts returning from the mainland established eight other mountain Sŏn sites, forming what came to be known as the Nine Mountains school of Sŏn (Kusan Sŏnmun). Of these eight, seven were affiliated with the Hongzhou lineage of the Middle Chan period, which eventually evolved into the Linji school of the mature Chan tradition; one, the Sumisan school, was derived from the lineage of Qingyuan Xingsi (d. 740), from which developed the Caodong school. Korean masters on the mainland, however, also played major roles in the development of Chinese Chan. Perhaps the most prominent of these Koreans was the monk Musang, also known as Kim Heshang (680–756; alt. 684–762), who was regarded as a patriarch of the Baotang school of the Sichuan region, and was the first Chan master known to the Tibetans. Despite the continued traffic of Sŏn adepts between China and Korea, the entrenched position of the scholastic schools within the Korean ecclesia thwarted the propagation of Nine Mountains Sŏn. Continued frustration at their inability to disseminate their message led such Sŏn adherents as Toŭi (d. 825) and Muyŏm (799–888) to attack the scholastic schools directly, leading ultimately to a bifurcation of the Korean Buddhist church into two vociferous factions.

Koryŏ Buddhism (937–1392). The principal contribution of Koryŏ Buddhists to the evolution of the Korean church was the reconciliation they effected between the Sŏn and scholastic schools. It was Ŭich'ŏn (1055–1101) who made the first such attempt, by seeking to combine both the Nine Mountains and scholastic schools into a revived Ch'ŏnt'ae school. Ch'ŏnt'ae teachings are known to have been present on the peninsula prior to Ŭich'ŏn's time. A century before, for example, Ch'egwan (d. 971), a renowned Korean Ch'ŏnt'ae adept, had been invited to Tang China to reintroduce long-lost Tiantai manuals; during his expatriation Ch'egwan systematized the school's philosophies in his *Tiantai sijiao yi,* one of the most important of Chinese Tiantai exegetical writings. Ŭich'ŏn's efforts to revitalize the school, however, have led to his being considered the effective founder of its Korean branch. It appears that Ŭich'ŏn regarded the meditative emphasis of the Ch'ŏnt'ae teachings as the ideal vehicle for accommodating the varying concerns of the Sŏn and scholastic schools. Unfortunately, his premature death at the age of forty-six brought a sudden end to his endeavor and left the sectarian scene still more unsettled.

Ŭich'ŏn's efforts were followed some three generations later by those of Chinul (1158–1210), a charismatic Sŏn master who was similarly motivated by a synthetic vision of the unity of Sŏn and the scholastic teachings. Unlike Ŭich'ŏn's scholastic orientation, however, Chinul sought to merge the various Buddhist schools of his time into a new Sŏn school that would synthesize a disparate variety of Buddhist soteriological approaches. Chinul introduced into Korean Sŏn practice the investigation of the "critical phrase" (Kor., *hwadu*; Chin., *huatou*), better known by the closely synonymous term *kongan* (Chin., *gong'an*; Jpn., *kōan*), as it had been developed in China by Dahui Zonggao (1089–1163). Chinul then sought to incorporate this investigation into the soteriological scheme of sudden awakening/gradual cultivation taught by Zongmi (780–841), and finally to amalgamate this approach to Sŏn with the interpretation of Hwaŏm thought given by Li Tongxuan (635–730). Chinul's synthesis of Sŏn and the scholastic teachings came to be regarded as a distinctively Korean school of Sŏn, called the Chogye-chong. His efforts revitalized the enervated Koryŏ church, and marked the ascendancy of Sŏn thought in the Korean Buddhist tradition.

It was Chinul's disciple, Chin'gak Hyesim (1178–1234), who assured the acceptance of *hwadu* practice as the principal meditative technique in Korean Sŏn Buddhism. Following the model of Chinese thinkers of the Song dynasty (960–1279), Hyesim examined the points of convergence between the three religions of Buddhism, Confucianism, and Daoism. This attempt to extend the embrace of Chinul's synthetic outlook so as to accommodate still other religions was to inspire a series of such investigations by later Korean authors. A Sŏn master of the later Koryŏ period, T'aego Pou (1301–1382), worked prodigiously to merge the remnants of the Nine Mountains Sŏn schools with the new Chogye-chong, and sought to graft onto this ecumenical school the Chinese Linji (Kor., Imje; Jpn., Rinzai) lineage, into which he had received transmission in Yuan-dynasty China. The efforts of these and other teachers assured that the Chogye-chong would remain the predominant school of Korean Buddhism, a position it has retained down to the present.

Chosŏn Buddhism (1392–1910). With the advent of the Chosŏn dynasty in 1392 the fortunes of Buddhism began to wane. While the official policies of the Chosŏn dynasty are commonly considered to have been Confucian in orientation, many of the kings continued to give munificent personal support to Buddhism. For example, the founder of the dynasty, Yi T'aejo (r. 1392–1398), appointed the renowned monk, Muhak Chach'o (1327–1398), to the official post of preceptor to the royal family (*wangsa*), and the account of T'aejo's reign in the *Yijo sillŏk* (Veritable record of the

Chosŏn dynasty) teems with references to his sponsorship of temple construction projects, maigre offerings to monks, and various Buddhist rites. Confucian bureaucrats, however, continued to pressure the throne for stricter selection procedures for Buddhist monks, limits on the number of monasteries and hermitages, reduction in the number of officially sanctioned sects, and reorganization of the ecclesiastical system, all in order to effect more centralized supervision of the religion. Such policies were formally adopted by T'aejong (r. 1400–1418), the third Chosŏn sovereign, and carried out on a massive scale by his successor, King Sejong (r. 1418–1450). In Sejong's proclamation of 1424, the Chogye, Ch'ŏnt'ae, and Vinaya schools were amalgamated into a single Sŏn (Meditative) school, and the remaining scholastic schools were merged into the Kyo (Doctrinal) school. New regulations were adopted for obtaining monk's certificates, making ordination much more difficult, and many monks already ordained were defrocked. The official ranks of national master (*kuksa*) and royal master (*wangsa*) were abolished. Temple paddy lands and forest properties were confiscated by the state and the legions of serfs retained by the monasteries were drafted into the army. Buddhist monasteries were no longer permitted within the capital or major cities. It is not surprising that during this dire period, Buddhist activities were as much concerned with the very survival of the tradition as with novel scholarly and meditative endeavors.

During this extremely difficult period in Korean Buddhist history, it is Sŏsan Hyujŏng (1520–1604) who epitomizes the continued Sŏn orientation of the church. Drawing his inspiration from Chinul's earlier vision of the unity of the Sŏn and scholastic schools, Hyujŏng produced a succinct manual of practice, titled the *Sŏn'ga kugam* (Mirror of the Sŏn School). His other guides to Confucianism and Daoism were intended to sustain the reconciliation between Buddhism and its rival religions that was begun during the mid-Koryŏ and to outline their many similarities of purpose. Despite all the attempts of Hyujŏng's lineage, however, Buddhism's creative drive continued to wane.

BUDDHISM DURING THE MODERN ERA. Japanese inroads on the peninsula from the late nineteenth century onward presented both new opportunities and new pressures for the Korean Buddhist tradition. Following the ratification of the Korea-Japan treaty of 1876, Japanese Buddhist sects, beginning with the Higashi Honganji sect of Pure Land, began to proselytize among the increasing number of Japanese immigrants resident in Korea, an activity that soon spread to the native Korean populace as well. Remonstrations by Japanese Nichiren missionaries compelled the impotent Chosŏn court in 1895 to lift the centuries-old prohibition against the presence of Buddhist monks in the capital of Seoul. During the same period, a resurgence of Sŏn practice was catalyzed by the Korean Sŏn master Kyŏnghŏ (1857–1912) and his disciples, and successors in his lineage continue to teach today.

After the annexation of Korea in 1910, some Korean monks felt that the fortunes of the religion were dependent upon arranging a merger with a major Japanese sect. Yi Hoegwang went so far as to negotiate a combination of the Korean church with the Japanese Sōtō sect, but most Korean Sŏn monks regarded the gradualistic teachings of the Sōtō sect as anathema to the subitist orientation of their own tradition, and managed to block the merger. Another movement threatened to further divide the Buddhist church. As early as 1913, Han Yongun (1879–1944), a Buddhist signatory to the 1919 Korean independence declaration and major literary figure, had shocked his contemporaries by advocating that monks be allowed to marry, a move he felt was necessary if Buddhism were to maintain any viable role in modern secular society. While this position was diametrically opposed to the traditional celibate orientation of the Korean ecclesia, the Japanese colonial government ultimately sustained it in 1926 with its promulgation of new monastic regulations that legalized matrimony for monks. Within a decade, virtually all monastery abbots were married, thereby producing a dramatic change in the traditional moral discipline of the Korean church. Other reform movements designed to present Buddhism in a way that would be more relevant to modern concerns arose with increasing frequency. Among the most prominent of these was Wŏn Buddhism, founded in 1916 by Pak Chung-bin, Sot'aesan (1891–1943), which combined Buddhist teachings with a disparate variety of elements drawn from Confucianism, Daoism, Tonghak, and even Christianity.

After independence in 1945, Korean Buddhism was badly split between two irreconcilable sects. The T'aego-chong, a liberal sect of married monks, had flourished under Japanese patronage and was based principally in the cities where it catered to the lay Buddhist population. The Chogye-chong was a smaller, religiously conservative faction of monks who had managed to maintain their celibacy during the long years of Japanese occupation; their concern was to restore the meditative, scholastic, and disciplinary orientations of traditional Korean Buddhism. Only after years of intense conflict did the Chogye-chong finally win government support for its position in 1954 and virtually all of major monasteries have reverted to its control. Now the predominant sect of Buddhism in Korea, the Chogye-chong has had considerable success in attracting a new generation of lay believers and monastic postulants to the teachings and practices of Buddhism.

SEE ALSO Chan; Chinul; Confucianism in Korea; Fazang; Huayan; Korean Religion; Tathāgata-garbha; Tiantai; Ŭichŏn; Ŭisang; Wŏnhyo; Worship and Devotional Life, article on Buddhist Devotional Life in East Asia; Xuanzang; Zongmi.

BIBLIOGRAPHY

Buswell, Robert E., Jr. *The Korean Approach to Zen: The Collected Works of Chinul.* Honolulu, 1983.

Buswell, Robert E., Jr. *The Formation of Ch'an Ideology in China and Korea: The Vajrasamādhi-Sūtra, a Buddhist Apocryphon.* Princeton, 1989.

Buswell, Robert E., Jr. *Tracing Back the Radiance: Chinul's Korean Way of Zen.* Honolulu, 1991.

Buswell, Robert E., Jr. *The Zen Monastic Experience: Buddhist Practice in Contemporary Korea.* Princeton, 1992.

Buswell, Robert E., Jr., ed. *Currents and Countercurrents: Korean Influences on the East Asian Buddhist Traditions.* Honolulu, 2005.

Buzo, Adrian and Tony Prince, trans. *Kyunyŏ-jŏn: The Life, Times and Songs of a Tenth Century Korean Monk.* Sydney, 1993.

Chappell, David W., and Ichishima Masao. *T'ien-t'ai Buddhism: An Outline of the Fourfold Teachings.* Honolulu, 1984.

Chun, Shin-Yong, ed. *Buddhist Culture in Korea.* Seoul, 1974.

Chung, Bongkil. *The Scriptures of Won Buddhism: A Translation of the Wŏnbulgyo Kyojŏn with Introduction.* Honolulu, 2003.

Cleary, J. C., trans. *A Buddha from Korea: The Zen Teachings of T'aego.* Boston, 1988.

Grayson, James Huntley. *Korea: A Religious History.* Oxford, 1989.

Ha, Tae-hung, and Grafton K. Mintz, trans. *Samguk Yusa: Legends and History of the Three Kingdoms of Ancient Korea.* Seoul, 1972.

Han, Sung Yang, Yün-hua Jan, and Shotarō Iida. *The Hye Ch'o Diary: Memoir of the Pilgrimage to the Five Regions of India.* Berkeley, 1984.

Kamstra, J. H. *Encounter or Syncretism: The Initial Growth of Japanese Buddhism.* Leiden, 1967.

Keel, Hee-sung. *Chinul: Founder of the Korean Sŏn Tradition.* Berkeley, 1984.

Kim, Han-Kyo, ed. *Studies on Korea: A Scholar's Guide.* Honolulu, 1980.

Kusan Sunim. *The Way of Korean Zen.* Translated by Martine Fages. New York, 1985.

Lancaster, Lewis R., and Chai-shin Yu, eds. *Assimilation of Buddhism in Korea: Religious Maturity and Innovation in the Silla Dynasty.* Berkeley, 1991.

Lancaster, Lewis R., and Chai-shin Yu, eds. *Buddhism in the Early Chosŏn: Suppression and Transformation.* Berkeley, 1996.

Lancaster, Lewis R., and Chai-shin Yu, eds. *Introduction of Buddhism to Korea: New Cultural Patterns.* Berkeley, 1989.

Lancaster, Lewis R., Kikun Suh, and Chai-shin Yu, eds. *Buddhism in Koryŏ: A Royal Religion.* Berkeley, 1995.

Lee, Peter H. *Anthology of Korean Literature: From Early Times to the Nineteenth Century.* Honolulu, 1981.

Lee, Peter H., trans. *Lives of Eminent Korean Monks: The Haedong Kosŭng Chŏn.* Cambridge, 1969.

Lee, Peter H., ed. *Sourcebook of Korean Civilization,* Volume 1: *From Early Times to the Sixteenth Century.* New York, 1993.

Mueller, Mark, trans. *Mirror of Zen: A Korean Buddhism Classic, Grand Master Sosan.* Seoul, n.d.

Muller, A. Charles. *The Sutra of Perfect Enlightenment: Korean Buddhism's Guide to Meditation (With Commentary by the Sŏn Monk Kihwa).* Albany, N.Y. 1999.

Odin, Steve. *Process Metaphysics and Hua-yen Buddhism: A Critical Study of Cumulative Penetration vs. Interpenetration.* Albany, 1982.

Park, Sung Bae. *Buddhist Faith and Sudden Enlightenment.* Albany, N.Y., 1983.

The Principal Book of Won-Buddhism, Korean-English (Wonbulgyo Chongjon). Iksan, Korea, 2000.

Shim, Jae-ryong. *Korean Buddhism: Tradition and Transformation.* Seoul, 1999.

Takeuchi, Yoshinori, et al., eds. *Buddhist Spirituality II: Later China, Korea, Japan, and the Modern World.* New York, 1999.

ROBERT EVANS BUSWELL, JR. (1987 AND 2005)

BUDDHISM: BUDDHISM IN JAPAN

Use of the phrase "Buddhism in Japan" suggests in part that, on the one hand, the modern terminology of the nation-state of Japan can be appropriately used throughout discussions of Buddhist belief and practice in the geographic area usually referred to as the "Japanese isles." On the other hand, the use of the language of "Buddhism" might suggest that Buddhist beliefs and practices developed as a singular phenomenon bearing internal consistency. Use of either of these concepts has limitations, since the nation-state of Japan developed only in the late nineteenth century, and Buddhism does not connote a singular institution or way of life followed in the Japanese isles. In particular, while we speak of "Buddhism" in the Japanese case, Buddhistic beliefs and practices did not historically constitute a creedal faith of the kind common to monotheistic religions; neither did it historically feature universally agreed-upon weekly liturgies (a Buddhist "Sabbath") nor, until the last few centuries, did it feature adherence to exclusively defined or otherwise well-defined sectarian organizations.

EARLY HISTORICAL CONTEXTS. The initial introduction of Buddhist images and implements to the Japanese isles is extremely difficult to date. Moreover, we are limited to later representations produced by members of the royal court of Yamato, the first literate and highly organized government in the isles, and those associated with them; and archaeological studies have only marginally helped us to gain access to the very earliest era of Buddhist influence. The mythohistory *Nihonshoki* (720 CE), produced by the Yamato court, as well as temple legends (e.g., *Gangōji garan engi narabi ni ruki shizai chō,* probably a Heian era [794–1185 CE] compilation, yet based on a no longer extant eighth-century *Gangōji engi*) variously depicted the introduction of such figures in the form of gifts from the Korean kingdom of Paekche to the Japanese court in 552 CE or 538 CE.

Continental Asian influences. The Soga family, which drew upon the support of the large number of immigrant families in the capital area (and may have also had immigrant origins), was the most powerful clan of the court and sponsored the introduction of Buddhist clerics and objects, as well Buddhist construction, from the late sixth to mid-seventh centuries. In addition, in this connection the immigrant family of the Hata and, apparently, other immigrant families also constructed Buddhist temples at the time.

Prince Shōtoku. Although some of the other prominent families of the court drew their support from older families of the Japanese isles and argued that worship of Buddhist divinities would antagonize indigenous deities (*kami*), the Soga's efforts may have been bolstered through patronage by Prince Taishi Shōtoku (574?–622?), who is represented from the early eighth century on as having became an ardent supporter of the faith. The Sogas and Shōtoku seem to have seen buddhas and *bodhisattvas* as beings who offered a variety of benefits so long as they were approached through appropriate ritual. Moreover, the fact that all of the temples constructed prior to the mid-seventh century were erected in connection with efforts to protect specific clans—Asukadera, possessing the character of a "clan temple" of the Sogas, being most prominent—illustrates the extent to which the reception varied depending on the group, that there was no consensus in the larger court concerning its relevance, and that the thaumaturgical capacities of Buddhist ritual were central to their concerns more than enlightenment.

The Yamato Court in the late seventh century. Recent excavations have indicated that the government began to establish large temples in the seventh century. It is clear that in the late seventh century the court patronized Buddhist temples at the same time that it began also to promote a notion of the ruler as *tennō* ("heavenly thearch") and high priest of the court, with the ancestral *kami* (deity) of his family represented as the highest in the realm. The offering of reverence to *kami,* on the one hand, and veneration of buddhas/ *bodhisattvas,* on the other, seem to have been accepted and, presumably, openly supported by the larger court. Indeed, it would seem that most in the court saw the buddhas and *bodhisattvas* as similar to the native *kami* in their perceived capacity to offer a variety of benefits (*riyaku*). Discourses concerning *karma,* rebirth, and enlightenment seem to have been virtually absent during this early era.

BUDDHISM IN THE NARA AND EARLY HEIAN PERIODS. It was during the Nara period (710–784 CE) that Buddhist institutions began to flourish on a much larger scale and Buddhist practices came to have an impact on the general populace in the isles. Japanese monks' travel to China to study under eminent Buddhist clerics became increasingly prominent in the Nara and Early Heian (794–1185) periods, among which the most prominent were Saichō (c. 767–822) and Kūkai (774–835), who respectively founded the lineages of Tendai and Shingon.

The impact of the ruling family. The reign of the ruler Shōmu (r. 724–749) and his wife Kōmyō constituted a clear shift toward ever more visible support of Buddhist temples and clerics. Shōmu began to establish a set of temples and convents in every province of the realm: in this case, a provincial temple that included, among its features, a *stūpa* of seven stories, in which were to be installed copies of the realm-protecting sūtras, the *Golden Light Scripture of Victorious Kings* and *Scripture of the Lotus Blossom of the Wonderful Law,* together with part of the first sūtra written in the sovereign's own hand; an accompanying nunnery was to be referred to as "convent for the *Lotus Sūtra* expiation rite," in which nuns would perform regular repentance rites on behalf of the realm—evoking memories that the first Japanese Buddhist clerics had been nuns and had obvious ritual and thematic connections with native shamanistic traditions, associated generally with *kami* worship.

Shōmu and the court were supportive on a personal and broader level of the Nara Buddhist temples and to small Buddhist lineages that were developing in Nara. The well-known six lineages within the larger temples of Nara included: Sanron, Hossō, Ritsu (Skt., Vinaya), Jōjitsu (*satyasiddhi*), Kusha (*abhidharma*), and Kegon (Skt. Avatamsaka), the last of which seems to have been added only with the ongoing completion of construction of the head temple of the provincial system, Tōdaiji, in the 750s. In actuality, these lineages included only a small percentage of the monks residing in the great temples; for example, in the case of Tōdaiji, they included only roughly 2 percent of the some three thousand monks.

Shōmu's wife, Kōmyō, was an equally fervent patron of Buddhists. Her sponsorship of a sūtra-copying bureau, Tōdaiji administration, and convent construction indicate at least two important points about Buddhism in early Japan. First, it is clear that women of the court, particularly during the Nara period, were powerful sponsors of Buddhist activities. Second, such sponsorship, associated with efforts throughout continental Asia to collect Buddhist scriptures, constituted a forerunner of later efforts of Japanese sovereigns and temples to acquire newly copied or printed versions of the Buddhist canon (*daizōkyō*) and, in that connection, to establish large collections of Buddhist and related materials (*kyōzō, hōzō*).

The personal interest of Shōmu and the ruling house in Buddhism, while made problematic by his daughter's later relationship as *tennō* with the monk Dōkyō, also illustrates the close relationship leading families of the court had with Buddhist clerics from the Nara period onwards. Recent scholarship has made it clear that much of the vibrancy of Buddhism in the era was constituted in the employ of monks (or, sometimes, nuns) as family ritual practitioners or teachers. That is, monks were often invited, often for lengthy periods, to take up residence in the homes of leading aristocratic families; it is believed that such clerics spent most of their time engaged in rituals for the purpose of healing, bodily protection, and sometimes the more general avoidance of calamity *(sokusai),* and that such activities foreshadowed those of the guardian palace monks *(gojisō)* of the Heian period.

The increasing prominence of Buddhist discourses on karma, rebirth, and enlightenment. During the Nara period, beliefs in karma, rebirth, and occasionally enlightenment became prominent in the court as well as in regional families, especially those close to the capital area. The earliest Japanese didactic story collection, *Nihon ryōiki* (*Anomalous Tales of Japan*) by the Yakushiji monk Kyōkai (fl. 823), indicates that many in the capital as well as regional areas believed in karma and related discourses like rebirth and indebtedness. Such developments may have been related to the activities of figures like Gyōki (668–749), who worked among the larger populace and was especially known for his help in the construction of landmarks such as bridges and water projects.

Thus, karma, rebirth, and notions of enlightenment were increasingly prominent among the larger populace, while the court, given its patronage of official Nara Buddhism, was clearly cognizant of such teachings and the Buddhist cosmology, which was distinct from that represented in the court mytho-histories concerning the ancestral *kami* of the ruling family. Moreover, Chinese Buddhist works depicting the lives of eminent monks commonly featured tensions between buddhas/*bodhisattvas* and native divinities, which may suggest a general parallel if not knowledge of earlier patterns of assimilation of native religiosity. Given such awareness, there were efforts, evident first through ritual practice and construction, to explain or resolve such ambiguity. First, small Buddhist temples called *jingūji* were constructed at shrine compounds like Ise and Usa from the eighth century on, in which clerics venerated buddhas/*bodhisattvas* on behalf of the *kami,* who were apparently seen as inferior and unenlightened beings in need of aid. Second, the ruling house itself incorporated Buddhist figures into its own ancestral veneration, as the shrine at Usa came to match Ise in its landholdings and prominence during the eighth century as a shrine of the ruling family; in particular, the main *kami* came, by the late eighth century, to be seen as not merely the spirit of the fifth-century ruler Ōjin but at the same time as the *bodhisattva* Hachiman (Yahata).

Nara Buddhism and the advent of new Buddhist lineages. A radical break did not actually occur in Japanese Buddhism with the move of the capital from Nara to Nagaoka and, shortly thereafter, Heian (Kyōto). The great Nara temples authorized by the government remained large institutions, and the lineages within them remained the province of a small number of monks.

The ruler Kanmu (r. 781–806) moved the capital and made efforts to strengthen the authority of the sovereign. He also sponsored new monastic and other envoys to China and welcomed the related advent of new lineages of Japanese Buddhism. The monks Saichō and Kūkai were the first monks to introduce major new lineages after their respective studies in Tang China in the early ninth century.

Tendai lineages. Saichō, who trained primarily in Tian-tai Buddhism there, with some studies of esoteric Buddhism as well, returned first in 805 and gained the patronage of Kanmu. Saichō succeeded in convincing Kanmu to introduce a new system of ordination the next year; the system based the distribution of annual ordinands granted to temples on their affiliation with specific lineages, which increased the prominence of the lineages while at the same time, insofar as it was limited to males, producing a gendered framework that would continue throughout the history of Buddhism in Japan. In this way, as scholars have recently noted, the novel production of male lineages at the same time seems to have constituted a major source of the precipitous decline that occurred in nuns' ordinations in the Heian periods.

Based on his studies in China, especially at Mount Tiantai, Saichō created in his Tendai lineage a catholic study program that allowed for four major areas of concentration while promoting the *Lotus Sūtra* as the greatest scripture in Mahāyāna Buddhism: esoteric Buddhism (Tantra), meditation, precepts, and the "perfect teaching" (Tendai). With the permission of the court, Saichō established a precepts platform at the temple complex he had established at Mount Hiei, not far from the capital of Heian. There, he used the Mahāyāna *bodhisattva* precepts based on the *Fan wang ching* scripture in clerical ordinations as an alternative to the traditional precepts, which had been carried over from early Buddhist into Mahāyāna Buddhist ordinations throughout East Asia. Saichō, drawing on Chinese Tian-tai doctrine, divided Buddhist teachings into classifications of scriptures, with the *Lotus Sūtra* and *Mahānīrvāna Sūtra* at the apex, and added new classifications conferring priority on scriptures (*sūtra*) over clerics' treatises (*śāstra*); he especially criticized Hossō and Sanron for their dependence on treatises. His acquisition of a precepts platform, teachings, as well as debates he had with monks of the Nara temples, illustrate that Saichō was not on good terms with the leading Nara Buddhist institutions.

Shingon lineages. Kūkai also went to China in 804 but returned a year later than Saichō, in 806. Kūkai studied esoteric Buddhist (Tantric) discourse and practice in the Chinese imperial capital of Chang-an under the monk Hui-kuo, and given his master's death, he was given a large number of esoteric Buddhist scriptures, ritual implements, and Buddha relics to take with him back to Japan. Kūkai initially found himself in a disadvantageous position vis-à-vis the Heian court, but he emphasized his unique possession of esoteric ritual knowledge and made a sustained effort to demonstrate it through performing esoteric Buddhist consecrations (*kanjō;* Skt. *abhiseka*) on behalf of large numbers of people, including the retired ruler Heizei (r. 806–809) and the leading clerics of the Nara Buddhist establishment. Kūkai's teaching emphasized that proper initiation into and practice of three mysteries lead to realization of buddhahood in this very body (*sokushin jōbutsu*): body (use of appropriate hand gestures), speech (sacred verbal formulae, *mantras*), and mind (use of *maṇḍalas*).

Given that the court believed his claims to ritual knowledge, Kūkai was often called upon to perform rites such as rain prayer. His increasingly close relationship with the court culminated in its granting him the temple Tōji in 822. From 834, the Shingon lineage received annual ordinands from the government. Although Kūkai introduced esoteric Buddhist precepts, he did so in collaboration with the official system of ordination, centered at Tōdaiji in Nara; thus, Shingon monks' ordinations would always be conducted only at Tōdaiji, guaranteeing an ongoing relationship between Shingon and the Nara lineages, especially Kegon and Sanron. In his later years, Kūkai retired to his remote temple complex at Mount Kōya, where he continued to write major treatises on esoteric Buddhism.

BUDDHISM IN THE MID-HEIAN AND KAMAKURA (1192–1333) PERIODS. From the mid-ninth century on, the royal court and those surrounding it underwent fundamental changes that made the Ritsuryō legal system, developed in the eighth century, increasingly irrelevant to the lives of the aristocrats and Buddhist clerics. The advent in 859 CE of the domination of the court by the northern Fujiwara family in the form of the system of chancellors and regents (*sekkan taisei*) governing on behalf of the *tennō* meant that the latter was increasingly reduced to primarily symbolic, ritual roles.

Annual court ceremonies and temple-shrine patronage. This development was also intimately related to the increasingly prominent series of annual court ceremonies (*nenjū gyōji*), the fuller outlines of which became apparent by the 840s and that included some major Buddhist rites, including the Latter Seven-Day Rite, the Misai-e Assembly, the Buddha's Birthday Assembly (Kanbutsu-e), the Buddha-Names Assembly (Butsumyō-e), and the Seasonal Sūtra Recitation (of the Greater Prajñāpāramitā Sūtra), the last of which would be performed first in 859 CE, corresponding to the beginning of the regent-chancellor system. Meanwhile, Buddhist ordinands were granted to pray for the salvation of the *kami* even at great shrines like Kamo and Kasuga, beginning the very same year; on the occasion of the petition, the Hiei monk Eryō (c. 802–860) employed, as the very first historical instance, the explanation that the *kami* were "traces" (*suijaku*) of the Buddha (*honji*, "essence"), a discourse that would become increasingly common from the eleventh century on.

Ritual knowledge, transmission, and the increasing prominence of esoteric Buddhist lineages. From the tenth to twelfth centuries, mid-ranking aristocratic families typically tried to acquire ritual knowledge that would be useful at court, often through trying to gain their sons employ in record keeping on behalf of the government. At the same time, of course, the northern Fujiwaras themselves attempted to gain unparalleled access to knowledge of such ritual, and in the era just after the unrivaled leadership of the great Fujiwara no Michinaga (966–1027), established the first of many great treasuries of the era: Uji (no) Hōzō, which included great quantities of documents, objects, and Buddhist scriptures.

Indeed, the introduction of esoteric Buddhist lineages, which emphasized the importance of initiation into—access to—secret rituals and the related possession of ritual knowledge, was undoubtedly also related to this trend in the court. The esoteric Buddhist lineages, while partially influenced by earlier examples of temples' amassing of large collections of Buddhist scriptures, especially attempted to increase their collections of not merely Buddhist scriptures but also ritual treatises as well as oral transmissions (*kuden*) concerning ritual practice.

Shingon traditions drew upon the charisma associated uniquely with Kūkai's image to emphasize their esoteric lineages. Monks of Shingon lineage produced over time many biographies of Kūkai (*Kūkaiden*), though it is apparent that they wrote little along the lines of the treatises that Kūkai had himself produced; indeed, only one major treatise was written about Kūkai's works in the first two centuries after his death. From the late eleventh century on, when the larger aristocracy made increasing efforts to recover the high level of Chinese studies of the early Heian period, Shingon monks began to produce new editions of Kūkai's works and treatises on them, while the court scholar Fujiwara no Atsumitsu (1063–1144) wrote treatises about Kūkai's esoteric Buddhist writings.

Shingon lineages also increasingly began to splinter into lines of ritual and textual interpretation, particularly demonstrated in varied oral transmissions that usually claimed special access to knowledge of the "original teaching" (*honsetsu*) of Kūkai—interpreted as orthodox Shingon instruction. Partially in an effort to explain the oral transmissions concerning esoteric ritual practice, Shingon monks began to compile copious iconographic commentaries and other works, eventually producing extremely large manuscript treasuries.

The advent of Pure Land Buddhist discourses and practices. From early on, Tendai featured monks interested not only in esoteric Buddhist practice but also in the practice of the *nenbutsu,* that is, of chanting the name of the Buddha Amida (Sanskrit, Amitābha) in hopes of birth in his Pure Land at the time of death—or to help enable unsettled spirits find peace. Although there were clearly esoteric Buddhist elements in the Hiei monk Genshin's (942–1017) *Ōjō yōshū* (*Essentials for Birth in the Pure Land,* written in 985 CE), the work featured as its main theme the reasons for and means by which one can be born in the Pure Land of the Buddha Amida, and had a great influence on the aristocracy.

Meanwhile, semi-independent clerics increasingly inhabited areas adjacent to and sometimes distant from the major Buddhist monasteries, and they were referred to most commonly as ascetics or "holy ones" (*hijiri*). Perhaps influenced in part by the precedent of Gyōki, such figures typically had much more interaction with those in the general populace than other monks. They were commonly associated with one or the other of the major temple complexes, so they seem most often to have not been completely independent.

Since even the early ninth century veneration of prominent *bodhisattvas* such as Kannon, Miroku (Skt. Maitreya), and Jizō, and sometimes of resident holy men or mountain ascetics (*shugenja*) was increasingly common not only among aristocrats and the populace in the area in or near the capital but also in outlying regions. For many in the aristocracy and in the larger populace, Buddhist practice had little to do with scholastic study or participation in a school of Buddhism but rather with the perceived powers of divinities in specific temples—such as at Kumano, where multiple divinities, identified as local manifestations of buddha figures like the Pure Land Buddha and Kannon, were prominent objects of pilgrimage and veneration throughout premodern times.

Tendai lineages and shifts in Heian Buddhism. The major Tendai temples at Mount Hiei and Onjōji (Miidera) profited from the combination of their locale in the mountains and comparative geographical nearness to the capital and, in that context, especially close relationship with leading aristocrats such as those in the northern Fujiwaras, the family that dominated court politics from the mid-ninth to mid-eleventh centuries.

Ryōgen (912–985) was in many ways a paradigmatic and particularly early example of a monk at Hiei who negotiated the difficult path to clerical success through parlaying personal skills and alliances with powerful figures of his era. Following his impressive performance at a debate on the occasion of the Yuima-e Assembly at Kōfukuji in Nara, Ryōgen became known to members of the court and, eventually, Fujiwara no Tadahira (880–949) and Fujiwara no Morosuke (908–960), the most powerful aristocrats of the day, became his patrons in exchange for a variety of ritual services. Two of the sons of Morosuke were ordained under Ryōgen. One, Jinzen (943–990), eventually became head of the complex at Hiei, where he not only engaged in regular rituals on behalf of his family but also received large private donations of estates directed to monastic halls he controlled; in this way, Jinzen amassed many estates and effectively directed their earnings to halls where members of his family would, ideally, continue to reside as monks in perpetuity.

By the late Heian era, in a manner similar to Shingon, Tendai lineages increasingly splintered along lines of distinct ritual and textual transmission. It was, in particular, monks of Tendai lineages who in this connection introduced more and more discourses related to "original enlightenment" (*hongaku*), which were originally rooted in Chinese commentarial works that concerned the dichotomy between gradual or ascending approaches to the Buddhist path and those based on initial acknowledgement of the practitioner's inherently awakened status as "buddha."

Buddhist knowledge, proselytization, and the rise of "new Kamakura Buddhisms." Consideration of this explosion of literatures in the so-called established *kenmitsu* (exoteric-esoteric) lineages, apparent in Tendai discussions on *hongaku* and in Shingon efforts to uncover the "original teaching" (*honsetsu*) of the twelfth century and thereafter, indicates that what scholars have referred to as the "new Kamakura schools" of Japanese Buddhism did not, in any sense, exclusively demonstrate intellectual and religious vibrancy during the Kamakura and later eras.

For example, in connection with the explosion of literatures in the *kenmitsu* lineages, it is clear that they established preaching traditions even before the advent of the new Kamakura schools. One occasion for such practice was that of esoteric ritual (*shuhō*), in which a ritual pronouncement (*hyōbyaku*) would be made, and the texts of such pronouncements came to be commonly assembled in collections by the mid-twelfth century; soon after, liturgical prayers (*kōshiki*) also became increasingly common, as they were read on the occasion of Buddhist assemblies. Another series of prominent examples of such traditions included the Agui preaching lines, which began with one of the sons of the illustrious scholar and politician Fujiwara no Michinori (Shinzei; d. 1159), the Tendai monk Chōken (c. 1126–1203).

Moreover, lay aristocrats were also intimately involved in the "popularization" and intellectual activities of Buddhism in the late Heian period. Such activity was often connected with aristocratic or royal cloisters (*monzeki*) following the same general pattern as represented by the halls Jinzen established at Hiei. Lay involvement was registered not merely in the writing by figures like Ōe no Masafusa (1041–1111) of ritual pronouncements and Fujiwara no Atsumitsu's commentaries on Kūkai's esoteric treatises, but also in figures such as the aristocrat Fujiwara no Yorinaga (1120–1156), who studied Buddhist logic under the tutelage of masters at the Nara temples Tōdaiji and, especially, Kōfukuji. Moreover, Ōe no Masafusa and other aristocrats continued the practice of compiling hagiographical accounts (*ōjōden*) of those thought to have been born in the Pure Land at the times of their deaths.

Meanwhile, warriors who proclaimed themselves Fujiwaras and governed at the autonomous area of Hiraizumi to the northeast in the twelfth century followed patterns established by the northern Fujiwaras and retired emperors, establishing complexes of temples where they were entombed and the objects of Pure Land mortuary practice; thus, even lay believers who were apparently of cultural backgrounds distinct from the population of the capital area appropriated Buddhist practices to embolden their authority and improve their destinies in the afterlife.

The prince-monk Shukaku (1150–1202) drew upon his privileged access to multiple lineages of Buddhist and court ritual, clerical and general scholarship, and poetry to inaugurate the construction of a vast manuscript collection at the main Omuro cloister of the Shingon temple Ninnaji. Indeed, cultural salons or enclaves such as that at Shukaku's cloister, or those of certain other mountain temples in the area near the capital, brought together monks and aristocrats (sometimes disillusioned with capital politics) to engage in conversations (*kōdan, zōtan*), and thus helped give rise over time to a variety of aesthetic lineages. For example, Shingon and Tendai cloisters had a great impact on the development of literary treatises and poetry houses. Meanwhile, the powerful Tendai cleric Jien (1155–1225), in this connection, was not only a famous poet and rhetorician but also the author of the first treatise on Japanese history, *Gukan shō.*

The Nara Buddhist community, in fact, was also increasingly active. Although individual figures of Hossō lineage were prominent, such as the important scholar- and preacher-monk Jōkei (1155–1213), a grandson of Fujiwara no Michinori (Shinzei) who was well known in his day for his ritual pronouncements and liturgical prayers, practice of recitation of the historical Buddha's name (*shaka nenbutsu*), criticisms of Hōnen's (1133–1212) new Pure Land lineage, as well as faith in the *bodhisattvas* Miroku and Kannon, the lineages associated with Tōdaiji were most active, especially Kegon and Shingon. (Precept lineages also developed, which will be discussed in the next section.) Among the figures especially active were Chōgen (1121–1206), Myōe (1170–1232), Sōshō (1202–1278), and his disciple Gyōnen (1240–1321). Chōgen, a semi-independent holy man (*hijiri*) of Shingon lineage, was appointed the fundraiser for the rebuilding of Tōdaiji following its burning in the 1180s and supported Pure Land Buddhist practice through establishing a series of subsidiary temples—in that connection, acquiring buddha relics and promoting their veneration. Myōe attempted to restore Shingon and Kegon lineages to what he saw as their appropriate prominence—and like Jōkei openly opposed Hōnen's lineage; however, he is also known for his preoccupation with revelatory dreams, his establishment of the temple Kōzanji in Kyōto, related amassing of a large manuscript collection, authorship of a treatise on the esoteric *kōmyō shingon* death rite, and establishment of a convent for female survivors of the Hōjō family following the Jōkyū war.

Sōshō was especially eminent in Kegon studies, although he also had a broad background in the study of Buddhist logic, Yogācāra (J. Yuishiki), and *abhidharma* (J. Kusha). He was thus associated with the developing eclectic study tradition at Tōdaiji and left a massive corpus of commentaries and other works. Moreover, Sōshō, apparently in connection with the precedent of the recent Jōkei, became devoted to the *bodhisattva* Miroku, a topic about which he also wrote. His disciple Gyōnen became just as influential in the scholastic tradition at Tōdaiji, writing the famous work *Combined Study of the Eight Lineages* (*Hasshū kōyō*).

Thus, the monastic lineages of Tendai, Shingon, and the major Nara temples featured within their complexes and in their relationships with the court, aristocracy, and the larger population aspects often associated with the "new" Kamakura lineages. Temples of Nara as well as the Tendai complex at Hiei, moreover, sponsored buddha-relic assemblies open to women from the tenth century; in the latter case, such activity was undertaken especially with monks' mothers in mind, yet it also featured large processions in the capital that were attended by great numbers of the local populace. Female members of imperial house, especially retired empresses of the northern Fujiwaras, would be especially involved in relic veneration during the era of retired sovereigns. At the same time, fully ordained nuns became increasingly rare during the Heian period, and the major mountain complexes of the Tendai and Shingon lineages prohibited the presence of women; and while female aristocrats would often take varying levels of tonsure as household nuns, particularly in their old age, such activities were most often taken after the death of a spouse or even in desperation and thus did not suggest that the conditions of female Buddhist practice in any sense matched that achieved in the Nara era.

Kamakura Buddhisms. Given that those involved with "new" movements of the Kamakura period possessed a variety of relationships with their respective groups, it is useful to use the general category of "lineage" rather than "school" to analyze their activities.

The first Pure Land Buddhist lineage was that of Hōnen (1133–1212), who was trained at Mount Hiei but came to teach that only the chanting of the name of the Buddha Amida was appropriate to the Final Age of the Buddhist *dharma* (*mappō*), an ancient discourse introduced many centuries earlier that taught that the world would enter a darker era with increasing temporal distance from the life of the historical Buddha. The appeal of the Pure Land Buddha Amida was already especially associated with his ability to transform believers to his realm despite the problems of the Final Age, and such discourse was increasingly common not only in Tendai but also Shingon lineages. However, with the virtual absence of social mobility during Fujiwara preeminence as well as the increasing decentralization of power since the ascendance of the retired emperors—including the multiple power blocs all the more evident with the rise of the Kamakura shogunate—many in the aristocracy and greater populace realized the remarkably unstable character of their era and associated it all the more with the dire straits of *mappō.* Hōnen and his promotion of the exclusive practice (*senju*) of the *nenbutsu* chant thus gained a ready audience, especially among the aristocracy. Given that Hōnen called for such exclusive practice, high-ranking Tendai clerics of Hiei and of other *kenmitsu* temples were incensed, so he not only originally had to leave Hiei but would eventually be exiled and repeatedly denounced. His numerous disciples developed multiple lineages of belief and practice, including that of Shinran (1173–1262) whose would become, like Hōnen's, one of the main schools delineated by the government among the major Buddhist institutions of the Tokugawa period. Another prominent yet unrelated Pure Land lineage developing from the late thirteenth century on was that of the Jishū, based on the beliefs and practices of the itinerant monk Ippen (1239–1289).

Among other novel lineages that began to emerge in the early Kamakura period were those focused on sitting meditation (Zen; Chinese, Chan), which particularly drew upon beliefs and practices of contemporary Buddhism in Song Dynasty China. The monk Eisai (alternatively, Yōsai; 1141–1215) was also initially trained at Mount Hiei and went to China, where he studied Tendai and Zen, the latter of which flourished in the Song. Eisai returned from China and established Zen temples from the 1190s on, and he freely drew upon Tendai and esoteric Buddhist teachings and practices in his exploration of Rinzai Zen practice; though opposed by many in Nara and at Hiei, Eisai was supported by the Kamakura shogunate. Not long after, a Hiei monk named Dōgen (1200–1253) also traveled to China and studied the strict Zen of a contemporary master of the Cao-dong (J. Sōtō) lineage. Dōgen stressed the importance of "just sitting" (*shikan taza*) meditation as itself an end—attempting thereby to especially undercut any division between discourses of gradual and sudden attainment of enlightenment. It was, however, only with the developing Five Mountains (*gozan*) temple system of the Rinzai lineage, patronized by the Kamakura and then, especially, by the Ashikaga shogunates, that meditation lineages became increasingly prominent; from the late medieval era on, Zen temples would also become extremely prominent among the more general populace and were especially known for their performance of funerals, including the bestowal of posthumous ordinations (*kaimyō*). In the case of each of these kinds of temples, contrary to the images that would develop after Rinzai and Sōtō were assigned the designation of distinct schools in the Tokugawa period, it was common for temples to include monks affiliated with both lineages.

The Zen lineages spawned a number of convents. In fact, a system of Five Mountains Rinzai convents developed in Kyōto and Kamakura that complemented the more famous monastic system of the same name. A prominent nunnery was Tōkeiji in Kamakura. The wife of the late military ruler Hōjō Tokimune, who took the name of Kakusan (1252–1305) after her ordination, had studied with her husband under the Chinese Zen master Wu-xue (1226–1286), established Tōkeiji with her son in 1282; the convent, as a unique site outside of state restrictions, became prominent as a "divorce" nunnery for women who sought sanctuary from the seventeenth century on. In Sōtō Zen lineages, there were only a few convents, although fairly large groups of nuns were often trained in hermitages outside the gates of monasteries. At the same time, women were the object of the majority of recorded Sōtō Zen funerals in the late medieval era, which may be related to their status as lay patrons and, perhaps, to increasing associations of women with impurity in late medieval society, given the introduction of the Chinese *"Blood-bowl" Sūtra* (*ketsubonkyō*): the work depicted women's assignment to birth in a blood hell due to menstrual blood and the necessity of performing rites for their salvation.

Another series of new lineages that developed were those of *Nichiren* or Lotus Buddhism, which were based on the teachings and practices associated with the monk Nichiren (1222–1282), who seems to have believed that he would reform Tendai lineages through returning them to exclusive practice of devotion to the *Lotus Sūtra.* Nichiren promoted the chanting of the title of the scripture and called for the establishment of a Buddhocracy, whereupon the world would be realized as a Buddha Realm. Nichiren's lineages were also distinct insofar as Nichiren was himself from the eastern region (*Kantō*) of the main island rather than the western area, which was where most of the other new lineages initially developed. A series of lineages would develop based on the teachings of his leading disciples; two of these lineages, Nichirenshū and Nichiren Shōshū, would become particularly prominent in later eras.

Over the course of the Kamakura period, Precept lineages also developed within *kenmitsu* Buddhism. Although the Sennyūji monk Shunjō (1166–1227), the Kōfukuji monk Kakujō (1194–1249), and Tōdaiji's Enshō (1221–1277) were prominent figures, it was Eison (1201–1290) who had the greatest impact on the development of such lineages.

Eison, trained originally at the Shingon temple Daigoji in Kyōto and at Mount Kōya, inaugurated a Precept lineage (Risshū; later called Shingon Risshū) after developing a conviction concerning the importance of proper observance of the precepts and studying at the Nara Precepts temple Saidaiji in the 1230s. Eison also received instruction, at the time, in the "self-administered precepts" (*jisei jukai*) from the monk Kakujō at nearby Kōfukuji, in which one could administer one's own clerical precepts rite—in cases where qualified precepts masters were absent—through taking a vow directly in front of an image of the Buddha. Eison established the Precept lineage at Saidaiji, where he engaged in large-scale ordinations for both lay and monastic believers; in this connection, he was especially devoted to the historical buddha Śākyamuni. Eison also helped revive the convent of Hokkeji in Nara when he administered the Precepts to nuns there in 1245, leading to the nunnery's flourishing and reclassification as a subtemple of Saidaiji. Later, Eison, especially together with his active disciple Ninshō (1217–1303), came to engage in a variety of charitable activities for groups of so-called non-persons, or *hinin,* disadvantaged lepers and others at the margins of society (sometimes represented as having sacred powers to dissolve defilement).

In addition, *kenmitsu* Buddhist lineages spawned the beginnings of literatures and rituals of "Shintō" (originally pronounced Jindō) by giving rise in the late Kamakura period to new lineages that concerned themselves with understanding and appropriating the true character and power of the *kami,* which were understood in specifically Buddhist terms. It was, particularly, in Shingon Jingi (*kami*-worship) lineages and Tendai Jingi lineages that esoteric *kami* initiation developed. In particular, these lineages conducted so-called *shintō kanjō* consecrations patterned on initiatory *denbō kanjō* consecration rites. Just as the ruler began to undergo Buddhist consecration at the time of his accession (*sokui kanjō*) from the late thirteenth century on—and clearly related to its development—the Buddhist Jingi lineages developed such consecrations to enable initiates such as mountain ascetics (*shugenja*) and monks at shrines to ritually and symbolically acquire rulership in imitation of the *tennō.* In terms of ceremonial space, such activities ritually activated the trace essence (*honji-suijaku*) associations between *kami* and Buddha.

There were also discourses that cut across a large number of the new lineages that developed. As noted above, *hongaku* discourses in Tendai lineages and similar discourses in Shingon lineages (*honsetsu*, etc.) constituted important aspects of the explosion of Buddhist literatures of the era, especially from the twelfth century on. For example, discourses associated with the new lineages, such as attainment of enlightenment in an instant, focus on a single factor as the key to salvation, the universally encompassing character of enlightenment, and the fluidity of the relationship between moral causality and salvation all found expression in *hongaku* discussions.

BUDDHISM IN THE MUROMACHI AND TOKUGAWA PERIODS. Buddhist lineages and their temples underwent a series of fundamental changes over the course of the Muromachi (1336–1573) and Tokugawa (1600–1867) periods. At the same time, larger trends occurred in Buddhist belief and practice that, when considered with larger societal developments, provide insight into the extent and character of the "popularization" and, eventually, "nationalization" of Buddhism. Insofar as the Muromachi era witnessed the most unstable series of wars and related events in Japanese history, resulting in decentralized rule on an unprecedented level, it is not surprising that Buddhist lineages and their temples experienced varying combinations of growth and instability. Early on, divided imperial lines struggled mutually for political legitimacy. In this and related contexts, theories elaborating the meaning of *kami* within Buddhist cosmology reached new levels of complexity. The discourse of "origin trace" (*honji suijaku*), which had arisen in *kenmitsu* Buddhist circles from the Heian period on and positioned buddhas/ *bodhisattvas* as essences with *kami* manifestations, became a linchpin not only for Buddhist Shintō initiations but also for all manner of "Shintō" theories within the *kenmitsu* temple complexes.

Changes in the *Kenmitsu* lineages. Meanwhile, institutionally, *kenmitsu* Buddhist lineages continued to thrive and prosper in a number of regions, while a number of the newer lineages continued to spread their practices, accompanied by their messages. The impetus to create larger and larger manuscript treasuries, increasingly accompanied by interest in continental Asian materials, particularly evident from the twelfth century on, continued throughout the Kamakura period and into the Muromachi period. Printing technology was appropriated to produce canons at Shingon's Mount Kōya, and temples in areas such as Kamakura and Nara printed Buddhist scriptures, Zen literature, and other works from the continent. At the same time, the production and hand copying (*shosha*) of vast quantities of works continued especially in the Shingon, Tendai, multiple Nara, and most of the newer Buddhist lineages; although substantially produced even from the twelfth century on, legends of the origins of temples (*engimono*), temple documentary or ritual records (*monjo, kikigaki, kirigami*, etc.), a variety of commentaries (*zuzō sho, shō, shōmono*), compilations (*shū, ruiju*), and biographies (*den*) increased dramatically in the thirteenth and fourteenth centuries. Several of the major monasteries of the *kenmitsu* lineages, especially Enryakuji (Mount Hiei: Tendai), Onjōji (Tendai), Kōfukuji (Nara: Hossō), Tōdaiji (Nara: Kegon, Shingon), and Kongōbuji (Mount Kōya: Shingon), took advantage of the extremely decentralized conditions to not merely improve their economic conditions through attempting to acquire all manner of new lands and often engage in overseas trade, but to commonly establish fighting forces to serve on behalf of their interests. In connection with offerings of land, branch temples and shrines were often constructed, in which the resident Buddhist divinities or *kami* were commonly seen by those in the area as arbiters of natural forces and in need of propitiation or veneration. They routinely also established new temples, including sometimes relatively large manuscript collections, to spread ritual knowledge and, sometimes, monastic learning.

Zen and the culture of learning. At the same time, Zen lineages increasingly took unique positions among the newer lineages with their success at winning the patronage of the Ashikaga (Muromachi) shogunate, which came particularly to promote Rinzai Zen lineages and the Five Mountains system from the late fourteenth century on. The Zen traditions, similar to the relationship between the *kenmitsu* lineages and the larger aristocracy, began in their patronage by the shogunate to influence the production of new cultural practices and, eventually, aesthetic lineages. The leaders of the shogunate were especially interested in cultivating the cultural traits of the aristocracies of Japan as well as China, and certain arts associated with Zen presumably carried such traits (and, in part, Buddhist meaning as well). The development of Japanese landscape arts—especially landscape paintings and rock gardens—from the late fourteenth century on was especially indebted to those in the cultural enclaves of the Five Mountains Zen temples and convents. This culture of learning, commonly represented in the form of paintings of and literary references to the Zen monk's study (*shosai*), included Buddhist contemplation, analysis, and discussion of continental Asian scholarship. Moreover, the shogunate academy Ashikaga Gakkō, which developed by the 1420s, was directly indebted to those in the Five Mountains institutions. In addition, beginning in the fourteenth century, the shogunate supported the inception of tea parties reminiscent of similar events in China. The monk Murata Shukō (1423–1502), who studied under the unconventional Zen cleric Ikkyū at Daitokuji, developed the first form of the later tea ceremony, which would eventually blend the influence of such aristocratic practice with those of the general populace.

Developments in other newer lineages. Meanwhile, recluses associated with Jishū and Precept lineages were heavily involved in Linked Poetry (*renga*) gatherings, which were similar to the cultural enclaves yet were marked by bringing together persons of different status on common ground. These figures were thus connected also with the "nonhumans" (*hinin*)—itinerant priests, entertainers, traders, and lepers often living in liminal riverbank areas (*kawara*), where cadavers were commonly left. The origins of such gatherings may have also been related to Eison's and Ninshō's activities of the self-administered precepts, which also brought together persons of differing classes in activity marked by equality, and constituted leagues (*ikki*) that would transform into groups challenging authorities from the fifteenth century on. Other of the newer lineages of Buddhism variously made inroads into rural areas. Although lineages such as Shinran's and Nichiren's had moved to some degree into the rural areas of the eastern area (Kantō) of the main island as early as the late Kamakura era and the Jishū and Precept lineages were comparatively mobile, most of the newer lineages had little success in rural areas before well into the Muromachi period. It was particularly with the increasing decentralization of power and social mobility from the mid-fifteenth century on that the newer lineages became especially successful in attracting larger numbers of adherents, and such conversions were often made in connection with leagues (*ikki*) that these lineages offered—that is, related to efforts to challenge the authority of local lords, their retainers, and governors. Shinran's True Pure Land lineage (Jōdo shinshū, or Ikkō shū) became especially prominent from the fifteenth century, when the eighth patriarch Rennyo (1415–1499) led it. Shinran's teaching especially appealed to the general populace through its emphasis on the Final Age of the Buddhist *dharma* and, in that context, the notion that all, whether monk or lay, are equally incapable of contributing in any way to their own salvation; Shinran had indeed himself said he was "neither monk nor layman" and went so far as to take a wife (based on an instruction in vision from the *bodhisattva* Kannon)—the precedent for True Pure Land priests' marriage from that time forward. Arguing that only one recitation of the *nenbutsu* with faith was sufficient for birth in Amida's Pure Land, Shinran and his successors gradually developed a willing audience among the population, especially over the course of the Muromachi period, when traditionally accepted class distinctions were increasingly seen by some as fundamentally arbitrary in character. Rennyo, after his persecution by Hiei and move to the Hokuriku region of northern Japan, transformed the lineage by appealing especially to all classes of rural villagers (especially peasants and low-level samurai) and emphasizing the universal and simple character of Amidist beliefs and practices; in doing so, and given the gradual rise in literacy, Rennyo attempted to expand the number of people who could read monks' sermons in the lineage by encouraging use of the syllabary rather Chinese characters in their recording. He also promoted the use of parishes or confraternities (*kō*), where villagers met in the local place of practice (*dōjō*), located in a temple or in the home of a supporting layman, who was usually a low-level samurai. The *ikkō ikki* leagues that rebelled against local governors beginning in the 1570s, featuring the low-level samurai and large numbers of peasants—the latter of which did not want to pay rents to local lords—were often at variance with Rennyo's wishes, but following successes in Hokuriku in 1488 Rennyo went on to take advantage of the new wealth, land, and military strength to establish the Honganji temple in the capital of Kyōto in 1496. The Nichiren lineage (Hokke shū) also became similarly powerful through the development of leagues, although in this case it converted its followers increasingly in urban areas, especially in Kyōto during the 1530s.

The arrival of Europeans and the nationalization of Buddhist "schools." Following the mid-sixteenth-century appearance of the Europeans and their religion, the leading samurai destroyed the military powers of the Buddhists within decades. The newly formed ruling Tokugawa shogunate (1600–1867) then decided to incorporate Buddhists into its administrative structure. It first ordered each major "school" of Japanese Buddhism to have a main temple for the training of clerics and a strictly hierarchical system of main and branch temples, as well as possess rules for monks' status, discipline, and clothing within the organization. By order of the shogunate, a national system of main-branch temples (*honmatsu seido*) was developed, which forced all temples to affiliate with one or other of the nationally designated schools. The shogunate eventually required that all Japanese households (*ie*) register with and become parishioners of their local temple, a system that became universal by roughly the 1660s. The development of this national system of congregations or parishes (*danka seido*) meant that Buddhist institutions, which had directly or indirectly affected much of Japanese cultural and social life for a millennium, became even more pervasive. Each household, through its membership, could not easily change its affiliation from one temple or school of Buddhism to another, while it at the same time was required to support the temple, particularly through donating to clerics on the occasions of family funerals or related memorial rites. In this way, the members of most households came increasingly to associate Buddhist temples with death or mortuary rites. At the same time, it is clear that Buddhism thereby became an integral part of ritual life for virtually all Japanese. The traditional *kenmitsu* and the newer lineages tended to profit financially from the national system set in place by the shogunate. True Pure Land lineages, given the wealth of the Honganji, continued despite early subjugation efforts by the first shogun of the era, Tokugawa Ieyasu (1542–1616), to enjoy special privileges vis-à-vis the military government, such as the continuing right to marry. Most of the major temples increasingly offered a whole variety of ritual services on behalf of the local populations. Those with famous buddha, *bodhisattva,* or other images increasingly offered regular displays (*kaichō*) of their sacred icons. Buddhist monks typically asked, as had commonly been the case throughout history, for donations when they conducted occasional rituals, though in this case they also enjoyed the increasing benefit of the new series of required funerary and memorial rites. Meanwhile, temples of Shingon and other lineages undertook to reorganize and expand their manuscript collections not so much in connection with record-keeping requirements as an effort to revive their intellectual life, which had particularly suffered with the breakdown of shogunal authority from the late fifteenth century on. Although the shogunate tried to retain control over religious practice, transinstitutional practices such as pilgrimage became more vibrant than ever. Meanwhile, various groups of so-called Kumano nuns traveled the isles and preached, sometimes promoting a physical pilgrimage but more often using "Kumano Ten-Realms *Maṇḍala*" (*kumano jikkai mandara*) paintings to endorse a spiritual pilgrimage to salvation—avoiding the torments of the blood hell, which they taught awaited most women at death. Moreover, the fact that print had become a virtually universal medium in the burgeoning merchant economy meant that a whole variety of easily accessible publications appeared in connection with practices like pilgrimage. Guidebooks to pilgrimage sites, literary descendants in part of the earlier temple legend collections, flourished as such sites grew more popular than ever before, despite the shogunate's efforts to limit physical movement.

Buddhism in the Meiji Period (1868–1912) and Modern Japan. Given the increasing intellectual current of "nativism" (*kokugaku*), which was not only connected with movement toward the development of a nation-state and modernization but also increasingly with a call for the return to full sovereignty of the *tennō* and the rejection of foreign influences, it is not surprising that Buddhist institutions, long gateways to continental learning and civilization, came to be subjected to all manner of criticisms.

Following patterns established on a small scale from the mid-seventeenth century on by lords of certain local domains, the new government immediately decided to separate *kami*-worshipping shrines from Buddhist temples by force, taking a policy of "Separation of *Kami* and Buddhas" (*shinbutsu bunri*) and producing what would come to be called "State Shintō" *(kokka shintō).* The sharply anti-Buddhist policies and tone of government statements created an atmosphere rife for exploitation, whereupon a virtual cultural revolution occurred in which Buddhist images and temples were purged throughout the Japanese isles. This purge, which came to known as "Expelling Buddhism and Destroying Śākyamuni" (*haibutsu kishaku*), began as soon as the new government policy was announced: a *kami*-worshipping priest led an armed group that stormed the Hie Shrine, part of the larger Enryakuji temple complex at Mount Hiei, and burned several hundred Buddhist images and scriptures. From this point on, violence against Buddhist institutions became rampant.

By 1871, the worst remnants of the purge were over, and Buddhist clerics, sometimes together with and sometimes in opposition to the government, began to make efforts to reconceive of and newly represent the relevance of Buddhist belief and practice to Japanese society. In response to the most prominent ideological attacks on institutional Buddhists—that monks and temples did not contribute to the nation, that their faith was foreign and counter to that of the nation, and that they held to ahistorical and mythic beliefs—they responded by engaging, increasingly along transsectarian (ecumenical) lines, in working on behalf of the population by constructing hospitals, aiding the poor, helping those in prison, feeding the ill of other lands, and also using their organizations to aid the Japanese military overseas.

For institutional Buddhists, the national and international unity of their faith was mediated by a transnational Asian Buddhism. Speaking of the "Three Realms" (India, China, Japan), a Japanese term originally used prior to nation-states (which also appropriated the same Japanese word, *koku/kuni*), they drew upon premodern discourses of the Tōdaiji monk Gyōnen and others who had attempted to legitimate Buddhist belief and practice in the Japanese isles through appealing to the presumed unified transmission of a singular and authentic Buddhist tradition. In the same period, Daisetsu Teitarō ("D.T.") Suzuki's (1870–1966) translation of *The Awakening of Faith* attempted to establish a "common ground" for all "true Buddhists" beyond attachment to "sectarian tenets," in this case an essential Mahāyāna doctrine represented as in no way inferior to the presumably more scientific early Buddhism. While Suzuki's work would later find a larger readership in Europe and the United States and come to stress discourses on buddha-nature in the context of Zen belief, *The Awakening of Faith* would be studied by modern Japanese scholars because of its influence on Tendai and other discourses concerning "original enlightenment" (*hongaku*) and interpreted by some as having reached its flowering in Japanese Buddhism. Such interpretations, combined with the emphasis on the Three Nations, are thought to have also contributed conceptually to pan-Asianism, which in the form of the Japanese policy of the "Greater East Asian Co-Prosperity Sphere" rhetorically helped to legitimize military aggression on the continent during the Pacific war. Recently, however, some other Japanese scholars would argue that Japanese Buddhism, especially in its emphasis on "original enlightenment," was especially prone to antinomianism.

Another aspect of institutional Buddhism of the late nineteenth and early twentieth centuries that should be noted was the universalizing of clerical marriage. While monks sometimes possessed wives and children but did not speak openly of their presence (this was frequent enough that children had rights to a deceased monk's property in the Heian period), it was only with Shinran and the True Pure Land lineages he founded that Buddhist clerics began to openly marry. However, Buddhist clerics as a whole now lost whatever privileges or exceptional aspects that had marked them; as a key part of this process, the government dismantled in 1872 all laws differentiating clergy from others in the populace—including official proscriptions against clerical marriage and meat eating (*nikujiki saitai*)—so most monks married. At the same time, almost all nuns, who unlike their male counterparts were not bequeathed family temples by their fathers and did not feel pressure to themselves bequeath—instead "left home" to enter the clergy—are unmarried to this day.

While monastic Buddhists were generally supportive of the war effort—and on peaceful terms with the militarists—the government was particularly distrustful of those in "new religions," including Buddhist ones like Sōka Kyōiku Gakkai (later called Sōka Gakkai), Reiyūkai, Risshō Kōseikai, Shinnyoen, Gedatsukai, and Honmon Butsuryūshū. Members of many of the new religions were observed on a regular basis and often imprisoned. With the destruction of the major metropolitan centers and the freeing of the leaders of the new religions, the latter enjoyed tremendous successes during the early postwar era. All of the new religions, including those Buddhist in character, offered this-worldly benefits of various sorts (often healing) as well as related resolutions to spiritual/emotional problems.

Sōka Gakkai, a lay organization that began within the Nichiren Shōshū sect, grew from an organization of a few thousand at the beginning of the 1950s to a membership of more than 7 million by the early 1970s. This and other of the new religions were particularly successful in urban areas, where residents were often geographically separated from their larger families; one member of an urban family, often the wife or mother in the household, would commonly enter the movement, attend regular meetings, and eventually bring in other members. Sōka Gakkai featured regular group meetings for Buddhist practice featuring recitation of the title of the *Lotus Sūtra,* belief in the essential importance of active proselytization, and, in that connection, political action to promote world peace and salvation. Other Buddhist new religions tended to emphasize ancestor veneration as a major component, including Reiyūkai, out of which other new religions, such as Risshō Kōseikai, have developed.

From the 1970s on so-called "new-new religions" (*shinshin shūkyō*) have developed, which generally share characteristics different from those of the new religions, and of which those of Buddhist character have also been active. While the growth of most of the earlier new religions slowed, these groups attempted to offer new responses to the changing conditions in contemporary Japan. For the most part, groups like Agonshū and Aum Shinrikyō, like their non-Buddhist counterparts, tended to appeal to youth through not merely this-worldly benefits but also a more critical stance vis-à-vis the current social and political situation.

Recently, institutional Buddhists have faced charges of social-class and gender discrimination. With regard to social discrimination, research during the last decades of the twentieth century clarified that some major sects of Japanese Buddhism, such as Zen, were involved historically in the use of "discriminatory precept names" (*sabetsu kaimyō*)—the application of discriminatory religious titles to those deceased of the outcast class (*burakumin*). Finally, the creation and increased use of *mizuko kuyō* rites, veneration of the *bodhisattva* Jizō (*mizuko jizō*) practiced on behalf of the spirits of aborted fetuses, from the 1970s on in some Buddhist temples had an integral relationship with advertising campaigns and broader temple efforts to increase profits; the motives of the temples have been particularly called into question, and some have argued that such practices target young women by producing fear of the curses (*tatari*) of unsettled fetus spirits—thus constituting an unfair and discriminatory practice.

Institutional Buddhists have also been challenged by recent changes in death practices. The image of greedy monks has led some Japanese to prefer to forgo such funerals, choosing options such as common graves and the free scattering of the dead's ashes.

However, alongside the growth of new practices transinstitutional rites of more traditional vintage like the Obon day of the dead as well as pilgrimage have been retained if not reinvigorated. Moreover, the New Year's pilgrimage, while associated with Shintō shrines, is often made instead to Buddhist temples, where Buddhas and *bodhisattvas* are likewise approached with prayers. In addition, Buddhist pilgrimage circuits vibrant since the Tokugawa period, such as the eighty-eight-temple route undertaken to match the piety of the great Shingon master Kūkai, have become as prominent as ever.

Finally, we should note that the influence of Buddhist discourses on society has accompanied the vast increase in media. The development of the internet as well as the popularity of *manga* (comics), *anime* (animation), and films have contributed to a wide diffusion of Buddhist images and ideas. Buddhist temples, new (and "new-new") Buddhist religions, and a variety of other Buddhist groups have taken advantage of the web to explain their teachings and offer other services. From the 1970s on, *manga* series such as the great Tezuka Osamu's series entitled *Buddha* and *anime* series such as *Ikkyū-san* have enjoyed great popularity. Buddhist themes also figured prominently in novels and other literature. The prominence of Buddhist figures, themes, images, and teachings in these media indicates the extent to which Buddhism continues to have a vibrant and multiple influence on Japanese culture, while its institutional presence perdures despite a variety of challenges.

SEE ALSO Buddhism, Schools of, article on Japanese Buddhism; Japanese Religions, overview article; Missions, article on Buddhist Missions; Pilgrimage, article on Buddhist Pilgrimage in East Asia; Shintō; Shugendō.

BIBLIOGRAPHY

Studies in English

The volume of Western-language materials concerning Buddhism in Japan has recently increased dramatically, as has the volume of the research. Prominently, relevant articles appear in *Japanese Journal of Religious Studies, Japanese Religions,* and a series of other journals on religion or Japan. Surprisingly, there is not as yet an up-to-date standard reference on Buddhism in Japan or Japanese religion, whereas specialized studies are numerous. The work edited by Kazuo Kasahara, *A History of Japanese Religion* (Tokyo, 2001), is a useful set of essays by prominent scholars of Japanese religion, though it remains a translation of a much earlier two-volume set published in Japanese. Comparatively more introductory works include H. Byron Earhart, *Japanese Religion: Unity and Diversity*, 3rd ed. (Belmont, Calif., 2004) and Ian Reader, Esben Andreasen, and Finn Stefansson, eds., *Japanese Religions Past and Present* (Honolulu, Hawaii, 1993). Daigan Matsunaga and Alicia Matsunaga, *Foundation of Japanese Buddhism*, 2 vols. (Los Angeles and Tokyo, 1974–1976), is a detailed yet dated overview of the historical transmission of the best known lineages of Japanese Buddhism.

Specialized Studies

Most of the promising work on Buddhism in Japan has been conducted in specialized studies or edited volumes. The following discussion constitutes an incomplete list, due to the volume of materials recently published. Early Japanese Buddhism remains little studied, although Ryūichi Abé, *The Weaving of Mantra: Kūkai and the Construction of Esoteric Buddhist Discourse* (New York, 1999) offers a useful overview of Buddhism in the Nara period. For a discussion of women in Nara period Buddhism, see Hongō Masatsugu, "State Buddhism and Court Buddhism: The Role of Court Women in the Development of Buddhism from the Seventh to the Ninth Centuries," in *Enduring Faith: Women and Buddhism in Premodern Japan,* edited by Barbara Ruch (Ann Arbor, Mich, 2002); the Ruch work includes a broad array of studies on women's involvement in both lay and monastic Buddhism prior to the modern era. For studies of Saichō and Kūkai, see Paul Groner, *Saichō: The Establishment of the Tendai School* (Honolulu, Hawaii, 2000), and the Abé work noted above, as well as the older Yoshito Hakeda, *Kūkai: Major Works* (New York, 1972). There are a number of important studies of Buddhism from the mid-Heian to the Kamakura period. William LaFleur's *The Karma of Words: Buddhism and the Literary Arts in Medieval Japan* (Princeton, N.J., 1983) examined the introduction of karmic cosmology into Japanese literature. With regard to Buddhist activities or lineages that existed prior to the advent of the new Kamakura period lineages, see Mark L. Blum, *The Origins and Development of Pure Land Buddhism: A Study and Translation of Gyōnen's Jōdo Hōmon Genrushō* (New York, 2002); Paul Groner, *Ryōgen and Mount Hiei: Japanese Tendai in the Tenth Century* (Honolulu, Hawaii, 2002); Janet Goodwin, *Alms and Vagabonds: Buddhist Temples and Popular Patronage in Medieval Japan* (Honolulu, Hawaii, 1994); Brian D. Ruppert, *Jewel in the Ashes: Buddha Relics and Power in Early Medieval Japan* (Cambridge, U.K., 2000); Jacqueline I. Stone, *Original Enlightenment and the Transformation of Medieval Japanese Buddhism* (Honolulu, Hawaii, 1999); George J. Tanabe, *Myōe the Dreamkeeper: Fantasy and Knowledge in Early Kamakura Buddhism* (Cambridge, U.K., 1992), and Mimi Hall Yiengpruksawan, *Hiraizumi: Buddhist Art and Regional Politics in Twelfth-Century Japan* (Cambridge, U.K., 1998). With regard to studies of new Kamakura period lineages, James Dobbins, *Jōdo Shinshū: Shin Buddhism in Medieval Japan* (Honolulu, Hawaii, 2002) remains the standard work on Shinran's lineage, as does William Bodiford, *Sōtō Zen in Medieval Japan* (Honolulu, Hawaii, 1993) concerning Sōtō Zen; the *Senchakushū* English Translation Project, trans. and ed., *Hōnen's Senchakushū* (Honolulu, Hawaii, 1998), provides the best translation of Hōnen's most famous work while offering a useful introduction. There are also a number of translations of works by Nichiren. Other works increasingly establish the commonalities between the previously existing lineages and those newly developed in the Kamakura period, including relevant Shintō lineages. These include Mikael S. Adolphson, *The Gates of Power: Monks, Courtiers, and Warriors in Premodern Japan* (Honolulu, Hawaii, 2000); Bernard Faure, *Visions of Power: Imagining Medieval Japanese Buddhism* (Princeton, N.J., 1996); Richard K. Payne, ed., *Re-Visioning "Kamakura" Buddhism* (Honolulu, Hawaii, 1998); Mark Teeuwen and Fabio Rambelli, eds., *Buddhas and Kami in Japan:* Honji Suijaku *as a Combinatory Paradigm* (London, 2003); and Robert H. Sharf and Elizabeth Horton Sharf, eds., *Living Images: Japanese Buddhist Icons in Context* (Stanford, Calif., 2001). While the last of these works includes studies of Buddhism from the Muromachi and Tokugawa periods, the number of other prominent works remains comparatively few, and typically concern particular figures or institutions of the period or popular religious practices. Studies of figures include Peter Haskel and Ryūichi Abé, *Great Fool: Zen Master Ryōkan—Poems, Letters, and Other Writings* (Honolulu, Hawaii, 1996) and James H. Sanford, *Zen-man Ikkyū* (Chico, Calif., 1981). Prominent works on institutions or popular practices include Helen J. Baroni, *Ōbaku Zen: The Emergence of the Third Sect of Zen in Tokugawa Japan* (Honolulu, Hawaii, 2000); Martin Collcutt, *Five Mountains: The Rinzai Zen Monastic Institution in Medieval Japan* (Cambridge, U.K., 1981); Helen Hardacre, *Religion and Society in Nineteenth-Century Japan: A Study of the Southern Kanto Region, Using Late Edo and Early Meiji Gazetteers* (Ann Arbor, Mich., 2002); Nam-Lin Hur, *Prayer and Play in Late Tokugawa Japan: Asakusa Sensōji and Edo Society* (Cambridge, U.K., 2000); Neil McMullin, *Buddhism and the State in Sixteenth Century Japan* (Princeton, N.J., 1984); D. Max Moerman, *Localizing Paradise: Kumano Pilgrimage and the Religious Landscape of Premodern Japan* (Cambridge, U.K., 2004); Joseph D. Parker, *Zen Buddhist Landscape Arts of Early Muromachi Japan (1336–1573)* (Albany, N.Y., 1999); and Duncan Ryūken Williams, *The Other Side of Zen: A Social History of Soto Zen Buddhism in Tokugawa Japan* (Princeton, N.J., 2005). There are numerous studies of Buddhism in the modern era, of which the most prominent are: Paula Kane Robinson Arai, *Women Living Zen* (New York, 1999); Helen Hardacre, *Lay Buddhism in Contemporary Japan: Reiyūkai Kyōdan* (Princeton, N.J., 1984); Helen Hardacre, *Marketing the Menacing Fetus in Japan* (Berkeley, Calif., 1999); Richard M. Jaffe, *Neither Monk Nor Layman: Clerical Marriage in Modern Japanese Buddhism* (Princeton, N.J., 2001); James Edward Ketelaar, *Of Heretics and Martyrs in Meiji Japan: Buddhism and Its Persecution* (Princeton, N.J., 1990); William LaFleur, *Liquid Life: Abortion and Buddhism in Japan* (Princeton, N.J., 1991); Ian Reader and George Tanabe, *Practically Religious: Worldly Benefits and the Common Religion of Japan* (Honolulu, Hawaii, 1998); Brian Daizen Victoria, *Zen at War* (New York, 1997); and Judith Snodgrass, *Presenting Japanese Buddhism to the West: Orientalism, Occidentalism, and the Columbian Exposition* (Chapel Hill, N.C., 2003) on the "new" Buddhism of the Meiji period and the interaction with the West and Western Buddhologists. Jamie Hubbard and Paul L. Swanson, eds., *Pruning the Bodhi Tree: The Storm over Critical Buddhism* (Honolulu, Hawaii, 1997), focuses on the debate concerning contemporary Japanese scholars who have criticized original enlightenment discourses in Japanese Buddhism.

Studies in Japanese

The great bulk of publications in the study of Japanese Buddhism has and remains in Japanese, and the volume of publication has dramatically increased in recent years. The most useful reference with which to consider the broader history of Japanese Buddhism has long been Tsuji Zennosuke, *Nihon bukkyōshi,* 10 vols. (Tokyo, 1944–1953), although there have been a large number of recent general works that address developments in theory and research. More recently, a series edited by Nihon Bukkyō Kenkyūkai entitled *Nihon no bukkyō,* 6 vols. (Kyōto, 1994–1996) and a volume edited by the same group called *Nihon bukkyō no kenkyūhō* (Kyōto, 2000) have offered the most rigorous series of general articles by leading contemporary scholars as well as the most up-to-date bibliographical essays on significant research that has been conducted on Japanese Buddhism in recent decades; the topics covered include not only the major historical periods, lineages of Japanese Buddhism, and *kami*-Buddha amalgamation but also the fields of Buddhist folklore, Buddhist literature, women in Buddhism, Buddhist art, and Buddhist architecture. For verification of the existence or historical validity of Buddhist texts, Ono Genmyō, ed., *Bussho kaisetsu daijiten,* 13 vols. (Tokyo, Supplementary vols. 12–13 ed. Maruyama Takao, rev. ed. 1964–1967) remains the best resource.

Specialized Studies

All of the major traditional sects of Japanese Buddhism have collected their own textual corpuses. However, careful study of any group or individual in Japanese Buddhism requires consultation of a broad range of both primary and secondary sources in Japanese. In terms of primary sources, initial collections that should be consulted are the sections including Japanese Buddhist works in *Taishō shinshū daizōkyō,* 100 vols. (Tokyo, 1924–1932), *Dainihon zokuzōkyō,* 750 vols. (Kyōto, 1905–1912), and *Dainihon bukkyō zensho,* 151 vols. (Tokyo, 1912–1922). Important sources for the study of early Buddhism include, of course, court chronicles, archaeological records, *Shōsō'in monjo* records, temple stories, and official temple collection records (*shizaichō*). As for major lineages that developed in the early period, only Tendai and Shingon feature large collections, which include: Tendai Shūten Kankōkai, ed., *Tendaishū zensho,* 25 vols. (Tokyo, 1935–1937), and Tendai Shūten Hensanjo, ed., *Zoku Tendaishū zensho,* 15+ vols. (Tokyo: 1987–); Shingonshū Zensho Kankōkai, ed., *Shingonshu zensho,* 44 vols. (Kōyasan, 1933–1939), and Zoku Shingonshū Zensho Kankōkai, ed., *Zoku Shingonshū zensho,* 42 vols. (Kōyasan, 1973–1988). As for the newer Kamakura period lineages, some of the major Pure Land Buddhist collections are Jōdoshū Shūten Kankōkai, ed., *Jōdoshū zensho,* 21 vols. (Tokyo, 1929–1931); Shūsho Hozonkai, ed., *Zoku Jōdoshū zensho,* 20 vols. (Tokyo, 1940–1942); Tsumaki Naoyoshi, ed., *Shinshū zensho,* 74 vols. (Tokyo, 1913–1916); Shinshū Tenseki Kankōkai, ed., *Shinshū taikei,* 37 vols. (Tokyo, 1974–1976) and *Zoku Shinshū taikei,* 24 vols. plus *Bekkan,* 4 vols. (Tokyo, 1976–1977). Some major Zen collections include: Sōtōshū Zensho Kankōkai, ed., *Sōtōshū zensho* (Tokyo, 1929–1935); Zoku Sōtōshū Zensho Kankōkai, ed., *Zoku Sōtōshū zensho* (Tokyo, 1974–1977). Prominent Nichiren lineage collections are Risshō Daigaku Nichiren Kyōgaku Kenkyūjo, ed., *Nichirenshū shūgaku zensho* (Tokyo, 1968–1978) and *Shōwa teihon Nichiren Shōnin ibun* (Minobusan, 1988). In the case of virtually all of the major lineages, collections of works by the founders and other major figures of the traditions have been published and should be consulted; recent research has resulted in the publication of large new collections of works attributed to figures lesser-known to scholarship, like the monk Shukaku of Shingon lineage. Collections of materials of the Tokugawa, Meiji, and modern periods can often be found in those of entire lineages, noted above. However, work of contemporary scholars such as scholars at the Historiographical Institute, University of Tokyo, and Tamamuro Fumio have also made great quantities of previously unpublished materials available for research. Relevant materials such as diaries and various genres of temple records should also be consulted regularly.

BRIAN O. RUPPERT (2005)

BUDDHISM: BUDDHISM IN THE WEST

During the twentieth century Buddhism became globally distributed and established. Buddhists have set foot in Australia and New Zealand, in the southern region of Africa, and in most countries of Europe, as well as in South and North America. Buddhism outside of Asia is marked by a heterogeneity and diversity that is observable in all thus-denoted "Western" countries. The entire range of Buddhism's main traditions and subtraditions can be found outside of Asia, often in one country and sometimes even in one major city, with some forty, fifty, or more different Buddhist groups in a single place. Buddhists of divergent traditions and schools have become neighbors—a rarity in Asia itself. Additionally, new Western Buddhist orders and organizations have been founded, signaling ambitious moves to create indigenized variations of Buddhist forms, practices, and interpretations. As the Western institutionalization of Buddhism rapidly accelerated in the closing three decades of the twentieth century, its research matured and became a recognized subject with numerous studies.

EARLY ENCOUNTERS. Very early information about Buddhist concepts can be traced to the records of the Greek philosopher Plutarch (first century CE). Plutarch writes about the Indo-Greek king Menander (Menandros, c. 155–130 BCE) and his conversation with the Buddhist monk Nāgasena, documented in the Pali text *Milindapañha* (Questions of King Milinda). The rise of Christianity and later of Islam blocked further exchange until Franciscan friars traveled to Mongolia in the thirteenth century. From the sixteenth century onwards, travelers and Jesuit missionaries to Tibet, China, and Japan left fragmentary accounts of Buddhist rituals and concepts. In the course of European colonial expansion, information was gathered about the customs and history of the peoples and regions that were subjected to British, Portuguese, and Dutch domination. Texts and descriptions began to be collected and translated in the late eighteenth century, although a distinction had not yet been clearly made between Hindu and Buddhist treatises. Simultaneously, in Europe the Romantic movement gave rise to a glorifying enthusiasm for the East and for India in particular. The Asian world and its religious and philosophical traditions were discovered along with efforts aimed at tracing a genuine and pure spirituality that was supposedly lost in Europe through the victory of rationalism.

Discovery of Buddhism through texts. The credit for first systematizing the increasing amount of information on Buddhist texts and concepts goes to the Paris philologist Eugène Burnouf (1801–1852). His *L'introduction à l'histoire du buddhisme indien* (1844) presented a scientific survey of Buddhist history and doctrines. Burnouf imposed a rational order on ideas hitherto perceived as unrelated, in this way creating the prototype of the European concept of Buddhism. In the 1850s, Europe witnessed a boom of studies and translations, paving the way for an enhanced knowledge of and interest in the teachings. At this time Asian religion was essentially treated as a textual object located in books, Oriental libraries, and institutes of the West.

The writings of the German philosopher Arthur Schopenhauer (1788–1860) inspired wide interest in Buddhist philosophy and ethics among intellectuals, academics, and artists. In the United States, the nineteenth-century transcendentalists Ralph Waldo Emerson, Henry David Thoreau, and Walt Whitman praised Indian philosophy and introduced translations, produced in Europe, to members of the American middle- and upper classes. Circles of aesthetic conversation and textual sources were the mediators that initiated the spread of and provided for the public presence of Buddhist ideas in Europe and the United States. The appeal of Indian spirituality was strengthened by the intervention of the Theosophical Society, founded by Helena P. Blavatsky (1831–1891) and Henry Steel Olcott (1832–1907) in 1875 in New York. In addition, Sir Edwin Arnold (1832–1904) published his famous poem *The Light of Asia* in 1879, followed by Olcott's *Buddhist Catechism* in 1881. Both works praised the Buddha and his teaching. Echoing this overt glorification of the Asian religion, a few Europeans became the first self-converted followers of the teaching in the early 1880s.

Though more Westerners took up Buddhist teachings as their new orientation in life, another twenty years passed before the first Buddhist organizations outside of Asia were formed. The Indologist Karl Seidenstücker (1876–1936) established the Society for the Buddhist Mission in Germany in 1903 in Leipzig. Likewise, the first British monk, Ananda Metteyya (Allen Bennett McGregor, 1872–1923), formed the Buddhist Society of Great Britain and Ireland in 1907 in London. By means of lectures, pamphlets, and books, the first professed Western Buddhists tried to win recruits from the educated middle- and upper social strata of society. These and related activities were polemically commented on by Christian clergy, who criticized the "nihilism" of Buddhism and the "foreignness" of the Asian religion to European society. This debate was strengthened when a few committed men, including Anton Güth (1878–1957), ordained as Nyānatiloka, became monks in the Theravāda tradition in the early twentieth century and temporarily remained in Europe.

Internationalization: Toward a global Buddhism. To a certain extent the incipient Buddhist activities in Western countries relied on reformist approaches and modernist reinterpretations of Asian Buddhist concepts. In Ceylon (Sri Lanka), the center of South Asian Buddhist revival, educated urban Buddhists who had been influence by Orientalist concepts emphasized the rational and scientific aspects of Buddhist teachings. These modernist Buddhists portrayed Buddhism as text-based, pragmatic, rational, universal, and socially active. Both European scholarship and the Western glorification of Buddhist ideas strengthened national and religious self-confidence in South Asia, further generating ideas of a missionary outreach. In addition, in 1880 Olcott and Blavatsky visited Colombo, Ceylon, and publicly took refuge in the Buddha, *dharma,* and *saṃgha,* becoming the first Westerners to do so in an Asian country.

In the two decades that followed, Olcott and the Ceylonese Anagārika Dharmapāla (1864–1933) worked together to renew the importance of Buddhism. In 1891, Dharmapāla set up the Mahā Bodhi Society, its aim being to restore the neglected site of Bodh Gayā in North India and to resuscitate Buddhism in India. These activities led to Dharmapāla's invitation to the World's Parliament of Religions in Chicago in 1893. His well-received speech at this paramount event for the formal debut of Asian religions in the United States established Dharmapāla as the main spokesman of Buddhist revival in South Asia. It was in Chicago in 1893 as well that Carl Theodor Strauss (1852–1937) became the first American to formally convert to Buddhism on American soil. In the years to come Strauss and Dharmapāla worked jointly and traveled extensively around the world to spread Buddhist teachings. Overseas branches of the Mahā Bodhi Society were formed in the United States (1897), Germany (1911), and Great Britain (1926), in this way establishing the society as the first international Buddhist organization and its founder as the first global Buddhist missionary or propagandist.

Buddhism brought by immigrants. A different, nonmodernist, and religiously more tradition-oriented line of Buddhism reached Western countries with the arrival of Chinese and Japanese migrants to the U.S. West Coast and later to South America. Gold had been discovered in California in 1848, and miners from China came in hopes of unearthing a fortune. By the 1880s the number of Chinese in California, Montana, and Idaho had grown to over 100,000 people. Upon their arrival, the immigrants built Chinese temples, the first two in San Francisco in 1853. During the next fifty years hundreds of so-called joss-houses, where Buddhist, Daoist, and Chinese folk traditions mingled, appeared throughout the western United States.

In striking contrast to the high esteem that Buddhist texts and ideas had gained among East Coast intellectuals, Americans on the West Coast devalued East Asian culture as exotic, strange, and incomprehensible. The Chinese laundrymen, cooks, and miners were regarded as unwelcome immigrants. In 1882, the Chinese Exclusion Act restricted further immigration of Chinese nationals. In a similar way, Japanese who had come to the United States in search of work beginning in the 1870s faced racism and social exclusion. Buddhism was regarded as a foreign religion, causing a threat to the relationship between Japanese and American people. Nevertheless, two Jōdo Shinshū priests were sent in 1899 to support the spiritual needs of Japanese laborers, and the Buddhist Mission to North America became formally established in 1914.

More migrants from Japan arrived in Central and South America around the turn of the century. Japanese workers traveled to Mexico and Peru in 1897 and to São Paulo in Brazil in 1908. The laborers intended to work for only a few years on the plantations and then return to Japan. Most often, however, their stay turned into long-term residence. During the first forty years of residence in Brazil, only one Japanese Buddhist temple was established, in Cafelândia in São Paulo in 1932. Japanese workers were expected to assimilate as quickly as possible to Brazilian culture, an expectation that included, among other things, abandoning their "heathen practices" and converting to Roman Catholicism. A fair number did, as the Japanese saw conversion as necessary to the process of Brazilianization. On the other hand, the decision to change their status from sojourner to immigrant resulted in efforts to ensure the preservation of Japanese culture and identity. It was from the 1950s onward, after Japan's defeat in World War II brought an end to the migrants' hopes for return, that Buddhist and Shintō temples became established in Brazil. The Mission of Sōtō Zenshū in Brazil founded Busshinji temple in 1956, followed by the influx of other Buddhist traditions since the 1970s.

As in Brazil, World War II was a watershed for Japanese people in the United States. Acculturative processes had begun during the 1920s and 1930s to meet the needs of the American-born generation; these processes included education programs and such adaptations as referring to Buddhist temples as *churches* and to priestly personnel as *minister* or *reverend.* Paradoxically, adaptation accelerated tremendously during the time of the internment camps. From 1942 to 1945, some 111,000 people of Japanese ancestry were interned, almost 62,000 of them being Buddhists, the majority Jōdo Shinshū. Religious services in the camps were conducted in English, a demand that was later established as the norm. Of similar importance, formerly tight bonds with the mother temples in Japan dissolved. This emancipation from the normative Japanese model was expressed in the organization's new name: No longer a "Mission [from Japan] to North America," it became reincorporated as the Buddhist Churches of America in 1944.

Chinese in the United States remained mostly concentrated in Chinatowns along the West Coast. As the numbers of Chinese dropped due to the Chinese Exclusion Act, so did the number of temples. The other strand of Buddhism in the United States—made up of those who had converted to Buddhism—was no more successful at initiating Buddhist activities during the first half of the twentieth century. The appearance of the Japanese Rinzai Zen monk Sōen Shaku (1859–1919) at the World's Parliament of Religions gave momentum to the practice of Zen meditation, which was strengthened by two disciples sent by Sōen Shaku to the United States: Zen masters Nyōgen Senzaki (1876–1958) and Sokei-an Sasaki (1882–1945). Although they stayed in the United States for years, the meditation groups they set up were met with little interest. It was not until D. T. Suzuki (1870–1966) returned to North America for a long stay in the 1950s that a psychologically reshaped Zen became popular.

BUDDHISM IN EUROPE DURING THE FIRST HALF OF THE TWENTIETH CENTURY. World War I brought an end to the incipient Buddhist movements in Europe. But Buddhism was taken up again immediately after the war, especially in Britain and Germany. In contrast to the early period, Buddhism was now beginning to be practiced, at least by its leading proponents. The teachings were not only to be conceived by the mind, but also applied to the whole person. Religious practices such as spiritual exercises and devotional acts became part of German and British Buddhist life during the 1920s and 1930s.

In 1921 Georg Grimm (1868–1945) and Seidenstücker initiated the Buddhist Parish in Germany. The committed group saw itself expressly as a religious community of Buddhist lay followers. Lectures by Grimm were attended by five hundred to one thousand listeners. In Berlin, Paul Dahlke (1865–1928) built the famous Buddhist House in 1924. In this house, which served as both residence and monastery, Dahlke led the same kind of ascetic and religious life as South Asian Buddhist monks. The divergent interpretations of the teachings of the Pali canon by Grimm and Dahlke led to the formation of two independent schools, which polemically disputed the central teaching of *anattā* (Pali, "no-self"). Both schools continued their work during the Nazi period (1933–1945), albeit restricted to small, private circles that were at times under Nazi political control. Buddhists were regarded by the Nazis as pacifists and eccentrics. With the exception of those who had abandoned their Jewish faith and become Buddhists—about a third of all Buddhists in German-speaking areas during the 1920s—no official or public persecution of Buddhism took place.

In London, Christmas Humphreys (1901–1983) formed the Buddhist Lodge of the Theosophical Society in 1924. A Buddhist shrine room was opened in 1925, and Buddhist festivals were celebrated. As a result of Anagārika Dharmapāla's missionary efforts in Britain during the mid-1920s, British Buddhists founded a branch of the Mahā

Bodhi Society (1926) and established a Buddhist monastery with three resident Theravāda *bhikkhus* (monks) in London (1928–1940, reopened in 1954). It was the first time that several monks resided for an extended period outside of Asia.

In Europe, it was undoubtedly those who had adopted Buddhism as their new orientation in life who dominated the small Buddhist scene. Except for a few Buddhist activists, such as Anagārika Dharmapāla and some Japanese Zen Buddhists, no Buddhist migrants from Asia came to Europe during this time. However, there is an important exception to this pattern: In the early twentieth century, Mongolian Tibetan Buddhists from Kalmykia and Buryatia in Russia established sizeable communities in Saint Petersburg, the czarist Russian capital until 1917. They built a Dge lugs (Geluk) style temple and monastery in Saint Petersburg in 1909 to 1915. The first Buddhist monastery on European soil thus became established not by European convert Buddhists but by so-called ethnic or migrant Buddhists led by the Buryat-Mongol lama Agvan Dorzhev. During the Communist Revolution in 1917, however, the temple was desecrated. Following the comparative calm of the 1920s, Buddhists and scholars were persecuted and murdered under Joseph Stalin's dictatorship (1930s–1953). It was not until the 1980s that conditions improved for Buddhists in Russia, and they were able to establish small communities and centers for different Buddhist traditions.

THE 1950S AND 1960S: SPREAD AND PLURALIZATION. In contrast to the first half of the twentieth century, the second half witnessed a boom of Buddhism outside of Asia. Western countries experienced a heavy influx of Asian immigrants and a tremendously expanded interest in Buddhist meditation, liturgy, and teachings among Westerners. World War II had brought an end to most public Buddhist activities in Europe. However, after 1945 Buddhists reestablished former Theravāda groups or founded new ones. Buddhist lectures were well attended and Buddhist books and journals well received. From the 1950s onwards, new Buddhist traditions were brought to Europe. Japanese Jōdo Shinshū was established in Britain (1952) and Germany (1956). The writings of Suzuki and Eugen Herrigel (1884–1955) popularized Zen meditation and art. Tibetan Buddhism won its first Western converts in Berlin in 1952 through the establishment of the Western branch of the order Arya Maitreya Mandala, founded by the German-born Lama Govinda in 1933 in India. In addition, the activities of Buddhist missionary organizations from South Asia gained momentum, an example being the Lanka Dharmaduta Society, founded in 1952, which sent Theravāda *bhikkhus* to the Berlin Buddhist House with the aim of spreading the *dharma.*

Buddhism spread more and more widely in various European countries as attractive books and translations became more readily available. Simultaneously, Asian teachers began visiting new Buddhist groups to lecture and conduct courses on a regular basis. During the 1960s a considerable change occurred in the way that members and interested people wanted to experience Buddhism both spiritually and physically. Meditation became popular, and Buddhists and sympathizers filled courses in Theravāda *vipassanā* meditation and Japanese Zen meditation. Zen seminars (Jpn., *sesshin*) took place in increasing numbers, with teachers coming from Japan to guide newly formed groups.

In the United States, lecture tours by Suzuki instigated an upsurge of interest in Zen concepts and meditation. At the same time, "Beat Zen" and "Square Zen" created by Allan Watts, Allen Ginsberg, and Jack Kerouac, popularized Zen and attracted members of the emerging counterculture. Japanese teachers such as Sōtō Zen master Shunryu Suzuki settled in the United States as immigration regulations were relaxed during the mid-1950s and 1960s. In addition, various meditation centers were founded as young Americans returned from Japan having received a traditional religious education. Notable among these was Philip Kapleau (1912–2004), author of the instrumental *The Three Pillars of Zen* (1965) and founder of the Rochester Zen Center in New York (1966), and Robert Aitken (b. 1917), founder of the Diamond Sangha in the 1960s. Both were disciples of Zen master Hakuun Yasutani (1885–1974), founder of the Zen school Sanbo Kyodan in 1954. In addition to the explosive interest in Zen meditational practice, further Buddhist traditions arrived from Asia with Sri Lankan, Thai, Chinese, Taiwanese, Korean, and Japanese teachers. Among these traditions and schools, one of the most vigorous turned out to be the Sōka Gakkai from Japan, which claimed a membership of 500,000 people in the mid-1970s.

The first Australian Buddhist organization was founded in 1952, with a membership of mainly well-educated citizens. Leading Australian Buddhists, such as Charles F. Knight (1890–1975) and Natasha Jackson (1902–1990), regarded Buddhism as a triumph of rationalism and used it as a foil in their attacks on Christianity. Their specific approach was strongly intellectualized, and they went to great lengths to prove that Buddhism was fully consonant with scientific thinking. As in Europe and the United States, Zen, Pure Land, and Sōka Gakkai were also imported into Australia during the 1960s.

In general, during this time two characteristics stand out in contrast to the previous phases: Buddhism was no longer dominated by a single main tradition, as had been the case in Europe with Theravāda and in the United States with Mahāyāna Buddhism. Rather, since the 1950s, Buddhist teachers of various traditions arrived from Asia to win converts and to found centers. A plurality of Buddhist traditions emerged, substantially supplemented by the various Buddhist strands formed by immigrant Buddhists. Secondly, the shift from intellectual interest to practical application deepened and spread through increased interest in meditation.

FROM THE 1970S ONWARD: RAPID INCREASE AND ONGOING PLURALIZATION. The Zen boom of the 1960s was followed by an upsurge of interest in Tibetan Buddhism. Tibetan teachers such as Tarthang Tulku (b. 1935) and Chögyam

Trungpa (1939–1987) arrived in the United States in 1969 and 1970 and formed organizations that established European branches during the 1980s. Beginning in the mid-1970s, high-ranking lamas conducted preaching tours in Europe, North America, and Australia, as well in South Africa and South America in later years. Many Westerners who were involved in the protest movements and counterculture of the late 1960s became fascinated by Tibetan Buddhist rituals and symbols and the lives of the lamas. Within two decades, converts to Tibetan Buddhism were able to found a multitude of centers and groups, which at times outnumbered those of all other Buddhist traditions in a given country.

This rapid increase, accompanied by an expansion of existing institutions, led to a considerable rise in the number of Buddhist groups and centers associated with convert Buddhists. In Great Britain, for example, the number of Buddhist organizations nearly quintupled from seventy-four to four hundred between 1979 and 2000. In Germany, interest in Buddhism resulted in an increase from approximately forty to more than six hundred groups, meditation circles, centers, and societies between 1975 and 2004. In North America, Don Morreale's *Complete Guide to Buddhist America* (1998) listed 1,062 meditation centers in 1997, the majority having been founded since the mid-1980s. Similar patterns are observable in Australia, where the number of Buddhist groups rose from 167 to 308 between 1991 and 1998. As a result of large-scale immigration, especially of Vietnamese people, the number of Buddhists in Australia multiplied more than six times from 35,000 to 200,000 from 1981 to 1996. As in Europe and North America, numerous schools, branches, and traditions of Theravāda, Mahāyāna, Tibetan, and nonsectarian Buddhism have gained a firm standing in Australia, and in New Zealand as well.

In a parallel development, considerable numbers of Buddhists from Asian countries have come to Western Europe, North America, and Australia since the 1960s. In Europe, and France in particular, large communities of refugees from Vietnam, Laos, and Cambodia have emerged. Paris has become the center for Southeast Asian Buddhist migrants, although the largest Vietnamese pagoda in Europe was inaugurated in Hanover, Germany, in 1991. Furthermore, many refugees, migrants, and business people from Asian countries have found asylum or a place to work in Western Europe. Similarly, in Canada and the United States hundreds of thousands of migrants arrived after immigration regulations were relaxed in the mid-1960s.

Whether in North America, Western Europe, or Australia, in the process of settling down, migrants established their own religious and cultural institutions to preserve their identity and heritage. By visiting pagodas and temples, performing customary acts of devotional worship, and jointly celebrating Buddhist festivals, immigrant Asian Buddhists gained a home away from home. Most Asian migrant communities have turned out to be markedly conservative, presenting a primarily stable and familiar environment for their members in the socioculturally foreign and often discriminatory environment. With the rise of second and third generations of immigrants from Asia, established role models and hierarchies are changing, and Asians in the West are pointing to language issues and calling for acculturated rituals, forms, and contents. Estimates of the total numbers of Buddhists in Europe at the beginning of the twenty-first century amount to around one million, two thirds of them Asian immigrants. In North America the number may be four to five times higher than in Europe, with Buddhists of Asian ancestry making up the vast majority.

Buddhism grew as well in both South America and South Africa beginning in the 1970s. Zen has captured the interest of non-Japanese Brazilians since the late 1970s, resulting in the establishment of numerous local meditation groups and centers. Likewise, Japanese traditions of Nichiren, Shingon, and Pure Land have gained followings. Tibetan Buddhism, arriving in Brazil the late 1980s, also experienced a boom during the 1990s. As in other non-Asian countries to which Buddhism spread, a plurality of schools and traditions has become established.

In South Africa, after an attempt to convert Indian migrant Hindus to Buddhism beginning in 1917, small Buddhist groups were formed during the 1970s in metropolitan centers. The emphasis was a nondenominational one, although followers of Tibetan, Zen, or Theravāda came together for joint meetings. One of South Africa's main Buddhist reference points became the Buddhist Retreat Center near Ixopo, formally inaugurated in 1980. In contrast to a prevalent ecumenical spirit, since the mid-1980s the various groups have begun sharpening their doctrinal identity and lineage adherence, and in many cases hitherto loose bonds with the Asian parent tradition or headquarters were strengthened. During the 1990s, Tibetan Buddhism gained a strong following as teachers started to stay permanently in South Africa. Likewise, Zen teachers and Theravāda *bhikkhus* settled in the country and firmly established their traditions.

Plurality and Global Interconnectedness. Buddhism outside of Asia is deeply marked by its plurality and heterogeneity. A multitude of schools and traditions have successfully settled in urbanized, industrialized settings. The general traditions of Theravāda, Mahāyāna, and Tibetan Buddhism are internally heavily subdivided according to country of origin (e.g., Theravāda from Sri Lanka, Thailand, Myanmar, or Laos); lineage (e.g., Tibetan Buddhism following Dge lugs [Geluk], Karma Bka' brgyud [Kagyu], Sa skya [Sakya], or Rnying ma [Nyingma]; teacher (Asian and Western, manifold); and emphasis on specific Buddhist concepts and practices. Flourishing in the West, these various Asian-derived schools and traditions did not remain unchanged, and various subschools have evolved. In addition, a second generation of Western teachers who are disciples to Western, not Asian masters, is maturing. These multifold developments have given birth to both traditionally oriented centers and to independent centers favoring innovation and the creation of a "Western Buddhism." Noteworthy examples of the latter include the Insight Meditation Society in the United States and the Friends of the Western Buddhist Order, founded by the British Sangharakshita in 1967.

The marked plurality of Buddhism outside of Asia has been intensified by the globalization of once local organizations. The British-based Friends of the Western Buddhist Order has spread worldwide. Organizations formerly restricted to the United States, such as the Insight Meditation Society or Aitken's Diamond Sangha, have established branch centers in Europe, Australia, and elsewhere. This global reach also came to apply to American Zen teachers, including Richard Baker Rōshi, Bernard Glassman Rōshi, and Prabhasadharma Rōshi, as well as to prominent Vietnamese and Korean meditation masters, including Thich Nhat Hanh and Seung Sahn. Tibetan Buddhist organizations have created similar global networks. Lamas and teachers tour the globe untiringly, and they visit the multitude of local groups and centers, including Chögyam Trungpa's Vajradhātu organization (renamed Shambhala International), the Karma Kagyu centers affiliated with Ole Nydahl from Denmark, Sogyal Rinpoche's Rigpa organization, or the New Kadampa Tradition of Geshe Kelsang Gyatso.

Global interconnectedness has become greatly intensified as a result of the World Wide Web. Buddhist centers maintain their own websites, linked to sister centers and parent organizations, and facilitating the exchange and spread of information. Numerous so-called cyber-*saṃghas* are available online, thus establishing a new form of Buddhist community. In these ways Buddhism adapts, as it has done continuously during its 2,600 years of history, to new cultural, political, and technological environments.

BIBLIOGRAPHY

On ancient and premodern encounters between Buddhism and the West, see the following instructive studies: Raymond Schwab, *The Oriental Renaissance: Europe's Discovery of India and the East, 1680–1880* (New York, 1984); Wilhelm Halbfass, *India and Europe: An Essay in Understanding* (Albany, N.Y., 1988), and the introductory chapters in Stephen Batchelor, *The Awakening of the West: The Encounter of Buddhism and Western Culture* (Berkeley, Calif., 1994).

Due to the wide-ranging institutionalization and explosive growth of Buddhism in the closing decades of the twentieth century, the 1990s saw an increase of descriptive and analytical studies focusing on specific countries outside of Asia. Developments in the United States have been covered by numerous studies. The first encompassing overviews by Charles S. Prebish, *American Buddhism* (North Scituate, Mass., 1979), and Rick Field, *How the Swans Came to the Lake: A Narrative History of Buddhism in America* (Boulder, Colo., 1981; 3d rev. ed., 1992), were enriched by Thomas A. Tweed's historical and analytical account in *The American Encounter with Buddhism 1844–1912: Victorian Culture and the Limits of Dissent* (Bloomington, Ind., 1992; reprint, 2000). Insightful overviews and analyses of Buddhism's plurality and processes of Americanization include Charles S. Prebish and Kenneth K. Tanaka, eds., *The Faces of Buddhism in America* (Berkeley, Calif., 1998); Charles S. Prebish, *Luminous Passage: The Practice and Study of Buddhism in America* (Berkeley, Calif., 1999); Richard Hugh Seager, *Buddhism in America* (New York, 1999); and Duncan Ryūken Williams and Christopher S. Queen, eds., *American Buddhism: Methods and Findings in Recent Scholarship* (Richmond, Va., 1999). Further research focusing on specific traditions includes a portrait of prominent American Zen teachers by Helen Tworkow, *Zen in America: Five Teachers and the Search for an American Buddhism* (New York, 1989; reprint, 1994); an instructive study by Jane D. Hurst, *Nichiren Shoshu Buddhism and the Soka Gakkai in America: The Ethos of a New Religious Movement* (New York, 1992); and an analytical description of immigrant temples built by South Asian Buddhists by Paul David Numrich, *Old Wisdom in the New World: Americanization in Two Immigrant Theravada Buddhist Temples* (Knoxville, Tenn., 1996).

Compared to this wealth of studies, Buddhism in Canada has been covered only in a chapter by Bruce Matthew in Charles S. Prebish and Martin Baumann, eds., *Westward Dharma: Buddhism beyond Asia* (Berkeley, Calif., 2002), and in Janet McLellan's study on immigrant communities and temples, *Many Petals of the Lotus: Five Asian Buddhist Communities in Toronto* (Toronto, 1999).

Most studies of Buddhism in Europe have focused on specific countries. The early history of Buddhism in Great Britain was covered by one of its key figures, Christmas Humphreys, in *Sixty Years of Buddhism in England (1907–1967): A History and a Survey* (London, 1968). This was followed by the more scholarly study by Ian Oliver, *Buddhism in Britain* (London, 1979). Helen Waterhouse's *Authority and Adaptation: A Case Study in British Buddhism* (Leeds, U.K., 1997) provides in-depth studies of the various Buddhist groups in Bath, whereas Bryan Wilson and Karel Dobbelaere offer a profound sociological investigation of the Sōka Gakkai in *A Time to Chant: The Soka Gakkai Buddhists in Britain* (Oxford, 1994).

The history of Buddhism in Germany is covered in Martin Baumann's detailed study *Deutsche Buddhisten: Geschichte und Gemeinschaften* (Marburg, Germany, 1993; 2d ed., 1995). Various articles by Baumann provide information in English of Buddhism's past and present in Germany. A mine of information can be found in two volumes on the lives of about 130 early German Buddhists by Hellmuth Hecker, *Lebensbilder deutscher Buddhisten: Ein bio-bibliographisches Handbuch* (Konstanz, Germany, 1996/1997). A valuable addition to these are interviews with ten contemporary leading German Buddhists by Detlef Kantowsky, *Wegzeichen-Gespräche über buddhistische Praxis* (Konstanz, Germany, 1991; rev. ed., Ulm, Germany, 1994).

Buddhism in France with a focus on Tibetan Buddhism was treated by Lionel Obadia, *Bouddhisme et Occident: La diffusion du bouddhisme tibétan en France* (Paris, 1999). A sociological study of convert Buddhists is Frédéric Lenoir, *Le bouddhisme en France* (Paris, 1999); the same author describes the encounter of Buddhism and the West in *La rencontre du bouddhisme et de l'Occident* (Paris, 1999). Catherine Choron-Baix provides one of the rare studies on immigrant Laotian Buddhists in France in *Bouddhisme et migration: La reconstitution d'une paroisse bouddhiste Lao en banlieue parisienne* (Paris, 1986).

Further country-specific documentation exists, for example, for Italy, Switzerland, Austria, the Netherlands, Norway, and Russia. The online annotated bibliography by Martin Baumann, "Buddhism in Europe," listed about 380 titles in 2001. It is available from http://www.globalbuddhism.org/bib-bud.html.

The history of Buddhism in Australia is well documented in Paul Croucher's *Buddhism in Australia, 1848–1988* (Kensington, U.K., 1989). Enid Adam and Philip J. Hughes give a picture of Buddhism's growth and composition by an analysis of census data in *Religious Community Profiles: The Buddhists in Australia* (Canberra, Australia, 1996). Michelle Spuler's *Facets of the Diamond: Developments in Australian Buddhism* (Richmond, U.K., 2002) describes the history and modes of adaptation of Robert Aitken's Diamond Sangha in Australia.

Buddhism in South Africa is covered by a small informative book edited by Michel Clasquin and Kobus Krüger, *Buddhism and Africa* (Pretoria, South Africa, 1999). Cristina Moreira da Rocha has set up an online bibliography on "Buddhism in Brazil," which is linked to the *Journal of Global Buddhism*, available from http://www.globalbuddhism.org. This journal also provides bibliographies on Buddhism in Australia, South Africa, Europe, the United States, and Canada.

Two prominent themes in studies on Western Buddhism are engaged Buddhism and the role and importance of women in establishing Buddhism in the West. Kenneth Kraft's *The Wheel of Engaged Buddhism: A New Map of the Path* (New York, 1999) focuses on Buddhism and sociopolitical engagement, as does Christopher S. Queen, ed., *Engaged Buddhism in the West* (Boston, 2000). Edited by one of the leading Buddhist women in the West, Karma Lekshe Tsomo's *Buddhism through American Women's Eyes* (Ithaca, N.Y., 1995) provides thirteen first-person accounts of Buddhist lives in the United States. Valuable additions are Marianne Dresser, ed., *Buddhist Women on the Edge: Contemporary Perspectives from the Dharma Frontier* (Berkeley, Calif., 1996), which includes twenty-five essays by American convert Buddhist women; and Sandy Boucher's *Opening the Lotus: A Women's Guide to Buddhism* (Boston, 1997).

Finally, comprehensive analyses of Buddhism in the West can be found in Stephen Batchelor's masterfully written narrative, *The Awakening of the West: The Encounter of Buddhism and Western Culture* (Berkeley, Calif., 1994), as well as in the broad-based scholarly volume edited by Charles S. Prebish and Martin Baumann, *Westward Dharma: Buddhism Beyond Asia* (Berkeley, 2002). Online sources on Buddhism in the West multiplied during the 1990s and early 2000s; notable online resources include the Australia-based BuddhaNet, available from http://www.buddhanet.net; the online *Journal of Buddhist Ethics*, available from http://jbe.gold.ac.uk; and the *Journal of Global Buddhism*, available from http://www.globalbuddhism.org. All provide links to the multitude of homepages on specific Buddhist traditions, schools, and centers.

MARTIN BAUMANN (2005)

BUDDHISM, SCHOOLS OF

This entry consists of the following articles:

EARLY DOCTRINAL SCHOOLS OF BUDDHISM
MAHĀYĀNA PHILOSOPHICAL SCHOOLS OF BUDDHISM
TANTRIC RITUAL SCHOOLS OF BUDDHISM [FIRST EDITION]
TANTRIC RITUAL SCHOOLS OF BUDDHISM [FURTHER CONSIDERATIONS]
TIBETAN AND MONGOLIAN BUDDHISM
HIMALAYAN BUDDHISM
CHINESE BUDDHISM
JAPANESE BUDDHISM
EAST ASIAN BUDDHISM

BUDDHISM, SCHOOLS OF: EARLY DOCTRINAL SCHOOLS OF BUDDHISM

The term *Hīnayāna* refers to the group of Buddhist schools or sects that appeared before the beginning of the common era and those directly derived from them. The word *Hīnayāna*, which means "small vehicle," that is, "lesser means of progress" toward liberation, is pejorative. It was applied disdainfully to these early forms of Buddhism by the followers of the great reformist movement that arose just at the beginning of the common era, which referred to itself as the Mahāyāna, or "large vehicle," that is, "greater means of progress" toward liberation. Indeed, the adherents of the Mahāyāna charged those of the Hīnayāna with selfishly pursuing only their own personal salvation, whereas they themselves claimed an interest in the liberation of all beings and vowed to postpone their own deliverance until the end of time. In other words, the ideal of the practitioners of the Hīnayāna was the *arhat* (Pali, *arahant*), the saint who has attained *nirvāṇa*, while that of the Mahāyāna was the *bodhisattva*, the all-compassionate hero who, resolving to become a Buddha in some far-distant future, dedicated the course of his innumerable lives to saving beings of all kinds. It would be more correct to give the name "early Buddhism" to what is called Hīnayāna, for the term denotes the whole collection of the most ancient forms of Buddhism: those earlier than the rise of the Mahāyāna and those that share the same inspiration as these and have the same ideal, namely the *arhat.*

Although it is directly descended from the earliest Buddhism—that originally preached by the Buddha himself—this early Buddhism is distinguished from it by the continual additions and reformulations of its adherents and teachers in their desire to deepen and perfect the interpretation of the ancient teaching. This constant, and quite legitimate, effort gave rise to many debates, controversies, and divisions that resulted in the appearance of a score of sects or schools. The actual, original teaching of the Buddha is accessible to us only through the canonic texts of these schools, texts that were set down in writing only about the beginning of the common era and reflect the divergences that already existed among these sects. Moreover, only a very small part of this vast canonic literature has survived, either in its original Indian language or in Chinese or Tibetan translation, and for this reason our knowledge of the doctrine taught by the Buddha himself still remains rather vague and conjectural. We do not possess all the documents necessary to recover it with certainty: even by compiling all the doctrinal and other elements common to the canonic texts we do have, we can reach, at best, only a stage of Buddhist doctrine immediately prior to the divergence of these schools. Their texts have been preserved for us by the mere chances of history.

The Indic word, both Sanskrit and Pali, that we translate here as "school" or "sect" is *nikāya,* meaning, properly, "group." In our context, it refers to a group of initiates, most likely monks (*bhikṣus*) rather than laymen, who sincerely profess to be faithful disciples of the Buddha but are distinguishable from other similar groups in that they base their beliefs on a body of canonic texts that differs from others to a greater or lesser extent. These differences between canonic texts involve not only their wording or written form but also a certain number of doctrinal elements and rules of monastic discipline. Despite the disaggregative pressures to which they were exposed (the same pressures, indeed, that created them), despite their geographical expansion and sometimes considerable dispersion, and notwithstanding the vicissitudes of history, which often posed new problems for them, most of these groups preserved a remarkable internal cohesiveness throughout several centuries. Still, schisms did occur within many of them, leading to the formation of new schools. Moreover, to judge from the documents we have—though these are unfortunately very scarce—it seems that relations among these various groups were generally good. Their disputes remained at the level of more or less lively discussion and degenerated into more serious conflicts only when involving questions of economics or politics.

Several factors account for these divisions and for the formation of these sects or schools. First of all, the Buddhist monastic community (*saṃgha*) never knew a supreme authority, imposing its unity by powerful and diverse methods, as was long the case in Christianity with its papacy. If we believe some canonic texts that seem to faithfully reflect reality, the Buddha himself was probably faced with several instances of insubordination on the part of certain groups of his monks and was not always able to overcome them. The oldest traditions, furthermore, agree that he did not designate a successor to head the community but only counseled his followers to remain faithful to his Doctrine (Dharma). This was a fragile defense against the forces that tried to break up the community once it was "orphaned" by the death of its founder.

For at least five centuries, the Buddha's teaching was actually preserved by oral transmission alone, very probably in different, though related, dialects. This, and the absence of an authoritative ecclesiastical hierarchy in the *saṃgha,* constitute two obvious sources of progressive distortion and alteration of the message left by the Blessed One to his immediate disciples. Furthermore, this message was not entirely clear or convincing to everyone it addressed, leading Buddhist preachers to furnish explanations and interpretations of the teaching. Finally, the teaching given by the Buddha was far from a complete system containing solutions to all the problems that might occur to the minds of people as diverse as those it was destined to reach. Thus, monks and lay disciples, as well as people outside Buddhism but curious and interested in its doctrine—*brahman* opponents, Jains, and others—easily found numerous flaws, errors, and contradictions in the teaching. These troubled the *saṃgha* but pleased those who were determined to refute or discredit it. Although the Buddhist preachers who improvised answers to these varied questions and objections were guided by what they knew and understood of the Buddha's teaching, their attempts expanded upon the original teaching and at the same time inevitably created new causes for differences and disputes within the heart of the community itself.

According to some eminent scholars, we must distinguish Buddhist "sects" from "schools." Sects, under this interpretation, were invariably born from serious dissent over issues of monastic discipline. Such dissent resulted in a fracturing of the community, a *saṃghabheda,* or schism, the participants in which ceased to live together or carry on a common religious life. By contrast, schools were differentiated by divergences of opinion on doctrinal points, but their dissension in these matters never gave rise to actual schisms or open hostility. This interpretation is certainly attractive, but it must be mitigated somewhat by the recognition that the actual situation prevailing between the various communities of the early church was somewhat more complex and variable than that indicated by the theory advanced here.

ORIGIN AND RELATIONSHIP OF THE SECTS AND SCHOOLS. All the documents from which we can draw information about the origin of the early Buddhist groups were written after the beginning of the common era and are therefore unreliable. Nevertheless, since the oldest of these texts generally agree on the main points, we can attempt to restore with a certain amount of confidence the common tradition from which they derive. This should provide a fairly accurate reflection of the true interrelationships among the sects and schools.

The first division of the community probably occurred toward the middle of the fourth century BCE, some time after the council of Vaiśālī but having no direct connection with this event, the claims of the Sinhala (Theravāda) tradition notwithstanding. The schism was probably caused by a number of disagreements on the nature of the *arhat*s, who, according to some authorities, retained imperfections even though they had attained *nirvāṇa* in this world. Because they were more numerous, the supporters of these ideas formed a group called the Mahāsāṃghikas, "those of the larger community"; their opponents, who claimed to remain faithful to the teaching of the Buddha's first disciples and denied that the *arhat* could retain any imperfections, took the name Sthaviravādins, "those who speak as the elders" or "those who teach the doctrine of the old ones."

Each of these two groups were then, in turn, divided progressively into several sects or schools. Although we are in little doubt about their origins as Mahāsāṃghikas or

Sthaviravādins, we often do not know precisely how these subsequent sects were linked with the first two groups, nor do we know the circumstances or time in which they appeared. We are particularly bereft of information about the sects and schools that arose directly or indirectly from the Mahāsāṃghika.

Among the groups that developed from the Mahāsāṃghika were the Ekavyāvahārika, then the Gokulika, and finally the Caitika schools. The Ekavyāvahārika probably gave rise, in turn, to the Lokottaravādins, but it may be that the Lokottaravādins were simply a form taken by the Ekavyāvahārikas at a particular time because of the evolution of their doctrine. From the Gokulikas came the Bahuśrutīyas and the Prajñaptivādins. At least a part of the Caitika school settled in southern India, on the lower Krishna River, shortly before the beginning of the common era. From them two important sects soon arose: the Pūrvaśailas and the Aparaśailas, then a little later the Rājagirikas and the Siddhārthikas. Together, the four sects formed Andhraka group, which took its name from the area (Andhra) where they thrived during the first few centuries CE.

The Sthaviravāda group seems to have remained united until about the beginning of the third century BCE, when the Vātsīputrīyas, who maintained the existence of a quasi-autonomous "person" (*pudgala*), split off. A half century later, probably during the reign of Aśoka (consecrated c. 268 BCE), the Sarvāstivādins also separated from the non-Vātsīputrīya Sthaviravādins and settled in northwest India. This time the dispute was over the Sarvāstivādin notion that "everything exists" (*sarvam asti*). In the beginning of the second century, the remaining Sthaviravādins, who appear to have taken at this time the name Vibhajyavādins, "those who teach discrimination," to distinguish themselves from the Sarvāstivādins, found themselves divided once again. Out of this dispute were born the Mahīśāsakas and the Dharmaguptakas, who opposed each other over whether the Buddha, properly speaking, belonged to the monastic community and over the relative value of offerings made to the Blessed One and those made to the community. At an unknown date about the beginning of the common era four new groups sprang from the Vātsīputrīyas: the Dharmottarīyas, the Bhadrayānīyas, the Ṣaṇṇagarikas, and the Sammatīyas. The Sammatīyas, who were very important in Indian Buddhism, later gave rise to the Avantaka and the Kurukulla schools. One group broke from the Sarvāstivādins: the Sautrāntikas, who can be identified with the Dārṣṭāntikas and the Saṃkrāntivādins.

Some of the Vibhajyavādins settled in southern India and Lanka in the mid-third century BCE and seem to have maintained fairly close relations for some time with the Mahīśāsakas, whose presence is attested in the same area. Adopting Pali as a canonical language and energetically claiming their teaching to be the strict orthodoxy, they took the name Theravādins, a Pali form of the Sanskrit Sthaviravādins. Like the Sthaviravādins, they suffered from internal squabbles and divisions: some years before the common era, the Abhayagirivāsins split from the Mahāvihāras, founded at the time of the arrival of Buddhism in Lanka; later, in the fourth century, the Jetavanīyas appeared.

Finally, three sects derived from the Sthaviravādins present some problems regarding their precise relationship and identity. The Kāśyapīyas, whose basic position was a compromise between those of the Sarvāstivādins and the Vibhajyavādins, apparently broke from the latter shortly after the split that created the Sarvāstivāda and Vibhajyavāda *nikāyas*. More mysterious are the Haimavatas, about whom the facts are both scarce and contradictory. As for the Mūlasarvāstivādins, or "radical Sarvāstivādins," they appeared suddenly at the end of the seventh century with a huge "basket of discipline" (Vinaya Piṭaka) in Sanskrit, much different in many respects from that of the earlier Sarvāstivādins. It is impossible to determine exactly what connection the Mūlasarvāstivādins had with the Sarvāstivādins.

Except for a few of the more important of these sects and schools—such as the Theravādins, who left us the treasure of their celebrated Sinhala chronicles—we know nothing of the history of these different groups. Their existence is nevertheless assured, thanks to the testimony of a fair number of inscriptions and other substantial documents. To judge from the information given by Xuanzang and Yijing, by the time they made their long visits to India in the seventh century, most of the sects had already disappeared. Of all the many groups descended from the original Mahāsāṃghikas, only the Lokottaravādins were still numerous and thriving, but only in a very specific location, Bamian (Bāmiyān, in present-day Afghanistan).

Here arises an important question, one whose answer is still uncertain: what connections existed between these early Buddhist sects and schools, known as Hīnayāna, and the groups formed by the followers of the Mahāyāna? Were any of them—in particular those of Mahāsāṃghika origin—converted in large numbers to the Mahāyāna, or did they perhaps give birth to it through the natural evolution of their doctrine? Should we interpret in this sense the expression Mahāyāna-Sthaviravādin, which Xuanzang used to refer to numerous Buddhist communities he encountered throughout India, and deduce from it that their followers were Sthaviravādins converted to the Mahāyāna? Or did believers of both groups live together, without mingling, in the areas where they were found? This second interpretation strikes one as more satisfactory; nevertheless, the first cannot be rejected definitively.

Geographical Distribution. Two types of records inform us about the geographical distribution of the sects and schools: inscriptions and the reports of a number of Chinese pilgrims who came to India. Numbering only a few tens and ranging in time between the second century BCE and the sixth century CE, the inscriptions that mention early sects give us only spotty and very insufficient data. Although they may actually attest to the presence of a given group in a specific place at a particular date, they leave us completely ignorant about the presence or absence of this sect in other places and at other times. The information supplied by the Chinese travelers, principally Xuanzang and to a lesser extent Yijing, is incomparably more complete, but it is valid only for the seventh century, when their journeys took place.

The study of these two kinds of sources—like that of the Sinhala chronicles, which are concerned mostly with Sri Lankan Buddhism—reveals some important general features about the early Buddhist schools. None of the groups was present everywhere throughout India and its neighboring countries; on the other hand, no area was the exclusive domain of any one group. For reasons that unfortunately nearly always escape us, certain groups were in the majority in some places, in the minority in others, and completely absent in still others but, as far as we can tell, coexisted in varying proportions with other groups wherever they were found. For example, in a number of places—especially those that history or legend made holy in the eyes of Buddhist devotees and were important places of pilgrimage—the monks of various sects lived together in neighboring monasteries and often venerated the same sacred objects—topes (*stūpas*), bodhi trees, and others. This was the case not only in the holy places in the Ganges Basin, where the major events in the Buddha's life occurred, but also far from there, in Sāñchī, Karlī, Amarāvatī, Nāgārjunikoṇḍa, and elsewhere. In Sri Lanka, the three great monasteries that became the centers of the three subsects of the Theravāda, the Mahāvihāra, the Abhaya-giri, and the Jetavana, were located on the outskirts of the island's ancient capital, Anuradhapura.

All of the sects and schools seem to have been present in the middle Ganges Basin, which is easily understandable since the principal places of pilgrimage were located there. The more important ones, which originated in both the Mahāsāṃghika and Sthaviravāda groups, also appear to have coexisted in eastern India, Bengal, and nearby areas, at least in the seventh century, as reported by both Xuanzang and Yijing.

The Theravādins always dominated most of Sri Lanka and still do today. In the eleventh century, they also largely converted the Burmese, followed a little later by the people of Thailand, Cambodia, and Laos, where they continue to exercise religious dominion today. In the seventh century, the Vibhajyavāda Sthaviravādins, who were very close, if not identical, to the Theravādins, likewise controlled all the Tamil country, the part of India nearest to Sri Lanka, and were also extremely numerous in the coastal region north of Bombay and near Buddhist holy places on the Ganges from which people embarked on journeys to Lanka and southern India.

Very little is known about the location of the sects most closely related to these. The presence of the Mahīśāsakas is recorded both in the Indian northwest, on the banks of the Krishna, and in Sri Lanka; that of the Dharmaguptakas in the Indian northwest only; and that of the Kāśyapīyas mostly in the Indian northwest but also around Bombay. The Sarvāstivādins were clearly in a majority over all of northwest India, from the upper Ganges Basin to Kashmir, from the mid-third century BCE to at least the seventh century CE.

In the seventh century, the Sammatīyas formed the sect comprising the largest number of monks and generally controlled all of western India, from the middle Indus Valley to southeast of Bombay. They were also very numerous throughout the Ganges Basin and in eastern India. Several inscriptions testify to the presence, at the beginning of the common era, of Dharmottarīyas and Bhadrayānīyas in the area of Bombay.

Data concerning the Mahāsāṃghika proper, and most of the sects that developed from it, are rare and widely scattered. We know for certain that the Mahāsāṃghika existed in northwestern India, around Bombay and on the banks of the lower Krishna. Caitikas also inhabited these last two areas but primarily the second, where Bahuśrutīyas also resided. By the seventh century, the Lokottaravādins had made Bamian, in the heart of present-day Afghanistan, one of the main centers of Buddhism in the Indo-Iranian realms and were still very numerous there, as Xuanzang reports. The Pūrvaśailas, Aparaśailas, Rājagirikas, and Siddhārtikas prospered during the first centuries of the common era in the lower Krishna Valley, which they covered with magnificent monuments, but by the beginning of the seventh century they had almost disappeared.

MAJOR DOCTRINAL DIFFERENCES. We are well acquainted with the principal doctrinal differences that gave rise to many of these schools, the basic ideas that distinguish them, and the reactions and rebuttals the various sects offered each other. In most cases, though, and particularly with regard to the apparently less important sects, our information is unfortunately too vague, and sometimes even contradictory or nonexistent, to tell us anything about the specifics of their doctrine.

Although many questions divided all or some of the schools, they did not provoke the formation of new sects. These debates were sometimes very important for the evolution of Buddhism as a whole. Often, various of the early sects that we might expect to hold similar views given their genesis in fact adopted doctrinal opinions at great variance with one another. Thus, there often came about, among schools with similar opinions on specific questions, entirely different regroupings from those one would expect in light of their traditional relationships. Let us first examine the fundamental ideas that appear to have brought about the formation of the principal sects.

The Mahāsāṃghikas probably separated from the Sthaviravādins over the belief that certain *arhats*, although they had attained *nirvāṇa* in this world, could be subject to nocturnal defilements as a result of erotic dreams; that they still harbored vestiges of ignorance; that they had areas of doubt on matters outside Buddhist doctrine; that they could be informed, indeed saved, by other people; and, finally, that they utter certain words when they meditated on the Path of Liberation. The Sthaviravādins denied these five possibilities, arguing that the *arhat* is completely free of all imperfections.

The Vātsīputrīyas and the schools that later developed from them, the Sammatīyas and others, believed in the existence of a "person" (*pudgala*) who is neither identical to the five aggregates (*skandhas*) that make up the living being nor different from them; neither within these five aggregates nor outside them. Although differing from the Brahmanic "soul" (*ātman*), denied unanimously by Buddhist doctrine, this "person" lives on from one existence to the next, thus ensuring the continuing identities of the agent of an act and of the being who suffers its effects in this life or the next. All the other schools rejected this hypothesis, maintaining the logical impossibility of conceptualizing this "person" and seeing in it simply a disguised form of the *ātman.*

The Sarvāstivādins claimed that "everything exists" (*sarvam asti*), that is, that the past and the future have real and material existence. This belief enabled them to explain several phenomena that were very important to Buddhists: the act of consciousness, which is made up of several successive, individual mental actions; memory or consciousness of the past; foresight or consciousness of the future; and the "ripening" (*vipāka*) of "actions" (*karman*), which takes place over a longer or shorter span of time, often exceeding the length of a single life. For the other sects, however, it was perfectly clear that what is past exists no longer and that what is to come does not yet exist.

The Kāśyapīyas, also called Suvarsṣkas, maintained a position between these two, namely, that a past action that has not yet borne fruit exists, but the rest of the past does not. This approach, however, satisfied neither the Sarvāstivādins nor their critics.

The Sautrāntikas distinguished themselves from the Sarvāstivādins insofar as they considered the canonic "basket of sermons" (Sūtra Piṭaka) to be the only one to contain the authentic words of the Buddha, whereas the "basket of higher teaching" (Abhidharma Piṭaka) is the work of the Blessed One's disciples. According to some of our sources, the Sautrāntikas were also called Saṃkrāntivādins because they held that the five aggregates (*skandhas*) constituting the living being "transmigrate" (*saṃkrānti*) from one existence to the next; probably this should be understood to mean that, in their view, four of these aggregates were absorbed at the moment of death into the fifth, a subtle consciousness. It also seems that the Sautrāntikas can be identified with the Dārṣṭāntikas, who were often criticized in the Sarvastivada writings and apparently gained their name because of their frequent use of comparisons or parables (*dṛṣṭātas*) in their discussions.

An important disagreement separated the Mahīśāsakas from the Dharmaguptakas. For the former, the Buddha is part of the monastic community (*saṃgha*); hence a gift given to the community produces a "great fruit" (*māhaphalam*), but one directed specifically to the Buddha does not. The Dharmaguptakas, on the other hand, held that the Buddha is separate from the community, and as he is far superior to it—since it is composed only of his followers—only the gift given to the Buddha produces a great fruit. These two opposing views had considerable influence on the religious practices of early Buddhism.

The Lokottaravādins differed from other Mahāsāṃghika schools in holding that the Buddhas are "otherworldly" (*lokottara*), a word having several very different senses but which they employed loosely to attribute an extraordinary nature to the Buddhas. According to them, the Buddhas are otherworldly not only because their thought is always perfectly pure but also because they remain outside and above the world. Thus it would seem to be among the Lokottaravādins that we should seek the origin of Buddhist docetism, that is, the distinction between the real, transcendent, and infinite Buddha, the "body of doctrine" (*dharmakāya*), and the apparent Buddha, the "body of magical creation" (*nirmāṇakāya*)—a kind of phantom emanating from the real one. To rescue beings, the *nirmāṇakāya* becomes incarnate, taking on their form and thus seeming to be born, to grow up, to discover and preach the doctrine of enlightenment, and to finally die and become completely extinguished. The Lokottaravādins must have also extolled the extraordinary character of the *bodhisattva,* undoubtedly on account of their supernatural conception of the Buddhas. These singular notions lead one to believe that this sect played an important part in the formation of the Mahāyāna, whose teaching adopted and developed similar ideas.

As their name seems to indicate, the Prajñaptivādins were probably distinguished from the other schools that arose from the Mahāsāṃghika group because they taught that all things are mere products of linguistic convention (*prajñapti*) and, hence, are devoid of actual existence. One might see here the origin of the famous theory of the universal "void" (*śūnyatā*), which is one of the basic elements of the Mahāyāna doctrine and is the main theme, reiterated with the greatest insistence, of its oldest works, the first Prajñāpāramitā Sūtras.

Unfortunately, we do not know the basic premises of the other schools, whether they arose from the Sthaviravāda group or the Mahāsāṃghika. The data that have come down to us concerning a few of them, such as the Gokulikas (also called Kukkuṭikas), the Bahuśrutīyas, the Sammatīyas, and some others, are very doubtful, vague, or extremely obscure, even contradictory. For others, we possess no information at all.

As noted above, hundreds of controversies also set the various schools apart from one another without provoking new divisions of the community. Most of these debates apparently concerned only two or three sects and lasted for a short time—unless this impression is due solely to our lack of information. On the other hand, certain of these arguments affected, and even impassioned, a large number of schools for long periods, sometimes for centuries, as evidenced by the treatises and commentaries on canonic texts that have come down to us. In these more important controversies the distribution of the sects between the two opposing camps is often independent of their derivational connections. It may be that relations of good neighborliness and, hence, ties based on geographical distribution favored such doctrinal alliances. In any case, I will point out the most significant of these divergences of opinion, which are important features in the history of early Buddhist thought.

The Sarvāstivādins, the Sammatīyas, and the Pūrvaśailas firmly believed in an "intermediate existence" (*antarābhava*) that linked death and rebirth. This concept was rejected by the Theravādins and the Mahāsāṃghikas. The latter, along with the Andhakas and the Sarvāstivādins, maintained that the *bodhisattva* may be born in the so-called evil existences *(durgati),* even in the various hells, to lighten the sufferings of the beings who live in them. The Theravādins denied that this was possible because, in their view, of the automatic retribution consequent upon all actions, a retribution that completely determines the circumstances of rebirths. According to the Vātsīputrīyas, the Sammatīyas, the Sarvāstivādins, and the Pūrvaśailas, the *arhats* could backslide in varying degrees and even lose *nirvāṇa,* but the Theravādins, Mahāsāṃghikas, and Sautrāntikas refused to accept this idea. The Theravādins, the Sarvāstivādins, and the Dharmaguptakas agreed that it was possible for the gods to practice the sexual abstinence (*brahmacarya*) of ascetics, whereas the Sammatīyas and the Mahīśāsakas judged this impossible. For the Theravādins and the Sarvāstivādins, there were only five fates (*gatis*), namely, those of gods, men, animals, starving ghosts (*pretas*), and the damned, but the Andhakas and the Vātsīputrīyas added another, that of the *asuras,* the superhuman beings who were adversaries of the gods (*devas*) yet were not devils in the Christian sense.

The Mahāsāṃghikas, the Theravādins, and the Mahīśāsakas taught that the clear understanding (*abhisamaya*) of the four noble truths (*catvāry āryasatyāni*) was instantaneous, whereas the Andhakas, the Sarvāstivādins, and the Sammatīyas believed that it happened gradually. So important was this dispute that it was still the central theme of the council of Lhasa (held in the eighth century), where Chinese and Tibetan Buddhist teachers opposed each other in doctrinal debate. The Sarvāstivādins seem to have been alone in denying that "thought" (*citta*) is inherently pure and contaminated only by accidental impurities, a belief held by the Mahāsāṃghikas, the Theravādins, and the neighboring schools.

The Theravādins, the Vātsīputrīyas, and the Sammatīyas recognized only one absolute, or "unconditioned" (*asaṃskṛta*) *dharma,* namely, *nirvāṇa,* but the majority of schools also considered empty space (*ākāśa*) an unconditioned *dharma.* Several of them taught that "dependent origination" (*pratītya-samutpāda*), the path (*mārga*) of enlightenment, and sometimes other entities as well, in particular the "suchness" (*tathatā*) or "permanence" (*sthitatā*) of things, were equally absolute and unconditioned. Thus, the ideas of these schools were quite close to those of the Mahāyāna.

Several important debates centered on the nature of the passions, more specifically, latent passions or tendencies (*anuśaya*) and active passions or obsessions (*paryavasthāna*). The Mahāsāṃghikas, the Andhakas, and the Mahīśāsakas set up a very precise distinction between them, while the Theravādins and Sarvāstivādins chose to see in them only two aspects of the same passions. For the Theravādins and the Sarvāstivādins, tendencies and obsessions alike were connected, or cofunctioned, with thought (*cittasaṃprayukta*), whereas for the Mahāsāṃghikas, the Vātsīputrīyas, the Sammatīyas, and the Mahīśāsakas, tendencies were unconnected, did not cofunction, with thought (*cittaviprayukta*), while obsessions were connected with it. As for the Andhakas, they held that obsessions and tendencies were equally separate from thought.

According to the Sarvāstivādins and the Vātsīputrīyas, ascetics of other, non-Buddhist beliefs (*tīrthika*) could, through their efforts, obtain the five lesser supernatural faculties (*abhijñā*) and thus work various miracles—perceiving the thoughts of others, recollecting their past lives, seeing the rebirths of creatures as conditioned by their past actions, and so forth. The Mahīśāsakas and the Dharmaguptakas, however, declared that the five supernatural faculties—like the sixth, the cleansing of impurities, that is, the attainment of *nirvāṇa*—could be acquired only by Buddhist ascetics treading the Path of Enlightenment.

The relation between "matter" (*rūpa*) and the mechanism of the ripening (*vipāka*) of actions (*karman*) also gave rise to disagreements. For the Theravādins, matter is independent of the ripening of actions, and it is not the fruit of this ripening. It is morally neither good nor bad but inherently neutral. In contrast, the Sarvāstivādins, Sammatīyas, and Mahīśāsakas taught that matter can be good or bad when it participates, through the body of man, in a good or bad act. Matter is also the fruit of ripening when it becomes the body—be it handsome or ugly, robust or sickly—received by a person at birth as a consequence of past deeds.

According to the Sarvāstivādins, the five forms of sensory perception are always associated with passionate desires (*rāgas*). The Mahāsāṃghikas and the Mahīśāsakas thought that they were sometimes associated and sometimes unassociated with them, while the Vātsīputrīyas rejected both these possibilities, declaring that the five forms of sensory perception are morally neutral by nature and thus can never be either good or bad.

LITERATURE. The literature of early Buddhism must have been very important in extent and interest because what has been preserved for us, even though it represents only a small part of the whole, is considerable. The great majority of this literature vanished with the sects that produced it; let us recall that only one, the Theravāda, still flourishes today in Sri Lanka and Southeast Asia. Most of the schools have left us nothing, save perhaps a few fragments, isolated sūtras, and other brief works in the original Indian language or more often in Chinese translation. Which sects they belonged to nearly always remains undetermined.

Roughly half of what has been handed down to us is in the original Indian language, in a more or less "hybrid" Sanskrit, in various Middle Indic dialects, and above all in Pali. It is in Pali that the body of Theravāda literature, which we possess practically in its entirety, was written. The remainder, of approximately the same size, has come down to us only in Chinese or Tibetan translations. The scope of what was preserved in the Tibetan version, as far as the Hīnayāna in particular is concerned, is much more limited than that of the Chinese translation and, moreover, is confined almost solely to works of the Sarvāstivādins and Mūlasarvāstivādins. In Mahāyāna literature, in contrast, the enormous amount of material translated into Tibetan is virtually equal to what was translated into Chinese.

Thus, it seems that a greater proportion of the canonical literature—properly speaking, that which belonged to the Tripiṭaka ("three baskets")—than of the postcanonical literature has been passed on to us. It comprises, primarily, the complete Pali Tipiṭaka, made up of its Sutta Piṭaka ("basket of sermons"), its Vinaya Piṭaka ("basket of discipline"), and its Abhidhamma Piṭaka ("basket of higher teaching").

The Sutta Piṭaka, in turn, is composed of five Nikāyas, or "groupings," bringing together the "long" (*dīgha*), "medium" (*majjhima*), and "grouped" (*saṃyutta*) sermons; those arranged according to number of categories (*aṅguttara*); and, lastly, the "minor" (*khuddaka*) sermons, the longest and most varied section of all. The *Khuddaka Nikāya* assembles the legends of the former "births" (*jātaka*) of the Buddha, legends recounting the "deeds" (*apadāna*; Skt., *avadāna*) of the great disciples, didactic stanzas (*gāthā*) attributed to them, a famous but anonymous collection of other instructional stanzas called the *Dhammapada*, and ten or so other equally varied works.

Like the other Baskets of Discipline that have survived, the Pali Vinaya Piṭaka essentially contains three parts. These provide detailed definitions and explanations of the numerous rules of discipline imposed on monks (*bhikkus*), those to be observed by nuns (*bhikkunīs*), and specific rules concerning the material life of both: the correct use of objects they were allowed to own, ceremony, sentencing of offenders, settling of disputes, and so on.

The Pali Abhidhamma Piṭaka consists of seven different works, in which the doctrine set forth in no particular order in the sermons (*suttas*) is reorganized, classified systematically, and fleshed out at numerous points. One of these seven books, the *Kathāvatthu* (Points of controversy), refutes more than two hundred opinions held by other Buddhist schools and in the process reveals the doctrines peculiar to the Theravāda.

Sadly, we do not possess a complete Tripiṭaka from any other early sect, but more or less significant parts of several of them have been preserved. Thus, five Vinaya Piṭakas have come to us intact: those of the Mahāsāṃghikas, Mahīśāsakas, Dharmaguptakas, Sarvāstivādins, and Mūlasarvāstivādins, all in Chinese translation, plus more or less extensive fragments of the last two in the original Sanskrit. We have an entire Tibetan translation of the Mūlasarvāstivādins Vinaya Piṭaka, which is much more voluminous and written later than the others. In addition, we have a detached portion of the Lokottaravāda Vinaya Piṭaka under the name Mahāvastu (Great Tale) in Hybrid Sanskrit. This is actually a traditional and partial biography of the Buddha, heavily encrusted with legendry.

The non-Theravāda sects used the term *āgama* ("tradition") for the four or five parts that made up their Sūtra Piṭakas, which correspond to the Pali Nikāyas. Five of these Āgamas, evidently complete, have survived in Chinese translation: the Dirghagama of the Dharmaguptakas; the Madhyamagama of the Sarvāstivādins; the Samyuktagamas of the Sarvāstivādins and the Kāśyapīyas; and, finally, an *Ekottarāgama* that most probably belongs to a sect derived from the Mahāsāṃghikas but different from the Lokottaravādins. There are also more than 150 isolated sūtras, nearly all preserved in Chinese and a few in their original Indian language, but it is generally impossible to determine what school they come from. No collection corresponding to the Pali *Khuddaka Nikāya* survives, but we do have the Chinese translations of some seventy works similar to those that make up the Theravāda collection, as well as the Indian originals of a number of others.

Two complete Abhidharma Piṭakas have survived in Chinese translation: that of the Sarvāstivādins (one part of this also exists in Tibetan) and one entitled Śāriputra-abhidharma, which seems to have belonged to the Dharmaguptakas but was perhaps also influenced by the Mahāsāṃghika. Like the Abhidharma Piṭaka of the Theravādins, that of the Sarvāstivādins comprises seven works, but its overall structure is very different, as is its doctrine, although there are notable similarities between some parts of the two works. The Śāriputra-abhidharma, which is made up of four main sections, differs even more from the Theravādins text. For the most part these three collections definitely postdate the first appearance of the sects that composed them and defended their own positions in them. The teaching given by the sermons in the various Nikāyas or Āgamas of the Sūtra Piṭakas, in contrast, presents a truly remarkable consistency, whatever their school of origin, and, thus, a great fidelity to the common early Buddhist base, predating the community's division into sects. The same is true for most of the monastic rules contained in the various

Vinaya Piṭaka, which are distinguished mainly by details of secondary or minor aspects of the ascetic life.

The postcanonical literature was undoubtedly very important, but even less of it remains than of the canonic material, and it is more unevenly distributed. Luckily, we possess in Pali the greater part of what was written by the Theravādins—commentaries on the canonic texts, treatises on doctrine, collections of legends, and devotional poems. We have also the principal Sarvāstivāda treatises, several commentaries on these works and on the major portion of their Abhidharma Piṭaka, as well as a few other late works. Unfortunately, the postcanonic literature available to us from all the other schools is limited to a half-dozen works.

The whole series of commentaries in Pali on the Theravāda canonic texts was composed in the fourth and fifth centuries CE by Buddhadatta, Buddhaghosa, and Dhammapala, who made use of ancient commentaries, now lost, in Old Sinhala. We also owe to Buddhaghosa, the wisest and most renowned of all the Theravāda masters, a substantial treatise entitled *Visuddhimagga* (The path of purity), in which the Mahāvihāra school's entire doctrine is set forth. Another famous treatise is the *Abhidhammatthasangaha* (Collection of interpretations of the higher doctrine), written by the Sinhala monk Anuruddha about the eleventh century. Other, less important treatises of the Mahāvihāra school were composed by various authors between the fourth and fifteenth centuries. Each of these works was the subject of one or more commentaries, most of which have not survived. Only one non-Mahāvihāra Theravāda work—strangely, in Chinese translation—is extant: a large treatise called *Vimuttimagga* (The path of liberation), attributed to Upatissa, who must have lived some time before Buddhaghosa and was probably a master of the Abhayagiri school.

To the treatises may be added the *Lokapaññatti* (Description of the world), a fourteenth-century adaptation by the Burmese monk Saddhammaghosa of a lost Sanskrit work, and especially the well-known *Milindapañha* (Questions of King Milinda), likewise inspired by a lost work. This seems to have been a little Buddhist propaganda manual aimed at the Greeks and Eurasians, such as King Menander (Milinda), who lived in northwestern India in the second century BCE. Besides the Pali version, there are two Chinese translations of the *Milindapañha* that rather differ from each other and even more so from the Theravāda text.

The postcanonic Theravāda literature also includes instructional poems and collections of legends in verse or prose. Among the instructional poems are the *Anāgatavaṃsa* (History of the future), in which the monk Kassapa recounts the life of the next Buddha, named Metteyya, and the *Jinacarita* (Story of the conqueror), Medhaṃkara's account of the miraculous life of the historical Buddha. The *Rasavāhinī* (Transportress of flavors), translated into Pali by Vedeha from an Old Sinhala poem, is a collection of some one hundred legends meant to encourage a life of piety.

However, it is its famous chronicles, a genre almost entirely abandoned in ancient India, that make Theravāda literature stand apart from that of the other sects. The series of the *Dīpavaṃsa* (History of the island), *Mahāvaṃsa* (Great history), and *Cūḷavaṃsa* (Lesser history) records in verse the whole history of Sri Lanka, from its beginning to the end of the eighteenth century, from the very specific point of view of the "elders" (*theras*) of the Mahāvihāra, the principal Sinhala Theravāda school. Other chronicles recount, in grandiose verse style, the stories of sacred relics: the *Bodhivaṃsa* tells the story of the bodhi tree, the *Thūpavaṃsa* that of the principal mound of Anurādhapura, and the *Dāṭhāvaṃsa* that of the Buddha's tooth.

The main works of the Sarvāstivādin postcanonic literature have generally survived in Chinese or Tibetan translation. Complete or partial Sanskrit originals of several of them have also been found.

Only two commentaries on the postcanonic literature of the Sarvāstivādins have come down to us. One concerns the rules of monastic discipline and is entitled *Sarvāstivāda-vinaya-vibhāṣā*; the other, called *Abhidharma-mahāvibhāṣā*, comments on the *Jñānaprasthāna*, the principal work of the Abhidharma Piṭaka of this sect. This *Mahāvibhāṣā* (Great commentary) is an immense summation of the doctrine of the Sarvāstivādins or, more precisely, of their most important school, known as the Vaibhāṣika, "supporter of the (*Mahā-*) *Vibhāṣā*." It is one of the most voluminous works in all Buddhist literature.

The Sarvāstivādins left several treatises written in Sanskrit during the first few centuries of the common era. The principal and best known is the *Abhidharmakośa* (Treasury of higher doctrine), written by Vasubandhu in the fifth century and the subject of numerous commentaries, many of which are extant in the Sanskrit original or in Chinese or Tibetan translation. Vasubandhu was accused of holding Sautrāntika views by his contemporary Saṃghabhadra, a strictly orthodox Sarvāstivādin. Saṃghabhadra refuted these views in a large treatise entitled *Abhidharma-nyāyānusāra* (Consistent with the logic of the further doctrine) and in a long commentary on the didactic stanzas (*kārikās*) of the *Abhidharmakośa*. The Sarvāstivādins also composed a *Lokaprajñapti* (Description of the world) according to Buddhist ideas, which has survived in Chinese and Tibetan translations.

The other schools have left only Chinese translations of a few treatises and commentaries, often very short and of unknown origin. Among the commentaries, which all correspond to complete or partial Vinaya Piṭakas, we may mention the *Vinayasaṃgraha* (Collection of Discipline) by the Mūlasarvāstivādins Viśeṣamitra and the *Vinayamātṛkā* (Summary of discipline), the sectarian affinity of which is uncertain.

All that remains of the literature of the Vātsīputrīyas and related schools, which must have been considerable, are the Chinese translations, sadly inferior and obscure, of two small treatises summarizing their teaching. The most important of these is entitled *Sammatīya-nikāya-śāstra* (Treatise of the Sammatīya sect).

Two other works of the same type have also survived in Chinese translation, but although they are better translated and are much longer, their sectarian origin presents some difficulty. One, called *Satyasiddhi* (Realization of the truths), written by Harivarman around the third century CE, teaches and defends the doctrine of a Mahāsāṃghika-derived school, probably the Bahuśrutīyas. The other is the *Vimuttimagga,* mentioned above, whose author, Upatissa, probably belonged to the Sinhala Abhayagiri school; its Pali original was recently rediscovered.

The literary genre of devotional legends in verse or prose was also a great inspiration to authors of all sects, most of whom remained as anonymous as those of the canonic texts. Some of these works recounted the life of the historical Buddha, embellishing it with numerous miracles for the sake of greater glory. Two of the three most famous were preserved by chance in their Indian originals. These were composed in Hybrid Sanskrit, which is to say greatly influenced by the Prakrit dialects: the *Mahāvastu* (Great tale) and the *Lalitavistara* (Account of the sport), both important sources for the development of the Buddha legend. The first is a detached portion of the Lokottaravāda Vinaya Piṭaka, but in scope, as well as in specific subject matter, it can be considered a distinct and, moreover, rather late work. The *Lalitavistara* was first compiled by the Sarvāstivādins but later revised by followers of the Mahāyāna. In contrast with these two, the *Buddhacarita* (Story of the Buddha) was written in classical Sanskrit by one of the greatest Indian poets, Aśvaghoṣa, who lived around the second century CE; only half of the Sanskrit text has been recovered, but the Chinese translation is complete.

The collections of legendary material recounting the edifying deeds of Buddhist saints, or the previous incarnations of these or the future Buddha, are numerous, whether in Hybrid Sanskrit originals or in Chinese versions. We shall mention here only the best known, the *Avadāaśataka* (Hundred exploits) and the *Divyāvadana* (Divine exploits).

NOTABLE PERSONALITIES. Be they Buddhists, *brahmans,* or otherwise, the Indians of ancient times had practically no interest in history as we understand it, with its concern for the exact recording of events, dates, names, and biographies of important figures in order to preserve a precise record of them. This is especially true for the history of Indian Buddhism and the lives of its great masters. With very rare exceptions, to us the masters are only names attached to one or more literary works or, much less often, to an important item or event in the history of Buddhism—such as an idea that was declared heretical, a dispute, or a council. Nearly always, we know nothing whatever of the lives of these people, including the regions where they were born or lived and the centuries in which they were active. Moreover, the scant information that tradition has preserved about them is either vague, contradictory, or obviously distorted by legend, obliging us to make use of it with great skepticism. Even the biographies of the principal Sinhala elders (*theras*) of the Theravāda sect, whose history is told at length and in detail by the chronicles of Sri Lanka, are hardly better known to us than those of the masters of other groups and schools of early Indian Buddhism. In any case, we possess infinitely less detail about the lives of these *theras* than about those of the kings, princes, and generals who studded the history of Sri Lanka and protected the island's monastic community for two thousand years. Nonetheless, these chronicles permit us to know the names of a much larger number of these Sinhala Theravāda elders than of the masters of other sects, and thanks to them we are generally informed with some precision about the time and place in which many of them lived.

Among the most noteworthy figures of the Theravāda, we must first point out the three great scholars to whom all of the commentaries on the Pali canon and several important treatises on doctrine are attributed. The most famous is certainly Buddhaghosa, author of the *Visuddhimagga.* According to tradition, Buddhaghosa was an Indian *brahman* from Bihar who converted to Buddhism, then probably came to live in the Tamil country and afterward in the Sri Lankan capital, Anurādhapura, during the reign of Mahānāma (409–431). Buddhadatta, who was, it seems, a little older than Buddhaghosa, was probably born in the Tamil country, on the banks of the Kāverī, and spent most of his life there, but he probably sojourned in Anurādhapura as well. Finally, Dhammapāla was probably also a Tamil, born in Kāñcīpuram in the late fourth century, and most likely lived mainly in his native land but also journeyed to Lanka. Thus, it would seem that in the early fifth century, Tamil India was an important seat of Buddhist—or, more precisely, Theravāda—culture, on a par with Sri Lanka and perhaps even more active.

The reign of Parakkamabāhu (Parakramabāhu) I (1153–1186), an especially prosperous epoch for the Sinhala Theravādins, was made illustrious by a number of scholar-monks. The most famous was Sāriputta, a pupil of Kassapa of Udumbaragiri, who had played a pivotal role in the reform of the community ordered by the king and was himself a great scholar. Sāriputta turned his residence, the new monastery of Jetavana at Polonnaruwa, into the major center of knowledge and Buddhist learning of his time. Author of several authoritative subcommentaries on canonic texts, highly esteemed grammarian and poet, he was as well versed in Sanskrit as in Pali and composed his works in both languages. Several of his many students became learned monks and authors of valued literary works, notably Dhammakitti, Saṅgharakkhita, Sumaṅgala, Buddhanāga, Medaṅkara, and Vācissara.

In modern times, mention must be made of one first-rank figure whose influence on the evolution of Theravāda Buddhism was both decisive and extensive. Prince Mongkut, the youngest son of the Siamese king Rama II, became a monk and, during the quarter-century that he spent in yellow robes, undertook a great reform of the community in his country. In particular, he founded a new monastic order, the Thammayut, which observed the rules of discipline more strictly than did its contemporaries, but he also kept abreast of the social realities of Siam and enthusiastically studied the culture and religions of the West. Becoming king on the death of his elder brother, he ruled under the name Rama IV (1851–1868), completing his work and transforming his country into a modern state largely open to trade and external influence. He is one of the principal architects of the great reform of Theravāda Buddhism that took place after the mid-nineteenth century not only in Siam but also in the neighboring kingdoms and in Sri Lanka. This movement was characterized by a return to the sources of the religion, namely the Pali Tipiṭaka, and also by a necessary and rational adaptation to modern circumstances.

The best-known figure of the Sarvāstivādins is certainly Vasubandhu, the author of the *Abhidharmakośa.* Unfortunately, our information about this great master is suspect and seemingly contradictory, so that his life remains a subject of debate. Is Vasubandhu the Sarvāstivādin identical with Vasubandhu the Yogācāra, the brother of Aśanga? Did he live in the fourth or the fifth century of our era? Was he born at Purusapura (present-day Peshawar) into a *brahman* family? Did he live in Kashmir, and then Ayodhya (present-day Faizābād), where he probably died? No agreement has been reached on these or other, lesser points of his biography.

We know even less about his principal adversary, Saṃghabhadra, except that he was Vasubandhu's contemporary, a Kashmiri, and a staunch defender of Vaibhasika Sarvāstivāda orthodoxy. As for other great teachers of this sect, to whom are attributed various interpretations of the notion of *sarvam asti* or the treatises that have come down to us in Chinese translation, they are hardly more than names to us: Vasumitra (one or several?), Kātyāyanīputra, Dharmaśrī, Ghoṣaka, Upaśānta, Dharmatrāta. . . . Indeed, the Sarvāstivāda's founder, Madhyāntika, who probably settled with his disciples in Kashmir during the reign of Aśoka, seems himself to belong more to legend than to history.

The founders of other schools are also nothing but names to us, and even these have been handed down: Mahādeva for the Mahāsāṃghikas, Vātsīputra for the Vātsīputrīyas, Uttara for the Sautrāntikas, and so on. We only know two or three other masters, whose names have been preserved by chance, such as Śrīlāta of the Sautrāntika and Harivarman, the author of the *Satyasiddhi.* Of Śrīlāta we know nothing more than his opinions, as these were criticized in Sarvāstivādin tracts. Harivarman was probably a *brahman* from the middle Ganges Basin, who most likely lived around the third century CE and was converted to Buddhism as a follower of one of the Mahāsāṃghika sects, probably the Bahuśrutīya, to judge from the study of his long treatise.

Expansion of the Schools Outside of India. Owing to the pious zeal of the emperor Aśoka, from the mid-third century BCE Buddhism began to expand outside of India proper, southeastward into Sri Lanka and northwestward into what is now Afghanistan. Numerous important epigraphic and archaeological monuments show that it soon prospered in both these areas. From this evidence and from the Sinhala chronicles we know that the Theravādins very quickly became, and remained, the dominant group in Sri Lanka, but we do not know exactly which sects flourished at the same time—during the last three centuries BCE—in the mountainous areas of the northwest, then called Gandhara and Kapiśa. It seems, however, that the Sarvāstivādins, traditionally believed to have originated in nearby Kashmir during the reign of Aśoka, began the conversion of these lands to Buddhism and were joined somewhat later by schools of the Mahāsāṃghika group.

A few very scarce inscriptions, but especially the reports of the famous Chinese pilgrims Xuanzang and Yijing, as well as the numerous discoveries of Buddhist manuscripts in Central Asia, provide information on the presence of various early sects outside India. Sects were found in Southeast Asia, Indonesia, Central Asia, and China in the first few centuries of the common era, especially in the seventh century.

At this same time, the Theravādins had found their way into Indonesia, where the Sarvāstivādins or Mūlasarvāstivādins were a strong majority. These two groups were extremely numerous and nearly alone in all of Central Asia, and they also flourished in southern China, where the Mahīśāsakas, Dharmaguptakas, and Kāśyapīyas prospered as well. These last three sects thrived in Indonesia, and Dharmaguptakas were also found in eastern China as well as in Shensi province. As for the Sammatīyas, they were in the majority in Champa, in the center of present-day Vietnam. Such is the information provided by Yijing.

The Chinese translations of three different works of early Indian Buddhist sects formed the basis of an equal number of distinctively Chinese schools, which were introduced shortly afterward into Japan. The oldest is known by the name Chengshi, which is the title of Kumārajīva's Chinese translation (411–412) of Harivarman's *Satyasiddhi.* The main doctrine of this treatise, which attracted and held the attention of its Chinese followers, distinguishes two truths: a mundane or relative truth and a supreme or absolute truth. It teaches that all things are empty of substance, not only the individual person made up of the five aggregates of phenomena, but also the whole of the external world. Thus, the teaching of this work would seem to lie between those of the Hīnayāna and the Mahāyāna or, more precisely, the Mādhyamika. The Chengshi school was in fact founded by two direct disciples of Kumārajīva, Sengdao and Sengsong, who each headed a different branch, one centered in Anhui and the other in Jiangsu. These two masters and some of their disciples composed many commentaries on the *Satyasiddhi* or, more exactly, on its Chinese translation, which helped make it widely known throughout southern China. The leaders of the Chinese Mahāyānist Sanlun sect, who were faithful followers of the Mādhyamikas, vigorously combatted this teaching, insisting that its concept of the void was mistaken. Their attacks resulted in the decline of the Chengshi school in the mid-seventh century and in its disappearance shortly afterward. Still, in 625, a Korean monk introduced the Chinese translation of the *Satyasiddhi* and its teaching to Japan, but the sect, which received the name Jōjitsu (after the Japanese pronunciation of Chengshi), found less success there than in China and was quickly absorbed by the rival school of Sanron, the Japanese form of San-lun.

The second sect was called Jushe, a transliteration of the Sanskrit *kośa,* because it was based on the famous *Abhidharmakośa* of Vasubandhu, translated into Chinese by Paramārtha in 563–567 and by Xuanzang in 651–654. The Sarvāstivāda realism expounded in this treatise was not very successful in China, where Mahāyāna doctrines were then dominant; consequently, the Jushe school died out in the late eighth century, when it was absorbed by the Chinese form of Yogācāra known as Faxiang. Previously, as early as 658, two Japanese monks, Chitsu and Chitatsu, had introduced the sect to Japan, where it bacame known as the Kusha. There it had less success and longevity as an independent school than in China, for Chitsu and Chitatsu themselves were followers of Faxiang, called Hossō in Japan. Hossō had already attained considerable importance, and it soon absorbed the Kusha school.

The third and final Chinese school derived from early Buddhism was quite different from the other two. Called Lü ("discipline"), it was established in the mid-seventh century by the eminent monk Daoxuan as a reaction against the doctrinal disputes that preoccupied Chinese Buddhists of the time. He maintained that moral uprightness and strict monastic discipline were much more necessary for the religious life than empty intellectual speculations. Consequently, he imposed on his followers the well-defined rules in the *Sifen lü,* a Chinese translation of the Vinaya Piṭaka of the Dharmaguptakas made by Buddhayaśas and Zhu Fonian in 412. Although his school never had many adherents of its own, it had a clear and lasting influence on Chinese Buddhism. Thanks to the school's activities, the *Sifen lü* became, and remains, the sole collection of disciplinary rules to be followed by all Chinese Buddhist monks regardless of their school, including followers of the Mahāyāna. The school was introduced to Japan in 753 by the Chinese monk Jianzhen (Jpn., Ganjin), who was welcomed with open arms at the court of Nara. Known by the name of Ritsu (not to be confused with a homophonous branch of the Shingon sect), it is still active in Japan today (it also existed in China early in this century) but no longer has many adherents.

However, the only early Buddhist sect to thrive after spreading outside of India is the Theravāda. Its lasting success (it still flourishes today) can be explained by the fact that it was established well before the common era in Sri Lanka, a relatively isolated region, and that it has almost always maintained a strongly preferential relationship with the island's political authorities and has known how best to profit from it. Much less certain was the extension of this phenomenon to a compact group of countries of mainland Southeast Asia from the eleventh century, a time when Buddhism, especially the early, so-called Hīnayāna Buddhism, was dying out throughout India itself. At that time, Hīnayāna Buddhism could claim only a very few followers, scattered among small and failing communities, in the whole vast territory of India. We can understand how the effect of such a happy chance could have seemed miraculous to Buddhist devotees.

This process began in Burma, in the mid-eleventh century, when Anorātha, who ruled the central and northern parts of the country, conquered the southern, maritime region, where Theravāda monks had recently converted the ruler. Anorātha, too, soon adopted the Buddhist faith of the Theravādins. Driven by religious zeal, he compelled all of his subjects to follow his example. From that time on, Theravāda has remained the religion of the majority of the Burmese people.

Two centuries later, when the Thai descended from the mountains to the north and took control of the entire country known today as Thailand, the same process took place. Their king converted to the Theravāda and exercised all his authority to promote its extension to the whole of the population.

In the following century, under circumstances that are still poorly known, neighboring Cambodia, where Mahāyāna Buddhism and Hinduism had flourished until then, became completely Theravādin in a short space of time and has remained so to the present day. The petty kingdoms of Laos, stretched out along the middle Mekong, were not long in following suit.

In contrast to what had happened in India, this distribution of Theravāda Buddhism among a number of different countries, which were (except for Sri Lanka) in close proximity to each other, helped ensure the sect's lasting prosperity. Indeed, when a monastic community in one of these countries found itself in difficulty or in decline, which happened a number of times here and there, the pious Buddhist king would ask for and receive help from another country's ruler, who would then send him a group of knowledgeable, respected monks to resolve the problems in question and restore the Theravāda to its full value and strength. Similarly, whatever reforms and progress were made in one country quickly spread to the Theravāda communities in others. Such was the case in the last century, when the prince-monk Mongkut, who became King Rama IV of Siam, instituted great transformations that allowed the Theravāda to adapt to the modern world at the same time that he carried out a return to its distant canonic sources.

SEE ALSO Arhat; Buddhaghosa; Buddhism, articles on Buddhism in India, Buddhism in Southeast Asia; Buddhist

Books and Texts; Buddhist Philosophy; Councils, article on Buddhist Councils; Dharma, article on Buddhist Dharma and Dharmas; Eightfold Path; Four Noble Truths; Ganjin; Karman, article on Buddhist Concepts; Mahāsāṃghika; Missions, article on Buddhist Missions; Mongkut; Nirvāṇa; Pratītya-samutpāda; Saṃgha, overview article; Sarvāstivāda; Sautrāntika; Sinhala Religion; Soteriology; Southeast Asian Religions, overview article; Vasubandhu.

BIBLIOGRAPHY

Aung, Schwe Zan, and C. A. F. Rhys Davids, trans. *Points of Controversy* (1915). London, 1969. A translation of the Pali *Kathāvatthu,* a text treating the doctrinal controversies between the various Hīnayāna sects from the Theravāda point of view.

Bareau, André. *Les sectes bouddhiques du Petit Véhicule.* Publications de l'École Français d'Extrême-Orient, vol. 38. Saigon, 1955. An exhaustive survey based on all available documents.

Bechert, Heinz, and Richard Gombrich. *The World of Buddhism.* London, 1984. This excellent work includes a discussion of schisms on page 82.

Ch'en, Kenneth. *Buddhism in China; a Historical Survey.* Princeton, 1964. See pages 129–131 and 301–303 for information on the Hīnayāna-derived Chinese sects.

Demiéville, Paul. "L'origine des sectes bouddhiques d'après Paramartha." In *Mélanges chinois et bouddhiques,* vol. 1, pp. 15–64. Brussels, 1932. A masterfully annotated French translation of one of the principal documents on the subject.

Dube, S. N. *Cross Currents in Early Buddhism.* New Delhi, 1980. Interesting study of doctrinal disputes among early sects, but based primarily on the *Kathāvatthu.*

Dutt, Nalinaksha. *Buddhist Sects in India.* 2d ed. Calcutta, 1978. Good general description of the history and, especially, the doctrines of the Hīnayāna sects.

Fujishima Ryauon. *Les bouddhisme japonais: Doctrines et histoire de douze sectes bouddhiques du Japon* (1889). Reprint, Paris, 1983. This old book is the most complete description in a Western language of Japanese Buddhist sects, particularly the three derived from the Hīnayāna.

Hajime, Nakamura. *Indian Buddhism: A Survey with Bibliographical Notes.* Hirakata, 1980. This large work brings into focus our knowledge of the whole of Indian Buddhism and contains an extremely rich and up-to-date bibliography. A long chapter concerns the Hīnayāna sects (pp. 90–140).

Lamotte, Étienne. *Histoire du bouddhisme indien: Des origines à l'ère Saka.* Louvain, 1958. A large part (pp. 571–705) of this excellent work discusses early sects, their origins and distribution, Buddhist languages, and the sects' doctrinal evolution.

La Vallée Poussin, Louis de, trans. *L'Abhidharmakośa de Vasubandhu* (1923–1931). 6 vols. Reprint, Brussels, 1971. This French translation of the famous treatise includes copious notes and a very long introduction by the great Belgian scholar. It is rich in information on the doctrinal controversies that concerned the Sarvāstivādins.

Law, Bimala Churn. *A History of Pali Literature.* London, 1933. Complete, very detailed description of Theravāda literature.

Masuda Jiryo. "Origins and Doctrines of Early Indian Buddhist Schools." *Asia Major* 2 (1925): 1–78. English translation, with notes, of the *Samayabhedoparacanacakra,* an account of the Hīnayāna sects and their main tenets.

Renou, Louis, and Jean Filliozat. *L'Inde classique.* Paris, 1953. Volume 2, pages 315–608, deals especially with the Hīnayāna sects, their literature, and doctrines. The collaboration of the Sinologist Paul Demiéville and the Tibetologist Marcelle Lalou is invaluable.

Shizutani Masao. *Shōjō bukkyōshi no kenkyū; Buha bukkyō no seiritsu to hensen.* Kyoto, 1978. The most recent work on the origin and evolution of the Hīnayāna sects. Detailed and complete study of literary and epigraphic sources.

Takakusu Junjirō, trans. *A Record of the Buddhist Religion as Practiced in India and the Malay Archipelago (A.D. 671–695)* (1896). Reprint, Dehli, 1966. English translation of Yijing's account of his pilgrimage to South and Southeast Asia.

Warder, A. K. *Indian Buddhism.* 2d rev. ed. Dehli, 1980. Treats Hīnayāna sects at length, offering interesting solutions to the problems they pose.

Watters, Thomas, trans. *On Yuan Chwang's Travels in India, 629–645 A.D.* 2 vols. London, 1904–1905. English translation of numerous extracts from the accounts of Xuanzang's journey, with excellent commentary correcting most of the many errors of earlier translations (those of Stanislas Julien, Samuel Beal, etc.), which are today unusable.

New Sources

Cohen, Richard S. "Discontented Categories: Hinayana and Mahayana in Indian Buddhist History." *Journal of the American Academy of Religion* 63 (1995): 1–25.

Egge, J. R. *Religious Giving and the Invention of Karma in Theravada Buddhism.* Richmond, 2001.

Hoffman, F. J., and M. Deegalle, *Pali Buddhism.* Richmond, 1996.

Holt, J., J. N. Kinnard, and J. S. Walters. *Constituting Communities: Theravada Buddhism and the Religious Cultures of South and Southeast Asia.* Albany, 2003

Hsüan, T., and S. Ganguly. *Treatise on Groups of Elements; The Abhidharma-dhatukaya-padasastra: English Translation of Hsüan-tsang's Chinese Version.* Delhi, 1994.

Ray, N. *An Introduction to the Study of Theravada Buddhism in Burma: A Study in Indo-Burmese Historical and Cultural Relations from the Earliest Times to the British Conquest.* Bangkok, 2002.

Soda, K. *Theravada Buddhist Studies in Japan.* Calcutta, 1998.

Thien, C. *The Literature of the Personalists of Early Buddhism.* Delhi, 1999.

Weber, C. *Wesen und Eigenschaften des Buddha in der Tradition des Hinayana-Buddhismus.* Wiesbaden, 1994.

André Bareau (1987)
Translated from French by David M. Weeks
Revised Bibliography

BUDDHISM, SCHOOLS OF: MAHĀYĀNA PHILOSOPHICAL SCHOOLS OF BUDDHISM

Mahāyāna Buddhists in India developed numerous theories on a wide range of topics, and according to Buddhist thinkers, all such theories must relate in principle to reaching *nirvāṇa*, the highest goal toward which Buddhists are meant to strive. Usually a theory prescribes a specific contemplative practice that will lead the Buddhist to that highest goal, and it is understood that the practice will lead to *nirvāṇa* only when guided by the theory that recommends it. Indian Mahāyāna Buddhists who accepted the soteriological importance of theory thus faced some critical interpretive tasks: select, defend, and articulate the correct (i.e., soteriologically efficacious) theory among competing theories.

As Mahāyāna Buddhist thought develops, these interpretive tasks focus on philosophical texts (*śāstras*) that become, for one reason or another, the inviolable sources of a theoretical system. The main Mahāyāna texts of this kind were composed by three Buddhist thinkers: Nāgārjuna (c. 150 CE), Asaṅga (c. 325 CE), and Vasubandhu (c. 325 CE). Although other thinkers' works also received considerable attention, the works of these three thinkers form the core of the Mahāyāna philosophical schools. Their texts and ideas are studied and interpreted again and again by each generation of Indian Mahāyāna thinkers until the virtual disappearance of Mahāyāna philosophy in India (c. 1400 CE).

As each generation's commentators take up the study of these foundational figures, they invariably employ a kind of dialectical method: arguments are couched as discussions between the proponent and the opponent of a particular notion. These dialectical arguments respond to a wide range of views, both Buddhist and non-Buddhist. Hence, formulating its own retorts and criticisms, each generation develops new and often multiple interpretations of seminal texts and concepts.

By the sixth century, the rapid accumulation of competing interpretations leads Mahāyāna thinkers such as Bhāvaviveka (c. 525 CE) to systematically employ terms for what are often called "philosophical schools." One obvious circumstance underlies this move: commentators fall into well-defined camps that adopt a particular moniker to identify their position. Followers of Nāgārjuna, for example, speak of their philosophy as Madhyamaka (the "Middle Way"), a term that Nāgārjuna himself coins. Subsequent generations of Madhyamaka thinkers are always concerned to defend and articulate the works of Nāgārjuna and, to some degree, the commentaries on Nāgārjuna composed by their predecessors. One thus encounters an unambiguous cohesion within Madhyamaka texts, as evinced by their intertextuality, the continuity of their ideas, their appeal to the same authorities, and so on. Hence, in using a single moniker to refer to many thinkers and their texts, Bhāvaviveka is simply reflecting the obvious cohesiveness of their textual traditions.

In describing Buddhist thought as "schools," however, another motivation is the confusion caused by the multiplicity of views that develop over generations. By Bhāvaviveka's time, Buddhist thought exhibits many variations, and if one adds the opinions of non-Buddhist philosophers, one arrives at a tangled knot of theory. Parsing authors and texts into specific schools allows Buddhist thinkers to unravel that knot and present its various strands in a straightforward fashion. Instead of unpacking endless arguments between individual authors, one instead interprets them as debates between philosophical traditions.

The need to sort and classify the bewildering variety of Mahāyāna philosophical views becomes especially acute when Buddhism spreads to other regions, such as China and Tibet. Indeed, in Tibet an entire literature develops around the term *school*, and most Tibetan monastic libraries hold several dozen texts that are devoted to minutely parsing and classifying Indian philosophical systems. This literature, called *doxography*, has heavily influenced the academic study of Indian Mahāyāna thought. The success and influence of Tibetan doxographies stems in part from their ability to elaborate a general classification found in Indian doxographical texts. Enumerated in these terms, all Buddhist thought falls into the hierarchy of the "four schools": the lowest two, the Vaibhāṣika and the Sautrāntika, are not part of the Mahāyāna, but they provide the foundation for the higher schools; the latter two, Yogācāra and Madhyamaka, are considered Mahāyāna schools. This schema, along with its numerous subcategories, has become standard in the academic study of Mahāyāna philosophy.

Since it is so prominent, the model of the four schools will guide the discussion presented below. It will be useful, however, to begin with the problems inherent in the notion of "philosophical schools." An overview of the first two schools will then provide the overall context of Mahāyāna thought. After a concise historical synopsis, this entry focuses on the earliest historical forms of the two Mahāyāna schools, namely Madhyamaka and Yogācāra, along with a brief consideration of later developments.

"SCHOOLS" AND "PHILOSOPHY." The notion of a philosophical "school" is a difficult one, even in its English usage. In rough terms, a "school" is a voluntary association of various thinkers who articulate and defend a particular set of theories that are deliberately traced through a series of commentators to one or more original thinkers. A main concern in speaking of schools is the need to distinguish the mere avowal of a position from the systematic articulation and defense of that position within a tradition. To refer clearly to that type of systematic articulation, Indian Buddhist authors eventually settle on the term *siddhānta,* literally, the "conclusion" or outcome of one's theoretical arguments. It is this term that is often translated as "school."

Although clearly useful for Buddhist exegetes and academic interpreters, the concept of a *siddhānta* or school holds several problems. For example, if a taxonomy of schools is to be of any use, one must sort each thinker and his works into one school or another. In this sorting process, however, the way in which a thinker may resist or reinterpret his own school is all too easily lost. The sorting of thinkers into this or that school may also lead one to ignore noteworthy differences and create false boundaries. Candrakīrti (c. 625 CE) and Śāntideva (c. 650 CE), for example, diverge significantly in their views, but since they are lumped together into the same school, their important differences may be ignored. Likewise, Dharmakīrti (c. 650 CE) and Śāntarakṣita (c. 750 CE) are sorted into distinct schools, but their thought may converge in ways that are not apparent in terms of their schools' definitions. Along these same lines, the taxonomy of schools does not fare well when confronted with liminal cases, where a thinker's allegiances are difficult to discern.

The English term *school* may also suggest a type of institutional coherence that does not apply to these philosophical traditions. It appears that only men wrote Buddhist philosophical texts, and nearly all were monks. As such, they received their sustenance through a monastic institution, and they held property in common with that institution. The practical circumstances of a monk's life and the norms that regulated his behavior were also guided by the rules passed to him upon ordination. If issues such as sustenance and behavioral norms lie at the core of a monk's institutional identity, then one must identify nearly every Buddhist philosopher first and foremost as a monk from a particular monastery regulated by the rules of a particular monastic tradition. Monastic traditions, moreover, were not distinguished by their philosophies; instead, each tradition was set apart primarily by its regional origin and the often mundane details of its rules. Hence, in institutional terms, an Indian Buddhist philosopher is first distinguished not by a particular philosophy, but rather by the regional affiliation and rules of his monastery's code. To put it another way, in some cases the color of a monk's robe indicated unambiguously the monastic tradition that he followed, but no such visible cue ever marked the philosophical school that he upheld.

Nevertheless, it would be a mistake to suppose that allegiance to a Mahāyāna philosophical school had no impact on a monk's life. Certainly, that allegiance located the philosopher within an intellectual community, one that extended across many monasteries in many monastic traditions; and it is clear that these intellectual communities engaged in both censure and approval of a thinker's works. A thinker's commitment to a Mahāyāna philosophical school also located him within a wider discourse on philosophy conducted by many traditions, both Buddhist and non-Buddhist. That is, although many Indian Buddhist thinkers did not compose their works in Sanskrit, Mahāyāna philosophers did use Sanskrit, and they thus shared a literary language with a wide range of non-Buddhist theorists. This may be one reason for the remarkable number of extended debates between Mahāyāna philosophy and these other, non-Buddhist traditions. In those debates, Mahāyāna Buddhist thinkers acted as intellectual defenders of the faith against philosophical critiques originating outside the Buddhist community, and this role probably impacted their lives in terms of patronage and prestige.

Another practical impact of allegiance to a school was the Mahāyāna notion of philosophy itself. Mahāyāna philosophical texts cover many of the same topics and use many of the same methods found in Euro-American philosophical traditions. And, as in classical Greece, *philosophy* here must not be interpreted as dry theory, but rather as systematic thought that is meant to explain, guide, and sustain contemplative practices. This does not mean that every argument correlates straightforwardly with a contemplative practice—consciously or not, Indian Buddhist thinkers often made philosophical decisions that have no obvious relation to such practices. Nevertheless, in a fundamental way Buddhist thinkers link their arguments to specific contemplative practices, such as meditations that analyze personal identity. This linkage reflects the avowed soteriological context of all Buddhist thought, namely, the cultivation of meditative experiences that allegedly eliminate suffering and lead to *nirvāṇa*. Indeed, from the traditional view, the Buddhist thinker's philosophical work was itself a kind of spiritual practice that moved the thinker closer to these final goals. Philosophy is therefore called "seeing" (*darśana*), a metaphor that evokes a central goal of Buddhist contemplative practice: an experience (*anubhava*) in which one sees things as they truly are (*yathābhūtadarśana*). Thus, in speaking of Mahāyāna "philosophy," one must recall that it is implicated deeply in this type of contemplative goal.

Despite the problems noted above, the schema of the four philosophical schools remains useful. The usual procedure is to begin by discussing the first two schools: the Vaibhāṣika and the Sautrāntika. Doxographers maintain that these schools do not embody any Mahāyāna philosophy, and it is precisely for this reason that they are presented first. In doing so, doxographers are able to present the shared, foundational notions that run through all Buddhist thought.

FOUNDATIONAL THEORIES. From its earliest period, Buddhist thought rested on a straightforward set of claims about human goals and the means to achieve those goals. In brief, the main human goal is the elimination of suffering, and the means to that end is the elimination of the causes of suffering. The strands of early Buddhist thought that develop into Mahāyāna philosophy specify that suffering's cause is a type of "ignorance" (*avidyā*), a distorted way of seeing the world that stems especially from misconceptions about personal identity. Ignorance creates and sustains mental dispositions that motivate and guide actions, and since those dispositions are rooted in a fundamental error, the actions guided by them are doomed to failure. Ignorance, moreover, permeates the minds of all unenlightened beings; hence, all of their actions—including those aimed at their highest goal of eliminating suffering—end in frustration.

The solution is to eliminate the fundamental misconceptions about one's personal identity that fuel ignorance, and one does so by demonstrating that their object, an essentially real and immutable "self" or *ātman*, does not exist. The procedure is to engage in a type of reductive analysis whereby, with the aid of contemplative practices, one searches through the constituents of body and mind in order to determine whether any of them—singly or in combination—could be such a self. Having seen that there is no such self to be found, one uses meditation to deepen that experience and explore all its implications. Eventually one becomes free of the misconceptions that create suffering; hence, one attains *nirvāṇa,* utter freedom from suffering.

This basic theory, which also lies at the core of Mahāyāna philosophy, is the main concern of the *abhidharma,* a style of Buddhist thought presented in great detail by the Vaibhāṣika school. The most basic of the four schools according to Indian and Tibetan doxographers, the Vaibhāṣikas derive their name from the *Mahāvibāṣa* (Great commentary) that is their inspiration. Their principal task is to articulate an elaborate taxonomy of all the truly real constituents of the body and mind in order to facilitate an exhaustive search for the self. These psychophysical constituents, called *dharmas,* are discovered through analysis to be the irreducibly real building blocks of the universe, and when one knows them as such, one is seeing mind and body as they truly are (*yathābhūtadarśana*). Since a person is nothing other than those irreducible constituents of mind and body, and since no essential self or immutable identity is numbered among those constituents, one concludes that this alleged essential self (*ātman*) is not truly real.

This theory of "no-self" (*anātman*) is meant to demonstrate that no fixed essence lies at the core of personal identity, but it does not deny that in a contingent way, one can speak intelligibly of persons or selves. A traditional example is a chariot: when one performs the Vaibhāṣikas' reductive analysis of a chariot, one finds only the parts, such as the wheels, axle, and so on. At the same time, one knows that there is no chariot separate from those parts; if there were, it would absurdly follow that the chariot would still exist even after its parts were removed. Hence, even though it may seem that a chariot exists, if one accepts irreducibility as a criterion of true existence, one must admit that no such chariot truly exists. Nevertheless, one is still able to use the word "chariot" intelligibly when engaged in the practical task of, for example, driving the chariot. Thus, in terms of practical actions and use of language, a chariot does exist.

Codifying these two ways of existing, the Vaibhāṣika refers to another key concept for the Mahāyāna: the "two truths" or "two realities," namely the "ultimate" (*paramārtha*) and the "conventional" (*saṃvṛtti*). According to the Vaibhāṣikas, if one wishes to know whether an entity exists ultimately, then one employs their analytical techniques; if, at the end of that reductive analysis, the entity in question has not been reduced to some more fundamental constituents, one concludes that it is *ultimately* real. On the other hand, even if the entity is reducible to more fundamental constituents, one may decide that from a practical or linguistic point of view, it still appears to be existent. In such a case, the entity will be considered *conventionally* real because, although it does not withstand analysis, it does conform to the conventions that govern the use of language and practical actions. Thus, since it can be reduced to more fundamental constituents, a chariot is not ultimately real. Nevertheless, in terms of the conventions that govern the use of the word *chariot,* it appears to be real for practical purposes; hence, a chariot is conventionally real. Likewise, since a person can be reduced to more fundamental constituents, no person is ultimately real; nevertheless, in practical and linguistic terms, one can speak of a person as conventionally real.

In order for the schema of the two realities to make sense, the Vaibhāṣika must explain precisely what it means for one to know that an entity exists ultimately. Their view amounts to a kind of taxonomic atomism: an ultimately real entity is irreducible, and one has full knowledge of this fact when one sees that the entity, due to its essence or nature (*svabhāva*), belongs to one or another of the irreducible categories that exhaustively account for all the stuff of the universe. In other words, the endpoint of the Vaibhāṣika analysis is not just that the thing in question cannot be broken down further, but also that one knows in an affirmative sense what it truly is by virtue of its nature; and one arrives at this knowledge by correctly categorizing the irreducible thing in question.

In emphasizing this taxonomic approach, the Vaibhāṣikas' method betrays a realist attitude toward categories. This realism attracts the criticism of the second non-Mahāyāna school, the Sautrāntikas, who critique it by pointing to its naïve assumptions. One such assumption is the belief that categories—or more generally, words and concepts—refer in some direct and straightforward way to real entities in the world, such that the things expressed by a particular word or concept are understood to be the same. For example, when one uses the word or concept *blue,* one appears to be referring to a thing that is somehow, by its nature, the same as all other blue things. In fact, say the Sautrāntikas, words and concepts do not refer in this way to real things. Thus, the seeming sameness of each thing called "blue" is an illusion; in actuality, each thing is utterly unique, and its unique identity or nature cannot be fully expressed through words or concepts.

The Sautrāntika critique resorts to complex and technical arguments, but to appreciate its relevance to the development of Mahāyāna thought, one need only attend to a main outcome: namely, that the Sautrāntika view moves away from the notion that all things are fixed in categorical identities. For the Vaibhāṣikas, the universe is composed of irreducible elements, each of which belongs by its very nature to a particular category. But according to the Sautrāntikas, the nature of a thing cannot be fully captured by a categorical identity. This leaves open the explicit possibility that any given thing is susceptible to multiple interpretations at the level of words and concepts.

GENERAL TRENDS AND PROBLEMS IN MAHĀYĀNA THOUGHT. Examined through the traditional schema of the four schools, the first two schools—Vaibhāṣika and

Sautrāntika—are usually discussed in the somewhat contrived and ahistorical manner presented just above. Such an approach scarcely does justice to these two "lower" schools, but it does capture an important facet of Mahāyāna thought: namely, that it is explicitly rooted in non-Mahāyāna Buddhism. Mahāyāna thinkers accept all of the elements discussed above: namely, that the elimination of suffering is a main spiritual goal; that ignorance is the primary cause of suffering; that ignorance is eliminated by knowing things as they truly are; that on the theory of no-self, persons are not ultimately real; and that an entity that is not ultimately real may nevertheless be considered conventionally real. Rather than rejecting these basic theories, Mahāyāna thinkers modify them in a way that creates a conceptual transition—not a radical discontinuity—from the non-Mahāyāna to the Mahāyāna.

A key element in this conceptual transition is a fundamental change in the notion of *nirvāṇa.* In non-Mahāyāna thought, *nirvāṇa,* the state in which suffering has utterly ceased, stands in strict opposition to *saṃsāra,* the world of suffering. *Saṃsāra,* moreover, is literally created by ignorance, and on most accounts, this means that everything within *saṃsāra* is tainted by ignorance. For the Vaibhāṣika, this taint is an irreversible and indisputable fact about the *dharmas* or fundamental building blocks that constitute *saṃsāra. Nirvāṇa,* on the other hand, is utterly free not only of suffering, but also of the ignorance that causes suffering. Hence, on the Vaibhāṣika view, *saṃsāra* and *nirvāṇa* must be entirely distinct.

In both literature and philosophy, Mahāyāna moves away from this strict distinction between *saṃsāra* and *nirvāṇa.* In a literary work such as the *Vimalakīrtinirdeśa Sūtra,* one learns that those close to true *nirvāṇa* are capable of seeing this world as a blissful paradise called a *buddhafield,* while those farther from that state still see it as a world of suffering. In the systematic texts of the first Mahāyāna philosopher, Nāgārjuna, one reads that in ontological terms, there is no difference whatsoever between *saṃsāra* and *nirvāṇa.* And in other systematic Mahāyāna works, *nirvāṇa* is redefined as "unlocated" *(apratiṣṭhita)* in that it is situated neither within the world of suffering that is *saṃsāra,* nor in a quietistic *nirvāṇa* that is diametrically opposed to that world. This new, nondualistic paradigm for *nirvāṇa* accompanies a redefinition of the highest goal for Buddhists. In short, for the Mahāyāna, the proper and highest goal of a Buddhist is not only the elimination of one's own suffering, but rather the attainment of buddhahood: a state of perfect bliss in which, while still active in a world that appears to be one of suffering, one is maximally efficient at leading other beings to *nirvāṇa.* Buddhahood is the goal that guides the *bodhisattva* ideal, the Mahāyāna's central ethical motif, which is based on a strong sense of compassion for all beings.

The Mahāyāna's new paradigm emphasizes the nonduality of *saṃsāra* and *nirvāṇa,* and to make good philosophical sense, it must be accompanied by a revision of the Vaibhāṣika ontology. It can no longer be the case that the fundamental building blocks of reality are fixed by their very nature in immutable identities; that is, it can no longer be the case that the stuff of the world of suffering must always remain what it has always been, namely, the direct or indirect product of ignorance. Instead, it must be the case that the world appears as it does—as wracked with suffering or as a blissful buddhafield—not because of some fixed and essential nature of things, but instead due to the minds of the beings that are experiencing that world. Here is the relevance of the Sautrāntika's critique of Vaibhāṣika thought: the nature of a thing cannot be fully captured by a categorical identity, and multiple interpretations of its identity are possible. It is crucial for Mahāyāna theory that the Sautrāntika critique be correct.

From a doxographical perspective, the Mahāyāna's ontological revision is facilitated by extending the doctrine of no-self. The doctrine of no-self rejects the notion that persons have a fixed, essential identity: one may seem to be an ultimately real person, but in fact, one is not truly or ultimately a person because one is reducible to the real, fundamental elements of which one is composed. For the Mahāyāna, a similar critique applies to the fundamental elements or *dharmas* that supposedly make up the person: an infinitesimal particle of matter, for example, seems to be an infinitesimal particle, but it is not truly or ultimately an infinitesimal particle. Indeed, according to the Mahāyāna, all of the Vaibhāṣikas' allegedly fundamental elements of the universe lack any fixed, essential identity as elements. All things are therefore completely mutable, and the world of suffering that is *saṃsāra* is not fixed in its nature: it can be the very locus of *nirvāṇa.*

By extending the critique of essential identity from persons to all the elements of the universe, Mahāyāna thinkers encounter three main issues. First, they must present a new style of critique that is not simply reductive; in other words, the claim that irreducible entities are not ultimately real cannot be supported by reducing them once more, since one will just arrive at the same problem. Instead, some other kind of analysis must be brought to bear. Second, Mahāyāna thinkers must specify what it means for one to see the true identity of things—to "see them as they truly are" *(yathābhūtadarśana)*—when that new analysis reaches its culmination. In other words, the Vaibhāṣika analysis leads to a straightforward and even intuitive conclusion: when one is looking at a chair, in fact what one is seeing is a bunch of irreducible particles of matter; the notion of a "chair" is just a convenient fiction. But if, as Mahāyāna thinkers maintain, even those irreducible elements are not truly real, what then is left for one to be seeing? This problem relates to the third issue: namely, that if even the fundamental building blocks of the world are not truly real, how then does one give an account of conventional reality? For the Vaibhāṣika, an entity such as a chair is not ultimately real because it can be reduced to its more fundamental parts. Nevertheless, in conventional terms one may speak of a "chair" as real, and one can do so because the term *chair* actually refers to those irreducible parts that are functioning together in a particular way. Thus, for the Vaibhāṣika, the warrant for claiming that a chair or a person is conventionally real is precisely the fact that one can point to the ultimately real elements of which it is composed. Mahāyāna thinkers, however, deny the ultimately reality even of those elements. Of what, then is conventional reality constructed?

These three issues—the need for a new style of analysis, a new account of knowing things as they are, and a new approach to conventional reality—all raise another issue: namely, that Mahāyāna thinkers seem to be arguing that, to at least some degree, the Vaibhāṣikas and other non-Mahāyāna philosophers are just plain wrong. Not only do they seem to argue that many Buddhists are wrong, but since Mahāyāna thinkers accept the Vaibhāṣikas' claim that their theories come from words of the Buddha, they seem to say that the Buddha was wrong too. To deal with this problem, followers of the Mahāyāna do not reject most of the previous canonical texts, perhaps in part because causing such a schism was considered as heinous as matricide. Instead, Mahāyāna thinkers sought a method to reconcile their innovations with the long established Buddhist community in which they were embedded. They settled on the notion of "skill in means" (*upāyakauśalya).*

Strictly speaking, "skill in means" may not be a philosophical concept, but it certainly functions as a philosophical method. In its most basic form, it amounts to this: the teaching must be tailored to the audience. That is, one presents theories and arguments at a level that the audience is capable of understanding, and if the audience cannot understand (or will inevitably reject) the highest level of one's philosophy, one uses a lower level of analysis that will prepare the audience to understand or accept the higher level. In part this means that arguments must be couched in such a way that they fit into a hierarchy of levels, and as Mahāyāna thought develops in India, this attention to levels of analysis becomes the central motif of late Mahāyāna thought.

HISTORICAL SYNOPSIS. Considered in historical terms, the two Mahāyāna schools—Madhyamaka and Yogācāra—develop through the following stages: Nāgārjuna (c. 150 CE) composes the early Madhyamaka texts; Asaṅga and Vasubandhu (both c. 350 CE) compose the early Yogācāra texts; Dignāga (c. 450 CE) and Dharmakīrti (c. 625 CE), with the help of Bhāvaviveka (c. 500 CE), integrate a set of theories known as "Buddhist epistemology"into Mahāyāna thought; from the seventh century onward, Madhyamaka and Yogācāra subschools develop in reaction to the developments of Buddhist epistemology, and later Madhyamaka thinkers such as Śāntarakṣita and Kamalaśīla (both c. 750 CE) create a synthesis that explicitly employs a hierarchy of schools representing levels of analysis. The discussion below focuses especially on early Madhyamaka and Yogācāra, and it concludes with a brief examination of their later subschools.

Early Madhyamaka: Nāgārjuna. The first systematic Mahāyāna thinker was Nāgārjuna, and his historical primacy is matched by his philosophical importance. As noted earlier, to move beyond early Buddhist thought Mahāyāna thinkers confront three main needs: a new style of analysis that moves beyond reductionism, a new account of knowing things as they are, and a new approach to the definition of conventional reality. Nāgārjuna's approach to these issues sets the stage for all subsequent Mahāyāna thought.

To formulate a new style of analysis, Nāgārjuna must critique the claim that through a strictly reductive analysis, one comes upon things that are ultimately real. The early Buddhist style of reductive analysis is straightforward: one analyzes an entity by attempting to break it into its component parts, and if it cannot be broken down further, the entity is ultimately real. A chair, for example, is not ultimately real because it can be broken down into more fundamental parts; and when the analytical process is brought to its conclusion, one eventually arrives at irreducible, partless particles that are the basic stuff of the chair.

Thus, when a reductive thinker such as a Vaibhāṣika completes the analysis of a chair, he concludes that a chair is actually just many particles. Hence, in ultimate terms, a chair exists as something other than itself: what seems to be a chair is not ultimately a chair; instead, it is actually irreducible particles. But, for these reductive thinkers, an irreducible entity such as a particle does ultimately exist as itself because it cannot be reduced to anything more fundamental. As such, that entity has *svabhāva,* literally, "own-existence." To speak of a thing's *svabhāva,* therefore, is to speak of what a thing is in and of itself; in other words, it is to speak of its "essence," the best translation of *svabhāva.*

To move beyond reductive analysis, Nāgārjuna focuses on this notion of essence. He accepts that, for an entity to exist ultimately, it must have an essence (*svabhāva*), but for him, to have an essence is not just a matter of being irreducible. Instead, he maintains that the notion of an essence is a way of indicating that the entity's identity is utterly devoid of any dependence on other entities. In short, he understands the notion of essence as independent or nonrelational existence. Hence, in lieu of reduction, his analysis examines the ways in which an entity might be dependent on other entities. If the entity is found to be dependent, then one must conclude that it lacks essence (*svabhāva*) and is thus not ultimately real.

For Nāgārjuna, dependence comes in various forms. For example, he begins his most influential work by arguing that causally produced entities cannot have essences because they depend on their causes. His analysis of causality, however, is only part of a larger strategy: namely, the analysis of relations. Even entities that are not causally produced are susceptible to this analysis. Perhaps the most radical example is *nirvāṇa* itself, which reductionists such as the Vaibhāṣika consider to be an ultimately real element that is free of any causal conditioning. Nāgārjuna, however, maintains that it is conditioned in another sense: one cannot give an account of what *nirvāṇa* is in itself without referring to its opposite, the world of suffering that is *saṃsāra*. In other words, *nirvāṇa* has no meaning without *saṃsāra*, just as "long" is meaningless without "short." Nāgārjuna thus concludes that "*nirvāṇa* is not at all different from *saṃsāra*" (*Mūlamadhyamaka-kārikā* 25.19).

When Nāgārjuna radically rejects any distinction between *saṃsāra* and *nirvāṇa,* he is not espousing some type of monism. Instead, he is drawing a consequence from a more fundamental point, namely, that *saṃsāra* and *nirvāṇa* lack essence. That is, in order to draw a distinction between them in ultimate terms, one must do so in terms of their essences—what each is in itself without depending on anything else. *Saṃsāra* and *nirvāṇa,* however, both lack essence because the identity of each is dependent on the other. Hence, any attempt to draw any ultimate distinction between them must fail.

More important is another conclusion of Nāgārjuna's analysis: since only an entity with an essence can be ultimately real, *saṃsāra* and *nirvāṇa* are not ultimately real. Nāgārjuna goes on to extend this analysis not just to *saṃsāra* and *nirvāṇa,* but to all things, and the upshot of his critique is that they all lack essence. In other words, to have an essence is to have some fixed, nonrelational identity, and no entity can fulfill this requirement. Moreover, since only a nonrelational entity—that is, one with an essence—could be ultimately existent, Nāgārjuna maintains that no entities whatsoever exist ultimately. To know all things as they are truly or ultimately is therefore to recognize that none exist ultimately.

Here one encounters the second issue that all Mahāyāna thinkers must face, namely, the need for a new account of "seeing things as they truly are." As with the Vaibhāṣika, Nāgārjuna accepts that suffering can only be stopped by eliminating ignorance, and that to eliminate ignorance one must see things as they truly are. For the Vaibhāṣika, to see things as they truly are is to experience what is ultimately real, namely, the foundational elements of the universe. In doing so, one can eliminate ignorance: the confused belief that somewhere among those elements one will find one's absolute, fixed identity or self (*ātman*). For Nāgārjuna, however, ignorance is not just a confusion about one's personal identity; instead, it is the deeply ingrained cognitive habit that makes beings see *all things* as if they had some fixed, absolute identity or essence (*svabhāva*). Thus, to eliminate ignorance one must realize that that no entity has any such essence, and this means that one must realize that no entity is ultimately real. But if no entity is ultimately real, what does it mean to see things as they truly are? At the end of the analysis, what is left that one could see?

To answer this question, Nāgārjuna employs a metaphor that runs throughout Mahāyāna thought. Inasmuch as no entity can have a nonrelational identity, every entity lacks essence, and Nāgārjuna speaks of this lack of essence as "emptiness" (*śūnyatā*). Thus, to know an entity in ultimate terms is to know its emptiness, which is a metaphor for its utter lack of essence. The danger, however, is that one will construe this as some kind of absolute nothingness at every entity's core. In that case, Nāgārjuna would be wrong to say that all things lack essence because they would have an essence, namely, that absolute nothingness. Responding to the danger of this type of nihilistic interpretation, Nāgārjuna points out that even emptiness lacks essence and is thus ultimately unreal. Thus, just as a person is empty of really being a person, emptiness is empty of really being emptiness. By understanding this "emptiness of emptiness" (*śūnyatāśūnyatā*), one avoids nihilism.

Nāgārjuna may avoid nihilism, but many questions remain concerning the realization of things as they truly are. Here one should recall that such a realization comes not only through Nāgārjuna's arguments, but also through their integration into a contemplative practice. But what sort of practice would it be? What kind of meditative experience would the arguments help to induce? It should already be clear that the meditation on things as they truly are—that is, the meditation on emptiness—cannot be an experience of some absolute nothingness or any other negative content. It would also seem problematic to hold that the meditation has positive content, such as an object. That is, the meditative experience of emptiness is an experience of any entity's ultimate reality, and if that experience is of some object, then one might conclude that the object experienced was the fixed, ultimate essence of that entity. This would seem to contradict Nāgārjuna's notion that all things lack essence. Hence, the meditative experience of emptiness apparently can be neither of something, nor of nothing.

This conundrum of emptiness clearly vexes subsequent Mahāyāna thinkers, and it leads to many developments in Mahāyāna thought. It also points to problems in the third issue that Nāgārjuna faces: an account of the conventional. As noted above, on Nāgārjuna's view, if one seeks the fixed, nonrelational essence that would constitute the ultimate identity of an entity, one fails to find any such essence. And to exist ultimately, a thing must have such an essence; hence, one concludes that no entity exists ultimately. But as with the Vaibhāṣika, Nāgārjuna maintains that an entity that does not exist ultimately may nevertheless exist conventionally. Hence, even though he denies the ultimate reality of all things, including the Buddhist path, he does not at all mean to deny that many such things, most especially the Buddhist path, are real and valuable in a conventional sense.

Concerning the conventional, the Vaibhāṣikas are straightforward: it is just a matter of recognizing that words such as "chair" are convenient fictions that allow us to speak easily of what is really there, namely, many irreducible particles. Thus, conventionally real things are composed of the irreducible, ultimately real stuff of the universe. But for Nāgārjuna, there is no such stuff, nor does one find anything else that is "really there" in the case of a chair or anything else. How then does one make sense of conventional reality?

To answer this question, Nāgārjuna must redefine the notion of conventionality. For the Vaibhāṣika, a conventional entity depends on the ultimate because it is made from ultimately real stuff, but for Nāgārjuna the conventional and the ultimate define and depend upon each other through their mutual exclusion, as in other dyads such as "long" and "short" or *saṃsāra* and *nirvāṇa.* And since an ultimately real entity has an utterly independent or nonrelational identity, a conventionally real entity must be its antithesis: its identity is utterly dependent or relational. As Nāgārjuna puts it, "We say that emptiness is that which is interdependence" (*Mūlamadhyamaka-kārikā* 8.24). In other words, when one sees that all entities fail the test of ultimacy because they are all empty of any nonrelational identity, one should also realize that if they have identities even conventionally, those identities must be rooted in the radical relationality that is "interdependence" (*pratītya-samutpāda*).

In seeing the conventional as interdependence, Nāgārjuna sets a theme for all subsequent Mahāyāna thought, but as with the notion of emptiness, he leaves many questions unanswered. For example, he has not addressed the Vaibhāṣikas' basic intuition that the conventional is made up from ultimate stuff. In other words, the modality of conventional reality may indeed be interdependence, but does not such a concept presuppose that there are things standing in the relation of interdependence? A relation cannot exist without *relata,* so how could it make sense to speak of the relation that is interdependence if there are not really any entities to be related? These questions, along with the problems of knowing emptiness, create fertile ground for the growth of Mahāyāna thought.

Early Yogācāra: Asaṅga and Vasubandhu. Not long after Nāgārjuna, Asaṅga and Vasubandhu develop the other major strand of Mahāyāna thought, the Yogācāra (literally, "Practice of Yoga"). Also called *citta-mātra* ("mind only"), this school emphasizes mind (*citta*) or consciousness (*vijñāna*) in its responses to the three issues mentioned above, namely, style of analysis, seeing things as they truly are, and an account of the conventional.

In terms of analysis, Asaṅga and Vasubandhu largely follow Nāgārjuna's lead. Asaṅga's main style of analysis is also relational, but his focus is different. He begins with the assumption that the notion of an ultimately real personal identity is rooted in one's sense of subjectivity. His analysis is relational because on his view, the reality of that subjectivity is tied to the reality of the objects that it allegedly knows. Hence, in order to follow previous Buddhist thinkers in demonstrating that there is no such fixed, ultimately real personal identity, he must show that all the objects allegedly perceived by this subjectivity are ultimately unreal. Therefore, the subjectivity must also be ultimately unreal because it can truly be a subjectivity only if it perceives objects.

Focusing on the relation between subject and object in this way, Asaṅga follows Nāgārjuna in extending the critique of essence beyond persons to the fundamental elements of the universe, but unlike Nāgārjuna, his approach creates a more obvious bridge between non-Mahāyāna and Mahāyāna thought. That is, as with non-Mahāyāna thought, the main goal is still to refute one's notion of an ultimately real self (*ātman*), but Asaṅga suggests that this goal is best reached by critiquing the self's alleged objects. The intuition here is that the false impression of ultimately real selfhood is rooted in one's sense of subjectivity as a perceiver of objects. Thus, in showing that there are no ultimately real elements that could serve as objects, Asaṅga is just offering a more profound and effective rejection of any fixed, absolute personal identity.

Asaṅga's strategy requires some means to refute the reality of any entities that could be construed as objects existing in distinction from the subjectivity that perceives them. For the Vaibhāṣikas, those objects basically consist of the irreducible elements that they take to be ultimately real; hence, Asaṅga's critique must demonstrate that all those elements are not ultimately real. Buddhist models of consciousness require that his analysis cover two general types of objects: mental objects, which are immaterial, and sense objects, which, being material, are allegedly composed of irreducible particles.

In terms of mental objects, Asaṅga develops a critique elaborated further by Vasubandhu. As with Nāgārjuna, the critique employs a relational analysis whereby an entity could be ultimately existent only if it is utterly free of dependence on other entities. Exploring an area not systematically addressed by Nāgārjuna, Asaṅga and Vasubandhu refute the ultimate reality of mental objects by demonstrating that their allegedly independent existence is contradicted by the linguistic and conceptual relationality that enables them to be mental objects in the first place. Their detailed arguments demonstrate that the referent of a word or concept is necessarily mind-dependent to at least some degree, and being dependent, that referent cannot be ultimately real.

The critique of sense objects, which thinkers such as the Vaibhāṣika take to be composed of irreducible particles, is developed especially by Vasubandhu. Here too the continuity with non-Mahāyāna thought is striking, for Vasubandhu chooses to employ a reductive analysis to demonstrate the ultimate irreality of such particles. But in contrast to reductionists such as the Vaibhāṣika, Vasubandhu is willing to reduce matter to the point where it no longer exists. In short, he demonstrates that irreducibility is incompatible with material existence: if material particles were irreducible, then they could have no size, but if they have no size, then how could an accumulation of them form gross objects such as jars or chairs? On the other hand, if they do have size, then they clearly are not irreducible, since they then must have parts, such as front, back, left, right, top, and bottom. The conclusion of this analysis is a philosophical idealism that totally denies the existence of matter. And although a few academic interpreters maintain that Vasubandhu does not mean to refute the reality of matter, such an interpretation ignores all subsequent Indian commentators and all Tibetan doxographers.

The critique of mental and physical objects developed by Asaṅga and Vasubandhu differs in an important respect from Nāgārjuna's approach. For Nāgārjuna, when one reaches the conclusion of the analysis, one's "seeing things as they truly are" is just seeing emptiness, which is not readily construed as seeing anything at all; indeed, later Indian Madhyamakas will speak of it as the "seeing that is non-seeing." Asaṅga and Vasubandhu, however, see their analysis as ending in a realization that has a far more affirmative content. The positive nature of that realization is shown by the way they redefine emptiness. For Nāgārjuna, emptiness is utter lack of essence, and since all things are empty, all things lack essence; hence, they are all ultimately unreal. For Asaṅga and Vasubandhu, emptiness is the absence of subject-object duality in the mind of the perceiver. Thus, although ultimately real objects do not stand in opposition to some ultimately real subject, there remains nevertheless the undeniable fact of consciousness itself.

Asaṅga and Vasubandhu explain their new notion of emptiness through the theory of the "three natures" (*trisvabhāva*). The usual order of enumeration is: the constructed nature (*parikalpitasvabhāva*), the dependent nature (*paratantrasvabhāva*), and the perfect nature (*pariniṣpannasvabhāva*). It is helpful to place the dependent nature at the head of this list because the other two—the constructed and the perfect—are actually two different modes of the dependent nature. That is, the dependent nature is the causal flow of consciousness itself: it is the sequence of one moment of consciousness produced by its own previous moment and going on to produce its own subsequent moment. This ongoing stream of consciousness can appear in two different modes. For ordinary persons, it appears with a dizzying variety of sensory and mental objects, and each mental moment except for the deepest sleep is replete with such an object. Asaṅga's and Vasubandhu's analysis of mental and sensory objects, however, demonstrates that none of these objects is ultimately real. Nevertheless—and this is the key ontological claim—the conclusion that the objects are ultimately unreal does not adequately account for the fact that those objects are appearing. Instead, one must see that denying the ultimate, independent reality of those objects is the same as affirming their conventional, dependent existence within the mind itself. To put it another way, when one sees the color blue, the apparent existence of the blue object as an external, independent object is false. But the fact that it is appearing to consciousness is undeniable, and since the Yogācāra analysis shows that it could not be external and independent of the mind, it must be within the mind itself. Seeing that flow of mind in that way—namely, as devoid of the apparent subject-object duality—is to see the perfect nature. Thus all objects and all subjects are not distinct, but this is not to deny their reality altogether. Rather, the denial of subject-object duality still leaves intact the causal flow of mind in which all those apparently dualistic experiences are occurring.

This critique of subject-object duality leads to a redefinition of emptiness. The "dependent nature" is a way of referring to the causal flow of mind that is "dependent" since each moment of consciousness is contingent upon its own previous moment, which acts as its cause. The "constructed nature" refers to the objects that appear in the mind such that they seem distinct from the subjectivity that apprehends them. It is "constructed" in that this dualistic distinction between subject and object is not innate; instead, it is created by ignorance. In this system, "emptiness" describes the causal flow of mind in terms of its ultimate mode, the perfect nature. That is, ultimately the causal flow of consciousness (the dependent nature) is *empty* or devoid of the seeming subject-object duality (the constructed nature) that appears in the ordinary experience that is the constructed nature. Thus, to see "emptiness" or the perfect nature is to see the causal flow of mind as it truly is, namely, utterly devoid of the subject-object duality that is the constructed nature.

A metaphor used in Yogācāra texts is helpful here. Suppose that a magician casts a spell on some stones such that his audience now sees them as elephants. The stones themselves represent the causal flow of mind. Those stones appear to the tricked audience as elephants, and this represents the constructed nature, namely, the fact that the mind itself (the stones) is appearing as something other than the mind (i.e., as elephants). The realization of the perfect nature is embodied by the magician who knows indubitably that he is actually seeing stones, which are empty of being elephants.

By redefining emptiness in this way, Asaṅga and Vasubandhu respond to a problem in Nāgārjuna's thought, namely, that he left no clear account of the conventional beyond a vague appeal to interdependence. Although they do not directly quote Nāgārjuna, Asaṅga and Vasubandhu seem disturbed by this vagueness, especially in terms of their concern for a "basis for affliction and purification" (*saṃkleśavyavadānāśraya*), that is, an ontological foundation for the fact that one can be afflicted by ignorance or liberated into *nirvāṇa.* For them, that basis is consciousness itself.

Turning to the issue of conventional reality, Asaṅga and Vasubandhu's theory of the three natures also enables them to give a more elaborate account than Nāgārjuna's. The conventional for these thinkers consists of the seemingly dualistic experiences that are the constructed nature. These would include all ordinary perceptions, as when one sees colors such as red and yellow. Such perceptions are driven by ignorance, in that the red and yellow colors seem distinct from the subjectivity that perceives them. These perceptions are not caused by material objects, since matter does not in fact exist. What, then, could cause such perceptions?

The answer is "foundational consciousness" or *ālayavijñāna.* Also translated as "storehouse consciousness," this form of awareness is entirely unconscious, but within it lie all the "seeds" (*bīja*) of experience, such as the perceptions of a red apple or of yellow corn. When one sees the red apple or the yellow corn, it is not that one's perception is caused by some material object. Instead, various circumstances have come together to allow the seeds of those perceptions to ripen. One's world, in short, is just a projection of mind.

In arguing that the world is a projection of mind, however, Asaṅga and Vasubandhu are not proposing some kind of mental monism where everything is reducible to one universal mind. Their rejection of monism becomes evident when one asks: if the world is just a projection of one's mind, why is it that a perceptual object (such as an unpleasant smell) cannot become something else (the bouquet of a rose) merely by the intention of one's mind to make it so? Part of the answer is the conditioning of each individual's mind, whereby one's reality is incapable of such radical and immediate alterations. But part of the answer is also the influence of an infinite number of other minds. In other words, the "seeds" that ripen into experiences in one's own mind have been created not only by one's own previous experiences, but also by the experiences of all the minds of the beings around one. This notion of intersubjectivity, which in Yogācāra literature is tied to the workings of *karma,* enables the Yogācāra to surpass Nāgārjuna in their account of the conventional.

Later Yogācāra. From the standpoint of traditional doxography, all Mahāyāna thinkers after Nāgārjuna, Asaṅga, and Vasubandhu fall into one of two camps: Madhyamaka or Yogācāra. These two schools, however, are retroactively split into several subschools by doxographers in India and Tibet in an attempt to give some structure to the great variety of debates and disagreements that arise within both Madhyamaka and Yogācāra.

The divergent strands of Madhyamaka and Yogācāra arise largely in relation to a major development among a group of thinkers that, while not technically forming a "school," exhibit considerable coherence and continuity. This new philosophical approach was developed especially by the Yogācāra thinkers Dignāga (c. 450 CE) and Dharmakīrti (c. 625 CE), but Bhāvaviveka, a Madhyamaka thinker, also plays a major role. In terms of its overall concern, this new style of philosophy can be called "Buddhist epistemology," since its central aim is to give a detailed account of how one gains reliable knowledge, and how one justifies one's claims to knowledge. This epistemic focus arises in part due to interactions with non-Buddhist thinkers who, at Dignāga's time, were well ahead of their Buddhist counterparts in the study of such issues. One main topic was the analysis of oral arguments, and one way to trump an opponent in debate was simply to point out that his proofs were not well formed. Since formal debates within and between traditions may have been relatively common, Buddhist thinkers needed to come up with their own positions in this regard so as to defend their arguments against such a tactic.

The concern with justification of knowledge, however, also reflects the ongoing interest of Mahāyāna thinkers in providing an adequate account of conventional reality. For example, Buddhist epistemology texts discuss perception in detail, and they thus give Yogācāra thinkers the tools to explore a central question left unanswered by Asaṅga and Vasubandhu: namely, what is the status of one's mental content? This question may seem abstruse, but it is unavoidable in Yogācāra thought.

As noted above, on the theory of the three natures, to see things as they truly are is to see emptiness, and in this system this means seeing that the causal flow of mind is ultimately empty of subject-object duality. Hence, when seeing the color red, the color appears to be external to one's mind, and it seems that one is "inside" looking out at the world; but these are illusions created by ignorance. In fact, the color and the subjectivity perceiving it are both nothing but occurrences in the causal flow of mind itself. By developing a detailed account of perception, Buddhist epistemology uncovers an obvious question here that relates to seeing things as they truly are, that is, seeing things without the influence of ignorance. Specifically: when one sees the causal flow of mind as empty of subject-object duality, does one still see the color red, for example, but now in some nondualistic way? In other words, if a perception's duality is produced by ignorance, does this mean that even its sheer content is also contaminated by ignorance?

Employing the tools of Buddhist epistemology, some later Yogācāra thinkers such as Devendrabuddhi (c. 650 CE) answer this question by denying that ignorance contaminates all mental content. In other words, when one is seeing things as they truly are, one is indeed just seeing the mind itself empty of subject-object duality, but the perceptual content—such as a color or shape—can still appear in one's cognition; it is just that one experiences that content as identical to the mind. This position develops into the subschool known as "Proponents of True Content" (Satyākāravāda). One implication is that, for them, the perceptions of a buddha can include the type of content found in the mind of ordinary persons, with the exception that a buddha's perceptions will be free of subject-object duality.

Other Yogācāra thinkers, such as Śākyabuddhi (c. 675 CE), take the opposite tack. As "Proponents of False Content" (Alīkākāravāda), they maintain that not just the duality of the perception, but even the content itself is contaminated by ignorance. Hence, to be free of ignorance and see things as they truly are, one must experience the mind itself devoid not only of duality, but of any perceptual content at all. The implications for buddhahood are clear: since a buddha is utterly free of ignorance and always seeing the world as it truly is, a buddha cannot ever perceive the world that an ordinary person sees.

Later Madhyamaka and levels of analysis. As with Yogācāra, Buddhist epistemology also significantly impacts Madhyamaka thought. After Dignāga develops the early form of Buddhist epistemology, the Madhyamaka thinker Bhāvaviveka applies it to Nāgārjuna's arguments. In doing so, he critiques the commentator Buddhapālita (c. 500 CE) for failing to employ well-formed proofs or "independent inferences" (*svatantrānumāna*) that follow the rules of Buddhist epistemology. Candrakīrti (c. 625 CE) later responds to Bhāvaviveka, and he does so by claiming that by insisting on well-formed arguments Bhāvaviveka is introducing a subtle form of essentialism into Nāgārjuna's critique of essence.

Candrakīrti's critique addresses a basic principle in Buddhist epistemology: in order for a proof to be well formed, the entity that is being analyzed must be perceptible to both participants in the debate. For example, to present a well-formed proof that a chair is not ultimately real, the chair itself must be perceptible to the person presenting the proof and to the person that is the target of the proof. Hence, when Bhāvaviveka refutes essentialist positions by using well-formed proofs, he must maintain that both he and his essentialist opponent can perceive the entity that they are discussing. On Candrakīrti's view, however, a Madhyamaka thinker should not use this procedure because it would require him to agree that the entity has some form of independent existence, and such an admission is anathema to a Madhyamaka.

Although it is not usually expressed in this way, the upshot of Candrakīrti's criticism is that a Madhyamaka thinker cannot fully inhabit the same perceptual world as the essentialist that he is critiquing. To do so would require that both the Madhyamaka and the opponent see the same thing, and this would require that the thing in question be somehow independent of the minds that are perceiving it. Being independent in that fashion, the thing would be essentially real, albeit in a subtle way. Candrakīrti therefore maintains that the only proper method for a Madhyamaka is to point out the "unacceptable consequences" (*prasaṅga*) that follow from the opponent's position, rather than attempting to present arguments based upon what both the Madhyamaka and his opponent can perceive.

Tibetan doxographers coin terms to categorize these two streams of Madhyamaka thought. Those who follow Bhāvaviveka in his use of Buddhist epistemology are called *Svātantrika*, that is, those who use well-formed inferences in their arguments. And thinkers who follow Candrakīrti are known to the Tibetans as *Prāsaṅgika*, namely, those who argue by pointing out unacceptable consequences.

For most Tibetan doxographers, Candrakīrti's Prāsaṅgika subschool is the highest form of Madhyamaka, but historically Bhāvaviveka's use of Buddhist epistemology became the norm for Indian Madhyamaka thinkers. Part of the reason for the enthusiastic adoption of Buddhist epistemology by later Madhyamakas may well have been their interest in a strategy first employed systematically by the Buddhist epistemologist Dharmakīrti. Dharmakīrti develops Buddhist epistemology in such a way that he can readily argue from multiple philosophical perspectives; indeed, large portions of his texts can be accepted equally well by Vaibhāṣika, Sautrāntika, and Yogācāra thinkers. Dharmakīrti is thus able to establish a common ground for debate and then introduce a wrinkle into his argument that suddenly points to a uniquely Yogācāra concept as if it were the natural conclusion to an analysis that even Vaibhāṣikas and Sautrāntikas accept. This technique, which clearly rests on the notion of "skill in means" discussed above, creates levels of analysis within Dharmakīrti's work, and it enables him to address multiple audiences with great ease. Later Madhyamaka thinkers, most prominently Śāntarakṣita and Kamalaśīla (both c. 750 CE) employ this method in nearly all their works, with the exception that their highest level of analysis is not Yogācāra, but rather Madhyamaka. Their use of levels of analysis also enables later Indian Madhyamakas to speak with greater precision and coherence about the relations among various schools of Buddhist thought, and it inspires the Tibetan doxographical enterprise that has encouraged the study of Mahāyāna thought in terms of schools.

SEE ALSO Abhinavagupta; Ālaya-vijñāna; Asaṅga; Buddhist Books and Texts; Buddhist Philosophy; Dharmakirti; Dignāga; Mādhyamika; Mahasamghika; Nāgārjuna; Sakya Pandita (Sa skya Pandita); Śūnyam and Śūnyatā; Vasubandhu.

BIBLIOGRAPHY

Anacker, Stefan. *Seven Works of Vasubandhu: The Buddhist Psychological Doctor.* Delhi, 1984. A translation of several major texts in the Yogācāra tradition.

Burton, David F. *Emptiness Appraised: A Critical Study of Nāgārjuna's Philosophy.* Richmond, U.K., 1999. A useful critique of Nāgārjuna.

Dreyfus, Georges, and Sara L. McClintock, eds. *The Svātantrika-Prāsaṅgika Distinction: What Difference Does a Difference Make?* Boston, 2002. Focuses on the debate between the two forms of Madhyamaka thought.

Dunne, John D. *Foundations of Dharmakīrti's Philosophy.* Boston, 2004. A study of the major figure in Buddhist epistemology, including a discussion of levels of analysis.

Garfield, Jay L., trans. and commentator. *The Fundamental Wisdom of the Middle Way: Nāgārjuna's Mūlamadhyamakakārikā.* Oxford, 1995. A complete translation of Nāgārjuna's main text along with a philosophical commentary.

Kapstein, Matthew. *Reason's Traces: Identity and Interpretation in Indian and Tibetan Buddhist Thought.* Boston, 2001. Includes a set of essays on the issue of identity along with an important piece on the notion of "Buddhist philosophy."

Nagao, G. M. *Mādhyamika and Yogācāra, a Study of Mahāyāna Philosophies: Collected Papers of G. M. Nagao* Edited by L. S. Kawamura. Albany, N.Y., 1991. Includes an especially useful essay on Yogācāra entitled "What Remains in *Śūnyatā*."

Ruegg, David Seyfort. *The Literature of the Madhyamaka School of Philosophy in India.* Wiesbaden, Germany, 1981. An exhaustive history of the Madhyamaka school in India, including some information on Yogācāra thinkers.

Williams, Paul, and Anthony Tribe. *Buddhist Thought: A Complete Introduction to the Indian Tradition.* London, 2000. An accessible presentation of Mahāyāna thought structured in terms of the four schools.

JOHN D. DUNNE (2005)

BUDDHISM, SCHOOLS OF: TANTRIC RITUAL SCHOOLS OF BUDDHISM [FIRST EDITION]

[*This entry was originally titled "Buddhism, Schools of: Esoteric Buddhism" in the first edition of the Encyclopedia.*]

Buddhist esotericism is an Indian movement obscure in its beginnings. Combining yoga and ritual, it calls itself the Diamond Vehicle (Vajrayāna)—where *diamond* means "the unsplittable"—or the Mantra Vehicle (Mantrayāna)—where *mantra* means "magical speech." The revealed texts of the tradition are called *tantra*, in contrast to sūtra (the generic name of the non-Tantric Buddhist scriptures), but both these words have the implication "thread" or "continuous line." In the case of the Tantras, the "continuous line" can be understood in various ways: the lineage of master-disciple, the continuity of vows and pledges in the practitioner's stream of consciousness, or the continuity of practice leading to a religious goal.

Much of Tantric literature is ritualistic in nature, manifesting Brahmanic influence by the use of incantations (*mantra*) and the burnt offering (*homa*), both of which were employed for magical purposes as far back as Vedic times. Similarly, the notion of the "five winds" found in certain of the Tantras dates back to some of the Upaniṣads. Many of the hand gestures and foot stances of Buddhist Tantric practice are also found in Indian dance. However, as specifically Buddhist Tantras, such texts are colored both by Buddhist theories and practices and by the typical terminology of Mahāyāna Buddhism. These texts regularly employ such ancient Buddhist formulations as the triad body, speech, and mind, and draw upon such common Mahāyāna notions as the pair "means" (*upāya*) and "insight" (*prajñā*). The Tantras accept the old Buddhist ontology of three worlds filled with deities and demons, and contribute the premise that one can relate to these forces by ritualistic manipulation of one's nature (body, speech, and mind), thereby attaining "success" (*siddhi*) in such mundane forms as appeasing the deities, or the supermundane success of winning complete enlightenment (Buddhahood), possibly in a single lifetime. The old Buddhist terminology "son or daughter of the family," here the Buddhist family, was extended to refer to Buddha families. Initially, the texts propose a triad of three Buddhas or Tathāgatas: Vairocana, Amitābha, and Akṣobhya. Later, Ratnasambhava and Amoghasiddhi are added to make up a family of five, and Vajrasattva to make a family of six. A supreme Buddha, referred to variously as Mahā-Vajradhara, Heruka, or Ādibuddha ("Primordial Buddha"), is also mentioned. But the texts do not use the term "Dhyāni Buddhas" that is sometimes found in Western books on the subject.

INFLUENCE IN TIME AND PLACE. Buddhist Tantrism appears to have originated in eastern India and to have been transmitted orally in private circles from around the third century CE. When we speak of the period of the origination of the tradition, however, we refer only to that era in which Buddhist Tantras arose in syncretism with an already extant lore non-Buddhist in character, and not to some hypothetic origin of Tantrism per se. The first textual evidence of this current is found in chapters bearing the title *dhāraṇī* (a kind of *mantra*) within certain Mahāyāna scriptures. The ninth chapter of the *Laṅkāvatāra Sūtra* (fourth century CE), for example, is devoted to magical formulas of supposedly meaningless sounds, which, when recited for one hundred and eight times, are claimed to ward off demons. The earliest Tantras are those that still give a leading role to Śākyamuni, the historical founder of Buddhism, perhaps placing him at the center of a *maṇḍala*. By comparing the names of the five Buddhas in the *Durgatipariśodhana Tantra* (i.e., Vairocana, Durgatipariśodhana, Ratnaketu, Śākyamuni, and Saṃkusumita) with those of the five Buddhas of the Mahākaruṇāgarbha Maṇḍala, which is derived from the *Vairocanābhisaṃbodhi Tantra* (i.e., Mahāvairocana, Dundubhinirghoṣa, Ratnaketu, Amitāyus, and Samkusumitarāja) and with the five of the Vajradhātu Maṇḍala, derived from the *Tattvasaṃgraha Tantra* (i.e., Mahāvairocana, Akṣobhya, Ratnasambhava, Amitābha, and Amoghasiddhi), we can observe that the name Śākyamuni is still employed in the earliest Tantras but is later replaced by the name Amitāyus, and finally by Amitābha, resulting in the standard set of Buddha names of later times.

Between the third and the eighth centuries, these cults, with their "revealed" scriptures, were transmitted secretly from master to disciple, but by the eighth and ninth centuries a remarkable change had occurred in the fortunes of Buddhist Tantrism. Evidence of the growing influence of the movement may be seen in the fact that a king called Great Indrabhūti of Uḍḍiyāna is said to have been initiated into the Tantric mysteries at about this time. Other important evidence of the growth of the tradition is found in the texts of the period. Whereas the revealed Tantric works of earlier centuries were written in strict anonymity and attributed to divine authorship, now historical figures begin to attach their names to commentarial literature. Buddhaguhya (second half of the eighth century) wrote learned commentaries on the three Tantras mentioned above. A host of commentaries also arose on the *Guhyasamāja Tantra* and the *Śrī-Cakrasaṃvara Tantra* cycles by such celebrated writers as Saraha and the Tantric Nāgārjuna (author of the *Pañcakrama*). While some Tantric works had been translated in Chinese earlier, it was not until the eighth century that Tantrism would take hold in China, owing largely to the efforts of the monk Vajrabodhi and his disciple Amoghavajra. Their kind of Tantrism was transmitted to the talented Japanese monk Kūkai (posthumously called Kōbō Daishi, 774–835), who introduced to Japan an elaborate cult based on the "two Tantras," the *Vairocanābhisaṃbodhi* and the *Tattvasaṃgraha*. This cult, a fusion of art, mysterious rituals, colorful costumes, religious music, and handsome calligraphy, would have a great cultural impact on Japan.

In this period certain Tantras were also translated into Tibetan. Tibet eagerly embraced these cults, and in time would produce native works on the most popular Tantras.

While a vast number of Tantric texts was translated into Tibetan, a lesser amount was preserved in Chinese translation. Chinese Buddhism generally disliked the Tantras, partly for their intricate ritualism, but more for the sexual symbolism, offensive to the Chinese mind, found in Tantras such as the *Guhyasamāja*. In Java, construction of the Borobaḍur monument, begun in the eighth century, shows Tantric influence in its use of *maṇḍalas* at its central stupa. It is also known that Atīśa, who arrived in Tibet in 1042 and became a towering figure in Tibetan Buddhism, had earlier studied for twelve years in the celebrated Tantric college of Śrīvijaya (now part of Indonesia). Thus it is clear that after the eighth century, Buddhist Tantrism was strongly entrenched in eastern India from Bengal north, had advanced to Nepal and Tibet, flourished for a time in China, became highly influential in Japan, and would establish a great school in the "Golden Isles" (Indonesia).

Tibet became an extraordinary center for Tantrism as well as the major storehouse of Tantric literature. The Indian *guru* Nā ro pa (956–1040?) was an important link in this development. It was Nā ro pa who transmitted Buddhist esotericism to the translator Mar pa, who in turn taught it to the poet Mi la ras pa. Thereafter, from this lineage arose the Bka' brgyud pa school, continuing the Great Seal *(mahāmudrā)* teachings and the six yoga doctrines that had been taught by Nā ro pa. In modern times, the Tibetan tragedy has resulted in a number of Tibetan monk refugees transplanting their Tantric lineages to Europe and the United States.

BUDDHIST TANTRIC LITERATURE. The Tibetan canon classifies the Tantras into four groups, the Kriyā Tantras, the Caryā Tantras, the Yoga Tantras, and the Anuttarayoga Tantras. The translations of the revealed Tantras were included under the four headings in a section of the canon called the Bka' 'gyur (Kanjur); the commentaries are grouped in a section of exegetical works called the Bstan-'gyur (Tanjur). The Sino-Japanese canon does not so group them. In the Tibetan canon, the two chief works of the Japanese Tantric school (Shingonshū), the *Vairocanābhisaṃbodhi* and the *Tattvasaṃgraha*, are the principal works of the Caryā and Yoga Tantras, respectively. The *Hevajra Tantra* and the *Guhyasamāja Tantra*, works well known to Western scholars, belong to the Anuttarayoga Tantra class, and are respectively a "Mother" and a "Father" Tantra of this class. The status of the popular *Kālacakra Tantra*, definitely an Anuttarayoga class text, has been disputed. There is also a host of small works called *sādhana*, which set forth methods of evoking a given deity. The *Sādhanamālā* is a well-known collection of such works. Since in the Tantric tradition deities are arrayed in designs called *maṇḍalas*, there are also treatises devoted to *maṇḍalas* and their associated rituals. The *Niṣpannayogāvalī* is a work on twenty-six of these *maṇḍalas*. During the last period of Buddhism in India the popularity of Tantrism gave rise to a group of Tantric heroes called *mahāsiddhas* ("great adepts"), and tales were compiled concerning their superhuman exploits. Their Tantric songs are collected in a work called the *Caryāgiti*. Other well-known Tantras include the *Mañjuśrī-mūla-kalpa* (a Kriyā Tantra), the *Sarvadurgatipariśodhana* (a Yoga Tantra), and the *Mañjuśrī-nāma-saṃgiti*, which was commented upon both as a Yoga Tantra and as an Anuttarayoga Tantra.

The editor of the Tibetan canon, Bu ston (1290–1364), arranged the Tantras in their respective four classes according to a theory that in order for a Tantra to be a Buddhist one, it should be in some Buddhist family, headed by one of the Buddhas. In the case of the Anuttarayoga Tantras, the Mother Tantras were classified under one or another of seven Buddhas, in order: "Teacher" (Tib., *ston pa*, probably referring to Vajrasattva), Heruka (i.e., Akṣobhya), *Vairocana*, Vajraprabha (i.e., Ratnasambhava), Padmanarteśvara (i.e., Amitābha), Paramāśva (i.e., Amogha*siddhi*), and Vajradhara. The *Śrī-Cakrasaṃvara* and the *Hevajra* were included under Heruka. The Father Tantras were classified under six Buddhas, identical to those used to classify the Mother Tantras except that the first, "Teacher," is omitted. The *Guhyasamāja Tantra* was classified under Akṣobhya and the *Yamāri* (or *Yamāntaka*) *Tantra* under Vairocana. The *Mañjuśrī-nāma-saṃgīti Tantra* and the *Kālacakra Tantra* were not included in this classification, presumably because they were classed under Ādibuddha, "Primordial Buddha."

In the case of the Yoga Tantras, the basic scripture, called *Tattvasaṃgraha*, is itself divided into four sections corresponding to four Buddha families. Explanatory Tantras of the Yoga Tantra class could thus be classed in one of those four sections or families, or could emphasize either "means" (*upāya*) or "insight" (*prajñā*). For example, the *Paramādya* is classed chiefly as an "insight" scripture.

The Caryā Tantras were classified under three Buddha families, the Tathāgata family (under Vairocana), the Padma family (under Amitābha), and the Vajra family (under Akṣobhya). The *Vairocanābhisaṃbodhi* is classed under the Tathāgata family; the *Vajrapāṇyabhiṣeka* is classed under the Vajra family; but the Padma family has no corresponding text among the Caryā Tantras.

The arrangement of the Kriyā Tantras is rather complicated. Using the same three families that govern the Caryā Tantras, the Kriyā Tantras make further subdivisions for the Lord of the Family, the Master, the Mother, Wrathful Deities, Messengers, and Obedient Ones. In addition, the Tathāgata family is subdivided into Uṣṇīṣa, *Bodhisattvas*, and Gods of the Pure Abode. For example, the *Suvarṇaprabhāsottama*, which was also quite popular as a Mahāyāna sūtra, is included under the Mother of the Tantras family. The Kriyā Tantras also include a category "Worldly Families" as well as "General" Kriyā Tantras, a category that includes the *Subāhuparipṛcchā*.

Naturally, there was always a considerable degree of arbitrariness in such categorizations; in fact, certain Tantras had a disputed status. The traditions carried to Tibet also classified the four divisions of Tantras according to their respective deities and according to the preferences of the human performers. When classed in terms of deities, the division reflects degrees of courtship: laughing for the Kriyā Tantras, mutual gazing for the Caryā Tantras, holding hands for the Yoga Tantras, and the pair united for the Anuttarayoga Tantras. When arranged according to human performers, the respective preference for outer ritual or inner *samādhi* is the determining factor. Kriyā Tantras appeal to those with a preference for ritual over *samādhi.* In the Caryā Tantras, ritual and *samādhi* are balanced; in the Yoga Tantras *samādhi* prevails over ritual; and in the Anuttarayoga Tantras *samādhi* alone is the requisite practice. An unorthodox explanation of these four classes is found in Smṛti's commentary on the *Vajravidāraṇā-nāma-dhāraṇī* (Kriyā Tantra, Master of the Family class). This author claims the four classes correspond to four kinds of Buddhist followers and the way in which they "cleanse with voidness." For the *śrāvaka*s (i.e., Hīnayāna monks) external cleansing purifies the body. For the *pratyekabuddha*s (*ṛṣi*s, "seers") inner cleansing purifies speech. For the Yogācāras (the Mind Only school) secret cleansing purifies the mind, and for the Mādhyamikas "reality cleansing" with a diamondlike *samādhi* unifies body, speech, and mind.

THE LANGUAGE OF BUDDHIST ESOTERICISM. Opponents of the Tantras have based their condemnations on what they read in such works. Since works of the Anuttarayoga Tantra class, the *Hevajra* and *Guhyasamāja Tantra*s in particular, are still preserved in the original Sanskrit, modern scholars have consulted these for their conclusions about Tantrism and are usually unable to consult the Tibetan or Sino-Japanese versions of a wide range of Tantras. Some scholars accordingly have referred to Buddhist Tantrism by names such as the Vāmācāra ("left-handed path") or the Sahajayāna ("together-born path"), but the Tantras themselves do not use such terms, and in fact such designations fail to throw light on their contents. It should be recognized that the followers of the Tantric cults, including many Tibetan monks, would *never* presume to interpret a Tantra from the language of the revealed text alone. These invariably require the assistance of a commentary, perhaps one written by their *guru.* On such grounds a number of Tantras translated into Tibetan have traditionally been considered "off-limits" precisely because they were not transmitted with their "lineage," the authoritative explanation, or with "permission" (*anujñā*) to evoke the deity of the Tantra. Commenting on the *Guhyagarbha Tantra,* the Tantric Līlavajra observes that the literal interpretation of Tantric texts is the basis for misunderstanding them and practically admits that some of his contemporaries not only misunderstand the texts but also appeal to them in order to justify their own corrupt practices. In the same way, modern authors who are outsiders to the cult assume that the literal meaning is the only meaning, and thus wrongly explain fragments of Tantras available to them.

A commentary on the *Guhyasamāja Tantra* by the Tantric Candrakīrti sets forth four kinds of explanation of the sense of a given passage (cf. Wayman, 1977, pp. 116–117): (1) the invariant sense (*akṣarārtha*), or literal meaning; (2) the shared sense (*samastāṅgārtha*), or sense of the text that is shared either with non-Tantric traditions or with Tantras of the three lower classes; (3) the pregnant sense (*garbhyartha*), by which is meant a meaning that either clarifies the doctrine of lust (*rāgadharma*), reveals conventional truth (*samvṛtisatya*), or considers the three gnoses (*jñānatraya*; i.e., Light, Spread of Light, Culmination of Light); and (4) the ultimate sense (*kolikārtha*), or the one that clarifies the Clear Light (*prabhāsvara*) or reveals the paired union (*yuganaddha*).

Equally important, the Tantras frequently use language that is deliberately obscure. In the Anuttarayoga Tantras this kind of arcane language is called *sandhyābhāṣā,* frequently rendered "twilight language" or "intentional language." In this highly metaphoric idiom the term "Diamond Body" (*vajrakāya*) is used to refer to menstrual blood, "Diamond Speech" (*vajravāk*) to refer to semen, and "Diamond Mind" (*vajracitta*) to refer to scented water. Clearly, Tantric language does not conform to our expectations of ordinary expository writing, where the clearer text is considered "better." In no other Buddhist tradition do the texts strive deliberately to conceal their meaning. But the Tantras have a synthetic character that combines such standard, and non-esoteric, practices as the contemplation of voidness (*śūnyatā*) with special secret practices all their own. The most basic meaning of "secret" in the Tantric tradition is that its theories and practices should be kept secret from those who are not fellow initiates, that is, from those who have not obtained initiation (*abhiṣeka*) or taken vows (*samvara*) and pledges (*samaya*). When these works explain the term "secret" (usually *guhya* in Sanskrit), they apply it to certain things that owe their secrecy to being inward or hidden, like the secret of female sexuality. A list of secret topics in this literature would comprise states of yoga, the circle of deities, and other experiences that are not accessible to ordinary consciousness and cannot be appreciated by the thoroughly mundane mind. Accordingly, it was never maintained that a person with initiation into a Tantric cult had thereby experienced such esoteric matters. Rather, it continues to be held that someone who had gone through such a ritual establishes a bond with a *guru* who will supply the lore of the particular Tantra and guide the disciple in its practice. Tantric language shares with many other Indian works a difficulty of interpretation. The compact style of Indian philosophical treatises, for example, is the cause for much dispute over their meaning. The Tantras compound this difficulty by the very nature of their contents, making interpretation of the texts all the more difficult.

TANTRIC PRACTICE AND ANALOGICAL THINKING. Tantric practice aims at relating man to supramundane forces or deities. In so doing, it makes use of two widely disparate systems of analogy. One procedure associates man and the divine by means of rules applicable to all practitioners. The other procedure assigns persons to one or another Buddha family according to the dominant personality traits of the individual practitioner. In terms of the four divisions of the Tantras, the first two, the Kriyā and Caryā, make use of the first system. The latter two, the Yoga and Anuttarayoga, generally employ the second. Each approach has its supporters who claim that it provides a way to become a *saṃbuddha* ("complete Buddha").

A preeminent Tantra of the first kind is the *Vairocanābhisaṃbodhi.* This Tantra stresses the basic triad Body, Speech, and Mind—the "three mysteries" of the Buddha—and the prescribed practices by which certain attainments may be generated. Here, the human performer affiliates with the Body by means of hand gestures (*mudrā*); with the Speech by means of incantations (*mantra*); and with the Mind by means of deep concentration (*samādhi*), especially on the *maṇḍala.* In this Tantra, the transcendental Buddha is Mahāvairocana, and the human Buddha is Śākyamuni. This correspondence agrees with the division of the bodies of the Buddha into *dharmakāya* and *rūpakāya* that is found in early Mahāyāna Buddhism. In the same light, Kūkai, the founder of the Japanese Shingon school, explicitly identifies Mahāvairocana with the *dharmakāya.* It is noteworthy that the practice in the Caryā Tantra, in fact the practice based on the *Vairocanābhisaṃbodhi,* has a twofold basis: "yoga with images" and "yoga without images." In the former, one contemplates the inseparability of "self reality" (*ātmatattva*) from "deity reality" (*devatātattva*), and in sequence the performer meditatively generates himself into Vairocana with one face and two hands, making the *samāpatti mudrā* ("seal of equipoise"). The process is called the "subjective ground." The performer then contemplates the Buddha Vairocana, like himself, in front of himself. This step is termed the "objective ground."

In the "yoga without images" the mind is understood to have two sides, one mundane-directed (the *manas* face), the other supramundane-directed (the *buddhi* face). Upon reaching the limit of "yoga with images" one perceives as though before the eyes a configuration of the body of the deity on the mundane-directed side of the mind. The practitioner then follows this with a contemplation in which the deity body appears as a bright illusion on the supramundane-directed side of the mind. Through this process one achieves the same result as do practitioners of the early Buddhist meditations on "calming the mind" (*śamatha*) and "discerning the real" (*vipaśyanā*). This approach is directed to an ultimate goal indicated by the term "arising of the Tathāgata," and chapters bearing this title are found both in the *Vairocanābhisaṃbodhi* and in the Mahāyāna scripture collection called the *Avataṃsaka Sūtra.* The multiple Buddhas in this tradition of Tantric analogies are on the mental level; they may also be understood to refer indiscriminately to "all Buddhas" rather than to particular Buddha families.

The fasting cult of Avalokiteśvara, which uses the *mantra* "Oṃ mani padme hūṃ," employs a similar system of analogies. The famous six-syllabled formula is correlated with six Buddhas, six colors, and six realms of sentient beings. It is also recited during six times of the day and the night. The individual performer must pass ritually through the six syllables. The situation is comparable to the youth Sudhana's tenure of study under many different teachers in sequence, as portrayed in the *Gaṇḍavyūha Sūtra* (part of the *Avataṃsaka*).

The second analogical system is formulated in the Yoga Tantra *Tattvasaṃgraha.* It consists of four sections. Persons of different predominant vices in their stream of consciousness are affiliated respectively with these sections, each presided over by a Buddha. The commentator Buddha*guhya* explains that the fourth of these sections results from a merger of the Ratna family (as agent) and the Karman family (as the fulfilling action), but for convenience, the *Tattvasaṃgraha* usually mentions only Ratnasambhava as the presiding Buddha here. The correlation of persons with particular Buddha families indicates which of the predominant mind-based vices is to be eliminated by the "purification path" of the particular Buddha family. Each of the four paths in turn requires four kinds of *mudrā* ("seal"), but each path emphasizes one of the four and subordinates the other three. The first path emphasizes the Great Seal *(mahāmudrā);* the second, the Symbolic or Linkage Seal *(samayamudrā);* the third, the Dharma Seal *(dharmamudrā);* and the fourth, the Action Seal *(karmamudrā).* The paths have been expanded by the addition of four corresponding *maṇḍalas.*

According to Mkhas grub rje's *Fundamentals of the Buddhist Tantras* the practice of these purificatory paths commences with an effort by the practitioner to generate the Symbolic Being, the practitioner's own symbolization of the deity with whom he has established a link or bond. One then draws in (usually through the crown of the head) the Knowledge Being (*jñānasattva*), the deity in the absolute sense, who is usually said to emanate "from the sky." Mkhas grub rje explains: "The purpose of executing the seals of the Four Seals is to merge and unify the body, speech, mind, and acts of the Knowledge Being with the body, speech, mind, and acts of the Symbolic Being. There would be no foundation for merger if either were present by itself."

The Japanese school of Tantra called Shingon is based on the Vairocana scripture (mainly its first chapter) and the *Tattvasaṃgraha* (mainly its first section, "The Diamond Realm"). Thus, this school ignores the real clash between these two scriptures. Shingon employs two *maṇḍala* realms, that of the Vajradhātu Maṇḍala (Jpn., Kongōkai), an unchanging "diamond" knowledge realm derived from the *Tattvasaṃgraha,* and that of the Mahākaruṇāgarbha Maṇḍala (Jpn., Taizō-kai), the changing realm of becoming that makes possible the "arising of the Tathāgata." This latter *maṇḍala* is derived from the Vairocana scripture. In the terminology of Tibetan Tantrism, this theory and practice of becoming a Buddha is classified as Caryā Tantra because the scripture from which the Mahākaruṇāgarbha Maṇḍala derives is so classified. This is so because there is no attempt here to relate performers to particular Buddha families according to dominant fault as is the case in the Yoga Tantras.

The Yoga Tantra *Tattvasaṃgraha* serves here to add a further dimension of knowledge in the form of commentarial additions and related practices, so as to preserve consistency between the two *maṇḍala* (Jpn., *mandara*) cycles.

The Anuttarayoga Tantras continue the procedure of the Yoga Tantras, and, in the Father Tantras, allot distinct character to the five Buddhas for the purpose of a fivefold correspondence with five different kinds of persons. The Mother Tantras of this class raise the correspondences to six. The Anuttarayoga Tantras also have a basic division into two stages, a stage of generation (*utpattikrama*) and a stage of completion or consummation (*saṃpannakrama*). Indeed, the stage of generation overlaps the Yoga Tantra by way of what it calls the "three *samādhis*," named "preliminary praxis," "triumphant *maṇḍala*," and "victory of the rite." Tsong kha pa's *Snags rim chen mo* (Great treatise on the mantra path) elucidates the stage of generation in terms of six consecutive members, each of which corresponds to one of the three *samādhis*. These three *samādhis* can be used as a classification in Yoga Tantra practice as well. In fact, when generalized, the three are the three parts of every Buddhist Tantric ritual: the preliminaries, the main part, and the concluding acts.

The second stage of the Anuttarayoga Tantra, the "stage of completion," deals with more concrete matters like the centers in the body (*cakras*) and five mysterious winds (first mentioned centuries earlier in the *Chāndogya* and other Upaniṣads). This stage comprises a six-membered yoga (*ṣaḍaṅgayoga*), also classified in five steps (*pañcakrama*). The five steps are accomplished in members three through six, while the first and second members represent a link with the stage of generation.

The Anuttarayoga Tantras also contain passages on the "higher initiations," the practice of which includes elements often referred to by modern writers as "sexo-yogic." Briefly speaking, these have to do with worship of the female, and, perhaps, a rite of sexual union in which the male performer does not emit semen. Before attempting any explanation of this topic, it would be well to mention that historically there were lay as well as renunciant Tantrics, just as there were lay as well as renunciant *bodhisattvas* in the Mahāyāna tradition. Among the Tibetan sects that practice Tantrism, it is only the Dge lugs pa that observes the Vinaya code of monastic morality. This does not mean, however, that the Dge lugs pa practices a "cleaned-up" Tantrism with the objectionable passages expurgated from the texts. As we have noted before, it is not necessary to read the Tantras in the literal manner without benefit of commentaries, as some modern scholars are wont to do.

The four initiations (*abhiṣeka*) of the Anuttarayoga Tantras begin with the "initiations of the flask," rites taken in common with the three lower classes of Tantras. To this is added a "secret initiation," an "insight-knowedge initiation," and an initiation known as the "fourth" (also called *akṣara*, denoting "syllable" or "the incessant"). The secret initiation involves a mysterious "red and white element," an experience of "bliss-void," and the implication that the initiation takes place in the *cakras* of the body (those centers ranged along the spine but said to exist as well in a subtle body). Treatises such as that by Mkhas grub rje distinguish between a *karmamudrā* (the female partner) and a *jñānamudrā* ("seal of knowledge"). The insight-knowledge initiation involves a sequence of four joys (*ānanda*) associated with the downward progress of the "melted white element": descending from the forehead to the neck there is joy; descending to the heart there is "super joy" (*paramānanda*); descending to the navel there is the "joy of exhaustion" (*viramānanda*); and upon reaching the sex center there is "together-born joy" (*sahajānanda*), on which occasion the element is not to be emitted. If we are to assume that the element in question is indeed semen, how was it able to descend from the forehead?

There is also an Anuttarayoga Tantra explanation of the "four seals," but it differs from that found in the Yoga Tantras. In the Anuttarayoga Tantra, two separate sequences of *mudrā* are employed, one for the stage of generation, the other for the stage of completion. These are discussed in chapter 36 of the Mother Tantra *Śrī-Cakrasaṃvara* and in Tsoṅ kha pa's commentary to this text, the *Sbas don*. For the stage of generation the sequence is as follows:

1. *Karmamudrā*: one imagines the external *prajñā* woman in the form of an attractive goddess.
2. *Dharmamudrā*: sacred seed syllables such as *hūṃ* are imagined in that body.
3. *Samayamudrā*: the radiation from the seed syllables is drawn back together in the circle of the completed *maṇḍala*.
4. *Mahāmudrā*: one imagines oneself as having the body of the principal deity.

The version for the stage of completion reverses the position of the *samayamudrā* and the *mahāmudrā*.

Particularly worthy of note is the difference in the description of the *prajñā* woman in the stage of generation and in the stage of completion. In the former, the practitioner approaches the *prajñā* woman only through his imagination, that is, he imagines that she is a goddess with radiating germ syllables in her body. He imagines drawing back the radiation into his own body as a *maṇḍala*, and finally imagines himself as the chief deity. In the stage of completion this woman can confer concrete joy in the four degrees of courtship previously mentioned in correlation with the four classes of Tantras (laughing, mutual gazing, holding hands, the two united). But there is also another *prajñā* woman, the one of the central channel (among the three said to be in the position of the spine). When the texts speak of a *prajñā* consort, which one is intended? Nā ro pa has some important information about this in his commentary on the *Hevajra Tantra*. He cites a verse from the *Mañjuśrī-nāma-saṃgiti* (10.14) referring to the four *mudrās*, and gives their order in agreement with the stage of completion described above, substituting *jñānamudrā* for *dharmamudrā*. He then makes this revealing statement:

> The *karmamudrā* [i.e., the external woman] is the causal one, being initial, from which there is the together-born [*sahaja*] non-transiting joy. While this is indeed a truth [*satya*], there are two truths [conventional and ultimate], and [the *prajñā* woman of the *karmamudrā*] is true in a conventional sense, like a reflection in a mirror, but is not true in the absolute sense. Thus, one of keen intelligence should not embrace the *karmamudrā*. One should cultivate the *jñānamudrā* by such means as purifying the personal aggregates [*skandhas*], elements [*dhātus*], and sense bases [*āyatanas*] into images of deities, as the ritual of the *maṇḍala* reveals. By working them with continual friction one ignites the fire of wisdom [*jñāna*]. What is to be attained is the Great Seal [*mahāmudrā*]. How is it attained? Through that fire when the ham syllable is burnt [as is stated in the final verse of chapter 1 of the *Hevajra Tantra*]. The Great Seal is like a dream, a hallucination, and the nature of mind. One should embrace this [the Great Seal] until one realizes directly the Symbolic Seal [*samayamudrā*], which is not a perishing thing. (*Vajrapada-sāra-saṃgraha-pañjikā*, Peking Tanjur, Jpn. photo ed., vol. 54, p. 248–255.)

Nā ro pa thus acknowledges that some male Tantrics (presumably laymen) resort to the concrete woman as both "initial" (mother) and "together" (wife) in this part of the stage of completion. But he goes on to insist that one of keen faculty, striving for the high goal, will skip this *mudrā* and go directly to the inner *prajñā* consort, the ignited "fire of wisdom" that brings on the Great Seal. Staying on this Great Seal, which introspects mental processes as a hallucination, one realizes directly the *samayamudrā*, the *mahāsukhakāya*, or "body of great bliss."

The above remarks should lend a more benign interpretation to the Tantras than has been the case in the past, when judgments such as "ghastly" were often passed on this literature. The style, of course, is quite unlike that of the older Buddhist scriptures.

Ritual in the Tantras. The *maṇḍala* rites of the *Guhyasamāja Tantra* cycle may be seen in outline form in the following sequence:

1. Rites of the Site: clearing the site; seizing (contemplatively) the site; elimination of the obstructing demons
2. Preparatory Acts: pitching the (initial) lines (in the *maṇḍala*) with chalk; preparing the flask (i.e., placement of the flask by the *maṇḍala*); beseeching the gods; preparation of the disciple
3. The Main Rite, beginning with *maṇḍala* construction: placement of the five colored threads (representing the five Buddhas); putting in the colors (in the colored areas of the *maṇḍala*); invitation of the gods (to take residence in the *maṇḍala*)
4. Initiations of the Flask: drawing the disciple into the *maṇḍala*; diadem initiation; diamond initiation; mirror initiation (ater initiation); name initiation; emblem initiation (=bell initiation)
5. Offerings: offerings to the gods; offerings to the *guru*
6. Permission and Drawing Together: conferral of permission on the disciple to invoke the deity; drawing together of the deities who are in the *maṇḍala*
7. Concluding Acts: release of the magic nail, that is, dismissal of the deities along with a burnt offering (*homa*)

In order to work, each of these rituals must be accompanied by an intense awareness, referred to as *samādhi*, that could also be termed *yoga*. By "working" is meant that at all times the performer maintains a connection with the divine, as is confirmed by the *mantra* "Samayas tvam" ("You are the symbol").

These rituals are replete with details that would take much space to set forth properly. A few details can be given about one that is especially interesting, the disciple's entrance into the *maṇḍala*. The first phase is divided into "entrance outside of the screen" and "entrance inside of the screen." While outside the screen, the disciple ties on a red or yellow blindfold. This is not removed until later in the ceremony, when the initiate receives a superintending deity by throwing a flower into the *maṇḍala*, after which it will be proper to view the complete *maṇḍala*. The preceptor tells the disciple to imagine in his heart a *vajra*, thereon a sun, and on this a black *hūṃ* syllable. He is then to imagine in his throat a lotus, thereon a sun, and on this a red *āḥ* syllable; and in his head a wheel, thereon a moon, and on this a white *oṃ* syllable. He should also imagine that rays from those syllables make his body full of light. The preceptor guides the disciple to the east gate of the *maṇḍala*. Now, in the phase inside the screen, the disciple recites *mantras*. He begins with the east gate, reciting to both the deity of the center and the deity of the east gate. The east gate deity is addressed in order to empower oneself; the south gate deity, to confer initiation on oneself; the west gate deity, to turn the wheel of the Dharma for oneself; and the north gate deity, to make the ritual acts effective. He also bows at each gate: for the east, he bows with all the limbs, the diamond palms (i.e., adamantine and thus unassailable by demons) advanced; for the south, he bows with the forehead, the palms joined at the heart; for the west, he bows with the mouth, the diamond palms joined at the top of the head; for the north, he touches the earth with the head, the diamond palms having been lowered from the top of the head and placed at the heart. Then at the east gate, the preceptor sets forth the pledge(s), contacting the disciple by taking his hand, or else by touching the disciple on the head with the *vajra*, and saying, "Today you may enter the family of all the Tathāgatas," in recognition of the fact that entrance into the *maṇḍala* makes one their progeny; and that having seen the *maṇḍala* means the deities are revealed to the initiate.

The disciple is not to disclose the rituals he has undergone to others who have not entered the *maṇḍala*. Dire consequences are threatened for violating the pledge; guarding it yields magical success. Among the pledges is one requiring that the initiate avoid the fourteen transgressions, especially the first one, disparaging one's master, and the seventh one, revealing the secrets to immature persons (that is, persons who have not been initiated). Both are transgressions of Dharma. After taking the pledge, the officiant goes through an imaginative process, the aim of which is to have the gnosis deity (*jñāna-sattva*) descend from the sky into the disciple. It begins with the officiant imagining the disciple in voidness, then generating him into a Buddha from a germ syllable, and then going through a sequence of *sādhanas* (evocations) in which he imagines the disciple's body filled with light. The disciple is induced to circumambulate the *maṇḍala* carrying a *vajra* in his right hand and doing a dance. The second phase is entering, in the sense of viewing, the *maṇḍala*. Still wearing the blindfold, the disciple is directed to throw a flower onto an area with five pictures representing Buddha families. The throwing of the flower constitutes entrance into the *maṇḍala*. The deity on whom the flower then falls is the superintendent deity (*adhideva*) for the disciple. The preceptor imagines that the Diamond Being is opening the Diamond Eye of the disciple; the disciple performs the same act of imagination and removes the blindfold, reciting the *mantra* "*Oṃ jñānacaksuḥ Hūṃ Āḥ Svāhā*," where *jñānacaksuḥ* denotes the eye of knowledge. Then the preceptor says, "Now, by virtue of faith, may you see the reality of this *maṇḍala!* May you be born in the family of the Buddha, be empowered by *mudrā* and *mantra*, be endowed with all *siddhis* (magical success), be the best pledge (*samaya*)! May you realize the *mantras* with the sport of the *vajra* and lotus!" Thus the disciple is given the "initiation of the flower wreath," a process that establishes whether the disciple should receive other initiations. When it is the case of conferring permission on the disciple to evoke a particular deity, a different procedure is followed. Such evocations are undertaken after examining dreams and other omens.

The burnt offering is among the concluding acts of the ritual. There are four kinds of burnt offering, each corresponding to a different type of magical art: the worldly aims of appeasing the deities (*śāntika*), winning material prosperity (*pauṣṭika*), subduing demons (*vaśīkaraṇa*), and overpowering enemies (*abhicāruka*).

Judging from these various indications, one may conclude that Buddhist esotericism has considerable appeal to Buddhists who find fulfillment in ritual participation, who prefer a secret life that is religiously motivated, and who believe that by exercising all avenues of one's being (body, speech, and mind) one is speeding up the progress to enlightenment. The performer must be strong in imagination of images and in belief, and resolute in daily service to the presiding or tutelary deity.

SEE ALSO Avalokiteśvara; Buddhism, article on Buddhism in Tibet; Buddhist Books and Texts; Language, article on Buddhist Views of Language; Mahāsiddhas; Maṇḍalas; Mantra; Mar pa; Mi la ras pa (Milarepa); Mudrā; Nā ro pa; Prajñā; Samādhi; Shingonshū; Upāya; Zhenyan.

BIBLIOGRAPHY

Bhattacharyya, Benoytosh. *The Indian Buddhist Iconography.* 2d ed., rev. & enl. Calcutta, 1958.

Chou, Yi-liang. "Tantrism in China." *Harvard Journal of Asiatic Studies* 8 (March 1945): 241–332.

Eliade, Mircea. "Yoga and Tantrism." In *Yoga: Immortality and Freedom*, pp. 200–273. New York, 1958.

Evans-Wentz, W. Y. *Tibetan Yoga and Secret Doctrines.* 2d ed. London, 1967.

First Panchen Lama. *The Great Seal of Voidness.* Prepared by the Translation Bureau of the Library of Tibetan Works and Archives. Dharamsala, 1976.

George, Christopher S., ed. and trans. *The Caṇḍamahāroṣaṇa Tantra, Chapters 1–8.* American Oriental Series, vol. 56. New Haven, 1974. In English and Sanskrit.

Guenther, Herbert V., ed. and trans. The *Life and Teachings of Nāropa.* Oxford, 1963.

Guenther, Herbert V., ed. and trans. *Yuganaddha: The Tantric View of Life.* Chowkhamba Sanskrit Studies, vol. 3. 2d rev. ed. Varanasi, 1969.

Hakeda, Yoshito S., ed. and trans. *Kūkai: Major Works.* New York, 1972. With an account of his life and study of his thought.

Kvaerne, Per. "On the Concepts of Sahaja in Indian Buddhist Tantric Literature." *Temenos* (Helsinki) 11 (1975): 88–135.

Kvaerne, Per. *An Anthology of Buddhist Tantric Songs.* New York, 1977.

Lessing, Ferdinand D. *Yung-ho-kung: An Iconography of the Lamaist Cathedral in Peking.* Stockholm, 1942.

Lessing, Ferdinand D., and Alex Wayman, eds. and trans. *Fundamentals of the Buddhist Tantras.* Indo-Iranian Monographs, vol. 8. The Hague, 1968. A translation of Mkhas grub rje's *Rgyud sde spyi'i rnam par bźag pa rgyas par bśad pa.*

Snellgrove, David L., ed. and trans. *The Hevajra Tantra: A Critical Study.* 2 vols. London Oriental Series, vol. 6. London, 1959.

Tajima, Ryūjun. *Étude sur le Mahāvairocana-sūtra.* Paris, 1936.

Tajima, Ryūjun. *Les deux grands maṇḍalas et la doctrine de l'esoterisme Shingon.* Paris, 1959.

Tsuda, Shin'ichi. *The Saṁvarodaya-tantra: Selected Chapters.* Tokyo, 1974.

Tsuda, Shin'ichi. "A Critical Tantrism." *Memoirs of the Research Department of the Tōyō Bunkō* 36 (1978): 167–231.

Tucci, Giuseppe. "The Religious Ideas: Vajrayāna." In *Tibetan Painted Scrolls*, vol. 1, pp. 209–249. Translated by Virginia Vacca. Rome, 1949.

Wayman, Alex. *The Buddhist Tantras: Light on Indo-Tibetan Esotericism.* New York, 1973.

Wayman, Alex. "The Ritual in Tantric Buddhism of the Disciple's Entrance into the Maṇḍala." *Studia Missionalia* 23 (1974): 41–57.

Wayman, Alex. *Yoga of the Guhyasamājatantra: The Arcane Lore of Forty Verses.* Delhi, 1977.

Wayman, Alex. "Reflections on the Theory of Barabuḍur as a Maṇḍala." In *Barabuḍur: History and Significance of a Buddhist Monument*, edited by Hiram W. Woodward, pp. 139–172. Berkeley, 1981.

Wayman, Alex. "The Title and Textual Affiliation of the Guhyagarbhatantra." In *Daijō Bukkyō kara Mikkyō e* [From Mahāyāna Buddhism to Tantra: Honorary Volume for Dr. Katsumata Shunkyō], pp. 1320–1334 (Japanese order), pp. 1–15 (English order). Tokyo, 1981.

Wayman, Alex, ed. and trans. *Chanting the Names of Mañjuśrī: The Mañjuśrī-nāma-saṁgiti (Sanskrit and Tibetan Texts).* Boston, 1985.

ALEX WAYMAN (1987)

BUDDHISM, SCHOOLS OF: TANTRIC RITUAL SCHOOLS OF BUDDHISM [FURTHER CONSIDERATIONS]

When Alex Wayman's article, entitled "Buddhism, Schools of: Esoteric Buddhism," appeared in the first edition of *The Encyclopedia of Religion* in 1987, the study of Tantric and esoteric forms of Buddhism was just beginning to emerge from the margins of Buddhist studies in general. Since that time, it has come to occupy (or at least to share) center stage in most special areas of Buddhist studies. Accordingly, a thorough overview of the study of Buddhist esotericism as it now stands is a desideratum, but one that could not be realized in time for the present publication. The following brief remarks, together with the additions to the bibliography, must in the event serve to offer the reader an orientation to the present state of the field.

Just what is Tantric Buddhism? Though several definitions have been proposed, none has so far won universal acceptance. Several of the characteristics most frequently mentioned—recitation of *mantra*-like formulae, the practice of protective ritual, visualization, the ritual invitation of a divinity performed in conformity to the traditional Indian welcome of an honored guest—all of these are to be found in non-esoteric forms of Buddhism to varying degrees. At the same time, some practices that do seem to be exclusively Tantric, at least in the Buddhist context—for instance, internal systems of yoga relying on the subtle physiology, "Tantric sex," and the ritual ingestion of forbidden meats and intoxicants—cannot serve as the basis for a definition because they are absent from many forms of Buddhist Tantrism. The most plausible definitional feature that has been adduced is perhaps the requirement of *abhiṣeka,* the initiatory consecration, literally "aspersion," that is derived from early Indian coronation rites. Though referred to also in the sūtra literature of the Mahāyāna in connection with the Buddha's consecration of the highest *bodhisattvas,* the actual performance of such a rite on behalf of ordinary human aspirants seems to be uniquely characteristic of the major Buddhist esoteric traditions.

As this suggests, much of what has been considered typically Tantric in Buddhism is part and parcel of the ritual repertoire of non-Tantric Buddhism, chiefly (but not at all exclusively) within the Mahāyāna. Accordingly, some have expressed skepticism regarding the appropriateness of the notion of peculiarly Tantric Buddhist "schools." The clearest example of a particular Buddhist sect or order defining itself as esoteric, over and against rival orders, is no doubt the Japanese Shingon sect. Whether or not distinctly Tantric schools existed in India and China remains a contested question, while in Tibet, because all Buddhist orders transmitted both Tantric and non-Tantric forms of Buddhism, Tantrism per se hardly serves to define any particular school. Esotericism thus may be best regarded as a widely ramified current within the Mahāyāna, and just what counts as esoteric is in most respects relative to the particular religious milieu being considered. The study of esoteric forms of Buddhism has thus tended to renounce the effort to locate essential characteristics that apply to all such traditions and to focus instead on specific developments in particular places and times. At the same time, genetic connections among differing Buddhist esoteric traditions may be noted—the cult of the cosmic Buddha Vairocana throughout much of Buddhist Asia is a case in point—and the rigorous, comparative study of these has yet to be undertaken.

Despite the popular image of Tantrism as a libertine and iconoclastic form of religiosity, scholars of Buddhism in many Asian countries have remarked on the striking relationship between Tantric Buddhism and monarchy, with its attendant interest in hierarchies of power, protection of the realm, and public order. Far from providing a vehicle of expression for radical free spirits (though perhaps it has been sometimes that), Buddhist Tantrism seems more often to have served the interests of conservative forces within religious orders and society at large.

Finally, owing to the strongly erotic component associated with some forms of Buddhist Tantrism—primarily the *anuttarayoga* traditions of India and Tibet (though eroticized elements of Japanese esotericism have also been noted)—there has been considerable interest in this aspect of Buddhism in relation to issues of sex and gender. While some have found a sort of proto-feminism in the Buddhist Tantras, a means to acknowledge and liberate feminine energies and perhaps real women as well, others have regarded this element of Tantrism as primarily a projection of masculine archetypes of the feminine. Social historical and anthropological research, clarifying the roles and status of women in actual communities adhering to the various forms of esoteric Buddhism, will enable scholars to interpret more precisely the discourses pertaining to women in particular Tantric texts.

SEE ALSO Avalokiteśvara; Mahāsiddhas; Maṇḍalas, article on Buddhist Maṇḍalas; Mar pa; Mi la ras pa (Milarepa); Nā ro pa; Prajñā; Samādhi; Shingonshū; Upāya.

BIBLIOGRAPHY

Abe Ryūichi. *The Weaving of Mantra: Kūkai and the Construction of Esoteric Buddhist Discourse.* New York, 1999. Far reaching examination of the thought of Kūkai (774–835), founder of the Shingon sect of Japanese Buddhism.

Davidson, Ronald M. *Indian Esoteric Buddhism: A Social History of the Tantric Movement.* New York, 2002. A major reassessment of our understanding of Indian Buddhist Tantrism, elaborated in the light of the social historical context in which it developed.

Faure, Bernard. *Visions of Power: Imagining Medieval Japanese Buddhism.* Translated by Phyllis Brooks. Princeton, 1996. Study of the imaginal world of Japanese esoteric Buddhism, as seen through the life and work of Keizan (1264–1325).

Frank, Bernard. *Le panthéon bouddhique au Japon: Collections d'Émile Guimet.* Paris, 1991. Detailed description of the pantheon of esoteric Buddhism in Japan.

Gellner, David N. *Monk, Householder, and Tantric Priest: Newar Buddhism and its Hierarchy of Ritual.* New York and Cambridge, U.K., 1992. Excellent anthropological study of Newar Buddhism in the Kathmandu Valley, with close attention to the social role of Tantrism.

Jessup, Helen I., and Thierry Zéphir. *Angkor et dix siècles d'art Khmer.* Paris, 1997. Offers fine examples of Khmer Buddhist Tantric sculpture.

Kapstein, Matthew T. *Reason's Traces: Identity and Interpretation in Indian and Tibetan Buddhism.* Boston, 2001. Includes studies of textual evidence for the development of esoteric Buddhism in India and of rituals for the production of Tantric art.

Lopez, Donald S., Jr. *Elaborations on Emptiness: Uses of the Heart Sūtra.* Princeton, 1996. Detailed consideration of the *Heart Sūtra* as a Tantric text.

Malandra, Geri Hockfield. *Unfolding a Maṇḍala: The Buddhist Cave Temples at Ellora.* Albany., N.Y., 1993. The early development of Indian Buddhist Tantrism, as seen through the sculptural programs of the Ellora caves of western India.

Nāropa. *Iniziazione: Kālacakra.* Translated by Raniero Gnoli and Giacomella Orofino. Milan, Italy, 1994. Annotated translation of an important Indian Buddhist treatise on the initiatory consecration.

Nihom, Max. *Studies in Indian and Indo-Indonesian Tantrism: The Kuñjarakarṇadharmakathana and the Yogatantra.* Vienna, 1994. Most recent and most thorough among the rare studies of the surviving textual record of Indonesian Tantrism.

Orzech, Charles D. *Politics and Transcendent Wisdom: The Scripture for Humane Kings in the Creation of Chinese Buddhism.* University Park, Pa., 1998. On Tantric rituals for the protection of the state in Tang dynasty China.

Sharf, Robert H. *Coming to Terms with Chinese Buddhism: A Reading of the Treasure Store Treatise.* Honolulu, 2002. Includes a provocative appendix on the conception of esoteric Buddhist "schools" in East Asia.

Shaw, Miranda Eberle. *Passionate Enlightenment: Women in Tantric Buddhism.* Princeton, 1994.

Skilling, Peter. "The Raksā Literature of the Śrāvakayāna" *Journal of the Pali Text Society* 16 (1992). On the protective rites of early Buddhism.

Slusser, Mary Shepherd. *Nepal Mandala: A Cultural Study of the Kathmandu Valley.* Princeton, 1982. Magisterial study of the cultural geography of Kathmandu, with much reference to Buddhist Tantric art and architecture.

Snellgrove, David L. *Indo-Tibetan Buddhism: Indian Buddhists and Their Tibetan Successors.* Boston, 1987. Extensive synthesis of sources on Tantric Buddhism. Magnificent collection of articles, including contributions to the study of Buddhist Tantrism in many parts of Asia.

Strickmann, Michel. *Mantras et mandarins: Le bouddhisme tantrique en Chine.* Paris, 1996. Groundbreaking work on diverse facets of the Tantric contribution to Chinese and East Asian religious culture.

Tanabe, George J., Jr. *Myōe the Dreamkeeper: Fantasy and Knowledge in Early Kamakura Buddhism.* Cambridge, Mass., 1992. Investigation of the dream-world of the Japanese esoteric master Myōe (c. 1173–1232).

Wallace, Vesna. *The Inner Kālacakratantra: A Buddhist Tantric View of the Individual.* New York, 2001. Study of a major Buddhist Tantra's chapter on the subtle nature of the human body, its development and potentials.

White, David Gordon, ed. *Tantra in Practice.* Princeton, 2000. Includes translated selections from a wide variety of Buddhist Tantric works.

MATTHEW T. KAPSTEIN (2005)

BUDDHISM, SCHOOLS OF: TIBETAN AND MONGOLIAN BUDDHISM

In introducing the "schools" of Tibetan and Mongolian Buddhism, several different phenomena in the formation of religious traditions must be distinguished. One may speak, for instance, of distinct orders or sects (*chos lugs,* or more specifically *rang rkang btsugs pa'i chos brgyud),* religious traditions that are set apart from others by virtue of their institutional independence, that is to say, whose unique character is embodied outwardly in the form of an independent hierarchy and administration, independent properties, and an identifiable membership of some sort. Such corporate religious bodies are of great importance in the Tibetan religious world, but they must not be confounded with lineages (*brgyud pa*), continuous successions of spiritual teachers who have transmitted a given body of knowledge over a period of generations but who need not be affiliated with a common order. Lineages may be highly specific, for instance, the line of teachers through which the study of a particular text or ritual method has been transmitted, or they may be of broader reach, as is the case when one speaks of the "lineages of practice" *(sgrub brgyud),* which have conserved significant bodies of religious tradition, including textual learning, liturgy, practical disciplines, iconographical knowledge, and so on. In this latter sense, lineages have often been the basis for the formation of the distinct orders. Finally, orders and lineages must both be differentiated from schools of thought, *grub mtha'* ("philosophical systems," equivalent to *siddhānta* in Sanskrit). The adherent of a given Tibetan Buddhist order will, in the course of his career, usually receive instruction in (or at least derived from) a number of differing lineages and be exposed to several schools of thought. It should be noted, however, that the terminology introduced here is not used in Tibetan with perfect regularity. At least one major author, Thu'u bkwan Chos kyi nyi ma (1737–1802), adopts the expression *grub mtha'* to refer to the major orders and lineages of Tibetan Buddhism. Nevertheless, even in this case, the term is chosen precisely because Thu'u bkwan's primary interest is the doctrinal and philosophical orientation of each of the religious traditions he considers.

These apparent complexities of usage had their origins in the very beginnings of the Tibetan Buddhist tradition under the Tibetan Empire of the seventh to ninth centuries. At that time, there was only one Buddhist order active in Tibet, that of the Mūlasarvāstivāda (Tibetan, *gzhi thams cad yod par smra ba),* one of the eighteen orders of early Indian Buddhism, whose monastic code, or Vinaya, was uniquely adopted by the Tibetans. At the same time, Tibetan Buddhists became familiar with several Indian Buddhist schools of thought, though the Madhyamaka, and in particular the Yogācāra Madhyamaka of the philosopher Śāntarakṣita (fl. c. 775), appears to have quickly become predominant. In this period too, lineages of instruction in contemplative practice, including some representing Chinese Chan and others associated with Tantric esotericism, began to disseminate their teachings among Tibetans.

Institutional, lineage-based, and philosophical or doctrinal ways of thinking about religious adherence in Tibet were thus from the beginning complementary, and in time they began increasingly to intersect with or to diverge from one another. Hence, the exact classification of the schools of Tibetan Buddhism has posed something of a problem, not only for modern researchers but for traditional Tibetan authorities as well. Thus, for example, Thu'u bkwan (Thuken, 1737–1802) recognizes eighteen distinct Buddhist traditions in Tibet—in this he is no doubt numerologically influenced by the stereotypical division of early Indian Buddhism into eighteen orders—but nevertheless he considers only seven of these as meriting treatment in depth. By contrast, the renowned fifteenth-century historian 'Gos lo tsā ba Gzhon nu dpal (Gö Lotsawa) organizes his great work, the *Deb ther sngon po* (Blue annals) on the principle of lineage, of which he treats about a dozen as particularly important but discusses many others inter alia. The eclectic master of the nineteenth century, 'Jam mgon kong sprul Blo gros Mtha' yas (Jamgön Kongtrül, 1813–1899), arranges his encyclopedia of the major lines of teaching, the *Gdams ngag mdzod* (Treasury of instructions), according to the scheme of the "eight great lineages of practice," following the enumeration proposed by 'Phreng po gter ston Shes rab 'od zer (Trhengpo tertön, 1517–1584). Finally, in the system best known in the West, the Tibetan government of the Dalai Lamas from the seventeenth century through 1959 recognized four major orders, though in fact several others continued to be active, even if not granted the status of independent orders by the central Tibetan government.

THE EIGHT MAJOR "LINEAGES OF PRACTICE." For present purposes, this article considers the major lineages and their roles in the formation of the orders following the scheme of the "eight lineages of practice." Mongolian Buddhist orders have generally been derived directly from their Tibetan antecedents. Accordingly, this article refers to Buddhism among the Mongols where appropriate, to indicate the lines of Tibetan Buddhist transmission to them that were most influential. One must note too that the Tibetan Bon religion, which in its institutional dimensions must be considered a Buddhist order, is generally left out of the classificatory schemes mentioned here, though some writers—Thu'u bkwan is perhaps the best-known example—have also considered it in this context. As Bon is treated in the present work in a separate article, it will not be discussed here.

The "Ancient Translation Tradition" (Snga 'gyur rnying ma pa) includes all of those lines of teaching that maintain that their esoteric and Tantric traditions were derived from the texts and instructions transmitted during the time of the Tibetan monarchs of the eighth to ninth centuries, Khri Srong lde'u btsan (Trhi Songdetsen, 742–c. 797) above all. By the late tenth century such lineages were continued primarily by a lay priesthood that increasingly came to be attacked by proponents of the "new *mantra* traditions" (*gsang sngags gsar ma*) for adhering to esoteric teachings that, so the critics declared, had been corrupted. The formation of a distinctive Rnying ma pa (Nyingmapa) tradition was in some respects a reaction to such charges and involved both the elaboration of historical apologetics and the codification of the older Tantric transmissions, their special doctrines, and the rites connected with them.

Historically, the Rnying ma pa asserted the preeminence of the Indian Tantric master Padmasambhava, who came to be effectively deified. Other Indian and Tibetan masters of the eighth to ninth centuries, notably Vimalamitra and the translator Vairocana, were also claimed as forebearers. The teaching of these figures was considered to emphasize the organization of the whole gamut of Buddhist doctrine and practice into nine sequential vehicles (*theg pa rim pa dgu*), of which the last three, comprising the esoteric instructions of the highest Tantras, represented the distinctive heritage of the Rnying ma pa. The pinnacle of the system was taken to be the abstract and visionary approach to contemplation known as the Great Perfection (rdzogs chen [dzogchen]), the authenticity of which was sometimes contested by adherents of the newer schools. From the twelfth century onward, the Rnying ma pa came to rely increasingly on a tradition of renewed revelation, mostly of Padmasambhava's teachings, referred to as "treasure doctrines" (*gter chos*). Though widely contested, these came to play a major role in the formation of Tibetan religious culture generally.

The Rnying ma pa have always had an important following among lay Tantric adepts (*sngags pa*), sometimes organized in village-based communities. Though identifiable Rnying ma pa monastic institutions existed during the twelfth century and perhaps earlier, the organization of the Rnying ma pa as a distinct monastic order seems largely to have emerged during the seventeenth century and reflects in part the political reforms of Tibetan religious organization under the government of the fifth Dalai Lama (1617–1682). At the same time, important lines of Rnying ma pa teaching have been preserved among the non–Rnying ma pa orders, including, for instance, the rites of the Tantric deities Vajrakīla and Yang dag Heruka among the Sa skya pa (Sakyapa), the "exceptionally secret" form of the deity Hayagrīva (*Rta mgrin yang gsang*) among the Dge lugs pa (Gelukpa), and the traditions of the *Tibetan Book of the Dead* and many other teachings derived from the treasure doctrines among the Bka' brgyud pa (Kagyupa).

Despite its emphasis on the practice of Tantric esotericism and though it has relied during much of its history on familial lineages of lay priests, the Rnying ma pa traditions have sometimes given rise to masters of the monastic traditions of Buddhist scholarship who have formulated distinctive doctrinal syntheses inspired by the special features of the Rnying ma pa teaching. Among the foremost are the lay adept Bsnubs Sangs rgyas ye shes (Nup Sangye Yeshe, c. tenth century), Rong zom Chos kyi bzang po (Rongzom Chözang, eleventh century), Klong chen Rab 'byams pa (Longchen Rabjampa, 1308–1363), Lo chen Dharmaśrī (1654–1717), 'Jigs med gling pa (Jikme Lingpa, 1730–1798), and Mi pham rgya mtsho (Mipham Gyatso, b1846–1912).

The "Tradition of [the Buddha's] Transmitted Precepts and Instructions" (Bka' gdams pa [Kadampa]) is traced to the activity of the Bengali master Atīśa (982–1054) and his leading Tibetan disciples, notably 'Brom ston Rgyal ba'i 'byung gnas (Dromtön, 1104–1163). As the first of the new orders formed beginning in the eleventh century, it had its immediate antecedents in the late-tenth-century Buddhist revival in the Gu ge kingdom of western Tibet, spearheaded by the monk-king of Gu ge, Ye shes 'od (Yeshe-ö), and the celebrated translator Rin chen bzang po (Rinchen Zangpo, 958–1055). By 1042, when Atīśa accepted the invitation of the former's successor, Byang chub 'od (Changcup-ö), to proceed to Tibet from the Vikramaśīla monastery in northeastern India, the renewal of Buddhism had been an ongoing concern in Gu ge for almost a century. After three years in residence there, where he composed his famous treatise on the Mahāyāna path, the *Byang chub lam gyi sgron ma* (Lamp for the path of enlightenment), Atīśa traveled to central Tibet and remained there for the last decade of his life. The Bka' gdams pa, as a distinctive order embodying his tradition of teaching, received institutional form after his lay disciple, 'Brom ston, founded the monastery of Rwa sgreng (Reting) in 1057.

The Bka' gdams pa were distinguished by a marked concern for moral rigor in the pursuit of the *bodhisattva*'s path. In some branches of the tradition, this resulted in an extreme emphasis on spiritual cultivation to the exclusion of the pursuit of learning. At the same time, Atīśa's own scholarly proclivities meant that some of his successors tended by contrast to emphasize study, so that the Bka' gdams pa were equally associated with the development of scholasticism at Gsang phu (Sangphu, founded 1071) and other monastic colleges. In the thirteenth and fourteenth centuries the Bka' gdams pa monastery of Snar thang (Narthang) emerged as a prominent scholastic center, renowned in particular for its traditions of learning in the *abhidharma* and other fields of Buddhist philosophy.

Owing to Atīśa's association with the Gu ge kings, who were suspicious of the moral excesses attributed to certain adherents of the Tantras, and owing to certain cautions expressed in Atīśa's own writings, the Bka' gdams pa are sometimes regarded as a non-Tantric lineage of Tibetan Buddhism. Atīśa himself, however, was a Tantric adept and, despite the concerns expressed by some among his more puritanical Tibetan disciples, he did teach aspects of Tantrism in Tibet. His role in the promotion of the cults of Avalokiteśvara and Tārā was particularly great, and he is widely associated as well with an important tradition of instruction in the *Guhyasamāja Tantra*. Nevertheless, the characteristic emphasis of his teaching was upon the exoteric Mahāyāna doctrine of "emptiness imbued with compassion" (*stong nyid snying rje'i snying po can*; Sanskrit, *śunyatā karuṇāgarbhā*), his insistence on which came to be emulated by all Tibetan Buddhist traditions. His Bka' gdams pa successors created a remarkable corpus of literature concerning spiritual exercise, called "training (or purification) of the mind" (*blo sbyong*), in which such common acts as eating and drinking, walking, going to sleep, and even breathing serve as focal points for the cultivation of spiritual love and a keen sense of the relativity of transient things.

The Bka' gdams pa tradition was therefore diverse in its nature, embodying elements of Mahāyāna ethical teaching, Tantrism, and formal Buddhist scholasticism. Its legacy was very widespread, and all of the later Tibetan orders, including the post-eleventh-century Rnying ma pa, reflect this to a great degree. Nevertheless, it was the Dge lugs pa order, whose foundation was inspired by Rje Tsong kha pa during the fifteenth century, that most self-consciously took up the Bka' gdams pa mantle, even adopting "new Bka' gdams pa" as a proper designation.

The "Tradition of the Path with Its Fruit" (Lam 'bras bu dang bcas pa) was derived ultimately from the teachings of the Indian *mahāsiddha* Virūpa as introduced into Tibet by 'Brog mi Lo tsā ba Śākya Ye shes (Drokmi, 992–1072) on the basis of the instructions of the *paṇḍita* Gayadhara. This way of esoteric practice was based primarily upon the *Hevajra Tantra*, and though it enjoyed a very wide diffusion, giving rise to a great many lines of transmission, it became from early on a special concern of the Sa skya pa order, which, with its suborders, has remained the particular guardians of the "Path and Fruit." In its fundamentals, the teaching of the Path and Fruit emphasizes as foundational an understanding of the "three visions" (*snang gsum*): the impure vision of ordinary beings immersed in *saṃsāra*, the vision of spiritual experience that characterizes the *bodhisattva* progressing on the path, and the pure vision of enlightenment. On this basis, one may embark upon the actual practice of the *Hevajra Tantra,* conceived in terms of "three continua" (*rgyud gsum*): the continuum of the ground, the nature of mind as forming a basis for spiritual progress; the continuum of the methodical path of yoga; and the continuum of the result, that is, the attainment of the gnosis of buddhahood.

The founding figure of the Sa skya pa was 'Khon Dkon mchog rgyal po (Khön Könchog Gyalpo, 1034–1102), who abandoned his clan's hereditary Rnying ma pa affiliations to become a disciple of 'Brog mi and in 1073 established the temple of Go rum at Sa skya, henceforth the family seat of the 'Khon clan. His family line produced, during the generations that followed, a succession of masters, the "five forebearers" (*gong ma lnga*), of capital importance for the entire later history of Tibetan Buddhism. Sa chen Kun dga' snying po (Sachen Kunga Nyingpo, 1092–1158), Dkon mchog rgyal po's son, did much to impart a distinctive character to the early Sa skya tradition, that of an aristocratic household that patronized the Buddhist religion generally, valued the refinement of learning, and maintained a special proficiency in Tantric ritual and yoga. One of 'Brog mi's chief successors, Zhang ston Chos 'bar (Zhangdön Chöbar, 1053–1135) became Sa chen's tutor, nurturing his charge to be a preeminent exponent of the system of the "Path and Fruit." Two of Sa chen's sons, Bsod nams rtse mo (Sönam Tsemo, 1142–1182) and Grags pa rgyal mtshan (Trakpa Gyaltsen, 1147–1216), while following their father in remaining laymen, exclusively dedicated themselves to the family's religious and ritual tradition. It is in the writings of Grags pa rgyal mtshan that the Path and Fruit was definitively codified. He also was tutor to his nephew, Sa skya Paṇḍita Kun dga' rgyal mtshan (Sakya Paṇḍita Kunga Gyaltsen, 1182–1251), a monk who came to be recognized as one of the leading scholars of his day. Besides his numerous contributions to many branches of Tibetan learning, it was under his leadership that the Sa skya pa emerged as a major monastic order. His famous journey in 1246 to meet the ruler of the Mongol Empire, Godan Khan, came to be seen as the precedent for the Mongols' adoption of Buddhism, and his nephew, Chos rgyal 'Phags pa (Chögyal Phakpa, 1235–1280), the last of the five forebearers, became the spiritual preceptor of the Mongol ruler of China, Kublai Khan.

As a monastic order, the Sa skya pa have continued to emphasize training in refined textual scholarship, balanced with the practice of the esotericism of the *Hevajra Tantra* as taught in the Path and Fruit tradition. Of their two leading suborders, the Ngor pa (Ngorpa), founded by Ngor chen Kun dga' bzang po (Ngorchen Kunga Zangpo, 1382–1456), and Tshar pa (Tsarpa), the former has enjoyed an extensive following, particularly in far eastern Tibet. The Sa skya pa produced a long line of outstanding doctrinal writers, who may be counted among the leading contributors to the development of Tibetan Buddhist philosophy. Noteworthy are Red mda' ba Gzhon nu blo gros (Remdawa, 1349–1412), Rong ston Shes bya kun gzigs (Rongtön, 1367–1449), Gser mdog Paṇchen Śākya mchog ldan (Serdok Panchen, 1428–1507), and Go rams pa Bsod nams seng ge (Gorampa, 1429–1489). Far from representing a unitary school dogma, these figures show considerable diversity in their approaches to the interpretation of Buddhist philosophical perspectives.

The "Succession of the Transmitted Precepts of Mar pa" (Mar pa bka' brgyud), most often referred to as Bka' brgyud pa, had as its particular domain the teachings of the Indian masters Tilopa (c. 988–1069), Nāropa (1016–1100), and Maitrīpa (1007–1085) as transmitted to Mar pa Chos kyi blo gros (Marpa, 1002/1012–1097). His tradition stressed the six doctrines (*chos drug*) of yogic practice and the culminating meditations of the great seal (*phyag rgya chen po*; Sanskrit, *mahāmudrā*), whereby the limits of all phenomena of *saṃsāra* and *nirvāṇa* are determined (hence, "sealed") in the realization of the ultimate nature of mind. The six yogas are:

1. Inner Heat (*gtum mo*), whereby the adept learns to master the subtle physical energies of the body;
2. Body of Apparition (*sgyu lus*), through which the illusion-like nature of ordinary experience becomes known;
3. Dream (*rmi lam*), in which one achieves the ability to consciously explore and to transform the possibilities that are revealed during dreams;
4. Radiant Light (*'od gsal*), referring to the luminous dimension of the mind;
5. Transference (*'pho ba*), the means to cause one's consciousness to leave the body abruptly at the moment of death and to seek rebirth in a pure realm;
6. Intermediate State (*bar do*), which here refers primarily to the state of consciousness in the course of migration between death and rebirth.

The first four enable one to attain enlightenment swiftly during this very lifetime, the last two to achieve it at death.

The proliferation of lineages adhering to the teachings of Mar pa was extensive, and the many lines of instruction that arose among his followers and their successors almost all created their own distinctive formulations of the Bka' brgyud teaching. As Mar pa and his major disciples were laymen, these were initially transmitted primarily within familial lineages. Of these, the line of the Rngog (Ngok) clan enjoyed a particular eminence for their mastery of the esoteric lore of the *maṇḍala,* while the Mes specialized in the exegetical traditions of the *Guhyasamāja Tantra.*

Mar pa's foremost disciple was the yogin Mi la ras pa (Milarepa, 1028/1040–1111/1123), who came to be regarded as Tibet's greatest poet and as a cultural hero exemplifying the ideal of the Tantric adept. His many students, such as Ras chung pa Rdo rje grags (Rechungpa Dorje Drak, 1084–1161), mostly adhered to his model, but one, Sgam po pa

Bsod nams rin chen (Gampopa Sonam Rinchen, 1079–1153), was a former physician who had been ordained as a monk in the Bka' gdams pa order following his young wife's tragic passing. It was Sgam po pa who formed the Bka' brgyud pa into a monastic order, and by stressing the path of gradual ethical self-cultivation as taught by the Bka' gdams pa, he created a unique synthesis of that teaching with the properly Bka' brgyud pa systems of yoga. Known as the "blending of the two streams" (*chu bo gnyis 'dres*), this synthesis has remained the normative teaching of all of the Bka' brgyud pa suborders. These are usually referred to as the "four great Bka' brgyud orders" (*bka' brgyud che bzhi*) founded by Sgam po pa's immediate disciples, among whom the leading disciples of Phag mo gru pa Rdo rje rgyal po (Phakmotrupa, 1110–1170) founded eight "lesser" orders (*chung brgyad*). (The terms *great* and *lesser* refer solely to their relative proximity to Sgam po pa and imply neither a quantitative nor a qualitative judgment.) The first Karma pa hierarch, Dus gsum mkhyen pa (Dusum Khyenpa, 1110–1193), is numbered among the four "greats," whereas 'Bri gung Skyob pa 'Jig rten gsum mgon (Drigung Kyopa, 1143–1217) was prominent among the founders of the eight "lesser" orders. Among the eight is also counted Gling rje ras pa Padma rdo rje (Lingje Repa, 1128–1188), whose disciple Gtsang pa Rgya ras (Tsangpa Gyare, 1161–1211) founded the 'Brug pa (Drukpa) Bka' brgyud pa order, which in turn gave rise to several major suborders of its own. (The 'Brug pa later established itself as the religion of the state in Bhutan, a position it retains in the early twenty-first century.)

Some branches of the Bka' brgyud pa began to "internationalize" with patronage from the Xixia (or Tangut) Kingdom during the twelfth to thirteenth centuries, resulting in their competing with the Sa skya pa for Mongol support after the fall of Xixia in 1227. The second and third Karma pa hierarchs, Karma Pakshi (1204–1283) and Rang byung rdo rje (Rangjung Dorje, 1284–1339), both charismatic teachers and prolific writers, were among those who received imperial honors in China, whereas the 'Bri gung pa branch of the Bka' brgyud pa allied itself with the Mongol dynasty of Iran. Following the decline of Mongol power in Tibet during the mid-fourteenth century, given the loss of patronage this entailed for the Sa skya pa, it was the Phag mo gru pa Bka' brgyud pa order that came to dominate Tibetan affairs. The formal institution of Bka' brgyud pa colleges, emphasizing Buddhist scholastic study, dates from this time. For the next two centuries, Bka' brgyud pa masters made considerable contributions to the ongoing development of Tibetan philosophy, literature, and art. Examples include the seventh and eighth Karma pa hierarchs, Chos grags rgya mtsho (Chodrak Gyatso, 1450/1454–1506) and Mi bskyod rdo rje (Mikyo Dorje, 1507–1554), and theorists of the Tantras, Dwags po Bkra shis rnam rgyal (Dakpo Tashi Namgyal, 1512–1587) and the fourth 'Brug chen hierarch, Padma dkar po (Pemakarpo, 1527–1592). Later luminaries of the Bka' brgyud traditions include Karma Chags med (Karma Chakme, d. 1678), who elaborated an original synthesis of the *mahāmudrā* and Great Perfection approaches to contemplation, and Ta'i Si tu Chos kyi 'byung gnas (Situ Chöki Jungne, 1699–1774), editor of the famed Sde dge edition of the Kanjur and a renowned scholar of linguistics. Mar pa Bka' brgyud pa teachings have been widely transmitted among non–Bka' brgyud pa orders, for instance among the Dge lugs pa, a considerable portion of whose esoteric traditions originated in Mar pa's lineage.

The "Succession of the Transmitted Precepts of Shangs" (Shangs pa bka' brgyud) took its name from the Shangs Valley, where the early-twelfth-century master Khyung po Rnal 'byor, "the yogin of the Eagle clan," founded his community. Though there is considerable uncertainty about his precise dates and traditional chronologies generally assign his birth to the year 990, he appears in fact to have been born half a century or so later. Originally an adherent of the Bon religion, he converted to Buddhism and became at first a follower of the Rnying ma pa tradition. Like many others of his generation, however, he regarded India as the source of uniquely authoritative Buddhist teachings and so left Tibet to pursue his path in the Kathmandu Valley of Nepal and in India proper.

During his travels in India Khyung po Rnal 'byor is supposed to have met numerous Tantric masters, including some who were at that time famed throughout the Tibetan Buddhist world. His foremost teachers, however, were two remarkable women, Niguma and Sukhasiddhi, the first of whom is referred to in his biography as Nāropa's "lady," a term that in this context is usually taken to mean "elder sister," though some say that Niguma had been Nāropa's wife. From Niguma, Khyung po learned a system of six yogas resembling the system taught by Nāropa as transmitted by Mar pa but differing primarily in its notable emphasis upon the topics of apparition and dream. The "six doctrines of Niguma" (*ni gu chos drug*), as they are known, continue to be practiced by Tibetan Buddhist adepts in the early twenty-first century. Khyung po's teaching as a whole was analogized to a tree, with the six doctrines as its roots, the "great seal" for its truck, the "three means for integrating ordinary experience with the path" as branches, the red and white forms of the sky-faring goddess, Khecarī, for flowers, and as the fruit, the realization that body and mind are deathless and without deviation.

The line of Khyung po Rnal 'byor's disciples—Rmog lcog pa (Mokcokpa), Dbon ston Skyer sgang pa (Öntön Kyergangpa), Gnyan ston (Nyentön), down to Sangs rgyas ston pa (Sangye Tönpa, 1219–1290)—uniquely transmitted the entire body of these precepts in a strictly secret lineage until the last mentioned began to disseminate them among practitioners of Tantric yoga. The early secrecy of the lineage contributes to considerable historical obscurity, though hagiographies of Khyung po and his successors do exist. Though there were a small number of properly Shangs pa hermitages at times, the Shangs pa were never established as an independent order and their doctrinal lineage was transmitted in later times among the Karma Bka' brgyud, Dge lugs pa, Sa skya pa, Jo nang pa, Rnying ma pa, and Zhwa lu pa orders. More recently, the Shangs pa teachings have aroused considerable interest among Buddhists in the West owing to the widespread activity of their leading twentieth-century representative, Kalu Rinpoche Rang byung kun khyab (1905–1989).

Zhi byed and Gcod. The related lineages of Zhi byed (zhije) ("Pacification") and Gcod (cö) ("Severance") originated respectively with the enigmatic Indian yogin Pha Dam pa Sangs rgyas (Phadampa Sangye, d. 1117) and his remarkable Tibetan successor, the *yoginī* Ma gcig lab sgron (Machig Labdron, c. 1055–1149). Although schools specializing in Pacification—as exemplified by the lineages of Rma Chos kyi shes rab (Ma Chöki Sherab, b. 1055), So chung Dge 'dun 'bar (Sochung Gendünbar, 1062–1128), and Kaṃ Ye shes rgyal mtshan (Kam Yeshe Gyaltsen, d. 1119)—were very widespread during the twelfth to fourteenth centuries, the teaching all but disappeared in later times. Pha Dam pa continued to be revered as a cultural hero, and the verse aphorisms attributed to him—*Ding ri brgya rtsa* (Century for the people of Ding ri)—is a popular classic of Tibetan gnomic literature. Severance, by contrast, permeated the entire Tibetan Buddhist tradition and is in the early twenty-first century preserved by all orders. Both of these systems of instruction seek to bring about realization as it is understood in the "Perfection of Wisdom" (Sanskrit, *Prajñāpāramitā*) sūtras by means inspired by esoteric Buddhist practice. This takes particularly dramatic form in the traditions of Severance, whose exquisite liturgies involve the adept's symbolic offering of his or her own body as food for all beings throughout the universe.

The "Yoga of Indestructible Reality" (Rdo rje'i rnal 'byor) designates the system of yoga associated with the *Kālacakra Tantra*, the "Wheel of Time," which was transmitted in Tibet initially by Gyi jo Lo tsā ba Zla ba'i 'od zer during the early eleventh century. A great many other lineages specializing in this Tantra also arose, so that it became one of the dominant esoteric traditions of the early second millennium.

The Kālacakra proposes in effect a system of universal knowledge, including astronomical calculation, medical tradition, and above all mastery of the internal disciplines of yoga. Indeed, these three domains—that of the universe without, the body within, and the esoteric realm of yoga—are treated homologously here, mapped onto one and the same divine *maṇḍala*. The Kālacakra became the basis for the Tibetan calendrical system among other branches of learning.

As a system of Tantric contemplative practice, the Kālacakra stresses a system of six yogas (*sbyor drug*): "withdrawal" and "absorption" are the yogas of body, whereby the purification of the subtle, central channel is achieved; "breath-control" and "restraint" are the yogas of speech, whereby the vital energies are caused to enter the central channel and to be stabilized; "recollection" is the yoga of mind, whereby the incorruptibility of the enlightened mind is attained; and finally, "concentration" is the refinement of gnosis, whereby the coalescence of bliss and emptiness is realized.

During the fourteenth century, two approaches to the interpretation and practice of the Kālacakra became predominant. The first was that of Zhwa lu Monastery, which was given its decisive formulation in the writings of the celebrated scholar and editor of the canon, Bu ston Rin chen grub (Butön Rinchendrub, 1290–1364). Though Bu ston's background was in the Bka' brgyud tradition, Zhwa lu was a clan-based monastery tied to the Lce family, so that it was regarded as representing a small but independent order. The second major Kālacakra tradition emerged at the monastery of Jo nang, which in its origins was in essence a Kālacakra hermitage. Its chief representative was the philosophically controversial master Dol po pa Shes rab rgyal mtshan (Dölpopa, 1292–1361). While these two contemporaries were both widely revered, they arrived at opposing conclusions regarding the Kālacakra's teaching in relation to Buddhist philosophy. For Dol po pa, the Tantra supported the controversial view that the definitive doctrine of Mahāyāna Buddhism was that of buddha-nature, not emptiness, so that the absolute could be considered not as empty in itself but only as extrinsically empty (*gzhan stong*) with respect to relative phenomena. In its own nature it was, rather, a plenitude of the qualities of the highest enlightenment. But, by contrast, Bu ston held that the discourse of buddha-nature was itself a relative way of speaking of the emptiness that stood as the true heart of the doctrine. The latter came to be favored in the Dge lugs pa order, and it is the "Bu ston tradition" (*bu lugs*) of the Kālacakra that continues to be transmitted in that order in the early twenty-first century, above all by the fourteenth Dalai Lama (b. 1935). The Jo nang pa order, which was suppressed for political reasons by the government of the fifth Dalai Lama during the seventeenth century, continued nevertheless to thrive in some parts of far eastern Tibet. Its controversial teaching of extrinsic emptiness became an important element in the nineteenth-century eclectic movement in Khams. The greatest of the Jo nang pa masters following Dol po pa was Rje btsun Tāranātha (1575–1634), a celebrated historian and Tantric commentator, whose later incarnation was recognized within the Dge lugs pa order in Mongolia. Known as the Jebtsundampa Hutukhtu, he was regarded as the "Dalai Lama of the Mongols" in pre-Communist society.

The "Service and Attainment of the Three Indestructible Realities" (Rdo rje gsum gyi bsnyen sgrub) represents what is in the early twenty-first century an extremely rare lineage of instruction, focusing upon the internal yoga of the subtle energy channels and vital energy and stemming from the teaching of the divine Vajrayoginī, as gathered by the Tibetan adept O rgyan pa Rin chen dpal (Orgyenpa Rinchenpal, 1230–1309) during his extensive travels in the northwestern quarters of the Indian subcontinent. The teaching was popularized by O rgyan pa's successors during the fourteenth century, when several commentaries on it were composed, but subsequently it seems to have lapsed into obscurity. O rgyan pa also figures prominently as a transmitter of several of the major Bka' brgyud pa lineages, notably the 'Brug pa and Karma pa traditions.

The Emergence of the Dge lugs pa Order. During the fourteenth and fifteenth centuries, the religious life of Tibet was dominated by the Sa skya pa and by the proliferation of Bka' brgyud pa suborders, most of which were, like the Sa skya pa, closely associated with important aristocratic households. The Bka' gdams pa maintained their prominence, whereas several smaller orders, especially the Jo nang pa and the Zhwa lu pa, had achieved considerable renown. Though the other lines of teaching discussed above—Shangs pa, Zhi byed, and Gcod—were also widely transmitted at this time, it is less clear that well-defined monastic orders had been formed on their basis. In addition, there were some monasteries—for example, Gnas rnying not far from Rgyal rtse (modern Gyantse)—which must be considered as representing unique orders in their own right and as sometimes enjoying considerable local influence. A further example along these lines is offered by the monastery of Bo dong, near the Yam 'brog lake, whose great master Phyogs las rnam rgyal (Chokle Namgyal, 1376–1451) created his own vast synthesis of Buddhist learning comprising over 130 volumes.

The most important development, however, was the emergence of an altogether new order, the Dga' ldan pa (Gandenpa), later best known as Dge lugs pa, the "Virtuous Ones." The founder of the Dge lugs pa was the great scholar Rje Tsong kha pa Blo bzang grags pa (Je Tsongkhapa, 1357–1419), who, however, certainly had no intention to create a new order. He saw himself, rather, as a custodian and rectifier of received tradition. Born in the far northeastern Tibetan province of Amdo (modern Qinghai), he came to central Tibet as a teenager and pursued rigorous studies with all the foremost luminaries of the age, including teachers of the Bka' gdams pa, Sa skya pa, Bka' brgyud pa, Zhwa lu pa, and Jo nang pa traditions. His dedication to the Bka' gdams pa teaching of the progressive path of the *bodhisattva* was such that he and his successors often came to be thought of as "new Bka' gdams pa" (Bka' gdams gsar ma), and his treatise *Lam rim chen mo* (Great progression of the path) is renowned as a definitive expression of this approach. From his main Sa skya pa teacher, Red mda' ba Gzhon nu blo gros (1349–1412), he acquired a special concern for the interpretation of the Prāsaṅgika-Mādhyamika philosophy of the Indian master Candrakīrti (c. 600–650) as well as an orientation to Tantrism that emphasized the primacy of the *Guhyasamāja Tantra.*

Moreover, it was in collaboration with Red mda' ba that Tsong kha pa undertook his celebrated reform of the practice of the monastic code, or Vinaya. In his Tantric teachings, Tsong kha pa to a great extent continued Bka' brgyud pa traditions as well as the yoga of the *Kālacakra Tantra* as taught in the Jo nang pa and Zhwa lu pa orders. Nevertheless, he thoroughly rejected the "extrinsic emptiness" doctrine of Dol po pa, regarding it as an extreme representative of persistent Tibetan misunderstandings of the Yogācāra philosophy of India, and though accepting the authority of the Prāsaṅgika-Mādhyamika, he developed his own distinctive interpretation thereof, which in many respects was not anticipated in the work of Red mda' ba. In short, though drawing on earlier tradition, Tsong kha pa formulated a novel synthesis of the Indian Buddhist legacy, strongly emphasizing careful textual study and the demands of logic.

Tsong kha pa attracted large numbers of talented disciples, who began at some point to refer to themselves after the name of the monastery their master had founded in 1409, Dga' ldan. This was soon replaced by the near-homonym Dge ldan pa ("virtuous"), which in turn gave way to the synonym Dge lugs pa. Because Tsong kha pa had followed the tradition of Bu ston in adopting a yellow ceremonial hat, in contrast to the red that was widely favored, his successors became known popularly as "yellow hats" (*zhwa ser*).

Tsong kha pa's followers appear to have shared a strong sense of corporate identity, reflected doctrinally in the writings of his leading students, including Rgyal tshab rje Dar ma rin chen (Gyaltsapje, 1364–1432), Mkhas grub rje Dge legs dpal bzang (Khedrupje, 1385–1438), and Dge 'dun grub pa (Gendün Drupa, 1391–1474), posthumously considered to be the first Dalai Lama. At the same time, a large number of new monastic centers emphasizing adherence to the Vinaya and rigorous programs of study based on the sustained practice of debate were established to promulgate his teaching. Examples include Se ra (1419) and 'Bras spungs (1416), in the vicinity of Lhasa. The latter, with as many as ten thousand monks, was, prior to 1959, considered to be the largest monastic community in the world. With the conversion by Bsod nams rgya mtsho (Sonam Gyatso, the third Dalai Lama) of the Mongol leader Altan Khan in 1578, the Dge lugs pa order became the predominant Tibetan Buddhist tradition among the Mongols, a position it continued to enjoy in the early twenty-first century.

Mongol intervention in Tibetan affairs brought about the consolidation of political power by the fifth Dalai Lama in 1642, so that the Dge lugs pa became, from this point on, the effective masters of Tibet. Coming in the wake of the preceding decades of civil strife, in which warring factions were generally allied with different orders, the Dalai Lama's regime sought to consolidate their control in part by a reorganization of religion. Numerous new Dge lugs pa monasteries were established throughout the country. Some older centers, particularly those of orders, such as the Karma pa and 'Brug pa Bka' brgyud pa, that had been allied with the Dge lugs pa's rivals, were forcibly converted. The Jo nang pa were altogether suppressed except for one nunnery within the Dalai Lama's domains. (The Bka' gdams pa by this time had been mostly absorbed into the Dge lugs pa order and so no longer had an independent existence.) Despite these politically impelled changes and despite the insistence by some of the more extreme sectarian proponents that only one order need be recognized, it was generally agreed that some degree of plurality was nevertheless desirable. This came to be expressed in the notion that there were but four Tibetan Buddhist orders—Rnying ma pa, Sa skya pa, Bka' brgyud pa, and Dge lugs pa—a conception formalized by the official ranks and titles conferred by the government upon the hierarchs of these traditions.

SEE ALSO Bon; Buddhism, articles on Buddhism in Mongolia, Buddhism in Tibet; Dge lugs pa; Mādhyamika; Tibetan Religions, overview article; Yogācāra.

BIBLIOGRAPHY

Aziz, Barbara Nimri. "Indian Philosopher as Tibetan Folk Hero." *Central Asiatic Journal* 23, nos. 1–2 (1979): 19–37. On Pha dam pa Sangs rgyas, founder of the Zhi byed lineage, as known in the folklore of the Ding ri region.

Batchelor, Stephen, ed. *The Jewel in the Lotus: A Guide to the Buddhist Traditions of Tibet.* Boston and London, 1987. Useful introductory anthology of readings from the major traditions.

Chang, Garma Chen Chi. *The Hundred Thousand Songs of Milarepa.* 2 vols. New Hyde Park, N.Y., 1962. Translation of a key text of the Bka' brgyud pa tradition.

Chattopadhyaya, Alaka. *Atiśa and Tibet: Life and Works of Dīpamkara Śrījñāna in Relation to the History and Religion of Tibet.* 2d ed. Delhi, 1981. Study of the life, works, and legacy of the eleventh-century Bengali master.

Dreyfus, Georges. *The Sound of Two Hands Clapping.* Berkeley, Calif., 2003. Invaluable exploration of Tibetan monastic education in the Dge lugs pa order.

Dudjom Rinpoche, Jigdrel Yeshe Dorje. *The Nyingma School of Tibetan Buddhism: Its Fundamentals and History.* Translated by Gyurme Dorje and Matthew Kapstein. Boston, 1991. A leading twentieth-century master's summation of the traditions of his order.

Edou, Jérôme. *Machig Labdrön and the Foundations of Chöd.* Ithaca, N.Y., 1996. Accessible introduction to the teachings of the Gcod lineage.

Kapstein, Matthew. "The Shangs-pa bKa'-brgyud: An Unknown Tradition of Tibetan Buddhism." In *Tibetan Studies in Honour of Hugh Richardson,* edited by Michael Aris and Aung San Suu Kyi, pp. 136–143. Warminster, U.K., 1979. Historical introduction to the Shangs pa Bka' brgyud pa.

Kapstein, Matthew. "The Illusion of Spiritual Progress." In *Paths to Liberation: The Marga and Its Transformations in Buddhist Thought,* edited by Robert Buswell and Robert Gimello, pp. 193–224. Honolulu, 1991. Study of the Shangs pa founder Khyung po rnal 'byor's revelations in India.

Kapstein, Matthew T. "gDams-ngag: Tibetan Technologies of the Self." In *Tibetan Literature: Studies in Genre,* edited by José Ignacio Cabezón and Roger R. Jackson. Ithaca, N.Y., 1996. Introduction to the eight major lineages.

Kapstein, Matthew T. *The Tibetan Assimilation of Buddhism: Conversion, Contestation, and Memory.* Oxford, 2000. Includes studies of the formation of some of the major lineages.

Karma Thinlay (Karma phrin las). *The History of the Sixteen Karmapas of Tibet.* Boulder, Colo., 1978. Lives of the hierarchs of the Karma Bka' brgyud pa.

Khenpo Rinpoche Könchog Gyaltsen, with Katherine Rogers. *The Garland of Mahamudra Practices.* Ithaca, N.Y., 1986; 2d ed., 2002.

Lhalungpa, Lobsang, trans. *The Life of Milarepa.* New York, 1977; reprint, Boulder, Colo., 1984. Translation of Gtsang smyon's influential biography of the great Bka' brgyud pa saint.

Lhalungpa, Lobsang, trans. and ed. *Mahāmudrā: The Quintessence of Mind and Meditation.* Boston and London, 1985. Translation of an important treatise on the key Bka' brgyud pa contemplative teaching.

Nālandā Translation Committee. *The Life of Marpa the Translator.* Boulder, Colo., 1982; reprint, 1995. Translation of Gtsang smyon's biography of the Bka' brgyud pa founder.

Nālandā Translation Committee. *The Rain of Wisdom.* Boulder, Colo., 1980; reprint, 1999. Translation of a noted anthology of Bka' brgyud pa religious poems.

Orofino, Giacomella. *Contributo allo studio dell'insegnamento di Ma gcig lab sgron.* Naples, Italy, 1987. On the teachings attributed to Ma gcig lab sgron, founder of the Gcod tradition.

Riggs, Nicole. *Like an Illusion: Lives of the Shangpa Kagyu Masters.* Eugene, Ore., 2001. Abridged translation of the hagiographies of the Shangs pa bka' brgyud pa.

Roerich, George, trans. *The Blue Annals.* 2d ed. Delhi, 1976. Translation of 'Gos lo tsā ba's magisterial record of Tibetan Buddhist lineage histories.

Ruegg, David S. "The Jo-naṅ-pas: A School of Buddhist Ontologists according to the *Grub-mtha' sel-gyi-me-lon.*" *Journal of the American Oriental Society* 83 (1963): 73–91. The Jo nang pa philosophy as seen by its Dge lugs pa opponents.

Ruegg, David S. *The Life of Bu ston Rin po che.* Rome, 1966. Translation of the biography of the leading representative of the Zhwa lu pa order.

Sherburne, Richard, trans. *A Lamp for the Path and Commentary of Atīśa.* London, 1983. Translation of Atīśa's fundamental treatise on the path of the *bodhisattva.*

Smith, E. Gene. *Among Tibetan Texts.* Boston, 2001. See pp. 53–57. Collected studies by the leading authority on the general history of Tibetan religious literature.

Snellgrove, David L. *Indo-Tibetan Buddhism: Indian Buddhists and Their Tibetan Successors.* Boston, 1987. Far-ranging overview of the history of esoteric Buddhism.

Sopa, Geshe Lhundub, Roger Jackson, and John Newman. *The Wheel of Time: The Kalachakra in Context.* Madison, Wis., 1985; reprint, Ithaca, N.Y., 1991. Useful introduction to the Kālacakra system.

Stearns, Cyrus. *Buddha from Dolpo.* Albany, N.Y., 1999. Biographical study of the leading Jo nang pa master, Dol po pa, with extracts from his writings.

Thurman, Robert A. F. *Tsong Khapa's Speech of Gold in the Essence of True Eloquence.* Princeton, N.J., 1984. Study and translation of one of Tsong kha pa's major philosophical contributions.

MATTHEW T. KAPSTEIN (2005)

BUDDHISM, SCHOOLS OF: HIMALAYAN BUDDHISM

The historical Buddha Śākyamuni, born in Lumbinī and raised in Kapilavastu, both in present-day Nepal, must have often set his eyes on the slopes and peaks of the Himalaya, the "abode of snow," which can be seen on clear days from either of these places. Some 2,500 years after his birth, the Himalayan regions from Ladakh in the northwest across to Bhutan in the southeast are still suffused with the cultural practices of the Buddhist religion—its manifold rites, practices, and doctrines, its symbols and institutions, all reflecting with great clarity the different waves of the spread of the Buddha's teaching to the Himalaya.

PATRONS AND PRECEPTORS. The region of Kashmir, where Buddhism was first diffused about 250 BCE, on the orders of King Aśoka, later became one of the gateways through which monastic and tantric lineages entered Tibet, especially during the so-called second spread (*phyi dar*), from the end of the tenth century onwards. Particularly instrumental in this phase of the introduction of Buddhism into the western Himalayas were the early kings of Guge Purang (a confederation whose territory included what is today known as Ladakh), who selected a group of young men and sent them to Kashmir to be trained as "translators" (*lo tsā ba*). One such link between the Indian and Tibetan cultures was Rin chen bzang po (958–1055), later preceptor to King Ye shes 'od and his family. Due to efforts like his, Western Tibet became a center of Buddhist thought and practice based on a direct knowledge of Indian canonical and philosophical literature. Royal patronage was continued by later kings, one of whom financed, for example, the Indian journey of Rngog Lo tsā ba Blo ldan Shes rab (1059–1109). Another key figure, for having established a famous Vinaya ordination lineage in Tibet, was the Kashmiri Mahāpaṇḍita Śākyaśrībhadra (d. 1225), who was the last head of the Buddhist university of Vikramaśīla in Magadha and one of the teachers of Sa skya Paṇḍita Kun dga' rgyal mtshan (1182–1251).

Vikramaśīla was already seeking out contact with Tibet and other Himalayan regions during its peak period in the second half of the tenth century, the most notable example being in the person of Atiśa Dīpaṃkaraśrījñāna (982–1054), another one of its heads to reach Tibet. In his case it was the family of the early kings of Guge Purang who issued the invitation, the monk-scholar from present-day Bengal arriving at their royal court in the year 1042. The influence of Atiśa was far-reaching, especially his insistence on the observance of the monastic rule and a restricted use of the Tantras. After his death this Buddhist school became known as the Bka' gdams pa, which in turn served as the model for the "New Bka' gdams pa," or Dge lugs pa, founded by Tsong kha pa Blo bzang grags pa (1357–1419). This latter tradition was spread in the western Himalayas by a group of Tsong kha pa's disciples called the "six great diffusers of the teachings to the borders." It became prominent from the fifteenth century onward, with monastic lineages being established in Guge and Ladakh.

At about the same time, the Ngor pa tradition, a subsect of the Sa skya pa school, which had been founded by members of the 'Khon family to whom Sa skya Paṇḍita belonged, became influential in Purang. This religious shift was the result of Purang having become a dependency of Glo bo, another Himalayan kingdom (what is now Mustang in northern Nepal). Although this dominance of Glo bo over Purang was short-lived, it shows that the spread of Buddhist schools in the Himalayan region relied heavily on royal support for the definition and maintenance of their monastic institutions. This was true also in the next period in the history of the western Himalayas, when the rulers of Ladakh became the dominant political power and the twin countries of Guge and Purang faded into the background. The most popular Buddhist teacher during that time was Stag tshang ras pa (1574–1651), a religious figure still of great significance for the Ladakhi people. He was a member of the 'Brug pa subsect of the Bka' brgyud pa school, and he was generously supported by the king of Ladakh, from whom he received a number of estates while acting as his preceptor.

A significant role in the diffusion of Buddhist traditions in the western Himalayas was also played by another subsect of the Bka' brgyud pa school, the 'Bri gung pa, whose major zone of activity was the area around Lake Manasarovar and Mount Kailash. The hermitages around the sacred mountain were established by yogins following the example of their great fellow yogin Mi la ras pa (1028/40–1111/23), and were later occupied mainly by followers of the 'Brug pa, founded by Gling ras pa Padma rdo rje (1128–1188), and of the 'Bri gung pa, founded by Skyob pa 'Jig rten mgon po (1143–1217). These two schools left the strongest imprint on the tradition of Buddhist pilgrimages to Kailash, the "Snow Mountain Ti se" (*gangs ti se*), the legends surrounding their representatives being mainly responsible for the drive to idealize and spiritualize this Himalayan region. The 'Bri gung pa are said to have fostered innumerable numbers of "hermits" (*ri pa*), headed by what may be called a "rector" (*rdor 'dzin*), who supervised their spiritual life at the sacred mountain. In the fifteenth century the influence of the 'Bri gung pa in the Kailash area declined, doubtless under that of the Ngor pa tradition. In Ladkah, the 'Bri gung pa had become influential at the beginning of the thirteenth century, but when the ruling house became patrons of the 'Brug pas they lost their former standing there too, never to recover it.

A TRANSLATOR'S JOURNEY. The last Buddhist *mahāpaṇḍita* to reach Tibet during the second spread was the yogin Vanaratna (1384–1458) of present-day Bengal. He undertook three journeys to the plateau, where he assumed the role of preceptor of the Phag mo gru family, the rulers of Central Tibet before the Rin spungs pa took over. Vanaratna promulgated tantric transmissions, mainly from the cycles of the *Kālacakra Tantra*, the *Hevajra Tantra*, and the *Cakrasaṃvara Tantra*. Among his Tibetan disciples were two translators, 'Gos Lo tsā ba Gzhon nu dpal (1392–1481) and Khrims khang Lo tsā ba Bsod nams rgya mtsho (1424–1482), the former well known as the author of the famous

"Blue Annals," a comprehensive historiographical work of Tibetan Buddhism written in the years 1476 to 1478.

Bsod nams rgya mtsho, also called the "Great Translator" (*lo chen*), had met Vanaratna during the latter's final journey to Tibet in the years 1453 to 1454 and assisted him on the return trip to Nepal, where Vanaratna had taken up residence in a Buddhist *vihāra* in Patan. More than ten years later the translator undertook the daring journey to the south on his own in order to receive further tantric transmissions. This journey is a late case of a *lo tsā ba*'s quest for authentic Buddhist teaching, showing how the natural barrier of the Himalaya was overcome by these motivated travelers.

The mountain chain was approached in the region of Chu bar, close to the Gaurīśankar peak (7,146 m), which is known to Tibetans as the "glaciers of the Goddess of Long Life" (*tshe ring ma'i gangs rnams*). This area and its landscape is suffused, like the Kailash region, with the memory of Mi la ras pa, following whose example the translator is said to have appeased the local deities. Two routes could be taken from there onwards to the Nepal Valley. Bsod nams rgya mtsho chose the one passing through Dolakhā, a small independent kingdom to the northeast of the valley. Walking on treacherous paths through narrow gorges, he eventually reached Bhaktapur, the royal center of Nepal, ruled by King Jaya Yakṣamalla (r. 1424–1482). In the Govicandra Mahāvihāra in Patan the spiritual relationship with Vanaratna was renewed, and the Tibetan disciple obtained special tantric transmissions revealed to the Mahāpaṇḍita. One of these encounters took place in Śāntipura in the surroundings of the Buddhist stupa known today as Svayaṃbhūnāth. After a pilgrimage to the different sacred sites of the Nepal Valley, including a triad of celebrated statues of Padmapāṇi Lokeśvara located within the cultural boundaries of fifteenth-century Nepal, Bsod nams rgya mtsho then left his teacher and Newar hosts and once again made his way through the dangerous gorges. Later he merely complained that he had not been able to collect medicinal plants growing in the Himalayan valleys in abundance, and compared his difficulties with the ones faced by an earlier Buddhist traveler.

In later times a second route, passing from Chu bar to Listi (to the west of Dolakhā), was normally taken by Tibetan priests making the journey to Nepal. Among these we find the Sixth Zhva dmar pa Chos kyi dbang phyug (1584–1630) and the Eighth Si tu Chos kyi 'byung gnas (1699–1774). Like Bsod nams rgya mtsho, in whose footsteps they followed, these hierarchs of the Bka' brgyud pa school were warmly welcomed by Malla rulers, including Jagajjyotirmalla (r. 1614–1637) and Jagajjayamalla (r. 1722–1736).

"The Himalayan Experience." A widely used cultural corridor through which monastic and tantric lineages of the Buddhist religion entered the Tibetan plateau was Mang yul Gung thang, a kingdom in southwest Tibet located to the north of the Nepal Valley. During the time of the so-called earlier spread (*snga dar*) from the seventh to the ninth centuries, the great adept Padmasambhava was the most notable person to have traveled through the region, where he subdued mountain gods and local spirits on his way to the court of the Yarlung kings in Central Tibet. The same route was used by Śantarakṣita, the abbot who introduced the first Vinaya lineage into Tibet. Even Srong btsan sgam po, the first Buddhist ruler of the Yarlung dynasty, is believed to have undertaken a journey from Mang yul Gung thang to the Kathmandu Valley in order to bring back a statue of Padmapāṇi Lokeśvara to Tibet. This legend accounts for the importance of the Newar culture in the transmission of Buddhist religious and artistic traditions to the north, and points at the same time to the widespread circulation of these kind of narratives centering on Srong btsan sgam po, and their relevance to what has been called "the Himalayan experience" in the diffusion of Buddhism.

The introduction of the Buddha's teaching to Tibet and neighboring Himalayan regions is a recurring theme within the cult of the Bodhisattva Avalokiteśvara, to whom is credited the conversion of uncivilized humans to the new religion. Instrumental in this scheme are a group of temples said to have been built during the reign of Srong btsan sgam po, and located for the most part in or near the southern valleys; these temples were held to be able "to tame the borders and areas beyond the borders" and thus secure the center, namely the Jokhang temple in Lhasa, for Buddhism. The whole process of "taming" (*'dul ba*) took on a special character when directed toward the Himalayan regions which, according to the Buddhist texts glorifying the deeds of Srong btsan sgam po, were wild and uncultivated. This notion was counterbalanced by authors who looked to the remote Himalayan regions in the south as a sort of earthly paradise, whose hillsides provided an ideal location for monasteries, and which was imbued with all the resources of nature needed for leading a life of Buddhist spirituality.

Both these cultural attitudes of viewing the Himalayan valleys as regions to be tamed and—especially in times of political turmoil—as sanctuaries to be sought out were cultivated and refined within the Rnying ma pa school, the followers of the great adept Padmasambhava. One of the most prolific writers in this respect was the "treasure-discoverer" (*gter ston*) Rig 'dzin Rgod ldem (1337–1408), whose texts describe various "hidden valleys" (*sbas yul*) ranging from the region of Mang yul Gung thang in the west to the Chumbi Valley between Sikkim and Bhutan in the east. This master acted as preceptor to the royal court of Mang yul Gung thang. Indeed the prophecies of Padmasambhava regarding its future rulers show that the idea of saving this royal branch of the Yarlung dynasty was a theme of central importance in the hidden-valley literature. These kind of texts state explicitly that sanctuaries in the Himalayan valleys are to be searched for during times when foreign armies threaten the security of Tibet. They can thus be understood as a reaction of the traumatized Rnying ma pas to the invasion by the Mongols in the thirteenth century and to their subsequent political dominion.

The supremacy of the Dge lugs pa school in Central Tibet four hundred years later, achieved with the help of their Mongol patrons, resulted once more in an increased production of this kind of literature and a more intense search for sacred abodes in the Himalayan borderlands. During this period, in the seventeenth century, the border-taming temple in Mang yul Gung thang functioned as one starting point for expeditions of Rnying ma pa treasure-discoverers to the south. The diffusion of Buddhist institutions and rites in such neighboring valleys as Glang 'phrang and Yol mo, located in present-day Nepal, must be seen as an outcome of these kinds of practices.

BUDDHIST MONARCHIES. The country of Sikkim, now part of the confederation of Indian states, was known to Rig 'dzin Rgod ldem under the name "Rice Land" (*'bras mo ljongs*). One of the monasteries that he founded, ruins of which still can be seen today, was within its borders. The greatest propagator of Buddhism in Sikkim appeared later: Lha btsun Nam mkha' 'jigs med (1587–1650), another treasure-discoverer of the Rnying ma pa school and follower of the Great Perfection doctrine. In the year 1641 he, together with Kaḥ thog Rig 'dzin chen po and Mnga' bdag Sems dpa' chen po, installed the first Buddhist king in Sikkim. The names of the latter two masters allude to the earlier spread of further Rnying ma pa lineages in the country, namely to the Kaḥ thog pa of Eastern Tibet and to the Mnga' bdag pa, who followed in the tradition of the treasure-discoverer Zhig po gling pa (1524–1583) from Central Tibet. The epitome of the hidden valley transformed into a Buddhist kingdom was Brag dkar bkra shis ldings, a sacred site surrounded in the style of a *maṇḍala* by four miraculous caves in the four cardinal directions; these places continue to be pilgrimage destinations for all Sikkimese Buddhists.

During the rule of the next *dharmarāja* or *chos rgyal*, a strong connection was established with the teachers of Smin grol gling, an influential Rnying ma pa monastery in Central Tibet, and this led to the foundation of Padma yang rtse, a monastery which later supervised all the Rnying ma pa institutions in Sikkim. 'Jigs med dpa' bo (b. 1682), the second incarnation of Lha btsun Nam mkha' 'jigs med, received his spiritual training under Rig 'dzin Gter bdag gling pa (1646–1714), the hierarch of Smin grol gling, and following an invitation to Sikkim became the preceptor of the Sikkimese king. His activities at the beginning of the eighteenth century coincided with the suppression of the Rnying ma pa school in Central Tibet due to the Dzungar invasions and an edict of the Manchu ruler Yung chen. In the year 1718 Rje btsun Mi 'gyur dpal sgron (1699–1769), the daughter of Rig 'dzin Gter bdag gling pa, escaped the Dzungar armies and traveled to Sikkim; there she was welcomed by the king and by 'Jigs med dpa' bo. The "Rice Land," too, thus offered refuge in troubled times to the followers of Padmasambhava.

Parts of northern Bhutan, the modern Buddhist monarchy bordering on Assam, were regarded as hidden sanctuaries as well, as can be seen from the writings of Rig 'dzin Padma gling pa (1450–1521). It was Zhabs drung Ngag dbang rnam rgyal (b. 1595) who founded a central government and established the borders of the "Land of the Thunder-Dragon" (*'brug yul*). A member of the Rgya family from Rva lung, from which family Rgyal ba'i dbang po (1428–1476), the second 'Brug chen hierarch of the 'Brug pa school, issued, he was forced to flee to the southern Himalaya upon claiming to be the incarnation of the fourth 'Brug chen Padma dkar po (1527–1592). The teaching tradition of the 'Brug pa school had already been introduced earlier to Bhutan, one of its representatives before the unification of the country being Kun dga' legs pa (1455–1529), the famous "Madman from Bhutan" (*'brug smyon*). Later on the country was ruled by a nominal head of state, an incarnate lama, while the secular administration was entrusted to a regent; these persons were known respectively as the Zhabs drung Rin po che and the Sde srid.

The fourth regent, Bstan 'dzin rab rgyas (1638–1696) was one key figure in the early phase of the 'Brug pa state, which lasted more than two hundred years before being replaced in 1907 by a modern monarchy. It was this regent who created a religious edifice at the famous cliff-side meditation cave of the great adept Padmasambhava at Stag tshang to the north of the Paro Valley (the site had earlier been in the hands of the Kaḥ thog pa), and he was also responsible for popularizing such religious practices as the display of massive appliqué hangings draped from monastery courtyard walls and the seasonal dance festivals dedicated to Padmasambhava. The forty-ninth regent, 'Jigs med rnam rgyal (1825–1881), is generally remembered for being the father of O rgyan dbang phyug (1862–1926), the founder of the modern monarchy. The latter's rise to political power was largely due to the encouragement shown and the rituals conferred upon him by his teacher Byang chub brtson 'grus (1817–1856). This lama from Central Tibet had traveled widely in Kashmir, Western Tibet, and Nepal, and he had conceived a special crown for his disciple: a magical battle helmet, which later became a symbol of royalty. Imbued with the essence of two forms of the great protector Mahākala, it was a conscious allusion to the role played by the raven-headed Mahākala in the first unification of Bhutan by Zhabs drung Ngag dbang rnam rgyal.

CRAFTSMEN AND ARTISTS. The legends concerning the enlightened activity of the bodhisattva Avalokiteśvara as the spiritual protector of the Himalayan region and the Buddhist king as his incarnation formed the ideological basis for monarchies like Sikkim and Bhutan from the very beginning. It is known, for example, that the first ruler of Sikkim held the teaching transmission of the "Hundred Thousand Proclamations of the Maṇi [Mantra]" (*maṇi bka' 'bum*), a heterogeneous collection of teachings ascribed to Srong btsan sgam po, and that in the seventeenth century prints of this collection were executed in the newly founded state of Bhutan.

This particular version can be traced back to an earlier edition, which is the oldest xylograph of this work after its dissemination in the form of manuscripts for a period of about four hundred years. It was in Mang yul Gung thang that a first block print of the collection had been produced, and the person responsible for this and other large-scale printing projects in that region was a monk of the Bo dong pa school by the name of "The Incomparable" (*mnyam med*) Chos dbang rgyal mtshan (1484–1549). An expert in the field of Buddhist art and craftsmanship, he oversaw the first carved edition of the teachings associated with Srong btsan sgam po at the royal court of Mang yul Gung thang upon the death of his teacher Btsun pa Chos legs (1437–1521), another influential member of the Bo dong pa community. The workshop of Chos dbang rgyal mtshan produced further xylographs of writings of the 'Brug pa and 'Ba' ra ba Bka' brgyud pa schools, and also carved on wood blocks the oldest edition of the *Theg mchog mdzod* (a classic of the Great Perfection doctrine) and of the *bKa' gdams glegs bam* (a collection of texts comprising hagiographical material and the esoteric teachings of the Bka' gdams pa school). Chos dbang rgyal mtshan's legacy to the monastic institutions of the Bo dong pa was a printed edition of a "stages of the path" (*lam rim*) manual by Bo dong Paṇ chen Phyogs las rnam rgyal (1375–1451), the founder of the school. This project, which occupied sixteen carvers for a period of over six months, was completed in Btsum, a hidden valley located in present-day Nepal. Chos dbang rgyal mtshan became involved in the popularization of this cultural phenomenon by virtue of being a disciple of such treasure-discoverers of the Rnying ma pa school as Rig 'dzin Mchog ldan mgon po (1497–1531) and Rig 'dzin bstan gnyis gling pa (1480–1553), both of whose collected writings he executed as block prints. This increased production of xylograph editions of Buddhist classics in southwestern Tibet, including the famous biography and spiritual songs of the great yogin Mi la ras pa, greatly enhanced the spread of these different literary traditions in the Himalayan valleys. It is possible to identify the individual carvers of such block print editions along with the artists who beautifully depicted the deities on their front and back pages.

One main seat of the Bo dong pa school was located in Porong, a nomadic region in the northern part of Mang yul Gung thang ruled by a local whose ancient capital was a place called "Big Tent" (*sbra chen*). In the 1960s, after the end of the rule of this family, the Porong area underwent dramatic change, but today the community has reorganized itself, its main monastery has been rebuilt, and the old block xylograph of Bo dong Paṇ chen has been reprinted.

Female Incarnations. Incarnate religious teachers have played an important role in the Himalaya, as hierarchs of Buddhist schools, as preceptors to royal families, or as "representatives" (*tshab*) of the great adept Padmasambhava in troubled times. In contrast to the great number of male "reincarnations" (*sprul sku*), the principle of female incarnate lineages seems to have been not very widely accepted. As *ḍākinīs*, or "sky-goers" (*mkha' 'gro ma*), women are nevertheless held in high esteem, both as symbols of divinity and as religious practitioners, especially among followers of the Rnying ma pa school. Once they achieve the status of holy women, they can thus become the legitimating source of male incarnate lineages; this can be seen, for example, in the cases of Rig 'dzin Padma gling pa, Rig 'dzin Bstan gnyis gling pa, and Rig 'dzin Jigs med gling pa (1730–1798), all of whom are regarded as reincarnations of female disciples of Padmasambhava (of the princesses Padma gsal, Nu 'byin sa le, and Ye shes mtsho rgyal respectively).

Although the number of female reincarnations has been relatively small, a few cases are still remembered among Himalayan Buddhists. The most well-known one is the so-called Rdo rje phag mo incarnation of Bsam sdings monastery near the lake Yar brog mtsho in Central Tibet. This divine lady is viewed as an emanation of Tārā, who for protective purposes assumed the appearance of a menacing animal, the "Diamond Sow" (*rdo rje phag mo*). The first member of this lineage was the youngest daughter of King Lha dbang rgyal mtshan (1401–1464) from Mang yul Gung thang, who later became the spiritual partner of Bo dong Paṇ chen Phyogs las rnam rgyal. In 1440 this princess, named Chos kyi sgron me, founded the monastery of Bsam sdings, a convent of the Bo dong pa school, with the support of the local ruler of Sna dkar rtse. The ruling family of this principality also cared for the next incarnation, the "Noble One" (*rje btsun ma*) Kun dga' bzang mo (b. 1459). The translator Bsod nams rgya mtsho met her in Sna dkar rtse not long after his return from Nepal. In the following years this female incarnation is known to have actively promoted teaching traditions of the Bo dong Paṇ chen across the Himalayan region. Her role as a charismatic religious teacher was accepted by the great Buddhist masters of her time, including the second 'Brug chen Rgyal ba'i dbang po and Lha btsun Kun dga' Chos kyi rgya mtsho (1432–1505), the teacher of Kun dga' legs pa, the Madman from Bhutan. The lineage of the Rdo rje phag mo incarnation continues down to the present time, with its twelfth member still residing at its place of origin.

Another female incarnate lineage is that of the Gung ru mkha' 'gro ma from Eastern Tibet, which is known from literary sources but has not survived as a living institution. The reason for this may be sought in unflattering political prophecies that Gung ru mkha' 'gro ma (also known as Lha rtse dpon mo) uttered with regard to the newly founded government of the fifth Dalai Bla ma Ngag dbang blo bzang rgya mtsho (1617–1682); as a result, the Dalai Bla ma expressed doubts about her spiritual authority, as stated in his autobiography. The divine lady was nevertheless credited with all signs of authenticity by Rong po Skal ldan rgya mtsho (1607–1677), a great master from Amdo. These events should not be interpreted as signs of misogynous behavior on the part of the religious and political head of seventeenth-century Tibet (he spoke without bitterness of the fourth incarnation of the Bsam sdings rDo rje phag mo). In any case, they are suggestive of an atmosphere of religious tolerance prevailing in Eastern Tibet (Khams and Amdo), the border regions of Lho kha and the Himalayan valleys in the south.

Pilgrimages and Stupas. Schools of Himalayan Buddhism developed following the spread of the Buddha's teaching to the mountainous region, and reflected the monastic lineages and tantric transmissions associated with places like Kashmir, Magadha, and Nepal. This process of religious transmission was completed by the fifteenth century, after which a reversed movement can be observed, with the now established religious traditions crossing back over the cultural boundaries to the south. One can trace this transition in the journeys of individual Buddhist travelers and in the practice of large-scale pilgrimages to sacred sites located in the Himalayan valleys. A conspicuous example of the latter is the migration of the Sherpa people from Eastern Tibet to the land south of Mount Everest in the sixteenth century, their search for a hidden valley leading to a permanent resettlement after they were displaced from their home country.

Sherpa Buddhism is characterized, like most local Buddhist cultures in the Himalaya, by foundings of temples and monasteries, the last major ones being under the inspiration of Ngag dbang bstan 'dzin nor bu (1867–1940), the great abbot of Rdza rong phu. Both this monastery, located on the northern side of the Everest massif, and the well-known Steng po che monastery (founded in the years 1915 to 1919) follow the teaching tradition of Smin grol gling. The rituals of this Rnying ma pa monastery in Central Tibet are kept alive in the Sherpa country through village festivals and the construction of stupas, which latter are recognized by the people as the containers of relics and as commemorative monuments.

Buddhist stupas like the ones of Svayaṃbhūnāth and Bodhnāth in the Kathmandu Valley of Nepal have been popular destinations of pilgrims for centuries. In the course of time, the upkeep of these religious shrines came into the hands of Tibetan priests. This led in turn to the construction of administrative buildings near the pilgrimage sites; in the case of Svayaṃbhūnāth and Bodhnāth, these buildings date from the eighteenth century. The exodus of the Tibetan people from their homeland after the revolt in Lhasa in 1959 was one main reason for the subsequent increased construction of monasteries near the stupas. In these places one can witness a revival of the cultural and religious traditions of Himalayan Buddhism. This holds true as well for regions like Ladakh, Sikkim, and Bhutan, where the Tibetan diaspora has found refuge and is able to maintain its religious and cultural identity.

Pilgrimages to sacred sites associated with the life of the historical Buddha Śākyamuni have a long tradition in India, and this cultural practice was also taken up by Himalayan Buddhists. One interesting example is the pilgrimage to a spurious Kuśinagara (the place of Buddha's *parinirvāṇa*) in Assam, as advocated by followers of the 'Brug pa school in the sixteenth century. The archaeological site of Lumbinī, the birthplace of Śākyamuni Buddha, was discovered only in 1896; modern pilgrimages to this spot are a quite recent phenomenon. A stupa of impressive height has just been completed there by the 'Bri gung pa school—a sign of the continuing definition and maintenance of Himalayan Buddhism in the place where its founder was born.

See Also Buddhism, overview article.

Bibliography

Aris, Michael. *The Raven Crown: The Origins of Buddhist Monarchy in Bhutan.* London, 1994. The Himalayan kingdom of Bhutan and the hereditary monarchy of O rgyan dbang phyug are presented as one of the few kingships to have reemerged in the twentieth century. The narrative is based on the Bhutanese chronicles.

Buffetrille, Katia, and Hildegard Diemberger, eds. *Territory and Identity in Tibet and the Himalayas.* Leiden, 2002. The articles explain notions of territory and identity in Tibetan and Tibeto-Burman communities using a fundamentally empirical method. Two essays deal with the nomadic principality of Porong.

Cadonna, Alfredo, and Ester Bianchi, eds. *Facets of Tibetan Religious Tradition and Contacts with Neighbouring Cultural Areas.* Florence, 2002. Results of the latest research in the field of Tibetan religious traditions at the Venetian institute Venezia e l'Oriente. One contribution investigates the theme of female reincarnations and the case of the Gung ru mkha' 'gro ma.

Ehrhard, Franz-Karl. *Early Buddhist Block Prints from Mang-yul Gung-thang.* Lumbinī, Nepal, 2000. Monograph surveying the history of a number of sixteenth-century xylographs produced by a local school of calligraphy and printing. One of the literary sources is the biography of the monk-artist Chos dbang rgyal mtshan.

Ehrhard, Franz-Karl. *Life and Travels of Lo-chen bSod-nams rgya-mtsho.* Lumbinī, Nepal, 2002. Assessment of the biographical tradition of a fifteenth-century translator mainly active in Lho kha on the basis of a work written by the Fourth Zhva dmar pa. A list of the translations of Mahāpaṇḍita Vanaratna and his interpreters is included.

Gutschow, Niels, Axel Michaels, Charles Ramble, and Ernst Steinkellner, eds. *Sacred Landscape of the Himalaya: Proceedings of an International Conference at Heidelberg.* Vienna, 2003. Contributions cover the entire range of the Himalaya, from Ladakh to Bhutan, reconstructing the historical topography of the predominantly Buddhist northern region. Contains maps of Mang yul Gung thang as a destination for Buddhist pilgrims.

Gyatso, Janet. *Apparitions of the Self: The Secret Autobiographies of a Tibetan Visionary.* Princeton, 1998. Examines autobiographical writing in Tibet from a comparative perspective. This literary genre is frequently met with in the study of Himalayan Buddhism. The book concludes with a study of the figure of the *ḍākinī* in these kind of texts.

Huber, Toni, ed. *Sacred Spaces and Powerful Places in Tibetan Culture: A Collection of Essays.* Dharamsala, India, 1999. Collection of essays on narrative, social identity and territory, ritual spaces and places, and hidden lands and holy domains. Two of the essays deal with the search for Himalayan sacred territories.

Klimburg-Salter, Deborah E. *Tabo: A Lamp for the Kingdom: Early Indo-Tibetan Buddhist Art in the Western Himalaya.* Milan,

Italy, 1997. Documentation of the royal monastery of Tabo, founded by King Ye shes 'od of Guge Purang, and still the largest monastery in the western part of the country. Includes a historical introduction to Western Tibet by Luciano Petech.

McKay, Alex, ed. *Pilgrimage in Tibet.* Richmond, U.K., 1998. Conference papers dealing with pilgrimage as a core element of religious practice in the Tibetan cultural world. Three articles cover Mount Kailash; one describes the opening of the hidden valley 'Bras mo ljongs.

Ortner, Sherry B. *High Religion: A Cultural and Political History of Sherpa Buddhism.* Princeton, 1989. The founding of Sherpa monasteries is analyzed as a "cultural scheme" by combining social and historical modes of analysis. The book draws no comparisons with other local cultures in the Himalaya.

Smith, E. Gene. *Among Tibetan Texts: History and Literature of the Himalayan Plateau.* Boston, 2001. These famous essays cover Buddhist texts representing all lineages, histories, and biographical and literary arts—among them studies on the diaries of the Eighth Si tu and on secular arts and sciences as presented by Bo dong Paṇ chen.

Vitali, Roberto. *The Kingdoms of Gu.ge Pu.hrang according to mNga'.ris rgyal-rabs by Gu.ge mKhan.chen Ngag.dbang grags.pa.* Dharamsala, India, 1996. Translation of the "Royal Genealogy of Western Tibet," written by one of Tsong kha pa's disciples. Part 2 provides details on the diffusion of the different Buddhist schools in Guge Purang.

FRANZ-KARL EHRHARD (2005)

BUDDHISM, SCHOOLS OF: CHINESE BUDDHISM

Chinese Buddhism is typically described in terms of *schools*, a word used variously to refer to lineages of exegetical interpretation, styles of devotional or cultivational practice, or combinations of both. The earliest schools to emerge, from the fifth century onward, were exegetical lineages devoted to the interpretation of individual scriptures or groups of scriptures. Early examples include traditions based on Chinese translations of Mādhyamika or Yogācāra treatises, as well as on individual scriptures such as the *Nirvāṇa Sūtra.* A tendency to greater conceptual inclusiveness culminated in the development of the systematic schools, often referred to as Sui-Tang schools because of the timing of their emergence during those dynasties (sixth to eighth centuries); primary examples are the Tiantai and Huayan (Flower Garland) traditions. At about the same time or slightly later there also developed identifiable modes of practice or modal traditions, so named because of the centrality of different forms of religious praxis to their identities; this refers to Pure Land devotionalism, Chan (Zen) meditation and dialogue practices, and esoteric Buddhist ritual endeavor.

TERMINOLOGY. The English term *school* evokes the philosophical traditions of ancient Greece, in which individual teachers guided small assemblies of (predominately male) students in different styles of intellectual discourse. This usage privileges individual founders and doctrinal content over social features and religious praxis, and it implies a historical model that is of limited application to the exegetical schools and individual monastic communities of Chinese Buddhism, and is at best unwieldy when used for other types of Buddhist schools.

Japanese scholarship and the Japanese denominational model have had a significant and often unrecognized influence on Western-language interpretations of Chinese Buddhism since the late nineteenth century. Japanese scholars such as Nanjō Bun'yū (1849–1927) and Takakusu Junjirō (1866–1945) worked as students and research assistants with major scholars such as Max Müller (1823–1900) and Sylvain Lévi (1863–1935), respectively, during the formative years of European Buddhist studies and religious studies. Adopting their mentors' perspective on the importance of the Buddha as founder and of doctrine as his primary contribution, these Japanese authors and their later colleagues described Chinese Buddhism in terms of the founders, doctrines, and characteristic practices of the separate denominational entities that had crystallized in Japan during the Tokugawa period (1600–1868), when the Japanese government had imposed a fixed administrative structure on the religion there. Although this was an understandable projection of early Japanese Buddhology, it is important to remember that nothing like a Japanese "school," as an integrated denominational organization with prescribed doctrines and practices and clearly defined institutional assets, priestly specialists, and lay membership, ever existed in Chinese Buddhism.

There are also profound differences between the "schools" of Chinese Buddhism and those of the parent Indian tradition, where the various *nikāyas* (e.g., Dharmaguptaka, Sarvāstivāda) functioned as ordination lineages and only secondarily as exponents of particular doctrinal stances. It is somewhat more appropriate to use the philosophical identifiers Mādhyamika, Yogācāra, and so on to identify pan-Asian styles of interpretation, although there were no institutional links between Indian and Chinese adherents of such philosophical "schools," and participants in these philosophical traditions in the two cultures worked from very different sets of texts.

In contrast, ordination lineage was rarely if ever used as a sectarian identifier in China. Only a few different sets of Vinaya regulations were ever in use there, and from at least the seventh century on all Chinese Buddhist monks and nuns were ordained under the same set of monastic regulations translated from those of the Indian Dharmaguptaka ordination lineage. In addition, as far as we can tell, virtually all Chinese Buddhists, even those who specialized in the study of treatises labeled *Hīnayānist* in the East Asian tradition (such as the widely read *Abhidharmakośa* of the Sautrāntika-Sarvāstivāda authority Vasubandhu, for example), identified themselves with the Mahāyāna. In addition, the number of foreign missionaries who identified strongly with the non-Mahāyāna was extremely small. Thus, using the terminology commonly applied to Indian Buddhism, all Chinese Buddhists belong to a single "school"—not a particularly helpful usage.

Finally, the rhetoric of *sect*, which is used in the literatures of sociology and religious studies to refer either to nonmainstream movements that challenge the status quo or to highly organized entities that prescribe totalistic programs of religious involvement for their members, is entirely inappropriate for the description of Chinese Buddhism prior to the emergence of the White Lotus Teaching and other popular movements of the fourteenth century and after.

EXEGETICAL LINEAGES. During the first four centuries of the common era, there was a gradually increasing number of Buddhist adherents and communities in China, but nothing that achieved the continuity or impact to be recognized as a distinctive school. This is true even of the highly esteemed Huiyuan (334–416), whose community on Mount Lu represented the ideal of early monastic life but did not continue to function as a coherent group after the master's death. Thus, even though Huiyuan is famous for having led a group of 123 clergy and laypeople in meditative devotions to the Buddha Amitābha of the Pure Land, this was but one event within a broader fabric of activities. Although important as a historical precedent to the later Pure Land tradition, which dogmatically claims him as a founding "patriarch," this cannot be considered the beginning of a Chinese Pure Land "school."

Given the foundation of those first four centuries, the early fifth-century output of the great translator and exegete Kumārajīva (d. 409) provided Chinese Buddhists with the textual resources for the sophisticated understanding of their chosen tradition. In addition, Kumārajīva attracted a number of gifted monks, who studied with him and assisted with the editing and explanation of the newly translated texts. Many of his texts thus became the foci of significant exegetical activity, with his own students writing widely read interpretive essays and commentaries. Such lineages of study constitute the earliest hints of sectarian differentiation in Chinese Buddhism.

As Stanley Weinstein (1987) has observed, of the ten texts most commonly studied in south China during the fifth century, seven had been translated by Kumārajīva. Four of these were sūtras: the *Lotus of the Wondrous Dharma* (*Miaofa lianhua jing, Saddharmapuṇḍarīka-sūtra*); *Teaching of Vimalakīrti* (*Weimojie jing, Vimalakīrtinirdeśa-sūtra*); *Perfection of Wisdom* (in two versions: *Bore jing, Prajñāpāramitā-sūtra*); and *Ten Stages* [*of the Bodhisattva*] (*Shizhu jing, Daśabhūmika-sūtra*). In addition, Kumārajīva produced a recension of the Vinaya known in Chinese as the *Ten-Recitation Vinaya* (*Shisong lü*), which derived from that of his own Sarvāstivāda ordination lineage. He also translated scholastic discourses, including an exposition of Buddhist analytical philosophy called *Treatise on the Perfection of Truth* (*Chengshi lun, Satyasiddhi-śāstra*), which later came to be viewed as anomalous because of its simplistic explanation of *śūnyatā* or "emptiness," and three Mādhyamika texts that came to be known collectively as *San lun* or *Three Treatises.* Kumārajīva's translation of the *Commentary on the Great Perfection of Wisdom* (*Da zhidu lun*, popularly called *Da lun*, **Mahāprajñāpāramitopadeśa*), although completed in 405, was largely ignored until the second half of the sixth century, when its study was taken up by scholars in the San lun tradition. The three other major texts studied in fifth-century south China were the *Nirvāṇa Sūtra* (*Niepan jing*), translated by Dharmakṣema in 421 and revised slightly by southern scholars shortly thereafter; the *Treatise on the Essence of the Abhidharma* (*Za apitan xin lun*, popularly referred to as *Pitan*, **Saṃyuktābhidharmahṛdaya-[śāstra]*), translated by Saṃghavarman around 435; and the *Sūtra of the Lion's Roar of Queen Śrīmālā* (*Shengman jing, Śrīmālādevīsiṃhanāda-sūtra*), translated by Guṇabhadra in 436.

In the north, dynastic wars in the 420s and 430s and a persecution of Buddhism in the 440s made continued scholarly activity difficult. When lecturing on the scriptures and commentarial writing resumed in the last decades of the fifth century, monks there focused primarily on texts that had been ignored in the south or which had only recently been translated. The most prominent exception was the *Nirvāṇa Sūtra*, which was the subject of massive commentarial attention both in the north and at the court of Liang Emperor Wu (r. 501–549) in southern China. Texts studied in the north but largely ignored in the south include the *Flower Garland Sūtra* (*Huayan jing, Avataṃsaka*) translated by Buddhabhadra in 420; the *Sūtra on the Bodhisattva Stages* (*Pusadichi jing, Bodhisattvabhūmi Sūtra*), translated by Dharmakṣema in 418; and the *Four-Part Disciplinary Code* (*Sifen lü*), the Vinaya recension deriving from the Dharmaguptaka ordination lineage and translated by Buddhayaśas and Zhu Fonian in 405 or 408. Of the texts appearing for the first time in translation in the first half of the sixth century, the one that attracted the greatest attention in north China was the *Commentary on the Sūtra of the Ten Stages* (*Shidi jing lun*, commonly called *Di lun*), translated by Bodhiruci and others in 511. Learned monks in south China in the second half of the sixth century were similarly attracted by the *Compendium of the Mahāyāna* (*She dasheng lun, Mahāyānasaṃgraha*, commonly called *She lun*) and the *Treasury of the Abhidharma* (*Apidamo jushe shi lun, Abhidharmakośa*), both translated by Paramārtha in 563.

The exegetical lineages devoted to each of these texts (or sets of texts, in the case of the San lun) constituted "schools" only in the most minimal sense. In the first place, although individual monks were known as specialists in particular scriptures, most seem to have worked on multiple texts of various types. Second, although the lineage of study of any text might be traceable from one generation to the next, even when a student's interpretation borrowed heavily from his teachers such connections were overwhelmed by the fluctuations in popularity of different scriptures over the decades. Third, monks often studied with multiple teachers, so that exegetical lineages often "cross-pollinated" each other. Fourth, far from attempting to keep scriptural traditions distinct and independent, the interpretations of individual scriptures were played against each other, with the understanding of one scripture used as a guide for the analysis of totally different texts, and the understanding of Buddhism as a whole applied to the line-by-line interpretation of specific scriptures.

Weinstein concludes that for fifth- and sixth-century China there were five principle exegetical traditions based on Indian treatise literature: Chengshi lun, Di lun, San lun (including study of the *Commentary on the Great Perfection of Wisdom*), Pitan (Abhidharma), and She lun. To this we might add the exegetical traditions based on sūtra and Vinaya literature—Lü (Vinaya), Nirvāṇa, and Huayan—the result being the set most often referred to as "schools" in modern writings.

The term sometimes used in contemporaneous Chinese writings to describe these traditions of monkish learning, *zong* (which in Chinese originally referred to a clan temple, or the clan's primal ancestor or ancestral deity, and by extension the clan as a whole), referred not to any kind of sectarian identity but to the "underlying theme" or "essential doctrine" of the text in question. Indeed, at the very end of the sixth century several "[study] group leaders" (*zhongzhu*) specializing in particular texts were accorded formal recognition by the Sui dynasty (589–618) government, with Emperor Wen (r. 581–605) assigning eminent monks residence at different major temples in Chang'an as leaders of the Di lun, Vinaya, Da lun (i.e., Da zhidu lun), and Niepan study groups, respectively. Based in part on this precedent, the teachings of all these exegetical traditions were transmitted to Japan before or during the Nara period (710–784), where their use as sectarian labels became institutionalized within Japanese Buddhism. However, as Abé Ryūichi has shown, even the study groups of Nara Buddhism were very small assemblies with overlapping memberships and entirely without administrative authority or institutional identity, so that the rhetoric of "school" is problematic in this case as well.

SYSTEMATIC SCHOOLS. A qualitative change in the nature of Chinese Buddhist schools occurred through the efforts of Tiantai Zhiyi (538–597). Zhiyi's wide-ranging discussion of a number of major Chinese scriptures, integrated interpretation of Buddhism from the perspective of the very popular *Lotus Sūtra*, and intimate connections with the founders of the Sui dynasty led to the establishment of one of the most influential and long-lasting schools of East Asian Buddhism. The tradition he established came to be known as the Tiantai school, based on the name of the mountain in southeastern China (Zhejiang province) chosen as his major center; it also flourished in Korea (as the Ch'ŏnt'ae school) and Japan (as the Tendai school). Although the Tiantai school fell out of favor during the early years of the Tang dynasty (618–906), it was "revived" by Zhiyi's fifth-generation successor Zhanran, who was in fact the first to refer to his tradition as "Tiantai school." Later, Tiantai flourished to the extent of becoming effectively synonymous with all "teaching" monasteries (roughly 5 percent of all major public institutions) from the Song dynasty (960–1279) onward.

Zhiyi's innovation was to combine (1) a set of interpretative schema intended to govern all Buddhist doctrine (as available in the East Asian subcontinent at the time); (2) a similarly comprehensive system of meditation practice; and (3) a specific institutional center and teaching lineage. One of the core elements of his teachings was the philosophy of emptiness (*śūnyatā*) derived from Nāgārjuna's writings, particularly the *Mūla-madhyamaka-kārikā*, represented in Chinese as the *Zhong lun* (*Treatise on the Middle*), one of the San lun or "three treatises," and the *Commentary on the Great Perfection of Wisdom*, also attributed to Nāgārjuna but more likely a compilation by the translator Kumārajīva. This was combined with a multifaceted use of the *Lotus Sūtra*, both for its doctrinal implications and as inspiration for repentance ritual and meditation practice. From this scripture Zhiyi adopted the position that the various teachings of the Buddha were directed at sentient beings at different levels of spiritual capacity, using "skillful means" (*upāya, fangbian*) to adapt his message to the listener. Given this theoretical basis, and drawing extensively on the work of earlier Chinese commentators, Zhiyi outlined the "five times"—five separate periods of the Buddha's teaching career—as well as different types of doctrine and methods of teaching used by the Buddha in different contexts. Although the details of this formulation cannot be included here, its implications were immense: Zhiyi provided a comprehensive explanation for the sometimes jarring differences between Buddhist scriptures, claiming that each different doctrinal message was intended to lead diverse congregations of followers upward to the single goal of buddhahood. In generating this schema Zhiyi built on earlier interpretations to signal the importance of such widely used texts as the *Flower Garland*, *Perfection of Wisdom*, *Vimalakīrti*, and *Nirvāṇa* sūtras, even while according his favored *Lotus Sūtra* pride of place as the very pinnacle of the Buddha's teachings. Zhiyi was similarly inclusive and systematic in the realm of meditation practice, defining four categories of *samādhi* that covered virtually all possible approaches: constantly seated, constantly walking, mixed seated and walking, and neither seated nor walking. Indeed, his concrete prescriptions for so many different types of meditation practice became the standard set of guidelines for all Chinese Buddhists for the next several centuries.

In terms of lineage identity, Zhiyi considered himself to represent, not one of multiple sectarian units within Buddhism, but the most profound teachings of Buddhism itself, as transmitted from Śākyamuni through the Indian Mādhyamika philosopher Nāgārjuna (fl. 2nd c. CE) to his own Chinese teachers and then himself. Zhiyi's fifth-generation successor, Zhanran, was the first to use the term "Tiantai school" (Tiantai *zong*), defending its superiority over other emergent schools of his day, and here the word *zong* takes on a new connotation of the essential teaching of Buddhism as transmitted through a specific lineage from the Buddha Śākyamuni. The sense of transmission from one "golden-mouthed" master to another in this system was notably abstract, and it was only with the development of the Chan school (see below) that a much more concrete and straightforward succession of patriarchs emerged. Later developments in Chinese Tiantai include the emergence of "home-mountain" and "off-mountain" factions in the Song dynasty, with monks based either on Mount Tiantai or elsewhere generating different interpretations of Zhiyi's teachings. Korean scholar-monks in the eleventh and twelfth centuries combined Zhiyi's various formulations into a neatly organized doctrinal system, and this system came to be widely accepted in medieval Japan and later Chinese Buddhism.

Inspired by Zhiyi's example, Chinese representatives of the Yogācāra and Huayan (Flower Garland) traditions sought to attract imperial support through similarly comprehensive interpretations of Buddhist doctrine. The great pilgrim and translator Xuanzang (600?–664) and his disciple Ci'en (Dasheng Ji, often referred to, probably inaccurately, as Kuiji; 632–682) introduced a substantial body of new texts as the basis of the so-called Faxiang school, while Fazang (643–712) built upon a tradition of scholarly and inspirational writing based on the *Huayan* or *Flower Garland Sūtra* to attract the support of Empress Wu (r. 690–705). The Faxiang (a widely used label in modern times, although it actually derives from the Japanese name Hossō) and Huayan (Jpn. Kegon) schools were extremely important in Nara-period Japan, and they remained important in different ways on the continent as well. Yogācāra was recognized for its doctrinal innovations regarding the nature of human consciousness and phenomenal reality, even though its specific positions never achieved widespread currency (in part through their philosophical complexity and in part through their contrast with Chinese preferences for more inclusive, even universalistic, doctrines). The Huayan school was similarly recognized for its elaboration of the mutual interpenetration of all phenomena (often using lists of mind-numbingly abstruse distinctions), but unlike Chinese Yogācāra it had a continuing legacy of visionary meditation and ritual practice that was accessible to accomplished scholars and ordinary people alike.

The systematic schools that appeared in the sixth to eighth centuries had enduring presences throughout the balance of Chinese (and, indeed, East Asian) Buddhist history. What sets these schools apart from the earlier exegetical lineages, as well as from other contemporaneous movements, was their particular combination of imperial support, religious breadth, and position within the textual tradition. In the first place, the founders of these schools all received unique levels of attention from the imperial rulers of their day. Zhiyi, for example, received special attention from the Sui dynasts as part of their campaign to conquer south China, while Xuanzang merited extraordinary acclaim because of his knowledge of the "western regions" and prodigious output as a translator. Fazang, for his part, was recognized as a precocious young monk and actively promoted by Empress Wu.

Second, although the Tiantai, Faxiang, and Huayan systems all had their distinctive emphases, each possessed a certain capaciousness that allowed for participation in different ways. The primary example of this is Zhiyi, whose encyclopedic attentions to the grand variety of Buddhist doctrine and meditation practice seemed to make a place for everyone and every approach. With his mastery of the latest trends in Indian Yogācāra, Xuanzang (and Ci'en) felt empowered to generate a comprehensive interpretation of Buddhist doctrine, which specified different alternatives available for those at different stages on the spiritual path. For his part, Fazang's presentations of abstract tenets proved highly attractive to Chinese Buddhists at the time and in subsequent generations, allowing both highly intellectual philosophical responses and strongly visionary approaches to meditation practice.

Third, the capacious quality just described was made possible in each case by magisterial control of a given body of Buddhist scripture. The *Lotus* and *Flower Garland* sūtras were arguably the most popular large scriptures in China during the preceding several centuries, and the various texts of the Yogācāra made it one of the most important modes of intellectual interpretation. Although Zhiyi was not directly involved with the enterprise of translation, and Fazang only to a limited degree, the connection of all three men with the imperially sponsored domain of Buddhist scriptural production should not be overlooked.

Thus each of the systematic Sui-Tang schools represented a comprehensive doctrinal system, complete with a lineage-based justification of its transmission from the Buddha, and a characteristic set of positions regarding spiritual cultivation. We should remember, though, that the elite monks identified with these systematic schools were but a tiny fraction of the Chinese monastic community.

Modal Traditions. In the seventh and eighth centuries, three modes of religious practice emerged that were to become enduring features of Chinese Buddhism: Pure Land devotionalism, Chan (better known by the Japanese pronunciation "Zen") meditation, and esoteric Buddhist (*mijiao*) visualization ritual. While very different from each other in terms of soteriological goals, devotional procedures, and ritual styles, these three modal traditions all (1) emphasized selected approaches to religious practice rather than attempting to be theoretically comprehensive; (2) allowed for great practical variation and participation by a wide range of individuals, from ordinary laypeople to sophisticated monks; and (3) had much more limited, and sometimes even antagonistic, relationships with Buddhist scriptural traditions.

The Chinese Pure Land tradition is based on a set of translated scriptures describing the Buddha Amitābha

("Infinite Light," also given as Amitāyus, "Infinite Lifespan") and his paradise, the "pure land" (*jingtu*) or "land of bliss" (reflecting the Sanskrit *sukhāvatī*). Through his aeons of religious cultivation as the Bodhisattva Dharmākara, Amitābha created a realm totally unlike the ordinary world-systems of Buddhist cosmology, including their heavens, in making it easy for those reborn there to achieve enlightenment. Amitābha promised that those who were "mindful" (*nian*, "remember, think," from the Sanskrit *anusmṛti*) of him for a mere ten moments of thought were guaranteed rebirth in his Pure Land. This was initially understood as an easy form of meditative visualization, in which one was aided by the graphic concreteness of the Buddha's image. As mentioned above, this type of visualization was practiced at one time at Huiyuan's community on Mount Lu.

During the sixth and seventh centuries, at Xuanzhongsi in north China (Shanxi province), there appeared a succession of monks who transformed the understanding of Pure Land practice, expanding it from the original visualization meditation just described to include ever greater emphasis on the oral recitation of the Buddha Amitābha's name. Tanluan (c. 488–c. 554) emphasized that Pure Land practice was an easy path suitable for people living in a corrupt world, while Daochuo (562–645) argued that this practice was particularly appropriate for the final period of the Buddhist teachings (*mofa*; Jpn. *mappō*), since it would result in a face-to-face meeting with Amitābha at death. Since he also held that it was impossible to know when one achieved the requisite ten moments of pure sincerity in performing the *nianfo* (literally, "mindfulness of the Buddha," almost always indicating Amitābha), Daochuo also directed his followers to perform as many oral repetitions as possible. Although Shandao (613–682) recommended the combined practice of sūtra recitation, visualization of Amitābha, and worshiping Buddha images, his primary emphases were that Pure Land practice was intended precisely for the ignorant and sinful, rather than the spiritually gifted or advanced, and that it consisted primarily of oral recitation. He also provided detailed instructions for how *nianfo* retreats were to be undertaken, either as ordinary religious practice aimed at liberation or as deathbed observations aimed at ensuring immediate rebirth.

Although these and other Chinese Pure Land masters were accomplished scholars, their commentaries and treatises argued that devotion to Amitābha could substitute for, rather than encompass and incorporate, other forms of Buddhist religiosity. Shandao in particular also promoted this style of devotionalism by the widespread distribution of painted images of Pure Land scenes and the sponsorship of sculpted images of Amitābha and his attendant *bodhisattvas*. Nor were these the only Tang-dynasty proponents of Pure Land Buddhism. Meditation on Amitābha was included within Zhiyi's "constantly walking" *samādhi*, which thus became the most widely practiced of the four categories in his system, and the increasing popularity of the recitation of Amitābha's name led to the development of musical styles of recitation. This occurred most notably on Mount Wutai in Shanxi, from which the melodic recitation of Amitābha's name was transmitted to Japan by the famous pilgrim Ennin (794–864) and others. Since the Pure Land represented a paradise that could be reached after death, this practice became a key ingredient of deathbed observances, and there soon developed stories depicting devoted individuals who had achieved rebirth in Amitābha's land of bliss. Since there was no clear-cut distinction between meditative and recitative *nianfo*, ordained and lay Buddhists of widely different social and educational backgrounds could all take part in the practice.

The word *Chan* transcribes the Sanskrit *dhyāna*, meaning "concentration meditation." Chan has its roots in the meditation traditions of fifth-century Kashmir, but it first emerged as a discernable religious movement in the sixth and early seventh centuries as a north China group of ascetic practitioners who recognized the south Indian monk Bodhidharma (d. circa 530) as their progenitor. Then, after three-quarters of a century of incubation at various locations in central China, in 701 the movement emerged on the national scene at the court of Empress Wu. Many of the basic doctrines now associated with Chan were formulated in the early years of the eighth century, and the most famous of the school's masters were active in central and south China in the late eighth and ninth centuries. It was not until after the fall of the Tang, however, in the Min regime of the far southeast (in what is now Fujian province), that the most distinctive features of the school—chiefly, its devotion to spontaneous repartée between masters and students, known as "encounter dialogue"—became public. Then, with the founding of the Song dynasty in 960, Chan became one of the dominant voices of Chinese Buddhism, its teachers monopolizing the position of abbot in nine-tenths of the largest monasteries throughout the country and its genealogically based style of self-understanding becoming the default mode of religious discourse.

The key to understanding Chinese Chan is its lineage schema, which proved to be far more compelling than the Tiantai school's abstract and discontinuous list of sages introduced above. Based in part on Indian notions of master-student succession, Chan held that the true teaching of Buddhism was passed down from the Buddha Śākyamuni through a succession of Indian patriarchs to Bodhidharma, and then by a succession of Chinese patriarchs to the teachers of the present day. Since the doctrinal elaborations of the scriptures were unable to capture the true essence of this teaching, Chan rejected the textual tradition that had been so important in Chinese Buddhism for all previous schools, defining itself instead as a "separate transmission outside the scriptures" (*jiaowai bie zhuan*; Jpn. *kyōge betsuden*). This genealogical model is also the key to understanding Chan religious praxis, which was undertaken largely according to two different models. In the Caodong (Jpn. Sōtō) tradition, one was to nourish the buddha-mind within one (i.e., one's buddha-nature, or the quality of originary or fundamental enlightenment in all sentient beings) to illuminate with its full potential, unhampered by the illusions of ordinary existence, a process known sometimes as "silent illumination" (*mozhao*; Jpn. *mokushō*). In the Linji (Jpn. Rinzai) tradition one was to demonstrate the active functioning of that buddha-mind in spontaneous interaction between enlightened master and aspiring student or, in later years, to interrogate famous examples of such interaction in one's meditation practice. The type of spontaneous and often nonverbal interaction depicted in Chan texts is known as "encounter dialogue," and the contemplation of pithy examples of encounter dialogue is known as "viewing the critical phrase" (*kanhua*; Jpn. *kanna*) Chan (often referred to, using the Japanese pronunciation, as *kōan* Zen), where the "critical phrase" is the climactic line of an anecdote that can only be understood by transcending ordinary thinking.

As an ideology of self-cultivation by religious professionals, Chan (unlike Pure Land) always remained centered within monastic institutions. Nevertheless, it attracted substantial literati interest, and its unique style of repartée was celebrated in diverse contexts of art and poetry, so that the image of the iconoclastic Chan master entered the shared repertoire of Chinese culture. Its genealogical model and iconoclastic tropes placed it in contrast with traditional forms of Buddhism, and Chan was able to flourish in part because it filled a vacuum left by the collapse of the state-supported translation enterprise after the end of the eighth century.

Esoteric Buddhism (*mijiao*) was introduced to China by three foreign missionaries in the eighth century: Śubhākarasiṃha (637–735), who arrived in Chang'an in 716; Vajrabodhi (671–741), who arrived in Guangzhou (Canton) in 720; and Amoghavajra (705–774), who became a disciple of Vajrabodhi's at age fifteen in China, traveled to India after his master's death, and returned to China in 746. Whereas magic-like techniques of recitation, visualization, and ritual had long been known from Indian sources, it was only from this period onward that there was introduced a comprehensive system of these techniques organized by the spatial metaphor of the *maṇḍala* (literally "circle," here referring to concentric configurations of buddhas, *bodhisattvas*, and other deities). Promising both speedy achievement of enlightenment and the empowerment for ritual action by the most profound and awesome forces of the universe, esoteric Buddhism overwhelmed the imaginations of eighth-century Chinese and received lavish support from the imperial court.

Although the texts and ritual procedures introduced by these three masters, with the assistance of their gifted Chinese disciple Yixing (683–727), made a massive contribution to the ritual vocabulary of Chinese Buddhism that permeated the entire tradition, esoteric Buddhism gained only a limited acceptance in China as a distinct and separate school. Its advocates never produced intellectually substantial doctrinal statements, either of Indian or native Chinese origin (although there was a brief flurry of new texts introduced in the last two decades of the tenth century), and even its two separate initiation lineages seem not to have been transmitted after the ninth century. Where Chan effectively benefited from the collapse of the translation enterprise, as an incipient systematic school (which it became in Japan, through the creative efforts of Kūkai) esoteric Buddhism floundered in China.

LATER DEVELOPMENTS. From the Song dynasty (960–1279) onward new subschools emerged in Chinese Buddhism, and some of the major schools took on each other's characteristics. First, various "houses" and other sublineages developed with Chan, which retained its dominance in monastic institutions throughout the country. Second, Pure Land Buddhism began to describe itself by means of a lineage succession, a style of presentation adopted from Chan. Third, the Tiantai school witnessed competition between "home-mountain" (*shanjia*) and "off-mountain" (*shanwai*) factions, identified by their residence on Mount Tiantai or elsewhere and characterized by different understandings of Zhiyi's teachings. Fourth, Tibetan Buddhism flourished for a time during the Yuan dynasty (1206–1368) and again during the Qing (1644–1911), especially at court, though anti-Mongol sentiments limited its more widespread dissemination. Fifth, there were numerous vectors of religious activity in Chinese Buddhism not normally considered discrete sectarian entities but which might usefully be considered in the same context; a primary example is the diffuse but extremely popular cult devoted to the salvific Bodhisattva Avalokiteśvara (known as Guanyin, Guanshiyin, Guanzizai, and other names in Chinese). Even granting these features, however, the sectarian labels that emerged during the Tang dynasty have remained in widespread use throughout the rest of Chinese history.

SEE ALSO Bodhidharma; Buddhism, article on Buddhism in China; Fazang; Huayan; Kuiji; Kumārajīva; Mādhyamika; Tiantai; Yogācāra; Zhiyi.

BIBLIOGRAPHY

The most important source for the understanding of Chinese Buddhist schools is Stanley Weinstein's masterful article on the subject in the first *Encyclopedia of Religion* (New York, 1987), vol. 2, pp. 482–487, which also provides useful references to Chinese and Japanese secondary works. For background information on the systematic schools and other topics, readers should also consult Weinstein's *Buddhism under the T'ang* (Cambridge, U.K., 1987). Although outdated, Kenneth K. S. Ch'en's *Buddhism in China: A Historical Survey* (Princeton, N.J., 1964) contains a wealth of generally reliable information. For an example of the early Japanese presentation of East Asian Buddhist schools, see Takakusu Junjirō, *The Essentials of Buddhist Philosophy*, edited by Wing-tsit Chan and Charles A. Moore (Honolulu, 1947; reprint, New Delhi, 1975). The best guide to interpreting Chinese exegetical lineages may be found in Ryūichi Abé's *The Weaving of Mantra: Kūkai and the Construction of Esoteric Buddhist Discourse* (New York, 1999). For Song-dynasty Buddhism, see the articles in Peter N. Gregory and Daniel A. Getz, Jr., eds., *Buddhism in the Sung* (Honolulu, 1999).

For issues in later Chinese Buddhism, see Yü Chün-fang, *The Renewal of Buddhism in China: Chu-hung and the Late Ming Synthesis* (New York, 1981, and Marsha Smith Weidner, ed., *Latter Days of the Law: Images of Chinese Buddhism, 850–1850* (Lawrence, Kans., and Honolulu, 1994).

JOHN R. MCRAE (2005)

BUDDHISM, SCHOOLS OF: JAPANESE BUDDHISM

Prior to its official introduction into the court in 552 CE, Buddhism had been brought to Japan by Chinese and Korean immigrants and was presumably practiced widely among their descendants. According to the *Nihongi*, an envoy of the king of Paekche presented Buddhist statues, sūtras, and other artifacts to the Japanese court in 552 (other sources give 538). The official introduction of Buddhism exacerbated the antagonism that had been developing between the internationalist Soga clan, which supported the court's recognition of Buddhism, and the more parochial clans, which considered the Buddha a *banshin* (foreign deity). To avoid further dissension, the court entrusted the administration of Buddhism to the Soga clan. The Buddhism promulgated by the Soga was primarily magical. However, aristocrats and court nobles were initially attracted to Buddhism as an intrinsic part of the highly advanced continental (i.e., Chinese and Korean) culture and civilization, which also encompassed Confucianism, Daoism, medicine, astronomy, and various technological skills. As it developed on the continent, Buddhism was not exclusively a religion, for it was also associated with a new, esoteric culture that included colorful paintings, statues, buildings, dance, and music.

Although Japanese understanding of Buddhism was superficial and fragmented in the early stages of assimilation, it gained religious depth through the course of history. The rise of Japanese Buddhism and the growth of schools or sects were closely related to and influenced by the structure of the state bureaucracy, which was itself in the initial stages of development. Yōmei (r. 585–587) was the first emperor officially to accept Buddhism, but it was his son, the prince regent Shōtoku (574–622), who was responsible for creating Japan's first great age of Buddhism. Although the sources provide very little precise information about his activities, Shōtoku is said to have been a great patron of Buddhism. In addition to building many Buddhist temples and sending students and monks to study in China, he wrote commentaries on three texts—the *Saddharmapuṇḍarīka (Lotus Sūtra)*, the *Vimalakīrti Sūtra*, and the *Śrīmala Sūtra*—and is supposed to have promulgated the famous "Seventeen-Article Constitution" based on Buddhist and Confucian ideas. Later, Shōtoku was worshiped as the incarnation of the *bodhisattva* Avalokiteśvara. His promotion of Buddhism fell strictly within the bounds of the existing religio-political framework of Japanese sacral kingship: he upheld the imperial throne as the central authority and envisioned a "multireligious system" in which Shintō, Confucianism, and Buddhism would maintain a proper balance under the divine authority of the emperor as the "son of Heaven." Shōtoku's religious policies, his indifference to the doctrinal and ecclesiastical divisions of Buddhism, his dependence on the universalistic soteriology of the *Lotus Sūtra*, and his emphasis on the path of the lay devotee significantly influenced the later development of Japanese Buddhism.

BUDDHISM IN THE NARA PERIOD. During the Nara period (710–784) the Ritsuryō state, based upon the principle of the mutual dependence of imperial law (*ōbō*) and Buddhist law (*buppō*), recognized Buddhism as a state religion and incorporated it into the bureaucratic system of the central government. Under these conditions Buddhism enjoyed royal favor, and temples and monks became wealthy. However, the state's sponsorship of Buddhism was not entirely altruistic. Throughout the Nara period the government was concerned with the political power held by the Buddhists. The state promoted Buddhism as a religion that could civilize, solidify, and protect the nation. Monks were encouraged to engage in the academic study of Buddhist texts, probably in the hope that they would settle in the government-controlled temples. These temples were presumably subordinate to the state and functioned as an intrinsic part of the state bureaucracy: priests were expected to perform rites and ceremonies to ensure the peace and order of the state, and monks and nuns were ordained under the state authority and thus were considered bureaucrats. The Ritsuryō government prohibited monks from concerning themselves with the needs and activities of the masses. However, those who were not granted official status as monks became associated with folk Buddhist activities. Movements of *ubasoku* (Skt., *upāsaka*; laymen), *hijiri* (holy men), and *yamabushi* (mountain ascetics) emerged spontaneously, integrating indigenous Shintō, Buddhist, and other religious and cultural elements. At the center of these movements were unordained magician-priests who lived in mountainous regions and who had acquired, through ascetic practices, shamanistic techniques and the art of healing. Later, these groups were to inspire powerful popular movements and would influence the development of Japanese Buddhism.

Prior to the Nara period Buddhism had remained nonsectarian. However, as the study of texts and commentaries on the sūtras became more intense and sophisticated, groups of scholar-monks organized themselves into schools or sects. Here, the term *sect* (*shū*) does not refer to an organized school but, rather, to a philosophical position based on the various sūtras. Differences between the sects were based solely on the particular text chosen as the focus of study: the ecclesiastical, doctrinal, or religious orientations of the individual sects were not mutually exclusive. Often, these sects were housed in a single temple and, under the restrictions imposed by the Ritsuryō government, they remained dependent on both the state and each other.

Of the six most noteworthy sects of Nara Buddhism, two were affiliated with the Hīnayāna tradition and four with the Mahāyāna tradition. In the first category were the Kusha, based on Vasubandhu's *Abhidharmakośa* (Jpn., *Kusharon*; Treasury of Higher Law), and the Jōjitsu, based on Harivarman's *Satyasiddhi* (Jpn., *Jōjitsuron*; Completion of truth). The Mahāyāna-affiliated sects included Sanron (Chin., *San-lun*), based on the *Mādhyamika Śāstra* (Jpn., *Chūron*; Treatise on the middle way) and on the *Dvādaśadvāra* (Jpn., *Jūnimon*; Treatise on twelve gates), both of which were written by Nāgārjūna, as well as on the *Śataśāstra* (Jpn., *Hyakuron*; One hundred verse treatise), written by Āryadeva; the Hossō sect (Skt., Yogācāra), principally based on the *Vijñaptimātratāsiddhi* (Jpn., *Jōyushikiron*; Completion of mere ideation) by Dharmapāla; the Kegon sect, based on the *Avataṃsaka Sūtra* (Jpn., *Kegongyō; Flower Garland Sūtra);* and the Ritsu sect (Vinaya), based on the so-called Southern Mountain tradition of Chinese Vinaya studies, represented chiefly by the work of Daoxuan (596–667). In the early years of the Nara, the most prominent and prestigious of these sects was the Hossō, which was transmitted by Dōshō, a Japanese monk who had studied in China. The prestige of the Hossō gradually waned, to be replaced by the Kegon sect under the leadership of Roben. The Ritsu sect provided the codes and external formalities of monastic discipline. The remaining three sects represented, for the most part, academic and political alternatives to the more powerful temples.

Schools of the Heian: Tendai and Shingon. The government's decision to move the capital from Nara to Kyoto was motivated in part by the need to regain the power held by the large, wealthy Buddhist temples. Toward the end of the Nara period, the effort to integrate Buddhism and temporal politics resulted in the accumulation of wealth and the acquisition of large tracts of private land by the Buddhist temples and the involvement in state politics by the more ambitious monks. This trend culminated in the so-called Dōkyō incident, which was, in effect, an attempt to make the religious authority of Buddhism supreme. Under the sponsorship of Empress Kōken (later, Shōtoku), Dōkyō, a monk in the Hossō sect, was promoted rapidly through the ranks of the state bureaucracy. In 766 Dōkyō was appointed "king of the Law" (*hō-ō*), and several years later he attempted to usurp the throne, an action that was quickly crushed by the court aristocracy. The government responded to this affair by once again affirming Buddhism's subordination to the state and enforcing traditional Buddhist discipline. Throughout the Heian period (794–1185), Buddhism continued to be promoted as the religion that would ensure the safety of the state (*chingo kokka*). The sects that arose in the Heian, however, were considerably different from the six Nara sects. Like their predecessors, the Heian sects depended on teachings recently brought back from China as a source of their religious authority. But rather than relying on Japanese and Chinese commentaries, as had their Nara counterparts, Heian-period monks began to focus their study on the actual sūtras, allegedly the words of the Buddha himself. In addition, the schools of the Heian were established by individuals who were considered de facto "founders" of sectarian lineages. They also tended to be centered in the mountains, that is, at a symbolic distance from political authority, and had their own systems of ordination. The two most important schools of this period were Tendai and Shingon (Chin., Zhenyan). Both stressed the importance of learning, meditation, and esoteric cults and mysteries. Most significantly, however, both schools attempted to establish a united center for Buddhism that would encompass all sects and unite Buddhism and the state.

Tendaishu. The founder of this sect, Saichō (767–822, also known by his posthumous title, Dengyō daishi), was a descendant of Chinese immigrants. In his youth, Saichō was trained in the Hossō, Kegon, and Sanron traditions; at the age of nineteen he was ordained at Tōdaiji in Nara. Thereafter, he withdrew from the capital city and opened a hermitage on Mount Hiei. Here, he began to study the writings of Zhiyi, the systemaizer of Chinese Tiantai. During his travels in China, Saichō received the *bodhisattva* ordination (*bosatsukai*) from Daosui, was initiated into *mantra* practices (*mikkyō*) by Shunxiao, studied Zen (Chin., Chan) meditation under Xiaoran, and trained in the Chinese Vinaya traditions. Upon his return to Japan, Saichō established a Tendai school that synthesized these four traditions within the framework of the *Lotus Sūtra.* Saichō adhered to the T'ien-t'ai doctrine that recognized universal salvation, that is, the existence of the absolute nature of Buddhahood in all beings, and stressed the meaning and value of the phenomenal world. These teachings stood in opposition to the standard philosophical position of the Nara schools, best represented by the Hossō doctrine that claimed that buddhahood was accessible only to the religious elite.

Saichō's ecumenical approach won the approval of the court. With the death of his patron, Emperor Kammu, and the rise of Kūkai and the Shingon sect, Saichō's influence at court diminished. One of his dreams—that the court approve the establishment of an independent center for Tendai ordination—was granted only after Saichō's death. The Tendai sect continued to exercise a profound influence on Japanese Buddhist life for centuries after the death of its founder. Under Ennin (794–864), a disciple of Saichō, the full flowering of Tendai Esotericism (Taimitsu) took place. Ennin was also responsible for the transmission of the Nembutsu cult (i.e., the practice of invoking the name of Amida Buddha) from China. Enchin (814–891), another prominent Tendai monk, also propagated the Taimitsu tradition and was responsible for the formation of the so-called Jimon subsect of Tendai, a group that vied for ecclesiastical power with Ennin's Sanmon subsect. Additionally, many of the most prominent Buddhist figures of the Kamakura period studied at the Tendai monastic center on Mount Hiei, including Hōnen of the Pure Land sect, Shinran of True Pure Land, Eisai of Rinzai, Dōgen of Sōtō Zen, and Nichiren, whose school bears his name. Through them the Tendai legacy was firmly, if subtly, maintained in Japanese Buddhism.

Shingonshū. Kūkai (774–835, also known by his posthumous title, Kōbō daishi), the founder of the Shingon school, was originally a student of Confucianism and hoped to enter government service. According to various legends, he experienced a compelling desire to leave the capital and live in the mountains, where, it is said, he trained with shamanistic Buddhist priests. He was inspired by the *Mahāvairocana Sūtra* (Jpn., *Dainichikyō*; Sūtra of the great sun buddha), which eventually led him to the tradition of Esoteric Buddhism (Vajrayāna). Between 804 and 806 he traveled in China, where he studied under Huiguo, the direct disciple of the Tantric master Amoghavajra. On his return to Japan he began to promote Shingon (i.e., Tantric) doctrine. At this time he wrote the *Jūjūshinron* (Ten stages of religious consciousness), in which he systematized the doctrines of Esoteric Buddhism and critically appraised the existing Buddhist teachings and literature. Under the patronage of Emperor Saga, Kūkai established a monastic center of Mount Kōya and was appointed abbot of Tōji (Eastern Temple) in Kyoto, which was granted the title Kyōō Gokokuji (Temple for the Protection of the Nation). In return for these favors, Kūkai performed various rites for the court and aristocracy.

According to the Shingon teachings, all the doctrines of Śākyamuni, the historical, manifested Buddha, are temporal and relative. Absolute truth is personified in the figure of Mahāvairocana (Jpn., Dainichi), the Great Sun Buddha, through the "three secrets"—the body, speech, and thought—of the Buddha. To become a Buddha—that is, to bring one's own activities of body, speech, and thought into accord with those of Mahāvairocana—one depends on *mudrās* (devotional gestures), *dhāraṇī* (mystical verse), and yoga (concentration). The Shingon school developed a system rich in symbolism and ritual, employing *maṇḍalas* and icons to meet the needs of people on all levels of society. Like the Tendai sect, Shingon produced many outstanding monks in subsequent generations.

Owing to the support of the court and aristocracy, the Esoteric Buddhism of Tendai (Taimitsu) and Shingon (also called Tōmitsu; "Eastern Esotericism," after its chief monastery, Tōji) prospered. While each school had its own principle of organization and its own doctrinal position, both sought the official authorization and support of the court. Therefore, as the power of the state declined, Tendai and Shingon evolved into religions associated solely with the elite, for whom they offered various magico-religious rites.

BUDDHIST SCHOOLS IN THE KAMAKURA PERIOD. The decline of the Ritsuryō system and the rise of military feudalism brought many changes to the organization and practice of Buddhism, although the basic ideology of the Ritsuryō persisted until the Ōnin War (1467–1477). It has been argued that the new Buddhist schools that emerged in the Kamakura period (1185–1333) transformed Buddhism in Japan into Japanese Buddhism. Unlike the schools of the Nara and Heian, which identified the religious sphere with the national community, the schools of the Kamakura attempted to establish specifically religious societies. The earlier schools had never seriously questioned the soteriological dualism that divided the path of monks from that of the laity, nor had they developed an independent community governed by normative principles other than the precepts. In spite of its otherworldly beliefs, Buddhism, as practiced in Nara and Heian Japan, was a religion grounded firmly in this world. The founders of the new schools in the Kamakura period had all studied at the Tendai center on Mount Hiei but had become dissatisfied with the emphasis on ceremonies and dogma, the perceived corruption of monastic life, and the rigid transmission of ecclesiastical office. In their stead, these religious leaders stressed personal religious experience, simple piety, spiritual exercise, intuition, and charisma. In many respects the practices and doctrines of the new schools reflect the eschatological atmosphere that had emerged toward the end of the Heian, when the country had experienced a series of crises, including famine, epidemics, war, and a deadlock of economy and politics. This sense of apocalypse found its expression in the widespread belief in *mappō*, the notion that Buddhism and society as a whole had entered an era of irreversible decline, and in the resultant popularity of the cult of Amida, which offered a religious path expressly intended to provide for beings living during *mappō*. In one way or another, these popular beliefs were incorporated into the most representative schools of the Kamakura period—Jōdoshū (Pure Land school), Jōdo Shinshū (True Prue Land school), Nichirenshū, and the Rinzai and Sōtō schools of Zen.

Jōdoshū. Prior to Hōnen (1133–1212), the founder of the Jōdo sect, most Buddhist schools incorporated the belief in the Pure Land and the practice of Nembutsu as adjuncts to their other practices. It was only with Hōnen, however, that absolute faith in Amida (Skt., Amitābha) Buddha became a criterion for sectarian affiliation. Like many of his contemporaries, Hōnen had become disillusioned with his early training in the Nara and Tendai schools. He turned to the charismatic teachings of such masters as Eiku, who promoted the belief in *mappō* and the efficacy of the cult of Amida. Under their tutelage, Hōnen came to realize the impossibility of attaining salvation and sanctification through the practice of precepts, meditation, and knowledge. Instead, Hōnen held that one must seek the path to salvation in the Pure Land and the saving grace of Amida. In this, Hōnen was much influenced by Genshin's *Ojoyoshu* (The essentials of rebirth, tenth century), a work that provides the theoretical basis for faith in the Pure Land. However, in his own work *Senchaku hongan nembutsushu* (Collection of passages on the original vow in which Nembutsu is chosen above all), Hōnen clearly departs from earlier forms of the cult of Amida. Here, Hōnen claims that one's salvation depends exclusively on one's "choice" (i.e., one's willingness) to place absolute faith in the salvific power of Amida Buddha. The community Hōnen established in the capital city was structured on the notions of egalitarianism and faith and, thus, was able to transcend the social distinctions of kinship and class. Such organizing principles made Hōnen's school a paradigm for the later development of Buddhism.

Jōdo Shinshū. Little is known of the formative influences in the life of Shinran (1173–1263), the founder of the Jōdo Shin school, except that he entered the Tendai monastery on Mount Hiei at the age of eight. When he was twenty-nine, Shinran met Hōnen, with whom he studied for six years. Shinran's notion of Amida Buddha's salvific power went far beyond that of his master. In holding that one's faith in Amida must be absolute, Shinran denied the efficacy of relying on one's own capacity to bring about redemption. His teachings went to the extreme of claiming that the recitation of the Nembutsu was an expression of gratitude to Amida rather than a cause of one's salvation. Shinran further stated that it is not man who "chooses" to have faith in Amida, but that it is Amida's Original Vow that "chooses" all beings to be saved. Therefore, even those who lead lives of crime and sin are saved.

Shinran's teachings represent a radical departure from traditional Buddhist doctrine. He reduced the Three Treasures (i.e., Buddha, Dharma, and Sangha) to one (i.e., Amida's Original Vow) and rejected the accepted methods of spiritual exercises and meditation as paths to enlightenment. He was critical of the government's persecution of Hōnen and argued that the secular authority of the state was subordinate to the eternal law of the Dharma. In the religious communities that surrounded Shinran, distinctions between the clergy and laity were eliminated; Shinran himself was married and had children. Although Shinran never formally established an independent sect, his daughter began to build a True Pure Land sectarian organization. This was the first time in the history of Buddhism in Japan that the continuity of a school was based on heredity.

Nichirenshū. Nichiren (1222–1282), eponymous founder of the sect, is perhaps one of the most charismatic and prophetic personalities in Japanese history. In the time he spent on Mount Hiei between 1242 and 1253, Nichiren came to believe that the *Saddharmapuṇḍarīka Sūtra (Lotus Sūtra)* contained the ultimate and complete teaching of the Buddha. In many respects, Nichiren's thought is based on Tendai doctrine: he upheld the notion of *ichinen sanzen* (all three thousand spheres of reality are embraced in a single moment of consciousness) and advocated universal salvation, urging the nation to return to the teachings of the *Lotus Sūtra.* However, Nichiren was also a reformer. Rather than accept the traditional concept of the transmission of the *Lotus Sūtra* through ecclesiastical offices, Nichiren argued that it was transmitted through "spiritual succession." Thus, he saw himself as the successor to the transmission that began with Śākyamuni and passed to Zhiyi and Saichō. He also identified himself as the incarnation of Viśiṣṭacāritra (Jpn., Jōgyō), the *bodhisattva* to whom the Buddha is said to have entrusted the *Lotus Sūtra.* Other of his reforms included the attempt to discredit the established Buddhist sects, in particular, Pure Land and Zen. At the same time, however, Nichiren incorporated many of their key notions and practices. With Shingon he shared the use of the *maṇḍala* and the concept of *sokushin jōbutsu* ("becoming a Buddha in this very body"), and with Pure Land he shared the practice of chanting (in this case, the title of the *Lotus Sūtra*) and the concept of the salvation of women and people whose natures are evil. Although Nichiren promoted the doctrine of universal salvation, his school developed into the most exclusivist and often militant group in Japanese religious history. Several modern Japanese movements trace their inspiration to Nichiren.

Zen Buddhism. In the Nara and Heian periods, Zen (Chin., Chan) meditation was a spiritual and mental discipline practiced in conjunction with other disciplines by all Buddhist sects. It was not until the Kamakura period, when the Linji (Jpn., Rinzai) and Caodong (Jpn., Sōtō) schools of Chan were brought from Song-dynasty China, that Zen emerged as a distinct movement.

Rinzaishū. The establishment of Rinzai Zen in Japan is associated with Eisai (1141–1215). Discouraged by the corruption of Buddhism in the late Heian, Eisai was initially concerned with the restoration of the Tendai tradition. He traveled to China, first in 1168 and again between 1187 and 1191, hoping to study the true Tendai tradition. In China, Eisai was introduced to the Linji school of Chinese Chan. At that time Chan was noted for its purist approach—its emphasis on a transmission that stood outside the classical Buddhist scriptures and what is termed the "direct pointing to the mind and perceiving one's own nature." In addition, the Chan monks in Song China refused to pay obeisance to the secular authorities. Eisai, however, was more conciliatory. He studied the practices, ceremonies, and texts of other schools and willingly paid obeisance to the Kamakura regime, which in return favored him with its patronage. Eisai strongly believed that one of the central tasks of Buddhism was to protect the nation and that Zen was a state religion. Far from approaching the common people, Eisai's form of Zen was elitist. Rinzai was established by Eisai's followers as an independent school, and while it remained an elitist group throughout the Kamakura period, its contributions to the cultural life of Japan were significant.

Sōtōshū. Dōgen (1200–1253), the transmitter of the Caodong school of Chinese Chan to Japan, entered the Tendai monastery on Mount Hiei when he was thirteen years old. His intense search for the certainty of attaining buddhahood drove him from Mount Hiei, first to a Pure Land teacher and later to Myōzen, a disciple of Eisai. Finally, in 1223, Dōgen traveled to China, where he attained enlightenment under the guidance of Rujing, a Chan master of the Caodong school. In 1227 Dōgen returned to Japan and began to expound Sōtō doctrine, eventually establishing an independent sect. As a student of the Caodong sect, Dōgen emphasized the gradual attainment of enlightenment through the practice of *zazen* (sitting in meditation), a meditative discipline that entailed sitting without any thought or any effort to achieve enlightenment. Dōgen's notion of *zazen* (also called *shikantaza*) stood in marked contrast to Eisai's use of the *kōan* as a means to attaining sudden enlightenment.

In spite of his adherence to Caodong tradition, Dōgen is known for his independence and self-reliance. He was convinced that the truth of Buddhism is applicable to everyone—regardless of sex, intelligence, or social status—and that enlightenment could be attained even in secular life. This doctrine is best expressed in Dōgen's dictum that all beings *are* the buddha-nature. Dōgen also rejected the theory of *mappō* popular among other Kamakura Buddhists. He held that the "perfect law" of the Buddha was always present and could be attained by a true practitioner at any time. Dōgen's emphasis on faith in the Buddha represents yet another departure from traditional Zen teachings that stress self-realization. Because he claimed that the Zen practitioner must have faith not only in the Buddha but also in scriptures and one's masters, Dōgen's school is often characterized as sacerdotal and authoritarian. However, after his death, Dōgen's school was institutionalized and grew to be one of the most politically and socially powerful movements in later periods.

BUDDHISM IN THE MODERN ERA. As a result of the Ōnin War and the Sengoku period (a period of incessant wars among feudal lords), the political system was destined to undergo formal changes. Oda Nobunaga (1534–1582), Toyotomi Hideyoshi (1536–1598), and Tokugawa Ieyasu (1542–1616), the three men who unified the nation, rejected the Ritsuryō system's principle of the mutual dependence of imperial and Buddhist law. The Tokugawa regime (1600–1868) instead adopted neo-Confucianism as the guiding principle of the nation, manipulating Buddhist institutions to strengthen its systems and policies. It maintained strict control over the development, organization, and activities of religious sects. The Tokugawa government continued to recognize and support all the Buddhist schools including those that the Muromachi government had deemed official religions. However, many of its policies toward Buddhism were stimulated by its persecutions of Christianity and its adoption of Confucianism as the state ideology. New sects and doctrinal developments were prohibited, forcing new movements, such as folk Nembutsu to go underground or suffer suppression. Existing schools forfeited their autonomy, and temples, monks, and nuns were institutionalized and routinized within the political structure. In many temples and local temple schools, particularly those associated with Zen, monks studied and taught the Confucian classics.

Along with political and economic modernizations, the Meiji restoration of 1868 brought significant changes to religious institutions. The Meiji government (1868–1912), which attempted to restore the actual rule of the emperor in a modern context, rejected some aspects of the religious policies of the feudal Tokugawa. It rejected the religious institution of Buddhism as a state religion and devised the hitherto nonexistent State Shintō as a "nonreligious" national cult. The loss of government patronage and the decline in prestige, power, and security experienced by institutionalized sects of Buddhism forced them to cooperate with the government. The various sects worked within the structure of the imperial regime by performing ancestral and life-cycle rituals. However, the absence of government favor also brought about a spiritual awakening within Buddhism. Buddhist intellectuals attempted to integrate Buddhist thought and tradition into the newly acquired Western culture and technology. Throughout the Meiji and into the Shōwa period (1912–), popular Buddhism continued to thrive. Such movements as Kokuchūkai (Nation's Pillar Society), led by the ex-Nichiren priest Tanaka Chigaku, gained popularity in the nationalist fervor of the 1890s. Another folk movement to grow out of Nichiren was the Honmon Butsuryūkō (Association to Exalt the Buddha), founded by the former monk Ōji Nissen and concerned primarily with faith healing. The increased popularity of new religions and lay Buddhist associations such as Sōka Gakkai, Reiyūkai, and Risshō Kōseikai continues in post–World War II Japan.

SEE ALSO Amitābha; Amoghavajra; Buddhism, article on Buddhism in Japan; Dōgen; Enchin; Ennin; Genshin; Hijiri; Hōnen; Huayan; Japanese Religions, overview article; Jōdo Shinshū; Jōdoshū; Mādhyamika; Mappō; New Religious Movements, article on New Religious Movements in Japan; Nianfo; Nichiren; Nichirenshū; Saichō; Shingonshū; Shinran; Shōtoku Taishi; Tendaishū; Tiantai; Yogācāra; Zen; Zhenyan; Zhiyi.

BIBLIOGRAPHY

Anesaki Masaharu. *History of Japanese Religion* (1935). Reprint, Tokyo and Rutland, Vt., 1963.

Ienaga Saburō, Akamatsu Toshihide, and Tamamura Taijō, eds. *Nihon bukkyōshi.* Kyoto, 1972.

Kitagawa, Joseph M. *Religion in Japanese History.* New York, 1966.

Saunders, E. Dale. *Buddhism in Japan.* Philadelphia, 1964.

Takakusu Junjirō. *The Essentials of Buddhist Philosophy.* Edited by Wing-tsit Chan and Charles A. Moore. Honolulu, 1947.

Tsuji Zennosuke. *Nihon bukkyōshi.* 10 vols. Tokyo, 1944–1955.

New Sources

Goodwin, Janet R. *Alms and Vagabonds: Buddhist Temples and Popular Patronage in Medieval Japan.* Honolulu, 1994.

Jaffe, Richard M. *Neither Monk nor Layman: Clerical Marriage in Modern Japanese Buddhism.* Honolulu, 1999.

Ketelaar, James Edmund. *Of Heretics and Martyrs in Meiji Japan: Buddhism and Its Persecution.* Princeton, 1990.

Payne, Richard K., ed. *Re-visioning "Kamakura" Buddhism.* Honolulu, 1998.

Pilgrim, Richard B. *Buddhism and the Arts of Japan.* New York, 1998.

Ruch, Barbara, ed. *Engendering Faith: Women and Buddhism in Premodern Japan.* Ann Arbor, Mich., 2002.

Stone, Jacqueline. *Original Enlightenment and the Transformation of Medieval Japanese Buddhism.* Honolulu, 1999.

MICHIO ARAKI (1987)
Revised Bibliography

BUDDHISM, SCHOOLS OF: EAST ASIAN BUDDHISM

The Japanese monk Gyōnen (1240–1321 CE) is well-known for his detailed work describing the origins of Buddhist schools and their transmission from India to East Asia. Because Gyōnen's understanding of these schools is clearly defined and is representative, in key respects, of other premodern East Asian sources, it will serve as a useful starting point from which to develop an understanding of the category "school" in the context of East Asian Buddhism. It will also serve as a basis for examining basic questions and relationships modern scholars face when trying to understand the development and transmission of these schools. Gyōnen's definition of "school" is also useful because modern Japanese Buddhist scholarship—a dominant intellectual force in the study of East Asian Buddhism—developed out of the sectarian tradition and institutions of scholar-monks like Gyōnen, and a number of Japanese universities are affiliated with modern Buddhist schools. His work also draws attention to relationships among East Asian schools of Buddhism, as well as to their collective relationship to Indian Buddhist schools, particularly their perceived fidelity to a "pure" or "original" Indian Buddhism.

TRANSMISSION OF BUDDHIST SCHOOLS IN THE "THREE LANDS." Among Gyōnen's collected works are general historical overviews of Buddhist schools and their lineages, including the *Sangoku buppō denzū engi* (Transmission of Buddhism in the Three Lands) and the *Hasshū kōyō* (Essentials of the Eight Schools). The former describes the transmission of Buddhist schools in the "three lands," or *sangoku,* of India, China, and Japan, and the latter details the eight "schools," or *shū,* of Japanese Buddhism. In these and other general works, Gyōnen understands "school" to be a lineage of masters and disciples united by their study of particular texts and doctrines. As such, both works contain detailed lists recounting these texts and doctrines, and describing the central figures from individual schools who have interpreted, lectured on, and propagated them.

In the *Sangoku buppō denzū engi,* Gyōnen identifies thirteen principal schools of Chinese Buddhism, including the Tiantai, Sanlun, and Chan, and traces their "uninterrupted transmission" through the "three lands," beginning with founding Indian figures and patriarchs such as Śākyamuni Buddha and Nāgārjuna, continuing through a line of Indian and Chinese masters, and eventually ending with Japanese teachers. Of these thirteen Chinese schools, he classifies eight as the traditional schools of Japanese Buddhism, which developed in Japan's Nara (710–794 CE) and Heian periods (794–1185 CE).

In these texts, Gyōnen generally uses *shū* (Chin. *zong,* Kor. *chong*) to refer to a school, but Mark Blum notes that he also refers to them as *ryū* ("stream") and *ke* ("house") (2002). Although *shū* is commonly used among premodern East Asian authors, other Chinese terms, often associated with particular schools or groups of schools, can be found: the Chinese character *bu,* "group" or "division," is generally used to refer to the schools of Hīnayāna Buddhism, whereas multiple words including *zong* appear in premodern East Asian sources to indicate the Mahāyāna schools that have predominated in the region. "Gate," "house," and "mountain," for example, are common designations for Chinese Chan, Korean *Son,* and Japanese Zen.

DEFINING "FULL-FLEDGED" CHINESE BUDDHIST SCHOOLS. These semantic problems have been compounded, moreover, not only because these individual words can have multiple meanings, but also because there is a lack of standardization in translation and usage in modern scholarly works. Even a cursory reading of the academic literature reveals scholars generally do not distinguish carefully among a number of terms used to translate *zong* and these other terms, including "school," "sect," "lineage," and "tradition," among others. Leo Pruden, for example, translates the term *shū,* appearing in the title of Gyōnen's *Hasshū kōyō,* as "tradition" (1994), whereas Mark Blum opts instead for "school" (2002). This ambiguity leads Blum to leave *shū* untranslated in some sections of his work, *The Origins and Development of Pure Land Buddhism: A Study and Translation of Gyōnen's Jōdo Hōmon Genrushō,* whereas John McRae adopts "school" in *Seeing through Zen: Encounter, Transformation, and Genealogy in Chinese Chan Buddhism* precisely because its ambiguity fits his interpretive framework.

In his description of Chinese schools of Buddhism in the first edition of *The Encyclopedia of Religion,* Stanley Weinstein seeks to clarify some of these ambiguities by distinguishing among three principal meanings of *zong* in premodern Chinese Buddhist sources: a doctrine, the teaching of a text, and a school. He writes that the tendency of scholars to automatically translate *zong* as "school" has produced "persistent misconceptions about what actually constitutes a school in Chinese Buddhism" (p. 257).

As a doctrine, *zong* appears in statements such as "the doctrine of emptiness," or in the *panjiao* systems devised by Chinese Buddhists to rank the large number of sometimes contradictory doctrines they received from South Asia. The second meaning of *zong,* the teaching of a text, is tied to the work of Kumārajīva (344–413 CE), a central figure in the translation of Buddhist texts from Sanskrit into Chinese. The translations of Kumarajiiva and later scholar-monks from the fifth and sixth centuries led to the development in China of "exegetical traditions" focusing on particular texts such as the *Dilun, Shelun,* and *Dalun,* whose members studied, lectured on, and commented on these works. Weinstein notes that monks of these traditions specialized in the interpretation of a particular text, and thus explicated its *zong,* which he describes as the "essential doctrine" or "underlying theme."

From among these exegetical traditions, Weinstein claims that only the Sanlun of Jizang (549–623 CE), which studies the *Dalun* and other texts, approaches what he defines as a "full-fledged school": "a tradition that traces its origin back to a founder, usually designated 'first patriarch,' who is believed to have provided the basic spiritual insights that were then transmitted through an unbroken line of successors or '*dharma* heirs'" (p. 260). Because Jizang's line ended only two generations after his death, however, Weinstein argues that it is only with the emergence of the Tiantai, Huayan, and Chan in the second half of the Tang dynasty (618–907 CE) that such schools could be found.

From among this group, Chan, for example, describes itself as an unbroken lineage of *dharma* heirs that can be traced from the figure of Bodhidharma—considered to be the twenty-eighth Indian patriarch and first figure to teach Chan in China—back to Śākyamuni Buddha. From the figure of Bodhidharma, moreover, Chan genealogical charts trace the development of these schools forward in time through a series of Chinese *dharma* heirs, whose lines were eventually transmitted to Korea and Japan. During Japan's Kamakura period (1185–1333 CE), Gyōnen's contemporaries Eisai (1145–1215 CE) and Dōgen (1200–1253 CE) traveled to China where they received certificates attesting their enlightenment and authorizing them to propagate the Linji (J. Rinzai) and Caodong (J. Sōto) Chan lineages. After returning to Japan, they transmitted these teachings to disciples who thus continued the tradition as an uninterrupted lineage of Japanese *dharma* heirs.

But even if the definition of school is restricted as Weinstein suggests, he and other scholars point out that the independent identities of Chan and these other schools were often after the fact creations of the disciples of their purported founders, sometimes a number of generations removed from the "first patriarch." Thus, although they may be described as discrete lineages by later members, and often accepted as such by scholar-monks like Gyōnen, these schools were not necessarily seen in this way during the lifetime of the founder and possibly not even for generations thereafter. Despite these and other issues taken up below, critics claim that modern scholars have often accepted the descriptions of these schools in the work of Gyōnen and other premodern sources at face value, and have thus understood them to be self-contained entities that have been "transmitted without interruption" and that can be clearly distinguished from the doctrines and practices of other schools of Buddhism, other religious traditions, and society at large.

"Textuality Overrides Actuality." Gregory Schopen asserts that the tendency to confuse such accounts in premodern sources like those of Gyōnen for actual conditions and practices has led to a situation in which "textuality overrides actuality" (p. 7). Schopen claims that texts serve as unreliable witnesses to the actual behavior of Buddhist monastics because they often reflect sectarian commitments and polemical agendas, and are thus likely to present idealized accounts of particular schools, as well as the Buddhist community more generally. In response to these perceived deficiencies, Schopen has turned to the study of epigraphic data, and has produced results that challenge widely accepted images of monastic behavior. He asserts, for example, that this evidence proves that Buddhist monks and nuns in India held money, transferred merit, and engaged in other activities that contravene the rules of monastic conduct or that do not accord with basic tenets of Buddhism.

Although Schopen's work centers on South Asia, other studies of East Asian schools of Buddhism reveal a similar disjuncture between idealized accounts of monastic behavior and actual practices. This body of scholarship covers a broad range of topics, including Bernard Faure's research on Buddhism and sexuality, as well as Brian Victoria's work on the connection between Zen and war. In *Zen at War,* Victoria argues that Zen Buddhist institutions and intellectuals helped create the ideological justification for the Japanese military's aggression on the East Asian continent from the early to mid-1900s. He asserts that D.T. Suzuki and other such figures forged a close connection between the principles of Zen and the "warrior spirit," or *bushidō,* and that these ideas were incorporated into the military's rhetoric portraying its aggression as a "just war" meant to liberate East Asians from Western colonial domination, and unite them as "Asian brethren" within the Greater East Asian Co-prosperity Sphere. In *Pruning the Bodhi Tree: The Storm over Critical Buddhism* (1997), Hakamaya Noriaki and Matsumoto Shirō make a similar argument of a close connection among Zen, Japanese nationalism, and the military, and also assert that Sōtō Zen institutions and leaders have contributed to social discrimination in Japan against the *burakumin,* Koreans, and women, among other minority groups.

The "Classical Paradigm" of Buddhist Studies. Other studies seek to reveal the processes by which commonly accepted images of Buddhist schools have been shaped by the assumptions, methods, and frames of reference of traditional Buddhist studies, often described as its "classical paradigm." Frank Reynolds states that this paradigm generally adopts "a positivistic view of historical methods and historical facts" (1999, p. 462), and, like Gyōnen, takes lineages, doctrines, and texts, which are often abstracted from their historical and social contexts, to be the central defining elements of Buddhist schools. Reynolds adds that this approach focuses on "origins," and thus privileges Sanskrit and Pali texts, as well as Indian schools and doctrines, as the chief arbiters for judging the legitimacy of non-Indian texts and forms of Buddhism, including those of East Asia. Much like Gyōnen's focus on "lands" in the *sangoku* paradigm, moreover, modern scholars often rely on "nation" as a key frame of reference for understanding the transmission and development of these schools, and are thus concerned with distinguishing among "national" varieties of East Asian Buddhism, or with judging the legitimacy of East Asian Buddhist schools, texts, and doctrines as a group based on their perceived fidelity to Indian "originals."

Robert Buswell asserts that the institutional history of North American Buddhist studies, an outgrowth of "area studies," and other factors have contributed to the former tendency, and that this focus on the distinctiveness of modern, national varieties of East Asian Buddhism inhibits a fuller understanding of premodern East Asian Buddhist schools and their members. By viewing these schools anachronistically through the lens of the modern notion of nation, observers may fail to recognize the complex of factors through which premodern East Asian Buddhists would have "imagined" their individual identities, identities which Buswell notes were connected simultaneously to both translocal Sino-Indian Buddhist "macroculture" and to local relationships and commitments. He claims that these tendencies have also reinforced what have been historically uncertain geographic borders and precluded academic "cross-fertilization," thereby preventing observers from viewing the development of these East Asian schools as part of broader processes of intercultural interaction. Buswell adds that this "national" approach has become so thoroughly ingrained in the academic training of Buddhist studies that it has rarely been questioned, and scholars thus "continue to hypostatize into inviolate traditions complex religious phenomena that involved multivalent levels of cultural interaction and symbiosis and intricate series of personal identities" (p. 73).

***Nihonjinron* and Japanese Sectarian Scholarship.** The structure of the *sangoku* paradigm also draws attention to the relations among the schools of these East Asian nations, particularly the differential treatment accorded Chinese Buddhist schools relative to those of the Korean peninsula. Whereas Gyōnen ascribes a central position to China as the bridge between Japanese and Indian Buddhism, he does not describe Korean schools of Buddhism in any detail. Although he does note that Buddhism was transmitted to Japan from the Korean peninsula in the sixth century CE, and that it was propagated by Shōtoku Taishi (574–622 CE) whose Buddhist tutors were peninsular monks, these schools were not seen to be of sufficient value to be included in the *sangoku* paradigm. And, whereas Blum makes a reasoned argument that Gyōnen's omission in this regard was linguistic—that is, Chinese, but not Korean, was a sacred, canonical language of Buddhism—rather than racial, this omission is complicated by the history of modern relations that exists between Japan and its East Asian neighbors, particularly the events described by Victoria.

Some critics contend that common images of these "national" East Asian Buddhist schools have been shaped in fundamental ways by Japan's racial attitudes and theories and by the intellectual paradigms and social structures of Japanese Buddhist scholarship. This body of work examines, for example, the ways in which the notion of a unified and unchanging Japanese "essence," often referred to as *nihonjinron* ("discourse on Japaneseness"), informs studies in a broad spectrum of Japanese cultural areas, including the works of National Learning (J. *kokugaku*), the Kyoto school of philosophy, and Zen and other schools of Buddhism.

A number of such studies also question how the institutional affiliations and agendas of Japanese Buddhist scholars, as well as the requirements for progressing within their scholarly communities, have delimited the range of acceptable topics and interpretive methods. T. Griffith Foulk writes that whereas Western scholars of Japanese Buddhism are deeply indebted to the research, guidance, and methods of their Japanese counterparts or mentors, there is a growing awareness that the latter's scholarship often reflects the interests of sectarian institutions that developed out of those of Gyōnen and other such premodern monk-scholars, and which he describes as normative traditions. These observers claim that such interests have led scholars to focus on the history of particular Japanese Buddhist schools and lineages, as well as on the thought and lives and of their central figures, and thereby limited the breadth of scholarly inquiry by isolating scholars of Buddhism from other academic disciplines. The influence of these theories and methods extends, moreover, to the study of Chinese and Korean Buddhist schools. In the case of the former, for example, McRae, Sharf, and others point out that understanding of Chan and other Chinese Buddhist schools has been deeply influenced by these Japanese methods and attitudes.

Korean Buddhist Identity and "Cultural Self-Sufficiency." To overcome the limits of these received methods, and to thereby bring the study of Buddhism into a broader-based discourse in the humanities, a number of scholars have applied the methods and theories of outside disciplines such as archaeology, anthropology, cultural studies, and literary criticism. These efforts include studies that investigate the interests and processes by which these premodern narratives have been created and transmitted, and identify the ideological and other functions they have played in the process of inventing schools as part of tradition.

One such example is Buswell's study, "Imagining 'Korean Buddhism': The Invention of a National Religious Tradition," which offers an alternative angle of vision for understanding the development of Korean Buddhist tradition by incorporating a number of these methods and theories, including Benedict Anderson's "imagined communities." In so doing, he reveals the limits of the traditional paradigm's focus on "nation" by showing the complexity of Buddhist identity, particularly, the ways in which premodern Buddhist monastics of the Korean peninsula imagined themselves as actors within a number of translocal and local relationships and commitments.

Buswell claims that for much of the history of Buddhism on the Korean peninsula, it would have been "patently absurd" for monastics to view themselves in national terms as there was "no independent sense of a 'Korean' national tradition of Buddhism distinct from the broader Sino-Indian tradition during the premodern era" (p. 85). Rather, their identities would have been defined by sectarian commitments, ordination lineages, functional positions (disciples of A, teachers of B, or as proselytists, doctrinal specialists, meditators, and so on), or local tribal or clan membership. Just as important, however, is that these monastics would also have imagined themselves to be participants in a pan-Asian Buddhist "macroculture." Buswell notes that these groups tried to integrate peninsular Buddhism into this macroculture by forging connections to India's King Aśoka, the Dragon King, and other translocal Buddhist models and authorizing mechanisms.

At the same time, however, these monastics actively sought to create a sense of their own "cultural self-sufficiency" by "inventing" legitimate local practices, figures, and texts, including the *Vajrasamādhi-sūtra.* Buswell asserts that the narrative describing the discovery of this text by a Silla envoy in the palace of the Dragon King was meant to establish the self-sufficiency and legitimacy of peninsular Buddhism relative to China by proving it was no longer in need of a constant influx of their texts and teachers. The *Vajrasamādhi-sūtra* also became a basic text in the development of Chinese Chan, and thus offers an important example of reversing the established direction of the flow of religious and cultural products from China eastward.

JAPANESE "CULTURAL SELF-SUFFICIENCY." Even in Japan where governmental authorities have often exerted greater control over Buddhist schools compared to China and Korea, the identities of individual monastics have not always been clearly defined along either strict national or sectarian lines. Although state control created greater institutional separation and sectarian awareness—evident in the harsh and sometimes violent sectarian debates of Gyōnen's Kamakura period—Buswell's approach is still instructive. Gyōnen, for example, is known primarily for his affiliation with the Kegon and Vinaya schools, but also "imagined" himself as a Brahmā, or Buddhist "striver," associated with teachers from the Pure Land and other schools. And much like the identities of premodern Korean monks described by Buswell, Gyōnen defined himself in both translocal and local terms. According to Blum, Gyōnen saw himself recording the transmission of transhistorical Buddhist truth embedded in "homogeneous time," but that manifested in particular times and places—which Blum describes as the "particularity of the Japanese experience" (2002, p. 90). Within this "particularity," Gyōnen imagined his identity in terms of his sectarian commitments to the Kegon school and position at Tōdaiji temple, as well as in functional terms—particularly as a commentator on the *Sangyō-gisho,* a collection of three Buddhist commentaries attributed to Japan's Shōtoku Taishi.

This process described by Buswell of establishing and bolstering local "cultural self-sufficiency" is evident in the valorization and transmission of these commentaries, and in the evolution of the figure of Shōtoku as father of Japanese Buddhism and Buddhist exegete. Shōtoku is depicted in accounts from the eighth century as a devout practitioner and generous patron of Buddhism, who later was linked to important Japanese Buddhist figures such as Kūkai (774–835 CE), Saichō (767–822 CE), and Shinran (1173–1263 CE), and was identified as the "first patriarch" or central figure in a number of Japanese Buddhist schools. These accounts relate that his keen intellectual interest and understanding of Buddhist doctrine, honed under the instruction of continental tutors, led to lectures at court on the *Śrīmālādevī Sūtra* and the *Lotus Sūtra.* These lectures are thought to constitute the basis for the composition of the *Shōmangyō-gisho* and the *Hokke-gisho,* two of the three commentaries attributed to him.

As Shōtoku's image evolved and religious authority expanded, his human ties to continental teachers were downplayed, whereas his synchronic ties to translocal Buddhist figures increased. Over time, Shōtoku came to be seen as the reincarnation of a number of central Buddhist figures such as Śākyamuni Buddha, Queen Śrīmālā, Avalokiteśvara, and the Chinese Tiantai monk Huisi (515–577 CE). Among these previous births, Shōtoku's former life as Queen Śrīmālā of India naturally authorized him to compose the *Shōmangyō-gisho* as it was an exegesis on the very text that she had proclaimed in Ayodhyā through the eloquence granted her by the Buddha himself.

The Japanese historian Tsuda Sōkichi argues that the compilers of these early Japanese texts sought to remake Yamato, or early Japan, in the image of China as described in its dynastic histories, and that accounts of Shōtoku's lectures were fabricated as part of this greater effort. Tsuda believes that Shōtoku's lectures, as well as other aspects of his Buddhist identity, were modeled on those given by Emperor Wu of the Liang dynasty (r. 502–549 CE) and other Chinese sovereigns. Although Shōtoku's authorship of the *Sangyō-gisho* is contested by Tsuda and a small number of other modern Japanese scholars, it has been seen by most observers as a crucial event in Japanese Buddhist history that served to create the "cultural self-sufficiency" of local Japanese schools and traditions. Regardless of the authenticity of their attribution to Shōtoku, they were accepted as genuine and were studied and transmitted by Gyōnen and other eminent Japanese Buddhist figures. Although Shōtoku's Buddhist teachers from the Korean peninsula were not written out of the historical record, there was a gradual diminution in their influence on his development as a Buddhist practitioner and exegete. Over time, a body of myths emerged that portrayed Shōtoku in an equal, and sometimes superior, position to his teachers.

Two of the three commentaries begin with a declaration stating that the text is the work of King Jōgū (Shōtoku Taishi) "of the Great Land of Yamato," and that it was not composed by anyone from across the sea. In 772 CE, a group of Buddhist monks accompanied a diplomatic mission to Tang China, where they presented copies of the *Shōmangyō-gisho* and *Hokke-gisho* to their Chinese hosts as proof of Shōtoku's profound understanding of Buddhist doctrine and the high standard of the traditions they represented. Based on this copy of the *Shōmangyō-gisho,* moreover, the Tang dynasty monk Mingkong (dates unknown) composed the *Shengmanjing shuyi sichao,* which was later copied and brought back to Japan by the Tendai school's Ennin (794–864 CE) and cited as proof of the value of the *Shōmangyō-gisho* and Shootoku's greatness as a Buddhist exegete. In a postscript to a copy of Mingkong's commentary presented by the Japanese monk Eizon (1201–1290 CE) to Hōryūji in March 1256, he wrote that the text was by "an eminent monk from the Great [Land of] Tang" and that it added prestige to the "sublime text" of Japan's Shōtoku Taishi.

THE "ENCOUNTER PARADIGM." Sharf asserts that Chinese Buddhism has often been viewed by modern scholars through the lens of the "encounter paradigm," in which its schools, texts, and doctrines have been understood as the product of a protracted "encounter" between "Indian Buddhism" and "Chinese civilization." He traces the formalization of this paradigm to the work of Arthur Wright, whose study, *Buddhism in Chinese History,* divides this process into four distinctive periods: preparation, domestication, independent growth, and appropriation. Although subsequent scholarship has argued over the details, Sharf contends that this view still prevails, and cites the influential work of Richard Robinson, which compares the Chinese Sanlun school of Jizang to its Indian "original" and finds the former to be, in some ways, "wanting" (p. 288, n. 15). Sharf believes that this paradigm, with its emphasis on "domestication and transformation," has often led scholars to compare Chinese Buddhism to an imagined sense of "original" Indian Buddhism, and thus to question whether the Chinese "got it right" (pp. 7–11). This attitude has led in turn to suspicions of Chinese "apocryphal" texts, like the influential *Awakening of Mahāyāna Faith,* and the consequent devaluation of the schools and doctrines of East Asian Buddhism that developed in reliance on them.

These attitudes are evident in the arguments of the Japanese scholars Hakamaya Noriaki and Matsumoto Shirō, the central figures of "Critical Buddhism," who harshly criticize a group of related Buddhist doctrines, including Buddha nature, *tathāgatagarbha,* and original enlightenment. These doctrines have been particularly popular in East Asian schools and have served as central topics in a number of Chinese Buddhist texts, including the *Awakening of Mahāyāna Faith.* In his article, "The Doctrine of *Tathāgata-garhba* Is Not Buddhist," Matsumoto rejects these doctrines because, he claims, they posit an essential, underlying substratum to reality, which contravenes basic Buddhist tenets such as dependent origination, emptiness, and no-self.

In "Critical Buddhism and Returning to the Sources," Dan Lusthaus states that this intellectual movement was an inevitable development that emerged, in part, because Japanese scholars of Buddhism like Hakamaya and Matsumoto have begun paying greater attention to Tibetan and Sanskrit materials, and reevaluating East Asian Buddhist schools and teachings in light of these efforts. Lusthaus contends that Chinese Buddhists of the Tang dynasty deliberately attempted to separate Chinese Buddhism from Indian interpretations and methodologies. He identifies the choice by the Chinese of Paramārtha's (499–569 CE) sixth-century translations of Buddhist texts from Sanskrit into Chinese over those of Xuanzang's (600–664 CE) in the following century as a key moment in Chinese Buddhist history, a moment in which "East Asian Buddhism returned with deliberateness and passion to its own earlier misconceptions instead of returning to the trajectory of Indian Buddhism from which it believed it had been spawned" (p. 35). As such, Chinese Buddhism paid little attention to Indian Buddhist philosophers and logicians, and turned instead to a "Chinese hierarchical system and a crypto-Taoist dialectical reasoning" (p. 38).

This debate over the possible deviation of East Asian schools from "original" or "pure" Buddhism represents a basic division in the field over how to view the processes of the transmission and assimilation of Buddhism in local conditions. Whereas the Critical Buddhists and others focus on the perceived deviation or degeneration of Buddhism as it has been transmitted over time and space, others contend that such attempts to reconstruct "original" Indian Buddhism face not only insurmountable hermeneutical obstacles but also replicate the very "essentialization" that they decry. Peter Gregory responds to the arguments of Hakamaya and Matsumoto in his essay, "Is Critical Buddhism Really Critical," by invoking the logic of Buddhist tenets, writing, "Only when we acknowledge that Buddhism lacks any defining, unalterable essence (an *ātman,* so to speak) and is itself the product of a complex set of interdependent and ever-changing conditions (*pratītyasamutpāda*), will we have a proper framework for understanding the process of its historical and cultural transformation and recognizing our own location in that stream we would call the 'tradition'" (1997, p. 297).

Gregory and others argue that determining "true Buddhism" is a normative, theological issue, and scholars should not simply ignore or dismiss the beliefs of East Asian Buddhist figures, like Gyōnen, who were convinced of the authenticity of the teachings and texts they engaged and transmitted. In a similar way, Sharf writes that his study is "an argument for treating Chinese Buddhism as the legitimate, if misunderstood scion of sinitic culture. Whatever else it may be, Buddhism is the product of Buddhists, and the Buddhists in the case at hand were Chinese" (p. 2). He argues that instead of trying to establish fixed or normative definitions of basic categories of Buddhism, scholars are better served by trying to understand their shifting and often hazy borders as well as their "rhetorical deployments." Sharf suggests that the Chinese schools of Buddhism detailed by Gyōnen are better understood as "organizational categories applied after the fact by medieval Buddhist historians and bibliographers" (p. 7). And the term "Buddhism," he writes, functions as a "placeholder," and pure Buddhism is "an analytic abstraction posited by Buddhist polemicists, apologists, reformers, and now scholars" (p. 16).

SEE ALSO Buddhism, overview article and articles on Buddhism in China, Buddhism in Japan, and Buddhism in Korea; Buddhist Meditation, article on East Asian Buddhist Meditation.

BIBLIOGRAPHY

Abe, Ryūichi. *Weaving of Mantra: Kūkai and the Construction of Esoteric Buddhist Discourse.* New York, 1999.

Blum, Mark L. *The Origins and Development of Pure Land Buddhism: A Study and Translation of Gyōnen's Jōdo Hōmon Genrushō.* Oxford, 2002.

Buswell, Robert E. Jr. *The Formation of Ch'an Ideology in China and Korea: The Vajrasamādhi-Sūtra, a Buddhist Apocryphon.* Princeton, N.J., 1989.

Buswell, Robert E. Jr. *Chinese Buddhist Apocrypha.* Honolulu, 1990.

Buswell, Robert E. Jr. "Imagining 'Korean Buddhism': The Invention of a National Religious Tradition." In *Nationalism and the Construction of Korean Identity,* edited by Hyung Il Pai and Timothy R. Tangherlini, pp. 73–107. Berkeley, Calif., 1998.

Ch'en, Kenneth K. S. *The Chinese Transformation of Buddhism.* Princeton, N.J., 1973.

Faure, Bernard. *Chan Insights and Oversights: An Epistemological Critique of the Chan Tradition.* Princeton, N.J., 1993.

Faure, Bernard. *The Red Thread: Buddhist Approaches to Sexuality.* Princeton, N.J., 1998.

Faure, Bernard. *The Power of Denial: Buddhism, Purity, and Gender.* Princeton, N.J., 2003.

Foulk, T. Griffith. "Issues in the Field of East Asian Buddhist Studies: An Extended Review of *Sudden and Gradual: Approaches to Enlightenment in Chinese Thought,* ed. Peter N. Gregory." In *Journal of the International Association of Buddhist Studies* 16, no. 1 (1993): 93–114.

Gregory, Peter. "Is Critical Buddhism Really Critical?" In *Pruning the Bodhi Tree: The Storm over Critical Buddhism,* edited by Jamie Hubbard and Paul Swanson, pp. 286–297. Honolulu, 1997.

Hakamaya, Noriaki. "Thoughts on the Ideological Background of Social Discrimination," translated by Jamie Hubbard. In *Pruning the Bodhi Tree: The Storm over Critical Buddhism,* edited by Jamie Hubbard and Paul Swanson, pp. 339–355. Honolulu, 1997.

King, Sallie B. "The Doctrine of Buddha-Nature Is Impeccably Buddhist." In *Pruning the Bodhi Tree: The Storm over Critical Buddhism,* edited by Jamie Hubbard and Paul L. Swanson, pp. 174–192. Honolulu, 1997.

Lancaster, Lewis, and C. S. Yu, eds. *Introduction of Buddhism to Korea: New Cultural Patterns.* Berkeley, Calif., 1989.

Lancaster, Lewis, and C. S. Yu, eds. *Assimilation of Buddhism in Korea: Religious Maturity and Innovation in the Silla Dynasty.* Berkeley, Calif., 1991.

Matsumoto Shirō. "The Doctrine of *Tathāgata-garbha* Is Not Buddhist," translated by Jamie Hubbard. In *Pruning the Bodhi Tree: The Storm over Critical Buddhism,* edited by Jamie Hubbard and Paul L. Swanson, pp. 165–173. Honolulu, 1997.

McRae, John. *Seeing through Zen: Encounter, Transformation, and Genealogy in Chinese Chan Buddhism.* Berkeley, Calif., 2003.

Muller, Charles A. *The Sūtra of Perfect Enlightenment: Korean Buddhism's Guide to Meditation.* Albany, N.Y., 1999.

Pruden, Leo M., trans. *The Essentials of the Eight Traditions.* Berkeley, Calif., 1994.

Reynolds, Frank. "Coming of Age: Buddhist Studies in the United States from 1972 to 1997." In *Journal of the International Association of Buddhist Studies* 2, no. 22 (1999): 457–483.

Robinson, Richard. *Early Mādhyamika in India and China.* Madison, Wis., 1967.

Schopen, Gregory. *Bones, Stones, and Buddhist Monks: Collected Papers on the Archaeology, Epigraphy, and Texts of Monastic Buddhism in India.* Honolulu, 1997.

Schopen, Gregory. "The Mahāyāna and the Middle Period in Indian Buddhism: Through a Chinese Looking-glass." *The Eastern Buddhist* 32, no. 2 (2001): 6–12.

Sharf, Robert H. "The Zen of Japanese Nationalism." In *Curators of the Buddha: The Study of Buddhism under Colonialism.* Chicago, 1995.

Sharf, Robert H. *Coming to Terms with Chinese Buddhism: A Reading of the Treasure Store Treatise.* Honolulu, 2002.

Stone, Jacqueline. "Some Reflections on Critical Buddhism." *Japanese Journal of Religious Studies* 26, nos. 1-2 (1999): 159–188.

Tsuda Sōkichi. *Nihon koten no kenkyū.* Tokyo, 1950.

Victoria, Brian. *Zen at War.* New York, 1997.

Wright, Arthur F. *Buddhism in Chinese History.* Stanford, Calif., 1959.

MARK DENNIS (2005)

BUDDHIST BOOKS AND TEXTS

This entry consists of the following articles:

CANON AND CANONIZATION
CANON AND CANONIZATION—VINAYA
RITUAL USES OF BOOKS
TRANSLATION
EXEGESIS AND HERMENEUTICS

BUDDHIST BOOKS AND TEXTS: CANON AND CANONIZATION

The canonical literature of Buddhism has a number of characteristics that make it unique among the religious scriptures of the world. First, the literature is not contained within a single canon: various regional, linguistic, and sectarian divisions have brought about the compilation of a number of separate canons. The scriptural collections that can be identified by language (e.g., Chinese, Tibetan, and Pali) vary from one another in significant ways, with few texts that found across all traditions. In addition to the multiplicity of canons, the various versions are marked by their sizes. Each canon contains a large number of texts, some of which are of great length. The Chinese canon alone covers nearly 100,000 pages in its printed form, whereas Buddhist sacred texts might be more adequately described as libraries, for these collections bear little resemblance to the single volumes that make up the canons of the religions of western Asia.

The function of these canons within the different traditions indicates that they were not just used for reading and study. The process of preservation of hundreds of texts required sizable resources that could only be secured by large groups of cooperating believers or by the governments. For many Buddhists, the canons were seen a source of merit making through donations for the process of printing, copying, and housing the texts. In most areas a few texts were then selected for use in ritual. The chanting of these chosen works was another way to acquire merit and was also a spiritual practice performed as part of the central activities of the public halls of monasteries. Monastics studied the content of the texts and taught both lay and ordained followers by using passages from the books as a structural element of the discourses.

INTRODUCTION. While it is possible to witness the widespread uses of the Buddhist canons, the more difficult matter is the way in which such a massive amount of information was assembled and codified. The sophistication of the content indicates that the canons were produced as part of an intensive training and study environment. The complexity of the content has led scholars to conclude that only a small percentage of Buddhists ever read and assimilated the whole of the intellectual and religious issues within the canons. These texts are often seen as "elite" documents that cannot be used to adequately describe the "popular" practices and beliefs of the majority of Buddhists. However, it is impossible to describe the practices of beliefs of Buddhists without taking into account the importance they placed on the canonic collections as objects of veneration. Over the centuries the communities have copied and preserved the texts as an integral part of their heritage and have put forward enormous efforts in the construction, writing, printing, and digitizing of their canons—indications of the canons' importance in a variety of popular as well as elite arenas.

In order to study the history of the Buddhist canons and to interpret the actions of those who contributed to that story, it is necessary to have a picture of the ways in which the appearance and preservation of the canons occurred in the different cultural spheres of Asia. For example, Buddhism in India was diversified by its expansion into regions far separated from one another. Because there was never any proscription against the use of local languages for transmitting the discourses of the Buddha, the identification of the list of texts to be included in a canon remained unfixed. In the beginning the texts were preserved orally and were recited for the followers by monks called *bhanakas.* These recitations were probably of two types. The first was the recitation of the *dharma*—the remembered words of the Buddha—identified by the preamble, "Thus have I heard." The hearer referred to in this case was the disciple Ananda. Tradition holds that he was asked to give the first recitation of the remembered teachings at an assembly known as the First Council of arhats immediately following the *parinirvāṇa,* or death of the Buddha. In addition to these types of teachings, later to be codified as the sūtra literature, there was a second division that related to the rules of conduct (Vinaya) for those who lived by monastic rule.

Eventually the canon was expanded to include a third category called *abhidharma,* a special exegetic literature that organized the teachings found in the sūtras into numerical categories. These lists were originally referred to as *matrka* (mother). It may be that the list of the topics taught by the Buddha was one way of guarding against the later introduction of items that did not belong to the earlier versions of the texts. Given this tripartite division, the Buddhists referred to the canon as a whole as the *Tripiṭaka* (Three baskets).

While the division of the texts into three types is the most common way of referring to the Buddhist canon structure, there were alternate groupings, such as the twelve textual genres: sūtra, *geya, vyakarana, gatha, udana, nidana, itivrttaka, jātaka, vaipulya, Adbutadharma, avadana,* and *upadesa.* In some cases these groupings were used as part of the titles of texts. It is no longer possible, however, to have a complete definition for how each of these types was differentiated from others.

As Buddhism grew, it developed a number of sectarian groups, recognized in the histories as the "Eighteen Schools." These schools contended with one another for support and argued over which texts were canonical. Because most of these groups have disappeared as distinct communities, leaving behind no full description of lists of accepted texts, it is also not possible to have a full inventory of the variety of Buddhist canons in India.

WRITING IT DOWN. It was some centuries before the canon was preserved in written form. In the Theravāda tradition of South and Southeast Asia, it is alleged that the canon was kept in its oral form until 29 BCE, when the Fourth Council was held in Sri Lanka under the aegis of King Vattagamani. At the council—similar to the story of the First Council—a single monk was called to recite the entire teaching of the Buddha; in this case it was a monk called Mahendra, who had been sent to Sri Lanka by King Aśoka (r. c. 270–230 BCE). King Vattagamani had five hundred scribes and reciters set to commit the canon to written form. (Whereas this is the traditional view, it should be noted that it was not until the fifth century CE that the final list of texts for the Theravāda canon could be agreed upon, and even then the material to be included in the *Khuddaka Nikaya* remained unsettled.)

The Pali language canon of the Theravāda tradition has been preserved and maintained in areas such as Burma, Sri

Lanka, Thailand, and Cambodia. These areas faithfully preserved the Indic form and did not attempt to put the texts into vernacular translations. Instead, the Pali was rendered in local script for the representation of the sounds. A similar pattern was followed in Korea and Japan, where the Chinese-character version was accepted as the standard; translations into Korean and Japanese language formats have only taken place in modern times. The maintenance of the Pali and Chinese as international canonic languages is tied to the history of literacy in Asia, where Indian and Chinese sources were often the first examples of written texts.

The Pali canon has been preserved in several forms. In Burma the so-called Fifth Council was held in 1871 under the patronage of King Mindon Min. During that council, the canon was reedited by comparison of text variants and at the end of the process was engraved on 729 stones that have been placed in a monastery near Mandalay. A Sixth Council was opened in Rangoon in 1954, and the canon was chanted by an assembly of twenty-five hundred monks. After two years the council was concluded, and a printed version of the Pali canon, approved by the gathering, appeared in Burmese script.

While Theravāda Buddhists have held that Pali is the official canonical language, they have been willing to transcribe the canon into various local scripts, reproducing the Pali sounds without translating. In Cambodia the royal court ordered that the Khmer edition of the canon be published; work on it began in 1929 and was completed in 1969. In this case the Cambodians broke with the older tradition and not only put the Pali into Khmer script but added a vernacular translation that paralleled it. In Europe a major effort, mounted under the direction of the Pali Text Society, sought to preserve and translate the Pali canon. The preparation of a modern critical edition began in 1882; by the early twenty-first century eighty-nine volumes had been edited and printed in roman transliteration. While this version had no official support from the *sangha* (Sanskrit, *saṃgha*; the Buddhist religious community)—as did the Burmese and the Khmer editions—it is a major contribution to the study of the Pali canon.

The Thai Buddhists have also been active in the work of editing and preserving the canon. In the eighteenth century King Rāma I (1737–1809 CE) convened a council of several hundred monks to restore the canon that was destroyed when the Burmese pillaged the capital at Ayutthaya. The Thai Buddhists then prepared a palm-leaf edition and presented it to King Rāma in 1788. His grandson, Rāma III (1788–1851 CE), had several additional copies of the leaves made. Much later their descendant King Chulalongkorn Rāma V (1868–1910) set in motion the project of having the canon printed in Thai script, an activity completed in 1893.

Mahāyāna Texts. The emergence of the Mahāyāna tradition around the beginning of the common era brought about a burst of creative literary energy within Buddhism. Based on the premise that "whatever is well-spoken is the word of the Buddha" (A. iv 164; Sn 450, 454), Mahāyāna communities began to produce new works they called sūtra, to which they affixed the preamble, "Thus have I heard," indicating that these texts, like their counterparts in the Eighteen Schools, were originally spoken by the Buddha. The Mahāyāna texts severely attacked the other schools and called them the "Lesser Vehicle" (Hīnayāna), thereby claiming that they understood only a portion of the higher teaching.

The Mahāyāna, along with the other schools, added to the canon commentaries on the sūtras called *śastra, vyakhya,* and *tika.* Such commentaries kept the canon open and made it possible for the incorporation of later teachings over the centuries.

In modern times the extant Sanskrit manuscripts are few in number compared to other Buddhist canonical collections. Some palm-leaf manuscripts still survive in India, several from the ninth-century Pala dynasty. The Nepalese manuscripts exist in greater number than those in India; through the centuries an active scribal tradition continued to ensure the preservation of materials. The Nepalese copies date mostly from the eighteenth or nineteenth centuries and show all the marks of many scribes, including a large number of errors that have accumulated. Some Sanskrit documents are kept in Tibet, and the Potala Palace in Lhasa still houses thousands of palm leaves in its archives.

Translation. As Buddhism began to spread outside of the Indian cultural sphere, canonical texts were carried along in both written form and in the memories of the missionary monks. Because there was no restriction regarding the language to be used for the texts, many were eventually translated. The most important development in this regard took place in China, where the task of translating was indeed a formidable one. The Sanskrit and other Indic texts presented the Chinese with a complex grammatical configuration of nouns in three numbers and three genders, verbs in three persons and numbers, and the designations for such inflections as present, imperfect, imperative, and optative. This was difficult for the Chinese, who had to render these texts into their own language using characters rather than a syllabary, with a written language that lacked inflections for case, number, tense, mood, or voice, and where the relationship between characters—by position, stress, or particles—established the nature of syntax. Notwithstanding these problems, for over a thousand years the Chinese continued translating the canon, in the process preserving hundreds of texts that have disappeared in other areas. Ironically some of these Chinese versions of the texts (a number of which were translated as early as the second century CE) may be closer in content to the ur-text than the extant Sanskrit manuscripts of India and Nepal, which date from a late period in Buddhist history. The translated canons played a major role in the promulgation of Buddhism. From Sanskrit came the Chinese as well as a major portion of the Tibetan canon, and from the Chinese came the Manchu and Tangut canons. The

Tibetan would in turn be used as the source for the Mongolian canon.

The preservation of the Chinese canon followed a different course than that of India or Southeast Asia. Whereas the Buddhist canon was one of the first collections to use the new technology of printing in China in the tenth century, the rest of the Buddhist world maintained the palm or birch-bark manuscript formats until modern printed versions were completed and published. (At first the Chinese also made manuscripts using manufactured surfaces of silk or paper with strips pasted together to form long scrolls.)

Canonic lists were established by the fourth century in China, largely through the compilation of catalogs of the holdings of various monastic libraries. In one sense the Chinese canonic list was started as a library shelf list. Biographies of eminent Chinese monks, travelogues, histories, and apologetic literature were also included in these. As the canon—now literally a library—continued to grow, the problem of recopying the whole collection became severe and expensive. Unlike the Pali canon (which, although large, was still of a size that could be copied with support from devoted laity), the Chinese canon, with its more than five thousand scrolls, was too massive to be copied without great effort.

The Fang Shan stones. One of the early attempts to preserve the growing number of translations in Chinese was the project of having the texts inscribed on stone. The largest assemblage of these engraved stones is in the caves of the Fang Shan district, which houses over fifteen thousand milled stone slabs, incised on both sides with the Buddhist texts.

The Fang Shan stones were produced in two distinct fashions over a six-century period. The first stones, from the Sui (581–618 CE) and Tang (618–907 CE) dynasties, were prepared as donations from lay groups. There was some attempt to fashion a sequential group of texts in the order found in ancient library catalogs. However, the donors often chose to reproduce multiple copies of popular texts rather than follow a set order. Initially begun by a local monk named Jing-wan—just before the founding of the Tang dynasty—the project continued until the last days of the Jin dynasty (1115–1234).

Because many of the Fang Shan stones carry inscriptions regarding the donors and the dates, it has been possible to reconstruct the process by which the carvings were accomplished. Hundreds of believers from that region formed associations to raise money for the carving of single or multiple blocks each year. On Buddha's birthday celebration the laity gathered at the site and carried the stones up the mountainside, placing them in caves for safekeeping. The first type of stones, some weighing hundreds of pounds, are dated 631 to 863 CE, the largest extant collection of manuscripts from the Tang dynasty. The rituals and the support given to the Fang Shan stones is a striking example of how important the Buddhist canon was for ordinary groups of people.

The nature of the stones at Fang Shan changed when the Khitan people established their reign over the area. In 1042 CE the court of the Liao dynasty (916–1125) took over the stone engraving process, and until 1110 it was a royal project. Few stones from laypeople were permitted in the caves. As the Liao dynasty lost power to the growing might of the Jurchen, people who called their dynasty Jin picked up the project that had come to a halt because of the political upheavals. For fifty years (1132–1182 CE) new stones were produced as part of the Jin dynasty's support of Buddhism. Because the project was under the control of officials, all stones were of standard size, and the sequence of the canonic list was followed in making new stones. Not much is mentioned about these stones in the histories outside of that particular region. In 1957 the Chinese Buddhist Association undertook the task of removing all stones from the caves to make rubbings of them and publish a full catalog. In the process they found that the Jin stones had been buried underneath the pagoda in a nearby monastery rather than in the caves cut from the stone cliff on the mountain.

The importance of the Fang Shan stones to the study of Chinese Buddhist canon is twofold: as the source for a study of the ancient manuscripts and as an example of the practices followed by the community of believers in those centuries. In many cases these stones are the oldest dated textual witness for Chinese manuscript study of the canon. Although the Fang Shan stones contain a large number of texts, it is not a complete set of the Chinese Buddhist canon. The canon was not produced in its entirety until the Song dynasty (960–1279 CE) undertook the revolutionary project of using the new technology of printing. In the year 972 a commission was given by the court to carve the entire canon onto wooden printing blocks in the city of Cheng du (in Sichuan), the wood carving center for China. This work went forward until 983, during which time 130,000 blocks were carved, containing the material of more than 5,000 rolls of manuscripts, each one 15 pages in length.

DISTRIBUTING THE CANON. When the printed edition of the Chinese canon was made available, it became the standard for official manuscript copying centers. This ensured a more fixed canon because identical xylographic copies could be made and distributed throughout China. The making of manuscripts continued, but now they had a printed version for reference. It would be some centuries before the Chinese began to think of printing as a way of making hundreds of copies for wide distribution rather than as a special copy that stood as a standard for the older method of manual reproduction.

One set of the prints made from the Northern Song blocks was sent to Korea. The court saw the printed technology as a sign of national development and recognized it as a powerful tool for merit-making. The king initiated a project for the Buddhist canon that transferred the tracings of the outlines of the Chinese volumes onto wooden blocks. The stated purpose of this project was to secure help and good fortune for the nation. This first Koryŏ dynasty (Korean dynasty, 918–1392 CE) xylograph collection, constructed during the period 1010 to 1030 CE, remained in use and continued to expand as new texts arrived from China until the invasion of the Mongols in the thirteenth century. The occupying troops saw the wooden plates as a potential powerful talisman for the Koreans and burned the Hungwang Monastery where the plates were stored. During this difficult period, the court was exiled to the island of Kanghwa, and although his kingdom faced the rule of Mongols, King Kojong (r. 1213–1259) ordered that a second set of blocks be made. He saw the act of preparing wooden blocks for the Buddhist canon as a defensive measure against the invaders.

The work of creating the second set of Koryŏ printing blocks took place from 1236 to 1251 CE under the direction of Sugi, an ordained monk and scholar. Fortunately Sugi did not content himself with merely reproducing a facsimile of the first set of blocks. He wrote an account of the process, titled *Koryo-kuk sinjo taejang kyogjon pyollok,* and had it included in the set of plates. His descriptions indicate that he used a number of sources to check the readings of the Northern Song edition and made many editorial changes. At the conclusion of the second set, more than eighty-one thousand blocks had been carved with the new Sugi edition.

The new Sugi edition relied heavily on another national project of the Khitan people of the Liao dynasty. The Khitan canon has long been a mystery because so little of it has been preserved for study. But when twelve rolls from this version were discovered in Shanxi province and removed to Beijing in the 1980s, scholars had material with which to judge the readings and the approach used by the Khitan redactors. These two versions of the blocks provide proof that the scholars of China and Korea were not merely scribal copiers; they felt free to make corrections and to pick alternate readings when the text witness appeared to be in error.

A second canon was produced outside Chinese borders by the Jurchen people, who were for a time in a confederation with the Khitan. When the Jurchen defeated the Liao dynasty of the Khitans, they followed the practice of having a xylograph set made for the Buddhist canon. Fortunately a sizable portion of rubbings from this set were found in Shaanxi province and were published in a facsimile edition in Beijing. It appears this version was made in the same way as the first Koryŏ by transferring traced characters to the new blocks.

PRESERVING THE CANON. Preserving the largest Buddhist canon was not left to the royal courts alone. As with the Fang Shan rock-cut canon, private resources were also used with printing. Local monasteries began producing sets of blocks that could be used to make large numbers of prints for distribution, and new xylograph copies are still being discovered. From the remaining prints scholars now have a better idea of the enormity of the task undertaken to preserve and disseminate the canon. The private editions are usually identified by the location of the blocks. In some cases, the blocks received royal support from the Ming court (1368–1644) and the Qing dynasty (1644–1911).

1. Chong ning edition (eleventh to twelfth centuries): Dong-chan Monastery in Fu-zhou.
2. Pi-lu edition (twelfth century): Kai-yuan Monastery in Fu-zhou.
3. Sixi edition (1126–1132 CE): Yuan-jue chueh Monastery in Hu-zhou. This is the so-called Song edition.
4. Zi-fu edition (1237–1252 CE): from Hu-zhou; thought to be a copy of the Sixi edition.
5. Ji-sha edition (thirteenth to fourteenth centuries): prepared in Ping-jiang chiang-fu in Jiangsu. A copy of the major portions of this edition was discovered in Shanxi province in 1929 and was published in facsimile in 1932 in Shanghai using the Yong-lo edition to supply the missing portions.
6. Pu-ning edition (thirteenth century): Pu-ning Monastery in Hang-zhou. This is the so-called Yuan edition. There are a handful of volumes from a fourteenth-century Yuan version discovered in Yunnan in 1979.
7. Hong-wu edition (1368–1398 CE): the first version of the canon done in Southern Ming in Nanjing. The blocks were destroyed in 1408.
8. Yong-lo edition (completed 1419 CE):): the second version prepared in Nanjing, usually referred to as the Southern Ming edition.
9. Yong-lo edition (fifteenth century; supplement in 1584 CE): prepared in Beijing and called the Northern Ming edition.
10. Wu-lin edition (fifteenth century): portions recoved in 1982 of this Hang-zhou edition.
11. Wan-li edition (sixteenth century): recovered in 1983. This is a recarving of number 8 above.
12. Jia-xing/Jing-shan edition (sixteenth to eighteenth century): notable for its format of sewn volumes rather than folded ones.
13. Qing edition (1733–1738 CE): a court project, often referred to as the Dragon edition.
14. Pin-jia edition (1909–1914 CE): a movable type edition done in Shanghai. Based on the Shukusatsu edition of Japan, this version is sometimes called the Hardoon canon because of the support of the Hardoon family.

Whereas a large part of the Chinese Buddhist canon was translated, it in turn was also rendered into other language forms. For example, among the Tangut people and the Hsihsia Kingdom, the ruler Yuan Hao started the process of moving the Chinese over to the Tangut script in the eleventh century. By the twelfth century the Chinese technology of printing blocks was used to make reproductions of the Tangut version.

When the Mongols took control of the central government of China, they turned attention away from the Chinese canon and supported efforts to make the scripture available to non-Chinese. Because of their support of the Tibetan form of Buddhism, they paid attention to the preservation and dissemination of the Tibetan translation of the Sanskrit and Chinese texts rather than relying solely on the Chinese canon.

THE TIBETAN CANON. The Tibetans had several problems to overcome in the construction of a canon in their own language. When Buddhism was introduced, no written form of the language could be easily used for the work of translation. In the seventh century King Sron bstan sgam po (d. 649 CE) set in motion the creation of a Tibetan alphabet. Tradition says that the work of translation began by the eighth century with help of such Indian masters as Śāntarakṣita (c. 725–790) and Padmasambhava. Studies show, however, that it was not until the thirteenth century that the translations were collected together and classified into a set that could be called a canon. The monastery at Snar than undertook this task and made the first catalog, dividing the texts into the Bka' 'gyur (*Kanjur*), which included all of the sūtras (the words attributed to the Buddha), and the Bstan 'gyur (*Tanjur*), or commentaries. The Yuan court undertook to make a printing block set for the Tibetan translations. In 1410 in Beijing the Bka' 'gyur was put on blocks shaped in the long, narrow format used by the Tibetans, which copied the style of the palm-leaf manuscripts of India. A second set of blocks, added as a supplement to the earlier ones, was produced in the seventeenth century. In the latter part of the same century another carving was done, followed in 1724 by a set of Bstan 'gyur blocks.

The set of rubbings taken from the blocks made during the reign of the Kangxi emperor and from the 1724 set are known collectively as the "Beijing edition." In the eighteenth century blocks were carved in areas occupied by Tibetan-speaking peoples. Sets were made at Snar than, Co ne, and Sde dge. Of these the Sde dge (Derge) is the favorite among scholars because of its careful editing. The last major editing task, commissioned by the thirteenth Dalai Lama, resulted in the production of the "Lhasa edition" of the Bka' 'gyur in 1931. This later edition is a comparison of the Sde dge and Snar than editions.

The translation of the Tibetan into Mongolian was started in the Yuan dynasty by imperial command. Lidgam Khan (1604–1634) supported this project, resulting in the translation of the Bstan 'gyur in 113 volumes. These volumes containing the Mongolian language version were written in gold and silver ink. The Kangxi emperor decided to have the translation revised and edited and engraved on printing blocks. The first rubbings of the Mongolian blocks were made in 1720, and because red ink was used, the 108 volumes of the printed set became known as the "Imperial Red edition." The complex story of how the ruling court of China used the Buddhist canon for political and religious purposes is further indication that the canon had many functions in societies.

THE CANON IN JAPANESE. Japanese versions of the Chinese canon have come to play an important role in Buddhist scholarship. By the early twenty-first century most scholars used printed editions from Japan made from movable metal type. Prior to the modern versions, however, woodblock editions were also made in Japan, which reportedly received a copy of the rubbings from the North Song edition in the eleventh century. However, the Japanese did not immediately produce their own woodblocks. It was not until the monk Tenkai made the first set of blocks in the seventeenth century that the Japanese obtained their own local print edition.

In 1681 Tetsugen produced a second set of blocks based on the Ming editions. In the nineteenth century the "Tokyo canon" was printed (1800–1885), and punctuation was introduced. The second Koryŏ edition was the basis for this Tokyo version. A "Kyoto canon" appeared between 1902 and 1905 based on the Koryŏ prints as well as some of the Ming readings from the Tetsugen edition. A critically edited version of the Chinese Buddhist canon printed from 1922 to 1933 is known as the "Taisho canon." This edition is used by most scholars when making footnote references to the Chinese canon. The basic text of the Taisho canon is from the Tokyo canon, which in turn copied the Koryŏ edition.

THE CANON IN THE COMPUTER AGE. In addition to these "received" versions of the canons, there are still occasionally some important archaeological finds, especially in regions of Central Asia. The discoveries of documents in cave 17 at Dunhuang, the cache of birch-bark manuscripts found in the stupa at Gilgit, and the texts written on wood in the ruins of the Tarim Basin have all contributed to knowledge of the way in which the Buddhist canon spread throughout Asia.

The translation of the canons is an ongoing process. The twentieth century saw an increase in the efforts to have vernacular versions available in printed form. Continued interest in the Buddhist scripture is indicated by the 1969 Cambodian translation of the Pali canon, the two modern Korean translations of the Chinese into the *hangul* script in both North Korea and South Korea, and the translation of much of the Chinese into a form of classical Japanese. Active translation projects have involved the English language. The Pali Text Society completed a major portion of the Pali canon into English, along with critical editions and aids, such as dictionaries and studies, and with funding from the Yehan Numata Foundation, a translation bureau has been established for the purpose of translating the Chinese canon into English (plans call for the translation and publication of 139 texts in the first phase of the project).

Buddhist communities that wish to move the canon from printed form to computerized versions have taken advantage of the digital age. In the late 1980s Mahidol University began the process of digitizing the Thai edition completed in the nineteenth century—the first full canon to appear in the new technology. Other groups followed the strategy, producing full digital versions of the Burmese "Sixth Council" edition, the Singhalese edition, and the Pali Text Society edition. The work of digitizing the Chinese Buddhist canon was more difficult, however; it required software development for the input of the ancient characters. The first complete digital version, the Koryŏ canon, is based on the printing blocks at Haein Monastery, followed by the input of the Japanese "Taisho" edition, the first internet-accessible form of the Chinese canon. In the early twenty-first century work began on the Tibetan canon as well with the intention of creating a database that contains many of the extant Sanskrit texts. The acceptance of the computer as a method for dissemination has been universal among the major Buddhist communities, and the willingness to expend funds for the creation of these databases indicates the esteem and value that the canon still possesses.

THE FUTURE OF THE CANON. From this survey of the history of the Buddhist canon it should be clear that, long before such activities were prevalent in the West, the Buddhists were editing, translating, and printing their scriptures. Because the canons remained open for such a long period (in a sense, the Chinese canon is still open), the size and nature of the collections of texts were unique among the religions of the world. No one group has ever controlled the development of the canons or exercised dominion over the decision about the inventory of texts to be included. In China especially the canon was lengthened because of a willingness to accept a great variety of texts into it. Scholars of popular religions point out that the texts most often used in East Asia are mainly written and compiled in China. These texts purport to be translations from Sanskrit, when in fact they originate from East Asia. Because the texts are supposedly from India, they have been described in ancient Chinese catalogs as "spurious" or in modern times as "apocryphal."

In some cases the East Asian texts have been readily assimilated into the canonic lists, but in others they have been rejected. It is understandable that the Chinese religious heritage would find an avenue of expression in new texts. The canonic listing was important for such works because the preservation of texts required the copy centers and the distribution network of the monasteries and government agencies. Whereas the East Asian texts deserve closer study, it is also the case that the canonic texts from Indic sources were continually cited by commentators and teachers over the centuries. These citations have yet to be fully documented, but they are important for the study of the canon because they will provide an insight into what texts were read by the scholar-monks in their writings and oral teachings.

As the Chinese Buddhist monastics achieved a degree of assurance about their understanding of the teachings, by the Tang dynasty they were less fixed on the translations from India. A shift occurred, and monastics moved away from reliance on the older canonic texts—although they did not fully reject them. Among the Chan schools, new literature appeared as the teachings of great masters, whose insights were taken to be the equal of any Indian exegete. Much of this literature used the translated canon as the authority for the masters, who did not claim to be dependent on the texts; rather, they acquired their understanding from meditation. The use of the older canon indicated that what the masters had experienced was in no way distant from the insights of the Buddha himself.

Later in the Chan movement the growing influence and popularity of certain great teachers, such as Mazu, helped create a situation in which the texts central to the school came from the records of these Chinese masters. They no longer felt the need to claim Indian origin for the teachings; it was now seen as coming directly from the Chinese culture and the Buddhist community. Instead of the "apocryphal" text of the past, the Chinese volumes were prized beyond all others and were seen as originating within the Chinese environment.

One can see that the use of the canon was multifaceted. At a time when the Chan school was distancing itself from the Chinese Buddhist canon, the large monasteries in China continued to make hundreds of thousands of printing blocks. The canon could thus be revered as an object and used for merit-making, whereas in other cases it served as a source of authority for the teachings of the Chinese masters.

CONCLUSION. Buddhist texts offer the scholarly world excellent examples of material that can be used to study the ways a text can change and be reformatted over time. A major problem for the editor or translator of a Buddhist text is that of making decisions based on a multiplicity of versions, sometimes in several languages and dating from different periods. The usual object of the editor is to achieve a reading that is as close as possible to the ur-text. However, this search is nearly impossible because the texts have been in a fluid state for centuries, and the received versions may have come from a stemma that includes multiple contending versions. Indeed some of the sūtras are compilations of set formulas that can be put together in any number of arrangements, altering from one time or place to another. Thus the collating of various codices from a number of stemmas does not lead to an autograph from which all witnesses have emerged.

If one could reconstruct the edition in such a fashion as to remove all the conflations, additions, and expansions of the doctrine, the resulting text would lose much of its value. Buddhist texts exhibit the changing modes of the tradition. Just as literary criticism focuses on the reader as much as it does on the author's intent, so too does Buddhist canonic literature represent the changes made by readers who left behind small traces of their contributions to the modern text.

The modern interest in canon is based primarily on European and North American literature. The Buddhist canon offers another pattern for exploration. It is a canon that has shifted and changed over time, a canon that has included contemporary work—even when it masquerades as the work of another time and place, a canon with texts that expand and contract and translations that preserve one or another version as well as the possibility of adding new texts in the future. Thus the potential has existed and often been realized for the addition of whole new sets of texts in the canon of Buddhism—such as the later Tantric tradition, the Mahāyāna writings, a variety of commentarial approaches, versions of texts appearing in new translations, and finally, an acceptance of East Asian texts as equal if not superior to the Indian ones.

Because the Buddhist canons represent the written part of a religion that teaches the constant availability of the insights of enlightenment and holds that the teaching of its founder, Śākyamuni, need not be the only expression of the highest teaching, it is not surprising to find canons of large size. The Buddhist canons provide a valid source for the study of the religion. The hundreds of texts represent all levels of the ideas and concepts. Even though maintained by the "elite" monastic community, the canons are filled with expressions of "popular" practices over the centuries. The Chinese canon's inclusion of works created in East Asia is an example of the complexity of the sources and the history of the world's largest scriptural collection.

See Also Councils, article on Buddhist Councils.

Bibliography

Buswell, Robert. *Chinese Buddhist Apocrypha.* Honolulu, 1990.

Collins, Steven. "On the Very Idea of the Pali Canon." *Journal of the Pali Text Society* 15 (1990): 89–126.

Davidson, Ronald. *Indian Esoteric Buddhism: Social History of the Tantric Movement.* New York, 2002.

Goodrich, L. Carrington. "Earliest Printed Editions of the *Tripiṭaka.*" *Visva Bharati Quarterly* 19 (Winter 1953–1954): 215–220.

Jong, J. W. D. "Notes a propose des colophons du Kanjur." *Zentralasiatische Studien* 6 (1972): 505–559.

Kychanov, Evgeniy I. "From the History of the Tangut Translation of the Buddhist Canon." In *Tibetan and Buddhist Studies Commemorating the 200th Anniversary of the Birth of Alexander Csoma de Körös,* edited by Louis Ligeti, vol. 1, pp. 377–387. Bibliotheca Orientalis Hungarica, vol. 28. Budapest, 1984.

Lancaster, Lewis R. "Editing of Buddhist Texts." In *Buddhist Thought and Asian Civilization,* edited by Leslie Kawamura and Leslie Scott, pp. 145–151. Emeryville, Calif., 1977.

Lancaster, Lewis R. "Buddhist Literature: Its Canons, Scribes, and Editors." In *The Critical Study of Sacred Texts,* edited by Wendy Doniger O'Flaherty, pp. 215–229. Berkeley Buddhist Studies Series, vol. 2. Berkeley, Calif., 1978.

Mitra, Rajendralala. *TheSanskrit Buddhist Literature of Nepal.* Calcutta, 1971.

Poceski, Mario. "Attitudes toward Canonicity and Religious Authority in Tang Chan." In *American Academy of Religion Abstracts.* Atlanta, 2002.

Ray, A. K., ed. *Sacred Texts of Buddhism: A Catalogue of Works Held in the Australian National University Library.* Canberra, 1981.

Simonsson, Nils. *Indo-Tibetische Studien: Die Methoden der tibetischen Uversetzer, untersucht im Hinblick auf die Bedeutung ihrer Ubersetzung fur die Sanskritpilologie,* vol. 1. Uppsala, 1957.

Lewis R. Lancaster (1987 and 2005)

BUDDHIST BOOKS AND TEXTS: CANON AND CANONIZATION—VINAYA

The earliest Buddhist literature is divided into the doctrinal teachings, the *dharma,* and the rules for ethical behavior, the Vinaya. The Vinaya is divided into the *Sūtravibhaṅga,* case studies of each individual rule, and the *Skandhaka,* essays on important topics, for example ordination, monastic clothing, medicine, adjudication of disputes, the conduct of community meetings, and so on. The Vinaya rules are collected in a separate list called the *Prātimokṣa,* and there is a summary of the *Skandhaka* called the *Karmavācanā.* Taken together, the Vinaya literature outlines the core Buddhist ethical teachings, ordination procedures, and community ritual guidelines. While the ethical and social behavior models have been consistent, the expression and structure of the Vinaya literature have been reformulated, expanded and interpreted. The pressures of rapid growth and social involvement brought about changes in Vinaya literature. These changes mark significant differences in Buddhist intellectual and social history in different cultures, times, and places.

From its beginning and through its history the Vinaya rules and the entire corpus of literature have been established in response to monks' and nuns' encounters with the ordained and the lay communities. The four fundamental rules (*pārājika*) of the Buddhist monastic code prohibit engaging in sexual activity, killing living beings, stealing, and lying (given in this order in the texts). The details of these prohibitions in the Vinaya literature show that they were actively discussed and applied; the four transgressions are demonstrated in a broad spectrum of case studies used to establish moral and legal precedents. The Vinaya literature covers a wide range of possible violations of each rule, classifies transgressions according to severity, and designates specific penalties for each type of violation.

The detailed nature of Buddhist ethical and legal codes is made clear in the descriptions of the first major transgression in the Vinaya, the prohibition of sexual activity for ordained monks and nuns. Along with the prohibitions against taking life, stealing, and lying, the attention given to sexuality shows that preserving the integrity of the celibate community was a top priority. Eighteen Vinaya rules of varying importance are concerned with sexuality, and intentional sexual relations is the first in the list of the most serious offenses, resulting in expulsion from the community. The related rules for monks and nuns prohibit sexual activity with men, women, hermaphrodites, eunuchs, any living being, and the dead and dying and whether intoxicated or sober. All varieties of intentional sexual activity are described and prohibited for monks and nuns and are grounds for expulsion from the community. The Pali Vinaya goes on to prohibit sexual relations while "awake, asleep, intoxicated, mad, drunk, [or with] dead . . . and decomposed partners" (Horner, 1938–1952, vol. 1, p. 49). Sexual relations are prohibited whether one is sleeping, awake, a novice monk or nun, or in any way compliant. All further varieties of sexual activity are explicitly described and prohibited, including incest, masturbation, or activity with any artificial device. Verbal allusions to sex acts and related abusive language are prohibited. In contrast to these descriptions of violations and penalties and in a demonstration of the extensive nature of this legal literature, the Vinaya does not hold female or male victims of sex abuse guilty of any violation, nor are such victims to be penalized. The penalties for each kind of transgression are included, beginning with dismissal from the community for intentional acts and confinement to quarters, suspension of privileges, and restrictions on interaction with the community for lesser violations.

The Vinaya literature is rich with descriptions of all varieties of each kind of transgression, their contexts, and their penalties. The rules against taking life include detailed case studies and legal precedents. The Vinaya literature prohibits intentionally killing any living being and specifies that human life is of greater value than animal life. Inciting anyone to injure any living being is a violation, and there are strict prohibitions against the slaughter of any living being on behalf of a monk or a nun. Intentional and unintentional activities that result in death are presented in detail, and penalties are assigned according to the severity of the transgression. Other rules prohibit physical violence motivated by anger or displeasure, and threats of violence are classified as violations.

For monks and nuns, taking anything not given is explained as stealing. Lying, especially about one's spiritual attainment or status, is particularly weighty for ordained monks and nuns. Infractions even remotely related to all four cardinal rules are illustrated in anecdotes and case studies, and the penalties for each type of transgression are specified. This literature is a rich source of Buddhist canonical law, and in addition to monastic rules, it served as a guideline for lay law in many cultures.

In addition to the four cardinal rules, six other community rules were included in an early list of ten. Monks and nuns were not to take alcoholic beverages, they were not to take meals after midday, and they were not to engage in dancing, music, or such entertainment. They were not to use ornamental jewelry or perfumes, they were not to sleep in luxurious bedding, and they were prohibited from handling gold and silver.

THE RULES. The Pali Vinaya, the oldest extant Vinaya, contains 227 rules for monks and 311 for nuns. The core list of rules is called the *Pātimokkha* (*Prātimokṣa*), and the list is memorized and recited by Buddhist monks during their monthly meetings into the early twenty-first century. Most scholars agree that this list of rules was compiled before the canonical versions with the stories and commentaries in the *Sūtravibhaṅga.* The separate list of rules, the *Prātimokṣa,* is, however, not included in any early version of the Vinaya Piṭaka.

The Vinaya rules are attributed to the historical Buddha, who is said to have made the rules as his group of followers grew. The gradual development of the lists of Vinaya rules shows that Buddhist monastic law was not conceived of as a predetermined or revealed moral agenda given in total to the ordained community. The rules were rather practical measures designed gradually to preserve what were thought to be mental and physical conditions appropriate to the practice of Buddhism. The historical Buddha made rules for the community as the occasions presented themselves, and it is likely that rules were collected and added after the Buddha's lifetime. The variations in size of the extant Vinaya collections show the dynamism of the community and the tension between preservation of the inherited rules and the need to adapt to unprecedented new conditions.

The original list of rules formulated in the Buddha's lifetime for his original community expanded as the Buddhist monastic community grew and spread to different places. Soon different Vinayas were collected and regarded as authoritative scripture. As far as is known, these were collected and transmitted orally. Fragments of written Vinaya documents dating to the first century BCE survive in several languages, but the first complete written Vinaya is in Pali language, dating to the fifth century CE. From text fragments and inscriptions, it is known that after the third century BCE at least six collections of Vinaya rules were produced in different cultural contexts. These Vinaya collections are generally associated with geographic regions and sect affiliation. They are the Sarvāstivādin, Dharmaguptaka, Mahīśāsaka, Mūlasarvāstivādin (the largest Vinaya), Pali, and Mahāsaṃghika. Of these the Vinayas of the Sarvāstivādin, Dharmaguptaka, Mahīśāsaka, and Mahāsaṃghika exist in Chinese translations, the Pali Vinaya in its language of composition, and the Vinaya of the Mūlasarvāstivādin in Chinese and Tibetan translations.

The literal meaning of the word *Prātimokṣa* is a rule or rules that lead one to liberation. The *Prātimokṣa* is the core of the *Sūtravibhaṅga,* which contains the explanatory stories or contexts for each rule. The rules are divided into eight sections, expulsion (*pārājika*)—four; community meeting (*saṅghādisesa*)—thirteen; undetermined (*aniyata*)—two; forfeiture (*niḥsargika*)—thirty; expiation (*pātayantika*)—ninety-two; confession (*pratideśanīya*)—four; and civility (*śaikṣa*)—seventy-five; adjudication (*adhikaraṇaśamatha*)—seven, adding up to a total, in the Pali version, of 227 rules. Eighty-four more rules dealing with sexual propriety and community behavior are added for nuns.

SKANDHAKA. The second part of the Vinaya is the *Skandhaka.* This section, like the rules (*Sūtravibhaṅga*) section, has an abbreviated summary called the *Karmavācanā,* which, like the *Prātimokṣa* list of rules, is not included in the Pali Vinaya. The *Skandhaka* section of the Vinaya is largely concerned with community issues, giving descriptions of rituals, procedures, monastic life, and materials. Instead of setting out rules and penalties, this section of the Vinaya deals with ordination procedures, monastic authority, community ritual observances, clothing styles, cosmetic styles, healthcare, adjudication of disputes, and so on.

There are two sections in the *Skandhaka*, the Main Section (*Mahāvagga*) and the Lesser Section (*Cullavagga*). The entire *Skandhaka* is set in the context of stories from the life and teachings of the Buddha, first including major components of monastic life in the Main Section and minor points in the Lesser Section. The Main Section begins with a brief account of the Buddha's enlightenment experience, the theory of the twelve links of causal interdependent origination, the eightfold path, the four noble truths and the theory of the nonexistence of the self. The first major section is on ordination. The Buddha's original procedure is described, then the specifics of the evolution of the ceremony and the requirements for ordination are set out. These descriptions of receiving monastic robes, having one's head shaved, and taking vows are preserved in all versions of the Vinaya.

The next two sections of the *Skandhaka* deal with feeding, housing, and occupying thousands of Buddhist monks and nuns during the Indian monsoon season. The Vinaya records that monks and nuns used to wander from place to place even through the rainy season. Farmers began to complain about crops destroyed by Buddhists wandering in the monsoon, undernourished and weaker monks and nuns began to develop illnesses, and travel became difficult. The Buddha and monastic authorities therefore instructed the communities to set up shelters and temporary residences for the duration of the monsoon season. With so many monks and nuns living together, the community was soon faced with the problems of retreat conduct and an effective method to propagate the teachings during the monsoon retreat time.

These sections of the Vinaya literature contain a rich collection of sociological, economic, and anthropological data. Mundane matters under the heading of "Leather Accessories" describe health and hygiene problems in ancient India, and the descriptions of the commodities in common use give information about the regional economy, including the use of wooden products, palm, bamboo, wool, gold, silver, gems, bronze, glass, tin, lead, and copper. Ethical and community definition issues follow in the section prohibiting the slaughter of cattle and animals and the problems that arise from use of their skins. Monks and nuns are not to kill animals, in particular cattle, which in addition to being living beings were considered sacred by many of the Buddhists' Indian brethren.

The section on medicine contains allowances to treat illness and provide hospice care. The foundations of Indian medicine were located in Buddhist monasteries, and these are evident here, for example, in the descriptions of acceptable medicines and their administration. The *Skandhaka* includes medical diagnostic information, food warnings, hygiene information, and information on medical procedures. It goes on to detail information about monks' and nuns' robes, the acceptable material for making monastic clothing, and the rituals for acquiring and distributing new robes. Again, the *Skandhaka* provides much information about ancient India's commodities economy. Here there are descriptions of the use of linen, cotton, silk, wool, hemp and canvas.

The *Skandhaka* continues with sections about the Campā and Kośāmbī communities and general descriptions of community interaction with the Buddhist legal system. Violations of Buddhist monastic rules, for example, the case of quarreling among the Kośāmbīs, are judged and sentences specified. These two sections mark the end of the Main Section of the *Skandhaka*. The remainder of the *Skandhaka* is the Lesser Section and it is packed with applications of Buddhists rules. The basic rules are stated in the texts, always with the Buddha present or on his authority, and the rules used are summarized at the end of each section. These long case histories describe the interface of the Buddhist worldview with everyday human life. The extensive deliberations in the Lesser Section show monks and nuns confronting and coping with basic human needs and shortcomings in accord with Buddhist guidelines.

LATER VINAYA LITERATURE. The Pali Vinaya and other Vinaya collections are preserved in the Buddhist canonical collections and are regarded as sacred and inviolable. However, as described here, the canonical collections were themselves products of processes of disputation and retrospective compilation. A good example of this process is the controversy between the Sthavira and Mahāsaṃghika sects, which likely produced slightly different versions of the Vinaya rules. Similarly the processes that produced and caused the revisions of the ancient collections continued, and the Vinaya was recast in later cultural and religious contexts.

There are good examples, particularly in Sri Lanka, India, and China, of the ongoing process of preserving the ancient rules and community rituals and at the same time building new text collections around them. In twelfth-century Sri Lanka, the Vinaya literary canon was recanonized in the *Katikāvata* (Regulations of the order) literature, which addressed new conditions and concerns of the monastic community. In India in about the seventh-century, after the end of the Gupta dynasty, the scholar Guṇaprabha composed the *Vinaya Sūtra* and commentary, based on the ancient *Skandhaka* literature. These texts were commented on extensively in India and became core documents for later Tibetan Buddhists, who produced a large corpus of Tibetan commentaries on Guṇaprabha's Indian texts. Similarly in China the Vinaya was recast in Chan monasteries to accommodate Chinese Confucian traditions in the *Chanyuan Qinggui* (Rules for purity in Chan monasteries). These and other compositions are careful to preserve inherited canonical rules and regulations, but they include innovations designed for each respective environment. The Vinaya canonical literature is thus preserved and at the same time carefully recast.

In addition to these well-known and widely circulated compositions, major Buddhist monasteries composed manuals that addressed their communities' special concerns, setting out ritual schedules and etiquette for their local communities. The ancient Vinaya rules were again preserved and rituals observed; ordination, monthly meetings, recitation of rules, and ethical parameters were kept intact. In sum, though definitely preserved intact, canonization of the Vinaya literature was not a procedure that set up lists of rules to be mechanically and literally followed in all circumstances. Canonization was rather a dynamic creative process that functioned to meet the needs of a growing and changing community and did not preclude later addition and reformulation.

See Also Law and Religion, article on Law and Religion in Buddhism; Monasticism, article on Buddhist Monasticism.

Bibliography

Frauwallner, Erich. *The Earliest Vinaya and the Beginnings of Buddhist Literature.* Rome, 1956. Translated by L. Petech. A useful early study of the history of the different versions of the Vinaya.

Hirakawa, Akira, trans. and ed. *Monastic Discipline for the Buddhist Nuns: An English Translation of the Chinese text of the Mahāsāṅghika Bhikṣuṇī Vinaya.* Patna, India, 1982. A good example of the Vinaya literature in translation.

Horner, Isaline B. *The Book of the Discipline (Vinayapiṭaka).* 6 vols. London, 1938–1952. A translation of the Pali Vinaya.

Kabilsingh, Chatsumarn. *A Comparative Study of Bhikkhunī Pāṭimokkha.* Vārāṇasī, India, 1984.

Lamotte, Étienne. *History of Indian Buddhism: From the Origins to the Śaka Era.* Translated by Sarah Webb-Boin. Louvain and Paris, 1988. A dated but useful reference for Vinaya literature.

Prebish, Charles S. *Buddhist Monastic Discipline: The Sanskrit Prātimokṣa Sūtras of the Mahāsāṅghikas and Mūlasarvāstivādins.* University Park, Pa., 1975.

Ratnapāla, Nandasēna. *The Katikāvatas: Laws of the Buddhist Order of Ceylon from the Twelfth Century to the Eighteenth Century.* Munich, 1971.

Thera, Ñāṇamoli, trans. *The Pāṭimokkha: 227 Fundamental Rules of a Bhikkhu.* Bangkok, 1966.

Wijayaratna, Mohan. *Buddhist Monastic Life: According to the Texts of the Theravāda Tradition.* Translated by Claude Grangier and Steven Collins. Cambridge, U.K., 1990.

Yifa. *The Origins of Buddhist Monastic Codes in China: An Annotated Translation and Study of the Chanyuan Qinggui.* Honolulu, Hawaii, 2002.

Paul K. Nietupski (2005)

BUDDHIST BOOKS AND TEXTS: RITUAL USES OF BOOKS

A written text can be a vehicle for the conveyance of meaning, but it is always also a material object with a physical presence in the world. In many Buddhist communities, the material presence of texts has been viewed as a crucial aspect of their nature and function. Buddhist texts are powerful, and their power is thought to reside not only in their message, but also (and sometimes especially) in the physical embodiment of that message.

The Buddha's Textual Body. The texts that are conceived of as having the greatest potential power and ritual efficacy are those that contain the word of the Buddha (*buddhavacana*), primarily sūtras or excerpts therefrom. Whereas the profundity of the Buddha's teachings provides one reason for the reverence accorded to such works, their ritual functions rely perhaps more heavily on the notion that they are embodiments of the Buddha himself, relics of his physical presence in which are invested the miraculous powers that he possessed. The origins of this notion remain unclear, but, following the work of Gregory Schopen (1975), most scholars have agreed that many ritual practices involving texts were developed by analogy with (and possibly in tension with) practices involving the bodily relics of the Buddha. Passages equating the Buddha with his teachings are not uncommon in Buddhist literature; among the most often cited is the Buddha's statement that "one who sees the dhamma, Vakkali, sees me; one who sees me, sees the dhamma" (*Samyutta Nikāya* III, 120). Whereas this passage has often been read as deemphasizing the importance of the Buddha's physical presence in favor of the teachings, it also offers precedent for the identification of the Buddha's body with the body of the teachings. Buddhist texts preserve not only the Buddha's wisdom, but also his powerful physical presence.

Numerous Mahāyāna sūtras make the equation explicit: the teachings of the Buddha (especially the sūtras in question) are his *dharma* body (*dharmakāya*) made present through recitation or inscription and worthy of the highest veneration. According to such sūtras, reading, writing, reciting, and worshiping them generates even greater merit than worshiping the bodily relics of the Buddha. Schopen and others see in such passages an attempt to establish the superiority of this "cult of the book" to the worship of physical relics. Moreover, as Schopen points out, bodily relics are (at least theoretically) limited in number, and are housed in specific shrines; they resist replication and transportation, whereas *dharma* relics can be reproduced endlessly and enshrined anywhere. As the Buddhist tradition spread to new communities, this portability ensured that the Buddha could be made physically present anywhere.

Several practices involving texts stem from the notion that the Buddha is embodied in the teachings. Throughout the Buddhist world, texts are enshrined, like the physical remains of the Buddha, in stupas (reliquary structures) and in images of the Buddha, objects of veneration that are vivified and rendered powerful in part by the texts and other varieties of relics that they contain. Whereas complete texts have often been interred, particular verses or formulae have been favored to serve this function in particular times and places, such as the well-known verse on interdependent origination (*pratītyasamutpādagāthā*), which encapsulates the Buddha's teaching on arising and cessation. Small clay tablets and miniature stupas stamped with this verse have been found in great number interred in stupas across Central, South, East, and Southeast Asia. Images inscribed with the verse are also ubiquitous. As Daniel Boucher's study indicates, from roughly the seventh to the thirteenth centuries, the *pratītyasamutpādagāthā* was perhaps the *dharma* relic par excellence. It made the Buddha physically present—not through its meaning so much as through its material embodiment of the *dharma.* A relic, whether of the Buddha's body or his speech, is not an inert object, but the potent presence of the Buddha himself. Together with other textual relics, the tablets marked with this verse suggest a conception of Buddha-speech (and perhaps language in general) as having an active, transformative presence in the world that is connected with—but by no means subordinate to—its capacity to convey meaning.

The textual embodiment of the Buddha is not exclusively a Mahāyāna phenomenon, although perhaps the phenomenon is most fully elaborated in that context. Some Theravāda systematizations of the bodies of the Buddha include the *dharma* body; some classifications of relics include *dharma* relics together with bodily relics, associative relics (objects he used, his footprints, or the bodhi tree), and relics by convention (images of the Buddha or of the places and things associated with him). It seems that Theravāda communities have placed greater emphasis on other varieties of relics than on *dharma* relics, but this conclusion may be reflective of different emphases in scholarship on the Theravāda as much as different emphases within Theravādin practice. Texts play a crucial role in the rituals through which images and other objects are imbued with the presence of the Buddha. In the Thai ceremony for consecrating Buddha images, for instance, the image is vivified through "hearing" the recitation of the life story and core teachings of the Buddha. In such rituals, the creation and transfer of power is achieved in no small part by the recitation of texts.

Text Production as Ritual Practice. Perhaps the most fundamental ritual practice associated with texts is text production itself, for this practice ensures the preservation and further use of a text—no small matter, especially in a manuscript culture, where access to texts is by no means assured. It would appear, however, that the impetus for having texts copied (or printed) in many Buddhist communities was not only preservation and dissemination of the teachings; the act of production is also an end in and of itself, for it is claimed to be a potent practice for generating merit. Such claims are sometimes made in the very texts to be copied. Several Mahāyāna sūtras, such as the *Prajñapāramitā* (Perfection of Wisdom) sūtras, the *Saddharmapuṇḍarīkasūtra* (*Lotus Sūtra*), and the *Suvarṇa(pra)bhāsottamasūtra* (*Sūtra of Golden Light*), explicitly and strongly encourage their own reproduction. Whereas Theravāda writings tend to be less overt and self-referential in this regard, stories exist that similarly recommend the production and worship of texts. One story in the *Paññasajātaka* (an "apocryphal" Thai collection of stories of the Buddha's previous lives), for instance, tells of a previous life in which the Buddha was a wise man who lived during the life of a former Buddha; because he wrote down and encouraged others to write down the teachings of that Buddha, he received plentiful worldly gifts from the deities, as well as a prediction from the former Buddha that he would himself become the Buddha Gautama.

These textual affirmations of the material rewards and great merit to be gained from the production of texts were clearly taken to heart in Buddhist communities. Among the manuscripts found at Dunhuang, for instance, numerous dedicatory colophons are preserved that specify the personal motivations of the Buddhists who copied, or sponsored the copying of, Buddhist texts. These motivations are commonly related to death and rebirth; copying a sūtra could generate the merit necessary to ensure that a recently deceased loved one would gain a good rebirth, or to mitigate against wrongdoings committed by oneself. Other motivations are attested as well, and almost all manuscripts include the dedication of merit to all beings. Similar dedications of merit are found in manuscripts throughout the Buddhist world.

The production of Buddhist texts could generate not only merit, but also political authority, as is especially evident in the periodic editing and reproduction of the Pali canon. As Stanley Tambiah has demonstrated, revising and "purifying" the canon established a ruler as a protector of the *dharma*—a role with significant political as well as religious capital. The Fifth Buddhist Council, held in 1871 in Burma, provides a striking example: the canon, revised under the direction of King Mindon, was inscribed not only on palm leaves, but also on 729 marble slabs—an undertaking that established the king's authority as well as the text of the *Tipiṭaka.*

Whereas producing a Buddhist text in any form would be meritorious, manuscript remains suggest that the material qualities of the text were of great significance in Buddhist communities. Formats vary according to cultural context and the function of the text. Texts produced primarily for the merit gained thereby reflect their status as objects of devotion: some are richly illustrated, or written in gold on beautifully dyed papers. One Japanese manuscript of the *Lotus Sūtra,* for instance, enshrines each character of the text in a small stupa, whereas another is embroidered in silk thread of different colors. Manuscripts are often enclosed in elaborately carved and painted manuscript covers, sūtra cases, or cloth wrappings. Texts inscribed in stone (including not only the Burmese Pali canon described above, but also most of the Chinese canon, carved between the seventh and the twelfth centuries and stored in caves at Fang Shan) promise to preserve the *dharma* beyond its predicted decline in the world. Texts meant to function in ritual contexts were produced in more practical formats, such as booklets containing what appear to be collections of liturgical texts found at

Dunhuang. Whereas manuscripts would frequently be produced by professional scribes paid by donors, there also exist numerous texts inscribed personally by the devotee. A few extant manuscripts are written in ink mixed with the blood of the writer, forging a bodily connection with the powerful physical text, and thus with the Buddha.

Since the more frequently a text was produced, the greater was the merit obtained. Thus, various technologies of text production developed, the most central of which is block printing. The earliest dated printed text (868 CE), found at Dunhuang, is the *Diamond Sūtra* (*Vajracchedika*), a text that explicitly exhorts its readers to reproduce it (its colophon indicates that copies were intended for free distribution). Indeed, it is likely that Buddhist practices of producing texts for merit were a central impetus in the development of print technology in China. Several Mahāyāna sūtras, including the *Diamond Sūtra*, are not only found in written form at Dunhuang, but are also depicted in wall murals—most not primarily as narratives, but as icons, in which the Buddha, preaching the sūtra, gazes directly at the viewer. Such representations again suggest a conception of sūtras as physical embodiments of the speech of the Buddha—and this physical embodiment takes precedence over the denotative content of the sūtras in their depiction. The sūtras are icons of the Buddha that, in the case of the paintings, literally make his body manifest.

Other practices that similarly aim to make a text "present" can also be understood as technologies of text production. The Tibetan prayer wheel, for instance, contains paper on which a *mantra* is written thousands of times. With each turning of the wheel, every one of the written *mantras* is made manifest, thereby generating tremendous merit for the practitioner. Some contemporary practitioners have adapted this practice to digital technology, saving numerous copies of a *mantra* to a computer hard drive that spins hundreds of thousands of times per hour. Prayer flags function similarly, the efficacy of the words written upon them being released with each breeze.

Such examples suggest a way to understand yet another mode of text production: recitation. Both in Theravāda and in Mahāyāna textual traditions, exhortations to recite or hear Buddhist literature are ubiquitous, often eclipsing exhortations to write. In manuscript cultures, especially—cultures in which access to the written text was often extremely limited—most Buddhists were likely to encounter the text in the context of recitation. Whereas recitation seldom leaves material traces for historians, some sūtras describe the effects of recitation on audiences and their worlds in distinctly physical terms. The oral/aural text is represented as a potent substance that enters and transforms its listeners and their environments. It is clear in such descriptions that preaching the sūtra indeed makes it manifest in the world in a manner strongly reminiscent of other, more obviously material, practices of text production. Take, for instance, the Tibetan practice of reciting the entire canon with great rapidity, a practice that might be understood as something like an oral prayer wheel: a large number of monks are given different sections of the canon, and each recites his portion simultaneously. Oral recitation makes the transformative power of the text present in the world, like the flapping of a prayer flag in the wind.

TEXTS AS AGENTS OF TRANSFORMATION. As is evident in the different technologies of text production, Buddhist texts are not only instruments of communication, but also agents of transformation; as manifestations of the Buddha, they have the capacity to radically transform the lives of devotees who interact with them in prescribed ways. In the ritual practices through which devotees access this power, the meaning-bearing aspects of a text—while surely related to its transformative capacity—recede, whereas the material qualities of language—whether oral or written—come to the fore. The language of Buddhist texts becomes a tangible, fully present force that can change the conditions of persons and their environments.

Rituals that provide access to the power of texts involve oral performance and/or the manipulation of written texts. In Theravādin communities, one of the principal rituals employed is the chanting of *paritta*, collections of Pali sūtras and other texts thought to have particularly potent protective powers or the capacity to render circumstances auspicious. These texts may be chanted by devotees or by monks in a formal ceremony that can last up to several days. The ceremonies are held to provide protection from hardship and malignant forces, and to promote beneficial conditions for specific ventures—from weddings to business deals.

In more formal ceremonies, the potency of the chanted texts is rendered materially accessible through substances that are themselves imbued with power through the recitation. A thread that connects all who are present during the chanting is later broken into pieces and distributed to devotees, who then wear the strands on their wrists or arms. Devotees wet their faces and heads with—and drink water blessed through—the ceremony. The Pali texts are comprehensible only to a few laypeople and to some monks, but the protective and beneficial power of chanting them or hearing them chanted depends not on comprehension, but on texts' materialization and on the ability of devotees to interact with the texts in material ways.

The relationship between meaning and transformative agency is most tenuous in practices involving *mantra* and *dhāraḥī*. These strings of Sanskrit (or Pali) syllables are employed in a wide variety of practices, from chanting to turning prayer wheels to meditation, but also recited at key points within numerous ceremonies that are not primarily focused on the texts—such as rites for the dying or the consecration of images in order to bless or empower a person or object. Many of these formulae are given in sūtras, bestowed by particular deities with the promise of protection, benefit, or awakening for the devotee who employs them. Some explicitly invoke a celestial being, but most barely gesture towards meaning. Instead, the power of the formulae resides in their materialization in sound or writing. Indeed, the elusiveness of meaning in these formulae is a crucial component of their transformative capacity, whether they are used for worldly ends or as meditative aids. Beyond conceptualization, formulae evoke a mysterious power to transform the mundane world or to lead the meditator beyond concepts.

Those Mahāyāna sūtras that proclaim their own transformative agency might be said to function in an analogous manner: the content of such texts is fundamentally concerned with articulating repeatedly the power of the form of the text itself when it is made manifest through writing or recitation. Rather than locating their potency in a conceptually graspable core revelation, these Mahāyāna sūtras draw attention to their own materiality, instructing their audiences on how to interact with them in physical, material, and ritualized ways. The literal interpretation of these instructions is indicated by traces of sandalwood powder and other ritual substances found on wooden manuscript covers from Northern India and Central Asia dating from the ninth century and later; several of the sūtras specifically encourage the devotee to offer such substances. And, as enjoined by the texts themselves, such texts were (and are) widely recited for the benefit and protection of individuals, communities, nations, and the world.

The amuletic function of texts perhaps best epitomizes the material manifestation of transformative agency. Tiny scrolls enclosed in ornaments, miniature texts, or amulets stamped with potent words are carried on the body of the devotee. Such textual objects—relics of the Buddha—both remind the practitioner of Buddhist teachings and offer wearable, tangible protection and benefit in daily life. The Southeast Asian practice of tattooing *yantra* (powerful diagrams in which *mantras* and Buddhist verses figure prominently) on the body to protect against weapons and malevolent forces, or to generate good will in others, provides a striking instance of making the power of language physically manifest; the human body itself becomes the powerful material text. Like manuscripts written in blood, tattoos forge a strong physical connection between the body of the devotee and the textual body of the Buddha.

THE RITUAL CONTEXT OF TEXTUAL PRACTICES. Rituals involving texts have in turn engendered further practices of text production. Throughout the Buddhist world, anthologies of texts or parts of texts employed in particular rituals—such as *paritta* ceremonies—have been produced. These anthologies are not merely functional; they are venerated bodies of literature in their own right. In China and Japan, the worship of Mahāyāna sūtras gave rise to a popular genre of secondary literature: miracle tales about the sûtras. These stories describe the miraculous intercession of the texts (and the celestial buddhas, *bodhisattvas,* and deities brought to life in their pages) in the lives of their devotees, as well as the dire consequences of treating the sūtras with disrespect. They model appropriate ritual behavior with regard to the sūtras, and serve as testimonials to the transformative powers that the texts themselves claim. Finally, given the conception of Buddhist texts as the embodiment of the Buddha and his power, the production of scholarly commentaries and translations cannot be neatly separated from more overtly devotional or apotropaic practices. The sophisticated theories and uses of language developed by thinkers across the Buddhist world emerged from contexts in which texts were materializations of tremendous, transformative power.

SEE ALSO Buddha; Buddhism, overview article.

BIBLIOGRAPHY

Abe, Ryūichi. *The Weaving of Mantra: Kūkai and the Construction of Esoteric Buddhist Discourse.* New York, 1999. Examines Kūkai's conception of language in relation to ritual practices involving sûtra, mantra, and *dhāraṇī.*

Bentor, Yael. "On the Indian Origins of the Tibetan Practice of Depositing Relics and *Dhāraṇīs* in Stupas and Images." *Journal of the American Oriental Society* 115, no. 2 (1995): 248–261.

Bodhi, Bikkhu. *The Connected Discourses of the Buddha: A New Translation of the Saāyutta Nikāya.* Somerville, Mass., 2000.

Boucher, Daniel. "The *Pratītyasamutpādagāthā* and Its Role in the Medieval Cult of the Relics." *Journal of the International Association of Buddhist Studies* 14, no. 1 (1991): 1–27.

Cabezón, José Ignacio, and Roger R. Jackson. *Tibetan Literature: Studies in Genre.* Ithaca, N.Y., 1996. See especially the essays in the sections on "Canonical Texts" and "Ritual."

Campany, Robert F. "Notes on the Devotional Uses and Symbolic Functions of Sūtra Texts as Depicted in Early Chinese Buddhist Miracle Tales and Hagiographies." *Journal of the International Association of Buddhist Studies* 14, no. 1 (1991): 28–69. A survey of miracle tales about sūtras.

Jaini, Padmanabh S., trans. "Akkharalikhitajâtaka." In *Apocryphal Birth-Stories (Panññasa-jātaka),* vol. 2, 198–209. London, 1986.

Klimburg-Salter, Deborah. "The Gilgit Manuscript Covers and the 'Cult of the Book.'" In *South Asian Archaeology, 1987: Proceedings of the Ninth International Conference of the Association of South Asian Archaeologists in Western Europe,* edited by Maurizio Taddei, pp. 815–830. Rome, 1990. Examines evidence in material culture for the "cult of the book."

Pal, Pratapaditya and Julia Meech-Pekarik. *Buddhist Book Illuminations.* New York, 1988. An art-historical study of illustrated Buddhist manuscripts.

Schopen, Gregory. "The Phrase '*sa pṭhivīpradeúaú caityabhūto bhavet*' in the *Vajracchedikā*: Notes on the Cult of the Book in Mahāyāna." *Indo-Iranian Journal* 17 (1975): 147–181. The germinal study of the "cult of the book."

Silva, Lily de. "Paritta: A Historical and Religious Study of the Buddhist Ceremony for Peace and Prosperity in Sri Lanka." In *Spolia Zeylanica,* vol. 36, part 1. Colombo, Sri Lanka, 1981.

Skilling, Peter. "The Rakṣā Literature of the Úrāvakayāna." *Journal of the Pali Text Society* 16 (1992): 109–182. Surveys varieties of Buddhist literature used for protective and beneficial purposes.

Tambiah, Stanley J. *World Conqueror and World Renouncer: A Study of Buddhism and Polity in Thailand against a Historical*

Background. Cambridge, U.K., 1976. Includes consideration of historical and modern revisions of the Pali canon and Buddhist practice by rulers of Theravādin states.

Tambiah, Stanley J. *The Buddhist Saints of the Forest and the Cult of Amulets: A Study in Charisma, Hagiography, Sectarianism, and Millennial Buddhism.* Cambridge, U.K., 1984. On conceptions of relics and the materialization of power, see 195–207; on the consecration of Buddha images and amulets, see 243–257.

Tannenbaum, Nicola. "Tattoos: Invulnerability and Power in Shan Cosmology." *American Ethnologist* 14, no. 4 (1987): 693–711.

Teiser, Stephen. *The Scripture on the Ten Kings and the Making of Purgatory in Medieval Chinese Buddhism.* Honolulu, 1994. A case study of Dunhuang manuscripts in relation to form, content, ritual function and text production.

Wu, Hung. "What Is *Bianxiang*? On the Relationship between Dunhuang Art and Dunhuang Literature." *Harvard Journal of Asiatic Studies* 52, no.1 (1992): 111–192. An art-historical analysis of the representations of sūtras at Dunhuang.

NATALIE GUMMER (2005)

BUDDHIST BOOKS AND TEXTS: TRANSLATION

Translation practices have been central to the ongoing reinterpretation and transformation of the Buddhist tradition. Translation ensures both continuity—through the transmission of the vast sacred literature of the tradition—and change, as different ways of interpreting Buddhist thought and practice are opened up or closed off in the process of translation. As an interpretive practice, translation depends upon and illuminates historical conceptions of Buddhist literature and of the process of translation itself, neither of which necessarily coincide with contemporary English conceptions. The translation of Buddhist literature reveals the different ways in which various Buddhist communities have located and recreated the value and power of their textual traditions in light of their individual cultural and historical contexts.

A frequently cited passage in the Pali canon (Vinaya 2.139) both prescribes and exemplifies the complex and crucial role that translation has played in the transmission of the Buddhist tradition. In this passage, two monks of the Brāhmaṇ class report to the Buddha that the teachings are being disseminated by monks of widely varying backgrounds *sakāya niruttiyā*, "in own language," and suggest to him that his words be rendered in *chandaso* (usually interpreted to mean "Sanskrit meter"). No, he replies to them, they should be disseminated "in own language." Numerous interpreters, ancient and modern, have viewed this passage as clearly defining the normative stance on the question of whether or not to translate texts, but they have not agreed on just what stance is being prescribed.

How one interprets this passage determines and is determined by one's opinion on whether to translate the word of the Buddha. Does the phrase "in own language" refer to the language of the preaching monk, or to the language of the Buddha himself? The passage admits multiple interpretations (not all of which have been summarized here). Thus, whereas many interpreters see here the Buddha's stamp of approval for translation practices, others, including the highly influential fifth century commentator Buddhaghosa—thought to be responsible for the translation of Theravādin commentarial literature from Sinhalese into Pali—view "in own language" as referring to the Buddha's own language. According to Buddhaghosa, that language was Pali.

The different historical interpretations of this putatively normative passage mirror the multiple approaches to and conceptions of translation taken in different times and places. The preservation of the Theravādin *tipiṭaka* in Pali, as compared to the translation of the *tripiṭaka* into Chinese and Tibetan, for instance, would appear to demarcate one of the most significant distinctions among Buddhist conceptions of translation. If one looks beyond general preferences regarding canonical language, however, the situation becomes considerably more complicated: Theravādin Buddhist communities have translated numerous texts into local languages, and have produced bilingual versions of canonical texts in which Pali is interspersed with local languages. Conversely, certain texts or parts of texts (like *mantra* and *dhāraṇī*) have been preserved in Buddhist Sanskrit by the same communities that chose, for the most part, to translate the canon. Buddhist conceptions of translation are reflected not simply in the question of whether to translate, but what—and how, and why—to translate.

The practices of premodern Buddhist translators clearly indicate that the answers to these questions were multiple. One stands a better chance of understanding the multiplicity of Buddhist conceptions of translation if one begins with the premise that the practice of translation in the vast majority of premodern Buddhist communities was a religious practice. Much of Buddhist literature is thought to embody not only meaning, but also tremendous efficacy and transformative power—the power to heal, bring prosperity, or even enlighten audiences. The production of translations is thus closely related to other religious—and even devotional—practices. Situating the questions of whether, how, and why Buddhists translated their sacred literature within this context of religious practice illuminates possible motivations and explanations that might otherwise remain obscure.

TECHNIQUES OF TRANSLATION. Whereas the conceptions of translation that inform Buddhist translation practices are only rarely examined explicitly by translators, the techniques used in translation can shed considerable light on diverse answers not only to the question of how to translate, but also to the question of why. The approach taken by a translator or community of translators is not arbitrary; it is shaped by the conception of Buddhist literature and its translation that is held by the translator. On the other hand, interpreting techniques of translation with the aim of understanding conceptions of translation is by no means straightforward. For instance, the late-eighth-century Tibetan king Khri Srong-lde'u-bstan (742–c. 800 CE) is credited with normalizing previously idiosyncratic translation practices, prescribing methods for rendering Sanskrit syntax and dictating precise one-to-one correspondences between Sanskrit and Tibetan terms. The result is a highly artificial style, a kind of "translationese," that had been adopted by Tibetan translators to such an extent that some modern scholars of Buddhism have thought that Tibetan translations could be used to produce "back-translations," reconstructions of Sanskrit texts that are no longer extant.

One can attempt to derive from this translation technique, employed in all editions of the Tibetan canon, the conception of translation that informs it. Any such attempt is itself, however, a kind of back-translation: an interpretive reconstruction that is necessarily flawed even though potentially illuminating. Does the deep concern for establishing equivalence between the two languages indicate that, despite the practice of translation, the power of the text was still thought to reside in the Sanskrit forms of the language, or does it suggest an extreme skepticism regarding a translator's ability to correctly grasp and render the meaning and transformative power of a text? Techniques of translation can indeed suggest the concerns and conceptions of the translator(s), but the techniques themselves are open to interpretation.

In contrast to the regularization of translation techniques in Tibet, Chinese translations exhibit a wide range of approaches. Early Chinese translators, such as An Shigao (second century CE), tended to borrow Daoist vocabulary for the rendering of Buddhist ideas. Many texts were produced by translation teams, in which different members assumed specific roles in the interpretive and editorial processes under the leadership of an illustrious translator. Particular translators cultivated distinctive techniques. Some, such as the monk Hsüan-tsang (602–664 CE), actively preserved the foreign flavor of a text through literal renderings. Others, most famously Kumārajīva (344–413 CE), attempted to convey the core significance of a text through free translations in elegant literary Chinese. Foreignness and familiarity both breed their own kinds of power, and these different techniques of translation can be interpreted as indicators of where different translators located the power of the religious texts they were translating.

Moreover, several different translations of the "same" text are frequently preserved side-by-side in the Chinese canon, a practice which itself invites interpretation. Perhaps Chinese Buddhist scholars conceived of different translations as illuminating different aspects or functions of a given text, or simply as representing part of a textual history worthy of preservation. This multiplicity provides an important contrast to the Tibetan practice of attempting to determine a single definitive translation, one that suggests a strikingly different conception of Buddhist literature and its translation.

LANGUAGE CHOICE. The translation of Buddhist literature is not simply a matter of rendering texts from one vernacular into another. Many of the languages in which Buddhist literature is preserved are literary languages distinct from those spoken by people who produced and used Buddhist literature. These literary languages have their own complex histories of transformation and codification. Thus, "Buddhist Sanskrit" describes a literary language (or, better, a range of language use) closely related to, but not identical with, classical Sanskrit in the normative sense. Indeed, some scholars maintain that the form of Sanskrit in which some Buddhist literature is preserved is itself a kind of translation, an amalgam of *prakritic* literary languages and Sanskrit, where the former is thought to be the original language of composition. Other scholars counter that Buddhists chose to compose and preserve texts in these "hybrid" literary forms. Likewise, the Pali in which Theravādan canonical texts are preserved was never a vernacular language; whatever its progenitors might have been, it has distinct features that indicate its deliberate construction as a literary language.

As noted above, Tibetan translations employ a highly artificial form of "translationese" that would be abstruse for the uninitiated reader. It is difficult to make generalizations about the language of the Chinese translations, which varies considerably in terms of its conformity with the norms of literary Chinese, itself a form of language very distinct from vernaculars. It is safe to say, however, that even the most colloquially inflected translations became, in the course of a few hundred years, distant from vernacular usage (as, for instance, the language of Shakespeare is for most contemporary English speakers).

Buddhist Sanskrit, Pali, Tibetan, and Chinese all functioned not only as literary languages, but also as translocal languages—languages in which Buddhist literature was preserved and studied by communities whose spoken language was different. Thus Pali functioned as a translocal language in South and Southeast Asia, Sanskrit in South and Central Asia, Chinese in East Asia and parts of Southeast Asia, and Tibetan in the Himalayas and in Mongolian communities. In this respect, these languages are distinct from local languages that, whether literary or vernacular, did not function beyond the borders of their linguistic communities. Note, however, that "local" and "translocal" are shifting categories. When Tibetan translations were made of Sanskrit Buddhist texts, they were rendered in a local literary language; when Mongolian Buddhists chose to use the Tibetan Buddhist canon, Tibetan was being used as a translocal language.

In addition to the distinctions between literary and vernacular and between local and translocal, a third distinction, between languages from which and languages into which translations were made, is relevant to an examination of Buddhist translation practices. Sanskrit, Pali, Tibetan, and Chinese all functioned as sources for translations into local languages. Sogdians, for instance, chose to translate Buddhist texts from the Chinese, whether due to access or to presumed authority. Once again, however, these categories are flexible and overlapping. Sinhalese commentaries on the *tipiṭaka* were translated into Pali, in part to make them accessible to a translocal audience.

Like the techniques of translation employed in different times and places, language choice admits various interpretations. The preservation of the canon in a foreign language does not suggest that translation did not take place. For example, the entire Tibetan canon was translated into Mongolian in the first half of the seventeenth century, but the Tibetan version came to be preferred for liturgical purposes. Preserving canonical texts in a translocal language like Pali can be understood in terms of the reverence for and power invested in what was thought to be the language of the Buddha, but it can also be understood as an element in the construction of a shared translocal culture, or as an attempt to restrict access to canonical texts to a powerful monastic elite. The translation of a massive corpus of texts into Chinese or Tibetan might be interpreted as a sign of the populist nature of the Buddhist movement in a particular time and place, but, since the variety of language employed in the translation is, in most cases, far from the vernacular, the charge of elitism might just as easily be applied. Regardless, it is safe to say that in the vast majority of Buddhist communities both local and translocal languages were employed, the choice between one or the other in the case of a given text being dictated by a complex and fluctuating conjunction of social, literary, and soteriological factors.

Take, for instance, the Thai ceremony for imbuing life in a Buddha image, in which monks chant the biography of the Buddha to the image in Pali. Translations of the text in local languages exist and are used in preaching, but only the Pali version is deemed to have the potency to enliven an image. A similar linguistic "division of labor" might well inform language choice in Khotanese Buddhism. While manuscript evidence suggests that Sanskrit sutras were produced in Khotan, Khotanese translations or summaries of the same texts are also attested. One possible explanation might be derived from the Thai case: perhaps Sanskrit texts served a different function from translated texts. Another explanation, provided by Jan Nattier (1990), suggests that, through the influence of Chinese Buddhist textual practices, a shift in language choice towards a preference for the vernacular took place in Central Asia after the sixth century, prior to which only Buddhist Sanskrit texts were produced. Both the functional and the temporal explanation have merit, and are not mutually exclusive options.

TRANSLATION AND ACCULTURATION. The complex choices regarding language use outlined above—whether, what, and how to translate—have profound implications for understanding the acculturation of Buddhism in particular places and times. Translation is a crucial moment in the life of a text; a translator (or team of translators) functions as both reader and author, shaping the text through the interpretive process of translation for all its future readers. This complex intercultural moment, which embodies the paradox of translation—the simultaneous sameness and difference of the translated text from the original—is both a central factor in and a powerful metaphor for processes of acculturation. Particularly in a tradition with so strong a textual orientation as Buddhism, translators' interpretations of key texts can have profound effects on the development of the tradition in its new locales. Central concepts and practices are shaped by the terminology employed to describe them; the influence of a particular text is dependent upon the poetic and rhetorical devices through which its message is rendered. Translation closes certain avenues of interpretation and development, while opening up others that may not have been fully present in the original. These dynamics can be seen not only in textual translation practices, but also in broader processes of adaptation, such as the "translation" of an Indic ritual employing cow dung as a sacred substance into a different cultural context where the substance is viewed as unclean excrement.

The choice to preserve a text in a translocal language, rather than translating it, by no means suggests a refusal of acculturating processes, although a desire to maintain the original purity of the teachings might be part of the motivation. Instead, preserving a body of religious literature in a translocal language forges particular ties to the context of origin. The acculturation of the tradition to a particular locale occurs through the production of new literature—in the translocal as well as in the local language—rather than through rendering a preexistent literary corpus in the local language. The preexistent literature itself can take on a somewhat esoteric (and potentially powerful) quality as a result of its incomprehensibility to the vast majority of practitioners. Preserving a canon in a translocal language also provides the conditions for the maintenance of a clerical elite, as well as for the creation of a translocal community connected by the bonds of religious language and practice. The Theravādan Buddhist world, for all the highly distinctive local variations it encompasses, shares deep relationships born in part from the shared preservation of Pali Buddhist literature and ritual and the maintenance of a monastic elite educated in that language.

This is not to suggest that contexts where translation into local languages was preferred were lacking in translocal relationships, esotericism, or institutional elites, but rather that such factors of acculturation were generated by means other than the preservation of religious literature in a translocal language. In China, translations themselves, with their distinctive locutions, became powerful markers of the context of origin and of the legitimation it imparted to texts. Indeed, the names of illustrious translators alone could lend the stamp of authority; the Chinese canon ascribes to Kumārajīva more texts than he could possibly have translated. By adopting the style and phrasings characteristic of a translation in the composition of a new work, and attributing it to a respected translator, one could create the legitimizing aura of Indic origin, thereby introducing new literature into a corpus whose boundaries were defined by the ostensible origin of texts. Indigenous "transcreations" of this sort occur in the Chinese canon; literature that was later excised from the canon due to its questionable authenticity has been preserved among the manuscripts found at Dunhuang. Transcreations were produced in other Buddhist communities, as well, although the legitimating strategies employed vary. Translations established new genres of literature that could subsequently be employed in the creation and legitimation of indigenous compositions, enabling Buddhist literature to address more directly the pressing questions of particular cultural and historical communities. In this way, translations have provided not only a means of preservation, but also a pretext for innovation within the tradition.

CONCLUSION. The conceptions of translation that underlie the practices outlined above are multiple, and clearly do not always coincide with the concept invoked by the English term. "Translation" tends to be used narrowly, such that only a text that attempts to render "faithfully" the meaning of another in a different language is usually deemed to be a translation. This contemporary conception of translation has generally guided scholarly studies of Buddhist translation practices. Did premodern Buddhist translators conceive of translation in such a manner, or were some Buddhist conceptions of translation more fluid? For instance, two Sanskrit terms for translation, *anuvāda* and *vivaraṇa*, both refer to exegetical as well as translation practices; how clear is the distinction between what English designates as two separate practices? Might some Buddhist translators have conceived of processes of summarization, excerption and anthologizing as processes of "translation"? Both because these questions depend on conceptions of textuality more broadly, and because they have so seldom been asked, no clear answers are yet possible.

It is clear, however, that translation is an interpretive practice. Any translation will privilege the aspects of a text that the translator perceives to be of central importance. Much of Buddhist literature is conceived of as not only conveying meaning, but also possessing transformative potential. The translation of such texts in Buddhist communities, then, involves rendering those qualities of a text that a particular translator or tradition of translation deems to be powerful. In this sense, translation practices have played and continue to play a central role in the ongoing transmission and transformation of the Buddhist tradition, not only in making texts accessible to different cultural and linguistic communities, but also in recreating the interpretive possibilities for Buddhist thought and practice.

BIBLIOGRAPHY

No general study of Buddhist translation practices has yet been published in English. Most available case studies tend to focus on the technical aspects of translation, and have therefore been omitted from the following list. While several of the works listed are not specifically focused on translation, all address issues central to its study.

Buswell, Robert E., Jr., ed. *Chinese Buddhist Apocrypha.* Honolulu, 1990.

Gómez, Luis O. *The Land of Bliss: The Paradise of the Buddha of Measureless Light.* Honolulu, 1996. Includes separate English translations of Sanskrit and Chinese versions of two sūtras, as well as a discussion of their differences.

Harrison, Paul. "A Brief History of the Tibetan Bka' 'Gyur." In *Tibetan Literature: Studies in Genre,* edited by Jose' Ignacio Cabezón and Roger R. Jackson, pp. 70–94. Ithaca, N.Y., 1995.

Mair, Victor. "Buddhism and the Rise of the Written Vernacular in East Asia: The Making of National Languages." *Journal of Asian Studies* 53 (3): 707–751.

Mizuno, Kogen. *Buddhist Sūtras: Origin, Development, Transmission.* Tokyo, 1982. One of the most accessible historical treatments of the transmission and translation of sūtras in China (although unfortunately lacking citations).

Nattier, Jan. "Church Language and Vernacular Language in Central Asian Buddhism." *Numen* 37 (1990): 195–219.

Pollock, Sheldon. "The Sanskrit Cosmopolis, 300–1300: Transculturation, Vernacularization, and the Question of Ideology." In *Ideology and Status of Sanskrit: Contributions to the History of the Sanskrit Language,* edited by Jan E. M. Houben, pp. 197–247. Leiden, 1996.

Pollock, Sheldon, ed. *Literary Cultures in History: Reconstructions from South Asia.* Berkeley, Calif., 2003. The essays by Sheldon Pollock, Steven Collins, Charles Hallisey, and Matthew Kapstein, in particular, examine questions of language choice relevant to the transmission of Buddhist literature.

Ruegg, David Seyfort. "On Translating the Buddhist Canon." In *Studies in Indo-Asian Art and Culture* 3, edited by P. Ratnam, pp. 243–261. New Delhi, 1973.

NATALIE GUMMER (2005)

BUDDHIST BOOKS AND TEXTS: EXEGESIS AND HERMENEUTICS

In the Buddhist tradition the practice and theory of scriptural interpretation faced conflicting sources and concepts of authority, a voluminous canon of relatively late compilation, and a complex history of interpretations that may be described as "hermeneutic pluralism." Furthermore, for some Buddhist traditions an emphasis on *dharma* (the eternal truths discovered by the Buddha) rather than on *buddhavacana* (the literal content of his message) reduces the significance of textual and historical constraints as part of a method of interpretation.

According to tradition, the Buddha was not the sole preacher of *dharma.* Even during the Buddha's life his disciples acted as missionaries, and their words were considered part of the "original" message of Buddhism. The texts affirm that at the Buddha's own behest the disciples began each sermon with the words "Evaṃ mayā śrutam ekasmin samaye" ("Thus have I heard on one occasion"). This formula presumably served as a guarantee of authenticity, or rather, of faithfulness to the teaching of the Master. Yet, the same introductory formula came to be used indistinctly for sermons attributed to the Master, to his disciples, or to mythical sages and deities.

It was also believed that there had also been previous buddhas, who had their own disciples, all of whom could have preached the *dharma.* These "Buddhists" from the mythical past could speak to human beings. Their words, as well as the "inspired speech" (*pratibhāṇa*) of ancient and contemporary *ṛṣis,* gods, and spirits, could be regarded as *dharma,* and thus be prefaced by the famous formula.

Even traditions that believe that the canon was redacted and closed during the First Council at Rājagṛha, shortly after the Buddha's death (c. 483 BCE), concede that not all Buddhist elders were present at that gathering, and that at least one group of "five hundred monks" insisted on keeping their own version of the teachings as they remembered them. All available evidence indicates that most of the canons were never closed. The Theravāda school, proud of its conservatism in scriptural matters, was still debating the content of its canon at least as late as the fifth century CE. Even today there is no complete agreement among Theravādins regarding the *Khuddaka Nikāya* section of their canon. Thus, it is not always possible to distinguish clearly between canonical, postcanonical, and paracanonical Buddhist literature.

All schools believe that at least some texts have been lost, truncated, or altered, and that a number of false or late texts have been incorporated into the canons of various schools. Even if occasionally these statements are used to bolster the position of one school over another, they probably represent an accurate description of the general state of things by the time the first scriptural collections were formally constituted. It is not difficult to see the impact that such a perception, combined with the mythology of revelation outlined above, would have on the tradition's view of the meaning of the scriptures and on the principles that should guide their interpretation.

BUDDHIST EXEGESIS: METHODS OF INTERPRETATION. The Buddhist canons were the result of a long process of compilation and redaction that we can no longer reconstruct. For many centuries the task of interpretation was complicated by a shifting definition of canonicity. The first steps in understanding scriptural traditions—identifying the limits and forms of scripture—were slow and hesitant.

It took roughly three centuries before the oral texts of specialized schools of reciters (*bhāṇakas*) were brought together into collections (*piṭakas*). Another century went by before the first canons were committed to writing (an early Theravāda canon was written down under King Vaṭṭagāmaṇī of Sri Lanka, c. 32 BCE). Even then the canons were not closed; some of the extant collections (i.e., the Tibetan and Chinese "canons"), were not compiled until more than a millennium had passed since the life of the founder, and they have remained open to the introduction of new literature until recent times.

The canon. Most Buddhists came to accept the theoretical division of scripture into three sections, metaphorically called "baskets" (*piṭaka*)—Sūtra (Pali, Sutta); Vinaya; and Abhidharma (Pali, Abhidhamma)—hence the name *tripiṭaka* (Pali, *tipiṭaka*), or "three baskets." But in practice the corpus of authoritative Buddhist texts is not always divided into these three categories. This division is in itself of secondary importance for the history of Buddhist exegesis, whereas the variety of canons that seem to have existed in ancient India, and their flexibility, are important factors in the development of Buddhist attitudes toward canonical authority and interpretation.

The earliest system of this type was the classification of Buddhist teachings (and texts) into two main divisions: *dharma* (instruction on doctrine and meditation) and Vinaya (monastic rules and discipline). This early classification of genres probably was followed closely in time by the introduction of a third type of sacred text—the *mātṛkā,* or numerical list.

Also ancient, and obviously precanonical, is a system of "genres" (*aṅga*). The Theravāda tradition distinguishes nine such genres, whereas the Sanskrit tradition counts twelve (sūtra, *geya, vyākaraṇa, gāthā, udāna, nidāna, ityukta, jātaka, vaipulya, adbhutadharma, avadāna,* and *upadeśa*). Although some of these terms are well known as words for literary genres or forms of canonical literature, the exact meaning of the items in these lists is not always transparent. The list clearly shows, however, an early interest in analyzing scripture by literary forms, themes, and, presumably, speaker and audience.

By the time Buddhists began compiling their "canons," several forms of exegesis had developed within the body of literature transmitted as sacred scripture. Beyond the implicit exegetical work of the redactors, which is more obvious in Buddhist scripture than it is in the Judeo-Christian Bible, important sections of the canons are composed of exegetical material. Some works considered to derive directly from the Master's mouth are, in structure and reference, major acts of interpretation or statements on the nature of interpretation. Such, for instance, are the *Mahāpadesa Suttanta,* on forms of appealing to authority; the *Kālāma Sutta,* a critique of authority and an affirmation of the hermeneutical value of meditation; the *Alagaddūpama Sutta,* on the instrumental value of doctrine; and the *Pratisaraṇa Sūtra,* on the criteria of interpretation. These texts reflect an early concern with the problems of transmission and interpretation. Other texts included in the *tripiṭakas* are frankly exegetical in character (although they may be of more recent vintage); these include two commentaries (the *Niddesas*) incorporated into the Sutta Piṭaka of the Theravādins, two works of theoretical hermeneutics included in the Sutta sections of the Burmese *tipiṭaka,* the *Sūtravibhaṅga* section of the Vinaya Piṭaka (an exegesis of the *prātimokṣa*), and of course the totality of the Abhidharma Piṭaka.

The *abhidharma* as exegesis. The *abhidharma* played a central role in the development of the practice and theory of exegesis in all schools of Indian Buddhism. The hermeneutical strategy of the *abhidharma* was itself derived from a practice attested frequently by the sūtras: dogmatic lists known as "matrices" (*mātṛkā*). These may appear to be mere catechistic or numerical lists; but more than topical indices or lists defining the limits of canonicity they are digests or exegetical guides. Some, evidently the oldest, are preserved in the Sūtra Piṭaka (e.g., *Saṅgīti Suttanta, Daśottara Sūtra*), and were the object of commentaries (e.g., Mahākauṣṭhila's *Saṅgītiparyāya*).

The role of *mātṛkās* as early canons of orthodoxy and interpretation is revealed by a legend, according to which the Buddha's disciple Śāriputra composed the *Saṅgīti Suttanta* in order to prevent a division in the Buddhist order similar to the one he had seen in the Jain community. The basic list, however, is not only a model for a definition of orthodoxy, it is also a pattern for exegetical coherence. The *mātṛkās* provide the structure for abhidharmic exegesis; each text must fit one or more of the categories contained in a traditional "matrix" or sets thereof. The "matrices" provided a simple logic of classification; all items of doctrine can be understood by opposites (the *dukas* of Pali *abhidhamma*: anything is *a* or not *a*) or by contraries (the *ṭīkā: x* is *a,* or *x* is *b,* or *x* is neither *a* nor *b*). Some of the earliest works of *abhidharma,* organized on this model (for instance, the Pali *Dhammasaṅgaṇī*), purport to reveal the underlying logic and structure of the *suttas*.

Non-Mahāyāna exegetical literature. The *abhidharma* can be understood as a series of attempts at an exegesis of the whole body of Buddhist teachings (texts and practices). Some books, therefore, tried to preserve an explicit connection with the sūtras. But the *abhidharma* was more a work of philosophical hermeneutics than of exegesis. Accordingly, a different genre of literature was developed to carry out the difficult task of preserving, recovering, or eliciting the meaning of individual texts.

Two of the earliest Buddhist works of conscious exegesis have been incorporated into the canon in the Sutta Piṭaka. These are the *Mahāniddesa* and the *Cullaniddesa,* commentaries on the fourth and fifth books of the *Suttanipāta.* They date from approximately the third century CE. However, two other works of early but uncertain date occupy a much more important position in the development of Buddhist exegetical theories: the *Nettippakaraṇa* and the *Peṭakopadesa,* both attributed to a (Mahā) Kaccāyana (of uncertain date). These works may have been composed in South India or Sri Lanka. The *Nettippakaraṇa* formulates the principles of interpretation (*netti*) common to both works on the basis of twelve techniques classified under the headings of "interpretation as to sense" (*byañjana*) and "interpretation as to meaning" (*attha*).

Earlier, at the beginning of the Common Era, the compilation of canonical collections and the explosion of *abhidharma* literature had created great works of synthesis on the Indian Peninsula. The most famous and influential of these was the *Mahāvibhāṣā* (c. 150–200 CE), a work of collective scholarship that attempted to make sense of the complex *abhidharma* literature of the Sarvāstivādins, in particular the *Jñānaprasthāna* of Kātyāyanīputra (or Kātyāyana; c. first century CE). Although it resulted in an equally abstruse work of doctrinal systematics, the *Mahāvibhāṣā* became an important source for doctrinal and interpretive categories, even for those who criticized it—especially the Mahāyāna.

Mahāyāna exegetical literature. In addition to playing the more obvious roles of criticism, reform, and systematic construction, the Mahāyāna sūtras fulfilled an exegetical role as well. It is common for a Mahāyāna sūtra to attempt a redefinition or reinterpretation of a classical formula from pre-Mahāyāna literature. The *Vajracchedikā-prajñāpāramitā,* for instance, presents the Mahāyāna reinterpretation of the "Parable of the Raft." The same text, in fact, the entire body of *prajñāpāramitā* literature, is devoted to what amounts to an all-out criticism of pre-Mahāyāna *abhidharma.* The traditional order established by orthodox exegesis is deconstructed in a search for the "ultimate meaning" behind the words of the older doctrines. The *Laṅkāvatāra Sūtra* and the *Tathāgataguhya Sūtra*—to quote another example—radically change the meaning of a classical passage by identifying truth with "holy silence." The earlier, canonical passage stated that "from the night of his enlightenment to the night of his *parinirvāṇa*. . .every word uttered by the Buddha was true." The two Mahāyāna sūtras changed the phrase to read "from the night of his enlightenment, to the night of his *nirvāṇa,* the Blessed One did not utter a single word."

These new departures, however, are not wholly the creation of Mahāyāna, for some of them are found in the literature of the Mahāsāṃghikas, one of the early *nikāya* schools. Some members of this school or community held that buddhas never pronounce a single word, yet living beings hear them preach. It was also claimed by some Mahāsāṃghikas that the Buddha can preach all things with a single word.

Another form of continuity within innovation occurs in Mahāyāna texts that follow the pattern of the *abhidharma mātṛkās* as a way of redefining or expanding on earlier doctrine. Some of these sūtras may be rightly called "abhidharmic" Mahāyāna sūtras. Such are, for instance, the *Dharmasaṃgīti* and the *Akṣayamatinirdeśa.*

Some texts make explicit pronouncements on the principles of interpretation or evaluation of Buddhist scripture in general. For instance, the *Laṅkāvatāra Sūtra*'s statement on the silence of the Buddha is extended to mean that all words of the Buddha have only a provisional value. They are pronounced only in response to the needs of living beings who cannot penetrate directly into the mystery of the Tathāgata's silence. The *Mahāyāna-mahāparinirvāṇa Sūtra* offers a model for a hierarchy in scriptural study and understanding. At the first level, one becomes "learned" in scriptural study by studying all of the twelve genres (*aṅga*) of scripture. Subsequently, one may study only one *aṅga*—the *vaipulya* (here equivalent to Mahāyāna) sūtras. Then one may study only the most subtle passages of the *vaipulya* section. But one may also study only one stanza of two lines from these sūtras and still be learned. Last, one becomes learned in scripture by understanding "that the Buddha never taught anything." The last of these is clearly, by implication, the most "learned."

Other statements with obvious implications for the interpretation of texts are those dealing with the relative value of various transmissions. Perhaps the best known of these formulations are those of the *Saddharmapuṇḍarīka Sūtra* (*Lotus Sūtra*), which asserts that the Buddha has been in *nirvāṇa* eternally and denies that the Buddha ever "entered *nirvāṇa*," as claimed by earlier scriptural tradition. The *Lotus* also reduces the meaning of the human lives of the Buddha to a mere teaching device, developing the theory of "skillful means" (*upāya*) as an explanation for the competing claims of its own brand of Mahāyāna and those of non-Mahāyāna Buddhists. Other texts establish criteria for authenticity that open doors to the new creative efforts of the Mahāyāna. The *Adhyāśayasaṃcodana Sūtra,* for example, establishes the well-known principle that "whatever has been well said has been said by the Buddha." Such statements are evident signs of a break with tradition and became seeds for further, perhaps dangerously limitless, innovation.

***Śāstras* and commentaries.** In India the methodology used in the composition of technical treatises (*śāstras*) was modeled on the commentarial tradition of Indian linguistics, heavily influenced by Patañjali's *Mahābhāṣya.* But the disciplines of poetics and logic also played an important role in the creation of standards for the composition of commentaries.

As Indian technical literature evolved through commentaries, continuity was preserved by reference to a common "root" text, which could be a scriptural text (sūtra) or the conscious work of an individual (*śāstra*). A certain latitude for variation was allowed in the commentaries of each school of thought, but the root text was authoritative. That is, the commentary had to be verbally faithful to the root text and had to recognize its authoritative status. But the *śāstras* themselves required commentaries, and some of the *śāstras* that became the object of commentaries acquired quasi-canonical status almost equivalent to that of the sūtras.

The system of authoritative texts followed by authoritative commentaries also produced a plethora of subcommentaries. The hierarchy was not always well-defined and the terminology not always consistent, but it was normally assumed that a sūtra would be the object of a commentary called a *bhāṣya,* or a more detailed gloss known as *vyākhyā* or *ṭīkā.* The root text of a *śāstra,* on the other hand, was often a versified treatise written in *kārikās* or mnemonic verses (functionally parallel to the Hindu sūtras or prose aphorisms), and explicated in a *bhāṣya* or *vṛtti* (sometimes by the author of the root text).

The beginnings of the Mahāyāna commentarial literature seem to be coterminous with the development of independent philosophical or dogmatic treatises (*śāstras*). But the exact dates of these events cannot be fixed with any certainty because an exact chronology depends in part on establishing the authorship of what may be the earliest major work in the genre, the commentary on the *Pañcaviṃśatisāhasrikā-prajñāpāramitā Sūtra* (Perfection of wisdom in twenty-five thousand lines), traditionally attributed to Nāgārjuna, whose dates are equally uncertain. This work, the *Mahāprajñāpāramitā-upadeśa Śāstra* (preserved only in Chinese translation under the title *Ta-chih-tu lun*), set the tone for Chinese exegesis, and defined some of the most important issues of Buddhist exegetical and hermeneutical theory for East Asia.

The genres of commentary and treatise flourished in India beginning (approximately) in the fourth century of the Common Era with Asaṅga and Vasubandhu. Although the tendency was to force the text into established scholastic molds, or to use it as a pretext for the formulation of independent philosophical dogmatics, commentators sometimes showed unusual sensitivity to the forms and structures of the text (e.g., Kamalaśīla's commentary on the *Avikalpapraveśa*). There was also room for the development of independent criteria and exegetical guides. A valuable example of this type of work is Vasubandhu's extensive treatise on the mechanics of the commentary, *Vyākhyayukti* (preserved only in Tibetan translation).

Exegetical categories. Outside of India the exegetical issue perhaps became more critical as communities lost some of the sense of continuity with the authoritative tradition of the land of origins. The need for exegetical and hermeneutical principles was especially acute in China. An exegetical schema attributed to an early scholar of Chinese Buddhism, Dao'an (312–385), was based on three categories that supposedly reflected accurately the structure of all sūtras: the setting (*nidāna*), the doctrinal and narrative core, and the transmission (*parīndāna*). This basic schema was widely used in China (where it was known as the *san-fen k'e-ching* and was adopted by Zhiyi (538–597) in his classical analysis of the *Lotus Sūtra,* the *Miaofa lianhua jing su.* The schema is not attested in India until later, as, for example, in Bandhuprabha's (sixth century CE) *Buddhabhūmi Śāstra,* a commentary on the *Buddhabhūmi Sūtra.* In practice, each of the three parts was itself subdivided to account for obvious and important elements of style, narrative development, and so forth, but also to signal those passages considered core or defining statements. The text was expected to satisfy the traditional requirements for a definition of the audience (in the *nidāna* section) and for a positive assessment of the value of the faith and practice inspired by it (usually in the transmission section). Other schemas, some evidently inspired by a similar conception, developed one or more of the three parts. For instance, the sixfold division of the introductory formula of the sūtras (*evaṃ mayā śrutam. . .*) according to the manner proposed in the *Mahāprajñāpāramitā-upadeśa Śāstra* was extremely popular among East Asian exegetes. This led to multiple variations in the division of the text of the sūtras, such as Shandao's (613–682) threefold introduction and Zhiyi's five parts of the introduction.

The most fruitful and innovative, though perhaps less rigorous, strategies were those that tried to discover metaphysical meanings in the structure of texts. Such was Zhiyi's "twofold approach"—by way of the deep structure and by way of the surface structure (*pen-chi erh men*) —to a text. This doctrine was part of a more complex exegetical plan, the four exegetical methods of the Tiantai tradition (*T'ien-t'ai ta-ssu-shih*), which brings us closer to broader hermeneutical issues. According to this doctrine, any scriptural passage can be treated from four perspectives: (1) the passage as expression of a particular relationship between the audience and the Buddha (the circumstances determining the intention); (2) the passage as embodying one of four methods of teaching; (3) classification of the passage into one of the categories of absolute or relative statement; and (4) the introspective readings of the passage (*guanxin*). In this methodological schema one can see in outline some of the salient features of Mahāyāna hermeneutics: contextual meaning, levels of meaning, and meditation as a tool of understanding.

BUDDHIST HERMENEUTICS: THEORIES OF INTERPRETATION AND CANONICITY. In traditional terms the fundamental questions of Buddhist hermeneutics can be classified into three broad categories:

1. If enlightenment (*bodhi*) is at least theoretically open to all (or most) sentient beings, what is the role of sacred words and authoritative texts? How does one distinguish the exegesis of sacred texts from the actual transmission or realization of the *dharma*?
2. Since the Buddha preached in so many different ways, adapting his language, style, and even doctrine to the spiritual disposition and maturity of his audience, did he have a plurality of messages or did he have a single truth to offer? If the latter, what was it, and, if the former, how is one to choose among his many teachings?
3. If Buddhism rejects conventional concepts of substance, self, possession, property, and referentiality, so fundamental to our conception of the world, is there a "higher language" that can be used to describe accurately reality as seen from the point of view of enlightenment?

From a modern perspective, one could characterize these three problems as defining the main subfields of Buddhist hermeneutics: the first statement addresses issues of Buddhist soteriology—the conflict between the ascetic-contemplative ideal and the institutional realities of Buddhism, between orthopraxy and orthodoxy. The second problem is that of Buddhist exegetical hermeneutics. Awareness of the late date and the diversity of "canonical" sources generates a "hermeneutical pluralism" that compounds the problem of determining the meaning of diversity and unity in tradition. The third item summarizes the problems of Buddhist philosophical hermeneutics: what are the relative positions and meanings of conventional language, its Buddhist critique, and "the silence of the sages"?

A better perception of the tone underlying the discussion of these issues can be derived from representative traditional responses to the problems:

1. The Buddhist *dharma* is not dependent on the historical event of Śākyamuni's enlightenment, ministry, and *nirvāṇa.* Whether a Tathāgata arises in the world or not, the basic teachings of Buddhism—impermanence, suffering, no-self, and liberation—remain facts of existence. Although the tradition initiated by Śākyamuni is a necessary aid to enlightenment, it is (in the metaphor of the *Laṅkāvatāra Sūtra*) only a finger pointing at the moon. The moon is always there, waiting to be seen (whether there is a finger to point at it or not); the finger is not the moon. Nevertheless, some Buddhists, the Theravādins, for instance, would insist on the historical significance of Śākyamuni's life and ministry, and on the close connection between exact literal meaning of doctrinal statements and effective practice.
2. The diversity of teachings is not due to confusion or weakness in the transmission. On the contrary, it is proof of Śākyamuni's wisdom and compassion, of his ability to adapt to the needs, capacities, and dispositions of living beings. According to the *Mahāprajñāpāramitā-upadeśa Śāstra,* his teachings were of four types, according to their definite purport (*siddhānta*): worldly (*laukika*), or surface meaning; therapeutic (*prātipakṣika*), or meaning intended as an antidote to mental afflictions and passion; personal (*prātipauruṣika*), or meaning intended for particular individuals; and absolute (*pāramārthika*), or ultimate meaning. This second point is further complicated by the Mahāyāna belief in multiple buddhas and in the timeless *saṃbhogakāya* ("body of bliss") of the buddhas, which eternally preaches in the heavens, and beyond, and is seen and heard in the visions of *bodhisattvas* and sages. Other Buddhists, however, (the Theravādins, for instance) emphasize canonical integrity, rejecting both the doctrine of multiple meanings and the doctrine of multiple buddhas. The Mahāsāṃghikas seem to have wanted to forestall exegetical pluralism and protect the integrity of scripture by claiming that all sūtras have only one explicit meaning.
3. The above attitudes toward the sacred word are inseparable from Buddhist views on levels of meaning, whatever the historical or causal connections between these three problems may have been. The creation of abhidharmic technical language was the first step in separating two orders of truth and expression. Speculation about the nature of the path and the state of perfect freedom of buddhas further contributed to a theory of levels of meaning, since a progression in spiritual insight was

taken to imply an increased capacity to penetrate behind the words of the doctrine.

The Mahāyāna insists that the higher sphere is only embodied in the silence of the *āryas.* The highest stage in the path, and, therefore, the highest order of meaning, can only be expressed in apophatic statements such as "appeasing all discursive thinking" (*sarvaprapañcopaśama*) and "cutting out all doctrines and practices" (*sarvavādacaryoccheda*). Still, all traditions, including the Mahāyāna, develop a language of the sacred (whether or not it is directly inspired by abhidharmic path theories), for it is necessary to explain holy silence in order to lead living beings to it. Thus, the culmination of this sort of speculation comes with the recognition that language, with all its limitations, is an important vehicle for salvation: language is *upāya* (e.g., in the Mādhyamika treatises, the *Laṅkāvatāra,* and the Tantras).

Criteria of authenticity. Early concepts of orthodoxy were based on doctrines of confirmation or inspiration, rather than on a literal definition of "the word of Buddha" (*buddhavacana*). A disciple could preach, then receive the Buddha's approval, or the authority of his words could be implicit in the Buddha's request or inspiration. Although it may seem difficult to have maintained this fiction when the Buddha was no longer living among his followers, Buddhists did not always see things this way. Since the *dharma* is, after all, the Buddha's true body, and since it exists whether or not there is a human Buddha to preach it, one could assume that the preaching of *dharma* would continue after his death. This justification formed part of the context for the proliferation of texts and the elasticity of concepts of canonical authenticity. It may also explain in part why the *abhidharma* and, later, the commentarial literature achieved such a prominent role in the development of Buddhist doctrine.

Such flexibility does not mean, however, that no attempt was made to establish criteria or rules for determining the genuineness of any particular statement of doctrine. The *Mahāpadesa Suttanta* of the *Dīgha Nikāya* (and its parallel in the *Aṅguttara Nikāya* and in the Āgamas) recognizes four possible ways of appealing to or arguing on the basis of authority: one may appeal to the authority of the Buddha, a community of monks, several elders, or a single elder. The validity of these appeals and their potential sources of authority, however, must be confirmed by comparing the doctrinal statements attributed to these persons against the "sūtra" and the "Vinaya."

The Sanskrit recensions of the *Mahāpadeśa Sūtra* add a third criterion: statements of doctrine must conform "to the reality or nature of things" (*dharmatā*). The same expansion is found in Pali literature in the *Nettippakaraṇa,* where the principles are actually applied to the analysis and evaluation of particular texts, and the three criteria are summarized in very suggestive language: "Which is the sūtra with whose approach [phrases and words] must agree? The four noble truths. Which is the Vinaya in which they must be seen? The Vinaya restraining covetousness, aversion, and delusion. Which is the *dharma* with which they must conform? The *dharma* of conditioned arising" (paras. 122–124).

The principle implies, of course, that whatever agrees with sūtra, Vinaya, and *dharma* (i.e., conditioned arising) carries authority for the Buddhist. If applied to texts this could mean that any new creation that is perceived as a continuation of the tradition (*secundum evangelium,* as it were) could have canonical authority. Indeed, the Mahāyāna used it in just this way to justify the development and expansion of earlier teachings. Theravādins, on the other hand, would understand the broad definitions of the *Nettippakaraṇa* as references to the letter of the canon, not to its spirit. Ultimately, then, the issue remained one of setting the limits of the interpretability of scriptural tradition.

What then is *buddhavacana*? The *Nettippakaraṇa* passage epitomizes the Buddhist tendency to use philosophical rather than historical arguments for authority. But the three tests do not form a complete system of criteria for textual authenticity. In the canonical versions they seem to refer to statements of doctrine and appeals to authority, not to texts. Most certainly if they were meant to constitute a system for establishing canonical authenticity their value would be limited, if not totally inexistent, for as tests of canonical authority the first (and original) two criteria would be tautological. One must accept that the teaching on the "four appeals to authority" was originally a method for determining orthodoxy, not a criterion of authenticity. Still, since Buddhist notions of the "word of Buddha" were elastic, the principle must have been ambiguous. That is to say, the circularity of the argument that "a genuine sūtra is one that agrees with the sūtra" may not be so obvious in the context of Buddhist notions of canonicity—at least in the early stages in the formation of the corpus of scriptures.

Some Buddhists, the Mahāyānists in particular, came to consider "agreement with the sūtras," rather than "inclusion in the Sūtra Piṭaka," the ultimate test of authority. Thus, in China a distinction is made between, on the one hand, pseudepigrapha, or "spurious sūtras" (*weijing*) that are nevertheless "canonical" (that is, in agreement with the spirit of the *dharma* and therefore to be accepted in the canon) and, on the other, those sūtras that are "false" (that is, in conflict with established Buddhist teaching) and therefore to be excluded from the canon. Both types of sūtra are not "genuine" only when contrasted to the "original" sūtras composed in India (which were themselves obviously much later than the time of the Buddha). Thus, given the history of the canon and the broad definition of "authoritative sūtra" current among all Buddhists, it must have been difficult to find any good reason for excluding a text only on historical grounds—to say nothing of establishing those grounds.

Interpretation. Three major sets of principles become central to the latter development of Buddhist hermeneutics. These are the "four reliances" or strategies for understanding a text; the "four types of intentional and metaphoric language;" and the "four modes of reasoning." Since the last of these three doctrines falls more under the rubric of philosophy, we shall omit it from this discussion.

Authority and interpretation. The problem of establishing criteria of interpretation cannot be completely separated from that of the hierarchy of authority. The interaction of both spheres of hermeneutics is seen clearly in the doctrine of the four "points of reliance" (*pratisaraṇa*). This doctrine is found in several Mahāyāna versions, the most popular of which is the *Pratisaraṇa Sūtra,* a text no longer preserved in the original Sanskrit except in quotations. According to this text there are four criteria of interpretation: (1) relying on the nature of things (*dharma*), not on the opinion of a person; (2) relying on the meaning or purport (*artha*) of a text, not its letter; (3) relying on those passages that explicitly express the higher doctrine (*nītārtha*), not on those that do not express it explicitly; and (4) understanding by intuitive realization (*jñāna*), not by conceptual thought (*vijñāna*).

Some of these principles are restatements of the Buddhist tendency to emphasize personal realization as the ultimate source of understanding. But this tendency is not without significant implications for a theory of shared or communicable meaning. A sūtra now lost in the original Sanskrit but preserved in Chinese and Tibetan translations, the *Adhyāśayasaṃcodana Sūtra,* says, "whatever is well spoken [*subhāṣita*], has been spoken by the Buddha." This is perhaps the most extreme formulation of the Mahāyāna's view of the historical roots of its traditions. The system, nevertheless, is not totally open, for implicit in it are the earlier notions of the meaningfulness and appropriateness of the words of the Buddha (and by extension, of scripture). Conversely, then, "whatever is spoken by the Buddha has been well spoken" (as stated, for instance, by King Aśoka in his Bhābrā Rock Edict). Therefore, all passages of scripture must be meaningful—as well as agreeing with the *dharma* and leading to liberation. But it is not always apparent that scripture meets these standards. It is not evident that scripture speaks with one voice. The interpreter must therefore explain the hidden meanings that reveal the underlying unity of intention in scripture, whatever may be the grounds for its authenticity.

Types of intention. In his major works, Asaṅga mentions several methods of understanding that can be applied to scripture. Among these, the four types of explicit intention and the four types of implicit intention suggest the outlines of a hermeneutical theory. Implicit or contextual meanings (*abhiprāya*) appear to be alternatives for decoding a passage—words intending an analogy, words intending another time frame, words intending a shift in referent, and words intended only for a specific individual. The four types of hidden intention (*abhisaṃdhi*) show another aspect of the process of decoding the sacred text: introductory hidden intention (where the meaning is relevant only for the beginner), metaphysical hidden intention (where the meaning is a statement on the nature of reality), therapeutic hidden intention (where the meaning is realized by following the instructions in combating unhealthy actions or states of mind), and metaphorical intention (where the meaning is not the literal meaning, and often is paradoxical in character; e.g., referring to a virtue as a vice).

The concept of intentional speech brings to mind the third of the four points of reliance and the third principle of Tiantai exegesis. The common problem in these doctrines is best expressed by the classical theory of the two levels of meaning: the implicit or interpretable meaning (*neyārtha*) and the explicit or self-evident meaning (*nītārtha*). This is perhaps the most important doctrine of Buddhist hermeneutics. Under this doctrine, passages or complete texts can be taken at face value as statements of the "ultimate" teaching of the Buddha or they can be understood as teachings preached in response to provisional or individual needs, and hiding the core teacher under the textual surface, which then requires interpretation or clarification. If a passage is considered to be of the first type, then it is in no need of further elucidation. Its meaning (*artha*) has already been brought out (*nīta*) by the text itself. If a passage belongs to the second group, then the higher meaning can be found only through interpretation. It must be brought out (*neya*) from underneath the surface meaning, so to speak.

Only the Mahāsāṃghikas seem to have rejected this distinction, claiming that all words of the Buddha mean what they literally mean, and therefore need no interpretation. But this extreme position was rejected by other schools, including the more conservative Sthaviras (Theravādins, Sarvāstivādins, etc.).

This hermeneutical schema is closely related to the doctrine of the two levels of truth, the relative or conventional *saṃvṛtti* and the absolute or ultimate *paramārtha,* arguably first developed in the Mādhyamika school. But the fundamental distinction in the case of implicit and explicit meaning is between modes of intention and meaning, rather than between levels of reality. The point at issue is not whether the words of the text are the ultimate truth (they are not), but whether or not they point directly and unambiguously to it.

Upāya. Also central to Mahāyāna understanding of the religious text is the concept that all forms of discourse are ultimately *saṃvṛtti-satya* (or at best a lower level of *paramārtha*). This is based on both a radical critique of language (as in the Mādhyamika doctrine of "emptiness") and a revaluation of language as a means to an end. In the case of religious language, the end is liberation—the ultimate purpose and the ultimate meaning of all religious discourse. On the lips of the enlightened speaker, language becomes a "skillful means" (*upāya*), pointing at or eliciting (*udbhāvanā*) realization of the goal. The doctrine finds mythological expression when it is stated that the Buddha's preaching always conforms to the aspirations and maturity of his audience and that his pronouncements are instruments to guide sentient beings, not propositions expressing absolute truth. The religious text is *upāya* in at least three ways: it is a compassionate concession to the diversity, aspirations, and faculties of sentient beings; it is an instrument to be used in attaining the goal; and it is the expression of the liberating techniques of the Buddha.

Hermeneutics in the Tantras. Tantric hermeneutics presupposes Mahāyāna hermeneutics. Among other Mahāyāna principles, it accepts the four reliances and Asaṅga's eight types of intention. Of course, Tantric theories of interpretation also retain the fundamental distinction between implicit and explicit meaning. However, the intention is now clearly determined by the context of Esoteric practices. Thus we find again the close connection between interpretation and religious practice that characterizes much of Buddhist hermeneutics and that is also evident in scholastic speculations on the path (as in the *abhidharma*); but here orthopraxy becomes central to textual interpretation. Here too, the traditions consider that the "root" text (*mūlatantra*) requires an explanation (*ākhyānatantra*), but as each text and school has specific practical contexts it is never assumed that a given hermeneutical scheme can be applied to all texts.

The Tantric Candrakīrti (c. 650 CE) explains in his *Pradīpoddyotanā* the basic principles of his school's hermeneutical system as applied to the *Guhyasamāja Tantra.* He explains this "root" text by means of seven analytic procedures called "ornaments" or "preparations" (*saptaalaṃkāra*). All seven are used directly or indirectly to bring out the meaning of the text in interpretation or practice, but only two sets appear to bear directly on the issue of interpretation, being at the same time exegetical topics, hermeneutical tools, and levels of meaning. These are the six alternative interpretations of the meaning of words in a passage (*ṣaṭkoṭikaṃ vyākhyānam*; Tib., *mtha' drug* or *rgyas bshad mtha' rnam pa drug*), and the "fourfold explanation" (*caturvidham ākhyānam*; Tib., *tshul bzhi* or *bshad pa rnam pa bzhi*).

The six alternatives (with slight alterations to the order of the original) are: (1) standard terms used in a literal sense (*yathāruta*); (2) nonstandard or nonnatural terms (*aruta* or *na yathāruta*; i.e. esoteric jargon); (3) implicit meaning requiring interpretation (*neyārtha*); (4) explicit or evident meaning (*nītārtha*); (5) intentional or metaphoric language (*saṃdhyāya bhāṣitam, saṃdhyā bhāṣā*); and (6) nonintentional language (*no saṃdhyā*). Western scholars are not in agreement as to the hermeneutical function of this "ornament," but the Tibetan tradition considers the six alternatives an integral part of the interpretation theory unique to Tantra.

The "fourfold explanation," on the other hand, is generally accepted as a hermeneutical schema. In this case Candrakīrti makes an explicit connection between levels of meaning and the stages of spiritual growth (particularly according to the schema of *utpattikrama* and *sampannakrama,* the latter being divided into five stages or *pañcakrama*). The four explanations are: (1) literal, surface, or natural meaning (*akṣarārtha*); (2) shared meaning (*samastāṅgam*); (3) hidden (*garbhī*) meaning; and (4) ultimate (*kolikam*) meaning. The first type of meaning is shared by those on the path and those who have not entered it. The second type is shared by the Mahāyāna and the Tantra (specifically those in the "initial" or *utpatti* stage). The third type is open only to those in the first three stages of the fivefold higher path. The last level of meaning is open only to those who have advanced to the fourth and fifth stages.

This schema is a subtle application of the basic principle of the explicit and the interpretable meanings. One must note, however, that in Tantric exegesis a single text or passage can be both *nīta* and *neya,* depending on the receptor of the message. This entails not only a complex hermeneutics, but also the possibility that the so-called direct meaning (*nīta*) of one level requires interpretation (i.e., is *neyārtha*) for those who are at another level of the path.

Progressive revelation. The Tantric hermeneutical schema manifests, even more transparently than earlier theories, one of the basic assumptions of Buddhist views of meaning: meanings (and "truths") are a function of the audience as much as, or more than, a function of the intention of the author. If this principle is extended into the cosmic or historical dimension, then new hermeneutical concepts can be derived from the doctrine that the Buddha can preach simultaneously to various assemblies of celestial *bodhisattvas*, adapt his teaching to the needs and faculties of diverse living beings, or preach only one message (in words or silence) yet be understood in different ways. This doctrine, applied to the historical reality of the conflict of authorities, transmissions, and interpretations, provides reasons, albeit ex post facto, for choosing and justifying any particular version of the many "teachings of the Buddha."

The turnings of the wheel. In context, statements about relative teaching and ultimate teaching are more sectarian and polemical in spirit than their mere abstract formulations suggest. When a text states that all teachings of the Buddha are only skillful means or empty sounds there is always a conflicting claim to the ultimate validity of the text's own interpretation of the "one true teaching" underlying the "provisional teachings." This is evident in all the classical statements—the *Lotus Sūtra,* the *Laṅkāvatāra Sūtra,* the *Saṃdhinirmocana Sūtra,* and others. In some of these texts we see attempts to formulate a historical argument in favor of doctrinal claims. The Buddha, the argument goes, preached in two (or three) major periods that divide his ministry as to location, audience, and depth of the teaching. These major divisions in the Buddha's ministry are called "turnings of the wheel of *dharma.*" According to the most widely accepted doctrine (as presented in the *Saṃdhinirmocana Sūtra*), there were three "turnings": the Buddha first preached the Hīnayāna teachings in Deer Park in Banaras. Then he preached the doctrine of "emptiness" (i.e., the Mādhyamika teachings) at Vulture Peak in Rājagṛha. Last, he preached, in the same place but when his disciples were more mature, the doctrine of "mind-only" (i.e., the Yogācāra doctrines).

There is, of course, a Mādhyamika version of this story in which the third turning is in fact that of emptiness and the second the "idealistic" doctrine of the *Saṃdhinirmocana Sūtra.* There is also a late Tantric version that adds a fourth turning: the revelation of Mantrayāna at Dhānyakaṭaka. Nevertheless, the scriptural weight of the *Saṃdhinirmocana* was such that the scholastics could not ignore its clear statement. Thus, Tsong kha pa (1357–1419), in his *Legs bshad snying po,* goes through the most subtle arguments to show that the sūtra's ordering of the turnings does not imply a privileged position for the doctrine of mind-only.

The formulation of pseudohistorical apologetics and hermeneutical strategies became popular in China. The Indian schema of the Three Turnings was adopted in the schools of Sanlun and Faxiang, while others developed autonomous systems: Huayan and Niepan (The Teachings of the Five Periods) and Tiantai (The Eight Teachings in Five Periods). The last of these, a synthesis created by the Tiantai monk Zhanran (711–782), divided and interpreted the scriptures according to the four types of doctrine used in the Buddha's preaching (*huafa*: the doctrines of the *tripiṭaka,* the common doctrines, the special doctrines, and the perfect or complete doctrine) and his four teaching styles (*huayi*: direct, gradual, secret, and indeterminate or variable). These eight forms of teaching were used in different proportions and combinations during five periods (*wushi*) in the Buddha's ministry: the Buddhāvataṃsaka cycle, the Deer Park cycle, the Vaipulya cycle, the Prajñāpāramitā cycle, and the cycle of the *Lotus* and *Nirvāṇa* sūtras.

This is traditionally taken to imply that a given passage or statement can have multiple levels of meaning. But the function of these "classifications of the teachings" (*jiaopan*) was apologetic as well as hermeneutic. The method served as much to establish the preeminence of a particular school as to make sense of the diversity of teachings.

The ages of the dharma. A parallel development, based on Indian scriptures but characteristic of East Asian Buddhism, is the doctrine of the "Latter Age of the *Dharma*" (Chin., *mofa*; Jpn., *mappō*). The use of this doctrine as a hermeneutical device consists in proposing that changes in historical circumstances require a different interpretation of the tradition or a new definition of orthopraxy. This doctrine developed in China during the turbulent sixth century CE, which culminated in the persecutions of 574 and 578 and led many Buddhists to believe they were living in the last days of the Buddhist *dharma.*

Daochuo (562–645), for instance, believed that the "difficult" practices that were at the heart of traditional Buddhist ascetic and contemplative discipline had become meaningless in the "Latter Age." He therefore proposed that the scriptures prophesying this age justified a new dispensation that would only require the "easier" practices of Pure Land devotion. Matching Indian prophecies on the future of the Buddhist religion with his historical circumstances, he felt he could derive the authority for doctrinal change from the canonical prophecies on the decline of the *dharma,* and indirectly from changing historical circumstances themselves.

Zen demythologization. A different form of adaptation, responding nevertheless occasionally to the issue of the "decay" of *dharma,* was the Chan (Zen) emphasis on a "return" to orthopraxy. Here the general four principles of the *Adhyāśayasaṃcodana* are used in their most extreme forms. Partially inspired by Chinese interpretations of the Mādhyamika critique of language, partially moved by Daoist rhetoric, this was a movement that emphasized "ultimate meaning," "direct experience," and "freedom from words" to the point of appearing—if not becoming—iconoclastic. One can understand the movement as a process of adaptation of foreign ideas by demythologization (or, arguably, remythologization), assisted by the deconstructive tendencies built into Buddhist hermeneutical doctrines.

The basic object of meditation, the *gong'an* (Jpn., *kōan*), stands for the sacred utterance of enlightened beings, an *upāya,* a finger pointing at the moon, and the embodiment of different aspects of the putatively single realization common to all buddhas. This is, after all, a tradition that claims "a transmission outside the scriptures, not relying on words." Nevertheless, the Chan (Zen) tradition continues, in its *kōan* collections, the Buddhist predilection for the classification and collection of words "well spoken." Furthermore, these collections, like the ancient sūtras, require commentaries, and in them Chan also revives, albeit in a new form, the tendency to develop numerical frames of reference. The *Jen-t'ien yen-mu* (compiled by Zhizhao, 1188 CE) contains a number of classificatory systems that can be understood as either guides to meditation or hermeneutical grids to interpret the student's progress in practice. Many of these "matrices" remain in use today. For instance, the elusive teachings of Linji Yixuan (d. 867 CE) are presented in formulas such as "Linji's Three Phrases," extrapolated from his *Linji lu* (Recorded sayings). Modern Zen masters still study the "Eighteen Questions of Fenyang" (*Fengyang shih-pa wen*), a terse guide to the various ways one can "handle" (treat, investigate, and answer) a *kōan,* devised by the Song dynasty master Fenyang Shanzhao (947–1024). Also central to modern-day practice, and outlined in the *Jen-t'ien yen-mu,* are the "Five Ranks" (*wuwei*) of Dongshan (910–990) and Caoshan (840–901). One can see in these schemas a certain parallel to the techniques of *abhidharma.*

However, Zen also preserves the opposite Buddhist tendency, best represented by the teachings of the Japanese master Dōgen Kigen (1200–1253). Dōgen echoes a particularly novel interpretation of the doctrine of "whatever is well spoken" in his writings on sūtra (*Shōbōgenzō*; "Okyō" and "Dōtoku"): all things are sūtras, in all things is manifested the enlightenment of the buddhas of all times. This vision, inspired by the *Buddhāvataṃsaka Sūtra,* also raises the question of how this "sūtra," which is found in all things, can be opened, read, and understood. The Zen tradition of Dōgen has tended to find the answer in silent meditation.

Dōgen also summarizes much of what is characteristic of the Zen view on interpreting the tradition in a few terse lines in his *Gakudōyōshinshū*: reliance on scripture only leads to confusion, to projecting one's own preferences on the text. The only way to correct understanding is by divesting oneself of the self.

Other approaches to Zen practice are not necessarily as distant as they seem from Dogen's deceptively simple recommendation. Traditional Chinese and Japanese classifications and methods of "handling" or "studying" *kōan* were systematized by Hakuin Ekaku (1686–1768) and his disciples. The resulting system of *kōans* (five levels of miscellaneous *kōans*, plus the five *goi kōans*, and the Ten Precepts) has all the marks of Buddhist catechistic instincts; Hakuin himself, in his essay "Goi kōketsu" in the *Keisō dokuzui*, established exact correlations between some of these stages and Indian scholastic categories. Still, the system also emphasizes the quest for meaning in practice and a gradual detachment from doctrinal conceptions, as well as from meditation experiences. The crowning piece of the system, the last *kōan* (*matsugo no rōkan*) asks the disciple to reflect on the meaning of "completing" a system of *kōans*—that is, what should be the last question, once the adept has answered all questions?

Hermeneutics and apologetics. All Buddhists tend, even today, to claim a certain immunity from history, partly justified by the emphasis on the presence of *dharma* in all things and all times, by the plurality of buddhas, and by the obvious diversity and plasticity of the tradition. When first faced with historical criticism, coming from non-Buddhists such as Tominaga Nakamoto (1715–1746) in his *Shutsujō kōgo* (1745), some Japanese Buddhists (e.g., Murakami Senshō [1851–1929] in *Bukkyō tōitsu ron*) readily admitted that the Mahāyāna scriptures could not be the *ipsissima verba* of the Master. They based the orthodoxy of their tradition on concepts outlined above: the unity of the spirit, consistency in the goal, and the development of "skillful means." Some, for instance, Maeda Eun (1855–1930), also appealed to the doctrine that all teachings are implicit in the one, original, and ineffable teaching. The concept of levels of meaning is also used to preserve some form of religious discourse while claiming that the ultimate is beyond language and history. Mahāyāna Buddhists continue to appeal to these principles, relying fundamentally on the ancient apologetic and hermeneutic strategies outlined in this article. The Theravāda tradition, on the other hand, tends to build its hermeneutics on the reaffirmation of its conviction that its canon contains the words of the Buddha.

Buddhist hermeneutics and Western thought. At present, Buddhists in Asia tend to argue for their interpretations of traditional doctrines and texts using one or another of the above strategies. Attempts to develop or adapt more contemporary notions of hermeneutic theory or practice are generally rare. An interesting exception to this generalization is the adoption of positivistic notions of textual integrity and authenticity in a movement known as the "critical Buddhism" doctrine (*Hihan Bukkyō*). Developed by a small group of Japanese scholars in the last decades of the twentieth century, the movement appeared at times to hide an apologetic favoring a philosophical and scholastic reading of the tradition based on Madhyamaka principles. The movement has remained primarily an intellectual curiosity. Some Western scholars, on the other hand, have made a few faint incursions into a postmodern reading of Buddhist thought; but, again, without persuading most of their colleagues, and certainly with, so far, a very limited impact, or no influence, on their Asian colleagues. It is too early to predict in which direction living Buddhist interpretive practices will move in the near future.

SEE ALSO Buddhism, Schools of, article on Mahāyāna Philosophical Schools of Buddhism; Buddhist Philosophy; Hermeneutics; Language, article on Buddhist Views of Language; Treasure Tradition.

BIBLIOGRAPHY

Bharati, Agehananda. "Intentional Language in the Tantras." *Journal of the American Oriental Society* 81 (1961): 261–270. Interpretation of the meaning of *saṃdhyā bhāṣā*.

Bond, George D. "*Word of the Buddha*": *The Tipiṭaka and its Interpretation in Theravāda Buddhism.* Colombo, Sri Lanka, 1982. This is a survey of Theravāda theories of exegesis, based primarily, but not exclusively on the *Nettippakaraṇa*.

Buddhadāsa. "Everyday Language and Dhamma Language." In *Toward the Truth,* edited by Donald K. Swearer, pp. 56–86. Philadelphia, 1971. A modern Theravāda view on levels of language.

Cabezón, José I. "The Concepts of Truth and Meaning in the Buddhist Scriptures." *Journal of the International Association of Buddhist Studies* 4 (1981): 7–23. Deals mostly with Mahāyāna views of levels of truth and meaning.

Chappell, David W. "Introduction to the 'T'ien-t'ai ssu-chiao-i'." *Eastern Buddhist,* new series 9 (1976): 72–86. Although this paper is a survey of the content and history of a Tiantai scholastic manual, much of the discussion centers on the nature of Tiantai hermeneutical schemata.

Doherty, Gerald. "Form is Emptiness: Reading the Diamond Sutra." *Eastern Buddhist,* n. s. 16 (1983): 114–123. A bold analysis of this famous sūtra from the point of view of deconstructive theory.

Gregory, Peter N. "Chinese Buddhist Hermeneutics: The Case of Hua-yen." *Journal of the American Academy of Religion* 51 (1983): 231–249. On the philosophical presuppositions of Huayan hermeneutics.

Ishizu Teruji. "Communication of Religious Inwardness and a Hermeneutic Interpretation of Buddhist Dogma." In *Religious Studies in Japan,* edited by the Nihon Shukyo Gakkai, pp. 3–21. Tokyo, 1959. This paper is a good example of an extreme ahistorical view on the meaning of Buddhist doctrines.

Lamotte, Étienne. *Saṃdhinirmocana Sūtra: L'explication des mystéres.* Louvain, Belgium, 1935. Translation of one of the most important sources for the doctrine of the Three Turnings and the distinction of explicit and implicit meanings. Lamotte also translated the first and most important half of the *Mahāprajñāpāramitā-upadeśa-śāstra* as *Le traité de la grande vertu de sagesse*, 5 vols. (Louvain, Belgium, 1944–1980). This work is attributed to a Mahāyānist Nāgārjuna, who was evidently trained in the Sarvāstivāda tradition. Lamotte also has two studies on questions in Buddhist hermeneutics: "La critique d'authenticité dans le bouddhisme," in *Indian antiqua*, edited by F. D. K. Bosch, pp. 213–222 (Leiden, 1947); and "La critique d'interprétation dans le bouddhisme," *Annuaire de l'institut de philologie et d'histoire orientales et slaves*, vol. 9: *Mélanges Henri Grégoire*, pp. 341–361 (Brussels, 1949).

Lopez, Donald S., Jr. *Elaborations on Emptiness: Uses of the Heart Sūtra*. Princeton, 1996.

Lopez, Donald S., Jr., ed. *Buddhist Hermeneutics*. Honolulu, 1988.

MacQueen, Graeme. "Inspired Speech in Early Mahāyāna Buddhism." *Religion* 11 (1981): 303–319; 12 (1982): 49–65. An exploration of the importance of *pratibhāṇa* for Mahāyāna notions of canonical authenticity.

Ñāṇamoli, Bhikkhu, trans. *The Guide*. London, 1962. A translation of Kaccāyana's *Nettippakaraṇa*, the classical Theravāda manual of exegesis. The attribution of this work to Kaccāyana, the Buddha's disciple, has been questioned by modern scholarship.

Pye, Michael, and Robert Morgan, eds. *The Cardinal Meaning: Essays in Comparative Hermeneutics; Buddhism and Christianity*. The Hague, 1973.

Ray, Reginald. "Buddhism: Sacred Text Written and Realized." In *The Holy Book in Comparative Perspective*, edited by Frederick M. Denny and Rodney L. Taylor, pp. 148–180. Columbia, S.C., 1985

Schoening, J. D. "Sutra Commentaries in Tibetan Translation." In *Tibetan Literature: Studies in Genre*, edited by José I. Cabezón and Roger R. Jackson, pp. 118ff. Ithaca, N.Y., 1996.

Steinkellner, Ernst. "Remarks on Tantristic Hermeneutics." In *Proceedings of the Csoma de Kőrös Memorial Symposium*, edited by Louis Ligeti, pp. 445–458. Budapest, 1978. Outline of some aspects of Candrakīrti's exegetical and hermeneutical theory.

Thurman, Robert A. F. "Buddhist Hermeneutics." *Journal of the American Academy of Religion* 46 (1978): 19–39. This is an outline of the principles of Buddhist hermeneutics based on the *Legs bhsad snying po*, a work translated by Thurman as *Tsong Khapa's Speech of Gold in the Essence of True Eloquence* (Princeton, 1984).

Wayman, Alex. "Concerning *Saṃdhā-bhāṣā/saṃdhibhāṣā/samdhyā bhāṣā*." In *Mélanges d'indianisme à la mémoire de Louis Renou*, pp. 789–796. Paris, 1968. Summarizes much of the debate on this technical term. Wayman's own thesis was developed further in "Twilight Language and a Tantric Song," in his *The Buddhist Tantra* (London, 1973), pp. 128–135.

Luis O. Gómez (1987 and 2005)

BUDDHIST ETHICS.

Buddhist ethics is a term of convenience that we may use here to describe systems of morality as well as styles of moral reasoning that have emerged in Buddhist traditions. Moral reflection has taken various forms in Buddhist civilizations, beginning with Buddhism's origins in South Asia two and a half millennia ago to its gradual spread across most of Asia through very diverse cultural contexts. While several patterns in moral thinking broadly shared by most or all forms of Buddhism may be suggested at the outset, deeper investigation must attend to particular expressions of Buddhist ethics in their historical and contextual diversity.

Enduring Patterns across Buddhist Traditions. From one perspective, Buddhist moral theorists are concerned with actions (*karma*), which are deemed to determine one's future experiences in this and future lives in the round of rebirths (*saṃsāra*). Actions that are prompted by virtuous and discerning intentions yield beneficial results both in this life and in the next. Conversely, actions that are rooted in bad states of mind—in particular, greed, hatred, and delusion—are harmful to self and others and thus result in unfortunate rebirths for those who commit them. This concern with action and its consequences is reflected in a list of basic norms known as the "five precepts" (*śīla*), to which Buddhists often commit formally in religious ceremonies; these prohibit taking life, theft, sexual misconduct, false speech, and the consumption of intoxicants. More positively, Buddhists have looked for moral guidance to the noble eightfold path, which, in addition to describing key elements of wisdom and contemplation crucial for the soteriological path, also articulates a positive description of ideal moral conduct in terms of right action, right speech, and right livelihood. Such descriptions enjoin truthfulness and nonviolence as defining "right" practice.

The emphasis on actions, however, should not obscure the intensive interest Buddhist thinkers have taken in the virtues and dispositions that produce them. Since Buddhists locate moral culpability in intention and volition rather than solely in the action itself, the operations of moral choice are central to ethical reflection. Buddhism offers a close analysis of mind, investigating the emotions, dispositions, and tendencies that drive our action and shape the world. Early Buddhism produced a very sophisticated moral psychology called *abhidharma*, which articulated an analysis of the constituents of the mind and their relationships that are crucial for the development of virtuous dispositions. This moral psychology, as well as other discourses on the mind, assert that the key to developing moral character is to replace negative and harmful mental states and emotions with positive and other-regarding mental states.

In many traditions of Buddhism, meditation practices are deployed to generate beneficial emotions and dispositions, providing practitioners with techniques that allow them to "abide" in particularly morally efficacious states, in particular, compassion (trembling at and allaying the distress of others), loving kindness (seeking the happiness of others), sympathetic joy (celebrating others' success), and equanimity (acquiring impartiality). By developing through introspection and contemplation one's mental culture one becomes sensitive to one's emotional life and can then change habitual and harmful states of mind. Thus one cultivates a developed moral subjectivity, a new awareness of oneself as a moral agent.

For example, a meditation practice widely attested in diverse Buddhist traditions aims to cultivate loving kindness towards others (including enemies) through the"mother contemplation." This meditation involves reflecting upon the nature of the endless chain of rebirths, wherein we have all, given the vast infinity of time in *saṃsāra,* been related to one another in previous lives. In beginning the contemplation, one should consider the tender ministrations of one's mother when one was an infant in this life. Tsong kha pa (1357–1419), an important Tibetan authority on meditation and morality, describes this recollection:

> The first thing I did was take a long period in her womb. Thereafter, in the time of my rearing, my downy baby hair pressed against her warm flesh. Her ten fingers gave me recreation. She suckled me with the milk from her breast. With her mouth she fed me. My snivel she wiped from my mouth. Wiping away with her hand my filth, she succored me wearilessly by diverse means. Moreover, my own capacity falling short, she gave me food and drink in the time of hunger and thirst; clothes when I shivered; money when I was "broke." (Wayman, 1991, p. 47)

In the practice one considers one's incapacity and vulnerability as an infant and the crucial acts of care that one's mother (or other caregiver) rendered. Such reflections create a subjectivity of gratitude and loving appreciation for one's parent. From these contemplations, the practice is extended to consider that all beings have at one time been one's mother and have partaken in this role of caregiving and generosity. Thus, it would be unbecoming to harbor angry or hostile thoughts against so-called enemies now, and instead one comes to be suffused with gratitude and loving kindness towards them.

The facts of our interconnected relationships with other beings often provide the resources from which moral disposition and character are seen to develop. Of great concern for Buddhists is the importance of seeking out wise and good friends and teachers for guidance. The Buddha once asserted that "in fact the whole of the holy life is friendship, closeness, and association with good people" (*Saṃyutta Nikāya,* vol. 2), and an essential ingredient in the development of character is seeking out a "good friend" (*kalyāna-mitra*), a wise counselor who can direct one in one's moral and religious progress. The supreme "good friend" of course is the Buddha himself, and we find in his story Buddhism's attentiveness to matters of character through studies of moral heroism. The Buddha's life story provides a locus for investigation into the development of moral agency. In traditional accounts his life story begins many eons ago when he first makes the aspiration to become a buddha, and then embarks upon a long and arduous spiritual journey across many lives as a *bodhisattva* in which he masters ten "perfections"—generosity, the precepts of morality (*śīla*), renunciation, wisdom, effort, patience, truth, resolution, loving-kindness, and equanimity. The dénouement of this moral and religious quest culminates in his "awakening" (*bodhi,* or *nirvāṇa*) in his life as Siddhārtha Gautama and his establishing of the *dharma* in our era. Buddhists admire this image of human perfection and hold it up as a model for contemplation on the Buddha's qualities and the narrative contexts in which his character was forged. Morality here is envisioned not as a matter of simply adhering to duties and obligations to avoid wrong action, but as aiming ever upwards in developing one's character and virtue.

Since the Buddha, as fully awakened, is no longer accessible as a living guide, one may turn to other resources for community support of one's moral development. In many forms of Buddhism, the best place to find a good friend is the monastic community (*saṃgha*), a group of men and women dedicating their lives to the religious quest in cooperation with others. They are governed by the monastic code *(vinaya),* which functions as a normative guide for an ideal community. The monastic discipline and its commentaries comprise critical ethical reflection in considering how this community works together harmoniously, how it garners through its exemplary behavior the support of lay Buddhists, and how it deals with breaches in its code of conduct. In its scholastic exegesis on discerning the criteria for determining culpability in violations of the monastic rules, the *vinaya* literature produces a legalistic style of ethical reasoning that carefully parses the nuances of action and intention.

Philosophical doctrines about the nature of personhood are also crucial to Buddhist moral thought. Buddhists deny any notion of a permanent, autonomous selfhood or soul that withstands the changes to which all things in *saṃsāra* are subject; a person is nothing more than a collection of constantly changing, but causally connected physical and mental phenomena comprised of five "aggregates": physical form, perception, feeling, mental activities, and consciousness. The refusal to grant any notion of a permanent, unchanging personal identity or selfhood has important ethical implications. First, the no-self (*anātman*) doctrine can undermine the selfishness and false sense of individual autonomy that is at the root of much wrongdoing and harmful action. Secondly, this view of personhood affirms one's interconnected dependence on the world, the conditionality and contingency of one's identity, and the pliability of personhood and capacity for change that are vital for a strong sense of moral agency.

This view of the person is accompanied by an understanding of reality that emphasizes the interrelatedness and mutual dependence of all life (*pratītya-samutpāda*), which is both the cause of our suffering and yet reveals the opportunities for emancipation. As part of an intricate web of relationships with other beings (including nonhuman animals and beings beyond those whom we know in this life alone) we find ourselves in networks of reciprocal obligations. Buddhist thinkers also argue that our interconnectedness with all beings reveals a basic sympathy natural to our condition, in which our fate is intimately tied up with that of others. This doctrine is thus a key resource for decentering self-interest and nurturing compassion.

With these shared patterns briefly sketched we turn now to particular expressions of Buddhist moral thinking as they have developed historically in specific Buddhist traditions.

THERAVĀDA ETHICS. Theravāda, the dominant form of Buddhism present today in Sri Lanka, Thailand, Burma (Myanmar), Cambodia, and Laos, is one of the earliest traditions of Buddhism and has an ancient canonical literature associated with it in the Pali language. As a great intellectual civilization centered in Sri Lanka for well over two thousand years, Theravāda has much to contribute to questions of ethics. One schema of the moral life that achieved sustained scholarly reflection among both ancient and modern commentators is the framework of the eightfold path, which articulates moral and spiritual progress through three stages: moral precepts (*sīla*), concentration (*samādhi*), and wisdom (*paññā*). The great fifth-century commentator Buddhaghosa framed his vision of the ideal Buddhist life in these terms, depicting morality as the basis and foundation of all religious progress, even while it continues to find fuller expression as one advances into the highest reaches of spiritual awakening and becomes an *arhat*, an awakened one. The *arhat* is entirely free of the three "defilements" (greed, hatred, and delusion), and is thus considered morally perfect.

While Buddhaghosa intends his model to apply principally to monastics—those who have dedicated their lives to this pursuit—Theravāda offers other resources for describing and reflecting on lay morality and the features of a broad social ethic. One text, very well-known throughout the Theravāda world, that speaks to a range of moral goods is the *Maṅgala Sutta*. The text records thirty-eight diverse prima facie values ranging from avoiding fools and associating with the wise, caring for one's mother and father, and practicing a blameless livelihood, to moral and ascetic practices associated with the monastic life. No single person would be capable of practicing all of these in a single life, as some of them mutually conflict (such as engaging in a blameless livelihood and being a monastic), yet the text and its extensive commentarial tradition refuse to rank these values and insist that each is "the highest auspiciousness." The text thus affirms different human social roles and moral capacities, sketching the contours of a model human society. The commentaries engage a "particularist" mode of moral reasoning, refusing to proceed from general principles or criteria, but instead treating a range of diverse moral values on their own distinct terms and in a manner highly sensitive to context (see Hallisey, 1996).

An important element of both personal and social morality is gift giving (*dāna*). Generosity to monks and nuns, as well as to the poor and needy, is a key Buddhist value, as it simultaneously sustains the community and dislodges greed and attachment to material things. Scholastic reflections on gift giving provide sophisticated ethical treatment of the motivations and intentions prompting gifts, the face-to-face relationships gifts forge, and the proper use of material wealth. Theravadins have also considered moral values associated with the just administration of state power. The ideal of the righteous king (*dhammarāja, cakkavatti*), promotes practices of governance that adhere to the precepts, prohibit onerous taxation, limit state violence, establish a viable justice system, and secure protection, prosperity, and peace for the people. When such a righteous king sits in power, order and harmony will naturally prevail at every level of society.

MAHĀYĀNA AND VAJRAYĀNA ETHICS. The emergence of Mahāyāna in India and Central Asia in the second century CE created a paradigm shift in Buddhist approaches to morality. Moreover, when Chinese pilgrims came to India to explore Buddhism and bring it back to China, they were drawn primarily to Mahāyāna teachings, and thus it was predominantly Mahāyāna that spread to China, and thence to Korea, Japan, and Vietnam, where it took diverse forms as it developed and adapted to East Asian civilizations. As Mahāyāna eventually gained ascendancy in India, it gave rise to yet another reformulation of the Buddhist path, known as Vajrayāna, traditions of which took root predominantly in Tibet, Nepal, and their neighboring Himalayan kingdoms.

The early Indian Mahāyāna thinkers were not satisfied with what they interpreted as the narrow ideal of the *arhat*, that is, the pursuit of one's own spiritual awakening and perfection through following the Buddha's teaching as a *śrāvaka*, a "hearer" or mere follower. Mahāyāna critics preferred instead the model of the Buddha himself, who, through countless eons from the moment of his aspiration for buddhahood, strove for a height of perfection that entailed not only his own release from *saṃsāra*, but also the teaching and saving of countless others. Thus the ideal of the *bodhisattva* came to be regarded as the pinnacle of Buddhist practice and teaching. Laypeople and monastics alike could strive to become *bodhisattvas*, taking a vow not to rest until they had secured the salvation of all beings as they practiced perfections over innumerable lifetimes.

This exalted ethic was advanced through a critique of non-Mahāyāna traditions, which were construed as providing a morality limited in both scope and conception. Mahāyāna theorists posited three tiers of morality that demonstrated the supposed shortcomings of non-Mahāyāna ethics: (1) The ethics of restraint, which includes the precepts and the monastic code; (2) the ethics of cultivating good states, through the practice of the perfections; and (3) the ethics of altruism, the tireless effort of striving for all beings (Keown, 1992, pp. 137–142). In the Mahāyāna view, the path of the *śrāvaka*, the follower, does not advance beyond the first tier, the mere refraining from harmful actions through rules of constraint. The *bodhisattva*, in contrast, strives to master the perfections and embrace a self-abnegating generosity toward all beings. The altruism described in Mahāyāna texts knows no limits. The eighth-century philosopher Śāntideva, for example, describes this practice as a willingness to offer oneself up entirely for the benefit of others: "I make over this body to all embodied beings to do with as they please. . . . May I be sustenance of many kinds for the realm of beings throughout space, until all have attained release" (Crosby and Skilton, 1995, p. 21). Upon taking the vow for awakening, the aspiring *bodhisattva* is committed to working unceasingly for the benefit of others through renunciation of his or her own interests; indeed awakening itself is conceived as renunciation of self through love of others.

While the overarching moral value associated with this vision is compassion, the *bodhisattva* works gradually—across many lives—to master ten distinct perfections. The list of perfections differs to some degree from the standard list of the Buddha's perfections, and includes the stages of the *bodhisattva* path: generosity, moral precepts, patience, vigor, meditation, wisdom, skillful means, vows, power, and omniscient knowledge. According to some formulations, the first six may be perfected in human states, but the last four require the supernatural range of a celestial being; in stage seven, one is reborn as a celestial *bodhisattva* endowed with superior powers of skillful means and knowledge that expand one's sphere of influence.

The perfection of skillful means (*upāya*) is particularly interesting from the ethical point of view. This virtue involves the mastery of a kind of situational intelligence and beneficial expedience whereby a *bodhisattva* is sometimes authorized, or even obliged, to violate the precepts in order to bring about a greater good. A classic example is a *bodhisattva* who kills a murderous thief on board a ship who designs to kill the passengers and rob them. The *bodhisattva* reasons that it would be heinous to allow the robber to carry out his design, but if he were to alert the passengers they would kill the robber, effecting their own bad karmic results. Thus the *bodhisattva* kills the robber himself, saving all present from the effects of their own murderous intentions. Of course, the *bodhisattva* is prepared to suffer in hell for countless eons as a result of breaking the precept that prohibits taking life; this is regarded as the price of his altruistic and self-denying impulse to take on the sufferings of others through prevent ing them from committing any harmful deeds. Discussions of skillful means thus demonstrate not only the far reaches of a *bodhisattva*'s compassion, but also a principled resistance to an absolutist moral code, perceiving instead moral demands that take in the complexities of circumstances in such a way that may require subverting normally universal moral rules. Of course, only advanced *bodhisattvas*, well established in insight and compassion, are enjoined to practice skillful means, and breaching the precepts willy-nilly is not sanctioned.

In addition to the *bodhisattva* ideal, developments in philosophy undergirded new approaches to morality in Mahāyāna traditions. Mahāyāna wisdom literature and philosophical discourses expounded the doctrines of "emptiness" (*śūnyatā*), the awareness that all factors of existence are interdependent and empty of their own, independent reality, and "suchness" (*tathatā*), the experience of things as they truly are, without any conceptual superimposition on them. *Nirvāṇa* comes to be seen as not so much as an independent state apart from *saṃsāra*, but as true awareness that embraces all things in their emptiness and suchness. Since true insight into reality transcends ordinary conceptions of good and bad, these religious teachings sometimes relativized conventional ethical distinctions.

As Buddhism spread eastward, many of these ideas were institutionalized in the tradition of Chan, or Zen as it was known in Japan. In addition, Zen embraced a doctrine that had first appeared in the Indian sūtras of the *tathāgata-garbha*, the seed or potentiality (or, in some formulations, the actuality) of awakening that is said to reside in all beings. Awakening is then not a matter of gradual ascent, but rather becoming aware of one's already awakened buddha-nature. Morality is thus conceived not as a disciplined path to spiritual progress, but rather as a manifestation of one's true awakened state.

The lofty Mahāyāna ideal of the *bodhisattva* followed two contrasting trajectories as it spread eastward. On the one hand, we see in this ideal a tremendous and perhaps unequaled exaltation of human possibility and agency. On the other hand, with the emergence of celestial *bodhisattvas*, certain traditions within Mahāyāna take on the flavor of savior religions. One might come to perceive oneself not as an aspiring *bodhisattva*, but conversely, as the beneficiary of the exertions of powerful *bodhisattvas*. The Mahāyāna sūtras depict a new pantheon of savior beings in an expanded cosmology that includes not only celestial *bodhisattvas*, but also multiple buddhas residing in other realms in the cosmos. The historical Buddha Gautama was reconceived to be one of many, indeed, infinite buddhas, many of whom preside in Pure Lands. These Pure Lands come to be objects of wonder and hope, with Buddhists in East Asia sometimes aspiring not so much to become *bodhisattvas*, but to be reborn, often through the intercession of *bodhisattvas* and buddhas, in these bliss realms wherein awakening is easily attained through direct access to the compassion and wisdom of a buddha.

These alternative visions of human agency spawned by the early Mahāyāna teachings come to be articulated and fully crystallized in sharp contrast to one another in Japanese sectarian traditions. Zen offers what has been described as a "self-power" practice, wherein moral and spiritual agency is found through one's own resources. In contrast, the Pure Land tradition initiated by Hōnen (1133–1212) and his disciple Shinran (1173–1262), advocates a religiosity devoid entirely of self-power and human agency, instead requiring only that one embrace one's incapacity and look for salvation to the agency of an "other-power," in this case that of the Buddha Amida. For Shinran, humans are helpless and depraved, too deeply mired in passion, hatred, and delusion to effect their own salvation, at least not in our age in which the *dharma* is in decline. One's only hope is to say the *nembutsu*, that is, evoke Amida Buddha's saving grace and compassion, whereby one may be reborn in Amida's Pure Land. Salvation is thus not a matter of morality and good works, and in fact it has particular relevance to the "sinner." In the *Tannisho*, Shinran is said to assert: "Even a good person can attain birth in the Pure Land, so it goes without saying that an evil person will" (Hirota, 1982, p. 23). Shinran is here exalting the faith of the depraved evil person who has no pretence of good works and thus must rely solely on faith in the grace of other-power.

Perhaps not surprisingly, this religiosity based on other-power came to have widespread appeal and has come to be one of the most popular forms of Buddhism in Japan, as it opens salvation to those who are unable or unwilling to embrace the arduous practices of monastic life, meditation, ritual, and so on that have often been the privilege of the elite. Perhaps also not surprisingly, the teachings of Hōnen and Shinran sometimes gave rise to those who embraced "licensed evil," since good works are irrelevant to salvation and the wicked are saved through merely saying the *nembutsu*. Very subtle and sophisticated scholastic traditions of ethical reflection and religious doctrine grew out of these developments in which Pure Land thinkers sought to respond to antinomian challenges and construe morality not as a means of salvation to be sure, but nevertheless as a valuable expression of gratitude for it.

Another important Japanese sectarian tradition is Nichiren Buddhism, named after its thirteenth-century founder. Like the other traditions of his day, Nichiren (1222–1282) adopted a view of history based on a notion of the "degeneration of the *dharma*" (*mappō*). This view of history provides a pessimistic account of human capacity with regard to following the precepts. But Nichiren's response differs from the Pure Land's in that he advocates active devotion to the *Lotus Sūtra*, an important Mahāyāna text. This devotion to the *Lotus Sūtra*, expressed in chanting "*Namu Myōhō-renge-kyō*," aligns oneself with the essence of Buddhist truth and awakening, and thus is thought to bring peace, justice, and spiritual renewal to the world.

Vajrayāna is sometimes conceived as being contiguous with Mahāyāna, and other times to transcend it as the fulfillment and highest level of Buddhism. It accepts Mahāyāna's philosophical ideas and its pantheon of savior deities (and indeed adds to them), but evinces some impatience with the long and arduous path of the *bodhisattva*. Instead Vajrayāna offers, sometimes through dramatic ritual and meditative techniques under the tutelage of a trusted teacher, a "fast path" to awakening. The fast path involves transcending dualities and conventional distinctions, including that between good and evil, thus exhibiting certain Mahāyāna impulses to downplay the value of renunciation and preceptive discipline in favor of seeking direct realization.

In Tibet, Vajrayāna Buddhism became a central, if not the central, element of the political culture, bringing to bear ethical questions of how Buddhist power should be configured. Buddhism in Tibet developed among sectarian traditions that often vied with one another over matters of ethical concern, particularly over the matter of whether, and in what ways, monastic and ethical discipline contributes to the advancement of mystical insight. The establishment of vast monastic universities, which Tibet inherited from India, contributed to an advanced intellectual climate conducive for debating these and other matters of religious import.

BUDDHIST ETHICS IN MODERN CONTEXTS. Buddhism's encounters with modernity provide occasion for examining applied ethics, as Buddhist values and principles come to be applied to situations that traditional authorities may not have fully anticipated. We might think of modernity's impact in Asia as generating several distinct but related transformations: the rise and preeminence of a scientific rationality and the fruits of scientific and technological inquiry (in medicine, warfare, and industry); new alignments of power, beginning with colonialism through much of Asia and yielding eventually to nationalism and independent nation-states; the advent of new political and economic ideologies and sometimes bloody experimentation with communism, socialism, and totalitarianism; the rise of Western hegemony through global capitalism and consumerism, with their often exploitative relationship to human labor and ecosystems; and new ideas from the West about gender equality, human rights, and democracy. These challenges and opportunities have given rise to much creative work in recent Buddhist ethical thought.

Efforts to modernize Buddhism arose as reformist movements in the nineteenth and twentieth centuries, primarily in Theravāda countries. Modernizing Buddhism was taken to mean excising its supernatural and mythical elements and downplaying the importance of devotional worship, while emphasizing Buddhism's rational, rule-oriented practices for monastics, and the purity of its ethical norms for all Buddhists. In the decades following Indian independence in 1947, Buddhism was configured in almost entirely social-ethical terms by the leader of India's untouchables, B. R. Ambedkar (1891–1956), who turned to Buddhism as an ideology of social liberation for his people. Another example of such a modernizing effort that shaped Buddhism into primarily a social ethic was promulgated by the Sinhala reformer Anagārika Dharmapāla (1864–1933) as part of his vision of a purified Sinhala Buddhist nationalism. He emphasized new pastoral roles for monks as caretakers of their communities, and new roles for the laity that entailed a bourgeois "this-worldly asceticism." These developments bore the imprint of the colonial government and Christian missionary influences they were seeking to displace. Other expressions of Buddhist modernism arose through the new literary genre of the novel, wherein multiple and conflicting perspectives may be explored simultaneously, new senses of national, ethnic, and religious communities may be developed, and new forms of social critique and prospects for social change may be voiced.

Today Buddhists from across the Buddhist world (which now includes the West as Buddhism spreads across the globe) are retooling traditional Buddhist thought and practice to address contemporary problems through social activism. This movement has been termed *engaged Buddhism* by one its foremost proponents, Thich Nhat Hanh (b. 1926), an activist monk promoting peace and nonviolence both in his country during the Vietnam War and globally. The various expressions of engaged Buddhism share the view that Buddhism requires a moral engagement with the world rather than a retreat from it; moreover, Buddhism's deep sensitivity to suffering properly yields political, economic, and social activism to bring Buddhist contributions to rectifying the major ills of our time. In addition to Thich Nhat Hanh, prominent engaged Buddhists include Buddhadāsa Bhikkhu (1906–1993), a Thai reformist monk whose social teachings critique materialism, advocate a Buddhist socialism, and promote harmonious relationships with nature; Sulak Sivaraksa (b. 1933), a Thai lay intellectual who challenges the structures and ideologies of international capitalism and consumerism that exploit people and resources particularly in developing countries like Thailand; and A. T. Ariyaratna (b. 1931), whose Sarvodaya Shramadana movement in Sri Lanka promotes social regeneration in rural and village contexts through active lay Buddhist commitments to service. In addition, there are a number of activists working to redress the role of women in contemporary Buddhism by organizing to reestablish the Theravāda order of fully ordained nuns (*bhikkhunīs*) and confronting traditional patriarchal structures and institutions that limit or devalue the roles and contributions of women in Buddhist societies.

The conferring of the Nobel Peace Prize on two Buddhist figures—in 1989 to the Dalai Lama (b. 1935), the spiritual and political head of the Tibetan people in exile since the Chinese invasion of Tibet in the 1950s, and in 1991 to Aung San Suu Kyi (b. 1945), the leader of the nonviolent democratic movement against the repressive military regime in Burma—has brought international attention and respect to these exemplars of Buddhist leadership and their causes. In addition, contemporary Buddhist scholars are engaging the political and social discourses of our time in Buddhist terms, in ways that challenge and critique existing paradigms for democracy, economics, and scientific and technological development. The work of Venerable P. A. Payutto (b. 1939), in particular, expresses very sophisticated ideals of liberty, democracy, and economic activity informed by Buddhist ethical principles.

Another promising avenue of research in Buddhist ethics that has gained considerable momentum in the last few years involves a collaboration of Buddhist scholars and cognitive scientists, under the leadership of the Dalai Lama. The collaboration brings to the international and scientific community insights from Buddhist contemplative practice, as well as the intellectual resources Buddhism offers in how it parses mental and affective phenomena. Of particular pertinence for ethics is the collaborators' conviction that Buddhism can contribute to understanding and better management of mental states and emotions, which in the Buddhist view, lie at the root of action. The collaboration is intended to yield practical advances in moral psychology, human development, prisoner rehabilitation, and education.

See Also Buddhas and Bodhisattvas, article on Ethical Practices Associated with Buddhas and Bodhisattvas.

Bibliography

Fine overviews of Buddhist ethics may be found in Peter Harvey's *An Introduction to Buddhist Ethics* (Cambridge, U.K., 2000) and Hammalawa Saddhatissa's *Buddhist Ethics* (London, 1997). Phra Prayudh Payutto's *Buddhadhamma: Natural Laws and Values for Life*, translated by Grant Olson (Albany, N.Y., 1995), is a brilliant account of Buddhist ethics from a modern Theravāda authority; his *Buddhist Economics: A Middle Way for the Market Place* (Bangkok, 1998), is an important application of Buddhist ideas to economic justice. The international online *Journal of Buddhist Ethics* (http://jbe.gold.ac.uk/), started in 1994, has done much to expand the field of Buddhist ethics. On questions of metaethics, consult Damien Keown's *The Nature of Buddhist Ethics* (New York, 1992), and for a contrasting approach through a discussion of the *Maṅgala Sutta*, see Charles Hallisey's "Ethical Particularlism in the Theravāda," *Journal of Buddhist Ethics* 3 (1996). Anthropologists, working especially in Theravāda societies, led the study of Buddhist ethics a generation ago in ways that still frame much scholarly work in the field; see Melford Spiro, *Buddhism and Society: A Great Tradition and Its Burmese Vicissitudes*, 2d ed. (Berkeley, 1982); Richard Gombrich, *Precept and Practice: Traditional Buddhism in the Rural Highlands of Ceylon* (Oxford, 1971); and Winston King, *In the Hope of Nibbana* (La Salle, Ill., 1964).

For useful translations of important Mahāyāna texts on the *bodhisattva* ideal consult Tsong kha pa in *The Ethics of Tibet*, translated by Alex Wayman (Albany, N.Y., 1991), and *The Bodhicaryāvatāra of Śāntideva,* translated by Kate Crosby and Andrew Skilton (Oxford, 1995). On Zen ethics see T. P. Kasulis, *Zen Action/Zen Person* (Honolulu, 1981), and for an accessible Pure Land text, consult *Tannisho: A Primer*, translated by Dennis Hirota (Kyoto, 1982). A useful anthology of studies of contemporary movements of Buddhist activism is *Engaged Buddhism: Buddhist Liberation Movements in Asia*, edited by Christopher Queen and Sallie King (Albany, N.Y., 1996); on Buddhist women's activism see Karma Lekshe Tsomo, *Buddhist Women and Social Justice: Ideals, Challenges, and Achievements* (Albany, N.Y., 2004). On Buddhist modernisms consult *Modern Buddhism*, edited by Donald Lopez (London, 2004). See *Contemporary Buddhist Ethics*, edited by Damien Keown (Surrey, U.K., 2000), for work on contemporary issues such as human rights, euthanasia, and the environmental crisis. On the collaboration between Buddhists and Western neuroscientists, see the Mind and Life Institute website at www.mindandlife.org for further resources.

MARIA HEIM (2005)

BUDDHIST MEDITATION

This entry consists of the following articles:

TIBETAN BUDDHIST MEDITATION
EAST ASIAN BUDDHIST MEDITATION

BUDDHIST MEDITATION: TIBETAN BUDDHIST MEDITATION

Buddhist contemplative traditions have thrived in Tibet since at least the seventh century CE, and have taken an astonishing variety of forms ranging over the entire spectrum of Indian and Central Asian Buddhist traditions. This diversity is usually organized under the rubric of "three vehicles" in Buddhism—the Lesser (Hīnayāna), Great (Mahāyāna), and Adamantine (Vajrayāna) vehicles. The historical challenge was to integrate this diversity into cogent systems of practice, and especially how to integrate exoteric Buddhist contemplation based on canonical sūtras, and esoteric forms of Buddhist meditation derived from canonical Tantras. Most Tibetan traditions came to see the Tantric methods as intrinsically superior in their capacity to generate more rapid realization due to their directness. By the thirteenth century, Tibet had established itself as the international center of esoteric Buddhism, and alone developed the full spectrum of Buddhist esoteric contemplative practices. We have thus structured the present survey of Tibetan Buddhist contemplative traditions in terms of traditional categories that proceed through the three vehicles from "lower" to "higher" in terms of the traditional explicit ranking of Tibetan sectarian traditions. The demarcation between "contemplation" and "ritual" is artificial and often of limited use, but we have still relied upon it based on similar distinctions in Tibetan literature.

SŪTRA. Our survey begins with the exoteric traditions of contemplation, the canonical basis of which is Sūtras believed to have been spoken by buddhas. In the present context, Sūtra is short hand for the entire array of literature, institutions and practices that marked exoteric Buddhism in India and Tibet.

Analytical meditation and stabilizing meditation. Meditation in Tibetan traditions is usually presented as being part of a therapeutic impulse to resolve the dissatisfactory nature of embodied existence for oneself and others. This enterprise has three main phases: listening (*thos*), which includes all forms of study and learning pertaining to normative Buddhist doctrine; reflection or contemplation (*bsam*), the phase in which the meditator processes those teachings in order to arrive at an understanding of their import; and finally meditation (*sgom*), the process by which these concepts become integrated into one's experience.

The third stage of meditation (bhāvana) is thus focused on deepening the individual's experience of the insights gained through the first two stages. In traditional presentations, meditation in this context is often described as being either "analytical meditation" (*dpyad sgom*) or "stabilizing meditation" (*'jog sgom*). Initially, the practitioner performs analytical meditation on some doctrinal aspect of the teachings, for example, impermanence, emptiness (*stong pa nyid;* Skt., *śūnyatā*), or compassion (*snying rje;* Skt., *karuṇā*), carefully scrutinizing the different explanations, and finally arriving at an inferential understanding of the topic. These "analytical" meditations often involve formal processes of reasoning that are carried out in reliance upon scriptural or oral guidance. Having arrived at such a clear understanding, one then employs the techniques of stabilizing meditation to reach a firm conviction and nondiscursive intuition of the validity of the teaching or doctrine under investigation. Alternatively, initially it is necessary to settle the mind so that it can remain calm and focused in its pursuit of knowledge and realization. This "calming" practice may in fact be the first form of meditation in which the beginning practitioner engages.

Calm abiding and insight meditation. A related presentation of the general meditative process is that of "calming" (*zhi gnas;* Skt., *śamatha;* literally, "calm abiding"), and "insight" (*lhag mthong;* Skt., *vipaśyanā;* literally, "higher seeing"). This is not unique to Tibetan Buddhism, but is frequently invoked within Tibet to explain basic Buddhist meditation. The practice of calming is designed to build the mind's capacity for concentration to such a degree that it can remain single-pointed (*rtse gcig*) and undistracted for long periods of time. Such techniques proliferated in Tibet, with the main variance being the object of focus, which could be a candle flame, one's breathing, a statue of a buddha, a song, a visualized syllable, or a waterfall. Most accounts of calming practices thus outline the object of focus, and then provide detailed accounts of the deepening levels of concentration, as well as pitfalls to avoid. In this way, contemplative calming serves as the meditative basis for the attainment of incisive insight into the nature of reality, specifically into the selflessness of persons and the selflessness of phenomena, realization of which are said to result ultimately in liberation or enlightenment. The practice of calming thus clears a mental space for the acquisition of the ability to see the world in accordance with Buddhist doctrinal analysis of its final reality, while the practice of insight cultivates and deepens that perception with an incisiveness based upon the newly acquired capacity for concentration. The practice of calm abiding is thus roughly equivalent to "stabilizing meditation," while the practice of insight meditation is roughly equivalent to "analytical meditation."

Meditation on emptiness. While earlier forms of Buddhism stressed the ultimate object of contemplation as "no-self," namely the lack of any permanent identity in people or things, the Great Vehicle instead stressed the notion of universal "emptiness," which came to be a dominant motif in Tibet. In a sense, all forms of analytical and insight meditation have "emptiness" as their ultimate object. Meditation on emptiness is highly valued in Tibetan Buddhist traditions since a nonconceptual realization of emptiness is considered to be the antidote to the ignorance that is the root cause of suffering. In general, emptiness is said to be absence of inherent existence, and is equivalent to the selflessness of persons and selflessness of phenomena discussed above. It is a fundamental Buddhist tenet that suffering arises in dependence on the misapprehension of the true nature and identity of persons and phenomena, mistaking them for independent, permanent, autonomous entities rather than the concatenation of various factors, events, and conditions they truly are. In reality, these entities are empty of this mistaken imputed identity, and need to be recognized as such in order to attain liberation or enlightenment (*byang chub;* Skt., *bodhi*).

There are many forms of emptiness meditation in the various Tibetan traditions. One such typical meditation associated with the "sūtra" stream of Tibetan Buddhism is the so-called "sevenfold reasoning" drawn from Candrakīrti's (c. 600–650) *Guide to the Middle Way (dbu ma la 'jug pa;* Skt., *Madhyamakāvatāra*). The gist of the reasoning concerns itself with the analysis of a chariot and its parts, and recalls the famous dialogue between Nāgasena and Milinda in the *Questions of King Milinda (milindapanha).* The seven analyses are: (1) there is no chariot other than its parts; (2) there is no chariot that is the same as its parts; (3) there is no chariot that inherently possesses its parts; (4) there is no chariot that inherently depends on its parts; (5) there is no chariot upon which its parts inherently depend; (6) there is no chariot that is the mere collection of its parts; and (7) there is no chariot that is the shape of its parts. These same reasonings may be applied to the existence of the "self" (*bdag;* Skt., *ātman*), whether it is of a person or a phenomenon (e.g., a chariot), and its relation to their aggregates (*phung po;* Skt., *skandha*).

Although emptiness meditation often has this rational character such that it resembles deconstructive analysis rehearsed according to scripts, it is also possible to meditate on emptiness in a less formal, systematic way. For instance, practitioners might employ images, symbols, and language such as the eight similes of illusion to induce an intuitive understanding of the nature of emptiness. In such a loosely structured meditation, one might reflect on phenomena being like a dream, an optical illusion, a mirage, a reflection of the moon in water, an echo, a castle in the sky, or a phantom. Having thus established a sense of emptiness on the basis of what is essentially an aesthetic mood, one rests in that state for a time. Regardless of the technique employed, immersion in emptiness during the formal meditative session is usually contrasted to the practice of maintaining that awareness after the session as one reengages with the social world of appearances and activities. The relationship between these two phases of "meditative equanimity" (*mnyam gzhag*) and "post-contemplative awareness" (*rjes thob*), a duality that ultimately must be dissolved, is an important topic within emptiness yoga.

Meditation on compassion. Tibetan Buddhism also possesses many meditation practices specifically concerned with the cultivation of compassion for living beings in accordance with the Great Vehicle's primary contemplative and ideological motif of the integration of emptiness and compassion. If emptiness deconstructs the world, compassion is what pulls us back into engagement within its illusory appearances. One of the most famous forms of compassion meditation found in Tibetan Buddhism is the "giving and taking" meditation (*gtong len*). This is done in conjunction with the meditator's breathing and in relation to all beings, including family members, friends, enemies, and strangers, all of whom are visualized seated around the meditator. As the meditator breathes out, the meditator imagines that all of his or her personal happiness, comfort, wealth, and resources transform into white light and go out to all the beings seated there. When the light strikes the beings that are visualized surrounding the meditator, he or she imagines that the light fulfills all their wishes, heals all illnesses, and bestows all happiness. With the inhalation of the breath, the meditator is directed to visualize all the suffering and causes for suffering present within the beings' mental continua being drawn back into the meditator in the form of black smoky light rays. These beams then merge with the meditator, who imagines that he or she has taken on all the sufferings and misery of all others. Most compassion contemplative techniques involve such guided reveries including scripted liturgy and visualizations.

Such meditation helps the meditator adopt an attitude that inverts the normal pattern of viewing oneself and one's own concerns as preeminent, and it instills the habit of seeing others as being more important. The significance of this in Buddhist terms is easy to discern. First, it inculcates in the practitioner compassion toward others, and slowly habituates one to sacrifice one's own interest in order to benefit others. Second, on the ultimate level, one is undermining and dismantling the structures of ego that are the underlying cause for all of one's suffering through exchanging one's own interests and happiness for those of others. In this way compassion both inculcates a realization of emptiness through dissolving boundaries, but also offers an essential complement to realization of emptiness by instilling a sense of the value of others, as illusory as their identity may ultimately be.

Stages of the Path and ordinary preliminaries. One of the most distinctive contributions to Buddhist meditation practice made by Tibetans is the category or genre of "Stages of the Path" (Lam rim). There have been countless practice-oriented texts written in this genre in all major traditions of Tibetan Buddhism. The precursor to most of these texts was a short work written by the Indian scholar Atīśa (982–1054) called *The Lamp for the Path (byang chub gyi sgron ma* (Skt., *bodhipathapradīpa*). This text is noted for its reference to the three spiritual levels of beings, as well as the notion that a solid foundation in the sūtra practices is essential to the practice of Tantra. Inspired by this brief text, later Tibetan scholars and meditators composed their own elaborations on the themes introduced in it. Among the most famous of these texts is Tsongkhappa's (tsong kha pa, 1357–1419) *Great Exposition of the Stages of the Path (lam rim chen mo),* and Gampopa's (sgam po pa, 1079–1153) *Jewel Ornament of Liberation (thar rgyan).* The type of meditation practice described in texts of this genre is what is usually referred to as "mind training" or "mental development" (*blo sbyong*).

Such meditation is, in a sense, intended to "reprogram" the practitioner, guiding him or her to new attitudes or views through the force of constant habituation. The core practices associated with this genre are sometimes referred to as "the four thoughts that turn the mind." These are thinking about the value of human rebirth, death and impermanence, the law of *karma* and cause and effect, and the disadvantages of living in cyclic existence. These four practices are designed to encourage the practitioner to recognize the unique opportunity for spiritual progress inherent in human existence, while realizing that the body is fragile and transient, and hence that the opportunity will not last forever. By recognizing that if one does not take advantage of this chance by engaging in virtuous actions one will be compelled to experience the resultant suffering, the practitioner is motivated to practice only *dharma* (virtue) henceforward. These practices comprise what are referred to as the four "ordinary preliminary practices" (*sngon 'gro*), which are considered prerequisites to the higher practices associated with Tantra. They essentially use guided imagination and analysis to rehearse and habituate the basic worldview of exoteric Buddhism—life is impermanent, selves are not what they seem to be, ordinary life will not fulfill us, and the moral consequences of our actions shape all.

TANTRA. Buddhist Tantra is marked throughout by a rhetorical focus on practice over intellectual studies. Its origins are defined by ritual practice, including complex ritual consecrations initiating one into ideal communities known as *maṇḍalas* and the self-transfiguration of the individual practitioner into a divine buddha. Subsequently, the rise of *yoginī* Tantras involved antinomian behavioral practices deconstructing social codes, as well as new contemplative practices focused on the body's interior with the goal of reproducing and transforming extreme experiences such as death and orgasm. A strong rhetorical tradition developed stressing the absolute centrality of personal contemplative experience, and there was a profusion of yogic techniques ranging over sleep, diet, death, sacrifice, and physical movements. This led to the phenomenon of large anthologies of integrated practices, such that many innovations lay as much in the packaging as in new techniques. The radicalization of Tantric practice led to tensions with exoteric forms of practice, such that their integration in overarching systems came to be a dominant theme of Tibetan Buddhist contemplation. The means of classification of the main Tantric contemplations are numerous and varied, but the most common includes two "phases": generation phase (*bskyed rim*) and perfection phase (*rdzogs rim*). Generation phase signifies deity yoga practices involving the visualization of one's self as a Buddhist deity, whereas perfection phase signifies both practices of radical nonconceptuality and somatic yogas involving the visualization, sensation, and manipulation of subtle currents of bodily energy.

Extraordinary preliminary practices. Most sects of Tibetan Buddhism embraced a packaged integration of exoteric and basic esoteric practices under the header of "preliminaries" (*sngon 'gro*) to serve as an introduction to advanced Tantric contemplation. As discussed above, their "ordinary" forms rehearsed basic Buddhist doctrine, while their "extraordinary" practices introduced basic Tantric contemplation: going for refuge, generating the altruistic aspiration for enlightenment, Vajrasattva purification, *maṇḍala* offerings, and Guru Yoga.

"Going for refuge" is done by reciting a short prayer while prostrating to a visualized "assembly tree" (*tshogs shing*), a *maṇḍala*-like vertical array of one's lineage. The refuge prayers themselves often encode specifically Tantric versions of the three jewels of Buddhism—the Buddha, his community, and his teachings. "Generating the altruistic aspiration for enlightenment" (*sems bskyed*) is the core Great Vehicle practice integrating compassion and emptiness, and here involves the recitation of a short prayer while visualizing the assembly tree. "Vajrasattva purification" is the visualization of the Buddha Adamantine Hero (Skt., Vajrasattva) above the crown of one's head, while reciting his hundred-syllable *mantra* revolving around his heart. The practitioner confesses downfalls, and visualizes that luminous ambrosia flows from Vajrasattva's heart to transform the practitioner's negativity into sustenance for suffering beings. "*Maṇḍala* offerings" is a practice of repeatedly creating small *maṇḍalas* using heaps of rice and three concentric discs placed on top of the other, and then offering these with visualized enhancements to the buddhas. "Guru Yoga" contemplation requires the visualization of one's guru as a divine buddha. Practitioners perform each 100,000 times, and thus rehearse the basic Tantric elements of visualization, *mantra* repetition, somatic sensations, constructions of *maṇḍalas,* the divinity and primacy of the guru, transformation, offerings, and the importance of divinities.

Generation phase practices: Deity yoga and *maṇḍala* meditation. The most famous, and often defining, Tantric practice is deity yoga (*lha'i rnal 'byor*), the ritual evocation of oneself as a Buddhist deity. The practice is often described as involving three principal factors—vivid visualization, divine pride in identifying oneself with the deity, and "recollection of purity" (*dag dran*) signifying the need to cognitively understand the symbolic import of each visualized element. The deities evoked are varied in character, and include buddhas, *bodhisattvas,* and others, male and female, different colors, different numbers of heads, arms, and legs, and different types of apparel or ritual objects. These practices can involve single deities or the visualization of symmetrically arrayed configurations of multiple deities known as *maṇḍalas*. *Maṇḍalas* are typically organized around a central deity or deity pair known as the *primary ones(s),* with whom a practitioner identifies in visualizing the *maṇḍala*. Visualized deities can be either serene in demeanor and appearance, or wrathful, in which case their visage is scowling, their appearance demonic, and their apparel and backdrop often drawn from a chaotic charnel ground.

These evocations are done according to handbooks termed "techniques for evocation" (*grub thabs;* Skt., *sādhana*), which provide visual detail for visualization, the verbal formula or *mantra* for recitation, the symbolic gestures known as "seals" (*phyag rgya;* Skt., *mudrā*) for performance with one's hands, and liturgy. Thus the eyes are trained to see the divinity in visual form as one's own body; the speech is conditioned to recite the sonic form of the divinity; and the hands form gestures embodying the deity and its activities. These practices can be done with variable locus for the visualization, namely, in front, as self, or in an object such as a ritual vase. Self-visualization is the primary form that has soteriological force, whereas visualization-in-front is for the purpose of making offerings and petitions, and visualization-in-an-object is utilized for various ritual purposes. It is thought that by imaginatively imitating all physical, verbal, and mental activities of a buddha, one creates powerful momentum for the rapid attainment of actual buddhahood. This process is termed "taking the result as the cause," and is one of the key distinguishing features of Tantra.

Retreats involve massive accumulations of *mantra* recitation by an individual practitioner. However, these practices of deity visualization, *mantra* repetition, and *maṇḍala* construction can also be done in communal practices as well. Deity yoga is closely related to "empowerment" rituals (*dbang;* Skt., *abhiṣeka*), which ritually introduce a practitioner into the *maṇḍala* or community of a specific deity. These empowerment rituals are a necessary precursor to doing yoga for a given deity, while deity yoga practices often repeat empowerment ritual processes within their own contemplative structure.

Perfection phase practices: Somatic yogas and other techniques. Perfection phase practices involve three distinct bodies of practices. The most important category involves somatic yogas in which subtle bodies are contemplatively manipulated to recreate extreme experiences, especially sexual and death-related experiences. This is consonant with the late Tantric emphasis on liminal and intense experiences—sexuality, dying, violence, transgression, sleep—and the transformation of these potent experiences into yogic processes. Secondly, it includes practices of nonconceptuality, and thirdly, the perfection phase came to be a catch-all term to embrace a variety of practices, including physical exercises, dietary prescriptions, and other topics. These are typically transmitted in Tibet in anthologies, the most famous example being perhaps *The Six Yogas of Nāropa*. Visceral experience is strongly stressed, and is often summarized in terms of bliss (*bde ba*), clarity and radiance (*gsal ba*), and nonconceptuality (*mi rtog*).

The most central is the "fierce woman" (*gtum mo;* Skt., Caṇḍali) practice based upon the "adamantine body", a subtle body of channels, winds, and nuclei forming an experiential configuration within the coarse physical body. The core sequence of contemplative events mimics sexual experience, but harnesses it for the sake of enlightenment. Three subtle channels run up the torso's center from the head to the genitals, branching out to pervade the body with "wheels" (*cakra*) at the crown, throat, heart, navel, and genitals. One visualizes a triangle of solar fire at the navel that causes a white lunar *haṃ* syllable at the crown to drip. The resultant flow downwards of ambrosial nuclei causes experiences of increasing joy known as "four joys," clearly modeled upon male sexual arousal. The emphasis on bliss is integrated with the Mahayana focus on emptiness, such that the yoga rightly pursued involves a potent realization of emptiness enhanced by the intensity of experience engendered by the bliss. It is famous for its testing procedure, in which an initiate is expected to utilize contemplatively generated heat to dry wet clothes while sitting naked on a glacier at night. Such public displays could be utilized to mobilize human and financial capital in support of their own social and religious agendas.

This is closely linked to sexual yoga, which involves a similar process in partnership with a visualized or real consort. The white nuclei descends into the genitals, but then is reversed without ejaculation and raised upwards back through the torso. The lunar nuclei are then distributed through the body, and finally one's whole body is deconstructed into luminous emptiness. Practitioners thus use this exceptionally powerful state of blissful consciousness to realize emptiness, with the intensity of experience magnifying the consequences of this realization. In the context of discussing this practice as sexual, there are many additional particulars relating to male and female genitalia, positions, herbs, and the like.

The yoga of "radiant light" (*'od gsal;* Skt., *prabhāsvara*) is based upon the human body and mind possessing an innate luminous buddha-nature occluded by karmic sedimentations and emotional distortions. The mind is interdependent with "winds," that is, the breath as well as other currents of energy flowing through the body on the model of a rider and horse. Subtle body praxis deconstructs conditioning and knots of emotional distortion, thereby enabling more subtle layers of consciousness and luminosity to emerge. The yogic technique of "vase breathing" confines the breath and internal winds in the area around the navel, thereby helping facilitate the dissolution of ordinary conceptuality by penning up its mounts. The goal is to bring all the winds into the body's central channel, where they become transformed into winds of primordial gnosis (*ye shes;* Skt., *jñāna*). This is described as a phased dissolution of the psychophysical winds, thereby causing their associated cognitive activities to collapse, and rehearsing the process of dying. A practitioner experiences various flashes of light, the subjective correlate of more subtle levels of consciousness, that gradually proceed to an immersion in the radiant light at the heart. Phenomenologies of such experiences include the eight or ten "signs" (*rtags*) and "four appearances" (*snang ba bzhi*), which are described as resembling smoke, mirages, moonlight, and the like, and culminate in an experience of radiant light.

Sleep and dream yogas are closely related to the esoteric meditations upon light, and exoteric contemplations on emptiness and illusion. Falling asleep involves the intertwined dissolution of winds, conceptuality, and consciousness similar to dying, and likewise culminating in an experience of radiant light and deep unconsciousness; dreaming involves the reversal of this process as manifestation, conceptuality, and experience revive out of the emptiness of radiant light. The goal is to preserve reflexive self-awareness throughout so as to bypass unconsciousness and instead fully experience the ultimate radiant light of consciousness. One visualizes an inner luminosity or syllable representing one's consciousness moving up and down the central axis of the body's interior, until finally with sleep it settles into a lotus flower at the heart. The practice facilitates lucid dreaming, namely the retention of a sense of awareness that one is dreaming even as one dreams. Such awareness—and the consequent sense of the malleability and fluidity of appearances—precisely parallels the Great Vehicle contemplation of emptiness and its focus on the illusory nature of appearances. Specific dreaming practices tend to be grouped into three principles—recognizing dreams as dreams, experimenting with the transformation of dream appearances, and enabling this awareness of recognized dreams to permeate daytime experience as well.

Magical devices (*phrul 'khor;* Skt., *yantra*) constitute a type of yogic practice focused on bodily postures and movements, and often named evocatively after animals, birds, types of people, ritual implements, and the like. Different traditions stress physical movement and static postures to different degrees, though usually they remain within a fairly small space of movement rather than involving broad movements across a large area. The magical-devices practices can also involve specific breathing practices and visualizations conjoined with bodily postures and movements, as well as exercises in the cultivation of awareness.

"Transference" of consciousness (*pho ba*) involves learning to shoot one's consciousness out of the body toward rebirth in a Pure Land. One visualizes one's consciousness as a luminous sphere or syllable moving up and down the central channel of one's subtle body in conjunction with respiration and the enunciation of the mantric syllables *hrik* and *pheṭ*. Often the Buddha Immeasurable Light ('Od dpag med [Öpakme]; Skt., Amitābha), who presides over the most popular Pure Land of choice, is visualized blocking off the top of one's skull. This practice is usually done during specialized retreats (often large lay gatherings) in which practitioners aim to create a small hole in their scalp where the consciousness is being targeted. In addition to enabling a practitioner to instinctively shoot his or her consciousness into a Pure Land in the case of accidental death, the same technique can be deployed in funerary ceremonies by the presiding lama to forcibly shoot the deceased person's consciousness out of the body into a Pure Land by force of his or her own visualization. The "intermediate process" (*bar do*) is the famous Tibetan religious conception of life, death, and rebirth as a never-ending series of transitions, including a period of tumultuous visions experienced between death and rebirth. The actual practices, however, are generally practices derived from elsewhere rather than constituting an entirely new set of practices.

The "extraction of essences" (*bcud len*) involves alchemical techniques for contemplatively generating dietary nourishment without relying on ordinary sources, and engendering and deepening realization. One set of practices involves ingesting specially prepared juices, meats, stones, herbs, precious substances (mercury, gold, etc.), or excrement, which may also be accompanied by special yogic recitations, breathing, visualization, and postures. It is believed that such special pills can help a retreatant sustain himself or herself for months during solitary retreat in isolated wilderness, as well as engender long life, physical vitality, and facilitation of special contemplative experiences. Other such practices include "eating winds," where sustenance is ingested from space via breath, and utilizing visualization-enhanced inhalation, which imagines waves of blue space, or red and white nuclei, flowing into one's body.

POST-TANTRA PRACTICES AND BEYOND. One of the most distinctive attributes of Tibetan Buddhist contemplation was the evolution of independent traditions out of perfection-phase praxis that embraced a radical rhetoric of the transcendence of practice along with a proclivity for naturalism, spontaneity, and nonconceptuality rather than the esoteric motifs of transgression, sexuality, and power. *Post-Tantra* is not an indigenous label, but expresses their simultaneous grounding in Tantra and the rejection of many of its fundamental paradigms. The most famous are the Great Perfection (*dzokchen, rdzogs chen*) in Nyingma (Rnying ma) and Bon lineages, and the Great Seal (*chakchen, phyag chen;* Skt., *mahāmudrā*), found in the Kagyü, Sakya, and Geluk schools. Their texts decline to specify contemplative procedures such as breathing, posture, concentration, visualization, or guided reveries, and consist of philosophical and poetic meditations on the nature of enlightenment. Such rhetoric left many wondering as to whether they formed contemplative paths, or instead were merely descriptions of realization. They are often characterized by a rhetoric of supremacy beyond sūtra and Tantra, while at times they are self-characterized as belonging to sūtra or Tantra. However, these traditions can be viewed as symbiotic with other contemplative traditions both in terms of being deconstructions of preoccupation with technique, and a type of aesthetic gazing and poetics of contemplative experiences. The recitation and reading of such texts offered subtle guides to contextualize the various meditative experiences to which other practices had given rise. Thus they came to have a strong association with the somatic body yogas, including sexual forms, but focused on the experiences unfolding from those practices toward final enlightenment rather than their techniques per se.

Many such texts and lineages however did set forth contemplative techniques, even if such prescriptive passages were still accompanied by a transcendentalist rhetoric that negated all practice. These techniques tend to be recognizable variations of exoteric practices of calming, insight, and emptiness yogas, but they focus on cultivating deconstruction of such states of concentration to foster an open and free-flowing awareness without negating appearances, emotions, and thoughts. The techniques themselves are often distinctive in terms of modifications in line with the rhetoric of simplicity, spontaneity, naturalness, and innate divinity. In this context the Great Seal tradition discusses four yogas—the one pointed (*rtse gcig*), the non-elaborate *(spros bral),* the single flavor (*ro gcig*), and nonmeditation *(sgom med).* The emphasis throughout is on contemplation of the nature of one's mind, the realization of which is blocked by contemplations that are too bound up with the mind's discursive operations.

The Great Perfection also underwent a series of transformations in which a variety of late Tantric contemplative practices were explicitly assimilated in accordance with the traditional focus on simplicity, spontaneity, release, and naturalness. The most influential of these was the Seminal Heart (Snying thig [Nyingthik]), which created anthologies of Tantric and non-Tantric Buddhist contemplations. The most distinctive innovations were the two principal practices of "breakthrough" *(khregs chod)* and "direct transcendence" (*thod rgal*). The former represents a cultivation of one's own naked self-awareness as directed by intensely poetic guided reveries, whereas the latter is a transmutation of perfection-phase techniques contemplating a spontaneous flow of light imagery. The flashes of light appear through staring at the light of the sun or moon or gazing within complete darkness, and then slowly increase in intensity, extent, and complexity of form to become vast arrays of *maṇḍalas* of buddhas.

These traditions are often grouped with other yogic traditions that share a tendency to blur the boundaries between sūtra and Tantra, embrace a rhetoric of transcendental superiority, and focus on nondual contemplative experiences. The Great Middle Way (Dbu ma chen po; [Uma chenpo]; Skt., Mahāmadhyamaka) appropriates the prestigious rubric of Mādhyamaka to disseminate traditional contemplative practices of calming, insight, and emptiness yoga in association with an emphasis on yoga rather than study, and luminous rather than austere conceptions of emptiness. The Path and the Fruit (Lam 'bras [Lamdré]), the supreme contemplative system of the Sakya school, involves tummo and sexual yoga with an innovative third practice named the "adamantine wave" (*rdo rje rba labs*). Peace-making (*zhi byed*) and "cutting" (*gcod*) stem from the eleventh-century Indian Phadampa Sangyé (Pha dam pa sangs rgyas, d. 1117). Cutting involves going to a remote and frightening location, such as a charnel grounds at night, and visualizing that the Adamantine Yoginī (Rdo rje rnal 'byor ma; Vajrayoginī), one of the main esoteric goddesses, cuts one's body into small pieces for offering to surrounding demons and spirits. The motif of disintegration evokes the exoteric realization of emptiness, while the sacrificial gift of one's body to others blends that realization with radical compassion.

COMMUNAL CONCLUSIONS. There are at least two major communal contexts for specialized practice of Buddhist contemplation: the monastery or temple, and retreat centers in isolated networks of sacred sites. While it is impossible to classify practices in any strict fashion based upon these communal centers, it is clear that exoteric techniques and deity yoga/*maṇḍala* meditation thrived in the monastic institutions with their deep doctrinal content, highly structured character, and institutional messages. Likewise, esoteric techniques focused on body yogas and post-Tantra contemplative systems particularly thrived in yogic circles outside such institutions. This is not surprising, given their strong experiential focus, relative resistance to doctrinal conditioning, and commitment to internal, solitary realization and transgressive experiences. In addition, yogic circles tend to be critical of intellectual pursuits as interfering with contemplative practice, while monastic institutions on the whole stress their integration and in actuality tend to stress far more the intellectual, ritual, and social sides of religion rather than solitary contemplation. However, such lines were only tendencies, not sedimented differences. In both contexts, extended retreats—including durations of years—were common in all sectors of Tibetan religion, though by no means widely practiced as such even within monasteries. The rhetoric of the centrality of sustained contemplative practice is pervasive, and both historical and ethnographic evidence point to this being far more than simple rhetoric, even within ordinary lay members of society. Tibetan Buddhist hagiographies frequently portray in narrative form a strong tension between solitary contemplation and social responsibilities, with retreatants feeling pulled back, often against their will, toward the communal responsibilities of life in the monastery or village.

BIBLIOGRAPHY

Beyer, Stephen. *The Cult of Tārā: Magic and Ritual in Tibet.* Berkeley, 1973. This brilliant study of the intersection of ritual and contemplation in Tantric Buddhism analyzes how "deity yoga" functions in diverse contexts to bind together a broad array of goals, processes, and agendas within soteriological and pragmatic contexts.

Cozort, Daniel. *Highest Yoga Tantra.* Ithaca, N.Y., 1986. This offers a concise but detailed introduction to the esoteric practices in the Geluk tradition of Tibetan Buddhism with a focus on perfection phase techniques.

Dreyfus, Georges B. J. *The Sound of Two Hands Clapping: The Education of a Tibetan Buddhist Monk.* Berkeley, Calif., 2003. This contains an excellent discussion of the relationship between the rhetoric and praxis of meditation in monastic traditions.

Dudjom Jigdrel Yeshe Dorje (Dudjom Rinpoche). *The Nyingma School of Tibetan Buddhism: Its Fundamentals and History.* Translated and edited by Gyurme Dorje and Matthew Kapstein. Boston, 1991. This encyclopedic work by a famous Tibetan author covers a vast range of Nyingma topics from the perspective of the twentieth century.

Germano, David F. "Architecture and Absence in the Secret Tantric History of rDzogs Chen." *The Journal of the International Association of Buddhist Studies* 17, no. 2 (1994): 203–335. This surveys the various forms of the Great Perfection with a special concern for their contemplative practices.

Guenther, Herbert V., trans. *Jewel Ornament of Liberation.* London, 1959. A translation of the classic Stages of the Path text by Gampopa, a disciple of Milarepa (Mi la ras pa).

Guenther, Herbert V., trans. *The Life and Teachings of Nāropa.* Oxford, 1963. This text and interpretation offers a systematic view of the *Six Yogas of Nāropa,* one of the most famous anthologies of perfection phase practice.

Gyatso, Geshe Kelsang. *Clear Light of Bliss: Mahāmudrā in Vajrayāna Buddhism.* London, 1982. This provides an exceptionally detailed description of the perfection phase practices from a Geluk point of view.

Hopkins, P. Jeffrey. *Emptiness Yoga: The Tibetan Middle Way.* Ithaca, N.Y., 1987. A clear description of emptiness meditation, especially as it is practiced in the monastic context.

Lopez, Donald, ed. *Religions of Tibet in Practice.* Princeton, 1997. This is a compilation of many translations with introductions of Tibetan texts dealing with meditation and ritual.

Patrul Rinpoche. *Words of My Perfect Teacher.* Translated by the Padmakara Translation Group. Boston, 1998. This is a translation of one of the most famous examples of Tantric preliminaries (*kun bzang bla ma'i zhal lung*); composed in the nineteenth century.

Rabten, Geshe, and Geshe Ngawang Dhargyey. *Advice from a Spiritual Friend.* Translated and edited by Brian Beresford. London, 1984. This is an excellent introduction to the practice of mind training (*blo sbyong*), with translations of several short exemplary texts.

Sherburne, Richard, trans. *A Lamp for the Path and Commentary of Atīśa.* London, 1983. This is a translation of one of the most influential Indian prototypes for the Stages of the Path and in general for Tibetan compendia of exoteric contemplative practices.

Takpo Tashi Namgyal. *Mahāmudrā: The Quintessence of Mind and Meditation.* Translated by Lhalungpa, Lobsang. Boston, 1986. This is a translation of an encyclopedic Kagyü survey of *mahāmudrā.*

Tsong kha pa, and Dalai Lama XIV (Tenzin Gyatso). *Deity Yoga.* Translated by P. Jeffrey Hopkins. Ithaca, N.Y., 1987. This is a partial translation of Tsong ka pa's important survey of Tantra, *The Great Stages of Mantra* (*sngags rim chen mo*), with commentary by the Dalai Lama.

Willis, Janice D. *The Diamond Light of the Eastern Dawn: A Collection of Tibetan Buddhist Meditations.* New York, 1972. This is a compilation of translations of various Buddhist meditational manuals with a focus on esoteric rites of evocation.

Wilson, Joe B. *Candrakīrti's Sevenfold Reasoning: Meditation on the Selflessness of Persons.* Dharmsala, India, 1980. This is a presentation of classical emptiness meditation based on analytical reasoning.

Zahler, Leah, trans. and ed. *Meditative States in Tibetan Buddhism.* Rev. ed. Boston, 1997. This offers a clear survey of the traditional processes and states discussed in the context of "calming" and "insight" contemplative techniques.

David Germano (2005)
Gregory A. Hillis (2005)

BUDDHIST MEDITATION: EAST ASIAN BUDDHIST MEDITATION

Meditation was of ultimate importance in early Buddhism, and has remained so in East Asian Buddhism. Although not all Buddhists in East Asia have meditated on a daily basis, they have always recognized meditation as one of the three trainings (*śīla, samādhi,* and *prajñā*) leading to buddhahood. *Śīla* (morality), *samādhi* (concentration), and *prajñā* (wisdom) are mutually supportive and indispensable, though achieving buddhahood ultimately depends more on *prajñā.*

In theory, the importance of meditation became less certain in East Asian Buddhist intellectual positions emphasizing inherent buddhahood (Chan/Zen or Tiantai/Tendai Buddhism) or utter reliance on Amitābha's grace (Pure Land Buddhism). In practice, however, meditation retained its central place in monastic life. Laypeople were not expected to meditate in early Buddhism, but in East Asian Buddhism there have always been male and female laypersons seeking buddhahood through meditation.

The distinction between *śamatha* (calming meditation) and *vipaśyanā* (insight meditation), or between *samādhi* and *prajñā,* can be helpful for analyzing the various forms of meditation, but most East Asian forms of meditation combine both aspects. Even theorists such as Zhiyi (538–597) who explicitly mention the distinction between *śamatha* and *vipaśyanā,* say that the two aspects are inseparable.

Meditation in the Formative Period. Chinese Buddhism has been Mahāyānist for nearly all of its history, but the earliest Buddhist teachings brought to China included both Nikāya and Mahāyāna Buddhist teachings, which the Chinese did not initially distinguish as separate vehicles. (The term Nikāya Buddhism is preferred to the term Hīnayāna Buddhism.)

One of the earliest translators, the Parthian An Shigao (active from 148), translated texts from the Sarvāstivāda tradition of Nikāya Buddhism. An Shigao translated materials on *dhyāna* (concentration) meditation, including the *Scripture of Mindfulness of Breathing* (T 602), which teaches counting the breaths as a preparation for entering concentration. This was an important text in Chinese Buddhism for the next several hundred years, and mindfulness of breathing was one of the main forms of meditation in early Chinese Buddhism.

Another early translator, the Kushan Lokakṣema (fl. 166–180s), translated the *Pratyutpanna samādhi sūtra* (T 418), a sūtra containing both Pure Land and *prajñāpāramitā* ideas (see Harrison, 1988). This sūtra teaches a form of *samādhi* called the "meditation of direct encounter with the buddhas of the present age," a form of *buddhānusmṛti* (keeping a buddha in mind, Ch. *nianfo*). In this practice, the meditator concentrates on a cosmic buddha such as Amitābha Buddha for a whole day and night, or a whole week, day and night, until the buddha appears to the meditator and preaches the *dharma* to him or her, and establishes the meditator as a nonreturning *bodhisattva*, a buddha-to-be. While this appearance is a sacred revelation and not a mere hallucination, it is at the same time "empty" of ultimate reality. This practice is recommended for monks, nuns, and laypeople. Other figures important for the development of Buddhist meditation in China during this period include Dao'an (312–385) and his disciple Huiyuan (334–416), who taught mindfulness of breathing and *buddhānusmṛti;* and Kumārajīva (350–409), who translated texts on meditation important in the Tiantai tradition and other traditions.

Because many of the earliest Buddhist translations were related to meditation, Henri Maspero (1971/1981) has argued that the translators were meeting the needs of a Chinese audience with an especial interest in meditation, perhaps an audience already familiar with Daoist meditation (pp. 400–412).

MEDITATION IN TIANTAI/TENDAI TRADITION. Tiantai Buddhism, founded by Zhiyi of Mt. Tiantai (in present-day Zhejiang province, southeast China), synthesizes the earlier theory-oriented Buddhism of south China with the practice-oriented Buddhism of north China. Zhiyi's greatest work on meditation is the *Mohe zhiguan* (Great calming and contemplation, T 1911; see Donner and Stevenson, 1993). The *Mohe zhiguan* discusses four kinds of *samādhi,* and ten modes and ten spheres of discernment. The four kinds of *samādhi* provided the ritual structure for all later Tiantai meditative practice in East Asia, whereas the ten modes and ten spheres of discernment involve mental exercises to be carried out within that structure. Tiantai Buddhism attempts to find a place for all Buddhist teachings within its systems (in contrast to the single-minded and exclusivist perspective of traditions such as Chan), and the framework of the four kinds of *samādhi* could encompass any form of Buddhist meditation. Even so, in the *Mohe zhiguan* the four categories are identified with six specific ritual meditation regimens. Tiantai monasteries were built with halls especially for these meditation regimens.

In the ninety-day constantly-sitting *samādhi,* the meditator contemplates the visionary body of the Buddha in emptiness, or indeed any other *dharma* (any thing), in order to identify the mind with the *dharmadhātu,* and realize the interpenetration of all dharmas.

The constantly walking *samādhi* is the "meditation of direct encounter with the buddhas of the present age" of the *Pratyutpanna samādhi sūtra* (see Harrison, 1988). The meditator circumambulates an altar to Amitābha for ninety days, chanting Amitābha's name and visualizing his form. The meditator will gain enough merit to be reborn in Amitābha's realm, or he or she may receive a personal visitation from Amitābha during the meditation period.

The category of part-walking and part-sitting includes the *vaipulya* repentance and the lotus *samādhi.* In the *vaipulya* repentance, the meditator installs a set of twenty-four deities in the meditation chamber, confesses his or her transgressions "with utmost sincerity and tears of lament" (Donner and Stevenson, 1993, p. 254), and then alternates between circumambulating while chanting *dhāraṇīs* and doing seated meditation. This regimen lasts only seven days, and laypersons may participate. The lotus *samādhi* involves confession before an altar to the *bodhisattva* Samantabhadra, circumambulation while reciting the *Lotus Sūtra,* and seated meditation.

For the category of neither walking nor sitting, Zhiyi offers the example of a repentance focused on the *bodhisattva* Avalokiteśvara (Guanyin), involving ritual offerings, confession, chanting *dhāraṇīs,* sitting, and sūtra recitation. This category also includes the "*samādhi* of freely following one's thoughts" (*sui ziyi sanmei*), which became especially important for some later Tiantai Buddhists who wished to rid Tiantai practice of its ritual aspect and pursue formless practices. In this approach, the meditator can use any form of physical activity or sense-perception as a basis for cultivating *samādhi,* including "evil" activities or sense-perceptions.

These practices have a double salvific effect. In each of these practices (except the last one) the meditator invokes the blessing of buddhas or *bodhisattvas* who may aid the meditator along the path to buddhahood with teachings and support. However, each practice is also an exercise in cultivating a buddha's vision of reality. In this vision, all ten *dharma*-realms, from the realm of hell-beings to the realm of perfect buddhahood, are mutually coextensive in all of their aspects, resulting in a "middle" state that synthesizes both existence and emptiness. This is what is meant by Zhiyi's famous phrase "three-thousand realms in an instant of thought" (*yinian sanqian*). For Zhiyi, *nirvāṇa* is not different from the world of common experience: it is this world seen through a refined pair of eyes. While the four kinds of *samādhi* are practiced in order to invoke the blessings of holy beings, they also are used to cultivate this *prajñā* (wisdom). The ten modes and ten spheres of discernment also discussed in the *Mohe zhiguan* make up a system of mental exercises that may be carried out within the four kinds of *samādhi.*

Later developments. Tiantai subitism, as it developed in Japanese Tendai Buddhism from the twelfth century on, has been termed *hongaku shisō* (original enlightenment thought). *Hongaku* texts emphasized that all people are perfect buddhas already—in fact, all things possess perfect buddhahood, even insentients such as plants or trees. Some *hongaku* texts rejected the idea of "attaining" buddhahood at all, and argued that buddhahood is none other than worldly experience. *Hongaku* thought has been criticized as rejecting religious practice, but some *hongaku* texts did give instructions for contemplative practice, and Habito has argued that *hongaku* texts were studied in a context of meditative practice.

MEDITATION IN CHAN/ZEN TRADITION. The name "Chan" comes from the word *dhyāna,* known in China as *channa.* Chan is the "meditation" school of Buddhism, yet Chan Buddhists have sometimes been critical of meditation. After the eighth century, the sudden approach to enlightenment became dominant, and the idea of gradually cultivating the mind over time through meditation became problematic. Seated meditation—known in China as *zuochan* and in Japan as *zazen*—itself became a problem. However, it is unlikely that those who criticized seated meditation ceased doing it.

Early Chan. The first record of Chan meditation comes from the end of the sixth century, where monastics and laypeople in north China compiled the *Erru sixing lun* (Treatise on the two entrances and four practices), recording teachings on mental cultivation attributed to Bodhidharma and his student Huike. This text teaches that one must discover the buddha-nature, which is within oneself but is obscured by false sense-impressions. The text teaches a form of meditation called "wall contemplation" (*biguan*) that dispenses with all stages of progress and aims at pacifying the mind and achieving a state in which all things are one and the same. The term "wall contemplation" is not explained in the text, but may refer to *śamatha* (McRae, 2003, p. 31). Some of the teachings of the *Erru sixing lun,* such as striving to realize one's inherent buddhahood through seated meditation, dispensing with stages of progress, and turning everyday activity into an exercise in mental cultivation, also are characteristic of later Chan/Zen meditation.

Shenxiu and Shenhui. In the seventh century, Chan Buddhism came to the public eye in the persons of Shenxiu (606–706) and Shenhui (684–758). Shenxiu's teachings relentlessly emphasized contemplation of the mind in seated meditation and throughout daily life. He taught his many students to contemplate their minds with perfect equanimity, make their minds penetrate all realms of the cosmos, realize nonbeing, and achieve the consciousness of a buddha in this lifetime. After Shenxiu's death, Shenhui attacked Shenxiu's students' legitimacy and teachings on meditation. Shenhui criticized seated meditation as an obstruction to enlightenment, and exhorted students to achieve enlightenment immediately, as opposed to becoming distracted by a gradualistic regimen of meditation. Shenhui did not invent the teaching of sudden enlightenment or the critique of seated meditation: his innovation was the critique of purifying and concentrating the mind. Shenhui probably did not intend for meditation to become taboo, and meditation continued to be taught by Shenhui's students. However, after Shenhui, Chan Buddhists could no longer admit to a concern for purifying the mind or speak of meditation as a gradualistic process. Chan/Zen Buddhists hardly dared to commit instructions on seated meditation to writing until the twelfth century.

Kōans. *Kōans,* perhaps the most distinctive aspect of Chan/Zen Buddhism, were first composed in the ninth or tenth centuries. *Kōan* practice involving meditation was systematized in China during the Song dynasty (960–1279), and further systematized in Japan thereafter.

Steven Heine (2002) defines a *kōan,* known in China as *gong'an,* as "a brief, enigmatic anecdote or dialogue between two contesting parties" (p. 1), usually recording an encounter between Chan master and student. *Kōan* literally means "public case," and the underlying image is of a legal case: the master interrogates the student like a magistrate interrogating the accused. Scholars such as D. T. Suzuki have presented *kōans* as authentic records of the irrational, spontaneous behavior of enlightened masters, ultimately incomprehensible to Western readers. Rather than viewed as authentic records of the ancient masters, however, *kōans* should be recognized as literary products with their own literary patterns, cultural themes, and social functions. Although *kōans* are intentionally enigmatic and have special uses within the context of Chan/Zen training, they need not be regarded as fundamentally impenetrable to a reader standing outside the tradition.

Kōans sometimes appear to reject meditation *per se,* but they are actually only warning against attachment to meditation, or criticizing a particular approach to meditation. In a famous eleventh-century *kōan* about an encounter between Nanyue Huairang (677–744) and Mazu Daoyi (709–788), Huairang chides Mazu for his attachment to seated meditation, telling Mazu that achieving buddhahood by practicing seated meditation would be as impossible as grinding a tile to make a mirror.

> Mazu said, "How does one do it right?" Huairang said, "Are you training in seated meditation, or training in sitting as the Buddha? If you are training in seated meditation, then meditation is neither seated nor lying down. . . . Your sitting as the Buddha is to kill the Buddha; if you are attached to the characteristic of sitting, you have not penetrated the principle involved." When Mazu heard this teaching he felt ecstatic. (*Jingde chuandeng lu,* T 2076, 51:240c; translation from McRae, p. 87, with alterations)

This anecdote, more likely a legend than the record of an actual event, was composed and reworked not to deny that meditation has a place in Chan training, but to warn the meditator against a subtle attachment to meditation. In a typical Chan move, "meditation" is redefined as a way of being, rather than a formal practice. Here, encountering a master, rather than meditation, is presented as the primary means to enlightenment.

***Kōan* meditation.** *Kōans* themselves were used as a focus of meditation. Dahui Zonggao (1089–1163), from the Linji Chan lineage, developed a training method called *kan-*

hua, "contemplating the [critical] phrase," which he taught to monastics and laypersons alike. According to this method, the student zeroes in on the *huatou,* the punch line of a *kōan,* which may be only a single word. The student concentrates upon the *huatou,* both in seated meditation and throughout all daily activities. Abstracted from its original context, the *huatou* is inscrutable, and the student becomes sorely troubled by doubt and frustration. Eventually, the student is consumed by doubt, "becoming" the doubt, and his or her dualistic thinking is replaced by one-pointedness of mind. Finally this great doubt shatters, bringing great enlightenment and recapturing the enlightened state of mind of the master in the *kōan.* Although *kanhua* meditation is a distinctively Chan form of meditation with its use of *kōans* and doubt, it also can be understood as a combination of *śamatha* and *vipaśyanā.*

Chan has often been described as a form of Buddhism uniquely influenced by Daoism, but this is difficult to substantiate historically. It would be more accurate to say that Chan Buddhists drew upon a common literati culture already imbued with ideas from Daoist classics such as *Laozi* (*Dao de jing*), *Zhuangzi,* and *Liezi.* Chan Buddhists over the past millennium also have come to include Daoist *qi*-circulation (*qigong*) techniques among their meditation practices, as these techniques have become more widely practiced in Chinese society in general.

Japanese Zen. The two main schools of Zen in Japan are Rinzai, known in China as Linji, and Sōtō, known in China as Caodong. While Buddhists of each school have always both practiced *zazen* (seated meditation) and studied *kōans,* the Rinzai school is known for *kōan* training, and the Sōtō school for *zazen.*

Kōan training was first brought to Japan in the twelfth century. The language of Chinese Chan presented difficulties for many Japanese monks, who coped by developing *kōan* training systems. Students studied *kōans* in standard sequences and drew their answers to *kōans* from lists of approved capping-phrases (*jakugo*). The *kōan* training systems of the Rinzai school, as practiced today, were established by Hakuin Ekaku (1686–1769) and his disciples. A student in a Rinzai training monastery today practices *kanna* meditation, working on his *kōan* during *zazen* and other activities, and using *jakugo* to express his understanding to his teacher (*rōshi*) during daily interviews (*dokusan*). Women and laymen do not usually have access to this training. In China, *kanna* meditation (*kanhua* in Japan and Korea) is practiced in Chan monasteries. This approach also is practiced in contemporary Korean Sŏn monasteries.

The Sōtō school was brought to Japan by Dōgen Kigen (1200–1253). Although he also was a brilliant master of *kōan* literature, Dōgen emphasized *zazen* over *kōan* training and wrote one of the first manuals on *zazen.* In Dōgen's *zazen,* one sits fixedly and practices "nonthinking." Dōgen taught that *zazen* is not merely a method by which one reaches enlightenment, *zazen* is itself enlightenment. The monk must not practice *zazen* for the sake of becoming a buddha, because all beings are buddhas already. Instead, the monk must practice *zazen* without any thought of attaining enlightenment experience, "just sitting," merely expressing his inherent buddhahood. This is a creative resolution to Chan/Zen's perennial problem of harmonizing the doctrine of sudden enlightenment with the real need for meditation practice.

Meditation in Pure Land Tradition. Pure Land Buddhism involves devotion to Amitābha Buddha (Amitāyus)—known in China as Amituo Fo and in Japan as Amida Butsu, or other buddhas or *bodhisattvas* such as Avalokiteśvara (Guanyin, Kannon). Most practitioners strive for rebirth in Sukhāvatī, Amitābha's paradisiacal world-system far to the west of our own world, though some practitioners believe that the Pure Land is an effect of enlightened consciousness rather than a place. A practitioner's rebirth in Sukhāvatī is made possible through Amitābha's infinite store of merit. Pure Land Buddhism in East Asia is based on four main texts, the *Longer* and *Shorter Sukhāvatī-vyūha sūtras, Amitāyur-dhyāna sūtra,* and *Sukhāvatī-vyūhopadeśa,* all known in China by the sixth century.

With the exception of Japanese Pure Land denominations, Pure Land Buddhism in the East Asian cultural sphere has been more a style of religiosity than an independent school. Although there have been masters who taught Pure Land exclusively, monastics usually have practiced Pure Land together with other forms of Buddhism, such as Tiantai or even Chan. Pure Land has also been one of the most practiced forms of Buddhism among laypeople.

Pure Land practice may involve recitation, visualization, and ritual. The main Pure Land practice is *nianfo* (Jp. *nembutsu,* Skt. *buddhānusmṛti*), which means "keeping (Amitābha) Buddha in mind" or "reciting (Amitābha) Buddha's name." In China, Pure Land devotees began to claim that ten recitations of the phrase "Honor to Amitābha Buddha," or even one recitation, are enough to bring about rebirth in the Pure Land, though most devotees recite Amitābha's name millions of times throughout their lives. Devotees hope to be rewarded with a vision or visitation from Amitābha, a sign that their rebirth in the Pure Land is assured. Even as simple recitation, *nianfo* can become a form of meditation.

Nianfo practice may also include visualizing and contemplating Amitābha's physical body (*rūpakāya*) with its major and minor marks, or his abstract cosmic body (*dharmakāya*) as the ground of reality. One text, the *Amitāyur-dhyāna sūtra,* teaches a series of sixteen *dhyāna* meditations. In these meditations, the meditator develops an impossibly complex and detailed vision of Amitābha and his Pure Land, with its lotus throne, jewel-trees, and so on. Whereas practitioners reciting Amitābha's name hoped to be rewarded with a vision of the Pure Land, the meditator here builds this vision for him- or herself. Because the meditator gains insight into Amitābha as the ground of reality, this *dhyāna* meditation has the aspect of *vipaśyanā* as well as *śamatha.*

Nianfo is often practiced in a ritual context. In everyday lay practice, this may involve incense offerings, prostration, and circumambulation of an image of Amitābha or another deity. One example of a Pure Land ritual meditation historically practiced by monastics is the constantly walking *samādhi* described in the above section on Tiantai Buddhism. Monastics and laypeople alike also may take part in Pure Land repentance rites. In these rites, Amitābha and other buddhas are invited to the ritual space to receive the worshipers' veneration and hear their confession of sins. Following this, the worshipers dedicate the merit gained from the rite to all beings, and vow their intent to be reborn in the Pure Land.

Hōnen and Shinran. In Pure Land Buddhism, as in Chan, meditation became problematic in light of doctrinal developments. Pure Land masters in medieval China taught that a single sincere recitation of Amitābha's name was sufficient to guarantee rebirth in his Pure Land. However, for many practitioners they still recommended meditation; that is, formal visualization practices. The situation changed in Japan, where the two most influential Pure Land masters, Hōnen (1133–1212) and Shinran (1173–1263), taught that the difficult meditation practices were not only not necessary, but could even threaten a practitioner's salvation. Japanese Pure Land Buddhism teaches that the practitioner must rely completely on the "other-power" (*tariki*) of Amitābha, but that a meditator might develop the false belief that he or she could achieve salvation based on the "self-power" (*jiriki*) of meditation.

MEDITATION IN ESOTERIC TRADITION. Esoteric Buddhism, also called Tantric or Vajrayāna Buddhism, was a relatively late form of Indian Buddhism transmitted to China in the Tang (618–907) and Southern Song (1127–1279) dynasties. Although Esoteric Buddhism as an institution flourished only briefly in China, Esoteric rituals and symbols can still be found in Chinese Buddhism and Daoism. Esoteric Buddhism was first established in Japan by Kūkai (774–835) and Saichō (767–822). Kūkai founded the esoteric Shingon school, and Saichō incorporated Esoteric Buddhism in his Tendai school. Although the following account describes Shingon meditation, the same general description also would apply to Tendai esoteric practice.

In Shingon practice, the three human activities of body, speech, and mind manifest the three sacred "secrets" of *mudrā, mantra,* and visualization *samādhi.* Shingon practices involve physical actions, chanting, and visualization, and thus straddle the categories of ritual and meditation. While Shingon practices cannot be pigeonholed into two exclusive categories of ritual and meditation, some practices are relatively more communal and ritual, and some are more individual and meditative. *Ajikan,* contemplation of the syllable *A,* is one such meditative practice, set within a ritual framework.

Today, *Ajikan* is practiced by monks, as well as male and female laypeople. In one version of *Ajikan,* as described by Zōei in the seventeenth century, the practitioner begins with prostrations, protective mantras, the Five Great Vows (such as to save all sentient beings), and a *mantra* to invite the cosmic buddha Mahāvairocana, known in Japan as Dainichi, to attend the ritual. He or she then visualizes the Sanskrit letter *A* resting on a white lotus flower, within a full moon, within the heart. The letter *A* is then visualized alternatively within the heart and before the eyes, and finally as expanding to fill the whole cosmos before contracting back into the heart. The syllable *A* represents the cosmos in its many aspects: *A* is the primary seed syllable, the origin of all existence, and the "ungraspable void" (as the negative prefix "a-"). After practicing these visualizations for between ten minutes and one hour, the practitioner bids Mahāvairocana return to his Pure Land and performs closing rites to finish the practice. If the practitioner is able to dwell in the thought of Great Compassion, visualize the syllable *A* in his or her heart at all times, and understand what is represented or manifested by this, he or she can achieve buddhahood in the present body. This practice combines aspects of both *śamatha* and *vipaśyanā,* and the practitioner appropriately forms a hand-position symbolizing the union of *dhyāna* and *prajñā* during the practice.

MODERN TENDENCIES. Over the past millennium, Chan has become the dominant monastic Buddhist institution in the East Asian cultural sphere (as Chan in China, Zen in Japan, Sŏn in Korea, and Thiền in Vietnam), and Pure Land has remained the dominant form of lay Buddhist practice. Chan and Pure Land meditation as described above are now practiced equally by laypeople and monastics, and Chan and Pure Land are often combined. Chan/Zen meditation is now practiced worldwide, but so is Pure Land. The greater involvement of laypeople has led to an overall simplification of meditative techniques. In some cases, such as in Taiwan, monastics may now freely choose which form of meditation they wish to practice. Buddhists have more international contacts now, and laypeople and monastics alike may choose to practice Theravāda or Tibetan forms of meditation in addition to or instead of traditional East Asian forms.

SEE ALSO Buddhas and Bodhisattvas, article on Ethical Practices associated with Buddhas and Bodhisattvas; Buddhism, overview article; Buddhism, Schools of, article on East Asian Buddhism; Chan; Daoism, overview article; Dharma, article on Buddhist Dharma and Dharmas; Sūtra Literature.

BIBLIOGRAPHY

Bielefeldt, Carl. *Dōgen's Manuals of Zen Meditation.* Berkeley and Los Angeles, 1988. A study of Dōgen's teachings on *zazen* within the context of Chan history, with translation.

Buswell, Robert E., Jr. "The 'Short-cut' Approach of *K'an-hua* Meditation: The Evolution of a Practical Subitism in Chinese Ch'an Buddhism." In *Sudden and Gradual: Approaches to Enlightenment in Chinese Thought,* edited by Peter N.

Gregory, pp. 321–377. Honolulu, 1987. The best discussion of *kanhua* Chan in a Western language.

Buswell, Robert E., Jr. *The Zen Monastic Experience: Buddhist Practice in Contemporary Korea.* Princeton, N.J., 1992. The best ethnography on contemporary Zen (Sŏn) monastic life, including chapters on meditation.

Donner, Neal, and Daniel B. Stevenson. *The Great Calming and Contemplation: A Study and Annotated Translation of the First Chapter of Chih-i's "Mo-ho chih-kuan."* Honolulu, 1993. A translation of the first quarter of the *Mohe zhiguan,* with a nearly one-hundred-page introduction.

Gregory, Peter N., ed. *Traditions of Meditation in Chinese Buddhism.* Honolulu, 1986. Includes articles on Tiantai *samādhi,* early Chan *samādhi,* Faxiang visualization of Maitreya, and so on.

Habito, Ruben L. *Originary Enlightenment: Tendai Hongaku Doctrine and Japanese Buddhism.* Studia Philologica Buddhica Occasional Paper Series XI. Tokyo, 1996. Argues that Tendai *hongaku* texts were studied in a context of meditative practice.

Harrison, Paul, trans. into English; Lokakṣema, trans. into Chinese. *The Pratyutpanna Samādhi Sutra.* Berkeley, Calif., 1988. The English translation of an important sūtra on meditation.

Harvey, Peter. "Buddhist Practice: Meditation and the Development of Wisdom." In *An Introduction to Buddhism: Teachings, History and Practices,* pp. 244–279. New York, 1990. An overview of Buddhist meditation, including sections on East Asia.

Heine, Steven. *Opening a Mountain: Kōans of the Zen Masters.* New York, 2002. A study of cultural symbols in *kōans,* with translations and discussions of *kōans* concerning encounters with mountain spirits, "Zen grannies," and so on.

Hori, Victor Sōgen. *Zen Sand: The Book of Capping Phrases for Kōan Practice.* Honolulu, 2003. The introduction offers the best discussion of contemporary Rinzai Zen *kōan* practice.

Hsing Yun. *Only a Great Rain: A Guide to Chinese Buddhist Meditation.* Boston, 1999. An overview of Chinese meditation teachings by a contemporary Taiwanese Chan master, with an introduction by John R. McRae.

Lü K'uan Yü (Charles Luk). *The Secrets of Chinese Meditation.* 1964; reprint, New York, 1969. Includes translations and discussions of Chan, Pure Land, and Tiantai meditation practices.

Maspero, Henri. *Taoism and Chinese Religion.* Paris, 1971; translated into English by Frank A. Kierman, Jr., Amherst, Mass., 1981.

McRae, John R. *Seeing through Zen: Encounter, Transformation, and Genealogy in Chinese Chan Buddhism.* Berkeley and Los Angeles, 2003. A critical overview of Chan history with hermeneutical guidelines for studying Chan.

Payne, Richard K. "*Ajikan:* Ritual and Meditation in the Shingon Tradition." In *Re-Visioning "Kamakura" Buddhism,* edited by Richard K. Payne, pp. 219–248. Honolulu, 1998. A discussion of the history and practice of *Ajikan.*

Sheng-yen. *Hoofprint of the Ox: Principles of the Chan Buddhist Path as Taught by a Modern Chinese Master.* New York, 2001. A handbook for practitioners by a contemporary Taiwanese Chan master, with a preface and introduction by Dan Stevenson.

Stevenson, Daniel B. "Pure Land Buddhist Worship and Meditation in China." In *Buddhism in Practice,* edited by Donald S. Lopez, Jr., pp. 359–379. Princeton, N.J., 1995. Translations with an invaluable introduction.

Stevenson, Daniel B. "Visions of Mañjuśrī on Mount Wutai." In *Religions of China in Practice,* edited by Donald S. Lopez, Jr., pp. 203–222. Princeton, N.J., 1996. Translation and discussion of the Tang monk Fazhao's *nianfo* practice and visions of the *bodhisattva.*

Stone, Jacqueline I. *Original Enlightenment and the Transformation of Medieval Japanese Buddhism.* Kuroda Institute Studies in East Asian Buddhism, 12. Honolulu, 1999. A comprehensive and penetrating discussion of *hongaku* thought.

Suzuki, Shunryu. *Zen Mind, Beginner's Mind.* New York, 1970. A Sōtō Zen master's informal talks to students in San Francisco; illustrates Sōtō Zen teachings on "just sitting."

Yamasaki, Taikō. *Shingon: Japanese Esoteric Buddhism.* Boston, 1988. An overview of Shingon Buddhism by a contemporary Shingon master of the Chūin-ryū lineage of Mt. Kōya. Includes a section on *Ajikan.*

CLARKE HUDSON (2005)

BUDDHIST PHILOSOPHY. When Buddhism first became known in the West, many historians of philosophy were reluctant to call it "philosophy." Philosophy in the strict sense was viewed as a legacy of the Greeks, who learned to cultivate a critical and theoretical attitude that was free from the limitations of tradition, mythology, and dogma. By the end of the twentieth century, this restrictive approach has begun to change. We now know much more about the critical precision of Buddhist philosophy, and Western philosophers are more favorably inclined toward the practical concerns that inspired Greek philosophy. As theoretical as Greek speculation may have been, it was never far from the practical challenge of living a good or happy life. The same is true of Buddhist philosophy. Even the most rarefied and theoretical analysis is related to a process of moral discipline and liberation from suffering.

In India the word most often translated as "philosophy" is *darśana,* whose root meaning is simply "to see." As a metaphor, *darśana* is close to the Greek word *theoria,* which is the source of our word *theoretical* and also means "to see." *Darśana* can be used to name a system or school of Indian philosophy, as in the title of Mādhava's famous *Sarvadarśanasamuccaya* (Compendium of all systems), or it can be used to name philosophy itself. Some Indian philosophers play on the metaphorical associations of the word to picture philosophy as way of ascending a mountain to get a clear vision of the world. Bhāvaviveka (also known as Bhavya or Bhāviveka) described the practitioner of philosophy as someone "who climbs the mountain peak of wisdom and is free from grief, but looks with compassion on people who are burned by grief." This verse echoes an earlier Buddhist verse about a wise person who ascends the "palace of wisdom" and, without grief or sorrow, sees the suffering of life spread out below. Hans Jonas has pointed out that the metaphor of vision plays a crucial role in Western philosophy, because it suggests distance, detachment, and the ability to perceive all of reality in a single, inclusive act of understanding. Jonas's point applies equally well to Buddhist philosophy. Whether it involves an Indian scholar climbing a mountain, a Chinese master polishing the mirror of the mind, or a Japanese philosopher gazing at the moon reflected in a dewdrop, Buddhist philosophy functions metaphorically as a form of vision.

The idea of vision suggests another important metaphor for the practice of Buddhist philosophy. To get to the top of the mountain, a philosopher has to follow a path. At a crucial moment in his life, Siddhārtha Gautama, the man who became the Buddha, realized that fasting and self-denial were not leading him where he wanted to go. He accepted a gift of food and took up a mode of discipline that is known in Buddhist tradition as a Middle Way, avoiding the extremes of self-denial and self-indulgence. Once he had found the Middle Way, he began to make progress toward the awakening (*bodhi*) that made him a buddha. For Buddhist philosophers, the Middle Way is more an intellectual discipline than a discipline of desire, but it is equally fundamental to their practice: their philosophical practice charts a Middle Way between the extremes of affirmation (in which things are treated as permanent entities) and negation (in which they are treated as utterly nonexistent).

The most fundamental way of understanding Buddhist philosophy, however, is simply as a pursuit of knowledge. From the earliest stages of Buddhist tradition, wisdom (*prajñā*) played a central role in Buddhist practice. Wisdom involved an ability to see through appearances of things and understand them correctly. By a grammatical accident that had enormous influence on the development of Buddhist thought, it also involved a certain way of "going." The word *way* (*pratipad*), in one of its forms, functions as a verbal noun that means "to go." For the philosophers of classical India, "to go" can always mean "to know." This means that the philosophy of the Middle Way is a way of knowing the world without illusion, grief, or suffering. While the metaphors of vision and the path have become attenuated in the long history of Western philosophy, the Buddhist view of the philosopher's path is not far from Plato's parable of the cave, where the challenge is to ascend from the dark world of mere appearances to the bright light of truth.

EARLY BUDDHIST THOUGHT. It is difficult to separate the teachings of the historical Buddha from the complex layers of oral tradition about his life, but several fundamental themes seem to have been established early in Buddhist history and have given decisive shape to the rest of Buddhist thought.

Early canonical literature tells a story about an encounter between the Buddha and a man named Mālunkyaputta. According to the story, Mālunkyaputta asked the Buddha a series of questions: Is the universe eternal or not? Is it finite or infinite? Is the soul identical to the body or not? Does the Buddha exist after death or not? Does he both exist and not exist after death? Does he neither exist nor not exist? Mālunkyaputta said that, if he did not get answers to these questions, he would leave the order. The Buddha responded with a story about a man who was wounded by a poisoned arrow. When someone tried to take out the arrow, the man said: "Wait! Until you tell me who shot the arrow, what kind of person he was, what the bow and arrow were made of, and so forth, I will not let you remove the arrow." The Buddha said that Mālunkyaputta was like the man shot by the arrow. His speculative questions did not have anything to do with the practical challenge of removing suffering. Buddhists interpret this story as meaning that the Buddha's teaching has a practical goal. Buddhist philosophy is not averse to questions about the nature of reality, even questions that are quite abstruse, but in the end their purpose is to remove suffering.

Another story compares the Buddha's teaching to a raft. The Buddha explains that his teaching should help people cross the river of suffering and should not be treated as a source of attachment. Someone who becomes attached to the words of the teaching is like a man who builds a raft to cross a river, gets to the other side, and is so fond of the raft that he puts it on his back and carries it wherever he goes. The right attitude toward the raft is to use it to cross a river then let it go. Once again, the teaching has a practical function, but out if its practicality grows a critical principle. This story challenges anyone who reveres tradition for its own sake, even when that tradition is the teaching of the Buddha. When the Buddha's teaching is no longer useful, or when it is not effective in removing suffering, it should be left behind. If "philosophy," in the strict sense of term, requires a critical spirit toward dogma, myth, and other forms of tradition, as it often does in the Western tradition, then a distinguishable Buddhist "philosophy" is beginning to stir in these early stories.

One of the most important systematic accounts of early Buddhist thought is found in the *Dhammacakkappavattana Sutta* (Discourse on the turning of the wheel of the teaching). According to Buddhist tradition, this discourse contains the Buddha's first sermon and summarizes the content of his awakening. It begins with the Middle Path, then presents a teaching about four noble truths: the truths of suffering (Skt., *duḥkha*; Pali, *dukkha*), the arising of suffering (*samudaya*), the cessation of suffering (*nirodha*), and the path to the cessation of suffering (Skt. *mārga*; Pali, *magga*). Although these truths need to be elaborated before their significance can become clear, they contain an outline of the major topics of Buddhist thought.

The truth of suffering is related to two other important aspects of Buddhist thought: the doctrines of impermanence (Skt., *anitya*; Pali, *anicca*) and no-self (Skt., *nairātmyam*; Pali, *anattā*). Buddhists argue that, while some things are painful in an obvious sense, other things become painful when they change and pass away, and eventually everything changes and passes away. Someone who holds onto changeable things will eventually experience them as suffering. Buddhists carry this point further and argue that, because things change, they lack the permanent identity or "self" that we normally attribute to them. They are nothing but a series of "aggregates" (Skt., *skandha*; Pali, *khandha*) or momentary phenomena that give the illusion of continuity, like momentary flickers in a flame or moments in the flow of a river. The doctrine of impermanence became a major point of controversy between Buddhist and Hindu philosophers, and the doctrine of no-self produced some of the most important debates within the Buddhist tradition itself.

According to the second noble truth, suffering comes from desire, and desire comes from ignorance through a causal sequence known as "dependent co-arising" (Skt., *pratītya-samutpāda*; Pali, *paṭicca-samuppāda*). The most fundamental form of ignorance is the misconception that there is a self. When someone realizes that nothing has any permanent identity, the chain of dependent co-arising unravels, and suffering begins to cease. The third noble truth, the cessation of suffering, is also known as *nirvāṇa* (Pali, *nibbāna*), a word that means simply to "blow out" the fire of ignorance and craving. In its traditional form, the concept of *nirvāṇa* has a negative flavor that sometimes puzzles Western interpreters, but it is not difficult to understand if it is read against the background of Indian views of reincarnation. Like their Hindu and Jain counterparts, Buddhists assume that a person's life follows a cycle of death and rebirth, known in Indian tradition as *saṃsāra* (literally, "wandering"). The goal of the Buddhist path is to bring this cycle to an end. *Nirvāṇa* is not merely the cessation of desire and ignorance; it is liberation from the cycle of reincarnation.

Traditional outlines of the path to *nirvāṇa*, the fourth noble truth, divide it into eight parts, beginning with "right understanding" and ending with "right concentration." In a formula attributed to the nun Dhammadinnā, the eight parts of the eightfold path can be grouped into three: moral conduct (Skt., *śīla*; Pali, *sīla*), concentration (*samādhi*), and wisdom (Skt., *prajñā*; Pali, *paññā*). Moral precepts for laypeople include no killing, no stealing, no lying, no abusing sex, and no taking of intoxicants. The practice of concentration involves a variety of disciplines that often are referred to in the general category of "meditation." Of these the most basic is to sit in a stable posture and concentrate on the movement of the breath. This practice is meant to let the negative tendencies of the mind pass away so that the mind can be clearly aware of the flow of experience. Finally this clear mind should be infused with the wisdom, or the understanding of no-self, that unravels the chain of suffering. It is here, in the cultivation and practice of wisdom, that philosophy finds its place in the path to *nirvāṇa*.

BUDDHIST SECTARIANISM. According to Buddhist literature, the leaders of the early community convened a council about a hundred years after the Buddha's death. While the sources do not agree about the exact nature of the disputes that led to this council, they do show that the community began to divide into different sects or schools (*nikāya*) at a relatively early date. A close study of the sources shows that these divisions initially involved questions of discipline in the Vinaya Piṭaka or "Basket of Discipline" in the Buddhist canon. Later disputes focused on doctrinal questions found in the Sutta Piṭaka and the Abhidhamma Piṭaka. Eventually these disputes produced eighteen separate schools.

The disputes that separated the eighteen schools are too complex and often too obscure to summarize, but one particular dispute had wide influence in later Buddhist thought. This is the "Personalist Controversy." Some of the early schools, such as the Vātsīputrīyas and Sammitīyas, affirmed the existence of a "person" (*pudgala*) that continued from one moment to the next and gave continuity to the personality. These schools said that the "person" was neither identical to nor different from the "aggregates" (*skandha*) that constitute the personality as it was understood by other Buddhist schools. The doctrine of the person (*pudgala-vāda*) was eventually rejected by the majority of Buddhist schools, but not without considerable controversy.

Judging from an account of the personalist doctrine in Vasubandhu's *Abhidharmakośa* (Treasury of the *abhidharma*), there were two reasons for the personalists' position. One was a scriptural text (the *Burden Sūtra*) that spoke of a "person" who took up and laid down the burden of *karma.* The other was that the personalists felt that a "person" was necessary to guarantee moral accountability. They seem to have understood the "person" as the shape or configuration (*saṃsthāna*) of the aggregates. While the shape of the aggregates is not different from the aggregates themselves, it continues while the aggregates themselves come and go. Vasubandhu's criticism of this position takes the form of a dilemma. If the "person" is just a conventional way of speaking about the aggregates, then it is not ultimately real. If it is ultimately real, then it cannot change and cannot be related to the aggregates. This dilemma is common in Buddhist philosophy and plays a crucial role in the Madhyamaka view of the two truths to be discussed below.

THE *ABHIDHARMA*. The systematic elaboration of Buddhist thought took a major step forward with the development of the *abhidharma* (Pali, *abidhamma*). The *abhidharma* tradition began as lists, known as *mātṛkās* ("matrices"), of the fundamental constituents (*dharmas*) of reality. As Vasubandhu explained in his *Abhidharmakośa*, *abhidharma* has to do with cultivating pure wisdom through the discrimination of these fundamental constituents. Eventually these lists of fundamental constituents were developed into a third "basket" of scripture. The *abhidharma* schools attributed these lists to the Buddha himself, although their attribution was not universally shared. An important early school known as the Sautrāntikas ("those who follow the discourses") challenged the claim that the *abhidharma* could be traced to the Buddha. This school based its doctrine solely on the Buddha's discourses (*sūtrānta*).

A good way to become acquainted with the questions that occupied the *abhidharma*, without having to deal with the complexity of the matrices, is to read the *Milindapañha* (The questions of King Milinda). This text presents a discussion between the monk Nāgasena and King Milinda, who is identified as Menander, an Indo-Greek king who ruled in northern India around 150–130 BCE. In one of its best known chapters, Milinda asks Nāgasena about the idea of "no-self." Does it mean that Nāgasena himself does not exist? Nāgasena responds by asking the king about his chariot. Does the word *chariot* refer to the wheel, the axle, the pole, or some other part of the chariot? The king says: No, the word *chariot* is just a conventional designation that depends for its meaning on these separate parts. Nāgasena then says that the word *Nāgasena* functions in the same way. It is just a conventional designation that depends on the momentary constituents of the personality. This comparison shows what Vasubandhu meant when he said that *abhidharma* is "the discrimination of fundamental constituents." The process of discrimination implies not only a theory of language but an epistemology: the knowledge of reality has to penetrate beneath the level of conventional designations to the momentary constituents in the flow of experience.

The most influential of the *abhidharma* schools belonged to the Sarvāstivādins ("who hold the doctrine that everything exists"), also known as the Vaibhāṣikas after the title of their greatest work, the *Mahāvibhāṣā* (Great commentary). The school began in the central region of the Ganges basin and eventually migrated to Kashmir where it flourished for several centuries and had wide impact on the transmission of Buddhism to Central and East Asia. Its influence was so great in China that the *Mahāvibhāṣā* has been preserved in several different recensions in the Chinese canon, including a translation made in 659 by the renowned Chinese scholar Xuanzang.

The most distinctive Sarvāstivādin theory, and the one from which the school gets its name, is the idea that "everything exists" not merely in the present, but in the past and future. This position was first developed in the first century CE in a text known as the *Vijñānakāya* (The body of consciousness) and seems to have responded to two problems associated with the concept of impermanence: How can an act of cognition "know" something in the past or future if that object does not exist, and how can past actions have any effect in the present, if the actions have ceased to exist? In the *Mahāvibhāṣā* there is an elaborate discussion of the mental factors that lead to awakening, along with the factors that hold a person back. As is often the case throughout Buddhist philosophy, epistemology plays a key part in the process of liberation.

THE MAHĀYĀNA. The appearance of the Mahāyāna (Great Vehicle), near the beginning of the Common Era, led to a reinterpretation of many of the basic values of Buddhist thought. Mahāyāna texts refer to the teachings of earlier schools as Hīnayāna (Lesser Vehicle) and claim that the Mahāyāna represents a transmission of the Buddha's most profound teaching. For modern scholars, the origins of the Mahāyāna are quite obscure. What is certain is that by the second century of the Common Era, when the first Buddhist translations appeared in China, Mahāyāna texts were actively circulating through the Indian Buddhist community. As the Mahāyāna movement gathered momentum, it transformed the Buddhism of India and became the dominant tradition in China, Korea, Japan, Tibet, and Vietnam.

Early Mahāyāna literature, particularly the *Prajñāpāramitā* (Perfection of Wisdom) *Sūtras*, introduced two key new ideas into the tradition of Buddhist thought. The first of these, the doctrine of emptiness, presented a bold and radical application of the traditional doctrine of no-self. The second, the ideal of the *bodhisattva*, placed this view of reality in a distinctive system of ethical practice and reflection. Neither of these two ideas was unprecedented in Buddhist tradition, but they were presented in such new ways that they precipitated a major reconsideration of the fundamental concepts of Buddhist thought.

According to the *bodhisattva* ideal, the goal of Buddhist life is not to achieve *nirvāṇa* in this life, as it had been in earlier tradition; it is to return in the cycle of reincarnation to help others on the path. While the *bodhisattva* ideal does not exclude monks and nuns, Mahāyāna texts like the *Vimalakīrtinirdeśa* (The teaching of Vimalakīrti) *Sūtra* speak positively about the lay life and draw lay people into the center of the teaching. *Bodhisattvas* are encouraged to practice the active virtue of compassion (*karuṇā*), along with the traditional virtue of wisdom (*prajñā*). This practice involves the cultivation of six "perfections" (*pāramitā*)—generosity, moral conduct, patience, fortitude, concentration, and wisdom (a list that was later expanded to ten)—and proceeds through a process of ten stages (*bhūmi*). In the last stages of this process, *bodhisattvas* acquire such extraordinary powers from their practice of merit and wisdom that they function almost like the Hindu gods.

While the *abhidharma* focused on the discrimination of *dharmas* as the momentary but real constituents of reality, the early Mahāyāna sūtras called the reality of these *dharmas* into question. In the first chapter of *The Perfection of Wisdom in Eight Thousand Lines*, for example, Śāriputra poses a question: "What *dharma* does the word *bodhisattva* refer to?" The answer is that he cannot "find, apprehend, or see" any *dharma* corresponding to the word *bodhisattva*. The sūtra extends the same analysis to all of the categories of Buddhist thought: no matter what the word, no *dharma* can be "apprehended" that corresponds to it. This view of reality can be distilled into the claim that all *dharmas* are "empty" of identity. In other words, the nature of all things is their emptiness.

While the Mahāyāna doctrine of emptiness is easy to state, its implications are complex. One obvious consequence is the concept of nonduality: no matter how different two things may seem, in the end there is no distinction between them. There is no difference between one moment and the next, between one person and another, and between *nirvāṇa* and *saṃsāra*. To the critics of the Mahāyāna, this view often seems to be a form of nihilism, but it has important positive implications. The *bodhisattva* ideal, for example, is not based merely on a sense of altruism or compassion. While the *bodhisattva* may wish to help others, and this desire may be an important motivation for starting out on the *bodhisattva* path, the *bodhisattva* also realizes that there is no way to separate his or her fate from the fate of others, and there is no way to escape into *nirvāṇa* apart from *saṃsāra* itself. The doctrine of emptiness leads inevitably to the *bodhisattva* practice. Emptiness may seem negative, but it leads to an expansive and affirmative philosophy of Buddhist practice.

THE MADHYAMAKA. The first systematic attempt to organize Mahāyāna thought is associated with the philosopher Nāgārjuna. Reliable historical information about Indian philosophers is rare, and the figure of Nāgārjuna is even more elusive than most. Scholars generally agree that he lived in south-central India sometime in the second or third century of the Common Era. Otherwise what we know of him comes only through his works. Of these, the most important is the *Mūlamadhyamaka-kārikā* (Root verses on the Middle Way), the text that served as the source of the Madhyamaka ("Middle Way") school. Nāgārjuna also was the author of a number of independent treatises on problems in logic and the philosophy of language, including the *Vigrahavyāvartanī* (Avoidance of disputes), a work on the *bodhisattva* path (the *Ratnāvalī* [Jewel garland]), and several well-known hymns.

Nāgārjuna makes the direction of his argument clear in the first verse of the *Mūlamadhyamaka-kārikā*: "Nothing ever arises anywhere from itself, from something else, from both, or from nothing at all." To say that nothing arises by any possible causal mechanism depends on a particular assumption about the nature of identity: if something has an "own-being" or "identity of its own" (*svabhāva*), then it cannot be produced by anything else and cannot give rise to itself. The only way something can "arise" is to be empty of any identity. In other words, for Nāgārjuna, the Buddhist view of impermanence expressed in the doctrine of dependent co-arising required that everything be empty of identity. Nāgārjuna expressed this point in two key verses in the *Mūlamadhyamaka-kārikā*: "We call dependent co-arising emptiness; it is a metaphorical designation, and it is the Middle Path"; and "Everything is possible for someone for whom emptiness is possible, and nothing is possible for someone for whom emptiness is not possible."

How can something be possible, if it has no identity? Is the doctrine of emptiness any different from saying that nothing exists at all? The answer to these questions requires another key Madhyamaka concept: the distinction between the two truths. Nāgārjuna said: "When buddhas teach the *dharma*, they depend on two truths: ordinary relative truth and ultimate truth. . . . It is impossible to teach the ultimate without depending on the conventional, and it is impossible to understand *nirvāṇa* without understanding the ultimate." The distinction between the two truths begins with a particular truth about language: a person has to depend on the distinctions of ordinary language in order to show that ordinary language does not apply. But the distinction has important metaphysical and epistemological implications: a person has to depend on an ordinary understanding of things in order to seek *nirvāṇa*. From the ultimate point of view distinctions fall away, but any action or thought that is directed toward ultimate truth gains its meaning by its dependence on relative (*saṃvṛti*) or conventional (*vyavahāra*) truth. The combination of the two truths—a conventional affirmation and an ultimate negation—constitutes the "middle way" that gives the school its name. It also allows Nāgārjuna to appropriate the basic categories of Buddhist life in a positive way without treating them as ultimately real.

The distinction between the two truths was fundamental to Madhyamaka thought, but it posed troubling philosophical problems for Nāgārjuna's followers. These problems emerged in a series of commentaries on the *Mūlamadhyamaka-kārikā*, written two or three centuries after the time of Nāgārjuna and focused on a disagreement about the logical form of Nāgārjuna's arguments. The commentator Buddhapālita (c. 470–540) interpreted Nāgārjuna's arguments as a *prasaṅga* or reductio ad absurdum in which the opponent's position is shown to lead to absurd conclusions. Buddhapālita formulated the argument against arising from self and other as two separate claims: If someone says that things cannot arise from themselves, this is impossible, because their arising would be useless, and if someone says that things cannot arise from something else, this too is impossible, because then anything could be produced by anything else. This interpretation of Nāgārjuna is known as *Prāsaṅgika* from its style of reasoning. Bhāvaviveka (c. 500–570) argued that the rules of Indian logic require Mādhyamikas not merely to defeat their opponent's position but to establish a position of their own. He restated the first part of Nāgārjuna's argument as an "independent syllogism" (*svatantra anumāna*) with his own independent assertion and reason: "Things do not arise from themselves, because they already exist." Because of his fondness for independent (*svatantra*) arguments, Bhāvaviveka's position is known as *Svātantrika*. Candrakīrti (c. 600–650) came to Buddhapālita's defense and provided the classic statement of the Prāsaṅgika approach. For Tibetan tradition and for modern scholars, Bhāvaviveka's Svātantrika and Candrakīrti's Prāsaṅgika represent the two major, competing options in the interpretation of Madhyamaka thought.

This dispute about logical procedure gives a glimpse of the problems that occupied Buddhist philosophers in what might be called the classical period of Buddhist philosophy in India. By the fourth and fifth centuries Buddhist monasteries had become sophisticated centers of learning and were drawn into debate not only with other Buddhists but with competing schools of Hindus and Jains. Bhāvaviveka himself played a crucial role in this inter-traditional dialogue by producing the *Tarkajvālā* (Flame of reason), the first systematic chapter-by-chapter account of the doctrines of competing Indian schools. It was natural for him to insist that Buddhists play by the accepted rules of debate and defend their own positions. It fell to Candrakīrti to reassert the austerity and simplicity of Nāgārjuna's vision of ultimate truth. Behind the argument about the procedure for debate, however, lay an argument about the nature of conventional truth. Bhāvaviveka felt that it was necessary to "accept" (*siddha*) conventional things before analyzing them from the ultimate perspective; Candrakīrti refused to attribute such independent reality to the subject of his arguments.

In addition to commentaries on Nāgārjuna, Bhāvaviveka and Candrakīrti wrote major works on the *bodhisattva* path. Both works, Candrakīrti's *Madhyamakāvatāra* (Introduction to the Middle Way) and the first three chapters of Bhāvaviveka's *Tarkajvālā*, present their analysis of Madhyamaka philosophy as part of the path to buddhahood. The same is true of the *Bodhicaryāvatāra* (Introduction to the practice of awakening) by Śāntideva (eighth century). In a widely-quoted scriptural text, wisdom (*prajñā*) is pictured as a way of giving sight to the other perfections and leading them to the city of *nirvāṇa*. While the practice of Buddhist philosophy became more and more concerned with issues of logic and epistemology, it did not lose its intimate relationship to the discipline of Buddhist life.

Madhyamaka continued to develop after the dispute between Candrakīrti and Bhāvaviveka. Bhāvaviveka's Svātantrika approach was taken up and extended by the eighth-century scholars Jñānagarbha, Śāntarakṣita, and Kamalaśīla, who shared the definition of conventional truth as "arising dependently, capable of effective action, and satisfying only when it is not analyzed." The concept of "effective action" (*artha-kriyā*) in this definition shows the influence of the Buddhist logician Dharmakīrti (seventh century). Both Śāntarakṣita and Kamalaśīla played important roles in the introduction of Buddhism to Tibet. On the Prāsaṅgika side, the philosopher Atīśa (eleventh century) helped reestablish the Buddhist intellectual tradition in Tibet after a period of persecution. His Prāsaṅgika convictions, along with his well-known work on the *bodhisattva* path, *Bodhipathapradīpa* (Lamp for the path to awakening), had immense influence on the shape of philosophy in Tibet. One of the least known areas of Madhyamaka thought in the last period of Indian Buddhist history has to do with the relationship between Madhyamaka and Tantra. Two works by the Tantric saint Vimalamitra are included in the Madhyamaka section of the Tibetan canon, and it is clear from later Tibetan history, as well as from the lives of Tantric saints, that Madhyamaka played an important role in developing the radical concept of nonduality on which Tantra was based.

THE YOGĀCĀRA. A century or two after the time of Nāgārjuna, a second school emerged to challenge its interpretation of the Mahāyāna. This school is known by the name Yogācāra or "Practice of Discipline." The origin of the Yogācāra is obscured by an old tradition that attributes several of the school's fundamental texts to the celestial *bodhisattva* Maitreya. The school's most important early exponents, if not its actual founders, were Asaṅga and Vasubandhu (fourth or fifth century), two philosophers who were possibly brothers. Like the Madhyamaka, the Yogācāra grew from the interpretation of a distinctive body of Mahāyāna sūtras. These included not merely the *Perfection of Wisdom Sūtras*, but sūtras that spoke of a "third turning of the wheel of the teaching" intended to interpret and move beyond the teaching of the Perfection of Wisdom. The *Sandhinirmocana* (Releasing the hidden meaning) *Sūtra* describes the *Perfection of Wisdom Sūtras* as *neyārtha* (requiring further interpretation) as opposed to the *Sandhinirmocana* itself, which *is nītārtha* (its meaning is definitive and does not need further interpretation).

Instead of two truths, the Yogācāra tradition developed a doctrine of three natures (*svabhāva*): imagined (*parikalpita*) nature, dependent (*paratantra*) nature, and perfected (*pariniṣpanna*) nature. The first of these natures has to do with distinctions between subject and object and between one object and another. When the mind distinguishes things and gives them names, the nature it attributes to them is "imagined": it is as unreal as a magic trick or a dream. The mind itself, in its imaginative capacity, constitutes "dependent nature." When it creates imaginative fantasies about the nature of the world, it is like the mind that creates a dream: its concepts are not real, but the mind itself is real. Perfected nature is defined as the absence of imagined nature in dependent nature. In this sense it is identical to emptiness itself, but it also can be equated with the mind when all its illusory concepts have been removed.

This Yogācāra picture of reality appears in different forms in different texts, including the *Madhyāntavibhāga* (Distinction between the middle and the extremes), the *Viṃśatikā* (Twenty verses) and the *Triṃśikā* (Thirty verses), but the basic picture remains the same. In all these texts, the three natures function not only as an ontology, to distinguish real from unreal, but as an epistemology and a roadmap for meditation. The first step in the meditative process is to grasp the concept of "mind-only" (*citta-mātra*) in order to eliminate attachment to external objects. Once a person has understood that there is nothing but mind, it is possible to free the mind from the idea that it is a separate subject, different from its objects. The goal of this process is to develop the nondual awareness that constitutes the Buddha's awakening. The concept of "mind-only" is widely understood to mean that the Yogācāra is a form of Indian idealism. There is much in Yogācāra literature to support this view, particularly the sophisticated Yogācāra analysis of the transformations (*pariṇāma*) of consciousness. But it is important to note that the concept of "mind-only" is used to remove attachment not only to objects but also to the mind as a separate subject.

After the time of Asaṅga and Vasubandhu, the Yogācāra school developed a complex commentarial tradition like the tradition of the Madhyamaka. Philosophers like Sthiramati (510–570) and Dharmapāla (c. 530–561) developed distinctive and influential interpretations of the school in the monasteries of North India. This was the intellectual milieu that Xuanzang (c. 600–664) encountered when he traveled from China in the early decades of the seventh century. After studying in Yogācāra circles for several years, he returned to China and introduced the Yogācāra tradition to Chinese Buddhism. While the school did not maintain a separate identity in China long after the death of Xuanzang, its influence was felt throughout the history of Chinese Buddhist thought.

BUDDHIST LOGIC. One of the most important legacies of the Yogācāra in India was the epistemological tradition known as Buddhist logic. Beginning in the sixth century in the works of Dignāga (c. 480–540), the tradition produced some of the greatest philosophers in the Indian tradition. There is a legend that the Hindu logician Udayana went to a temple one day and found the door locked. In frustration, he addressed God in the following words: "Drunk with the wine of your own divinity, you ignore me; but when the Buddhists are here, your existence depends on me." The Buddhists he was referring to were not the Mādhyamikas or the early Yogācāras, but the philosophical heirs of Dignāga who kept up their controversies with their Hindu opponents until the Buddhist monasteries were destroyed at the end of the twelfth century.

In his major work, the *Pramāṇasamuccaya* (A compendium of the means of knowledge), Dignāga argued that there are only two acceptable ways to know: perception (*pratyakṣa*) and inference (*anumāna*). Perception gives access to momentary particulars (*svalakṣaṇa*), which are ultimately real, while inference gives access to universals (*sāmānya-lakṣaṇa*), which are only conventionally real. Absent from this list is knowledge based on scripture or verbal testimony. Verbal testimony played a crucial epistemic role in Hindu exegesis of the Vedas, but Dignāga cast verbal testimony aside in favor of perception and the logical analysis of experience based on perception. In this respect, he represented a more sophisticated version of the critical approach that animated the teaching of the Buddha himself.

With Dignāga's austere two-part epistemology came not only a complex analysis of the types of perception but also a thorough study of the forms of inference and, with the theory of inference, a view of language as *anyāpoha* ("exclusion of the other"). Dignāga recognized that it was impossible for a word like *cow* to refer directly to the universal "cowness," since such an entity was nothing more than an intellectual construct. Instead, he argued that the word gained its meaning by excluding particulars that did not belong to a cow, such as the distinguishing characteristics of a horse.

Dignāga's successors included Dharmakīrti, who wrote the *Pramāṇavārttika*, the authoritative commentary on Dignāga's major work, and two philosophers, Ratnakīrti and Jñānaśrīmitra, who carried the Buddhist-Hindu controversy into the tenth and eleventh centuries on such topics as the existence of God and the self and the doctrine of momentariness.

BUDDHIST PHILOSOPHY OUTSIDE INDIA. The history of Buddhist philosophy outside India is a complex topic in its own right and cannot be treated simply as an extension of controversies and schools borrowed from India. In the earliest stages of Buddhist philosophical activity in Tibet and East Asia, the challenge was to interpret and absorb the Indian traditions, but it was not long before scholars in both areas generated distinctive traditions of philosophical reasoning.

In Tibet, the Indian Buddhist philosophical tradition became part of the standard monastic curriculum in all the Tibetan schools. Students received the texts from their teachers, memorized them, and then debated their meaning with their peers. In the Dge lugs (Geluk) pa tradition that is represented by the lineage of the Dalai Lamas, the curriculum included Candrakīrti's *Madhyamakāvatāra*, Dharmakīrti's *Pramāṇavārttika*, a summary of the *Perfection of Wisdom Sūtras*, and a text on the monastic discipline. While Tibetan philosophers had a traditional focus, they were capable of impressive originality and creative insight, as anyone who has encountered the work of a scholar like Tsong kha pa (1357–1419) can attest. The study of Indian Buddhist philosophy today would not be the same without the insights generated by the Tibetan exegetical tradition.

The earliest attempts to formulate Buddhist thought in China began in the second and third centuries CE and were strongly influenced by indigenous Chinese traditions, particularly Daoism. The neo-Daoist concept of "original nonbeing" came tantalizingly close to the Mahāyāna concept of emptiness and helped give Chinese Buddhist philosophy a Daoist flavor that never entirely disappeared. One of the finest examples of the Daoist turn in early Chinese Buddhism was the brilliant fifth-century commentator Sengzhao. As a pupil of the influential translator Kumārajīva (c. 350–409/413), Sengzhao had access to the text of Nāgārjuna's *Mūlamadhyamaka-kārikā* and understood its Indian characteristics, but he transformed its argument in a distinctively Chinese way, depicting the Buddhist sage in a way that would have been very much at home in Daoist circles in the same period.

In the sixth and seventh centuries, as Chinese thinkers became more adept at interpreting Indian texts in their original languages, Madhyamaka and Yogācāra went through a brief period of efflorescence. Jizang (549–623) made a bold attempt to articulate the Madhyamaka, while Xuandang (600–664) did the same for the Yogācāra. With the arrival of the Tang dynasty (618–907), however, Chinese Buddhism developed its own distinctive, indigenous philosophical schools. One of the most influential was the Tiantai, founded by Zhiyi (538–597) on Mount Tiantai ("Heavenly Terrace"). Zhiyi's thought can be summarized in three key doctrines: the nature of all *dharmas*, the harmony of three levels of truth, and the three thousand worlds immanent in an instant of thought. Tiantai had an inclusive, eirenic character that gave it great influence, not only in China but also in Japan where, as the Tendai school, it gave rise to the three major Buddhist movements of the Kamakura period (1185–1333): Pure Land Buddhism, the tradition of Nichiren, and Zen. Another key school associated with the Tang dynasty was the Huayan, founded by Fazang (643–712). The Huayan was based on the *Avataṃsaka Sūtra*, an Indian Mahāyāna text that compared the world to a network of jewels, with every individual jewel reflecting the light of every other jewel. This vision of the interconnectedness of the cosmos had important influence in Chinese philosophy, including neo-Confucianism, and in the philosophical literature of Japan.

Whether the Chan ("Meditation") school (referred to in Japan as *Zen*) should be called "philosophical" in the strict sense of the word might be debated. It could just as well be called "anti-philosophical," in the sense that it challenges discursive logic and favors direct experience over "words and letters," but it had so much influence on the development of Buddhist thought that it cannot be excluded. One of the key documents in the history of Chan is *The Platform Sūtra of the Sixth Patriarch* by Huineng (638–713). In this text the master Hongren (601–674) asks his disciples to write verses expressing the basic point of the Buddha's teaching. The master then uses the verses to decide who should carry on the mantle of his authority. One student writes a verse saying that the body is the tree of wisdom and the mind is the stand of a mirror: the purpose of meditation is to wipe the mirror and not allow it to become dusty. Huineng responds with a strict application of the concept of emptiness: "The mirror of the mind is always clear and pure. How can it be defiled by dust?" Out of Huineng's teaching grew the Southern school of Chan, with an emphasis on sudden awakening. The Northern school, which traced its origin to Huineng's rival, Shenxiu (c. 606–706), stressed a view of gradual awakening.

The intellectual strength of the Chan tradition shows itself vividly in the work of the Japanese Zen master and philosopher Dōgen (1200–1253). Dōgen was born in the family of an influential courtier but lost his family at an early age and entered the Tendai monastery on Mount Hiei in Kyoto to become a monk. Not satisfied with his studies, he traveled to China and received what he later called "the *dharma*-gate of face-to-face transmission." Returning to Japan, he founded the Sōtō school of Japanese Zen, a school that is known for its practice of "just sitting." Dōgen's major work, the *Shōbōgenzō* (Treasury of the true *dharma* eye), crosses the line between poetry and philosophy with its eloquent and paradoxical explorations of the concept of emptiness. It is relentlessly analytical, while it constantly subverts the linear process of logical analysis; it also is intensely intellectual, while it dissolves the intellect in a quest for pure experience.

RECENT BUDDHIST PHILOSOPHY. The history of Buddhist philosophy since the mid-nineteenth century has been dominated in one form or another by the encounter with the West. The Theravāda tradition felt Western influence as early as the end of the nineteenth century, when the Theosophists Henry Steel Olcott (1832–1907) and H. P. Blavatsky (1831–1891) arrived in Sri Lanka, converted to Buddhism, and attempted to create a modern, rational Buddhism. They criticized practices that they considered corrupt or superstitious, like the worship of local deities, and they argued that Buddhists should return to the tradition's pragmatic, down-to-earth, experiential roots. This interpretation of the Buddhist tradition continues to have enormous influence in contemporary accounts of the Buddha's teaching.

One of the most influential attempts to bring Buddhism into dialogue with Western philosophy took place in the Kyoto school in Japan. The Kyoto school began in the departments of philosophy and religion at Kyoto State University under the influence of Nishida Kitarō (1870–1945). Nishida attempted to be loyal to Japanese traditions, especially Buddhism, and to synthesize Japanese traditions with the philosophical tradition of the West. Nishida's project was taken up by his successor in Kyoto, Tanabe Hajime (1885–1962), and by his student Nishitani Keiji (1900–1990). Nishida felt a deep affinity between Japanese thought and certain currents of German idealism, especially its use of dialectical logic and its openness toward mysticism. His concept of absolute nothingness involved a dialectical relationship of being and nonbeing and yielded a view of the self in which the self is "made nothing" so that it can open up to its true identity. In *Religion and Nothingness* (English translation 1982), Nishitani related this process to the history of Western philosophy and argued that Western thought had to pass through a stage of nihility to achieve a state of absolute nothingness, where it could embrace both being and nothingness. After the death of Nishitani, the Kyoto school has been less of a force in Japanese philosophy, but it remains one of the boldest attempts to cross the boundaries between philosophy and religion and between Buddhism and the tradition of Western philosophy.

SEE ALSO Dharma, article on Buddhist Dharma and Dharmas; Eightfold Path; Four Noble Truths; Mādhyamika; Nirvāṇa; Prajña; Pratītya-samutpāda; Soteriology; Soul, article on Buddhist Concepts; Tathāgata-garbha; Yogācāra.

BIBLIOGRAPHY

Wilhelm Halbfass gives a thorough and illuminating account of nineteenth- and twentieth-century European responses to Indian philosophy in *India and Europe: An Essay in Understanding* (Albany, N.Y., 1988). Bimal Krishna Matilal makes the analytical and critical dimension of Indian thought clear in *Epistemology, Logic, and Grammar in Indian Philosophical Analysis* (The Hague, 1971) and *Perception: An Essay on Classical Indian Theories of Knowledge* (Oxford, 1986). On the relationship between theory and practice in Indian literature, see Sheldon Pollock, "The Theory of Practice and the Practice of Theory in Indian Intellectual History," *Journal of the American Oriental Society* 105 (1985): 499–519. Studies of the same issue in Classical Greek and Roman philosophy include Pierre Hadot, *Philosophy as a Way of Life* (Oxford, 1995), and Martha C. Nussbaum, *The Fragility of Goodness: Luck and Ethics in Greek Tragedy and Philosophy* (Cambridge, U.K., 1986). On the role of vision as a metaphor for philosophy in the Western tradition, see Han Jonas, "The Nobility of Sight: A Study in the Phenomenology of the Senses," in *The Phenomenon of Life: Toward a Philosophical Biology* (1966; reprint, Evanston, Ill., 2001).

There are many helpful introductions to Buddhist thought. Three of the best are Walpola Rahula, *What the Buddha Taught* (New York, 1974); Paul Williams, *Buddhist Thought: A Complete Introduction to the Indian Tradition* (London, 2000); and Donald W. Mitchell, *Buddhism: Introducing the Buddhist Experience* (New York, 2002). Karl H. Potter's *Presuppositions of India's Philosophies* (Englewood Cliffs, N.J., 1963) still provides one of the most useful ways of understanding the relationship of the doctrine of reincarnation to Indian theories of causation and epistemology. Steven Collins wrote an important study of the no-self doctrine in *Selfless Person* (Cambridge, U.K., 1982).

For a summary of scholarship on the Buddhist councils, see André Bareau, *Les premiers conciles bouddhiques* (Paris, 1955); Charles S. Prebish, "A Review of Scholarship on the Buddhist Councils," *Journal of Asian Studies* 33 (1974): 239–254; and Janice J. Nattier and Charles S. Prebish, "Mahāsaṃghika Origins: The Beginnings of Buddhist Sectarianism," *History of Religions* 16 (1977). On the doctrines of the eighteen *nikāyas*, see André Bareau, "Trois traités sur les sectes bouddhiques attribués à Vasumitra, Bhavya, et Vinītadeva," *Journal Asiatique* 242 (1954): 229–265; 244 (1956): 167–199. Vasubandhu's discussion of the personalist doctrine (*pudgala-vāda*) is available in Edward Conze's *Buddhist Scriptures* (London, 1959), pp. 192–97.

The most inclusive account of the *abhidharma* is Karl H. Potter's *Abhidharma Buddhism to 150 A.D., Encyclopedia of Indian Philosophies*, vol. 7 (Delhi, 1996). Vasubandhu's *Abidharmakośa* has been translated into French by Louis de La Vallée Poussin in *L'Abhidharmakośa de Vasubandhu* (Brussels, 1971).

For an account of the Perfection of Wisdom literature and its role in the development of the Mahāyāna, see Edward Conze's *The Perfection of Wisdom Literature*, 2d ed. (Tokyo, 1978). Conze's translation of *The Perfection of Wisdom in Eight Thousand Lines and Its Verse Summary* (Bolinas, Calif., 1973) gives a clear picture of the scriptural sources of the Mahāyāna. Another important Mahāyāna sūtra in translation is Etienne Lamotte's *The Teaching of Vimalakīrti (Vimalakīrtinirdeśa)* (London, 1976).

The best source for a history of Madhyamaka thought is David Seyfort Ruegg's *The Literature of the Madhyamaka School in India* (Wiesbaden, Germany, 1981). No single translation of Nāgārjuna's *Mūlamadhyamaka-kārikā* is considered definitive, but Jay L. Garfield, trans., *The Fundamental Wisdom of the Middle Way* (New York, 1995) provides a useful orientation to this fundamental text. A translation of the *Vigrahavyāvartanī*, one of Nāgārjuna's most important works on logic and epistemology, can be found in Kamaleswar Bhattacharya, "The Dialectical Method of Nāgārjuna," *Journal of Indian Philosophy* 1 (1971): 217–261. To study the disputes that divided the Madhyamaka tradition in India and Tibet, there is no better source than *The Svatantrika-Prasangika Distinction: What Difference Does a Difference Make?* edited by Georges B. J. Dreyfus and Sara L. McClintock (Boston, 2003). The most accessible translation of a Madhyamaka work on the *bodhisattva* path is Śāntideva's *Bodhicaryāvatāra*, translated by Kate Crosby and Andrew Skilton (Oxford, 1996).

The basic sources of the Yogācāra tradition are available in Thomas A. Kochmuttom's *A Buddhist Doctrine of Experience: A New Translation and Interpretation of the Works of Vasubandhu the Yogācārin* (Delhi, 1989) and Stefan Anacker's *Seven Works of Vasubandhu* (Delhi, 1998). For scholarly accounts of Dignāga's thought, see Masaaki Hattori's Dignāga, *On Perception* (Cambridge, Mass., 1968), and Richard P. Hayes, *Dignāga on the Interpretation of Signs* (Dordrecht, Netherlands, 1988). Tom J. F. Tillemans gives a good example of the excellent scholarship being done today on Dharmakīrti's epistemology in *Scripture, Logic, and Language: Essays on Dharmakīrti and His Tibetan Successors* (Somerville, Mass., 1999). One of the most helpful surveys of the issues that dominated the later tradition of Buddhist logic is Yuichi Kajiyama's translation of Mokṣākaragupta's *Tarkabhāṣā*, in *An Introduction to Buddhist Philosophy* (Vienna, 1998).

Georges Dreyfus has written an engaging account of the scholar's life in a Tibetan monastery in *The Sound of One Hand Clapping: The Education of a Tibetan Monk* (Berkeley, Calif., 2003). There is no single source to turn to for an introduction to Chinese Buddhist philosophy. Wing-tsit Chan provides excerpts from major texts with helpful commentary in *A Sourcebook in Chinese Philosophy* (Princeton, N.J., 1963). Brook Ziporyn has written two important studies of Tiantai philosophy: *Evil and/or/as the Good: Omnicentrism, Intersubjectivity, and Value Paradox in Tiantai Buddhist Thought* (Cambridge, Mass., 2000), and *Being and Ambiguity: Philosophical Experiments with Tiantai Buddhism* (Chicago, 2004). For a philosophical reflection on Zen, see Dale S. Wright, *Philosophical Meditations on Zen Buddhism* (Cambridge, U.K., 1998). Important selections from Dōgen's writings are available in Kazuaki Tanahashi, ed., *Moon in a Dewdrop: Writings of Zen Master Dōgen* (New York, 1985).

James W. Heissig has written a useful history of the Kyoto school in *Philosophers of Nothingness: An Essay on the Kyoto School* (Honolulu, 2001). Keiji Nishitani's most important work in English translation is *Religion and Nothingness*, translated by Jan van Bragt (Berkeley, Calif., 1982).

MALCOLM DAVID ECKEL (2005)

BUDDHIST RELIGIOUS YEAR. The Buddhist religious year celebrates seminal events in the life of the founder and the early religious community and sanctifies the annual changes of the seasons and the cyclical passage of time in which the life of the community is embedded. Particular cultural traditions adjust and amplify both dimensions of the Buddhist calendar according to their own histories and circumstances.

Each Buddhist culture developed its own religious calendar punctuated by particular ceremonies, rituals, and festivals. Chinese Buddhists, for example, celebrated the life of the Buddha and various *bodhisattvas*, the death anniversaries of certain figures in Chinese Buddhist history, various celestial beings (*tian gong*), the emperor's birthday, and such seasonal events as the celebration of the new year and the end of summer. In Tibet, the religious year included not only celebrations for the Buddha and major religious figures such as Padmasambhava, but also monthly commemorations of a wide variety of deities and saints and the celebration of the new year. Within any given cultural tradition the specifically Buddhist events of the year—the life of the Buddha, the observance of the rains retreat (*vassa*), and so forth—are likely to be articulated with the agricultural cycle. Thus, in much of Southeast Asia, Buddha's Day occurs at the onset of the monsoon rains in May; the *kaṭhina* ceremonies, in which gifts are presented to the monks, comes at the end of *vassa*, the end of the planting season; and the merit-making ceremony in honor of the Buddha's appearance as Prince Vessantara comes in February–March, after the rice harvest. In short, the Buddhist religious year is closely integrated with the cycle of rice cultivation and its accompanying economic activities.

For the purposes of this article we shall not divide the Buddhist religious year chronologically, in part because of the variance among Buddhist calendars from culture to culture. Rather, we shall first examine the major observances of the Buddhist year as defined by the events in the life of the Buddha and the founding of his religion (*sāsana*), and then seasonal celebrations, in particular, the New Year. Although these two dimensions of the Buddhist religious year are separable for analytical purposes, within the lives of Chinese, Tibetan, Japanese, Thai, Sri Lankan and Burmese Buddhists the distinction is, at best, moot. From the perspective of the individual, furthermore, the religious year is also marked by life-transition ceremonies of an annual (e.g., birth and death anniversaries) or occasional nature, for instance, house consecrations. In traditional Buddhist societies, then, the religion essentially sanctified and made meaningful all aspects of life, whether cosmic, communal, or individual.

In short, the experience of the tradition calibrates the religious year, its founding, the major events within its early history, its most significant turning points. The major annual observances of the Buddhist year include, but are not limited to, the life of the Buddha, the proclamation of the Buddha's teaching, or *dharma*, the founding of the monastic order, the beginning and end of the monsoon rains retreat (*vassa*), founder's celebrations, and saint's anniversaries. Observances celebrated more frequently, monthly or bimonthly, weekly or daily, include sabbath ceremonies, the fortnightly monastic confessional, or Prātimokṣa, and daily monastic rituals.

CELEBRATING THE BUDDHA. Buddhist doctrine traditionally divides the Buddha's life into eight or twelve acts, many of which are commemorated in various ways in particular Buddhist cultures. These acts include the Buddha's birth, enlightenment, first discourse, entry into *nirvāṇa*, descent from Trāyastriṃśa Heaven, where he had instructed his mother in the Abhidharma, the simultaneous appearance of the 1,250 arhats at Veḷuvana monastery in Rājagṛha, and the miracle of Śrāvastī, where the Buddha miraculously multiplied himself into an infinite number of flaming manifestations, thereby vanquishing the heretics who had challenged him to a magical competition.

Buddha's Day. Buddha's Day, or Visākhā Pūjā in the Theravāda tradition, is considered by many to be the most holy day in the Buddhist year, as it commemorates the birth, enlightenment, and death (i.e., *parinirvāṇa*) of the Buddha, believed by Theravāda Buddhists to have occurred miraculously on the same day of the week. In Theravāda countries this celebration, known as Vesak in Sri Lanka, occurs on the full-moon day of Visākhā (Skt., Vaiśākha; April–May). Vesak celebrations in Southeast Asia focus on the monastery. Devotees observe the precepts and listen to sermons on the life of the Buddha. In Thailand, the traditional Vesak sermon, the *pathama-sambodhi*, continues throughout the entire night. It begins with the wedding of Suddhodana and Mahāmāyā, the Buddha's parents, and concludes with the distribution of the Buddha's relics and an accounting of the reasons for the decline of Buddhism in India. The text is a composite of scripture and popular commentary in which the Buddha is depicted as a teacher and miracle worker. In addition to attendance at monastery services, other common Vesak practices include watering bodhi trees within monastery compounds, circumambulation of the *cetiya* reliquary at night with incense and candles, acts of social service such as feeding the poor and treating the sick in hospitals, pilgrimage to sacred sites, and the bathing of Buddha images.

The celebration of Buddha's Day is both ancient and widespread. The seminal events of the Buddha's career coalesced into Vesak by the Theravādins are acknowledged independently in other Buddhist cultures. In Tibet, for example, the traditional religious year included celebration of the Buddha's conception or incarnation on the fifteenth day of the first lunar month, the attainment of Buddhahood on the eighth day of the fourth month, the Buddha's death, or *parinirvāṇa*, on the fifteenth day of the fourth month, and the Buddha's birth on the fourth day of the sixth month of the Tibetan year. The first of these events, the Buddha's incarnation, occupied a preeminent place in the Tibetan religious year, in part because of its assimilation into the New Year carnival. It was a day when special respects were paid to the Dalai Lāma, and the Buddha's mother, Mahādevī, was solicited for special boons. In China, Korea, and Japan, the Buddha's birthday has been marked, in particular, by a procession of Buddha images and the bathing of these images. These traditions associated with Buddha's Day or Buddha's Birthday appear to be of early origin.

The Mahāvaṃsa mentions a procession of Buddha images during the reign of Duṭṭhagāmaṇī (Sinhala,

Duṭugämunu; r. 101–77 BCE), for which the prototype may well have been a ceremony described in Aśoka's Fourth Rock Edict. Faxian observed a similar procession in India during his visit in the fifth century of the common era. The tradition of bathing Buddha images appears to be symbolized by the *Lalitavistara* episode of the two *nāga* serpents, Nanda and Upananda, bathing the *bodhisattva* after his birth, an episode depicted at such far-flung sites as Tun-huang and Borobudur. The *Mahāsattva Sūtra* describes a similar event where the Buddha is bathed by Indra and the four *deva* kings. It designates the eighth day of the fourth lunar month as the time when all devotees should wash his images in respect of the Buddha's power to grant boons.

Buddha's Day ceremonies and festivities embody both normative and popular dimensions of the Buddhist tradition, as do other celebrations marking the Buddhist religious year. Although relatively free of non-Buddhist elements, the focus on the Buddha image—whether through consecration, procession, or lustration—has primarily a mythic and/or magical significance. The Buddha is honored as a being greater than any other deity, and as a granter of boons. On the popular level, this aspect of Buddha's Day has assumed a greater importance than remembrance of the Buddha as the Enlightened One and great teacher.

The commemoration of Buddha relics. According to the *Mahāparinibbāna Sutta*, after the Buddha's death his relics were divided among the eight *cakkavatti* (Skt., *cakravartin*) rulers of India, who enshrined them in *cetiya* (Skt., *caitya*, reliquary mounds) at eight locations throughout India. While the obvious symbolic nature of this story belies its historicity, by the Mauryan period in India (fourth to second century BCE) *caitya* the likes of Sāñcī and Bhārhut had become important centers of pilgrimage and popular piety. The early association of Buddha relics with kingship in India points to a pattern perpetuated throughout much of Buddhist Asia: the enshrinement of a major Buddha relic as a monarch's attempt to legitimate his rule through the appropriation of the *buddhasāsana* (the Buddhist religion), and, even more importantly, to base his realm around a center of magical, sacred power. Buddhist chronicles often make no clear distinction between the sacred boundary of a Buddhist sanctuary housing a major Buddhist relic and jurisdictional limits of towns or larger political units. Both temple and kingdom, in one sense, derive their identity from the Buddha relic. Consequently, ceremonies commemorating the enshrinement of a Buddha relic are often major annual celebrations honoring the person of the Buddha that empower both the religion and the state. An outstanding example of such an annual celebration is found in Sri Lanka.

In Sri Lanka, the most elaborate national festival celebrates the arrival of the eyetooth relic of the Buddha, which is enshrined as the palladium of the kingdom in the Daladā Māligāwa (Temple of the Tooth) in Kandy. The *Dhātuvaṃsa* (Chronicle of the tooth relic) states that the relic was brought to Sri Lanka from Kaliṅga in India during the reign of King Kitsirimeghavaṇṇa (352–377). The king enshrined the relic in the capital, Anurādhapura, ordered that a grand festival celebrate its arrival, and dedicated the whole of Sri Lanka to it. Faxian, who visited Sri Lanka in the ninth century, gives us a record of the annual festival celebrating the tooth relic, reputed to have been brought to Sri Lanka only ten days after the Buddha's *parinirvāṇa.* He reports that the procession of the relic around the precincts of the capital occurred in the middle of the third lunar month. The procession he witnessed passed between five hundred people costumed to represent the five hundred lives (*jātaka*) of the *bodhisattva* according to the Theravāda tradition. The *Daladāsirita* (History of the tooth relic), written in the fourteenth century, describes in great detail the annual circumambulation of the tooth relic around the capital. The procession was marked by the sprinkling of holy water throughout the city sanctified by the chanting of the *paritta.* Today, the festival takes place during the month of Āsāḷha (Skt., Āṣādha; the lunar month of July–August) in the town of Kandy. The festival, which has taken on a carnival atmosphere, goes on for eleven nights, culminating in the twelfth day with a water cutting ceremony.

Similar festivals occurred in East Asia, as well. During the Tang dynasty (618–907) the festival that attracted the largest crowds in the capital, Xi'an, centered around Buddha relics. During the second or third lunar month, tooth relics from four temples and a fingerbone relic from the Famen Si were put on display for a week. The Famen Si relic was, on occasion, put on public view inside the royal palace. A ninth-century memorial by Han Yu claimed that the display of the relic produced such a frenzy on the part of the viewers that they burned their heads, roasted their fingers, and threw away their clothes and money. Such annual festivals honoring Buddha relics calibrate the religious year not so much in terms of the life of the Buddha but in terms of the magical power of his bodily presence, a presence fraught with political as well as religious significance.

Honoring the Buddha's dharma. The Buddha's teaching, or more narrowly conceived, particular Buddhist texts, are often honored in annual ceremonies and ritual celebrations. In Tibet, the feast of the First Discourse was traditionally held on the fourth day of the sixth lunar month. In modern Thailand, the commemoration of the *Dhammacakkappavattana Sutta* occurs on the full moon of Āsāḷha, the eighth lunar month, at the beginning of the monsoon rains retreat (*vassa*). In addition to the first discourse, the tradition also celebrates the Buddha's preaching of the Abhidharma to his mother and the teaching of the Prātimokṣa, the core of the monastic discipline (Vinaya), which the tradition holds took place three months before the Buddha's *parinirvāṇa.* These celebrations may be assimilated into other parts of the Buddhist year, as, for example, in Tibet, where the Buddha's descent from Trāyastriṃśa Heaven marks the end of the monsoon rains retreat.

As an example of an annual popular ceremony celebrating a particular text we look to the preaching of the *Vessan-*

tara Jātaka in the Theravāda countries of Southeast Asia. This ceremony is known in Thailand as Thet Mahāchāt. To be sure, the occasion focuses on the Buddha's perfection of the virtue of *dāna* (generosity) and on the efficacy of *puñña* (religious merit), but it also clearly demonstrates the power of the *dharma* as a text, not only as a teaching or narrative, but as something with special potency in both its written and oral form. Thus, as with the annual celebrations focusing on the Buddha, which remember not only the seminal events of his life but also the magical power of his physical presence, annual celebrations remembering the *dharma* refer not simply to the Buddha's teaching of Dharma, Abhidharma, and Vinaya but to the power of the text, especially as chanted.

In northeastern Thailand the preaching of the *Vessantara Jātaka,* which recounts a former life of the Buddha as Prince Vessantara, occurs in February–March after the rice harvest. While the ceremony includes various animistic and Brahmanic elements, the celebration focuses on the preaching of the thirteen chapters of the Thai version of the story. Monks famed for preaching particular chapters may be invited by sponsors whose donations to the *sangha* (Skt., *saṃgha;* the monastic order) are thought to be particularly meritorious. Prior to the recitation of the text the laity may enact the journey of Vessantara from the kingdom of Sivi and back again, having passed the tests to his generosity arranged by the god Indra. When the entire story is preached the ceremony, which begins in the morning, lasts well into the night.

In China, Korea, and Japan texts such as the *Saddharmapuṇḍarīka Sūtra* (Lotus sūtra) were the objects of major ceremonies. In Japan the *Ninnōkyō,* or *Sūtra of the Benevolent Kings,* was from the seventh to the thirteenth century one of the most important scriptures in Japanese Buddhism. It became the object of a public cult (*ninnō-e*), and ceremonies celebrating it were frequent at the Japanese court in order to ensure the maintenance of the dynasty and the welfare of the state. In Tibet, the fifteenth day of the third lunar month commemorated the preaching of the *Kālacakra Tantra;* each monastery also annually celebrated the particular Tantra to which its school ascribed special importance.

Thus, while the Buddhist year celebrated the Tripiṭaka in terms of three events in the Buddha's legendary life, other texts, which often dealt with such popular topics as the *bodhisattva,* miracles, and, more specifically, magical protection of the state, were often the occasion of annual ceremonies. In short, on the level at which the *dharma* enters into the popular perception of sacred time, it too, like the figure of the Buddha, takes on magical significance that protects the individual and guarantees social and political wellbeing.

CELEBRATING THE RELIGION. The religious year not only celebrates the person and life of the Buddha and his teaching, but the founding of the Buddha's community or monastic order, the establishment of the Buddha's religion in various parts of Asia, the monastic year as focused on the period of the monsoon rains retreat, and particularly important religious figures such as holy founders and reformers of the tradition.

The founding of the Saṃgha. The founding of the *saṃgha* is tied to the miraculous event of the Buddha's appearance before the 1,250 arhats at Veḷuvana Mahāvihāra in Rājagṛha. All had received ordination from the Buddha with the words "Ehi bhikkhu" ("Come, O monk"); according to tradition, the Buddha used this occasion to hand down the Prātimokṣa to his assembled followers. In short, the unannounced, miraculously simultaneous gathering of over a thousand monks ordained by the Buddha himself became the occasion for establishing the rule of order for the Buddhist monastic life.

In Thailand this event in the religious year is celebrated on the full moon sabbath of the third lunar month (Māgha) and is known as Māgha Pūjā. The celebration follows a relatively simple pattern. At about dusk crowds of laity gather in temple compounds to circumambulate the temple *cetiya* before entering the preaching hall for an evening of chanting and a sermon. The traditional text used for the occasion is a *gāthā* on the Prātimokṣa composed in the early nineteenth century by King Rama IV when he was a monk. It encourages the *sangha* to be a field of merit through constant attention and heedfulness, a teaching similar to the Buddha's instructions to the monks at Veḷuvana to do no evil of any kind, be established in the good, and to maintain a clear mind.

Establishing the tradition. Various types of annual events celebrate the establishment of Buddhism in a particular location or cultural area. These events range from commemorations of the arrival of Buddhist missionaries to the founding of particular temples or monasteries, often with royal support, for instance, the Shōmusai festival of the Tōdaiji in Nara held in May in commemoration of the death of the Japanese emperor Shōmu (701–756) and his patronage of Buddhism.

Temple or pagoda festivals and holy days commemorating events in the life of the Buddha are the most often observed Buddhist ceremonies in Myanmar. Nearly every Myanmari will attend at least one pagoda festival annually. Unlike observances connected with the life of the Buddha, Myanmar temple and pagoda anniversaries are much more in the nature of a country fair. At larger temples the event may last a week with a temporary bazaar featuring commercial goods for sale, games of chance, and of course, numerous makeshift restaurants. Evenings will be filled with various kinds of dramatic performances, including traditional plays and dances and the showing of films. Temple anniversary celebrations also provide an opportunity to solicit donations, often as part of merit-making ceremonies. As in the case of the annual festival at Wat Cedi Luang in Chiangmai, northern Thailand, ceremonies may also include significant non-Buddhist elements such as propitiation of the guardian spirits of the area or region. In the case of Wat Cedi Luang, the anniversary celebration in May includes propitiation of the foundation pillar of the city (identified with the Hindu god Indra) as well as offerings to the autochonous guardian spirits of Chiangmai, a ceremony performed somewhat surreptitiously outside of the city.

In Sri Lanka the establishment of Buddhism on the island is celebrated about a month after Vesak with the Poson festival. The major activities take place at Anurādhapura and Mahintale, where thousands of people come to honor Mahinda, the patron saint of Sri Lanka, who is reputed to have brought the *dharma* to the island at the request of his father, King Aśoka. Later, Mahinda's sister, Sanghamittā, came to the island to establish a Buddhist order of nuns. She brought a branch of the sacred bodhi tree with her, which was planted in the capital. Paying homage to the sacred bodhi tree is an important part of the festivities that take place.

The rains retreat. The earliest form of Buddhist monastic organization seems to have been mendicancy. In the *Mahāvagga* of the Vinaya Piṭaka monks are encouraged to adopt a peripatetic existence. During the monsoon rains, however, the Buddha's disciples gathered in more stable communities. Indeed, assuming that mendicancy characterized the earliest Buddhist monastic practice, cenobitism may well have grown out of the tradition of rains-retreat residence (*vassāvasa*).

Practical explanations for the origin of the observance of a rains retreat fail to take account of its more archaic, magical nature, which is associated with ascetic practice. Various aspects of early Buddhist monastic life and discipline can be interpreted as contrasting the sexual continence of the monk with its polar opposite, the feminine principle of life, gestation, and generation. This principle is embodied not only by women, whose contact with celibate monks is highly circumscribed, but by mother earth, who gives birth to life-sustaining crops. Monastic confinement during the monsoon rains-retreat period might be interpreted as protecting the life-generating power of the earth from the ascetic power of the monk and, correspondingly, defending the monk from the potencies of the earth during the most crucial gestation period of the cycle of plant life. Such an interpretation of the symbolic-magical significance of the origin of the rains-retreat period provides insight into one of the most important annual calendric rituals in Theravāda Buddhist countries, celebrations at the onset and, in particular, at the conclusion of the rains retreat, or Buddhist lenten period.

Both the beginning and end of the rains-retreat period are marked by auspicious rituals held on the full-moon sabbaths of July and October. The onset of *vassa* often witnesses many ordination ceremonies, for in Myanmar, Thailand, Cambodia, and Laos many young men observed the custom of accepting ordination for one lenten period only. On the July full-moon sabbath the laity will process to the monastery bearing gifts (*dāna*) for the monks. During the sabbath service monks and laity will be exhorted to observe an austere lent, thereby emphasizing the primary theme of the rains-retreat period. Especially for monks, the lenten period is a religiously observant time. More time is spent inside the monastery in study, meditation, and monastic devotions. In short, *vassa* epitomizes the lifestyle of the monk as an ascetic, *nirvāṇa*-seeking follower of the Buddha. On a magical level, his more rigorous practice during this period charges the monk with power, to which the laity gain access through the rituals marking the end of the rains retreat.

In Theravāda countries the end of the Buddhist lenten period provides the occasion for the most significant merit-making ceremonies. In Myanmar, the full-moon day of October marks the reemergence of the Buddha himself from Trāyastriṃśa Heaven. Oil lamps ringing monastery pagodas represent the mythic heavenly torches that lit his descent to earth. During the ceremonies that take place over the month following the October full-moon sabbath the laity give generously to the *sangha*, especially gifts of new robes (*kaṭhina*). In Myanmar, Thailand, Laos, and Cambodia *kaṭhina* ceremonies were and are often marked by processions to the monastery compound highlighted by the gift of a "wishing tree" (*padesa*) reminiscent of the trees in the Southern Island of the Buddhist cosmology that supplied the populace with all their needs simply for the asking. Symbolically, this annual celebration provides a ritual mechanism whereby the laity can gain access to the magical-spiritual power of the monks generated during the rains retreat. Thus, even this most exemplary period of the monastic life has a parochialized, magical significance that serves the immediate needs of the laity.

Celebrating the saints. The Buddhist year not only commemorates the Buddha and his teaching, the monastic order and its institutionalization at various times and in various places, but also the lives of saints. In Mahāyāna and Tantrayāna cultures *bodhisattva* days honor popular mythic savior figures, for instance, Guanyin (Avalokiteśvara), as well as legendary patriarchs (e.g., Bodhidharma) and historic reformers such as Hakuin. Some Buddhist figures are celebrated at the national level (e.g., Padmasambhava in Tibet) while others are of regional or more local significance.

Traditionally, the Chinese celebrated Guanyin's birthday on the nineteenth day of the second lunar month. In addition, her enlightenment and entry into *nirvāṇa* were also celebrated on the nineteenth day of the sixth month, and nineteenth day of the ninth month, respectively. Guanyin is celebrated as a merciful savior, the granter of intelligent sons and virtuous daughters, and the dispeller of natural catastrophies. In popular Chinese accounts of Guanyin's origins she is depicted as having been a royal princess from Sichuan Province by the name of Miao-shan who, as a consequence of her ascetic piety, was reborn as a *bodhisattva* destined to return to the human realm as the merciful Guanyin.

Bodhidharma is looked upon as the founder of the Chan (Jpn., Zen) school of Buddhism in China and the first of six traditional Chan patriarchs. His death anniversary is celebrated on the fifth day of the tenth lunar month. Other annual celebrations commemorating founders of Buddhist schools honor, among others, Baijiang, a noted Chan master of the Tang dynasty (nineteenth day of the first month) and Zhiyi, founder of the Tiantai school (the twenty-fourth day of the eleventh lunar month).

In Tibet saint-founders were the object of annual celebrations. The Rnying ma pa school, for instance, established a sequence of monthly ceremonies commemorating various aspects of Padmasambhava's life; the tenth day of the first month celebrates his flight from the world; the tenth day of the second month, his taking religious vows; the tenth day of the third month, his changing fire into water having been consigned to the flames by the king of Zahor, taking the name Padmasambhava, and so on.

In short, the lives of saints, founders, patriarchs, and reformers, whether deified in myth or valorized in legend, provide a special definition to the year in various Buddhist cultures. In the case of Padmasambhava episodes from the guru's biography provide a narrative structure of sacred time to the religious year. In other Buddhist traditions, death anniversaries commemorating key figures in patriarchial lineages integrate the year into a sacral continuum that includes the Buddha, the originator of the sect or school, the father of the subtradition, and so on down to the founder of the local monastery.

Seasonal Celebrations. The Buddhist religious year celebrates the seasonal changes, the agricultural calendar, and the seasons of human life and death. In Japan, for example, seasonal celebrations include New Year's Eve Day (Joya-e) and New Year's Day (Oshōgatsu), December 31 and January 1; the heralding of spring (Setsubun-e), February 3; spring and fall equinox (Higan-e), March 21 and September 21; Festival of the Dead (Obon), July 15; and Buddhist Thanksgiving Day (Segaki-e), sometime in the summer. Seasonal celebrations tend to be highly syncretic, with the Buddhist dimension competing with various non-Buddhist elements.

In Tibet, the New Year festival (Lo gsar) incorporated a Buddhist element, the great miracle of Śrāvastī, but its fundamental meaning is the exorcism of evil influences from the old year and the calling up of good fortune for the year to come. The elaborate ritual performances held during the New Year festival aimed not only at the welfare of the individual, but, even more so, at the good of the community. In Japan, New Year may be celebrated by visiting well-known Buddhist temples and shrines, but the traditional custom of eating pounded rice cakes (*mochi*) and drinking sweetened wine (*toso*) symbolized the hope for good health and longevity.

In Thailand, the New Year celebration (Songkrān) falls in the middle of April at the end of the dry season just prior to the coming of the monsoon rains. Although Buddhist temples and monasteries are the site of many New Year ceremonies, the New Year festival, as in Tibet and Japan, seems to have more to do with good luck and a healthy life in the year to come than with specifically Buddhist concerns. In the Thai case, elements of the New Year celebration are obviously intended as acts of sympathetic magic to abet the onset of the monsoon rains, necessary for the planting of the rice crop.

Seasons in the agricultural year are demarcated in various ways in the Buddhist religious calendar. In some cases, agricultural transition may be subsumed into specifically Buddhist events, such as the close relationship between Buddha's Day in monsoon, Theravāda countries, and the planting of rice. In other instances, however, these transitions may simply be made more meaningful by the Buddhist dimension of the culture in which they are embedded. For example, in Sri Lanka the seed-sowing festival (Vap Magula) traditionally held for the prosperity of the nation, is given Buddhist legitimation through the legend of Siddhārtha's presence at the plowing ceremony held by the future Buddha's father, King Suddhodana. In the modern period, all-night *pirit* (Pali, *paritta*) ceremonies will be held before the festival, attended by ministers of state who play the role of traditional Buddhist kings. The harvest festival in Sri Lanka (Aluth Sahal Maṅgalya) and Theravāda Southeast Asia focuses on the offering of first fruits in gratitude to the Buddha and the gods. In Sri Lanka, the contemporary harvest ceremony is held in Anurādhapura under the leadership of the minister of agriculture and development. Both the seed festival and the harvest festival undoubtedly represent Buddhist transformations of Brahmanic ceremonies.

Although individual life-transitions ordinarily do not define a community's religious year unless the person occupies a position of signal importance in China, Korea, and Japan, annual festivals for the deceased achieved national significance. While the festival represents the pervasive significance of the propitiation of ancestral spirits in these cultures, the Buddhist tradition provided its own distinctive validation. According to legend, the Buddha's disciple Maudgalyāyana descended to the deepest hell to rescue his mother from its torments. The Buddha advised Maudgalyāyana that by making offerings of food, clothing, and other necessities to the monks on behalf of the denizens of hell they would be relieved of their suffering. In China it became the custom that offerings made at the Ullambana All Soul's Feast held during the seventh lunar month were believed to rescue ancestors for seven preceding generations. In Japan the Obon festival takes place over three days, July 13–15. Activities will include special services at the home altar, visits to temple graveyards in order to welcome the ancestral spirits back to their home, and special vegetarian feasts. On the last day of the celebration the spirits will be sent off in miniature boats (*shōryōbune*) filled with food and lighted lanterns.

Concluding Remark. The Buddhist religious year sanctifies the life of the individual and the community in all of its aspects. Through annual ritual ceremonials and festivals mundane life is transfigured and the seemingly chaotic nature of existence finds meaning in an ordered sequence of paradigmatic events. While the life of the founder and the events of the early Buddhist community provide the central focus of the Buddhist religious year, its comprehensive scope incorporates all aspects of life from the beginning (the New Year festival) to the end (the All Souls' Feast).

SEE ALSO Avalokiteśvara; Kingship, article on Kingship in East Asia; Stupa Worship; Worship and Devotional Life, articles on Buddhist Devotional Life in East Asia, Buddhist Devotional Life in Southeast Asia, Buddhist Devotional Life in Tibet.

BIBLIOGRAPHY

Information on the Buddhist religious year or on Buddhist calendric rituals and festivals can be found in numerous books treating Buddhism in particular cultural contexts. Material on this subject in Theravāda Buddhist cultures is somewhat more recent than that for Central and East Asia. For Sri Lanka, Lynn de Silva's *Buddhism, Beliefs and Practices in Sri Lanka*, 2d rev. ed. (Colombo, 1980), provides an extensive, concise description of major calendric festivals. H. L. Seneviratne's "The Äsala Perahära in Kandy," *Ceylon Journal of Historical and Social Studies* 6 (1963): 169–180, is a detailed treatment of the major annual Buddhist festival in Sri Lanka. James G. Scott (Shway Yoe) discusses various calendric festivals (e.g., pagoda, harvest, and end of the rains retreat) in *The Burman, His Life and Notions*, 3d ed. (London, 1910). Melford E. Spiro has a brief section on annual ceremonies in *Buddhism and Society: A Great Tradition and Its Burmese Vicissitudes*, 2d ed. (Berkeley, 1982). Many studies of Thai Buddhism touch on the ceremonies of the Buddhist religious year. Stanley J. Tambiah's *Buddhism and the Spirit Cults in North-East Thailand* (Cambridge, U.K., 1970) is a gold mine of information, as is Kenneth E. Wells's earlier study, *Thai Buddhism: Its Rites and Activities* (Bangkok, 1939). More specialized contributions include my *Wat Haripuñjaya: A Study of the Royal Temple of the Buddha's Relic, Lamphun, Thailand* (Missoula, Mont., 1976), which has a chapter on calendric ceremonies, and Charles F. Keyes's "Buddhist Pilgrimage Centers and the Twelve Year Cycle: Northern Thai Moral Orders in Space and Time," *History of Religions* 15 (1975): 71–89. For Laos, Henri Deydier's *Introduction à la connaissance du Laos* (Saigon, 1952) provides a concise introductory survey to the Laotian calendar and religious festivals. A more focused and interpretative work is Frank E. Reynolds's "Ritual and Social Hierarchy: An Aspect of Traditional Religion in Buddhist Laos," *History of Religions* 9 (August 1969): 78–89. For Cambodia, Adhémard Leclère's *Le bouddhisme au Cambodge* (Paris, 1899) contains a section that concisely surveys the annual festivals in Cambodia.

For China, Joseph Edkins's *Chinese Buddhism*, 2d rev. ed. (London, 1893), provides a brief sketch of the Buddhist calendar. Kenneth Chʿen's *Buddhism in China: A Historical Survey* (Princeton, 1964) is also a useful introduction to annual festivals. Wolfram Eberhard's *Chinese Festivals* (New York, 1952) does little more than list the festivals of the Buddhist calendar. Other important studies include C. K. Yang's *Religion in Chinese Society* (Berkeley, 1961) and Emily Ahern's *The Cult of the Dead in a Chinese Village* (Stanford, Calif., 1973). All Souls' festivals are treated in J. J. L. Duyvendak's "The Buddhistic Festival of All-Souls in China and Japan," *Acta Orientalia* 5 (1926): 39–48; J. J. M. de Groot's "Buddhist Masses for the Dead in Amoy," in *Actes du Sixième Congrès International des Orientalistes* (Leiden, 1885), sec. 4, pp. 1–120; and Karl Ludvig Reichelt's *Truth and Tradition in Chinese Buddhism*, 4th ed. (Shanghai, 1934), pp. 77–126. See also Marinus Willem de Visser's *Ancient Buddhism in Japan*, 2 vols. (Leiden, 1928–1935), which treats a variety of Japanese Buddhist festivals, including Obon. For Korea, see Roger L. Janelli and Dawnhee Yim Janelli's *Ancestor Worship and Korean Society* (Stanford, Calif., 1982).

For Central Asia, three classic studies on Tibet provide brief descriptions of the religious calendar and annual festivals: L. Austine Waddell's *The Buddhism of Tibet*, 2d ed. (Cambridge, U.K., 1934); Giuseppe Tucci's *The Religions of Tibet*, translated by Geoffrey Samuel (Berkeley, 1980); and Rolf A. Stein's *Tibetan Civilization*, translated by J. E. Stapleton Driver (Stanford, Calif., 1972). Mary M. Anderson's *The Festivals of Nepal* (London, 1971) treats thirty-six annual festivals. For Mongolia, see Walther Heissig's *The Religions of Mongolia*, translated by Geoffrey Samuel (Berkeley, 1970).

New Sources

Cohen, E. *The Chinese Vegetarian Festival in Phuket: Religion, Ethnicity, and Tourism on a Southern Thai Island.* Bangkok, 2001.

Holzman, D. *Immortals, Festivals, and Poetry in Medieval China: Studies in Social and Intellectual History.* Brookfield, Vt., 1998.

Kohn, R. J. *Lord of the Dance: The Mani Rimdu Festival in Tibet and Nepal.* Albany, N.Y., 2001.

Qi, X. *Folk Customs at Traditional Chinese Festivities.* Beijing, 1988.

Ramble, C., and M. Brauen. *Proceedings of the International Seminar on the Anthropology of Tibet and the Himalaya: September 21–28 1990 at the Ethnographic Museum of the University of Zurich.* Zürich, 1993.

Singapore Federation of Chinese Clan Associations. *Chinese Customs and Festivals in Singapore.* Singapore, 1989.

Teiser, S. F. *The Ghost Festival in Medieval China.* Princeton, 1988.

Vogel, Claus. "On the Date of the Posadha Ceremony as Taught by the Mulasarvastivadins." *Bauddhavidyasudhakarah* (1997): 673–688.

DONALD K. SWEARER (1987)
Revised Bibliography

BUDDHIST STUDIES. Buddhism is considered to be a historical religion, that is, a religion with a founder who appeared at a specific moment in human history. This founder is, of course, the Buddha, who lived for some eighty years in what is today northern India and southern Nepal, sometime between the sixth and fourth centuries BCE. Buddhist texts would reject any claim that Buddhism originated at that time; Śākyamuni was only the most recent of a series of buddhas who have appeared in the past and will appear in the future. Yet, Buddhists across the centuries of Buddhist history would agree that he was the buddha for the present age, and that his life and teachings constitute an epochal event in the history of the universe. The study of Buddhism, whether by Buddhist monks in the monasteries of Asia or by scholars in the European and American academy, has therefore consistently looked back to the Buddha and to the teachings attributed to him as the defining point of origin.

TRADITIONAL STUDY OF BUDDHISM. If by "Buddhism," one means the teachings of the Buddha, then a history of the study of Buddhism would begin in India, almost 2,500 years ago. According to traditional accounts, shortly after the Buddha's passage into *nirvāṇa,* a council of monks was convened in order to recite, remember, and thereby retain his teachings for the future. Regardless of whether this first council was a historical event, its description in a variety of texts points to persistent concerns with issues of canon throughout the history of Buddhism. What should be judged as the word of the Buddha? What did the Buddha teach? And among the many things he must have taught over his long career, which represented his own view and which were an accommodation to suit the needs of a given audience? Such questions are not merely the concern of the modern secular scholar. They have been asked, and answered, over the course of more than two millennia by Buddhist monks and scholars from across Asia, who developed sophisticated methods—some historical, some textual—for determining what is to be accepted as the authentic teaching of the Buddha.

Thus, the writings of the sixth-century Indian monk Bhāvaviveka, for example, include a detailed list of arguments made by non-Mahāyāna Buddhist scholastics in support of their claim that the Mahāyāna sūtras are spurious, that is, that they are not the word of the Buddha. In Tibet, in the fourteenth century, the Buddhist monk Bu ston (1290–1364) compiled what is known as the *bka' 'gyur,* "the translation of the word" [of the Buddha], and explained the principles according to which he included some texts and excluded others. In Tokugawa Japan, where the Mahāyāna sūtras were regarded as the word of the Buddha, Tominaga Nakamoto (1715–1746) used historical analysis to identify numerous discrepancies among these texts; he argued that the Mahāyāna sūtras were not various manifestations of the Buddha's skillful means, but rather were composed long after his death during struggles for scholastic superiority. The Thai king Mongkut (Rāma IV, 1804–1868) made a detailed study of Buddhist literature in an effort to establish the authentic Pali canon, excluding what he deemed legendary elements such as the well-known stories of the Buddha's previous lives.

As Buddhism spread across Asia, the texts, whether they were judged canonical or non-canonical, required translation from various Indic languages (notably Sanskrit and Pali) into a wide variety of vernaculars. Translation has therefore long been central to the study of Buddhism and has been a preoccupation of Buddhist scholars, who have consistently sought the most complete and accurate editions of Indian texts, who have developed and debated the principles for producing the most accurate translations, and who have compiled glossaries and other translation tools that continue to be used by modern scholars.

The energies of Buddhist scholars have not, however, been directed solely to textual exegesis; they have been directed toward other domains of the study of their tradition. For example, the famous Chinese Buddhist pilgrims to India, Faxian (c. 337–422) and Xuanzang (602–664), wrote detailed accounts of their travels, attempting to link the places that they visited with the legendary and historical sites mentioned in Buddhist scriptures, while also describing the Buddhist doctrines and practices they encountered; Xuanzang provided information on both the size and the sectarian affiliation of a large number of Buddhist monasteries in India and Central Asia.

Buddhism is a religion in which primary importance is given to lineage—the ability to trace a teaching from one's teacher back to India and to the Buddha himself. It is from lineage, as much as from texts, that authority and authenticity derive. A great deal of historical investigation has traditionally been devoted, therefore, to establishing lines of transmission. Buddhist scholars have often gone to great lengths, spanning the historical and the mythological, in an effort to chart the passage of specific doctrines back across centuries in time and across mountains and oceans in space in order to claim authority and legitimation for their particular sect.

To note some of the concerns of Asian scholars of Buddhism, over the course of two millennia, is meant to suggest that any history of the study of Buddhism must take into full account the developments in the modes of analysis of their religion by scholars who were also adherents of that religion. These scholars, in most cases Buddhist monks, produced editions of texts, dictionaries, digests of philosophical tenets, catalogues of scriptures, as well as numerous chronicles and histories—both local and global—all products of a sustained tradition of historical reflection. The relationship between their concerns and methods and those of academic scholars of Buddhism is one of continuity rather than sharp disjunction, and the network of relations between the "traditional" and the "modern" remains a fruitful subject for analysis. It is nonetheless the case that the terms "the study of Buddhism" or "Buddhist studies," most commonly evoke the "academic" or "scientific" study of Buddhism that began in Europe in the nineteenth century.

EARLY EUROPEAN ENCOUNTERS. Prior to the thirteenth century, European contact with Buddhist societies was limited. Reports of Buddhism in classical antiquity appear as early as Clement of Alexandria (200 CE), who mentions the Buddha as one of the deities of India. Some two centuries later, Hieronymus (fourth–fifth century) stated that the Buddha was born from the side of a virgin. Elements of a biography of the Buddha became the basis for the lives of two Christian saints, Barlaam and Josaphat, although the Buddhist source of the narrative was not noted until the mid-nineteenth century.

The study of Buddhism by professional scholars in Europe was preceded by a number of encounters with Buddhist peoples by a wide variety of European travelers, missionaries, and diplomats, and European knowledge of Buddhism into the early nineteenth century derived largely from their reports. These include, among others, the accounts of Marco Polo (1254–1324), who reported on the religions of the Mongol Empire as well as Sri Lanka, the Flemish Franciscan friar Willem van Ruysbroek (c. 1215–c. 1295; also known as William of Rubruck), who visited the Mongol court in 1253 and 1255, and the Czech Franciscan friar Odoric (c. 1286–1331), who traveled extensively in China and Mongolia in the early fourteenth century. The travels of Roman Catholic priests during this period were motivated, at least in part, by the search for the kingdom of Prester John, a legendary Christian realm believed to exist somewhere in Asia. Simon de la Loubère (1642–1729), envoy of Louis XIV to the court of Siam, provided a detailed description of Thai Buddhism, including the monastic code, in his 1691 *Du Royaume de Siam,* published in English in 1693 as *New Historical Relation of the Kingdom of Siam.* The Jesuit missionary Ippolito Desideri (1684–1733) spent five years in Tibet beginning in 1716. He lived in a monastery in Lhasa and learned to read and write Tibetan well, producing refutations of Buddhist doctrines written in classical Tibetan. He also wrote an extensive description of Tibetan religion and culture, entitled *Notizie Istoriche del Thibet.*

These figures are just a few of many Europeans to describe their encounters with Buddhists—in China, in Japan, in Tibet, in Mongolia, in Sri Lanka, in Thailand, in Burma—prior to the nineteenth century. It is important to note, however, that none of these figures, regardless of the extent of the knowledge they gained, described the tradition they encountered with the term *Buddhism.* Prior to the eighteenth century, Europeans recognized only four religions in the world: Christianity, Judaism, Islam, and Idolatry (or Paganism). What is identified today as "Buddhism" was regarded then as so many local versions of idolatry. It is only at the end of the eighteenth century that Europeans began to conclude that the various images of the Buddha, with various local names, encountered across Asia in fact represented the same figure and that his followers were thus widely dispersed across the continent. One of the first to make this observation was Dr. Francis Buchanan (1762–1829) in his 1799 article "On the Religion and Literature of the Burmas" published in *Asiatick Researches.* According to the *Oxford English Dictionary,* the term *Buddhism* (or *Boudhism*) is first attested in 1801.

EUROPEAN STUDIES IN THE NINETEENTH CENTURY. It can therefore be said that the history of the study of Buddhism, understood as a single tradition that began with the Buddha in India and subsequently spread across Asia, does not begin in Europe until the nineteenth century. The development of this knowledge in the nineteenth century was the result of a number of factors, including the rise of the science of philology and the study of Asian languages in the academies of Europe, and of particular importance, European colonial projects in Asia. Articles on a wide variety of topics related to Buddhism appeared in scholarly journals such as *Asiatick Researches* and *Journal Asiatique.* In 1823, the German scholar Julius von Klaproth (1783–1835) published a life of the Buddha from Mongol sources. In 1833 and 1834, George Turnour (1799–1843), a British civil servant, published in Ceylon *Epitome of the History of Ceylon, and the Historical Inscriptions.* This contained a translation of "the first twenty chapters of the Mahawanso [the *Mahāvaṁsa,* a famous Sinhalese chronicle] and a prefatory essay on Pali Buddhistical literature." In 1837, Isaak Jakob Schmidt (1779–1847) published the first complete translation of a Buddhist sūtra into a European language with his translation of the *Diamond Sūtra,* from Tibetan into German. The Transylvanian scholar Alexander Csoma de Kőrös (1784–1842) published a series of articles on the Tibetan canon, based on his studies in Ladakh. One of the most important works of this period was that of the great French sinologist Jean Pierre Abel-Rémusat (1788–1832). His unfinished translation of the account of the Chinese monk Faxian's fifth-century pilgrimage to India was completed and heavily annotated by Klaproth and Charles Landresse and published in 1836 as *Foé Koué Ki, ou Relation des royaumes bouddhiques.*

It is notable that none of this important scholarship dealt directly with the land of Buddhism's birth, India. Buddhism had essentially disappeared from India by the fourteenth century CE. When the officials of the British East India Company undertook their various research projects in India, all that was found of Buddhism were various monuments and ruins, and the presence of the Buddha in the Hindu pantheon, where he had become the ninth incarnation of the god Viṣṇu. There were no Buddhist institutions, nor any Buddhists, to be found. This absence of Buddhism in India during the period of European colonialism, and its survival only in the form of archaeological and textual remains, proved an important factor in the European construction of Buddhism.

An official of the East India Company, Brian Houghton Hodgson (1800–1894), was stationed in Nepal, where he found Buddhism to be thriving. Hodgson published a number of widely read articles on Buddhism, but he is remembered for another reason: Beginning in 1824, with the assistance of a Nepalese Buddhist pundit, Hodgson accumulated a large number of Buddhist Indian Sanskrit (and some Tibetan) manuscripts that had been preserved in Nepal. Between 1827 and 1845, he dispatched more than four hundred works to libraries in Calcutta, London, Oxford, and Paris. They included many of the most important sūtras and Tantras of Sanskrit Buddhism. The manuscripts attracted little attention initially, except in Paris, where Eugène Burnouf (1801–1852) held the chair of Sanskrit at the Collège de France. Burnouf immediately recognized their importance, and after reading through scores of manuscripts, selected one, the *Lotus Sūtra,* for translation. He planned a three-volume study of Buddhist literature (a volume on Sanskrit texts, a volume on Pali texts, and a volume on the history of Indian Buddhism) to precede its publication, and in 1844 published the first volume, *Introduction à l'histoire du Buddhisme indien.* This massive work (647 pages in the original edition) was the first scholarly book-length study of Buddhism in a European language. For the depth and breadth of its analysis and for the quality of its translations from numerous Buddhist texts (he consulted Sanskrit, Pali, Chinese, and Tibetan sources), it is regarded by many as the foundational text for the European study of Buddhism. Burnouf died before he was able to complete the remaining volumes of his study, and his translation of the *Lotus Sūtra* (*Le Lotus de la bonne loi*) was published after his death. Burnouf was also the first scholar to make a detailed study of the rock edicts of the emperor Aśoka. The study of Buddhist epigraphy has remained an important source for the social history of Buddhism.

For the remainder of the nineteenth century, India became the primary focus of Buddhist studies in Europe, and Sanskrit (together with Pali) became the lingua franca of the field. A great deal of attention was focused on the life of the Buddha and on the early history of Buddhism in India, prior to its demise there. There was particular interest, parallel to the quest for the historical Jesus, in a quest for the historical Buddha and his teachings, which was referred to by such terms as "original Buddhism," "primitive Buddhism," sometimes "pure Buddhism." This Buddhism was regarded by many as a complete philosophical and psychological system, based on reason and restraint, opposed to ritual, superstition, and the priest-craft and caste prejudice of the *brahmans.* Standing in sharp contrast to what was perceived as the spiritual and sensuous exoticism of colonial India where Buddhism was long dead, this ancient Buddhism, derived from the textual studies of scholars in the libraries of Europe, could be regarded as the authentic form of this great world religion, against which the various Buddhisms of the modern Orient could be judged, and generally found to be lacking. Buddhism thus came to regarded as a tradition that resided most authentically in its texts, such that it could be effectively studied from the libraries of Europe; many of the most important scholars of the nineteenth century never traveled to Asia.

The Life of the Buddha. As might be expected, the life and teachings of the Buddha have remained a persistent topic of scholarly investigation. Sir William Jones of the East India Company knew of the Buddha only as one of the incarnations of the Hindu deity Viṣṇu, and speculated on his origin, considering both Scandinavia and Ethiopia as possible sites. By the late nineteenth century and early twentieth century, a sufficient number of texts had become available to allow scholars to analyze a wide variety of sources on the life of the Buddha. Émile Senart (1847–1928) sought to understand the events of the life of the Buddha within the context of Indian mythology. Hermann Oldenberg (1854–1920) used text critical methods in an attempt to identify the oldest stratum of Buddhist literature and to derive from that the historical (as opposed to mythological) elements of the Buddha's life and original teachings. During the late nineteenth century, scholars also sought to determine the relationship of Buddhist concepts to those found in other contemporary Indian philosophical systems, such as Sāṃkhya and Yoga. Work on the life of the Buddha continued in the twentieth century with the publication of E. J. Thomas's 1927 *Life of the Buddha as Legend and History,* which examined the structural and doctrinal relationships among various biographical fragments. Since then, scholars have identified a number of biographical cycles of the Buddha and connected them to specific discourses in the sutra and vinaya literature. Important biographical studies have been produced by Erich Frauwallner (1898–1974), Étienne Lamotte (1903–1983), and André Bareau (1921–1993). Albert Foucher (1865–1952) made extensive use of art historical and archaeological evidence to link the development of the Buddha's biography to pilgrimage sites in India. Even the dates of the Buddha's birth and death remained a topic of scholarly inquiry in the late twentieth century, with Heinz Bechert arguing that the Buddha may have lived as much as a century later than the once widely accepted dates of 563–483 BCE.

The Role of Colonialism. The history of the study of Buddhism in the nineteenth century is closely linked to the history of European (and later, Japanese) colonialism, with the domains of scholarly investigation often directly related to domains of colonial possession. Thus, the British provided much of the early archaeological and art historical scholarship on Indian Buddhism. The island of Sri Lanka was at that time the British colony of Ceylon, and much of the work of the translation of the Pali canon was carried out under the direction of Thomas W. Rhys Davids (1843–1922), a former colonial official in Ceylon. In 1881, he founded the Pali Text Society, currently based in Oxford, which, over the subsequent century, published scholarly editions and translations of a large number of important works of the Theravāda tradition of Southeast Asia. The French scholar Paul Mus (1902–1969), based in Vietnam (at that time the French colony of Indochina), produced a groundbreaking study of Borobudur, the monumental stone complex located in Java. Tibetan Buddhism was the dominant form of Buddhism in Mongolia and the Kalmykia. The authority of the Russian Empire and, later, the Soviet Union, in these regions gave Russian scholars easy access to a large corpus of Tibetan Buddhist materials.

This is not to suggest that European scholars limited their studies to the traditions of their nation's colonies. As more and more Buddhist texts became available in the libraries of Europe, access was provided to those who learned the necessary languages. The tradition of Sanskrit studies begun in Paris by Burnouf was continued by his scholarly descendents. This lineage included Sylvain Lévi (1863–1935), who produced new editions, translations, and studies on a wide range of subjects. In his travels in Nepal, Lévi found a number of important Mahāyāna texts that had not been previously available in Europe, including central texts of the Yogācāra school. Lévi's most prominent student was the Belgian scholar, Louis de la Vallée Poussin (1869–1938), perhaps the most important European scholar of Buddhism of the late nineteenth and early twentieth centuries. He translated key texts from a number of genres and Buddhist languages. Perhaps his greatest work was his translation from Chinese of Vasubandhu's *Abhidharmakośa* (relying, it should be noted, on an annotated Japanese edition), but he also published editions, translations, and studies of central Yogācāra, Madhyamaka, and tantric texts, in addition to a number of significant topical studies. Another of Lévi's pupils, Jean Przyluski (1885–1944), joined Marcelle Lalou (1890–1967) in founding the *Bibliographie bouddhique* (1930–1967), which provided an annotated reference to all important scholarship on Buddhism published between 1928 and 1958. The Belgian Roman Catholic priest Étienne Lamotte, a student of la Vallée Poussin, provided translations of important Mahāyāna sūtras, including the *Vimalakırti.* He also wrote an influential *History of Indian Buddhism.* His copiously annotated five-volume translation from Chinese of the *Dazhi dulun,* Kumārajīva's translation of a massive commentary on the *Perfection of Wisdom in 25,000 Stanzas,* was published between 1944 and 1980 under the title *Le traité de la grande vertu de sagesse.* Lamotte's student, Hubert Durt for many years directed the *Hōbōgirin* encyclopedia project of the École Française d'Extrême Orient, located in Kyoto.

Although Buddhist studies have been a predominantly text-centered enterprise since its inception, this is not to suggest that there have not been important anthropological studies, especially in the postwar period. For reasons that are not entirely clear (apart from the early translation of many of its canonical texts), much of the most important anthropological work has focused on the Theravāda traditions of Sri Lanka and Thailand. Here, the studies of Richard Gombrich, Gananath Obeyesekere, and Stanley Tambiah have been influential. Important contributions to Pali textual studies have continued through the twentieth century, including those made by K. R. Norman and by the team of scholars in the ongoing Critical Pali Dictionary project in Denmark, begun in 1924.

TRANSLATIONS FOR THE PUBLIC. As is clear, Buddhist studies in the west is very much a descendant of Indology, in the sense that prior to the Second World War, the study of Buddhism in the western academy was carried out largely by Sanskritists (or sometimes Sinologists) who also read Buddhist texts. However, the translations and studies produced by these scholars did not circulate only within a closed academic circle. The gradual accumulation of knowledge of a wide variety of Buddhist texts led to publication of translations and anthologies that played a significant role in bringing Buddhism to a wide audience of readers around the world, including in Asian societies. Some of these translations were made or overseen by scholars of Buddhism. In 1894, the Sacred Books of the East series was published, edited by Friedrich Max Müller (1823–1900), a student of Burnouf. Ten of the forty-nine volumes of the series were devoted to Buddhist works. Reflecting the opinion of the day that Pali texts of the Theravāda tradition represented the most accurate record of what the Buddha taught, seven of these volumes were devoted to Pali works. Among other Indian works, Aśvaghoṣa's famous life of the Buddha appeared twice, translated in one volume from Sanskrit and in another from Chinese. The *Lotus Sūtra* was included in another volume. The final volume of the series is entitled *Buddhist Mahāyāna Texts* and contains such famous works as the *Diamond Sūtra,* the *Heart Sūtra,* and the three Pure Land sūtras, all Indian works (or at least so regarded at the time) but included because of their importance for Japanese Buddhism. In 1895, Thomas W. Rhys Davids initiated the Sacred Books of the Buddhists series, which provided English translations of dozens of texts. Some of the most widely read translations and anthologies were produced by enthusiasts of Buddhism who were not trained in Asian languages. Thus, in 1894, Paul Carus (1852–1919) published *The Gospel of Buddha According to Old Records.* The American Theosophist Walter Y. Evans-Wentz (1878–1965) published his study of a translation of a Tibetan text in 1927 as *The Tibetan Book of the Dead.* In 1938, Dwight Goddard (1861–1939) published an anthology of mostly Chinese Buddhist texts as *A Buddhist Bible.*

Such works played an important role in a phenomenon that scholars have retrospectively dubbed "Buddhist modernism." Beginning in the late nineteenth century, through the efforts of Asian Buddhists (including such figures as Anagarika Dharmapala in Sri Lanka, Taixu in China, and Shaku Sōen in Japan) as well as European and American enthusiasts (including early members of the Theosophical Society), Buddhist modernists sought to defend Buddhism against the attacks of secularists and Christian missionaries by portraying Buddhism as an ancient system of rational and ethical philosophy that was at the same time entirely modern, in that it dispensed with the ritualistic trappings of religion, was compatible with science, and promoted an egalitarian society. Buddhist modernism has had a significant influence on the development of the study of Buddhism, especially in the case of those figures who have been both scholars of Buddhism and Buddhist modernists. Perhaps the most influential of these figures was D. T. Suzuki (1870–1966), who sought to portray the Zen tradition as above all concerned with an "experience" that is unbound by time or culture. This interaction of the "academic" and the "popular" has remained a constant component in the modern study of Buddhism.

EXPEDITIONS TO ASIA. At the end of the nineteenth century and the beginning of the twentieth, a large number of Buddhist manuscripts were discovered by European and Japanese expeditions at sites along the former Silk Road in Central

Asia. An important cache of Sanskrit texts, some of the most ancient yet identified, were found at Gilgit in modern Pakistan. Beginning with Aurel Stein (1862–1943) in 1907, a series of European and Japanese scholars visited the huge cave temple complex at Dunhuang in the desert of western China. Over the course of a decade, they removed tens of thousands of bamboo slips, scrolls, and manuscripts in a wide range of languages and deposited them in libraries in London, Paris, Saint Petersburg, Kyoto, and New Delhi. These texts remain the subject of detailed study and continue to provide insights into the practices of Central Asian, Chinese, and Tibetan Buddhism. The caves at Dunhuang, a site of Buddhist activity from the fourth to the fourteenth centuries, have been identified as a World Heritage site, and their remarkable paintings are being digitally photographed and catalogued. Manuscripts continued to be discovered throughout the twentieth century at sites across Asia, from Afghanistan to Tibet to Japan.

THE STUDY OF BUDDHISM IN JAPAN. The fact that Japanese expeditions were dispatched in search of ancient Buddhist manuscripts suggests that the academic study of Buddhism was not limited to Europe and North America in the late nineteenth and early twentieth centuries. Japan has played a central role in the history of the study of Buddhism. Japan is perhaps unique in the Buddhist world as a society possessing a long heritage of traditional Buddhist studies, which moved to a European style "scientific study" of Buddhist traditions (both its own and others) beginning in the late nineteenth century, with Japanese scholars eventually making significant contributions to all fields of study. Among the reasons for Japanese eminence in the field of Buddhist studies is the fact that Japan never came under European or American colonial domination and became a colonial power in its own right. During the Tokugawa period, Japanese scholars participated in a tradition of critical scholarship that produced excellent editions of a number of canonical Buddhist texts central to the major sects of Japanese Buddhism. During the Meiji period, students in a wide range of academic disciplines were encouraged to study abroad. Among these students was Nanjō Bun' yū (1849–1927), who traveled to Oxford to study Sanskrit with Max Müller. He produced a catalogue of the Chinese Buddhist canon that made reference to Sanskrit and Tibet editions and was instrumental in establishing Sanskrit studies in Japan. Another Japanese student at Oxford, Takakusu Junjirō (1866–1945), provided Müller with a translation from the Chinese of a Pure Land sūtra for inclusion in Sacred Books of the East. Fujishima Ryōon (1853–1918) studied with French scholars and wrote the first history of Japanese Buddhism to appear in a European language. The Taisho edition of the Chinese Buddhism canon, published in Japan between 1924 and 1935, has provided the standard version of thousands of texts. Japanese scholars also produced a large number of invaluable reference works, including Mochizuki Shinkō's encyclopedia of Buddhism, the *Bukkyō daijiten,* published between 1932 and 1936. In the period following the Second World War, Japanese Buddhist scholars produced influential studies on a wide range of topics in Indian, Chinese, Tibetan, and Japanese Buddhism. Among the many scholars who might be mentioned are Ui Hakuju, Kamata Shigeo, Sekiguchi Shindai, Nakamura Hajime, Nagao Gadjin, Takasaki Jikidō, Yanagida Seizan, and Hirakawa Akira. Buddhist studies remain a vibrant academic discipline in Japan, with most scholars drawn from the families of Japanese Buddhist priests.

THE STUDY OF CHINESE BUDDHISM. The study of Chinese Buddhism has differed from the study of Buddhism in India (from which Buddhists were absent after the fourteenth century) or Tibet (where the possibility of European travel was restricted in the nineteenth and much of the twentieth centuries). By the end of the nineteenth century, China was the object of intensive missionary activity from both Europe and North America, and much of the early study of the Chinese Buddhist community was undertaken by missionaries such as Samuel Beal (1825–1899). The importance of Chinese translations of Indian Buddhist texts had been recognized by Burnouf, but texts composed in Chinese, apart from the accounts of the Chinese pilgrims to India, attracted little scholarly attention until the twentieth century. The institutional practice of Chinese Buddhism became the subject of a number of important studies in the decades prior to the Communist Revolution. Notable among these are the work of Jan J. M. de Groot (1854–1921), the Danish architectural historian Johannes Prip-Møller (1889–1943), and Holmes Welch, who documented the Buddhist revival in China in the early twentieth century, as well as Buddhism under Mao. Buddhist texts and doctrines have been the object of important studies by scholars such as Paul Demiéville (1894–1979), but also within the context of social and institutional history, where the studies of Jacques Gernet have been highly influential. Erik Zürcher wrote a detailed study of early Chinese Buddhism and explored some of the relations between Daoist and Buddhist terminology. This is not to suggest that there has not been a strong and influential tradition of Chinese Buddhist studies among Chinese scholars. Beginning in the early twentieth century and continuing until the Cultural Revolution, important historical studies were produced by such scholars as Tang Yongtong (1893–1964), Chen Yinke (1890–1969), and Hu Shi (1891–1962). The philosopher Feng Youlan (1895–1990) also wrote extensively on Buddhism. Since the end of the Cultural Revolution, both the practice and study of Buddhism have begun to reemerge in China.

Crucial scholarship on Chinese Buddhist texts has been carried out by Japanese scholars. In part because of the historical links between the Japanese sects of Buddhism and China, in part because of the Japanese colonial presence in Taiwan, China, and Korea in the first half of the twentieth century, Japanese scholars have produced a range of important studies on all aspects of Chinese Buddhism, focusing especially on the key texts and lineages of the Chinese traditions that became established in Japan. With the growth of

Buddhist studies in North America in the last half of the twentieth century, knowledge of Japanese scholarship has been deemed essential for all work in East Asian Buddhism, and provided the focus for much graduate training. Stanley Weinstein at Yale was one of a number of scholars to insist on the importance of Japanese scholarship for the study of Chinese Buddhism. The study of Korean Buddhism has also become a distinct area of Buddhist studies (rather than a branch of Chinese Buddhism) through the efforts of a number of scholars, including Robert Buswell.

THE STUDY OF TIBETAN BUDDHISM. Prior to the Second World War, Tibetan Buddhism was valued above all for its preservation, in accurate translation, of a large canon of Indian Mahāyāna texts that had been lost in the original Sanskrit. With the notable exception of the work of such scholars as Eugene Obermiller (1901–1935) and Giuseppe Tucci (1894–1984), the vast corpus of autochthonous Tibetan Buddhist literature remained largely unexamined by European scholars. This situation changed dramatically as a result of the invasion of Tibet by the Peoples Republic of China and the subsequent flight into exile of the Dalai Lama in 1959. Over the course of the next decade, he was followed into exile by tens of thousands of Tibetan refugees, many of whom were highly educated monks and lamas. These refugees settled in India and Nepal, and later in Europe and North America. European and American scholars soon began to study Tibetan Buddhist texts in collaboration with refugee Tibetan scholars, thereby bringing the doctrines and practices of Tibetan Buddhism to a large audience in the West. Among the first scholars in this regard were David Snellgrove, Herbert Guenther, and David Seyfort Ruegg, who demonstrated the important contributions made by Tibetan Buddhist scholars to many of the key philosophical debates and concepts of Indian Buddhism. Beginning in 1961, under Public Law 480, the Government of India provided the U.S. Library of Congress with copies of all books published in India. The head of the Library of Congress in New Delhi from 1968–1985 was the eminent Tibetologist E. Gene Smith, who arranged for thousands of Tibetan texts, brought out of Tibet by refugees, to be published in India and sent to depository libraries across the United States. As a consequence, during the last decades of the twentieth century, Tibetan Buddhism became a major area of Buddhist studies, not only for the insight it can provide on the development of Indian Buddhism, but also, for the first time, as an important domain of investigation in its own right, with academic research in the Tibetan cultural regions of the PRC also becoming possible. The extensive Tibetan literature on Buddhist Tantra has also become a growing area of scholarly investigation. The close collaboration of European, American, and Japanese academics with traditionally trained Tibetan scholars has not only borne fruit in terms of the translation of texts; it has also raised important questions about the relation between the academic and the popular and between Buddhist scholarship and Buddhist practice.

THE STUDY OF BUDDHISM IN THE UNITED STATES. The first academic lecture on Buddhism to be delivered in the United States was "Memoir on the History of Buddhism," presented by Edward Eldridge Salisbury (1814–1901)—instructor of Sanskrit at Yale and recently returned from study with Burnouf in Paris—at the first annual meeting of the American Oriental Society on May 28, 1844. Buddhist studies did not become well established in the United States, however, until more than a century later. Two distinguished Pali scholars of the early period were Henry Clarke Warren (1854–1899) and Eugene W. Burlingame (1876–1932). Franklin Edgerton (1885–1963) coined the term "Buddhist Hybrid Sanskrit" to describe the deviations from classical Sanskrit that occur in many Indian Buddhist texts and in 1953 published a two-volume grammar and dictionary of Buddhist Hybrid Sanskrit.

The American academy saw enormous changes during the decades after the Second World War, especially in the 1960s and 1970s, with the explosion of two fields: area studies devoted to Asia and religious studies. Area studies provided federal funds (through the National Defense Education Act) for training in a wide range of Asian languages. At the same time, the study of religion moved from the seminary to the college and university, where departments of religion were formed, often on the model of the Christian seminary, with faculty in such areas as Old Testament, New Testament, Church History, Modern Religious Thought, Ethics, and perhaps, World Religions. Because of the pan-Asian scope of Buddhism, college and university positions in World Religions were often occupied by scholars of Buddhism.

In 1961, Richard Robinson (1926–1970) instituted the first doctoral program in Buddhist studies in the United States at the University of Wisconsin. Over the subsequent decades, other programs, some led by Robinson's students, were established in a range of area studies departments (at Berkeley, Michigan, British Columbia, and UCLA) and religious studies departments (Harvard, Yale, Princeton, Columbia, Chicago, and Virginia). In Europe, Buddhist studies were pursued at Oxford, the University of London, Hamburg, Lausanne, and Vienna. By 1976 and the founding of the International Association of Buddhist Studies, the study of Buddhism was taking place in Europe, North America, South America, Australia, and New Zealand, and across Asia.

Although broad trends can only be identified with a certain caution, it is probably accurate to say that in the decades following the Second World War, there was a strong interest in the study of what has been called Buddhist philosophy. In part because of the strong philological and philosophical training of the early European scholars in the field, in part because of the perceived need to justify the sophistication of Buddhist thought in American departments of religious studies, scholars tended to focus their attention on the elite scholastic traditions of Buddhism, especially the Abhidharma of the Theravāda, the Madhyamaka and logical traditions of India (with their Tibetan commentaries), and the Chan and Zen traditions of East Asia. In some cases, Buddhist texts and figures have been brought into the realm of comparative philosophy, where Nāgārjuna could be seen as Kantian at the beginning of the twentieth century, as Wittgensteinian in the middle, and as Derridian at its end. In the last decades of the twentieth century, as the humanities in general turned toward social history, there has been a turn away from scholastic Buddhist philosophy and toward institutional histories, employing a wide range of sources in an attempt to discern how Buddhism was practiced in the various cultures of Asia and among all levels of society, both monastic and lay. The more recent manifestations of Buddhism outside Asia are also beginning to be examined.

SEE ALSO Chinese Religion, article on History of Study; Tibetan Religions, article on History of Study.

BIBLIOGRAPHY

Almond, Philip C. *The British Discovery of Buddhism.* Cambridge, U.K., 1988. A study of the development of British attitudes toward Buddhism during the Victorian period.

Droit, Roger-Pol. *The Cult of Nothingness: The Philosophers and the Buddha.* Chapel Hill, N.C., 2003. Originally published in French in 1997, a study of the ways in which European philosophers of the nineteenth century understood Buddhism and the idea of *nirvāṇa.*

Halbfass, Wilhelm. *India and Europe: An Essay in Understanding.* Albany, N.Y., 1988. A study of the European encounter with India, and especially Indian philosophies and religions, from classical antiquity to the twentieth century.

Hanayama, Shinsho. *Bibliography of Buddhism.* Tokyo, 1961. A bibliography of works on Buddhism published in European languages from the seventeenth century up to 1932.

Jong, J. W. de. "A Brief History of Buddhist Studies in Europe and America." *Eastern Buddhist,* n.s. 7, no. 1 (May 1974): 55–106, and no. 2 (October 1974): 49–82. Reprinted in a single volume, Tokyo, 1997. The most detailed account of the development of Buddhist studies in the West, although with a strong focus on Indological studies and little discussion of the study of East Asian and Southeast Asian Buddhism.

Ketelaar, James Edward. *Of Heretics and Martyrs in Meiji Japan: Buddhism and Its Persecution.* Princeton, N.J., 1990. A study of the persecution of Buddhism by the Japanese government in the last decades of the nineteenth century, and the redefinitions of Buddhism that emerged as a result.

Leoshko, Janice. *Sacred Traces: British Explorations of Buddhism in South Asia.* Burlington, Vt., 2003. A study of nineteenth-century European investigations of Buddhist art and archaeology in India, and the legacy of these investigations for subsequent views of the Buddha and of Buddhism.

Lopez, Donald S., Jr., ed. *Curators of the Buddha: The Study of Buddhism under Colonialism.* Chicago, 1995. A collection of essays on several of the major figures in the development of Buddhist studies in Europe and North America.

Lubac, Henri de. *Le rencontre du bouddhisme et de l'Occident.* Paris, 1952. A history of European encounters with Buddhism from classical antiquity to the twentieth century, focusing especially on the work of Roman Catholic missionaries and on subsequent academic scholarship.

McRae, John R. "Chinese Religions: The State of the Field." Part 2: "Living Religious Traditions: Buddhism." *Journal of Asian Studies* 54, no. 2 (1995): 354–371. A bibliographical essay on the state of the field of Chinese Buddhist studies at the end of the twentieth century.

Nakamura, Hajime. *Indian Buddhism: A Survey with Bibliographical Notes.* Intercultural Research Institute Monograph, no. 9. Hirakata, Japan, 1980. A survey of the Japanese- and European-language scholarship on Indian Buddhism.

Przyluski, Jean, et al. *Bibliographie bouddhique.* Buddhica: Documents et travaux pour l'étude du bouddhisme, vols. 1–31. Paris, 1929–1961. An annotated listing of all major articles and books on Buddhism up to 1958, including both European- and Asian-language works.

Schwab, Raymond. *The Oriental Renaissance: Europe's Rediscovery of India and the East, 1680–1880.* New York, 1984. Originally published in French in 1950, a detailed study of the rise of Oriental studies in Europe and its influence on European arts and letters.

DONALD LOPEZ (2005)

BUGIS RELIGION.

The Bugis, sometimes referred to as the Buginese, are an Indonesian people numbering about three million, most of whom live in their homeland of Celebes (South Sulawesi). *Bugis* is an archaic form of their name retained by the Malay/Indonesian language; in fact they call themselves Ugi' or ToUgi'. Bugis emigrants have also established significant, mostly coastal, settlements throughout the Indonesian archipelago. They speak a language of the Western Austronesian family, the same family as their national language (Malay or Indonesian).

After a long period of contact with Muslim, mainly Malay, traders who had settled in their main trading harbors, and after some spontaneous but aborted attempts to adopt Christianity during the middle of the sixteenth century, the Bugis officially became Muslims between 1605 and 1610 under the initiative and pressure of the neighboring kingdom of Goa. But although they soon came to be considered among the most devout Muslims in the archipelago, they have retained in their traditions many pre-Islamic elements. These include the *bissu,* transvestite priests in charge of the regalia of the ruling house and of princely rituals; popular practitioners called *sanro;* sacred places, to which offerings are regularly brought; and the psalmody, on certain ceremonial occasions, of the sacred epic *La galigo,* which provides an interesting if incomplete view of pre-Islamic Bugis culture.

THE MYTH OF ORIGIN. The Bugis creation myth has been somewhat mixed with Islamic mysticism, but as far as it can be reconstituted, the early Bugis believed in a supreme deity called To Papunna ("the owner of everything") or Déwata

Sisiné, later Déwata Séuwaé ("the one God"). From this deity emanated a male and a female being, linked to some extent to the sun and the moon. From their separated seed were born a number of beings who were not clearly identified; then from their sexual union were born the main gods of the upper-world and the underworld, said to number either seven, fourteen, or nineteen, according to various versions of the myth. Of these gods, six married couples are described in *La galigo* as playing a significant role, and two couples are mentioned as being more important than the others: one at the depths of the Abyss, whose male partner was known as Guri ri Selle'; and the other at the summit of Heaven, whose male entity, Datu Patoto' ("the prince who fixes destinies") or Datu Palanro ("the princely smith"), was considered the highest god of all. These two couples had nine children each, seven of whom reigned over various strata of Heaven or the Abyss. The eldest son of Datu Patoto', La Toge'langi' (also known as Batara Guru), and Guru ri Selle's daughter were sent to the Middle World to establish there, in Luwu', the first human settlement. However, they are not the primeval ancestors of humankind, which rather descends from the servants who followed them from Heaven and the Abyss, as well as from the servants of other divine rulers, the children of the secondary heavenly and abyssal couples, who came later to establish other kingdoms in and around Sulawesi (Celebes).

THE POLITICAL MYTHS. The *La galigo* epic tells of the life and deeds of six generations of earthly descendants to these first divine rulers, and especially of Sawérigading, the Bugis cultural hero, a grandson of Batara Guru. Still considered sacred by a small group of non-Muslim Bugis, *La galigo* is a repository of princely rituals, performed by the *bissu*, and of princely conduct. The epic tells that after the sixth generation of rulers descended from Batara Guru and other children of the gods, all princes of divine origin had to leave this world to go back to Heaven or the Abyss, except for the princely couple in Luwu'. All Bugis nobility is said to be descended either from that Luwu' couple, or from other divine princes sent either from Heaven (Tomanurung) or from the Abyss (Totompo'). Most of the Bugis lordships and kingdoms claim to have been founded by a divine couple, and they keep as regalia various articles such as swords, banners, and ploughs, which are said to have been brought by these ancestors of their rulers.

THE CULT AND ITS OBJECTS. Two kinds of closely related Bugis rituals can be distinguished. One was performed by the *bissu* at princely courts; now, however, the number of *bissu* is rapidly declining and their activity is becoming more and more limited. The other ritual is enacted by the popular practitioners called *sanro*, who are still very active in Bugis country. Both kinds of rituals include sacrifices (of buffalo, goats, or chickens) and offerings of glutinous rice, usually presented in four (or, sometimes, two, seven, or eight) colors. The rituals are performed during rites of passage, house or boat building, first-use rites, anniversaries, and during certain phases of the rice cycle, as well as at community celebrations in order to obtain the welfare or protection of the people, of the lordship, or of the state, especially in case of bad crops, epidemics, or wars.

In *La galigo*, the objects of the cult are expressly said to be the gods of Heaven and the Abyss; they decided, in turn, to people the Middle World just because "one is no god when there is no one to pay homage to you." Nowadays, the average Bugis knows very little of pre-Islamic theology, which, moreover, was never recorded systematically but was only implicit in the tradition. Still, many Bugis continue to believe that besides Allāh, whom they call Puang Allataala or Déwata Séuwaé, there are many spiritual beings to whom one must pay homage and who, in turn, act as intercessors between humans and the supreme being, who is too far above humankind to be contacted directly. Sawérigading is sometimes named as one such intervening figure, but he seems to have been the object of a cult maintained more by the *bissu* than by laity. Likewise, a deity named Déwata Mattanru' Kati ("the god with golden horns"), to whom a special cult is rendered by the *bissu*, may be one of the heavenly gods of *La galigo*. Other divine beings who are, still today, the object of a general cult among all categories of Bugis include the rice goddess, Sangiang Serri. According to *La galigo* she was the first child born on earth to Bataru Guru, but she died after seven days, whereupon her body, once buried, transformed itself into the rice plant. Another revered being is Taddampali, an aquatic being who may be the same as La Punna Liung, the messenger of the Abyss in *La galigo*. Included here also are the local *tomanurung* ("descended [from heaven] beings"). Many Bugis still keep in their homes wooden tabernacles or miniature beds where the divine beings are said to descend during ceremonies.

Other kinds of spiritual or invisible beings (*totenrita*) also appear as divine-human intercessors. Among these are house and boat spirit guardians and local spirits dwelling in large stones, trees, or springs. Other spirits may be dangerous, as for example the *paddengngeng* ("hunters"), invisible horsemen who capture people's souls with their lassos, thereby provoking unexpected illness and death. Their kingdom, described in some of the oral traditions, seems to recall the Land of the Dead as described in *La galigo*.

THE AFTERWORLD. In *La galigo*, the afterworld is described as a distant island somewhere in the western seas. The dead come first to a land where they must wait until all the funerary rituals and required offerings have been accomplished by their living relatives; otherwise they cannot proceed further. In that place, sinners must also undergo various punishments. The dead must then take a ritual bath, pay their entrance to the keeper of the heartland, and cross a golden bridge. In the inner Land of the Dead, everything is the reverse of life among the living.

With Islamicization, most of these observances have been obliterated, and Muslim funerals have now replaced traditional ones. However, an ancestor cult still exists that features pilgrimages to sacred, non-Islamic graves and offerings brought to family ancestors in a special place in the home.

BIBLIOGRAPHY

Hamonic, Gilbert. "Pour une étude comparée des cosmogonies de Célèbes-Sud: À propos d'un manuscrit inédit sur l'origine des dieux bugis." *Archipel* 25 (1983): 35–62. The first translated edition, with commentary, of a hitherto secret text on creation and the genesis of the gods according to a Bugis view.

Hamonic, Gilbert. *Le langage des dieux: Cultes et rituels préislamiques du pays bugis (Célèbes-Sud, Indonésie).* Paris, 1987. An important work containing a corpus of about two thousand verses of *bissu* ritual chants, with translation and commentary.

Kern, Rudolph A. *Catalogus van de Boegineesche, tot den I La Galigo cyclus behoorende handschriften der Leidsche Universiteits Bibliotheek, alsmede van die in andere Europeesche bibliotheken.* Leiden, 1939.

Kern, Rudolph A. *Catalogus van de Boeginese, tot de I La Galigo-cyclus behorende handschriften van Jajasan Matthes (Matthesstichting) te Makassar (Indonesie).* Makassar, Indonesia, 1954. A complete compilation in two books of all manuscripts containing episodes of the *La galigo* epic. Includes lists of gods and heros appearing in the cycle.

Matthes, Benjamin F. *Boeginesche chresthomathie: Oorspronkelijke Boeginesche geschriften in proza en poëzij, uitgegeven, van aanteekeningen voorzien en ten deele vertaald.* 3 vols. Vol. 1, Makassar, Indonesia, 1864; vols. 2 and 3, Amsterdam, 1872. The only anthology thus far available of Bugis texts, including the beginning of the *La galigo* epic. Liberally annotated.

Matthes, Benjamin F. *Over de bissoe's of heidensche priesters en priesteessen der Boeginezen.* Amsterdam, 1872. An extremely valuable account of the *bissu* priests and their rituals.

Pelras, Christian. "'Herbe divine': Le riz chez les Bugis (Indonésie)." *Études rurales* 53–56 (1974): 357–374. A description of rice cultivation among the Bugis, including associated rituals.

Pelras, Christian. "Le panthéon des anciens Bugis, à travers les textes de *La galigo*." *Archipel* 25 (1983): 65–97. A reconstitution of the Bugis pantheon and worldview, according to the *La galigo* epic and other texts.

New Sources

Guillaumont, A., and C. Amiel. "Qu'est-ce qu'un dieu." *Revue de l'histoire des religions* 205 (1988): 339–465.

Hamonic, Gilbert. "God, Divinities and Ancestors for the Positive Representation of a Religious Plurality in Bugis Society, South Sulawesi, Indonesia." *Southeast Asian Studies (Tonan Ajia kenkyu [Kyoto])* 29, no. 1 (1991): 3–34.

Hamonic, Gilbert, and Christian Pelras. "En quete des dieux bugis: entre mythe et rituel, entre silence et parole." *Revue de l'histoire des religions* 205 (1988): 345–366.

Pelras, Christian. *The Bugis.* Oxford, 1996.

CHRISTIAN PELRAS (1987)
Revised Bibliography

BUKHĀRĪ, AL- Abū ʿAbd Allah Muḥammad b. Ismāʿīl al-Bukhārī (810–870) was a Muslim scholar of *ḥadīth.* Born in the central Asian city of Bukhāra, al-Bukhārī compiled one of the most authoritative collections on the words and deeds of the Prophet Muḥammad. According to the biographical accounts, he began the study of *ḥadīth* at the age of 10, and was soon correcting his own teachers. At age 16 he made the pilgrimage to Mecca, and from there he traveled throughout Iraq, Syria, Egypt, and Iran in the search for *ḥadīth* that was traditional among many scholars of the day. It is claimed that he heard or collected 600,000 reports and that he spent sixteen years reducing these to around 3,000 "sound" reports for his most renowned work, *al-Jāmiʿ al-ṣaḥīḥ* (The Sound and Comprehensive Exposition).

Al-Bukhārī lived during a time in which many collections of information regarding the Prophet were being collected and evaluated and an intellectual struggle obtained, especially in Iraq and lands to the east, between those who favored *ḥadīth* over and against individual reasoning (*raʾy*) as the main source of Islamic law. Anecdotes about Muḥammad were found in accounts of his military expeditions and life in general (*maghāzī, sīra*), as well as in books of jurisprudence that also contained legal discussions and nonprophetic material, but al-Bukhārī made his contribution to the collection of *ḥadīth* proper. In this venture, the most important aspect of the *ḥadīth* was not the content but rather the *isnād*, the list of names of informants who (preferably orally) passed on the saying. Many of the earliest works were *musnads*, that is, organized according to the transmitter. Al-Bukhārī's *Ṣaḥīḥ* was one of the first *muṣannafs*, in which materials were organized according to topic. Sunnī Muslims eventually recognized six canonical *ḥadīth* collections, of which the most authoritative are the two *Ṣaḥīḥ* books of al-Bukhārī and his fellow Iranian contemporary al-Hajjāj (d. 853). (The remaining four are known as *sunan*, and are more restricted to legal and everyday issues.)

Although al-Bukhārī did not provide any explanatory introduction to his collection, he divided the material into approximately one hundred chapters treating matters of law, ritual, and theology, with numerous subheadings for individual topics or questions, often drawn from phrases in the Qurʾān or the *ḥadīth* corpus itself. In some cases, subheadings appear without any corresponding *ḥadīth*, presumably to indicate that no sound *ḥadīth* existed on that topic. In many cases, al-Bukhārī inserted his own comments and opinions on the matters at hand, and frequently cited the same report (or a part thereof) under different subheadings as he saw fit. The ensemble was similar to a work of jurisprudence in aiming to provide a guide to all recognized aspects of Muslim dogma and praxis.

Al-Bukhārī's major work is not only vast but also meticulous. Although the work is arranged according to the content of the reports, the criteria for inclusion in the *Ṣaḥīḥ* was nevertheless squarely based on soundness of the *isnād*, the chain of names indicating the source of the anecdote. A typical *isnād* will be something like "I heard from A that B informed him that C said. . . ." *Ṣaḥīḥ*, or "sound," refers to a *ḥadīth* whose chain of transmitters extends uninterrupted back to the Prophet Muḥammad himself, and is composed entirely of men of well-established reliability and honesty. Opinions could differ significantly on the question of whether a transmitter was reliable or not, and even the two canonical *Ṣaḥīḥs* of al-Bukhārī and Muslim works contain different material. The compiler's efforts extended then not only to the collection of prophetic reports but to the evaluation of their transmitters and their links. In addition to judging the character and reliability of the transmitters, it had to be ascertained that they lived in the appropriate era, and al-Bukhārī is said to have insisted that there be evidence not only that the chronology was correct but that successive informants had actually met each other at some point. Muslim, compiler of the other great *Ṣaḥīḥ*, held that chronology sufficed.

According to an anecdote in the biographical accounts, a group of Baghdad scholars attempted to trick al-Bukhari into public error by changing the *isnāds* and contents of one hundred *ḥadīth*. He listened, admitted he had not heard of these particular reports, then recited the correct versions back to his interrogators and suggested they had been confused. Apocryphal or not, these and similar stories indicate the nature of al-Bukhārī's talent: the mastery and memorization of countless *ḥadīth,* with the precise wording of their contents and the details of their *isnāds*.

Like many classical Islamic works, the *Ṣaḥīḥ* was the object of numerous commentaries, and subsequent scholarship dealt with every aspect of al-Bukhārī's compilation. Commentary was one of the ways in which the community continued to engage with its canonical works, and the process served both to preserve and to renew the work for subsequent generations. It also served as a tool in various disputes, as an authoritative work could be shown to support a particular sectarian viewpoint. Commentary on the *Ṣaḥīḥ* has continued into the modern age.

However, his *Ṣaḥīḥ* was not above criticism. Some of his inclusions are said to be less "sound" than he claimed, and he included a large number of *ḥadīth* reports that did not meet his own standards, presenting them in part or without *isnād* in order to illustrate a point or support an argument. In the views of some commentators, these inclusions weakened the book's rigor and were even said to have helped contribute to the decline of rigorous *isnād* scholarship.

Whatever the comments on individual reports or on the details, the consensus of the Sunnī Muslim community has been that al-Bukhārī's *Ṣaḥīḥ* is the most authoritative text in Islam after the Qurʾān. Like the scripture, there are even premodern accounts of the veneration of the physical copy of the book, that it protects its owner against hardship, that oaths were sworn on it, or that no ship with a copy on board will sink, and so on.

He also compiled a number of other books, most notably a biographical dictionary of *ḥadīth* transmitters, but his renown rests mainly on his *Ṣaḥīḥ*.

BIBLIOGRAPHY

Burton, John. *An Introduction to the Hadith.* Edinburgh, U.K., 1994. Burton's book will not serve as an introduction to the *ḥadīth,* but it does have some useful pages on al-Bukhārī.

Goldziher, Ignaz. *Muslim Studies.* London, 1971. One of the most comprehensive introductory discussions of al-Bukhārī's methods.

Khan, Muhammad Muhsin. *The Translation of the Meanings of Sahih al-Bukhari,* 9 vols. Chicago, 1979. An English translation of the *Ṣaḥīḥ,* but as it omits the *isnāds* and other supporting information, it does not accurately reflect the nature of the whole work.

Sezgin, Fuat. *Geschichte des arabischen Schriftums. i, Qur'anwissenschaften, Hadit̲, Geschichte, Fiqh, Dogmatik, Mystik.* Leiden, Netherlands, 1967. Critical and extensive bio-bibliographical notice.

Siddiqi, Muhammad Zubayr. *Ḥadīth Literature: Its Origins, Development and Special Features.* Cambridge, U.K., 1993. Straightforward account of al-Bukhārī's life and scholarship, with very useful footnotes to more detailed primary and secondary sources.

BRUCE FUDGE (2005)

BULGAKOV, SERGEI (1871-1944), Russian economist, philosopher, theologian, and Russian Orthodox priest. Sergei Nikolaevich was born in Livny, province of Orel, less than fifty years before the revolutions of 1917. The son of a Russian Orthodox priest, Bulgakov was raised in a pious Orthodox home. Following his early formal education, he was enrolled in the theological seminary in Orel Province, which he left shortly thereafter for secular studies. A convinced atheist, at age nineteen he enrolled in the law school of the University of Moscow. By the time of his graduation in 1894 he was a committed and enthusiastic Marxist, with a special interest in political economy. His master's thesis on the relationship of capitalism and agriculture was published in 1900.

In 1901 Bulgakov was appointed to the faculty of the Polytechnic Institute of Kiev as a political economist. During his tenure there he began to have doubts about Marxism both as a philosophy and as an economic theory. The publication in 1903 of his *Ot Marksizma k idealizmu* (From Marxism to Idealism) signaled his definitive break with Marxism. In 1906 he was elected to the Second Duma and appointed to the faculty of the Institute of Commerce of Moscow. At this time, along with other members of the Russian intelligentsia, he began to turn from economics to philosophy, theology, and religion. He joined with thinkers such as Pavel Florenskii, Nikolai Berdiaev, and Vladimir Solov'ev in founding and writing for such periodicals as *Novyi put'* (New path) and *Voprosy zhizni* (Problems of life). Their movement, which developed in the direction of Eastern Orthodox Christianity, began as an angry attack on the radical intelligentsia through the journal *Vekhi.* Later, the movement took on a more positive orientation. Bulgakov expressed these emerging views in his works *Filosofiia khoziaistva* (Philosophy of economics; 1912); *Svet nevechernii* (The unending light; 1917); and *Tikhie dumy* (Quiet meditations; 1918).

Bulgakov became fully identified with the Russian Orthodox church after 1917 and was ordained a priest on June 11, 1918. He was elected to the newly formed Supreme Ecclesiastical Council, under the reconstituted patriarchate of Moscow. Because he was a clergyman, he lost the position that he held at the University of Simferopol. In 1922 he was expelled from the Soviet Union.

After a short stay in Prague, Bulgakov moved to Paris, where he spent the rest of his life as dean and professor of dogmatics at the Saint Sergius Theological Institute. He proved a creative and prolific author of theological works, many of which have a controversial and polemical character. Between 1926 and 1938 he produced seventeen major works. Six additional works were published posthumously, including *Die Tragödie der Philosophie* (The tragedy of philosophy; 1927), *The Social Teaching of Modern Russian Orthodox Theology* (1934), *Agnets Bozhii* (The lamb of God; 1933), and *Nevesta Agntsa* (The bride of the lamb; 1945). There remains a significant corpus of unpublished writings. In striving to present the basic doctrines of Eastern Orthodox Christianity in a contemporary light, Bulgakov provoked more conventional thinkers and became the center of theological controversy.

Bulgakov is remembered particularly for his controversial sophiological teachings, for which *Svet nevechernii* is a major early source. In 1936 and 1937 he published additional works on sophiology, which was the theological vehicle for his cosmology. In his formulation, Wisdom (*sophia*) is the all-inclusive concept of creation. It is the eternal female reality, the maternal womb of being, the "fourth hypostasis," the "world of ideas, the idealist basis of the created world." In Bulgakov's analysis, Wisdom is the pattern for divine creation. His sophiological teachings, which attempt to bring together the cosmological understandings of modern science and traditional theological understandings of creation, were accepted neither by the patriarchate of Moscow nor by the Karlovskii Synod, which represented Russian Orthodoxy outside the Soviet Union. The official Orthodox church condemned Bulgakov's sophiology, especially its conceptualization of the "fourth hypostasis," which was seen as a distortion of the received doctrine of the Holy Trinity. However, he was never excommunicated for this teaching. One of the most powerful and creative theological minds of his era, at his death Bulgakov was buried with full ecclesiastical honors.

BIBLIOGRAPHY

For a general understanding of Bulgakov's place in the theological climate of Russian Orthodoxy in Paris, see Donald A. Lowrie's *Saint Sergius in Paris: The Orthodox Theological Institute* (New York, 1951). For his general place in the range and dynamics of Russian intellectual history, see Nicolas Zernov's *The Russian Religious Renaissance of the Twentieth Century* (London, 1963) and N. O. Lossky's *History of Russian Philosophy* (New York, 1951). A full bibliography of his works is found in L. A. Zander's *Bog i mir: Mirosozertsanie Ottsa Sergiia Bulgakova*, 2 vols. (Paris, 1948).

The most helpful of his own writings in understanding his intellectual history is his autobiography, *Avtobiograficheskie zametki* (Paris, 1947). The following are representative writings in English translation: *A Bulgakov Anthology*, edited by Nicolas Zernov and James Pain (Philadelphia, 1976); *The Wisdom of God: A Brief Summary of Sophiology* (New York, 1937); and *Karl Marx as a Religious Type*, edited by Virgil Lang and translated by Luba Barna (Belmont, Mass., 1980).

STANLEY SAMUEL HARAKAS (1987)

BULL-ROARERS have been used as cult objects by various peoples from ancient times to the present day, usually in the context of male initiation ceremonies. They are generally made of wood (or ceramics, as in ancient Greece) and are generally flat, most commonly measuring sixty centimeters long and eight centimeters wide. Either through the whirring sound they make when swung or through the carved or painted marks they bear, they symbolize generalized powers of fertility, in particular those of male generative powers, of wind, and of rain.

In the mythology of ancient Greece, a bull-roarer was one of the toys with which the Titans distracted the child Dionysos before they slew him. As a cult object, the bull-roarer was used in rainmaking ceremonies, symbolizing Kronos as rainmaker, and in the Eleusinian mysteries, where the connection between Dionysos and Demeter as fertility deities was emphasized (Frazer, vol. 7, 1912). In present-day Europe the bull-roarer is still used among the Basques by boys to frighten women and girls during and after the Mass on Good Friday.

Through comparison with South American myths and rituals, where the bull-roarer's sound is associated with a giant snake, with the generative power of the phallus, and also with the period of food depletion and hunger, Lévi-Strauss (relying on the work of Otto Zerries and Geneviève Massignon) develops the following correlation: as the instrument is used during the absence of food and of fire (connected to European customs of extinguishing the fire before Easter), and thus with fasting, it indicates symbolically a time when man and nature are in close contact, a primordial time before the invention of fire, when food had to be consumed raw or warmed by the sun. The use of the bull-roarer's sound to separate women (nature-bound) from men (culture-bearers) seems to be corroborated by Australian Aboriginal usage of bull-roarers for fertility rituals or "increase-ceremonies" with secret-sacred character (Lévi-Strauss, 1966, pp. 354–357). However, there are also exceptions, as the Ungarinyin know of "female" bull-roarers. In general, Aboriginal devices of this sort are described under the Aranda term *tjurunga,* and in all tribal regions they embody the spirit, the essence, and the vital forces of the heroes and creator-spirits of the Dreaming. The spiritual power of these beings can be activated through ritual use of bull-roarers to affect procreation. Some tribal groups maintain that bull-roarers already exist in specific trees and have only to be "set free" through the ritual act of carving. Certain specific acts, such as shaving particles from a *tjurunga* and blowing them over the landscape or reciting and singing stories of the Dreaming featuring the totemic ancestors represented in and through a *tjurunga,* have the effect of continuing procreation of all nature (Petri and Worms, 1968).

Relying on New Guinean materials wherein bull-roarers symbolize phallic power, van Baal (1963) suggests that the secrecy surrounding the bull-roarer rituals in Australia points to the sacredness of the meaning of the sexual act. Without such rituals, sexual intercourse is too sacred to be practiced. As bull-roarer rituals take over the sacred meaning, intercourse can be performed as a profane act of pleasure.

SEE ALSO Tjurungas; Ungarinyin Religion.

BIBLIOGRAPHY

Baal, Jan van. "The Cult of the Bull-Roarer in Australia." *Bijdragen tot de Taal-, Land- en Volkenkunde* 119 (1963): 201–214. Provides an original interpretative framework for bull-roarer cults, relying on field experience in New Guinea and using Australian data for comparative purposes.

Frazer, James G. *The Golden Bough.* 3d ed., rev. & enl. London, 1911–1912. See especially part 1 (vols. 1–2), *The Magic Art and the Evolution of Kings,* an indispensable classic on means for the magical control of rain with primary sources on a global scale, and part 5 (vols. 7–8), *Spirits of the Corn and of the Wild,* an extensive discussion of fertility rituals in ancient Greece with cross-cultural comparisons.

Lévi-Strauss, Claude. *Mythologiques,* vol. 2, *Du miel aux cendres.* Paris, 1966. Translated as *From Honey to Ashes* (New York, 1973). An extensive structural analysis of myths and rituals of South American tribes in regard to culinary and musical coding.

Massignon, Geneviève. "La crécelle et les instruments des ténèbres en Corse." *Arts et traditions populaires* 7 (July-December, 1959): 274–280. The major European source of Lévi-Strauss's deductive hypothesis concerning aerophones and their symbolic connection with times of fasting, absence of fire, and male procreative powers.

Petri, Helmut, and Ernest A. Worms. *Australische Eingeborenen-Religionen.* Stuttgart, 1968. A comprehensive survey of Australian Aboriginal religious systems with a great amount of original data.

Zerries, Otto. "The Bull-Roarer among South American Indians." *Revista do Museo Paulista* 7 (1953). The main empirical data with which Lévi-Strauss supports his deductive theory that bull-roarers are instruments of darkness.

New Sources

Peek, Philip M. "The Sounds of Silence: Cross-World Communication and the Auditory Arts in African Societies." *American Ethnologist* 21, no. 3 (1984): 474–494.

Testart, Alain. "Rhombes et des tjurunga: la question des objets sacrés en Australie." *Homme* (Paris), no. 125 (1993): 31–65.

KLAUS-PETER KÖPPING (1987)
Revised Bibliography

BULTMANN, RUDOLF

BULTMANN, RUDOLF (1884–1976), Christian theologian and New Testament scholar. Born in Wiefelstede, in what was then the grand duchy of Oldenburg, Bultmann was the son of a Lutheran pastor, himself the son of a missionary to Africa, and also the grandson on the maternal side of a pastor in Baden. He attended the humanistic *Gymnasium* in Oldenburg before studying theology in Tübingen, Berlin, and Marburg. After receiving a scholarship to Marburg in 1907, he took his doctoral degree there in 1910 and qualified as university lecturer in 1912. He taught as instructor in Marburg until 1916, when he was appointed assistant professor in Breslau. In 1920 he was called to Giessen as full professor, only to return after one year to Marburg, where he taught as full professor until becoming professor emeritus in 1951, and where he continued to live until his death.

Bultmann's special field of competence as a theologian was the New Testament, and it is quite possible that he is the most influential scholar in this field in the twentieth century. His first major work, *Die Geschichte der synoptischen Tradition* (1921; *The History of the Synoptic Tradition,* 1963), established him as one of the cofounders of form criticism of the synoptic Gospels. Together with his book *Jesus* (1926; *Jesus and the Word,* 1934), it has been decisive for the ongoing quest of the historical Jesus as well as for subsequent critical study of the tradition redacted in the Gospels. Hardly less significant for research in the field are his studies of the Fourth Gospel, epitomized by the commentary that is perhaps his masterwork, *Das Evangelium des Johannes* (1941; *The Gospel of John: A Commentary,* 1971), and his interpretation of the theology of Paul, especially in his other major work, *Theologie des Neuen Testaments* (1948–1953; *Theology of the New Testament,* 1951, 1955). In any number of other respects as well, from the general problem of biblical hermeneutics to the special question of gnosticism and the New Testament, his work and the critical discussion of it continue to be determinative for serious study of the New Testament.

Yet it is not only or even primarily as a New Testament scholar that Bultmann is significant for theology and religious studies. In his own mind, certainly, he was, first and last, a Christian theologian, who did all of his historical work in service of the church and its witness, and it is in this capacity that he is now also widely regarded as one of the two or three Protestant theologians of the twentieth century whose impact on theology promises to be lasting. The warrants for this promise in his case are many, but two features of his thought in particular are basic to its significance.

First of all, Bultmann was distinctive among his contemporaries in clearly distinguishing and resourcefully addressing both of the essential tasks of Christian theology.

Thus, as much as he agreed with Karl Barth that theology's first task is to interpret the Christian witness appropriately, in accordance with the normative witness to Jesus Christ attested by scripture, he differed from Barth in insisting that theology also has the task of interpreting this witness understandably, in terms that men and women today can understand and find credible. On the other hand, if his efforts to deal with this second, apologetic task brought him into close proximity to Paul Tillich, his deep concern with the first, dogmatic task gave his thought a very different character from the more speculative, unhistorical cast of Tillich's kind of philosophical theology.

The other equally fundamental feature of Bultmann's thought was his thoroughgoing interpretation of Christian faith, as of religion generally, in existentialist terms. In this respect, there is no question of the formative influence on his theology of the existentialist philosophy of the early Martin Heidegger, who was his close colleague in Marburg from 1923 to 1928. But if Heidegger provided the conceptuality for Bultmann's existentialist theology, he had already learned from the Lutheran pietism out of which he came and, above all, from his teacher Wilhelm Herrmann, that faith can be understood only as an existential phenomenon. Consequently, while he never doubted that faith does indeed have to do with the strictly ultimate reality called God, he was convinced that faith always has to do with this reality, not in its being in itself, but in its meaning for us, and hence as authorizing our own authentic existence.

The first of the four volumes of Bultmann's collected essays, *Glauben und Verstehen* (1933; *Faith and Understanding*, 1969), shows that the theology defined by these two basic features had already taken shape during the 1920s. But it is also clear from the three later volumes (1952, 1960, 1965; Eng. trans. of vol. 2, 1955) as well as from his other writings during the so-called demythologizing debate, all of which appeared in the series edited by H. W. Bartsch, *Kerygma und Mythos* (1948–1955; *Kerygma and Myth*, partial Eng. trans., 1953, 1962), that the same theology found its classic expression in 1941 in his programmatic essay "New Testament and Mythology," which provoked this famous debate. If Bultmann was insistent in this essay that theology has no alternative but to demythologize the New Testament, he was also clear that the demand for demythologizing is not merely apologetic but, as he later formulated it, is also "a demand of faith itself." And when he explained the demythologizing he called for positively, as a procedure for interpreting rather than for eliminating myth, it proved to be nothing other than thoroughgoing existentialist interpretation now applied to the mythological formulations of the New Testament.

Even today, Bultmann's theology remains the most controversial of the twentieth century, and it is still uncertain whether he will be reckoned among the fathers of the modern church or among its arch heretics. But there seems little question now that this is the level at which his work must be judged, and its impact already confirms that the history of theology, no less than the history of philosophy, is never quite the same after the shock of a great thinker.

Bibliography

Works by Bultmann in English in addition to those cited above include his Gifford Lectures, *History and Eschatology* (Edinburgh, 1957), and the selection of his shorter writings I edited and translated in *Existence and Faith* (New York, 1960). His most important contributions to the demythologizing debate are all available in my edition and translation of *New Testament and Mythology and Other Basic Writings* (Philadelphia, 1984). Among works on his theology, the volume edited by Charles W. Kegley, *The Theology of Rudolf Bultmann* (New York, 1966), provides a useful orientation to the extensive critical discussion, while the best general introduction is Walter Schmithals's *An Introduction to the Theology of Rudolf Bultmann* (London, 1968).

Schubert M. Ogden (1987)

BUNYAN, JOHN

BUNYAN, JOHN (1628–1688), English Nonconformist and author of *The Pilgrim's Progress.* The son of a brazier, John Bunyan was born in the village of Elstow, near Bedford, and may have attended a local grammar school. During the Civil War he served with the parliamentary forces at Newport Pagnell, Buckinghamshire, where he came into contact with various religious sects. In the early 1650s he underwent prolonged spiritual turmoil, at the nadir of which he was convinced that he had betrayed Christ by allying himself with the devil. About 1655 Bunyan joined the open-communion Baptist church at Bedford, whose pastor was John Gifford, a former royalist officer. Some members of the congregation were sympathetic to the tenets of the Fifth Monarchists, a radical millenarian group to which Bunyan himself was apparently attracted for a time.

Bunyan launched his career as a preacher and prolific author before the monarchy and the Church of England were restored in 1660. For preaching illegally, he was arrested in November 1660 and imprisoned for twelve years in the county jail at Bedford. While imprisoned, he spent much of his time making laces to support his family and writing new books, but near the end of his incarceration he also worked closely with representatives of four other churches to organize a network of preachers and teachers in northern Bedfordshire and contiguous areas in order to resist the uniformity imposed by the Church of England and thus help to ensure the survival of Nonconformity during future periods of persecution. In January 1672 Bunyan was chosen pastor of the Bedford church, although he was not released from prison until the following September. The period of intense ministerial activity that ensued was threatened when a warrant for his arrest was issued in March 1675. Although Bunyan eluded this warrant by temporarily fleeing Bedford, he was rearrested late in 1676, only to be freed the following June. The last dozen years of his life were devoted to preaching in the Midlands and London, as well as to further writing. When the Roman Catholic monarch, James II, tried to win support by granting toleration to Nonconformists. Bunyan was cautious, although some members of his congregation accepted positions in the reorganized Bedford Corporation. Bunyan did not live to see James deposed in the Glorious Revolution, for he died in London on August 31, 1688.

Of Bunyan's approximately sixty works, the most popular is *The Pilgrim's Progress,* the first part of which was composed during his long imprisonment but not published until 1678. A virtual epic of the Christian life couched in Puritan ideals, the story of Christian's struggles from the Slough of Despond to the Eternal City draws heavily on Bunyan's own religious experience. The dramatic power of the narrative is enhanced by vivid symbolism, homely colloquialisms, and myriad human touches. The same ground is traversed in more quiescent fashion by Christiana and her children in the second part, published in 1684, in which Bunyan paid more attention to women. Both parts depend extensively on Bunyan's spiritual autobiography, *Grade Abounding to the Chief of Sinners* (1666), a sine qua non for understanding all his works. In its pages such psychologists as William James and Josiah Royce have sought the key to Bunyan's personality. Whether he was in fact troubled by psychotic disorders is difficult to ascertain, for *Grace Abounding,* like other works of this genre, follows a rather commonplace thematic pattern: the path to sainthood commences with denunciations of one's utter depravity.

Bunyan's attempt to repeat the success of *The Pilgrim's Progress* with *The Holy War* (1682), a ponderous albeit technically superior allegory, produced a sophisticated but less personal work. Its complex allegorical levels embrace world history, recent English events, the experience of the individual soul, and probably an apocalyptic vision. Bunyan abandoned allegory to depict the wayward reprobate in *The Life and Death of Mr. Badman* (1680), which, although it lacks the emotional intensity and dramatic tension of *The Pilgrim's Progress,* has captured the interest of both literary specialists, as a possible forerunner of the novel, and historians, for its incisive comments on English society.

Bunyan's theological views were substantially shaped by the Bible, John Foxe's *Book of Martyrs,* Martin Luther's commentary on *Galatians,* and works of two early seventeenth-century Puritans, Arthur Dent's *The Plaine Mans Pathway to Heaven* (1601) and Lewis Bayly's *The Practice of Piety* (1612). Bunyan's views were essentially compatible with those of other strict Calvinists of his period, such as the Nonconformists John Owen and Thomas Goodwin. This is notably manifest in his exposition of the key concept of the covenants, particularly as expounded in his major theological treatise, *The Doctrine of the Law and Grace Unfolded* (1659). Bunyan's emphasis on God's role in establishing the covenant of grace set him apart from such moderate Calvinists as Richard Baxter, who gave greater prominence to human responsibility, but Bunyan stopped short of the antinomians by insisting that the moral law has a valid and significant place in the covenant of grace. Unlike most strict Calvinists, however, Bunyan repudiated the idea of a baptismal covenant, for in his judgment water baptism was necessary neither for admission to the Lord's Supper nor for church membership. Bunyan hotly debated this subject with such traditional Baptists as Henry Danvers, Thomas Paul, and John Denne. As a controversialist he also engaged in literary debates with the Quakers Edward Burrough and William Penn and with the latitudinarian Edward Fowler. Another prominent theme in Bunyan's theology was millenarianism, the *loci classici* of which are *The Holy City* (1665) and *Of Antichrist and His Ruin* (1692, posthumous).

Although Bunyan achieved virtually instantaneous recognition with the publication of *The Pilgrim's Progress,* especially in lay Protestant religious circles, critical acclaim was slow to follow. Alexander Pope and Jonathan Swift referred kindly to his masterpiece, but Edmund Burke and David Hume sneered. With the onset of romanticism and the evangelical revivals, interest in Bunyan soared, and by the Victorian period he was commonly referred to in evangelical circles as a genius. Copies of *The Pilgrim's Progress* poured from the press—more than thirteen hundred editions by 1938—accompanied by numerous popular commentaries, nearly all from evangelicals. Predictions at the turn of the twentieth century of Bunyan's theological and literary obsolescence proved premature when the atrocities of World War I brought new relevance to his works. Although religious interest in him waned in the late twentieth century, his reputation is now firmly established among students of religion, history, literature, and psychology.

BIBLIOGRAPHY

The standard critical edition of Bunyan's works includes *The Pilgrim's Progress,* edited by James Blanton Wharey and revised by Roger Sharrock (Oxford, 1960); *Grace Abounding to the Chief of Sinners,* edited by Roger Sharrock (Oxford, 1962); *The Holy War,* edited by Roger Sharrock and James Forrest (Oxford, 1980); *The Life and Death of Mr. Badman,* edited by Roger Sharrock and James Forrest (Oxford, 1988); and *The Miscellaneous Works of John Bunyan* under the general editorship of Roger Sharrock (Oxford, 1976–). The best biography is still John Brown's enthusiastic *John Bunyan, 1628–1688: His Life, Times, and Work,* revised by Frank Mott Harrison (London, 1928). For Bunyan's thought and its antecedents, the standard account is Richard L. Greaves's *John Bunyan* (Abingdon, U.K., and Grand Rapids, Mich., 1969). A provocative analysis of Bunyan's relationship to his contemporaries is provided in William York Tindall's *John Bunyan: Mechanick Preacher* (New York, 1934). For a full bibliography of Bunyan studies, see James Forrest and Richard L. Greaves's *John Bunyan: A Reference Guide* (Boston, 1982).

RICHARD L. GREAVES (1987)

BURCKHARDT, TITUS. Titus Burckhardt (1908–1984) was born in Florence, Italy into a Protestant patrician family from Basle in the German-speaking part of Switzerland, the son of the sculptor Carl Burckhardt, and great-nephew of the famous art historian Jacob Burckhardt. A school friendship with Fritjhof Schuon (1907–1998), who had been one of the first expositors of the perennial philosophy in the second half of the 20th century, in Basle was to become a long spiritual and intellectual friendship, with both of them being interested in Eastern art from an early age. Burckhardt had intended to be a sculptor—following in his father's footsteps—and he attended several art schools in Switzerland and Italy. A stay in Morocco in the 1930s changed the course of his life. He studied Arabic literature and jurisprudence and followed the teachings of the Sufic masters Sidi Mohammed Bouchara at Salé and Moulay Ali ad-Darqāwī at Fez. The latter town of Fez had retained a great deal of its intellectual and spiritual luster and it is at the heart of the tradition that the young Westerner joined, under the name ʿIbrahīm, Abraham ʾIz al-Din, in the Shādhiliyya, a link in the great chain of Islamic esoteric mystic brotherhoods. He translated the principal texts of Sufism, the *Fusūs al-Hikam* ("pearls of wisdom from the prophets"), by Ibn Arabī, and the *Rasāʾil* ("letters"), by his master ad-Darqāwī. Schuon once again met him at Fez, in 1935. For his part, Schuon had been initiated in 1933 he had been initiated by Shaykh al-ʿAlawī in the Alawyia brotherhood of Mostaganem in Algeria, and their spiritual paths were never again to part. They had a common belief in the idea of a universal, perennial tradition, a *philosophia perennis,* which had been handed down unbroken from the beginning, just like the principles René Guénon (1886–1951) had set out from 1921 in a series of works published in Paris. *L'introduction générale à l'étude des doctrines hindoues* (1921), then *L'homme et son devenir selon le Vēdānta* (1925), set out the "non-dual" metaphysics of the Vedanta as the perfect expression of "traditional science"; Islam, Daoism, and ancient Christianity all shared in this great tradition. This science alone could oppose the modern decline denounced in *Orient et Occident* (1924) or *La crise du monde moderne* (1927), both edited by Réne Guénon, and the need to break away and reject this was an opinion shared by Burckhardt, Schuon, and the circle established around the neo-Traditionalist or Perennial movement. A westernized Indian put back in touch with his own tradition by reading Guénon, A. K. Coomaraswamy (1877–1947), who was in charge of the department of Asiatic art at the Museum of Fine Art in Boston, would also play an important part in the workings of this circle. They all sought harmony between their lives and their philosophy, but the question was posed differently for Easterners and for those from the West who lacked a regular initiation in the Christian tradition. Sufism, with its implication of conversion to Islam, was considered by Guénon to be the natural outcome of his writings, and he had taken that route himself. He therefore encouraged Schuon to found his own branch of a Ṣūfī brotherhood, or *ṭarīqah.* In 1935 Schuon became *moqqadem* (lieutenant) of the Master, the *shaykh* of Mostaganem. The following year Schuon, after a dream, claimed for himself the role of *shaykh.* Three centers were established, in Amiens, Lausanne, and Basle, and Burckhardt took particular charge of the last of these. Difficulties arose between Guénon and Schuon on doctrinal questions, especially regarding Christianity, and were made worse by different approaches—more cold and intellectual by the former, in the splendor of the truth of creation (according to Plato's famous expression) by the latter. Burckhardt was clearly inclined to Schuon's side of the debate. During the 1950s and 1960s he held the post of artistic director at the publisher Urs Graf at Olten, near Basle, working on the publication of beautiful illuminated mediaeval manuscripts such as the *Book of Durrow* and the *Book of Kells,* ancient Celtic gospels housed at Trinity College, Dublin. He was also in charge of a spiritual historical collection entitled *Stätten des Geistes,* which illustrated the multiple expressions behind the fundamental unity of the various traditions. He was personally responsible for three of the works: on the Gothic cathedral at Chartres; on Siena, the pride and joy of the Italian Renaissance; and his masterpiece, on the Islamic city of Fez. This global overview via a single town allowed him to link urbanism, architecture, and drawing and decorative arts to the class of artisans as they lived in the daily life of traditional societies and in modern Morocco. In this way Burckhardt developed a new concept of Islamic art, free from local influence and historical legacies, Andalusian or Persian art, thus revealing an expression of a spiritual feeling, of a search for truth. By rejecting the use of images, Islamic art dispensed with emotion, enhancing harmony and inner peace; the continuous presence of degrees of light led from the created world to its origin. The result of this investigation, carried out in parallel with his research into the fundamental tenets of Christian, Hindu, and Buddhist art, was published in *Principes et méthodes de l'art sacré* (1958), a work collecting many German, French, and English articles, and particularly those published in the journal inspired by Guénon, *Etudes traditionnelles.* In the same vein Burckhardt tackled the astrology of Ibn Arabī together with alchemy: the earthly symbolism of metals, the object of alchemy, corresponded to the heaven of the zodiac and the planets; the planets reflected "cosmic intelligence," metals "the first intelligent form of earthly matter" or *materia prima.* Cosmic harmony came about as a result of their connection, opening the way for the transformation of the person who was aware of them.

Burckhardt's talents were recognized, and between 1972 and 1977 the Moroccan government and UNESCO entrusted him with a mission to safeguard the architectural and cultural heritage, including the traditional arts and crafts, of the medina, the old town of Fez. He was formally honored by an international conference at Marrakesh in 1999.

SEE ALSO Coomaraswamy, Ananda; Guénon, René.

BIBLIOGRAPHY

Works by Burckhardt

"Considérations sur l'alchimie", *Etudes Traditionnelles,* Oct-Nov. 1948, pp. 288-300.

Clef spirituelle de l'astrologie musulmane. Paris, 1950.

Du Soufisme. Lyon, France, 1951.

De l'Homme universel. Lyon, France, 1953.

Vom Sufitum-Einführung in die Mystik des Islams. Munich, 1953.

La sagesse des Prophètes. Paris, 1955.

Principes et méthodes de l'art sacré. Lyon, France, 1958.

Siena, Stadt der Jungfrau. Olten and Freiburg-im Breisgau, Germany, 1958.

Alchemie, Sinn und Weltbild. Olten and Freiburg-im Breisgau, Germany, 1960.

Fes Stadt des Islams. Olten and Freiburg-im Breisgau, Germany, 1960.

Chartres und die Geburt des Kathedrale. Lausanne, Switzerland, 1962.

Lettres d'un Maître soufi. Milan, 1978.

L'art de l'Islam. Paris, 1985.

Mirror of the Intellect, translated by William Stoddart. Cambridge, U.K., and Albany, N.Y., 1987.

Works on Burckhardt

Kansoussi, Jaafar, ed. *Sagesse et splendeur des arts islamiques: Hommage à Titus Burckhardt.* Marrakech, 2000.

Nasr, Seyyed Hosein. "With Titus Burckhardt at the Tomb of Ibn Arabī." *Studies in Comparative Religion,* Titus Burckhardt memorial issue) 16, nos. 1 and 2 (1984): 17–20.

JEAN-PIERRE LAURANT (2005)
Translated from French by Paul Ellis

BURIAL SEE FUNERAL RITES

BURIAT RELIGION. The Buriats, northern Mongols, are the most significant minority native to eastern Siberia. They are not a homogeneous body; there are two cultural extremes, between which exists a range of intermediate groups.

The western or Cisbaikalian extreme is represented by the Ekhirit-Bulagat tribe, forest dwellers who are engaged in hunting and fishing. Although they were isolated from the Mongolian empire, they had begun to practice livestock breeding through the influence of Mongolian émigrés at the time of the arrival of Russian cossacks in the mid-seventeenth century. After colonization and sedentarization, their segmentary clan structure survived more ideologically than practically. Shamanism has remained strong there up to the present, successfully resisting the assaults of lamaist propaganda and affected only superficially by Orthodox Christianity.

The eastern or Transbaikalian extreme is represented by the Khori, who, as a result of Mongolian civil wars during the sixteenth and seventeenth centuries, settled with their herds in the steppes. They were treated favorably by the rulers of the Russian empire because of their strategic position in relation to the Chinese empire. Beginning in the eighteenth century, lamaism, which had come from Mongolia, spread rapidly. While lamaism favored the ideals of nomadic pastoralism and developed the tendency toward a centralizing hierarchy, it was forced to adapt its practice to traditional shamanic forms and to fight the power of the shamans themselves.

Shamanism is a constituent element of traditional Buriat society. Within the framework of the clan institution, due to its control of the spirits (which originate from souls), it assures a mediation between man and the supernatural concerning access to natural resources, thereby assuring a general regulation of societal life, transcending by far the individual shaman and his activity. Many authors have tended to exaggerate the role of the shaman's personality and to construct an independent and rigid pantheon of spirits fundamentally linked with daily tribal life. The shamanic institution and its practice varies according to the modes of subsistence and society and associated exterior influences. Three kinds can be distinguished, the second being the only well-documented one.

THE HUNTER'S SHAMANISM. The first type of shamanism is associated with hunting. Animals, conceived as being organized in exogamic clans maintain relations of alliance and vengeance that are analogous to those that obtain between humans. Hunter and shaman are each in his own way similar to the son-in-law who takes a wife and gives a sister: in return for the game meat taken from the forest spirits, the hunter feeds the animal spirits (*ongons*); in return for the living human and animal souls obtained from the corresponding spirits, the shaman restores the souls of the deceased to their world, whence his role in birth and death.

Any misbehavior or infraction entails sanctions that always affect biological life, resulting in such occurrences as intemperate weather, absence of game, sickness, and death. Because the soul is indispensable to bodily life, it is the shaman's lot to conduct preventative and restorative mediations. With the help of the personal allies he has made among human and animal spirits, he symbolically travels and meets the troublemaking spirits in order to negotiate a return to order. Invested to serve his clan, the shaman may be led to act against other clans (by diverting game away from them, afflicting them with sickness) and become the symbolic architect of wars.

THE CATTLE BREEDER'S SHAMANISM. The second and best-documented type of shamanism is found among those of the Ekhirit-Bulagat tribe who breed cattle. The essential part of relations between the human and spirit worlds consists of relations between the living and the dead. Subsistence is dependent upon one's ancestors *(übged),* who are "masters" *(ezen)* of the mountains dominating the clan territory. These ancestors legitimize and protect the economic life of their descendants and punish them with biological harm for every breach of clan ethics. In the *tailghan* sacrifices (of mares or sheep) offered by each clan to its ancestors, the shaman participates as a member of the clan.

The principal causes for recourse to shamanic mediation are accidents in the realm of filiation ties and rules, that is, anything that affects patrilineal continuity: sterility, difficult childbirth, childhood illness, and even conjugal disputes and women's flights or escapades that entail the risk, for a man, not to have any descendants. (According to legend, shamanism originated from a wife who ran off.) Those involved must both be cured during their lifetime and spared frustration that would incite them to inflict harm after their death. Private sacrifices *(khereg)* are offered to their souls after death, first to neutralize and soothe them and then to transform them into *zayaan.* These spirits are the exceptional dead (of which the positive examples are the great shamans, warriors, or hunters), who govern the fate of men and are of prime importance in the religious practice. The ordinary dead support their descendants in wars against other clans; a clan without a shaman to intervene by mediating with its dead takes recourse to flight rather than expose itself to combat. In the pastoral setting, however, the restorative activities of the shaman generally prevail over the offensive ones.

The shaman. Among the Ekhirit-Bulagats, in order to become a shaman *(böö)* one must have a shaman "essence" *(udkha),* that is, a genetically transmitted right, which is evidenced by the existence of shamans among one's ancestors. It is imperative for one of the descendants of a shamanic line to become a shaman so that the ancestor shamans can have a representative on earth. Equally important is that the candidate demonstrate his capability in order to be supported and invested by his people. Finally, although gender is proclaimed irrelevant, male shamans are much more numerous than female shamans (*udaghans*); patrilineal rule is compulsory.

A shaman's career generally is decided at adolescence, under a certain amount of pressure from the boy's relatives. Fainting fits, visions, flights or escapades, and anorexia called *khüdkhe* ("disordered state") are interpreted as signs that the shaman is familiarizing himself with the spirits under the aegis of his ancestors. He trains in the shamanic manner of singing and gesticulating (in a lugubrious voice with animal-like cries, sighs and gasping fits, leaping, swaying, etc., representing the voyage to the spirit world) and imitates or assists experienced shamans for several years. At the end of this apprenticeship, he is invested by his community through a rite (called *ughaalgha*) in which he receives his accoutrements (costume, drum, etc). This rite consists of symbolically "reanimating" the shaman, making him both spirit and human, dead and alive. It is this amalgamation of the two modes of being that permits him to ensure mediation. He then takes an oath to serve his people, who will monitor him closely in this work and who will not hesitate to replace or do away with him should they become dissatisfied.

Without an "essence" one still can become a shaman if one has numerous deceased relatives, particularly if one relative was struck dead by lightning, a process that energizes a new essence. His ability would then have to be demonstrated. Should the obligation to become a shaman be perceived as unbearable by the sole descendant of a line, the shamanic role nevertheless provides an excellent opportunity for an individual to emerge, especially for women. Female shamans whose vocations are thwarted become the most formidable "fates" *(zayaan)* upon death. In addition, those who are not shamans occasionally shamanize, either for their own psychic needs or within the framework of collective peregrinations *(böölööšen* or *naĭguur)* while trying to face natural disasters or pressures of acculturation.

The principal moments of the shamanic séance are (1) the censing of the area with the smoke of burning spruce bark (the spruce, known to the Buriats as *žodoo,* is the symbol of the shaman's function) in order to effect the shaman's entrance into sacred space-time; (2) the incorporation of auxiliary spirits; (3) the transcendent vision, in which the shaman identifies the spirit responsible for the disturbance; (4) the journey of the soul to the realm of the spirit in question in order to negotiate with him; (5) a sacrifice in accordance with his wishes; and (6) general divination. Following the séance, the shaman resumes his normal life.

The sky creators and their founding sons. If the spirits of the deceased rule over daily life, the *tengeris* (or *tengris*; "skies," a class of supernatural beings) creators and predestinators of humans, appear in the background. They are divided into opposite camps, the fifty-five White Tengeris of the West (or Right), whose leader is considered older, and the forty-four Black Tengeris of the East (or Left), whose leader is considered younger. This division, which illustrates the conflict between the Elder and the Younger, on the one hand denotes the principle of clan segmentation (and perhaps an ancient organization by moieties); on the other hand, it denotes the principle of dualistic power, viewed as a conflict between the established authority (symbolized by the elder) and the challenge to that authority (symbolized by the younger). The elder represents the clan institution, which has inherited legitimate authority but no real power; the younger represents the shamanic institution, which has real power but must subordinate the exercise of its function to the interests of the clan and which has a social position, resting on ability, that is always susceptible to being challenged (whence the fact that the shaman is both indispensable to the clan and feared by it at the same time on account of his ability to manipulate the powers of the spirits).

The first legendary shaman carried the adjective *khara* ("black") in his name. It seems that the notion of a white shaman is an artificial creation that resulted from religious acculturation or was a reaction against it: an examination of the facts reveals the nonexistence of white shamans as such. While the *tengeris* remain in the sky, expressing themselves through atmospheric phenomena, their sons descend to the earth, as did Buxa Noyon the Bull Lord, founder of the Ekhirit-Bulagat tribe; the epic hero Geser, founder of the rules of marriage; and the various "kings" *(khad)* of mountains and waters.

Marginalized Shamanism. The third kind of Buriat shamanism is that which survived in the lamaist regions in spite of persecution (which occurred at the beginning of the nineteenth century, primarily in the regions of Barguzin and Tunka). There the shaman is no longer a sort of "clan property." His role and status is marginalized; personal desire is the key motivator for becoming a shaman, and the door is open to women. Occasionally a family may have both a son who is a lama and a daughter who is a shaman. It is not unusual for one to contact a shaman to "call back the soul" *(hünehe kharyuulkha)* robbed from a sick person by a spirit after a lama's attempt has failed, for the shaman is still considered the more capable of succeeding.

The biggest changes affect the conception of the supernatural world (which continues to expand and develop as a hierarchy) and the social significance of rituals. The faces of the celestial *tengeri*s are becoming more individualistic, borrowing traits from lamaist deities and occasionally becoming merged with them. It is to them and no longer to ancestral spirits that milk offerings and prayers are directed in order to obtain an increase in offspring and livestock. Some new faces appear, such as that of Erlik, master of the world of the dead. Some are transformed, like the spirit of the hearth fire, represented west of Lake Baikal by a couple worshiped by all hearths of the same clan; in the east this couple becomes an independent woman, *tengeri* or khan of the fire, worshiped separately by each family.

To compete with the clan sacrifices *(tailghan),* the lamas organize great bloodless rituals *(oboo),* which are open to a large parochial community and are held on a mountain summit. The lamaist practice threatens to eliminate or at least to overtake the shamanic practice on all levels (through control over pastoral space and daily life, divination, medicine, and magical demonstrations). Judging from the actual relics, it is clear that the lamas have succeeded only superficially. The establishment of an actual Buriat Lamaist church in Transbaikalia was encouraged by the Russian Empire in order to avoid dependence on Mongolia and hence on China; in fact, lamaism obtained a strong sociopolitical position but was nearly emptied of all Buddhist content. Comparatively, in the agricultural regions of Cisbaikalia, Orthodox Christianity has had only a superficial influence over the ritual seasons (for example, the cults of Saint Nicholas and other saints). Along with the official existence of the lamaist monastery at Ivolga, the cult of Maydar (Maitreya), the future Buddha, seems to be the only living practice today; it is supported by a kind of nationalistic prophesying, but it is very limited geographically.

The Adaptation of Shamanism. Organically linked with a noncentralized type of society, pragmatic in its own principle, deriving its power from simple spirits, turning each shaman into a rival of others, shamanism is vulnerable to every centralizing influence and to the penetration of any dogma that implies transcendental entities and is represented by a constituent clerical body. This weakness is at the same time a strength: shamanism can adapt. The spirits are brought into line with current tastes (for example, the souls of revolutionaries who died tragically, victims of the Second World War), whereas in the sky, such a figure as Lenin deliberates with the *tengeri*s concerning world affairs. Despite these innovations, illness, especially children's illness, remains the principal occasion for true shamanic intervention. Free from all liturgy and cultural servitude, based on flexibility and individual innovation, the shaman's practice is all but formalist and may take place in secrecy. Communication with the dead plays a role in the awareness of ethnic identity; certain ritualistic details, like the drops of alcohol poured at the inauguration of all feasts, or like the ribbons hung on trees growing through a hill or near a thermal spring, have become true cultural traits of the Buriats.

See Also Erlik; Ongon; Shamanism; Southern Siberian Religions; Tengri.

Bibliography

Eliade, Mircea. *Shamanism: Archaic Techniques of Ecstasy* (1951). Princeton, 1964. The only general overview on shamanism covering a wide range of peoples. Includes extensive data on the Buriats.

Khangalov, M. N. *Sobranie sochinenii.* 3 vols. Ulan-Ude, 1958–1960. A remarkable compendium of data gathered at the end of the nineteenth and beginning of the twentieth century in the regions to the west of Lake Baikal by a highly learned Buriat authority on shamanism.

Lamaizm v Buriatii XVIII-nachala XX veka: Struktura i sotsial'naia rol' kul'tovoi sistemy. Novosibirsk, 1983. An excellent study of the conflicts and accommodations between lamaism and shamanism in Transbaikalia during the eighteenth, nineteenth, and twentieth centuries.

Manzhigeev, I. A. *Buriatskie shamanisticheskie i doshamanisticheskie terminy.* Moscow, 1978. Presents, in the form of a glossary, the notable personalities and concepts of Buriat shamanism and mythology.

Mikhailov, T. M. *Iz istorii buriatskogo shamanizma (s drevneishikh vremen po XVIII v.).* Novosibirsk, 1980. A history of Buriat shamanism, treated as a discrete religious system. Balances both critical and theoretical approaches.

Sandschejew, Garma. "Weltanschauung und Schamanismus der Alaren-Burjaten," *Anthropos* 22 (1927): 576–613, 933–955; 23 (1928): 538–560, 967–986. A richly informative panorama of the shamanism of the Alar Buriats (west of Lake Baikal) based on the personal observations of the author.

New Sources

Balzer, Marjorie Mandelstam, ed. *Shamanism: Soviet Studies of Traditional Religion in Siberia and Central Asia.* Armonk, N.Y., 1990.

Fridman, Eva Jane Neumann. "Sacred Geography: Shamanism in the Buddhist Republics of Russia." Ph.D. diss., Brown University, Providence, 1998.

Hamayon, Roberte. "Abuse of the Father, Abuse of the Husband: A Comparative Analysis of Two Buryat Myths of Ethnic Origin." In *Synkretismus in den Religionen Zentralasiens: Ergebnisse eines Kolloquiums vom 24.5. bis 26.5.1983 in St. Augustin bei Bonn,* edited by Walther Heissig and Hans-Joachim Klimkeit, pp. 91–107. Wiesbaden, 1987.

Hurelbaatar, A. "An Introduction to the History and Religion of the Buryat Mongols of Shinehen in China." *Inner Asia* 2, no. 1 (2000): 73–116.

Kiripolska, Marta. "The Twelve Deeds of the Buddha: A 19th Century Buriat Translation of the Hymn [Buriat Manuscript found in the Collection of Naprstek Museum in Prague]." *Mongolian Studies* 23 (2000): 17–42.

Tkacz, Virlana. *Shanar: Dedication Ritual of a Buryat Shaman in Siberia as Conducted by Bayir Rinchinov.* New York, 2002.

ROBERTE HAMAYON (1987)
Translated from French by Sherri L. Granka
Revised Bibliography

BURMESE RELIGION. The Burmese people, for the purpose of this article, are the majority population of the Socialist Republic of the Union of Burma, the westernmost country of mainland Southeast Asia. The language they speak is Burmese (or Arakanese, its most important dialect variant), and they are often called Burmans. The word *Burmese* is reserved for the total population of this country, including "tribal" minority peoples (chiefly residing in the mountains and practicing religions other than those of the Burmans), the Tai-speaking Shan of the eastern plateau (the Shan State), and the Austroasiatic-speaking Mon of southern Burma. The traditional religion of the Shan and Mon is the same Theravāda Buddhism as that of the Burmans, although with some variation peculiar to themselves. The Burmese made their first appearance in history about the tenth century of the common era.

Any Burman will tell you that the traditional religion is Theravāda Buddhism, although a small minority of Burmese are not Buddhists. It is sometimes alleged that to be Burmese is to be a Buddhist. What is really at issue is the fact that the traditional social and cultural institutions of the Burmese, now and historically, are found in large measure in the social, political, and ideological fabric of Buddhist doctrine, so that even non-Buddhist Burmese recognize the centrality of Buddhism to their social cultural identity.

There is a good deal about Burmese Buddhism that is distinctive. In the first place, there is a specifically Burmese tradition in the way Buddhism is interpreted and practiced. Burmese Buddhism is no more deviant from a supposed pristine scriptural norm than any past or present form of the religion. In addition, the Burmese also practice a cult of service to various spirits (Spiro, 1967). This cult exists both at the national level as a formal institution of the former Burmese monarchy (the cult of the Thirty-seven Lords [*nats*], the spirit guardians of the kingdom) and locally with regard to spirits associated with features of the landscape and with family lines and administrative jurisdictions as their proper domains (*nat*), as well as homeless ghosts, demons, and so on. Not only are the details of belief and practice of these cults (sometimes including the serving of killed animals and alcoholic spirits to these beings) not to be found in the Buddhist scriptures or commentaries, but it is also the case that the practices of this cult are often at odds with the Buddhist behavioral precepts. Burmese themselves, while insisting that they are committed Buddhists, see a contradiction between what some authors have therefore called these two different religions. It will be a major task of this article to try to resolve this issue.

Such facts have led many to speak of a syncretic Burmese religion rather than of Buddhism, some of them purporting to see Buddhism as a mere veneer. However, while Burmese religion consists of the two "cults," careful consideration of the full range of canonical Buddhism shows that the religion of the Burmese is simply Buddhism, and that the conflict between the two cults has a basis in paradoxes within canonical Buddhism itself. Nor is it sufficient to say that Buddhism, being ultimately concerned with longterm, transcendental goals, provides no means of immediately quelling one's fears and anxieties about wordly suffering, which the cult of spirits serves specifically to alleviate.

There is ample scriptural basis for the idea that it is the positive duty of authority, in particular of a proper Buddhist monarch, to subdue, by conversion, subversion, or other means, whatever spirit forces may be thought to exist as a threat to the conditions in which Buddhism, its doctrine, practice, and monastic order (Skt., *saṃgha*; Pali, *sangha*) may flourish in society. It is therefore the king's duty, and, by extension of his authority, that of all secular persons in his jurisdiction, to protect religion by dealing with potentially harmful spirit agencies. Buddhism presupposes the existence of various classes of spiritural beings, including, of course, gods (*devas*, *devatas*), in its brahmanically derived cosmology, so that it has no need to specify completely either their natures or how to deal with them. That is left to local tradition, and it is unsurprising that, consequently—since beliefs have to come from somewhere—there is in Burma a close relationship between the leading ideas of the spirit cult within Buddhism and the leading ideas of pre-Buddhist animism as evidenced in the traditional religions of neighboring non-Buddhist tribal peoples. Syncretism that may well be, but it is nevertheless canonically motivated, even positively enjoined. Here arises the first paradox.

The means for dealing with whatever spirit agencies may exist are to be arrived at according to what local tradition says of these various spirits. In fact, these demands often require one to act contrary to Buddhist precepts of Right Action. This is no more problematical than the inherent tension (Tambiah, 1976, pp. 22–23) in the role of a Buddhist monarch, who, creating and maintaining the conditions wherein religion can flourish, must be responsible for acts of violence, as in war and the punishment of crime. The consequence, in both cases, is ambivalence, defining Buddhism as the Middle Way.

In traditional Burma the king was expected ideally to conform to the Theravāda version of the *bodhisattva* idea. Yet the king was also one of the "five evils," along with war, pestilence, spirit *nats*, and the like; indeed, as a peremptory, if not arbitrary, "lord," a king was himself, not altogether metaphorically, a *nat.* Although he had to have earned enormous previous merit in order to now have the entire order as his field of merit (a field so productive that he might look forward to future Buddhahood), it was also incumbent upon him, as the *bodhisattva* (*hpaya:laun*) ideal might suggest, to take on a burden of demerit in the course of carrying out his obligations. This is so for the *cakravartin* (Pali, *cak-kavatti*), the Wheel-turning World Conqueror, that ideal *min:laung* (immanent king) or *hpaya:laung*, who serves as the model not so much for the general run of Buddhist kings as for what may be called a major Buddhist throne or monarchical lineage and for the *ekarāja*, the "sovereign king" who rules righteously, the actual model for the ordinary Buddhist monarch depicted in such Burmese court manuals as *Hywei Nan: Thoun: Wohara Abhidān* (Maung Maung Tin, 1979).

The cult of spirits is also at once enjoined and disparaged by Buddhism. On the one hand there are the aforementioned canonical precedents and injunctions. On the other hand, just as regional *nat* cults and messianic forms of Buddhism tend to be suppressed by the state because they imply the need to redress social disorder and constitute a challenge to a state and its moral legitimacy, so also from the point of view of an orthodox *sangha*, the need for extracanonical cult practices addressed to spirits is held to imply that religion is not flourishing, so that the world of spirits is not properly under control and religion is not, of itself, adequate for protection against them. This is not canonically unthinkable, but the order quite reasonably wishes to see itself as pure and vigorous, just as, indeed, government desires its own legitimacy to be upheld by the view that religion is in good order.

Then too, there is the positive injunction, fully canonical, to bring about the end of wrong action. Since much of what constitutes wrong action has to do with causing suffering to other beings (and the spirits are often cast in such a role), it is not only proper to try to get agents of suffering to desist, it is positively enjoined to do so. Thus, both the existence of spirit cults and the ambivalence with which Burmese Buddhists view these cults is well within the scope of canonical Buddhist motivation and rationalization.

THE NATS. The chief object of the cult of spirits in Burma are the *nats*, of which there are numerous kinds. The first distinction is that between the *upapāti nat* and the *meiʔhsa nat*, that is, between the *deva* and *devata*: respectively, denizens of the heavens atop Mount Meru, essentially of Brahmanic origin, and the many kinds of local spirits. The words *upapāti* and *meiʔhsa* derive from Pali terms meaning "well born" and "[born owing to] evildoing." This distinction does not indicate that all of the second kind are of purely indigenous origin. In fact, many of the *meiʔhsa nats* belong to Indian-derived categories of tree spirits (*youʔhka-zou*; from Pali, *rukkha*, "tree," and Burmese *sou:*, "to rule or govern," equivalent to Indian *yakkhas*) and demons (e.g., Burmese *goun-ban*, from Pali, *kumbhaṇḍa*), although technically, demons and ogres, being without fixed abodes or at least without proper domains, are not *nats*. Nor should it be thought that all *meiʔhsa nats* are inherently malevolent, in the sense of being anti-Buddhist. The potential malevolence of proper *nats* comes from two facts: the manner of their creation and/or the fact that they are lords of their perspective domains, either by nature or by royal appointment (*amein. do*). Indeed, most of the appointed *nats*, at least, are guardian spirits of the whole country, of regions, villages, families, households, and individuals. As such, they are expected to protect these various levels of jurisdiction of the nation as a Buddhist (originally monarchical) entity, and so they serve as guardians of religion. This is so to the extent that some *nats*, speaking through mediums, will take their "subjects" to task for not living according to Buddhist precepts.

The *nats* that are above all the objects of a formally organized cult are the Thirty-seven Lords. There are more than thirty-seven of these, but the number thirty-seven is dictated by the consideration that ideally a Buddhist kingdom should be organized as a microcosm of a proper portion of the Buddhist view of the universe as a whole in order that the proportion between merit and status-power characteristic of the universe as a whole be mirrored in the political and social hierarchies of a Buddhist kingdom. The reason for this organization appears to be that only thus will the economy of merit-seeking necessary to an orderly Buddhist society be effected. Viewed secularly, the king is to his domain as the god Indra (Pali, Sakka; Skt., Śakra; from which Burm. Thagya: [Min:]) is to his heaven, Tāvatiṃsa (Tawadeintha). Moreover, as Indra is ultimate secular ruler in the world at large, so a king aspiring to the state of *cakkavatti*, the ideal occupant of a Buddhist throne, should have kingdoms under him, on the same galactic principle of merit hierarchy. Hence, the hypothetical ideal organization of the kingdom, in the Burmese (and Mon) view, is a center surrounded by thirty-two subordinate realms, just as Indra at his ultimate cosmic center has thirty-two *devatas* and their realms as his subordinates. This makes thirty-three; to these are added the Four Kings (*cātummahārājā*, or *lokapāla*, Quarter Guardians) of the heaven immediately between Indra's and the world of men, yielding thirty-seven.

However, from the reign of Kyanzittha (fl. 1084–1113) the kings of Burma were *dhammarājika* monarchs. That is, while not entirely eschewing various sorts of symbolic identification with one or other Brahmanic god (Kyanzittha himself with Viṣṇu), as Buddhist kings they took as their ideal symbolic model a *cakkavatti* not after the fashion of a conquering king who (re)turns to the center of the cosmic wheel having reached to its rim (*cakkavāla*), but rather after the fashion of the Buddha, who, in preaching his doctrine to men, is said to have turned, or set in motion, the "Wheel of Dhamma" (ultimate principle or law). Nevertheless, the god-centered model for kingship had somehow to be realized. This was done by having a sort of spirit kingship of royally appointed guardians in parallel, so to speak, with human kingship, the system of Thirty-seven Lords.

It is Sakka himself who is chief among these thirty-seven, but, as he is in his paradise atop Mount Meru (Burm., Myin:mou Taun), the more immediate head of this group is Min: Maha-giri, the king or lord of the great mountain, who resides atop Mount Poppa, a prominent and sacred hill in the neighborhood of Pagan, the first Burmese capital (tenth to thirteenth century). Mount Poppa served as the local analog of Meru and its placement relative to the capital/center of the kingdom was in the sacred southeastern direction, the directional corner most proper, for instance, to Buddhist and *nat* shrines in a house. In spite of a great deal of literature suggesting that in the indianized kingdoms of Southeast Asia the symbolic sacred mountain was located in the center of the capitals, in Burma at least, the mountain's symbolic effectiveness required that it be outside, at the center of some even larger domain properly containing the kingdom. Min: Maha-giri serves as guardian of the kingdom as a whole, more particularly as the guardian of the palace, and, by extension, of every house in the kingdom, where, as Ein-hte: Min: Maha-giri ("lord of the great mountain within the house"), he is represented at a shrine in the form of a coconut (representing a head) bound with a red scarf.

The Maha-giri *nat* seems to have had an indigenous origin, perhaps overlain by brahmanic (specifically, Saiva) influences during the time of the Pyu, the people whose kingdom preceded that of the Burmans in central and upper Burma. All thirty-seven, save Thagya: min:, are filled by a set of royal appointees, mostly male. Each of these was given a fief, each has an elaborate mythological history recording his or her origin, characteristics, and manner of being served. These *nats* have various functions as guardian spirits, and most serve several of these. One at least has jurisdiction over certain fields in connection with her primary jurisdiction (shared with another) over Aungpinlei, the great artificial lake and former irrigation tank in the vicinity of present-day Mandalay, although generally, nature *nats*, including *nats* owning fields, local hills, trees, and the like, are not among the Thirty-seven Lords. Each town and its administrative jurisdiction (*myou.* refers to both without distinguishing between them) and each village has its official guardian *nat*, and every person has what is called a *mizainhpa-zain nat*, that is, a guardian inherited from parents (*mihpa*, "mother-father"). This should not be interpreted as one from the "side" of each parent; there ought to be only one for each person. Indeed, the parental *nats* derive their jurisdiction, as such, from their primary township charges.

In the time of the Burmese kingdom (until the final British conquest of 1885), virtually all persons belonged to one or other of three sumptuary classes: *kyun* (slaves, or rather, persons fully bound and without civil status), *athi* (persons whose duty of service to the king was essentially commutable by a head tax), and *ahmu. dan:* (persons hereditarily bound to specific civil or military state services—the so-called service classes, organized into "regiments"). *Athi* were generally under the civil jurisdiction of the place where they happened to live, hence under the jurisdiction of that place's guardian *nat*. *Ahmu. dan:* were supposed to be under the civil jurisdiction of the place where their regimental headquarters was located, a place where the lands assigned for their maintenance was also to be found. For the latter in particular, intermarriage with persons from different service groups was discouraged because it resulted in mixed civil and spirit jurisdictions, and of course, created difficulties in the proper keeping of the rolls of the service groups. For these reasons, for service people and even for *athi*, who were also subject to some service requirements, taxes, and census controls, there was a strong tendency toward local endogamy supported by numerous royal orders. These orders made it clear that part of what was intended was clear jurisdiction, and that unambiguous *nat* jurisdiction was included in this. The system of *mizainhpa-zain nats* has its origins in this set of considerations. Many people also have a wholly individual guardian *nat* (and in fact six *devas* and six other guardians who may or may not be of the Thirty-seven), but almost nothing is known about these *kou-zaun.* (self-protection) *nats*.

In order to understand how the Thirty-seven Lords were created, it is necessary to explain the concept of *asein-thei*, a "green" (i.e., unprepared) death, a widespread concept throughout both literate and tribal Southeast Asia. In ordinary circumstances, when someone is about to die he or she is expected to fix the mind upon his or her accumulated store of merit and demerit, and upon the teachings of religion. Friends, relatives and neighbors will, especially right after the funeral, read religious sermons aloud both to fix the minds of the bereaved so that their spirits will not wander from the body out of grief and shock, and so that the spirit of the deceased, if still about, may listen to *dhamma* (Skt., *dharma*) and so pass to a new birth according to his or her *kamma* (Skt., *karman*). When, however, someone dies violently, the spirit of the deceased will fly off in shock and anger and will be so unprepared that attention to merit, demerit, and *dhamma* will not be likely. In such a case, the deceased becomes a ghost, indeed a lost dissatisfied one, preying upon the living in its frustration (the most virulent perhaps are the women dying in childbirth).

When the person killed has been a person of great physical and/or charismatic power, and especially when he or she has been killed because of someone's deliberate treachery, the ghost created is especially dangerous. This type of ghost can, however, be dealt with if the king, who is in any event often the cause of the killing, issues a royal order (*amein. do*) appointing the spirit to an official position (in particular, one among the Thirty-seven Lords). The idea is no doubt related to the tribal notion that the virulent ghost created by the taking of an enemy's head can be converted to a servant of great power by the rites celebrating the head so taken. In any event, such was the origin of the Thirty-seven Lords; they were powerful guardian spirits of the kingdom and of religion, converted or subverted to the latter interests by royal appointment. They remain, however, a potential danger to the community, especially as lords, so that it remains necessary to placate them. It is to this end that the formal *nat* cult exists.

An additional function of this system of Thirty-seven Lords is that it replaces strictly local spirits that have regional jurisdiction with centrally appointed ones, thus replacing symbolic motivations to divisive regional loyalties with symbolic motivations to a sense of nationality for all Burmans. This is true not only because the lords are royal appointees, but also because the cult organization of all these *nats* is nationwide and because it replaces strictly local cults (understood as going back to pacts made with local spirits by the ancestors of the local inhabitants, hereditarily binding upon these descendents and open to no one else).

The cult consists essentially of a system of mediums, *nat kado* (wives—but see Lehman, 1984, for male *nat*-wives), who, for various reasons, psychological for the most part, enjoy a relationship with one or more of the lords that obligates the mediums to serve them by dancing for them periodically in offering rituals. Such behavior occurs especially at one of the several annual *nat* celebrations of national importance (e.g., the Taunbyoun festival devoted to the two Taunbyoun brothers among the Thirty-seven—they were Muslims, so even Buddhists who have them as their *mizainhpazain nat* must abstain from pork), pilgrimage to which tends to create a sense of Burmese national self-identification. This sense parallels that resulting from pilgrimage to such nationally important Buddhist shrines as the Shwei Dagon pagoda at Rangoon and the Maha Muni shrine, the shrine of the palladial Buddha image of the last several kings of Burma. These occasions, which, the great fairs aside, are often local and locally sponsored on an unscheduled basis, are known as *nat pwe:* (where *pwe:* refers to any show, display, or demonstration) or, especially in upper Burma, *nat kana:* (*kana:* refers to the temporary openwork bamboo shed in which these rites are held—*nat sin* in other places). The rituals consist of dances symbolic of the mythology of the lord in question, and of obeisances and offerings of fruits and other things at the altars upon which the figurines of various lords are ranged. It is common to speak of "worshiping" *nat* (*nat puzo*, from Pali, *pūjā*; *nat hyi. hkou:*, to bow down in adoration or homage). Technically, such terms are supposed to be reserved for the veneration of the Buddha, his order, and his relics, and obeisance to those persons (parents, elders, monks, teachers, and king and government as patron of religion) from whom one gets merit by example and by the act of merit sharing that follows all Buddhist rituals. This veneration is undertaken in order to validate their greater merit and apologize for possible offences (*gado*). But the act is also performed (at least in its modified form of salutation by raising hands, palms together, to the forehead) toward any powerful or exalted persons (*nats* included). The veneration is undertaken sometimes in flattery and out of fear of their power, but sometimes because all officials can be looked upon as extensions of government and because of the implicit correlation between charisma (*hpoun:*, from Pali, *puñña*, "merit-quality"), distinction (*goun*), and influence and authority (*o-za a-na*), on the one hand, and merit (*kuthou;* Pali, *kusala*), on the other. Properly speaking, *nat* are said to be "served" (*pa. tha.*) or "offered to" (*tin*). No Burmese Buddhist will ever talk of his involvement in *nat* service as *nat ba-tha* (from Pali, *bhāsa*, "doctrine").

MILLENARIANISM. Yet another strand in Burmese religion is millenarian Buddhism. It combines magical-alchemical practices with meditational exercises and has a strong association with the aforementioned notion of the *min:laun-hpaya:laun* as a messianic Buddhist figure heralding the coming of the future Buddha (Skt., Maitraya; Pali, Metteya). Devotees of one or other of these millenarian figures (sometimes appearing as royal pretenders replete with imitation royal courts and retinues, more often held to exist in some mystical state or realms) are frequently organized into *gain:* (*Pali, gaṇa*). *Gain:* is often rendered in the literature as "sect," but means "congregation" in this usage. (Within the *sangha*, Burmese usage maintains a blurred distinction between *gain:*, with their separate monasteries, ordination traditions, and Vinaya interpretations, and *nikāya*, sects, which may, in addition, refuse commensality and monastic coresidence with other groups of monks.

These *gain:* are semisecret congregations, no doubt partly owing to their millenarianism being perceived as defiance of constituted government, but also because of the nature of their practices. These practices, including the attempt to compound alchemical substances (*datloun:*, "lumps of power"—the essential ingredient is mercury) that are expected to make one invincible and to prolong one's existence indefinitely, are intended to ensure that the devotees will attain what amount to the fruits of the higher absorptions or meditation stages (Pali, *jhāna;* Burm., *zān*, colloquially understood as the possession of supernormal powers). In this way, the practitioners expect to be preserved until the arrival of Metteya, in order that they may hear him preach his dispensation and so be able "at once" to attain *nibbāna* (Skt., *nirvāṇa;* Burm., *neiˀpan*). The importance of the idea of congregation here is that the conjoint practice of these acts and rites will generate conjoint powers (rather on the analogy of a battery), a notion also employed in the chanting of the protective *paritta* (Burm. *payeiˀ) texts.*

The supreme adept in *gain:* practices is said to obtain *weiˀza* (Pali, *vijjā*, "wisdom"), or to be, more correctly *weiˀzadou* (Pali, *vijjādhara;* a knower of charms, a sorcerer). Technically, the point of becoming a *weiˀzadou* is to attain the highest *zān,* in which case one is said to exist in a sort of suspended state. This state, condition, or realm is known to the Burmese as *htweʔ yaʔ pauʔ*, which may be translated perhaps as "the point of going out." It seems not unlikely that there are connections here with the idea of "going beyond" in wisdom characteristic of the *prajñāpāramitā* view in Mahāyāna Buddhism. This is not impossible in view of the long history of mutual influences between the various schools of Buddhism and the complex history of pre-Pagan Mon Buddhism. It was from this latter that the Burmese supposedly got their Theravāda and earliest Pagan Buddhism in Burma, which, far from being pure Theravāda, was largely Sanskritic, partly Tantric, partly Sarvāstivada, and partly other, less clearly known things.

Another reason for the semiclandestine nature of millenarian Buddhism and the *gain:* is the profound ambivalence that in Theravāda countries has always attended emphasis on meditation practices and the associated study of *Abhidhamma,* owing to the suspicion that such adepts and students may be chiefly interested not in salvation but rather in securing and using the supernormal powers attendant upon such practices. The deliberate pursuit of such powers as an end in itself, and the overt claim to such powers, is prohibited by the Buddha for monks, and by implication at least, for Buddhists in general. Furthermore, the rise in popularity of both monastic and lay-oriented meditation movements and centers, and perhaps even the prominence in Burma of Abhidhamma *pariyatti* (scholarship), given the close canonical relationship between the two, may reflect a sort of domestication of millenarian tendencies in a country, and nowadays in an age, marked by a considerable amount of political instability, social change, and cultural malaise. Its popularity among Burma's westernized classes as part of an attempt to make it compatible with their notion of a modern worldview makes this likely. In particular, it may be significant that, as in most aspects of millenarian Buddhism, the organizations are lay only, so there also exists a considerable proliferation of purely lay meditation organizations; the absence of monks in these cases seems to represent a development distinct from traditional notions of Theravāda orthodoxy.

It would be a mistake to equate all aspects of magical Buddhism, however, with millenarian Buddhism. For, as ambivalent as orthodoxy, represented in particular by the Vinaya, is toward the practice by monks of the apotropaic use of Buddhist symbols in astrology, the casting of horoscopes, the provision of amulets, and the preparation of charms, and as common as it is for practitioners of these arts to be laymen, there are plenty of otherwise perfectly orthodox monks who practice them, too. Furthermore, those laymen who possess ability in this area tend overwhelmingly to learn their craft during periods of relatively prolonged monastic residence as monks or novices, presumably from monks.

One final matter requires an account, and that is the question why it is that millenarian movements, the intense and pervasive concern with acquiring merit, and all other attempts to be reborn as a male human being with wealth and status characterize so much of Burmese Buddhism. Is this an indication of a failure of the capacity to believe in the goal of *nibbāna,* of a noncanonical (if not positively unorthodox) tendency in Burmese religion? Is the fact, common in many Theravāda countries, that merit-making activities are occasions of public display of one's giving (*dāna*) unambiguously contrary to the scriptural adjuration that unpublicized giving is the most, if not the only, meritorious form? It seems not.

Consider some ambiguities connected with merit. First, there is the economic principle that it takes the fruits of previously earned merit to make greater merit, and that merit is to some extent proportional to the fruits of previous merit—because only then does one have the good fortune to be born into the position from which the greater merit may be made. Translated into practical action, this principle leads to the notion that the meritoriousness of any act is arguable. In particular, a person in a position of social or personal obligation with respect to any act of giving earns little merit from it, since only free, unobligated acts really earn merit for the actor. Consider also the principle that one rarely if ever knows where one stands in one's samsaric trajectory; one does not know, for instance, how much demerit may still have to be expiated or how much merit must still be made in order that one may be in the position to make a serious attempt towards transcendental goals, *nibbāna* above all.

Since the merit from an act is relative to the act's being done freely, and since a consequence of the uncertainty about one's overall store of merit and demerit is a pervasive uncertainty about relative social status and one's sumptuary obligations toward others, the only way one can be reasonably certain about one's *dāna* is to have its meritoriousness publicly acknowledged, hence publicly displayed. In the same vein, it must often seem canonically justifiable that one finds oneself psychologically incapable of giving serious positive commitment to purely religious goals. In such cases, it may seem perhaps wiser to aspire to a future human birth in which one's store of merit will be sufficient to motivate one toward transcendental objectives, or even to have such objectives taught to one by Metteya. The devotee hopes for greater personal, social, and economic stability at some future time as a better basis for ultimate accomplishments, and invests one's present resources in merit making accordingly. The measure of the practitioner's commitment to nibbanic soteriology is clearly the embarrassment people admit to when they shy away from trying for nibbanic extinction and the fervency with which they pray that they may in a better future life be able to try and attain *nibbāna.*

SEE ALSO Buddhism, article on Buddhism in Southeast Asia; Buddhist Religious Year; Cakravartin; Folk Religion, article on Folk Buddhism; Merit, article on Buddhist Concepts; Nats; Saṃgha, article on Saṃgha and Society in South and Southeast Asia; Theravāda; Worship and Devotional Life, article on Buddhist Devotional Life in Southeast Asia.

BIBLIOGRAPHY

Aung-Thwin, Michael. *Pagan: The Foundations of Modern Burma.* Honolulu, 1985. A trenchant analysis of the political economy of royal merit making.

Bizot, François. *Le figuier à cinq branches: Recherche sur le bouddhisme khmer.* Paris, 1976. Fine analysis of non-Theravāda aspects of Southeast Asian Buddhism and monasticism.

Ferguson, John P. "The Symbolic Dimensions of the Burmese Sangha." Ph.D. diss., Cornell University, 1975. The major study of monastic sectarianism and its history.

Ferguson, John P., and E. Michael Mendelson. "Masters of the Buddhist Occult: The Burmese Weikzas." *Contributions to Asian Studies* 16 (1981): 62–80. The one easy introduction to Burmese millenarian Buddhism.

Htin Aung, Maung. *Folk Elements in Burmese Buddhism.* London, 1962.

Lehman, Frederic K. "On the Vocabulary and Semantics of 'Field' in Theravada Buddhist Society." *Contributions to Asian Studies* 16 (1981): 101–111.

Lehman, Frederic K. "Remarks on Freedom and Bondage in Traditional Burma and Thailand." *Journal of Southeast Asian Studies* 15 (September 1984): 233–244.

Luce, Gordon H. *Old Burma, Early Pagán.* 3 vols. Locust Valley, N.Y., 1969. A great Burma scholar's monumental work; the standard source on earliest Burmese history.

Mendelson, E. Michael. *Sangha and State in Burma.* Ithaca, N.Y., 1975. To date, the definitive work on its subject.

Nash, Manning. *The Golden Road to Modernity.* New York, 1965. Probably the best modern village ethnography of Burma.

Ray, Nihar-Ranjan. *Sanskrit Buddhism in Burma.* Calcutta, 1936.

Schober, Juliane. "On Burmese Horoscopes." *South East Asian Review* 5 (1980): 43–56. The latest and most acute treatment of Burmese astrological concepts in a Western language.

Scott, James George. *The Burman: His Life and Notions* (1882). 3d ed. London, 1910. The standard general introduction to Burmese social and cultural life.

Shorto, H. L. "The Planets, the Days of the Week and the Points of the Compass: Orientation Symbolism in 'Burma.'" In *Natural Symbols in South East Asia,* edited by G. B. Milner, pp. 152–164. London, 1978. A unique and insightful treatment of Burmese ideas of temporality and directionality.

Spiro, Melford E. *Buddhism and Society: A Great Tradition and Its Burmese Vicissitudes.* New York, 1970. Spiro's books are the most thorough descriptions and analyses of Burmese religion, combining fine ethnography and fine anthropological analysis with sound use of philosophical and textual knowledge, although the author's psychoanalytical emphasis has been often criticized.

Spiro, Melford E. *Burmese Supernaturalism.* Philadelphia, 1978.

Steinberg, David I. *Burma: A Socialist Nation of Southeast Asia.* Boulder, Colo., 1982. A fine popular introduction to modern Burma, its peoples, history, politics, economics.

Temple, R. C. *The Thirty-seven Nats: A Phase of Spirit-Worship Prevailing in Burma.* London, 1906. The standard description of these figures, illustrated.

New Sources

Abdullah, Daud. "Fire in the Night: Wingate of Burma, Ethiopia, and Zion." *Muslim World Book Review* 21, no. 2 (2001): 38–40.

Boisvert, Mathieu. "La ceremonie de l'ordination mineure bouddhique (shin pyu) en Birmanie et ses ramifications sociales." *Sciences Religieuses* 30, no. 2 (2001): 131–149.

Case, Jay Riley. *Foreign Missionary Enterprise at Home.* London, 2003.

Harvey, Graham. *Indigenous Religions: A Companion.* New York, 2000.

Lindell, Kristina. "The Folk-tales of Burma: An Introduction." *Asian Folklore Studies* 60, no. 1 (2001): 179–180.

Strachan, Paul. *Pagan: Art and Architecture of Old Burma.* Edinburgh, 1989.

Win, Kanbawza. "Are Christians Persecuted in Burma?" *Asia Journal of Theology* 14, no. 1 (2000): 170–175.

Woodward, Mark R. "Gifts for the Sky People: Animal Sacrifice, Head Hunting and Power Among the Naga of Burma and Assam." *Indigenous Religions.* New York (2000): 219–229.

FREDERIC K. LEHMAN (CHIT HLAING) (1987)
Revised Bibliography

BURNOUF, EUGÈNE (1801–1852), French Sanskritist, Buddhologist, and Indologist. Son of the classicist Jean-Louis Burnouf, Eugène Burnouf was born in Paris on April 8, 1801. After distinguishing himself at the Lycée Louis-le-Grand and the École de Chartes, Eugène began the study of Sanskrit with his father and Leonard de Chézy in 1824, only one year after de Chézy's appointment to Europe's first Sanskrit chair. Just two years later, Burnouf, together with Christian Lassen, published *Essai sur le Pali* (1826), which identified and analyzed the sacred language of Theravāda Buddhism of Ceylon (now Sri Lanka) and mainland Southeast Asia.

If a single person can be credited with inaugurating the West's serious study of Buddhism according to primary sources, he is Eugène Burnouf. In less than three decades prior to the middle of the nineteenth century, Burnouf succeeded in establishing European Buddhist studies on solid footing through his own research and preparation of young scholars, and also in contributing significantly to the foundation of studies in the Veda and the Purāṇas, and to Avestan studies as well.

In 1833, a year that also saw publication of *Commentaire sur le Yaçna,* a landmark in modern Avestan studies, Eugène succeeded de Chézy as professor of Sanskrit at the Collège de France. About the same time, he began work on the Buddhist texts sent by Brian H. Hodgson, an East India Company resident in Katmandu, to the French Asiatic Society in Paris. By 1837, Burnouf had resolved to translate the *Saddharmapuṇḍarīka Sūtra* (Lotus Sūtra of the True Dharma), a text that he felt was most representative of the materials sent by Hodgson.

About 1840, Burnouf decided that the annotations needed to make a translation of the *Lotus Sūtra* intelligible to European audiences threatened to overwhelm the text. He thus set as a preliminary task the writing of an "introduction to Buddhism" that would provide the necessary context. His *Introduction à l'histoire du bouddhisme indien* was published in 1844. His *Lotus de la bonne loi*, the translation of the *Lotus Sūtra*, appeared posthumously in 1852.

Although Burnouf is deservedly celebrated for his own pathbreaking scholarship on Buddhism and the Avestan tradition, his importance to the history of religions does not end there. Among his students in Paris in the 1840s was the young Sanskritist F. Max Müller. "Went to Burnouf, [who is] spiritual, amiable, thoroughly French," Müller wrote in his journal in 1845, and continued,

> He received me in the most friendly way, talked a great deal, and all that he said was valuable, not on ordinary topics but on special [ones]. 'I am a Brahman, a Buddhist, a Zoroastrian; I hate the Jesuits' – that is the sort of man [he is]. His lectures were on the *Rigveda*, and they opened a new world to me. He explained to us his own research, he showed us new manuscripts that he had received from India, in fact he did all he could to make us his fellow-workers.

It was at Burnouf's urging that Müller undertook his own critical edition of the *Ṛgveda Saṃhita* (1849–1873).

In addition to Burnouf's teaching and his continuing research in Buddhist, Sanskrit, and Tibetan sources, he also worked on materials directly significant for the study of Hinduism, seeing a translation of the first nine books (in three volumes) of the *Bhāgavata Purāṇa* (1840–1847) into print before his death.

To his pioneering Buddhist studies Burnouf brought a calm and imperturbable attitude generally unruffled by the new and often puzzling ideas his research disclosed. Patient and thorough, this scholar, whose genius effectively introduced in Europe the scientific study of Hinayana and Mahayana Buddhist traditions, remained open throughout his lamentably brief career to information from all Buddhist sources. He set standards for Buddhist studies that few of his successors would match.

BIBLIOGRAPHY

Although by no means of merely antiquarian interest, Eugène Burnouf's scholarly writings have remained untranslated into English. *L'Introduction à l'histoire du bouddhisme indien* (Paris, 1844) and the translations *Le Lotus de la bonne loi* (Paris, 1852) and *Le Bhagavata Purāṇa*, 5 vols. (Paris, 1840–1898) are still important and provide the reader of French with eloquent testimony to the spirit and grace of Burnouf's judicious scholarship.

Appreciations of Burnouf's life and work are numerous. Among the more helpful are Sylvain Lévi's preface to the 1925 edition of *Le Lotus*; Raymond Schwab's *La renaissance orientale* (Paris, 1950), esp. pp. 309–316; and *Ernst Windisch's Geschichte der Sanskrit-Philologie und indischen Altertumskunde*, 2 vols. (Strasbourg, 1917–1920), pp. 123–140.

G. R. WELBON (1987 AND 2005)

BUSHIDŌ, the Japanese warrior's code, cannot be defined by a single neat formula. Every age can be said to have had notions of acceptable warrior behavior, but apart from certain core values—of which the most obvious were skill at arms, courage, hardihood, and a serious demeanor—the criteria varied substantially. It was until recent times an unwritten code, in the sense that no one document contained a complete formulation; rather, the code was reflected in literature, regulations, and decrees. Even when it was committed to writing, it was subject to periodic change.

ORIGIN AND DEVELOPMENT. The *bushi* emerged as a class during the tenth century, when a militia system controlled by the central government broke down in the provinces. Local bands brought together by blood ties and geographic propinquity were formed under the leadership of a provincial governor or large holder of land rights, with few exceptions sprung from the lower echelons of the aristocracy. A bond of mutual loyalty, heavily weighted in the leader's favor, emerged: unspecified protection in exchange for unlimited military service.

It has been plausibly suggested that these warriors inherited their fighting spirit from the continental immigrants who had established themselves as the dominant racial strain centuries earlier. These had been mounted fighting men, whose ethos may well have survived on the frontier during the Sinicization of the Japanese heartland. Certainly, the indomitable warrior spirit is portrayed in Japan's earliest surviving literature, which dates from the eighth century. During the eleventh century, however, although the silken aristocrats of the capital used them to settle their power contests, they looked down on them as inferior relations, rebels, or uneducated rustics. But by the end of the twelfth century, the *bushi* had become indispensable in keeping order in the capital. Eventually they took over the effective administration of the whole country, with a consequent enhancement of status.

Thenceforth, terms attesting the existence of a concept of Bushidō began to appear, although the word itself is not noted in literature until 1604. Phrases signifying "the warrior's charisma" and emphasizing the special fighting qualities of the warriors of the eastern provinces proliferated. These extolled their physical strength, superb skill at arms and daring horsemanship, resourcefulness, fearlessness, ferocity, readiness to die, and generosity of mind.

Not all *bushi* could have equaled the paragons depicted in the medieval war tales, but they all shared a clearly defined ideal. Most prominent was their obsession with the honor of the family name. This gave rise to the pre-battle ritual of self-identification, recital of ancestors' exploits, and boasts of personal valor. Expectation of personal reward earned in individual combat, attested by eyewitnesses or by trophies of severed enemy heads, was a concomitant phenomenon. Bestowal of rewards nurtured the notion of loyalty between lord and vassal that became the essence of Bushidō. But an attempt was made to separate the ethic of loyalty from material considerations by generous recognition of high-minded conduct, whether displayed by friend or by foe.

Inevitably, the age of civil war (1467–1568) led to an eclipse of the loyalty central to the unwritten code. A morally and financially bankrupt central government changed gradually to a system of decentralized administration, dangerously lacking in check or balance, and accompanied by gross disorder. The military prestige (*iegara*) of a family—its ability to afford protection—rather than possession of an ancient name became all-important. Traitors and turncoats abounded, for some *bushi* did not scruple to desert or oust an incompetent or unfortunate lord. The hereditary military classes were also diluted by the recruitment of peasants as infantry and by the rise of men of low birth to the ranks of feudal lords. Within a century most of the old leadership had been replaced by new blood.

To survive, a warlord had to mold his followers into an efficient, reliable fighting force. Discipline was upgraded and regulations issued enjoining frugality, vigilance, conscientiousness, and other useful virtues. An ideal of unremitting and self-sacrificing service was created, and the bond between lord and vassal was formalized by oaths of allegiance. New weapons and defense measures leading to the building of fortresses and castles made it necessary for the feudal lord to keep his vassals near at hand rather than domiciled on scattered holdings. The process of the separation of the *bushi* from the soil and his development into a full-time fighting man was under way.

This new spirit had been generally discernible from about 1500. From then on, the struggle for the acquisition of land gradually came to be motivated more by considerations of power politics than mere greed. National hegemony became a general dream.

The Tokugawa Bushi: New Functions, New Ideals. When unification was finally attained and peace firmly established, the function of the *bushi* changed. The Confucian scholar Yamaga Sokō (1622–1685) set out specifically to define an appropriate role for the *bushi* in peacetime. Concerned that they should earn their keep not only as a standing army and police force but as administrators, he urged the raising of their educational standard. Additionally, he saw them as eminently qualified to fulfill the function of political and intellectual leaders. Ingeniously, Yamaga grafted onto the traditional feudal virtues of self-sacrifice and readiness to die a selection of Confucian qualities: moral and intellectual superiority, prudence and good judgment, a cultivated mind and a humane heart. He thus produced a blend of the Confucian "superior man" with the traditional Japanese warrior temperament—what has been called "the heroic man." He did not merely codify hitherto unwritten notions of chivalrous conduct; he created a new ideal.

Of a more hectic temper was the thinking of Yamamoto Tsunetomo's manual for *bushi*, *Hagakure* (1716), which emphasized total self-dedication and constant preparedness. Because it was written during an age of peace, this work has been inappropriately labeled "escapist"; it was, in fact, essentially revivalist. Yamamoto's aim was the moral rearmament of the *bushi* by the cultivation of a resolute will to right action regardless of the consequences. The dangers inherent in such a fundamentalist attitude are obvious, but clearly it supplies a powerful stimulus to purposeful conduct.

An important aspect of Bushidō that now received special emphasis was its elitism. This had early emerged. During the twelfth century, the warrior's obsession with protecting the honor of his name had distinguished him sharply from the court nobles who hankered after high rank and title. Further, that canny general Minamoto Yoritomo (1147–1199) sought to burnish the warrior image by setting up criteria for the recruitment of vassals. Very early also, the *bushi* attempted to distance themselves from the populace by acquiring refinement. Devotion to aesthetic pursuits was particularly prominent during the period of the civil wars. A sword hunt in 1588, by disarming the populace, greatly strengthened the self-image of the "two-sworded" *bushi* as a superior caste. Similarly, the codification of Bushidō during the Tokugawa period (1600–1868) gave the warrior a sense of separation from the emerging commercial classes. The combination of the concept of *bun* (learning) with that of *bu* (martial arts) as the new Tokugawa ideal emphasized Confucian education as the monopoly of the military classes, and reinforced the cachet of elitism. Inevitably, arrogance was nurtured along with self-pride.

The central government and local lords employed Confucian scholars to lecture to the *bushi* on the ethic, and subsidized popular preachers to carry the same message to other classes in a form suitable to their station. *Bushi* values were thus widely disseminated throughout the whole Japanese people, so that the *bushi* ideal drew strength from its congruence with the core values of society.

Through such constant exhortation, the *bushi* were in some measure preserved from becoming parasites. They did not produce, but they provided essential services with a high degree of efficiency. For two and a half centuries they supplied administrators, magistrates, judges, police, firechiefs, supervisors of public works, and so on—functions they had been trained to perform since at least the thirteenth century. They also became doctors, teachers, researchers, advisers, theorists, and advocates of new ideas.

The recent wholesale denigration of the Tokugawa *bushi* as urbanized and emasculated, mere hirelings, is not supported by fact: they engineered the Meiji restoration and the dismantling of feudalism, and, as the bulk of the educated class, they contributed substantially to the modernization of the state. That a class comprising 6 percent of the population provided 23 percent of the Meiji entrepreneurs is significant.

MODERN BUSHIDŌ: AN ENDURING IDEAL. Debate on the relative positions of emperor and shogun in the body politic has been aroused by the application to the Japanese situation of the Confucian tenet that function should fit title. Also, Tokugawa encouragement of learning revived the study of ancient emperor-centered literature. The result was a movement honoring the emperor as the ultimate focus of loyalty. The amalgamation of this idea with the newly formulated bureaucratic *bushi* ethic penetrated the Japanese mind and prepared the way for Meiji Bushidō (after 1868).

This "new" Bushidō was created by the deliberate utilization of traditional values to strengthen the modern state. Though the *bushi* as a class were abolished, a Meiji statesman, Itō Hirobumi, described Bushidō as "our ancient feudal chivalry," which defined the conduct of "man as he ought to be" and constituted "moral education of the highest type." The discarding of the identification of Bushidō with the warrior made clear the intention to transform it into a mass religion.

By 1937 *Kokutai no hongi* (Fundamentals of our national polity), published by the Ministry of Education as the bible of nationalism, apotheosized Bushidō as the central tenet of morality and the mainstay of society, transcending Confucianism and Buddhism. This form of Bushidō enjoined total suppression of self-interest, with death as its supreme expression. It implied the shift of unquestioning loyalty from an immediate superior to the sovereign, substituting unconditional service to the state for a bond depending on personal gratitude, and Shinto mythology for Confucian rationalism. There were available exemplars of devotion to the legitimate imperial court in exile during its unsuccessful struggle (1336–1390) against a puppet court supported by the presiding military power. Of these, the general Kusunoki Masashige (1294–1336) was the most illustrious. Inevitably, he became the focus of a new cult.

Although loyalty to a superior had always been central to Bushidō, it had never been blind loyalty. Confucianism emphasized the necessity of thinking things out for oneself. This implied the duty of remonstrance if the conduct of superiors was considered culpable. Earlier ages had provided notable illustrations, but when this obligation was democratized during Meiji, it led to admonitory assassinations anticipating the horrors of modern terrorism.

The *bushi's* contempt for death, strongly reinforced by his predilection for Zen, had been constant throughout. Trained to kill or be killed, he made indifference to it a point of honor, giving the attitude its most succinct expression in the saying "Bushidō lies in dying." Translated into practical peacetime terms, this simply meant total and selfless dedication. Coincidentally, since death was always regarded as the final proof of sincerity, it gave rise to a cult of suicide. This could take the form of self-disembowelment to accompany one's lord in death or, when faced with defeat, the throwing away of life by a feat of reckless daring. Modern extreme extensions of this view were the hopeless charges of the so-called human bullets in the Russo-Japanese War (1904–1905) and the kamikaze pilots in World War II.

World War II imparted a sinister meaning to the idea of Bushidō. The code was identified with war atrocities, many of which arose from a fanatically held conviction that death was preferable to surrender. This engendered contempt for, and hence ill treatment of, prisoners of war. On the other hand, it also triggered gruesome mass suicides by captured Japanese soldiers.

Some say Bushidō expired with Japan's defeat in 1945. Yet not long after the war, historical novels elucidating the viewpoint of the *bushi* of the civil war period became best-sellers among businessmen. They saw the magnates of that competitive age as excellent models for successful leadership in the world of modern international commerce. The stage-managed suicide of the modern novelist Mishima Yukio (1925–1970) was a lurid example of how susceptible even a modern Japanese mind is to Bushidō's perennial glamour.

From the seventeenth century to modern times, Bushidō has come under sharp criticism as illogical, irrelevant, and morbid. It is true that excesses have been committed in its name through adherence to its anachronistic aspects. Yet it has by and large been a dynamic concept. To the original core values, others were added from time to time in a continuous process of merging and synthesizing. But always Bushidō carried the implication of some kind of sinewy superiority, of effort beyond the capabilities of the ordinary man. And the durability of its appeal surely furnishes some justification for the Meiji scholar Inazo Nitobe's claim in his famous essay of 1905: "Bushidō is the soul of Japan."

SEE ALSO War and Warriors, overview article; Yamaga Sokō.

BIBLIOGRAPHY

Three small books provide a simple historical background and a succinct introduction to the study of Bushidō: Peter Duus's *Feudalism in Japan* (New York, 1969); H. Paul Varley, Ivan Morris, and Nobuko Morris's *The Samurai* (London, 1970); and Conrad Totman's *Japan before Perry: A Short History* (Berkeley, 1982). Three large and lavishly illustrated volumes give detailed expositions of *bushi* lifestyle and way of thought: George Richard Storry's *The Way of the Samurai* (New York, 1978), Stephen R. Turnbull's *The Samurai: A Military History* (New York, 1977), and Oscar Ratti and Adele Westbrook's *Secrets of the Samurai* (Tokyo and Rutland, Vt., 1973). *Sources of the Japanese Tradition,* 2 vols. (New York, 1958), compiled by Ryusaku Tsunoda, Wm. Theodore de Bary, and Donald Keene, presents valuable source material on the formulation of Bushidō.

Finally, three essays throw additional light on significant aspects of the topic: Yamamoto Tsunetomo's *Hagakure: A Code of the Way of Samurai,* translated by Takao Mutoh (Tokyo,

1980); Mishima Yukio's *The Samurai Ethic in Modern Japan*, translated by Kathryn Sparling (Tokyo, 1978); and Inazo Nitobe's *Bushidō: The Soul of Japan* (Tokyo, 1980).

New Sources

Cleary, Thomas F. *The Japanese Art of War: Understanding the Culture of Strategy.* Boston, 1991.

Ikegami, Eiko. *The Taming of the Samurai: Honorific Individualism and the Making of Modern Japan.* Cambridge, U.K., 1995.

Katchmer, George A. *Professional Budo: Ethics, Chivalry, and the Samurai Code.* Jamaica Plains, Mass., 1995.

Newman, John. *Bushido: The Way of the Warrior: A New Perspective on the Japanese Military Tradition.* New York, 1989.

Turnbull, Stephen, ed. *The Samurai Tradition.* Surrey, U.K., 2000.

JOYCE ACKROYD (1987)
Revised Bibliography

BUSHMEN SEE KHOI AND SAN RELIGION

BUSHNELL, HORACE

BUSHNELL, HORACE (1802–1876), Congregational minister and theologian. Born in Bantam, Connecticut, and reared in nearby New Preston, Bushnell attended Yale College and the Law School in New Haven. Stirred by a revival that swept the college in 1831, he decided to enter Yale Divinity School. In 1833 he was ordained pastor of the North Church of Hartford. He experienced an extraordinary spiritual illumination in 1848, a year in which he was also invited to lecture at Harvard, Andover, and Yale. The books resulting from these lectures and from Bushnell's attempts to clarify and refine their content in the face of criticism (*God in Christ,* 1849, and *Christ in Theology,* 1851) stirred up a hornet's nest of controversy and brought charges of heresy from conservative churchmen. In 1858 Bushnell's *Nature and the Supernatural* was published, and *Christian Nurture,* probably his best-known work, appeared in 1861 (an earlier version had been published in 1847). Persistent health problems forced him to resign his North Church pastorate in April 1861, but he continued to be active during the last fifteen years of his life, preaching, lecturing, and producing such additional books as *Work and Play* (1864), *Christ and His Salvation* (1864), *The Vicarious Sacrifice* (1866), *Moral Uses of Dark Things* (1868), *Forgiveness and Law* (1874), and *Building Eras in Religion* (published posthumously in 1881).

Four traits of Bushnell's theological thought suggest something of the distinctive contribution he made to his times. The first is its high degree of originality. Bushnell did not prize originality for its own sake; he saw it as necessary for penetrating to the enduring heart of Christian teaching and rediscovering its relevance to the needs and concerns of human beings in a time of rapid change. Second, his theology was intended to be a mediating theology, one seeking grounds of consensus that could allay the spirit of divisiveness and contumely that marked so much of the theological debate of his day. Third, Bushnell held that religious doctrines are not meant to satisfy speculative curiosity. The decisive test of any doctrine is an experiential one, that is, the contributions it can make to the transformation of life and character. He insisted that divine revelation itself has this "instrumental" function (as he termed it), and that its import can be grasped only when it is approached with its practical end clearly in mind. Fourth, Bushnell tried to put theological discourse and method on a new footing by arguing that the language of religion, including that of the Bible, is the language of analogy, metaphor, and symbol, and that its function is to suggest and evoke truths and modes of awareness that cannot be literally expressed. Hence, its proper use and interpretation requires the imaginative skill of the poet or orator, not that of the abstract speculative reasoner. These ideas about theological language and method went much against the grain of the prevailing concept of theology in Bushnell's time, which was that theology should be an exact rational science, with precise definitions, finely drawn distinctions, and strict logical deductions.

Bushnell was one of the two most creative Protestant theologians in America prior to the twentieth century; the other was Jonathan Edwards (1703–1758). Bushnell's book on Christian nurture has exerted more influence on theories of Christian education among Protestants than any other work of recent times. His ideas on religious language anticipated much that is now being said about the crucial role of myth, symbol, story, and paradox in the discourse of the religions of the world. His fresh approaches sounded the death knell of the Edwardian Calvinism that was dominant in his day and had been so since the time of Jonathan Edwards, and they provided the point of departure for what came to be called the "new theology" of American Protestant liberalism. His critique of biblical literalism helped to pave the way for theological acceptance of the results of biblical criticism and for easier rapprochement between religion and science.

BIBLIOGRAPHY

Cherry, Conrad. *Nature and Religious Imagination: From Edwards to Bushnell.* Philadelphia, 1980. Explores Jonathan Edwards's symbolic vision of nature and its religious meanings, shows how this vision suffered sharp decline among religious thinkers in New England after Edwards's death, and then exhibits the resurgence of a similar vision in the thought of Bushnell.

Crosby, Donald A. *Horace Bushnell's Theory of Language.* The Hague, 1975. Investigates Bushnell's theory of language and religious language in the context of other philosophies of language in nineteenth-century America, discussing its implications for theological content and method. Examines and evaluates reactions to Bushnell's language theory from his theological peers.

Dorrien, Gary. *The Making of American Tribal Theology: Imagining Progressive Religion, 1805–1900.* Louisville, Ky., 2001. Makes a detailed case for the singular historical importance of Bushnell's contributions to the emergence of American

Protestant liberalism and argues that he should be recognized as America's greatest nineteenth-century theologian.

Edwards, Robert L. *Of Singular Genius, of Singular Grace: A Biography of Horace Bushnell.* Cleveland, Ohio, 1992. Engagingly written, thoroughly researched account of Bushnell's controversial life.

Smith, David L. *Symbolism and Growth: The Religious Thought of Horace Bushnell.* Chico, Calif., 1981. Argues that the principal focus of Bushnell's thought is his theory of how human beings influence each other through their social and linguistic interactions. Seeks to show how Bushnell used this theory to explain God's communications of himself for the purpose of nurturing and redeeming human character.

Smith, H. Shelton, ed. *Horace Bushnell.* New York, 1965. Valuable collection of some of Bushnell's most important writings, with informative general introduction and introductions to each selection. Includes an extensive bibliography of works by and about Bushnell.

DONALD A. CROSBY (1987 AND 2005)

BU STON (1290–1364), also known as Bu ston Rin poche and Bu Lo tsā ba; properly, Rin chen grub pa; Tibetan Buddhist monk-scholar, translator, redactor, historian, and architect. In the annals of Tibetan Buddhism, Bu ston holds a singular position. He is renowned as the codifier of the Tibetan Buddhist canon and as the last great translator and systematizer prior to the fourteenth-century reformer Tsong kha pa. Considered to have been an incarnation of the Kashmiri saint Śākyaśrī bhadra (Tib., Kha che pang chen), Bu ston showed a precocious and prodigious talent for translation. Furthermore, he mastered certain aspects of the Tantras and became known as a chief authority on the Yoga Tantra cycles and on the Kālacakra system in particular.

Bu ston wrote one of the earliest authoritative histories of Buddhism, covering its development both in India and Tibet up to the fourteenth century. He also compiled and produced detailed catalogs of all Buddhist scriptures translated into Tibetan up until his time, retranslating many and editing out of the official canon texts deemed spurious. It was Bu ston who first organized the Tibetan canon into the now famed subdivisions of "Sūtra translations" (Tib., Bka' 'gyur) and "Śāstra translations" (Tib., Bstan 'gyur). Although the texts constituting the Bka' 'gyur were fairly well established by his time, it was due exclusively to Bu ston's incredible zeal and effort that the Bstan 'gyur came to assume its present shape.

Bu ston was born into an illustrious line of Tantric practitioners. From age seven onward, he studied the Tantras under the guidance of both his grandfather and the renowned Bka' brgyud pa master Khro phu ba. (Bu ston's biography claims that he came to possess such mastery of Tantric ritual that even as a child people sought him out in preference to his grandfather.)

At the age of eighteen Bu ston left home and became a novice monk. For the next several years he studied under learned masters from all traditions; his teachers are said to have numbered some twenty-eight. In 1312 he took full ordination. Thereafter, he devoted himself to mastering Candragomin's works on grammar, and subsequently, the various languages of east and west India, including Kashmiri and Sanskrit. Henceforth, he became famed as an unparalleled translator of Indian Buddhist scripture. During this period he also made an intensive study of the Kālacakra, later earning the reputation of being a master of this particular Tantric cycle.

At age thirty Bu ston was invited to assume the see of the Źwa lu Monastery of the Sa skya order. This monastery remained his main seat throughout the rest of his life. From it he expounded the Kālacakra and other Tantric cycles along with numerous exoteric scriptures; he gave innumerable initiations and composed commentaries on the Sūtras and Tantras. It was during his tenure at Źwa lu that Bu ston wrote his famous *Chos 'byung* (*History of Buddhism*), completed about 1322. It was also at Źwa lu that Bu ston began to organize the first definitive Tibetan Buddhist canon. Applying his genius to systematizing the canon, Bu ston established a new method of classifying the scriptures. With regard to the Sūtra collection he introduced a threefold schema. He divided the collection philosophically and historically into what he called the "three *dharmacakras*," or "turnings of the wheel of the Law." Above all, he is revered for having given to the Tantra collection a fourfold schema, classifying these works into four distinct *rgyuds*, or classes: Kriya, Carya, Yoga, and Anuttarayoga. This method of treating the Tantra literature was later adopted and preserved by Tsong kha pa and his disciple Mkhas grub rje.

In addition to writing and teaching, Bu ston was an accomplished architect. In 1352 he composed a classic work on the construction of Buddhist stupas (reliquary mounds) called the *Shape and Dimensions of the Mahābodhi Stūpa*, and at the age of sixty-three he oversaw the construction at Źwa lu Ri phug of a stupa measuring almost thirty meters in height. This Ri phug stupa later served as the primary model for the great stupa raised at Rgyal rtse.

On reaching his sixty-seventh year, Bu ston handed on the see of Źwa lu. Still, for the next seven years he zealously continued to carry out the three chief activities performed by a true *bla ma* ("superior teacher")—namely, to study, to teach, and to write. He died peacefully in 1364.

SEE ALSO Buddhism, article on Buddhism in Tibet; Buddhism, Schools of, article on Tibetan and Mongolian Buddhism; Tibetan Religions, overview article.

BIBLIOGRAPHY

Bu ston. *Chos 'byuṅ.* Translated by Eugene Obermiller as *History of Buddhism*, 2 vols. (Heidelberg, 1931–1932). An invaluable resource for both Buddhist history and literature to the fourteenth century.

Ruegg, David S. *The Life of Bu ston Rinpoche.* Rome, 1966. A fine translation of the "liberative life story" (Tib., *rnam thar*) of Bu ston.

New Sources

Eimer, Helmut. *Der Tantra-Katalog des Bu ston im Vergleich mit der Abteilung Tantra des tibetischen Kanjur.* Bonn, 1989.

Luczanits, Christian. "The Sources for Bu ston's Introduction to the Acts of a Buddha." *Wiener Zeitschrift fur die Kunde Sudasiens und Archiv fur indische Philosophie* 37 (1993): 93–108.

Vogel, Claus. "Bu ston on the Date of the Buddha's Nirvana: Translated from His History of the Doctrine (Chos 'byun)." In *Die Datierung des historischen Buddha,* edited by Heinz Bechert, pp. 403–414. Gottingen, 1991.

JANICE D. WILLIS (1987)
Revised Bibliography

BUTLER, JOSEPH (1692–1752), English theologian and moral philosopher. Butler was born into a Presbyterian family in Berkshire. He began his studies at a dissenting academy, but changed his allegiance to the Church of England and entered Oriel College, Oxford University. After ordination, he held a succession of charges, including clerk of the closet to Queen Caroline, clerk of the closet to King George II, bishop of Bristol, and bishop of Durham. He died at Bath and is buried in the cathedral at Bristol.

The first part of Butler's only systematic work, *Analogy of Religion* (1736), argued against those deists of his day who, although rejecting the Christian scriptures, believed that God had created the universe and that a rational religion could be found in nature. These deists denied special revelation on the grounds of alleged rational difficulties. Butler attempted to show that the difficulties found in special revelation, rejected by deists, were analogous to the difficulties found in natural revelation, which deists accepted. To be consistent, deists should accept special revelation. Butler was aware—but did not think it probable—that one who accepts this analogy may reject both revelations. The second part of his *Analogy* is one of the classic defenses of Christian theism.

Butler's ethical theory is based on an analysis of the component parts of human nature. There are three levels operating harmoniously: the several passions, each directed at a particular desire; the rational principles of self-love and benevolence, concerned with the individual's general welfare; and conscience, the moral standard and decision maker. Butler considered ethics to be a subdivision of theology, presenting his theories in *Fifteen Sermons* (1726). Philosophers, however, generally treat his ethics independently of his theology. Butler is also known for his refutation of psychological egoism, based on his analysis of benevolence, a natural component of human nature.

SEE ALSO Deism.

BIBLIOGRAPHY

There have been many editions of Butler's two books: *Fifteen Sermons Preached at the Rolls Chapel* (1726) and *The Analogy of Religion, Natural and Revealed, to the Constitution and Course of Nature* (1736). The most readily available complete editions of his works (which also include a few additional sermons) are *The Works of Joseph Butler, D. C. L.*, 2 vols., edited by W. E. Gladstone (Oxford, 1896–1897), and *The Works of Bishop Butler*, 2 vols., edited by J. H. Bernard (London, 1900). Both texts have informative introductions.

The best general work on Butler is Ernest C. Mossner's *Bishop Butler and the Age of Reason* (New York, 1936), while the most penetrating analysis of Butler's ethics is Austin Duncan-Jones's *Butler's Moral Philosophy* (Harmondsworth, 1952). Recommended as a work integrating his natural theology and ethics is my own *Butler's Ethics* (The Hague, 1964).

P. ALLAN CARLSSON (1987)